THE NORTON ANTHOLOGY OF DRAMA

Second Edition

SHORTER EDITION

THE NORTON ANTHOLOGY OF DRAMA

Second Edition

J. ELLEN GAINOR
CORNELL UNIVERSITY

STANTON B. GARNER JR.
UNIVERSITY OF TENNESSEE

MARTIN PUCHNER
HARVARD UNIVERSITY

SHORTER EDITION

W. W. NORTON & COMPANY

NEW YORK · LONDON

W. W. Norton & Company has been independent since its founding in 1923, when William Warder Norton and Mary D. Herter Norton first published lectures delivered at the People's Institute, the adult education division of New York City's Cooper Union. The firm soon expanded its program beyond the Institute, publishing books by celebrated academics from America and abroad. By midcentury, the two major pillars of Norton's publishing program— trade books and college texts—were firmly established. In the 1950s, the Norton family transferred control of the company to its employees, and today—with a staff of four hundred and a comparable number of trade, college, and professional titles published each year—W. W. Norton & Company stands as the largest and oldest publishing house owned wholly by its employees.

Since this page cannot accommodate all the copyright notices, Permissions Acknowledgments constitutes an extension of the copyright page.

Editor: Peter Simon
Assistant Editor: Quynh Do
Managing Editor, College: Marian Johnson
Project Editor: Linda Feldman
Electronic Media Editor: Eileen Connell
Marketing Manager, Literature: Kimberly Bowers
Production Manager: Benjamin Reynolds
Photo Editor: Nelson Colón
Permissions Manager: Megan Jackson
Permissions Clearing: Nancy Rodwan
Text Design: Rubina Yeh
Art Director: Trish Marx

Composition: Westchester Book Composition
Manufacturing: LSC Communications—Crawfordsville, IN

Library of Congress has catalogued the full edition as follows:

The Norton Anthology of Drama / [edited by] J. Ellen Gainor, Stanton B. Garner Jr., Martin Puchner. — Second edition.
    pages cm.
    Includes bibliographical references and index.
    ISBN 978-0-393-92151-9 (pbk., v. 1) – ISBN 978-0-393-92152-6 (pbk., v. 2)
    1. Drama—Collections. I. Gainor, J. Ellen, editor of compilation. II. Garner, Stanton B., 1955– editor of compilation. III. Puchner, H. Martin, editor of compilation.
    PN6112.N67 2014
    808.2—dc23

                                                                        2013013971

This edition:
ISBN: 978-0-393-92340-7 (pbk.)

W. W. Norton & Company, Inc., 500 Fifth Avenue, New York, NY 10110-0017
                                    wwnorton.com
W. W. Norton & Company Ltd., 15 Carlisle Street, London W1D 3BS

4   5   6   7   8   9   0

Contents

COLOR INSERT

*Plays in Performance: *Oedipus the King*
*Plays in Performance: *Everyman*
*Plays in Performance: *Hamlet*
*Plays in Performance: *Tartuffe*
*Plays in Performance: *Machinal*
*Plays in Performance: *A Streetcar Named Desire*
*Plays in Performance: *Angels in America, Part I*

Preface

DRAMA, one of the oldest of the arts, is also the most multifaceted. Grounded in the different mediums of writing and physical enactment, it offers pleasures both to the spectators of its theatrical realizations and to the solitary reader. In preparing the Shorter Second Edition of *The Norton Anthology of Drama*, the editors have remained mindful of this dual allegiance, and we have continued to follow our guiding principle that drama is at once a literary document, speaking to us across a vast expanse of time and space, and a live event, taking place in the here and now. Most of the plays collected here can be experienced in theaters today, or at least be seen in a filmed performance. But even those that are rarely performed in the contemporary era are presented in *The Norton Anthology of Drama* with considerable attention to their life on the stage.

With several new features—including a "Plays in Performance" section designed to enrich the student's understanding of plays in production—this second edition builds on the strengths that distinguish *The Norton Anthology of Drama* from other available drama anthologies. Its plays and their presentation reflect a commitment to the richness and internationality of the dramatic tradition and to the dialogues that mark dramatic performance across languages, borders, and periods.

Most anthologies organize their plays into historical and geographical units with such headings as "Greek Drama," "Renaissance Drama," and "Contemporary Drama." We, on the other hand, rely on chronology to organize our plays (using actual or estimated dates of first performance, and substituting publication or composition dates for those plays not originally written for performance or plays whose performance was significantly delayed). This decision reflects our belief that theater is historically and geographically more fluid than unit "boxes" imply. It also enhances flexibility of course development and organization—*The Norton Anthology of Drama* makes possible many different courses while mandating no specific approach. At the same time, those who desire a presentation of theatrical history that emphasizes historical periods and national traditions will find this structure in the anthology's Introduction.

In determining the table of contents for this anthology, the editors were guided by the desire to select the most thematically rich, performatively engaging, and pedagogically compelling plays available—plays that respond to the historical, cultural, literary, and theatrical contexts in which they were written in new, often groundbreaking, ways. The Shorter Second Edition continues to feature three masterpieces of the twentieth-century stage for which *The Norton Anthology of Drama* holds exclusive anthology publication rights. Two of these—Eugene O'Neill's *Long Day's Journey into Night* and Tennessee Williams's *A Streetcar Named Desire*—are numbered in the greatest plays from the modern American theater, while the third—Samuel Beckett's *Waiting for Godot*—is widely considered the century's most important and influential dramatic work. This last inclusion is particularly significant. Since its publication in 1952, Beckett's greatest play has been available in English only in editions from its American and British publishers. It had never before appeared in a general drama anthology prior to its publication in the first edition of *The Norton Anthology of Drama*, complete with annotation and critical introduction. Our presentation of twentieth-century drama is immeasurably enriched by its presence.

To ensure that reading classic plays written in languages other than English is a lively experience for students, we have selected vibrant translations that speak in a modern idiom while respecting the spirit and sense of the original. When no existing version satisfied us, we commissioned a new one. Whether commissioned specifically for *The Norton Anthology of Drama* or published previously, the translations in this anthology are all not only engaging and accessible on the page but also eminently performable.

In balancing the literary with the theatrical, we have designed an anthology that will work in both English and theater classrooms. For the instructor of dramatic literature courses at the introductory and advanced levels, the plays in *The Norton Anthology of Drama* reward textual attention of a literary kind while also encouraging analysis of the play's performance possibilities. For the theater instructor, the anthology provides theatrically vibrant texts in actable editions and translations. Students encountering drama for the first time will discover how powerfully the language of these plays comes alive on the tongue, and experienced and inexperienced students alike will find the versions here to be ideal for in-class performance as well as for line and scene reading. The

teaching of drama can be conducted through a range of classroom activities, and *The Norton Anthology of Drama* has been designed to facilitate as many as possible.

Those familiar with the first Shorter Edition of *The Norton Anthology of Drama* will notice a number of changes and additions to the second. In response to comments from our readers, we have chosen Euripides' *Medea* and Henrik Ibsen's *A Doll House* as representative plays by these dramatists, and we have replaced Harold Pinter's *Old Times* and Caryl Churchill's *The Number* with the more frequently requested selections *The Homecoming* and *Cloud Nine*. In addition to the indigenous North American playwright Daniel David Moses' 1991 play *Almighty Voice and His Wife*, which was recently revived to great acclaim in Canada, we have added Sophie Treadwell's 1928 play *Machinal*, which deepens the anthology's representation of plays written by women. All told, the Shorter Second Edition includes seven new plays.

Like the Norton anthologies of British, American, and world literatures; *The Norton Anthology of Theory and Criticism*; and the other anthologies with which Norton has shaped classroom teaching over the years, *The Norton Anthology of Drama* provides students and instructors with a wealth of introductory and editorial support. The substantial Introduction opens by exploring the relationship between dramatic literature and theatrical performance, and it concludes with a discussion of the challenges and opportunities of reading plays as scripts for performance. This final section—"Reading Drama, Imagining Theater"—is designed to give students approaching drama for the first time the tools they need to understand a uniquely hybrid form. The "Short History of Theater," which makes up the central part of the introduction, provides a detailed yet brisk overview of the political, social, and theatrical contexts within which drama has been embedded through the ages and across the globe.

We illustrate this history—and the headnotes that accompany each play—with vivid images of theaters, playwrights, actors, and audiences; manuscript pages, woodcuts, early printings, and other illustrations representing the importance of manuscript and print culture to the development and dissemination of drama; pictures from acting manuals; and other images related to theatrical production. The performance dimension of the plays included in this anthology is further enlivened by dozens of new headnote photographs of legendary or contemporary performances of the plays under discussion and by a new "Plays in Performance" feature, which highlights the issues involved in bringing seven classic plays to the contemporary stage. This color insert expands students' understanding of the complex decision-making that informs the production of a play, and it gives students a glimpse of the creative work performed by actors and directors as they reframe and reimagine plays onstage. It also includes examples of critical responses to the productions selected for discussion. We believe that this addition speaks to the theatrical life of plays with greater vibrancy and immediacy.

Supplemented by the substantial yet concise historical survey that opens the anthology, the headnotes that accompany each selection offer detailed, accessible introductions to the plays. These headnotes include summaries of the author's life and career, the specific historical and cultural contexts of the play in question, production information (where pertinent), and consideration of the play's importance in terms of its historical period and the broader history of drama and theater. The headnotes also include a discussion of the plays themselves, though we have taken care not to "explain" the plays to students, instead raising issues that will enable them to interpret the works on their own. For those interested in delving more deeply into the subject matter, we provide a carefully chosen and annotated bibliography of books and articles on each play and author. Throughout the headnote and bibliography, the editors have emphasized usefulness, readability, and student interest.

Similar care has been taken with the dramatic texts and their annotations. We have done everything possible to ensure that the texts in *The Norton Anthology of Drama* are the most authoritative ones available; if competing versions of these texts exist, we have selected the ones that are endorsed by contemporary scholarly consensus. In cases in which there is more than one version of a play—Marlowe's *Doctor Faustus* and Shaw's *Pygmalion*, for instance—we have selected the text that reflects the playwright's earliest theatrical vision. Our edition of *Hamlet*—a play with one of the most complicated and contested textual histories in world drama—is accompanied by a brief summary of that textual history, an overview of recent attempts to establish or resist an "authoritative" text, and a rationale for the version of the text included here. At the levels of selection and copyediting, we have devoted an exceptional amount of attention to ensuring that the text as it appears here is the most correct published version available.

Whereas other drama anthologies occasionally present historically and linguistically challenging plays without any annotations at all, *The Norton Anthology of Drama* provides footnotes and marginal glosses whenever an unfamiliar word, phrase, or historical/cultural reference risks interfering with a student's understanding of the text. We have tried to avoid cluttering plays with such material—we assume that students have access to a dictionary—but we have worked to annotate those words and references whose significance is obscured or hidden by historical remoteness. A number of our plays—including *Godot*—are annotated here for the first time, and we hope that even those plays that have been annotated before have been given a fresh presentation through our footnotes and marginal glosses.

Anthologies of drama, students and instructors have long agreed, are unwieldy affairs, encompassing as they do twenty-five centuries of drama in phone-book-size volumes. *The Norton Anthology of Drama*, by contrast, has been published in volumes that fit comfortably in the hand and on a lap, with the play-texts appearing on easy-to-read, single-column pages.

Finally, the many resources in *The Norton Anthology of Drama*—the Introduction, individual headnotes, bibliographies, and textual annotations—are complemented by resources outside the anthology itself. An Instructor's Manual by Zander Brietzke, written in consultation with the editors, provides valuable material for teaching both large survey courses and smaller lectures and seminars. This guide presents the most important topics that might be covered in a lecture on a given play; it also suggests creative classroom exercises for students who want to explore the complexities of a scene by performing it in class. Topics and exercises focus on particular passages and scenes, yet also cover larger themes, as do the handy paper topics provided for each play. Teachers will also find a list of prominent productions in this Instructor's Manual, along with a list of the best film adaptations that might be used in class or for further study. Of additional help is the second edition's improved companion website, wwnorton.com/drama, which provides students with a supplementary ebook reader containing texts exploring the criticism and theory of drama. For the present edition the editors have written short headnotes for these critical texts and annotated them where appropriate. Other resources on the extensive companion website offer students review materials, a comprehensive glossary of terms, and a guide to writing about drama.

Coming from performing arts and literature departments, the editors of *The Norton Anthology of Drama* bring the perspectives of these overlapping disciplines to dramatic history and performance and to the project of compiling a comprehensive anthology of dramatic literature. We have been aided in our efforts by a number of contributing editors, who have taken responsibilities for plays and playwrights that require special expertise. Numerous other scholars have lent knowledge and experience to this project—reading drafts of the headnotes and Introduction; clarifying points of fact and interpretation; providing nuance, when needed, to prevent historical overgeneralization; and helping us track down and identify historical images for the anthology. *The Norton Anthology of Drama*, in short, has been a deeply collaborative process, in which scholars from a number of areas have pooled their expertise to produce the most complete, informative, and engaging anthology of its kind.

Acknowledgments

A project of this magnitude cannot reach its final form without the help and encouragement of many people beyond those whose names appear on the book's cover. Given our appreciation of and love for the collaborative art of theater, we editors of *The Norton Anthology of Drama* are especially sensitive to the countless ways in which we have been helped and inspired by others.

CONTRIBUTING EDITORS

First, we would like to acknowledge the following scholars, who lent us their expertise by editing and introducing specific plays:

Dina Ahmed Amin (University of Cairo), *Song of Death*

Art Borreca (University of Iowa), *The Homecoming; Angels in America: Millennium Approaches*

Karen Brazell (late of Cornell University), *Atsumori*

Thomas Cartelli (Muhlenberg College), *The Tragical History of Doctor Faustus*

Ivo Kamps (University of Mississippi), *Hamlet; Twelfth Night*

Evan Darwin Winet (independent scholar, Berkeley, Ca.), *Snow in Midsummer*

Each of these scholars has played a critical role in making the anthology what it is, and we are grateful to have had the opportunity to collaborate with them.

TRANSLATORS

Some of the texts in *The Norton Anthology of Drama* are works in translation that were commissioned specifically for the anthology. We thank the following translator, whose skillful work has provided our readers with a new translation that is both readable and performable:

Constance Congdon (Amherst College), *Tartuffe*

We remain grateful to all those who offered support and assistance with the first edition of the anthology. We would like to acknowledge here the following people and institutions who provided us with advice, encouragement, administrative support, research assistance, and constructive critiques as we prepared the second edition: Andrew Bielski, Zander Brietzke, Amanda

Claybaugh, Kerri Ann Considine, Jerry Dickey, Mary Dzon, David, St. John and Loie Faulkner, Helene Foley, Mary Gainor, Alison Maerker Garner, Helen Elizabeth Garner, Amy Gillingham, Laura L. Howes, Rebecca Kastleman, Mechele Leon, Shilo McGiff, Meagan Michelson, Fred Muratori and the Reference and Interlibrary Loan Staff of Cornell University Libraries, Virginia H. Murphy, Sarah Powers Norman, Gregary Racz, Jeffrey Rusten, Sabine Sörgel, Victoria Swanson, Thomas Robert Travers, Judith Welch, Katherine Young, and the staff of the University of Tennessee Library Interlibrary Loan and Library Express departments.

The publisher and editors are grateful to all of the educators who responded to surveys, questionnaires, and review requests during the planning stages of both the first and second editions. The anthology continues to be a popular and useful text in large part because of the good suggestions offered by the following people: Michael Abbott, Mara Amster, Gordon S. Armstrong, Wendy Arons, M. G. Aune, Yashdip S. Bains, Beulah Baker, John I. Baker III, Margaret Ball, Claudia Barnett, Jane Barnette, Maria Beach, Keri Behre, Susan Bennett, Linda Ben-Zvi, Robin Bernstein, Scott Blanks, Dallas Boggs, Scott Boltwood, Kimberley A. Bouchard, Sandra M. Boynton, Adrienne Macki Braconi, Owen E. Brady, Kazimierz Braun, Sybil Brinberg, Chris Brooks, Sarah Bryant-Bertail, Jackson R. Bryer, Doug Buchanan, Matthew Buckley, Mike Burnett, Tom Butler, Ruth Cantrell, Anne Cattaneo, Dorothy Chansky, Renee Charlow, Nick Clary, Angus Cleghorn, Thomas F. Connolly, Kenneth Cox, Margaret Croskery, Marsha Cummins, Richard Cunningham, Keith Cushman, Koos Daley, Lynda Del Valle, William Demastes, Brian Desmond, Carlos Dews, Betty Diamond, Lyn Dohaney, Elizabeth Lee Dollar, Maria-Elena Doyle, Lofton Durham, Robert Duxbury, Bill Dynes, David W. Engel, Michael Erickson, Jay Farness, Anne Fearman, Mary Field, Phyllis Fields, Nancy Finn, Chris Fisher, Theresa Flowers, Terezinha Fonseca, Ivan Fuller, Valerie L. Gager, Donald P. Gagnon, Jure Gantar, Steven Gilbert, Gary Gisselman, Daniel Gonzalez, Rebecca Gorman, Fanni Green, Elissa Guralnick, Janet Haedicke, Paul Hansom, Jerry Harris, Kevin J. Harty, David Hay, Christopher Herr, Jessica Hillman, Woody Hood, David Hopes, D. J. Hopkins, Glenn Hopp, Elisabeth Schulz Hostetter, Helen M. Housley, Tonya Howe, Keith N. Hull, William Hutchings, Bill Jenkins, David Johnson, Peggy Rae Johnson, Walter H. Johnson, Mark Johnston, Greg Jones, P. Pennington Jones, Karen Rae Keck, Helen Killoran, Michael King, Matthew Kinservik, Cindy Kistenberg, Robert Knopf, Michael Kohler, David Kramer, David Kranes, Damon Kupper, James H. Lake, Penne J. Laubenthal, Lisa Leibering, Bruce Leland, Paul M. Levitt, John L'Heureux, Mark Lococo, Stanley V. Longman, Wayne Luckman, Thomas Luddy, William Luhr, Kevin M. Lynch, Bonnie Lyons, Sue Mach, William MacLennan, Philip Manwell, Deborah Martinson, Irene Martyniuk, Cary Mazer, Joseph McCadden, Adrienne McCormick, Janet E. McLean, Kirk Melnikoff, Lorraine Mercer, Naomi Miller, Lamata Mitchell, Kathleen Monahan, Deborah J. Montuori, Robert Moore, Annissa Morgensen-Lindsay, Jonathan Morse, Wayne Narey, Joan Navarre, Emmanuel N. Ngwang, Lance Norman, I. Nunnari, Kevin Oakes, Leslie O'Dell, Deirdre O'Leary, Pat Onion, Lary Opitz, Terry Otten, Howard Pearce, Todd Pettigrew, Jen Plants, Michael Pogach, Ann Price, Ray Pritchard, June Pulliam, Marjean D. Purinton, Jason Radalin, Paige Reynolds, Elise Robinson, Korey Rothman, Elizabeth Rowse, Gene Ruffini, Rebecca Rumbo, Neil Kristian Scharnick, Owen W. Schaub, Joel Schechter, Samuel T. Shanks, Johanna M. Smith, Mark Spergel, N. J. Stanley, Sally Story, William Streitberger, Sharon Sullivan, Sherman Sutherland, Wilbur Thomas, David Thompson, Dean Thompson, Jon Tuttle, Randolph Umberger, Mardi Valgemae, Martine Van Elk, Ronald Wainscott, Brian Warren, Albert Wertheim, J. Chris Westgate, Kevin Wetmore, David Wheeler, Lisa Whitney, Kayla Wiggins, Heather Williams, Don B. Wilmeth, Janet S. Wolf, Whitney Womack Smith, Leigh Woods, Joyce Wszalek, Kate Wulle, Trisha Yarbrough, Yvonne Yaw, Rick Yeatman, Mary Yost-Rushton, John T. Young, Kelly Younger, and Toby Zinman.

Thank you, one and all.

THE NORTON ANTHOLOGY OF DRAMA

Second Edition

SHORTER EDITION

Introduction

DRAMA AND THEATER

Audiences gather in a hillside amphitheater under the eastern Mediterranean sun to watch the impersonated figures of Greek myth play out their heroic, terrifying stories. In Kyoto, Japan, the sweep of robes on a railed wooden bridge announces the entry of a masked noh actor, who moves and gestures in front of his aristocratic audience with stylized precision. In London, a group of traveling players are given advice on acting by a Danish prince while the spectators who crowd the theater—aldermen, midwives, apprentices—enjoy the irony of actors meditating on their craft. In Paris, two tramps sitting by a tree on a country road share conversation and stage routines that barely conceal their anguish; an audience, seated in the dark, bears witness to their starkly contemporary situation.

The history of theater and dramatic performance is, in many ways, the history of moments such as these. The collaborative product of actors, playwrights, designers, directors, and spectators, theater achieves its magic in the live moment, rich with its sounds, sights, and feelings. The immediacy of the audience-stage encounter renders the act of theater-making magical and unique. Like other

art forms—such as novels, paintings, and movies—theater constructs imaginative worlds that we can marvel at, be moved by, and learn from. Unlike these other forms, however, theater puts its worlds into live motion, in real time. In a kind of alchemy, theater takes the realm of fiction and brings it to life with living beings whose interactions take place before our eyes. At the same time, it takes the experiences of everyday life and transforms them through the magic of performance into something more powerful, deeply felt, and artful than the daily exchanges we witness and participate in. The actor stands in for us, embodies our hopes and fears, boldly enacts what is forbidden or only dreamed of. And like the theater itself, the actor introduces us to the pleasures inherent in recognition, imitation, and the intensity of a life passionately observed and lived.

Theater is the art of the moment, and its ability to captivate us with its illusion is linked to its magical but always precarious sleight of hand. Theater is the most ephemeral of vehicles—a performance, once finished, is lost to time—and the unrepeatability of its accomplishments is a major source of its power. Unlike film, which fixes action in celluloid or other media, theater takes place in the actual, in the here and now that it shares with its spectators, and its illusions are inseparable from its precariousness. Not surprisingly, the most memorable playgoing experiences are often those when something goes wrong—a stage chair collapses, a piece of stage machinery fails, an understudy is rushed on during the middle of a performance when the main actor falls ill—and the carefully constructed dramatic illusion hangs in the balance.

Central to the act of theater-making is the dramatic text, play-text, or script, which serves as the fictional and narrative foundation of the theatrical event. Whether these texts are loosely sketched, as in the improvisational performances of the Renaissance commedia dell'arte, or highly detailed in plot, setting, characterization, and dialogue, the use of scripted narratives is one of the principal features distinguishing theater from other performance types. With the invention of writing, these texts became artworks in and of themselves, and drama assumed its place as the first "literary" form, no longer exclusively dependent on performance for its realization. Plays were available in manuscript form to the educated elite of ancient Greece and Rome; classical India, China, and Japan; and medieval Europe; and after the invention of the printing press in the fifteenth century, they became available to an expanding popular readership. The plays of WILLIAM SHAKESPEARE and TENNESSEE WILLIAMS share space on twenty-first-century bookstore shelves with the novels of Jane Austen and Cormac McCarthy. But the literary dimension of dramatic works remains inseparable from performance—actual, possible, historical, imagined—with the result that drama has different aims and reference points than do more exclusively literary forms. To read a novel is to project characters, actions, and locations within an imaginative realm that is guided and limited by the words on the page; it is to undertake a mental and emotional activity that resembles dreaming more than it does the actions we engage in daily. To read a play, in contrast, is to encounter a text whose primary purpose, with rare exceptions, is to make something happen in real space and time with actors whose bodies and voices are the drama's principal instruments. In this sense, a play resembles a symphonic score, whose printed notations are directions for the production of musical sound. Even those plays that we refer to as "closet dramas," which were usually not performed when written—whether because of political, technical, or cultural barriers or because their authors preferred them to be read or recited rather than subjected to the stage's inherent limitations—often seem to have been created with some ideal performance in mind.

As the final section of this introduction ("Reading Drama, Imagining Theater") will discuss in more detail, drama invites the reader to put her- or himself in the position of a theater artist, alive to the possibilities and choices that bring a play to life, imagining the different ways that a scene, line, or gesture might look, sound, and feel when performed. Being attentive to the conditions of performance allows one to appreciate the features that characterize drama as a literary and theatrical form: the necessary economy of its action, setting, and characterization, which are denied the leisure of novelistic description; the centrality of spoken language, which provides access to offstage and subjective worlds; and the preoccupation with questions of role-playing, impersonation, and the many ways in which we perform for the benefit of others and ourselves. In the absence of an omniscient narrator or other guiding authorial consciousness, drama emerges through the interplay of its characters, who enact their stories in the theater and on the imagined stage of one's reading. The power of these stories resides in the immediacy of the actors and their interactions with the theater environment, which of course includes the audience.

Humans have always told each other stories. From the earliest times for which we have physical or documentary evidence, we have acted our stories for each other. We donned costumes and masks, wielded props, and later created designated places—theaters—where we use the immediacy of live performance to communicate the powerful experiences that have

Spectators watch a performance of Anton Chekhov's *Three Sisters* at the Guthrie Theater in Minneapolis, 1963.

shaped us. Like other forms of organized social performance—games, festivities, storytelling, athletic displays, civic ceremonies, political events, and rituals— these encounters are deeply embedded in specific historical, social, and cultural contexts. To study the history of theater and drama is to confront a range of historical junctures, social and institutional practices, and cultural forms. It is also to encounter one of the most enduring of human activities: make-believe, the act of making oneself other than oneself for purposes of entertainment, commemoration, communication, or devotion.

Through performance and its rituals, we confirm our shared humanity—we acknowledge the importance of each other's existence and suggest that our lives are of value. Collectively, we generate forms of community while articulating the meanings that lend shape to our lives. The sense of communion and reciprocal awareness engendered by live performance, and the dramatic texts written for it, transcends cultures and history; it is foundational to who we are as living beings. As prehistoric cave paintings indicate, imitation and ritual were part of the earliest human societies. We are performers by nature. Although theater and drama are relative latecomers to human history (having been around for a mere 2,500 years), the activities they draw on are as old as humanity itself.

A SHORT HISTORY OF THEATER

The origins of theater—and hence of drama—have long been a subject of scholarly debate. We possess little material evidence concerning the development of theatrical activity in most cultures, and what generalizations we might draw from it are complicated by the fact that the earliest forms of theater were the product of a variety of social, political, and religious forces. However, those studying different dramatic traditions have found theater to be closely connected to hunting, fertility, and other rituals in those early societies where it emerged. The nature of this connection has been debated by scholars, but the consensus view is that theatrical activity represented an extension of ritual's symbolic forms of representation into nonritual contexts. The rituals of early societies involved the enactment of religious and mythic narratives by privileged participants—shaman, priest, ruler, sacrificial victim—and these performances could become quite elaborate. In Egypt, rituals commemorating the death and resurrection of Osiris, a god associated with fertility, took place at the sacred site of Abydos as early as 2500 B.C.E. Evidence suggests that the dramatic events of Osiris's life may have been performed by priests and that these performances were accompanied by lavish spectacle.

Ritual differs from theater, of course, in that its prescribed actions, passed down from generation to generation, are designed to effect change in the natural or spiritual worlds. The ritual performances of Egypt remained tied to their religious and dynastic functions and never developed in the direction of theater. In those cultures in which theater did emerge, symbolic performance asserted itself as an object of interest in its own right, thereby paving the way for institutions, practitioners, and audiences who conceived of theater as a communal artistic activity. The earliest of these transitions—and one of the most important for the subsequent history of theater and drama—occurred in Greece in the fifth century B.C.E.

Greek Theater

ORIGINS OF GREEK THEATER

The theater of classical Greece looms large in the history of Western theater. Not only did the emergence of theater as an institution in Athens during the fifth century B.C.E. establish the world's first theatrical culture, but the characters who confronted their fate on the Greek stage—Orestes, Oedipus, Antigone, Medea—remain among the most imposing characters in the dramatic repertoire. Yet despite the importance of Greek theater to the history of Western drama, little is known about its origins. Scholars have depended, for the most part, on the scattered remarks of later classical writers who were themselves speculating about events hundreds of years in the past. Archaeological findings, the history of words associated with the theater, and vase paintings have since provided additional hints as to how the first Greek theaters came into existence. Most scholars subscribe to the notion that the origins of Greek theater lie in religious rituals. Ancient Greek religious life included many different types of ceremonies and public performances: funeral services, festivals celebrating the seasons or individual gods, processions and competitions. But which of these performances provided the decisive impulse is much harder to pinpoint. The Greek word for tragedy, *tragōidia*, originally meant "goat song" and therefore seems to associate tragedy with ritual practices involving the killing of a goat. Other theories hold that theater emerged from rituals performed at the tombs of heroes.

Though we know little about either the goat song or the ritual performances at tombs, other cultural practices that aided the development of theater are much better documented. Among them are the public performances of storytellers, or *rhapsōidoi*, who recited stories of gods and mythical humans to large audiences. The first theorist of theater, the philosopher Plato (ca. 427–ca. 347 B.C.E.), emphasized the similarities between public recitations of epic poetry and simple dramatic performances. What is still the most convincing theory about the origin of Greek theater was developed by Aristotle (384–322 B.C.E.), who wrote a generation after his teacher Plato. Aristotle claimed that theater emerged from a specific ceremony honoring Dionysus, a god associated with fertility, agriculture, wine, and (by extension) physical and spiritual intoxication. During the Attic ceremony honoring him, a chorus and a chorus leader (*koryphaios*) sang and danced a hymn composed in a particular form known as the *dithyrambos*. According to Aristotle, these ritual performances formed the basis for later dramatic performance. The Greek language reinforces Aristotle's claim, for

This image, a detail from a *kylix* (a wine cup) painted by the so-called Brygos Painter in the early fifth century B.C.E., depicts a devotee (a *bacchante* or *maenad*) of the god Dionysus performing a ritualized dance. In her right hand is a *thrysus*, an ivy-covered staff that was an important part of sacred rituals.

the choral performers of dithyrambs were called *tragōidoi*, pointing once again to the later word for tragedy.

The association of theater with the dithyrambs performed in the honor of Dionysus makes sense for many reasons. The first Greek playwright, Thespis (sixth century B.C.E.), whose plays have all been lost, is credited with adding an individual performer to the dithyrambic chorus and chorus leader, and thus enabling dramatic interaction to emerge. Because Thespis himself is said to have performed this newly individual role, he is considered by many to be the world's first actor, and his name has given us the word *thespian*. From this point on the chorus (or chorus leader) was not limited to reciting a hymn but could impersonate an imaginary figure by engaging in a dialogue with the newly introduced actor. The Greek word for actor, *hypokritēs*, by the way, still exists in the English word *hypocrite*, whose now largely negative meaning underscores that acting involves imitation

and pretense. Subsequent playwrights added more actors to increase the possibilities for dialogue between individuals, although the chorus remained an important component of Greek, and subsequently of Roman, theater.

Another reason for associating theater with the Dionysian dithyrambs is that the first known Greek plays were performed at the City Dionysia, one of four Athenian festivals (another was the Rural Dionysia) held during the winter in honor of the god. Over the course of the fifth century B.C.E., when Greek theater was at its height, other festivals incorporated dramatic performances, but the City Dionysia remained the most important event for theater. The City Dionysia, which attracted many visitors from other city-states and from outside Greece, was a multiday affair, whose focus was various competitions. The first was a competition of dithyrambs, first organized around 600 B.C.E., among the four (later ten) "tribes" (*phylai*)—the administrative and military divisions to which all Athenian citizens belonged. Each tribe sponsored two choruses, one consisting of fifty men, the other of fifty boys. Although these dithyrambic performances centered on the worship of Dionysus, they soon included other gods and myths as well. As early as 534 B.C.E., when Thespis became the first recorded winner of the prize for tragedy, plays were added to the program. By the beginning of the fifth century B.C.E, a system was in place: each dramatist had to compose three tragedies, which were followed by the performance of a short satirical work (called a *satyr play*). Somewhat later, around 486 B.C.E., another type of drama was added: comedy. The City Dionysia held a competition among the different playwrights for first prize, an honor that helped spark the explosive growth in the number of plays written for the occasion and raising the status of theater more generally.

GREEK TRAGEDY

One development necessary for drama to emerge from these various rituals and performances was the invention of writing and the spread of literacy. Greek rituals did not include written scripts but were instead based on formulaic and orally transmitted incantations, hymns, and performances. Likewise, dithyrambic and epic poems were originally memorized and improvised by the performers, but not composed as literature. The first epics to be preserved in writing were those attributed to Homer (ca. 750–700 B.C.E.), the *Iliad* and the *Odyssey*; and in the late seventh century B.C.E., Arion (active 628–625 B.C.E.) was apparently the first to write down his own dithyrambs (none of which have survived). Consequently, Homer and Arion are considered by some to be the first tragedians, though they did not actually write plays.

The earliest extant tragedies all date from the fifth century B.C.E. and were written by three playwrights: Aeschylus (ca. 525–456 B.C.E.), SOPHOCLES (ca. 496–406 B.C.E.), and EURIPIDES (ca. 480–406 B.C.E.). These plays are set in a mythical past (with one exception—Aeschylus's *Persians*, which takes place during the Persian Wars), using the stories of gods and heroic humans that had been transmitted orally by the early epic poets and subsequently written down. Because Greek audiences already knew the broad outlines of the stories dramatized on the stage, they were able to notice and appreciate subtle differences in the treatments of given myths.

At the center of tragedy is a conflict that eventually results in the downfall of a larger-than-life character. The protagonists of tragedy are socially and morally elevated beings, and the destruction they undergo results, in part, from what Aristotle called *hamartia*; though the term has sometimes been translated as "tragic flaw," it is more accurately understood as referring to a mistaken action or error of judgment. That tragic protagonists bear responsibility for their fate does not mean that they deserve the destruction inflicted on them, however, for their fate is also determined by forces, circumstances, and dilemmas outside their control. For example, while the decision of Antigone (in Sophocles' play of the same name) to bury her brother Polyneices follows the religious imperative, obeying that imperative brings her into conflict with her uncle Creon, the king of Thebes, who has declared him a traitor and therefore has forbidden his burial. Faced with this set of forces not of her making—one, a social and religious mandate; the other, a legal prohibition—Antigone has no alternative but to choose her tragic fate. Similarly, the protagonist of Sophocles' OEDIPUS THE KING (ca. 428 B.C.E.), who unknowingly killed his father and married his mother, must accept punishment for deeds performed not with malicious intent but with an overweening pride and belief in his own invulnerability. Ironically, the man of action and the solver of the Sphinx's riddle proves rash in his actions and blind to fate's riddle in his own life. Virtues and flaws, the notion of *hamartia* may also suggest, are intimately tied up in each other: we can trust our talents and strengths too much and learn, in the outcome of our actions, that they are both the reason for our good fortune and the cause of our demise.

As these tragic conflicts unfold, the protagonists find themselves in another contentious relation, namely with the chorus. Not surprisingly, given its origins in choral dithyrambs, tragedy retained the chorus as an important element. Reflecting the perspective of the community, this body observes and comments on the actions and entanglements of the protagonists, trying to rein in their excesses and restore order to the civic realm. The chorus also reminds the audience of the background story of a given myth and often engages the protagonists in a dialogue that draws out the motives of their actions. In keeping with the evolving nature of Greek tragedy during the fifth century B.C.E., the role of the chorus underwent changes. As dramatic characters grew in number, complexity, and importance, the role of the chorus lessened.

The complexity of the relations between individual actors and the chorus shaped the typical structure of Greek tragedy. Greek tragedies begin either with a prologue that sets the scene or with the entrance—*parodos*—of the chorus. The main body of the tragedy is then composed of a sequence of episodes—*epeisodia*, scenes in which the main actors talk to one another or to the chorus—and choral songs without dialogue, *stasima*. At the end of the play, the characters and the chorus leave the stage in what is called the *exodos*. Greek tragedy, in other words, was a highly structured and formalized art form in which dialogue between two individual actors, today the main component of drama, was relatively unimportant. Instead, choral lyrics and the dialogue between chorus and protagonist took up most of the play. Playwrights used different styles of language and meter to distinguish between the different sections of tragedy. Choral lyrics were a form of poetry highly elevated in diction and intricately composed, while the exchanges between the chorus and individual characters, though still quite stylized, were more conversational. The dialogues in iambic meter between the individual characters, though they too were artfully wrought, were closer still to everyday speech. Such differentiation can clearly be seen in the works of Euripides, who, writing slightly later than Aeschylus and Sophocles, attempted to bring the language of tragedy nearer to the language actually spoken by the audience.

As noted above, in its mature form the City Dionysia included a competition in

This detail from the so-called Pronomos Vase, painted in the late fifth century B.C.E., depicts actors preparing for a satyr play.

which each dramatist presented three tragedies followed by a satyr play. Unfortunately, because only one complete satyr play has survived—Euripides' *Cyclops*—it is difficult to generalize about the genre. The plays seem to have dealt with the same mythical and heroic figures and stories as tragedies but irreverently, as burlesque. Accordingly, their language was apparently more colloquial than that of tragedy. The satyr play remained closely connected to Dionysus, for in Greek mythology satyrs were half-human and half-bestial creatures who formed part of his retinue, and the leader of the chorus in satyr plays was Silenus, a satyr who was a constant companion of the god. The satyr play provided the audience with comic relief at the end of a daylong performance of tragedies.

GREEK COMEDY

The satyr play, despite its comic elements, belonged to a genre distinct from comedy. Although comedies had not originally been part of festival competitions, they were incorporated into the City Dionysia festival around 486 B.C.E. The origins of comedy also lie in ritual, most likely in rites that featured groups of men wearing representations of large *phalloi* (male sexual organs) and animal masks. A second source for Greek comedy was a form of mime—short, improvised sketches treating everyday situations humorously. These foundations are visible in what is called Old Comedy, which developed in the fifth century B.C.E.; its only remaining examples are the plays of ARISTOPHANES (ca. 450–ca. 385 B.C.E.), although the names of other comic playwrights are known to us, including Magnes (active 472 B.C.E.) and Aristophanes' main rival, Eupolis (ca. 445–ca. 411 B.C.E.). The choruses of comedy may well represent animals or inanimate objects—Aristophanes' plays have such titles as *The Frogs*, *The Wasps*, and *The Clouds*—and they often treat explicitly sexual themes. In contrast to both tragedy and the satyr play, comedies take as their subject matter not the gods and heroes of Greek mythology but rather the everyday life of contemporary Athenians, and the topics they engage range from the long Peloponnesian War with Sparta (which provides the background to *LYSISTRATA* [411 B.C.E.], Aristophanes' best-known play) to public personalities such as the philosopher Socrates. Like tragedy, Old Comedy begins with a prologue, which is followed by the entry of the chorus; it contains passages of dialogue; and it concludes with the exit of all the characters. It also features an added element: a section called the *parabasis* (literally, "digression") in which the chorus addresses the audience directly, discussing political and social problems and sometimes praising the playwright. In the *parabasis* and throughout each play, classical comedy engages with political and social issues much more directly than tragedy, although it does so comically, drawing on fantasy, humor that frequently is ribald, and farce.

THE GREEK STAGE

The main performance venue for Athenian theater was the Dionysus theater, located in the hill just below the Acropolis, an elevated area on which stood the Parthenon and which served as the city's religious and political center. Given the elaborate nature of later Greek and Roman theaters, the Dionysus theater in the fifth century B.C.E. was surprisingly simple. A large *amphitheatron*, holding between 14,000 to 17,000 audience members, was built into the hillside, with seating provided by temporary wooden benches. At the center of the amphitheater was the *orchēstra* (or "dancing place"), a semicircle in whose middle stood the *thymelē*, a raised stone used as an altar or a table. Behind the *orchēstra* stood a wooden structure, the *skēnē*, which served as a place where actors could change masks and costumes and, through one or more doors, appear and disappear from the stage. The area in front of the *skēnē* would later be known as the *paraskēnion*, a term from which the modern word *proscenium* derives. On either side of the *skēnē* were passageways.

This physical arrangement was used by the Greek dramatists in increasingly complex ways. The passageways aided the elaborate entrances and exits of the chorus, while the *orchēstra* was the place where the dances performed by the chorus and the interaction between chorus and individual actors took place. The altar or table could be used by individual actors to hide and suddenly appear. The *skēnē* at the back of the performance area provided even more theatrical possibilities. For example, playwrights placed messengers and other figures on its roof, where they could be on the lookout and describe battles and other scenes they pretended to see on its other side (a stage device called *teichoskopeia*, or "watching from a wall"). The doors in the *skēnē* were used not only to aid entrances and exits but also to suddenly reveal characters. To heighten the effect of the doors, a rolling platform, or *ekkyklēma*, was employed to roll the body of a killed character in front of the audience or to make other dramatic disclosures. Such a device was especially important since almost all physical violence—the blinding of Oedipus, for example, or Medea's murder of her children—occurred offstage, often (the audience was led to believe) within the scene building. A second mechanism became increasingly popular: a crane called a *mēchanē*, which could move characters through the air into the space in front of the scene building. Euripides, in particular, used such cranes to introduce gods, who would resolve the plot and mete out punishment at the end of his tragedies; this device became well-known by its Latin name, *deus ex machina* (god from a machine). Various forms of painted panels were probably employed on the stage as well, though little is known about their appearance and function.

Because theater was an integral part of civic and religious festivals, an elaborate system of rules and practices governed the production of plays. A leading figure of the Athenian government, an *archōn eponymos*, selected from among the wealthy citizens a *chorēgos*, or producer, who would provide the funds for the chorus, while the city government provided the funds for the playwright and the leading actors.

The playwrights were responsible for rehearsals and sometimes even performed in their own plays. The number of performers was strictly limited. The chorus probably contained twelve to fifteen members, although as many as fifty may have appeared in some early plays of Aeschylus. The number of individual actors was even more crucial, because it directly affected how many characters were available to the playwright. Aeschylus's early plays used two actors, who could take on different roles over the course of a play—but obviously, no more than two speaking parts could be present simultaneously. Either Aeschylus or, more likely, his younger rival Sophocles took the decisive step of introducing a third actor, thereby expanding the playwright's options considerably.

One reason why actors could change so easily from one role to the next was the relative simplicity of their costumes. A thick, richly colored garment covered their bodies; large, high boots made them appear larger than life; and a mask made from either fabric or wood covered their entire face. Given the size of the theater and the bulkiness of their costumes, the actors had

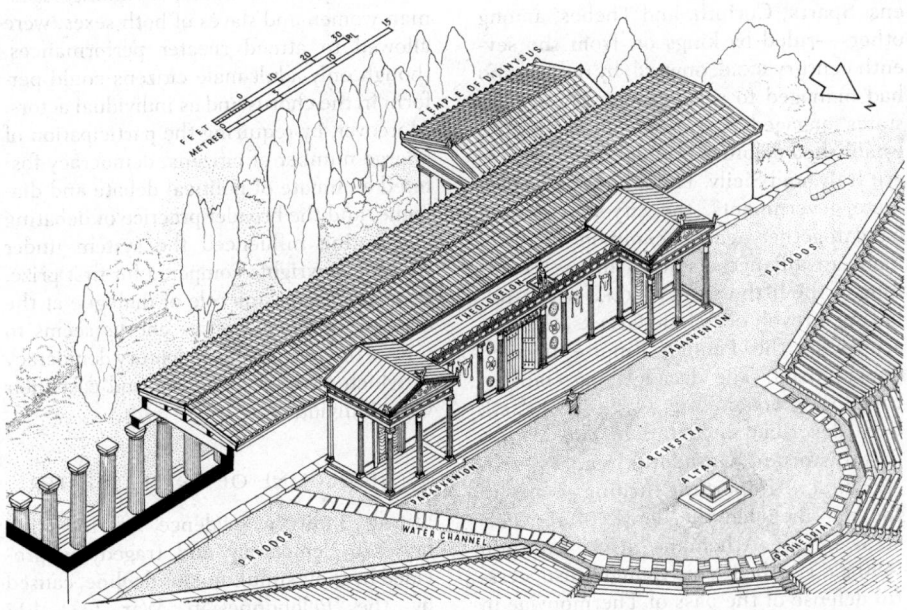

A reconstruction of the Dionysus theater by the theater and architectural scholar Richard Leacroft. An actor stands in the *orchēstra*, while another stands on the roof of the *skēnē*.

to rely on large gestures rather than on small, intimate reactions, and in masks they lacked any recourse to facial expressions. Scenes of dialogue alternated with the elaborate dances of the chorus. The performance of Greek plays was accompanied by music, provided mainly by the flute—it was a flute player who led the entrance of the chorus at the beginning of the play—but various other wind and percussion instruments were employed as well. Today's audiences and readers can easily overlook the significance of music, which is generally little used in contemporary revivals of Greek plays, but the scholars and artists who attempted to revive Greek tragedy during the European Renaissance were very conscious of its importance. Indeed, this awareness led to the creation of opera, a form of theater that relies primarily on music and song and only secondarily on spoken dialogue.

THEATER AND ATHENIAN DEMOCRACY

The emergence and rise of Greek theater is intimately tied to the political history of Greece. Greece was not a unified nation but rather a network of city-states—Athens, Sparta, Corinth, and Thebes, among others—ruled by kings or, from the seventh century B.C.E. onward, by nobles who had managed to seize power. These city-states engaged in various alliances and established colonies in Asia Minor, southern Italy, and Sicily. Though they had separate governments, the city-states could band together against common enemies. Such an alliance occurred in the beginning of the fifth century B.C.E., when, following a revolt of Asiatic Greeks, the vast armies of the Persian Empire invaded Greece itself. The decades-long conflict, called the Persian Wars (499–449 B.C.E.), were described in detail by the world's first historian, Herodotus (ca. 484–ca. 425 B.C.E.). Important turning points in the war included the defeat of the Persians by the Athenians near Marathon (490 B.C.E.), the heroic though unsuccessful defense of the pass of Thermopylae in central Greece by a small Spartan force (480 B.C.E.), and the destruction of the Persian fleet by Athens at Salamis (480

B.C.E.), a battle that was critical to Persia's subsequent defeat.

The crucial role of Athens in winning this victory led to its increasing dominance over the rest of Greece, and it built a largely seaborne empire consisting of allies, dependent states, and colonies. It was during this time of military dominance that Athens became a cosmopolitan center for the arts—the birthplace of Greek theater and the center of many other intellectual and cultural pursuits, such as philosophy (although many philosophers living in Athens were foreign-born). Equally important was the development in Athens of an early form of democracy that involved all adult male citizens in the governance of the Athenian empire, serving in the courts, military offices, and other administrative posts. Women, slaves, and foreigners, it is important to note, were not considered citizens. Moreover, though it was a predecessor of modern democracies, Athenian democracy included many features that might strike today's citizens as odd, such as the choosing of important positions by lot (to avoid favoritism). Many scholars consider the rise of Athenian theater and of democracy to be related developments. It is likely that most of the city's inhabitants, including Athenian women and slaves of both sexes, were allowed to attend theater performances, though only adult male citizens could perform in the chorus and as individual actors. Moreover, by requiring the participation of a large number of citizens, democracy fostered a climate of political debate and dialogue, and the broader practice of debating and voting influenced the system under which playwrights competed for first prize. Even the increasing role of dialogue at the expense of the collective chorus seems to mirror the rise of a participatory democracy in which citizens speak out and cast their votes individually.

THE DECLINE OF GREEK THEATER

Strong indirect evidence of the link between democracy and tragedy is provided by their simultaneous decline, caused by the Peloponnesian War (431–404 B.C.E.)—the long conflict between Athens and Sparta described by the Athenian historian Thucydides (ca. 455–ca. 400 B.C.E.).

The ruins of the theater at Epidaurus, Greece. The theater was built in the middle of the fourth century B.C.E.

By the war's end, Athens had lost its empire and, at least temporarily, its democracy. Though Greek theater continued to develop—chiefly through the emergence, in the following century, of New Comedy, whose main practitioner was the playwright Menander (ca. 342–ca. 292 B.C.E.) and whose plays depended much less on fantastic plots and conceits than had their Old Comedy predecessors—by the end of the fifth century B.C.E. the most important era of Greek theater had come to an end.

GREEK THEORIES OF DRAMA

The fourth century B.C.E.'s contribution to theater history was the work of two authors who together provided the first written theories of drama: Plato and Aristotle. Though Plato did not take up the subject separately, his philosophy as a whole is deeply engaged with the theater as medium and institution. All of his works were written as dialogues, and although there is no evidence of their performance before large audiences, they may have been recited by students in his Academy, the school that he founded (which took its name from its site, a park sacred to the legendary hero Academus). In these dialogues, Plato—or, more precisely, his main character, Socrates—is often critical of tragedy and comedy as well as of actors, arguing that drama and other works of art offer mere representations of the world and therefore stand in the way of the pursuit of truth, which consists of

knowledge of the things themselves. Drawn to the exchange of ideas but suspicious of the seductions of theatrical performance, Plato offered his own philosophical dialogues as an alternative form of drama.

Plato's student Aristotle, by contrast, devoted an entire treatise to the subject of tragedy, describing its classifications, elements, and structure and examining its effect on spectators. In his widely influential *Poetics*, probably composed around 330 B.C.E., Aristotle discusses the origin of tragedy in dithyrambic hymns, the nature of the heroic protagonist, the function of the chorus, and what he considers to be the six crucial elements of theater: plot, character, thought, diction, music, and spectacle (the last is accorded a marginal position in his descriptive hierarchy). He also emphasizes certain plot elements, such as sudden reversals (*peripeteiai*) and the moment of recognition (*anagnōrisis*), and insists that unlike epic poetry, with its meandering plots, tragedy should present a single, unified action. This focus mandates that the action of tragedy be confined to short periods of time, typically one day, and to a single place. Renaissance commentators on the *Poetics* turned these recommendations into the three unities—of time, place, and action—that, according to the strictures of what became known as neoclassical theory, must be maintained by playwrights.

In response to Plato's attack on theatrical representation, Aristotle defended actors by arguing that the drive to imitate, *mimēsis*, was a common human trait and served as a source of pleasure. Perhaps the most influential term introduced in this treatise was *katharsis*, the purging or cleansing of emotions that was the desired effect of tragedy on the audience. Whereas Plato had argued that the extreme emotions depicted in tragedy could have adverse effects on the audience and therefore recommended that playwrights, like other artists, be banished from his ideal republic, Aristotle held that tragedy provided a release, a *katharsis*, of those stirred-up emotions—particularly fear and pity—and that dramatic art thus served a socially therapeutic function. The disagreement between Plato and Aristotle about the value of theater, the reaction of the audience, and the status of actors has persisted to the present—in our debates, for instance, about depictions of violence onstage and on the screen. Much as the playwrights of the fifth century B.C.E. have continued to influence theater history, so the philosophers of the fourth century still shape our thinking about theater.

Roman Theater

The decline of Athens, which at its height had dependent colonies in Italy (where Greeks from several city-states had settled

as early as the eighth century B.C.E.), coincided with the rise and expanding influence of Rome. By the middle of the third century B.C.E., the city-state of Rome had managed to unify most of Italy under its leadership, and its victory over its North African rival, Carthage, in the First Punic War (264–241 B.C.E.) enabled Rome to extend its hegemony over Sicily as well as parts of Greece itself. One hundred years later, Rome had absorbed the entire Greek world, on its way to becoming one of the largest empires ever created.

Even though Rome was a rising military power, its art, literature, philosophy, and theater remained heavily influenced by those of Greece. Like Greek theater, Roman theater was performed in the context of civic festivals, here called *ludi*, which by 240 B.C.E. included both tragedies and comedies. The most important of these festivals were the *Ludi Romani*, which honored not Dionysus (or his Roman counterpart, Bacchus) but Jupiter, chief of the gods. This and other festivities differed from their Greek counterparts in significant ways. Influenced by the earlier performance practices of the Etruscans, who belonged to an earlier civilization (centered in present-day Tuscany and part of Umbria) that reached its height in the sixth century B.C.E., the festivities of early Rome included

Roman masks—one tragic, one comic—as depicted in a wall mosaic from the first century B.C.E.

a variety of nondramatic entertainments—chariot races, prizefighting, dance, farce—that vied with dramatic performance for the spectators' attention. Relatively few early Roman tragedies and comedies survive, although it is clear that most were adaptations of existing Greek plays, which were introduced to Rome in 240 B.C.E. The first known dramatists in Rome, Livius Andronicus (ca. 284–ca. 204 B.C.E.) and Gnaeus Naevius (ca. 270–201 B.C.E.), adapted both Greek tragedies and comedies into Latin, while later playwrights, including the tragedians Quintus Ennius (239–169 B.C.E.) and Lucius Accius (170–ca. 86 B.C.E.), specialized in one or the other genre. Even though Roman tragedies were mostly versions of Greek ones, Roman playwrights introduced considerable alterations, changes, and innovations; far from being a sign of unoriginality, adaptation thus became a special art form. Whereas the Greek playwrights had used known stories and characters in composing their plays, Roman playwrights perfected a more elaborate technique of imitation by working from established dramatic models.

ROMAN COMEDY

Though both tragedies and comedies were performed in Roman theaters, comedy was the genre in which Roman playwrights excelled. Roman comedians could look back at a long tradition of farce, and they drew especially on Atellan farce, a burlesque form based on improvisation and a small set of stock characters that took its name from Atella, a town near Naples in southern Italy. These improvised sketches and stock characters remained popular throughout the history of Rome and beyond, influencing such later theater traditions as Italy's commedia dell'arte. At the same time, a more literary form of comedy, based on Greek Old and New Comedy, was developing. The two most famous Roman playwrights—Titus Maccius Plautus (ca. 254–ca. 184 B.C.E.) and Terence (Publius Terentius Afer, ca. 190–159 B.C.E.)—were authors of such comedies. The most important changes Plautus and Terence made to their Greek models were eliminating the chorus and significantly expanding the use of music, thereby turning their comedies into a kind of musical theater.

EMPIRE AND SPECTACLE

The height of Roman drama, as represented by Plautus and Terence, occurred under the Roman Republic, a political system that allowed a limited number of citizens to participate in government and prevented any single individual from gaining supreme power. It was under the Republic that Rome established its dominance through the Second Punic War with Carthage (218–201

This detail from a Roman mosaic depicts a *venation*—a battle between a leopard and a gladiator.

B.C.E.) and finally defeated and destroyed Carthage in 146 B.C.E. at the end of the Third Punic War (149–146 B.C.E.). Rome now dominated not only Italy and Greece but also large parts of northern Africa. The resulting flow of wealth and power to Rome increasingly undermined republican institutions, and the Republic gave way to an empire with an absolute ruler. Under the emperors—beginning with Augustus (63 B.C.E.–14 C.E.)—Rome expanded its empire as far as England, Germany, France, Spain, and the Balkans and controlled the entire Mediterranean basin.

The increasing scale of the Roman Empire, and the unheard-of concentration of wealth and power in Rome itself, fueled a tendency toward expensive and lavish spectacles, comparable perhaps to blockbuster Hollywood action films today. These non-dramatic varieties of performance, most of them significantly more spectacular than anything seen on the dramatic stage, came to overshadow tragedy and comedy. Among these new public entertainments were chariot races held in sizable arenas, the largest of which, the Circus Maximus in Rome, accommodated more than 60,000 spectators. Other spectacles included elaborately orchestrated, and often lethal, sea battles, which sometimes involved thousands of participants; contests called *venationes,* in which wild animals fought against one another or against humans; and of course the most emblematic and notorious of Roman spectacles—gladiatorial contests, which featured hand-to-hand combat to the death. Although their appetite for staged (but real) violence was voracious, Romans weren't entirely bloodthirsty in their entertainment preferences; pantomime and short comic sketches of mime performances were also very popular.

CLOSET TRAGEDY

The overwhelming popularity of nondramatic entertainments led to a decline of traditional dramatic forms, especially tragedy and comedy. Writers with literary ambitions therefore began to create "closet dramas," plays designed to be recited at small, private gatherings or to be read in private. In fact, the most famous Roman tragic dramatist, Lucius Annaeus Seneca (4 B.C.E.–65 C.E.), wrote only closet dramas, and his plays were never performed on the great Roman stages of the time. Modeled on Greek tragedy, Seneca's tragedies are composed in an intricate, literary Latin that became a model for many subsequent writers. That these dramas were not written to be performed did not make them less violent. Indeed, unlike Greek tragedy, which had hidden most of its violence offstage, Seneca required that the audience or readers envision it as happening in their "sight." Though few in his own time would have known of his plays, they proved enormously influential on later playwrights, including the Elizabethan playwrights Thomas Kyd and WILLIAM SHAKESPEARE.

THE ROMAN STAGE

Although plays had been written in Latin since the third century B.C.E., the first permanent theater—erected at Pompeii—was not built until 55 B.C.E. Before that time, temporary stages (often quite stable and elaborate) were used for dramatic and other performances. Modeled on their Greek predecessors, Roman theaters included large amphitheaters for the audience; these could be built into hills, like Greek theaters, or erected on level ground. The amphitheater formed a semicircle similar to the Greek *orchēstra,* which was closed on one side by a building, the *scaena,* which was the counterpart of the Greek *skēnē.* In their adaptation from one society to another, however, the function and proportions of these elements changed significantly. For example, the *orchēstra* was used by the chorus, but its Roman equivalent was occupied—as it is in today's theaters—by the most privileged of the audience members. The action of the play took place on a raised stage, or *pulpitum,* located in front of the scene building, which was significantly larger and more elaborate than its Greek predecessor. Supported by several sets of columns and often ornately decorated, the scene building could be many stories high—a change that had profound implications. Unlike the audience of Greek theater, whose view of the stage was framed by landscape and sky, the Roman audience looked entirely at the artificial world created on a stage.

A digital reconstruction of the interior of the theater of Pompey in Rome. This image—based on a collaborative research project by Richard Beacham, James E. Packer, and John Burge—was generated by the King's Visualization Lab and is copyright © King's College London.

Even as playwrights such as Seneca withdrew from the stage, the Roman taste for spectacle—races, parades, festivals, and staged battles—led to the development of elaborate stage machinery. Roman theater producers not only instituted the stage curtain but also invented sliding panels, cranes, and a type of elevator with which actors or animals could be lifted onto the stage from below. They also introduced more complex, three-dimensional stage decorations, extensive stage props, and even live animals. The actors, called *histriones* in Latin, were not, as had originally been the case in Greece, talented citizen amateurs; instead, they were theater professionals, some of whom were slaves. Their acting style ranged from burlesque and conversational for comedy to more formal and declamatory for tragedy. Costumes and masks were mostly fashioned on Greek models.

THE DECLINE AND INFLUENCE OF ROMAN THEATER

Roman theater declined significantly with the rise of Christianity, which won official toleration in 313 C.E. when the emperor Constantine I issued the Edict of Milan; it soon became the dominant religion in the Roman Empire. Christian clergy were highly critical of theater and in particular its actors, declaring the attendance of theater cause for excommunication and denying actors the holy sacraments (a practice that remained in place in some parts of Europe well into the modern era). Yet despite the theater's waning under Christianity, the influence of classical theater would reverberate through the centuries. The architecture of Roman theater buildings helped shape Renaissance stage design, for example, and Roman comedy and tragedy were important models for English Renaissance playwrights, who often knew of Greek works only through their Roman adaptations and translations. Equally vital for Renaissance theater was Rome's most significant critic, the poet Quintus Horatius Flaccus, known as Horace (65–8 B.C.E.), whose *Ars Poetica* (*The Art of Poetry* [ca. 10 B.C.E.]) discusses the origins, forms, and ends of drama. Recommending such formal practices as the division of plays into five acts, Horace also offered a powerfully moral conception of drama's function. Not only should playwrights cater to their audiences, he asserted, they should also serve as moral instructors: their works, in other words, should prove useful (*utile*) as well as pleasing (*dulce*). In keeping with this conception of theater's social role, he argued against the more fantastic, spectacular, and violent aspects of Roman theater. Like those of Aristotle, his views on drama were taken up by later theorists of drama and theater.

Although Roman theater was in many ways derivative, the influence of its drama, architecture, and practice on subsequent theater history was even greater than that of its Greek predecessor and model. The plays of Plautus, Terence, and Seneca inspired the work of later playwrights, and Roman theater technology—much of it described in *De Architectura* (*On Architecture*), written in the first century B.C.E. by the architect and engineer Vitruvius—made important contributions to theater design during the European Renaissance. One of the most lasting legacies of Roman theater may be the division it opened up between drama as a literary genre and stage as a site of spectacle. In later centuries, in the great ages of world theater, drama and theater have often worked hand in hand; but at times they have become estranged, leading to forms of literary drama disconnected from a theater system mainly interested in extravagant spectacle. To the extent that this division still informs our theater today—when, for example, lavish Broadway spectacles divert attention from serious plays—we are still in the process of working through the inheritance of Roman theater.

Classical Indian Theater

During the millennium after Greece and Rome established the outlines of European theatrical culture, the foundations were being laid for separate traditions in Asia. The earliest, and arguably the most influential, form of Asian theater emerged in India, home to one of the world's oldest civilizations. By 2500 B.C.E. the Indus Valley civilization had introduced city-states and a technologically advanced agricultural society in northwestern and western India. Its decline was caused in part by internal weakness and in part by the incursions of the Aryans, a nomadic people from northern Iran or central Asia. By 1500 B.C.E., the Indian subcontinent had been settled by the Aryans, who developed the Vedic civilization that would subsequently shape Indian history and culture. Central to this culture were the Vedas, or scriptures, that constituted the founding texts of Hinduism (the earliest of these, the *Rig-Veda*, was composed between 1500 and 1000 B.C.E.). Written in Sanskrit, these texts inspired a number of further writings; among them were two epic poems, the *Mahabharata* and the *Ramayana* (both written between 500 and 200 B.C.E.), which exerted a vast influence on later literature and theater in India and Southeast Asia. The Aryans also introduced the system of caste, or social stratification, that divided Indian society into four groups: priests, warriors and rulers, traders and merchants, and workers and peasants. The caste system, which provided the social framework of classical Indian drama and the audience that attended it, remains influential in today's India despite laws mandating equality of treatment for all members of society.

ORIGINS OF INDIAN THEATER

The scarcity of available historical evidence prevents us from knowing much about the origins of Indian, or Sanskrit, theater. In some Vedic rituals priests performed symbolic gestures, and these actions occasionally involved impersonating a represented figure, but it is impossible to tell whether these rites were the seeds of a more purely theatrical tradition. The *Mahabharata* makes references to performers (*nata*), though it is not known if actors were among them. Unlike Greece, India has no surviving theater structures from this period. The earliest plays extant, which date from the first century C.E., display a sophistication that suggests a long period of prior development, but there is no way of determining when a literary theater was first established. What evidence we do have concerning the Sanskrit theater comes from the plays that have survived from later centuries and from the *Natyasastra* (*The Art of Theater*), a compendious treatise on the nature and purpose of dramatic performance ascribed to Bharata Muni and written sometime between 300 B.C.E. and 200 C.E. Longer and more detailed than Aristotle's *Poetics*, the *Natyasastra* includes information concerning acting, theater and stage structures, theater organization, music, dance, playwriting, and aesthetics.

AUDIENCE, PLAYHOUSE, AND ACTORS

Theatrical performances during the classical age of Sanskrit theater (100–900 C.E.) apparently were offered on occasions ranging from sacred festivals to the coronation of kings, marriages, births, or the return of travelers. Although Bharata writes that the ideal spectator for such performances was learned and of high birth, members of all four castes (seated separately) seem to have attended. The *Natyasastra* describes three types of playhouses (square, triangular, and rectangular) and three sizes that these buildings could assume (small, medium-sized, and large), but focuses mainly on a rectangular building measuring 96 by 48 feet. Such a playhouse should resemble a cave, so that the actors' voices would resonate. Its interior was divided into two equal areas, with one half (called the *prekshagriha*) devoted to seating an audience that would have probably included no more than 500 spectators. The other half was itself divided in two: its back half (the *nepathya*) served as a backstage and dressing room,

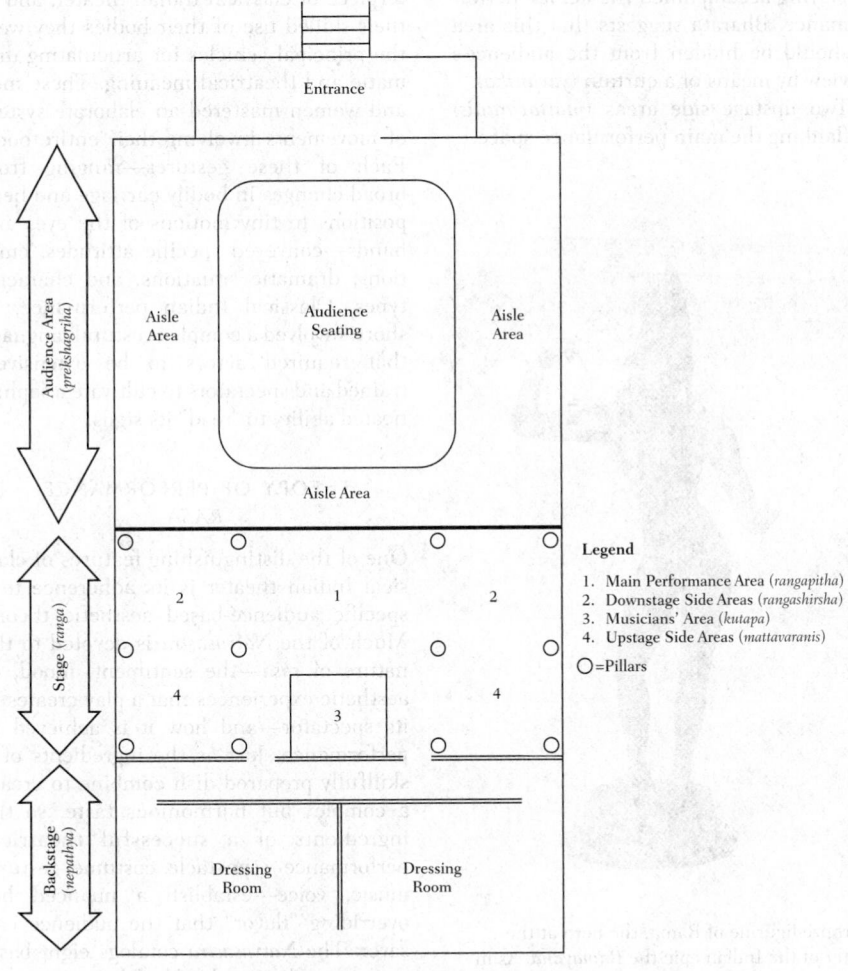

The Classical Indian Stage

A diagram of the Sanskrit stage, based on descriptions in the *Natyasastra* by Bharata.

and its front half (the *ranga*) represented the performance area. The performance area, in turn, contained a number of distinct zones:

1. The main performance space (*rangapitha*) at the center of the stage.
2. The upstage area (*rangashirsha*), which stretched across the width of the performance space, between the back wall and the front performance area. Demarcating the back of this area was an ornamented curtain, possibly held by two attendants, with two openings, one for entrances and the other for exits.
3. The space between these openings (the *kutapa*), an area for musicians, whose playing accompanied the actors' performance. Bharata suggests that this area should be hidden from the audience's view by means of a curtain (*yavanika*).
4. Two upstage side areas (*mattavaranis*) flanking the main performance space.

A bronze figurine of Rama, the hero at the center of the Indian epic the *Ramayana*. As in performance, the gestures and attitudes portrayed in Indian sculpture are highly stylized.

These separate but contiguous acting areas made possible the fluid narrative structure of Sanskrit drama, in which dramatic action shifts between different locations and events and encounters can be staged simultaneously.

Apart from general decorations, which could serve a symbolic function, there were few props and no scenery on the classical Indian stage. Location and specific actions were indicated through a fixed repertoire of highly stylized movements. Actors walked around the stage in a circle to indicate a journey, for example, and mimed actions such as stepping into and out of a carriage. To an even greater degree than most other theatrical traditions, actors were the centerpiece of classical Indian theater, and in their skilled use of their bodies they were the principal vehicles for articulating dramatic and theatrical meaning. These men and women mastered an elaborate system of movements involving their entire body. Each of these gestures—ranging from broad changes in bodily carriage and head positions to tiny motions of the eyes and hands—conveyed specific attitudes, emotions, dramatic situations, and character types. Classical Indian performance, in short, involved a complex gestural language that required actors to be extensively trained and spectators to cultivate a sophisticated ability to "read" its signs.

THEORY OF PERFORMANCE: *RASA*

One of the distinguishing features of classical Indian theater is its adherence to a specific audience-based aesthetic theory. Much of the *Natyasastra* is devoted to the nature of *rasa*—the sentiment, mood, or aesthetic experiences that a play creates in its spectator—and how it is achieved in performance. Just as the ingredients of a skillfully prepared dish combine to create a complex but harmonious taste, so the ingredients of a successful theatrical performance—spectacle, costume, gesture, music, voice—establish a nuanced but overriding "flavor" that the audience can savor. The *Natyasastra* catalogs eight basic *rasas* (a ninth was added by later commentators) and associates these with eight permanent (and thirty-three transitory) human emotions, or *bhavas*. As actors portray these emotions, the spectator experiences the corresponding *rasa*. The effect, akin to that of any good meal, is a sense of aesthetic fullness and satisfaction.

CLASSICAL INDIAN DRAMA

About two dozen Sanskrit plays have survived to the present day, and they demonstrate the formal richness of classical Indian drama. Though Bharata describes ten major categories of play, two types were dominant on the classical Indian stage: *nataka* plays, whose stories are drawn from mythology or history, deal with exploits of kings and heroes; and *prakarana* plays are characterized by invented stories and less exalted characters. All plays combine a central story with numerous subsidiary plots, interweaving the serious and the comic. Indian dramatists employed both verse and prose in their plays and a mixture of Sanskrit and the popular dialects collectively known as Prakrit. The former is reserved for characters of high social standing, whereas the latter is spoken by characters of lesser station.

Most of the finest Sanskrit plays were written during the Gupta dynasty (ca. 320–ca. 550 C.E.), a period that witnessed a golden age of science, mathematics, literature, and philosophy in India. Major playwrights during this period include Bhasa, the author of thirteen surviving plays; Kalidasa, whose epic romance *Shakuntala* is considered by many to be the finest Sanskrit play; and Shudraka, whose lengthy masterpiece *The Little Clay Cart* (ca. 100–300 C.E.) is excerpted in this anthology. Important Sanskrit drama continued to be written through the seventh century. Subsequent Indian history was marked by political instability as the court culture that helped sustain Sanskrit drama was threatened by a series of invasions by Muslim armies from the north from the tenth century onward. Sanskrit theater had largely disappeared as a cultural form by 1000 C.E.

Classical Chinese Theater

ORIGINS OF CHINESE THEATER

China, another of the world's oldest civilizations, has one of its richest performance and theater histories. Ancient Chinese scholars described performances synthesizing dance, music, and poetry as early as the reign of the legendary sage-ruler Yi Shun (2300–2205 B.C.E.), and shamanistic and court rituals involving dance and music were attributed to the Shang dynasty (1600–1045 B.C.E.). There are records dating to the first millennium B.C.E. of court entertainments—performed by jesters and others—that included music, dance, and mime. The integration of various activities in these earliest Chinese performances anticipates the capacious scope of later Chinese theater. The Chinese word that would later be used for "play" (*xi*) also meant "game," and it could be used to describe acrobatics, sports, and other kinds of entertainment. This highly theatrical synthesis of performance forms has flourished in Chinese theater to the present day, as the popularity of Beijing opera—a style of theater combining dance, music, storytelling, acrobatics, and martial arts—demonstrates.

THEATER DURING THE TANG AND SONG DYNASTIES

Theater and other forms of entertainment thrived during the Tang and Song dynasties, whose rulers held power in China between the seventh and thirteenth centuries C.E. During the Tang dynasty (618–907 C.E.), dance stories, skits, shadow and puppet plays, and a popular genre of play satirizing corrupt officials thrived at court and in the marketplace, as did circuslike performances and other forms of staged spectacle. Storytelling flourished as well, in forms that included the oral presentation of religious and secular stories by preachers attempting to disseminate Buddhism to nonliterate audiences. It was during the Tang period that Emperor Minghuang—considered the patron of Chinese theater—established the Pear Orchard Conservatory, the first academy in China devoted to the training of actors and other performers.

During the Song dynasty (960–1279), a period that saw a rise in commerce and the growth and social diversification of Chinese urban centers, amusement centers called "tile districts" (*wazi*) were organized in major cities. These centers, which provided a wide variety of entertainment, included theaters—as many as fifty in the tile districts of the northern capital Bianliang (modern-day Kaifeng)—that could seat up to several thousand spectators. The most accomplished players also performed at the emperor's palace, while itinerant players performed in villages and elsewhere on temporary stages. In addition to viewing such activities as tightrope walking, storytelling, and puppetry, audiences in the tile districts of northern China (a region that was taken over from the Song emperor by invaders from Manchuria in 1127 and ruled thereafter by the Jin dynasty) were entertained by the performance of *zaju*: variety shows that featured dramatic sketches accompanied by musical performance, comic routines, dancing, and acrobatics. In the southern provinces (which remained under Song rule), a separate form of theater known as *nanxi* developed during this period. Longer than their counterparts presented in the north and more intricate in story lines, *nanxi* made use of folk music and an array of familiar character types that influenced subsequent Chinese drama.

YUAN DRAMA: *ZAJU*

Though *nanxi* and the *zaju* have clear dramatic elements, it was not until the Yuan dynasty (1234–1368), when first part and later all of China was under Mongol occupation, that drama flourished as a literary genre. As the Venetian explorer Marco Polo (1254–1324) reported during his travels to the court of Kublai Khan (1215–1294), greatest of the Mongol emperors, China during the Yuan dynasty was a land of prosperity and cultural achievement, enjoying the fruits of increased trade and cultural exchange with western Asia and Europe. Contemporary records mention the titles of some 700 plays written during this period—of which 163 have been preserved, many of them in collections compiled during the late Ming dynasty (1368–1644)—and the names of roughly 550 dramatists, including GUAN HANQING (ca. 1245–ca. 1322), the most prolific and best known of the Yuan playwrights. In its quantity and sophistication, Yuan drama has often been compared to

that of Elizabethan and Jacobean England. One of the reasons for its flourishing is that Chinese scholars, who had traditionally served in government posts, found themselves excluded from civil service under Mongol rule; they therefore turned their attention to other careers, such as writing. To appeal to a popular audience, these scholars abandoned the classical Chinese of Confucius (Kong Fuzi, ca. 551–479 B.C.E.)—whose ethical teachings constituted a pillar of traditional Chinese society—and helped develop the vernacular as a dramatic language. The result was a richly poetic drama, literary in conception yet deeply grounded in the performance traditions of Chinese theater.

Most of this drama is referred to as "Yuan *zaju*," to distinguish it from the earlier form of northern theater. These plays treated subjects ranging from the historical, legendary, and supernatural to the contemporary. They told stories of love, war, political intrigue, adventure, religious conversion, domestic drama, crime, and judicial punishment. Their characters—covering a broad spectrum, from gods, emperors, and generals to hermits, outlaws, concubines, and ordinary people—derive from an array of popular types. Yuan *zaju* plays are typically four acts long, though shorter wedge acts (*xiezi*) may be added when additional plot material is required, and they include from ten to twenty songs, all performed by the main character. These songs, often of great poetic beauty, are the lyrical center of *zaju* plays. The remainder of the dramatic action is conveyed through speech and dialogue. In keeping with the Confucian emphasis on right and wrong and on the importance of correct conduct, *zaju* plays end with justice served, even when (as in Guan Hanqing's SNOW IN MIDSUMMER) a play's hero or heroine dies.

ACTORS AND STAGE

Yuan acting troupes included men and women performers, and both men and women played male and female roles. From the scattered evidence we possess—including a fourteenth-century colored mural from a temple in the northern province of Shanxi that depicts a Yuan acting

場作此在秀都忠樂散行大

Yuan troupe onstage, from a 1324 temple wall painting in the northern Chinese province of Shanxi.

troupe onstage—we know that actors wore ornate, colorful costumes and highly stylized makeup. Though the physical structure of the stage most likely varied with the venue and performance occasion, the stage depicted in the Shanxi mural—consisting of a bare tile floor with entrances on either side of a decorative wall painting in the rear—was probably typical. There was no formal scenery on the Yuan stage and props were minimal. Musicians performed onstage, and their instruments included the flute, gong, clapper, drum, and a lute-like instrument known as a *pipa*. The audience of these Yuan performers seems to have represented a wide range of Chinese society, from the Mongol emperors and their courts down to merchants, peasants, and poor laborers. Yuan *zaju* was a drama that appealed to educated and uneducated spectators alike.

THE RISE OF *NANXI*

Zaju continued to be popular into the Ming dynasty, which assumed power in 1368 after a rebellion drove the Yuan from power, but in the fourteenth century it was rivaled and eventually eclipsed by the reemergence of *nanxi* drama in the southern provinces and its development into a form markedly different from the theater found in the north. *Nanxi* plays are longer than *zaju* plays, and they contain a variable number of acts (as many as fifty or more, each with its own title). Singing is not restricted to a single character; instead, songs are performed by two or more singers, and sometimes by choruses. Acted to the accompaniment of a bamboo flute, *nanxi* plays drew on folk music, and their overall atmosphere in performance was elegiac. Although *zaju* is considered China's premier classical drama, the development of a "southern style" of drama proved to be more influential. A number of the distinctive character types of *nanxi* drama, in fact, remain popular on today's Chinese stage.

Classical Japanese Theater

When Westerners think of Asian theater, it is the theater of Japan that most often comes to mind. In part, this can be explained by the cultural distinctiveness of Japan's theatrical and dramatic traditions: the meditative dance theater of noh, the stylized acrobatics of kabuki, the sophisticated gestures of bunraku puppet theater. But it also has to do with the preservation of such theatrical traditions through centuries of political and social change. In a country devoted to ritual, ceremony, and other forms of tradition, theatrical practices have been handed down with the formal exactitude of the tea ceremony. As a result, we can come to understand the development of Japanese theater not only by reading histories of theater but by attending live performances.

ORIGINS OF JAPANESE THEATER

Although archaeologists have uncovered clay representations of singers, dancers, and musical instruments from as early as the third century B.C.E., the earliest manifestations of what we would consider theater in Japan were dance-based ritual celebrations collectively known as *kagura*. These performances were connected with Shintoism, a prehistoric religion devoted to the worship of gods and spirits who represented aspects of the natural world. Versions of *kagura* were performed at Shinto shrines by shamanistic priestesses, at the imperial court, and in villages during harvest and other annual festivals. Other theatrical forms emerged in the centuries after Buddhism was introduced to Japan between 538 and 552 C.E., a period during which continental Asian culture was embraced by the imperial court. In the seventh and eighth centuries, two forms of dance theater came from China via Korea: *gigaku*, a Buddhist dance play in which masked figures moved in procession, and *bugaku*, a stately court entertainment that eventually included dances from India, Tibet, and Vietnam in addition to those from China and Korea.

Other popular forms of entertainment also flourished during this time, involving music, dance, masked pantomime, and in some instances acrobatics, juggling, and tightrope walking. Several of these traditions had dramatic components, including *sarugaku* (monkey entertainment), a form of variety theater containing comic dialogues and short skits that came to be performed at Buddhist temples. By the thirteenth century, the dramatic and performance elements of these entertainments had become increasingly sophisticated, and the form was given the name *sarugaku noh*. The term *noh*, which means "skill" or "craft," eventually stood alone as a theatrical category.

THE EMERGENCE OF NOH THEATER: KANAMI AND ZEAMI

The emergence of noh theater reflected the political and social changes that Japan had undergone during the previous two centuries. In 1192 the Japanese emperor relinquished rule of the country to samurai generals, whose rising military and economic power had made them the country's dominant social class. These generals, who gave themselves the title *shogun*, presided over wealthy courts in Kamakura and later Kyoto and established a feudal society with rigidly demarcated social strata. Although many cultural forms that had found favor in the imperial court fell out of fashion, the shoguns patronized the arts, including the theater of sarugaku noh. In 1374, Kanami Kiyotsugu (1333–1384), head of one of the country's *sarugaku noh* troupes, performed before the young shogun Ashikaga Yoshimitsu (1358–1408). So impressed was the shogun that he became Kanami's patron and took the performer's son, ZEAMI MOTOKIYO (1363–1443), who was also an accomplished actor, as his companion and lover.

It was through the efforts of Kanami and Zeami that noh became an autonomous form. An innovator by temperament, Kanami combined elements of existing performance traditions into a dramatic form adapted to the tastes of the shogunate and lower warrior classes. Kanami amalgamated popular songs, dance, music, and poetry within an aesthetic of meditative deliberateness and restraint drawn from Zen Buddhism. Limiting his plays to a single protagonist, he advocated a style of acting based on authenticity of physical and vocal characterization. After Kanami's death, Zeami, who would become one of the most important figures in the history of Japanese theater, extended and refined his father's theatrical innovations. In a number of theoretical writings, including the seven-volume *Kadensho* (1400–02), Zeami discussed the intricacies of noh acting, the relationship of noh theater to its audience, and the aesthetic concepts underlying noh performance, such as *yugen*, which denotes suggestive beauty, gracefulness, and an awareness of life's impermanence. In addition to being noh's chief theoretician and one of its greatest actors, Zeami was also its most accomplished playwright, authoring nearly half of the 240 surviving plays that constitute the noh repertoire.

NOH DRAMA

The stories of noh plays are drawn from mythology, legend, and history, particularly (as in Zeami's *ATSUMORI* [ca. 1400]) the twelfth-century civil war between rival samurai clans. The main character (or *shite*) is often a ghost, demon, or tormented person who cannot find rest because of his or her past deeds. In the typical two-act structure, the central character appears disguised in the first act and is revealed in the second. He or she speaks an elevated, highly literary verse and frequently quotes classical Chinese and Japanese poetry. Other established roles include the main character's companion (*tsure*); a third party (*waki*), frequently a priest, who encounters the main character in the first act; and a servant or commoner (*kyogen*), whose language is colloquial and who often provides a narrative summary in the interlude between acts. An onstage chorus sings many of the characters' lines and narrates events within the dramatic action, while three or four onstage musicians accompany the play with drums and

The *shite*, or primary actor, in a contemporary performance of the noh drama *The Lady Aoi*. Note the mask, costume, folding fan, and stylized gesture of the performer. In the background sit the *hayashi-kata*, or musicians.

flute. The climax of a noh play takes the form of a ritualized dance.

Noh dramas fall into five categories: plays about gods; warrior plays; plays about women, or "wig plays"; miscellaneous plays, including plays about madness and plays about the present time; and demon plays, in which the main character is a good or evil supernatural being. In a traditional noh program, plays from each of these categories were performed, in the order given. Between the plays, farcical sketches known as *kyogen* (wild words) were performed by the same actors who took the colloquial roles in the noh drama. A *nohgaku* program (the term refers to the combination of *noh* and *kyogen* in performance) took seven or eight hours to complete.

ACTORS

The actors of noh drama, who were male—a tradition maintained in all but a few noh companies today—were dressed in elaborate, highly formal silk costumes. These costumes, which included kimonos for male characters, involved variously layered inner and outer garments. Actors were usually wigged. Among the most celebrated features of noh theater are the masks that the main character and his or her companion wore. Treasured for their craftsmanship and elegant yet simple design, these masks offered stylized representations of the established noh character types: male and female, old and young, human and supernatural. Actors in other roles wore masklike makeup. In contrast to the richness of visual presentation that characterized the actors thus attired, the physical setting and props in noh performance were minimal. Movable structures were used to represent a hut, boat, mountain, and other features, while handheld props served to represent emotional states and a range of other objects. A folding fan, for instance, one of the main props in noh theater, could be used to stand for a sword, a flute, or other item. The handling of physical objects formed part of the broader choreography of noh performance, which involved slow, deliberate movement and symbolic, meditative gestures. The acts of walking and dancing, for example, called for painstaking control of body posi-

tion and motion, and years of training were required for the actor to master such simple gestures as lifting an arm or raising a hand to the eyes, the symbol of weeping.

THE NOH STAGE

Drawn to its formal precision and ceremonial nature, later dramatists and theater artists have sought to appropriate elements of the noh for the modern theater (*Four Plays for Dancers*, published in 1921 by the Irish playwright and poet William Butler Yeats, represents one such attempt). To an extent unrivaled in world theater, however, traditional noh performance is inseparable from the stage for which it was written. The configuration, dimensions, and materials of this stage were standardized during the seventeenth century and have remained unchanged in noh theaters to the present day. The main stage, roughly 18 feet square and raised about 2½ feet above the ground, consists of a polished surface of Japanese cypress with four pillars, roughly 15 feet high, that support a temple-like roof. The audience sits in front of and to the left of this stage. A visible backstage area, at the front of which the musicians sit, features a wooden wall with painted pine trees, while an area to the audience's right of the main acting area is occupied by the chorus, who sit in two rows facing the stage.

One of the most characteristic features of the noh stage is the *hashigakiri*, a railed passageway or bridge that extends from the side of the backstage area on the audience's left to a dressing (or "mirror") room, from which actors make their entrances and to which they exit. A secondary exit to the right of the backstage area is used by the chorus and stage attendants. Reverberating jars are placed under the main stage, backstage, and bridge to provide additional resonance and to amplify the sound of characters walking and stomping their feet. Specific areas of the stage are associated with individual characters and with conventionally assigned functions. The pillar that stands where the bridge meets the stage, for instance, known as the *shite* pillar, is where the main character stops to announce his name upon entering the stage area.

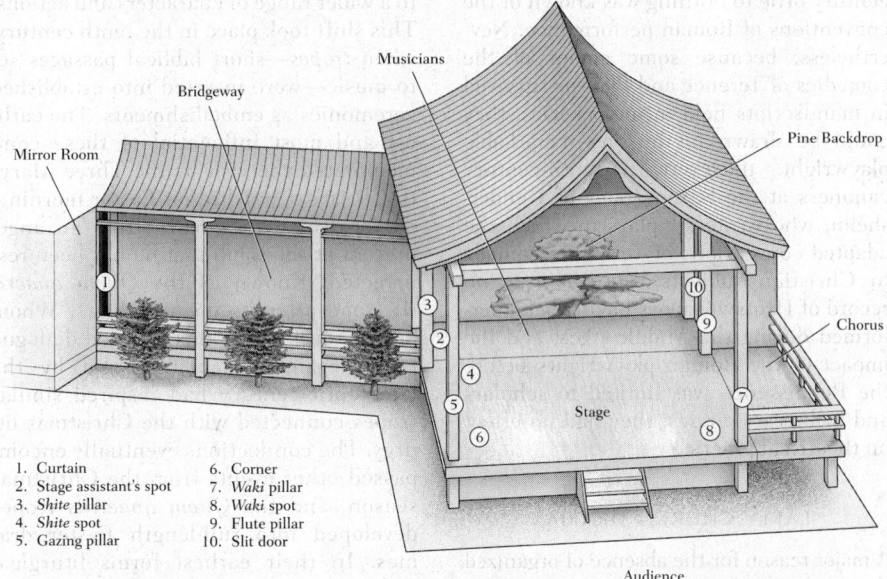

Musicians

Bridgeway

Mirror Room

Pine Backdrop

Chorus

Stage

1

3

2

4

5

6

10

9

7

8

1. Curtain
2. Stage assistant's spot
3. *Shite* pillar
4. *Shite* spot
5. Gazing pillar
6. Corner
7. *Waki* pillar
8. *Waki* spot
9. Flute pillar
10. Slit door

Audience

LATER NOH THEATER

The conventions of modern-day noh theater were standardized during the Tokugawa shogunate (1603–1867), a period when the center of government was moved to Edo (modern-day Tokyo) and the hierarchies of Japanese society were institutionalized to a greater extent. Noh theater companies assumed their modern form as hereditary heads (*iemoto*) were made responsible for preserving the traditions of the major schools of noh. Rooted in the practices and accomplishments of its early masters, noh became an art for connoisseurs; although amateur noh companies found support among the commoners, its principal audience was courtly and upper-class.

KABUKI AND BUNRAKU

By the early seventeenth century, other theatrical forms had emerged to satisfy the tastes of a rising urban middle class. Kabuki—a form of dramatic theater involving music, dance, and acrobatics; ornate costumes and makeup; extensive scenery; and spectacular tricks of stage technology—developed in the early decades of the 1600s from the lively, often erotic, dances that temple maidens performed at religious shrines. The performance of kabuki, which

was restricted to adult males in 1653, became a highly conventional and stylized art, and its practitioners—including the popular *onnagata*, or actor of female roles—require decades of training. Bunraku, an elaborate form of puppet (or doll) theater that developed out of earlier puppet and storytelling traditions, also became popular during this period. Like noh, which can be seen in specially built theaters throughout Japan, these centuries-old theater forms remain popular on today's stage.

Medieval European Theater

EUROPE AFTER THE ROMAN EMPIRE

The disintegration of the Roman Empire between the fifth and sixth centuries C.E. marked the end of organized theatrical activity in western and central Europe as it had been practiced in classical Rome. Itinerant groups of performers traveled through southern Europe offering such entertainments as storytelling, juggling, tumbling, and jesting; local popular festivals, many with origins in pagan rites surrounding the winter solstice and the earth's return to fertility in spring, contained a variety of performative elements. But although the abandoned amphitheaters across Europe gave evidence of an earlier theatrical culture, after the sixth century little to nothing was known of the conventions of Roman performance. Nevertheless, because some copies of the comedies of Terence and Plautus survived in manuscripts held in monasteries, they could be drawn on by one remarkable playwright: HROTSVIT, a tenth-century canoness at the Saxon abbey of Gandersheim, who wrote six plays in which she adapted conventions of Terentian comedy to Christian subjects. But there is no record of Hrotsvit's plays having been performed during the Middle Ages, and the impact of the Roman playwrights before the Renaissance was limited to scholars and to literary circles; they had no effect on theatrical practice.

EARLY CHURCH DRAMA

A major reason for the absence of organized theater during this era was the opposition of the Christian Church to all such activities. Throughout the Middle Ages (and much of the early modern period), church authorities and moralists denounced theater and other forms of spectacle and impersonation as idolatrous, obscene, and dangerous in their effects on the audience members' passions. Ironically, this same church served as the major site for the reemergence of theater in medieval Europe—but perhaps not surprisingly, since the Catholic liturgy is itself a performed spectacle. During the medieval mass, priests wearing ornate robes officiated before spectators gathered in designated locations within enclosed structures. Processions and other forms of ceremony marked holy days throughout the year, while each day's canonical "offices" or "hours" (such as matins and vespers) were marked by services of their own. Chanting during the liturgy was often antiphonal—with passages sung alternately by two choirs, much like dialogue—and singer-performers often gave voice to the words of Christ and others in the Bible. Individual dates throughout the Christian calendar commemorated biblical events and the figures who participated in them, and thus were inherently associated with a rich trove of narrative and potentially dramatic material.

But ritual and ceremony are not the same as drama, and the latter could emerge only when liturgical celebration gave way to a wider range of characters and actions. This shift took place in the tenth century, when *tropes*—short biblical passages set to music—were inserted into established ceremonies as embellishments. The earliest and most influential of these commemorated the visit by the Three Marys to Christ's sepulchre on Easter morning, during which they learn from an angel present at the tomb that he has been resurrected. Known as the *Quem quaeritis* trope after its opening line ("Whom are you seeking?"), this chanted dialogue rapidly gained popularity and by the late tenth century had inspired similar tropes connected with the Christmas liturgy. The connections eventually encompassed other events from the Christmas season, and the *Quem quaeritis* tropes developed into full-length Easter dramas. In their earliest forms liturgical tropes were performed in Benedictine monasteries for fellow monastics; but as cathedrals and other large church buildings were constructed in the eleventh

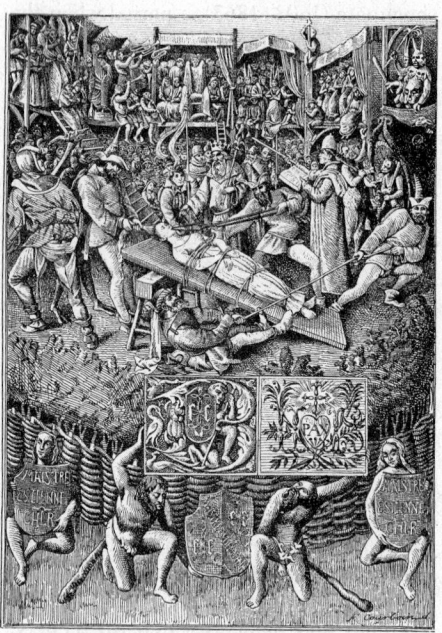

This engraving, a nineteenth-century copy of an original devotional miniature by Jean Fouquet (ca. 1415–1481), depicts the performance of a "miracle play" of the martyrdom of St. Apollonia of Alexandria.

and twelfth centuries, the lay congregations became audiences for these religious performances.

By the twelfth century, church drama had so expanded in scope and complexity that some works—the Christmas and Passion plays from the Benediktbeuern Abbey in Bavarian Germany, for example—were performed outside the context of the liturgy. Eventually, as part of this natural progression, the plays came to be performed outside the context of the church. The range of suitable dramatic subjects grew to include figures and events from the Old and the New Testament: the raising of Lazarus, Daniel in the lion's den, and the conversion of St. Paul, to name a few. Plays commemorating the lives of saints—often called "miracle plays" because they recounted the miracles or martyrdoms that led to the protagonist's conversion—mixed narratives of conflict and romantic adventure with moral exempla. Versions of these saints' plays were written and performed into the late Middle Ages.

CORPUS CHRISTI CYCLES

In a parallel development, religious plays began to be written in the national languages of central and western Europe (rather than the Latin of the church), and during the fourteenth and fifteenth centuries these vernacular forms developed into elaborate dramatic cycles of short plays, or pageants. The most notable of these cycle plays were performed in conjunction with the Feast of Corpus Christi (literally, "The Body of Christ"), a holy day—proposed by Pope Urban IV in 1264 and instituted by the church in 1311—celebrating the redemptive presence of the Holy Eucharist. This feast day, which occurred in late spring or early summer, included an outdoor procession in which the host was displayed; eventually, taking advantage of the generally favorable weather and the longer period of daylight, performers took an entire day and sometimes more to mount plays dramatizing events from biblical history. Though more limited versions of these cycles were performed on the Continent, the best-known achievements in this extended dramatic form were England's Corpus Christi plays, which dramatized the history of the world from the fall of the angels and the creation to the Last Judgment. Local records and the manuscripts of individual plays note performances in London, Coventry, Norwich, Newcastle-on-Tyne, and elsewhere in England, but the great majority of the surviving cycle plays come from just four towns, apparently all in the north: York, Wakefield, Chester, and N Town (where N stands for *nomen*—Latin for "name"—suggesting that this cycle was performed by touring players who would insert whatever name was appropriate as they traveled across the countryside). These cycles are quite extensive, containing between twenty-five pageants (the Chester cycle) to forty-eight (the York cycle). Although English cycle drama was performed as early as 1376, most Corpus Christi plays date from the fifteenth century. This distinctive form of drama continued to be performed—scholars have speculated that as a youth, WILLIAM SHAKESPEARE may have seen a performance of the Coventry cycle; by the late sixteenth century, however, it was effectively suppressed by the newly established Church of England.

The development of theatrical activity on such a scale was made possible by the growth of medieval towns and the formation of guilds: that is, associations governing the practice of individual crafts and trades, which participated in town government and played a major role in both the religious and nonreligious aspects of civic life. In northern England, guilds assumed primary responsibility for the production of the Corpus Christi plays, which therefore are also called "mystery cycles" (the word *mystery*, derived from the Latin *mysterium*, referred to a craft, trade, or profession known only to a few). This arrangement indicates that the cycle plays performed a civic as well as religious function. Given responsibility for individual pageants, guilds provided actors, scenery, costumes, props, and other theatrical elements and materials. In some cases guilds were assigned plays for which they seemed particularly suited: the shipwrights would be given the Noah plays, for instance, while the goldsmiths produced plays about the Three Kings.

STAGING

The manner in which individual Corpus Christi cycles were staged remains a matter of debate. Although practice varied from town to town, there is evidence of two forms of staging: processional and fixed. In certain cities, such as York and Coventry, plays were mounted on pageant wagons that performed, in procession, before spectators gathered at designated viewing sites throughout the town. Scholars disagree on the structure and appearance of these wagons: some speculate that they had two levels (the lower serving as a dressing room), while others argue for a single-platform structure. In addition to the acting area, performers occasionally acted in the street surrounding the pageant wagon; in the Nativity pageant, one of two surviving plays from Coventry, the actor playing Herod "rages in the pagond [pageant wagon] and in the street also." In the alternative staging method, all plays were performed at stationary locations. It is also possible that some combination of processional and fixed staging was practiced: for instance, pageant wagons may have paraded through the town with the actors arranged in tableaux, then gathered in a circle at an open place where they could serve as stages for an audience that stood within the circle's periphery and moved from play to play.

Whether presented on pageant wagons or at fixed locations, the Corpus Christi cycles drew on a staging convention that had characterized medieval drama since its liturgical beginnings. The acting area had two components: one or more structures called *sedes* (mansions) and a nonlocalized playing space adjacent to these that was known as the *platea* (courtyard, or place). The former, usually represented by decorative booths, oriented the dramatic action to specific locations (Heaven, Hell, palace, house, manger), while the latter allowed for extensions of the action into more indeterminate spaces beyond the *sedes*. Financed by prosperous guilds and engineered by skilled craftsmen, Corpus Christi performances could be awe-inspiring affairs,

This engraved illustration from Thomas Sharp's *Dissertation on the Pageants Anciently Performed at Coventry* (1825) presents an imaginative reconstruction of the performance of a pageant play in Coventry, England.

with special effects and elaborate technical devices. Cranes enabled characters to ascend, descend, and fly between locations, while the Hell's Mouth through which sinners were dragged relied on an elaborate contraption of pulleys and smoke-ejecting bellows. Costumes included everyday medieval garments, ecclesiastical vestments, and—in the case of heavenly beings, who wore gilded masks, and devils, who were given the features of grotesque animals—nonnaturalistic adornments.

DRAMATIC TEXTS

Individual plays, or pageants, within specific cycles vary in length, structure, and style. Some are very formal and rely heavily on long-standing conventions, while others combine biblical narratives with scenes and characters from medieval life. Because the authors of these plays often embellished the biblical accounts with more realistic incidents and characterizations, the Corpus Christi cycles established links between sacred history and the world of their audiences. Indeed, the plays reveal as much about the medieval world as they do about the biblical episodes they take as their subjects. Among the greatest of these works blending the sacred and everyday is by an author whom later scholars call the WAKEFIELD MASTER. This unidentified playwright, whose plays display a command of vernacular dialects, complex characterization, and realistic situations, wrote the SECOND SHEPHERDS' PLAY (ca. 1475), which parallels and contrasts the scene of the Nativity with a rustic sheep-stealing episode. By counterpointing the mystery of Christ's Incarnation with the earthiness of fallen humanity, this widely known play demonstrates the use of comedy in Corpus Christi drama. Its folk elements remind us of popular forms of entertainment and celebration—folk festivals, songs and stories, mummers' plays (i.e., seasonal folk plays)—and of the drama that emerged from them in the later Middle Ages. In this tradition are the farces of the German poet and dramatist Hans Sachs (1494–1576), written for the festivities of Shrovetide, the three days preceding Lent.

MORALITY PLAYS

At the same time that the mystery cycles were being organized in the late fourteenth century, a different form of religious drama was emerging in England and France: the morality play. Like the Corpus Christi pageants, this drama was concerned with human salvation—but rather than exploring sin and redemption across the vast landscape of human and divine history, as did the cycles, morality plays focused on the moral life of the individual Christian. Written in the mode of allegory, in which abstract ideas and categories of individuals are given concrete form, morality drama featured a representative figure of humanity—Mankind, Everyman, Well-Advised, Ill-Advised—whose identity is universal rather than historical, biblical, or individual. This character interacts with figures personifying virtues and vices, who typically seek to win his soul in a battle between temptation and spiritual obedience. Whereas Corpus Christi plays occasionally employed allegorical characters, morality drama derived neither from these plays nor from the liturgical drama that preceded them. In addition to reflecting the general fondness for allegory in the Middle Ages—Prudentius's poem *Psychomachia* (fourth century c.e.), which introduced the competition of virtues and vices, was widely influential throughout the medieval period—morality drama likely drew on Pater Noster (or Lord's Prayer) plays; these were dramatizations of the seven deadly sins, performed in England during the fourteenth and fifteenth centuries. Since no Pater Noster plays have survived, specific relationships between the two dramatic forms cannot be established.

The oldest extant English morality play is a dramatic fragment titled *The Pride of Life* (ca. 1350). Only a few plays from the following 160 years have survived, but they indicate the drama's variety of forms and staging practices. The longest and most complex of the English moralities, *The Castle of Perseverance* (ca. 1405–25), presents the life of its protagonist Mankind from birth to death, the struggle over his soul by virtues and vices, a debate

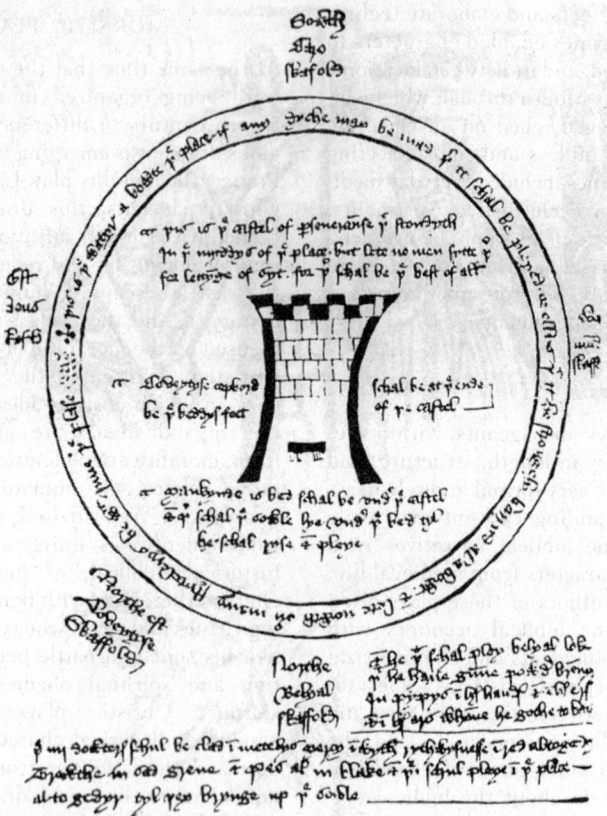

Diagram for staging *The Castle of Perseverance*, from a fifteenth-century manuscript.

between Body and Soul, the parliament of heaven, and the final judgment on Mankind's soul. The manuscript for this play, which includes a diagram, offers particular insight into its staging. Located outdoors, the performance area of *The Castle of Perseverance* consisted of a circular playing space with a structure indicating Mankind's castle in the center and five mansions on the periphery. The later *Mankind* (ca. 1465–70), by contrast, was performed before rural audiences by an itinerant group of professional or semiprofessional actors. The staging requirements were necessarily simple—a few props, a small booth for entrances and exits—and the play could be staged both in an open courtyard and indoors. The play itself combines the story of the farmer Mankind's temptation, fall, and repentance with wide-ranging comic business, most

having to do with the devil and his attendant mischief-figures. Finally, the best known of the moralities, EVERYMAN (ca. 1510, translated from a 1495 Dutch original), eschews the drama of temptation for the more somber story of Everyman's journey to death and final judgment. Although textual evidence suggests that the play was written for a playing area with fixed structures, there are no records of its actual performance.

During the sixteenth century, morality drama became broadly popular with audiences across the social spectrum. A growing number of morality plays were performed in public and private venues throughout England by troupes of professional actors—the direct precursors of the acting companies of Shakespeare's time. As the intellectual and religious climate of England changed in response to Renaissance humanism (a revival in the study of classical literature, science, and philosophy) and to the Reformation (a movement to reform the Catholic Church that led to the founding of Protestant religious denominations), morality drama evolved in its subject matter as well as its ideological function. In the hands of such Tudor humanist writers as Henry Medwall (1462–1501?) and John Skelton (ca. 1460–1529), morality plays engaged with increasingly secular subjects, addressing issues of philosophy, social relations, and politics in addition to moral and religious questions. In this form they frequently resembled Tudor interludes (indoor dramatic entertainments that were usually performed in noble households, guild halls, and schools). During the religious controversies of the English Reformation, morality drama was employed by Catholics and Protestants to dramatize their doctrinal and political divisions. Even more profoundly than the Corpus Christi cycles, which were cumbersome in structure and rooted in a medieval religious consensus that no longer applied in sixteenth-century England, morality plays helped shape subsequent English drama. Because their allegorical conventions were adaptable to a range of issues and ideologies, these plays provided a dramatic structure for such Elizabethan and Jacobean plays as CHRISTOPHER MARLOWE's *DOCTOR FAUSTUS* (ca. 1588). Certainly, the legacy of the Vice characters, with their conniving but theatrically appealing horseplay, can be seen clearly in such later dramatic masterpieces as Ben Jonson's *Volpone* (1606).

Theater in Early Modern Europe, 1500–1700

As European theater developed between 1500 and 1700, it was affected by a range of political, economic, social, artistic, and religious changes that were transforming the region and its relationship to the rest of the world. The term *early modern*, which is often used to designate the period in European history between the end of the Middle Ages and the beginning of the Industrial Revolution, focuses attention on those developments that inaugurated the world we know today: the rise of science and acceler-

ating technological innovation, the growth of cities and the emergence of mercantile economies, New World exploration and colonization, and the transformations of church and state through reformation, absolutism, and revolution. But as the competing term *Renaissance*—applied to the fifteenth and sixteenth centuries—suggests, this period is also characterized by a powerful look backward to the classical era of Greece and Rome and to the social, artistic, and intellectual values that scholars, newly given access to many of its rediscovered texts, found there. As they combined the new and the old in fruitful, and also volatile, ways, the years 1500–1700 were a period of unprecedented discovery and rediscovery in the visual, plastic, architectural, and musical arts. But arguably it was theater—where audiences in England, Spain, France, and elsewhere in Europe saw their world represented in action—that witnessed the greatest accomplishments during this extraordinary period.

THE EUROPEAN RENAISSANCE: HUMANISM AND THE CLASSICAL PAST

The European Renaissance played a crucial role in the transformations that Europe underwent in the fifteenth and sixteenth centuries. The term *Renaissance,* which means "rebirth," was first used in 1550 by the artist and critic Giorgio Vasari (1511–1574) to refer to the rediscovery of classical values—which, he claimed, had been eclipsed during the Middle Ages by Christianity and the "barbarian" cultures of northern Europe—in the paintings of Giotto (ca. 1267–1337) and later Florentine artists. This view of medieval civilization as a dark age compared to the civilizations of Greece and Rome is, of course, inaccurate, as is any absolute demarcation between the later Middle Ages and the Renaissance. Europe in the 1500s remained in many ways medieval. But the turn to the classical world represented a driving force behind humanism, the dominant intellectual movement in Renaissance Europe, and it effected a profound shift of cultural direction. Convinced that the civilizations of Greece and Rome represented the highest point of human achievement and that modern Europe should cultivate their ideals and emulate their accomplishments, scholars devoted themselves to the rediscovery, translation, and textual study of classical works, many of which had been preserved in European monasteries and in the libraries of the Byzantine Empire and Islamic Spain. The invention of the printing press in 1450 by Johann Gutenberg (ca. 1400–1468) accelerated the process by which these texts and Renaissance commentaries on them were disseminated.

The deepening understanding of Greek and Roman writers, and of classical civilization as a whole, revolutionized the fields of literature and the arts. The Italian writers Petrarch (Francesco Petrarca, 1304–1374) and Giovanni Boccaccio (1313–1375) urged their peers to study Greek and Roman writers, and the influence of authors, literary forms, historical subjects, and mythological characters from the classical period was widespread in the literature of the next three centuries. Though it is a mistake to see this expanding interest as a departure from the religious concerns of medieval literature—most Renaissance writers explored classical materials in the context of Christian belief—an intensifying concern with human experience and the things of the world makes itself felt throughout the literature of this period, including its finest: the essays of Michel de Montaigne (1533–1592), for example, and the picaresque fiction of Miguel de Cervantes (1547–1616). A similar interest in the world as it is lived and observed is apparent in the work of Leonardo da Vinci (1452–1519), Michelangelo (1475–1564), and other Renaissance artists, who abandoned the flat, often ornamental surfaces of medieval art for more lifelike representations of the human figure and the visible world.

PATRONAGE

The Renaissance as a cultural phenomenon was closely linked to the increasing urbanization and the changing economic and political landscapes of European society. The movement began in the city-states of Italy, where rulers competed with each other to be patrons of scholarship, literature, and the other arts. Here, as elsewhere in Europe, wealth and power were increasingly concentrated in the hands of princes and other monarchs, civic authorities, and an expanding merchant class, and these groups sought to enhance their prestige by funding art, architecture, literature, music, and lavish spectacles. The most prominent of the Italian cultural centers was Florence, which served—under the rule of Lorenzo de' Medici (1449–1492), "the Magnificent"—as a home for humanists, artists, poets, and philosophers. Later centers of patronage included the courts of England's Elizabeth I and James I, Spain's Philip II, and France's Louis XIV. Acting companies, whose members had previously operated on the margins of society, also benefited from the patronage system during the sixteenth and seventeenth centuries. Even as it earned money from the London playgoing public, for instance, the company to which WILLIAM SHAKESPEARE belonged—the Lord Chamberlain's Men, later renamed the King's Men—enjoyed the support, protection, and legitimation conferred by courtly patronage.

SCIENCE AND THE "NEW PHILOSOPHY"

As Renaissance humanism reevaluated medieval learning in light of earlier classical traditions, it profoundly altered established fields of knowledge and inquiry. In the field of political philosophy, for instance, the Italian theorist Niccolò Machiavelli (1469–1527) proposed a view of politics and government in which the maintenance and exercise of power, not moral authority, were the ultimate justification for political action. So controversial were these ideas that his very name became synonymous with cunning and ruthless self-interest. The argument between older and newer conceptions of the world was a defining feature of the scientific revolution that took place during the sixteenth and seventeenth centuries. In 1543 Nicolaus Copernicus (1473–1543) published his treatise demonstrating that the earth orbited the sun, thereby refuting the geocentric model that had dominated classical and medieval understanding of the heavens.

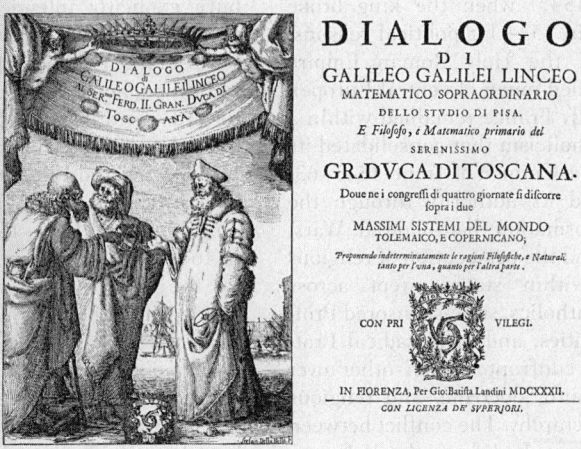

The title page and engraved frontispiece of Galileo's *Dialogue Concerning the Two Chief World Systems*, published in Florence in 1632. In the book, Galileo argued in favor of Copernicus's model of the solar system, in which the planets revolve around the sun, and against the older Ptolemaic system, which placed the earth at the center of the known universe. The engraving shows Aristotle (left), Ptolemy (center), and Copernicus (right).

Further astronomical discoveries were made by Galileo Galilei (1564–1642), who relied on an improved version of the recently invented telescope to make direct celestial observations. The use of empirical observation, experimentation, and inductive reasoning (i.e., drawing general conclusions from data) represented a shift from the more abstract procedures applied by medieval scholars of the natural world. While Aristotle and classical authorities continued to influence Renaissance science and its social practice—the theories of human physiology set forth by the Greek physician Galen (129–ca. 199 C.E.) remained popular during the period, for example—and while most early modern scientists reconciled their scientific methods and discoveries with a literal belief in the Bible, the scientific method worked to undermine traditional notions of authority. As the poet John Donne wrote of recent scientific discoveries in 1611, "[T]he new Philosophy calls all in doubt."

REFORMATION AND COUNTER-REFORMATION

By 1600, the spirits of inquiry and individualism had challenged the authority of the Catholic Church and, in the process, redrawn the political and religious map of Europe. The Protestant Reformation began as a call for reform within the church in 1517, when Martin Luther (1483–1546) wrote a series of theses protesting the sale of indulgences (the remission of temporal punishment for sins) on behalf of the pope. Luther's opposition to the abuses of the Catholic Church quickly expanded to include a broader challenge to its authority. Believing that the church had lost contact with the fundamental truths of Christianity, Luther rejected the doctrine that salvation required the intercession of a religious clergy, arguing instead that salvation was a function of faith alone and that the Bible was the sole authority on spiritual matters.

With the help of the newly invented printing press, Luther's ideas were widely disseminated throughout Europe, and other Protestant movements followed. Protestantism was adopted by states in Germany, Scandinavia, and elsewhere in northern Europe, many of which took advantage of this opportunity to assert their independence from Catholic Rome; the Church of England, for example, was established as a Protestant church under the head of Henry

VIII (1491–1547) when the king broke from Rome in 1534 for political reasons. Italy, Spain, the Holy Roman Empire (which included much of central Europe), and eventually France remained within a reviving Catholicism that consolidated its doctrine at the Council of Trent (1545–63) and extended its authority through the Counter-Reformation that followed. Wars, rebellions, and the persecution of religious minorities within states swept across Europe as Catholics, state-sponsored Protestant majorities, and more radical Protestant sects confronted each other over matters of faith, doctrine, and religious and social hierarchy. The conflict between nations that resulted from the Reformation would not begin to be resolved until the Peace of Westphalia, which ended Europe's devastating Thirty Years War (1618–48).

MONARCHY AND GOVERNMENT

Religious controversy and the political turmoil it precipitated contributed to the changing shapes of monarchy and government during the early modern period. In the late sixteenth and early seventeenth centuries, power was increasingly centralized in the hands of monarchs, who justified this movement toward absolutism by invoking the doctrine of the divine right of kings—the right to rule by virtue of birth, a right bestowed by God alone. France offers the most striking example of this development. Following the religious wars that divided the country in the 1500s and the continuation of civil disturbances and political intrigues in the first half of the 1600s, Louis XIV (1638–1715), the "Sun King," assumed the throne in 1643 and began a seventy-two-year reign that saw France and the French court achieve a position of dominance throughout Europe. The statement that is famously attributed to him—"L'état, c'est moi" ("I am the state")—reflects his power over the country's nobility, laws, military, and growing bureaucracy. His model was followed by other European monarchs such as Frederick William I (1688–1740) of Prussia and Peter the Great (1672–1725) of Russia; indeed, the latter built a palace in the recently founded city of St. Peters-

burg explicitly intended to rival Louis' monumental palace at Versailles.

Absolutism did not triumph everywhere in Europe, however. In England the moves toward centralized royal power undertaken by the Tudor monarchs Henry VII, Henry VIII, and Elizabeth I were checked by Parliament in the 1600s: the Stuart king Charles I (1600–1649) was beheaded in 1649 during the English Civil War, and for the following eleven years—a period divided into the Commonwealth and the Protectorate—England was subject to parliamentary and military rule. The Stuart monarchy was restored in 1660 with the crowning of Charles II (1630–1685), but the next forty years, known as the Restoration, witnessed the overthrow of his brother and successor, the Catholic James II (1633–1701), as a result of conflicts with his Protestant Parliament. Similar clashes awaited European monarchs in the eighteenth century.

NEW WORLD ENCOUNTERS

No overview of early modern Europe would be complete that failed to acknowledge the profound shift in European consciousness brought about by the encounter with the Western Hemisphere. In the Middle Ages Europeans had traveled through Asia by land as far east as Kublai Khan's China, and by 1500 the Portuguese had explored the west coast of Africa. But the "discovery" of an inhabited land across the ocean by the Italian-born Spanish explorer Christopher Columbus (1451–1506), who landed in the Caribbean in 1492 while seeking a western sea route to Asia, had consequences that reached much further. The success of this and subsequent expeditions prompted a race for conquest and settlement of the Americas by Spain and other European powers competing for resources, territorial possessions, and prestige. Over the next hundred years, the Spanish colonized an area stretching from eastern and southern South America to what is today Mexico and much of the United States, while Portugal, the Netherlands, France, and England also established colonies in the New World. The first permanent English settlement was Jamestown (located in the colony of Virginia) in 1607, and by the end of the seventeenth century England's colonial holdings encompassed a good deal of eastern North America.

The history of European colonialism in the Americas is, without doubt, a dark one. The indigenous peoples of South, Central, and North America suffered violence, exploitation, death by disease, and forced conversions, and the relationships between colonizer and colonized were shaped by military power, economic interests, and the religious fervor of missionaries. Europe's colonization of the New World inaugurated a transatlantic system of trade that would eventually bring African slaves to the Americas as part of a highly organized exchange of labor, resources, and commodities. At the same time, even as New World settlers may have sought to Europeanize the indigenous peoples and societies they encountered, their own world was transformed by the contact. Materially, Europe benefited from the introduction of new commodities, such as tobacco, corn, and previously unknown medications. But as Renaissance travel literature reveals, the encounter with the New World also fundamentally changed Europeans' awareness of their recently expanded world. When four delegates (or "kings," as they were called)

from the Iroquois Confederacy visited London and Queen Anne's court in 1710, they inspired a fascination whose intensity reveals how deeply their newly discovered hemisphere had penetrated the early modern imagination.

PROFESSIONAL THEATER, 1500–1700

Theater played an important part in the emergence of early modern Europe. As a medium of impersonation and display, theater spoke to a deeply theatricalized society where power was asserted through spectacles, performances, and rituals of display. The spirits of individualism and inquiry found a natural home in an art form in which characters grappled with their destinies on a public stage, and spectators who flocked to attend these performances saw the concerns of their world illuminated and explored. As defenders and critics debated its moral authority, European theater during this period exerted unprecedented social influence.

The years 1500–1700 saw wide-ranging developments in the institution and practices of theater. In addition to those performances that took place in court, private, and university settings, the first

An engraving from the mid-1600s showing actors onstage at the Hôtel de Bourgogne.

professional theaters, public and private, opened in Europe during the second half of the sixteenth century. Paris had the Hôtel de Bourgogne, built in 1548; London the short-lived Red Lion, in 1567; and Madrid the Corral de la Cruz, in 1579; and by 1600 these major cities—and several in Italy—had become thriving theatrical centers. Many of these early theater buildings employed staging arrangements used in courtyard and other outdoor performance venues—the major public theaters of London, such as the Globe, were open-air theaters and contained stages that extended into the audience. But the development of theater architecture and scenic practices during this period was also influenced by the rediscovery of the treatise on architecture by the Roman engineer and architect Vitruvius. Italian architects and theorists drew on it in determining the theater's shape, the relationship between stage and auditorium, and the design of tragic, comic, and pastoral scenes. During the seventeenth and eighteenth centuries, Italian stage design became influential throughout Europe, as such innovations were introduced as the use of perspective, a form of visual representation that creates the impression of three-dimensionality and distance. As it gained popularity, the simultaneous staging that characterized the medieval period and continued into early modern production was replaced by a spatially unified visual field. Italian designers also pioneered the use of the proscenium, an archway or a frame that would become characteristic of European stage design from the late sixteenth to nineteenth centuries.

As the sophistication of theater technology grew, stage design and scenic effects became increasingly elaborate. The spectacular staging for which the theaters of seventeenth-century Italy, France, and Spain became particularly well-known— multiple scenery changes, flying chariots, hidden grottoes, lavish pictorial effects— were manifestations of the baroque style that dominated European arts during this period. The baroque, which stresses exuberance, monumentality, and ornateness, achieved its highest realization in court performances, when royalty spent large sums for the work of Italy's leading designers and those who studied their innovations. This movement toward greater spectacle was accelerated by the development of opera during the 1600s.

COMMEDIA DELL'ARTE

The establishment of theater as a public, private, and courtly institution was paralleled by the professionalization of actors and others involved in theatrical productions. Acting companies operated in England and on the Continent throughout the sixteenth century, and these troupes often performed in other countries in addition to their own. The most widely known were the *commedia dell'arte* (literally, "comedy of art") players who emerged in Italy in the mid-1500s, performed throughout Europe, and occupied an important place in European theatrical history into the eighteenth century. These troupes—which consisted of ten to twelve actors, both male and female—presented comic scenarios centering on love and intrigue. While the narrative outlines of these scenarios were established in advance, their performance depended on improvisation and the use of comic routines or improvisational asides known as *lazzi*. Popular with audiences, *lazzi* were often ingenious bits of comic business that players used to enliven their performances, such as using a wooden arm to slip away from a beating or engaging in acrobatic contortions in order to catch a flea. Commedia dell'arte actors portrayed a range of stock characters—some masked and some unmasked—that included lovers, masters, and servants (known as *zanni*). Among the best known of the masked characters are Pantalone, a rich miser, and Arlecchino (or Harlequin), an acrobatic servant with a distinctive motley-colored costume.

Commedia dell'arte companies were organized on the sharing plan, an arrangement that enabled performers to share in the risks and profits of their companies. It was just one of the forms of economic organization that acting companies throughout Europe used as actors, managers, playwrights, and others participated in the expanding business of theater. Per-

Riciulina.   *Metzetin*

A sixteenth-century engraving of two commedia actors dancing.

forming at Europe's courts (often under the patronage of royalty and nobility) while also operating within a newly established network of public and private playhouses, theater companies in the late 1500s and 1600s began to enjoy some measure of economic security. At the same time, the life of theater professionals remained a hard one, with actors and playwrights often living on the edge of poverty and under the threat of debtors' prison. Theater and the profession of acting were regarded with the social ambivalence and antitheatrical prejudice that early modern Europe inherited from the medieval period. In Catholic and Protestant countries alike, the theater was regularly associated with immorality, and such charges came from secular as well as religious sources. Relationships with state and civic authorities were often equally fraught. Dramatic censorship was instituted in Spain and England, and the theater was subject to a range of restrictive laws throughout Europe. Although the licensing of theaters that took place during the 1600s conferred greater legitimacy on the companies that gained state approval, the implementation of such policies had the effect of bringing theatrical

activity even more firmly under government control.

THE DRAMA OF EARLY MODERN EUROPE

The profound changes in Europe between 1500 and 1700 and the accompanying theatrical developments helped ensure that the era would become one of the most prominent in the creation of dramatic literature. The rediscovery, translation, and publication of Greek and Roman plays spurred widespread interest in classical drama, and the translation into Italian of Aristotle's *Poetics* in 1549 helped ignite a debate over Aristotelian dramatic theory that lasted into the eighteenth century. Through the efforts of sixteenth-century Italian and French commentators, Aristotle's treatise was interpreted and codified into neoclassical precepts concerning decorum, verisimilitude, dramatic probability, concentrated action, and uniformity of subject and tone. The dramatic unities of time, place, and action, for example, dictated that the playwright not strain a spectator's credulity by having events take place over more than one day and in more than one location and that the play be restricted to a single, focused plotline. Noble characters were appropriate to tragedy, while those of lower social station belonged to the domain of comedy. Neoclassical theory had its greatest impact on the drama of Italy and France; but even in England and Spain, where dramatists generally eschewed its precepts for more episodic, stylistically varied dramatic styles, debates over classical authority took place.

Early in the sixteenth century, comedy, tragedy, tragicomedy, pastoral, and dramatic satire were strongly influenced by classical models. But as the academic performance of plays in Latin gave way to plays written in the vernacular, the drama of early modern Europe began drawing more strongly on native performance traditions inherited from the Middle Ages. The result was a rich tapestry of dramatic styles, ranging from the multiple, episodic plots of Elizabethan and Jacobean English drama to the classical simplicity of the plays of Jean Racine (1639–1699). As part of a larger theatrical field that included religious performances, royal pageants, civic commemorations, and such popular forms as mumming, drama during the period 1500–1700 entertained a variety of spectators in numerous venues. Concentrated in Europe's major cities, this drama reflected a lively urban culture and the early stirrings of national self-awareness. And although many of its most enduring technological, performative, and theoretical innovations arose in Italy, the theater of early modern Europe found its highest dramatic achievement in England, Spain, and France.

English Theater, 1576–1642

In 1576, when the actor, manager, and theatrical entrepreneur James Burbage (1531–1597) built the Theatre in Shoreditch (an area to the northeast of the City of London), the commercial theater was in its infancy in England. The performance of plays and other theatrical activity had, of course, enjoyed popularity earlier in the sixteenth century. Dramatists influenced by Renaissance humanism wrote comedies, tragedies, and moral interludes that made use of classical and medieval models alike; they were performed in a variety of places, including at court and in noble households, schools, universities, and London's legal societies, the Inns of Court. Among the best known of these earlier plays are *Ralph Roister Doister* (ca. 1553) and *Gammer Gurton's Needle* (1552–53), two early English comedies, and Thomas Norton and Thomas Sackville's *Gorboduc* (1561), generally considered the first English tragedy. Traveling actors brought mummings, farces, and other forms of popular dramatic entertainment to local communities, and Corpus Christi plays continued to be staged throughout England until the 1570s, when their performance was effectively halted by royal edict. But the expansion of dramatic activity that would make London one of the most vibrant theatrical centers in Europe did not occur until the commercial theater was established during the century's final quarter.

PUBLIC AND PRIVATE THEATERS

In England, as elsewhere in Europe, the construction of theater buildings was essential to the institutionalization of theater. Theater buildings in London were of two kinds: public and private. Burbage's Theatre established the model for subsequent public theaters. Polygonal in shape, it contained three tiers of audience galleries surrounding a roughly circular, unroofed yard. We have sufficient information about this and other public theaters built between 1577 and 1623—notably the Swan, the Rose, the Fortune, and the Globe, which was built in Southwark (on the southern side of the Thames) with timber from the dismantled Theatre in 1599—to know that the stage for these theaters extended into the yard at a height of approximately 5 feet. Partly roofed, this stage featured a structure at the rear known as the *tiring house*, which included two doors for entrances and exits and one or two balcony levels that could be used for audience seating, music, and scenes requiring actors to perform above stage level (the so-called balcony scene in SHAKESPEARE's *Romeo and Juliet* [1595], for example). A trapdoor on the stage floor allowed ghosts and other characters to ascend from a darkened cellar (sometimes referred to as *hell*), while pulleys on

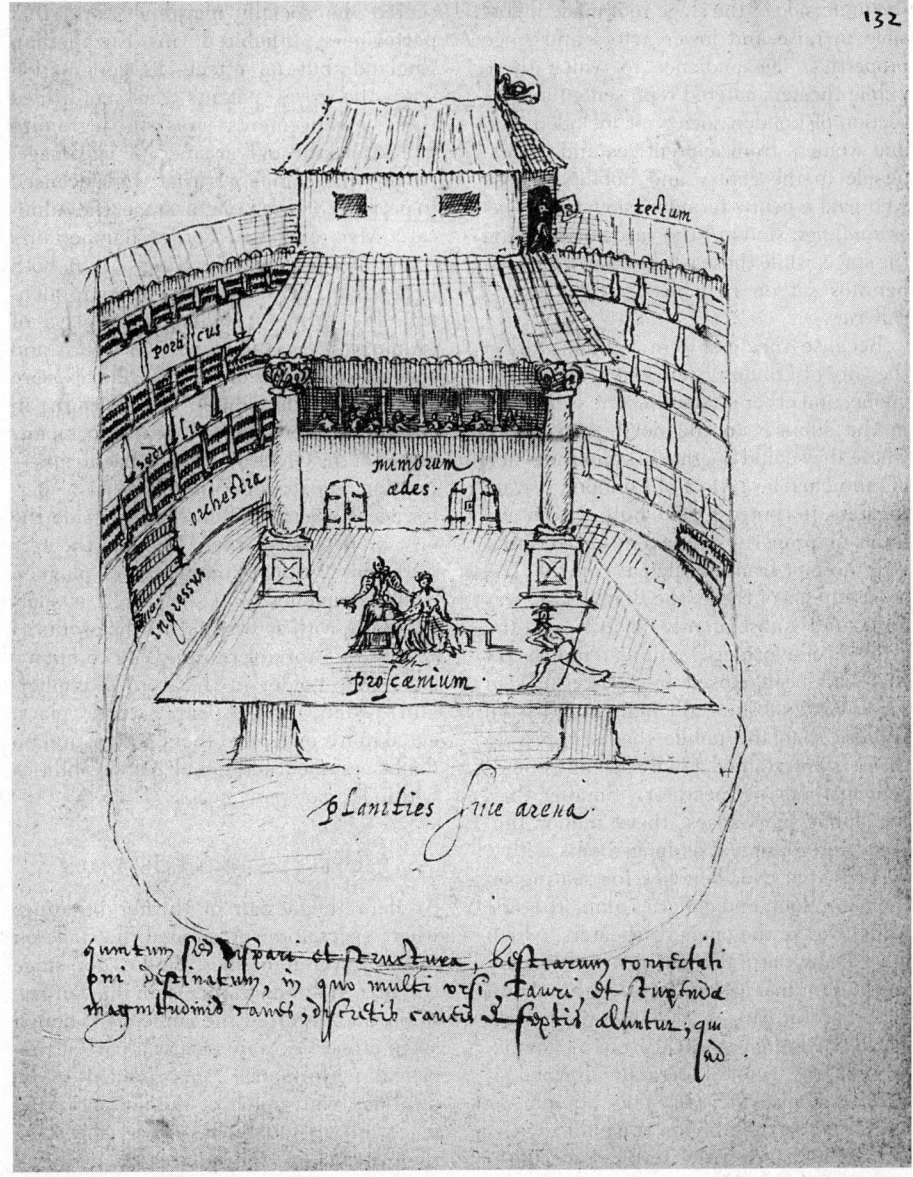

This sketch of the Swan Theater—a copy of an original by a late-sixteenth-century Dutch visitor to London named Johannes de Witt—is the only surviving contemporary likeness of the inside of an Elizabethan theater. Latin words or phrases identify the major parts of the theater: the *proscaenium* (the flat, open stage); the *mimorum aedes* (a dressing room for the actors); the *planities sive arena* (the "yard," in which spectators could stand in front of the stage); the *tectum* (the roof); the *porticus* (covered gallery); the *sedilia* (seats); the *orchestra* (seats for important spectators); and the *ingressus* (the entry into the various galleries).

the underside of the stage roof made it possible to raise and lower actors and stage properties. The audience to which these public theaters catered represented a cross section of London society; it included men and women, from apprentices and tradespeople to the gentry and nobility. Those who paid a penny for admission, known as *groundlings*, stood in the yard surrounding the stage, while those who paid two or three pennies sat on benches in the covered galleries.

Because theaters were banned within the City of London itself, the Theatre, the Globe, and other public theaters were built in the suburbs to the north and south, where they could operate beyond the reach of municipal law. Most of London's private theaters, in contrast, were built within city limits on properties known as *liberties* that were exempt from municipal control. The most famous of these, the Blackfriars, was built and subsequently rebuilt on the grounds of a former Dominican monastery that had been closed by Henry VIII in 1538. With substantially higher admission charges than the public theaters, private theaters entertained a more socially homogeneous body of spectators. Smaller than the public playhouses, these indoor theaters were designed as long rooms with a stage at one end, benches for seating on the main floor, and galleries along the side walls. Unlike the open-air theaters, which were lit by natural light, private theaters were illuminated by candlelight. Until 1609, performances at London's private theaters were given exclusively by companies of boy actors; originally formed at choir schools, they became popular at court and on the London stage during the late 1500s and early 1600s but subsequently fell out of favor.

ACTING COMPANIES

An essential contribution to the rise of professional theater in late-sixteenth-century England was a legal shift in the status of actors. In 1572 the government of Elizabeth I passed a law decreeing that itinerant actors and entertainers be arrested and punished as vagabonds if they could not demonstrate that they belonged to the household of a nobleman. The law under-

scored the socially marginal world that performers inhabited in Elizabethan England, but its effect—in conjunction with the royal patents that confirmed these arrangements—was to legitimize companies through aristocratic patronage. Among the companies that were licensed to perform on the London stage, the Admiral's Men and the Lord Chamberlain's Men (later renamed the King's Men), both licensed in 1594, were the most influential; the former produced the plays of CHRISTOPHER MARLOWE (1564–1593) and the latter the plays of William Shakespeare (1564–1616). In addition to performing in specific theaters—Shakespeare's company played at the Globe and, later, Blackfriars—London theatrical companies also performed at court and on tours outside the city (a necessity when London theaters were closed during outbreaks of plague). Adult companies were structured as sharing plans, with actors sharing the profits as well as the work of running the company. As a shareholder in the Lord Chamberlain's Men, Shakespeare wrote plays, acted in his own and others' works, and no doubt assumed additional responsibilities within the company.

PROPERTIES AND COSTUMES

As befit the design of theater buildings where spectators surrounded the stage on three or even four sides, the London stage was presentational rather than illusionistic in how it addressed the audience. Though stage properties were clearly a part of theatrical performance, they tended to be minimal, with much of the action taking place on an undefined area of the stage reminiscent of the *platea* of medieval drama. Setting, when it was specified, was established more through verbal description than through stage properties. Costumes, on the other hand, were often quite elaborate, with visually luxurious pieces provided by the nobility or purchased by the companies themselves. Whereas actresses were allowed to perform on the Continent, only male actors performed on the London stage before the closing of the theaters in 1642. Women's roles were usually played by boy actors within the companies, a practice that Shakespeare's

Cleopatra (played by a boy) alludes to when she imagines her story being performed on a Roman stage: "I shall see / Some squeaking Cleopatra boy my greatness / I'th' posture of a whore." But what may seem like limitations to the modern eye were opportunities for exceptional displays of acting skill by the period's many renowned performers, including the most celebrated actor of his day, Richard Burbage (James Burbage's son, 1568–1619).

PLAYWRIGHTS AND PLAYS

The proliferation of theaters and the rising demand for theatrical entertainment created intense competition for new plays, and a professional class of playwrights emerged to meet this demand. Shakespeare earned enough money from his playwriting and other theatrical efforts to purchase a large house and property in Stratford-upon-Avon, but not all playwrights had equal success, and they often turned their hands to pamphleteering and other activities in London's booming print market. Forced to work under the eye of the Master of the Revels, who in 1581 was granted the power to license plays (and thereby to act as government censor), playwrights were subject to arrest, imprisonment, and even torture if they addressed controversial subjects in their plays. Because plays belonged to the companies that purchased them, playwrights had no rights over their production or publication. Nor were plays accorded the literary standing of poetry and other more strictly literary forms. Company-authorized and pirated versions of plays occasionally appeared in inexpensive quarto editions (on small-sized paper), but it wasn't until 1616, when Ben Jonson (1572–1637) published his plays under the title *The Works of Benjamin Jonson,* that a dramatist presumed to accord his works the status of literary art. Like most of his contemporary dramatists, Shakespeare showed little interest in the publication of his plays, and it was only in 1623, seven years after his death, that two of his colleagues published his plays in a large-format edition, subsequently known as the First Folio.

The drama of Renaissance England was rich and varied, combining the eloquence of dramatic poetry with the vibrant particularity of contemporary life. During the 1580s and 1590s, the London stage offered a wealth of plays in the genres of comedy, tragedy, dramatic pastoral, and history play. With *The Spanish Tragedy* (1587), Thomas Kyd (1558–1594) inaugurated the genre of revenge tragedy that was to prove popular during the reigns of Elizabeth and James, and before his premature death (in 1593) Marlowe wrote a half-dozen or so tragedies and history plays that remain among the finest of their age. Elizabethan comedy ranged from the pastoral and romantic plays of Robert Greene (1558–1592) to Jonson's early satiric comedies. The exuberance that characterizes much of this drama reflected the optimism of an England that was asserting itself as a European power (the English defeat of the Spanish Armada occurred in 1588). This attitude changed in the years preceding Elizabeth's death in 1603, and the drama of the early seventeenth century was marked by a darkening of tone and subject matter. Shakespeare's greatest tragedies were written during this period, as were the plays of John Webster (1579–1630s?) and other tragic dramatists. In the area of comedy, the closing years of the sixteenth century and the first quarter of the seventeenth saw the sharpening of dramatic satire; a proliferation of city comedies (plays whose characters are drawn from London's urban classes) in the drama of Thomas Middleton (1580–1627), Thomas Dekker (ca. 1572–1632), and others; and the popularity of a hybrid genre—tragicomedy—in the plays of Francis Beaumont (ca. 1584–1616) and John Fletcher (1579–1625). The years of Charles I's reign (1625–49) saw the tragedies of John Ford (1586–1639?) and the genteel comedies of James Shirley (1596–1666).

COURT THEATER: MASQUES

The early seventeenth century also witnessed a flowering of theatrical activity in the courts of James I and Charles I. The Stuart court masque was an elaborate form of entertainment that featured lavish spectacle, music, singing, dance, and allegorical or mythological plots celebrating monarchical authority. Jonson was the leading writer of masques during this

Costume design by Inigo Jones for Ben Jonson's *The Masque of Queens* (1609).

period, and he worked in collaboration with the architect and stage designer Inigo Jones (1573–1652), who introduced important aspects of Italian stage design to the English theater. Like the court ballets that were performed in France during the reign of Louis XIV later in the century, the Stuart masques reflect the profound relationship between theatricality and the performance of power in the early modern state.

CIVIL WAR, COMMONWEALTH, AND THE CLOSING OF THE THEATERS

This relationship came to an end during the English Civil War (1642–49), which was followed by the Commonwealth and the Protectorate (1649–60); those eighteen years witnessed the overthrow of the English monarchy by a Puritan-dominated Parliament and the closing of the theaters by parliamentary decree in 1642. The Globe was torn down in 1644 to make room for tenements, and other theaters were subsequently dismantled or allowed to fall into disrepair. Theatrical activity was not entirely eliminated during these years—dramatic performances were given at private houses and other nontheatrical venues, and in the 1650s the musical dramas of William Davenant (1606–1668) marked the beginning of English opera—but the great age of Tudor and Stuart theater had come to a decisive end.

Spanish Theater, 1580–1700

During the sixteenth and seventeenth centuries, a period known as the "Golden Age" of Spanish literature and art, dramatic theater in Spain achieved a level of excellence that rivaled that of SHAKE-SPEARE's England. The rise of theater and the distinctive shapes it assumed reflected the history of Spain's emergence as a European and global power. During the medieval period much of Spain was under Muslim rule, and the slow reconquest of the Iberian peninsula by Christian armies was not completed until the Battle of Granada in 1492. The kingdoms of Aragon and Castile were joined by the marriage of Ferdinand II (1452–1516) and Isabella I (1451–1504) in 1469, and the resultant unified Spain extended its power through further dynastic alliances and an overseas empire that included vast areas of North, Central, and South America.

While other areas of Europe were feeling the initial shocks of the Protestant Reformation, the Catholic Church consolidated its authority in Spain and, through the office of the Spanish Inquisition, kept religious division beyond its borders. Spain's unique history strongly affected its theatrical development. The centuries of Muslim occupation gave Spanish drama and Spanish literature as a whole their most distinctive theme—that of honor; at the same time, the pervasive Catholicism of Spanish life during the later period ensured that the religious and secular theaters, which were diverging elsewhere in Europe, remained unusually close.

THEATERS AND AUDIENCE

Like the indoor tennis courts that preceded them and continued to be used as venues for theatrical productions, the public theaters of Paris were rectangular structures, typically long and narrow, with an auditorium for the public and a stage that included room, as the century progressed, for increasingly sophisticated technical machinery. The main floor of the auditorium consisted of a pit (*parterre*) for standing spectators with benches along the wall. The side and rear walls contained three rows of galleries, the first two of which were divided into boxes (*loges*). At the rear of the *parterre* and below the boxes rose the *amphithéâtre*, a section whose rows were raked to provide a better angle for viewing the stage. Both stage and auditorium were illuminated by candlelight. For much of the first half of the seventeenth century, scenic practice followed the conventions of medieval drama, with dramatic locales represented by the separate scenic structures called *mansions*. But as Italian scene design was adopted in the public theaters, the Parisian stage incorporated the spatially unifying principles of perspective staging. Any increase in dramatic illusion that might have resulted from perspective staging, though, was offset by the lively presence of the spectators, whose appearance and behavior in the Paris theater often constituted a performance in their own right. Perhaps more distracting to the actors than the unruly occupants of the *parterre* were those spectators who were allowed to sit onstage during performances. A cross section of Paris society, including the nobility and, on occasion, the king himself, made up the audience.

NEOCLASSICISM AND FRENCH DRAMA

The triumph of Italian scene design, with its concentration on single locations, was aided by the growing influence of neoclassicism on seventeenth-century French drama. During the 1630s and 1640s a number of French authors and intellectuals championed the "rules" that earlier Renaissance commentators had drawn from Aristotle's *Poetics*, and the principles advocated by neoclassical theory (including

An engraving showing the performance of Molière's *The Imaginary Invalid*, in 1664, before Louis XIV and his court.

the dramatic unities) were given official sanction by the newly formed Académie Française. The authority and validity of neoclassicism were fiercely debated, particularly as its strictures might apply to the genre of tragedy. The most passionately argued of these debates concerned *Le Cid* (1636–37), a tragedy written by France's leading playwright at the time, Pierre Corneille (1606–1684). Those who attacked Corneille's play for not observing the principles of verisimilitude, decorum, and purity of genre were supported by the Académie, which entered the debate at the request of Richelieu. Although some writers continued to resist, the principles of neoclassical theory became widely adopted by French playwrights. That these principles could be artistically enabling as well as prescriptive is demonstrated by the formally elegant, psychologically complex plays of Jean Racine (1639–1699), France's greatest tragic dramatist.

French comedy also attained a pinnacle of excellence in the later seventeenth century, chiefly through the plays of JEAN-BAPTISTE POQUELIN (1621?–1673), better known by his stage name, MOLIÈRE. Like SHAKESPEARE, Molière was a man of the theater as well as a writer, and his career as a dramatist is intertwined with the professions of actor and company manager. After years touring the French provinces, the theatrical troupe that Molière had helped found in 1643 settled in the French capital. By the 1660s the company had established itself in the Palais Royal, had been awarded an annual subsidy from Louis XIV, and was performing to great acclaim at court and before the Parisian public. Much of this acclaim resulted from Molière's dramatic contributions: farces influenced by the commedia dell'arte, court spectacles, ballets, and, most of all, the comedies of manners in which Molière offered lively and satirical portraits of French society. These plays were not without their controversies—*TARTUFFE* (1664–69), Molière's comic investigation of religious hypocrisy, was attacked on religious grounds and banned from performance for five years—but they quickly became standards of the classical French repertoire.

THE DECLINE OF COURT INFLUENCE

By the end of the seventeenth century, Paris had established itself as the theatrical capital of Europe. The Comédie Française was the leading theatrical company of its time, and under the influence of Jean-Baptiste Lully (1632–1687) French opera had become equally renowned. The brilliance of the theatrical arts in seventeenth-century France owed much to the splendor of the French court, which displayed its power through the culture of spectacle. After Louis XIV moved his court and France's nobility outside Paris to the newly built Palace of Versailles in 1682, however, the role in French theater of the court and its literary tastes declined. As in England at the turn of the eighteenth century, in France public theater was left to thrive on its own terms. That Paris continued to exert a strong influence on European theater in the centuries that followed is powerful testimony to the theater that Corneille, Racine, and Molière helped build.

English Theater, 1660–1700

RESTORATION AND THEATER

When Charles II, eldest son of the executed Charles I, made his triumphant return in 1660 after eighteen years of parliamentary rule, both the monarchy and the public theater were reestablished in England. But the intervening years ensured that both institutions looked very different than they had before the Civil War. Restoration theater (1660–1700) was the product of a largely aristocratic culture, and it catered to a much narrower audience than had the theater of Elizabeth I and James I. Rejecting the Puritanism of the Commonwealth and Protectorate, upper-class Restoration London was an intensely social world, and the licentiousness, materialism, social competition, and love of wit for which the elite society of this period is notorious found ample representation onstage.

The emergence of this theater owes much to broader European theatrical developments. During their exile in France, Charles II and members of his court grew familiar with the theatrical

An early-nineteenth-century engraving of the interior of the Duke's Theatre in Lincoln's Inn Fields during the reign of Charles II.

culture that flourished under Louis XIV, and the theater that they helped establish upon their return reflected their taste for Continental stagecraft. Shortly after Charles II was restored to the throne, he issued royal patents to William Davenant (1606–1668) and Thomas Killigrew (1612–1683) to form theatrical companies and purchase or build theaters. Because the few theaters that survived the Civil War were unable to meet the technical requirements of Italian scenic innovations—sliding upstage shutters and side wings that made possible rapid scene changes, trapdoors, and flying machinery, for instance—new theaters were built to accommodate the new technology. The King's Company (managed by Killigrew and sponsored by Charles II himself) first used an indoor tennis court but soon was performing at the newly built Theatre Royal on Bridges Street; when this burned down in 1672 they performed at a new structure on the same site, the Drury Lane Theatre. The Duke's Company (managed by Davenant and sponsored by the duke of York, the future king James II) used the Lincoln's Inn Fields Theatre (a converted tennis court) and, after 1671,

the Dorset Garden Theatre. Given that the patented companies held a monopoly over theatrical production in London—merging in 1682 (after the King's Company fell into dire financial straits) to form the United Company, an arrangement that lasted until 1695—these buildings were the center of London's theatrical life.

PLAYHOUSES, AUDIENCE, AND ACTORS

Restoration playhouses were small structures when compared with the open-air theaters that were built in London in the late sixteenth century. The stage featured a proscenium arch with a curved apron (or open floor) extending into the audience and to the side. The main floor of the auditorium (or pit) contained benches, and these were surrounded on the side and rear by box seats and galleries. The play-watching experience in this setting was intimate. Restoration theaters accommodated no more than 600 spectators, and all were seated within 35 feet or so of the stage. Boxes allowed spectators to sit above the sides of the stage (and hence be prominently displayed to the rest of the audience), and by the end of the century spectators were routinely seated onstage. Auditorium and stage were both lit by candelabra, with the result that actors and their spectators were equally illuminated. Restoration actors often played on the forestage (near the audience), and they delivered their lines as much to the spectators as to the play's other characters. It was not uncommon for spectators, who could be quite unruly in the Restoration theater, to interrupt a play by addressing the actors themselves.

As these practices and behaviors begin to suggest, the relationship between Restoration spectators and the performances they attended was marked by mutual interaction and display. Attending the theater was a popular activity for the upper classes of London society and for the king, and the theater became a microcosm of this aristocratic world, its relationships (overt and covert), and its social distinctions. Men and women came to the theater arrayed in the latest fashions, and the theater became an arena for displaying symbols of social distinction. Women— some of them prostitutes—often wore masks (or *vizards*) to disguise their identities, and the rendezvous that were arranged through this and other stratagems mirrored the sexual intrigue being performed onstage. The introduction of women actors for the first time on the English stage contributed to the sexually charged atmosphere of Restoration theaters. Charles II, who had seen actresses perform on the Continent, justified their inclusion in the name of moral reformation, since their presence would eliminate transvestism—boys dressing as women. But the theatrical display of female bodies onstage became an erotic attraction in its own right, particularly when women actors dressed as men, donning tight-fitting, knee-length pants in what were called *breeches roles*. Contemporary moralists viewed actresses as a symbol of the theater's licentiousness; and while their general accusation was unfair, it was certainly true that some actresses did have affairs with theatergoers. Charles II, a well-known libertine, numbered the actress Nell Gwynn (1650–1687) among his many mistresses.

RESTORATION DRAMA

The drama of Restoration England assumed a number of characteristic forms. Even the revivals of English plays written before the Civil War—chiefly, the works of Beaumont and Fletcher, Shakespeare, and Jonson— were often adapted to reflect contemporary tastes and conventions. During this period heroic tragedy flourished; it featured larger-than-life characters, exotic locales, and elevated—occasionally ranting—dramatic verse. Other tragedies written during this time observed the principles of French neoclassicism, such as the concentration of dramatic action according to the dramatic "unities." Adherence to these principles was not as strict in England as it was in France, however, and Restoration tragedy continued to be influenced by Shakespeare and by earlier English dramatic conventions. In his 1668 *An Essay of Dramatic Poesy*, the period's most significant work of dramatic theory, John Dryden (1611–1700)—a leading writer of tragic and other drama— defended "the honour of our *English* writers" against those who overvalued French dramatic models.

But it was in comedy that the Restoration's achievements were most dazzling. Set in contemporary London, the Restoration comedy of manners featured gallants (or rakes), ladies, jealous husbands, cast-off mistresses, unsophisticated country visitors, fops, and clever servants engaged in often predatory games of intrigue and seduction. The wit and wordplay that characterize these plays reflect the importance of language, innuendo, and verbal disguise to Restoration stage interactions. Many of the plays contain a secondary plot involving conventional lovers, but the theatrical energies of the finest Restoration comedies—*The Country Wife* (1675), by William Wycherley (1641–1716); *The Man of Mode* (1676), by George Etherege (1636–1692); THE ROVER (written in two parts, 1677, 1681), by APHRA BEHN (1640–1689), England's first professional woman playwright; and *The Way of the World* (1700), by William Congreve (1670–1729)—are located in the central, equally matched "wit" couple. The lens provided by these interactions enabled playwrights to investigate fashion, marriage as a social contract, authenticity, masculinity, and social difference. By the end of the century, however, Restoration comedy faced opposition from a growing middle-class audience that rejected its libertinism, amorality, and elitism. When Jeremy Collier (1650–1726), an English clergyman, published *A Short View of the Immorality and Profaneness of the English Stage* in 1698, his attack hastened the end of a comic form that had outlived the courtly world of Charles II.

Eighteenth-Century Theater

The eighteenth century in Europe was characterized by stability and change; it was a period when the new rubbed uncomfortably against the old, and the outlines of the modern world began to emerge with unprecedented clarity. Throughout the century many of the artistic forms that had traditionally been preferred by the social elite continued to thrive. However, the social and economic transformations that would lead, by century's end, to the beginning of the Industrial Revolution hastened the growth of a middle class with its own interests, moral expectations, and tastes. Neoclassicism retained considerable authority on the Continent throughout the century, and the influence of classical ideals was evident in movements in literature, art, architecture, and music late in the century, but these were countered by the growing middle-class demand for nonelite literary and cultural forms such as the novel, which—with the help of an expanding popular press—by 1800 had become a literary form in its own right.

THE ENLIGHTENMENT

The eighteenth century was also the period of the Enlightenment, a philosophical movement centered in France that stressed the authority of reason and universally valid principles in human affairs. While some of

the age's thinkers approved of the authoritarian rule of such "enlightened despots" as Frederick the Great (1712–1786) of Prussia and Catherine the Great (1729–1796) of Russia, the Enlightenment's main proponents challenged arbitrary authority and advocated limits to state power. The writings of such theorists as Jean-Jacques Rousseau (1712–1778), who argued that a social contract between individuals constitutes the only legitimate form of political order, established the foundations of modern democracy and were an important influence on the American Revolution (1775–83), the French Revolution (1789–99), and the Latin American revolutions of the early nineteenth century.

THEATERS AND ACTORS

The public theaters of eighteenth-century Europe offered a variety of entertainments—pantomime, comic opera, burlesque, and other popular performance forms in

A painting by William Hogarth of a scene from John Gay's popular ballad opera *The Beggar's Opera*. Note the audience members onstage in boxes.

addition to serious and comic drama—to an audience whose numbers grew throughout the century. To accommodate this increase in spectators and keep up with the latest trends in stage design and technology, the major theaters of the period were expanded, renovated, and sometimes replaced by newer, larger buildings. Established theaters and theatrical companies continued to dominate theatrical life in Europe's capitals, usually as a result of government licensing, though theatrical activity beyond these theaters enjoyed periods of popularity. In London (the capital of what was now known as Great Britain, following the union of England and Scotland in 1707), a number of unlicensed theaters operating in the 1720s and 1730s contributed to a lively theatrical scene that produced the long-running ballad opera *The Beggar's Opera* (1728), by John Gay (1685–1732), and satirical burlesques directed at the government of Sir Robert Walpole (1676–1745), who was in effect Britain's prime minister (a title not yet in official usage). In part as a reaction to this satirical activity, the Theatrical Licensing Act, which confirmed the Drury Lane and Covent Garden as London's only licensed theaters and empowered the Lord Chamberlain to approve plays for performance, was passed in 1737. In Paris, the monopoly of the Comédie Française and the Opéra was challenged by nonlicensed troupes that performed as part of the city's seasonal fairs. These troupes, which presented comic operas, pantomimes, and (by the end of the century) comic and noncomic drama, eventually established themselves as year-round companies housed on the fashionable Boulevard du Temple.

Although theater as an institution changed less in the eighteenth century than in earlier centuries, scenic practice underwent a number of modifications designed to intensify the stage's visual realism. The symmetries of classical perspective were relinquished in favor of angled perspectives, which allowed the scene to be viewed from varying points of view, and mid- and late-century designers introduced picturesque landscapes, historical and exotic locales, and increasingly sophisticated atmospheric settings made possible, in part, by advances in lighting and sound effects.

Another development that reinforced the increasing illusionism of the eighteenth-century stage in London and Paris was the removal from it of spectators, a change that was complete by the middle of the century.

Although by modern standards eighteenth-century acting remained stylized in gesture and vocal delivery, in this area, too, practitioners shifted toward realism—and away from rhetorical modes of delivery. David Garrick (1717–1779), the century's greatest English actor, was praised for his natural style of acting, and similar advances in realistic performance took place on the Continent. To be sure, these efforts to bring the stage closer to life were limited in their aspirations and accomplishments. But though realism would not become a fully formed theatrical aesthetic until the nineteenth century, the first steps toward it were taken in the eighteenth.

EIGHTEENTH-CENTURY DRAMA

In the eighteenth century, the genres of tragedy and comedy underwent a number of important modifications that reflected the tastes of a growing middle-class audience and its largely conservative moral outlook. Tragedy, which had traditionally been concerned with actions of the ruling classes, set in historical and mythological locales, was expanded to include the events and scenes of ordinary life. The pioneering play in the subgenre of domestic tragedy was *The London Merchant* (1731), by the English playwright George Lillo (1693–1739), which centered on the downfall and moral reclamation of a London apprentice. Comedy was similarly modified as the values of wit, ingenuity, and sexual titillation gave way to noble feeling, moral elevation, and what Sir Richard Steele (1672–1729), one of the new subgenre's earliest champions, called "a joy too exquisite for laughter." Sentimental comedy (known in France as *comédie larmoyante*, or "tearful comedy") became popular throughout Europe during the eighteenth century.

Traditional tragedy and comedy had their supporters and practitioners as well. For example, the French philosopher and writer Voltaire (François-Marie Arouet, 1694–1778) wrote intricate tragedies in the elevated style, and the Irish-born London playwrights Oliver Goldsmith (ca. 1730–1774) and Richard Brinsley Sheridan (1751–1816) championed "laughing comedy" against the drama of sentimentality. In Italy Carlo Goldoni (1707–1793) reformed Italian comedy by transforming the improvisational drama of the commedia dell'arte into a literary genre. While eliminating the bawdiness and nonrealistic devices of the commedia, he nonetheless succeeded in preserving the tradition's comic spirit. Overall, though, sentimental drama and the century's other dramatic innovations crossed and, because of their popularity, undermined the boundaries between the traditional genres. In the 1750s Denis Diderot (1713–1784), one of the leading figures of the French Enlightenment, advocated a genre midway between tragedy and comedy: the *drame bourgeois*, which would take the social and familial problems of the middle class as its subject. Though it produced few plays of note during the late eighteenth century, the *drame bourgeois* was an important precursor to the social problem plays of HENRIK IBSEN (1828–1906) and later modern dramatists.

GERMAN THEATER AND DRAMA

One of the most important theatrical developments in the eighteenth century was the rise of established theater beyond its traditional centers in Italy, Spain, England, and France. This expansion was most striking in the German states of northern and central Europe. Although Vienna was one of the leading centers of opera in the late seventeenth century and troupes of professional actors performed at courts and in public settings throughout German-speaking Europe, an organized German theater did not develop until the eighteenth century. The Thirty Years War, which was fought largely on German soil, had devastated the region in the seventeenth century, and the territories that in the late nineteenth century would become modern Germany consisted of numerous small states within a declining Holy Roman Empire. With the region's resources scattered over a large area rather than concentrated in a capital or in other urban centers, it fell to the individual states to establish and support public theaters.

The Hamburg National Theater, established in 1767, was a short-lived venture that paved the way for state-subsidized theaters elsewhere in German-speaking Europe. The Gotha Court Theater was founded in 1775, the Imperial and National Theater of Vienna in 1776, and the Court and National Theater of Mannheim in 1779. Of the numerous state theaters that followed these, the most significant were the Royal National Theater, established in Berlin in 1786, and the Weimar Court Theater (1791), which produced plays by two of the century's greatest dramatists, Johann Wolfgang von Goethe (1749–1832) and Friedrich von Schiller (1759–1805). Though these theaters operated independently of each other, their founding reflected a broad cultural concern with the expression of German national identity.

Despite being a relative newcomer to the European dramatic tradition, German drama of the mid- and late eighteenth century was significant in its experimentation and the range of its literary achievement. Gotthold Ephraim Lessing (1729–1781), an early advocate of sentimental drama, wrote plays that dealt with national, social, and philosophical themes and was instrumental in freeing German drama from the influence of French neoclassicism. His *Hamburg Dramaturgy,* a series of essays published in 1767 and 1768, was one of the century's most important works of dramatic theory. A more radical break with neoclassicism was achieved by the playwrights of the *Sturm und Drang* (storm and stress) movement, a revolt against Enlightenment rationalism that flourished between the late 1760s and early 1780s. The drama written as part of this movement—including early plays by Goethe and Schiller—explored intense emotion, nature, rebellion against society, and violent action in irregular, often episodic plots.

Goethe and Schiller eventually rejected *Sturm und Drang* for the "Weimar classicism" of their work created between the former's visit to Italy in 1786–88 and the latter's death in 1805. Ranging over modern European history, classical mythology, and philosophy, the plays of this period pursued the values of harmony, wholeness, and aesthetic distance. This desire to provide Germany with a classical tradition

An illustration of a scene from one of Schiller's *Sturm und Drang* dramas, *Kabale und Liebe* (1784).

reflected a revived interest in the classical world in late-eighteenth-century Europe—the ruins of Herculaneum and Pompeii, which offered Europeans a mesmerizing portrait of Roman life preserved in the ashes of Mount Vesuvius's eruption of 79 C.E., were discovered in Italy in 1709 and 1748. The resultant drama embodied the aesthetic values of beauty, harmony, and form rather than the prescriptive neoclassicism of earlier centuries. At the same time, this drama drew its subjects from a Europe facing a period of political and aesthetic changes. Indeed, Goethe's masterpiece, the poetic drama FAUST (written in two parts, 1808, 1831), owes as much to the Romanticism that flourished in the next century as it does to the classical past.

Romanticism and Melodrama, 1800–1880

THE AGE OF REVOLUTION

At the end of the eighteenth century, two events fundamentally changed the political and cultural landscape of the Western world: the American Revolution and the French Revolution. The American Revolution severed England from its most prosperous colony and launched a radical experiment in democracy in the New World. A few years later, the French Revolution showed that even in Europe the old order was not impervious to change. Begun as a relatively modest revolt against the excesses of a king seeking absolute power, the French Revolution became radical when the lower orders and their revolutionary leaders turned against the aristocracy with increasing violence. The twin revolutions had far-reaching consequences, as neighboring countries watched them and their aftermaths with astonishment, enthusiasm, and fear. Soon, they would be directly affected as well, when Napoleon Bonaparte (1769–1821) rose from the French revolutionary forces to conquer much of Europe, propelled by a powerful army and the promise of freedom from local tyranny. Even after Napoleon had been defeated and the political map of Europe reordered in 1815 at the Congress of Vienna, what historians now term the Age of Revolution would continue well into the second half of the nineteenth century.

ROMANTICISM AND THE THEATER

The two revolutions changed more than the political order of two countries: they also altered how Western societies thought about themselves, with marked effects on cultural institutions and the arts. The French and the American revolutions had been inspired by Enlightenment philosophers such as Voltaire (François-Marie Arouet, 1694–1778), Immanuel Kant (1724–1804), and Thomas Jefferson (1743–1826), who had advocated new social organizations based not on religious beliefs but on rational planning and thought. But as the social upheavals of these revolutions grew more and more violent and unsettling, the Enlightenment insistence on pure reason lost some of its currency. Reflecting these changing historical and intellectual currents, the generation of writers, artists, and thinkers following the revolutions articulated the movement known as Romanticism. The Romantics did not reject the Enlightenment and its social experiments entirely, but they considered its more extreme claims with skepticism. They consequently placed greater emphasis on subjective experience and even on irrational desires and beliefs, which had been rejected by the Enlightenment. By the same token, they turned against the restrained, rational movement in the arts known as classicism. Whereas artists adhering to classicism respected the boundaries between styles and poetic forms, the Romantics created unusual mixtures and sometimes left their works deliberately in fragments. Ruins of medieval architecture were prized over classical buildings, and folk arts such as fairy tales or rustic idylls over Greek and Roman models.

These developments changed the face of drama and theater as well. Indeed, the battles between the advocates of classicist theater and those of the new Romantic theater were often fierce. The French writer Victor Hugo (1802–1885), whose preface to the play *Cromwell* (1827) served as a manifesto of Romanticism, aroused the ire of traditionalists by rejecting the unities of time and place, advocating the use of historically accurate stage settings, and calling for a theatrical art that included the sublime and the grotesque. So intense were the passions of classicists

An illustration, by Jean Albert Grand-Carteret, of the audience disturbances that followed the final scene of Victor Hugo's *Hernani* at its premiere in 1830.

and romanticists over the future of French theater that the performances of Hugo's play *Hernani* (1830) at the Comédie Française were interrupted by sustained outbursts by supporters and detractors.

Like many of their contemporaries, Romantic playwrights developed an

This late-eighteenth-century engraving of King Lear in the storm indicates the passionate intensity with which Shakespeare was often performed on the Romantic stage.

ambivalent attitude toward the French Revolution. In the early nineteenth century Georg Büchner (1813–1837) wanted to bring the legacy of the French Revolution to Germany, where the political system was especially hierarchical and repressive. He even wrote a tragedy about one of the leaders of the French Revolution—*Danton's Death* (1835), a sympathetic portrait of Georges-Jacques Danton (1759–1774). Other Romantics, such as William Wordsworth (1770–1850) and Samuel Taylor Coleridge (1772–1834), became much more disenchanted with the French Revolution, foregrounding not its social gains but its violence. But though they were divided in their attitudes toward the political and social upheavals of their time, the Romantics could agree on many other things. One was the eminence of WILLIAM SHAKESPEARE, which led to a revival of the playwright across Europe; French and German Romantics treated the Elizabethan playwright as their most important predecessor. What the Romantics admired in Shakespeare was precisely what classicism had rejected: namely, the mixing of high and low characters and of comedy and tragedy, as well as the fantastic events depicted in Shakespeare's romances.

CLOSET DRAMA

Despite the fascination with theater in general and Shakespeare in particular, Romantic drama was characterized by an increasing distance from the theater audience. Although plays such as Hugo's *Hernani* enjoyed controversy and success on the popular stage, many dramas written by the great Romantic writers either were not performed during their lifetimes or received limited, private performances or readings. Such plays written for reading only, or *closet dramas*, form the most significant genre of dramatic literature during the Romantic era. Among them are *The Borderers* (1796), by Wordsworth; *The Death of Empedocles* (1798; unfinished), by Friedrich Hölderlin (1770–1843); *Remorse* (1813), by Coleridge; *Manfred* (1817), by Lord Byron (1788–1824); *The Cenci* (1819), by Percy Bysshe Shelley (1792–1822); and the plays of Alfred de Musset (1810–1857). The two plays from this era collected in the *Norton Anthology of Drama*—Goethe's *Faust* (part 1, 1808) and Büchner's *Woyzeck* (1836)—are closet dramas as well.

THEATERS AND ACTORS

The increasing division between dramatic literature and theatrical performance had to do both with the preferences of writers and with the state of the theater industry. Poets distrusted theater managers and actors, choosing instead to write for the reading public only. At the same time, theaters—which, throughout Europe, continued to expand in size during the nineteenth century—catered to the tastes of the general public by putting on lavish spectacles. (When a similar estrangement between dramatic authors and theater managers had occurred in imperial Rome, Seneca likewise wrote only for readers or small recitations and left the theater to the popular entertainments then dominating the stage.) The demand for such spectacles drove innovation, and thus nineteenth-century theater history is dominated by a series of technical developments—including the use of gaslights (first introduced around 1825) and limelights, an early form of spotlight that greatly enhanced designers' ability to create theatrical illusions and effects. The public also desired equestrian as well as nautical plays, as new traps, elevators, moving panoramas, and, later on, revolving stages expanded the range of theatrical possibilities. Other developments were more in tune with cultural tastes and ideas dominant in the Romantic era. As general interest in the distant past grew, audiences began to pay more attention to historically accurate costumes and sets. At the same time, celebrated actors such as England's Edmund Kean (1787–1833)—famous for his interpretation of Shakespeare—and France's Frédérick Lemaître (1800–1876) developed a Romantic acting style, based on the expression of strong emotions. Such performances may have seemed spontaneous and authentic, but in fact many Romantic actors, who were given little time for rehearsal, followed manuals of gesture and expression.

MELODRAMA

Though most poets refused to write plays for the stage, a second group of writers were only too willing to supply the theaters of Europe with the popular drama they needed. The most popular type of play during this period was melodrama, which suited the public's taste for spectacle, music, and easily digestible characters and plots. The term *melodrama* is taken from the French *melodrame*, which joins the Greek word for music (*melos*) to drama; it was first applied in the late eighteenth century to plays with musical interludes that employ an easily recognizable dramatic formula and unambiguous moral contrasts. Drawing on a set of stock characters—the villain, the hapless maiden in distress, and the hero—melodramatic plots involve extraordinary coincidences and hinge on sudden revelations and encounters. France was the birthplace of melodrama, and its king was René-Charles Guilbert de Pixérécourt (1773–1844). Another prominent author of melodrama was the Irish writer Dion Boucicault (1820?–1890). Boucicault not only wrote popular plays set in Ireland, such as *The Colleen Bawn* (1860), but after spending several years in the United States he set several notable plays there as well, including *The Octoroon; or, Life in Louisiana* (1859).

Both in England and in France, many melodramas were produced by adapting novels to the stage. It was a time when the novel experienced an unprecedented rise in status and appeal, and many of the era's most accomplished writers turned their hands to fiction. Prime candidates for adaptation were the immensely popular novels of Charles Dickens (1812–1870). In France, novels by Alexandre Dumas père (1802–1870) and his son, Alexandre Dumas fils (1824–1895), were adapted by the two authors themselves, among them the former's *The Three Musketeers* (1844) and *The Count of Monte Christo* (1845) and the latter's *La Dame aux camélias* (in English known as *Camille;* 1848), which also became the libretto for Giuseppe Verdi's opera *La Traviata* (1853). Because of Paris's dominant cultural position, nineteenth-century French melodramas were imported into many European countries and more distant lands.

THE WELL-MADE PLAY

Alongside melodrama, French playwrights perfected another, related form of drama, the so-called *well-made play* (a name borrowed from the French *pièce bien-fait*). The well-made play was based not on spectacle and music but on complicated, intricately constructed plots. Playwrights relied on well-known techniques such as overheard conversations, mistaken identities, sudden appearances and disappearances, and other forms of confusion that culminated in the main scene of the play—the confrontation of the main antagonists—followed by the final resolution. Because everything in a well-made play led up to such a scene, it was called *scène à faire*, the obligatory scene that "had to be done." Masters of the well-made play included Augustin-Eugène Scribe (1791–1861), who wrote more than 300 plays, and the even more popular Victorien Sardou (1831–1908), who composed several plays specifically for the greatest star of the French nineteenth-

Sarah Bernhardt in the title role of Victorien Sardou's *Theodora* (1884).

century stage, Sarah Bernhardt (1844–1923). Sardou so dominated the second half of the nineteenth century that GEORGE BERNARD SHAW (1856–1950), a radical reformer of the well-made play, referred to his drama as "sardoodledom." Like melodrama, the well-made play was an extremely popular export, imitated everywhere.

EUROPE AT MIDCENTURY

The ever-more-sophisticated spectacles, melodramas, and well-made plays were created in the context of Europe's larger economic and political developments. The Age of Revolution had come to a second climax with the Europe-wide revolution of 1848, during which the countries of Continental Europe suffered through protests, strikes, and overturned governments. The revolution of 1848 gave expression to the social consequences of rapid, though uneven, industrialization in various regions of Europe, including the large-scale movements of people to urban centers, the emergence of an industrial proletariat, and the triumph of a bourgeois class. What followed was a period of political reaction and a new focus on economic gains. It was a time when England and France in particular secured and expanded their empires, and from those holdings outside Europe they drew enormous resources. The financial speculation that attended such enterprises as the building of the railroads led a fortunate few to amass unheard-of fortunes, especially in the 1870s and 1880s. This new accumulation of wealth contributed to the development of extravagant and lavish spectacles, the expansion of theaters, and an emphasis on technical developments.

NATIONALISM AND THE THEATER

The nineteenth century was also the century of nationalism, as growing numbers of countries attempted to establish and affirm their own native traditions and values. Nationalists called for national theaters to showcase the new (or old) national self-consciousness, on the model of the Comédie Française, the foremost theater of France. Theatrically the most remarkable of those efforts was undertaken by Richard Wagner (1813–1883) in Germany. Wagner sought to integrate dramatic literature, music, and acting, as well as all the other components of theater such as set design and lighting, into a new and complete synthesis—what he labeled the *Gesamtkunstwerk* (total work of art). Single-handedly, he wrote the libretti, composed the music, and influenced the staging of his operas, which he called music-dramas, at the opera house in Bayreuth newly built under his supervision, the Festspielhaus (Festival Theater). Because Wagner wanted to immerse his spectators in the power of theatrical illusion, he inaugurated what are today common theatrical methods such as dimming the light in the auditorium and hiding the orchestra to encourage the audience to focus exclusively on the stage. Though Wagner himself relied on Romantic plots and folktales, many later theater practitioners, such as the Swiss designer Adolphe Appia (1862–1928), took their inspiration from him as they attempted to create a new and modern theater.

THEATER IN THE UNITED STATES, 1800–1900

The quest for national identity was no less urgent in the United States, but it took a very different form. Theatrical activity in colonial America was recorded in the 1600s, and the first theater was built in Williamsburg, Virginia, in 1716. Even after the American Revolution was over and independence from England had been won, many economic and cultural ties between the newly formed United States of America and its former mother country remained in place. One particularly strong connection was their theaters. In the United States in the late eighteenth century, theatrical activity was largely restricted to the cities of Philadelphia, New York, Boston, and Charleston, South Carolina, and the small but growing number of resident professional companies was dominated by English-born actors and actors who had been trained in England. While the United States produced its own playwrights—including Mercy Otis Warren (1728–1814) and Royall Tyler (1757–1826)—English plays constituted most of

The Astor Place Riot, New York City, 1849.

the dramatic repertoire well into the nineteenth century.

During the nineteenth century, a new and genuinely American theater culture appeared, owing in no small part to the country's first native-born acting star. Edwin Forrest (1806–1872) established an American school of acting based on a heroic style that relied on grand, physical gestures and speech that appealed to popular audiences. While Forrest stayed in America, Charlotte Cushman (1816–1876), the first famous American actress, moved to England once she had become well known, proving that England still had greater cachet and rewards for an ambitious actor. In 1849 the relation between the United States and England, and more specifically the difference between the English and the more physical American acting schools, led to violence. In New York City, both Forrest and the visiting English actor William Charles Macready (1793–1873) were playing Macbeth. The two men were longtime rivals, and when thousands of followers of Forrest invaded the Astor Place Opera House to stop Macready's performance, with thousands more outside, the mayor called out the National Guard. Guardsmen fired into the crowd, and at least twenty-two died in what has become known as the Astor Place Riot.

STAGING RACE

While Americans were fighting for cultural independence, there emerged in the United States another type of theater not found in England or any other part of Europe: the minstrel show. Initially its players were white performers in blackface, their skins darkened with burnt cork or shoe polish, but African American minstrel troupes soon appeared as well. Musicians and singers would form a semicircle, and they would alternate between songs, dances, and short bits of dialogue, mostly between two characters—Tambo (a player of the tambourine) and Bones (a player of the bones, a clacking folk instrument made of bones or wood)—seated at either end of the semicircle, or between them and an interlocutor who sat in the middle. The minstrel show relied on racial stereotypes, for whether whites represented African Americans, as was most often the case, or African Americans made up the troupe, they had to conform to the stereotyped routines that were initially established by white performers and demanded by the predominantly white audiences. In this way, the minstrel show, America's most popular form of theatrical entertainment in the nineteenth century, was part of the fabric of American racism even as it established an American, and especially an African American, performance tradition.

America's most popular play of the nineteenth century also dealt with race relations. Harriet Beecher Stowe's (1811–1896) immensely influential novel *Uncle Tom's Cabin* (1851–52), which some have credited with having helped to start the U.S. Civil War (1861–65) through its moving depiction of the plight of slaves, inspired numerous dramatic adaptations; the most famous was an 1852 version by George L. Aiken (1830–1876), which had the longest run—more than 300 performances—of any single production in nineteenth-century America. Aiken's dramatization was largely faithful to Stowe's antislavery stance, but many other adaptations simply reverted to racial stereotypes. These adaptations, known as Tom shows, helped establish "Uncle Tom" as a derogatory label for African Americans who appeared to make their peace with slavery and suppression rather than rebelling against them. While minstrel shows and the dramatizations of *Uncle Tom's Cabin* played a central role in nineteenth-century American theater, other representations of black life or slavery rarely appeared onstage. As so often in the history of drama, dramatists at odds with popular taste had to write for a smaller reading public instead, as the African American writer and former slave William Wells Brown (1814–1884) did with his play *The Escape; or, A Leap for Freedom* (1858).

Modern Theater, 1880–1945

THEATER AND THE MODERN WORLD

In the era of Romanticism, theatrical performance and dramatic literature had increasingly drifted apart. During the last two decades of the nineteenth century, however, serious writers were finally drawn to the theater once more. This did not mean that they sought to please the tastes of popular audiences. Indeed, modern drama was often characterized by a tension, even antagonism, between dramatists and audiences, an antagonism sometimes provoked by the playwrights themselves. Riling up audiences had been part of theater history for some time, as demonstrated by various nineteenth-century clashes in theaters, but now an adversarial relationship between producers and consumers became expected. The history of modern drama frequently involved confrontations between supporters of innovation and hostile audiences unprepared for new subjects, dramatic structures, and theatrical techniques. Whether by design or not, being controversial became the very condition for being modern.

Many modern dramatists earned their notoriety by engaging and often confronting audiences with challenging subjects and unusual forms. They wanted to restore theater's serious, moral function and to challenge, rather than please, their audience. To that end, they depicted the most vexing moral problems and dilemmas of their time. During the late nineteenth and early twentieth centuries, Europe and North America underwent a number of profound changes: new technologies, scientific advancement, urbanism, the proliferation of nationalist movements, changing class relationships, an accelerating economic transition from agriculture to industry, and new theories of human nature (including Marxism, Darwinism, and Freudianism).

Challenging the conventions and complacency of late nineteenth and early twentieth century society, modern playwrights addressed the impact of these and other changes. The Norwegian dramatist HENRIK IBSEN (1828–1906) depicted public hypocrisy, restrictive social conventions, and such taboo subjects as hereditary syphilis. His play *A DOLL HOUSE* (1879), which exposes the hypocrisies and inequalities of Victorian marriage, was denounced in newspapers, sermons, and books. GEORGE BERNARD SHAW (1856–1950), who championed his Norwegian contemporary in *The Quintessence of Ibsenism* (1891), wrote about prostitution and woman's emancipation in *Mrs. Warren's Profession* (1893) and expressed his idiosyncratic form of socialism in such plays as *Man and Superman* (1903). The German writer Gerhart Hauptmann (1862–1946) used his play *The Weavers* (1892) to call attention to the degrading conditions of weavers, while the Swedish playwright AUGUST STRINDBERG (1849–1912) depicted the ruthless battle between the sexes in *MISS JULIE* (1888). Even OSCAR WILDE (1854–1900), who delighted audiences with *THE IMPORTANCE OF BEING EARNEST* (1895) and

Eleonora Duse as Rebecca in the 1906 production of Ibsen's *Rosmersholm* at the National Theater of Christiana. Rebecca rejects not only the Christian religion but also the entire structure of Christian ethics.

other social comedies, violated conventional expectations with *Salomé* (1894), a play based on a sexually charged episode in the New Testament that describes the decapitation of St. John the Baptist. What united these playwrights was that all struggled with official censors; many of their plays could be presented only to small, private audiences because they were banned.

Though provocative themes and characters drew the most immediate hostile reaction, dramatists also deviated radically from the established rules governing dramatic forms. Many modernists criticized and ridiculed the most popular nineteenth-century dramas, such as melodramas and well-made plays. Ibsen and Shaw borrowed the conventions of the well-made play but interrupted its smooth, technically structured plots with lengthy dialogues, set speeches, and other devices that shifted

dramatic attention from incidents to social and psychological issues. In such later plays as *The Dream Play* (1902) and *The Ghost Sonata* (1907), Strindberg abandoned dramatic rules for the logic of dreams. Seeking to capture the nuances of everyday life, ANTON CHEKHOV (1860–1904) rejected the stock characters and heightened dramatic incidents of the contemporary Russian theater for a drama of understatement, indirection, and psychological nuance. Traditional forms, when they were used, were adapted to new purposes, and new forms were developed to respond to a changing modern world.

THE INDEPENDENT THEATER MOVEMENT: NATURALISM

These modern playwrights could present their work to the public because of the opening of small, independent theaters intended to provide an alternative to the larger commercial theaters. Particularly important in this respect was André Antoine's (1858–1943) Théâtre Libre in Paris, which introduced the plays of Ibsen, among others. In London the Independent Theatre, founded by J. T. Grein (1862–1935), was devoted to the same task, and later Shaw and Harley Granville-Barker (1877–1946) would find a home at the Court Theatre. In Berlin it was the Freie Bühne of Otto Brahm (1856–1912) and in Moscow the Moscow Art Theater of Konstanin Stanislavsky (1863–1938) that made available performance venues for modern drama. All the theaters named above were associated with naturalism, a movement that originated in France in the 1860s and advocated that literature and art must faithfully present reality, with the writer and artist assuming the position of an objective scientist.

In its concern with the accurate portrayal of human beings and the external world, naturalism represented an extension of the realist movement that came to dominate European and North American art and literature during the middle of the nineteenth century and remains a powerful aesthetic current in today's theater. A reaction against the idealizing tendencies of Romanticism, realism seeks to depict contemporary life and society directly, unmediated by art's distorting conventions. The plays of Ibsen and Chekhov and the early plays of Shaw, which address social realities in recognizably contemporary settings, fall under this rubric. Naturalism differs from realism in that it relies on a more scientifically grounded understanding of the relation between individuals and their environment. Inspired by Charles Darwin (1809–1882) and his theory of natural selection, naturalists believed that humans are not free agents choosing their own destiny but rather are creatures determined by their environment, their physiology, and the social conditions under which they live. In the arts, the chief proponent of naturalism was Émile Zola (1840–1902), who influenced Antoine, Grein, Brahm, and other directors associated with naturalism in the theater. Dramatists who were strongly affected by naturalism include Strindberg and Hauptmann.

MODERN ACTING

Naturalism changed not only the nature of plays but also the modes of staging them. The movement led to an increased emphasis on realistic stage props and décor and a rejection of the histrionic acting practiced in the nineteenth-century commercial theater. The Russian actor and director Konstantin Stanislavsky, for example, pioneered a new acting system based on the actor's psychology and emotions. For performances of Ibsen, he even imported Norwegian furniture to help the actors merge with their roles. What Stanislavsky did for individual roles, George II, the duke of Saxe-Meiningen (1826–1914), did for groups, introducing new systems of ensemble acting and bringing vivid crowds to the stage. Modern plays, with their new and daring female roles, also made it possible for a new generation of female stars to emerge and contribute to a truly modern acting style. Among them were Eleonora Duse (1958–1924) in Italy, Elizabeth Robins (1862–1952) in England, and Eva Le Gallienne (1899–1991) in the United States. In developing their signature roles, many of these actresses chose characters from Ibsen's plays.

AESTHETICISM AND SYMBOLISM

Naturalism was not the only movement that sought to break with the conventions of nineteenth-century theater. Indeed, the rapidity with which such movements followed one another, and their strenuous and public efforts to present a distinctive rationale for artistic innovation, became a distinctive feature of modernism. Aestheticism, which advocated the primacy of beauty over values such as social or political utility, was particularly associated with Oscar Wilde (although Wilde himself was well aware of the importance of societal forces; he expressed a commitment to socialism and suffered prosecution as a homosexual). Symbolism focused on rarified meanings, subjectivity, and suggestion rather than common idioms or everyday speech. Symbolist playwrights

A set-design sketch by Adolphe Appia, ca. 1910. Note the abstract
pattern of lines and angles.

included Maurice Maeterlinck (Belgium,
1862– 1949), Madame Rachilde (France,
1860–1953), William Butler Yeats (Ireland, 1865–1939), and Aleksandr Blok
(Russia, 1880–1921). Symbolism also
entailed a return to exalted and poetic
speeches and a preference for simple, symbolic designs over the cluttered stage sets
of naturalism. Symbolist design was championed especially in Paris, in Aurélien
Lugné-Poe's (1869–1940) Théâtre de
l'Œuvre. In England, the abstract sets of
Edward Gordon Craig (1872–1966) had
many affinities with symbolism, as did the
monumental and abstract designs of Adolphe Appia (1862–1928).

THEATER AND THE AVANT-GARDE

The battles between different movements
became more pronounced and complicated
in the first decades of the twentieth century. A host of "isms," often announced

through manifestos and declarations,
emerged virtually overnight, and many disappeared as quickly. Among those that
made a mark was expressionism, which
arose in Germany at the start of the century. Expressionists, who advocated the
externalization of psychic states instead of
the realistic representation of life, critiqued
the dehumanizing forces of industrialization in distorted, often nightmarish form.
Prominent expressionistic dramatists
included Georg Kaiser (1878–1945), Oskar
Kokoshka (1886–1980), and Ernst Toller
(1893–1939). These and other writers
championed technological advances that
supported their artistry, especially in scenic
design and stage lighting, as well as through
the expanding medium of cinema. *The
Cabinet of Dr. Caligari* (1920) was an especially influential expressionistic film. In the
late 1910s and 1920s, expressionism also
had an influence on such American playwrights as EUGENE O'NEILL (1888–1953),

A photograph of the original 1935 production of Antonin Artaud's *Les Cenci*. Based on an Italian story of incest, torture, and patricide, the play embodies the Theater of Cruelty that Artaud espoused in *The Theater and Its Double*. Artaud, in the role of Count Cenci, stands in front.

SUSAN GLASPELL (1876–1948), and SOPHIE TREADWELL (1885–1970).

A very different movement was futurism, which was initiated by F. T. Marinetti (1876–1944) and flourished largely in Italy and Russia. Inspired by an enthusiasm for technology and machines—the products of a belated but rapid industrialization in northern Italy—Marinetti sought to banish the human actor from the theater, relying instead on puppets, machines, and other inanimate objects. He also rejected well-structured plays in favor of short episodes of discontinuous actions and effects. Futurism was followed by Dadaism, which pushed the anarchic provocations of the futurists to an extreme. In the Cabaret Voltaire, which flourished in Zurich during World War I (1914–18), Tristan Tzara (1896–1963) and other Dadaists presented nonsense poems, manifestos, musical pieces, and masked performances of various kinds, often simultaneously. Like futurism, Dadaism quickly became an international movement with followers in the major European cities and beyond. When Dadaism declined in Paris in the early twenties, many of its adherents joined the movement of surrealism, which was led by André Breton (1896–1966). Influenced by the psychoanalytic theory of Sigmund Freud (1865–1939), surrealism focused on spontaneous associations, drifting thoughts, and dream images. The surrealists were also interested in earlier writers who shared their concerns, including the provocateur Alfred Jarry (1873–1907), who had written crude and funny plays violating almost all strictures of decency and proper form. His scatological, grotesque, and irreverent play *Ubu the King* (1896) became an icon of the surrealist movement. The most influential theater maker associated with surrealism (even though he left the movement after a quarrel with Breton) was Antonin Artaud (1896–1948), who, under the name Theater of Cruelty, advocated a primal, physical theater inspired not just by ancient rituals but also by the slapstick comedy of the Marx Brothers. Artaud's writings on theater, which were published in 1938 under the title *The Theater and Its Double*, drew on images such as the plague, primitive myths, and the "animated hieroglyphics" of Balinese theater to establish theater as an antidote to the decadence of modern life.

The increasingly strident movements of the early twentieth century are often grouped together under the classification *avant-garde*. Originally a military term used to designate the advance corps of an army, in the early nineteenth century *avant-garde* became a political label applied to radical and advanced groups seeking social change. It was only in the second half of the nineteenth century that the notion of the avant-garde infiltrated the arts, allowing artists of various movements to present themselves as ahead of everyone else. Yet because the avant-garde groups maintained ties to their political roots, their formation must be understood in the context of the political history of the early twentieth century, and they often strongly promoted socialism, anarchism, or, as in the case of the Italian futurists, fascism. Indeed, the Futurists were extreme Italian nationalists, advocating war as an end in itself as well as a form of self-aggrandizement. The Dadaists, by contrast, formed in opposition to World War I and came to embrace an international socialism as a way to destroy the old class-based societies. They shared that aim with surrealists, many of whom joined various communist parties. Even more closely linked to socialism were the Russian futurists, who participated in the Russian October Revolution of 1917 and strove through artistic means to help it succeed.

POLITICAL THEATER: BRECHT

Socialism had an immense effect on many artists and thinkers of the first half of the twentieth century and later, including those not associated with the more extreme avant-garde movements. The most influential political playwright was BERTOLT BRECHT (1898–1956), who developed a new form of drama and performance called Epic Theater, which relied on a number of techniques meant to interrupt the flow of plot and acting. Brecht believed that such interruptions would ensure that audiences actively ponder, rather than passively consume, the theatrical spectacle. He had also learned from the director Erwin Piscator (1893–1966) the value of bringing many art forms, including film (still relatively new at the time), into the theater, and he collaborated with composers such as Kurt Weill (1900–1950) on new, presentational forms

A scene from the original 1928 production of *The Threepenny Opera*, a collaboration between the composer Kurt Weill and Bertolt Brecht.

of opera and other forms of musical theater. Brecht, Piscator, and Weill, together with many other European writers and theater makers, fled to the United States during the Nazi era and exerted considerable influence on theater and music there. Besides these émigrés, the best-known political writer in the United States was Clifford Odets (1906–1963), whose plays depicted the plight of working-class families and often included rousing calls for a socialist society.

CULTURAL RENEWAL: IRELAND AND THE UNITED STATES

Not all theaters in the early twentieth century were dominated by avant-garde and socialist plays. The Abbey Theatre (1904) in Dublin, for example, was devoted to gaining the cultural independence of Ireland, which for centuries had been under England's control; it thus followed the nineteenth-century movement for national theaters in European countries other than those—England, France, Spain, and Italy—that had traditionally dominated theater. One of its founding members, Lady Augusta Gregory (1852–1932), advocated a return to the Irish language, which had long been marginalized by English colonizers and settlers. The playwrights associated with the theater took varied approaches to drama. While Ireland's leading poet William Butler Yeats composed dense, difficult plays filled with highly poetic language and mostly set in a mythical past, John Millington Synge (1871–1909) wrote in a more colloquial, highly lyrical idiom. His plays, which undercut romanticized views of the Irish peasantry, proved controversial with the theatergoing Dublin public; so jarring was his presentation of rural Ireland in *The Playboy of the Western World* (1907) that it sparked theatrical riots and a long dispute that threatened the existence of the Abbey Theatre and the Irish Theatre Movement of which it was part.

Cultural independence was also the purpose of the Provincetown Players in the United States, a small theater troupe devoted to presenting new and challenging plays by American playwrights such as Susan Glaspell and Eugene O'Neill. Founded in Cape Cod and then moved to

A photograph of the Provincetown Players' original production of Eugene O'Neill's *All God's Chill'un Got Wings* (1924). Paul Robeson, seated, played the lead role.

New York City, the company was part of the so-called Little Theatre Movement of the 1910s and 1920s in the United States. This movement, which was inspired by Europe's alternative theater movement of the late nineteenth century, provided the space for staging new and experimental plays without the financial constraints of the commercial theater, which by the late nineteenth century was dominated by New York's Broadway theaters and by touring productions of successful shows that took star performers to theaters in an extensive network across the United States. Some modern playwrights, such as O'Neill, both participated in the Little Theatre Movement and managed to have their plays performed on Broadway, where the largest and most elegant commercial theaters were located. Broadway still retains its unique status, as demonstrated by the distinction drawn today between Broadway, off-Broadway, and even off-off-Broadway theaters.

TRAGEDY, METATRAGEDY, METATHEATER

While the era of modern drama saw an unprecedented explosion of new forms of

In Eugène Ionesco's *The Bald Soprano*, a classic example of Theater of the Absurd, characters engage in nonsensical banter that calls into question the nature of communication in modern society. Pictured here is the 1950 production at the Théâtre Noctambules in Paris, directed by Nicolas Bataille.

itself to social and political critique in the hands of Eastern European dissidents such as the Czech playwright Václav Havel (1936–2011) and dramatists living under repressive regimes throughout the Third World.

POSTWAR GERMAN THEATER: THE BRECHTIAN LEGACY

Postwar drama followed a different trajectory in Germany and the other German-speaking countries of central Europe. Most of Germany's theaters had been destroyed during the war, and the governments of both West Germany and East Germany embarked on major efforts to rebuild their countries' cultural infrastructure. The drama that was written for these theaters in the 1950s dealt mainly with social and political issues, and the subjects of guilt and responsibility loomed particularly large for a people confronting their collective role in World War II. Aiding the development of political theater were Bertolt Brecht's return to East Germany after his self-imposed exile during the Nazi period and the founding of the

Berliner Ensemble in 1949 by Brecht and his wife, the actress Helene Weigel (1900–1971). The Berliner Ensemble put Brecht's theories of rehearsal and production into practice and in performing to audiences at home and abroad established Brecht's plays and the "Brechtian style" as major forces in the contemporary theater. In the German-speaking theater Brecht's influence was manifest in the drama of a new generation of playwrights, many of whom adopted the Brechtian focus on social and political issues and employed Brechtian techniques, though usually without the doctrinaire and, at times, utopian Marxism that often shaped Brecht's plays. The Swiss playwright Friedrich Dürrenmatt (1921–1990) made Brechtian and absurdist techniques part of his pessimistic dramatic vision of humanity in the postwar world, while the German playwright Peter Weiss (1916–1982) brought elements of Artaud's Theater of Cruelty to a Brechtian concern with history. Weiss's dramas of the mid- and late 1960s—such as *The Investigation* (1965), which examines the Holocaust through the theatrical recreation of war crimes testimony—were written in the style of documentary theater, a genre that other dramatists embraced during the decade.

POSTWAR BRITISH THEATER: THE WELFARE STATE AND ITS DISCONTENTS

In the ten years immediately following the war, the theater in Britain gave little evidence of the important role it would play in the history of contemporary drama. The country itself was undergoing historic changes: in 1945 Clement Attlee's (1883–1967) Labour Party achieved a landslide victory over the incumbent prime minister and wartime hero Winston Churchill (1874–1965), and the following six years saw the establishment of the British welfare state. One sign of the increasing role of government in society was the creation of the Arts Council of Great Britain, an independent, government-funded body that—for the first time in Britain—provided state subsidies for the arts. But these changes in society left little mark on the London theater, which for the most part was sustaining itself on an uninspiring diet of West End productions. Two events caused a seismic shift. In 1955 Beckett's *Waiting for Godot* was given its London premiere, and in the following year *Look Back in Anger*, by the playwright John Osborne (1929–1994), electrified the theater world; it was produced by the London Stage Company, a noncommercial company specifically formed to support new playwrights. Osborne's play expressed the restlessness and anger of a generation at odds with the materialism and oppressive class structure of Britain in the mid-1950s, and it reflected the disillusionment permeating an imperial power in the twilight of its ascendancy. Along with the work of the Theatre Workshop—a company in a working-class area in East London that, under the leadership of Joan Littlewood (1914–2002), produced plays by such working-class playwrights as Shelagh Delaney (1939–2011)—*Look Back in Anger* opened the door for a new generation of dramatists grappling with social class and other issues central to British national identity.

The subsequent development of social and political theater in Britain was influenced by Brecht's theories and practices; indeed, over the next two decades Brechtian dramaturgy and stagecraft found their widest application outside Germany in British theater. The Berliner Ensemble visited London in 1956 (the year of Brecht's death) and 1965, and its epic style influenced a number of left-wing directors, designers, and play-

Jimmy Porter (played by Kenneth Haigh) plays his trumpet to distract himself from his cramped quarters and the complacency of postwar Britain in the original 1956 Royal Court production of John Osborne's *Look Back in Anger*.

wrights. John Arden (1930–2012) and Edward Bond (b. 1934) belong to the first generation of British dramatists who employed the strategies and techniques of Brechtian theater to strikingly original ends. The Brechtian turn in British drama received greater impetus in the aftermath of 1968, when a new generation of socialist playwrights—inspired by the revolutionary events in Paris and elsewhere and aided by the abolition of government censorship, which had been in effect since the Theatrical Licensing Act of 1737—made Brechtian devices a cornerstone of their more radical political drama. John McGrath (1935–2002), Howard Brenton (b. 1942), and David Hare (b. 1947) are only a few of the many dramatists who drew on Brecht in the 1970s and early 1980s. Among the women playwrights who sought to adapt Brecht within the politics of an emerging feminist movement, CARYL CHURCHILL (b. 1938)—whose plays range with deliberate abandon through space and time in treating their historical and contemporary subjects—is the most accomplished and widely known. This intensification of political playwriting after the events of 1968 was matched by a proliferation of radical (or "fringe") theater groups throughout Britain and Northern Ireland.

PINTER, STOPPARD, ORTON

Other playwrights and dramatic currents helped define postwar British theater. The influence of Samuel Beckett was apparent in the drama of HAROLD PINTER (1930–2008) and Tom Stoppard (b. 1937), two of the country's leading contemporary playwrights. Pinter combined the indeterminacy and linguistic evasions of Beckettian drama with the often gritty realism of interactions within the lower, middle, and upper strata of Britain's class-based society. Stoppard, who was born in Czechoslovakia, drew on Beckett in a technically virtuoso, philosophically sophisticated drama that also has more than a passing kinship to GEORGE BERNARD SHAW's "drama of ideas." Joining Stoppard in reworking the English comic tradition was Joe Orton (1933–1967), whose plays of the mid-1960s exploited the farcical, the macabre, and the surface gentility of

English drawing-room comedy within an anarchic drama of sexual desire pursued across boundaries of gender, sexual identity, and class.

POSTWAR AMERICAN THEATER: EXPRESSIVE REALISM, METHOD ACTING

Theater in the United States achieved one of its greatest flowerings in the years immediately following World War II. While Europe found it necessary to revive—and in many cases, rebuild—its theatrical institutions, the Broadway theaters that represented the center of theatrical life in the United States had been left relatively untouched by the war. But with few exceptions—the plays of Thornton Wilder (1897–1975), for instance—this theater had produced little of substance since the mid-1930s. The rebirth of American theater that followed the end of the war resulted from the collaboration between a group of visionary theatrical practitioners and two emerging dramatists—TENNESSEE WILLIAMS (1911–1983) and ARTHUR MILLER (1915–2005)—whose innovative dramaturgy was put to work in plays that captured the aspirations and

Director Elia Kazan and playwright Arthur Miller sitting on Jo Mielziner's set for the 1949 Broadway production of *Death of a Salesman*.

anxieties of postwar America. The designer Jo Mielziner (1901–1976) pioneered an expressive or "subjective" stage realism that presented the theatrical categories of present and past, here and there, exterior and interior with poetic fluidity. Using the stage designs of Mielziner and under the direction of Elia Kazan (1909–2003), such plays as Williams's *A STREETCAR NAMED DESIRE* (1947) and Miller's *DEATH OF A SALESMAN* (1949) explored the shifting landscapes of memory and desire on a stage where the external world was at once materially real and evanescent. Such plays created a need for performers to convey greater psychological complexity, and it was met by contemporary developments in American acting. Continuing the interest in Konstantin Stanislavsky's psychological approach to acting that had marked the work of the Group Theater in the 1930s, the Actors Studio (founded in 1947 by members of the earlier company) promoted method acting, a performance style that emphasized psychological motivation, intention, and the importance of subtext in the presentation of dramatic characters. This approach, perhaps most famously realized in the theatrical and film performances of

Marlon Brando (1924–2004), dominated American acting through the 1950s.

OFF-BROADWAY AND OFF-OFF-BROADWAY THEATER

Even as Broadway played a central role in presenting a revitalized American drama, its historically dominant role in American theater was challenged during the postwar years. In an attempt to diversify and expand theatrical activity outside the city of New York, a number of regional theaters were formed with resident companies presenting an annual season of plays. Among the most prominent of these are the Alley Theatre (Houston, 1947), the Arena Stage (Washington, 1950), and the Guthrie Theater (Minneapolis, 1963). Within New York, the increasing conservatism of Broadway theaters in the face of rising production costs led to the opening of off-Broadway theaters. Like the Little Theater Movement of the 1910s, off-Broadway theater involved smaller buildings that often were some distance from the main commercial theater district, and because these spaces served smaller audiences—between 100 and 499 spectators—they could be used to produce plays that the larger

Playwright Luis Valdez, right, founder of El Teatro Campesino, with the United Farm Workers president, Cesar Chavez, in front of New York's Winter Garden Theater in 1979. *Zoot Suit*, by Valdez, was the first Chicano play to be performed on Broadway.

Broadway houses found too risky. European writers such as Beckett and Ionesco saw the first New York productions of their plays in off-Broadway theaters, as did a number of new American playwrights, including Edward Albee (b. 1928). Off-Broadway also played a significant role in the careers of more established American playwrights. The 1956 production of *The Iceman Cometh* by Circle in the Square, one of the decade's most important off-Broadway theaters, revived interest in the plays of EUGENE O'NEILL (1888–1953) and thus helped lead to the Broadway premiere of *LONG DAY'S JOURNEY INTO NIGHT* that same year.

But by the end of the 1950s, off-Broadway theaters were themselves dealing with rising costs; they therefore became more reluctant to gamble on experimental plays or on unproven writers and increasingly reliant on productions whose commercial success seemed guaranteed. In response, off-off-Broadway theaters were founded throughout New York. These low-budget theaters—which were located in coffeehouses, church buildings, various basements, and wherever else space was available—provided opportunities for a generation of younger dramatists with strong antiestablishment leanings and experimental creative interests. During the 1960s—in Caffe Cino (1958), La MaMa Experimental Theatre Club (1961), Judson Poets' Theater (1961), and elsewhere—they launched the careers of such prominent contemporary playwrights as Maria Irene Fornes (b. 1930) and Sam Shepard (b. 1943). The often radical plays produced in these venues took part in the experimentation more broadly under way in 1960s American theater. For example, under the leadership of Joseph Chaikin (1935–2003), the Open Theater rejected the psychological realism of method acting for a form of acting rooted in improvisation, role-playing, and transformation. Communal theater groups, such as the Living Theater (which had been founded as an off-Broadway company in 1947), explored a radically participatory theater in which the division between performer and audience became almost imperceptible. Other theater groups—the Free Southern Theater, the Bread and Puppet Theater, and El Teatro Campesino, to name a few—used agitprop techniques, puppetry, and populist theater traditions to engage with social issues such as civil rights, the conditions of migrant farmworkers, and the Vietnam War.

AFRICAN AMERICAN THEATER

The years 1945–70 also saw the rise of contemporary African American drama. Drama and theater, of course, had played a central role in the Harlem Renaissance during the 1920s and 1930s, most notably in the plays of Langston Hughes (1902–1967), and the government-funded Federal Theatre Project of the 1930s had provided work for African American theater professionals through the "Negro units" that were established in New York and other cities. But it was not until Lorraine Hansberry's (1930–1965) play *A Raisin in the Sun*, which had an acclaimed run on Broadway in 1959, that serious African American drama claimed the attention of mainstream audiences. A product of the 1950s civil rights movement, the play also anticipated the more radical political and cultural movements of the decade that followed. African American theater of the 1960s reflected a deepening militancy; the plays of Amiri Baraka (b. 1934), for instance, reveal the author's growing separatism and revolutionary convictions, while the Black Arts Repertory Theatre (1965) that Baraka helped establish in Harlem was at the forefront of the militant Black Arts Movement. These and other dramatists of the 1950s and 1960s laid the groundwork for such later African American playwrights as Ntozake Shange (b. 1948), AUGUST WILSON (1945–2005), and SUZAN-LORI PARKS (b. 1964).

Contemporary Theater

THE CONTEMPORARY WORLD

The term *contemporary*, always imprecise, is particularly elusive when applied to today's historical moment. In a world of accelerated change—where international events, technological developments, and cultural trends follow each other with dizzying speed—the past of even a few years ago can seem like another age. Much has transpired during the period from the end of the 1960s through the first decade of the twenty-first century, and these years could be subdivided into smaller segments, each with its defining issues and preoccupations. Over the time since 1970, a world has emerged markedly different from that of the postwar years, and the overall trends and transformations of those decades have led to a present whose outlines we are still coming to understand.

In the past forty years a number of pivotal events have remapped the international geopolitical landscape, and two have been particularly important in their immediate and long-range consequences. As the result of intensifying pressure from the outside and the weaknesses of their own economic and social systems, which were unable to adapt to a changing global economy, the Soviet Union and its satellite states rejected communism in favor of Western-style capitalist economies in the years 1989–91, thereby bringing an end to the cold war that had defined international relations since the end of World War II. The fall of the Berlin Wall in November 1989 was the most visual symbol of this rapid change that took the form of peaceful and violent revolutions

throughout the former Eastern Bloc, the unification of Germany, the dissolution of the Soviet Union in 1991, and the wars among the newly independent states of the former Yugoslavia. The second major shift was the rise of Islamist militancy as a social and political force. Islamic fundamentalists in Iran overthrew the monarchy of the shahs in 1979, replacing it with a revolutionary Islamic republic; in the 1980s, foreign volunteers joined an Afghan national resistance movement in what they viewed as a fight for Islam and drove the Soviet Union out of Afghanistan (1979–89). Such successes helped foster the growth of organized terrorist organizations, leading to the attacks on the World Trade Center and the Pentagon on September 11, 2001, and the subsequent wars in Afghanistan and Iraq.

THEATER AND GLOBALIZATION

Even more important in shaping the contemporary world than these geopolitical and ideological changes have been developments in the transnational spheres of capital and finance, corporate organization, information, communications, and culture. The world's economy has become

The 1987 production at the Theatre des Bouffes du Nord of *Mahabharata*, directed by Peter Brook.

drama. The growing political and cultural assertiveness of the continent's original inhabitants has also produced an impressive body of Native American drama. This drama is sometimes the product of theater groups, such as the U.S.-based Spiderwoman Theater, that draw on Native American storytelling and performance traditions.

More broadly, the theater has begun to include a wider range of voices and experiences that traditionally have been marginalized within, or excluded from, the stage. The roots of this expansion lie in the "identity" or "liberation" movements that have gathered strength in recent decades in Europe, North America, and other areas of the world. The contemporary women's movement, for example, which burgeoned in the 1970s, has produced a rich body of drama concerned with women's experience, the meaning of "woman" in traditional representations, and the changing manifestations of gender in the late twentieth and early twenty-first centuries. This drama has often formed part of an explicit feminist project to challenge male-directed theatrical practices, institutions, and notions of authorship, and it has sometimes been produced by companies employing newer, more collaborative forms of theatrical practice.

Gay and lesbian drama has also gained a prominent voice in the contemporary theater. Though homosexual rights groups existed in Europe and the United States earlier in the century, agitation for the rights and recognition of gay, lesbian, bisexual, and transgendered individuals did not come to the attention of the general public until the late 1960s. The Sexual Offenses Act of 1967 decriminalized most sexual acts between adults in Britain, and the 1969 Stonewall riots in New York galvanized the gay liberation movement in the United States. Perhaps because of its interest in role-playing and its tolerance for unconventional identities, the modern theater has attracted an impressive number of homosexual and bisexual playwrights, including OSCAR WILDE (1854–1900), Gertrude Stein (1874–1946), Federico García Lorca (1898–1936), TENNESSEE WILLIAMS (1911–1983), Jean Genet (1910–1986), Lorraine Hansberry (1930–

1965), Edward Albee (b. 1928), and Joe Orton (1933–1967). Yet only in the 1970s did an openly gay and lesbian drama emerge in its own right. Among the leading writers of this drama is the American playwright Tony Kushner, whose two-part dramatic fantasia *Angels in America* was one of a number of plays during the 1980s and 1990s that addressed the AIDS epidemic. Important authors of lesbian drama include the contemporary American playwright and performance artist Holly Hughes (b. 1955).

THEATER IN THE TWENTY-FIRST CENTURY

As the works of these and other contemporary playwrights indicate, theater remains deeply responsive to social movements, cultural developments, and historical shifts and transformations. As the twenty-first century unfolds, theater—a medium at once traditional and new—offers a unique perspective on the issues and preoccupations of a changing world. One of the oldest of the arts, theater brings nearly 2,500 years of performance forms and dramatic texts to the current historical moment. At the same time, theater is one of the most immediate of the representational arts, grounded in the physical presence of the actor's body and the irreproducible occasion of live performance. Old plays are performed in new contexts, and the resulting dialogue frames both present and past in mutually illuminating ways. *HAMLET* (1600–01) has been performed thousands of times, but every time the Danish prince picks up Yorick's skull—a stage prop—he does it for different audiences in a performance interaction that changes from moment to moment. Its sensitivity to audience and occasion makes theater exceptionally responsive to the complex web of issues, relationships, and interactions that make up the present moment. For this reason, many of the contemporary theater's most important activities have taken place not in traditional theater buildings but in the squares, community centers, and other sites where people gather and work. Health and theater workers have used theater as a vehicle for vaccination campaigns in South America, AIDS education in Africa, and trauma therapy for those victimized by violence around the world. In these and other forms, theater remains deeply important in regions that may not have access to other media, in cultures that rely for education less on print than on oral modes of transmitting information, and with marginalized social groups in other societies.

Theater is more international than it has ever been, and in its emerging and time-honored forms it constitutes an important part of the global cultural landscape. As the expansion and proliferation of media continue in this digitalizing age of multiple entertainment sources, theater and drama carry on traditions that have been handed down for centuries, reworking these conventions in often striking ways and making them responsive to a new century's changing realities.

READING DRAMA, IMAGINING THEATER

For those of us who are used to reading novels and short stories, opening the text of a play can come as something of a surprise. Characters are identified before the story ever begins, in a listing (often labeled *dramatis personae*) that seems more like the entries in an address book than the stuff of literature. Instead of the designations "he said" or "she said" that embed what these characters say within a novel's or short story's unfolding narrative, dialogue is presented directly, with the speakers' names indicated on the left-hand margin. Stage directions indicate when characters enter or exit the dramatic scene, how they move around in relation to each other, and how they handle the objects of their material world. The very world they inhabit feels constrained—even claustrophobic—next to the expansive, shifting settings of *Don Quixote* or *War and Peace*.

Features such as these point to the essential difference between drama and more strictly literary forms such as fiction and poetry. While the term *playwright* means "maker of plays," the written text that we pick up to read provides only a part of the larger phenomenon we call *performance*. Its meanings, in other words, are not limited to the private worlds created by readers as they encounter words on a page. Rather, the printed play is a blueprint for something that happens in real time and space before an audience. The dramatic text in performance thus depends not on a single literary author but on the collective artistry of actors, designers, directors, and others involved in theatrical production. Even those plays—known as "closet dramas"—that were written with the expectation that they would never (or could never) be performed in an actual theater generate imaginative scenarios that have more in common with an audience's experience of watching a play than with a solitary reader's enjoyment. The fact that plays are written with some form of theater in mind—that they exist as dramatic scripts as well as literary works—ensures that the pleasures associated with dramatic art are rich and complex.

As a consequence, to read drama well requires a theatrical imagination attuned to the possible realizations of the dramatic script onstage. The first time we encounter an unfamiliar play, we seek and respond to its narrative—the story it is telling us. But we cannot fully appreciate the impact of such a play unless we consider *how* that story is told and what kind of performance it suggests. Reading plays is an active process—a creative collaboration with the dramatist that takes place in the mind of the reader. As a way of conceiving the dramatic world of a play, it may be helpful to start by envisioning its physical environment, or setting. Where and when is the play set? What and where are the key markers in that location (a door, for example, or a throne)? Some playwrights—particularly those who write under the influence of theatrical realism—include a great deal of information about the play's physical environment, making the stage materialize by supplying a wealth of particular detail. Other dramatic texts provide minimal, or no, setting specifications; for example, SAMUEL BECKETT'S *WAITING FOR GODOT* (1952) includes the famously minimalist direction "A country road. A tree. Evening." Plays written before the nineteenth century often lack place descriptions and depend on the dramatic action and dialogue to establish what is onstage. The settings of Sanskrit drama, for instance, are suggested through dialogue and mimed actions, as when the courtesan Vasantasena mimes stepping into a carriage in Shudraka's *The Little Clay Cart* (ca. 100–300 C.E.), while the plays of SHAKESPEARE and his contemporaries establish location through economical, highly evocative verbal description. Knowing something about the production conventions in use during specific periods can help you re-create how a play might have looked to its original audience, but it should not limit your imagination. As the history of theatrical performance indicates, plays are adaptable to other kinds of theaters, stage resources, and production practices.

When visualizing this physical environment, you may wish to make a rough sketch of the scenic environment (or environments) indicated within the dramatic text, so that you can visualize how the characters and locale interact in each scene. Some theatrical terminology is useful here. In many theatrical traditions, locations and movement onstage are designated by a gridlike pattern. The section farthest away from the audience is considered *upstage*, while the area closest to them is *downstage*. Unless otherwise indicated, the sides of the stage are noted from the actor's perspective; hence, *stage right* will be to the actor's right, and *stage left* will be to the actor's left. The midpoint of the stage is called its *center*. Thus, for example, an actor might be told to enter through a door up right and to move (or "cross") to sit on a chair down left. When imagining the layout of a particular scene, it is important to be aware of who is onstage and where, at all times, even when these characters participate only silently in what is going on. Though the presence of such characters may be easy to forget, they may prove pivotal to the action of individual scenes.

Try to envision each character's appearance, as well as how much flexibility there may be in matching the bodily reality of a given actor to the physical description of the character. At some times and in some places, the correspondence between bodily appearance and role has been fairly conventionalized, with recognizable "types" recurring in similar dramatic performances. But even such roles can be taken by actors who vary in appearance, bearing, age, and manner, or even play against type. Throughout theater history, for example, what we now call cross-gender casting and cross-racial casting have been important elements of performance. As part of your effort to visualize the play in performance, you might cast known actors in your imaginary staging to make it more vivid, then substitute others to see how different personalities and styles of acting might shape a role differently. Here, too, the text can be your guide. Is the performance required by the text naturalistic or stylized, comic or serious? In some cases—the stylized theater of Japanese noh, for example—the answer is clear, and by imposing antithetical acting styles you may violate the play's aesthetic underpinnings. In most cases, however, access to a range of acting styles can liberate possibilities within the dramatic text, offering new perspectives and opening it up to new theatrical energies.

In addition, it is useful to pay close attention to what characters say and how they say it. Language is the playwright's principal means for revealing characters and their dramatic world, and the play relies mainly on the spoken word to communicate with its audience. Dramatic speech often reveals important information about the characters, including their class position, geographic origin (especially through dialect), and personality. In the absence of a narrator who might make known to us a character's inner thoughts and feelings, speech is the conduit through which the play's figures disclose their hopes, fears, and intentions. Such characterization rests not simply on what a specific character says but also on what is said about him or her. Indeed, the richness of a dramatic portrait is often the product of multiple—and differing—accounts, observations, and perspectives offered by a play's characters.

Language, of course, is more than information, and nowhere is this truer than in the theater, where language exists not to be read but to be spoken. The words on the page of a dramatic text are designed for the mouth, and as chosen by the best dramatists their sounds fill and guide the mouth, position the body in specific attitudes, and occupy the stage with their acoustic power. When the playwright John Millington Synge wrote that "in a good play every speech should be as fully flavored as a nut or apple," he was referring not just to his own use of Irish dialect but to the linguistic and syntactical richness that makes all great dialogue a kind of vocal music. When bringing a play to theatrical life in your mind, read its lines aloud, feel the emotions they stir in your body, and enjoy the music that they create within your room. By yourself or with a friend, read some of the dialogue, noticing the contrapuntal rhythms that characters establish when they speak together. Even when reading translations—such as the ones included in this anthology, which were selected with vocal and other forms of performability in mind—you can feel such cadences and musicality. Along with the other sounds that a play may require— the ritualized foot stamping of the noh actor, the swish of regal costumes, Feste's lute in Shakespeare's TWELFTH NIGHT (1600–01)—the spoken word makes up the soundscape of dramatic performance. Reading with an awareness of this aural power can enhance your understanding and appreciation of drama.

While noting that the spoken language is a primary determinant of dramatic and theatrical meaning, we must not ignore the other elements that reinforce or complicate the acts of expression, communication, and signification. Three texts, in fact, work together in performance: the spoken text, the action text, and the subtext. Whereas the *spoken text*, or dialogue, is what the characters say to each other (or to the audience) during the play, the *action text*— whether scripted by the playwright or created by the director, the actors, or both—is the physical language of the play: the gestures and movements that signifi-

cantly shape our understanding of the story. In highly conventionalized theater cultures, such as those of classical India and Japan, the actors' movements and gestures become intricate languages in their own right, signifying to an audience that understands their meaning specific relationships, emotions, and attitudes. But directors and actors of all eras have used the action text as a way of communicating meaning, even when the effect of such gestures and movements may be to undermine the sentiments expressed in the spoken text (as when the villain of nineteenth-century melodrama winks at the audience while professing his sincerity to an onstage character). *Subtext* consists of the unspoken thoughts, feelings, and intentions of the characters that underlie and prompt the action and spoken texts. The relationship between the subtext and its manifestation in word and action is as variable in the theater as it is in life. Sometimes language and gesture express the inner life directly and fully. "Language most shows the man; speak that I may see thee," wrote Ben Jonson in a prose collection published shortly after his death. But as *Volpone* (1606) and other plays by Jonson demonstrate, drama concerns itself more frequently with the discrepancy between private intention and public expression. Characters hide their meanings from others (and occasionally from themselves), feign indifference when they feel love, say only part of what they mean, pursue their designs under the unsuspecting eyes of those they interact with. Even silence—the choice not to speak—plays an important role in conveying contextual meaning.

The dynamic interplay of these three texts—and their interaction with set design, lighting, and the other elements of production—creates the depth and complexity of live theater. When we speak of an actor's interpretation of a role, or a director's concept for a production, we are thinking about the myriad choices that artists make, using these intersecting texts, to develop fully realized characters and to communicate with the audience through the play and its performance. The key word here is "interpretation," for the dramatic text as it exists on its own is fundamentally incomplete, suspended between possible realizations. Because plays are designed for performance, they depend on the activities of actors, directors, designers, stage managers, musicians, and the other theatrical practitioners who have served in different periods to usher them into life. And every choice that is made by these practitioners helps to realize, or interpret, the play in light of its possible range of meanings. Because the combinations of such choices are infinite, no two productions of a play are ever the same, and a great work of dramatic art has an endless capacity to surprise us with new experiences and insights whenever it is performed.

Because reading drama can and should resemble the process of actual production, you should approach the dramatic text as if you were a theater professional. Instead of reading a play to discern preexisting meanings, look for the places where a role, a scene, or a verbal exchange may be performed in different ways, and make choices as to how such components might be interpreted in the theater of your mind. What happens if an actor dwells on certain words in a speech as opposed to others? Where might he or she pause when delivering the lines, and what would be the effect of such vocal punctuation? What subtextual meanings do you see behind words and actions, and how might your actors bring them out? Consider the other elements of production as well. How would you light a production of your play, and what would be the effect of your decisions? How do the meaning and dynamics of a scene change if you focus your light on certain characters rather than others? What costumes do you imagine for your actors, and what would these tell us about the characters they play? Where would you position actors on the stage, and how would they move in relation to each other? Is the stage busy or relatively still during individual scenes? In those plays that lack detailed set descriptions, what theatrical environment do you envision for the action that takes place? Conversely, with plays that have extensive directions, what specific fixtures and objects might you choose to realize the desired effect? Although some dramatists have indicated that they expect their directions be followed exactly in production, would you want to modify the given directions in any way, either to accommodate different kinds of stages or to offer a more radical vision of the play and its dramatic possibilities? As you imagine your play in the theater, you can also consider how much—if any—of the direction provided by the playwright to employ and what possible impact on an audience such changes in direction might have. Finally, what stage might you choose for a production of your play: a traditional stage, with the audience seated directly in front of the action (the proscenium stage, for instance), or a different stage arrangement, such as one in which the audience is seated on three sides (i.e., "in the round")? How do the meanings and implications of your play change when the spectators are so close to the actors and can see each other as they look at the stage?

Though reading a play in this way does not require extensive familiarity with the theater, your ability to appreciate the theatrical possibilities of a given play will be greatly enriched by the experience of seeing plays performed onstage. Go to the theater when you can; immerse yourself in the moment when the audience grows quiet, the actors enter, and the stage is taken over by a spectacle that is illusory but feels, in its most powerful moments, more real than life itself. And while attending the theater will enhance your reading of dramatic texts, the reverse is also true. Readers who imagine the theater as part of their reading become more informed and responsive audience members, actively aware of the choices the artists have made in interpreting dramatic texts and better able to evaluate their effectiveness. One of the many pleasures of reading drama is measuring your interpretation against actual performances of the play and comparing those individual performances with each other. Like the aficionados of other arts, you may develop, over a lifetime, your own repertoire of remembered performances and texts. And as you deepen your awareness of the relationship between what is written and what takes place onstage, you may fall under the spell of drama, which—whether enacted in the theater or in your own mind—is timeless yet always new.

THE PLAYS

SOPHOCLES

ca. 496–406 B.C.E.

A GENERATION younger than Aeschylus, Sophocles is often regarded as the most accomplished author of Greek tragedy. He was certainly the most successful. Up to twenty-four victories at the Dionysus festival in Athens are recorded for him (in contrast to thirteen for Aeschylus and five for EURIPIDES), and it is said that he never finished lower than second. Aristotle, the first philosopher to write an extended work on Greek tragedy, singled out Sophocles' OEDIPUS THE KING as a model of what tragedy should look like. The Oedipus myth inspired Sophocles to write not just one but three masterpieces: *Antigone*, a play about Oedipus's daughter; *Oedipus the King*; and *Oedipus at Colonos*, a searching tragedy about the aging Oedipus. In Oedipus and his descendants, Sophocles recognized the subject most perfectly suited to the art of tragedy.

Although only scant information is available about Sophocles' life, we know that he was born into a wealthy family of Colonus and that he occupied some of the highest political positions in Athens. He served as treasurer of the Delian League, a network of allied and dependent states built by Athens after its victory over the Persians. Moreover, together with Pericles, the famed leader of Athens, he commanded the Athenian fleet in its campaign against Samos. During his adult life,

Sophocles watched Athens evolve from a small city-state to the greatest empire of the region, projecting its power far into Persia. The last decades of his life were dominated by a second war—the Peloponnesian War with a rival Greek city-state, Sparta. Toward the end of his life, he became a *proboulos*, one of ten advisors endowed with special powers of governance. Sophocles died at the age of ninety as a respected and admired citizen and civic leader, a few years before the Peloponnesian War would end in the final defeat of Athens and the demise of its empire.

Sophocles launched his career as a playwright in 468 B.C.E., when he won his first victory at the Dionysus festival in Athens by defeating the acknowledged master of tragedy, Aeschylus. He was enormously productive, writing more than one hundred plays, although only seven have been preserved: *Ajax* (ca. 450), *Antigone* (ca. 441), *Oedipus the King* (ca. 428), *Electra* (ca. 419), *The Trachian Women* (ca. 413), *Philoctetes* (ca. 409), and *Oedipus at Colonus* (ca. 406), as well as one comical satyr play, *The Trackers* (date unknown). Sophocles shaped the course of theater not only through his plays but also through his theatrical innovations. The philosopher Aristotle praised Sophocles for having established new techniques of scene painting; for having introduced a third actor (hitherto, only two actors had been permitted), thereby significantly expanding the possibilities for interaction among individual characters; and for having enlarged the tragic chorus from twelve to fifteen. At the same time, Sophocles accorded the chorus less room in his plays than the older playwright Aeschylus had done, foregrounding instead the conflicts among individual characters. As a consequence, his plays are much closer to the form of contemporary drama than any previous Greek tragedies extant.

Like his predecessor Aeschylus and his younger contemporary Euripides, Sophocles took the material for his plays from Greek myth. However, he used this material in his own distinct manner. Sophocles placed much more emphasis than did Aeschylus on turning the individual characters into complex, three-dimensional humans with conflicting motives and passions. One example is his version of the Electra myth—the sole myth whose dramatic adaptations by all three major Greek tragedians survive (though different playwrights often treated the same myth). Comparing Sophocles' version with Aeschylus's, *The Libation Bearers* (the middle part of the *Oresteia* trilogy; see the headnote on Aeschylus, above) is particularly instructive. Sophocles' version is much more dynamic, and it shifts emphasis from Orestes' act of matricide to the solitary suffering of his sister, Electra. Sophocles also uses much more suspense, postponing and drawing out the recognition scenes as long as possible, even though the audience was of course familiar with the basic outlines of the plot.

Emphasizing the individual was an innovation that allowed for a more nuanced form of characterization. But it also had a cultural and political dimension. The very structure of Greek tragedy—with individual characters, often the rulers, engaging in conflict with a chorus, usually composed of elders or representative citizens—dramatized for the Athenian audience the political history of their own city. During the emergence of Athenian tragedy, Athens had gone from autocratic rule to a democracy that involved a growing number of male citizens in the political process. The rule of the one versus the rule of the many was therefore a topic of immense political impor-

tance. Sophocles' tragedies, depicting complex individuals, thus reflected the struggle over the new political form of democracy.

Of all the characters Sophocles used to populate his plays, none fascinated him more than Oedipus, a tragic figure perfectly suited to Sophocles' interest in conflicted persons. From one perspective, the myth of Oedipus is that of an individual doomed by outside forces. The son of the king and queen of Thebes, Oedipus is condemned to death to avoid the terrible prediction of an oracle that he would kill his father. But a servant takes pity on the child, and the young Oedipus is simply cast out. He grows up in the city of Corinth, ignorant of his true parents, and as an adult he returns to Thebes, unwittingly killing his father at a crossroads after having been provoked by one of the attendants. The next set piece of the myth is the encounter with the Sphinx, which is holding the city in her thrall. Oedipus submits to her test, correctly answering the riddle. Hailed as liberator of Thebes, he now marries the widowed queen and becomes a good ruler. It is only when a pestilence devastates the city and the oracle declares the murderer of the late king to be still at large that Oedipus turns to the crime and begins a methodical manhunt that constitutes most of the play. Only gradually does the truth come out, and Oedipus must finally recognize himself as the murderer he has been hunting. He blinds himself and submits to a life in exile, enduring perpetual wandering until he finds a final resting place near Athens.

Sophocles first treated the Oedipus myth with an early play about Oedipus's daughter, *Antigone*; he then returned to the myth in his middle period with *Oedipus the King*. Toward the end of his life, he felt himself drawn to the figure of Oedipus once more, composing his very last play, *Oedipus at Colonus*, on the aging Oedipus. Containing almost no external action, it depicts the old, blinded Oedipus searching for a final resting place, which is finally granted to him by the liberal city of Athens. It is a ruminative and meditative play about an Oedipus reconciled to his fate and looking for a place to die. Rather than being conceived as interrelated, the three Oedipus plays are unconnected works, each exemplary in its own way.

OEDIPUS THE KING

Oedipus the King is Sophocles' most haunting play about the Oedipus myth, and for many it is among the most haunting plays of all time. Its power arises in part from its extraordinary structure and form. In a bold move that distinguishes this play from most other Greek tragedies, Sophocles set the entire action of the play in its past, thus presenting onstage a gradual revelation of events—conveyed by speeches and dialogue—that happened long before the onstage "present." The past dominates the lives of the characters, holding them firmly in its grip.

The emphasis on the revelation of the past also means that *Oedipus the King* directs attention mostly to the realm of language rather than to the action presented on the stage. At the beginning of the play, King Oedipus has consulted the oracle at Delphi, seeking a way to halt the plague devastating the city. The oracle declares that the reason for the pestilence is the continued presence in Thebes of the murderer of the former king, Laius, who must be cast out. Oedipus is most eager to find the murderer and to expel him. As various witnesses and messengers are brought before him, the play turns into a veritable detective story—a search for traces and clues of a past crime through the cross-examination of witnesses and the careful interpretation of various prophecies and oracles. Oedipus leaps at this challenge, not only because his own rule and power depend on his success but also because he is supremely confident in his skill at untangling puzzles and riddles. As the foreign visitor who freed Thebes from the clutches of the Sphinx by solving its famous riddle, Oedipus had previously demonstrated his talent for sharp and analytical thinking. And because he owes his current position as venerated tyrant of Thebes to this skillful feat, his pride in his intellect seems warranted. Faced with a new threat to his adopted home, he is ready to exercise his skill again, once again deciphering riddles to free the city from its plight.

This time, however, things are different. Despite his self-confidence, he has in fact become something of a riddle himself. The whole play revolves around this paradox: on the one hand Oedipus is the ideal ruler, a patient and responsive king who speaks to his people directly and listens intently to their pleas; but on the other hand, he is the very pestilence that has ruined the city. Oedipus is a riddle or puzzle in another sense as well: by having unwittingly killed his father and married his mother, he becomes, as the chorus points out repeatedly, both son and husband and, to the offspring of this incestuous union, both father and sibling. These are paradoxes Oedipus cannot fathom or solve; they are the web spun around him, leading to the final, cruel revelation at the end of the play.

The riddle of a person who is both husband and son, brother and father is ultimately based on kinship. Kinship is central to Greek mythology, with its family curses passed down from parents to children. In *Oedipus the King* this theme is pursued to its extreme. In its largest dimensions, kinship helps distinguish between citizens and foreigners. Oedipus had come to Thebes as a voluntary exile, fleeing the couple whom he thought were his real parents in the city of Corinth in order to escape the prophecy that he would kill his father and marry his mother. Only at the end of the play, as part of its tragic turn, does it become clear that he is in fact a citizen of Thebes, son of the late King Laius and his wife (and now Oedipus's wife), Jocasta. Oedipus is thus doubly ignorant: he knows neither what city-state he belongs to nor who his kin are. This, precisely, is his crime, or his failure, and for this he is punished.

Dominated by messengers, reports, rumors, oracles, and prophecies, *Oedipus the King* is also unusually rich in puns and plays on names. Oedipus is named after his swollen (*oidos*) foot, an injury caused when he was cast out by his parents in their attempt to thwart the prophecy attached to their child. But his name also contains the word *oida*, which means "I know." The play is full of references to and echoes of both meanings, punning on the word for swelling and the concept of knowledge as well as its opposite, ignorance. The most famous metaphor for the play's attention to knowledge and ignorance is light. From the beginning, Oedipus vows to shed light on the mysterious murder of the former king and insists that he will force the obscure truth out into the open, no matter at what cost. Well into the play, his wife begins to fathom the grim reality of his identity and begs him to halt his single-minded search for his own past. But Oedipus wants nothing to remain hidden and does not stop until he has brought the bitter truth into the bright daylight. Given the role of light and darkness played in the entire tragedy, it is only fitting that Oedipus would punish himself not only with exile but also with blinding, so that he may no longer set eyes on the terrible deeds he has done. That the blind seer Tiresias has been right all along underscores the play's singular fixation on this one assemblage of images and metaphors.

Oedipus the King, with its pestilence and foreign ruler, is also embedded in the cultural and political history of Athens. The historian Thucydides famously described the plague that devastated Athens during the Peloponnesian War, which the plague in Thebes inevitably brings to mind. The play is also remarkable in its attention to medical language, registering the emergence of medicine as a specialized discipline in the fifth century B.C.E. Finally, it should be remembered that the play was performed before Athenian audiences, which would naturally compare their own city to Thebes. This point is brought home in Sophocles' last play, *Oedipus at Colonus*, where the magnanimous Athenians protect the outcast Oedipus, thus gratifying the Athenian audience at the expense of their rival.

Modern audiences have been disturbed that Oedipus is punished for a deed he had not intended and which he had in fact done everything to avoid. But Oedipus is not merely a victim of fate. For one thing, he is overconfident in his own powers, in his ability to protect the city and to excise its pestilence. We see him pass rash judgment on those who want the truth to remain hidden in order to protect themselves and Oedipus. Yet he is not an unfair ruler. Rather, the play is a meditation on the concept of luck, *tuchē*, so central to Greek tragedy and morality. Oedipus had been an extraordinarily lucky man, as he himself admits. But he is revealed to be the unluckiest of all. That forces larger than human powers dominate these characters' lives is no reason to absolve them from responsibility and moral judgment, however. Indeed, Oedipus takes responsibility for all of it—for his actions, for his changing luck, for what he did not know, and also for what he had to learn.

Few plays have provoked the imagination and conscience of audiences as powerfully as this one, and few have inspired as many adaptations and interpretations. Julius Caesar wrote a version of *Oedipus the King*, as did the Roman playwright Seneca. A celebrated version by the French playwright Corneille (1659) was followed by that of the Enlightenment philosopher and playwright Voltaire (1718). Sigmund Freud coined the term "Oedipus complex," based in part on his interpretation of Sophocles' play, to describe one of his core psychological theories. Cultural anthropologists have used the play to explain features shared in different societies. The twentieth century brought an influential adaptation by Jean Cocteau (1934). *Oedipus the King* has also been set to music by Carl Orff (1959) and filmed by the influential Italian filmmaker Pier Paulo Pasolini (1967). Numerous performances and interpretations of Sophocles' play have ensured that the story of a man who killed his father and married his mother still captures our fears today.

In the end, however, what ensured the power of this play across centuries may not be its various adaptations or its focus on incest, a taboo across cultures and eras. Incest was in fact only one element in Sophocles' campaign to use the theater in a way that was startlingly new at the time: namely, as a vehicle for truth. The play depicts an uncompromising, even self-destructive, search for truth at all cost. Everything else—the well-being of Jocasta, of Kreon, and of Oedipus himself—is ignored. If you want the truth, the play says, you must be ready to sacrifice everything for it. Rarely has a play formulated this fundamental insight and shown its consequences with greater clarity than does Sophocles' unique and radical tragedy. To learn more about the staging of *Oedipus the King* and to view photographs from select performances of the play, see the "Plays in Performance" color insert near the center of this volume.

M.P.

Oedipus the King[1]

CHARACTERS

OEDIPUS, king of Thebes
A PRIEST of Zeus
KREON, brother of Jocasta
A CHORUS of Theban citizens
  and their LEADER
TIRESIAS, a blind prophet
JOCASTA, the queen, wife of Oedipus

A MESSENGER from Corinth
A SHEPHERD
A MESSENGER from inside the palace
ANTIGONE, ISMENE, daughters of
  Oedipus and Jocasta
GUARDS and attendants
PRIESTS of Thebes

[TIME AND SCENE: *The royal house of Thebes.*[2] *Double doors dominate the façade; a stone altar stands at the center of the stage.*

Many years have passed since OEDIPUS *solved the riddle of the Sphinx*[3] *and ascended the throne of Thebes, and now a plague has struck the city. A procession of priests enters; suppliants, broken and despondent, they carry branches wound in wool and lay them on the altar.*

The doors open. Guards assemble. OEDIPUS *comes forward, majestic but for a telltale limp, and slowly views the condition of his people.*]

OEDIPUS   Oh my children, the new blood of ancient Thebes,
why are you here? Huddling at my altar,
praying before me, your branches wound in wool.[4]
Our city reeks with the smoke of burning incense,
5   rings with cries for the Healer[5] and wailing for the dead.
I thought it wrong, my children, to hear the truth
from others, messengers. Here I am myself—
you all know me, the world knows my fame:
I am Oedipus.
        [*Helping a* PRIEST *to his feet.*]
            Speak up, old man. Your years,
10   your dignity—you should speak for the others.
Why here and kneeling, what preys upon you so?
Some sudden fear? some strong desire?

---

1. Translated by Robert Fagles.
2. Capital city of the region of Boeotia, in east-central Greece, famed throughout the ancient world for the seven gates in its fortifications.
3. A monster that had terrorized Thebes as long as no one could answer her riddle: "What walks on four feet in the morning, two at noon, and three in the evening?" When Oedipus correctly answered "Man," the monster killed herself, and Oedipus

was rewarded with both the Theban kingship and the hand of Thebes' queen, Jocasta, in marriage.
4. Emblems of supplication, laid on the altar and then taken up again after the suppliant's request is granted.
5. Apollo, god of medicine as well as light and prophecy.

You can trust me. I am ready to help,
I'll do anything. I would be blind to misery
15   not to pity my people kneeling at my feet.

PRIEST   Oh Oedipus, king of the land, our greatest power!
You see us before you now, men of all ages
clinging to your altars. Here are boys,
still too weak to fly from the nest,
20   and here the old, bowed down with the years,
the holy ones—a priest of Zeus[6] myself—and here
the picked, unmarried men, the young hope of Thebes.
And all the rest, your great family gathers now,
branches wreathed, massing in the squares,
25   kneeling before the two temples of queen Athena
or the river-shrine where the embers glow and die
and Apollo sees the future in the ashes.[7]

                              Our city—
look around you, see with your own eyes—
our ship pitches wildly, cannot lift her head
30   from the depths, the red waves of death . . .
Thebes is dying. A blight on the fresh crops
and the rich pastures, cattle sicken and die,
and the women die in labor, children stillborn,
and the plague, the fiery god of fever hurls down
35   on the city, his lightning slashing through us—
raging plague in all its vengeance, devastating
the house of Cadmus![8] And black Death luxuriates
in the raw, wailing miseries of Thebes.
Now we pray to you. You cannot equal the gods,
40   your children know that, bending at your altar.
But we do rate you first of men,
both in the common crises of our lives
and face-to-face encounters with the gods.
You freed us from the Sphinx, you came to Thebes
45   and cut us loose from the bloody tribute we had paid
that harsh, brutal singer. We taught you nothing,
no skill, no extra knowledge, still you triumphed.
A god was with you, so they say, and we believe it—
you lifted up our lives.

                              So now again,
50   Oedipus, king, we bend to you, your power—
we implore you, all of us on our knees:
find us strength, rescue! Perhaps you've heard
the voice of a god or something from other men,
Oedipus . . . what do you know?
55   The man of experience—you see it every day—
his plans will work in a crisis, his first of all.

---

6. Ruler of the Greek gods.
7. That is, the ashes of sacrificed animals: the priests of Apollo divined the future through
the patterns found in them. *Athena:* goddess of wisdom and war.
8. The mythical founder of Thebes.

Act now—we beg you, best of men, raise up our city!
Act, defend yourself, your former glory!
Your country calls you savior now
for your zeal, your action years ago.
Never let us remember of your reign:
you helped us stand, only to fall once more.
Oh raise up our city, set us on our feet.
The omens were good that day you brought us joy—
be the same man today!
Rule our land, you know you have the power,
but rule a land of the living, not a wasteland.
Ship and towered city are nothing, stripped of men
alive within it, living all as one.

OEDIPUS   My children,
I pity you. I see—how could I fail to see
what longings bring you here? Well I know
you are sick to death, all of you,
but sick as you are, not one is sick as I.
Your pain strikes each of you alone, each
in the confines of himself, no other. But my spirit
grieves for the city, for myself and all of you.
I wasn't asleep, dreaming. You haven't wakened me—
I've wept through the nights, you must know that,
groping, laboring over many paths of thought.
After a painful search I found one cure:
I acted at once. I sent Kreon,
my wife's own brother, to Delphi[9]—
Apollo the Prophet's oracle—to learn
what I might do or say to save our city.

Today's the day. When I count the days gone by
it torments me . . . what is he doing?
Strange, he's late, he's gone too long.
But once he returns, then, then I'll be a traitor
if I do not do all the god makes clear.

PRIEST   Timely words. The men over there
are signaling—Kreon's just arriving.

OEDIPUS [Sighting KREON, then turning to the altar.]
                                          Lord Apollo,
let him come with a lucky word of rescue,
shining like his eyes!

PRIEST   Welcome news, I think—he's crowned, look,
and the laurel wreath is bright with berries.[1]

---

9. Site of the shrine on the slope of Mount
Parnassus, in central Greece, where Apollo
prophesies through his priestess. *Kreon:* a
direct descendant of Cadmus, Thebes'
founder; it was Kreon who offered to share
the Theban throne with anyone who could
solve the riddle of the Sphinx.
1. The laurel crown is a sign that Kreon bears
good news.

OEDIPUS   We'll soon see. He's close enough to hear—

[*Enter* KREON *from the side; his face is shaded with a wreath.*]

Kreon, prince, my kinsman, what do you bring us?
What message from the god?

KREON   Good news.
I tell you even the hardest things to bear,
100   if they should turn out well, all would be well.

OEDIPUS   Of course, but what were the god's *words*? There's no hope
and nothing to fear in what you've said so far.

KREON   If you want my report in the presence of these . . .

[*Pointing to the priests while drawing* OEDIPUS *toward the palace.*]

I'm ready now, or we might go inside.

OEDIPUS   Speak out,
105   speak to us all. I grieve for these, my people,
far more than I fear for my own life.

KREON   Very well,
I will tell you what I heard from the god.
Apollo commands us—he was quite clear—
"Drive the corruption from the land,
110   don't harbor it any longer, past all cure,
don't nurse it in your soil—root it out!"

OEDIPUS   How can we cleanse ourselves—what rites?
What's the source of the trouble?

KREON   Banish the man, or pay back blood with blood.
115   Murder sets the plague-storm on the city.

OEDIPUS   Whose murder?
Whose fate does Apollo bring to light?

KREON   Our leader,
my lord, was once a man named Laius,[2]
before you came and put us straight on course.

OEDIPUS   I know—
or so I've heard. I never saw the man myself.

120   KREON   Well, he was killed, and Apollo commands us now—
he could not be more clear,
"Pay the killers back—whoever is responsible."

OEDIPUS   Where on earth are they? Where to find it now,
the trail of the ancient guilt so hard to trace?

125   KREON   "Here in Thebes," he said.
Whatever is sought for can be caught, you know,
whatever is neglected slips away.

OEDIPUS   But where,
in the palace, the fields or foreign soil,
where did Laius meet his bloody death?

130   KREON   He went to consult an oracle, Apollo said,
and he set out and never came home again.

---

2. Former king of Thebes and husband of Jocasta; he was on his way to Delphi to consult the
oracle of Apollo when he was killed.

OEDIPUS   No messenger, no fellow-traveler saw what happened?
    Someone to cross-examine?
KREON   No,
    they were all killed but one. He escaped,
135   terrified, he could tell us nothing clearly,
    nothing of what he saw—just one thing.
OEDIPUS   What's that?
    one thing could hold the key to it all,
    a small beginning give us grounds for hope.
KREON   He said thieves attacked them—a whole band,
140   not single-handed, cut King Laius down.
OEDIPUS   A thief,
    so daring, so wild, he'd kill a king? Impossible,
    unless conspirators paid him off in Thebes.
KREON   We suspected as much. But with Laius dead
    no leader appeared to help us in our troubles.
145 OEDIPUS   Trouble? Your *king* was murdered—royal blood!
    What stopped you from tracking down the killer
    then and there?
KREON   The singing, riddling Sphinx.
    She . . . persuaded us to let the mystery go
    and concentrate on what lay at our feet.
OEDIPUS   No,
150   I'll start again—I'll bring it all to light myself!
    Apollo is right, and so are you, Kreon,
    to turn our attention back to the murdered man.
    Now you have *me* to fight for you, you'll see:
    I am the land's avenger by all rights,
155   and Apollo's champion too.
    But not to assist some distant kinsman, no,
    for my own sake I'll rid us of this corruption.
    Whoever killed the king may decide to kill me too,
    with the same violent hand—by avenging Laius
160   I defend myself.
              [*To the priests.*]
              Quickly, my children.
    Up from the steps, take up your branches now.
              [*To the guards.*]
    One of you summon the city here before us,
    tell them I'll do everything. God help us,
    we will see our triumph—or our fall.
          [OEDIPUS *and* KREON *enter the palace, followed by the guards.*]
165 PRIEST   Rise, my sons. The kindness we came for
    Oedipus volunteers himself.
    Apollo has sent his word, his oracle—
    Come down, Apollo, save us, stop the plague.
          [*The priests rise, remove their branches and exit to the side. Enter a*
          CHORUS, *the citizens of Thebes, who have not heard the news that*
          KREON *brings. They march around the altar, chanting.*]

CHORUS   Zeus!
Great welcome voice of Zeus,[3] what do you bring?
170   What word from the gold vaults of Delphi
comes to brilliant Thebes? Racked with terror—
          terror shakes my heart
and I cry your wild cries, Apollo, Healer of Delos[4]
I worship you in dread . . . what now, what is your price?
175   some new sacrifice? some ancient rite from the past
come round again each spring?—
          what will you bring to birth?
Tell me, child of golden Hope
          warm voice that never dies!

180   You are the first I call, daughter of Zeus
deathless Athena—I call your sister Artemis,[5]
heart of the market place enthroned in glory,
          guardian of our earth—
I call Apollo, Archer astride the thunderheads of heaven—
185   O triple shield against death, shine before me now!
If ever, once in the past, you stopped some ruin
launched against our walls
          you hurled the flame of pain
far, far from Thebes—you gods
190   come now, come down once more!
                              No, no
the miseries numberless, grief on grief, no end—
too much to bear, we are all dying
O my people . . .
          Thebes like a great army dying
195   and there is no sword of thought to save us, no
and the fruits of our famous earth, they will not ripen
no and the women cannot scream their pangs to birth—
screams for the Healer, children dead in the womb
          and life on life goes down
200   you can watch them go
          like seabirds winging west, outracing the day's fire
down the horizon, irresistibly
          streaking on to the shores of Evening
                                        Death
so many deaths, numberless deaths on deaths, no end—
205   Thebes is dying, look, her children
stripped of pity . . .
          generations strewn on the ground
unburied, unwept, the dead spreading death
and the young wives and gray-haired mothers with them

3. That is, Apollo, who could speak for Zeus,   Sea that was central to his cult.
his father.   5. Goddess of the moon and the hunt; twin
4. Apollo's birthplace, an island in the Aegean   sister of Apollo.

210 cling to the altars, trailing in from all over the city—
     Thebes, city of death, one long cortege
             and the suffering rises
                 wails for mercy rise
         and the wild hymn for the Healer blazes out
215 clashing with our sobs our cries of mourning—
         O golden daughter of god, send rescue
         radiant as the kindness in your eyes!

     Drive him back!—the fever, the god of death
             that raging god of war[6]
220 not armored in bronze, not shielded now, he burns me,
     battle cries in the onslaught burning on—
     O rout him from our borders!
     Sail him, blast him out to the Sea-queen's chamber
             the black Atlantic gulfs
225   or the northern harbor, death to all
     where the Thracian[7] surf comes crashing.
     Now what the night spares he comes by day and kills—
     the god of death.

                     O lord of the stormcloud,
         you who twirl the lightning, Zeus, Father,
230 thunder Death to nothing!

     Apollo, lord of the light, I beg you—
         whip your longbow's golden cord
     showering arrows on our enemies—shafts of power
     champions strong before us rushing on!

235 Artemis, Huntress,
     torches flaring over the eastern ridges—
             ride Death down in pain!

     God of the headdress gleaming gold, I cry to you—
     your name and ours are one, Dionysus—
240   come with your face aflame with wine
             your raving women's[8] cries
         your army on the march! Come with the lightning
     come with torches blazing, eyes ablaze with glory!
     Burn that god of death[9] that all gods hate!
             [OEDIPUS enters from the palace to address the CHORUS, as if
             addressing the entire city of Thebes.]

6. Ares, son of Zeus and Hera, the god of savage warfare.
7. Ares was associated with Thrace, northeast
of Greece, whose inhabitants the Greeks
viewed as savage. Sea-queen: Amphitrite, consort of Poseidon, god of the sea.

8. The Maenads—frenzied women who worship Dionysus, the god of wine and of drama.
He is identified with Thebes (see line 239)
because his mother was Semele, a Theban
princess.
9. That is, Ares.

245 OEDIPUS   You pray to the gods? Let me grant your prayers.
Come, listen to me—do what the plague demands:
you'll find relief and lift your head from the depths.
I will speak out now as a stranger to the story,[1]
a stranger to the crime. If I'd been present then,
250 there would have been no mystery, no long hunt
without a clue in hand. So now, counted
a native Theban years after the murder,
to all of Thebes I make this proclamation:
if any one of you knows who murdered Laius,
255 the son of Labdacus, I order him to reveal
the whole truth to me. Nothing to fear,
even if he must denounce himself,
let him speak up
and so escape the brunt of the charge—
260 he will suffer no unbearable punishment,
nothing worse than exile, totally unharmed.

    [OEDIPUS *pauses, waiting for a reply.*]

                          Next,
if anyone knows the murderer is a stranger,
a man from alien soil, come, speak up.
I will give him a handsome reward, and lay up
265 gratitude in my heart for him besides.

    [*Silence again, no reply.*]

But if you keep silent, if anyone panicking,
trying to shield himself or friend or kin,
rejects my offer, then hear what I will do.
I order you, every citizen of the state
270 where I hold throne and power: banish this man—
whoever he may be—never shelter him, never
speak a word to him, never make him partner
to your prayers, your victims burned to the gods.
Never let the holy water touch his hands
275 Drive him out, each of you, from every home.
He is the plague, the heart of our corruption,
as Apollo's oracle has just revealed to me.
So I honor my obligations:
I fight for the god and for the murdered man.

280 Now my curse on the murderer. Whoever he is,
a lone man unknown in his crime
or one among many, let that man drag out
his life in agony, step by painful step—
I curse myself as well . . . if by any chance
285 he proves to be an intimate of our house,
here at my hearth, with my full knowledge,
may the curse I just called down on him strike me!

---

1. Oedipus was raised in Corinth, a Greek city-state south of Thebes.

These are your orders: perform them to the last.
I command you, for my sake, for Apollo's, for this country
290   blasted root and branch by the angry heavens.
Even if god had never urged you on to act,
how could you leave the crime uncleansed so long?
A man so noble—your king, brought down in blood—
you should have searched. But I am the king now,
295   I hold the throne that he held then, possess his bed
and a wife who shares our seed[2] . . . why, our seed
might be the same, children born of the same mother
might have created blood-bonds between us
if his hope of offspring hadn't met disaster—
300   but fate swooped at his head and cut him short.
So I will fight for him as if he were my father,
stop at nothing, search the world
to lay my hands on the man who shed his blood,
the son of Labdacus descended of Polydorus,
305   Cadmus of old and Agenor, founder of the line:[3]
their power and mine are one.

                                             Oh dear gods,
my curse on those who disobey these orders!
Let no crops grow out of the earth for them—
shrivel their women, kill their sons,
310   burn them to nothing in this plague
that hits us now, or something even worse.
But you, loyal men of Thebes who approve my actions,
may our champion, Justice, may all the gods
be with us, fight beside us to the end!

315 LEADER   In the grip of your curse, my king, I swear
I'm not the murderer, I cannot point him out.
As for the search, Apollo pressed it on us—
he should name the killer.

OEDIPUS   Quite right,
but to force the gods to act against their will—
320   no man has the power.

LEADER   Then if I might mention
the next best thing . . .

OEDIPUS   The third best too—
don't hold back, say it.

LEADER   I still believe . . .
Lord Tiresias[4] sees with the eyes of Lord Apollo.
Anyone searching for the truth, my king,
325   might learn it from the prophet, clear as day.

OEDIPUS   I've not been slow with that. On Kreon's cue
I sent the escorts, twice, within the hour.

---

2. Jocasta, queen of Thebes, was the widow   the city's founder, and Agenor, father of
of Laius.   Cadmus.
3. Here Oedipus traces the lineage of his   4. The blind prophet of Thebes.
predecessor, King Laius, back to Cadmus,

I'm surprised he isn't here.

LEADER   We need him—
without him we have nothing but old, useless rumors.

330 OEDIPUS   Which rumors? I'll search out every word.

LEADER   Laius was killed, they say, by certain travelers.

OEDIPUS   I know—but no one can find the murderer.

LEADER   If the man has a trace of fear in him
he won't stay silent long,

335   not with your curses ringing in his ears.

OEDIPUS   He didn't flinch at murder,
he'll never flinch at words.

> [*Enter* TIRESIAS, *the blind prophet, led by a boy with escorts in*
> *attendance. He remains at a distance.*]

LEADER   Here is the one who will convict him, look,
they bring him on at last, the seer, the man of god.

340   The truth lives inside him, him alone.

OEDIPUS   O Tiresias,
master of all the mysteries of our life,
all you teach and all you dare not tell,
signs in the heavens, signs that walk the earth!
Blind as you are, you can feel all the more

345   what sickness haunts our city. You, my lord,
are the one shield, the one savior we can find.
We asked Apollo—perhaps the messengers
haven't told you—he sent his answer back:
"Relief from the plague can only come one way.

350   Uncover the murderers of Laius,
put them to death or drive them into exile."
So I beg you, grudge us nothing now, no voice,
no message plucked from the birds, the embers
or the other mantic ways within your grasp.

355   Rescue yourself, your city, rescue me—
rescue everything infected by the dead.
We are in your hands. For a man to help others
with all his gifts and native strength:
that is the noblest work.

TIRESIAS   How terrible—to see the truth

360   when the truth is only pain to him who sees!
I knew it well, but I put it from my mind,
else I never would have come.

OEDIPUS   What's this? Why so grim, so dire?

TIRESIAS   Just send me home. You bear your burdens,

365   I'll bear mine. It's better that way,
please believe me.

OEDIPUS   Strange response . . . unlawful,
unfriendly too to the state that bred and reared you—
you withhold the word of god.

TIRESIAS   I fail to see
that your own words are so well-timed.

370   I'd rather not have the same thing said of me . . .

OEDIPUS   For the love of god, don't turn away,
　　　not if you know something. We beg you,
　　　all of us on our knees.
TIRESIAS　　　　　　　None of you knows—
　　　and I will never reveal my dreadful secrets,
375　　not to say your own.
OEDIPUS   What? You know and you won't tell?
　　　You're bent on betraying us, destroying Thebes?
TIRESIAS   I'd rather not cause pain for you or me.
　　　So why this . . . useless interrogation?
380　　You'll get nothing from me.
OEDIPUS　　　　　　　　　　Nothing! You,
　　　you scum of the earth, you'd enrage a heart of stone!
　　　You won't talk? Nothing moves you?
　　　Out with it, once and for all!
TIRESIAS   You criticize my temper . . . unaware
385　　of the one you live with, you revile me.
OEDIPUS   Who could restrain his anger hearing you?
　　　What outrage—you spurn the city!
TIRESIAS   What will come will come.
　　　Even if I shroud it all in silence.
390 OEDIPUS   What will come? You're bound to tell me that.
TIRESIAS   I'll say no more. Do as you like, build your anger
　　　to whatever pitch you please, rage your worst—
OEDIPUS   Oh I'll let loose, I have such fury in me—
　　　now I see it all. You helped hatch the plot,
395　　you did the work, yes, short of killing him
　　　with your own hands—and given eyes I'd say
　　　you did the killing single-handed!
TIRESIAS　　　　　　　　　　Is that so!
　　　I charge you, then, submit to that decree
　　　you just laid down: from this day onward
400　　speak to no one, not these citizens, not myself.
　　　You are the curse, the corruption of the land!
OEDIPUS   You, shameless—
　　　aren't you appalled to start up such a story?
　　　You think you can get away with this?
TIRESIAS　　　　　　　　　　I have already.
405　　The truth with all its power lives inside me.
OEDIPUS   Who primed you for this? Not your prophet's trade.
TIRESIAS   You did, you forced me, twisted it out of me.
OEDIPUS   What? Say it again—I'll understand it better.
TIRESIAS   Didn't you understand, just now?
410　　Or are you tempting me to talk?
OEDIPUS   No, I can't say I grasped your meaning.
　　　Out with it, again!
TIRESIAS   I say you are the murderer you hunt.
OEDIPUS   That obscenity, twice—by god, you'll pay.
415 TIRESIAS   Shall I say more, so you can really rage?
OEDIPUS   Much as you want. Your words are nothing—futile.

TIRESIAS   You cannot imagine . . . I tell you,
    you and your loved ones live together in infamy,
    you cannot see how far you've gone in guilt.

420 OEDIPUS   You think you can keep this up and never suffer?

TIRESIAS   Indeed, if the truth has any power.

OEDIPUS   It does
    but not for you, old man. You've lost your power,
    stone-blind, stone-deaf—senses, eyes blind as stone!

TIRESIAS   I pity you, flinging at me the very insults
425   each man here will fling at you so soon.

OEDIPUS   Blind,
    lost in the night, endless night that cursed you!
    You can't hurt me or anyone else who sees the light—
    you can never touch me.

TIRESIAS   True, it is not your fate
    to fall at my hands. Apollo is quite enough,
430   and he will take some pains to work this out.

OEDIPUS   Kreon! Is this conspiracy his or yours?

TIRESIAS   Kreon is not your downfall, no, you are your own.

OEDIPUS   O power—
    wealth and empire, skill outstripping skill
    in the heady rivalries of life,
435   what envy lurks inside you! Just for this,
    the crown the city gave me—I never sought it,
    they laid it in my hands—for this alone, Kreon,
    the soul of trust, my loyal friend from the start
    steals against me . . . so hungry to overthrow me
440   he sets this wizard on me, this scheming quack,
    this fortune-teller peddling lies, eyes peeled
    for his own profit—seer blind in his craft!

    Come here, you pious fraud. Tell me,
    when did you ever prove yourself a prophet?
445   When the Sphinx, that chanting Fury kept her deathwatch here,
    why silent then, not a word to set our people free?
    There was a riddle, not for some passer-by to solve[5]—
    it cried out for a prophet. Where were you?
    Did you rise to the crisis? Not a word,
450   you and your birds, your gods—nothing.
    No, but I came by, Oedipus the ignorant,
    I stopped the Sphinx! With no help from the birds,
    the flight of my own intelligence hit the mark.

    And this is the man you'd try to overthrow?
455   You think you'll stand by Kreon when he's king?
    You and the great mastermind—
    you'll pay in tears, I promise you, for this,

5. Oedipus was on his way to Apollo's oracle at Delphi when he came upon the Sphinx.

this witch-hunt. If you didn't look so senile
the lash would teach you what your scheming means!

460 LEADER   I would suggest his words were spoken in anger,
Oedipus . . . yours too, and it isn't what we need.
The best solution to the oracle, the riddle
posed by god—we should look for that.

TIRESIAS   You are the king no doubt, but in one respect,
465   at least, I am your equal: the right to reply.
I claim that privilege too.
I am not your slave. I serve Apollo.
I don't need Kreon to speak for me in public.

So,
you mock my blindness? Let me tell you this.
470   You with your precious eyes,
you're blind to the corruption of your life,
to the house you live in, those you live with—
who *are* your parents? Do you know? All unknowing
you are the scourge of your own flesh and blood,
475   the dead below the earth and the living here above,
and the double lash of your mother and your father's curse
will whip you from this land one day, their footfall
treading you down in terror, darkness shrouding
your eyes that now can see the light!

Soon, soon
480   you'll scream aloud—what haven won't reverberate?
What rock of Cithaeron[6] won't scream back in echo?
That day you learn the truth about your marriage,
the wedding-march that sang you into your halls,
the lusty voyage home to the fatal harbor!
485   And a crowd of other horrors you'd never dream
will level you with yourself and all your children.

There. Now smear us with insults—Kreon, myself,
and every word I've said. No man will ever
be rooted from the earth as brutally as you.

490 OEDIPUS   Enough! Such filth from him? Insufferable—
what, still alive? Get out—
faster, back where you came from—vanish!

TIRESIAS   I would never have come if you hadn't called me here.

OEDIPUS   If I thought you would blurt out such absurdities,
495   you'd have died waiting before I'd had you summoned.

TIRESIAS   Absurd, am I! To you, not to your parents:
the ones who bore you found me sane enough.

OEDIPUS   Parents—who? Wait . . . who is my father?

TIRESIAS   This day will bring your birth and your destruction.

500 OEDIPUS   Riddles—all you can say are riddles, murk and darkness.

TIRESIAS   Ah, but aren't you the best man alive at solving riddles?

6. The mountain range, south of Thebes, where the infant Oedipus was abandoned.

OEDIPUS   Mock me for that, go on, and you'll reveal my greatness.

TIRESIAS   Your great good fortune, true, it was your ruin.

OEDIPUS   Not if I saved the city—what do I care?

505 TIRESIAS   Well then, I'll be going.

[*To his attendant.*]

Take me home, boy.

OEDIPUS   Yes, take him away. You're a nuisance here.
Out of the way, the irritation's gone.

[*Turning his back on* TIRESIAS, *moving toward the palace.*]

TIRESIAS   I will go,
once I have said what I came here to say.
I'll never shrink from the anger in your eyes—

510 you can't destroy me. Listen to me closely:
the man you've sought so long, proclaiming,
cursing up and down, the murderer of Laius—
he is here. A stranger,
you may think, who lives among you,

515 he soon will be revealed a native Theban
but he will take no joy in the revelation.
Blind who now has eyes, beggar who now is rich,
he will grope his way toward a foreign soil,
a stick tapping before him step by step.

[OEDIPUS *enters the palace.*]

520 Revealed at last, brother and father both
to the children he embraces, to his mother
son and husband both—he sowed the loins
his father sowed, he spilled his father's blood!
Go in and reflect on that, solve that.

525 And if you find I've lied
from this day onward call the prophet blind.

[TIRESIAS *and the boy exit to the side.*]

CHORUS   Who—
who is the man the voice of god denounces
resounding out of the rocky gorge of Delphi?
The horror too dark to tell,

530 whose ruthless bloody hands have done the work?
His time has come to fly
to outrace the stallions of the storm
his feet a streak of speed—
Cased in armor, Apollo son of the Father

535 lunges on him, lightning-bolts afire!
And the grim unerring Furies[7]
closing for the kill.
Look,
the word of god has just come blazing
flashing off Parnassus'[8] snowy heights!

---

7. Monstrous female personifications of
vengeance.

8. Site of Delphi, where the oracular shrine
was a deep cave or chasm (see lines 546–47).

540   That man who left no trace—
        after him, hunt him down with all our strength!
        Now under bristling timber
            up through rocks and caves he stalks
                like the wild mountain bull—
545   cut off from men, each step an agony, frenzied, racing blind
        but he cannot outrace the dread voices of Delphi
        ringing out of the heart of Earth,
            the dark wings beating around him shrieking doom
                the doom that never dies, the terror—
550   The skilled prophet scans the birds and shatters me with terror!
        I can't accept him, can't deny him, don't know what to say,
        I'm lost, and the wings of dark foreboding beating—
        I cannot see what's come, what's still to come . . .
        and what could breed a blood feud between
555   Laius' house and the son of Polybus?[9]
        I know of nothing, not in the past and not now,
        no charge to bring against our king, no cause
        to attack his fame that rings throughout Thebes—
            not without proof—not for the ghost of Laius,
560   not to avenge a murder gone without a trace.
        Zeus and Apollo know, they know, the great masters
                of all the dark and depth of human life.
        But whether a mere man can know the truth,
        whether a seer can fathom more than I—
565   there is no test, no certain proof
            though matching skill for skill
        a man can outstrip a rival. No, not till I see
        these charges proved will I side with his accusers.
        We saw him then, when the she-hawk[1] swept against him,
570   saw with our own eyes his skill, his brilliant triumph—
            there was the test—he was the joy of Thebes!
            Never will I convict my king, never in my heart.
                    [Enter KREON from the side.]

        KREON   My fellow-citizens, I hear King Oedipus
        levels terrible charges at me. I had to come.
575   I resent it deeply. If, in the present crisis
        he thinks he suffers any abuse from me,
        anything I've done or said that offers him
        the slightest injury, why, I've no desire
        to linger out this life, my reputation in ruins.
580   The damage I'd face from such an accusation
        is nothing simple. No, there's nothing worse:
        branded a traitor in the city, a traitor
        to all of you and my good friends.

9. A reference to the rivalry between the cit-   1. That is, the Sphinx, which had the paws of a
ies of Thebes (formerly ruled by King Laius)   lion, the tail of a serpent, and the wings of an
and Corinth (ruled by Polybus, Oedipus's   eagle.
adoptive father).

LEADER   True,
　　but a slur might have been forced out of him,
585　　by anger perhaps, not any firm conviction.
　　KREON The charge was made in public, wasn't it?
　　　I put the prophet up to spreading lies?
　　LEADER Such things were said . . .
　　　I don't know with what intent, if any.
590　KREON Was his glance steady, his mind right
　　　when the charge was brought against me?
　　LEADER I really couldn't say. I never look
　　　to judge the ones in power.

　　　　　[*The doors open.* OEDIPUS *enters.*]

　　　　　　　　　　　　　　　　Wait,
　　here's Oedipus now.
　　OEDIPUS   You—here? You have the gall
595　to show your face before the palace gates?
　　You, plotting to kill me, kill the king—
　　I see it all, the marauding thief himself
　　scheming to steal my crown and power!

　　　　　　　　　　　　　　　　　　　　Tell me,
　　in god's name, what did you take me for,
600　coward or fool, when you spun out your plot?
　　Your treachery—you think I'd never detect it
　　creeping against me in the dark? Or sensing it,
　　not defend myself? Aren't you the fool,
　　you and your high adventure. Lacking numbers,
605　powerful friends, out for the big game of empire—
　　you need riches, armies to bring that quarry down!
　　KREON Are you quite finished? It's your turn to listen
　　　for just as long as you've . . . instructed me.
　　　Hear me out, then judge me on the facts.
610　OEDIPUS You've a wicked way with words, Kreon,
　　　but I'll be slow to learn—from you.
　　　I find you a menace, a great burden to me.
　　KREON Just one thing, hear me out in this.
　　OEDIPUS   Just one thing,
　　　don't tell *me* you're not the enemy, the traitor.
615　KREON Look, if you think crude, mindless stubbornness
　　　such a gift, you've lost your sense of balance.
　　OEDIPUS If you think you can abuse a kinsman,
　　　then escape the penalty, you're insane.
　　KREON Fair enough, I grant you. But this injury
620　you say I've done you, what is it?
　　OEDIPUS Did you induce me, yes or no,
　　　to send for that sanctimonious prophet?
　　KREON I did. And I'd do the same again.
　　OEDIPUS All right then, tell me, how long is it now
625　since Laius . . .
　　KREON   Laius—what did *he* do?

OEDIPUS   Vanished,
   swept from sight, murdered in his tracks.
KREON   The count of the years would run you far back . . .
OEDIPUS   And that far back, was the prophet at his trade?
KREON   Skilled as he is today, and just as honored.
630 OEDIPUS   Did he ever refer to me then, at that time?
KREON   No,
   never, at least, when I was in his presence.
OEDIPUS   But you did investigate the murder, didn't you?
KREON   We did our best, of course, discovered nothing.
OEDIPUS   But the great seer never accused me then—why not?
635 KREON   I don't know. And when I don't, *I* keep quiet.
OEDIPUS   You do know this, you'd tell it too—
   if you had a shred of decency.
KREON   What?
   If I know, I won't hold back.
OEDIPUS   Simply this:
   if the two of you had never put heads together,
640 we would never have heard about *my* killing Laius.
KREON   If that's what he says . . . well, you know best.
   But now I have a right to learn from you
   as you just learned from me.
OEDIPUS   Learn your fill,
   you never will convict me of the murder.
645 KREON   Tell me, you're married to my sister, aren't you?
OEDIPUS   A genuine discovery—there's no denying that.
KREON   And you rule the land with her, with equal power?
OEDIPUS   She receives from me whatever she desires.
KREON   And I am the third, all of us are equals?
650 OEDIPUS   Yes, and it's there you show your stripes—
   you betray a kinsman.
KREON   Not at all.
   Not if you see things calmly, rationally,
   as I do. Look at it this way first:
   who in his right mind would rather rule
655 and live in anxiety than sleep in peace?
   Particularly if he enjoys the same authority.
   Not I, I'm not the man to yearn for kingship,
   not with a king's power in my hands. Who would?
   No one with any sense of self-control.
660 Now, as it is, you offer me all I need,
   not a fear in the world. But if I wore the crown . . .
   there'd be many painful duties to perform,
   hardly to my taste.
             How could kingship
   please me more than influence, power
665 without a qualm? I'm not that deluded yet,
   to reach for anything but privilege outright,
   profit free and clear.

Now all men sing my praises, all salute me,
now all who request your favors curry mine.
670 I am their best hope: success rests in me.
Why give up that, I ask you, and borrow trouble?
A man of sense, someone who sees things clearly
would never resort to treason.
No, I've no lust for conspiracy in me,
675 nor could I ever suffer one who does.

Do you want proof? Go to Delphi yourself,
examine the oracle and see if I've reported
the message word-for-word. This too:
if you detect that I and the clairvoyant
680 have plotted anything in common, arrest me,
execute me. Not on the strength of one vote,
two in this case, mine as well as yours.
But don't convict me on sheer unverified surmise.
How wrong it is to take the good for bad,
685 purely at random, or take the bad for good.
But reject a friend, a kinsman? I would as soon
tear out the life within us, priceless life itself.
You'll learn this well, without fail, in time.
Time alone can bring the just man to light—
690 the criminal you can spot in one short day.

LEADER   Good advice,
my lord, for anyone who wants to avoid disaster.
Those who jump to conclusions may go wrong.

OEDIPUS   When my enemy moves against me quickly,
plots in secret, I move quickly too, I must,
695 I plot and pay him back. Relax my guard a moment,
waiting his next move—he wins his objective,
I lose mine.

KREON   What do you want?
You want me banished?

OEDIPUS   No, I want you dead.

KREON   Just to show how ugly a grudge can . . .

OEDIPUS   So,
700 still stubborn? you don't think I'm serious?

KREON   I think you're insane.

OEDIPUS   Quite sane—in my behalf.

KREON   Not just as much in mine?

OEDIPUS   You—my mortal enemy?

KREON   What if you're wholly wrong?

OEDIPUS   No matter—I must rule.

KREON   Not if you rule unjustly.

OEDIPUS   Hear him, Thebes, my city!

705 KREON   My city too, not yours alone!

LEADER   Please, my lords.

        [Enter JOCASTA from the palace.]

            Look, Jocasta's coming,

and just in time too. With her help
you must put this fighting of yours to rest.
JOCASTA   Have you no sense? Poor misguided men,
710   such shouting—why this public outburst?
Aren't you ashamed, with the land so sick,
to stir up private quarrels?
              [*To* OEDIPUS.]
Into the palace now. And Kreon, you go home.
Why make such a furor over nothing?
715   KREON   My sister, it's dreadful . . . Oedipus, your husband,
he's bent on a choice of punishments for me,
banishment from the fatherland or death.
OEDIPUS   Precisely. I caught him in the act, Jocasta,
plotting, about to stab me in the back.
720   KREON   Never—curse me, let me die and be damned
if I've done you any wrong you charge me with.
JOCASTA   Oh god, believe it, Oedipus,
honor the solemn oath he swears to heaven.
Do it for me, for the sake of all your people.
              [*The* CHORUS *begins to chant.*]
725   CHORUS   Believe it, be sensible
give way, my king, I beg you!
OEDIPUS   What do you want from me, concessions?
CHORUS   Respect him—he's been no fool in the past
and now he's strong with the oath he swears to god.
730   OEDIPUS   You know what you're asking?
CHORUS   I do.
OEDIPUS   Then out with it!
CHORUS   The man's your friend, your kin, he's under oath—
don't cast him out, disgraced
branded with guilt on the strength of hearsay only.
OEDIPUS   Know full well, if that is what you want
735   you want me dead or banished from the land.
CHORUS   Never—
no, by the blazing Sun, first god of the heavens!
   Stripped of the gods, stripped of loved ones,
let me die by inches if that ever crossed my mind.
But the heart inside me sickens, dies as the land dies
740   and now on top of the old griefs you pile this,
your fury—both of you!
OEDIPUS   Then let him go,
even if it does lead to my ruin, my death
or my disgrace, driven from Thebes for life.
It's you, not him I pity—your words move me.
745   He, wherever he goes, my hate goes with him.
KREON   Look at you, sullen in yielding, brutal in your rage—
you'll go too far. It's perfect justice:
natures like yours are hardest on themselves.
OEDIPUS   Then leave me alone—get out!

KREON   I'm going.
750   You're wrong, so wrong. These men know I'm right.
                   [*Exit to the side. The* CHORUS *turns to* JOCASTA.]
CHORUS   Why do you hesitate, my lady
   why not help him in?
JOCASTA   Tell me what's happened first.
CHORUS   Loose, ignorant talk started dark suspicions
755   and a sense of injustice cut deeply too.
JOCASTA   On both sides?
CHORUS   Oh yes.
JOCASTA   What did they say?
CHORUS   Enough, please, enough! The land's so racked already
   or so it seems to me . . .
   End the trouble here, just where they left it.
760 OEDIPUS   You see what comes of your good intentions now?
   And all because you tried to blunt my anger.
CHORUS   My king,
   I've said it once, I'll say it time and again—
      I'd be insane, you know it,
   senseless, ever to turn my back on you.
765   You who set our beloved land—storm-tossed, shattered—
   straight on course. Now again, good helmsman,
   steer us through the storm!
             [*The* CHORUS *draws away, leaving* OEDIPUS *and* JOCASTA *side by side.*]
JOCASTA   For the love of god,
   Oedipus, tell me too, what is it?
   Why this rage? You're so unbending.
770 OEDIPUS   I will tell you. I respect you, Jocasta,
   much more than these . . .
                   [*Glancing at the* CHORUS.]
   Kreon's to blame, Kreon schemes against me.
JOCASTA   Tell me clearly, how did the quarrel start?
OEDIPUS   He says *I* murdered Laius—I am guilty.
775 JOCASTA   How does he know? Some secret knowledge
   or simple hearsay?
OEDIPUS   Oh, he sent his prophet in
   to do his dirty work. You know Kreon,
   Kreon keeps his own lips clean.
JOCASTA   A prophet?
   Well then, free yourself of every charge!
780   Listen to me and learn some peace of mind:
   no skill in the world,
   nothing human can penetrate the future.
   Here is proof, quick and to the point.

   An oracle came to Laius one fine day
785   (I won't say from Apollo himself
   but his underlings, his priests) and it said
   that doom would strike him down at the hands of a son,

our son, to be born of our own flesh and blood. But Laius,
so the report goes at least, was killed by strangers,
790   thieves, at a place where three roads meet . . . my son—
he wasn't three days old and the boy's father
fastened his ankles, had a henchman fling him away
on a barren, trackless mountain.

                                    There, you see?
Apollo brought neither thing to pass. My baby
795   no more murdered his father than Laius suffered—
his wildest fear—death at his own son's hands.
That's how the seers and all their revelations
mapped out the future. Brush them from your mind.
Whatever the god needs and seeks
800   he'll bring to light himself, with ease.

OEDIPUS   Strange,
hearing you just now . . . my mind wandered,
my thoughts racing back and forth.

JOCASTA   What do you mean? Why so anxious, startled?

OEDIPUS   I thought I heard you say that Laius
805   was cut down at a place where three roads meet.

JOCASTA   That was the story. It hasn't died out yet.

OEDIPUS   Where did this thing happen? Be precise.

JOCASTA   A place called Phocis, where two branching roads,
one from Daulia,[2] one from Delphi,
810   come together—a crossroads.

OEDIPUS   When? How long ago?

JOCASTA   The heralds no sooner reported Laius dead
than you appeared and they hailed you king of Thebes.

OEDIPUS   My god, my god—what have you planned to do to me?

815 JOCASTA   What, Oedipus? What haunts you so?

OEDIPUS   Not yet.
Laius—how did he look? Describe him.
Had he reached his prime?

JOCASTA   He was swarthy,
and the gray had just begun to streak his temples,
and his build . . . wasn't far from yours.

OEDIPUS   Oh no no,
820   I think I've just called down a dreadful curse
upon myself—I simply didn't know!

JOCASTA   What are you saying? I shudder to look at you.

OEDIPUS   I have a terrible fear the blind seer can see.
I'll know in a moment. One thing more—

JOCASTA   Anything,
825   afraid as I am—ask, I'll answer, all I can.

OEDIPUS   Did he go with a light or heavy escort,
several men-at-arms, like a lord, a king?

JOCASTA   There were five in the party, a herald among them,

---

2. A Boeotian town not far from Thebes. *Phocis*: the region where Delphi is located, west of
Boeotia.

and a single wagon carrying Laius.

OEDIPUS   Ai—
830 now I can see it all, clear as day.
      Who told you all this at the time, Jocasta?

JOCASTA   A servant who reached home, the lone survivor.

OEDIPUS   So, could he still be in the palace—even now?

JOCASTA   No indeed. Soon as he returned from the scene
835 and saw you on the throne with Laius dead and gone,
      he knelt and clutched my hand, pleading with me
      to send him into the hinterlands, to pasture,
      far as possible, out of sight of Thebes.
      I sent him away. Slave though he was,
840 he'd earned that favor—and much more.

OEDIPUS   Can we bring him back, quickly?

JOCASTA   Easily. Why do you want him so?

OEDIPUS   I'm afraid,
      Jocasta, I have said too much already.
      That man—I've got to see him.

JOCASTA   Then he'll come.
845 But even I have a right, I'd like to think,
      to know what's torturing you, my lord.

OEDIPUS   And so you shall—I can hold nothing back from you,
      now I've reached this pitch of dark foreboding.
      Who means more to me than you? Tell me,
850 whom would I turn toward but you
      as I go through all this?

      My father was Polybus, king of Corinth.
      My mother, a Dorian,[3] Merope. And I was held
      the prince of the realm among the people there,
855 till something struck me out of nowhere,
      something strange . . . worth remarking perhaps,
      hardly worth the anxiety I gave it.
      Some man at a banquet who had drunk too much
      shouted out—he was far gone, mind you—
860 that I am not my father's son. Fighting words!
      I barely restrained myself that day
      but early the next I went to mother and father,
      questioned them closely, and they were enraged
      at the accusation and the fool who let it fly.
865 So as for my parents I was satisfied,
      but still this thing kept gnawing at me,
      the slander spread—I had to make my move.

                                              And so,
      unknown to mother and father I set out for Delphi,
      and the god Apollo spurned me, sent me away

---

3. From Doris, a region of central Greece.

870 denied the facts I came for,
     but first he flashed before my eyes a future
     great with pain, terror, disaster—I can hear him cry,
     "You are fated to couple with your mother, you will bring
     a breed of children into the light no man can bear to see—
875 you will kill your father, the one who gave you life!"
     I heard all that and ran. I abandoned Corinth,
     from that day on I gauged its landfall only
     by the stars, running, always running
     toward some place where I would never see
880 the shame of all those oracles come true.
     And as I fled I reached that very spot
     where the great king, you say, met his death.

     Now, Jocasta, I will tell you all.
     Making my way toward this triple crossroad
885 I began to see a herald, then a brace of colts
     drawing a wagon, and mounted on the bench . . . a man,
     just as you've described him, coming face-to-face,
     and the one in the lead and the old man himself
     were about to thrust me off the road—brute force—
890 and the one shouldering me aside, the driver,
     I strike him in anger!—and the old man, watching me
     coming up along his wheels—he brings down
     his prod, two prongs straight at my head!
     I paid him back with interest!
895 Short work, by god—with one blow of the staff
     in this right hand I knock him out of his high seat,
     roll him out of the wagon, sprawling headlong—
     I killed them all—every mother's son!

     Oh, but if there is any blood-tie
900 between Laius and this stranger . . .
     what man alive more miserable than I?
     More hated by the gods? I am the man
     no alien, no citizen welcomes to his house,
     law forbids it—not a word to me in public,
905 driven out of every hearth and home.
     And all these curses I—no one but I
     brought down these piling curses on myself!
     And you, his wife, I've touched your body with these,
     the hands that killed your husband cover you with blood.

910 Wasn't I born for torment? Look me in the eyes!
     I am abomination—heart and soul!
     I must be exiled, and even in exile
     never see my parents, never set foot
     on native ground again. Else I am doomed
915 to couple with my mother and cut my father down . . .

Polybus who reared me, gave me life.
                              But why, why?
Wouldn't a man of judgment say—and wouldn't he be right—
some savage power has brought this down upon my head?

Oh no, not that, you pure and awesome gods,
920   never let me see that day! Let me slip
from the world of men, vanish without a trace
before I see myself stained with such corruption,
stained to the heart.

LEADER   My lord, you fill our hearts with fear.
925   But at least until you question the witness,
do take hope.

OEDIPUS   Exactly. He is my last hope—
I am waiting for the shepherd. He is crucial.

JOCASTA   And once he appears, what then? Why so urgent?

OEDIPUS   I will tell you. If it turns out that his story
930   matches yours, I've escaped the worst.

JOCASTA   What did I say? What struck you so?

OEDIPUS   You said *thieves*—
he told you a whole band of them murdered Laius.
So, if he still holds to the same number,
I cannot be the killer. One can't equal many.
935   But if he refers to one man, one alone,
clearly the scales come down on me:
I am guilty.

JOCASTA   Impossible. Trust me,
I told you precisely what he said,
and he can't retract it now;
940   the whole city heard it, not just I.
And even if he should vary his first report
by one man more or less, still, my lord,
he could never make the murder of Laius
truly fit the prophecy. Apollo was explicit:
945   my son was doomed to kill my husband . . . my son,
poor defenseless thing, he never had a chance
to kill his father. They destroyed him first.

So much for prophecy. It's neither here nor there.
From this day on, I wouldn't look right or left.

950 OEDIPUS   True, true. Still, that shepherd,
someone fetch him—now!

JOCASTA   I'll send at once. But do let's go inside.
I'd never displease you, least of all in this.

      [OEDIPUS *and* JOCASTA *enter the palace.*]

CHORUS   Destiny guide me always
955   Destiny find me filled with reverence
      pure in word and deed.
Great laws tower above us, reared on high
born for the brilliant vault of heaven—

    Olympian Sky their only father,[4]
960   nothing mortal, no man gave them birth,
    their memory deathless, never lost in sleep:
    within them lives a mighty god, the god does not grow old.

    Pride breeds the tyrant
    violent pride, gorging, crammed to bursting
965   with all that is overripe and rich with ruin—
    clawing up to the heights, headlong pride
    crashes down the abyss—sheer doom!
      No footing helps, all foothold lost and gone.
    But the healthy strife that makes the city strong—
970   I pray that god will never end that wrestling:
    god, my champion, I will never let you go.

    But if any man comes striding, high and mighty
      in all he says and does,
    no fear of justice, no reverence
975   for the temples of the gods—
      let a rough doom tear him down,
    repay his pride, breakneck, ruinous pride!
    If he cannot reap his profits fairly
      cannot restrain himself from outrage—
980   mad, laying hands on the holy things untouchable!

    Can such a man, so desperate, still boast
    he can save his life from the flashing bolts of god?
      If all such violence goes with honor now
        why join the sacred dance?

985   Never again will I go reverent to Delphi,
      the inviolate heart of Earth
    or Apollo's ancient oracle at Abae
    or Olympia[5] of the fires—
    unless these prophecies all come true
990   for all mankind to point toward in wonder.
    King of kings, if you deserve your titles
      Zeus, remember, never forget!
    You and your deathless, everlasting reign.

    They are dying, the old oracles sent to Laius,
995   now our masters strike them off the rolls.
      Nowhere Apollo's golden glory now—
        the gods, the gods go down.

    [*Enter* JOCASTA *from the palace, carrying a suppliant's branch
    wound in wool.*]

4. Mount Olympus in Thessaly, in northern Greece, was believed to be the home of the gods.
5. Site in the western Peloponnesus of a major temple of Zeus (location of the quadrennial Olympic games). *Abae:* a town in Phocis, whose oracle of Apollo was older than that at Delphi.

JOCASTA   Lords of the realm,[6] it occurred to me,
just now, to visit the temples of the gods,
1000   so I have my branch in hand and incense too.

Oedipus is beside himself. Racked with anguish,
no longer a man of sense, he won't admit
the latest prophecies are hollow as the old—
he's at the mercy of every passing voice
1005   if the voice tells of terror.
I urge him gently, nothing seems to help,
so I turn to you, Apollo, you are nearest.

> [*Placing her branch on the altar, while an old herdsman enters
> from the side, not the one just summoned by the King but an
> unexpected* MESSENGER *from Corinth.*]

I come with prayers and offerings . . . I beg you,
cleanse us, set us free of defilement!
1010   Look at us, passengers in the grip of fear,
watching the pilot of the vessel go to pieces.

MESSENGER [*Approaching* JOCASTA *and the* CHORUS.]
Strangers, please, I wonder if you could lead us
to the palace of the king . . . I think it's Oedipus.
Better, the man himself—you know where he is?

1015 LEADER   This is his palace, stranger. He's inside.
But here is his queen, his wife and mother
of his children.

MESSENGER   Blessings on you, noble queen,
queen of Oedipus crowned with all your family—
blessings on you always!

1020 JOCASTA   And the same to you, stranger, you deserve it . . .
such a greeting. But what have you come for?
Have you brought us news?

MESSENGER   Wonderful news—
for the house, my lady, for your husband too.

JOCASTA   Really, what? Who sent you?

MESSENGER   Corinth.
1025   I'll give you the message in a moment.
You'll be glad of it—how could you help it?—
though it costs a little sorrow in the bargain.

JOCASTA   What can it be, with such a double edge?

MESSENGER   The people there, they want to make your Oedipus
1030   king of Corinth, so they're saying now.

JOCASTA   Why? Isn't old Polybus still in power?

MESSENGER   No more. Death has got him in the tomb.

JOCASTA   What are you saying? Polybus, dead?—dead?

MESSENGER   If not,
if I'm not telling the truth, strike me dead too.

---

6. That is, the chorus.

1035 JOCASTA [*To a servant.*]   Quickly, go to your master, tell him this!
        You prophecies of the gods, where are you now?
        This is the man that Oedipus feared for years,
        he fled him, not to kill him—and now he's dead,
        quite by chance, a normal, natural death,
1040   not murdered by his son.
      OEDIPUS [*Emerging from the palace.*]
                                              Dearest,
        what now? Why call me from the palace?
      JOCASTA [*Bringing the* MESSENGER *closer.*]
        Listen to *him*, see for yourself what all
        those awful prophecies of god have come to.
      OEDIPUS   And who is he? What can he have for me?
1045 JOCASTA   He's from Corinth, he's come to tell you
        your father is no more—Polybus—he's dead!
      OEDIPUS [*Wheeling on the* MESSENGER.]
        What? Let me have it from your lips.
      MESSENGER   Well,
        if that's what you want first, then here it is:
        Make no mistake, Polybus is dead and gone.
1050 OEDIPUS   How—murder? sickness?—what? what killed him?
      MESSENGER   A light tip of the scales can put old bones to rest.
      OEDIPUS   Sickness then—poor man, it wore him down.
      MESSENGER   That,
        and the long count of years he'd measured out.
      OEDIPUS   So!
        Jocasta, why, why look to the Prophet's hearth,
1055   the fires of the future? Why scan the birds
        that scream above our heads? They winged me on
        to the murder of my father, did they? That was my doom?
        Well look, he's dead and buried, hidden under the earth,
        and here I am in Thebes, I never put hand to sword—
1060   unless some longing for me wasted him away,
        then in a sense you'd say I caused his death.
        But now, all those prophecies I feared—Polybus
        packs them off to sleep with him in hell!
        They're nothing, worthless.
      JOCASTA   There.
1065   Didn't I tell you from the start?
      OEDIPUS   So you did. I was lost in fear.
      JOCASTA   No more, sweep it from your mind forever.
      OEDIPUS   But my mother's bed, surely I must fear—
      JOCASTA   Fear?
        What should a man fear? It's all chance,
1070   chance rules our lives. Not a man on earth
        can see a day ahead, groping through the dark.
        Better to live at random, best we can.
        And as for this marriage with your mother—
        have no fear. Many a man before you,
1075   in his dreams, has shared his mother's bed.

Take such things for shadows, nothing at all—
Live, Oedipus,
as if there's no tomorrow!

OEDIPUS   Brave words,
and you'd persuade me if mother weren't alive.
1080   But mother lives, so for all your reassurances
I live in fear, I must.

JOCASTA   But your father's death,
that, at least, is a great blessing, joy to the eyes!

OEDIPUS   Great, I know . . . but I fear *her*—she's still alive.

MESSENGER   Wait, who is this woman, makes you so afraid?

1085   OEDIPUS   Merope, old man. The wife of Polybus.

MESSENGER   The queen? What's there to fear in her?

OEDIPUS   A dreadful prophecy, stranger, sent by the gods.

MESSENGER   Tell me, could you? Unless it's forbidden
other ears to hear.

OEDIPUS   Not at all.
1090   Apollo told me once—it is my fate—
I must make love with my own mother,
shed my father's blood with my own hands.
So for years I've given Corinth a wide berth,
and it's been my good fortune too. But still,
1095   to see one's parents and look into their eyes
is the greatest joy I know.

MESSENGER   You're afraid of that?
That kept you out of Corinth?

OEDIPUS   My *father*, old man—
so I wouldn't kill my father.

MESSENGER   So that's it.
Well then, seeing I came with such good will, my king,
1100   why don't I rid you of that old worry now?

OEDIPUS   What a rich reward you'd have for that!

MESSENGER   What do you think I came for, majesty?
So you'd come home and I'd be better off.

OEDIPUS   Never, I will never go near my parents.

1105   MESSENGER   My boy, it's clear, you don't know what you're doing.

OEDIPUS   What do you mean, old man? For god's sake, explain.

MESSENGER   If you ran from *them*, always dodging home . . .

OEDIPUS   Always, terrified Apollo's oracle might come true—

MESSENGER   And you'd be covered with guilt, from both your parents.

1110   OEDIPUS   That's right, old man, that fear is always with me.

MESSENGER   Don't you know? You've really nothing to fear.

OEDIPUS   But why? If I'm their son—Merope, Polybus?

MESSENGER   Polybus was nothing to you, that's why, not in blood.

OEDIPUS   What are you saying—Polybus was not my father?

1115   MESSENGER   No more than I am. He and I are equals.

OEDIPUS   My father—
how can my father equal nothing? You're nothing to me!

MESSENGER   Neither was he, no more your father than I am.

OEDIPUS   Then why did he call me his son?

MESSENGER   You were a gift,
    years ago—know for a fact he took you
1120   from my hands.
    OEDIPUS   No, from another's hands?
    Then how could he love me so? He loved me, deeply . . .
    MESSENGER   True, and his early years without a child
    made him love you all the more.
    OEDIPUS   And you, did you . . .
    buy me? find me by accident?
    MESSENGER   I stumbled on you,
1125   down the woody flanks of Mount Cithaeron.
    OEDIPUS   So close,
    what were you doing here, just passing through?
    MESSENGER   Watching over my flocks, grazing them on the slopes.
    OEDIPUS   A herdsman, were you? A vagabond, scraping for wages?
    MESSENGER   Your savior too, my son, in your worst hour.
    OEDIPUS   Oh—
1130   when you picked me up, was I in pain? What exactly?
    MESSENGER   Your ankles . . . they tell the story. Look at them.
    OEDIPUS   Why remind me of that, that old affliction?
    MESSENGER   Your ankles were pinned together. I set you free.
    OEDIPUS   That dreadful mark—I've had it from the cradle.
1135 MESSENGER   And you got your name from that misfortune too,
    the name's still with you.[7]
    OEDIPUS   Dear god, who did it?—
    mother? father? Tell me.
    MESSENGER   I don't know.
    The one who gave you to me, he'd know more.
    OEDIPUS   What? You took me from someone else?
1140   You didn't find me yourself?
    MESSENGER   No sir,
    another shepherd passed you on to me.
    OEDIPUS   Who? Do you know? Describe him.
    MESSENGER   He called himself a servant of . . .
    if I remember rightly—Laius.
        [JOCASTA *turns sharply.*]
1145 OEDIPUS   The king of the land who ruled here long ago?
    MESSENGER   That's the one. That herdsman was *his* man.
    OEDIPUS   Is he still alive? Can I see him?
    MESSENGER   They'd know best, the people of these parts.
        [OEDIPUS *and the* MESSENGER *turn to the* CHORUS.]
    OEDIPUS   Does anyone know that herdsman,
1150   the one he mentioned? Anyone seen him
    in the fields, in the city? Out with it!
    The time has come to reveal this once for all.
    LEADER   I think he's the very shepherd you wanted to see,
    a moment ago. But the queen, Jocasta,

---

7. "Oedipus" literally means "swollen foot."

1155   she's the one to say.
        OEDIPUS   Jocasta,
        you remember the man we just sent for?
        Is *that* the one he means?
        JOCASTA   That man . . .
        why ask? Old shepherd, talk, empty nonsense,
        don't give it another thought, don't even think—
1160   OEDIPUS   What—give up now, with a clue like this?
        Fail to solve the mystery of my birth?
        Not for all the world!
        JOCASTA   Stop—in the name of god,
        if you love your own life, call off this search!
        My suffering is enough.
        OEDIPUS   Courage!
1165   Even if my mother turns out to be a slave,
        and I a slave, three generations back,
        you would not seem common.
        JOCASTA   Oh no,
        listen to me, I beg you, don't do this.
        OEDIPUS   Listen to you? No more. I must know it all,
1170   must see the truth at last.
        JOCASTA   No, please—
        for your sake—I want the best for you!
        OEDIPUS   Your best is more than I can bear.
        JOCASTA   You're doomed—
        may you never fathom who you are!
        OEDIPUS [*To a servant.*]   Hurry, fetch me the herdsman, now!
1175   Leave her to glory in her royal birth.
        JOCASTA   Aieeeeee—
                            man of agony—
        that is the only name I have for you,
        that, no other—ever, ever, ever!
                    [*Flinging through the palace doors. A long, tense silence follows.*]
        LEADER   Where's she gone, Oedipus?
1180   Rushing off, such wild grief . . .
        I'm afraid that from this silence
        something monstrous may come bursting forth.
        OEDIPUS   Let it burst! Whatever will, whatever must!
        I must know my birth, no matter how common
1185   it may be—I must see my origins face-to-face.
        She perhaps, she with her woman's pride
        may well be mortified by my birth,
        but I, I count myself the son of Chance,
        the great goddess, giver of all good things—
1190   I'll never see myself disgraced. She is my mother!
        And the moons have marked me out, my blood-brothers,
        one moon on the wane, the next moon great with power.
        That is my blood, my nature—I will never betray it,
        never fail to search and learn my birth!
1195   CHORUS   Yes—if I am a true prophet

        if I can grasp the truth,
      by the boundless skies of Olympus,
    at the full moon of tomorrow, Mount Cithaeron
    you will know how Oedipus glories in you—
1200 you, his birthplace, nurse, his mountain-mother!
    And we will sing you, dancing out your praise—
    you lift our monarch's heart!
        Apollo, Apollo, god of the wild cry
          may our dancing please you!
                                        Oedipus—
1205   son, dear child, who bore you?
    Who of the nymphs who seem to live forever
    mated with Pan,[8] the mountain-striding Father?
    Who was your mother? who, some bride of Apollo
    the god who loves the pastures spreading toward the sun?
1210   Or was it Hermes,[9] king of the lightning ridges?
    Or Dionysus, lord of frenzy, lord of the barren peaks—
    did he seize you in his hands, dearest of all his lucky finds?—
      found by the nymphs, their warm eyes dancing, gift
    to the lord who loves them dancing out his joy!

        [OEDIPUS *strains to see a figure coming from the distance. Attended by pal-
        ace guards, an old* SHEPHERD *enters slowly, reluctant to approach the King.*]

1215 OEDIPUS   I never met the man, my friends . . . still,
    if I had to guess, I'd say that's the shepherd,
    the very one we've looked for all along.
    Brothers in old age, two of a kind,
    he and our guest here. At any rate
1220 the ones who bring him in are my own men,
    I recognize them.
                [*Turning to the* LEADER.]
                    But you know more than I,
    you should, you've seen the man before.
    LEADER   I know him, definitely. One of Laius' men,
    a trusty shepherd, if there ever was one.
1225 OEDIPUS   You, I ask you first, stranger,
    you from Corinth—is this the one you mean?
    MESSENGER   You're looking at him. He's your man.
    OEDIPUS [*To the* SHEPHERD.]   You, old man, come over here—
    look at me. Answer all my questions.
1230 Did you ever serve King Laius?
    SHEPHERD   So I did . . .
    a slave, not bought on the block though,
    born and reared in the palace.

---

8. Son of Hermes and a nymph; the god of
woods and pastures and the companion of
Dionysus. *Nymphs:* female nature spirits,
long-lived but not immortal.

9. Greek god of boundaries and travelers,
Zeus's messenger and the gods' herald; like
Dionysus, he was associated with wild places,
especially mountains.

OEDIPUS   Your duties, your kind of work?

SHEPHERD   Herding the flocks, the better part of my life.

1235   OEDIPUS   Where, mostly? Where did you do your grazing?

SHEPHERD   Well,
Cithaeron sometimes, or the foothills round about.

OEDIPUS   This man—you know him? ever see him there?

SHEPHERD [*Confused, glancing from the* MESSENGER *to the King.*]
Doing what?—what man do you mean?

OEDIPUS [*Pointing to the* MESSENGER.]   This one here—ever have
1240   dealings with him?

SHEPHERD   Not so I could say, but give me a chance,
my memory's bad . . .

MESSENGER   No wonder he doesn't know me, master.
But let me refresh his memory for him.
1245   I'm sure he recalls old times we had
on the slopes of Mount Cithaeron;
he and I, grazing our flocks, he with two
and I with one—we both struck up together,
three whole seasons, six months at a stretch
1250   from spring to the rising of Arcturus[1] in the fall,
then with winter coming on I'd drive my herds
to my own pens, and back he'd go with his
to Laius' folds.

[*To the* SHEPHERD.]

Now that's how it was,
wasn't it—yes or no?

SHEPHERD   Yes, I suppose . . .
1255   it's all so long ago.

MESSENGER   Come, tell me,
you gave me a child back then, a boy, remember?
A little fellow to rear, my very own.

SHEPHERD   What? Why rake up that again?

MESSENGER   Look, here he is, my fine old friend—
1260   the same man who was just a baby then.

SHEPHERD   Damn you, shut your mouth—quiet!

OEDIPUS   Don't lash out at him, old man—
you need lashing more than he does.

SHEPHERD   Why,
master, majesty—what have I done wrong?

1265   OEDIPUS   You won't answer his question about the boy.

SHEPHERD   He's talking nonsense, wasting his breath.

OEDIPUS   So, you won't talk willingly—
then you'll talk with pain.

[*The guards seize the* SHEPHERD.]

SHEPHERD   No, dear god, don't torture an old man!

---

1. One of the brightest stars in the northern sky; its "rising" before dawn in September is a sign
of summer's end.

1270 OEDIPUS   Twist his arms back, quickly!

SHEPHERD   God help us, why?—
   what more do you need to know?

OEDIPUS   Did you give him that child? He's asking.

SHEPHERD   I did . . . I wish to god I'd died that day.

OEDIPUS   You've got your wish if you don't tell the truth.

1275 SHEPHERD   The more I tell, the worse the death I'll die.

OEDIPUS   Our friend here wants to stretch things out, does he?

   [*Motioning to his men for torture.*]

SHEPHERD   No, no, I gave it to him—I just said so.

OEDIPUS   Where did you get it? Your house? Someone else's?

SHEPHERD   It wasn't mine, no, I got it from . . . someone.

1280 OEDIPUS   Which one of them?

   [*Looking at the citizens.*]

OEDIPUS   Whose house?

SHEPHERD   No—
   god's sake, master, no more questions!

OEDIPUS   You're a dead man if I have to ask again.

SHEPHERD   Then—the child came from the house . . . of Laius.

OEDIPUS   A slave? or born of his own blood?

SHEPHERD   Oh no,

1285 I'm right at the edge, the horrible truth—I've got to say it!

OEDIPUS   And I'm at the edge of hearing horrors, yes, but I must hear!

SHEPHERD   All right! His son, they said it was—his son!
   But the one inside, your wife,
   she'd tell it best.

1290 OEDIPUS   My wife—
   she gave it to you?

SHEPHERD   Yes, yes, my king.

OEDIPUS   Why, what for?

SHEPHERD   To kill it.

1295 OEDIPUS   Her own child,
   how could she?

SHEPHERD   She was afraid—
   frightening prophecies.

OEDIPUS   What?

1300 SHEPHERD   They said—
   he'd kill his parents.

OEDIPUS   But you gave him to this old man—why?

SHEPHERD   I pitied the little baby, master,
   hoped he'd take him off to his own country,

1305 far away, but he saved him for this, this fate.
   If you are the man he says you are, believe me,
   you were born for pain.

OEDIPUS   O god—
   all come true, all burst to light!
   O light—now let me look my last on you!

1310 I stand revealed at last—
   cursed in my birth, cursed in marriage,

cursed in the lives I cut down with these hands!

> [*Rushing through the doors with a great cry. The Corinthian* MESSENGER,
> *the* SHEPHERD *and attendants exit slowly to the side.*]

CHORUS   O the generations of men
   the dying generations—adding the total
1315 of all your lives I find they come to nothing . . .
    does there exist, is there a man on earth
   who seizes more joy than just a dream, a vision?
   And the vision no sooner dawns than dies
   blazing into oblivion.
1320 You are my great example, you, your life
   your destiny, Oedipus, man of misery—
   I count no man blest.

     You outranged all men!
    Bending your bow to the breaking-point
   you captured priceless glory, O dear god,
1325 and the Sphinx came crashing down,
     the virgin, claws hooked
   like a bird of omen singing, shrieking death—
   like a fortress reared in the face of death
   you rose and saved our land.
1330 From that day on we called you king
   we crowned you with honors, Oedipus, towering over all—
   mighty king of the seven gates of Thebes.

   But now to hear your story—is there a man more agonized?
   More wed to pain and frenzy? Not a man on earth,
1335 the joy of your life ground down to nothing
   O Oedipus, name for the ages—
    one and the same wide harbor served you
     son and father both
   son and father came to rest in the same bridal chamber.
1340 How, how could the furrows your father plowed
   bear you, your agony, harrowing on
   in silence O so long?

    But now for all your power
   Time, all-seeing Time has dragged you to the light,
   judged your marriage monstrous from the start—
1345 the son and the father tangling, both one—
   O child of Laius, would to god
    I'd never seen you, never never!
     Now I weep like a man who wails the dead
   and the dirge comes pouring forth with all my heart!
1350 I tell you the truth, you gave me life
   my breath leapt up in you
   and now you bring down night upon my eyes.

> [*Enter a* MESSENGER *from the palace.*]

MESSENGER   Men of Thebes, always first in honor,
    what horrors you will hear, what you will see,
1355 what a heavy weight of sorrow you will shoulder . . .
    if you are true to your birth, if you still have
    some feeling for the royal house of Thebes.
    I tell you neither the waters of the Danube
    nor the Nile[2] can wash this palace clean.
1360 Such things it hides, it soon will bring to light—
    terrible things, and none done blindly now,
    all done with a will. The pains
    we inflict upon ourselves hurt most.
LEADER   God knows we have pains enough already.
1365 What can you add to them?
MESSENGER   The queen is dead.
LEADER   Poor lady—how?
MESSENGER   By her own hand. But you are spared the worst,
    you never had to watch . . . I saw it all,
    and with all the memory that's in me
1370 you will learn what that poor woman suffered.
    Once she'd broken in through the gates,
    dashing past us, frantic, whipped to fury,
    ripping her hair out with both hands—
    straight to her rooms she rushed, flinging herself
1375 across the bridal-bed, doors slamming behind her—
    once inside, she wailed for Laius, dead so long,
    remembering how she bore his child long ago,
    the life that rose up to destroy him, leaving
    its mother to mother living creatures
1380 with the very son she'd borne.
    Oh how she wept, mourning the marriage-bed
    where she let loose that double brood—monsters—
    husband by her husband, children by her child.
                               And then—
    but how she died is more than I can say. Suddenly
1385 Oedipus burst in, screaming, he stunned us so
    we couldn't watch her agony to the end,
    our eyes were fixed on him. Circling
    like a maddened beast, stalking, here, there,
    crying out to us—
                   Give him a sword. His wife,
1390 no wife, his mother, where can he find the mother earth
    that cropped two crops at once, himself and all his children?
    He was raging—one of the dark powers pointing the way,
    none of us mortals crowding around him, no,
    with a great shattering cry—someone, something leading him on—

2. The Greek original reads "Phasis," a river in Asia Minor; like the Danube, Europe's second-longest river, it empties into the Black Sea.

1395   he hurled at the twin doors and bending the bolts back
out of their sockets, crashed through the chamber.
And there we saw the woman hanging by the neck,
cradled high in a woven noose, spinning,
swinging back and forth. And when he saw her,
1400   giving a low, wrenching sob that broke our hearts,
slipping the halter from her throat, he eased her down,
in a slow embrace he laid her down, poor thing . . .
then, what came next, what horror we beheld!

He rips off her brooches, the long gold pins
1405   holding her robes—and lifting them high,
looking straight up into the points,
he digs them down the sockets of his eyes, crying, "You,
you'll see no more the pain I suffered, all the pain I caused!
Too long you looked on the ones you never should have seen,
1410   blind to the ones you longed to see, to know! Blind
from this hour on! Blind in the darkness—blind!"
His voice like a dirge, rising, over and over
raising the pins, raking them down his eyes.
And at each stroke blood spurts from the roots,
1415   splashing his beard, a swirl of it, nerves and clots—
black hail of blood pulsing, gushing down.
These are the griefs that burst upon them both,
coupling man and woman. The joy they had so lately,
the fortune of their old ancestral house
1420   was deep joy indeed. Now, in this one day,
wailing, madness and doom, death, disgrace
all the griefs in the world that you can name,
all are theirs forever.

LEADER   Oh poor man, the misery—
has he any rest from pain now?

    [*A voice within, in torment.*]

MESSENGER   He's shouting,
1425   "Loose the bolts, someone, show me to all of Thebes!
My father's murderer, my mother's—"
No, I can't repeat it, it's unholy.
Now he'll tear himself from his native earth,
not linger, curse the house with his own curse.
1430   But he needs strength, and a guide to lead him on.
This is sickness more than he can bear.

    [*The palace doors open.*]

                   Look,
he'll show you himself. The great doors are opening—
you are about to see a sight, a horror
even his mortal enemy would pity.

    [*Enter* OEDIPUS, *blinded, led by a boy. He stands at the palace steps,
as if surveying his people once again.*]

CHORUS   O the terror—

1435   the suffering, for all the world to see,
the worst terror that ever met my eyes.
What madness swept over you? What god,
what dark power leapt beyond all bounds,
beyond belief, to crush your wretched life?—

1440   godforsaken, cursed by the gods!
I pity you but I can't bear to look.
I've much to ask, so much to learn,
so much fascinates my eyes,
but you . . . I shudder at the sight.

OEDIPUS   Oh, Ohh—

1445   the agony! I am agony—
where am I going? where on earth?
    where does all this agony hurl me?
where's my voice?—
    winging, swept away on a dark tide—

1450   My destiny, my dark power, what a leap you made!

CHORUS   To the depths of terror, too dark to hear, to see.

OEDIPUS   Dark, horror of darkness
    my darkness, drowning, swirling around me
    crashing wave on wave—unspeakable, irresistible

1455   headwind, fatal harbor! Oh again,
    the misery, all at once, over and over
    the stabbing daggers, stab of memory
raking me insane.

CHORUS   No wonder you suffer
twice over, the pain of your wounds,

1460   the lasting grief of pain.

OEDIPUS   Dear friend, still here?
    Standing by me, still with a care for me,
    the blind man? Such compassion,
        loyal to the last. Oh it's you,
    I know you're here, dark as it is

1465   I'd know you anywhere, your voice—
it's yours, clearly yours.

CHORUS   Dreadful, what you've done . . .
how could you bear it, gouging out your eyes?
What superhuman power drove you on?

OEDIPUS   Apollo, friends, Apollo—

1470   he ordained my agonies—these, my pains on pains!
    But the hand that struck my eyes was mine,
    mine alone—no one else—
        I did it all myself!
    What good were eyes to me?

1475   Nothing I could see could bring me joy.

CHORUS   No, no, exactly as you say.

OEDIPUS   What can I ever see?
    What love, what call of the heart
    can touch my ears with joy? Nothing, friends.
    Take me away, far, far from Thebes,

1480   quickly, cast me away, my friends—
    this great murderous ruin, this man cursed to heaven,
        the man the deathless gods hate most of all!
CHORUS   Pitiful, you suffer so, you understand so much . . .
    I wish you'd never known.
OEDIPUS   Die, die—
1485   whoever he was that day in the wilds
    who cut my ankles free of the ruthless pins,
        he pulled me clear of death, he saved my life
        for this, this kindness—
        Curse him, kill him!
1490   If I'd died then, I'd never have dragged myself,
    my loved ones through such hell.
CHORUS   Oh if only . . . would to god.
OEDIPUS   I'd never have come to this,
        my father's murderer—never been branded
    mother's husband, all men see me now! Now,
1495   loathed by the gods, son of the mother I defiled
            coupling in my father's bed, spawning lives in the loins
    that spawned my wretched life. What grief can crown this grief?
        It's mine alone, my destiny—I am Oedipus!
CHORUS   How can I say you've chosen for the best?
1500   Better to die than be alive and blind.
OEDIPUS   What I did was best—don't lecture me,
    no more advice, I, with *my* eyes,
    how could I look my father in the eyes
    when I go down to death? Or mother, so abused . . .
1505   I have done such things to the two of them,
    crimes too huge for hanging.
                        Worse yet,
    the sight of my children, born as they were born,
    how could I long to look into their eyes?
    No, not with these eyes of mine, never.
1510   Not this city either, her high towers,
    the sacred glittering images of her gods—
    I am misery! I, her best son, reared
    as no other son of Thebes was ever reared,
    I've stripped myself, I gave the command myself.
1515   All men must cast away the great blasphemer,
    the curse now brought to light by the gods,
    the son of Laius—I, my father's son!

    Now I've exposed my guilt, horrendous guilt,
    could I train a level glance on you, my countrymen?
1520   Impossible! No, if I could just block off my ears,
    the springs of hearing, I would stop at nothing—
    I'd wall up my loathsome body like a prison,
    blind to the sound of life, not just the sight.
    Oblivion—what a blessing . . .
1525   for the mind to dwell a world away from pain.

O Cithaeron, why did you give me shelter?
Why didn't you take me, crush my life out on the spot?
I'd never have revealed my birth to all mankind.
O Polybus, Corinth, the old house of my fathers,
1530   so I believed—what a handsome prince you raised—
under the skin, what sickness to the core.
Look at me! Born of outrage, outrage to the core.
O triple roads—it all comes back, the secret,
dark ravine, and the oaks closing in
1535   where the three roads join . . .
You drank my father's blood, my own blood
spilled by my own hands—you still remember me?
What things you saw me do? Then I came here
and did them all once more!
                          Marriages! O marriage,
1540   you gave me birth, and once you brought me into the world
you brought my sperm rising back, springing to light
fathers, brothers, sons—one murderous breed—
brides, wives, mothers. The blackest things
a man can do, I have done them all!
                          No more—
1545   it's wrong to name what's wrong to do. Quickly,
for the love of god, hide me somewhere,
kill me, hurl me into the sea
where you can never look on me again.

        [*Beckoning to the* CHORUS *as they shrink away.*]
                          Closer,
it's all right. Touch the man of grief.
1550   Do. Don't be afraid. My troubles are mine
and I am the only man alive who can sustain them.

        [*Enter* KREON *from the palace, attended by palace guards.*]

LEADER   Put your requests to Kreon. Here he is,
just when we need him. He'll have a plan, he'll act.
Now that he's the sole defense of the country
in your place.
1555 OEDIPUS   Oh no, what can I say to him?
How can I ever hope to win his trust?
I wronged him so, just now, in every way.
You must see that—I was so wrong, so wrong.
KREON   I haven't come to mock you, Oedipus,
1560   or to criticize your former failings.

        [*Turning to the guards.*]
                          You there,
have you lost all respect for human feelings?
At least revere the Sun, the holy fire
that keeps us all alive. Never expose a thing
of guilt and holy dread so great it appalls
1565   the earth, the rain from heaven, the light of day!
Get him into the halls—quickly as you can.

Piety demands no less. Kindred alone
should see a kinsman's shame. This is obscene.

OEDIPUS   Please, in god's name . . . you wipe my fears away,
1570   coming so generously to me, the worst of men.
Do one thing more, for your sake, not mine.

KREON   What do you want? Why so insistent?

OEDIPUS   Drive me out of the land at once, far from sight,
where I can never hear a human voice.

1575   KREON   I'd have done that already, I promise you.
First I wanted the god to clarify my duties.

OEDIPUS   The god? His command was clear, every word:
death for the father-killer, the curse—
he said destroy me!

1580   KREON   So he did. Still, in such a crisis
it's better to ask precisely what to do.

OEDIPUS   So miserable—
you'd consult the god about a man like me?

KREON   By all means. And this time, I assume,
even you will obey the god's decrees.

OEDIPUS   I will,
1585   I will. And you, I command you—I beg you . . .
the woman inside, bury her as you see fit.
It's the only decent thing,
to give your own the last rites. As for me,
never condemn the city of my fathers
1590   to house my body, not while I'm alive, no,
let me live on the mountains, on Cithaeron,
my favorite haunt, I have made it famous.
Mother and father marked out that rock
to be my everlasting tomb—buried alive.
1595   Let me die there, where they tried to kill me.

Oh but this I know: no sickness can destroy me,
nothing can. I would never have been saved
from death—I have been saved
for something great and terrible, something strange.
1600   Well let my destiny come and take me on its way!
About my children, Kreon, the boys at least,
don't burden yourself. They're men,
wherever they go, they'll find the means to live.
But my two daughters, my poor helpless girls,
1605   clustering at our table, never without me
hovering near them . . . whatever I touched,
they always had their share. Take care of them,
I beg you. Wait, better—permit me, would you?
Just to touch them with my hands and take
1610   our fill of tears. Please . . . my king.
Grant it, with all your noble heart.
If I could hold them, just once, I'd think
I had them with me, like the early days

when I could see their eyes.

> [ANTIGONE *and* ISMENE, *two small children, are led in from
> the palace by a nurse.*]

                           What's that

1615 O god! Do I really hear you sobbing?—
my two children. Kreon, you've pitied me?
Sent me my darling girls, my own flesh and blood!
Am I right?

KREON   Yes, it's my doing.
I know the joy they gave you all these years,
1620 the joy you must feel now.

OEDIPUS   Bless you, Kreon!
May god watch over you for this kindness,
better than he ever guarded me.

                    Children, where are you?
Here, come quickly—

> [*Groping for* ANTIGONE *and* ISMENE, *who approach their father
> cautiously, then embrace him.*]

                Come to these hands of mine,
your brother's hands, your own father's hands
1625 that served his once bright eyes so well—
that made them blind. Seeing nothing, children,
knowing nothing, I became your father,
I fathered you in the soil that gave me life.
How I weep for you—I cannot see you now . . .
1630 just thinking of all your days to come, the bitterness,
the life that rough mankind will thrust upon you.
Where are the pubic gatherings you can join,
the banquets of the clans? Home you'll come,
in tears, cut off from the sight of it all,
1635 the brilliant rites unfinished.
And when you reach perfection, ripe for marriage,
who will he be, my dear ones? Risking all
to shoulder the curse that weighs down my parents,
yes and you too—that wounds us all together.
1640 What more misery could you want?
Your father killed his father, sowed his mother,
one, one and the selfsame womb sprang you—
he cropped the very roots of his existence.

Such disgrace, and you must bear it all!
1645 Who will marry you then? Not a man on earth.
Your doom is clear: you'll wither away to nothing,
single, without a child.

> [*Turning to* KREON.]

             Oh Kreon,
you are the only father they have now . . .
we who brought them into the world
1650 are gone, both gone at a stroke—

Don't let them go begging, abandoned,
men without men. Your own flesh and blood!
Never bring them down to the level of my pains.
Pity them. Look at them, so young, so vulnerable,
1655   shorn of everything—you're their only hope.
Promise me, noble Kreon, touch my hand!

       [*Reaching toward* KREON, *who draws back.*]

You, little ones, if you were old enough
to understand, there is much I'd tell you.
Now, as it is, I'd have you say a prayer.
1660   Pray for life, my children,
live where you are free to grow and season.
Pray god you find a better life than mine,
the father who begot you.

KREON   Enough.
You've wept enough. Into the palace now.

1665 OEDIPUS   I must, but I find it very hard.

KREON   Time is the great healer, you will see.

OEDIPUS   I am going—you know on what condition?

KREON   Tell me. I'm listening.

OEDIPUS   Drive me out of Thebes, in exile.

1670 KREON   Not I. Only the gods can give you that.

OEDIPUS   Surely the gods hate me so much—

KREON   You'll get your wish at once.

OEDIPUS   You consent?

KREON   I try to say what I mean; it's my habit.

OEDIPUS   Then take me away. It's time.

1675 KREON   Come along, let go of the children.

OEDIPUS   No—
don't take them away from me, not now! No no no!

       [*Clutching his daughters as the guards wrench them loose and take
       them through the palace doors.*]

KREON   Still the king, the master of all things?
No more: here your power ends.
   None of your power follows you through life.

       [*Exit* OEDIPUS *and* KREON *to the palace. The* CHORUS *comes forward
       to address the audience directly.*]

1680 CHORUS   People of Thebes, my countrymen, look on Oedipus.
He solved the famous riddle with his brilliance,
   he rose to power, a man beyond all power.
   Who could behold his greatness without envy?
   Now what a black sea of terror has overwhelmed him.
1685   Now as we keep our watch and wait the final day,
   count no man happy till he dies, free of pain at last.

                                       [*Exit in procession.*]

EURIPIDES

ca. 480–406 B.C.E.

THE last of the three important Greek tragedians, Euripides was also the most daring innovator of the classical stage. His startling and powerful plays quickly made him one of the most successful playwrights of Athens, a rival to the older and more established Aeschylus and SOPHO-CLES, and after his death, his fame continued to grow. Euripides managed to push the drama he had inherited to new extremes and to inaugurate a new form of tragedy, one attuned to a growing skepticism toward inherited truths. Although still based on mythic figures and events, Euripides' tragedies treat gods and heroes with suspicion, making them more human, exposing their frailties, and bringing them closer to everyday reality. Euripides' skepticism spoke not only to contemporaries but to later audiences. While some commentators, particularly in the nineteenth and twentieth centuries, celebrated Euripides as the great modernizer of tragedy, others blamed him for its demise—most famously the nineteenth-century philosopher Friedrich Nietzsche, who accused Euripides of having killed tragedy. But no matter whether one wishes to praise Euripides as innovator or fault him for excessive irreverence, there can be no doubt that he changed the course of drama, leaving an imprint on the form of tragedy that can be felt even today.

Although born into a wealthy family, Euripides did not participate in public life. He began to write tragedies when he was eighteen, but did not win first prize at the Dionysia until he was around forty years old; the titles of these winning plays are unknown. Euripides' oldest extant play is *Alcestis* (438 B.C.E.), a tragicomedy that took second place at the competition. *MEDEA*, his oldest tragedy, was presented in 431 B.C.E. Even though his tragedies found a following in Athens, they also made him enemies, who objected to his irreverent depiction of the gods. Probably because of the growing influence of these enemies, at an advanced age Euripides emigrated to Macedonia at the invitation of its king, Archelaus, and died there one year later. He won only four prizes at Athens during his lifetime, but the posthumous performance of his last play, *The Bacchae*, gained him a fifth; and soon his popularity was to surpass that of all other Greek tragedians—a status he still holds today, especially in the theater.

Euripides' popularity was due to a number of innovations. The most important is that his tragedies are much more realistic than those of his predecessors, both in their depiction of character and in their language. Expanding on the changes introduced by Sophocles, his older contemporary, Euripides further reduced the importance of the chorus, placing more emphasis on dramatic interaction and confrontation. Doing so enabled him to make his plots more complicated and his characterization more nuanced. In part to bring his complex plots to a final conclusion, Euripides often relied on the *deus ex machina* (literally, "god from a machine"), the conventional recourse to a god brought onto the stage by means of a crane at the end of the play to intervene in hopeless situations, to resolve dilemmas, and to deal out punishment. This dramaturgical strategy, especially as it appears in *Medea*, earned him a rebuke from Aristotle in *Poetics* (ca. 360–355 B.C.E.), who maintained that "the denouements of plots . . . should come out of the character . . . and not from the 'machine.'"[1] Critics have subsequently argued, however, that the *dea ex machina* in *Medea* reveal how we should ultimately understand this character as semi-divine and her horrific acts of violence as divine retribution. Shortly after Euripides' death, ARISTOPHANES' comedy *The Frogs* (405 B.C.E.) shows Euripides in competition with the first master of tragedy, Aeschylus. Even though Aeschylus finally wins, because his language and topics are weightier than those of Euripides, Aristophanes acknowledges Euripides' greater skill in developing plots and his more realistic approach.

Through a series of historical accidents, Euripides' is the largest existing corpus of plays of any Greek playwright. A number of his plays, like other Greek tragedies, survived through acting copies, which in turn became the basis for the collection of Greek tragedy at the Library of Alexandria during the second century B.C.E. But we are fortunate to have as well a portion of what may have been Euripides' collected works in alphabetical order: plays beginning with the Greek letters epsilon, eta, iota, or kappa.

Even a cursory look at Euripides' plays shows both the variety of his styles and his most typical techniques. His version of *Electra*, for example, was conceived in direct response to Aeschylus's treatment and probably also with Sophocles'. Of the three, Euripides' *Orestes* is the least heroic by far

and most prone to hesitation and doubt. All the characters are drawn more realistically; they are more rooted in common, everyday reality, even though the play is still set in the mythical past. Euripides' *Helen* follows the same pattern. Based on a common variant of the myth, according to which Helen resided in Egypt during the Trojan War while her double—created by the gods—caused all the trouble in Troy, Euripides' *Helen* depicts the secret arrival of Menelaus in Egypt, clad in rags and unimpressive in many other ways as well. Another innovation is also visible in this play: it ends not tragically but with the happy escape of Menelaus and Helen. Tragedy here becomes romance.

Euripides made tragedy more realistic, more concerned with individual character, and more flexible in its endings. But this approach did not render his tragedies less stark or brutal. On the contrary, he created some of the most extreme situations and events ever depicted on the Greek stage. He became notorious for treatments of sensational subject matter—such as the doomed passion of a woman for her stepson (in *Hippolytus*) or the murder of two children by their own mother in a desperate act of revenge on their father (in *Medea*)—that often culminated in lurid violence. Euripides was never one to compromise, and he constantly sought to find new avenues to take and new areas to explore even if they seemed to go against custom and common decency.

MEDEA

This strategy may well have cost him the prize in 431 B.C.E., when *Medea* shocked and dismayed audiences and judges alike with its grisly, murderous conclusion. Yet Euripides' uncompromising dramaturgy is arguably also responsible for the play's ongoing fascination. The character of Medea and the narratives of which she is a part have figured prominently in the performing arts for centuries. Seneca wrote his own dramatic version in the first century C.E.; the first ballet version was created in France in the mid-sixteenth century; and the first operatic version emerged a century later in Italy. Numerous addi-

1. Aristotle, *Poetics*, trans. Gerald F. Else (Ann Arbor: University of Michigan Press, 1970), p. 44.

tional dramatic, operatic, balletic, and filmic renditions, each famous in its own right, have followed. These include French playwright Jean Anouilh's 1953 adaptation; Italian composer Luigi Cherubini's 1787 opera, revived by opera diva Maria Callas in the mid-twentieth century; American choreographer Martha Graham's 1946 ballet; and Danish director Lars von Trier's 1988 film. In both classical and modern Greek, *Medea* remains a fixture in its native theater, and over the last century alone, leading actresses of each generation have tackled this demanding role in English translation, including Sybil Thorndike in 1919, Judith Anderson in 1947, Diana Rigg in 1992, and Fiona Shaw in 2000.

We know that Euripides had previously dramatized other episodes of the myth (now lost) before he crafted *Medea*, and his fifth-century B.C.E. audiences would certainly have had some familiarity with these stories, which had also been dramatized by SOPHOCLES and Aeschylus. The tale of Jason and the Golden Fleece, which the Nurse recounts at the opening of *Medea*, had long held a central place in Greek mythology. When Jason was a boy, his uncle Pelias usurped the throne of Iolcos from Jason's father, and the youth went into exile. Trained as a hero, Jason later returned to his homeland to reclaim his patrimony. Pelias agreed that he would give Jason the throne if he could capture the Golden Fleece, a treasure held in Colchis, across the Black Sea, and guarded by a fearful serpent. Jason, favored by the goddess Hera, arrives safely aboard the *Argo*. He receives critical help in his quest from Medea, daughter of the king of Colchis, who has fallen in love with him. To secure their escape with the Fleece, they kill her brother, and upon their return to Iolcos, Medea also arranges the unwitting murder of Pelias by his daughters. But instead of gaining his rightful throne, Jason and Medea are exiled, and they find refuge in Corinth, where Euripides sets his play.

While these core components of the myth were well established, it appears that there were multiple variants to the later Corinthian episodes in the Jason and Medea story. Euripides could thus exercise more originality and creativity with the plot of *Medea*, and it is clear that he

took full advantage of this opportunity to call into question received notions of character and morality embedded in the ancient tales. Specifically, he interrogates Jason's heroic stature by imagining for him motives and actions that seem to be only self-interested. Jason's decision to abandon Medea to marry the Corinthian princess and secure his standing in his new homeland, his relative inaction following his new father-in-law Creon's decree of exile for Medea and their children, and his unwillingness now to acknowledge Medea's pivotal role in the successful quest for the Golden Fleece all reveal a figure less admirable than the older versions of the legends might have us believe. Moreover, Euripides contrasts Jason's recent behavior to his earlier promises to Medea—the oaths of loyalty he swore to her in acknowledgment of her aid and her love that, by ancient custom, he should have held sacred. Jason's violation of these vows is akin to an act of *hubris* and thus merits punishment by the gods. These oaths are particularly significant because they bound together people from two nations, Jason the Greek prince and Medea the "barbarian" (meaning "foreign") princess. For an Athenian audience, potentially aware of the imminence of hostilities with Sparta and the onset of what became known as the Peloponnesian War (431–404 B.C.E.), these figures from two different cultures, locked in conflict, may well have taken on larger symbolic meanings.

Euripides underscores the importance of such oaths by putting one at the very center of the play—in the scene between Medea and Aegeus, mythic king of Athens. While his appearance at this middle point in the narrative may at first seem odd—he has not heretofore been a part of the immediate story—Athenian audiences would have understood that this episode ties the strands of the legend together and links it directly to them. Within the world of the play, it is not sufficient that Aegeus simply agrees to protect Medea in exchange for her assurance of his longed-for paternity; she explains that "[a] promise in words only . . . might not be strong enough" (lines 757–58). Instead, she insists that Aegeus "Swear by the Earth we stand on, and by Helios—my father's father—and the whole race of gods . . . Never to expel me from your land yourself, and never, as long as you live, to give me up willingly to any enemy" (lines 768–73). Medea, of course, does not divulge her larger plan to Aegeus while extracting this oath, and like so many other figures in the drama, Aegeus too plays an unwitting role in Medea's vengeful triumph.

Euripides' decision to question received notions of Jason's morality and heroic status through his broken oaths parallels the implicit requirement that we reexamine our ideas about Medea, the woman who demands such sacred vows. This "most theatrical of all Greek tragic characters" (Macintosh) and the figure most responsible for renewed interest in the performance of Greek tragedy, Medea remains a challenge for artists and scholars alike, who continue to grapple with the contradictions and complexities of her character. Her ongoing fascination is clearly linked to the range of emotional states she exhibits and the variety of tactics and personae she employs to realize her goals. As the Nurse tells us in the prologue, Medea has been "dishonored," but she is also "a terror" (lines 25, 50). Indeed, Euripides defines Medea through such binaries: she is mortal yet also divine; accepted by the Chorus as like them yet also considered a barbarian; ferocious as an animal yet also deeply human; wronged and sympathetic yet also frightening and unfathomable in her resolve to kill again and again.

Some critics have suggested that Medea's semidivine status as the granddaughter

Fiona Shaw as Medea and Jonathan Cake as Jason in the 2001 Abbey Theatre production of *Medea*, directed by Deborah Warner.

of Helios, god of the sun, sets her apart from other women, while others look to her acts throughout the legends and identify her as a sorceress or witch. Medea certainly appears to have some special powers; we know they played a role in Jason's quest for the Golden Fleece, in the death of Pelias before the action begins, and crucially in the deaths of King Creon and his daughter during the play. Critic B. M. W. Knox, however, deems her simply a *pharmakis*, a woman with expertise in love potions, drugs, and poisons but not necessarily in witchcraft. Regardless of label, she destabilizes our received understanding of female identity, and we may well ask why Euripides ultimately ascribes such horrific behavior to a woman.

Critics have often noted that thirteen of Euripides' eighteen extant plays feature a central female figure. Yet even as Euripides depicts the struggles of these figures to define their roles in Greek society, they do so within a cultural context focused on male selfhood. Theater in the classical era was part of the public sphere, the *polis*, defined and dominated by men. The *oikos*, women's domestic realm, was also shaped by patriarchal forces. Thus we may think of *Medea* as depicting the tensions between public and private life, as well as the more personal struggle between reason and emotion, rather than as a discourse on marriage per se or on relations between men and women in the classical era. We must not lose sight of the fact that Euripides, a male playwright, created Medea for a male actor to perform before a largely male audience.

The central conflicts depicted in Euripides' plays—attitudes toward the gods, responses to foreign influences, relations between the sexes—are as pressing and pertinent today as they were in the fifth century B.C.E. His contemporaries saw Euripides as modern, innovative, and daring, and he has remained so ever since. M.P., J.E.G

Medea[1]

CHARACTERS

NURSE

TUTOR, *of Medea and Jason's sons*

MEDEA

CHORUS, *of Corinthian women*

CREON, *king of Corinth*

JASON

AEGEUS, *king of Athens*

MESSENGER

TWO BOYS, *sons of Medea and Jason*

SCENE: *A normal house on a street in Corinth. The elderly* NURSE *steps out of its front door.*

NURSE   I wish the *Argo*[2] never had set sail,
  had never flown to Colchis[3] through the dark

---

1. Translated by Diane Arnson Svarlien.
2. Jason's ship for his quest of the Golden Fleece; see introduction.

3. Medea's birthplace, across the Black Sea from Jason's homeland of Iolcos, now called Volo.

Clashing Rocks; I wish the pines had never
been felt along the hollows on the slopes
5   of Pelion[4] to fit their hands with oars—
those heroes who went off to seek the golden
pelt for Pelias[5] My mistress then,
Medea, never would have sailed away
to reach the towers of Iolcus' land;
10   the sight of Jason never would have stunned
her spirit with desire. She would have never
persuaded Pelias' daughters to kill their father,[6]
never had to come to this land—Corinth.[7]
Here she's lived in exile with her husband
15   and children, and Medea's presence pleased
the citizens. For her part, she complied
with Jason in all things. There is no greater
security than this in all the world:
when a wife does not oppose her husband.
20   But now, there's only hatred. What should be
most loved has been contaminated, stricken
since Jason has betrayed them—his own children,
and my lady, for a royal bed.
He's married into power: Creon's daughter.
25   Poor Medea, mournful and dishonored,
shrieks at his broken oaths, the promise sealed
with his right hand (the greatest pledge there is)—
she calls the gods to witness just how well
Jason has repaid her. She won't touch food;
30   surrendering to pain, she melts away
her days in tears, ever since she learned
of this injustice. She won't raise her face;
her eyes are glued to the ground. Friends talk to her,
try to give her good advice; she listens
35   the way a rock does, or an ocean wave.
At most, she'll turn her pale neck aside,
sobbing to herself for her dear father,
her land, her home, and all that she betrayed
for Jason, who now holds her in dishonor.
40   This disaster made her realize:
a fatherland is no small thing to lose.
She hates her children, feels no joy in seeing them.
I'm afraid she might be plotting something.
Her mind is fierce, and she will not endure
45   ill treatment. I know her. I'm petrified
to think what thoughts she might be having now:
a sharpened knife-blade thrust right through the liver—

4. Mountain in northeastern Greece near   Iolcos.
Iolcos.   6. See introduction.
5. Jason's uncle, usurper of the throne of   7. City in southern Greece.

she could even strike the royal family, murder
the bridegroom too, make this disaster worse.
50 She's a terror. There's no way to be
her enemy and come out as the victor.
Here come the children, resting from their games,
with no idea of their mother's troubles.
A child's mind is seldom filled with pain.

[*Enter the* TUTOR *from the house with the two children of* JASON *and* MEDEA.]

55 TUTOR   Timeworn stalwart of my mistress' household,
why do you stand here by the gates, alone,
crying out your sorrows to yourself?
You've left Medea alone. Doesn't she need you?

NURSE   Senior attendant to the sons of Jason,
60 decent servants feel their masters' griefs
in their own minds, when things fall out all wrong.
As for me, my pain was so intense
that a desire crept over me to come out here
and tell the earth and sky my mistress' troubles.

65 TUTOR   Poor thing. Is she not done with weeping yet?

NURSE   What blissful ignorance! She's barely started.

TUTOR   The fool—if one may say such things of masters—
she doesn't even know the latest outrage.

NURSE   What is it, old man? Don't begrudge me that.

70 TUTOR   Nothing. I'm sorry that I spoke at all.

NURSE   By your beard, don't hide this thing from *me*,
your fellow servant. I can keep it quiet.

TUTOR   As I approached the place where the old men
sit and play dice, beside the sacred spring
75 Peirene, I heard someone say—he didn't
notice I was listening—that Creon,
the ruler of this land, intends to drive
these children and their mother out of Corinth.
I don't know if it's true. I hope it isn't.

80 NURSE   Will Jason let his sons be so abused,
even if he's fighting with their mother?

TUTOR   He has a new bride; he's forgotten them.
He's no friend to this household anymore.

NURSE   We are destroyed, then. Before we've bailed our boat
85 from the first wave of sorrow, here's a new one.

TUTOR   But please, don't tell your mistress. Keep it quiet.
It's not the time for her to know of this.

NURSE   Children, do you hear the way your father
is treating you? I won't say, *May he die!*
90 —he is my master—but it's obvious
he's harming those whom he should love. He's guilty.

TUTOR   Who isn't? Are you just now learning this,
that each man loves himself more than his neighbor?
If their father doesn't cherish them, because
95 he's more preoccupied with his own bed—

NURSE   Go inside now, children. Everything

will be all right.

[*The* TUTOR *turns the children toward the house.*]

And you, keep them away—
don't let them near their mother when she's like this.
I've seen her: she looks fiercer than a bull;
100 she's giving them the eye, as if she means
to do something. Her rage will not let up,
I know, until she lashes out at someone.
May it be enemies she strikes, and not her loved ones!

[*In the following passage,* MEDEA *sings and the* NURSE *chants.*]

MEDEA   [*From within the house, crying out in rage.*]
Aaaah!
Oh, horrible, horrible, all that I suffer,
105 *my unhappy struggles. I wish I could die.*[8]

NURSE   You see, this is it. Dear children, your mother
has stirred up her heart, she has stirred up her rage.
Hurry up now and get yourselves inside the house—
but don't get too close to her, don't let her see you:
110 her ways are too wild, her nature is hateful,
her mind is too willful.
Go in. Hurry up!

[*Exit the* TUTOR *and the boys.*]

It's clear now, it's starting: a thunderhead rising,
swollen with groaning, and soon it will flash
as her spirit ignites it—then what will she do?
115 Her heart is so proud, there is no way to stop her;
her soul has been pierced by these sorrows.

MEDEA   *Aaaah!*
The pain that I've suffered, I've suffered so much,
worth oceans of weeping. O children, accursed,
may you die—with your father! Your mother is hateful.
120 *Go to hell, the whole household! Every last one.*

NURSE   Oh, lord. Here we go. What have *they* done—the children?
Their father's done wrong—why should you hate *them*?
Oh, children, my heart is so sore, I'm afraid
you will come to some harm.
Rulers are fierce
125 in their temperament; somehow, they will not be governed;
they like to have power, always, over others.
They're harsh, and they're stubborn. It's better to live
as an equal with equals. I never would want
to be grand and majestic—just let me grow old
130 in simple security. Even the *word*
"moderation" sounds good when you say it. For mortals
the middle is safest, in word and in deed.
Too much is too much, and there's always a danger

---

8. Passages in italics indicate lyric sections that would have been sung with musical accompaniment.

a god may get angry and ruin your household.

[*Enter the* CHORUS *of Corinthian women from the right, singing.*]

135 CHORUS   *I heard someone's voice, I heard someone shout:*
the woman from Colchis: poor thing, so unhappy.
Is her grief still unsoftened? Old woman, please tell us—
I heard her lament through the gates of my hall.
Believe me, old woman, I take no delight
140   *when this house is in pain. I have pledged it my friendship.*
NURSE   This house? It no longer exists. It's all gone.
He's taken up with his new royal marriage.
She's in her bedroom, my mistress, she's melting
her life all away, and her mind can't be eased
145 by a single kind word from a single dear friend.
MEDEA   *Aaaah!*
May a fire-bolt from heaven come shoot through my skull!
What do I gain by being alive?
Oh, god. How I long for the comfort of death.
I hate this life. How I wish I could leave it.

[Strophe]

150 CHORUS   Do you hear, O Zeus, O sunlight and earth,
this terrible song, the cry
of this unhappy bride?
Poor fool, what a dreadful longing,
this craving for final darkness.
155 You'll hasten your death. Why do it?
Don't pray for this ending.
If your husband reveres a new bed, a new bride,
don't sharpen your mind against him.
You'll have Zeus himself supporting
160 your case. Don't dissolve in weeping
for the sake of your bedmate.
MEDEA   *Great goddess Themis and Artemis, holy one:*[9]
do you see what I suffer, although I have bound
my detestable husband with every great oath?
165 *May I see him, along with his bride and the palace*
scraped down to nothing, crushed into splinters.
He started it. He was the one with the nerve
to commit this injustice. Oh father, oh city,
I left you in horror—I killed my own brother.[1]
170 NURSE   You hear what she says, and the gods that she prays to:
Themis, and Zeus, the enforcer of oaths?
There's no way my mistress' rage will die down
into anything small.

9. Themis presided over petitions to the gods to ensure their reasonableness; Artemis, the Greek name for Diana, abjured marriage and protected women in childbirth.
1. See introduction.

[Antistrophe]

CHORUS How I wish she'd come outside, let us see
175   her face, let her hear our words
         and the sound of our voice.
         If only she'd drop her anger,
         unburden her burning spirit,
         let go of this weight of madness.
180   I'll stand by our friendship.
         Hurry up, bring her here, get her out, go inside,
         and bring her to us. Go tell her
         that we are her friends. Please hurry!
         She's raging—the ones inside may
185   feel the sting of her sorrow.

NURSE   I'll do as you ask, but I fear that my mistress
         won't listen to me.
         I will make the effort—what's one more attempt?
         But her glare is as fierce as a bull's, let me tell you—
190   she's wild like a lion who's just given birth
         whenever a servant tries telling her anything.

         You wouldn't go wrong, you'd be right on the mark,
         if you called them all half-wits, the people of old:
         they made lovely songs for banquets and parties,
195   but no one took time to discover the music
         that might do some good, the chords or the harmony
         people could use to relieve all the hateful
         pain and distress that leads to the downfall
         of houses, the deaths and the dreadful misfortunes.
200   Let me tell you, there would be some gain in that—music
         with the power to heal. When you're having a sumptuous
         feast, what's the point of a voice raised in song?
         Why bother with singing? The feast is enough
         to make people happy. That's all that they need.
              [Exit the NURSE into the house.]

205 CHORUS I heard a wail, a clear cry of pain;
         she rails at the betrayer of her bed,
         the bitter bridegroom.
         For the injustice she suffers, she calls on the gods:
         Themis of Zeus, protectress of oaths,
210   who brought her to Hellas,[2] over the salt water dark as night,
         through the waves of Pontus' forbidding gate.[3]
              [Enter MEDEA from the house, attended by the NURSE and other female
              servants.[4] Here spoken dialogue resumes.]

MEDEA   Women of Corinth, I have stepped outside
         so you will not condemn me. Many people
         act superior—I'm well aware of this.

---

2. Greece.
3. Another name for the Black Sea, the "gate"
of which is the narrow strait known as the
Bosporus.
4. Nonspeaking roles, and thus not part of
the character list.

215 Some keep it private; some are arrogant
    in public view. Yet there are other people
    who, just because they lead a quiet life,
    are thought to be aloof. There is no justice
    in human eyesight: people take one look
220 and hate a man, before they know his heart,
    though no injustice has been done to them.
    A foreigner must adapt to a new city,
    certainly. Nor can I praise a citizen
    who's willful, and who treats his fellow townsmen
225 harshly, out of narrow-mindedness.

    My case is different. Unexpected trouble
    has crushed my soul. It's over now; I take
    no joy in life. My friends, I want to die.
    My husband, who was everything to me—
230 how well I know it—is the worst of men.

    Of all the living creatures with a soul
    and mind, we women are the most pathetic.
    First of all, we have to buy a husband:[5]
    spend vast amounts of money, just to get
235 a master for our body—to add insult
    to injury. And the stakes could not be higher:
    will you get a decent husband, or a bad one?
    If a woman leaves her husband, then she loses
    her virtuous reputation. To refuse him
240 is just not possible. When a girl leaves home
    and comes to live with new ways, different rules,
    she has to be a prophet—learn somehow
    the art of dealing smoothly with her bedmate.
    If we do well, and if our husbands bear
245 the yoke without discomfort or complaint,
    our lives are admired. If not, it's best to die.
    A man, when he gets fed up with the people
    at home, can go elsewhere to ease his heart
    —he has friends, companions his own age.
250 We must rely on just one single soul.
    They say that we lead safe, untroubled lives
    at home while they do battle with the spear.
    They're wrong. I'd rather take my stand behind
    a shield three times than go through childbirth once.

255 Still, my account is quite distinct from yours.
    This is your city. You have your fathers' homes,
    your lives bring joy and profit. You have friends.
    But I have been deserted and outraged—
    left without a city by my husband,
260 who stole me as his plunder from the land

5. Ancient Greek custom dictated that the bride's family pay a dowry to the groom.

of the barbarians. Here I have no mother,
no brother, no blood relative to help
unmoor me from this terrible disaster.
So, I will need to ask you one small favor.

265   If I should find some way, some strategy
to pay my husband back, bring him to justice,
keep silent. Most of the time, I know, a woman
is filled with fear. She's worthless in a battle
and flinches at the sight of steel. But when

270   she's faced with an injustice in the bedroom,
there is no other mind more murderous.

CHORUS   I'll do as you ask. You're justified, Medea,
in paying your husband back. I'm not surprised
you grieve at your misfortunes.
                                    Look! I see Creon,

275   the lord of this land, coming toward us now.
He has some new decision to announce.

        [*Enter* CREON *from the right, with attendants.*]

CREON   You with the grim face, fuming at your husband,
Medea, I hereby announce that you
must leave this land, an exile, taking with you

280   your two children. You must not delay.
This is my decision. I won't leave
until I've thrown you out, across the border.

MEDEA   Oh, god. I'm crushed; I'm utterly destroyed.
My enemies, their sails unfurled, attack me,

285   and there's no land in sight, there's no escape
from ruin. Although I suffer, I must ask:
Creon, why do you send me from this land?

CREON   I'll speak plainly: I'm afraid of you.
You could hurt my daughter, even kill her.

290   Every indication points that way.
You're wise by nature, you know evil arts,
and you're upset because your husband's gone
away from your bedroom. I have heard reports
that you've made threats, that you've devised a plan

295   to harm the bride, her father, and the bridegroom.
I want to guard against that. I would rather
have you hate me, woman, here and now,
than treat you gently and regret it later.

MEDEA   Oh, god.
Creon, this is not the first time: often

300   I've been injured by my reputation.
Any man who's sensible by nature
will set a limit on his children's schooling
to make sure that they never grow too wise.
The wise are seen as lazy, and they're envied

305   and hated. If you offer some new wisdom
to half-wits, they will only think you're useless.
And those who are considered experts hate you

when the city thinks you're cleverer than they are.
I myself have met with this reaction.
310 Since I am wise, some people envy me,
some think I'm idle, some the opposite,
and some feel threatened. Yet I'm not all that wise.

And you're afraid of me. What do you fear?
Don't worry, Creon. I don't have it in me
315 to do wrong to a man with royal power.
What injustice have you done to me?
Your spirit moved you, and you gave your daughter
as you saw fit. My husband is the one
I hate. You acted well, with wise restraint.
320 And now, I don't begrudge your happiness.
My best to all of you—celebrate the wedding.
Just let me stay here. I know when I'm beaten.
I'll yield to this injustice. I'll submit
in silence to those greater than myself.
325 CREON   Your words are soothing, but I'm terrified
of what's in your mind. I trust you less than ever.
It's easier to guard against a woman
(or man, for that matter) with a fiery spirit
than one who's wise and silent. You must leave
330 at once—don't waste my time with talk. It's settled.
Since you are my enemy, and hate me,
no ruse of yours can keep you here among us.

> [MEDEA *kneels before* CREON *and grasps his hand and knees in supplication.*]

MEDEA   No, by your knees! By your new-married daughter!
CREON   You're wasting words. There's no way you'll persuade me.
335 MEDEA   You'll drive me out, with no reverence for my prayers?
CREON   I care more for my family than for you.
MEDEA   How clearly I recall my fatherland.
CREON   Yes, that's what *I* love most—after my children.
MEDEA   Oh, god—the harm Desire does to mortals!
340 CREON   Depending on one's fortunes, I suppose.
MEDEA   Zeus, do not forget who caused these troubles.
CREON   Just leave, you fool. I'm tired of struggling with you.
MEDEA   Struggles. Yes. I've had enough myself.
CREON   My guards will force you out in just a moment.
345 MEDEA   Oh, please, not that! Creon, I entreat you!
CREON   You intend to make a scene, I gather.
MEDEA   I'll leave, don't worry. That's not what I'm asking.
CREON   Why are you forcing me? Let go of my hand!
MEDEA   Please, let me stay just one more day, that's all.
350 I need to make arrangements for my exile,
find safe asylum for my children, since
their father doesn't give them any thought.
Take pity on them. You yourself have children.
It's only right for you to treat them kindly.

355 If we go into exile, I'm not worried
    about myself—I weep for their disaster.
    CREON   I haven't got a ruler's temperament;
    reverence has often led me into ruin.
    Woman, I realize this is all wrong,
360 but you shall have your wish. I warn you, though:
    if the sun god's lamp should find you and your children
    still within our borders at first rising,
    it means your death. I've spoken; it's decided.
    Stay for one day only, if you must.
365 You won't have time to do the things I fear.

    [*Exit* CREON *and attendants to the right.* MEDEA *rises to her feet.*]

    CHORUS   Oh, god! This is horrible, unhappy woman,
    the grief that you suffer. Where will you turn?
    Where will you find shelter? What country, what home
    will save you from sorrow? A god has engulfed you,
370 Medea—this wave is now breaking upon you,
    there is no way out.
    MEDEA   Yes, things are all amiss. Who could deny it?
    Believe me, though, that's not how it will end.
    The newlyweds have everything at stake,
375 and struggles await the one who made this match.
    Do you think I ever could have fawned
    on him like that without some gain in mind,
    some ruse? I never would have spoken to him,
    or touched him with my hands. He's such an idiot.
380 He could have thrown me out, destroyed my plans;
    instead he's granted me a single day
    to turn three enemies to three dead bodies:
    the father, and the bride, and my own husband.
    I know so many pathways to their deaths,
385 I don't know which to turn to first, my friends.
    Shall I set the bridal home on fire,
    creeping silently into their bedroom?

    There's just one threat. If I am apprehended
    entering the house, my ruse discovered,
390 I'll be put to death; my enemies
    will laugh at me. The best way is the most
    direct, to use the skills I have by nature
    and poison them, destroy them with my drugs.

    Ah, well.

    All right, they die. What city will receive me?
395 What host will offer me immunity,
    what land will take me in and give me refuge?
    There's no one. I must wait just long enough
    to see if any sheltering tower appears.
    Then I will kill in silence, by deceit.

400   But if I have no recourse from disaster,
        I'll take the sword and kill them, even if
        it means my death. I have the utmost nerve.
        Now, by the goddess whom I most revere,
        Hecate,[6] whom I choose as my accomplice,
405   who dwells within my inmost hearth, I swear:
        no one can hurt my heart and then fare well.
        I'll turn their marriage bitter, desolate—
        they'll regret the match, regret my exile.

        And now, spare nothing that is in your knowledge,
410   Medea: make your plan, prepare your ruse.
        Do this dreadful thing. There is so much
        at stake. Display your courage. Do you see
        how you are suffering? Do not allow
        these Sisyphean snakes[7] to laugh at you
415   on Jason's wedding day. Your father is noble;
        your grandfather is Helios. You have
        the knowledge, not to mention woman's nature:
        for any kind of noble deed, we're helpless;
        for malice, though, our wisdom is unmatched.
        CHORUS

                    [Strophe 1]

420   The streams of the holy rivers are flowing backward.
        Everything runs in reverse—justice is upside down.
        Men's minds are deceitful, and nothing is settled,
        not even oaths that are sworn by the gods.
        The tidings will change, and a virtuous reputation
425   will grace my name. The race of women will reap
        honor, no longer the shame of disgraceful rumor.

                    [Antistrophe 1]

        The songs of the poets of old will no longer linger
        on my untrustworthiness. Women were never sent
        the gift of divine inspiration by Phoebus
430   Apollo, lord of the elegant lyre,[8]
        the master of music—or I could have sung my own song
        against the race of men. The fullness of time
        holds many tales: it can speak of both men and women.

                    [Strophe 2]

        You sailed away from home and father,
435   driven insane in your heart; you traced a path

        ---

        6. Goddess of magic or enchantment.   thus an insult. See also note 8, p. 266.
        7. Derogatory reference to the Corinthians.   8. Apollo, god of the sun, was often figured
        Sisyphus was an early king of Corinth known   with this stringed instrument.
        for his cruelty; to be linked to Sisyphus was

between the twin cliffs of Pontus.[9]
The land you live in is foreign.
Your bed is empty, your husband
gone. Poor woman, dishonored,
440   sent into exile.

[Antistrophe 2]

The Grace of oaths is gone, and Reverence
flies away into the sky, abandoning
great Hellas. No father's dwelling
unmoors you now from this heartache.
445   Your bed now yields to another:
now a princess prevails,
greater than you are.

[Enter JASON from the right.]

JASON   This is not the first time—I have often
observed that a fierce temper is an evil
450   that leaves you no recourse. You could have stayed
here in this land, you could have kept your home
by simply acquiescing in the plans
of those who are greater. You are now an exile
because of your own foolish words. To me
455   it makes no difference. You can keep on calling
Jason the very worst of men. However,
the words you spoke against the royal family—
well, consider it a gain that nothing worse
than exile is your punishment. As for me,
460   I wanted you to stay. I always tried
to calm the king, to soothe his fuming rage.
But you, you idiot, would not let up
your words against the royal family. That's why
you are now an exile. All the same,
465   I won't let down my loved ones. I have come here
looking out for your best interests, woman,
so you won't be without the things you need
when you go into exile with the children.
You'll need money—banishment means hardship.
470   However much you hate me, I could never
wish you any harm.

MEDEA   You are the worst!
You're loathsome—that's the worst word I can utter.
You're not a man. You've come here—most detested
by the gods, by me, by all mankind.
475   That isn't courage, when you have the nerve
to harm your friends, then look them in the face.
No, that's the worst affliction known to man:
shamelessness.

9. An ancient region along the southern coast of the Black Sea.

And yet, I'm glad you've come.
Speaking ill to you will ease my soul,
480   and listening will cause you pain. I'll start
at the beginning. First, I saved your life—
as every single man who sailed from Hellas
aboard the *Argo* knows—when you were sent
to yoke the fire-breathing bulls, and sow
485   the deadly crop.[1] I killed the dragon, too:
the sleepless one, who kept the Golden Fleece
enfolded in his convoluted coils;[2]
I was your light, the beacon of your safety.
For my part, I betrayed my home, my father,
490   and went with you to Pelion's slopes, Iolcus
with more good will than wisdom—and I killed
Pelias, in the cruelest possible way:
at his own children's hands. I ruined their household.

And you—you *are* the very worst of men—
495   betrayed me, after all of that. You wanted
a new bed, even though I'd borne you children.
If you had still been childless, anyone
could understand your lust for this new marriage.

All trust in oaths is gone. What puzzles me
500   is whether you believe those gods (the ones
who heard you swear) no longer are in power,
or that the old commandments have been changed?
You realize full well you broke your oath.

Ah, my right hand, which you took so often,
505   clinging to my knees.[3] What was the point
of touching me? You are despicable.
My hopes have all gone wrong. Well, then! You're here:
I have a question for you, friend to friend.
(What good do I imagine it will do?
510   Still, I'll ask, since it makes you look worse.)
Where do I turn now? To my father's household
and fatherland, which I betrayed for you?
Or Pelias' poor daughters? Naturally
they'll welcome me—the one who killed their father!

515   Here is my situation. I've become
an enemy to my own family, those
whom I should love, and I have gone to war

---

1. Aeetes, king of Colchis, challenged Jason
with a series of tasks during his quest for the
Golden Fleece; among these were the requirements that he harness two fire-breathing
bulls, plow with them, and sow dragons' teeth

that sprouted warriors he then had to kill.
2. The Golden Fleece was guarded by a powerful serpent; see introduction.
3. Thus in a position of supplication.

with those whom I had no reason at all
to hurt, and all for your sake. In exchange,
520 you've made me the happiest girl in all of Hellas.
I have you, the perfect spouse, a marvel,
so trustworthy—though I must leave the country
friendless and deserted, taking with me
my friendless children! What a charming scandal
525 for a newlywed: your children roam
as beggars, with the one who saved your life.

Zeus! For brass disguised as gold, you sent us
reliable criteria to judge.
But when a man is base, how can we know?
530 Why is there no sign stamped upon his body?
CHORUS This anger is a terror, hard to heal,
when loved ones clash with loved ones in dispute.
JASON It seems that I must have a way with words
and, like a skillful captain, reef my sails
535 in order to escape this gale that blows
without a break—your endless, tired harangue.
The way I see it, woman (since you seem
to feel that I must owe you some huge favor),
it was Cypris,[4] no other god or mortal,
540 who saved me on my voyage. Yes, your mind
is subtle. But I must say—at the risk
of stirring up your envy and your grudges—
Eros[5] was the one who forced your hand:
his arrows, which are inescapable,
545 compelled you to rescue me. But I won't put
too fine a point on that. You *did* support me.
You saved my life, in fact. However, you
received more than you gave, as I shall prove.
First of all, you live in Hellas now
550 instead of your barbarian land. With us,
you know what justice is, and civil law:
not mere brute force. And every single person
in Hellas knows that you are wise. You're famous.
You'd never have that kind of reputation
555 if you were living at the edge of nowhere.
As for me, I wouldn't wish for gold
or for a sweeter song than Orpheus'[6]
unless I had the fame to match my fortune.

Enough about my struggles—you're the one
560 who started this debate. As for my marriage
to the princess, which you hold against me,

4. Another name for the Greek goddess   6. Orpheus received a lyre from Apollo, upon
Aphrodite.   which he played music of unparalleled beauty.
5. God of love.

I shall show you how I acted wisely
and with restraint, and with the greatest love
toward you and toward our children—Wait! Just listen!
565   When I moved here from Iolcus, bringing with me
disaster in abundance, with no recourse,
what more lucky windfall could I find
(exile that I was) than marrying
the king's own child? It's not that I despised
570   your bed—the thought that irritates you most—
nor was I mad with longing for a new bride,
or trying to compete with anyone—
to win the prize for having the most children.
I have enough—no reason to complain.
575   My motive was the best: so we'd live well
and not be poor. I know that everyone
avoids a needy friend. I wanted to raise
sons in a style that fits my family background,
give brothers to the ones I had with you,
580   and treat them all as equals. This would strengthen
the family, and I'd be blessed with fortune.
What do *you* need children for? For me, though,
it's good if I can use my future children
to benefit my present ones. Is that
585   bad planning? If you weren't so irritated
about your bed, you'd never say it was.
But you're a woman—and you're all the same!
If everything goes well between the sheets
you think you have it all. But let there be
590   some setback or disaster in the bedroom
and suddenly you go to war against
the things that you should value most. I mean it—
men should really have some other method
for getting children. The whole female race
595   should not exist. It's nothing but a nuisance.
CHORUS   Jason, you've composed a lovely speech.
But I must say, though you may disagree:
you have betrayed your wife. You've been unjust.
MEDEA   Now, this is where I differ from most people.
600   In my view, someone who is both unjust
and has a gift for speaking—such a man
incurs the greatest penalty. He uses
his tongue to cover up his unjust actions,
and this gives him the nerve to stop at nothing
605   no matter how outrageous. Yet he's not
all that wise. Take your case, for example.

Spare me this display of cleverness;
a single word will pin you to the mat.
If you weren't in the wrong, you would have told me
610   your marriage plans, not kept us in the dark—

your loved ones, your own family!

JASON   Yes, of course
    you would have been all for it! Even now
    you can't control your rage against the marriage.

MEDEA   That's not what you were thinking. You imagined
615   that for an older man, a barbarian wife
    was lacking in prestige.

JASON   No! Please believe me:
    It wasn't for the woman's sake I married
    into the king's family. As I have said,
    I wanted to save you, and give our children
620   royal brothers, a safeguard for our household.

MEDEA   May I not have a life that's blessed with fortune
    so painful, or prosperity so irritating.

JASON   Your prayer could be much wiser: don't consider
    what's useful painful. When you have good fortune,
625   don't see it as a hardship.

MEDEA   Go ahead—
    you have somewhere to turn!—commit this outrage.
    I am deserted, exiled from this land.

JASON   You brought that on yourself. Don't blame another.

MEDEA   Did I remarry? How did I betray you?

630 JASON   You blasphemously cursed the royal family.

MEDEA   And I'm a curse to your family as well.

JASON   I won't discuss this with you any further.
    If you'd like me to help you and the children
    with money for your exile, then just say so.
635   I'm prepared to give with an open hand,
    and make arrangements with my friends to show you
    hospitality. They'll treat you well.
    You'd be an idiot to refuse this offer.
    You'll gain a lot by giving up your anger.

640 MEDEA   I wouldn't stay with your friends, and I would never
    accept a thing from you. Don't even offer.
    There is no profit in a bad man's gift.

JASON   All the same, I call the gods to witness:
    I only want to help you and the children.
645   But you don't want what's good; you push away
    your friends; you're willful. And you'll suffer for it.

MEDEA   Get out of here. A craving for your new bride
    has overcome you—you've been away so long.
    Go, celebrate your wedding. It may be
650   (the gods will tell) a marriage you'll regret.

        [*Exit* JASON *to the right.*]

CHORUS

[Strophe 1]

Desire, when it comes on too forcefully, never bestows
excellence, never makes anyone prestigious.

When she comes with just the right touch, there's no goddess
    more gracious
than Cypris.
655   Mistress, never release from your golden bow
an inescapable arrow, smeared with desire
and aimed at my heart.

[Antistrophe 1]

Please, let me be cherished by Wisdom, be loved by Restraint,
loveliest gift of the gods. May dreadful Cypris
660   never stun my spirit with love for the bed of another
and bring on
anger, battles of words, endless fighting, strife.
Let her be shrewd in her judgment; let her revere
the bedroom at peace.

[Strophe 2]

665   O fatherland, O home, never allow
me to be without a city:
a grief without recourse, life that's hard to live through,
most distressing of all fates.
May I go to my death, my death
670   before I endure that; I'd rather face
my final day. There's no worse heartache
than to be cut off from your fatherland.

[Antistrophe 2]

We've seen it for ourselves; nobody else
gave me this tale to consider.
675   No city, no friend will treat you with compassion
in your dreadful suffering.
May he die, the ungracious man
who won't honor friends, who will not unlock
his mind to clear, calm thoughts of kindness.
680   I will never call such a man my friend.

    [*Enter* AEGEUS *from the left.*][7]

AEGEUS   Medea, I wish all the best to you.
There is no finer way to greet a friend.
MEDEA   All the best to you, Aegeus, son
of wise Pandion. Where are you traveling from?
685 AEGEUS   I've come from Phoebus' ancient oracle.[8]
MEDEA   What brought you to the earth's prophetic navel?
AEGEUS   Seeking how I might beget a child.

---

7. While the unanticipated arrival of the king of Athens at this part in the play may appear odd, Athenian audiences would have understood this episode as part of the larger Medea myth; see introduction.

8. The shrine of Phoebus Apollo, located in Delphi, was known as the "navel stone," where east and west meet, and was thus considered the center of the world.

MEDEA	By the gods, are you still childless?
AEGEUS	Still childless. Some god must be to blame.
690 MEDEA	Do you have a wife, or do you sleep alone?
AEGEUS	I'm married, and we share a marriage bed.
MEDEA	Well, what did Phoebus say concerning children?
AEGEUS	His words were too profound for human wisdom.
MEDEA	May I hear the oracle? Is it permitted?
695 AEGEUS	Yes, why not? This calls for a wise mind.
MEDEA	Then tell me, if indeed it is permitted.
AEGEUS	He said, "Don't loose the wineskin's hanging foot . . ."[9]
MEDEA	Before you do what thing? Or reach what place?
AEGEUS	Before returning to my paternal hearth.
700 MEDEA	And why have you sailed here? What do you need?
AEGEUS	There is a man named Pittheus, lord of Troezen . . .[1]
MEDEA	Pelops' son.[2] They say he's very pious.
AEGEUS	I want to bring this prophecy to him.
MEDEA	Yes. He's wise, and well-versed in such things.
705 AEGEUS	And most beloved of my war companions.
MEDEA	Good luck to you. May you get what you desire.
AEGEUS	But you—your eyes are melting. What's the matter?
MEDEA	My husband is the very worst of men.
AEGEUS	What are you saying? Why the low spirits? Tell me.
710 MEDEA	Jason treats me unjustly. I've done him no harm.
AEGEUS	What has he done? Explain to me more clearly.
MEDEA	He has another wife, who takes my place.
AEGEUS	No. He wouldn't dare. It's much too shameful.
MEDEA	It's true. His former loved ones are dishonored.
715 AEGEUS	Did he desire another? Or tire of you?
MEDEA	Oh yes, he felt desire. We cannot trust him.
AEGEUS	Let him go, if he's as bad as you say.
MEDEA	He desired a royal marriage-bond.
AEGEUS	Who's giving away the bride? Go on, continue.
720 MEDEA	Creon, the ruler of this land of Corinth.
AEGEUS	Woman, your pain is understandable.
MEDEA	I am destroyed. And that's not all—I'm exiled.
AEGEUS	By whom? This is new trouble on top of trouble.
MEDEA	By Creon. He is driving me from Corinth.
725 AEGEUS	And Jason is allowing it? Shame on him.
MEDEA	He claims to be against it, but he'll manage
	to endure it somehow.

[MEDEA *again assumes the supplicant position.*]

Listen, I entreat you;

9. An ambiguous prophecy based on the image of wine stored in the shank portion of an animal skin; see also next note.
1. In this Athenian legend, Pittheus knows that the prophecy means that Aegeus is not to drink wine until he returns to Athens. Pittheus, however, withholds this information,

allows Aegeus to drink to excess, and then allows him to sleep with his daughter Aethra. The Athenian hero Theseus is the product of this encounter.
2. The hero Pelops founded the Peloponnese, the peninsula in the south of Greece.

by your beard and by your knees, I beg you:
Have pity on me; pity my misfortune.
730 Don't let me go deserted into exile;
receive me in your home and at your hearth.
If you do it, may the gods grant your desire
for children; may you die a prosperous man.
You don't know what a windfall you have found!
735 I'll cure your childlessness, make you a father.
I know the drugs required for such things.
AEGEUS   For many reasons, woman, I am eager
to grant this favor to you: first, the gods;
and secondly, the children that you promise.
740 I'm at a total loss where that's concerned.
But this is how it is. When you arrive,
I'll treat you justly, try to shelter you.
However, you must know this in advance:
I'm not willing to escort you from this land.
745 If you can come to my house on your own,
I'll let you stay there—it will be your refuge.
I will not give you up to anyone.
But you must leave this land all by yourself.
My hosts here must have no complaint with me.
750 MEDEA   So be it. But if I had some assurance
that I could trust you, I'd have all I need.
AEGEUS   You don't believe me? Tell me, what's the problem?
MEDEA   Oh, I believe you. But I have enemies:
Creon, and the house of Pelias.
755 If they come for me, and you're not bound
by any oath, then you might let them take me.
A promise in words only, never sworn
by any gods, might not be strong enough
to keep you from befriending them, from yielding
760 to their delegations. I'm completely helpless;
they have prosperity and royal power.
AEGEUS   Your words show forethought. If you think it's best,
I'll do it without any hesitation.
In fact, this is the safest course for me:
765 I'll have a good excuse to turn away
your enemies. And things are settled well
for you, of course. I'll swear: just name the gods.
MEDEA   Swear by the Earth we stand on, and by Helios[3]—
my father's father—and the whole race of gods.
770 AEGEUS   To do or not do what? Just say the word.
MEDEA   Never to expel me from your land yourself,
and never, as long as you live, to give me up
willingly to any enemy.
AEGEUS   I swear by Earth, by Helios' sacred light,

3. The sun.

775   by all the gods: I'll do just as you say.

    MEDEA   Fine. And if you don't? What would you suffer?

    AEGEUS   Whatever an unholy man deserves.

        [MEDEA rises.]

    MEDEA   Farewell, then, on your voyage. This is good.

    I'll find you in your city very soon,

780   once I've done my will, and had my way.

        [*Exit* AEGEUS *to the left. The* CHORUS *address him as he leaves.*]

    CHORUS   May lord Hermes, the child of Maia,[4] escort you

    and bring you back home. May you do as you please,

    and have all you want. In my judgment, Aegeus,

    you're a good, noble man.

785   MEDEA   O Zeus, and Zeus's Justice, and the light

    of Helios, I now shall be the victor

    over my enemies. My friends, I've set my foot

    upon the path. My enemies will pay

    what justice demands—I now have hope of this.

790   This man, when I was at my lowest point,

    appeared, the perfect harbor for my plans.

    When I reach Pallas' city,[5] I shall have

    a steady place to tie my ship. And now

    I'll tell you what my plans are. Hear my words;

795   they will not bring you pleasure. I will send

    a servant to bring Jason here to see me.

    When he comes, I'll soothe him with my words:

    I'll say that I agree with him, that he

    was right to marry into the royal family,

800   betraying me—well done, and well thought out!

    "But let my children stay here!" I will plead—

    not that I would leave them in this land

    for my enemies to outrage—my own children.

    No: this is my deceit, to kill the princess.

805   I'll send them to her, bearing gifts in hand

    —a delicate robe, and a garland worked in gold.

    If she takes these fine things and puts them on,

    she, and anyone who touches her,

    will die a painful death. Such are the drugs

810   with which I will smear them.

                     But enough of that.

    Once that's done, the next thing I must do

    chokes me with sorrow. I will kill the children—

    my children. No one on this earth can save them.

    I'll ruin Jason's household, then I'll leave

815   this land, I'll flee the slaughter of the children

    I love so dearly. I will have the nerve

    for this unholy deed. You see, my friends,

---

4. The nymph Maia bore Hermes, who became the gods' messenger.

5. Another name for Athens, protected by Pallas Athene.

to his descendants. Take these wedding gifts
in your arms, my children; go and give them
to the lucky bride, the royal princess.

985 These are gifts that no one could find fault with.

    [*The attendant puts the gifts in the children's arms.*]

JASON   You fool! Why let these things out of your hands?
Do you think the royal household needs more robes,
more gold? Hold on to these. Don't give them up.
If my wife thinks anything of me,

990 I'm sure that I mean more to her than wealth.

MEDEA   Don't say that. Even the gods can be persuaded
by gifts. And gold is worth a thousand words.
She has the magic charm; the gods are helping
her right now: she's young, and she has power.

995 To save my children from exile, I'd give my life,
not merely gold. You, children, when you've entered
that wealthy house, must supplicate your father's
young wife, my mistress. You must plead with her
and ask her that you be exempt from exile.

1000 Give her these fine things. That is essential:
she must receive these gifts with her own hands.
Go quickly now, and bring back to your mother
the good news she desires—that you've succeeded.

    [*The children, bearing the gifts, leave with the* TUTOR *to the right.*]

CHORUS

[Strophe 1]

Now I no longer have hope that the children will live,
1005 no longer. They walk to the slaughter already.
The bride will receive the crown of gold;
she'll receive her horrible ruin.
Upon her golden hair, with her very own hands,
she'll place the fine circlet of Hades.[9]

[Antistrophe 1]

1010 She'll be persuaded; the grace and the heavenly gleam
will move her to try on the robe and the garland.
The bride will adorn herself for death,
for the shades below. She will fall
into this net; her death will be horrible. Ruin
1015 will be inescapable, fated.

[Strophe 2]

And you, poor thing, bitter bridegroom, in-law to
    royalty:
you don't know you're killing your children,

9. Death.

bringing hateful death to your bride.
How horrible: how unaware you are of your fate.

[Antistrophe 2]

1020   I cry for your pain in turn, poor thing; you're a
                mother, yet
          you will slaughter them, your own children,
          for the sake of your bridal bed,
          the bed that your husband now shares with somebody else.

                [The TUTOR *returns, at the right, from the palace with the
                children.]*

TUTOR   Mistress, your children are released from exile.
1025   The princess happily received the gifts
       with her own hands. As far as she's concerned,
       the children's case is settled; they're at peace.

       Ah!
       Why are you upset by your good fortune?
MEDEA   Oh, god.
TUTOR   Your cry is out of tune. This is good news!
1030 MEDEA   Oh god, oh god.
TUTOR   Have I made some mistake?
       Is what I've said bad news, and I don't know it?
MEDEA   You've said what you have said. I don't blame you.
TUTOR   So—why are you crying? Why are your eyes cast down?
MEDEA   Old man, I am compelled. The gods and I
1035   devised this strategy. What was I thinking?
TUTOR   Don't worry now. Your children will bring you home.
MEDEA   I'll send others home before that day.
TUTOR   You're not the only woman who's lost her children.
       We're mortals. We must bear disasters lightly.
1040 MEDEA   I'll do as you ask. Now, go inside the house
       and see to the children's needs, as usual.

                [Exit TUTOR *into the house.]*

       Oh, children, children, you two have a city
       and home, in which you'll live forever parted
       from your mother. You'll leave poor me behind.
1045   I'll travel to another land, an exile,
       before I ever have the joy of seeing
       you blessed with fortune—before your wedding days,
       before I prepare your beds and hold the torches.[1]
       My willfulness has cost me all this grief.
1050   I raised you, children, but it was no use;
       no use, the way I toiled, how much it hurt,
       the pain of childbirth, piercing like a thorn.
       And I had so much hope when you were born:
       you'd tend to my old age, and when I died,

---

1. Weddings were traditionally held at night, hence the need for lit torches in the ceremony.

1055 you'd wrap me in my shroud with your own hands:
     an admirable fate for anyone.
     That sweet thought has now been crushed. I'll be parted
     from both of you, and I will spend my years
     in sorrow and in pain. Your eyes no longer
1060 will look upon your mother. You'll move on
     to a different life.
                    Oh god, your eyes, the way
     you look at me. Why do you smile, my children,
     your very last smile? Aah, what will I do?
     The heart goes out of me, women, when I look
1065 at my children's shining eyes. I couldn't do this.
     Farewell to the plans I had before.
     I'll take my children with me when I leave.
     Why should I, just to cause their father pain,
     feel twice the pain myself by harming them?
1070 I will not do it. Farewell to my plans.
     But wait—what's wrong with me? What do I want?
     To allow my enemies to laugh at me?
     To let them go unpunished?
                       What I need
     is the nerve to do it. I was such a weakling,
1075 to let a soothing word enter my mind.
     Children, go inside the house.
              [The children start to go toward the house, but as MEDEA
              continues to speak, they continue to watch and listen
              to her, delaying their entry inside.]
                       Whoever
     is not permitted to attend these rites,
     my sacrifice, let that be his concern.
     I won't hold back the force that's in my hand.

     Aah!
1080 Oh no, my spirit, please, not that! Don't do it.
     Spare the children. Leave them alone, poor thing.
     They'll live with me there. They will bring you joy.

     By the avenging ones[2] who live below
     in Hades, no, I will not leave my children
1085 at the mercy of my enemies' outrage.
     Anyway, the thing's already done.
     She won't escape. The crown is on her head.
     The royal bride's destroyed, wrapped in her robes.
     I know it. Now, since I am setting foot
1090 on a path that will break my heart, and sending them
     on one more heartbreaking still, I want to speak
     to my children.
              [MEDEA reaches toward her children; they come back to her.]

2. The Eumenides, or Furies.

Children, give me your right hands,
give them to your mother, let me kiss them.
Oh, how I love these hands, how I love these mouths,
1095 the way the children stand, their noble faces!
May fortune bless you—in the other place.
Your father's taken all that once was here.
Oh, your sweet embrace, your tender skin,
your lovely breath, oh children.
                Go now—go.
    [*The children go inside.*]
1100 I cannot look at them. Grief overwhelms me.
I know that I am working up my nerve
for overwhelming evil, yet my spirit
is stronger than my mind's deliberations:
this is the source of mortals' deepest grief.
1105 CHORUS Quite often I've found myself venturing deeper
than women do normally into discussions
and subtle distinctions, and I would suggest
that we have our own Muse, who schools us in wisdom—
not every woman, but there are a few,
1110 you'll find one among many, a woman who doesn't
stand entirely apart from the Muses.

Here's my opinion: the childless among us,
the ones who have never experienced parenthood,
have greater good fortune than those who have children.
1115 They don't know—how could they?—if children
    are pleasant
or hard and distressing. Their lack of experience
saves them from heartache.
But those who have children, a household's sweet
    offshoot—
I see them consumed their whole lives with concern.
1120 They fret from the start: are they raising them well?
And then: will they manage to leave them enough?
Then finally: all of this toil and heartache,
is it for children who'll turn out to be
worthless or decent? That much is unclear.

1125 There's one final grief that I'll mention. Supposing
your children have grown up with plenty to live on,
they're healthy, they're decent—if fortune decrees it,
Death comes and spirits their bodies away
down to the Underworld. What is the point, then,
1130 if the gods, adding on to the pains that we mortals
endure for the sake of our children, send death,
most distressing of all? Tell me, where does that leave us?
    MEDEA My friends, I have been waiting for some time,
keeping watch to see where this will lead.
1135 Look now: here comes one of Jason's men

ARISTOPHANES

ca. 450–ca. 385 B.C.E.

COMEDY (a word derived from the Greek *kōmōidia*, "song of the *kōmos*," or band of revelers) officially joined its predecessor, tragedy, as part of the dramatic competitions in Athens in the fifth century B.C.E., first at the City Dionysia (ca. 486) and then at the Lenaea (ca. 442). While scholars estimate that several hundred plays that we now categorize as "Old Comedy" may have been produced at the festivals in the fifth century B.C.E. alone, only eleven relatively complete texts by Aristophanes remain to provide evidence of this important form of classical theater. Aristophanes' track record of success as a dramatist, with at least six first-place and four second-place awards in the competitions, may account in part for the preservation of his comedies across the centuries. Exuding energy and wit, his plays career from the depths of vulgarity to the heights of poetic sophistication. Although in some eras he has been faulted for the inconsistencies in his narratives and the implausibility of his scenarios, Aristophanes more recently has regained critical favor for his nuanced interplay of theme and action. *LYSISTRATA* stands out in this regard and has attracted sustained interest since the early twentieth century for its focus on women's roles at times of war.

Born in a region near Athens, Aristophanes appears to have been a landowner and also a political representative to the Athenian Council of 500, the group that helped establish the government's agenda. Plato's *Symposium* (ca. 384 B.C.E.) depicts Aristophanes as fitting in with the social and intellectual elite of Athens, and his plays certainly reflect familiarity with Attic politics and culture. Aristophanes is believed to have written more than forty plays, the first of which was produced in 427 B.C.E. and the last around 386 B.C.E. These works reflect the comparative freedom of expression granted to the comic playwrights of the era and are known for their pointed political critique, their frank sexuality, and their close engagement with the myths and social conventions of Attic culture. They blend the fantastic and the quotidian, often making the impossible seem plausible—as do the anthropomorphized choruses in *The Birds* (Dionysia, 414) and *The Frogs* (Lenaea, 405).

Produced at the Lenaea in 411, *Lysistrata* dealt directly with recent events in the Peloponnesian War, by then a twenty-year struggle between Athens (and its island and mainland dependencies) and Sparta (and its allies). The war would continue until 404, when the ultimate defeat of Athens' navy led to the end of its empire. This conflict spanned much of Aristophanes' career and recurred thematically in many of his plays. In *Lysistrata*, he was responding specifically to the disastrous loss of the

Athenian fleet in 413 at Sicily and its aftermath, including the appointment by the Athenian government of a board of executive councillors called "Probouloi" who could act quickly and could officially manage the city-state's finances without being subject to the usual democratic process.

With the men of Athens and Sparta at war, Aristophanes depicts the ongoing conflict's impact on the daily lives of others, especially women and the elderly men left in charge of the government. Lysistrata, an Athenian woman, decides that the best way to bring the hostilities to a quick end is for the women to refuse to have sex with the warriors. Calling together the women on both sides of the war, she persuades them to leave their homes and, in the case of the Athenians, to occupy the Acropolis—the main meeting place and market of Athens, as well as the site of the city's treasury. In this way, Lysistrata believes, the women will gain control over both the financial and the human resources integral to the war effort, forcing a declaration of peace and the return to the communities of domestic order, tranquillity, and economic security.

The dramatic structure of *Lysistrata* exemplifies the standard form of Old Comedy. The opening scene, or prologue, introduces us to the central concerns of the play: in this instance, the sex-strike plot for which the work is most remembered. During the entrance (*parados*) of the chorus, Aristophanes chooses to divide the standard group of twenty-four into two halves—twelve old men and twelve old women—whose antagonism contributes both to the humor of the work and to its themes of domestic and political upheaval; moreover, the *parados* sets up the grounds for the debate, or *agōn*, to follow. This rhetorical contest between Lysistrata and the Commissioner of Public Safety, a satiric portrait of one of the Probouloi, reflects the spirit of formal competition that pervaded classical Greek culture; it also enables Aristophanes to expand the scope of the play to incorporate additional social and political issues, including Lysistrata's heartfelt depiction of women's grief at the loss of their sons in war. In such moments, we see that Aristophanes distinguishes his title character from his satiric portraits of other figures, possibly because he modeled

her on Lysimache, priestess of Athena Polias, the most important of such positions in Athenian religious culture. The *parabasis*, or interlude, that follows the *agōn* again showcases the chorus and provides a transition to the series of episodes that will resolve the action. Notable among these is the highly comic scene with the Athenian couple Myrrhine and Kinesias that bawdily demonstrates, through the oversized, erect phallus the latter sports, the effectiveness of the women's deprivation tactics.

At such a great remove from the classical era, audiences and readers today may find both the structure and style of ancient comedy challenging. Moreover, although we have some general knowledge of how these plays were performed, we lack the specific understanding necessary to envision them with historical authenticity. We know, for example, that the plays combined spoken verse, recitative (verse declaimed rhythmically), and song; music and dance also contributed significantly to the overall theatrical effect. Our uncertainty about the exact nature of any of these performative elements has frustrated some interpreters of *Lysistrata*, but others have capitalized on it to create exciting and innovative productions. The absence of stage directions, the corruptions in ancient manuscripts, and lingering doubts about the exact meaning of topical references or allusions all complicate the work of translators and scholars, but they also extend the range of possibilities for contemporary performances.

Despite the gaps in our knowledge about Greek comedy generally and *Lysistrata* specifically, we know enough to recognize that some aspects of the play that seem strange to us would have been considered routine, or at least not unusual, to fifth-century Athenians. First, because the City Dionysia and the Lenaea were both civic and religious festivals, replete with ritual sacrifices to the gods in addition to the theatrical competition, the mingling of religious and political themes in *Lysistrata* not only would have been highly appropriate for the festival context but also would have mirrored the tenor of Athenian daily life. Second, although the frank representation of sexuality, especially the prominence of the phallus, might strike some contemporary

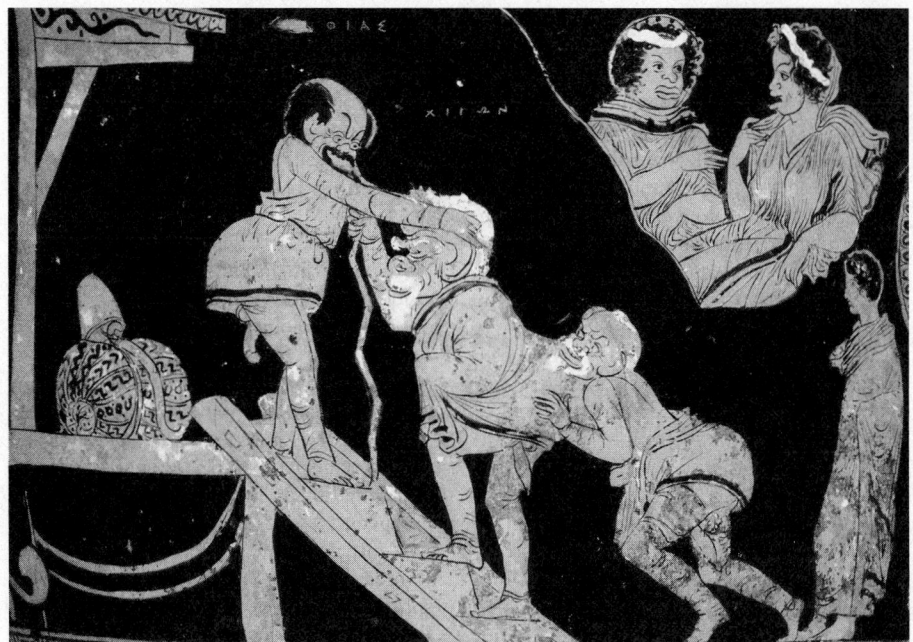

This detail from a painted bell-krater (large wine bowl) dating from the fourth century B.C.E. shows three actors performing in a comedy about the centaur Cheiron.

readers as antithetical to a religious ceremony, it was perfectly in keeping with Greek cultural traditions; such explicitness is even less surprising if we consider that comedy most likely is partly rooted in the rituals of cults that honored the fertility gods Dionysus and Demeter (among other deities). Finally, the play's sexually explicit banter and innuendo would have been matched by equally explicit costumery—not only the phalluses padded to indicate various degrees of erection but also the stuffed bodysuit worn by the character Reconciliation, overemphasizing the proportions of the female anatomy to render them visible to a large outdoor audience. *Lysistrata* thus illustrates vividly how comic writers perceptively capture, often through exaggeration, distinctive cultural practices as well as individuals' foibles.

An awareness of this connection between comedy and its original context is especially important to a clear understanding of the central role of female characters in *Lysistrata*. Although *Lysistrata* is believed to be the first Western comedy featuring a female heroine and incorporating varied images of women's lives and attributes, we

should also remember that this title character and all the other women in the play would have been portrayed by male performers, in a society in which the activities of well-off women were circumscribed and revolved exclusively around the home. Only male citizens participated in public endeavors, and Lysistrata's entry into the public sphere, although appearing potentially realistic to contemporary readers and audiences, should be seen in its Greek context as fantastical—as implausible as choruses of singing and dancing birds and frogs. Thus we should not interpret the play as proto-feminist, or as a critique of the "separate spheres" ideology that informed classical Greek society. Indeed, Lysistrata wants nothing more than to restore the status quo, with all citizens—male and female—returning to their established roles.

The implausibilities and inconsistencies in Aristophanes' dramaturgy have proven alienating to some contemporary readers and audiences, who are more comfortable with the conventions of dramatic realism that have dominated the theater since the nineteenth century. Yet if we can keep in mind that ideas about narrative cohesion and realistic action—our notions of what makes a play "good"—are themselves historical constructs, we may better appreciate Aristophanes' shifts between, for example, the farcical sex-strike plot of the *parados* and the *agōn*'s more serious treatment of financial concerns. Similarly, we might suspend our disbelief at the apparent contradiction between the warriors' absence from home and the women's plan to deny them sex.

More importantly, our openness to these unique qualities of Aristophanic dramaturgy may enable us to discern the metaphors he used to structure his fantasy of women's political intervention. First, the disjunctions in the "logical" flow of dramatic action parallel the war's disruption of civic and family life. The two-pronged strategy proposed by Lysistrata—withholding sex and blocking access to state funds—also helps make evident the foundational elements of marriage: the sexual relationship between husband and wife, and the economic transactions that similarly support the home environment. Lysistrata then works to establish the links between the women's world and the state, describing how domestic management mirrors core elements of governmental practices. Aristophanes further develops these associations through the implied staging, which visually

ties these domestic and civic worlds together. We assume that Lysistrata and her friend Kalonike first encounter each other outside their homes, but soon the central door in the *scaenae frons* (the wooden stage building used for entrances and exits) is also serving as the entrance to the Acropolis. Later, Myrrhine transforms the space just outside the Acropolis into a bedroom, furthering the linkage, and the play concludes with the women's hosting a banquet on the Acropolis to celebrate the peace. Aristophanes' utopian vision of harmony at home and abroad thus shapes a comedy that could at best work to influence the state's future strategies or at least temporarily divert an Athenian audience otherwise consumed by its increasingly grim political prospects.

Centuries later, Aristophanes' concept of women's leading the initiative for peace spurred a group of women actors to launch the *Lysistrata* Project, a global protest against the United States' invasion of Iraq. On March 3, 2003, artists around the world held more than 1,000 public readings of the play in fifty-nine countries to voice their opposition to this military action. That these artists and their audiences saw such relevance in a work almost 2,500 years old expresses volumes about the ongoing power of theater to speak of and to humanity.

—J.E.G.

Lysistrata[1]

CHARACTERS

LYSISTRATA, an Athenian woman
KALONIKE, Lysistrata's friend
MYRRHINE, an Athenian wife
LAMPITO, a Spartan wife
MAGISTRATE, one of the ten Probouloi
OLD WOMEN (three), allies of Lysistrata

WIVES (four), Lysistrata's conspirators
KINESIAS, Myrrhine's husband
BABY, son of Kinesias and Myrrhine
SPARTAN HERALD
SPARTAN AMBASSADOR
ATHENIAN AMBASSADORS (two)

1. Translated by Jeffrey Henderson.

MUTE CHARACTERS

ATHENIAN WOMEN

ISMENIA, a Theban woman

KORINTHIAN WOMAN

SPARTAN WOMEN

SKYTHIAN GIRL, Lysistrata's slave

MAGISTRATE'S SLAVES

SKYTHIAN POLICEMEN

OLD WOMEN, allies of Lysistrata

MANES, Kinesias' slave

SPARTAN DELEGATES

SPARTAN SLAVES, with the
    Spartan delegation

ATHENIAN DELEGATES

RECONCILIATION

DOORKEEPER

CHORUS

OLD ATHENIAN MEN (twelve)

OLD ATHENIAN WOMEN (twelve)

Prologue

[SCENE: *A neighborhood street in Athens, after dawn. The stage-building has a large central door and two smaller, flanking doors. From one of these* LYSISTRATA *emerges and looks expectantly up and down the street.*]

LYSISTRATA   Now if someone had invited the women to a revel for Bacchos, or to Pan's shrine, or to Genetyllis's at Kolias,[2] they'd be jamming the streets with their tambourines. But now there's not a single woman here. [*The far door opens.*] Except for my own neighbor there. Good morning, Kalonike.[3]

5 KALONIKE   You too, Lysistrata.[4] What's bothering you? Don't frown, child. Knitted brows are no good for your looks.

LYSISTRATA   But my heart's on fire, Kalonike, and I'm terribly annoyed about us women. You know, according to the men we're capable of all sorts of mischief—

10 KALONIKE   And that we are, by Zeus![5]

LYSISTRATA   but when they're told to meet here to discuss something that really matters, they're sleeping in and don't show up!

KALONIKE   Honey, they'll be along. For wives to get out of the house is a lot of trouble, you know: we've got to look after the husband or wake up a

15   slave or put the baby to bed, or give it a bath or feed it a snack.

LYSISTRATA   Sure, but there's other business they ought to take more seriously than that stuff.

KALONIKE   Well, Lysistrata dear, what exactly *is* this business you're calling us women together for? What's the deal? Is it a big one?

20 LYSISTRATA   Big!

KALONIKE   Not hard as well?

LYSISTRATA   It's big *and* hard, by Zeus.

KALONIKE   Then how come we're not all here?

LYSISTRATA   That's not what I meant! If it were, we'd all have shown up fast

2. Promontory near Athens where stood a statue of Aphrodite, the goddess of beauty and carnal love. *Bacchos*: also known as Dionysus, the god of wine and fertility. *Pan*: goat-footed god of woods and pastures, often worshipped with Dionysus. *Genetyllis*: pro-

tectress of childbirth (in some accounts, another name for Aphrodite; in others, her companion).

3. A name meaning "beautiful victory."

4. A name meaning "disbander of armies."

5. King of the Greek gods.

25   enough. No, it's something I've been thinking hard *about*, kicking it around,
      night after sleepless night.

      KALONIKE   All those kicks must have made it really smart.

      LYSISTRATA   Smart enough that the salvation of all Greece lies in the women's
      hands!

30   KALONIKE   In the *women's* hands? That's hardly reassuring!

      LYSISTRATA   It's true: our country's future depends on *us*: whether the Pelo-
      ponnesians[6] become extinct—

      KALONIKE   Well, that would be just fine with me, by Zeus!

      LYSISTRATA   and all the Boiotians[7] get annihilated—

35   KALONIKE   Not *all* of them, though: please spare the eels![8]

      LYSISTRATA   I won't say anything like that about the Athenians, but you know
      what I *could* say. But if the women gather together here—the Boiotian
      women, the Peloponnesian women, and ourselves—together we'll be able
      to rescue Greece!

40   KALONIKE   But what can mere *women* do that's intelligent or noble? We sit
      around the house looking pretty, wearing saffron dresses and makeup and
      Kimberic gowns and canoe-sized slippers.

      LYSISTRATA   Exactly! That's exactly what I think will rescue Greece: our fancy
      little dresses, our perfumes and our slippers, our rouge and our see-through
45   underwear!

      KALONIKE   How do you mean? I'm lost.

      LYSISTRATA   They'll guarantee that not a single one of the men who are still
      alive will raise his spear against another—

      KALONIKE   Then, by the Two Goddesses,[9] I'd better get my party dress dyed
50   saffron!

      LYSISTRATA   nor hoist his shield—

      KALONIKE   I'll wear a Kimberic gown!

      LYSISTRATA   nor even pull a knife!

      KALONIKE   I've got to buy some slippers!

55   LYSISTRATA   So shouldn't the women have gotten here by now?

      KALONIKE   By *now*? My god, they should have taken wing and flown here ages ago!

      LYSISTRATA   My friend, you'll see that they're typically Athenian: everything
      they do, they do too late. There isn't even a single woman here from the
      Paralia, nor from Salamis.[1]

60   KALONIKE   Oh, them: I just *know* they've been up since dawn, straddling
      their mounts.

      LYSISTRATA   And the women I reckoned would be here first, and counted on,
      the women from Acharnai,[2] they're not here either.

      KALONIKE   Well, Theogenes' wife, for one, was set to make a fast getaway.
65   [*Groups of women begin to enter from both sides.*] But look, here come some
      of your women now!

6. Inhabitants of Peloponnesos, the peninsula that forms the southern Greek mainland,
with whom Athens was at war; they were led
by Sparta.
7. That is, the Thebans in Boiotia, northwest
of Athens, its other main opponents in the
Peloponnesian War.
8. A delicacy native to Boiotia.
9. Demeter, goddess of agriculture, and her

daughter Persephone or Kore (the Maiden),
queen of the underworld; both were associated with fertility and women.
1. Island in the Aegean Sea near Athens.
Paralia: a district on the coast of Attica, the
region in which Athens is located (literally,
"seacoast").
2. A district near Athens.

LYSISTRATA   And here come some others, over there!

KALONIKE   Phew! Where are *they* from?

LYSISTRATA   From Dungstown.

70 KALONIKE   It seems they've got some sticking to their shoes.

MYRRHINE   I hope we're not too late, Lysistrata. What do you say? Why don't you say something?

LYSISTRATA   Myrrhine,[3] I've got no medal for anyone who shows up late for important business.

75 MYRRHINE   Look, I couldn't find my girdle; it was dark. But now we're here, so tell us what's so important.

LYSISTRATA   No, let's wait a little while, until the women from Boiotia and the Peloponnesos come.

MYRRHINE   That's a much better plan. And look, there's Lampito coming now!

[*Enter* LAMPITO, *accompanied by a group of other Spartan women, a Theban woman* (ISMENIA) *and a Korinthian woman.*]

80 LYSISTRATA   Greetings, my very dear Spartan Lampito! My darling, how dazzling is your beauty! What rosy cheeks, what firmness of physique! You could choke a bull!

LAMPITO   Is true, I think, by Twain Gods. Much exercise, much leaping to harden buttocks.[4]

85 KALONIKE   And what a beautiful pair of boobs you've got!

LAMPITO   Hey, you feel me up like sacrificial ox!

LYSISTRATA   And this other young lady here, where's *she* from?

LAMPITO   By Twain Gods, she come as representative of Boiotia.

MYRRHINE   She's certainly *like* Boiotia, by Zeus, with all her lush bottomland.

90 KALONIKE   Yes indeed, her bush has been most elegantly pruned.

LYSISTRATA   And who's this other girl?

LAMPITO   Lady of substance, by Twain Gods, from Korinth.[5]

KALONIKE   She's substantial all right, both frontside and backside.

LAMPITO   Who convenes this assembly of women here?

95 LYSISTRATA   I'm the one.

LAMPITO   Then please to tell what you want of us.

KALONIKE   That's right, dear lady, speak up. What's this important business of yours?

LYSISTRATA   I'm ready to tell you. But before I tell you, I want to ask you a small question; it won't take long.

100 KALONIKE   Ask away.

LYSISTRATA   Don't you all pine for your children's fathers when they're off at war? I'm sure that every one of you has a husband who's away.

KALONIKE   My husband's been away five months, my dear, at the Thracian front; he's guarding Eukrates.[6]

105 MYRRHINE   And *mine's* been at Pylos[7] *seven* whole months.

---

3. A name meaning "myrtle," which was also a slang term for the vulva.
4. Spartan women, unlike their counterparts in other polities, received an education similar to that of men, including physical training. Throughout, Aristophanes caricatures the Doric dialect of the Spartans, which differed notably from the Attic-Ionic Greek of the Athenians. *Twain Gods*: the twins Kastor and

Pollux, sons of Leda, Zeus, and Tyndareos, king of Sparta, and patrons of the Spartans.
5. A city-state in the northern Peloponnesos; like Sparta and Thebes, a rival of Athens.
6. An Athenian general; Thrace, a region in northeastern Greece, was an ally of Athens, and many battles were fought there during the war.
7. A district in the southern Peloponnesos, occupied by the Athenians since 425 B.C.E.

LAMPITO   And *mine*, soon as he come home from regiment, is strapping on
the shield and flying off.

KALONIKE   Even *lovers* have disappeared without a trace, and ever since the
Milesians[8] revolted from us, I haven't even seen a six-inch dildo, which
110   might have been a consolation, however small.

LYSISTRATA   Well, if I could devise a plan to end the war, would you be ready
to join me?

KALONIKE   By the Two Goddesses, I would, even if I had to pawn this dress
and on the very same day—drink up the proceeds!

115   MYRRHINE   And *I* think I would even cut myself in two like a flounder and
donate half to the cause!

LAMPTIO   And I would climb up to summit of Taÿgeton,[9] if I'm able to see
where peace may be from there.

LYSISTRATA   Here goes then; no need to beat around the bush. Ladies, if
120   we're going to force the men to make peace, we're going to have to give up—

KALONIKE   Give up what? Tell us.

LYSISTRATA   You'll do it, then?

KALONIKE   We'll do it, even if it means our death!

LYSISTRATA   All right. We're going to have to give up—cock. Why are you
125   turning away from me? Where are you going? Why are you all pursing your
lips and shaking your heads? What means thine altered color and tearful
droppings?[1] Will you do it or not? What are you waiting for?

KALONIKE   Count me out; let the war drag on.

MYRRHINE   Me too, by Zeus; let the war drag on.

130   LYSISTRATA   This from you, Ms. Flounder? Weren't you saying just a moment
ago that you'd cut yourself in half?

KALONIKE   Anything else you want, anything at all! I'm even ready to walk
through fire; *that* rather than give up cock. There's nothing like it, Lysistrata dear.

135   LYSISTRATA   And what about you?

WOMAN   I'm ready to walk through fire too.

LYSISTRATA   Oh what a low and horny race are we! No wonder men write
tragedies about us: we're nothing but Poseidon and a bucket.[2] Dear Spartan, if you alone would side with me we might still salvage the plan; give
140   me your vote!

LAMPITO   By Twain Gods, is difficult for females to sleep alone without the
hard-on. But anyway, I assent; is need for peace.

LYSISTRATA   You're an absolute dear, and the only real woman here!

KALONIKE   Well, what if we *did* abstain from, uh, what you say, which heaven
145   forbid: would peace be likelier to come on account of *that*?

LYSISTRATA   Absolutely, by the Two Goddesses. If we sat around at home all
made up, and walked past them wearing only our see-through underwear

---

8. The inhabitants of Miletus, a Greek city-
state on the coast of Asia Minor (present-day
Turkey) that revolted from Athens in 412 B.C.E.
9. A mountain range near Sparta.
1. The elevated language characteristic of
tragedy is here (as often in Greek comedy)

used for comic effect.
2. An allusion to the myth of Tyro; after being
seduced by Poseidon, god of the sea, she gave
birth to twin boys whom she left in a tub by
the edge of a river.

Victory,[9] be our ally, help us win a trophy over the women on the Akropolis
55   and their present audacity!

> [*As the men crouch down to light their torches the second semichorus
> enters on the run. It is composed of twelve old women, nicely dressed and
> carrying pitchers of water on their heads.*]

WOMEN'S LEADER   I think I can see sparks and smoke, fellow women, as if a
fire were ablaze. We must hurry all the faster!

WOMEN (*strophe*)
Fly, fly, Nikodike,
before Kalyke and Kritylla are incinerated,
60   blown from all directions
by nasty winds and old men who mean death!
I'm filled with dread: am I too late to help?
I've just come from the well with my pitcher;
it was hard to fill by the light of dawn,
65   in the throng and crash and clatter of pots,
fighting the elbows of housemaids and branded slaves.
I hoisted it onto my head with zeal, and carry the water here
to assist the women, my fellow citizens faced with burning.

(*antistrophe*)
I've heard that some frantic old men
70   are on the loose with three talents[1] of logs,
like furnace-men at the public bathhouse.
They're coming to the Akropolis, screaming
the direst threats, that they mean to use their fire
"to turn these abominable women into charcoal."
75   Goddess, may I never see these women in flames;
instead let them rescue Greece and her citizens from war and madness!
O golden-crested Guardian of the citadel, that is why
they occupy your shrine. I invite thee to be our ally, Tritogeneia,[2]
defending it with water, should any man set it afire.

80 WOMEN'S LEADER   Hold on! Hey! What's this? Men! Awful, nasty men! No
gentlemen, no god-fearing men would ever be caught doing this!

MEN'S LEADER   This here's a complication we didn't count on facing: this
swarm of women outside the gates is here to help the others!

WOMEN'S LEADER   Fear and trembling, eh? Don't tell me we seem a lot to
85   handle: you haven't even seen the tiniest fraction of our forces yet!

MEN'S LEADER   Phaidrias, are we going to let these women go on jabbering
like this? Why hasn't somebody busted a log over their heads?

WOMEN'S LEADER   Let's ground our pitchers then; if anyone attacks us they
won't get in our way.

90 MEN'S LEADER   By Zeus, if someone had socked them in the mouth a couple
of times, like Boupalos,[3] they wouldn't still be talking!

---

9. Probably a reference to Athena Nike (Victory), whose temple also stood on the
Akropolis.
1. About 175 pounds.

2. An ancient name of Athena.
3. A sculptor (6th c. B.C.E.), born on the
island of Chios, who was subjected to severe
satire and invective by the poet Hipponax.

WOMEN'S LEADER   OK, here's my mouth; someone take a sock at it; I'll stand here and take it. But then I'm the bitch who gets to grab you by the balls!

MEN'S LEADER   If you don't shut up, I'll knock you right out of your old hide!

95   WOMEN'S LEADER   Come over here and just touch Stratyllis with the tip of your finger.

MEN'S LEADER   What if I give you the one-two punch? Got anything scary to counter with?

WOMEN'S LEADER   I'll rip out your lungs and your guts with my fangs.

100   MEN'S LEADER   There isn't a wiser poet than Euripides: no beast exists so shameless as women!

WOMEN'S LEADER   Let's pick up our pitchers of water, Rhodippe.

MEN'S LEADER   Why did you bring water here, you witch?

WOMEN'S LEADER   And why have *you* got fire, you tomb? To burn yourself up?

105   MEN'S LEADER   *I'm* here to build a pyre and burn up your friends.

WOMEN'S LEADER   And *I've* come to put it out with this.

MEN'S LEADER   *You're* going to put out *my* fire?

WOMEN'S LEADER   That's what you soon will see.

MEN'S LEADER   I think I might barbecue you with this torch of mine.

110   WOMEN'S LEADER   Got any soap with you? I'll give you a bath.

MEN'S LEADER   *You* give *me* a bath, you crone?

WOMEN'S LEADER   A bath fit for a bridegroom!

MEN'S LEADER   What insolence!

WOMEN'S LEADER   I'm a free woman!

115   MEN'S LEADER   I'll put a stop to your bellowing.

WOMEN'S LEADER   You're not on a jury now, you know.[4]

MEN'S LEADER   Torch her hair! [*The men advance.*]

WOMEN'S LEADER   Acheloos,[5] do your thing! [*The women douse them.*]

MEN'S LEADER   Oh! Damn!

120   WOMEN'S LEADER   It wasn't too hot, was it?

MEN'S LEADER   Hot? Stop it! What do you think you're doing?

WOMEN'S LEADER   I'm watering you, so you'll bloom.

MEN'S LEADER   But I'm already dried out from shivering!

WOMEN'S LEADER   You've got fire there; why not sit by it and get warm?

Episode[6]

[*Enter the* MAGISTRATE, *an irascible old man, accompanied by two slaves carrying crowbars and four Skythian policemen.*]

MAGISTRATE   So the women's depravity bursts into flame again: beating drums, chanting "Sabazios!", worshiping Adonis on the rooftops.[7] I heard it all once before while sitting in Assembly. Demostratos[8] (bad luck to him!) was moving that we send an armada to Sicily, while his wife was dancing and yelling "Poor young Adonis!" Then Demostratos moved that we sign up

5

---

4. Paid jury duty provided old men with some financial support.
5. A large river in central Greece.
6. In ancient Greek drama, a scene of action between choral sections.
7. The cults of Sabazios and Adonis, which

had come to Athens relatively recently from the east, were especially favored by women.
8. An Athenian orator and proponent of the expedition launched against Syracuse, on the island of Sicily, in 415 B.C.E.; the outcome was a disastrous loss for Athens.

some Zakynthian[9] infantry, but his wife up on the roof was getting drunk and going "Beat your breast for Adonis!" But he just went on making his motions, that godforsaken, disgusting Baron Bluster! From women, I say, you get this kind of riotous extravagance!

10 MEN'S LEADER [*Pointing to the* CHORUS OF WOMEN]   Save your breath till you hear about *their* atrocities! They've committed every kind, even doused us with those pitchers. Now we get to shake water out of our clothes as if we'd peed in them!

MAGISTRATE   By the salty sea-god it serves us right! When we ourselves are
15   accomplices in our wives' misbehavior and teach them profligacy, these are the sort of schemes they bring to flower! Aren't *we* the ones who go to the shops and say stuff like, "Goldsmith, about that necklace you made me: my wife was having a ball the other night, and now the prong's slipped out of its hole. Me, I've got to cruise over to Salamis. So if you've got time, by all means
20   visit her in the evening and fit a prong in her hole." Another husband says this to a teenage shoemaker with a very grown-up cock, "Shoemaker, my wife's pinky-toe hurts. It seems the top-strap is cramping the bottom, where she's tender. So why don't you drop in on her some lunchtime and loosen it up so there's more play down there?" That's the sort of thing that's led to *this*, when
25   I, a Magistrate, have lined up timber for oars and now come to get the necessary funds, and find myself standing at the gate, locked out by women! But I'm not going to stand around. [*To the two slaves*] Bring the crowbars; I'll put a stop to their arrogance. What are *you* gaping at, you sorry fool? And where are *you* staring? I said crowbar, not winebar! Come on, put those crowbars under the gates and start jimmying on that side; I'll help out on this side.

30 LYSISTRATA [*Emerging from the gates*]   Don't jimmy the gates; I'm coming out on my very own. Why do you need crowbars? It's not crowbars you need; it's rather brains and sense.

MAGISTRATE   Really! You witch! Where's a policeman? Grab her and tie both hands behind her back! [*One of the policemen advances on* LYSISTRATA.]

35 LYSISTRATA   If he so much as touches me with his fingertip, by Artemis[1] he'll go home crying, public servant or not! [*The policeman retreats.*]

MAGISTRATE   What, are you scared? [*To a second policeman*] You there, help him out; grab her around the waist and tie her up, on the double!

[*A large* OLD WOMAN *emerges from the gates.*]

FIRST OLD WOMAN   If you so much as lay a hand on her, by Pandrosos[2] I'll
40   beat the shit out of you! [*Both policemen retreat.*]

MAGISTRATE   Beat the shit out of me! Where's another policeman? [*A third policeman steps forward.*] Tie *her* up first, the one with the dirty mouth!

[*A* SECOND OLD WOMAN *emerges from the gates.*]

SECOND OLD WOMAN   If you raise your fingertip to her, by our Lady of Light[3] you'll be begging for an eye-cup! [*The third archer retreats.*]

45 MAGISTRATE   What's going on? Where's a policeman? [*The fourth policeman steps forward.*] Arrest her. I'll foil *one* of these sallies of yours!

[*A* THIRD OLD WOMAN *emerges from the gates.*]

9. From Zakynthos, an island in the Ionian Sea (west of the Peloponnesos) allied to Athens.
1. Virgin goddess of the hunt and the wilds, twin sister of Apollo; she also brings release

to women in childbirth.
2. Daughter of the legendary first king of Athens; she was worshipped on the Akropolis.
3. Hekate, goddess of the moon and childbirth.

THIRD OLD WOMAN   If you come near her, by Eastern Artemis[4] I'll rip out your
hair till it screams! [*The fourth policeman retreats.*]

MAGISTRATE   What a terrible setback! I'm out of policemen. But men must
50 never, ever be worsted by women! Skythians, let's charge them *en masse*;
form up ranks!

[*The four policemen prepare to charge.*]

LYSISTRATA   By the Two Goddesses, you'll soon discover that we also have
four squadrons of fully armed combat-women, waiting inside!

MAGISTRATE   Skythians, twist their arms behind their backs!

[*The policemen advance.*]

55 LYSISTRATA [*Calling into the Akropolis like a military commander*]   Women of
the reserve, come out double-time! Forward, you spawn of the marketplace, you soup and vegetable mongers! Forward, you landladies, you
hawkers of garlic and bread! [*Four squadrons of tough old market-women
rush out of the Akropolis and, together with the women already onstage,
attack the four policemen.*] Tackle them! Hit them! Smash them! Call them
60 names, the nastier the better! [*The policemen run away howling.*] That's
enough! Withdraw! Don't strip the bodies!

[*The women of the reserve go back into the Akropolis.*]

MAGISTRATE   Terrible! What a calamity for my men!

LYSISTRATA   Well, what did you expect? Did you think you were going up
against a bunch of slave-girls? Or did you think women lack gall?

65 MAGISTRATE   They've got it aplenty, by Apollo, provided there's a wineshop
nearby.

MEN'S LEADER   You've little to show for all your talk, Magistrate of this country! What's the point of fighting a battle of words with these beasts? Don't
you comprehend the kind of bath they've given us just now—when we were
70 still in our clothes, and without soap to boot?

WOMEN'S LEADER   Well, sir, you shouldn't lift your hand against your neighbors just anytime you feel like it. If you do, you're going to end up with a
black eye. I'd rather be sitting at home like a virtuous maiden, making no
trouble for anyone here, stirring not a single blade of grass. But if anyone
75 annoys me and rifles my nest, they'll find a wasp inside!

Onstage Debate

MEN (*strophe*)
Zeus, how in the world are we going to deal with these monsters?
They've gone beyond what I can bear! Now it's time for a trial:
together let's find out
what they thought they were doing
5 when they occupied Kranaos'[5] citadel
and the great crag of the Akropolis,
a restricted, holy place.

MEN'S LEADER   Question her and don't give in; cross-examine what she says.
It's scandalous to let this sort of behavior go unchallenged.

---

4. Artemis was worshipped throughout the
Greek world. To the east, in Tauris (the
present-day Crimean Peninsula), that worship involved orgiastic rites.
5. A mythical king of Athens.

10 MAGISTRATE   Here's the first thing I'd like to know, by Zeus: what do you
      mean by barricading our Akropolis?

    LYSISTRATA   To keep the money safe and to keep *you* from using it to finance
      the war.

    MAGISTRATE   So we're at war on account of the money?

15 LYSISTRATA   Yes, and the money's why everything else got messed up too.
      Peisandros[6] and the others aiming to hold office were always fomenting
      some kind of commotion so that they'd be able to steal it. So let them keep
      fomenting to their hearts' content: they'll be withdrawing no more money
      from *this* place.

20 MAGISTRATE   But what do you plan to do?

    LYSISTRATA   Don't you see? We'll manage it for you!

    MAGISTRATE   *You'll* manage the money?

    LYSISTRATA   What's so strange in that? Don't we manage the household finances
      for you already?

25 MAGISTRATE   That's different!

    LYSISTRATA   How so?

    MAGISTRATE   These are *war* funds!

    LYSISTRATA   But there shouldn't even *be* a war.

    MAGISTRATE   How else are we to protect ourselves?

30 LYSISTRATA   We'll protect you.

    MAGISTRATE   *You?*

    LYSISTRATA   Yes, us.

    MAGISTRATE   What brass!

    LYSISTRATA   You'll be protected whether you like it or not!

35 MAGISTRATE   You're going too far!

    LYSISTRATA   Angry, are you? We've got to do it anyway.

    MAGISTRATE   By Demeter, you've got no right!

    LYSISTRATA   You must be saved, dear fellow.

    MAGISTRATE   Even if I don't ask to be?

40 LYSISTRATA   All the more so!

    MAGISTRATE   And where do *you* get off taking an interest in war and peace?

    LYSISTRATA   We'll tell you.

    MAGISTRATE   Well, make it snappy, unless you want to get hurt.

    LYSISTRATA   Listen then, and try to control your fists.

45 MAGISTRATE   I can't; I'm so angry I can't keep my hands to myself.

    FIRST OLD WOMAN   Then *you're* the one'll get hurt!

    MAGISTRATE   Croak those curses at yourself, old bag! [*To* LYSISTRATA] Start
      talking.

    LYSISTRATA   Gladly. All along, being proper women, we used to suffer in
50   silence no matter what you men did, because you wouldn't let us make a
      sound. But you weren't exactly all we could ask for. No, we knew only too
      well what you were up to, and too many times we'd hear in our homes
      about a bad decision you'd made on some great issue of state. Then, mask-
      ing the pain in our hearts, we'd put on a smile and ask you, "How did the
55   Assembly go today? Any decision about a rider to the peace treaty?" And my
      husband would say, "What's that to you? Shut up!" And I'd shut up.

6. Athenian politician, often attacked in comedy for corruption. Soon after the first performance of *Lysistrata*, Peisandros joined an
oligarchic faction that seized power, with
widespread violence and confiscations (by
410 B.C.E., democracy was restored).

FIRST OLD WOMAN *I* wouldn't have shut up!

MAGISTRATE If you hadn't shut up you'd have got a beating!

LYSISTRATA Well, that's why I *did* shut up. Later on we began to hear about
60 even worse decisions you'd made, and then we would ask, "Husband, how
come you're handling this so stupidly?" And right away he'd glare at me and
tell me to get back to my sewing if I didn't want major damage to my head:
"War shall be the business of menfolk,"[7] unquote.

MAGISTRATE He was right on the mark, by Zeus.

65 LYSISTRATA How could he be right, you sorry fool, when we were forbidden
to offer advice even when your policy was *wrong?* But *then*—when we began
to hear you in the streets openly crying, "There isn't a man left in the land,"
and someone else saying, "No, by Zeus, not a one"—after *that* we women
decided to lose no more time and to band together to save Greece. What
70 was the point of waiting any longer? So, if you're ready to take your turn at
listening, we have some good advice, and if you shut up, as we used to, we
can put you back on the right track.

MAGISTRATE *You* put *us*—outrageous! I won't stand for it!

LYSISTRATA Shut up!

75 MAGISTRATE *Me* shut up for *you?* A damned woman, with a veil on your face
too?[8] I'd rather die!

LYSISTRATA If the veil's an obstacle, here, take mine, it's yours, put it on *your* face
[*She removes her veil and puts it on the* MAGISTRATE'S *head*], and *then* shut up!

FIRST OLD WOMAN And take this sewing-basket too.

80 LYSISTRATA Now hitch up your clothes and start sewing; chew some beans[9]
while you work. War shall be the business of womenfolk!

WOMEN'S LEADER Come away from your pitchers, women: it's our turn to
pitch in with a little help for our friends!

WOMEN (*antistrophe*)
Oh yes! I'll dance with unflagging energy;
85 the effort won't weary my knees.
I'm ready to face anything
with women courageous as these:
they've got character, charm and guts,
they've got intelligence and heart
90 that's both patriotic and smart!

WOMEN'S LEADER Now, most valiant of prickly mommies and spikey gran-
nies, attack furiously and don't let up: you're still running with the wind!

LYSISTRATA If Eros of the sweet soul and Cyprian Aphrodite imbue our thighs
and breasts with desire, and infect the men with sensuous rigidity and club-
95 cock, then I believe all Greece will one day call us Disbanders of Battles.[1]

MAGISTRATE What's your plan?

LYSISTRATA First of all, we can stop people going to the market fully armed
and acting crazy.

---

7. Words spoken by Hector to his wife, Andromache, in the *Iliad* (6.492).
8. Respectable women wore veils in public.
9. The ancient equivalent of gum chewing.
1. In Greek, *Lusimachas*, an allusion to Lysi-mache (literally, "Battle Settler"), then priest-ess of Athena in Athens; possibly also a pun

on the title character's name. *Eros:* son of Aphrodite and, like his mother, a deity of carnal love. *Cyprian:* of Cyprus, the island onto which the newly born Aphrodite emerged from the sea and an important center of her cult.

FIRST OLD WOMAN   Paphian[2] Aphrodite be praised!

100 LYSISTRATA   At this very moment, all around the market, in the pottery shops
and the grocery stalls, they're walking around in arms like Korybantes![3]

MAGISTRATE   By Zeus, a man's got to act like a man!

LYSISTRATA   But it's totally ridiculous when he takes a shield with a Gorgon-
blazon[4] to buy sardines!

105 FIRST OLD WOMAN   Yes, by Zeus, I saw a long-haired fellow,[5] a cavalry captain, on
horseback, getting porridge from an old women and sticking it into his brass
hat. Another one, a Thracian, was shaking his shield and spear like Tereus;[6]
he scared the fig-lady out of her wits and gulped down all the ripe ones!

110 MAGISTRATE   So how will you women be able to put a stop to such a complicated international mess, and sort it all out?

LYSISTRATA   Very easily.

MAGISTRATE   How? Show me.

[LYSISTRATA uses the contents of the basket which the MAGISTRATE was
given to illustrate her demonstration.]

LYSISTRATA   It's rather like a ball of yarn when it gets tangled up. We hold it
this way, and carefully wind out the strands on our spindles, now this way,
115 now that way. That's how we'll wind up this war, if allowed, unsnarling it by
sending embassies, now this way, now that way.

MAGISTRATE   You really think your way with wool and yarnballs and spindles
can stop a terrible crisis? How brainless!

LYSISTRATA   I do think so, and if *you* had any brains you'd handle *all* the polis'
120 business the way we handle our wool!

MAGISTRATE   Well, how then? I'm all ears.

LYSISTRATA   Imagine the polis as fleece just shorn. First, put it in a bath and
wash out all the sheep-dung; spread it on a pallet and beat out the riff-raff
with a stick and pluck out the thorns; as for those who clump and knot them-
125 selves together to snag government positions, card them out and pluck off
their heads. Next, card the wool into a basket of unity and goodwill, mixing
in everyone. The resident aliens and any other foreigner who's your friend,
and anyone who owes money to the people's treasury, mix them in there too.
And by Zeus, don't forget the cities that are colonies of this land: they're like
130 flocks of your fleece, each one separated from the others. So take all these
flocks and bring them together here, joining them all and making one big
bobbin. And from this weave a fine new cloak for the people!

MAGISTRATE   Isn't it awful how these women go like this with their sticks and
like this with their bobbins, when they share none of the war's burdens!

135 LYSISTRATA   None? You monster! We bear more than our fair share, first of all
by giving birth to sons and sending them off to the army—

MAGISTRATE   Enough of that! Let's not open old wounds.

2. Of Paphos, a city on Cyprus that was the
site of a famous temple of Aphrodite.

3. Eastern worshippers of the Phrygian goddess Cybele, known for ecstatic dancing.

4. Emblem depicting one of the three snake-
haired sisters (common on warriors' shields);
the sight of a Gorgon turned all who looked
at her to stone.

5. That is, a Spartan; Spartan men traditionally wore their hair long.

6. A mythical Thracian king whose story was
told in a tragedy by Sophocles. He raped his
sister-in-law Philomela and cut out her
tongue, but his wife, Prokne, still learned of
the deed and fed him their own son in
revenge. All three were turned into birds.

LYSISTRATA   Then, when we ought to be having fun and enjoying our bloom of
youth, we sleep alone because of the campaigns. And to say no more about
140   *our* case, it pains me to think of the maidens growing old in their rooms.
MAGISTRATE   Men grow old too, don't they?
LYSISTRATA   That's quite a different story. When a man comes home he can
quickly find a girl to marry, even if he's a greybeard. But a woman's prime is
brief; if she doesn't seize it no one wants to marry her, and she sits at home
145   looking for good omens.
MAGISTRATE   But any man who can still get a hard-on—
LYSISTRATA   Why don't you just drop dead? Here's a grave-site; buy a coffin;
I'll start kneading you a honeycake.[7] [*Taking off her garland*] Use these as a
wreath.
FIRST OLD WOMAN [*Handing him ribbons*]   You can have these from me.
150   SECOND OLD WOMAN   And this garland from me.
LYSISTRATA   All set? Need anything else? Get on the boat, then. Charon[8] is
calling your name and you're holding him up!
MAGISTRATE   Isn't it shocking that I'm being treated like this? By Zeus, I'm
going straight to the other magistrates to display myself just as I am![9]
155   LYSISTRATA [*As* MAGISTRATE *exits with his slaves*]   I hope you won't complain
about the funeral we gave you. I tell you what: the day after tomorrow, first
thing in the morning, we'll perform the third-day offerings at your grave!
[*The women exit into the Akropolis.*]

Choral Debate

MEN'S LEADER   No free man should be asleep now! Let's strip for action,
men, and meet this emergency! [*The men remove their jackets.*]
MEN (*strophe a*)
   I think I smell much bigger trouble in this
   a definite whiff of Hippias[1] tyranny!
5   I'm terrified that certain men from Sparta
   have gathered at the house of Kleisthenes[2]
   and scheme to stir up our godforsaken women
   to seize the Treasury and my jury-pay,
   my very livelihood.
10   MEN'S LEADER   It's shocking, you know, that they're lecturing the citizens now,
and running their mouths—mere women!—about brazen shields. And to top
it all off they're trying to make peace between us and the men of Sparta, who
are no more trustworthy than a starving wolf. Actually, this plot they weave
against us, gentlemen, aims at tyranny! Well, they'll never tyrannize over *me*:
15   from now on I'll be on my guard, I'll "carry my sword in a myrtle-branch" and
go to market fully armed right up beside Aristogeiton.[3] I'll stand beside him
like this [*assuming the posture of Aristogeiton's statue*]: that way I'll be ready to

---

7. Traditionally given to the dead as an offering to Cerberus, the three-headed dog that
guarded the entrance to the underworld.
8. The boatman who ferried dead souls across
the river Styx to the underworld.
9. That is, dressed as both a woman and a
corpse.
1. A tyrant expelled from Athens in 510 B.C.E.,

with the help of the Spartan king Kleomenes.
2. A contemporary of Aristophanes, frequently ridiculed in his plays as effeminate.
3. One of the assassins of Hipparchos (d. 514
B.C.E.), brother of Hippias; their statues
stood in the Agora, or marketplace. The Men's
Leader quotes a popular drinking song celebrating this killing.

smack this godforsaken old hag right in the jaw! [*He advances on the* WOM-
EN'S LEADER *with fist raised.*]

WOMEN'S LEADER   Just try it, and your own mommy won't recognize you
20   when you get home! Come on, fellow hags, let's start by putting *our* jackets
on the ground. [*The women remove their jackets.*]

WOMEN (*antistrophe a*)
    Citizens of Athens, we want to start
    by offering the polis some good advice,
    and rightly, for she raised me in splendid luxury.
25   As soon as I turned seven I was an Arrephoros;
    then I was a Grinder; when I was ten I shed
    my saffron robe for the Foundress at the Brauronia.
    And once, when I was a beautiful girl, I carried the Basket,
    wearing a necklace of dried figs.[4]

30 WOMEN'S LEADER   Thus I *owe* it to the polis to offer some good advice. And
even if I *was* born a woman, don't hold it against me if I manage to suggest
something better than what we've got now. I have a stake in our community: my contribution is *men*. You miserable geezers have *no* stake, since
you've squandered your paternal inheritance, won in the Persian Wars,[5]
35   and now pay no taxes in return. On the contrary, we're all headed for bankruptcy on account of you! Have you anything to grunt in rebuttal? Any
more trouble from you and I'll clobber you with this rawhide boot right in
the jaw! [*She raises her foot at the Men's Leader.*]

MEN (*strophe b*)
    This behavior of theirs amounts to extreme hubris,
40   and I do believe it's getting aggravated.
    No man with any balls can let it pass.

MEN'S LEADER   Let's doff our shirts, 'cause a man's gotta smell like a man
from the word go and shouldn't be all wrapped up like souvlaki.
        [*The men remove their shirts.*]

MEN   Come on, Whitefeet!
45   We went against Leipsydrion[6]
    when we still were something;
    now we've got to rejuvenate, grow wings
    all over, shake off these old skins of ours!

MEN'S LEADER   If any man among us gives these women the tiniest thing to
50   grab on to, there's no limit to what their nimble hands will do. Why, they'll
even be building frigates and launching naval attacks, cruising against us
like Artemisia.[7] And if they turn to horsemanship, you can scratch our cavalry: there's nothing like a woman when it comes to mounting and riding;
even riding hard she won't slip off. Just look at the Amazons in Mikon's[8]
55   painting, riding chargers in battle against men. Our duty is clear: grab each

4. A symbol of fertility. The women list the religious duties of upper-class Athenian girls, serving Athena and, in the case of the Brauronia, honoring Artemis.
5. The conclusion of the wars with Persia by 448 B.C.E. left Athens in control of an empire, from which it exacted tribute.
6. A stronghold in northern Attica, used by those who sought unsuccessfully to over-

throw the tyrant Hippias in 513 B.C.E.
7. Ruler of Caria (in present-day Turkey), an ally of the Persians; she led five ships against the Greeks at Salamis in 480 B.C.E.
8. Athenian sculptor and painter (5th c. B.C.E.); his frescoes included one in the temple of Theseus that represented Athenians fighting Amazons, a nation of warrior women believed to live on the southeastern shore of the Black Sea.

woman's neck and lock it in the wooden stocks! [*He moves toward the* WOMEN'S LEADER.]

WOMEN (*antistrophe b*)
By the Two Goddesses, if you fire me up
I'll come at you like a wild sow and clip you bare,
and this very day you'll go bleating to your friends for help!

60 WOMEN'S LEADER   Quickly, women, let's also take off our tunics; a woman's gotta smell like a woman, mad enough to bite! [*The women remove their shirts.*]

WOMEN   All right now, someone attack me!
He'll eat no more garlic
and chew no more beans.
65 If you so much as curse at me, I boil over with such rage,
I'll be the beetle-midwife to your eagle's eggs.[9]

WOMEN'S LEADER   You men don't worry me a bit, not while my Lampito's around and my Ismenia, the noble Theban girl. You'll have no power to do anything about us, not even if you pass seven decrees: that's how much every 70 one hates you, you good-for-nothing, and especially our neighbors. Why, just yesterday I threw a party for the girls in honor of Hekate, and I invited my friend from next door, a fine girl who's very special to me: an eel from Boiotia. But they said she couldn't come because of *your* decrees. And you'll *never* stop passing these decrees until someone grabs you by the leg and throws you 75 away and breaks your neck! [*She makes a grab for the* MEN'S LEADER'*s leg.*]

Episode

[LYSISTRATA *comes out of the Akropolis and begins to pace.*]

WOMEN'S LEADER
O mistress of this venture and strategem,
why com'st thou from thy halls so dour of mien?

LYSISTRATA
The deeds of ignoble women and the female heart
do make me pace dispirited to and fro.

WOMEN'S LEADER
5 What say'st thou? What say'st thou?

LYSISTRATA
'Tis true, too true!

WOMEN'S LEADER
What dire thing? Pray tell it to thy friends.

LYSISTRATA
'Twere shame to say and grief to leave unsaid.

WOMEN'S LEADER
Hide not from me the damage we have taken.

LYSISTRATA
10 The story in briefest compass: we need to fuck!

WOMEN'S LEADER
Ah, Zeus!

LYSISTRATA
Why rend the air for Zeus? You see our plight.

---

9. That is, testicles. In a fable by Aesop, a dung beetle avenges itself on an eagle by repeatedly breaking the bird's eggs.

The truth is, I can't keep the wives away from their husbands any longer;
they're running off in all directions. The first one I caught was over there
15   by Pan's Grotto,[1] digging at her hole, and another was trying to escape by
clambering down a pulley-cable. And yesterday another one mounted a
sparrow and was about to fly off to Orsilochos' house when I pulled her off
by her hair. They're coming up with every kind of excuse to go home. [*A
wife comes out of the Akropolis, looks around, and begins to run offstage.*]
Hey you! What's your hurry?
20   FIRST WIFE   I want to go home. I've got some Milesian wool in the house,
and the moths are chomping it all up.
LYSISTRATA   Moths! Get back inside.
FIRST WIFE   By the Two Goddesses, I'll be right back; just let me spread it on
the bed!
25   LYSISTRATA   You won't be spreading anything, nor be going anywhere.
FIRST WIFE   So I'm supposed to let my wool go to waste?
LYSISTRATA   If that's what it takes. [*As the first wife walks back toward*
LYSISTRATA *a second runs out of the Akropolis.*]
SECOND WIFE   Oh my god, my god, the flax! I forgot to shuck it when I left
the house!
30   LYSISTRATA   Here's another one off to shuck her flax. March right back here.
SECOND WIFE   By our Lady of Light, I'll be back in a flash; just let me do a
little shucking.
LYSISTRATA   No! No shucking! If *you* start doing it, some other wife will want
to do the same. [*While the second wife walks back toward* LYSISTRATA *a third
runs out of the Akropolis, holding her bulging belly.*]
35   THIRD WIFE   O Lady of Childbirth, hold back the baby till I can get to a more
profane spot![2]
LYSISTRATA   What are you raving about?
THIRD WIFE   I'm about to deliver a child!
LYSISTRATA   But you weren't pregnant yesterday.
40   THIRD WIFE   But today I am. Please, Lysistrata, send me home to the midwife, and right away!
LYSISTRATA   What's the story? [*She feels the wife's belly.*] What's this? It's hard.
THIRD WIFE   It's a boy.
LYSISTRATA [*Knocking on it*]   By Aphrodite, it's obvious you've got something
45   metallic and hollow in there. Let's have a look. [*She lifts up the wife's dress,
exposing a large bronze helmet.*] Ridiculous girl! You're big with the sacred
helmet, not with child!
THIRD WIFE   But I *am* with child, by Zeus!
LYSISTRATA   Then what were you doing with this?
50   THIRD WIFE   Well, if I began to deliver here in the citadel, I could get into the
helmet and have my baby there, like a pigeon.
LYSISTRATA   What kind of story is that? Excuses! It's obvious what's going on.
You'll have to stay here till your—helmet has its naming-day.
THIRD WIFE   But I can't even *sleep* on the Akropolis, ever since I saw the
55   snake[3] that guards the temple.

1. A cave on the Akropolis containing a shrine
to Pan, goat-footed god of woods, pastures,
and wild places.
2. Sacred locations such as the Akropolis

would be polluted by birth or death.
3. The snake sacred to Athena, believed to
live in the foundations of the Erechtheum,
had never been seen.

FOURTH WIFE   And what about poor me—listening to the owls[4] go *woo woo* all night is killing me!

LYSISTRATA   You nutty girls, enough of your horror stories! I guess you do miss your husbands; but do you think they don't miss *you?* They're spending
60   some very rough nights, I assure you. Just be patient, good ladies, and put up with this, just a little bit longer. There's an oracle predicting victory for us, *if* we stick together. Here's the oracle right here. [*She produces a scroll.*]

THIRD WIFE   Tell us what it says.

LYSISTRATA   Be quiet, then.
65   Yea, when the swallows hole up in a single home,
       fleeing the hoopoes[5] and leaving the penis alone,
       then are their problems solved, what's high is low:
       so says high-thundering Zeus—

THIRD WIFE   You mean *we'll* be lying on top?

70 LYSISTRATA   But:
       if the swallows begin to argue and fly away
       down from the citadel holy, all will say,
       no bird more disgustingly horny lives today!

THIRD WIFE   A pretty explicit oracle. Ye gods!

75 LYSISTRATA   So let's hear no more talk of caving in. Let's go inside. Dear comrades, it would be a real shame if we betray the oracle. [*All enter the Akropolis.*]

Choral Songs

MEN (*strophe*)
       I want to tell you all a tale
       that once I heard when but a lad.
       In olden times there lived a young man,
       his name was Melanion.[6]
5   He fled from marriage until
       he got to the wilderness.
       And he lived in the mountains
       and he had a dog,
       and he wove traps and hunted rabbits,
10   but never went home again
       because of his hatred.
       That's how much *he* loathed women.
       And, being wise, *we* loathe them just
       as much as Melanion did.

15 MEN'S LEADER   How about a kiss, old bag?

WOMEN'S LEADER   Try it, and you've eaten your last onion!

MEN'S LEADER   How about I haul off and kick you? [*He kicks up his leg.*]

WOMEN'S LEADER [*Laughing*]   That's quite a bush you've got down there!

MEN'S LEADER   Well, Myronides too was rough down there,
20   and hairy-assed to all his enemies;
       so too was Phormion.[7]

---

4. Birds sacred to Athena.
5. The bird into which Tereus was transformed, known for its erectile crest.
6. In the myth featuring Melanion, the young man wins and marries Atalanta through a

trick; she is the one fleeing marriage, having sworn to accept only the man who could defeat her in a footrace.
7. A successful Athenian general, as was Myronides (both 5th c. B.C.E.).

WOMEN (*antistrophe*)
    I also want to tell you all a tale,
    a reply to your Melanion.
    There once was a drifter named Timon,
25 who fenced himself off with impregnable thorns,
    as implacable as a Fury.[8]
    So this Timon too
    left home because of his hatred
    <and lived in the mountains,>[9]
30 constantly cursing and railing
    against the wickedness of men.
    That's how much *he* loathed *you*,
    wicked men, ever and always.
    But he was a dear friend to women.
35 WOMEN'S LEADER   How would you like a punch in the mouth?
    MEN'S LEADER   No way! You're really scaring me!
    WOMEN'S LEADER   Then how about a good swift kick?
    MEN'S LEADER   If you do you'll be flashing your twat!
    WOMEN'S LEADER   Even so you'll never see
40 any hair down there on me:
    I may be getting antiquated
    but I keep myself well depilated.

> [*The* WOMEN'S CHORUS *picks up their and the men's discarded clothing and both semichoruses withdraw from the center of the orchestra to sit along its edges; during the ensuing episode the women put their clothing back on.*]

Episode

[LYSISTRATA *appears on the roof of the stage-building, which represents the Akropolis ramparts, and walks to and fro, looking carefully in all directions; suddenly she stops and peers into the distance.*]

LYSISTRATA   All right! Yes! Ladies, come here, quick!

[MYRRHINE *and several other wives join* LYSISTRATA.]

WIFE   What is it? What's all the shouting?

LYSISTRATA   A man! I see a man coming this way, stricken, in the grip of Aphrodite's mysterious powers. Lady Aphrodite, mistress of Cyprus and
5   Kythera[1] and Paphos, make thy journey straight and upright!

WIFE   Where is he, whoever he is?

LYSISTRATA   He's by Chloe's[2] shrine.

WIFE   By Zeus, I see him now! But who is he?

LYSISTRATA   Take a good look. Anyone recognize him?

10 MYRRHINE   Oh God, I do. He's my own husband Kinesias![3]

---

8. One of the Eumenides, monstrous female personifications of vengeance. *Timon:* a legendary misanthrope, depicted by Shakespeare in *Timon of Athens* (1607–8); nowhere else is he portrayed as a friend to women (see line 34, below).
9. The words inside angled brackets are supplied by the translator for a line missing in the Greek text.

1. The island, off the southern tip of the Peloponnesos, near which Aphrodite was born in the sea foam.
2. An epithet of the goddess Demeter (literally, "Verdant").
3. Common Greek name; in this play, also a sexual pun on the Greek verb *kinein*, "to move, to arouse."

LYSISTRATA All right, it's your job to roast him, to torture him, to bamboozle him, to love him and not to love him, and to give him anything he wants—except what you swore over the bowl not to.

MYRRHINE Don't you worry, I'll do it!

15 LYSISTRATA Great! I'll stick around here and help you bamboozle him and roast him. Now everyone get out of sight!

[All the wives go back inside except LYSISTRATA. Enter KINESIAS, wearing a huge erect phallus and accompanied by a male slave holding a baby. He is in obvious pain.]

KINESIAS [To himself] Oh, oh, evil fate! I've got terrible spasms and cramps. It's like I'm being broken on the rack!

LYSISTRATA [Leaning down from the ramparts] Who's that who's standing up
20 within our defense perimeter?

KINESIAS Me.

LYSISTRATA A man?

KINESIAS [Brandishing his phallus] Of course a man!

LYSISTRATA In that case please depart.

25 KINESIAS And who are you to throw me out?

LYSISTRATA The daytime guard.

KINESIAS Then in the gods' name call Myrrhine out here to me.

LYSISTRATA Listen to him, "call Myrrhine"! And who might you be?

KINESIAS Her husband, Kinesias, from Paionidai.[4]

30 LYSISTRATA Well, hello, dear chum! Among us your name is hardly unknown or without celebrity. Your wife always has you on her lips; she'll be eating an egg or an apple and she'll say, "This one's for Kinesias."

KINESIAS Oh gods!

LYSISTRATA Yes, by Aphrodite. And whenever the conversation turns to men,
35 your wife speaks up forthwith and says, "Compared to Kinesias, everything else is trash!"

KINESIAS Come on now, call her out!

LYSISTRATA Well? Got anything for me?

KINESIAS [Indicating his phallus] Indeed I do, if you want it. [LYSISTRATA
40 looks away.] What about this? [He tosses her a purse.] It's all I've got, and you're welcome to it.

LYSISTRATA OK then, I'll go in and call her for you. [She leaves the ramparts.]

KINESIAS Make it quick, now! [Alone] I've had no joy or pleasure in my life since the day Myrrhine left the house. I go into the house and feel agony;
45 everything looks empty to me; I get no pleasure from the food I eat. Because I'm horny!

MYRRHINE [Still out of sight, speaking to LYSISTRATA] I love that man, I love him! But he doesn't want my love. Please don't make me go out to him!

KINESIAS Myrrhinikins, dearest, why are you doing this? Get down here!

50 MYRRHINE [Appearing at the ramparts] By Zeus I'm not going down there!

KINESIAS You won't come down even when I ask you, Myrrhine?

MYRRHINE You're asking me, but you don't want me at all.

KINESIAS Me not want you? Why, I'm desolate!

MYRRHINE I'm leaving.

4. A deme or village in Attica.

55 KINESIAS   No, wait! At least listen to the baby! [*He grabs the baby from the*
       slave and holds it up towards MYRRHINE.] Come on you, yell for mommy!
    BABY   Mommy! Mommy! Mommy!
    KINESIAS [*To* MYRRHINE]   Hey, what's wrong with you? Don't you feel sorry
       for the baby, unwashed and unsuckled for six days now?
60 MYRRHINE   *Him* I feel sorry for. Too bad his *father* doesn't care about him!
    KINESIAS: Get down here, you screwy woman, and see to your child!
    MYRRHINE   How momentous is motherhood! I've got no choice but to go
       down there. [*She leaves the ramparts.* KINESIAS *returns the baby to the slave.*]
    KINESIAS   <Absence really does make the heart grow fonder!> She seems much
65   younger than I remember, and she has a sexier look in her eyes. She acted
       prickly and very stuck-up too, but that just makes me want her even more!

            [MYRRHINE *enters from the Akropolis gates and goes over to the baby,*
            ignoring KINESIAS.]

    MYRRHINE   Poor sweetie pie, with such a lousy father, let me give you a kiss,
       mommy's little dearest!
    KINESIAS [*To* MYRRHINE's *back*]   What do you think you're doing, you naughty
70   girl, listening to those other women and giving me a hard time and hurting
       yourself as well? [*He puts a hand on her shoulder.*]
    MYRRHINE [*Wheeling around*]   Don't you lay your hands on me!
    KINESIAS   You know you've let our house, your things and mine, become an
       utter mess?
75 MYRRHINE   It doesn't bother me.
    KINESIAS   It doesn't bother you that the hens are pulling your woollens apart?
    MYRRHINE   Not a bit.
    KINESIAS   And what a long time it's been since you've celebrated Aphrodite's
       holy mysteries.[5] Won't you come home?
80 MYRRHINE   Not me, by Zeus; I'm going nowhere until you men agree to a
       settlement and stop the war.
    KINESIAS   Well, if that's what's decided, then that's what we'll do.
    MYRRHINE   Well, if that's what's decided, I'll be going home. But for the time
       being I've sworn to stay here.
85 KINESIAS   But at least lie down here with me; it's been so long.
    MYRRHINE   No way. But I'm not saying I don't love you.
    KINESIAS   Love me? So why won't you lie down, Myrrhine?
    MYRRHINE   Right here in front of the baby? You must be joking!
    KINESIAS   Zeus no! Boy, take him home. [*Exit slave.*] There you are, the kid's
90   out of our way. Now, why don't you just lie down?
    MYRRHINE   Lie down *where,* you silly man?
    KINESIAS [*Looking around*]   Where? Pan's Grotto will do fine.
    MYRRHINE   But I need to be pure before I can go back up to the Akropolis.
    KINESIAS   Very easily done: just wash off in the Klepsydra.[6]
95 MYRRHINE   You're telling me, dear, that I should go back on the oath I swore?
    KINESIAS   Don't worry about any oath; let me take the consequences.
    MYRRHINE   All right then, I'll get us a bed.
    KINESIAS   No, don't; the ground's OK for us.

---

5. That is, had sexual intercourse.   6. A spring on the slope of the Akropolis.

MYRRHINE Apollo no! I wouldn't dream of letting you lie on the ground, no
100   matter what kind of man you are. [MYRRHINE *goes into one of the flanking*
       doors, which represents Pan's Grotto.]
       KINESIAS She really loves me, that's quite obvious!
       MYRRHINE [*Returning with a cot*] There you are! Lie right down while I
       undress. [KINESIAS *lies on the cot.*] But wait, I forgot, what is it, yes, a mat-
       tress! Got to get one.
105 KINESIAS A mattress? Not for me, thanks.
       MYRRHINE By Artemis, it's shabby on cords.
       KINESIAS Well, give me a kiss.
       MYRRHINE [*Kissing him*] There. [*She returns to the Grotto.*]
       KINESIAS Oh lordy! Get the mattress quick!
110 MYRRHINE [*Returning with a mattress*] There we are! Lie back down and I'll
       get my clothes off. But wait, what is it, a pillow, you haven't got a pillow!
       KINESIAS I don't need a pillow!
       MYRRHINE I do. [*She returns to the Grotto.*]
       KINESIAS Is this cock of mine supposed to be Herakles waiting for his dinner?[7]
115 MYRRHINE [*Returning with a pillow*] Lift up now, upsy daisy. There, is that
       everything?
       KINESIAS Everything I need. Come here, my little treasure!
       MYRRHINE Just getting my breastband off. But remember: don't break your
       promise about a peace-settlement.
120 KINESIAS May lightning strike me, by Zeus!
       MYRRHINE You don't have a blanket.
       KINESIAS It's not a blanket I want—I want to fuck!
       MYRRHINE That's just what you're going to get. Back in a flash. [*She returns*
       to the Grotto.]
       KINESIAS That woman drives me nuts with all her bedding!
125 MYRRHINE [*Returning with a blanket*] Get up.
       KINESIAS [*Pointing to his phallus*] I've already got it up! [MYRRHINE *carefully*
       arranges the blanket while KINESIAS *fidgets.*]
       MYRRHINE Want some scent?
       KINESIAS Apollo[8] no, none for me.
       MYRRHINE But I will, by Aphrodite, whether you like it or not.
130 KINESIAS [*As* MYRRHINE *returns to the Grotto*] Then let the scent flow! Lord
       Zeus!
       MYRRHINE [*Returning with a round bottle of perfume*] Hold out your hand.
       Take some and rub it in.
       KINESIAS I don't like this scent, by Apollo; it takes a long time warming up
135   and it doesn't smell like conjugal pleasures.
       MYRRHINE Oh silly me, I brought the Rhodian[9] brand!
       KINESIAS No, wait, I like it! Let it go, you screwy woman!
       MYRRHINE What are you talking about? [*She returns to the Grotto.*]
       KINESIAS Goddamn the man who first decocted scent!
140 MYRRHINE [*Returning with a long, cylindrical bottle*] Here, try this tube.
       KINESIAS [*Pointing to his phallus*] Got one already! Now lie down, you slut,
       and don't bring me anything more.

---

7. The hero was routinely portrayed as having great appetites.

8. Greek god of prophecy, light, and healing.

9. From the Aegean island of Rhodes.

MYRRHINE   By Artemis I will. Just getting my shoes off. But remember, darling,
you're going to vote for peace. [*At this,* KINESIAS *averts his eyes from* MYRRHINE
and fiddles with the blanket; MYRRHINE *dashes off into the Akropolis.*]

145 KINESIAS   I'll give it serious consideration. [*He looks up again, only to find*
MYRRHINE *gone.*] The woman's destroyed me, annihilated me! Not only
that: she's pumped me up and dropped me flat!

> [*During the ensuing duet both semichoruses return to the center of the*
> *orchestra; the women carry the shirts that the men had removed earlier.*]

Now what shall I do? Whom shall I screw?
I'm cheated of the sexiest girl I knew!
150 How will I raise and rear this orphaned cock?
Is Fox Dog[1] out there anywhere?
I need to rent a practical nurse!
MEN'S LEADER   Yea frightful agony, thou wretch,
dost rack the soul of one so sore bediddled.
155 Sure I do feel for thee, alack!
What kidney could bear it,
what soul, what balls,
what loins, what crotch,
thus stretched on the rack
160 and deprived of a morning fuck?
KINESIAS   Ah Zeus! The cramps attack anew!
MEN'S LEADER   And *this* is what she's done to you,
the detestable, revolting shrew!
WOMEN'S LEADER   No, she's totally sweet and dear!
165 MEN'S LEADER   Sweet, you say! She's wicked, wicked!
KINESIAS   You're right: wicked is what she is!
O Zeus, Zeus, raise up a great tornado,
with lightning bolts and all,
to sweep her up like a heap of grain
170 and twirl her into the sky,
and then let go and let her fall
back down to earth again,
and let her point of impact be
this dick of mine right here!

Episode

[*Enter a Spartan* HERALD, *both arms hidden beneath a long travelling cloak and*
pushing it out in front.]

HERALD   [*To* KINESIAS]   Where be the Senate of Athens or the Prytanies?[2]
Have some news to tell them.
KINESIAS   And what might you be? Are you human? Or a Konisalos?[3]
HERALD   Am Herald, youngun, by the Twain, come from Sparta about
5 settlement.
KINESIAS   And that's why you've come hiding a spear in your clothes?

---

1. Nickname of the famous pimp Philostratos.
2. That portion of the Athenian council responsible for the day-to-day business of the

state; its membership rotated.
3. A phallic fertility spirit associated with a Spartan dance.

HERALD   Not I, by Zeus, no spear!

KINESIAS   Why twist away from me? And why hold your coat out in front of
you? You've got a swollen groin from the long ride, maybe?

10 HERALD   By Kastor, this guy crazy! [*He accidently reveals his erect phallus.*]

KINESIAS   Hey, that's hard-on, you rascal!

HERALD   No, by Zeus, is not! Don't be silly!

KINESIAS   Then what do you call *that*?

HERALD   Is Spartan walking-stick.

15 KINESIAS [*Pointing to his own phallus*]   Then *this* is a Spartan walking-stick
too. Listen, I know what's up; you can level with me. How are things going
in Sparta?

HERALD   All Sparta rise, also allies. All have hard-on. Need Pellana.[4]

KINESIAS   What caused this calamity to hit you? Was it Pan?

20 HERALD   Oh no. Was Lampito started it, yes, and then other women in
Sparta, they all start together like in footrace, keep men away from their
hair-pies.

KINESIAS   So how are you faring?

HERALD   Hard! Walk around town bent over, like men carrying oil-lamp in
25 wind. The women won't permit even to touch the pussy till all of us unanimously agree to make peace-treaty with rest of Greeks.

KINESIAS   So this business is a global conspiracy by all the women! Now I get
it! OK, get back to Sparta as quick as you can and arrange to send ambassadors here with full powers to negotiate a treaty. And I'll arrange for *our* Coun
30 cil to choose their own ambassadors; this cock of mine will be Exhibit A.

HERALD   I fly away. You offer capital advice. [*He exits by the way he entered;*
KINESIAS *exits in the opposite direction.*]

MEN'S LEADER   A woman's harder to conquer than any beast,
than fire, and no panther is quite so ferocious.

WOMEN'S LEADER   You understand that, but then you still resist us?

35 It's possible, you rascal, to have our lasting friendship.

MEN'S LEADER   I'll never cease to loathe women!

WOMEN'S LEADER   Well, whenever you like. But meanwhile I'll not stand
for you to be undressed like that. Just look how ridiculous you are!
I'm coming over to put your shirt back on.

[*She walks over and replaces his shirt, and the other women each follow
suit for one of the men.*]

40 MEN'S LEADER   By god, that's no mean thing you've done for us.
And now I'm sorry I got mad and took it off.

WOMEN'S LEADER   And now you look like a man again, not so ridiculous.
And if you weren't so hostile I'd have removed
that bug in your eye, that's still in there, I see.

45 MEN'S LEADER   So *that's* what's been driving me nuts! Here, take my ring;
please dig it out of my eye, then show it to me;
by god, it's been biting my eye for quite some time.

WOMEN'S LEADER   All right, I will, though you're a grumpy man.
Great gods, what a humongous gnat you've got in there!

50 There, take a look. Isn't it positively Trikorysian?[5]

---

4. A city south of Sparta; here, the name
appears to have obscure sexual connotations.

5. From Trikorythos, a marshy district in
Attica.

MEN'S LEADER   By god, you've helped me; that thing's been digging wells,
    and now it's out my eyes are streaming tears.
WOMEN'S LEADER   Then I'll wipe them away, though you're a genuine rascal,
    and kiss you.
55 MEN'S LEADER   Don't kiss me!
WOMEN'S LEADER   I'll kiss you whether you like it or not!
    [*She does so, and the other women follow suit as before.*]
MEN'S LEADER   The worst of luck to you! You're born sweet-talkers.
    The ancient adage gets it in a nutshell:
    "Can't live *with* the pests or without 'em either."
    But now I'll make peace, and promise nevermore
60   to mistreat you or to take mistreatment *from* you.
    Let's get together, then, and start our song.
    [*The semichoruses become one and for the remainder of the play perform
    as a single chorus.*]

CHORUS (*strophe*)
    We don't intend to say anything
    the least bit slanderous about
    any citizen, you gentlemen out there,
65   but quite the opposite: to say and do
    only what's nice, because the troubles
    you've got already are more than enough.

    So let every man and woman tell us
    if they need to have a little cash,
70   say two or three minas;[6] we've got it at home
    and we've got some purses for it too.
    And if peace should ever break out,
    everyone that we lent money to
    can forget to repay—if they got anything!

(*antistrophe*)
75   We're getting set to entertain
    some visitors from Karystos[7] today;
    they're fine and handsome gentlemen.
    There'll be a special soup, and that piglet
    of mine, I've sacrificed it on the grill,
80   and it's turning out to be fine and tender meat.
    So come on over to my house today:
    get up early and take a bath,
    and bathe the kids, and walk right in.
    You needn't ask anyone's permission,
85   just go straight on inside like it was yours,
    because the door will be locked!

---

6. A substantial sum of money. *So let every
man and woman tell us*: a line unique in suggesting that women attended the performances of ancient comedy.
7. A small town on the Aegean island of Euboea,
north of Athens, that was an ally of Athens.

Episode

[*The* SPARTAN AMBASSADORS *enter, their clothes concealing conspicuous bulges. They are accompanied by slaves.*]

CHORUS-LEADER   Hey! Here come ambassadors from Sparta, dragging long beards and wearing something around their waists that looks like a pig-pen. [*To the Spartans*] Gentlemen of Sparta: first, our greetings! Then tell us how you all are doing?

5 SPARTAN AMBASSADOR   No use to waste a lot of time describing. Is best to *show* how we're doing. [*The Spartans open their cloaks to reveal their erect phalli.*]

CHORUS-LEADER   Gosh! Your problem's grown very hard, and it seems to be even more inflamed than before.

SPARTAN AMBASSADOR   Unspeakable! What can one say? We wish for some
10 one to come, make peace for us on any terms he like.

[ATHENIAN AMBASSADORS *enter from the opposite direction, with cloaks bulging.*]

CHORUS-LEADER   Look, I see a party of native sons approaching, like men wrestling, holding their clothes away from their bellies like that! Looks like a bad case of prickly heat.

FIRST ATHENIAN AMBASSADOR [*To the* CHORUS-LEADER.]   Who can tell us
15 where Lysistrata is? The men are here, and we're . . . as you see. [*They reveal their own erect phalli.*]

CHORUS-LEADER   *Their* syndrome seems to be the same as *theirs*. These spasms: do they seize you in the wee hours?

FIRST ATHENIAN AMBASSADOR   Yes, and what's worse, we're worn totally raw by being in this condition! If someone doesn't get us a treaty pretty soon,
20 there's no way we won't be fucking Kleisthenes!

CHORUS-LEADER   If you've got any sense, you'll cover up there: you don't want one of the Herm-Dockers[8] to see you like this.

FIRST ATHENIAN AMBASSADOR   By god, that's good advice. [*The Athenians rearrange their cloaks to cover their phalli.*]

SPARTAN AMBASSADOR   By the Twain Gods, yes indeed. Come, put cloaks
25 back on! [*The Spartans follow suit.*]

FIRST ATHENIAN AMBASSADOR   Greetings, Spartans! We've had an awful time.

SPARTAN AMBASSADOR   Dear colleague, we've had a *fearful* time, if those men saw us fiddling with ourselves.

FIRST ATHENIAN AMBASSADOR   Come on, then, Spartans, let's talk details. The
30 reason for your visit?

SPARTAN AMBASSADOR   Are ambassadors, for settlement.

FIRST ATHENIAN AMBASSADOR   That's very good; us too. So why not invite Lysistrata to our meeting, since she's the only one who can settle our differences?

SPARTAN AMBASSADOR   Sure, by the Twain Gods, Lysistrata, and Lysistratos[9]
35 too if ye like!

[LYSISTRATA *emerges from the Akropolis gate.*]

8. The unknown individuals who, just before the great expedition was to leave for Sicily (in 415 B.C.E.), broke the erect phalluses off statues of Hermes. These representations of the messenger god, the patron of travelers, stood outside houses and public buildings throughout the city.
9. The masculine form of the name Lysistrata, perhaps also mocking the Spartans as homosexuals.

FIRST ATHENIAN AMBASSADOR   It looks as if we don't have to invite her: she
must have heard us, for here she comes herself.

CHORUS-LEADER   Hail, manliest of all women! Now is your time: be forceful
and flexible, high-class and vulgar, haughty and sweet, a woman for all sea-
40   sons; because the head men of Greece, caught by your charms, have gathered together with all their mutual complaints and are turning them over
to you for settlement.

LYSISTRATA   Well, it's an easy thing to do if you get them when they're hot for
it and not testing each other for weaknesses. I'll soon know how ready they
45   are. Where's Reconciliation? [*A naked girl comes out of the Akropolis.*] Take
hold of the Spartans first and bring them here; don't handle them with a
rough or mean hand, or crudely, the way our husbands used to handle us,
but use a wife's touch, like home sweet home. [*The* SPARTAN AMBASSADOR
refuses to give his hand.] If he won't give you his hand, lead him by his
50   weenie. [*The* SPARTAN AMBASSADOR *complies, and she leads him and his colleagues to* LYSISTRATA, *where they stand to her left.*] Now go and fetch those
Athenians too; take hold of whatever they give you and bring them here.
[RECONCILIATION *escorts the Athenians to* LYSISTRATA'S *right.*] Spartans, move
in closer to me, and you Athenians too; I want you to listen to what I have to
55   say. I *am* a woman, but still I've got a mind: I'm pretty intelligent in my own
right, and because I've listened many a time to the conversations of my father
and the older men I'm pretty well educated too. Now that you're a captive
audience I'm ready to give you the tongue-lashing you deserve—both of you.
        Don't both of you sprinkle altars from the same cup like kinsmen, at the
60   Olympic Games, at Thermopylai, at Delphi,[1] and so many other places I
could mention if I had to make a long list? Yet with plenty of enemies available with their barbarian armies, it's *Greek* men and *Greek* cities you're
determined to destroy! That's the first point I wanted to make.

FIRST ATHENIAN AMBASSADOR   [*Gazing at* RECONCILIATION]   My cock is burst-
65   ing out of its skin and killing me!

LYSISTRATA   Next I'm going to turn to *you*, Spartans. Don't you remember the
time when Perikleidas the Spartan came here on bended knee and sat at
Athenian altars, white-faced in his scarlet uniform, begging for a military
contingent? That time when Messenia was up in arms against you and the
70   god was shaking you with an earthquake? And Kimon came with four thousand infantrymen and rescued all Lakedaimon?[2] And after that sort of treatment from the Athenians, you're now out to ravage their country, who've
treated you so well?

FIRST ATHENIAN AMBASSADOR   By Zeus they *are* guilty, Lysistrata!

75   SPARTAN AMBASSADOR   We're guilty—[*looking at* RECONCILIATION] but what
an unspeakably fine ass!

---

1. Sites revered by all Greeks. At the Olympic
Games, held quadrennially in Olympia, on the
Peloponnesian Peninsula, a truce was observed;
Thermopylae, in central Greece, was the site of
the Spartans' heroic stand against the Persians
in 480 B.C.E.; Delphi, in central Greece, was
the site of the most important oracle of Apollo
and of the Panhellenic games.

2. That is, Sparta. Kimon, an Athenian general and statesman, brought aid to Sparta in
464 B.C.E. after a devastating earthquake
was followed by a rebellion of their serfs.
(Lysistrata refrains from adding that the
Spartans abruptly sent the Athenians away,
an affront to Athenian pride that resulted in
Kimon's exile.)

LYSISTRATA Do you Athenians think I'm going to let *you* off? Don't you remember the time when you were dressed in slaves' rags and the Spartans came in force and wiped out many Thessalian fighters, many friends and
80   allies of Hippias?[3] That day when they were the only ones helping you to drive him out? How they liberated you, and replaced your slaves' rags with a warm cloak, as suits a free people?

SPARTAN AMBASSADOR [*Still gazing at* RECONCILIATION] I never saw such a classy woman!

85 FIRST ATHENIAN AMBASSADOR *I've* never seen a lovelier cunt!

LYSISTRATA So after so many good deeds done, why are you at war? Why not stop this terrible behavior? Why not make peace? Come on, what's in the way?

[*During the following negotiations* RECONCILIATION*'s body serves as a map of Greece.*]

SPARTAN AMBASSADOR We are ready, if they are ready to return to us this abutment.

90 LYSISTRATA Which one, sir?

SPARTAN AMBASSADOR Back Door[4] here, that we for long time count on having, and grope for.

FIRST ATHENIAN AMBASSADOR By Poseidon, that you *won't* get!

LYSISTRATA Give it to them, good sir.

95 FIRST ATHENIAN AMBASSADOR Then who will *we* be able to harrass?

LYSISTRATA Just ask for some other place in return for that one.

FIRST ATHENIAN AMBASSADOR Well, let's see now. First of all give us Echinous here and the Malian Gulf behind it and both Legs.[5]

SPARTAN AMBASSADOR By Twain Gods, we will not give *everything*, dear fellow!

100 LYSISTRATA Let it go: don't be squabbling about legs.

FIRST ATHENIAN AMBASSADOR Now I'm ready to strip down and do some ploughing!

SPARTAN AMBASSADOR Me first, by Twain Gods: before one ploughs one spreads manure!

105 LYSISTRATA You may do that when you've ratified the settlement. If, after due deliberation, you do decide to settle, go back and confer with your allies.

FIRST ATHENIAN AMBASSADOR *Allies*, dear lady? We're too hard up for that! Won't our allies, all of them, come to the same decision *we* have, namely, to fuck?

110 SPARTAN AMBASSADOR *Ours* will, by Twain Gods!

FIRST ATHENIAN AMBASSADOR And so will the Karystians,[6] by Zeus!

LYSISTRATA You make a strong case. For the time being see to it you remain pure, so that we women can host you on the Akropolis with what we brought in our boxes. There you may exchange pledges of mutual trust,
115   and after that each of you may reclaim his wife and go home.

FIRST ATHENIAN AMBASSADOR What are we waiting for?

SPARTAN AMBASSADOR [*To* LYSISTRATA] Lead on wherever you wish.

---

3. The Spartans came to the aid of Athenian democrats and expelled the tyrant Hippias in 510 B.C.E. (Again, Lysistrata leaves out the acrimonious end of the story—the Spartans' later attempt to overthrow the democracy.) *Thessalian*: from Thessaly, in northern Greece.

4. Pylos; also a joke at the Spartans' supposed preference for anal sex.
5. Echinous is a town in Thessaly; the Malian Gulf is near Thermopylae; the "Legs" here are the walls that connected the city of Megara, west of Athens, and its seaport, Nisaia.
6. The inhabitants of Karystos.

FIRST ATHENIAN AMBASSADOR   By Zeus yes, as quick as you can!

[LYSISTRATA *escorts* RECONCILIATION *inside, followed by the* SPARTAN *and* ATHENIAN AMBASSADORS; *the Spartans' slaves sit down outside the door, which is attended by a doorkeeper.*]

CHORUS (*strophe*)
Intricate tapestries,
120 nice clothes and fine gowns
and gold jewellery: all that I own
is yours for the asking
for your sons and for your daughter too,
when she's picked to march with the basket.[7]
125 I declare my home open to everyone
to take anything you want.
Nothing is sealed up so tight
that you won't be able to break the seals
and take away what you find inside.
130 But you won't see anything
unless your eyes are sharper than mine.
(*antistrophe*)
If anyone's out of bread
but has slaves and lots of little kids to feed,
you can get flour from my house:
135 puny grains, but a pound of them
grow up to be a loaf
that looks very hearty.
Any of you poor people are welcome
to come to my house with sacks and bags
140 to carry the flour away; my houseboy will load them up.
A warning though: don't knock at my door—
beware of the watchdog there!

Episode

FIRST ATHENIAN AMBASSADOR [*Still inside, knocking at the door and yelling to the doorkeeper*]   Open the door, you! [*He bursts through the door, sending the doorkeeper tumbling down the steps. He wears a garland and carries a torch, as from a drinking-party.*] You should have got out of the way. [*Other Athenians emerge, similarly equipped. To the slaves*] You there, why are you sitting around? Want me to singe you with this torch?
5   What a stale routine! I refuse to do it. [*Encouragement from the spectators.*] Well, if it's absolutely necessary we'll go the extra mile, to do you all a favor. [*He begins to chase the slaves with his torch.*]
SECOND ATHENIAN AMBASSADOR [*Joining the* FIRST]   And we'll help you go that extra mile! [*To the slaves*] Get lost! You'll cry for your hair if you don't!
10 FIRST ATHENIAN AMBASSADOR   Yes, get lost, so the Spartans can come out after their banquet without being bothered. [*The slaves are chased off.*]
SECOND ATHENIAN AMBASSADOR   I've never been at a better party! The Spartans were really great guys, and we made wonderful company ourselves over the drinks.

7. That is, during a religious festival.

15   FIRST ATHENIAN AMBASSADOR   Stands to reason: when we're sober we're not
     ourselves. If the Athenians will take my advice, from now on we'll do all our
     ambassadorial business drunk. As it is, whenever we go to Sparta sober, we
     start right in looking for ways to stir up trouble. When they say something
     we don't hear it, and when they don't say something we're convinced that
20   they did say it, and we each return with completely different reports. But
     this time everything turned out fine. When somebody sang the Telamon
     Song when he should have been singing the Kleitagora Song,[8] everybody
     would applaud and even swear up and down what a fine choice it was.
     [*Some of the slaves approach the door again.*] Hey, those slaves are back!
25   Get lost, you whip-fodder! [*They chase the slaves away.*]
     SECOND ATHENIAN AMBASSADOR   Yes, by Zeus, here they come out of the door.
     [*The* SPARTAN AMBASSADORS *file out; their leader carries bagpipes.*]
     SPARTAN AMBASSADOR [*To the stage-piper or to a piper who accompanies the
     Spartans*]   Take pipes, my good man, and I dance two-step and sing nice
     song for Athenians and ourselves.
     FIRST ATHENIAN AMBASSADOR   God yes, take the pipes: I love to watch you
30   people dance!
     SPARTAN AMBASSADOR   Memory, speed to this lad
           your own Muse, who knows
           about us and the Athenians,
           about that day at Artemision
35   when *they* spread sail like gods
           against the armada
           and whipped the Medes,
           while Leonidas[9] led *us*,
           like wild boars we were, yes,
40   gnashing our tusks, our jaws running
           streams of foam, and our legs too.
           The enemy, the Persians,
           outnumbered the sand on the shore.

           Goddess of the Wilds, Virgin Beast-Killer,[1]
45   come this way, this way to the treaty,
           and keep us together for a long long while.
           Now let friendship in abundance
           attend our agreement always,
           and may we ever abandon
50   foxy strategems.
           Come this way, this way,
           Virgin Huntress!
                    [*A mute* LYSISTRATA *comes out of the Akropolis, followed by the Athenian
                    and Spartan wives.*]

----

8. Evidently songs of war and of love (Telamon
was a legendary hero of the generation before
the Trojan War, and Kleitagora was a Spartan
woman poet).
9. The Spartan king and general who led the
small band against the Persians ("the Medes")

at Thermopylae in 480 B.C.E.; at the same
time, an indecisive naval battle took place
nearby at Cape Artemision. *Muse*: a goddess
of art and learning, conventionally invoked
for inspiration.
1. Artemis.

FIRST ATHENIAN AMBASSADOR   Well! Now that everything else has been wrapped
up so nicely, it's time for you Spartans to reclaim these wives of yours; and
55   you Athenians, these here. Let's have husband stand by wife and wife by
husband; then to celebrate our great good fortune let's have a dance for the
gods. And let's be sure never again to make the same mistakes! [*The couples
descend into the orchestra to dance to the* AMBASSADOR'*s song; around them
dance the members of the chorus, who are also paired in couples.*]

   Bring on the dance, include the Graces,
   and invite Artemis,
60   and her twin brother, the benign Healer,[2]
   and the Nysian whose eyes flash
   bacchic among his maenads,
   and Zeus alight with flame
   and the thriving Lady his consort;[3]
65   and invite the divine powers
   we would have as witnesses
   to remember always
   this humane peace,
   which the goddess Kypris[4] has fashioned.
70 CHORUS   Alalai, yay Paian![5]
   Shake a leg, iai!
   Dance to victory, iai!
   Evoi evoi,[6] evai evai!

FIRST ATHENIAN AMBASSADOR Now, my dear Spartan, *you* give us some music:
75   a new song to match the last one!

SPARTAN AMBASSADOR   Come back again from fair Taÿgetos,
   Spartan Muse, and distinguish this occasion
   with a hymn to the God of Amyklai[7]
   and Athena of the Brazen House[8]
80   and Tyndareos' fine sons,
   who gallop beside the Eurotas.[9]
   Ho there, hop!
   Hey there, jump!
   Let's sing a hymn to Sparta,
85   home of dance divine
   and stomping feet,
   where by the Eurotas' banks
   young girls frisk like fillies,
   raising dust-clouds underfoot
90   and tossing their tresses
   like maenads waving their wands and playing,

2. Apollo. *Graces*: the incarnations of beauty
and grace, daughters of Zeus.
3. The goddess Hera, sister and wife of Zeus.
Maenads: the women who worship Dionysus,
god of wine and of an emotional cult who was
raised on Mount Nysa (whose location was a
matter of dispute).
4. Aphrodite.

5. A title of Apollo ("Healer").
6. The ecstatic cry of worshippers of Dionysus.
7. Site south of Sparta of a major shrine to
Apollo.
8. Sparta's bronze-plated temple to Athena.
9. The river that runs by Sparta. *Tyndareos'
fine sons*: Kastor and Pollux.

led by Leda's daughter,[1]
their chorus-leader pure and pretty.

[*To the* CHORUS] Come on now, hold your hair in your hand, get your feet

95 hopping like a deer and start making some noise to spur the dance! And
sing for the goddess who's won a total victory, Athena of the Brazen House!

[*All exit dancing, the* CHORUS *singing a traditional hymn to Athena.*]

---

1. Helen, the daughter of Leda and Zeus; she was worshipped as a goddess in Sparta.

HROTSVIT OF GANDERSHEIM

935?–1002?

Hrotsvit, a canoness in the tenth-century abbey of Gandersheim, in north-central Germany, lays claim to several significant firsts in the history of Western literature. She is the first known Christian dramatist, the first Saxon poet, and the first female historian of Europe. Her plays are the first performable plays of the Middle Ages, and her epic poems are the only extant Latin epics composed by a woman. Her sophisticated output has been a puzzle and anomaly for literary scholars and historians for centuries, and opinions about the works have often been shaped by an unwillingness to acknowledge that a medieval woman could possibly know as much or write with as much skill as Hrotsvit did. Only during the last decades of the twentieth century were Hrotsvit's achievements given the sort of attention that they deserve; and even now, there is much that we don't know and can't fully appreciate about this remarkable woman.

What little we do know of Hrotsvit's life comes from clues in her own writing. Scholars suspect that she was born around 935. Although nothing is certain about her activities before she entered the abbey at Gandersheim in 955, we can say a few things confidently about the nature of her education and religious service once she chose to live in that Christian community. First, she would have had access to many classical Latin texts. During the medieval period, the major centers of learning in Europe were the monastic and cathedral schools, whose libraries amassed major collections of philosophical and theological writings. The Benedictine nunnery at Gandersheim was one of the most prominent of these centers. Such libraries collected manuscripts drawn not only from the Christian era but also from the classical Roman era that had preceded it. Because early Christian theologians believed that the pagan Latin texts were useful preparation for the more difficult challenge of reading Holy Scripture in Latin, students in monastic settings had access to much of the classical canon as well as to writings on church doctrine and biblical texts. Judging from clues in her own writings, it appears that Hrotsvit read Virgil, Ovid, and Terence among classical authors; she was also familiar with such early Christian philosophers as Augustine and Boethius. She was particularly well versed in saints' lives—the hagiographic texts that underlie many of her legends and dramas.

We also assume that Hrotsvit, like most canonesses who entered Gandersheim and other monasteries, was of noble birth. We know that she joined the community at about the same time that Gerberga II, a niece of Otto I (the German king and Holy Roman Emperor), came to the monastery.

In her writings, Hrotsvit credits Gerberga with much of her education. This connection to one of the most powerful families in Saxony suggests that either before or during her years at Gandersheim, Hrotsvit may have spent time at court, which would have given her further access to broad cultural influences.

Hrotsvit's oeuvre remained completely unknown to scholars for nearly five hundred years after her death; then, in 1494, the German humanist Conrad Celtis found what is now known as the Emmeram-Munich Codex, which he published in 1501. While German scholars, in a spirit of cultural nationalism, were quick to embrace Hrotsvit, critics elsewhere found her writing so advanced compared to other manuscripts from that period that they questioned its authenticity. In 1867, the Viennese scholar Joseph von Aschbach asserted that Celtis had forged the codex, arguing that no medieval woman could possibly have possessed Hrotsvit's knowledge of either the world or of classical literature. Aschbach's theories have subsequently been definitively refuted by the discovery of additional copies of Hrotsvit's writing, in their original Latin as well as in early vernacular translation. But the confirmation of the legitimacy of her oeuvre—which comprises eight verse legends; six plays in rhymed, rhythmic prose; two verse epics; and a short poem—has not resolved fundamental questions, particularly in the case of the plays, surrounding their genesis or historical significance.

Although we cannot definitively date Hrotsvit's work, most recent scholarship posits that she was at the height of her creative powers from 965 to 975. Scholars believe she began writing legends based on saints' lives soon after her arrival at the abbey, and her collection of plays followed. If these assumptions are true, then she may well have written her dramas at about the same time that the *Quem quaeritis* (Whom do you seek?) trope came to be added to the Easter Mass. This precursor to full-fledged medieval liturgical drama consisted of a short series of simple questions and answers between an angel and the women who come to Christ's tomb following the resurrection, sung by two halves of a church choir. Hrotsvit's work could thus predate the first extant mystery plays, or dramas based on scriptural incidents, by about seventy-five years. This revised history would then throw into question the long-held theory about how drama "reemerged" in the West after the end of the classical era.

In the standard explanation, dramatic arts declined precipitously after the collapse of Rome—essentially lying dormant for six centuries, only to be reborn in the tenth century. This rebirth was the product of growing theatricality in the rituals of the Catholic Mass, starting with the *Quem quaeritis* trope. Liturgical drama eventually broke free of the confines of the Mass, evolving into the mystery cycles that were sponsored and performed by professional guilds. From that point, scholars have generally believed, it was merely a matter of time before the drama would fully reflower, as it eventually did during the Renaissance.

Hrotsvit's dramas disrupt the prevailing narrative of medieval theater history because her plays are much more sophisticated than the rudimentary seed from which the revived Western drama was traditionally thought to have grown. In addition, the plays of Hrotsvit, which the playwright herself describes as imitations of the Roman comic dramatist Terence, demonstrate a continuity between classical and medieval theater, not the revival of a dead form.

Even among scholars who recognize that Hrotsvit's work complicates the standard history, there is considerable disagreement about the influence of her plays on medieval drama generally. Some have characterized Hrotsvit's work as an "isolated experiment," or a mere "literary exercise," implying that her plays were neither widely known nor intended for performance. While the discovery of copies of her manuscripts in different locations suggests that her works were known within the Christian community in Europe and thus could indeed have had some impact on medieval drama, the current evidence allows no more than conjecture about what, and how extensive, that impact might have been. Whether her plays were works of theater or just literary exercises has proven a more vexing question. We cannot conclude from the form of these six works that they were composed for theatrical performance. Like Seneca's plays in late antiquity, Hrotsvit's plays may simply have been examples of closet drama— pieces never staged, or never intended to be staged. But regardless of Hrotsvit's intentions, the plays themselves are undeniably theatrical, and can be performed.

The extent of Hrotsvit's understanding of theatrical performance is difficult to gauge, as many historians believe that Europeans in the tenth century had little knowledge of classical stage practice. In this era, written dialogues with speech prefixes (sometimes names of real people) were considered valuable pedagogical tools, but it is unclear whether they were meant to be read silently or aloud. Nor is it certain that such texts that we now understand to be dramatic or theatrical were distinguished from others in any way. Some scholars have speculated that dialogues may have been read aloud, either by a single person or by a number voicing the different "characters," with the suggested action silently dramatized by a mime, but there is little evidence to support or disprove this theory. What we can say is that of all of Hrotsvit's plays, DUL-CITIUS most strongly suggests its author's sense of performance. For this reason, it has emerged as a crucial text for historians seeking to explore the possible conjunction of dialogue and action in medieval drama.

Further complicating our interpretation of Hrotsvit's intentions is the self-deprecating tone of the prefaces and epistles that introduce many of her works. Initially, Hrotsvit's own prose was taken as evidence of her negligibility as a writer, but scholars have more recently acknowledged that it simply adheres to a common medieval Christian convention that gives God, not the writer, credit for whatever genius might be found in the work. A better clue to her sense of self and of her earthly mission may reside in the Latin nom de plume she adopted: Clamor Validus Gandeshemensis, or "the strong voice of Gandersheim." Perhaps, like some modern critics, she saw her own strength in a bold and daring design in her writings that was unmatched by any efforts of her contemporaries, either in literature or visual art. Or perhaps she was thinking that representing wise, strong, and virtuous Christian women in texts to be shared within communities like her own would have the power to transform cultural stereotypes.

In the preface to her dramas, Hrotsvit explains her goals, declaring a debt to and a quarrel with the Latin playwright Terence:

> Many Catholics one may find, and we are also guilty of charges of this kind, who for the beauty of their eloquent style, prefer the use of pagan guile to the usefulness of Sacred Scripture. There are also others, who, devoted to sacred reading and scorning the works of other pagans, yet frequently read Terence's fiction, and as they delight in the sweetness of his style and diction, they are stained by learning of wicked things in his depiction. Therefore I, the strong voice of Gandersheim, have not refused to imitate him in writing whom others laud in reading, so that in that selfsame form of composition in which the shameless acts of lascivious women were phrased the laudable chastity of sacred virgins may be praised within the limits of my little talent.

From this brief statement, Hrotsvit's plan is clear: she will revise Terence for Christendom. While borrowing his compositional style, she will correct his misogynistic portrayal of women and instead promote images of female virtue and chastity.

Although critics are divided about the extent and nature of Hrotsvit's debt to Terence, they generally agree that *Dulcitius* is the most Terentian of her plays. The influence of classical comedy may be seen in the play's lighter moments, such as the scene in which the Roman governor Dulcitius makes a lunge at pots and pans, thinking they are the young Christian virgins whom he wishes to ravish, ends up with soot all over his face, and is then mistaken for a demon. Comparisons can likewise be made between Terence's use of established classical character types, such as bombastic fathers, and Hrotsvit's adaptation of them as Roman figures of

COMEDIA SECVNDA DVLCICVS

An illustration from the 1501 edition of Hrotsvit's
complete works showing the virgins Agape (love), Chionia
(purity), and Hirena (peace) being burned alive.

authority. We may also observe a shared predilection for love conflicts as plot devices, and such motifs as scheming and disguise figuring in the works of both dramatists. Some critics, however, argue that these resemblances are isolated parallels, and that the spirit and content of Hrotsvit's plays much more thoroughly reflect medieval sensibilities. In their view, the comic scene and the conflicts between typed characters illustrate the use of Christian symbolism, as Hrotsvit pits the pagan forces of evil against the blessedness of Christian virtue and martyrdom.

Hrotsvit is remarkably faithful in *Dulcitius* to her source material, which is taken from the *Acta Sanctorum* (*Acts of the Saints*), a sixty-eight-volume compendium of exemplary tales of Christian saints' lives. The story that serves as the basis for *Dulcitius* describes the martyr-

dom of the holy virgins Agape (love), Chionia (purity), and Hirene (peace), all put to death by order of the Roman emperor Diocletian in Thessalonica in the year 290. In her careful schema, Hrotsvit opposes the idealized women to the pagan male authorities Dulcitius (who represents lust), Diocletian (arrogance), and Sissinus (cruelty). The virgins' death at the hands of torturers ensures their Christian salvation, while their pagan persecutors secure eternal damnation—made literal by Dulcitius's representation as the soot-faced devil—for their evil deeds. Like Christ, the women are tempted to abandon their religious beliefs and sense of mission, but they resist. They withstand torture and death, thereby overpowering their male aggressors, whom they show to be impotent in the face of Christian faith. Through these trials, Hrotsvit throws into question the image of women as the weaker sex. Moreover, by celebrating female chastity she strongly links women not with Eve—the dominant association—but with the idealized Virgin Mary.

These themes of female fortitude and faith recur in Hrotsvit's other dramas, *Gallicanus*, *Calimachus*, *Abraham*, *Pafnutius*, and especially *Sapientia*, her last drama, which also depicts the martyrdom of three young virgins. The works not only were thematically innovative but also reflected an astounding facility with Latin rhetorical structures, including *stichomythia*, the use of alternating lines of dialogue to dramatize a dispute. By including doxologies (short hymns of praise to God) at the close of most of her works and in other ways, Hrotsvit demonstrated her clear understanding of the role her works might play in the broader arena of Christian education, as well as her knowledge of the liturgy. And her skill at characterization remains unprecedented in early medieval dramaturgy.

While scholars may never be able fully to determine how Hrotsvit's work may have influenced the development of the medieval drama, her growing significance in the modern period is indisputable. Her plays have been translated and performed steadily from the late nineteenth century forward. Especially noteworthy is the 1914 production of *Pafnutius* in London by the Pioneer Players, which showcased the talents of three prominent women of the Edwardian theater. Edith Craig directed, using the English translation of Christabel Marshall (under the pseudonym Christopher St. John), and the performance featured the legendary actor Ellen Terry in the role of the Nun. The study of Hrotsvit's plays from the mid-twentieth century onward has forced scholars both to carefully reexamine foundational assumptions in theater history and to reconsider dismissive attitudes toward women's writing throughout the Western tradition. The rediscovery of other medieval women authors—most notably the twelfth-century dramatist and musician-composer Hildegard of Bingen, writer of the earliest extant liturgical morality play, *Ordo virtutum*—will surely help fuel this important critical dialogue.   J.E.G.

The Martyrdom of the Holy Virgins Agape, Chionia, and Hirena[1]

DULCITIUS

CHARACTERS

DIOCLETIAN, a Roman emperor
AGAPE, a holy virgin
CHIONIA, a holy virgin
HIRENA, a holy virgin
DULCITIUS, a Roman governor

DULCITIUS'S WIFE
SISSINUS, a Roman count
SOLDIERS
GUARDS

The martyrdom of the holy virgins Agape, Chionia, and Hirena whom, in the silence of the night, Governor Dulcitius secretly visited, desiring to delight in their

1. Translated by Katharina M. Wilson.

embrace.[2] *But as soon as he entered, he became demented and kissed and hugged the pots and pans, mistaking them for the girls until his face and his clothes were soiled with disgusting black dirt. Afterward Count Sissinus, acting on orders, was given the girls so he might put them to tortures. He, too, was deluded miraculously but finally ordered that Agape and Chionia be burnt and Hirena be slain by an arrow.*

DIOCLETIAN[3]   The renown of your free and noble descent and the brightness of your beauty demand that you be married to one of the foremost men of my court. This will be done according to our command if you deny Christ and comply by bringing offerings to our gods.

5   AGAPE   Be free of care, don't trouble yourself to prepare our wedding because we cannot be compelled under any duress to betray Christ's holy name, which we must confess, nor to stain our virginity.

DIOCLETIAN   What madness possesses you? What rage drives you three?

AGAPE   What signs of our madness do you see?

10   DIOCLETIAN   An obvious and great display.

AGAPE   In what way?

DIOCLETIAN   Chiefly in that renouncing the practices of ancient religion you follow the useless, newfangled ways of the Christian superstition.

AGAPE   Heedlessly you offend the majesty of the omnipotent God. That is

15   dangerous . . .

DIOCLETIAN   Dangerous to whom?

AGAPE   To you and to the state you rule.

DIOCLETIAN   She is mad; remove the fool!

CHIONIA   My sister is not mad; she rightly reprehended your folly.

20   DIOCLETIAN   She rages even more madly; remove her from our sight and arraign the third girl.

HIRENA   You will find the third, too, a rebel and resisting you forever.

DIOCLETIAN   Hirena, although you are younger in birth, be greater in worth!

HIRENA   Show me, I pray, how?

25   DIOCLETIAN   Bow your neck to the gods, set an example for your sisters, and be the cause for their freedom!

HIRENA   Let those worship idols, Sire, who wish to incur God's ire. But I won't defile my head, anointed with royal unguent by debasing myself at the idols' feet.

30   DIOCLETIAN   The worship of gods brings no dishonor but great honor.

HIRENA   And what dishonor is more disgraceful, what disgrace is any more shameful than when a slave is venerated as a master?

DIOCLETIAN   I don't ask you to worship slaves but the mighty gods of princes and greats.

---

2. The story of the martyrdom of the holy virgins in 290 c.e. derives from the *Acta Sanctorum* (*Acts of the Saints*), an encyclopedia of the saints recognized by the Roman Catholic Church. The virgins' Greek names mean Love, Purity, and Peace, respectively. Although there was an actual Dulcitius, a Roman military leader who in 369 c.e. was appointed *Dux Britanniarum* (commander of Britain; Latin), he lived nearly a century after the events depicted in the play. Hrotsvit may have chosen the name simply for the irony of its link to the Latin *dulcis*, which means "sweet, charming."

3. Gaius Aurelius Valerius Diocletianus (ca. 245–316 c.e.), Roman emperor from 284 to 305 c.e. He was zealous in the persecution of Christians.

35 HIRENA   Is he not anyone's slave who, for a price, is up for sale?

DIOCLETIAN   For her speech so brazen, to the tortures she must be taken.

HIRENA   This is just what we hope for, this is what we desire, that for the love of Christ through tortures we may expire.

DIOCLETIAN   Let these insolent girls who defy our decrees and words be put
40   in chains and kept in the squalor of prison until Governor Dulcitius can examine them.[4]

*

DULCITIUS   Bring forth, soldiers, the girls whom you hold sequestered.

SOLDIERS   Here they are whom you requested.

DULCITIUS   Wonderful, indeed, how beautiful, how graceful, how admirable
45   these little girls are!

SOLDIERS   Yes, they are perfectly lovely.

DULCITIUS   I am captivated by their beauty.

SOLDIERS   That is understandable.

DULCITIUS   To draw them to my heart, I am eager.

50 SOLDIERS   Your success will be meager.

DULCITIUS   Why?

SOLDIERS   Because they are firm in faith.

DULCITIUS   What if I sway them by flattery?

SOLDIERS   They will despise it utterly.

55 DULCITIUS   What if with tortures I frighten them?

SOLDIERS   Little will it matter to them.

DULCITIUS   Then what should be done, I wonder?

SOLDIERS   Carefully you should ponder.

DULCITIUS   Place them under guard in the inner room of the pantry, where
60   they keep the servants' pots.

SOLDIERS   Why in that particular spot?

DULCITIUS   So that I may visit them often at my leisure.

SOLDIERS   At your pleasure.

DULCITIUS   What do the captives do at this time of night?

65 SOLDIERS   Hymns they recite.

DULCITIUS   Let us go near.

SOLDIERS   From afar we hear their tinkling little voices clear.

DULCITIUS   Stand guard before the door with your lantern but I will enter and satisfy myself in their longed-for embrace.

70 SOLDIERS   Enter. We will guard this place.

*

AGAPE   What is that noise outside the door?

HIRENA   That wretched Dulcitius coming to the fore.

CHIONIA   May God protect us!

AGAPE   Amen.

75 CHIONIA   What is the meaning of this clash of the pots and the pans?

HIRENA   I will check. Come here, please, and look through the crack!

AGAPE   What is going on?

---

4. The asterisks have been added by the translator to denote changes in locale or the passage of time; Hrotsvit's extant manuscripts contain no such scene divisions.

HIRENA   Look, the fool, the madman base, he thinks he is enjoying our
embrace.

AGAPE   What is he doing?

80 HIRENA   Into his lap he pulls the utensils, he embraces the pots and the
pans, giving them tender kisses.

CHIONIA   Ridiculous!

HIRENA   His face, his hands, his clothes, are so soiled, so filthy, that with all
the soot that clings to him, he looks like an Ethiopian.

85 AGAPE   It is only right that he should appear in body the way he is in his
mind: possessed by the Devil.

HIRENA   Wait! He prepares to leave. Let us watch how he is greeted, and
how he is treated by the soldiers who wait for him.

*

SOLDIERS   Who is coming out? A demon without doubt. Or rather, the Devil
90 himself is he; let us flee!

DULCITIUS   Soldiers, where are you taking yourselves in flight? Stay! Wait!
Escort me home with your light!

SOLDIERS   The voice is our master's tone but the look the Devil's own. Let us
not stay! Let us run away; the apparition will slay us!

95 DULCITIUS   I will go to the palace and complain, and reveal to the whole
court the insults I had to sustain.

*

DULCITIUS   Guards, let me into the palace; I must have a private audience.

GUARDS   Who is this vile and detestable monster covered in torn and despicable rags? Let us beat him, from the steps let us sweep him; he must not
100 be allowed to enter.

DULCITIUS   Alas, alas, what has happened? Am I not dressed in splendid garments? Don't I look neat and clean? Yet anyone who looks at my mien
loathes me as a foul monster. To my wife I shall return, and from her learn
what has happened. But there is my spouse, with disheveled hair she leaves
105 the house, and the whole household follows her in tears.

WIFE   Alas, alas, my Lord Dulcitius, what has happened to you? You are not
sane; the Christians have made a laughingstock out of you.

DULCITIUS   Now I know at last. I owe this mockery to their witchcraft.

WIFE   What upsets me so, what makes me more sad, is that you were igno
110 rant of all that happened to you.

DULCITIUS   I command that those insolent girls be led forth, and that they be
publicly stripped of all their clothes, so that they experience similar mockery in retaliation for ours.

*

SOLDIERS   We labor in vain; we sweat without gain. Behold, their garments
115 stick to their virginal bodies like skin, and he who urged us to strip them
snores in his seat, and he cannot be awakened from his sleep. Let us go to
the Emperor and report what has happened.

*

DIOCLETIAN   It grieves me very much to hear that Governor Dulcitius has
been so greatly deluded, so greatly insulted, so utterly humiliated. But
120 these vile young women shall not boast with impunity of having made a

mockery of our gods and those who worship them. I shall direct Count Sissinus to take due vengeance.

*

SISSINUS   Soldiers, where are those insolent girls who are to be tortured?

SOLDIERS   They are kept in prison.

125 SISSINUS   Leave Hirena there, bring the others here.

SOLDIERS   Why do you except the one?

SISSINUS   Sparing her youth. Perchance, she may be converted easier, if she
is not intimidated by her sisters' presence.

SOLDIERS   That makes sense.

*

130 SOLDIERS   Here are the girls whose presence you requested.

SISSINUS   Agape and Chionia, give heed, and to my council accede!

AGAPE   We will not give heed.

SISSINUS   Bring offerings to the gods.

AGAPE   We bring offerings of praise forever to the true Father eternal, and to
135   His Son co-eternal, and also to the Holy Spirit.

SISSINUS   This is not what I bid, but on pain of penalty prohibit.

AGAPE   You cannot prohibit it; neither shall we ever sacrifice to demons.

SISSINUS   Cease this hardness of heart, and make your offerings. But if you
persist, then I shall insist that you be killed according to the Emperor's
140   orders.

CHIONIA   It is only proper that you should obey the orders of your Emperor,
whose decrees we disdain, as you know. For if you wait and try to spare us,
then you could be rightfully killed.

SISSINUS   Soldiers, do not delay, take these blaspheming girls away, and
145   throw them alive into the flames.

SOLDIERS   We shall instantly build the pyre you asked for, and we will cast
these girls into the raging fire, and thus we'll put an end to these insults at
last.

AGAPE   O Lord, nothing is impossible for Thee; even the fire forgets its
nature and obeys Thee; but we are weary of delay; therefore, dissolve the
150   earthly bonds that hold our souls, we pray, so that as our earthly bodies die,
our souls may sing your praise in Heaven.

*

SOLDIERS   Oh, marvel, oh stupendous miracle! Behold their souls are no
longer bound to their bodies, yet no traces of injury can be found; neither
their hair, nor their clothes are burnt by the fire, and their bodies are not at
all harmed by the pyre.

155 SISSINUS   Bring forth Hirena.

*

SOLDIERS   Here she is.

SISSINUS   Hirena, tremble at the deaths of your sisters and fear to perish
according to their example.

HIRENA   I hope to follow their example and expire, so with them in Heaven
160   eternal joy I may acquire.

SISSINUS   Give in, give in to my persuasion.

HIRENA   I will never yield to evil persuasion.

SISSINUS   If you don't yield, I shall not give you a quick and easy death, but multiply your sufferings.

165   HIRENA   The more cruelly I am tortured, the more gloriously I'll be exalted.

SISSINUS   You fear no tortures, no pain? What you abhor, I shall ordain.

HIRENA   Whatever punishment you design, I will escape with help Divine.

SISSINUS   To a brothel you will be consigned, where your body will be shamefully defiled.

170   HIRENA   It is better that the body be dirtied with any stain than that the soul be polluted with idolatry.

SISSINUS   If you are so polluted in the company of harlots, you can no longer be counted among the virginal choir.

HIRENA   Lust deserves punishment, but forced compliance the crown. With
175   neither is one considered guilty, unless the soul consents freely.

SISSINUS   In vain have I spared her, in vain have I pitied her youth.

SOLDIERS   We knew this before; for on no possible score can she be moved to adore our gods, nor can she be broken by terror.

SISSINUS   I shall spare her no longer.

180   SOLDIERS   Rightly you ponder.

SISSINUS   Seize her without mercy, drag her with cruelty, and take her in dishonor to the brothel.

HIRENA   They will not do it.

SISSINUS   Who can prohibit it?

185   HIRENA   He whose foresight rules the world.

SISSINUS   I shall see . . .

HIRENA   Sooner than you wish, it will be.

SISSINUS   Soldiers, be not afraid of what this blaspheming girl has said.

SOLDIERS   We are not afraid, but eagerly follow what you bade.

*

190   SISSINUS   Who are those approaching? How similar they are to the men to whom we gave Hirena just then. They are the same. Why are you returning so fast? Why so out of breath, I ask?

SOLDIERS   You are the one for whom we look.

SISSINUS   Where is she whom you just took?

195   SOLDIERS   On the peak of the mountain.

SISSINUS   Which one?

SOLDIERS   The one close by.

SISSINUS   Oh you idiots, dull and blind. You have completely lost your mind!

SOLDIERS   Why do you accuse us, why do you abuse us, why do you threaten
200   us with menacing voice and face?

SISSINUS   May the gods destroy you!

SOLDIERS   What have we committed? What harm have we done? How have we transgressed against your orders?

SISSINUS   Have I not given the orders that you should take that rebel against
205   the gods to a brothel?

SOLDIERS   Yes, so you did command, and we were eager to fulfill your demand, but two strangers intercepted us saying that you sent them to us to lead Hirena to the mountain's peak.

SISSINUS   That's new to me.

210   SOLDIERS   We can see.

SISSINUS   What were they like?

SOLDIERS   Splendidly dressed and an awe-inspiring sight.

SISSINUS   Did you follow?

SOLDIERS   We did so.

215 SISSINUS   What did they do?

SOLDIERS   They placed themselves on Hirena's left and right, and told us to
be forthright and not to hide from you what happened.

SISSINUS   I see a sole recourse, that I should mount my horse and seek out
those who so freely made sport with us.

*

220 SISSINUS   Hmm, I don't know what to do. I am bewildered by the witchcraft
of these Christians. I keep going around the mountain and keep finding
this track, but I neither know how to proceed nor how to find my way back.

SOLDIERS   We are all deluded by some intrigue; we are afflicted with a great
fatigue; if you allow this insane person to stay alive, then neither you nor

225 we shall survive.

SISSINUS   Anyone among you, I don't care which, string a bow, and shoot an
arrow, and kill that witch!

SOLDIERS   Rightly so.

HIRENA   Wretched Sissinus, blush for shame, and proclaim your miserable

230 defeat because without the help of weapons, you cannot overcome a tender
little virgin as your foe.

SISSINUS   Whatever the shame that may be mine, I will bear it more easily
now because I know for certain that you will die.

HIRENA   This is the greatest joy I can conceive, but for you this is a cause to

235 grieve, because you shall be damned in Tartarus[5] for your cruelty, while I
shall receive the martyr's palm and the crown of virginity; thus I will enter
the heavenly bridal chamber of the Eternal King, to whom are all honor
and glory in all eternity.

5. In Greek and Roman mythology, a realm of punishment and torment beneath the underworld;
in the Christian context of *Dulcitius*, Tartarus refers to hell.

GUAN HANQING

ca. 1245–ca. 1322

HAILED as the most original pioneer of the form of dramatic theater called *zaju* (Northern variety drama), Guan Hanqing holds a position similar to that of SHAKESPEARE: a prolific writer during a pivotal historical era whose writings have been accorded unrivaled cultural status. While the critical reputations of his contemporaries have waxed and waned over the centuries, Guan's literary and theatrical standing remains unchallenged even today. Chinese critics and audiences alike have praised his works for their sympathetic portrayals of ordinary human life and suffering, their skillful balance of realism and dramatic poetry, and their remarkably powerful women characters. These qualities are exemplified in *Dou E Yuan*—literally *Injustice to Dou E*, but sometimes (as here) published in English as *SNOW IN MIDSUMMER*, the title of a well-known later adaptation—which remains one of the best-loved of Guan's *zaju* plays. In the centuries since it was written it has become one of the most frequently performed and adapted works in Chinese theater.

Guan was born in the mid-thirteenth century and lived out his life in the northern district of Yen-ching, which in 1267 became Kublai Khan's "great capital," Ta-tu, on the site of modern-day Beijing. He began writing around 1260 and did not stop until his death in the late thirteenth or early fourteenth century. His long career spanned the entire period of Kublai Khan's reign as Khan from 1260 to 1294 and as first ruler of the Mongol (or Yuan) dynasty (1271–1368). Official court records of the time make no specific reference to Guan, suggesting that he did not hold an official post there. Though this may at first seem surprising, given his celebrity as a respected writer, playwrights were rarely granted positions at court under Kublai Khan. It is also unlikely that

Guan had sympathetic ties with the old Han Chinese aristocracy. He would never have known the court of the Song dynasty (960–1279), which the Mongol khans overthrew; and during his lifetime north China under Kublai Khan was relatively peaceful and prosperous. A more probable explanation is that Guan favored more mundane pleasures over those of the court. Because Guan lived in a physician's household (where he himself may have worked as a practicing physician), he was protected from mandatory public service and taxation and enjoyed considerable freedom to live as he pleased. Indeed, he was known as the "Playboy of the Grand Capital" and focused his attention on gambling, drinking, and romance. By all accounts, he preferred the teahouse to the palace and would rather spend time with public entertainers and their commoner clientele than with courtly entertainers and their aristocratic patrons.

Although the performance traditions and techniques of Chinese theater have developed and changed considerably since the fourteenth century, Chinese still tend to view *zaju* plays as their "classical" drama, a corpus of works of higher poetic and literary quality than the drama of other eras. This lofty status is even more remarkable when we consider that there are more than three millennia of recorded theater history in China prior to the Yuan era. Accounts from court histories of the first millennium B.C.E. describe early theatrical performances in the time of the mythical King Yu Shun (2300–2205 B.C.E.). According to the scholars of the East Zhou dynasty (770–256 B.C.E.), theatrical rituals and musical performances occurred in China from the Shang dynasty (1760–1066 B.C.E.) onward. Imperial patronage during the first millennium B.C.E. supported jesters, puppeteers, storytellers, and other theatrical entertainers; Chinese actors today trace their art back to these various performative traditions, as well as to the famous Pear Orchard Conservatory, China's first known academy of music, which was established during the Tang dynasty (618–907 C.E.). Building on the various theatrical and musical forms that preceded them, early *zaju* of the Song dynasty in northern China arranged acrobatics, musical performances, and other entertainments around a short theatrical sketch, usually of a satirical nature. The growing popularity of theatrical entertainments coincided with the emergence of a vibrant middle class. To meet the increased demand for

staged performances, numerous permanent theaters were built, some of them in the form of grand entertainment venues similar to today's film megaplexes.

This long tradition of performing arts in China might have been abruptly cut short had the Han intellectuals at the center of power during the Song dynasty held theatrical entertainments in high esteem, for the Mongol khans were keen to reject the cultural values of their predecessors and to keep the Han Chinese out of court. They therefore dismantled many crucial Chinese institutions after their conquest, casting many artists and intellectuals—who favored literary and philosophical pursuits dedicated to elucidating and

The ghost of Dou E appears to her father in this woodblock illustration from a Ming Dynasty publication of *Snow in Midsummer*.

expanding on the Confucian classics—
out of positions of power and respect.
Theatrical entertainers, who had enjoyed
little respect from the Han elite, actually
found their fortunes improved under
Mongol rule: because they were officially
classified with skilled technicians, they
were protected from some of the more
brutal state policies that affected intellectuals previously rewarded during the Song
dynasty. It was the genius of Guan Hanqing and his contemporaries to take this
cultural opportunity to transform the dramatic elements from various theatrical
traditions, including early *zaju*, into cohe-
sive dramatic texts—into a new form of
zaju drama—much as the first great Greek
theater artists, Thespis and Aeschylus,
crafted tragedies from the looser frameworks of Dionysian rituals. As a result, during the Yuan dynasty *zaju* performances
finally became high culture, and their
scripts gained new literary respectability.

Guan's most admired *zaju* play, *Dou E
Yuan*, concerns Dou E, who as a seven-
year-old girl is given by her father, a poor
Confucian scholar, to the widow Cai as
payment for a debt. Ten years later, Dou E
marries Cai's son but soon finds herself a
widow. When another debtor, Doctor Lu,
attempts to strangle Cai instead of repaying what he owes, she is rescued by Old
Zhang and his son Donkey, who seek to
marry the women. Dou E refuses Donkey's proposal out of loyalty to her dead
husband, and the spurned suitor attempts
to poison Cai, believing that the older
woman's death will force Dou E to accept
him. When instead Old Zhang drinks the
poisoned soup and dies, Donkey accuses
Dou E of murder and presents her with
the choice of marrying him or going to
court. Taken before the Prefect and beaten,
Dou E maintains her innocence; but to
spare her mother-in-law a beating, she
falsely confesses to the crime and is sentenced to death. Dou E promises that her
death will be followed by several signs that
she has suffered an injustice, including a
snowfall during the hottest part of the
summer. Three years after her execution,
her father returns as a court-appointed
judicial official. Dou E's ghost appears to
him, and when he hears her story he vows
to avenge the wrong done to her.

Snow in Midsummer consists of four
sequences of song sets (marked here as
acts), each of which—as in Yuan *zaju*
generally—contains about a dozen songs or
verse passages connected by prose dialogue
and action. In keeping with the dramatic
convention of Yuan *zaju*, one major character—in this case, Dou E—sings the most
morally and emotionally sympathetic lines
of the play in lyric poetry. The other characters convey their feelings and opinions
in various forms of spoken verse, while
those passages whose principal function is
to advance the story are spoken in simple
prose. Because the Yuan stage had no formal scenery and minimal props, Guan's
play relies heavily on language to underscore onstage movements, the passage of
time, and the arc of its dramatic action.
Characters identify and reidentify themselves, repeatedly recounting the events
that have taken place. For example, Act 2
opens with an actor declaring: "I am Dr.
Lu. I lured Mistress Cai outside the town
and was just going to strangle her when two
men rescued her. Today I am opening shop.
I wonder who will turn up." This technique
creates a story that is as much narrative as
dramatic, and the sketch of past and present acquires an almost ceremonial clarity
of presentation. It is the outline of moral
illustration, but it is also the outline of a
tragedy at once individual, social, and—in
the face of death—cosmological.

Unifying these levels of meaning is the
play's concern with justice in human
affairs. *Snow in Midsummer* belongs to
the popular genre of Chinese crime and
detective fiction known in the sixteenth
century as *kung-an*. *Zaju* plays written in
this mode involve the commission of a
crime and its prosecution under the legal
system of the period. Within the courtroom, a judge or clerk ultimately solves
the crime and dispenses justice. In almost
all "courtroom" plays, the crime is murder,
and the conflict is presented as a metaphysical struggle between good and evil.
Snow in Midsummer also falls into a more
specialized category: the "judgment-
reversal" *zaju*, in which the verdict of a
first judge is discovered to be erroneous
and overturned by a second judge. The
main points of interest in this subgenre
are the difference between the corrupt

judge and the honest judge and the process by which the latter undoes the damage caused by the former. Any Yuan courtroom play requires a villain, and the judgment-reversal plays call for two: the person who actually commits the crime and the dishonest judge. In *Snow in Midsummer* and other plays of this type, the victim is initially given a choice between a private and court settlement. The victim always chooses the court, confident that justice will prevail, but is proved terribly wrong. So it plays out in *Snow in Midsummer*, as the Prefect completes the cycle of injustice by sentencing Dou E to death.

The notion of justice portrayed in courtroom *zaju* is broadly in accordance with the principles of Confucius (551–479 B.C.E.), a philosopher whose teachings on government, justice, social relationships, and individual ethical conduct exerted a powerful influence on Chinese thought and literature for millennia. During the Song dynasty, which preceded the Mongol occupation, the *Analects* and other writings of the *Ru* philosophical school that Confucius founded were required study for those, like Dou E's father, who took the imperial civil service examinations. The principles of Confucianism—loyalty, proper observance of ritual, duty, justice, and benevolence—permeated every aspect of Chinese intellectual and cultural life. In the area of social relationships, Confucius stressed that cruelty should be redressed with justice, and all Yuan courtroom dramas, including *Snow in Midsummer*, meet that requirement in their conclusions. The judgment-reversal plays portray an especially stark imbalance in what a Confucian would view as the just equilibrium of human society, an imbalance epitomized in the disgraceful figure of the first judge and set right by his replacement in the second trial. From a Confucian perspective, the results are morally satisfying: the social, natural, and divine order is restored and an injustice redressed. Guan complicates these moral polarities that underlie Confucian thought and conventional judgment-reversal drama, however. In *Snow in Midsummer*, the second judge—Dou E's father—is not simply the inverse of the first judge. His methods appear no less brutal than those

of his predecessor, and his powers of investigation little better. Moreover, it takes the otherworldly intercession of Dou E's ghost for her father even to pay attention to the case, and he discovers nothing that she does not explain to him.

Confucian principles also underlie the play's characterizations, though here, too, Guan's dramatic writing imbues Confucian models with human realism and complexity. Confucianism places a high value on filial duty and piety, for instance, and Dou E is clearly motivated by duty to her father (and, later, Cai). Yet rather than being a Confucian archetype, she is clearly an individual, motivated by passion and subject to historical social conditions. Throughout the play, she is the victim of misfortune and exploitation, and the social dimensions of her life's sorrows are recapitulated several times throughout the play, first by Cai and later with more personal bitterness by herself. The young widow's fierce denunciation of Cai's acceptance of a husband is fueled at least partly by her knowledge that fate has denied her the pleasures and protections of marriage. Medieval Chinese women were often powerless in the face of male desires, as demonstrated in the play by Cai's inability to fend off Zhang's advances despite her economic independence. Unmarried women and widows were especially vulnerable to such abuses, and Dou E's calamities are closely related to her status as a woman without a husband.

The personal difficulties of widowhood, of course, do not obscure the fact that Dou E acts at every turn in accordance with Confucian family values. Given the bitterness of her attack on Cai's inappropriate marriage, her willingness to sacrifice herself for her adoptive mother in court is stunning. But what appears in the abstract to be a noble act in the name of filial piety can also be understood as a welcome release from the tribulations of a miserable life. Similarly, while the miracles granted by Heaven at Dou E's execution and the circumstances of her return as a ghost to demand justice frame her story as a divine restoration of the natural Confucian order, the dramatic emphasis is on the final appeal from a daughter to her father to redress her personal tragedy.

Justice may triumph at the end of *Snow in Midsummer*, but Guan's play remains haunted by Dou E's earlier protest and lament, sung before her execution:

> The good are poor, and die before their
>   time;
> The wicked are rich, and live to a great
>   old age.
> The gods are afraid of the mighty and
>   bully the weak;
> They let evil take its course.
> Ah, Earth! You will not distinguish
>   good from bad,
> And, Heaven! You let me suffer this
>   injustice!
> Tears pour down my cheeks in vain!

By calling into question Confucian notions of divine justice, lines such as these challenge the certainties of Confucian belief. Indeed, Dou E's redemption at the conclu-sion of the play seems as much a product of her will, indomitable even after death, as it is of heavenly or earthly justice.

Later adaptations of *Dou E Yuan* by the literati of the Ming dynasty (1368–1644) altered the work in ways that deepened its adherence to Confucian thought. But Guan's original play, which appealed to a wider, populist audience, emphasizes the ordinary passions and frustrations of Dou E and the other characters. Thus Dou E, who might be seen as a universal representation of conservative Confucian moral values, is at the same time a compellingly individual character, forceful in personality and artic-ulate in her protests against the injustice she faces. Such complexity has led critics to variously interpret *Snow in Midsummer* as a Chinese tragedy, a piece of historical social realism, a parable of Confucian justice, and a proto-feminist work.

EVAN DARWIN WINET

Snow in Midsummer[1]

CHARACTERS

MISTRESS CAI, a widow
DOU TIANZHANG, a poor scholar,
   later a government inspector
DOU E, Dou Tianzhang's daughter
DUANYUN
DOCTOR LU

OLD ZHANG
DONKEY, his son
PREFECT
ATTENDANT
The OFFICER in charge of executions
EXECUTIONER

Act 1

[*Enter* MISTRESS CAI.]

MRS. CAI   A flower may blossom again,
    But youth never returns.

I am Mistress Cai of Chuzhou.[2] There were three of us in my family; but
unluckily my husband died, leaving me just one son who is eight years old.

5 We live together, mother and son, and are quite well off. A scholar named
Dou of Shanyang Prefecture borrowed five taels[3] of silver from me last
year. Now the interest and capital come to ten taels,[4] and I've asked several
times for the money; but Mr. Dou cannot pay it. He has a daughter, and
I've a good mind to make her my daughter-in-law;[5] then he won't have to

10 pay back the ten taels. Mr. Dou chose today as a lucky day, and is bringing
the girl to me; so I won't ask him to pay me back, but wait for him at home.
He should be here soon.

[*Enter* DOU TIANZHANG, *leading his daughter* DUANYUN.]

DOU   I am master of all the learning in the world,
    But my fate is worse than that of other men.

15 My name is Dou Tianzhang, and the home of my ancestors is Chang-an.[6] I
have studied the classics since I was a child and read a good deal; but I

---

1. Translated by Yang Xianyi and Gladys Yang.
2. A city in Anhui province, southeast China.
In the original Chinese, Cai identifies herself
here as an older woman with a humble term
meaning "mother-in-law."
3. Chinese unit of weight, slightly more than
an English ounce. *Scholar*: the original Chinese term here was used during the Tang
dynasty (618–907 C.E.) to specify one who
had passed the state examination to become a
civil servant; later, under the Song (907–
1279) and Yuan (1271–1368) dynasties, it
referred more generally to a scholar or candidate for the examination. *Shanyang Prefecture*:

an administrative subdivision of Liaoning
province in northeast China.
4. An interest rate that doubles the original
loan is outrageously usurious, a recurring
theme in the play.
5. It was customary for a family to take in a
girl, usually from a poor family, to raise as a
future daughter-in-law. Before marriage, she
would be referred to as a "child-daughter-in-
law" (in this translation, "child-bride").
6. Several times the capital of ancient China.
Dou Tianzhang identifies himself humbly
here with a traditional self-reference for a
young man.

haven't yet taken the examinations.[7] Unfortunately my wife has died, leaving me this only daughter, Duanyun. She lost her mother when she was three, and now she is seven. Living from hand to mouth, I moved to Shanyang Prefecture in Chuzhou and took lodgings here. There is a widow in this town named Cai, who lives alone with her son and is fairly well off, and as I had no money for traveling I borrowed five taels from her. Now, with the interest, I owe her ten taels; but though she has asked several times for the money, I haven't been able to pay her. And recently she has sent to say she would like my daughter to marry her son. Since the spring examinations will soon be starting, I should be going to the capital; but I have no money for the road. So I am forced to take Duanyun to Widow Cai as her future daughter-in-law. I'm not marrying my daughter but selling her! For this means the widow will cancel my debt and give me some cash for my journey. This is all I can hope for. Ah, child, your father does this against his will! While talking to myself I've reached her door. Mistress Cai! Are you at home?

       [*Enter* MISTRESS CAI.]

MRS. CAI   So it's Mr. Dou! Come in, please. I've been waiting for you.

       [*They greet each other.*]

DOU   I've brought you my daughter, ma'am, not to be your daughter-in-law— that would be asking too much—but to serve you day and night. I must be going to take the examination. I hope you will look after her.

MRS. CAI   Well, you owed me ten taels including interest. Here is your promissory note back and another two taels for your journey. I hope you don't think it too little.

DOU   Thank you, ma'am! Instead of asking for what I owe you, you have given me money for the road. Someday I shall repay your kindness in full. My daughter is a foolish child. Please take care of her, ma'am, for my sake.

MRS. CAI   Don't worry, Mr. Dou. I shall look after your daughter as if she were my own.

DOU [*kneeling to her*]   If the child deserves a beating, ma'am, for my sake just scold her! And if she deserves a scolding, for my sake speak gently to her! As for you, Duanyun, this isn't like at home, where your father used to put up with your whims. If you're naughty here, you'll be beaten and cursed. When shall I see you again, child? [*He sighs.*]

    I drum sadly on my sheath;
      I have studied the Confucian classics;
      My unhappy wife died young,
      And now I am parted from my only daughter.

       [*Exit.*]

MRS. CAI   Now Mr. Dou has left me his daughter, and gone to the capital for the examination. I must see to the house.

       [*Exeunt.*[8]]

       [*Enter* DOCTOR LU.]

---

7. That is, the state examinations to demonstrate literary proficiency; successful candidates were admitted to the civil bureaucracy, a primary means of climbing the social ladder. *The classics*: the works of Confucius (551–449 B.C.E.), which were the basis of a Chinese classical education.
8. They exit (Latin).

55 DOCTOR   I diagnose all diseases with care,
     And prescribe as the Herbal[9] dictates;
     But I cannot bring dead men back to life,
     And the live ones I treat often die.[1]

I am Doctor Lu. I own a drug shop[2] here. I've borrowed ten taels of silver
60 from Mistress Cai of this town, and with interest now owe her twenty taels.
She keeps coming for the money; but I haven't got it. If she doesn't come
back, so much the better. If she does, I have a plan. I'll sit in my shop now,
and wait to see who turns up.

     [*Enter* MISTRESS CAI.]

MRS. CAI   I am Mistress Cai. Thirteen years ago Mr. Dou Tianzhang left his
65 daughter Duanyun with me to marry my son, and I changed her name to
Dou E. But after their marriage my son died, so now she's a widow. That
was nearly three years ago, and she'll soon be out of mourning.[3] I've told
her that I'm going to town to collect a debt from Doctor Lu. Now I've
reached his house. Is Doctor Lu in?

70 DOCTOR   Yes, ma'am, come in.

MRS. CAI   You've kept my money for a long time, doctor. You must pay me back.

DOCTOR   I've no money at home, ma'am. If you'll come with me to the village, I'll get money for you.

MRS. CAI   Very well. I'll go with you.

     [*They start walking.*]

75 DOCTOR   Now we are outside the city. Here's a good spot, with no one about.
Why not do it here? I've got the rope ready. Who's that calling you, ma'am?

MRS. CAI   Where?

     [*The* DOCTOR *strangles the widow with the rope. Enter* OLD ZHANG *and
     his son* DONKEY. *As they rush forward the* DOCTOR *takes to his heels.* OLD
     ZHANG *revives* MISTRESS CAI.]

DONKEY   It's an old woman, dad, nearly strangled to death.

ZHANG   Hey, you! Who are you? What's your name? Why did that fellow try
80 to strangle you?

MRS. CAI   My name is Cai and I live in town with my widowed daughter-in-law.
Doctor Lu owes me twenty taels so he lured me here and tried to strangle
me. If not for you and this young man,[4] it would have been all up with me!

DONKEY   Did you hear that, dad? She has a daughter-in-law at home!
85 Suppose you take her as your wife and I take the daughter-in-law? Propose
it to her, dad!

ZHANG   Hey, widow! You've no husband and I've no wife. How about the two
of us getting married?

MRS. CAI   What an idea! I shall give you a handsome sum of money to thank
you.

90 DONKEY   So you refuse! I'd better strangle you after all.

MRS. CAI   Wait! Let me think a moment, brother!

---

9. An early Chinese pharmaceutical treatise.
1. Some translators interpret these ambiguous lines to mean "I uselessly treat the dead, and kill the living."
2. That is, a pharmacy, where raw medicinal herbs are sold.

3. That is, Dou E has faithfully observed the protocols of widowhood and will soon be able to stop wearing mourning clothes (and thus will become eligible for remarriage).
4. Mrs. Cai uses a courteous form of address that literally means "older brother."

DONKEY   What do you need to think for? You take my dad, and I'll take your daughter-in-law.

MRS. CAI [aside]   If I don't agree he'll strangle me! [To them.] Very well.
95   Come home with me, both of you.

DONKEY   Let's go.

[Exeunt.]

[Enter DOU E.]

DOU E   I am Duanyun,[5] and my home was in Chuzhou. When I was three I lost my mother; and when I was seven I had to leave my father, for he sent me to Mistress Cai as her son's child-bride, and she changed my name to
100   Dou E. At seventeen I married; but unluckily my husband died three years ago. Now I am twenty. There is a Doctor Lu in town who owes my mother-in-law twenty taels including interest; and though she has asked him several times for the money, he hasn't paid her back. She's gone today to try to collect the debt. Ah, when shall I escape from my misery?

105   My heart is full of grief,
        I have suffered for so many years!
        Morning or evening it is all the same:
        From dawn to dusk I can neither eat nor sleep,
        Racked by sad dreams at night, sad thoughts by day,
110   Unending sorrow which I cannot banish,
        Unceasing reasons for fresh misery.
        Wretchedness makes me weep, grief makes me frown;
    Will this never come to an end?
    Is it my fate to be wretched all my life?
115   Who else knows grief like mine?
        For my sorrow, like flowing water, never ceases.
        At three I lost my mother, at seven was torn from my father;
        Then the life of the husband I married was cut short;
        So my mother-in-law and I are left as widows,
120   With no one to care for us or see to our needs.
        Did I burn too little incense in my last life[6]
        That my marriage was unlucky?
        We should all do good betimes;
        So I mourn for my husband and serve my mother-in-law,
125   Obedient to all her bidding.
    My mother-in-law has been gone a long time to collect that debt. What can be keeping her?

[Enter MISTRESS CAI with OLD ZHANG and DONKEY.]

MRS. CAI   Wait here at the door while I go in.

DONKEY   All right, mother. Go in and tell her her husband is at the door.

[MISTRESS CAI sees DOU E.]

130 DOU E   So you're back, mother. Have you had a meal?

MRS. CAI [crying]   Ah, poor child! How am I going to break this to you?

DOU E   I see her in floods of tears,

---

5. Dou E identifies herself with a humble self-reference for a young woman.
6. A reference to the Buddhist belief in

karma, the doctrine that one's actions determine one's destiny in future incarnations.

Hiding some grief in her heart;
Greeting her quickly, I beg her to tell me the reason.

135 MRS. CAI   How can I say this?

DOU E   She's shilly-shallying and looks ashamed.
What has upset you, mother? Why are you crying?

MRS. CAI   When I asked Doctor Lu for the silver, he lured me outside the town, then tried to strangle me; but an old man called Zhang and his son
140 Donkey saved my life. Now Old Zhang is going to marry me: that's why I'm upset.

DOU E   That would never do, mother! Please think again! We're not short of money. Besides, you are growing old—how can you take another husband?

MRS. CAI   Child, I couldn't do anything else!

145 DOU E   Mother, listen to me!
What will become of you
If you choose a day and solemnize a wedding?[7]
Now your hair is as white as snow,
How can you wear the bright silk veil of a bride?
150 No wonder they say it is hard to keep women at home,[8]
If at sixty, when all thought of love should be over,
You've forgotten your former husband,
And taken a fancy to another man!
This will make others split their sides with laughter!
155 Yes, split their sides with laughter!
Like the widow who fanned her husband's tomb,
You're no tender bamboo shoot, no tender shoot.
How can you paint your eyebrows and remarry?
Your husband left you his property,
160 Made provision for the future,
For daily food and a good livelihood,
So that you and your son could remain beholden to no one,
And live to a ripe old age.
Did he go to such trouble for nothing?

165 MRS. CAI   Since it has come to this, I think you'd better take a husband too, and today can be the wedding day.

DOU E   You take a husband if you must. I won't!

MRS. CAI   The date is fixed, and they are already here.

DONKEY   Now we shall marry into their family. Our hats are brushed as good
170 as new, and have narrow brims like bridegrooms'! Good! Fine!

DOU E   Stand back, you fellows!
Women should not believe all men say;
Such a marriage could not last.
Where did she find this old yokel,
175 And this other ruffian here?
Have you no feeling left for the dead?
You must think this over again.
Your husband worked in different cities and counties
To amass a well-earned fortune, and lack nothing.

7. That is, by burning incense in ancestral halls.
8. According to a Chinese proverb, "A grown girl is not to be kept at home; if you try, you only make an enemy out of her."

180   How can you let his estate go to Donkey Zhang?
       He tilled the land, but others are reaping the harvest.
            [*Exit.*]

ZHANG [*to* MRS. CAI]   Let us go and drink, ma'am.
            [*Exeunt.*]

DONKEY   Dou E refuses to have me, but I shan't let her get away: she will
       have to be my wife. Now I'll drink with my old man! [*Exit.*]

Act 2

[*Enter* DOCTOR LU.]

DOCTOR   I am Doctor Lu. I lured Mistress Cai outside the town and was just
       going to strangle her when two men rescued her. Today I am opening shop.
       I wonder who will turn up.
            [*Enter* DONKEY.]

DONKEY   I am Donkey Zhang. Dou E still refuses to marry me. Now the old
5   woman is ill, I'm going to poison her; for once the old one is dead, the young
       one will have to be my wife.[9] Ah, here is a drug shop. Doctor! I want a drug!

DOCTOR   What drug do you want?

DONKEY   I want some poison.

DOCTOR   Who dares sell you poison? How can you ask such a thing?

10 DONKEY   You won't let me have it then?

DOCTOR   I won't. What are you going to do about it?

DONKEY [*seizing him*]   Fine! Fine! Aren't you the man who tried to murder
       Mistress Cai? Do you think I don't recognize you? I'll take you to court.

DOCTOR [*in panic*]   Let me go, brother! I've got it! I've got it!
            [*Gives him the poison.*]

15 DONKEY   Now that I've got the poison, I'm going home.
            [*Exit.*]

DOCTOR   So that man who came to buy poison was one of the men who res-
       cued the widow. Since I've given him poison, he may get me into further
       trouble later. I'd better close my shop and go to Zhuozhou[1] to sell drugs.
            [*Exit.*]

[*Enter* MISTRESS CAI, *supported by* OLD ZHANG *and* DONKEY.]

20 ZHANG   I came to Mistress Cai's house hoping to be her second husband.
       Who would have thought that the widow would fall ill? I am really too
       unlucky. If there's anything you fancy to eat, ma'am, just let me know.

MRS. CAI   I'd like some mutton tripe soup.

ZHANG   Son, go and tell Dou E to make some mutton tripe soup for her
       mother-in-law.

25 DONKEY   Dou E! Your mother-in-law wants some mutton tripe soup. Look
       sharp about it!
            [*Enter* DOU E.]

DOU E   I am Dou E. My mother-in-law is unwell and wants some mutton tripe
       soup, so I've made her some. When you think of it, some women are too fickle!
       She wants to lie with a husband all her life,

---

9. That is, social and economic necessity will
force Dou E to accept him as a husband.

1. A city in Hebei province, northeastern
China.

30   Unwilling to sleep alone;
       First she married one, and now she has picked another.
       Some women never speak of household matters,
       But pick up all the gossip,
       Describe their husbands' adventures,
35   And are always up to some low tricks themselves.
       Is there one like Lady Zhuo[2] who stooped to serve in a tavern?
       Or like Meng Guang[3] who showed such respect to her husband?
       The women today are different:
       You can neither tell their character from their speech,
40   Nor judge them by their actions.
       They're all of them faithless, all run after new lovers;
       And before their husband's graves are dry
       They set aside their mourning for new clothes.
       Where is the woman whose tears for her husband
45   Caused the Great Wall to crumble?[4]
       Where is she who left her washing
       And drowned herself in the stream?[5]
       Where is she who changed into stone
       Through longing for her husband?[6]
50   How shameful that women today are so unfaithful,
       So few of them are chaste, so many wanton!
       All, all are gone, those virtuous women of old;
       For wives will not cleave to their husbands!
     Now the soup is ready. I had better take it in.

    DONKEY   Let me take it to her. [*He takes the bowl.*] This hasn't much flavor.
55   Bring some salt and vinegar.

             [DOU E *goes out.* DONKEY *puts poison in the soup.* DOU E *comes back.*]

    DOU E   Here are the salt and vinegar.

    DONKEY   Put some in.

    DOU E   You say that it lacks salt and vinegar,
60   Adding these will improve the flavor.
       I hope my mother will be better soon,
       And the soup will serve as a cordial.
       Then the three of you can live happily together.

    ZHANG   Son, is the soup ready?

---

2. Zhuo Wenjun, the daughter of a rich man, who eloped with Sima Xiangru (179–117 B.C.E.), a famous Han Dynasty scholar. Since they were poor, they kept a small tavern in Chengdu where she served as barmaid [translator's note].

3. Wife of Liang Hung of the Later Han dynasty. She showed her respect and love for her husband by raising the dinner tray as high as her eyebrows when she brought it to him.

4. According to a folktale, Meng Jiang-nu's husband, a conscript laborer, died while building the Great Wall during the reign of the First Emperor of Qin. She went to the wall to find her missing husband and wept so bitterly that part of it collapsed, revealing his dead body.

5. During the Spring and Autumn Period (770–475 B.C.E.), Wu Zixu, a minister of Chu, fled to Wu. He came upon a woman doing her laundry by a river, who fed him and then drowned herself in the river—both to prove that she would not betray him to his pursuers and because she had compromised her chastity by taking in a man who was a stranger.

6. A reference to a legend about a faithful wife who, during her husband's absence from home, climbed a hill every day to watch for his return. Finally she turned into a boulder, which was called *wang-fu shi* (watching-for-husband stone).

65 DONKEY   Here it is. Take it.
    ZHANG [*taking the soup*]   Have some soup, ma'am.
    MRS. CAI   I am sorry to give you so much trouble. You have some first.
    ZHANG   Won't you try it?
    MRS. CAI   No, I want *you* to drink it first.
        [OLD ZHANG *drinks the soup.*]
70 DOU E   One says: "Won't you try it?"
        The other says: "You have it!"
        What a shameful way to talk!
        How can I help being angry?
        The new couple is in transports;
75   Forgetting her first husband,
        She listens to this new man's lightest word.
        Now her heart is like a willow seed in the breeze,
        Not steadfast as a rock.
        Old love is nothing to new love:
80   She wants to live with this new man forever,
        Without a thought for the other man far away.
    ZHANG   Why has this soup made me dizzy?
        [*He falls to the ground.*]
    MRS. CAI   Why should you feel unwell after that soup? [*Panic-stricken.*] Take
    a grip on yourself, old man! Don't give up so easily! [*Wails.*]
85 DOU E   It's no use grieving for him;
        All mortal men must die when their time is up.
        Some fall ill, some meet with accidents;
        Some catch a chill, some are struck down by heat;
        Some die of hunger, surfeit, or overwork;
90   But every death has its cause,
        Human life is ruled by fate,[7]
        And no man can control it,
        For our span of life is predestined.
        He has been here a few days only;
95   He is not of your family,
        And he never sent you wedding gifts:
        Sheep, wine, silk, or money.
        For a time you stayed together,
        But now he is dead and gone!
100   I am not an unfilial daughter,
        But I fear what the neighbors may say;
        So stop your moaning and wailing:
        He is not the man you married as a girl.
        [OLD ZHANG *dies.*]
    MRS. CAI   What shall we do? He's dead!
105 DOU E   He's no relation—I have no tears for him.
        There's no need to be so overcome with grief,
        Or to cry so bitterly and lose your head!

---

7. Human affairs are subject to the authority of Heaven and Earth, which is often invoked in this play when human judgment falters.

DONKEY   Fine! You've poisoned my father! What are you going to do about it?

MRS. CAI   Child, you had better marry him now.

110 DOU E   How can you say such a thing, mother?
This fellow forced my mother-in-law to keep him;
Now he's poisoned his father,
But whom does he think he can frighten?

MRS. CAI   You'd better marry him, child.

115 DOU E   A horse can't have two saddles;[8]
I was your son's wife when he was alive,
Yet now you are urging me to marry again.
This is unthinkable!

120 DONKEY   Dou E, you murdered my old man. Do you want to settle this in private or settle it in public?

DOU E   What do you mean?

DONKEY   If you want it settled in public, I'll drag you to the court, and you'll have to confess to the murder of my father! If you want it settled in private, agree to be my wife. Then I'll let you off.

125 DOU E   I am innocent. I'll go with you to the prefect.[9]

[DONKEY *drags* DOU E *and* MISTRESS CAI *out.*]

Act 3

[*Enter the* PREFECT *with an* ATTENDANT.]

PREFECT   I am a hard-working official;
I make money out of my lawsuits;
But when my superiors come to investigate,
I pretend to be ill and stay at home in bed.

5   I am prefect of Chuzhou. This morning I am holding court.
Attendant, summon the court!

[*The* ATTENDANT *gives a shout.*]

[*Enter* DONKEY, *dragging in* DOU E *and* MISTRESS CAI.]

DONKEY   I want to lodge a charge.

ATTENDANT   Come over here.

[DONKEY *and* DOU E *kneel to the* PREFECT, *who kneels to them.*][1]

PREFECT [*kneeling*]   Please rise.

10 ATTENDANT   Your Honor, this is a citizen who's come to ask for justice. Why should you kneel to him?

PREFECT   Why? Because such citizens are food and clothes to me!

[*The* ATTENDANT *assents.*]

PREFECT   Which of you is the plaintiff, which the defendant? Out with the truth now!

15 DONKEY   I am the plaintiff. I accuse this young woman, Dou E, of poisoning my father with soup. Let justice be done, Your Honor!

PREFECT   Who poisoned the soup?

DOU E   Not I!

---

8. A proverb meaning that a wife cannot serve two husbands.
9. The presiding judicial magistrate.

1. A stylized self-presenting gesture of humility that is appropriate for Donkey and Dou E, but ironic for a prefect.

MRS. CAI   Not I!

20 DONKEY   Not I!

PREFECT   If none of you did it, I wonder if I could have done it?

DOU E   Your Honor is as discerning as a mirror,
    And can see my innermost thoughts.
    There was nothing wrong with the soup,
25   I know nothing about the poison;
    He made a pretense of tasting it,
    Then his father drank it and fell down dead.
    It is not that I want to deny my guilt in court;
    But I cannot confess to a crime I have not committed!

30 PREFECT   Low characters are like that: they'll only confess when put to
torture. Attendant! Bring the bastinado to beat her.

       [The ATTENDANT *beats* DOU E. *Three times she faints and he has to sprinkle
       her with water to bring her round.*]

DOU E   This terrible beating is more than I can bear.
    You brought this on yourself, mother. Why complain?
    May all women in the world who marry again
35   Be warned by me!
    Why are they shouting so fiercely?
    I groan with pain;
    I come to myself, then faint away again.
    A thousand strokes: I am streaming with blood!
40   At each blow from the bastinado
    My blood spurts out and my skin is torn from my flesh;
    My spirit takes flight in fear,
    Approaching the nether regions.[2]
    Who knows the bitterness in my heart?
45   It was not I who poisoned the old man;
    I beg Your Honor to find out the truth!

PREFECT   Will you confess now?

DOU E   I swear it was not I who put in the poison.

PREFECT   In that case, beat the old woman.

50 DOU E [*hastily*]   Stop, stop! Don't beat my mother-in-law!
    Rather than that, I'll say I poisoned the old man.

PREFECT   Fasten her in the cangue[3] and throw her into the gaol for the condemned. Tomorrow she shall be taken to the marketplace to be executed.

MRS. CAI [*weeping*]   Dou E, my child! It's because of me you are losing your
55 life. Oh, this will be the death of me!

DOU E   When I am a headless ghost, unjustly killed,
    Do you think I will spare that scoundrel?
    Men cannot be deceived forever,
    And Heaven will see this injustice.
60   I struggled as hard as I could, but now I am helpless;
    I was forced to confess that I poisoned the old man;
    How could I let you be beaten, mother?
    How could I save you except by dying myself?

       [*She is led off.*]

2. That is, nearing death.
3. A frame used to confine the neck and hands in a portable pillory or stocks.

DONKEY   If she's to be killed tomorrow, I'll hang around.
     [*Exit.*]

65   MRS. CAI   Poor child! Tomorrow she will be killed in the marketplace. This
will be the death of me! [*Exit.*]

PREFECT   Tomorrow Dou E will be executed. Today's work is done. Bring me
my horse; I am going home to drink.
     [*Exeunt.*]

     [*Enter the* OFFICER *in charge.*]

OFFICER   I am the officer in charge of executions. Today we are putting a
70   criminal to death. We must stand guard at the end of the road, to see that
no one comes through.

     [*Enter the* ATTENDANTS. *They beat the drum and the gong three times;
then the* EXECUTIONER *enters, sharpens his sword, and waves a flag.* DOU
E *is led on in a cangue. The gong and drum are beaten.*]

EXECUTIONER   Get a move on! Let no one pass this way.

DOU E   Through no fault of mine I am called a criminal,
     And condemned to be beheaded—
75   I cry out to Heaven and Earth of this injustice!
     I reproach both Earth and Heaven
     For they would not save me.
     The sun and moon give light by day and by night,
     Mountains and rivers watch over the world of men;
80   Yet Heaven cannot tell the innocent from the guilty;
     And confuses the wicked with the good!
     The good are poor, and die before their time;
     The wicked are rich, and live to a great old age.
     The gods are afraid of the mighty and bully the weak;
85   They let evil take its course.
     Ah, Earth! you will not distinguish good from bad,
     And, Heaven! you let me suffer this injustice!
     Tears pour down my cheeks in vain!

EXECUTIONER   Get a move on! We are late.

90   DOU E   The cangue round my neck makes me stagger this way and that,
     And I'm jostled backward and forward by the crowd.
     Will you do me a favor, brother?

EXECUTIONER   What do you want?

DOU E   If you take me the front way, I shall bear you a grudge;
95   If you take me the back way, I shall die content.
     Please do not think me willful!

EXECUTIONER   Now that you're going to the execution ground, are there any
relatives you want to see?

DOU E   I am going to die. What relatives do I need?

100   EXECUTIONER   Why did you ask me just now to take you the back way?

DOU E   Please don't go by the front street, brother,
     But take me by the back street.
     The other way my mother-in-law might see me.

EXECUTIONER   You can't escape death, so why worry if she sees you?

105   DOU E   If my mother-in-law were to see me in chains being led to the
execution ground—
     She would burst with indignation!

She would burst with indignation!
Please grant me this comfort, brother, before I die!

[*Enter* MISTRESS CAI.]

110 MRS. CAI   Ah, Heaven! Isn't that my daughter-in-law? This will be the death of me!

EXECUTIONER   Stand back, old woman!

DOU E   Let her come closer so that I can say a few words to her.

EXECUTIONER   Hey, old woman! Come here. Your daughter-in-law wants to 115 speak to you.

MRS. CAI   Poor child! This will be the death of me!

DOU E   Mother, when you were unwell and asked for mutton tripe soup, I prepared some for you. Donkey Zhang made me fetch more salt and vinegar so that he could poison the soup, and then told me to give it to you. He didn't 120 know his old man would drink it. Donkey Zhang poisoned the soup to kill you, so that he could force me to be his wife. He never thought his father would die instead. To take revenge, he dragged me to court. Because I didn't want you to suffer, I had to confess to murder, and now I am going to be killed. In future, mother, if you have gruel to spare, give me half a bowl; and if you have 125 paper money to spare, burn some for me, for the sake of your dead son![4]

Take pity on one who is dying an unjust death;
Take pity on one whose head will be struck from her body;
Take pity on one who has worked with you in your home;
Take pity on one who has neither mother nor father;
130 Take pity on one who has served you all these years;
And at festivals offer my spirit a bowl of cold gruel.

MRS. CAI [*weeping*]   Don't worry. Ah, this will be the death of me!

DOU E   Burn some paper coins to my headless corpse,
For the sake of your dead son.
135 We wail and complain to Heaven:
There is no justice! Dou E is wrongly slain!

EXECUTIONER   Now then, old woman, stand back! The time has come.

[DOU E *kneels, and the* EXECUTIONER *removes the cangue from her neck.*]

DOU E   I want to say three things, officer. If you will let me, I shall die content. I want a clean mat and a white silk streamer twelve feet long to hang 140 on the flagpole. When the sword strikes off my head, not a drop of my warm blood will stain the ground. It will all fly up instead to the white silk streamer. This is the hottest time of summer, sir. If injustice has indeed been done, three feet of snow will cover my dead body. Then this district will suffer from drought for three whole years.

145 EXECUTIONER   Be quiet! What a thing to say!

[*The* EXECUTIONER *waves his flag.*]

DOU E   A dumb woman was blamed for poisoning herself;
A buffalo is whipped while it toils for its master.

EXECUTIONER   Why is it suddenly so overcast? It is snowing!

[*He prays to Heaven.*]

---

4. By the time of the play's composition, the ancient Chinese custom of offering burnt sacrifices for the newly dead had been superseded by the burning of paper symbols of worldly wealth—coins, livestock, luxury goods, etc.—to help ensure prosperity in the afterlife.

DOU E   Once Zou Yan[5] caused frost to appear

150   Now snow will show the injustice done to me!

> [*The* EXECUTIONER *beheads her, and the* ATTENDANT *sees to her body.*]

EXECUTIONER   A fine stroke! Now let us go and have a drink.

> [*The* ATTENDANTS *assent, and carry the body off.*]

Act 4

> [*Enter* DOU TIANZHANG.][6]

DOU   I am Dou Tianzhang. It is thirteen years since I left my child Duanyun. I went to the capital, passed the examination and was made a counsellor.[7] And because I am able, just, and upright, the emperor appointed me Inspector of the Huai River Area.[8] I have traveled from place to place investigating cases,

5   and I have the sword of authority and golden tally[9] so that I can punish corrupt officials without first reporting to the throne. My heart is torn between grief and happiness. I am glad because I am a high official responsible for seeing that justice is done. I am sad, though, because when Duanyun was seven I gave her to Mistress Cai; and after I became an official and sent for

10   news of the widow to Chuzhou, the neighbors said she had moved away—to what place they did not know—and there has been no word since. I have wept for my child till my eyes are dim and my hair is white. Now I have come south of the Huai River, and am wondering why this district has had no rain for three years. I shall rest in the district office, boy. Tell the local officers

15   they need not call today. I shall see them early tomorrow.

SERVANT [*calling out*]   The officers and secretaries are not to call on His Excellency today. He will see them early tomorrow.

DOU   Tell the secretaries of the different departments to send all their cases here for my inspection. I shall study some under the lamp.

> [*The* SERVANT *brings him the files.*]

20 DOU   Light the lamp for me. You have been working hard, and you may rest now. But come when I call you.

> [*The* SERVANT *lights the lamp and leaves.*]

DOU   I shall go through a few cases. Here is one concerning Dou E, who poisoned her father-in-law. Curious that the first culprit's surname should be the same as mine! To murder one's father-in-law is one of the unpardonable

25   crimes;[1] so it seems there are lawless elements among my clan. Since this case has been dealt with, I need not read it. I'll put it at the bottom of the pile

---

5. A loyal official serving the prince of Yan during the Warring States period (475–221 B.C.E.). When the prince imprisoned him on the strength of an enemy's accusation, Zou Yan cried out to heaven, which exhibited displeasure by bringing frost in midsummer.

6. His new status is indicated by a cap and a sash. He is accompanied by his servant (a role that would be played as a clown).

7. Specifically, a counsellor for state affairs in the Imperial Secretariat.

8. That is, a provincial surveillance commissioner for two adjacent judicial circuits north of the Yangtze River: one to the west of the Huai River, and the other to the east of the Huai River.

9. Symbols of authority, given by the emperor. The sword empowered the receiver to deliver the death penalty without the usual mandatory review by a central authority (an extraordinary sanction); the golden tablet was worn by high-ranking Yuan officials.

1. The Criminal Law Section in the *History of Yuan* lists ten unpardonable crimes: to contemplate rebellion, to contemplate a greatly subversive act, to contemplate treason, to commit a detestable or subversive act (Dou E's crime), to lack moral rules, to be extremely disrespectful, to lack filial piety, to abuse one for whom one would be obliged to mourn, to behave unrighteously, and to commit incest.

and look at another. Wait, I suddenly feel drowsy. I suppose I am growing old, and am tired after traveling. I will take a short nap on the desk. [*He sleeps.*]

[*Enter* DOU E's *ghost.*]

DOU E   Day after day I weep in the underworld,[2]
30   Waiting impatiently for my revenge.
      I pace on slowly in darkness,
      Then am borne along by the whirlwind;
      Enveloped by mist I come swiftly in ghostly form.
[*She looks about her.*] Now the door-gods[3] will not let me pass. I am the
35   daughter of Inspector Dou. Though I died unjustly, my father does not know it; so I have come to visit him in his dreams.

[*She enters the room and weeps.*]

DOU [*shedding tears*]   Duanyun, my child! Where have you been?

[DOU E's *spirit leaves,*[4] *and* DOU *wakes up.*]

How odd! I fell asleep and dreamed that I saw my daughter coming towards me; but where is she now? Let me go on with these cases.

[DOU E's *spirit enters and makes the lamp burn low.*]

40   Strange! I was just going to read a case when the light flickered and dimmed. My servant is asleep; I must trim the wick myself. [*As he trims the lamp,* DOU E's *spirit rearranges the file.*] Now the light is brighter, I can read again. "This concerns the criminal Dou E, who poisoned her father-in-law." Strange! I read this case first, and put it under the others. How has it come to the top?
45   Since this case has already been dealt with let me put it at the bottom again and study a different one. [*Once more* DOU E's *spirit makes the lamp burn low.*] Strange! Why is the light flickering again? I must trim it once more. [*As* DOU *trims the light,* DOU E's *spirit once more turns over the file.*] Now the lamp is brighter, I can read another case. "This concerns the criminal Dou E, who
50   poisoned her father-in-law." How extraordinary! I definitely put this at the bottom of the pile just before I trimmed the lamp. How has it come to the top again? Can there be ghosts in this office? Well, ghost or no ghost, an injustice must have been done. Let me put this underneath and read another. [DOU E's *spirit makes the lamp burn low again.*] Strange! The lamp is flickering again.
55   Can there actually be a ghost here tampering with it? I'll trim it once more. [*As he trims the wick,* DOU E's *spirit comes up to him and he sees her. He strikes his sword on the desk.*] Ah, there's the ghost! I warn you, I am the emperor's inspector of justice. If you come near, I'll cut you in two. Hey, boy! How can you sleep so soundly? Get up at once! Ghosts! Ghosts! This is terrifying!

DOU E   Fear is making him lose his head;
60   The sound of my weeping has frightened him more than ever.
      Here, Dou Tianzhang, my old father,
      Will you let your daughter Dou E bow to you?

DOU   You say I am your father, ghost, and offer to bow to me as my daughter. Aren't you mistaken? My daughter's name is Duanyun. When she was

---

2. That is, she weeps at "the Home-gazing Terrace" to which, according to Chinese folklore, the dead ascend in order to watch their families in the human world.
3. At New Year's, pictures of the gods of the left and right doors are hung to ward off spirits.

4. A "false exit," as it is known in classical Chinese theater: the actor turns his or her back toward the audience to indicate an absence, and then simply turns around again to "reenter."

65 seven she was given to Mistress Cai as a child-bride. You call yourself by a different name, Dou E. How can you be my child?

DOU E   After you gave me to Mistress Cai, father, she changed my name to Dou E.

DOU   So you say you are my child Duanyun. Let me ask you this: Are you the 70 woman accused of murdering her father-in-law and executed?

DOU E   I am.

DOU   Hush, girl! I've wept for you till my eyes grew dim, and worried for you till my hair turned white. How did you come to be condemned for this most heinous of crimes? I am a high official now, whose duty it is to see 75 that justice is done. I have come here to investigate cases and discover corrupt officials. You are my child, but you are guilty of the worst crime of all. If I could not control you, how can I control others? When I married you to the widow's son, I expected you to observe the Three Duties and Four Virtues.[5] The Three Duties are obedience to your father before marriage, 80 obedience to your husband after marriage, and obedience to your son after your husband's death. The Four Virtues are to serve your parents-in-law, to show respect to your husband, to remain on good terms with your sisters-in-law, and to live in peace with your neighbors. But regardless of your duties, you have committed the gravest crime of all! The proverb says: Look 85 before you leap, or you may be sorry too late. For three generations no son of our clan has broken the law; for five generations no daughter has married again. As a married woman, you should have studied propriety and morality; but instead you perpetrated the most terrible crime. You have disgraced our ancestors and injured my good name. Tell me the whole 90 truth at once, and nothing but the truth! If you utter one false word, I shall send you to the tutelary god; then your spirit will never reenter human form, but remain a hungry ghost forever in the shades.[6]

DOU E   Don't be so angry, father. Don't threaten me like an angry wolf or tiger! Let me explain this to you. At three, I lost my mother; at seven, I was 95 parted from my father, when you sent me to Mistress Cai as her future daughter-in-law, and my name was changed to Dou E. At seventeen, I married; but unhappily two years later my husband died, and I stayed as a widow with my mother-in-law. In Chuzhou there lived a certain Doctor Lu, who owed my mother-in-law twenty taels of silver. One day when she went 100 to ask him for the money, he lured her outside the town and tried to strangle her; but Donkey Zhang and his father came by and saved her life. Old Zhang asked: "Whom do you have in your family, ma'am?" My mother-in-law said: "No one but a widowed daughter-in-law." Old Zhang said: "In that case, I will marry you. What do you say?" When my mother-in-law refused, 105 the two men said: "If you don't agree, we shall strangle you again!" So she was frightened into marrying him. Donkey tried to seduce me several times, but I always resisted him. One day my mother-in-law was unwell and wanted some mutton tripe soup. When I prepared it, Donkey told me to let him taste it. "It's good," he said. "But there's not enough salt and vinegar." When I

5. Fundamental Confucian principles. For a gentleman, the Three Duties are to cultivate nonviolence and gravity of bearing, to serve the truth, and to speak only what is worthy and just; the Four Virtues are sincerity, benevolence, filial piety, and propriety.

6. In Chinese folklore, ghosts are restless souls that wander forever in a perpetual state of unfulfilled desire. *To the tutelary god*: that is, to the temple of the city's guardian god.

110 went to fetch more, he secretly poisoned the soup and told me to take it to her. But my mother-in-law gave it to Old Zhang. Then blood spurted from the old man's mouth, nose, ears and eyes, and he died. At that Donkey said, "Dou E, you poisoned my father. Do you want to settle this in public or in private?" "What do you mean?" I asked. "If you want it settled in public," he

115 said, "I shall take the case to court, and you will pay for my father's death—with your life. If you want it settled in private, then be my wife." "A good horse won't have two saddles," I told him. "A good woman won't remarry. For three generations no son of our clan has broken the law; for five generations no daughter has married again. I'd rather die than be your wife. I am inno-

120 cent. I'll go to court with you." Then he dragged me before the prefect. I was tried again and again, stripped and tortured; but I would rather have died than make a false confession. When the prefect saw that I wouldn't confess, he threatened to have my mother-in-law tortured; and because she was too old to stand the torture, I made a false confession. Then they took me to the

125 execution ground to kill me. I made three vows before my death. First, I asked for a twelve-foot white silk streamer and swore that, if I was innocent, when the sword struck off my head no drop of my blood would stain the ground—it would all fly up to the streamer. Next I vowed that, though it was midsummer, Heaven would send down three feet of snow to cover my body.

130 Last, I vowed that this district would suffer three years' drought. All these vows have come true, because of the crime against me.

> I complained not to any official but to Heaven,
> For I could not express the injustice that was done me;
> And to save my mother from torture

135
> I confessed to a crime of which I was innocent,
> And remained true to my dead husband.
> Three feet of snow fell on my corpse;
> My hot blood gushed to the white silk streamer;
> Zou Yan called down frost,

140
> And snow showed the injustice done me.
> Your child committed no crime,
> But suffered a great wrong:
> For resisting seduction I was executed!
> I would not disgrace my clan, so I lost my life!

145
> Day after day in the shades
> My spirit mourns alone.
> You are sent by the emperor with authority;
> Consider this case and this man's wickedness;
> Cut him in pieces and avenge my wrong!

150 DOU [weeping]   Ah, my wrongly slain daughter, how this wrings my heart! Let me ask you this: Is it because of you that this district has suffered for three years from drought?

DOU E   It is.

DOU   So! This reminds me of a story. In the Han Dynasty[7] there was a virtu-

155 ous widow whose mother-in-law hanged herself, and whose sister-in-law accused her of murdering the old woman. The governor of Donge[8] had her

---

7. 206 B.C.E.–220 C.E.
8. Unclear reference; Shih Chung-wen trans-

lates this title instead as the governor of Tung-hai, or the prefect of the East Sea.

executed, but because of her unjust death there was no rain in that district for three years. When Lord Yu came to investigate, he saw the dead woman's ghost carrying a plea and weeping before the hall; and after he changed the verdict, killed a bull, and sacrificed at her grave there was a great downpour of rain. This case is rather similar to that. Tomorrow I shall right this wrong for you.

> I bow my white head in sorrow
> Over the innocent girl who was wrongly slain.
> Now dawn is breaking, you had better leave me;
> Tomorrow I shall set right this miscarriage of justice.

DOU E [*bowing*]   With sharp sword of authority and tally of gold,
> You will kill all evil and corrupt officials,
> To serve your sovereign and relieve the people!

[*She turns back.*] There's one thing I nearly forgot, father. My mother-in-law is old now, and has no one to look after her.

DOU   This is dutiful, my child.

DOU E   I ask my father to care for my mother-in-law,
> For she is growing old. My father now
> Will reopen my case and change the unjust verdict.
>
> > [*Exit.*]

DOU   Dawn is breaking. Call the local officers, and all those concerned in the case of Dou E.

SERVANT   Yes, Your Excellency.

> [*The* PREFECT, MISTRESS CAI, DONKEY ZHANG *and* DOCTOR LU *are sent in. They kneel before* DOU.]

DOU   Mistress Cai, do you recognize me?

MRS. CAI   No, Your Excellency.

DOU   I am Dou Tianzhang. Listen, all of you, to the verdict! Donkey Zhang murdered his father and blackmailed good citizens. He shall be executed in public. Let him be taken to the marketplace to be killed. The prefect passed a wrong sentence. He shall be given one hundred strokes and have his name struck off the official list.[9] Doctor Lu is guilty of selling poison. Let him be beheaded in the marketplace. Mistress Cai shall be lodged in my house. The wrong sentence passed on Dou E shall be rescinded.

> Let the Donkey be killed in public,
> The prefect dismissed from office;
> Then let us offer a great sacrifice
> So that my daughter's spirit may go to heaven.

9. That is, he will never again be eligible for government employment; hence, he will never be able to improve his social standing.

SNOW IN MIDSUMMER, ACT 3

ZEAMI MOTOKIYO

1363–1443

A MONG the numerous theatrical forms and dramatic genres developed in Japan, none has been more revered than the stately yet elusive noh theater that became a high art form in the fourteenth century. While kabuki theater would later dazzle the senses with extravagant costumes, acrobatic movements, and elaborate scenic effects, noh achieved its dramatic and theatrical effects through understatement, ritualistic gesture, and a poetic conception of language, character, and the stage. In the evolution of noh from earlier forms of theater to a courtly entertainment of the samurai, or warrior, class, Zeami Motokiyo is a celebrated and central figure. Actor, head of an acting troupe, and playwright, Zeami refined the art of noh into a theatrical form combining songs, dance, music, and poetry. During his long and productive career, Zeami articulated the aesthetics of this newly crafted art and its performance in a series of treatises that rank among the world's most important works of dramatic theory.

Born in 1363, Zeami was the son of Kanami Kiyotsugu (1333–1384), who was an accomplished actor and playwright and the head of an acting troupe specializing in *sarugaku* (or *sarugaku noh*, as the theatrical form was then called). In 1374, Kanami and his eleven-year-old son performed at the Imakumano Shrine in Kyoto, the imperial capital of medieval Japan. As the result of this performance, they won the patronage of the young shogun (or military ruler) Ashikaga Yoshimitsu (1358–1408), who, as part of his successful attempt to enhance his legitimacy, aided the arts as the earlier nobility had always done. With Yoshimitsu's support and with the benefit of a highly cultured audience, Kanami brought a number of innovations to *sarugaku* that furthered its development

into the sophisticated art we recognize as noh.

His son became a favorite of the shogun, serving him as both artist and companion/ lover, and upon Kanami's death the young Zeami took over as head of his father's troupe. Consolidating and extending his father's theatrical innovations, Zeami became one of the noh theater's most accomplished actors, playwrights, and theorists. In a number of studies—including *Fushikadensho* (*Teachings on Style and the Flower,* 1400–02), *Shikado* (*The True Path to the Flower,* 1420), and *Nosakusho* (*On Writing Noh Plays,* 1423)—Zeami discussed the origins of noh and its defining features, the intricacies of acting, and the principles of noh composition. About fifty plays are now ascribed to him, including some that are extensive revisions of earlier texts, and the greatest of these—such plays as *Komachi at Sekidera* and *ATSUMORI*—stand as crowning achievements in the canon of noh drama. With the death of Yoshimitsu in 1408, however, Zeami lost his privileged position at court; and though he continued to act and write for the noh theater, the shoguns who followed Yoshimitsu extended their patronage to other individuals and rival theatrical traditions. In 1422, Zeami passed the leadership of his acting troupe to his eldest son, Motomosa, and became a Buddhist monk. Greater disappointment and hardship awaited him. Under the shogun Yoshinori, who assumed power in 1429, Zeami and Motomosa were relieved of their official responsibilities; and in 1434 Zeami was banished to the remote island of Sado, where he composed *Kintōsho* (*Book of the Golden Island*) about his exile. When he returned—most likely following the general amnesty declared after the assassination of Yoshinori in 1441—he probably lived until

75 dampened by the waves that
drench our rocky pillows,
in seaside shacks we huddle together
befriended only by Suma folk—
bent like wind-bent pines on the strands
　　　　[Circles left to the shite spot.]
80 of evening smoke rising from the fires—
　　　　[Waving his fan in his left hand, the SHITE *moves forward.]*
brushwood, it's called,
　　　　[Holding out his fan parallel to the floor.]
this stuff piled up to sleep upon.
Our worries, too, pile up in rustic Suma,
where we're forced to play out our lives
　　　　[Pointing his fan to the right, he looks up.]
85 becoming simple Suma folk—
　　　　[Circles to the left.]
such is our clan's fate; how forlorn we are!
　　　　[Stops at backstage center.]

　　　　[The chanting changes from the melodic to the dynamic mode.]

SHITE　And then, on the night of the sixth day of the second month,
Tsunemori, my father, gathered us together
to enjoy ourselves with song and dance.
90 WAKI　And your entertainment that night,
the elegant flute music from your encampment,
was clearly heard by us on the opposing side.
SHITE　It was indeed Atsumori,
awaiting the end, his bamboo flute
95 WAKI　accompanying a variety of
SHITE　ballads and songs,
WAKI　many voices
　　　　[The SHITE *circles right to the shite spot.]*
CHORUS　arise, creating steady cadences.
　　　　[Medium tempo dance. The SHITE *performs a sprightly yet elegant dance to
　　　　the music of the flute and hand drums. This dance, unusual in a warrior
　　　　play, emphasizes Atsumori's artistic sensitivity. The context also foregrounds
　　　　the flute music, which is the normal accompaniment to the dance.]*

SHITE *[Raising his fan]*　And so it is,
100 the royal barque sets forth
　　　　*[The dynamic song becomes strongly rhythmical, matching the steady beats of
　　　　the drums.]*
CHORUS　and all the members of the clan
　　　　[The SHITE *stamps his feet.]*
board their ships to sail.
　　　　[Making a sweeping point with his fan, he turns to the right.]
Not wanting to be late
　　　　[Goes to the front of the stage.]

Atsumori races to the shore;
105   the royal barque and troopships, too,
have already put out to sea.
      [*Raises his fan over his head and looks out into the distance.*]

SHITE   It's hopeless! Reining in his horse
      [*Mimes pulling on the reins with his left hand.*]

amidst the breakers, he stands bewildered.
      [*Waves his fan to indicate agitation.*]

CHORUS   At that very moment
      [*The* SHITE *stamps his feet.*]

110 from behind comes
      [*He turns and faces the bridgeway.*]

Kumagae no Jirō Naozane.
"Don't flee!"
      [*Hurries to the shite spot.*]

he shouts and charges.
Atsumori too
      [*Moves quickly to center front.*]

115 turns about his horse, and
      [*Mimes reining in his horse and races backstage.*]

in the breakers they draw swords
      [*Mimes drawing a sword (represented by his fan) and goes to the front right corner.*]

and exchange blows, twice, thrice,
      [*Strikes with his fan.*]

they are seen to strike;
on horseback they grapple,
      [*Wraps his arms around himself.*]

120 then fall onto the wave-swept shore,
      [*Twirls around and kneels.*]

one atop the other; finally
struck down, Atsumori dies;
      [*Points his fan at his head and looks down.*]

the wheel of fate turns, and they meet.
      [*Stands, goes to center back, and draws his sword.*]

"The enemy's right here!"
      [*Hurries toward the* WAKI.]

125 he cries and is about to strike.
      [*Raises his sword to strike.*]

Returning good for evil,
      [*Kneels.*]

the priest performs services and prays
      [*Stands and returns to backstage.*]

that in the end they will be reborn together
      [*Spreads his arms, moves toward the* WAKI *again, and drops his sword.*]

Fortaxed,° and rammed,°   *Overtaxed / beaten down*
25 We are made hand-tamed
    With these gentlery-men.[3]

Thus they reave us° our rest—   *rob us of*
Our Lady them wary!°   *curse*
These men that are lord-fest,°   *bound to lords*
30 They cause the plow tarry.
That, men say, is for the best—
We find it contrary.
Thus are husbands oppressed
In point to miscarry
35   On live.[4]
Thus hold they us under,
Thus they bring us in blunder,°   *trouble*
It were a great wonder
    And° ever should we thrive.   *If*

40 There shall come a swain
As proud as a po.[5]
He must borrow my wain,°   *wagon*
My plow also;
Then I am full fain°   *glad*
45 To grant ere he go.
Thus live we in pain,
Anger, and woe,
    By night and by day.
He must have if he lang it,
50 If I should forgang it.[6]
I were better be hanged
    Than once say him nay.

For may he get a paint-sleeve[7]
Or brooch nowadays,
55 Woe is him that him grieve
Or once again-says.°   *gainsays*
Dare no man him reprieve,°   *reprove*
What mastery he maes.[8]
And yet may no man lieve°   *believe*
60 One word that he says,
    No letter.
He can make purveyance[9]

3. By these gentry folks (here the retainers, or supervisors, employed by absentee landlords to manage an estate).
4. Thus are farmworkers oppressed to the point of perishing.
5. There shall come a retainer, as proud as a peacock. Here (and in the following lines) Coll refers to the ostentatious livery worn by the "gentlery-men."

6. If he desires (something) he must have it, even if I have to do without (forgo) it.
7. Painted sleeve. This and the brooch in line 54 refer to the badges of authority worn by the landlord's officers.
8. No matter what force he uses.
9. The requisitioning of food or vehicles in the name of the lord or king.

With boast and bragance,°   *bragging*
And all is through maintenance°   *protection*
65   Of men that are greater.

It does me good, as I walk
Thus by mine one,°   *myself*
Of this world for to talk
In manner of moan.
70   To my sheep I will stalk,
And hearken anon,
There abide on a balk,[1]
Or sit on a stone,
    Full soon;
75 For I trow,° pardie,°   *believe / by God*
True men if they be,[2]
We get more company
    Ere it be noon.

        [Enter GIB, *who at first does not see* COLL.*]*

GIB   Benste and Dominus,[3]
80 What may this bemean?°   *mean*
Why fares this world thus?
Such have we not seen.
Lord, these weathers are spiteous°   *spiteful*
And the winds full keen,
85 And the frosts so hideous
They water mine een,°   *eyes*
    No lie.
Now in dry, now in wet,
Now in snow, now in sleet,
90 When my shoon° freeze to my feet   *shoes*
    It is not all easy.

But as far as I ken,
Or yet as I go,[4]
We sely wedmen°   *poor married men*
95 Dree° mickle° woe;   *Suffer / much*
We have sorrow then and then°— *time and time again*
It falls oft so.
Sely Copple,[5] our hen,
Both to and fro
100   She cackles;
But begin she to croak,
To groan or to cluck,

---

1. A ridge of rough grassland dividing two plowed portions of a common field.
2. That is, if the other shepherds, whom Coll has arranged to meet, keep their promise.
3. Bless us and Lord (a corruption of the Latin blessing *Benedicite Dominus*, "Bless us, Lord").
4. That is, as I know from experience.
5. Literally, the crest on a bird's head.

Woe is him is our cock,
 For he is in the shackles.

105 These men that are wed
Have not all their will:
When they are full hard stead°   *hard put to it*
They sigh full still;°   *unceasingly*
God wot° they are led   *knows*
110 Full hard and full ill;
In bower nor in bed
They say nought theretill.°   *thereto*
 This tide°   *time*
My part have I fun;°   *found, learned*
115 I know my lesson:
Woe is him that is bun,°   *bound (in marriage)*
 For he must abide.

But now late in our lives—
A marvel to me,
120 That I think my heart rives°   *breaks*
Such wonders to see;
What that destiny drives
It should so be[6]—
Some men will have two wives,
125 And some men three
 In store.[7]
Some are woe° that has any,   *miserable*
But so far can° I,   *know*
Woe is him that has many,
130 For he feels sore.

But young men a-wooing,
For God that you bought,°   *redeemed*
Be well ware of wedding
And think in your thought:
135 "Had I wist"° is a thing   *known*
That serves of nought.
Mickle° still° mourning   *Much / constant*
Has wedding home brought,
 And griefs,
140 With many a sharp shower,°   *pang*
For thou may catch in an hour
That° shall sow° thee full sour° *That which / vex / bitterly*
 As long as thou lives.

For as ever read I 'pistle,[8]
145 I have one to my fere°   *for my mate*

6. What destiny compels must come to pass.
7. That is, because they remarry after being widowed.
8. That is, epistle—a scriptural reading in the Mass, often from the epistles of St. Paul.

As sharp as a thistle,
As rough as a brere;°   *briar*
She is browed like a bristle,
With a sour-loten cheer,[9]
150 Had she once wet her whistle
She could sing full clear
   Her Pater Noster.[1]
She is great as a whale;
She has a gallon of gall:
155 By him that died for us all,
   I would I had run to° I lost her.   *until*

COLL   God look over the raw![2]
[*to* GIB] Full deafly ye stand!
GIB   Yea, the devil in thy maw°   *belly*
160 So tariand!°   *For tarrying so*
Saw thou awhere of Daw?[3]
COLL   Yea, on a lea-land°   *fallow ground*
Heard I him blaw.°   *blow (his horn)*
He comes here at hand,
165   Not far.
Stand still.
GIB   Why?
COLL   For he comes, hope° I.   *think*
GIB   He will make us both a lie
   But if° we be ware.   *Unless*

[*Enter* DAW,[4] *who does not see the others.*]

170 DAW   Christ's cross me speed°   *help me*
And Saint Nicholas![5]
Thereof had I need:
It is worse than it was.
Whoso could take heed
175 And let the world pass,
It is ever in dread°   *fear*
And brickle° as glass,   *brittle*
   And slithes.°   *slides away*
This world foor° never so,   *fared*
180 With marvels mo° and mo,   *more*
Now in weal, now in woe,
   And all thing writhes.°   *everything changes*

Was never sin° Noah's flood   *since*
Such floods seen,

9. She has bristly brows and a sour-looking expression.
1. Our Father (Latin); that is, the Lord's prayer, which begins with this phrase (see Matthew 6.9–13 and Luke 11.2–4).
2. God watch over the audience (row)! As the next line suggests, Coll accuses Gib of lecturing the audience while he has tried to get his attention.
3. Have you seen Daw anywhere?
4. Daw, whose name is both a nickname for *David* and a word meaning "simpleton," is a boy who works for one of the older shepherds.
5. The patron saint of young people.

But this will I borrow.
   [*Moves with the sheep to his cottage and calls from outside.*]
425 How, Gill, art thou in?
Get us some light.
GILL [*inside*]   Who makes such a din
This time of the night?
I am set for to spin;
430 I hope not I might
Rise a penny to win²—
I shrew° them on height!   curse
   So fares
A housewife that has been
435 To be raised thus between:³
Here may no note° be seen   work
   For° such small chares.°   Because of / chores

MAK   Good wife, open the hek!°   inner door
Sees thou not what I bring?
440 GILL   I may thole° thee draw the sneck.°   let / latch
Ah, come in, my sweeting.
MAK   Yea, thou thar not reck
Of my long standing.⁴
   [*She opens the door.*]
GILL   By the naked neck
445 Art thou like for to hing.°   hang
MAK   Do way!°   Enough
I am worthy° my meat,°   worthy of / food
For in a strait° I can get   in a fix
More than they that swink° and sweat   toil
450 All the long day.

Thus it fell to my lot,
Gill, I had such grace.°   luck
GILL   It were a foul blot
To be hanged for the case.°   deed
455 MAK   I have 'scaped,° Jelot,⁵   escaped
Of as hard a glase.°   blow
GILL   But "So long goes the pot
To the water," men says,
   "At last
460 Comes it home broken."
MAK   Well know I the token,°   portent

2. I don't see how I can earn a penny (from my spinning) by so much getting up like this.
3. This is what it's like for any woman who has been a housewife: to be gotten up (i.e., interrupted) continually.
4. Yes, you needn't mind about keeping me standing here so long.
5. An affectionate nickname for Gill.

But let it never be spoken!
    But come and help fast.

        I would he were flain,°   skinned
465   I list° well eat: wish (to)
        This twelvemonth was I not so fain°   glad
        Of one sheep-meat.
    GILL   Come they° ere he be slain,   If they come
        And hear the sheep bleat—
470 MAK   Then might I be ta'en°—   taken
        That were a cold sweat!
            Go spar°   fasten
        The gate-door.°   outer door
    GILL   Yes, Mak,
        For and° they come at thy back—   if
475 MAK   Then might I buy, for all the pack,
        The devil of the war.[6]

    GILL   A good bourd° have I spied,   trick
        Sin° thou can° none.   Since / know
        Here shall we him hide
480   To° they be gone,   Until
        In my cradle. Abide!
        Let me alone,
        And I shall lie beside
        In childbed and groan.
485 MAK   Thou red,°   get ready
        And I shall say thou was light°   delivered
        Of a knave-child° this night.   male child
    GILL   Now well is me day bright
        That ever I was bred.[7]

490   This is a good guise°   method
        And a far-cast:°   cunning trick
        Yet a woman's advice
        Helps at the last.
        I wot° never who spies: know
495   Again° go thou fast.   Back
    MAK   But° I come ere they rise,   Unless
        Else blows a cold blast.
        I will go sleep.   [Returns to the shepherds.]
        Yet° sleeps all this meny,°   Still / company
500   And I shall go stalk privily,
        As it had never been I
            That carried their sheep.   [Lies down among them.]
                [The shepherds are waking.]

6. Then I might receive a devil of a hard time   7. Now lucky for me the bright day on which
from the pack of them.   I was born.

COLL   *Resurrex a mortruus!*[8]
   Have hold my hand!
505 *Judas carnas dominus!*[9]
   I may not well stand.
   My foot sleeps, by Jesus,
   And I walter° fastand.°   *stagger / (from) hunger*
   I thought we had laid us
510 Full near England.
   GIB   Ah, yea?
   Lord, what° I have slept weel!   *how*
   As fresh as an eel,
   As light I me feel
515   As leaf on a tree.

   DAW   Benste° be herein!   *A blessing*
   So my body quakes,
   My heart is out of skin,
   What-so it makes.[1]
520 Who makes all this din?
   So my brows blakes,[2]
   To the door will I win.[3]
   Hark, fellows, wakes!
     We were four:
525 See ye aywhere of Mak now?
   COLL   We were up ere thou.
   GIB   Man, I give God avow
     Yet yede° he naw're.°   *went / nowhere*

   DAW   Methought he was lapped°   *wrapped*
530 In a wolfskin.
   COLL   So are many happed°   *covered*
   Now, namely° within.   *especially*
   DAW   When we had long napped,
   Methought with a gin°   *snare*
535 A fat sheep he trapped,
   But he made no din.
   GIB   Be still!
   Thy dream makes thee wood.°   *mad*
   It is but phantom, by the rood.
540 COLL   Now God turn all to good,
     If it be his will.
     [*They wake up* MAK, *who pretends to have been asleep.*]
   GIB   Rise, Mak, for shame!
   Thou lies right lang.°   *long*
   MAK   Now Christ's holy name

8. Corruption of *resurrexit a mortuis* (He rose from the dead), from the Latin Creed.
9. "Judas flesh lord," possibly a corruption of *laudes canas Domino* (sing praises to the Lord).

1. Whatever (may) cause it.
2. My brow grows pale (with fear).
3. I'll head to the door. (Daw is so disoriented by his nightmare he forgets that he is sleeping outdoors.)

545 Be us amang!°   *among*
    What is this? For Saint Jame,
    I may not well gang.°   *walk*
    I trow° I be the same.   *suppose*
    Ah, my neck has lain wrang.°   *wrong, crookedly*
    [*One of them twists his neck.*]
550   Enough!
    Mickle° thank! Sin° yestereven   *Much / Since*
    Now, by Saint Stephen,
    I was flayed with a sweven—
        My heart out of slough.[4]

555 I thought Gill began to croak
    And travail° full sad,°   *labor / heavily*
    Well-near at the first cock,[5]
    Of a young lad,
    For to mend° our flock—   *increase*
560 Then be I never glad:
    I have tow on my rock[6]
    More than ever I had.
        Ah, my head!
    A house full of young tharms!°   *bellies*
565 The devil knock out their harns!°   *brains*
    Woe is him has many barns,°   *children*
        And thereto little bread.

    I must go home, by your leave,
    To Gill, as I thought.°   *intended*
570 I pray you look° my sleeve,   *inspect*
    That I steal nought.
    I am loath you to grieve
    Or from you take aught.
    DAW   Go forth! Ill might thou chieve!°   *fare*
575 Now would I we sought
        This morn,
    That we had all our store.[7]
    COLL   But I will go before.
    Let us meet.
    GIB   Whore?°   *Where*
580 DAW   At the crooked thorn.
        [*They go off in search of their sheep.*]
        [MAK's *house.* MAK *arrives at the door.*]
    MAK   Undo this door!
    GILL   Who is here?
    MAK   How long shall I stand?
    GILL   Who makes such a bere?°   *noise*

---

4. I was terrified by a dream—My heart (jumped) out of my skin.
5. When the cock first crows (i.e., midnight).
6. I have flax on my distaff (i.e., I'm in trouble).
7. I'd like us to check this morning (to be sure) that we have all our stock.

Now walk in the weniand![8]

585 MAK   Ah, Gill, what cheer?
It is I, Mak, your husband.
GILL   Then may we see here
The devil in a band,°   noose
Sir Guile!
590 Lo, he comes with a lote°   noise
As° he were holden in° the throat: As if / held by
I may not sit at my note°   work (weaving)
A hand-long° while.   brief

MAK   Will ye hear what fare° she makes   commotion
595 To get her a glose?°   excuse (for not working)
And does nought but lakes°   plays
And claws° her toes?   scratches
GILL   Why, who wanders? Who wakes?
Who comes? Who goes?
600 Who brews? Who bakes?
What makes me thus hose?°   hoarse
And than°   then
It is ruth° to behold,   pity
Now in hot, now in cold,
605 Full woeful is the household
That wants° a woman.   lacks

But what end has thou made
With the herds,° Mak?   shepherds
MAK   The last word that they said
610 When I turned my back,
They would look that they had
Their sheep all the pack.
I hope° they will not be well paid°   expect / pleased
When they their sheep lack.
615 Pardie!°   By God
But how-so the game goes,
To me they will suppose,[9]
And make a foul nose,°   noise
And cry out upon me.
620 But thou must do as thou hight.°   promised
GILL   I accord me theretill.[1]
I shall swaddle him right
In my cradle
   [*She wraps up the sheep and puts it in the cradle.*]
If it were a greater sleight,
625 Yet could I help till.[2]

8. The waning of the moon, thought to be a
time of bad luck. (Gill is cursing.)
9. However the game goes, they'll suspect me.

1. I agree to that.
2. Even if it were a greater trick, I could still
help with it.

    I will lie down straight.°   *at once*
    Come hap° me.   *cover*
MAK   I will.   [*Covers her.*]
GILL   Behind!
    Come Coll and his marrow,°   *mate*
630   They will nip us full narrow.°   *hard*
MAK   But I may cry "Out, harrow,"[3]
    The sheep if they find.

GILL   Hearken ay when they call—
    They will come anon.
635   Come and make ready all,
    And sing by thine one.°   *self*
    Sing "lullay"° thou shall,   *lullaby*
    For I must groan
    And cry out by the wall
640   On Mary and John
      For sore.°   *pain*
    Sing "lullay" on fast
    When thou hears at the last,[4]
    And but I play a false cast,[5]
645   Trust me no more.
            [*The shepherds meet again.*]
DAW   Ah, Coll, good morn.
    Why sleeps thou not?
COLL   Alas, that ever I was born!
    We have a foul blot:
650   A fat wether° have we lorn.°   *ram / lost*
DAW   Marry, God's forbot!°   *God forbid*
GIB   Who should do us that scorn?
    That were a foul spot!°   *disgrace*
COLL   Some shrew.°   *rascal*
655   I have sought with my dogs
    All Horbury[6] shrogs,°   *thickets*
    And of fifteen hogs
      Found I but one ewe.[7]

DAW   Now trow me, if ye will,
660   By Saint Thomas of Kent,
    Either Mak or Gill
    Was at that assent.[8]
COLL   Peace, man, be still!
    I saw when he went.

---

3. A cry of distress or alarm.
4. When you finally hear (them).
5. And if I don't play a false trick.
6. A village near Wakefield.
7. And among fifteen hogs (i.e., young sheep),

I found only an ewe. (That is, the ram, or "fat wether," is missing.)
8. Was a party to it. *Saint Thomas of Kent*: Thomas à Becket (ca. 1118–1170), the martyred archbishop of Canterbury.

665 Thou slanders him ill—
     Thou ought to repent
         Good speed.°   speedily
     GIB Now as ever might I thee,°   thrive
     If I should even here dee,°   die
670 I would say it were he
         That did that same deed.

     DAW Go we thither, I read,°   advise
     And run on our feet.
     Shall I never eat bread
675 The sooth to I weet.⁹
     COLL Nor drink in my head,¹
     With him till I meet.
     GIB I will rest in no stead°   place
     Till that I him greet,
680   My brother.
     One I will hight:²
     Till I see him in sight
     Shall I never sleep one night
         There I do another.³

         [*The shepherds approach* MAK's *house.* MAK *and* GILL *within,
         she in bed, groaning, he singing a lullaby.*]

685 DAW Will ye hear how they hack?⁴
     Our sire list° croon.   *is pleased to*
     COLL Heard I never none crack°   *bawl*
     So clear out of tune.
     Call on him.
     GIB   Mak!
690 Undo your door soon!°   *immediately*
     MAK Who is that spake,
         As° it were noon,   *As if*
         On loft?°   *Loudly*
     Who is that, I say?
695 DAW Good fellows, were it day.⁵
     MAK As far as ye may,
         [*opening*] Good,° speaks soft   *Good sirs*

     Over a sick woman's head
     That is at malease.⁶
700 I had liefer° be dead   *rather*
     Ere she had any disease.°   *disturbance*
     GILL Go to another stead!

9. Until I know the truth.   4. Trill (used sarcastically).
1. That is, in my mouth.   5. Good friends, if it were daylight (i.e., they
2. One thing I will promise.   are not good friends, since it is night).
3. I'll never sleep two nights in the same   6. Who is unwell.
place.

I may not well wheeze:°   *breathe*
Each foot that ye tread
705   Goes through my nese°   *nose*
            So hee!°   *loudly*
COLL   Tell us, Mak, if you may,
        How fare ye, I say?
MAK   But are ye in this town today?
710   Now how fare ye?

        Ye have run in the mire
        And are wet yit.
        I shall make you a fire
        If you will sit.
715   A nurse would I hire.
        Think ye on yit?[7]
        Well quit is my hire—
        My dream this is it—
            A season.[8]
720   I have barns,° if ye knew,   *children*
        Wel mo than enew:°   *enough*
        But we must drink as we brew,
            And that is but reason.

        I would ye dined ere ye yode.°   *go*
725   Methink that ye sweat.
GIB   Nay, neither mends our mood,
        Drink nor meat.[9]
MAK   Why sir, ails you aught but good?[1]
DAW   Yea, our sheep that we get°   *tend*
730   Are stolen as they yode:°   *wandered*
        Our loss is great.
MAK   Sirs, drinks!
        Had I been thore,°   *there*
        Some should have bought° it full sore.   *paid for*
735 COLL   Marry, some men trows° that ye wore,°   *believe / were*
            And that us forthinks.°   *displeases*

GIB   Mak, some men trows,
        That it should be ye.
DAW   Either ye or your spouse,
740   So say we.
MAK   Now if you have suspouse°   *suspicion*
        To Gill or to me,
        Come and ripe° the house   *ransack*

7. Do you remember it (i.e., my dream about   9. Neither drink nor food will mend our
childbirth)?   mood.
8. My wages have been well paid for a while   1. Does anything not good trouble you? (i.e.,
(i.e., I've got what was coming to me). My   is something wrong?)
dream has come true.

And then may ye see
745 Who had her²
If I any sheep fot,° *fetched, stole*
Either cow or stot° *heifer*
And Gill my wife rose not
Here sin° she laid her.° *since / lay down*

750 As I am true and leal,° *honest*
To God here I pray
That this be the first meal
That I shall eat this day.
COLL Mak, as I have sele,³
755 Advise thee, I say:
He learned timely to steal
That could not say nay.⁴ [*They begin to search.*]
GILL I swelt!° *die*
Out, thieves, from my wones!° *dwelling*
760 Ye come to rob us for the nones.⁵
MAK Hear ye not how she groans?
Your hearts should melt.

GILL Out, thieves, from my barn!° *child*
Nigh him not thore!⁶
765 MAK Wist ye how she had farn,⁷
Your hearts would be sore.
You do wrong, I you warn,
That thus comes before° *in the presence*
To° a woman that has farn°— *Of / been in labor*
770 But I say no more.
GILL Ah, my middle!
I pray to God so mild,
If ever I you beguiled,
That I eat this child
775 That lies in this cradle
MAK Peace, woman, for God's pain,
And cry not so!
Thou spills° thy brain *You injure*
And makes me full woe.
780 GIB I trow our sheep be slain.
What find ye two?
DAW All work we in vain;
As well may we go.
But hatters!⁸
785 I can find no flesh,
Hard nor nesh,° *soft*

---

2. Who took the sheep.
3. As I hope to have the happiness (of salvation).
4. He who could not say no (to another's property) learned early to steal (proverbial).
5. You come for the purpose of robbing us.
6. Don't come near him there!
7. If you knew how she had labored.
8. Confound it! (an oath of unclear origin).

Salt nor fresh,
But two tome° platters.   *empty*

Quick cattle but this,
790   Tame nor wild,
None, as I have bliss,
As loud as he smiled.[9]   [*Approaches the cradle.*]

   GILL   No, so God me bliss,°   *bless*
And give me joy of my child!
795   COLL   We have marked° amiss—   *aimed*
I hold° us beguiled.   *consider*
   GIB   Sir, don!°   *completely*
[*to* MAK] Sir—Our Lady him save!—
Is your child a knave?°   *boy*
800   MAK   Any lord might him have,
This child, to° his son.   *as*

When he wakens he kips,°   *snatches, grabs*
That joy is to see.
   DAW   In good time to his hips,
805   And in sely.[1]
But who were his gossips,°   *godparents*
So soon ready?
   MAK   So fair fall their lips[2]
   COLL   Hark, now, a lee,°   *lie*
810   MAK   So God them thank,
Perkin, and Gibbon Waller, I say,
And gentle John Horne, in good fay°—   *faith*
He made all the garray°   *commotion*
With the great shank.[3]

815   GIB   Mak, friends will we be,
For we are all one.°   *at one, agreed*
   MAK   We? Now I hold for me,
For mends get I none.[4]
Farewell all three,
820   All glad were ye gone.[5]
   DAW   Fair words may there be,
But love is there none
This year.   [*They go out the door.*]
   COLL   Gave ye the child anything?
825   GIB   I trow not one farthing.

9. (I can find) no livestock but this (i.e., the baby), neither tame nor wild, that smelled—as I (hope to) have bliss—as strong as he (i.e., the missing ram).
1. Good luck to him, and happiness.
2. May good luck come to them.
3. Long legs; an allusion to a dispute among the shepherds in the *First Shepherds' Play*.
4. I'll look out for myself, for I'll get no amends.
5. I'd be very glad if you were gone (probably spoken as an aside).

DAW   Fast again will I fling.°   *run*
      Abide ye me there.   *[He runs back.]*

      Mak, take it no grief
      If I come to thy barn.°   *child*
830 MAK   Nay, thou does me great reprief,°   *shame*
      And foul has thou farn.°   *done*
    DAW   The child it will not grief,
      That little day-starn.°   *day star*
      Mak, with your leaf,°   *leave, permission*
835 Let me give your barn
        But sixpence.
    MAK   Nay, do way! He sleeps.
    DAW   Methinks he peeps.
    MAK   When he wakens he weeps.
840   I pray you go hence.
            [The other shepherds reenter.]
    DAW   Give me leave him to kiss,
      And lift up the clout.°   *cloth*
      [lifts the cover]
      What the devil is this?
      He has a long snout!
845 COLL   He is marked amiss.
      We wot ill about.[6]
    GIB   Ill-spun weft, ywis,°   *certainly*
      Ay comes foul out.[7]
        Aye, so!
850   He is like to our sheep.
    DAW   How, Gib, may I peep?
    COLL   I trow kind will creep
      Where it may not go.[8]

    GIB   This was a quaint gaud°   *cunning trick*
855 And a far-cast.°   *clever device*
      It was high fraud.
    DAW   Yea, sirs, was't.°   *it was*
      Let bren° this bawd   *Let's burn*
      And bind her fast.
860   A false scaud°   *scold*
      Hang at the last.[9]
        So shall thou.
      Will you see how they swaddle
      His four feet in the middle?
865   Saw I never in the cradle
      A horned lad[1] ere now.

---

6. He's deformed. We do wrong to pry around.
7. Ill-spun threads always make bad cloth (proverbial); that is, evil always reveals itself in its results.
8. Nature will creep where it can't walk (pro-
verbial); that is, nature will reveal itself one way or another.
9. Will hang at the end.
1. That is, the devil.

MAK   Peace bid I! What,
    Let be your fare!°   *commotion*
    I am he that him gat.°   *begot*
870 And yond woman him bare.
    COLL   What devil shall he hat?[2]
    Lo, God, Mak's heir!
    GIB   Let be all that!
    Now God give him care°—   *sorrow*
875   I sawgh![3]
    GILL   A pretty child is he
    As sits on a woman's knee,
    A dillydown,° pardie,   *darling*
       To gar° a man laugh.   *make*

880 DAW   I know him by the earmark—
    That is a good token.
    MAK   I tell you, sirs, hark,
    His nose was broken.
    Sithen° told me a clerk[4]   *Afterward*
885 That he was forspoken.°   *bewitched*
    COLL   This is a false wark.°   *work, deed*
    I would fain be wroken.°   *avenged*
    Get wapen.°   *(a) weapon*
    GILL   He was taken with° an elf   *by*
890 I saw it myself—
    When the clock struck twelf
    Was he forshapen.°   *transformed*

    GIB   Ye two are well feft
    Sam in a stead.[5]
895 DAW   Sin° they maintain their theft,   *Since*
    Let do° them to dead.°   *Let's put / death*
    MAK   If I trespass eft,°   *again*
    Gird° off my head.   *Strike*
    With you will I be left.[6]
900 COLL   Sirs, do° my read:°   *follow / advice*
    For this trespass
    We will neither ban° ne flite,°   *curse / quarrel*
    Fight nor chite,°   *chide*
    But have done as tite,°   *quickly*
905   And cast him in canvas.
        [*They toss* MAK *in a blanket.*]

---

2. What in the devil will he be named?
3. I saw (the sheep).
4. A literate, learned person, possibly a local church or government official (in England pronounced "clark," as the rhyme scheme requires).

5. You two are well provided for in the same way; that is, you are as clever a pair of rogues as ever lived.
6. I leave myself with you (as a judge); that is, I put myself at your mercy.

[*The fields.*]

COLL　Lord, what° I am sore, — *how*
In point for to brist!° — *burst*
In faith, I may no more—
Therefore will I rist.° — *rest*

910　GIB　As a sheep of seven score[7]
He weighed in my fist:
For to sleep aywhore° — *anywhere*
Methink that I list.° — *desire*

DAW　Now I pray you
915　Lie down on this green.

COLL　On these thieves yet I mean.° — *think*

DAW　Whereto should ye teen?° — *be angry*
Do as I say you.　　　　　　[*They lie down.*]

[*An* ANGEL *sings* Gloria in Excelsis[8] *and then speaks.*]

ANGEL　Rise, herdmen hend,° — *gentle*
920　For now is he born
That shall take fro the fiend
That Adam had lorn;[9]
That warlock° to shend,° — *devil / destroy*
This night is he born.
925　God is made your friend
Now at this morn,
He behestys.° — *promises*
At Bedlem° go see: — *Bethlehem*
There lies that free,° — *noble one*
930　In a crib full poorly,
Betwixt two bestys.° — *beasts*

[*The* ANGEL *withdraws.*]

COLL　This was a quaint° steven° — *exquisite / voice*
That ever yet I hard.° — *heard*
It is a marvel to neven° — *speak of*
935　Thus to be scar'd.° — *scared*

GIB　Of God's Son of heaven
He spake upward.° — *from above*
All the wood on a leven
Methought that he gard
940　Appear.[1]

DAW　He spake of a barn° — *child*
In Bedlem, I you warn.° — *tell*

COLL　That betokens yond starn.[2]
Let us seek him there.

---

7. That is, 140 pounds.
8. Glory [to God] in the highest (Latin), the title and first words of the "great doxology," used in the Roman Catholic Mass (a variation of the words in the Vulgate Bible with which angels announce the birth of Jesus to shepherds; see Luke 2.14).
9. What Adam lost.
1. I thought he made the woods appear as if lit up in a flash of lightning.
2. That's what yonder star signifies.

945 GIB Say, what was his song?
       Heard ye not how he cracked° it?   *sang*
       Three breves° to a long?   *short notes*
    DAW Yea, marry, he hacked° it.   *trilled*
       Was no crochet° wrong,   *note*
950   Nor nothing that lacked it.°   *that it lacked*
    COLL For to sing us among,
       Right as he knacked° it,   *sang*
         I can.°   *know how*
    GIB Let see how ye croon!
955 Can ye bark at the moon?
    DAW Hold your tongues! Have done!
    COLL Hark after, than!   [*Sings.*]

    GIB To Bedlem he bade
       That we should gang:°   *go*
960 I am full fard°   *afraid*
       That we tarry too lang.°   *long*
    DAW Be merry and not sad;
       Of mirth is our sang:
       Everlasting glad°   *joy*
965 To meed° may we fang.°   *As reward / get*
    COLL Without nose°   *noise*
       Hie we thither forthy°   *therefore*
       To that child and that lady;
       If° we be wet and weary,   *Even if*
970   We have it not to lose.³

    GIB We find by the prophecy—
       Let be your din!—
       Of David and Isay,°   *Isaiah*
       And mo° than I min,°   *more / remember*
975 That prophesied by clergy°   *learnedly*
       That in a virgin
       Should he light° and lie,   *alight*
       To sloken° our sin   *quench*
         And slake° it,   *relieve*
980 Our kind,° from woe,   *humankind*
       For Isay said so:
       Ecce virgo
         *Concipiet*⁴ a child that is naked.

    DAW Full glad may we be
985 And abide° that day   *look forward to*
       That lovely to see,
       That all mights may.⁵

---

3. We must not forget it.
4. Behold, a virgin shall conceive (Vulgate;
Isaiah 7.14).
5. To see that lovely one who is almighty.

Lord, well were me
For once and for ay
990 Might I kneel on my knee,
Some word for to say
    To that child.
But the angel said
In a crib was he laid,
995 He was poorly arrayed,
    Both meaner° and mild.   *lowly*

COLL   Patriarchs that has been,
And prophets beforn,°   *in the past*
That desired to have seen
1000 This child that is born,
They are gone full clean°—   *completely*
That have they lorn.[6]
We shall see him, I ween,°   *think*
Ere it be morn,
1005   To token.[7]
When I see him and feel,
Then wot I full weel
It is true as steel
    That° prophets have spoken: *What*

1010 To so poor as we are
That he would appear,
First find and declare[8]
By his messenger.
GIB   Go we now, let us fare,
1015 The place is us near.
DAW   I am ready and yare;°   *eager*
Go we in fere°   *together*
    To that bright.°   *bright one*
Lord, if thy wills be—
1020 We are lewd° all three—   *unlearned*
Thou grant us some kins glee
    To comfort thy wight.[9]
        [*They go to Bethlehem and enter the stable.*]
COLL   Hail, comely and clean!°   *pure*
1025 Hail, young child!
Hail Maker, as I mean,°   *believe*
Of° a maiden so mild!   *Born of*
Thou has waried,° I ween,°   *cursed / believe*
The warlock° so wild.   *devil*
The false guiler of teen,[1]

6. That opportunity have they lost.
7. As a sign.
8. Find (us) first and declare (his coming).
9. Grant us some joyful means of comforting thy child.
1. The false and malevolent beguiler.

1030   Now goes he beguiled.
        Lo, he merries!°   *is merry*
    Lo, he laughs, my sweeting!
    A well fair meeting!
    I have holden° my heting:°   *kept / promise*
1035   Have a bob° of cherries.   *bunch*

    GIB   Hail, sovereign Saviour,
    For thou has us sought!
    Hail freely food° and flour,°   *noble child / flower*
    That all thing has wrought!
1040   Hail, full of favour,
    That made all of nought!
    Hail! I kneel and I cower.
    A bird have I brought
        To my barn.°   *child*
1045   Hail, little tiny mop!°   *baby*
    Of our creed thou art crop.°   *head*
    I would drink on thy cup,
        Little day-starn.

    DAW   Hail, darling dear,
1050   Full of Godhead!
    I pray thee be near
    When that I have need.
    Hail, sweet is thy cheer°—   *face*
    My heart would bleed
1055   To see thee sit here
    In so poor weed,°   *clothing*
        With no pennies.
    Hail, put forth thy dall!°   *hand*
    I bring thee but a ball:
1060   Have and play thee withal,
        And go to the tennis.[2]
    MARY   The Father of heaven,
    God omnipotent,
    That set all on seven,[3]
1065   His Son has he sent.
    My name could he neven,
    And light ere he went.[4]
    I conceived him full even°   *indeed*
    Through might as he meant.[5]
1070   And now is he born.
    He° keep you from woe!   *May he*
    I shall pray him so.
    Tell forth as ye go,
        And min on° this morn.   *remember*

---

2. The sport of tennis was identified with the court and nobility in the late Middle Ages.
3. Who created everything in seven (days).
4. He named my name and alighted (in me) before he went.
5. Through (God's) might, as he intended.

1075 COLL   Farewell, lady,
       So fair to behold,
       With thy child on thy knee.
     GIB   But he lies full cold.
       Lord, well is me.
1080   Now we go, thou behold.
     DAW   Forsooth, already
       It seems to be told
          Full oft.
     COLL   What grace we have fun!°   *found*
1085 GIB   Come forth, now are we won!°   *redeemed*
     DAW   To sing are we bun:°   *bound*
       Let take on loft.[6]
          [*They sing.*]

6. Let us begin (to sing) loudly.

EVERYMAN

ca. 1510

*E*VERYMAN, the most widely read and frequently produced play written in English before the Elizabethan age, forms part of the tradition of morality drama that flourished in England during the fifteenth and early sixteenth centuries. A play about sin, repentance, and death, it reflects the religious and moral worldview of the late Middle Ages. Appearing at the turn of the sixteenth century, however, *Everyman* is also a transitional play in the history of English dramatic literature. As one of the first plays to be published in England, *Everyman* owes much of its popularity during its time to a new reading public that emerged after the invention of the printing press by the German Johannes Gutenberg around 1450. Such a readership had been unavailable to the dramatists of earlier centuries, whose plays were available only in manuscript. In addition, while this drama of Everyman's final reckoning reflects the theology of orthodox Catholicism, its insistence on certain doctrinal points suggests an awareness of the burgeoning reform movement that would profoundly divide Christian Europe during the Protestant Reformation. The allegorical structure of *Everyman* and other morality plays—in which characters, objects, and actions represent abstract concepts or principles in a narrative that conveys a moral lesson—provided English playwrights with a useful framework for examining these and other social and philosophical issues in the turbulent years that followed.

Everyman survives in four different editions, two of them incomplete, which appeared between 1510 and 1535. No manuscript of the play exists. The play bears close similarities to an earlier Dutch play titled *Elckerlijc,* which was written by a Petrus Diesthemius, or Peter from the [Flemish city of] Diest, frequently identified as the theologian and Carthusian priest Peter of Doorlandt. *Elckerlijc* was printed in 1495 in Delft; it was subsequently published in Antwerp, where it was awarded first prize at a *landjuweel,* or rhetorical contest. For a number of decades, scholars argued over which play came first, but the weight of recent evidence—textual and otherwise—has established beyond reasonable doubt that the English *Everyman* was a translation of the Dutch original. As A. C. Cawley points out, Antwerp was an important printing center at the turn of the sixteenth century, regularly publishing English translations of books originally written in Dutch for sale in the English market. In London, foreign printers enjoyed privileges not granted to their domestic counterparts and were frequently accorded royal patronage. One of these printers, a Norman named Richard Pynson, published the first extant edition of *Everyman*; though we do not know the identity of the translator, we can infer the play's popularity from the number of surviving editions.

It has become a critical commonplace that while *Everyman* is the most famous of English morality plays, it is in many ways the least typical. In earlier moralities, such as *The Castle of Perseverence* (ca. 1405–25) and *Mankind* (ca. 1465–70), figures representing Virtue and Vice contend for the soul of humankind in often elaborate allegorical settings rife with incident and encounter. Moral conflict in these plays is frequently dramatized through comic horseplay, as the Vice figures demonstrate the distractions posed by earthly temptation. By focusing on words over action, in contrast, *Everyman* concentrates on the closing moments of life and on the moral crisis that occurs when Death calls the sinner to account. As Everyman undergoes his final journey, learning that the earthly things in which he had put his faith will fail him in his hour of extremity and that the path to salvation lies through good deeds and repentance, the distractions of earthly temptation and the diversions of horseplay are relegated to the past. No Vice figures prance across the stage in *Everyman*; instead, the play's moral allegory unfolds with a simplicity verging on parable. This theatrical asceticism may owe something to its sources, for scholars have determined that one of *Everyman*'s core narrative elements—the testing of friends in an hour of need—is Buddhist rather than Western in origin. This story was introduced to medieval Europe through the eleventh-century Greek text *Barlaam and Josaphat*, a collection of Christianized tales from the East.

In its focus on mortality, *Everyman* reflects a broader literary and social preoccupation with death in the fifteenth century. In his 1924 study *The Waning of the Middle Ages*, Johan Huizinga wrote: "No other epoch has laid so much stress as the expiring Middle Ages on the thought of death." *Memento mori* (remember that you must die) was a regular theme in the sermons of mendicant preachers since the thirteenth century, and its lesson resonated in a Europe that lost one-third of its population to the Black Death in the mid-1300s. Personifications of Death were common in fifteenth-century woodcuts, and the spectacle of Death choosing his victims indiscriminately from all stations of life formed the subject of the Dance of Death (or *Danse Macabre*), a dramatic form that originated in Germany and was performed in England in the fifteenth century. Of even greater relevance to *Everyman* were the treatises on the art of holy dying or *Ars moriendi*, widely known throughout Europe in the 1400s. The *Ars moriendi* dealt with the process of death and the techniques (meditations, prayers, questions) that would help one die in a state of holiness. Particular attention was given to the temptations that threaten to divert the virtuous mind at the hour of death: heresy, despair, rage, spiritual pride, and an attachment to the things of the world.

This last temptation, elaborated in William Caxton's 1490 translation (from a French work) *The Art and Craft to Know Well to Die*—"the over-great occupation of outward things and temporal, as toward his wife his children and his friends carnal, toward his riches or toward other things which he hath most loved in his life"—finds particularly strong echoes in *Everyman*. To find strength in the face of death, the dying individual is instructed to meditate on the death of Christ.

Like Moriens (literally, "The Dying One"), the protagonist at the center of the *Ars moriendi*, Everyman stands as the representative of a broader humanity that must come to terms with the inevitability of death and the impermanence of earthly life. The Messenger's speech that opens the play underscores the identification between Everyman on stage and Everyman in the audience—"Here shall you see how fellowship and jollity, / Both strength, pleasure, and beauty, / Will fade from thee as flower in May." God's speech, which follows it, extends this allegorical identification. As V. A. Kolve has noted, Everyman is spoken of as both singular and plural in number in God's opening speech: as a consequence of this linguistic slippage, "We are implicated collectively as well as individually." Like Death's victims in the Dance of Death, the character Everyman is caught unawares by calls of mortality and judgment. Immersed in a life of pleasure and possessions, he has elevated the temporal order over the spiritual; and as he embarks on this final journey, or "pilgrimage," he must revalue his life according to its higher moral law. *Everyman*'s many references to "reckoning" and to rendering "account," which recall the parable of the talents in Matthew 25.14–30, emphasize the need for spiritual industry and proper discernment of what is transitory and what is eternal.

As he prepares to undertake Death's journey, Everyman seeks the company and support of his friends, kindred, and material possessions from which he derived pleasure in more carefree days. That Fellowship, Kindred, Cousin, and Goods abandon him in his hour of greatest need despite their earlier promises never to for-

This woodcut from the fifteenth-century, *Ars moriendi*, shows Moriens, at the end of his struggle with earthly temptations, being welcomed into paradise.

sake him comes as no surprise to the audience; their departures are both inevitable and accompanied by a certain humor, as when Cousin protests that he cannot accompany Everyman because he has a cramp in his toe. The popular sayings that Everyman repeats in soliciting their help—"For it is said ever among / That money maketh all right that is wrong," for instance—are shown to be empty. When Everyman turns to his Good Deeds, he finds her willing to accompany him but too enfeebled by his sins to rise from the ground and do so. His encounter with her is a turning point both in the play's narrative and in his theological development, for

he learns the steps by which he may render his spiritual account clean and adequate. He is introduced to Knowledge, whose name denoted a number of related understandings to the play's medieval audience: knowledge of God, acknowledgment of sin, and an awareness of its remedies. Knowledge, in turn, introduces him to Confession, who instructs him in contrition and encourages him to punish his offending flesh with the scourge of Penance. When Everyman has purified himself through these penitential acts, Good Deeds rises from the ground, restored, to accompany him on the remainder of his pilgrimage. The morally rejuvenated Everyman is also joined on his final pilgrimage by four "persons of great might": Discretion, Strength, Beauty, and Five-Wits (the personification of the five physical senses). Unlike Everyman's unreliable earlier companions, who signify the attachments of the external world, the allegorical figures in this last group represent the individual's personal attributes redeemed by grace.

Before he reaches his grave, Everyman departs to receive the sacraments of Holy Communion and extreme unction, or last rites, and his brief exit affords Knowledge and Five-Wits the opportunity for an extended digression on the importance of priesthood. Because they administer the seven sacraments, these two insist, priests stand even "above angels in degree." Though some priests violate their divine responsibilities, priesthood offers the only "remedy we find under God." The emphasis on sacraments is important to the play's doctrinal foundations, for in Roman Catholic belief and observance, they represent the vehicles by which God's grace is manifested in human life. Everyman has expressed contrition for his sins, but it is not until he receives the sacraments that his reconciliation with God is complete.

The closing sequence, in which Everyman meets his death and is received into heaven, achieves a surprisingly emotional effect in a play that is otherwise marked by the contemplative distance and processional formality of allegory. As Everyman stands before his grave—so weak he "may not stand"—he is successively abandoned by Beauty, Strength, Discretion, and Five-Wits. Unlike his earlier abandonment by his companions and worldly goods, which this scene mirrors, this last-minute departure comes as something of a jolt to the play's audience as well as to its protagonist. Although Strength may promise Everyman that "we will not from you go / Till ye have done this voyage long," the support of Everyman's attributes and faculties necessarily but painfully fail at the moment of death. Even Knowledge, whose support proved crucial to Everyman's transition into a state of grace, must abandon the dying individual in the end. When Everyman exclaims "O all thing faileth save God alone," he expresses the anguish that marks the loss of these deeply per-

Frontispiece of the 1528–29 edition of *Everyman* printed by John Skot.

sonal companions. But this anguish also affirms a faith in the constancy embodied in God's promise of salvation. Accompanied by Good Deeds, his lone companion into the afterlife, Everyman echoes Christ's dying words: "*In manus tuas . . . commendo spiritum meum*" ("Into thy hands I commend my spirit"; Luke 23.46). As reward for his moral regeneration he is welcomed by an Angel to heaven and eternal life. His reckoning, which was earlier described as "blotted and blind," is now "crystal clear."

The epilogue of *Everyman*, which is delivered by a theological Doctor, underscores the play's moral lesson: "And he that hath his account whole and sound, / High in heaven he shall be crowned." As he redirects the play's attention from Everyman onstage to Everyman in the audience—"Ye hearers"—he reminds us that this play about dying right is equally, in the end, about the importance of living right. Like other visual and literary wor¹ in the *memento mori* tradition, *Every* seeks to impress upon its audiei.

awareness of life's impermanence, an ability to discern the eternal in the midst of the transitory, and a commitment to live life as if every day might be one's last.

No evidence has survived concerning sixteenth-century performances of *Everyman*; indeed, there is no record of performance before the nineteenth century. Because the title page of the 1528–29 edition of the play printed by John Skot (upon which the present text is based) opens with the words "HERE BEGINNETH A TREATISE . . . IN MANNER OF A MORAL PLAY," some critics have concluded that—in contrast with its Dutch counterpart, for which performance records exist—*Everyman* was translated and printed primarily for a reading public. But while the number of editions in which it appeared supports the claim that *Everyman* had a wide readership, the play's success in twentieth-century theaters, churches, and schools attests to its theatrical qualities, and the simplicity of its theatrical requirements encourages the belief that it was known to audiences as well as readers.

Whether *Everyman* was performed outdoors, like the earlier English moralities, or indoors, like the Tudor interludes it also resembles, is open to conjecture, and the absence of stage directions from the printed text makes precise reconstruction of a sixteenth-century performance impossible. But some of the play's central theatrical features are evident from textual indications, and others can be inferred from contemporary theatrical practice. The play's setting observes the dual structure characteristic of other medieval drama, in which a localized structure (or *sedes*) is contrasted with an unlocalized acting area (or *platea*). The House of Salvation—Confession's abode—looms over the action of *Everyman* as the site of the allegorical protagonist's pivotal transformations. As Cawley suggests, it is reasonable to assume that this structure had a battlement height from which God addresses sinful humanity at the start of the play and into which Everyman's soul is received at its conclusion. Placement of Everyman's grave in front of this structure would allow Everyman to exit his grave and ascend to heaven with

requisite speed. Distinguished as they are by their initial immobility, both Goods and Good Deeds no doubt require their own acting areas. The text of *Everyman* provides evidence of additional theatrical elements. Props, while few in number, figure prominently in the play's dramatic and theological action: Everyman's account book, the penitential scourge, the crucifix that Everyman presents after receiving the sacraments. Costume also contributes to the play's meaning. Everyman, who is dressed "gaily" at the beginning of the play, exchanges these clothes for a penitential robe in the play's second half. He certainly would not have been the only character whose allegorical significance is marked by dress: if productions of *Everyman* followed Tudor theatrical practice, its costumes would have been vividly emblematic—most notably in the case of Death, whose representation would have drawn from an extensive repertoire of medieval woodcuts and other illustrations.

The history of Everyman's emergence in our own time as a classic of the early English theater is almost as striking as the play itself. After several centuries' absence from the stage, *Everyman* became the first medieval play to appear on the modern stage in July 1901, when William Poel, founder of the Elizabethan Stage Society, mounted a production of this supposedly "primitive" drama in the courtyard of a former London monastery. The production was an immediate sensation: by the following season it had reached the commercial theaters, and it subsequently toured abroad. An observation by one of the play's initial reviewers suggests both the success of Poel's production and the power that *Everyman* must have held for its Tudor audience as well: "In the open air in a courtyard and enclosed with antiquated buildings with no distinction of lighting to differentiate between performers and auditors . . . the essential human vitality of the whole thing was what most strongly appeared." To learn more about the staging of *Everyman* and to view photographs from select performances of the play, see the "Plays in Performance" color insert near the center of this volume.　　　　s.g.

Everyman[1]

CHARACTERS

MESSENGER	KNOWLEDGE
GOD	CONFESSION
DEATH	BEAUTY
EVERYMAN	STRENGTH
FELLOWSHIP	DISCRETION
KINDRED	FIVE-WITS
COUSIN	ANGEL
GOODS	DOCTOR
GOOD DEEDS	

HERE BEGINNETH A TREATISE HOW THE HIGH FATHER OF HEAVEN SENDETH DEATH
TO SUMMON EVERY CREATURE TO COME AND GIVE ACCOUNT OF THEIR
LIVES IN THIS WORLD, AND IS IN MANNER OF A MORAL PLAY.

[*Enter* MESSENGER.]

MESSENGER   I pray you all give your audience,
And hear this matter with reverence,
By figure° a moral play.   *In its form*
The Summoning of Everyman called it is,
5   That of our lives and ending shows
How transitory we be all day.°   *always*
The matter is wonder precious,
But the intent of it is more gracious
And sweet to bear away.
10   The story saith: Man, in the beginning
Look well, and take good heed to the ending,
Be you never so gay.
You think sin in the beginning full sweet,
Which in the end causeth the soul to weep,
15   When the body lieth in clay.
Here shall you see how fellowship and jollity,
Both strength, pleasure, and beauty,
Will fade from thee as flower in May.
For ye shall hear how our Heaven-King
20   Calleth Everyman to a general reckoning.
Give audience and hear what he doth say.

[*Exit* MESSENGER.—*Enter* GOD.]

1. The text is based on the earliest printing of the play (no manuscript is known) by John Skot, about 1530, as reproduced by W. W. Greg (1904). The spelling has been modernized except where modernization would spoil the rhyme, and modern punctuation has been added. The stage directions have been amplified.

GOD   I perceive, here in my majesty,
    How that all creatures be to me unkind,[2]
    Living without dread in worldly prosperity.
25   Of ghostly sight[3] the people be so blind,
    Drowned in sin, they know me not for their God.
    In worldly riches is all their mind:
    They fear not of my righteousness the sharp rod;
    My law that I showed when I for them died
30   They forget clean, and shedding of my blood red.
    I hanged between two,[4] it cannot be denied:
    To get them life I suffered to be dead.
    I healed their feet, with thorns hurt was my head.
    I could do no more than I did, truly—
35   And now I see the people do clean forsake me.
    They use the seven deadly sins damnable,
    As pride, coveitise,° wrath, and lechery[5]   *covetousness*
    Now in the world be made commendable.
    And thus they leave of angels the heavenly company.
40   Every man liveth so after his own pleasure,
    And yet of their life they be nothing sure.
    I see the more that I them forbear,
    The worse they be from year to year:
    All that liveth appaireth° fast.   *degenerates*
45   Therefore I will, in all the haste,
    Have a reckoning of every man's person.
    For, and° I leave the people thus alone   *if*
    In their life and wicked tempests,
    Verily they will become much worse than beasts;
50   For now one would by envy another up eat.
    Charity do they all clean forgeet.
    I hoped well that every man
    In my glory should make his mansion,°   *dwelling place*
    And thereto I had them all elect.°   *chosen*
55   But now I see, like traitors deject,°   *debased*
    They thank me not for the pleasure that I to° them meant,   *for*
    Nor yet for their being that I them have lent.
    I proffered the people great multitude of mercy,
    And few there be that asketh it heartily.°   *sincerely*
60   They be so cumbered° with worldly riches   *encumbered*
    That needs on them I must do justice—
    On every man living without fear.
    Where art thou, Death, thou mighty messenger?
        [*Enter* DEATH.]
  DEATH   Almighty God, I am here at your will,
65 Your commandment to fulfill.
  GOD   Go thou to Everyman,

2. Lacking in natural filial affection or duty.
3. In spiritual vision.
4. That is, the two thieves between whom

Jesus was crucified.
5. The other deadly sins are gluttony, sloth, and envy.

And show him, in my name,
A pilgrimage he must on him take,
Which he in no wise may escape;
70 And that he bring with him a sure reckoning
Without delay or any tarrying.
DEATH   Lord, I will in the world go run over all,°   *throughout*
And cruelly° out-search both great and small.   *rigorously*
[*Exit* GOD.]
Everyman will I beset that liveth beastly
75 Out of God's laws, and dreadeth not folly.
He that loveth riches I will strike with my dart,
His sight to blind, and from heaven to depart°   *cut off*
Except that Almsdeeds be his good friend—
In hell for to dwell, world without end.
80 Lo, yonder I see Everyman walking:
Full little he thinketh on my coming;
His mind is on fleshly lusts and his treasure,
And great pain it shall cause him to endure
Before the Lord, Heaven-King.
[*Enter* EVERYMAN.]
85 Everyman, stand still! Whither art thou going
Thus gaily? Hast thou thy Maker forgeet?°   *forgotten*
EVERYMAN   Why askest thou?
Why wouldest thou weet?°   *know*
DEATH   Yea, sir, I will show you:
90 In great haste I am sent to thee
From God out of his majesty.
EVERYMAN   What! sent to me?
DEATH   Yea, certainly.
Though thou have forgot him here,
95 He thinketh on thee in the heavenly sphere,
As, ere we depart, thou shalt know.
EVERYMAN   What desireth God of me?
DEATH   That shall I show thee:
A reckoning he will needs have
100 Without any longer respite.
EVERYMAN   To give a reckoning longer leisure I crave.
This blind° matter troubleth my wit.°   *obscure / understanding*
DEATH   On thee thou must take a long journay:
Therefore thy book of count° with thee thou bring,   *accounts*
105 For turn again thou cannot by no way.
And look thou be sure of thy reckoning,
For before God thou shalt answer and shew
Thy many bad deeds and good but a few—
How thou hast spent thy life and in what wise,
110 Before the Chief Lord of Paradise.
Have ado that we were in that way,[6]
For weet thou well thou shalt make none attornay.[7]

6. That is, let's get going.   7. No one (your) advocate.

EVERYMAN   Full unready I am such reckoning to give.
          I know thee not. What messenger art thou?
115 DEATH   I am Death that no man dreadeth,[8]
          For every man I 'rest,° and no man spareth;   *arrest*
          For it is God's commandment
          That all to me should be obedient.
EVERYMAN   O Death, thou comest when I had thee least in mind.
120   In thy power it lieth me to save:
          Yet of my good° will I give thee, if thou will be kind,   *goods*
          Yea, a thousand pound shalt thou have—
          And defer this matter till another day.
    DEATH   Everyman, it may not be, by no way.
125   I set nought by[9] gold, silver, nor riches,
          Nor by pope, emperor, king, duke, nor princes,
          For, and° I would receive gifts great,   *if*
          All the world I might get.
          But my custom is clean contrary:
130   I give thee no respite. Come hence and not tarry!
EVERYMAN   Alas, shall I have no longer respite?
          I may say Death giveth no warning.
          To think on thee it maketh my heart sick,
          For all unready is my book of reckoning.
135   But twelve year and I might have a biding,[1]
          My counting-book I would make so clear
          That my reckoning I should not need to fear.
          Wherefore, Death, I pray thee, for God's mercy,
          Spare me till I be provided of remedy.
140 DEATH   Thee availeth not to cry, weep, and pray;
          But haste thee lightly° that thou were gone that journay   *quickly*
          And prove° thy friends, if thou can.   *put to the test*
          For weet° thou well the tide° abideth no man,   *know / time*
          And in the world each living creature
145   For Adam's sin must die of nature.[2]
EVERYMAN   Death, if I should this pilgrimage take
          And my reckoning surely make,
          Show me, for saint° charity,   *holy*
          Should I not come again shortly?
150 DEATH   No, Everyman. And thou be once there,
          Thou mayst never more come here,
          Trust me verily.
EVERYMAN   O gracious God in the high seat celestial,
          Have mercy on me in this most need!
155   Shall I have company from this vale terrestrial
          Of mine acquaintance that way me to lead?
    DEATH   Yea, if any be so hardy
          That would go with thee and bear thee company.
          Hie thee that thou were gone[3] to God's magnificence,

8. Who is afraid of no man.   2. In the course of nature.
9. I set no store by.   3. Hurry up and go.
1. If I might have a respite for twelve years.

160 Thy reckoning to give before his presence.
What, weenest° thou thy life is given thee,   suppose
And thy worldly goods also?

EVERYMAN   I had weened so, verily.

DEATH   Nay, nay, it was but lent thee.

165 For as soon as thou art go,°   gone
Another a while shall have it and then go therefro,
Even as thou hast done.
Everyman, thou art mad! Thou hast thy wits° five,   senses
And here on earth will not amend thy live!⁴

170 For suddenly I do come.

EVERYMAN   O wretched caitiff!° Whither shall I flee   unfortunate wretch
That I might 'scape this endless sorrow?
Now, gentle Death, spare me till tomorrow,
That I may amend me

175 With good advisement.⁵

DEATH   Nay, thereto I will not consent,
Nor no man will I respite,
But to the heart suddenly I shall smite,
Without any advisement.

180 And now out of thy sight I will me hie:
See thou make thee ready shortly,
For thou mayst say this is the day
That no man living may 'scape away.

            [*Exit* DEATH.]

EVERYMAN   Alas, I may well weep with sighs deep:

185 Now have I no manner of company
To help me in my journey and me to keep.°   protect
And also my writing° is full unready—   account
How shall I do now for to excuse me?
I would to God I had never be geet!°   been born

190 To my soul a full great profit it had be.
For now I fear pains huge and great.
The time passeth: Lord, help, that all wrought!
For though I mourn, it availeth nought.
The day passeth and is almost ago:°   gone

195 I wot° not well what for to do.   know
To whom were I best my complaint to make?
What and° I to Fellowship thereof spake,   if
And showed him of this sudden chance?
For in him is all mine affiance,°   trust

200 We have in the world so many a day
Be good friends in sport and play.
I see him yonder, certainly.
I trust that he will bear me company.
Therefore to him will I speak to ease my sorrow.

            [*Enter* FELLOWSHIP.]

4. In your life.   5. With proper reflection.

205   Well met, good Fellowship, and good morrow!
    FELLOWSHIP Everyman, good morrow, by this day!
    Sir, why lookest thou so piteously?
    If anything be amiss, I pray thee me say,
    That I may help to remedy.
210 EVERYMAN Yea, good Fellowship, yea:
    I am in great jeopardy.
    FELLOWSHIP My true friend, show to me your mind.
    I will not forsake thee to my life's end
    In the way of good company.
215 EVERYMAN That was well spoken, and lovingly!
    FELLOWSHIP Sir, I must needs know your heaviness.°   *sorrow*
    I have pity to see you in any distress.
    If any have you wronged, ye shall revenged be,
    Though I on the ground be slain for thee,
220 Though that I know before that I should die.
    EVERYMAN Verily, Fellowship, gramercy.°   *many thanks*
    FELLOWSHIP Tush! by thy thanks I set not a stree.°   *straw*
    Show me your grief and say no more.
    EVERYMAN If I my heart should to you break,°   *open*
225 And then you to turn your mind fro me,
    And would not me comfort when ye hear me speak,
    Then should I ten times sorrier be.
    FELLOWSHIP Sir, I say as I will do, indeed.
    EVERYMAN Then be you a good friend at need.
230 I have found you true herebefore.
    FELLOWSHIP And so ye shall evermore.
    For, in faith, and° thou go to hell,   *if*
    I will not forsake thee by the way.
    EVERYMAN Ye speak like a good friend. I believe you well.
235 I shall deserve° it, and° I may.   *repay / if*
    FELLOWSHIP I speak of no deserving, by this day!
    For he that will say and nothing do
    Is not worthy with good company to go.
    Therefore show me the grief of your mind,
240 As to your friend most loving and kind.
    EVERYMAN I shall show you how it is:
    Commanded I am to go a journey,
    A long way, hard and dangerous,
    And give a strait° count,° without delay,   *strict / account*
245 Before the high judge Adonai.[6]
    Wherefore I pray you bear me company,
    As ye have promised, in this journay.
    FELLOWSHIP This is matter indeed! Promise is duty—
    But, and° I should take such a voyage on me,   *if*
250 I know it well, it should be to my pain.
    Also it maketh me afeard, certain.
    But let us take counsel here, as well as we can—

6. A Hebrew name for God.

For your words would fear° a strong man.   *frighten*
EVERYMAN   Why, ye said if I had need,
255 Ye would me never forsake, quick ne° dead,   *alive nor*
Though it were to hell, truly.
FELLOWSHIP   So I said, certainly,
But such pleasures° be set aside, the sooth° to say.   *pleasantries / truth*
And also, if we took such a journey,
260 When should we again come?
EVERYMAN   Nay, never again, till the day of doom.[7]
FELLOWSHIP   In faith, then will not I come there!
Who hath you these tidings brought?
EVERYMAN   Indeed, Death was with me here.
265 FELLOWSHIP   Now by God that all hath bought,°   *redeemed*
If Death were the messenger,
For no man that is living today
I will not go that loath° journey—   *loathsome*
Not for the father that begat me!
270 EVERYMAN   Ye promised otherwise, pardie.°   *by God*
FELLOWSHIP   I wot well I said so, truly.
And yet, if thou wilt eat and drink and make good cheer,
Or haunt to women the lusty company,[8]
I would not forsake you while the day is clear,
275 Trust me verily!
EVERYMAN   Yea, thereto ye would be ready—
To go to mirth, solace,° and play: *enjoyment*
Your mind to folly will sooner apply°   *attend*
Than to bear me company in my long journey.
280 FELLOWSHIP   Now in good faith, I will not that way.
But, and° thou will murder or any man kill,   *if*
In that I will help thee with a good will.
EVERYMAN   O that is simple° advice, indeed!   *foolish*
Gentle fellow, help me in my necessity:
285 We have loved long, and now I need—
And now, gentle Fellowship, remember me!
FELLOWSHIP   Whether ye have loved me or no,
By Saint John, I will not with thee go!
EVERYMAN   Yet I pray thee take the labor and do so much for me,
290 To bring me forward,° for saint charity,   *escort me*
And comfort me till I come without° the town.   *outside*
FELLOWSHIP   Nay, and° thou would give me a new gown,   *even if*
I will not a foot with thee go.
But, and° thou had tarried, I would not have left thee so.   *if*
295 And as° now, God speed thee in thy journey!   *as for*
For from thee I will depart as fast as I may.
EVERYMAN   Whither away, Fellowship? Will thou forsake me?
FELLOWSHIP   Yea, by my fay!° To God I betake° thee.   *faith / commend*
EVERYMAN   Farewell, good Fellowship! For thee my heart is sore.
300 Adieu forever—I shall see thee no more.

7. That is, Judgment Day.   8. Or frequent the lusty company of women.

FELLOWSHIP   In faith, Everyman, farewell now at the ending:
　　　For you I will remember that parting is mourning.
　　　　　　[*Exit* FELLOWSHIP.]

EVERYMAN   Alack, shall we thus depart° indeed—　　　　　　　　*part*
　　　Ah, Lady,[9] help!—without any more comfort?
305　　Lo, Fellowship forsaketh me in my most need!
　　　For help in this world whither shall I resort?
　　　Fellowship herebefore with me would merry make,
　　　And now little sorrow for me doth he take.
　　　It is said, "In prosperity men friends may find
310　　Which in adversity be full unkind."
　　　Now whither for succor shall I flee,
　　　Sith° that Fellowship hath forsaken me?　　　　　　　　　*Since*
　　　To my kinsmen I will, truly,
　　　Praying them to help me in my necessity.
315　　I believe that they will do so,
　　　For kind will creep where it may not go.[1]
　　　I will go 'say°—for yonder I see them—　　　　　　　　*assay, try*
　　　Where° be ye now my friends and kinsmen.　　　　　　　*Whether*
　　　　　　[*Enter* KINDRED *and* COUSIN.]

KINDRED   Here be we now at your commandment:
320　　Cousin, I pray you show us your intent
　　　In any wise, and not spare.
COUSIN   Yea, Everyman, and to us declare
　　　If ye be disposed to go anywhither.
　　　For, weet° you well, we will live and die togither.　　　*know*
325 KINDRED   In wealth and woe we will with you hold,
　　　For over his kin a man may be bold.[2]
EVERYMAN   Gramercy, my friends and kinsmen kind.
　　　Now shall I show you the grief of my mind.
　　　I was commanded by a messenger
330　　That is a high king's chief officer:
　　　He bade me go a pilgrimage, to my pain—
　　　And I know well I shall never come again.
　　　Also I must give a reckoning strait,°　　　　　　　　　*strict*
　　　For I have a great enemy that hath me in wait,[3]
335　　Which intendeth me to hinder.
KINDRED   What account is that which ye must render?
　　　That would I know.
EVERYMAN   Of all my works I must show
　　　How I have lived and my days spent;
340　　Also of ill deeds that I have used
　　　In my time sith life was me lent,
　　　And of all virtues that I have refused.
　　　Therefore I pray you go thither with me

9. The Virgin Mary.

1. For kinship will crawl where it cannot walk
(proverbial); that is, kinsmen will find a way to
help each other no matter what the circum-

stance.

2. That is, for a man may count on his
kinsmen.

3. That is, Satan, who lies in wait for me.

To help me make mine account, for saint charity.

345 COUSIN   What, to go thither? Is that the matter?
    Nay, Everyman, I had liefer° fast° bread and water   *rather / fast on*
    All this five year and more!

EVERYMAN   Alas, that ever I was bore!°   *born*
    For now shall I never be merry
350   If that you forsake me.

KINDRED   Ah, sir, what? Ye be a merry man:
    Take good heart to you and make no moan.
    But one thing I warn you, by Saint Anne,[4]
    As for me, ye shall go alone.

355 EVERYMAN   My Cousin, will you not with me go?

COUSIN   No, by Our Lady! I have the cramp in my toe:
    Trust not to me. For, so God me speed,
    I will deceive° you in your most need.   *betray*

KINDRED   It availeth you not us to 'tice.°   *entice*
360   Ye shall have my maid with all my heart:
    She loveth to go to feasts, there to be nice,°   *wanton*
    And to dance, and abroad to start.[5]
    I will give her leave to help you in that journey,
    If that you and she may agree.

365 EVERYMAN   Now show me the very effect° of your mind: *tenor*
    Will you go with me or abide behind?

KINDRED   Abide behind? Yea, that will I and I may!
    Therefore farewell till another day.

           [*Exit* KINDRED.]

EVERYMAN   How should I be merry or glad?
370   For fair promises men to me make,
    But when I have most need they me forsake.
    I am deceived. That maketh me sad.

COUSIN   Cousin Everyman, farewell now,
    For verily I will not go with you;
375   Also of mine own an unready reckoning
    I have to account—therefore I make tarrying.°   *stay behind*
    Now God keep thee, for now I go.

           [*Exit* COUSIN.]

EVERYMAN   Ah, Jesus, is all come hereto?°   *to this*
    Lo, fair words maketh fools fain:°   *glad*
380   They promise and nothing will do, certain.
    My kinsmen promised me faithfully
    For to abide with me steadfastly,
    And now fast away do they flee.
    Even so Fellowship promised me.
385   What friend were best me of to provide?[6]
    I lose my time here longer to abide.
    Yet in my mind a thing there is:

4. The mother of the Virgin Mary.   6. To provide myself with.
5. And to run around.

All my life I have loved riches;
If that my Good° now help me might,   *Goods*
390   He would make my heart full light.
I will speak to him in this distress.
Where art thou, my Goods and riches?
GOODS [*within*]   Who calleth me? Everyman? What, hast thou haste?
I lie here in corners, trussed and piled so high,
395   And in chests I am locked so fast—
Also sacked in bags—thou mayst see with thine eye
I cannot stir, in packs low where I lie.
What would ye have? Lightly° me say.   *Quickly*
EVERYMAN   Come hither, Good, in all the haste thou may,
400   For of counsel I must desire thee.

      [*Enter* GOODS.]

GOODS   Sir, and° ye in the world have sorrow or adversity,   *if*
That can I help you to remedy shortly.
EVERYMAN   It is another disease° that grieveth me: *trouble*
In this world it is not, I tell thee so.
405   I am sent for another way to go,
To give a strait count general
Before the highest Jupiter° of all.   *God*
And all my life I have had joy and pleasure in thee:
Therefore I pray thee go with me,
410   For, peradventure, thou mayst before God Almighty
My reckoning help to clean and purify.
For it is said ever among[7]
That money maketh all right that is wrong.
GOODS   Nay, Everyman, I sing another song:
415   I follow no man in such voyages.
For, and° I went with thee,   *if*
Thou shouldest fare much the worse for me;
For because on me thou did set thy mind,
Thy reckoning I have made blotted and blind,°   *illegible*
420   That thine account thou cannot make truly—
And that hast thou for the love of me.
EVERYMAN   That would grieve me full sore
When I should come to that fearful answer.
Up, let us go thither together.
425 GOODS   Nay, not so, I am too brittle, I may not endure.
I will follow no man one foot, be ye sure.
EVERYMAN   Alas, I have thee loved and had great pleasure
All my life-days on good and treasure.
GOODS   That is to thy damnation, without leasing,[8]
430   For my love is contrary to the love everlasting.
But if thou had me loved moderately during,[9]
As to the poor to give part of me,
Then shouldest thou not in this dolor° be,   *distress*

---

7. For it is commonly said.   9. That is, during your lifetime.
8. Without a lie (i.e., truly).

Nor in this great sorrow and care.

435 EVERYMAN   Lo, now was I deceived ere I was ware,
And all I may wite° misspending of time.   *blame on*

GOODS   What, weenest° thou that I am thine?   *suppose*

EVERYMAN   I had weened so.

GOODS   Nay, Everyman, I say no.

440 As for a while I was lent thee;
A season thou hast had me in prosperity.
My condition° is man's soul to kill;   *nature*
If I save one, a thousand I do spill.°   *destroy*
Weenest thou that I will follow thee?

445 Nay, from this world, not verily.

EVERYMAN   I had weened otherwise.

GOODS   Therefore to thy soul Good is a thief;
For when thou art dead, this is my guise°—   *custom*
Another to deceive in the same wise

450 As I have done thee, and all to his soul's repreef.°   *shame*

EVERYMAN   O false Good, cursed thou be,
Thou traitor to God, that hast deceived me
And caught me in thy snare!

GOODS   Marry, thou brought thyself in care,[1]

455 Whereof I am glad:
I must needs laugh, I cannot be sad.

EVERYMAN   Ah, Good, thou hast had long my heartly° love;   *heartfelt*
I gave thee that which should be the Lord's above.
But wilt thou not go with me, indeed?

460 I pray thee truth to say.

GOODS   No, so God me speed!
Therefore farewell and have good day.

[*Exit* GOODS.]

EVERYMAN   Oh, to whom shall I make my moan
For to go with me in that heavy° journay?   *sorrowful*

465 First Fellowship said he would with me gone:°   *go*
His words were very pleasant and gay,
But afterward he left me alone.
Then spake I to my kinsmen, all in despair,
And also they gave me words fair—

470 They lacked no fair speaking,
But all forsake me in the ending.
Then went I to my Goods that I loved best,
In hope to have comfort; but there had I least
For my Goods sharply did me tell

475 That he bringeth many into hell.
Then of myself I was ashamed,
And so I am worthy to be blamed:
Thus may I well myself hate.
Of whom shall I now counsel take?

1. That is, you brought sorrow on yourself.

480   I think that I shall never speed
        Till that I go to my Good Deed.
        But alas, she is so weak
        That she can neither go° nor speak.   *walk*
        Yet will I venture° on her now.   *gamble*
485   My Good Deeds, where be you?
        GOOD DEEDS [*speaking from the ground*]   Here I lie, cold in the ground:
        Thy sins hath me sore bound
        That I cannot stear.°   *stir*
        EVERYMAN   O Good Deeds, I stand in fear:
490   I must you pray of counsel,
        For help now should come right well.[2]
        GOOD DEEDS   Everyman, I have understanding
        That ye be summoned, account to make,
        Before Messiah of Jer'salem King.
495   And you do by me,[3] that journey with you will I take.
        EVERYMAN   Therefore I come to you my moan to make:
        I pray you that ye will go with me.
        GOOD DEEDS   I would full fain,° but I cannot stand, verily.   *gladly*
        EVERYMAN   Why, is there anything on you fall?°   *fallen*
500 GOOD DEEDS   Yea, sir, I may thank you of all:
        If ye had perfectly cheered me,
        Your book of count full ready had be.
        [GOOD DEEDS *shows him the account book.*]
        Look, the books of your works and deeds eke,°   *also*
        As how they lie under the feet,
505   To your soul's heaviness.°   *distress*
        EVERYMAN   Our Lord Jesus help me!
        For one letter here I cannot see.
        GOOD DEEDS   There is a blind° reckoning in time of distress![4]   *illegible*
        EVERYMAN   Good Deeds, I pray you help me in this need,
510   Or else I am forever damned indeed.
        Therefore help me to make reckoning
        Before the Redeemer of all thing
        That King is and was and ever shall.
        GOOD DEEDS   Everyman, I am sorry of° your fall   *for*
515   And fain would help you and° I were able.   *if*
        EVERYMAN   Good Deeds, your counsel I pray you give me.
        GOOD DEEDS   That shall I do verily,
        Though that on my feet I may not go;
        I have a sister that shall with you also,
520   Called Knowledge, which shall with you abide
        To help you to make that dreadful reckoning.
        [*Enter* KNOWLEDGE.]
        KNOWLEDGE   Everyman, I will go with thee and be thy guide,
        In thy most need to go by thy side.

---

2. For help would be most welcome now.
3. If you do as I advise.

4. That is, for the sinful person, the book of
reckoning is hard to read in the hour of distress.

EVERYMAN   In good condition I am now in everything,
525   And am whole content with this good thing,
      Thanked be God my Creator.
GOOD DEEDS   And when she hath brought you there
      Where thou shalt heal thee of thy smart,°   *pain*
      Then go you with your reckoning and your Good Deeds together
530   For to make you joyful at heart
      Before the blessed Trinity.[5]
EVERYMAN   My Good Deeds, gramercy!
      I am well content, certainly,
      With your words sweet.
535 KNOWLEDGE   Now go we together lovingly
      To Confession, that cleansing river.
EVERYMAN   For joy I weep—I would we were there!
      But I pray you give me cognition,°   *knowledge*
      Where dwelleth that holy man Confession?
540 KNOWLEDGE   In the House of Salvation:
      We shall find him in that place,
      That shall us comfort, by God's grace.
              [KNOWLEDGE *leads* EVERYMAN *to* CONFESSION.]
      Lo, this is Confession: kneel down and ask mercy,
      For he is in good conceit° with God Almighty.   *esteem*
545 EVERYMAN [*kneeling*]   O glorious fountain that all
              uncleanness doth clarify,°   *purify*
      Wash from me the spots of vice unclean,
      That on me no sin may be seen.
      I come with Knowledge for my redemption,
      Redempt° with heart and full contrition,   *Redeemed*
550   For I am commanded a pilgrimage to take
      And great accounts before God to make.
      Now I pray you, Shrift,° mother of Salvation,   *Confession*
      Help my Good Deeds for my piteous exclamation.
CONFESSION   I know your sorrow well, Everyman:
555   Because with Knowledge ye come to me,
      I will you comfort as well as I can,
      And a precious jewel I will give thee,
      Called Penance, voider° of adversity.   *expeller*
      Therewith shall your body chastised be—
560   With abstinence and perseverance in God's service.
      Here shall you receive that scourge of me,
      Which is penance strong that ye must endure,
      To remember thy Saviour was scourged for thee
      With sharp scourges, and suffered it patiently.
565   So must thou ere thou 'scape that painful pilgrimage.
      Knowledge, keep° him in this voyage,   *guard*
      And by that time Good Deeds will be with thee.
      But in any wise be secure° of mercy—   *certain*
      For your time draweth fast—and ye will saved be.

5. That is, God as existing in three persons: the Father, Son, and Holy Spirit.

570   Ask God mercy and he will grant, truly.
        When with the scourge of penance man doth him° bind,   *himself*
        The oil of forgiveness then shall he find.
    EVERYMAN   Thanked be God for his gracious work,
        For now I will my penance begin.
575   This hath rejoiced and lighted my heart,
        Though the knots be painful and hard within.[6]
    KNOWLEDGE   Everyman, look your penance that ye fulfill,
        What pain that ever it to you be;
        And Knowledge shall give you counsel at will
580   How your account ye shall make clearly.
    EVERYMAN   O eternal God, O heavenly figure,
        O way of righteousness, O goodly vision,
        Which descended down in a virgin pure
        Because he would every man redeem,
585   Which Adam forfeited by his disobedience;
        O blessed Godhead, elect and high Divine,°   *divinity*
        Forgive my grievous offense!
        Here I cry thee mercy in this presence:[7]
        O ghostly Treasure, O Ransomer and Redeemer,
590   Of all the world Hope and Conduiter,°   *Conductor, Guide*
        Mirror of joy, Foundator° of mercy,   *Founder*
        Which enlumineth° heaven and earth thereby,   *illuminates*
        Hear my clamorous complaint, though it late be;
        Receive my prayers, of thy benignity.
595   Though I be a sinner most abominable,
        Yet let my name be written in Moses' table.[8]
        O Mary, pray to the Maker of all thing°   *things*
        Me for to help at my ending,
        And save me from the power of my enemy,
600   For Death assaileth me strongly.
        And Lady, that I may by mean of thy prayer
        Of your Son's glory to be partner—
        By the means of his passion I it crave.
        I beseech you help my soul to save.
605   Knowledge, give me the scourge of penance:
        My flesh therewith shall give acquittance.°   *satisfaction for sins*
        I will now begin, if God give me grace.
    KNOWLEDGE   Everyman, God give you time and space!°   *opportunity*
        Thus I bequeath you in the hands of our Saviour:
610   Now may you make your reckoning sure.
    EVERYMAN   In the name of the Holy Trinity
        My body sore punished shall be:
        Take this, body, for the sin of the flesh!
        Also° thou delightest to go gay and fresh,°   *As / finely dressed*

---

6. Though the knots (of the scourge) are hard and painful to my senses.
7. That is, in the presence of Knowledge and Confession.

8. That is, the tablets that God gave Moses on Mount Sinai on which the Ten Commandments were written. In the Middle Ages these tablets were associated with baptism and penance.

615   And in the way of damnation thou did me bring,
      Therefore suffer now strokes of punishing!
      Now of penance I will wade the water clear,
      To save me from purgatory, that sharp fire.
      GOOD DEEDS   I thank God, now can I walk and go,
620   And am delivered of my sickness and woe.
      Therefore with Everyman I will go, and not spare:
      His good works I will help him to declare.
      KNOWLEDGE   Now, Everyman, be merry and glad:
      Your Good Deeds cometh now, ye may not be sad.
625   Now is your Good Deeds whole and sound,
      Going° upright upon the ground.   *Walking*
      EVERYMAN   My heart is light, and shall be evermore.
      Now will I smite faster than I did before.
      GOOD DEEDS   Everyman, pilgrim, my special friend,
630   Blessed be thou without end!
      For thee is preparate° the eternal glory.   *prepared*
      Ye have me made whole and sound
      Therefore I will bide by thee in every stound.°   *trial*
      EVERYMAN   Welcome, my Good Deeds! Now I hear thy voice,
635   I weep for very sweetness of love.
      KNOWLEDGE   Be no more sad, but ever rejoice:
      God seeth thy living in his throne above.
      Put on this garment to thy behove,°   *advantage*
      Which is wet with your tears—
640   Or else before God you may it miss
      When ye to your journey's end come shall.
      EVERYMAN   Gentle Knowledge, what do ye it call?
      KNOWLEDGE   It is a garment of sorrow;
      From pain it will you borrow:°   *protect*
645   Contrition it is
      That getteth forgiveness;
      It pleaseth God passing° well.   *exceedingly*
      GOOD DEEDS   Everyman, will you wear it for your heal?° *well-being*
      EVERYMAN   Now blessed be Jesu, Mary's son,
650   For now have I on true contrition.
      And let us go now without tarrying.
      Good Deeds, have we clear our reckoning?
      GOOD DEEDS   Yea, indeed, I have it here.
      EVERYMAN   Then I trust we need not fear.
655   Now friends, let us not part in twain.
      KNOWLEDGE   Nay, Everyman, that will we not, certain.
      GOOD DEEDS   Yet must thou lead with thee
      Three persons of great might.
      EVERYMAN   Who should they be?
660   GOOD DEEDS   Discretion and Strength they hight,°   *are called*
      And thy Beauty may not abide behind.
      KNOWLEDGE   Also ye must call to mind
      Your Five-Wits° as for your counselors.   *senses*
      GOOD DEEDS   You must have them ready at all hours.

665 EVERYMAN   How shall I get them hither?
   KNOWLEDGE   You must call them all togither,
   And they will be here incontinent.°   *immediately*
   EVERYMAN   My friends, come hither and be present,
   Discretion, Strength, my Five-Wits, and Beauty!
       [*They enter.*]
670 BEAUTY   Here at your will we be all ready.
   What will ye that we should do?
   GOOD DEEDS   That ye would with Everyman go
   And help him in his pilgrimage.
   Advise you:° will ye with him or not in that voyage?   *Consider*
675 STRENGTH   We will bring him all thither,
   To his help and comfort, ye may believe me.
   DISCRETION   So will we go with him all togither.
   EVERYMAN   Almighty God, loved° might thou be!   *praised*
   I give thee laud that I have hither brought
680 Strength, Discretion, Beauty, and Five-Wits—lack I nought—
   And my Good Deeds, with Knowledge clear,
   All be in my company at my will here:
   I desire no more to my business.
   STRENGTH   And I, Strength, will by you stand in distress,
685 Though thou would in battle fight on the ground.
   FIVE-WITS   And though it were through the world round,
   We will not depart for sweet ne sour.
   BEAUTY   No more will I, until death's hour,
   Whatsoever thereof befall.
690 DISCRETION   Everyman, advise you first of all:
   Go with a good advisement° and deliberation.   *reflection*
   We all give you virtuous° monition°   *confident / prediction*
   That all shall be well.
   EVERYMAN   My friends, hearken what I will tell;
695 I pray God reward you in his heaven-sphere;
   Now hearken all that be here,
   For I will make my testament,
   Here before you all present:
   In alms half my good° I will give with my hands twain,   *goods*
700 In the way of charity with good intent;
   And the other half, still° shall remain,   *which still*
   I 'queath° to be returned there° it ought to be.   *bequeath / where*
   This I do in despite of the fiend of hell,
   To go quit out of his perel,
705 Ever after and this day.⁹
   KNOWLEDGE   Everyman, hearken what I say:
   Go to Priesthood, I you advise,
   And receive of him, in any wise,°   *at all costs*
   The holy sacrament and ointment¹ togither;

9. To be free of his power today and ever after.   unction (anointing of the sick).
1. The Eucharist (see line 724) and extreme

710 Then shortly see ye turn again hither:
We will all abide you here.

FIVE-WITS   Yea, Everyman, hie you that ye ready were.
There is no emperor, king, duke, ne baron,
That of God hath commission

715 As hath the least priest in the world being:
For of the blessed sacraments pure and bening°   *benign*
He beareth the keys,[2] and thereof hath the cure°   *care*
For man's redemption—it is ever sure—
Which God for our souls' medicine

720 Gave us out of his heart with great pine,°   *suffering*
Here in this transitory life for thee and me.
The blessed sacraments seven there be:
Baptism, confirmation, with priesthood° good,   *ordination*
And the sacrament of God's precious flesh and blood,

725 Marriage, the holy extreme unction, and penance:
These seven be good to have in remembrance,
Gracious sacraments of high divinity.

EVERYMAN   Fain° would I receive that holy body,   *Gladly*
And meekly to my ghostly° father I will go.   *spiritual*

730 FIVE-WITS   Everyman, that is the best that ye can do:
God will you to salvation bring.
For priesthood exceedeth all other thing:°   *things*
To us Holy Scripture they do teach,
And converteth man from sin, heaven to reach;

735 God hath to them more power given
Than to any angel that is in heaven.
With five words[3] he may consecrate
God's body in flesh and blood to make,
And handleth his Maker between his hands.

740 The priest bindeth and unbindeth all bands,[4]
Both in earth and in heaven.
Thou ministers° all the sacraments seven;   *administers*
Though we kiss thy feet, thou were worthy;
Thou art surgeon that cureth sin deadly;

745 No remedy we find under God
But all° only priesthood.   *Except*
Everyman, God gave priests that dignity
And setteth them in his stead among us to be.
Thus be they above angels in degree.

[*Exit* EVERYMAN.]

750 KNOWLEDGE   If priests be good, it is so, surely.
But when Jesu hanged on the cross with great smart,°   *pain*
There he gave out of his blessed heart
The same sacrament in great torment,
He sold them not to us, that Lord omnipotent:

---

2. Spiritual power or authority. See Matthew 16.19.
3. *Hoc est enim corpus meum* ("For this is my body"; Latin), words for the consecration of bread in the Roman Catholic liturgy.
4. Bonds (of sin). See Matthew 16.19.

755　Therefore Saint Peter the Apostle doth say
　　　That Jesu's curse hath all they
　　　Which God their Saviour do buy or sell[5]
　　　Or they for any money do take or tell.[6]
　　　Sinful priests giveth the sinners example bad:
760　Their children sitteth by other men's fires, I have heard;[7]
　　　And some haunteth women's company
　　　With unclean life, as lusts of lechery.
　　　These be with sin made blind.
　　FIVE-WITS　I trust to God no such may we find.
765　Therefore let us priesthood honor,
　　　And follow their doctrine for our souls' succor.
　　　We be their sheep and they shepherds be
　　　By whom we all be kept in surety.
　　　Peace, for yonder I see Everyman come,
770　Which hath made true satisfaction.
　　GOOD DEEDS　Methink it is he indeed.
　　　　　　[Re-enter EVERYMAN.]
　　EVERYMAN　Now Jesu be your alder speed![8]
　　　I have received the sacrament for my redemption,
　　　And then mine extreme unction.
775　Blessed be all they that counseled me to take it!
　　　And now, friends, let us go without longer respite.
　　　I thank God that ye have tarried so long.
　　　Now set each of you on this rood° your hond°   cross / hand
　　　And shortly follow me:
780　I go before there I would be.[9] God be our guide!
　　STRENGTH　Everyman, we will not from you go
　　　Till ye have done this voyage long.
　　DISCRETION　I, Discretion, will bide by you also.
　　KNOWLEDGE　And though this pilgrimage be never so strong,°   wearisome
785　I will never part you fro.
　　STRENGTH　Everyman, I will be as sure by thee
　　　As ever I did by Judas Maccabee.[1]
　　EVERYMAN　Alas, I am so faint I may not stand—
　　　My limbs under me doth fold!
790　Friends, let us not turn again to this land,
　　　Not for all the world's gold.
　　　For into this cave must I creep
　　　And turn to earth, and there to sleep.
　　BEAUTY　What, into this grave, alas?
795　EVERYMAN　Yea, there shall ye consume,° more and lass.[2]   decay
　　BEAUTY　And what, should I smother here?

5. An allusion to simony, the buying or selling of sacraments, sacred objects, or ecclesiastical offices. See Acts 8.18–21.
6. Or who for (any sacrament) take or pay money. *Tell:* to count out.
7. That is, they have illegitimate children.

8. Now may Jesus favor you all.
9. I lead (the way to) where I wish to be.
1. The leader of the Jews in their successful revolt against the Syrians in the 2nd century B.C.E.
2. More and less (i.e., all of you).

EVERYMAN   Yea, by my faith, and nevermore appear.
　　In this world live no more we shall,
　　But in heaven before the highest Lord of all.
800 BEAUTY   I cross out all this!³ Adieu, by Saint John—
　　I take my tape in my lap and am gone.⁴
EVERYMAN   What, Beauty, whither will ye?
BEAUTY   Peace, I am deaf—I look not behind me,
　　Not and° thou wouldest give me all the gold in thy chest.　　*if*
　　　　　[*Exit* BEAUTY.]
805 EVERYMAN   Alas, whereto may I trust?
　　Beauty goeth fast away fro me—
　　She promised with me to live and die!
STRENGTH   Everyman, I will thee also forsake and deny.
　　Thy game liketh° me not at all.　　　　　　　　　　*pleases*
810 EVERYMAN   Why then, ye will forsake me all?
　　Sweet Strength, tarry a little space.°　　　　　　　*while*
STRENGTH   Nay, sir, by the rood of grace,
　　I will hie me from thee fast,
　　Though thou weep till thy heart tobrast.°　　*break into pieces*
815 EVERYMAN   Ye would ever bide by me, ye said.
STRENGTH   Yea, I have you far enough conveyed!
　　Ye be old enough, I understand,
　　Your pilgrimage to take on hand:⁵
　　I repent me that I hither came.
820 EVERYMAN   Strength, you to displease I am to blame,⁶
　　Yet promise is debt, this ye well wot.°　　　　　　*know*
STRENGTH   In faith, I care not:
　　Thou art but a fool to complain;
　　You spend your speech and waste your brain.
825 Go, thrust thee into the ground.
　　　　　[*Exit* STRENGTH.]
EVERYMAN   I had weened° surer I should you have found.　*supposed*
　　He that trusteth in his Strength
　　She him deceiveth at the length.
　　Both Strength and Beauty forsaketh me—
830 Yet they promised me fair and lovingly.
DISCRETION   Everyman, I will after Strength be gone:
　　As for me, I will leave you alone.
EVERYMAN   Why Discretion, will ye forsake me?
DISCRETION   Yea, in faith, I will go from thee.
835 For when Strength goeth before,
　　I follow after evermore.
EVERYMAN   Yet I pray thee, for the love of the Trinity,
　　Look in my grave once piteously.

---

3. I cancel all this (i.e., my promise to stay with you).
4. I'll gather up my knitting or spinning and be on my way (proverbial).

5. To take responsibility for your own pilgrimage.
6. I am to blame for displeasing you.

DISCRETION   Nay, so nigh° will I not come.   *near*
840   Farewell everyone!

        [*Exit* DISCRETION.]

EVERYMAN   O all thing faileth save God alone—
    Beauty, Strength, and Discretion.
    For when Death bloweth his blast
    They all run fro me full fast.
845 FIVE-WITS   Everyman, my leave now of thee I take.
    I will follow the other, for here I thee forsake.
EVERYMAN   Alas, then may I wail and weep,
    For I took you for my best friend.
FIVE-WITS   I will no longer thee keep.°   *watch over*
850   Now farewell, and there an end!

        [*Exit* FIVE-WITS.]

EVERYMAN   O Jesu, help, all hath forsaken me!
GOOD DEEDS   Nay, Everyman, I will bide with thee:
    I will not forsake thee indeed;
    Thou shalt find me a good friend at need.
855 EVERYMAN   Gramercy, Good Deeds! Now may I true friends see.
    They have forsaken me every one—
    I loved them better than my Good Deeds alone.
    Knowledge, will ye forsake me also?
KNOWLEDGE   Yea, Everyman, when ye to Death shall go,
860   But not yet, for no manner of danger.
EVERYMAN   Gramercy, Knowledge, with all my heart!
KNOWLEDGE   Nay, yet will I not from hence depart
    Till I see where ye shall become.[7]
EVERYMAN   Methink, alas, that I must be gone
865   To make my reckoning and my debts pay,
    For I see my time is nigh spent away.
    Take example, all ye that this do hear or see,
    How they that I best loved do forsake me,
    Except my Good Deeds that bideth truly.
870 GOOD DEEDS   All earthly things is but vanity.
    Beauty, Strength, and Discretion do man forsake,
    Foolish friends and kinsmen that fair spake—
    All fleeth save Good Deeds, and that am I.
EVERYMAN   Have mercy on me, God most mighty,
875   And stand by me, thou mother and maid, holy Mary!
GOOD DEEDS   Fear not: I will speak for thee.
EVERYMAN   Here I cry God mercy!
GOOD DEEDS   Short° our end, and 'minish° our pain.   *Shorten / diminish*
    Let us go, and never come again.
880 EVERYMAN   Into thy hands, Lord, my soul I commend:
    Receive it, Lord, that it be not lost.
    As thou me boughtest,° so me defend,   *redeemed*
    And save me from the fiend's boast,

---

7. What shall become of you.

That I may appear with that blessed host
885 That shall be saved at the day of doom.
In manus tuas, of mights most,
Forever *commendo spiritum meum*.[8]

> [EVERYMAN *and* GOOD DEEDS *descend into the grave.*]

KNOWLEDGE Now hath he suffered that° we all shall endure,   *that which*
The Good Deeds shall make all sure.
890 Now hath he made ending,
Methinketh that I hear angels sing
And make great joy and melody
Where Everyman's soul received shall be.

ANGEL [*within*] Come, excellent elect° spouse to Jesu![9]   *chosen*
895 Here above thou shalt go
Because of thy singular virtue.
Now the soul is taken the body fro,
Thy reckoning is crystal clear:
Now shalt thou into the heavenly sphere—
900 Unto the which all ye shall come
That liveth well before the day of doom.

> [*Enter* DOCTOR.[1]]

DOCTOR This moral men may have in mind:
Ye hearers, take it of worth,° old and young,   *prize it highly*
And forsake Pride, for he deceiveth you in the end.
905 And remember Beauty, Five-Wits, Strength, and Discretion,
They all at the last do Everyman forsake,
Save° his Good Deeds there doth he take—   *Only*
But beware, for and° they be small,   *if*
Before God he hath no help at all—
910 None excuse may be there for Everyman.
Alas, how shall he do than?°   *then*
For after death amends may no man make,
For then mercy and pity doth him forsake.
If his reckoning be not clear when he doth come,
915 God will say, *"Ite, maledicti, in ignem eternum!"*[2]
And he that hath his account whole and sound,
High in heaven he shall be crowned,
Unto which place God bring us all thither,
That we may live body and soul togither.
920 Thereto help, the Trinity!
Amen, say ye, for saint° charity.   *holy*

---

8. Into thy hands, greatest of powers, I commend my spirit forever; the Latin directly quotes the last words of Jesus on the cross, according to Luke 23.46 (in the Vulgate).
9. Marriage was a common medieval metaphor for the soul's union with Christ.
1. A doctor of theology.
2. Go, ye cursed, into everlasting fire (slightly misquoting Matthew 25.41).

CHRISTOPHER MARLOWE

1564–1593

A LANDMARK event in the development of the Faust myth, Christopher Marlowe's *DOCTOR FAUSTUS* also served, at its moment of production (ca. 1590–93), as a legend of its own time. The play's representation of a consummate scholar's embrace of necromancy (or black magic) to gain a "world of profit and delight," the sale of his soul to the devil, and the consequent loss of both body and soul placed it at the heart of the age's religious controversies and debates. However, Marlowe's casting of his protagonist in the role of a Renaissance *magus*—a blend of scientist, physician, dabbler in the occult, and seeker of spiritual truths—also evoked that age's fascination with gaining mastery over the material world, probing the secrets of nature, and extending human experience to the frontiers of the globe. At a time when Spanish ships were returning from the Americas freighted down with gold and silver, travelers on new trade routes to the East were bringing back daily reports of exotic places and people, and great wealth was being created that could serve new tastes and desires, Marlowe's audience would understandably be drawn to a scholar born of "parents base of stock" who decided to employ forbidden means to realize his most extravagant dreams and ambitions.

Born the son of a shoemaker in 1564 in the cathedral city of Canterbury, Christopher Marlowe could surely be compared to such a character. Unlike most sons of tradesmen, who could at best expect to follow in their fathers' footsteps after a few years of schooling, Marlowe not only attended the King's School, having won a place set aside for gifted children of the poor, but was also awarded a prestigious scholarship to study at Corpus Christi College, Cambridge, where he joined a mix of the wealthiest and most "forward wits" of his time. Marlowe took up residence there in December 1580, earned his B.A. in 1584, and, despite notable unexplained absences, received his M.A. in 1587 at the special urging of Queen Elizabeth's Privy Council for having "done her Majesty good service . . . in matters touching the benefit of his country." This "service" almost surely involved spying on English Catholics in France on behalf of the Elizabethan secret service. Yet the very same year he received his M.A., Marlowe also emerged as the author of *Tamburlaine the Great*—one of the most successful, provocative, and influential plays to be performed on the Elizabethan stage.

Although Marlowe was one of several Cambridge graduates to turn their study of the classics, and their painstaking emulation of Latin verse forms, to positive artistic and commercial advantage in London, he was the first to make the leap from mannered imitation to the creation of an English blank-verse line answerable to the challenges of public playhouse performance. In *Tamburlaine*, Marlowe dramatizes the rise to unlimited worldly power of a former shepherd, who struts across the stage celebrating his successive triumphs with conquering looks and words, unconstrained by any moral misgiving or religious qualm. Urged on by the "strong enchantments" of what BEN JONSON would later call Marlowe's "mighty line," the London audience clamored for more; and Marlowe supplied it in an equally successful sequel to *Tamburlaine*, with Edward Alleyn, the leading actor of the time, again playing the featured role. Marlowe would go on to write four more plays—*The Jew of Malta, Edward II, Doctor Faustus,* and *The Massacre at Paris*—each one of which could have earned him the early death that in fact befell him had he directly identified himself with the pronouncements and

professions of his protagonists: a "bottle-nosed" Jew bent on murder and mayhem; a lovesick English monarch, willing to trade his kingdom in order to "frolic" with his male lover; a renowned scholar who sells his soul to the devil; and a ruthless Machiavellian Catholic responsible for fomenting the notorious St. Bartholomew's Day massacre of French Protestants in 1572. Uncertain as the chronology of these plays' composition is, their intention to court controversy could not be clearer.

A study in mystery and contradiction from first to last, this remarkably gifted, mercurial poet-playwright—who was accounted "the Muses' darling" soon after his death—would meet his end in the town of Deptford on the evening of May 29, 1593, when one Ingram Frizer plunged a knife into his forehead. Marlowe was in the company of the same shady customers—debtors, money brokers, intriguers, spies—with whom he had been consorting for some time. No one knows whether Frizer acted in drunkenness, in self-defense, or in furtherance of a well-laid plan, or if Marlowe was a victim of his own violent temperament or scandalous opinions. Those opinions, including his supposed denial of Christ's divinity, had prompted the Privy Council on May 18 to issue a warrant for Marlowe's arrest. Nine days later, they featured prominently in a deposition from Richard Baines, another of Marlowe's suspect companions, claiming that Marlowe had denied Christ's divinity and made other blasphemous statements. The clock appears to have been counting down for Marlowe much as it did in the last minutes of Doctor Faustus's life, though a number of scholars argue that his former sponsors on the Privy Council are far more likely to have been responsible for his demise than the devil or despair.

Tempting as it is to bring Marlowe's notorious life and death to bear on that of his most famous protagonist, *Doctor Faustus* diverged considerably from the unerringly heterodox direction he pursued in his other plays. In a seeming departure from the "atheist lecture" he was reported to have delivered, Marlowe had Faustus entertain a series of grandiose fantasies

The Tragicall Hiſtory
of the Life and Death
of *Doctor Fauſtus.*
Written by *Ch. Marklin.*

LONDON,
Printed for *Iohn Wright*, and are to be ſold at his ſhop Without Newgate, at the ſ...... ...of the Bib..... 1616.

Title page of the 1616 B-text of *Doctor Faustus*.

only to bring the full weight of the medieval Christian cosmos—with its angels and devils whispering messages of mercy and despair in the wavering soul's ear—down upon the magus's head for daring to do "more than heavenly power permits." And he did so by situating Faustus within the framework of a medieval morality play presided over by a Chorus that influences the audience's impressions of Faustus from first to last, conflating Faustus's daring with the foolhardiness of the mythical Icarus and the presumption of Lucifer in the very first speech of the play. The plot, as Marlowe's Chorus proclaims it, could not be simpler. A brilliant scholar becomes so "swoll'n" with pride at his attainments that "Nothing so sweet as magic is to him, / Which he prefers before [what should be] his chiefest bliss." The stages of Faustus's conversion to the black arts are detailed in the play's first act and almost immediately consummated in his first transactions with Lucifer's agent, Mephistopheles. The rest of the play dramatizes how little Faustus receives in return for his investment and how fiercely he strives to repent before the clock runs out on the twenty-four years of pleasure he has bargained for and Mephistopheles comes to claim him.

The dramatic foreshortening of Faustus's necromantic career is much more pronounced in the 1604 A-text of *Doctor Faustus* (reprinted here) than it is in the considerably longer 1616 B-text. Since neither version was published during Marlowe's lifetime, neither has the kind of authority scholars look for in making determinations about authorship. But since the disproportionate number of tricks and other comic business found in the B-text are symptomatic of the additions that the theatrical impresario Philip Henslowe commissioned after Marlowe's death, most scholars believe that the A-text is closer to the author's intentions. Like most cinematic remakes, the B-text lacks both the bite and integrity of its supposed original, which often bears the imprint of a dramatist composing in the white heat of artistic concentration. Marlowe seems to have written the haunting postscript—*"Terminat hora diem, terminat Author opus"* ("The hour ends the day, the author

ends his work")—to his career-defining play just as the clock struck twelve.

Marlowe's comparatively orthodox treatment of his subject matter likely owes much to the critical tone taken toward Faustus's exploits by his source, *The History of the Damnable Life and Deserved Death of Doctor John Faustus,* a recent English translation (ca. 1589–92) of what has come to be known as the *Faustbook,* which was first published in German in 1587. However, Marlowe also took pains to transform the itinerant magician of his English and German sources into a universally accomplished scholar who makes the tragically momentous decision to risk everything to achieve godlike power. Marlowe signals at every turn the fatal (and foolish) mistakes Faustus makes. Indeed, nature itself rebels against Faustus's bargain, as when his blood congeals and refuses to flow long enough to allow him to deed his body and soul to Lucifer. In the end Faustus attempts to revolt against his devil's reckoning and tries to repent, but he is bullied back into submission by Mephistopheles. He concludes that his transgressions have rendered him unforgivable, forever incapable of sincerely asking for, much less receiving, God's saving grace.

Doctor Faustus is a study in paradox and contradiction, the product not only of colliding medieval and early modern worldviews but of competing religious professions and doctrinal debates. Though a strong case has been made for Calvinism—with its strict division of humanity into the elect and the damned—as the religious system of belief that informs Faustus's conception of himself as unredeemable and of God as vengeful and remote, the play presents a shifting array of religious signs and markers, making it difficult to determine which specific Christian ordering of nature presides over the scholar's fall. Faustus is, for example, told by Mephistopheles in the space of eight lines that hell lies "Within the bowels of these elements, / Where we are tortured and remain forever," as well as that "Hell hath no limits, nor is circumscribed / In one self place, for where we are is hell / And where hell is must we ever be." He is subsequently invited by Lucifer himself to view hell, as if it were a geo-

Paul Hilton as Doctor Faustus (left) and Arthur Darvill as Mephistopheles in the 2011 production of *Doctor Faustus* at Shakespeare's Globe, London.

graphically demarcated place on a tour map. To delight his mind, he's even given a command performance of a parade of the seven deadly sins: a standard piece of the medieval theological and iconographic repertory that had fallen out of fashion by Marlowe's time. Other seeming contradictions present themselves with a devilishly deadly irony that the savvy Faustus should have anticipated from the very first appearance of the devil at his door when summoned, an indication that the worlds of good and evil, heaven and hell, angels on one side and demons on the other are both intact and fixed in opposition to one another. This dichotomy is clearly exemplified when Mephistopheles denies Faustus's seemingly modest request for a wife, claiming that "marriage is but a ceremonial toy"; what he really means is that marriage has a sacramental status that places it beyond the pale of the devil's control or authority.

Ironically, given the price he has paid for it, the twenty-four years of Faustus's supernatural power turn out to be uneventful, even tedious. For someone who dreamed of becoming "great emperor of the world," Faustus spends a disproportionate amount of time conjuring spirits, playing jokes, and trading quips. The end of the play finds him in the same place as its beginning: at home in Wittenberg with his servant Wagner and his fellow scholars. Whereas Robin, the clownish but practical fool, says he would never bargain his soul for a joint of lamb unless it were well roasted, Faustus appears to have traded "eternal joy" for a banquet that never gets served, much less eaten. In the end he finds himself alone, facing the ultimate penalty laid out in his signed agreement. Imagine the last hour of Faustus's life, abbreviated in Marlowe's play to the time it takes an actor to speak 58 lines—no more than two or three minutes. In a play in which so much else is rendered uncertain or ambiguous, death and damnation are facts that Faustus knows will arrive on schedule. The penalty for his life has been set: "the clock will strike; / The devil will come, and Faustus must be damned." Faustus tries to hope, tries to make time stop and the planets "stand still," tries to beg Christ for mercy. He asks the earth to "gape" so that he may run into it, asks that his body dissolve "like a foggy mist" into the clouds, and imagines his soul transmigrating into that of "some brutish beast" or metamorphosing "into little waterdrops / [That] fall into the ocean, ne'er [to] be found." All to no avail. God "bends his ireful brows," the devil pulls him down, and his last expedient, a promise to burn his books, falls on deaf ears. If it is true that there is nothing like the prospect of death to concentrate the mind, then it may well be said that nothing in dramatic literature concentrates the mind on the imminence of death as intensely as does the last scene of *Doctor Faustus*.

Yet what sin has Faustus committed that he must be damned? Is it pride, the deadliest of the seven deadly sins? Is it the unforgivable sin of despair, which prevents an individual from harboring any hope of redemption? Or is it Faustus's conviction that he has been singled out as one of the reprobates who, unlike the "elect," can do nothing to make himself worthy of God's grace? Apart from playing several crude practical jokes and asking Mephistopheles to torment the Old Man (who apparently has been sent on a mission of mercy from God), Faustus does nothing in the course of the drama to harm others; and on his last night on earth, he appears to be well-loved and regarded by those who know him best, Wagner and his students. Could (or should) God have made Faustus stronger, more capable of resisting the temptations and power of the devil? Or has God spoken through the words and ministrations of the Good Angel and Old Man, and given Faustus as much of a chance to redeem himself as he gives anyone?

As Faustus is spirited offstage by Mephistopheles and his crew of devils at the end of the play, it may well seem that the odds have worked against Faustus from the start and that while conscientiously cultivating his damnation, he has gotten precious little help or protection from on high. Indeed, the last image of God provided by Faustus is of a punishing, wrathful deity to whom he desperately pleads, "My God, my God, look not so fierce on me!" Faustus, the foolish, deluded, profoundly overmatched victim, as opposed to the arrogant, overreaching Faustus of the play's first two acts, is the final version of the character we see before the Chorus reenters to shut off controversy with the authority of a slammed door:

> *Cut is the branch that might have*
>   *grown full straight,*
> *And burnèd is Apollo's laurel bough*
> *That sometime grew within this*
>   *learnèd man.*
> *Faustus is gone. Regard his hellish fall,*
> *Whose fiendful fortune may exhort*
>   *the wise*
> *Only to wonder at unlawful things,*
> *Whose deepness doth entice such*
>   *forward wits*
> *To practice more than heavenly*
>   *power permits.*

A branch that might have grown straight has been cut, a laurel bough bespeaking divinely appointed inspiration has been burned, and the fault is Faustus's own for failing to take advantage of "learning's golden gifts." A hard verdict, no doubt, but one that may, in retrospect, remind us of another "Muses' darling" cut down in his prime.
                                          THOMAS CARTELLI

The Tragical History of Doctor Faustus

CHARACTERS

The CHORUS
Doctor John FAUSTUS
WAGNER, his servant
The GOOD ANGEL
The EVIL ANGEL
VALDES ⎱
CORNELIUS ⎰ famous magicians
Three SCHOLARS
MEPHISTOPHELES
ROBIN, the clown, a stableman
Devils
RAFE, a stableman, another clown
LUCIFER
Beelzebub

PRIDE ⎫
COVETOUSNESS ⎪
WRATH ⎪
ENVY ⎬ the Seven Deadly Sins
GLUTTONY ⎪
SLOTH ⎪
LECHERY ⎭

The POPE
The Cardinal of LORRAINE
FRIARS
A VINTNER
The EMPEROR of Germany, Charles V
A KNIGHT
Attendants
Alexander the Great ⎱
His paramour ⎰ spirits
A HORSE-COURSER
The DUKE of Vanholt
The DUCHESS of Vanholt
Helen of Troy, a spirit
An OLD MAN

SCENE: *Doctor Faustus's study at Wittenberg, and on his travels.*

Prologue

[*Enter* CHORUS.]

CHORUS   Not marching now in fields of Trasimene,[1]
　　　　Where Mars° did mate° the Carthaginians,　　　　*Roman god of war / defeat*
　　　　Nor sporting in the dalliance of love
　　　　In courts of kings where state is overturned,
5　　　Nor in the pomp of proud audacious deeds,
　　　　Intends our muse to vaunt his heavenly verse.[2]

---

1. The lake in Italy where the Carthaginian general Hannibal destroyed two Roman legions in 217 B.C.E.
2. "Our muse" appears to refer to Marlowe himself, with the preceding lines alluding to

earlier plays of his, including *Edward II* and the first and second parts of *Tamburlaine the Great*. The reference to a play about Hannibal remains obscure.

Only this, gentlemen: we must perform
The form of Faustus' fortunes, good or bad.
To patient judgments we appeal our plaud,°   *seek approval*
10   And speak for Faustus in his infancy.
Now is he born, his parents base of stock,
In Germany, within a town called Rhode.
Of riper years to Wittenberg he went,
Whereas° his kinsmen chiefly brought him up.   *Where*
15   So soon he profits in divinity,
The fruitful plot of scholarism graced,
That shortly he was graced with doctor's name,
Excelling all whose sweet delight disputes
In heavenly matters of theology;
20   Till, swoll'n with cunning° of a self-conceit,   *learning; cleverness*
His waxen wings did mount above his reach,[3]
And, melting, heavens conspired his overthrow.
For, falling to a devilish exercise,
And glutted more with learning's golden gifts,
25   He surfeits upon cursèd necromancy;
Nothing so sweet as magic is to him,
Which he prefers before his chiefest bliss.[4]
And this the man that in his study sits.   [*Exit.*]

1.1

[*Enter* FAUSTUS *in his study.*]
FAUSTUS   Settle thy studies, Faustus, and begin
To sound the depth of that° thou wilt profess.   *that which*
Having commenced, be a divine in show,[5]
Yet level at the end° of every art,   *aim at the goal*
5   And live and die in Aristotle's works.
Sweet *Analytics*,[6] 'tis thou hast ravished me!
[*He reads.*] "*Bene disserere est finis logices.*"[7]
Is to dispute well logic's chiefest end?
Affords this art no greater miracle?
10   Then read no more; thou hast attained the end.
A greater subject fitteth Faustus' wit.
Bid *On kai me on*[8] farewell. Galen,[9] come!
Seeing *ubi desinit philosophus, ibi incipit medicus*,[1]
Be a physician, Faustus. Heap up gold,

3. An allusion to the mythological figure Icarus, whose "waxen wings" (devised by his father, Daedalus), melted when he flew too close to the sun.
4. That is, the hope of salvation.
5. A theologian in appearance.
6. Two of the treatises on logic by the Greek philosopher Aristotle (384–322 B.C.E.) are the *Prior Analytics* and the *Posterior Analytics*.

7. Quoted (Latin) from Peter Ramus's *Dialectica* (1576) and translated in the following line.
8. Being and not being (Greek).
9. Greek physician (129–ca. 199 C.E.), the standard authority on medicine for centuries.
1. Where the philosopher ends, there the physician begins (Latin).

15   And be eternized° for some wondrous cure.   *made forever famous*
       [*He reads.*] "*Summum bonum medicinae sanitas*":[2]
       "The end of physic° is our body's health."   *medicine*
       Why, Faustus, hast thou not attained that end?
       Is not thy common talk sound aphorisms?°   *established wisdom*
20   Are not thy bills° hung up as monuments,   *prescriptions*
       Whereby whole cities have escaped the plague
       And thousand desp'rate maladies been eased?
       Yet art thou still but Faustus, and a man.
       Wouldst thou make man to live eternally,
25   Or, being dead, raise them to life again,
       Then this profession were to be esteemed.
       Physic, farewell. Where is Justinian?[3]
       [*He reads.*] "*Si una eademque res legatur duobus,*
       Alter rem, alter valorem rei,"[4] etc.
30   A pretty° case of paltry legacies!   *petty*
       [*He reads.*] "*Exhaereditare filium non potest pater nisi*[5]—"
       Such is the subject of the Institute
       And universal body of the church.°   *canon law*
       His study fits a mercenary drudge
35   Who aims at nothing but external trash—
       Too servile and illiberal° for me.   *ungentlemanly*
       When all is done, divinity is best.
       Jerome's Bible,[6] Faustus, view it well.
       [*He reads.*] "*Stipendium peccati mors est.*"° Ha!   *(see Romans 6.23)*
40   "*Stipendium,*" etc.
       "The reward of sin is death." That's hard.
       [*He reads.*] "*Si peccasse negamus, fallimur,*
       Et nulla est in nobis veritas."°   *(see 1 John 1.8)*
       "If we say that we have no sin,
45   We deceive ourselves, and there's no truth in us."
       Why then belike we must sin,
       And so consequently die.
       Ay, we must die an everlasting death.
       What doctrine call you this? Che serà, serà,°   *(Spanish)*
50   "What will be, shall be"? Divinity, adieu!
           [*He picks up a book of magic.*]
       These metaphysics° of magicians   *This occult lore*
       And necromantic books are heavenly,
       Lines, circles, signs, letters, and characters°—   *astrological signs*
       Ay, these are those that Faustus most desires.
55   Oh, what a world of profit and delight,
       Of power, of honor, of omnipotence

2. An Aristotelian claim (see *Nicomachean Ethics* 1.7, 1097a).
3. Roman emperor (r. 527–65 C.E.); he codified Roman law in a series of publications, including the *Institutes* (533), the textbook quoted below.
4. If one thing is willed to two persons, one gets the thing, the other the value of the thing (Latin).
5. A father cannot disinherit his son unless (Latin).
6. The Latin (or Vulgate) version of the Bible, translated by Saint Jerome (ca. 347–419/420 C.E.).

Is promised to the studious artisan!°   *cultivator of the arts*
All things that move between the quiet° poles   *unmoving*
Shall be at my command. Emperors and kings
60   Are but obeyed in their several provinces,
Nor can they raise the wind or rend the clouds;
But his dominion that exceeds° in this   *excels*
Stretcheth as far as doth the mind of man.
A sound magician is a mighty god.
65   Here, Faustus, try° thy brains to gain a deity.°   *test / godhood*
    [*Calling*] Wagner!
        [*Enter* WAGNER.]
            Commend me to my dearest friends,
    The German Valdes and Cornelius.
    Request them earnestly to visit me.
    WAGNER   I will, sir.   [*Exit.*]
70 FAUSTUS   Their conference will be a greater help to me
    Than all my labors, plod I ne'er so fast.
        [*Enter the* GOOD ANGEL *and the* EVIL ANGEL.]
    GOOD ANGEL   O Faustus, lay that damnèd book aside
    And gaze not on it, lest it tempt thy soul
    And heap God's heavy wrath upon thy head!
75   Read, read the Scriptures. That° is blasphemy.   *(the book of magic)*
    EVIL ANGEL   Go forward, Faustus, in that famous art
    Wherein all nature's treasury is contained.
    Be thou on earth as Jove° is in the sky,   *Jupiter (i.e., God)*
    Lord and commander of these elements.
        [*Exeunt*° ANGELS.]   *They exit (Latin)*
80 FAUSTUS   How am I glutted with conceit° of this!   *the idea*
    Shall I make spirits fetch me what I please,
    Resolve me of° all ambiguities,   *Free me from*
    Perform what desperate° enterprise I will?   *reckless*
    I'll have them fly to India° for gold,   *the Indies*
85   Ransack the ocean for orient pearl,
    And search all corners of the newfound world°   *(i.e., America)*
    For pleasant fruits and princely delicates.°   *delicacies*
    I'll have them read° me strange philosophy   *teach*
    And tell the secrets of all foreign kings.
90   I'll have them wall all Germany with brass
    And make swift Rhine circle fair Wittenberg.
    I'll have them fill the public schools° with silk,   *university lecture halls*
    Wherewith the students shall be bravely° clad.   *smartly*
    I'll levy soldiers with the coin they bring
95   And chase the Prince of Parma[7] from our land,
    And reign sole king of all our provinces;
    Yea, stranger engines° for the brunt° of war   *machines / assault*
    Than was the fiery keel at Antwerp's bridge[8]

7. The Spanish governor-general in the Netherlands from 1579 to 1592 and commander of the Spanish Armada in 1588.

8. Those defending Antwerp against the Spanish in 1585 used a fireship to destroy Parma's bridge over the Scheldt River.

I'll make my servile spirits to invent.
100 Come, German Valdes and Cornelius,
And make me blest with your sage conference!

[*Enter* VALDES *and* CORNELIUS.]

Valdes, sweet Valdes, and Cornelius,
Know that your words have won me at the last
To practice magic and concealèd arts.
105 Yet not your words only, but mine own fantasy,
That will receive no object,° for my head   other idea; objection
But° ruminates on necromantic skill.   Only
Philosophy is odious and obscure;
Both law and physic are for petty wits;
110 Divinity is basest of the three,
Unpleasant, harsh, contemptible, and vile.
'Tis magic, magic that hath ravished me.
Then, gentle° friends, aid me in this attempt,   wellborn
And I, that have with concise syllogisms
115 Graveled° the pastors of the German church   Floored, confounded
And made the flow'ring pride of Wittenberg
Swarm to my problems° as the infernal spirits   disputations, lectures
On sweet Musaeus when he came to hell,[9]
Will be as cunning as Agrippa[1] was,
120 Whose shadows° made all Europe honor him.   spirits

VALDES Faustus, these books, thy wit, and our experience
Shall make all nations to canonize us.
As Indian Moors[2] obey their Spanish lords,
So shall the subjects° of every element   servant-spirits
125 Be always serviceable to us three.
Like lions shall they guard us when we please,
Like Almaine rutters° with their horsemen's staves,° German cavalry / lances
Or Lapland giants, trotting by our sides;
Sometimes like women, or unwedded maids,
130 Shadowing more beauty in their airy° brows   heavenly
Than in the white breasts of the Queen of Love.°   Venus
From Venice shall they drag huge argosies,°   large merchant ships
And from America the golden fleece[3]
That yearly stuffs old Philip's treasury,
135 If learnèd Faustus will be resolute.

FAUSTUS Valdes, as resolute am I in this
As thou to live. Therefore object it not.°   do not object

CORNELIUS The miracles that magic will perform
Will make thee vow to study nothing else.

9. Marlowe is apparently confusing the mythical poet Musaeus (described as standing in
the midst of a large number of spirits in the
underworld; Virgil, *Aeneid* 6.666–68) with
his predecessor Orpheus, who descended to
Hades in an unsuccessful attempt to retrieve
his dead wife, Eurydice.
1. Henry Cornelius Agrippa (1486–1535),
famous German physician and alchemist.

2. That is, the indigenous residents of the
Americas, such as the Aztecs of Mexico and
Incas of Peru.
3. That is, the huge amounts of gold the
Spanish were transporting over the Atlantic
to the king of Spain, Philip II (r. 1556–98). In
classical mythology, a literal golden fleece
was the object of the quest by Jason and the
Argonauts.

140 He that is grounded in astrology,
Enriched with tongues,° well seen° in minerals,   *languages / versed*
Hath all the principles magic doth require.
Then doubt not, Faustus, but to be renowned
And more frequented° for this mystery°   *resorted to / art*
145 Than heretofore the Delphian oracle.[4]
The spirits tell me they can dry the sea
And fetch the treasure of all foreign wrecks—
Ay, all the wealth that our forefathers hid
Within the massy entrails of the earth.
150 Then tell me, Faustus, what shall we three want?°   *lack*
FAUSTUS Nothing, Cornelius. Oh, this cheers my soul!
Come, show me some demonstrations magical,
That I may conjure in some lusty° grove   *pleasant*
And have these joys in full possession.
155 VALDES Then haste thee to some solitary grove,
And bear wise Bacon's and Albanus' works,[5]
The Hebrew Psalter, and New Testament;
And whatsoever else is requisite
We will inform thee ere our conference cease.
160 CORNELIUS Valdes, first let him know the words of art,°   *magical incantations*
And then, all other ceremonies learned,
Faustus may try his cunning by himself.
VALDES First I'll instruct thee in the rudiments,
And then wilt thou be perfecter than I.
165 FAUSTUS Then come and dine with me, and after meat°   *food*
We'll canvass every quiddity° thereof,   *scrutinize every detail*
For ere I sleep I'll try what I can do.
This night I'll conjure, though I die therefore. [*Exeunt.*]

1.2

[*Enter two* SCHOLARS.]

FIRST SCHOLAR I wonder what's become of Faustus, that
was wont to make our schools ring with *"sic probo."*°   *I prove it thus (Latin)*
SECOND SCHOLAR That shall we know, for see, here comes
his boy.°   *servant*

[*Enter* WAGNER *carrying wine.*]

5 FIRST SCHOLAR How now, sirrah,[6] where's thy master?
WAGNER God in heaven knows.
SECOND SCHOLAR Why, dost not thou know?
WAGNER Yes, I know, but that follows not.
FIRST SCHOLAR Go to, sirrah! Leave your jesting, and tell
10 us where he is.
WAGNER That follows not necessary by force of argument

4. Apollo's shrine at Delphi, in lower central Greece, was the site of the most authoritative oracle in the ancient world.
5. The English scientist Roger Bacon (ca.

1220–1292) and the Italian physician Pietro d'Abano (ca. 1250–1316) were both philosophers accused of heresy and black magic.
6. A form of address to male social inferiors.

that you, being licentiate,° should stand upon't. There   *advanced scholars*
fore, acknowledge your error, and be attentive.

SECOND SCHOLAR   Why, didst thou not say thou knew'st?

15 WAGNER   Have you any witness on't?

FIRST SCHOLAR   Yes, sirrah, I heard you.

WAGNER   Ask my fellow if I be a thief.

SECOND SCHOLAR   Well, you will not tell us.

WAGNER   Yes, sir, I will tell you. Yet if you were not dunces,
20 you would never ask me such a question. For is not he
corpus naturale?° And is not that *mobile?* Then, where   *a natural body (Latin)*
fore should you ask me such a question? But that I
am° by nature phlegmatic,[7] slow to wrath, and prone to   *Were I not*
lechery—to love, I would say—it were not for you to
25 come within forty foot of the place of execution,°   *dining room, gallows*
although I do not doubt to see you both hanged
the next sessions.° Thus, having triumphed over you,   *sitting of the court*
I will set my countenance like a precisian° and begin to   *Puritan*
speak thus: Truly, my dear brethren, my master is
30 within at dinner with Valdes and Cornelius, as this
wine, if it could speak, it would inform Your Worships.
And so the Lord bless you, preserve you, and keep you,
my dear brethren, my dear brethren.   [*Exit.*]

FIRST SCHOLAR   Nay, then, I fear he is fall'n into that
35 damned art for which they two are infamous through the
world.

SECOND SCHOLAR   Were he a stranger, and not allied° to me,   *a companion*
yet should I grieve for him. But come, let us go and
inform the rector,° and see if he, by his grave counsel, can   *head of the university*
40 reclaim him.

FIRST SCHOLAR   Oh, but I fear me nothing can reclaim him.

SECOND SCHOLAR   Yet let us try what we can do.   [*Exeunt.*]

1.3

[*Enter* FAUSTUS *to conjure.*]

FAUSTUS   Now that the gloomy shadow of the earth,
Longing to view Orion's drizzling look,[8]
Leaps from th'Antarctic world unto the sky
And dims the welkin° with her pitchy breath,   *sky*
5 Faustus, begin thine incantations,
And try if devils will obey thy hest,°   *behest, command*
Seeing thou hast prayed and sacrificed to them.
Within this circle is Jehovah's name,
Forward and backward anagrammatized,
10 The breviated names of holy saints,
Figures of every adjunct to the heavens,

7. Sluggish or dull. According to early modern accounts of human emotion, imbalances in the four bodily humors (fluids)—black bile (melancholic), blood (sanguine), yellow bile (choleric), and phlegm—determined one's personality.
8. Because in the Northern Hemisphere the constellation Orion rises in November, it was associated with winter storms.

And characters of signs° and erring stars°   the zodiac / planets
By which the spirits are enforced to rise.
Then fear not, Faustus, but be resolute,
15   And try the uttermost magic can perform.
Sint mihi dei Acherontis propitii! Valeat numen triplex
Jehovae! Ignei, aerii, aquatici, terreni, spiritus, salvete! Ori-
entis princeps Lucifer, Beelzebub, inferni ardentis monar-
cha, et Demogorgon, propitiamus vos, ut appareat et surgat
20   *Mephistopheles. Quid tu moraris? Per Jehovam, Gehennam,*
et consecratam aquam quam nunc spargo, signumque cru-
cis quod nunc facio, et per vota nostra, ipse nunc surgat
*nobis dicatus Mephistopheles!*⁹

> [FAUSTUS *sprinkles holy water and makes a sign of the*
> *cross.*]

> [*Enter a devil* (MEPHISTOPHELES).]

I charge thee to return and change thy shape.
25   Thou art too ugly to attend on me.
Go, and return an old Franciscan friar;
That holy shape becomes a devil best.

> [*Exit devil* (MEPHISTOPHELES).]

I see there's virtue° in my heavenly words.   power
Who would not be proficient in this art?
30   How pliant is this Mephistopheles,
Full of obedience and humility!
Such is the force of magic and my spells.
Now, Faustus, thou art conjurer laureate,
That canst command great Mephistopheles.
35   *Quin redis, Mephistopheles, fratris imagine!*¹

> [*Enter* MEPHISTOPHELES *dressed as a friar.*]

MEPHISTOPHELES   Now, Faustus, what wouldst thou have me do?
FAUSTUS   I charge thee wait upon me whilst I live,
To do whatever Faustus shall command,
Be it to make the moon drop from her sphere
40   Or the ocean to overwhelm the world.
MEPHISTOPHELES   I am a servant to great Lucifer
And may not follow thee without his leave.
No more than he commands must we perform.
FAUSTUS   Did not he charge thee to appear to me?
45   MEPHISTOPHELES   No, I came now hither of mine own accord.
FAUSTUS   Did not my conjuring speeches raise thee? Speak.
MEPHISTOPHELES   That was the cause, but yet *per accidens.*°   incidentally (Latin)
For when we hear one rack° the name of God,   torture, tear

9. May the gods of Acheron be propitious to me. Away with the threefold godhead of Jehovah! Hail, spirits of fire, air, water, and earth! Lucifer, Prince of the East, Beelzebub, monarch of burning hell, and Demogorgon, we invoke you, that Mephistopheles may appear and rise. Why do you delay? By Jehovah, Gehenna, and the holy water that I now sprin-kle, by the sign of the cross that I now make, and by our vows, may Mephistopheles himself, invoked by us, now rise! (Latin). *Acheron*: a river of the underworld. *Beelzebub, Demogorgon*: devils. *Gehenna*: hell.
1. Why not return in the image of a friar, Mephistopheles! (Latin).

Abjure the Scriptures and his Savior Christ,
50 We fly in hope to get his glorious soul,
Nor will we come unless he use such means
Whereby he is in danger to be damned.
Therefore, the shortest cut for conjuring
Is stoutly to abjure the Trinity[2]
55 And pray devoutly to the prince of hell.

FAUSTUS So Faustus hath
Already done, and holds this principle:
There is no chief but only Beelzebub,
To whom Faustus doth dedicate himself.
60 This word "damnation" terrifies not him,
For he confounds hell in Elysium.[3]
His ghost be with the old philosophers![4]
But leaving these vain trifles of men's souls,
Tell me what is that Lucifer thy lord?

65 MEPHISTOPHELES Archregent and commander of all spirits.

FAUSTUS Was not that Lucifer an angel once?

MEPHISTOPHELES Yes, Faustus, and most dearly loved of God.

FAUSTUS How comes it then that he is prince of devils?

MEPHISTOPHELES Oh, by aspiring pride and insolence,
70 For which God threw him from the face of heaven.

FAUSTUS And what are you that live with Lucifer?

MEPHISTOPHELES Unhappy spirits that fell with Lucifer,
Conspired against our God with Lucifer,
And are forever damned with Lucifer.

75 FAUSTUS Where are you damned?

MEPHISTOPHELES In hell.

FAUSTUS How comes it then that thou art out of hell?

MEPHISTOPHELES Why, this is hell, nor am I out of it.
Think'st thou that I, who saw the face of God
80 And tasted the eternal joys of heaven,
Am not tormented with ten thousand hells
In being deprived of everlasting bliss?
O Faustus, leave these frivolous demands,
Which strike a terror to my fainting soul!

85 FAUSTUS What, is great Mephistopheles so passionate
For being deprived of the joys of heaven?
Learn thou of° Faustus manly fortitude,   *from*
And scorn those joys thou never shalt possess.
Go bear these tidings to great Lucifer:
90 Seeing Faustus hath incurred eternal death
By desp'rate thoughts against Jove's deity,
Say he surrenders up to him his soul,
So° he will spare him four-and-twenty years,   *Provided that*
Letting him live in all voluptuousness,
95 Having thee ever to attend on me,

2. That is, God as existing in three persons: the Father, the Son, and the Holy Spirit.
3. He conflates the Christian Hell with the Elysian fields, the abode of the blessed in the underworld in Greek and Roman mythology.
4. That is, pre-Christian philosophers.

To give me whatsoever I shall ask,
To tell me whatsoever I demand,
To slay mine enemies and aid my friends,
And always be obedient to my will.
100 Go and return to mighty Lucifer,
And meet me in my study at midnight,
And then resolve me of° thy master's mind.   *explain to me*

MEPHISTOPHELES   I will, Faustus.   [*Exit.*]

FAUSTUS   Had I as many souls as there be stars,
105 I'd give them all for Mephistopheles.
By him I'll be great emperor of the world
And make a bridge through the moving air
To pass the ocean with a band of men;
I'll join the hills that bind° the Afric shore   *surround, encircle*
110 And make that land continent to° Spain,   *contiguous with*
And both contributory to my crown.
The emp'ror shall not live but by my leave,
Nor any potentate of Germany.
Now that I have obtained what I desire,
115 I'll live in speculation° of this art   *contemplation*
Till Mephistopheles return again.   [*Exit.*]

1.4

[*Enter* WAGNER *and* ROBIN *the clown.*]

WAGNER   Sirrah boy, come hither.
ROBIN   How, "boy"? 'Swounds,° "boy"! I hope you have seen   *By God's wounds (oath)*
many boys with such pickedevants° as I have. "Boy,"   *pointed beards*
quotha?[5]
5 WAGNER   Tell me, sirrah, hast thou any comings in?°   *income*
ROBIN   Ay, and goings out[6] too, you may see else.
WAGNER   Alas, poor slave,° see how poverty jesteth in his   *rogue, servant*
nakedness! The villain is bare and out of service,[7] and so
hungry that I know he would give his soul to the devil for
10 a shoulder of mutton, though it were blood raw.
ROBIN   How? My soul to the devil for a shoulder of mutton, though 'twere blood raw? Not so, good friend. By'r
Lady,[8] I had need have it well roasted, and good sauce to
it, if I pay so dear.
15 WAGNER   Well, wilt thou serve me, and I'll make thee go
like *Qui mihi discipulus*?[9]
ROBIN   How, in verse?
WAGNER   No, sirrah, in beaten silk and stavesacre.[1]
ROBIN   How, how, knave's acre?[2] [*Aside*] Ay, I thought that

---

5. That is, "You call *me* 'boy'?"
6. Expenses (with a possible reference to what can be seen through Robin's tattered clothing).
7. The wretch is poor and unemployed.
8. By our Lady—that is, the Virgin Mary (an oath).

9. You who are my pupil (Latin).
1. In embroidered silk anointed with larkspur (whose seeds were used to make a delousing concoction).
2. The name of a poor, narrow street in London.

20   was all the land his father left him. [*To* WAGNER] Do ye
     hear? I would be sorry to rob you of your living.

  WAGNER   Sirrah, I say in stavesacre.

  ROBIN   Oho, oho, "stavesacre"! Why then, belike,° if I were   *probably*
     your man,° I should be full of vermin.   *servant*

25 WAGNER   So thou shalt, whether thou be'st with me or
     no. But, sirrah, leave your jesting, and bind° yourself   *apprentice*
     presently° unto me for seven years, or I'll turn all the lice   *now*
     about thee into familiars,[3] and they shall tear thee in
     pieces.

30 ROBIN   Do you hear, sir? You may save that labor. They are
     too familiar with me already. 'Swounds, they are as bold
     with my flesh as if they had paid for my meat and drink.

  WAGNER   Well, do you hear, sirrah? [*Offering money*] Hold,
     take these guilders.°   *Dutch coins*

35 ROBIN   Gridirons?° What be they?   *Griddles*

  WAGNER   Why, French crowns.°   *coins*

  ROBIN   Mass,° but for the name of French crowns a man were   *By the Mass (oath)*
     as good have as many English counters.[4] And what should I
     do with these?

40 WAGNER   Why now, sirrah, thou art at an hour's warning°   *notice*
     whensoever or wheresoever the devil shall fetch thee.

  ROBIN   No, no, here, take your gridirons again.

     [*He attempts to return the money.*]

  WAGNER   Truly, I'll none of them.

  ROBIN   Truly, but you shall.

45 WAGNER [*to the audience*]   Bear witness I gave them him.

  ROBIN   Bear witness I gave them you again.

  WAGNER   Well, I will cause two devils presently to fetch
     thee away. [*Calling*] Baliol and Belcher!

  ROBIN   Let your Balio and your Belcher come here and I'll
50   knock them. They were never so knocked since they
     were devils. Say I should kill one of them, what would
     folks say? "Do ye see yonder tall° fellow in the round   *valiant*
     slop?° He has killed the devil." So I should be called "Kill   *baggy breeches*
     devil" all the parish over.

     [*Enter two devils, and* ROBIN *the clown runs up and
     down crying.*]

55 WAGNER   Baliol and Belcher! Spirits, away!

               [*Exeunt devils.*]

  ROBIN   What, are they gone? A vengeance on them! They
     have vile long nails. There was a he-devil and a she-
     devil. I'll tell you how you shall know them:° all he-devils   *tell them apart*
     has horns,[5] and all she-devils has clefts° and cloven feet.   *cleft hooves; vulvas*

60 WAGNER   Well, sirrah, follow me.

  ROBIN   But do you hear? If I should serve you, would you
     teach me to raise up Banios and Belcheos?

---

3. Attendant evil spirits, which take the shape   exchange.
of animals.   5. Devils' horns; cuckolds' horns.
4. Valueless tokens used in computation and

WAGNER   I will teach thee to turn thyself to anything, to
a dog, or a cat, or a mouse, or a rat, or anything.
65 ROBIN   How? A Christian fellow to a dog or a cat, a mouse
or a rat? No, no, sir. If you turn me into anything, let it
be in the likeness of a little, pretty, frisking flea, that I
may be here and there and everywhere. Oh, I'll tickle the
pretty wenches' plackets!° I'll be amongst them, i'faith!   *slits in petticoats*
70 WAGNER   Well, sirrah, come.
ROBIN   But do you hear, Wagner?
WAGNER   How? [*Calling*] Balioll and Belcher!
ROBIN   Oh, Lord, I pray sir, let Banio and Belcher go sleep.
WAGNER   Villain, call me Master Wagner, and let thy left
75 eye be diametarily° fixed upon my right heel, with *quasi*   *diametrically*
vestigiis nostris insistere.[6]   [*Exit.*]
ROBIN   God forgive me, he speaks Dutch fustian.° Well, I'll   *bombast*
follow him, I'll serve him, that's flat.°   [*Exit.*]   *for certain*

2.1

[*Enter* FAUSTUS *in his study.*]

FAUSTUS   Now, Faustus, must thou needs be damned,
And canst thou not be saved.
What boots° it then to think of God or heaven?   *avails*
Away with such vain fancies, and despair!
5 Despair in God and trust in Beelzebub.
Now go not backward. No, Faustus, be resolute.
Why waverest thou? Oh, something soundeth in mine ears:
"Abjure this magic, turn to God again!"
Ay, and Faustus will turn to God again.
10 To God? He loves thee not.
The god thou servest is thine own appetite,
Wherein is fixed the love of Beelzebub.
To him I'll build an altar and a church,
And offer lukewarm blood of newborn babes.
[*Enter* GOOD ANGEL *and* EVIL ANGEL.]
15 GOOD ANGEL   Sweet Faustus, leave that execrable art.
FAUSTUS   Contrition, prayer, repentance—what of them?
GOOD ANGEL   Oh, they are means to bring thee unto heaven.
EVIL ANGEL   Rather illusions, fruits of lunacy,
That makes men foolish that do trust them most.
20 GOOD ANGEL   Sweet Faustus, think of heaven and heavenly things!
EVIL ANGEL   No, Faustus, think of honor and wealth.
[*Exeunt* ANGELS.]
FAUSTUS   Of wealth?
Why, the seigniory of Emden° shall be mine.   *(port in north Germany)*
When Mephistopheles shall stand by me,
25 What god can hurt thee, Faustus? Thou art safe;

6. As if to walk in our (my) footsteps (Latin).

Cast° no more doubts. Come, Mephistopheles,   *Entertain*
And bring glad tidings from great Lucifer.
Is't not midnight? Come, Mephistopheles!
Veni, veni,° Mephistophile!   *Come, come (Latin)*
    [*Enter* MEPHISTOPHELES.]

30   Now tell, what says Lucifer, thy lord?
MEPHISTOPHELES   That I shall wait on Faustus whilst he lives,
    So° he will buy my service with his soul.   *Provided that*
FAUSTUS   Already Faustus hath hazarded that for thee.
MEPHISTOPHELES   But, Faustus, thou must bequeath it solemnly

35   And write a deed of gift with thine own blood,
    For that security° craves great Lucifer.   *guarantee*
    If thou deny it, I will back to hell.
FAUSTUS   Stay, Mephistopheles, and tell me, what good Will
    my soul do thy lord?
MEPHISTOPHELES   Enlarge his kingdom.

40 FAUSTUS   Is that the reason he tempts us thus?
MEPHISTOPHELES   *Solamen miseris socios habuisse doloris.*[7]
FAUSTUS   Have you any pain, that tortures° others?   *you who torture*
MEPHISTOPHELES   As great as have the human souls of men.
    But tell me, Faustus, shall I have thy soul?

45   And I will be thy slave, and wait on thee,
    And give thee more than thou hast wit to ask.
FAUSTUS   Ay, Mephistopheles, I give it thee.
MEPHISTOPHELES   Then stab thine arm courageously,
    And bind thy soul that at some certain day

50   Great Lucifer may claim it as his own,
    And then be thou as great as Lucifer.
FAUSTUS [*cutting his arm*]   Lo, Mephistopheles, for love of thee
    I cut mine arm, and with my proper° blood   *own*
    Assure my soul to be great Lucifer's,

55   Chief lord and regent of perpetual night.
    View here the blood that trickles from mine arm,
    And let it be propitious for my wish.
MEPHISTOPHELES   But, Faustus, thou must
    Write it in manner of a deed of gift.

60 FAUSTUS   Ay, so I will. [*He writes.*] But Mephistopheles,
    My blood congeals, and I can write no more.
MEPHISTOPHELES   I'll fetch thee fire to dissolve it straight.°   *immediately*
        [*Exit.*]
FAUSTUS   What might the staying of my blood portend?
    Is it unwilling I should write this bill?°   *legal document*

65   Why streams it not, that I may write afresh?
    "Faustus gives to thee his soul"—ah, there it stayed!
    Why shouldst thou not? Is not thy soul thine own?
    Then write again: "Faustus gives to thee his soul."
    [*Enter* MEPHISTOPHELES *with a chafer*° *of coals.*]   *chafing dish*
MEPHISTOPHELES   Here's fire. Come, Faustus, set it on.

---

7. It is a comfort to the wretched to have companions in their sorrows (i.e., misery loves company; Latin).

70 FAUSTUS   So. Now the blood begins to clear again.
      Now will I make an end immediately.   [*He writes.*]
MEPHISTOPHELES [*aside*]   Oh, what will not I do to obtain his soul?
FAUSTUS   *Consummatum est.*[8] This bill is ended,
      And Faustus hath bequeathed his soul to Lucifer.
75   But what is this inscription on mine arm?
      "*Homo, fuge!*"° Whither should I fly?   *Flee, o man! (Latin)*
      If unto God, he'll throw thee down to hell.—
      My senses are deceived; here's nothing writ.—
      I see it plain. Here in this place is writ
80   "*Homo, fuge!*" Yet shall not Faustus fly.
MEPHISTOPHELES [*aside*]   I'll fetch him somewhat° to delight   *something*
      his mind.   [*Exit.*]
            [*Enter* MEPHISTOPHELES *with devils, giving crowns and
            rich apparel to* FAUSTUS, *and dance and then depart.*]
FAUSTUS   Speak, Mephistopheles. What means this show?
MEPHISTOPHELES   Nothing, Faustus, but to delight thy mind withal°   *with*
      And to show thee what magic can perform.
85 FAUSTUS   But may I raise up spirits when I please?
MEPHISTOPHELES   Ay, Faustus, and do greater things than these.
FAUSTUS   Then there's enough for° a thousand souls.   *to pay for*
      Here, Mephistopheles, receive this scroll,
      A deed of gift of body and of soul—
90   But yet conditionally that thou perform
      All articles prescribed between us both.
MEPHISTOPHELES   Faustus, I swear by hell and Lucifer
      To effect all promises between us made.
FAUSTUS   Then hear me read them.
95   "On these conditions following:
         First, that Faustus may be a spirit in form and substance.
         Secondly, that Mephistopheles shall be his servant,
      and at his command.
         Thirdly, that Mephistopheles shall do for him and bring
100   him whatsoever.°   *anything at all*
         Fourthly, that he shall be in his chamber or house invisible.
         Lastly, that he shall appear to the said John Faustus at
      all times in what form or shape soever he please.
         I, John Faustus of Wittenberg, Doctor, by these pres-
105   ents° do give both body and soul to Lucifer, Prince of the   *this document*
      East, and his minister Mephistopheles; and furthermore
      grant unto them that, four-and-twenty years being ex-
      pired, the articles above written inviolate,° full power to   *not violated*
      fetch or carry the said John Faustus, body and soul, flesh,
110   blood, or goods, into their habitation wheresoever.
                                          By me, John Faustus."
MEPHISTOPHELES   Speak, Faustus. Do you deliver this as
      your deed?

---

8. It is finished (Latin), the last words of Jesus on the cross, according to John 19.30 (Vulgate).

FAUSTUS [*giving the deed*]   Ay. Take it, and the devil give
115 thee good on't.

MEPHISTOPHELES   Now, Faustus, ask what thou wilt.

FAUSTUS   First will I question with thee about hell.
Tell me, where is the place that men call hell?

MEPHISTOPHELES   Under the heavens.

FAUSTUS   Ay, but whereabout?

120 MEPHISTOPHELES   Within the bowels of these elements,
Where we are tortured and remain forever.
Hell hath no limits, nor is circumscribed
In one self° place, for where we are is hell,   *one and the same*
And where hell is must we ever be.
125 And, to conclude, when all the world dissolves,
And every creature shall be purified,
All places shall be hell that is not heaven.

FAUSTUS   Come, I think hell's a fable.

MEPHISTOPHELES   Ay, think so still, till experience change thy mind.

130 FAUSTUS   Why, think'st thou then that Faustus shall be damned?

MEPHISTOPHELES   Ay, of necessity, for here's the scroll
Wherein thou hast given thy soul to Lucifer.

FAUSTUS   Ay, and body too. But what of that?
Think'st thou that Faustus is so fond°   *foolish*
135 To imagine that after this life there is any pain?
Tush, these are trifles and mere old wives' tales.

MEPHISTOPHELES   But, Faustus, I am an instance to prove the
contrary,
For I am damned and am now in hell.

FAUSTUS   How? Now in hell? Nay, an° this be hell,   *if*
140 I'll willingly be damned here. What? Walking, disputing,
etc.?[9] But leaving off this, let me have a wife, the fairest
maid in Germany, for I am wanton and lascivious and cannot live without a wife.

MEPHISTOPHELES   How, a wife? I prithee, Faustus, talk not
145 of a wife.

FAUSTUS   Nay, sweet Mephistopheles, fetch me one, for I
will have one.

MEPHISTOPHELES   Well, thou wilt have one. Sit there till I
come. I'll fetch thee a wife, in the devil's name.   [*Exit.*]

[*Enter* MEPHISTOPHELES *with a devil dressed like
a woman, with fireworks.*]

150 MEPHISTOPHELES   Tell, Faustus, how dost thou like thy wife?

FAUSTUS   A plague on her for a hot whore!

MEPHISTOPHELES   Tut, Faustus, marriage is but a ceremonial toy.°   *amusement*
If thou lovest me, think no more of it.   [*Exit devil.*]
I'll cull thee out the fairest courtesans
155 And bring them ev'ry morning to thy bed.
She whom thine eye shall like thy heart shall have,
Be she as chaste as was Penelope,

9. "Etc." signals a moment of improvisation.

As wise as Saba,[1] or as beautiful
As was bright Lucifer before his fall.
160   [*Presenting a book*] Hold, take this book. Peruse it thoroughly.
    The iterating° of these lines brings gold;   *repeating, reciting*
    The framing° of this circle on the ground   *inscribing*
    Brings whirlwinds, tempests, thunder, and lightning.
    Pronounce this thrice devoutly to thyself,
165   And men in armor shall appear to thee,
    Ready to execute what thou desir'st.
    FAUSTUS   Thanks, Mephistopheles. Yet fain° would I have   *gladly*
    a book wherein I might behold all spells and incanta-
    tions, that I might raise up spirits when I please.
170 MEPHISTOPHELES   Here they are in this book.
                                [*There turn to them.*]
    FAUSTUS   Now would I have a book where I might see all
    characters° and planets of the heavens, that I might   *astrological symbols*
    know their motions and dispositions.
    MEPHISTOPHELES   Here they are too.   [*Turn to them.*]
175 FAUSTUS   Nay, let me have one book more—and then I
    have done—wherein I might see all plants, herbs, and
    trees that grow upon the earth.
    MEPHISTOPHELES   Here they be.   [*Turn to them.*]
    FAUSTUS   Oh, thou art deceived.
180 MEPHISTOPHELES   Tut, I warrant thee.   [*Exeunt.*]

2.2

    [*Enter* ROBIN *the ostler° with a book in his hand.*]   *stable boy*
    ROBIN   Oh, this is admirable! Here I ha' stol'n one of
    Doctor Faustus' conjuring books, and, i'faith, I mean
    to search some circles[2] for my own use. Now will I
    make all the maidens in our parish dance at my plea-
5   sure stark naked before me, and so by that means I
    shall see more than e'er I felt or saw yet.
                [*Enter* RAFE, *calling* ROBIN.]
    RAFE   Robin, prithee, come away. There's a gentleman
    tarries to have his horse, and he would have his things[3]
    rubbed and made clean; he keeps such a chafing with
10   my mistress about it, and she has sent me to look thee
    out.° Prithee, come away.   *look for you*
    ROBIN   Keep out, keep out, or else you are blown up,
    you are dismembered, Rafe! Keep out, for I am about a
    roaring piece of work.
15 RAFE   Come, what dost thou with that same book?° Thou   *that book there*
    canst not read?

1. The queen of Sheba, who greatly admired   2. Conjuring circles; vaginas.
Solomon's wisdom (Kings 10.1–9). *Penelope*:   3. His leather riding gear (with sexual
the wife of Odysseus and in classical myth a   suggestion).
model of faithfulness.

ROBIN Yes, my master and mistress shall find that I can read—he for his forehead, she for her private study.[4] She's born to bear with me,[5] or else my art fails.

20 RAFE Why, Robin, what book is that?

ROBIN What book? Why the most intolerable[6] book for conjuring that e'er was invented by any brimstone devil.

RAFE Canst thou conjure with it?

ROBIN I can do all these things easily with it: first, I can 25 make thee drunk with hippocras° at any tavern in Europe   *spiced wine* for nothing. That's one of my conjuring works.

RAFE Our Master Parson says that's nothing.

ROBIN True, Rafe; and more, Rafe, if thou hast any mind to° Nan Spit,[7] our kitchen maid, then turn her and   *any liking for* 30 wind her to thy own use as often as thou wilt, and at midnight.

RAFE Oh, brave,° Robin! Shall I have Nan Spit, and to   *splendid* mine own use? On that condition I'll feed thy devil with horse-bread° as long as he lives, of free cost.   *horse feed, fodder*

35 ROBIN No more, sweet Rafe. Let's go and make clean our boots, which lie foul upon our hands, and then to our conjuring, in the devil's name.   [*Exeunt.*]

2.3

[*Enter* FAUSTUS *in his study, and* MEPHISTOPHELES.]

FAUSTUS When I behold the heavens, then I repent
And curse thee, wicked Mephistopheles,
Because thou hast deprived me of those joys.

MEPHISTOPHELES Why, Faustus,
5 Think'st thou heaven is such a glorious thing?
I tell thee, 'tis not half so fair as thou
Or any man that breathes on earth.

FAUSTUS How provest thou that?

MEPHISTOPHELES It was made for man; therefore is man
10 more excellent.

FAUSTUS If it were made for man, 'twas made for me.
I will renounce this magic and repent.

[*Enter* GOOD ANGEL *and* EVIL ANGEL.]

GOOD ANGEL Faustus, repent yet, God will pity thee.

EVIL ANGEL Thou art a spirit. God cannot pity thee.

15 FAUSTUS Who buzzeth in mine ears I am a spirit?
Be I a devil,[8] yet God may pity me;

---

4. That is, in sex with her, which will put a cuckold's horns on his forehead.
5. Put up with me; support my body in sex; bear my child.
6. Malapropism for "incomparable."

7. Named for the spit on which cooking meat is turned.
8. A notoriously ambiguous phrase, which may mean "Even if I *am* a devil" or "Even if I *were* a devil."

Ay, God will pity me if I repent.

EVIL ANGEL   Ay, but Faustus never shall repent.

[*Exeunt* ANGELS.]

FAUSTUS   My heart's so hardened I cannot repent.
20   Scarce can I name salvation, faith, or heaven
But fearful echoes thunders in mine ears:
"Faustus, thou art damned!" Then swords and knives,
Poison, guns, halters° and envenomed steel°   *nooses / swords*
Are laid before me to dispatch myself;
25   And long ere this I should have slain myself
Had not sweet pleasure conquered deep despair.
Have not I made blind Homer sing to me
Of Alexander's love and Oenone's death?[9]
And hath not he that built the walls of Thebes
30   With ravishing sound of his melodious harp[1]
Made music with my Mephistopheles?
Why should I die, then, or basely despair?
I am resolved Faustus shall ne'er repent.
Come, Mephistopheles, let us dispute again
35   And argue of divine astrology.
Tell me, are there many heavens above the moon?
Are all celestial bodies but one globe,
As is the substance of this centric earth?[2]

MEPHISTOPHELES   As are the elements, such are the spheres,
40   Mutually folded in each others' orb;
And, Faustus, all jointly move upon one axletree,°   *axle, pole*
Whose terminine° is termed the world's wide pole.   *limit*
Nor are the names of Saturn, Mars, or Jupiter
Feigned, but are erring stars.°   *wandering planets*
45 FAUSTUS   But tell me, have they all one motion, both *situ*
et tempore?°   *in space and time (Latin)*

MEPHISTOPHELES   All jointly move from east to west in
four-and-twenty hours upon the poles of the world,
but differ in their motion upon the poles of the zodiac.°   *i.e., along the zodiac*
50 FAUSTUS   Tush, these slender trifles Wagner can decide.
Hath Mephistopheles no greater skill?
Who knows not the double motion of the planets?
The first is finished in a natural day,
The second thus, as Saturn in thirty years, Jupiter in
55   twelve, Mars in four,° the Sun, Venus, and Mercury in a   *(in fact, two)*
year, the moon in twenty-eight days. Tush, these are
freshmen's suppositions.° But tell me, hath every sphere   *arguing points*
a dominion or intelligentia?°   *controlling spirit*

---

9. The story of the love of Paris (Alexander) for Helen, whom the Greeks waged the Trojan War to retrieve, forms the backdrop of Homer's *Iliad;* and Oenone, the daughter of a river god who was Paris's first love, killed herself after his death.

1. In Greek mythology Amphion, a son of Zeus, was famous for his musical talent; after he became king of Thebes, he built the city walls by playing his lyre to move their stones.
2. That is, this earth at the center of the universe (the Ptolemaic view).

MEPHISTOPHELES Ay.

60 FAUSTUS How many heavens or spheres are there?

MEPHISTOPHELES Nine: the seven planets, the firmament,
and the empyreal° heaven.   *highest*

FAUSTUS Well, resolve me in this question: why have we
not conjunctions, oppositions, aspects, eclipses all at one

65 time,° but in some years we have more, in some less?   *at regular intervals*

MEPHISTOPHELES *Per inaequalem motum respectu totius.*³

FAUSTUS Well, I am answered. Tell me who made the world.

MEPHISTOPHELES I will not.

FAUSTUS Sweet Mephistopheles, tell me.

70 MEPHISTOPHELES Move° me not, for I will not tell thee.   *Anger*

FAUSTUS Villain, have I not bound thee to tell me anything?

MEPHISTOPHELES Ay, that is not against our kingdom, but
this is. Think thou on hell, Faustus, for thou art damned.

FAUSTUS Think, Faustus, upon God, that made the world.

75 MEPHISTOPHELES Remember this.°   [*Exit.*]   *You will pay for this*

FAUSTUS Ay, go, accursèd spirit, to ugly hell!
'Tis thou hast damned distressèd Faustus' soul.
Is't not too late?

[*Enter* GOOD ANGEL *and* EVIL ANGEL.]

EVIL ANGEL Too late.

80 GOOD ANGEL Never too late, if Faustus can repent.

EVIL ANGEL If thou repent, devils shall tear thee in pieces.

GOOD ANGEL Repent, and they shall never raze thy skin.

[*Exeunt* ANGELS.]

FAUSTUS Ah, Christ, my Savior,
Seek to save distressèd Faustus' soul!

[*Enter* LUCIFER, BEELZEBUB, *and* MEPHISTOPHELES.]

85 LUCIFER Christ cannot save thy soul, for he is just.
There's none but I have int'rest in the same.

FAUSTUS Oh, who art thou that look'st so terrible?

LUCIFER I am Lucifer,
And this is my companion prince in hell.

90 FAUSTUS O Faustus, they are come to fetch away thy soul!

LUCIFER We come to tell thee thou dost injure us.
Thou talk'st of Christ, contrary to thy promise.
Thou shouldst not think of God. Think of the devil,
And of his dame,⁴ too.

95 FAUSTUS Nor will I henceforth. Pardon me in this,
And Faustus vows never to look to heaven,
Never to name God or to pray to him,
To burn his Scriptures, slay his ministers,
And make my spirits pull his churches down.

100 LUCIFER Do so, and we will highly gratify° thee. Faustus,   *reward, satisfy*

3. Because of unequal motion in respect to
the whole (Latin).
4. Dam, wife. Witchcraft manuals attribute

to the devil (Lucifer) many sexual partners
and, occasionally, a long-term female consort
or wife.

we are come from hell to show thee some pastime.
Sit down, and thou shalt see all the Seven Deadly
Sins appear in their proper° shapes.   *own*

FAUSTUS   That sight will be as pleasing unto me as Para-
105   dise was to Adam the first day of his creation.

LUCIFER   Talk not of Paradise nor creation, but mark this
show. Talk of the devil, and nothing else.—Come away!

[FAUSTUS *sits.*]

[*Enter the Seven Deadly Sins.*]

Now, Faustus, examine them of° their several° names   *about / different*
and dispositions.

110   FAUSTUS   What art thou, the first?

PRIDE   I am Pride. I disdain to have any parents. I am like
to Ovid's flea:[5] I can creep into every corner of a wench.
Sometimes like a periwig I sit upon her brow, or like a
fan of feathers I kiss her lips. Indeed I do. What do I
115   not? But fie, what a scent is here! I'll not speak another
word except° the ground were perfumed and covered with   *unless*
cloth of arras.°   *rich tapestry*

FAUSTUS   What art thou, the second?

COVETOUSNESS   I am Covetousness, begotten of an old
120   churl in an old leathern bag;° and might I have my   *money bag*
wish, I would desire that this house and all the people
in it were turned to gold, that I might lock you up in
my good chest. O my sweet gold!

FAUSTUS   What art thou, the third?

125   WRATH   I am Wrath. I had neither father nor mother. I
leaped out of a lion's mouth when I was scarce half an
hour old, and ever since I have run up and down the
world with this case of rapiers,° wounding myself when I   *pair of swords*
had nobody to fight withal.° I was born in hell, and   *with*
130   look to it,° for some of you shall be my father.   *be advised*

FAUSTUS   What art thou, the fourth?

ENVY   I am Envy, begotten of a chimney sweeper and an
oyster-wife.° I cannot read, and therefore wish all   *oyster seller*
books were burnt. I am lean with seeing others eat.
135   Oh, that there would come a famine through all the
world, that all might die, and I live alone! Then thou
shouldst see how fat I would be. But must thou sit and
I stand? Come down, with a vengeance!°   *with a curse (on you)*

FAUSTUS   Away, envious rascal!—What are thou, the fifth?

140   GLUTTONY   Who, I, sir? I am Gluttony. My parents are all
dead, and the devil a penny° they have left me but   *not even a penny*
a bare pension, and that is thirty meals a day, and
ten bevers°—a small trifle to suffice nature.° Oh, I come   *snacks / bodily nature*
of a royal parentage. My grandfather was a gammon
145   of bacon,° my grandmother a hogshead° of claret   *ham / large cask*

5. The medieval "Elegy of a Flea" was wrongly attributed to the Roman poet Ovid (43 B.C.E.–17
C.E.).

wine. My godfathers these: Peter Pickle-herring° and *pickled herring*
Martin Martlemas-beef.[6] Oh, but jolly gentlewoman,
and well beloved in every good town and city; her name
was Mistress Margery March-beer.° Now, Faustus, *strong beer*
150 thou hast heard all my progeny, wilt thou bid me to
supper?

FAUSTUS   No, I'll see thee hanged. Thou wilt eat up all my
victuals.

GLUTTONY   Then the devil choke thee!

155 FAUSTUS   Choke thyself, glutton!—What art thou, the
sixth?

SLOTH   I am Sloth. I was begotten on a sunny bank, where
I have lain ever since, and you have done me great injury
to bring me from thence. Let me be carried thither again
160 by Gluttony and Lechery. I'll not speak another word for a
king's ransom.

FAUSTUS   What are you, Mistress Minx, the seventh and
last?

LECHERY   Who, I, sir? I am one that loves an inch of raw
165 mutton better than an ell of fried stockfish,[7] and the first
letter of my name begins with lechery.

LUCIFER   Away, to hell, to hell!   [*Exeunt the Sins.*]
Now, Faustus, how dost thou like this?

FAUSTUS   Oh, this feeds my soul!

170 LUCIFER   Tut, Faustus, in hell is all manner of delight.

FAUSTUS   Oh, might I see hell and return again, how happy
were I then!

LUCIFER   Thou shalt. I will send for thee at midnight. [*He
presents a book.*] In meantime, take this book. Peruse it
175 throughly,° and thou shalt turn thyself into what shape *thoroughly*
thou wilt.

FAUSTUS [*taking the book*] Great thanks, mighty Lucifer. This
will I keep as chary° as my life. *carefully*

LUCIFER   Farewell, Faustus, and think on the devil.

180 FAUSTUS   Farewell, great Lucifer. Come, Mephistopheles.

[*Exeunt omnes*° FAUSTUS *and* MEPHISTOPHELES *by one* *all (Latin)*
way, LUCIFER *and* BEELZEBUB *by another.*]

3. Chorus

[*Enter* WAGNER *solus.*°] *alone (Latin)*

WAGNER   Learnèd Faustus,
To know the secrets of astronomy
Graven° in the book of Jove's high firmament, *Engraved*
Did mount himself to scale Olympus'[8] top,
5   Being seated in a chariot burning bright

6. Beef slaughtered on the Feast of St. Martin
(November 11).
7. One who prefers raw meat to dried cod—

that is, hot sex to cold chastity.
8. A mountain in northern Greece and, in
classical mythology, the home of the gods.

Drawn by the strength of voky° dragons' necks.   *yoked*
He now is gone to prove° cosmography,   *make trial of*
And, as I guess, will first arrive at Rome
To see the Pope and manner of his court
10   And take some part of° holy Peter's feast[9]   *in*
That to this day is highly solemnized.   [*Exit* WAGNER.]

3.1

[*Enter* FAUSTUS *and* MEPHISTOPHELES.]

FAUSTUS   Having now, my good Mephistopheles
Passed with delight the stately town of Trier°   *(in western Germany)*
Environed round with airy mountaintops,
With walls of flint and deep intrenchèd lakes°   *moats*
5   Not to be won by any conquering prince;
From Paris next, coasting° the realm of France,   *skirting*
We saw the river Maine fall into Rhine,
Whose banks are set with groves of fruitful vines.
Then up to Naples, rich Campania,
10   Whose buildings, fair and gorgeous to the eye,
The streets straight forth° and paved with finest brick,   *perfectly straight*
Quarters the town in four equivalents.
There saw we learned Maro's[1] golden tomb,
The way he cut an English mile in length
15   Thorough° a rock of stone in one night's space[2]   *through*
From thence to Venice, Padua, and the rest,
In midst of which a sumptuous temple[3] stands
That threats° the stars with her aspiring top.   *threatens, challenges*
Thus hitherto hath Faustus spent his time.
20   But tell me now, what resting place is this?
Hast thou, as erst° I did command,   *earlier*
Conducted me within the walls of Rome?
MEPHISTOPHELES   Faustus, I have. And because° we will   *in order that*
not be unprovided, I have taken up His Holiness's privy°   *private*
25   chamber for our use.
FAUSTUS   I hope His Holiness will bid us welcome.
MEPHISTOPHELES   Tut, 'tis no matter, man. We'll be bold
with his good cheer.
And now, my Faustus, that thou mayst perceive
30   What Rome containeth to delight thee with,
Know that this city stands upon seven hills
That underprops the groundwork of the same.
Just° through the midst runs flowing Tiber's stream,   *Right*
With winding banks that cut it in two parts,

9. In the Roman Catholic Church, the main feast (or festival) of St. Peter and St. Paul takes place on June 29.
1. The Roman poet Virgil (70–19 B.C.E.), whose full name was Publius Vergilius Maro.
2. This tunnel through volcanic tufa, about a half mile long, was probably constructed in the 1st century C.E.; in the Middle Ages, it was credited to Virgil and his magic.
3. That is, St. Mark's Basilica in Venice, consecrated in 1094.

35 Over the which four stately bridges lean,
   That makes safe passage to each part of Rome.
   Upon the bridge called Ponte Angelo
   Erected is a castle passing° strong,   *surpassingly*
   Within whose walls such store of ordnance are,
40 And double cannons, framed° of carvèd brass   *made*
   As match the days within one complete year[4]
   Besides the gates and high pyramides°   *obelisks*
   Which Julius Caesar[5] brought from Africa.
FAUSTUS   Now, by the kingdoms of infernal rule,
45 Of Styx, Acheron, and the fiery lake
   Of ever-burning Phlegethon[6] I swear
   That I do long to see the monuments
   And situation of bright splendent Rome.
   Come, therefore, let's away!
50 MEPHISTOPHELES   Nay, Faustus, stay. I know you'd fain see
       the Pope
   And take some part of holy Peter's feast,
   Where thou shalt see a troupe of bald-pate friars
   Whose *summum bonum*° is in belly cheer.   *highest good (Latin)*
55 FAUSTUS   Well, I am content to compass° then some sport,   *devise*
   And by their folly make us merriment.
   Then charm° me, that I may be invisible, to do what I   *put a spell on*
   please unseen of any whilst, stay in Rome.
MEPHISTOPHELES [*placing a robe on* FAUSTUS]   So, Faustus,
60 now do what thou wilt, thou shalt not be discerned.

       [*Sound a sennet.° Enter the* POPE *and the Cardinal of*   *trumpet call*
       LORRAINE *to the banquet, with* FRIARS *attending.*]

POPE   My lord of Lorraine, will't please you draw near?
FAUSTUS   Fall to, and the devil choke you an you spare.°   *if you hold back*
POPE   How now, who's that which spake?—Friars, look
   about.

       [*Some* FRIARS *attempt to search.*]

65 FRIAR   Here's nobody, if it like° Your Holiness.   *please*
POPE [*presenting a dish*]   My lord, here is a dainty dish was°   *that was*
   sent me from the Bishop of Milan.
FAUSTUS [*snatching it*]   I thank you, sir.
POPE   How now, who's that which snatched the meat from
70 me? Will no man look? [*Some* FRIARS *search about.*] My
   lord, this dish was sent me from the Cardinal of Florence.
FAUSTUS [*snatching the dish*]   You say true. I'll ha't.
POPE   What, again?—My lord, I'll drink to Your Grace.
75 FAUSTUS [*snatching the cup*]   I'll pledge Your Grace.
LORRAINE   My lord, it may be some ghost, newly crept out of
   purgatory, come to beg a pardon of Your Holiness.

---

4. That is, there are 365 cannons.
5. During the civil war precipitated by Caesar
(100–44 B.C.E.), the Roman general fought in
Egypt and Africa; however, the first ruler to

bring Egyptian obelisks to Rome was his successor, Augustus.
6. A river of fire in the classical underworld;
Styx and Acheron are also rivers in Hades.

POPE   It may be so.—Friars, prepare a dirge to lay° the fury   *allay*
   of this ghost.—Once again, my lord, fall to.°   *partake of the feast*
     [*The* POPE *crosseth himself.*]

80 FAUSTUS   What, are you crossing of yourself?
   Well, use that trick no more, I would advise you.
     [*The* POPE *crosses himself again.*]

   Well, there's a second time. Aware° the third,   *Beware*
   I give you fair warning.
     [*The* POPE *crosses himself again, and* FAUSTUS *hits
     him a box of the ear, and they all* (*except* FAUSTUS
     and MEPHISTOPHELES) *run away.*]

   Come on, Mephistopheles. What shall we do?
85 MEPHISTOPHELES   Nay, I know not. We shall be cursed
   with bell, book, and candle.[7]
   FAUSTUS   How? Bell, book, and candle, candle, book, and
   bell, Forward and backward, to curse Faustus to hell.
   Anon you shall hear a hog grunt, a calf bleat, and an ass
90 bray, Because it is Saint Peter's holy day.
     [*Enter all the* FRIARS *to sing the dirge.*]

   FRIAR   Come, brethren, let's about our business with good
   devotion.
     [*The* FRIARS *sing this.*]

   Cursèd be he that stole away His Holiness's meat from
   the table.
95   *Maledicat Dominus!*[8]
   Cursèd be he that struck His Holiness a blow on the
   face.
     Maledicat Dominus!
   Cursèd be he that took° Friar Sandelo a blow on the pate.°   *gave / head*
100   *Maledicat Dominus!*
   Cursèd be he that disturbeth our holy dirge.
     Maledicat Dominus!
   Cursèd be he that took away His Holiness's wine.
     Maledicat Dominus!
105 *Et omnes sancti.*[9] Amen.
     [FAUSTUS *and* MEPHISTOPHELES *beat the* FRIARS,
     and fling fireworks among them, and so exeunt.]

3.2

     [*Enter* ROBIN *with a conjuring book and* RAFE *with
     a silver goblet.*]

   ROBIN   Come, Rafe, did not I tell thee we were forever
   made by this Doctor Faustus' book? *Ecce signum.*° Here's   *Behold the proof (Latin)*
   a simple purchase° for horse-keepers! Our horses shall   *acquisition*

---

7. A form of excommunication that involved
ringing a bell, closing a holy book, and snuff-
ing out a candle.

8. May the Lord curse him! (Latin).
9. And all the saints (Latin); that is, may all
the saints curse him too.

eat no hay[1] as long as this lasts.

      [*Enter the* VINTNER.°]   *innkeeper*

5 RAFE   But, Robin, here comes the Vintner.

    ROBIN   Hush, I'll gull° him supernaturally.—Drawer,° I hope   *trick / Bartender*
    all is paid. God be with you. Come, Rafe. [*They start to go.*]

    VINTNER [*to* ROBIN]   Soft,° sir, a word with you. I must yet   *Wait*
    have a goblet paid from you ere you go.

10 ROBIN   I, a goblet? Rafe, I, a goblet? I scorn you, and you are
    but a etc. I, a goblet? Search me.

    VINTNER   I mean so, sir, with your favor.°   *permission*

      [*The* VINTNER *searches* ROBIN.]

    ROBIN   How say you now?

    VINTNER   I must say somewhat° to your fellow.—You, sir.   *something*

15 RAFE   Me, sir? Me, sir? Search your fill.

      [*He tosses the goblet to* ROBIN; *then the* VINTNER
      searches RAFE.]

    Now, sir, you may be ashamed to burden honest men with
    a matter of truth.°   *question of honesty*

    VINTNER   Well, t'one of you hath this goblet about you.

    ROBIN   You lie, drawer, 'tis afore° me. Sirrah, you, I'll teach   *in front of*

20 ye to impeach° honest men. Stand by. I'll scour° you   *accuse / beat*
    for a goblet. Stand aside, you had best, I charge you in the
    name of Beelzebub. [*He tosses the goblet to* RAFE.]

    [*Aside to* RAFE] Look to the goblet, Rafe.

    VINTNER   What mean you, sirrah?

25 ROBIN   I'll tell you what I mean. [*He reads.*] "Sanctobulorum
    Periphrasticon!"°—Nay, I'll tickle you, Vintner. [*Aside to*   *(Latin gibberish)*
    Rafe] Look to the goblet, Rafe.—"Polypragmos Belseborams
    framanto pacostiphos tostu Mephistopheles!" etc.°   *(Latin gibberish)*

      [*Enter to them* MEPHISTOPHELES.]

             [*Exit the* VINTNER, *running.*]

    MEPHISTOPHELES   Monarch of hell, under whose black survey

30 Great potentates do kneel with awful° fear,   *awe-filled*
    Upon whose altars thousand souls do lie,
    How am I vexèd with these villains' charms!°   *spells*
    From Constantinople am I hither come
    Only for pleasure of these damnèd slaves.

35 ROBIN   How, from Constantinople? You have had a great
    journey. Will you take sixpence in your purse to pay for
    your supper and be gone?

    MEPHISTOPHELES   Well, villains, for your presumption I
    transform thee [*to* ROBIN] into an ape, and thee [*to* RAFE]

40 into a dog. And so, begone!

      [*They are transformed in shape.*]

            [*Exit* MEPHISTOPHELES.]

    ROBIN   How, into an ape? That's brave.° I'll have fine sport   *excellent*
    with the boys; I'll get nuts and apples enough.

---

1. That is, they will eat like kings.

RAFE   And I must be a dog.

ROBIN   I'faith, thy head will never be out of the pottage° pot.   *porridge*

[*Exeunt.*]

4. Chorus

[*Enter* CHORUS.]

CHORUS   When Faustus had with pleasure ta'en the view
　　　Of rarest things and royal courts of kings,
　　　He stayed his course° and so returnèd home,   *stopped traveling*
　　　Where such as bear his absence but with grief—
5　　I mean his friends and nearest companions—
　　　Did gratulate° his safety with kind words.   *rejoice at*
　　　And in their conference of what befell,
　　　Touching° his journey through the world and air,   *Regarding*
　　　They put forth questions of astrology,
10　　Which Faustus answered with such learnèd skill
　　　As° they admired and wondered at his wit.   *That*
　　　Now is his fame spread forth in every land.
　　　Amongst the rest the Emperor[2] is one,
　　　Carolus the Fifth, at whose palace now
15　　Faustus is feasted 'mongst his noblemen.
　　　What there he did in trial° of his art°   *demonstration / skill*
　　　I leave untold, your eyes shall see performed.   [*Exit.*]

4.1

[*Enter* EMPEROR, FAUSTUS, MEPHISTOPHELES, *and
a* KNIGHT, *with attendants.*]

EMPEROR   Master Doctor Faustus, I have heard strange° re-   *unusual,*
port of thy knowledge in the black art—how that none in   *wondrous*
my empire, nor in the whole world, can compare with thee
for the rare effects of magic. They say thou hast a familiar
5   spirit by whom thou canst accomplish what thou list.° This,   *desire, want*
therefore, is my request: that thou let me see some proof of
thy skill, that mine eyes may be witnesses to confirm what
mine ears have heard reported. And here I swear to thee,
by the honor of mine imperial crown, that whatever thou
10   dost, thou shalt be no ways prejudiced or endamaged.

KNIGHT   [*aside*]   I'faith, he looks much like a conjurer.°   *(ironic)*

FAUSTUS   My gracious sovereign, though I must confess
myself far inferior to the report men have published,° and   *spread abroad*
nothing answerable° to the honor of Your Imperial Majesty,   *suitable*
15   yet, for that° love and duty binds me there unto, I am   *because*
content to do whatsoever Your Majesty shall command me.

2. Charles (Carolus) V (1500–1558), king of Spain (r. 1516–56) and emperor of the Holy
Roman Empire (r. 1519–56).

EMPEROR   Then, Doctor Faustus, mark what I shall say.
    As I was sometime° solitary set   recently
    Within my closet,° sundry thoughts arose   private room
20 About the honor of mine ancestors—
    How they had won by prowess such exploits,
    Got such riches, subdued so many kingdoms
    As we that do succeed or they that shall
    Hereafter possess our throne shall,
25 I fear me, never attain to that degree
    Of high renown and great authority.
    Amongst which kings is Alexander the Great,³
    Chief spectacle of the world's preeminence,
    The bright shining of whose glorious acts
30 Lightens the world with his reflecting beams—
    As° when I hear but motion° made of him,   so that / mention
    It grieves my soul I never saw the man.
    If, therefore, thou by cunning of thine art
    Canst raise this man from hollow vaults below
35 Where lies entombed this famous conqueror,
    And bring with him his beauteous paramour,
    Both in their right shapes, gesture, and attire
    They used to wear during their time of life,
    Thou shalt both satisfy my just desire
40 And give me cause to praise thee whilst I live.
FAUSTUS   My gracious lord, I am ready to accomplish your
    request, so far forth as by art and power of my spirit I am
    able to perform.
KNIGHT [aside]   I'faith, that's just nothing at all.
45 FAUSTUS   But if it like° Your Grace, it is not in my ability to   please
    present before your eyes the true substantial bodies of those
    two deceased princes, which long since are consumed to
    dust.
KNIGHT [aside]   Ay, marry,° Master Doctor, now there's a sign   by Mary (an oath)
    of grace in you, when you will confess the truth.
50 FAUSTUS   But such spirits as can lively° resemble Alexander   in a lifelike
    and his paramour shall appear before Your Grace in that   manner
    manner that they best lived in, in their most flourishing
    estate—which I doubt not shall sufficiently content Your
    Imperial Majesty.
55 EMPEROR   Go to,° Master Doctor. Let me see them presently.°   Proceed / at once
KNIGHT   Do you hear, Master Doctor? You bring Alexander
    and his paramour before the Emperor?
FAUSTUS   How then, sir?
KNIGHT   I'faith, that's as true as Diana⁴ turned me to a stag.

---

3. Alexander III of Macedon (356–323   4. The Roman huntress goddess (the Greek
B.C.E.); the greatest of all Greek generals, he   Artemis).
unified Greece and conquered much of Asia.

60 FAUSTUS   No, sir, but when Actaeon died,[5] he left the horns
     for you. [*Aside to* MEPHISTOPHELES] Mephistopheles,
     begone!

                                    [*Exit* MEPHISTOPHELES.]

KNIGHT   Nay, an you go to conjuring,° I'll be gone.   *if you play mere tricks*

                                    [*Exit* KNIGHT.]

FAUSTUS [*aside*]   I'll meet with° you anon for interrupting   *get even with*
     me so.—Here they are, my gracious lord.

          [*Enter* MEPHISTOPHELES *with Alexander and his
          paramour.*]

65 EMPEROR   Master Doctor, I heard this lady while she lived
     had a wart or mole in her neck. How shall I know
     whether it be so or no?

FAUSTUS   Your Highness may boldly go and see.

          [*The* EMPEROR *makes an inspection, and then exit
          Alexander with his paramour.*]

EMPEROR   Sure these are no spirits, but the true substantial
70   bodies of those two deceased princes.

FAUSTUS   Will't please Your Highness now to send for the
     knight that was so pleasant° with me here of late?   *humorous*

EMPEROR   One of you call him forth.

          [*An attendant goes to summon the* KNIGHT.]

          [*Enter the* KNIGHT *with a pair of horns on his head.*]

     How now, Sir Knight? Why, I had thought thou hadst been a
75   bachelor, but now I see thou hast a wife, that not only gives
     thee horns but makes thee wear them.[6] Feel on thy head.

KNIGHT [*to* FAUSTUS]   Thou damnèd wretch and execrable dog,
     Bred in the concave° of some monstrous rock,   *hollow*
     How dar'st thou thus abuse a gentleman?
80   Villain, I say, undo what thou hast done.

FAUSTUS   Oh, not so fast, sir. There's no haste but good.°   *Don't be too hasty*
     Are you remembered° how you crossed me in my confer-   *Do you remember*
     ence with the Emperor? I think I have met with you for it.

EMPEROR   Good Master Doctor, at my entreaty release
85   him. He hath done penance sufficient.

FAUSTUS   My gracious lord, not so much for the injury° he   *insult*
     offered me here in your presence as to delight you
     with some mirth hath Faustus worthily requited this
     injurious knight; which being all I desire, I am con-
90   tent to release him of his horns.—And, Sir Knight,
     hereafter speak well of scholars. [*Aside to* MEPHISTOPH-
     ELES] Mephistopheles, transform him straight.° [*The*   *at once*
     horns are removed.] Now, my good lord, having
     done my duty, I humbly take my leave.

EMPEROR   Farewell, Master Doctor. Yet, ere you go,

---

5. Because Acteon saw the goddess naked, Artemis/Diana turned him into a stag, and he was torn to pieces by his own dogs.

6. Cuckolds were traditionally represented as wearing horns.

95   Expect from me a bounteous reward.

          [Exeunt EMPEROR, KNIGHT, *and attendants.]*

  FAUSTUS   Now, Mephistopheles, the restless course

      That time doth run with calm and silent foot,

      Short'ning my days and thread of vital life,

      Calls for the payment of my latest° years.   *last, final*

100   Therefore, sweet Mephistopheles, let us make haste

      To Wittenberg.

  MEPHISTOPHELES   What, will you go on horseback or on foot?

  FAUSTUS   Nay, till I am past this fair and pleasant green,

      I'll walk on foot.

          [Enter a HORSE-COURSER.[7]*]*

105 HORSE-COURSER   I have been all this day seeking one Master

      Fustian.° Mass,° see where he is.—God save you, Master   *Bombast / By the Mass*

      Doctor.

  FAUSTUS   What, Horse-courser! You are well met.[8]

  HORSE-COURSER *[offering money]* Do you hear, sir? I have

110   brought you forty dollars for your horse.

  FAUSTUS   I cannot sell him so. If thou lik'st him for fifty, take

      him.

  HORSE-COURSER   Alas, sir, I have no more.

      [To MEPHISTOPHELES*]* I pray you, speak for me.

115 MEPHISTOPHELES *[to* FAUSTUS*]*   I pray you, let him have him.

      He is an honest fellow, and he has a great charge,° neither   *financial burden*

      wife nor child.

  FAUSTUS   Well, come, give me your money. *[He takes the*

      money.] My boy° will deliver him to you. But I must tell   *servant*

120   you one thing before you have him: ride him not into the

      water, at any hand.°   *on any account*

  HORSE-COURSER   Why, sir, will he not drink of all waters?[9]

  FAUSTUS   Oh, yes, he will drink of all waters. But ride him

      not into the water. Ride him over hedge, or ditch, or where

125   thou wilt, but not into the water.

  HORSE-COURSER   Well, sir. *[Aside]* Now am I made man for-

      ever! I'll not leave my horse for forty. If he had but the

      quality of hey, ding, ding, hey, ding, ding, I'd make a

      brave living on him; he has a buttock as slick as an eel.[1]

130   *[To* FAUSTUS*]* Well, good-bye, sir. Your boy will deliver him

      me? But hark ye, sir: if my horse be sick or ill at ease, if I

      bring his water[2] to you, you'll tell me what it is?

  FAUSTUS   Away, you villain! What, dost think I am a horse

      doctor?

          [Exit HORSE-COURSER.*]*

135   What art thou, Faustus, but a man condemned to die?

      Thy fatal time doth draw to final end.

---

7. A horse dealer (stereotypically a shrewd or
dishonest bargainer).
8. An expression of greeting.
9. That is, go anywhere (proverbial).

1. That is, he is sleek and well-formed. *Hey,
ding, ding:* a virile quality (to generate stud
fees).
2. That is, his urine (to diagnose the illness).

Despair doth drive distrust unto my thoughts.
Confound° these passions with a quiet sleep.   *Allay, alleviate*
Tush! Christ did call the thief upon the cross;[3]
140   Then rest thee, Faustus, quiet in conceit.°   *in thought*

[FAUSTUS *sleeps in his chair.*]

[*Enter* HORSE-COURSER *all wet, crying.*]

HORSE-COURSER   Alas, alas! "Doctor" Fustian, quotha!° Mass,   *indeed*
Doctor Lopus[4] was never such a doctor. He's given me a
purgation, he's purged me of forty dollars. I shall never
see them more. But yet, like an ass as I was, I would not
145   be ruled by him, for he bade me I should ride him into no
water. Now I, thinking my horse had had some rare
quality that he would not have had me known of, I, like
a venturous youth, rid him into the deep pond at the
town's end. I was no sooner in the middle of the pond
150   but my horse vanished away and I sat upon a bottle° of   *bundle*
hay, never so near drowning in my life. But I'll seek out
my doctor and have my forty dollars again, or I'll make
it the dearest horse! Oh, yonder is his snippersnapper.°—   *mouthy fellow*
Do you hear? You, hey-pass,[5] where's your master?
155   MEPHISTOPHELES   Why, sir, what would you? You cannot
speak with him.
HORSE-COURSER   But I will speak with him.
MEPHISTOPHELES   Why, he's fast asleep. Come some
other time.
160   HORSE-COURSER   I'll speak with him now, or I'll break his
glass windows° about his ears.   *eyeglasses*
MEPHISTOPHELES   I tell thee he has not slept this eight nights.
HORSE-COURSER   An° he have not slept this eight weeks,   *Even if*
I'll speak with him.
165   MEPHISTOPHELES   See where he is, fast asleep.
HORSE-COURSER   Ay, this is he.—God save ye, Master
Doctor. Master Doctor, Master Doctor Fustian! Forty
dollars, forty dollars for a bottle of hay!
MEPHISTOPHELES   Why, thou see'st he hears thee not.
170   HORSE-COURSER [*hollers in his ear*]   So-ho, ho! So-ho, ho! No?
Will you not wake? I'll make you wake ere I go.

[*The* HORSE-COURSER *pulls him by the leg, and
pulls it away.*]

Alas, I am undone! What shall I do?
FAUSTUS   Oh, my leg, my leg! Help, Mephistopheles!
Call the officers! My leg, my leg!
175   MEPHISTOPHELES [*seizing the* HORSE-COURSER]   Come,
villain, to the constable.

---

3. Jesus said to the thief who feared the judgment of God, "Verily I say unto thee, Today shalt thou be with me in paradise" (Luke 23.43).
4. Roderigo Lopez (ca. 1525–1594), Queen Elizabeth's private physician; a Portuguese Jew, he was implicated in a plot to poison her and was executed.
5. An exclamation of conjurors or jugglers commanding objects to move.

HORSE-COURSER   Oh, Lord, sir, let me go, and I'll give you
  forty dollars more.

MEPHISTOPHELES   Where be they?

180 HORSE-COURSER   I have none about me. Come to my hostry°   *hostelry, inn*
  and I'll give them you.

MEPHISTOPHELES   Begone, quickly. [HORSE-COURSER *runs away.*]

FAUSTUS   What, is he gone? Farewell, he!° Faustus has his leg   *Good riddance to him*
  again, and the Horse-courser, I take it, a bottle of hay for
185 his labor. Well, this trick shall cost him forty dollars more.

> [*Enter* WAGNER.]

  How now, Wagner, what's the news with thee?

WAGNER   Sir, the Duke of Vanholt° doth earnestly entreat   *Anhalt (in Germany)*
  your company.

190 FAUSTUS   The Duke of Vanholt! An honorable gentleman, to
  whom I must be no niggard of° my cunning.° Come,   *unsparing with / skill*
  Mephistopheles, let's away to him.   [*Exeunt.*]

4.2

> [*Enter* FAUSTUS *with Mephistopheles. Enter to them
> the* DUKE *of Vanholt and the pregnant* DUCHESS. *The*
> DUKE *speaks.*]

DUKE   Believe me, Master Doctor, this merriment hath
  much pleased me.

FAUSTUS   My gracious lord, I am glad it contents you so
  well.—But it may be, madam, you take no delight in this.
5 I have heard that great-bellied women do long for some
  dainties or other. What is it, madam? Tell me, and you
  shall have it.

DUCHESS   Thanks, good Master Doctor. And, for° I see your   *because*
  courteous intent to pleasure me, I will not hide from you
10 the thing my heart desires. And were it now summer, as it
  is January and the dead time of the winter, I would desire
  no better meat° than a dish of ripe grapes.   *food*

FAUSTUS   Alas, madam, that's nothing. [*Aside to* MEPHISTOPHE-
  LES] Mephistopheles, begone!   [*Exit* MEPHISTOPHELES.]
15 Were it a greater thing than this, so° it would content   *provided that*
  you, you should have it.

> [*Enter* MEPHISTOPHELES *with the grapes.*]

  Here they be, madam. Will't please you taste on them?

> [*The* DUCHESS *tastes the grapes.*]

DUKE   Believe me, Master Doctor, this makes me wonder
  above the rest, that, being in the dead time of winter and in
20 the month of January, how you should come by these grapes.

FAUSTUS   If it like Your Grace, the year is divided into two circles over the whole world, that when it is here winter with
  us, in the contrary circle it is summer with them, as in
  India, Saba,[6] and farther countries in the East; and by

---

6. Sheba, an ancient kingdom on the Red Sea.

25   means of a swift spirit that I have, I had them brought
     hither, as ye see.—How do you like them, madam? Be they
     good?
     DUCHESS   Believe me, Master Doctor, they be the best grapes
     that e'er I tasted in my life before.
30   FAUSTUS   I am glad they content you so, madam.
     DUKE   Come, madam, let us in,
     Where you must well reward this learnèd man
     For the great kindness he hath showed to you.
     DUCHESS   And so I will, my lord, and whilst I live
35   Rest beholding° for this courtesy.   *Remain beholden*
     FAUSTUS   I humbly thank Your Grace.
     DUKE   Come, Master Doctor, follow us and receive your reward.
          [*Exeunt.*]

                              5.1

          [*Enter* WAGNER *solus.*]
     WAGNER   I think my master means to die shortly,
     For he hath given to me all his goods.
     And yet methinks if that death were near
     He would not banquet and carouse and swill
5   Amongst the students, as even now he doth,
     Who are at supper with such belly-cheer
     As Wagner ne'er beheld in all his life.
     See where they come. Belike° the feast is ended.   [*Exit.*]   *Apparently*
          [*Enter* FAUSTUS *with two or three* SCHOLARS *and*
          MEPHISTOPHELES.]
     FIRST SCHOLAR   Master Doctor Faustus, since our confer-
10   ence about fair ladies—which was the beautifull'st in all
     the world—we have determined with° ourselves that   *among*
     Helen of Greece was the admirablest lady that ever
     lived. Therefore, Master Doctor, if you will do us that
     favor as to let us see that peerless dame of Greece,
15   whom all the world admires for majesty, we should
     think ourselves much beholding unto you.
     FAUSTUS   Gentlemen,
     For that° I know your friendship is unfeigned,   *Because*
     And Faustus' custom is not to deny
20   The just requests of those that wish him well,
     You shall behold that peerless dame of Greece,
     No otherways° for pomp and majesty   *otherwise*
     Than when Sir Paris crossed the seas with her
     And brought the spoils to rich Dardania.°   *Troy*
25   Be silent then, for danger is in words.
          [*Music sounds and Helen led in by* MEPHISTOPHE-
          LES *passeth over the stage.*]
     SECOND SCHOLAR   Too simple is my wit to tell her praise,

The stars move still; time runs; the clock will strike;
The devil will come, and Faustus must be damned.
Oh, I'll leap up to my God! Who pulls me down?
See, see where Christ's blood streams in the firmament!
75 One drop would save my soul, half a drop. Ah, my Christ!
Ah, rend not my heart for naming of my Christ!
Yet will I call on him. Oh, spare me, Lucifer!
Where is it now? 'Tis gone; and see where God
Stretcheth out his arm and bends his ireful brows!
80 Mountains and hills, come, come and fall on me,
And hide me from the heavy wrath of God!
No, no!
Then will I headlong run into the earth.
Earth, gape! Oh, no, it will not harbor me.
85 You stars that reigned at my nativity,
Whose influence hath allotted death and hell,
Now draw up Faustus like a foggy mist
Into the entrails of yon laboring cloud,
That when you vomit forth into the air,°   *hurl a thunderbolt*
90 My limbs may issue from your smoky mouths,
So that my soul may but ascend to heaven.
        [*The watch strikes.*]
Ah, half the hour is past!
'Twill all be past anon.
O God,
95 If thou wilt not have mercy on my soul,
Yet for Christ's sake, whose blood hath ransomed me,
Impose some end to my incessant pain.
Let Faustus live in hell a thousand years,
A hundred thousand, and at last be saved!
100 Oh, no end is limited to damnèd souls.
Why wert thou not a creature wanting° soul?   *lacking a*
Or why is this immortal that thou hast?
Ah, Pythagoras' metempsychosis,[3] were that true,
This soul should fly from me and I be changed
105 Unto some brutish beast.
All beasts are happy, for, when they die,
Their souls are soon dissolved in elements;
But mine must live still° to be plagued in hell.   *always*
Curst be the parents that engendered me!
110 No, Faustus, curse thyself. Curse Lucifer,
That hath deprived thee of the joys of heaven.
        [*The clock striketh twelve.*]
Oh, it strikes, it strikes! Now, body, turn to air,
Or Lucifer will bear thee quick° to hell.   *alive*
        [*Thunder and lightning.*]

---

3. The passage of the soul at death into another body (human or animal), a theory espoused by the Greek philosopher Pythagoras (6th c. B.C.E.).

O soul, be changed into little waterdrops,
115 And fall into the ocean, ne'er be found!
My God, my God, look not so fierce on me!

    [*Enter* LUCIFER, MEPHISTOPHELES, *and other devils.*]

Adders and serpents, let me breathe awhile!
Ugly hell, gape not. Come not, Lucifer!
I'll burn my books. Ah, Mephistopheles!

       [*The devils exeunt with him.*]

Epilogue

    [*Enter* CHORUS.]

CHORUS   Cut is the branch that might have grown full straight,
    And burnèd is Apollo's laurel bough[4]
    That sometime° grew within this learnèd man.   *formerly*
    Faustus is gone. Regard his hellish fall,
5   Whose fiendful fortune may exhort the wise
    Only to wonder at[5] unlawful things,
    Whose deepness doth entice such forward° wits   *daring, presumptuous*
    To practice more than heavenly power permits.   [*Exit.*]

Terminat hora diem; terminat author opus.[6]

---

4. The laurel, sacred to Apollo, the god of wisdom, is associated with poetry and victory.
5. That is, to wonder at without partaking of.

6. The hour ends the day; the author ends his work (Latin).

WILLIAM SHAKESPEARE

1564–1616

"HE was not of an age, but for all time"
—so wrote Ben Jonson, William
Shakespeare's contemporary and rival playwright, in a commendatory poem included
in the first collected edition of Shakespeare's plays, the so-called First Folio
(published in 1623). Almost 400 years later,
these words must seem prophetic to us.
Shakespeare's plays and poetry have been
translated into every conceivable language,
his plays have been performed on stages
the world over, and his influence on generations of writers and poets, on popular culture and media, and on the English
language itself has been incalculable. What
accounts for Shakespeare's enormous and
lasting success? Is it the rich density and
complexity of his verse, his keen insight
into human nature, or his talent for cap-
turing in words the energies, hopes, and
anxieties of his time? One factor stands
out above all others: from his earliest
plays—the farcical *Comedy of Errors*
(1589–93), the sprawling historical tetral-
ogy about the English Wars of the Roses
(1589–94), and the bloody Roman tragedy
Titus Andronicus (1589–91)—Shakespeare demonstrated an unfailing sense of
theater, both its ability to hold an audience and its power as a medium for social
and psychological exploration. Shakespeare's plays have remained at the center
of the theatrical repertoire through periods of changing dramatic tastes, and they
have adapted themselves to different cultures and theatrical traditions. The success of such contemporary Hollywood
movies as Kenneth Branagh's *Henry V*
(1989), Baz Luhrmann's *Romeo+Juliet*
(1996), Richard Loncraine's *Richard III*
(1995), and Josh Madden's *Shakespeare in
Love* (1998)—the Oscar-winning film
about Shakespeare's life—demonstrates
how fully this man of the theater has been
embraced by new audiences and media.

William Shakespeare was born in 1564
in the small market town of Stratford-
upon-Avon, to a glove maker named John
Shakespeare and Mary Arden, a member
of a distinguished Warwickshire family.
Though a commoner and a craftsman,
John Shakespeare must have been an
ambitious man. He acquired real estate
and held a series of increasingly important
positions in local government, culminat-
ing in the office of bailiff (mayor) in 1569.
Companies of traveling actors visited
Stratford on a number of occasions during
William's childhood, and it is almost certain that the young Shakespeare, perhaps
because of his father's standing in the
community, witnessed his first dramatic
performances in the town's Guild Hall.
The young boy's imagination may have
been sparked by Corpus Christi or morality plays, or by early Tudor humanist plays,

all of which left traces of influence in Shakespeare's dramas. In the late 1570s, however, when William was six years old, his father's financial and political fortunes took a steep downward turn, and the coat of arms for which he had applied, and which would have granted him the appellation of "gentleman," was held up (until William paid the remaining balance on the application in 1596).

It is likely that William Shakespeare attended Stratford's grammar school, where Latin and the classics were taught. He married at the age of eighteen. His bride, Anne Hathaway, was his senior by some eight years. Their first child, Susanna, was born in May 1583, about six months after the wedding. Two more children, the twins Judith and Hamnet, were born in 1585. After that the picture of Shakespeare's activities gets murky. There are apocryphal stories about him working as a schoolmaster, a lawyer's aide, a sailor, and a soldier, but there is no firm evidence to support any of them. A traveling company of actors, the Earl of Leicester's Men (which later was to become the Lord Chamberlain's Men), came through Stratford in 1587. It is tempting to imagine that the young Shakespeare, taken with the acting craft, found employment with them and accompanied them back to London, where he was to make his fortune as a dramatist. Unfortunately, there is nothing in the historical record to validate such musings.

The next thing we know for certain is that Shakespeare was a working playwright in London by 1592. The rival dramatist Robert Greene refers to him in that year as an "upstart crow" and parodies a line from Shakespeare's early history play *Henry VI, Part 3*. Around 1594, Shakespeare joined the Lord Chamberlain's Men (the same troupe that had visited Stratford in 1587). Shakespeare was to stay with the Lord Chamberlain's Men, renamed the King's Men in 1603 when King James I assumed patronage over the company, until his retirement from the theater and return to Stratford around 1613. The Lord Chamberlain's Men had been the proud owners of the first permanent London playhouse, the Theatre, located in the district of Shoreditch—just northeast of the city walls and outside the jurisdiction of the city fathers, whose Puritan leanings made them aggressive opponents of stage plays. Following a financial dispute with their landlord, the Lord Chamberlain's Men pulled down their playhouse and reassembled it on the south bank of the river Thames; they named their new home, which opened for business in 1599, the Globe. It is in this theater that the comedy *TWELFTH NIGHT; OR, WHAT YOU WILL* and *THE TRAGEDY OF HAMLET, PRINCE OF DENMARK,* both anthologized here, were first presented to the public.

The conditions of performance at the Globe theater differed substantially from those on today's stages. First, all performances had to take place during daytime, as they were illuminated only by the sunlight pouring in through the open roof. The stage, a rectangular wooden scaffold some 5.5 feet high and believed to have measured roughly 43 feet wide by 27 feet deep, did not have a proscenium arch (as many stages do today), was covered by a roof, and protruded into the audience area of the theater known as the pit. The underside of the stage's roof, which was painted with the signs of the zodiac and was referred to as "the heavens," gave some protection to the actors during bad weather, a comfort not afforded to the "groundlings" who stood packed in the pit, exposed to the elements. Customers who paid more had seats in the covered, multitiered galleries surrounding the pit and the stage. The stage itself had a gallery above (which was used for such occasions as Romeo and Juliet's "balcony" scene), as well as a small inner stage or discovery space (used, for example, to reveal Miranda and Ferdinand playing chess in Shakespeare's late play *The Tempest*). The stage also had a trapdoor that could serve as the exit into hell (as in CHRISTOPHER MARLOWE's *Doctor Faustus*) or as the point of entry for the ghost of Hamlet's father. With "the heavens" above and the netherworld below, Shakespeare's Globe symbolically encompassed the entire cosmos within the "wooden O" (*Henry V*) that was the theater. The manner of performance itself was in some ways deeply symbolic in that the actors did not employ elaborate scenery or complicated special effects to

A detail from Claes Jansz Visscher's engraved panorama of London, *Londinum Florentissima Britanniae Urbs* (1616). The Globe theater is in the center foreground.

create a sense of realism, though they did don sumptuous costumes.

Audiences of Shakespeare's *Hamlet*, for instance, were asked to accept that the Ghost appeared on the castle walls "in the dead waste and middle of the night," while the actor before them stood on a wooden stage, surrounded by spectators, on a bright, sunny afternoon. What is more, a prohibition against the appearance of female actors on the stage (which was not repealed until shortly after the restoration of the monarchy in 1660) meant that all female roles were acted by boys. Whether such cross-dressing undermined the "realism" of the performance, or exactly how Elizabethan audiences experienced it, is a matter of some controversy. More than anything, however, it is fair to say that actors relied heavily on Shakespeare's amazingly rich and allusive language to spark the imagination and hold the attention of their paying spectators.

HAMLET

By the time Shakespeare wrote *The Tragedy of Hamlet, Prince of Denmark* (1600–1601) he had reached the height of his powers as a dramatist. During the 1590s, Shakespeare had written a sonnet sequence,

carefully crafted narrative poems, and a number of highly successful comedies, tragedies, and history plays, including *The Taming of the Shrew* (1592), *Richard II* (1595), *Romeo and Juliet* (1595), *A Midsummer Night's Dream* (1594–96), *The Merchant of Venice* (1596–97), *Henry IV, Part 1* (1596–97), *Henry V* (1598–99), *Julius Caesar* (1599), *Much Ado about Nothing* (1598), and *As You Like It* (1599–1600). With the composition of *Hamlet* he initiated a period of less than ten years during which he composed his greatest tragedies. Among these, *Hamlet* has probably captivated our interest the most; for more than four centuries, its titular hero has been a magnetic figure for actors, critics, and audiences alike. The Romantic poet Samuel Taylor Coleridge so deeply admired Hamlet's courage, skill, and ability for abstract and rational thought that he proclaimed, "I have a smack of Hamlet myself." Hamlet has been hailed not only as the quintessential Renaissance courtier and prince, but also as the first literary character who is like us: that is, one who dramatizes what Harold Bloom calls the "internalization of the self" so strikingly that it rivals or even exceeds the complex inner life we encounter in the thought of such early modern giants as Martin Luther, Desiderius Erasmus, and Michel de Montaigne. For some, Hamlet has become such an iconic figure that he has outgrown the play in which he appears. Whether or not this is true, many of us find ourselves attracted to and fascinated by Hamlet, even though we seem so far to have been unable to "pluck out the heart of [his] mystery."

Composed near the end of Elizabeth I's reign, *Hamlet* tells a story that is not original with Shakespeare. It may be based on a number of sources, the so-called *Ur-Hamlet* (a play that no longer exists), Saxo Grammaticus's *Historia Danica* (1180–1208), and François de Belleforest's *Histories Tragiques* (1576, a French translation of Grammaticus) chief among them. Although

Shakespeare's play differs in many significant aspects from Grammaticus's narrative history, there are also similarities that appear too striking to be accidental. Grammaticus's account describes a fratricide (which, as in *Hamlet,* is also a regicide), an incestuous marriage, feigned madness (Hamlet's "antic disposition"), a spying courtier, the use of a woman (*Hamlet*'s Ophelia) as a lure, and a voyage to England.

A number of these elements are also vital to a group of Elizabethan revenge plays to which *Hamlet* certainly belongs, and which includes Thomas Kyd's *The Spanish Tragedy* and works by John Webster, Thomas Middleton, John Marston,

Frontispiece illustration for Christiern Pedersen's 1514 edition of Saxo Grammaticus's *Historia Danica.*

and others. Harkening back to the "trage-dies of blood" created by the Roman play-wright Seneca, Elizabethan revenge plays typically contain an act of murder that can-not be redressed by the authorities (usually because the highest authority in the play is complicit in the crime), an appearance of a ghost who demands just revenge (usually from a son or father), madness (feigned or actual), a great deal of intrigue, a hesita-tion or delay on the part of the avenger, and a set of actions that leads to the death of the murderer but simultaneously contami-nates the avenger and typically results in his death. Shakespeare's *Hamlet* certainly puts most of these elements on display, but it handles them creatively in ways that enrich the genre and deeply complicate our understanding of the play.

The question of Hamlet's "delay" has long vexed critics and audiences. Why does Hamlet not simply kill Claudius after his initial meeting with his father's ghost? Hamlet is adamant that the spec-ter is a trustworthy, "honest ghost," and he surely seems to have opportunities to kill Claudius. Yet considerable time passes, and Hamlet neither slays his uncle nor develops a plan to do so. The truth is that, like the critics who have tried to solve the riddle of his delay, Hamlet him-self seems confused and perturbed by his inaction. Watching with admiration and bewilderment an impromptu performance of the fall of Troy by a troupe of traveling players who visit Elsinore, Hamlet won-ders why it is that an actor can muster such intense passion in acting out a fiction—for "What's Hecuba to him, or he to Hecuba, / That he should weep for her?" —while he, who has a real "cue for passion," does nothing, "not for a king / Upon whose property and most dear life / A damned defeat was made." Hamlet never provides us with a satisfactory answer to his own question, which is all the more puzzling given that he despises Claudius and would not for a moment regret his death. Even when Hamlet appears to set-tle on a course of action by putting on "The Murder of Gonzago" to "catch the conscience of the King," his actions appear erratic and confused. This play-within-a-play sequence, as devised by Hamlet, has attracted critical interest as a prime example of metatheatricality, a dra-maturgical device in which a play's char-acters take on various theatrical functions. In this scene, as well as in the "nunnery" scene with Ophelia, Hamlet embodies both directorial and playwriting roles in his orchestration of others' words and actions. Yet these scenes also demonstrate that actors and directors cannot com-pletely control their audiences' reactions. While watching a loose reenactment of the murder of King Hamlet, Claudius does have a response that could be con-strued as guilt, but his calling an abrupt halt to the performance occurs not when the king is killed by a brother but when Lucianus, his nephew, pours poison into the sleeping king's ear. We may expect that Hamlet will now finally "sweep to [his] revenge," but instead he answers a summons from his mother. When, on his way to Gertrude's chambers, he comes upon Claudius at prayer, he fails to seize this opportunity to dispatch the king and instead takes his anger out on his mother in an unstoppable flood of words.

The depth and subtlety of Hamlet's trauma over the revenge question stand in sharp contrast with Shakespeare's han-dling of two other young princes, Laertes and Fortinbras, who also suffer the loss of a father. Fortinbras's father was killed in single combat by Hamlet's father before the start of the play, and Laertes' father, Polonius, is stabbed to death by Hamlet. Neither Fortinbras nor Laertes lacks the necessary passion for swift vengeance. In the first scene, we hear that Fortinbras is readying a military invasion of Denmark, and when Laertes learns of his father's death he rushes back from France to kill whoever is responsible, even if it turns out to be King Claudius. "That drop of blood that's calm proclaims me bastard," Laertes says, suggesting that avenging a father's death is an instinctive act for an honorable son. Such an act requires no deliberation or concern for consequences, and it is this reckless liberty that Hamlet longs for but, as a result of his self-reflective nature, is unable to achieve.

Yet Hamlet finds it impossible to be more like Laertes or Fortinbras, and it is precisely in his inability to be a one-dimensional man of action that we

368 | WILLIAM SHAKESPEARE

encounter the depth and complexity of his character. He lacks the passion and single-ness of purpose to act on his father's command. Maybe it is because he perceives too great a disjunction between the straightfor-wardness of the Ghost's call for justice and the widespread disorder and corruption that render Denmark an "unweeded garden / That grows to seed." Maybe Hamlet real-izes that killing Claudius would be nothing more than an isolated and ambiguous act of revenge in a fundamentally unjust world. But whatever his reasons, Hamlet's inabil-ity to balance the Ghost's command with the corrupt world of Elsinore is precisely what intensifies and expands the inner life of his character. His inability to live in and accept the world as he finds it drives him inward, rendering him significantly more introspective and self-conscious, and there-fore more recognizably modern, than other characters who walked across the Elizabe-than public stage. It is as if the character of Hamlet allows Shakespeare to explore recesses of the human mind of which other poets and dramatists had at best only been dimly aware.

But the depth of Hamlet's interiority, insofar as it is promoted by his frustration over not killing the king, comes at a heavy price. When the play comes to a close, not only Claudius but also Gertrude, Rosen-crantz, Guildenstern, Laertes, Polonius, Ophelia, and Hamlet himself are dead, and one could argue that the swift execu-tion of justice on Claudius by Hamlet in the first act would have saved the lives of all of them. The madness and death of Ophelia are particularly distressing to audiences because the young woman is wholly a victim of others' machinations, including those of Hamlet.

Ophelia's plight and the gender dynam-ics that shape it draw attention to the lim-ited number of options aristocratic young women had available to them in the early modern period. During her premarriage days, Ophelia would have been expected to guard her reputation and chastity zealously, to be an obedient daughter to her father and an obedient sister to her brother. Her identity in Danish aristo-cratic society is defined largely in relation to the men in her life and in terms of her exchangeability on the marriage market.

As limiting as this life trajectory may seem to us, it was a reality for most aristo-cratic women of the time, and Ophelia apparently does not possess the inner strength to resist this model (as some of Shakespeare's other heroines attempt to do). What is more, it is the vital responsi-bility of the men who control Ophelia's destiny to facilitate her transition from one position to the next. Laertes' strong admonition to Ophelia to rebuff Hamlet's courtship reflects his guardianship of his sister's chastity as well as his recognition of the importance of her purity to the state. In practical terms, Laertes is guarding his sis-ter's reputation; yet his action also hinders her transition from the role of sister and daughter to that of wife. Her father, Polo-nius, is equally anxious about Hamlet's intentions, and he forbids her from seeing Hamlet any further. Claudius, who, like Elizabeth I, has a fundamental interest in shaping aristocratic marriages, completely fails in his role as kingly guardian of one of his noble subjects when he goes along with Polonius's plan to use Ophelia as a pawn in a spying game to learn more about the cause of Hamlet's odd behavior. None of the men show any concern for how their words and actions destroy Ophelia's future in Danish society.

Hamlet also contributes significantly to Ophelia's anguish when he elects to inflict his "antic disposition" on her. The genu-ine distress that this performance causes Ophelia seems of no concern to Hamlet. Betrayed by her father, brother, king, and potential husband, there is literally noth-ing for Ophelia to be anymore. The "nun-nery" to which a cruel Hamlet tries to consign her at one point might be a socially acceptable choice for Ophelia, but the option is never pursued.

Critics have long argued over whether Ophelia's madness speech gives us clues that she and Hamlet might have con-summated their relationship. While her song about love betrayed and loss of maidenhead (4.5) need not imply physical consummation, her emotional and psy-chological commitment to a life with Hamlet is so complete that she is unable to imagine or reconstitute another role for herself in the world of Elsinore, whether she is physically a virgin or not.

The dismantling of Ophelia's identity has led to the dissolution of her psychological coherence, and it results, following a cruel logic, in the loss of her very being in death.

It is possible that Hamlet's dying endorsement of the Norwegian warrior Prince Fortinbras as Denmark's new ruler is an acknowledgment that action, even reckless and violent action, is preferable to Hamlet's own propensity for delay and indecision. The rise of Fortinbras can be read as a return to power of Hamlet's father, a return of the feudal warrior-king. It functions as a rejection not only of the Machiavellian Claudius but also of Hamlet himself; indeed, it is difficult to imagine Hamlet as an effective ruler, given his style of decision making. But even so, despite the human cost associated with Hamlet's delay, it is precisely this delay, and more specifically Hamlet's anxious

pondering of its meaning, that yields us a character of uncommon psychological depth, self-scrutiny, and complexity.

To learn more about the staging of *Hamlet* and to view photographs from select performances of the play, see the "Plays in Performance" color insert near the center of this volume.

TWELFTH NIGHT

Twelfth Night; or, What You Will (1600–1601) is one of Shakespeare's most provocative, captivating, and complex romantic comedies, and yet it appears to be the last that he composed in this form. Around 1601, at the height of his dramatic powers, Shakespeare entered an artistic phase that produced his so-called problem plays (or "dark comedies") and his mature tragedies,

The King Drinks (ca. 1640), by David Teniers the Younger, depicts a popular ritual associated with Twelfth Night throughout Europe: the person who finds a dried bean in his serving of the "Three Kings cake" is pronounced king for the evening.

including *Hamlet*. The explanations of why Shakespeare abandoned romantic comedy at this time are necessarily speculative, but it appears likely that the dramatist was growing increasingly dissatisfied with the form's inability to accommodate the complexities of real life. In the midst of its festive spirit, *Twelfth Night* reveals the beginning of this dissatisfaction.

We know that *Twelfth Night* was performed at the Inns of Court (the residences in London of the city's legal societies) on the occasion of Candlemas Day, February 2, 1602. A witness to the performance noted a similarity between *Twelfth Night* and one of the mistaken-identity farces of the Roman playwright Plautus (which had also influenced an earlier Shakespeare play, *The Comedy of Errors*). The year 1602 marks the earliest *recorded* performance of the play, but it is possible that Shakespeare's acting company, the Lord Chamberlain's Men, had already staged it at the Globe. It has been suggested that a performance took place in 1601 at the court of Queen Elizabeth to coincide with the visit to England of the duke of Bracciano, Don Virginio Orsino. But as tempting as it is to tease out possible analogies between *Twelfth Night*'s Duke Orsino and the historical Don Virginio Orsino, there is no indication that Shakespeare wrote *Twelfth Night* or any of his plays for special court occasions.

Twelfth Night—which is based on Barnabe Riche's story "Of Apolonius and Silla" (1581) and, indirectly, on the anonymous Italian comedy *Gl'Ingannati* (1537)—offers a compelling tale of look-alike twins separated by shipwreck. Characterized by a festive atmosphere and a preoccupation with love, romantic comedies exhibit a drive toward social unity, marriage, and happiness. Typically, Shakespeare starts his romantic comedies by presenting us with a group of young, single men and women who are eligible for marriage but who encounter obstacles to the fulfillment of their personal desires. What is more, the obstacles stand in the way not only of personal happiness but, more importantly, of socially acceptable unions that enable the orderly reproduction of existing social classes and family structures (both of which are of vital concern to the genre of romantic comedy). The impediment can take a variety of forms, including obstructionist parents, an antagonist who wishes the lovers ill, misguided desire, grief over the loss of a loved one, or fear of the opposite sex. The middle acts of romantic comedies are commonly taken up with the younger generation's clumsy but sometimes endearing attempts to overcome these obstacles, an endeavor in which they ultimately succeed, though sometimes only because of good fortune, outside aid from their elders, or supernatural intervention. The resolution of the story's dramatic conflicts is generally harmonious, mostly satisfying (to the characters as well as the audience), and life-affirming. *Twelfth Night*—perhaps reflecting the growing strain between realism and romance in Shakespearean comedy—withholds some of that satisfaction and admits disturbances to that harmony.

Shakespeare signals his interest in the social energies associated with those disturbances in the title of his play. Loosely connected to the Roman festival of Saturnalia—which marked the winter solstice with feasting, revelry, playful disrespect for authority, and sensual indulgences—"twelfth night," also known as Epiphany, marks the end of the holiday season that lasts from Christmas through January 6. The carnivalesque spirit that prevailed during these days was sometimes channeled into ritualized lampoonings of Elizabethan civil and church authorities. The Feast of Fools and such figures as the Boy Bishop, the Lords of Misrule, and the Boy King inverted the established social order and allowed ordinary men and women to release (in a controlled fashion) any resentments and hostilities that might have accrued from living and working in an oppressive, hierarchical society with sharp divisions between the haves and have nots. Although Shakespeare neither mentions "twelfth night" in the body of his text nor dramatizes any of the popular rituals associated with it, the play is permeated on all levels with a carnivalesque spirit and energy that produces significant upheaval and reversal in the traditional social order.

The second part of the play's title—*What You Will*—connects the theme of disorder through *mis*directed desire more specifically to individual events and characters. According to the *Oxford English Dictionary,* the word *will* can mean "desire, wish, [or] longing," with a sexual connotation. Virtually all the characters in the play engage in forms of desire that conflict for one reason or another with the established social order and therefore impede the proper and orderly reproduction of the play's social structure, which is an essential element of a successful romantic comedy.

The hard-drinking Sir Toby Belch and the professional jester Feste, whose name implies festivity and who declares himself to be a deliberate "corrupter of words," are of course the most obvious representatives of a type of Saturnalian disorder; but the aristocrats themselves, because they insist on following their "will" or desire, appear equally at odds with the normative social order. Duke Orsino, for instance, wallows in an obsessive and self-indulgent love for the Countess Olivia, even though we quickly gather that she will never have him. His misdirected desire prevents him from marrying and producing an heir, thereby putting the processes of generational renewal and social reproduction, as well as the future governance of Illyria, in limbo. Olivia, in turn, decides to mourn her recently deceased brother and father for the uncommonly long period of seven years, thus endangering the future of her estate and blocking the timely reproduction of the aristocratic class of Illyria. She further complicates things by unwittingly falling in love with an unobtainable partner, a woman named Viola who has disguised herself as a man (named Cesario). Viola herself falls in love with her employer, Duke Orsino, but her male disguise makes it impossible for her to pursue her desire in overt ways. Adding to the confusion, Toby and Maria (Olivia's gentlewoman) trick Malvolio into believing that Olivia is in love with him, prompting the sour but ambitious steward who dreams of becoming "Count Malvolio" to behave ridiculously and upend the very principles of decorum and propriety he is supposed to uphold. Sir Andrew Aguecheek, a foolish knight who spends his time in the company of Sir Toby, also has his heart set on the Countess Olivia, but it becomes clear almost immediately that he has no chance of winning her. His desire is fruitless; all he is good for is paying Toby's liquor bills.

Antonio the sea captain, who saves Viola's twin brother, Sebastian, after the shipwreck, has very strong, homoerotic feelings for Sebastian, but the latter does not seem interested in reciprocating, giving rise to another instance of misdirected desire within a comic world where heterosexuality is the norm.

The expectation—created by the genre of romantic comedy—is that disorder gives way to order and harmony by play's end. These are ordinarily achieved by a repositioning of characters to their proper place within the social fabric of the play, either by confirming their proper social rank or gender or by having them enter into socially acceptable marriages. *Twelfth Night* certainly attempts to achieve such harmony through a repositioning of characters, but the effort is not entirely successful—a failure that is surely deliberate. On the surface, matters appear resolved. Viola is reunited with her look-alike twin brother, Sebastian. Viola's female gender is confirmed, and she will become Orsino's wife. The Countess Olivia realizes that she inadvertently fell for another woman, but this mistake is rectified when she equally inadvertently marries Sebastian (whom she believes to be Cesario at the time the couple exchanges their vows). Even the riotous Toby appears to leave behind his self-indulgent ways when he enters into a union with the sensible Maria. After all the disorder, it appears that the ruling class of Illyria may be settling down to a calmer family life and the business of biological and social reproduction.

But when we look just below its surface, we recognize that this newfound harmony may be only superficial. Olivia is now married to a man she has known for only a few hours, and their compatibility could well become an issue later. What is more, Olivia's same-sex desire for Viola cannot have magically evaporated. When Orsino describes Cesario's physical appearance, he stresses "his" feminine qualities: "Diane's lip / Is not more smooth and rubious; thy small pipe / Is as the maiden's organ, shrill and sound, / And all is semblative a woman's part." In other words, you sound like a woman, you look like a woman, and you resemble a woman in every way. Because the part of Viola was played by a boy actor in Shakespeare's theater, there is

Indira Varma (left) as Olivia and Victoria Hamilton (right) as Viola in the 2011 Donmar Warehouse (London) production of *Twelfth Night*.

no doubt that the "woman's part" could have been removed from the performance. A boy could simply act as a boy would. But Shakespeare appears determined that Olivia shall fall madly in love with a character whose "woman's part" breaks through the masculine disguise. No matter how surprised Olivia is when she finally learns that Cesario is a woman, we cannot discount that she fell in love with "him" in part because of those female qualities. Sebastian tries to explain to Olivia what has transpired, saying, "lady, you have been mistook. / But nature to her bias drew in that. / You would have been contracted to a maid." Sebastian's metaphor is taken from the game of bowls, which was played with a ball with an off-center weight that made it curve from a straight path. These lines are generally interpreted as intended to quiet fears of Olivia's homoeroticism by suggesting that "nature" redirected her affections from Cesario to Sebastian. But if we take "that" to refer to what is "mistook," then nature's "bias" in fact drew Olivia to her mistake, to another woman.

An element of homoeroticism also remains part of the Orsino-Viola relation-

ship. Viola's female gender has been verbally established at the time that Orsino proposes marriage, but Viola never removes her masculine disguise, meaning that we are visually presented with a union between two men. No doubt Viola will soon again don her "maiden weeds," but who is to say that Orsino will not one day remember the time he fell in love with "her" and ask, "Would you like to try on again those breeches and doublet you used to wear?" This question and the broader issue of how these couples will fare in the future are not openly addressed amid the festiveness of the play's conclusion, but they are implied or encouraged by the "o'erhasty marriage[s]"—to borrow a phrase from *Hamlet*.

We may not care very much that the marriage between Toby and Maria is equally hasty and unprepared for, nor may we feel very sorry that the foolish Sir Andrew is left without a mate at play's end, but we may be disturbed by Illyria's inability to find a place for Captain Antonio. Elizabethan culture strongly disapproved of sodomy, but writers often idealized male-male friendship, especially between aristocratic males, and described it in passionate and erotic language. We cannot be certain that Antonio is what we would today call a homosexual, but his complete devotion to Sebastian leaves him without an obvious partner when Sebastian marries. Yet Shakespeare makes it clear that Antonio does not deserve to be excluded from a newly harmonious Illyrian society. Antonio is a thoroughly noble and admirable character who unselfishly risks his life for Sebastian (and Viola) on more than one occasion. If anything, Shakespeare gives us reason to lament that a character as worthy as Antonio cannot find a place for himself within the society's social structure. It is as if in 1601 or 1602, when Shakespeare writes *Twelfth Night*, he no longer feels that the comedic resolution—which calls for heterosexual marriages—can adequately contain the complexities of human desire and social reality. And even the marriages that do occur seem somehow less plausible than we would want them to be. Of course it would be misleading to suggest that Shakespeare's earlier romantic comedies tie up all the loose ends neatly—they do not—but *Twelfth Night* seems to anticipate the even more problematic endings of his "dark comedies" to follow.

Audiences may be less troubled by the fate of Olivia's steward Malvolio, who, like Antonio and Andrew, is left unintegrated into the play's multiple unions, but his vow to "be revenged on the whole pack of you" strikes a jarring note at play's end. Such a tone does not seem to fit the supposedly conciliatory spirit of comedy. There is no doubt that Malvolio is an unpleasant person, and his rigid opposition to the spirit of carnival embraced by Toby, Andrew, and Maria makes him a killjoy, but we cannot forget that he is ultimately only doing the bidding of his employer, the Countess Olivia. To an English audience living in a class-based society, it may indeed have seemed mad for the commoner Malvolio to think he could marry a countess; but such marriages were becoming increasingly common in Shakespeare's time, as many aristocratic families could not sustain themselves and their estates in the new economy and wealthy merchants and traders were increasingly willing to part with vast sums of money for the privilege of marrying into the upper class. Audiences may have disliked Malvolio as a man, but his ambition may well have been their fantasy.

The trend toward a darker, more pessimistic view of life, glimpsed at in *Twelfth Night* and fully realized in *Hamlet*, becomes increasingly persistent in the plays written in the first decade of the seventeenth century. Critics have speculated that the death of Shakespeare's father in 1601 may have led the playwright to contemplate his own mortality. The "problem" plays *Troilus and Cressida* (1602), *Measure for Measure* (1603), and *All's Well That Ends Well* (1604–05) contain elements of such earlier romantic comedies as *A Midsummer Night's Dream*, *Much Ado about Nothing*, and *As You Like It*, but they do not offer the same satisfying, life-affirming resolutions as those prior plays. The writing of *Hamlet* marks the beginning of a period in which Shakespeare wrote his greatest tragedies: *Othello* (1603–04), *King Lear* (1605), *Macbeth* (1606), and *Anthony and Cleopatra* (1606). In the final years of his career as a playwright, Shakespeare wrote four plays that are listed among the comedies in the First Folio but are more commonly referred to today as "romances": *Pericles* (1607–08), *Cymbeline* (1609–10), *The Winter's Tale* (1609), and *The Tempest* (1610–11). As we might expect from an aging author who harbors no illusions about the ways of the world yet is not without hope, these final plays tackle some of the same issues that dominate the tragedies—family crisis, destructive jealousy, political betrayal—but they rely on magical or miraculous interventions to produce endings that, while not unequivocally happy, avoid outright tragedy. In their self-conscious allusions to characters and dramatic situations from earlier in Shakespeare's career, these late plays reveal a playwright, on the eve of his retirement from the theater, looking back over his own artistic achievement and recombining elements from it in new, often magical configurations. Indeed, many critics have seen Prospero—the magician who stage-manages the events and transformations of *The Tempest*—as a figure of Shakespeare himself. In Prospero's decision to "abjure" his "rough magic" at the play's end, audiences, readers, and scholars have sometimes seen Shakespeare's farewell to his own dramatic art and to the stage—"this insubstantial pageant"—that he

brought to life with such dazzling power. It is a measure of this power that centuries later, his plays continue to define the theater he took as his own.   IVO KAMPS

TEXTUAL NOTE FOR *HAMLET*

The earliest versions of Shakespeare's *Hamlet* exist in three printed forms: a quarto dated 1603, another quarto dated 1604, and the text printed in the First Folio of 1623. The consensus is that the 1603 text (known as Q1) is what scholars call a "bad quarto." It is most likely a reconstruction based on the memories of one or more of the actors who performed in the play. For that reason it may give us valuable insights into stage directions, and it may also offer accurate versions of speeches as delivered by the particular actor(s) in question, but it tends to be unreliable in most other ways. The second quarto is probably based on Shakespeare's own manuscript or on a scribal version of that manuscript. The Folio text is presumably based on a promptbook (a version of the play authorized for performance by the Master of the Revels, the government's censor). The promptbook, rather than the author's manuscript, was the basis for the play's performance and therefore the version of the play that Shakespeare's audiences actually witnessed.

The survival of the second quarto (Q2) and the First Folio (F1) texts creates a dilemma for today's editors of Shakespeare's text. While the two texts are identical in many respects, they are also different in important ways. F1 deletes about 230 lines that appear in Q2, but F1 adds 83 different lines that are not present in Q2. F1, for instance, does not have Hamlet's famous final soliloquy, "How all occasions do inform against me." The crux, of course, lies in the reasons that account for the differences between the two texts. Are these differences the product of interventions by actors or by the printer, or do they represent Shakespeare's own revision of the play? Textual scholars have offered a range of answers to this question, but none is conclusive.

What is more, we have to decide what our objective is in editing the play: do we want to get as close as possible to the

Shakespearean "original," or do we want to reconstruct the text as it was performed in Shakespeare's theater in his time? If we seek the former, we should focus on Q2 as our primary text; if we want the theater-based text, we must turn to F1.

Some editors have addressed the textual instability of *Hamlet* by providing all three texts rather than resolving their discrepancies and producing a composite version. In their 2003 edition, Bernice W. Kliman and Benjamin Bertram printed Q1, Q2, and F1 in parallel columns, while Ann Thompson and Neil Taylor published separate editions of the three versions in two volumes (2006). Other editors have produced digital versions of *Hamlet* that allow users to navigate among different versions. Bernice W. Kliman's *Enfolded Hamlet* (1996), for instance, presents Q2 and F1 embedded on the same screen; users can click on one version or the other, or both, as a way of exploring the textual variants.

The current edition, which consists of the text edited by Robert S. Miola for the Norton Critical Edition of *Hamlet*, takes a more conservative editorial approach. Miola uses Q2, the text closest to Shakespeare's manuscript, or "foul papers," as its copy text and makes changes to it only when a reading doesn't make sense or makes less sense than a variant reading present in one of the other texts. The explanatory notes and the introduction to the current edition are new.

TEXTUAL NOTE FOR
TWELFTH NIGHT

Because the only authoritative text of *Twelfth Night* is the one that appears in F1, all editions of this play derive from this source. The current edition consists of the text edited by Barbara A. Mowat and Paul Werstine, which appears in the *Norton Anthology of English Literature*. The explanatory notes and the introduction to the current edition are new.

The Tragedy of Hamlet, Prince of Denmark

THE PERSONS OF THE PLAY

GHOST of Hamlet, the late King of
    Denmark
KING CLAUDIUS, his brother
QUEEN GERTRUDE of Denmark, widow
    of King Hamlet, now
    wife of Claudius
Prince HAMLET, son of King Hamlet
    and Queen Gertrude
POLONIUS, a lord
LAERTES, son of Polonius
OPHELIA, daughter of Polonius
REYNALDO, servant of Polonius
HORATIO ⎫
ROSENCRANTZ ⎬ friends of Prince
GUILDENSTERN ⎭ Hamlet
FRANCISCO ⎫
BARNARDO ⎬ soldiers
MARCELLUS ⎭

VALTEMAND
CORNELIUS ⎫
OSRIC   ⎬ courtiers
GENTLEMEN ⎭
A SAILOR
Two CLOWNS, a gravedigger and his
    companion
A PRIEST
FORTINBRAS, Prince of Norway
A CAPTAIN in his army
AMBASSADORS from England
PLAYERS, who play the parts of
    the PROLOGUE, PLAYER KING,
    PLAYER QUEEN, and LUCIANUS, in
    The Mousetrap
Lords, messengers, attendants, guards,
    soldiers, followers of Laertes, sailors

1.1

Enter [separately] BARNARDO *and* FRANCISCO, *two sentinels*
[at several° doors].   *separate*

BARNARDO Who's there?
FRANCISCO Nay, answer me.[1] Stand and unfold yourself.°   *make yourself known*
BARNARDO Long live the King!
FRANCISCO Barnardo?
5 BARNARDO He.
FRANCISCO You come most carefully° upon your hour.   *precisely*
BARNARDO 'Tis now struck twelve. Get thee to bed, Francisco.
FRANCISCO For this relief much thanks. 'Tis bitter cold,
And I am sick at heart.
10 BARNARDO Have you had quiet guard?
FRANCISCO Not a mouse stirring.
BARNARDO Well, good night.
If you do meet Horatio and Marcellus,
The rivals° of my watch, bid them make haste.   *partners*

1.1 Location: The guard platform of Elsinore Castle at midnight.
1. As the sentry on duty, Francisco has the right to challenge anyone who approaches.

Enter HORATIO *and* MARCELLUS.

15 FRANCISCO   I think I hear them.—Stand, ho! Who is there?

HORATIO   Friends to this ground.°   *i.e, this country*

MARCELLUS   And liegemen to the Dane.°   *the Danish King*

FRANCISCO   [*Leaving*] Give° you good night.   *May God give*

MARCELLUS   O, farewell, honest soldier. Who hath relieved you?

FRANCISCO   Barnardo hath my place. Give you good night.

                                                              Exit.

20 MARCELLUS   Holla, Barnardo.

BARNARDO   Say, what, is Horatio there?

HORATIO   A piece of him.²

BARNARDO   Welcome, Horatio. Welcome, good Marcellus.

HORATIO   What, has this thing appeared again tonight?

BARNARDO   I have seen nothing.

25 MARCELLUS   Horatio says 'tis but our fantasy,
   And will not let belief take hold of him
   Touching° this dreaded sight twice seen of° us.   *Regarding / by*
   Therefore I have entreated him along
   With us to watch the minutes of this night,
30 That if again this apparition come
   He may approve° our eyes and speak to it.³   *confirm*

HORATIO   Tush, tush, 'twill not appear.

BARNARDO   Sit down awhile,
   And let us once again assail your ears,
   That are so fortified against our story,
   What we have two nights seen.

35 HORATIO   Well, sit we down,
   And let us hear Barnardo speak of this.

BARNARDO   Last night of all,°   *this very last night*
   When yond same star that's westward from the pole°   *the North Star*
   Had made his° course t'illume that part of heaven   *its*
40 Where now it burns, Marcellus and myself,
   The bell then beating one—

         Enter GHOST [*in armor*].

MARCELLUS   Peace, break thee off! Look where it comes again!

BARNARDO   In the same figure like the King that's dead.

MARCELLUS   Thou art a scholar; speak to it, Horatio.

45 BARNARDO   Looks 'a° not like the King? Mark it, Horatio.   *he*

HORATIO   Most like. It harrows me with fear and wonder.

BARNARDO   It would° be spoke to.   *wants to*

MARCELLUS   Speak to it, Horatio.

HORATIO   What art thou that usurp'st⁴ this time of night,
   Together with that fair and warlike form

---

2. Horatio may mean that the only part of him that is visible in the dark is the hand he offers in greeting.
3. It was popularly held that a ghost could not speak unless spoken to. Marcellus thinks that Horatio, a man of learning, is the appropriate

person to address the ghost (see line 48).
4. As a creature belonging to another realm, the ghost has entered the natural world and seized a shape belonging to the King of Denmark.

50   In which the majesty of buried Denmark[5]
     Did sometimes° march? By heaven, I charge thee, speak!   *formerly*
   MARCELLUS   It is offended.
   BARNARDO   See, it stalks away.
   HORATIO   Stay, speak, speak! I charge thee speak!

                                  Exit GHOST.

   MARCELLUS   'Tis gone and will not answer.
55 BARNARDO   How now, Horatio, you tremble and look pale.
    Is not this something more than fantasy?
    What think you on't?°   *of it*
   HORATIO   Before my God I might not this believe
     Without the sensible° and true avouch°   *sensory / guarantee*
     Of mine own eyes.
60 MARCELLUS   Is it not like the King?
   HORATIO   As thou art to thyself.
     Such was the very armor he had on
     When he the ambitious Norway° combated;   *King of Norway*
     So frowned he once when, in an angry parle,°   *discussion*
65 He smote the sledded Polacks[6] on the ice.
     'Tis strange.
   MARCELLUS   Thus twice before and jump at this dead hour,
     With martial stalk hath he gone by our watch.
   HORATIO   In what particular thought to work[7] I know not,
70 But in the gross and scope of mine opinion,[8]
     This bodes some strange eruption° to our state.   *disruption*
   MARCELLUS   Good now,° sit down, and tell me, he that   *(an entreaty; "Please")*
       knows,
     Why this same strict and most observant watch
     So nightly toils the subject of the land,[9]
75 And why such daily cost of brazen cannon
     And foreign mart° for implements of war,   *trade*
     Why such impress° of shipwrights, whose sore task   *forced service*
     Does not divide the Sunday from the week.
     What might be toward,° that this sweaty haste   *imminent*
80 Doth make the night joint-laborer with the day?
     Who is't that can inform me?
   HORATIO   That can I.
     At least the whisper goes so: our last King,
     Whose image even but now appeared to us,
     Was, as you know, by Fortinbras of Norway,
85 Thereto pricked° on by a most emulate° pride,   *urged / competitive*
     Dared to the combat; in which our valiant Hamlet[1]—
     For so this side of our known world esteemed him—
     Did slay this Fortinbras; who, by a sealed compact°   *contract, agreement*

---

5. That is, the recently deceased King of Denmark.
6. Poles (who traveled by sled).
7. Exactly how to comprehend this.
8. But in the general sense of my opinion (in

contrast with my "particular thought" [line 69]).
9. Causes the subjects of this country to toil.
1. That is, the recently deceased king, not the young prince.

Well ratified by law and heraldry,°   *practices pertaining to rank,*
90 Did forfeit with his life all these his lands   *pedigree, and precedence*
    Which he stood seized[2] of to the conqueror.
    Against the which a moiety competent°   *an equal portion*
    Was gagèd° by our King, which had return°   *pledged / would have reverted*
    To the inheritance° of Fortinbras,   *possession*
95 Had he been vanquisher, as by the same cov'nant
    And carriage of the article designed,°   *drawn up*
    His fell to Hamlet. Now, sir, young Fortinbras,[3]
    Of unimprovèd° mettle hot and full,   *untested, unrestrained*
    Hath in the skirts° of Norway here and there   *outlying territories*
100 Sharked up a list[4] of lawless resolutes
    For food and diet to some enterprise
    That hath a stomach in't;° which is no other—   *appetite for it*
    As it doth well° appear unto our state—   *clearly*
    But to recover of us, by strong hand
105 And terms compulsatory, those foresaid lands
    So by his father lost. And this, I take it,
    Is the main motive of our preparations,
    The source of this our watch, and the chief head°   *source*
    Of this post-haste and rummage° in the land.   *turmoil*
110 BARNARDO   I think it be no other but e'en so.
    Well may it sort that this portentous figure
    Comes armèd through our watch so like the King
    That was and is the question° of these wars.   *cause*
    HORATIO   A mote° it is to trouble the mind's eye.   *speck of dust*
115 In the most high and palmy° state of Rome,   *triumphant*
    A little ere the mightiest Julius[5] fell,
    The graves stood tenantless, and the sheeted° dead   *shrouded*
    Did squeak and gibber in the Roman streets
    At stars with trains of fire[6] and dews of blood,
120 Disasters[7] in the sun; and the moist star,°   *the moon*
    Upon whose influence Neptune's empire stands,[8]
    Was sick almost to doomsday with eclipse.[9]
    And even the like precurse° of feared events,   *precursor*
    As harbingers° preceding still° the Fates   *heralds / always*
125 And prologue to the omen[1] coming on,
    Have heaven and earth together demonstrated
    Unto our climatures° and countrymen.   *regions*
    Enter GHOST.

2. Which he held in possession.
3. Son of the slain King of Norway.
4. Hastily and indiscriminately collected a band.
5. Julius Caesar (100–44 B.C.E.), Roman general and statesman, stabbed to death by a band of conspirators.
6. That is, comets, traditionally seen as ominous portents.
7. Signs of ill omen.
8. The seas depend (as by the currents and tides). *Neptune:* Roman god of the sea.
9. In 1598, England witnessed both solar and lunar eclipses. Many believed that the Second Coming and Final Judgment were close at hand, citing prophesies in the biblical Book of Revelation (6.12) of the sun "as black as dark sackcloth" and the moon "like blood."
1. Usually, an "omen" is a sign that presages of a future good or evil event, but here it appears to refer to the event itself.

But, soft,° behold, lo, where it comes again!   *be quiet*
I'll cross² it though it blast° me.—Stay, illusion!   *injure; curse*
[*The* GHOST *spreads his arms.*]
130   If thou hast any sound or use of voice,
Speak to me!
If there be any good thing to be done,
That may to thee do ease and grace to me,
Speak to me!
135   If thou art privy to thy country's fate,
Which, happily,° foreknowing may avoid,   *perhaps*
Oh, speak!
Or if thou hast uphoarded° in thy life   *heaped up*
Extorted treasure in the womb of earth,
140   For which, they say, your spirits oft walk in death,
Speak of it!   *The cock crows.*
    Stay, and speak!—Stop it, Marcellus!
MARCELLUS   Shall I strike it with my partisan?°   *long-handled spear*
HORATIO   Do, if it will not stand. [*They strike at it.*]
BARNARDO   'Tis here!
145 HORATIO   'Tis here!   [*Exit* GHOST.]
MARCELLUS   'Tis gone.
We do it wrong, being so majestical,
To offer it the show of violence,
For it is as the air invulnerable,
150   And our vain blows malicious mockery.°   *pretended violence*
BARNARDO   It was about to speak when the cock crew.
HORATIO   And then it started like a guilty thing
Upon a fearful summons. I have heard
The cock, that is the trumpet to the morn,
155   Doth with his lofty and shrill-sounding throat
Awake the god of day,° and at his warning,   *the sun god Apollo*
Whether in sea or fire, in earth or air,
Th'extravagant and erring³ spirit hies°   *hastens*
To his confine;° and of the truth herein   *territory*
160   This present object° made probation.°   *sight / proof*
MARCELLUS   It faded on the crowing of the cock.
Some say that ever 'gainst° that season comes   *just before*
Wherein our Savior's birth is celebrated,
This bird of dawning singeth all night long.
165   And then they say no spirit dare stir abroad,
The nights are wholesome, then no planets strike,° *exert evil influence*
No fairy takes,° nor witch hath power to charm—   *bewitches*
So hallowed and so gracious° is that time.   *full of grace, blessed*
HORATIO   So have I heard, and do in part believe it.
170   But look, the morn in russet mantle clad
Walks o'er the dew of yon high eastward hill.

2. Encounter; also, make the sign of the cross (as a defense against its potentially evil power).

3. That is, wandering outside of its proper boundaries.

Break we our watch up and by my advice
Let us impart what we have seen tonight
Unto young Hamlet, for upon my life
175 This spirit, dumb to us, will° speak to him.   *wishes to*
Do you consent we shall acquaint him with it,
As needful in our loves,[4] fitting our duty?
MARCELLUS   Let's do't, I pray, and I this morning know
Where we shall find him most convenient.

                                                                   Exeunt.° (They) exit. (Latin)

1.2

Flourish. Enter CLAUDIUS, *King of Denmark,* GERTRUDE
the Queen, COUNCIL, *as°* POLONIUS *and his son* LAERTES,   *including*
HAMLET, *cum aliis [including* CORNELIUS, VOLTEMAND,
and ATTENDANTS].

KING   Though yet of Hamlet our[5] dear brother's death
The memory be green, and that it us befitted
To bear our hearts in grief, and our whole kingdom
To be contracted in one brow of woe,
5 Yet so far hath discretion fought with nature[6]
That we with wisest sorrow think on him,
Together with remembrance of ourselves.
Therefore our sometime° sister, now our queen,   *former*
Th'imperial jointress° to this warlike state,   *joint owner*
10 Have we—as 'twere with a defeated joy,
With an auspicious° and a dropping° eye,   *joyful / tearful*
With mirth in funeral, and with dirge in marriage,
In equal scale weighing delight and dole°—   *sorrow*
Taken to wife. Nor have we herein barred
15 Your better wisdoms, which have freely gone
With this affair along. For all, our thanks.
Now follows that you know° young Fortinbras,   *be informed that*
Holding a weak supposal° of our worth,   *estimation*
Or thinking by our late dear brother's death
20 Our state to be disjoint and out of frame,°   *order*
Colleagued° with this dream of his advantage,   *Coupled*
He hath not failed to pester us with message
Importing° the surrender of those lands   *Regarding*
Lost by his father, with all bands° of law,   *binding terms*
25 To our most valiant brother—so much for him.
Now for ourself and for this time of meeting,
Thus much the business is: we have here writ
To Norway, uncle of young Fortinbras—
Who, impotent and bedrid, scarcely hears
30 Of this his nephew's purpose—to suppress
His further gait° herein, in that the levies,   *course*

---

4. As necessitated by the love we bear him.   5. My (Claudius often uses the royal "we").
1.2 Location: Elsinore Castle.   6. Natural inclination (to mourn the dead king).

The lists, and full proportions are all made
Out of his subject.[7] And we here dispatch
You, good Cornelius, and you, Voltemand,
35 For bearers of this greeting to old Norway,
Giving to you no further personal power
To business with the King more than the scope
Of these dilated° articles allow. [*He gives them a paper.*]   detailed
Farewell, and let your haste commend your duty.[8]

COR. ⎫
40 VOL. ⎬ In that and all things will we show our duty.
      ⎭

KING   We doubt it nothing.° Heartily farewell.   not at all
                    [*Exeunt* CORNELIUS *and* VOLTEMAND.]
And now, Laertes, what's the news with you?
You told us of some suit; what is't, Laertes?
You cannot speak of reason to the Dane[9]
45 And lose your voice.° What wouldst thou beg, Laertes,   *i.e., waste your words*
That shall not be my offer, not thy asking?[1]
The head is not more native[2] to the heart,
The hand more instrumental to the mouth,
Than is the throne of Denmark to thy father.
What wouldst thou have, Laertes?

50 LAERTES   My dread lord,
Your leave° and favor° to return to France,   *consent / approval*
From whence, though willingly, I came to Denmark
To show my duty in your coronation.
Yet now I must confess, that duty done,
55 My thoughts and wishes bend again toward France,
And bow them to your gracious leave and pardon.°   *permission to depart*

KING   Have you your father's leave? What says Polonius?
POLONIUS   He hath, my lord, wrung from me my slow leave
By laborsome petition, and at last
60 Upon his will° I sealed my hard° consent.   *wish / grudging*
I do beseech you, give him leave to go.

KING   Take thy fair hour,[3] Laertes. Time be thine,
And thy best graces spend it at thy will.
But now, my cousin[4] Hamlet, and my son—
65 HAMLET   A little more than kin and less than kind.[5]
KING   How is it that the clouds still hang on you?
HAMLET   Not so, my lord. I am too much in the sun.[6]
QUEEN   Good Hamlet, cast thy nighted color[7] off,

---

7. That is, because the expenses and troops
are drawn from his subjects.
8. Let your haste in this matter be worthy of
your duty (to Denmark).
9. The King of Denmark; that is, Claudius
himself.
1. That I will not grant you before you even
ask it.
2. Closely and naturally related (an allusion
to the "body politic").
3. Seize the moment (of your youth).

4. Kinsman (a term used for relatives more
distant than one's brother or sister).
5. As Claudius's stepson, Hamlet is now more
than "kin"; but because he is Claudius's
nephew he is also less than "kind" (son).
Hamlet is also punning that he feels less than
kindly toward Claudius.
6. In the sunlight of Claudius's favor (with a
pun on "son").
7. His melancholy behavior as well as his
black mourning attire.

And let thine eye look like a friend on Denmark.
70 Do not forever with thy vailèd° lids   *downcast*
Seek for thy noble father in the dust.
Thou know'st 'tis common—all that lives must die,
Passing through nature to eternity.
HAMLET   Ay, madam, it is common.[8]
QUEEN   If it be,
75 Why seems it so particular° with thee?   *personal, special*
HAMLET   "Seems," madam, nay, it is. I know not "seems."
'Tis not alone my inky cloak, good mother,°   *stepmother*
Nor customary suits of solemn black,
Nor windy suspiration° of forced breath,   *sighing*
80 No, nor the fruitful° river in the eye,   *productive (of tears)*
Nor the dejected havior° of the visage,   *expression*
Together with all forms, moods, shapes of grief,
That can denote me truly. These indeed "seem,"
For they are actions that a man might play;
85 But I have that within which passes show,
These but the trappings and the suits of woe.
KING   'Tis sweet and commendable in your nature, Hamlet,
To give these mourning duties to your father,
But you must know your father lost a father,
90 That father lost, lost his, and the survivor bound
In filial obligation for some term
To do obsequious sorrow.[9] But to persever
In obstinate condolement° is a course   *lamentation*
Of impious stubbornness; 'tis unmanly grief.
95 It shows a will most incorrect to° heaven,   *defiant of*
A heart unfortified or mind impatient,
An understanding simple° and unschooled.   *childish, ignorant*
For what we know must be and is as common
As any the most vulgar thing to sense,[1]
100 Why should we in our peevish opposition
Take it to heart? Fie, 'tis a fault to heaven,
A fault against the dead, a fault to nature,
To reason most absurd, whose common theme
Is death of fathers, and who still° hath cried   *always*
105 From the first corpse[2] till he that died today,
"This must be so." We pray you, throw to earth
This unprevailing° woe and think of us   *ineffective*
As of a father. For, let the world take note,
You are the most immediate° to our throne,   *next in succession*
110 And with no less nobility of love
Than that which dearest father bears his son,

8. Generally true; Hamlet may also be implying that it is vulgar.
9. To mourn in a manner appropriate to
funeral rites.
1. As common as any of the ordinary things

we perceive through our senses.
2. An infelicitous reference to the biblical
character Abel, who, like Hamlet's father, was
killed by his brother.

Do I impart toward you. For your intent
In going back to school in Wittenberg,[3]
It is most retrograde° to our desire,   *contrary*
115   And we beseech you bend you° to remain   *submit yourself*
Here in the cheer and comfort of our eye,
Our chiefest courtier, cousin, and our son.
        QUEEN   Let not thy mother lose her prayers, Hamlet.
        I pray thee, stay with us; go not to Wittenberg.
120   HAMLET   I shall in all my best obey you, madam.
        KING   Why, 'tis a loving and a fair reply.
        Be as ourself in Denmark. Madam, come,
        This gentle and unforced accord of Hamlet
        Sits smiling° to my heart; in grace° whereof   *Pleases / honor*
125   No jocund health that Denmark° drinks today   *the King of Denmark*
        But the great cannon to the clouds shall tell,°   *proclaim, sound*
        And the King's rouse[4] the heaven shall bruit° again,   *loudly sound*
        Respeaking earthly thunder. Come away.
                                Flourish. Exeunt all but HAMLET.

        HAMLET   Oh, that this too, too solid[5] flesh would melt,
130   Thaw, and resolve° itself into a dew,   *dissolve*
        Or that the Everlasting had not fixed
        His canon° gainst self-slaughter. O God, God,   *law*
        How weary, stale, flat, and unprofitable
        Seem to me all the uses° of this world!   *employments; customs*
135   Fie on't, ah, fie. 'Tis an unweeded garden
        That grows to seed; things rank and gross in nature
        Possess it merely.° That it should come thus,   *utterly*
        But two months dead—nay, not so much, not two!
        So excellent a king that was to this,°   *(Claudius)*
140   Hyperion to a satyr,[6] so loving to my mother,
        That he might not beteem° the winds of heaven   *permit*
        Visit her face too roughly. Heaven and earth,
        Must I remember? Why, she would hang on him
        As if increase of appetite had grown
145   By what it fed on, and yet within a month—
        Let me not think on't. Frailty, thy name is woman!
        A little month, or ere° those shoes were old   *before*
        With which she followed my poor father's body,
        Like Niobe, all tears,[7] why she—
150   O God, a beast that wants discourse of reason[8]
        Would have mourned longer!—married with my uncle,
        My father's brother, but no more like my father

3. A university town in Germany.
4. A bout of drinking or a toast.
5. Instead of "solid," Q1 has "sallied," which is probably an obsolete form of "sullied": contaminated, soiled, polluted.
6. In classical myth, a woodland creature part man and part goat, known for lechery and

love of wine. *Hyperion:* the sun god (a Titan).
7. In Greek myth, Niobe wept so ceaselessly for her children, killed by the gods Apollo and Artemis to punish her for boasting, that she was turned into a stone from which water endlessly flows.
8. That is, that lacks the capacity to reason.

Than I to Hercules.[9] Within a month,
Ere yet the salt of most unrighteous° tears   *hypocritical*
155   Had left the flushing° in her gallèd° eyes,   *redness / inflamed*
She married. Oh, most wicked speed, to post°   *hasten*
With such dexterity° to incestuous sheets![1]   *nimbleness, eagerness*
It is not, nor it cannot come to good.
But break,° my heart, for I must hold my tongue.   *stop*

     Enter HORATIO, MARCELLUS, *and* BARNARDO.

160   HORATIO   Hail to your lordship.
HAMLET   I am glad to see you well. Horatio!—or I do forget myself.
HORATIO   The same, my lord, and your poor servant ever.
HAMLET   Sir, my good friend. I'll change° that name with   *exchange*
    you.
    And what make you from[2] Wittenberg, Horatio?
165   —Marcellus!
MARCELLUS   My good lord.
HAMLET   I am very glad to see you. [*To* BARNARDO] Good
    even, sir.
    —But what, in faith, make you from Wittenberg?
HORATIO   A truant° disposition, good my lord.   *idle*
170   HAMLET   I would not hear your enemy say so,
Nor shall you do my ear that violence
To make it truster of your own report
Against yourself. I know you are no truant.
But what is your affair in Elsinore?
175   We'll teach you for to drink ere you depart.
HORATIO   My lord, I came to see your father's funeral.
HAMLET   I prithee, do not mock me, fellow-student;
I think it was to see my mother's wedding.
HORATIO   Indeed, my lord, it followed hard upon.°   *soon after*
180   HAMLET   Thrift, thrift, Horatio. The funeral baked meats
Did coldly° furnish forth the marriage tables.   *when coldly*
Would I had met my dearest° foe in heaven   *most bitter*
Or ever I had seen that day, Horatio.
My father, methinks I see my father.
HORATIO   Where, my lord?
185   HAMLET   In my mind's eye, Horatio.
HORATIO   I saw him once. 'A° was a goodly king.   *He*
HAMLET   'A was a man. Take him for all in all,
I shall not look upon his like again.
HORATIO   My lord, I think I saw him yesternight.
HAMLET   Saw who?
190   HORATIO   My lord, the King your father.
HAMLET   The King my father?
HORATIO   Season your admiration[3] for a while

---

9. In classical mythology, the greatest of all heroes.
1. Both the Catholic Church and the Church of England condemned as incest the marriage between a man and his deceased brother's wife.
2. That is, what are you doing away from.
3. Temper your astonishment.

With an attent° ear till I may deliver   *attentive*
Upon the witness of these gentlemen
This marvel to you.
195 HAMLET   For God's love, let me hear!
    HORATIO   Two nights together had these gentlemen,
      Marcellus and Barnardo, on their watch
      In the dead waste and middle of the night,
      Been thus encountered: a figure like your father,
200   Armèd at point° exactly, cap-à-pie,[4]   *in readiness*
      Appears before them, and with solemn march
      Goes slow and stately by them. Thrice he walked
      By their oppressed and fear-surprisèd eyes
      Within his truncheon's length, whilst they, distilled°   *melted*
205   Almost to jelly with the act° of fear,   *effect*
      Stand dumb and speak not to him. This to me
      In dreadful secrecy impart they did,
      And I with them the third night kept the watch.
      Where, as they had delivered, both in time,
210   Form of the thing, each word made true and good,
      The apparition comes. I knew your father;
      These hands are not more like.[5]
    HAMLET   But where was this?
    MARCELLUS   My lord, upon the platform where we watch.
    HAMLET   Did you not speak to it?
    HORATIO   My lord, I did,
215   But answer made it none. Yet once methought
      It lifted up its head and did address
      Itself to motion, like as it would speak;[6]
      But even° then the morning cock crew loud,   *just*
      And at the sound it shrunk in haste away
      And vanished from our sight.
220 HAMLET   'Tis very strange.
    HORATIO   As I do live, my honored lord, 'tis true.
      And we did think it writ down° in our duty   *stipulated*
      To let you know of it.
    HAMLET   Indeed, sirs, but this troubles me.
      Hold you the watch tonight?
225 ALL   We do, my lord.
    HAMLET   Armed, say you?
    ALL   Armed, my lord.
    HAMLET   From top to toe?
    ALL   My lord, from head to foot.
    HAMLET   Then saw you not his face.
    HORATIO   O, yes, my lord, he wore his beaver° up.   *faceguard of a helmet*
230 HAMLET   What looked he, frowningly?
    HORATIO   A countenance more in sorrow than in anger.

---

4. Head to foot (French).
5. That is, my hands resemble each other as
much as the apparition resembled your father.

6. That is, it made a gesture as if it wanted to
speak.

HAMLET   Pale or red?

HORATIO   Nay, very pale.

HAMLET   And fixed his eyes upon you?

HORATIO   Most constantly.

HAMLET   I would I had been there.

HORATIO   It would have much amazed you.

235 HAMLET   Very like.
        Stayed it long?

HORATIO   While one with moderate haste might tell°   *count to*
        ahundred.

MAR. ⎱
BAR. ⎰ Longer, longer.

HORATIO   Not when I saw't.

HAMLET   His beard was grizzled°—no?   *gray*

240 HORATIO   It was as I have seen it in his life,
        A sable silvered.[7]

HAMLET   I will watch tonight.
        Perchance 'twill walk again.

HORATIO   I warr'nt° it will.   *guarantee*

HAMLET   If it assume my noble father's person,
        I'll speak to it, though hell itself should gape

245   And bid me hold my peace. I pray you all,
        If you have hitherto concealed this sight,
        Let it be tenable° in your silence still;   *withheld*
        And whatsoever else shall hap° tonight,   *happen*
        Give it an understanding but no tongue.

250   I will requite your loves. So, fare you well.
        Upon the platform twixt eleven and twelve,
        I'll visit you.

ALL   Our duty to your honor.

HAMLET   Your loves, as mine to you; farewell.

                Exeunt [HORATIO, MARCELLUS, *and* BARNARDO].
        My father's spirit in arms? All is not well;

255   I doubt° some foul play. Would the night were come.   *susupect*
        Till then sit still, my soul. Foul deeds will rise,
        Though all the earth o'erwhelm them, to men's eyes.   *Exit.*

                            1.3

            Enter LAERTES *and* OPHELIA, *his sister.*

LAERTES   My necessaries are embarked.° Farewell.   *aboard ship*
        And, sister, as the winds give benefit
        And convey is assistant,[8] do not sleep
        But let me hear from you.

OPHELIA   Do you doubt that?

5 LAERTES   For Hamlet, and the trifling of his favor,
        Hold it a fashion and a toy in blood,[9]

---

7. Black and gray (or white).
1.3 Location: Unlocalized, perhaps the home
of Polonius.

8. That is, a means of transport is available.
9. That is, consider it a passing enthusiasm
and an amorous flirtation.

A violet in the youth of primy nature,
Forward,° not permanent, sweet, not lasting,   *Precocious*
The perfume and suppliance° of a minute—   *diversion*
No more.
OPHELIA   No more but so.
10 LAERTES   Think it no more.
For nature crescent° does not grow alone   *growing*
In thews° and bulks, but as this temple° waxes,   *muscles / body*
The inward service° of the mind and soul   *duty*
Grows wide withal.° Perhaps he loves you now,   *along with it*
15 And now no soil° nor cautel° doth besmirch   *blemish / trickery*
The virtue of his will,° but you must fear,   *desires*
His greatness weighed,° his will is not his own.   *considered*
He may not, as unvalued persons° do,   *commoners*
20 Carve for himself,[1] for on his choice depends
The safety and health of this whole state,
And therefore must his choice be circumscribed
Unto the voice° and yielding° of that body[2]   *vote / consent*
Whereof he is the head. Then if he says he loves you,
It fits° your wisdom so far to believe it   *befits*
25 As he in his particular act and place[3]
May give his saying deed,[4] which is no further
Than the main° voice of Denmark goes withal.   *general*
Then weigh what loss your honor may sustain
If with too credent° ear you list° his songs,   *credulous / listen to*
30 Or lose your heart, or your chaste treasure open
To his unmastered° importunity.   *unrestrained*
Fear it, Ophelia, fear it, my dear sister,
And keep you in the rear of your affection,[5]
Out of the shot° and danger of desire.   *range*
35 "The chariest° maid is prodigal enough   *most circumspect*
If she unmask her beauty to the moon;"[6]
"Virtue itself scapes not calumnious strokes";
"The canker galls the infants[7] of the spring"
Too oft before their buttons be disclosed,°   *are open*
40 And in the morn and liquid dew of youth
Contagious blastments° are most imminent.   *blights*
Be wary then; best safety lies in fear.
Youth to itself rebels though none else near.
OPHELIA   I shall th'effect of this good lesson keep
45 As watchman to my heart. But, good my brother,
Do not, as some ungracious° pastors do,   *graceless; ungodly*
Show me the steep and thorny way to heaven
Whiles, a puffed° and reckless libertine,   *bloated, proud*

1. That is, choose for himself.
2. The body politic, the state.
3. His particular rank and power.
4. That is, may turn his words into actions.
5. That is, stay behind the front line of your feelings (a military metaphor).
6. The moon (identified in classical mythology with the virgin huntress goddess Artemis / Diana) here symbolizes chastity.
7. That is, the cankerworm damages the young plants.

Himself the primrose path of dalliance treads,
And recks° not his own rede.°   *heeds / advice*

50   LAERTES   Oh, fear me not.°   *don't worry about me*
I stay too long.

     Enter POLONIUS.

         But here my father comes.
A double blessing is a double grace;
Occasion smiles upon a second leave.[8]

    POLONIUS   Yet here, Laertes? Aboard, aboard, for shame!
55   The wind sits in the shoulder° of your sail,   *billow*
And you are stayed° for. There—my blessing with thee.   *waited*
And these few precepts in thy memory
Look thou character.° Give thy thoughts no tongue,   *inscribe*
Nor any unproportioned° thought his act.   *disorderly*
60   Be thou familiar,° but by no means vulgar.[9]   *friendly*
Those friends thou hast, and their adoption tried,[1]
Grapple them unto thy soul with hoops of steel,
But do not dull thy palm with entertainment[2]
Of each new-hatched, unfledged courage.° Beware   *high-spirited youth*
65   Of entrance to a quarrel, but, being in,
Bear't° that th'opposèd may beware of thee.   *Handle it so*
Give every man thy ear, but few thy voice.
Take each man's censure,° but reserve thy judgment.   *opinion*
Costly thy habit° as thy purse can buy,   *clothing*
70   But not expressed in fancy;° rich not gaudy,   *frivolous fashion*
For the apparel oft proclaims the man,
And they in France of the best rank and station
Are of a most select and generous chief in that.[3]
Neither a borrower nor a lender be,
75   For loan oft loses both itself and friend,
And borrowing dulls the edge of husbandry.°   *thrift*
This above all—to thine own self be true,
And it must follow, as the night the day,
Thou canst not then be false to any man.
80   Farewell. My blessing season° this in thee.   *ripen, mature*

    LAERTES   Most humbly do I take my leave, my lord.

    POLONIUS   The time invests° you. Go, your servants tend.°   *presses / await*

    LAERTES   Farewell, Ophelia, and remember well
What I have said to you.

    OPHELIA   'Tis in my memory locked,
85   And you yourself shall keep the key of it.

    LAERTES   Farewell.   *Exit* LAERTES.

    POLONIUS   What is't, Ophelia, he hath said to you?

    OPHELIA   So please you, something touching the Lord
Hamlet.

---

8. That is, it is a happy opportunity that affords
a second farewell.
9. Indiscriminate in friendship.
1. Their friendship tested.

2. That is, do not make the palm of your hand
callous by shaking the hand.
3. The nobles of France are first in displaying
their rank through their fine apparel.

POLONIUS   Marry,[4] well bethought.

90   'Tis told me he hath very oft of late
Given private time to you, and you yourself
Have of your audience° been most free and bounteous.   *attention*
If it be so—as so 'tis put on° me,   *to*
And that in way of caution—I must tell you

95   You do not understand yourself so clearly
As it behooves my daughter and your honor.
What is between you? Give me up the truth.

OPHELIA   He hath, my lord, of late made many tenders°   *offers*
Of his affection to me.

100 POLONIUS   "Affection"? Pooh, you speak like a green girl,
Unsifted° in such perilous circumstance.   *Inexperienced*
Do you believe his "tenders," as you call them?

OPHELIA   I do not know, my lord, what I should think.

POLONIUS   Marry, I will teach you. Think yourself a baby

105   That you have ta'en these tenders for true pay,
Which are not sterling.° Tender° yourself more dearly,   *genuine / Price*
Or—not to crack the wind of the poor phrase,
Wronging it thus—you'll tender me a fool.[5]

OPHELIA   My lord, he hath importuned me with love

110   In honorable fashion.

POLONIUS   Ay, "fashion" you may call it. Go to,[6] go to.

OPHELIA   And hath given countenance° to his speech, my   *authority*
lord,
With almost all the holy vows of heaven.

POLONIUS   Ay, springes° to catch woodcocks.[7] I do know,   *snares*

115   When the blood burns, how prodigal° the soul   *generously; wastefully*
Lends the tongue vows. These blazes, daughter,
Giving more light than heat, extinct° in both,   *extinguished*
Even in their promise as it is a-making,
You must not take for fire. From this time

120   Be something scanter of your maiden presence;
Set your entreatments at a higher rate
Than a command to parle.[8] For Lord Hamlet,
Believe so much in° him, that he is young,   *about*
And with a larger tether may he walk

125   Than may be given you. In few,° Ophelia,   *short*
Do not believe his vows, for they are brokers,°   *go-betweens*
Not of that dye which their investments[9] show,
But mere implorators° of unholy suits,   *implorers*
Breathing° like sanctified and pious bawds,   *Whispering*

130   The better to beguile. This is for all:

4. By the Virgin Mary (a mild oath).
5. You will make me look like a fool; you will present me with a grandchild ("fool" was often used as a synonym for "child"). *Crack . . . thus:* wear out the phrase by overusing it.
6. Come now (i.e., "don't be so naïve"). *Fashion:* flattery resulting from a passing and

youthful fancy (see line 6).
7. Proverbially stupid birds.
8. That is, value your favors more highly than to grant every request for an interview.
9. Clerical vestments (i.e., they are not what they seem).

I would not, in plain terms, from this time forth
Have you so slander° any moment leisure   *disgrace*
As to give words or talk with the Lord Hamlet.
Look to't, I charge you. Come your ways.°   *Come along*
135 OPHELIA   I shall obey, my lord.

                                                                    Exeunt.

1.4

               Enter HAMLET, HORATIO, *and* MARCELLUS.

HAMLET   The air bites shrewdly;° it is very cold.   *sharply*
HORATIO   It is a nipping and an eager° air.   *biting*
HAMLET   What hour now?
HORATIO   I think it lacks of twelve.
MARCELLUS   No, it is struck.
HORATIO   Indeed? I heard it not.
5   It then draws near the season°   *time*
     Wherein the spirit held his wont° to walk.   *was accustomed*
               A flourish of trumpets, and two pieces go off.°   *(cannons fire offstage)*
     What does this mean, my lord?
HAMLET   The King doth wake tonight and takes his rouse,°   *drinks*
     Keeps wassail, and the swagg'ring upspring reels,[1]
10   And as he drains his drafts of Rhenish° down,   *Rhine wine*
     The kettledrum and trumpet thus bray out
     The triumph of his pledge.[2]
HORATIO   Is it a custom?
HAMLET   Ay, marry, is't,
     But to my mind, though I am native here
15   And to the manner° born, it is a custom   *custom*
     More honored in the breach than the observance.
     This heavy-headed revel east and west
     Makes us traduced and taxed of° other nations;   *criticized by*
     They clepe° us drunkards and with swinish phrase°   *call / calling us pigs*
20   Soil our addition;° and indeed it takes   *reputation*
     From our achievements, though performed at height,°   *most excellently*
     The pith° and marrow of our attribute.°   *heart / reputation*
     So, oft it chances in particular men
     That for some vicious mole of nature[3] in them,
25   As in their birth°—wherein they are not guilty,   *Inherited at birth*
     Since nature cannot choose his° origin—   *its*
     By their o'ergrowth of some complexion,[4]
     Oft breaking down the pales° and forts of reason,   *fences, boundaries*
     Or by some habit that too much o'erleavens
30   The form of plausive manners[5]—that these men,

1.4 Location: The guard platform of Elsinore
Castle at midnight.
1. Staggers through a vigorous dance. *Was-
sail*: carousal, health drinking.
2. The triumph of his toast (achieved by emptying his cup at a single draught).
3. A blemish in some men's nature that leads
to vice.

4. That is, by the domination of one of the
four humors, thought to determine character:
black bile was held responsible for a melancholy disposition; blood, sanguine; yellow
bile, choleric; and phlegm, phlegmatic.
5. That is, exerts its negative influence over
pleasing manners (as too much leavening can
ruin a batch of bread dough).

Carrying, I say, the stamp of one defect,
Being nature's livery or fortune's star,[6]
His virtues else,° be they as pure as grace,   *other virtues*
As infinite as man may undergo,°   *sustain*
35 Shall in the general censure° take corruption *public opinion*
From that particular fault. The dram of evil[7]
Doth all the noble substance often dout
To his own scandal.°   *disgrace*

  Enter GHOST.

HORATIO   Look, my lord, it comes!
HAMLET Angels and ministers of grace defend us!
40 Be thou a spirit of health or goblin° damned, *demon*
Bring with thee airs from heaven or blasts[8] from hell,
Be thy intents wicked or charitable,
Thou com'st in such a questionable° shape *question-provoking*
That I will speak to thee. I'll call thee Hamlet,
45 King, father, royal Dane. Oh, answer me!
Let me not burst in ignorance, but tell
Why thy canonized° bones, hearsèd° in death, *sanctified / coffined*
Have burst their cerements,° why the sepulcher, *grave clothes*
Wherein we saw thee quietly interred,
50 Hath oped his ponderous and marble jaws
To cast thee up again. What may this mean,
That thou, dead corpse, again in complete steel° *full armor*
Revisits thus the glimpses of the moon,° *shimmering moonlight*
Making night hideous, and we fools of nature[9]
55 So horridly to shake our disposition°   *state of mind*
With thoughts beyond the reaches of our souls?
Say, why is this? Wherefore? What should we do?

  [GHOST] *beckons* [HAMLET].

HORATIO It beckons you to go away with it,
As if it some impartment° did desire   *communication*
To you alone.
60 MARCELLUS Look with what courteous action
It waves you to a more removèd ground.
But do not go with it.
HORATIO   No, by no means.
HAMLET It will not speak; then I will follow it.
HORATIO Do not, my lord.
HAMLET   Why, what should be the fear?
65 I do not set my life at a pin's fee,°   *the worth of a pin*
And for my soul, what can it do to that,
Being a thing immortal as itself?
It waves me forth again. I'll follow it.
HORATIO What if it tempt you toward the flood,° my lord, *sea*

---

6. Either by a defect in their nature or the
influence of ill fortune.
7. Minuscule amount of evil, punning on
"evil" and "eale," or yeast (see line 29).
8. Foul, malignant airs that spread infection.

Airs: wholesome breezes.
9. Accustomed to the natural order of things
(and therefore shaken by supernatural
phenomena).

70 Or to the dreadful summit of the cliff
That beetles o'er° his base into the sea,   *overhangs*
And there assume some other horrible form
Which might deprive your sovereignty of reason,[1]
And draw you into madness? Think of it.
75 The very place puts toys of desperation,°   *desperate fancies*
Without more motive, into every brain
That looks so many fathoms to the sea
And hears it roar beneath.

HAMLET   It waves me still.—Go on. I'll follow thee.

MARCELLUS   You shall not go, my lord. [*They hold him.*]

80 HAMLET   Hold off your hands!

HORATIO   Be ruled. You shall not go.

HAMLET   My fate cries out,
And makes each petty artery in this body
As hardy as the Nemean lion's[2] nerve.

     [GHOST *beckons.*]

Still am I called. Unhand me, gentlemen!
85 By heaven, I'll make a ghost of him that lets° me!   *hinders*
[*Breaking free*] I say, away!—Go on. I'll follow thee.

                     Exeunt GHOST *and* HAMLET.

HORATIO   He waxes desperate with imagination.

MARCELLUS   Let's follow. 'Tis not fit thus to obey him.

HORATIO   Have after.° To what issue° will this come?   *Go on / end*

90 MARCELLUS   Something is rotten in the state of Denmark.

HORATIO   Heaven will direct it.°   *(the outcome)*

MARCELLUS   Nay, let's follow him.

                            Exeunt.

1.5

   Enter GHOST *and* HAMLET.

HAMLET   Whither wilt thou lead me? Speak, I'll go no
   further.

GHOST   Mark me.

HAMLET   I will.

GHOST   My hour is almost come,
When I to sulf'rous and tormenting flames
Must render up myself.

HAMLET   Alas, poor ghost!

5 GHOST   Pity me not, but lend thy serious hearing
To what I shall unfold.

HAMLET   Speak. I am bound to hear.

GHOST   So art thou to revenge, when thou shalt hear.

HAMLET   What?

---

1. Deprive reason of its sovereignty over your
mind.
2. In classical mythology, a lion whose skin
was impervious to weapons; killing it was the

first of Hercules' twelve labors.
1.5 Location: The battlements of Elsinore
Castle.

GHOST   I am thy father's spirit,

10   Doomed for a certain term to walk the night,
     And for the day confined to fast° in fires,   *do penance*
     Till the foul crimes done in my days of nature°   *my natural life*
     Are burnt and purged away.³ But that I am forbid
     To tell the secrets of my prison house,
15   I could a tale unfold whose lightest word
     Would harrow up° thy soul, freeze thy young blood,   *lacerate, tear*
     Make thy two eyes like stars start from their spheres,
     Thy knotted and combinèd locks to part,
     And each particular hair to stand an end
20   Like quills upon the fearful porpentine.
     But this eternal blazon⁴ must not be
     To ears of flesh and blood. List,° list, oh, list!   *Listen*
     If thou didst ever thy dear father love—
     HAMLET   O God!
25   GHOST   Revenge his foul and most unnatural murder.
     HAMLET   Murder?
     GHOST   Murder most foul, as in the best it is,
     But this most foul, strange, and unnatural.
     HAMLET   Haste me to know't, that I with wings as swift
30   As meditation or the thoughts of love
     May sweep to my revenge.
     GHOST   I find thee apt;
     And duller shouldst thou be than the fat° weed   *gross*
     That roots itself in ease on Lethe wharf,⁵
     Wouldst thou not stir in this. Now, Hamlet, hear:
35   'Tis given out that, sleeping in my orchard,°   *garden*
     A serpent stung me; so the whole ear of Denmark
     Is by a forgèd process° of my death   *false account*
     Rankly abused.° But know, thou noble youth,   *deceived*
     The serpent that did sting thy father's life
40   Now wears his crown.
     HAMLET   O my prophetic soul! My uncle!
     GHOST   Ay, that incestuous, that adulterate° beast,   *adulterous*
     With witchcraft of his wit, with traitorous gifts°—   *talents*
     O wicked wit and gifts that have the power
45   So to seduce—won to his shameful lust
     The will of my most seeming-virtuous queen.
     O Hamlet, what falling off was there
     From me, whose love was of that dignity
     That it went hand in hand even with the vow
50   I made to her in marriage, and to decline
     Upon a wretch whose natural gifts were poor
     To° those of mine.   *Compared to*
     But virtue, as it never will be moved,

3. A description that suggests purgatory, the place, mainly associated with Catholicism, where the dead expiate their sins by suffering.

4. Revelation of eternal things.
5. The bank of Lethe, the river in the classical underworld whose waters cause forgetfulness.

Though lewdness court it in a shape of heaven,
55 So lust, though to a radiant angel linked,
Will sate itself in a celestial bed
And prey on garbage.
But soft.° Methinks I scent the morning air;   wait
Brief let me be. Sleeping within my orchard,
60 My custom always of the afternoon,
Upon my secure hour thy uncle stole,
With juice of cursèd hebona[6] in a vial,
And in the porches° of my ears did pour   entrances
The leperous distilment,° whose effect   extracted essence
65 Holds such an enmity with blood of man
That swift as quicksilver it courses through
The natural gates and alleys of the body,
And with a sudden vigor it doth possess
And curd, like eager° droppings into milk,   sour, acid
70 The thin and wholesome blood. So did it mine,
And a most instant tetter barked about,[7]
Most lazar-like,° with vile and loathsome crust,   like a leper
All my smooth body.
Thus was I, sleeping, by a brother's hand,
75 Of life, of crown, of queen, at once dispatched,°   dispossessed
Cut off even in the blossoms of my sin,[8]
Unhouseled, disappointed, unaneled,[9]
No reck'ning° made, but sent to my account   settling of spiritual accounts
With all my imperfections on my head.   (by confession of sins)
80 O horrible, O horrible, most horrible!
If thou hast nature° in thee, bear it not;   natural feeling
Let not the royal bed of Denmark be
A couch for luxury° and damned incest.   lust
But, howsoever thou pursues this act,
85 Taint not thy mind,[1] nor let thy soul contrive
Against thy mother aught.° Leave her to heaven,   anything whatsoever
And to those thorns that in her bosom lodge
To prick and sting her. Fare thee well at once.
The glow-worm shows the matin° to be near,   morning
90 And 'gins° to pale his uneffectual fire.   begins
Adieu, adieu, adieu. Remember me.   [Exit.]
HAMLET   O all you host of heaven! O earth! What else?
And shall I couple° hell? Oh, fie! Hold, hold, my heart,   add
And you, my sinews, grow not instant old,
95 But bear me swiftly up. Remember thee?
Ay, thou poor ghost, whiles memory holds a seat

---

6. A poison; possibly a confusion for "hen-
bane," a plant with poisonous properties.
7. That is, a pustular eruption of the skin ("tetter") covered the body as bark covers a tree.
8. That is, before there was an opportunity to
confess and repent sins.

9. Without the Eucharist ("unhouseled");
unprepared ("disappointed"), because uncon-
fessed and unrepentant; and without receiving
extreme unction or anointing ("unaneled").
1. Do not become corrupted yourself.

In this distracted globe.[2] Remember thee?
Yea, from the table° of my memory   *tablet*
I'll wipe away all trivial, fond° records,   *foolish*
100 All saws of books, all forms, all pressures past[3]
That youth and observation copied there,
And thy commandment all alone shall live
Within the book and volume of my brain,
Unmixed with baser matter. Yes, by heaven.
105 O most pernicious woman!
O villain, villain, smiling, damnèd villain!
My tables°—meet° it is I set it down   *writing tablets / fitting*
That one may smile and smile and be a villain.
At least, I am sure, it may be so in Denmark.
110 So, uncle, there you are. Now to my word.[4]
It is "Adieu, adieu. Remember me."
I have sworn't.

         Enter HORATIO *and* MARCELLUS *[calling].*

HORATIO   My lord, my lord!
MARCELLUS   Lord Hamlet!
115 HORATIO   Heavens secure him.
HAMLET   *[Aside]* So be it.
MARCELLUS   Illo,[5] ho, ho, my lord!
HAMLET   Hillo, ho, ho, boy! Come and come.
MARCELLUS   How is't, my noble lord?
120 HORATIO   What news, my lord?
HAMLET   Oh, wonderful!°   *astonishing*
HORATIO   Good my lord, tell it.
HAMLET   No, you will reveal it.
HORATIO   Not I, my lord, by heaven.
125 MARCELLUS   Nor I, my lord.
HAMLET   How say you, then? Would heart of man once
      think it?
But you'll be secret?
HOR. ⎫
MAR. ⎭   Ay, by heaven.
HAMLET   There's never a villain dwelling in all Denmark
130 But he's an arrant° knave.   *out-and-out*
HORATIO   There needs no ghost, my lord, come from the
      grave
To tell us this.
HAMLET   Why, right, you are in the right.
And so without more circumstance° at all,   *ceremony*
I hold it fit that we shake hands and part,
135 You, as your business and desire shall point you—
For every man hath business and desire,

2. Troubled earth; perhaps, confused head; also perhaps a reference to the Globe theater in which *Hamlet* was performed.
3. That is, all wise sayings from books, all

shape or customs, all past impressions.
4. Perhaps, watchword; or the ghost's command; or oath.
5. A falconer's cry to his hawk.

Such as it is—and for my own poor part,
I will go pray.

HORATIO   These are but wild and whirling words, my lord.

140 HAMLET   I am sorry they offend you, heartily;
Yes, faith, heartily.

HORATIO   There's no offense, my lord.

HAMLET   Yes, by Saint Patrick, but there is, Horatio,
And much offense too. Touching this vision here,
It is an honest° ghost, that let me tell you.   truthful, reliable

145 For your desire to know what is between us,
O'ermaster't as you may. And now, good friends,
As you are friends, scholars, and soldiers,
Give me one poor request.

HORATIO   What is't, my lord? We will.

HAMLET   Never make known what you have seen tonight.

150 HOR.⎱ My lord, we will not.
MAR.⎰

HAMLET   Nay, but swear't.

HORATIO   In faith, my lord, not I.[6]

MARCELLUS   Nor I, my lord, in faith.

HAMLET   [Holding out his sword] Upon my sword.

155 MARCELLUS   We have sworn, my lord, already.

HAMLET   Indeed, upon my sword, indeed.

GHOST (Cries under the stage)   Swear.

HAMLET   Ha, ha, boy, sayst thou so? Art thou there,
truepenny?°—   honest fellow
Come on, you hear this fellow in the cellarage;
Consent to swear.

160 HORATIO   Propose the oath, my lord.

HAMLET   Never to speak of this that you have seen,
Swear by my sword.

GHOST [Beneath] Swear.

HAMLET   Hic et ubique?[7] Then we'll shift our ground.
[He moves to another place.]

165 Come hither, gentlemen,
And lay your hands again upon my sword.
Swear by my sword
Never to speak of this that you have heard.

GHOST   [Beneath] Swear by his sword.

170 HAMLET   Well said, old mole! Canst work i' th' earth so fast?
A worthy pioner.°—Once more remove,° good friends.   miner / move
[He moves again.]

HORATIO   O day and night, but this is wondrous strange!

HAMLET   And therefore as a stranger give it welcome.[8]
There are more things in heaven and earth, Horatio,

175 Than are dreamt of in your philosophy.[9] But come.
Here, as before, never, so help you mercy,

---

6. Indeed, I will not reveal it.
7. Here and everywhere (Latin).
8. That is, welcome it with the courtesy due

to a stranger.
9. Natural philosophy (i.e., science).

How strange or odd soe'er I bear myself—
As I, perchance, hereafter shall think meet
To put an antic disposition on[1]—
180   That you, at such times seeing me, never shall,
With arms encumbered° thus, or this headshake,   folded
Or by pronouncing of some doubtful° phrase   ambiguous
As "Well, well, we know," or "We could an if° we would,"   if only
Or "If we list° to speak," or "There be, an if they might,"[2]   liked
185   Or such ambiguous giving out, to note
That you know aught° of me—this do swear,   anything
So grace and mercy at your most need help you.
GHOST [Beneath] Swear. [They swear.]
HAMLET   Rest, rest, perturbèd spirit.—So, gentlemen,
190   With all my love I do commend me to you,
And what so poor a man as Hamlet is
May do t'express his love and friending° to you,   friendship
God willing, shall not lack.° Let us go in together;   be deficient
And still° your fingers on your lips, I pray.   always
195   The time is out of joint.° O cursèd spite,   in complete disorder
That ever I was born to set it right!
Nay, come, let's go together.[3]
                                                        Exeunt.

2.1

Enter old POLONIUS *with his man* [REYNALDO].
POLONIUS   Give him this money and these notes, Reynaldo.
        [*He gives money and papers.*]
REYNALDO   I will, my lord.
POLONIUS   You shall do marvelous wisely, good Reynaldo,
Before you visit him, to make inquire
Of his behavior.
5   REYNALDO   My lord, I did intend it.
POLONIUS   Marry, well said, very well said. Look you, sir,
Inquire me° first what Danskers° are in Paris,   for me / Danes
And how, and who, what means,° and where they keep,°   means of income / reside
What company, at what expense; and finding
10   By this encompassment and drift of question[4]
That they do know my son, come you more nearer
Than your particular demands will touch it.[5]
Take you,° as 'twere, some distant knowledge of him,   Pretend
As thus, "I know his father and his friends,
15   And in part him"—do you mark this, Reynaldo?
REYNALDO   Ay, very well, my lord.

1. To behave fantastically, to act like a madman.
2. There are those who would say this or that if they could so do safely.
3. Hamlet tells the others to depart with him (rather than to follow him, as befitting his rank).
2.1 Location: Polonius's chambers
4. By this roundabout manner of questioning.
5. You will come nearer to the truth than if you make direct inquiries.

POLONIUS   "And in part him, but," you may say, "not well.
    But if't be he I mean, he's very wild,
    Addicted so and so," and there put on him°   *accuse him of*
20   What forgeries[6] you please—marry, none so rank°   *heinous*
    As may dishonor him, take heed of that—
    But, sir, such wanton,° wild, and usual slips   *unrestrained*
    As are companions noted and most known
    To youth and liberty.
REYNALDO   As gaming, my lord.
25 POLONIUS   Ay, or drinking, fencing, swearing,
    Quarreling, drabbing°—you may go so far.   *whoring*
REYNALDO   My lord, that would dishonor him.
POLONIUS   Faith, no, as you may season° it in the charge.   *moderate*
    You must not put another scandal on him,
30   That he is open° to incontinency;°   *given to / sexual excess*
    That's not my meaning. But breathe his faults so quaintly° *delicately*
    That they may seem the taints of liberty,[7]
    The flash and outbreak of a fiery mind,
    A savageness in unreclaimèd° blood,   *untamed*
35   Of general assault.[8]
REYNALDO   But, my good lord—
POLONIUS   Wherefore° should you do   *Why*
    this?
REYNALDO   Ay, my lord, I would know that.
POLONIUS   Marry, sir, here's my drift,
    And I believe it is a fetch of wit:
40   You laying these slight sullies° on my son   *stain*
    As 'twere a thing a little soiled wi' the working,[9]
    Mark you, your party° in converse, him you would sound,° *partner / sound out*
    Having° ever seen in the prenominate crimes[1]   *If he has*
    The youth you breathe of guilty, be assured
45   He closes with° you in this consequence:[2]   *discloses to*
    "Good sir," or so, or "friend," or "gentleman,"
    According to the phrase° or the addition[3]   *expression*
    Of man and country—
REYNALDO   Very good, my lord.
POLONIUS   And then, sir, does 'a° this—'a does—What was I   *he*
    about to say?
50   By the mass,° I was about to say something. Where did I *(a mild oath)*
    leave?
REYNALDO   At "closes in the consequence."
POLONIUS   At "closes in the consequence"—ay, marry.
    He closes thus: "I know the gentleman;
    I saw him yesterday," or "th'other day"
55   —Or then or then with such or such—and, "as you say,

---

6. False accusations.
7. The blemishes that result from freedom without discipline.
8. To which all young men are prone.
9. Shopworn (i.e., slightly soiled while com-

ing to maturity).
1. Aforementioned transgressions.
2. In the following manner.
3. Title; customary style of address.

There was 'a° gaming," "there o'ertook in's rouse,"°   *he / drunk from his carousal*
"There falling out° at tennis," or perchance,   *quarreling*
"I saw him enter such a house of sale,"
Videlicet,° a brothel, or so forth. See you now   *That is to say (Latin)*
60 Your bait of falsehood takes this carp° of truth,   *fish*
And thus do we of wisdom and of reach,°   *understanding*
With windlasses, and with assays of bias,[4]
By indirections find directions out.[5]
So, by my former° lecture and advice   *previous*
65 Shall you my son. You have me,° have you not?   *have my meaning*

REYNALDO   My lord, I have.

POLONIUS   God be wi'ye; fare ye well.

REYNALDO   Good my lord.

POLONIUS   Observe his inclination in° yourself.   *for*

REYNALDO   I shall, my lord.

70 POLONIUS   And let him ply° his music.   *practice*

REYNALDO   Well, my lord.

POLONIUS   Farewell.

                        Exit REYNALDO.

    Enter OPHELIA.

             How now, Ophelia, what's the matter?

OPHELIA   Oh, my lord, my lord, I have been so affrighted!

POLONIUS   With what, i'the name of God?

75 OPHELIA   My lord, as I was sewing in my closet,
Lord Hamlet, with his doublet all unbraced,°   *his jacket unlaced*
No hat upon his head, his stockings fouled,
Ungartered, and down-gyvèd to his ankle,[6]
Pale as his shirt, his knees knocking each other,
80 And with a look so piteous in purport
As if he had been loosèd out of hell
To speak of horrors—he comes before me.

POLONIUS   Mad for thy love?

OPHELIA   My lord, I do not know,
But truly I do fear it.

POLONIUS   What said he?

85 OPHELIA   He took me by the wrist and held me hard,
Then goes he to the length of all his arm,
And with his other hand thus o'er his brow,
He falls to such perusal of my face
As 'a° would draw it. Long stayed he so.   *As if he*
90 At last, a little shaking of mine arm,
And thrice his head thus waving up and down,
He raised a sigh so piteous and profound
As it did seem to shatter all his bulk°   *body*
And end his being. That done, he lets me go,
95 And, with his head over his shoulder turned,

---

4. That is, indirect efforts: a "windlass" is a roundabout approach to intercept the game in hunting; "bias" is the curve taken by the ball toward its target in the game of bowls.

5. That is, by indirect means find out the truth.
6. Fallen down around his ankles like shackles (gyves).

He seemed to find his way without his eyes,
For out o' doors he went without their helps,
And to the last bended their light[7] on me.

POLONIUS   Come, go with me: I will go seek the King.

100 This is the very ecstasy° of love,   *insanity*
Whose violent property fordoes° itself   *destrays*
And leads the will to desperate undertakings,
As oft as any passion under heaven
That does afflict our natures. I am sorry.

105 What, have you given him any hard words of late?

OPHELIA   No, my good lord, but, as you did command,
I did repel his letters and denied
His access to me.

POLONIUS   That hath made him mad.
I am sorry that with better heed and judgment

110 I had not quoted° him: I feared he did but trifle,   *observed*
And meant to wrack thee. But beshrew my jealousy![8]
By heaven, it is as proper to our age
To cast beyond ourselves[9] in our opinions
As it is common for the younger sort

115 To lack discretion. Come, go we to the King.
This must be known, which, being kept close,° might move   *secret*
More grief to hide than hate to utter love.[1]
Come.

                                        Exeunt.

2.2

Flourish. Enter KING *and* QUEEN, ROSENCRANTZ *and*
GUILDENSTERN [*and* ATTENDANTS].

KING   Welcome, dear Rosencrantz and Guildenstern.
Moreover° that we much did long to see you,   *Besides*
The need we have to use you did provoke
Our hasty sending.° Something have you heard   *summons*

5 Of Hamlet's transformation—so call it,
Sith° nor th'exterior nor the inward man   *Since*
Resembles that° it was. What it should be,   *what*
More than his father's death, that thus hath put him
So much from th'understanding of himself,

10 I cannot dream of. I entreat you both
That, being of so young days° brought up with him,   *from childhood*
And sith so neighbored to[2] his youth and havior,°   *behavior*
That you vouchsafe your rest° here in our court   *agree to remain*
Some little time, so by your companies

15 To draw him on to pleasures, and to gather,
So much as from occasion° you may glean,   *opportunities*

7. That is, the light that eyes were thought to
emit.
8. Curse my suspicious nature. *Wrack thee:*
take your virginity.
9. Go too far (by way of caution). *Proper to
our age:* i.e., characteristic of men of Poloni-

us's own (advanced) age.
1. That is, might cause more grief if kept
secret than it would incur hatred (or disapproval) if revealed.
2.2 Location: The castle.
2. Familiar with.

Whether aught° to us unknown afflicts him thus   *anything*
That, opened,° lies within our remedy.   *if revealed*
QUEEN   Good gentlemen, he hath much talked of you,
20   And sure I am two men there is not living
To whom he more adheres.° If it will please you   *is more attached*
To show us so much gentry° and good will   *courtesy*
As to expend your time with us awhile,
For the supply and profit³ of our hope,
25   Your visitation shall receive such thanks
As fits a king's remembrance.
ROSENCRANTZ   Both Your Majesties
Might, by the sovereign power you have of° us,   *over*
Put your dread° pleasures more into command   *revered*
Than to entreaty.
GUILDENSTERN   But we both obey,
30   And here give up ourselves in the full bent°   *to our utmost*
To lay our service freely at your feet,
To be commanded.
KING   Thanks, Rosencrantz and gentle Guildenstern.
QUEEN   Thanks, Guildenstern and gentle Rosencrantz.
35   And I beseech you instantly to visit
My too much changèd son.—Go, some of you,
And bring these gentlemen where Hamlet is.
GUILDENSTERN   Heavens make our presence and our   *doings; stratagems*
practices°
Pleasant and helpful to him.
QUEEN   Ay, amen.
Exeunt ROSENCRANTZ, GUILDENSTERN
[*and some* ATTENDANTS].

Enter POLONIUS.

40   POLONIUS   Th'ambassadors from Norway, my good lord,
Are joyfully returned.
KING   Thou still° hast been the father of good news.   *always*
POLONIUS   Have I, my lord? I assure my good liege
I hold my duty as I hold my soul,
45   Both to my God and to my gracious king;
And I do think—or else this brain of mine
Hunts not the trail of policy° so sure   *statecraft*
As it hath used to do—that I have found
The very cause of Hamlet's lunacy.
50   KING   Oh, speak of that; that do I long to hear.
POLONIUS   Give first admittance to th'ambassadors;
My news shall be the fruit° to that great feast.   *dessert*
KING   Thyself do grace to them and bring them in.
[*Exit* POLONIUS.]
He tells me, my dear Gertrude, he hath found
55   The head° and source of all your son's distemper.   *chief reason*
QUEEN   I doubt° it is no other but the main,°.   *suspect / main cause*
His father's death and our hasty marriage.

3. Support and advancement.

KING   Well, we shall sift him.°   *question (Polonius)*

    Enter AMBASSADORS [VOLTEMAND *and* CORNELIUS, *with*
    POLONIUS].

                    —Welcome, my good friends.

    Say, Voltemand, what from our brother° Norway?   *fellow monarch*

60 VOLTEMAND   Most fair return of greetings and desires.°   *good wishes*

    Upon our first,[4] he sent out to suppress

    His nephew's levies, which to him appeared

    To be a preparation 'gainst the Polack,°   *the King of Poland*

    But, better looked into, he truly found

65   It was against Your Highness; whereat grieved

    That so his sickness, age, and impotence

    Was falsely borne in hand,[5] sends out arrests

    On Fortinbras;[6] which he, in brief, obeys,

    Receives rebuke from Norway, and, in fine,°   *conclusion*

70   Makes vow before his uncle never more

    To give th'assay of arms[7] against Your Majesty.

    Whereon old Norway, overcome with joy,

    Gives him three-score° thousand crowns in annual fee,°   *sixty / payment*

    And his commission to employ those soldiers,

75   So levied as before, against the Polack,

    With an entreaty, herein further shown, [*He gives a paper.*]

    That it might please you to give quiet pass

    Through your dominions for this enterprise,

    On such regards of safety and allowance[8]

    As therein are set down.

80 KING   It likes° us well,   *pleases*

    And at our more considered time[9] we'll read,

    Answer, and think upon this business.

    Meantime we thank you for your well-took labor.

    Go to your rest; at night we'll feast together.

    Most welcome home!

                       Exeunt AMBASSADORS.

85 POLONIUS   This business is well ended.

    My liege, and madam, to expostulate°   *reason earnestly*

    What majesty should be, what duty is,

    Why day is day, night, night, and time is time,

    Were nothing but to waste night, day, and time.

90   Therefore, since brevity is the soul of wit,°   *wisdom*

    And tediousness the limbs and outward flourishes,°   *rhetorical flourishes*

    I will be brief. Your noble son is mad,

    "Mad" call I it, for to define true madness,

    What is't but to be nothing else but mad?

    But let that go.

---

4. When we first broached the matter (of young Fortinbras's military preparations).
5. That is, was deceitfully taken advantage of.
6. Orders to Fortinbras to stop his military action against Denmark.
7. To undertake military action.
8. With such safeguards and stipulations.
9. A convenient time for further consideration.

95 | QUEEN More matter with less art.° | *rhetorical art* |

POLONIUS   Madam, I swear I use no art at all.
That he's mad, 'tis true; 'tis true, 'tis pity,
And pity 'tis, 'tis true—a foolish figure,°   *figure of speech*
But farewell it,° for I will use no art.   *to it*
100   Mad let us grant him then, and now remains
That we find out the cause of this effect,
Or rather say, the cause of this defect,
For this effect defective comes by cause.[1]
Thus it remains, and the remainder thus.
105   Perpend.°   *Consider*
I have a daughter—have while she is mine°—   *until she marries*
Who, in her duty and obedience, mark,
Hath given me this. Now gather and surmise.
       [*He reads a letter.*]
"To the celestial, and my soul's idol, the most beautified°   *beautiful*
110   Ophelia"—that's an ill phrase, a vile phrase, "beautified" is
a vile phrase; but you shall hear. Thus: [*He reads.*]
"In her excellent white bosom,[2] these," etc.
QUEEN   Came this from Hamlet to her?
POLONIUS   Good madam, stay° awhile; I will be faithful.°   *wait/read faithfully*
       [*He reads the letter.*]
115   "Doubt thou the stars are fire,
                     Doubt that the sun doth move,
                     Doubt° truth to be a liar,   *Suspect*
                     But never doubt I love.
Oh, dear Ophelia, I am ill at these numbers.[3] I have not
120   art to reckon my groans.[4] But that I love thee best, oh,
most best, believe it. Adieu.
Thine evermore, most dear lady, whilst this machine is to°   *body belongs*
him, Hamlet."
This in obedience hath my daughter shown me,
125   And, more above,° hath his solicitings,   *moreover*
As they fell out° by time, by means, and place,   *came to pass*
All given to mine ear.
KING   But how hath she
Received his love?
POLONIUS   What do you think of me?
KING   As of a man faithful and honorable.
130   POLONIUS   I would fain° prove so. But what might you think,   *gladly*
When I had seen this hot love on the wing—
As I perceived it, I must tell you that,
Before my daughter told me—what might you,
Or my dear Majesty your queen here, think,
135   If I had played the desk or table book,[5]
Or given my heart a winking,° mute and dumb,   *closing of the eyes*

---

1. That is, this effect, which in Hamlet is a
defect (i.e., his madness), has a cause.
2. Where love letters should be kept.

3. Bad at writing verses.
4. Count my groans (in metrical verse).
5. That is, if I had kept this knowledge secret.

Or looked upon this love with idle sight?
What might you think? No, I went round° to work,   straightaway
And my young mistress thus I did bespeak:°   address
140 "Lord Hamlet is a prince out of thy star.[6]
This must not be." And then I prescripts gave her
That she should lock herself from his resort,°   company
Admit no messengers, receive no tokens.
Which done, she took the fruits of my advice;
145 And he, repellèd—a short tale to make—
Fell into a sadness, then into a fast,
Thence to a watch,° thence into a weakness,   insomnia
Thence to lightness,° and by this declension°   light-headedness / decline
Into the madness wherein now he raves,
And all we° mourn for.   of us
150 KING   Do you think this?
QUEEN   It may be very like.°   likely
POLONIUS   Hath there been such a time—I would fain
    know that—
That I have positively said "'Tis so,"
When it proved otherwise?
KING   Not that I know.
155 POLONIUS   Take this from this, if this be otherwise.
If circumstances lead me, I will find
Where truth is hid, though it were hid indeed
Within the center.[7]
KING   How may we try° it further?   test
POLONIUS   You know sometimes he walks four hours
    together
Here in the lobby.
160 QUEEN   So he does indeed.
POLONIUS   At such a time I'll loose my daughter to him.
[To the KING] Be you and I behind an arras° then.   a hanging tapestry
Mark the encounter. If he love her not,
And be not from his reason fall'n thereon,°   for that reason
165 Let me be no assistant for a state,
But keep a farm and carters.°   cart drivers
KING   We will try it.

        Enter HAMLET [reading a book].

QUEEN   But look where sadly the poor wretch comes
    reading.
POLONIUS   Away, I do beseech you, both away.
I'll board him presently.[8] Oh, give me leave.

        Exeunt KING and QUEEN [with ATTENDANTS].

170 How does my good Lord Hamlet?
HAMLET   Well, God-a-mercy.[9]
POLONIUS   Do you know me, my lord?
HAMLET   Excellent well. You are a fishmonger.°   fish dealer

6. Above your sphere (a reference to the concentric spheres of the Ptolemaic universe).
7. The center of the earth (which, in the Ptolemaic system, is also the center of the

universe).
8. I'll approach him immediately.
9. God have mercy (on you); a courteous
response to a greeting.

POLONIUS   Not I, my lord.

175 HAMLET   Then I would you were so honest a man.

POLONIUS   Honest, my lord?

HAMLET   Ay, sir. To be honest, as this world goes, is to be
one man picked out of ten thousand.

POLONIUS   That's very true, my lord.

180 HAMLET   For if the sun breed maggots in a dead dog, being
a good kissing carrion[1]—Have you a daughter?

POLONIUS   I have, my lord.

HAMLET   Let her not walk i'the sun. Conception[2] is a bless-
ing, but as your daughter may conceive, friend, look to't.°   be careful about that

185 POLONIUS   [Aside] How say you by that? Still harping on my
daughter. Yet he knew me not at first; 'a° said I was a fish   he
monger. 'A is far gone. And truly in my youth I suffered
much extremity for love, very near this. I'll speak to him
again.—What do you read, my lord?

190 HAMLET   Words, words, words.

POLONIUS   What is the matter,[3] my lord?

HAMLET   Between who?

POLONIUS   I mean the matter that you read, my lord.

HAMLET   Slanders, sir; for the satirical rogue says here
195 that old men have gray beards, that their faces are wrin-
kled, their eyes purging° thick amber° and plum-tree   discharging / resin
gum, and that they have a plentiful lack of wit, together
with most weak hams.° All which, sir, though I most   thighs
powerfully and potently believe, yet I hold it not hon-
200 esty° to have it thus set down; for yourself, sir, shall grow   proper, honorable
old as I am, if, like a crab, you could go backward.

POLONIUS   [Aside] Though this be madness, yet there is
method in't.—Will you walk out of the air,[4] my lord?

HAMLET   Into my grave.

205 POLONIUS   Indeed, that's out of the air. [Aside] How
pregnant° sometimes his replies are—a happiness° that   full of meaning / An aptness
often madness hits on, which reason and sanity could not
so prosperously° be delivered of. I will leave him and my   successfully
daughter.—My lord, I will take my leave of you.

210 HAMLET   You cannot take from me anything that I will not
more willingly part withal°—except my life, except my   with
life, except my life.

POLONIUS   Fare you well, my lord.

HAMLET   These tedious old fools.

        Enter GUILDENSTERN and ROSENCRANTZ.

215 POLONIUS   You go to seek the Lord Hamlet. There he is.

ROSENCRANTZ   [To POLONIUS]   God save you, sir.

                    [Exit POLONIUS.]

1. Flesh good enough for the sun to "kiss."
"Carrion" most often refers to a dead carcass,
but it can also refer contemptuously to living
flesh, with a sexual connotation.
2. The power to form ideas; pregnancy. Let . . .
sun: have her avoid public spaces; keep her

away from me (with a pun on "sun" / "son," and
the use of the sun as an emblem of royalty).
3. Subject (but Hamlet takes it as a conflict
between two parties).
4. Fresh air was thought harmful to the sick.

GUILDENSTERN   My honored lord.

ROSENCRANTZ   My most dear lord.

HAMLET   My excellent good friends! How dost thou, Guil-
220   denstern? Ah, Rosencrantz. Good lads, how do you both?

ROSENCRANTZ   As the indifferent children° of the earth.   *ordinary men*

GUILDENSTERN   Happy° in that we are not overhappy. On   *Fortunate*
    Fortune's cap we are not the very button.°   *top*

HAMLET   Nor the soles of her shoe?

225   ROSENCRANTZ   Neither, my lord.

HAMLET   Then you live about her waist, or in the middle of
    her favors?

GUILDENSTERN   Faith, her privates[5] we.

HAMLET   In the secret parts of Fortune? Oh, most true, she
230   is a strumpet.° What news?   *whore*

ROSENCRANTZ   None, my lord, but the world's grown honest.

HAMLET   Then is doomsday near. But your news is not
    true. But in the beaten way[6] of friendship, what make
    you at° Elsinore?   *brings you to*

235   ROSENCRANTZ   To visit you, my lord; no other occasion.

HAMLET   Beggar that I am, I am ever poor in thanks; but I
    thank you, and sure, dear friends, my thanks are too dear
    a halfpenny.[7] Were you not sent for? Is it your own
    inclining? Is it a free° visitation? Come, come, deal justly   *voluntary*
240   with me; come, come. Nay, speak.

GUILDENSTERN   What should we say, my lord?

HAMLET   Anything but to the purpose. You were sent for,
    and there is a kind of confession in your looks, which
    your modesties have[8] not craft enough to color.° I know   *conceal*
245   the good King and Queen have sent for you.

ROSENCRANTZ   To what end, my lord?

HAMLET   That you must teach me. But let me conjure° you,   *implore*
    by the rights of our fellowship, by the consonancy° of our   *concord, friendship*
    youth, by the obligation of our ever-preserved love, and
250   by what more dear a better proposer° can charge you   *speaker*
    withal,° be even° and direct with me whether you were   *besides / honest*
    sent for or no.

ROSENCRANTZ [To GUILDENSTERN] What say you?

HAMLET   Nay, then, I have an eye of° you. If you love me,   *on*
255   hold not off.°   *speak freely*

GUILDENSTERN   My lord, we were sent for.

HAMLET   I will tell you why. So shall my anticipation pre-
    vent your discovery,[9] and your secrecy to the King and
    Queen molt no feather.° I have of late, but wherefore I   *i.e., remain intact*
260   know not, lost all my mirth, forgone all custom of°   *customary*
    exercises, and indeed it goes so heavily with my disposi-
    tion that this goodly frame,° the earth, seems to me a   *structure*

---

5. Private parts; close friends; ordinary subjects (without title or office).
6. Well-worn, familiar way.
7. That is, too expensively priced at a half-

penny (i.e., my gratitude is of little worth).
8. Your personal integrity has.
9. Your having to betray the confidence (of
the king and queen).

sterile promontory,° this most excellent canopy, the air, look   *land jutting out into water*
you, this brave o'erhanging¹ firmament, this majestical roof
265 fretted° with golden fire, why, it appeareth nothing to me   *decorated*
but a foul and pestilent congregation of vapors. What a
piece of work° is a man! How noble in reason, how infinite   *masterpiece*
in faculties,° in form and moving how express² and   *natural aptitude*
admirable, in action how like an angel, in apprehension
270 how like a god! The beauty of the world, the paragon of
animals! And yet to me, what is this quintessence³ of
dust? Man delights not me; nor women neither, though
by your smiling you seem to say so.
ROSENCRANTZ My lord, there was no such stuff in my
275 thoughts.
HAMLET Why did ye laugh then, when I said "man delights
not me"?
ROSENCRANTZ To think, my lord, if you delight not in
man, what Lenten entertainment⁴ the players shall
280 receive from you. We coted them° on the way, and hither   *passed them by*
are they coming to offer you service.
HAMLET He that plays the king shall be welcome. His
Majesty shall have tribute of me, the adventurous knight
shall use his foil and target,⁵ the lover shall not sigh gra-
285 tis,° the humorous man shall end his part in peace,⁶ and   *without payment*
the lady shall say her mind freely—or the blank verse
shall halt for't.⁷ What players are they?
ROSENCRANTZ Even those you were wont to take such
delight in, the tragedians° of the city.   *actors*
290 HAMLET How chances it they travel? Their residence,⁸
both in reputation and profit, was better both ways.
ROSENCRANTZ I think their inhibition⁹ comes by the
means of the late innovation.¹
HAMLET Do they hold the same estimation° they did   *good reputation*
295 when I was in the city? Are they so followed?
ROSENCRANTZ No, indeed, are they not.

1. This splendid overhang; that is, the roof or "heavens" overhanging the Elizabethan stage, decorated with stars or the signs of the zodiac.
2. Well framed, well designed.
3. The most essential part of a substance; literally, the "fifth essence" of which the heavenly bodies were supposedly composed, thought to be actually latent in the four elements (air, water, earth, fire).
4. Meager reception (with an allusion to the prohibition of plays during Lent).
5. Sword and shield.
6. That is, the man who is governed by one of the four humors shall be allowed to play his part without interruption. (The "humorous Man," the "adventurous knight," and the other figures mentioned in this speech are stock characters in Elizabethan plays.)
7. That is, she shall be allowed to speak her

mind (without censoring her words?), or else her blank verse (unrhymed iambic pentameter) will not scan properly.
8. That is, residence in the city, presumably in their permanent theater.
9. Ban on the performance of stage plays (perhaps a reference to a Privy Council order of 1600 limiting performances to two a week, in only two theaters.)
1. If "the late innovation" means "recent political insurrection," then this could refer to a ban on stage plays possibly resulting from the performance of *Richard II* during the earl of Essex's rebellion in 1601 against Elizabeth I. "Innovation" may also refer to the emergence of the very popular company of boy actors that performed at the private Blackfriars theater and provided stiff competition for the adult companies.

HAMLET   It is not very strange; for my uncle is King of Denmark, and those that would make mouths° at him while my   *faces*
father lived give twenty, forty, fifty, a hundred ducats apiece
300   for his picture in little.° 'Sblood,[2] there is something in this   *miniature*
more than natural,° if philosophy° could find it out.   *unnatural / science*
     A flourish.

GUILDENSTERN   There are the players.

HAMLET   Gentlemen, you are welcome to Elsinore. Your
hands, come then. Th'appurtenance° of welcome is   *accessory*
305   fashion and ceremony. Let me comply with you in this
garb,[3] lest my extent° to the players, which I tell you must   *what I show*
show fairly° outwards, should more appear like enter-   *plainly*
tainment° than yours.° You are welcome. But my uncle-   *more welcoming /*
father and aunt-mother are deceived.   *to you*

310   GUILDENSTERN   In what, my dear lord?

HAMLET   I am but mad north-north-west;[4] when the wind
is southerly I know a hawk from a handsaw.[5]
     Enter POLONIUS.

POLONIUS   Well be with you, gentlemen.

HAMLET   Hark you, Guildenstern, and you too, at each ear
315   a hearer: that great baby you see there is not yet out of
his swaddling clouts.

ROSENCRANTZ   Haply° he is the second time come to them,   *Perhaps*
for they say an old man is twice° a child.   *for the second time*

HAMLET   I will prophesy he comes to tell me of the play-
320   ers; mark it. [*Loudly*] You say right, sir; o' Monday
morning, 'twas then indeed.

POLONIUS   My lord, I have news to tell you.

HAMLET   My lord, I have news to tell you. When Roscius[6]
was an actor in Rome—

325   POLONIUS   The actors are come hither, my lord.

HAMLET   Buzz, buzz.

POLONIUS   Upon my honor—

HAMLET   Then came each actor on his ass.

POLONIUS   The best actors in the world, either for tragedy,
330   comedy, history, pastoral, pastoral-comical, historical-
pastoral, scene individable, or poem unlimited.[7] Seneca
cannot be too heavy nor Plautus too light.[8] For the law of
writ and the liberty,[9] these are the only men.

---

2. By God's blood (a common oath).
3. Use courteous action with you in the
appropriate fashion (by shaking hands).
4. That is, I am mad only when the wind
blows from the north-northwest; or, I am
only a little bit mad (because the north-
northwesterly direction on a compass is only
a little bit removed from true north).
5. That is, one tool from another (a "hawk" is
a pickaxe in addition to being a bird of prey).
6. Quintus Roscius Gallus (d. ca. 62 B.C.E.), a

famous Roman actor.
7. That is, scenes and plays that observe the
unities of time, place, and action (individable) and those that ignore them (unlimited).
8. Lucius Annaeus Seneca (ca. 4 B.C.E.–65
C.E.), Roman writer of tragedy and philosophy; Titus Macchius Plautus (ca. 254–184
B.C.E.), Roman writer of comedies.
9. For plays that are written according to the
rules and those that are not.

HAMLET   O Jephthah, judge of Israel,[1] what a treasure hadst
335   thou!
POLONIUS   What a treasure had he, my lord?
HAMLET   Why,

> "One fair daughter, and no more,
>   The which he lovèd passing° well."   *surpassing*

340 POLONIUS   [*Aside*] Still on my daughter.
HAMLET   Am I not i'the right, old Jephthah?
POLONIUS   If you call me Jephthah, my lord, I have a
   daughter that I love passing well.
HAMLET   Nay, that follows not.
345 POLONIUS   What follows, then, my lord?
HAMLET   Why,

> "As by lot,° God wot"°   *chance / knows*

and then, you know,

> "It came to pass, as most like° it was"—   *likely*

350 the first row° of the pious chanson° will show you more, for   *stanza / song*
   look where my abridgment[2] comes.

   Enter the PLAYERS.

You are welcome, masters, welcome all.—I am glad to
see thee well. Welcome, good friends.—Oh, old friend!
Why, thy face is valanced[3] since I saw thee last. Com'st
355 thou to beard° me in Denmark?—What, my young lady   *oppose (with pun)*
and mistress![4] By'r lady, your ladyship is nearer to heaven
than when I saw you last by the altitude of a chopine.°   *i.e., a thick cork sole*
Pray God, your voice, like a piece of uncurrent gold, be
not cracked within the ring.[5]—Masters, you are all wel-
360 come. We'll e'en to't° like French falconers, fly at any-   *go at it*
thing we see.[6] We'll have a speech straight.° Come, give   *immediately*
us a taste of your quality.° Come, a passionate speech.   *abilities*
FIRST PLAYER   What speech, my good lord?
HAMLET   I heard thee speak me a speech once, but it was
365 never acted, or if it was, not above once, for the play, I
remember, pleased not the million; 'twas caviar to the
general.° But it was—as I received it, and others, whose   *common people*
judgments in such matters cried in the top of° mine—an   *superseded*
excellent play, well digested° in the scenes, set down   *shaped*
370 with as much modesty° as cunning. I remember one said   *restraint*
there were no sallets[7] in the lines to make the matter
savory, nor no matter in the phrase that might indict the

---

1. Title of a popular ballad (quoted by Hamlet
in later lines). Jephthah vowed that if he
defeated the Ammonites, he would sacrifice
the first living thing that met him on his return
home—which was his daughter (Judges
11.30–40).
2. Those who interrupt me; also, entertainments.
3. Fringed (with facial hair).
4. The boy who played female characters.

5. That is, your voice is still suitable for acting female roles. Coins that were clipped
(cracked) so deeply around the edges (to
obtain small amounts of metal) that the circle
around the monarch's head was broken were
"uncurrent" (no longer legal tender).
6. That is, undertake anything, no matter
how difficult and without much forethought.
7. Literally, salads, something mixed or
savory; that is, spicy or vulgar words.

author of affection, but called it an honest method, as
wholesome as sweet, and by very much more handsome
375 than fine.[8] One speech in't I chiefly loved: 'twas
Aeneas's talk to Dido and thereabout of it, especially
when he speaks of Priam's slaughter.[9] If it live in your
memory, begin at this line—let me see, let me see—

"The rugged° Pyrrhus, like th'Hyrcanian beast"[1]—   *savage*

380 'Tis not so. It begins with Pyrrhus—

"The rugged Pyrrhus, he whose sable° arms,   *black*
Black as his purpose, did the night resemble
When he lay couchèd° in th'ominous horse,[2]   *hidden*
Hath now this dread and black complexion° smeared   *appearance*
385 With heraldry° more dismal. Head to foot   *heraldic colors*
Now is he total gules,° horridly tricked°   *red / sketched*
With blood of fathers, mothers, daughters, sons,
Baked and impasted with° the parching° streets   *encrusted by / blazing*
That lend a tyrannous and a damnèd light
390 To their lord's murder. Roasted in wrath and fire,
And thus o'ersized[3] with coagulate gore,
With eyes like carbuncles,[4] the hellish Pyrrhus
Old grandsire Priam seeks."
So, proceed you.

395 POLONIUS 'Fore God, my lord, well spoken, with good
accent and good discretion.

FIRST PLAYER   "Anon° he finds him,   *Soon*
Striking too short at Greeks. His antique sword,
Rebellious to his arm, lies where it falls,
Repugnant° to command. Unequal matched,   *Resistant*
400 Pyrrhus at Priam drives, in rage strikes wide.
But with the whiff and wind of his fell° sword   *fierce; deadly*
Th'unnervèd° father falls. Then senseless Ilium,[5]   *unmanned*
Seeming to feel this blow, with flaming top
Stoops to his° base, and with a hideous crash   *its*
405 Takes prisoner Pyrrhus' ear. For lo, his sword,
Which was declining° on the milky° head   *descending / white*
Of reverend Priam, seemed i'th'air to stick;
So as a painted tyrant[6] Pyrrhus stood,
And, like a neutral to his will and matter,[7]
410 Did nothing.
But as we often see against° some storm   *before*

8. More graceful than ostentatious.
9. In book 2 of Virgil's *Aeneid* (19 B.C.E.), the
Trojan Aeneas tells Dido, queen of Carthage,
stories of the fall of Troy, including the death
of its king, Priam.
1. The tiger (the region of Hyrcania in the Cau-
casus was associated in the *Aeneid* with tigers).
Pyrrhus: the son of the Greek warrior Achilles,
who came to Troy to avenge his father's death.
2. The wooden horse within which Greek sol-

diers hid to gain entry into Troy.
3. Covered with size, a glutinous substance
used to prepare a porous surface for painting.
4. Red jewels believed to shine in the dark.
5. The citadel of Troy.
6. That is, as a tyrant in a painting, unable to
move.
7. As one indifferent to his intention and
circumstance.

A silence in the heavens, the rack° stand still,   *mass of clouds*
The bold winds speechless, and the orb° below   *sphere (earth)*
As hush as death, anon the dreadful thunder
415 Doth rend the region,° so, after Pyrrhus' pause,   *sky*
A rousèd vengeance sets him new a-work,
And never did the Cyclops'[8] hammers fall
On Mars's armor, forged for proof eterne,[9]
With less remorse° than Pyrrhus' bleeding sword   *pity*
420 Now falls on Priam.
Out, out, thou strumpet, Fortune! All you gods
In general synod,° take away her power!   *assembly*
Break all the spokes and fellies from her wheel,[1]
And bowl the round nave° down the hill of heaven,[2]   *hub*
425 As low as to the fiends!"
POLONIUS   This is too long.
HAMLET   It shall to the barber's with your beard.—Prithee,
say on. He's for a jig[3] or a tale of bawdry, or he sleeps.
Say on; come to Hecuba.[4]
430 FIRST PLAYER   "But who—ah woe!—had seen the moblèd°   *muffled*
queen"—
HAMLET   "The moblèd queen"?
POLONIUS   That's good.
FIRST PLAYER   "Run barefoot up and down, threat'ning the
435   flames
With bisson rheum,° a clout° upon that head   *blinding tears / cloth*
Where late the diadem° stood, and for a robe,   *crown*
About her lank and all o'erteemèd[5] loins,
A blanket, in the alarm of fear caught up—
440 Who this had seen, with tongue in venom steeped,
'Gainst Fortune's state° would treason have pronounced.   *rule*
But if the gods themselves did see her then,
When she saw Pyrrhus make malicious sport
In mincing with his sword her husband's limbs,
445 The instant burst of clamor that she made,
Unless things mortal move them not at all,
Would have made milch° the burning eyes of heaven,   *moist*
And passion° in the gods."   *strong emotion*
POLONIUS   Look whe'er° he has not turned his color and   *whether*
450 has tears in's eyes.—Prithee, no more.
HAMLET   'Tis well. I'll have thee speak out the rest of this
soon.—Good my lord, will you see the players well
bestowed?° Do you hear, let them be well used° for they   *lodged / treated*
are the abstract° and brief chronicles of the time.   *summary account*

8. In classical mythology, one-eyed giants who forged weapons for the gods.
9. To be eternally impenetrable. *Mars his:* Mars's (the Roman god of war).
1. The goddess Fortune is often pictured with a wheel whose turning controls human fate. *Fellies:* segments of the wheel's rim.
2. Perhaps Mount Olympus, by tradition the home of the classical gods.
3. A comic song and dance (usually performed at the end of a play).
4. The wife of Priam, queen of Troy.
5. Worn out with bearing children (more than a dozen, according to traditional accounts).

455   After your death you were better have a bad epitaph
        than their ill report while you live.
    POLONIUS My lord, I will use them according to their
        desert.
    HAMLET God's bodikins,[6] man, much better. Use every
460   man after° his desert, and who shall scape whipping?   *according to*
        Use them after your own honor and dignity; the less they
        deserve, the more merit is in your bounty. Take them in.
    POLONIUS Come, sirs.
    HAMLET Follow him, friends. We'll hear a play tomorrow.
        [*As they start to leave,* HAMLET *speaks aside to the* FIRST
        PLAYER.]
465   Dost thou hear me, old friend? Can you play *The Murder*
        of Gonzago?
    FIRST PLAYER Ay, my lord.
    HAMLET We'll ha't° tomorrow night. You could, for need,°   *have it / if necessary*
        study a speech of some dozen lines, or sixteen lines,
470   which I would set down and insert in't, could you not?
    FIRST PLAYER Ay, my lord.
    HAMLET Very well. Follow that lord, and look you mock
        him not.
                          Exeunt POLONIUS *and* PLAYERS.
    My good friends, I'll leave you till night. You are wel-
475   come to Elsinore.
    ROSENCRANTZ Good my lord.
                Exeunt [ROSENCRANTZ *and* GUILDENSTERN].
    HAMLET Ay, so, good-bye to you.—Now I am alone.
        Oh, what a rogue and peasant slave am I!
        Is it not monstrous that this player here,
480   But° in a fiction, in a dream of passion,   *Merely*
        Could force his soul so to his own conceit[7]
        That from her° working all the visage wanned,°   *(his soul's) / grew pale*
        Tears in his eyes, distraction in his aspect,
        A broken voice, and his whole function° suiting   *all his gestures*
485   With forms to his conceit?° And all for nothing.   *imagination*
        For Hecuba.
        What's Hecuba to him, or he to her,
        That he should weep for her? What would he do,
        Had he the motive and the cue for passion
490   That I have? He would drown the stage with tears
        And cleave the general ear[8] with horrid speech,
        Make mad the guilty and appall the free,°   *innocent*
        Confound the ignorant, and amaze,° indeed,   *perplex*
        The very faculties of eyes and ears. Yet I,
495   A dull and muddy-mettled° rascal, peak°   *dull-spirited / mope*
        Like John-a-dreams,[9] unpregnant of° my cause,   *not quickened by*

---

6. By God's little body (a mild oath).   8. The ears of all who heard him.
7. That is, could conform his very being to   9. A proverbial name for a dreamy fellow.
the character he was playing.

And can say nothing—no, not for a king
Upon whose property[1] and most dear life
A damned defeat[2] was made. Am I a coward?
500 Who calls me villain, breaks my pate° across,   *head*
Plucks off my beard and blows it in my face,
Tweaks me by the nose, gives me the lie i'the throat
As deep as to the lungs?[3] Who does me this,
Ha? 'Swounds,° I should take it; for it cannot be   *By God's wounds (an oath)*
505 But I am pigeon-livered, and lack gall[4]
To make oppression bitter, or ere this
I should ha'fatted all the region kites[5]
With this slave's offal. Bloody, bawdy villain!
Remorseless, treacherous, lecherous, kindless° villain!   *unnatural*
510 Why, what an ass am I. This is most brave,°   *splendid*
That I, the son of a dear father murdered,
Prompted to my revenge by heaven and hell,
Must like a whore unpack my heart with words
And fall a-cursing like a very drab,°   *whore*
515 A scullion.° Fie upon't, foh!   *kitchen servant*
About,[6] my brains! Hum, I have heard
That guilty creatures sitting at a play
Have by the very cunning° of the scene   *artfulness*
Been struck so to the soul that presently°   *instantly*
520 They have proclaimed their malefactions;°   *crimes*
For murder, though it have no tongue, will speak
With most miraculous organ. I'll have these players
Play something like the murder of my father
Before mine uncle. I'll observe his looks;
525 I'll tent° him to the quick. If 'a° do blench,   *probe / he*
I know my course. The spirit that I have seen
May be the devil, and the devil hath power
T'assume a pleasing shape; yea, and perhaps
Out of my weakness and my melancholy,
530 As he is very potent with such spirits,[7]
Abuses° me to damn me. I'll have grounds   *Tricks*
More relative° than this. The play's the thing   *pertinent*
Wherein I'll catch the conscience of the King.   *Exit.*

3.1

Enter KING, QUEEN, POLONIUS, OPHELIA, ROSENCRANTZ,
GUILDENSTERN, LORDS.

KING   And can you, by no drift of conference,[8]
Get from him why he puts on this confusion,

1. Crown and queen; also, Claudius's essential character qualities.
2. A destructive crime worthy of damnation.
3. Calls me an egregious liar.
4. Pigeons or doves were thought to be mild because they did not secrete gall (believed to cause anger).

5. All the kites (birds of prey) in the air.
6. Get going; turn about.
7. It was thought that those given to melancholy and despair were more easily manipulated by the devil.
3.1 Location: The castle.
8. By no carefully directed conversation.

Grating so harshly all his days of quiet
With turbulent and dangerous lunacy?

5 ROSENCRANTZ   He does confess he feels himself distracted,
But from what cause 'a° will by no means speak.   *he*

GUILDENSTERN   Nor do we find him forward° to be   *willing*
    sounded,°   *questioned*
But, with a crafty madness, keeps aloof
When we would bring him on to some confession

10 Of his true state.

QUEEN   Did he receive you well?

ROSENCRANTZ   Most like a gentleman.

GUILDENSTERN   But with much forcing of his disposition.°   *mood*

ROSENCRANTZ   Niggard of question,⁹ but of° our demands   *to*
Most free in his reply.

15 QUEEN   Did you assay° him to any pastime?   *try to win*

ROSENCRANTZ   Madam, it so fell out that certain players
We o'erraught° on the way. Of these we told him,   *overtook*
And there did seem in him a kind of joy
To hear of it. They are here about the court,

20 And, as I think, they have already order
This night to play before him.

POLONIUS   'Tis most true.
And he beseeched me to entreat Your Majesties
To hear and see the matter.

KING   With all my heart, and it doth much content me
25 To hear him so inclined.
Good gentlemen, give him a further edge,°   *encouragement*
And drive his purpose into these delights.

ROSENCRANTZ   We shall, my lord.

             Exeunt ROSENCRANTZ *and* GUILDENSTERN [*and* LORDS].

KING   Sweet Gertrude, leave us two,
30 For we have closely° sent for Hamlet hither,   *privately*
That he, as 'twere by accident, may here
Affront° Ophelia. Her father and myself,   *Meet*
We'll so bestow ourselves that, seeing, unseen,
We may of their encounter frankly judge,
35 And gather by him, as he is behaved,
If't be th'affliction of his love or no
That thus he suffers for.

QUEEN   I shall obey you.
And for your part, Ophelia, I do wish
That your good beauties be the happy cause
40 Of Hamlet's wildness. So shall I hope your virtues
Will bring him to his wonted° way again,   *usual*
To both your honors.

OPHELIA   Madam, I wish it may.

                                          [*Exit* QUEEN.]

POLONIUS   Ophelia, walk you here.—Gracious,° so please   *Your Grace*
    you,

9. Sparing of conversation.

We will bestow ourselves.
　　[*To* OPHELIA, *giving a book*] Read on this book,
45　That show of such an exercise[1] may color
　　Your loneliness.[2] We are oft to blame in this—
　　'Tis too much proved°—that with devotion's visage　　*too often made plain*
　　And pious action we do sugar o'er
　　The devil himself.
50　KING [*Aside*]　Oh, 'tis too true!
　　How smart° a lash that speech doth give my conscience.　　*stinging*
　　The harlot's cheek, beautied with plast'ring° art,　　*cosmetic*
　　Is not more ugly to° the thing that helps it[3]　　*compared to*
　　Than is my deed to my most painted word.
55　Oh, heavy burden!
　　POLONIUS　I hear him coming. Withdraw, my lord.
　　　　　　　　　　　　　　　　　　　　[*They withdraw.*]

　　　Enter HAMLET. [OPHELIA *pretends to read.*]

　　HAMLET　To be or not to be—that is the question.
　　Whether 'tis nobler in the mind to suffer
　　The slings and arrows of outrageous fortune,
60　Or to take arms against a sea of troubles
　　And by opposing end them. To die, to sleep—
　　No more—and by a sleep to say we end
　　The heartache and the thousand natural shocks
　　That flesh is heir to. 'Tis a consummation°　　*final ending*
65　Devoutly to be wished. To die, to sleep,
　　To sleep, perchance to dream—ay, there's the rub,[4]
　　For in that sleep of death what dreams may come
　　When we have shuffled° off this mortal coil°　　*cast / turmoil; flesh*
　　Must give us pause. There's the respect°　　*consideration*
70　That makes calamity of so long life.°　　*so long-lived*
　　For who would bear the whips and scorns of time,
　　Th'oppressor's wrong, the proud man's contumely,°　　*insolent abuse*
　　The pangs of despised love, the law's delay,
　　The insolence of office,[5] and the spurns°　　*insults*
75　That patient merit of th'unworthy takes,[6]
　　When he himself might his quietus make[7]
　　With a bare bodkin?° Who would fardels° bear,　　*dagger / burdens*
　　To grunt and sweat under a weary life,
　　But that the dread of something after death,
80　The undiscovered country, from whose bourn°　　*boundary*
　　No traveler returns, puzzles° the will,　　*perplexes*
　　And makes us rather bear those ills we have
　　Than fly to others that we know not of?
　　Thus conscience° does make cowards of us all,　　*moral judgment; knowledge*

---

1. Act of devotion (the book is a prayer book).
2. That is, may give a credible appearance to your solitude.
3. That is, the cosmetic.
4. In the game of bowls, an obstacle that hinders or diverts a bowl from its intended course.

5. That is, of officeholders; bureaucrats.
6. That is, that the worthy have to endure patiently from the unworthy.
7. Gain his discharge—here, death. Paid-off debts were marked *quietus est*, "he is quit" (Latin).

85 And thus the native hue° of resolution   *natural (sanguine) color*
    Is sicklied o'er with the pale cast° of thought,   *tinge, shade*
    And enterprises of great pitch[8] and moment,°   *importance*
    With this regard,° their currents° turn awry,   *respect / courses*
    And lose the name of action.—Soft you now,
90 The fair Ophelia.—Nymph, in thy orisons°   *prayers*
    Be all my sins remembered.

OPHELIA   Good my lord,
    How does your honor for this many a day?

HAMLET   I humbly thank you; well.

OPHELIA   My lord, I have remembrances of yours
95 That I have longèd long to redeliver.
    I pray you, now receive them.

HAMLET   No, not I. I never gave you aught.

OPHELIA   My honored lord, you know right well you did,
    And with them words of so sweet breath composed
100 As made these things more rich. Their perfume lost,
    Take these again, for to the noble mind
    Rich gifts wax° poor when givers prove unkind.   *grow*
    There, my lord. [*She returns gifts.*]

HAMLET   Ha, ha, are you honest?°   *chaste; truthful*
105 OPHELIA   My lord?

HAMLET   Are you fair?

OPHELIA   What means your lordship?

HAMLET   That if you be honest and fair, your honesty
    should admit no discourse to° your beauty.   *conversation with*

110 OPHELIA   Could beauty, my lord, have better commerce°   *dealings*
    than with honesty?

HAMLET   Ay, truly, for the power of beauty will sooner
    transform honesty from what it is to a bawd than the
    force of honesty can translate beauty into his° likeness.   *its*
115 This was sometime a paradox, but now the time° gives it   *the present time*
    proof. I did love you once.

OPHELIA   Indeed, my lord, you made me believe so.

HAMLET   You should not have believed me; for virtue
    cannot so inoculate our old stock but we shall relish of
120 it.[9] I loved you not.

OPHELIA   I was the more deceived.

HAMLET   Get thee to a nunnery.[1] Why wouldst thou be a
    breeder of sinners? I am myself indifferent honest,° but   *reasonably virtuous*
    yet I could accuse me of such things that it were better
125 my mother had not borne me. I am very proud, revenge-
    ful, ambitious, with more offenses at my beck° than I   *command*
    have thoughts to put them in, imagination to give them
    shape, or time to act them in. What should such fellows

---

8. That is, height (the high point of a bird's flight).

9. That is, we will always taste ("relish") our original sin because a graft of virtue, no mat-

ter how strong in us, is unable to overcome it (a metaphor from horticulture).

1. A convent (requiring Ophelia to take a vow of chastity); also, in slang, a brothel.

as I do crawling between earth and heaven? We are
130 arrant° knaves; believe none of us. Go thy ways to a · · · · · · · · · · · · · · · · · · *out-and-out*
nunnery. Where's your father?

OPHELIA   At home, my lord.

HAMLET   Let the doors be shut upon him that he may play
the fool nowhere but in's own house. Farewell.

135 OPHELIA   Oh, help him, you sweet heavens!

HAMLET   If thou dost marry, I'll give thee this plague for
thy dowry: be thou as chaste as ice, as pure as snow,
thou shalt not escape calumny.° Get thee to a nunnery, · · · · · · · · · · · · · · · · · · *slander*
farewell. Or if thou wilt needs marry, marry a fool, for
140 wise men know well enough what monsters² you° make of · · · · · · · · · *you women*
them. To a nunnery, go, and quickly too. Farewell.

OPHELIA   Heavenly powers, restore him!

HAMLET   I have heard of your paintings well enough. God
hath given you one face, and you make yourselves another.
145 You jig and amble, and you lisp,° you nickname God's · · · · · · · · *speak affectedly*
creatures³ and make your wantonness ignorance.⁴ Go
to, I'll no more on't;° it hath made me mad. I say we will · · · · · · · · · · · · · · · · · · *of it*
have no more marriage. Those that are married already—
all but one—shall live. The rest shall keep as they are. To
150 a nunnery, go!   *Exit.*

OPHELIA   Oh, what a noble mind is here o'erthrown!
The courtier's, soldier's, scholar's, eye, tongue, sword,
Th'expectation and rose of the fair state,
The glass° of fashion and the mold of form,⁵ · · · · · · · · · · · · · · · *mirror image*
155 Th'observed of all observers—quite, quite down!
And I, of ladies most deject and wretched,
That sucked the honey of his music vows,
Now see that noble and most sovereign reason
Like sweet bells jangled out of time and harsh,
160 That unmatched form and stature of blown° youth · · · · · · · · · · *in full bloom*
Blasted° with ecstasy.° Oh, woe is me, · · · · · · · · · · · · · · *Blighted / madness*
T'have seen what I have seen, see what I see!

Enter KING *and* POLONIUS.

KING   Love—his affections° do not that way tend; · · · · · · · · · · · · · · *feelings*
Nor what he spake, though it lacked form a little,
165 Was not like madness. There's something in his soul
O'er which his melancholy sits on brood,
And I do doubt° the hatch and the disclose° · · · · · · · · · · · · · *fear / disclosure*
Will be some danger; which for to prevent,
I have in quick determination
170 Thus set it down:° he shall with speed to England · · · · · · · · · · · *determined it*
For the demand of our neglected tribute.⁶
Haply the seas and countries different

---

2. Cuckolds, who were said to grow horns on
their forehead.
3. That is, as if the true names of God's creatures are not good enough.
4. Excuse your illicit and seductive behavior

as ignorance.
5. The pattern of courtly decorum.
6. Between 886 and 1066, considerable parts
of England were under Danish control.

With variable objects[7] shall expel
This something settled° matter in his heart,   *somewhat established*
175 Whereon his brains still° beating puts him thus   *always*
From fashion of himself.[8] What think you on't?

POLONIUS   It shall do well. But yet do I believe
The origin and commencement of his grief
Sprung from neglected° love.—How now, Ophelia?   *unrequited*
180 You need not tell us what Lord Hamlet said;
We heard it all.—My lord, do as you please,
But if you hold it fit, after the play
Let his queen-mother all alone entreat him
To show his grief. Let her be round° with him;   *frank*
185 And I'll ᵛbe placed, so please you, in the ear°   *within earshot*
Of all their conference. If she find him not,[9]
To England send him, or confine him where
Your wisdom best shall think.

KING   It shall be so.
Madness in great ones° must not unwatched go.   *those of high rank*

                         Exeunt.

3.2

Enter HAMLET *and three of the* PLAYERS.

HAMLET   Speak the speech, I pray you, as I pronounced it
to you, trippingly on the tongue. But if you mouth it[1] as
many of our players do, I had as lief° the town crier spoke   *soon*
my lines. Nor do not saw the air too much with your
5 hand, thus, but use all gently, for in the very torrent, tempest, and, as I may say, whirlwind of your passion, you
must acquire and beget a temperance that may give it
smoothness. Oh, it offends me to the soul to hear a robus-
tious° periwig-pated° fellow tear a passion to tatters,   *bombastic / wig-wearing*
10 to very rags, to split the ears of the ground lings,[2] who for
the most part are capable of° nothing but inexplicable   *able to understand*
dumb shows[3] and noise. I would have such a fellow
whipped for o'erdoing Termagant. It out-Herods Herod;[4]
pray you, avoid it.
15 PLAYER   I warrant your honor.[5]
HAMLET   Be not too tame neither, but let your own discretion be your tutor. Suit the action to the word, the word
to the action, with this special observance, that you
o'erstep not the modesty° of nature. For anything so   *moderation*
20 o'erdone is from° the purpose of playing, whose end,   *contrary to*

---

7. With various (new) objects of interest.
8. Puts him out of his normal conduct.
9. If she fails to uncover the truth.
3.2 Location: The castle.
1. If you speak in a pompously oratorical style.
2. Those who paid the least to see plays; they stood in the yard of the theater (in front of the stage).

3. Pantomime episodes that perform the plot of the next scene.
4. The Herod of the New Testament was portrayed in medieval mystery plays as a raging tyrant. *Termagant:* an imaginary deity, presented in mystery plays as a violent and raging character worshipped by Muslims.
5. I promise your lordship (that we will avoid it).

both at the first and now, was and is to hold, as 'twere,
the mirror up to nature, to show virtue her feature, scorn
her own image, and the very age and body of the time his
form and pressure.[6] Now this overdone or come tardy

25 off,° though it makes the unskillful° laugh, cannot but   *done poorly / ignorant*
make the judicious grieve—the censure of which one[7] must
in your allowance o'erweigh a whole theater of others. Oh,
there be players that I have seen play and heard others
praise—and that highly—not to speak it profanely, that,

30 neither having th'accent of Christians, nor the gait of
Christian, pagan, nor man, have so strutted and bel-
lowed that I have thought some of Nature's journeymen[8]
had made men, and not made them well, they imitated
humanity so abominably.

35 PLAYER   I hope we have reformed that indifferently° with us.   *tolerably*
HAMLET   Oh, reform it altogether. And let those that play
your clowns speak no more than is set down for them,
for there be of° them that will themselves laugh to set   *some of*
on° some quantity of barren° spectators to laugh too,   *provoke / witless*

40 though in the meantime some necessary question of
the play be then to be considered. That's villainous, and
shows a most pitiful ambition in the fool that uses it.
Go make you ready.

                                     [Exeunt PLAYERS.]

        Enter POLONIUS, GUILDENSTERN, and ROSENCRANTZ.

How now, my lord, will the King hear this piece of work?
45 POLONIUS   And the Queen too, and that presently.°   *immediately*
HAMLET   Bid the players make haste.

                                     [Exit POLONIUS.]

Will you two help to hasten them?
ROSENCRANTZ   Ay, my lord.

                                  Exeunt they two.

HAMLET   What, ho, Horatio!
       Enter HORATIO.
50 HORATIO   Here, sweet lord, at your service.
HAMLET   Horatio, thou art e'en as just a man
As e'er my conversation coped withal.[9]
HORATIO   Oh, my dear lord—
HAMLET   Nay, do not think I flatter,
For what advancement may I hope from thee,
55 That no revenue hast but thy good spirits
To feed and clothe thee? Why should the poor be
    flattered?
No, let the candied° tongue lick absurd pomp,   *flattering*

---

6. That is, a play shows the imprint of the
truth of the present time in the same way that
a stamp imprints itself on wax.
7. The judgment of even one of them (the

judicious).
8. Hirelings, not yet masters of their trade.
9. As ever I encountered in my dealings
("conversation") with people.

And crook the pregnant° hinges of the knee   *ready (to bend)*
Where thrift may follow fawning.[1] Dost thou hear?

60 Since my dear soul was mistress of her choice[2]
And could of° men distinguish her election,   *between*
Sh'hath sealed° thee for herself, for thou hast been   *set a mark on; claimed*
As one, in suffering all, that° suffers nothing,   *who*
A man that Fortune's buffets and rewards

65 Hast ta'en with equal thanks; and blest are those
Whose blood° and judgment are so well commeddled°   *passions / commingled*
That they are not a pipe for Fortune's finger
To sound what stop[3] she please. Give me that man
That is not passion's slave, and I will wear him

70 In my heart's core, ay, in my heart of heart,
As I do thee.—Something too much of this.—
There is a play tonight before the King.
One scene of it comes near the circumstance
Which I have told thee of my father's death.

75 I prithee, when thou seest that act afoot,
Even with the very comment of thy soul[4]
Observe my uncle. If his occulted° guilt   *hidden*
Do not itself unkennel[5] in one speech,
It is a damnèd ghost that we have seen,

80 And my imaginations are as foul
As Vulcan's stithy.[6] Give him heedful note,
For I mine eyes will rivet to his face,
And after we will both our judgments join
In censure of his seeming.[7]

85 HORATIO   Well, my lord.
If 'a steal aught the whilst this play is playing
And scape detecting, I will pay the theft.[8]

[*Flourish.*] *Enter trumpets and kettledrums,* KING,
QUEEN, POLONIUS, OPHELIA[, ROSENCRANTZ, GUILDEN-
STERN, *and others*].

HAMLET   They are coming to the play. I must be idle.° Get   *unoccupied; incoherent*
you a place.

90 KING   How fares[9] our cousin° Hamlet?   *kinsman*

HAMLET   Excellent, i'faith, of the chameleon's dish: I eat
the air,[1] promise-crammed. You cannot feed capons[2] so.

KING   I have nothing with this answer, Hamlet. These
words are not mine.

---

1. Where profit may result from flattery.
2. Was able to discriminate.
3. Finger hole in a wind instrument.
4. With your most acute critical faculty.
5. That is, reveal (as a fox is driven from its hole).
6. Blacksmith's shop. Vulcan was the Roman god of fire and metalworking.
7. To judge his appearance or reaction.
8. That is, make restitution for the stolen goods.
9. Does. *Fare* also means "food" or "to feed," a meaning on which Hamlet plays in his response.
1. Chameleons were believed to feed on air.
2. Castrated roosters, fattened or "crammed" for eating; also, dull men. *Promise-crammed:* possibly a reference to Claudius's promise that Hamlet will succeed to the throne, perhaps with a play on "air" / "heir."

95 HAMLET No, nor mine now, my lord. [*To* POLONIUS] You
played once i'th'university, you say?

POLONIUS That did I, my lord, and was accounted a good
actor.

HAMLET What did you enact?

100 POLONIUS I did enact Julius Caesar. I was killed i'the
Capitol; Brutus killed me.

HAMLET It was a brute part of him to kill so capital a calf°   *fool*
there.—Be the players ready?

ROSENCRANTZ Ay, my lord. They stay° upon your patience.   *wait*

105 QUEEN Come hither, my dear Hamlet, sit by me.

HAMLET [*Approaching* OPHELIA] No, good mother,° here's   *stepmother*
metal more attractive.[3]

POLONIUS [*To the* KING] Oho, do you mark that?

HAMLET Lady, shall I lie in your lap?

110 OPHELIA No, my lord.

HAMLET Do you think I meant country matters?[4]

OPHELIA I think nothing, my lord.

HAMLET That's a fair thought to lie between maids' legs.

OPHELIA What is, my lord?

115 HAMLET Nothing.

OPHELIA You are merry, my lord.

HAMLET Who, I?

OPHELIA Ay, my lord.

HAMLET O God, your only jig-maker.[5] What should a man
120 do but be merry? For look you how cheerfully my mother
looks, and my father died within's° two hours.   *within this*

OPHELIA Nay, 'tis twice two months, my lord.

HAMLET So long? Nay then, let the devil wear black, for
I'll have a suit of sables.[6] O heavens, die two months
125 ago, and not forgotten yet? Then there's hope a great
man's memory may outlive his life half a year. But, by'r
Lady, 'a° must build churches then or else shall 'a suffer   *he*
not thinking on,[7] withthe hobby-horse,[8] whose epitaph
is "For O, for O, the hobby-horse is forgot."

> *The trumpets sound. Dumb show follows.*
>
> *Enter a* KING *and a* QUEEN, *the* QUEEN *embracing him
> and he her. He takes her up, and declines his head upon
> her neck. He lies him down upon a bank of flowers. She,
> seeing him asleep, leaves him. Anon comes in another
> man, takes off his crown, kisses it, pours poison in the
> sleeper's ears, and leaves him. The* QUEEN *returns, finds*

3. Metal (also "temperament") with greater magnetic powers.
4. Vulgar doings (with a pun on "cunt").The sexual puns continue with "nothing" (vagina) and "thing" (penis).
5. The performer or creator of a farcical song and dance, frequently performed right after the end of a play. *Only*: peerless, best.
6. A suit trimmed with (black) sable fur (not

an appropriate garment for a mourner).
7. Endure not being thought of.
8. The performer in morris dances and May Day festivities who wore the figure of a horse (also called a hobbyhorse) around his waist. The "epitaph" for the hobbyhorse—which disapproving Puritans sought to ban—is probably a line from a song.

the KING *dead, makes passionate action. The* POISONER *with some three or four come in again, seem to condole with her. The dead body is carried away. The* POISONER *woos the* QUEEN *with gifts; she seems harsh awhile, but in the end accepts love.*

[*Exeunt* PLAYERS.]

130 OPHELIA What means this, my lord?

HAMLET Marry, this is mitching malicho;[9] it means mischief.

OPHELIA Belike this show imports the argument° of the   *plot*
play.

Enter PROLOGUE.

135 HAMLET We shall know by this fellow. The players cannot keep counsel;° they'll tell all.   *a secret*

OPHELIA Will 'a° tell us what this show meant?   *he*

HAMLET Ay, or any show that you will show him. Be not you ashamed to show, he'll not shame to tell you what it means.

140 OPHELIA You are naught,° you are naught. I'll mark the   *indecent*
play.

PROLOGUE For us and for our tragedy,
Here stooping to your clemency,
We beg your hearing patiently.   [*Exit.*]

145 HAMLET Is this a prologue or the posy of a ring?[1]

OPHELIA 'Tis brief, my lord.

HAMLET As woman's love.

Enter [*two players as*] KING *and* QUEEN.

PLAYER KING Full thirty times hath Phoebus' cart[2] gone round
Neptune's salt wash and Tellus' orbèd ground,[3]

150 And thirty dozen moons with borrowed° sheen   *reflected*
About the world have times twelve thirties been,
Since love our hearts and Hymen° did our hands   *god of marriage*
Unite commutual in most sacred bands.

PLAYER QUEEN So many journeys may the sun and moon

155 Make us again count o'er ere love be done.
But, woe is me, you are so sick of late,
So far from cheer and from our former state,
That I distrust° you. Yet, though I distrust,   *am worried about*
Discomfort° you, my lord, it nothing must,   *Disturb*

160 For women fear too much, even as they love,
And women's fear and love hold quantity,°   *are of equal proportion*
Either none, in neither aught, or in extremity.[4]
Now what my love is, proof° hath made you know,   *experience*
And as my love is sized,° my fear is so.   *proportioned*

165 Where love is great, the littlest doubts are fear;
Where little fears grow great, great love grows there.

---

9. Sneaking misdeed ("*malicho*" is Spanish).
1. The motto inscribed in a ring.
2. The chariot of the sun god Apollo (i.e., the sun).

3. Tellus is the Roman goddess of the earth ("orbè ground"); Neptune is the Roman god of the sea.
4. Either not existing at all or extremely strong.

PLAYER KING   Faith, I must leave thee, love, and shortly too;
    My operant° powers their functions leave° to do,   *active / cease*
    And thou shalt live in this fair world behind,
170   Honored, beloved; and haply° one as kind   *perhaps*
    For husband shalt thou—
PLAYER QUEEN   Oh, confound° the rest!   *bring to nought*
    Such love must needs be treason in my breast.
    In second husband let me be accurst!
    None wed the second but who killed the first.
175 HAMLET   That's wormwood.[5]
PLAYER QUEEN   The instances° that second marriage move°   *reasons / motivate*
    Are base respects of thrift,° but none of love.   *desires for profit*
    A second time I kill my husband dead
    When second husband kisses me in bed.
180 PLAYER KING   I do believe you think what now you speak,
    But what we do determine oft we break.
    Purpose is but the slave to memory,[6]
    Of violent birth, but poor validity,°   *durability*
    Which now, like fruit unripe, sticks on the tree,
185   But fall unshaken when they mellow be.
    Most necessary 'tis that we forget
    To pay ourselves what to ourselves is debt.[7]
    What to ourselves in passion we propose,
    The passion ending, doth the purpose lose.
190   The violence of either grief or joy
    Their own enactures with themselves destroy.[8]
    Where joy most revels, grief doth most lament,
    Grief joys, joy grieves, on slender accident.[9]
    This world is not for aye, nor 'tis not strange
195   That even our loves should with our fortunes change;
    For 'tis a question left us yet to prove
    Whether love lead fortune or else fortune love.
    The great man down, you mark his favorite flies;
    The poor, advanced,° makes friends of enemies;   *promoted*
200   And hitherto° doth love on fortune tend,°   *thus for / attend*
    For who not needs shall never lack a friend,
    And who in want a hollow friend doth try,°   *test*
    Directly seasons him° his enemy.   *trains him (to be)*
    But, orderly to end where I begun,
205   Our wills and fates do so contrary run
    That our devices still° are overthrown;   *our plans always*
    Our thoughts are ours, their ends° none of our own.   *outcomes*
    So think thou wilt no second husband wed,
    But die thy thoughts when thy first lord is dead.
210 PLAYER QUEEN   Nor earth to me give food, nor heaven light,
    Sport and repose lock from me day and night,

---

5. A proverbially bitter-tasting plant whose oil was used in medicine.
6. That is, (carrying out) an intention depends on memory.
7. That is, it is natural that we forget the promises that we made to ourselves.
8. Extreme grief or joy destroy themselves in their fulfillment.
9. Because of a small, unanticipated event.

To desperation turn my trust and hope,
And anchor's cheer in prison be my scope,[1]
Each opposite[2] that blanks° the face of joy   *makes pale*
215 Meet what I would have well, and it destroy,
Both here and hence pursue me lasting strife,
If, once I be a widow, ever I be a wife.
HAMLET   If she should break it° now—   *her oath*
PLAYER KING   'Tis deeply sworn. Sweet, leave me here awhile.
220 My spirits grow dull, and fain° I would beguile   *gladly*
The tedious day with sleep.
PLAYER QUEEN   Sleep rock thy brain,
And never come mischance between us twain.
                    [*He sleeps.*] *Exit* [PLAYER QUEEN].
HAMLET   Madam, how like you this play?
QUEEN   The lady doth protest too much, methinks.
225 HAMLET   Oh, but she'll keep her word.
KING   Have you heard the argument?° Is there no offense   *plot*
in't?
HAMLET   No, no, they do but jest, poison in jest; no offense
i'the world.
230 KING   What do you call the play?
HAMLET   *The Mousetrap.* Marry, how? Tropically.[3] This play
is the image of a murder done in Vienna. Gonzago is the
Duke's name, his wife, Baptista. You shall see anon. 'Tis a
knavish piece of work, but what of that? Your Majesty
235 and we that have free° souls, it touches° us not. Let   *innocent / concerns*
the galled jade winch, our withers are unwrung.[4]
                    Enter LUCIANUS.
This is one Lucianus, nephew to the King.
OPHELIA   You are as good as a chorus,[5] my lord.
HAMLET   I could interpret between you and your love, if I
240 could see the puppets dallying.[6]
OPHELIA   You are keen,° my lord, you are keen.   *sharp-witted*
HAMLET   It would cost you a groaning to take off mine edge.[7]
OPHELIA   Still better, and worse.[8]
HAMLET   So you mis-take your husbands.[9]—Begin, mur-
245 derer. Leave thy damnable faces[1] and begin. Come, "the
croaking raven doth bellow for revenge."[2]

1. The extent of my happiness. *Anchor's cheer:* a hermit's (anchorite's) fare.
2. Each adverse event.
3. Figuratively (i.e., as a trope).
4. Let the inferior horse ("jade") whose hide is sore from chafing wince, our shoulders (literally, the portion of the horse's back between the shoulder blades) are not rubbed sore ("unwrung").
5. A character (named "Chorus") who describes or interprets the action of the play (see Shakespeare's *Henry V* and *Romeo and Juliet*).
6. Flirting. In a puppet show, the actor who

narrates the dialogue was known as the "interpreter."
7. To satisfy my sexual desire (Hamlet puns on "keen" as "sexually aroused") leading to "groaning" in sexual intercourse, childbirth, or both.
8. More sharp-witted and less well-mannered.
9. So you take husbands under false pretenses ("for better and for worse") and subsequently betray them.
1. Facial expressions.
2. Misquoted from the anonymous *The True Tragedy of Richard III* (ca. 1591).

LUCIANUS   Thoughts black, hands apt, drugs fit, and time
    agreeing,
    Confederate° season, else no creature seeing,   *Conniving*
    Thou mixture rank° of midnight weeds collected,   *foul*
250   With Hecate's ban[3] thrice blasted, thrice infected,
    Thy natural magic and dire property°   *quality*
    On wholesome life usurps immediately.
    [*He pours the poison into the* SLEEPER'S *ear.*]

HAMLET   'A° poisons him i'the garden for his estate.° His   *He / state, kingdom*
    name's Gonzago. The story is extant and written in very
255   choice Italian; you shall see anon how the murderer gets
    the love of Gonzago's wife.
    [CLAUDIUS *stands.*]

OPHELIA   The King rises.

QUEEN   How fares my lord?

POLONIUS   Give o'er° the play.   *Stop*

260 KING   Give me some light. Away!

POLONIUS   Lights, lights, lights!

                  Exeunt all but HAMLET *and* HORATIO.

HAMLET   "Why, let the strucken deer go weep,[4]
    The hart ungallèd° play;   *unwounded*
    For some must watch,° while some must sleep,   *stay awake*
265   Thus runs the world away."[5]
    Would not this, sir, and a forest of feathers[6]—if the rest of
    my fortunes turn Turk[7] with me—with Provincial roses on
    my razed shoes,[8] get me a fellowship in a cry of players?[9]

HORATIO   Half a share.

270 HAMLET   A whole one, ay.
    "For thou dost know, O Damon[1] dear,
    This realm dismantled° was   *stripped*
    Of Jove[2] himself, and now reigns here
    A very, very—pajock."[3]

275 HORATIO   You might have rhymed.

HAMLET   O good Horatio, I'll take the ghost's word for a
    thousand pound. Didst perceive?

HORATIO   Very well, my lord.

HAMLET   Upon the talk of the poisoning?

280 HORATIO   I did very well note him.

HAMLET   Aha! Come, some music, come, the recorders!
    "For if the King like not the comedy,

3. Curse of Hecate, Greek goddess of childbirth and later witchcraft.
4. A deer was thought to weep when mortally
hurt. Lines 262–65 are probably from a lost
ballad.
5. That's the way things go (in the world).
6. Plumes, often worn by Elizabethan actors
onstage. *This:* the play just performed.
7. Become a renegade (literally, convert to
Islam).
8. Shoes with decorative slashes. *Provincial*

roses: rosettes of ribbon (resembling French
roses).
9. Part ownership in a theatrical company
(literally, a pack of players).
1. A figure in Greek mythology, legendary for
his friendship with Pythias.
2. Jupiter, the king of the Roman gods.
3. Peacock (here used as a term of contempt).
"Pajock" appears in the place of the expected
rhyme word, "ass."

Why then, belike, he likes it not, perdy."°   *by God; indeed*
Come, some music!

    Enter ROSENCRANTZ *and* GUILDENSTERN.

285   GUILDENSTERN   Good my lord, vouchsafe me a word with
       you.
    HAMLET   Sir, a whole history.
    GUILDENSTERN   The King, sir—
    HAMLET   Ay, sir, what of him?
290   GUILDENSTERN   Is in his retirement° marvelous distem-   *withdrawal*
       pered.
    HAMLET   With drink, sir?
    GUILDENSTERN   No, my lord, with choler.[4]
    HAMLET   Your wisdom should show itself more richer° to sig-   *of greater value*
295   nify this to the doctor, for for me to put him to his pur-
    gation[5] would perhaps plunge him into more choler.
    GUILDENSTERN   Good my lord, put your discourse into some
       frame,° and start° not so wildly from my affair.   *order / leap away*
    HAMLET   I am tame, sir. Pronounce.
300   GUILDENSTERN   The Queen, your mother, in most great
       affliction of spirit, hath sent me to you.
    HAMLET   You are welcome.
    GUILDENSTERN   Nay, good my lord, this courtesy is not of
       the right breed.° If it shall please you to make me a whole-   *kind*
305   some° answer, I will do your mother's commandment; if   *sane; beneficial*
    not, your pardon° and my return shall be the end of   *permission to depart*
    business.
    HAMLET   Sir, I cannot.
    ROSENCRANTZ   What, my lord?
310   HAMLET   Make you a wholesome answer; my wit's dis-
    eased. But, sir, such answer as I can make, you shall
    command, or rather, as you say, my mother. Therefore
    no more, but to the matter: my mother, you say—
    ROSENCRANTZ   Then thus she says: your behavior hath
315   struck her into amazement and admiration.°   *astonishment*
    HAMLET   Oh, wonderful son that can so stonish° a mother!   *astonish*
    But is there no sequel at the heels of this mother's admi-
    ration? Impart.
    ROSENCRANTZ   She desires to speak with you in her closet°   *private chamber*
320   ere you go to bed.
    HAMLET   We shall obey were she ten times our mother.
    Have you any further trade with us?
    ROSENCRANTZ   My lord, you once did love me.
    HAMLET   And do still, by these pickers and stealers.[6]
325   ROSENCRANTZ   Good my lord, what is your cause of dis-
    temper? You do surely bar the door upon your own lib-
    erty if you deny your griefs to your friend.

4. Anger; also, a bilious disorder requiring the
attentions of a physician (the meaning to
which Hamlet responds).
5. Bloodletting; spiritual purging.

6. Hands. (The catechism in the Book of
Common Prayer contains the promise "to
keep my hands from picking and stealing.")

HAMLET   Sir, I lack advancement.

ROSENCRANTZ   How can that be, when you have the voice
330   of the King himself for your succession in Denmark?

HAMLET   Ay, sir, but "While the grass grows"[7]—the prov-
erb is something° musty.   *somewhat*

> *Enter the PLAYERS with recorders.*

Oh, the recorders. Let me see one. [*He takes a recorder.*]
To withdraw° with you, why do you go about to recover   *speak privately*
335   the wind[8] of me, as if you would drive me into a toil?°   *trap*

GUILDENSTERN   O my lord, if my duty be too bold, my love
is too unmannerly.[9]

HAMLET   I do not well understand that. Will you play
upon this pipe?°   *(the recorder)*

340   GUILDENSTERN   My lord, I cannot.

HAMLET   I pray you.

GUILDENSTERN   Believe me, I cannot.

HAMLET   I do beseech you.

GUILDENSTERN   I know no touch of it, my lord.

345   HAMLET   It is as easy as lying: govern these ventages° with   *finger holes*
your fingers and thumb, give it breath with your mouth,
and it will discourse most eloquent music. Look you,
these are the stops.

GUILDENSTERN   But these cannot I command to any
350   utt'rance of harmony; I have not the skill.

HAMLET   Why, look you now how unworthy a thing you
make of me. You would play upon me, you would seem
to know my stops, you would pluck out the heart of my
mystery. You would sound me[1] from my lowest note to
355   my compass,° and there is much music, excellent voice,   *range (of musical pitch)*
in this little organ,° yet cannot you make it speak.   *musical instrument*
'Sblood, do you think I am easier to be played on than a
pipe? Call me what instrument you will, though you fret[2]
me, you cannot play upon me.

> *Enter POLONIUS.*

360   God bless you, sir.

POLONIUS   My lord, the Queen would speak with you, and
presently.°   *immediately*

HAMLET   Do you see yonder cloud that's almost in shape
of a camel?

365   POLONIUS   By the mass, and 'tis like a camel indeed.

HAMLET   Methinks it is like a weasel.

POLONIUS   It is backed like a weasel.

HAMLET   Or like a whale.

POLONIUS   Very like a whale.

---

7. "While the grass grows, the horse starves."
Hamlet means that he may not live long
enough to gain the crown of Denmark.
8. Move to the leeward side.
9. That is, if I am too presumptuous (with

you) it is only because of my love (for you).
1. Ascertain my depth; play on me.
2. Vex. Also, to furnish with frets, the bars on
the fingerboard of stringed instruments that
regulate the fingering.

370 HAMLET   Then I will come to my mother by and by.° [*Aside*]   *right away*
        They fool me to the top of my bent.[3]—I will come by and
        by. Leave me, friends. I will. Say so. "By and by" is easily
        said.

                     [*Exeunt all but* HAMLET.]

        'Tis now the very witching time of night,
375 When churchyards yawn, and hell itself breathes out
        Contagion to this world. Now could I drink hot blood,
        And do such business as the bitter day
        Would quake to look on. Soft, now to my mother.
        O heart, lose not thy nature!° Let not ever   *natural affection*
380 The soul of Nero[4] enter this firm° bosom.   *resolute*
        Let me be cruel, not unnatural.
        I will speak daggers to her but use none.
        My tongue and soul in this be hypocrites,[5]
        How in my words soever she be shent,[6]
385 To give them seals[7] never my soul consent.   *Exit.*

3.3

     Enter KING, ROSENCRANTZ, *and* GUILDENSTERN.

    KING   I like him not, nor stands it safe with us
        To let his madness range. Therefore prepare you.
        I your commission will forthwith dispatch,°   *prepare*
        And he to England shall along with you.
5 The terms of our estate° may not endure   *My position as king*
        Hazard so near's as doth hourly grow
        Out of his brows.
   GUILDENSTERN   We will ourselves provide.°   *make ready*
        Most holy and religious fear° it is   *care*
        To keep those many many bodies safe
10 That live and feed upon Your Majesty.
   ROSENCRANTZ   The single and peculiar° life is bound   *individual and private*
        With all the strength and armor of the mind
        To keep itself from noyance°, but much more   *harm*
        That spirit upon whose weal° depends and rests   *well-being*
15 The lives of many. The cess° of majesty   *decease*
        Dies not alone, but like a gulf° doth draw   *whirlpool*
        What's near it with it; or it is a massy° wheel[8]   *massive*
        Fixed on the summit of the highest mount,
        To whose huge spokes ten thousand lesser things
20 Are mortised° and adjoined, which,° when it falls,   *attached / so that*
        Each small annexment, petty consequence,
        Attends° the boist'rous ruin. Never alone   *Accompanies*

---

3. They make me play the madman to the limits of my skill.
4. The Roman emperor Nero (r. 54–68 C.E.) murdered his mother, Agrippina.
5. That is, let my words and appearance misleadingly suggest that I mean to do her violence.
6. However my words put her to shame.
7. To validate them with actions.
3.3 Location: The castle.
8. That is, Fortune's wheel (usually depicted with the king at its top).

Did the king sigh, but with a general groan.

25 KING Arm you,° I pray you, to this speedy voyage,   *Prepare yourself*
For we will fetters put about this fear
Which now goes too free-footed.

ROSENCRANTZ   We will haste us.

Exeunt GENTLEMEN [ROSENCRANTZ *and*
GUILDENSTERN].

Enter POLONIUS.

POLONIUS My lord, he's going to his mother's closet.
Behind the arras° I'll convey myself   *wall tapestry*
To hear the process;° I'll warrant she'll tax him home.[9]   *proceedings*
30 And, as you said, and wisely was it said,
'Tis meet° that some more audience than a mother,   *proper*
Since nature makes them partial, should o'erhear
The speech, of vantage.[1] Fare you well, my liege.
I'll call upon you ere you go to bed
And tell you what I know.

35 KING   Thanks, dear my lord.

Exit [POLONIUS].

Oh, my offense is rank, it smells to heaven;
It hath the primal eldest curse[2] upon't,
A brother's murder. Pray can I not,
Though inclination be as sharp as will;[3]
40 My stronger guilt defeats my strong intent,
And like a man to double business bound[4]
I stand in pause where I shall first begin,
And both neglect. What if this cursèd hand
Were thicker than itself with brother's blood?[5]
45 Is there not rain enough in the sweet heavens
To wash it white as snow? Whereto serves mercy
But to confront the visage of offense?[6]
And what's in prayer but this twofold force,
To be forestallèd° ere we come to fall,   *prevented (from sinning)*
50 Or pardoned being down? Then I'll look up.
My fault is past. But, oh, what form of prayer
Can serve my turn? "Forgive me my foul murder"?
That cannot be since I am still possessed
Of those effects for which I did the murder—
55 My crown, mine own ambition, and my queen.
May one be pardoned and retain th'offense?
In the corrupted currents of this world
Offense's gilded° hand may shove by justice,   *bribing*
And oft 'tis seen the wicked prize[7] itself

9. Scold him sternly.
1. To (our) profit or benefit.
2. The curse God put on Cain for committing the first murder, of his brother, Abel (Genesis 4.11–12).
3. Though my desire is as strong as my resolve.

4. That is, committed to divergent goals.
5. What if this hand had on it a layer of blood thicker than the hand itself.
6. That is, what function does mercy have other than to confront sin face-to-face?
7. The fruits of wickedness.

60 Buys out the law; but 'tis not so above.
There is no shuffling,° there the action lies   *evasive conduct*
In his° true nature,[8] and we ourselves compelled,   *its*
Even to the teeth and forehead of° our faults,   *face-to-face with*
To give in evidence.[9] What then? What rests?°   *remains*
65 Try what repentance can. What can it not?
Yet what can it when one cannot repent?
Oh, wretched state, oh, bosom black as death!
Oh, limèd[1] soul that, struggling to be free,
Art more engaged!° Help, angels, make assay.°   *restricted / an attempt*
70 Bow, stubborn knees, and heart with strings of steel,
Be soft as sinews of the new-born babe.
All may be well. [*He kneels.*]

    Enter HAMLET.

HAMLET Now might I do it. But now 'a° is a-praying.   *he*
And now I'll do't. [*He draws his sword.*]
          And so 'a goes to heaven,
75 And so am I revenged. That would be scanned:[2]
A villain kills my father and for that,
I, his sole son, do this same villain send
To heaven.
Why, this is hire and salary, not revenge.
80 'A took my father grossly, full of bread,[3]
With all his crimes broad blown,[4] as flush as May,
And how his audit stands who knows save heaven?
But in our circumstance and course of thought,[5]
'Tis heavy with him. And am I then revenged,
85 To take him in the purging of his soul,
When he is fit and seasoned° for his passage?   *suitably prepared*
No.
Up, sword, and know thou a more horrid hent.°   *occasion*
    [*He sheathes his sword.*]
When he is drunk asleep, or in his rage,
90 Or in th'incestuous pleasure of his bed,
At game a-swearing, or about some act
That has no relish° of salvation in't—   *tinge*
Then trip him that his heels may kick at heaven,
And that his soul may be as damned and black
95 As hell, whereto it goes. My mother stays.°   *awaits*
This physic[6] but prolongs thy sickly days.   *Exit.*
KING My words fly up, my thoughts remain below.
Words without thoughts never to heaven go.   *Exit.*

---

8. The deed (literally, the legal proceeding) is truly revealed.
9. To testify. Unlike in an English court, in heaven one is compelled to give evidence against oneself.
1. Caught as with birdlime, a sticky substance used for snaring birds.
2. That needs to be examined.
3. In full enjoyment of worldly pleasures.

"Behold, this was the iniquity of thy sister Sodom, pride, fullness of bread, and abundance of idleness was in her and in her daughters" (Ezekiel 16.49).
4. With all his sins in full bloom.
5. That is, in the context of our limited understanding here on earth.
6. Medicine (i.e., both Hamlet's delay in revenging and Claudius's prayer).

3.4

Enter [QUEEN] GERTRUDE *and* POLONIUS.

POLONIUS 'A° will come straight.° Look you lay home to   *He / right away*
    him.[7]

    Tell him his pranks have been too broad° to bear with,   *unrestrained; indecent*
    And that Your Grace hath screened and stood between
    Much heat° and him. I'll silence me even here.   *anger*
    Pray you, be round.°   *blunt*

5 QUEEN   I'll warrant you. Fear° me not.   *Doubt*
    Withdraw, I hear him coming.

              [POLONIUS *hides behind the arras.*]

    Enter HAMLET.

HAMLET   Now, Mother, what's the matter?

QUEEN   Hamlet, thou hast thy father° much offended.   *(stepfather, Claudius)*

HAMLET   Mother, you have my father° much offended.   *(old Hamlet)*

10 QUEEN   Come, come, you answer with an idle° tongue.   *foolish*

HAMLET   Go, go, you question with a wicked tongue.

QUEEN   Why, how now,° Hamlet?   *what's this*

HAMLET   What's the matter now?

QUEEN   Have you forgot me?[8]

HAMLET   No, by the rood,° not so.   *cross (of Christ)*
    You are the Queen, your husband's brother's wife,
15   And, would it were not so, you are my mother.

QUEEN   Nay, then, I'll set those to you that can speak.[9]

HAMLET   Come, come, and sit you down; you shall not
    budge.
    You go not till I set you up a glass°   *mirror*
    Where you may see the inmost part of you.

20 QUEEN   What wilt thou do? Thou wilt not murder me?
    Help, ho!

POLONIUS [*Behind the arras*]   What ho! Help!

HAMLET [*Drawing*]   How now, a rat?

    [*He thrusts his rapier through the arras.*]

                  Dead for a ducat, dead![1]

POLONIUS   Oh, I am slain!   [*He falls and dies.*]

25 QUEEN   O me, what hast thou done?

HAMLET   Nay, I know not. Is it the King?

QUEEN   Oh, what a rash and bloody deed is this!

HAMLET   A bloody deed—almost as bad, good Mother,°   *stepmother*
    As kill a king and marry with his brother.

30 QUEEN   As kill a king!

HAMLET   Ay, lady, it was my word.

    [*He discovers* POLONIUS.]

    Thou wretched, rash, intruding fool, farewell.

3.4 Location: The Queen's private chamber.
7. Be sure you admonish him ("lay" means "thrust").
8. Have you forgotten to whom you are speaking?

9. That is, who can speak to someone as ill-mannered as you.
1. I'll wager a ducat he is dead; or, I'll kill him for a ducat.

I took thee for thy better;° take thy fortune.   *(i.e., Claudius)*
Thou find'st to be too busy° is some danger.   *prying*
35 —Leave wringing of your hands. Peace, sit you down,
And let me wring your heart, for so I shall,
If it be made of penetrable stuff,
If damnèd custom° have not brazed[2] it so   *habitual sinfulness*
That it be proof and bulwark against sense.[3]
40 QUEEN What have I done, that thou dar'st wag thy tongue
In noise so rude against me?
HAMLET   Such an act
That blurs the grace and blush of modesty,
Calls virtue hypocrite, takes off the rose[4]
From the fair forehead of an innocent love
45 And sets a blister there,[5] makes marriage vows
As false as dicers' oaths. Oh, such a deed
As from the body of contraction° plucks   *the marriage contract*
The very soul, and sweet religion makes
A rhapsody[6] of words. Heaven's face does glow°   *blush*
50 O'er this solidity and compound mass[7]
With heated visage, as against the doom,[8]
Is thought-sick at the act.
QUEEN   Ay me, what act
That roars so loud, and thunders in the index?[9]
HAMLET *[Showing her two likenesses]*
Look here upon this picture, and on this,
55 The counterfeit presentment° of two brothers. *painted representation*
See what a grace was seated on this brow,
Hyperion's curls, the front° of Jove himself,   *brow*
An eye like Mars to threaten and command,
A station° like the herald Mercury[1]   *stance*
60 New-lighted° on a heaven-kissing hill—   *Newly alighted*
A combination and a form indeed
Where every god did seem to set his seal°   *to authenticate*
To give the world assurance of a man.
This was your husband. Look you now what follows:
65 Here is your husband, like a mildewed ear°   *ear of grain*
Blasting° his wholesome brother. Have you eyes?   *Infecting*
Could you on this fair mountain leave° to feed   *cease*
And batten on this moor?[2] Ha, have you eyes?
You cannot call it love, for at your age
70 The heyday in the blood° is tame, it's humble,   *sexual desire*
And waits upon° the judgment, and what judgment *is subservient to*
Would step from this to this? Sense,[3] sure, you have,

---

2. Brazened, hardened.
3. Armed and fortified against natural feeling.
4. The emblem of ideal love.
5. Prostitutes were branded on the forehead.
6. A disconnected string.
7. The earth itself (a compound of the four elements believed to constitute all matter).
8. As if doomsday were at hand.
9. Table of contents; preface.
1. The winged messenger of the Roman gods.
2. Gorge yourself on this barren wasteland.
3. Perception through the five senses (sight, smell, hearing, taste, and touch).

Else could you not have motion,° but sure that sense   *locomotion*
Is apoplexed,° for madness would not err,   *paralyzed*
75   Nor sense to ecstasy° was ne'er so thrilled   *madness*
But it reserved some quantity of choice
To serve in such a difference.⁴ What devil was't
That thus hath cozened you at hoodman-blind?°   *blindman's buff*
Eyes without feeling, feeling without sight,
80   Ears without hands or eyes, smelling sans all,⁵
Or but a sickly part of one true sense
Could not so mope.° Oh, shame! Where is thy blush?   *be so stupefied*
Rebellious hell,
If thou canst mutine° in a matron's bones,   *mutiny*
85   To flaming youth let virtue be as wax,
And melt in her° own fire. Proclaim no shame   *(youth's)*
When the compulsive ardor gives the charge,°   *orders the attack*
Since frost itself as actively doth burn,
And reason pardons will.⁶

QUEEN   O Hamlet, speak no more.
90   Thou turn'st my very eyes into my soul.
And there I see such black and grainèd° spots   *ingrained*
As will leave there their tinct.°   *color*

HAMLET   Nay, but to live
In the rank sweat of an enseamèd° bed,   *a greasy*
Stewed⁷ in corruption, honeying and making love
Over the nasty sty—

95 QUEEN   Oh, speak to me no more.
These words like daggers enter in my ears;
No more, sweet Hamlet.

HAMLET   A murderer and a villain,
A slave that is not twentieth part the tithe°   *tenth part*
Of your precedent° lord, a vice⁸ of kings,   *former*
100 A cutpurse° of the empire and the rule,   *pickpocket*
That from a shelf the precious diadem stole
And put it in his pocket—

QUEEN   No more!

HAMLET   A king of shreds and patches⁹—

     Enter GHOST.

Save me and hover o'er me with your wings,
105 You heavenly guards!—What would your gracious figure?

QUEEN   Alas, he's mad!

HAMLET   Do you not come your tardy son to chide,
That, lapsed in time and passion,¹ lets go by

---

4. That is, the difference between Hamlet's father and Claudius.
5. Without the other senses.
6. When mature passion ("frost") burns as intensely as does youthful passion, and when reason, which is supposed to counsel the will with restraint, instead acts as a pimp to desire.
7. Boiled (with a pun on *stew*, meaning "brothel").
8. The comic character in a morality play presenting a vice.
9. The multicolored outfit of the vice character.
1. Having allowed time to elapse and my passion (for revenge) to cool.

Th'important° acting of your dread command?   *urgent*
110 Oh, say!

GHOST   Do not forget. This visitation
    Is but to whet thy almost blunted purpose.
    But look, amazement° on thy mother sits.   *bewilderment*
    Oh, step between her and her fighting° soul.   *struggling, conflicted*
115 Conceit° in weakest bodies strongest works.   *Imagination*
    Speak to her, Hamlet.

HAMLET   How is it with you, lady?

QUEEN   Alas, how is't with you,
    That you do bend your eye on vacancy,
    And with th'incorporal° air do hold discourse?   *immaterial*
120 Forth at your eyes your spirits wildly peep,
    And, as the sleeping soldiers in th'alarm,°   *call to arms*
    Your bedded hair, like life in excrements,[2]
    Start up and stand an end. O gentle son,
    Upon the heat and flame of thy distemper°   *disordered mind*
125 Sprinkle cool patience. Whereon do you look?

HAMLET   On him, on him! Look you how pale he glares!
    His form and cause conjoined,[3] preaching to stones
    Would make them capable.° [*To* GHOST] Do not look upon   *receptive*
    me,
    Lest with this piteous action you convert°   *turn aside*
130 My stern effects.° Then what I have to do   *purpose*
    Will want true color—tears perchance for blood.[4]

QUEEN   To whom do you speak this?

HAMLET   Do you see nothing there?

QUEEN   Nothing at all, yet all that is I see.

135 HAMLET   Nor did you nothing hear?

QUEEN   No, nothing but ourselves.

HAMLET   Why, look you there, look how it steals away,
    My father in his habit as he lived.[5]
    Look where he goes even now out at the portal!

                         Exit GHOST.

140 QUEEN   This is the very coinage of your brain.
    This bodiless creation ecstasy
    Is very cunning in.[6]

HAMLET   My pulse as yours doth temperately keep time,
    And makes as healthful music. It is not madness
145 That I have uttered. Bring me to the test,
    And I the matter will reword,° which madness   *repeat verbatim*
    Would gambol° from. Mother, for love of grace,   *leap away*
    Lay not that flattering unction[7] to your soul

2. In outgrowths (such as hair and nails). *Bedded:* laid flat.
3. His appearance joined with his purpose for appearing.
4. That is, then my purpose (i.e., revenge) will lack true passion or motivation; I will instead produce colorless tears and not shed red blood.
5. In his typical attire and appearance as if (or when) he lived.
6. Madness is especially crafty in the creation of hallucinations like this.
7. An ointment that appears to heal (by lessening or removing discomfort) but does not cure the disease.

That not your trespass but my madness speaks.
It will but skin° and film the ulcerous place,   *thinly cover*
Whiles rank corruption, mining° all within,   *undermining*
Infects unseen. Confess yourself to heaven,
Repent what's past, avoid what is to come,
And do not spread the compost on the weeds,
To make them ranker. Forgive me this my virtue,°   *my virtuous entreaty*
For in the fatness° of these pursy° times   *grossness / fat*
Virtue itself of vice must pardon beg,
Yea, curb° and woo for leave° to do him good.   *bow / permission*

QUEEN   O Hamlet, thou hast cleft my heart in twain.

HAMLET   Oh, throw away the worser part of it,
And live the purer with the other half.
Good night. But go not to my uncle's bed.
Assume° a virtue, if you have it not.   *Act out*
That monster, Custom, who all sense doth eat,
Of habits devil, is angel yet in this,
That to the use° of actions fair and good   *habit*
He likewise gives a frock or livery
That aptly° is put on. Refrain tonight,   *fittingly*
And that shall lend a kind of easiness
To the next abstinence, the next more easy;
For use almost can change the stamp of nature,
And either shame the devil, or throw him out
With wondrous potency. Once more, good night.
And when you are desirous to be blessed,
I'll blessing beg of you. [*He gestures to* POLONIUS.]
                For this same lord,°   *(Polonius)*
I do repent; but heaven hath pleased it so
To punish me with this, and this with me,
That I must be their scourge and minister.[8]
I will bestow° him and will answer well[9]   *dispose of*
The death I gave him. So again, good night.
I must be cruel only to be kind.
This bad begins, and worse remains behind.°   *to come*
One word more, good lady.

QUEEN   What shall I do?

HAMLET   Not this by no means that I bid you do:
Let the bloat° king tempt you again to bed,   *bloated*
Pinch wanton on your cheek, call you his mouse,
And let him, for a pair of reechy° kisses   *filthy*
Or paddling° in your neck with his damned fingers,   *playing fondly*
Make you to ravel° all this matter out   *unwind (i.e., reveal)*
That I essentially am not in madness,

8. "Scourge" and "minister" were sometimes used interchangeably to refer to one who punishes sin on God's behalf. "Scourge" is also applied to tyrants, who may still be serving God's justice when they kill, but who appear to contaminate or condemn themselves in the process because they kill cruelly or for personal reasons. God's "minister," by contrast, acts as God's servant and does not become an independent agent of revenge.
9. Assume responsibility for.

But mad in craft.° 'Twere good you let him know,   *by design*
For who that's but° a queen—fair, sober, wise—   *only*
Would from a paddock,° from a bat, a gib,°   *toad / tomcat*
Such dear concerning° hide? Who would do so?   *important matters*
195 No, in despite of sense and secrecy,
    Unpeg the basket on the house's top,
    Let the birds fly, and, like the famous ape,
    To try conclusions,° in the basket creep   *To experiment*
    And break your own neck down.[1]
200 QUEEN   Be thou assured, if words be made of breath,
    And breath of life, I have no life to breathe
    What thou hast said to me.
  HAMLET   I must to England. You know that?
  QUEEN   Alack,
    I had forgot. 'Tis so concluded on.
205 HAMLET   There's letters sealed, and my two schoolfellows,
    Whom I will trust as I will adders° fanged,   *venomous snakes*
    They bear the mandate; they must sweep my way
    And marshal me to knavery.[2] Let it work.
    For 'tis the sport to have the enginer[3]
210 Hoist with his own petard,[4] and't shall go hard
    But I will delve one yard below their mines°   *military tunnels*
    And blow them at the moon. Oh, 'tis most sweet,
    When in one line two crafts directly meet.[5]
    This man shall set me packing.
215 I'll lug the guts into the neighbor room.
    Mother, good night. Indeed, this counselor
    Is now most still, most secret, and most grave,
    Who was in life a most foolish, prating knave.
    —Come, sir, to draw toward an end with you.[6]
220 —Good night, Mother.   *Exit* [HAMLET *dragging* POLONIUS].

4.1

Enter KING *to* QUEEN, *with* ROSENCRANTZ *and*
GUILDENSTERN.

  KING   There's matter in these sighs, these profound heaves,
    You must translate. 'Tis fit we understand them.
    Where is your son?
  QUEEN   Bestow this place on us a little while.
                  [*Exeunt* ROSENCRANTZ *and* GUILDENSTERN.]
5 Ah, mine own lord, what have I seen tonight!
  KING   What, Gertrude? How does Hamlet?
  QUEEN   Mad as the sea and wind when both contend

1. In a story now lost, an ape apparently enters a cage on top of a house that has been opened (unpegged), allowing birds to escape. The ape falls to its death, perhaps because it tries to fly.
2. Prepare the way for me and lead me into a trap.
3. The designer of military devices.
4. Blown up by his own explosive.
5. When two cunning plots come together.
6. To conclude matters between us (with a pun on "draw," pull).
4.1 Location: The castle.

Which is the mightier. In his lawless fit,
Behind the arras hearing something stir,
10 Whips out his rapier, cries "A rat, a rat!"
And in this brainish apprehension° kills   headstrong delusion
The unseen good old man.
   KING   Oh, heavy deed!
It had been so with us,° had we been there.   me (the royal "we")
His liberty is full of threats to all—
15 To you yourself, to us, to everyone.
Alas, how shall this bloody deed be answered?°   explained satisfactorily
It will be laid to° us, whose providence°   blamed on / foresight
Should have kept short,° restrained, and out of haunt[7]   controlled
This mad young man. But so much was our love,
20 We would not understand what was most fit,
But, like the owner° of a foul disease,   carrier
To keep it from divulging,° let it feed   being known
Even on the pith° of life. Where is he gone?   vital substance
   QUEEN To draw apart the body he hath killed,
25 O'er whom his very madness, like some ore°   vein of gold
Among a mineral° of metals base,   mine
Shows itself pure: 'a° weeps for what is done.   he
   KING O Gertrude, come away!
The sun no sooner shall the mountains touch
30 But we will ship him hence, and this vile deed
We must with all our majesty and skill
Both countenance° and excuse.   authorize
        Enter ROSENCRANTZ *and* GUILDENSTERN.
             —Ho, Guildenstern!
Friends both, go join you with some further aid.
Hamlet in madness hath Polonius slain,
35 And from his mother's closet hath he dragged him.
Go seek him out, speak fair, and bring the body
Into the chapel. I pray you, haste in this.
       [*Exeunt* ROSENCRANTZ *and* GUILDENSTERN.]
Come, Gertrude, we'll call up our wisest friends
And let them know both what we mean to do
40 And what's untimely done. So, haply, slander,[8]
Whose whisper o'er the world's diameter°   whole extent
As level as the cannon to his blank[9]
Transports his poisoned shot, may miss our name
And hit the woundless° air. Oh, come away.   invulnerable
45 My soul is full of discord and dismay.
                        Exeunt.

---

7. Away from places frequented by others.
8. The phrase "So, haply, slander" is supplied
by earlier editors because half a verse line is

missing from Q2.
9. As straight as the cannon to its target (i.e.,
point-blank).

4.2

Enter HAMLET.

HAMLET   Safely stowed. But soft, what noise? Who calls
on Hamlet? Oh, here they come.

[*Enter* ROSENCRANTZ, GUILDENSTERN, *and others.*]

ROSENCRANTZ   What have you done, my lord, with the
dead body?

5   HAMLET   Compound° it with dust, whereto 'tis kin.   *United*

ROSENCRANTZ   Tell us where 'tis, that we may take it
thence, and bear it to the chapel.

HAMLET   Do not believe it.

ROSENCRANTZ   Believe what?

10   HAMLET   That I can keep your counsel and not mine own.[1]
Besides, to be demanded of° a sponge! What replication°   *questioned by / reply*
should be made by the son of a king?

ROSENCRANTZ   Take you me for a sponge, my lord?

HAMLET   Ay, sir, that soaks up the King's countenance,° his   *favor*

15   rewards, his authorities. But such officers do the King
best service in the end. He keeps them, like an ape, in the
corner of his jaw, first mouthed to be last swallowed.
When he needs what you have gleaned, it is but squeezing you, and, sponge, you shall be dry again.

20   ROSENCRANTZ   I understand you not, my lord.

HAMLET   I am glad of it. A knavish speech sleeps in a foolish ear.

ROSENCRANTZ   My lord, you must tell us where the body is
and go with us to the King.

25   HAMLET   The body is with the King, but the King is not with
the body.[2] The King is a thing.

GUILDENSTERN   A thing, my lord?

HAMLET   Of nothing. Bring me to him.

Exeunt.

4.3

Enter KING, *and two or three.*

KING   I have sent to seek him and to find the body.
How dangerous is it that this man goes loose!
Yet must not we put the strong law on him;
He's loved of° the distracted° multitude,   *by / fickle*

5   Who like not in their judgment, but their eyes,[3]
And where 'tis so, th'offender's scourge° is weighed,   *punishment*
But never the offense. To bear° all smooth and even,   *manage*
This sudden sending him away must seem

4.2 Location: The castle.
1. That I can follow your advice ("counsel")
and keep my secret ("counsel").
2. The theory of "the king's two bodies" distinguished the monarch's mortal body from

the sacred and eternal body of his royal office.
4.3 Location: The castle.
3. Who judge not with their rational faculties
but by outward appearance.

Deliberate pause.[4] Diseases desperate grown

10 By desperate appliance° are relieved,   *remedy*
Or not at all.

Enter ROSENCRANTZ, [GUILDENSTERN,] *and all the rest.*

How now, what hath befall'n?

ROSENCRANTZ   Where the dead body is bestowed, my lord,
We cannot get from him.

KING   But where is he?

ROSENCRANTZ   Without, my lord, guarded, to know your
pleasure.

KING   Bring him before us.

15 ROSENCRANTZ   Ho! Bring in the lord.

They enter [with HAMLET].

KING   Now, Hamlet, where's Polonius?

HAMLET   At supper.

KING   At supper? Where?

HAMLET   Not where he eats, but where 'a° is eaten. A   *he*
20 certain convocation of politic[5] worms are e'en° at him.   *now*
Your worm is your only emperor for diet.[6] We fat all creatures else to fat us, and we fat ourselves for maggots.
Your fat king and your lean beggar is but variable
service°—two dishes, but to one table. That's the end.   *different courses*

25 KING   Alas, alas!

HAMLET   A man may fish with the worm that hath eat of
a king, and eat of the fish that hath fed of that worm.

KING   What dost thou mean by this?

HAMLET   Nothing but to show you how a king may go a
30 progress[7] through the guts of a beggar.

KING   Where is Polonius?

HAMLET   In heaven. Send thither to see. If your messenger
find him not there, seek him i'th'other place yourself.
But, indeed, if you find him not within this month, you
35 shall nose him as you go up the stairs into the lobby.

KING   [*To some* ATTENDANTS] Go seek him there.

HAMLET   'A will stay till you come.

[*Exeunt* ATTENDANTS.]

KING   Hamlet, this deed, for thine especial safety—
Which we do tender,° as we dearly grieve   *value*
40 For that which thou hast done—must send thee hence.
Therefore prepare thyself.
The bark is ready, and the wind at help,
Th'associates tend,° and everything is bent°   *companions wait / ready*
For England.

45 HAMLET   For England?

4. A carefully considered decision (to interrupt the action).
5. Crafty; skilled in statecraft.
6. Food; perhaps also a pun on the Diet (council) at the German city of Worms in 1521, at

which the reform-minded theologian Martin
Luther, in the presence of Emperor Charles V,
was condemned for religious heresy.
7. On a state journey made by a royal or noble.

KING   Ay, Hamlet.

HAMLET   Good.

KING   So is it, if thou knew'st our purposes.

HAMLET   I see a cherub[8] that sees them. But come, for
50   England. Farewell, dear Mother.

KING   Thy loving father, Hamlet.

HAMLET   My mother. Father and mother is man and wife;
man and wife is one flesh,[9] so, my mother. Come, for
England.

Exit.

55   KING   Follow him at foot;° tempt him with speed aboard.   *at his heels*
Delay it not. I'll have him hence tonight.
Away, for everything is sealed and done
That else leans° on th'affair. Pray you, make haste.   *bears*

[Exeunt all but the KING.]

And, England,[1] if my love thou hold'st at aught°—   *at any value*
60   As my great power thereof may give thee sense,[2]
Since yet thy cicatrice° looks raw and red   *scar*
After the Danish sword, and thy free awe[3]
Pays homage to us—thou mayst not coldly set°   *regard with indifference*
Our sovereign process,° which imports at full,[4]   *royal command*
65   By letters congruing° to that effect,   *appealing earnestly*
The present° death of Hamlet. Do it, England,   *immediate*
For like the hectic° in my blood he rages,   *consumptive fever*
And thou must cure me. Till I know 'tis done,
Howe'er my haps,° my joys will ne'er begin.   *Exit.*   *fortunes*

4.4

Enter FORTINBRAS with his army over the stage.

FORTINBRAS   Go, Captain, from me greet the Danish king.
Tell him that by his license° Fortinbras   *permission*
Craves the conveyance of° a promised march   *escort*
Over his kingdom. You know the rendezvous.
5   If that His Majesty would aught with us,
We shall express our duty° in his eye;°   *respect / presence*
And let him know so.

CAPTAIN   I will do't, my lord.

FORTINBRAS   Go softly on.

[Exeunt all but the CAPTAIN.]

Enter HAMLET, ROSENCRANTZ, [GUILDENSTERN,] etc.

HAMLET   Good sir, whose powers° are these?   *forces*
10   CAPTAIN   They are of Norway, sir.

HAMLET   How purposed, sir, I pray you?

CAPTAIN   Against some part of Poland.

HAMLET   Who commands them, sir?

CAPTAIN   The nephew to old Norway, Fortinbras.

15 HAMLET   Goes it against the main° of Poland, sir,   *the main part*
    Or for some frontier?

CAPTAIN   Truly to speak, and with no addition,°   *exaggeration*
    We go to gain a little patch of ground
    That hath in it no profit but the name.

20   To pay five ducats, five, I would not farm° it.   *lease*
    Nor will it yield to Norway or the Pole
    A ranker rate,° should it be sold in fee.°   *higher return / outright*

HAMLET   Why, then the Polack never will defend it.

CAPTAIN   Yes, it is already garrisoned.

25 HAMLET   Two thousand souls and twenty thousand ducats
    Will not debate the question of this straw.°   *trifling matter*
    This is th'imposthume° of much wealth and peace   *abscess*
    That inward breaks and shows no cause without°   *on the outside*
    Why the man dies. I humbly thank you, sir.

30 CAPTAIN   God be wi'you, sir.   [*Exit.*]

ROSENCRANTZ   Will't please you go, my lord?

HAMLET   I'll be with you straight. Go a little before.

[*Exeunt all but* HAMLET.]

    How all occasions do inform against° me   *accuse*
    And spur my dull revenge! What is a man,
35   If his chief good and market° of his time   *profit*
    Be but to sleep and feed? A beast, no more.
    Sure he that made us with such large discourse,°   *powers of reasoning*
    Looking before and after,[5] gave us not
    That capability° and godlike reason   *intelligence*
40   To fust° in us unused. Now, whether it be   *Became moldy*
    Bestial oblivion,[6] or some craven scruple°   *cowardly qualm*
    Of° thinking too precisely on th'event—   *From*
    A thought which, quartered, hath but one part wisdom
    And ever three parts coward—I do not know
45   Why yet I live to say "This thing's to do,"
    Sith° I have cause, and will, and strength, and means   *Since*
    To do't. Examples gross° as earth exhort me: *obvious*
    Witness this army of such mass and charge,°   *expense*
    Led by a delicate and tender° prince,   *skillful and young*
50   Whose spirit with divine ambition puffed°   *swollen*
    Makes mouths at the invisible event,[7]
    Exposing what is mortal and unsure
    To all that fortune, death, and danger dare,
    Even for an eggshell. Rightly to be great
55   Is not to stir without great argument,
    But greatly to find quarrel in a straw

---

5. With an understanding of the past and the future.
6. Animal-like forgetfulness.

7. Makes disdainful faces at unforeseeable consequences.

When honor's at the stake.[8] How stand I then,
That have a father killed, a mother stained,
Excitements of° my reason and my blood,   *Events that excite*
60 And let all sleep, while to my shame I see
Th'imminent death of twenty thousand men
That for a fantasy and trick° of fame,   *trifle; sham*
Go to their graves like beds, fight for a plot
Whereon the numbers cannot try the cause,[9]
65 Which is not tomb enough and continent°   *container*
To hide the slain? Oh, from this time forth,
My thoughts be bloody or be nothing worth!   *Exit.*

4.5

Enter HORATIO, [QUEEN] GERTRUDE, *and a* GENTLEMAN.

QUEEN   I will not speak with her.
GENTLEMAN   She is importunate,
Indeed distract. Her mood will needs be pitied.
QUEEN   What would she have?
GENTLEMAN   She speaks much of her father, says she hears
5 There's tricks° i'the world, and hems, and beats her heart,°   *dishonesty / breast*
Spurns enviously at straws,[1] speaks things in doubt°   *obscurely*
That carry but half sense. Her speech is nothing,
Yet the unshapèd use° of it doth move   *confused manner*
The hearers to collection;° they yawn° at it,   *inference / gape*
10 And botch° the words up fit to their own thoughts,   *patch*
Which,° as her winks, and nods, and gestures yield them,   *(i.e., the words)*
Indeed would make one think there might be thought,
Though nothing sure, yet much unhappily.
HORATIO   'Twere good she were spoken with, for she may strew
15 Dangerous conjectures in ill-breeding minds.
Let her come in.

                            [*Exit* GENTLEMAN.]

QUEEN   [*Aside*] To my sick soul, as sin's true nature is,
Each toy° seems prologue to some great amiss.°   *trifle / misfortune*
So full of artless jealousy° is guilt,   *crude suspicion*
20 It spills itself in fearing to be spilt.

        Enter OPHELIA.

OPHELIA   Where is the beauteous majesty of Denmark?
QUEEN   How now, Ophelia?
OPHELIA   (*She sings.*) "How should I your true love know
From another one?
25   By his cockle hat and staff

---

8. That is, to be truly great is not to start a war without outstanding reasons, but nobly ("greatly") to find conflict in a trifling matter when honor hangs in the balance.

9. That is, not large enough for the armies to fight on.
4.5 Location: The castle.
1. Takes offense angrily at trifles.

And his sandal shoon."[2]

QUEEN Alas, sweet lady, what imports° this song?   *means*

OPHELIA Say you? Nay, pray you, mark.°   *listen*

"He is dead and gone, lady,   *Song.*

30   He is dead and gone;

At his head a grass green turf,

    At his heels a stone."

Oho!

QUEEN Nay, but Ophelia—

35 OPHELIA Pray you, mark.

[*Sings*] "White his shroud as the mountain snow"—

    Enter KING.

QUEEN Alas, look here, my lord.

OPHELIA "Larded° all with sweet flowers;   *Song.*   *Bedecked*

Which bewept to the ground did not[3] go

40   With true-love showers."°   *tears*

KING How do you, pretty lady?

OPHELIA Well, God 'ild° you. They say the owl was a baker's   *God yield (repay)*
daughter.[4] Lord, we know what we are, but know not
what we may be. God be at your table.

45 KING Conceit° upon her father.   *Morbid thoughts*

OPHELIA Pray, let's have no words of this; but when they
ask you what it means, say you this:

"Tomorrow is Saint Valentine's day,[5]   *Song.*

    All in the morning betime,°   *early*

50 And I a maid at your window,

    To be your Valentine.

Then up he rose and donned his clothes,

    And dupped° the chamber door,   *opened*

Let in the maid, that out a maid°   *a virgin*

55   Never departed more."

KING Pretty Ophelia.

OPHELIA Indeed, without an oath, I'll make an end on't:°   *of it*

[*Sings*] "By Gis° and by Saint Charity,[6]   *Jesus*

    Alack, and fie for shame!

60 Young men will do't° if they come to't;   *i.e., have sex*

    By Cock,[7] they are to blame.

Quoth she, 'Before you tumbled me,

    You promised me to wed.'"

He answers:

---

2. The "sandal shoon" (shoes) and the "cockle hat" were typical attributes of a pilgrim (the cockleshell was attached to the hats of those who had returned from the shrine of St. James in Compostella, Spain).

3. The insertion of "not" interrupts the meter and changes the expected meaning.

4. In an old folktale, a baker's daughter who gave ungenerously when Christ asked for bread was turned into an owl. In Wales, the owl's cry was thought to signify an unmarried girl's loss of virginity.

5. The song hints at the notion that the first girl seen by a man on Valentine's day will be his true love.

6. That is, Holy Charity (not an actual saint).

7. A common corruption of "God" in mild oaths (with an obvious pun on "penis").

65   "'So would I ha' done, by yonder sun,
            An° thou hadst not come to my bed.'"   *If*
      KING   How long hath she been thus?
      OPHELIA   I hope all will be well. We must be patient, but I
      cannot choose but weep to think they would lay him
70   i'the cold ground. My brother shall know of it. And so I
      thank you for your good counsel.—Come, my coach!
      Good night, ladies, good night. Sweet ladies, good night,
      good night.

                                                            [*Exit.*]

      KING   Follow her close; give her good watch, I pray you.

                                                    [*Exit* HORATIO.]

75   Oh, this is the poison of deep grief; it springs
      All from her father's death—and now behold!
      O Gertrude, Gertrude,
      When sorrows come, they come not single spies,°   *scouts*
      But in battalions. First, her father slain;
80   Next, your son gone, and he most violent author
      Of his own just remove; the people muddied,°   *confused*
      Thick and unwholesome in thoughts and whispers
      For good Polonius' death—and we have done but greenly°   *foolishly*
      In hugger-mugger° to inter him; poor Ophelia,   *Secretly*
85   Divided from herself and her fair judgment,
      Without the which we are pictures or mere beasts;
      Last, and as much containing° as all these,   *as pertinent*
      Her brother is in secret come from France,
      Feeds on this wonder, keeps himself in clouds,[8]
90   And wants° not buzzers° to infect his ear   *lacks / rumormongers*
      With pestilent speeches of his father's death,
      Wherein necessity, of matter beggared,°   *lacking facts*
      Will nothing stick our person to arraign
      In ear and ear.[9] O my dear Gertrude, this,
95   Like to a murdering piece,[1] in many places
      Gives me superfluous[2] death.
          A noise within.
      KING   Attend!
      Where is my Switzers?[3] Let them guard the door.
          Enter a MESSENGER.
      What is the matter?
      MESSENGER   Save yourself, my lord!
100   The ocean, overpeering of his list,[4]
      Eats not the flats° with more impiteous° haste   *flatlands / ruthless; unpifying*
      Than young Laertes, in a riotous head,°   *armed force*
      O'erbears your officers. The rabble call him lord,

8. Obscure, hidden; or, perhaps, in clouds of suspicion.
9. That is, will not fail to accuse me in every ear.
1. A cannon that scattered its shot.
2. Superfluous because one death would be enough.
3. Swiss mercenaries (employed as royal guards at a number of European courts).
4. Rising above its shore (boundary).

And, as the world were now but⁵ to begin,
105 Antiquity forgot, custom not known,
The ratifiers and props of every word,⁶
They cry, "Choose we! Laertes shall be king!"
Caps, hands, and tongues applaud it to the clouds,
"Laertes shall be king! Laertes king!" *A noise within.*
110 QUEEN   How cheerfully on the false trail they cry.⁷
Oh, this is counter,⁸ you false Danish dogs!

       Enter LAERTES *with* OTHERS.

KING   The doors are broke.
LAERTES   Where is this king?—Sirs, stand you all without.
ALL   No, let's come in.
115 LAERTES   I pray you, give me leave.
ALL   We will, we will.
LAERTES   I thank you. Keep the door. [OTHERS *retire.*]
                       O thou vile king,
Give me my father!
QUEEN [*Holding him*]   Calmly, good Laertes.
LAERTES   That drop of blood that's calm proclaims me
    bastard,
120 Cries cuckold to my father, brands the harlot
Even here, between the chaste unsmirchèd brows
Of my true mother.
KING   What is the cause, Laertes,
That thy rebellion looks so giant-like?
Let him go, Gertrude; do not fear our° person.   *fear for my*
125 There's such divinity doth hedge° a king,   *protect*
That treason can but peep to what it would,⁹
Acts little of his° will. Tell me, Laertes,   *its*
Why thou art thus incensed. Let him go, Gertrude.
Speak, man.
LAERTES   Where is my father?
KING   Dead.
130 QUEEN   But not by him.
KING   Let him demand his fill.
LAERTES   How came he dead? I'll not be juggled with.°   *deceived*
To hell, allegiance! Vows, to the blackest devil!
Conscience and grace, to the profoundest pit!
I dare damnation. To this point I stand,¹
135 That both the worlds I give to negligence.²
Let come what comes, only I'll be revenged
Most throughly° for my father.   *thoroughly*
KING   Who shall stay° you?   *stop*

---

5. That is, as if the world were only now beginning.
6. The ancient traditions and customs, which ratify the meaning of every word, have been forgotten (by the rabble).
7. That is, as if they were hounds baying after their prey.

8. Following the trail of game in the reverse (here, the wrong) direction.
9. That is, that treason can only glimpse at what it would like to do.
1. This I insist on.
2. That I do not care about the consequences in this world or the ones after death.

LAERTES   My will, not all the world's.
    And for my means, I'll husband them so well,
140 They shall go far with little.
KING   Good Laertes,
    If you desire to know the certainty
    Of your dear father, is't writ in your revenge
    That, swoopstake,[3] you will draw° both friend and foe,   *take from*
    Winner and loser?
LAERTES   None but his enemies.
145 KING Will you know them, then?
LAERTES   To his good friends thus wide I'll ope my arms,
    And like the kind life-rend'ring pelican
    Repast them with my blood.[4]
KING   Why, now you speak
    Like a good child and a true gentleman.
150 That I am guiltless of your father's death,
    And am most sensibly° in grief for it,   *intensely*
    It shall as level° to your judgment 'pear   *plain*
    As day does to your eye. *A noise within.*
       Enter OPHELIA [*singing, meeting* LAERTES' *followers*].
LAERTES   Let her come in.
    How now, what noise is that?
155 O heat, dry up my brains![5] Tears seven times salt,
    Burn out the sense and virtue° of mine eye!   *power*
    By heaven, thy madness shall be paid with weight,
    Till our scale turn the beam.[6] O rose of May,
    Dear maid, kind sister, sweet Ophelia!
160 O heavens, is't possible a young maid's wits
    Should be as mortal as a poor man's life?
OPHELIA   "They bore him barefaced on the bier   *Song.*
        And in his grave rained many a tear"—
    Fare you well, my dove.
165 LAERTES   Hadst thou thy wits, and didst persuade° revenge,   *argue for*
    It could not move thus.
OPHELIA   You must sing "A-down, a-down,"[7] and you "call
    him a-down-a." Oh, how the wheel[8] becomes it! It is the
    false steward that stole his master's daughter.
170 LAERTES   This nothing's more than matter.[9]
OPHELIA   There's rosemary, that's for remembrance; pray you,
    love, remember. And there is pansies, that's for thoughts.[1]

---

3. Indiscriminately (literally, taking all the stakes in a game of chance).
4. The pelican mother was thought to feed ("repast") its young with blood from a wound she pecked in her own breast.
5. According to the humoral theory of physiology, the brain was a cold and moist organ. In this line and the next, Laertes expresses the wish that his rational and sensory abilities perish so that he would not have to bear witness to Ophelia's madness.
6. The image is of the scales of justice, in which

madness will be outweighed by vengeance.
7. A common refrain in popular ballads.
8. Refrain; possibly also a reference to Fortune's wheel.
9. That is, this nonsense means more than coherent speech does.
1. Rosemary was thought to strengthen memory, and it was commonly associated with remembrance at weddings and at funerals. Pansies symbolize love; Ophelia puns on *pensées* (thoughts; French), from which the flower's name derives.

LAERTES A document° in madness, thoughts and remem-   *lesson*
    brance fitted.°   *conferred fittingly*

175 OPHELIA There's fennel for you, and columbines.[2]
    There's rue for you, and here's some for me; we may
    call it "herb of grace" o' Sundays. You may wear your
    rue with a difference.[3] There's a daisy. I would give you
    some violets,[4] but they withered all when my father
180   died. They say 'a° made a good end.   *he*
    [*Sings*] "For bonny sweet Robin is all my joy."

LAERTES Thought and afflictions, passion,° hell itself   *suffering*
    She turns to favor° and to prettiness.   *grace*

OPHELIA "And will 'a not come again?   *Song.*
185   And will 'a not come again?
      No, no, he is dead,
      Go to thy deathbed,
    He never will come again.
    "His beard was as white as snow,
190   Flaxen° was his poll.°   *white / head*
      He is gone, he is gone,
      And we cast away moan.
    God ha' mercy on his soul."
    And of all Christians' souls. God be wi'you.   [*Exit.*]

195 LAERTES Do you see this, O God?

KING Laertes, I must commune with° your grief,   *share in*
    Or you deny me right. Go but apart,
    Make choice of whom° your wisest friends you will,   *whichever of*
    And they shall hear and judge twixt you and me.
200   If by direct or by collateral° hand   *indirect*
    They find us touched,° we will our kingdom give,   *touched with guilt*
    Our crown, our life, and all that we call ours
    To you in satisfaction;° but if not,   *compensation*
    Be you content to lend your patience to us,
205   And we shall jointly labor with your soul
    To give it due content.

LAERTES   Let this be so.
    His means of death, his obscure funeral—
    No trophy,° sword, nor hatchment[5] o'er his bones,   *memorial*
    No noble rite, nor formal ostentation°—   *display, ceremony*
210   Cry to be heard, as 'twere from heaven to earth,
    That I must call't in question.

KING   So you shall.
    And where th'offense is, let the great axe fall.
    I pray you, go with me.

                           Exeunt.

---

2. Fennel signifies flattery; columbine was known for its horned shape and here may signify cuckoldry. Rue (an aromatic herb) suggests regret and repentance.
3. Perhaps Ophelia means that she and the recipient (the King or Queen?) of the imagi-nary rue have different reasons for wearing it.
4. The daisy may signify dissembling or faith-lessness; the violets, faithfulness.
5. A square or lozenge-shaped tablet exhibit-ing the armorial bearings of the deceased.

4.6

Enter HORATIO[, *a* GENTLEMAN,] *and others.*

HORATIO What are they that would speak with me?

GENTLEMAN Seafaring men, sir. They say they have letters for you.

HORATIO Let them come in.

[*Exit* GENTLEMAN.]

5   I do not know from what part of the world I should be
greeted, if not from Lord Hamlet.

Enter SAILORS.

SAILOR God bless you, sir.

HORATIO Let him bless thee too.

SAILOR 'A° shall, sir, an't° please him. There's a letter for you,   *He / if it*
10   sir—it came from th'ambassador that was bound for Eng-
land—if your name be Horatio, as I am let to know it is.

[*He gives a letter.*]

HORATIO [*Reads*] "Horatio, when thou shalt have over-
looked° this, give these fellows some means° to the King;   *read / access*
they have letters for him. Ere we were two days old at
15   sea, a pirate of very warlike appointment° gave us chase.   *equipment*
Finding ourselves too slow of sail, we put on a compelled
valor, and in the grapple I boarded them. On the instant
they got clear of our ship, so I thieves of mercy, but they
knew what they did;[6] I am to do a turn for them. Let the
20   King have the letters I have sent and repair° thou to me   *come*
with as much speed as thou wouldst fly° death. I have   *flee*
words to speak in thine ear will make thee dumb, yet are
they much too light for the bore of the matter.[7] These good
fellows will bring thee where I am. Rosencrantz and Guil-
25   denstern hold their course for England; of them I have
much to tell thee. Farewell.

He that thou knowest
thine, Hamlet."

Come, I will give you way° for these your letters,   *a means of delivery*
30   And do't the speedier that you may direct me
To him from whom you brought them.

Exeunt.

4.7

Enter KING *and* LAERTES.

KING Now must your conscience my acquittance seal,[8]
And you must put me in your heart for friend,

4.6 Location: The castle.
6. That is, the pirates showed mercy to Hamlet
with the expectation of some reward or compensation. *Thieves of mercy:* merciful thieves.
7. A firearms metaphor: the caliber or importance ("bore") of this subject ("the matter")

requires more than the light-gauge shot
("words") Hamlet has at his disposal.
4.7 Location: The castle.
8. That is, your conscience must confirm my
innocence.

Sith° you have heard, and with a knowing ear,   *Since*
That he which hath your noble father slain
Pursued my life.

5 LAERTES   It well appears. But tell me
Why you proceed not against these feats,°   *acts*
So criminal and so capital° in nature,   *punishable by death*
As by your safety, greatness, wisdom, all things else,
You mainly° were stirred up.   *greatly*

10 KING   Oh, for two special reasons,
Which may to you, perhaps, seem much unsinewed,°   *very feeble*
But yet to me they're strong. The Queen his mother
Lives almost by his looks, and for myself—
My virtue or my plague, be it either which—
15 She is so conjunctive° to my life and soul,   *closely joined*
That, as the star moves not but in his sphere,⁹
I could not but by her. The other motive
Why to a public count° I might not go   *accounting*
Is the great love the general gender° bear him,   *common people*
20 Who, dipping all his faults in their affection,
Work like the spring that turneth wood to stone,¹
Convert his gyves° to graces, so that my arrows,   *shackles*
Too slightly timbered° for so loud° a wind,   *light / strong*
Would have reverted to my bow again,
25 But not where I have aimed them.

LAERTES   And so have I a noble father lost,
A sister driven into desp'rate terms,°   *circumstances*
Whose worth, if praises may go back again,²
Stood challenger on mount of all the age
30 For her perfections.³ But my revenge will come.

KING   Break not your sleeps for that. You must not think
That we are made of stuff so flat and dull°   *tame and spiritless*
That we can let our beard be shook with danger⁴
And think it pastime. You shortly shall hear more.
35 I loved your father, and we love ourself,
And that, I hope, will teach you to imagine—

Enter a MESSENGER *with letters.*

MESSENGER   [*Giving letters*] These to Your Majesty, this to
the Queen.

KING   From Hamlet! Who brought them?

MESSENGER   Sailors, my lord, they say. I saw them not:
40 They were given me by Claudio. He received them
Of him that brought them.

KING   Laertes, you shall hear them.
—Leave us.   [*Exit* MESSENGER.]

---

9. According to Ptolemaic astronomy, planets (stars) circled around the earth, each confined to a specific sphere.
1. The spring whose water contains so much lime that it petrifies fallen branches or exposed roots.

2. May refer to the past (i.e., to Ophelia's former virtues).
3. Challenged the world, in the sight of all ("on mount"), to match her virtues.
4. That I will let myself be affronted by someone powerful.

[*Reads*] "High and mighty, you shall know I am set naked° on   *destitute; defenseless*
      your kingdom. Tomorrow shall I beg leave to see your
45   kingly eyes, when I shall, first asking you pardon,°   *permission*
      thereunto recount the occasion of my sudden return."
      What should this mean? Are all the rest come back?
      Or is it some abuse,° and no such thing?   *trickery*
LAERTES   Know you the hand?
KING   'Tis Hamlet's character.° "Naked,"   *handwriting*
50   And in a postscript here, he says "alone."
      Can you devise° me?   *explain to*
LAERTES   I am lost in it, my lord. But let him come.
      It warms the very sickness in my heart
      That I shall live and tell him to his teeth,
      "Thus didst thou."
55 KING   If it be so, Laertes—
      As how should it be so, how otherwise?⁵—
      Will you be ruled by me?
LAERTES   Ay, my lord,
      So you will not o'errule me to a peace.
KING   To thine own peace. If he be now returned,
60   As checking at⁶ his voyage, and that° he means   *if*
      No more to undertake it—I will work him
      To an exploit, now ripe in my device,°   *planning*
      Under the which he shall not choose but fall,
      And for his death no wind of blame shall breathe,
65   But even his mother shall uncharge° the practice°   *not accuse / scheme*
      And call it accident.
LAERTES   My lord, I will be ruled,
      The rather° if you could devise it so   *All the more quickly*
      That I might be the organ.°   *instrument*
KING   It falls right.
      You have been talked of since your travel much,
70   And that in Hamlet's hearing, for a quality
      Wherein they say you shine. Your sum of parts°   *abilities combined*
      Did not together pluck such envy from him
      As did that one, and that, in my regard,
      Of the unworthiest siege.°   *lowest rank*
75 LAERTES   What part is that, my lord?
KING   A very ribbon in the cap of youth,
      Yet needful too, for youth no less becomes°   *is suited by*
      The light and careless livery that it wears
      Than settled age his sables° and his weeds,°   *furred gowns / garments*
80   Importing health and graveness.° Two months since°   *seriousness, sobriety / ago*
      Here was a gentleman of Normandy—
      I have seen myself, and served against, the French,
      And they can well° on horseback, but this gallant   *are skilled*
      Had witchcraft in't; he grew unto his seat,
85   And to such wondrous doing brought his horse,

---

5. That is, how can Hamlet have returned (despite the order for his execution), but how else to explain the letter?

6. Turning away from (as a falcon abandons the prey it was sent to pursue).

As had he been incorpsed and demi-natured[7]
With the brave beast. So far he topped° my thought   surpassed
That I in forgery of shapes and tricks[8]
Come short of what he did.

90 LAERTES   A Norman was't?

KING   A Norman.

LAERTES   Upon my life, Lamord.

KING   The very same.

LAERTES   I know him well. He is the brooch° indeed   ornament
And gem of all the nation.

KING   He made confession° of you,   acknowledgment
95 And gave you such a masterly report
For art and exercise in your defense,
And for your rapier most especial,
That he cried out 'twould be a sight indeed
If one could match you. Th'escrimers° of their nation   fencers
100 He swore, had neither motion, guard, nor eye,
If you opposed them. Sir, this report of his
Did Hamlet so envenom with his envy
That he could nothing do but wish and beg
Your sudden° coming o'er, to play° with you.   prompt / fence
Now, out of this—

105 LAERTES   What out of this, my lord?

KING   Laertes, was your father dear to you?
Or are you like the painting of a sorrow,
A face without a heart?

LAERTES   Why ask you this?

KING   Not that I think you did not love your father,
110 But that I know love is begun by time,°   by circumstances
And that I see in passages of proof°   actual instances
Time qualifies° the spark and fire of it.   tempers
There lives within the very flame of love
A kind of wick or snuff[9] that will abate it,
115 And nothing is at a like° goodness still,°   an identical / always
For goodness, growing to a pleurisy,[1]
Dies in his own too much.[2] That we would do,
We should do when we would; for this "would" changes,
And hath abatements° and delays as many   decreases
120 As there are tongues, are hands, are accidents,°   occurrences
And then this "should" is like a spendthrift sigh,
That hurts by easing.[3] But to the quick° o' th'ulcer   life, core
Hamlet comes back. What would you undertake
To show yourself in deed your father's son
More than in words?

125 LAERTES   To cut his throat i'the church.

---

7. As if he had been made into one body and
had half the nature (like a centaur).
8. That my ability to imagine his maneuvers
and feats of skill.
9. The burned part of the wick (which must be
removed to allow the candle to burn brightly).

1. An excess (the inflammatory lung disease
pleurisy was believed to be caused by an
excess of humors).
2. Of its own overabundance.
3. Each sigh was believed to cost a drop of
blood.

KING No place, indeed, should murder sanctuarize;[4]
Revenge should have no bounds. But good Laertes,
Will you do this, keep close within your chamber.
Hamlet returned shall know you are come home.
130 We'll put on° those shall praise your excellence   *encourage*
And set a double varnish on the fame
The Frenchman gave you, bring you in fine° together,   *conclusion*
And wager o'er your heads. He, being remiss,°   *inattentive*
Most generous,° and free from all contriving,   *noble in nature*
135 Will not peruse the foils, so that with ease,
Or with a little shuffling, you may choose
A sword unbated,° and in a pass of practice[5]   *unblunted*
Requite him for your father.
LAERTES   I will do't.
And for that purpose I'll anoint my sword.
140 I bought an unction° of a mountebank°   *ointment / quack doctor*
So mortal that, but dip a knife in it,
Where it draws blood no cataplasm° so rare,   *poultice*
Collected from all simples° that have virtue°   *herbs / healing powers*
Under the moon,[6] can save the thing from death
145 That is but scratched withal.° I'll touch my point   *with it*
With this contagion, that if I gall° him slightly,   *wound*
It may be death.
KING   Let's further think of this.
Weigh what convenience both of time and means
May fit us to our shape.[7] If this should fail,
150 And that our drift look° through our bad performance,   *purpose become visible*
'Twere better not assayed.° Therefore this project   *attempted*
Should have a back or second° that might hold   *back-up position*
If this did blast in proof.[8] Soft, let me see.
We'll make a solemn wager on your cunnings°—   *skills*
155 I ha't!
When in your motion° you are hot and dry—   *exercise*
As make your bouts more violent to that end—
And that he calls for drink, I'll have prepared him
A chalice for the nonce,° whereon but sipping,   *occasion*
160 If he by chance escape your venomed stuck,°   *thrust*
Our purpose may hold there. [*A noise within*] But stay,
what noise?

Enter QUEEN.

QUEEN One woe doth tread upon another's heel,
So fast they follow. Your sister's drowned, Laertes.
LAERTES Drowned! Oh, where?
165 QUEEN There is a willow[9] grows askant the brook,
That shows his hoary° leaves in the glassy stream;   *gray; white*

---

4. Shield a murderer from punishment. In England, criminals who took refuge in a church were protected from arrest for all crimes except sacrilege and treason.
5. With a treacherous sword thrust.
6. Herbs picked by moonlight were believed to be especially potent.
7. May make us ready for the roles we will assume (in our plan).
8. Should blow up in our faces (like a cannon).
9. The willow is an emblem of forsaken love and of mourning.

Therewith fantastic garlands did she make
Of crowflowers, nettles, daisies, and long purples,°   *purple orchids*
That liberal° shepherds give a grosser¹ name,   *free-spoken*
170   But our cold° maids do dead men's fingers call them.   *chaste*
There on the pendent boughs her crownet° weeds   *made into a crown*
Clamb'ring to hang,² an envious sliver° broke,   *a malicious branch*
When down her weedy trophies and herself
Fell in the weeping brook. Her clothes spread wide,
175   And mermaid-like awhile they bore her up,
Which time she chanted snatches of old lauds,°   *hymns*
As one incapable° of her own distress,   *unaware*
Or like a creature native and endued°   *adopted*
Unto that element. But long it could not be
180   Till that her garments, heavy with their drink,
Pulled the poor wretch from her melodious lay°   *song*
To muddy death.

LAERTES   Alas, then she is drowned.

QUEEN   Drowned, drowned.

LAERTES   Too much of water hast thou, poor Ophelia,
185   And therefore I forbid my tears. But yet
It is our trick;° nature her custom holds,   *natural tendency*
Let shame say what it will. [*He weeps.*] When these are
     gone,
The woman will be out.³ Adieu, my lord.
I have a speech o' fire that fain° would blaze,   *eagerly*
But that this folly drowns it.   *Exit.*
190 KING   Let's follow, Gertrude.
How much I had to do to calm his rage!
Now fear I this will give it start again.
Therefore let's follow.

                              Exeunt.

5.1

Enter two CLOWNS⁴ [*one a* GRAVEDIGGER].

GRAVEDIGGER   Is she to be buried in Christian burial when
she willfully seeks her own salvation?⁵

OTHER   I tell thee she is; therefore make her grave straight.°   *immediately*
The crowner° hath sat on her and finds it Christian burial.⁶   *coroner*

5 GRAVEDIGGER   How can that be, unless she drowned herself in her own defense?

OTHER   Why, 'tis found so.

---

1. More lewd (e.g., "priest's-pintle" [penis]; "dog's cullions" [testicles]).
2. Forsaken lovers were said to hang garlands in willow trees.
3. That is, when I am done crying the woman in me will also be gone.
5.1 Location: A churchyard.
4. Men from the country, rustics.
5. Possibly a mistake for "damnation"; suicide was considered a mortal sin that disqualified

one from a "Christian burial" in consecrated ground. Or the clown may be suggesting that Ophelia is speeding her "salvation" by going to her reward "willfully" rather than by waiting for nature to take its course.
6. The coroner has investigated the case of her death and concluded that it merits a Christian burial (i.e., that her drowning was not a suicide).

GRAVEDIGGER It must be *se offendendo*;[7] it cannot be else.
For here lies the point: if I drown myself wittingly, it argues
10 an act, and an act hath three branches—it is to act, to
do, to perform. Argal,[8] she drowned herself wittingly.

OTHER Nay, but hear you, goodman delver°—   *Master Digger*

GRAVEDIGGER Give me leave. Here lies the water—good.
Here stands the man—good. If the man go to this water
15 and drown himself, it is, will he, nill he,° he goes. Mark   *willy-nilly*
you that. But if the water come to him and drown him, he
drowns not himself. Argal, he that is not guilty of his own
death shortens not his own life.

OTHER But is this law?

20 GRAVEDIGGER Ay, marry, is't—crowner's quest° law.   *inquest*

OTHER Will you ha' the truth on't? If this had not been a
gentlewoman, she should have been buried out o' Christian burial.

GRAVEDIGGER Why, there thou sayst.° And the more pity   *that's right*
25 that great folk should have countenance° in this world to   *privilege*
drown or hang themselves more than their even°-   *fellow*
Christian. Come, my spade. There is no ancient gentlemen but gardeners, ditchers, and grave-makers. They hold
up° Adam's profession.   *continue in*

30 OTHER Was he a gentleman?

GRAVEDIGGER 'A° was the first that ever bore arms.[9] I'll   *He*
put another question to thee. If thou answerest me not
to the purpose, confess thyself—[1]

OTHER Go to.[2]

35 GRAVEDIGGER What is he that builds stronger than either
the mason, the shipwright, or the carpenter?

OTHER The gallows-maker, for that outlives a thousand
tenants.

GRAVEDIGGER I like thy wit well, in good faith. The gallows
40 does well.° But how does it well? It does well to those   *is a good answer*
that do ill. Now thou dost ill to say the gallows is built
stronger than the church. Argal, the gallows may do well
to thee. To't again, come.

OTHER Who builds stronger than a mason, a shipwright,
45 or a carpenter?

GRAVEDIGGER Ay, tell me that, and unyoke.[3]

OTHER Marry,° now I can tell.   *By the Virgin Mary*

GRAVEDIGGER To't.

OTHER Mass,° I cannot tell.   *By the Mass*

50 GRAVEDIGGER Cudgel thy brains no more about it, for
your dull ass will not mend° his pace with beating. And   *quicken*

7. In self-offense; an error for the Latin
legal phrase *se defendendo*, "[killing] in self-
defense."
8. A corruption of the Latin *ergo* (therefore).
9. Was given the heraldic insignia that entitled a man to call himself a "gentleman"
(punning on "arms," meaning "limbs").
1. Proverbial: "Confess thyself and be hanged."
2. An exclamation of impatience.
3. Cease (your joking), as an ox stops working
at the end of the day when unyoked.

when you are asked this question next, say "a grave-
maker." The houses he makes lasts till doomsday. Go get
thee in and fetch me a stoup° of liquor.   *flagon*

[*Exit* OTHER.]

[GRAVEDIGGER *digs.*]

55   "In youth when I did love, did love,   *Song.*
       Methought it was very sweet,
To contract°—oh—the time for—a—my behove,°   *shorten / advantage*
Oh, methought there—a—was nothing—a—meet."[4]

       Enter HAMLET *and* HORATIO.

HAMLET   Has this fellow no feeling of his business? 'A°   *He*
60   sings in grave-making.

HORATIO   Custom hath made it in him a property of
easiness.[5]

HAMLET   'Tis e'en so. The hand of little employment
hath the daintier sense.[6]

65   GRAVEDIGGER   "But age, with his stealing steps,   *Song.*
       Hath clawed me in his clutch,
And hath shipped me into the land,
       As if I had never been such."[7]

       [*He throws up a skull.*]

HAMLET   That skull had a tongue in it and could sing
70   once. How the knave jowls° it to the ground, as if 'twere   *dashes*
Cain's jawbone, that did the first murder. This might be
the   pate   of   a   politician°—which   this   ass   now   *schemer*
o'erreaches[8]—one that would circumvent God, might it
not?

75   HORATIO   It might, my lord.

HAMLET   Or of a courtier, which could say, "Good morrow,
sweet lord. How dost thou, sweet lord?" This might be
my Lord Such-a-one, that praised my Lord Such-a-one's
horse when 'a° went to beg it, might it not?   *he*

80   HORATIO   Ay, my lord.

HAMLET   Why, e'en so, and now my Lady Worm's, chapless,°   *without a lower jaw*
and knocked about the mazard° with a sexton's spade.   *head*
Here's fine revolution, an we had the trick[9] to see't. Did
these bones cost no more the breeding but to play at
85   loggets with them?[1] Mine ache to think on't.

GRAVEDIGGER   "A pickaxe and a spade, a spade,   *Song.*
       For and° a shrouding sheet;   *And also*
Oh, a pit of clay for to be made

---

4. That is, nothing so suitable. The clown's
song is a garbled version of lines from Lord
Thomas Vaux's poem "The Aged Lover
Renounceth Love," which appears in *Tottel's
Miscellany* (1557).
5. Something he can do easily, without emotional distress.
6. Is more sensitive (because it is not
calloused).

7. Perhaps, been such in youth.
8. Lords it over (as if he were of superior rank).
9. If we had the ability. *Revolution*: a turning
of Fortune's wheel.
1. That is, did these bones mature for no
other purpose than to be used in loggets (a
game played by throwing sticks as closely as
possible to a stake)?

For such a guest is meet."

[*He throws up another skull.*]

90 HAMLET   There's another. Why may not that be the skull
of a lawyer? Where be his quiddities° now, his quillities,°   subtleties / quibbles
his cases, his tenures,° and his tricks? Why does he suffer   property titles
this mad knave now to knock him about the sconce°   head
with a dirty shovel, and will not tell him of his action of
95   battery?° Hum, this fel low might be in's time a great   prosecution for assault
buyer of land, with his statutes, his recognizances, his
fines, his double vouchers, his recoveries.[2] To have his fine°   excellent
pate full of fine dirt! Will vouchers vouch° him no more of   assure
his purchases and doubles than the length and breadth of
100 a pair of indentures?° The very conveyances of his lands   contracts
will scarcely lie in this box,° and must th'inheritor°   coffin / owner
himself have no more, ha?

HORATIO   Not a jot more, my lord.

HAMLET   Is not parchment made of sheepskins?

105 HORATIO   Ay, my lord, and of calves' skins too.

HAMLET   They are sheep and calves° which seek out   simpletons and dolts
assurance[3] in that. I will speak to this fellow.—Whose
grave's this, sirrah?[4]

GRAVEDIGGER   Mine, sir.

110   [*Sings.*] "Oh, a pit of clay for to be made"—

HAMLET   I think it be thine, indeed, for thou liest in't.

GRAVEDIGGER   You lie out on't, sir, and therefore 'tis not
yours. For my part, I do not lie in't, yet it is mine.

HAMLET   Thou dost lie in't, to be in't and say it is thine.

115   'Tis for the dead not for the quick;° therefore thou liest.   living

GRAVEDIGGER   'Tis a quick° lie, sir; 'twill away again from   lively
me to you.

HAMLET   What man dost thou dig it for?

GRAVEDIGGER   For no man, sir.

120 HAMLET   What woman then?

GRAVEDIGGER   For none neither.

HAMLET   Who is to be buried in't?

GRAVEDIGGER   One that was a woman, sir, but, rest her
soul, she's dead.

125 HAMLET   How absolute° the knave is! We must speak by   precise, literal
the card[5] or equivocation will undo us. By the Lord,
Horatio, this three years I have took note of it: the age is
grown so picked° that the toe of the peasant comes so   refined
near the heel of the courtier he galls his kibe.°—How   chafes his heel
130   long hast thou been grave-maker?

2. All legal terms: "statutes" and "recognizances" are documents in which portions of
land or properties were pledged as surety in a
contractual agreement; "double vouchers"
are summons of two persons into court to
attest to the title to a property; "recoveries"
are processes by which an entailed estate is

transferred from one party to another.
3. Who seek security (in legal documents).
4. Term of address to a social inferior.
5. With utmost clarity (Hamlet may be referring to the mariner's card, on which were
marked the points of a compass).

GRAVEDIGGER   Of the days i'the year, I came to't that day
that our last king Hamlet overcame Fortinbras.
HAMLET   How long is that since?
GRAVEDIGGER   Cannot you tell that? Every fool can tell
135   that. It was that very day that young Hamlet was born,
he that is mad and sent into England.
HAMLET   Ay, marry, why was he sent into England?
GRAVEDIGGER   Why, because 'a° was mad. 'A shall recover   *he*
his wits there, or if 'a do not, 'tis no great matter there.
140   HAMLET   Why?
GRAVEDIGGER   'Twill not be seen in him there. There the
men are as mad as he.
HAMLET   How came he mad?
GRAVEDIGGER   Very strangely, they say.
145   HAMLET   How strangely?
GRAVEDIGGER   Faith, e'en with losing his wits.
HAMLET   Upon what ground?°   *For what reason*
GRAVEDIGGER   Why, here in Denmark. I have been sexton
here, man and boy, thirty years.
150   HAMLET   How long will a man lie i'the earth ere he rot?
GRAVEDIGGER   Faith, if 'a be not rotten before 'a die—as
we have many pocky⁶ corpses that will scarce hold the
laying in⁷—'a° will last you some eight year or nine year.   *he*
A tanner will last you nine year.
155   HAMLET   Why he more than another?
GRAVEDIGGER   Why, sir, his hide is so tanned with his
trade that 'a will keep out water a great while, and your
water is a sore decayer of your whoreson⁸ dead body.
Here's a skull now hath lien you i'th'earth three-and-
160   twenty years.
HAMLET   Whose was it?
GRAVEDIGGER   A whoreson mad fellow's it was. Whose do
you think it was?
HAMLET   Nay, I know not.
165   GRAVEDIGGER   A pestilence on him for a mad rogue! 'A
poured a flagon of Rhenish° on my head once. [*He picks   *Rhine wine*
up a skull.*] This same skull, sir, was, sir, Yorick's skull,
the King's jester.
HAMLET   This?
170   GRAVEDIGGER   E'en that.
HAMLET   [*He takes the skull.*] Alas, poor Yorick. I knew
him, Horatio, a fellow of infinite jest, of most excellent
fancy. He hath bore me on his back a thousand times,
and now how abhorred in my imagination it is! My gorge
175   rises at it. Here hung those lips that I have kissed I know
not how oft. Where be your gibes now, your gambols,°   *tricks*

6. Infected with the pox (a term that usually   during the burial ceremony.
referred to syphilis).   8. Vile (a general term of contempt).
7. That is, that will scarcely hold together

your songs, your flashes of merriment that were wont to
set the table on a roar? Not one now, to mock your own
grinning? Quite chopfallen?[9] Now, get you to my lady's
180 table and tell her, let her paint° an inch thick, to this   *wear makeup*
favor° she must come. Make her laugh at that. Prithee,   *appearance*
Horatio, tell me one thing.

HORATIO   What's that, my lord?

HAMLET   Dost thou think Alexander[1] looked o' this fashion
185 i'th'earth?

HORATIO   E'en so.

HAMLET   And smelt so? Pah! [*He puts down the skull.*]

HORATIO   E'en so, my lord.

HAMLET   To what base uses we may return, Horatio! Why
190 may not imagination trace the noble dust of Alexander
till 'a find it stopping a bunghole?

HORATIO   'Twere to consider too curiously° to consider so.   *minutely*

HAMLET   No, faith, not a jot, but to follow him thither with
modesty° enough, and likelihood to lead it: Alexander   *moderation*
195 died, Alexander was buried, Alexander returneth to dust,
the dust is earth, of earth we make loam,[2] and why of
that loam whereto he was converted might they not stop
a beer barrel?

Imperious Caesar, dead and turned to clay,
200 Might stop a hole to keep the wind away.
Oh, that that earth which kept the world in awe
Should patch a wall t'expel the winter's flaw!°   *gust of wind*

    Enter KING, QUEEN, LAERTES, *and the corpse* [*of* OPHE-
    LIA, *with a* DOCTOR OF DIVINITY, *and* ATTENDANTS.]

But soft, but soft awhile. Here comes the King,
The Queen, the courtiers. Who is this they follow?
205 And with such maimed rites?[3] This doth betoken
The corpse they follow did with desp'rate hand
Fordo° its own life. 'Twas of some estate.°   *Destroy / rank*
Couch we° awhile and mark.   *Let us hide*

    [*They withdraw.* OPHELIA's *body is taken to the grave.*]

LAERTES   What ceremony else?

210 HAMLET [*To* HORATIO]   That is Laertes, a very noble youth.
    Mark.

LAERTES   What ceremony else?

DOCTOR   Her obsequies have been as far enlarged
As we have warranty.° Her death was doubtful,[4]   *authority*
And but that great command o'ersways the order[5]
215 She should in ground unsanctified been lodged
Till the last trumpet.° For° charitable prayers,   *Judgment Day / Instead of*

---

9. Dejected; with lower jaw fallen away.
1. Alexander the Great (356–323 B.C.E.), King
of Macedon, who conquered a great empire.
2. A mixture of clay, sand, and other materials
used to make bricks and plaster.
3. A curtailed ceremony (rather than an elab-

orate court funeral).
4. Questionable (because it may have been a
suicide.)
5. If the power of the court had not overruled
church practice.

Flints and pebbles should be thrown on her.
Yet here she is allowed her virgin crants,°   *garland*
Her maiden strewments,° and the bringing home   *strewn flowers*
220   Of bell and burial.[6]

LAERTES   Must there no more be done?

DOCTOR   No more be done.
We should profane the service of the dead
To sing a requiem and such rest to her
As to peace-parted° souls.   *peacefully departed*

LAERTES   Lay her i'th'earth,
225   And from her fair and unpolluted flesh
May violets spring. I tell thee, churlish priest,
A minist'ring angel shall my sister be
When thou liest howling.°   *(in hell)*

HAMLET [*To* HORATIO]   What, the fair Ophelia?

QUEEN [*Strewing flowers*]   Sweets to the sweet. Farewell.
230   I hoped thou shouldst have been my Hamlet's wife.
I thought thy bride-bed to have decked, sweet maid,
And not have strewed thy grave.

LAERTES   Oh, treble woe
Fall ten times double on that cursèd head
Whose wicked deed thy most ingenious sense°   *keen intellect*
235   Deprived thee of!—Hold off the earth awhile,
Till I have caught her once more in mine arms.

> [*He leaps into the grave and embraces* OPHELIA.]

Now pile your dust upon the quick and dead,
Till of this flat a mountain you have made,
T'o'ertop old Pelion[7] or the skyish head
240   Of blue Olympus.

HAMLET [*Advancing*]   What is he whose grief
Bears such an emphasis, whose phrase° of sorrow   *particular expression*
Conjures the wand'ring stars,° and makes them stand   *planets*
Like wonder-wounded° hearers? This is I,   *awestruck*
Hamlet the Dane![8]

LAERTES [*Grappling with him*]   The devil take thy soul!

245   HAMLET   Thou pray'st not well.
I prithee, take thy fingers from my throat,
For though I am not splenitive° and rash,   *hot-tempered*
Yet have I in me something dangerous,
Which let thy wisdom fear. Hold off thy hand.

250   KING   Pluck them asunder.

QUEEN   Hamlet, Hamlet!

ALL   Gentlemen!

HORATIO   Good my lord, be quiet.

> [*The* ATTENDANTS *part them.*]

---

6. The burial procession and interment to the sound of church bells.
7. The highest mountain of a range in Thessaly, in northern Greece; in Greek mythology, the Titans piled Mount Ossa on Pelion in an attempt to scale Mount Olympus and defeat the gods.
8. The title normally given to the King of Denmark.

HAMLET   Why, I will fight with him upon this theme
255   Until my eyelids will no longer wag.°   *blink*
QUEEN   O my son, what theme?
HAMLET   I loved Ophelia. Forty thousand brothers
    Could not with all their quantity of love
    Make up my sum.—What wilt thou do for her?
260 KING   Oh, he is mad, Laertes.
QUEEN   For love of God, forbear him.°   *leave him alone*
HAMLET   'Swounds,° show me what thou'lt do.   *By God's wounds*
    Woo't° weep? Woo't fight? Woo't fast? Woo't tear thyself?   *Wilt thou*
    Woo't drink up eisel?° Eat a crocodile?   *vinegar*
265   I'll do't. Dost come here to whine,
    To outface me with leaping in her grave?
    Be buried quick° with her, and so will I.   *alive*
    And if thou prate of mountains, let them throw
    Millions of acres on us till our ground,
270   Singeing his pate against the burning zone,[9]
    Make Ossa like a wart! Nay, an° thou'lt mouth,°   *if / rant, rage*
    I'll rant as well as thou.
QUEEN   This is mere madness,
    And this awhile the fit will work on him.
    Anon,° as patient as the female dove,   *Soon*
275   When that her golden couplets[1] are disclosed,°   *hatched*
    His silence will sit drooping.
HAMLET   Hear you, sir.
    What is the reason that you use me thus?
    I loved you ever. But it is no matter.
    Let Hercules himself do what he may,
280   The cat will mew, and dog will have his day.[2]   *Exit.*
KING   I pray thee, good Horatio, wait upon° him.   *accompany*
                     [*Exit* HORATIO.]
[*To* LAERTES]   Strengthen your patience in° our last night's   *with*
    speech;
    We'll put the matter to the present push.°   *to immediate trial*
    —Good Gertrude, set some watch over your son.—
285   This grave shall have a living° monument.   *lasting*
    An hour of quiet thereby shall we see;
    Till then in patience our proceeding be.
                         Exeunt.

5.2

Enter HAMLET *and* HORATIO.

HAMLET   So much for this, sir; now shall you see the other.°   *other matter*
    You do remember all the circumstance?
HORATIO   Remember it, my lord!
HAMLET   Sir, in my heart there was a kind of fighting

---

9. In the Ptolemaic system, the sphere of the
sun.
1. Two yellow chicks.

2. That is, even if mighty Hercules were to
stand in the way, each will do what he must.
5.2 Location: The castle.

5 That would not let me sleep. Methought I lay
  Worse than the mutines in the bilboes.[3] Rashly,°   *Impulsively*
  And praised be rashness for it—let us know°   *acknowledge*
  Our indiscretion sometime serves us well,
  When our deep plots do pall° and that should learn us   *weaken*
10 There's a divinity that shapes our ends,
  Rough-hew° them how we will—   *Roughly form*
HORATIO   That is most certain.
HAMLET   Up from my cabin,
  My sea-gown scarfed about me, in the dark
  Groped I to find out them, had my desire,
15 Fingered° their packet, and in fine° withdrew   *Filched / finally*
  To mine own room again, making so bold,
  My fears forgetting manners, to unfold
  Their grand commission, where I found, Horatio,
  A royal knavery, an exact command,
20 Larded° with many several° sorts of reasons,   *Enriched / different*
  Importing° Denmark's health and England's too,   *Relating to*
  With—ho!—such bugs and goblins in my life,[4]
  That on the supervise,° no leisure bated,°   *reading / delay permitted*
  No, not to stay° the grinding of the axe,   *await*
  My head should be struck off.
25 HORATIO   Is't possible?
HAMLET [*Giving a paper*] Here's the commission. Read it
    at more leisure.
  But wilt thou hear now how I did proceed?
HORATIO   I beseech you.
HAMLET   Being thus benetted round° with villains—   *hemmed in*
30 Ere I could make a prologue to my brains,
  They had begun the play[5]—I sat me down,
  Devised a new commission, wrote it fair.[6]
  I once did hold it, as our statists° do,   *states men, politicians*
  A baseness° to write fair, and labored much   *lower-class skill*
35 How to forget that learning, but, sir, now
  It did me yeoman's service.° Wilt thou know   *served me well*
  Th'effect of what I wrote?
HORATIO   Ay, good my lord.
HAMLET   An earnest conjuration° from the King,   *request*
  As England was his faithful tributary,
40 As love between them like the palm might flourish,
  As peace should still her wheaten garland[7] wear
  And stand a comma° 'tween their amities,   *link*
  And many suchlike "as"es of great charge,[8]
  That on the view and knowing of these contents,
45 Without debatement further more or less,
  He should those bearers put to sudden death,

3. The mutineers in the shackles.
4. Such things to be dreaded if I were allowed to live. *Bugs:* bugbears.
5. That is, Hamlet began to devise a plan before he consciously intended to do so.

6. That is, in the clear handwriting of the clerks who prepared official documents.
7. A symbol of agricultural prosperity and peace.
8. Important clauses beginning with "as" (with a pun on "asses").

Not shriving time⁹ allowed.

HORATIO   How was this sealed?

HAMLET   Why, even in that was heaven ordinant.°   *guiding*
I had my father's signet in my purse,
50 Which was the model of that Danish seal,
Folded the writ up in the form of th'other,
Subscribed° it, gave't th'impression,¹ placed it safely,   *Signed*
The changeling² never known. Now, the next day
Was our sea fight, and what to this was sequent°   *subsequent*
55 Thou knowest already.

HORATIO   So Guildenstern and Rosencrantz go to't.

HAMLET   They are not near my conscience; their defeat°   *destruction*
Does by their own insinuation° grow.   *interference*
'Tis dangerous when the baser nature comes
60 Between the pass and fell incensèd points
Of mighty opposites.³

HORATIO   Why, what a king is this!

HAMLET   Does it not, think thee, stand me now upon?⁴
He that hath killed my king and whored my mother,
Popped in between th'election⁵ and my hopes,
65 Thrown out his angle° for my proper° life,   *fishing hook / own*
And with such coz'nage°—is't not perfect conscience?   *deceit*

Enter [OSRIC], a courtier.

OSRIC   Your lordship is right welcome back to Denmark.

HAMLET   I humbly thank you, sir. [Aside to HORATIO] Dost
know this water-fly?

70 HORATIO [Aside] No, my good lord.

HAMLET [Aside] Thy state is the more gracious,° for 'tis a vice   *blessed*
to know him. He hath much land and fertile. Let a beast be
lord of beasts, and his crib shall stand at the King's mess.⁶
'Tis a chough,° but, as I say, spacious in the possession of   *crow or jackdaw*
75 dirt.   *(noisy bird)*

OSRIC   Sweet lord, if your lordship were at leisure, I
should impart a thing to you from His Majesty.

HAMLET   I will receive it, sir, with all diligence of spirit.
Your bonnet° to his right use; 'tis for the head.   *hat*

80 OSRIC   I thank your lordship; it is very hot.

HAMLET   No, believe me, 'tis very cold; the wind is northerly.

OSRIC   It is indifferent° cold, my lord, indeed.   *somewhat*

HAMLET   But yet methinks it is very sultry and hot for my
complexion.°   *constitution*

85 OSRIC   Exceedingly, my lord. It is very sultry, as 'twere—I
cannot tell how. My lord, His Majesty bade me signify

---

9. No time for confession and absolution (as ordinarily granted to the condemned).
1. Imprinted the seal in wax.
2. The substituted letter (literally, an elf child substituted for a human child by fairies).
3. Between the thrust and fiercely angry rapiers ("points") of mighty adversaries.

4. Rest incumbent on me.
5. In Denmark, the king was elected.
6. A man of wealth and property (possessing many herds) shall find himself at the king's table, even if he is no better than his animals. *Crib:* feed box, manger.

to you that 'a° has laid a great wager on your head. Sir,   *he*
this is the matter—

HAMLET I beseech you, remember.[7]

[HAMLET *gestures to* OSRIC *to put on his hat.*]

90 OSRIC Nay, good my lord, for my ease, in good faith. Sir,
here is newly come to court Laertes—believe me, an
absolute gentleman, full of most excellent differences,°   *superior qualities*
of very soft society and great showing.[8] Indeed, to speak
feelingly° of him, he is the card° or calendar of gentry,[9]   *discerningly / map*
95 for you shall find in him the continent of what part[1] a
gentleman would see.

HAMLET Sir, his definement suffers no perdition in you,[2]
though I know to divide him inventorially° would dozy°   *by way of inventory /*
th'arithmetic of memory, and yet but yaw neither in respect   *make dizzy*
100 of his quick sail.[3] But, in the verity of extolment,° I take   *future praise*
him to be a soul of great article,[4] and his infusion° of such   *inborn essence*
dearth° and rareness as, to make true diction° of him, his   *dearness / to speak truly*
semblable° is his mirror, and who else would trace him, his   *likeness*
umbrage, nothing more.[5]

105 OSRIC Your lordship speaks most infallibly of him

HAMLET The concernancy,° sir? Why do we wrap the gentle-   *relevance*
man in our more rawer breath?°   *words*

OSRIC Sir?

HORATIO Is't not possible to understand in another
110 tongue? You will do't, sir, really.[6]

HAMLET What imports the nomination° of this gentleman?   *mention*

OSRIC Of Laertes?

HORATIO [*To* HAMLET] His purse is empty already; all's
golden words are spent.

115 HAMLET Of him, sir.

OSRIC I know, you are not ignorant—

HAMLET I would you did, sir. Yet, in faith, if you did, it
would not much approve° me. Well, sir?   *recommend*

OSRIC You are not ignorant of what excellence Laertes is—

120 HAMLET I dare not confess that, lest I should compare
with him in excellence.[7] But to know a man well were to
know himself.

---

7. That is, remember your courtesy (i.e., put
your hat back on).
8. Of pleasing manners and noble appearance.
9. That is, the model of gentlemanly behavior.
Calendar: guide, register.
1. Embodiment of all qualities. ("Continent"
continues the geographical metaphor begun
in line 93.)
2. He loses nothing in your definition of him.
Hamlet mimics Osric's affected style of
speech to acknowledge that Osric's description does Laertes justice.
3. Still mocking Osric's mode of speech,
Hamlet employs a nautical metaphor: any

such tediously verbose attempt to list all of
Laertes' virtues would tend to swerve ("yaw")
off course in comparison with Laertes' rapid
forward motion ("quick sail").
4. Of great moment.
5. That is, anyone who imitates him becomes
only his shadow, nothing more.
6. That is, is it not possible to understand
your own (Osric's) manner of speech when
spoken by another (Hamlet)? You can if you
will try, sir, splendidly.
7. That is, I dare not confirm his excellence,
because I would have to assert my own equal
excellence to recognize his.

OSRIC   I mean, sir, for his weapon. But in the imputation
laid on him by them in his meed,° he's unfellowed.° — merit / unequaled
125 HAMLET   What's his weapon?
OSRIC   Rapier and dagger.
HAMLET   That's two of his weapons—but well.
OSRIC   The King, sir, hath wagered with him six Barbary
horses, against the which he has impawned,° as I take it, six — wagered
130 French rapiers and poniards, with their assigns,[8] as girdle,
hanger,[9] and so. Three of the carriages, in faith, are very
dear to fancy,[1] very responsive to the hilts, most delicate° — charming
carriages, and of very liberal conceit.° — elaborate design
HAMLET   What call you the "carriages"?
135 HORATIO   [To HAMLET] I knew you must be edified by the
margent[2] ere you had done.
OSRIC   The carriages, sir, are the hangers.
HAMLET   The phrase would be more germane to the matter if we could carry a cannon by our sides.[3] I would it
140 might be "hangers" till then. But, on: six Barbary horses
against six French swords, their assigns, and three
liberal-conceited carriages; that's the French bet against
the Danish. Why is this all "impawned," as you call it?
OSRIC   The King, sir, hath laid,° sir, that in a dozen passes — wagered
145 between yourself and him, he shall not exceed you three
hits.[4] He hath laid on twelve for nine,[5] and it would come
to immediate trial if your lordship would vouchsafe the
answer.° — accept the challenge
HAMLET   How if I answer no?
150 OSRIC   I mean, my lord, the opposition of your person in
trial.
HAMLET   Sir, I will walk here in the hall. If it please His
Majesty, it is the breathing time of day[6] with me; let the
foils be brought. The gentleman willing, and the King
155 hold his purpose, I will win for him an I can; if not, I will
gain nothing but my shame and the odd hits.
OSRIC   Shall I deliver you so?
HAMLET   To this effect, sir, after what flourish your nature
will.
160 OSRIC   I commend my duty° to your lordship. — offer my service
HAMLET   Yours.

[Exit OSRIC.]

'A° does well to commend° it himself; there are no tongues — He / recommend
else for's turn.[7]

8. With their paraphernalia ("assigns"), such as sword belt ("girdle") and the loop or strap on a sword belt from which the sword was hung (often richly ornamented).
9. A pretentious way of saying "hangers."
1. That is beautifully made.
2. That is, by a gloss, as in the margin of a book.
3. Hamlet refers to a gun carriage (the wheeled frame on which a cannon is mounted).
4. That is, the King has wagered that in twelve bouts Laertes will outscore Hamlet by no more than three hits.
5. The meaning of this phrase is unclear. Perhaps Osric is saying that in the twelve bouts Laertes must score twelve hits against Hamlet's nine to win.
6. That is, the time for exercise.
7. That is, no one else will do it for him.

HORATIO   This lapwing runs away with the shell on his head.[8]

165 HAMLET   'A did comply so, sir, with his dug[9] before 'a
sucked it. Thus has he—and many more of the same
breed that I know the drossy° age dotes on—only got the   *worthless*
tune of the time and, out of an habit of encounter,[1] a kind
of yeasty collection,° which carries them through and   *set of frothy phrases*
170 through the most profane and winnowed opinions;[2] and
do but blow them to their trial, the bubbles are out.[3]

    Enter a LORD.

LORD   My lord, His Majesty commended him to you by
young Osric, who brings back to him that you attend
him in the hall. He sends to know if your pleasure hold
175 to play with Laertes, or that you will take longer time.

HAMLET   I am constant to my purposes; they follow the
King's pleasure. If his fitness speaks, mine is ready,[4] now
or whensoever, provided I be so able as now.

LORD   The King and Queen and all are coming down.

180 HAMLET   In happy time.[5]

LORD   The Queen desires you to use some gentle entertainment to Laertes[6] before you fall to play.

HAMLET   She well instructs me.

    [*Exit* LORD.]

HORATIO   You will lose, my lord.

185 HAMLET   I do not think so. Since he went into France, I
have been in continual practice. I shall win at the odds.°   *(see 5.2.140–43)*
Thou wouldst not think how ill all's here about my heart,
but it is no matter.

HORATIO   Nay, good my lord.

190 HAMLET   It is but foolery, but it is such a kind of gaingiv-
ing° as would perhaps trouble a woman.   *misgiving*

HORATIO   If your mind dislike anything, obey it. I will forestall their repair° hither and say you are not fit.   *arrival*

HAMLET   Not a whit, we defy augury. There is special provi-
195 dence in the fall of a sparrow.[7] If it be now, 'tis not to
come; if it be not to come, it will be now; if it be not now,
yet it will come. The readiness is all. Since no man of
aught he leaves knows, what is't to leave betimes?[8] Let be.

---

8. Elizabethans frequently alluded to the notion that the newly hatched plover lapwing (plover) runs from the nest with its shell on its head. The suggestion here is that Osric has finally replaced his bonnet. Also, his gait may resemble the lapwing's wavering flight.
9. He did bow politely to his mother's breast.
1. The style of speech ("tune") of the time and the conventions ("habit") of polite social intercourse.
2. The most well-aired and well-sifted opinions.
3. Put them to the test ("blow them") and their ignorance will be exposed (the "bubbles" will burst).

4. That is, if this is a good time for him, it is also for me.
5. At an opportune time (a polite phrase).
6. To receive Laertes with some sign of respect or courtesy.
7. Elizabethans distinguished between general providence (God's overarching plan for human history) and special providence (God's guidance in particular events, such as the fall of a single sparrow, which, according to Matthew 10.29, shall not happen without God's knowledge).
8. That is, because no man truly owns what he leaves behind (i.e., earthly possessions), what does it matter if he leaves this world early?

A table prepared. [ENTER] *trumpets, drums, and officers*
with cushions, KING, QUEEN, *and all the state, foils,*
daggers, [*cups of wine,* OSRIC,] *and* LAERTES

KING Come, Hamlet, come, and take this hand from me.
[*The* KING *puts* LAERTES's *hand into* HAMLET's.]

200 HAMLET Give me your pardon, sir. I have done you wrong,
But pardon't, as you are a gentleman.
This presence° knows,   *royal assembly*
And you must needs have heard, how I am punished
With a sore distraction. What I have done
205 That might your nature, honor, and exception°   *displeasure*
Roughly awake, I here proclaim was madness.
Was't Hamlet wronged Laertes? Never Hamlet.
If Hamlet from himself be ta'en away,
And when he's not himself does wrong Laertes,
210 Then Hamlet does it not. Hamlet denies it.
Who does it, then? His madness. If't be so,
Hamlet is of the faction that is wronged;
His madness is poor Hamlet's enemy.
Let my disclaiming from° a purposed evil   *disavowing any part in*
215 Free me so far in your most generous thoughts
That I have shot my arrow o'er the house
And hurt my brother.
LAERTES   I am satisfied in nature,[9]
Whose motive in this case should stir me most
To my revenge. But in my terms of honor
220 I stand aloof, and will no reconcilement
Till by some elder masters of known honor
I have a voice° and precedent of peace   *authoritative declaration*
To keep my name ungored.° But till that time   *unblemished*
I do receive your offered love like love,
And will not wrong it.
225 HAMLET   I embrace it freely,
And will this brother's wager frankly° play.   *freely*
—Give us the foils.
LAERTES   Come, one for me.
HAMLET I'll be your foil,[1] Laertes. In mine ignorance
Your skill shall, like a star i'the darkest night,
Stick° fiery off indeed.   *Stand out; thrust*
230 LAERTES   You mock me, sir.
HAMLET No, by this hand.
KING Give them the foils, young Osric. Cousin Hamlet,
You know the wager?
HAMLET   Very well, my lord;
Your Grace has laid the odds o' the weaker side.
235 KING I do not fear it; I have seen you both.

9. That is, according to natural personal
feeling.
1. Flattering contrast (from the metal foil

placed under a gem to add to its brilliance),
with a pun on fencing foils.

But since he is better,° we have therefore odds.[2]   *favored*

LAERTES   This is too heavy. Let me see another.

HAMLET   This likes° me well. These foils have all a° length?   *pleases / the same*

[*They prepare to play.*]

OSRIC   Ay, my good lord.

240   KING   Set me the stoups° of wine upon that table.   *flagons*
      If Hamlet give the first or second hit,
      Or quit in answer of the third exchange,[3]
      Let all the battlements their ordnance fire.
      The King shall drink to Hamlet's better breath,°   *improved energy*

245   And in the cup an union° shall he throw,   *a pearl*
      Richer than that which four successive kings
      In Denmark's crown have worn. Give me the cups,
      And let the kettle° to the trumpet speak,   *kettledrum*
      The trumpet to the cannoneer without,

250   The cannons to the heavens, the heaven to earth,
      "Now the King drinks to Hamlet." Come, begin.

      Trumpets the while.

      And you, the judges, bear a wary eye.

HAMLET   Come on, sir.

LAERTES   Come, my lord.

      [*They play.* HAMLET *scores a hit.*]

255   HAMLET   One.

LAERTES   No.

HAMLET   Judgment?

OSRIC   A hit, a very palpable hit.

      Drum, trumpets, and shot. Flourish. A piece goes off.

LAERTES   Well, again.

260   KING   Stay,° give me drink. Hamlet, this pearl is thine.   *Stop*
      Here's to thy health. [*He drinks.*] Give him the cup.

HAMLET   I'll play this bout first. Set it by awhile.
      Come. [*They play.*] Another hit; what say you?

LAERTES   I do confess't.

KING   Our son shall win.

265   QUEEN   He's fat° and scant of breath.   *sweaty; out of shape*
      Here, Hamlet, take my napkin,° rub thy brows.   *handkerchief*
      The Queen carouses° to thy fortune, Hamlet.   *drinks a toast*

HAMLET   Good madam.

KING   Gertrude, do not drink.

270   QUEEN   I will, my lord. I pray you pardon me. [*She drinks.*]

KING [*Aside*]   It is the poisoned cup; it is too late.

HAMLET   I dare not drink yet, madam; by-and-by.

QUEEN   Come, let me wipe thy face.

LAERTES [*Aside*]   My lord, I'll hit him now.

KING [*Aside*]   I do not think't.

275   LAERTES [*Aside*]   And yet it is almost against my conscience.

HAMLET   Come, for the third, Laertes; you do but dally.

---

2. That is, I have arranged the terms in your favor (referring to Hamlet's advantage of three hits).

3. Repay ("quit") Laertes with a hit in the third bout (presumably having lost the first two).

I pray you pass° with your best violence;   *thrust*
I am sure you make a wanton of me.[4]

LAERTES Say you so? Come on.

[*They play.*]

280 OSRIC Nothing neither way.

LAERTES Have at you now!

[LAERTES *wounds* HAMLET; *then, in scuffling, they
change rapiers, and* HAMLET *wounds* LAERTES.]

KING Part them! They are incensed.

HAMLET Nay, come again!

[*The* QUEEN *falls.*]

OSRIC   Look to the Queen there, ho!

HORATIO They bleed on both sides. How is it, my lord?

285 OSRIC How is't, Laertes?

LAERTES Why, as a woodcock[5] to my own springe,° Osric;   *trap*
I am justly killed with mine own treachery.

HAMLET How does the Queen?

KING   She swoons to see them bleed.

QUEEN No, no, the drink, the drink—O my dear Hamlet!—

290 The drink, the drink! I am poisoned. [*She dies.*]

HAMLET O villainy! Ho, let the door be locked!
Treachery! Seek it out!

[LAERTES *falls. Exit* OSRIC.]

LAERTES It is here, Hamlet, thou art slain.
No med'cine in the world can do thee good;

295 In thee there is not half an hour's life;
The treacherous instrument is in thy hand,
Unbated° and envenomed. The foul practice   *Not blunted*
Hath turned itelf on me. Lo, here I lie,
Never to rise again. Thy mother's poisoned.

300 I can no more. The King, the King's to blame.

HAMLET The point envenomed too? Then, venom, to thy work!

[*He stabs the* KING.]

ALL Treason! treason!

KING Oh, yet defend me, friends! I am but hurt.

HAMLET [*Forcing the* KING *to drink*]
Here, thou incestuous, damnèd Dane,

305 Drink off this potion! Is thy union[6] here?
Follow my mother.

[*The* KING *dies.*]

LAERTES   He is justly served;
It is a poison tempered° by himself.   *mixed*
Exchange forgiveness with me, noble Hamlet.
Mine and my father's death come not upon thee,[7]

310 Nor thine on me. [*He dies.*]

---

4. You play with me as if I were a spoiled child.
5. A proverbially stupid bird.
6. Pearl (with a pun on "marriage").

7. That is, you are not responsible for our
deaths.

HAMLET   Heaven make thee free of it. I follow thee.
 I am dead, Horatio. Wretched Queen, adieu.
 You that look pale and tremble at this chance,
 That are but mutes° or audience to this act,   *silent witnesses*
315 Had I but time—as this fell sergeant,[8] Death,
 Is strict in his arrest—oh, I could tell you—
 But let it be. Horatio, I am dead;
 Thou livest. Report me and my cause aright
 To the unsatisfied.
HORATIO   Never believe it.
320 I am more an antique Roman than a Dane.[9]
 Here's yet some liquor left.
    [*He attempts to drink from the poisoned cup but* HAMLET
    restrains him.]
HAMLET   As thou'rt a man,
 Give me the cup! Let go! By heaven, I'll ha't.
 O God, Horatio, what a wounded name,
 Things standing thus unknown, shall I leave behind me.
325 If thou didst ever hold me in thy heart,
 Absent thee from felicity awhile,
 And in this harsh world draw thy breath in pain,
 To tell my story. *A march afar off* [*and shot within*].
    What warlike noise is this?
   Enter OSRIC.
OSRIC   Young Fortinbras, with conquest come from Poland,
330 To th'ambassadors of England gives
 This warlike volley.°   *military salute*
HAMLET   Oh, I die, Horatio.
 The potent poison quite o'ercrows° my spirit.   *triumphs over*
 I cannot live to hear the news from England,
 But I do prophesy th'election lights
335 On Fortinbras. He has my dying voice.°   *vote*
 So tell him, with th'occurrents° more and less,   *events*
 Which have solicited[1]—the rest is silence. [*He dies.*]
HORATIO   Now cracks a noble heart. Good night, sweet
  prince,
 And flights of angels sing thee to thy rest. [*March within.*]
340 Why does the drum come hither?
   Enter FORTINBRAS, *with the* [*English*] AMBASSADORS
   [*with drums, colors, and* ATTENDANTS].
FORTINBRAS   Where is this sight?
HORATIO   What is it you would see?
 If aught of woe or wonder, cease your search.
FORTINBRAS   This quarry cries on havoc.[2] O proud Death,
 What feast is toward° in thine eternal cell,   *in preparation*

---

8. This dread sheriff's officer.
9. The ancient Romans (unlike the Christian Danes) viewed suicide as sometimes honorable.
1. Incited (this sentence seems to be incom-

plete, possibly broken off as Hamlet realizes he is about to die).
2. This heap of game ("quarry") proclaims a massacre.

345   That thou so many princes at a shot
      So bloodily hast struck?

AMBASSADOR   The sight is dismal,
    And our affairs from England come too late.
    The ears are senseless that should give us hearing
350   To tell him° his commandment is fulfilled,   (*Claudius*)
      That Rosencrantz and Guildenstern are dead.
      Where should we have our thanks?

HORATIO   Not from his mouth,
    Had it th'ability of life to thank you.
    He never gave commandment for their death.
    But since, so jump° upon this bloody question,°   *immediately / quarrel*
355   You from the Polack wars, and you from England,
      Are here arrived, give order that these bodies
      High on a stage be placèd to the view,
      And let me speak to th'yet unknowing world
      How these things came about. So shall you hear
360   Of carnal, bloody, and unnatural acts,
      Of accidental judgments,° casual° slaughters,   *retributions / chance*
      Of deaths put on° by cunning, and for no cause,   *instigated*
      And, in this upshot, purposes mistook
      Fall'n on th'inventors' heads. All this can I
      Truly deliver.
365 FORTINBRAS   Let us haste to hear it,
    And call the noblest to the audience.
    For me, with sorrow I embrace my fortune.
    I have some rights of memory in this kingdom,
    Which now to claim my vantage doth invite me.
370 HORATIO   Of that I shall have also cause to speak,
    And from his mouth whose voice will draw on more.[3]
    But let this same be presently performed,
    Even while men's minds are wild, lest more mischance
    On° plots and errors happen.   *On top of*

FORTINBRAS   Let four captains
375   Bear Hamlet like a soldier to the stage,
      For he was likely, had he been put on,[4]
      To have proved most royal; and for his passage,
      The soldiers' music and the rite of war
      Speak loudly for him.
380   Take up the bodies. Such a sight as this
      Becomes the field,[5] but here shows° much amiss.   *appears*
      Go bid the soldiers shoot.

                Exeunt [marching, with the bodies;
           after which a peal of ordnance is shot off].

                       FINIS.

---

3. Whose vote will draw more votes (in Fortinbras's favor).

4. Put to the test (as King of Denmark).

5. Is fitting for a battlefield.

Twelfth Night;
or, What You Will

THE PERSONS OF THE PLAY

ORSINO, duke of Illyria

VALENTINE ⎫
CURIO ⎭ attending on Orsino

FIRST OFFICER

SECOND OFFICER

VIOLA, a lady, later disguised as
  Cesario

A CAPTAIN

SEBASTIAN, Viola's twin brother

ANTONIO, another sea-captain

OLIVIA, a countess

MARIA, Olivia's waiting-gentlewoman

SIR TOBY Belch, Olivia's kinsman

SIR ANDREW Aguecheek, companion of
  Sir Toby

MALVOLIO, Olivia's steward

FABIAN, a member of Olivia's
  household

FESTE the clown, Olivia's jester

A PRIEST

A SERVANT of Olivia

Musicians, sailors, lords, attendants

1.1

Enter ORSINO, *Duke of Illyria,*[1] CURIO, *and other*
  lords, with musicians playing.

ORSINO If music be the food of love, play on.
  Give me excess of it, that, surfeiting,
  The appetite may sicken and so die.
  That strain° again! It had a dying fall.°   *(of music) / cadence*
5 O, it came o'er my ear like the sweet sound
  That breathes upon a bank of violets,
  Stealing and giving odor. Enough; no more.
  'Tis not so sweet now as it was before.
  O spirit of love, how quick and fresh[2] art thou,
10 That, notwithstanding thy capacity,
  Receiveth as the sea,° naught enters there,   *without limit*
  Of what validity° and pitch[3] soe'er,   *value*
  But falls into abatement° and low price   *decreased value*
  Even in a minute. So full of shapes° is fancy°   *fanciful forms / love*
15 That it alone is high fantastical[4]
CURIO Will you go hunt, my lord?
ORSINO   What, Curio?
CURIO   The hart.

1.1 Location: Orsino's palace.
1. An imaginary dukedom on the eastern
coast of the Adriatic Sea.
2. Lively and eager to devour.

3. High worth (in falconry, "pitch" is the
highest point in a hawk's flight).
4. That is, love reigns supreme in the imagination of the lover.

ORSINO   Why, so I do, the noblest that I have.⁵
        O, when mine eyes did see Olivia first,
        Methought she purged the air of pestilence.⁶
20   That instant was I turned into a hart,
        And my desires, like fell° and cruel hounds,   fierce
        E'er since pursue me.⁷

        Enter VALENTINE

                How now, what news from her?
VALENTINE   So please my lord, I might not be admitted,°   was not granted entry
        But from her handmaid do return this answer:
25   The element itself, till seven years' heat,⁸
        Shall not behold her face at ample° view,   full
        But like a cloistress° she will veilèd walk,   nun
        And water once a day her chamber round
        With eye-offending brine°—all this to season°   salty tears / preserve
30   A brother's dead love,⁹ which she would keep fresh
        And lasting in her sad remembrance.
ORSINO   O, she that hath a heart of that fine frame¹
        To pay this debt of love but to a° brother,   to a mere
        How will she love when the rich golden shaft²
35   Hath killed the flock of all affections else°   all other feelings
        That live in her; when liver, brain, and heart,³
        These sovereign thrones, are all supplied, and filled
        Her sweet perfections⁴ with one self° king!   one and the same
        Away before me to sweet beds of flowers!
40   Love thoughts lie rich when canopied with bowers.

                                Exeunt.°   They exit (Latin)

                        1.2

        Enter VIOLA, *a* CAPTAIN, *and sailors.*

VIOLA   What country, friends, is this?
CAPTAIN   This is Illyria, lady.
VIOLA   And what should I do in Illyria?
        My brother he is in Elysium.⁵
        Perchance° he is not drowned. What think you, sailors?   Perhaps
5 CAPTAIN   It is perchance° that you yourself were saved.   by chance
VIOLA   O my poor brother! And so perchance may he be.
CAPTAIN   True, madam. And to comfort you with chance,°   that possibility
        Assure yourself, after our ship did split,°   break up
        When you and those poor number saved with you

5. Orsino puns on "hart" and "heart."
6. Serious epidemic diseases were thought to be caused by bad air.
7. Orsino compares himself to Actaeon, a hunter in classical mythology who was turned into a stag and torn apart by his own dogs after he saw the goddess Diana (Artemis) bathing naked.
8. The sky ("element") itself for seven hot summers.
9. That is, her love for her dead brother.

1. Such excellent construction.
2. The arrow of Cupid, Roman god of love.
3. In the Renaissance, the liver, brain, and heart were often identified as the seats of, respectively, love, the rational soul, and feeling or emotion.
4. And her sweet perfections are filled.
1.2 Location: The coast of Illyria.
5. In classical mythology, the abode of the blessed after death.

10 Hung on our driving boat,[6] I saw your brother,
    Most provident in peril, bind himself—
    Courage and hope both teaching him the practice—
    To a strong mast that lived° upon the sea,   *floated*
    Where, like Arion[7] on the dolphin's back,
15 I saw him hold acquaintance with the waves[8]
    So long as I could see.
    VIOLA [*giving him money*] For saying so, there's gold.
    Mine own escape unfoldeth to° my hope,   *encourages*
    Whereto thy speech serves for authority,°   *corroboration*
    The like° of him. Know'st thou this country?   *The same (news)*
20 CAPTAIN Ay, madam, well, for I was bred and born
    Not three hours' travel from this very place.
    VIOLA Who governs here?
    CAPTAIN A noble duke, in nature as in name.
    VIOLA What is his name?
25 CAPTAIN Orsino.
    VIOLA Orsino. I have heard my father name him.
    He was a bachelor then.
    CAPTAIN And so is now, or was so very late;°   *recently*
    For but a month ago I went from hence,
30 And then 'twas fresh in murmur°—as, you know,   *rumor*
    What great ones do the less will prattle of—
    That he did seek the love of fair Olivia.
    VIOLA What's she?
    CAPTAIN A virtuous maid, the daughter of a count
35 That died some twelvemonth since, then leaving her
    In the protection of his son, her brother,
    Who shortly° also died, for whose dear love,   *shortly thereafter*
    They say, she hath abjured° the sight   *renounced*
    And company of men.
    VIOLA   O, that I served that lady,
40 And might not be delivered° to the world   *made known*
    Till I had made mine own occasion mellow,°   *ripe (to be known)*
    What my estate° is.   *rank, social position*
    CAPTAIN   That were hard to compass,°   *achieve*
    Because she will admit no kind of suit,°   *petition*
    No, not the Duke's.
45 VIOLA There is a fair behavior[9] in thee, captain,
    And though that nature with a beauteous wall
    Doth oft close in pollution,[1] yet of thee
    I will believe thou hast a mind that suits
    With this thy fair and outward character.
50 I prithee°—and I'll pay thee bounteously—   *pray thee*
    Conceal me what I am, and be my aid
    For such disguise as haply° shall become   *possibly*

6. Our boat being driven before the wind.
7. Greek poet and singer (late 7th c. B.C.E.).
According to legend, to avoid being murdered
by pirates, he jumped into the sea and was
rescued by dolphins enchanted by his music.

8. That is, stay above water.
9. Manner of conduct; external appearance.
1. Though nature often conceals a person's
inward corruption with outward beauty.

The form of my intent.[2] I'll serve this duke.
Thou shalt present me as an eunuch[3] to him.
55 It may be worth thy pains,° for I can sing   *troubles*
And speak to him in many sorts of music
That will allow me very worth his service.[4]
What else may hap, to time I will commit.
Only shape thou thy silence to my wit.°   *plan*
60 CAPTAIN   Be you his eunuch, and your mute° I'll be.   *silent servant*
When my tongue blabs, then let mine eyes not see.
VIOLA   I thank thee. Lead me on.   *Exeunt.*

1.3

Enter SIR TOBY *[Belch] and* MARIA.[5]

SIR TOBY   What a plague° means my niece to take the   *(an oath)*
death of her brother thus? I am sure care's an enemy
to life.
MARIA   By my troth, Sir Toby, you must come in earlier o'
5   nights. Your cousin,° my lady, takes great exceptions to   *kinswoman*
your ill hours.
SIR TOBY   Why, let her except before excepted![6]
MARIA   Ay, but you must confine yourself within the
modest limits of order.
10 SIR TOBY   Confine? I'll confine myself no finer[7] than I
am. These clothes are good enough to drink in, and so
be these boots too. An° they be not, let them hang them-   *If*
selves in their own straps!
MARIA   That quaffing and drinking will undo you. I heard
15   my lady talk of it yesterday, and of a foolish knight that
you brought in one night here to be her wooer.
SIR TOBY   Who, Sir Andrew Aguecheek?[8]
MARIA   Ay, he.
SIR TOBY   He's as tall[9] a man as any's in Illyria.
20 MARIA   What's that to th' purpose?
SIR TOBY   Why, he has three thousand ducats a year!
MARIA   Ay, but he'll have but a year in all these ducats.[1]
He's a very° fool and a prodigal.   *an absolute*
SIR TOBY   Fie that you'll say so! He plays o' th' viol-de-
25   gamboys,[2] and speaks three or four languages word for

---

2. The outward appearance of my plan.
3. A castrato, a male soprano. While this disguise would explain Viola's feminine voice,
she ultimately chooses the disguise of a
young (male) page whose voice has not yet
changed.
4. That will prove me very worthy to serve him.
1.3 Location: The Countess Olivia's residence.
5. Usually pronounced "Ma-RYE-uh."
6. A play on a Latin legal phrase (*exceptis
excipiendis*) meaning "with the necessary
exceptions having been made." Thus Toby

sidesteps Olivia's criticism.
7. A pun: he will dress ("confine") himself
neither more strictly (because of his girth)
nor more elegantly.
8. Usually pronounced "AY-gyoo-cheek."
9. Brave (Maria understands the word in its
usual modern sense).
1. That is, he will spend his money in a year.
2. The viola da gamba, a bowed stringed
instrument played while held between the
legs (as is the modern cello).

word without book,° and hath all the good gifts of nature.

from memory

MARIA He hath indeed, almost natural,[3] for besides that he's a fool, he's a great quarreler, and but that he hath the gift° of a coward to allay the gust° he hath in quarreling, 'tis thought among the prudent he would quickly have the gift of a grave.

talent / relish

SIR TOBY By this hand, they are scoundrels and sub-stractors° that say so of him. Who are they?

i.e., detractors

MARIA They that add, moreover, he's drunk nightly in your company.

SIR TOBY With drinking healths to my niece. I'll drink to her as long as there is a passage in my throat and drink in Illyria. He's a coward and a coistrel° that will not drink to my niece till his brains turn o'th' toe, like a parish top.[4] What, wench! *Castiliano, vulgo,*[5] for here comes Sir Andrew Agueface.[6]

horse groom, knave

Enter SIR ANDREW [*Aguecheek*].

SIR ANDREW Sir Toby Belch! How now, Sir Toby Belch?

SIR TOBY Sweet Sir Andrew!

SIR ANDREW [*to* MARIA] Bless you, fair shrew.[7]

MARIA And you too, sir.

SIR TOBY Accost, Sir Andrew, accost![8]

SIR ANDREW What's that?

SIR TOBY My niece's chambermaid.°

lady-in-waiting

SIR ANDREW Good Mistress Accost, I desire better acquaintance.

MARIA My name is Mary, sir.

SIR ANDREW Good Mistress Mary Accost—

SIR TOBY You mistake, knight. "Accost" is front her, board her, woo her, assail[9] her.

SIR ANDREW By my troth, I would not undertake[1] her in this company.° Is that the meaning of "accost"?

this audience

MARIA Fare you well, gentlemen. [*begins to exit*]

SIR TOBY An° thou let part so, Sir Andrew, would thou mightst never draw sword again.[2]

If

SIR ANDREW An you part so, mistress, I would I might never draw sword again. Fair lady, do you think you have fools in hand?°

are dealing with fools

3. Naturally deficient in intellect. (Idiots were called "naturals.")
4. A large top that parishioners could whip into spinning for their entertainment and exercise.
5. The meaning of this phrase is unknown; perhaps "speak of the devil," because Castil-ians were considered devilish.
6. With a face pale and thin, as if he were suf-fering from the cold stage of an ague.
7. A woman given to scolding; here, probably used in a benign and playful sense.

8. Greet (Maria), possibly with a kiss as was Elizabethan fashion.
9. A series of nautical terms with double meanings, beginning with "accost," or sail alongside (which is also a meaning of "board"). *Front:* meet face-to-face; *board:* make advances to; *assail:* make trial of, woo.
1. Attempt her (with sexual implication).
2. That is, to part with her in this fashion is unworthy of a knight (but also with sexual implication).

MARIA   Sir, I have not you by th' hand.

65 SIR ANDREW   Marry,[3] but you shall have, and here's my hand.

MARIA [*taking his hand*]   Now sir, thought is free.[4] I pray you, bring your hand to th' butt'ry-bar,[5] and let it drink.

SIR ANDREW   Wherefore,° sweetheart? What's your meta-   Why

70 phor?

MARIA   It's dry,[6] sir.

SIR ANDREW   Why, I think so. I am not such an ass but I can keep my hand dry.[7] But what's your jest?

MARIA   A dry jest,[8] sir.

75 SIR ANDREW   Are you full of them?

MARIA   Ay, sir, I have them at my fingers' ends.[9] Marry, now I let go your hand, I am barren.°   *Exit.*   (of jokes)

SIR TOBY   O knight, thou lack'st° a cup of canary![1] When   are in need of did I see thee so put down?[2]

80 SIR ANDREW   Never in your life, I think, unless you see canary put me down.° Methinks sometimes I have no   lay me low more wit than a Christian° or an ordinary man has. But   an ordinary human I am a great eater of beef,[3] and I believe that does harm to my wit.

85 SIR TOBY   No question.

SIR ANDREW   An I thought that, I'd forswear it. I'll ride home tomorrow, Sir Toby.

SIR TOBY   *Pourquoi,*° my dear knight?   Why (French)

SIR ANDREW   What is "*pourquoi*"? Do, or not do? I would

90 I had bestowed that time in the tongues[4] that I have in fencing, dancing, and bear-baiting. O, had I but fol- lowed the arts!°   i.e., liberal arts

SIR TOBY   Then hadst thou had an excellent head of hair.

SIR ANDREW   Why, would that have mended° my hair?   improved

95 SIR TOBY   Past question, for thou seest it will not curl by nature.

SIR ANDREW   But it becomes me well enough, does't not?

SIR TOBY   Excellent! It hangs like flax on a distaff,[5] and I hope to see a housewife take thee between her legs and

100 spin it off.[6]

---

3. By the Virgin Mary (a mild oath).

4. I may think whatever I like (proverbial).

5. The ledge on top of the half-door to the buttery, a storeroom for liquor and provisions, over which such items were served.

6. Unproductive of its intended meaning. Dryness of the palm of Sir Andrew's hand (which Maria is holding) is also a sign of sex- ual impotence.

7. A reference to the proverb "fools have wit enough to keep themselves out of the rain."

8. A joke about dryness; a joke that displays a dry or sharp wit; a joke that partially fails because of Sir Andrew's obtuseness.

9. Ready at hand; she also refers to Sir

Andrew, whom she holds at her fingers' ends.

1. A sweet wine (originally from the Canary Islands).

2. Defeated verbally, made a fool of.

3. Eating too much beef was believed to lower intelligence.

4. The study of languages; Sir Toby answers as if he had meant (curling) tongs.

5. A staff that holds the wool or flax being spun into thread.

6. That is, remove his hair both by using it as if it were flax to be spun and by infecting him with venereal disease (which will result in baldness). One meaning of "housewife" (hus- wife) is prostitute.

SIR ANDREW Faith,° I'll home tomorrow, Sir Toby. Your   *By my faith*
niece will not be seen, or if she be, it's four to one she'll
none of me. The Count[7] himself here hard by° woos her.   *nearby*

SIR TOBY She'll none o' th' Count. She'll not match above

105 her degree,° neither in estate,° years, nor wit. I   *social rank / status*
have heard her swear't. Tut, there's life in't,[8] man.

SIR ANDREW I'll stay a month longer. I am a fellow o' th'
strangest mind i' th' world. I delight in masques and
revels sometimes altogether.

110 SIR TOBY Art thou good at these kickshawses,[9] knight?

SIR ANDREW As any man in Illyria, whatsoever he be,
under the degree of my betters; and yet I will not com-
pare with an old man.°   *expert*

SIR TOBY What is thy excellence in a galliard,[1] knight?

115 SIR ANDREW Faith, I can cut a caper.[2]

SIR TOBY And I can cut the mutton° to't.   *cooked sheep; whore*

SIR ANDREW And I think I have the back-trick[3] simply as
strong as any man in Illyria.

SIR TOBY Wherefore are these things hid? Wherefore

120 have these gifts a curtain[4] before 'em? Are they like to
take dust, like Mistress Mall's[5] picture? Why dost thou
not go to church in a galliard and come home in a cor-
anto?[6] My very walk should be a jig. I would not so
much as make water but in a cinquepace.[7] What dost

125 thou mean? Is it a world to hide virtues in? I did think,
by the excellent constitution of thy leg, it was formed
under the star of a galliard.[8]

SIR ANDREW Ay, 'tis strong, and it does indifferent° well in   *reasonably*
a flame-colored stock.° Shall we set about some revels?   *multicolored stockings*

130 SIR TOBY What shall we do else? Were we not born under
Taurus?[9]

SIR ANDREW Taurus? That's sides and heart.

SIR TOBY No, sir, it is legs and thighs. Let me see thee
caper.

[SIR ANDREW *dances.*]

135 Ha, higher! Ha, ha, excellent.   *Exeunt.*

---

7. That is, Duke Orsino (sometimes referred
to as "Count" in the play).
8. Where there's life, there's hope (proverbial).
9. Trifles (from the French *quelque chose*).
1. A quick, lively dance in triple time.
2. Dance or leap in a frolicsome way. Also,
capers (the buds or berries of a plant used as
a condiment) were employed in mutton
sauces.
3. Backward step in the galliard.
4. Paintings were sometimes hidden behind
curtains to protect them from dust and
sunlight.
5. "Mall" was a nickname for "Mary." It has
been suggested that this is a reference to

Queen Elizabeth's lady-in-waiting, Mary Fit-
ton, who was pregnant with Sir William Knol-
lys's illegitimate child at the time Shakespeare
wrote *Twelfth Night*.
6. A "running dance" (*courante*) of French
origin.
7. A galliard-like dance whose steps were reg-
ulated by the number five.
8. That is, under a star conducive to dancing.
9. The second sign of the zodiac, the Bull,
was associated with the neck and the throat
and, less commonly, with the legs and thighs,
but never with the sides and the heart (as Sir
Andrew suggests).

1.4

Enter VALENTINE, *and* VIOLA *in man's attire [as Cesario].*

VALENTINE   If the Duke continue these favors towards you, Cesario, you are like to be much advanced. He hath known you but three days, and already you are no stranger.

5 VIOLA   You either fear his humor° or my negligence, that you call in question the continuance of his love. Is he inconstant, sir, in his favors?   *changeable mood*

VALENTINE   No, believe me.

VIOLA   I thank you. Here comes the Count.

Enter ORSINO, CURIO, *and attendants*

10 ORSINO   Who saw Cesario, ho?

VIOLA   On your attendance,° my lord, here.   *At your service*

ORSINO [*to* CURIO *and attendants*]   Stand you a while
      aloof.° [*to* VIOLA] Cesario,   *to the side*
Thou know'st no less but all.° I have unclasped   *i.e., everything*
To thee the book even of my secret soul.

15 Therefore, good youth, address thy gait unto her.°   *go to (Olivia)*
Be not denied access, stand at her doors
And tell them, there thy fixèd foot shall grow°   *take root*
Till thou have audience.

VIOLA   Sure, my noble lord,
If she be so abandoned to her sorrow

20 As it is spoke, she never will admit me.

ORSINO   Be clamorous and leap all civil bounds[1]
Rather than make unprofited° return.   *unsuccessful*

VIOLA   Say I do speak with her, my lord, what then?

ORSINO   O, then unfold the passion of my love.

25 Surprise her with discourse of my dear° faith.[2]   *heartfelt*
It shall become thee well to act my woes—
She will attend it better in thy youth
Than in a nuncio's° of more grave aspect.°   *messenger's / appearance*

VIOLA   I think not so, my lord.

ORSINO   Dear lad, believe it;

30 For they shall yet° belie thy happy years   *thus far*
That say thou art a man. Diana's lip
Is not more smooth and rubious,° thy small pipe°   *ruby red / treble voice*
Is as the maiden's organ, shrill° and sound,°   *high-pitched / uncracked*
And all is semblative° a woman's part.   *similar to*

35 I know thy constellation[3] is right apt
For this affair. [*to* CURIO *and attendants*] Some four or
      five attend him,
All, if you will, for I myself am best
When least in company. [*to* VIOLA] Prosper well in this

1.4 Location: Orsino's palace.
1. Exceed the norms of courtesy.
2. Take her unawares with speech of my

heartfelt love.
3. That is, your nature (as determined by the stars).

And thou shalt live as freely as thy lord,
To call his fortunes thine.

40 VIOLA   I'll do my best
To woo your lady. [*aside*] Yet a barful strife!⁴
Whoe'er I woo, myself would be his wife.   *Exeunt.*

1.5

Enter MARIA *and* [FESTE,⁵ *the*] *clown.*

MARIA   Nay, either tell me where thou hast been or I will
not open my lips so wide as a bristle may enter in° way of   *by*
thy excuse. My lady will hang thee for thy absence.

FESTE   Let her hang me. He that is well hanged⁶ in this
5   world needs to fear no colours.⁷

MARIA   Make that good.°   *Explain that*

FESTE   He shall see none to fear.

MARIA   A good Lenten⁸ answer. I can tell thee where
that saying was born, of "I fear no colors."

10 FESTE   Where, good Mistress Mary?

MARIA   In the wars; and that may you be bold to say in
your foolery.

FESTE   Well, God give them wisdom that have it, and
those that are fools, let them use their talents.⁹

15 MARIA   Yet you will be hanged for being so long absent, or
to be turned away°—is not that as good as a hanging to   *dismissed*
you?

FESTE   Many a good hanging¹ prevents a bad marriage,
and, for turning away, let summer bear it out.²

20 MARIA   You are resolute, then?

FESTE   Not so, neither, but I am resolved on two points.°   *issues; laces*

MARIA   That if one break, the other will hold, or, if both
break, your gaskins° fall.   *wide breeches*

FESTE   Apt, in good faith, very apt. Well, go thy way. If
25   Sir Toby would leave drinking, thou wert as witty a
piece of Eve's flesh° as any in Illyria.³   *a woman*

MARIA   Peace, you rogue. No more o' that. Here comes my
lady. Make your excuse wisely, you were best.°   [*Exit*]   *it would be best for you*

Enter Lady OLIVIA *with* MALVOLIO⁴ [*and attendants*]

FESTE [*aside*]   Wit,° an't° be thy will, put me into good   *Intelligence / if it*
30   fooling! Those wits that think they have thee do very oft
prove fools, and I that am sure I lack thee may pass for a

---

4. A task full of hindrances.
1.5 Location: Orsino's residence.
5. Usually pronounced "FESS-tee."
6. Hanged to death. Feste also implies that he is "well hung" (i.e., well-endowed sexually), a trait regularly attributed to fools (as supposed to accompany mental deficiency).
7. Fear no foe (literally, military flags); punning on "collars," the hangman's noose.
8. Lean or meager (i.e., appropriate to Lent).
9. Abilities, with a punning allusion to the

parable of the talents (coins) in Matthew 25.14–30.
1. A reference to both capital punishment and sexual endowment.
2. That is, let mild weather make it bearable (for the newly homeless).
3. Feste appears to say that Toby is as likely to give up drinking as Maria is to be witty.
4. Usually pronounced "Mal-VOE-lee-o" (a name meaning "ill will").

wise man. For what says Quinapalus?[5] "Better a witty
Fool than a foolish wit." God bless thee, lady.

OLIVIA [*to attendants*]   Take the fool away.

35 FESTE   Do you not hear, fellows? Take away the lady.

OLIVIA   Go to,[6] you're a dry° fool. I'll no more of you.   dull
Besides, you grow dishonest.[7]

FESTE   Two faults, madonna,° that drink and good counsel   my lady (Italian)
will amend. For give the dry fool drink, then is the fool
40 not dry. Bid the dishonest man mend° himself: if he   reform
mend, he is no longer dishonest; if he cannot, let the
botcher° mend him. Anything that's mended is but   mender of old clothes
patched; virtue that transgresses is but patched with
sin, and sin that amends is but patched with virtue.[8] If
45 that this simple syllogism will serve, so; if it will not,
what remedy? As there is no true cuckold but calamity,
so beauty's a flower.[9] The lady bade take away the fool.
Therefore, I say again, take her away.

OLIVIA   Sir, I bade them take away you.

50 FESTE   Misprision[1] in the highest degree! Lady, *cucullus
non facit monachum.*[2] That's as much to say as, I wear
not motley[3] in my brain. Good madonna, give me leave
to prove you a fool.

OLIVIA   Can you do it?

55 FESTE   Dexteriously,° good madonna.   Dexterously

OLIVIA   Make your proof.

FESTE   I must catechize you for it, madonna. Good my
mouse° of virtue, answer me.   (term of endearment)

OLIVIA   Well, sir, for want of other idleness° I'll bide° your   diversion / await
60 proof.

FESTE   Good madonna, why mournest thou?

OLIVIA   Good fool, for my brother's death.

FESTE   I think his soul is in hell, madonna.

OLIVIA   I know his soul is in heaven, fool.

65 FESTE   The more fool, madonna, to mourn for your
brother's soul, being in heaven. Take away the fool,
gentlemen.

OLIVIA   What think you of this fool, Malvolio? Doth he
not mend?[4]

70 MALVOLIO   Yes, and shall do till the pangs of death
shake him. Infirmity, that decays the wise, doth ever
make the better fool.

---

5. An invented philosopher whose wisdom
Feste pretends to quote.
6. An expression of impatience.
7. Unreliable (because unaccountably absent
from the house).
8. In this passage, Feste caricatures formal
logic (the syllogism).
9. That is, the cuckold is the misfortune that
Olivia has wed, to which she must be unfaithful so that her beauty can bloom and find love

(before it fades).
1. Misunderstanding; wrongful arrest.
2. The cowl does not make the monk (Latin
proverb).
3. The multicolored tunic of professional
jesters.
4. Improve (by becoming more entertaining);
Malvolio takes the improvement to lie in
becoming more foolish.

OLIVIA   Give me my veil. Come, throw it o'er my face.
We'll once more hear Orsino's embassy.°   *ambassador's message*

Enter VIOLA [*as Cesario*]

VIOLA   The honorable lady of the house, which is she?

160 OLIVIA   Speak to me. I shall answer for her. Your will?

VIOLA   Most radiant, exquisite, and unmatchable
beauty—I pray you, tell me if this be the lady of the
house, for I never saw her. I would be loath to cast
away° my speech, for, besides that it is excellently well   *waste*
165 penned, I have taken great pains to con° it. Good beau-   *memorize*
ties, let me sustain° no scorn. I am very comptible,°   *endure / sensitive*
even to the least sinister usage.[8]

OLIVIA   Whence came you, sir?

VIOLA   I can say little more than I have studied,° and   *committed to memory*
170 that question's out of my part. Good gentle one, give
me modest° assurance if you be the lady of the house,   *reasonable*
that I may proceed in my speech.

OLIVIA   Are you a comedian?°   *an actor*

VIOLA   No, my profound heart.[9] And yet, by the very fangs
175 of malice, I swear I am not that I play.° Are you the lady   *what I act*
of the house?

OLIVIA   If I do not usurp° myself, I am.   *impersonate*

VIOLA   Most certain, if you are she, you do usurp yourself,
for what is yours to bestow is not yours to reserve.[1] But
180 this is from° my commission.° I will on with my speech   *beyond / instructions*
in your praise, and then show you the heart of my
message.

OLIVIA   Come to what is important in't, I forgive you° the   *excuse you from reciting*
praise.

185 VIOLA   Alas, I took great pains to study it, and 'tis poetical.

OLIVIA   It is the more like to be feigned. I pray you keep
it in. I heard you were saucy° at my gates, and allowed   *impertinent*
your approach rather to wonder at you than to hear
you. If you be not mad, be gone. If you have reason, be
190 brief. 'Tis not that time of moon with me to make one
in so skipping a dialogue.[2]

MARIA   Will you hoist sail, sir? Here lies your way.

VIOLA   No, good swabber, I am to hull[3] here a little longer. —Some mollification for your giant,[4] sweet lady.
195 Tell me your mind, I am a messenger.

OLIVIA   Sure you have some hideous matter to deliver,
when the courtesy[5] of it is so fearful. Speak your office.°   *commission*

---

8. The smallest discourtesy.
9. My most wise lady.
1. That is, a woman usurps a husband's rightful role if she bestows herself not on a man
but on herself (by "reserving" herself).
2. That is, I am not so under the moon's influence (literally, so lunatic) that I am willing to

participate in such a fantastic conversation.
3. Lie at anchor, with furled sails. *Swabber:*
one who mops the decks of a ship.
4. Maria, who is small of stature, is here
mockingly identified as one of the giants who
protected ladies in medieval romances.
5. The courteous preamble.

VIOLA   It alone concerns your ear. I bring no overture° of   *declaration*
war, no taxation of homage.[6] I hold the olive° in my hand.   *olive branch*
200   My words are as full of peace as matter.°   *meaning*

OLIVIA   Yet you began rudely. What are you? What would
you?

VIOLA   The rudeness that hath appeared in me have I
learned from my entertainment.° What I am and what I   *reception*
205   would are as secret as maidenhead:° to your ears, divin-   *virginity*
ity; to any other's, profanation.

OLIVIA   [*to* MARIA *and attendants*]   Give us the place alone.
We will hear this divinity.°   MARIA *and attendants exit.*   *religious discourse*
Now sir, what is your text?[7]

210   VIOLA   Most sweet lady—

OLIVIA   A comfortable° doctrine, and much may be said   *comforting*
of it. Where lies your text?

VIOLA   In Orsino's bosom.

OLIVIA   In his bosom? In what chapter of his bosom?

215   VIOLA   To answer by the method,° in the first of his heart.   *in the same style*

OLIVIA   O, I have read it; it is heresy. Have you no more
to say?

VIOLA   Good madam, let me see your face.

OLIVIA   Have you any commission from your lord to nego-
220   tiate with my face? You are now out of° your text. But we   *straying from*
will draw the curtain and show you the picture. [*She*
removes her veil.] Look you, sir, such a one I was this
present.[8] Is't not well done?

VIOLA   Excellently done, if God did all.[9]

225   OLIVIA   'Tis in grain,° sir; 'twill endure wind and weather.   *It is dyed fast*

VIOLA   'Tis beauty truly blent,° whose red and white   *blended*
Nature's own sweet and cunning° hand laid on.   *skillful*
Lady, you are the cruel'st she° alive   *woman*
If you will lead these graces to the grave
230   And leave the world no copy.[1]

OLIVIA   O sir, I will not be so hard-hearted! I will give out
divers schedules° of my beauty. It shall be inventoried   *inventory*
and every particle and utensil labeled[2] to my will: as,
item, two lips, indifferent° red; *item,* two gray eyes,   *moderately*
235   with lids to them; *item,* one neck, one chin, and so
forth. Were you sent hither to praise° me?   *appraise*

VIOLA   I see you what you are. You are too proud.
But if° you were the devil, you are fair.   *Even if*
My lord and master loves you. O, such love
240   Could be but recompensed though[3] you were crowned

6. Demand for payment of tribute.
7. That is, the passage on which "Cesario's" sermon will expound.
8. That is, this is a current ("present") likeness of me (as though she were revealing a portrait of herself).

9. If it is your natural face, without cosmetics.
1. That is, no child; Olivia, however, takes "copy" to mean "written record."
2. Every individual part and article described and added as a codicil.
3. Should be equally returned even if.

The nonpareil of beauty.°   *An unsurpassed beauty*

OLIVIA   How does he love me?

VIOLA   With adorations, fertile° tears,   *plentiful*
With groans that thunder love, with sighs of fire.[4]

OLIVIA   Your lord does know my mind. I cannot love him.

245   Yet I suppose him virtuous, know him noble,
Of great estate, of fresh and stainless youth;
In voices well divulged,° free,° learned, and valiant,   *well spoken of / noble*
And in dimension and the shape of nature°   *physical appearance*
A gracious° person. But yet I cannot love him.   *An attractive*

250   He might have took his answer long ago.

VIOLA   If I did love you in° my master's flame,°   *with / passion*
With such a suff'ring, such a deadly° life,   *deathlike*
In your denial I would find no sense,
I would not understand it.

OLIVIA   Why, what would you?

255   VIOLA   Make me a willow[5] cabin at your gate
And call upon my soul° within the house,   *(i.e., Olivia)*
Write loyal cantons° of contemnèd° love   *songs / despised*
And sing them loud even in the dead of night,
Hallow° your name to the reverberate° hills   *Shout / echoing*

260   And make the babbling gossip of the air[6]
Cry out "Olivia!" O, you should not rest
Between the elements of air and earth
But you should pity me.

OLIVIA   You might do much.

265   What is your parentage?

VIOLA   Above my fortunes,[7] yet my state° is well.   *social standing*
I am a gentleman.

OLIVIA   Get you to your lord.
I cannot love him. Let him send no more—
Unless perchance you come to me again

270   To tell me how he takes it. Fare you well.
I thank you for your pains. Spend this for me.

[*She offers money.*]

VIOLA   I am no fee'd post,° lady. Keep your purse.   *hired messenger*
My master, not myself, lacks recompense.
Love make his heart of flint that you shall love.[8]

275   And let your fervor, like my master's, be
Placed in contempt. Farewell, fair cruelty.   *Exit.*

OLIVIA   "What is your parentage?"
"Above my fortunes, yet my state is well.
I am a gentleman." I'll be sworn thou art.

---

4. The "tears," "groans," and "sighs of fire" are all clichés of romantic melancholy, fashionable in Elizabethan sonnet writing.
5. The willow was a symbol of grief for unrequited love.
6. Echo, in classical mythology. In love with but rejected by Narcissus, the nymph Echo was eventually reduced to nothing but a voice.
7. My (current) circumstances.
8. That is, may love harden the heart of the man you fall in love with.

280   Thy tongue, thy face, thy limbs, actions, and spirit
       Do give thee fivefold blazon.[9] Not too fast! Soft,° soft—   *Wait*
       Unless the master were the man.° How now?   *servant*
       Even so quickly may one catch the plague?
       Methinks I feel this youth's perfections
       With an invisible and subtle stealth
285   To creep in at mine eyes. Well, let it be.—
       What ho, Malvolio!

             Enter MALVOLIO

MALVOLIO   Here, madam, at your service.
OLIVIA   Run after that same peevish messenger,
       The County's° man. He left this ring behind him,   *Count's (i.e., Duke's)*
290   Would I° or not. Tell him I'll none of it.   *Whether I wished it*
       Desire him not to flatter with° his lord,   *encourage*
       Nor hold him up with hopes. I am not for him.
       If that the youth will come this way tomorrow,
       I'll give him reasons for't. Hie thee,° Malvolio.   *Hurry*
295 MALVOLIO   Madam, I will.   *Exit.*
OLIVIA   I do I know not what, and fear to find
       Mine eye too great a flatterer for my mind.[1]
       Fate, show thy force. Ourselves we do not owe.°   *own*
       What is decreed must be, and be this so.

                    [*Exit at another door.*]

                          2.1

            Enter ANTONIO *and* SEBASTIAN.

ANTONIO   Will you stay no longer? Nor will° you not that   *wish*
       I go with you?
SEBASTIAN   By your patience, no. My stars shine darkly
       over me. The malignancy of my fate[2] might perhaps
5   distemper° yours. Therefore I shall crave of you your   *disturb; infect*
       leave that I may bear my evils alone. It were a bad
       recompense for your love to lay any of them on you.
ANTONIO   Let me yet know of you whither you are bound.
SEBASTIAN   No, sooth,° sir. My determinate° voyage is   *truly / determined-on*
10   mere extravagancy.° But I perceive in you so excellent a   *aimless wandering*
       touch of modesty° that you will not extort from me   *civility; reserve*
       what I am willing to keep in. Therefore it charges me
       in manners° the rather to express myself. You must   *in courteous fashion*
       know of me then, Antonio, my name is Sebastian, which
15   I called Roderigo. My father was that Sebastian of Mes-
       saline[3] whom I know you have heard of. He left behind
       him myself and a sister, both born in an hour.°   *in the same hour*
       If the

---

9. That is, your natural attributes—tongue, face, limbs, etc.—proclaim you a gentleman as well as any coat of arms would.
1. That is, my eye has seduced my reason.
2.1 Location: Somewhere near the Illyrian coast.

2. The malevolent influence of the stars (which shape my future); "malignancy" also has its medical sense.
3. Possibly Messina (in Sicily) or Massila (modern-day Marseille), or a fictional town.

heavens had been pleased, would we had so ended!
But you, sir, altered that, for some hour before you took
20   me from the breach° of the sea was my sister drowned.   *surf*
ANTONIO Alas the day!
SEBASTIAN A lady, sir, though it was said she much resembled me, was yet of many accounted beautiful. But
though I could not with such estimable wonder° overfar   *appreciative judgment*
25   believe that, yet thus far I will boldly publish° her: she   *declare*
bore a mind that envy° could not but call fair. She is   *envy itself; the envious*
drowned already, sir, with salt water, though I seem to
drown her remembrance again with more.
ANTONIO Pardon me, sir, your bad entertainment.[4]
30 SEBASTIAN O good Antonio, forgive me your trouble.[5]
ANTONIO If you will not murder me[6] for my love, let me
be your servant.
SEBASTIAN If you will not undo what you have done—
that is, kill him whom you have recovered°—desire it   *rescued*
35   not. Fare ye well at once. My bosom is full of kind-
ness,° and I am yet° so near the manners of my mother   *tender feelings / still*
that, upon the least occasion more, mine eyes will tell
tales of me.[7] I am bound to the Count Orsino's court.
Farewell.   *Exit.*
40 ANTONIO The gentleness of all the gods go with thee!
I have many enemies in Orsino's court,
Else would I very shortly see thee there.
But come what may, I do adore thee so
That danger shall seem sport, and I will go.   *Exit.*

2.2

Enter VIOLA *and* MALVOLIO, *at several° doors.*   *different*

MALVOLIO Were not you even° now with the Countess   *just*
Olivia?
VIOLA Even now, sir. On° a moderate pace I have since   *At*
arrived but hither.°   *traveled only this far*
5 MALVOLIO She returns this ring to you, sir. You might have
saved me my pains to have taken it away yourself. She
adds, moreover, that you should put your lord into a desperate assurance° she will none of him. And one thing   *hopeless certainty*
more, that you be never so hardy° to come again in his   *bold*
10   affairs, unless it be to report your lord's taking of this.[8]
Receive it so.
VIOLA She took the ring of me.[9] I'll none of it.
MALVOLIO Come, sir, you peevishly threw it to her, and
her will is it should be so returned.

---

4. That is, the inadequate hospitality I have
offered you.
5. The trouble I have put you through (by
being my guest).
6. That is, cause my death by insisting that I
depart.

7. That is, my tears will betray my feelings.
2.2 Location: Somewhere between Olivia's
estate and Orsino's palace.
8. Reaction to Olivia's rejection.
9. From me (Viola plays along with Olivia's
story).

[*He throws down the ring.*]

15 If it be worth stooping for, there it lies, in your eye;° if   *within your view*
    not, be it his that finds it.   *Exit.*

VIOLA I left no ring with her. What means this lady?

[*She picks up the ring.*]

    Fortune forbid my outside° have not charmed her!   *outward appearance*
    She made good view of° me, indeed so much   *examined me closely*
20 That sure methought her eyes had lost° her tongue,   *had made her lose*
    For she did speak in starts distractedly.
    She loves me, sure! The cunning of her passion
    Invites me in° this churlish messenger.   *by means of*
    None of my lord's ring? Why, he sent her none!
25 I am the man.[1] If it be so, as 'tis,
    Poor lady, she were better love a dream.
    Disguise, I see thou art a wickedness
    Wherein the pregnant° enemy° does much.   *resourceful / (Satan)*
    How easy is it for the proper false[2]
30 In women's waxen hearts to set their forms![3]
    Alas, our frailty is the cause, not we,
    For such as we are made of, such we be.[4]
    How will this fadge?° My master loves her dearly,   *turn out*
    And I, poor monster,[5] fond° as much on him,   *dote*
35 And she, mistaken, seems to dote on me.
    What will become of this? As I am man,
    My state is desperate for my master's love.
    As I am woman (now, alas the day!),
    What thriftless° sighs shall poor Olivia breathe!   *unprofitable*
40 O Time, thou must untangle this, not I.
    It is too hard a knot for me t'untie.   [*Exit*]

2.3

Enter SIR TOBY *and* SIR ANDREW.

SIR TOBY Approach, Sir Andrew. Not to be abed after
    midnight is to be up betimes,° and "*diluculo surgere*,"[6]   *early*
    thou knowest.

SIR ANDREW Nay, by my troth,° I know not. But I know to   *by my faith (a mild oath)*
5 be up late is to be up late.

SIR TOBY A false conclusion. I hate it as an unfilled can.°   *drinking vessel, tankard*
    To be up after midnight and to go to bed then is early, so
    that to go to bed after midnight is to go to bed betimes.
    Does not our lives consist of the four elements?[7]

10 SIR ANDREW Faith, so they say, but I think it rather con-
    sists of eating and drinking.

---

1. That is, the man of Olivia's affections.
2. Men who are handsome and duplicitous.
3. To make strong impressions in women's
soft hearts (the seat of their passions).
4. That is, we are frail because we are made
of frail flesh.
5. That is, both a man and a woman.

6. An abbreviated form of the Latin phrase
Diluculo surgere saluberrimum est (To rise at
dawn is most healthful).
7. The four elements—fire, water, earth, and
air—thought to constitute all matter.

2.3 Location: Olivia's house.

SIR TOBY Thou'rt a scholar. Let us therefore eat and
drink. Marian, I say, a stoup° of wine!   *drinking vessel*

Enter [FESTE, *the*] *clown.*

SIR ANDREW Here comes the fool, i'faith.

15 FESTE How now, my hearts? Did you never see the picture of "We Three"?[8]

SIR TOBY Welcome, ass. Now let's have a catch.°   *sing a round*

SIR ANDREW By my troth, the fool has an excellent breast.°   *voice*
I had rather than forty shillings I had such a leg,° and so   *(for dancing)*
20 sweet a breath to sing, as the fool has.—In sooth, thou
wast in very gracious fooling last night when thou
spokest of Pigrogromitus, of the Vapians passing the
equinoctial of Queubus.[9] 'Twas very good, i'faith. I sent
thee sixpence for thy leman.° Hadst it?   *sweetheart*

25 FESTE I did impeticos thy gratillity,[1] for Malvolio's nose
is no whipstock,° my lady has a white hand, and the Myr-   *whip handle*
midons[2] are no bottle-ale houses.°   *low-class taverns*

SIR ANDREW Excellent! Why, this is the best fooling,
when all is done. Now a song.

30 SIR TOBY [*to* FESTE] Come on, there is sixpence for you.
Let's have a song.

SIR ANDREW [*to* FESTE] There's a testril[3] of me, too. If
one knight give a—

FESTE Would you have a love song or a song of good° life?   *virtuous*

35 SIR TOBY A love song, a love song.

SIR ANDREW Ay, ay, I care not for good life.

FESTE *sings*

O mistress mine, where are you roaming?
O, stay and hear! Your truelove's coming,
That can sing both high and low.
40 Trip° no further, pretty sweeting.   *Go*
Journeys end in lovers meeting,
Every wise man's son doth know.

SIR ANDREW Excellent good, i' faith.

SIR TOBY Good, good.

45 FESTE What is love? 'Tis not hereafter.
Present mirth hath present laughter.
What's to come is still° unsure.   *always*
In delay there lies no plenty,
Then come kiss me, sweet and twenty.[4]
50 Youth's a stuff will not endure.

SIR ANDREW A mellifluous voice, as I am true knight.

SIR TOBY A contagious breath.[5]

---

8. A picture, inscribed "we three," of two fools or ass heads, the third being the viewer.
9. Examples of Feste's mock learning.
1. That is, impetticoat (pocket) your gratuity (a small tip).
2. Followers of the Greek warrior Achilles at Troy; here, possibly the name of a tavern (the obscurity of Feste's meaning is probably intentional).
3. That is, a tester, a sixpence coin.
4. Sweet and twenty more times sweet.
5. A catchy voice; also, foul or infectious breath.

SIR ANDREW   Very sweet and contagious, i' faith.

SIR TOBY   To hear by the nose, it is dulcet in contagion.[6]

55   But shall we make the welkin° dance indeed? Shall we   *heavens*
rouse the night owl in a catch that will draw three
souls out of one weaver?[7] Shall we do that?

SIR ANDREW   An° you love me, let's do't. I am dog° at a   *If / expert*
catch.

60   FESTE   By'r Lady, sir, and some dogs will catch well.

SIR ANDREW   Most certain. Let our catch be "Thou Knave."

FESTE   "Hold thy peace, thou knave," knight? I shall be
constrained in't to call thee "knave," knight.

SIR ANDREW   'Tis not the first time I have constrained
65   one to call me "knave." Begin, Fool. It begins "Hold thy
peace."

FESTE   I shall never begin if I hold my peace.

SIR ANDREW   Good, i' faith. Come, begin. [*They sing the
catch.*]

    Enter MARIA.

MARIA   What a caterwauling do you keep here! If my
70   lady have not called up her steward Malvolio and bid
him turn you out of doors, never trust me.

SIR TOBY   My lady's a Cathayan,[8] we are politicians,° Mal-   *connivers*
volio's a Peg-a'-Ramsey,[9] and [*sings*] "Three merry men
be we." Am not I consanguineous?[1] Am I not of her
75   blood? Tillyvally!° "Lady"! [*sings*] "There dwelt a man in   *Fiddlesticks*
Babylon, lady, lady."[2]

FESTE   Beshrew° me, the knight's in admirable fooling.   *Curse me (a mild oath)*

SIR ANDREW   Ay, he does well enough if he be disposed,
and so do I, too. He does it with a better grace, but I do
80   it more natural.[3]

SIR TOBY [*sings*]   "O' the twelfth day of December"[4]—

MARIA   For the love o' God, peace!

    Enter MALVOLIO

MALVOLIO   My masters, are you mad? Or what are you?
Have you no wit,° manners, nor honesty° but to gabble   *sense / decency*
85   like tinkers at this time of night? Do ye make an ale-
house of my lady's house, that you squeak out your
coziers'° catches without any mitigation or remorse° of   *cobblers' / intermission*
voice? Is there no respect of place, persons, nor time in
you?

90   SIR TOBY   We did keep time, sir, in our catches. Sneck up!°   *Go hang yourself*

---

6. If we heard with our noses, the sound would be sweetly infectious.
7. Weavers, commonly associated with the singing of psalms, would presumably be resistant to most simple catches. Music was believed able to draw the soul from the body.
8. Chinese; but also a slang term for "cheat."
9. A line from an old song. *Peg-a'-Ramsey*: a character in a popular ballad (here used scornfully).
1. That is, a blood relative of Olivia.
2. The first line ("There dwelt a man in Babylon") and the refrain ("Lady, lady") of the ballad "Constant Susanna."
3. Effortlessly; "natural" also means "idiot."
4. Probably the first line of another ballad or possibly a version of "the twelfth day of Christmas," hence *Twelfth Night.*

MALVOLIO   Sir Toby, I must be round° with you. My lady   *direct*
bade me tell you that, though she harbors you as her
kinsman, she's nothing allied° to your disorders. If you   *no kin*
can separate yourself and your misdemeanors, you are
95   welcome to the house; if not, an° it would please you to   *if*
take leave of her, she is very willing to bid you farewell.

SIR TOBY [*sings*]   "Farewell, dear heart, since I must needs
be gone."5

MARIA   Nay, good Sir Toby.

100   FESTE   "His eyes do show his days are almost done."

MALVOLIO   Is't even so?

SIR TOBY   "But I will never die."

FESTE   "Sir Toby, there you lie."

MALVOLIO   This is much credit to you.

105   SIR TOBY   "Shall I bid him go?"

FESTE   "What an if° you do?"   *an if=if*

SIR TOBY   "Shall I bid him go, and spare not?"

FESTE   "O no, no, no, no, you dare not."

SIR TOBY   Out o' tune, sir? Ye lie. Art° any more than a   *Are you*
110   steward? Dost thou think because thou art virtuous
there shall be no more cakes and ale?6

FESTE   Yes, by Saint Anne, and ginger7 shall be hot i' th'
mouth, too.

SIR TOBY   Thou'rt i' th' right.—Go, sir, rub your chain
115   with crumbs.8—A stoup of wine, Maria!

MALVOLIO   Mistress Mary, if you prized my lady's favor at
anything more than contempt you would not give
means° for this uncivil rule.° She shall know of it, by this   *drink / uncivilized behavior*
hand.   *Exit.*

120   MARIA   Go shake your ears!°   *(i.e., your ass's ears)*

SIR ANDREW   'Twere as good a deed as to drink when a
man's a-hungry to challenge him the field° and then to   *to a duel*
break promise with him and make a fool of him.

SIR TOBY   Do't, knight. I'll write thee a challenge. Or I'll
125   deliver thy indignation to him by word of mouth.

MARIA   Sweet Sir Toby, be patient for tonight. Since the
youth of the Count's was today with my lady, she is
much out of quiet. For Monsieur Malvolio, let me
alone with him. If I do not gull him into a nayword and
130   make him a common recreation,9 do not think I have
wit enough to lie straight in my bed. I know I can do it.

SIR TOBY   Possess° us, possess us, tell us something of him.   *Inform*

---

5. A line from the ballad "Corydon's Farewell to Phyllis."
6. That is, good things. Cakes and ale were often served at church fairs, a practice frowned on by the Puritans (with whom Malvolio is associated by Maria in line 133, below).
7. A root used to flavor drinks such as ale. *Saint*

Anne: mother of the Virgin Mary (the veneration of whom was offensive to Puritans).
8. That is, mind your own business (literally, "go shine your steward's chain").
9. One who provides recreation or entertainment for all (by becoming a laughingstock). *Nayword:* a byword (for "gull" or "fool").

MARIA   Marry, sir, sometimes he is a kind of puritan.[1]

SIR ANDREW   O, if I thought that, I'd beat him like a dog!

135   SIR TOBY   What, for being a puritan? Thy exquisite° rea-   *ingenious*
son, dear knight?

SIR ANDREW   I have no exquisite reason for't, but I have
reason good enough.

MARIA   The devil a puritan that he is, or anything con-
140   stantly but a time-pleaser;° an affectioned° ass that cons   *flatterer / affected*
state without book[2] and utters it by great swathes;° the   *in long stretches*
best persuaded of himself,[3] so crammed, as he thinks,
with excellencies, that it is his grounds of faith° that all   *unyielding belief*
that look on him love him. And on that vice in him will
145   my revenge find notable cause to work.

SIR TOBY   What wilt thou do?

MARIA   I will drop in his way some obscure epistles of
love, wherein by the color of his beard, the shape of his
leg, the manner of his gait, the expressure° of his eye,   *expression*
150   forehead, and complexion,° he shall find himself most   *appearance*
feelingly personated.° I can write very like my lady your   *represented*
niece; on a forgotten matter, we can hardly make distinction of our hands.°   *handwriting*

SIR TOBY   Excellent! I smell a device.°   *scheme, plot*

155   SIR ANDREW   I have't in my nose, too.

SIR TOBY   He shall think, by the letters that thou wilt
drop, that they come from my niece, and that she's in
love with him.

MARIA   My purpose is indeed a horse of that color.

160   SIR ANDREW   And your horse now would make him an ass.

MARIA   Ass° I doubt not.   *(punning on "as")*

SIR ANDREW   O, 'twill be admirable!

MARIA   Sport° royal, I warrant you. I know my physic° will   *Amusement / medicine*
work with him. I will plant you two, and let the fool
165   make a third, where he shall find the letter. Observe his
construction° of it. For this night, to bed, and dream on   *interpretation*
the event.° Farewell.   *Exit.*   *outcome*

SIR TOBY   Good night, Penthesilea.[4]

SIR ANDREW   Before me,[5] she's a good wench.

170   SIR TOBY   She's a beagle true bred, and one that adores
me. What o' that?

SIR ANDREW   I was adored once, too.

SIR TOBY   Let's to bed, knight. Thou hadst need send for
more money.

175   SIR ANDREW   If I cannot recover° your niece, I am a foul   *win*
way out.°   *at a financial loss*

---

1. That is, he is puritanical in his strictness
and moral conduct (though not necessarily a
member of a Puritan sect).
2. Memorizes high-flown language.

3. Having the highest opinion of himself.
4. Queen of the Amazons (another playful
allusion to Maria's small size).
5. A play on the common oath "before God."

SIR TOBY   Send for money, knight. If thou hast her not i'
th' end, call me "Cut."[6]
SIR ANDREW   If I do not, never trust me, take it how you
180   will.
SIR TOBY   Come, come, I'll go burn some sack.° 'Tis too   warm some Spanish wine
late to go to bed now. Come, knight; come, knight.
Exeunt.[7]

2.4

Enter ORSINO, VIOLA, CURIO, *and others.*

ORSINO   Give me some music. Now good morrow,° friends.   morning
Now good Cesario, but° that piece of song,   (give us) just
That old and antique° song we heard last night.   quaint
Methought it did relieve my passion° much,   suffering
5   More than light airs and recollected° terms   studied; artificial
Of these most brisk and giddy-pacèd times.
Come, but one verse.
CURIO   He is not here, so please your lordship, that
should sing it.
10   ORSINO   Who was it?
CURIO   Feste the jester, my lord, a fool that the Lady Oliv-
ia's father took much delight in. He is about the house.
ORSINO   Seek him out, and play the tune the while.
[*Exit* CURIO]
Music plays.
[*To* VIOLA] Come hither, boy. If ever thou shalt love,
15   In the sweet pangs of it remember me,
For such as I am, all true lovers are,
Unstaid° and skittish in all motions° else   Unsteady / emotions
Save in the constant image of the creature
That is beloved. How dost thou like this tune?
20   VIOLA   It gives a very echo to the seat
Where love is throned.°   (i.e., the heart)
ORSINO   Thou dost speak masterly.°   masterfully
My life upon't, young though thou art, thine eye
Hath stayed upon some favor° that it loves.   face
Hath it not, boy?
VIOLA   A little, by your favor.°   leave; face
ORSINO   What kind of woman is't?
25   VIOLA   Of your complexion.
ORSINO   She is not worth thee, then. What years, i' faith?
VIOLA   About your years, my lord.
ORSINO   Too old, by heaven. Let still° the woman take   always
An elder than herself. So wears° she to him;   she slowly adapts
30   So sways she level° in her husband's heart.   she holds steady

6. Dock-tailed, as a workhorse; also, slang
term for a gelding.
7. Feste has no lines after line 113; thus, he
may exit with Maria above, or even earlier.
2.4 Location: Orsino's palace.

For, boy, however we do praise ourselves,
Our fancies° are more giddy and unfirm,   affections
More longing, wavering, sooner lost and worn,°   spent, exhausted
Than women's are.

VIOLA   I think° it well, my lord.   believe
35 ORSINO   Then let thy love be younger than thyself,
Or thy affection cannot hold the bent.°   remain steady
For women are as roses, whose fair flower,
Being once displayed, doth fall that very hour.

VIOLA   And so they are. Alas, that they are so,
40 To die even° when they to perfection grow!   just

Enter CURIO *and* [FESTE, *the*] *clown.*

ORSINO   O, fellow, come, the song we had last night.—
Mark it, Cesario. It is old and plain;
The spinsters° and the knitters in the sun   spinners
And the free° maids that weave their thread with bones⁸   carefree
45 Do use° to chant it. It is silly sooth,   Are accustomed
And dallies with° the innocence of love   lingers lovingly on
Like the old age.⁹

FESTE   Are you ready, sir?
ORSINO   Ay, prithee, sing.

Music.

50 FESTE [*sings*]   Come away,° come away, death,   hither
              And in sad cypress¹ let me be laid.
          Fly away, fly away, breath,
              I am slain by a fair cruel maid.
          My shroud of white, stuck all with yew,°   yew sprigs
55   O prepare it.
          My part of death, no one so true
              Did share it.²

          Not a flower, not a flower sweet
          On my black coffin let there be strewn;
60   Not a friend, not a friend greet
              My poor corpse, where my bones shall
                  be thrown.
          A thousand thousand sighs to save,
              Lay me, O, where
          Sad true lover never find my grave,
65   To weep there.

ORSINO [*giving money*]   There's for thy pains.°   efforts
FESTE   No pains, sir. I take pleasure in singing, sir.
ORSINO   I'll pay thy pleasure, then.
FESTE   Truly, sir, and pleasure will be paid,³ one time or
70 another.
ORSINO   Give me now leave to leave° thee.   permission to dismiss

8. Use bone bobbins (to weave "bone lace").   and death.
9. As in the good old days.   2. That is, no one died so true to love as I.
1. A coffin made of cypress wood, or a bier   3. That is, pleasure must be paid for
covered with cypress boughs. The cypress,   (proverbial).
like the yew (line 54), symbolized mourning

FESTE   Now the melancholy god[4] protect thee, and the
tailor make thy doublet° of changeable taffeta,[5] for thy   *jacket*
mind is a very opal.[6] I would have men of such con-
75   stancy put to sea, that their business might be everything and their intent° everywhere, for that's it that   *destination*
always makes a good voyage of nothing.[7] Farewell.
                                                                    Exit.

ORSINO   Let all the rest give place.°   *leave us*

        [*Exeunt all but* ORSINO *and* VIOLA.]
                    Once more, Cesario,
Get thee to yond same sovereign cruelty.
80   Tell her my love, more noble than the world,
Prizes not quantity of dirty lands.
The parts° that fortune hath bestowed upon her,   *rank and riches*
Tell her, I hold as giddily° as fortune.   *lightly*
But 'tis that miracle and queen of gems°   *(i.e., her beauty)*
85   That nature pranks° her in attracts my soul.   *dresses*
VIOLA   But if she cannot love you, sir—
ORSINO   I cannot be so answered.
VIOLA   Sooth,° but you must.   *In truth*
Say that some lady, as perhaps there is,
Hath for your love as great a pang of heart
90   As you have for Olivia. You cannot love her;
You tell her so. Must she not then be answered?
ORSINO   There is no woman's sides
Can bide° the beating of so strong a passion   *endure*
As love doth give my heart; no woman's heart
95   So big, to hold so much; they lack retention.°   *capacity, constancy*
Alas, their love may be called appetite,
No motion° of the liver, but the palate,[8]   *impulse*
That suffer surfeit, cloyment,° and revolt;°   *satiety / revulsion*
But mine is all as hungry as the sea,
100   And can digest as much. Make no compare
Between that love a woman can bear me
And that I owe° Olivia.   *have for*
VIOLA   Ay, but I know—
ORSINO   What dost thou know?
105   VIOLA   Too well what love women to men may owe.
In faith, they are as true of heart as we.
My father had a daughter loved a man
As it might be, perhaps, were I a woman,
I should your lordship.
ORSINO   And what's her history?

4. Saturn, the god and planet associated by
astrology with melancholy.
5. A thin silk, whose color appears to change
when viewed from different perspectives.
6. An iridescent gemstone that appears to
change color when viewed from different
perspectives.

7. That is, an aimless sea voyage is a good
experience for the fickle lover because he has
no specific goal.
8. That is, their love originates not in the liver
(the seat of real, lasting love) but in the palate
(and thus is a matter of casual taste).

110 VIOLA   A blank, my lord. She never told her love,
　　　But let concealment, like a worm i' th' bud,
　　　Feed on her damask° cheek. She pined in thought,　　　*pink and white*
　　　And with a green and yellow⁹ melancholy
　　　She sat like Patience on a monument,¹
115　　Smiling at grief. Was not this love indeed?
　　　We men may say more, swear more, but indeed
　　　Our shows are more than will;² for still° we prove　　　*always*
　　　Much in our vows but little in our love.
　　ORSINO   But died thy sister of her love, my boy?
120 VIOLA   I am all the daughters of my father's house,
　　　And all the brothers, too—and yet I know not.
　　　Sir, shall I to this lady?
　　ORSINO　　　　　　　　Ay, that's the theme.
　　　To her in haste. Give her this jewel. Say
　　　My love can give no place, bide no denay.°　　　*cannot abide denial*
　　　　　　　　　　　　　　Exeunt [severally].

2.5

Enter SIR TOBY, SIR ANDREW, *and* FABIAN.

SIR TOBY   Come thy ways,° Signior Fabian.　　　*Come along*
FABIAN   Nay, I'll come. If I lose a scruple° of this sport let　　*the least bit*
　me be boiled to death with melancholy.³
SIR TOBY   Wouldst thou not be glad to have the niggardly
5　rascally sheep-biter⁴ come by some notable shame?
FABIAN   I would exult, man. You know he brought me out
　o' favor with my lady about a bearbaiting⁵ here.
SIR TOBY   To anger him, we'll have the bear again, and we
　will fool° him black and blue, shall we not, Sir Andrew?　　*mock*
10 SIR ANDREW   An° we do not, it is pity of our lives.　　*If*
　　Enter MARIA [*with a letter*].
SIR TOBY   Here comes the little villain.—How now, my
　metal of India?⁶
MARIA   Get ye all three into the boxtree.° Malvolio's com-　　*boxwood hedge*
　ing down this walk. He has been yonder i' the sun prac-
15　ticing behavior to his own shadow this half hour. Observe
　him, for the love of mockery, for I know this letter will
　make a contemplative⁷ idiot of him. Close,° in the name　　*Hide*
　of jesting! [*The men hide.*] Lie thou there, [*putting
　down the letter*] for here comes the trout that must be
20　caught with tickling.⁸　　　　　　　　　　*Exit.*

9. Pale and sallow in complexion.
1. That is, like a sculpted figure of Patience atop a gravestone.
2. Our displays of passion are greater than the love we feel.
2.5 Location: Olivia's garden.
3. In the humoral theory of physiology, melancholy was a cold humor, caused by a preponderance of bile, on which "boiled" may pun.
4. A sneaking fellow (literally, a dog that bites sheep); also, a whoremonger (someone who chases after "mutton" or whores).
5. A pursuit frowned on by Puritans.
6. Gold (implying that Maria is worth her weight in gold).
7. Meditative (a word with religious overtones).
8. That is, flattery; trout can be caught by gently stroking beneath them until they back into one's hand.

Enter MALVOLIO.

MALVOLIO 'Tis but fortune, all is fortune. Maria once told
me she did affect° me, and I have heard herself come   (Olivia) was fond of
thus near, that should she fancy,° it should be one of my   fall in love
complexion. Besides, she uses me with a more exalted
25 respect than anyone else that follows her. What should
I think on't?

SIR TOBY   Here's an overweening rogue.

FABIAN   O, peace! Contemplation makes a rare turkey-
cock of him. How he jets° under his advanced° plumes!   struts / pulled up

30 SIR ANDREW   'Slight,° I could so beat the rogue!   By God's light (an oath)

SIR TOBY   Peace, I say.

MALVOLIO   To be Count Malvolio!

SIR TOBY   Ah, rogue!

SIR ANDREW   Pistol him, pistol him!

35 SIR TOBY   Peace, peace!

MALVOLIO   There is example° for't. The Lady of the   precedent
Strachy married the yeoman of the wardrobe.[9]

SIR ANDREW   Fie on him, Jezebel![1]

FABIAN   O, peace, now he's deeply in. Look how imagi-
40 nation blows him.°   puffs him up

MALVOLIO   Having been three months married to her,
sitting in my state°—   chair of state

SIR TOBY   O, for a stone-bow,[2] to hit him in the eye!

MALVOLIO   Calling my officers° about me, in my branched[3]   household staff
45 velvet gown, having come from a daybed,° where I have   sofa
left Olivia sleeping—

SIR TOBY   Fire and brimstone!

FABIAN   O, peace, peace!

MALVOLIO   And then to have the humor of state;[4] and
50 after a demure travel of regard,[5] telling them I know
my place, as I would they should do theirs, to ask for
my kinsman Toby—

SIR TOBY   Bolts and shackles!

FABIAN   O, peace, peace, peace! Now, now.

55 MALVOLIO   Seven of my people, with an obedient start,
make out° for him. I frown the while, and perchance   go forth
wind up my watch, or play with my—some rich jewel.[6]
Toby approaches; curtsies° there to me—   bows

SIR TOBY   Shall this fellow live?

60 FABIAN   Though our silence be drawn from us with
cars,[7] yet peace.

---

9. The person in charge of the linen and
clothing in a wealthy household (this Lady
has not been identified).
1. A proud, immoral woman (from the wife of
King Ahab of Israel; see especially 1 Kings
21).
2. A crossbow used to shoot stones.
3. Embroidered in a figured pattern.
4. To adopt the manner of the great.
5. Casting my eye about the room with proper

gravity.
6. Malvolio probably begins to say "my chain"
(the symbol of his rank as steward in the
household), but then remembers that as Olivia's husband he will have replaced it with a
more appropriate ornament, a jewel.
7. That is, by torture (a prisoner might be tied
to two carts, or "cars," which then pulled in
opposite directions).

MALVOLIO   I extend my hand to him thus, quenching my
  familiar° smile with an austere regard of control—   *friendly*
SIR TOBY   And does not Toby take° you a blow o' the lips   *give*
65   then?
MALVOLIO   Saying "Cousin Toby, my fortunes, having
  cast me on your niece, give me this prerogative of
  speech"—
SIR TOBY   What, what?
70 MALVOLIO   "You must amend your drunkenness."
SIR TOBY   Out, scab!
FABIAN   Nay, patience, or we break the sinews of our plot.
MALVOLIO   "Besides, you waste the treasure of your time
  with a foolish knight"—
75 SIR ANDREW   That's me, I warrant you.
MALVOLIO   "One Sir Andrew."
SIR ANDREW   I knew 'twas I, for many do call me fool.
MALVOLIO [*seeing the letter*]   What employment° have we   *business*
  here?
80 FABIAN   Now is the woodcock near the gin.[8]
SIR TOBY   O, peace, and the spirit of humors intimate[9]
  reading aloud to him.
MALVOLIO [*taking up the letter*]   By my life, this is my lady's
  hand. These be her very *c*'s, her *u*'s, and her *t*'s,[1] and thus
85   makes she her great *P*'s. It is in contempt of° question   *beyond*
  her hand.
SIR ANDREW   Her *c*'s, her *u*'s, and her *t*'s? Why that?
MALVOLIO [*reads*]   "To the unknown beloved, this, and my
  good wishes."—Her very phrases! By your leave, wax.°
90   Soft.° And the impressure her Lucrece,[2] with which she   *sealing wax*
  uses to seal—'tis my lady! [*He opens the letter.*] To   *Wait*
  whom should this be?
FABIAN   This wins him, liver[3] and all.
MALVOLIO [*reads*]   "Jove knows I love,
95   But who?
                Lips, do not move;
                No man must know."
  "No man must know." What follows? The numbers°   *meter*
  altered.
  "No man must know." If this should be thee, Malvolio!
100 SIR TOBY   Marry, hang thee, brock![4]
MALVOLIO [*reads*]   "I may command where I adore,
                But silence, like a Lucrece knife,
              With bloodless stroke my heart doth gore;
              M.O.A.I. doth sway my life."

---

8. Snare. The woodcock is a proverbially stupid and easily caught bird.
9. May the spirit of whimsy suggest.
1. Malvolio unwittingly spells "cut," slang for
the vagina.
2. The image of Lucretia, the Roman model

of chastity (who stabbed herself to death after
being raped), was printed in the wax.
3. The seat of love (see 1.1.36n).
4. Badger, conventionally labeled "stinky"; so
dirty fellow, skunk.

105 FABIAN A fustian° riddle!   *pompous*

SIR TOBY Excellent wench, say I.

MALVOLIO "M.O.A.I. doth sway my life." Nay, but first
let me see, let me see, let me see.

FABIAN What dish o' poison has she dressed° him!   *prepared for*

110 SIR TOBY And with what wing the staniel checks at it!⁵

MALVOLIO "I may command where I adore." Why, she may
command me; I serve her, she is my lady. Why, this is
evident to any formal capacity.⁶ There is no obstruction°   *difficulty*
in this. And the end—what should that alphabetical posi-
115 tion° portend? If I could make that resemble something   *ordering of letters*
in me! Softly! "M.O.A.I."—

SIR TOBY O, ay make up that.—He is now at a cold scent.

FABIAN Sowter will cry upon't for all this, though it be as
rank as a fox.⁷

120 MALVOLIO "M"—Malvolio. "M"—why, that begins my
name!

FABIAN Did not I say he would work it out? The cur is
excellent at faults.⁸

MALVOLIO "M." But then there is no consonancy in the
125 sequel.⁹ That suffers under probation.° "A" should   *close scrutiny*
follow, but "O" does.

FABIAN And "O"¹ shall end, I hope.

SIR TOBY Ay, or I'll cudgel him and make him cry "O."

MALVOLIO And then "I" comes behind.

130 FABIAN Ay, an° you had any eye behind you, you might   *if*
see more detraction° at your heels than fortunes before   *defamation*
you.

MALVOLIO "M.O.A.I." This simulation° is not as the   *riddle*
former, and yet to crush° this a little, it would bow² to   *force*
135 me, for every one of these letters are in my name.
Soft, here follows prose. [*He reads.*] "If this fall into
thy hand, revolve.° In my stars° I am above thee, but be   *consider / fortunes*
not afraid of greatness. Some are born great, some
achieve greatness, and some have greatness thrust
140 upon 'em. Thy fates open their hands.° Let thy blood   *offer their bounty*
and spirit embrace them. And, to inure° thyself to what   *accustom*
thou art like° to be, cast thy humble slough³ and appear   *likely*
fresh. Be opposite° with a kinsman, surly with servants. *contrary, quarrelsome*
Let thy tongue tang arguments of state.⁴ Put thyself
145 into the trick of singularity.° She thus advises thee that *act eccentrically*

---

5. That is, with what speed does this inferior
hawk fly after it.
6. Normal understanding.
7. "Sowter" (the name of a hound) will cry
out when it loses the scent of its quarry, even
though that scent is as strong ("rank") as a
fox's.
8. That is, good at following his quarry (literally, excellent at lost scents, or "faults").

9. No pattern to the letters that follow.
1. That is, the hangman's noose (perhaps also
a cry of pain or lamentation).
2. Yield (its meaning).
3. Cast off your humble deportment, as a
snake sheds (sloughs) its old skin.
4. Let your tongue ring loudly with arguments about politics or statecraft.

sighs for thee. Remember who commended thy yellow
stockings and wished to see thee ever cross-gartered.[5] I
say, remember. Go to,° thou art made, if thou desirest   *Get going*
to be so. If not, let me see thee a steward still, the fel-
150 low of servants, and not worthy to touch Fortune's fingers. Farewell. She that would alter services[6] with thee.
                        The Fortunate-Unhappy."
Daylight and champaign discovers[7] not more! This is
open.° I will be proud, I will read politic° authors, I will   *clear / political*
155 baffle° Sir Toby, I will wash off gross acquaintance,[8] I   *disgrace*
will be point-device the very man.[9] I do not now fool
myself, to let imagination jade° me; for every reason   *trick*
excites to this, that my lady loves me. She did commend my yellow stockings of late, she did praise my
160 leg being cross-gartered, and in this she manifests
herself to my love and, with a kind of injunction, drives
me to these habits° of her liking. I thank my stars, I am   *this attire*
happy. I will be strange,° stout,° in yellow stockings,   *aloof / proud*
and cross-gartered, even with the swiftness of putting
165 on. Jove and my stars be praised! Here is yet a postscript. [*He reads.*] "Thou canst not choose but know
who I am. If thou entertainest° my love, let it appear in   *accept*
thy smiling; thy smiles become thee well. Therefore in
my presence still° smile, dear my sweet, I prithee." Jove,   *always*
170 I thank thee. I will smile, I will do everything that thou
wilt have me.   *Exit.*

FABIAN   I will not give my part of this sport for a pension of thousands to be paid from the Sophy.°   *Shah of Persia*

SIR TOBY   I could marry this wench for this device.

175 SIR ANDREW   So could I, too.

SIR TOBY   And ask no other dowry with her but such
another jest.

SIR ANDREW   Nor I neither.

    Enter MARIA

FABIAN   Here comes my noble gull-catcher.°   *fool catcher*

180 SIR TOBY   Wilt thou set thy foot o' my neck?[1]

SIR ANDREW   Or o' mine either?

SIR TOBY   Shall I play° my freedom at tray-trip[2] and   *gamble*
become thy bondslave?

SIR ANDREW   I' faith, or I either?

185 SIR TOBY   Why, thou hast put him in such a dream that
when the image of it leaves him he must run mad.

MARIA   Nay, but say true, does it work upon him?

---

5. The fashion (possibly outmoded by the
time of the play) of wearing the garters so
that in front they pass above as well as below
the knee.
6. Exchange places (of mistress and servant).
7. Open country reveals.
8. Rid myself of acquaintances of low social

rank.
9. That is, I will become, to the smallest
detail, the man described in the letter.
1. An act symbolizing a conqueror's triumph.
2. A game of dice in which three (trey) was a
winning roll.

SIR TOBY   Like aqua vitae° with a midwife.   *strong liquor*

MARIA   If you will then see the fruits of the sport, mark
190   his first approach before my lady. He will come to her
in yellow stockings, and 'tis a color she abhors, and
cross-gartered, a fashion she detests; and he will smile
upon her, which will now be so unsuitable to her disposition, being addicted to a melancholy as she is, that it
195   cannot but turn him into a notable contempt.³ If you
will see it, follow me.

SIR TOBY   To the gates of Tartar,⁴ thou most excellent
devil of wit!

SIR ANDREW   I'll make one,° too.   *Exeunt.*   *go along*

3.1

Enter VIOLA *and* [FESTE, *the*] *clown* [*with pipe and
tabor*].°   *small drum*

VIOLA   Save° thee, friend, and thy music. Dost thou live   *God save*
by thy tabor?

FESTE   No, sir, I live by° the church.   *near*

VIOLA   Art thou a churchman?°   *clergyman*

5   FESTE   No such matter, sir. I do live by the church, for I do
live at my house, and my house doth stand by the church.

VIOLA   So thou mayst say the king lies by⁵ a beggar if a
beggar dwell near him, or the church stands° by thy   *is maintained*
tabor if thy tabor stand by the church.

10   FESTE   You have said, sir. To see this age! A sentence° is   *saying*
but a chev'ril° glove to a good wit. How quickly the   *kidskin*
wrong side may be turned outward!

VIOLA   Nay, that's certain. They that dally nicely° with   *play cleverly*
words may quickly make them wanton.⁶

15   FESTE   I would therefore my sister had had no name, sir.

VIOLA   Why, man?

FESTE   Why, sir, her name's a word, and to dally with
that word might make my sister wanton. But, indeed,
words are very rascals since bonds⁷ disgraced them.

20   VIOLA   Thy reason, man?

FESTE   Troth, sir, I can yield you none without words,
and words are grown so false I am loath to prove reason with them.

VIOLA   I warrant thou art a merry fellow and carest for
25   nothing.

FESTE   Not so, sir. I do care for something. But in my
conscience, sir, I do not care for you. If that be to care
for nothing, sir, I would it would make you invisible.

VIOLA   Art not thou the Lady Olivia's fool?

---

3. A notable object of contempt.
4. Tartarus (that part of the classical underworld where the wicked were punished).
3.1 Location: Olivia's garden.
5. Dwells near; also, lies with sexually.

6. Equivocal; also, lewd.
7. Written contracts, which replaced a man's
simple promise; Feste puns on the meaning
"fetters."

30 FESTE   No indeed, sir. The Lady Olivia has no folly. She
      will keep no fool, sir, till she be married, and fools are
      as like husbands as pilchards° are to herrings: the   *small fish*
      husband's the bigger. I am indeed not her fool but her
      corrupter of words.

35 VIOLA   I saw thee late° at the Count Orsino's.   *recently*

    FESTE   Foolery, sir, does walk about the orb[8] like the
      sun; it shines everywhere. I would be sorry, sir, but°   *unless*
      the fool should be as oft with your master as with my
      mistress. I think I saw your wisdom[9] there.

40 VIOLA   Nay, an thou pass upon me,[1] I'll no more with thee.
      Hold, there's expenses for thee. [*giving a coin*]

    FESTE   Now Jove in his next commodity° of hair send   *parcel, supply*
      thee a beard!

    VIOLA   By my troth I'll tell thee, I am almost sick° for   *eager; lovesick*
45   one, [*aside*] though I would not have it grow on *my*   *(for Orsino)*
      chin.—Is thy lady within?

    FESTE   Would not a pair of these° have bred,° sir?   *(coins) / multiplied*

    VIOLA   Yes, being kept together and put to use.[2]

    FESTE   I would play Lord Pandarus[3] of Phrygia, sir, to
50   bring a Cressida to this Troilus.

    VIOLA   I understand you, sir. 'Tis well begged. [*giving
      another coin*]

    FESTE   The matter I hope is not great, sir, begging but a
      beggar: Cressida was a beggar.[4] My lady is within, sir.
      I will conster° to them whence you come. Who you   *explain*
55   are and what you would are out of my welkin°—I might   *sky; air (an element)*
      say "element," but the word is overworn.   *Exit.*

    VIOLA   This fellow is wise enough to play the fool,
      And to do that well craves° a kind of wit.°   *requires / intelligence*
      He must observe their mood on whom he jests,
60   The quality° of persons, and the time,   *social rank; character*
      And, like the haggard,° check at every feather[5]   *wild hawk*
      That comes before his eye. This is a practice°   *skill*
      As full of labor as a wise man's art,
      For folly that he wisely shows is fit,°   *appropriate*
65   But wise men, folly-fall'n, quite taint their wit.[6]

        Enter SIR TOBY *and* SIR ANDREW

    SIR TOBY   Save you, gentleman.

    VIOLA   And you, sir.

    SIR ANDREW   *Dieu vous garde, monsieur.*[7]

---

8. The earth (around which, in the Ptolemaic
system, all heavenly bodies orbited).
9. "Your wisdom" is a form of address, here
sarcastic.
1. If you attack me (literally, make a fencing
pass at me).
2. Invested; lent out at interest.
3. The go-between in the love story of Troilus
and Cressida. Feste will bring two coins
together, as Pandarus would lovers, and have

them reproduce.
4. In Robert Henryson's version of the story,
Testament of Cresseid (though not in Shakespeare's own *Troilus and Cressida*), Cressida
becomes a leprous beggar.
5. Fly after every bird.
6. That is, wise men, having fallen into folly,
tarnish their innate intelligence or wisdom.
7. God protect you, sir (French).

VIOLA   *Et vous aussi. Votre serviteur!*[8]

70 SIR ANDREW   I hope, sir, you are, and I am yours.

SIR TOBY   Will you encounter° the house? My niece is   *approach; enter*
desirous you should enter, if your trade be to her.

VIOLA   I am bound to° your niece, sir; I mean, she is the   *for*
list° of my voyage.   *limit; destination*

75 SIR TOBY   Taste° your legs, sir; put them to motion.   *Try, test*

VIOLA   My legs do better understand° me, sir, than I under-   *stand under*
stand what you mean by bidding me taste my legs.

SIR TOBY   I mean, to go, sir, to enter.

VIOLA   I will answer you with gait and entrance.[9]

Enter OLIVIA *and* [MARIA, *her*] *gentlewoman*

80 But we are prevented.° Most excellent accomplished   *anticipated*
lady, the heavens rain odors on you!

SIR ANDREW [*to* SIR TOBY]   That youth's a rare° courtier.   *an excellent*
"Rain odors," well.

VIOLA   My matter hath no voice,° lady, but to your own   *must not be spoken*
85 most pregnant° and vouchsafed[1] ear.   *receptive*

SIR ANDREW [*to* SIR TOBY]   "Odors," "pregnant," and
"vouchsafed." I'll get 'em all three all ready.°   *committed to memory*

OLIVIA   Let the garden door be shut, and leave me to my
hearing.   [*Exeunt* SIR TOBY, SIR ANDREW, *and* MARIA.]

90 Give me your hand, sir.

VIOLA   My duty, madam, and most humble service.

OLIVIA   What is your name?

VIOLA   Cesario is your servant's name, fair princess.

OLIVIA   My servant, sir? 'Twas never merry world
95 Since lowly feigning was called compliment.[2]
You're servant to the Count Orsino, youth.

VIOLA   And he is yours, and his must needs be yours.
Your servant's servant is *your* servant, madam.

OLIVIA   For° him, I think not on him. For his thoughts,   *As for*
100 Would they were blanks rather than filled with me.

VIOLA   Madam, I come to whet your gentle thoughts
On his behalf.

OLIVIA   O, by your leave,[3] I pray you.
I bade you never speak again of him;
But would you undertake another suit,
105 I had rather hear you to solicit that
Than music from the spheres.[4]

VIOLA   Dear lady—

OLIVIA   Give me leave, beseech you. I did send,
After the last enchantment you did here,
A ring in chase of you. So did I abuse°   *dishonor*

---

8. And you, also; (I am) your servant (French).
9. Going and entering, with a pun on "gate."
1. Graciously offered.
2. That is, the world has not been a happy place since flattery came to be called courtesy.
3. Permit me to interrupt (a courteous expres-

sion, as is "give me leave," line 108).
4. In the Ptolemaic system, the planets and other heavenly bodies were thought to be affixed to concentric spheres, whose turning made glorious music inaudible to human ears.

110 Myself, my servant, and, I fear me, you.
Under your hard construction must I sit,[5]
To force° that on you in a shameful cunning   *For forcing*
Which you knew none of yours. What might you think?
Have you not set mine honor at the stake,
115 And baited it with all th' unmuzzled thoughts[6]
That tyrannous heart can think? To one of your
    receiving°   *perceptiveness*
Enough is shown. A cypress,[7] not a bosom,
Hides my heart. So let me hear you speak.

VIOLA   I pity you.

OLIVIA   That's a degree to° love.   *step toward*

120 VIOLA   No, not a grize,° for 'tis a vulgar proof°   *step / common experience*
That very oft we pity enemies.

OLIVIA   Why then methinks 'tis time to smile again.[8]
O world, how apt° the poor are to be proud!   *ready*
If one should be a prey, how much the better
125 To fall before the lion than the wolf.[9]

    Clock strikes.
The clock upbraids me with the waste of time.
Be not afraid, good youth, I will not have you.
And yet when wit and youth is come to harvest,
Your wife is like to reap a proper° man.   *handsome; worthy*
There lies your way, due west.

130 VIOLA   Then westward ho![1]
Grace and good disposition° attend your ladyship.   *frame of mind*
You'll nothing, madam, to my lord by me?

OLIVIA   Stay. I prithee, tell me what thou think'st of me.

VIOLA   That you do think you are not what you are.

135 OLIVIA   If I think so, I think the same of you.[2]

VIOLA   Then think you right. I am not what I am.

OLIVIA   I would you were as I would have you be.

VIOLA   Would it be better, madam, than I am?
I wish it might, for now I am your fool.[3]

140 OLIVIA [*aside*]   O, what a deal of scorn looks beautiful
In the contempt and anger of his lip!
A murd'rous guilt shows not itself more soon
Than love that would seem hid. Love's night is noon.—[4]
Cesario, by the roses of the spring,
145 By maidhood, honor, truth, and everything,
I love thee so, that, maugre° all thy pride,   *despite*
Nor° wit nor reason can my passion hide.   *Neither*

5. I must be judged harshly by you.
6. An allusion to bearbaiting, in which a bear is chained to a stake and attacked by hungry dogs.
7. A piece of light, transparent material, often used (when black) for mourning.
8. That is, to leave melancholy behind (because we are not enemies).
9. That is, to fall before a noble foe like Ors-

ino rather than unyielding Cesario.
1. The cry of Thames boatmen as they depart from London toward Westminster.
2. Here, apparently rebuffed by "Cesario," Olivia switches back to the polite "you" after having used the familiar "thou" (line 134).
3. That is, you made a fool of me.
4. That is, love shines out brightly at all times.

Do not extort thy reasons from this clause,
For that I woo, thou therefore hast no cause;[5]
150 But rather reason thus with reason fetter:[6]
Love sought is good, but given unsought is better.
VIOLA By innocence I swear, and by my youth,
I have one heart, one bosom, and one truth,
And that no woman has, nor never none
155 Shall mistress be of it, save I alone.
And so adieu, good madam. Nevermore
Will I my master's tears to you deplore.°   *lament*
OLIVIA Yet come again, for thou perhaps mayst move
That heart, which now abhors, to like his love.

Exeunt [severally].

3.2

Enter SIR TOBY, SIR ANDREW, *and* FABIAN.

SIR ANDREW No, faith, I'll not stay a jot longer.
SIR TOBY Thy reason, dear venom,° give thy reason.   *venomous one*
FABIAN You must needs yield your reason, Sir Andrew.
SIR ANDREW Marry, I saw your niece do more favors to the
5 Count's servingman than ever she bestowed upon me.
I saw't i' th' orchard.°   *garden*
SIR TOBY Did she see thee the while, old boy? Tell me
that.
SIR ANDREW As plain as I see you now.
10 FABIAN This was a great argument° of love in her toward   *proof*
you.
SIR ANDREW 'Slight, will you make an ass o' me?
FABIAN I will prove it legitimate, sir, upon the oaths of
judgment and reason.
15 SIR TOBY And they have been grand-jurymen[7] since
before Noah was a sailor.
FABIAN She did show favor to the youth in your sight
only to exasperate you, to awake your dormouse[8] valor,
to put fire in your heart and brimstone° in your liver.   *heat*
20 You should then have accosted her, and with some
excellent jests, fire-new from the mint,° you should   *newly minted*
have banged the youth into dumbness. This was looked
for at your hand, and this was balked.[9] The double gilt°   *gold plating*
of this opportunity you let time wash off, and you are
25 now sailed into the north of my lady's opinion,[1] where
you will hang like an icicle on a Dutchman's[2] beard,

---

5. That is, do not extract reasons from what I
have just said to argue that because ("for that")
I woo, you need not reciprocate my love.
6. But instead restrain your reasoning with
the following reason.
3.2 Location: Olivia's house.
7. Experts at evaluating evidence.
8. Sleeping (dormice are small rodents known

for their long periods of hibernation).
9. This opportunity was ignored.
1. That is, out of the warmth of her favor.
2. An allusion to the Dutch Arctic explorer Wil-
lem Barents (ca. 1550–1597), who made several attempts to discover a navigable passage to
the East along the northern coast of Russia.

unless you do redeem it by some laudable attempt either of valor or policy.° — *crafty device*

SIR ANDREW   An't° be any way, it must be with valor, for 30 policy I hate. I had as lief° be a Brownist as a politician.[3] — *If it* / *soon*

SIR TOBY   Why then, build me thy fortunes upon the basis of valor. Challenge me° the Count's youth to fight with him. Hurt him in eleven places. My niece shall take note of it, and assure thyself, there is no love-broker° in the 35 world can more prevail in man's commendation with woman than report of valor. — *for me* / *go-between*

FABIAN   There is no way but this, Sir Andrew.

SIR ANDREW   Will either of you bear me a challenge to him?

40 SIR TOBY   Go, write it in a martial hand. Be curst° and brief. It is no matter how witty, so it be eloquent and full of invention.° Taunt him with the license of ink.[4] If thou "thou'st" him[5] some thrice, it shall not be amiss, and as many lies as will lie in thy sheet of paper, although the 45 sheet were big enough for the bed of Ware[6] in England, set 'em down. Go, about it. Let there be gall enough in thy ink, though thou write with a goose-pen,[7] no matter. About it.° — *abusive* / *imagination* / *Get on with it*

SIR ANDREW   Where shall I find you?

50 SIR TOBY   We'll call thee at the cubiculo.° Go. — *little chamber*

Exit SIR ANDREW.

FABIAN   This is a dear manikin° to you, Sir Toby. — *puppet*

SIR TOBY   I have been dear° to him, lad, some two thousand strong, or so. — *costly*

FABIAN   We shall have a rare letter from him. But you'll 55 not deliver't?

SIR TOBY   Never trust me, then. And by all means stir on the youth to an answer. I think oxen and wainropes° cannot hale° them together. For Andrew, if he were opened and you find so much blood in his liver[8] as 60 will clog° the foot of a flea, I'll eat the rest of th' anatomy.° — *wagon ropes* / *pull* / *burden* / *cadaver*

FABIAN   And his opposite,° the youth, bears in his visage no great presage of cruelty. — *rival*

Enter MARIA

SIR TOBY   Look where the youngest wren of nine[9] comes.

---

3. An intriguer. *Brownist:* a follower of the Puritan sect founded by Robert Browne (ca. 1550–1633).
4. With the freedom that writing allows (when compared to conversation).
5. That is, address him discourteously (to use the familiar "thou" to a relative stranger was an insult).
6. A famous bedstead built in 1590, almost

11 feet square (twice the normal size of beds of the period).
7. A quill pen made from the feather of a goose, a proverbially foolish bird. *Gall:* an ingredient of ink; bitterness, acrimony.
8. Cowards were believed to have little or no blood in their liver.
9. The smallest wren in a nest of nine; that is, the smallest of the small.

65 MARIA If you desire the spleen,[1] and will laugh yourselves into stitches, follow me. Yond gull° Malvolio is   *dupe*
turned heathen, a very renegado;[2] for there is no Christian that means to be saved by believing rightly can
ever believe such impossible passages of grossness.[3]
70 He's in yellow stockings.

SIR TOBY And cross-gartered?

MARIA Most villainously,° like a pedant° that keeps a   *atrociously / teacher*
school i' th' church.[4] I have dogged him like his mur-
derer. He does obey every point of the letter that I
75 dropped to betray him. He does smile his face into
more lines than is in the new map with the augmenta-
tion of the Indies.[5] You have not seen such a thing as
'tis. I can hardly forbear hurling things at him. I know
my lady will strike him. If she do, he'll smile and take't
80 for a great favor.

SIR TOBY Come, bring us, bring us where he is. *Exeunt.*

3.3

Enter SEBASTIAN *and* ANTONIO.

SEBASTIAN I would not by my will have troubled you,
But, since you make your pleasure of your pains,
I will no further chide you.

ANTONIO   I could not stay behind you. My desire,
5 More sharp than filèd steel, did spur me forth;
And not all° love to see you—though so much   *not entirely (out of)*
As might have drawn one to a longer voyage—
But jealousy° what might befall your travel,   *anxiety about*
Being skill-less in° these parts, which to a stranger,   *unfamiliar with*
10 Unguided and unfriended, often prove
Rough and unhospitable. My willing love,
The rather° by these arguments of fear,   *All the more*
Set forth in your pursuit.

SEBASTIAN   My kind Antonio,
I can no other answer make but thanks,
15 And thanks, and ever [thanks; and] oft° good turns   *very often*
Are shuffled off° with such uncurrent[6] pay.   *shrugged off*
But were my worth, as is my conscience,° firm,   *awareness of my debt*
You should find better dealing. What's to do?
Shall we go see the relics° of this town?   *antiquities; memorials*
20 ANTONIO Tomorrow, sir. Best first go see your lodging.

SEBASTIAN I am not weary, and 'tis long to night.

---

1. Thought to be the seat of immoderate laughter.
2. Renegade (Spanish); apostate.
3. Such obvious absurdities (as the planted letter contains; see 2.5).
4. The practice of holding classes in church buildings was disappearing in Shakespeare's time.
5. Possibly a reference to a new map (published ca. 1599) that showed the Earth's surface crisscrossed by rhumb lines and that was "augmented" with recent discoveries in both the Americas and the East Indies.
3.3 Location: A street.
6. No longer current; that is, worthless.

I pray you let us satisfy our eyes
With the memorials and the things of fame
That do renown this city.

ANTONIO   Would you'd pardon me.
25 I do not without danger walk these streets.
Once in a sea fight 'gainst the Count his° galleys   *(the Count's)*
I did some service, of such note indeed
That were I ta'en° here it would scarce be answered.[7] *captured*

SEBASTIAN Belike° you slew great number of his people? *Perhaps*

30 ANTONIO Th' offense is not of such a bloody nature,
Albeit the quality° of the time and quarrel   *circumstances*
Might well have given us bloody argument.° *reason for bloodshed*
It might have since been answered in repaying
What we took from them, which, for traffic's° sake, *trade's*
35 Most of our city did. Only myself stood out,° *refused to go along*
For which if I be latchèd° in this place,   *captured*
I shall pay dear.

SEBASTIAN   Do not then walk too open.

ANTONIO It doth not fit° me. Hold, sir, here's my purse. *is not fitting for*
In the south suburbs at the Elephant°   *(an inn)*
40 Is best to lodge. I will bespeak our diet°   *order our food*
Whiles you beguile° the time and feed your knowledge *pass*
With viewing of the town. There shall you have me.

SEBASTIAN Why I your purse?

ANTONIO Haply° your eye shall light upon some toy° *Perhaps / trifle*
45 You have desire to purchase, and your store,° *supply of money*
I think, is not for idle markets,[8] sir.

SEBASTIAN I'll be your purse-bearer and leave you
For an hour.

ANTONIO   To th' Elephant.

SEBASTIAN   I do remember.

Exeunt [severally].

3.4

Enter OLIVIA *and* MARIA.

OLIVIA *[aside]* I have sent after him. He says he'll come.
How shall I feast him? What bestow of° him?   *on*
For youth is bought more oft than begged or borrowed.
I speak too loud.—
5 *[To* MARIA*]* Where's Malvolio? He is sad° and civil° *serious / respectful*
And suits well for a servant with my fortunes.
Where is Malvolio?

MARIA He's coming, madam, but in very strange manner.
He is sure possessed,[9] madam.

---

7. That is, it would be hard for me to defend myself or make reparations.
8. Sufficient to buy unnecessary luxuries.
3.4 Location: Olivia's garden.

9. That is, insane; possession by a demon or the devil was a common explanation for madness.

10 OLIVIA   Why, what's the matter? Does he rave?

MARIA   No, madam, he does nothing but smile. Your
ladyship were best to have some guard about you if he
come, for sure the man is tainted in's° wits.   *in his*

OLIVIA   Go call him hither.   [*Exit* MARIA.]

I am as mad as he,

15   If sad and merry madness equal be.

Enter [MARIA *with*] MALVOLIO [*cross-gartered and
wearing yellow stockings*].

How now, Malvolio?

MALVOLIO   Sweet lady, ho, ho!

OLIVIA   Smil'st thou? I sent for thee upon a sad occasion.°   *serious matter*

MALVOLIO   Sad, lady? I could be sad. This does make
20   some obstruction in the blood, this cross-gartering, but
what of that? If it please the eye of one, it is with me as
the very true sonnet° is: "Please one, and please all."[1]   *short poem; song*

OLIVIA   Why, how dost thou, man? What is the matter
with thee?

25 MALVOLIO   Not black in my mind, though yellow in my
legs.[2] It did come to his hands, and commands shall be
executed. I think we do know the sweet Roman hand.[3]

OLIVIA   Wilt thou go to bed,[4] Malvolio?

MALVOLIO [*kissing his hand*]   To bed? "Ay, sweetheart,
30   and I'll come to thee."[5]

OLIVIA   God comfort thee! Why dost thou smile so, and
kiss thy hand so oft?

MARIA   How do you, Malvolio?

MALVOLIO   At your request? Yes, nightingales answer daws![6]

35 MARIA   Why appear you with this ridiculous boldness
before my lady?

MALVOLIO   "Be not afraid of greatness." 'Twas well writ.

OLIVIA   What meanest thou by that, Malvolio?

MALVOLIO   "Some are born great"—

40 OLIVIA   Ha?

MALVOLIO   "Some achieve greatness"—

OLIVIA   What sayst thou?

MALVOLIO   "And some have greatness thrust upon them."

OLIVIA   Heaven restore thee!

45 MALVOLIO   "Remember who commended thy yellow
stockings"—

OLIVIA   Thy yellow stockings?

MALVOLIO   "And wished to see thee cross-gartered."

OLIVIA   Cross-gartered?

1. That is, "If I please you, then I please
everyone I care to please" (a line from a popular ballad).
2. Black indicated melancholy; yellow, both
jealousy and choler.
3. The Italian-style handwriting then coming
into use.
4. That is, to cure your madness with sleep.
5. A line from a popular song.
6. That is, should I answer you? A nightingale
(whose song is proverbially beautiful) does
not respond to a crow.

50 MALVOLIO   "Go to, thou art made, if thou desirest to be
       so"—
    OLIVIA   Am I made?
    MALVOLIO   "If not, let me see thee a servant still."
    OLIVIA   Why, this is very midsummer madness!⁷

           Enter a SERVANT.

55 SERVANT   Madam, the young gentleman of the Count
       Orsino's is returned. I could hardly entreat him
       back. He attends° your ladyship's pleasure.   *awaits*
    OLIVIA   I'll come to him.   [*Exit* SERVANT.]
       Good Maria, let this fellow be looked to. Where's my
60   cousin Toby? Let some of my people have a special
       care of him. I would not have him miscarry° for the   *come to harm*
       half of my dowry.

           [*Exeunt* OLIVIA *and* MARIA, *severally.*]

    MALVOLIO   O ho, do you come near° me now? No worse   *understand*
       man than Sir Toby to look to me. This concurs directly
65   with the letter. She sends him on purpose that I may
       appear stubborn to him, for she incites me to that in
       the letter: "Cast thy humble slough," says she. "Be
       opposite with a kinsman, surly with servants; let thy
       tongue tang with arguments of state; put thyself the
70   into trick of singularity," and consequently° sets   *thereafter*
       down the manner how: as, a sad face, a reverend car-
       riage, a slow tongue,° in the habit° of some sir of   *deliberate speech / clothing*
       note,° and so forth. I have limed her,⁸ but it is Jove's   *a gentleman*
       doing, and Jove make me thankful! And when she
75   went away now, "Let this fellow be looked to." "Fel-
       low."⁹ Not "Malvolio," nor after my degree, but "fel-
       low." Why, everything adheres together, that no dram
       of a scruple, no scruple of a scruple,¹ no obstacle, no
       incredulous° or unsafe circumstance—what can be   *incredible*
80   said? Nothing that can be can come between me and
       the full prospect of my hopes. Well, Jove, not I, is the
       doer of this, and he is to be thanked.

           Enter SIR TOBY, FABIAN, *and* MARIA.

    SIR TOBY   Which way is he, in the name of sanctity?° If all *of all that is sacred*
       the devils of hell be drawn in little,° and Legion²   *in miniature*
85   himself possessed him, yet I'll speak to him.
    FABIAN   Here he is, here he is.—How is't with you, sir?
       How is't with you, man?
    MALVOLIO   Go off, I discard you. Let me enjoy my pri-
       vate.° Go off.   *privacy*

---

7. The midsummer moon was thought to
cause insanity.
8. Caught her, like a bird trapped by sticky
birdlime spread on a branch.
9. Malvolio gives "fellow" the meaning (unintended by Olivia) "consort" or "counterpart."

1. That is, no bit of doubt; as apothecaries'
weights, a dram is 60 grains and a scruple is
one-third of a dram.
2. The name of an "unclean spirit" exorcised
by Jesus (Mark 5.8–9).

90 MARIA [*to* SIR TOBY] Lo, how hollow° the fiend speaks   *resoundingly*
    within him! Did not I tell you? Sir Toby, my lady prays
    you to have a care of him.

    MALVOLIO Aha, does she so?

    SIR TOBY Go to, go to! Peace, peace. We must deal gently
95 with him. Let me alone.°—How do you, Malvolio? How   *Leave him to me*
    is't with you? What, man, defy the devil! Consider, he's
    an enemy to mankind.

    MALVOLIO Do you know what you say?

    MARIA La° you, an° you speak ill of the devil, how he   *Look / if*
100 takes it at heart! Pray God he be not bewitched!

    FABIAN Carry his water to th' wise woman.[3]

    MARIA Marry, and it shall be done tomorrow morning if I
    live. My lady would not lose him for more than I'll say.

    MALVOLIO How now, mistress?

105 MARIA O Lord!

    SIR TOBY Prithee, hold thy peace. This is not the way.
    Do you not see you move° him? Let me alone with him.   *excite; anger*

    FABIAN No way but gentleness, gently, gently. The fiend
    is rough° and will not be roughly used.   *violent*

110 SIR TOBY Why, how now, my bawcock?[4] How dost thou,
    chuck?°   *chick (endearment)*

    MALVOLIO Sir!

    SIR TOBY Ay, biddy,° come with me.—What, man, 'tis not   *hen; chicken*
    for gravity to play at cherry-pit[5] with Satan. Hang him,
115 foul collier![6]

    MARIA Get him to say his prayers, good Sir Toby; get
    him to pray.

    MALVOLIO My prayers, minx?°   *insolent girl*

    MARIA No, I warrant you, he will not hear of godliness.

120 MALVOLIO Go hang yourselves all! You are idle,° shallow   *foolish*
    things. I am not of your element.° You shall know more   *social sphere*
    hereafter.   *Exit.*

    SIR TOBY Is't possible?

    FABIAN If this were played upon a stage now, I could
125 condemn it as an improbable fiction.

    SIR TOBY His very genius° hath taken the infection of   *spirit; soul*
    the device,° man.   *scheme*

    MARIA Nay, pursue him now, lest the device take air and
    taint.[7]

130 FABIAN Why, we shall make him mad indeed.

    MARIA The house will be the quieter.

    SIR TOBY Come, we'll have him in a dark room and bound.[8]

---

3. The female healer, herbalist. *Water*: urine
(used to diagnose illness).
4. Fine fellow (from the French *beau coq*,
"fine bird").
5. It is not fitting for a dignified man to play a
children's game (pitching cherry stones into a
small hole).

6. Coal miner or carrier (the devil was commonly portrayed as pitch black).
7. Be exposed to the effects of the air (i.e.,
become public knowledge) and therefore
spoil.
8. A standard treatment of the insane.

My niece is already in the belief that he's mad. We may
carry it thus, for our pleasure and his penance, till our
135   very pastime, tired out of breath, prompt us to have
merc on him, at which time we will bring the device to
the bar⁹ and crown thee for a finder of madmen. But
see, but see!

       Enter SIR ANDREW.

FABIAN   More matter for a May morning.¹
140 SIR ANDREW *[presenting a paper]*   Here's the challenge.
Read it. I warrant there's vinegar and pepper in't.
FABIAN   Is't so saucy?
SIR ANDREW   Ay, is't? I warrant him. Do but read.
SIR TOBY   Give me. *[He reads.]* "Youth, whatsoever thou
145   art, thou art but a scurvy fellow."
FABIAN   Good, and valiant.
SIR TOBY,   "Wonder not, nor admire° not in thy mind, why   *marvel*
I do call thee so, for I will show thee no reason for't."
FABIAN   A good note, that keeps you from the blow of
150   the law.²
SIR TOBY   "Thou comest to the Lady Olivia, and in my sight
she uses thee kindly. But thou liest in thy throat;° that is   *deeply; egregiously*
not the matter I challenge thee for."
FABIAN   Very brief, and to exceeding good sense—less.
155 SIR TOBY   "I will waylay thee going home, where if it be
thy chance to kill me"—
FABIAN   Good.
SIR TOBY   "Thou killest me like a rogue and a villain."
FABIAN   Still you keep o' th' windy side³ of the law. Good.
160 SIR TOBY   "Fare thee well, and God have mercy upon
one of our souls. He may have mercy upon mine, but
my hope is better, and so look to thyself. Thy friend,
as thou usest him, and thy sworn enemy,

                              Andrew Aguecheek."
165 If this letter move° him not, his legs cannot. I'll give't him.   *incite*
MARIA   You may have very fit occasion for't. He is now in
some commerce° with my lady, and will by and by depart.   *dealings*
SIR TOBY   Go, Sir Andrew. Scout me° for him at the   *Look out*
corner of the orchard like a bum-baily.⁴ So soon as
170   ever thou seest him, draw, and as thou drawest, swear
horrible, for it comes to pass oft that a terrible oath,
with a swaggering accent sharply twanged off, gives
manhood more approbation° than ever proof° itself   *confirmation /*
would have earned him. Away!   *demonstration; deed*
175 SIR ANDREW   Nay, let me alone for swearing.⁵   *Exit.*

---

9. That is, the bar of judgment; to a court.
1. Entertainment for May Day (i.e., a holiday).
2. That safeguards you from legal action (for
slander or disturbing the peace).
3. To windward and thus out of the reach of

the law.
4. A contemptuous term for a bailiff, an officer charged with making arrests.
5. That is, I am unsurpassed at swearing.

SIR TOBY   Now will not I deliver his letter, for the behavior of the young gentleman gives him out to be of good
capacity° and breeding; his employment between his   *ability*
lord and my niece confirms no less. Therefore, this let-
180   ter, being so excellently ignorant, will breed no terror in
the youth. He will find it comes from a clodpoll.° But,   *blockhead*
sir, I will deliver his challenge by word of mouth, set
upon Aguecheek a notable report of valor, and drive
the gentleman—as I know his youth will aptly receive
185   it[6]—into a most hideous° opinion of his rage, skill, fury,   *terrifying*
and impetuosity. This will so fright them both that they
will kill one another by the look, like cockatrices.[7]

     Enter OLIVIA *and* VIOLA.

FABIAN   Here he comes with your niece. Give them way°   *Stay out of their way*
till he take leave, and presently° after him.   *immediately go*
190   SIR TOBY   I will meditate the while upon some horrid
message for a challenge.

     [*Exeunt* SIR TOBY, FABIAN, *and* MARIA.]

OLIVIA   I have said too much unto a heart of stone
And laid mine honor too unchary[8] on't.
There's something in me that reproves my fault,
195   But such a headstrong potent fault it is
That it but mocks reproof.
VIOLA   With the same 'havior that your passion bears
Goes on my master's griefs.[9]
OLIVIA   Here, wear this jewel[1] for me. 'Tis my picture.
200   Refuse it not, it hath no tongue to vex you.
And I beseech you come again tomorrow.
What shall you ask of me that I'll deny,
That honor, saved, may upon asking give?[2]
VIOLA   Nothing but this: your true love for my master.
205   OLIVIA   How with mine honor may I give him that
Which I have given to you?
VIOLA   I will acquit you.[3]
OLIVIA   Well, come again tomorrow. Fare thee well.
A fiend like thee might bear my soul to hell.   [*Exit.*]

     Enter [SIR] TOBY *and* FABIAN.

SIR TOBY   Gentleman, God save thee.
210   VIOLA   And you, sir.
SIR TOBY   That defense thou hast, betake thee to't. Of
what nature the wrongs are thou hast done him, I
know not, but thy intercepter, full of despite,° bloody   *defiance*
as the hunter,[4] attends° thee at the orchard end.   *awaits*

---

6. That is, his inexperience will cause him to
believe the report of Sir Andrew's valor.
7. Basilisks, mythical monsters that killed
with a look.
8. Risked my honor too incautiously.
9. With the same behavior that marks your

passion, my master's griefs persist.
1. That is, a jeweled locket.
2. That honor, uncompromised, may give
when asked.
3. Release you (from your promise to me).
4. Bloodthirsty as a hunting dog or a huntsman.

215   Dismount thy tuck,° be yare° in thy preparation, for thy   *Draw your rapier / quick*
    assailant is quick, skillful, and deadly.
    VIOLA   You mistake, sir, I am sure no man hath any quarrel
    to° me. My remembrance° is very free and clear from any   *with / memory*
    image of offense done to any man.
220 SIR TOBY   You'll find it otherwise, I assure you. There-
    fore, if you hold your life at any price, betake you to
    your guard, for your opposite° hath in him what youth,   *opponent*
    strength, skill, and wrath can furnish man withal.°   *with*
    VIOLA   I pray you, sir, what is he?
225 SIR TOBY   He is knight dubbed with unhatched[5] rapier
    and on carpet consideration,[6] but he is a devil in pri-
    vate brawl. Souls and bodies hath he divorced three,
    and his incensement at this moment is so implacable
    that satisfaction can be none but by pangs of death and
230   sepulcher. "Hob, nob"[7] is his word;° "give't or take't."   *motto*
    VIOLA   I will return again into the house and desire some
    conduct° of the lady. I am no fighter. I have heard of   *protective escort*
    some kind of men that put quarrels purposely on oth-
    ers, to taste° their valor. Belike° this is a man of that   *test / Perhaps*
235   quirk.
    SIR TOBY   Sir, no. His indignation derives itself out of a
    very competent° injury. Therefore get you on and give   *sufficient*
    him his desire. Back you shall not to the house, unless
    you undertake that° with me which with as much   *(a duel)*
240   safety you might answer him. Therefore on, or strip
    your sword stark naked, for meddle° you must, that's   *fight a duel*
    certain, or forswear to wear iron about you.[8]
    VIOLA   This is as uncivil as strange. I beseech you, do me
    this courteous office, as to know of° the knight what my   *from*
245   offense to him is. It is something of my negligence,
    nothing of my purpose.
    SIR TOBY   I will do so.—Signior Fabian, stay you by this
    gentleman till my return.   *Exit.*
    VIOLA   Pray you, sir, do you know of this matter?
250 FABIAN   I know the knight is incensed against you even to
    a mortal arbitrement,° but nothing of the circumstance   *fight to the death*
    more.
    VIOLA   I beseech you, what manner of man is he?
    FABIAN   Nothing of that wonderful promise, to read° him   *judge*
255   by his form° as you are like to find him in the proof of his   *appearance*
    valor. He is indeed, sir, the most skillful, bloody, and
    fatal opposite that you could possibly have found in
    any part of Illyria. Will you° walk towards him, I will   *If you will*
    make your peace with him if I can.

5. Unused in battle.
6. "Carpet knights" won their titles not in battle but in the carpeted ease of the court.
7. Have or have not; that is, give it or take it, or kill or be killed.
8. Or give up your right to wear a sword.

260 VIOLA I shall be much bound to you for't. I am one
that had rather go with Sir Priest than Sir Knight, I
care not who knows so much of my mettle.° *Exeunt.*   *temperament; courage*
      Enter SIR TOBY *and* SIR ANDREW.

SIR TOBY Why, man, he's a very devil. I have not seen such
a virago.[9] I had a pass[1] with him, rapier, scabbard, and
265 all, and he gives me the stuck-in[2] with such a mortal
motion that it is inevitable; and on the answer,° he pays   *return hit*
you as surely as your feet hits the ground they step on.
They say he has been fencer to the Sophy.°   *Shah of Persia*

SIR ANDREW Pox on't! I'll not meddle with him.

270 SIR TOBY Ay, but he will not now be pacified. Fabian can
scarce hold him yonder.

SIR ANDREW Plague on't! An° I thought he had been val-   *If*
iant and so cunning in fence, I'd have seen him damned
ere I'd have challenged him. Let him let the matter
275 slip, and I'll give him my horse, gray Capilet.

SIR TOBY I'll make the motion.° Stand here, make a good   *offer*
show on't. This shall end without the perdition of souls.°   *loss of lives*
[*aside*] Marry, I'll ride your horse as well as I ride
you.
      Enter FABIAN *and* VIOLA.

280 [*aside to* FABIAN] I have his horse to take up° the quarrel.   *settle*
I have persuaded him the youth's a devil.

FABIAN [*aside to* SIR TOBY] He is as horribly conceited[3]
of him, and pants and looks pale as if a bear were at
his heels.

285 SIR TOBY [*to* VIOLA] There's no remedy, sir; he will fight
with you for's° oath' sake. Marry, he hath better bethought   *for his*
him of his quarrel, and he finds that now scarce to be
worth talking of. Therefore, draw for the supportance
of his vow.[4] He protests° he will not hurt you.   *solemnly declares*

290 VIOLA [*aside*] Pray God defend me. A little thing[5] would
make me tell them how much I lack of a man.

FABIAN [*to* SIR ANDREW] Give ground if you see him
furious.

SIR TOBY Come, Sir Andrew, there's no remedy. The gen-
295 tleman will, for his honor's sake, have one bout with
you. He cannot by the duello° avoid it. But he has prom-   *code of dueling*
ised me, as he is a gentleman and a soldier, he will not
hurt you. Come on, to't.

SIR ANDREW [*drawing his sword*] Pray God he keep his
300 oath.

VIOLA [*drawing his sword*] I do assure you, 'tis against
my will.

9. Female warrior (suggesting both ferocity and
feminine appearance).
1. Bout of fencing.
2. The stoccado, a thrust or stab (from the

Italian *stoccata*).
3. He has as horrifying a conception of him.
4. So that he may keep his oath.
5. Possibly a sexual innuendo.

Enter ANTONIO.

ANTONIO [*to* SIR ANDREW] Put up your sword. If this
    young gentleman
Have done offense, I take the fault on me.

305   If you offend him, I for him defy you.

SIR TOBY You, sir? Why, what are you?

ANTONIO [*drawing his sword*] One, sir, that for his love
    dares yet do more
Than you have heard him brag to you he will.

SIR TOBY [*drawing his sword*] Nay, if you be an under-

310   taker,⁶ I am for° you.   *I will fight*

Enter OFFICERS.

FABIAN O, good Sir Toby, hold. Here come the officers.

SIR TOBY [*to* ANTONIO] I'll be with you anon.

VIOLA [*to* SIR ANDREW] Pray, sir, put your sword up, if
    you please.

315 SIR ANDREW Marry, will I, sir. And for that° I promised   *that which*
    you, I'll be as good as my word. He° will bear you easily,   *the horse*
    and reins well.   *(Capilet, line 275)*

[SIR ANDREW *and* VIOLA *put up their swords.*]

FIRST OFFICER This is the man. Do thy office.

SECOND OFFICER Antonio, I arrest thee at the suit of

320   Count Orsino.

ANTONIO You do mistake me, sir.

FIRST OFFICER No, sir, no jot. I know your favor° well,   *face*
    Though now you have no sea-cap on your head.—
    Take him away. He knows I know him well.

325 ANTONIO I must obey. [*to* VIOLA] This comes with seeking
    you.
But there's no remedy. I shall answer° it.   *defend myself*
What will you do, now my necessity
Makes me to ask you for my purse? It grieves me
Much more for what I cannot do for you

330   Than what befalls myself. You stand amazed,
But be of comfort.

SECOND OFFICER   Come, sir, away.

ANTONIO [*to* VIOLA] I must entreat of you some of that
    money.

VIOLA What money, sir?
For the fair kindness you have showed me here,

335   And part° being prompted by your present trouble,   *partly*
Out of my lean and low ability
I'll lend you something. My having is not much.
I'll make division of my present° with you.   *i.e., what I now have*
Hold, there's half my coffer.° [*offering him money*]   *funds*

340 ANTONIO   Will you deny me now?
Is't possible that my deserts to you

6. One who takes up a challenge.

Can lack persuasion?[7] Do not tempt my misery,
Lest that it make me so unsound° a man   *weak*
As to upbraid you with those kindnesses
That I have done for you.

345 VIOLA   I know of none,
Nor know I you by voice or any feature.
I hate ingratitude more in a man
Than lying, vainness, babbling drunkenness,
Or any taint of vice whose strong corruption
Inhabits our frail blood—

350 ANTONIO   O heavens themselves!
SECOND OFFICER   Come, sir, I pray you go.
ANTONIO   Let me speak a little. This youth that you see
    here
I snatched one half out of the jaws of death,
Relieved him with such sanctity° of love,   *purity*
355 And to his image,[8] which methought did promise
Most venerable worth,[9] did I devotion.
FIRST OFFICER   What's that to us? The time goes by. Away!
ANTONIO   But O, how vile an idol proves this god!
Thou hast, Sebastian, done good feature shame.°   *shamed physical beauty*
360 In nature there's no blemish but the mind;
None can be called deformed but the unkind.
Virtue is beauty, but the beauteous evil
Are empty trunks o'er-flourished[1] by the devil.
FIRST OFFICER   The man grows mad. Away with him.—
    Come, come, sir.
365 ANTONIO   Lead me on.   *Exit [with* OFFICERS].
VIOLA [*aside*]   Methinks his words do from such passion
    fly
That he believes himself; so do not I.[2]
Prove true, imagination, O, prove true,
That I, dear brother, be now ta'en for you!
370 SIR TOBY   Come hither, knight; come hither, Fabian. We'll
    whisper o'er a couplet or two of most sage saws.°   *sayings*
      [SIR TOBY, FABIAN, *and* SIR ANDREW *move aside*.]
VIOLA   He named Sebastian. I my brother know
    Yet living in my glass.° Even such and so   *mirror*
    In favor° was my brother, and he went   *appearance*
375 Still° in this fashion, color, ornament,   *Always*
For him I imitate. O, if it prove,
Tempests are kind, and salt waves fresh in love!   *Exit.*
SIR TOBY   A very dishonest,° paltry boy, and more a coward   *disgraceful*
    than a hare. His dishonesty appears in leaving his
380   friend here in necessity, and denying him; and for his
    coward-ship, ask Fabian.

---

7. Is it possible that my former acts of kindness toward you cannot persuade you?
8. Outward appearance; also, a religious icon.
9. Which appeared to me worthy of veneration.

1. Chests (or bodies) elaborately decorated.
2. That is, I cannot quite dare to believe what
these words suggest to me.

FABIAN A coward, a most devout coward, religious in it.

SIR ANDREW 'Slid,° I'll after him again and beat him.   *By God's eyelid*

SIR TOBY Do, cuff him soundly, but never draw thy sword.   *(an oath)*

SIR ANDREW An° I do not—   [*Exit.*]   *If*

385 FABIAN Come, let's see the event.°   *outcome*

SIR TOBY I dare lay any money 'twill be nothing yet.°   *after all*

                    Exeunt.

4.1

        Enter SEBASTIAN *and* [FESTE, *the*] *clown.*

FESTE Will you° make me believe that I am not sent for   *Are you attempting to*
    you?

SEBASTIAN Go to, go to, thou art a foolish fellow.
    Let me be clear° of thee.   *free*

5 FESTE Well held out,° i' faith. No, I do not know you, nor   *maintained*
    I am not sent to you by my lady to bid you come speak
    with her, nor your name is not Master Cesario, nor
    this is not my nose neither. Nothing that is so is so.

SEBASTIAN I prithee, vent° thy folly somewhere else.   *air; utter*

10 Thou know'st not me.

FESTE Vent my folly? He has heard that word of some
    great man and now applies it to a fool. Vent my folly?
    I am afraid this great lubber° the world will prove a cock-   *lout*
    ney.³ I prithee now, ungird thy strangeness⁴ and tell

15 me what I shall vent to my lady. Shall I vent to her
    that thou art coming?

SEBASTIAN I prithee, foolish Greek,° depart from me.   *buffoon*
    There's money for thee. If you tarry longer,
    I shall give worse payment.

20 FESTE By my troth, thou hast an open hand. These
    wise men that give fools money get themselves a good
    report—° after fourteen years' purchase.⁵   *reputation*

        Enter SIR ANDREW, SIR TOBY, *and* FABIAN

SIR ANDREW [*to* SEBASTIAN] Now, sir, have I met you again?
    [*striking him*] There's for you.

25 SEBASTIAN [*returning the blow*] Why, there's for thee,
    and there, and there.—Are all the people mad?

SIR TOBY Hold, sir, or I'll throw your dagger o'er the house.

FESTE [*aside*] This will I tell my lady straight.° I would   *immediately*
    not be in some of your coats for twopence.   [*Exit.*]

30 SIR TOBY [*seizing Sebastian*] Come on, sir, hold!

SIR ANDREW Nay, let him alone. I'll go another way to
    work with him. I'll have an action of battery° against   *charges of assault*
    him, if there be any law in Illyria. Though I struck him
    first, yet it's no matter for that.

35 SEBASTIAN [*to* SIR TOBY] Let go thy hand!

4.1 Location: Somewhere near Olivia's house.
3. A pampered, foppish child.
4. Drop the pretense that you are a stranger.

5. That is, at too high a price (a piece of land was usually valued at twelve times its annual rent).

SIR TOBY   Come, sir, I will not let you go. Come, my young
    soldier, put up your iron. You are well fleshed.° Come on.   *experienced in combat*
SEBASTIAN   I will be free from thee.
    [*He pulls free and draws his sword.*]
                                  What wouldst thou now?
    If thou dar'st tempt me further, draw thy sword.
40 SIR TOBY   What, what? Nay, then, I must have an ounce
    or two of this malapert° blood from you.   *impudent*
    [*He draws his sword.*]
    Enter OLIVIA.
OLIVIA   Hold, Toby! On thy life I charge thee, hold!
SIR TOBY   Madam.
OLIVIA   Will it be ever thus? Ungracious wretch,
45 Fit for the mountains and the barbarous caves,
    Where manners ne'er were preached! Out of my
    sight!—
    Be not offended, dear Cesario.—
    Rudesby,° be gone!   *Ruffian*
    [*Exeunt* SIR TOBY, SIR ANDREW, *and* FABIAN.]
                       I prithee, gentle friend,
    Let thy fair wisdom, not thy passion, sway
50 In this uncivil and unjust extent°   *attack*
    Against thy peace. Go with me to my house,
    And hear thou there how many fruitless pranks
    This ruffian hath botched up,° that thou thereby   *badly put together*
    Mayst smile at this. Thou shalt not choose but go.
55 Do not deny. Beshrew° his soul for me!   *Curse*
    He started one poor heart of mine, in thee.[6]
SEBASTIAN [*aside*]   What relish° is in this? How runs the   *taste; meaning*
    stream?
    Or° I am mad, or else this is a dream.   *Either*
    Let fancy° still my sense in Lethe[7] steep;   *imagination*
60 If it be thus to dream, still° let me sleep!   *always*
OLIVIA   Nay, come, I prithee. Would thou'dst be ruled
    by me!
SEBASTIAN   Madam, I will.
OLIVIA   O, say so, and so be!   *Exeunt.*

4.2

Enter MARIA *and* [FESTE, *the*] *clown.*

MARIA   Nay, I prithee, put on this gown and this beard;
    make him believe thou art Sir Topas[8] the curate. Do it
    quickly. I'll call Sir Toby the whilst.°   [*Exit.*]   *in the meantime*

---

6. That is, he has frightened my heart, which
I have given to you. Because "start" (to force
from a hiding place) is also a hunting term,
there may be a pun on "heart" and "hart."
7. The river of forgetfulness in the classical
underworld.

4.2 Location: Olivia's house.
8. Perhaps an allusion to Chaucer's burlesque
knight of the "Rime of Sir Topas" in *The Canterbury Tales.* Also, the semiprecious stone
topaz was thought to cure a variety of ailments, including madness.

FESTE Well, I'll put it on, and I will dissemble° myself in't,   *disguise*

5 and I would I were the first that ever dissembled° in such   *deceived*

a gown. [*He puts on gown and beard.*] I am not tall°   *stout*

enough to become the function well,[9] nor lean enough

to be thought a good student,° but to be said° an honest   *(of divinity) / known as*

man and a good housekeeper° goes as fairly as[1] to   *household manager*

10 say a careful man and a great scholar. The competi-

tors° enter.   *My partners*

        Enter SIR TOBY [*and* MARIA].

SIR TOBY Jove bless thee, Master Parson.

FESTE *Bonos dies*, Sir Toby; for, as the old hermit of

Prague,[2] that never saw pen and ink, very wittily said to

15 a niece of King Gorboduc,[3] "That that is, is," so I,

being Master Parson, am Master Parson; for what is

"that" but "that" and "is" but "is"?

SIR TOBY To him, Sir Topas.

FESTE [*disguising his voice*] What ho, I say! Peace in

20 this prison!

SIR TOBY The knave counterfeits well. A good knave.

     [MALVOLIO *within*]

MALVOLIO Who calls there?

FESTE Sir Topas the curate, who comes to visit Malvo-

lio the lunatic.

25 MALVOLIO Sir Topas, Sir Topas, good Sir Topas, go to

my lady—

FESTE Out, hyperbolical° fiend![4] How vexest thou this   *ranting*

man! Talkest thou nothing but of ladies?

SIR TOBY [*aside*] Well said, Master Parson.

30 MALVOLIO Sir Topas, never was man thus wronged.

Good Sir Topas, do not think I am mad. They have laid

me here in hideous darkness—

FESTE Fie, thou dishonest Satan! I call thee by the most

modest° terms, for I am one of those gentle ones that   *mildest*

35 will use the devil himself with courtesy. Sayst thou

that house° is dark?   *room*

MALVOLIO As hell, Sir Topas.

FESTE Why, it hath bay windows transparent as barri-

cadoes,[5] and the clerestories° toward the south-north   *windows in the upper wall*

40 are as lustrous as ebony;[6] and yet complainest thou of

obstruction?

MALVOLIO I am not mad, Sir Topas. I say to you this

house is dark.

---

9. To grace the role of priest (priests were stereotypically fat and students underfed).
1. Sounds as good as.
2. Probably another of Feste's invented
authorities. *Bonos dies:* good day (corruption
of Latin *bonus dies*).

3. Legendary king of ancient Britain.
4. Feste addresses the devil that supposedly
possesses Malvolio.
5. As barricades (i.e., not transparent at all).
6. A hard wood that is a dull black (i.e., not at
all "lustrous" or bright).

FESTE   Madman, thou errest. I say there is no darkness
45   but ignorance, in which thou art more puzzled than
the Egyptians in their fog.[7]
MALVOLIO   I say this house is as dark as ignorance,
though ignorance were as dark as hell. And I say there
was never man thus abused. I am no more mad than
50   you are. Make the trial of it in any constant question.°   rational discourse
FESTE   What is the opinion of Pythagoras[8] concerning
wildfowl?
MALVOLIO   That the soul of our grandam might haply°   perhaps
inhabit a bird.
55   FESTE   What thinkest thou of his opinion?
MALVOLIO   I think nobly of the soul, and no way approve
his opinion.
FESTE   Fare thee well. Remain thou still in darkness.
Thou shalt hold th' opinion of Pythagoras ere I will
60   allow of thy wits,° and fear to kill a woodcock[9] lest thou   certify your sanity
dispossess the soul of thy grandam. Fare thee well.
MALVOLIO   Sir Topas, Sir Topas!
SIR TOBY   My most exquisite Sir Topas!
FESTE   Nay, I am for all waters.[1]
65   MARIA   Thou mightst have done this without thy beard
and gown. He sees thee not.
SIR TOBY   To him in thine own voice, and bring me word
how thou findest him. I would we were well rid of this
knavery. If he may be conveniently delivered,° I would   set free
70   he were, for I am now so far in offense with my niece
that I cannot pursue with any safety this sport to the
upshot.° Come by and by to my chamber.   conclusion

> [*Exeunt* SIR TOBY *and* MARIA.]

FESTE [*sings*][2]   "Hey, Robin, jolly Robin,
                        Tell me how thy lady *does*."
75   MALVOLIO   Fool!
FESTE [*sings*]   "My lady is unkind, perdy."[3]
MALVOLIO   Fool!
FESTE   "Alas, why is she so?"
MALVOLIO   Fool, I say!
FESTE   "She loves another"—
80   Who calls, ha?
MALVOLIO   Good fool, as ever thou wilt deserve well at my
hand, help me to a candle, and pen, ink, and paper. As I
am a gentleman, I will live to be thankful to thee for't.
FESTE   Master Malvolio?

---

7. One of the biblical plagues was a "darkness
over the land of Egypt" (see Exodus 10.21–23).
8. Greek philosopher (6th c. B.C.E.), well-
known for his belief in the transmigration of
souls between living things.
9. A proverbially stupid bird.

1. I can sail any sea (i.e., I am able to handle
all situations).
2. Feste's sung lines are fragments of an old
song.
3. Certainly; indeed (from the French *par-
dieu*, "by God").

85 MALVOLIO Ay, good fool.

FESTE Alas, sir, how fell you besides° your five wits?[4]   *out of*

MALVOLIO Fool, there was never man so notoriously°   *outrageously*
  abused. I am as well in my wits, fool, as thou art.

FESTE But° as well? Then you are mad indeed, if you be   *Only*
90 no better in your wits than a fool.

MALVOLIO They have here propertied me,[5] keep me in
  darkness, send ministers to me—asses!—and do all
  they can to face me[6] out of my wits.

FESTE Advise you° what you say. The minister is here.   *Be careful*
95 [*as Sir Topas*] Malvolio, Malvolio, thy wits the heavens
  restore. Endeavor thyself to sleep and leave thy vain
  bibble-babble.°   *idle chatter*

MALVOLIO Sir Topas!

FESTE [*as Sir Topas*] Maintain no words with him, good
100 fellow. [*as fool*] Who, I, sir? Not I, sir. God buy you,° good   *God be with you*
  Sir Topas. [*as Sir Topas*] Marry, amen. [*as fool*] I will,
  sir, I will.

MALVOLIO Fool! Fool! Fool, I say!

FESTE Alas, sir, be patient. What say you, sir? I am shent°   *reproved*
105 for speaking to you.

MALVOLIO Good fool, help me to some light and some
  paper. I tell thee, I am as well in my wits as any man
  in Illyria.

FESTE Welladay° that you were, sir!   *Alas*
110 MALVOLIO By this hand, I am. Good fool, some ink,
  paper, and light; and convey what I will set down to my
  lady. It shall advantage thee more than ever the bearing
  of letter did.

FESTE I will help you to't. But tell me true, are you not
115 mad indeed, or do you but counterfeit?

MALVOLIO Believe me, I am not. I tell thee true.

FESTE Nay, I'll ne'er believe a madman till I see his brains.
  I will fetch you light and paper and ink.

MALVOLIO Fool, I'll requite it in the highest degree. I
120 prithee, be gone.

FESTE [*sings*]   I am gone, sir,
        And anon, sir,
          I'll be with you again,
        In a trice,
125   Like to the old Vice,[7]
          Your need to sustain.
        Who with dagger of lath,
        In his rage and his wrath,
          Cries "aha!" to the devil;
130   Like a mad lad,

4. The five wits are common sense, fantasy, memory, judgment, and imagination.
5. Treated me like a piece of property.
6. Falsely portray me as.
7. A stock comic character in morality plays and interludes.

"Pare thy nails, dad!
    Adieu, goodman⁸ devil."   *Exit.*

4.3

Enter SEBASTIAN.

SEBASTIAN   This is the air; that is the glorious sun.
This pearl she gave me, I do feel't and see't.
And though 'tis wonder that enwraps me thus,
Yet 'tis not madness. Where's Antonio, then?
5   I could not find him at the Elephant.
Yet there he was;° and there I found this credit,°   *he had been / report*
That he did range° the town to seek me out.   *wander*
His counsel now might do me golden service.
For though my soul disputes well with my sense⁹
10   That this may be some error, but no madness,
Yet doth this accident and flood of fortune
So far exceed all instance,° all discourse,°   *precedent / reason*
That I am ready to distrust mine eyes
And wrangle with my reason that persuades me
15   To any other trust° but that I am mad—   *conviction*
Or else the lady's mad. Yet if 'twere so,
She could not sway° her house, command her followers,   *rule*
Take and give back affairs and their dispatch¹
With such a smooth, discreet, and stable bearing
20   As I perceive she does. There's something in't
That is deceivable.° But here the lady comes.   *deceptive*

Enter OLIVIA *and* PRIEST.

OLIVIA   Blame not this haste of mine. If you mean well,
Now go with me and with this holy man
Into the chantry by.° There, before him   *nearby private chapel*
25   And underneath that consecrated roof,
Plight me the full assurance of your faith,²
That my most jealous° and too doubtful soul   *anxious*
May live at peace. He shall conceal it
Whiles° you are willing it shall come to note,°   *Until / become public*
30   What° time we will our celebration keep   *At which*
According to my birth.° What do you say?   *social rank*
SEBASTIAN   I'll follow this good man and go with you
And, having sworn truth, ever will be true.
OLIVIA   Then lead the way, good father, and heavens so
    shine
35   That they may fairly note° this act of mine.   *Exeunt.*   *look favorably on*

---

8. A vague title of dignity for one of low social
rank, thus an insult to Malvolio.
4.3 Location: Olivia's garden.
9. My reason agrees with my other senses.
1. That is, receive reports on household matters and issue orders for their management.
2. That is, enter into a betrothal (a binding
contract), to be followed with a marriage ceremony at a later date (lines 30–31).

5.1

Enter [FESTE, *the*] *clown and* FABIAN.

FABIAN   Now, as thou lovest me, let me see his letter.

FESTE   Good Master Fabian, grant me another request.

FABIAN   Anything.

FESTE   Do not desire to see this letter.

5 FABIAN   This is to give a dog and in recompense desire
my dog again.[3]

Enter ORSINO, VIOLA, CURIO, *and lords.*

ORSINO   Belong you to the Lady Olivia, friends?

FESTE   Ay, sir, we are some of her trappings.°   ornaments; i.e., entourage

ORSINO   I know thee well. How dost thou, my good fellow?

10 FESTE   Truly, sir, the better for my foes and the worse for
my friends.

ORSINO   Just the contrary: the better for thy friends.

FESTE   No, sir, the worse.

ORSINO   How can that be?

15 FESTE   Marry, sir, they praise me and make an ass of
me.[4] Now my foes tell me plainly I am an ass; so that
by my foes, sir, I profit in the knowledge of myself, and
by my friends I am abused.° So that, conclusions to be   misled
as kisses, if your four negatives make your two affirma-
20 tives,[5] why then the worse for my friends and the better
for my foes.

ORSINO   Why, this is excellent.

FESTE   By my troth, sir, no—though it please you to be
one of my friends.

25 ORSINO [*giving a coin*]   Thou shalt not be the worse for
me; there's gold.

FESTE   But° that it would be double-dealing,[6] sir, I would   Except for the fact
you could make it another.

ORSINO   O, you give me ill counsel.

30 FESTE   Put your grace in your pocket,[7] sir, for this
once, and let your flesh and blood obey it.

ORSINO   Well, I will be so much a sinner to° be a double-   as to
dealer. [*giving a coin*] There's another.

FESTE   *Primo, secundo, tertio*[8] is a good play,° and the old   game
35 saying is, the third pays for all.[9] The triplex,° sir, is a   triple time in music

---

5.1 Location: Near Olivia's house.
3. Perhaps a reference to a story about Elizabeth I, related in the diary of John Man-
ningham (ca. 1575–1622): the queen asked
for a dog from a man named Dr. Bullein;
granted a request in return, he asked for the
dog back.
4. That is, they flatter me into thinking better
of myself than I deserve, which makes me
look foolish.
5. That is, because a grammatical double

negative is a positive, a woman who says "no,
no, no, no" in response to a request for kisses
is really saying "yes, yes."
6. Duplicity (because he is asking for a double donation).
7. That is, pocket up your virtue; also, let
your grace (the proper address to a duke)
reach into your purse (to bring out an additional coin).
8. First, second, third (Latin).
9. The third time is the charm.

good tripping measure, or the bells of Saint Bennet,[1]
sir, may put you in mind—one, two, three.

ORSINO You can fool no more money out of me at this
40 throw.° If you will let your lady know I am here to speak   *(of the dice)*
with her, and bring her along with you, it may awake
my bounty° further.   *generosity*

FESTE Marry, sir, lullaby to your bounty till I come
again. I go, sir, but I would not have you to think
that my desire of having is the sin of covetousness.
45 But, as you say, sir, let your bounty take a nap. I will
awake it anon.   *Exit.*

      Enter ANTONIO *and* OFFICERS.

VIOLA Here comes the man, sir, that did rescue me.

ORSINO That face of his I do remember well.
Yet when I saw it last, it was besmeared
50 As black as Vulcan[2] in the smoke of war.
A baubling° vessel was he captain of,   *paltry*
For shallow draft and bulk unprizable,[3]
With which such scatheful° grapple did he make   *destructive*
With the most noble bottom° of our fleet   *ship*
55 That very envy and the tongue of loss[4]
Cried fame and honor on him.—What's the matter?

FIRST OFFICER Orsino, this is that Antonio
That took the *Phoenix* and her freight from Candy,°   *Candia, capital of Crete*
And this is he that did the *Tiger* board
60 When your young nephew Titus lost his leg.
Here in the streets, desperate of shame and state,[5]
In private brabble° did we apprehend him.   *brawl*

VIOLA He did me kindness, sir, drew on my side,[6]
But in conclusion put strange speech upon° me.   *spoke strangely to*
65 I know not what 'twas but distraction.°   *except madness*

ORSINO Notable° pirate, thou salt-water thief,   *Notorious*
What foolish boldness brought thee to their mercies
Whom thou, in terms so bloody and so dear,°   *costly*
Hast made thine enemies?

ANTONIO   Orsino, noble sir,
70 Be pleased that I shake off these names you give me.
Antonio never yet was thief or pirate,
Though, I confess, on base° and ground enough,   *foundation*
Orsino's enemy. A witchcraft drew me hither.
That most ingrateful boy there by your side
75 From the rude sea's enraged and foamy mouth
Did I redeem; a wrack° past hope he was.   *castaway*

His life I gave him and did thereto add
My love, without retention° or restraint,   reservation
All his in dedication.° For his sake   dedicated to him
80 Did I expose myself, pure° for his love,   purely
Into the danger of this adverse° town;   hostile
Drew to defend him when he was beset;
Where, being apprehended, his false cunning—
Not meaning to partake with me in danger—
85 Taught him to face me out of his acquaintance[7]
And grew a twenty years' removèd thing
While one would wink;[8] denied me mine own purse,
Which I had recommended° to his use   committed
Not half an hour before.
90 VIOLA   How can this be?
ORSINO [to Antonio]   When came he to this town?
ANTONIO   Today, my lord; and for three months before,
No int'rim, not a minute's vacancy,°   interval
Both day and night did we keep company.

            Enter OLIVIA *and attendants.*

95 ORSINO   Here comes the Countess. Now heaven walks on
            earth!—
But for thee, fellow: fellow, thy words are madness.
Three months this youth hath tended upon me—
But more of that anon. [to an OFFICER] Take him aside.
OLIVIA   What would my lord, but that[9] he may not have,
100 Wherein Olivia may seem serviceable?°—   be of service
Cesario, you do not keep promise with me.
VIOLA   Madam?
ORSINO   Gracious Olivia—
OLIVIA   What do you say, Cesario?—Good my lord—
105 VIOLA   My lord would speak; my duty hushes me.
OLIVIA   If it be aught° to the old tune, my lord,   anything
It is as fat and fulsome° to mine ear   gross and repugnant
As howling after music.
ORSINO   Still so cruel?
110 OLIVIA   Still so constant, lord.
ORSINO   What, to perverseness? You, uncivil lady,
To whose ingrate and unauspicious[1] altars
My soul the faithful'st off'rings hath breathed out
That e'er devotion tendered—what shall I do?
115 OLIVIA   Even what it please my lord that shall become°   befit
him.
ORSINO   Why should I not, had I the heart to do it,
Like to th' Egyptian thief at point of death,
Kill what I love?[2]—a savage jealousy

---

7. To shamelessly deny knowing me.
8. In the time it takes to blink.
9. Except that (my love) which.
1. Ungrateful and unfavorable.
2. In Heliodorus's prose romance *Ethiopica*

(3rd c. C.E.; translated from Greek into English in 1569), an Egyptian robber named Thyamis tries to kill Chariclea (his captive, with whom he has fallen in love) when they are attacked by a larger band of robbers.

That sometime savors nobly.° But hear me this: *has nobility in it*
120 Since you to non-regardance° cast my faith,   *neglect*
And that I partly know the instrument
That screws° me from my true place in your favor,   *forces*
Live you the marble-breasted tyrant still.
But this your minion,° whom I know you love,   *favorite*
125 And whom, by heaven I swear, I tender° dearly,   *regard*
Him will I tear out of that cruel eye
Where he sits crownèd in his master's spite—³
Come, boy, with me. My thoughts are ripe in mischief.
I'll sacrifice the lamb that I do love
130 To spite a raven's heart within a dove.
VIOLA   And I, most jocund,° apt,° and willingly,   *happily / readily*
To do you rest a thousand deaths would die.
OLIVIA   Where goes Cesario?
VIOLA   After him I love
More than I love these eyes, more than my life,
135 More by all mores° than e'er I shall love wife.   *(such) comparisons*
If I do feign, you witnesses above,
Punish my life for tainting of my love.
OLIVIA   Ay me, detested!° How am I beguiled!   *rejected*
VIOLA   Who does beguile you? Who does do you wrong?
140 OLIVIA   Hast thou forgot thyself? Is it so long?
Call forth the holy father.   [*Exit an attendant.*]
ORSINO [*to* VIOLA]   Come, away!
OLIVIA   Whither, my lord?—Cesario, husband, stay.
ORSINO   Husband?
OLIVIA   Ay, husband. Can he that deny?
ORSINO   Her husband, sirrah?⁴
VIOLA   No, my lord, not I.
145 OLIVIA   Alas, it is the baseness of thy fear
That makes thee strangle thy propriety.⁵
Fear not, Cesario. Take thy fortunes up.
Be that° thou know'st thou art, and then thou art   *that which*
As great as that° thou fear'st.   *he whom (i.e., Orsino)*
    Enter PRIEST.
          O, welcome, father.
150 Father, I charge thee by thy reverence
Here to unfold—though lately we intended
To keep in darkness what occasion° now   *necessity*
Reveals before 'tis ripe—what thou dost know
Hath newly° passed between this youth and me.   *recently*
155 PRIEST   A contract of eternal bond of love,
Confirmed by mutual joinder° of your hands,   *joining*
Attested by the holy close° of lips,   *meeting*
Strengthened by interchangement of your rings,

3. Notwithstanding the opposition of his master.
4. Customary form of address to a male social inferior.
5. That is, kill your own identity (as my husband).

And all the ceremony of this compact

160 Sealed in my function,[6] by my testimony;
Since when, my watch hath told me, toward my grave
I have traveled but two hours.

ORSINO [*to* VIOLA] O thou dissembling cub! What wilt
thou be
When time hath sowed a grizzle on thy case?[7]

165 Or will not else thy craft° so quickly grow   *cunning*
That thine own trip shall be thine overthrow?[8]
Farewell, and take her, but direct thy feet
Where thou and I henceforth may never meet.

VIOLA My lord, I do protest—

OLIVIA   O, do not swear.

170 Hold little° faith, though thou hast too much fear.   *Keep a little*

Enter SIR ANDREW

SIR ANDREW For the love of God, a surgeon! Send one
presently° to Sir Toby.   *immediately*

OLIVIA What's the matter?

SIR ANDREW He's broke° my head across, and has given   *cut*

175 Sir Toby a bloody coxcomb[9] too. For the love of God,
your help! I had rather than forty pound I were at home.

OLIVIA Who has done this, Sir Andrew?

SIR ANDREW The Count's gentleman, one Cesario. We took
him for a coward, but he's the very devil incardinate.°   *(incarnate)*

180 ORSINO My gentleman Cesario?

SIR ANDREW 'Od's lifelings,[1] here he is!—You broke my
head for nothing, and that that I did, I was set on to
do't by Sir Toby.

VIOLA Why do you speak to me? I never hurt you.

185 You drew your sword upon me without cause,
But I bespake you fair[2] and hurt you not.

SIR ANDREW If a bloody coxcomb be a hurt, you have
hurt me. I think you set nothing by° a bloody coxcomb.   *think nothing of*

Enter SIR TOBY *and* [FESTE, *the*] *clown.*

Here comes Sir Toby halting.° You shall hear more. But   *limping*

190 if° he had not been in drink, he would have tickled°   *if only / chastised*
you othergates° than he did.   *otherwise*

ORSINO How now, gentleman? How is't with you?

SIR TOBY That's all one.° He's hurt me, and there's th'   *irrelevant*
end on't. [*to* FESTE] Sot,° didst see Dick Surgeon,   *Fool; drunkard*

195 sot?

FESTE O, he's drunk, Sir Toby, an hour agone. His eyes
were set° at eight i 'th' morning.   *closed*

6. That is, ratified by my priestly authority.
7. Gray hairs on your hide.
8. That your attempt to take down another shall be your own downfall ("trip" is a wrestling term).
9. Head; also, a fool's hat, which resembles the crest of a cock.
1. By God's little lives (an oath).
2. I spoke to you with all courtesy.

SIR TOBY   Then he's a rogue and a passy-measures pavan.³
I hate a drunken rogue.
200 OLIVIA   Away with him! Who hath made this havoc with
them?
SIR ANDREW   I'll help you, Sir Toby, because we'll be
dressed⁴ together.
SIR TOBY   Will *you* help?—an ass-head, and a coxcomb,°   *fool*
205 and a knave, a thin-faced knave, a gull?°   *dupe*
OLIVIA   Get him to bed, and let his hurt be looked to.

[*Exeunt* SIR TOBY, SIR ANDREW, FESTE, *and* FABIAN.]

Enter SEBASTIAN.

SEBASTIAN   I am sorry, madam, I have hurt your kinsman,
But, had it been the brother of my blood,
I must have done no less with wit and safety.⁵
210 You throw a strange regard upon me,⁶ and by that
I do perceive it hath offended you.
Pardon me, sweet one, even for the vows
We made each other but so late ago.
ORSINO   One face, one voice, one habit, and two persons!
215 A natural perspective,⁷ that is and is not!°   *(an illusion)*
SEBASTIAN   Antonio, O, my dear Antonio!
How have the hours racked and tortured me
Since I have lost thee!
ANTONIO   Sebastian are you?
220 SEBASTIAN   Fear'st thou that,° Antonio?   *Do you doubt that*
ANTONIO   How have you made division of yourself?
An apple cleft in two is not more twin
Than these two creatures. Which is Sebastian?
OLIVIA   Most wonderful!°   *amazing*
225 SEBASTIAN [*looking at* VIOLA]   Do I stand there? I never
had a brother,
Nor can there be that deity° in my nature   *divine power*
Of here and everywhere.° I had a sister,   *omnipresence*
Whom the blind° waves and surges have devoured.   *indiscriminate*
Of charity,° what kin are you to me?   *Kindly (tell me)*
230 What countryman? What name? What parentage?
VIOLA   Of Messaline. Sebastian was my father.
Such a Sebastian was my brother, too.
So went he suited° to his watery tomb.   *dressed; in appearance*
If spirits can assume both form and suit,
You come to fright us.
235 SEBASTIAN   A spirit I am indeed,
But am in that dimension grossly clad

3. A slow, stately dance of Italian origin (*pas-samezzo pavana* [Italian]). Sir Toby may think that its swaying movements resemble the unsteadiness of a drunk.
4. We'll have our wounds tended to.
5. With reasonable prudence for my own safety.
6. That is, you look at me as if I were a stranger.
7. An optical illusion produced by nature (and not by a mirror).

Which from the womb I did participate.[8]
Were you a woman, as the rest goes even,[9]
I should my tears let fall upon your cheek
240 And say "Thrice welcome, drownèd Viola."
VIOLA   My father had a mole upon his brow.
SEBASTIAN   And so had mine.
VIOLA   And died that day when Viola from her birth
Had numbered thirteen years.
245 SEBASTIAN   O, that record is lively[1] in my soul!
He finishèd indeed his mortal act
That day that made my sister thirteen years.
VIOLA   If nothing lets° to make us happy both   *prevents*
But this my masculine usurped attire,
250 Do not embrace me till each circumstance
Of place, time, fortune, do cohere and jump°   *agree*
That I am Viola; which to confirm,
I'll bring you to a captain in this town,
Where lie my maiden weeds;° by whose gentle help   *clothes*
255 I was preserved to serve this noble count.
All the occurrence of my fortune[2] since
Hath been between° this lady and this lord.   *as messenger between*
SEBASTIAN [to OLIVIA]   So comes it, lady, you have been
mistook.
But nature to her bias drew in that.[3]
260 You would have been contracted° to a maid.   *betrothed*
Nor are you therein, by my life, deceived:
You are betrothed both to a maid and man.[4]
ORSINO [to OLIVIA]   Be not amazed; right noble is his
blood.
If this be so, as yet the glass seems true,[5]
265 I shall have share in this most happy wrack.°—   *fortunate shipwreck*
Boy, thou hast said to me a thousand times
Thou never shouldst love woman like to me.°   *as much as (you love) me*
VIOLA   And all those sayings will I overswear°   *swear again*
And all those swearings keep as true in soul
270 As doth that orbèd continent the fire[6]
That severs day from night.
ORSINO   Give me thy hand,
And let me see thee in thy woman's weeds.
VIOLA   The captain that did bring me first on shore
Hath my maid's garments. He, upon some action,°   *legal charge*
275 Is now in durance° at Malvolio's suit,   *prison*
A gentleman and follower of my lady's.

---

8. That is, I am a spirit, yes, but one, like all
humans, dressed in flesh from the time I was
in the womb.
9. As everything else indicates.
1. The memory of that is vivid.
2. That is, all that has happened to me.
3. That is, but nature caused you to swerve to

me in that matter. (The image is from the
game of bowls, played with a weighted ball
that curves from a straight path.)
4. That is, a man who is a virgin.
5. That is, the "natural perspective" (of line
215) continues to seem real.
6. That is, as the sun's sphere contains the fire.

OLIVIA He shall enlarge° him. Fetch Malvolio hither.   *release*
And yet, alas, now I remember me,
They say, poor gentleman, he's much distract.

Enter [FESTE, the] clown with a letter, and FABIAN.

280   A most extracting frenzy° of mine own   *distracting madness*
From my remembrance clearly banished his.°   *his madness*
How does he, sirrah?

FESTE Truly, madam, he holds Beelzebub at the stave's
end[7] as well as a man in his case may do. He's here writ
285 a letter to you. I should have given't you today morning. But as a madman's epistles are no gospels,[8] so it
skills° not much when they are delivered.   *matters*

OLIVIA Open't and read it.

FESTE Look then to be well edified, when the fool deliv-
290 ers° the madman. [*He reads.*] "By the Lord, madam"—   *speaks the words of*

OLIVIA How now, art thou mad?

FESTE No, madam, I do but read madness. An° your lady-   *If*
ship will have it as it ought to be, you must allow *vox.*[9]

OLIVIA Prithee, read i' thy right wits.

295 FESTE So I do, madonna. But to read his right wits[1] is
to read thus. Therefore, perpend,° my princess, and   *pay attention*
give ear.

OLIVIA [*giving letter to Fabian*] Read it you, sirrah.

FABIAN "By the Lord, madam, you wrong me, and the
300 world shall know it. Though you have put me into
darkness and given your drunken cousin rule over me,
yet have I the benefit of my senses as well as your
Ladyship. I have your own letter that induced me to
the semblance I put on, with the which I doubt not but
305 to do myself much right or you much shame. Think of
me as you please. I leave my duty[2] a little unthought of
and speak out of my injury.

                        The madly-used Malvolio."

OLIVIA Did he write this?

310 FESTE Ay, madam.

ORSINO This savors not much of distraction.°   *madness*

OLIVIA See him delivered,° Fabian. Bring him hither.   *released*
                                [*Exit FABIAN.*]

My lord, so please you, these things further thought on,
To think me as well a sister as a wife,[3]
315 One day shall crown th' alliance on't,[4] so please you,
Here at my house, and at my proper cost.°   *own expense*

ORSINO Madam, I am most apt° t' embrace your offer.   *ready*

---

7. Keeps the devil at a distance (proverbial).
8. The letters of a madman are not to be taken as gospel truths.
9. The voice (Latin); Feste is using a voice he thinks appropriate for a madman.
1. To read his state of mind correctly.

2. The duty I owe you (as your servant).
3. That is, think of me as favorably as your sister-in-law as you would have had I been your wife.
4. That is, be the occasion of the two marriages that will cement this new relationship.

[*to* VIOLA] Your master quits° you; and for your service   *releases*
   done him,
320 So much against the mettle° of your sex,   *temperament*
   So far beneath your soft and tender breeding,
   And since you called me "master" for so long,
   Here is my hand. You shall from this time be
   Your master's mistress.
OLIVIA [*to* VIOLA]
                     A sister! You are she.

     Enter MALVOLIO [*and* FABIAN.]

ORSINO   Is this the madman?
OLIVIA   Ay, my lord, this same.—
   How now, Malvolio?
325 MALVOLIO   Madam, you have done me wrong,
   Notorious wrong.
OLIVIA   Have I, Malvolio? No.
MALVOLIA [*handing her a paper*]   Lady, you have. Pray
   you peruse that letter.
   You must not now deny it is your hand.°   *handwriting*
   Write from° it if you can, in hand or phrase,   *differently from*
330 Or say 'tis not your seal, not your invention.°   *composition*
   You can say none of this. Well, grant it then,
   And tell me, in the modesty of honor,[5]
   Why you have given me such clear lights° of favor?   *signs*
   Bade me come smiling and cross-gartered to you,
335 To put on yellow stockings, and to frown
   Upon Sir Toby and the lighter° people?   *lesser*
   And, acting° this in an obedient hope,   *after doing*
   Why have you suffered° me to be imprisoned,   *allowed*
   Kept in a dark house, visited by the priest,
340 And made the most notorious geck° and gull   *fool*
   That e'er invention° played on? Tell me why.   *trickery*
OLIVIA   Alas, Malvolio, this is not my writing,
   Though I confess much like the character.°   *(my) handwriting*
   But out of question, 'tis Maria's hand.
345 And now I do bethink me, it was she
   First told me thou wast mad; then cam'st° in smiling,   *you came*
   And in such forms which here were presupposed°   *previously suggested*
   Upon thee in the letter. Prithee, be content.
   This practice° hath most shrewdly passed° upon thee.   *trick / cleverly played*
350 But when we know the grounds and authors of it,
   Thou shalt be both the plaintiff and the judge
   Of thine own cause.
FABIAN   Good madam, hear me speak,
   And let no quarrel nor no brawl to come
   Taint the condition of this present hour,
355 Which I have wondered at. In hope it shall not,

5. As an honorable person would.

Most freely I confess myself and Toby
Set this device against Malvolio here,
Upon some stubborn and uncourteous parts
We had conceived against him.[6] Maria writ
360   The letter, at Sir Toby's great importance,°   *importuning*
In recompense whereof he hath married her.
How with a sportful malice it was followed°   *carried through*
May rather pluck on° laughter than revenge,   *encourage*
If that the injuries be justly weighed
365   That have on both sides passed.

OLIVIA [*to* MALVOLIO]   Alas, poor fool, how have they
   baffled° thee!   *disgraced*

FESTE   Why, "Some are born great, some achieve greatness, and some have greatness thrown upon them." I
was one, sir, in this interlude,° one Sir Topas, sir, but   *comedy*
370   that's all one. "By the Lord, fool, I am not mad"—
but, do you remember "Madam, why laugh you at
such a barren rascal; an° you smile not, he's gagged"?   *if*
And thus the whirligig° of time brings in his revenges.   *spinning top*

MALVOLIO   I'll be revenged on the whole pack of you!
                                                [*Exit.*]

375 OLIVIA   He hath been most notoriously abused.

ORSINO   Pursue him and entreat him to a peace.
                                   [*Exit one or more.*]

He hath not told us of the captain yet.
When that is known, and golden time convents,°   *suits*
A solemn combination shall be made
380   Of our dear souls. Meantime, sweet sister,
We will not part from hence.° Cesario, come—   *here (Olivia's house)*
For so you shall be while you are a man.
But when in other habits° you are seen,   *attire*
Orsino's mistress, and his fancy's° queen.   *imagination's; love's*
                        Exeunt [*all but* FESTE].

385 FESTE *sings*   When that I was and a little tiny boy,
        With hey, ho, the wind and the rain,
      A foolish thing was but a toy,
        For the rain it raineth every day.

      But when I came to man's estate,
390   With hey, ho, the wind and the rain,
      'Gainst knaves and thieves men shut their gate,
        For the rain it raineth every day.

      But when I came, alas, to wive,
        With hey, ho, the wind and the rain,

6. That is, because of some rude and uncivil qualities that we discerned in him and held against him.

395 By swaggering° could I never thrive, *blustering; bullying*
     For the rain it raineth every day.

     But when I came unto my beds,
       With hey, ho, the wind and the rain,
     With tosspots° still had drunken heads, *drunkards*
400   For the rain it raineth every day.

     A great while ago the world begun,
       With hey, ho, the wind and the rain,
     But that's all one, our play is done,
       And we'll strive to please you every day.

                                             Exit.

MOLIÈRE (JEAN-BAPTISTE POQUELIN)

1621?–1673

FRANCE'S greatest comic dramatist, Molière (born Jean-Baptiste Poquelin) has remained, since the seventeenth century, among the world's most frequently produced and widely studied playwrights. An actor, a director, and a manager as well, Molière was a consummate man of the theater, completely dedicated to art; his thirty-year career coincided with, and significantly contributed to, the flowering of French dramaturgy. A contemporary of the renowned tragic dramatists Pierre Corneille (1606–1684) and Jean Racine (1639–1699), Molière joined his colleagues in catapulting the French theater to European prominence. Under the leadership of Louis XIV (r. 1643–1715), whose appreciation for and support of the arts defined his reign, France emerged at the cultural vanguard in the baroque era, setting standards for dramatic composition and production that lasted until the advent of modernism.

Born into a family of bourgeois artisan merchants, Jean-Baptiste was baptized on January 15, 1622. His father, Jean Poquelin, and mother, Marie Cressé, worked in the bedding trade, and in 1631 Jean was named *tapissier ordinaire du roi*, a royal appointment that involved caring for the king's furniture. Their gain in economic security and prestige enabled them to send their son to the Collège de Clermont, the most fashionable school in Paris at the

time. This Jesuit institution introduced Jean-Baptiste to a study of the humanities, which included classical languages and literatures, rhetoric, theology, and philosophy. Very probably he acted in Latin comedies and tragedies as part of his education; the works of the Roman comic dramatists Plautus and Terence, replete with narratives of frustrated young lovers, overbearing parents, and cunning slaves, clearly informed his development as a writer. He likely also saw the popular folk theater of the day.

When Jean-Baptiste reached age fifteen, Jean Poquelin conveyed his royal appointment to his son, securing for the youth a solid future in the family trade. Though the young man may have accompanied the king in this capacity on a military campaign in 1642, he apparently continued his studies, including a new focus in law. In any case, in 1643 Jean-Baptiste's career took a novel and decisive turn. In exchange for 630 livres from his father, he gave up his royal office and with a small group of colleagues formed the Illustre Théâtre. The creation of the company benefited the actors in a number of ways: they gained control of their employment, the profits, and the kinds of work produced, as they moved away from older dramatic traditions. About a year later, Jean-Baptiste assumed the stage name Molière.

It was a challenging time to embark on a theatrical career. Elsewhere in Europe, dramatic writing had already blossomed in the Renaissance, but France lagged behind. Theatrical activity there in the early decades of the seventeenth century consisted mainly of productions of scripts from other countries as well as the lively Italian farces performed in the streets of Paris and in the provinces. A native. variant of this latter tradition had also developed after liturgical drama was secularized in the late medieval period. Equally popular were the traveling companies specializing in the Italian commedia dell'arte, with its repertoire of stock characters, familiar plots, and improvised comic business called *lazzi* that surmounted the language barrier. We can trace the direct impact of all these traditions on a play like TARTUFFE (1664–69), one of Molière's greatest and most controversial comedies.

Just a decade before the founding of the Illustre Théâtre, the shape of French literature had been transformed by the establishment of the French Academy (*Académie Française*), under the sponsorship of the influential minister Cardinal Richelieu. The Academy created rules for the composition of French literature and national standards for literary taste. Drawing on Aristotle's *Poetics,* the Academy emphasized the importance of adhering to the unities of time, place, and action for the drama and stressed that tragedy should depict the lives of kings and the aristocracy, while comedy should portray those of lower social status. Under the Academy's direction, verse drama prevailed. The twelve-syllable line called the *alexandrine* dominated French dramaturgy, and Molière frequently utilized the rhyming couplets that were standard for his era. (The translation of *Tartuffe* included here renders the couplets in the pentameter line more natural in English.) The Academy also established that plausibility (*vraisemblance*) and propriety (*bienséance*) should inform all dramatic writing. Many of Molière's works display the tension between his efforts to conform to these rules and his appreciation of the bawdier farce traditions that had proven so popular with the audiences he now sought to attract. He also recognized that his plays had to somehow acknowledge and win the king's invaluable ongoing patronage.

Before he could pen the masterpieces that define his theatrical legacy, Molière and his colleagues struggled for more than a decade just to make ends meet. Finding it impossible to pay its bills in Paris, the Illustre Théâtre survived for almost fifteen years by touring the provinces. During this period, the company members honed their skills as actors, and Molière began to compose some short, comic plays for the group to perform before their main productions—for the most part, tragic dramas from the emerging French repertoire. His first full-length work, *L'Étourdi* (*The Blockhead*), based on a commedia scenario, dates from about 1655. The troupe returned to Paris in 1658, under the patronage of the king's brother; the successful production of Molière's *Les Précieuses ridicules* (*The Affected Young Ladies*) the following year secured their standing both at court and with the Parisian public. In 1660 the king granted them the right to perform at the Palais Royal theater. New challenges soon arose, however. Beginning with his companion pieces *L'École des maris* and *L'École des femmes* (*The School for Husbands* and *The School for Wives*, 1661–62), Molière repeatedly found himself embroiled in public controversy, as his comedies assailed the mores and exposed the foibles of Parisian society. Yet these disputes pale in comparison to the religious furor that erupted over *Tartuffe.*

The Protestant reform movement that had swept over much of Europe during the sixteenth century had little effect on France owing mainly to the Catholic Church's brutal suppression of the Protestant Huguenots, which began with the St. Bartholomew's Day Massacre in 1572. Henry IV's Edict of Nantes, issued in 1598, officially ended France's half century of religious wars and placed the country firmly within the control of a moderate but decidedly Catholic monarchy. Although Catholic rule by Molière's time was more tolerant than the bloody repression that had preceded it, the church's oversight of many aspects of French life remained largely unchecked throughout the seventeenth century. At the same time, a wide range of ideological positions existed within French Catholicism, from the strict asceticism of the Jansenists to the more worldly open-mindedness of the Christian humanists to the scholastics' focus on doctrine. Adding to this sometimes fractious mix were religious organizations such as the Compagnie du Saint-Sacrement (Society of the Blessed Sacrament), whose members—many powerful laypeople among them—combined charitable work with efforts to enforce a strict moral code. Such internal frictions did not affect the church's hostility to the theater, especially the profession of acting; its opposition had been strong since the late Middle Ages. Because the church viewed theatrical representation, or pretense to another identity, as inherently sinful, actors lived under the constant threat of excommunication. Indeed, because Molière died suddenly—within hours after coughing up blood while performing in his *Le Malade imaginaire* (*The Imaginary Invalid*, 1673)—as an unrepentant actor he was denied a full Christian burial.

Even Louis XIV had to approach such matters carefully. Far from devout, he nevertheless recognized the enormous political power of the clergy in his country. Within his own household, he had to deal with the exacting religious strictures of his mother, the Dowager Queen Anne d'Autriche—a model, scholars believe, for Mme Pernelle, *Tartuffe*'s overbearing mother figure. Yet the king, like Molière, well understood that some individuals used declarations of faith for personal gain; with royal acquiescence or perhaps even encouragement, Molière could expose their hypocrisy and turn the tables on those who defamed his profession. In *Tartuffe,* the vices long attributed to the theater are ascribed to the character who would have been among the theater's most vocal opponents: Tartuffe himself.

Molière quickly establishes the conflict that will dominate the play's action. The well-to-do but gullible Monsieur Orgon and his domineering mother have fallen under the influence of Monsieur Tartuffe, a man who pretends to great humility, self-sacrifice, and religious devotion. Orgon takes Tartuffe into his home and begins to treat him as his most valued relation. Although Orgon's wife and children see through Tartuffe, they cannot convince Orgon or his mother of the pretense. Events take a more serious turn when Orgon decides to marry his daughter to the hypocrite rather than the man to whom she is betrothed, Valère. This decision in turn threatens the happiness of his son, Damis, who is engaged to Valère's sister. Indeed, Orgon endangers the well-being of his entire family by entrusting Tartuffe with secret information and even his property. Ultimately, through the efforts of his resourceful wife, Elmire, and the intervention of the king, Tartuffe's true nature is revealed, and the family is saved from disaster.

Molièristes have long argued inconclusively about whether the playwright based the figure of Tartuffe on any particular individual or on features of any specific Catholic faction. Just as plausibly, Tartuffe may be a composite portrait drawn from Molière's keen observations of false devotion. Realistic yet indeterminate, the characterization incensed a number of religious leaders, precisely because its subtle inclusion of elements of many different groups' ideologies enabled it to be interpreted as an attack on widely disparate religious individuals and their affiliations. As Molière noted in a letter to the king in 1667,

> The men whom I depict in my comedy [*Tartuffe*] . . . know how to display all of their aims in the most favorable light; yet, no matter how pious they may seem, it is surely not the interests of God which stir them; they have proven this often enough in the comedies they have allowed to be performed hundreds of times without making the least objection. Those plays attacked only piety and religion, for which they care very little; but this play attacks and makes fun of them, and that is what they cannot bear.

Already in 1664, after the king—clearly under pressure from religious leaders or powerful members of the Compagnie du Saint-Sacrement—had banned the play following its initial performance, Molière was warning Louis XIV that "the Tartuffes have skillfully gained Your Majesty's favor, and the models [i.e., the religious hypocrites] have succeeded in eliminating the copy [i.e., the play]." In both letters, Molière tried to alert the king to the connections between what was represented in the play itself and what was going on at court and in

Frontispiece of a 1682 printing of *Tartuffe ou L'Imposteur*.

Parisian society, and to persuade him to allow the play to be staged once again.

Complicating our understanding of these issues and the elements of the play that initially spawned the controversy is the script's history: only the last of its three different versions still exists. On May 12, 1664, at the request of Louis XIV, Molière presented at Versailles a new three-act play titled *Tar-*

tuffe, ou L'Hypocrite. While we will never know how closely the final play corresponds to this first performance, many scholars believe that it contained what in our text are acts 1, 3, and 4—those scenes focusing on Tartuffe and his increasing dominance in Orgon's household. Over the next five years, Molière would make numerous attempts to have the ban on *Tartuffe* lifted;

to appease his opponents, he also significantly revised and expanded the play. Molière hints in his second letter to the king that Tartuffe was originally costumed as a cleric, but that he was attired later as a lay figure, with long hair and lace on his clothing. In the second version Molière also changed the character's name to Panulphe, making him a sword-carrying man of the world. But these alterations satisfied no one, and Molière subsequently dropped them. In his preface to the final version, Molière explains that in revising the play, he had

> used all the art and skill that I could to distinguish clearly the character of the hypocrite from that of the truly devout man. For that purpose I used two whole acts to prepare the appearance of my scoundrel. Never is there a moment's doubt about his character; he is known at once from the qualities I have given him; and from one end of the play to the other, he does not say a word, he does not perform an action which does not depict to the audience the character of a wicked man.

Finally, in February 1669, the king acceded to the playwright's requests, allowing the work now titled *Tartuffe, ou L'Imposteur* to be performed in public. The reason for his change of heart remains a mystery, but scholars believe that the death of the dowager queen may have removed one major obstacle; other likely factors were Molière's revisions and his persuasive arguments that by exposing and ridiculing hypocrisy, the comedy could benefit the public. Audiences responded with wild enthusiasm; *Tartuffe* became the most popular play of its era and beyond, with more than 2,000 performances at the Comédie Française, the French national theater, between 1680 and 1900.

One of the keys to the work's success is its timelessness: the bourgeois family narrative of generational conflict and endangered love relationships transcends the play's origins in the specific religious and political context of the 1660s. *Tartuffe* weaves together time-honored characters and plot elements, popular since the heyday of Roman comedy, with enduring concerns about the law, justice, leadership, and the relationship between the family and the state.

To be sure, the second act, with its extended quarrel between Mariane and her lover Valère over their true feelings for each other, and the fifth act, with its whirlwind of events leading up to the ultimately happy ending, may at first strike some as tacked on and having little relation to the play's central concern—Tartuffe and his duplicitous

Brian Bedford (left) as Orgon and Henry Goodman (right) in the title role of the 2003 Roundabout Theater Company (New York) production of *Tartuffe*.

nature. Yet a common theme of illusion versus reality ties the marriage plot to the revelation of Tartuffe's deceptions. Just as the lovers must work through their false assumptions to rediscover the truth of their mutual devotion, so Orgon and his mother must be made to see Tartuffe for who he really is. In addition, Mariane's understanding of her father's control of her marital destiny resonates with other questions of power and appropriate social behavior in the play. Orgon rules the home as the king rules the state; Orgon must learn from his monarch how to exercise that authority wisely. Tartuffe thus emerges as a threat not only to the family of Orgon but also to the entire kingdom.

Molière builds his resolution around the political trope "L'état, c'est moi" (I am the state), which equates monarch and realm. The somewhat fantastical denouement—which some scholars have called a "rex ex machina" on the model of the classical deus ex machina—certainly stretches the limits of verisimilitude, or *vraisemblance.* But as an extended tribute to Louis XIV, the ending did realize the Academy's principle of propriety (*bienséance*) and appears to have contributed to the work's ultimate success. Molière, here as in many of his plays, walks a fine line between following the dictates of the French Academy and realizing his own dramatic goals. His calculated decision to acknowledge the king's beneficence within *Tartuffe,* as well as to represent an idealized monarchy, provides a space that also enables him to remind Louis XIV of how to best deploy royal power to the benefit of all France.

Molière continued to explore the issues of hypocrisy, authority, and benevolence in many of his later works, including *Dom Juan, ou le Festin de pierre* (*Dom Juan, or the Feast with the Statue,* 1665), *Le Misanthrope* (1666), and *Le Bourgeois gentilhomme* (*The Bourgeois Gentleman,* 1670). Written for actors by an actor, the plays have sparked some of the theater's most legendary performances and productions. And because the timelessness of his themes ensures their timeliness across the ages, Molière's comedies have continued to serve as vehicles for social commentary. Since the seventeenth century, directors have repeatedly found these works able to critique the present moment and to reveal the vagaries and varieties of human behavior. To learn more about the staging of *Tartuffe* and to view photographs from select performances of the play, see the "Plays in Performance" color insert near the center of this volume.   J.E.G.

Tartuffe[1]

CHARACTERS

MADAME PERNELLE, mother of Orgon
ORGON, husband of Elmire
ELMIRE, wife of Orgon
DAMIS, son of Orgon
MARIANE, daughter of Orgon
VALÈRE, fiancé of Mariane
CLÉANTE, brother-in-law of Orgon

TARTUFFE,[2] a religious hypocrite
DORINE, lady's maid to Mariane
MONSIEUR LOYAL, a bailiff
THE EXEMPT, an officer of the king
FLIPOTE, lady's maid to Madame Pernelle
LAURENT, a servant of Tartuffe

---

1. Versification by Constance Congdon, from a translation by Virginia Scott.
2. The name Tartuffe is similar both to the Italian word *tartufo,* meaning "truffle," and to the French word for truffle, *truffe,* from which is derived the French verb *truffer*—one meaning of which in Molière's day was "to deceive or cheat."

The scene is Paris, in ORGON's *house.*

1.1

[MADAME PERNELLE, FLIPOTE, ELMIRE, MARIANE,
DORINE, DAMIS, CLÉANTE]

MADAME PERNELLE[3]   Flipote, come on! My visit here is through!

ELMIRE   You walk so fast I can't keep up with you!

MADAME PERNELLE   Then stop! That's your last step! Don't take another.
After all, I'm just your husband's mother.

5   ELMIRE   And, as his wife, I have to see you out—
Agreed? Now, what is this about?

MADAME PERNELLE   I cannot bear the way this house is run—
As if I don't know how things should be done!
No one even thinks about my pleasure,

10   And, if I ask, I'm served at someone's leisure.
It's obvious—the values here aren't good
Or everyone would treat me as they should.
The Lord of Misrule here has his dominion.

DORINE   But—

MADAME PERNELLE   See? A servant with an opinion.

15   You're the former nanny, nothing more.
Were I in charge here, you'd be out the door.

DAMIS   If—

MADAME PERNELLE   —You—be quiet. Now let Grandma spell
Her special word for you: "F-O-O-L."
Oh yes! Your dear grandmother tells you that,

20   Just as I told my son, "Your son's a brat.
He won't become a drunkard or a thief,
And yet, he'll be a lifetime full of grief."

MARIANE   I think—

MADAME PERNELLE   —Oh, don't do that, my dear grandchild.
You'll hurt your brain. You think that we're beguiled

25   By your quietude, you fragile flower,
But as they say, still waters do run sour.

ELMIRE   But Mother—

MADAME PERNELLE   —Daughter-in-law, please take this well—
Behavior such as yours leads straight to hell.
You spend money like it grows on trees

30   Then wear it on your back in clothes like these.
Are you a princess? No? You're dressed like one!
One wonders whom you dress for—not my son.
Look to these children whom you have corrupted
When their mama's life was interrupted.

35   She spun in her grave when you were wed;
She's still a better mother, even dead.

CLÉANTE   Madame, I do insist—

MADAME PERNELLE   —You do? On what?

---

3. The role of Madame Pernelle was originally played by a male actor, a practice that was already
a comic convention in Molière's time.

That we live life as you do, caring not
For morals? I hear each time you give that speech
40   Your sister memorizing what you teach.
I'd slam the door on you. Forgive my frankness.
That is how I am! And it is thankless.

DAMIS   Tartuffe would, from the bottom of his heart,
If he had one, thank you.

MADAME PERNELLE   Oh, now you start.
45   Grandson, it's "Monsieur Tartuffe" to you.
And he's a man who should be listened to.
If you provoke him with ungodly chat,
I will not tolerate it, and that's that.

DAMIS   Yet I should tolerate this trickster who
50   Has become the voice we answer to.
And I'm to be as quiet as a mouse
About this tyrant's power in our house?
All the fun things lately we have planned,
We couldn't do. And why? Because they're banned—

55 DORINE   By him! Anything we take pleasure in
Suddenly becomes a mortal sin.

MADAME PERNELLE   Then "he's here just in time" is what I say!
Don't you see? He's showing you the way
To heaven! Yes! So follow where he leads!
60   My son knows he is just what this house needs.

DAMIS   Now Grandmother, listen. Not Father, not you,
No one can make me follow this man who
Rules this house, yet came here as a peasant.
I'll put him in his place. It won't be pleasant.

65 DORINE   When he came here he wasn't wearing shoes.
But he's no village saint—it's all a ruse.
There was no vow of poverty—he's poor!
And he was just some beggar at the door
Whom we should have tossed. He's a disaster!
70   To think this street bum now plays the master.

MADAME PERNELLE   May God have mercy on me. You're all blind.
A nobler, kinder man you'll never find.

DORINE   So you think he's a saint. That's what he wants.
But he's a hypocrite and merely flaunts
75   This so-called godliness.

MADAME PERNELLE   Will you be quiet!?

DORINE   And that man of his—I just don't buy it—
He's supposed to be his servant? No.
They're in cahoots, I bet.

MADAME PERNELLE   How would you know?
When, clearly, you don't understand, in fact,
80   How a servant is supposed to act?
This holy man you think of as uncouth,
Tries to help by telling you the truth
About yourself. But you can't hear it.
He knows what heaven wants and that you fear it.

85 DORINE   So "heaven" hates these visits by our friends?
       I see! And that's why Tartuffe's gone to any ends
       To ruin our fun? But it is he who's zealous
       About "privacy"—and why? He's jealous.
       You can't miss it, whenever men come near—
90   He's lusting for our own Madame Elmire.
    MADAME PERNELLE   Since you, Dorine, have never understood
       Your place, or the concepts of "should"
       And "should not," one can't expect you to see
       Tartuffe's awareness of propriety.
95   When these men visit, they bring noise and more—
       Valets and servants planted at the door,
       Carriages and horses, constant chatter.
       What must the neighbors think? These things matter.
       Is something going on? Well, I hope not.
100   You know you're being talked about a lot.
    CLÉANTE   Really, Madame, you think you can prevent
       Gossip? When most human beings are bent
       On rumormongering and defamation,
       And gathering or faking information
105   To make us all look bad—what can we do?
       The fools who gossip don't care what is true.
       You would force the whole world to be quiet?
       Impossible! And each new lie—deny it?
       Who in the world would want to live that way?
110   Let's live our lives. Let gossips have their say.
    DORINE   It's our neighbor, Daphne. I just know it.
       They don't like us. It's obvious—they show it
       In the way they watch us—she and her mate.
       I've seen them squinting at us, through their gate.
115   It's true—those whose private conduct is the worst
       Will mow each other down to be the first
       To weave some tale of lust, so hearts are broken
       Out of a simple kiss that's just a token
       Between friends—just friends and nothing more.
120   See—those whose trysts are kept behind a door
       Yet everyone finds out? Well, then, they need
       New stories for the gossip mill to feed
       To all who'll listen. So they must repaint
       The deeds of others, hoping that a taint
125   Will color others' lives in darker tone
       And, by this process, lighten up their own.
    MADAME PERNELLE   Daphne and her mate are not the point.
       But when Orante says things are out of joint,
       There's a problem. She's a person who
130   Prays every day and should be listened to.
       She condemns the mob that visits here.
    DORINE   This good woman shouldn't live so near
       Those, like us, who run a bawdy house.
       I hear she lives as quiet as a mouse—

135   Devout, though. Everyone applauds her zeal.
      She needed that when age stole her appeal.
      Her passion is policing—it's her duty
      And compensation for her loss of beauty.
      She's a reluctant prude. And now, her art,
140   Once used so well to win a lover's heart,
      Is gone. Her eyes, that used to flash with lust,
      Are steely from her piety. She must
      Have seen that it's too late to be a wife,
      And so she lives a plain and pious life.
145   This is a strategy of old coquettes.
      It's how they manage once the world forgets
      Them. First, they wallow in a dark depression,
      Then see no recourse but in the profession
      Of a prude. They criticize the lives of everyone.
150   They censure everything, and pardon none.
      It's envy. Pleasures that they are denied
      By time and age, now, they just can't abide.
      MADAME PERNELLE   You do go on and on. [*To* ELMIRE] My dear Elmire,
      This is all your doing. It's so clear
155   Because you let a servant give advice.
      Just be aware—I'm tired of being nice.
      It's obvious to anyone with eyes
      That what my son has done is more than wise
      In welcoming this man who's so devout;
160   His very presence casts the devils out.
      Or most of them—that's why I hope you hear him.
      And I advise all of you to stay near him.
      You need his protection and advice.
      Your casual attention won't suffice.
165   It's heaven sent him here to fill a need,
      To save you from yourselves—oh yes, indeed.
      These visits from your friends you seem to want—
      Listen to yourselves! So nonchalant!
      As if no evil lurks in these events.
170   As if you're blind to what Satan invents.
      And dances! What are those but food for slander!
      It's to the worst desires these parties pander.
      I ask you now, what purpose do they serve?
      Where gossip's passed around like an hors-d'oeuvre.
175   A thousand cackling hens, busy with what?
      It takes a lot of noise to cover smut.
      It truly is the tower of Babylon,[4]
      Where people babble on and on and on.
      Ah! Case in point—there stands Monsieur Cléante,

---

4. That is, the biblical Tower of Babel (the Hebrew equivalent of the Akkadian Bab-ilu, or Babylon—a name explained by the similar sounding but unrelated Hebrew verb *balal*, "confuse"), described in Genesis 11.1–9; to prevent it from being constructed and reaching heaven, God scattered all the people and confused their language, creating many tongues where there had been only one.

180 Sniggering and eyeing me askant,
As if this has nothing to do with him,
And nothing that he does would God condemn.
And so, Elmire, my dear, I say farewell.
Till when? When it is a fine day in hell.
185 Farewell, all of you. When I pass through that door,
You won't have me to laugh at anymore.
Flipote! Wake up! Have you heard nothing I have said?
I'll march you home and beat you till you're dead.
March, slut, march.

1.2[5]

[DORINE, CLÉANTE]

CLÉANTE   I'm staying here. She's scary,
That old lady—
DORINE   I know why you're wary.
Shall I call her back to hear you say,
"That *old* lady"? That would make her day.
5 CLÉANTE   She's lost her mind, she's—now we have the proof—
Head over heels in love with whom? Tartuffe.
DORINE   So here's what's worse and weird—so is her son.
What's more—it's obvious to everyone.
Before Tartuffe and he became entwined,
10 Orgon once ruled this house in his right mind.
In the troubled times,[6] he backed the prince,
And that took courage. We haven't seen it since.
He is intoxicated with Tartuffe—
A potion that exceeds a hundred proof.
15 It's put him in a trance, this devil's brew.
And so he worships this imposter who
He calls "brother" and loves more than one—
This charlatan—more than daughter, wife, son.
This charlatan hears all our master's dreams,
20 And all his secrets. Every thought, it seems,
Is poured out to Tartuffe, like he's his priest!
You'd think they'd see the heresy, at least.
Orgon caresses him, embraces him, and shows
More love for him than any mistress knows.
25 Come for a meal and who has the best seat?
Whose preferences determine what we eat?
Tartuffe consumes enough for six, is praised,
And to his health is every goblet raised,
While on his plate are piled the choicest bites.

---

5. In classical French drama, a new scene begins whenever a character enters or leaves the stage, even if the action continues without interruption; this convention has become known as "French scenes." Characters remaining onstage are listed; others from the previous scene can be assumed to have exited.

6. That is, during the Fronde (literally, "sling"; 1648–53), a civil war that took place while France was being ruled by a regent for Louis XIV—"the prince" whom Orgon supported—as various factions of the nobility sought to limit the growing authority of the monarchy.

30   Then when he belches, our master delights
      In that and shouts, "God bless you!" to the beast,
      As if Tartuffe's the reason for the feast.
      Did I mention the quoting of each word,
      As if it's the most brilliant thing we've heard?
35   And, oh, the miracles Tartuffe creates!
      The prophecies! We write while he dictates.
      All that's ridiculous. But what's evil
      Is seeing the deception and upheaval
      Of the master and everything he owns.
40   He hands him money. They're not even loans—
      He's giving it away. It's gone too far.
      To watch Tartuffe play him like a guitar!
      And this Laurent, his man, found some lace.
      Shredded it and threw it in my face.
45   He'd found it pressed inside *The Lives of Saints*,[7]
      I thought we'd have to put him in restraints.
      "To put the devil's finery beside
      The words and lives of saintly souls who died—
      Is action of satanical transgression!"
50   And so, of course, I hurried to confession.

1.3

[ELMIRE, MARIANE, DAMIS, CLÉANTE, DORINE]

ELMIRE [*to* CLÉANTE]   Lucky you, you stayed. Yes, there was more,
      And more preaching from Grandma, at the door.
      My husband's coming! I didn't catch his eye.
      I'll wait for him upstairs. Cléante, good-bye.
5 CLÉANTE   I'll see you soon. I'll wait here below,
      Take just a second for a brief hello.
    DAMIS   While you have him, say something for me?
      My sister needs for Father to agree
      To her marriage with Valère, as planned.
10   Tartuffe opposes it and will demand
      That Father break his word, and that's not fair;
      Then I can't wed the sister of Valère.
      Listening only to Tartuffe's voice,
      He'd break four hearts at once—
    DORINE   He's here.

1.4

[ORGON, CLÉANTE, DORINE]

ORGON   Rejoice!
    I'm back.
    CLÉANTE   I'm glad to see you, but I'm on my way.
    Just stayed to say hello.
    ORGON   No more to say?
    Dorine! Come back! And Cléante, why the hurry?

---

7. A text (*Flos Sanctorum*, 1599–1601) by the Spanish Jesuit Pedro de Ribadeneyra, available in French translation by 1646.

5   Indulge me for a moment. You know I worry.
     I've been gone two days! There's news to tell.
     Now don't hold back. Has everyone been well?
    DORINE   Not quite. There was that headache Madame had
     The day you left. Well, it got really bad.
10   She had a fever—
    ORGON   And Tartuffe?
    DORINE   He's fine—
     Rosy-nosed and red-cheeked, drinking your wine.
    ORGON   Poor man!
    DORINE   And then, Madame became unable
     To eat a single morsel at the table.
    ORGON   Ah, and Tartuffe?
    DORINE   He sat within her sight,
15   Not holding back, he ate with great delight,
     A brace of partridge, and a leg of mutton.
     In fact, he ate so much, he popped a button.
    ORGON   Poor man!
    DORINE   That night until the next sunrise,
     Your poor wife couldn't even close her eyes.
20   What a fever! Oh, how she did suffer!
     I don't see how that night could have been rougher.
     We watched her all night long, worried and weepy.
    ORGON   Ah, and Tartuffe?
    DORINE   At dinner he grew sleepy.
     After such a meal, it's not surprising.
25   He slept through the night, not once arising.
    ORGON   Poor man!
    DORINE   At last won over by our pleading,
     Madame agreed to undergo a bleeding.[8]
     And this, we think, has saved her from the grave.
    ORGON   Ah, and Tartuffe?
    DORINE   Oh, he was very brave.
30   To make up for the blood Madame had lost
     Tartuffe slurped down red wine, all at your cost.
    ORGON   Poor man!
    DORINE   Since then, they've both been fine, although
     Madame needs me. I'll go and let her know
     How anxious you have been about her health,
35   And that you prize it more than all your wealth.

1.5

     [ORGON, CLÉANTE]

    CLÉANTE   You know that girl was laughing in your face.
     I fear I'll make you angry, but in case
     There is a chance you'll listen, I will try
     To say that you are laughable and why.
5   I've never known of something so capricious

---

8. Bloodletting (whether by leeches or other means), for centuries a standard medical treatment for a wide range of diseases.

As letting this man do just as he wishes
In your home and to your family.
You brought him here, relieved his poverty,
And, in return—

ORGON   Now you listen to me!
10   You're just my brother-in-law, Cléante. Quite!
You don't know this man. And don't deny it!

CLÉANTE   I don't know him, yes, that may be so,
But men like him are not so rare, you know.

ORGON   If you only could know him as I do,
15   You would be his true disciple, too.
The universe, your ecstasy would span.
This is a man . . . who . . . ha! . . . well, such a man.
Behold him. Let him teach you profound peace.
When first we met, I felt my troubles cease.
20   Yes, I was changed after I talked with him.
I saw my wants and needs as just a whim!
Everything that's written, all that's sung,
The world, and you and me, well, it's all dung!
Yes, it's crap! And isn't that a wonder!
25   The real world—it's just some spell we're under!
He's taught me to love nothing and no one!
Mother, father, wife, daughter, son—
They could die right now, I'd feel no pain.

CLÉANTE   What feelings you've developed, how humane.

30 ORGON   You just don't see him in the way I do,
But if you did, you'd feel what I feel, too.
Every day he came to church and knelt,
And from his groans, I knew just what he felt.
Those sounds he made from deep inside his soul,
35   Were fed by piety he could not control.
Of the congregation, who could ignore
The way he humbly bowed and kissed the floor?
And when they tried to turn away their eyes,
His fervent prayers to heaven and deep sighs
40   Made them witness his deep spiritual pain.
Then something happened I can't quite explain.
I rose to leave—he quickly went before
To give me holy water at the door.
He knew what I needed, so he blessed me.
45   I found his acolyte, he'd so impressed me,
To ask who he was and there I learned
About his poverty and how he spurned
The riches of this world. And when I tried
To give him gifts, in modesty, he cried,
50   "That is too much," he'd say, "A half would do."
Then gave a portion back, with much ado.
"I am not worthy. I do not deserve
Your gifts or pity. I am here to serve
The will of heaven, that and nothing more."

55   Then takes the gift and shares it with the poor.
    So heaven spoke to me inside my head.
    "Just bring him home with you" is what it said
    And so I did. And ever since he came,
    My home's a happy one. I also claim
60   A moral home, a house that's free of sin,
    Tartuffe's on watch—he won't let any in.
    His interest in my wife is reassuring,
    She's innocent of course, but so alluring,
    He tells me whom she sees and what she does.
65   He's more jealous than I ever was.
    It's for my honor that he's so concerned.
    His righteous anger's all for me, I've learned,
    To the point that just the other day,
    A flea annoyed him as he tried to pray,
70   Then he rebuked himself, as if he'd willed it—
    His excessive anger when he killed it.
    CLÉANTE   Orgon, listen. You're out of your mind.
    Or you're mocking me. Or both combined.
    How can you speak such nonsense without blinking?
75 ORGON   I smell an atheist! It's that freethinking!
    Such nonsense is the bane of your existence.
    And that explains your damnable resistance.
    Ten times over, I've tried to save your soul
    From your corrupted mind. That's still my goal.
80 CLÉANTE   You have been corrupted by your friends,
    You know of whom I speak. Your thought depends
    On people who are blind and want to spread it
    Like some horrid flu, and, yes, I dread it.
    I'm no atheist. I see things clearly.
85   And what I see is loud lip service, merely,
    To make exhibitionists seem devout.
    Forgive me, but a prayer is not a shout.
    Yet those who don't adore these charlatans
    Are seen as faithless heathens by your friends.
90   It's as if you think you'd never find
    Reason and the sacred intertwined.
    You think I'm afraid of retribution?
    Heaven sees my heart and their pollution.
    So we should be the slaves of sanctimony?
95   Monkey see, monkey do, monkey phony.
    The true believers we should emulate
    Are not the ones who groan and lay prostrate.
    And yet you see no problem in the notion
    Of hypocrisy as deep devotion.
100   You see as one the genuine and the spurious.
    You'd extend this to your money? I'm just curious.
    In your business dealings, I'd submit,
    You'd not confuse the gold with counterfeit.
    Men are strangely made, I'd have to say.

105   They're burdened with their reason, till one day,
       They free themselves with such force that they spoil
       The noblest of things for which they toil.
       Because they must go to extremes. It's a flaw.
       Just a word in passing, Brother-in-law.
110 ORGON   Oh, you are the wisest man alive, so
       You know everything there is to know.
       You are the one enlightened man, the sage.
       You are Cato the Elder[9] of our age.
       Next to you, all men are dumb as cows.
115 CLÉANTE   I'm not the wisest man, as you espouse,
       Nor do I know—what—all there is to know?
       But I do know, Orgon, that quid pro quo
       Does not apply at all to "false" and "true,"
       And I would never trust a person who
120   Cannot tell them apart. See, I revere
       Everyone whose worship is sincere.
       Nothing is more noble or more beautiful
       Than fervor that is holy, not just dutiful.
       So nothing is more odious to me
125   Than the display of specious piety
       Which I see in every charlatan
       Who tries to pass for a true holy man.
       Religious passion worn as a facade
       Abuses what's sacred and mocks God.
130   These men who take what's sacred and most holy
       And use it as their trade, for money, solely,
       With downcast looks and great affected cries,
       Who suck in true believers with their lies,
       Who ceaselessly will preach and then demand
135   "Give up the world!" and then, by sleight of hand,
       End up sitting pretty at the court,
       The best in lodging and new clothes to sport.
       If you're their enemy, then heaven hates you.
       That's their claim when one of them berates you.
140   They'll say you've sinned. You'll find yourself removed
       And wondering if you'll be approved
       For anything, at all, ever again.
       Because so heinous was this fictional "sin."
       When these men are angry, they're the worst,
145   There's no place to hide, you're really cursed.
       They use what we call righteous as their sword,
       To coldly murder in the name of the Lord.
       But next to these imposters faking belief,
       The devotion of the true is a relief.
150   Our century has put before our eyes
       Glorious examples we can prize.

9. Roman statesman and author (234–149 B.C.E.), famous as a stern moralist devoted to traditional Roman ideals of honor, courage, and simplicity.

Look at Ariston, and look at Periandre,
Oronte, Alcidamas, Polydore, Clitandre:[1]
Not one points out his own morality,
155 Instead they speak of their mortality.
They don't form cabals,[2] they don't have factions,
They don't censure other people's actions.
They see the flagrant pride in such correction
And know that humans can't achieve perfection.
160 They know this of themselves and yet their lives
Good faith, good works, all good, epitomize.
They don't exhibit zeal that's more intense
Than heaven shows us in its own defense.
They'd never claim a knowledge that's divine
165 And yet they live in virtue's own design.
They concentrate their hatred on the sin,
And when the sinner grieves, invite him in.
They leave to others the arrogance of speech.
Instead they practice what others only preach.
170 These are the men who show us how to live.
Their lives, the best example I can give.
These are my men, the ones whom I would follow.
Your man and his life, honestly, are hollow.
I believe you praise him quite sincerely,
175 I also think you'll pay for this quite dearly.
He's a fraud, this man whom you adore.

ORGON   Oh, you've stopped talking. Is there any more?

CLEANTE   No.

ORGON   I am your servant, sir.

CLÉANTE   No! wait!
There's one more thing—no more debate—
180 I want to change the subject, if I might.
I heard that you said the other night,
To Valère, he'd be your son-in-law.

ORGON   I did.

CLÉANTE   And set the date?

ORGON   Yes.

CLÉANTE   Did you withdraw?

ORGON   I did.

CLÉANTE   You're putting off the wedding? Why?

185 ORGON   Don't know.

CLÉANTE   There's more?

ORGON   Perhaps.

CLÉANTE   Again I'll try:
You would break your word?

ORGON   I couldn't say.

CLÉANTE   Then, Orgon, why did you change the day?

1. Made-up names.
2. A possible allusion to the Compagnie de Saint-Sacrement, a tightly knit group of prominent French citizens known for public works as well as strict morality; they were pejoratively referred to as the *cabale*.

ORGON Who knows?

CLÉANTE   But we need to know, don't we now?
Is there a reason you would break your vow?

190 ORGON That depends.

CLÉANTE   On what? Orgon, what is it?
Valère was the reason for my visit.

ORGON Who knows? Who knows?

CLÉANTE   So there's some mystery there?

ORGON Heaven knows.

CLÉANTE   It does? And now, Valère—
May he know, too?

ORGON   Can't say.

CLÉANTE   But, dear Orgon,
195 We have no information to go on.
We need to know—

ORGON   What heaven wants, I'll do.

CLÉANTE Is that your final answer? Then I'm through.
But your pledge to Valère? You'll stand by it?

ORGON Good-bye.

                            [ORGON *exits.*]

CLÉANTE   More patience, yes, I should try it.
200 I let him get to me. Now I confess
I fear the worst for Valère's happiness.

2.1

[ORGON, MARIANE]

ORGON Mariane.

MARIANE   Father.

ORGON   Come. Now. Talk with me.

MARIANE Why are you looking everywhere?

ORGON   To see
If everyone is minding their own business.
So. Child, I've always loved your gentleness.

5 MARIANE And for your love, I'm grateful, Father dear.

ORGON Well said. And so to prove that you're sincere,
And worthy of my love, you have the task
Of doing for me anything I ask.

MARIANE Then my obedience will be my proof.

10 ORGON Good. What do you think of our guest, Tartuffe?

MARIANE Who, me?

ORGON   Yes, you. Watch what you say right now.

MARIANE Then, Father, I will say what you allow.

ORGON Wise words, Daughter. So this is what you say:
"He is a perfect man in every way;
15 In body and soul, I find him divine."
And then you say, "Please Father, make him mine."
Huh?

MARIANE Huh?

ORGON   Yes?

MARIANE   I heard . . .

ORGON   Yes.

MARIANE   What did you say?
    Who is this perfect man in every way,
    Whom in body and soul I find divine
20 And ask of you, "Please, Father, make him mine?"

ORGON   Tartuffe.

MARIANE   All that I've said, I now amend
    Because you wouldn't want me to pretend.

ORGON   Absolutely not—that's so misguided.
    Have it be the truth, then. It's decided.

25 MARIANE   What?! Father, you want—

ORGON   Yes, my dear, I do—
    To join in marriage my Tartuffe and you.
    And since I have—

2.2

[DORINE, ORGON, MARIANE]

ORGON   Dorine, I know you're there!
    Any secrets in this house you don't share?

DORINE   "Marriage"—I think, yes, I heard a rumor,
    Someone's failed attempt at grotesque humor,
5   So when I heard the story, I said, "No!
    Preposterous! Absurd! It can't be so."

ORGON   Oh, you find it preposterous? And why?

DORINE   It's so outrageous, it must be a lie.

ORGON   Yet it's the truth and you will believe it.

10 DORINE   Yet as a joke is how I must receive it.

ORGON   But it's a story that will soon come true.

DORINE   A fantasy!

ORGON   I'm getting tired of you.
    Mariane, it's not a joke—

DORINE   Says he,
    Laughing up his sleeve for all to see.

15 ORGON   I'm telling you—

DORINE   —more make-believe for fun.
    It's very good—you're fooling everyone.

ORGON   You have made me really angry now.

DORINE   I see the awful truth across your brow.
    How can a man who looks as wise as you
20 Be such a fool to want—

ORGON   What can I do
    About a servant with a mouth like that?
    The liberties you take! Decorum you laugh at!
    I'm not happy with you—

DORINE   Oh sir, don't frown.
    A smile is just a frown turned upside down.
25 Be happy, sir, because you've shared your scheme,
    Even though it's just a crazy dream.
    Because, dear sir, your daughter is not meant
    For this zealot—she's too innocent.

She'd be alarmed by his robust desire
30   And question heaven's sanction of this fire
And then the gossip! Your friends will talk a lot,
Because you're a man of wealth and he is not.
Could it be your reasoning has a flaw—
Choosing a beggar for a son-in-law?
35 ORGON   You, shut up! If he has nothing now
Admire that, as if it were his vow,
This poverty. His property was lost
Because he would not pay the deadly cost
Of daily duties nibbling life away,
40   Leaving him with hardly time to pray.
The grandeur in his life comes from devotion
To the eternal, thus his great emotion.
And at those moments, I can plainly see
What my special task has come to be:
45   To end the embarrassment he feels
And the sorrow he so nobly conceals
Of the loss of his ancestral domain.
With my money, I can end his pain.
I'll raise him up to be, because I can,
50   With my help, again, a gentleman.
DORINE   So he's a gentleman. Does that seem vain?
Then what about this piety and pain?
Those with "domains" are those of noble birth.
A holy man's domain is not on earth.
55   It seems to me a holy man of merit
Wouldn't brag of what he might inherit—
Even gifts in heaven, he won't mention.
To live a humble life is his intention.
Yet he wants something back? That's just ambition
60   To feed his pride. Is that a holy mission?
You seem upset. Is it something I said?
I'll shut up. We'll talk of her instead.
Look at this girl, your daughter, your own blood.
How will her honor fare covered with mud?
65   Think of his age. So from the night they're wed,
Bliss, if there is any, leaves the marriage bed,
And she'll be tied unto this elderly person.
Her dedication to fidelity will worsen
And soon he will sprout horns,[3] your holy man,
70   And no one will be happy. If I can
Have another word, I'd like to say
Old men and young girls are married every day,
And the young girls stray, but who's to blame
For the loss of honor and good name?
75   The father, who proceeds to pick a mate,
Blindly, though it's someone she may hate,

3. The traditional sign of the cuckold.

Bears the sins the daughter may commit,
Imperiling his soul because of it.
If you do this, I vow you'll hear the bell,
80   As you die, summoning you to hell.
ORGON   You think that you can teach me how to live.
DORINE   If you'd just heed the lessons that I give.
ORGON   Can heaven tell me why I still endure
This woman's ramblings? Yet, of this I'm sure,
85   I know what's best for you—I'm your father.
I gave you to Valère, without a bother.
But I hear he gambles and what's more,
He thinks things that a Christian would abhor.
It's from free thinking that all evils stem.
90   No wonder, then, at church, I don't see him.
DORINE   Should he race there, if he only knew
Which Mass you might attend, and be on view?
He could wait at the door with holy water.
ORGON   Go away. I'm talking to my daughter.
95   Think, my child, he is heaven's favorite!
And age in marriage? It can flavor it,
A sweet comfit suffused with deep, deep pleasure.
You will be loving, faithful, and will treasure
Every single moment—two turtledoves—
100   Next to heaven, the only thing he loves.
And he will be the only one for you.
No arguments or quarrels. You'll be true.
Like two innocent children, you will thrive,
In heaven's light, thrilled to be alive.
105   And as a woman, surely you must know
Wives mold husbands, like making pies from dough.
DORINE   Four and twenty cuckolds baked in a pie.
ORGON   Ugh! What a thing to say!
DORINE   Oh, really, why?
He's destined to be cheated on, it's true.
110   You know he'd always question her virtue.
ORGON   Quiet! Just be quiet. I command it!
DORINE   I'll do just that, because you do demand it!
But your best interests—I will protect them.
ORGON   Too kind of you. Be quiet and neglect them.
115 DORINE   If I weren't fond of you—
ORGON   —Don't want you to
DORINE   I will be fond of you in spite of you.
ORGON   Don't!
DORINE   But your honor is so dear to me,
How can you expose yourself to mockery?
ORGON   Will you never be quiet!
DORINE   Oh, dear sir,
120   I can't let you do this thing to her,
It's against my conscience—
ORGON   You vicious asp!

DORINE Sometimes the things you call me make me gasp.
　　　And anger, sir, is not a pious trait.
ORGON It's your fault, girl! You make me irate!
125　I am livid! Why won't you be quiet!
DORINE I will. For you, I'm going to try it.
　　　But I'll be thinking.
ORGON　　　　　　　Fine. Now, Mariane,
　　　You have to trust—your father's a wise man.
　　　I have thought a lot about this mating.
130　I've weighed the options—
DORINE　　　　　　　It's infuriating
　　　Not to be able to speak.
ORGON　　　　　　　And so
　　　I'll say this. Of up and coming men I know,
　　　He's not one of them, no money in the bank,
　　　Not handsome.
DORINE　　　　That's the truth. Arf! Arf! Be frank.
135　He's a dog!
ORGON　　　He has manly traits.
　　　And other gifts.
DORINE　　　　And who will blame the fates
　　　For failure of this marriage made in hell?
　　　And whose fault will it be? Not hard to tell.
　　　Since everyone you know will see the truth:
140　You gave away your daughter to Tartuffe.
　　　If I were in her place, I'd guarantee
　　　No man would live the night who dared force me
　　　Into a marriage that I didn't want.
　　　There would be war with no hope of détente.
145 ORGON I asked for silence. This is what I get?
DORINE You said not to talk to *you*. Did you forget?
ORGON What do you call what you are doing now?
DORINE Talking to myself.
ORGON　　　　　　　You insolent cow!
　　　I'll wait for you to say just one more word.
150　I'm waiting . . .
　　　　　　[ORGON *prepares to give* DORINE *a smack but each time he
　　　　　　looks over at her, she stands silent and still.*]
　　　　　　　　Just ignore her. Look at me.
　　　I've chosen you a husband who would be,
　　　If rated, placed among the highest ranks.
　　　[*To* DORINE] Why don't you talk?
DORINE　　　　　　　　　　　Don't feel like it, thanks.
ORGON I'm watching you.
DORINE　　　　　　　Do you think I'm a fool?
155 ORGON I realize that you may think me cruel.
　　　But here's the thing, child, I will be obeyed,
　　　And this marriage, child, will not be delayed.
DORINE [*running from* ORGON, DORINE *throws a line to* MARIANE]
　　　You'll be a joke with Tartuffe as a spouse.

[ORGON *tries to slap her but misses.*]

ORGON   What we have is a plague in our own house!
160   It's her fault that I'm in the state I'm in,
         So furious, I might commit a sin.
         She'll drive me to murder. Or to curse.
         I need fresh air before my mood gets worse.   [ORGON *exits.*]

2.3

[DORINE, MARIANE]

DORINE   Tell me, have you lost the power of speech?
          I'm forced to play your role and it's a reach.
          How can you sit there with nothing to say
          Watching him tossing your whole life away?
5   MARIANE   Against my father, what am I to do?
    DORINE   You want out of this marriage scheme, don't you?
    MARIANE   Yes.
    DORINE   Tell him no one can command a heart.
          That when you marry, you will have no part
          Of anyone unless he pleases you.
10   And tell your father, with no more ado,
          That you will marry for yourself, not him,
          And that you won't obey his iron whim.
          Since he finds Tartuffe to be such a catch,
          He can marry him himself. There's a match.
15 MARIANE   You know that fathers have such sway
          Over our lives that I've nothing to say.
          I've never had the strength.
    DORINE   Let's think. All right?
          Didn't Valère propose the other night?
          Do you or don't you love Valère?
20 MARIANE   You know the answer, Dorine—that's unfair.
          Just talking about it tears me apart.
          I've said a hundred times, he has my heart.
          I'm wild about him. I know. And I've told you.
    DORINE   But how am I to know, for sure, that's true?
25 MARIANE   Because I told you. And yet you doubt it?
          See me blushing when I speak about it?
    DORINE   So you do love him?
    MARIANE   Yes, with all my might.
    DORINE   He loves you just as much?
    MARIANE   I think that's right.
    DORINE   And it's to the altar you're both heading?
30 MARIANE   Yes.
    DORINE   So what about this other wedding?
    MARIANE   I'll kill myself. That's what I've decided.
    DORINE   What a great solution you've provided!
          To get out of trouble, you plan to die!
          Immediately? Or sometime, by and by?
35 MARIANE   Oh, really, Dorine, you're not my friend,
          Unsympathetic—

DORINE   I'm at my wit's end,
  Talking to you whose answer is dying,
  Who, in a crisis, just gives up trying.
MARIANE   What do you want of me, then?
DORINE   Come alive!
40   Love needs a resolute heart to survive.
MARIANE   In my love for Valère, I'm resolute.
  But the next step is his.
DORINE   And so, you're mute?
MARIANE   What can I say? It's the job of Valère,
  His duty, before I go anywhere,
45   To deal with my father—
DORINE   —Then, you'll stay.
  "Orgon was born bizarre" is what some say.
  It there were doubts before, we have this proof—
  He is head over heels for his Tartuffe,
  And breaks off a marriage that he arranged.
50 Valère's at fault if your father's deranged?
MARIANE   But my refusal will be seen as pride
  And, worse, contempt. And I have to hide
  My feelings for Valère, I must not show
  That I'm in love at all. If people know,
55   Then all the modesty my sex is heir to
  Will be gone. There's more: how can I bear to
  Not be a proper daughter to my father?
DORINE   No, no, of course not. God forbid we bother
  The way the world sees you. What people see,
60   What other people think of us, should be
  Our first concern. Besides, I see the truth:
  You really want to be Madame Tartuffe.
  What was I thinking, urging opposition
  To Monsieur Tartuffe! This proposition,
65   To merge with him—he's such a catch!
  In fact, for you, he's just the perfect match.
  He's much respected, everywhere he goes.
  And his ruddy complexion nearly glows.
  And as his wife, imagine the delight
70   Of being near him, every day and night.
  And vital? Oh, my dear, you won't want more.
MARIANE   Oh, heaven help me!
DORINE   How your soul will soar,
  Savoring this marriage down to the last drop,
  With such a handsome—
MARIANE   All right! You can stop!
75 Just help me. Please. And tell me there's a way
  To save me. I'll do whatever you say.
DORINE   Each daughter must choose always to say yes
  To what her father wants, no more and no less.
  If he wants to give her an ape to marry,
80   Then she must do it, without a query.

But it's a happy fate! What is this frown?
You'll go by wagon to his little town,
Eager cousins, uncles, aunts will greet you
And will call you "sister" when they meet you,
85 Because you're family now. Don't look so grim.
You will so adore chatting with them.
Welcomed by the local high society,
You'll be expected to maintain propriety
And sit straight, or try to, in the folding chair
90 They offer you, and never, ever stare
At the wardrobe of the bailiff's wife
Because you'll see her every day for life.[4]
Let's not forget the village carnival!
Where you'll be dancing at a lavish ball
95 To a bagpipe orchestra of locals,
An organ grinder's monkey doing vocals—
And your husband—

MARIANE   —Dorine, I beg you, please,
    Help me. Should I get down here on my knees?

DORINE   Can't help you.

MARIANE   Please, Dorine, I'm begging you!

100 DORINE   And you deserve this man.

MARIANE   That just not true!

DORINE   Oh yes? What changed?

MARIANE   My darling Dorine . . .

DORINE   No.

MARIANE   You can't be this mean.
    I love Valère. I told you and it's true.

DORINE   Who's that? Oh. No, Tartuffe's the one for you.

105 MARIANE   You've always been completely on my side.

DORINE   No more. I sentence you to be Tartuffified!

MARIANE   It seems my fate has not the power to move you,
    So I'll seek my solace and remove to
    A private place for me in my despair.
110 To end the misery that brought me here.

        [MARIANE starts to exit.]

DORINE   Wait! Wait! Come back! Please don't go out that door.
    I'll help you. I'm not angry anymore.

MARIANE   If I am forced into this martyrdom,
    You see, I'll have to die, Dorine.

DORINE   Oh come,
115 Give up this torment. Look at me—I swear.
    We'll find a way. Look, here's your love, Valère.

        [DORINE moves to the side of the stage.]

4. Dorine's description reflects the stereotypes associated with rural pretensions to culture.

2.4

[VALÈRE, MARIANE, DORINE]

VALÈRE   So I've just heard some news that's news to me,
And very fine news it is, do you agree?
MARIANE   What?
VALÈRE   You have plans for marriage I didn't know.
You're going to marry Tartuffe. Is this so?
5 MARIANE   My father has that notion, it is true.
VALÈRE   Madame, your father promised—
MARIANE   —me to you?
He changed his mind, announced this change to me,
Just minutes ago . . .
VALÈRE   Quite seriously?
MARIANE   It's his wish that I should marry this man.
10 VALÈRE   And what do you think of your father's plan?
MARIANE   I don't know.
VALÈRE   Honest words—better than lies.
You don't know?
MARIANE   No.
VALÈRE   No?
MARIANE   What do you advise?
VALÈRE   I advise you to . . . marry Tartuffe. Tonight.
MARIANE   You advise me to . . .
VALÈRE   Yes.
MARIANE   Really?
VALÈRE   That's right.
15 Consider it. It's an obvious choice.
MARIANE   I'll follow your suggestion and rejoice.
VALÈRE   I'm sure that you can follow it with ease.
MARIANE   Just as you gave it. It will be a breeze.
VALÈRE   Just to please you was my sole intent.
20 MARIANE   To please you, I'll do it and be content.
DORINE   I can't wait to see what happens next.
VALÈRE   And this is love to you? I am perplexed.
Was it a sham when you—
MARIANE   That's in the past
Because you said so honestly and fast
25 That I should take the one bestowed on me.
I'm nothing but obedient, you see,
So, yes, I'll take him. That's my declaration,
Since that's your advice and expectation.
VALÈRE   I see, you're using me as an excuse,
30 Any pretext, so you can cut me loose.
You didn't think I'd notice—I'd be blind
To the fact that you'd made up your mind?
MARINE   How true. Well said.
VALÈRE   And so it's plain to see,
Your heart never felt a true love for me.

35 MARIANE If you want to, you may think that is true.
It's clear this thought has great appeal for you.
VALÈRE If I want? I will, but I'm offended
To my very soul. But your turn's ended,
And I can win this game we're playing at:
40 I've someone else in mind.
MARIANE   I don't doubt that.
Your good points—
VALÈRE   Oh, let's leave them out of this.
I've very few—in fact, I am remiss.
I must be. Right? You've made that clear to me.
But I know someone, hearing that I'm free,
45 To make up for my loss, will eagerly consent.
MARIANE The loss is not that bad. You'll be content
With your new choice, replacement, if you will.
VALÈRE I will. And I'll remain contented still,
In knowing you're as happy as I am.
50 A woman tells a man her love's a sham.
The man's been fooled and his honor blighted.
He can't deny his love is unrequited,
Then he forgets this woman totally,
And if he can't, pretends, because, you see,
55 It is ignoble conduct and weak, too,
Loving someone who does not love you.
MARIANE What a fine, noble sentiment to heed.
VALÈRE And every man upholds it as his creed.
What? You expect me to keep on forever
60 Loving you after you blithely sever
The bond between us, watching as you go
Into another's arms and not bestow
This heart you've cast away upon someone
Who might welcome—
MARIANE   I wish it were done.
65 That's exactly what I want, you see.
VALÈRE That's what you want?
MARIANE   Yes.
VALÈRE   Then let it be.
I'll grant your wish.
MARIANE   Please do.
VALÈRE   Just don't forget,
Whose fault it was when you, filled with regret,
Realize that you forced me out the door.
70 MARIANE True.
VALÈRE   You've set the example and what's more,
I'll match you with my own hardness of heart.
You won't see me again, if I depart.
MARIANE That's good!

[VALÈRE *goes to exit, but when he gets to the door, he
returns.*]

VALÈRE	What?
MARIANE	What?
VALÈRE	You said . . . ?
MARIANE	Nothing at all.
VALÈRE	Well, I'll be on my way, then.

[*He goes, stops.*]

Did you call?

75　MARIANE　Me? You must be dreaming.

VALÈRE　I'll go away.
　　Good-bye, then.

MARIANE　Good-bye.

DORINE　I am here to say,
　　You both are idiots! What's this about?
　　I left you two alone to fight it out,
　　To see how far you'd go. You're quite a pair
80　In matching tit for tat— Hold on, Valère!
　　Where are you going?

VALÈRE　What, Dorine? You spoke?

DORINE　Come here.

VALÈRE　I'm upset and will not provoke
　　This lady. Do not try to change my mind.
　　I'm doing what she wants.

DORINE　You are so blind.
85　Just stop.

VALÈRE　No. It's settled.

DORINE　Oh, is that so?

MARIANE　He can't stand to look at me, I know.
　　He wants to go away, so please let him.
　　No, I shall leave so I can forget him.

DORINE　Where are you going?

MARIANE　Leave me alone.
90　DORINE　Come back here at once.

MARIANE　No. Even that tone
　　Won't bring me. I'm not a child, you see.

VALÈRE　She's tortured by the very sight of me.
　　It's better that I free her from her pain.

DORINE　What more proof do you need? You are insane!
95　Now stop this nonsense! Come here both of you.

VALÈRE　To what purpose?

MARIANE　What are you trying to do?

DORINE　Bring you two together! And end this fight.
　　It's so stupid! Yes?

VALÈRE　No. It wasn't right
　　The way she spoke to me. Didn't you hear?
100　DORINE　Your voices are still ringing in my ear.

MARIANE　The way he treated me—you didn't see?

DORINE　Saw and heard it all. Now listen to me.
　　The only thing she wants, Valère, is you.
　　I can attest to that right now. It's true.

105   And Mariane, he wants you for his wife,
       And only you. On that I'll stake my life.
   MARIANE   He told me to be someone else's bride!
   VALÈRE   She asked for my advice and I replied!
   DORINE   You're both impossible. What can I do?
110   Give your hand—
   VALÈRE   What for?
   DORINE   Come on, you.
    Now yours, Mariane—don't make me shout.
    Come on!
   MARIANE   All right. But what is this about?
   DORINE   Here. Take each other's hand and make a link.
    You love each other better than you think.
115 VALÈRE   Mademoiselle, this is your hand I took,
    You think you could give me a friendly look?

               [MARIANE *peeks at* VALÈRE *and smiles.*]

   DORINE   It's true. Lovers are not completely sane.
   VALÈRE   Mariane, haven't I good reason to complain?
    Be honest. Wasn't it a wicked ploy?
120   To say—
   MARIANE   You think I told you that with joy?
    And you confronted me.
   DORINE   Another time.
    This marriage to Tartuffe would be a crime,
    We have to stop it.
   MARIANE   So, what can we do?
    Tell us.
125 DORINE   All sorts of things involving you.
    It's all nonsense and your father's joking.
    But if you play along, say, without choking,
    And give your consent, for the time being,
    He'll take the pressure off, thereby freeing
130   All of us to find a workable plan
    To keep you from a marriage with this man.
    Then you can find a reason every day
    To postpone the wedding, in this way:
    One day you're sick and that can take a week.
135   Another day you're better but can't speak,
    And we all know you have to say "I do,"
    Or the marriage isn't legal. And that's true.
    Now bad omens—would he have his daughter
    Married when she's dreamt of stagnant water,
140   Or broken a mirror or seen the dead?
    He may not care and say it's in your head,
    But you will be distraught in your delusion,
    And require bed rest and seclusion.
    I do know this—if we want to succeed,
145   You can't be seen together. [*To* VALÈRE] With all speed,
    Go, and gather all your friends right now,
    Have them insist that Orgon keep his vow.

Social pressure helps. Then to her brother.
All of us will work on her stepmother.
150   Let's go.
　　　VALÈRE   Whatever happens, can you see?
　　　My greatest hope is in your love for me.
MARIANE   Though I don't know just what Father will do,
　　　I do know I belong only to you.
　　　VALÈRE   You put my heart at ease! I swear I will . . .
155 DORINE   It seems that lovers' tongues are never still.
　　　Out, I tell you.
　　　VALÈRE [taking a step and returning]   One last—
DORINE   No more chat!
　　　You go out this way, yes, and you go that.

3.1

[DAMIS, DORINE]

DAMIS   May lightning strike me dead, right here and now,
　　　Call me a villain, if I break this vow:
　　　Forces of heaven or earth won't make me sway
　　　From this my—
DORINE   Let's not get carried away.
5   Your father only said what he intends
　　　To happen. The real event depends
　　　On many things and something's bound to slip,
　　　Between this horrid cup and his tight lip.
DAMIS   That this conceited fool Father brought here
10   Has plans? Well, they'll be ended—do not fear.
DORINE   Now stop that! Forget him. Leave him alone.
　　　Leave him to your stepmother. He is prone,
　　　This Tartuffe, to indulge her every whim.
　　　So let her use her power over him.
15   It does seem pretty clear he's soft on her,
　　　Pray God that's true. And if he will concur
　　　That this wedding your father wants is bad,
　　　That's good. But he might want it, too, the cad.
　　　She's sent for him so she can sound him out
20   On this marriage you're furious about,
　　　Discover what he feels and tell him clearly
　　　If he persists that it will cost him dearly.
　　　It seems he can't be seen while he's at prayers,
　　　So I have my own vigil by the stairs
25   Where his valet says he will soon appear.
　　　Do leave right now, and I'll wait for him here.
DAMIS   I'll stay to vouch for what was seen and heard.
DORINE   They must be alone.
DAMIS   I won't say a word.
DORINE   Oh, right. I know what you are like. Just go.
30   You'll spoil everything, believe me, I know.
　　　Out!

DAMIS   I promise I won't get upset.

[DORINE *pinches* DAMIS *as she used to do when he was a child.*]

Ow!

DORINE   Do as I say. Get out of here right *now!*

3.2

[TARTUFFE, LAURENT, DORINE]

TARTUFFE [*noticing* DORINE]   Laurent, lock up my scourge and hair shirt,[5] too.
And pray that our Lord's grace will shine on you.
If anyone wants me, I've gone to share
My alms at prison with the inmates there.

5   DORINE   What a fake! What an imposter! What a sleaze!

TARTUFFE   What do you want?

DORINE   To say—

TARTUFFE [*taking a handkerchief from his pocket*]   Good heavens, please,
Do take this handkerchief before you speak.

DORINE   What for?

TARTUFFE   Cover your bust. The flesh is weak.
Souls are forever damaged by such sights,

10   When sinful thoughts begin their evil flights.

DORINE   It seems temptation makes a meal of you—
To turn you on, a glimpse of flesh will do.
Inside your heart, a furnace must be housed.
For me, I'm not so easily aroused.

15   I could see you naked, head to toe—
Never be tempted once, and this I know.

TARTUFFE   Please! Stop! And if you're planning to resume
This kind of talk, I'll leave the room.

DORINE   If someone is to go, let it be me.

20   Yes, I can't wait to leave your company.
Madame is coming down from her salon,
And wants to talk to you, if you'll hang on.

TARTUFFE   Of course. Most willingly.

DORINE [*aside*]   Look at him melt.
I'm right. I always knew that's how he felt.

25   TARTUFFE   Is she coming soon?

DORINE   You want me to leave?
Yes, here she is in person, I believe.

3.3

[ELMIRE, TARTUFFE]

TARTUFFE   Ah, may heaven in all its goodness give
Eternal health to you each day you live,
Bless your soul and body, and may it grant
The prayerful wishes of this supplicant.

---

5. Implements to mortify his flesh (penitential practices of religious ascetics).

5 ELMIRE   Yes. Thank you for that godly wish, and please,
     Let's sit down so we can talk with ease.
  TARTUFFE   Are you recovered from your illness now?
  ELMIRE   My fever disappeared, I don't know how.
  TARTUFFE   My small prayers, I'm sure, had not the power,
10   Though I was on my knees many an hour.
     Each fervent prayer wrenched from my simple soul
     Was made with your recovery as its goal.
  ELMIRE   I find your zeal a little disconcerting.
  TARTUFFE   I can't enjoy my health if you are hurting.
15   Your health's true worth, I can't begin to tell.
     I'd give mine up, in fact, to make you well.
  ELMIRE   Though you stretch Christian charity too far,
     Your thoughts are kind, however strange they are.
  TARTUFFE   You merit more, that's in my humble view.
20 ELMIRE   I need a private space to talk to you.
     I think that this will do—what do you say?
  TARTUFFE   Excellent choice. And this is a sweet day,
     To find myself here tête-à-tête with you,
     That I've begged heaven for this, yes, is true,
25   And now it's granted to my great relief.
  ELMIRE   Although our conversation will be brief,
     Please open up your heart and tell me all.
     You must hide nothing now, however small.
  TARTUFFE   I long to show you my entire soul,
30   My need for truth I can barely control.
     I'll take this time, also, to clear the air—
     The criticisms I have brought to bear
     Around the visits that your charms attract,
     Were never aimed at you or how you act,
35   But rather were my own transports of zeal,
     Which carried me away with how I feel,
     Consumed by impulses, though always pure,
     Nevertheless, intense in how—
  ELMIRE   I'm sure
     That my salvation is your only care.
40 TARTUFFE [grasping her fingertips]   Yes, you're right, and so my fervor there—
  ELMIRE   Ouch! You're squeezing too hard.
  TARTUFFE   —comes from this zeal . . .
     I didn't mean to squeeze. How does this feel?
     [He puts his hand on ELMIRE's knee.]
  ELMIRE   Your hand—what is it doing . . . ?
  TARTUFFE   So tender,
     The fabric of your dress, a sweet surrender
45   Under my hand—
  ELMIRE   I'm quite ticklish. Please, don't.
     [She moves her chair back, and TARTUFFE moves his forward.]
  TARTUFFE   I want to touch this lace—don't fret, I won't.
     It's marvelous! I so admire the trade
     Of making lace. Don't tell me you're afraid.

ELMIRE   What? No. But getting back to business now,
50 It seems my husband plans to break a vow
    And offer you his daughter. Is this true?
TARTUFFE   He mentioned it, but I must say to you,
    The wondrous gifts that catch my zealous eye,
    I see quite near in bounteous supply.
55 ELMIRE   Not earthly things for which you would atone.
TARTUFFE   My chest does not contain a heart of stone.
ELMIRE   Well, I believe your eyes follow your soul,
    And your desires have heaven as their goal.
TARTUFFE   The love that to eternal beauty binds us
60 Doesn't stint when temporal beauty finds us.
    Our senses can as easily be charmed
    When by an earthly work we are disarmed.
    You are a rare beauty, without a flaw,
    And in your presence, I'm aroused with awe
65 But for the Author of All Nature, so,
    My heart has ardent feelings, even though
    I feared them at first, questioning their source.
    Had I been ambushed by some evil force?
    I felt that I must hide from this temptation:
70 You. My feelings threatened my salvation.
    Yes, I found this sinful and distressing,
    Until I saw your beauty as a blessing!
    So now my passion never can be wrong,
    And, thus, my virtue stays intact and strong.
75 That is how I'm here in supplication,
    Offering my heart in celebration
    Of the audacious truth that I love you,
    That only you can make this wish come true,
    That through your grace, my offering's received,
80 And accepted, and that I have achieved
    Salvation of a sort, and by your grace,
    I could be content in this low place.
    It all depends on you, at your behest—
    Am I to be tormented or be blest?
85 You are my welfare, solace, and my hope,
    But, whatever your decision, I will cope.
    Will I be happy? I'll rely on you.
    If you want me to be wretched, that's fine, too.
ELMIRE   Well, what a declaration! How gallant!
90 But I'm surprised you want the things you want.
    It seems your heart could use a talking to—
    It's living in the chest of someone who
    Proclaims to be pious—
TARTUFFE   —And so I am.
    My piety's a true thing—not a sham,
95 But I'm no less a man, so when I find
    Myself with you, I quickly lose my mind.
    My heart is captured and, with it, my thought.

Yet since I know the cause, I'm not distraught.
Words like these from me must be alarming,
100 But it is your beauty that's so charming,
I cannot help myself, I am undone.
And I'm no angel, nor could I be one.
If my confession earns your condemnation,
Then blame your glance for the annihilation
105 Of my command of this: my inmost being.
A surrender of my soul is what you're seeing.
Your eyes blaze with more than human splendor,
And that first look had the effect to render
Powerless the bastions of my heart.
110 No fasting, tears or prayers, no pious art
Could shield my soul from your celestial gaze
Which I will worship till the End of Days.[6]
A thousand times my eyes, my sighs have told
The truth that's in my heart. Now I am bold,
115 Encouraged by your presence, so I say,
With my true voice, will this be the day
You condescend to my poor supplication,
Offered up with devout admiration,
And save my soul by granting this request:
120 Accept this love I've lovingly confessed?
Your honor has, of course, all my protection,
And you can trust my absolute discretion.
For those men that all the women die for,
Love's a game whose object is a high score.
125 Although they promise not to talk, they will.
They need to boast of their superior skill,
Receive no favors not as soon revealed,
Exposing what they vowed would be concealed.
And in the end, this love is overpriced,
130 When a woman's honor's sacrificed.
But men like me burn with a silent flame,
Our secrets safe, our loves we never name,
Because our reputations are our wealth.
When we transgress, it's with the utmost stealth.
135 Your honor's safe as my hand in a glove,
So I can offer, free from scandal, love,
And pleasure without fear of intervention.
ELMIRE   Your sophistry does not hide your intention.
In fact, you know, it makes it all too clear.
140 What if, through me, my husband were to hear
About this love for me you now confess
Which shatters the ideals you profess?
How would your friendship fare, then, I wonder?
TARTUFFE   It's your beauty cast this spell I suffer under.
145 I'm made of flesh, like you, like all mankind.

6. That is, the final days before human history ends and the Kingdom of God is established.

And since your soul is pure, you will be kind,
And not judge me harshly for my brashness
In speaking of my love in all its rashness.
I beg you to forgive me my offense,
150   I plead your perfect face as my defense.
    ELMIRE   Some might take offense at your confession,
But I will show a definite discretion,
And keep my husband in the dark about
These sinful feelings for me that you spout.
155   But I want something from you in return:
There's a promised marriage, you will learn,
That supersedes my husband's recent plan—
The marriage of Valère and Mariane.
This marriage you will openly support,
160   Without a single quibble, and, in short,
Renounce the unjust power of a man
Who'd give his own daughter, Mariane,
To another when she's promised to Valère.
In return, my silence—

3.4

[ELMIRE, DAMIS, TARTUFFE]

DAMIS [jumping out from where he had been hiding]
              —Hold it right there!
No, no! You're done. All this will be revealed.
I heard each word. And as I was concealed,
Something besides your infamy came clear:
5   Heaven in its great wisdom brought me here,
To witness and then give my father proof
Of the hypocrisy of his Tartuffe,
This so-called saint anointed from above.
Speaking to my father's wife of love!
10   ELMIRE   Damis, there is a lesson to be learned,
And there is my forgiveness to be earned.
I promised him. Don't make me take it back.
It's not my nature to see as an attack
Such foolishness as this, or see the need
15   To tell my husband of the trivial deed.
    DAMIS   So, you have your reasons, but I have mine.
To grant this fool forgiveness? I decline.
To want to spare him is a mockery,
Because he's more than foolish, can't you see?
20   This fanatic in his insolent pride,
Brought chaos to my house, and would divide
Me and my father—unforgivable!
What's more, he's made my life unlivable,
As he undermines two true love affairs,
25   Mine and Valère's sister, my sister and Valère's!
Father must hear the truth about this man.
Heaven helped me—I must do what I can

To use this chance. I'd deserve to lose it,
If I dropped it now and didn't use it.
30 ELMIRE   Damis—
DAMIS   No, please, I have to follow through.
I've never felt as happy as I do
Right now. And don't try to dissuade me—
I'll have my revenge. If you forbade me,
I'd still do it, so you don't have to bother.
35 I'll finish this for good. Here comes my father.

3.5

[ORGON, DAMIS, TARTUFFE, ELMIRE]

DAMIS   Father! You have arrived. Let's celebrate!
I have a tale that I'd like to relate.
It happened here and right before my eyes,
I offer it to you—as a surprise!
5 For all your love, you have been repaid
With duplicity. You have been betrayed
By your dear friend here, whom I just surprised
Making verbal love, I quickly surmised,
To your wife. Yes, this is how he shows you
10 How he honors you—he thinks he knows you.
But as your son, I know you much better—
You demand respect down to the letter.
Madame, unflappable and so discreet,
Would keep this secret, never to repeat.
15 But, as your son, my feelings are too strong,
And to be silent is to do you wrong.
ELMIRE   One learns to spurn without being unkind,
And how to spare a husband's peace of mind.
Although I understood just what he meant,
20 My honor wasn't touched by this event.
That's how I feel. And you would have, Damis,
Said nothing, if you had listened to me.

3.6

[ORGON, DAMIS, TARTUFFE]

ORGON   Good heavens! What he said? Can it be true?
TARTUFFE   Yes, my brother, I'm wicked through and through.
The most miserable of sinners, I.
Filled with iniquity, I should just die.
5 Each moment of my life's so dirty, soiled,
Whatever I come near is quickly spoiled.
I'm nothing but a heap of filth and crime.
I'd name my sins, but we don't have the time.
And I see that heaven, to punish me,
10 Has mortified my soul quite publicly.
What punishment I get, however great,
I well deserve so I'll accept my fate.
Defend myself? I'd face my own contempt,

If I thought that were something I'd attempt.
15 What you've heard here, surely, you abhor,
So chase me like a criminal from your door.
Don't hold back your rage, please, let it flame,
For I deserve to burn, in my great shame.

ORGON [*to* DAMIS]   Traitor! And how dare you even try
20 To tarnish this man's virtue with a lie?

DAMIS   What? This hypocrite pretends to be contrite
And you believe him over me?

ORGON   That's spite!
And shut your mouth!

TARTUFFE   No, let him have his say.
And don't accuse him. Don't send him away.
25 Believe his story—why be on my side?
You don't know what motives I may hide.
Why give me so much loyalty and love?
Do you know what I am capable of?
My brother, you have total trust in me,
30 And think I'm good because of what you see?
No, no, by my appearance you're deceived,
And what I say you think must be believed.
Well, believe this—I have no worth at all.
The world sees me as worthy, yet I fall
35 Far below. Sin is so insidious.
[*To* DAMIS] Dear son, do treat me as perfidious,
Infamous, lost, a murderer, a thief.
Speak on, because my sins, beyond belief,
Can bring this shameful sinner to his knees,
40 In humble, paltry effort to appease.

ORGON [*to* TARTUFFE]   Brother, there is no need . . .
                                    [*To* DAMIS] Will you relent?

DAMIS   He has seduced you!

ORGON   Can't you take a hint?
Be quiet! [*To* TARTUFFE] Brother, please get up. [*To* DAMIS] Ingrate!

DAMIS   But father, this man

ORGON   —whom you denigrate.
45 DAMIS   But you should—

ORGON   Quiet!

DAMIS   But I saw and heard—

ORGON   I'll slap you if you say another word.

TARTUFFE   In the name of God, don't be that way.
Brother, I'd rather suffer, come what may,
Than have this boy receive what's meant for me.
50 ORGON [*to* DAMIS]   Heathen!

TARTUFFE   Please! I beg of you on bended knee.

ORGON [*to* DAMIS]   Wretch! See his goodness?!

DAMIS   But—

ORGON   No!

DAMIS   But—

ORGON   Be still!
And not another word from you until

You admit the truth. It's plain to see
Although you thought that I would never be
55 Aware and know your motives, yet I do.
You all hate him. And I saw today, you,
Wife, servants—everyone beneath my roof—
Are trying everything to force Tartuffe
Out of my house—this holy man, my friend.
60 The more you try to banish him and end
Our sacred brotherhood, the more secure
His place is. I have never been more sure
Of anyone. I give him as his bride
My daughter. If that hurts the family pride,
65 Then good. It needs humbling. You understand?
DAMIS You're going to force her to accept his hand?
ORGON Yes, traitor, and this evening. You know why?
To infuriate you. Yes, I defy
You all. I am master and you'll obey.
70 And you, you ingrate, now I'll make you pay
For your abuse of him—kneel on the floor,
And beg his pardon, or go out the door.
DAMIS Me? Kneel and ask the pardon of this fraud?
ORGON What? You refuse? Someone get me a rod!
75 A stick! Something! [To TARTUFE] Don't hold me.
        [To DAMIS] Here's your whack!
Out of my house and don't ever come back!
DAMIS Yes, I'll leave, but—
ORGON   Get out of my sight!
I disinherit you, you traitor, you're a blight
On this house. And you'll get nothing now
80 From me, except my curse!

3.7

[ORGON, TARTUFFE]

ORGON   You have my vow,
He'll never more question your honesty.
TARTUFFE [to heaven] Forgive him for the pain he's given me.
    [To ORGON] How I suffer. If you could only see
5 What I go through when they disparage me.
ORGON Oh no!
TARTUFFE   The ingratitude, even in thought,
Tortures my soul so much, it leaves me fraught
With inner pain. My heart's stopped. I'm near death,
I can barely speak now. Where is my breath?
ORGON [running in tears to the door through which he chased DAMIS]
10 You demon! I held back, you little snot
I should have struck you dead right on the spot!
    [To TARTUFFE] Get up, Brother. Don't worry anymore.
TARTUFFE Let us end these troubles, Brother, I implore.
For the discord I have caused, I deeply grieve,
15 So for the good of all, I'll take my leave.

ORGON   What? Are you joking? No!

TARTUFFE   They hate me here.
    It pains me when I see them fill your ear
    With suspicions.

ORGON   But that doesn't matter.
    I don't listen.

TARTUFFE   That persistent chatter
20   You now ignore, one day you'll listen to.
    Repetition of a lie can make it true.

ORGON   No, my brother. Never.

TARTUFFE   A man's wife
    Can so mislead his soul and ruin his life.

ORGON   No, no.

TARTUFFE   Brother, let me, by leaving here,
25   Remove any cause for doubt or fear.

ORGON   No, no. You will stay. My soul is at stake.

TARTUFFE   Well, then, a hefty penance I must make.
    I'll mortify myself, unless . . .

ORGON   No need!

TARTUFFE   Then we will never speak of it, agreed?
30   But the question of your honor still remains,
    And with that I'll take particular pains
    To prevent rumors. My absence, my defense—
    I'll never see your wife again, and hence—

ORGON   No. You spend every hour with her you want,
35   And be seen with her. I want you to flaunt,
    In front of them, this friendship with my wife.
    And I know how to really turn the knife
    I'll make you my heir, my only one,
    Yes, you will be my son-in-law and son.[7]
40   A good and faithful friend means more to me
    Than any member of my family.
    Will you accept this gift that I propose?

TARTUFFE   Whatever heaven wants I can't oppose.

ORGON   Poor man! A contract's what we need to write.
45   And let all the envious burst with spite.

4.1

[CLÉANTE, TARTUFFE]

CLÉANTE   Yes, everyone is talking and each word
    Diminishes your glory, rest assured.
    Though your name's tainted with scandal and shame,
    I'm glad I ran across you, all the same,
5   Because I need to share with you my view
    On this disaster clearly caused by you.
    Damis, let's say for now, was so misguided,
    He spoke before he thought. But you decided

7. In fact, French laws governing inheritance would have made such a change extremely difficult
to accomplish.

To just sit back and watch him be exiled
10 From his own father's house. Were he a child,
Then, really, would you dare to treat him so?
Shouldn't you forgive him, not make him go?
However, if there's vengeance in your heart,
And you act on it, tell me what's the part
15 That's Christian in that? And are you so base,
You'd let a son fall from his father's grace?
Give God your anger as an offering,
Bring peace and forgive all for everything.

TARTUFFE   I'd do just that, if it were up to me.
20 I blame him for nothing, don't you see?
I've pardoned him already. That's my way.
And I'm not bitter, but have this to say:
Heaven's best interests will have been served,
When wrongdoers have got what they deserved.
25 In fact, if he returns here, I would leave,
Because God knows what people might believe.
Faking forgiveness to manipulate
My accuser, silencing the hate
He has for me could be seen as my goal.
30 When I would only wish to save his soul.
What he said to me, though unforgivable,
I give unto God to make life livable.

CLÉANTE   To this conclusion, sir, I have arrived:
Your excuses could not be more contrived.
35 Just how did you come by the opinion
Heaven's business is in your dominion,
Judging who is guilty and who is not?
Taking revenge is heaven's task, I thought.
And if you're under heaven's sovereignty,
40 What human verdict would you ever be
The least bit moved by. No, you wouldn't care—
Judging other's lives is so unfair.
Heaven seems to say "live and let live,"
And our task, I believe, is to forgive.

45 TARTUFFE   I said I've pardoned him. I take such pains
To do exactly what heaven ordains.
But after his attack on me, it's clear,
Heaven does not ordain that he live here.

CLÉANTE   Does it ordain, sir, that you nod and smile,
50 When taking what is not yours, all the while?
On this inheritance you have no claim
And yet you think it's yours. Have you no shame?

TARTUFFE   That this gift was, in any way, received
Out of self-interest, would not be believed
55 By anyone who knows me well. They'd say,
"The world's wealth, to him, holds no sway."
I am not dazzled by gold nor its glitter,
So lack of wealth has never made me bitter.

If I take this present from the father,
60 The source of all this folderol and bother,
I am saving, so everyone understands,
This wealth from falling into the wrong hands.
Waste of wealth and property's a crime,
And that is what would happen at this time.
65 But I would use it as part of my plan:
For glory of heaven, and the good of man.

CLÉANTE Well, sir, I think these small fears that plague you,
In fact, may cause the rightful heir to sue.
Why trouble yourself, sir—couldn't you just
70 Let him own his property, if he must?
Let others say his property's misused
By him, rather than have yourself accused
Of taking it from its rightful owner.
Wouldn't a pious man be a donor
75 Of property? Unless there is a verse
Or proverb about how you fill your purse
With what's not yours, at all, in any part.
And if heaven has put into your heart
This obstacle to living with Damis,
80 The honorable thing, you must agree,
As well as, certainly, the most discreet,
Is pack your bags and, quickly, just retreat.
To have the son of the house chased away,
Because a guest objects, is a sad day.
85 Leaving now would show your decency,
Sir . . .

TARTUFFE Yes. Well, it is half after three;
Pious duties consume this time of day,
You will excuse my hurrying away.

CLÉANTE Ah!

4.2

[ELMIRE, MARIANE, DORINE, CLÉANTE]

DORINE   Please, come to the aid of Mariane.
She's suffering because her father's plan
To force this marriage, impossible to bear,
Has pushed her from distress into despair.
5 Her father's on his way here. Do your best,
Turn him around. Use subtlety, protest,
Whatever way will work to change his mind.

4.3

[ORGON, ELMIRE, MARIANE, CLÉANTE, DORINE]

ORGON Ah! Here's everyone I wanted to find!
[*To* MARIANE] This document I have here in my hand
Will make you very happy, understand?

MARIANE Father, in the name of heaven, I plead

5   To all that's good and kind in you, concede
     Paternal power, just in this sense:
     Free me from my vows of obedience.
     Enforcing that inflexible law today
     Will force me to confess each time I pray
10   My deep resentment of my obligation.
     I know, father, that I am your creation,
     That you're the one who's given life to me.
     Why would you now fill it with misery?
     If you destroy my hopes for the one man
15   I've dared to love by trying now to ban
     Our union, then I'm kneeling to implore,
     Don't give me to a man whom I abhor.
     To you, Father, I make this supplication.
     Don't drive me to some act of desperation,
20   By ruling me simply because you can.

ORGON [*feeling himself touched*]   Be strong! Human weakness shames a man!

MARIANE   Your affection for him doesn't bother me—
     Let it erupt, give him your property,
     And if that's not enough, then give him mine.
25   Any claim on it, I do now decline.
     But in this gifting, don't give him my life.
     If I must wed, then I will be God's wife,
     In a convent, until my days are done.

ORGON   Ah! So you will be a holy, cloistered nun,
30   Because your father thwarts your love affair.
     Get up! The more disgust you have to bear,
     The more of heaven's treasure you will earn.
     And the heaven will bless you in return.
     Through this marriage, you'll mortify your senses.
35   Don't bother me with any more pretenses.

DORINE   But . . . !

ORGON   Quiet, you! I see you standing there.
     Don't speak a single world! don't even dare!

CLÉANTE   If you permit, I'd like to say a word . . .

ORGON   Brother, the best advice the world has heard
40   Is yours—its reasoning, hard to ignore.
     But I refuse to hear it anymore.

ELMIRE [*to* ORGON]   And now, I wonder, have you lost your mind?
     Your love for this one man has made you blind.
     Can you stand there and say you don't believe
45   A word we've said? That we're here to deceive?

ORGON   Excuse me—I believe in what I see.
     You, indulging my bad son, agree
     To back him up in this terrible prank,
     Accusing my dear friend of something rank.
50   You should be livid if what you claim took place,
     And yet this look of calm is on your face.

ELMIRE   Because a man says he's in love with me,
     I'm to respond with heavy artillery?

I laugh at these unwanted propositions.
55 Mirth will quell most ardent ambitions.
Why make a fuss over an indiscretion?
My honor's safe and in my possession.
You say I'm calm? Well, that's my constancy—
It won't need a defense, or clemency.
60 I know I'll never be a vicious prude
Who always seems to hear men being rude,
And then defends her honor tooth and claw,
Still snarling, even as the men withdraw.
From honor like that heaven preserve me,
65 If that's what you want, you don't deserve me.
Besides, you're the one who has been betrayed.

ORGON   I see through this trick that's being played.

ELMIRE   How can you be so dim? I am amazed
How you can hear these sins and stay unfazed.
70 But what if I could show you what he does?

ORGON   Show?

ELMIRE   Yes.

ORGON   A fiction!

ELMIRE   No, the truth because
I am quite certain I can find a way
To show you in the fullest light of day . . .

ORGON   Fairy tales!

ELMIRE   Come on, at least answer me.
75 I've given up expecting you to be
My advocate. What have you got to lose,
By hiding somewhere, anyplace you choose,
And see for yourself. And then we can
Hear what you say about your holy man.

80 ORGON   Then I'll say nothing because it cannot be.

ELMIRE   Enough. I'm tired. You'll see what you see.
I'm not a liar, though I've been accused.
The time is now and I won't be refused.
You'll be a witness. And we can stop our rants.

85 ORGON   All right! I call your bluff, Miss Smarty Pants.

ELMIRE [to DORINE]   Tell Tartuffe to come.

DORINE   Watch out. He's clever.
Men like him are caught, well, almost never.

ELMIRE   Narcissism is a great deceiver,
And he has lots of that. He's a believer
90 In his charisma. [To CLÉANTE and MARIANE] Leave us for a bit.

4.4

[ELMIRE, ORGON]

ELMIRE   See this table? Good. Get under it.

ORGON   What!

ELMIRE   You are hiding. Get under there and stay.

ORGON   Under the table?

ELMIRE: Just do as I say.

5   I have a plan, but for it to succeed,
       You must be hidden. So are we agreed?
       You want to know? I'm ready to divulge it.
   ORGON   This fantasy of yours—I'll indulge it.
       But then I want to lay this thing to rest.
10 ELMIRE   Oh, that'll happen. Because he'll fail the test.
       You see, I'm going to have a conversation
       I'd never have—just as an illustration
       Of how this hypocrite behaved with me.
       So don't be scandalized. I must be free
15   To flirt. Clearly, that's what it's going to take
       To prove to you your holy man's a fake.
       I'm going to lead him on, to lift his mask,
       Seem to agree to anything he'll ask,
       Pretend to respond to his advances.
       It's for you I'm taking all these chances.
20   I'll stop as soon as you have seen enough;
       I hope that comes before he calls my bluff.
       His plans for me must be circumvented,
       His passion's strong enough to be demented,
       So the moment you're convinced, you let me know
25   That I've revealed the fraud I said I'd show.
       Stop him so I won't have a minute more
       Exposure to your friend, this lecherous boor.
       You're in control. I'm sure I'll be all right.
       And . . . here he comes—so hush, stay out of sight.

4.5

[TARTUFFE, ELMIRE, ORGON (*under the table*)]

   TARTUFFE   I'm told you want to have a word with me.
   ELMIRE   Yes. I have a secret but I'm not free
       To speak. Close that door, have a look around,
       We certainly do not want to be found
5   The way we were just as Damis appeared.
       I was terrified for you and as I feared,
       He was irate. You saw how hard I tried
       To calm him down and keep him pacified.
       I was so upset; I never had the thought
10   "Deny it all," which might have helped a lot,
       But as it turns out, we've nothing to fear.
       My husband's not upset, it would appear.
       Things are good, to heaven I defer,
       Because they're even better than they were.
15   I have to say I'm quite amazed, in fact,
       His good opinion of you is intact.
       To clear the air and quiet every tongue,
       And to kill any gossip that's begun—
       You could've pushed me over with a feather—
20   He wants us to spend all our time together!
       That's why, with no fear of a critical stare,

I can be here with you or anywhere.
Most important, I am completely free
To show my ardor for you, finally.

25 TARTUFFE   Ardor? This is a sudden change of tone
From the last time we found ourselves alone.

ELMIRE   If thinking I was turning you away
Has made you angry, all that I can say
Is that you do not know a woman's heart!
30 Protecting our virtue keeps us apart,
And makes us seem aloof, and even cold.
But cooler outside, inside the more bold.
When love overcomes us, we are ashamed,
Because we fear that we might be defamed.
35 We must protect our honor—not allow
Our love to show. I fear that even now,
In this confession, you'll think ill of me.
But now I've spoken, and I hope you see
My ardor that is there. Why would I sit
40 And listen to you? Why would I permit
Your talk of love, unless I had a notion
Just like yours, and with the same emotion?
And when Damis found us, didn't I try
To quiet him? And did you wonder why,
45 In speaking of Mariane's marriage deal,
I not only asked you, I made an appeal
That you turn it down? What was I doing?
Making sure I'd be the one you'd be wooing.

TARTUFFE   It is extremely sweet, without a doubt,
50 To watch your lips as loving words spill out.
Abundant honey there for me to drink,
But I have doubts. I cannot help but think,
"Does she tell the truth, or does she lie,
To get me to break off this marriage tie?
55 Is all this ardor something she could fake,
And just an act for her stepdaughter's sake?"
So many questions, yet I want to trust.
But need to know the truth, in fact, I must.
Pleasing you, Elmire, is my main task,
60 And happiness, and so I have to ask
To sample this deep ardor felt for me
Right here and now, in blissful ecstasy.

ELMIRE [coughing to alert ORGON]
You want to spend this passion instantly?
I've been opening my heart consistently,
65 But for you, it's not enough, this sharing.
Yet for a woman, it is very daring.
So why can't you be happy with a taste,
Instead of the whole meal consumed in haste?

TARTUFFE   We dare not hope, all those of us who don't
70 Deserve a thing. And so it is I won't

Be satisfied with words. I'll always doubt,
Assume my fortune's taken the wrong route
On its way to me. And that is why
I don't believe in anything till I
75 Have touched, partaken until satisfied.
ELMIRE   So suddenly, your love can't be denied.
It wants complete dominion over me,
And what it wants, it wants violently.
I know I'm flustered, I know I'm out of breath—
80 Your power over me could be the death
Of my reason. Does this seem right to you?
To use my weakness against me, just to
Conquer? No one's gallant anymore.
I invite you in. You break down the door.
85 TARTUFFE   If your passion for me isn't a pretense,
Then why deny me its best evidence?
ELMIRE   But, heaven, sir, that place that you address
So often, would judge us both if we transgress.
TARTUFFE   That's all that's in the way of my desires?
90 These judgments heaven makes of what transpires?
All you fear is heaven's bad opinion.
ELMIRE   But I am made to fear its dominion.
TARTUFFE   And I know how to exorcise these fears.
To sin is not as bad as it appears
95 If, and stay with me on this, one can think
That in some cases, heaven gives a wink

[*It is a scoundrel speaking.*][8]

When it comes to certain needs of men
Who can remain upright but only when
There is a pure intention. So you see,
100 If you just let yourself be led by me,
You'll have no worries, and I can enjoy
You. And you, me. Because we will employ
This way of thinking—a real science
And a secret, thus, with your compliance,
105 Fulfilling my desires without fear,
Is easy now, so let it happen here.

[ELMIRE *coughs.*]

That cough, Madame, is bad.
ELMIRE   I'm in such pain.
TARTUFFE   A piece of licorice might ease the strain.
ELMIRE [*directed to* ORGON]   This cold I have is very obstinate.
110 It stubbornly holds on. I can't shake it.
TARTUFFE   That's most annoying.
ELMIRE   More than I can say.
TARTUFFE   Let's get back to finding you a way,
Finally, to get around your scruples:

8. This stage direction, inserted by Molière himself, supports the playwright's assertion that he took pains to demonstrate Tartuffe's true nature.

Secrecy—I'm one of its best pupils
115 And practitioners. Responsibility
For any evil—you can put on me.
I will answer up to heaven if I must,
And give a good accounting you can trust.
There'll be no sins for which we must atone,
120 'Cause evil exists only when it's known.
Adam and Eve were public in their fall.
To sin in private is not to sin at all.

ELMIRE [after coughing again]   Obviously, I must give in to you,
Because, it seems, you are a person who
125 Refuses to believe anything I say.
Live testimony only can convey
The truth of passion here, no more, no less.
That it should go that far, I must confess,
Is such a pity. But I'll cross the line,
130 And give myself to you. I won't decline
Your offer, sir, to vanquish me right here.
But let me make one point extremely clear:
If there's a moral judgment to be made,
If anyone here feels the least betrayed,
135 Then none of that will be my fault. Instead,
The sin weighs twice as heavy on your head.
You forced me to this brash extremity.

TARTUFFE   Yes, yes, I will take all the sin on me.

ELMIRE   Open the door and check because I fear
140 My husband—just look—might be somewhere near.

TARTUFFE   What does it matter if he comes or goes?
The secret is, I lead him by the nose.
He's urged me to spend all my time with you.
So let him see—he won't believe it's true.

145 ELMIRE   Go out and look around. Indulge my whim.
Look everywhere and carefully for him.

4.6

[ORGON, ELMIRE]

ORGON [coming out from under the table]
I swear that is the most abominable man!
How will I bear this? I don't think I can.
I'm stupefied!

ELMIRE   What? Out so soon? No, no.
You can't be serious. There's more to go.
5 Get back under there. You can't be too sure.
It's never good relying on conjecture.

ORGON   That kind of wickedness comes straight from hell.

ELMIRE   You've turned against this man you know so well?
Good lord, be sure the evidence is strong
10 Before you are convinced. You might be wrong.

[She steps in front of ORGON.]

4.7

[TARTUFFE, ELMIRE, ORGON]

TARTUFFE   Yes, all is well; there's no one to be found,
And I was thorough when I looked around.
To my delight, my rapture, at last . . .

ORGON [*stopping him*]   Just stop a minute there! You move too fast!

5   Delight and rapture? Fulfilling desire?
Ah! Ah! You are a traitor and a liar!
Some holy man you are, to wreck my life,
Marry my daughter? Lust after my wife?
I've had my doubts about you, but kept quiet,

10   Waiting for you to slip and then deny it.
Well, now it's happened and I'm so relieved,
To stop pretending that I am deceived.

ELMIRE [*to* TARTUFFE]   I don't approve of what I've done today,
But I needed to do it, anyway.

15   TARTUFFE   What? You can't think . . .

ORGON   No more words from you.
Get out of here, you. . . . You and I are through.

TARTUFFE   But my intentions . . .

ORGON   You still think I'm a dunce?
You shut your mouth and leave this house at once!

TARTUFFE   You're the one to leave, you, acting like the master.

20   Now I'll make it known, the full disaster:
This house belongs to me, yes, all of it,
And I'll decide what's true, as I see fit.
You can't entrap me with demeaning tricks,
Yes, here's a situation you can't fix.

25   Here nothing happens without my consent.
You've offended heaven. You must repent.
But I know how to really punish you.
Those who harm me, they know not what they do.

4.8

[ELMIRE, ORGON]

ELMIRE   What was that about? I mean, the latter.

ORGON   I'm not sure, but it's no laughing matter.

ELMIRE   Why?

ORGON   I've made a mistake I now can see,
The deed I gave him is what troubles me.

5   ELMIRE   The deed?

ORGON   And something else. I am undone.
I think my troubles may have just begun.

ELMIRE   What else?

ORGON   You'll know it all. I have to race,
To see if a strongbox is in its place.

5.1

[ORGON, CLÉANTE]

CLÉANTE   Where are you running to?

ORGON   Who knows.

CLÉANTE   Then wait.

It seems to me we should deliberate,
Meet, plan, and have some family talks.

ORGON   I can't stop thinking about the damned box

5   More than anything, that's the loss I fear.

CLÉANTE   What about this box makes it so dear?

ORGON   I have a friend whom I felt sorry for,
Because he chose the wrong side in the war;[9]
Before he fled, he brought it to me,

10   This locked box. He didn't leave a key.
He told me it has papers, this doomed friend,
On which his life and property depend.

CLÉANTE   Are you saying you gave the box away?

ORGON   Yes, that's true, that's what I'm trying to say.

15   I was afraid that I would have to lie,
If I were confronted. That is why
I went to my betrayer and confessed
And he, in turn, told me it would be best
If I gave him the box, to keep, in case

20   Someone were to ask me to my face
About it all, and I might lie and then,
In doing so, commit a venial sin.[1]

CLÉANTE   As far as I can see, this is a mess,
And with a lot of damage to assess.

25   This secret that you told, this deed you gave,
Make the situation hard to save.
He's holding all the cards, your holy man,
Because you gave them to him. If you can,
Restrain yourself a bit and stay away.

30   That would be best. And do watch what you say.

ORGON   What? With his wicked heart and corrupt soul,
Yet I'm to keep my rage under control?
Yes, me who took him in, right off the street?
Damn all holy men! They're filled with deceit!

35   I now renounce them all, down to the man,
And I'll treat them worse than Satan can.

CLÉANTE   Listen to yourself! You're over the top,
Getting carried away again. Just stop.
"Moderation." Is that a word you know?

40   I think you've learned it, but then off you go,

---

9. That is, he opposed Louis in the Fronde (see 1.2.11 and note). Although Orgon supported the king, this act left him open to the charge of being a traitor to the throne—a capital offense.

1. Because Tartuffe had possession of the box, Orgon could deny that he had it without lying. A venial (or "pardonable") sin is relatively minor.

Always ignoring the strength in reason,
Flinging yourself from loyalty to treason.
Why can't you just admit that you were swayed
By the fake piety that man displayed?
45   But no. Rather than change your ways, you turned
Like that. [*Snaps fingers*] Attacking holy men who've earned
The right to stand among the true believers.
So now all holy men are base deceivers?
Instead of just admitting your delusion,
50   "They're all like that!" you say—brilliant conclusion.
Why trust reason, when you have emotion?
You've implied there is no true devotion.
Freethinkers are the ones who hold that view,
And yet, you don't agree with them, do you?
55   You judge a man as good without real proof.
Appearances can lie—witness: Tartuffe.
If your respect is something to be prized,
Don't toss it away to those disguised
In a cloak of piety and virtue.
60   Don't you see how deeply they can hurt you?
Look for simple goodness—it does exist.
And just watch for imposters in our midst,
With this in mind, try not to be unjust
To true believers, sin on the side of trust.

5.2

[DAMIS, ORGON, CLÉANTE]

DAMIS   Father, what? I can't believe it's true,
That scoundrel has the gall to threaten you?
And use the things you gave him in his case
'Gainst you? To throw you out? I'll break his face.
5 ORGON   My son, I'm in more pain than you can see.
DAMIS   I'll break both his legs. Leave it to me.
We must not bend under his insolence.
I'll finish this business, punish his offense,
I'll murder him and do it with such joy.
10 CLÉANTE   Damis, you're talking like a little boy,
Tantrums head the list of your main flaws.
We live in modern times, with things called "laws."
Murder is illegal. At least for us.

5.3

[MADAME PERNELLE, MARIANE, ELMIRE, DORINE,
DAMIS, ORGON, CLÉANTE]

MADAME PERNELLE   It's unbelievable! Preposterous!
ORGON   Believe it. I've seen it with my own eyes.
He returned kindness with deceit and lies.
I took in a man, miserable and poor,
5   Brought him home, gave him the key to my door,

I loaded him with favors every day,
To him, my daughter, I just gave away,
My house, my wealth, a locked box from a friend.
But to what depths this devil would descend.
10 This betrayer, this abomination,
Who had the gall to preach about temptation,
And know in his black heart he'd woo my wife,
Seduce her! Yes! And then to steal my life,
Using my property, which I transferred to him,
15 I know, I know—it was a stupid whim.
He wants to ruin me, chase me from my door,
He wants me as he was, abject and poor.

DORINE   Poor man!

MADAME PERNELLE   I don't believe a word, my son,
This isn't something that he could have done.

20 ORGON   What?

MADAME PERNELLE   Holy men always arouse envy.

ORGON   Mother, what are you trying to say to me?

MADAME PERNELLE   That you live rather strangely in this house;
He's hated here, especially by your spouse.

ORGON   What has this got to do with what I said?

25 MADAME PERNELLE   Heaven knows, I've beat into your head:
"In this world, virtue is mocked forever;
Envious men may die, but envy never."

ORGON   How does that apply to what's happened here?

MADAME PERNELLE   Someone made up some lies; it's all too clear.

30 ORGON   But I saw it myself, you understand.

MADAME PERNELLE   "Whoever spreads slander has a soiled hand."

ORGON   You'll make me, Mother, say something not nice.
I saw it for myself; I've told you twice.

MADAME PERNELLE   "No one can trust what gossips have to say,
35 Yet they'll be with us until Judgment Day."

ORGON   You're talking total nonsense, Mother!
I said I saw him, this man I called Brother!
I saw him with my wife, with these two eyes.
The word is "saw," past tense of "see." These "lies"
40 That you misnamed are just the truth.
I saw my wife almost beneath Tartuffe.

MADAME PERNELLE   Oh, is that all? Appearances deceive.
What we think we see, we then believe.

ORGON   I'm getting angry.

MADAME PERNELLE   False suspicions, see?
45 We are subject to them, occasionally,
Good deeds can be seen as something other.

ORGON   So I'm to see this as a good thing, Mother,
A man trying to kiss my wife?

MADAME PERNELLE   You must.
Because, to be quite certain you are just,
50 You should wait until you're very, very sure
And not rely on faulty conjecture.

ORGON   Goddammit! You would have me wait until . . . ?
And just be quiet while he has his fill,
Right before my very eyes, Mother, he'd—

55 MADAME PERNELLE   I can't believe that he would do this "deed"
Of which he's been accused. There is no way.
His soul is pure.

ORGON   I don't know what to say!
Mother!

DORINE   Just deserts, for what you put us through.
You thought we lied, now she thinks that of you.

60 CLÉANTE   Why are we wasting time with all of this?
We're standing on the edge of the abyss.
This man is dangerous! He has a plan!

DAMIS   How could he hurt us? I don't think he can.

ELMIRE   He won't get far, complaining to the law—

65 You'll tell the truth, and he'll have to withdraw.

CLÉANTE   Don't count on it; trust me, he'll find a way
To use these weapons you gave him today.
He has legal documents, and the deed.
To kick us out, just what else does he need?

70 And if he's doubted, there are many ways
To trap you in a wicked legal maze.
You give a snake his venom, nice and quick,
And after that you poke him with a stick?

ORGON   I know. But what was I supposed to do?

75 Emotions got the best of me, it's true.

CLÉANTE   If we could placate him, just for a while,
And somehow get the deed back with a smile.

ELMIRE   Had I known we had all this to lose,
I never would have gone through with my ruse.

80 I would've—

          [A knock on the door.]

ORGON   What does that man want? You go find out.
But I don't want to know what it's about.

5.4

[MONSIEUR LOYAL, MADAME PERNELLE, ORGON,
DAMIS, MARIANE, DORINE, ELMIRE, CLÉANTE]

MONSIEUR LOYAL [to DORINE]   Dear sister, hello. Please, I beg of you,
Your master is the one I must speak to.

DORINE   He's not receiving visitors today.

MONSIEUR LOYAL   I bring good news so don't send me away.

5 My goal in coming is not to displease;
I'm here to put your master's mind at ease.

DORINE   And you are . . . who?

MONSIEUR LOYAL   Just say that I have come
For his own good and with a message from
Monsieur Tartuffe.

DORINE [to ORGON]   It's a soft-spoken man,

10 Who says he's here to do just what he can
To ease your mind. Tartuffe sent him.

CLÉANTE   Let's see

What he might want.

ORGON   Oh, what's my strategy?

He's come to reconcile us, I just know.

CLÉANTE   Your strategy? Don't let your anger show,

15 For heaven's sake. And listen for a truce.

MONSIEUR LOYAL   My greetings, sir. I'm here to be of use.

ORGON   Just what I thought. His language is benign.
For the prospect of peace, a hopeful sign.

MONSIEUR LOYAL   Your family's dear to me, I hope you know.

20 I served your father many years ago.

ORGON   I humbly beg your pardon, to my shame,
I don't know you, nor do I know your name.

MONSIEUR LOYAL   My name's Loyal. I'm Norman by descent.
My job of bailiff is what pays my rent.

25 Thanks be to heaven, it's been forty years
I've done my duty free of doubts or fear.
That you invited me in, I can report,
When I serve you with this writ from the court.

ORGON   What? You're here . . .

MONSIEUR LOYAL   No upsetting outbursts, please.

30 It's just a warrant saying we can seize,
Not me, of course, but this Monsieur Tartuffe—
Your house and land as his. Here is the proof.
I have the contract here. You must vacate
These premises. Please, now, don't be irate.

35 Just gather up your things now, and make way
For this man, without hindrance or delay.

ORGON   Me? Leave my house?

MONSIEUR LOYAL   That's right, sir, out the door.
This house, at present, as I've said before,
Belongs to good Monsieur Tartuffe, you see,

40 He's lord and master of this property
By virtue of this contract I hold right here.
Is that not your signature? It's quite clear.

DAMIS   He's so rude, I do almost admire him.

MONSIEUR LOYAL   Excuse me. Is it possible to fire him?

45 My business is with you, a man of reason,
Who knows resisting would be seen as treason.
You understand that I must be permitted
To execute the orders as committed.

DAMIS   I'll execute him, Father, to be sure.

50 His long black nightgown won't make him secure.

MONSIEUR LOYAL   He's your son! I thought he was a servant.
Control the boy. His attitude's too fervent,
His anger is a bone of contention—
Throw him out, or I will have to mention

55 His name in this, my official report.

DORINE   "Loyal" is loyal only to the court.
MONSIEUR LOYAL   I have respect for all God-fearing men,
   So instantly I knew I'd come here when
   I heard your name attached to this assignment.
60 I knew you'd want a bailiff with refinement.
   I'm here for you, just to accommodate,
   To make removal something you won't hate.
   Now, if I hadn't come, then you would find
   You got a bailiff who would be less kind.
65 ORGON   I'm sorry, I don't see the kindness in
   An eviction order.
MONSIEUR LOYAL   Let me begin:
   I'm giving you time. I won't carry out
   This order you are so upset about.
   I've come only to spend the night with you,
70 With my men, who will be coming through.
   All ten of them, as quiet as a mouse.
   Oh, you must give me the keys to the house.
   We won't disturb you. You will have your rest—
   You need a full night's sleep—that's always best.
75 There'll be no scandal, secrets won't be bared;
   Tomorrow morning you must be prepared,
   To pack your things, down to the smallest plate,
   And cup, and then these premises vacate.
   You'll have helpers; the men I chose are strong,
80 And they'll have this house empty before long.
   I can't think of who would treat you better
   And still enforce the law down to the letter,
   Just later with the letter is my gift.
   So, no resistance. And there'll be no rift.
85 ORGON   From that which I still have, I'd give this hour,
   One hundred coins of gold to have the power
   To sock this bailiff with a punch as great
   As any man in this world could create.
CLÉANTE   That's enough. Let's not make it worse.
DAMIS   The nerve
90 Of him. Let's see what my right fist can serve.
DORINE   Mister Loyal, you have a fine, broad back,
   And if I had a stick, you'd hear it crack.
MONSIEUR LOYAL   Words like that are punishable, my love—
   Be careful when a push becomes a shove.
95 CLÉANTE   Oh, come on, there's no reason to postpone,
   Just serve your writ and then leave us alone.
MONSIEUR LOYAL   May heaven keep you, till we meet again!
ORGON   And strangle you, and him who sent you in!

5.5

[ORGON, CLÉANTE, MARIANE, ELMIRE, MADAME
PERNELLE, DORINE, DAMIS]

ORGON   Well, Mother, look at this writ. Here is proof
Of treachery supreme by your Tartuffe.
Don't jump to judgment—that's what you admonished.
MADAME PERNELLE   I'm overwhelmed, I'm utterly astonished.
5 DORINE   I hear you blaming him and that's just wrong.
You'll see his good intentions before long.
"Just love thy neighbor" is here on this writ,
Between the lines, you see him saying it.
Because men are corrupted by their wealth.
10   Out of concern for your spiritual health,
He's taking, with a pure motivation,
Everything that keeps you from salvation.
ORGON   Aren't you sick of hearing "Quiet!" from me?
CLÉANTE   Thoughts of what to do now? And quickly?
15 ELMIRE   Once we show the plans of that ingrate,
His trickery can't get him this estate.
As soon as they see his disloyalty,
He'll be denied, I hope, this property.

5.6

[VALÈRE, ORGON, CLÉANTE, ELMIRE, MARIANE, etc.]

VALÈRE   I hate to ruin your day—I have bad news.
Danger's coming. There's no time to lose.
A good friend, quite good, as it turns out,
Discovered something you must know about,
5   Something at the court that's happening now.
That swindler—sorry, if you will allow,
That holy faker—has gone to the king,
Accusing you of almost everything.
But here's the worst: he says that you have failed
10   Your duty as a subject, which entailed
The keeping of a strongbox so well hidden,
That you could deny knowledge, if bidden,
Of a traitor's whereabouts. What's more,
That holy fraud will come right through that door,
15   Accusing you. You can't do anything.
He had this box and gave it to the king.
So there's an order out for your arrest!
And evidently, it's the king's behest,
That Tartuffe come, so justice can be done.
20 CLÉANTE   Well, there it is, at last, the smoking gun.
He can claim this house, at the very least.
ORGON   The man is nothing but a vicious beast.
VALÈRE   You must leave now, and I will help you hide.
Here's ten thousand in gold. My carriage is outside.
25   When a storm is bearing down on you

Running is the best thing one can do.
I have a place where both of us can stay.

ORGON   My boy, I owe you more than I can say.
I pray to heaven that, before too long,
30   I can pay you back and right the wrong
I've done to you. [*To* ELMIRE] Good-bye. Take care, my dear.

CLÉANTE   We'll plan. You go while the way is still clear.

5.7

[THE EXEMPT, TARTUFFE, VALÈRE, ORGON, ELMIRE,
MARIANE, DORINE, *etc.*[2]]

TARTUFFE   Easy, just a minute, you move too fast.
Your cowardice, dear sir, is unsurpassed.
What I have to say is uncontested.
Simply put, I'm having you arrested.

5   ORGON   You villain, you traitor, your lechery
Is second only to your treachery.
And you arrest me—that's the crowning blow.

TARTUFFE   Suffering for heaven is all I know,
So revile me. It's all for heaven's sake.

10   CLÉANTE   Why does he persist when we know it's fake?

DAMIS   He's mocking heaven. What a loathsome beast.

TARTUFFE   Get mad—I'm not bothered in the least.
It is my duty, what I'm doing here.

MARIANE   You really think that if you persevere
15   In this lie, you'll keep your reputation?

TARTUFFE   My honor is safeguarded by my station,
As I am on a mission from the king.

ORGON   You dog, have you forgotten everything?
Who picked you up from total poverty?

20   TARTUFFE   I know that there were things you did for me.
My duty to our monarch is what stifles
Memory, so your past gifts are trifles.
My obligations to him are so rife,
That I would give up family, friends, and life.

25   ELMIRE   Fraud!

DORINE   Now there's a lie that beats everything,
His pretended reverence for our king!

CLÉANTE   This "duty to our monarch," as you say,
Why didn't it come up before today?
You had the box, you lived here for some time,
30   To say the least, and yet this crime
That you reported—why then did you wait?
Orgon caught you about to desecrate
The holy bonds of marriage with his wife.
Suddenly, your obligations are so "rife"
35   To our dear king, that you're here to turn in

2. Molière himself added "etc." to the list of speaking characters. Thus Laurent and Flipote may
return to the stage for this final scene.

Your former friend and "brother" and begin
To move into his house, a gift, but look,
Why would you accept gifts from a crook?
TARTUFFE [*to* THE EXEMPT] Save me from this whining! I have had my fill!
40   Do execute your orders, if you will.
THE EXEMPT I will. I've waited much too long for that.
I had to let you have your little chat.
It confirmed the facts our monarch knew,
That's why, Tartuffe, I am arresting you.[3]
45   TARTUFFE Who, me?
THE EXEMPT   Yes, you.
TARTUFFE   You're putting me in jail?
THE EXEMPT Immediately. And there will be no bail.
[*To* ORGON] You may compose yourself now, sir, because
We're fortunate in leadership and laws.
We have a king who sees into men's hearts,
50   And cannot be deceived, so he imparts
Great wisdom, and a talent for discernment.
Thus frauds are guaranteed a quick internment.
Our Prince of Reason sees things as they are,
So hypocrites do not get very far.
55   But saintly men and the truly devout,
He cherishes and has no doubts about.
This man could not begin to fool the king
Who can defend himself against the sting
Of much more subtle predators. And thus,
60   When this craven pretender came to us,
Demanding justice and accusing you,
He betrayed himself. Our king could view
The baseness lurking in his coward's heart.
Evil like that can set a man apart.
65   And so divine justice nodded her head,
The king did not believe a word he said.
It was soon confirmed, he has a crime
For every sin, but why squander the time
To list them or the aliases he used.
70   For the king, it's enough that he abused
Your friendship and your faith. And though we knew
Each accusation of his was untrue,
Our monarch himself, wanting to know
Just how far this imposter planned to go,
75   Had me wait to find this out, then pounce,
Arrest this criminal, quickly denounce
The man and all his lies. And now, the king
Orders delivered to you, everything
This scoundrel took, the deed, all documents,
80   This locked box of yours and all its contents,

3. In his capacity as officer of the king, The Exempt becomes both Louis's representative and his surrogate.

And nullifies the contract giving away
Your property, effective today.
And finally, our monarch wants to end
Your worries about aiding your old friend
85　Before he went into exile because,
In that same way, and in spite of the laws,
You openly defended our king's right
To his throne. And you were prepared to fight.
From his heart, and because it makes good sense
90　That a good deed deserves a recompense,
He pardons you. And wanted me to add:
He remembers good longer than the bad.

DORINE　May heaven be praised!

MADAME PERNELLE　　　　　I am so relieved.

ELMIRE　A happy ending!

MARIANE　　　　　　Can it be believed?

95　ORGON [to TARTUFFE]　Now then, you traitor . . .

CLÉANTE　　　　　　　　　　　Stop that, Brother, please.
You're sinking to his level. Don't appease
His expectations of mankind. His fate
Is misery. But it's never too late
To take another path, and feel remorse.
100　So let's wish, rather, he will change his course,
And turn his back upon his life of vice,
Embrace the good and know it will suffice.
We've all seen the wisdom of this great king,
Whom we should go and thank for everything.

105　ORGON　Yes, and well said. So come along with me,
To thank him for his generosity.
And then once that glorious task is done,
We'll come back here for yet another one—
I mean a wedding for which we'll prepare,
110　To give my daughter to the good Valère.

APHRA BEHN
1640?–1689

In her famous essay on women's writing, *A Room of One's Own* (1929), Virginia Woolf opines, "All women together ought to let flowers fall upon the tomb of Aphra Behn . . . , for it was she who earned them the right to speak their minds." As one of the first professional woman writers, Behn personifies for Woolf the struggles and triumphs attendant on living solely by one's pen. Yet the phenomenon of Behn as a professional writer, and the discovery of the circumstances that spawned her theatrical and literary career, initially drew more attention than her prodigious output itself. Indeed, even for Woolf, Behn's financial achievement "outweighs anything that she actually wrote." Ironically, Behn's unique professional status long allowed critics to dismiss her work as that of a hack and, more pointedly, of an immodest woman. Alexander Pope's notorious observation that Behn "fairly puts all characters to bed" reinforced the presumption that her dramas reflected personal licentiousness. Only in recent decades has her writing received a thorough analysis. That thoughtful reconsideration has established her importance as a Restoration dramatist and theater theorist, as a poet, and as a progenitor of the English novel.

Indisputably, the scarcity of concrete facts about her life combined with persistent insinuations of "irregular" behavior, including stories of her having spied for the English Crown, continues to tantalize us about Behn. No records exist to confirm her birth, but most biographers believe she was born in 1640, in the vicinity of Canterbury, to parents (possibly named Johnson) of uncertain social position. The biographer Angeline Goreau argues that the sophistication of Behn's writing, even in her earliest works, suggests a level of education available only to women of the gentry and higher social orders. Perhaps more significantly, we can see clear textual evidence in THE ROVER (1677) and elsewhere of Behn's keen understanding of class positions and their pervasive social impact. Moreover, as a child of a Royalist family, growing up in the periods of the English Civil War (1642–49) and the Commonwealth (1649–60), she developed an acute sensitivity to her country's shifting tides of power. Political concerns, and a sense of political commitment, underlie much of her dramaturgy.

It appears that in 1663 Aphra and her family embarked on a voyage to the then British colony of Surinam, where her father may have been assigned to a government post or may have hoped to profit as a planter. He died during the journey, however, and the surviving family members left Surinam in early 1664. Yet the brief stay made a strong impression; Aphra's observations of plantation life and the practices of slavery inform her best-known novel, *Oroonoko* (1688). Upon her return to England, she apparently married one Mr. Behn, who may have been a merchant. Some biographers conjecture that he soon died in the plague that swept London in 1664 to 1666, leaving her without financial support; others believe that the marriage was fictitious, created by Behn to provide herself social legitimacy.

During her time in Surinam, Aphra had met William Scot, whose father, Thomas Scot, had been executed for his role in the regicide of Charles I. Although the nature of their relationship is unknown, it seems likely that William introduced Aphra to the world of political intrigue, which would soon involve her directly. In 1666, Behn probably became a spy for the restored Charles II, traveling to Antwerp to reconnect with William Scot, who was living there in exile and was probably an informant in the Anglo-Dutch War. Behn, like many in government service at the time, quickly fell into financial distress when promised payments failed to materialize. When she returned to England in 1667, she was seriously in debt and was briefly held in debtor's prison. This experience of privation marked her indelibly, and the precarious financial status of women in Restoration society became one of her dominant concerns. Yet her time in Antwerp had also persuaded her of her self-sufficiency, even in dangerous and male-dominated arenas. In the preface to her late play *The Lucky Chance* (1687), she openly connected her creativity to her understanding of the masculine sphere in which she worked, claiming privilege "for my Masculine Part the Poet in me."

After her release from jail, Behn decided to embark on a career as a professional playwright. In September 1670, her first piece, *The Forced Marriage,* premiered at Lincoln's Inn Fields and ran for six nights—a solid performance record for the period. Behn followed with *The Amorous Prince* (1671), *The Dutch Lover* (1673), *Abdelazer* (1676), *The Town Fop* (1676), *The Debauchee* (later attributed to her, 1677), and in March 1677, the first part of *The Rover.*

Over the next twelve years, Behn's output included approximately a dozen more plays (attributions remain conjectural for some, produced anonymously), including the second part of *The Rover* (1681), numerous translations, several volumes of verse, the protonovelistic *Love Letters between a Nobleman and His Sister,* and the fictional prose works *Oroonoko* and *The Fair Jilt.* Two other plays and several other fictional works appeared posthumously. Behn died in April 1689, shortly after the coronation of William and Mary, and is buried in Westminster Abbey.

That Behn could maintain even a meager livelihood in the professional theater for more than twenty years clearly indicates that she was a popular dramatist. The reasons aren't hard to imagine. What is true of mass culture today was equally valid for the Restoration: though some degree of novelty may be welcome, the public enjoys entertainment forms that it already knows well. Behn had a quick wit and a ready hand at adaptation and translation, and she used these skills to create new plays that incorporated themes, dramatic structures, character types, and plot devices that had already proven their stageworthiness.

The closure of the theaters from 1642 to 1660 by the Puritan government had severely impeded but could not altogether quash the ongoing development of the English drama, which had flourished in the Renaissance. When Thomas Killigrew and Sir William Davenant received patents from Charles II to operate London's two licensed theaters, they looked to published drama, especially by WILLIAM SHAKESPEARE, Ben Jonson, and Francis Beaumont and John Fletcher, to remount. These revivals, as well as adaptations of established works and of closet dramas written during the interregnum (the time between the beheading of Charles I in 1649 and the restoration of the monarchy in 1660), constituted most of the early Restoration stage repertoire. The new dramas that had immediately preceded the Commonwealth period, such as the comedies of James Shirley, provided further inspiration for aspiring Restoration dramatists.

The Rover may be best understood within these complex political and theatrical contexts. Following common dramatic practice, Behn decided to adapt a lengthy unproduced work by Killigrew, written in 1654 and published a decade later, titled *Thomaso, or, The Wanderer.* By refashioning characters, streamlining action, and highlighting plot elements from *Thomaso* that she suspected would please her audience, Behn created in *The Rover* a play that could also carry her distinctive themes. Her subtle revisions of well-established patterns of stage dialogue and character types, which had been codified over the preceding decade through the dramas of Sir George Etherege, John Dryden, and William Wycherley, among others, enabled her both to develop these themes and to build upon her growing theatrical reputation.

Behn's first strategic choice in adapting *Thomaso* was to change its setting. She moves the action from the time of the Spanish Inquisition to the more recent past—the period of Royalist exile—and places her characters in Naples during the carnival season of revelry that precedes Lent. After the murder of Charles I, his son Prince Charles fled England, as did a good number of his supporters, who feared persecution under the Puritan regime. That Cromwell then confiscated many of the Royalists' estates may account for the impecunious state of characters like the "rover" Willmore, whose seaboard travels also associate him with the Prince. As the Royalists' friend Blunt avows, "I thank my stars I had more grace than to forfeit my estate by cavaliering." But he also admits that supporting his friends "is a greater crime to my conscience, gentlemen, than to the commonwealth."

Behn depicts the adventures of a band of these traveling Englishmen (her subtitle is "The Banished Cavaliers"), led by the rakish Willmore and his more earnest friend Belvile. They encounter the local women "of quality," Hellena, Florinda, and Valeria, as well as prostitutes, especially the courtesan Angellica. Although the setting is foreign and somewhat exotic, the narrative arc is traditional, centering on which of the characters will marry and how those relationships will be solidified. Behn thus brings together conventions from both the drama of intrigue and romantic comedy. She retains the swashbuckling flavor of Killigrew's Spanish setting and peppers her action with lively swordplay between rivals for the favors of

"Venetian" masquerades, such as the one pictured here that was held in Ranelagh Gardens, London, in April of 1749, were quite popular in England during the late seventeenth and early eighteenth centuries.

Angellica and protectors of the honor of the chaste Florinda. By removing the drama from a court setting, moreover, she participates in the Restoration theater's shift of focus away from the aristocracy and toward those in the growing middle ranks of society. By interweaving dramatic forms and broadening the range of characters, Behn can explore issues of class and gender frankly while simultaneously confirming her loyalty to the returned monarch and his supporters.

From the medieval era forward, Western literature has depicted the carnival season preceding Lent as a time of culturally sanctioned upheaval, when rigid social structures are briefly relaxed. Behn dramatizes just such a moment in *The Rover,* as the aristocratic young women of Naples disguise themselves and escape their sequestered home environment to join the revelry, where they meet the English cavaliers. Behn must have seen a direct link between her carnival setting and Restoration culture writ large, given their shared predilections for masking, posturing, and sexual license; we may assume that audiences for *The Rover* grasped these connections through such devices as the thinly disguised characterization of the libertine John Wilmot, earl of Rochester, as her libertine Willmore. At the same time, however, Behn demonstrates that even within the freedoms offered by masquerade, women remained subject to male power and assumed sexual privilege. Behn's viewers may also have perceived the metatheatrical quality of the play, as she repeatedly calls our attention to the donning of a series of costumes by Hellena, Florinda, and Valeria as well as to the highly staged yet ignominious duping of Blunt by the conniving Lucetta.

Behn signals her focus on the female characters from her opening scene, which introduces us to Florinda and her sister Hellena. We are privy to the sisters' exchanges about Florinda's multiple suitors and Hellena's desire to find a man and to avoid having to become a nun: "I'm resolved to provide myself this Carnival, if there be e'er a handsome proper fellow of my humour above ground, though I ask

first." Behn contrasts the sisters through their attitudes toward sexuality. While Hellena is willing to transcend traditional feminine passivity by "ask[ing] first," Florinda is the more conventional romantic heroine. We learn that Florinda has previously been rescued in Pamplona from the "licensed lust of common soldiers" by her admirer, Captain Belvile, but she will face three more threats of sexual assault before she is safely united with him. She must also outwit her brother Pedro and her father, each of whom has arranged for her marriage to an eligible, but undesired, suitor. The feistier Hellena soon develops an attraction for the rake Willmore, but finds she must plot to secure his complete attention and fidelity.

Through the play's opening dialogue, Behn establishes the competing tensions that will shape her comedy: between women's desire to make their own matrimonial choices and men's assumption of that privilege, between women's interest in reciprocal enjoyment of sex and men's single-minded lust, between women's financial dependence on men and their wish to gain some control over their economic future. Behn deploys the familiar trope of marriage and money central to Restoration comedy but refocuses it by realistically depicting the social and financial constraints affecting the female characters. The introduction of the courtesan Angellica Bianca and the "jilting wench" Lucetta, who play important roles in the play's examination of women's economic status, also enables Behn to explore the traditional depiction of women as either virgins or whores and to question the relationship of these opposing roles to the exchange economy she portrays.

Restoration comedy frequently critiqued marriages based solely on economic convenience, but Behn portrays the emotional and personal costs of such arrangements to women with real poignancy. Women of the era were legally considered the property of their fathers until, through the dowry system, they became the property of their husbands, who thereby gained complete control of their wealth and their person. Arranged marriages thus served to protect and enhance family fortunes. As Behn's contemporary Margaret Cavendish, duchess of Newcastle, once remarked, "Daughters are to be accounted but as Movable Goods or Furniture that wear out." In the opening scene of *The Rover*, Florinda implores her brother not to "follow the ill customs of our country and make a slave of his sister" by marrying her to a man she hates.

Where Behn departs from Restoration dramatic convention is in overtly connecting the financial networks of marriage and prostitution—especially in the absence of true affection. When Willmore tries to convince Angellica to favor him sexually for the sake of desire alone, chastising her, "Poor as I am I would not sell myself, / No, not to gain your charming high-prized person," Angellica exposes his hypocrisy:

> Pray tell me, sir, are not you guilty of
> the same mercenary crime? When a lady
> is proposed to you for a wife, you never
> ask how fair, discreet, or virtuous she is,
> but what's her fortune; which, if but

small, you cry "She will not do my business," and basely leave her, though she languish for you. Say, is not this as poor?

That Hellena and Florinda both possess fortunes, enhancing their suitability for marriage to the impecunious but noble cavaliers, underscores this irony. Behn does not attempt to overcome the power of dramatic (and moral) convention by disrupting the inevitable union of the "gay couple" Hellena and Willmore with a serious relationship between Willmore and Angellica. But she does, through the amorous triangulation of these three characters, resist typical structures of jealousy and opposition between women. Indeed, throughout the play, Behn provides multiple instances of women joining forces to achieve their economic and amatory goals.

However, a darker corollary to these associations among the play's women emerges from the male characters' repeated inability to distinguish between prostitutes

Jeremy Irons as Willmore ("the Rover") in the 1986 production of *The Rover* by the Royal Shakespeare Company.

and women "of quality." Blunt, after being tricked out of his belongings by Lucetta, whom he erroneously assumed was a lady of elevated social standing, displays open hostility to the female sex as a whole. For Blunt, virgins and whores are "as much one as t'other," and his plan to rape Florinda blatantly displays male sexuality as the exercise of power over women: "Cruel? Yes, I will kiss and beat thee all over, kiss and see thee all over; thou shalt lie with me, too, not that I care for the enjoyment, but to let thee see I have ta'en deliberated malice to thee, and will be revenged on one whore for the sins of another." Behn makes clear that no woman is immune to the potential for sexual violation in the carnivalesque culture she depicts.

In his rage, Blunt calls attention to the pretense he associates with prostitution, designating all whores "dissembling witches." He describes Florinda's tale of persecution by a group of unknown men she encounters while trying to flee to Belvile as if it were a performance—a calculated impersonation of the damsel in distress designed to fool him yet again. Such gestures point toward Behn's understanding of the increasingly complex interplay of women and theatricality in the Restoration. Behn's own entry into the theater as a playwright coincided with the appearance of the first professional English actresses. The display of women onstage quickly became associated with prostitution, a linkage made notorious by the actress Nell Gwynn, who was Charles II's mistress. But Behn realized that her own self-promotion, required of her as a playwright, drew a similar judgment; she very possibly retained the name Angellica Bianca from Killigrew and treated the character more sympathetically because she perceived that the courtesan character and she had much in common.

By deftly balancing sympathetic portraits of female characters with their frank display—particularly of Hellena, costumed in the breeches that allowed for more of the actress's body to be revealed—Behn calculatedly negotiated her position in the Restoration playhouse. She recognized that she could interject her own perspectives on women's lives as long as she also worked within established theatrical practices that appealed to the male patrons of the stage. Her combination of comic action, witty dialogue, bravado, romantic suspense, and titillation succeeded theatrically well into the eighteenth century. *The Rover* remained a regular part of the repertoire throughout the first half of that century and returned to popularity late in the twentieth, demonstrating its worth not only as an exemplar of Restoration drama but also as successful and timeless stage comedy.   J.E.G.

The Rover;
or, *The Banished Cavaliers*[1]

Prologue

Wits, like physicians, never can agree,
When of a different society.
And Rabel's drops[2] were never more cried down
By all the learned doctors of the town,
5   Than a new play whose author is unknown.[3]
Nor can those doctors with more malice sue
(And powerful purses) the dissenting few,
Than those, with an insulting pride, do rail
At all who are not of their own cabal.°   *clique*
10   If a young poet hit your humour° right,   *mood*
You judge him then out of revenge and spite.
So amongst men there are ridiculous elves,
Who monkeys hate for being too like themselves.
So that the reason of the grand debate
15   Why wit so oft is damned when good plays take,
Is that you censure as you love, or hate.
    Thus like a learned conclave poets sit,
Catholic° judges both of sense and wit,   *Universal*
And damn or save as they themselves think fit.
20   Yet those who to others' faults are so severe,
Are not so perfect but themselves may err.
Some write correct, indeed, but then the whole
(Bating° their own dull stuff i'th' play) is stole: *Excepting*
As bees do suck from flowers their honeydew,
25   So they rob others striving to please you.
    Some write their characters genteel and fine,
But then they do so toil for every line,
That what to you does easy seem, and plain,
Is the hard issue of their laboring brain.
30   And some th'effects of all their pains, we see,
Is but to mimic good extempore.°   *improvisation*
Others, by long converse about the town,
Have wit enough to write a lewd lampoon,
But their chief skill lies in a bawdy song.
35   In short, the only wit that's now in fashion,
Is but the gleanings of good conversation.
As for the author of this coming play,

---

1. The Royalist supporters of Charles I; as many went into exile during the English Civil War and interregnum of 1642–60, often their estates were confiscated by Oliver Cromwell.

2. A well-known patent medicine.
3. *The Rover* was initially produced and published anonymously.

I asked him[4] what he thought fit I should say
In thanks for your good company today:
40 He called me fool, and said it was well known
You came not here for our sakes, but your own.
New plays are stuffed with wits and with deboches,°   *debauchees*
That crowd and sweat like cits in May-Day coaches.[5]

WRITTEN BY A PERSON OF QUALITY

CHARACTERS

DON ANTONIO, the Viceroy's son
DON PEDRO, a noble Spaniard, his friend
BELVILE, an English colonel in love with Florinda
WILLMORE, the Rover
FREDERICK, an English gentleman, and friend to Belvile and Blunt
BLUNT, an English country gentleman
STEPHANO, servant to Don Pedro
PHILIPPO, Lucetta's gallant
SANCHO, pimp to Lucetta
BISKEY and SEBASTIAN, two bravos° to Angellica   *hired ruffians, henchmen*
OFFICER and SOLDIERS
DIEGO, Page to Don Antonio
FLORINDA, sister to Don Pedro
HELLENA, a gay young woman designed for[6] a nun, and sister to Florinda
VALERIA, a kinswoman to Florinda
ANGELLICA BIANCA, a famous courtesan
MORETTA, her woman
CALLIS, governess to Florinda and Hellena
LUCETTA, a jilting wench
SERVANTS, OTHER MASQUERADERS, MEN AND WOMEN

THE SCENE: *Naples, in Carnival time.*[7]

1.1

[SCENE: *A chamber.*]

     [*Enter* FLORINDA *and* HELLENA.]

FLORINDA   What an impertinent thing is a young girl bred
in a nunnery! How full of questions! Prithee no more,
Hellena; I have told thee more than thou understand'st
already.

5 HELLENA   The more's my grief. I would fain° know as much   *gladly*
as you, which makes me so inquisitive; nor is't enough
I know you're a lover, unless you tell me too who 'tis
you sigh for.

---

4. Behn used the masculine pronoun so that playgoers would not dismiss this work as written by a woman.
5. It was customary to ride around Hyde Park in coaches on May Day. *Cits:* urban males, but not gentlemen (slang).
6. That is, designated (by her family) to become.
7. The period of festival before the fasting and prayer of Lent, commonly celebrated in Roman Catholic countries.

FLORINDA   When you're a lover I'll think you fit for a
10 secret of that nature.

HELLENA   'Tis true, I never was a lover yet, but I begin to
have a shrewd guess what 'tis to be so, and fancy it very
pretty to sigh, and sing, and blush, and wish, and dream
and wish, and long and wish to see the man, and when I
15 do, look pale and tremble, just as you did when my
brother brought home the fine English colonel to see
you. What do you call him? Don Belvile?

FLORINDA   Fie, Hellena.

HELLENA   That blush betrays you. I am sure 'tis so. Or is it
20 Don Antonio the Viceroy's son? Or perhaps the rich old
Don Vincentio, whom my father designs you for a husband? Why do you blush again?

FLORINDA   With indignation; and how near soever my
father thinks I am to marrying that hated object, I shall let
25 him see I understand better what's due to my beauty,
birth, and fortune, and more to my soul, than to obey
those unjust commands.

HELLENA   Now hang me, if I don't love thee for that dear
disobedience. I love mischief strangely, as most of our
30 sex do who are come to love nothing else. But tell me,
dear Florinda, don't you love that fine *Anglese*?° For I   *Englishman (Italian)*
vow, next to loving him myself, 'twill please me most
that you do so, for he is so gay and so handsome.

FLORINDA   Hellena, a maid designed for a nun ought not
35 to be so curious in a discourse of love.

HELLENA   And dost thou think that ever I'll be a nun? Or
at least till° I'm so old I'm fit for nothing else? Faith no,   *before*
sister; and that which makes me long to know whether
you love Belvile, is because I hope he has some mad
40 companion or other that will spoil my devotion. Nay, I'm
resolved to provide myself this Carnival, if there be e'er a
handsome proper fellow of my humour above ground,
though I ask first.

FLORINDA   Prithee be not so wild.

45 HELLENA   Now you have provided yourself of a man you
take no care of poor me. Prithee tell me, what dost thou
see about me that is unfit for love? Have I not a world of
youth? A humour gay? A beauty passable? A vigor desirable? Well shaped? Clean limbed? Sweet breathed? And
50 sense enough to know how all these ought to be employed to the best advantage? Yes, I do and will; therefore
lay aside your hopes of my fortune by my being a devote,°   *nun*
and tell me how you came acquainted with this Belvile.
For I perceive you knew him before he came to Naples.

55 FLORINDA   Yes, I knew him at the siege of Pamplona;[8]
he was then a colonel of French horse, who when the

---

8. The capital of the Spanish province of Navarre, which was several times attacked by the
French during the Thirty Years War (1618–48) waged throughout Europe.

town was ransacked, nobly treated my brother and myself, preserving us from all insolences. And I must own,
besides great obligations, I have I know not what that
60   pleads kindly for him about my heart, and will suffer no
other to enter. But see, my brother.

> [*Enter* DON PEDRO, STEPHANO *with a masking habit,*°   masquerade costume
> *and* CALLIS.]

PEDRO   Good morrow, sister. Pray when saw you your
lover Don Vincentio?

FLORINDA   I know not, sir. Callis, when was he here? For I
65   consider it so little I know not when it was.

PEDRO   I have a command from my father here to tell you
you ought not to despise him, a man of so vast a fortune,
and such a passion for you. —Stephano, my things.

> [*Puts on his masking habit.*]

FLORINDA   A passion for me? 'Tis more than e'er I saw, or he
70   had a desire should be known. I hate Vincentio, sir, and I
would not have a man so dear to me as my brother follow
the ill customs of our country and make a slave of his sister. And, sir, my father's will I'm sure you may divert.

PEDRO   I know not how dear I am to you, but I wish only
75   to be ranked in your esteem equal with the English colonel Belvile. Why do you frown and blush? Is there any
guilt belongs to the name of that cavalier?

FLORINDA   I'll not deny I value Belvile. When I was exposed
to such dangers as the licensed lust of common soldiers
80   threatened, when rage and conquest flew through the city,
then Belvile, this criminal for my sake, threw himself into
all dangers to save my honor. And will you not allow him
my esteem?

PEDRO   Yes, pay him what you will in honor, but you
85   must consider Don Vincentio's fortune, and the jointure[9] he'll make you.

FLORINDA   Let him consider my youth, beauty, and fortune, which ought not to be thrown away on his age and
jointure.

90 PEDRO   'Tis true, he's not so young and fine a gentleman
as that Belvile. But what jewels will that cavalier present
you with. Those of his eyes and heart?

HELLENA   And are not those better than any Don Vincentio has brought from the Indies?

95 PEDRO   Why, how now! Has your nunnery breeding taught
you to understand the value of hearts and eyes?

HELLENA   Better than to believe Vincentio's deserve value
from any woman. He may perhaps increase her bags,°   wealth
but not her family.

100 PEDRO   This is fine! Go! Up to your devotion! You are not
designed for the conversation of lovers.

9. The property promised to a wife at marriage in the event of her husband's death.

HELLENA [*aside*]   Nor saints yet a while, I hope. —Is't not enough you make a nun of me, but you must cast my sister away too, exposing her to a worse confinement than
105   a religious life?

PEDRO   The girl's mad! It is a confinement to be carried into the country to an ancient villa belonging to the family of the Vincentios these five hundred years, and have no other prospect° than that pleasing one of seeing all   *view*
110   her own that meets her eyes: a fine air, large fields, and gardens where she may walk and gather flowers?

HELLENA   When, by moonlight? For I am sure she dares not encounter with the heat of the sun; that were a task only for Don Vincentio and his Indian breeding, who
115   loves it in the dog days.[1] And if these be her daily divertissements,° what are those of the night? To lie in a wide   *amusements*
moth-eaten bedchamber with furniture in fashion in the reign of King Sancho the First;[2] the bed, that which his forefathers lived and died in.

120   PEDRO   Very well.

HELLENA   This apartment, new furbished and fitted out for the young wife, he out of freedom makes his dressing room; and being a frugal and a jealous coxcomb,° instead   *fool*
of a valet to uncase° his feeble carcass, he desires you to   *undress*
125   do that office. Signs of favor, I'll assure you, and such as you must not hope for unless your woman be out of the way.

PEDRO   Have you done yet?

HELLENA   That honor being past, the giant stretches itself,
130   yawns and sighs a belch or two loud as a musket, throws himself into bed, and expects° you in his foul sheets; and   *waits for*
ere you can get yourself undressed, calls you with a snore or two. And are not these fine blessings to a young lady?

135   PEDRO   Have you done yet?

HELLENA   And this man you must kiss, nay you must kiss none but him too, and nuzzle through his beard to find his lips. And this you must submit to for threescore years, and all for a jointure.

140   PEDRO   For all your character of Don Vincentio, she is as like to marry him as she was before.

HELLENA   Marry Don Vincentio! Hang me, such a wedlock would be worse than adultery with another man. I had rather see her in the *Hostel de Dieu*,[3] to waste her youth
145   there in vows, and be a handmaid to lazars° and cripples,   *lepers*
than to lose it in such a marriage.

PEDRO   You have considered, sister, that Belvile has no

---

1. The hottest part of summer, when Sirius (the Dog Star) rises. *Indian breeding*: birth in the West Indies.
2. King of Pamplona (Navarre) in the 10th century.
3. A charitable hospital operated by a religious order.

fortune to bring you to; banished his country, despised at home, and pitied abroad.

150 HELLENA   What then? The Viceroy's son is better than that old Sir Fifty. Don Vincentio! Don Indian! He thinks he's trading to Gambo[4] still, and would barter himself— that bell and bauble—for your youth and fortune.

PEDRO   Callis, take her hence and lock her up all this Car-
155 nival, and at Lent she shall begin her everlasting pen-ance in a monastery.

HELLENA   I care not; I had rather be a nun than be obliged to marry as you would have me if I were designed for't.

PEDRO   Do not fear the blessing of that choice. You shall be
160 a nun.

HELLENA [aside]   Shall I so? You may chance to be mis-taken in my way of devotion. A nun! Yes, I am like to make a fine nun! I have an excellent humour for a grate![5] No, I'll have a saint of my own to pray to shortly, if I like
165 any that dares venture on me.

PEDRO   Callis, make it your business to watch this wildcat.
—As for you, Florinda, I've only tried° you all this while   tested
and urged my father's will; but mine is that you would love Antonio: he is brave and young, and all that can
170 complete the happiness of a gallant maid. This absence of my father will give us opportunity to free you from Vin-centio by marrying here, which you must do tomorrow.

FLORINDA   Tomorrow!

PEDRO   Tomorrow, or 'twill be too late. 'Tis not my friendship
175 to Antonio which makes me urge this, but love to thee and hatred to Vincentio; therefore resolve upon tomorrow.

FLORINDA   Sir, I shall strive to do as shall become your sister.

PEDRO   I'll both believe and trust you. Adieu.

[Exeunt° PEDRO and STEPHANO.]   They exit (Latin)

HELLENA   As becomes his sister! That is to be as resolved
180 your way as he is his.

[HELLENA goes to CALLIS.]

FLORINDA   I ne'er till now perceived my ruin near.
I've no defence against Antonio's love,
For he has all the advantages of nature,
The moving arguments of youth and fortune.

185 HELLENA   But hark you, Callis, you will not be so cruel to lock me up indeed, will you?

CALLIS   I must obey the commands I have. Besides, do you consider what a life you are going to lead?

HELLENA   Yes, Callis, that of a nun; and till then I'll be in-
190 debted a world of prayers to you if you'll let me now see what I never did, the divertissements of a Carnival.

---

4. The British colony of Gambia in West Africa, a center of the slave trade.
5. The framework of bars on a convent's doors and windows, separating nuns from the secular world.

CALLIS   What, go in masquerade? 'Twill be a fine farewell
to the world, I take it. Pray what would you do there?

HELLENA   That which all the world does, as I am told: be as
195   mad as the rest and take all innocent freedoms. Sister,
you'll go too, will you not? Come, prithee be not sad.
We'll outwit twenty brothers if you'll be ruled by me.
Come, put off this dull humour with your clothes, and
assume one as gay and as fantastic as the dress my cousin
200   Valeria and I have provided, and let's ramble.

FLORINDA   Callis, will you give us leave to go?

CALLIS [aside]   I have a youthful itch of going myself. —
Madam, if I thought your brother might not know it, and
I might wait on you; for by my troth I'll not trust young
205   girls alone.

FLORINDA   Thou seest my brother's gone already, and thou
shalt attend and watch us.

[Enter STEPHANO.]

STEPHANO   Madam, the habits° are come, and your cousin   costumes
Valeria is dressed and stays for you.

210   FLORINDA [aside]   'Tis well. I'll write a note, and if I
chance to see Belvile and want an opportunity to speak
to him, that shall let him know what I've resolved in favor
of him.

HELLENA   Come, let's in and dress us.

[Exeunt.]

1.2

[SCENE: A long street.]

[Enter BELVILE, melancholy; BLUNT and FREDERICK.]

FREDERICK   Why, what the devil ails the colonel, in a time
when all the world is gay, to look like mere° Lent thus?   pure
Hadst thou been long enough in Naples to have been in
love, I should have sworn some such judgment had be-
5   fallen thee.

BELVILE   No, I have made no new amours since I came to
Naples.

FREDERICK   You have left none behind you in Paris?

BELVILE   Neither.

10   FREDERICK   I cannot divine the cause then, unless the old
cause, the want of money.

BLUNT   And another old cause, the want of a wench.
Would not that revive you?

BELVILE   You are mistaken, Ned.

15   BLUNT   Nay, 'adsheartlikins,° then thou'rt past cure.   God's little heart (oath)

FREDERICK   I have found it out: thou hast renewed thy acquaintance with the lady that cost thee so many sighs at
the siege of Pamplona—pox on't,° what d'ye call her—her   (an oath)
brother's a noble Spaniard, nephew to the dead general.

20 Florinda. Ay, Florinda. And will nothing serve thy turn
    but that damned virtuous woman, whom on my con-
    science thou lov'st in spite too, because thou seest little
    or no possibility of gaining her.

   BELVILE Thou art mistaken; I have int'rest enough in that
25 lovely virgin's heart to make me proud and vain, were it
    not abated by the severity of a brother, who, perceiving
    my happiness—

   FREDERICK Has civilly forbid thee the house?

   BELVILE 'Tis so, to make way for a powerful rival, the
30 Viceroy's son, who has the advantage of me in being a
    man of fortune, a Spaniard, and her brother's friend;
    which gives him liberty to make his court, whilst I have
    recourse only to letters and distant looks from her win-
    dow, which are as soft and kind as those which heaven
35 sends down on penitents.

   BLUNT Heyday! 'Adsheartlikins, simile! By this light the
    man is quite spoiled. Fred, what the devil are we made of
    that we cannot be thus concerned for a wench? 'Ads-
    heartlikins, our Cupids[6] are like the cooks of the camp:
40 they can roast or boil a woman, but they have none of the
    fine tricks to set 'em off; no hogoes° to make the sauce   savory relishes
    pleasant and the stomach sharp.

   FREDERICK I dare swear I have had a hundred as young,
    kind, and handsome as this Florinda; and dogs eat me if
45 they were not as troublesome to me i'th' morning as they
    were welcome o'er night.

   BLUNT And yet I warrant he would not touch another
    woman if he might have her for nothing.

   BELVILE That's thy joy, a cheap whore.

50 BLUNT Why, 'adsheartlikins, I love a frank soul. When did
    you ever hear of an honest woman that took a man's
    money? I warrant 'em good ones. But gentlemen, you
    may be free; you have been kept so poor with parlia-
    ments and protectors that the little stock you have is not
55 worth preserving. But I thank my stars I had more grace
    than to forfeit my estate by cavaliering.[7]

   BELVILE Methinks only following the court should be suf-
    ficient to entitle 'em to that.

   BLUNT 'Adsheartlikins, they know I follow it to do it no
60 good, unless they pick a hole in my coat for lending you
    money now and then, which is a greater crime to my
    conscience, gentlemen, than to the commonwealth.

        [Enter WILLMORE.]

---

6. Cupid is the Roman god of love, often
depicted as winged; his arrows cause their
target to fall in love.
7. The estates of many Royalists (i.e., Cavaliers) were confiscated by Oliver Cromwell's
government following the Parliamentarian
victory in the English Civil War. The official
title of the country's leader during that period
was Lord Protector of the Commonwealth.

WILLMORE   Ha! Dear Belvile! Noble colonel!

BELVILE   Willmore! Welcome ashore, my dear rover! What
65   happy wind blew us this good fortune?

WILLMORE   Let me salute my dear Fred, and then command me. —How is't, honest lad?

FREDERICK   Faith, sir, the old compliment, infinitely the
better to see my dear mad Willmore again. Prithee, why
70   camest thou ashore? And where's the Prince?[8]

WILLMORE   He's well, and reigns still lord of the wat'ry element. I must aboard again within a day or two, and my
business ashore was only to enjoy myself a little this Carnival.

75   BELVILE   Pray know our new friend, sir; he's but bashful, a
raw traveler, but honest, stout, and one of us.

            [*Embraces* BLUNT.]

WILLMORE   That you esteem him gives him an int'rest here.

BLUNT   Your servant, sir.

WILLMORE   But well, faith, I'm glad to meet you again in a
80   warm climate, where the kind sun has its godlike power
still over the wine and women. Love and mirth are my
business in Naples, and if I mistake not the place, here's
an excellent market for chapmen° of my humour.   *merchants*

BELVILE   See, here be those kind merchants of love you
85   look for.

            [*Enter several men in masking habits, some playing on
            music, others dancing after; women dressed like cour-
            tesans, with papers pinned on their breasts, and baskets
            of flowers in their hands.*]

BLUNT   'Adsheartlikins, what have we here?

FREDERICK   Now the game begins.

WILLMORE   Fine pretty creatures! May a stranger have
leave to look and love? What's here? "Roses for every
90   month"?   [*Reads the papers.*]

BLUNT   Roses for every month? What means that?

BELVILE   They are, or would have you think they're courtesans, who here in Naples are to be hired by the month.

WILLMORE   Kind and obliging to inform us, pray where do
95   these roses grow? I would fain plant some of 'em in a bed
of mine.

WOMAN   Beware such roses, sir.

WILLMORE   A pox of fear: I'll be baked with thee between a
pair of sheets, and that's thy proper still;[9] so I might but
100   strew such roses over me and under me. Fair one, would
you would give me leave to gather at your bush this idle
month; I would go near to make somebody smell of it all
the year after.

---

8. The exiled son of Charles I, soon to be
crowned Charles II (1630–1685; r. 1660–85).

9. That is, apparatus for distilling rose petals
to make perfume.

BELVILE   And thou hast need of such a remedy, for thou
105   stink'st of tar and ropes' ends like a dock or pesthouse.[1]

[*The* WOMAN *puts herself into the hands of a man
and exeunt.*]

WILLMORE   Nay, nay, you shall not leave me so.
BELVILE   By all means use no violence here.
WILLMORE   Death!° Just as I was going to be damnably in   God's death (an oath)
love, to have her led off! I could pluck that rose out of
110   his hand, and even kiss the bed the bush grew in.
FREDERICK   No friend to love like a long voyage at sea.
BLUNT   Except a nunnery,° Fred.   convent; brothel
WILLMORE   Death! But will they not be kind? Quickly be
kind? Thou know'st I'm no tame sigher, but a rampant
115   lion of the forest.

[*Advances from the farther end of the scenes two men
dressed all over with horns[2] of several sorts, making
grimaces at one another, with papers pinned on their
backs.*]

BELVILE   Oh the fantastical rogues, how they're dressed!
'Tis a satire against the whole sex.
WILLMORE   Is this a fruit that grows in this warm country?
BELVILE   Yes, 'tis pretty to see these Italians start, swell,
120   and stab at the word *cuckold*, and yet stumble at horns
on every threshold.
WILLMORE   See what's on their back. [*Reads.*] "Flowers of
every night." Ah, rogue! And more sweet than roses of
every month! This is a gardener of Adam's own breeding.[3]

[*They dance.*]

125   BELVILE   What think you of these grave people? Is a wake
in Essex[4] half so mad or extravagant?
WILLMORE   I like their sober grave way; 'tis a kind of legal
authorized fornication, where the men are not chid for't,
nor the women despised, as amongst our dull English.
130   Even the monsieurs want that part of good manners.
BELVILE   But here in Italy, a monsieur is the humblest
best-bred gentleman: duels are so baffled by bravos° that   hired ruffians
an age shows not one but between a Frenchman and a
hangman, who is as much too hard for him on the Piazza
135   as they are for a Dutchman on the New Bridge.[5] But see,
another crew.

[*Enter* FLORINDA, HELLENA, *and* VALERIA, *dressed like
gipsies;* CALLIS *and* STEPHANO, LUCETTA, PHILIPPO
and SANCHO *in masquerade.*]

1. A hospital for victims of the plague.
2. The symbol of a cuckold.
3. An allusion to the Garden of Eden.
4. The location of Blunt's home in rural
southeastern England (see also 2.1).

5. Nieuwerbrug (New Bridge), in southern
Holland, was attacked by the French in the
Third Anglo-Dutch War (1672–74)—an
anachronistic reference, as the play is set
before 1660.

HELLENA   Sister, there's your Englishman, and with him a
handsome proper fellow. I'll to him, and instead of telling him his fortune, try my own.

140   WILLMORE   Gipsies, on my life. Sure these will prattle if a
man cross their hands. [*Goes to* HELLENA.] —Dear,
pretty, and, I hope, young devil, will you tell an amorous
stranger what luck he's like to have?

HELLENA   Have a care how you venture with me, sir, lest I
145   pick your pocket, which will more vex your English
humor than an Italian fortune will please you.

WILLMORE   How the devil cam'st thou to know my country
and humor?

HELLENA   The first I guess by a certain forward impu-
150   dence, which does not displease me at this time; and the
loss of your money will vex you because I hope you have
but very little to lose.

WILLMORE   Egad, child, thou'rt i'th' right; it is so little I
dare not offer it thee for a kindness. But cannot you di-
155   vine what other things of more value I have about me
that I would more willingly part with?

HELLENA   Indeed no, that's the business of a witch, and I
am but a gipsy yet. Yet without looking in your hand, I
have a parlous guess 'tis some foolish heart you mean, an
160   inconstant English heart, as little worth stealing as your
purse.

WILLMORE   Nay, then thou dost deal with the devil, that's
certain. Thou hast guessed as right as if thou hadst been
one of that number it has languished for. I find you'll be
165   better acquainted with it, nor can you take it in a better
time; for I am come from sea, child, and Venus not being
propitious to me in her own element,[6] I have a world of
love in store. Would you would be good-natured and take
some on't off my hands.

170   HELLENA   Why, I could be inclined that way, but for a foolish vow I am going to make to die a maid.

WILLMORE   Then thou art damned without redemption,
and as I am a good Christian, I ought in charity to divert
so wicked a design. Therefore prithee, dear creature, let
175   me know quickly when and where I shall begin to set a
helping hand to so good a work.

HELLENA   If you should prevail with my tender heart, as I
begin to fear you will, for you have horrible loving eyes,
there will be difficulty in't that you'll hardly° undergo for   *with hardship*
180   my sake.

WILLMORE   Faith, child, I have been bred in dangers, and
wear a sword that has been employed in a worse cause
than for a handsome kind woman. Name the danger; let
it be anything but a long siege, and I'll undertake it.

6. Venus, the Roman goddess of love, was born from the sea foam off the island of Cythera.

185 HELLENA Can you storm?

WILLMORE Oh, most furiously.

HELLENA What think you of a nunnery wall? For he that wins me must gain that first.

WILLMORE A nun! Oh, now I love thee for't! There's no sin-
190 ner like a young saint. Nay, now there's no denying me; the old law had no curse to a woman like dying a maid: witness Jeptha's daughter.[7]

HELLENA A very good text this, if well handled; and I per-ceive, Father Captain, you would impose no severe
195 penance on her who were inclined to console herself before she took orders.°   *became a nun*

WILLMORE If she be young and handsome.

HELLENA Ay, there's it. But if she be not—

WILLMORE By this hand, child, I have an implicit faith,
200 and dare venture on° thee with all faults. Besides, 'tis more   *dare to approach* meritorious to leave the world when thou hast tasted and proved the pleasure on't. Then 'twill be a virtue in thee, which now will be pure ignorance.

HELLENA I perceive, good Father Captain, you design
205 only to make me fit for heaven. But if, on the contrary, you should quite divert me from it, and bring me back to the world again, I should have a new man to seek, I find. And what a grief that will be; for when I begin, I fancy I shall love like anything; I never tried yet.

210 WILLMORE Egad, and that's kind! Prithee, dear creature, give me credit for a heart, for faith, I'm a very honest fel-low. Oh, I long to come first to the banquet of love! And such a swinging° appetite I bring. Oh, I'm impatient. Thy   *hearty* lodging, sweetheart, thy lodging, or I'm a dead man!

215 HELLENA Why must we be either guilty of fornication or murder if we converse with you men? And is there no dif-ference between leave to love me, and leave to lie with me?

WILLMORE Faith, child, they were made to go together.

LUCETTA [*pointing to* BLUNT] Are you sure this is the
220 man?

SANCHO When did I mistake your game?

LUCETTA This is a stranger, I know by his gazing; if he be brisk he'll venture to follow me, and then, if I understand my trade, he's mine. He's English, too, and they say that's
225 a sort of good-natured loving people, and have generally so kind an opinion of themselves that a woman with any wit may flatter 'em into any sort of fool she pleases.

[*She often passes by* BLUNT *and gazes on him; he struts and cocks, and walks and gazes on her.*]

BLUNT 'Tis so, she is taken; I have beauties which my false glass° at home did not discover.°   *mirror / reveal*

---

7. Sacrificed by Jephthah to fulfill his vow to God, after she was allowed two months to "bewail [her] virginity" (see Judges 11.30–39).

230 FLORINDA [aside] This woman watches me so, I shall get
no opportunity to discover myself to him, and so miss
the intent of my coming. —[To BELVILE.] But as I was
saying, sir, by this line you should be a lover.
[Looking in his hand.]

BELVILE I thought how right you guessed: all men are in
235 love, or pretend to be so. Come, let me go; I'm weary of
this fooling.
[Walks away.]

FLORINDA I will not, sir, till you have confessed whether
the passion that you have vowed Florinda be true or false.
[She holds him; he strives to get from her.]

BELVILE Florinda!
[Turns quick towards her.]

240 FLORINDA Softly.

BELVILE Thou hast nam'd one will fix me here forever.

FLORINDA She'll be disappointed then, who expects you this
night at the garden gate. And if you fail not, as— [Looks on
CALLIS, who observes 'em.] Let me see the other hand—you
245 will go near to do, she vows to die or make you happy.

BELVILE What canst thou mean?

FLORINDA That which I say. Farewell.
[Offers° to go.]   Attempts

BELVILE Oh charming sybil,° stay; complete that joy which   prophetess
as it is will turn into distraction! Where must I be? At
250 the garden gate? I know it. At night, you say? I'll sooner
forfeit heaven than disobey.
[Enter DON PEDRO and other maskers, and pass over
the stage.]

CALLIS Madam, your brother's here.

FLORINDA Take this to instruct you farther.
[Gives him a letter, and goes off.]

FREDERICK Have a care, sir, what you promise; this may
255 be a trap laid by her brother to ruin you.

BELVILE Do not disturb my happiness with doubts.
[Opens the letter.]

WILLMORE My dear pretty creature, a thousand blessings
on thee! Still in this habit, you say? And after dinner at
this place?

260 HELLENA Yes, if you will swear to keep your heart and not
bestow it between this and that.

WILLMORE By all the little gods of love, I swear; I'll leave
it with you, and if you run away with it, those deities of
justice will revenge me.
[Exeunt all the women except LUCETTA.]

265 FREDERICK Do you know the hand?°   handwriting

BELVILE 'Tis Florinda's. All blessings fall upon the virtuous
maid.

FREDERICK   Nay, no idolatry; a sober sacrifice I'll allow you.

BELVILE   Oh friends, the welcom'st news! The softest° letter!   *most tender*

270   Nay, you shall all see it! And could you now be serious, I might be made the happiest man the sun shines on!

WILLMORE   The reason of this mighty joy?

BELVILE   See how kindly she invites me to deliver her from the threatened violence of her brother. Will you not

275   assist me?

WILLMORE   I know not what thou mean'st, but I'll make one at any mischief where a woman's concerned. But she'll be grateful to us for the favor, will she not?

BELVILE   How mean you?

280 WILLMORE   How should I mean? Thou know'st there's but one way for a woman to oblige me.

BELVILE   Do not profane; the maid is nicely virtuous.

WILLMORE   Who, pox, then she's fit for nothing but a husband. Let her e'en go, colonel.

285 FREDERICK   Peace, she's the colonel's mistress, sir.

WILLMORE   Let her be the devil; if she be thy mistress, I'll serve her. Name the way.

BELVILE   Read here this postscript.

     [*Gives him a letter.*]

WILLMORE [*reads*]   "At ten at night, at the garden gate, of

290   which, if I cannot get the key, I will contrive a way over the wall. Come attended with a friend or two." —Kind heart, if we three cannot weave a string to let her down a garden wall, 'twere pity but the hangman wove one for us all.

295 FREDERICK   Let her alone for that; your woman's wit, your fair kind woman, will out-trick a broker or a Jew, and contrive like a Jesuit in chains.[8] But see, Ned Blunt is stolen out after the lure of a damsel.

     [*Exeunt* BLUNT *and* LUCETTA.]

BELVILE   So, he'll scarce find his way home again unless

300   we get him cried by the bellman° in the market place.   *town crier*
And 'twould sound prettily: "A lost English boy of thirty."

FREDERICK   I hope 'tis some common crafty sinner, one that will fit him. It may be she'll sell him for Peru:[9] the rogue's sturdy, and would work well in a mine. At least I hope

305   she'll dress him for our mirth, cheat him of all, then have him well-favoredly banged,° and turned out at midnight.   *beaten*

WILLMORE   Prithee what humor is he of, that you wish him so well?

BELVILE   Why, of an English elder brother's humour: edu-

310   cated in a nursery, with a maid to tend him till fifteen, and lies with his grandmother till he's of age; one that

---

8. A description that rests on stereotypes of Jews as cheating bargainers and Jesuits as equivocal and deceptive in argument.

9. That is, sell him for slave labor in the mines of Peru, then a Spanish colony.

knows no pleasure beyond riding to the next fair, or going up to London with his right worshipful father in par-liament time, wearing gay clothes, or making honorable
315 love to his lady mother's laundry maid; gets drunk at a hunting match, and ten to one then gives some proofs of his prowess. A pox upon him, he's our banker, and has all our cash about him; and if he fail, we are all broke.

FREDERICK   Oh, let him alone for that matter; he's of a
320 damned stingy quality that will secure our stock. I know not in what danger it were indeed if the jilt should pretend she's in love with him, for 'tis a kind believing coxcomb; otherwise, if he part with more than a piece of eight,° geld   *Spanish dollar* him—for which offer he may chance to be beaten if she
325 be a whore of the first rank.

BELVILE   Nay, the rogue will not be easily beaten; he's stout enough. Perhaps if they talk beyond his capacity he may chance to exercise his courage upon some of them, else I'm sure they'll find it as difficult to beat as to please him.

330 WILLMORE   'Tis a lucky devil to light upon so kind a wench!

FREDERICK   Thou hadst a great deal of talk with thy little gipsy; couldst thou do no good upon her? For mine was hardhearted.

WILLMORE   Hang her, she was some damned honest person
335 of quality, I'm sure, she was so very free and witty. If her face be but answerable to her wit and humor, I would be bound to constancy this month to gain her. In the mean-time, have you made no kind acquaintance since you came to town? You do not use to be honest so long, gentlemen.

340 FREDERICK   Faith, love has kept us honest: we have been all fir'd with a beauty newly come to town, the famous Paduana° Angellica Bianca.   *woman from Padua*

WILLMORE   What, the mistress of the dead Spanish general?

BELVILE   Yes, she's now the only ador'd beauty of all the
345 youth in Naples, who put on all their charms to appear lovely in her sight: their coaches, liveries, and them-selves all gay as on a monarch's birthday to attract the eyes of this fair charmer, while she has the pleasure to behold all languish for her that see her.

350 FREDERICK   'Tis pretty to see with how much love the men regard her, and how much envy the women.

WILLMORE   What gallant has she?

BELVILE   None; she's exposed to sale, and four days in the week she's yours, for so much a month.

355 WILLMORE   The very thought of it quenches all manner of fire in me. Yet prithee, let's see her.

BELVILE   Let's first to dinner, and after that we'll pass the day as you please. But at night ye must all be at my de-votion.

360 WILLMORE   I will not fail you.

[*Exeunt.*]

2.1

[SCENE: *The long street.*]

[*Enter* BELVILE *and* FREDERICK *in masking habits, and* WILLMORE *in his own clothes, with a vizard° in his hand.*]   mask

WILLMORE   But why thus disguised and muzzled?

BELVILE   Because whatever extravagances we commit in these faces, our own may not be obliged to answer 'em.

WILLMORE   I should have changed my eternal buff,° too; but   *habitual*
5   no matter, my little gipsy would not have found me out   *military jacket*
then. For if she should change hers, it is impossible I
should know her unless I should hear her prattle. A pox
on't, I cannot get her out of my head. Pray heaven, if
ever I do see her again, she prove damnably ugly, that I
10   may fortify myself against her tongue.

BELVILE   Have a care of love, for o' my conscience she was
not of a quality to give thee any hopes.

WILLMORE   Pox on 'em, why do they draw a man in then?
She has played with my heart so, that 'twill never lie still
15   till I have met with some kind wench that will play the
game out with me. Oh, for my arms full of soft, white,
kind woman—such as I fancy Angellica.

BELVILE   This is her house, if you were but in stock° to get   *possessed of capital*
admittance. They have not dined yet; I perceive the pic-
20   ture is not out.

[*Enter* BLUNT.]

WILLMORE   I long to see the shadow of the fair substance;
a man may gaze on that for nothing.

BLUNT   Colonel, thy hand. And thine, Fred. I have been an
ass, a deluded fool, a very coxcomb from my birth till this
25   hour, and heartily repent my little faith.

BELVILE   What the devil's the matter with thee, Ned?

BLUNT   Oh, such a mistress, Fred! Such a girl!

WILLMORE   Ha! Where?

FREDERICK   Ay, where?

30   BLUNT   So fond, so amorous, so toying,° and so fine! And   *flirting*
all for sheer love, ye rogue! Oh, how she looked and
kissed! And soothed my heart from my bosom! I cannot
think I was awake, and yet methinks I see and feel her
charms still. Fred, try if she have not left the taste of her
35   balmy kisses upon my lips.

[*Kisses him.*]

BELVILE   Ha! Ha! Ha!

WILLMORE   Death, man, where is she?

BLUNT   What a dog was I to stay in dull England so long!
How have I laughed at the colonel when he sighed for
40   love! But now the little archer° has revenged him! And by   *i.e., Cupid*
this one dart I can guess at all his joys, which then I took

for fancies, mere dreams and fables. Well, I'm resolved
to sell all in Essex and plant here forever.

BELVILE   What a blessing 'tis, thou hast a mistress thou
45 dar'st boast of; for I know thy humour is rather to have a
proclaimed clap° than a secret amour.   *gonorrhea*

WILLMORE   Dost know her name?

BLUNT   Her name? No, 'adsheartlikins. What care I for
names? She's fair, young, brisk and kind, even to ravish-
50 ment! And what a pox care I for knowing her by any
other title?

WILLMORE   Didst give her anything?

BLUNT   Give her? Ha! Ha! Ha! Why, she's a person of quality. That's a good one! Give her? 'Adsheartlikins, dost
55 think such creatures are to be bought? Or are we provided for such a purchase? Give her, quoth ye? Why, she
presented me with this bracelet for the toy of a diamond
I used to wear. No, gentlemen, Ned Blunt is not everybody. She expects me again tonight.

60 WILLMORE   Egad, that's well; we'll all go.

BLUNT   Not a soul! No, gentlemen, you are wits; I am a
dull country rogue, I.

FREDERICK   Well, sir, for all your person of quality, I shall
be very glad to understand your purse be secure; 'tis our
65 whole estate at present, which we are loath to hazard in
one bottom.[1] Come sir, unlade.°   *unload*

BLUNT   Take the necessary trifle useless now to me, that
am beloved by such a gentlewoman. 'Adsheartlikins,
money! Here, take mine too.

70 FREDERICK   No, keep that to be cozened,° that we may laugh.   *tricked, cheated*

WILLMORE   Cozened? Death! Would I could meet with one
that would cozen me of all the love I could spare tonight.

FREDERICK   Pox, 'tis some common whore, upon my life.

BLUNT   A whore? Yes, with such clothes, such jewels, such
75 a house, such furniture, and so attended! A whore!

BELVILE   Why yes, sir, they are whores, though they'll neither entertain you with drinking, swearing, or bawdry;
are whores in all those gay clothes and right jewels; are
whores with those great houses richly furnished with
80 velvet beds, store of plate,° handsome attendance, and fine   *silver or gold utensils*
coaches; are whores, and arrant°ones.   *thorough; notorious*

WILLMORE   Pox on't, where do these fine whores live?

BELVILE   Where no rogues in office, ycleped° constables, dare   *called*
give 'em laws, nor the wine-inspired bullies of the town
85 break their windows; yet they are whores though this Essex
calf° believe 'em persons of quality.   *fool*

BLUNT   'Adsheartlikins, y'are all fools. There are things
about this Essex calf that shall take with the ladies, beyond
all your wit and parts. This shape and size, gentlemen, are

---

1. In the hold of one ship; that is, in a single location.

90   not to be despised; my waist, too, tolerably long, with
      other inviting signs that shall be nameless.

WILLMORE   Egad, I believe he may have met with some
      person of quality that may be kind to him.

BELVILE   Dost thou perceive any such tempting things
95   about him that should make a fine woman, and of qual-
      ity, pick him out from all mankind to throw away her
      youth and beauty upon; nay, and her dear heart, too? No,
      no, Angellica has raised the price too high.

WILLMORE   May she languish for mankind till she die, and
100   be damned for that one sin alone.

> [*Enter two* BRAVOS *and hang up a great picture of*
> ANGELLICA'S *against the balcony, and two little ones
> at each side of the door.*]

BELVILE   See there the fair sign to the inn where a man
      may lodge that's fool enough to give her price.

> [WILLMORE *gazes on the picture.*]

BLUNT   'Adsheartlikins, gentlemen, what's this?

BELVILE   A famous courtesan, that's to be sold.

105 BLUNT   How? To be sold? Nay, then I have nothing to say
      to her. Sold? What impudence is practiced in this coun-
      try; with what order and decency whoring's established
      here by virtue of the Inquisition![2] Come, let's be gone;
      I'm sure we're no chapmen for this commodity.

110 FREDERICK   Thou art none, I'm sure, unless thou couldst
      have her in thy bed at a price of a coach in the street.

WILLMORE   How wondrous fair she is! A thousand crowns
      a month? By heaven, as many kingdoms were too little! A
      plague of this poverty, of which I ne'er complain but
115   when it hinders my approach to beauty which virtue
      ne'er could purchase.

> [*Turns from the picture.*]

BLUNT   What's this? [*Reads.*] "A thousand crowns a
      month"! 'Adsheartlikins, here's a sum! Sure 'tis a mis-
      take. —[*To one of the* BRAVOS.] Hark you, friend, does
120   she take or give so much by the month?

FREDERICK   A thousand crowns! Why, 'tis a portion° for the   *dowry*
      Infanta![3]

BLUNT   Hark ye, friends, won't she trust?

BRAVO   This is a trade, sir, that cannot live by credit.

> [*Enter* DON PEDRO *in masquerade, followed by*
> STEPHANO.]

125 BELVILE   See, here's more company; let's walk off a while.

> [*Exeunt English;* PEDRO *reads.*]

PEDRO   Fetch me a thousand crowns; I never wished to
      buy this beauty at an easier rate.   [*Passes off.*°]   *Departs*

---

2. A Roman Catholic tribunal set up to com-   3. The daughter of the king of Spain.
bat heresy.

[Enter ANGELLICA *and* MORETTA *in the balcony, and draw a silk curtain.]*

ANGELLICA   Prithee, what said those fellows to thee?

BRAVO   Madam, the first were admirers of beauty only, but
130   no purchasers; they were merry with your price and picture, laughed at the sum, and so passed off.

ANGELLICA   No matter, I'm not displeased with their rally-
ing; their wonder feeds my vanity, and he that wishes but°   *only wishes*
to buy gives me more pride than he that gives my price
135   can make my pleasure.

BRAVO   Madam, the last I knew through all his disguises
to be Don Pedro, nephew to the general, and who was
with him in Pamplona.

ANGELLICA   Don Pedro? My old gallant's nephew? When
140   his uncle died he left him a vast sum of money; it is he
who was so in love with me at Padua, and who used to
make the general so jealous.

MORETTA   Is this he that used to prance before our window,
and take such care to show himself an amorous ass? If I
145   am not mistaken, he is the likeliest man to give your price.

ANGELLICA   The man is brave and generous, but of a
humour so uneasy and inconstant that the victory over his
heart is as soon lost as won; a slave that can add little to
the triumph of the conqueror. But inconstancy's the sin
150   of all mankind, therefore I'm resolved that nothing but
gold shall charm my heart.

MORETTA   I'm glad on't; 'tis only interest that women of
our profession ought to consider, though I wonder what
has kept you from that general disease of our sex so long;
155   I mean, that of being in love.

ANGELLICA   A kind but sullen star under which I had the
happiness to be born. Yet I have had no time for love; the
bravest and noblest of mankind have purchased my favors at so dear a rate, as if no coin but gold were current
160   with our trade. But here's Don Pedro again; fetch me my
lute, for 'tis for him or Don Antonio the Viceroy's son
that I have spread my nets.

[Enter at one door DON PEDRO, STEPHANO; DON ANTO-
NIO *and* DIEGO *(his page) at the other door, with
people following him in masquerade, anticly° attired,*   *bizarrely*
some with music. They both go up to the picture.]

ANTONIO   A thousand crowns! Had not the painter flattered her, I should not think it dear.

165   PEDRO   Flattered her? By heaven, he cannot. I have seen
the original, nor is there one charm here more than
adorns her face and eyes; all this soft and sweet, with a
certain languishing air that no artist can represent.

ANTONIO   What I heard of her beauty before had fired my
170   soul, but this confirmation of it has blown it to a flame.

PEDRO   Ha!

DIEGO Sir, I have known you throw away a thousand
crowns on a worse face, and though y'are near your marriage, you may venture a little love here; Florinda will
175   not miss it.
PEDRO [aside] Ha! Florinda! Sure 'tis Antonio.
ANTONIO Florinda! Name not those distant joys; there's
not one thought of her will check my passion here.
PEDRO [aside] Florinda scorned! [A noise of a lute above.]
180   And all my hopes defeated of the possession of Angellica! [ANTONIO gazes up.] Her injuries, by heaven, he
shall not boast of!

       [Song to a lute above.]

SONG

I

    When Damon first began to love
    He languished in a soft desire,
185   And knew not how the gods to move,
    To lessen or increase his fire.
    For Caelia in her charming eyes
Wore all love's sweets, and all his cruelties.

II

    But as beneath a shade he lay,
190   Weaving of flowers for Caelia's hair,
    She chanced to lead her flock that way,
    And saw the am'rous shepherd there.
    She gazed around upon the place,
    And saw the grove, resembling night,
195   To all the joys of love invite,
Whilst guilty smiles and blushes dressed her face.
At this the bashful youth all transport grew,
And with kind force he taught the virgin how
To yield what all his sighs could never do.

      [ANGELLICA throws open the curtains and bows to
      ANTONIO, who pulls off his vizard and bows and blows
      up kisses. PEDRO, unseen, looks in's face.]

200 ANTONIO By heaven, she's charming fair!
PEDRO [aside] 'Tis he, the false Antonio!
ANTONIO [to a bravo] Friend, where must I pay my off'ring
of love?
My thousand crowns I mean.
PEDRO That off'ring I have designed to make,
205   And yours will come too late.
ANTONIO Prithee begone; I shall grow angry else,
And then thou art not safe.
PEDRO My anger may be fatal, sir, as yours,
And he that enters here may prove this truth.

210 ANTONIO   I know not who thou art, but I am sure thou'rt
worth my killing, for aiming at Angellica.

    [They draw and fight.]

    [Enter WILLMORE *and* BLUNT, *who draw and part'em.]*

BLUNT   'Adsheartlikins, here's fine doings.

WILLMORE   Tilting for the wench, I'm sure. Nay, gad, if that
would win her I have as good a sword as the best of ye.

215 Put up,° put up, and take another time and place, for this   *Sheathe (your swords)*
is designed for lovers only.

    [They all put up.]

PEDRO   We are prevented; dare you meet me tomorrow on the Molo?°   *pier*
For I've a title to a better quarrel,
That of Florinda, in whose credulous heart
220 Thou'st made an int'rest, and destroyed my hopes.

ANTONIO   Dare! I'll meet thee there as early as the day.

PEDRO   We will come thus disguised, that whosoever
chance to get the better, he may escape unknown.

ANTONIO   It shall be so.

    [Exeunt PEDRO *and* STEPHANO.]

225 —Who should this rival be? Unless the English colonel,
of whom I've often heard Don Pedro speak. It must be
he, and time he were removed who lays a claim to all my
happiness.

    *[*WILLMORE, *having gazed all this while on the
picture, pulls down a little one.]*

WILLMORE   This posture's loose and negligent;
230 The sight on't would beget a warm desire
In souls whom impotence and age had chilled.
This must along with me.

BRAVO   What means this rudeness, sir? Restore the picture.

ANTONIO   Ha! Rudeness committed to the fair Angellica!
235 —Restore the picture, sir.

WILLMORE   Indeed I will not, sir.

ANTONIO   By heaven, but you shall.

WILLMORE   Nay, do not show your sword; if you do, by this
dear beauty, I will show mine too.

240 ANTONIO   What right can you pretend to't?

WILLMORE   That of possession, which I will maintain. You,
perhaps, have a thousand crowns to give for the original.

ANTONIO   No matter, sir, you shall restore the picture.

ANGELLICA   Oh, Moretta, what's the matter?

    *[*ANGELLICA *and* MORETTA *above.]*

245 ANTONIO   Or leave your life behind.

WILLMORE   Death! You lie; I will do neither.

    [They fight. The Spaniards join with ANTONIO, BLUNT
laying on° like mad.]   *vigorously attacking*

ANGELLICA   Hold, I command you, if for me you fight.

    [They leave off and bow.]

WILLMORE [*aside*] How heavenly fair she is! Ah, plague of
her price!

250 ANGELICA You sir, in buff, you that appear a soldier, that
first began this insolence—

WILLMORE 'Tis true, I did so, if you call it insolence for a
man to preserve himself. I saw your charming picture
and was wounded; quite through my soul each pointed

255 beauty ran; and wanting a thousand crowns to procure
my remedy, I laid this little picture to my bosom, which,
if you cannot allow me, I'll resign.

ANGELICA No, you may keep the trifle.

ANTONIO You shall first ask me leave, and this.

[*Fight again as before.*]
[*Enter* BELVILE *and* FREDERICK, *who join with the*
English.]

260 ANGELICA Hold! Will you ruin me? —Biskey! Sebastian!
Part 'em!

[*The Spaniards are beaten off.*]

MORETTA Oh, madam, we're undone. A pox upon that
rude fellow; he's set on to ruin us. We shall never see
good days again till all these fighting poor rogues are

265 sent to the galleys.

[*Enter* BELVILE, BLUNT, FREDERICK, *and* WILLMORE
with's shirt bloody.]

BLUNT 'Adsheartlikins, beat me at this sport and I'll ne'er
wear sword more.

BELVILE [*to* WILLMORE] The devil's in thee for a mad fellow; thou art always one at an unlucky adventure. Come,

270 let's be gone whilst we're safe, and remember these are
Spaniards, a sort of people that know how to revenge an
affront.

FREDERICK You bleed! I hope you are not wounded.

WILLMORE Not much. A plague on your dons;° if they fight   ° *Spaniards*

275 no better they'll ne'er recover Flanders.[4] What the devil
was't to them that I took down the picture?

BLUNT Took it! 'Adsheartlikins, we'll have the great one
too; 'tis ours by conquest. Prithee help me up and I'll
pull it down.

280 ANGELICA [*to* WILLMORE] Stay, sir, and ere you affront
me farther let me know how you durst commit this outrage. To you I speak, sir, for you appear a gentleman.

WILLMORE To me, madam? —Gentlemen, your servant.[5]

[BELVILE *stays him.*]

BELVILE Is the devil in thee? Dost know the danger of

285 ent'ring the house of an incensed courtesan?

WILLMORE I thank you for your care, but there are other

---

4. The Low Countries, which largely revolted
from Spanish rule in the 16th century.

5. That is, "I am your servant," a polite
leave-taking.

matters in hand, there are, though we have no great
temptation. Death! Let me go!

FREDERICK Yes, to your lodging if you will, but not in here.
290 Damn these gay harlots; by this hand I'll have as sound
and handsome a whore for a patacoon.⁶ Death, man,
she'll murder thee!

WILLMORE Oh, fear me not. Shall I not venture where a
beauty calls? A lovely charming beauty! For fear of dan-
295 ger? When, by heaven, there's none so great as to long
for her whilst I want money to purchase her.

FREDERICK Therefore 'tis loss of time unless you had the
thousand crowns to pay.

WILLMORE It may be she may give a favor; at least I shall
300 have the pleasure of saluting° her when I enter and when   *kissing*
I depart.

BELVILE Pox, she'll as soon lie with thee as kiss thee, and
sooner stab than do either. You shall not go.

ANGELLICA Fear not, sir, all I have to wound with is my eyes.
305 BLUNT Let him go. 'Adsheartlikins, I believe the gentlewoman means well.

BELVILE Well, take thy fortune; we'll expect you in the
next street. Farewell, fool, farewell.

WILLMORE 'Bye, colonel.   [*Goes in.*]
310 FREDERICK The rogue's stark mad for a wench.

                                                            [*Exeunt.*]

2.2

[SCENE: *A fine chamber.*]

[*Enter* WILLMORE, ANGELLICA, *and* MORETTA.]

ANGELLICA Insolent sir, how durst you pull down my picture?

WILLMORE Rather, how durst you set it up to tempt poor
am'rous mortals with so much excellence, which I find
you have but too well consulted by the unmerciful price
5 you set upon't. Is all this heaven of beauty shown to
move despair in those that cannot buy? And can you
think th'effects of that despair should be less extravagant
than I have shown?

ANGELLICA I sent for you to ask my pardon, sir, not to ag-
10 gravate your crime. I thought I should have seen you at
my feet imploring it.

WILLMORE You are deceived. I came to rail at you, and rail
such truths too, as shall let you see the vanity of that
pride which taught you how to set such price on sin.
15 For such it is whilst that which is love's due is meanly
bartered for.

ANGELLICA Ha! Ha! Ha! Alas, good captain, what pity 'tis
your edifying doctrine will do no good upon me.

6. A Portuguese and Spanish coin of relatively little value.

Moretta, fetch the gentleman a glass, and let him survey
20   himself to see what charms he has. —[*Aside, in a soft*
tone.] And guess my business.

MORETTA   He knows himself of old: I believe those
breeches and he have been acquainted ever since he was
beaten at Worcester.[7]

25 ANGELLICA   Nay, do not abuse the poor creature.

MORETTA   Good weatherbeaten corporal, will you march
off? We have no need of your doctrine, though you have of
our charity. But at present we have no scraps; we can afford
no kindness for God's sake. In fine,° sirrah,[8] the price   *In conclusion*
30   is too high i'th' mouth for you, therefore troop,° I say.   *be off*

WILLMORE   Here, good forewoman of the shop, serve me
and I'll be gone.

[*Offers money.*]

MORETTA   Keep it to pay your laundress; your linen stinks
of the gun room. For here's no selling by retail.

35 WILLMORE   Thou hast sold plenty of thy stale ware at a
cheap rate.

MORETTA   Ay, the more silly kind heart I, but this is an age
wherein beauty is at higher rates. In fine, you know the
price of this.

40 WILLMORE   I grant you 'tis here set down, a thousand
crowns a month. Pray, how much may come to my share
for a pistole?° Bawd, take your black lead and sum it   *a gold coin*
up, that I may have a pistole's worth of this vain gay
thing, and I'll trouble you no more.

45 MORETTA   Pox on him, he'll fret me to death! Abominable
fellow, I tell thee we only sell by the whole piece.

WILLMORE   'Tis very hard, the whole cargo or nothing.
Faith, madam, my stock will not reach it; I cannot be
your chapman. Yet I have countrymen in town, mer-
50   chants of love like me; I'll see if they'll put in for a share.
We cannot lose much by it, and what we have no use for,
we'll sell upon the Friday's mart at "Who gives more?"—
I am studying, madam, how to purchase you, though at
present I am unprovided of money.

55 ANGELLICA [*aside*]   Sure this from any other man would
anger me; nor shall he know the conquest he has made.
—Poor angry man, how I despise this railing.

WILLMORE   Yes, I am poor. But I'm a gentleman,
And one that scorns this baseness which you practice.
60   Poor as I am I would not sell myself,
No, not to gain your charming high-prized person.
Though I admire you strangely for your beauty,

---

7. The site of Cromwell's 1651 defeat of   8. A form of address to male social inferiors,
Prince Charles in the final battle of the   and thus here indicating contempt.
English Civil War.

Yet I contemn° your mind.   *scorn, despise*

And yet I would at any rate enjoy you;

65   At your own rate; but cannot. See here

The only sum I can command on earth:

I know not where to eat when this is gone.

Yet such a slave I am to love and beauty

This last reserve I'll sacrifice to enjoy you.

70   Nay, do not frown, I know you're to be bought,

And would be bought by me. By me,

For a meaning trifling sum, if I could pay it down.

Which happy knowledge I will still repeat,

And lay it to my heart: it has a virtue in't,

75   And soon will cure those wounds your eyes have made.

And yet, there's something so divinely powerful there—

Nay, I will gaze, to let you see my strength.

       [*Holds her, looks on her, and pauses and sighs.*]

By heav'n, bright creature, I would not for the world

Thy fame° were half so fair as is thy face.   *reputation*

       [*Turns her away from him.*]

80 ANGELLICA [*aside*]   His words go through me to the very soul.—

If you have nothing else to say to me—

WILLMORE   Yes, you shall hear how infamous you are—

For which I do not hate thee—

But that secures my heart, and all the flames it feels

85   Are but so many lusts:

I know it by their sudden bold intrusion.

The fire's impatient and betrays; 'tis false.

For had it been the purer flame of love,

I should have pined and languished at your feet,

90   Ere found the impudence to have discovered it.

I now dare stand your scorn and your denial.

MORETTA [*aside*]   Sure she's bewitched, that she can stand

thus tamely and hear his saucy railing. —Sirrah, will you

be gone?

95 ANGELLICA [*to* MORETTA]   How dare you take this liberty!

Withdraw! —Pray tell me, sir, are not you guilty of the

same mercenary crime? When a lady is proposed to you

for a wife, you never ask how fair, discreet, or virtuous

she is, but what's her fortune; which, if but small, you cry

100   "She will not do my business," and basely leave her,

though she languish for you. Say, is not this as poor?

WILLMORE   It is a barbarous custom, which I will scorn to

defend in our sex, and do despise in yours.

ANGELLICA   Thou'rt a brave° fellow! Put up thy gold, and know,   *fine, handsome*

105   That were thy fortune as large as is thy soul,

Thou shouldst not buy my love.

Couldst thou forget those mean effects of vanity

Which set me out to sale,

And as a lover prize my yielding joys.
110 Canst thou believe they'll be entirely thine,
Without considering they were mercenary?

WILLMORE   I cannot tell, I must bethink me first.
[*Aside*.] Ha! Death, I'm going to believe her.

ANGELICA   Prithee confirm that faith, or if thou canst not,
115 Flatter me a little: 'twill please me from thy mouth.

WILLMORE [*aside*]   Curse on thy charming tongue! Dost thou return
My feigned contempt with so much subtlety?—
Thou'st found the easiest way into my heart,
Though I yet know that all thou say'st is false.

[*Turning from her in rage.*]

120 ANGELICA   By all that's good, 'tis real;
I never loved before, though oft a mistress.
Shall my first vows be slighted?

WILLMORE [*aside*]   What can she mean?

ANGELICA [*in an angry tone*]   I find you cannot credit me.

125 WILLMORE   I know you take me for an errant ass,
An ass that may be soothed into belief,
And then be used at pleasure;
But, madam, I have been so often cheated
By perjured, soft, deluding hypocrites,
130 That I've no faith left for the cozening sex,
Especially for women of your trade.

ANGELICA   The low esteem you have of me perhaps
May bring my heart again:
For I have pride that yet surmounts my love.

[*She turns with pride; he holds her.*]

135 WILLMORE   Throw off this pride, this enemy to bliss,
And show the power of love: 'tis with those arms
I can be only vanquished, made a slave.

ANGELICA   Is all my mighty expectation vanished?
No, I will not hear thee talk; thou hast a charm
140 In every word that draws my heart away,
And all the thousand trophies I designed
Thou hast undone. Why art thou soft?
Thy looks are bravely rough, and meant for war.
Couldst thou not storm on still?
145 I then perhaps had been as free as thou.

WILLMORE [*aside*]   Death, how she throws her fire about my soul!—
Take heed, fair creature, how you raise my hopes,
Which once assumed pretends to all dominion:
There's not a joy thou hast in store
150 I shall not then command.
For which I'll pay you back my soul, my life!
Come, let's begin th'account this happy minute!

ANGELICA   And will you pay me then the price I ask?

WILLMORE   Oh, why dost thou draw me from an awful° worship,   awe-filled
155 By showing thou art no divinity.

Conceal the fiend, and show me all the angel!
Keep me but ignorant, and I'll be devout
And pay my vows forever at this shrine.

[*Kneels and kisses her hand.*]

ANGELLICA   The pay I mean is but thy love for mine.
160 Can you give that?

WILLMORE   Entirely. Come, let's withdraw where I'll renew
my vows, and breathe 'em with such ardor thou shalt not
doubt my zeal.

ANGELLICA   Thou hast a power too strong to be resisted.

[*Exeunt* WILLMORE *and* ANGELLICA.]

165 MORETTA   Now my curse go with you! Is all our project fallen
to this? To love the only enemy to our trade? Nay, to love
such a shameroon,° a very beggar; nay, a pirate beggar,   phony, deceiver
whose business is to rifle and be gone; a no-purchase,
no-pay tatterdemalion, and English picaroon;° a rogue   rogue; pirate
170 that fights for daily drink, and takes a pride in being loy-
ally lousy? Oh, I could curse now, if I durst. This is the
fate of most whores.

Trophies, which from believing fops we win,
Are spoils to those who cozen us again.   [*Exit.*]

3.1

[SCENE: *A street.*]

[*Enter* FLORINDA, VALERIA, HELLENA, *in antic different dresses from what they were in before;* CALLIS
attending.]

FLORINDA   I wonder what should make my brother in so ill
a humor? I hope he has not found out our ramble this
morning.

HELLENA   No, if he had, we should have heard on't at both
5 ears, and have been mewed up° this afternoon, which I   pent up,
would not for the world should have happened. Hey ho,   confined
I'm as sad as a lover's lute.

VALERIA   Well, methinks we have learnt this trade of gipsies as readily as if we had been bred upon the road to
10 Loretto;⁹ and yet I did so fumble when I told the stranger
his fortune that I was afraid I should have told my own
and yours by mistake. But methinks Hellena has been
very serious ever since.

FLORINDA   I would give my garters she were in love, to
15 be revenged upon her for abusing me. How is't,
Hellena?

HELLENA   Ah, would I had never seen my mad monsieur.
And yet, for all your laughing, I am not in love. And yet

9. An Italian town near the Adriatic coast; it is the site of a shrine of the Virgin Mary visited by
many pilgrims.

this small acquaintance, o' my conscience, will never out
20 of my head.

VALERIA   Ha! Ha! Ha! I laugh to think how thou art fitted
with a lover, a fellow that I warrant loves every new face
he sees.

HELLENA   Hum, he has not kept his word with me here,
25 and may be taken up. That thought is not very pleasant
to me. What the deuce should this be now that I feel?

VALERIA   What is't like?

HELLENA   Nay, the Lord knows, but if I should be hanged
I cannot choose but be angry and afraid when I think that
30 mad fellow should be in love with anybody but me. What
to think of myself I know not: would I could meet with
some true damned gipsy, that I might know my fortune.

VALERIA   Know it! Why there's nothing so easy: thou wilt
love this wand'ring inconstant till thou find'st thyself
35 hanged about his neck, and then be as mad to get free
again.

FLORINDA   Yes, Valeria, we shall see her bestride his baggage horse and follow him to the campaign.

HELLENA   So, so, now you are provided for there's no care
40 taken of poor me. But since you have set my heart
a-wishing, I am resolved to know for what; I will not die
of the pip,[1] so I will not.

FLORINDA   Art thou mad to talk so? Who will like thee well
enough to have thee, that hears what a mad wench thou
45 art?

HELLENA   Like me? I don't intend every he that likes me
shall have me, but he that I like. I should have stayed in
the nunnery still if I had liked my lady abbess as well as
she liked me. No, I came thence not, as my wise brother
50 imagines, to take an eternal farewell of the world, but to
love and to be beloved; and I will be beloved, or I'll get
one of your men, so I will.

VALERIA   Am I put into the number of lovers?

HELLENA   You? Why, coz,[2] I know thou'rt too good-natured
55 to leave us in any design; thou wouldst venture a cast°   *i.e., roll the dice*
though thou comest off a loser, especially with such a
gamester. I observe your man, and your willing ear
incline that way; and if you are not a lover, 'tis an art
soon learnt—that I find.   [*Sighs.*]

60 FLORINDA   I wonder how you learnt to love so easily. I had
a thousand charms to meet my eyes and ears ere I could
yield, and 'twas the knowledge of Belvile's merit, not the
surprising person, took my soul. Thou art too rash, to
give a heart at first sight.

65 HELLENA   Hang your considering lover! I never thought

---

1. A vague, catchall term for human diseases;
here, heartache or depression.

2. Cousin, an affectionate term for any relative outside the speaker's immediate family.

beyond the fancy that 'twas a very pretty, idle, silly kind of pleasure to pass one's time with: to write little soft non-sensical billets,° and with great difficulty and danger receive answers in which I shall have my beauty praised, my wit admired, though little or none, and have the vanity and power to know I am desirable. Then I have the more inclination that way because I am to be a nun, and so shall not be suspected to have any such earthly thoughts about me; but when I walk thus—and sigh thus—they'll think my mind's upon my monastery, and cry, "How happy 'tis she's so resolved." But not a word of man.

brief notes

FLORINDA   What a mad creature's this!

HELLENA   I'll warrant, if my brother hears either of you sigh, he cries gravely, "I fear you have the indiscretion to be in love, but take heed of the honor of our house, and your own unspotted fame"; and so he conjures on till he has laid the soft-winged god in your hearts, or broke the bird's nest. But see, here comes your lover, but where's my inconstant? Let's step aside, and we may learn something.

[*Go aside.*]

[*Enter* BELVILE, FREDERICK, *and* BLUNT.]

BELVILE   What means this! The picture's taken in.

BLUNT   It may be the wench is good-natured, and will be kind gratis. Your friend's a proper handsome fellow.

BELVILE   I rather think she has cut his throat and is fled; I am mad he should throw himself into dangers. Pox on't, I shall want him, too, at night. Let's knock and ask for him.

HELLENA   My heart goes a-pit, a-pat, for fear 'tis my man they talk of.

[*Knock;* MORETTA *above.*]

MORETTA   What would you have?

BELVILE   Tell the stranger that entered here about two hours ago that his friends stay here for him.

MORETTA   A curse upon him for Moretta: would he were at the devil!

But he's coming to you.

[*Enter* WILLMORE.]

HELLENA   Ay, ay 'tis he. Oh, how this vexes me!

BELVILE   And how and how, dear lad, has fortune smiled? Are we to break her windows, or raise up altars to her, hah?

WILLMORE   Does not my fortune sit triumphant on my brow? Dost not see the little wanton god there all gay and smiling? Have I not an air about my face and eyes that distinguish me from the crowd of common lovers? By heaven, Cupid's quiver has not half so many darts as her eyes! Oh, such a *bona roba!*[3] To sleep in her arms is lying *in fresco,*° all perfumed air about me.

in fresh air (Italian)

3. Courtesan; literally, "good stuff" (*buonaroba,* Italian).

HELLENA [*aside*] Here's fine encouragement for me to fool
110 on!

WILLMORE Hark'ee, where didst thou purchase that rich
Canary[4] we drank today? Tell me, that I may adore the
spigot and sacrifice to the butt. The juice was divine; into
which I must dip my rosary, and then bless all things that
115 I would have bold or fortunate.

BELVILE Well, sir, let's go take a bottle and hear the story
of your success.

FREDERICK Would not French wine do better?

WILLMORE Damn the hungry balderdash! Cheerful sack[5]
120 has a generous virtue in't inspiring a successful confidence, gives eloquence to the tongue and vigor to the
soul, and has in a few hours completed all my hopes and
wishes! There's nothing left to raise a new desire in me.
Come, let's be gay and wanton. And, gentlemen, study;
125 study what you want, for here are friends that will supply
gentlemen. [*Jingles gold.*] Hark what a charming sound
they make! 'Tis the he and the she gold whilst here, and
shall beget new pleasures every moment.

BLUNT But hark'ee, sir, you are not married, are you?

130 WILLMORE All the honey of matrimony but none of the
sting, friend.

BLUNT 'Adsheartlikins, thou'rt a fortunate rogue!

WILLMORE I am so, sir: let these inform you! Ha, how
sweetly they chime! Pox of poverty: it makes a man a
135 slave, makes wit and honor sneak. My soul grew lean
and rusty for want of credit.

BLUNT 'Adsheartlikins, this I like well; it looks like my
lucky bargain! Oh, how I long for the approach of my
squire, that is to conduct me to her house again. Why,
140 here's two provided for!

FREDERICK By this light, y'are happy men.

BLUNT Fortune is pleased to smile on us, gentlemen, to
smile on us.

[*Enter* SANCHO *and pulls down* BLUNT *by the sleeve;
they go aside.*]

SANCHO Sir, my lady expects you. She has removed all
145 that might oppose your will and pleasure, and is impatient till you come.

BLUNT Sir, I'll attend you. —Oh the happiest rogue! I'll
take no leave, lest they either dog me or stay me.

[*Exit with* SANCHO.]

BELVILE But then the little gipsy is forgot?

150 WILLMORE A mischief on thee for putting her into my

---

4. A sweet wine from the Canary Islands.
5. A dry white wine from Spain and the Canary Islands.

thoughts! I had quite forgot her else, and this night's debauch had drunk her quite down.

HELLENA   Had it so, good captain!   [*Claps him on the back.*]

WILLMORE [*aside*]   Ha! I hope she did not hear me!

155 HELLENA   What, afraid of such a champion?

WILLMORE   Oh, you're a fine lady of your word, are you
not? To make a man languish a whole day—

HELLENA   In tedious search of me.

WILLMORE   Egad, child, thou'rt in the right. Hadst thou
160   seen what a melancholy dog I have been ever since I was
a lover, how I have walked the streets like a Capuchin,°   Franciscan monk
with my hands in my sleeves—faith, sweetheart, thou
wouldst pity me.

HELLENA [*aside*]   Now if I should be hanged I can't be
165   angry with him, he dissembles so heartily. —Alas, good
captain, what pains you have taken; now were I ungrateful not to reward so true a servant.

WILLMORE   Poor soul, that's kindly said; I see thou barest
a conscience. Come then, for a beginning show me thy
170   dear face.

HELLENA   I'm afraid, my small acquaintance, you have
been staying that swinging stomach you boasted of this
morning. I then remember my little collation° would   light meal
have gone down with you without the sauce of a hand
175   some face. Is your stomach so queasy now?

WILLMORE   Faith, long fasting, child, spoils a man's appetite.
Yet if you durst treat, I could so lay about me° still—   i.e., eat heartily

HELLENA   And would you fall to before a priest says grace?

WILLMORE   Oh fie, fie, what an old out-of-fashioned thing
180   hast thou named? Thou couldst not dash me more out of
countenance shouldst thou show me an ugly face.

> [*Whilst he is seemingly courting* HELLENA, *enter AN-*
> GELLICA, MORETTA, BISKEY, *and* SEBASTIAN, *all in*
> *masquerade.* ANGELLICA *sees* WILLMORE *and stares.*]

ANGELLICA   Heavens, 'tis he! And passionately fond to see
another woman!

MORETTA   What could you less expect from such a swag-
185   gerer?

ANGELLICA   Expect? As much as I paid him: a heart entire,
Which I had pride enough to think when'er I gave,
It would have raised the man above the vulgar,
Made him all soul, and that all soft and constant.

190 HELLENA   You see, captain, how willing I am to be friends
with you, till time and ill luck make us lovers; and ask
you the question first rather than put your modesty to
the blush by asking me. For alas, I know you captains
are such strict men, and such severe observers of your
195   vows to chastity, that 'twill be hard to prevail with your
tender conscience to marry a young willing maid.

WILLMORE   Do not abuse me, for fear I should take thee at thy word and marry thee indeed, which I'm sure will be revenge sufficient.

200 HELLENA   O' my conscience, that will be our destiny, because we are both of one humor: I am as inconstant as you, for I have considered, captain, that a handsome woman has a great deal to do whilst her face is good. For then is our harvesttime to gather friends, and should I in

205   these days of my youth catch a fit of foolish constancy, I were undone: 'tis loitering by daylight in our great journey. Therefore, I declare I'll allow but one year for love, one year for indifference, and one year for hate; and then go hang yourself, for I profess myself the gay, the kind, and

210   the inconstant. The devil's in't if this won't please you!

WILLMORE   Oh, most damnably. I have a heart with a hole quite through it too; no prison mine, to keep a mistress in.

ANGELLICA [aside]   Perjured man! How I believe thee now!

HELLENA   Well, I see our business as well as humors are

215   alike: yours to cozen as many maids as will trust you, and I as many men as have faith. See if I have not as desperate a lying look as you can have for the heart of you. [Pulls off her vizard; he starts.] How do you like it, captain?

WILLMORE   Like it! By heaven, I never saw so much

220   beauty! Oh, the charms of those sprightly black eyes! That strangely fair face, full of smiles and dimples! Those soft round melting cherry lips and small even white teeth! Not to be expressed, but silently adored! [She replaces her mask.] Oh, one look more, and strike

225   me dumb, or I shall repeat nothing else till I'm mad.

[He seems to court her to pull off her vizard; she refuses.]

ANGELLICA   I can endure no more. Nor is it fit to interrupt him, for if I do, my jealousy has so destroyed my reason I shall undo° him. Therefore I'll retire, and you, Sebastian   destroy [to one of her bravos], follow that woman and learn who

230   'tis; while you [to the other bravo] tell the fugitive I would speak to him instantly.   [Exit.]

[This while FLORINDA is talking to BELVILE, who stands sullenly; FREDERICK courting VALERIA.]

VALERIA [to BELVILE]   Prithee, dear stranger, be not so sullen, for though you have lost your love you see my friend frankly offers you hers to play with in the meantime.

235 BELVILE   Faith, madam, I am sorry I can't play at her game.

FREDERICK [to VALERIA]   Pray leave your intercession and mind your own affair. They'll better agree apart: he's a modest sigher in company, but alone no woman 'scapes him.

240 FLORINDA [aside]   Sure he does but rally.° Yet, if it should   banter be true? I'll tempt him farther. —Believe me, noble stranger, I'm no common mistress. And for a little proof

on't, wear this jewel. Nay, take it, sir, 'tis right, and bills
of exchange may sometimes miscarry.

245 BELVILE   Madam, why am I chose out of all mankind to be
the object of your bounty?

VALERIA   There's another civil question asked.

FREDERICK [aside]   Pox of's modesty; it spoils his own markets and hinders mine.

250 FLORINDA   Sir, from my window I have often seen you, and
women of my quality have so few opportunities for love
that we ought to lose none.

FREDERICK [to VALERIA]   Ay, this is something! Here's a
woman! When shall I be blest with so much kindness

255   from your fair mouth? —[Aside to BELVILE.] Take the
jewel, fool!

BELVILE   You tempt me strangely, madam, every way—

FLORINDA [aside]   So, if I find him false, my whole repose
is gone.

260 BELVILE   And but for a vow I've made to a very fair lady,
this goodness had subdued me.

FREDERICK [aside to BELVILE]   Pox on't, be kind, in pity to me
be kind. For I am to thrive here but as you treat her friend.

HELLENA   Tell me what you did in yonder house, and I'll

265   unmask.

WILLMORE   Yonder house? Oh, I went to a—to—why,
there's a friend of mine lives there.

HELLENA   What, a she or a he friend?

WILLMORE   A man, upon honor, a man. A she friend? No,

270   no, madam, you have done my business, I thank you.

HELLENA   And was't your man friend that had more darts
in's eyes than Cupid carries in's whole budget° of arrows?   quiver

WILLMORE   So—

HELLENA   "Ah, such a *bona roba!* To be in her arms is lying

275   *in fresco,* all perfumed air about me." Was this your man
friend too?

WILLMORE   So—

HELLENA   That gave you the he and the she gold, that
begets young pleasures?

280 WILLMORE   Well, well, madam, then you can see there are
ladies in the world that will not be cruel. There are,
madam, there are.

HELLENA   And there be men, too, as fine, wild, inconstant
fellows as yourself. There be, captain, there be, if you go

285   to that now. Therefore, I'm resolved—

WILLMORE   Oh!

HELLENA   To see your face no more—

WILLMORE   Oh!

HELLENA   Till tomorrow.

290 WILLMORE   Egad, you frighted me.

HELLENA   Nor then neither, unless you'll swear never to
see that lady more.

WILLMORE See her! Why, never to think of womankind again.

HELLENA Kneel, and swear.

> [*Kneels; she gives him her hand.*]

295 WILLMORE I do, never to think, to see, to love, nor lie, with any but thyself.

HELLENA Kiss the book.

WILLMORE Oh, most religiously. [*Kisses her hand.*]

HELLENA Now what a wicked creature am I, to damn a
300 proper fellow.

CALLIS [*to* FLORINDA] Madam, I'll stay no longer: 'tis e'en dark.

FLORINDA [*to* BELVILE] However, sir, I'll leave this with you, that when I'm gone you may repent the opportunity
305 you have lost by your modesty.

> [*Gives him the jewel, which is her picture, and exit. He gazes after her.*]

WILLMORE [*to* HELLENA] 'Twill be an age till tomorrow, and till then I will most impatiently expect you. Adieu, my dear pretty angel.

> [*Exeunt all the women.*]

BELVILE Ha! Florinda's picture! 'Twas she herself. What a
310 dull dog was I! I would have given the world for one minute's discourse with her.

FREDERICK This comes of your modesty. Ah, pox o' your vow; 'twas ten to one but we had lost the jewel by't.

BELVILE Willmore, the blessed'st opportunity lost! Florinda,
315 friends, Florinda!

WILLMORE Ah, rogue! Such black eyes! Such a face! Such a mouth! Such teeth! And so much wit!

BELVILE All, all, and a thousand charms besides.

WILLMORE Why, dost thou know her?

320 BEVILE Know her! Ay, ay, and a pox take me with all my heart for being so modest.

WILLMORE But hark'ee, friend of mine, are you my rival? And have I been only beating the bush all this while?

BELVILE I understand thee not. I'm mad! See here—

> [*Shows the picture.*]

325 WILLMORE Ha! Whose picture's this? 'Tis a fine wench!

FREDERICK The colonel's mistress, sir.

WILLMORE Oh, oh, here. [*Gives the picture back.*] I thought't had been another prize. Come, come, a bottle will set thee right again.

330 BELVILE I am content to try, and by that time 'twill be late enough for our design.

WILLMORE Agreed.

> Love does all day the soul's great empire keep,
> But wine at night lulls the soft god asleep.

> [*Exeunt.*]

3.2

[SCENE: LUCETTA's *house.*]

[*Enter* BLUNT *and* LUCETTA *with a light.*]

LUCETTA   Now we are safe and free: no fears of the coming home of my old jealous husband, which made me a
little thoughtful° when you came in first. But now love is   *preoccupied*
all the business of my soul.

5   BLUNT   I am transported!—[*Aside.*] Pox on't, that I had but
some fine things to say to her, such as lovers use. I was a
fool not to learn of° Fred a little by heart before I came.   *from*
Something I must say. —'Adsheartlikins, sweet soul, I
am not used to compliment, but I'm an honest gentle
10   man, and thy humble servant.

LUCETTA   I have nothing to pay for so great a favor, but
such a love as cannot but be great, since at first sight of
that sweet face and shape it made me your absolute
captive.

15   BLUNT [*aside*]   Kind heart, how prettily she talks! Egad, I'll
show her husband a Spanish trick: send him out of the
world and marry her; she's damnably in love with me,
and will ne'er mind settlements,[6] and so there's that
saved.

20   LUCETTA   Well, sir, I'll go and undress me, and be with you
instantly.

BLUNT   Make haste then, for 'adsheartlikins, dear soul,
thou canst not guess at the pain of a longing lover
when his joys are drawn within the compass of a few
25   minutes.

LUCETTA   You speak my sense, and I'll make haste to prove it.
[*Exit.*]

BLUNT   'Tis a rare girl, and this one night's enjoyment with
her will be worth all the days I ever passed in Essex.
Would she would go with me into England, though to
30   say truth, there's plenty of whores already. But a pox on
'em, they are such mercenary prodigal whores that they
want such a one as this, that's free and generous, to give
'em good examples. Why, what a house she has, how rich
and fine!

[*Enter* SANCHO.]

35   SANCHO   Sir, my lady has sent me to conduct you to her
chamber.

BLUNT   Sir, I shall be proud to follow.—[*Aside.*] Here's one
of her servants too; 'adsheartlikins, by this garb and gravity he might be a justice of peace in Essex, and is but a
40   pimp here.

[*Exeunt.*]

6. Property secured for a wife at marriage.

3.3

[SCENE: *The scene changes to a chamber with an alcove bed in't, a table, etc.;* LUCETTA *in bed.*]

> [*Enter* SANCHO *and* BLUNT, *who takes the candle of* SANCHO *at the door.*]

SANCHO   Sir, my commission reaches no farther.

BLUNT   Sir, I'll excuse your compliment.

> [*Exit* SANCHO.]

—What, in bed, my sweet mistress?

LUCETTA   You see, I still outdo you in kindness.

5 BLUNT   And thou shalt see what haste I'll make to quit scores. Oh, the luckiest rogue!

> [*He undresses himself.*]

LUCETTA   Should you be false or cruel now—

BLUNT   False! 'Adsheartlikins, what dost thou take me for, a Jew? An insensible heathen? A pox of thy old jealous

10 husband: an° he were dead, egad, sweet soul, it should be none of my fault if I did not marry thee.

LUCETTA   It never should be mine.

BLUNT   Good soul! I'm the fortunatest dog!

LUCETTA   Are you not undressed yet?

15 BLUNT   As much as my impatience will permit.

> [*Goes toward the bed in his shirt, drawers, etc.*]

LUCETTA   Hold, sir, put out the light; it may betray us else.

BLUNT   Anything; I need no other light but that of thine eyes.—[*Aside.*] 'Adsheartlikins, there I think I had it.

> [*Puts out the candle; the bed descends; he gropes about to find it.*]

Why, why, where am I got? What, not yet? Where are

20 you, sweetest? —Ah, the rogue's silent now. A pretty love-trick this; how she'll laugh at me anon! —You need not, my dear rogue, you need not! I'm all on fire already; come, come, now call me, in pity.—Sure I'm enchanted! I have been round the chamber, and can find neither

25 woman nor bed. I locked the door; I'm sure she cannot go that way, or if she could, the bed could not. — Enough, enough, my pretty wanton; do not carry the jest too far! [*Lights on a trap, and is let down.*] —Ha! Betrayed! Dogs! Rogues! Pimps! Help! Help!

> [*Enter* LUCETTA, PHILLIPO, *and* SANCHO *with a light.*]

30 PHILLIPO   Ha! Ha! Ha! He's dispatched finely.

LUCETTA   Now, sir, had I been coy, we had missed of this booty.

PHILLIPO   Nay, when I saw 'twas a substantial fool, I was mollified. But when you dote upon a serenading coxcomb, upon a face, fine clothes, and a lute, it makes me rage.

35 LUCETTA   You know I was never guilty of that folly, my dear Phillipo, but with yourself. But come, let's see what we have got by this.

if

PHILLIPO A rich coat; sword and hat; these breeches, too,
are well lined! See here, a gold watch! A purse—Ha!
40 Gold! At least two hundred pistoles! A bunch of diamond
rings, and one with the family arms! A gold box, with a
medal of his king, and his lady mother's picture! These
were sacred relics, believe me. See, the waistband of his
breeches have a mine of gold—old queen Bess's![7] We
45 have a quarrel to her ever since eighty-eight,[8] and may
therefore justify the theft: the Inquisition might have
committed it.
LUCETTA See, a bracelet of bowed gold! These his sisters
tied about his arm at parting. But well, for all this, I fear
50 his being a stranger may make a noise and hinder our
trade with them hereafter.
PHILLIPO That's our security: he is not only a stranger to
us, but to the country too. The common shore° into,   sewer
which he is descended thou know'st, conducts him into
55 another street, which this light will hinder him from ever
finding again. He knows neither your name, nor that of
the street where your house is; nay, nor the way to his
own lodgings.
LUCETTA And art thou not an unmerciful rogue, not to af-
60 ford him one night for all this? I should not have been
such a Jew.
PHILLIPO Blame me not, Lucetta, to keep as much of thee
as I can to myself. Come, that thought makes me wanton; let's to bed. —Sancho, lock up these.
65   This is the fleece which fools do bear,
              Designed for witty men to shear.
                              [*Exeunt.*]

3.4

[SCENE: *The scene changes, and discovers* BLUNT *creeping out of
a common shore; his face, etc., all dirty.*]

BLUNT [*climbing up*] Oh, Lord, I am got out at last, and,
which is a miracle, without a clue.[9] And now to damning
and cursing! But if that would ease me, where shall I
begin? With my fortune, myself, or the quean° that coz-   whore
5 ened me? What a dog was I to believe in woman! Oh, coxcomb! Ignorant conceited coxcomb! To fancy she could
be enamored with my person! At first sight enamored!
Oh, I'm a cursed puppy! 'Tis plain, fool was writ upon my
forehead! She perceived it; saw the Essex calf there. For
10 what allurements could there be in this countenance,
which I can endure because I'm acquainted with it.
Oh dull, silly dog, to be thus soothed into a cozening! Had

7. Queen Elizabeth I of England (r.
1558–1603).
8. That is, 1588, when the Spanish Armada
was defeated by the English navy.
9. A ball of thread used to guide one's way out
of a maze.

I been drunk, I might fondly have credited the young
quean; but as I was in my right wits to be thus cheated, con-
15 firms it: I am a dull believing English country fop. But my
comrades! Death and the devil, there's the worst of all! Then
a ballad will be sung tomorrow on the Prado,° to a lousy   *fashionable*
tune of the enchanted squire and the annihilated damsel.   *promenade*
But Fred—that rogue—and the colonel will abuse me be-
20 yond all Christian patience. Had she left me my clothes,
I have a bill of exchange at home would have saved my
credit. But now all hope is taken from me. Well, I'll
home, if I can find the way, with this consolation: that I
am not the first kind believing coxcomb; but there are,
25 gallants, many such good natures amongst ye.
    And though you've better arts to hide your follies,
    'Adsheartlikins, y'are all as arrant cullies.° [*Exit.*]   *dupes*

3.5

[SCENE: *The garden in the night.*]

  [*Enter* FLORINDA *in an undress, with a key and a
  little box.*]

FLORINDA Well, thus far I'm in my way to happiness. I
have got myself free from Callis; my brother too, I find
by yonder light, is got into his cabinet,° and thinks not of   *small private room*
me; I have by good fortune got the key of the garden back
5 door. I'll open it to prevent Belvile's knocking: a little
noise will now alarm my brother. Now am I as fearful as
a young thief. [*Unlocks the door.*] Hark! What noise is
that? Oh, 'twas the wind that played amongst the boughs.
Belvile stays long, methinks; it's time. Stay, for fear of a
10 surprise,° I'll hide these jewels in yonder jasmine.   *sudden attack*
  [*She goes to lay down the box.*]
  [*Enter* WILLMORE, *drunk.*]

WILLMORE What the devil is become of these fellows
Belvile and Frederick? They promised to stay at the next
corner for me, but who the devil knows the corner of a
full moon? Now, whereabouts am I? Ha, what have we
15 here? A garden! A very convenient place to sleep in. Ha!
What has God sent us here? A female! By this light, a
woman! I'm a dog if it be not a very wench!
FLORINDA He's come! Ha! Who's there?
WILLMORE Sweet soul, let me salute thy shoestring.
20 FLORINDA [*aside*] 'Tis not my Belvile. Good heavens, I know
him not!—Who are you, and from whence come you?
WILLMORE Prithee, prithee, child, not so many hard questions! Let it suffice I am here, child. Come, come kiss
me.

25   FLORINDA   Good gods! What luck is mine?

WILLMORE   Only good luck, child, parlous° good luck. Come   *extremely*
hither. —[*Aside.*] 'Tis a delicate shining wench. By this
hand, she's perfumed, and smells like any nosegay. —[*To*
FLORINDA.] Prithee, dear soul, let's not play the fool and

30   lose time—precious time. For as Gad shall save me, I'm as
honest a fellow as breathes, though I'm a little disguised°   *drunk*
at present. Come, I say. Why, thou mayst be free with me:
I'll be very secret. I'll not boast who 'twas obliged me, not
I; for hang me if I know thy name.

35   FLORINDA   Heavens! What a filthy beast is this!

WILLMORE   I am so, and thou ought'st the sooner to lie
with me for that reason. For look you, child, there will be
no sin in't, because 'twas neither designed nor premedi-
tated: 'tis pure accident on both sides. That's a certain

40   thing now. Indeed, should I make love to you, and you
vow fidelity, and swear and lie till you believed and
yielded—that were to make it wilful fornication, the crying sin of the nation. Thou art, therefore, as thou art a
good Christian, obliged in conscience to deny me noth-

45   ing. Now, come be kind without any more idle prating.

          [*He seizes her by the arm.*]

FLORINDA   Oh, I am ruined! Wicked man, unhand me!

WILLMORE   Wicked? Egad, child, a judge, were he young and
vigorous, and saw those eyes of thine, would know 'twas
they gave the first blow, the first provocation. Come, prithee

50   let's lose no time, I say. This is a fine convenient place.

FLORINDA   Sir, let me go, I conjure° you, or I'll call out.   *beseech*

WILLMORE   Ay, ay, you were best to call witness to see how
finely you treat me. Do!

FLORINDA   I'll cry murder, rape, or anything, if you do not

55   instantly let me go!

WILLMORE   A rape! Come, come, you lie, you baggage,° you   *whore*
lie. What! I'll warrant you would fain° have the world be-   *gladly*
lieve now that you are not so forward as I. No, not you.
Why at this time of night was your cobweb door set open,

60   dear spider, but to catch flies? Ha! Come, or I shall be
damnably angry. Why, what a coil° is here!   *fuss*

FLORINDA   Sir, can you think—

WILLMORE   That you would do't for nothing? Oh, oh, I
find what you would be at. Look here, here's a pistole for

65   you. Here's a work indeed! Here, take it, I say!

FLORINDA   For heaven's sake, sir, as you're a gentleman—

WILLMORE   So now, now, she would be wheedling me for
more! What, you will not take it then? You are resolved
you will not? Come, come, take it or I'll put it up again,

70   for look ye, I never give more. Why, how now, mistress,
are you so high i'th' mouth a pistole won't down with
you? Ha! Why, what a work's here! In good time! Come,

no struggling to be gone. But an° y'are good at a dumb   *if*
wrestle, I'm for ye. Look ye, I'm for ye.

[*She struggles with him.*]

[*Enter* BELVILE *and* FREDERICK.]

75 BELVILE   The door is open. A pox of this mad fellow! I'm
angry that we've lost him; I durst have sworn he had followed us.

FREDERICK   But you were so hasty, colonel, to be gone.

FLORINDA   Help! Help! Murder! Help! Oh, I am ruined!

80 BELVILE   Ha! Sure that's Florinda's voice! [*Comes up to
them.*] A man! —Villain, let go that lady!

[*A noise;* WILLMORE *turns and draws;* FREDERICK
interposes.]

FLORINDA   Belvile! Heavens! My brother too is coming,
and 'twill be impossible to escape. Belvile, I conjure you
to walk under my chamber window, from whence I'll give
85   you some instructions what to do. This rude man has
undone us.   [*Exit.*]

WILLMORE   Belvile!

[*Enter* PEDRO, STEPHANO, *and other servants, with lights.*]

PEDRO   I'm betrayed! Run, Stephano, and see if Florinda
be safe.

[*Exit* STEPHANO.]

[*They fight, and* PEDRO's *party beats 'em out.*]

90   —So, whoe'er they be, all is not well. I'll to Florinda's chamber.

[*Going out, meets* STEPHANO.]

STEPHANO   You need not, sir: the poor lady's fast asleep,
and thinks no harm. I would not awake her, sir, for fear
of frighting her with your danger.

PEDRO   I'm glad she's there. —Rascals, how came the gar-
95   den door open?

STEPHANO   That question comes too late, sir. Some of my
fellow servants masquerading, I'll warrant.

PEDRO   Masquerading! A lewd custom to debauch our
youth! There's something more in this than I imagine.

[*Exeunt.*]

3.6

[SCENE: *Scene changes to the street.*]

[*Enter* BELVILE *in rage,* FREDERICK *holding him,*
WILLMORE *melancholy.*]

WILLMORE   Why, how the devil should I know Florinda?

BELVILE   Ah, plague of your ignorance! If it had not been
Florinda, must you be a beast? A brute? A senseless swine?

WILLMORE   Well, sir, you see I am endued with patience: I
5   can bear. Though egad, y'are very free with me, methinks.
I was in good hopes the quarrel would have been on my
side, for so uncivilly interrupting me.

BELVILE   Peace, brute, whilst thou'rt safe. Oh, I'm distracted!

WILLMORE   Nay, nay, I'm an unlucky dog, that's certain.

10   BELVILE   Ah, curse upon the star that ruled my birth, or whatsoever other influence that makes me still so wretched.

WILLMORE   Thou break'st my heart with these complaints. There is no star in fault, no influence but sack, the

15   cursed sack I drunk.

FREDERICK   Why, how the devil came you so drunk?

WILLMORE   Why, how the devil came you so sober?

BELVILE   A curse upon his thin skull, he was always beforehand that way.

20   FREDERICK   Prithee, dear colonel, forgive him; he's sorry for his fault.

BELVILE   He's always so after he has done a mischief. A plague on all such brutes!

WILLMORE   By this light, I took her for an errant harlot.

25   BELVILE   Damn your debauched opinion! Tell me, sot, hadst thou so much sense and light about thee to distinguish her woman, and couldst not see something about her face and person to strike an awful reverence into thy soul?

WILLMORE   Faith no, I considered her as mere a woman as

30   I could wish.

BELVILE   'Sdeath, I have no patience. Draw, or I'll kill you!

WILLMORE   Let that alone till tomorrow, and if I set not all right again, use your pleasure.

BELVILE   Tomorrow! Damn it,

35   The spiteful light will lead me to no happiness.
Tomorrow is Antonio's, and perhaps
Guides him to my undoing. Oh, that I could meet
This rival, this powerful fortunate!

WILLMORE   What then?

40   BELVILE   Let thy own reason, or my rage, instruct thee.

WILLMORE   I shall be finely informed then, no doubt. Hear me, colonel, hear me; show me the man and I'll do his business.

BELVILE   I know him no more than thou, or if I did I

45   should not need thy aid.

WILLMORE   This you say is Angellica's house; I promised the kind baggage to lie with her tonight.

            [*Offers to go in.*]
            [*Enter* ANTONIO *and* DIEGO. ANTONIO *knocks on the hilt of's sword.*]

ANTONIO   You paid the thousand crowns I directed?

DIEGO   To the lady's old woman, sir, I did.

50   WILLMORE   Who the devil have we here?

BELVILE   I'll now plant myself under Florinda's window, and if I find no comfort there, I'll die.

            [*Exeunt* BELVILE *and* FREDERICK.]

      [*Enter* MORETTA.]

MORETTA   Page?

DIEGO   Here's my lord.

55 WILLMORE   How is this? A picaroon° going to board my   *pirate*
    frigate?— Here's one chase gun[1] for you!

           [*Drawing his sword, justles* ANTONIO, *who turns and
    draws. They fight;* ANTONIO *falls.*]

MORETTA   Oh, bless us! We're all undone!

           [*Runs in and shuts the door.*]

DIEGO   Help! Murder!

           [BELVILE *returns at the noise of fighting.*]

BELVILE   Ha! The mad rogue's engaged in some unlucky
60 adventure again.

           [*Enter two or three* MASQUERADERS.]

MASQUERADER   Ha! A man killed!

WILLMORE   How, a man killed? Then I'll go home to sleep.

           [*Puts up° and reels out. Exeunt* MASQUERADERS   *Sheathes his sword*
    another way.]

BELVILE   Who should it be? Pray heaven the rogue is safe,
    for all my quarrel to him.

           [*As* BELVILE *is groping about, enter an* OFFICER *and
    six* SOLDIERS.]

65 SOLDIER   Who's there?

OFFICER   So, here's one dispatched. Secure the murderer.

BELVILE   Do not mistake my charity for murder! I came to
    his assistance!

           [*Soldiers seize on* BELVILE.]

OFFICER   That shall be tried, sir. St. Jago![2] Swords drawn
70 in the Carnival time!

           [*Goes to* ANTONIO.]

ANTONIO   Thy hand, prithee.

OFFICER   Ha! Don Antonio! Look well to the villain there.
    —How is it, sir?

ANTONIO   I'm hurt.

75 BELVILE   Has my humanity made me a criminal?

OFFICER   Away with him!

BELVILE   What a curst chance is this!

                             [*Exeunt soldiers with* BELVILE.]

ANTONIO   [*aside*]   This is the man that has set upon me
    twice. —[*To the officer.*] Carry him to my apartment till
80 you have farther orders from me.

                             [*Exit* ANTONIO, *led.*]

---

1. A cannon mounted at a port in the bow or
stern of a ship.
2. St. James, revered in Spain (where, accord-

ing to tradition, he preached and his body
was brought).

4.1

[SCENE: *A fine room.*]

[*Discovers* BELVILE *as by dark alone.*]

BELVILE   When shall I be weary of railing on fortune, who is resolved never to turn with smiles upon me? Two such defeats in one night none but the devil and that mad rogue could have contrived to have plagued me with. I
5   am here a prisoner. But where, heaven knows. And if there be murder done, I can soon decide the fate of a stranger in a nation without mercy. Yet this is nothing to the torture my soul bows with when I think of losing my fair, my dear Florinda. Hark, my door opens. A light! A
10   man, and seems of quality. Armed, too! Now shall I die like a dog, without defense.

[*Enter* ANTONIO *in a nightgown, with a light; his arm in a scarf, and a sword under his arm. He sets the candle on the table.*]

ANTONIO   Sir, I come to know what injuries I have done you, that could provoke you to so mean an action as to attack me basely without allowing time for my defense?
15   BELVILE   Sir, for a man in my circumstances to plead innocence would look like fear. But view me well, and you will find no marks of coward on me, nor anything that betrays that brutality you accuse me with.

ANTONIO   In vain, sir, you impose upon my sense. You are
20   not only he who drew on me last night, but yesterday before the same house, that of Angellica. Yet there is something in your face and mien that makes me wish I were mistaken.

BELVILE   I own I fought today in the defense of a friend of
25   mine with whom you, if you're the same, and your party were first engaged. Perhaps you think this crime enough to kill me, but if you do, I cannot fear you'll do it basely.

ANTONIO   No sir, I'll make you fit for a defense with this.

[*Gives him the sword.*]

BELVILE   This gallantry surprises me, nor know I how to
30   use this present, sir, against a man so brave.

ANTONIO   You shall not need. For know, I come to snatch you from a danger that is decreed against you: perhaps your life, or long imprisonment. And 'twas with so much courage you offended, I cannot see you punished.
35   BELVILE   How shall I pay this generosity?

ANTONIO   It had been safer to have killed another than have attempted me. To show your danger, sir, I'll let you know my quality: and 'tis the Viceroy's son whom you have wounded.
40   BELVILE   The Viceroy's son! —[*Aside.*] Death and confusion! Was this plague reserved to complete all the rest? Obliged by him, the man of all the world I would destroy!

ANTONIO   You seem disordered, sir.

BELVILE   Yes, trust me, I am, and 'tis with pain that man
45   receives such bounties who wants° the power to pay 'em   *lacks*
back again.

ANTONIO   To gallant spirits 'tis indeed uneasy, but you may
quickly overpay me, sir.

BELVILE [*aside*]   Then I am well. Kind heaven, but set us
50   even, that I may fight with him and keep my honor safe.
—Oh, I'm impatient, sir, to be discounting° the mighty   *reducing*
debt I owe you. Command me quickly.

ANTONIO   I have a quarrel with a rival, sir, about the maid
we love.

55   BELVILE [*aside*]   Death, 'tis Florinda he means! That
thought destroys my reason, and I shall kill him.

ANTONIO   My rival, sir, is one has all the virtues man can
boast of—

BELVILE [*aside*]   Death, who should this be?

60   ANTONIO   He challenged me to meet him on the Molo as
soon as day appeared, but last night's quarrel has made
my arm unfit to guide a sword.

BELVILE   I apprehend you, sir. You'd have me kill the man
that lays a claim to the maid you speak of. I'll do't. I'll fly
65   to do't!

ANTONIO   Sir, do you know her?

BELVILE   No, sir, but 'tis enough she is admired by you.

ANTONIO   Sir, I shall rob you of the glory on't, for you must
fight under my name and dress.

70   BELVILE   That opinion must be strangely obliging that
makes you think I can personate the brave Antonio,
whom I can but strive to imitate.

ANTONIO   You say too much to my advantage. Come, sir,
the day appears that calls you forth. Within, sir, is the
75   habit.   [*Exit* ANTONIO.]

BELVILE   Fantastic fortune, thou deceitful light,
That cheats the wearied traveler by night,
Though on a precipice each step you tread,
I am resolved to follow where you lead.   [*Exit.*]

4.2

[SCENE: *The Molo.*]

[*Enter* FLORINDA *and* CALLIS *in masks, with*
STEPHANO.]

FLORINDA [*aside*]   I'm dying with my fears: Belvile's not
coming as I expected under my window makes me
believe that all those fears are true.—Canst thou not tell
with whom my brother fights?

5   STEPHANO   No, madam, they were both in masquerade. I
was by when they challenged one another, and they
had decided the quarrel then, but were prevented by

some cavaliers; which made 'em put it off till now. But I
am sure 'tis about you they fight.

10 FLORINDA [aside] Nay, then, 'tis with Belvile, for what
other lover have I that dares fight for me except Antonio,
and he is too much in favor with my brother. If it be he,
for whom shall I direct my prayers to heaven?

STEPHANO Madam, I must leave you, for if my master see
15 me, I shall be hanged for being your conductor. I escaped narrowly for the excuse I made for you last night
i'th' garden.

FLORINDA And I'll reward thee for't. Prithee, no more.

[Exit STEPHANO.]

[Enter DON PEDRO in his masking habit.]

PEDRO Antonio's late today; the place will fill, and we may
20 be prevented.

[Walks about.]

FLORINDA [aside] Antonio? Sure I heard amiss.

PEDRO But who will not excuse a happy lover
When soft fair arms confine the yielding neck,
And the kind whisper languishingly breathes
25 "Must you be gone so soon?"
Sure I had dwelt forever on her bosom—
But stay, he's here.

[Enter BELVILE dressed in Antonio's clothes.]

FLORINDA [aside] 'Tis not Belvile; half my fears are vanished.

30 PEDRO Antonio!

BELVILE [aside] This must be he.—You're early, sir; I do   am not accustomed
not use° to be outdone this way.

PEDRO The wretched, sir, are watchful, and 'tis enough
you've the advantage of me in Angellica.

35 BELVILE [aside] Angellica! Or° I've mistook my man, or   Either
else Antonio! Can he forget his interest in Florinda and
fight for common prize?

PEDRO Come, sir, you know our terms.

BELVILE [aside] By heaven, not I. —No talking; I am
40 ready, sir.

[Offers to fight; FLORINDA runs in.]

FLORINDA [to BELVILE] Oh, hold! Whoe'er you be, I do
conjure you hold! If you strike here, I die!

PEDRO Florinda!

BELVILE Florinda imploring for my rival!

45 PEDRO Away; this kindness is unseasonable.

[Puts her by; they fight; she runs in just as BELVILE
disarms PEDRO.]

FLORINDA Who are you, sir, that dares deny my prayers?

BELVILE Thy prayers destroy him; if thou wouldst preserve
him, do that thou'rt unacquainted with, and curse him.

[She holds him.]

FLORINDA   By all you hold most dear, by her you love,
50   I do conjure you, touch him not.

BELVILE   By her I love?
See, I obey, and at your feet resign
The useless trophy of my victory.
[*Lays his sword at her feet.*]

PEDRO   Antonio, you've done enough to prove you love
55   Florinda.

BELVILE   Love Florinda! Does heaven love adoration, prayer,
or penitence? Love her? Here, sir, your sword again.
[*Snatches up the sword and gives it to him.*]
Upon this truth I'll fight my life away.

PEDRO   No, you've redeemed my sister, and my friend-
60   ship.
[*He gives him* FLORINDA, *and pulls off his vizard to show his face, and puts it on again.*]

BELVILE   Don Pedro!

PEDRO   Can you resign your claims to other women, and
give your heart entirely to Florinda?

BELVILE   Entire, as dying saints' confessions are!
65   I can delay my happiness no longer:
This minute let me make Florinda mine.

PEDRO   This minute let it be. No time so proper: this night
my father will arrive from Rome, and possibly may hinder what we purpose.

70   FLORINDA   Oh, heavens! This minute?
[*Enter masqueraders and pass over.*]

BELVILE   Oh, do not ruin me!

PEDRO   The place begins to fill, and that we may not be
observed, do you walk off to St. Peter's church, where I
will meet you and conclude your happiness.

75   BELVILE   I'll meet you there. —[*Aside.*] If there be no more
saints' churches in Naples.

FLORINDA   Oh, stay, sir, and recall your hasty doom!
Alas, I have not yet prepared my heart
To entertain so strange a guest.

80   PEDRO   Away; this silly modesty is assumed too late.

BELVILE   Heaven, madam, what do you do?

FLORINDA   Do? Despise the man that lays a tyrant's claim
To what he ought to conquer by submission.

BELVILE   You do not know me. Move a little this way.
[*Draws her aside.*]

85   FLORINDA   Yes, you may force me even to the altar,
But not the holy man that offers° there   *worships*
Shall force me to be thine.
[PEDRO *talks to* CALLIS *this while.*]

BELVILE   Oh, do not lose so blest an opportunity!
[*Pulls off his vizard.*]

See, 'tis your Belvile, not Antonio,
90 Whom your mistaken scorn and anger ruins.

FLORINDA   Belvile!
Where was my soul it could not meet thy voice,
And take this knowledge in.

[*As they are talking, enter* WILLMORE, *finely dressed,
and* FREDERICK.]

WILLMORE   No intelligence? No news of Belvile yet? Well, I
95 am the most unlucky rascal in nature. Ha! Am I deceived,
or is it he? Look, Fred! 'Tis he, my dear Belvile!

[*Runs and embraces him;* BELVILE'S *vizard falls out
on's hand.*]

BELVILE   Hell and confusion seize thee!

PEDRO   Ha! Belvile! I beg your pardon, sir.

[*Takes* FLORINDA *from him.*]

BELVILE   Nay, touch her not. She's mine by conquest, sir;
100 I won her by my sword.

WILLMORE   Didst thou so? And egad, child, we'll keep her
by the sword.

[*Draws on* PEDRO; BELVILE *goes between.*]

BELVILE   Stand off!
Thou'rt so profanely lewd, so curst by heaven,
105 All quarrels thou espousest must be fatal.

WILLMORE   Nay, an° you be so hot, my valor's coy,   *if*
And shall be courted when you want it next.

[*Puts up his sword.*]

BELVILE [*to* PEDRO]   You know I ought to claim a victor's right,
But you're the brother to divine Florinda,
110 To whom I'm such a slave. To purchase her
I durst not hurt the man she holds so dear.

PEDRO   'Twas by Antonio's, not by Belvile's sword
This question should have been decided, sir.
I must confess much to your bravery's due,
115 Both now and when I met you last in arms;
But I am nicely punctual° in my word,   *punctilious*
As men of honor ought, and beg your pardon:
For this mistake another time shall clear.

[*Aside to* FLORINDA *as they are going out*]

—This was some plot between you and Belvile,
120 But I'll prevent you.

[*Exeunt* PEDRO *and* FLORINDA.]

[BELVILE *looks after her and begins to walk up and
down in rage.*]

WILLMORE   Do not be modest now and lose the woman.
But if we shall fetch her back so—

BELVILE   Do not speak to me!

WILLMORE   Not speak to you? Egad, I'll speak to you, and
125 will be answered, too.

BELVILE Will you, sir?

WILLMORE I know I've done some mischief, but I'm so
dull a puppy that I'm the son of a whore if I know how or
where. Prithee inform my understanding.

130 BELVILE Leave me, I say, and leave me instantly!

WILLMORE I will not leave you in this humor, nor till I
know my crime.

BELVILE Death, I'll tell you, sir—

[Draws and runs at WILLMORE; he runs out, BELVILE
after him, FREDERICK interposes.]

[Enter ANGELLICA, MORETTA, and SEBASTIAN.]

ANGELLICA Ha! Sebastian, is that not Willmore? Haste!
135 haste and bring him back.

[Exit SEBASTIAN.]

FREDERICK [aside] The colonel's mad: I never saw him
thus before. I'll after 'em lest he do some mischief, for I
am sure Willmore will not draw on him.   [Exit.]

ANGELLICA I am all rage! My first desires defeated!
140 For one for aught he knows that has no
Other merit than her quality,
Her being Don Pedro's sister. He loves her!
I know 'tis so. Dull, dull, insensible,
He will not see me now, though oft invited,
145 And broke his word last night. False perjured man!
He that but yesterday fought for my favors,
And would have made his life a sacrifice
To've gained one night with me,
Must now be hired and courted to my arms.

150 MORETTA I told you what would come on't, but Moretta's
an old doting fool. Why did you give him five hundred
crowns, but to set himself out for other lovers? You should
have kept him poor if you had meant to have had any
good from him.

155 ANGELLICA Oh, name not such mean trifles! Had I given
him all
My youth has earned from sin,
I had not lost a thought nor sigh upon't.
But I have given him my eternal rest,
160 My whole repose, my future joys, my heart!
My virgin heart, Moretta! Oh, 'tis gone!

MORETTA Curse on him, here he comes. How fine she has
made him, too.

[Enter WILLMORE and SEBASTIAN; ANGELLICA turns
and walks away.]

WILLMORE How now, turned shadow?
165 Fly when I pursue, and follow when I fly?
[Sings.]

Stay, gentle shadow of my dove,
And tell me ere I go,

Whether the substance may not prove
A fleeting thing like you.

[*As she turns she looks on him.*]

170   There's a soft kind look remaining yet.

ANGELLICA   Well, sir, you may be gay: all happiness, all
joys pursue you still. Fortune's your slave, and gives you
every hour choice of new hearts and beauties, till you are
cloyed with the repeated bliss which others vainly lan-
175   guish for. But know, false man, that I shall be revenged.

[*Turns away in rage.*]

WILLMORE   So, gad, there are of those faint-hearted lovers,
whom such a sharp lesson next their hearts would make as
impotent as fourscore.° Pox o' this whining; my business   *as an 80-year-old man*
is to laugh and love. A pox on't, I hate your sullen lover:
180   a man shall lose as much time to put you in humor now
as would serve to gain a new woman.

ANGELLICA   I scorn to cool that fire I cannot raise,
Or do the drudgery of your virtuous mistress.

WILLMORE   A virtuous mistress? Death, what a thing thou
185   hast found out for me! Why, what the devil should I do
with a virtuous woman, a sort of ill-natured creatures that
take a pride to torment a lover. Virtue is but an infirmity in
woman, a disease that renders even the handsome ungrateful; whilst the ill-favored, for want of solicitations and ad-
190   dress, only fancy themselves so. I have lain with a woman
of quality who has all the while been railing at whores.

ANGELLICA   I will not answer for your mistress's virtue,
Though she be young enough to know no guilt;
And I could wish you would persuade my heart
195   'Twas the two hundred thousand crowns you courted.

WILLMORE   Two hundred thousand crowns! What story's
this? What trick? What woman, ha?

ANGELLICA   How strange you make it. Have you forgot the
creature you entertained on the Piazzo last night?

200 WILLMORE [*aside*]   Ha! My gipsy worth two hundred thousand crowns! Oh, how I long to be with her! Pox, I knew
she was of quality.

ANGELLICA   False man! I see my ruin in thy face.
How many vows you breathed upon my bosom
205   Never to be unjust. Have you forgot so soon?

WILLMORE   Faith, no; I was just coming to repeat 'em. But
here's a humor indeed would make a man a saint. —
[*Aside.*] Would she would be angry enough to leave me,
and command me not to wait on her.

[*Enter* HELLENA *dressed in man's clothes.*]

210 HELLENA   This must be Angellica: I know it by her mump-
ing° matron here. Ay, ay, 'tis she. My mad captain's with   *grimacing*
her, too, for all his swearing. How this unconstant humor
makes me love him! —Pray, good grave gentlewoman, is
not this Angellica?

215 MORETTA   My too young sir, it is. —[*Aside.*] I hope 'tis one
from Don Antonio.

> [*Goes to* ANGELLICA.]

HELLENA [*aside*]   Well, something I'll do to vex him for this.

ANGELLICA   I will not speak with him. Am I in humor to
receive a lover?

220 WILLMORE   Not speak with him? Why, I'll be gone, and
wait your idler minutes. Can I show less obedience to
the thing I love so fondly?

> [*Offers to go.*]

ANGELLICA   A fine excuse this! Stay—

WILLMORE   And hinder your advantage? Should I repay
225 your bounties so ungratefully?

ANGELLICA [*to* HELLENA]   Come hither, boy. —[*To* WILLMORE.]
That I may let you see
How much above the advantages you name
I prize one minute's joy with you.

WILLMORE [*impatient to be gone*]   Oh, you destroy me
230 with this endearment.—[*Aside.*] Death, how shall I get
away?—Madam, 'twill not be fit I should be seen with
you. Besides, it will not be convenient. And I've a friend—
that's dangerously sick.

ANGELLICA   I see you're impatient. Yet you shall stay.

235 WILLMORE [*aside*]   And miss my assignation with my
gipsy.

> [*Walks about impatiently;* MORETTA *brings* HELLENA,
> *who addresses herself to* ANGELLICA.]

HELLENA   Madam,
You'll hardly pardon my intrusion
When you shall know my business,
240 And I'm too young to tell my tale with art;
But there must be a wondrous store of goodness
Where so much beauty dwells.

ANGELLICA   A pretty advocate, whoever sent thee.
Prithee proceed.

> [*To* WILLMORE, *who is stealing off.*]

—Nay, sir, you shall not go.

245 WILLMORE [*aside*]   Then I shall lose my dear gipsy forever.
Pox on't, she stays me out of spite.

HELLENA   I am related to a lady, madam,
Young, rich, and nobly born, but has the fate
To be in love with a young English gentleman.
250 Strangely she loves him, at first sight she loved him,
But did adore him when she heard him speak;
For he, she said, had charms in every word
That failed not to surprise, to wound and conquer.

WILLMORE [*aside*]   Ha! Egad, I hope this concerns me.

255 ANGELLICA [*aside*]   'Tis my false man he means. Would he were gone:
This praise will raise his pride, and ruin me.

[*To* WILLMORE.] —Well,
Since you are so impatient to be gone,
I will release you, sir.

WILLMORE [*aside*]   Nay, then I'm sure 'twas me he spoke
260   of: this cannot be the effects of kindness in her. —No,
Madam, I've considered better on't, and will not give you
cause of jealousy.

ANGELLICA   But sir, I've business that—

WILLMORE   This shall not do; I know 'tis but to try me.

265 ANGELLICA   Well, to your story, boy. —[*Aside*]. Though
'twill undo me.

HELLENA   With this addition to his other beauties,
He won her unresisting tender heart.
He vowed, and sighed, and swore he loved her dearly;
270   And she believed the cunning flatterer,
And thought herself the happiest maid alive.
Today was the appointed time by both
To consummate their bliss:
The virgin, altar, and the priest were dressed;
275   And whilst she languished for th'expected bridegroom,
She heard he paid his broken vows to you.

WILLMORE [*aside*]   So, this is some dear rogue that's in
love with me, and this way lets me know it. Or, if it be
not me, she means someone whose place I may
280   supply.

ANGELLICA   Now I perceive
The cause of thy impatience to be gone,
And all the business of this glorious dress.

WILLMORE   Damn the young prater; I know not what he
285   means.

HELLENA   Madam,
In your fair eyes I read too much concern
To tell my farther business.

ANGELLICA   Prithee, sweet youth, talk on: thou mayst perhaps
290   Raise here a storm that may undo my passion,
And then I'll grant thee anything.

HELLENA   Madam, 'tis to entreat you (oh unreasonable)
You would not see this stranger.
For if you do, she vows you are undone;
295   Though nature never made a man so excellent,
And sure he 'ad been a god, but for inconstancy.

WILLMORE [*aside*]   Ah, rogue, how finely he's instructed!
'Tis plain, some woman that has seen me *en passant.*°   in passing (French)

ANGELLICA   Oh, I shall burst with jealousy! Do you know
300   the man you speak of?

HELLENA   Yes, madam, he used to be in buff and scarlet.

ANGELLICA [*to* WILLMORE]   Thou false as hell, what canst
thou say to this?

WILLMORE   By heaven—

305 ANGELLICA   Hold, do not damn thyself—

HELLENA   Nor hope to be believed.

    [*He walks about; they follow.*]

ANGELLICA   Oh perjured man!

    Is't thus you pay my generous passion back?

HELLENA   Why would you, sir, abuse my lady's faith?

310 ANGELLICA   And use me so unhumanely.

HELLENA   A maid so young, so innocent—

WILLMORE   Ah, young devil!

ANGELLICA   Dost thou not know thy life is in my power?

HELLENA   Or think my lady cannot be revenged?

315 WILLMORE   [*aside*]   So, so, the storm comes finely on.

ANGELLICA   Now thou art silent: guilt has struck thee dumb.

    Oh, hadst thou still been so, I'd lived in safety.

       [*She turns away and weeps.*]

WILLMORE   [*aside to* HELLENA]   Sweetheart, the lady's name
    and house—quickly! I'm impatient to be with her.

       [*Looks toward* ANGELLICA *to watch her turning, and*
       as she comes towards them he meets her.]

320 HELLENA   [*aside*]   So, now is he for another woman.

WILLMORE   The impudent'st young thing in nature: I can-
    not persuade him out of his error, madam.

ANGELLICA   I know he's in the right; yet thou'st a tongue
    That would persuade him to deny his faith.

       [*In rage walks away.*]

325 WILLMORE   [*said softly to* HELLENA]   Her name, her name,
    dear boy!

HELLENA   Have you forgot it, sir?

WILLMORE   [*aside*]   Oh, I perceive he's not to know I am a
    stranger to his lady. —Yes, yes, I do know, but I have forgot
330   the—[ANGELLICA *turns.*] —By heaven, such early confi-
    dence I never saw.

ANGELLICA   Did I not charge you with this mistress, sir?
    Which you denied, though I beheld your perjury.
    This little generosity of thine has rendered back my
335   heart.   [*Walks away.*]

WILLMORE   [*to* HELLENA]   So, you have made sweet work
    here, my little mischief. Look your lady be kind and
    good-natured now, or I shall have but a cursed bargain
    on't. [ANGELLICA *turns toward them.*] — The rogue's bred
340   up to mischief; art thou so great a fool to credit him?

ANGELLICA   Yes, I do, and you in vain impose upon me.
    Come hither, boy. Is not this he you spake of?

HELLENA   I think it is. I cannot swear, but I vow he has
    just such another lying lover's look.

       [HELLENA *looks in his face; he gazes on her.*]

345 WILLMORE   [*aside*]   Ha! Do I not know that face? By
    heaven, my little gipsy! What a dull dog was I: had I but
    looked that way I'd known her. Are all my hopes of a new

woman banished?—Egad, if I do not fit° thee for this,   *punish*
hang me. —[*To* ANGELLICA.] Madam, I have found out
350 the plot.

HELLENA [*aside*]   Oh lord, what does he say? Am I discovered now?

WILLMORE   Do you see this young spark here?

HELLENA [*aside*]   He'll tell her who I am.

355 WILLMORE   Who do you think this is?

HELLENA [*aside*]   Ay, ay, he does know me. —Nay, dear
captain, I am undone if you discover me.

WILLMORE   Nay, nay, no cogging°; she shall know what a   *deceit; wheedling*
precious mistress I have.

360 HELLENA   Will you be such a devil?

WILLMORE   Nay, nay, I'll teach you to spoil sport you will
not make. — This small ambassador comes not from a
person of quality, as you imagine and he says, but from a
very errant° gipsy: the talking'st, prating'st, canting'st   *good-for-nothing*
365 little animal thou ever saw'st.

ANGELLICA   What news you tell me, that's the thing I
mean.

HELLENA [*aside*]   Would I were well off the place! If ever I
go a-captain-hunting again—

370 WILLMORE   Mean that thing? That gipsy thing? Thou
mayst as well be jealous of thy monkey or parrot as of
her. A German motion° were worth a dozen of her, and   *puppet*
a dream were a better enjoyment—a creature of a constitution fitter for heaven than man.

375 HELLENA [*aside*]   Though I'm sure he lies, yet this vexes me.

ANGELLICA   You are mistaken: she's a Spanish woman
made up of no such dull materials.

WILLMORE   Materials? Egad, an she be made of any that
will either dispense or admit of love, I'll be bound to con-
380 tinence.

HELLENA [*aside to him*]   Unreasonable man, do you
think so?

WILLMORE   You may return, my little brazen head, and tell
your lady, that till she be handsome enough to be
385 beloved, or I dull enough to be religious, there will be
small hopes of me.

ANGELLICA   Did you not promise, then, to marry her?

WILLMORE   Not I, by heaven.

ANGELLICA   You cannot undeceive my fears and torments,
390 till you have vowed you will not marry her.

HELLENA [*aside*]   If he swears that, he'll be revenged on
me indeed for all my rogueries.

ANGELLICA   I know what arguments you'll bring against
me: fortune and honor.

395 WILLMORE   Honor! I tell you, I hate it in your sex; and those
that fancy themselves possessed of that foppery are
the most impertinently troublesome of all womankind,

and will transgress nine commandments to keep one.[3]
And to satisfy your jealousy, I swear—

400 HELLENA [*aside to him*]   Oh, no swearing, dear captain.

WILLMORE   If it were possible I should ever be inclined to
marry, it should be some kind young sinner: one that has
generosity enough to give a favor handsomely to one that
can ask it discreetly, one that has wit enough to manage
405 an intrigue of love. Oh, how civil such a wench is to a
man that does her the honor to marry her.

ANGELLICA   By heaven, there's no faith in anything he says.

[*Enter* SEBASTIAN.]

SEBASTIAN   Madam, Don Antonio—

ANGELLICA   Come hither.

410 HELLENA [*aside*]   Ha! Antonio! He may be coming hither,
and he'll certainly discover me. I'll therefore retire without a ceremony.   [*Exit* HELLENA.]

ANGELLICA   I'll see him. Get my coach ready.

SEBASTIAN   It waits you, madam.

415 WILLMORE [*aside*]   This is lucky. —What, madam, now
I may be gone and leave you to the enjoyment of my
rival?

ANGELLICA   Dull man, that canst not see how ill, how poor,
That false dissimulation looks. Be gone,
420 And never let me see thy cozening face again,
Lest I relapse and kill thee.

WILLMORE   Yes, you can spare me now. Farewell, till you're
in better humor. —[*Aside*.] I'm glad of this release. Now
for my gipsy:
425 For though to worse we change, yet still we find
New joys, new charms, in a new miss that's kind.

[*Exit* WILLMORE.]

ANGELLICA   He's gone, and in this ague of my soul
The shivering fit returns.
Oh, with what willing haste he took his leave,
430 As if the longed-for minute were arrived
Of some blest assignation.
In vain I have consulted all my charms,
In vain this beauty prized, in vain believed
My eyes could kindle any lasting fires;
435 I had forgot my name, my infamy,
And the reproach that honor lays on those
That dare pretend a sober passion here.
Nice° reputation, though it leave behind   Strict in conduct
More virtues than inhabit where that dwells,
440 Yet that once gone, those virtues shine no more.
Then since I am not fit to be beloved,

---

3. That is, the commandment forbidding adultery (Exodus 20.14; Deuteronomy 5.18).

I am resolved to think on a revenge
On him that soothed° me thus to my undoing.   *flattered*

[*Exeunt.*]

4.3

[SCENE: *A street.*]

[*Enter* FLORINDA *and* VALERIA *in habits different
from what they have been seen in.*]

FLORINDA   We're happily escaped, and yet I tremble still.

VALERIA   A lover, and fear? Why, I am but half an one, and
yet I have courage for any attempt. Would Hellena were
here: I would fain have had her as deep in this mischief
5   as we; she'll fare but ill else, I doubt.

FLORINDA   She pretended a visit to the Augustine nuns; but
I believe some other design carried her out; pray heaven
we light on her. Prithee, what didst do with Callis?

VALERIA   When I saw no reason would do good on her, I
10   followed her into the wardrobe,° and as she was looking   *dressing room*
for something in a great chest, I toppled her in by the
heels, snatched the key of the apartment where you were
confined, locked her in, and left her bawling for help.

FLORINDA   'Tis well you resolve to follow my fortunes, for
15   thou darest never appear at home again after such an
action.

VALERIA   That's according as the young stranger and I
shall agree. But to our business. I delivered your note to
Belvile when I got out under pretense of going to Mass. I
20   found him at his lodging, and believe me it came season-
ably, for never was man in so desperate a condition. I told
him of your resolution of making your escape today if your
brother would be absent long enough to permit you; if
not, to die rather than be Antonio's.

25   FLORINDA   Thou should'st have told him I was confined to
my chamber upon my brother's suspicion that the business on the Molo was a plot laid between him and I.

VALERIA   I said all this, and told him your brother was now
gone to his devotion; and he resolves to visit every
30   church till he find him, and not only undeceive him in
that, but caress him so as shall delay his return home.

FLORINDA   Oh heavens! He's here, and Belvile with him,
too.

[*They put on their vizards.*]

[*Enter* DON PEDRO, BELVILE, WILLMORE; BELVILE *and*
DON PEDRO *seeming in serious discourse.*]

VALERIA   Walk boldly by them, and I'll come at a distance,
35   lest he suspect us.

[*She walks by them and looks back on them.*]

WILLMORE   Ha! A woman, and of excellent mien!

PEDRO   She throws a kind look back on you.

WILLMORE   Death, 'tis a likely wench, and that kind look
shall not be cast away. I'll follow her.

40 BELVILE   Prithee do not.

WILLMORE   Do not? By heavens, to the antipodies,[4] with
such an invitation.

[*She goes out, and* WILLMORE *follows her.*]

BELVILE   'Tis a mad fellow for a wench.

[*Enter* FREDERICK.]

FREDERICK   Oh, colonel, such news!

45 BELVILE   Prithee what?

FREDERICK   News that will make you laugh in spite of
fortune.

BELVILE   What, Blunt has had some damned trick put
upon him? Cheated, banged, or clapped?[5]

50 FREDERICK   Cheated, sir, rarely° cheated of all but his shirt   *superbly*
and drawers; the unconscionable whore too turned him
out before consummation, so that, traversing the streets
at midnight, the watch found him in this *fresco* and conducted him home. By heaven, 'tis such a sight, and yet I

55 durst as well been hanged as laughed at him or pity him:
he beats all that do but ask him a question, and is in
such an humour.

PEDRO   Who is't has met with this ill usage, sir?

BELVILE   A friend of ours whom you must see for mirth's

60 sake. — [*Aside.*] I'll employ him to give Florinda time for
an escape.

PEDRO   What is he?

BELVILE   A young countryman of ours, one that has been
educated at so plentiful a rate he yet ne'er knew the

65 want of money; and 'twill be a great jest to see how simply
he'll look without it. For my part, I'll lend him none: and
the rogue know not how to put on a borrowing face and
ask first, I'll let him see how good 'tis to play our parts
whilst I play his. Prithee, Fred, do you go home and keep

70 him in that posture till we come.

[*Exeunt.*]

[*Enter* FLORINDA *from the farther end of the scene,
looking behind her.*]

FLORINDA   I am followed still. Ha! My brother too
advancing this way! Good heavens defend me from
being seen by him!   [*She goes off.*]

[*Enter* WILLMORE, *and after him* VALERIA, *at a little
distance.*]

WILLMORE   Ah, there she sails! She looks back as she were

75 willing to be boarded; I'll warrant her prize.°   *a ship legally captured*

[*He goes out,* VALERIA *following.*]

[*Enter* HELLENA, *just as he goes out, with a page.*]

HELLENA   Ha, is not that my captain that has a woman in
chase? 'Tis not Angellica.—Boy, follow those people at a
distance, and bring me an account where they go in.

[*Exit page.*]

—I'll find his haunts, and plague him everywhere. Ha!
80   My brother!

[BELVILE, WILLMORE, PEDRO *cross the stage*; HELLENA
runs off.]

4.4

[SCENE: *Scene changes to another street.*]

[*Enter* FLORINDA.]

FLORINDA   What shall I do? My brother now pursues me.
Will no kind power protect me from his tyranny? Ha!
Here's a door open; I'll venture in, since nothing can be
worse than to fall into his hands. My life and honor are
5   at stake, and my necessity has no choice.   [*She goes in.*]

[*Enter* VALERIA, *and* HELLENA'S PAGE *peeping after*
FLORINDA.]

PAGE   Here she went in; I shall remember this house.

[*Exit boy.*]

VALERIA   This is Belvile's lodging; she's gone in as readily
as if she knew it. Ha! Here's that mad fellow again; I
dare not venture in. I'll watch my opportunity.

[*Goes aside.*]

[*Enter* WILLMORE, *gazing about him.*]

10   WILLMORE   I have lost her hereabouts. Pox on't, she must
not 'scape me so.   [*Goes out.*]

4.5

[SCENE: *Scene changes to* BLUNT'S *chamber, discovers him sitting on a couch in his shirt and drawers, reading.*]

BLUNT   So, now my mind's a little at peace, since I have
resolved revenge. A pox on this tailor, though, for not
bringing home the clothes I bespoke.° And a pox of all   ordered
poor cavaliers: a man can never keep a spare suit for 'em,
5   and I shall have these rogues come in and find me naked,
and then I'm undone. But I'm resolved to arm myself: the
rascals shall not insult over me too much. [*Puts on an old
rusty sword and buff belt.*] Now, how like a morris dancer[6]
I am equipped! A fine ladylike whore to cheat me thus
10   without affording me a kindness for my money! A pox
light on her, I shall never be reconciled to the sex more;

6. That is, costumed in white, like an English folk dancer.

she has made me as faithless as a physician, as unchari-
table as a churchman, and as ill-natured as a poet. Oh,
how I'll use all womankind hereafter! What would I give
to have one of 'em within my reach now! Any mortal
thing in petticoats, kind fortune, send me, and I'll forgive
thy last night's malice. —Here's a cursed book, too—a
warning to all young travelers—that can instruct me how
to prevent such mischiefs now 'tis too late. Well, 'tis a
rare convenient thing to read a little now and then, as
well as hawk and hunt.

[*Sits down again and reads.*]

[*Enter to him* FLORINDA.]

FLORINDA This house is haunted, sure: 'tis well furnished,
and no living thing inhabits it. Ha! A man! Heavens,
how he's attired! Sure 'tis some rope dancer,° or fencing
master. I tremble now for fear, and yet I must venture
now to speak to him. —Sir, if I may not interrupt your
meditations—

[*He starts up and gazes.*]

BLUNT Ha, what's here? Are my wishes granted? And is
not that a she creature? 'Adsheartlikins, 'tis. —What
wretched thing art thou, ha?

FLORINDA Charitable sir, you've told yourself already what
I am: a very wretched maid, forced by a strange unlucky
accident to seek a safety here, and must be ruined if you
do not grant it.

BLUNT Ruined! Is there any ruin so inevitable as that
which now threatens thee? Dost thou know, miserable
woman, into what den of mischiefs thou art fallen; what
abyss of confusion, ha? Dost not see something in my
looks that frights thy guilty soul, and makes thee wish to
change that shape of woman for any humble animal, or
devil? For those were safer for thee, and less mischievous.

FLORINDA Alas, what mean you, sir? I must confess, your
looks have something in 'em makes me fear, but I
beseech you, as you seem a gentleman, pity a harmless
virgin that takes your house for sanctuary.

BLUNT Talk on, talk on; and weep, too, till my faith return. Do, flatter me out of my senses again. A harmless
virgin with a pox; as much one as t'other, 'adsheartlikins. Why, what the devil, can I not be safe in my
house for you, not in my chamber? Nay, not even being
naked too cannot secure me? This is an impudence
greater than has invaded me yet. Come, no resistance.

[*Pulls her rudely.*]

FLORINDA Dare you be so cruel?

BLUNT Cruel? 'Adsheartlikins, as a galley slave, or a Spanish whore. Cruel? Yes, I will kiss and beat thee all over,

tightrope walker

kiss and see thee all over; thou shalt lie with me too, not
that I care for the enjoyment, but to let thee see I have
ta'en deliberated malice to thee, and will be revenged on
one whore for the sins of another. I will smile and deceive
60 thee; flatter thee, and beat thee; embrace thee and rob
thee, as she did me; fawn on thee, and strip thee stark
naked; then hang thee out at my window by the heels,
with a paper of scurvy verses fastened to thy breast in
praise of damnable women. Come, come, along.

65 FLORINDA   Alas, sir, must I be sacrificed for the crimes of
the most infamous of my sex? I never understood the
sins you name.

BLUNT   Do, persuade the fool you love him, or that one of you
can be just or honest; tell me I was not an easy coxcomb, or
70 any strange impossible tale: it will be believed sooner than
thy false showers or protestations. A generation of damned
hypocrites! To flatter my very clothes from my back! Dissembling witches! Are these the returns you make an honest
gentleman that trusts, believes, and loves you? But if I be
75 not even with you—Come along, or I shall—

[*Pulls her again.*]

[*Enter* FREDERICK.]

FREDERICK   Ha, what's here to do?

BLUNT   'Adsheartlikins, Fred, I am glad thou art come, to
be a witness of my dire revenge.

FREDERICK   What's this, a person of quality too, who is
80 upon the ramble to supply the defects of some grave impotent husband?

BLUNT   No, this has another pretense: some very unfortunate accident brought her hither, to save a life pursued by
I know not who or why, and forced to take sanctuary here
85 at fool's haven. 'Adsheartlikins, to me of all mankind for
protection? Is the ass to be cajoled again, think ye? No,
young one, no prayers or tears shall mitigate my rage;
therefore prepare for both my pleasures of enjoyment
and revenge. For I am resolved to make up my loss here
90 on thy body: I'll take it out in kindness and in beating.

FREDERICK   Now, mistress of mine, what do you think of
this?

FLORINDA   I think he will not, dares not be so barbarous.

FREDERICK   Have a care, Blunt, she fetched a deep sigh;
95 she is enamoured with thy shirt and drawers. She'll strip
thee even of that; there are of her calling such unconscionable baggages and such dexterous thieves, they'll
flay a man and he shall ne'er miss his skin till he feels
the cold. There was a countryman of ours robbed of a
100 row of teeth whilst he was a-sleeping, which the jilt
made him buy again when he waked. You see, lady, how
little reason we have to trust you.

BLUNT   'Adsheartlikins, why this is most abominable!

FLORINDA   Some such devils there may be, but by all
105   that's holy, I am none such. I entered here to save a life
in danger.

BLUNT   For no goodness, I'll warrant her.

FREDERICK   Faith, damsel, you had e'en confessed the
plain truth, for we are fellows not to be caught twice in
110   the same trap. Look on that wreck: a tight vessel when
he set out of haven, well trimmed and laden. And see
how a female picaroon of this island of rogues has shattered him, and canst thou hope for any mercy?

BLUNT   No, no, gentlewoman, come along; 'adsheartlikins,
115   we must be better acquainted.—We'll both lie with her,
and then let me alone to bang° her.   beat

FREDERICK   I'm ready to serve you in matters of revenge
that has a double pleasure in't.

BLUNT   Well said.—You hear, little one, how you are con-
120   demned by public vote to the bed within; there's no
resisting your destiny, sweetheart.
                    [Pulls her.]

FLORINDA   Stay, sir. I have seen you with Belvile, an English
cavalier. For his sake, use me kindly. You know him, sir.

BLUNT   Belvile? Why yes, sweeting, we do know Belvile, and
125   wish he were with us now. He's a cormorant[7] at whore and
bacon: he'd have a limb or two of thee, my virgin pullet.
But 'tis no matter; we'll leave him the bones to pick.

FLORINDA   Sir, if you have any esteem for that Belvile, I
conjure you to treat me with more gentleness; he'll
130   thank you for the justice.

FREDERICK   Hark'ee, Blunt, I doubt° we are mistaken in   fear
this matter.

FLORINDA   Sir, if you find me not worth Belvile's care, use
me as you please. And that you may think I merit better
135   treatment than you threaten, pray take this present.
                    [Gives him a ring; he looks on it.]

BLUNT   Hum, a diamond! Why, 'tis a wonderful virtue now
that lies in this ring, a mollifying virtue. 'Adsheartlikins,
there's more persuasive rhetoric in't than all her sex can
utter.

140   FREDERICK   I begin to suspect something, and 'twould
anger us vilely to be trussed up for a rape upon a maid of
quality, when we only believe we ruffle[8] a harlot.

BLUNT   Thou art a credulous fellow, but 'adsheartlikins, I
have no faith yet. Why, my saint prattled as parlously° as   excessively
145   this does; she gave me a bracelet, too, a devil on her! But
I sent my man to sell it today for necessaries, and it
proved as counterfeit as her vows of love.

7. That is, he is insatiably greedy; cormorants   8. Handle with rude familiarity.
are voracious seabirds.

FREDERICK   However, let it reprieve her till we see Belvile.

BLUNT   That's hard, yet I will grant it.

> [Enter a SERVANT.]

150 SERVANT   Oh, sir, the colonel is just come in with his new
friend and a Spaniard of quality, and talks of having you
to dinner with 'em.

BLUNT   'Adsheartlikins, I'm undone! I would not see 'em
for the world. Hark'ee, Fred, lock up the wench in your
155 chamber.

FREDERICK   Fear nothing, madam: whate'er he threatens,
you are safe whilst in my hands.

> [Exeunt FREDERICK and FLORINDA.]

BLUNT   And sirrah, upon your life, say I am not at home, or
that I'm asleep, or—or—anything. Away; I'll prevent their
160 coming this way.

> [Locks the door, and exeunt.]

5.1

[SCENE: BLUNT's chamber.]

> [After a great knocking as at his chamber door, enter
> BLUNT softly crossing the stage, in his shirt and draw-
> ers as before.]

VOICES [call within]   Ned! Ned Blunt! Ned Blunt!

BLUNT   The rogues are up in arms. 'Adsheartlikins, this
villainous Frederick has betrayed me: they have heard of
my blessed fortune.

5 VOICES [and knocking within]   Ned Blunt! Ned! Ned!

BELVILE [within]   Why, he's dead, sir, without dispute
dead; he has not been seen today. Let's break open the
door. Here, boy—

BLUNT   Ha, break open the door? 'Adsheartlikins, that
10 mad fellow will be as good as his word.

BELVILE [within]   Boy, bring something to force the door.

> [A great noise within, at the door again.]

BLUNT   So, now must I speak in my own defense; I'll try
what rhetoric will do.—Hold, hold! What do you mean,
gentlemen, what do you mean?

15 BELVILE [within]   Oh, rogue, art alive? Prithee open the
door and convince us.

BLUNT   Yes, I am alive, gentlemen, but at present a little busy.

BELVILE [within]   How, Blunt grown a man of business?
Come, come, open and let's see this miracle.

20 BLUNT   No, no, no, no, gentlemen, 'tis no great business.
But—I am—at—my devotion. 'Adsheartlikins, will you
not allow a man time to pray?

BELVILE [within]   Turned religious? A greater wonder than
the first! Therefore open quickly, or we shall unhinge, we
25 shall.

BLUNT [*aside*]   This won't do.—Why hark'ee, colonel, to
tell you the truth, I am about a necessary affair of life:
I have a wench with me. You apprehend me?—The devil's in't if they be so uncivil as to disturb me now.

30   WILLMORE [*within*]   How, a wench? Nay then, we must
enter and partake. No resistance. Unless it be your lady
of quality, and then we'll keep our distance.

BLUNT   So, the business is out.

WILLMORE [*within*]   Come, come, lend's more hands to

35   the door. Now heave, all together. [*Breaks open the door.*]
So, well done, my boys.

> [*Enter* BELVILE *and his* PAGE, WILLMORE, FREDERICK,
> *and* PEDRO. BLUNT *looks simply,*° *they all laugh at*   foolish
> *him; he lays his hand on his sword, and comes up to*
> WILLMORE.]

BLUNT   Hark'ee, sir, laugh out your laugh quickly, d'ye
hear, and be gone. I shall spoil your sport else, 'adsheartlikins, sir, I shall. The jest has been carried on too

40   long.—[*Aside.*] A plague upon my tailor!

WILLMORE   'Sdeath, how the whore has dressed him! Faith,
sir, I'm sorry.

BLUNT   Are you so, sir? Keep't to yourself then, sir, I advise
you, d'ye hear, for I can as little endure your pity as his

45   mirth.

> [*Lays his hand on's sword.*]

BELVILE   Indeed, Willmore, thou wert a little too rough
with Ned Blunt's mistress. Call a person of quality whore,
and one so young, so handsome, and so eloquent? Ha,
ha, he.

50   BLUNT   Hark'ee, sir, you know me, and know I can be
angry. Have a care, for 'adsheartlikins, I can fight, too, I
can, sir. Do you mark me? No more.

BELVILE   Why so peevish, good Ned? Some disappointments, I'll warrant. What, did the jealous count, her

55   husband, return just in the nick?

BLUNT   Or the devil, sir. [*They laugh.*] D'ye laugh? Look ye
settle me a good sober countenance, and that quickly,
too, or you shall know Ned Blunt is not—

BELVILE   Not everybody, we know that.

60   BLUNT   Not an ass to be laughed at, sir.

WILLMORE   Unconscionable sinner! To bring a lover so
near his happiness—a vigorous passionate lover—and
then not only cheat him of his movables,° but his very   personal property
desires, too.

65   BELVILE   Ah, sir, a mistress is a trifle with Blunt; he'll have
a dozen the next time he looks abroad. His eyes have
charms not to be resisted; there needs no more than to
expose that taking person to the view of the fair, and he
leads 'em all in triumph.

70 PEDRO   Sir, though I'm a stranger to you, I am ashamed at
         the rudeness of my nation; and could you learn who did
         it, would assist you to make an example of 'em.

   BLUNT   Why ay, there's one speaks sense now, and hand-
         somely. And let me tell you, gentlemen, I should not have
75   showed myself like a jack pudding° thus to have made you   *clown, buffoon*
         mirth, but that I have revenge within my power. For
         know, I have got into my possession a female, who had
         better have fallen under any curse than the ruin I design
         her. 'Adsheartlikins, she assaulted me here in my own
80   lodgings, and had doubtless committed a rape upon me,
         had not this sword defended me.

   FREDERICK   I know not that, but o' my conscience thou had
         ravished her, had she not redeemed herself with a ring.
         Let's see't, Blunt.

         [*Blunt shows the ring.*]

85 BELVILE   [*aside*] Ha! The ring I gave Florinda when we
         exchanged our vows!—Hark'ee, Blunt—

         [*Goes to whisper to him.*]

   WILLMORE   No whispering, good colonel, there's a woman
         in the case. No whispering.

   BELVILE   [*aside to* BLUNT] Hark'ee, fool, be advised, and
90   conceal both the ring and the story for your reputation's
         sake. Do not let people know what despised cullies we
         English are; to be cheated and abused by one whore, and
         another rather bribe thee than be kind to thee, is an in-
         famy to our nation.

95 WILLMORE   Come, come, where's the wench? We'll see
         her; let her be what she will, we'll see her.

   PEDRO   Ay, ay, let us see her. I can soon discover whether
         she be of quality, or for your diversion.

   BLUNT   She's in Fred's custody.

100 WILLMORE   Come, come, the key—

         [*To* FREDERICK, *who gives him the key; they are going.*]

   BELVILE [*aside*]   Death, what shall I do?—Stay, gentlemen.—
         [*Aside.*] Yet if I hinder 'em, I shall discover all.—Hold, let's
         go one at once. Give me the key.

   WILLMORE   Nay, hold there, colonel, I'll go first.

105 FREDERICK   Nay, no dispute, Ned and I have the propriety°   *right of possession*
         of her.

   WILLMORE   Damn propriety! Then we'll draw cuts.°   *draw lots*
         [BELVILE *goes to whisper* WILLMORE.] Nay, no corruption,
         good colonel. Come, the longest sword carries her.

         [*They all draw, forgetting* DON PEDRO, *being a Span-
         iard, had the longest.*⁹]

110 BLUNT   I yield up my interest to you, gentlemen, and that
         will be revenge sufficient.

9. The English commonly fought with a shorter sword than the Spanish.

WILLMORE [*to* PEDRO] The wench is yours. —[*Aside.*] Pox
of his Toledo,[1] I had forgot that.

FREDERICK Come, sir, I'll conduct you to the lady.

[*Exeunt* FREDERICK *and* PEDRO.]

115 BELVILE [*aside*] To hinder him will certainly discover her.
—Dost know, dull beast, what mischief thou hast done?

[WILLMORE *walking up and down, out of humor.*]

WILLMORE Ay, ay, to trust our fortune to lots! A devil on't,
'twas madness, that's the truth on't.

BELVILE Oh, intolerable sot—

[*Enter* FLORINDA *running, masked,* PEDRO *after her;*
WILLMORE *gazing round her.*]

120 FLORINDA [*aside*] Good heaven defend me from discovery!

PEDRO 'Tis but in vain to fly me; you're fallen to my lot.

BELVILE [*aside*] Sure she's undiscovered yet, but now I
fear there is no way to bring her off.°   rescue her

WILLMORE [*aside*] Why, what a pox, is not this my woman,
125 the same I followed but now?

[PEDRO *talking to* FLORINDA, *who walks up and down.*]

PEDRO As if I did not know ye, and your business here.

FLORINDA [*aside*] Good heaven, I fear he does indeed!

PEDRO Come, pray be kind; I know you meant to be so
when you entered here, for these are proper gentlemen.

130 WILLMORE But sir, perhaps the lady will not be imposed
upon: she'll choose her man.

PEDRO I am better bred than not to leave her choice free.

[*Enter* VALERIA, *and is surprised at sight of* DON PEDRO.]

VALERIA [*aside*] Don Pedro here! There's no avoiding him.

FLORINDA [*aside*] Valeria! Then I'm undone.

135 VALERIA [*to* PEDRO, *running to him*] Oh, I have found you,
sir! The strangest accident—if I had breath—to tell it.

PEDRO Speak! Is Florinda safe? Hellena well?

VALERIA Ay, ay, sir. Florinda is safe. —[*Aside.*] From any
fears of you.

140 PEDRO Why, where's Florinda? Speak!

VALERIA Ay, where indeed, sir; I wish I could inform you.
But to hold you no longer in doubt—

FLORINDA [*aside*] Oh, what will she say?

VALERIA She's fled away in the habit—of one of her pages,
145 sir. But Callis thinks you may retrieve her yet, if you
make haste away. She'll tell you, sir, the rest. —[*Aside.*]
If you can find her out.

PEDRO Dishonorable girl, she has undone my aim. —[*To*
BELVILE.] Sir, you see my necessity of leaving you, and I
150 hope you'll pardon it. My sister, I know, will make her
flight to you; and if she do, I shall expect she should be
rendered back.

1. A sword made in Toledo, a city in Spain famous for the quality of its steel blades.

BELVILE   I shall consult my love and honor, sir.

[*Exit* PEDRO.]

FLORINDA [*to* VALERIA]   My dear preserver, let me embrace
155   thee.

WILLMORE   What the devil's all this?

BLUNT   Mystery, by this light.

VALERIA   Come, come, make haste and get yourselves
married quickly, for your brother will return again.

160   BELVILE   I'm so surprised with fears and joys, so amazed to
find you here in safety, I can scarce persuade my heart
into a faith of what I see.

WILLMORE   Hark'ee, colonel, is this that mistress who has
cost you so many sighs, and me so many quarrels with
165   you?

BELVILE   It is. —[*To* FLORINDA.] Pray give him the honor of
your hand.

WILLMORE   Thus it must be received, then. [*Kneels and
kisses her hand.*] And with it give your pardon, too.

170   FLORINDA   The friend to Belvile may command me
anything.

WILLMORE [*aside*]   Death, would I might; 'tis a surprising
beauty.

BELVILE   Boy, run and fetch a father° instantly.   *priest*

[*Exit* BOY.]

175   FREDERICK   So, now do I stand like a dog, and have not a
syllable to plead my own cause with. By this hand,
madam, I was never thoroughly confounded before, nor
shall I ever more dare look up with confidence, till you
are pleased to pardon me.

180   FLORINDA   Sir, I'll be reconciled to you on one condition:
that you'll follow the example of your friend in marrying
a maid that does not hate you, and whose fortune, I believe, will not be unwelcome to you.

FREDERICK   Madam, had I° no inclinations that way, I   *even if I had*
185   should obey your kind commands.

BELVILE   Who, Fred marry? He has so few inclinations for
womankind that had he been possessed of paradise he
might have continued there to this day, if no crime but
love could have disinherited him.

190   FREDERICK   Oh, I do not use to boast of my intrigues.

BELVILE   Boast! Why, thou dost nothing but boast. And I
dare swear, wert thou as innocent from the sin of the
grape as thou art from the apple,[2] thou might'st yet claim
that right in Eden which our first parents lost by too
195   much loving.

FREDERICK   I wish this lady would think me so modest a
man.

---

2. That is, the fruit of the tree of knowledge; the disobedience of Adam and Eve in eating it (not
"too much loving") led to their expulsion from Eden (Genesis 2.15–17, 3.1–24).

664 | APHRA BEHN

VALERIA   She would be sorry then, and not like you half so
well. And I should be loath to break my word with you,
200   which was, that if your friend and mine agreed, it should
be a match between you and I.
  [*She gives him her hand.*]
FREDERICK   Bear witness, colonel, 'tis a bargain.
  [*Kisses her hand.*]
BLUNT [*to* FLORINDA]   I have a pardon to beg, too; but 'ads-
heartlikins, I am so out of countenance° that I'm a dog   *abashed*
205   if I can say anything to purpose.
FLORINDA   Sir, I heartily forgive you all.
BLUNT   That's nobly said, sweet lady.—Belvile, prithee
present her her ring again, for I find I have not courage
to approach her myself.
  [*Gives him the ring; he gives it to* FLORINDA.]
  [*Enter* BOY.]
210   BOY   Sir, I have brought the father that you sent for.
                                                    [*Exit* BOY.]
BELVILE   'Tis well. And now, my dear Florinda, let's fly to
complete that mighty joy we have so long wished and
sighed for.—Come, Fred, you'll follow?
FREDERICK   Your example, sir, 'twas ever my ambition in
215   war, and must be so in love.
WILLMORE   And must not I see this juggling° knot tied?   *cheating, deceptive*
BELVILE   No, thou shalt do us better service and be our
guard, lest Don Pedro's sudden return interrupt the cer-
emony.
220   WILLMORE   Content; I'll secure this pass.
  [*Exeunt* BELVILE, FLORINDA, FREDERICK, *and* VALERIA.]
  [*Enter* BOY.]
BOY [*to* WILLMORE]   Sir, there's a lady without would speak
to you.
WILLMORE   Conduct her in; I dare not quit my post.
BOY [*to* BLUNT]   And sir, your tailor waits you in your
225   chamber.
BLUNT   Some comfort yet: I shall not dance naked at the
wedding.
  [*Exeunt* BLUNT *and* BOY.]
  [*Enter again the* BOY, *conducting in* ANGELLICA *in a*
  masking habit and a vizard. WILLMORE *runs to her.*]
WILLMORE [*aside*]   This can be none but my pretty gipsy.—
Oh, I see you can follow as well as fly. Come, confess
230   thyself the most malicious devil in nature; you think you
have done my business with Angellica—
ANGELLICA   Stand off, base villain!
  [*She draws a pistol and holds it to his breast.*]
WILLMORE   Ha, 'tis not she! Who art thou, and what's
thy business?

235 ANGELLICA   One thou hast injured, and who comes to kill
    thee for't.
WILLMORE   What the devil canst thou mean?
ANGELLICA   By all my hopes to kill thee—
        [*Holds still the pistol to his breast; he going back, she
        following still.*]
WILLMORE   Prithee, on what acquaintance? For I know
240   thee not.
ANGELLICA   Behold this face so lost to thy remembrance,
        [*Pulls off her vizard.*]

    And then call all thy sins about thy soul,
    And let 'em die with thee.
WILLMORE   Angellica!
245 ANGELLICA   Yes, traitor! Does not thy guilty blood run
    shivering through thy veins? Hast thou no horror at this
    sight, that tells thee thou hast not long to boast thy
    shameful conquest?
WILLMORE   Faith, no, child. My blood keeps its old ebbs
250   and flows still, and that usual heat too, that could oblige
    thee with a kindness, had I but opportunity.
ANGELLICA   Devil! Dost wanton with my pain? Have at thy
    heart!
WILLMORE   Hold, dear virago!° Hold thy hand a little; I am   *warrior woman*
255   not now at leisure to be killed. Hold and hear me. —
    [*Aside.*] Death, I think she's in earnest.
ANGELLICA   [*aside, turning from him*] Oh, if I take not
    heed, my coward heart will leave me to his mercy. —
    What have you, sir, to say? —But should I hear thee,
260   thoud'st talk away all that is brave about me, and I have
    vowed thy death by all that's sacred.
        [*Follows him with the pistol to his breast.*]
WILLMORE   Why then, there's an end of a proper hand-
    some fellow, that might 'a lived to have done good service
    yet. That's all I can say to't.
265 ANGELLICA   [*pausingly*] Yet—I would give thee time
    for—penitence.
WILLMORE   Faith, child, I thank God I have ever took care
    to lead a good, sober, hopeful life, and am of a religion
    that teaches me to believe I shall depart in peace.
270 ANGELLICA   So will the devil! Tell me,
    How many poor believing fools thou hast undone?
    How many hearts thou hast betrayed to ruin?
    Yet these are little mischiefs to the ills
    Thou'st taught mine to commit: thou'st taught it love.
275 WILLMORE   Egad, 'twas shrewdly hurt the while.
ANGELLICA   Love, that has robbed it of its unconcern,
    Of all that pride that taught me how to value it.
    And in its room
    A mean submissive passion was conveyed,

280   That made me humbly bow, which I ne'er did
     To anything but heaven.
     Thou, perjured man, didst this; and with thy oaths,
     Which on thy knees thou didst devoutly make,
     Softened my yielding heart, and then I was a slave.
285   Yet still had been content to've worn my chains,
     Worn 'em with vanity and joy forever,
     Hadst thou not broke those vows that put them on.
     'Twas then I was undone.
           [*All this while follows him with the pistol to his breast.*]

WILLMORE   Broke my vows? Why, where hast thou lived?
290   Amongst the gods? For I never heard of mortal man that
has not broke a thousand vows.

ANGELLICA   Oh, impudence!

WILLMORE   Angellica, that beauty has been too long tempting, not to have made a thousand lovers languish; who, in
295   the amorous fever, no doubt have sworn like me. Did they
all die in that faith, still adoring? I do not think they did.

ANGELLICA   No, faithless man; had I repaid their vows, as
I did thine, I would have killed the ingrateful that had
abandoned me.

300 WILLMORE   This old general has quite spoiled thee: nothing makes a woman so vain as being flattered. Your old
lover ever supplies the defects of age with intolerable
dotage, vast charge, and that which you call constancy;
and attributing all this to your own merits, you domineer,
305   and throw your favors in's teeth, upbraiding him still with
the defects of age, and cuckold him as often as he de-
ceives your expectations. But the gay, young, brisk lover,
that brings his equal fires, and can give you dart for dart,
he'll be as nice° as you sometimes.   *wanton*

310 ANGELLICA   All this thou'st made me know, for which I
     hate thee.
     Had I remained in innocent security,
     I should have thought all men were born my slaves,
     And worn my power like lightning in my eyes,
315   To have destroyed at pleasure when offended.
     But when love held the mirror, the undeceiving glass
     Reflected all the weakness of my soul, and made me know
     My richest treasure being lost, my honor,
     All the remaining spoil could not be worth
320   The conqueror's care or value.
     Oh, how I fell, like a long-worshiped idol,
     Discovering all the cheat.
     Would not the incense and rich sacrifice
     Which blind devotion offered at my altars
325   Have fallen to thee?
     Why wouldst thou then destroy my fancied power?

WILLMORE   By heaven, thou'rt brave, and I admire thee
     strangely.°   *to an exceptional degree*

I wish I were that dull, that constant thing

330 Which thou wouldst have, and nature never meant me.

I must, like cheerful birds, sing in all groves,

And perch on every bough,

Billing the next kind she that flies to meet me;

Yet, after all, could build my nest with thee,

335 Thither repairing when I'd loved my round,

And still reserve a tributary flame.

To gain your credit, I'll pay you back your charity,

And be obliged for nothing but for love.

[*Offers her a purse of gold.*]

ANGELLICA   Oh, that thou wert in earnest!

340 So mean a thought of me

Would turn my rage to scorn, and I should pity thee,

And give thee leave to live;

Which for the public safety of our sex,

And my own private injuries, I dare not do.

345 Prepare—   [*Follows still, as before.*]

I will no more be tempted with replies.

WILLMORE   Sure—

ANGELLICA   Another word will damn thee! I've heard thee
talk too long.

[*She follows him with the pistol ready to shoot; he
retires, still amazed. Enter* DON ANTONIO, *his arm in a
scarf, and lays hold on the pistol.*]

350 ANTONIO   Ha! Angellica!

ANGELLICA   Antonio! What devil brought thee hither?

ANTONIO   Love and curiosity, seeing your coach at door.
Let me disarm you of this unbecoming instrument of
death. [*Takes away the pistol.*] Amongst the number of

355 your slaves was there not one worthy the honor to have
fought your quarrel? —[*To* WILLMORE.] Who are you, sir,
that are so very wretched to merit death from her?

WILLMORE   One, sir, that could have made a better end of
an amorous quarrel without you, than with you.

360 ANTONIO   Sure 'tis some rival. Ha! The very man took
down her picture yesterday; the very same that set on me
last night! Blessed opportunity—

[*Offers to shoot him.*]

ANGELLICA   Hold, you're mistaken, sir.

ANTONIO   By heavens, the very same!—Sir, what preten-

365 sions have you to this lady?

WILLMORE   Sir, I do not use° to be examined, and am ill at   *am not accustomed*
all disputes but this—

[*Draws;* ANTONIO *offers to shoot.*]

ANGELLICA [*to* WILLMORE]   Oh, hold! You see he's armed
with certain death.

370 —And you, Antonio, I command you hold,

By all the passion you've so lately vowed me.
[*Enter* DON PEDRO, *sees* ANTONIO, *and stays.*]

PEDRO [*aside*]   Ha! Antonio! And Angellica!

ANTONIO   When I refuse obedience to your will,
May you destroy me with your mortal hate.
375   By all that's holy, I adore you so,
That even my rival, who has charms enough
To make him fall a victim to my jealousy,
Shall live; nay, and have leave to love on still.

PEDRO [*aside*]   What's this I hear?

380   ANGELLICA [*pointing to* WILLMORE]   Ah thus, 'twas thus he
talked, and I believed.
Antonio, yesterday
I'd not have sold my interest in his heart
For all the sword has won and lost in battle.
385   —But now, to show my utmost of contempt,
I give thee life; which, if thou wouldst preserve,
Live where my eyes may never see thee more.
Live to undo someone whose soul may prove
So bravely constant to revenge my love.
[*Goes out.* ANTONIO *follows, but* PEDRO *pulls him back.*]

390   PEDRO   Antonio, stay.

ANTONIO   Don Pedro!

PEDRO   What coward fear was that prevented thee from
meeting me this morning on the Molo?

ANTONIO   Meet thee?

395   PEDRO   Yes, me; I was the man that dared thee to't.

ANTONIO   Hast thou so often seen me fight in war, to find
no better cause to excuse my absence? I sent my sword
and one to do thee right, finding myself uncapable to use
a sword.

400   PEDRO   But 'twas Florinda's quarrel that we fought, and
you, to show how little you esteemed her, sent me your
rival, giving him your interest. But I have found the cause
of this affront, and when I meet you fit for the dispute,
I'll tell you my resentment.

405   ANTONIO   I shall be ready, sir, ere long, to do you
reason.   [*Exit* ANTONIO.]

PEDRO   If I could find Florinda, now whilst my anger's
high, I think I should be kind, and give her to Belvile in
revenge.

410   WILLMORE   Faith, sir, I know not what you would do, but I
believe the priest within has been so kind.

PEDRO   How? My sister married?

WILLMORE   I hope by this time he is, and bedded too, or
he has not my longings about him.

415   PEDRO   Dares he do this? Does he not fear my power?

WILLMORE   Faith, not at all; if you will go in and thank
him for the favor he has done your sister, so; if not, sir,

my power's greater in this house than yours: I have a
damned surly crew here that will keep you till the next
420 tide, and then clap you on board for prize.° My ship lies   *as a captive of*
but a league off the Molo, and we shall show your don-
ship a damned Tramontana[3] rover's trick.

[*Enter* BELVILE.]

BELVILE This rogue's in some new mischief. Ha! Pedro
returned!

425 PEDRO Colonel Belvile, I hear you have married my sister.

BELVILE You have heard truth then, sir.

PEDRO Have I so? Then, sir, I wish you joy.

BELVILE How?

PEDRO By this embrace I do, and I am glad on't.

430 BELVILE Are you in earnest?

PEDRO By our long friendship and my obligations to thee,
I am; the sudden change I'll give you reasons for anon.
Come, lead me to my sister, that she may know I now
approve her choice.

[*Exit* BELVILE *with* PEDRO.]

[WILLMORE *goes to follow them. Enter* HELLENA, *as
before in boy's clothes, and pulls him back.*]

435 WILLMORE Ha! My gipsy! Now a thousand blessings on
thee for this kindness. Egad, child, I was e'en in despair
of ever seeing thee again; my friends are all provided for
within, each man his kind woman.

HELLENA Ha! I thought they had served me some such
440 trick!

WILLMORE And I was e'en resolved to go aboard, and condemn myself to my lone cabin, and the thoughts of thee.

HELLENA And could you have left me behind? Would you
have been so ill natured?

445 WILLMORE Why, 'twould have broke my heart, child. But
since we are met again, I defy foul weather to part us.

HELLENA And would you be a faithful friend now, if a
maid should trust you?

WILLMORE For a friend I cannot promise: thou art of a
450 form so excellent, a face and humour too good for cold
dull friendship. I am parlously afraid of being in love,
child; and you have not forgotten how severely you have
used me?

HELLENA That's all one; such usage you must still look
455 for: to find out all your haunts, to rail at you to all that
love you, till I have made you love only me in your own
defense, because nobody else will love you.

WILLMORE But hast thou no better quality to recommend
thyself by?

---

3. Barbarous (literally, "north wind" in Italian—i.e., across the mountains).

460 HELLENA   Faith, none, captain. Why, 'twill be the greater
        charity to take me for thy mistress. I am a lone child, a
        kind of orphan lover; and why I should die a maid, and in
        a captain's hands too, I do not understand.

    WILLMORE   Egad, I was never clawed away with broad
465   sides from any female before. Thou hast one virtue I
        adore—good nature. I hate a coy demure mistress, she's
        as troublesome as a colt; I'll break none. No, give me a
        mad mistress when mewed,° and in flying, one I dare   *confined (as a hawk)*
        trust upon the wing, that whilst she's kind will come to
470   the lure.

    HELLENA   Nay, as kind as you will, good captain, whilst it
        lasts. But let's lose no time.

    WILLMORE   My time's as precious to me as thine can be.
        Therefore, dear creature, since we are so well agreed,
475   let's retire to my chamber; and if ever thou wert treated
        with such savory love! Come, my bed's prepared for such
        a guest all clean and sweet as thy fair self. I love to steal
        a dish and a bottle with a friend, and hate long graces.
        Come, let's retire and fall to.

480 HELLENA   'Tis but getting my consent, and the business is
        soon done. Let but old gaffer Hymen[4] and his priest say
        amen to't, and I dare lay my mother's daughter by as proper
        a fellow as your father's son, without fear or blushing.

    WILLMORE   Hold, hold, no bug° words, child. Priest and   *terrifying*
485   Hymen? Prithee add a hangman to 'em to make up the
        consort. No, no, we'll have no vows but love, child, nor
        witness but the lover: the kind deity enjoins naught but
        love and enjoy. Hymen and priest wait still upon portion
        and jointure; love and beauty have their own cere-
490   monies. Marriage is as certain a bane to love as lending
        money is to friendship. I'll neither ask nor give a vow,
        though I could be content to turn gipsy and become a
        left-handed bridegroom[5] to have the pleasure of working
        that great miracle of making a maid a mother, if you
495   durst venture. 'Tis upse° gipsy that, and if I miss I'll lose   *in the manner of*
        my labor.

    HELLENA   And if you do not lose, what shall I get? A cradle
        full of noise and mischief, with a pack of repentance at
        my back? Can you teach me to weave incle° to pass my   *linen thread*
500   time with? 'Tis upse gipsy that, too.

    WILLMORE   I can teach thee to weave a true love's knot
        better.

    HELLENA   So can my dog.

    WILLMORE   Well, I see we are both upon our guards, and I
505   see there's no way to conquer good nature but by yielding.
        Here, give me thy hand: one kiss, and I am thine.

---

4. The classical god of marriage, usually represented not as an old man ("gaffer") but as
youthful.

5. That is, a "bridegroom" in a wedding not
properly solemnized and thus not fully legal.

HELLENA   One kiss! How like my page he speaks! I am resolved you shall have none, for asking such a sneaking sum.
He that will be satisfied with one kiss will never die of that
510 longing. Good friend single-kiss, is all your talking come to
this? A kiss, a caudle!⁶ Farewell, captain single-kiss.

[*Going out; he stays her.*]

WILLMORE   Nay, if we part so, let me die like a bird upon a
bough, at the sheriff's charge. By heaven, both the Indies shall not buy thee from me. I adore thy humour and
515 will marry thee, and we are so of one humour it must be
a bargain. Give me thy hand. [*Kisses her hand.*] And now
let the blind ones, love and fortune, do their worst.

HELLENA   Why, god-a-mercy, captain!

WILLMORE   But hark'ee: the bargain is now made, but is it
520 not fit we should know each other's names, that when we
have reason to curse one another hereafter, and people
ask me who 'tis I give to the devil, I may at least be able to
tell what family you came of?

HELLENA   Good reason, captain; and where I have cause, as
525 I doubt not but I shall have plentiful, that I may know at
whom to throw my—blessings, I beseech ye your name.

WILLMORE   I am called Robert the Constant.

HELLENA   A very fine name! Pray was it your faulkner° or   *hawk keeper*
butler that christened you? Do they not use to whistle
530 when they call you?

WILLMORE   I hope you have a better, that a man may name
without crossing himself—you are so merry with mine.

HELLENA   I am called Hellena the Inconstant.

[*Enter* PEDRO, BELVILE, FLORINDA, FREDERICK, VALERIA.]

PEDRO   Ha! Hellena!

535 FLORINDA   Hellena!

HELLENA   The very same. Ha! My brother! Now, captain,
show your love and courage; stand to your arms and
defend me bravely, or I am lost forever.

PEDRO   What's this I hear? False girl, how came you hither,
540 and what's your business? Speak!

[*Goes roughly to her.*]

WILLMORE   Hold off, sir; you have leave to parley° only.   *speak; negotiate*

[*Puts himself between.*]

HELLENA   I had e'en as good tell it, as you guess it. Faith,
brother, my business is the same with all living creatures
of my age: to love and be beloved—and here's the man.

545 PEDRO   Perfidious maid, hast thou deceived me too;
deceived thyself and heaven?

HELLENA   'Tis time enough to make my peace with that.
Be you but kind, let me alone with heaven.

6. A warm drink (of thin gruel mixed with ale or wine) for an invalid, given especially to women
after childbirth.

PEDRO Belvile, I did not expect this false play from you.
550 Was't not enough you'd gain Florinda, which I pardoned,
but your lewd friends too must be enriched with the
spoils of a noble family?
BELVILE Faith, sir, I am as much surprised at this as you
can be. Yet, sir, my friends are gentlemen, and ought to
555 be esteemed for their misfortunes, since they have the
glory to suffer with the best of men and kings. 'Tis true,
he's a rover of fortune, yet a prince aboard his little
wooden world.
PEDRO What's this to the maintenance of a woman of her
560 birth and quality?
WILLMORE Faith, sir, I can boast of nothing but a sword
which does me right where'er I come, and has defended a
worse cause than a woman's; and since I loved her before
I either knew her birth or name, I must pursue my reso-
565 lution and marry her.
PEDRO And is all your holy intent of becoming a nun
debauched into a desire of man?
HELLENA Why, I have considered the matter, brother, and
find the three hundred thousand crowns my uncle left me,
570 and you cannot keep from me, will be better laid out in
love than in religion, and turn to as good an account. Let
most voices carry it: for heaven or the captain?
ALL CRY A captain! A captain!
HELLENA Look ye, sir, 'tis a clear case.
575 PEDRO Oh, I am mad! —[Aside.] If I refuse, my life's in
danger. —Come, there's one motive induces me. Take her;
I shall now be free from fears of her honor. Guard it you
now, if you can; I have been a slave to't long enough.
    [Gives her to him.]
WILLMORE Faith, sir, I am of a nation that are of opinion
580 a woman's honor is not worth guarding when she has a
mind to part with it.
HELLENA Well said, captain.
PEDRO [to VALERIA] This was your plot, mistress, but I
hope you have married one that will revenge my quar-
585 rel to you.
VALERIA There's no altering destiny, sir.
PEDRO Sooner than a woman's will; therefore I forgive
you all, and wish you may get my father's pardon as easily, which I fear.
    [Enter BLUNT dressed in a Spanish habit, looking
    very ridiculously; his MAN adjusting his band.°]

collar

590 MAN 'Tis very well, sir.
BLUNT Well, sir! 'Adsheartlikins, I tell you 'tis damnable
ill, sir. A Spanish habit! Good Lord! Could the devil and
my tailor devise no other punishment for me but the
mode of a nation I abominate?
595 BELVILE What's the matter, Ned?

BLUNT   Pray view me round, and judge.

       [*Turns round.*]

BELVILE   I must confess thou art a kind of an odd figure.

BLUNT   In a Spanish habit with a vengeance! I had rather
be in the Inquisition for Judaism than in this doublet
600   and breeches; a pillory were an easy collar to this, three
handfuls high; and these shoes, too, are worse than the
stocks, with the sole an inch shorter than my foot. In
fine, gentlemen, methinks I look like a bag of bays[7]
stuffed full of fool's flesh.

605 BELVILE   Methinks 'tis well, and makes thee look e'en
cavalier. Come, sir, settle your face and salute our
friends. Lady—

BLUNT [*to* HELLENA]   Ha! Sayst thou so, my little rover?
Lady, if you be one, give me leave to kiss your hand, and
610   tell you, 'adsheartlikins, for all I look so, I am your humble servant. A pox of my Spanish habit!

       [*Music is heard to play.*]

WILLMORE   Hark! What's this?

       [*Enter* BOY.]

BOY   Sir, as the custom is, the gay people in masquerade,
who make every man's house their own, are coming up.

       [*Enter several men and women in masking habits,
with music; they put themselves in order and dance.*]

615 BLUNT   'Adsheartlikins, would 'twere lawful to pull off
their false faces, that I might see if my doxy° were not   *prostitute*
amongst 'em.

BELVILE [*to the maskers*]   Ladies and gentlemen, since you
are come so *a propos*,° you must take a small collation   *opportunely (French)*
620   with us.

WILLMORE [*to* HELLENA]   Whilst we'll to the good man
within, who stays to give us a cast of his office.[8] Have
you no trembling at the near approach?

HELLENA   No more than you have in an engagement or a
625   tempest.

WILLMORE   Egad, thou'rt a brave girl, and I admire thy
love and courage.

       Lead on; no other dangers they can dread,
       Who venture in the storms o'th' marriage bed.

                              [*Exeunt.*]

             The End

---

7. Perhaps "baize," a thick cloth; or perhaps a bag containing bay leaves, used in cooking.
8. A taste of his customary function.

Epilogue

The banished cavaliers! A roving blade!
A popish carnival! A masquerade!
The devil's in't if this will please the nation
In these our blessed times of reformation,
5   When conventickling[9] is so much in fashion.
And yet—
That mutinous tribe less factions do beget,
Than your continual differing in wit.
Your judgment's, as your passion's, a disease:
10   Nor° muse nor miss your appetite can please;   *Neither*
You're grown as nice° as queasy consciences,   *fastidious*
Whose each convulsion, when the spirit moves,
Damns everything that maggot° disapproves.   *capricious person*
    With canting rule you would the stage refine,
15   And to dull method all our sense confine.
With th'insolence of commonwealths you rule,
Where each gay fop and politic grave fool
On monarch wit impose, without control.
As for the last, who seldom sees a play,
20   Unless it be the old Blackfriars[1] way;
Shaking his empty noddle o'er bamboo,°   *cane*
He cries, "Good faith, these plays will never do!
Ah, sir, in my young days, what lofty wit,
What high-strained scenes of fighting there were writ.
25   These are slight airy toys. But tell me, pray,
What has the House of Commons done today?"
Then shows his politics, to let you see
Of state affairs he'll judge as notably
As he can do of wit and poetry.
30   The younger sparks, who hither do resort,
Cry,
"Pox o' your genteel things! Give us more sport!
Damn me, I'm sure 'twill never please the court."
    Such fops are never pleased, unless the play
35   Be stuffed with fools as brisk° and dull as they.   *pert*
Such might the half-crown spare, and in a glass°   *mirror*
At home behold a more accomplished ass.
Where they may set their cravats, wigs, and faces,
And practice all their buffoonry grimaces:
40   See how this huff becomes, this damny,° stare,   *damn me!*
Which they at home may act because they dare,
But must with prudent caution do elsewhere.
Oh that our Nokes, or Tony Lee,[2] could show
A fop but half so much to th' life as you.

---

9. Holding meetings of religious noncon-
formists.
1. A London theater that closed in 1642, at
the onset of the English Civil War.

2. James Nokes (1642–1696) and Anthony
Leigh (d. 1692), popular comic actors of the
1670s who often appeared together.

Postscript

This play had been sooner in print, but for a report about the town (made by some either very malicious or very ignorant) that 'twas *Thomaso*[3] altered; which made the booksellers fear some trouble from the proprietor of that admirable play, which indeed
5 has wit enough to stock a poet, and is not to be pieced or mended by any but the excellent author himself. That I have stolen some hints from it, may be a proof that I valued it more than to pretend to alter it, had I the dexterity of some poets, who are not more expert in stealing than in the art of concealing, and who even that
10 way outdo the Spartan boys.[4] I might have appropriated all to myself; but I, vainly proud of my judgment, hang out the sign of Angellica (the only stolen object) to give notice where a great part of the wit dwelt; though if the *Play of the Novella*[5] were as well worth remembering as *Thomaso*, they might (bating the name)
15 have as well said I took it from thence. I will only say the plot and business (not to boast on't) is my own; as for the words and characters, I leave the reader to judge and compare 'em with *Thomaso*, to whom I recommend the great entertainment of reading it. Though had this succeeded ill, I should have had no need of
20 imploring that justice from the critics, who are naturally so kind to any that pretend to usurp their dominion, especially of our sex:[6] they would doubtless have given me the whole honor on't. Therefore I will only say in English what the famous Virgil[7] does in Latin: I make verses, and others have the fame.

Finis

3. The 1654 play by Thomas Killigrew on which *The Rover* is largely based.
4. In ancient Sparta, boys were deliberately underfed so that they would learn to steal food; but if caught, they were disgraced.
5. The 1632 play by Richard Brome that inspired some elements of *The Rover*.
6. This acknowledgment of female author-

ship did not appear in the first issue of the first quarto or in some copies of the second issue.
7. Roman poet (70–19 B.C.E.), author of the *Aeneid;* according to the Roman grammarian Donatus (4th c. C.E.), a couplet he wrote anonymously in praise of the emperor Augustus was claimed by another.

AUGUST STRINDBERG

1849–1912

WHEN scholars try to decide who invented modern drama, their arguments focus on two Scandinavian playwrights: the Norwegian HENRIK IBSEN and the Swede Johan August Strindberg. Ibsen is the more classical writer of the two: his plays are tightly constructed, formally controlled, and carefully paced. Strindberg, by contrast, is a modernist rebel: his plays are flights of fancy, manifestations of a wild imagination that created characters engaged in a perpetual struggle of wills and desires. Strindberg refused to have anything to do with inherited forms of drama. Instead, he reinvented drama from scratch. In order to find new models for his plays, he turned to the most unlikely places. He read contemporary philosophy—for example, the German philosopher Friedrich Nietzsche. He explored the logic of dreams. He studied Eastern religions such as Hinduism. At the same time, he made a name for himself as a painter and wrote a voluminous geographical and cultural history of Sweden as well as a large number of essays, pamphlets, and books on a great variety of subjects, including the occult, magic, and science. Strindberg's career was littered with ill-conceived and quixotic projects, such as his attempts to synthesize gold, which nearly cost him his sanity. Even more disturbing, and notorious, were his anti-Semitic pamphlets and his attacks on the women's rights movement. But somehow out of this volatile life and mind emerged a number of modernism's most compelling and revolutionary plays.

Strindberg was born into a lower-middle-class family, but his mother had been a servant. The stigma attached to this parentage, which Strindberg captured and exaggerated in his first autobiographical novel, *The Son of a Servant* (1886), continued to haunt him to the end of his life. So did his lack of economic resources. He was financially dependent on his friends as early as his student days in Upsala, and even after he had established himself as a writer he could barely make ends meet. His precarious finances forced him to give up his university studies and take jobs as a teacher and also, briefly, as an actor. Eventually he landed a somewhat more secure position as a librarian, which allowed him enough free time to start his career as a writer. But the uneventful and quiet periods in Strindberg's life were few, in part because of his difficult relations with women. His first marriage—to Siri von Essen, an independent and freethinking Finnish aristocrat—lasted for seven tumultuous years and became the subject of his autobiographical novel *A Madman's Defense* (1888). At the same time, his professional life was in almost as much turmoil. Some of his early plays were staged with relative success, but Strindberg felt attacked by critics and ignored by the theater establishment, a sense that persisted throughout his life. This perceived lack of appreciation was also why he left Sweden in 1883, beginning a long self-imposed exile in France, Germany, Switzerland, and Denmark, interrupted only briefly by returns home.

Many of Strindberg's best-known plays, including *The Father* (1887) and MISS JULIE (1888), were first produced outside Sweden, where he first achieved fame as a dramatist. Most of the important influences on Strindberg were likewise European. He engaged in a long correspondence with the influential Danish critic and philosopher Georg Brandes and had less extensive exchanges with Friedrich Nietzsche and Émile Zola. While living in Berlin, he met the director Max Reinhardt, who produced several of Strindberg's plays to great acclaim. Strindberg made friends, but he had a greater talent for making enemies, and he often broke with friends and supporters for no good reason. One of the targets of Strindberg's ire was Ibsen, the older and more established of the two Scandinavian playwrights.

Even though Strindberg had been a professed atheist for much of his life, in the 1890s he increasingly turned to religion, occultism, and pseudoscience. This period also coincided with the end of his volatile second marriage, to Frida Uhl, an Austrian writer. In 1895, after separating from her, he found himself in desolate circumstances in Paris and stopped writing literature entirely. Instead he spent his scant funds purchasing chemical equipment with which he attempted to produce gold. Paranoid delusions, illness, and failed experiments, together with the mystical writings of Emanuel Swedenborg (1688–1772), fueled his mental instability. The autobiographical *Inferno* (ca. 1898) and his *Occult Diary* (written 1896–1908) sadly testify to this physical and mental decline. In 1897, when he was close to fifty years old, he finally returned permanently to Sweden.

Upon his return to Sweden, Strindberg started to write plays again but in a very different mode. Whereas his earlier plays had concentrated on single events and

encounters, these new, symbolist and expressionist plays, including *The Road to Damascus* (1898) and *The Dream Play* (1901), unfold in loosely connected scenes and episodes. Characters are fluid and shifting, mysterious encounters lead to unforeseen consequences, and the dialogue is infused with religious figures and expressions. These later plays—which also include his so-called chamber plays, among them *The Ghost Sonata* (1907) and *The Pelican* (1907)—revolve around suffering, sin, and redemption. Back in Stockholm Strindberg had also gotten married a third time, to Harriet Bosse, an actress much younger than he. But this marriage was brief, and Strindberg spent his last years alone, in a modest apartment in Stockholm known as the Blue Tower. He never became popular, but in the last years of his life he achieved something of a literary reputation. Although he failed to win the Nobel Prize in Literature—one of the five prizes endowed by the final bequest of the Swedish chemist and armaments manufacturer Alfred Nobel, first awarded in 1901—he was finally honored with a state pension and a so-called Anti-Nobel Prize, a large sum raised by national subscription, one year before his death.

Miss Julie belongs to Strindberg's naturalist period, which also includes *The Father* and *Creditors* (1889). Naturalist drama was a rebellion against the bombastic history plays of Romanticism, the simplistic division between good and evil characters in melodrama, and the neatly constructed drawing-room comedies that flourished in the middle of the century. Naturalism, by contrast, privileged contemporary, and particularly lower-class, settings, which had rarely been seen on the stage except for comic effect. Strindberg's naturalist plays are interested in class differences, especially their effect on the relations between men and women. Like his autobiographical novels and short stories, Strindberg's naturalist plays depict the sexes as engaged in an all-out war. Whether vampires or degenerate creatures, women are always seeking the subjection of men. *The Father* pushes such irrational misogyny to an extreme: it portrays a man who, surrounded by his wife, daughter, mother-in-law, and old nurse, is slowly but surely being driven mad by these vengeful women; finally, he collapses dead in the arms of his nurse. The dramatist's auto-biographical novels, as well as his letters and essays, suggest that Strindberg experienced his own marriages as similarly assaultive. But in his plays, at least, he was able to treat his own bitter experiences and paranoid obsessions with more detachment, thereby turning them into more compelling artistic forms.

Miss Julie strives for verisimilitude in its form. The play, confined to a single setting and one long act, represents a single, continuous action that lasts precisely as long as the play itself; it thus strictly obeys the neo-Aristotelian unities of time, place, and action. It is set not in some elaborate drawing room but in the kitchen of an estate, the domain of a cook and her apparent fiancé, another servant in the house in which a count lives with his daughter. Though its opening scene depicts the two servants, the play soon turns to its primary interest: the relation between the emancipated and freethinking mistress of the house, Miss Julie, and the ambitious, virile valet, Jean. The play describes a simple dramatic arc. At first Miss Julie has the upper hand. She flirts with her servant and finally persuades him to dance with her. After a sexual encounter, the dynamics change: now the servant is the dominant one. The play shows in detail the shifting power balance as Jean suggests to Miss Julie that they flee together and fantasizes about setting up a hotel in Italy. But nothing comes of the plan: they are trapped in the kitchen and trapped by their deed. Miss Julie finds herself in the hands of a power-hungry but volatile man, and by the end of the play she has lost her social position and her honor and has nowhere to turn.

As is to be expected from a self-declared opponent of the New Woman such as Strindberg, Miss Julie does not fare well in this play precisely because she is too emancipated. In keeping with naturalist doctrine, her stance is caused by her parents' corrupting influence; one sign of their moral failings is their initial refusal to be lawfully wedded. Her mother's descent into adultery and arson also helps explain the transformation of the seem-ingly self-confident and articulate mistress into a moral wreck. Nowhere is Strindberg's reactionary view on marriage and emancipation clearer than in the back-story of Miss Julie, which serves to justify her ultimate downfall. Like many other naturalists, Strindberg was deeply influenced by "social Darwinists," who misapplied evolutionary theory to explain and justify social inequities; here, bad parentage necessarily dooms her. Such plots of social rising and falling are common in naturalist novels and plays alike.

Even though the emancipated aristocrat Miss Julie may in some ways be reminiscent of Strindberg's first wife, the play itself is based not on his own marriage but rather on an account Strindberg had heard of a servant who ended up dominating his former mistress both sexually and socially. In Strindberg's moral universe, the degenerate aristocrat must ultimately be brought down, just as the servant Jean, of humble birth but possessing a forceful will, must rise. The relation between Miss Julie and Jean, couched in a language of dominance,

Siri von Essen, Strindberg's first wife and the first to play the lead role in the 1889 production of *Miss Julie* at the Scandinavian Experimental Theater.

servitude, and struggle, is indebted to Nietzsche, especially those aspects of his philosophy that now seem most troubling.

All the characters in *Miss Julie* are measured in terms of their power and their will to dominate others, but the backdrop of their struggle for dominance is a fixed class structure. Even though in the second part of the play Jean presents himself as the strong servant who will triumph over his mistress, he wavers between arrogance and submission, falling into the latter attitude especially toward Miss Julie's absent father. Throughout the play, the count's return is expected and with it the resumption of Jean's duties, epitomized in the task of polishing his master's shoes. Miss Julie, too, fears the return of her father, who has wholly rejected his former liberal attitudes and now rules sternly and justly, conforming to Strindberg's own conservative ideal. The battle between Jean and Miss Julie is waged in the oppressive atmosphere of the servants' quarters, a setting that underscores the constant threat of retribution. Despite Strindberg's belief in social Darwinism and the survival of the stronger, the determining power of social class can never be entirely overcome in *Miss Julie*: the play and its protagonist remain mired in class resentment. Jean may despise Miss Julie and manage to bring her into his power, but part of him remains a servant.

The oscillation between dominance and subservience within an individual is part of the theory of characterization that Strindberg articulates in his famous preface to the play. He rejects the traditional stage characters, who often manifest a single dominant trait—such stock figures as the hapless victim, the scheming villain, and the trusted friend. Clear motivations and distinct types may be useful in the construction of plots, but in Strindberg's view they fail to represent the conflicted and shifting forces that actually drive human action. Like modernist novelists such as James Joyce and Virginia Woolf, Strindberg wanted to replicate the irregular workings of the human mind. While other naturalists placed great emphasis on external detail of costume and dialect, Strindberg was more interested in interiority and psychology. His characters change their minds constantly, and when they express their thoughts, they are allowed to be inconsistent, shifting, and inarticulate. Strindberg also insisted on abolishing many of the artificial aspects

Aisling O'Sullivan as Miss Julie and Christopher Eccleston as Jean in the 2000 Theatre Royal Haymarket (London) production of *Miss Julie*.

of stagecraft, including painted scenes, makeup, unnatural lighting effects such as those caused by footlights, and the practice of playing to the audience. At the same time, he made no attempt to do away with all elements of theatrical artifice. Even in his naturalist plays, he included theatrical set pieces such as dance, music, and ballet. They often take the place of crowd scenes, which Strindberg did not believe could be staged naturalistically in the theater. He thus pragmatically opted for established theatrical techniques when necessary.

Miss Julie has remained a central play in the canon of modern drama. Early productions were mounted in Copenhagen, Berlin, and, most famously, Paris at André Antoine's Théâtre Libre in 1893, a production that confirmed Strindberg's standing as a leading naturalist playwright. In Sweden, the play was not produced until 1906, when it was staged at the Intima Teater. Upon his return to Sweden, Strindberg had founded this theater with the director August Falck, and many of his late chamber plays were written for it. Decorated in green and white draperies, with a bust of Strindberg in the small foyer, the Intima Teater was in fact modeled on Antoine's Théâtre Libre. But even though Strindberg had control over this theater, he was never entirely content with its productions of his plays. The quality of the acting was mixed, and the theater was under constant

financial strain. In 1910 it had to be closed for good. Despite his efforts, Strindberg thus never found a company that could adequately translate his theories and plays into theatrical reality. And not until shortly before his death did he receive the enthusiastic support from the press, publishers, and the theatergoing public that had eluded him for decades.

Strindberg's life was a struggle against the world and against himself. His plays, likewise, are full of struggles among characters, even as they fight for a new type of drama. While Strindberg's struggles were mostly destructive in his life, they were immensely productive in his art. His plays never take anything for granted, and in each play he sought to invent drama anew. In the process, he first created an unusual form of naturalism; then, in his later work, he pioneered what would be known as expressionism—plays full of enigmatic characters, religious language, and episodic plots. But neither label can entirely capture the essence of Strindberg's plays, which are among the most personal and singular in the history of modern drama. Even though readers today are, if anything, more shocked than his contemporaries at his racist, misogynist, and strange religious opinions, Strindberg's unusual plays have continued to compel generations of readers, theatergoers, and critics, and his varied and rich work remains one of the pillars of modern drama.   M.P.

Miss Julie[1]

Preface

Like the arts in general, the theater has for a long time seemed to me a *Biblia Pauperum*,[2] a picture Bible for those who cannot read, and the playwright merely a lay preacher who hawks the latest ideals in popular form, so popular that the middle classes—the bulk of the audiences—can grasp them without racking their brains too much. That explains why the theater has always been an elementary school for

1. Translated by Evert Sprinchorn.   2. Bible of the Poor (Latin).

youngsters and the half-educated, and for women, who still retain a primitive capacity for deceiving themselves and for letting themselves be deceived, that is, for suc-
cumbing to illusions and responding hypnotically to the suggestions of the author.
Consequently, now that the rudimentary and undeveloped mental processes that
operate in the realm of fantasy appear to be evolving to the level of reflection,
research, and experimentation, I believe that the theater, like religion, is about to be
replaced as a dying institution for whose enjoyment we lack the necessary qualifications. Support for my view is provided by the theater crisis through which all of
Europe is now passing, and still more by the fact that in those highly cultured lands
which have produced the finest minds of our time—England and Germany—the
drama is dead, as for the most part are the other fine arts.

Other countries, however, have thought to create a new drama by filling the old
forms with new contents. But since there has not been enough time to popularize the
new ideas, the public cannot understand them. And in the second place, controversy
has so stirred up the public that they can no longer look on with a pure and dispassionate interest, especially when they see their most cherished ideals assailed or hear
an applauding or booing majority openly exercise its tyrannical power, as can happen
in the theater. And in the third place, since the new forms for the new ideas have not
been created, the new wine has burst the old bottles.

In the play that follows I have not tried to accomplish anything new—that is
impossible. I have only tried to modernize the form to satisfy what I believe up-to-
date people expect and demand of this art. And with that in mind I have seized
upon—or let myself be seized by—a theme that may be said to lie outside current
party strife, since the question of being on the way up or on the way down the social
ladder, of being on the top or on the bottom, superior or inferior, man or woman, is,
has been, and will be of perennial interest. When I took this theme from real life—I
heard about it a few years ago and it made a deep impression on me—I thought it
would be a suitable subject for a tragedy, since it still strikes us as tragic to see a happily favored individual go down in defeat, and even more so to see an entire family
line die out. But perhaps a time will come when we shall be so highly developed and
so enlightened that we can look with indifference upon the brutal, cynical, and
heartless spectacle that life offers us, a time when we shall have laid aside those
inferior and unreliable mechanical apparatuses called emotions, which will become
superfluous and even harmful as our mental organs develop. The fact that my heroine wins sympathy is due entirely to the fact that we are still too weak to overcome
the fear that the same fate might overtake us. The extremely sensitive viewer will of
course not be satisfied with mere expressions of sympathy, and the man who believes
in progress will demand that certain positive actions be taken for getting rid of the
evil, a kind of program, in other words. But in the first place absolute evil does not
exist. The decline of one family is the making of another, which now gets its chance
to rise. This alternate rising and falling provides one of life's greatest pleasures, for
happiness is, after all, relative. As for the man who has a program for changing the
disagreeable circumstance that the hawk eats the chicken and that lice eat up the
hawk, I should like to ask him why it should be changed. Life is not prearranged
with such idiotic mathematical precision that only the larger gets to eat the smaller.
Just as frequently the bee destroys the lion (in Aesop's[3] fable)—or at least drives him
wild.

If my tragedy makes most people feel sad, that is their fault. When we get to be as
strong as the first French Revolutionists were, we shall be perfectly content and
happy to watch the forests being cleared of rotting, superannuated trees that have
stood too long in the way of others with just as much right to grow and flourish for a
while—as content as we are when we see an incurably ill man finally die.

---

3. Greek storyteller (early 6th c. B.C.E.), known especially for his moralizing animal fables
(Strindberg is here apparently thinking of "The Gnat and the Lion").

Recently my tragedy *The Father*[4] was censured for being too unpleasant—as if one wanted merry tragedies. "The joy of life" is now the slogan of the day. Theater managers send out orders for nothing but farces, as if the joy of living lay in behaving like a clown and in depicting people as if they were afflicted with St. Vitus's dance[5] or congenital idiocy. I find the joy of living in the fierce and ruthless battles of life, and my pleasure comes from learning something, from being taught something. That is why I have chosen for my play an unusual but instructive case, an exception, in other words—but an important exception of the kind that proves the rule—a choice of subject that I know will offend all lovers of the conventional. The next thing that will bother simple minds is that the motivation for the action is not simple and that the point of view is not single. Usually an event in life—and this is a fairly new discovery—is the result of a whole series of more or less deep-rooted causes. The spectator, however, generally chooses the one that puts the least strain on his mind or reflects most credit on his insight. Consider a case of suicide. "Business failure," says the merchant. "Unhappy love," say the women. "Physical illness," says the sick man. "Lost hopes," says the down-and-out. But it may be that the reason lay in all of these or in none of them, and that the suicide hid his real reason behind a completely different one that would reflect greater glory on his memory.

I have motivated the tragic fate of Miss Julie with an abundance of circumstances: her mother's basic instincts, her father's improper bringing-up of the girl, her own inborn nature, and her fiancé's sway over her weak and degenerate mind. Further and more immediately: the festive atmosphere of Midsummer Eve, her father's absence, her period, her preoccupation with animals, the erotic excitement of the dance, the long summer twilight, the highly aphrodisiac influence of flowers, and finally chance itself, which drives two people together in an out-of-the-way room, plus the boldness of the aroused man.

As one can see, I have not been entirely the physiologist, not been obsessively psychological, not traced everything to her mother's heredity, not found the sole cause in her period, not attributed everything to our "immoral times," and not simply preached a moral lesson. Lacking a priest, I have let the cook handle that.

I am proud to say that this complicated way of looking at things is in tune with the times. And if others have anticipated me in this, I am proud that I am not alone in my paradoxes, as all new discoveries are called. And no one can say this time that I am being one-sided.

As far as the drawing of characters is concerned, I have made the people in my play fairly "characterless" for the following reasons. In the course of time the word *character* has acquired many meanings. Originally it probably meant the dominant and fundamental trait in the soul complex and was confused with temperament. Later the middle class used it to mean an automaton. An individual who once and for all had found his own true nature or adapted himself to a certain role in life, who in fact had ceased to grow, was called a man of character, while the man who was constantly developing, who, like a skillful sailor on the currents of life, did not sail with close-tied sheets but who fell off before the wind in order to luff again, was called a man of no character—derogatorily of course, since he was so difficult to keep track of, to pin down and pigeonhole. This middle-class conception of a fixed character was transferred to the stage, where the middle class has always ruled. A character there came to mean someone who was always one and the same, always drunk, always joking, always melancholy, and who needed to be characterized only by some physical defect such as a club foot, a wooden leg, or a red nose, or by the repetition of some such phrase as, "That's capital," or "Barkis is willin'."[6] This uncomplicated

---

4. Published one year earlier, in 1887.
5. Chorea, a disease characterized by involuntary spasmodic movements.
6. A phrase repeated by Mr. Barkis, a character in Charles Dickens's *David Copperfield*

(1849–50), to indicate his desire to marry Clara Peggotty; that novel, like many other works by Dickens, was successfully adapted to the stage.

way of viewing people is still to be found in the great Molière. Harpagon[7] is nothing but a miser, although Harpagon could have been both a miser and an exceptional financier, a fine father, and a good citizen. Worse still, his "defect" is extremely advantageous to his son-in-law and his daughter, who will be his heirs and who therefore should not find fault with him, even if they do have to wait a while to jump into bed together. So I do not believe in simple stage characters. And the summary judgments that writers pass on people—he is stupid, this one is brutal, that one is jealous, this one is stingy, and so on—should not pass unchallenged by the naturalists who know how complicated the soul is and who realize that vice has a reverse side very much like virtue.

Since the persons in my play are modern characters, living in a transitional era more hectic and hysterical than the previous one at least, I have depicted them as more unstable, as torn and divided, a mixture of the old and the new. Nor does it seem improbable to me that modern ideas might also have seeped down through newspapers and kitchen talk to the level of the servants. Consequently the valet may belch forth from his inherited slave soul certain modern ideas. And if there are those who find it wrong to allow people in a modern drama to talk Darwin and who recommend the practice of Shakespeare to our attention, may I remind them that the gravedigger in *Hamlet* talks the then-fashionable philosophy of Giordano Bruno (Bacon's philosophy),[8] which is even more improbable, seeing that the means of spreading ideas were fewer then than now. And besides, the fact of the matter is that Darwinism has always existed, ever since Moses' history of creation[9] from the lower animals up to man, but it was not until recently that we discovered it and formulized it.

My souls—or characters—are conglomerations from various stages of culture, past and present, walking scrapbooks, shreds of human lives, tatters torn from old rags that were once Sunday best—hodgepodges just like the human soul. I have even supplied a little source history into the bargain by letting the weaker steal and repeat words of the stronger, letting them get ideas (suggestions as they are called) from one another, from the environment (the songbird's blood), and from objects (the razor). I have also arranged for *Gedankenübertragung*[1] through an inanimate medium to take place (the count's boots, the servant's bell). And I have even made use of "waking suggestions" (a variation of hypnotic suggestion), which have by now been so popularized that they cannot arouse ridicule or skepticism as they would have done in Mesmer's[2] time.

I say Miss Julie is a modern character not because the man-hating half-woman has not always existed but because she has now been brought out into the open, has taken the stage, and is making a noise about herself. Victim of a superstition (one that has seized even stronger minds) that woman, that stunted form of human being, standing with man, the lord of creation, the creator of culture, is meant to be the equal of man or could ever possibly be, she involves herself in an absurd struggle with him in which she falls. Absurd because a stunted form, subject to the laws of propagation, will always be born stunted and can never catch up with the one who has the lead. As follows: A (the man) and B (the woman) start from the same point C, A with a speed of let us say 100 and B with a speed of 60. When will B overtake A?

7. The protagonist in *The Miser* (1668), a play by the French dramatist Molière (1622–1673).
8. Perhaps a reference to the extreme logical precision of the gravedigger's wordplay in Shakespeare's *Hamlet* (1600–01), 5.1. Francis Bacon (1561–1626), an English philosopher and essayist, promoted the use of the inductive method of modern science; Bruno (1548–1600), an Italian philosopher, challenged dogmatism (he was burned at the stake for heresy). The major idea of the English naturalist Charles Darwin (1809–1882)—the theory of evolution through natural selection, or Darwinism—was gaining wider acceptance at the end of the 19th century.
9. That is, the account given in Genesis, whose authorship was traditionally ascribed to Moses.
1. Telepathy (German).
2. Franz Anton Mesmer (1734–1815), German physician who devised a therapeutic technique, based on "animal magnetism," that was developed into hypnosis.

Answer: never. Neither with the help of equal education or equal voting rights—nor by universal disarmament and temperance societies—any more than two parallel lines can ever meet. The half-woman is a type that forces itself on others, selling itself for power, medals, recognition, diplomas, as formerly it sold itself for money. It represents degeneration. It is not a strong species for it does not maintain itself, but unfortunately it propagates its misery in the following generation. Degenerate men unconsciously select their mates from among these half-women, so that they breed and spread, producing creatures of indeterminate sex to whom life is a torture, but who fortunately are overcome eventually either by a hostile reality, or by the uncontrolled breaking loose of their repressed instincts, or else by their frustration in not being able to compete with the male sex. It is a tragic type, offering us the spectacle of a desperate fight against nature; a tragic legacy of romanticism, which is now being dissipated by naturalism—a movement that seeks only happiness, and for that strong and healthy species are required.

Miss Julie, however, is also a vestige of the old warrior nobility that is now being superseded by a new nobility of nerve and brain. She is a victim of the disorder produced within a family by a mother's "crime," of the mistakes of a whole generation gone wrong, of circumstances, of her own defective constitution—all of which put together is equivalent to the fate or universal law of the ancients. The naturalists have banished guilt along with God, but the consequences of an act—punishment, imprisonment, or the fear of it—cannot be banished for the simple reason that they remain whether or not the naturalist dismisses the case from his court. Those sitting on the sidelines can easily afford to be lenient; but what of the injured parties? And even if her father were compelled to forgo taking his revenge, Miss Julie would take vengeance on herself, as she does in the play, because of that inherited or acquired sense of honor that has been transmitted to the upper classes from—well, where does it come from? From the age of barbarism, from the first Aryans,[3] from the chivalry of the Middle Ages. And a very fine code it was, but now inimical to the survival of the race. It is the aristocrat's form of hara-kiri, a law of conscience that bids the Japanese to slice his own stomach when someone else dishonors him. The same sort of thing survives, slightly modified, in that exclusive prerogative of the aristocracy, the duel. (Example: the husband challenges his wife's lover to a duel; the lover shoots the husband and runs off with the wife. Result: the husband has saved his *honor* but lost his wife.) Hence the servant Jean lives on; but not Miss Julie, who cannot live without honor. The advantage that the slave has over his master is that he has not committed himself to this defeatist principle. In all of us Aryans there is enough of the nobleman, or of the Don Quixote,[4] to make us sympathize with the man who takes his own life after having dishonored himself by shameful deeds. And we are all of us aristocrats enough to be distressed at the sight of a great man lying like a dead hulk ready for the scrap pile, even, I suppose, if he were to raise himself up again and redeem himself by honorable deeds.

The servant Jean is the beginning of a new species in which noticeable differentiation has already taken place. He began as a child of a poor worker and is now evolving through self-education into a future gentleman of the upper classes. He is quick to learn, has highly developed senses (smell, taste, sight), and a keen appreciation of beauty. He has already come up in the world, for he is strong enough not to hesitate to make use of other people. He is already a stranger to his old friends, whom he despises as reminders of past stages in his development, and whom he fears and avoids because they know his secrets, guess his intentions, look with envy on his rise and with joyful expectation toward his fall. Hence his character is unformed and

3. Hypothetical ancient speakers of Indo-European, progenitors of European (especially the Germanic) peoples.
4. The eponymous hero of Miguel de Cer-

vantes's novel (1605, 1615), here invoked as a symbol of unflagging devotion to chivalric ideals.

divided. He wavers between an admiration of high positions and a hatred of the men who occupy them. He is an aristocrat—he says so himself—familiar with the ins and outs of good society. He is polished on the outside, but coarse underneath. He wears his frock coat with elegance but offers no guarantee that he keeps his body clean.

Although he respects Miss Julie, he is afraid of Christine, because she knows his innermost secrets. Yet he is sufficiently hard-hearted not to let the events of the night upset his plans for the future. Possessing both the coarseness of the slave and the toughmindedness of the born ruler, he can look at blood without fainting, shake off bad luck like water, and take calamity by the horns. Consequently he will escape from the battle unwounded, probably ending up as proprietor of a hotel. And if he himself does not get to be a Rumanian count, his son will doubtless go to college and possibly end up as a government official.

Now his observations about life as the lower classes see it, from below, are well worth listening to—that is, they are whenever he is telling the truth, which is not too often, because he is more likely to say what is advantageous to him than what is true. When Miss Julie supposes that everyone in the lower classes must feel greatly oppressed by the weight of the classes above, Jean naturally agrees with her since he wants to win her sympathy. But he promptly takes it all back when he finds it expedient to separate himself from the mob.

Apart from the fact that Jean is coming up in the world, he is also superior to Miss Julie in that he is a man. In the sexual sphere, he is the aristocrat. He has the strength of the male, more highly developed senses, and the ability to take the initiative. His inferiority is merely the result of his social environment, which is only temporary and which he will probably slough off along with his livery.

His slave nature expresses itself in his awe of the count (the boots) and his religious superstitions. But he is awed by the count mainly because the count occupies the place he wants most in life; and this awe is still there even after he has won the daughter of the house and seen how empty that beautiful shell was.

I do not believe that any love in the "higher" sense can be born from the union of two such different souls; so I have let Miss Julie's love be refashioned in her imagination as a love that protects and purifies, and I have let Jean imagine that even his love might have a chance to grow under other social circumstances. For I suppose love is very much like the hyacinth that must strike roots deep in the dark earth *before* it can produce a vigorous blossom. Here it shoots up, bursts into bloom, and turns to seed all at once. Such plants can only be short-lived.

Christine—finally to get to her—is a female slave, spineless and phlegmatic after years spent at the kitchen stove, bovinely unconscious of her own hypocrisy, and with a full quota of moral and religious notions that serve as scapegoats and cloaks for her sins—which a stronger soul does not require since he is able either to carry the burden of his own sins or to rationalize them out of existence. She attends church regularly where she deftly unloads unto Jesus her household thefts and picks up from him another load of innocence. She is only a secondary character, and I have deliberately done no more than sketch her in—just as I treated the country doctor and parish priest in *The Father* where I only wanted to draw ordinary everyday people such as most country doctors and parsons are. That some have found my minor characters one-dimensional is due to the fact that ordinary people while at work are to a certain extent one-dimensional and do lack an independent existence, showing only one side of themselves in the performance of their duties. And as long as the audience does not feel it needs to see them from different angles, my abstract sketches will pass muster.

Now as far as the dialogue is concerned, I have broken somewhat with tradition in refusing to make my characters into interlocutors who ask stupid questions to elicit witty answers. I have avoided the symmetrical and mathematical design of the artfully constructed French dialogue and have let minds work as irregularly as they do in real life, where no subject is quite exhausted before another mind engages at random some cog in the conversation and governs it for a while. My dialogue wanders here and there, gathers material in the first scenes which is later picked up, repeated, reworked, developed, and expanded like the theme in a piece of music.

The action of the play poses no problem. Since it really involves only two people, I have limited myself to these two, introducing only one minor character, the cook, and keeping the unhappy spirit of the father brooding over the action as a whole. I have chosen this course because I have noticed that what interests people most nowadays is the psychological action. Our inveterately curious souls are no longer content to see a thing happen; we want to see how it happens. We want to see the strings, look at the machinery, examine the double-bottom drawer, put on the magic ring to find the hidden seam, look in the deck for the marked cards.

In treating the subject this way I have had in mind the case-history novels of the Goncourt brothers,[5] which appeal to me more than anything else in modern literature.

As far as play construction is concerned, I have made a stab at getting rid of act divisions. I was afraid that the spectator's declining susceptibility to illusion might not carry him through the intermission, when he would have time to think about what he has seen and to escape the suggestive influence of the author-hypnotist. I figure my play lasts about ninety minutes. Since one can listen to a lecture, a sermon, or a political debate for that long or even longer, I have convinced myself that a play should not exhaust an audience in that length of time. As early as 1872 in one of my first attempts at the drama, The Outlaw, I tried out this concentrated form, although with little success. I had finished the work in five acts when I noticed the disjointed and disturbing effect it produced. I burned it, and from the ashes there arose a single, complete reworked act of fifty pages that would run for less than an hour. Although this play form is not completely new, it seems to be my special property and has a good chance of gaining favor with the public when tastes change. My hope is to educate a public to sit through a full evening's show in one act. But this whole question must first be probed more deeply. In the meantime, in order to establish resting places for the audience and the actors without destroying the illusion, I have made use of three arts that belong to the drama: the monologue, the pantomime, and the ballet, all of which were part of classic tragedy, the monody having become the monologue and the choral dance, the ballet.

The realists have banished the monologue from the stage as implausible. But if I can motivate it, I make it plausible, and I can then use it to my advantage. Now it is certainly plausible for a speaker to pace the floor and read his speech aloud to himself. It is plausible for an actor to practice his part aloud, for a child to talk to her cat, a mother to babble to her baby, an old lady to chatter to her parrot, and a sleeping man to talk in his sleep. And in order to give the actor a chance to work on his own for once and for a moment not be obliged to follow the author's directions, I have not written out the monologues in detail but simply outlined them. Since it makes very little difference what is said while asleep, or to the parrot or the cat, inasmuch as it does not affect the main action, a gifted player who is in the midst of the situation and mood of the play can probably improvise the monologue better than the author, who cannot estimate ahead of time how much may be said and for how long before the illusion is broken.

Some theaters in Italy have, as we know, returned to the art of improvisation[6] and have thereby trained actors who are truly inventive—without, however, violating the intentions of the author. This seems to be a step in the right direction and possibly the beginning of a new, fertile form of art that will be genuinely creative.

In places where the monologue cannot be properly motivated, I have resorted to pantomime. Here I have given the actor even more freedom to be creative and win

---

5. Edmond de Goncourt (1822–1896) and Jules de Goncourt (1830–1870), coauthors of six novels set in 18th-century France.

6. That is, the commedia dell'arte, which relies on improvisation by stock characters along conventional plotlines.

honor on his own. Nevertheless, not to try the audience beyond its limits, I have relied on music—well motivated by the Midsummer Eve dance—to exercise its hypnotic powers during the pantomime scene. I beg the music director to select his tunes with great care, so that associations foreign to the mood of the play will not be produced by reminders of popular operattas or current dance numbers or by folk music of interest only to ethnologists.

The ballet that I have introduced cannot be replaced by a so-called crowd scene. Such scenes are always badly acted, with a pack of babbling fools taking advantage of the occasion to "gag it up," thereby destroying the illusion. Inasmuch as country people do not improvise their taunts but make use of material already to hand by giving it a double meaning, I have not composed an original lampoon but have made use of a little-known round dance that I noted down in the Stockholm district. The words do not fit the situation exactly, which is what I intended, since the slave in his cunning (that is, weakness) never attacks directly. At any rate, let us have no comedians in this serious story and no obscene smirking over an affair that nails the lid on a family coffin.

As far as the scenery is concerned, I have borrowed from impressionistic painting the idea of asymmetrical and open composition, and I believe that I have thereby gained something in the way of greater illusion. Because the audience cannot see the whole room and all the furniture, they will have to surmise what's missing; that is, their imagination will be stimulated to fill in the rest of the picture. I have gained something else by this: I have avoided those tiresome exits through doors. Stage doors are made of canvas and rock at the slightest touch. They cannot even be used to indicate the wrath of an angry father who storms out of the house after a bad dinner, slamming the door behind him "so that the whole house shakes." (In the theater it sways and billows.) Furthermore, I have confined the action to one set, both to give the characters a chance to become part and parcel of their environment and to cut down on scenic extravagance. If there is only one set, one has a right to expect it to be as realistic as possible. Yet nothing is more difficult than to make a room look like a room, however easy it may be for the scene painter to create waterfalls and erupting volcanos. I suppose we shall have to put up with walls made of canvas, but isn't it about time that we stopped painting shelves and pots and pans on the canvas? There are so many other conventions in the theater that we are told to accept in good faith that we should be spared the strain of believing in painted saucepans.

I have placed the backdrop and the table at an angle to force the actors to play face to face or in half profile when they are seated opposite each other at the table. In a production of *Aida*[7] I saw a flat placed at such an angle, which led the eye out in an unfamiliar perspective. Nor did it look as if it had been set that way simply to be different or to avoid those monotonous right angles.

Another desirable innovation would be the removal of the footlights. I understand that the purpose of lighting from below is to make the actors look more full in the face. But may I ask why all actors should have full faces? Doesn't this kind of lighting wipe out many of the finer features in the lower part of the face, especially around the jaws? Doesn't it distort the shape of the nose and throw false shadows above the eyes? If not, it certainly does something else: it hurts the actor's eyes. The footlights hit the retina at an angle from which it is usually shielded (except in sailors who must look at the sunlight reflected in the water), and the result is the loss of any effective play of the eyes. All one ever sees on stage are goggle-eyed glances sideways at the boxes or upward at the balcony, with only the whites of the eyes being visible in the latter case. And this probably also accounts for that tiresome fluttering of the eyelashes that the female performers are particularly guilty of. If an actor nowadays wants to express something with his eyes, he can only do it looking right at the

7. An Italian opera by Giuseppe Verdi (1871), set in ancient Egypt.

audience, in which case he makes direct contact with someone outside the proscenium arch—a bad habit known, justifiably or not, as "saying hello to friends."

I should think that the use of sufficiently strong side lights (through the use of reflectors or something like them) would provide the actor with a new asset: an increased range of expression made possible by the play of the eyes, the most expressive part of the face.

I have scarcely any illusions about getting actors to play for the audience and not directly at them, although this should be the goal. Nor do I dream of ever seeing an actor play through all of an important scene with his back to the audience. But is it too much to hope that crucial scenes could be played where the author indicated and not in front of the prompter's box as if they were duets demanding applause? I am not calling for a revolution, only for some small changes. I am well aware that transforming the stage into a real room with the fourth wall missing and with some of the furniture placed with backs to the auditorium would only upset the audience, at least for the present.

If I bring up the subject of makeup, it is not because I dare hope to be heeded by the ladies, who would rather be beautiful than truthful. But the male actor might do well to consider if it is an advantage to paint his face with character lines that remain there like a mask. Let us imagine an actor who pencils in with soot a few lines between his eyes to indicate great anger, and let us suppose that in that permanently enraged state he finds he has to smile on a certain line. Imagine the horrible grimace! And how can the old character actor wrinkle his brows in anger when his false bald pate is as smooth as a billiard ball?

In a modern psychological drama, in which every tremor of the soul should be reflected more by facial expressions than by gestures and grunts, it would probably be most sensible to experiment with strong side lighting on a small stage, using actors without any makeup or a minimum of it.

And then, if we could get rid of the visible orchestra with its disturbing lights and the faces turned toward the public; if the auditorium floor could be raised so that the spectator's eyes are not level with the actor's knees; if we could get rid of the proscenium boxes and their occupants, arriving giggling and drunk from their dinners; and if we could have it dark in the auditorium during the performance; and if, above everything else, we could have a *small* stage and an *intimate* auditorium—then possibly a new drama might arise and at least one theater become a refuge for cultured audiences. While we are waiting for such a theater, we shall have to write for the dramatic stockpile and prepare the repertory that one day shall come.

Here is my attempt. If I have failed, there is still time to try again!

CHARACTERS

MISS JULIE, twenty-five years old

JEAN, valet, thirty years old

CHRISTINE, cook, thirty-five years old

THE CHORUS, a party of country folk

The scene is a country estate in Sweden.

The time: A Midsummer Night in the 1880s. The hours after midnight, June 24, St. John the Baptist's Day.

The Set

The scene is the kitchen of the estate belonging to the count, MISS JULIE's father. It is a large kitchen, situated along with the servants' quarters in the basement of the manor house. The side walls and the ceiling of the kitchen are masked by the tormentors[8] and borders of the set. The rear wall runs obliquely upstage from the left. On this wall to the left are two shelves with pots and pans of copper, iron, and pewter. The shelves are decorated with goffered[9] paper. A little to the right can be seen three-fourths of a deep arched entry with two glass doors, and through them can be seen a fountain with a statue of a cupid,[1] lilac bushes in bloom, and the tops of some Lombardy poplars.

From the left of the stage the corner of a large, Dutch-tile kitchen stove protrudes with part of the hood showing.

Projecting from the right side of the stage is one end of the servants' dining table of white pine, with a few chairs around it.

The stove is decorated with branches of birch leaves; the floor is strewn with juniper twigs.

On the end of the table is a large Japanese spice jar filled with lilacs.

An icebox, a sink, a washbasin.

Over the door a big old-fashioned bell; and to the left of the door the gaping mouth of a speaking tube.[2]

[CHRISTINE *is standing at the stove, frying something in a pan. She is wearing a light-colored cotton dress and an apron.*]

[JEAN *enters, dressed in livery and carrying a pair of high-top boots with spurs. He sets them where they are clearly visible.*]

JEAN   What a night! She's wild again! Miss Julie's absolutely wild!

CHRISTINE   You sure took your time getting back!

JEAN   I took the count down to the station, and on my way back, I passed the barn and went in for a dance. And there was Miss Julie leading the dance
5   with the game warden. Then she noticed me. And she ran right into my arms and chose me for the ladies' waltz. And she's been dancing ever since like—like I don't know what. Wild, I tell you, absolutely wild!

CHRISTINE   That's nothing new. But she's been worse than ever during the last two weeks, ever since her engagement was broken off.

10   JEAN   Yes. I never did hear all there was to that. He was a good man, too, even if he wasn't rich. Well, they've got such crazy ideas. [*He sits down at the end of the table.*] Tell me, isn't it strange that a young girl like her—all right, young woman—prefers to stay home here with the servants rather than go with her father to visit her relatives?

15   CHRISTINE   I suppose she's ashamed to face them after that fiasco with her young man.

JEAN   No doubt. He wouldn't take any nonsense from her. Do you know what happened, Christine? I saw the whole thing. Of course, I didn't let on.

CHRISTINE   You were there? I don't believe it.

20   JEAN   Well, I was. They were in the stable yard one evening—and she was training him, that's what she called it. Do you know what? She was making him jump over her riding whip—training him like a dog. He jumped over

---

8. Curtains or doors on the sides of a stage set that hide the wings from the view of the audience.
9. Embossed to produce patterns of raised figures.

1. A representation of the Roman god of love.
2. A hollow pipe connecting two cones, used in businesses and upper-class homes in the 19th century for communicating over distances.

twice, and she whipped him both times. But the third time, he grabbed the whip from her, [scratched her face with it—long scratch on her left
25 cheek;][3] then broke it in a thousand pieces—and walked off.

CHRISTINE   I don't believe it! What do you know!

JEAN   Yes, that put an end to that affair. —What have you got for me that's really good, Christine?

CHRISTINE [*serving him from the frying pan*]   Just a little bit of kidney. Cut it
30 from the veal roast.

JEAN [*smelling it*]   Wonderful! One of my special *délices!*[4] [*Feeling the plate*] Hey, you didn't warm the plate!

CHRISTINE   You're more fussy than the count himself when you set your mind to it. [*She rumples his hair affectionately.*]

35 JEAN [*irritated*]   Cut it out! Don't muss up my hair. You know how particular I am!

CHRISTINE   Oh, don't get mad. Can I help it if I like you?

[JEAN *eats.* CHRISTINE *gets out a bottle of beer.*]

JEAN   Beer on Midsummer Eve! No thank you! I've got something much bet- ter than that. [*He opens a drawer in the table and takes out a bottle of red
40 wine with a gold seal.*] Do you see that? Gold Seal. Now give me a glass.

[*She hands him a tumbler.*]

—No, a wineglass of course. This has to be drunk properly. No water.

CHRISTINE [*goes back to the stove and puts on a small saucepan*]   Lord help the woman who gets you for a husband. You're an old fussbudget!

JEAN   Talk, talk! You'd consider yourself lucky if you got yourself a man as
45 good as me. It hasn't done you any harm to have people think I'm your fiancé. [*He tastes the wine.*] Very good. Excellent. But warmed just a little too little. [*Warming the glass in his hands*] We bought this in Dijon. Four francs a liter, unbottled—and the tax on top of that. . . . What on earth are you cooking? It stinks like hell!

50 CHRISTINE   Some damn mess that Miss Julie wants for her Diana, that damn dog of hers.

JEAN   You should watch your language, Christine. . . . Why do you have to stand in front of the stove on a holiday, cooking for that mutt? Is it sick?

CHRISTINE   Oh, she's sick, all right! She sneaked out to the gatekeeper's pug
55 and—got herself in a fix. And you know Miss Julie, she can't stand anything like that.

JEAN   She's too stuck-up in some ways and not proud enough in others. Just like her mother. The countess felt right at home in the kitchen or down in the barn with the cows, but when she went driving, one horse wasn't
60 enough for her, she had to have a pair. Her sleeves were always dirty, but her buttons had the royal crown on them. As for Miss Julie, she doesn't give a hoot in hell how she looks and acts. I mean, she's not really refined, not really. Just now, down at the barn, she grabbed the game warden right from under Anna's eyes and asked him to dance. You wouldn't see anybody
65 in our class behaving like that. But that's what happens when the gentry try to act like the common people—they become common! . . . However, I'll

---

3. The passage in brackets was deleted in Strindberg's manuscript, probably by Strind- berg himself [translator's note].
4. Pleasures, delights (French).

say one thing for her: she *is* beautiful! Statuesque! Ah, those shoulders—those—and so forth, and so forth!

CHRISTINE Oh, don't exaggerate. Clara tells me all about her, and Clara
70 dresses her.

JEAN Clara, pooh! You women are always jealous of each other. I've been out riding with her. . . . And how she can dance . . . !

CHRISTINE Listen, Jean, you *are* going to dance with me, aren't you, when I'm finished here?

75 JEAN Certainly! Of course I am.

CHRISTINE Promise?

JEAN Promise! Listen—if I say I'm going to do a thing, I do it. . . . Christine, I thank you for a delicious meal. Superb! [*He shoves the cork back into the bottle.*]

[MISS JULIE *appears in the entry, talking to someone outside.*]

MISS JULIE I'll be right back. Don't wait for me.

[JEAN *slips the bottle into the table drawer quickly and rises respectfully.* MISS JULIE *comes in and crosses over to* CHRISTINE, *who is at the stove.*]

80 MISS JULIE Did you get it ready?

[CHRISTINE *signals that* JEAN *is present.*]

JEAN [*polite and charming*] Are you ladies sharing secrets?

MISS JULIE [*flipping her handkerchief in his face*] Don't be nosy!

JEAN Oh, that smells good! Violets.

MISS JULIE [*flirting with him*] Don't be impudent! And don't tell me you're
85 an expert on perfumes, too. I love the way you dance!—No, mustn't look! Go away!

JEAN [*cocky but pleasant*] What are the ladies cooking up? A witches' brew for Midsummer Eve? So they can tell the future?[5] Read what's in the cards for them, and see who they'll marry?

90 MISS JULIE [*curtly*] You'd have to have good eyes to see that. [*To* CHRISTINE] Pour it into a small bottle, and seal it tight. . . . Jean, come and dance a schottische[6] with me.

JEAN [*hesitating*] I hope you don't think I'm being rude, but I've already promised this dance to Christine.

95 MISS JULIE She can always find someone. Isn't that so, Christine? You don't mind if I borrow Jean for a minute, do you?

CHRISTINE It ain't up to me. If Miss Julie is gracious enough to invite you, it ain't right for you to say no, Jean. You go on, and thank her for the honor.

100 JEAN Frankly, Miss Julie, I don't want to hurt your feelings, but I wonder if it's wise—I mean for you to dance twice in a row with the same partner. Especially since the people around here love to talk.

MISS JULIE [*bridling*] What do you mean? What kind of talk? What are you trying to say?

105 JEAN [*retreating*] I wish you wouldn't misunderstand me, Miss Julie. It just doesn't look right for you to prefer one of your servants to the others who are hoping for the same unusual honor.

MISS JULIE Prefer! What an idea! I'm really surprised. I, the mistress of the house, am good enough to come to their dance, and when I feel like

5. In Swedish folklore, Midsummer Eve is a time of fortune-telling.

6. Literally, "Scottish" (German), a country dance similar to the polka.

110 dancing, I want to dance with someone who knows how to lead. After all I don't want to look ridiculous.

JEAN   As you wish, Miss Julie. I am at your orders.

MISS JULIE [*gently*]   Don't take it as an order. Tonight we're all just having a good time. There's no question of rank. Now give me your arm. —Don't
115 worry, Christine. I won't run off with your boyfriend.

[JEAN *gives her his arm and leads her out.*]

Pantomime Scene

This should be played as if the actress were actually alone. She turns her back on the audience when she feels like it; she does not look out into the auditorium; she does not rush through the scene as if afraid the audience will grow impatient.

CHRISTINE *alone. In the distance the sound of the violins playing the schottische.* CHRISTINE, *humming in time with the music, cleans up after* JEAN, *washes the dishes, dries them, and puts them away in a cupboard. Then she takes off her apron, takes a little mirror from one of the table drawers, and leans it against the jar of lilacs on the table. She lights a tallow candle, heats a curling iron, and curls the bangs on her forehead. Then she goes to the doorway and stands listening to the music. She comes back to the table and finds the handkerchief that* MISS JULIE *left behind. She smells it, spreads it out, and then, as if lost in thought, stretches it, smooths it out, and folds it in four.*

[JEAN *enters alone.*]

JEAN   Wild! I told you she was wild! You should have seen the way she was dancing. Everyone was peeking at her from behind the doors and laughing at her. What's the matter with her, Christine?

CHRISTINE   You might know it's her monthlies, Jean. She always acts peculiar
5 then. . . . Well, are you going to dance with me?

JEAN   You're not mad at me because I broke my promise?

CHRISTINE   Of course not. Not for a little thing like that, you know that. I know my place.

JEAN [*grabs her around the waist*]   You're a sensible girl, Christine. You're
10 going to make somebody a good wife—

[MISS JULIE, *coming in, sees them together. She is unpleasantly surprised.*]

MISS JULIE [*with forced gaiety*]   Well, aren't you the gallant beau—running away from your partner!

JEAN   On the contrary, Miss Julie. As you can see, I've hurried back to the partner I deserted.

15 MISS JULIE [*changing tack*]   You know, you're the best dancer I've met. — Why are you wearing livery on a holiday? Take it off at once.

JEAN   I'd have to ask you to leave for a minute. My black coat is hanging right here—[*He moves to the right and points.*]

MISS JULIE   You're not embarrassed because I'm here, are you? Just to
20 change your coat? Go in your room and come right back again. Or else stay here and I'll turn my back.

JEAN   If you'll excuse me, Miss Julie.

[*He goes off to the right. His arm can be seen as he changes his coat.*]

MISS JULIE [*to* CHRISTINE]   Tell me something, Christine. Is Jean your fiancé? He acts so familiar with you.

25 CHRISTINE   Fiancé? I suppose so. At least we say we are.

MISS JULIE   What do you mean?

CHRISTINE   Well, Miss Julie, you have had fiancés yourself, and you know—

MISS JULIE   But we were properly engaged—!

CHRISTINE   I know, but did anything come of it?

[JEAN *comes back, wearing a black cutaway coat and derby.*]

30   MISS JULIE   *Très gentil, monsieur Jean! Très gentil!*

JEAN   *Vous voulez plaisanter, madame.*

MISS JULIE   *Et vous voulez parler français!*[7] Where did you learn to speak French?

JEAN   In Switzerland. I was *sommelier*[8] in one of the biggest hotels in
35   Lucerne.

MISS JULIE   My! but you look quite the gentleman in that coat! *Charmant!*[9]

[*She sits down at the table.*]

JEAN   Flatterer!

MISS JULIE [*stiffening*]   Who said I was flattering you?

JEAN   My natural modesty would not allow me to presume that you were
40   paying sincere compliments to someone like me, and therefore I could only
assume that you were exaggerating, which, in this case, means flattering
me.

MISS JULIE   You certainly have a way with words. Where did you learn to talk
like that? Seeing plays?

45   JEAN   And other places. You don't think I stayed in the house for six years
when I was a valet in Stockholm, do you?

MISS JULIE   I thought you were born in this district. Weren't you?

JEAN   My father worked as a farmhand on the district attorney's estate, next
door to yours. I used to see you when you were little. Of course you didn't
50   notice me.

MISS JULIE   Did you really?

JEAN   Yes. I remember one time in particular—. But I can't tell you about
that!

MISS JULIE   Of course you can. . . . Oh, come on. Just this once—for me.

55   JEAN   No. No, I really couldn't. Not now. Some other time maybe.

MISS JULIE   Some other time? That means never. What's the harm in telling
me now?

JEAN   There's no harm. I just don't feel like it. —Look at her.

[*He nods at* CHRISTINE, *who has fallen asleep in a chair by the stove.*]

MISS JULIE   Won't she make somebody a pretty wife! I'll bet she snores, too.

60   JEAN   No, she doesn't. But she talks in her sleep.

MISS JULIE [*archly*]   Now how could you know she talks in her sleep?

JEAN [*coolly*]   I've heard her . . .

[*Pause. They look at each other.*]

MISS JULIE   Why don't you sit down?

JEAN   I wouldn't take the liberty in your presence.

65   MISS JULIE   Not even if I ordered you?

JEAN   Of course I'd obey.

MISS JULIE   Well then: sit down. —Wait a minute. Could you get me something to drink?

7. "Very nice, Mister Jean! Very nice!" "You
are trying to flatter me, madam." "And you
are trying to speak French!" (French).

8. Wine steward.
9. Charming (French).

JEAN   I don't know what there is in the icebox. Only beer, I suppose.

70 MISS JULIE   Only beer?! I have simple tastes. I prefer beer to wine.

[JEAN *takes a bottle of beer from the icebox and opens it. He looks in the cupboard for a glass and a plate, and serves her.*]

JEAN   At your service, *mademoiselle*.[1]

MISS JULIE   Thank you. What about you?

JEAN   I'm not much of a beer-drinker, thank you, but if it's your wish—

MISS JULIE   My wish! I should think a gentleman would want to keep his lady

75 company.

JEAN   A point well taken! [*He opens another bottle and takes a glass.*]

MISS JULIE   Now drink a toast to me!

[JEAN *hesitates.*]

You're not shy, are you? A big, strong man like you?

[*Playfully,* JEAN *kneels and raises his glass in mock gallantry.*]

JEAN   To my lady's health!

80 MISS JULIE   Bravo! Now you have to kiss my shoe, too. Then you will have hit it off perfectly.

[JEAN *hesitates, then boldly grasps her foot and touches it lightly with his lips.*]

Superb! You should have been an actor.

JEAN [*rising*]   This has got to stop, Miss Julie! Someone might come in and see us.

85 MISS JULIE   So what?

JEAN   People would talk, that's what! If you knew how their tongues were wagging out there just a few minutes ago!

MISS JULIE   What did they say? Tell me. Sit down and tell me.

JEAN   I don't want to hurt your feelings. . . . They used expressions that—

90 that hinted at certain—you know what I mean. You're not a child. And when they see a woman drinking, alone with a man—and a servant at that—in the middle of the night—well . . .

MISS JULIE   Well what?! Besides, we're not alone. Christine is here.

JEAN   Sleeping!

95 MISS JULIE   I'll wake her up. [*She goes over to* CHRISTINE.] Christine! Are you asleep? [CHRISTINE *babbles in her sleep.*] Christine! —My, how sound she sleeps!

CHRISTINE [*talking in her sleep*]   Count's boots are brushed . . . put on the coffee . . . right away, right away, right . . . mm—mm . . . poofff . . .

[MISS JULIE *shakes* CHRISTINE.]

100 MISS JULIE   Wake up, will you!

JEAN [*sternly*]   Let her alone! Let her sleep!

MISS JULIE [*sharply*]   What?

JEAN   She's been standing over the stove all day. She's worn out when night comes. Anyone asleep is entitled to some consideration.

105 MISS JULIE [*changing her tone*]   That's a very kind thought. It does you credit, Jean. You're right, of course. [*She offers* JEAN *her hand.*] Now come on out and pick some lilacs for me.

---

1. Miss (French).

[*During the following,* CHRISTINE *wakes up and, drunk with sleep, shuffles off to the right to go to bed. A polka can be heard in the distance.*]

JEAN   With you, Miss Julie?

MISS JULIE   Yes, with me.

110   JEAN   That's no good. Absolutely not.

MISS JULIE   I don't know what you're thinking. Aren't you letting your imagination run away with you?

JEAN   No. Other people are.

MISS JULIE   How? Imagining that I'm—*verliebt*[2] with a servant?

115   JEAN   I'm not conceited, but it's been known to happen. And to these people nothing's sacred.

MISS JULIE   "These people!" Why, I do believe you're an aristocrat!

JEAN   Yes, I am.

MISS JULIE   I'm climbing down—

120   JEAN   Don't climb down, Miss Julie! Take my advice. No one will believe that you climbed down deliberately. They'll say you fell.

MISS JULIE   I have a higher opinion of these people than you do. Let's see who's right! Come on! [*She gives him a long, steady look.*]

JEAN   You know, you're very strange.

125   MISS JULIE   Perhaps. But then so are you. . . . Besides, everything is strange. Life, people, everything. It's all scum, drifting and drifting on the water until it sinks—drowns. There's a dream I have every now and then. It's coming back to me now. I'm sitting on top of a pillar. I've climbed up it somehow and I don't know how to get back down. When I look down I get

130   dizzy. I have to get down but I don't have the courage to jump. I can't hold on much longer and I want to fall; but I don't fall. I know I won't have any peace until I get down; no rest until I get down, down on the ground. And if I ever got down on the ground, I'd want to go farther down, right down into the earth. . . . Have you ever felt anything like that?

135   JEAN   Never! I used to dream that I'm lying under a tall tree in a dark woods. I want to get up, up to the very top, to look out over the bright landscape with the sun shining on it, to rob the bird's nest up there with the golden eggs in it. And I climb and I climb, but the trunk is so thick, and so smooth, and it's such a long way to that first branch. But I know that if I could just

140   reach that first branch, I'd go right to the top as if on a ladder. I've never reached it yet, but someday I will—even if only in my dreams.

MISS JULIE   Here I am talking about dreams with you. Come out with me. Only into the park a way. [*She offers him her arm, and they start to go.*]

JEAN   Let's sleep on nine midsummer flowers, Miss Julie, and then our

145   dreams will come true![3]

[MISS JULIE *and* JEAN *suddenly turn around in the doorway.* JEAN *is holding his hand over one eye.*]

MISS JULIE   You've caught something in your eye. Let me see.

JEAN   It's nothing. Just a bit of dust. It'll go away.

MISS JULIE   The sleeve of my dress must have grazed your eye. Sit down and I'll help you. [*She takes him by the arm and sits him down. She takes his*

2. In love (German).
3. A girl would pick in silence on Midsummer Eve nine different sorts of flowers, make a bouquet of them, and place them under her pillow. The man who appeared in her dreams would be the man she would marry [translator's note].

head and leans it back. With the corner of her handkerchief she tries to get
150 *out the bit of dust.*] Now sit still, absolutely still. [*She slaps his hand.*] Do as
you're told. Why, I believe you're trembling—a big, strong man like you.
[*She feels his biceps.*] With such big arms!

JEAN [*warningly*] Miss Julie!

MISS JULIE Yes, *Monsieur Jean?*

155 JEAN *Attention! Je ne suis qu'un homme!*[4]

MISS JULIE Sit still, I tell you! . . . There now! It's out. Kiss my hand and
thank me!

JEAN [*rising to his feet.*] Listen to me, Miss Julie—Christine has gone to
bed! —Listen to me, I tell you!

160 MISS JULIE Kiss my hand first!

JEAN Listen to me!

MISS JULIE Kiss my hand first!

JEAN All right. But you'll have no one to blame but yourself.

MISS JULIE For what?

165 JEAN For what! Are you twenty-five years old and still a child? Don't you
know it's dangerous to play with fire?

MISS JULIE Not for me, I'm insured!

JEAN [*boldly*] Oh, no, you're not! And even if you are, there's inflammable
stuff next door.

170 MISS JULIE Meaning you?

JEAN Yes. Not just because it's me, but because I'm young and—

MISS JULIE And irresistibly handsome? What incredible conceit! A Don Juan,
maybe! Or a Joseph![5] Yes, bless my soul, that's it: you're a Joseph!

JEAN You think so?!

175 MISS JULIE I'm almost afraid so!

[JEAN *boldly steps up to her, grabs her around the waist, tries to kiss her.
She slaps his face.*]

None of that!

JEAN More games? Or are you serious?

MISS JULIE I'm serious.

JEAN Then you must have been serious a moment ago, too! You take your
180 games too seriously; that's dangerous. Well, I'm tired of your games, and if
you'll excuse me, I'll return to my work. [*Takes up the boots and starts to
brush them.*] The count will be wanting his boots on time, and it's long past
midnight.

MISS JULIE Put those boots down.

185 JEAN No! This is my job. It's what I'm here for. I never undertook to be your
playmate. That's something I could never be. I consider myself too good for
that.

MISS JULIE You are proud.

JEAN In some ways. Not in others.

190 MISS JULIE Have you ever been in love?

4. Be careful! I am just a man! (French).
5. In the Bible, a son of Jacob: after Joseph
was sold into slavery by his brothers, his good
looks led his master's wife to make sexual
advances toward him; when he refused her,
she falsely accused him of rape (Genesis
39.6–18). *Don Juan:* the legendary Spanish
seducer of women, whose story is told in a
number of European dramas and in Mozart's
opera *Don Giovanni* (1787).

JEAN We don't use that word around here. But I've hankered after some girls, if that's what you mean. . . . I even got sick once because I couldn't have the one I wanted—really sick, like the princes in the Arabian Nights[6]— who couldn't eat or drink for love.

195 MISS JULIE Who was she?

[JEAN *does not reply.*]

Who was the girl?

JEAN You can't get that out of me.

MISS JULIE Even if I ask you as an equal—ask you—as a friend? . . . Who was she?

200 JEAN You.

MISS JULIE [*sitting down*] How—amusing . . .

JEAN Yes, maybe so. Ridiculous. . . . That's why I didn't want to tell you about it before. Want to hear the whole story? . . . Have you any idea what you and your people look like from down below? Of course not. Like hawks

205 or eagles, that's what: you hardly ever see their backs because they're always soaring so high up. I lived with seven brothers and sisters—and a pig—out on the wasteland where there wasn't even a tree growing. But from my window I could see the wall of the count's garden with the apple trees sticking up over it. That was the Garden of Eden for me, and there

210 were many angry angels with flaming swords standing guard over it.[7] But in spite of them, I and the other boys found a way to the Tree of Life. . . . How contemptible, that's what you're thinking.

MISS JULIE For stealing apples? All boys do that.

JEAN That's what you say now. All the same, you think me contemptible.

215 Never mind. One day I went with my mother into this paradise to weed the onion beds. Next to the vegetable garden stood a Turkish pavilion, shaded by jasmine and hung all over with honeysuckle. I couldn't imagine what it was used for; I only knew I had never seen such a beautiful building. People went in, and came out again. And then one day the door was left open.

220 I sneaked in. The walls were covered with portraits of kings and emperors, and the windows had red curtains with tassels on them. —Recognize it? Yes, the count's private privy. . . . I— [*He breaks off a lilac and holds it under* MISS JULIE's *nose.*] I had never been inside a castle, never seen anything besides the church. This was more beautiful. And no matter what I

225 tried to think about, my thoughts always came back—to that little pavilion. And little by little there arose in me a desire to experience just for once the whole pleasure of—. *Enfin,*[8] I sneaked in, looked about, and marveled. And just then I heard someone coming! There was only one way out—for the upper-class people. But for me there was one more—a lower one.[9] And I

230 had no other choice but to take it. [MISS JULIE, *who has taken the lilac from* JEAN, *lets it fall to the table.*] Then I began to run like mad, plunging through the raspberry bushes, plowing through the strawberry patches, and came up on the rose terrace. And there I caught sight of a pink dress and a pair of white stockings. You! I crawled under—well, you can imagine

---

6. *The Thousand and One Nights,* a collection of ancient tales in Arabic, arranged in its present form in the 15th century.
7. See Genesis 3.24.

8. Finally (French).
9. That is, through the pit or trench under the outhouse.

235   what it was like—under thistles that pricked me and wet dirt that stank to high heaven. And all the while I could see you walking among the roses. I said to myself, "If it's true that a thief can enter heaven and be with the angels,[1] isn't it strange that a poor man's child here on God's green earth can't enter the count's park and play with the count's daughter."

240 MISS JULIE [*sentimentally*]   Do you think all poor children have felt that way?

JEAN [*hesitatingly at first, then with mounting conviction*]   If all poor ch—? Yes—yes, naturally. Of course!

MISS JULIE   It must be terrible to be poor.

JEAN [*with exaggerated intensity*]   Oh, Miss Julie! You don't know! A dog can
245   lie on the sofa with its mistress; a horse can have its nose stroked by the hand of a countess; but a servant—! [*Changing his tone*] Of course, now and then you meet somebody with guts enough to work his way up in the world, but how often? —Anyway, you know what I did afterward? I threw myself into the millstream with all my clothes on. Got fished out and spanked. But the
250   following Sunday, when Pa and everybody else in the house went to visit Grandma, I arranged things so I'd be left behind. Then I washed myself all over with soap and warm water, put on my best clothes, and went off to church—just to see you there once more. I saw you, and then I went home determined to die. But I wanted to die beautifully and comfortably, without
255   pain. I remembered some stories I had heard about how fatal it was to sleep under an elderberry bush. And we had a big one that had just blossomed out. I stripped it of every leaf and blossom it had and made a bed of them in a bin of oats. Have you ever noticed how smooth oats are? As smooth to the touch as human skin. . . . So I pulled the lid of the bin shut and closed my eyes.
260   Fell asleep. And when they woke me I was really very sick. However, I didn't die, as you can see. —What was I trying to prove? I don't know. There was no hope of winning you. It was just that you were a symbol of the absolute hopelessness of my ever getting out of the class I was born in.

MISS JULIE   You know, you have a real gift for telling stories. Did you go to
265   school?

JEAN   A little. But I've read a lot of novels and gone to the theater. And I've also listened to educated people talk. That way I learned the most.

MISS JULIE   You mean to tell me you stand around listening to what we're saying!

270 JEAN   Certainly! And I've heard an awful lot, I can tell you—sitting on the coachman's seat or rowing the boat. One time I heard you and a girlfriend talking—

MISS JULIE   Really? . . . And just what did you hear?

JEAN   Well, now, I don't know if I can repeat it. I can tell you I was a little
275   amazed. I couldn't imagine where you had learned such words. Maybe at bottom there isn't such a big difference as you might think, between people and people.

MISS JULIE   How vulgar! At least people in my class don't behave like you when we're engaged.

280 JEAN [*looking her in the eye*]   Are you sure? —Come on now, it's no use playing the innocent with me.

---

1. According to 1 Corinthians 6.9–10, the thief cannot enter heaven.

MISS JULIE   He was a beast. The man I offered my love was a beast.

JEAN   That's what you all say—afterward.

MISS JULIE   All?

285 JEAN   I'd say so. I've heard the same expression used several times before in similar circumstances.

MISS JULIE   What kind of circumstances?

JEAN   The kind we're talking about. I remember the last time I—

MISS JULIE [*rising*]   That's enough! I don't want to hear any more.

290 JEAN   How strange! Neither did she! . . . Well, now if you'll excuse me, I'll go to bed.

MISS JULIE [*softly*]   Go to bed on Midsummer Eve?

JEAN   That's right. Dancing with that crowd up there really doesn't amuse me.

295 MISS JULIE   Jean, get the key to the boathouse and row me out on the lake. I want to see the sun come up.

JEAN   Do you think that's wise?

MISS JULIE   You sound as if you were worried about your reputation.

JEAN   Why not? I don't particularly care to be made ridiculous, or to be kicked out without a recommendation just when I'm trying to establish

300   myself. Besides, I have a certain obligation to Christine.

MISS JULIE   Oh, I see. It's Christine now.

JEAN   Yes, but I'm thinking of you, too. Take my advice, Miss Julie. Go up to your room.

MISS JULIE   When did you start giving me orders?

305 JEAN   Just this once. For your own sake! Please! It's very late. You're so tired, you're drunk; you don't know what you're doing. Go to bed, Miss Julie. — Besides, if my ears aren't deceiving me, they're coming this way, looking for me. If they find us here together, you're done for!

THE CHORUS [*is heard coming nearer, singing*]

> Said Jill to Jack, "Soil needs a tilling."
310 > Tri-di-ri-di-ralla, tri-di-ri-di-ra.
> Said Jack to Jill, "Time's a-spilling."
> Tri-di-ri-di-ralla-la.
> Said Jill to Jack, "Gold's a-hoarding."
> Tri-di-ri-di-ralla, tri-di-ri-di-ra.
315 > Said Jack to Jill, "Tell not my lording."
> Tri-di-ri-di-ralla-la.
> Said Jill to Jack, "Hair is for plaiting."
> Tri-di-ri-di-ralla, tri-di-ri-di-ra.
> "But Jill for Jack is not waiting."
320 > Tri-di-ri-di-ralla-la![2]

MISS JULIE   I know these people. I love them just as they love me. Let them come. You'll see.

JEAN   Oh, no, Miss Julie, they don't love you! They take the food you give them, but they spit on it as soon as your back is turned. Believe me! Just

325 listen to them. Listen to what they're singing. —No, you'd better not listen.

---

2. A peasants' folk song.

MISS JULIE [*listening*]   What are they singing?

JEAN   A nasty song—about you and me!

MISS JULIE   How disgusting! Oh, what cowardly, sneaking—

JEAN   That's what the mob always is—cowards! You can't fight them; you can
330   only run away.

MISS JULIE   Run away? Where? There's no way out of here. And we can't go
in to Christine.

JEAN   What about my room? What do you say? Rules don't count in a situation like this. You can trust me. —You said, let's be friends. Remember?
335   Well, I'm your friend—your true, devoted, respectful friend.

MISS JULIE   But suppose—suppose they looked for you there?

JEAN   I'll bolt the door. If they try to break it down, I'll shoot. Come, Miss
Julie! [*On his knees*] Please, Miss Julie!

MISS JULIE [*meaningfully*]   You promise me that you won't—

340   JEAN   I swear to you!

[MISS JULIE *goes out quickly to the right. Jean follows her impetuously.*]

The Ballet

*The country people enter in festive costumes, with flowers in their hats. The fiddler is
in the lead. A keg of small beer and a little keg of liquor, decorated with greenery, are
set up on the table. Glasses are brought out. They all drink. Then they form a circle and
sing "Said Jill to Jack," dancing the round dance as they sing. At the end of the dance,
they all leave singing.*

MISS JULIE *comes in alone; looks at the devastated kitchen; clasps her hands together;
then takes out a powder puff and powders her face.* JEAN *enters. He is in high spirits.*

JEAN   You see! You heard them, didn't you? You've got to admit it's impossible
to stay here.

MISS JULIE   No, I don't. But even if I did, what could we do?

JEAN   Go away, travel, get away from here!

5   MISS JULIE   Travel? Yes—but where?

JEAN   Switzerland, the Italian lakes. You've never been there?

MISS JULIE   No. Is it beautiful?

JEAN   Eternal summer, oranges, laurel trees, ah . . . !

MISS JULIE   What do we do when we get there?

10   JEAN   I'll set up a hotel—a first-class hotel with a first-class clientele.

MISS JULIE   Hotel?

JEAN   I tell you that's the life! Always new faces, new languages. Not a minute to think about yourself or worry about your nerves. No looking for
something to do. The work keeps you busy. Day and night the bells ring,
15   the trains whistle, the buses come and go. And all the while the money
comes rolling in. I tell you it's the life!

MISS JULIE   Yes, that's the life. But what about me?

JEAN   The mistress of the whole place, the star of the establishment! With
your looks—and your personality—it can't fail. It's perfect! You'll sit in the
20   office like a queen, setting your slaves in motion by pressing an electric button. The guests will file before your throne and timidly lay their treasures on
your table. You can't imagine how people tremble when you shove a bill in
their face! I'll salt the bills and you'll sugar them with your prettiest smile.
Come on, let's get away from here—[*He takes a timetable from his pocket.*]—

25 right away—the next train! We'll be in Malmö at six-thirty, Hamburg eight-forty in the morning; Frankfurt to Basel in one day, and to Como[3] by way of the Gotthard tunnel in—let me see—three days! Three days!

MISS JULIE   You make it sound so wonderful. But, Jean, you have to give me strength. Tell me you love me. Come and put your arms around me.

30 JEAN [hesitates]   I want to . . . but I don't dare. Not anymore, not in this house. I do love you—without a shadow of a doubt. How can you doubt that, Miss Julie?

MISS JULIE [shyly, very becomingly]   You don't have to be formal with me, Jean. You can call me Julie. There aren't any barriers between us now. Call
35 me Julie.

JEAN [agonized]   I can't! There are still barriers between us, Miss Julie, as long as we stay in this house! There's the past, there's the count. I've never met anyone I feel so much respect for. I've only got to see his gloves lying on a table and I shrivel up. I only have to hear that bell ring and I shy like a fright-
40 ened horse. I only have to look at his boots standing there so stiff and proud and I feel my spine bending. [He kicks the boots.] Superstitions, prejudices that they've drilled into us since we were children! But they can be forgotten just as easily! Just get us to another country where they have a republic! They'll crawl on their hands and knees when they see my uniform. On their
45 hands and knees, I tell you! But not me! Oh, no. I'm not made for crawling. I've got guts, backbone. And once I grab that first branch, you just watch me climb. I may be a valet now, but next year I'll be owning property; in ten years, I'll be living off my investments. Then I'll go to Rumania, get myself some decorations, and maybe—notice I only say maybe—end up as a count!

50 MISS JULIE   How wonderful, wonderful.

JEAN   Listen, in Rumania you can buy titles. You'll be a countess after all. My countess.

MISS JULIE   But I'm not interested in that. I'm leaving all that behind. Tell me you love me, Jean, or else—or else what difference does it make what
55 I am?

JEAN   I'll tell you a thousand times—but later! Not now. And not here. Above all, let's keep our feelings out of this or we'll make a mess of everything. We have to look at this thing calmly and coolly, like sensible people. [He takes out a cigar, clips the end, and lights it.] Now you sit there and I'll sit here,
60 and we'll talk as if nothing had happened.

MISS JULIE [in anguish]   My God, what are you? Don't you have any feelings?

JEAN   Feelings? Nobody's got more feelings than I have. But I've learned to control them.

MISS JULIE   A few minutes ago you were kissing my shoe—and now—!

65 JEAN [harshly]   That was a few minutes ago. We've got other things to think about now!

MISS JULIE   Don't speak to me like that, Jean!

JEAN   I'm just trying to be sensible. We've been stupid once; let's not be stupid again. Your father might be back at any moment, and we've got to decide our
70 future before then. —Now what do you think about my plans? Do you approve or don't you?

---

3. A city on the southwest end of Lake Como, in northern Italy; Jean outlines the journey there from Sweden through Germany and Switzerland.

MISS JULIE   I don't see anything wrong with them. Except one thing. For a big undertaking like that, you'd need a lot of capital. Have you got it?

JEAN [*chewing on his cigar*]   Have I got it? Of course I have. I've got my
75   knowledge of the business, my vast experience, my familiarity with languages. That's capital that counts for something, let me tell you.

MISS JULIE   You can't even buy the railway tickets with it.

JEAN   That's true. That's why I need a backer—someone to put up the money.

MISS JULIE   Where can you find him on a moment's notice?

80   JEAN   You'll find him—if you want to be my partner.

MISS JULIE   I can't. And I don't have a penny to my name.

   [*Pause.*]

JEAN   Then you can forget the whole thing.

MISS JULIE   Forget—?

JEAN   And things will stay just the way they are.

85   MISS JULIE   Do you think I'm going to live under the same roof with you as your mistress? Do you think I'm going to have people sneering at me behind my back? How do you think I'll ever be able to look my father in the face after this? No, no! Take me away from here, Jean—the shame, the humiliation. . . . What have I done? Oh, my God, my God! What have I done! [*She bursts into tears.*]

90   JEAN   Now don't start singing that tune. It won't work. What have you done that's so awful? You're not the first.

MISS JULIE [*crying hysterically*]   Now you think me contemptible—I'm falling, falling!

JEAN   Fall down to me, and I'll lift you up again!

95   MISS JULIE   What awful hold did you have over me? What drove me to you? The weak to the strong? The falling to the rising! Or maybe it was love? Love? This? You don't know what love is!

JEAN   Want to bet? Did you think I was a virgin?

MISS JULIE   You're coarse—vulgar! The things you say, the things you think!

100   JEAN   That's the way I was brought up. It's the way I am! Now don't get hysterical. And don't play the fine lady with me. We're eating off the same platter now. . . . That's better. Come over here and be a good girl and I'll treat you to something special. [*He opens the table drawer and takes out the wine bottle. He pours the wine into two used glasses.*]

MISS JULIE   Where did you get that wine?

105   JEAN   From the wine cellar.

MISS JULIE   My father's burgundy!

JEAN   Should be good enough for his son-in-law.

MISS JULIE   I was drinking beer and you—!

JEAN   Shows I have better taste than you.

110   MISS JULIE   Thief!

JEAN   You going to squeal on me?

MISS JULIE   Oh, God! Partner in crime with a petty house thief! I must have been drunk; I must have been walking in my sleep. Midsummer Night! Night of innocent games—

115   JEAN   Yes, very innocent!

MISS JULIE [*pacing up and down*]   Is there anyone here on earth as miserable as I am?

JEAN   Why be miserable? Look at the conquest you've made! Think of poor Christine in there. Don't you think she's got any feelings?

120 MISS JULIE   I thought so a while ago; I don't now. A servant's a servant—

JEAN   And a whore's a whore!

MISS JULIE [*falls to her knees and clasps her hands together*]   Oh, God in heaven, put an end to my worthless life! Lift me out of this awful filth I'm sinking in! Save me! Save me!

125 JEAN   I feel sorry for you, I have to admit it. When I was lying in the onion beds, looking up at you on the rose terrace, I—I'm telling you the truth now—I had the same dirty thoughts that all boys have.

MISS JULIE   And you said you wanted to die for me!

JEAN   In the oat bin? That was only a story.

130 MISS JULIE   A lie, you mean.

JEAN [*getting sleepy*]   Practically. I think I read it in a paper about a chimney sweep who curled up in a wood-bin with some lilacs because they were going to arrest him for nonsupport of his child.

MISS JULIE   Now I see you as you really are.

135 JEAN   What did you expect me to do? It's always the fancy talk that gets the women.

MISS JULIE   You dog!

JEAN   You bitch!

MISS JULIE   Well, now you've seen the eagle's back—

140 JEAN   Wasn't exactly its back—!

MISS JULIE   I was going to be the window dressing for your hotel—!

JEAN   And I the hotel—!

MISS JULIE   Sitting at the desk, attracting your customers, padding your bills—!

JEAN   I could manage that myself—!

145 MISS JULIE   How can a human soul be so dirty and filthy?

JEAN   Then why don't you clean it up?

MISS JULIE   You lackey! You shoeshine boy! Stand up when I talk to you!

JEAN   You lackey lover! You bootblack's tramp! Shut your mouth and get out of here! Who do you think you are telling me I'm coarse? I've never seen
150 anybody in my class behave as crudely as you did tonight. Have you ever seen any of the girls around here grab at a man like you did? Do you think any of the girls of my class would throw themselves at a man like that? I've never seen the like of it except in animals and prostitutes!

MISS JULIE [*crushed*]   That's right! Hit me! Walk all over me! It's all I deserve.
155 I'm rotten. But help me! Help me to get out of this—if there is any way out for me!

JEAN [*less harsh*]   I'd be doing myself an injustice if I didn't admit that part of the credit for this seduction belongs to me. But do you think a person in my position would have dared to look twice at you if you hadn't asked for
160 it? I'm still amazed—

MISS JULIE   And still proud.

JEAN   Why not? But I've got to confess the victory was a little too easy to give me any real thrill.

MISS JULIE   Go on, hit me again!

165 JEAN [*standing up*]   No. . . . I'm sorry I said that. I never hit a person who's down, especially a woman. I can't deny that, in one way, it was good to find

out that what I saw glittering up above was only fool's gold, to see that the eagle's back was as gray as its belly, that the smooth cheek was just powder, and that there could be dirt under the manicured nails, that the handker-
170 chief was soiled even though it smelled of perfume. But, in another way, it hurts to find that everything I was striving for wasn't very high above me after all, wasn't even real. It hurts me to see you sink far lower than your own cook. Hurts, like seeing the last flowers cut to pieces by the autumn rains and turned to muck.

175 MISS JULIE   You talk as if you already stood high above me.

JEAN   Well, don't I? Don't forget I could make you a countess but you can never make me a count.

MISS JULIE   I have a father for a count. You can never have that!

JEAN   True. But I might father my own counts—that is, if—

180 MISS JULIE   You're a thief! I'm not!

JEAN   There are worse things than being a thief. A lot worse. And besides, when I take a position in a house, I consider myself a member of the family—in a way, like a child in the house. It's no crime for a child to steal a few ripe cherries when they're falling off the trees, is it? [He begins to feel
185 passionate again.] Miss Julie, you're a beautiful woman, much too good for the likes of me. You got carried away by your emotions and now you want to cover up your mistake by telling yourself that you love me. You don't love me. Maybe you were attracted by my looks—in which case your kind of love is no better than mine. But I could never be satisfied to be just an ani-
190 mal for you, and I could never make you love me.

MISS JULIE   How do you know that for sure?

JEAN   You mean there's a chance? I could love you, there's no doubt about that. You're beautiful, you're refined—[He goes up to her and takes her hand.]—educated, lovable when you want to be, and once you set a man's
195 heart on fire, I'll bet it burns forever. [He puts his arm around her waist.] You're like hot wine with strong spices. One of your kisses is enough to—

[He attempts to lead her out, but she rather reluctantly breaks away from him.]

MISS JULIE   Let me go. You don't get me that way.

JEAN   Then how? Not by petting you and not with pretty words, not by plan-ning for the future, not by saving you from humiliation! Then how, tell me
200 how?

MISS JULIE   How? How? I don't know how! I don't know at all! —I hate you like I hate rats, but I can't get away from you.

JEAN   Then come away with me!

MISS JULIE   [pulling herself together]   Away? Yes, we'll go away! —But I'm so
205 tired. Pour me a glass of wine, will you?

[JEAN pours the wine, MISS JULIE looks at her watch.]

Let's talk first. We still have a little time. [She empties the glass of wine and holds it out for more.]

JEAN   Don't overdo it. You'll get drunk.

MISS JULIE   What difference does it make?

JEAN   What difference? It looks cheap. —What did you want to say to me?

210 MISS JULIE   We're going to run away together, right? But we'll talk first—that is, I'll talk. So far you've done all the talking. You've told me your life, now

I'll tell you mine. That way we'll know each other through and through before we become . . . traveling companions.

JEAN   Wait a minute. Are you sure you won't regret this afterward—surrendering your secrets to me?

MISS JULIE   I thought you were my friend.

JEAN   I am—sometimes. Just don't count on it.

MISS JULIE   You don't mean that. Anyway, everybody knows my secrets. —My mother's parents were very ordinary people, just commoners. She was brought up, according to the theories of her time, to believe in equality, the independence of women, and all that. And she had a strong aversion to marriage. When my father proposed to her, she swore she would never become his wife but that she might possibly consent to become his mistress. So he told her he didn't want to see the woman he loved enjoy less respect than he did. But she said she didn't care what the world thought—and he, believing that he couldn't live without her, accepted her conditions. That did it. From then on he was cut off from his old circle of friends and left without anything to do in the house, which couldn't have kept him occupied anyway. Then I came into the world—against my mother's wishes, as far as I can make out. My mother decided to bring me up as a nature child. And on top of that I had to learn everything a boy learns, so I could be living proof that women were just as good as men. I had to wear boy's clothes, learn to handle horses—but not to milk the cows! Girls did that! I was made to groom the horses and harness them, and learn farming and go hunting—I even had to learn how to slaughter the animals. It was disgusting. Awful! And on the estate all the men were set to doing women's chores, and the women to doing men's work—with the result that the whole place fell to pieces, and we became the local laughing-stock. Finally, my father must have come out of his trance. He rebelled, and everything was changed according to his wishes. They got married—very quietly. Then my mother got sick. I don't know what kind of sickness it was, but she often had convulsions, and she would hide herself in the attic or in the garden, and sometimes she would stay out all night. Then there occurred that big fire you've heard about. The house, the stables, the cowsheds, all burned down—and under very peculiar circumstances that led one to suspect arson. You see, the accident occurred the day after the insurance expired, and the premiums on the new policy, which my father had sent in, were delayed through the messenger's carelessness, and didn't arrive in time. [*She refills her glass and drinks.*]

JEAN   You've had enough.

MISS JULIE   Who cares! —We were left without a penny to our name. We had to sleep in the carriages. My father didn't know where to turn for money to rebuild the house. Then Mother suggested to him that he might try to borrow money from an old friend of hers, who owned a brick factory not far from here. Father took out a loan, but there wasn't any interest charged, which surprised him. So the place was rebuilt. [*She drinks some more.*] Do you know who set fire to the place?

JEAN   Your honorable mother!

MISS JULIE   Do you know who the brick manufacturer was?

JEAN   Your mother's lover?

260 MISS JULIE Do you know whose money it was?

JEAN Let me think a minute. . . . No, I give up.

MISS JULIE It was my mother's!

JEAN The count's, you mean. Or was there a marriage settlement?[4]

MISS JULIE There wasn't a settlement. My mother had a little money of her
265 own which she didn't want under my father's control, so she invested it
with her—friend.

JEAN Who pinched it!

MISS JULIE Right! He kept it for himself. Well, my father found out what
happened. But he couldn't go to court, couldn't pay his wife's lover, couldn't
270 prove that it was his wife's money. That was how my mother got her
revenge because he had taken control of the house. He was on the verge of
shooting himself. There was even a rumor that he tried and failed. But
somehow he took a new lease on life and he forced my mother to pay for
her mistakes. Can you imagine what those five years were like for me? I
275 loved my father, but I took my mother's side because I didn't know the
whole story. She had taught me to hate all men—I'm sure you've heard how
she hated men—and I swore to her that I'd never be slave to any man.

JEAN You got engaged to the attorney, didn't you?

MISS JULIE Only to make him my slave.

280 JEAN I guess he didn't go for that, did he?

MISS JULIE Oh, he wanted to well enough. I didn't give him the chance. I got
bored with him.

JEAN Yes, so I noticed—in the stable yard.

MISS JULIE What did you notice?

285 JEAN I saw how he—. [Still see it on your cheek.

MISS JULIE What!

JEAN The stripe on your cheek.][5] He broke it off.

MISS JULIE It's a lie! I broke it off! Did he tell you that? He's beneath
contempt!

JEAN Come on now, as bad as that? So you hate men, hm?

290 MISS JULIE Yes, I do. . . . Most of the time. But sometimes, when I can't help
myself—oh . . . [She shudders in disgust.]

JEAN Then you hate me, too?

MISS JULIE You have no idea how much! I'd like to see you killed like an animal—

295 JEAN Like when you're caught having sex with an animal: you get two years
at hard labor and the animal is killed. Right?

MISS JULIE Right.

JEAN But there's no one to catch us—and no animal!—So what are we going
to do?

300 MISS JULIE Go away from here.

JEAN To torture ourselves to death?

MISS JULIE No. To enjoy ourselves for a day or two, or a week, for as long as
we can—and then—to die—

JEAN Die? That's stupid! I've got a better idea: start a hotel!

---

4. An agreement, made before a marriage, to
transfer some property to the wife.
5. The passage in brackets was deleted in

Strindberg's manuscript, probably by Strindberg himself [translator's note].

305 MISS JULIE [*continuing without hearing* JEAN]   —on the shores of Lake Como, where the sun is always shining, where the laurels bloom at Christmas, and the golden oranges glow on the trees.

JEAN   Lake Como is a stinking wet hole, and the only oranges I saw there were on the fruit stands. But it's a good tourist spot with a lot of villas and
310   cottages that are rented out to lovers. Now there's a profitable business. You know why? They rent the villa for the whole season, but they leave after three weeks.

MISS JULIE [*naively*]   Why after only three weeks?

JEAN   Because that's about as long as they can stand each other. Why else?
315   But they still have to pay the rent. You see? Then you rent it out again to another couple, and so on. There's no shortage of love—even if it doesn't last very long.

MISS JULIE   Then you don't want to die with me?

JEAN   I don't want to die at all! I enjoy life too much. And moreover, I con
320   sider taking your own life a sin against the Providence that gave us life.

MISS JULIE   You believe in God? You?

JEAN   Yes, certainly I do! I go to church every other Sunday—. Honestly, I've had enough of this talk. I'm going to bed.

MISS JULIE   Really? You think you're going to get off that easy? Don't you
325   know that a man owes something to the woman he's dishonored?

JEAN [*takes out his purse and throws a silver coin on the table*]   There you are. I don't want to owe anybody anything.

MISS JULIE [*pretending not to notice*]   Do you know what the law says—?

JEAN   Lucky for you the law says nothing about women who seduce men!

330 MISS JULIE [*as before*]   What else can we do but go away from here, get married, and get divorced?

JEAN   Suppose I refuse to enter into this *mésalliance?*[6]

MISS JULIE   *Mésalliance?*

JEAN   For me! I've got better ancestors than you. I don't have a female arson
335   ist in my family.

MISS JULIE   You can't prove that.

JEAN   You can't prove the opposite—because we don't have any family records—except in the police files. But I've read the whole history of your family in that peerage book in the drawing room. Do you know who the
340   founder of your family line was? A miller—who let his wife sleep with the king one night during the Danish war.[7] I don't have any ancestors like that. I don't have any ancestors at all! But I can become an ancestor myself.

MISS JULIE   This is what I get for baring my heart and soul to someone too low to understand, for sacrificing the honor of my family—

345 JEAN   Dishonor! —I warned you, remember? Drinking makes one talk, and talking's bad.

MISS JULIE   Oh, how sorry I am! . . . If only it had never happened! . . . If only you at least loved me!

JEAN   For the last time—what do you want me to do? Cry? Jump over your
350   whip? Kiss you? Lure you to Lake Como for three weeks and then—? What

6. Literally, "misalliance" (French), an ill-advised marriage.
7. That is, the war begun by Denmark in 1657 that ended with the Treaty of Copenhagen (1660), which restored to Sweden its southern provinces.

am I supposed to do? What do you want? I've had more than I can take. This is what I get for involving myself with women. . . . Miss Julie, I can see that you're unhappy; I know that you're suffering; but I simply cannot understand you. My people don't behave like this. We don't hate each

355 other. We make love for the fun of it, when we can get any time off from our work. But we don't have time for it all day and all night like you do. If you ask me, you're sick, Miss Julie. Your mother's mind was affected, you know. There are whole counties affected with pietism. That was your mother's trouble—pietism. It's spreading like the plague.

360 MISS JULIE   You can be understanding, Jean. You're talking to me like a human being now.

JEAN   Well, be human yourself. You spit on me, but you don't let me wipe it off—on you.

MISS JULIE   Help me, Jean. Help me. Tell me what I should do, that's all—

365 which way to go.

JEAN   For Christ's sake, if only I knew myself!

MISS JULIE   I've been crazy—I've been out of my mind—but does that mean there's no way out for me?

JEAN   Stay here as if nothing had happened. Nobody knows anything.

370 MISS JULIE   Impossible! Everybody who works here knows. Christine knows.

JEAN   They don't know a thing. Anyhow they'd never believe it.

MISS JULIE [slowly, significantly]   But . . . it might happen again.

JEAN   That's true!

MISS JULIE   And one time there might be . . . consequences.

375 JEAN [stunned]   Consequences!! What on earth have I been thinking of! You're right. There's only one thing to do: get away from here! Immediately! I can't go with you—that would give the whole game away. You'll have to go by yourself. Somewhere—I don't care where!

MISS JULIE   By myself? Where? —Oh, no, Jean, I can't. I can't!

380 JEAN   You've got to! Before the count comes back. You know as well as I do what will happen if you stay here. After one mistake, you figure you might as well go on—the damage is already done. Then you get more and more careless until—finally you're exposed. I tell you, you've got to get out of the country. Afterward you can write to the count and tell him everything—

385 leaving me out, of course. He'd never figure it was me. He wouldn't even let himself think it was me.

MISS JULIE   I'll go—if you'll come with me!

JEAN   Lady, are you out of your mind? "Miss Julie elopes with her footman." The day after tomorrow it would be in all the papers. The count would

390 never live it down.

MISS JULIE   I can't go away. I can't stay. Help me. I'm so tired, so awfully tired. . . . Tell me what to do. Order me. Start me going. I can't think anymore, can't move anymore . . .

JEAN   Now do you realize how weak you all are? What gives you the right to

395 go strutting around with your noses in the air as if you owned the world? All right, I'll give you your orders. Go up and get dressed. Get some traveling money. And come back down here.

MISS JULIE [almost in a whisper]   Come up with me!

JEAN   To your room? . . . You're going crazy again! [He hesitates a moment.]

400 No! No! Go! Right now! [He takes her hand and leads her out.]

MISS JULIE [*as she is leaving*]   Don't be so harsh, Jean.

JEAN   Orders always sound harsh. You've never had to take them.

> [JEAN, *left alone, heaves a sigh of relief and sits down at the table. He takes out a notebook and a pencil and begins to calculate, counting aloud now and then. The pantomime continues until* CHRISTINE *enters, dressed for church, and carrying* JEAN's *white tie and shirtfront in her hand.*]

CHRISTINE   Lord in Heaven, what a mess! What on earth have you been doing?

JEAN   It was Miss Julie. She dragged the whole crowd in here. You must have
405   been sleeping awfully sound if you didn't hear anything.

CHRISTINE   I slept like a log.

JEAN   You already dressed for church?

CHRISTINE   Yes, indeed. Don't you remember you promised to go to communion with me today?

410   JEAN   Oh, yes. Of course, I remember. I see you've brought my things. All right. Come on, put it on me. [*He sits down, and* CHRISTINE *starts to put the white tie and shirtfront on him. Pause.*]

JEAN [*yawning*]   What's the lesson for today?

CHRISTINE   The beheading of John the Baptist, what else? It's Midsummer. It's his feast day.

415   JEAN   My God, that will go on forever. —Hey, you're choking me! . . . Oh, I'm so sleepy, so sleepy.

CHRISTINE   What were you doing up all night? You look green in the face.

JEAN   I've been sitting here talking with Miss Julie.

CHRISTINE   That girl! She doesn't know how to behave herself!

> [*Pause.*]

420   JEAN   Tell me something, Christine . . .

CHRISTINE   Well, what?

JEAN   Isn't it strange when you think about it? Her, I mean.

CHRISTINE   What's so strange?

JEAN   Everything!

> [*Pause.* CHRISTINE *looks at the half-empty glasses on the table.*]

425   CHRISTINE   Have you been drinking with her?

JEAN   Yes!

CHRISTINE   Shame on you! —Look me in the eyes! You haven't . . . ?

JEAN   Yes!

CHRISTINE   Is it possible? Is it really possible?

430   JEAN [*thinking about it*]   Yes. It is.

CHRISTINE   Oh, how disgusting! I could never have believed anything like this would happen! No. No. This is too much!

JEAN   Don't tell me you're jealous of her?

CHRISTINE   No, not of her. If it had been Clara—or Sophie—I would have
435   scratched your eyes out! But her—? That's different. I don't know why. . . . But it's still disgusting!

JEAN   You're not mad at her?

CHRISTINE   No. Mad at you. You were mean and cruel to do a thing like that, very mean. The poor girl! . . . Let me tell you, I'm not going to stay in this
440   house a moment longer, not when I can't have any respect for my employers.

JEAN   Why do you want to respect them?

CHRISTINE   Don't try to be smart. You don't want to work for people who behave like pigs, do you? Well, do you? If you ask me, you'd be lowering yourself by doing that.

445 JEAN   Oh, I don't know. I think it's rather comforting to find out that they're not one damn bit better than we are.

CHRISTINE   Well, I don't. If they're not any better, there's no point in us trying to be like them. —And think of the count. Think of all the sorrows he's been through in his time. My God! I won't stay in this house any longer. . . .

450   Imagine! You, of all people! If it had been the attorney fellow; if it had been somebody respectable—

JEAN   Now just a minute—!

CHRISTINE   Oh, you're all right in your own way. But there's a big difference between one class and another. You can't deny that. —No, this is some-

455   thing I can never get over. She was so proud, and so sarcastic about men, you'd never believe she'd go and throw herself at one. And at someone like you! And she was going to have Diana shot because the poor thing ran after the gatekeeper's mongrel! —Well, I tell you, I've had enough! I'm not going to stay here any longer. When my term's up, I'm leaving.

460 JEAN   Then what'll you do?

CHRISTINE   Well, since you brought it up, it's about time that you got yourself a decent place, if we're going to get married.

JEAN   Why should I go looking for another place? I could never get a job like this if I'm married.

465 CHRISTINE   Well, I know that! But you could get a job as a porter, or maybe try to get a government job as a caretaker somewhere. A square deal and a square meal, that's what you get from the government—and a pension for the wife and children.

JEAN [wryly]   Fine, fine! But I'm not the kind of guy who thinks about dying

470   for his wife and children this early in the game. Let me tell you, I've got slightly bigger plans than that.

CHRISTINE   Plans! Ha! What about your obligations? You'd better start giving them a little thought!

JEAN   Don't start nagging me about obligations! I know what I have to do

475   without you telling me. [He hears a sound upstairs.] Anyhow, we'll have plenty of chance to talk about this later. You just go and get yourself ready, and we'll be off to church.

CHRISTINE   Who is that walking around up there?

JEAN   I don't know. Clara, I suppose. Who else?

480 CHRISTINE [starting to leave]   It can't be the count, can it? Could he have come back without anybody hearing him?

JEAN [frightened]   The count? No, it can't be. He would have rung.

CHRISTINE [leaving]   God help us! I've never heard the like of this.

[The sun has now risen and strikes the tops of the trees in the park. As the scene progresses, the light shifts gradually until it is shining very obliquely through the windows. JEAN goes to the door and signals. MISS JULIE enters, dressed for travel, and carrying a small birdcage, covered with a towel. She sets the cage down on a chair.]

MISS JULIE   I'm ready now.

485 JEAN   Shh! Christine's awake.

MISS JULIE [extremely tense and nervous during the following]   Did she suspect anything?

JEAN   She doesn't know a thing. —My God, what happened to you?

MISS JULIE   What do you mean? Do I look so strange?

490   JEAN   You're white as a ghost, and you've—excuse me—you've got dirt on your face.

MISS JULIE   Let me wash it off. [*She goes over to the washbasin and washes her face and hands.*] There! Do you have a towel? . . . Oh, look, the sun's coming up!

495   JEAN   That breaks the magic spell!

MISS JULIE   Yes, we were spellbound last night, weren't we? Midsummer madness . . . Jean, listen to me! Come with me. I've got the money!

JEAN [*suspiciously*]   Enough?

MISS JULIE   Enough for a start. Come with me, Jean. I can't travel alone today.
500   Midsummer Day on a stifling hot train, packed in with crowds of people, all staring at me—stopping at every station when I want to be flying. I can't, Jean, I can't! . . . And everything will remind me of the past. Midsummer Day when I was a child and the church was decorated with leaves—birch leaves and lilacs . . . the table spread for dinner with friends and relatives . . .
505   and after dinner, dancing in the park, with flowers and games. Oh, no matter how far you travel, the memories tag right along in the baggage car . . . and the regrets and the remorse.

JEAN   All right, I'll go with you! But it's got to be now—before it's too late! This very instant!

510   MISS JULIE   Hurry and get dressed! [*She picks up the birdcage.*]

JEAN   No baggage! It would give us away.

MISS JULIE   Nothing. Only what we can take to our seats.

JEAN [*as he gets his hat*]   What in the devil have you got there? What is that?

MISS JULIE   It's only my canary. I can't leave it behind.

515   JEAN   A canary! My God, do you expect us to carry a birdcage around with us? You're crazy. Put that cage down!

MISS JULIE   It's the only thing I'm taking with me from my home—the only living thing who loves me since Diana was unfaithful to me! Don't be cruel, Jean. Let me take it with me.

520   JEAN   I told you to put that cage down! —And don't talk so loud. Christine can hear us.

MISS JULIE   No, I won't leave it with a stranger. I won't. I'd rather have you kill it.

JEAN   Give it here, the little pest. I'll wring its neck.

MISS JULIE   Oh, don't hurt it. Don't—. No, I can't do it!

525   JEAN   Don't worry, I can. Give it here.

[MISS JULIE *takes the bird out of the cage and kisses it.*]

MISS JULIE   Oh, my little Serena, must you die and leave your mistress?

JEAN   You don't have to make a scene of it. It's a question of your whole life and future. You're wasting time!

[JEAN *grabs the canary from her, carries it to the chopping block, and picks up a meat cleaver.* MISS JULIE *turns away.*]

You should have learned how to kill chickens instead of shooting revolvers—
530   [*He brings the cleaver down.*]—then a drop of blood wouldn't make you faint.

MISS JULIE [*screaming*]   Kill me too! Kill me! You can kill an innocent creature without turning a hair—then kill me. Oh, how I hate you! I loathe you!

There's blood between us. I curse the moment I first laid eyes on you! I curse the moment I was conceived in my mother's womb.

535 JEAN   What good does your cursing do? Let's get out of here!

MISS JULIE [*approaches the chopping block, drawn to it against her will*].   No, I don't want to go yet. I can't. —I have to see. —Shh! [*She listens but keeps her eyes fastened on the chopping block and cleaver.*] You don't think I can stand the sight of blood, do you? You think I'm so weak, don't you? Oh, how I'd love to see your blood, your brains on that chopping block. I'd
540   love to see the whole of your sex swimming in a sea of blood just like that. I could drink blood out of your skull. Use your chest as a foot bath, dip my toes in your guts! I could eat your heart roasted whole! —You think I'm weak! You think I loved you because my womb hungered for your semen. You think I want to carry your brood under my heart and feed it with my
545   blood? Bear your child and take your name? —Come to think of it, what is your name? I've never even heard your last name. I'll bet you don't have one. I'd be Mrs. Doorman or Madame Garbageman. You dog with *my* name on your collar—you lackey with *my* initials on your buttons! Do you think I'm going to share you with my cook and fight over you with my
550   maid?! Ohh! —You think I'm a coward who's going to run away! No, I'm going to stay—come hell or high water. My father will come home—find his desk broken into—his money gone. He'll ring—on that bell—two rings for the valet. And then he'll send for the sheriff—and I'll tell him everything. Everything! Oh, what a relief it'll be to have it all over . . . over and
555   done with . . . if only it will be over. . . . He'll have a stroke and die . . . and there'll be an end to all of us. There'll be peace . . . and quiet . . . forever. . . . The coat of arms will be broken on his coffin; the count's line will be extinct—while the valet's breed will continue in an orphanage, win triumphs in the gutter, and end in jail!

[CHRISTINE *enters, dressed for church and with a hymnbook in her hand.* MISS JULIE *rushes over to her and throws herself into her arms as if seeking protection.*]

560 MISS JULIE   Help me, Christine! Protect me against this man!

CHRISTINE [*cold and unmoved*]   This is a fine way to behave on a holy day! [*She sees the chopping block.*] Just look at the mess you've made there! How do you explain that? And what's all this shouting and screaming about?

565 MISS JULIE   Christine, you're a woman, you're my friend! I warn you, watch out for this—this monster!

JEAN [*feeling awkward*]   If you ladies are going to talk, you won't want me around. I think I'll go and shave. [*He slips out to the right.*]

MISS JULIE   You've got to understand, Christine! You've got to listen to me!

570 CHRISTINE   No, I don't. I don't understand this kind of shenanigans at all. Where do you think you're going dressed like that? And Jean with his hat on? —Well? —Well?

MISS JULIE   Listen to me, Christine! If you'll just listen to me, I'll tell you everything.

575 CHRISTINE   I don't want to know anything.

MISS JULIE   You've got to listen to me—!

CHRISTINE   What about? About your stupid behavior with Jean? I tell you that doesn't bother me at all, because it's none of my business. But if you

have any silly idea about talking him into skipping out with you, I'll soon
580 put a stop to that.

MISS JULIE [*extremely tense*]   Christine, please don't get upset. Listen to me.
I can't stay here, and Jean can't stay here. So you see, we have to go away.

CHRISTINE   Hm, hm, hm.

MISS JULIE [*suddenly brightening up*]   Wait! I've got an idea! Why couldn't all
585 three of us go away together?—out of the country—to Switzerland—and
start a hotel? I've got the money, you see. Jean and I would be responsible
for the whole affair—and Christine, you could run the kitchen, I thought.
Doesn't that sound wonderful! Say you'll come, Christine, then everything
will be settled. Say you will! Please! [*She throws her arms around* CHRISTINE
and pats her.]
590 CHRISTINE [*remaining aloof and unmoved*]   Hm. Hm.

MISS JULIE [*presto tempo*[8]]   You've never been traveling, Christine. You have to
get out and see the world. You can't imagine how wonderful it is to travel by
train—constantly new faces, new countries. We'll go to Hamburg, and stop
over to look at the zoo—it's famous, has everything—you'll love that. And
595 we'll go to the theater and the opera. And then when we get to Munich,
we'll go to the museums, Christine. They have Rubenses and Raphaels
there—those great painters, you know. Of course you've heard about
Munich where King Ludwig[9] lived—you know, the king who went mad. And
then we can go and see his castles—they're just like the ones you read about
600 in fairy tales. And from there it's just a short trip to Switzerland—with the
Alps. Think of the Alps, Christine, covered with snow in the middle of summer. And oranges grow there, and laurel trees that are green the whole year
round—

> [JEAN *can be seen in the wings at the right, sharpening his straight razor
> on a strop held between his teeth and his left hand. He listens to* MISS
> JULIE *with a satisfied expression on his face, now and then nodding
> approvingly.* MISS JULIE *continues tempo prestissimo.*[1]]

—and that's where we'll get a hotel. I'll sit at the desk while Jean stands at
605 the door and receives the guests, goes out shopping, writes the letters. What
a life that will be! The train whistle blowing, then the bus arriving, then a
bell ringing upstairs, then the bell in the restaurant rings—and I'll be making
out the bills—and I know just how much to salt them—you can't imagine
how timid tourists are when you shove a bill in their face! —And you, Chris-
610 tine, you'll run the whole kitchen—there'll be no standing at the stove for
you—of course not. If you're going to talk to the people, you'll have to dress.
And with your looks—I'm not trying to flatter you, Christine—you'll run off
with some man one fine day—a rich Englishman, that's who it'll be, they're
so easy to—[*Slowing down*]—to catch. —Then we'll all be rich. —We'll build
615 a villa on Lake Como. —Maybe it does rain there sometimes, but—[*More
and more lifelessly*]—the sun has to shine sometimes, too—even if it looks

---

8. Quick time (Italian), a musical direction.
9. King Ludwig II of Bavaria (1845–1886;
r. 1864–86), known as "the Fairy-Tale King,"
built several extravagant palaces—most
famously Neuschwanstein, the so-called Cinderella castle; he was declared insane in

1886. Peter Paul Rubens (1577–1640) was a
Flemish baroque painter; Raphael (Raffaello
Sanzio, 1483–1520), a master of the Italian
Renaissance.
1. At a very rapid tempo (Italian).

cloudy. —And—then . . . or else we can always travel some more—and come back . . . [*Pause*]—here . . . or somewhere else . . .

CHRISTINE   Do you really believe a word of that yourself, Miss Julie?

620 MISS JULIE [*completely beaten*]   Do I believe a word of it myself?

CHRISTINE   Do you?

MISS JULIE [*exhausted*]   I don't know. I don't believe anything anymore. [*She sinks down on the bench and lays her head between her arms on the table.*] Nothing. Nothing at all.

CHRISTINE [*turns to the right and faces* JEAN]   So! You were planning to run

625 away, were you?

JEAN [*taken aback, lays his razor down on the table*]   We weren't exactly going to run away! Don't exaggerate. You heard Miss Julie's plans. Even if she's tired now after being all night, her plans are perfectly practical.

CHRISTINE   Well, just listen to you! Did you really think you could get me to

630 cook for that little—!

JEAN [*sharply*]   You keep a respectful tongue in your mouth when you talk to your mistress! Understand?

CHRISTINE   Mistress!

JEAN   Yes, mistress!

635 CHRISTINE   Well of all the—! I don't have to listen—

JEAN   Yes, you do! You need to listen more and blabber less. Miss Julie is your mistress. Don't you forget that! And if you're going to despise her for what she did, you ought to despise yourself for the same reason.

CHRISTINE   I've always held myself high enough to—

640 JEAN   High enough to make you look down on others!

CHRISTINE   —enough to keep from lowering myself beneath my station. Don't you dare say that the count's cook has ever had anything to do with the stable groom or the swineherd. Don't you dare!

JEAN   Yes, you got yourself a decent man. Lucky you!

645 CHRISTINE   What kind of a decent man is it who sells the oats from the count's stables?

JEAN   Listen to who's talking! You get the gravy on the groceries and take bribes from the butcher!

CHRISTINE   How dare you say a thing like that!

650 JEAN   And you say you can't respect your employers. You of all people! You!

CHRISTINE   Are you going to church or aren't you? You need a good sermon after your great exploits.

JEAN   No, I'm not going to church! Go yourself. Go tell God how bad you are.

655 CHRISTINE   Yes, I'll do just that. And I'll come back with enough forgiveness for your sins, too. Our Redeemer suffered and died on the cross for all our sins, and if we come to Him in faith and with a penitent heart, He will take all our sins upon Himself.

JEAN   Rake-offs[2] included?

MISS JULIE   Do you really believe that, Christine?

660 CHRISTINE   With all my heart, as sure as I'm standing here. It was the faith I was born into, and I've held on to it since I was a little girl, Miss Julie. Where sin aboundeth, there grace aboundeth also.[3]

2. Cuts; money or goods skimmed off the top.   3. Romans 5.20.

MISS JULIE   If I had your faith, Christine, if only—

CHRISTINE   But you see, that's something you can't have without God's spe-
665   cial grace. And it is not granted to everyone to receive it.

MISS JULIE   Then who receives it?

CHRISTINE   That's the secret of the workings of grace, Miss Julie, and God is
no respecter of persons. With Him the last shall be first[4]—

MISS JULIE   In that case, he does have respect for the last, doesn't he?

670   CHRISTINE [continuing]   —and it is easier for a camel to go through the eye
of a needle than for a rich man to enter the kingdom of God.[5] That's how
things are, Miss Julie. I'm going to leave now—alone. And on my way out
I'm going to tell the stable boy not to let any horses out, in case anyone has
any ideas about leaving before the count comes home. Goodbye.

[She leaves.]

675   JEAN   She's a devil in skirts! —All because of a canary!

MISS JULIE [listlessly]   Never mind the canary. . . . Do you see any way out of
this, any end to it?

JEAN [after thinking for a moment]   No.

MISS JULIE   What would you do if you were in my place?

680   JEAN   In your place? Let me think. . . . An aristocrat, a woman, and—
fallen. . . . I don't know. —Or maybe I do.

MISS JULIE [picks up the razor and makes a gesture with it]   Like this?

JEAN   Yes. But I wouldn't do it, you understand. That's the difference between
us.

685   MISS JULIE   Because you're a man and I'm a woman? What difference does
that make?

JEAN   Just the difference that there is—between a man and a woman.

MISS JULIE [holding the razor in her hand]   I want to! But I can't do it. My
father couldn't do it either, that time when he should have.

690   JEAN   No, he was right not to. He had to get his revenge first.

MISS JULIE   And now my mother is getting her revenge again through me.

JEAN   Didn't you ever love your father, Miss Julie?

MISS JULIE   Yes, enormously. But I must have hated him too. I must have
hated him without knowing it. It was he who brought me up to despise
695   my own sex, to be half woman and half man. Who's to blame for what
has happened? My father, my mother, myself? Myself? I don't have a self
that's my own. I don't have a single thought I didn't get from my father,
not an emotion I didn't get from my mother. And that last idea—about
all people being equal—I got that from him, my fiancé. That's why I say
700   he's beneath contempt. How can it be my own fault? Put the blame on
Jesus, like Christine does? I'm too proud to do that—and too intelligent,
thanks to what my father taught me. . . . A rich man can't get into
heaven? That's a lie. But at least Christine, who's got money in the savings bank, won't get in. . . . Who's to blame? What difference does it
705   make who's to blame? I'm still the one who has to bear the guilt, suffer
the consequences—

JEAN   Yes, but—

[The bell rings sharply twice. MISS JULIE jumps up. JEAN changes his coat.]

4. Matthew 19.30, 20.16; Luke 13.30; Mark   5. Matthew 19.24.
10.31.

JEAN   The count's back! What if Christine—[*He goes to the speaking tube, taps on it, and listens.*]

MISS JULIE   Has he looked in his desk yet?

710 JEAN   This is Jean, sir! [*Listens. The audience cannot hear what the count says.*] Yes, sir! [*Listens.*] Yes, sir! Yes, as soon as I can. [*Listens.*] Yes, at once, sir! [*Listens.*] Very good, sir! In half an hour.

MISS JULIE [*trembling with anxiety*]   What did he say? For God's sake, what did he say?

715 JEAN   He ordered his boots and his coffee in half an hour.

MISS JULIE   Half an hour then! . . . Oh, I'm so tired. I can't bring myself to do anything. Can't repent, can't run away, can't stay, can't live . . . can't die. Help me, Jean. Command me, and I'll obey like a dog. Do me this last favor. Save my honor, save his name. You know what I ought to do but can't force
720   myself to do. Let me use your willpower. You command me and I'll obey.

JEAN   I don't know—. I can't either, not now. I don't know why. It's as if this coat made me—I can't give you orders in this. And now, after the count has spoken to me, I—I can't really explain it—but—I've got the backbone of a damned lackey! If the count came down here now and ordered me to cut
725   my throat, I'd do it on the spot.

MISS JULIE   Then pretend you're him. Pretend I'm you. You were such a good actor just a while ago, when you were kneeling before me. You were the aristocrat then. Or else—have you been to the theater and seen a hypnotist?

[JEAN *nods.*]

He says to his subject, "Take this broom!" and he takes it. He says, "Now
730   sweep!" and he sweeps.

JEAN   The person has to be asleep!

MISS JULIE [*ecstatic, transported*]   I'm already asleep. The whole room has turned to smoke. You seem like an iron stove, a stove that looks like a man in black with a high hat. Your eyes are glowing like fading coals in a dying
735   fire. Your face is a white smudge, like ashes.

[*The sun is now shining in on the floor and falls on* JEAN.]

It's so good and warm—[*She rubs her hands together as if warming them at a fire.*]—and so bright—and so peaceful.

JEAN [*takes the razor and puts it in her hand*]   There's the broom. Go now, when the sun is up—out into the barn—and—[*He whispers in her ear.*]

740 MISS JULIE [*waking up*]   Thanks! I'm going to get my rest. But tell me one thing. Tell me that the first can also receive the gift of grace. Tell me that, even if you don't believe it.

JEAN   The first? I can't tell you that. —Wait a moment, Miss Julie. I know what I can tell you. You're no longer one of the first. You're one of—the last.

745 MISS JULIE   That's true! I'm one of the last. I am the very last! —Oh! —Now I can't go! Tell me just once more, tell me to go!

JEAN   Now I can't either. I can't!

MISS JULIE   And the first shall be the last . . .

JEAN   Don't think—don't think! You're taking all my strength from me. You're
750   making me a coward. . . . What?! I thought I saw the bell move. No. . . . Let me stuff some paper in it. —Afraid of a bell! But it isn't just a bell. There's somebody behind it. A hand that makes it move. And there's some-

thing that makes the hand move. —Stop your ears, that's it, stop your ears! But it only rings louder. Rings louder and louder until you answer it. And then it's too late. Then the sheriff comes—and then—[*There are two sharp rings on the bell.* JEAN *gives a start, then straightens himself up.*] It's horrible! But there's no other way for it to end. —Go!

[MISS JULIE *walks resolutely out through the door.*]

HENRIK IBSEN

1828–1906

WRITING in an era when the theater had become a second-rate occupation, with most gifted writers turning instead to novels or poetry, Henrik Johan Ibsen restored to drama its prestige and relevance. During the nineteenth century, the invention of new theatrical machinery and techniques had turned theater into spectacle. Producers spent their time and money on special effects, dazzling audiences with lighting, horses, or even sea battles to add to—and sometimes replace—the appeal of popular actors. Nineteenth-century theater was in some ways comparable to present-day Hollywood and its focus on blockbuster action movies filled with special effects and big-name stars. Ibsen showed Europe that drama could be more than just spectacle: it could be an art form addressing the most serious moral and social questions of the time. The theatergoing public was first shocked, and later thrilled, to have controversial figures and themes presented on the stage, in plays that relied not on special effects but on carefully drawn characters and well-constructed dramatic situations. Honing his dramatic technique over half a century, Ibsen almost single-handedly brought a new seriousness to drama, and in doing so he won enduring acclaim as the originator of modern drama.

Ibsen achieved his unparalleled success against all odds. He was born in Skien, a small town in Norway, far removed from the cultural centers of Europe both physically and linguistically. When Ibsen left his provincial home at the age of fifteen, he was apprenticed to a pharmacist for more than six years; during that time he began to write occasional pieces, including his first play, *Catiline* (written 1848–49). Only at the age of twenty-two was he able to free himself from his apprenticeship—as well as from a liaison with a maid that had resulted in an illegitimate child—and move to the capital, Christiania (now Oslo), to study for the university entrance exam, which he failed. His efforts as a dramatist were better received, as one of his plays—the one-act *The Burial Mound* (1850)—was performed. The true beginning of his career occurred several years later, however, when he moved to Bergen to take his first job in the theater. After a few years spent learning the craft, he assumed positions of greater responsibility—as artistic director and dramatist—at a theater back in Christiania, where in 1857 he also married and had another child. By the time Ibsen was thirty-five, the foundation for his subsequent success as a dramatist had been laid.

While working at the theaters in Bergen and Christiania, Ibsen got to know the standard dramatic form of the time, the so-called well-made play (a literal translation of the French *pièce bien-fait*). Popularized by the French playwrights Victorien Sardou (1831–1908) and Augustin-Eugène Scribe (1791–1861), well-made plays were formulaic dramas focused less on well-developed characters than on complicated plots and well-timed confrontations. They offered fast-moving action, intrigues, alliances, and sudden revelations. Immensely popular at the time, the genre was also attacked by proponents of modern drama for favoring cheap suspense and empty entertainment over social relevance and meaningful art.

Ibsen's own drama can be viewed as an evolving series of reactions to the well-made play, beginning with *Brand* (1866) and *Peer Gynt* (1867). They mark Ibsen's rejection not only of the well-made play but also of the theater as such, for they were "dramatic poems"—plays written exclusively to be read, not performed. All the rules that governed stage action, the rules of the well-made play, could thus be ignored entirely. Both plays were built around a single character on a singular and willful mission. *Brand* is the more tragic of the two; it presents a fanatical preacher who seeks to impose an uncompromising religion on his small parish high up in the Norwegian mountains, demanding increasingly large sacrifices of his congregants and of himself until he finally dies in utter isolation. In *Peer Gynt*, the protagonist's quest is cast in a more satirical form. The adventures of the title character, a notorious liar, take him from the fairy-tale realm of the Norwegian mountain trolls to the Moroccan desert and then back to Norway, where he dies not as a hero but as a mediocrity, even in his sinning. Drawing on literary models such as Goethe's *Faust* (1808, 1832) and Byron's *Don Juan* (1819–24), *Peer Gynt* freely mixes fantasy and reality, conjuring mountain trolls, mad German philosophers, and the devil himself.

By the time he wrote *Brand* and *Peer Gynt*, Ibsen had left Norway. He would spend twenty-seven years on the Continent, mostly in Italy and Germany, before returning to his homeland in 1891, at the age of sixty-three. Exile became the condition in which he thrived and from which he suffered. After *Brand* and *Peer Gynt*

had secured his reputation, Ibsen started writing for the stage once more, but in an entirely different style. Whereas his earliest dramas had dealt with history, he now chose to write, once and for all, about the contemporary world he knew best—namely, the contemporary Norwegian middle class—in prose, not verse. His single purpose was to lay bare the ugly reality behind the facade of middle-class respectability, to expose the lies of bourgeois characters and indeed of bourgeois society as a whole. The five plays of this period—*The Pillars of Society* (1877), A DOLL HOUSE (1879), *Ghosts* (1881), *An Enemy of the People* (1882), and *The Wild Duck* (1884)—made Ibsen notorious throughout Europe and established him as an author of shock, confrontation, and revolt: in short, as a modern. With these plays, Ibsen struck a nerve and secured his place in the pantheon of world drama.

The main cause of audiences' consternation also explains why these plays are now seen as the beginning of modern drama: they introduced realism, long established in the novel, to the theater. Using idiomatic language, Ibsen created a drama devoted to unveiling hidden motives and past misdeeds so that the truth would shine forth on the stage. In this way, Ibsen campaigned not only against a theater of special effects but also against a theater of convention. Realism, for Ibsen, required a theater of emotional and moral truth, a theater centered on understanding the subjective experience and objective conditions of modern life.

A DOLL HOUSE

Within this group of plays, *A Doll House* made the biggest splash. Its initial sales in Scandinavia numbered in the thousands and led to theatrical productions both there and abroad, including Germany and the United States; soon the play was translated into many other languages, inaugurating an unparalleled global career. One reason for this success was the play's notorious ending, which violated nineteenth-century views of marriage and the family. Nora is oppressed by a domineering husband who belittles her from the very opening lines of the play and who is revealed as callous at a moment of crisis. In response, Nora leaves him and her children, banging the door behind her. Her husband and contemporary audiences were shocked. This unexpected turn of events alone sufficed to establish Ibsen as a bold critic of gender relations or, in the views of his growing number of enemies, as a muckraker singularly intent on assaulting audiences with indecency. So unusual was this ending that George Bernard Shaw even coined a new term, "discussion play," to capture how this plot-driven drama suddenly changes course and engages in a lengthy discussion about marriage before the final bang. With a single stroke, Ibsen had scandalized Europe and the United States and turned himself into a controversial public figure.

Shortly after the play's publication, a German theater manager decided the play's ending was more than his audience could stomach and had Nora return to her husband in remorse; he even managed to force Ibsen into writing the bowdlerized ending himself. Ibsen probably wanted to do dam-

age control, fearing that a hack writer would do worse. More recently, a new production has Nora return to her husband as well, but only to shoot him with a pistol. Through eccentric decisions like these, the play's ending has remained the most famous in theater history.

Given all this notoriety, it may be surprising to recognize that for the most part, the play is quite conventionally and carefully crafted. It is driven forward by a blackmail plot and includes all the tricks of the trade for creating suspense that Ibsen had learned from French well-made plays during his long apprenticeship in the theater, including the gradual revelation of secrets, overheard threats, and surprising revelations about past events; we even have the blackmail letter waiting in a mailbox right onstage, threatening to reveal Nora's secret, while she desperately tries to distract her husband, hoping to keep him from opening it.

But beyond its plot devices, the enduring power of this play is due to the skill with which Ibsen weaves together several threads and themes that give nuance to its abrupt ending. Ibsen is an expert at han-

Hattie Morahan as Nora Helmer and Dominic Rowan as Torvald Helmer in the 2012 production at the Young Vic Theatre, London, directed by Carrie Cracknell.

dling stage props, beginning with the macaroons that Nora secretly savors and that are also harbingers of other, more consequential, secrets. The Christmas tree that greets us in the first scene with a homey atmosphere soon gives way to an excessive Tarantella dance, suggesting that the play will spiral out of control. The nicely set-up home is nothing but a doll's house that will end up being utterly destroyed.

Like Ibsen's other famous plays, *A Doll House* is set among the bourgeoisie, the world of lawyers, doctors, architects, professors, and above all, bankers. Tovald is a banker, and Ibsen never lets us forget it. The questions Ibsen wants us to ask are specific to this social group: What kind of houses do they live in? Did they borrow money to buy them? Can they meet their mortgage payments? How about the furniture: did they buy that on credit as well? In order to get credit, or to advance in the banking business, the characters in this world must inspire trust. Trust in turn requires them to keep up appearances, both financial and moral. As soon as Torvald sees his appearance threatened, he begins to treat Nora with unvarnished roughness, ultimately causing Nora's departure. Keeping up appearances is not just a matter of social respectability but goes to the heart of bourgeois life. In peeling back layer after layer of pretense, Ibsen's plays aim at this heart with surgical precision.

Ibsen's greatest topic is inheritance. This theme, too, is tied to money and credit, but in keeping with the spirit of the time, Ibsen pursues it much further. Inspired by lively scientific debates about evolution and inheritance, Ibsen has his characters inherit medical diseases that turn out to be moral ones as well, as with Dr. Ranke in *A Doll House,* who is the family friend and commentator on the action almost in the manner of a Greek chorus. Moral and immoral features are passed down through the generations, and Ibsen's characters often struggle in vain to rid themselves of these various inheritances.

By weaving together questions of credit, trust, appearance, and inheritance, Ibsen became the great dramatist of the bourgeoisie, the poet of bourgeois capitalism. No one managed to capture the fears, but also the fantasies, of the bourgeoisie quite like him.

While the ending of the play continues to be its most famous feature, it has long ceased to be shocking. Ibsen's scandalous reputation, his apparent embrace of radical projects such as women's liberation, placed him in the company of political radicals, some of whom, like the British playwright and pamphleteer George Bernard Shaw, were eager to adopt him in their cause. But Ibsen did not seek to replace the world of bourgeois capitalism with a socialist system. Rather, he became an expert at diagnosing the bourgeoisie. It is to this diagnosis that *A Doll House* owes its enduring power and significance.

Ibsen is a dramatist of singular importance in part because he has consistently inspired the most important actors and directors. In England, Ibsen initially owed his influence to GEORGE BERNARD SHAW and William Archer, writers who led what some have called the Ibsen campaign. Shaw's defense of Ibsen against the scornful reception given his drama in the popular press and Archer's translations and productions of Ibsen's plays turned the Norwegian into the most important figure in British modern drama. Directors and playwrights elsewhere soon championed Ibsen as well. André Antoine, whose Théâtre Libre had pioneered a naturalist style of acting and design, played Oswald in *Ghosts* in 1890, and the influential Russian director Konstantin Stanislavski, whose Moscow Art Theater promoted an acting style based on authentic emotional responses, played Doctor Stockman in *An Enemy of the People* in 1900. Ibsen's later plays attracted a different set of directors, more interested in symbolism and poetry than in naturalism and truth. Aurélien Lugné-Poe, who had attacked realist drama and instead pioneered a symbolist theater full of ominous allusions and hieratic moods, staged *Rosmersholm* (1893) and *The Master Builder* (1894) in Paris, and directors interested in surrealism and suggestive stagecraft, such as Ingmar Bergman, have continued to be attracted first and foremost to Ibsen's late plays.

Ibsen is acknowledged as a founder of modern drama, but his place in theater history is full of enigmas and contradictions. He started his career with historical dramas that were typical nineteenth-century fare, yet he became the herald of modern drama. Rather than simply rejecting the dramatic techniques of his time, he transformed them into a drama that seemed new, shocking, and modern to his audience. He received the most attention for his realist plays but later turned realism in a more poetic and symbolist direction. In the end, Ibsen created a dramatic oeuvre of variety and complexity. His plays could be many things to many people, viewed as

stirring manifestos against social injustice or modern tragedies of striking poetic and dramatic force. This versatility, more than anything else, is responsible for Ibsen's having remained one of the most popular dramatists of all time. Today, he ranks second only after SHAKESPEARE as the world's most-performed playwright, a position that testifies to Ibsen's dramatic art: shocking and novel when it was first presented to audiences, it has stood the test of time.

M.P.

A Doll House[1]

CHARACTERS

TORVALD HELMER, a lawyer
NORA, his wife
DR. RANK
MRS. LINDE
NILS KROGSTAD, a bank clerk

THE HELMERS' THREE SMALL CHILDREN
ANNE-MARIE, their nurse
HELENE, a maid
A DELIVERY BOY

Act 1

A comfortable, tasteful, but not expensively furnished room. A door to the right in the back wall leads out to the hall; another door to the left leads in to Helmer's study. Between these doors is a piano. In the middle of the left wall, a door, and farther back, a window. Near the window a round table with armchairs and a small sofa. In the right wall, upstage, a door and, on this same side nearer the foreground, a porcelain stove with a pair of armchairs and a rocking chair. Between the stove and the door, a little table. Engravings on the walls. An étagère[2] with porcelain figures and other small art objects; a small bookcase with books in rich bindings. Carpet on the floor; the fire burns in the stove. A winter's day.

[*A bell rings in the hallway; soon after, we hear the door being opened. Nora, cheerfully humming, enters the room; she is dressed in outdoor clothes and carries a great number of packages, which she sets down on the table, right. She lets the door to the hall stand open and we see a Porter carrying a Christmas tree and a basket, which he hands to the Maid, who had opened the door for them.*]

1. Translated by Rick Davis and Brian Johnston.

2. A shelf for the display of objects.

NORA Be sure you hide the tree, Helene. We can't let the children see it before it's decorated tonight. [*To the Porter as she takes out her purse.*] How much—? Oh yes, I know, half a krone—here's one—no, keep the change.

[*The Porter thanks her and leaves. Nora closes the door. She continues laughing softly to herself while she takes off her outdoor clothes. She takes a bag of macaroons from her pocket and eats a couple; then she walks cautiously and listens outside her husband's door.*]

He's home, all right.

[*Humming again, she goes over to the table, right.*]

5 HELMER [*From within the study.*] Do I hear a skylark singing out there?

NORA [*Busy opening some packages.*] Yes, you do.

HELMER Is there by any chance a squirrel rummaging around?

NORA Yes!

HELMER When did the squirrel get home?

10 NORA Just this second. [*She puts the bag of macaroons in her pocket and wipes her mouth.*] Come out here, Torvald, and look at what I've bought.

HELMER Can't be disturbed! [*After a moment, he opens the door and looks in, his pen in his hand.*] Did you say bought? All that? Has the little spendthrift been out wasting money again?

15 NORA Oh, Torvald—this year we really ought to let ourselves go a little bit. It's the first Christmas we haven't had to watch our money.

HELMER But we still can't go around wasting it, you know.

NORA Yes, Torvald, now we can afford to waste a little bit here and there. Isn't that right? Just a teeny little bit. Now that you've got such a big salary

20 and we've got heaps and heaps of money coming in?

HELMER Yes, after New Year's. And then it's three whole months before the first paycheck.

NORA Fuff! We can borrow till then.

HELMER Nora! [*Goes over to her and takes her playfully by the ear.*] Is that

25 dizzy little head of yours spinning around again? Suppose I borrowed a thousand today, and you wasted it all on Christmas, and then on New Year's Eve I got hit in the head by a falling brick and lay there—

NORA [*Covering his mouth.*] Ugh! Don't say awful things like that!

HELMER Well, suppose it happened—what then?

30 NORA If anything that awful happened, some silly loan would be the least of my worries.

HELMER What about the people I'd borrowed from?

NORA Them? Who cares about them! They're only strangers.

HELMER Nora, Nora, you are such a woman! Seriously, Nora, you know

35 what I think about these things. No debts! Never borrow! Some freedom's lost, and because of that some beauty too, from a home that's built on borrowing and debt. The two of us have managed to hold out bravely until now; and we'll stay the course for the little time remaining.

NORA [*Goes over to the stove.*] All right, Torvald, whatever you want.

40 HELMER [*Following.*] Now, now; the little songbird mustn't droop its wings. Right? Is the squirrel standing there sulking? [*Taking out his wallet.*] Nora, guess what I have?

NORA [*Turning quickly.*] Money!

HELMER There, see? [*Handing her some bills.*] For heaven's sake, I know

45 how much a house goes through at Christmastime.

NORA [*Counting.*] Ten—twenty—thirty—forty—Oh, thank you, thank you, Torvald. This will help me no end.

HELMER It had certainly better.

NORA Yes, yes, I'll make sure it does. But come here so I can show you what
50 I've bought. And so cheap! Look—new clothes for Ivar, also a sword. Here's a horse and trumpet for Bob. And for Emmy, a doll and a doll bed. They're pretty plain, but she'll just tear them to pieces anyway before you know it. And here's some dress material and some handkerchiefs for the maids— even though old Anne-Marie really deserves a little more.

55 HELMER And what's in that package there?

NORA [*With a cry.*] No, Torvald! Not till tonight!

HELMER Aha! But tell me, you little spendthrift, what did you think of for yourself?

NORA For me? Oh, I don't need anything.

60 HELMER You most certainly do. Tell me what you'd like most of all—within reason.

NORA Oh, I really don't know. Yes—listen, Torvald—

HELMER Well?

NORA [*Fumbling with his button; not looking at him.*] If you want to give me
65 something, you could—you could—

HELMER Well, say it.

NORA [*Quickly.*] You could give me money, Torvald. Only what you can spare; then one of these days I could buy something with it.

HELMER No, but Nora—

70 NORA Yes, do it, Torvald, darling. I'm begging you. And I'll hang the money in pretty gilt paper on the tree. Wouldn't that be lovely?

HELMER What do we call those little birds that are always spending their money?

NORA Spendthrifts—yes, I know, I know. But let's do what I say, Torvald;
75 then I'll have time to think about what I really need. That's pretty practical, isn't it?

HELMER [*Smiling.*] Absolutely—if you could only hold on to the money I give you, and if you actually bought something for yourself with it. But it will go for the house, for a lot of things we don't need, and I'll just have to
80 shell out again.

NORA Oh, Torvald—

HELMER Can't be denied, my dear little Nora. [*Puts his arm around her waist.*] Spendthrifts are sweet; but they go through an awful lot of money. It's unbelievable how expensive it is to keep a spendthrift.

85 NORA Oh, fuff—how can you say that? I save absolutely everything I can.

HELMER [*Laughing.*] Yes, that's true—everything you *can*. But the trouble is, you *can't*.

NORA [*Humming and smiling with quiet complacency.*] Hmm. You just can't imagine what kinds of expenses larks and squirrels have, Torvald.

90 HELMER You are a strange little one. Just like your father was. You'll try anything you can think of to get hold of some money; but the moment you get some, it slips through your fingers. You never know what you've done with it. But you are what you are. It's in your blood—these things are hereditary, Nora.

NORA I wish I'd inherited a lot of Papa's qualities.

95 HELMER Well I don't want you to be anything but what you are: my sweet little songbird. But listen—I'm getting the distinct impression—you've got a sort of a—what can I call it—a kind of a guilty look today.

NORA   I do?

HELMER   You certainly do. Look me straight in the eye.

100 NORA [*Looking at him.*]   Well?

HELMER [*Wagging his finger.*]   Our sweet tooth wouldn't have been running wild in town today, would it?

NORA   No, what makes you think that?

HELMER   You're sure that sweet tooth didn't make a little stop at the
105   bakery?

NORA   No, Torvald, I swear—

HELMER   Didn't nibble a little candy?

NORA   No, absolutely not.

HELMER   Not even munched on a macaroon or two?

110 NORA   No, Torvald, honestly, I promise—

HELMER   Now, now—of course I'm only joking.

NORA [*Going to the table, right.*]   I'd never dream of going against you.

HELMER   No, I know that. And after all, you've given me your word. [*Goes to her.*] Well, you keep your little Christmas secrets to yourself, then, my
115   dearest Nora. I guess everything will be revealed this evening when we light the tree.

NORA   Did you remember to invite Doctor Rank?

HELMER   No—there's no need; it's taken for granted. But I'll ask him again when he stops in this morning. I've ordered the very best wine. Nora, you
120   can't imagine how excited I am about tonight.

NORA   Me too! And the children are just going to love it!

HELMER   Ah, it's so marvelous to have a secure position and a comfortable income. Isn't it fun just to think about that?

NORA   Oh, it's wonderful!

125 HELMER   Do you remember last Christmas? Three whole weeks beforehand, you locked yourself up every evening, till way past midnight, making flowers for the Christmas tree, and all the other little surprises you had for us. Uch—I've never been so bored in my whole life.

NORA   I wasn't bored at all.

130 HELMER [*Smiling.*]   But it didn't amount to much after all, Nora.

NORA   Oh, are you going to tease me with that again? I couldn't help it that the cat came in and tore everything to bits.

HELMER   No, that's right, you couldn't, my poor little Nora. You worked so hard to make us happy, that's the main thing. But it's good that those hard
135   times are behind us.

NORA   Yes, it's really wonderful.

HELMER   Now I don't have to sit here all alone boring myself, and you don't have to torture your precious eyes and your delicate little fingers—

NORA [*Clapping her hands.*]   No, is that true, Torvald, I really don't have to?
140   How wonderful to hear that! [*Takes his arm.*] Now I'll tell you what I thought we should do—as soon as Christmas is over—[*The doorbell rings.*] Oh, that doorbell. [*Tidying up the room.*] That means a visitor—what a bore!

HELMER   I'm not at home to visitors, remember that.

145 MAID [*In the doorway.*]   Madam, there's a strange lady here to see you.

NORA   Show her in.

MAID [*To Helmer.*]   And the Doctor arrived at the same time.

HELMER   He went straight to my study?

MAID Yes, sir, he did.

> [*Helmer goes into his room. The Maid shows Mrs. Linde, dressed in traveling clothes, into the room and closes the door after her.*]

150 MRS. LINDE [*Timidly and somewhat hesitantly.*] Good day, Nora.

NORA [*Uncertainly.*] Good day—

MRS. LINDE You don't recognize me.

NORA No; I don't know—I think—[*Bursting out.*] Kristine! Is it really you?

MRS. LINDE Yes, it is.

155 NORA Kristine! How could I not recognize you? But then how could I—? [*Quieter.*] You've changed, Kristine.

MRS. LINDE Yes, I expect I have. In nine—ten—long years—

NORA Is it that long? Yes, that's right. Oh, the last eight years have been happy ones, believe me. And now you've come to town as well. Made the
160 long trip in winter. That was brave.

MRS. LINDE I just got here this morning on the steamer.

NORA To enjoy yourself at Christmas, of course. That's a lovely idea! Yes, enjoy ourselves—we will certainly do that. But take off your coat. You're not too cold? [*Helps her.*] That's it; now let's settle down and be cozy here
165 by the stove. No, take the armchair there. I'll sit here in the rocking chair. [*Gripping her hands.*] Yes, now you look more like yourself again; it was just those first few moments—you have gotten a bit paler, Kristine—and maybe a little thinner.

MRS. LINDE And much, much older, Nora.

170 NORA Well, maybe a little older, a tiny little bit; but not too much. [*Drawing back, suddenly serious.*] Oh, I can't believe how thoughtless I am, sitting here chattering—Kristine, can you forgive me?

MRS. LINDE What do you mean, Nora?

NORA [*Quietly.*] Poor Kristine, you're a widow.

175 MRS. LINDE Yes, for three years now.

NORA I knew it of course, I read it in the paper. Oh, Kristine, you have to believe me, I was always going to write you at the time, but I kept putting it off, and things kept getting in the way.

MRS. LINDE Nora, dear, I understood completely.

180 NORA No, it was horrible of me. You poor thing, it must have been so hard for you—and he didn't leave you anything to live on?

MRS. LINDE No.

NORA And no children?

MRS. LINDE No.

185 NORA So, nothing at all.

MRS. LINDE No—not even a sense of grief to hold on to.

NORA [*Looking at her in disbelief.*] Kristine, how is that possible?

MRS. LINDE [*Smiles sadly, stroking Nora's hair.*] Ah, sometimes it happens that way, Nora.

190 NORA So completely alone. That must be terribly sad for you. I have three lovely children—you can't see them right now, they're out with Anne-Marie. But now you have to tell me everything.

MRS. LINDE No, no, I'd rather hear about you.

NORA No, you have to go first. Today I'm not going to be selfish. Today I'm
195 only going to think about you. But I have to tell you *one* thing. Did you hear about the great luck we just had?

MRS. LINDE No, what is it?

NORA   My husband has been made manager of the Bank.

MRS. LINDE   Your husband? That is lucky!

200   NORA   Isn't it? The law is such a chancy business, especially when you won't take the ugly cases. Torvald would never do that, of course, and I agree with him completely. So you can imagine how happy we are! He starts at the Bank right after New Year's, and then he'll be getting a huge salary and lots of commissions. From now on we'll be able to live quite differently—we

205   can actually do what we want. Oh, Kristine, I feel so light and happy! Isn't it lovely to have lots of money, and not have to worry about anything?

MRS. LINDE   It's lovely just to have enough.

NORA   No, not just enough, but lots and lots of money!

MRS. LINDE   [Smiling.]   Nora, Nora, haven't you gotten over that yet? You

210   were such a spendthrift in school.

NORA   [Laughing softly.]   Yes, Torvald still says the same thing. [Wagging her finger.] But "Nora, Nora" hasn't been as wild as you all think. We haven't exactly been in a position where I could waste any money. We've both had to work.

215   MRS. LINDE   You too?

NORA   Yes, odd jobs—sewing, embroidery, work like that—[Casually.] and also other things. You know Torvald left the government when we got married; he saw he'd never be promoted, and he needed to earn more money than before. In that first year he worked himself to the bone, always looking for

220   extra income, day and night. But he couldn't keep it up, and he got deathly sick. The doctor said he absolutely had to move south.

MRS. LINDE   Didn't you stay a whole year in Italy?

NORA   That's right. It wasn't that easy to get away, as you can imagine. Ivar had just been born. But we had to go, there was no question about it. Ah,

225   it was a wonderful trip, and it saved Torvald's life. But it was incredibly expensive.

MRS. LINDE   I believe you.

NORA   Four thousand, eight hundred kroner. That's a lot of money.

MRS. LINDE   It's just lucky you had it when the emergency came up.

230   NORA   Well, I can tell you, we had to get it from Papa.

MRS. LINDE   So that's how. That was about the time your father died, I think.

NORA   Yes, Kristine, it was right then. Just think, I couldn't go and be with him. I stayed right here and waited every day for little Ivar to come into the world. And I had my poor, sick Torvald to take care of. Dear, sweet Papa!

235   I never saw him again, Kristine. That was the saddest time in my whole marriage.

MRS. LINDE   I know how much he meant to you. But then you left for Italy?

NORA   Yes, we had the money then, and the doctors insisted. So we left in a month.

240   MRS. LINDE   And your husband came back completely cured?

NORA   Right as rain!

MRS. LINDE   But—the doctor—?

NORA   What do you mean?

MRS. LINDE   I thought the maid said the man who came in with me was a

245   doctor.

NORA   Yes, Doctor Rank. He's not here on a house call, he's our best friend—he comes by at least once a day. No, Torvald hasn't been sick a day since then. And the children are strong and sound and so am I. [Jumping

up and clapping her hands.] Oh God, oh God, Kristine, it's so wonderful to
250 live and be happy! But I'm being hateful here, only talking about myself.
[*Sits on a stool close by Kristine and lays her arms on her knees.*] Please don't
be mad at me! Tell me something—is it really true that you didn't love your
husband? So why did you marry him?

MRS. LINDE   My mother was still alive, but she was bedridden and couldn't
255 take care of herself; and I also had to look after my two younger brothers.
I couldn't justify refusing his offer.

NORA   No, no, you were right. He was rich at the time, wasn't he?

MRS. LINDE   He was pretty well-off, I think. But the business wasn't very
solid, Nora: when he died it all went to pieces, nothing was left.

260 NORA   And then—?

MRS. LINDE   Well, I had to do what I could for myself—a little shop, a few
students, whatever else I could find. These last three years have been like
one long workday without a break. But now it's over, Nora. My poor mother
doesn't need me anymore, she's gone. And the boys are working now,
265 they're on their own.

NORA   You must feel such relief—

MRS. LINDE   No, not at all. Only inexpressibly empty. Nothing more to live
for. [*Stands uneasily.*] So I couldn't stand it any longer out in that little
backwater. It's got to be easier here to find something to do, something to
270 keep my mind working. If only I could be lucky enough to find a steady job,
some office work—

NORA   But Kristine, that's so exhausting, and you're tired enough to begin
with. You'd be better off if you could get away to a spa for a while.

MRS. LINDE [*Going over to window.*]   I don't have a papa to send me on a trip,
275 Nora.

NORA [*Getting up.*]   Oh, don't be mad at me!

MRS. LINDE   Nora, dear, don't you be mad at me. That's the worst thing
about this situation of mine; it leaves you with so much bitterness. You've
got nothing to work for, but you still have to watch out for every opportu-
280 nity. You have to live, so you become selfish. When you told me your news,
I was more excited for my own sake than yours.

NORA   Why? Oh, I see—you mean maybe Torvald can do something for you.

MRS. LINDE   That's exactly what I was thinking.

NORA   And so he will, Kristine! Leave it to me—I'll suggest it so beautifully,
285 so beautifully—find something charming that he'll really appreciate. Oh, I
can't wait to help you.

MRS. LINDE   You're so kind, Nora, to take such an interest in me—doubly
kind, since you don't know much about life's hardships yourself.

NORA   I—? Don't know much—?

290 MRS. LINDE [*Smiling.*]   Well, good Lord, a little sewing and things like that—
you're such a child, Nora.

NORA [*Tosses her head, walks across the room.*]   You shouldn't be so sure
about that.

MRS. LINDE   Oh?

295 NORA   You're like everyone else. You all think I'm not capable of anything serious—

MRS. LINDE   Now, now—

NORA   That I've never been put to the test in the cold, hard world.

MRS. LINDE   Nora, you've just been telling me all about your troubles.

NORA   Fuff! Trifles! [*Quietly.*] I haven't told you the big thing.

300 MRS. LINDE   What big thing? What do you mean?

NORA   You look down on me an awful lot, Kristine, but you really shouldn't. You're proud that you've worked so hard for your mother all these years.

MRS. LINDE   I don't look down on anyone. But it's true that I'm proud—and happy—that I was given the chance to ease my mother's sorrow in her last
305   days.

NORA   And when you think about what you've done for your brothers, you're proud of that as well.

MRS. LINDE   I think I'm entitled to that.

NORA   So do I. But now you'll hear, Kristine. I also have something to be
310   proud and happy about.

MRS. LINDE   I don't doubt it. But how do you mean?

NORA   Let's talk quietly. What if Torvald heard? He mustn't, not for anything in the world. Nobody can find out about this, nobody but you.

MRS. LINDE   What is it?

315 NORA   Come over here. [*Pulls her down on the sofa beside her.*] Now then: here's what I have to be proud and happy about. I saved Torvald's life.

MRS. LINDE   Saved—? How did you save—?

NORA   I told you about the trip to Italy. Torvald would never have survived if he hadn't gone down there—

320 MRS. LINDE   Yes, well, your father gave you all the money you needed—

NORA [*Smiling.*]   Yes, that's what Torvald and everyone else believe, but—

MRS. LINDE   But—?

NORA   Papa never gave anything. I got the money myself.

MRS. LINDE   You? That was a lot of money.

325 NORA   Four thousand, eight hundred kroner. What do you say to that?

MRS. LINDE   But Nora, how was that possible? Did you win the lottery?

NORA [*Disdainfully.*]   The lottery. [*Snorting.*] What kind of art would *that* have taken?

MRS. LINDE   Then where did you get it from?

330 NORA [*Humming and smiling secretively.*]   Hmm; tra la la la la!

MRS. LINDE   Because you certainly couldn't have borrowed it.

NORA   Oh? Why not?

MRS. LINDE   No, a wife can't get a loan without her husband's permission.

NORA [*Tossing her head.*]   Well, but a wife with a head for business, a wife
335   who knows how to be a little clever—

MRS. LINDE   Nora, I just don't understand—

NORA   And you don't need to. Nobody said anything about *borrowing* the money. Maybe I got it some other way. [*Throwing herself back on the sofa.*] Maybe I got it from one of my admirers. When you're as alluring as I am—

340 MRS. LINDE   You're crazy.

NORA   I've got you really curious now, haven't I?

MRS. LINDE   Listen to me, Nora: you haven't done anything foolish, have you?

NORA [*Sitting up again.*]   Is it foolish to save your husband's life?

MRS. LINDE   I think it's foolish that without his knowledge you—

345 NORA   But that's just it—he mustn't know anything! Good Lord, can't you see that? He can never know how bad off he was. The doctors came to *me* to say his life was in jeopardy—that only a trip south could save him. At first I tried to coax him into it—I told him how lovely it would be to take a

trip abroad like other young wives—then I begged and cried—I said he
350 should be kind and indulge a woman in my condition—and I hinted that he
could easily take out a loan. That really set him off, Kristine. He told me I
was being frivolous, and that it was his duty as a husband not to indulge my
every whim and caprice—I think that's what he called them. Well, well, I
thought, saved you must be and saved you shall be—and that's when I came
355 up with my plan.

MRS. LINDE Didn't your husband ever find out that the money wasn't your
father's?

NORA Never. Papa died right after that. I thought about letting him in on it
and asking him not to say anything. But with him lying there so sick—and
360 finally it wasn't necessary.

MRS. LINDE And you've never confided in your husband?

NORA No, for heaven's sake, how can you even imagine that? He's so strict
about those things. And besides, Torvald's a man—he'd be so humiliated if
he knew he owed me anything. It could even spoil our relationship; it
365 would be the end of our beautiful, happy home.

MRS. LINDE So you'll never tell him?

NORA [Reflectively, half-smiling.] Yes, maybe someday; years from now, when
I can't count on my looks anymore. Don't laugh! I mean when Torvald's not
as attracted to me as he is now—when my dancing and dressing-up and
370 reciting for him don't interest him any more. Then it'll be good to have
something to fall back on. [Breaking off.] Dumb, dumb, dumb! That'll
never happen. So what do you think of my big secret, Kristine? I can do
things after all, can't I? But as you can imagine, it's been a big worry for
me. It hasn't been that easy to make the payments on time. So I had to save
375 a little, here and there, whenever I could. I couldn't really take anything
out of the housekeeping budget, because Torvald has to live in a certain
style. And I couldn't scrimp on the children's clothes; I used up whatever I
got for them—the angels!

MRS. LINDE Poor Nora! So it came out of your allowance?

380 NORA Yes, of course. But then it was mostly my problem. Whenever
Torvald gave me money for new clothes or whatever, I'd only use half;
I always bought the simplest, cheapest things. I'm lucky that everything looks good on me, so Torvald never noticed. But it made me sad
sometimes, Kristine—because it's so nice to dress up now and then, isn't
385 it?

MRS. LINDE Yes it is.

NORA But I found other ways to make some money too. Last winter I was
lucky enough to get a big copying job to do. So I shut myself in and wrote
every evening till late at night. Ah, I'd get so tired, so tired—but it was also
390 great fun, sitting and working and earning money like that. Almost like
being a man.

MRS. LINDE How much have you managed to pay off like that?

NORA Well, I can't really say exactly. This kind of account is very hard to
keep track of. I only know that I've paid back everything I can scrape
395 together. A lot of times I didn't know which way to turn. [Smiling.] I'd sit
here and imagine that a rich old man had fallen in love with me.

MRS. LINDE What? Which man?

NORA   Oh, come on! And that he'd just died and when they read his will,
there it was in big letters: "My entire fortune is to be paid in cash, immedi-
400   ately, to the delightful Mrs. Nora Helmer."

MRS. LINDE   But Nora, who is he?

NORA   Good Lord, don't you get it? There never was any such person; it was
just something I'd sit here and dream about when I couldn't think of any
other way to get the money. But now it doesn't matter, the old bore can go
405   back where he came from; I don't need him or his will, because my troubles
are over. Oh, God, it's so lovely to think of, Kristine! Carefree! To be carefree, completely carefree! To run around and play with the children; to
make everything in the house warm and beautiful, just the way Torvald
likes it! Then maybe we can travel a little. Maybe I'll get down to the ocean
410   again. Oh yes, it is so wonderful to live and be happy!

[The bell rings in the hallway.]

MRS. LINDE   [Rising.]   The bell—maybe I should go.

NORA   No, stay here. It won't be for me. It's probably for Torvald.

MAID   [From the hall doorway.]   Excuse me, ma'am. There's a gentleman here
to speak with the lawyer.

415   NORA   With the Bank Manager, you mean.

MAID   Yes, with the Bank Manager. But I didn't know if—since the Doctor's
in there—

NORA   Who is the gentleman?

KROGSTAD   [From the doorway.]   It's me, Mrs. Helmer.

[Mrs. Linde starts, checks herself, and turns toward the window.]

420   NORA   [A step towards him, tense, in a low voice.]   You? What is it? What do
you want to talk to my husband about?

KROGSTAD   Bank matters—more or less. I have a minor position on the bank
staff, and I hear your husband is our new chief.

NORA   And so it's—

425   KROGSTAD   Just dry business, Mrs. Helmer. Absolutely nothing else.

NORA   Then would you please be good enough to step into his study?

[She nods indifferently and shuts the hallway door; then she goes and
tends the stove.]

MRS. LINDE   Nora—who was that man?

NORA   That was a lawyer named Krogstad.

MRS. LINDE   So it really was him.

430   NORA   Do you know that man?

MRS. LINDE   I used to know him—a long time ago. He was a law clerk for a
while up in our area.

NORA   Yes, that's right, he was.

MRS. LINDE   He certainly has changed.

435   NORA   He had a very unhappy marriage.

MRS. LINDE   And now he's a widower?

NORA   With several children. There we go, now it's burning. [She closes the
stove door and moves the rocking chair a little to the side.]

MRS. LINDE   He's got himself involved in all kinds of businesses, they say.

NORA   Oh yes? Probably; I really wouldn't know. But let's not think about
440   business—it's so boring!

[Doctor Rank comes out from Helmer's study.]

RANK [*Still in the doorway.*]   No, no, Torvald: I don't want to be in the way; I'd just as soon go talk to your wife for a while. [*Closing the door and noticing Mrs. Linde.*] I'm sorry—I'm in the way here too.

NORA   You certainly are not. [*Introducing him.*] Doctor Rank, Mrs. Linde.

445   RANK   Aha! That's an oft-mentioned name in this house. I think I passed you on the stairs when I arrived.

MRS. LINDE   Yes, I don't handle stairs very well.

RANK   Aha—are you having some kind of trouble?

MRS. LINDE   Probably just overwork.

450   RANK   Nothing more? So you've probably come to town to catch your breath in the holiday parties.

MRS. LINDE   I'm looking for a job.

RANK   Is that the prescription for overwork?

MRS. LINDE   One has to live, Doctor.

455   RANK   Yes, there's general agreement on that point.

NORA   Oh, come on now, Doctor Rank, you want to live as much as anyone.

RANK   Yes, I really do. Wretched as I am, I really want to stretch my torment to the limit. All my patients feel the same way. And it's the same with the morally diseased—right now there's a terminal moral case in there with

460   Helmer—

MRS. LINDE [*Quietly.*]   Ah—!

NORA   Who's that?

RANK   Oh, just a certain lawyer Krogstad, no one you'd know anything about. His character, my ladies, is rotten right down to the roots—but even he

465   began making speeches—as if it were self-evident—that he had to *live*.

NORA   Oh? What did he want to talk to Torvald about?

RANK   I don't know for sure. All I heard was something about the bank.

NORA   I didn't know Krog—that this lawyer Krogstad had anything to do with the bank.

470   RANK   Yes, he's got some kind of position down there. [*To Mrs. Linde.*] I don't know if you have, in your part of the country, any of these moral detectives, these investigators who go around sniffing out moral corruption and then get their victims into a safe place where they can keep them under constant surveillance—it's a lucrative business these days. The healthy ones

475   get left out in the cold—no room for them!

MRS. LINDE   And yet it's the sick ones who need to be brought inside.

RANK [*Shrugs his shoulders.*]   There you have it. That's the philosophy that's turning our whole world into a hospital.

   [*Nora, lost in thought, breaks into quiet laughter, clapping her hands.*]

RANK   Why do you laugh? Do you really know what the world is?

480   NORA   What do I care about the boring old world? I was laughing at something else—something terribly funny. Tell me, Doctor Rank, all those people who work at the bank—are they all under Torvald now?

RANK   Is *that* what's so terribly funny to you?

NORA [*Smiling and humming.*]   Never mind! Never mind! [*Walking around

485   the room.*] Yes, it is extremely amusing that we—that Torvald has so much influence over so many people. [*Takes a bag from her pocket.*] Doctor Rank, how about a little macaroon?

RANK   Aha! Macaroons! I thought they were illegal here.

NORA   Yes, but Kristine gave me these—

490 MRS. LINDE   What? I—?

NORA   Now, now, now, don't worry. How could you know that Torvald made a
law against them? You see, he's afraid they'll rot my teeth. But, fuff—just
this once—don't you agree, Doctor Rank? There you are! [*She pops a macaroon into his mouth.*] You too, Kristine. And I'll have one too, just a little
495   one—or two at the most. [*Walking around again.*] Yes, now I am really tremendously happy. There's just one last thing in the world I have a tremendous desire to do.

RANK   Oh? What's that?

NORA   I have this tremendous desire to say something so that Torvald can
500   hear it.

RANK   So why can't you say it?

NORA   No, I don't dare. It's too horrible.

MRS. LINDE   Horrible?

RANK   Well, then, maybe you'd better not. But with us—can't you? What do
505   you want to say so Torvald can hear?

NORA   I have a tremendous desire to say: To hell with everything!

RANK   Are you crazy?

MRS. LINDE   For heaven's sake, Nora.

RANK   Say it—here he is.

510 NORA [*Hiding the macaroons.*]   Shh, shh, shh!

[*Helmer enters from his study, hat in hand and overcoat on his arm.*]

NORA   Well, my dear, are you through with him?

HELMER   Yes, he just left.

NORA   Let me introduce you—this is Kristine, who's just come to town.

HELMER   Kristine? I'm sorry, but I don't know—

515 NORA   Mrs. Linde, Torvald dear, Mrs. Kristine Linde.

HELMER   Oh, I see. A childhood friend?

MRS. LINDE   Yes, we knew each other back then.

NORA   And just think, she made the long trip here just to talk to you.

MRS. LINDE   Well, actually, I didn't—

520 NORA   Kristine, you see, is extremely good at office work, and so she's tremendously eager to place herself under the direction of a capable man so
that she can learn even more than she—

HELMER   Very sensible, Mrs. Linde.

NORA   So that when she heard you'd been made bank manager—there was a
525   bulletin about it in all the papers—she started out as fast as she could,
and—it's true, isn't it, Torvald? You could do something for Kristine for my
sake, yes?

HELMER   It's not completely out of the question. You are, I suppose, a widow?

MRS. LINDE   Yes.

530 HELMER   And you have experience in office work?

MRS. LINDE   Yes, quite a bit.

HELMER   Well then, it's entirely possible that I can offer you a position—

NORA [*Clapping her hands.*]   You see, you see!

HELMER   You appeared at a lucky moment, Mrs. Linde.

535 MRS. LINDE   How can I thank you—

HELMER   Not at all necessary. [*Puts on overcoat.*] But today I'll have to ask
you to excuse me—

RANK   Wait—I'll go with you.

[*Rank gets his fur coat from the hall and warms it at the stove.*]

NORA Don't be out long, Torvald my dear.

540 HELMER Just an hour, no more.

NORA Are you leaving too, Kristine?

MRS. LINDE [*Putting on her outdoor things.*] Yes, now I've got to find myself a room.

HELMER Then maybe we can all walk together for a while.

545 NORA [*Helping her.*] It's so boring that we don't have space here, but it's just impossible for us to—

MRS. LINDE Don't even think of it! Goodbye, Nora, and thank you for everything.

NORA Goodbye for now. But I'll see you again this evening. You too, Doctor
550 Rank. What? If you feel well? Of course you will! Wrap yourself up nice and warm.

[*They all go out together into the hall. Children's voices are heard on the stairs.*]

NORA There they are! There they are!

[*She runs to open the front door. Anne-Marie, their nanny, enters with the children.*]

NORA Come in, come in! [*Bends down and kisses them.*]
Oh, you sweet little darlings! Look at them, Kristine, aren't they lovely!

555 RANK No loitering out here in the draft!

HELMER Let's go, Mrs. Linde; this place is unbearable now for anyone but mothers.

[*Doctor Rank, Helmer, Mrs. Linde go down the stairs. The nursemaid goes into the living room with the children. Nora goes in also, after shutting the door to the hallway.*]

NORA You look so clean and healthy! Your cheeks are all red! Like apples and roses. [*The children chatter away to her throughout the following.*] Was it
560 fun? That's great. Really? You pulled both Emmy and Bob on the sled? My goodness, both of them together! You're a clever boy, Ivar. Here, let me hold her for a little while, Anne-Marie. My sweet little doll-baby! [*Takes the smallest child from Anne-Marie and dances with her.*] Yes, yes, Mommy will dance with Bob too. What? A snowball fight? Oh, I wish I was there with
565 you! No, don't bother, I'll undress them myself, Anne-Marie. Yes, let me do it, it's so much fun. Go in for a while—you look frozen. There's warm coffee for you on the stove. [*Anne-Marie goes into the room on the left. Nora takes off the children's outdoor clothes and throws them around while the children all talk at the same time.*] Is that so? A great big dog came running after you? But it didn't bite? No, dogs never bite lovely little doll-babies.
570 Stop peeking into the packages, Ivar! What is it? Oh, wouldn't you like to know? No, it's something awful! Well? Do you want to play? What'll we play? Hide-and-seek. Yes, let's play hide-and-seek. Bob, you hide first. Me? All right, I'll hide first.

[*She and the children play, laughing and shouting, in the living room and the adjoining room to the right. At last Nora hides under the table; the children come storming in, searching, not finding her; then, hearing her muffled laughter, rush to the table, lift the tablecloth, and discover her. A storm of delight. Meanwhile, there has been a knocking at the front door; no one has noticed it. Now the door half opens, and Krogstad appears. He waits a little while the game continues.*]

KROGSTAD   I beg your pardon, Mrs. Helmer.

575   NORA [*Turns, with a stifled cry, half jumps up.*]   Ah! What do you want?

KROGSTAD   Excuse me. The front door was open—somebody must have forgotten to shut it.

NORA [*Rising.*]   My husband's not here, Mr. Krogstad.

KROGSTAD   I know that.

580   NORA   Well—what do you want?

KROGSTAD   A word with you.

NORA   With—? [*To the children, quietly.*] Go in with Anne-Marie. No, the strange man won't hurt Mama. When he's gone we can play some more. [*She leads the children in to the room on the left and closes the door after them. Now, tense and nervous.*] You want to speak with me?

585   KROGSTAD   Yes, I do.

NORA   Today—? But it's not the first of the month yet—

KROGSTAD   No, it's Christmas Eve. It's up to you how much Christmas cheer you'll have.

NORA   What do you want? Today I can't possibly—

590   KROGSTAD   We won't talk about that right now. It's something else. I suppose you have a moment?

NORA   Well, yes; all right—though—

KROGSTAD   Good. I was sitting over at Olsen's Restaurant and I saw your husband going down the street—

595   NORA   Oh yes.

KROGSTAD   With a lady.

NORA   So?

KROGSTAD   I wonder if you'll allow me to ask if that lady was Mrs. Linde?

NORA   Yes.

600   KROGSTAD   Just arrived in town?

NORA   Yes, today.

KROGSTAD   She's a good friend of yours?

NORA   Yes, she is. But I can't see—

KROGSTAD   I also knew her at one time.

605   NORA   I'm aware of that.

KROGSTAD   Really? That's what I thought. Well, then, let me get right to the point: Is Mrs. Linde getting a job at the bank?

NORA   Why do you think you can cross-examine me, Mr. Krogstad? You, who's just one of my husband's employees? But since you ask, you might as

610   well know: yes, Mrs. Linde got a job. And I arranged it all for her, Mr. Krogstad. Now you know.

KROGSTAD   As I thought.

NORA [*Pacing the floor.*]   Oh, I should hope that one always has a little bit of influence. Just because one is a woman, it doesn't follow that—when one

615   is in an inferior position, Mr. Krogstad, one ought to be very careful with somebody who—

KROGSTAD   Who has influence?

NORA   Exactly.

KROGSTAD [*Changing tone.*]   Mrs. Helmer, would you be good enough to use

620   your influence on my behalf?

NORA   What? What do you mean?

KROGSTAD   Would you be kind enough to make sure that I keep my inferior position at the bank?

NORA   What do you mean? Who's trying to take it away from you?

625 KROGSTAD   Oh, you don't have to play the innocent with me. I understand perfectly well that your friend doesn't want to run the risk of seeing me again; and now I also understand who to thank for being let go.

NORA   But I promise you—

KROGSTAD   Yes, yes, yes. But here's the point: there's still time, and I'd advise
630   you to use your influence to prevent it.

NORA   But, Mr. Krogstad, I have no influence at all.

KROGSTAD   No? I thought a minute ago you said—

NORA   I didn't mean it that way. What makes you think I've got any sort of influence over my husband in things like that?

635 KROGSTAD   Oh, I've known your husband since we were students together— and I don't believe our Bank Manager has any more willpower than any other married man.

NORA   You talk like that about my husband and I'll show you the door.

KROGSTAD   The lady has courage.

640 NORA   I'm not afraid of you any more. Soon after New Year's I'll be done with the whole business.

KROGSTAD   Now listen to me, Mrs. Helmer. If it becomes necessary, I'll fight to the death for my little job at the bank.

NORA   Yes, it looks that way.

645 KROGSTAD   And not just for the money—that's the least of my concerns. It's something else—well, all right—you know, of course, like everyone else, that some years ago I was guilty of an indiscretion.

NORA   I think I heard something about it.

KROGSTAD   The case never came to trial, but even so every door was closed to
650   me. So I had to go into the sort of business you're familiar with. I had to find something—and I think I can say that I've been far from the worst in that line of work. But now I want to put all of it behind me. My sons are growing up. For their sake I want to win back as much respect as I can in the community. That position in the bank was the first rung in the ladder
655   for me. Now your husband wants to kick me right back off the ladder and into the mud again.

NORA   But for God's sake, Mr. Krogstad, it's just not in my power to help you.

KROGSTAD   That's because you don't have the will to do it—but I can force you to.

660 NORA   You wouldn't tell my husband that I owe you money?

KROGSTAD   Hmm—what if I did?

NORA   That would be shameful. [Choking with tears.] That secret—my pride and my joy—if he learned about it in such a horrible way—learned it from you—. You'd put me through such an incredibly unpleasant scene—

665 KROGSTAD   Only unpleasant?

NORA [Vehemently.]   Just try it! It'll only be worse for you. Because then my husband will really get to see what kind of man you are, and you'll have no chance of keeping your job.

KROGSTAD   I asked you if all you were afraid of was this unpleasant scene
670   here at home?

NORA   If my husband finds out about it, of course he'll pay you off immediately, and we'd have nothing more to do with you.

KROGSTAD [*A step nearer.*] Listen, Mrs. Helmer: either you've got a terrible memory or a very shaky grasp of business. Let me get a few facts straight
675 for you.

NORA How do you mean?

KROGSTAD When your husband was sick, you came to me for four thousand, eight hundred kroner.

NORA I didn't know where else to go.

680 KROGSTAD I promised to get it for you—

NORA And you did.

KROGSTAD I promised to get it for you on certain conditions. At the time you were so wrapped up in your husband's illness that I suppose you didn't think through all the details. Maybe I'd better remind you of them. Now:
685 I promised to get you the money based on a note that I drafted.

NORA Yes, which I signed.

KROGSTAD Very good. But below your signature I added some lines to the effect that your father would guarantee the loan. Your father was to sign there.

NORA Was to—? He signed it.

690 KROGSTAD I left out the date. Your father was supposed to date his own signature. Do you remember that?

NORA Yes, I think so—

KROGSTAD Then I handed the note over to you so you could mail it to your father. Isn't that the case?

695 NORA Yes.

KROGSTAD And of course you did that right away—because only about five, six days later, you brought me the note, with your father's signature. And then you got your money.

NORA Well? Haven't I been meeting my payments?

700 KROGSTAD Yes, more or less. But to return to the question: that was a difficult time for you, wasn't it, Mrs. Helmer?

NORA Yes, it was.

KROGSTAD Your father was very ill, I believe.

NORA He was very near the end.

705 KROGSTAD He died soon after that?

NORA Yes.

KROGSTAD Tell me, Mrs. Helmer, do you by any chance recall the date of your father's death? Which day of the month, I mean.

NORA Papa died on the twenty-ninth of September.

710 KROGSTAD Quite correct; I've already confirmed that. That brings us to an oddity that I simply cannot account for.

NORA What kind of oddity? I don't understand—

KROGSTAD Here's the oddity, Mrs. Helmer: your father countersigned the note three days after his death.

715 NORA How? I don't understand—

KROGSTAD Your father died on the twenty-ninth of September. But look at this. Here your father has dated his signature "October 2nd." Isn't that odd, Mrs. Helmer? [*Nora is silent.*] Can you explain it to me? [*Nora remains silent.*] Here's another remarkable thing: the date "October 2nd" and the
720 year are not written in your father's hand, but in a hand that I ought to know. Now, that could be explained; your father forgot to date his signature,

and someone else did it for him, somewhat carelessly, before anyone knew of his death. Nothing wrong with that. Everything hinges on the signature. And that *is* genuine, isn't it, Mrs. Helmer? It really was your father himself

725 who signed his name there?

NORA [*After a short silence, throws back her head and looks firmly at him.*] No, it wasn't. *I* signed Papa's name.

KROGSTAD Listen, Mrs. Helmer—do you understand that this is a dangerous confession?

730 NORA Why? You'll get your money soon enough.

KROGSTAD Can I ask you—why didn't you send the note to your father?

NORA Impossible. Papa was so sick. If I had asked him for his signature, I'd have had to tell him what the money was for. I just couldn't tell him, in his condition, that my husband was dying. It was just impossible.

735 KROGSTAD Then it would have been better for you to give up the trip.

NORA No, impossible again. That trip was to save my husband's life. I couldn't give that up.

KROGSTAD But didn't it occur to you that you were committing a fraud against me?

740 NORA I couldn't worry about that. I certainly wasn't concerned about you. I could hardly stand you, making up all those cold conditions when you knew perfectly well how much danger my husband was in.

KROGSTAD Mrs. Helmer, you obviously don't have any idea what you've implicated yourself in. But let me tell you this: what I once did was nothing

745 more, and nothing worse, and it destroyed me.

NORA You? Are you trying to get me to believe that you risked everything to save your wife?

KROGSTAD Laws don't much care about motives.

NORA Then they must be very bad laws.

750 KROGSTAD Bad or not, if I produce this paper in court, you'll be judged by those laws.

NORA I don't believe it. Doesn't a daughter have the right to spare her dying father from worry and anxiety? Shouldn't a wife have the right to save her husband's life? I don't know the law very well, but I'm sure it must say

755 somewhere in there that these things are legal. You must be a very bad lawyer, Mr. Krogstad.

KROGSTAD Maybe so. But business—this kind of business we're in—don't you think I know something about that? Good. Do what you want. But hear this: if I get thrown down a second time, you're coming with me. [*He bows and goes out through the hall door.*]

760 NORA [*Stands for a moment, reflecting, then tosses her head.*] Nonsense! He's trying to frighten me! I'm not all that naïve. [*Starts gathering up the children's clothes, but soon stops.*] But—? No, impossible. I did it out of love.

CHILDREN [*In the doorway, left.*] Mama, the strange man's going down the street.

765 NORA Yes, I know. But don't mention the strange man to anyone. You hear? Not even Papa.

CHILDREN No, Mama. Now can we play again?

NORA No, no. Not now.

CHILDREN But Mama, you promised.

770 NORA Yes, but right now I can't. Go inside; I've got too much to do. Go in, go in, my dear, sweet little ones. [*She herds them carefully into the room and*

closes the door after them. She sits on the sofa, takes up her embroidery, makes some stitches, but soon stops.] Helene! Let me have the tree in here. [*Goes to the table at left and opens a drawer, pauses again.*] No, that's completely impossible!

775 MAID [*With the spruce tree.*]   Where should I put it, Ma'am?

NORA   There—in the middle of the floor.

MAID   Anything else?

NORA   No, thank you. I have what I need.

[*The Maid, having set the tree down, goes out.*]

NORA [*Busy decorating the tree.*]   Candles here, flowers here—that horrible
780 man! Talk, talk, talk. Nothing's going to happen. The Christmas tree will be just lovely. I'll do anything you want me to, Torvald—I'll sing for you, dance for you—

[*Helmer, with a packet of papers under his arm, comes in through the hall.*]

NORA   Ah! Back already?

HELMER   Yes. Has someone been here?

785 NORA   Here? No.

HELMER   That's strange. I just saw Krogstad going out the door.

NORA   Really? Oh, of course. Krogstad was here for a moment.

HELMER   Nora, I can see it in your eyes, he's been here asking you to put in a good word for him.

790 NORA   Yes.

HELMER   And you were going to pretend it was your own idea. You'd pretend he'd never been here. Did he ask you to do that as well?

NORA   Yes, Torvald, but—

HELMER   Nora, Nora, you could go along with that? Do business with that sort
795 of person, and make promises to him? And then, on top of it all, tell me a lie!

NORA   A lie?

HELMER   Didn't you tell me no one had been here? [*Wagging his finger.*] My little songbird mustn't ever do a thing like that again. A songbird needs a clean beak to chirp with. No false notes. [*Takes her by the waist.*] Isn't that
800 the way it should be? Yes, of course it is. So let's not talk about it any more. [*Sits by the stove.*] Ah, it's so snug and cozy here.

NORA [*Working on the tree; after a short pause.*]   Torvald!

HELMER   Yes?

NORA   I'm terribly excited about the Stenborg's party the day after tomorrow.

805 HELMER   And I'm terribly curious to see what you'll surprise me with.

NORA   Oh, that stupid nonsense!

HELMER   What?

NORA   I can't find anything I like; everything seems so pointless, so idiotic.

HELMER   Is that what little Nora thinks?

810 NORA [*Behind his chair, her arms on its back.*]   Are you very busy, Torvald?

HELMER   Well—

NORA   What are those papers?

HELMER   Bank business.

NORA   Already?

815 HELMER   I've convinced the retiring manager to give me full authority to make changes in personnel and procedure. I'll have to use Christmas week for that. I want everything in order for the New Year.

NORA   So that's why this poor Krogstad—

HELMER Hm.

NORA [*Still leaning on the back of his chair, stroking the hair on his neck.*]
820   If you weren't so busy, I would ask you for a terribly big favor.

HELMER Let's hear it. What can it be?

NORA No one has your good taste. I really want to look my best at the cos-
       tume party. Torvald, couldn't you take over from me and advise me what to
       wear and how to design my costume?

825 HELMER So our little rebel's ready for a cease-fire?

NORA Yes, Torvald. I can't get anywhere without your help.

HELMER All right. I'll think about it. We'll come up with something.

NORA How sweet of you! [*Goes over to the Christmas tree; pause.*] These red
       flowers are so pretty—But tell me, was what that Krogstad did really such
830   a crime?

HELMER He forged people's names. Do you know what that means?

NORA Maybe he did it out of need.

HELMER Yes, or thoughtlessness, like so many others. And I wouldn't con-
       demn a man categorically because of one isolated incident.

835 NORA No, you wouldn't, would you, Torvald?

HELMER Men can often redeem themselves by openly confessing their guilt
       and accepting their punishment.

NORA Punishment?

HELMER But Krogstad didn't do that. He got himself off the hook with tricks
840   and loopholes. That's what's corrupted him.

NORA Do you think that would—?

HELMER Imagine what life is like for a man like that: he has to lie and dis-
       semble and cheat everyone he meets—has to wear a mask in front of his
       nearest and dearest—yes, even his wife and children. And the children—
845   that's the most terrible part of it.

NORA Why?

HELMER Because an atmosphere so filled with lies brings pestilence and
       disease into every corner of a home. Every breath the children take carries
       the infection.

850 NORA [*Closer behind him.*] Are you sure about that?

HELMER Ah, my dear, I'm a lawyer—I've seen it often enough. Almost every-
       one who turns bad as a youth has had a compulsive liar for a mother.

NORA Why just—a mother?

HELMER Usually you can trace it to the mother, but fathers have the same
855   effect; it's something every lawyer knows. And yet this Krogstad has been
       living at home, poisoning his children with lies and deceit; that's why I
       call him morally corrupt. And that's why my sweet little Nora must promise
       me not to plead his case. Your hand on that. Now, now, what's this?
       Give me your hand. There. That's settled. And let me tell you, it would be
860   impossible for me to work with him; I literally feel sick when I'm around
       someone like that.

NORA [*Withdraws her hand and goes over to the other side of the Christmas
       tree.*] It's so hot in here! And I've got so much to pull together!

HELMER [*Rising and gathering his papers.*] Yes, I've got to try to get through
       some of these before dinner. I'll also give some thought to your costume.
865   And I might also be thinking about something to hang on the tree in gilt
       paper—. [*Lays his hand on her head.*] Oh, my sweet little songbird. [*He goes
       into his room and closes the door.*]

NORA [*Softly, after a silence.*]   No, no! It's not true. It's impossible. It just can't be possible.

ANNE-MARIE [*In doorway, left.*]   The children are asking if they can come in
870 to Mama.

NORA   No, no, no, don't let them in here with me! You stay with them, Anne-Marie.

ANNE-MARIE   Very well, Ma'am.

NORA [*Pale with terror.*]   Harm my children—! Poison my home? [*Short
875 pause; she tosses her head.*] It's not true. It could never be true!

Act 2

The same room in the corner by the piano stands the Christmas tree, stripped, bedraggled, with its candle-stumps all burned down. Nora's outdoor clothing lies on the sofa.

[*Nora, alone, walks restlessly around the room. Finally she stands by the sofa and picks up her coat.*]

NORA [*Dropping the coat again.*]   Somebody's coming! [*Goes to the door, listens.*] No, nobody there. Naturally—nobody's coming on Christmas Day—or tomorrow either. But maybe— [*She opens the door and looks out.*] No, nothing in the mailbox—perfectly empty: [*Comes forward.*] Oh, nonsense!
5 Of course he wasn't serious about it. Nothing like that could happen. After all, I have three small children.

[*Anne-Marie, carrying a large carton, comes in from the room on the left.*]

ANNE-MARIE   Well, I finally found the box of masquerade costumes.

NORA   Thanks. Put it on the table.

ANNE-MARIE [*Does so.*]   But it's a terrible mess.

10 NORA   Ah, I wish I could rip them into a million pieces.

ANNE-MARIE   Lord bless us—they can be fixed up again. Just have a little patience.

NORA   Yes, I'll go and get Mrs. Linde to help.

ANNE-MARIE   You're not going out again now? In this horrible weather? Mrs.
15 Nora will catch cold—get sick.

NORA   Worse things could happen. How are the children?

ANNE-MARIE   The poor little things are playing with their Christmas presents, but—

NORA   Are they always asking for me?

20 ANNE-MARIE   They're so used to having their Mama with them.

NORA   Yes, Anne-Marie, but I can't be with them as much as before.

ANNE-MARIE   Well, little children get used to anything.

NORA   Do you think so? Do you think they'd forget their mama if she were really gone?

25 ANNE-MARIE   Lord help us—gone?

NORA   Listen—tell me, Anne-Marie—I've wondered about this a lot—how could you ever, in your heart of hearts, stand to give your child away to strangers?

ANNE-MARIE   But I just had to when I became little Nora's wet nurse.

30 NORA   Yes, but how could you actually do it?

ANNE-MARIE   When I could get such a good place? A poor girl in trouble has to jump at a chance like that. Because that slick good-for-nothing wouldn't do anything for me.

NORA But your daughter's completely forgotten you.

35 ANNE-MARIE Oh no, not really. She wrote to me when she was confirmed, and when she got married.

NORA [*Clasps her around the neck.*] Dear old Anne-Marie—you were a good mother for me when I was little.

ANNE-MARIE Poor little Nora, with me as her only mother.

40 NORA And if my little ones didn't have a mother, I know that you—stupid, stupid, stupid! [*Opening the carton.*] Go to them. Right now I have to—tomorrow you'll see how beautiful I look.

ANNE-MARIE Yes, Mrs. Nora will be the most beautiful woman at the party.

[*Anne-Marie goes into the room on the left.*]

NORA [*Begins to unpack the box, but soon throws the whole thing aside.*] Ah,
45 if I had the nerve to go out. If only nobody would come. If only nothing happened here at home in the meantime. Stupid talk; nobody's coming. Just don't think. I have to brush out this muff. Beautiful gloves, beautiful gloves. Get it out, get it out! One, two, three, four, five, six, [*Screams.*] Oh, here they come. [*Goes toward the door, but stops, irresolute. Mrs. Linde*
50 *comes in from the hall where she has removed her outdoor clothes.*] So it's you, Kristine. No one else out there? I'm glad you're here.

MRS. LINDE I heard you were asking for me.

NORA Yes, I happened to be passing by. I need your help with something. Come sit with me by the sofa. Look at this. There's going to be a costume
55 party tomorrow over at Consul Stenborg's, and Torvald wants me to go as a Neapolitan[3] fisher girl and dance the tarantella[4]—I learned it in Capri.[5]

MRS. LINDE Well, well—you're giving a real performance?

NORA Yes, Torvald says I should. Look—here's my costume. Torvald had it made for me down there. But it's all torn now and I just don't know—

60 MRS. LINDE We'll get that fixed up in no time; the trimmings are just coming loose here and there, that's all. Needle and thread? There, now we have what we need.

NORA This is so nice of you.

MRS. LINDE [*Sewing.*] So you're going in disguise tomorrow. Nora? You know
65 what? I'll come by for a minute and look at you when you're all dressed up. You know I've completely forgotten to thank you for the lovely evening yesterday.

NORA [*Gets up and crosses the floor.*] Oh, I don't think it was as nice yesterday as it usually is. You should have gotten here a little earlier, Kristine.
70 Torvald really knows how to make a home charming and elegant.

MRS. LINDE So do you, just as much, I'd say. You're not your father's daughter for nothing. Tell me—is Doctor Rank always so depressed?

NORA No, yesterday he was particularly low. But he's got a very serious illness—tuberculosis of the spine, poor man. You know his father was a
75 disgusting creature who kept mistresses and things like that—that's how poor Doctor Rank got to be so sickly.[6]

---

3. An inhabitant of Naples, a city in Southern Italy.
4. An Italian folk dance named after the tarantula, a venomous spider. It was believed that victims of the bite needed to keep danc-

ing to stay alive.
5. An island off the coast of Italy, near Naples.
6. Nora expresses the popular, but false, belief that immoral conduct leads to the disease.

MRS. LINDE [*Dropping her sewing to her lap.*]   Nora, my dear, how do you know about these things?

NORA [*Walking around.*]   Fuff. When you've had three children you end up
80 meeting some women who know a little about medicine, and they tell you a few things.

MRS. LINDE [*Sewing again, short silence.*]   Does Doctor Rank come to the house every day?

NORA   Every single day. He's Torvald's best friend ever since they were chil-
85 dren, and he's my good friend too. Doctor Rank sort of belongs to the house.

MRS. LINDE   But tell me this—is he honest? I mean, doesn't he like to tell people what they want to hear?

NORA   No, not at all. What makes you think that?

90 MRS. LINDE   When you introduced us yesterday he said he'd heard my name here so often—but then I noticed that your husband didn't have any idea who I was. So how could Doctor Rank—

NORA   That's right, Kristine. Torvald is so unbelievably devoted to me—he says he wants me all to himself. When we were first married he'd get
95 jealous if I so much as mentioned any of my old friends from back home. So, of course, I stopped. But with Doctor Rank I can talk about all those things, because he enjoys hearing about them.

MRS. LINDE   Listen to me, Nora: in many ways you're still a child. I'm quite a bit older than you and I have a little more experience. Let me tell you
100 something: you should put an end to all this with Doctor Rank.

NORA   What should I put an end to?

MRS. LINDE   All of it, I think. Yesterday you said something about a rich admirer who was going to give you money—

NORA   Yes, but unfortunately he doesn't exist. So what?

105 MRS. LINDE   Is Doctor Rank rich?

NORA   Yes.

MRS. LINDE   No one to care for?

NORA   No, no one—but—?

MRS. LINDE   And he comes by every day?

110 NORA   Yes, that's what I told you.

MRS. LINDE   How can such a cultivated man be so obvious?

NORA   I really don't understand you.

MRS. LINDE   Don't play games, Nora. Don't you think I know who lent you the money?

115 NORA   Are you out of your mind? How can you even think that? A good friend of ours, who comes over here every single day! That would have been horrible!

MRS. LINDE   So it really wasn't him?

NORA   No, I promise you. I would never have thought of that—anyway, he
120 didn't have any money to lend back then—he inherited it all later.

MRS. LINDE   Well, that was just as well for you, I think.

NORA   No, I would never have thought of asking Doctor Rank. Even though I'm sure that if I did—

MRS. LINDE   But of course you wouldn't.

125 NORA   No, of course not. I can't imagine how it would be necessary. On the other hand, I'm sure that if I even mentioned it to him—

MRS. LINDE   Behind your husband's back?

NORA   I've got to get out of this other thing—that's also behind his back. I've really got to get out of that.

130 MRS. LINDE   Yes, that's what I said yesterday. But—

NORA [Walking up and down.]   A man can deal with these things so much better than a woman—

MRS. LINDE   Your own husband can, yes.

NORA   Nonsense. [Stopping.] When you pay back everything you owe you get

135   your note back.

MRS. LINDE   That's right.

NORA   And you can tear it up in a hundred thousand pieces and burn it—that disgusting piece of paper!

MRS. LINDE [Looking straight at her, putting the sewing down, rising slowly.]   Nora—you're hiding something from me.

140 NORA   Can you see that?

MRS. LINDE   Something's happened since yesterday morning. Nora, what is it?

NORA [Going to her.]   Kristine! [Listens.] Ssh! Torvald's home. Look—go in there with the children for a while. Torvald can't stand to see people sewing. Let Anne-Marie help you.

145 MRS. LINDE [Gathering some of her things.]   Yes, all right, but I'm not leaving before we talk all this through. [She goes into the room at left; at the same time, Helmer comes in from the hall.]

NORA [Goes to meet him.]   Oh, I've been waiting for you, Torvald my dear.

HELMER   Was that the dressmaker?

NORA   No, it's Kristine; she's helping me with my costume. You know, I think

150   I'm going to outdo myself this time.

HELMER   Yes, that was a pretty good idea I had, wasn't it?

NORA   Brilliant. But wasn't it also nice of me to agree to it?

HELMER [Taking her under the chin.]   Nice of you? Agreeing with your husband? All right, you crazy thing, I know you didn't mean it that way. But I

155   don't want to disturb you; I suppose you'll want to try it on.

NORA   Will you be working?

HELMER   Yes. [Shows her a bundle of papers.] See. I've been down to the bank— [He is about to go into his study.]

NORA   Torvald.

160 HELMER   Yes.

NORA   If your little squirrel were to beg you ever so nicely for something—?

HELMER   Well?

NORA   Would you do it?

HELMER   First, of course, I'd need to know what it is.

165 NORA   The squirrel would romp around and do tricks if you'd be sweet and say yes.

HELMER   Come on, what is it?

NORA   The lark would sing high and low in every room—

HELMER   So what, she does that anyway.

170 NORA   I'd pretend I was a fairy child and dance for you in the moonlight, Torvald.

HELMER   Nora, I hope this isn't that same business from this morning.

NORA [Coming closer.]   Yes, Torvald, please, I beg you!

HELMER   You really have the nerve to drag that up again.

175 NORA   Yes, yes, you've got to do what I say; you've got to let Krogstad keep his job in the bank.

HELMER   But Nora, I'm giving his job to Mrs. Linde.

NORA   That's very sweet of you; but can't you get rid of another clerk, someone besides Krogstad?

180 HELMER   I can't believe how stubborn you're being! Just because you went ahead and made a foolish promise to speak up for him, now I'm supposed to—

NORA   That's not why, Torvald. It's for your own sake. That man writes articles for some horrible newspapers; you've said so yourself. He can do you an awful lot of harm. I'm scared to death of him—

185 HELMER   Aha—I understand. You're frightened of the old memories.

NORA   What do you mean by that?

HELMER   You're thinking about your father.

NORA   That's right. Remember how those horrible people wrote about Papa in the papers and slandered him so terribly. I believe they'd have gotten

190 him fired if the government hadn't sent you up there to investigate and if you hadn't been so kind and fair to him.

HELMER   My little Nora, there is a considerable difference between your father and me. Your father's public life was not exactly beyond reproach—but mine is. And that's how I plan to keep it for as long as I hold my position.

195 NORA   Oh, you can never tell what spiteful people might do. It could be so nice and quiet and happy in our home—so peaceful and carefree—you and me and the children, Torvald—

HELMER   And precisely by continuing to plead for him like this you're making it impossible for me to keep him on. It's already known around the

200 bank that I'm letting Krogstad go. What if the rumor got around that the new bank manager was letting himself be overruled by his wife—

NORA   Yes, so what?

HELMER   Oh, of course—as long as our little rebel here gets her way—I should make myself look silly in front of my whole staff—make people think I can be

205 influenced by all kinds of outside pressures—you can bet that would come back to haunt me soon enough. Besides—there's one thing that makes it impossible to have Krogstad in the bank as long as I'm the manager.

NORA   What's that?

HELMER   I might be able to overlook his moral failings if I had to—

210 NORA   Yes, Torvald, isn't that right?

HELMER   And I hear he's quite good at his job too. But he was a boyhood friend of mine—one of those stupid friendships you get into without thinking, and end up regretting later in life. I might just as well tell you—we're on a first-name basis. And that tactless idiot makes no secret of it in front

215 of people. The opposite, in fact—he thinks it entitles him to take a familiar tone with me, so he's always coming out with "Hey, Torvald—Torvald, can I talk to you, Torvald—" and I can tell you I find it excruciating. He'll make my life at the bank completely intolerable.

NORA   Torvald, you can't be serious.

220 HELMER   Oh? Why not?

NORA   No, because these are such petty things.

HELMER   What are you saying? Petty? Do you think I'm petty?

NORA   Not at all, Torvald, and that's just the reason—

HELMER   All right; you call me petty, I might as well be just that. Petty!
225   Very well! Now we'll put a stop to all of this. [*Goes to the door and calls.*]
Helene!

NORA   What are you doing?

HELMER   [*Searching through his papers.*]   A decision. [*The Maid enters.*] See
this letter? Find a messenger right away and have him deliver it. Quickly.
230   The address is on the envelope. There—here's some money.

MAID   Yes sir. [*She leaves with the letter.*]

HELMER   [*Tidying up his papers.*]   So that's that, my little Miss Stubborn.

NORA   [*Breathless.*]   Torvald, what was that letter?

HELMER   Krogstad's notice.

235   NORA   Get it back, Torvald! There's still time. Oh, Torvald, get it back! Do it
for my sake—for your own sake—for the children's sake! Listen, Torvald,
do it! You don't realize what can happen to all of us.

HELMER   Too late.

NORA   Yes, too late.

240   HELMER   Nora, I forgive you for being nervous about this, even though
you're really insulting me. Yes, you are. Isn't it insulting to think that *I*
would be afraid of what some hack journalist might do for revenge? But I
forgive you, all the same, because it shows so beautifully how much you
love me. That's how it should be, my own darling Nora. Come what may!
245   When things get tough, I've got the courage—and the strength, you can
believe it. I'm the kind of man who can take it all on himself.

NORA   [*Terrified.*]   What do you mean by that?

HELMER   The whole thing, like I said.

NORA   [*Resolutely.*]   You'll never have to do that, never.

250   HELMER   Good—so we'll share it, Nora, as man and wife. That's the way it
should be. [*Fondling her.*] Happy now? Well, well, well—enough of those
frightened dove's eyes. It's nothing but empty fantasy. Now you should run
through your tarantella and try the tambourine. I won't hear a thing in the
office, so you can make all the noise you want. [*Turning in the doorway.*]
255   And when Rank comes, tell him where he can find me. [*He nods to her, goes
to his study with his papers, and closes the door behind him.*]

NORA   [*Distracted with fear, standing as though glued to the spot, whispering.*]
He's really going to do it. He will do it. He'll do it in spite of everything—No,
never, never in this world! Anything but that—escape! A way out—[*The bell
rings in the hall.*] Doctor Rank! Anything but that! Whatever else happens!

[*She brushes her hands over her face, pulls herself together and goes to
open the door in the hall. Doctor Rank is standing outside hanging up
his fur coat. During the following, it begins to grow dark.*]

NORA   Doctor Rank, I recognized your ring. But you can't see Torvald quite
260   yet; I think he's busy.

RANK   And you?

NORA   [*While he comes into the room and she closes the door after him.*]   Oh,
as you know perfectly well, I always have an hour to spare for you.

RANK   Thanks. I shall make use of it as long as I can.

265   NORA   What do you mean? As long as you can?

RANK   Yes, does that worry you?

NORA   Well, it's such a strange way to talk. Is anything going to happen?

RANK   Something that I've been expecting for a long time. But I didn't think
it would come so soon.

270 NORA [*Gripping his arm.*]   What have you found out? Doctor Rank, you have
　　to tell me!

RANK [*Sitting by the stove.*]   It's all over. There's no point in lying to myself.

NORA [*Breathing easier.*]   Is it you—?

RANK   Who else? I'm the worst of all my patients, Mrs. Helmer. Over the last
275　few days I've done a general audit of my internal account. Bankrupt. Within
　　a month I'll probably be rotting in the churchyard.

NORA   Oh, really. What a horrible thing to say.

RANK   It *is* a horrible thing. But the worst of it all is the horror beforehand.
　　There's one more examination to go; when I've done that I'll know when
280　the disintegration will begin. There is something I want to ask you. Helmer
　　is so sensitive; he can't stand to be around anything ugly. I won't let him
　　come to my sickroom.

NORA   Oh, but Doctor Rank—

RANK   I won't allow him in there. Under any circumstances. I'll lock the door
285　to him. As soon as I'm absolutely certain of the worst, I'll send you my card
　　with a black cross on it; then you'll know that it's begun.

NORA   No, you are completely unreasonable today. And I especially wanted
　　you to be in a really good mood.

RANK   When I hold death in my hands? And to suffer like this for someone
290　else's guilt? Is there any justice in that? In every family—every single one—
　　somehow this inexorable retribution is taking its course.

NORA [*Stopping her ears.*]   La la la la la! Cheer up! Cheer up!

RANK   Yes, finally even I can only laugh at the whole thing. My poor, inno-
　　cent back has to pay for my father's career as a lascivious lieutenant.

295 NORA [*By the table to the left.*]   Was he that addicted to asparagus and *pâté
　　de foie gras?*[7]

RANK   Yes, and truffles.

NORA   Truffles, yes. And also oysters, I believe.

RANK   Yes, oysters, oysters, of course.

300 NORA   And port and champagne too. It's so sad that all these delicious things
　　have to go and attack our bones.

RANK   Especially when they attack the unfortunate bones that never got the
　　slightest pleasure from them.

NORA   Ah, yes—that's the greatest sadness of all.

305 RANK [*Looks searchingly at her.*]   Hmm—

NORA [*Shortly after.*]   Why did you smile?

RANK   No, no—you laughed.

NORA   No, you smiled, Doctor Rank!

RANK [*Getting up.*]   You're an even bigger flirt than I thought!

310 NORA   I'm full of crazy ideas today.

RANK   So it seems.

NORA [*With both hands on his shoulders.*]   Dear, dear Doctor Rank: for Tor-
　　vald and me, you simply will not die.

RANK   Oh, you'll soon get over that loss. Those who go away are soon
315　forgotten.

NORA [*Looking anxiously at him.*]   Do you think so?

RANK   You make new relationships, and then—

NORA   Who makes new relationships?

7. French. A paté made from goose liver.

RANK   Both you and Helmer will, after I'm gone. You're well on your way
320   already, I'd say. What was that Mrs. Linde doing here last night?

NORA   Come on now—you're not telling me you're jealous of poor Kristine?

RANK   Yes I am. She'll be my successor here in this house. When my time is
up, I'll bet that woman will—

NORA   Ssh—don't talk so loud—she's in there.

325 RANK   Again today! There, you see?

NORA   She's just fixing my costume. Good Lord, you're unreasonable today.
[*Sits on the sofa.*] Now be nice, Doctor Rank. Tomorrow you'll see how
beautifully I'll dance—and you can imagine I'm doing it just for you—yes,
for Torvald too, of course. [*Takes various things out of a carton.*] Doctor
330   Rank, sit here. I want to show you something.

RANK   [*Sitting.*]   What is it?

NORA   Look here. Look!

RANK   Silk stockings.

NORA   Flesh-colored. Lovely, aren't they? It's so dark in here now, but in the
335   morning—no, no, no, only the feet. Oh, well, you might as well go ahead
and look higher up.

RANK   Hmm.

NORA   What's this critical stare? Don't you think they'll fit?

RANK   I couldn't possibly have an accurate opinion on that.

340 NORA.   [*Glancing at him for a moment.*]   Shame on you. [*Hits him lightly on
the ear with the stockings.*] That's what you get. [*Puts them away again.*]

RANK   And what other splendors do I get to see?

NORA   Not a thing—you're being bad. [*She hums a little and rummages through
her things.*]

RANK   [*After a short pause.*]   When I'm sitting here like this, so close to you,
345   I can't imagine—I can't begin to comprehend—what would have become
of me if I had never found my way to this house.

NORA   [*Smiling.*]   Yes, I believe you really enjoy being here with us.

RANK   [*Quietly, looking ahead.*]   And to have to leave it all behind—

NORA   Nonsense, you're not leaving us behind.

350 RANK   [*As before.*]   And to think that nothing remains after you're gone—no
little gesture of gratitude—hardly even a passing regret—just a vacant
place that the first person who comes along can fill.

NORA   And what if I were to ask you now for—? No—

RANK   For what?

355 NORA   For a great proof of your friendship.

RANK   Yes, yes?

NORA   I mean a tremendously big favor—

RANK   Would you really let me be so happy, just this once?

NORA   You have no idea what it is.

360 RANK   All right—so tell me.

NORA   No, Doctor Rank, I can't. It's too big, too unreasonable. It's advice,
and help, and a great service too.

RANK   So much the better. I can't imagine what you mean. But keep talking.
Don't you have confidence in me?

365 NORA   Yes, in you before anyone else. You're my best and truest friend, you
know that. That's why I can tell you. All right, Doctor Rank: there's something you've got to help me prevent. You know how intensely, how inde-

scribably deeply Torvald loves me—he'd give his life for my sake without a moment's thought.

370 RANK [*Bending toward her.*]   Nora—do you think he's the only one?

NORA [*With a slight start.*]   Who—?

RANK   Who would gladly give his life for you?

NORA [*Heavily.*]   I see.

RANK   I promised myself that you'd know before the end. I'll never find a bet-
375 ter chance than this. Yes, Nora, now you know. And you also know that you can trust me like nobody else.

NORA [*Rises and speaks, evenly and calmly.*]   Let me through.

RANK [*Makes way for her, but remains seated.*]   Nora—

NORA [*In the hall doorway.*]   Helene, bring in the lamp. [*She goes over to the
380 stove.*] Ah, dear Doctor Rank, that was really awful of you.

RANK [*Rising.*]   That I've loved you just as much as anyone? Was *that* awful?

NORA   No, but that you felt you had to tell me. That was just not necessary.

RANK   What do you mean? You mean that you knew—?

[*The Maid enters with the lamp, sets it on the table, and goes out again.*]

RANK   Nora—Mrs. Helmer—I'm asking you. Did you know?

385 NORA   Oh, how do I know what I knew or didn't know? I can't say. How could you be so clumsy, Doctor Rank! When everything was so nice.

RANK   Well, in any case now you know that I'm at your service with body and soul. So please go on.

NORA [*Looking at him.*]   After this?

390 RANK   Please, please tell me what it is.

NORA   Now I can't tell you anything.

RANK   Yes, yes. Don't torment me like this. Let me do whatever is humanly possible for you.

NORA   You can't do anything for me now. In fact, I really don't need any help.
395 You'll see—it was just my imagination. It really is. Of course! [*Sits in the rocking chair, looks at him, smiling.*] Well, you are a piece of work, Doctor Rank. Don't you think you should be a little ashamed, now that the lamp is here?

RANK   No, not really. But maybe I'd better go—for good?

400 NORA   No, you certainly will not do that. Of course you'll keep coming here just like before. You know perfectly well that Torvald can't do without you.

RANK   Yes, but what about you?

NORA   Oh, I always enjoy your visits very much.

RANK   That's exactly what set me off on the wrong track. You're an enigma to
405 me. I've often felt you'd almost rather be with me than with Helmer.

NORA   Well, you see, there are the people you love the most, and the people you'd almost rather be with.

RANK   Ah yes, you're on to something there.

NORA   When I was at home, of course I loved Papa the most. But I always
410 had the most fun sneaking into the maids' rooms, because they never tried to teach me anything and they always had so much fun talking to each other.

RANK   Ah—so *they're* the ones that I've replaced.

NORA [*Jumping up and going to him.*]   Oh, dear Doctor Rank, I didn't mean
415 that at all. But you can see that with Torvald it's a lot like it was with Papa—

[*The Maid enters from the hall.*]

MAID   Ma'am. [*Whispers and hands Nora a card.*]

NORA [*Glancing at the card.*] Ah! [*Puts it in her pocket.*]

RANK   Something wrong?

NORA   No, no, not at all. It's just—it's about my new costume.

420 RANK   How could that be? Your costume's in there.

NORA   Oh, yes—that one. But this is a different one, I ordered it—Torvald can't find out—

RANK   Aha—there's our great secret.

NORA   That's right. Go on in to him. He's working in the inner room. Keep

425   him there as long as—

RANK   Don't worry—he won't get by me. [*He goes into Helmer's study.*]

NORA [*To the Maid.*] And he's waiting in the kitchen?

MAID   Yes, he came up the back stairs.

NORA   Did you tell him somebody was here?

430 MAID   I did, but that didn't help.

NORA   He won't go away?

MAID   No, he won't leave until he's talked to you.

NORA   Let him come in then; but quietly. Helene, not a word of this to anyone; it's a surprise for my husband.

435 MAID   Oh, yes, I understand. [*She goes out.*]

NORA   This terrible thing is really happening. It's coming no matter what. No, no, no. It can't happen. It must not happen.

> [*She goes and bolts Helmer's door. The Maid opens the hall door for Krogstad and closes it after him. He's dressed in traveling clothes, a fur coat, overshoes, and a fur cap.*]

NORA [*Goes toward him.*] Talk quietly—my husband's home.

KROGSTAD   I don't care.

440 NORA   What do you want from me?

KROGSTAD   Some answers.

NORA   Quick, then. What?

KROGSTAD   You know, of course, I got my notice.

NORA   I couldn't stop it, Mr. Krogstad. I fought for you as hard as I could,

445   but it was no use.

KROGSTAD   Does your husband really love you so little? He knows what I can do to you, and he still dares—

NORA   How can you imagine he knows about it?

KROGSTAD   No, I didn't think he did. It's not like my fine Torvald Helmer to

450   show that kind of strength.

NORA   Mr. Krogstad, I demand respect for my husband.

KROGSTAD   Good Lord, of course, all due respect. But since the lady has kept all this so carefully hidden, might I ask if you've also come to understand a little better than yesterday what you've actually done?

455 NORA   Better than you could ever teach me.

KROGSTAD   Yes, I'm such a terrible lawyer—

NORA   What do you want with me?

KROGSTAD   Just to see how things are with you, Mrs. Helmer. I couldn't stop thinking about you all day. A cashier, a hack journalist, a—well, a man like

460   me also has a little of what is commonly called heart, you know.

NORA   Then show it. Think of my little children.

KROGSTAD Have you or your husband given any thought to mine? But that's not the issue right now. I just wanted to tell you that you don't need to take this business too seriously. For the time being I'm not taking any
465 action.

NORA Oh, that's true, I was sure of it.

KROGSTAD The whole thing can be settled amicably. No one else needs to know about it, just the three of us.

NORA My husband can never find out.

470 KROGSTAD How can you stop that? Can you pay off the balance?

NORA No, not right now.

KROGSTAD Maybe you can find a way to raise the money in a few days?

NORA No way that I'd use.

KROGSTAD Well, it wouldn't do you any good anyway. Even if you were standing
475 there with a pile of cash in your hands you still wouldn't get your note back.

NORA Tell me what you're going to do with it.

KROGSTAD Just keep it—just hold it in my custody. No one else needs to know anything about it. So if you happen to be thinking of some desperate remedy—

480 NORA Which I am.

KROGSTAD If you're thinking of running away from home—

NORA Which I am.

KROGSTAD Or something worse—

NORA How did you know?

485 KROGSTAD Then give it up right now.

NORA How could you know I was thinking of *that*?

KROGSTAD Most of us think of *that* to begin with. I thought about it too—but I didn't have the courage.

NORA [*Lifelessly.*] I don't either.

490 KROGSTAD [*Relieved.*] That's true?

NORA I don't have it; I don't have it.

KROGSTAD It'd be pretty silly anyway. As soon as the first big storm blows over—I have here in my pocket a letter to your husband—

NORA Which tells everything?

495 KROGSTAD As nicely as possible.

NORA [*Quickly.*] He must never get that letter. Tear it up. I'll get the money somehow.

KROGSTAD Excuse me, Mrs. Helmer, but I think I just told you—

NORA I'm not talking about what I owe you. Just let me know how much you
500 demand from my husband and I'll get you the money.

KROGSTAD I'm not demanding any money from your husband.

NORA So what then?

KROGSTAD I'll tell you. I want to get back on my feet, Mrs. Helmer; I want to move up. And your husband is going to help me. For the last year and a half
505 I haven't gone near anything disreputable—all the time fighting to make ends meet—but I was happy to work my way up, step by step. Now I'm being driven out again and I'm not in a very forgiving mood, I'm ready to climb, I tell you. I'll get back in the bank, and in a higher position than before. Your husband will set me up.

510 NORA He'll never do that!

KROGSTAD   He'll do it. I know him; he won't even dare to argue. And once I'm in there with him, you'll see how it goes. In a year I'll be the manager's right-hand man. Nils Krogstad will be running that bank, not Torvald Helmer.

NORA   You'll never live to see that.

515 KROGSTAD   You think you might—

NORA   Now I have the courage.

KROGSTAD   Forget it—a pampered, spoiled woman like you?

NORA   You'll see—you'll see.

KROGSTAD   Under the ice, maybe? Down in the freezing black water? Float-520 ing up in the spring, ugly, unrecognizable, your hair falling out—

NORA   You don't frighten me.

KROGSTAD   You don't frighten me either. People don't do such things, Mrs. Helmer. Besides, what would be the point? I'd have him in my pocket just the same.

525 NORA   After—? Even when I'm no longer—?

KROGSTAD   Are you forgetting? In that case I'll be in charge of your reputation. [*Nora stares speechless at him.*] Well, I've warned you. Don't do anything stupid. When Helmer gets my letter, I'll wait for a word from him. Just keep in mind that it's your husband who has forced me back onto 530 these old roads of mine. I'll never forgive him for that. Goodbye, Mrs. Helmer. [*He goes out through the hallway.*]

NORA   [*Goes to the hall door, opens it a fraction, and listens.*]   Gone. He didn't leave the letter. No, no, no, that would be impossible! [*Opening the door farther.*] What? He's waiting outside. Not going downstairs. Changing his 535 mind? Maybe he'll—?

[*A letter drops into the mailbox; then Krogstad's footsteps are heard receding as he walks downstairs. Nora, with a stifled cry, runs across the room to the sofa table; short pause.*]

NORA   In the mailbox. [*Creeps cautiously to the hall door.*]   Lying there. Torvald, Torvald—no saving us now!

[*Mrs. Linde enters with the costume from the room at the left.*]

MRS. LINDE   Well, I think that's it for the repairs. Should we try it—

NORA   [*In a low, hoarse voice.*]   Kristine, come here.

540 MRS. LINDE   [*Throws the dress onto the sofa.*]   What's the matter—you're upset!

NORA   Come here. See that letter? There—see it, through the window in the mailbox?

MRS. LINDE   Yes, I see it.

NORA   It's from Krogstad.

545 MRS. LINDE   Nora—Krogstad's the one who lent you the money!

NORA   Yes. And now Torvald will know everything.

MRS. LINDE   Believe me, Nora, that's best for both of you.

NORA   There's more to it. I forged a signature.

MRS. LINDE   Oh for heaven's sake—

550 NORA   I'm just telling you this, Kristine, so that you can be my witness.

MRS. LINDE   What do you mean, witness? How can I—?

NORA   If I were to lose my mind—that could easily happen—

MRS. LINDE   Nora!

NORA   Or if anything else happened to me, if I couldn't be here—

555 MRS. LINDE   Nora, you're beside yourself!

NORA   And if someone wanted to try to take the whole thing onto himself, all the blame, you see—

MRS. LINDE   Yes, but how can you think—

NORA   You've got to swear it isn't true, Kristine. I'm in my perfect mind; I
560   understand exactly what I'm saying; and I'm telling you: no one else knew
about it. I did it all alone. Remember that.

MRS. LINDE   I will. But I don't understand any of it.

NORA   How could you understand? A wonderful thing is about to happen.

MRS. LINDE   Wonderful?

565   NORA   Yes, a wonderful thing. But also terrible, Kristine, and it just can't
happen, not for all the world.

MRS. LINDE   I'm going to talk to Krogstad right away.

NORA   Don't: he'll only hurt you some way.

MRS. LINDE   Once upon a time he'd have gladly done anything for me.

570   NORA   Him?

MRS. LINDE   Where does he live?

NORA   How should I know? Wait—[Searches her pocket.] Here's his card.
But what about the letter, the letter—?

HELMER   [In his study, knocking on the door.]   Nora!

575   NORA   [Screams in panic.]   What is it? What do you want?

HELMER   Now, don't be frightened. We're not coming in. The door's locked;
are you trying on your costume?

NORA   Yes, I'm trying it on. I'm going to be so beautiful, Torvald.

MRS. LINDE   [Having read the card.]   He lives right around the corner.

580   NORA   Yes, but that's no help. We're lost. The letter's in the box.

MRS. LINDE   Your husband has the key?

NORA   Always.

MRS. LINDE   Krogstad will have to ask for his letter back unopened—he'll
have to find some excuse—

585   NORA   But this is the time when Torvald usually—

MRS. LINDE   Stall him. Go in there and stay with him. I'll get back as fast as
I can. [She goes out hurriedly through the hall door. Nora goes to Helmer's
door and opens it, looking in.]

NORA   Torvald!

HELMER   Well—can I finally come back into my own living room? Come on,
590   Rank, now we'll get to see— [In the doorway.] But—?

NORA   What, Torvald my dear?

HELMER   Rank had me all set for a great dress parade.

RANK   [In the doorway.]   That's what I was expecting, but I guess I was wrong.

NORA   No one gets to bask in my full glory until tomorrow.

595   HELMER   But Nora, you look so tired. Have you been practicing too hard?

NORA   No, I haven't practiced at all yet.

HELMER   You know it's essential—

NORA   Absolutely essential. But I can't possibly do it without your help; I've
forgotten everything.

600   HELMER   We'll get it back quick enough.

NORA   Yes, take care of me right to the end, Torvald. Do you promise? Ah, I'm
so nervous. That big party—you have to give up everything for me tonight.
Not one bit of business, don't even go near your work. All right, Torvald.
Promise?

605   HELMER   I promise. Tonight I'll be completely at your service—you helpless
little thing. Hmm—just one item to take care of first—[Goes toward the
hall door.]

NORA   What do you want out there?

HELMER   Just seeing if there's any mail.

NORA   No, no, Torvald, don't do that!

610 HELMER   What now?

NORA   Torvald, please, there's nothing there.

HELMER   Just let me have a look. [*About to go; Nora, at the piano, plays the opening notes of the tarantella. Helmer stops at the door.*]

NORA   I can't dance tomorrow if I don't rehearse with you.

HELMER   [*Going to her.*]   Nora, are you really so frightened of it?

615 NORA   Tremendously frightened. Let's rehearse right now; there's still time before dinner. Oh, Torvald, sit down and play for me. Show me how it goes; direct me, like you always do.

HELMER   I'd be glad to, if you want.

[*Nora snatches the tambourine out of the box, and also a long, multicolored shawl which she drapes around herself; then she springs forward and calls out.*]

NORA   Play for me! Now I'll dance!

[*Helmer plays and Nora dances; Doctor Rank stands behind Helmer and watches.*]

620 HELMER   [*Playing.*]   Slower, slower—

NORA   I can't help it.

HELMER   Not so violent, Nora!

NORA   That's how it has to be.

HELMER   [*Stopping.*]   No, no—that's not it at all.

625 NORA   [*Laughing, swinging the tambourine.*]   What did I tell you?

RANK   Let me play for her.

HELMER   [*Getting up.*]   Yes, good idea. That way I can be a better teacher.

[*Rank sits at the piano and plays. Nora dances with increasing wildness. Helmer has placed himself by the stove, continually directing dancing instructions to her; she seems not to hear him; her hair loosens and falls over her shoulders; she doesn't notice, but keeps on dancing. Mrs. Linde enters.*]

MRS. LINDE   [*As though spellbound in the doorway.*]   Ah—!

NORA   [*Still dancing.*]   See, Kristine, what fun!

630 HELMER   But Nora, you're dancing as if your life were at stake.

NORA   It is, it is!

HELMER   Rank, stop. This is absolute madness. Stop it!

[*Rank stops playing and Nora suddenly comes to a halt.*]

HELMER   [*Goes to her.*]   I would never have believed this—you've forgotten everything I taught you.

635 NORA   [*Throwing down the tambourine.*]   As you can see.

HELMER   Some extra work's in order here.

NORA   Yes, you see how important it is. You've got to keep teaching me right up to the last minute. Promise, Torvald?

HELMER   Depend on it.

640 NORA   You can't even think—today or tomorrow—about anything but me— don't open any letters, don't even touch the mailbox—

HELMER   Ah—you're still afraid of that man.

NORA   Yes, yes, that too.

HELMER   Nora, I can see it in your face, there's a letter from him out there.

645 NORA   I don't know. I think there is. But you can't read things like that now; there can't be anything horrible between us till all this is over.

RANK [*Softly to Helmer.*]   You shouldn't go against her.

HELMER   The child will have its way. But tomorrow night—after you've danced—

NORA   Then you're free.

650 MAID [*In the doorway, right.*]   Ma'am, dinner's on the table.

NORA   We'll have champagne, Helene.

MAID   Very good, ma'am. [*Goes out.*]

HELMER   Hey, hey—a whole banquet?

NORA   Yes—a champagne supper right through till dawn! [*Calling out.*] And
655   some macaroons, Helene—lots of them—just this once.

HELMER [*Taking her hands.*]   There, there, there—not so wild, not so scared—be my little skylark again.

NORA   Oh, yes, I certainly will. But go to dinner—you too, Doctor Rank. Kristine, I need you to help me with my hair.

660 RANK [*Softly as they go.*]   There wouldn't be anything—anything on the way?

HELMER   No, my friend, not a thing; nothing more than these silly fears I've been telling you about. [*They go out, right.*]

NORA   Well?

MRS. LINDE   Gone to the country.

665 NORA   I saw it in your face.

MRS. LINDE   He gets back tomorrow night. I left him a note.

NORA   You shouldn't have done that. You can't stop it now. Behind it all there's this great joy—waiting for a wonderful thing to happen.

MRS. LINDE   What are you waiting for?

670 NORA   You can't understand that. Go in with them—I'll be there in a minute.

[*Mrs. Linde goes into the dining room. Nora stands for a moment as if to compose herself; then she looks at her watch.*]

NORA   Five. Seven hours to midnight. Then twenty-four hours to the next midnight. Then the tarantella will be done. Twenty-four plus seven— thirty-one hours to live.

HELMER [*In the doorway, right.*]   What happened to the skylark?

675 NORA [*Going to him with open arms.*]   Here's your skylark!

Act 3

Same room. The sofa-table, with chairs around it, has been moved to the middle of the room. A lamp is burning on the table. The door to the hall stands open. Dance music can be heard from the apartment above.

[*Mrs. Linde is sitting by the table, desultorily turning the pages of the book; she attempts to read but seems unable to fix her attention. Once or twice she listens, tensely, for a sound at the door.*]

MRS. LINDE   Not here yet. And it's now or never. If he'd only—[*Listens again.*] Ah—there he is. [*She goes out into the hall and cautiously opens the outer door; quiet footsteps are heard on the stairs. She whispers.*] Come in. Nobody's here.

5 KROGSTAD [*In the doorway.*]   I found a note from you at home. What does it mean?

MRS. LINDE   I had to talk to you.

KROGSTAD   Oh yes? And it had to be here, in this house?

MRS. LINDE   My place is impossible—there's no private entrance to my room.
10   Come in; we're all alone. The maid's asleep and the Helmers are at a party upstairs.

KROGSTAD   [*Comes into the room.*]   Well, well, well—so the Helmers are dancing tonight. How about that?

MRS. LINDE   Why shouldn't they?

15   KROGSTAD   True enough—why shouldn't they.

MRS. LINDE   Well, Krogstad, let's talk.

KROGSTAD   Do the two of us have anything more to talk about?

MRS. LINDE   We have a lot to talk about.

KROGSTAD   I wouldn't have thought so.

20   MRS. LINDE   No, because you've never really understood me.

KROGSTAD   What was there to understand, more than the usual thing? A heartless woman sends a man packing as soon as she gets a better offer.

MRS. LINDE   Do you think I'm that heartless? Do you think it was easy for me to break up with you?

25   KROGSTAD   Wasn't it?

MRS. LINDE   Krogstad, did you really think that?

KROGSTAD   Then how could you have written to me that way?

MRS. LINDE   I couldn't do anything else. If I had to make the break, it was my duty to try to stamp out whatever feelings you had for me.

30   KROGSTAD   [*Clenching his hands.*]   So that was it! And this—all this for money's sake!

MRS. LINDE   Don't forget that I had a helpless mother and two little brothers. We couldn't wait for you, Krogstad; your prospects were so cloudy then.

35   KROGSTAD   Maybe. But you had no right to abandon me for somebody else's sake.

MRS. LINDE   Yes—I don't know. I've asked myself over and over if I had any right to do that.

KROGSTAD   [*More quietly.*]   When I lost you I felt the ground dissolve under
40   my feet. Look at me: I'm a man adrift on a wreck.

MRS. LINDE   Help could be close by.

KROGSTAD   It was—until you appeared and blocked the way.

MRS. LINDE   I didn't know, Krogstad. I only learned today that I'm replacing you at the bank.

45   KROGSTAD   Since you say so, I believe it. But now you know—so won't you pull out?

MRS. LINDE   No, because that wouldn't do you the least bit of good.

KROGSTAD   Oh, who cares? I'd do it anyway.

MRS. LINDE   I've learned to act rationally. Life and bitter necessity have
50   taught me that.

KROGSTAD   And life has taught me not to believe in empty phrases.

MRS. LINDE   Then life has taught you a very rational lesson. But you do believe in deeds, don't you?

KROGSTAD   What do you mean?

55   MRS. LINDE   You said that you were like a man adrift, standing on a wreck.

KROGSTAD   I said that with good reason.

MRS. LINDE   Well I'm a woman adrift; I'm hanging on to a wreck as well.

KROGSTAD   That was your choice.

MRS. LINDE   There was no other choice at the time.

60 KROGSTAD   So?

MRS. LINDE   Krogstad, what if these two shipwrecks could reach across to one another?

KROGSTAD   What are you saying?

MRS. LINDE   Two on one raft stand a better chance than each one alone.

65 KROGSTAD   Kristine!

MRS. LINDE   Why do you suppose I came to town?

KROGSTAD   Were you really thinking about me?

MRS. LINDE   For me to go on living, I need to work. All my life, as long as I can remember, I've worked—it's given me my only real joy. But now I'm
70 completely alone in the world, completely empty and desolate. Working for yourself—well, there's no joy in that. Krogstad: give me someone and something to work for.

KROGSTAD   I don't believe all this. This is just some hysterical feminine urge for self-sacrifice.

75 MRS. LINDE   Have you ever known me to be hysterical?

KROGSTAD   Can you really mean all this? Do you know about my past—the whole story?

MRS. LINDE   Yes.

KROGSTAD   And you know what people think of me here?

80 MRS. LINDE   You hinted just now that you thought you could have been a different person with me.

KROGSTAD   I know that for sure.

MRS. LINDE   Couldn't it still happen?

KROGSTAD   Kristine—you're serious about this? Yes, you are. I can see it in
85 you. Do you have the courage as well?

MRS. LINDE   I need someone to be a mother to, and your children need a mother. The two of us need each other. Krogstad, I have faith in you, in what's there deep down in your heart. I could risk anything together with you.

90 KROGSTAD   [Seizing her hands.]   Thank you, Kristine, thank you—now I know I can bring myself up in people's eyes—ah, I forgot—

MRS. LINDE   [Listening.]   The tarantella! Go, go, go!

KROGSTAD   What's going on?

MRS. LINDE   Do you hear the music up there? When it's over, they'll be
95 down.

KROGSTAD   All right, I'll go. It's all pointless. Of course you don't know what I've done with the Helmers.

MRS. LINDE   Yes, Krogstad, I know all about it.

KROGSTAD   And you still have the courage to—

100 MRS. LINDE   I know very well how far despair can drive a man like you.

KROGSTAD   If I could only undo what I've done!

MRS. LINDE   That's easy. Your letter's still in the mailbox.

KROGSTAD   Are you sure?

MRS. LINDE   Absolutely. But—

105 KROGSTAD   [Looks searchingly at her.]   Is that what this is all about? Would you save your friend at any price? Tell me honestly, tell me straight—is that it?

MRS. LINDE   Krogstad: when you've sold yourself once for someone else's sake, you don't do it a second time.

KROGSTAD   I'll demand my letter back.

110 MRS. LINDE   No, no.

KROGSTAD   Yes, of course I will. I'll stay here until Helmer comes down; I'll tell him to give me back my letter—that it's only about my dismissal—that he shouldn't read it.

MRS. LINDE   No, Krogstad. Don't take back your letter.

115 KROGSTAD   But wasn't that exactly why you got me over here?

MRS. LINDE   Yes, in the first panic. But in the twenty-four hours between then and now, I've seen some incredible things in this house. Helmer has to learn everything; this awful secret has to come to light; those two have to come to a clear understanding—they can't go on with all this hiding, all these

120 lies.

KROGSTAD   Well, if you're willing to take the risk—. But there's one thing I can do right away.

MRS. LINDE [*Listening.*]   Hurry! Go, go! The dance is over. We're not safe another second!

125 KROGSTAD   I'll wait for you downstairs.

MRS. LINDE   Yes, do that. You'll have to see me home.

KROGSTAD   This incredible happiness—I've never felt anything like it!

[*He goes out by the front door; the door between the living room and the hall stays open.*]

MRS. LINDE [*Tidies the room a little and gets her outer garments ready.*]   What a change! What a change! People to work for, to live for—a home to make.

130 That's something worth doing. If only they'd come soon. [*Listens.*] Ah— there they are. Get dressed.

[*Helmer's and Nora's voices are heard outside; a key is turned and Helmer leads Nora almost forcibly into the hall. She is wearing the Italian costume with a large black shawl over it; he is in evening dress with an open black domino[8] over it.*]

NORA [*Still in the doorway, resisting.*]   No, no, no, not in there! I'm going up again. I don't want to leave so early!

HELMER   But Nora, my dearest—

135 NORA   Oh, I beg you, I implore you, from the bottom of my heart Torvald— just one more hour!

HELMER   Not another minute, Nora, my sweet. You know we had an agreement. Come on now, into the drawing room; you're catching cold out here. [*He leads her gently into the drawing room against her resistance.*]

MRS. LINDE   Good evening.

140 NORA   Kristine!

HELMER   Well, Mrs. Linde—here so late?

MRS. LINDE   Yes, forgive me. I really wanted to see Nora in her costume.

NORA   So you've been sitting here waiting for me?

MRS. LINDE   Yes, I didn't get here in time—you'd all gone upstairs. And I just

145 thought I couldn't leave without seeing you.

HELMER [*Taking off Nora's shawl.*]   Well, get a good look at her. I think she's worth looking at. Isn't she lovely, Mrs. Linde?

MRS. LINDE   Yes, I have to say—

8. A hooded robe usually worn to a costume party.

HELMER   Isn't she incredibly lovely? That was the general consensus at the
150   party, too—but also incredibly stubborn, the sweet thing. What to do about
that? Would you believe it, I almost had to use force to get her down here.

NORA   Ah, Torvald, you're going to regret that you didn't let me have my way
just a half-hour more.

HELMER   Hear that, Mrs. Linde? She danced her tarantella to thunderous
155   applause—well-deserved applause, too—even though there was something
a little too naturalistic about the whole thing—I mean, something that
went beyond the strict requirements of art. But so what? The main thing is,
she was a success—a tremendous success. Should I let her stay around
after that? Spoil the effect? No, thank you! I took my lovely Capri girl—my
160   capricious little Capri girl, I could say—on my arm; made a quick trip
around the ballroom—a curtsy to all sides—and as they say in novels, the
lovely apparition vanished. Exits are tremendously important, Mrs. Linde—
they should always be effective; but that's what I can't get Nora to see.
Uch, it's hot in here. [*Throws his domino on a chair and opens the door to*
165   *his room.*] What? it's dark—oh, yes, of course—excuse me—[*Goes in and
lights candles.*]

NORA   [*Whispering quickly and breathlessly.*]   Well?

MRS. LINDE   [*Quietly.*]   I talked to him.

NORA   And—?

MRS. LINDE   Nora, you have to tell your husband everything.

170   NORA   [*Dully.*]   I knew it.

MRS. LINDE   You've got nothing to worry about from Krogstad—but you have
to speak out.

NORA   I won't do it.

MRS. LINDE   Then the letter will.

175   NORA   Thank you, Kristine. Now I know what I have to do. Sssh!—

HELMER   [*Coming in again.*]   Now, Mrs. Linde—have you had a chance to
admire her?

MRS. LINDE   Yes, and now I'll say good night.

HELMER   So soon? Is this yours, this knitting?

180   MRS. LINDE   [*Taking it.*]   Oh yes.

HELMER   So you also knit.

MRS. LINDE   Yes.

HELMER   Know what? You should embroider instead.

MRS. LINDE   Really? Why?

185   HELMER   Much prettier. Want to see? You hold the embroidery like this with
your left hand, and guide the needle with your right—like this—lightly, in
and out, in a sweeping curve—right?

MRS. LINDE   I suppose so—

HELMER   Now knitting, on the other hand—so ugly to watch—see here, the
190   arms jammed together, the needles going up and down—there's something
Chinese about it. Ah—that was a tremendous champagne up there.

MRS. LINDE   Well, Nora, good night! And no more stubbornness!

HELMER   Well said, Mrs. Linde!

MRS. LINDE   Good night, Mr. Helmer.

195   HELMER   [*Following her to the door.*]   Good night, good night. I hope you're
all right getting home. I would, of course—but you don't have far to go.
Good night, good night. [*She leaves; he closes the door after her and comes*

in again.] Well, well. We finally got her out the door. What an incredible
bore that woman is.

200 NORA   Aren't you tired, Torvald?

HELMER   No, not a bit.

NORA   Not sleepy at all?

HELMER   Absolutely not—in fact, I'm exhilarated! You, on the other hand,
are looking very tired and sleepy.

205 NORA   Yes, I'm tired. I'll get to sleep soon.

HELMER   See, see! I was right! It was time to go home.

NORA   Oh, everything you do is right.

HELMER [*Kisses her on the brow.*]   Now my little lark is talking like a real person. Say—did you notice how lively Rank was tonight?

210 NORA   Was he? I didn't get to talk to him.

HELMER   I barely did myself, but I haven't seen him in such a good mood in
a long time. [*Looks at Nora a while, then comes closer to her.*] Hmm—my
God, it's glorious to be back in our own home again, completely alone with
you—you enchanting young woman!

215 NORA   Don't look at me like that, Torvald!

HELMER   Shouldn't I look at my most precious possession? All this magnificence, and it's mine, mine alone, completely and utterly mine!

NORA   You shouldn't talk this way to me tonight.

HELMER [*Following her.*]   The tarantella's still in your blood. I understand.
220   And that makes me want you even more. Listen! Now the guests are
beginning to leave. [*More softly.*] Nora—soon the whole house will be
silent.

NORA   I hope so.

HELMER   Yes, my own darling Nora, that's right. Ah—do you know why,
225   whenever I'm out at a party with you—do you know why I barely speak to
you, why I keep my distance, hardly even shoot you a stolen glance? Do
you know why I do that? Because I'm imagining you're my secret lover, my
young, secret sweetheart, and that no one in the room guesses there's anything going on between us.

230 NORA   Oh yes, yes, yes—I know you're always thinking of me.

HELMER   And when it's time to go, and I place the shawl over your smooth
young shoulders, around this wonderful curve of your neck—then I pretend you're my young bride, that we've come straight from the wedding,
that I'm bringing you home for the first time, alone with you for the first
235   time, completely alone with you, you young, trembling, delicious—ah,
I've done nothing but long for you all night! When I saw you doing the
tarantella—like a huntress, luring us all to your trap—my blood started to
boil. I couldn't stand it any longer. That's why I got you down here so early—

NORA   Get away, Torvald! Please get away from me. I don't want all this.

240 HELMER   What are you saying? Still playing the lark with me, Nora? You
want, you don't want? Aren't I your husband?

[*There's a noise outside.*]

NORA [*Startled.*]   Did you hear that?

HELMER [*Going to the door.*]   Who's there?

RANK [*Outside.*]   Just me. May I come in for a moment?

245 HELMER [*Softly, irritated.*]   What can he possibly want now? [*Aloud.*] Just a
second. [*Goes to the door and opens it.*] I'm so glad you didn't pass us by on
your way out.

RANK I thought I heard voices, and I really wanted to stop in. [*Looking around.*] Oh, yes—the old haunts. What a warm little nest you've got here.

250 HELMER Speaking of which, you were having a pretty warm time upstairs—almost hot, I'd say.

RANK Absolutely. And why not? You have to get the most out of life—everything you can, anyway, for as long as you can. That was excellent wine.

HELMER And the champagne!

255 RANK You thought so too? My thirst for it was amazing—even to me.

NORA Torvald also had his share of champagne tonight.

RANK Oh yes?

NORA Yes, and that makes him so entertaining.

RANK And why shouldn't you enjoy an evening like this after a productive
260 day?

HELMER Productive? I can't exactly say that for myself.

RANK [*Slaps him on the back.*] Ah, but you see, I can!

NORA Doctor Rank, it sounds like you've done some medical research today.

RANK That's right.

265 HELMER Oh come on—here's little Nora talking about medical research!

NORA And may I congratulate you on the results?

RANK Yes indeed.

NORA Were they good?

RANK The best kind—for doctor and patient alike—certainty.

270 NORA [*Quickly, inquisitively.*] Certainty.

RANK Absolute certainty. So haven't I earned a festive night out?

NORA Yes, Doctor Rank, you have.

HELMER I'm all for that—as long as the morning after's not too bad.

RANK Well, you never get something for nothing in this world.

275 NORA Doctor Rank, do you like masquerade balls?

RANK Oh yes—especially when the disguises are good and strange—

NORA So tell me. At the next one, how should the two of us appear?

HELMER You little noodlehead! You're already on to the next one?

RANK The two of us? I can tell you that: you'll go as Charmed Life—

280 HELMER All right, but what's the costume for that?

RANK Your wife can go just as she always is.

HELMER Well said. Now have you decided on something for yourself?

RANK Yes, Helmer, my mind's made up.

HELMER Well?

285 RANK At the next masquerade, I will be—invisible.

HELMER That's pretty funny.

RANK I hear there's a hat—a huge, black hat—called the Hat of Invisibility. You put it on, and no one on earth can see you.

HELMER [*Stifling a grin.*] Oh, yes, of course.

290 RANK But I've forgotten what I really came for. Helmer, how about a cigar—a dark Havana.

HELMER With pleasure. [*Holds out the case to him.*]

RANK Thanks. [*Takes one and cuts the tip.*]

NORA Let me give you a light.

295 RANK Thank you. [*She holds the match as he lights the cigar.*] Now, goodbye.

HELMER Old friend—goodbye, goodbye.

NORA Sleep well, Doctor.

RANK   Thank you for that wish.

300   NORA   Now wish me the same.

RANK   Wish you?—All right, if you want—sleep well. And thanks for the light. [*He exits, nodding to both of them.*]

HELMER [*Quietly.*]   He's drunk.

NORA [*Vaguely.*]   Maybe.

[*Helmer takes his keys from his pocket and goes out into the hall.*]

305   NORA   What are you doing, Torvald?

HELMER   I've got to empty the mailbox—it's so full, there's no room for the morning papers.

NORA   Are you working tonight?

HELMER   You know I'm not. What's this? Someone's been fiddling with the
310   lock.

NORA   The lock?

HELMER   Yes, definitely. Who could it be? I can't believe the maids—? Wait, here's a broken hairpin—Nora, this is yours—

NORA [*Quickly.*]   Then it must be the children.

315   HELMER   Well you've really got to break them of that. Hmm—there we go, finally got it open. [*Takes out the contents and shouts into the kitchen.*] Helene? Helene—put out the hall lamp. [*He comes back into the room and shuts the door. He holds the letters in his hand.*] Look—see how it piled up? [*Sorts through them.*] What's this?

320   NORA [*By the window.*]   The letter! No, no, Torvald!

HELMER   Two cards, from Rank.

NORA   From Doctor Rank?

HELMER [*Looking at them.*]   Doctor Rank, Physician and Surgeon. They were on top. He must have dropped them in as he left.

325   NORA   Is there anything on them?

HELMER   There's a black cross over the name. Look. That's gruesome. It's like he's announcing his own death.

NORA   That's exactly what he's doing.

HELMER   What? Did he tell you anything?

330   NORA   Yes. He said that when these cards arrived, it meant he's saying goodbye to us. Now he'll shut himself in and die.

HELMER   My poor friend. Of course I knew I wouldn't have him for long. But so soon—and now he's hiding himself away like a wounded animal.

NORA   If it has to happen, it's best to let it happen quietly. Isn't that right,
335   Torvald?

HELMER [*Pacing up and down.*]   He'd grown to be a part of us. I don't think I can imagine myself without him. His loneliness—his suffering was like a cloudy background to our sunlit happiness. Well, maybe it's best this way—at least for him. [*Stands still.*] And maybe for us too, Nora. Now we
340   only have each other. [*Puts his arms around her.*] Ah, you—my darling wife. I don't think I'll ever be able to hold you close enough. You know, Nora—so many times I've wished that you were in some terrible danger, so I could risk my life, my blood, everything, everything for you.

NORA [*Tears herself free and says firmly and resolutely.*]   Read your mail now,
345   Torvald.

HELMER   No, not tonight. Tonight I want to be with you—

NORA   With your friend's death on your mind?

HELMER   You're right. We're both a little shaken by this. This ugliness has
come between us—thoughts of death and decay. We have to try to get rid of
350   them; until then, we go our separate ways.

NORA [*Her arms around his neck.*]   Torvald—good night! Good night!

HELMER [*Kissing her forehead.*]   Good night, little songbird. Sleep well,
Nora. Now I'll read the mail. [*He goes in with the letters, shuts the door
behind him.*]

[*Nora, with wild eyes, fumbles around, seizes Helmer's domino, wraps it
around herself, and whispers quickly, hoarsely, spasmodically.*]

NORA   Never see him again—never, never, never. [*Throws the shawl over her
355   head.*] Never see the children again either—not even the children—never,
never—the icy black water—the bottomless—that—if only it weren't all
over—now he has it, he's reading it now—no, no, not yet. Torvald, good-
bye, children, good-bye—

[*She starts to go into the hall; at the same moment Helmer flings open his
door and stands there, an open letter in his hand.*]

HELMER   Nora!

360   NORA [*Screams.*]   Ahh—!

HELMER   What is this? Do you know what's in this letter?

NORA   Yes. Yes I know. Let me go. Let me out!

HELMER [*Holding her back.*]   Where are you going?

NORA [*Trying to break loose.*]   Don't try to save me, Torvald!

365   HELMER [*Staggers back.*]   It's true?! What he said is the truth? Horrible!
No—it's impossible—this can't be true.

NORA   It is true. I have loved you more than anything in the world.

HELMER   Don't start with your silly excuses.

NORA [*Taking a step toward him.*]   Torvald!

370   HELMER   You miserable—what have you done?

NORA   Let me go. You won't have to take the blame for me. You're not going
to take it on yourself.

HELMER   No more playacting! [*Locking the hall door.*]   You'll stay right here
and explain yourself. Do you understand what you've done? Answer me! Do
375   you understand?

NORA [*Looking fixedly at him, her face hardening.*]   Yes. Now I'm beginning
to understand everything.

HELMER [*Pacing up and down.*]   Ah!—what a rude awakening for me! For
eight years—my pride and joy, a hypocrite, a liar,—even worse, a criminal!
380   There's so much ugliness at the bottom of all this—indescribable ugliness!
Uccch! [*Nora remains silent, looking fixedly at him.*] I should have seen it
coming. Every one of your father's disgusting values—quiet!—every disgusting value is coming out in you. No religion, no morals, no sense of
duty—this is my punishment for being so easy on him up there. I did it for
385   your sake; and you repay me like this!

NORA   Yes, like this.

HELMER   You've destroyed my happiness. My whole future—thrown away!
It's horrible when you think about it. I'm totally at the mercy of some
amoral animal who can do whatever he wants with me—demand anything
390   he wants, order me around, command me however he pleases, and I can't
so much as squeak in protest. And this is how I'll go down, right to the bottom, all for the sake of some frivolous woman.

NORA   When I'm gone from this world, then you'll be free.

HELMER   Stop playacting! You sound like your father—he always had one of
395   those phrases on the tip of his tongue. How would it help me if you were gone
from this world, as you put it? Not in the least. He can still reveal everything,
and if he does I'd be suspected of being an accomplice to your crimes! People
might think I was behind it all, that it was my idea! And I have you to thank
for all this—after I've carried you along, taken you and led you by the hand
400   ever since we were married. Do you understand what you have done to me?

NORA   [Coldly and calmly.]   Yes.

HELMER   I can't grasp this—it's just unbelievable to me. But we have to try to
set things right. Take off that shawl. I said take it off! I've got to find some
way to appease him—this thing has to be covered up, whatever it costs. As
405   for you and me, things will seem just like before. For public consumption
only, of course. You'll stay in the house, that's understood. But I can't trust
you to bring up the children. Oh God—to have to say that to the one
I—even now—well, that's over. After today there's no happiness, only holding the wreckage together, the scraps and shards—[The doorbell rings.
410   Helmer starts.] What's that? It's so late! Is this it? Is he going to—? Nora,
hide yourself! Say you're sick. [Nora stands motionless. Helmer goes and
opens the hall door.]

MAID   [Half-dressed in the hall doorway.]   A letter for Mrs. Helmer.

HELMER   Give it here. [Takes the letter and closes the door.] Yes, it's from him.
You're not getting it. I'll read it myself.

415   NORA   Read it.

HELMER   [By the lamp.]   I hardly dare. It could be the end for both of us. I've
got to know. [Tears open the letter; scans a few lines; looks at an enclosed
paper and gives a cry of joy.] Nora! [Nora looks enquiringly at him.] Nora!
No, let me read it again—yes, yes, it's true. I'm saved! Nora, I'm saved!

420   NORA   And I?

HELMER   You too, of course. We're both saved, both of us. See? He sent you
back your note—he writes that he's sorry and ashamed—that a happy
change in his life—oh, what does it matter what he writes? We're saved,
Nora! Now no one can hurt you. Oh, Nora, Nora—no: first, let's get all this
425   ugliness out of here. Let me see. [Glances at the note for a moment.] No, I
won't look at it. It'll be nothing more than a dream I had. [He tears both letters in pieces and throws them both into the stove, watching them burn.] So,
nothing left. He wrote that ever since Christmas Eve—God, these must
have been three terrible days for you, Nora.

430   NORA   I have fought a hard battle these last three days.

HELMER   And suffered, not seeing any way out but—no, we won't think
about this ugly thing any more. We'll just rejoice and keep telling ourselves
"it's over—it's all over." Do you hear me, Nora? It seems like you haven't
quite got it yet—it's over! What's this about, this cold stare? Ah, poor little
435   Nora, I understand—you can't bring yourself to believe I've forgiven you.
But I have, Nora, I swear. I've forgiven everything. I know perfectly well
that you did all this out of love for me.

NORA   That's true.

HELMER   You've loved me like a wife should love her husband. You just
440   couldn't judge how to do it. But do you think that makes me love you any
the less, because you couldn't manage by yourself? No, no—just lean on
me. I'll counsel you, I'll direct you. I wouldn't be much of a man if this

female helplessness didn't make you doubly attractive to me. Forget what I said in those first few terrible moments, when I thought I was
445 going to lose everything. I've forgiven you, Nora—I swear, I've forgiven you.

NORA Thank you for your forgiveness. [*She goes out through the door on the right.*]

HELMER No, stay—[*Looking in.*] What are you doing?

NORA Taking off my costume.

450 HELMER [*By the open door.*] Yes, do that. Try to calm down, collect your thoughts, my little, shivering songbird. If you need protection, I have broad wings to shelter you with. [*Walks around near the door.*] Oh, Nora—our home is so snug, so cozy. This is your nest, where I can keep you like a dove that I've snatched, unharmed, from the falcon's claws; I'll bring peace and
455 rest to your beating heart. Little by little it will happen, Nora, believe me. Tomorrow, this will all seem different to you; and soon everything will be back to normal. I won't need to keep saying I forgive you—you'll feel it, you'll know it's true. How could you ever think I could bring myself to disown you, or even punish you? You don't know how a man's heart works,
460 Nora. There's something indescribably sweet and satisfying for a man in knowing he's forgiven his wife—forgiven her from the bottom of his heart. It's as if he possesses her doubly now—as if she were born into the world all over again—and she becomes, in a way, his wife and his child at the same time. And that's what you'll be for me from now on, you little, help-
465 less, confused creature. Don't be frightened of anything—just open your heart to me and I'll be both your conscience and your will. What's this—? You've changed your dress?

NORA Yes, Torvald, I've changed my dress.

HELMER But why now, so late?

470 NORA I'm not sleeping tonight.

HELMER But Nora, dear—

NORA [*Looking at her watch.*] It's not all that late. Sit down, Torvald. We have a great deal to talk about together. [*She sits at one end of the table.*]

HELMER Nora—what's going on? That hard expression—

475 NORA Sit down. This will take time. I have a lot to say to you.

HELMER [*Sits at table directly opposite her.*] You're worrying me, Nora. I don't understand you.

NORA No, that's just it. You don't understand me. And I have never understood you—not until tonight. No—no interruptions. You have to hear me
480 out. We're settling accounts, Torvald.

HELMER What do you mean by that?

NORA [*After a short silence.*] Doesn't *one* thing strike you about the way we're sitting here?

HELMER What might that be?

485 NORA We've been married for eight years. Doesn't it strike you that this is the first time that the two of us—you and I, man and wife—have ever talked seriously?

HELMER Well—"seriously"—what does that mean?

NORA In eight whole years—no, longer—right from the moment we met, we
490 haven't exchanged one serious word on one serious subject.

HELMER Should I constantly be involving you in problems you couldn't possibly help me solve?

NORA   I'm not talking about problems. I'm saying that we've never sat down together and seriously tried to get to the bottom of anything.

495 HELMER   But Nora, dearest—would you have wanted that?

NORA   Yes, of course, that's just it. You've never understood me. A great wrong has been done me, Torvald. First by Papa, then by you.

HELMER   What! By us—who've loved you more than anyone in the world.

NORA [*Shaking her head.*]   You've never loved me. You just thought it was a 500 lot of fun to be in love with me.

HELMER   Nora, how can you say that?

NORA   It's a fact, Torvald. When I was at home with Papa, he told me all his opinions; so of course I had the same opinions. And if I had any others, I kept them hidden, because he wouldn't have liked that. He called me his 505 doll-child, and he played with me like I played with my dolls. Then I came to your house—

HELMER   What kind of way is that to describe our marriage?

NORA [*Undisturbed.*]   I mean, I went from Papa's hands into yours. You set up everything according to your taste; so of course I had the same taste, or 510 I pretended to, I'm not really sure. I think it was half-and-half, one as much as the other. Now that I look back on it, I can see that I've lived like a beggar in this house, from hand to mouth; I've lived by doing tricks for you, Torvald. But that's how you wanted it. You and Papa have committed a great sin against me. It's your fault that I've become what I am.

515 HELMER   Nora—this is unreasonable, and it's ungrateful! Haven't you been happy here?

NORA   No, never. I thought so, but I never really was.

HELMER   Not—not happy!

NORA   No, just having fun. You've always been very nice to me. But our home 520 has never been anything but a playpen. I've been your doll-wife here, just like I was Papa's doll-child at home. And my children, in turn, have been my dolls. It was fun when you came and played with me, just like they had fun when I played with them. That's what our marriage has been, Torvald.

HELMER   There's some truth in this—as exaggerated and hysterical as it is. 525 But from now on, things will be different. Playtime is over: now the teaching begins.

NORA   Who gets this teaching? Me or the children?

HELMER   Both you and the children, my dearest Nora.

NORA   Ah, Torvald: you're not the man to teach me how to be a good wife to you.

530 HELMER   You can say that!

NORA   And me—how can I possibly teach the children?

HELMER   Nora!

NORA   Didn't you say that yourself, not too long ago? You didn't dare trust them to me?

535 HELMER   In the heat of the moment! How can you take that seriously?

NORA   Yes, but you spoke the truth. I'm not equal to the task. There's another task I have to get through first. I have to try to teach myself. And you can't help me there. I've got to do it alone. And so I'm leaving you.

HELMER [*Springing up.*]   What did you say?

540 NORA   If I'm going to find out anything about myself—about everything out there—I have to stand completely on my own. That's why I can't stay with you any longer.

HELMER Nora, Nora!

NORA I'll leave right away. Kristine can put me up for tonight—

545 HELMER You're out of your mind! I won't allow it—I forbid you!

NORA It's no use forbidding me anything any more. I'll take what's mine with me. I won't take anything from you, now or later.

HELMER What kind of madness is this?

NORA Tomorrow I'm going home—back to my old hometown, I mean. It'll
550 be easier for me to find something to do up there.

HELMER You blind, inexperienced creature!

NORA I have to try to get some experience, Torvald.

HELMER Abandon your home, your husband, your children! Do you have any idea what people will say?

555 NORA I can't worry about that. I only know what I have to do.

HELMER It's grotesque! You're turning your back on your most sacred duties!

NORA What do you think those are—my most sacred duties?

HELMER I have to tell you? Aren't they to your husband and children?

NORA I have other duties, equally sacred.

560 HELMER No, you don't! Like what?

NORA Duties to myself.

HELMER You're a wife and mother, first and foremost.

NORA I don't believe that any more. I believe that, first and foremost, I'm a human being—just as much as you—or at least I should try to become one.
565 I'm aware that most people agree with you, Torvald, and that your opinion is backed up by plenty of books. But I can't be satisfied any more with what most people say, or what's written in the books. Now I've got to think these things through myself, and understand them.

HELMER What don't you understand about your place in your own home?
570 Don't you have an infallible teacher for questions like this? Don't you have your religion?

NORA Oh, Torvald, I really don't know what religion is.

HELMER What are you saying?

NORA I only know what Pastor Hansen said when I was confirmed. He told
575 me that religion was this and that and the other thing. When I get away from here, when I'm alone, I'll look into that subject too. I'll see if what Pastor Hansen said is true—or at least, if it's true for me.

HELMER These things just aren't right for a young woman to be saying. If religion can't get through to you, let me try your conscience. You do have
580 some moral feeling? Or—answer me—maybe not?

NORA Well, Torvald, it's not easy to answer that. I really don't know. I'm actually quite confused about these things. I only know that my ideas are totally different from yours. I find out that the law is not what I thought it was—but I can't get it into my head that the law is right. A woman has no
585 right to spare her dying father's feelings, or save her husband's life! I just can't believe these things.

HELMER You're talking like a child. You don't understand the society you live in.

NORA No, I don't. But now I'm going to find out for myself. I've got to figure
590 out who's right—the world or me.

HELMER You're ill, Nora—you have a fever. I almost think you're out of your mind.

NORA   I've never been so clear—and so certain—about so many things as I am tonight.

595   HELMER   You're clear and certain that you'll desert your husband and children?

NORA   Yes, I will.

HELMER   There's only one explanation left.

NORA   What is it?

HELMER   You no longer love me.

600   NORA   No. That's precisely it.

HELMER   Nora!—you can say that!

NORA   Oh, it hurts so much, Torvald. Because you've always been so kind to me. But I can't help it. I don't love you any more.

HELMER [*Struggling to control himself.*]   Are you also clear and certain about
605   that?

NORA   Yes, absolutely clear and certain. That's why I can't live here any more.

HELMER   Can you tell me how I lost your love?

NORA   Yes, I can. It was this evening, when the wonderful thing didn't happen—then I saw that you weren't the man I thought you were.

610   HELMER   Say more—I'm not following this.

NORA   I've waited so patiently for ten years now—good Lord. I know that these wonderful things don't come along every day. Then this disaster broke over me, and I was absolutely certain: now the wonderful thing is coming. While Krogstad's letter was lying out there, I never imagined you'd
615   give in to his terms, even for a minute. I was so certain you'd say to him: tell your story to the whole world! And when that was done—

HELMER   Yes, then what? When I'd given my wife up to shame and disgrace—!

NORA   When that was done, I was completely certain that you would step
620   forward and take everything on yourself—you'd say "I am the guilty one."

HELMER   Nora!

NORA   You're thinking that I'd never accept such a sacrifice from you? No, of course I wouldn't. But what good would my protests be over yours? *That* was the wonderful thing I was hoping for, and in terror of. And to prevent
625   it, I was willing to end my life.

HELMER   I'd work for you night and day, Nora—gladly—suffer and sacrifice for your sake. But no one gives up his honor even for the one he loves.

NORA   That's exactly what millions of women have done.

HELMER   Oh—! You're thinking and talking like an ignorant child.

630   NORA   Maybe. But you don't think—or talk—like the man I could choose to be with. When your big fright was over—not the danger I was in, but what might happen to you—when that threat was past, then it was like nothing happened to you. I was just what I was before, your little songbird, your doll, and you'd have to take care of it twice as hard as before, since it was
635   so frail and fragile. In that moment, Torvald, it dawned on me that I'd been living with a stranger—that I'd borne three children with him—. Aah—I can't stand the thought of it! I could tear myself to pieces.

HELMER [*Heavily.*]   I see. I see. A gulf has really opened up between us. But Nora, can't we fill it in somehow?

640   NORA   The way I am now, I'm no wife for you.

HELMER   I can transform myself—I have the strength for it.

NORA   Maybe—if your doll is taken away from you.

HELMER   To live without—without you! Nora, I can't bear the thought of it!

NORA   All the more reason it has to happen. [*Having gone in to the right, she returns with her outdoor clothes and a little traveling bag, which she sets on a chair by the table.*]

645 HELMER   Nora, Nora, not now! Wait until tomorrow.

NORA [*Puts on her coat.*]   I can't spend the night in a strange man's house.

HELMER   Can't we live here like brother and sister?

NORA [*Tying her hat.*]   You know very well how long that would last. [*Throws her shawl around her.*] Good-bye, Torvald. I won't see the children. They're

650 in better hands than mine, that much I know. The way I am now, I can't do anything for them.

HELMER   But some day, Nora—some day—?

NORA   How do I know? I have no idea what will become of me.

HELMER   But you're my wife, right now and always, no matter what becomes

655 of you.

NORA   Listen, Torvald; when a wife deserts her husband's house, as I'm doing now, I've heard that the law frees him from any responsibility to her. And anyway, I'm freeing you. From everything. Complete freedom on both sides. See, here's your ring. Give me mine.

660 HELMER   Even that.

NORA   Even that.

HELMER   Here it is.

NORA   So. Well, now it's finished. I'm putting the keys here. As far as the household goes, the maids know all about it—better than I do. Tomorrow,

665 after I'm gone, Kristine will come and pack the things I brought from home. I'll have them sent.

HELMER   All finished, all over! Nora—will you never think about me after this?

NORA   Of course I'll think about you often—and the children, and the

670 house—.

HELMER   Could I write to you, Nora?

NORA   No, never. You can't do that.

HELMER   But I'll have to send you—

NORA   Nothing; nothing.

675 HELMER   —help you, if you need—

NORA   No. I'm telling you, I accept nothing from strangers.

HELMER   Nora—can't I ever be anything more than a stranger to you?

NORA [*Taking her traveling bag.*]   Oh, Torvald—not unless the most wonderful thing of all were to happen—

680 HELMER   Name it—what is this most wonderful thing?

NORA   It's—both you and I would have to transform ourselves to the point that—oh, Torvald, I don't know if I believe in it any more—

HELMER   But I will. Name it! Transform ourselves to the point that—

NORA   That our living together could become a marriage. Good-bye. [*She goes through the hall door.*]

HELMER [*Sinking down into a chair by the door and burying his face in his

685 hands.*]   Empty. She's not here. [*A hope flares up in him.*] The most wonderful thing of all—?

[*From below, the sound of a door slamming shut.*]

OSCAR WILDE

1854–1900

Oscar Wilde cut a remarkable figure within the literary, cultural, and theatrical worlds of late nineteenth-century Britain. Dandy, man of letters, public speaker, proponent of aestheticism (the movement championing "Art for Art's Sake"), and prolific author of poetry, fiction, essays, children's stories, criticism, and drama, he entertained London high society with his epigrammatic wit even as he flouted some of the most deeply held values of late-Victorian society. His 1890 novel, *The Picture of Dorian Gray,* scandalized many of its readers with its decadence and perceived amorality, and his society comedies of the early 1890s both entertained and satirized their West End audience. Something of an outsider by virtue of his Irishness and homosexuality, he fashioned a distinctly modern form of celebrity that challenged the norms of Victorian respectability. But Wilde's position in the society of his day was, it turned out, a precarious one. In 1895, even as two of his dramas played on the West End, he was convicted and imprisoned on the charge of "gross indecency" after three sensational trials that represent, to this day, a landmark in the public perception of homosexuality. "I'll be a poet, a writer, a dramatist," he wrote to a friend before leaving Oxford University in 1878. "Somehow or other, I'll be famous, and if not famous, notorious."

One of the most accomplished writers for the theater in fin de siècle London, Oscar Wilde became, in the end, his own greatest drama.

Oscar Fingal O'Flahertie Wills Wilde was born in Dublin on October 16, 1854, to William Wilde, an eye and ear surgeon, and the former Jane Francesca Elgee, who wrote Irish Nationalist poetry under the pseudonym "Speranza." After graduating from Portora Royal School in Enniskillen, he attended Trinity College, Dublin, where he distinguished himself as a student of the classics; he won a number of awards, including the prestigious Berkeley Prize for Greek. In 1874 he was awarded a scholarship to Magdalen College, Oxford, which he attended for the next four years. Wilde later referred to two great turning points in his life: "the first when my father sent me to Oxford, the second when Society sent me to prison." At Oxford Wilde studied with John Ruskin and Walter Pater, two leading scholars of aesthetics. Pater exerted the most lasting influence on the young Irishman. In his recently published *Studies in the History of the Renaissance* (1873), Pater celebrated "poetic passion, the desire for beauty, and the love of art for art's sake." Wilde, who had been attracted to aestheticism even before he arrived in Oxford, adopted the movement's beliefs, manners, and poses. He wore his hair long, dressed flamboyantly, and decorated his room in the aesthetic mode, with such accessories as lilies (associated with the Pre-Raphaelite painters) and studiously artistic furnishings. "I find it harder and harder every day to live up to my blue china," he famously stated, and the mannered self-consciousness of such sentiments would make him one of England's most visible aesthetes. During this time Wilde also wrote many of the poems that would appear in an 1881 collection of verse.

When Wilde moved from Oxford to London in 1878, he quickly established himself in high society through his brilliant conversation and wit. Within two years the newspaper *Punch* was regularly caricaturing him as a figurehead of the aesthetic movement, and in 1881 W. S. Gilbert and Sir Arthur Sullivan's comic opera *Patience* satirized aestheticism through the "perfectly precious" Wilde-like character Bunthorne. When the producer of *Patience* took the opera on tour in the United States and Canada the following year, Wilde accompanied the production as a lecturer and representative aesthete. Wilde traveled from coast to coast; met Ulysses S. Grant, Walt Whitman, and other prominent Americans; and registered his impressions of the New World in such epigrams as this: "When good Americans die they go to Paris; when bad Americans die they stay in America." Back in England, Wilde toured the British Isles as lecturer, worked as a journalist and book reviewer, and assumed the editorship of *Woman's World,* a popular late-Victorian periodical. In 1884 Wilde married Constance Mary Lloyd, with whom he had two sons over the next two years. But while Wilde continued to entertain the fashionable society of London with his witty conversation, and while his marriage established a degree of social respectability, he was known for little beyond being a celebrity. That began to change in 1888 with the publication of *The Happy Prince and Other Tales,* the first of two collections of original fairy tales. Over the next seven years, Wilde published a collection of critical essays (which included "The Artist as Critic" [1890]); two additional collections of stories; *The Picture of Dorian Gray,* his novel about a hedonistic aristocrat that shocked the Victorian public; and his five major plays.

An avid theatergoer since his college days and a friend of such theater luminaries as the actresses Lillie Langtry and Sarah Bernhardt, Wilde first tried his hand at drama with *Vera; or, The Nihilists* and *The Duchess of Padua,* which were written in the early 1880s and given short runs in New York. In 1891 Wilde agreed to write a social comedy for George Alexander, manager of the St. James's Theatre, and it was this play that would catapult him to the forefront of the London theater scene. *Lady Windermere's Fan,* produced in 1892, uses the narrative frame of the "problem play"—a nineteenth-century dramatic genre that dealt with controversial social issues—but deploys provocative social commentary and witty epigram to undermine the comfortable moral conclusions that plays in this genre frequently adopted. The play was widely popular, and the attention it received was intensified by Wilde himself, who strolled onstage, cigarette in hand, to greet the opening night applause and congratulate the audience for thinking as highly of his play as he did. *Lady Windermere's Fan* was followed by three more extremely successful social comedies: *A Woman of No Importance* (1893), *An Ideal Husband* (1895), and— Wilde's greatest play—THE IMPORTANCE OF BEING EARNEST (1895). *Salomé,* which Wilde wrote in 1891, dramatized the love of Salomé, Herodias's daughter, for John the Baptist (or Iokanaan) and her incantatory dance with his severed head. Deeply influenced by the symbolist drama of Stéphane Mallarmé (1842–1898) and Maurice Maeterlinck (1862–1949), *Salomé* was refused production by the Lord Chamberlain, who invoked a centuries-old law that prohibited the theatrical depiction of biblical figures. Wilde's poetic tragedy would not be seen on the English stage until after the playwright's death.

But even as Wilde was establishing himself as London's leading literary figure, the elements of his precipitous change in fortune were being set in place. In 1891 he met Lord Alfred Douglas, third son of the ninth marquess of Queensberry, and the two became inseparable. It is not clear when Wilde first became involved in homosexual relationships, but by the 1890s he was leading an active hidden life in London and abroad. The antagonism of Douglas's father toward what he understood to be a scandalous connection came to a head in February 1895 when Queensberry delivered a card to the London club of which Wilde was a member with the inscription "To Oscar Wilde, posing Somdomite [sic]." Wilde took out a warrant charging Queensberry with criminal libel, and in April the case went to trial. When Queensberry presented a list of male prostitutes who would testify concerning Wilde's illegal activities, however, Wilde withdrew the prosecution and the marquess was acquitted. Wilde, who was quickly arrested, now found himself the defendant, and after two trials (the first ended with a hung jury), he was sentenced to two years' hard labor for homosexual conduct. Over the next twenty-four months he suffered the misery and deprivations of the Victorian prison system. Initially allowed only a Bible, hymnbook, and prayerbook, he was eventually able to obtain other books and writing materials. Under these somewhat more lenient conditions he wrote De Profundis (published in part in 1905; unexpurgated, in 1962), a book-length letter to Douglas that included a meditation on his own life and fate. When Wilde was released from prison in May 1897, he left for France and never again set foot in England. In 1898 Wilde published The Ballad of Reading Gaol—inspired by his experience in prison—but his career as a writer was effectively over. He died in Paris on November 30, 1900, at the age of forty-six.

In De Profundis, which became his own eulogy, Wilde summed up what he felt to be the nature of his contribution to the cultural and philosophical life of his times:

> I made art a philosophy, and philosophy an art: I altered the minds of men and the colors of things: there was nothing I said or did that did not make people wonder: I took the drama, the most objective form known to art, and made it as personal a mode of expression as the lyric or the sonnet, at the same time that I widened its range and enriched its characterization. . . . I treated Art as the supreme reality, and life as a mere mode of fiction: I awoke the imagination of my century so that it created myth and legend around me: I summed up all systems in a phrase, and all existence in an epigram.

Wilde's conception of art resists both the moral seriousness of much nineteenth-century literature and what he considered to be the Philistine tendencies of the Victorian middle and upper classes. Writing that "all art is quite useless," he sought to dissociate artistic creation from traditional notions of social usefulness and moral edification. The result of this creative principle was a sophisticated manipulation of literary and social form. Indeed, Wilde became one of his age's most visible celebrities by also serving as its most clever critic. Even as his writing detailed the rituals and conventions of Victorian high society, Wilde subverted the hierarchy of values that structured this world.

Nowhere is this transgressive impulse more evident than in the famous Wildean epigrams, which invert traditional platitudes through clever turns of phrase. Take one example: "Ignorance is like a delicate exotic fruit; touch it and the bloom is gone." The immediate effect of such a remark is studied frivolity: as Algernon says of another epigram, similarly found in The Importance of Being Earnest, "It is perfectly phrased! and quite as true as any observation in civilized life should be." At the same time, the line offers a pointed commentary on those segments of the British upper class who value privilege over education. Wilde's plays draw on the manners tradition of social comedy, but in their boundary-assaulting wit they bear more than passing kinship to the more explicitly political drama of his fellow Irishman GEORGE BERNARD SHAW.

The Importance of Being Earnest, which opened to widespread acclaim at the St. James's Theatre on February 14, 1895, is the epitome of Wilde's subversive mode of playwriting. Its philosophy, as Wilde defined it, is straightforward: "That we should treat all the trivial things of life seriously, and all the serious things of life with sincere and studied triviality." Unlike

Wilde's earlier comedies, which borrowed the situations and plot devices of contemporary popular drama and were occasionally marred by the uneasy blend of melodrama and wit, *The Importance of Being Earnest* embraces the logic of a thoroughly stylized world in which action borders on farce, epigram rules the day, and even the butler speaks with exceptional propriety. Its world is ruthlessly superficial—"In matters of grave importance," Gwendolen insists, "style, not sincerity is the vital thing"—and its irreverent wit satirizes the institutions and ideals of Victorian society: marriage, religion, gender roles, family, the class system, colonialism, English country living, science, education, romantic idealism, and (of course) earnestness, the habit of taking oneself and one's cherished beliefs quite seriously.

Algernon and Jack, the play's central male characters, pursue a life of leisure and pleasure untroubled by the codes of respectability and responsibility that govern the society around them. Wilde's audience would have recognized them as "dandies" within a nineteenth-century tradition of mannered individualism that included the fashionable man-about-town Beau Brummell (1778–1840). The dandy, as Alan Sinfield observes, rejected the middle-class values of work and purity through a display of "conspicuous idleness, moral skepticism, and effeminacy." As much an attitude toward life as a manner and style of dress, dandyism called attention to its originality even as it embraced the outward forms of aristocratic society. Unlike Wilde's earlier comedies, which introduce dandy characters in conventional social settings, *The Importance of Being Earnest* presents a world in which wit, pleasure, and studied superficiality are the moral norm. It is a world of erased distinctions and inverted expectations, where smoking

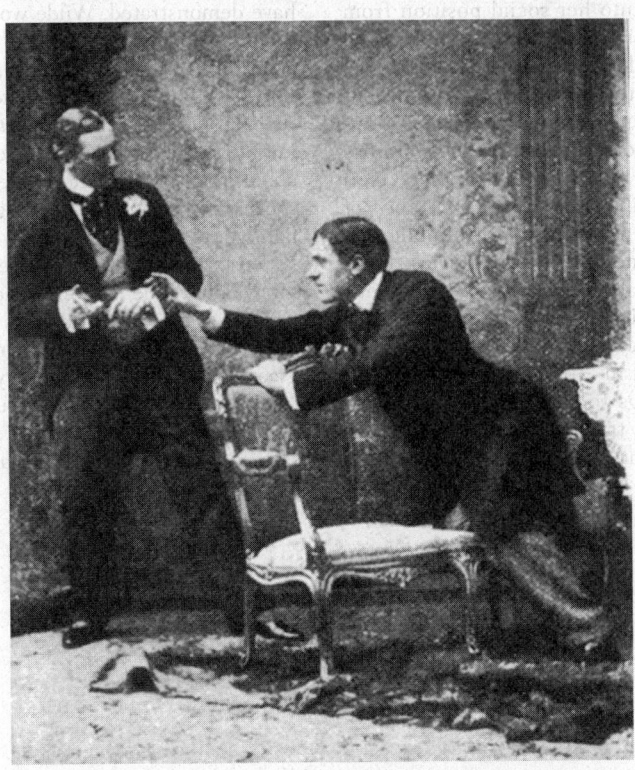

Allan Aynesworth as Algernon and George Alexander as Jack in the original 1895 production of *The Importance of Being Earnest*.

is as good an occupation for a man as any other and the most important thing to do in a moment of crisis is eat a muffin in the proper manner. Even Lady Bracknell, that most formidable representative of British social propriety, carries the observance of appearance and form to a dandiacal level of irreverence: "To lose one parent may be regarded as a misfortune—to lose *both* seems like carelessness."

In "The Critic as Artist" Wilde wrote: "Man is least himself when he talks in his own person. Give him a mask, and he will tell you the truth." Few characters in *The Importance of Being Earnest* are what they appear. Jack Worthing takes on his alter ego, Ernest, when he slips away to the city to see his nonexistent brother, and Algernon assumes the same name when he visits Cecily on the pretense of visiting his imaginary friend Bunbury. Gwendolen hides the secret of her romance with Jack from her mother, Cecily creates an imaginary engagement, and Lady Bracknell's authoritarian manner hides the fact that she married into her social position from decidedly nonaristocratic origins. Even Lane, the butler, and Miss Prism, the governess, have their secrets. In a play that pivots on the question of who one is, "Bunburying" becomes a metaphor for more fundamental shifts of identity. As Neil Sammells points out, *The Importance of Being Earnest* is obsessed with public and private documents—letters, diaries, birth certificates, Army Lists, novels—and with "their fallibility as a means of establishing 'authenticity,' whether of person or incident." But in "an age of surfaces" (the phrase belongs to Lady Bracknell), such categories as truth and identity remain elusive, caught in the play of social conventions and outward forms. The play on the word "Earnest" in the comedy's title reflects a society where who one is may hinge on a name and where Sincerity is the stepchild of Accident. "It is a terrible thing," Jack laments, "for a man to find out suddenly that all his life he has been speaking nothing but the truth."

In the end, Victorian earnestness had its revenge, and for those who know the playwright's biography it is hard not to view Wilde's final comedy in light of the events that followed shortly upon its premiere. When Wilde was arrested after the first trial, his name was taken off the billboards for *The Ideal Husband* and *The Importance of Being Earnest,* and in view of the author's sudden notoriety the two productions were soon canceled. The Bunburying in which Wilde's protagonists engage must have felt, to many in his audience, uncomfortably close to the secret life of which he was accused and for which he was convicted. In fact, the connections are more than coincidental. As recent scholars have demonstrated, Wilde wove a series of homosexual allusions within the play: in addition to its other meanings, for instance, *earnest* was a Victorian code word for homosexual. But though *The Importance of Being Earnest* engages and is framed by the trenchant realities of late-nineteenth-century society, its strategy of taking seriousness lightly and lightness seriously ensures that its world maintains the studied refinement for which Wilde strove. Dandyism, Wilde wrote, "is the assertion of the absolute modernity of beauty." What dominates this greatest of nineteenth-century comedies— "written by a butterfly for butterflies" (as Wilde wrote a friend)—is the power of wit, satire, and unscrupulous elegance.   S.G.

The Importance of Being Earnest
A Trivial Comedy for Serious People

CHARACTERS

JOHN WORTHING, J.P.[1]
ALGERNON MONCRIEFF
REV. CANON CHASUBLE, D.D.[2]
MERRIMAN, butler
LANE, manservant

LADY BRACKNELL
HON. GWENDOLEN FAIRFAX
CECILY CARDEW
MISS PRISM, governess

Time
The Present.

First Act

[SCENE: *Morning-room in Algernon's flat in Half Moon Street.*[3] *The room is luxuriously and artistically furnished. The sound of a piano is heard in the adjoining room.*]

[LANE *is arranging afternoon tea on the table, and after the music has ceased,* ALGERNON *enters.*]

ALGERNON   Did you hear what I was playing, Lane?

LANE   I didn't think it polite to listen, sir.

ALGERNON   I'm sorry for that, for your sake. I don't play accurately—anyone can play accurately—but I play with wonderful expression. As far as the
5   piano is concerned, sentiment is my forte. I keep science for Life.

LANE   Yes, sir.

ALGERNON   And, speaking of the science of Life, have you got the cucumber sandwiches cut for Lady Bracknell?

LANE   Yes, sir. [*Hands them on a salver.*]

10   ALGERNON [*inspects them, takes two, and sits down on the sofa*]   Oh! . . . by the way, Lane, I see from your book that on Thursday night, when Lord Shoreham and Mr Worthing were dining with me, eight bottles of champagne are entered as having been consumed.

LANE   Yes, sir; eight bottles and a pint.

15   ALGERNON   Why is it that at a bachelor's establishment the servants invariably drink the champagne? I ask merely for information.

LANE   I attribute it to the superior quality of the wine, sir. I have often observed that in married households the champagne is rarely of a first-rate brand.

ALGERNON   Good Heavens! Is marriage so demoralizing as that?

20   LANE   I believe it *is* a very pleasant state, sir. I have had very little experience of it myself up to the present. I have only been married once. That was in consequence of a misunderstanding between myself and a young person.

---

1. Justice of the Peace.
2. Doctor of Divinity.
3. Located off Piccadilly Street in Mayfair, a fashionable district of London's West End.

Morning-room: an informal room for receiving morning visitors. Later visitors would be received in the more formal drawing room.

ALGERNON [*languidly*] I don't know that I am much interested in your family
life, Lane.

25 LANE No, sir; it is not a very interesting subject. I never think of it myself.

ALGERNON Very natural, I am sure. That will do, Lane, thank you.

LANE Thank you, sir.   [LANE *goes out.*]

ALGERNON Lane's views on marriage seem somewhat lax. Really, if the lower
orders don't set us a good example, what on earth is the use of them? They
30 seem, as a class, to have absolutely no sense of moral responsibility.

        [*Enter* LANE.]

LANE Mr Ernest Worthing.

        [*Enter* JACK.]   [LANE *goes out.*]

ALGERNON How are you, my dear Ernest? What brings you up to town?

JACK Oh, pleasure, pleasure! What else should bring one anywhere? Eating
as usual, I see, Algy!

35 ALGERNON [*stiffly*] I believe it is customary in good society to take some slight
refreshment at five o'clock. Where have you been since last Thursday?

JACK [*sitting down on the sofa*] In the country.

ALGERNON What on earth do you do there?

JACK [*pulling off his gloves*] When one is in town one amuses oneself. When
40 one is in the country one amuses other people. It is excessively boring.

ALGERNON And who are the people you amuse?

JACK [*airily*] Oh, neighbours, neighbours.

ALGERNON Got nice neighbours in your part of Shropshire?[4]

JACK Perfectly horrid! Never speak to one of them.

45 ALGERNON How immensely you must amuse them! [*Goes over and takes
sandwich.*] By the way, Shropshire is your county, is it not?

JACK Eh? Shropshire? Yes, of course. Hallo! Why all these cups? Why
cucumber sandwiches? Why such reckless extravagance in one so young?
Who is coming to tea?

50 ALGERNON Oh! merely Aunt Augusta and Gwendolen.

JACK How perfectly delightful!

ALGERNON Yes, that is all very well; but I am afraid Aunt Augusta won't quite
approve of your being here.

JACK May I ask why?

55 ALGERNON My dear fellow, the way you flirt with Gwendolen is perfectly
disgraceful. It is almost as bad as the way Gwendolen flirts with you.

JACK I am in love with Gwendolen. I have come up to town expressly to propose to her.

ALGERNON I thought you had come up for pleasure? . . . I call that business.

60 JACK How utterly unromantic you are!

ALGERNON I really don't see anything romantic in proposing. It is very
romantic to be in love. But there is nothing romantic about a definite proposal. Why, one may be accepted. One usually is, I believe. Then the
excitement is all over. The very essence of romance is uncertainty. If ever I
65 get married, I'll certainly try to forget the fact.

---

4. A county of England in the west Midlands, adjoining the Welsh border (about 150 miles
northwest of London).

JACK   I have no doubt about that, dear Algy. The Divorce Court was specially invented for people whose memories are so curiously constituted.

ALGERNON   Oh! there is no use speculating on that subject. Divorces are made in Heaven——[JACK *puts out his hand to take a sandwich.* ALGERNON
70   *at once interferes.*] Please don't touch the cucumber sandwiches. They are ordered specially for Aunt Augusta. [*Takes one and eats it.*]

JACK   Well, you have been eating them all the time.

ALGERNON   That is quite a different matter. She is my aunt. [*Takes plate from below.*] Have some bread and butter. The bread and butter is for Gwendo-
75   len. Gwendolen is devoted to bread and butter.

JACK   [*advancing to table and helping himself*]   And very good bread and butter it is too.

ALGERNON   Well, my dear fellow, you need not eat as if you were going to eat it all. You behave as if you were married to her already. You are not married
80   to her already, and I don't think you ever will be.

JACK   Why on earth do you say that?

ALGERNON   Well, in the first place girls never marry the men they flirt with. Girls don't think it right.

JACK   Oh, that is nonsense!

85   ALGERNON   It isn't. It is a great truth. It accounts for the extraordinary num- ber of bachelors that one sees all over the place. In the second place, I don't give my consent.

JACK   Your consent!

ALGERNON   My dear fellow, Gwendolen is my first cousin. And before I allow
90   you to marry her, you will have to clear up the whole question of Cecily. [*Rings bell.*]

JACK   Cecily! What on earth do you mean? What do you mean, Algy, by Cecily? I don't know anyone of the name of Cecily.

[*Enter* LANE.]

ALGERNON   Bring me that cigarette case Mr Worthing left in the smoking- room the last time he dined here.

95   LANE   Yes, sir.   [LANE *goes out.*]

JACK   Do you mean to say you have had my cigarette case all this time? I wish to goodness you had let me know. I have been writing frantic letters to Scotland Yard[5] about it. I was very nearly offering a large reward.

ALGERNON   Well, I wish you would offer one. I happen to be more than usu-
100   ally hard up.

JACK   There is no good offering a large reward now that the thing is found.

[*Enter* LANE *with the cigarette case on a salver.* ALGERNON *takes it at once.* LANE *goes out.*]

ALGERNON   I think that is rather mean of you, Ernest, I must say. [*Opens case and examines it.*] However, it makes no matter, for, now that I look at the inscription inside, I find that the thing isn't yours after all.

105   JACK   Of course it's mine. [*Moving to him*] You have seen me with it a hun- dred times, and you have no right whatsoever to read what is written inside. It is a very ungentlemanly thing to read a private cigarette case.

5. The headquarters of the London Metropolitan Police Force.

ALGERNON   Oh! it is absurd to have a hard-and-fast rule about what one should read and what one shouldn't. More than half of modern culture
110   depends on what one shouldn't read.

JACK   I am quite aware of the fact, and I don't propose to discuss modern culture. It isn't the sort of thing one should talk of in private. I simply want my cigarette case back.

ALGERNON   Yes; but this isn't your cigarette case. This cigarette case is a
115   present from someone of the name of Cecily, and you said you didn't know anyone of that name.

JACK   Well, if you want to know, Cecily happens to be my aunt.

ALGERNON   Your aunt!

JACK   Yes. Charming old lady she is, too. Lives at Tunbridge Wells.[6] Just give
120   it back to me, Algy.

ALGERNON   [retreating to back of sofa]   But why does she call herself little Cecily if she is your aunt and lives at Tunbridge Wells. [Reading] 'From little Cecily with her fondest love.'

JACK   [moving to sofa and kneeling upon it]   My dear fellow, what on earth is
125   there in that? Some aunts are tall, some aunts are not tall. That is a matter that surely an aunt may be allowed to decide for herself. You seem to think that every aunt should be exactly like your aunt! That is absurd! For Heaven's sake give me back my cigarette case. [Follows ALGERNON round the room.]

ALGERNON   Yes. But why does your aunt call you her uncle? 'From little
130   Cecily, with her fondest love to her dear Uncle Jack.' There is no objection, I admit, to an aunt being a small aunt, but why an aunt, no matter what her size may be, should call her own nephew her uncle, I can't quite make out. Besides, your name isn't Jack at all; it is Ernest.

JACK   It isn't Ernest; it's Jack.

135   ALGERNON   You have always told me it was Ernest. I have introduced you to everyone as Ernest. You answer to the name of Ernest. You look as if your name was Ernest. You are the most earnest looking person I ever saw in my life. It is perfectly absurd your saying that your name isn't Ernest. It's on your cards. Here is one of them. [Taking it from case] 'Mr Ernest Worthing, B. 4, The
140   Albany.'[7] I'll keep this as a proof that your name is Ernest if ever you attempt to deny it to me, or to Gwendolen, or to anyone else. [Puts the card in his pocket.]

JACK   Well, my name is Ernest in town and Jack in the country, and the cigarette case was given to me in the country.

ALGERNON   Yes, but that does not account for the fact that your small Aunt
145   Cecily, who lives at Tunbridge Wells, calls you her dear uncle. Come, old boy, you had much better have the thing out at once.

JACK   My dear Algy, you talk exactly as if you were a dentist. It is very vulgar to talk like a dentist when one isn't a dentist. It produces a false impression.

ALGERNON   Well, that is exactly what dentists always do. Now, go on! Tell me
150   the whole thing. I may mention that I have always suspected you of being a confirmed and secret Bunburyist, and I am quite sure of it now.

JACK   Bunburyist? What on earth do you mean by a Bunburyist?

ALGERNON   I'll reveal to you the meaning of that incomparable expression as soon as you are kind enough to inform me why you are Ernest in town and
155   Jack in the country.

6. A fashionable spa town in Kent, about 30 miles southeast of London.

7. Popular bachelors' quarters near Piccadilly Street, in central London.

JACK   Well, produce my cigarette case first.

ALGERNON   Here it is. [*Hands cigarette case.*] Now produce your explanation, and pray make it improbable. [*Sits on sofa.*]

JACK   My dear fellow, there is nothing improbable about my explanation at
160   all. In fact it's perfectly ordinary. Old Mr Thomas Cardew, who adopted me when I was a little boy, made me in his will guardian to his grand-daughter, Miss Cecily Cardew. Cecily who addresses me as her uncle from motives of respect that you could not possibly appreciate, lives at my place in the country under the charge of her admirable governess, Miss Prism.

165   ALGERNON   Where is that place in the country, by the way?

JACK   That is nothing to you, dear boy. You are not going to be invited. . . . I may tell you candidly that the place is not in Shropshire.

ALGERNON   I suspected that, my dear fellow! I have Bunburyed all over Shropshire on two separate occasions. Now, go on. Why are you Ernest in
170   town and Jack in the country?

JACK   My dear Algy, I don't know whether you will be able to understand my real motives. You are hardly serious enough. When one is placed in the position of guardian, one has to adopt a very high moral tone on all subjects. It's one's duty to do so. And as a high moral tone can hardly be said to
175   conduce very much to either one's health or one's happiness, in order to get up to town I have always pretended to have a younger brother of the name of Ernest, who lives in the Albany, and gets into the most dreadful scrapes. That, my dear Algy, is the whole truth pure and simple.

ALGERNON   The truth is rarely pure and never simple. Modern life would be
180   very tedious if it were either, and modern literature a complete impossibility!

JACK   That wouldn't be at all a bad thing.

ALGERNON   Literary criticism is not your forte, my dear fellow. Don't try it. You should leave that to people who haven't been at a University. They do it so well in the daily papers. What you really are is a Bunburyist. I was quite
185   right in saying you were a Bunburyist. You are one of the most advanced Bunburyists I know.

JACK   What on earth do you mean?

ALGERNON   You have invented a very useful younger brother called Ernest, in order that you may be able to come up to town as often as you like. I have
190   invented an invaluable permanent invalid called Bunbury, in order that I may be able to go down into the country whenever I choose. Bunbury is perfectly invaluable. If it wasn't for Bunbury's extraordinary bad health, for instance, I wouldn't be able to dine with you at Willis's[8] tonight, for I have been really engaged to Aunt Augusta for more than a week.

195   JACK   I haven't asked you to dine with me anywhere tonight.

ALGERNON   I know. You are absurdly careless about sending out invitations. It is very foolish of you. Nothing annoys people so much as not receiving invitations.

JACK   You had much better dine with your Aunt Augusta.

200   ALGERNON   I haven't the smallest intention of doing anything of the kind. To begin with, I dined there on Monday, and once a week is quite enough to dine with one's own relations. In the second place, whenever I do dine

---

8. A fashionable restaurant on King Street, near Piccadilly, frequented by Wilde and his companion Alfred Lord Douglas.

there I am always treated as a member of the family, and sent down[9] with either no woman at all, or two. In the third place, I know perfectly well
205 whom she will place me next to, tonight. She will place me next Mary Farquhar, who always flirts with her own husband across the dinner-table. That is not very pleasant. Indeed, it is not even decent . . . and that sort of thing is enormously on the increase. The amount of women in London who flirt with their own husbands is perfectly scandalous. It looks so bad.
210 It is simply washing one's clean linen in public. Besides, now that I know you to be a confirmed Bunburyist I naturally want to talk to you about Bunburying. I want to tell you the rules.

JACK   I'm not a Bunburyist at all. If Gwendolen accepts me, I am going to kill my brother, indeed I think I'll kill him in any case. Cecily is a little too
215 much interested in him. It is rather a bore. So I am going to get rid of Ernest. And I strongly advise you to do the same with Mr . . . with your invalid friend who has the absurd name.

ALGERNON   Nothing will induce me to part with Bunbury, and if you ever get married, which seems to me extremely problematic, you will be very glad
220 to know Bunbury. A man who marries without knowing Bunbury has a very tedious time of it.

JACK   That is nonsense. If I marry a charming girl like Gwendolen, and she is the only girl I ever saw in my life that I would marry, I certainly won't want to know Bunbury.

225 ALGERNON   Then your wife will. You don't seem to realize, that in married life three is company and two is none.

JACK [*sententiously*]   That, my dear young friend, is the theory that the corrupt French Drama[1] has been propounding for the last fifty years.

ALGERNON   Yes; and that the happy English home has proved in half the time.
230 JACK   For heaven's sake, don't try to be cynical. It's perfectly easy to be cynical.

ALGERNON   My dear fellow, it isn't easy to be anything nowadays. There's such a lot of beastly competition about. [*The sound of an electric bell is heard.*] Ah! that must be Aunt Augusta. Only relatives, or creditors, ever ring in that Wagnerian[2] manner. Now, if I get her out of the way for ten
235 minutes, so that you can have an opportunity for proposing to Gwendolen, may I dine with you tonight at Willis's?

JACK   I suppose so, if you want to.

ALGERNON   Yes, but you must be serious about it. I hate people who are not serious about meals. It is so shallow of them.

[*Enter* LANE.]

240 LANE   Lady Bracknell and Miss Fairfax.

[ALGERNON *goes forward to meet them. Enter* LADY BRACKNELL *and* GWENDOLEN.]

LADY BRACKNELL   Good afternoon, dear Algernon, I hope you are behaving very well.

ALGERNON   I'm feeling very well, Aunt Augusta.

9. Directed to accompany someone to dinner. Victorian dinner guests would gather upstairs in the drawing room, and then gentlemen would escort ladies to the dining room in arranged couples.
1. Because its plots frequently involved adultery and infidelity, French drama was often viewed by the English as immoral.
2. Loud and imposing, like the operas of the German composer Richard Wagner (1813–1883).

LADY BRACKNELL   That's not quite the same thing. In fact the two things
245   rarely go together. [*Sees* JACK *and bows to him with icy coldness.*]

ALGERNON [*to* GWENDOLEN]   Dear me, you are smart![3]

GWENDOLEN   I am always smart! Aren't I, Mr Worthing?

JACK   You're quite perfect, Miss Fairfax.

GWENDOLEN   Oh! I hope I am not that. It would leave no room for develop-
250   ments, and I intend to develop in many directions. [GWENDOLEN *and* JACK
   sit down together in the corner.]

LADY BRACKNELL   I'm sorry if we are a little late, Algernon, but I was obliged
   to call on dear Lady Harbury. I hadn't been there since her poor husband's
   death. I never saw a woman so altered; she looks quite twenty years
   younger. And now I'll have a cup of tea, and one of those nice cucumber
255   sandwiches you promised me.

ALGERNON   Certainly, Aunt Augusta. [*Goes over to tea-table.*]

LADY BRACKNELL   Won't you come and sit here, Gwendolen?

GWENDOLEN   Thanks, mamma, I'm quite comfortable where I am.

ALGERNON [*picking up empty plate in horror*]   Good heavens! Lane! Why are
260   there no cucumber sandwiches? I ordered them specially.

LANE [*gravely*]   There were no cucumbers in the market this morning, sir. I
   went down twice.

ALGERNON   No cucumbers!

LANE   No, sir. Not even for ready money.[4]

265 ALGERNON   That will do, Lane, thank you.

LANE   Thank you, sir.   [*Goes out.*]

ALGERNON   I am greatly distressed, Aunt Augusta, about there being no
   cucumbers, not even for ready money.

LADY BRACKNELL   It really makes no matter, Algernon. I had some crumpets
270   with Lady Harbury, who seems to me to be living entirely for pleasure now.

ALGERNON   I hear her hair has turned quite gold from grief.

LADY BRACKNELL   It certainly has changed its colour. From what cause I, of
   course, cannot say. [ALGERNON *crosses and hands tea.*] Thank you. I've quite
   a treat for you tonight, Algernon. I am going to send you down with Mary
275   Farquhar. She is such a nice woman, and so attentive to her husband. It's
   delightful to watch them.

ALGERNON   I am afraid, Aunt Augusta, I shall have to give up the pleasure of
   dining with you tonight after all.

LADY BRACKNELL [*frowning*]   I hope not, Algernon. It would put my table
280   completely out.[5] Your uncle would have to dine upstairs. Fortunately he is
   accustomed to that.

ALGERNON   It is a great bore, and, I need hardly say, a terrible disappointment to me, but the fact is I have just had a telegram to say that my poor
   friend Bunbury is very ill again. [*Exchanges glances with* JACK.] They seem
285   to think I should be with him.

LADY BRACKNELL   It is very strange. This Mr Bunbury seems to suffer from
   curiously bad health.

ALGERNON   Yes; poor Bunbury is a dreadful invalid.

---

3. Neatly stylish in appearance.
4. Immediate cash payment (the well-off often bought goods on credit).

5. That is, ruin the seating arrangement, which was always carefully planned to balance male and female guests.

LADY BRACKNELL   Well, I must say, Algernon, that I think it is high time that
290   Mr Bunbury made up his mind whether he was going to live or to die. This
shilly-shallying with the question is absurd. Nor do I in any way approve of
the modern sympathy with invalids. I consider it morbid. Illness of any kind
is hardly a thing to be encouraged in others. Health is the primary duty of
life. I am always telling that to your poor uncle, but he never seems to take
295   much notice . . . as far as any improvement in his ailments goes. I should be
much obliged if you would ask Mr Bunbury, from me, to be kind enough not
to have a relapse on Saturday, for I rely on you to arrange my music for me.
It is my last reception, and one wants something that will encourage conversation, particularly at the end of the season[6] when everyone has practically
300   said whatever they had to say, which, in most cases, was probably not much.
ALGERNON   I'll speak to Bunbury, Aunt Augusta, if he is still conscious, and I
think I can promise you he'll be all right by Saturday. Of course the music is
a great difficulty. You see, if one plays good music, people don't listen, and if
one plays bad music people don't talk. But I'll run over the programme I've
305   drawn out, if you will kindly come into the next room for a moment.
LADY BRACKNELL   Thank you, Algernon. It is very thoughtful of you. [*Rising, and following* ALGERNON] I'm sure the programme will be delightful,
after a few expurgations. French songs I cannot possibly allow. People
always seem to think that they are improper, and either look shocked,
310   which is vulgar, or laugh, which is worse. But German sounds a thoroughly respectable language, and indeed, I believe is so. Gwendolen, you
will accompany me.
GWENDOLEN   Certainly, mamma.

> [LADY BRACKNELL *and* ALGERNON *go into the music-room,* GWENDOLEN
> *remains behind.*]

JACK   Charming day it has been, Miss Fairfax.
315   GWENDOLEN   Pray don't talk to me about the weather, Mr Worthing. Whenever people talk to me about the weather, I always feel quite certain that
they mean something else. And that makes me so nervous.
JACK   I do mean something else.
GWENDOLEN   I thought so. In fact, I am never wrong.
320   JACK   And I would like to be allowed to take advantage of Lady Bracknell's
temporary absence . . .
GWENDOLEN   I would certainly advise you to do so. Mamma has a way of coming back suddenly into a room that I have often had to speak to her about.
JACK [*nervously*]   Miss Fairfax, ever since I met you I have admired you more
325   than any girl . . . I have ever met since . . . I met you.
GWENDOLEN   Yes, I am quite aware of the fact. And I often wish that in public, at any rate, you had been more demonstrative. For me you have always
had an irresistible fascination. Even before I met you I was far from
indifferent to you. [JACK *looks at her in amazement.*] We live, as I hope you
330   know, Mr Worthing, in an age of ideals. The fact is constantly mentioned
in the more expensive monthly magazines, and has reached the provincial
pulpits I am told: and my ideal has always been to love some one of the
name of Ernest. There is something in that name that inspires absolute

---

6. That is, the social season in London, which began in May and lasted through July; during this
time fashionable society attended balls, dinners, and other entertainments.

confidence. The moment Algernon first mentioned to me that he had a
335   friend called Ernest, I knew I was destined to love you.

JACK   You really love me, Gwendolen?

GWENDOLEN   Passionately!

JACK   Darling! You don't know how happy you've made me.

GWENDOLEN   My own Ernest!

340   JACK   But you don't really mean to say that you couldn't love me if my name
wasn't Ernest?

GWENDOLEN   But your name is Ernest.

JACK   Yes, I know it is. But supposing it was something else? Do you mean to
say you couldn't love me then?

345   GWENDOLEN   [glibly]   Ah! that is clearly a metaphysical speculation, and like
most metaphysical speculations has very little reference at all to the actual
facts of real life, as we know them.

JACK   Personally, darling, to speak quite candidly, I don't much care about
the name of Ernest . . . I don't think the name suits me at all.

350   GWENDOLEN   It suits you perfectly. It is a divine name. It has a music of its
own. It produces vibrations.

JACK   Well, really, Gwendolen, I must say that I think there are lots of other
much nicer names. I think Jack, for instance, a charming name.

GWENDOLEN   Jack? . . . No, there is very little music in the name Jack, if any
355   at all, indeed. It does not thrill. It produces absolutely no vibrations. . . . I
have known several Jacks, and they all, without exception, were more than
usually plain. Besides, Jack is a notorious domesticity[7] for John! And I pity
any woman who is married to a man called John. She would probably never
be allowed to know the entrancing pleasure of a single moment's solitude.
360   The only really safe name is Ernest.

JACK   Gwendolen, I must get christened at once—I mean we must get married at once. There is no time to be lost.

GWENDOLEN   Married, Mr Worthing?

JACK   [astounded]   Well . . . surely. You know that I love you, and you led me
365   to believe, Miss Fairfax, that you were not absolutely indifferent to me.

GWENDOLEN   I adore you. But you haven't proposed to me yet. Nothing has
been said at all about marriage. The subject has not even been touched on.

JACK   Well . . . may I propose to you now?

GWENDOLEN   I think it would be an admirable opportunity. And to spare you
370   any possible disappointment, Mr Worthing, I think it only fair to tell you
quite frankly beforehand that I am fully determined to accept you.

JACK   Gwendolen!

GWENDOLEN   Yes, Mr Worthing, what have you got to say to me?

JACK   You know what I have got to say to you.

375   GWENDOLEN   Yes, but you don't say it.

JACK   Gwendolen, will you marry me? [Goes on his knees.]

GWENDOLEN   Of course I will, darling. How long you have been about it! I am
afraid you have had very little experience in how to propose.

JACK   My own one, I have never loved anyone in the world but you.

380   GWENDOLEN   Yes, but men often propose for practice. I know my brother
Gerald does. All my girl-friends tell me so. What wonderfully blue eyes you

7. A domestic or familiar expression.

have, Ernest! They are quite, quite, blue. I hope you will always look at me just like that, especially when there are other people present.

[*Enter* LADY BRACKNELL.]

LADY BRACKNELL   Mr Worthing! Rise, sir, from this semi-recumbent posture.
385   It is most indecorous.

GWENDOLEN   Mamma! [*He tries to rise; she restrains him.*] I must beg you to retire. This is no place for you. Besides, Mr Worthing has not quite finished yet.

LADY BRACKNELL   Finished what, may I ask?

390   GWENDOLEN   I am engaged to Mr Worthing, mamma. [*They rise together.*]

LADY BRACKNELL   Pardon me, you are not engaged to anyone. When you do become engaged to some one, I, or your father, should his health permit him, will inform you of the fact. An engagement should come on a young girl as a surprise, pleasant or unpleasant, as the case may be. It is hardly a
395   matter that she could be allowed to arrange for herself. . . . And now I have a few questions to put to you, Mr Worthing. While I am making these inquiries, you, Gwendolen, will wait for me below in the carriage.

GWENDOLEN [*reproachfully*]   Mamma!

GWENDOLEN   In the carriage, Gwendolen! [GWENDOLEN *goes to the door. She and* JACK *blow kisses to each other behind* LADY BRACKNELL's *back.* LADY BRACKNELL *looks vaguely about as if she could not understand what the noise*
400   *was. Finally turns round.*] Gwendolen, the carriage!

GWENDOLEN   Yes, mamma.   [*Goes out, looking back at* JACK.]

LADY BRACKNELL [*sitting down*]   You can take a seat, Mr Worthing.

[*Looks in her pocket for note-book and pencil.*]

JACK   Thank you, Lady Bracknell, I prefer standing.

LADY BRACKNELL [*pencil and note-book in hand*]   I feel bound to tell you that
405   you are not down on my list of eligible young men, although I have the same list as the dear Duchess of Bolton has. We work together, in fact. However, I am quite ready to enter your name, should your answers be what a really affectionate mother requires. Do you smoke?

JACK   Well, yes, I must admit I smoke.

410   LADY BRACKNELL   I am glad to hear it. A man should always have an occupation of some kind. There are far too many idle men in London as it is. How old are you?

JACK   Twenty-nine.

LADY BRACKNELL   A very good age to be married at. I have always been of
415   opinion that a man who desires to get married should know either everything or nothing. Which do you know?

JACK [*after some hesitation*]   I know nothing, Lady Bracknell.

LADY BRACKNELL   I am pleased to hear it. I do not approve of anything that tampers with natural ignorance. Ignorance is like a delicate exotic fruit;
420   touch it and the bloom is gone. The whole theory of modern education is radically unsound. Fortunately in England, at any rate, education produces no effect whatsoever. If it did, it would prove a serious danger to the upper classes, and probably lead to acts of violence in Grosvenor Square.[8] What is your income?

8. A Mayfair neighborhood east of Speakers' Corner in Hyde Park.

425 JACK   Between seven and eight thousand[9] a year.

LADY BRACKNELL [makes a note in her book]   In land, or in investments?

JACK   In investments, chiefly.

LADY BRACKNELL   That is satisfactory. What between the duties expected of one during one's lifetime, and the duties exacted from one after one's death,[1]
430   land has ceased to be either a profit or a pleasure. It gives one position, and prevents one from keeping it up. That's all that can be said about land.

JACK   I have a country house with some land, of course, attached to it, about fifteen hundred acres, I believe; but I don't depend on that for my real income. In fact, as far as I can make out, the poachers are the only people
435   who make anything out of it.

LADY BRACKNELL   A country house! How many bedrooms? Well, that point can be cleared up afterwards. You have a town house, I hope? A girl with a simple, unspoiled nature, like Gwendolen, could hardly be expected to reside in the country.

440 JACK   Well, I own a house in Belgrave Square,[2] but it is let by the year to Lady Bloxham. Of course, I can get it back whenever I like, at six months' notice.

LADY BRACKNELL   Lady Bloxham? I don't know her.

JACK   Oh, she goes about very little. She is a lady considerably advanced in years.

445 LADY BRACKNELL   Ah, nowadays that is no guarantee of respectability of character. What number in Belgrave Square?

JACK   149.

LADY BRACKNELL [shaking her head]   The unfashionable side. I thought there was something. However, that could easily be altered.

450 JACK   Do you mean the fashion, or the side?

LADY BRACKNELL [sternly]   Both, if necessary, I presume. What are your politics?

JACK   Well, I am afraid I really have none. I am a Liberal Unionist.[3]

LADY BRACKNELL   Oh, they count as Tories. They dine with us. Or come in
455   the evening, at any rate. Now to minor matters. Are your parents living?

JACK   I have lost both my parents.

LADY BRACKNELL   Both? To lose one parent may be regarded as a misfortune—to lose both seems like carelessness. Who was your father? He was evidently a man of some wealth. Was he born in what the Radical
460   papers call the purple of commerce, or did he rise from the ranks of the aristocracy?

JACK   I am afraid I really don't know. The fact is, Lady Bracknell, I said I had lost my parents. It would be nearer the truth to say that my parents seem to have lost me . . . I don't actually know who I am by birth. I was . . . well,
465   I was found.

LADY BRACKNELL   Found!

JACK   The late Mr Thomas Cardew, an old gentleman of a very charitable and kindly disposition, found me, and gave me the name of Worthing, because

---

9. That is £7,000 to £8,000, roughly equivalent to $1 million today.
1. That is, inheritance taxes, a play on the secondary meaning of "duties."
2. The center of Belgravia, a fashionable neighborhood just west of Buckingham Palace.

3. The Liberal Unionists were a splinter group of the Liberal Party that joined with the Conservatives (known as the Tories) to defeat William Gladstone's Home Rule Bill of 1886, which would have granted political autonomy to Ireland.

he happened to have a first-class ticket for Worthing in his pocket at the
470 time. Worthing is a place in Sussex.[4] It is a seaside resort.

LADY BRACKNELL   Where did the charitable gentleman who had a first-class
ticket for this seaside resort find you?

JACK [gravely]   In a hand-bag.

LADY BRACKNELL   A hand-bag?

475 JACK [very seriously]   Yes, Lady Bracknell. I was in a hand-bag—a somewhat
large, black leather hand-bag, with handles to it—an ordinary hand-bag in
fact.

LADY BRACKNELL   In what locality did this Mr James, or Thomas, Cardew
come across this ordinary hand-bag?

480 JACK   In the cloak-room at Victoria Station.[5] It was given to him in mistake
for his own.

LADY BRACKNELL   The cloak-room at Victoria Station?

JACK   Yes. The Brighton line.[6]

LADY BRACKNELL   The line is immaterial. Mr Worthing, I confess I feel some
485 what bewildered by what you have just told me. To be born, or at any rate
bred, in a hand-bag, whether it had handles or not, seems to me to display
a contempt for the ordinary decencies of family life that reminds one of the
worst excesses of the French Revolution. And I presume you know what
that unfortunate movement led to? As for the particular locality in which
490 the hand-bag was found, a cloak-room at a railway station might serve to
conceal a social indiscretion—has probably, indeed, been used for that
purpose before now—but it could hardly be regarded as an assured basis
for a recognized position in good society.

JACK   May I ask you then what you would advise me to do? I need hardly say
495 I would do anything in the world to ensure Gwendolen's happiness.

LADY BRACKNELL   I would strongly advise you, Mr Worthing, to try and
acquire some relations as soon as possible, and to make a definite effort to
produce at any rate one parent, of either sex, before the season is quite
over.

500 JACK   Well, I don't see how I could possibly manage to do that. I can produce
the hand-bag at any moment. It is in my dressing-room at home. I really
think that should satisfy you, Lady Bracknell.

LADY BRACKNELL   Me, sir! What has it to do with me? You can hardly imagine
that I and Lord Bracknell would dream of allowing our only daughter—a
505 girl brought up with the utmost care—to marry into a cloak-room, and
form an alliance with a parcel? Good morning, Mr Worthing!

[LADY BRACKNELL sweeps out in majestic indignation.]

JACK   Good morning! [ALGERNON, from the other room, strikes up the Wedding March.[7] JACK looks perfectly furious, and goes to the door.] For goodness' sake don't play that ghastly tune, Algy! How idiotic you are!

[The music stops, and ALGERNON enters cheerily.]

---

4. Wilde, who frequently named characters
after places, wrote *The Importance of Being
Earnest* while vacationing with his family in
the coastal town of Worthing. Sussex is a
county south of London.
5. One of London's main rail stations, located
in Belgravia.
6. The rail line to Brighton, a popular seaside
resort in Sussex on England's south coast.
7. The recessional often played at weddings,
from Felix Mendelssohn's *A Midsummer
Night's Dream* (1842).

510 ALGERNON   Didn't it go off all right, old boy? You don't mean to say Gwendolen refused you? I know it is a way she has. She is always refusing people.
   I think it is most ill-natured of her.

   JACK   Oh, Gwendolen is as right as a trivet.[8] As far as she is concerned,
   we are engaged. Her mother is perfectly unbearable. Never met such a
515 Gorgon[9] . . . I don't really know what a Gorgon is like, but I am quite sure
   that Lady Bracknell is one. In any case, she is a monster, without being
   a myth, which is rather unfair . . . I beg your pardon, Algy, I suppose I
   shouldn't talk about your own aunt in that way before you.

   ALGERNON   My dear boy, I love hearing my relations abused. It is the only
520 thing that makes me put up with them at all. Relations are simply a tedious
   pack of people, who haven't got the remotest knowledge of how to live, nor
   the smallest instinct about when to die.

   JACK   Oh, that is nonsense!

   ALGERNON   It isn't!

525 JACK   Well, I won't argue about the matter. You always want to argue about
   things.

   ALGERNON   That is exactly what things were originally made for.

   JACK   Upon my word, if I thought that, I'd shoot myself . . . [A pause] You
   don't think there is any chance of Gwendolen becoming like her mother in
530 about a hundred and fifty years, do you Algy?

   ALGERNON   All women become like their mothers. That is their tragedy. No
   man does. That's his.

   JACK   Is that clever?

   ALGERNON   It is perfectly phrased! and quite as true as any observation in
535 civilized life should be.

   JACK   I am sick to death of cleverness. Everybody is clever nowadays. You
   can't go anywhere without meeting clever people. The thing has become an
   absolute public nuisance. I wish to goodness we had a few fools left.

   ALGERNON   We have.

540 JACK   I should extremely like to meet them. What do they talk about?

   ALGERNON   The fools? Oh! about the clever people, of course.

   JACK   What fools!

   ALGERNON   By the way, did you tell Gwendolen the truth about your being
   Ernest in town, and Jack in the country?

545 JACK [in a very patronizing manner]   My dear fellow, the truth isn't quite the
   sort of thing one tells to a nice sweet refined girl. What extraordinary ideas
   you have about the way to behave to a woman!

   ALGERNON   The only way to behave to a woman is to make love to her,[1] if she
   is pretty, and to someone else if she is plain.

550 JACK   Oh, that is nonsense.

   ALGERNON   What about your brother? What about the profligate Ernest?

   JACK   Oh, before the end of the week I shall have got rid of him. I'll say he died
   in Paris of apoplexy. Lots of people die of apoplexy, quite suddenly, don't they?

   ALGERNON   Yes, but it's hereditary, my dear fellow. It's a sort of thing that
555 runs in families. You had much better say a severe chill.

---

8. Proverbial expression for steadiness; a
trivet is a three-footed stand used to support
cooking vessels over a fire.
9. In Greek mythology, one of three snake-
haired sisters, the sight of whom turned all
who looked at them to stone.
1. That is, flirt with her, court her.

JACK   You are sure a severe chill isn't hereditary, or anything of that kind?

ALGERNON   Of course it isn't!

JACK   Very well, then. My poor brother Ernest is carried off suddenly in Paris, by a severe chill. That gets rid of him.

560 ALGERNON   But I thought you said that . . . Miss Cardew was a little too much interested in your poor brother Ernest? Won't she feel his loss a good deal?

JACK   Oh, that is all right. Cecily is not a silly romantic girl, I am glad to say. She has got a capital appetite, goes on long walks, and pays no attention at 565 all to her lessons.

ALGERNON   I would rather like to see Cecily.

JACK   I will take very good care you never do. She is excessively pretty, and she is only just eighteen.

ALGERNON   Have you told Gwendolen yet that you have an excessively pretty 570 ward who is only just eighteen?

JACK   Oh! one doesn't blurt these things out to people. Cecily and Gwendolen are perfectly certain to be extremely great friends. I'll bet you anything you like that half an hour after they have met, they will be calling each other sister.

575 ALGERNON   Women only do that when they have called each other a lot of other things first. Now, my dear boy, if we want to get a good table at Willis's, we really must go and dress. Do you know it is nearly seven?

JACK [irritably]   Oh! it always is nearly seven.

ALGERNON   Well, I'm hungry.

580 JACK   I never knew you when you weren't. . . .

ALGERNON   What shall we do after dinner? Go to a theatre?

JACK   Oh no! I loathe listening.

ALGERNON   Well, let us go to the Club?[2]

JACK   Oh, no! I hate talking.

585 ALGERNON   Well, we might trot round to the Empire[3] at ten?

JACK   Oh no! I can't bear looking at things. It is so silly.

ALGERNON   Well, what shall we do?

JACK   Nothing!

ALGERNON   It is awfully hard work doing nothing. However, I don't mind 590 hard work where there is no definite object of any kind.

[Enter LANE.]

LANE   Miss Fairfax.

[Enter GWENDOLEN. LANE goes out.]

ALGERNON   Gwendolen, upon my word!

GWENDOLEN   Algy, kindly turn your back. I have something very particular to say to Mr Worthing.

595 ALGERNON   Really, Gwendolen, I don't think I can allow this at all.

GWENDOLEN   Algy, you always adopt a strictly immoral attitude towards life. You are not quite old enough to do that.

[ALGERNON retires to the fireplace.]

2. Any one of a number of exclusive, members-only clubs for men.
3. The Empire Theatre of Varieties, a well-
known music hall in Leicester Square, a center of entertainments in London's West End.

JACK   My own darling!

GWENDOLEN   Ernest, we may never be married. From the expression on
600   mamma's face I fear we never shall. Few parents nowadays pay any regard
to what their children say to them. The old-fashioned respect for the young
is fast dying out. Whatever influence I ever had over mamma, I lost at the
age of three. But although she may prevent us from becoming man and
wife, and I may marry someone else, and marry often, nothing that she can
605   possibly do can alter my eternal devotion to you.

JACK   Dear Gwendolen!

GWENDOLEN   The story of your romantic origin, as related to me by mamma,
with unpleasing comments, has naturally stirred the deeper fibres of my
nature. Your Christian name has an irresistible fascination. The simplicity
610   of your character makes you exquisitely incomprehensible to me. Your
town address at the Albany I have. What is your address in the country?

JACK   The Manor House, Woolton, Hertfordshire.[4]

[ALGERNON, *who has been carefully listening, smiles to himself, and
writes the address on his shirt-cuff. Then picks up the Railway Guide.*]

GWENDOLEN   There is a good postal service, I suppose? It may be necessary
to do something desperate. That of course will require serious considera-
615   tion. I will communicate with you daily.

JACK   My own one!

GWENDOLEN   How long do you remain in town?

JACK   Till Monday.

GWENDOLEN   Good! Algy, you may turn round now.

620   ALGERNON   Thanks, I've turned round already.

GWENDOLEN   You may also ring the bell.

JACK   You will let me see you to your carriage, my own darling?

GWENDOLEN   Certainly.

JACK   [*to LANE, who now enters*]   I will see Miss Fairfax out.

625   LANE   Yes, sir.

[JACK *and* GWENDOLEN *go off.*]

[LANE *presents several letters on a salver to Algernon. It is to be surmised
that they are bills, as* ALGERNON, *after looking at the envelopes, tears
them up.*]

ALGERNON   A glass of sherry, Lane.

LANE   Yes, sir.

ALGERNON   Tomorrow, Lane, I'm going Bunburying.

LANE   Yes, sir.

630   ALGERNON   I shall probably not be back till Monday. You can put up my dress
clothes, my smoking jacket,[5] and all the Bunbury suits . . .

LANE   Yes, sir. [*Handing sherry*]

ALGERNON   I hope tomorrow will be a fine day, Lane.

LANE   It never is, sir.

635   ALGERNON   Lane, you're a perfect pessimist.

LANE   I do my best to give satisfaction, sir.

[*Enter* JACK. LANE *goes off.*]

---

4. A rural county just northeast of London.   usually in the evening. *Put up*: pack.
5. A loose-fitting casual jacket worn at home,

JACK   There's a sensible, intellectual girl! the only girl I ever cared for in my
life. [ALGERNON *is laughing immoderately.*] What on earth are you so
amused at?

640   ALGERNON   Oh, I'm a little anxious about poor Bunbury, that is all.

JACK   If you don't take care, your friend Bunbury will get you into a serious
scrape some day.

ALGERNON   I love scrapes. They are the only things that are never serious.

JACK   Oh, that's nonsense, Algy. You never talk anything but nonsense.

645   ALGERNON   Nobody ever does.

[JACK *looks indignantly at him, and leaves the room.* ALGERNON *lights a
cigarette, reads his shirt-cuff, and smiles.*]

Act Drop.[6]

Second Act

[SCENE: *Garden at the Manor House. A flight of gray stone steps leads up to the house.
The garden, an old-fashioned one, full of roses. Time of year, July. Basket chairs, and
a table covered with books, are set under a large yew tree.*]

[MISS PRISM *discovered seated at the table.* CECILY *is at the back watering
flowers.*]

MISS PRISM [*calling*]   Cecily, Cecily! Surely such a utilitarian occupation as
the watering of flowers is rather Moulton's duty[7] than yours? Especially
at a moment when intellectual pleasures await you. Your German grammar is on the table. Pray open it at page fifteen. We will repeat yesterday's
5   lesson.

CECILY [*coming over very slowly*]   But I don't like German. It isn't at all a
becoming language. I know perfectly well that I look quite plain after my
German lesson.

MISS PRISM   Child, you know how anxious your guardian is that you should
10   improve yourself in every way. He laid particular stress on your German,
as he was leaving for town yesterday. Indeed, he always lays stress on your
German when he is leaving for town.

CECILY   Dear Uncle Jack is so very serious! Sometimes he is so serious that I
think he cannot be quite well.

15   MISS PRISM [*drawing herself up*]   Your guardian enjoys the best of health, and
his gravity of demeanour is especially to be commended in one so comparatively young as he is. I know no one who has a higher sense of duty and
responsibility.

CECILY   I suppose that is why he often looks a little bored when we three are
20   together.

MISS PRISM   Cecily! I am surprised at you. Mr Worthing has many troubles in
his life. Idle merriment and triviality would be out of place in his conversation. You must remember his constant anxiety about that unfortunate
young man his brother.

25   CECILY   I wish Uncle Jack would allow that unfortunate young man, his
brother, to come down here sometimes. We might have a good influence
over him, Miss Prism. I am sure you certainly would. You know German,

6. The painted curtain lowered to indicate
divisions between acts or scenes.

7. The gardener Moulton appears in Wilde's
earlier, four-act version of the play.

and geology, and things of that kind influence a man very much. [CECILY *begins to write in her diary.*]

MISS PRISM [*shaking her head*]   I do not think that even I could produce any
effect on a character that according to his own brother's admission is
irretrievably weak and vacillating. Indeed I am not sure that I would desire
to reclaim him. I am not in favour of this modern mania for turning bad
people into good people at a moment's notice. As a man sows so let him
reap.[8] You must put away your diary, Cecily. I really don't see why you should
keep a diary at all.

CECILY   I keep a diary in order to enter the wonderful secrets of my life. If I
didn't write them down I should probably forget all about them.

MISS PRISM   Memory, my dear Cecily, is the diary that we all carry about
with us.

CECILY   Yes, but it usually chronicles the things that have never happened,
and couldn't possibly have happened. I believe that Memory is responsible
for nearly all the three-volume novels that Mudie[9] sends us.

MISS PRISM   Do not speak slightingly of the three-volume novel, Cecily. I
wrote one myself in earlier days.

CECILY   Did you really, Miss Prism? How wonderfully clever you are! I hope
it did not end happily? I don't like novels that end happily. They depress me
so much.

MISS PRISM   The good ended happily, and the bad unhappily. That is what
Fiction means.

CECILY   I suppose so. But it seems very unfair. And was your novel ever
published?

MISS PRISM   Alas! no. The manuscript unfortunately was abandoned. I use
the word in the sense of lost or mislaid.[1] To your work, child, these speculations are profitless.

CECILY [*smiling*]   But I see dear Dr Chasuble coming up through the garden.

MISS PRISM [*rising and advancing*]   Dr Chasuble! This is indeed a pleasure.

[*Enter* CANON CHASUBLE.]

CHASUBLE   And how are we this morning? Miss Prism, you are, I trust, well?

CECILY   Miss Prism has just been complaining of a slight headache. I think
it would do her so much good to have a short stroll with you in the Park,
Dr Chasuble.

MISS PRISM   Cecily, I have not mentioned anything about a headache.

CECILY   No, dear Miss Prism, I know that, but I felt instinctively that you had
a headache. Indeed I was thinking about that, and not about my German
lesson, when the Rector came in.

CHASUBLE   I hope Cecily, you are not inattentive.

CECILY   Oh, I am afraid I am.

CHASUBLE   That is strange. Were I fortunate enough to be Miss Prism's pupil,
I would hang upon her lips. [MISS PRISM *glares.*] I spoke metaphorically.—My

---

8. A New Testament proverb: "Be not deceived; God is not mocked: for whatsoever a man soweth, that shall he also reap" (Galatians 6.7).
9. Charles Edward Mudie (1818–1890), an English publisher who in 1842 founded a lending library that charged subscribers to borrow books; most Victorian fiction was published in three volumes (a practice that benefited for-fee libraries).
1. That is, not in the sense of "licentious" or "unrestrained."

metaphor was drawn from bees.[2] Ahem! Mr Worthing I suppose, has not
70   returned from town yet?

MISS PRISM   We do not expect him till Monday afternoon.

CHASUBLE   Ah yes, he usually likes to spend his Sunday in London. He is not
one of those whose sole aim is enjoyment, as, by all accounts, that unfortunate young man his brother seems to be. But I must not disturb Egeria
75   and her pupil any longer.

MISS PRISM   Egeria? My name is Lætitia,[3] Doctor.

CHASUBLE   [bowing]   A classical allusion merely, drawn from the Pagan
authors. I shall see you both no doubt at Evensong?[4]

MISS PRISM   I think, dear Doctor, I will have a stroll with you. I find I have a
80   headache after all, and a walk might do it good.

CHASUBLE   With pleasure, Miss Prism, with pleasure. We might go as far as
the schools and back.

MISS PRISM   That would be delightful. Cecily, you will read your Political
Economy in my absence. The chapter on the Fall of the Rupee[5] you may
85   omit. It is somewhat too sensational. Even these metallic problems have
their melodramatic side.[Goes down the garden with DR CHASUBLE.]

CECILY   [picks up books and throws them back on table]   Horrid Political
Economy! Horrid Geography! Horrid, horrid German!

[Enter MERRIMAN with a card on a salver.]

MERRIMAN   Mr Ernest Worthing has just driven over from the station. He
90   has brought his luggage with him.

CECILY [takes the card and reads it]   'Mr Ernest Worthing, B.4 The Albany,
W.' Uncle Jack's brother! Did you tell him Mr Worthing was in town?

MERRIMAN   Yes, Miss. He seemed very much disappointed. I mentioned that
you and Miss Prism were in the garden. He said he was anxious to speak to
95   you privately for a moment.

CECILY   Ask Mr Ernest Worthing to come here. I suppose you had better talk
to the housekeeper about a room for him.

MERRIMAN   Yes, Miss.   [MERRIMAN goes off.]

CECILY   I have never met any really wicked person before. I feel rather fright-
100   ened. I am so afraid he will look just like everyone else.

[Enter ALGERNON, very gay and debonnair.]

He does!

ALGERNON   [raising his hat]   You are my little cousin Cecily, I'm sure.

CECILY   You are under some strange mistake. I am not little. In fact, I believe
I am more than usually tall for my age. [ALGERNON is rather taken aback.]
105   But I am your cousin Cecily. You, I see from your card, are Uncle Jack's
brother, my cousin Ernest, my wicked cousin Ernest.

ALGERNON   Oh! I am not really wicked at all, cousin Cecily. You mustn't
think that I am wicked.

2. A reference to the honey of Miss Prism's
instruction.
3. A Latin name (literally, "beauty, grace, joy").
Egeria: in Roman mythology, one of the Cam-
enae (prophetic nymphs), said to have counseled Numa Pompilius, the legendary second
king of Rome; thus, any female adviser or
patron.
4. Evening church services.
5. India's currency had been declining in
value for a number of years. Political Economy: that is, an economics textbook.

CECILY   If you are not, then you have certainly been deceiving us all in a
110   very inexcusable manner. I hope you have not been leading a double life,
pretending to be wicked and being really good all the time. That would be
hypocrisy.

ALGERNON   [*looks at her in amazement*]   Oh! Of course I have been rather
reckless.

115   CECILY   I am glad to hear it.

ALGERNON   In fact, now you mention the subject, I have been very bad in my
own small way.

CECILY   I don't think you should be so proud of that, although I am sure it
must have been very pleasant.

120   ALGERNON   It is much pleasanter being here with you.

CECILY   I can't understand how you are here at all. Uncle Jack won't be back
till Monday afternoon.

ALGERNON   That is a great disappointment. I am obliged to go up by the
first train on Monday morning. I have a business appointment that I am
125   anxious . . . to miss.

CECILY   Couldn't you miss it anywhere but in London?

ALGERNON   No: the appointment is in London.

CECILY   Well, I know, of course, how important it is not to keep a business
engagement, if one wants to retain any sense of the beauty of life, but still
130   I think you had better wait till Uncle Jack arrives. I know he wants to speak
to you about your emigrating.

ALGERNON   About my what?

CECILY   Your emigrating. He has gone up to buy your outfit.

ALGERNON   I certainly wouldn't let Jack buy my outfit. He has no taste in
135   neckties at all.

CECILY   I don't think you will require neckties. Uncle Jack is sending you to
Australia.[6]

ALGERNON   Australia! I'd sooner die.

CECILY   Well, he said at dinner on Wednesday night, that you would have to
140   choose between this world, the next world, and Australia.

ALGERNON   Oh, well! The accounts I have received of Australia and the next
world, are not particularly encouraging. This world is good enough for me,
cousin Cecily.

CECILY   Yes, but are you good enough for it?

145   ALGERNON   I'm afraid I'm not that. That is why I want you to reform me. You
might make that your mission, if you don't mind, cousin Cecily.

CECILY   I'm afraid I've no time, this afternoon.

ALGERNON   Well, would you mind my reforming myself this afternoon?

CECILY   It is rather Quixotic[7] of you. But I think you should try.

150   ALGERNON   I will. I feel better already.

CECILY   You are looking a little worse.

ALGERNON   That is because I am hungry.

CECILY   How thoughtless of me. I should have remembered that when one
is going to lead an entirely new life, one requires regular and wholesome
155   meals. Won't you come in?

---

6. While Australia was no longer a penal colony in Wilde's day, it was still widely seen as a
place where disreputable family members

might be sent.
7. Impulsively idealistic, like the hero of Miguel
de Cervantes's *Don Quixote* (1605, 1615).

ALGERNON   Thank you. Might I have a buttonhole[8] first? I never have any appetite unless I have a buttonhole first.

CECILY   A Maréchal Niel?[9] [*Picks up scissors.*]

ALGERNON   No, I'd sooner have a pink rose.

160 CECILY   Why? [*Cuts a flower.*]

ALGERNON   Because you are like a pink rose, Cousin Cecily.

CECILY   I don't think it can be right for you to talk to me like that. Miss Prism never says such things to me.

ALGERNON   Then Miss Prism is a short-sighted old lady. [CECILY *puts the rose*
165 *in his buttonhole.*] You are the prettiest girl I ever saw.

CECILY   Miss Prism says that all good looks are a snare.

ALGERNON   They are a snare that every sensible man would like to be caught in.

CECILY   Oh! I don't think I would care to catch a sensible man. I shouldn't know what to talk to him about.

[*They pass into the house.* MISS PRISM *and* DR CHASUBLE *return.*]

170 MISS PRISM   You are too much alone, dear Dr Chasuble. You should get married. A misanthrope I can understand—a womanthrope, never!

CHASUBLE [*with a scholar's shudder*]   Believe me, I do not deserve so neologistic a phrase.[1] The precept as well as the practice of the Primitive Church was distinctly against matrimony.[2]

175 MISS PRISM [*sententiously*]   That is obviously the reason why the Primitive Church has not lasted up to the present day. And you do not seem to realize, dear Doctor, that by persistently remaining single, a man converts himself into a permanent public temptation. Men should be more careful; this very celibacy leads weaker vessels astray.

180 CHASUBLE   But is a man not equally attractive when married?

MISS PRISM   No married man is ever attractive except to his wife.

CHASUBLE   And often, I've been told, not even to her.

MISS PRISM   That depends on the intellectual sympathies of the woman. Maturity can always be depended on. Ripeness can be trusted. Young
185 women are green.[3] [DR CHASUBLE *starts.*] I spoke horticulturally. My metaphor was drawn from fruits. But where is Cecily?

CHASUBLE   Perhaps she followed us to the schools.

[*Enter* JACK *slowly from the back of the garden. He is dressed in the deepest mourning, with crape hat-band[4] and black gloves.*]

MISS PRISM   Mr Worthing!

CHASUBLE   Mr Worthing?

190 MISS PRISM   This is indeed a surprise. We did not look for you till Monday afternoon.

---

8. A flower worn in the lapel of a man's jacket.
9. A fragrant yellow rose, developed in France and first grown in England in 1864; it was named after Adolphe Niel, marshal of France under Napoleon III.
1. Chasuble is pained by the illogical coinage "womanthrope," which mixes Old English and Greek roots.
2. That is, the marriage of clergy (permitted in the Church of England). *The Primitive Church*: the Early Christian church. As his comment on celibacy indicates, the High Church Anglicanism practiced by Chasuble—whose name evokes a vestment worn during services—saw itself as maintaining that tradition.
3. Unripe, and thus inexperienced, easily deceived; understood by Chasuble as suffering from greensickness, an anemic condition found especially in adolescent girls and long believed to be caused by celibacy.
4. A band of crepe material, worn to signify mourning.

JACK [*shakes* MISS PRISM's *hand in a tragic manner*]   I have returned sooner than I expected. Dr Chasuble, I hope you are well?

CHASUBLE   Dear Mr Worthing, I trust this garb of woe does not betoken
195   some terrible calamity?

JACK   My brother.

MISS PRISM   More shameful debts and extravagance?

CHASUBLE   Still leading his life of pleasure?

JACK [*shaking his head*]   Dead!

200 CHASUBLE   Your brother Ernest dead?

JACK   Quite dead.

MISS PRISM   What a lesson for him! I trust he will profit by it.

CHASUBLE   Mr Worthing, I offer you my sincere condolence. You have at least the consolation of knowing that you were always the most generous
205   and forgiving of brothers.

JACK   Poor Ernest! He had many faults, but it is a sad, sad blow.

CHASUBLE   Very sad indeed. Were you with him at the end?

JACK   No. He died abroad; in Paris, in fact. I had a telegram last night from the manager of the Grand Hotel.[5]

210 CHASUBLE   Was the cause of death mentioned?

JACK   A severe chill, it seems.

MISS PRISM   As a man sows, so shall he reap.

CHASUBLE [*raising his hand*]   Charity, dear Miss Prism, charity! None of us are perfect. I myself am peculiarly susceptible to draughts. Will the inter-
215   ment take place here?

JACK   No. He seemed to have expressed a desire to be buried in Paris.

CHASUBLE   In Paris! [*Shakes his head.*] I fear that hardly points to any very seri-ous state of mind at the last. You would no doubt wish me to make some slight allusion to this tragic domestic affliction next Sunday. [JACK *presses his*
220   *hand convulsively.*] My sermon on the meaning of the manna in the wilder-ness[6] can be adapted to almost any occasion, joyful, or, as in the present case, distressing. [*All sigh.*] I have preached it at harvest celebrations, chris-tenings, confirmations, on days of humiliation and festal days. The last time I delivered it was in the Cathedral, as a charity sermon on behalf of the Soci-
225   ety for the Prevention of Discontent among the Upper Orders. The Bishop, who was present, was much struck by some of the analogies I drew.

JACK   Ah! that reminds me, you mentioned christenings I think, Dr Chasu-ble? I suppose you know how to christen all right? [DR CHASUBLE *looks astounded.*] I mean, of course, you are continually christening, aren't you?

230 MISS PRISM   It is, I regret to say, one of the Rector's most constant duties in this parish. I have often spoken to the poorer classes on the subject. But they don't seem to know what thrift is.

CHASUBLE   But is there any particular infant in whom you are interested, Mr Worthing? Your brother was, I believe, unmarried, was he not?

235 JACK   Oh, yes.

MISS PRISM [*bitterly*]   People who live entirely for pleasure usually are.

---

5. A luxurious Paris hotel.
6. The food said to have miraculously fallen

from heaven for the hungry Israelites when
they wandered in the wilderness (Exodus 16).

JACK   But it is not for any child, dear Doctor. I am very fond of children. No! the fact is, I would like to be christened myself, this afternoon, if you have nothing better to do.

240   CHASUBLE   But surely, Mr Worthing, you have been christened already?

JACK   I don't remember anything about it.

CHASUBLE   But have you any grave doubts on the subject?

JACK   I certainly intend to have. Of course I don't know if the thing would bother you in any way, or if you think I am a little too old now.

245   CHASUBLE   Not at all. The sprinkling, and, indeed, the immersion of adults is a perfectly canonical practice.

JACK   Immersion!

CHASUBLE   You need have no apprehensions. Sprinkling is all that is necessary, or indeed I think advisable. Our weather is so changeable. At what

250   hour would you wish the ceremony performed?

JACK   Oh, I might trot round about five if that would suit you.

CHASUBLE   Perfectly, perfectly! In fact I have two similar ceremonies to perform at that time. A case of twins that occurred recently in one of the outlying cottages on your own estate. Poor Jenkins the carter, a most hard-working man.

255   JACK   Oh! I don't see much fun in being christened along with other babies. It would be childish. Would half-past five do?

CHASUBLE   Admirably! Admirably! [*Takes out watch.*] And now, dear Mr Worthing, I will not intrude any longer into a house of sorrow. I would merely beg you not to be too much bowed down by grief. What seem to us

260   bitter trials are often blessings in disguise.

MISS PRISM   This seems to me a blessing of an extremely obvious kind.

[*Enter* CECILY *from the house.*]

CECILY   Uncle Jack! Oh, I am pleased to see you back. But what horrid clothes you have got on! Do go and change them.

MISS PRISM   Cecily!

265   CHASUBLE   My child! my child!

[CECILY *goes towards* JACK; *he kisses her brow in a melancholy manner.*]

CECILY   What is the matter, Uncle Jack? Do look happy! You look as if you had toothache, and I have got such a surprise for you. Who do you think is in the dining-room? Your brother!

JACK   Who?

270   CECILY   Your brother Ernest. He arrived about half an hour ago.

JACK   What nonsense! I haven't got a brother.

CECILY   Oh, don't say that. However badly he may have behaved to you in the past he is still your brother. You couldn't be so heartless as to disown him. I'll tell him to come out. And you will shake hands with him, won't

275   you, Uncle Jack?   [*Runs back into the house.*]

CHASUBLE   These are very joyful tidings.

MISS PRISM   After we had all been resigned to his loss, his sudden return seems to me peculiarly distressing.

JACK   My brother is in the dining-room? I don't know what it all means. I

280   think it is perfectly absurd.

[*Enter* ALGERNON *and* CECILY *hand in hand. They come slowly up to* JACK.]

JACK   Good heavens! [*Motions* ALGERNON *away.*]

ALGERNON   Brother John, I have come down from town to tell you that I am very sorry for all the trouble I have given you, and that I intend to lead a better life in the future.

[JACK *glares at him and does not take his hand.*]

285 CECILY   Uncle Jack, you are not going to refuse your own brother's hand?

JACK   Nothing will induce me to take his hand. I think his coming down here disgraceful. He knows perfectly well why.

CECILY   Uncle Jack, do be nice. There is some good in everyone. Ernest has just been telling me about his poor invalid friend Mr Bunbury whom he 290 goes to visit so often. And surely there must be much good in one who is kind to an invalid, and leaves the pleasures of London to sit by a bed of pain.

JACK   Oh! he has been talking about Bunbury has he?

CECILY   Yes, he has told me all about poor Mr Bunbury, and his terrible state of health.

295 JACK   Bunbury! Well, I won't have him talk to you about Bunbury or about anything else. It is enough to drive one perfectly frantic.

ALGERNON   Of course I admit that the faults were all on my side. But I must say that I think that Brother John's coldness to me is peculiarly painful. I expected a more enthusiastic welcome, especially considering it is the first 300 time I have come here.

CECILY   Uncle Jack, if you don't shake hands with Ernest I will never forgive you.

JACK   Never forgive me?

CECILY   Never, never, never!

305 JACK   Well, this is the last time I shall ever do it. [*Shakes hands with* ALGER-NON *and glares.*]

CHASUBLE   It's pleasant, is it not, to see so perfect a reconciliation? I think we might leave the two brothers together.

MISS PRISM   Cecily, you will come with us.

CECILY   Certainly, Miss Prism. My little task of reconciliation is over.

310 CHASUBLE   You have done a beautiful action today, dear child.

MISS PRISM   We must not be premature in our judgments.

CECILY   I feel very happy.

[*They all go off.*]

JACK   You young scoundrel, Algy, you must get out of this place as soon as possible. I don't allow any Bunburying here.

[*Enter* MERRIMAN.]

315 MERRIMAN   I have put Mr Ernest's things in the room next to yours, sir. I suppose that is all right?

JACK   What?

MERRIMAN   Mr Ernest's luggage, sir. I have unpacked it and put it in the room next to your own.

320 JACK   His luggage?

MERRIMAN   Yes, sir. Three portmanteaus, a dressing-case,[7] two hat-boxes, and a large luncheon-basket.

ALGERNON   I am afraid I can't stay more than a week this time.

7. A case for toiletries.

JACK   Merriman, order the dog-cart[8] at once. Mr Ernest has been suddenly
325   called back to town.

MERRIMAN   Yes, sir.   [*Goes back into the house.*]

ALGERNON   What a fearful liar you are, Jack. I have not been called back to
town at all.

JACK   Yes, you have.

330 ALGERNON   I haven't heard anyone call me.

JACK   Your duty as a gentleman calls you back.

ALGERNON   My duty as a gentleman has never interfered with my pleasures
in the smallest degree.

JACK   I can quite understand that.

335 ALGERNON   Well, Cecily is a darling.

JACK   You are not to talk of Miss Cardew like that. I don't like it.

ALGERNON   Well, I don't like your clothes. You look perfectly ridiculous in
them. Why on earth don't you go up and change? It is perfectly childish to
be in deep mourning for a man who is actually staying for a whole week
340   with you in your house as a guest. I call it grotesque.

JACK   You are certainly not staying with me for a whole week as a guest or
anything else. You have got to leave . . . by the four-five train.

ALGERNON   I certainly won't leave you so long as you are in mourning. It
would be most unfriendly. If I were in mourning you would stay with me, I
345   suppose. I should think it very unkind if you didn't.

JACK   Well, will you go if I change my clothes?

ALGERNON   Yes, if you are not too long. I never saw anybody take so long to
dress, and with such little result.

JACK   Well, at any rate, that is better than being always over-dressed as you are.

350 ALGERNON   If I am occasionally a little over-dressed, I make up for it by being
always immensely over-educated.

JACK   Your vanity is ridiculous, your conduct an outrage, and your presence
in my garden utterly absurd. However, you have got to catch the four-five,
and I hope you will have a pleasant journey back to town. This Bunburying,
355   as you call it, has not been a great success for you.   [*Goes into the house.*]

ALGERNON   I think it has been a great success. I'm in love with Cecily, and
that is everything.

> [*Enter* CECILY *at the back of the garden. She picks up the can and begins
> to water the flowers.*]

But I must see her before I go, and make arrangements for another Bunbury. Ah, there she is.

360 CECILY   Oh, I merely came back to water the roses. I thought you were with
Uncle Jack.

ALGERNON   He's gone to order the dog-cart for me.

CECILY   Oh, is he going to take you for a nice drive?

ALGERNON   He's going to send me away.

365 CECILY   Then have we got to part?

ALGERNON   I am afraid so. It's a painful parting.

CECILY   It is always painful to part from people whom one has known for a
very brief space of time. The absence of old friends one can endure with

---

8. A light, two-wheeled open carriage, originally designed with a small rear compartment to hold
sportsmen's dogs.

equanimity. But even a momentary separation from anyone to whom one
370   has just been introduced is almost unbearable.

ALGERNON   Thank you.

       [*Enter* MERRIMAN.]

MERRIMAN   The dog-cart is at the door, sir.

       [ALGERNON *looks appealingly at* CECILY.]

CECILY   It can wait, Merriman . . . for . . . five minutes.

MERRIMAN   Yes, Miss.   [*Exit* MERRIMAN.]

375 ALGERNON   I hope, Cecily, I shall not offend you if I state quite frankly and
openly that you seem to me to be in every way the visible personification of
absolute perfection.

CECILY   I think your frankness does you great credit, Ernest. If you will allow
me I will copy your remarks into my diary. [*Goes over to table and begins
writing in diary.*]

380 ALGERNON   Do you really keep a diary? I'd give anything to look at it. May I?

CECILY   Oh no. [*Puts her hand over it.*] You see, it is simply a very young girl's
record of her own thoughts and impressions, and consequently meant for
publication. When it appears in volume form I hope you will order a copy.
But pray, Ernest, don't stop. I delight in taking down from dictation. I have
385   reached 'absolute perfection'. You can go on. I am quite ready for more.

ALGERNON [*somewhat taken aback*]   Ahem! Ahem!

CECILY   Oh, don't cough, Ernest. When one is dictating one should speak
fluently and not cough. Besides, I don't know how to spell a cough. [*Writes
as* ALGERNON *speaks.*]

ALGERNON [*speaking very rapidly*]   Cecily, ever since I first looked upon your
390   wonderful and incomparable beauty, I have dared to love you wildly, passionately, devotedly, hopelessly.

CECILY   I don't think that you should tell me that you love me wildly, passionately, devotedly, hopelessly. Hopelessly doesn't seem to make much
sense, does it?

395 ALGERNON   Cecily!

       [*Enter* MERRIMAN.]

MERRIMAN   The dog-cart is waiting, sir.

ALGERNON   Tell it to come round next week, at the same hour.

MERRIMAN [*looks at* CECILY, *who makes no sign*]   Yes, sir. [MERRIMAN *retires.*]

CECILY   Uncle Jack would be very much annoyed if he knew you were stay-
400   ing on till next week, at the same hour.

ALGERNON   Oh, I don't care about Jack. I don't care for anybody in the whole
world but you. I love you, Cecily. You will marry me, won't you?

CECILY   You silly boy! Of course. Why, we have been engaged for the last
three months.

405 ALGERNON   For the last three months?

CECILY   Yes, it will be exactly three months on Thursday.

ALGERNON   But how did we become engaged?

CECILY   Well, ever since dear Uncle Jack first confessed to us that he had a
younger brother who was very wicked and bad, you of course have formed
410   the chief topic of conversation between myself and Miss Prism. And of
course a man who is much talked about is always very attractive. One feels
there must be something in him after all. I daresay it was foolish of me, but
I fell in love with you, Ernest.

ALGERNON Darling! And when was the engagement actually settled?

415 CECILY On the 14th of February last.[9] Worn out by your entire ignorance of my existence, I determined to end the matter one way or the other, and after a long struggle with myself I accepted you under this dear old tree here. The next day I bought this little ring in your name, and this is the little bangle with the true lovers' knot I promised you always to wear.

420 ALGERNON Did I give you this? It's very pretty, isn't it?

CECILY Yes, you've wonderfully good taste, Ernest. It's the excuse I've always given for your leading such a bad life. And this is the box in which I keep all your dear letters. [*Kneels at table, opens box, and produces letters tied up with blue ribbon.*]

ALGERNON My letters! But my own sweet Cecily, I have never written you 425 any letters.

CECILY You need hardly remind me of that, Ernest. I remember only too well that I was forced to write your letters for you. I wrote always three times a week, and sometimes oftener.

ALGERNON Oh, do let me read them, Cecily?

430 CECILY Oh, I couldn't possibly. They would make you far too conceited. [*Replaces box.*] The three you wrote me after I had broken off the engagement are so beautiful, and so badly spelled, that even now I can hardly read them without crying a little.

ALGERNON But was our engagement ever broken off?

435 CECILY Of course it was. On the 22nd of last March. You can see the entry if you like. [*Shows diary.*] 'Today I broke off my engagement with Ernest. I feel it is better to do so. The weather still continues charming.'

ALGERNON But why on earth did you break it off? What had I done? I had done nothing at all. Cecily, I am very much hurt indeed to hear you broke 440 it off. Particularly when the weather was so charming.

CECILY It would hardly have been a really serious engagement if it hadn't been broken off at least once. But I forgave you before the week was out.

ALGERNON [*crossing to her, and kneeling*] What a perfect angel you are, Cecily.

CECILY You dear romantic boy. [*He kisses her, she puts her fingers through his* 445 *hair.*] I hope your hair curls naturally, does it?

ALGERNON Yes, darling, with a little help from others.

CECILY I am so glad.

ALGERNON You'll never break off our engagement again, Cecily?

CECILY I don't think I could break it off now that I have actually met you. 450 Besides, of course, there is the question of your name.

ALGERNON Yes, of course. [*Nervously*]

CECILY You must not laugh at me, darling, but it had always been a girlish dream of mine to love some one whose name was Ernest. [ALGERNON *rises,* CECILY *also.*] There is something in that name that seems to inspire absolute 455 confidence. I pity any poor married woman whose husband is not called Ernest.

ALGERNON But, my dear child, do you mean to say you could not love me if I had some other name?

CECILY But what name?

9. Valentine's Day, also the date when *The Importance of Being Earnest* premiered at St. James's Theatre in 1895.

460 ALGERNON   Oh, any name you like—Algernon—for instance . . .

CECILY   But I don't like the name of Algernon.

ALGERNON   Well, my own dear, sweet, loving little darling, I really can't see why you should object to the name of Algernon. It is not at all a bad name. In fact, it is rather an aristocratic name. Half of the chaps who get into the 465 Bankruptcy Court are called Algernon. But seriously, Cecily . . . [*Moving to her*] . . . if my name was Algy, couldn't you love me?

CECILY [*rising*]   I might respect you, Ernest, I might admire your character, but I fear that I should not be able to give you my undivided attention.

ALGERNON   Ahem! Cecily! [*Picking up hat*] Your Rector here is, I suppose, 470 thoroughly experienced in the practice of all the rites and ceremonials of the Church?

CECILY   Oh yes. Dr Chasuble is a most learned man. He has never written a single book, so you can imagine how much he knows.

ALGERNON   I must see him at once on a most important christening—I mean 475 on most important business.

CECILY   Oh!

ALGERNON   I shan't be away more than half an hour.

CECILY   Considering that we have been engaged since February the 14th, and that I only met you today for the first time, I think it is rather hard that 480 you should leave me for so long a period as half an hour. Couldn't you make it twenty minutes?

ALGERNON   I'll be back in no time.   [*Kisses her and rushes down the garden.*]

CECILY   What an impetuous boy he is! I like his hair so much. I must enter his proposal in my diary.

[*Enter* MERRIMAN.]

485 MERRIMAN   A Miss Fairfax has just called to see Mr Worthing. On very important business Miss Fairfax states.

CECILY   Isn't Mr Worthing in his library?

MERRIMAN   Mr Worthing went over in the direction of the Rectory some time ago.

490 CECILY   Pray ask the lady to come out here; Mr Worthing is sure to be back soon. And you can bring tea.

MERRIMAN   Yes, Miss.   [*Goes out.*]

CECILY   Miss Fairfax! I suppose one of the many good elderly women who are associated with Uncle Jack in some of his philanthropic work in 495 London. I don't quite like women who are interested in philanthropic work. I think it is so forward of them.

[*Enter* MERRIMAN.]

MERRIMAN   Miss Fairfax.

[*Enter* GWENDOLEN.]   [*Exit* MERRIMAN.]

CECILY [*advancing to meet her*]   Pray let me introduce myself to you. My name is Cecily Cardew.

500 GWENDOLEN   Cecily Cardew? [*Moving to her and shaking hands*] What a very sweet name! Something tells me that we are going to be great friends. I like you already more than I can say. My first impressions of people are never wrong.

CECILY   How nice of you to like me so much after we have known each other 505 such a comparatively short time. Pray sit down.

GWENDOLEN [*still standing up*]   I may call you Cecily, may I not?

CECILY   With pleasure!

GWENDOLEN   And you will always call me Gwendolen, won't you.

CECILY   If you wish.

510 GWENDOLEN   Then that is all quite settled, is it not?

CECILY   I hope so.

[*A pause. They both sit down together.*]

GWENDOLEN   Perhaps this might be a favourable opportunity for my mentioning who I am. My father is Lord Bracknell. You have never heard of
515 papa, I suppose?

CECILY   I don't think so.

GWENDOLEN   Outside the family circle, papa, I am glad to say, is entirely unknown. I think that is quite as it should be. The home seems to me to be the proper sphere for the man.[1] And certainly once a man begins to neglect his domestic duties he becomes painfully effeminate, does he not? And I
520 don't like that. It makes men so very attractive. Cecily, mamma, whose views on education are remarkably strict, has brought me up to be extremely short-sighted; it is part of her system; so do you mind my looking at you through my glasses?

CECILY   Oh! not at all, Gwendolen. I am very fond of being looked at.

525 GWENDOLEN [*after examining* CECILY *carefully through a lorgnette*]   You are here on a short visit I suppose.

CECILY   Oh no! I live here.

GWENDOLEN [*severely*]   Really? Your mother, no doubt, or some female relative of advanced years, resides here also?

530 CECILY   Oh no! I have no mother, nor, in fact, any relations.

GWENDOLEN   Indeed?

CECILY   My dear guardian, with the assistance of Miss Prism, has the arduous task of looking after me.

GWENDOLEN   Your guardian?

535 CECILY   Yes, I am Mr Worthing's ward.

GWENDOLEN   Oh! It is strange he never mentioned to me that he had a ward. How secretive of him! He grows more interesting hourly. I am not sure, however, that the news inspires me with feelings of unmixed delight. [*Rising and going to her*] I am very fond of you, Cecily; I have liked you ever
540 since I met you! But I am bound to state that now that I know that you are Mr Worthing's ward, I cannot help expressing a wish you were—well just a little older than you seem to be—and not quite so very alluring in appearance. In fact, if I may speak candidly——

CECILY   Pray do! I think that whenever one has anything unpleasant to say,
545 one should always be quite candid.

GWENDOLEN   Well, to speak with perfect candour, Cecily, I wish that you were fully forty-two, and more than usually plain for your age. Ernest has a strong upright nature. He is the very soul of truth and honour. Disloyalty would be as impossible to him as deception. But even men of the noblest
550 possible moral character are extremely susceptible to the influence of the physical charms of others. Modern, no less than Ancient History, supplies

---

1. The 19th-century doctrine of separate spheres divided life into two domains: public (male) and private (female).

us with many most painful examples of what I refer to. If it were not so, indeed, History would be quite unreadable.

CECILY I beg your pardon, Gwendolen, did you say Ernest?

555 GWENDOLEN Yes.

CECILY Oh, but it is not Mr Ernest Worthing who is my guardian. It is his brother—his elder brother.

GWENDOLEN [*sitting down again*] Ernest never mentioned to me that he had a brother.

560 CECILY I am sorry to say they have not been on good terms for a long time.

GWENDOLEN Ah! that accounts for it. And now that I think of it I have never heard any man mention his brother. The subject seems distasteful to most men. Cecily, you have lifted a load from my mind. I was growing almost anxious. It would have been terrible if any cloud had come across a friend-
565 ship like ours, would it not? Of course you are quite, quite sure that it is not Mr Ernest Worthing who is your guardian?

CECILY Quite sure. [*A pause*] In fact, I am going to be his.

GWENDOLEN [*enquiringly*] I beg your pardon?

CECILY [*rather shy and confidingly*] Dearest Gwendolen, there is no reason
570 why I should make a secret of it to you. Our little county newspaper is sure to chronicle the fact next week. Mr Ernest Worthing and I are engaged to be married.

GWENDOLEN [*quite politely, rising*] My darling Cecily, I think there must be some slight error. Mr Ernest Worthing is engaged to me. The announce-
575 ment will appear in the 'Morning Post'[2] on Saturday at the latest.

CECILY [*very politely, rising*] I am afraid you must be under some misconcep-
tion. Ernest proposed to me exactly ten minutes ago. [*Shows diary.*]

GWENDOLEN [*examines diary through her lorgnette carefully*] It is certainly very curious, for he asked me to be his wife yesterday afternoon at 5.30.
580 If you would care to verify the incident, pray do so. [*Produces diary of her own.*] I never travel without my diary. One should always have something sensational to read in the train. I am so sorry, dear Cecily, if it is any disappointment to you, but I am afraid *I* have the prior claim.

CECILY It would distress me more than I can tell you, dear Gwendolen, if it
585 caused you any mental or physical anguish, but I feel bound to point out that since Ernest proposed to you he clearly has changed his mind.

GWENDOLEN [*meditatively*] If the poor fellow has been entrapped into any foolish promise I shall consider it my duty to rescue him at once, and with a firm hand.

590 CECILY [*thoughtfully and sadly*] Whatever unfortunate entanglement my dear boy may have got into, I will never reproach him with it after we are married.

GWENDOLEN Do you allude to me, Miss Cardew, as an entanglement? You are presumptuous. On an occasion of this kind it becomes more than a moral duty to speak one's mind. It becomes a pleasure.

595 CECILY Do you suggest, Miss Fairfax, that I entrapped Ernest into an engagement? How dare you? This is no time for wearing the shallow mask of manners. When I see a spade I call it a spade.

GWENDOLEN [*satirically*] I am glad to say that I have never seen a spade. It is obvious that our social spheres have been widely different.

---

2. The London *Morning Post*, a conservative daily newspaper.

[*Enter* MERRIMAN, *followed by the footman. He carries a salver, table cloth, and plate stand.* CECILY *is about to retort. The presence of the servants exercises a restraining influence, under which both girls chafe.*]

600 MERRIMAN Shall I lay tea here as usual, Miss?

CECILY [*sternly, in a calm voice*] Yes, as usual.

[MERRIMAN *begins to clear table and lay cloth. A long pause.* CECILY *and* GWENDOLEN *glare at each other.*]

GWENDOLEN Are there many interesting walks in the vicinity, Miss Cardew?

CECILY Oh! yes! a great many. From the top of one of the hills quite close one can see five counties.

605 GWENDOLEN Five counties! I don't think I should like that. I hate crowds.

CECILY [*sweetly*] I suppose that is why you live in town?

[GWENDOLEN *bites her lip, and beats her foot nervously with her parasol.*]

GWENDOLEN [*looking round*] Quite a well-kept garden this is, Miss Cardew.

CECILY So glad you like it, Miss Fairfax.

GWENDOLEN I had no idea there were any flowers in the country.

610 CECILY Oh, flowers are as common here, Miss Fairfax, as people are in London.

GWENDOLEN Personally, I cannot understand how anybody manages to exist in the country, if anybody who is anybody does. The country always bores me to death.

615 CECILY Ah! This is what the newspapers call agricultural depression,[3] is it not? I believe the aristocracy are suffering very much from it just at present. It is almost an epidemic amongst them, I have been told. May I offer you some tea, Miss Fairfax?

GWENDOLEN [*with elaborate politeness*] Thank you. [*Aside*] Detestable girl!
620 But I require tea!

CECILY [*sweetly*] Sugar?

GWENDOLEN [*superciliously*] No, thank you. Sugar is not fashionable any more.

[CECILY *looks angrily at her, takes up the tongs and puts four lumps of sugar into the cup.*]

CECILY [*severely*] Cake or bread and butter?

625 GWENDOLEN [*in a bored manner*] Bread and butter, please. Cake is rarely seen at the best houses nowadays.

CECILY [*cuts a very large slice of cake, and puts it on the tray*] Hand that to Miss Fairfax.

[MERRIMAN *does so, and goes out with footman.* GWENDOLEN *drinks the tea and makes a grimace. Puts down cup at once, reaches out her hand to the bread and butter, looks at it, and finds it is cake. Rises in indignation.*]

GWENDOLEN You have filled my tea with lumps of sugar, and though I asked
630 most distinctly for bread and butter, you have given me cake. I am known for the gentleness of my disposition, and the extraordinary sweetness of my nature, but I warn you, Miss Cardew, you may go too far.

CECILY [*rising*] To save my poor, innocent, trusting boy from the machinations of any other girl there are no lengths to which I would not go.

3. British agriculture had been in an economic slump since the 1870s.

635 GWENDOLEN   From the moment I saw you I distrusted you. I felt that you were false and deceitful. I am never deceived in such matters. My first impressions of people are invariably right.

CECILY   It seems to me, Miss Fairfax, that I am trespassing on your valuable time. No doubt you have many other calls of a similar character to make in
640   the neighbourhood.

[*Enter* JACK.]

GWENDOLEN [*catching sight of him*]   Ernest! My own Ernest!

JACK   Gwendolen! Darling! [*Offers*⁴ to kiss her.]

GWENDOLEN [*drawing back*]   A moment! May I ask if you are engaged to be married to this young lady? [*Points to* CECILY.]

645 JACK [*laughing*]   To dear little Cecily! Of course not! What could have put such an idea into your pretty little head?

GWENDOLEN   Thank you. You may! [*Offers her cheek.*]

CECILY [*very sweetly*]   I knew there must be some misunderstanding, Miss Fairfax. The gentleman whose arm is at present round your waist is my
650   dear guardian, Mr John Worthing.

GWENDOLEN   I beg your pardon?

CECILY   This is Uncle Jack.

GWENDOLEN [*receding*]   Jack! Oh!

[*Enter* ALGERNON.]

CECILY   Here is Ernest.

655 ALGERNON [*goes straight over to* CECILY *without noticing anyone else*]   My own love! [*Offers to kiss her.*]

CECILY [*drawing back*]   A moment, Ernest! May I ask you—are you engaged to be married to this young lady?

ALGERNON [*looking round*]   To what young lady? Good heavens! Gwendolen!

660 CECILY   Yes, to good heavens, Gwendolen, I mean to Gwendolen.

ALGERNON [*laughing*]   Of course not! What could have put such an idea into your pretty little head?

CECILY   Thank you. [*Presenting her cheek to be kissed*] You may.

[ALGERNON *kisses her.*]

GWENDOLEN   I felt there was some slight error, Miss Cardew. The gentleman
665   who is now embracing you is my cousin, Mr Algernon Moncrieff.

CECILY [*breaking away from* ALGERNON]   Algernon Moncrieff! Oh!

[*The two girls move towards each other and put their arms round each other's waists as if for protection.*]

CECILY   Are you called Algernon?

ALGERNON   I cannot deny it.

CECILY   Oh!

670 GWENDOLEN   Is your name really John?

JACK [*standing rather proudly*]   I could deny it if I liked. I could deny anything if I liked. But my name certainly is John. It has been John for years.

CECILY [*to* GWENDOLEN]   A gross deception has been practised on both of us.

GWENDOLEN   My poor wounded Cecily!

675 CECILY   My sweet wronged Gwendolen!

GWENDOLEN [*slowly and seriously*]   You will call me sister, will you not?

4. Attempts.

[*They embrace.* JACK *and* ALGERNON *groan and walk up and down.*]

CECILY [*rather brightly*]   There is just one question I would like to be allowed to ask my guardian.

GWENDOLEN   An admirable idea! Mr Worthing, there is just one question I
680   would like to be permitted to put to you. Where is your brother Ernest? We are both engaged to be married to your brother Ernest, so it is a matter of some importance to us to know where your brother Ernest is at present.

JACK [*slowly and hesitatingly*]   Gwendolen—Cecily—it is very painful for me
685   to be forced to speak the truth. It is the first time in my life that I have ever been reduced to such a painful position, and I am really quite inexperienced in doing anything of the kind. However I will tell you quite frankly that I have no brother Ernest. I have no brother at all. I never had a brother in my life, and I certainly have not the smallest intention of ever having
690   one in the future.

CECILY [*surprised*]   No brother at all?

JACK [*cheerily*]   None!

GWENDOLEN [*severely*]   Had you never a brother of any kind?

JACK [*pleasantly*]   Never. Not even of any kind.

695 GWENDOLEN   I am afraid it is quite clear, Cecily, that neither of us is engaged to be married to anyone.

CECILY   It is not a very pleasant position for a young girl suddenly to find herself in. Is it?

GWENDOLEN   Let us go into the house. They will hardly venture to come
700   after us there.

CECILY   No, men are so cowardly, aren't they?

[*They retire into the house with scornful looks.*]

JACK   This ghastly state of things is what you call Bunburying, I suppose?

ALGERNON   Yes, and a perfectly wonderful Bunbury it is. The most wonderful Bunbury I have ever had in my life.

705 JACK   Well, you've no right whatsoever to Bunbury here.

ALGERNON   That is absurd. One has a right to Bunbury anywhere one chooses. Every serious Bunburyist knows that.

JACK   Serious Bunburyist! Good heavens!

ALGERNON   Well, one must be serious about something, if one wants to have
710   any amusement in life. I happen to be serious about Bunburying. What on earth you are serious about I haven't got the remotest idea. About everything, I should fancy. You have such an absolutely trivial nature.

JACK   Well, the only small satisfaction I have in the whole of this wretched business is that your friend Bunbury is quite exploded. You won't be able to
715   run down to the country quite so often as you used to do, dear Algy. And a very good thing too.

ALGERNON   Your brother is a little off colour,[5] isn't he, dear Jack? You won't be able to disappear to London quite so frequently as your wicked custom was. And not a bad thing either.

720 JACK   As for your conduct towards Miss Cardew, I must say that your taking in a sweet, simple, innocent girl like that is quite inexcusable. To say nothing of the fact that she is my ward.

---

5. That is, in poor health.

ALGERNON   I can see no possible defence at all for your deceiving a brilliant, clever, thoroughly experienced young lady like Miss Fairfax. To say nothing
725   of the fact that she is my cousin.

JACK   I wanted to be engaged to Gwendolen, that is all. I love her.

ALGERNON   Well, I simply wanted to be engaged to Cecily. I adore her.

JACK   There is certainly no chance of your marrying Miss Cardew.

ALGERNON   I don't think there is much likelihood, Jack, of you and Miss
730   Fairfax being united.

JACK   Well, that is no business of yours.

ALGERNON   If it was my business, I wouldn't talk about it. [*Begins to eat muffins.*] It is very vulgar to talk about one's business. Only people like stock-brokers do that, and then merely at dinner parties.

735   JACK   How you can sit there, calmly eating muffins when we are in this horrible trouble, I can't make out. You seem to me to be perfectly heartless.

ALGERNON   Well, I can't eat muffins in an agitated manner. The butter would probably get on my cuffs. One should always eat muffins quite calmly. It is the only way to eat them.

740   JACK   I say it's perfectly heartless your eating muffins at all, under the circumstances.

ALGERNON   When I am in trouble, eating is the only thing that consoles me. Indeed, when I am in really great trouble, as anyone who knows me intimately will tell you, I refuse everything except food and drink. At the
745   present moment I am eating muffins because I am unhappy. Besides, I am particularly fond of muffins. [*Rising*]

JACK [*rising*]   Well, that is no reason why you should eat them all in that greedy way. [*Takes muffins from* ALGERNON.]

ALGERNON [*offering tea-cake*]   I wish you would have tea-cake instead. I
750   don't like tea-cake.

JACK   Good heavens! I suppose a man may eat his own muffins in his own garden.

ALGERNON   But you have just said it was perfectly heartless to eat muffins.

JACK   I said it was perfectly heartless of you, under the circumstances. That
755   is a very different thing.

ALGERNON   That may be. But the muffins are the same. [*He seizes the muffin-dish from* JACK.]

JACK   Algy, I wish to goodness you would go.

ALGERNON   You can't possibly ask me to go without having some dinner. It's absurd. I never go without my dinner. No one ever does, except vegetarians
760   and people like that. Besides I have just made arrangements with Dr Chasuble to be christened at a quarter to six under the name of Ernest.

JACK   My dear fellow, the sooner you give up that nonsense the better. I made arrangements this morning with Dr Chasuble to be christened myself at 5.30, and I naturally will take the name of Ernest. Gwendolen would
765   wish it. We can't both be christened Ernest. It's absurd. Besides, I have a perfect right to be christened if I like. There is no evidence at all that I ever have been christened by anybody. I should think it extremely probable I never was, and so does Dr Chasuble. It is entirely different in your case. You have been christened already.

770   ALGERNON   Yes, but I have not been christened for years.

JACK   Yes, but you have been christened. That is the important thing.

ALGERNON Quite so. So I know my constitution can stand it. If you are not quite sure about your ever having been christened, I must say I think it rather dangerous your venturing on it now. It might make you very unwell.

775 You can hardly have forgotten that someone very closely connected with you was very nearly carried off this week in Paris by a severe chill.

JACK Yes, but you said yourself that a severe chill was not hereditary.

ALGERNON It usen't to be, I know—but I daresay it is now. Science is always making wonderful improvements in things.

780 JACK [picking up the muffin-dish] Oh, that is nonsense; you are always talking nonsense.

ALGERNON Jack, you are at the muffins again! I wish you wouldn't. There are only two left. [Takes them.] I told you I was particularly fond of muffins.

JACK But I hate tea-cake.

785 ALGERNON Why on earth then do you allow tea-cake to be served up for your guests? What ideas you have of hospitality!

JACK Algernon! I have already told you to go. I don't want you here. Why don't you go!

ALGERNON I haven't quite finished my tea yet! and there is still one muffin
790 left.

[JACK groans, and sinks into a chair. ALGERNON still continues eating.]

Act Drop.

Third Act

[SCENE: Morning-room at the Manor House.]

[GWENDOLEN and CECILY are at the window, looking out into the garden.]

GWENDOLEN The fact that they did not follow us at once into the house, as anyone else would have done, seems to me to show that they have some sense of shame left.

CECILY They have been eating muffins. That looks like repentance.

5 GWENDOLEN [after a pause] They don't seem to notice us at all. Couldn't you cough?

CECILY But I haven't got a cough.

GWENDOLEN They're looking at us. What effrontery!

CECILY They're approaching. That's very forward of them.

10 GWENDOLEN Let us preserve a dignified silence.

CECILY Certainly. It's the only thing to do now.

[Enter JACK followed by ALGERNON. They whistle some dreadful popular air from a British Opera.[6]]

GWENDOLEN This dignified silence seems to produce an unpleasant effect.

CECILY A most distasteful one.

GWENDOLEN But we will not be the first to speak.

15 CECILY Certainly not.

GWENDOLEN Mr Worthing, I have something very particular to ask you. Much depends on your reply.

6. Possibly a reference to the comic operas of W. S. Gilbert (1836–1911) and Sir Arthur Sullivan (1842–1900), whose 1881 Patience satirized Wilde and the aesthetic movement.

CECILY   Gwendolen, your common sense is invaluable. Mr Moncrieff, kindly answer me the following question. Why did you pretend to be my guard-
20   ian's brother?

ALGERNON   In order that I might have an opportunity of meeting you.

CECILY [to GWENDOLEN]   That certainly seems a satisfactory explanation, does it not?

GWENDOLEN   Yes, dear, if you can believe him.

25 CECILY   I don't. But that does not affect the wonderful beauty of his answer.

GWENDOLEN   True. In matters of grave importance, style, not sincerity is the vital thing. Mr Worthing, what explanation can you offer to me for pretend-ing to have a brother? Was it in order that you might have an opportunity of coming up to town to see me as often as possible?

30 JACK   Can you doubt it, Miss Fairfax?

GWENDOLEN   I have the gravest doubts upon the subject. But I intend to crush them. This is not the moment for German scepticism.[7] [*Moving to* CECILY] Their explanations appear to be quite satisfactory, especially Mr Worthing's. That seems to me to have the stamp of truth upon it.

35 CECILY   I am more than content with what Mr Moncrieff said. His voice alone inspires one with absolute credulity.

GWENDOLEN   Then you think we should forgive them?

CECILY   Yes. I mean no.

GWENDOLEN   True! I had forgotten. There are principles at stake that one
40   cannot surrender. Which of us should tell them? The task is not a pleasant one.

CECILY   Could we not both speak at the same time?

GWENDOLEN   An excellent idea! I nearly always speak at the same time as other people. Will you take the time from me?

45 CECILY   Certainly.

[GWENDOLEN *beats time with uplifted finger.*]

GWENDOLEN and CECILY [*speaking together*]   Your Christian names are still an insuperable barrier. That is all!

JACK and ALGERNON [*speaking together*]   Our Christian names! Is that all? But we are going to be christened this afternoon.

50 GWENDOLEN [*to* JACK]   For my sake you are prepared to do this terrible thing?

JACK   I am.

CECILY [*to* ALGERNON]   To please me you are ready to face this fearful ordeal?

ALGERNON   I am!

GWENDOLEN   How absurd to talk of the equality of the sexes! Where ques-
55   tions of self-sacrifice are concerned, men are infinitely beyond us.

JACK   We are. [*Clasps hands with* ALGERNON.]

CECILY   They have moments of physical courage of which we women know absolutely nothing.

GWENDOLEN [*to* JACK]   Darling!

60 ALGERNON [*to* CECILY]   Darling! [*They fall into each other's arms.*]

[*Enter* MERRIMAN. *When he enters he coughs loudly, seeing the situation.*]

---

7. German biblical scholars of the 19th century were notorious among the British for their skepticism toward scriptural authority and claims of divine revelation.

MERRIMAN Ahem! Ahem! Lady Bracknell!

JACK Good heavens!

[*Enter* LADY BRACKNELL. *The couples separate in alarm.*]

[*Exit* MERRIMAN.]

LADY BRACKNELL Gwendolen! What does this mean?

GWENDOLEN Merely that I am engaged to be married to Mr Worthing,
65 mamma.

LADY BRACKNELL Come here. Sit down. Sit down immediately. Hesitation of
any kind is a sign of mental decay in the young, of physical weakness in the
old. [*Turns to* JACK.] Apprised, sir, of my daughter's sudden flight by her
trusty maid, whose confidence I purchased by means of a small coin, I fol-
70 lowed her at once by a luggage train.[8] Her unhappy father is, I am glad to
say, under the impression that she is attending a more than usually lengthy
lecture by the University Extension Scheme[9] on the Influence of a permanent income on Thought. I do not propose to undeceive him. Indeed I have
never undeceived him on any question. I would consider it wrong. But of
75 course, you will clearly understand that all communication between yourself and my daughter must cease immediately from this moment. On this
point, as indeed on all points, I am firm.

JACK I am engaged to be married to Gwendolen, Lady Bracknell!

LADY BRACKNELL You are nothing of the kind, sir. And now, as regards Alger-
80 non! . . . Algernon!

ALGERNON Yes, Aunt Augusta.

LADY BRACKNELL May I ask if it is in this house that your invalid friend Mr
Bunbury resides?

ALGERNON [*stammering*] Oh! No! Bunbury doesn't live here. Bunbury is
85 somewhere else at present. In fact, Bunbury is dead.

LADY BRACKNELL Dead! When did Mr Bunbury die? His death must have
been extremely sudden.

ALGERNON [*airily*] Oh! I killed Bunbury this afternoon. I mean poor Bunbury died this afternoon.

90 LADY BRACKNELL What did he die of?

ALGERNON Bunbury? Oh, he was quite exploded.

LADY BRACKNELL Exploded! Was he the victim of a revolutionary outrage? I
was not aware that Mr Bunbury was interested in social legislation. If so,
he is well punished for his morbidity.

95 ALGERNON My dear Aunt Augusta, I mean he was found out! The doctors
found out that Bunbury could not live, that is what I mean—so Bunbury
died.

LADY BRACKNELL He seems to have had great confidence in the opinion of his
physicians. I am glad, however, that he made up his mind at the last to some
100 definite course of action, and acted under proper medical advice. And now
that we have finally got rid of this Mr Bunbury, may I ask, Mr Worthing,
who is that young person whose hand my nephew Algernon is now holding
in what seems to me a peculiarly unnecessary manner?

JACK That lady is Miss Cecily Cardew, my ward.

[LADY BRACKNELL *bows coldly to* CECILY.]

---

8. Freight train.
9. An extramural education program in which

university instructors delivered lectures to
students not pursuing regular degrees.

105 ALGERNON   I am engaged to be married to Cecily, Aunt Augusta.

LADY BRACKNELL   I beg your pardon?

CECILY   Mr Moncrieff and I are engaged to be married, Lady Bracknell.

LADY BRACKNELL [*with a shiver, crossing to the sofa and sitting down*]   I do not
know whether there is anything peculiarly exciting in the air of this partic-
110   ular part of Hertfordshire, but the number of engagements that go on
seems to me considerably above the proper average that statistics have laid
down for our guidance. I think some preliminary enquiry on my part would
not be out of place. Mr Worthing, is Miss Cardew at all connected with any
of the larger railway stations in London? I merely desire information. Until
115   yesterday I had no idea that there were any families or persons whose
origin was a Terminus.[1]

[JACK *looks perfectly furious, but restrains himself.*]

JACK [*in a clear, cold voice*]   Miss Cardew is the granddaughter of the late
Mr Thomas Cardew of 149, Belgrave Square, S.W.; Gervase Park, Dorking,
Surrey; and the Sporran, Fifeshire, N.B.[2]

120   LADY BRACKNELL   That sounds not unsatisfactory. Three addresses always
inspire confidence, even in tradesmen. But what proof have I of their
authenticity?

JACK   I have carefully preserved the Court Guides[3] of the period. They are
open to your inspection, Lady Bracknell.

125   LADY BRACKNELL [*grimly*]   I have known strange errors in that publication.

JACK   Miss Cardew's family solicitors are Messrs[4] Markby, Markby, and
Markby.

LADY BRACKNELL   Markby, Markby, and Markby? A firm of the very highest
position in their profession. Indeed I am told that one of the Mr Markbys
130   is occasionally to be seen at dinner parties. So far I am satisfied.

JACK [*very irritably*]   How extremely kind of you, Lady Bracknell! I have also
in my possession, you will be pleased to hear, certificates of Miss Cardew's
birth, baptism, whooping cough, registration, vaccination, confirmation,
and the measles; both the German and the English variety.[5]

135   LADY BRACKNELL   Ah! A life crowded with incident, I see; though perhaps
somewhat too exciting for a young girl. I am not myself in favour of premature experiences. [*Rises, looks at her watch.*] Gwendolen! the time
approaches for our departure. We have not a moment to lose. As a matter
of form, Mr Worthing, I had better ask you if Miss Cardew has any little
140   fortune?

JACK   Oh! about a hundred and thirty thousand pounds in the Funds.[6] That
is all. Goodbye, Lady Bracknell. So pleased to have seen you.

LADY BRACKNELL [*sitting down again*]   A moment, Mr Worthing. A hundred
and thirty thousand pounds! And in the Funds! Miss Cardew seems to me

---

1. The station at the end of a railway line.
2. That is, with residences in Belgravia, in a
county south of London, and in Scotland
("North Britain").
3. Annual publications listing the names and
addresses of those presented at court—that
is, the British nobility, gentry, and anyone else
of social importance.

4. The plural of "Mister." *Solicitors:* British
lawyers who advise and represent clients but
do not argue cases in court.
5. That is, both rubeola and rubella.
6. Interest-bearing government bonds—and a
considerable fortune (roughly equivalent to
$20 million today).

145 a most attractive young lady, now that I look at her. Few girls of the present day have any really solid qualities, any of the qualities that last, and improve with time. We live, I regret to say, in an age of surfaces. [*To* CECILY] Come over here, dear. [CECILY *goes across.*] Pretty child! your dress is sadly simple, and your hair seems almost as Nature might have left it. But we

150 can soon alter all that. A thoroughly experienced French maid produces a really marvellous result in a very brief space of time. I remember recommending one to young Lady Lancing, and after three months her own husband did not know her.

JACK [*aside*] And after six months nobody knew her.[7]

LADY BRACKNELL [*glares at* JACK *for a few moments. Then bends, with a practised*

155 *smile, to* CECILY] Kindly turn round, sweet child. [CECILY *turns completely round.*] No, the side view is what I want. [CECILY *presents her profile.*] Yes, quite as I expected. There are distinct social possibilities in your profile. The two weak points in our age are its want of principle and its want of profile. The chin a little higher, dear. Style largely depends on the way the chin is

160 worn. They are worn very high, just at present. Algernon!

ALGERNON Yes, Aunt Augusta!

LADY BRACKNELL There are distinct social possibilities in Miss Cardew's profile.

ALGERNON Cecily is the sweetest, dearest, prettiest girl in the whole world.

165 And I don't care twopence about social possibilities.

LADY BRACKNELL Never speak disrespectfully of Society, Algernon. Only people who can't get into it do that. [*To* CECILY] Dear child, of course you know that Algernon has nothing but his debts to depend upon. But I do not approve of mercenary marriages. When I married Lord Bracknell I had no

170 fortune of any kind. But I never dreamed for a moment of allowing that to stand in my way. Well, I suppose I must give my consent.

ALGERNON Thank you, Aunt Augusta.

LADY BRACKNELL Cecily, you may kiss me!

CECILY [*kisses her*] Thank you, Lady Bracknell.

175 LADY BRACKNELL You may also address me as Aunt Augusta for the future.

CECILY Thank you, Aunt Augusta.

LADY BRACKNELL The marriage, I think, had better take place quite soon.

ALGERNON Thank you, Aunt Augusta.

CECILY Thank you, Aunt Augusta.

180 LADY BRACKNELL To speak frankly, I am not in favour of long engagements. They give people the opportunity of finding out each other's character before marriage, which I think is never advisable.

JACK I beg your pardon for interrupting you, Lady Bracknell, but this engagement is quite out of the question. I am Miss Cardew's guardian, and

185 she cannot marry without my consent until she comes of age. That consent I absolutely decline to give.

LADY BRACKNELL Upon what grounds may I ask? Algernon is an extremely, I may almost say an ostentatiously, eligible young man. He has nothing, but he looks everything. What more can one desire?

190 JACK It pains me very much to have to speak frankly to you, Lady Bracknell, about your nephew, but the fact is that I do not approve at all of his moral character. I suspect him of being untruthful.

---

7. Acknowledged her socially (i.e., her behavior had become scandalous).

[ALGERNON *and* CECILY *look at him in indignant amazement.*]

LADY BRACKNELL   Untruthful! My nephew Algernon? Impossible! He is an Oxonian.[8]

195 JACK   I fear there can be no possible doubt about the matter. This afternoon, during my temporary absence in London on an important question of romance, he obtained admission to my house by means of the false pretense of being my brother. Under an assumed name he drank, I've just been informed by my butler, an entire pint bottle of my Perrier-Jouet, Brut, '89;[9] a

200 wine I was specially reserving for myself. Continuing his disgraceful deception, he succeeded in the course of the afternoon in alienating the affections of my only ward. He subsequently stayed to tea, and devoured every single muffin. And what makes his conduct all the more heartless is, that he was perfectly well aware from the first that I have no brother, that I never had a

205 brother, and that I don't intend to have a brother, not even of any kind. I distinctly told him so myself yesterday afternoon.

LADY BRACKNELL   Ahem! Mr Worthing, after careful consideration I have decided entirely to overlook my nephew's conduct to you.

JACK   That is very generous of you, Lady Bracknell. My own decision, how-

210 ever, is unalterable. I decline to give my consent.

LADY BRACKNELL   [*to* CECILY]   Come here, sweet child. [CECILY *goes over.*] How old are you, dear?

CECILY   Well, I am really only eighteen, but I always admit to twenty when I go to evening parties.

215 LADY BRACKNELL   You are perfectly right in making some slight alteration. Indeed, no woman should ever be quite accurate about her age. It looks so calculating. . . . [*In a meditative manner*] Eighteen, but admitting to twenty at evening parties. Well, it will not be very long before you are of age and free from the restraints of tutelage. So I don't think your guardian's con-

220 sent is, after all, a matter of any importance.

JACK   Pray excuse me, Lady Bracknell, for interrupting you again, but it is only fair to tell you that according to the terms of her grandfather's will Miss Cardew does not come legally of age till she is thirty-five.

LADY BRACKNELL   That does not seem to me to be a grave objection. Thirty-

225 five is a very attractive age. London society is full of women of the very highest birth who have, of their own free choice, remained thirty-five for years. Lady Dumbleton is an instance in point. To my own knowledge she has been thirty-five ever since she arrived at the age of forty, which was many years ago now. I see no reason why our dear Cecily should not be

230 even still more attractive at the age you mention than she is at present. There will be a large accumulation of property.

CECILY   Algy, could you wait for me till I was thirty-five?

ALGERNON   Of course I could, Cecily. You know I could.

CECILY   Yes, I felt it instinctively, but I couldn't wait all that time. I hate wait-

235 ing even five minutes for anybody. It always makes me rather cross. I am not punctual myself, I know, but I do like punctuality in others, and waiting, even to be married, is quite out of the question.

ALGERNON   Then what is to be done, Cecily?

CECILY   I don't know, Mr Moncrieff.

8. A student at or graduate of Oxford University.   9. A particularly fine vintage of dry champagne.

240 LADY BRACKNELL   My dear Mr Worthing, as Miss Cardew states positively
that she cannot wait till she is thirty-five—a remark which I am bound to
say seems to me to show a somewhat impatient nature—I would beg of you
to reconsider your decision.

JACK   But my dear Lady Bracknell, the matter is entirely in your own hands.
245 The moment you consent to my marriage with Gwendolen, I will most
gladly allow your nephew to form an alliance with my ward.

LADY BRACKNELL [*rising and drawing herself up*]   You must be quite aware
that what you propose is out of the question.

JACK   Then a passionate celibacy is all that any of us can look forward to.
250 LADY BRACKNELL   That is not the destiny I propose for Gwendolen. Algernon,
of course, can choose for himself. [*Pulls out her watch.*] Come, dear;
[GWENDOLEN *rises.*] we have already missed five, if not six, trains. To miss
any more might expose us to comment on the platform.

[*Enter* DR CHASUBLE.]

CHASUBLE   Everything is quite ready for the christenings.
255 LADY BRACKNELL   The christenings, sir! Is not that somewhat premature?

CHASUBLE [*looking rather puzzled, and pointing to* JACK *and* ALGERNON]   Both
these gentlemen have expressed a desire for immediate baptism.

LADY BRACKNELL   At their age? The idea is grotesque and irreligious! Algernon, I forbid you to be baptized. I will not hear of such excesses. Lord
260 Bracknell would be highly displeased if he learned that that was the way in
which you wasted your time and money.

CHASUBLE   Am I to understand then that there are to be no christenings at
all this afternoon?

JACK   I don't think that, as things are now, it would be of much practical
265 value to either of us, Dr Chasuble.

CHASUBLE   I am grieved to hear such sentiments from you, Mr Worthing.
They savour of the heretical views of the Anabaptists,[1] views that I have
completely refuted in four of my unpublished sermons. However, as your
present mood seems to be one peculiarly secular, I will return to the
270 church at once. Indeed, I have just been informed by the pew-opener[2] that
for the last hour and a half Miss Prism has been waiting for me in the
vestry.

LADY BRACKNELL [*starting*]   Miss Prism! Did I hear you mention a Miss
Prism?
275 CHASUBLE   Yes, Lady Bracknell. I am on my way to join her.

LADY BRACKNELL   Pray allow me to detain you for a moment. This matter
may prove to be one of vital importance to Lord Bracknell and myself.
Is this Miss Prism a female of repellent aspect, remotely connected with
education?
280 CHASUBLE [*somewhat indignantly*]   She is the most cultivated of ladies, and
the very picture of respectability.

LADY BRACKNELL   It is obviously the same person. May I ask what position
she holds in your household?

---

1. Members of a radical Protestant sect, established in Germany in the 16th century, that advocated the baptism only of adult believers (*Anabaptist* literally means "one who baptizes over again"); the label was sometimes applied pejoratively to Baptists or to others who rejected Anglican doctrine.

2. An usher who unlocked the private pews provided by many churches.

PLAYS IN PERFORMANCE

OEDIPUS THE KING

Gerard Murphy (Oedipus), Joanne Pearce (Antigone) with Chorus at the Royal Shakespeare Company production of Sophocles' *Oedipus at Colonus* (part of the so-called Theban cycle, of which *Oedipus the King* is also a part) at the Swan Theatre, Stratford-upon-Avon, England (October 25, 1991). Members of the Chorus in this production wear masks, mimicking the conventions of classical productions. © Donald Cooper / Photostage

Oedipus the King is one of the most important plays in Western drama, and it continues to inspire directors, playwrights, and audiences around the world. At the same time, it is a Greek tragedy that was written for a theater that is very different from ours. No matter whether directors modernize the play or hark back to the very origins of theater, they must first study the particular type of Greek theater for which this play was originally written.

Classical Greek tragedy was performed in massive outdoor theaters (there were up to 20,000 seats at the theater at Epidaurus, for example) during annual civic festivals. The scale of the theaters required a highly stylized form of acting that in no way resembles modern realistic performance. Three performers played all the speaking parts, a feat achieved by having actors play multiple roles distinguished by the use of large masks. While the episodes composed of dialogue, such as Oedipus's confrontations with Tiresias and Creon, may resemble contemporary drama, modern audiences often have difficulty appreciating the Greek chorus. Perhaps that barrier becomes more manageable if one recognizes that the classical chorus has many similarities with a modern musical theater chorus: both provide background information that clarifies past events and relationships; both comment on the actions of the principal characters; and both move rhythmically around the stage.

Greek audiences also knew the myths and legends dramatized by the playwrights. In addition to participating in a civic and religious occasion, audiences could also appreciate a particular playwright's variation or take on an old story, noticing nuances and new emphases.

Tragedies like *Oedipus the King* confront many of the most basic questions of human existence: Why does the universe seem so cruel and indifferent to human

The National Theatre of Greece's 2000 production of *Oedipus the King*.
© Alberto Pizzoli / Sygma / Corbis

Ralph Fiennes (as Oedipus, standing) and Alan Howard (as Tiresias, lying on table) perform with artists of the company (as the Chorus) in England's Royal National Theatre's 2008 production. © Robbie Jack / Corbis

suffering? What is our responsibility in this unfolding drama of life? The audience's identification with these universal dilemmas evokes a primal sense of pity and fear.

To assess modern productions, one can ask if those primal emotions are evoked and how that is accomplished. In 1954, director Tyrone Guthrie, founder of the Stratford Shakespeare Festival in Ontario, Canada, chose to create a highly stylized version of *Oedipus the King* in order to re-create the solemn, religious nature of the drama. He got the audience's attention at the beginning of the production by having a violent explosion shake the theater. The stage filled with smoke and incense, and eventually the chorus emerged from this cloud. Dressed in earth-toned rags, their faces were covered with gray, skeletal masks that one reviewer compared to Edvard Munch's painting *The Scream*.[1] The principal characters all wore heavily padded and draped costumes, gloves, masks, and elevated boots (*kothurni*), making them appear larger than life. In place of possessing individual qualities, each character became an abstraction: King, Queen, Prophet.

Guthrie's interpretation of the play as a primitive, tribal ritual was, by all

1. Laurel Bowman, "Sophocles' Oedipus Rex," *Didaskalia* 4.1 (Spring 1997), www.didaskalia.net /issues/vol4no1/bowmana.html, (accessed 4/16/13).

accounts, highly effective. Oedipus's transition from the golden, powerful king to a blood-stained exile led away by his daughters at the play's end managed to evoke pity and terror in audiences.

The National Theatre of Greece's 2000 production of *Oedipus the King* used the physical immensity of the Roman Colosseum as its backdrop. This production, marking the reopening of that formidable space after a partial restoration, was the first drama to be performed in the colosseum in fifteen hundred years. After its world premiere in Rome, the production then toured to other sites, including the ancient theater at Epidaurus and New York's City Center.

In contrast to Guthrie's ritualized production with its emphasis on the Chorus, the National Theatre's production focused on the figure of Oedipus himself. Through staging and costume choices, Oedipus was entirely separated from those around him: as king he is distinct from the chorus, and as outcast he is isolated from both family and society. It was this existential isolation that evoked pity and fear in audiences.

After more than twenty-four hundred years, *Oedipus the King* remains the ultimate detective story capable of stirring strong emotions in modern audiences. Whether the director chooses to focus on religious ceremony or on individual isolation as a strategy for seeking answers to Oedipus's mystery, Sophocles' masterpiece still resonates with modern audiences searching for their own place in the world.

M.P.

EVERYMAN

The Royal Shakespeare Company's 1996 production of *Everyman*, directed by Kathryn Hunter and Marcello Magni, featuring Joseph Mydell (center, holding staff) as the eponymous central character. © Donald Cooper / Photostage

Everyman, a staple of university, community, and professional productions, has established itself as the most popular medieval play in the modern theatrical repertoire. After a period of several centuries during which *Everyman* was not produced, twentieth-century audiences were reintroduced to the play in 1901, when William Poel, founder of the English Stage Company, presented an outdoor production of *Everyman* in the courtyard of the Charterhouse, a former Carthusian monastery in London. The production, which was taken on tour under different directors in Britain and the United States between 1901 and the 1930s, was enormously successful, although some audience members were scandalized by the representation of God onstage, which many considered sacrilegious.

Originating in the medieval morality play tradition, *Everyman* presents unique challenges to modern directors, actors, and audiences. With characters named "Everyman," "Fellowship," and "Good Deeds," the play employs an allegorical structure largely at odds with the realism that dominates modern characterization,

Everyman, played by Ajay Naidu, undergoes penance for his sins in the 1995 production staged by Chicago's Steppenwolf Theatre Company and directed by Frank Galati. © Michael Brosilow / Steppenwolf Theatre

plot, and setting. Its action lacks the stage or diversions that characterize other English morality plays, and the theological doctrine it advances reflects a late medieval, rather than a contemporary, belief system. The task of modern productions, therefore, is to bring *Everyman* to life for contemporary spectators.

The 1993 Broadway debut of *Angels in America*. © Joan Marcus

Throughout this development and production process in the United States, several key cast members remained in place: Stephen Spinella as Prior Walter, Kathleen Chalfant as Hannah Pitt, and Ellen McLaughlin as The Angel. The continuity provided by these actors must surely have anchored the productions and contributed markedly to their success in so many different theaters and with so many creative teams. Yet some critics who saw the play in both small and large venues also expressed a preference for the simpler productions on smaller stages, which made the theatrical experience more immediate. Michael Feingold of the *Village Voice* felt Wolfe's production exuded "flat, neat efficiency."[6] And Frank Rich clearly preferred the National's version to that of the Taper, which he deemed "plodding."[7] Yet, despite such quibbles, critics unanimously championed Kushner's writing and the scope of the drama. As Malcolm Rutherford of London's *Financial Times* concluded, "You should see this play, for even if you loathe it, you will love discussing it afterwards."[8]

J.E.G.

6. Michael Feingold, "Building the Monolith," *Village Voice*, May 18, 1993.

7. Frank Rich, "Marching Out of the Closet, into History," *New York Times*, Nov. 10, 1992.

8. Malcolm Rutherford, "Arts: A Drama Out of a Crisis," *Financial Times*, Jan. 25, 1992.

CHASUBLE [*severely*]   I am a celibate, madam.

285 JACK [*interposing*]   Miss Prism, Lady Bracknell, has been for the last three years Miss Cardew's esteemed governess and valued companion.

LADY BRACKNELL   In spite of what I hear of her, I must see her at once. Let her be sent for.

CHASUBLE [*looking off*]   She approaches; she is nigh.

[*Enter* MISS PRISM *hurriedly.*]

290 MISS PRISM   I was told you expected me in the vestry, dear Canon. I have been waiting for you there for an hour and three quarters. [*Catches sight of* LADY BRACKNELL *who has fixed her with a stony glare.* MISS PRISM *grows pale and quails. She looks anxiously round as if desirous to escape.*]

LADY BRACKNELL [*in a severe, judicial voice*]   Prism! [MISS PRISM *bows her head in shame.*] Come here, Prism! [MISS PRISM *approaches in a humble manner.*] Prism! Where is that baby? [*General consternation. The* CANON *starts back in horror.* ALGERNON *and* JACK *pretend to be anxious to shield* CECILY *and* GWENDOLEN *from hearing the details of a terrible public scan-* 295 *dal.*] Twenty-eight years ago, Prism, you left Lord Bracknell's house, Number 104, Upper Grosvenor Street, in charge of a perambulator[3] that contained a baby, of the male sex. You never returned. A few weeks later, through the elaborate investigations of the Metropolitan police, the perambulator was discovered at midnight, standing by itself in a remote corner of 300 Bayswater.[4] It contained the manuscript of a three-volume novel of more than usually revolting sentimentality. [MISS PRISM *starts in involuntary indignation.*] But the baby was not there! [*Everyone looks at* MISS PRISM.] Prism! Where is that baby? [*A pause.*]

MISS PRISM   Lady Bracknell, I admit with shame that I do not know. I only 305 wish I did. The plain facts of the case are these. On the morning of the day you mention, a day that is for ever branded on my memory, I prepared as usual to take the baby out in its perambulator. I had also with me a somewhat old, but capacious hand-bag in which I had intended to place the manuscript of a work of fiction that I had written during my few unoccu- 310 pied hours. In a moment of mental abstraction, for which I never can forgive myself, I deposited the manuscript in the bassinette, and placed the baby in the hand-bag.

JACK [*who has been listening attentively*]   But where did you deposit the hand-bag?

315 MISS PRISM   Do not ask me, Mr Worthing.

JACK   Miss Prism, this is a matter of no small importance to me. I insist on knowing where you deposited the hand-bag that contained that infant.

MISS PRISM   I left it in the cloak-room of one of the larger railway stations in London.

320 JACK   What railway station?

MISS PRISM [*quite crushed*]   Victoria. The Brighton line. [*Sinks into a chair.*]

JACK   I must retire to my room for a moment. Gwendolen, wait here for me.

GWENDOLEN   If you are not too long, I will wait here for you all my life.

[*Exit* JACK *in great excitement.*]

3. Baby carriage (pram).
4. A fashionable residential area of west London, north of Kensington Gardens.

CHASUBLE   What do you think this means, Lady Bracknell?

325 LADY BRACKNELL   I dare not even suspect, Dr Chasuble. I need hardly tell you that in families of high position strange coincidences are not supposed to occur. They are hardly considered the thing.

[*Noises heard overhead as if someone was throwing trunks about. Everyone looks up.*]

CECILY   Uncle Jack seems strangely agitated.

CHASUBLE   Your guardian has a very emotional nature.

330 LADY BRACKNELL   This noise is extremely unpleasant. It sounds as if he was having an argument. I dislike arguments of any kind. They are always vulgar, and often convincing.

CHASUBLE [*looking up*]   It has stopped now. [*The noise is redoubled.*]

LADY BRACKNELL   I wish he would arrive at some conclusion.

335 GWENDOLEN   This suspense is terrible. I hope it will last.

[*Enter* JACK *with a hand-bag of black leather in his hand.*]

JACK [*rushing over to* MISS PRISM]   Is this the hand-bag, Miss Prism? Examine it carefully before you speak. The happiness of more than one life depends on your answer.

MISS PRISM [*calmly*]   It seems to be mine. Yes, here is the injury it received
340   through the upsetting of a Gower Street omnibus[5] in younger and happier days. Here is the stain on the lining caused by the explosion of a temperance beverage, an incident that occurred at Leamington.[6] And here, on the lock, are my initials. I had forgotten that in an extravagant mood I had had them placed there. The bag is undoubtedly mine. I am delighted to have it
345   so unexpectedly restored to me. It has been a great inconvenience being without it all these years.

JACK [*in a pathetic voice*]   Miss Prism, more is restored to you than this hand-bag. I was the baby you placed in it.

MISS PRISM [*amazed*]   You?

350 JACK [*embracing her*]   Yes . . . mother!

MISS PRISM [*recoiling in indignant astonishment*]   Mr Worthing! I am unmarried!

JACK   Unmarried! I do not deny that is a serious blow. But after all, who has the right to cast a stone[7] against one who has suffered? Cannot repentance
355   wipe out an act of folly? Why should there be one law for men, and another for women. Mother, I forgive you. [*Tries to embrace her again.*]

MISS PRISM [*still more indignant*]   Mr Worthing, there is some error. [*Pointing to* LADY BRACKNELL] There is the lady who can tell you who you really are.

JACK [*after a pause*]   Lady Bracknell, I hate to seem inquisitive, but would
360   you kindly inform me who I am?

LADY BRACKNELL   I am afraid that the news I have to give you will not altogether please you. You are the son of my poor sister, Mrs Moncrieff, and consequently Algernon's elder brother.

5. Public carriage (bus). *Gower Street*: a street in the Bloomsbury section of central London (where the University of London and the British Museum are located).
6. Royal Leamington Spa, in Warwickshire, about 100 miles northwest of London. *Tem-* *perance beverage*: in the 1890s, carbonated soda drinks were marketed as wholesome alternatives to alcohol.
7. That is, condemn a sinner—in the phrase's original context, a woman caught committing adultery (see John 8.7).

JACK   Algy's elder brother! Then I have a brother after all. I knew I had a
365   brother! I always said I had a brother! Cecily—how could you have ever
doubted that I had a brother. [*Seizes hold of* ALGERNON.] Dr Chasuble, my
unfortunate brother. Miss Prism, my unfortunate brother. Gwendolen,
my unfortunate brother. Algy, you young scoundrel, you will have to treat
me with more respect in the future. You have never behaved to me like a
370   brother in all your life.

ALGERNON   Well, not till today, old boy, I admit. I did my best, however, though
I was out of practice. [*Shakes hands.*]

GWENDOLEN [*to* JACK]   My own! But what own are you? What is your Christian
name, now that you have become someone else?

375 JACK   Good heavens! . . . I had quite forgotten that point. Your decision on
the subject of my name is irrevocable, I suppose?

GWENDOLEN   I never change, except in my affections.

CECILY   What a noble nature you have, Gwendolen!

JACK   Then the question had better be cleared up at once. Aunt Augusta, a
380   moment. At the time when Miss Prism left me in the hand-bag, had I been
christened already?

LADY BRACKNELL   Every luxury that money could buy, including christening,
had been lavished on you by your fond and doting parents.

JACK   Then I was christened! That is settled. Now, what name was I given?
385   Let me know the worst.

LADY BRACKNELL   Being the eldest son you were naturally christened after
your father.

JACK [*irritably*]   Yes, but what was my father's Christian name?

LADY BRACKNELL [*meditatively*]   I cannot at the present moment recall what
390   the General's Christian name was. But I have no doubt he had one. He was
eccentric, I admit. But only in later years. And that was the result of the
Indian climate, and marriage, and indigestion, and other things of that kind.

JACK   Algy! Can't you recollect what our father's Christian name was?

ALGERNON   My dear boy, we were never even on speaking terms. He died
395   before I was a year old.

JACK   His name would appear in the Army Lists[8] of the period, I suppose, Aunt
Augusta?

LADY BRACKNELL   The General was essentially a man of peace, except in his
domestic life. But I have no doubt his name would appear in any military
400   directory.

JACK   The Army Lists of the last forty years are here. These delightful records
should have been my constant study. [*Rushes to bookcase and tears the
books out.*] M. Generals . . . Mallam, Maxbohm, Magley, what ghastly
names they have—Markby, Migsby, Mobbs, Moncrieff! Lieutenant 1840,
405   Captain, Lieutenant-Colonel, Colonel, General 1869, Christian names,
Ernest John. [*Puts book very quietly down and speaks quite calmly.*] I always
told you, Gwendolen, my name was Ernest, didn't I? Well, it is Ernest after
all. I mean it naturally is Ernest.

LADY BRACKNELL   Yes, I remember now that the General was called Ernest.
410   I knew I had some particular reason for disliking the name.

8. The official lists of all the commissioned officers in the army.

GWENDOLEN   Ernest! My own Ernest! I felt from the first that you could have
no other name!

JACK   Gwendolen, it is a terrible thing for a man to find out suddenly that all
his life he has been speaking nothing but the truth. Can you forgive me?

415   GWENDOLEN   I can. For I feel that you are sure to change.

JACK   My own one!

CHASUBLE [to MISS PRISM]   Lætitia! [Embraces her.]

MISS PRISM [enthusiastically]   Frederick! At last!

ALGERNON   Cecily! [Embraces her.] At last!

420   JACK   Gwendolen! [Embraces her.] At last!

LADY BRACKNELL   My nephew, you seem to be displaying signs of triviality.

JACK   On the contrary, Aunt Augusta, I've now realized for the first time in
my life the vital Importance of Being Earnest.

Tableau.[9]

Curtain.

---

9. That is, a tableau vivant: having characters freeze in a final pose as the curtain fell was a vogue
in 19th-century theater.

ANTON CHEKHOV
1860–1904

Anton Chekhov, who died four years after the dawn of the new century, casts a long shadow over the history of modern theater. The greatest dramatist the Russian stage has ever seen, he stands as a central figure in the emergence of twentieth-century drama. At first glance, Chekhov may seem an unlikely candidate for this historical role. Inheriting a tradition of Russian fiction that included such literary monuments as Fyodor Dostoevsky's novel *Crime and Punishment* (1866) and Leo Tolstoy's *War and Peace* (1865–89), Chekhov achieved his initial literary reputation through the writing of novellas and short stories rather than drama. Of the dozen and a half plays that he wrote, the majority are comic one acts, and those on which his reputation chiefly rests—*The Seagull, Uncle Vanya, The Three Sisters*, and THE CHERRY ORCHARD—are only four in number and were written relatively late in his career. In Chekhov's case, though, numbers are misleading, for the dramatic terrain that these plays opened up proved so innovative that their influence can be felt more than a century after his death. Rewriting the aesthetic of theatrical realism through a drama of understatement, indirection, and psychological nuance, Chekhov's major plays offer a new vision of the relationship between theater and everyday life.

Chekhov was born on January 17, 1860, in Taganrog, a small seaport on the Sea of Azov (a northern arm of the Black Sea) in southern Russia. His father was a merchant and his paternal grandfather a serf who had purchased his freedom and that of his family in 1841. Only one generation removed from serfdom, Chekhov remained acutely aware of his background: in an autobiographical letter to his friend and publisher Alexei Suvorin in 1889, he described an imaginary character who, after squeezing the slave blood out of himself "drop by drop," awakes one day to find that "the blood coursing through his veins is no longer that of a slave but that of a real human being." After attending local schools, he graduated in 1879 with a scholarship for university study. Chekhov's father had moved the rest of his family to Moscow three years earlier in order to escape debtor's prison, and when Anton joined them he enrolled at the Moscow University School of Medicine, from which he earned a degree at the age of twenty-four. Although Chekhov soon gave up private practice to focus on writing, his medical training remained an essential part of his personal and professional identity. "Medicine is my lawful wife and literature is my mistress," he later commented. "When I get tired of one I go to the other." He continued to treat patients, often for free, and he demonstrated a lifelong interest in matters of public health. During the famine and cholera epidemic of 1892–93, he served as head of a district sanitary committee and treated many of the epidemic's poorest victims.

Chekhov began writing in his teens. He edited a school newspaper and, encouraged by his older brothers, wrote humorous anecdotes and sketches. By the time he graduated from medical school, he was publishing comic sketches, parodies, dialogues, and short stories in small-press periodicals. As the popularity of his fiction grew, Chekhov's stories began appearing in more established periodicals and newspapers, and in 1884 he published his first collection of short stories, *Fairy Tales of Melpomene.* Dmitri Grigorovich, a leading short-story writer and a prominent figure in Russia's literary establishment, praised Chekhov as the most talented writer of his generation; the young writer's accomplishment was given official recognition when his second collection of stories, *In the Twilight,* was awarded the Pushkin Prize by the Imperial Academy of Science in 1888. Although Chekhov attempted unsuccessfully to write a novel, he was attracted—and his artistic temperament was suited—to more condensed fictional forms. Focusing on the particularities of character, social class, and setting while maintaining the authorial objectivity for which he became renowned, he developed the short story into a vehicle of unprecedented psychological complexity and acute social observation. His finest stories—such as "Ward No. 6" (1892), "My Life" (1896), and "Peasants" (1897)—are considered masterpieces of the genre.

Chekhov's interest in the theater also developed at an early age. As a schoolboy, he participated in amateur theatrical skits with his siblings (he had four brothers and one sister), and he and his friends saw professional plays at the Taganrog theater. In his late teens he composed two plays that have not survived, a one-act farce and a full-length drama titled *Fatherlessness,* and during his first two years of medical school he produced a cumbersome four-act drama that may have been a reworked version of the latter play. Though he subsequently destroyed this play, a copy was discovered after his death and has been published under the title *Platonov.* Chekhov's first theatrical production did not occur until 1887, when *Ivanov,* a play about a bored and disillusioned landowner, premiered in Moscow to critical and popular acclaim. It was followed in 1889 by *The Wood Demon,* a full-length comedy, and by a series of one-act comedies that Chekhov wrote between 1887 and 1901. Conceived in the tradition of vaudeville farce, these "airy trifles" (as Chekhov called them) were little more than curtain-raisers, though *The Bear* (1888) proved popular throughout Russia and *The Proposal* (1889) entertained a St. Petersburg audience that included Czar Alexander III.

A gap of five years separates this early drama from the earliest of the four mature plays that figure so prominently in the history of modern drama. In 1895 Chekhov wrote *The Seagull,* a play about art, disappointed love, and the psychology of survival. Set, like his other major plays, on a provincial Russian estate, it explores the shifting relationships in a quartet of central characters: Arkádina, an aging actress; her son Tréplev, an avant-garde writer; Trigórin, an established novelist; and Nína, a young actress whose aspirations, hardships, and disappointments identify her with a seagull that Tréplev has shot. At the play's premiere in St. Petersburg on October 17, 1896, the audience responded so negatively that Chekhov fled the auditorium during the second act and vowed never to write another play. However, when Konstantin Stanislavsky and Vladimir Nemirovich-Danchenko, founders of the newly formed Moscow Art Theatre, revived *The Seagull* two years later, the play proved so popular that the theater company adopted its title bird as their emblem. With Stanislavsky as director, the MAT staged the Moscow premieres of Chekhov's remaining plays: *Uncle Vanya,* a reworked version of *The Wood Demon,* in 1899; *The Three Sisters* in 1901; and *The Cherry Orchard* in 1904. Six months after *The Cherry Orchard* opened, Chekhov died of tuberculosis at the age of forty-four.

The innovations of dramaturgy and stagecraft in these plays are both subtle and wide-ranging. Late nineteenth-century Russian theater was dominated by farce and melodrama, genres that relied on stock characters and heightened dramatic incident. Reacting against these theatrical conventions, Chekhov insisted that drama imitate the textures, issues, and actions of everyday life and that its characters reflect the complexity of human experience. In a statement of his artistic principles, Chekhov wrote:

> The demand is made that the hero and heroine should be dramatically effective. But in life people do not shoot themselves, or hang themselves, or fall in love, or deliver themselves of clever sayings every minute. They spend most of their time eating, drinking, running after women or men, talking nonsense. It is therefore necessary that this should be shown on the stage. A play ought to be written in which the people should come and go, dine, talk of the weather, or play cards, not because the author wants it but because that is what happens in real life. Life on the stage should be as it really is, and the people, too, should be as they are and not on stilts.

In order to accomplish this objective, Chekhov reduced the importance of traditional dramatic climaxes by minimizing their impact or eliminating them altogether. His characters resist dramatic stereotype, and the stage they occupy generates multiple points of attention rather than central protagonists and antagonists. These characters talk, do ordinary things, and are defined more by the actions they don't take than those they do. In keeping with Chekhov's belief that a dramatist's job is not to judge the characters created but to present them in the light of dispassionate observation, his plays give little evidence of their author's point of view. The result is a drama of understatement, indirection, and nuance, where action and emotion lie beneath the words. Chekhov famously observed: "People are having a meal, just having a meal, but at the same time their happiness is being created, or their lives are being destroyed."

The Cherry Orchard is one of the finest examples of Chekhov's "drama of the undramatic" (in the critic Richard Gilman's phrase). Its plot hinges on the fate of the Ranyévskaya estate, famed for its beautiful cherry orchard but no longer able to support its occupants or their privileged lifestyle. Its threatened sale is the stuff of French "mortgage melodramas," which often hinged on the possible or actual loss of property at the hands of a villainous manipulator; but the climactic event of Chekhov's play—the auction at which the estate is sold—occurs offstage, and its outcome is recounted after the fact. In a similar undermining of expectations, the participants in this crisis do not fit the moral categories of conventional melodrama. Liubóv (Madame Ranyévskaya) and her brother Gáyev, who cling to their childhood memories of the orchard, lose the estate through a mixture of paralysis and fecklessness, not victimization; indeed, their inaction in the face of the imminent loss of their property is the play's most sustained narrative thread. For his part, Lopákhin—the former serf who eventually buys the estate—is a far cry from the stock villain of melodrama. He urges Liubóv and Gáyev to sell the orchard as a way of saving the estate, and in the giddiness of having bought the property he speaks movingly (if somewhat thoughtlessly) about his social transformation. In terms of dramatic technique, the moment in act 3 when he delivers this speech is a rare example in Chekhov's play of a character's dominating the stage and claiming attention. The rest of the time characters engage in conversation with each other, sometimes listening, sometimes not. In keeping with its muted sphere of action, *The Cherry Orchard* opens with the arrival of characters and ends with their departure.

Chekhov wrote *The Cherry Orchard* while living as a semi-invalid in Yalta, and its composition was long and difficult. Yet the play is the most comic of his mature dramas. In September 1903 he wrote to his wife, Olga Knipper, who would play the role of Madame Ranyévskaya, "My play . . . hasn't turned out as a drama, but as a comedy, at times almost a farce." Subtitling his play "A Comedy in Four Acts," Chekhov insisted on this view of the play throughout its rehearsals and found himself in frequent disagreement

The Moscow Art Theater's original 1904 production of *The Cherry Orchard*, directed by Constantin Stanislavsky. Stanislavsky, who performed the role of Gayev in this production, is on the far left, gesturing toward the bookcase.

with his director, Stanislavsky, who considered the play a tragedy and accentuated the atmosphere of pathos and loss. In Chekhov's hands, comedy is central to the play's mixture of tones. In addition to the obvious moments of slapstick—Liubóv's adopted daughter Várya swings a stick at the accountant Yepikhódov in anger but hits Lopákhin instead, while "the eternal student" Trofímov falls noisily down the stairs after an argument with Liubóv—Chekhov employs comedy as a vehicle of irony and distance. His use of comedy is particularly evident in those moments when the physical world intrudes on private emotion and in those tics and mannerisms that signal a character's self-absorption. When the governess Carlotta laments that she doesn't own a birth certificate at the start of the play's second act—"Where I'm from . . .

who I am . . . no idea"—the painful undertones of her meditation are deflected when she reaches into her pocket and absentmindedly takes a bite out of a cucumber pickle. And when Gáyev plays his imaginary billiards game or delivers an oration to the family bookcase, these humorous moments measure the extent to which he, like all the play's characters, inhabits a world of his own.

The problem in Stanislavsky's "tearful" direction of *The Cherry Orchard*, in other words, was that he sought to reveal the play's emotions through overt gesture rather than through the ironic counterpoint of surface activity and emotional undercurrents. In Chekhovian drama the weight of emotion lies in what is not said, as when the forced gaiety of the ball in act 3 is undercut by the audience's awareness

that the auction is taking place offstage. And few scenes in all of Chekhov's plays hold the emotional power of Várya's exchange with Lopákhin near the play's end, when the two exchange small talk while failing to address the life-deciding issue that hangs over them.

As elsewhere in Chekhov's writing, individual psychology in *The Cherry Orchard* is deeply embedded within the social, economic, and political landscape of turn-of-the-century Russia. In the sale of the Ranyévskaya estate, Chekhov dramatizes the historical eclipse of the landowning class that had formed the historical pillar of feudal Russia. Semyónov-Píshchik, a neighboring landowner, must borrow money from Liubóv to meet his financial needs, and he pays her back only after selling the rights to extract the white clay that

has been discovered on his property. In Lopákhin's plan to cut down the cherry orchard and build vacation homes we feel the emerging class of others, like him, who have grown prosperous through acquired wealth. Social mobility defines *The Cherry Orchard,* and as the contrasting destinies of Chekhov's central characters demonstrate, this mobility extends in both directions. Beyond the circle of property and money, of course, is the vast number of Russia's poor and uneducated. Firs, the family's aging house servant, recalls the emancipation of the serfs in 1861, and Chekhov's play provides ample evidence of the poverty and social dislocation that this class has had to endure. Indigent peasants have been staying in the old servants' quarters, and a homeless man intrudes upon the pastoral quiet of act 2. The student

Trofímov addresses this poverty and its history in a speech to Liubóv's daughter Ánya: "Your grandfather, and his father, and his father's fathers, they *owned* the people who slaved away for them all over this estate, and now the voices and faces of human beings hide behind every cherry in the orchard, every leaf, every tree trunk." Envisioning a future of happiness and social justice, he calls on Ánya to devote her life to working in the cause of human progress. "This whole country is our orchard," he proclaims, widening the scope of the play's issues to include czarist Russia as a whole.

In view of subsequent Russian history—in 1917 the Communist-led Russian Revolution overthrew Czar Nicholas II and proclaimed an era of social equality—Trofímov's speeches in act 2 have sometimes been taken as Chekhov's own call for transformative social change. Not surprisingly, Soviet productions of *The Cherry Orchard* made Trofímov the herald of a new revolutionary order. To be sure, Chekhov's Trofímov articulates the revolutionary sentiment that had gained increasing

force in Russia by the turn of the century. Universities were major sites of antigovernment agitation, and (as Chekhov indicated in a letter to his wife) Trofímov's extended career as a graduate student reflects the fact that he has been expelled more than once for political reasons. At the same time, though Trofímov's rhetoric is stirring, his vision of a future that will redeem the present resembles the beautiful dreams that other Chekhov characters use to escape the drabness and disappointment of their lives. Trofímov does little to translate language into action, and this character who likes the sound of his own voice cuts a somewhat ridiculous figure at times. The optimism of his predictions exist in ironic counterpoint with the present, just as the historical evolution represented by change in *The Cherry Orchard* coexists with the painfulness of individual loss. To push the tone of *The Cherry Orchard* in one direction at the expense of another—to stress its resignation or its desire for something better, its comedy or its tears—is to deny the multiple perspectives that Chekhov so masterfully calls into play.

s.g.

The Cherry Orchard
A Comedy in Four Acts[1]

CHARACTERS

LIUBÓV RANYÉVSKAYA [Lyúba, Liúba
  Andréyevna], who owns the estate
ÁNYA, her daughter, seventeen years old
VÁRYA, her adopted daughter, twenty-four
  years old
LEONÍD GÁYEV [Lonya, Lyónya
  Andréyich], Liubóv's brother
YERMOLÁI LOPÁKHIN [Yermolái Alexéyich],
  a businessman
PÉTYA TROFÍMOV, a graduate student
BORÍS SEMYÓNOV-PÍSHCHIK, who owns
  land in the neighborhood

CARLOTTA, the governess
SEMYÓN YEPIKHÓDOV, an accountant
DUNYÁSHA [Avdótya Fyódorovna,
  Dunyáhsa Kozoyédov], the maid
FIRS, the butler, eighty-seven years old
YÁSHA, the valet
A HOMELESS MAN
The STATIONMASTER
The POSTMASTER
Guests, servants

1. Translated by Paul Schmidt.

The action takes place on Ranyévskaya's estate.

Act 1

[*A room they still call the nursery. A side door leads to* ÁNYA's *room. Almost dawn; the sun is about to rise. It's May; the cherry orchard is already in bloom, but there's a chill in the air. The windows are shut. Enter* DUNYÁSHA *with a lamp, and* LOPÁKHIN *with a book in his hand.*]

LOPÁKHIN   The train's finally in, thank God. What time is it?

DUNYÁSHA   Almost two. [*She blows out the lamp.*] It's getting light.

LOPÁKHIN   How late is the train this time? Must be at least two hours. [*He yawns and stretches.*] That was dumb. I came over on purpose just to meet
5   them at the station, and then I fell asleep. Sat right here and fell asleep. Too bad. You should have woke me up.

DUNYÁSHA   I thought you already left. [*She listens.*] Listen, that must be them.

LOPÁKHIN   [*he listens*]   No, they still have the luggage to get, and all that. [*Pause*] She's been away five years now; no telling how she's changed. She
10   was always a good person. Very gentle, never caused a fuss. I remember one time when I was a kid, fifteen or so, they had my old man working in the store down by the village, and he hit me, hard, right in the face; my nose started to bleed. And we had to come up here to make a delivery or something; he was still drunk. And Liubóv Andréyevna—she wasn't much
15   older than I was, kind of thin—she brought me inside the house, right into the nursery here, and washed the blood off my face for me. "Don't cry," she told me. "Don't cry, poor boy; you'll live long enough to get married." [*Pause*] Poor boy . . . Well, my father was poor, but take a look at me now, all dressed up, brand-new suit and tan shoes. Silk purse out of a sow's ear,
20   I guess . . . I'm rich now, got lots of money, but when you think about it, I guess I'm still a poor boy from the country. [*He flips the pages of the book.*] I tried reading this book, couldn't figure out a word it said. Put me to sleep.

   [*Pause.*]

DUNYÁSHA   The dogs were barking all night long; they know their mistress is coming home.

25   LOPÁKHIN   Don't be silly.

DUNYÁSHA   I'm so excited I'm shaking. I may faint.

LOPÁKHIN   You're getting too full of yourself, Dunyásha. Look at you, all dressed up like that, and that hairdo. You watch out for that. You got to remember who you are.

   [*Enter* YEPIKHÓDOV *with a bunch of flowers; he wears a jacket and tie and brightly polished boots, which squeak loudly. As he comes in, he drops the flowers.*]

30   YEPIKHÓDOV   [*picking up the flowers*]   Here. The gardener sent these over; he said put them on the dining room table. [*He gives the flowers to* DUNYÁSHA.]

LOPÁKHIN   And bring me a beer.

DUNYÁSHA   Right away.

   [*She goes out.*]

YEPIKHÓDOV   It's freezing this morning—it must be in the thirties—and
35   the cherry blossoms are out already. I cannot abide the climate here. [*He*

sighs.] I never have abided it, ever. [*Beat*][2] Yermolái Alexéyich, would you examinate something for me, please? Day before yesterday I bought myself a new pair of boots, and listen to them squeak, will you? I just cannot endear it. Do you know anything I can put on them?

40 LOPÁKHIN   Will you shut up? You drive me crazy.

YEPIKHÓDOV   Every day something awful happens to me. It's like a habit. But I don't complain. I just try to keep smiling.

   [*Enter* DUNYÁSHA; *she brings* LOPÁKHIN *a beer.*]

YEPIKHÓDOV   I'm going. [*He bumps into a chair, which falls over.*] You see? [*He seems proud of it.*] You see what I was referring about? Excuse my
45 expressivity, but what a concurrence. It's almost uncanny, isn't it?

   [*He leaves.*]

DUNYÁSHA   You know what? That Yepikhódov proposed to me!

LOPÁKHIN   Oh?

DUNYÁSHA   I just don't know what to think. He's kind of nice. . . . He's a real quiet boy, but then he opens his mouth, and you can't ever understand
50 what he's talking about. I mean, it sounds nice, but it just doesn't make any sense. I do like him, though. Kind of. And he's crazy about me. It's funny, you know, every day something awful happens to him. People around here call him Double Trouble.

LOPÁKHIN [*he listens*]   That must be them.

55 DUNYÁSHA   It's them! Oh, I don't know what's the matter with me! I feel so funny; I'm cold all over.

LOPÁKHIN   It really is them this time. Let's go; we should be there at the door. You think she'll recognize me? It's been five years.

DUNYÁSHA [*excited*]   Oh, my God! I'm going to faint! I think I'm going to
60 faint!

   [*The sound of two carriages outside the house.* LOPÁKHIN *and* DUNYÁSHA *hurry out. The stage is empty. The sound outside gets louder.* FIRS, *leaning heavily on his cane, crosses the room, heading for the door; he wears an old-fashioned butler's livery and a top hat; he says something to himself, but you can't make out the words. The offstage noise and bustle increases. A voice: "Here we are . . . this way." Enter* LIUBÓV ANDRÉYEVNA, ÁNYA, *and* CARLOTTA, *dressed in traveling clothes.* VÁRYA *wears an overcoat, and a kerchief on her head.* GÁYEV, SEMYÓNOV-PÍSHCHIK, LOPÁKHIN, DUNYÁSHA *with a bundle and an umbrella, Servants with the luggage—all pass across the stage.*]

ÁNYA   Here we are. Oh, Mama, do you remember this room?

LIUBÓV ANDRÉYEVNA   The nursery!

VÁRYA   It's freezing; my hands are like ice. We kept your room exactly as you left it, Mama. The white and lavender one.

65 LIUBÓV ANDRÉYEVNA   The nursery! Oh, this house, this beautiful house! I slept in this room when I was a child. . . . [*She weeps.*] And I feel like a child again! [*She hugs* GÁYEV, VÁRYA, *then* GÁYEV *again.*] And Várya hasn't changed at all—still looks like a nun! And Dunyásha dear! Of course I remember you! [*She hugs* DUNYÁSHA.]

70 GÁYEV   The train was two hours late. What kind of efficiency is that? Eh?

CARLOTTA   And my dog loves nuts.

2. Pause.

SEMYÓNOV-PÍSHCHIK Really! I don't believe it!

[*Everyone leaves, except* ÁNYA *and* DUNYÁSHA.]

DUNYÁSHA We've been up all night, waiting. . . . [*She takes* ÁNYA's *coat and hat.*]

ÁNYA I've been up for four nights now. . . . I didn't sleep the whole trip. And
75 now I'm freezing.

DUNYÁSHA When you went away it was still winter, it was snowing, and now look! Oh, sweetie, you're back! [*She laughs and hugs* Ánya.] I've been up all night, waiting to see you. Sweetheart, I just can't wait—I've got to tell you what happened. I can't wait another minute!

80 ÁNYA [*wearily*] Now what?

DUNYÁSHA Yepikhódov proposed the day after Easter! He wants to marry me!

ÁNYA That's all you ever think about. . . . [*She fixes her hair.*] I lost all my hairpins. . . .

DUNYÁSHA I just don't know what to do about him. He really, really loves me!

85 ÁNYA [*looking through the door to her room*] My own room, just as if I'd never left. I'm back home! Tomorrow I'll get up and go for a walk in the orchard. I just wish I could get some sleep. I didn't sleep the whole trip, I was so worried.

DUNYÁSHA Pétya's here. He got here day before yesterday.

90 ÁNYA [*joyfully*] Pétya!

DUNYÁSHA He's staying out in the barn. Said he didn't want to bother anybody. [*She looks at her watch.*] He told me to get him up, but Várya said not to. You let him sleep, she said.

[*Enter* VÁRYA. *She has a big bunch of keys attached to her belt.*]

VÁRYA Dunyásha, go get the coffee. Mama wants her coffee.

95 DUNYÁSHA Oh, I forgot!

[*She goes out.*]

VÁRYA You're back. Thank God! You're home again! [*She embraces* Ánya.] My angel is home again! My beautiful darling!

ÁNYA You won't believe what I've been through!

VÁRYA I can imagine.

100 ÁNYA I left just before Easter; it was cold. Carlotta never shut up the whole trip; she kept doing those silly tricks of hers. I don't know why you had to stick me with her.

VÁRYA Darling, you couldn't go all that way by yourself! You're only seventeen!

105 ÁNYA We got to Paris, it was cold and snowy, and my French is just awful! Mama was living in this fifth-floor apartment, we had to walk up, we get there and there's all these French people, some old priest reading some book, and it was crowded, and everybody was smoking these awful cigarettes—and I felt so sorry for Mama, I just threw my arms around her
110 and couldn't let go. And she was so glad to see me, she cried—

VÁRYA [*almost crying*] I know, I know . . .

ÁNYA And she sold the villa in Mentón,[3] and the money was already gone, all of it! And I spent everything you gave me for the trip; I haven't got a thing left. And Mama still doesn't understand! We have dinner at the

___

3. A resort town on the French Mediterranean coast.

115 train station, and she orders the most expensive things on the menu, and then she tips the waiters a ruble[4] each! And Carlotta does the same! And Yásha expects the same treatment—he's just awful. You know, Yásha, that flunky of Mama's—he came back with us.

VÁRYA   I saw him, the lazy good-for-nothing.

120 ÁNYA   So what happened? Did you get the interest paid?

VÁRYA   With what?

ÁNYA   Oh, my God, my God . . .

VÁRYA   The place goes up for sale in August.

ÁNYA   Oh, my God.

[LOPÁKHIN *sticks his head in the doorway and makes a mooing sound, then goes away.*]

125 VÁRYA   Oh, that man! I'd like to—[*She shakes her fist.*]

ÁNYA [*she hugs her*]   Várya, did he propose yet? [VÁRYA *shakes her head no.*] But you know he loves you! Why don't the two of you just sit down and be honest with each other? What are you waiting for?

VÁRYA   I don't think anything will ever come of it. He's always so busy, he

130 never has time for me. He just isn't interested! It's hard for me when I see him, but I don't care anymore. Everybody talks about us getting married, people even congratulate me, but there's nothing. . . . I mean, it's all just a dream. [*A change of tone*] Oh, you've got a new pin, a little bee. . . .

135 ÁNYA [*with a sigh*]   I know. Mama bought it for me. [*She goes into her room and starts to giggle, like a little girl.*] You know what? In Paris I went for a ride in a balloon!

VÁRYA   Oh, darling, you're back! My angel is home again!

[DUNYÁSHA *comes in, carrying a tray with coffee things, and begins setting them out on the table.* VÁRYA *stands at the doorway and talks to* ÁNYA *in the other room.*]

You know, dear, I spend the livelong day trying to keep this house going,

140 and all I do is dream. I want to see you married off to somebody rich, then I can rest easy. And I think then I'll go away by myself, maybe live in a convent, or just go traveling: Kiev, Moscow . . . spend all my time making visits to churches. I'd start walking and just go and go and go. That would be heaven!

145 ÁNYA   Listen to the birds in the orchard! What time is it?

VÁRYA   It must be almost three. You should get some sleep, darling. [*She goes into* ÁNYA'*s room.*] Yes, that would be heaven!

[*Enter* YÁSHA *with a suitcase and a lap robe. He walks with an affected manner.*]

YÁSHA   I beg pardon! May I intrude?

DUNYÁSHA   I didn't even recognize you, Yásha. You got so different there in

150 France.

YÁSHA   *I'm sorry*—who are you exactly?

DUNYÁSHA   When you left, I wasn't any higher than this. [*She holds her hand a distance from the floor.*] I'm Dunyásha. You know, Dunyásha Kozoyédov. Don't you remember me?

4. Roughly equivalent to $20 today.

155 YÁSHA   Well! You sure turned out cute, didn't you? [*He looks around carefully, then grabs and kisses her; she screams and drops a saucer;* YÁSHA *leaves in a hurry.*]

VÁRYA [*at the door, annoyed*]   Now what happened?

DUNYÁSHA [*almost in tears*]   I broke a saucer.

VÁRYA [*ironically*]   Well, isn't that lucky!

ÁNYA [*entering*]   Somebody should let Mama know Pétya's here.

160 VÁRYA   I told them to let him sleep.

ÁNYA [*lost in thought*]   Father died six years ago, and a month later our little brother, Grísha, drowned. Sweet boy, he was only seven. And Mama couldn't face it, that's why she went away, just went away and never looked back. [*Shivers.*] And I understand exactly how she felt. I wish she knew that.
         [*Pause.*]
165   And Pétya Trofímov was Grísha's tutor. He might remind her . . .
         [*Enter* FIRS *in his old-fashioned butler's livery. He crosses to the table and begins looking over the coffee things.*]

FIRS   The missus will have her breakfast here. [*He puts on a pair of white gloves.*] Is the coffee ready? [*To* DUNYÁSHA, *crossly*] Where's the cream? Go get the cream!

DUNYÁSHA   Oh, my God, I'm sorry. . . .
         [*Hurries off.*]

170 FIRS [*he starts fussing with the coffee things*]   Young flibbertigibbet . . . [*He mumbles to himself.*] They're all back from Paris. . . . In the old days they went to Paris too . . . had to go the whole way in a horse and buggy. [*He laughs.*]

VÁRYA   Firs, what are you talking about?

FIRS   Beg pardon? [*Joyfully*] The missus is home! Going to see her at last!
175   Now I can die happy. . . . [*He starts to cry with joy.*]
         [*Enter* LIUBÓV, GÁYEV, LOPÁKHIN, *and* SEMYÓNOV-PÍSHCHIK, *who wears a crumpled linen suit. As* GÁYEV *enters, he gestures as if he were making a billiard shot.*]

LIUBÓV ANDRÉYEVNA   How did it go? I'm trying to remember. . . . Yellow ball in the side pocket! Bank shot off the corner!

GÁYEV   And right down the middle! Oh, sister, sister, just think . . . when you and I were little we used to sleep in this room, and now I'm almost
180   fifty-one! Strange, isn't it?

LOPÁKHIN   Time sure passes. . . .

GÁYEV [*beat*]   Say again?

LOPÁKHIN   I said, time sure passes.

GÁYEV [*looking at* LOPÁKHIN]   Who's wearing that cheap cologne?

185 ÁNYA   I'm going to bed. Good night, Mama. [*She kisses her mother.*]

LIUBÓV ANDRÉYEVNA   Oh, my darling little girl, my baby! Are you glad you're home? I still can't quite believe I'm here.

ÁNYA   Good night, Uncle.

GÁYEV [*he kisses her*]   God bless you, dear. You're getting to look so much like
190   your mother! Liúba, she looks just like you when you were her age. She really does.
         [ÁNYA *says good night to* LOPÁKHIN *and* PÍSHCHIK, *goes into her room, and closes the door behind her.*]

LIUBÓV ANDRÉYEVNA She's tired to death.

PÍSHCHIK Well, that's such a long trip!

VÁRYA Gentlemen, please. It's almost three; time you were going.

195 LIUBÓV ANDRÉYEVNA [laughs] You're the same as ever, Várya. [Hugs and kisses her.] Just let me have my coffee, then we'll all be going.

[FIRS puts a pillow beneath her feet.]

Thank you, dear. I've really gotten addicted to coffee; I drink it day and night. You old darling, you! Thank you.

VÁRYA I'll just go make sure they've got everything unloaded.

[Goes out.]

200 LIUBÓV ANDRÉYEVNA I can't believe I'm really here! [Laughs.] I feel like jumping up and waving my arms in the air! [Covers her face with her hands.] It's still like a dream. I love this country, really I do, I adore it. I started to cry every time I looked out the train windows. [Almost in tears] But I do need my coffee! Thank you, Firs, thank you, darling. I'm so glad
205 you're still alive.

FIRS Day before yesterday.

GÁYEV He doesn't hear too well anymore.

LOPÁKHIN Time for me to go. I have to leave for Hárkov[5] at five. I'm really disappointed; I was looking forward to seeing you, have a chance to
210 talk. . . . You look wonderful, just the way you always did.

PÍSHCHIK [breathes hard] Better than she always did. That Paris outfit. . . . She makes me feel young again!

LOPÁKHIN Your brother here thinks I'm crude, calls me a money grubber. That doesn't bother me; he can call me whatever he wants. I just hope
215 you'll trust me the way you used to, look at me the way you used to. . . . My God, my father slaved for your father and grandfather, my whole family worked for yours; but you, you treated me different. You did so much for me I forgot about all that. Fact is, I . . . I love you like you were family . . . more, even.

220 LIUBÓV ANDRÉYEVNA I can't sit still; I'm just not in the mood! [Gets up excitedly, moves about the room.] I'm so happy I could die! I know I sound stupid—go ahead, laugh. . . . Dear old bookcase. . . . [Kisses the bookcase.] My little desk . . .

GÁYEV Did I tell you Nanny died while you were away?

225 LIUBÓV ANDRÉYEVNA [sits back down and drinks her coffee] Yes, you wrote me. God rest her.

GÁYEV Stásy died too. And Petrúsha Kosói quit and moved into town; he works at the police station. [Takes out a little box of hard candies and puts one in his mouth.]

PÍSHCHIK Dáshenka—you remember Dáshenka? My daughter? Anyway, she
230 sends her regards. . . .

LOPÁKHIN Well, I'd like to give you some very good news. [Looks at his watch.] Afraid there's no time to talk now, though; I've got to go. Well, just to make it short, you know you haven't kept up the mortgage payments on your place here. So now they foreclosed and your estate is up for sale.
235 At auction. They set a date already, August twenty-second, but don't you worry, you can rest easy. We can take care of this—I've got a great idea.

---

5. That is, Kharkov, the second-largest city in Ukraine (then part of the Russian Empire).

Now listen, here's how it works: your place here is fifteen miles from town, and it's only a short drive from the train station. All you've got to do is clear out the old cherry orchard, plus that land down by the river, and subdivide!
240 You lease the plots, build vacation homes, and I swear that'll bring you in twenty-five thousand[6] a year, maybe more.

GÁYEV What an outrageous thing to say!

LIUBÓV ANDRÉYEVNA Excuse me . . . Excuse me, I don't think I quite understand. . . .

245 LOPÁKHIN You'll get at least twenty-five hundred an acre! And if you start advertising right away, I swear to God come this fall you won't have a single plot left. You see what I'm saying? Your troubles are over! Congratulations! The location is terrific; the river's a real selling point. Only thing is, you've got to start clearing right away. Get rid of all the old buildings. This house,
250 for instance, will have to go. You can't get people to live in a barn like this anymore. And you'll have to cut down that old cherry orchard.

LIUBÓV ANDRÉYEVNA Cut down the cherry orchard? My dear man, you don't understand! Our cherry orchard is a landmark! It's famous for miles around!

255 LOPÁKHIN The only thing famous about it is how big it is. You only get cherries every two years, and even then you can't get rid of them. Nobody buys them. It's just not a commercial crop.

GÁYEV Our cherry orchard is mentioned in the encyclopedia![7]

LOPÁKHIN [looks at his watch] We have to think of something to do and then
260 do it. Otherwise the cherry orchard will be sold at auction on August twenty-second, this house and all the land with it. Make up your minds! Believe me, I've thought this through; there isn't any other way to do it. There just isn't.

FIRS Back in the old days, forty, fifty years ago, they used to make dried
265 cherries, pickled cherries, preserved cherries, cherry jam, and sometimes—

GÁYEV Oh, Firs, just shut up.

FIRS —sometimes they sent them off to Moscow by the wagonload. People paid a lot for them! Back then the dried cherries were soft and juicy and sweet, and they smelled just lovely; back then they knew how to fix
270 them. . . .

LIUBÓV ANDRÉYEVNA Does anybody know how to fix them nowadays?

FIRS Nope. They all forgot.

PÍSHCHIK Tell us about Paris. What was it like? Did you eat frogs?

LIUBÓV ANDRÉYEVNA I ate crocodiles.

275 PÍSHCHIK Crocodiles? Really! I don't believe it!

LOPÁKHIN You see, it used to be out here in the country there were only landlords and poor farmers, but now all of a sudden there are summer people moving in; they want vacation homes. Every town you can name is surrounded by them—it's the coming thing. In twenty years they'll expand and
280 multiply! Right now maybe they're only places to relax on the weekend, but I bet you eventually people will put down roots out here, they'll create neighborhoods, and then your cherry orchard will blossom and bear fruit once again—and even bring in a profit!

---

6. Roughly equivalent to $500,000 today (all references to money are in rubles).
7. Probably a reference to the *Great Russian*

Encyclopedic Dictionary (1890–1906), an authoritative 86-volume reference work published by F. A. Brockhaus and I. A. Efron.

GÁYEV [*indignantly*] That's outrageous!

[*Enter* VÁRYA *and* YÁSHA.]

285 VÁRYA Mama, a couple of telegrams came for you. [*Takes a key and opens the old bookcase; the lock creaks.*] Here they are.

LIUBÓV ANDRÉYEVNA They're from Paris. [*She tears them up without opening then.*] I'm through with Paris.

GÁYEV Liúba, have you any idea how old this bookcase is? Last week I pulled
290 out the bottom drawer, and there was the date on the back, burned right into the wood. A hundred years! This bookcase is exactly a hundred years old! What do you say to that, eh? We should have a birthday celebration. Of course, it's an inanimate object, any way you look at it, but still, it's a . . . well, it's a . . . a bookcase.

295 PÍSHCHIK A hundred years old! Really! I don't believe it!

GÁYEV Yes, yes, it is. [*He caresses the bookcase.*] Dear old bookcase! Wonderful old bookcase! I rejoice in your existence. For a hundred years now you have borne the shining ideals of goodness and justice, a hundred years have not dimmed your silent summons to useful labor. To generations of our
300 family [*Almost in tears*] you have offered courage, a belief in a better future, you have instructed us in ideals of goodness and social awareness. . . .

[*Pause.*]

LOPÁKHIN Right. Well . . .

LIUBÓV ANDRÉYEVNA Oh, Lonya, you're still the same as ever!

GÁYEV [*somewhat embarrassed*] Yellow ball in the side pocket! Bank shot off
305 the center!

LOPÁKHIN Well, I've got to be off.

YÁSHA [*gives* LIUBÓV *a pillbox*] Isn't it perhaps time for your pills?

PÍSHCHIK No, no, no, dear lady! Never take medicine! Won't do any good! Won't do any harm either, though. Watch! [*Takes the pillbox, dumps the*
310 *contents into his hand, puts them in his mouth, and swallows them with a swig of beer.*] There! All gone!

LIUBÓV ANDRÉYEVNA [*alarmed*] Are you out of your mind?

PÍSHCHIK I have just taken all your pills for you.

LOPÁKHIN What a glutton.

[*Everybody laughs.*]

315 FIRS He was here over the holidays, ate half a crock of pickles. . . . [*Mumbles.*]

LIUBÓV ANDRÉYEVNA What's he mumbling about?

VÁRYA He's been going on like that for the last three years. We're used to it by now.

YÁSHA He's getting senile.

[*Enter* CARLOTTA, *in a white dress with a lorgnette on a chain. She starts to cross the room.*]

320 LOPÁKHIN Oh, excuse me, Carlotta, I didn't get a chance to say hello yet. [*Tries to kiss her hand.*]

CARLOTTA [*takes her hand away*] I let you kiss my hand, first thing I know, you'll want to kiss my elbow, then my shoulder . . .

LOPÁKHIN This isn't my lucky day.

[*Everybody laughs.*]

Carlotta, show us a trick!

325 LIUBÓV ANDRÉYEVNA Yes, do, Carlotta—show us a trick!

CARLOTTA Not now. I'm off to bed.

> [*Leaves.*]

LOPÁKHIN Well, I'll see you in three weeks. [*Kisses* LIUBÓV's *hand.*] Goodbye now. I've got to be off. [*To* GÁYEV] Goodbye. [*Hugs* PÍSHCHIK.] So long. [*Shakes hands with* VÁRYA, *then with* FIRS *and* YÁSHA.] I sort of hate to leave.

330 [*To* LIUBÓV] Think over what I said about subdividing the place. You decide to do it, let me know, and I'll take care of everything. I'll get you a loan of fifty thousand. Think it over now, seriously.

VÁRYA [*angry*] Will you please just go?

LOPÁKHIN I'm going, I'm going.

> [*Leaves.*]

335 GÁYEV What a bore. Oh, excuse me, *pardon,*[8] I forgot—that's Várya's boyfriend. He's going to marry our Várya.

VÁRYA Uncle, will you please not talk nonsense?

LIUBÓV ANDRÉYEVNA Oh, but Várya, that's wonderful! He's a fine man!

PÍSHCHIK One of the finest, in fact . . . the very, very finest . . . My Dáshenka

340 always says . . . she says . . . she says a lot of things. [*Snores, but immediately wakes up.*] Dear lady, yes, always respected you, hmm. . . . You think you could lend me, say, two hundred and forty rubles? Mortgage payment, you know, due tomorrow . . .

VÁRYA [*terrified*] We can't; we don't have any!

345 LIUBÓV ANDRÉYEVNA I'm afraid that's the truth. We haven't any money.

PÍSHCHIK I'll get it somewhere. [*Laughs.*] I never give up hope. There was that time I thought I was finished, it was all over, and all of a sudden—boom! The railroad cut across some of my land and paid me for it. You'll see, something will turn up tomorrow or the next day. Dáshenka will win two

350 hundred thousand in the lottery; she just bought a ticket.

LIUBÓV ANDRÉYEVNA Well, the coffee's gone. We might as well go to bed.

FIRS [*takes out a clothes brush and brushes* GÁYEV's *clothes; scolds him*] You've got on the wrong trousers again. What am I supposed to do with you?

VÁRYA [*softly*] Ánya's asleep. [*Quietly opens the window.*] The sun's coming

355 up; it's not as cold as it was. Look, Mama, what wonderful trees! Smell the perfume! Oh, Lord! And the orioles are singing!

GÁYEV [*opens another window*] The whole orchard is white. You remember, Liúba? That long path, stretched out like a ribbon, on and on, the way it used to shine in the moonlight? You remember? You haven't forgotten?

360 LIUBÓV ANDRÉYEVNA Oh, my childhood! My innocence! I slept in this room, I could look out over the orchard, when I woke up in the morning I was happy, and it all looked exactly the same as this! Nothing has changed! [*Laughs delightedly.*] White, white, all white! My whole orchard is white! Autumn was dark and drizzly, and winter was cold, but now you're young

365 again, flowering with happiness—the angels of heaven have never abandoned you. If only I could shake off this weight I've been carrying so long. If only I could forget my past!

GÁYEV Yes, and now they're selling the orchard to pay our debts. Strange, isn't it?

---

8. Gáyev's interjection of the French word *pardon* (excuse me) is typical of the upper classes, who in pre-Soviet Russia spoke French as a second language.

370 LIUBÓV ANDRÉYEVNA   Look! There . . . in the orchard . . . it's Mother! In her white dress! [*Laughs delightedly.*] It's Mother!

GÁYEV   Where?

VÁRYA   Oh, Mama, for God's sake . . .

LIUBÓV ANDRÉYEVNA   It's all right; I was just imagining things. There to the
375   right, by the path to the summerhouse, that little white tree all bent over . . . it looked just like a woman.

> [*Enter* TROFÍMOV. *He is dressed like a student and wears wire-rimmed glasses.*]

What a glorious orchard! All those white blossoms, and the blue sky—

TROFÍMOV   Liubóv Andréyevna!

> [*She turns to look at him.*]

I don't mean to disturb you; I just wanted to say hello. [*Shakes her hand*
380   *warmly.*] They told me to wait until later, but I couldn't. . . .

> [LIUBÓV *stares at him, bewildered.*]

VÁRYA   It's Pétya Trofímov. . . .

TROFÍMOV   Pétya Trofímov—I was your little boy Grísha's tutor. . . . Have I really changed all that much?

> [LIUBÓV *embraces him and begins to weep softly.*]

GÁYEV [*embarrassed*]   Liúba, that'll do, that'll do. . . .

385 VÁRYA [*weeps*]   Oh, Pétya, I told you to wait till tomorrow.

LIUBÓV ANDRÉYEVNA   Grísha . . . my little boy. Grísha . . . my son . . .

VÁRYA   Oh, Mama, don't; it was God's will.

TROFÍMOV [*gently, almost in tears*]   There, there . . .

LIUBÓV ANDRÉYEVNA [*weeps softly*]   My little boy drowned, lost forever . . .
390   Why? What for? My dear boy, why? [*Quiets down.*] Ánya's asleep, and here I am carrying on like this. . . . Pétya, what's happened to you? You used to be such a nice-looking boy. What happened? You look dreadful. You've gotten so old!

TROFÍMOV   Some lady on the train called me a high-class tramp.

395 LIUBÓV ANDRÉYEVNA   You were only a boy then, just out of high school, you were adorable, and now you've got glasses and you're losing your hair. And haven't you graduated yet? [*Goes to the door.*]

TROFÍMOV   I suppose I'm what you'd call a permanent graduate student.

LIUBÓV ANDRÉYEVNA [*kisses* GÁYEV, *then* VÁRYA]   Time for bed. You've gotten
400   old too, Leoníd.

PÍSHCHIK [*follows* LIUBÓV]   Time for bed, time to go . . . Ooh, my gout! I'd better stay the night. Now, dear, look, look . . . Liubóv Andréyevna, tomorrow morning I need . . . two hundred and forty rubles. . . .

GÁYEV   He never gives up, does he?

405 PÍSHCHIK   Two hundred and forty rubles; my mortgage payment due. . . .

LIUBÓV ANDRÉYEVNA   Darling, I simply have no money.

PÍSHCHIK   But, dear, I'll give it right back. . . . It's such a *trivial* amount. . . .

LIUBÓV ANDRÉYEVNA   Oh, all right. Leoníd will get it for you. Leoníd, you give him the money.

410 GÁYEV   I should give him money? That'll be the day.

LIUBÓV ANDRÉYEVNA   We have to give it to him; he needs it. He'll give it back.

> [*Exit* LIUBÓV, TROFÍMOV, PÍSHCHIK, *and* FIRS. GÁYEV, VÁRYA, *and* YÁSHA *remain.*]

GÁYEV She still thinks money grows on trees. [*To* YÁSHA] My good man, will you leave us, please? Go back to the barn, where you belong.

YÁSHA [*smiles*] Leoníd Andréyich, you're the same as you always were.

415 GÁYEV What say? [*To* VÁRYA] What did he just say?

VÁRYA [*to* YÁSHA] Your mother came in from the country to see you. She's been sitting in the kitchen for two days now, waiting.

YÁSHA Oh, for God's sake, can't she leave me alone?

VÁRYA You are really disgraceful!

420 YÁSHA That's all I need right now. Why couldn't she wait till tomorrow?
[*Goes out.*]

VÁRYA Mama hasn't changed; she's the same as she always was. If it were up to her, she'd give away everything.

GÁYEV Yes. . . . [*Pause*] Someone gets sick, you know, and the doctor tries one thing after another, that means there's no cure. I've been thinking and 425 thinking, racking my brains, I come up with one thing, then another, but the truth is, none of them will work. It would be wonderful if somebody left us a lot of money, it would be wonderful if we could marry off Ánya to somebody with a lot of money, it would be wonderful if we could go see Ánya's godmother in Yároslavl,[9] try to borrow the money from her. She's 430 very, very rich.

VÁRYA [*weeps*] If only God would help us!

GÁYEV Oh, stop crying. She's very, very rich, but she doesn't like us. Because in the first place, my sister married a mere lawyer instead of a man with a title. . . .
[ÁNYA *appears in the doorway.*]

435 She married a lawyer, and then her behavior has not been—how shall I put it?—particularly exemplary. She's a lovely woman, goodhearted, charming, and of course she's my sister and I love her very much, and there are extenuating circumstances and such, but the fact is, she's what you'd have to call a . . . a loose woman. And she doesn't care who knows it; you can 440 feel it in every move she makes.

VÁRYA [*whispers*] Ánya's here.

GÁYEV What say? [*Pause*] Funny, I must have gotten something in my eye: I can't see too well. . . . Did I tell you what happened Thursday, when I was at the county courthouse?
[ÁNYA *comes into the room.*]

445 VÁRYA Why aren't you asleep?

ÁNYA I tried. I couldn't sleep.

GÁYEV Kitten . . . [*Kisses* ÁNYA's *cheek, then her hands.*] My dear child . . . [*Almost in tears*] You're more than just my niece, you're my angel, you know that? You're my whole world, believe me, believe me. . . .

450 ÁNYA I believe you, Uncle. And I love you; we all love you. . . . But, Uncle dear, you should learn not to talk so much. The things you were saying just now about Mama, about your own sister . . . What were you saying all that for?

GÁYEV I know, I know. . . . [*Covers his face with her hand.*] It's awful, I know. 455 My God, a few minutes ago I made a speech to a piece of furniture. . . . It

9. A city on the Volga River, about 160 miles northeast of Moscow.

was so stupid! The thing is, I never realize how stupid I sound until I'm done.

VÁRYA   She's right, Uncle. You just have to learn to keep still, that's all.

ÁNYA   If you do, you'll feel much better about yourself, you know you will. . . .

460 GÁYEV   I will, I will, I promise. [*Kisses* ÁNYA's *and* VÁRYA's *hands.*] I'll keep still. Only right now I have to talk a little more. Business! On Thursday I was at the county courthouse; there was a group of us talking—just this and that—and it turns out I might be able to arrange a promissory note for enough money to pay off the mortgage.

465 VÁRYA   If only God would help us!

GÁYEV   I'm going in on Tuesday, I'll talk to them again. [*To* VÁRYA] Don't whine! [*To* ÁNYA] Your mother will talk to Lopákhin; he can't refuse to help her. And you, as soon as you're rested, you go to Yároslavl, go talk to your godmother. There. We'll be operating on three fronts at once; we're sure to
470 succeed. We *will* pay off this mortgage, I know we will. . . . [*He pops a hard candy into his mouth.*] I swear by my honor, I swear by anything you want, the estate will not be sold! [*Excitedly*] I swear by my own happiness! Here, you have my hand on it. You may call me . . . dishonorable, call me anything you will, if I ever let this estate go on the auction block! I swear by my
475 entire existence!

ÁNYA   [*her calm mood has returned; she is happy*]   You're so smart, Uncle! You're such a wonderful man! [*Hugs* GÁYEV.] Now I feel better! So much better! I'm happy again!

[*Enter* FIRS.]

FIRS   [*reproachfully*]   Leoníd Andréyich, why aren't you in bed, like decent
480 God-fearing people?

GÁYEV   I'm coming, I'm coming. You go to bed, Firs. I can get undressed by myself. All right, children, nighty-night. We can talk about the details tomorrow, now it's time for bed. [*Kisses* ÁNYA *and* VÁRYA.] I am a man of the eighties, you know. People don't think much of that era now, but I can tell
485 you frankly that I have had the courage of my convictions and often had to pay the price.[1] But these local peasants all love me. You have to get to know them, that's all. You have to get to know them, and—

ÁNYA   Uncle. You're at it again.

VÁRYA   Just be quiet, Uncle.

490 FIRS   [*angrily*]   Leoníd Andréyich!

GÁYEV   I'm coming, I'm coming. . . . Go to bed now. Yellow ball in the side pocket! Clean shot!

[*Goes out;* FIRS *follows him, limping.*]

ÁNYA   I feel much better. I don't much want to go to Yároslavl, I don't like my godmother, but I feel better now. Thanks to Uncle [*Sits down.*]

495 VÁRYA   We've got to get some sleep. I'm going to bed. Oh, there's something came up since you left. You know we've got all those old retired servants living out back—Paulina, old Karp, and the rest of them. And what happened, they started inviting people in to spend the night. Well, it's annoying, but I never said a thing. Then what happened was, they started telling everybody
500 all they were getting to eat was beans. Because I was so cheap, you see. It

---

1. When Alexander III (1845–1894) became czar in 1881, he initiated a series of repressive measures designed to combat liberal and revolutionary elements in Russian society.

was that old Karp was doing it. So I said to myself, All right, that's the way you want it, all right, just wait, and I sent for him [*Yawns*], and in he comes, so I say, Karp, you're such an idiot—[*Looks at* ÁNYA.] Ánya!

[*Pause.*]

She's asleep. [*Lifts* ÁNYA *by the arms.*] Come on, time for bed. . . . Come on,
505 let's go. . . . [*Leads her off.*] My angel fell asleep! Come on. . . . [*They start out.*]

> [*In the distance, beyond the orchard, a shepherd plays a pipe.* TROFÍMOV *enters, sees* ÁNYA *and* VÁRYA, *stops.*]

VÁRYA Shh! She's asleep. . . . Come on, darling, let's go. . . .

ÁNYA [*softly, half asleep*] I was so tired. . . . All those bells . . . Uncle dear . . . and Mama. Uncle and Mama.

VÁRYA Come on, darling, come on. . . .

> [*They go off into* ÁNYA'*s room.*]

510 TROFÍMOV [*deeply moved*] My sunshine! My springtime!

Curtain.

Act 2

[*An open space. The overgrown ruin of an abandoned chapel. There is a well beside it and some large stones that must once have been grave markers. An old bench. Beyond, the road to the Gáyev estate. On one side a shadowy row of poplar trees; they mark the limits of the cherry orchard. A row of telegraph poles, and on the far distant horizon, on a clear day, you can just make out the city. It's late afternoon, almost sunset.* CAR-LOTTA, YÁSHA, *and* DUNYÁSHA *are sitting on the bench;* YEPIKHÓDOV *stands nearby, strumming his guitar; each seems lost in his own thoughts.* CAR-LOTTA *wears an old military cap and is adjusting the strap on a hunting rifle.*]

CARLOTTA [*meditatively*] I haven't got a birth certificate, so I don't know how old I really am. I just think of myself as young. When I was a little girl, Mama and my father used to travel around to fairs and put on shows, good ones. I did back flips, things like that. And after they died this German
5 woman brought me up, taught me a few things. And that was it. Then I grew up and had to go to work. As a governess. Where I'm from . . . who I am . . . no idea. Who my parents were—maybe they weren't even married—no idea. [*Takes a large cucumber pickle out of her pocket and takes a bite.*] No idea at all.

[*Pause.*]

10 And I feel like talking all the time, but there's no one to talk to. No one.

YEPIKHÓDOV [*plays the guitar and sings*]

"What do I care for the rest of the world,
or care what it cares for me . . ."[2]

Very agreeable, playing a mandolin.

DUNYÁSHA That's not a mandolin, it's a guitar. [*Takes out a compact with a mirror and powders herself.*]

15 YEPIKHÓDOV When a man is madly in love, a guitar is a mandolin.

---

2. Words from a popular turn-of-the-century ballad.

[*Sings.*]

"As long as my heart is on fire with love,
and the one I love loves me."

[YÁSHA *sings harmony.*]

CARLOTTA   Oof! You people sound like hyenas.

DUNYÁSHA   But it must have been just lovely, being in Europe.

20 YÁSHA   Oh, it was. Quite, quite lovely. I have to agree with you there. [*Yawns, then lights a cigar.*]

YEPIKHÓDOV   That's understandable. In Europe, things have already come to a complex.

YÁSHA [*beat*]   I suppose you could say that.

YEPIKHÓDOV   I'm a true product of the educational system; I read all the
25   time. All the right books too, but I have no chosen directive in life. For me, strictly speaking, it's live or shoot myself. That's why I always carry a loaded pistol. See? [*Takes out a revolver.*]

CARLOTTA   All done. Time to go. [*Slings the rifle over her shoulder.*] You're a very smart man, Yepikhódov, and a very scary one. Ooh! The women must
30   adore you. [*Starts off.*] They're all so dumb, these smart boys. Never anyone to talk to . . . Always alone, all by myself, no one to talk to . . . and I still don't know who I am. Or why. No idea.

[*Walks slowly off.*]

YEPIKHÓDOV   I should explain, by the way, for the sake of expressivity, that fate has been, ah, *rigorous* to me. I am, strictly speaking, tempest-tossed.
35   Always have been. Now, you may say to me, Oh, you're imagining things, but then why, when I wake up this morning—here's an example—and I look down, why is there this spider on my stomach? Detrimentally large too. [*Makes a circle with his two hands.*] Big as that. Or take a beer, let's say. I go to drink it, what do I see floating around in it? Something highly
40   unappreciative, like a cockroach.

[*Pause.*]

Have you ever read Henry Thomas Buckle?[3]

[*Pause.*]

May I design to disturb you, Avdótya Fyódorovna, with something I have to say?

DUNYÁSHA   So say it.

45 YEPIKHÓDOV   Preferentially alone. [*Sighs.*]

DUNYÁSHA [*embarrassed*]   All right. . . . Only first get me my wrap; it's by the kitchen door. It's getting kind of damp.

YEPIKHÓDOV   Ah, I see. Yes, get the wrap, of course. Now I know what to do with my gun.

[*Takes his guitar and goes off, strumming.*]

50 YÁSHA   Double Trouble. He's an idiot, if you ask me. [*Yawns.*]

DUNYÁSHA   I hope to God he doesn't shoot himself.

[*Pause.*]

I get upset over every little thing anymore. Ever since I started working for them here, I've gotten used to their *lifestyle*. Just look at my hands. Look at

---

3. English historian (1821–1862), author of *History of Civilization in England* (1857–61), an unfinished attempt to present history as an exact science.

how white they are, just like I was rich. I'm different now from like I was.
55 I'm more delicate, I'm more sensitive; everything upsets me. . . . It's just
awful how things upset me. So if you cheat on me, Yásha, I may just have a
nervous breakdown.

YÁSHA [*kisses her*]   Oh, you little cutie! Just remember, though: a girl has to
watch her step. What I'm after is a *nice* girl.

60 DUNYÁSHA   I really love you, Yásha, I really do. You're so smart, you know so
many things. . . .
   [*Pause.*]

YÁSHA [*yawns*]   Yeah. . . . But my theory is, a girl says she loves you, she's not
a nice girl.
   [*Pause.*]

Nothing like smoking a cigar out here in the fresh air. . . . [*Listens.*] Some-
65 body's coming. . . . It's them. . . .
   [DUNYÁSHA *hugs him impulsively.*]

YÁSHA   Go on back to the house. Go back the other way, make believe
you've been swimming down by the river, so they don't think we've
been . . . we've been getting together out here like this. I don't want them
to think that.

70 DUNYÁSHA [*a little cough*]   That cigar smoke is giving me a headache. . . .
   [*Goes out.*]

[YÁSHA *sits beside the chapel wall. Enter* LIUBÓV, GÁYEV, *and* LOPÁKHIN.]

LOPÁKHIN   You have to make up your mind one way or the other; time's running out. There's no argument left. You want to subdivide or don't you? Just
give me an answer, one word, yes or no.

LIUBÓV ANDRÉYEVNA   Who's been smoking those cheap cigars? [*Sits down.*]

75 GÁYEV   Everything's so convenient, now that there's the railroad. We went
into town just to have lunch. Yellow ball in the side pocket! What do
you say—why don't we go back to the house, eh? Have ourselves a little
game . . .

LIUBÓV ANDRÉYEVNA   Let's wait till later.

80 LOPÁKHIN   Just one word! [*Imploringly*] Why don't you give me an answer?

GÁYEV [*yawns*]   To what?

LIUBÓV ANDRÉYEVNA [*rummages in her purse*]   Yesterday I had a lot of money,
today it's all gone. My poor Várya feeds us all on soup to economize, the
poor old people get nothing but beans, and I just spend and spend. . . .
85 [*Drops her purse; gold coins spill out.*] Oh, I've spilled everything. . . .

YÁSHA   Here, allow me. [*Picks up the money.*]

LIUBÓV ANDRÉYEVNA   Oh, please do, Yásha; thank you. And why I had to go
into that town for lunch—that stupid restaurant of yours, those stupid
musicians, those stupid tablecloths; they smelled of soap. . . . Why do we
90 drink so much, Lyónya? And eat so much? Why do we talk so much? The
whole time we were in the restaurant, you kept talking, and none of it
made any sense. Talking about the seventies, about Symbolism.[4] And to
who? The waiters! Talking about Symbolism to waiters!

---

4. A movement in literature and art that
began in France in the last third of the 19th
century; it emphasized the evocation of subjective emotion, via symbol and metaphor,
rather than objective description, and it had
its greatest influence in Russia in the 1880s.
The seventies: a time of widespread populist
agitation among Russia's peasant population.

LOPÁKHIN Yes.

95 GÁYEV [*makes a deprecating gesture*] I'm incorrigible, I suppose. . . . [*To* YÁSHA, *irritably*] What are *you* doing here? Why are you always underfoot every time I turn around?

YÁSHA [*laughs*] Because every time I hear your voice it makes me laugh.

GÁYEV Either he goes or I do!

100 LIUBÓV ANDRÉYEVNA Yásha, please . . . just go 'way, will you?

YÁSHA [*gives* LIUBÓV *her purse*] I'm going. Right now. [*Barely containing his laughter*] Right this very minute . . .

[*Goes out.*]

LOPÁKHIN You know who Derigánov is? You know how much money he has? You know he's planning to buy your property? They say he's coming to the auction himself.

105

LIUBÓV ANDRÉYEVNA Who told you that?

LOPÁKHIN Everybody in town knows about it.

GÁYEV The old lady in Yároslavl promised to send money. . . . But when, and how much, she didn't say.

110 LOPÁKHIN How much will she send? A hundred thousand? Two hundred?

LIUBÓV ANDRÉYEVNA Ten or fifteen thousand. And we're lucky to get that much.

LOPÁKHIN Excuse me, but you people . . . I have never met anyone so unbusinesslike, so impractical, so . . . so *crazy* as the pair of you! Somebody tells

115 you flat out your land is about to be sold, you don't even seem to understand!

LIUBÓV ANDRÉYEVNA But what should we do? Just tell us what we should do!

LOPÁKHIN I tell you every day what you should do! Every day I come out here and say the same thing. The cherry orchard and the rest of the land

120 has to be subdivided and developed for leisure homes, and it has to be done right away. The auction date is getting closer! Can't you understand? All you have to do is make up your mind to subdivide, you'll have more money than even you can spend! Your troubles will be over!

LIUBÓV ANDRÉYEVNA Subdivide, leisure homes . . . excuse me, but it's all so

125 hopelessly vulgar.

GÁYEV I couldn't agree more.

LOPÁKHIN You people drive me crazy! Another minute, I'll be shouting my head off! Oh, I give up, I give up! Why do I even bother? [*To* GÁYEV] You're worse than an old lady!

130 GÁYEV What say?

LOPÁKHIN I said you're an old lady! [*Starts to leave.*]

LIUBÓV ANDRÉYEVNA [*fearfully*] No, no, no, please, my dear, don't go. Please. I'm sure we'll think of something.

LOPÁKHIN What's there to think of?

135 LIUBÓV ANDRÉYEVNA Please. Don't go. Things are easier when you're around. . . .

[*Pause.*]

I keep waiting for something to happen. It's as if the house were about to fall down around our ears or something. . . .

GÁYEV [*meditatively*] Yellow ball in the side pocket . . . Clean shot down the

140 middle . . .

LIUBÓV ANDRÉYEVNA We're guilty of so many sins, I know—

LOPÁKHIN   Sins? What are you talking about?

GÁYEV [*pops a hard candy into his mouth*]   People say I've eaten up my entire
inheritance in candy. [*Laughs.*]

145   LIUBÓV ANDRÉYEVNA   All my sins . . . I've always wasted money, just thrown it
away like a madwoman, and I married a man who never paid a bill in his life.
He was an alcoholic; he drank himself to death—on champagne. And I was
so unhappy I fell in love with another man, *unfortunately,* and had an affair
with him, and that was when—that was the first thing, my first punishment,
150   right down there, in the river, my little boy drowned, and I left, I went to
France, I left and never wanted to come back, I never wanted to see that
river again, I just closed my eyes and *ran,* forgot about everything, and that
man followed me. He just wouldn't let up. And he was so mean to me, so
cruel! I bought a villa in Mentón because he got sick while we were there,
155   and for the next three years I never had a moment's peace, day or night. He
tormented me from his sickbed. I could feel my soul dry up. And last year I
couldn't afford the villa anymore, so I sold it and we moved to Paris, and
once we were in Paris he took everything I had left and ran off with another
woman, and I tried to kill myself. It was so stupid, and so shameful! Finally
160   all I wanted was to come back home, to where I was born, to my daughter.
[*Wipes away her tears.*] Oh, dear God, dear God, forgive me! Forgive me my
sins! Don't punish me again! [*Takes a telegram from her purse.*] This came
today, from Paris. . . . He says he's sorry, he wants me back. . . . [*Tears up the
telegram.*] Where's [*Listens.*] . . . where's that music coming from?

165   GÁYEV   That's our famous local orchestra. Those Jewish musicians, you
remember? Four fiddles, a clarinet, and a double bass.

LIUBÓV ANDRÉYEVNA   Are they still around? We should have them over some
evening and throw a party.

LOPÁKHIN [*listens*]   I don't hear anything. [*Sings to himself.*]

170   "Ooh-la-la . . .
         Just a little bit of money
         makes a lady very French . . ."

[*Laughs.*] I went to the theater last night, saw this musical. Very funny.

LIUBÓV ANDRÉYEVNA   I doubt there was anything funny about it. You ought to
175   stop going to see playacting and take a good look at your own reality. What
a boring life you lead! And what uninteresting things you talk about.

LOPÁKHIN   Well . . . yeah, there's some truth to that. It is a pretty dumb life
we lead. . . .

       [*Pause.*]

My father was a . . . he was a dirt farmer, an idiot, never understood me,
180   never taught me anything, just got drunk and beat me up. With a stick.
Fact is, I'm not much better myself. Never did well in school, my writing's
terrible, I'm ashamed if anybody sees it. I write like a pig.

LIUBÓV ANDRÉYEVNA   My dear man, you should get married.

LOPÁKHIN   Yes. . . . Yes, I should.

185   LIUBÓV ANDRÉYEVNA   And you should marry our Várya. She's a wonderful girl.

LOPÁKHIN   She is.

LIUBÓV ANDRÉYEVNA   Her people were quite ordinary, but she works like a
dog, and the main thing is, she loves you. And you like her, I know you do.
You always have.

190 LOPÁKHIN   Look, I've got nothing against it. I . . . She's a wonderful girl.
       [*Pause.*]

GÁYEV   They offered me a position at the bank. Six thousand a year. Did I tell you?

LIUBÓV ANDRÉYEVNA   Don't be silly! You stay right here where you belong.
       [*Enter* FIRS, *carrying an overcoat.*]

FIRS   Sir, sir, please put this on. It's getting damp.

195 GÁYEV [*puts it on*]   Firs, you're getting to be a bore.

FIRS   That so? Went out this morning, didn't even tell me. [*Tries to adjust* GÁYEV's *clothes.*]

LIUBÓV ANDRÉYEVNA   Poor Firs! You've gotten so old!

FIRS   Beg pardon?

LOPÁKHIN   She said you got very old!

200 FIRS   I've lived a long time. They were trying to marry me off way back before your daddy was born. [*Laughs.*] By the time we got our freedom back,[5] I was already head butler. I had all the freedom I needed, so I stayed right here with the masters.
       [*Pause.*]
       I remember everybody got all excited about it, but they never even knew
205   what they were getting excited about.

LOPÁKHIN   Oh, sure, things were wonderful back in the good old days! They had the right to beat you if they wanted, remember?

FIRS [*doesn't hear*]   That's right. Masters stood by the servants, servants stood by the masters. Nowadays it's all mixed up; you can't tell who's who.

210 GÁYEV   Shut up, Firs. . . . I have to go into town tomorrow. A friend promised to introduce me to someone who might be able to arrange a loan. Some general.

LOPÁKHIN   That's never going to work. Trust me, you won't get enough even for the interest payments.

215 LIUBÓV ANDRÉYEVNA   He's imagining things. There's no general.
       [*Enter* ÁNYA, VÁRYA, *and* TROFÍMOV.]

GÁYEV   Here come our young people.

ÁNYA   Mama's resting.

LIUBÓV ANDRÉYEVNA [*tenderly*]   Here we are, dears, over here. [*Kisses* ÁNYA *and* Várya.] If you only knew how much I love you both. Come sit here by
220   me . . . that's right.
       [*They all sit down.*]

LOPÁKHIN   Our permanent graduate student seems to spend all his time studying the ladies.

TROFÍMOV   Mind your own business.

LOPÁKHIN   Almost in his fifties, he's still in school.

225 TROFÍMOV   Just stop the silly jokes, will you?

LOPÁKHIN   Oh, the *scholar* is losing his temper!

TROFÍMOV   Will you please just leave me alone?

LOPÁKHIN [*laughs*]   Let me ask you a question: You look at me, what do you see?

5. That is, 1861, when the serfs—feudal agricultural workers bound to their lord's land,
who made up one-third of Russia's total
population—were freed by Alexander II's
Edict of Emancipation.

230 TROFÍMOV   When I look at you, Yermolái Alexéyich, what I see is a rich man.
One who will soon be a millionaire. You are as necessary a part of the evolution of the species as the wild animal that eats up anything in its path.

   [*Everybody laughs.*]

VÁRYA   Forget biology, Pétya. You should stick to counting stars.

LIUBÓV ANDRÉYEVNA   I want to hear more about what we were talking about
235   last night.

TROFÍMOV   What were we talking about?

GÁYEV   About human dignity.

TROFÍMOV   We talked about a lot last night, but we never got anywhere. You
people talk about human dignity as if it were something mystical. I suppose
240   it is, in a way, for you anyway, but when you really get down to it, what have
humans got to be proud of? Biologically we're pretty minor specimens—
besides which, the great majority of human beings are vulgar and unhappy
and totally *un*dignified. We should stop patting ourselves on the back and
get to work.

245 GÁYEV   You still have to die.

TROFÍMOV   Who says? Anyway, what does that mean, to die? Maybe we have
a hundred senses, and all we lose when we die are the five we're familiar
with, and the other ninety-five go on living.

LIUBÓV ANDRÉYEVNA   Oh, Pétya, you're so smart!

250 LOPÁKHIN [*with irony*]   Oh, yes, very.

TROFÍMOV   Remember, human beings are constantly progressing, and their
power keeps growing. Things that seem impossible to us nowadays, the
day will come when they're not a problem at all, only we have to work
toward that day. We have to seek out the truth. We don't do that, you
255   know. Most of the people in this country aren't working toward anything.
People I come in contact with—at the university, for instance—they're
supposed to be educated, but they're not interested in the truth. They're
not interested in much of anything, actually. They certainly don't *do*
much. They call themselves intellectuals and think that gives them the
260   right to look down on the rest of the world. They never read anything
worthwhile, they're completely ignorant where science is concerned, they
talk about art and they don't even know what it is they're talking about.
They take themselves so seriously, they're full of theories and ideas, but
just go look at the cities they live in. Miles and miles of slums, where
265   people go hungry and where they live packed into unheated tenements
full of cockroaches and garbage, and their lives are full of violence and
immorality. So what are all the theories for? To keep people like us from
seeing all that. Where are the day-care centers they talk so much about,
and the literacy programs? It's all just talk. You go out to the parts of town
270   where the poor people live, you can't find them. All you find is dirt and
ignorance and crime. That's why I don't like all this talk, all these theories.
Bothers me, makes me afraid. If that's all our talk is good for, we'd better
just shut up.

LOPÁKHIN   I get up at five and work from morning to night, and you know,
275   my business involves a lot of money, my own and other people's, so I see
lots of people, see what they're like. And you just try to get anything accomplished: you'll see how few decent, honest people there really are. Sometimes at night I can't sleep, and I think: Dear God, you gave us this

beautiful earth to live on, these great forests, these wide fields, the broad
280 horizons . . . by rights we should be giants.
LIUBÓV ANDRÉYEVNA   What do you want giants for? The only good giants are
in fairy tales. Real ones would scare you to death.
[*Upstage,* YEPIKHÓDOV *strolls by, playing his guitar.*]
[*Dreamily*] There goes Yepikhódov. . . .
ÁNYA [*dreamily*]   There goes Yepikhódov. . . .
285 GÁYEV   The sun, ladies and gentlemen, has just set.
TROFÍMOV   Yes.
GÁYEV [*as if reciting a poem, but not too loud*]   O wondrous nature, cast upon
us your eternal rays, forever beautiful, forever indifferent. . . . Mother, we
call you; life and death reside within you; you bring forth and lay waste—
290 VÁRYA [*pleading*]   Uncle, please!
ÁNYA   Uncle, you're doing it again.
TROFÍMOV   We'd rather have the yellow ball in the side pocket.
GÁYEV   Sorry, sorry. I'll keep still.
[*They all sit in silence. The only sound we hear is old* FIRS *mumbling.
Suddenly a distant sound seems to fall from the sky, a sad sound, like a
harp string breaking. It dies away.*]
LIUBÓV ANDRÉYEVNA   What was that?
295 LOPÁKHIN   Can't tell. Sounds like it could be an echo from a mine shaft. But
it must be far away.
GÁYEV   Or some kind of bird . . . like a heron.
TROFÍMOV   Or an owl.
LIUBÓV ANDRÉYEVNA [*shivers*]   Makes me nervous.
[*Pause.*]
300 FIRS   It's like just before the trouble started. They heard an owl screech, and
the kettle wouldn't stop whistling. . . .
GÁYEV   Before what trouble?
FIRS   The day we got our freedom back.
[*Pause.*]
LIUBÓV ANDRÉYEVNA   My dears, it's getting dark; we should be going in.
305 [*To* ÁNYA] You've got tears in your eyes, darling. What's the matter? [*Hugs*
ÁNYA.]
ÁNYA   Nothing, Mama. It's all right.
TROFÍMOV   Someone's coming.
[*Enter a* HOMELESS MAN *in a white cap and an overcoat; he's slightly
drunk.*]
HOMELESS MAN   Can anyone please tell me, can I get to the train station this
way?
310 GÁYEV   Of course you can. Just follow this road.
HOMELESS MAN   Much obliged. [*Bows.*] Wonderful weather we're having . . .
[*Recites.*] "Behold one of the poor in spirit, just trying to inherit a little of
the earth. . . ."[6] [*To* VÁRYA] Listen, you think you could spare some money
for a hungry man?

6. An allusion to two of the beatitudes from Jesus's Sermon on the Mount: "Blessed are the poor in spirit, for theirs is the kingdom of heaven. . . . Blessed are the meek, for they shall inherit the earth" (Matthew 5.3, 5).

[VÁRYA *is terrified; she screams.*]

315 LOPÁKHIN [*angrily*]   Now hold on just a minute!

LIUBÓV ANDRÉYEVNA [*panicked*]   Here . . . here . . . take this. [*Fumbles in her purse.*] Oh, I don't seem to have anything smaller. Here, take this. [*Gives him a gold piece.*]

HOMELESS MAN   Very much obliged!

[*Goes out.*]

[*Everybody laughs.*]

VÁRYA   Get me out of here! Oh, please get me out! Mama, how could you!
320   We can't even feed the servants, and you go and give him a gold piece!

LIUBÓV ANDRÉYEVNA   I know, darling, I'm just stupid about money. When we get home I'll give you whatever I've got left; you can take care of it. Yermo-lái Alexéyich, can you lend me some money?

LOPÁKHIN   Of course.

325 LIUBÓV ANDRÉYEVNA   My darlings, it really is time to go in. Várya dear, we've just gotten you engaged. Congratulations.

VÁRYA [*almost in tears*]   Mama, that's nothing to joke about!

LOPÁKHIN   Amelia, get thee to a nunnery![7]

GÁYEV   Look how my hands shake. I don't know if I could play billiards
330   anymore. . . .

LOPÁKHIN   Nymph, in thy horizons be all my sins remembered!

LIUBÓV ANDRÉYEVNA   Please, let's go. It's almost suppertime.

VÁRYA   He scared me half to death. I can feel my heart pounding.

LOPÁKHIN   But keep in mind, the cherry orchard is going to be sold. On
335   August twenty-second! You hear what I'm saying? You've got to think about this! You've got to!

[*They all go off except* ÁNYA *and* TROFÍMOV.]

ÁNYA [*laughs*]   I'm so glad that tramp scared Várya off. Now we can be alone.

TROFÍMOV   Várya's afraid we're going to fall in love; that's why she never leaves us alone. She's so narrow-minded; she simply can't understand that
340   we are above love. Our goal is to get rid of the silly illusions that keep us from being free and happy. We are moving forward, toward the future! Toward one bright star that burns ahead of us! Forward, friends! Come join us in our journey!

ÁNYA [*claps her hands*]   Oh, you talk so beautifully!

[*Pause.*]

345   It's just heavenly out here today!

TROFÍMOV   Yes, the weather's been really good lately.

ÁNYA   I don't know what it is you've done to me, Pétya, but I don't love the cherry orchard anymore, not the way I used to. I used to think there was no place on earth like our orchard.

350 TROFÍMOV   This whole country is our orchard. It's a big country and a beauti-ful one; it has lots of wonderful places in it.

[*Pause.*]

Just think, Ánya: your grandfather, and his father, and his father's fathers, they *owned* the people who slaved away for them all over this estate, and

---

7. Hamlet's charge to Ophelia in Shakespeare's *Hamlet* (1600–01; 3.1.122). Lopákhin's next line also quotes Hamlet though he substitutes "horizons" for "orisons" 3.1.91–92).

now the voices and faces of human beings hide behind every cherry in the
355 orchard, every leaf, every tree trunk. Can't you see them? And hear them?
And owning human beings has left its mark on all of you. Look at your
mother and your uncle! They live off the labor of others, they always have,
and they've never even noticed! They owe their entire lives to those other
people, people they wouldn't even let walk through the front gate of their
360 beloved cherry orchard! This whole country has fallen behind; it'll take us
at least two hundred years to catch up. The thing is, we don't have any real
sense of our own history; all we do is sit around and talk, talk, talk, then
we feel depressed, so we go out and get drunk. If there's one thing that's
clear to me, it's this: if we want to have any real life in the present, we
365 have to do something to make up for our past, we have to get over it, and
the only way to do that is to make sacrifices, get down to work, and work
harder than we've ever worked before. Do you understand what I mean,
Ánya?

ÁNYA The house we live in isn't our house anymore. It hasn't ever been,
370 really. And I'll leave it all behind, I promise you I will.

TROFÍMOV Yes, you will! Throw away your house keys and go as far away as
you can! You'll be free as the wind.

ÁNYA [*radiant*] I love the way you say things!

TROFÍMOV You have to understand me, Ánya. I'm not thirty yet, I'm still
375 young; I may still be in school, but I've learned a lot. Winter comes, sometimes I get cold and hungry, or sick and upset, I don't have a cent to my
name; things work out or they don't. . . . But no matter what, my heart and
soul are always full of feelings, all kinds . . . I can't even explain them. And
I feel happiness coming, Ánya, I can feel it, I can almost see it—

380 ÁNYA [*dreamily*] Look, the moon's rising.

[*The sound of* YEPIKHÓDOV's *guitar, still playing the same mournful song.
The moon rises. Somewhere beyond the poplar trees,* VÁRYA *can be heard
calling.*]

VÁRYA [*off*] Anya! Ánya, where are you?

TROFÍMOV Yes, the moon is rising.

[*Pause.*]

It's happiness, that's what it is: it's rising, it's coming closer and closer, I
can hear it. And even if we miss it, if we never find it, that's all right!
385 Someone will!

VÁRYA [*off*] Ánya! Ánya, where are you?

TROFÍMOV [*angrily*] That Várya! Why won't she let us alone!

ÁNYA Don't let her bother you. Let's take a walk by the river. It's so nice
there.

390 TROFÍMOV All right, let's go.

[*They leave. The stage is empty.*]

VÁRYA [*off*] Ánya! Ánya!

Curtain.

Act 3

[*A sitting room, separated from the ballroom in back by an archway. The
chandeliers are lit. From the entrance hall comes the sounds of an
orchestra, the Jewish musicians* GÁYEV *mentioned in Act 2. Evening. In
the ballroom, everyone is dancing a grande ronde.* SEMYÓNOV-PÍSHCHIK's

voice is heard calling the figures of the dance: "Promenade à une paire!"[8]
*The dancers dance through the sitting room in pairs in the following
order:* PÍSHCHIK *and* CARLOTTA, TROFÍMOV *and* LIUBÓV ANDREYÉVNA, ÁNYA
and the POSTMASTER, VÁRYA *and the* STATIONMASTER, *etc.* VÁRYA *is in
tears, which she tries to wipe away as she dances. The final pair includes*
DUNYÁSHA. *As the dancers return to the ballroom,* PÍSHCHIK *calls out:
"Grande ronde, balancez!" and "Les cavaliers à genoux et remercier vos
dames."*[9] FIRS *in his butler's uniform crosses the stage, carrying a seltzer
bottle on a tray.* PÍSHCHIK *and* TROFÍMOV *come into the sitting room.*]

PÍSHCHIK   I'm prone to strokes, already had two of 'em, I really shouldn't be
dancing, but you know what they say: When in Rome. Besides, I'm really
strong as a horse. Speaking of Romans, my father—what a joker he was—he
used to claim our family was descended from the emperor Caligula's
5   horse—you know, the one he made a senator?[1] [*Sits down.*] The only problem is we have no money. [*His head nods, he snores, then immediately wakes
up.*] So the only thing I ever think about is money.
TROFÍMOV   Your father was right. You do look a little like a horse.
PÍSHCHIK   Nothing wrong with horses. Wonderful animals. If I had one, I
10   could sell it. . . .
    [*From the adjacent billiard room come the sounds of a game.* VÁRYA
    appears in the archway.]
TROFÍMOV [*teases her*]   Mrs. Lopákhin! Mrs. Lopákhin!
VÁRYA [*angrily*]   High-class tramp!
TROFÍMOV   Yes, I'm a high-class tramp, and I'm proud of it!
VÁRYA [*bitterly*]   We've hired an orchestra! And what are we supposed to pay
15   them with?
    [*Goes out.*]
TROFÍMOV [*to* PÍSHCHIK]   All the energy you've used trying to find money to
pay your mortgage, if you'd spent that energy on something else, you could
have moved the world.
PÍSHCHIK   Nietzsche,[2] you know, the philosopher—a great thinker, Nietz-
20   sche, a man of genius, one of the great minds of the century—now Nietzsche,
you know, says, in his memoirs, that counterfeit money's just as good as
real. . . .
TROFÍMOV   I didn't know you'd read Nietzsche.
PÍSHCHIK   Well . . . actually, Dáshenka told me. And I'm desperate enough.
25   I'm ready to start counterfeiting. I need three hundred and ten rubles, day
after tomorrow. All I've got so far is a hundred and thirty. . . . [*He feels in
his pockets anxiously.*] It's gone! My money's gone! [*Almost in tears*] I've lost
my money! [*Joyfully*] Oh, here it is! It slipped down into the lining of my
coat! God, I'm all in a sweat!
    [*Enter* LIUBÓV *and* CARLOTTA.]
30   LIUBÓV ANDREYÉVNA [*she hums a dance tune*]   Why is it taking so long?
What's Leoníd doing all this time in town? He should be back by now.

8. "Promenade with your partner!" (French).
9. "Large circle, swing with your arms!";
"Gentlemen, kneel down and thank your
ladies" (French).
1. According to the Roman historian Sueto-
nius, the emperor Caligula (r. 37–41 C.E.)
considered making his favorite racehorse a
consul; the version in popular lore is that he
appointed the animal a senator.
2. Friedrich Nietzsche (1844–1900), German
philosopher who was among the most influential of modern thinkers.

848 | ANTON CHEKHOV

[*Calls to* DUNYÁSHA *in the ballroom.*] Dunyásha, tell the musicians they can take a break.

TROFÍMOV   They probably postponed the auction.

35   LIUBÓV ANDREYÉVNA   I suppose it was a mistake to hire an orchestra. Or to have a party in the first place. Oh, well . . . what difference does it make? [*Sits down and hums quietly.*]

CARLOTTA [*hands* PÍSHCHIK *a deck of cards*]   Here's the deck. Pick a card, any card. . . . No, no, just think of one.

PÍSHCHIK   All right, I'm thinking of one.

40   CARLOTTA   Good. Now shuffle the deck. Very good. Now give it to me. Observe, my dear Píshchik! *Eins, zwei, drei!*[3] Now look in your jacket pocket, and you will find your card.

PÍSHCHIK [*takes a card from his jacket pocket*]   That's it, the eight of spades! [*Amazed*] Really! I don't believe it!

45   CARLOTTA [*holds out the deck to* TROFÍMOV]   Quick, what's the top card?

TROFÍMOV   The top card? Oh . . . uh . . . the queen of spades.

CARLOTTA   Correct! [*To* PÍSHCHIK] Now which card's on top?

PÍSHCHIK   Ace of hearts!

CARLOTTA   Correct! [*Claps her hands, and the deck disappears.*] Well, isn't this
50   a lovely day we're having?

[*A mysterious woman's voice answers; it seems to come from the floorboards: "A lovely day indeed. I couldn't agree more."*]

Whoever you are, I adore you!

[*The voice: "I adore you too!"*]

STATIONMASTER [*applauds*]   Bravo! A lady ventriloquist!

PÍSHCHIK [*amazed*]   Really! I don't believe it! Carlotta, you are amazing! I'm completely in love with you!

55   CARLOTTA   In love? [*Shrugs her shoulders.*] What do you know about love? *Guter Mensch aber schlechter Musikant.*[4]

TROFÍMOV [*slaps* PÍSHCHIK *on the shoulder*]   You're just an old horse!

CARLOTTA   All right, everybody, watch closely! One more trick! [*Takes a lap robe from a chair.*] See, what a lovely blanket! I'm thinking of selling it.
60   [*Shakes out the lap robe and holds it up.*] Who wants to buy?

PÍSHCHIK [*amazed*]   Really! I don't believe it!

CARLOTTA   *Eins, zwei, drei!* [*Quickly raises the lap robe.*]

[ÁNYA *appears behind the lap robe; she curtsies, runs to her mother and kisses her, then runs back into the ballroom. General applause and cries of delight.*]

LIUBÓV ANDREYÉVNA [*applauding*]   Bravo! Bravo!

CARLOTTA   Now one more! *Eins, zwei, drei!*

[*She raises the lap robe;* VÁRYA *appears; she takes a bow.*]

65   PÍSHCHIK   Really! I don't believe it!

CARLOTTA   That's all. The show is over.

[*Throws the lap robe to* PÍSHCHIK, *takes a bow, goes through the ballroom and out.*]

PÍSHCHIK [*goes after her*]   Enchanting! What a woman! What a woman! [*Goes out.*]

3. One, two, three! (German).
4. A good man but a bad musician (German); that is, an incompetent.

LIUBÓV ANDREYÉVNA   Leoníd still isn't back from town yet. I don't understand
what could be taking him so long! It's got to be all over by now: either the
70   estate has been sold or they've postponed the auction. Why does he have to
keep us in suspense like this?

VÁRYA [*tries to comfort her*]   Uncle bought the estate, I'm sure he has.

TROFÍMOV [*ironically*]   Oh, I'm sure.

VÁRYA   Ánya's godmother sent him a power of attorney to buy the estate in
75   her name; she agreed to take over the mortgage. She did it for Ánya. So
God *has* helped us. Uncle has saved the estate.

LIUBÓV ANDREYÉVNA   The old lady in Yároslavl sent us fifteen thousand to
buy the place in her name—she doesn't trust us—but that's not even
enough to pay the interest. [*Covers her face with her hands.*] My fate . . .
80   my entire life . . . It's all being decided today.

TROFÍMOV [*teases* VÁRYA]   Mrs. Lopákhin! Mrs. Lopákhin!

VÁRYA [*angrily*]   And you're a permanent graduate student! Who's been suspended twice!

LIUBÓV ANDRÉYEVNA   Don't get so angry, Várya; he's only teasing you. What's
85   wrong with that? And what's wrong with Lopákhin? If you want to marry
him, do; he's a nice man. Interesting, even. If you don't want to marry him,
don't; nobody's forcing you.

VÁRYA   It's not a joking matter, Mama, believe me. I'm serious about him. He
is a nice man, and I like him.

90   LIUBÓV ANDRÉYEVNA   Then go ahead and marry him! I don't understand what
you're waiting for!

VÁRYA   Mama, I can't propose to him myself! For two years now everybody's
been telling me to marry him, everybody, but he never mentions it. Or he
jokes about it! Look, I understand, he's busy getting rich, he doesn't have
95   time for me. Oh, if I had just a little money—I don't care how much, even
a couple of hundred—I'd get out of here and go someplace far away. I'd go
join a convent.

TROFÍMOV   Now, there's an exalted idea!

VÁRYA [*to* TROFÍMOV]   I thought students were supposed to be smart! [*Her
100   tone softens; almost crying.*] Oh, Pétya, you used to be so nice-looking,'
and now you're getting old! [*To* LIUBÓV, *in a normal tone*] It's just that I need
something to do all the time, Mama; it's the way I am. I can't sit around and
do nothing.

[*Enter* YÁSHA.]

YÁSHA [*barely controlling his laughter*]   Yepikhódov broke a billiard cue!
[*Goes out.*]

105   VÁRYA   What is Yepikhódov doing here? Who asked him to come? And what's
he doing playing billiards? I just don't understand these people. . . .
[*Goes out.*]

LIUBÓV ANDRÉYEVNA   Pétya, don't tease her like that; you can see she's upset
already.

TROFÍMOV   Oh, she's such a busybody, always poking her nose into other
110   people's business. She hasn't left Ánya and me alone the whole summer;
she's afraid we're having a . . . an *affair*. What business is it of hers? Besides,
it's not true. I'd never do anything so sordid. We're above love!

LIUBÓV ANDRÉYEVNA   And I, I suppose, am beneath love. [*Upset*] Why isn't
Leoníd back yet? I just want to know: has the estate been sold or not? The

115 whole disaster seems so impossible to me, I don't know what to think, or
do. . . . Oh, God, I'm losing my mind! I want to scream, or do something completely stupid . . . Help me, Pétya! Save me! Say something, say
something!

TROFÍMOV Whether they sell it or not, does it make any difference really?
120 You can't go back to the past. Everything here came to an end a long time
ago. Try to calm down. You can't go on deceiving yourself; at least once in
your life you have to look the truth straight in the eye.

LIUBÓV ANDRÉYEVNA What truth? You seem so sure what's truth and what
isn't, but I'm not. I've lost any sense of it, I've lost sight of the truth. You're
125 so sure of yourself, aren't you, so sure you have all the answers to everything, but darling, have you ever really had to live with one of your answers?
You're too young. Of course *you* look into the future and see a brave new
world, you don't expect any difficulties, but that's because you know nothing about life! Yes, you have more courage than my generation has, and
130 better morals, and you're better educated, but for God's sake have a little
sense of what it's like for me, and be easier on me. Pétya, I was born here!
My parents lived here all their lives; so did my grandfather. I love this
house! Without the cherry orchard my life makes no sense, and if you have
to sell it, you might as well sell me with it. [*She embraces* TROFÍMOV *and*
135 *kisses his forehead.*] And it was here my son drowned, you know that. . . .
[*Weeps.*] Have some feeling for me, Pétya, you're such a good, sweet boy.

TROFÍMOV I pity you. [*Beat*] I do, from the bottom of my heart.

LIUBÓV ANDRÉYEVNA You should have said that differently, just a little differently. . . . [*Takes out her handkerchief; a telegram falls to the floor.*] You can't
140 imagine how miserable I am today. All this noise, and every new sound
makes me shake. I can't get away from it, but then when I'm alone in my
room I can't stand the silence. Don't judge me, Pétya! I love you like one of
my own family; I'd be very happy to see you and Ánya married, you know I
would, only, darling, you must finish school first! You have *got* to graduate!
145 You don't do anything except drift around from place to place—what kind
of life is that? It's true, isn't it? Isn't that the truth? And we have to do
something about that beard of yours; it's so scraggly. . . . [*Laughs.*] You've
gotten so funny-looking!

TROFÍMOV [*picks up the telegram*] I have no desire to be good-looking.

150 LIUBÓV ANDRÉYEVNA The telegram's from Paris. I get a new one every day.
One yesterday, now again today. That madman is sick again and in trouble. . . . He wants me to forgive him, he wants me back . . . and I suppose I
should go back to Paris to be with him. Now see, Pétya, you're giving me
that superior look, but darling, what am I supposed to do? He's sick, he's
155 alone, he's unhappy, and who has he got to look after him? To give him his
medicine and keep him out of trouble? And I love him—why do I have to
pretend I don't, or not talk about it? I love him. That's just the way it is: I
love him. I love him! He's a millstone around my neck, and he'll drown me
with him, but he's *my* millstone! I love him and I can't live without him!
160 [*Grabs* TROFÍMOV'S *hand.*] Don't judge me, Pétya, don't think badly of me,
just don't say anything, please just don't say anything. . . .

TROFÍMOV [*almost in tears*] But for God's sake, you have to face the facts! He
robbed you blind!

LIUBÓV ANDRÉYEVNA No, no, please, you mustn't say that, you mustn't—

165 TROFÍMOV He doesn't care a thing for you—you're the only person who doesn't seem to understand that! He's rotten!

LIUBÓV ANDRÉYEVNA [*gets angry but tries to control it*] And you, you're what? Twenty-six, twenty-seven? Listen to you: you sound like you'd never even graduated to long pants!

170 TROFÍMOV That's fine with me!

LIUBÓV ANDRÉYEVNA You're supposed to be a man; at your age you ought to know something about love. You ought to be in love yourself! [*Angrily*] Really! You think you're so smart, you're just a kid who doesn't know the first thing about it, you're probably a virgin, you're ridiculous, you're
175 grotesque—

TROFÍMOV [*horrified*] What are you saying!

LIUBÓV ANDREYÉVNA "I'm above love!" You're not above love; you've just never gotten down to it! You're all wet, like Firs says. At your age, you ought to be sleeping with someone!

180 TROFÍMOV [*horrified*] What a terrible thing to say! That's terrible! [*He runs toward the ballroom, covering his ears.*] That's just horrible. . . . I can't listen to that; I'm leaving. [*Goes out, but reappears immediately.*] All is over between us!

[*Goes out into the entrance hall.*]

LIUBÓV ANDRÉYEVNA [*calls after him*] Pétya, wait a minute! Come back! I was
185 just joking, Pétya, don't be so silly! Pétya!

[*A great clatter from the entrance hall; someone has fallen downstairs. ÁNYA and VÁRYA scream.*]

What happened?

[*ÁNYA and VÁRYA suddenly howl with laughter.*]

ÁNYA [*runs in, laughing*] Pétya just fell headfirst down the stairs!

[*Runs out.*]

LIUBÓV ANDRÉYEVNA Oh, what a silly boy!

[*The STATIONMASTER in the ballroom gets on a chair and begins declaiming the opening lines of "The Magdalen" by Alexei Tolstoy.[5]*]

STATIONMASTER "The splendid ballroom gleams with gold and candles,
190   a crowd of dancers whirls around the room;
    and there apart, an empty glass beside her,
    behold the fallen beauty, the lost, the doomed.

    Her lavish gown and jewels make all eyes wonder,
    her shameless glance bespeaks a life of sin;
195   young men and old cast longing glances at her—
    see, how her fatal beauty draws them in!"

[*Everyone gathers to listen, but soon the orchestra returns and the strains of a waltz are heard from the entrance hall. The reading breaks off, and everybody begins to dance. TROFÍMOV, ÁNYA, and VÁRYA come in from the entrance hall.*]

5. Russian novelist, poet, and playwright (1817–1875), a distant relative of the more famous novelist Leo Tolstoy. "The Magdalen" is sometimes translated "The Sinful Woman" (a *magdalen* is a reformed prostitute).

LIUBÓV ANDRÉYEVNA   Pétya . . . oh, darling, I'm *so* sorry. . . . You sweet thing, please forgive me. . . . Come on, let's dance. [*Dances with* TROFÍMOV.]

> [ÁNYA *and* VÁRYA *dance together.* FIRS *enters, leans his walking stick against the side door.* YÁSHA *appears and stands watching the dancers.*]

YÁSHA   What's the matter, pops?

200 FIRS   I don't feel so good. The old days, we had a dance, we had generals and barons and admirals; nowadays we have to send out for the postmaster and the stationmaster. And they're none too eager to come, either. Oh, I'm getting old and feeble. The old master, their grandfather, anybody got sick, he used to dose 'em all with sealing wax. Didn't matter what they had, they all

205 got sealing wax. I've been taking sealing wax myself now for nigh onto twenty years. Take some every day. That's probably why I'm still alive.

YÁSHA   You're getting boring, pops. [*Yawns.*] Time for you to crawl off and die.

FIRS   Oh, you . . . you young flibbertigibbet. [*Mumbles.*]

> [TROFÍMOV *and* LIUBÓV *dance through the ballroom, into the sitting room.*]

210 LIUBÓV ANDRÉYEVNA   *Merci.*[6] I need to sit down and rest a bit. . . . [*Sits.*] I'm so tired.

> [*Enter* ÁNYA.]

ÁNYA [*upset*]   There was a man in the kitchen just now, he said the cherry orchard's already been sold!

LIUBÓV ANDRÉYEVNA   Who bought it?

215 ÁNYA   He didn't say. And he's gone now. [*Dances with* TROFÍMOV; *they dance off across the ballroom.*]

YÁSHA   That was just some old guy talking crazy. It wasn't anybody from around here.

FIRS   And Leoníd Andréyich still isn't back. All he had on was his topcoat; you watch, he'll catch cold. He's all wet, that one.

220 LIUBÓV ANDRÉYEVNA   I'll never live through this. Yásha, go out and see if anybody knows who bought it.

YÁSHA   It was just some old guy. He left long ago. [*Laughs.*]

LIUBÓV ANDRÉYEVNA [*somewhat annoyed*]   What are you laughing at? What's so funny?

225 YÁSHA   That Yepikhódov. What a dope. Old Double Trouble.

LIUBÓV ANDRÉYEVNA   Firs, suppose the estate is sold—where are you going to go?

FIRS   I'll go wherever you tell me to.

LIUBÓV ANDRÉYEVNA   What's the matter? Your face looks so funny. . . . Are

230 you sick? You should go to bed.

FIRS   Yes . . . [*Smirks.*] Yes, sure, go to bed, and then who'll take care of things? I'm the only one you've got.

YÁSHA   Liubóv Andréyevna, there's a favor I have *got* to ask you; it's very important. If you go back to Paris, please take me with you. Please! You've

235 got to! I positively cannot stay around here. [*Looks around, lowers his voice.*] You can see for yourself this place is hopeless. The whole country's a mess, nobody has any culture, it's boring, the food is lousy, and there's that old Firs drooling all over the place and talking like an idiot. Please, take me with you—you've just got to!

> [*Enter* PÍSHCHIK.]

---

6. Thank you (French).

240 PÍSHCHIK Beautiful lady, what about a waltz? Just one little waltz! [LIUBÓV crosses to him.] You dazzler, you! And what about a loan, just one little loan, just a hundred and eighty, that's all I need. [They begin to dance.] Just a hundred and eighty . . .

[They dance off into the ballroom.]

YÁSHA [sings to himself] "Can't you see my heart is breaking . . ."

[In the ballroom, a figure appears dressed in checkered trousers and a gray top hat, jumping and waving its arms. We hear shouts of "Bravo, Carlotta!"]

245 DUNYÁSHA [stops to powder her nose] The missus told me to dance—there's too many gentlemen and not enough ladies—so I did, I've been dancing all night and my heart won't stop beating, and you know what, Firs? Just now, the postmaster, you know? He said something almost made me faint.

[The orchestra stops playing.]

FIRS What did he say?

250 DUNYÁSHA That I was like a flower. That's what he said.

YÁSHA [yawns] What does he know about it?

[Goes out.]

DUNYÁSHA Just like a flower. I'm a very romantic girl, really. I just adore that kind of talk.

FIRS You're out of your mind.

[Enter YEPIKHÓDOV.]

255 YEPIKHÓDOV [to DUNYÁSHA] Why are you deliberating not to notice me? You act as if I wasn't here, like I was a bug or something [Sighs.] Ah, life!

DUNYÁSHA Excuse me?

YEPIKHÓDOV Of course, you may be right. [Sighs.] But if you look at it, let's say, from a . . . a point of view, then you're the faulty one—excuse my
260 expressivity—because you led me on. Into this predictament. Look at me! Every day something awful happens to me. It's like a habit. But I can look disaster in the face and keep smiling. You gave me your word, you know, and you even—

DUNYÁSHA Do you mind? Let's talk about it later. Right now I'd rather be left
265 alone. With my dreams. [Plays with a fan.]

YEPIKHÓDOV Every day. Something awful. But all I do—excuse my expressivity—is try to keep smiling. Sometimes I even laugh.

[Enter VÁRYA from the ballroom.]

VÁRYA [to YEPIKHÓDOV] Are you still here? I thought I told you to go home. Really, you have no consideration. [To DUNYÁSHA] Dunyásha, go back to
270 the kitchen! [To YEPIKHÓDOV] You come in here and start playing billiards, you break one of our cues, now you hang around in here as if we'd invited you.

YEPIKHÓDOV Excuse my expressivity, but you have no right to penalize me.

VÁRYA I'm not penalizing you, I'm telling you! All you do here is wander
275 around and bump into the furniture. You're supposed to be working for us, and you don't do a thing. I don't know why we hired you in the first place.

YEPIKHÓDOV [offended] Whether I work or not or wander around or not or play billiards or not is none of your business! You do not have the know-it-all to make my estimation!

280 VÁRYA How dare you talk to me like that! [In a rage] How dare you! What do you mean, I don't have the know-it-all? You get yourself out of here right this minute! Right this minute!

YEPIKHÓDOV [*apprehensively*]   I wish you wouldn't use language like that—
VÁRYA [*beside herself*]   Get out of here right this minute! Out! [*He goes to the*
door; she follows him.] Double Trouble! I don't want to see hide or hair of
you, I don't want to lay eyes on you ever again! [YEPIKHÓDOV *goes out; from*
behind the door we hear him screech: "I'll call the police on you!"] Oh, you
coming back for more? [*Grabs the stick that* FIRS *has left by the door.*] Come
on . . . Come on . . . Come on, I'll show you! All right, all right, you asked
for it—[*Swings the stick; the door opens, and she hits* LOPÁKHIN *over the*
head as he enters.]
LOPÁKHIN   Thanks a lot.
VÁRYA [*still angry, sarcastic*]   Oh, I'm so sorry!
LOPÁKHIN   S'all right. Always appreciate a warm welcome.
VÁRYA   I don't need appreciation. [*Walks off, then turns and asks gently.*] I
didn't hurt you, did I?
LOPÁKHIN   No, I'm fine. Just a whopping big lump, that's all.

> [*Voices from the ballroom: "Lopákhin! Lopákhin's here! He's back!*
> *Lopákhin's back!" People crowd into the sitting room.*]

PÍSHCHIK   The great man in person! [*Hugs* LOPÁKHIN.] Is that cognac I smell?
It is! You've been celebrating! Well, so have we. Join the party!
LIUBÓV ANDRÉYEVNA   It's you, Yermolái Alexéyich. Where have you been all
this time? Where's Leoníd?
LOPÁKHIN   He's coming; we took the same train.
LIUBÓV ANDRÉYEVNA   What happened? Did they have the auction? Tell me!
LOPÁKHIN [*embarrassed, afraid to show his joy*]   The auction was all over by
four this afternoon, but we missed the train. We had to wait for the nine-
thirty. [*Exhales heavily.*] Oof! My head is really spinning. . . .

> [*Enter* GÁYEV; *he holds a wrapped package in one hand, wipes his eyes*
> *with the other.*]

LIUBÓV ANDRÉYEVNA   Lyónya, what's the matter? Lyónya! [*Impatiently, begin-*
ning to cry] For God's sake, what happened!
GÁYEV [*weeps and can't answer her; makes a despairing gesture with his free*
hand and turns to FIRS] Here, take these . . . some anchovies . . . imported.
I haven't eaten a thing all day. You have no idea what I've been through!
[*The door to the billiard room is open; we hear the click of billiard balls and*
YÁSHA's *voice: "Seven ball in the left pocket!"* GÁYEV's *expression changes; he*
stops crying.] I'm all worn out. Firs, come help me get ready for bed.

> [*Goes through the ballroom and out;* FIRS *follows him.*]

PÍSHCHIK   What about the auction? Tell us what happened!
LIUBÓV ANDRÉYEVNA   Is the cherry orchard sold?
LOPÁKHIN   It's sold.
LIUBÓV ANDRÉYEVNA   Who bought it?
LOPÁKHIN   I did.

> [*Pause.* LIUBÓV *is overcome; she would fall, if she weren't standing beside*
> *a table and the armchair.* VÁRYA *takes the keys from her belt, throws them*
> *on the floor, crosses the room, and goes out.*]

I did! I bought it! No, wait, don't go, please. I'm still a little mixed up
about it, I can't talk yet. . . . [*Laughs.*] We get to the auction, and there's
Derigánov, all ready and waiting. Leoníd Andréyich only had fifteen thousand, so right away Derigánov raises the bid to thirty, that's on top of the
balance on the mortgage. So I see what he's up to, and I bid against him.

Raise it to forty. He bids forty-five. I bid fifty-five. See, he was raising by five, and I double him, I raise him ten each time. Anyway, finally it's all over, and I got it! Ninety thousand plus the balance on the mortgage.[7] And now the cherry orchard is mine! Mine! [*A loud laugh*] My God, the cherry orchard belongs to me! Tell me I'm drunk, tell me it's all a dream, I'm making this up—[*Stomps on the floor.*] And don't anybody laugh! My God, if my father and my grandfather could be here now and see this, see *me,* their Yermolái, the boy they beat, who went barefoot in winter and never went to school, see how that poor boy just bought the most beautiful estate in the whole world! I bought the estate where my father and my grandfather slaved away their lives, where they wouldn't even let them in the kitchen! My God, I must be dreaming—I can't believe all this is happening! [*Picks up* VÁRYA's *keys; smiles gently.*] See, she threw away her keys; she knows she isn't running the place anymore. . . . [*Jingles the keys.*] Well, that's all right.

[*The orchestra starts tuning up again.*]

That's it, let's have some music—come on, I want to hear it! Everybody come watch! Come on and watch what I do! I'm going to chop down every tree in that cherry orchard, every goddamn one of them, and then I'm going to develop that land! Watch me! I'm going to do something our children and grandchildren can be proud of! Come on, you musicians, play!

[*The orchestra begins to play.* LIUBÓV *curls up in the armchair and weeps bitterly.*]

LOPÁKHIN [*reproachfully*]   Oh, why didn't you listen to me? You dear woman, you dear good woman, you can't ever go back to the past. [*With tears in his eyes*] Oh, if only we could change things, if only life were different, this unhappy, messy life . . .

PÍSHCHIK [*takes his arm; quietly*]   She's crying. Come on, we'll go in the other room, leave her alone for a while. Come on. . . . [*Leads him into the ballroom.*]

LOPÁKHIN   What's the matter? Tell the band to keep playing! Louder! [*Ironic*] It's my house now! The cherry orchard belongs to me! I can do what I want to! [*Bumps into a small table, almost knocking over a candlestick.*] Don't worry about that: I can pay for it! I can pay for everything!

[*Goes out with* PÍSHCHIK.]

[*The sitting room is empty except for* LIUBÓV, *who sits tightly clenched and weeping bitterly. The orchestra plays softly. Suddenly* ÁNYA *and* TROFÍMOV *enter.* ÁNYA *goes and kneels before her mother.* TROFÍMOV *remains by the archway.*]

ÁNYA   Mama! Mama, you're crying. Mama dear, I love you, I'll take care of you. The cherry orchard is sold, it's gone now, that's the truth, Mama, that's the truth, but don't cry. You still have your life to lead, you're still a good person. . . . Come with me, Mama, we'll go away, someplace far away from here. We'll plant a new orchard, even better than this one, you'll see, Mama, you'll understand, and you'll feel a new kind of joy, like a light in your soul. . . . Let's go, Mama. Let's go!

Curtain.

7. The winning bid for the estate was equivalent to nearly $2 million today—about twice what Lopákhin had offered to lend Liubóv and her family to save the estate (act 1).

Act 4

[*The same room as Act 1. The curtains have been taken down, the pictures are gone from the walls, and there are only a few pieces of furniture shoved into a corner, as if for sale. The place feels empty. By the doorway, a pile of trunks, suitcases, etc. The door on the right is open; we hear* ÁNYA *and* VÁRYA *talking in the room beyond.* LOPÁKHIN *stands waiting. Beside him,* YÁSHA *holds a tray of glasses filled with champagne. Through the door we see* YEPIKHÓDOV *in the front hall, fastening the straps on a trunk. The sound of murmured voices offstage; some of the local people have come to say goodbye.* GÁYEV's *voice: "Thank you all, good people, thanks, thanks very much for coming."*]

YÁSHA   It's some of these poor yokels, come to say goodbye. I'm of the opinion, you know, these people around here . . . ? They're okay, but they're . . . they're just a bunch of know-nothings.

[*The murmur of voices dies away.* LIUBÓV *and* GÁYEV *come in from the entrance hall; she has stopped crying, but she is shaking slightly, and her face is pale. She cannot speak.*]

GÁYEV   You gave them all the money you had, Liúba. You can't do that! You
5   can't do that anymore!

LIUBÓV ANDREYÉVNA   I couldn't help it! I just couldn't help it!

[*They both go out.* LOPÁKHIN *follows them to the door.*]

LOPÁKHIN   Wait, please. How about a little glass of champagne, just to celebrate? I forgot to bring some from town, but I got this one bottle at the station. It was all they had.

[*Pause.*]

10   No? What's the matter, don't you want any? [*Comes back from the door.*] If I'd known that, I wouldn't have bought it. I don't feel like any myself.

[YÁSHA *carefully puts the tray down on a chair.*]

Go on, Yásha, you might as well have one.

YÁSHA   Bon voyage! And here's to the girls we leave behind! [*Drinks.*] This is not your real French champagne, I can tell.

15   LOPÁKHIN   Cost me enough.

[*Pause.*]

It's cold as hell in here.

YÁSHA   They figured they were going away today anyway—they decided not to heat the place. [*Laughs.*]

LOPÁKHIN   What's with you?

20   YÁSHA   I'm laughing because everything worked out just the way I wanted.

LOPÁKHIN   It's October already, but the sun's out; it feels like summer. Good weather for home builders. [*Looks at his watch, then at the door.*] Listen, everybody, you got forty-six minutes till train time! And it's twenty minutes from here to the station, so you better get a move on.

[*Enter* TROFÍMOV *from outside; he's wearing an overcoat.*]

25   TROFÍMOV   It must be time to go. The carts are here. Where the hell are my galoshes? I've lost them somewhere. [*At the door*] Ánya, where are my galoshes? I can't find them anyplace!

LOPÁKHIN   I'm off to Hárkov. I'll be taking the same train as you. Off to Hárkov, spend the winter there. I've been hanging around here too long,

30 doing nothing; I can't stand that. I got to keep working, otherwise I don't know what to do with my hands; if they're not doing something, they feel like they don't belong to me.

TROFÍMOV So. We're leaving, and you're going back to your useful labors in the real world.

35 LOPÁKHIN Have a glass of champagne.

TROFÍMOV No, thanks.

LOPÁKHIN So you're off to Moscow?

TROFÍMOV Yes. I'll go into town with them today, and then leave tomorrow for Moscow.

40 LOPÁKHIN Sure. I'll bet all those professors are waiting for you to show up, wouldn't want to start their lectures without you!

TROFÍMOV Mind your own business.

LOPÁKHIN How long you say you've been at that university?

TROFÍMOV Come on! Think up something new, will you? You're getting bor-
45 ing. [*Pokes around, looking for his galoshes.*] You know, we probably won't ever see each other again, so you mind my giving you a little advice? As a farewell present? Don't wave your arms around so much. Bad habit. And this development you're putting in out here—you think that's going to improve the world? You think your leisure home buyers are going to turn
50 into yeoman farmers? That's a lot of arm waving too. Well, what the hell. I like you anyway. You've got nice hands. Gentle and sensitive. You could have been an artist. And you're like that inside too—gentle and sensitive.

LOPÁKHIN [*hugs him*] Goodbye, boy. Thanks for everything. Here, let me give you a little money. You may need it for the trip.

55 TROFÍMOV What for? I don't need money!

LOPÁKHIN What *for*? You don't have any!

TROFÍMOV I do too. Thanks all the same. I got paid for a translation I did. I have money right here in my pocket. [*Worried*] I just wish I could find my galoshes!

60 VÁRYA [*from the next room*] Here they are! The smelly things . . . [*Throws a pair of galoshes into the room.*]

TROFÍMOV What are you always getting mad for? Hmm . . . These aren't my galoshes.

LOPÁKHIN This past spring I planted a big crop of poppies. Three hundred acres. Sold the poppy seed, made forty thousand clear. And when those
65 poppies were all in flower, what a picture that was! So look, I just made forty thousand, I can afford to loan you some money. Why turn up your nose at it? Because you think I'm just a dirt farmer?

TROFÍMOV So your father was a dirt farmer. Mine worked in a drugstore. What does that prove?

[*LOPÁKHIN takes out his wallet.*]

70 Forget it, forget it. Look, you could give me a couple of hundred thousand, I still wouldn't take it. I'm a free man. And you people, everything you think is so valuable, it doesn't mean a thing to me. I don't care whether you're rich or poor; you've got no power over me. I can do without you, I can go right on past you, because I am proud and I am strong. Humanity is
75 moving onward, toward a higher truth and a higher happiness, higher than anyone can imagine. And I'm ahead of the rest!

LOPÁKHIN You think you'll ever get there?

TROFÍMOV I'll get there.

> [*Pause.*]

I'll get there. Or I'll make sure the rest of them get there.

> [*From the orchard comes the sound of axes; they've started chopping down the cherry trees.*]

80 LOPÁKHIN Well, boy, goodbye. Time to go. You and I don't see eye to eye, but life goes on anyway. Whenever I work real hard, round the clock practically, that clears my mind somehow, and for a minute I think maybe I know what we're all here for. But God, boy, think of the thousands of people in this country who don't know what they're doing or why they're doing it.
85 But . . . I guess that doesn't have much to do with the price of eggs. They told me Leoníd Andréyich got a job at the bank, six thousand a year. He won't last; he's too lazy.

ÁNYA [*at the door*] Mama asks you to please wait until she's gone before you start cutting down the orchard.

90 TROFÍMOV I agree. That isn't very tactful, you know.

> [*Goes out into the front hall.*]

LOPÁKHIN All right, all right, I'll take care of it. God, these people . . .

> [*Goes out after him.*]

ÁNYA Have they taken Firs to the nursing home?

YÁSHA I told them about it this morning. So I imagine they have.

ÁNYA [*to* YEPIKHÓDOV, *who crosses the room*] Yepikhódov, could you please go
95 and make sure they've taken Firs to the nursing home?

YÁSHA [*offended*] I already told them this morning! Why keep asking?

YEPIKHÓDOV The aged Firs, in my ultimate opinion, is beyond nursing. They ought to take him to the cemetery. And I can only envy him. [*Sets a suitcase down on a cardboard hatbox and crushes it.*] There. Finally. Wouldn't you
100 know.

> [*Goes out.*]

YÁSHA [*snickers*] Old Double Trouble.

VÁRYA [*from the next room*] Have they taken Firs to the nursing home?

ÁNYA They took him this morning.

VÁRYA Then why didn't they take the letter for the doctor?

105 ÁNYA They must have forgotten. We'll have to send someone after them with it.

VÁRYA Where's Yásha? Tell him his mother is here; she wants to say goodbye.

YÁSHA [*with a dismissive gesture*] What a bore! Why can't she just leave me alone?

> [DUNYÁSHA *has been drifting in and out, fussing with the baggage; now that she sees* YÁSHA *alone, she goes to him.*]

110 DUNYÁSHA Oh . . . oh, Yásha, why won't you even look at me? You're going away . . . you're leaving me behind. . . . [*Starts to cry and throws her arms around his neck.*]

YÁSHA What are you crying about? [*Drinks some champagne.*] Six days from now, I'll be back in Paris. Tomorrow we get on the express train, and we're off! And that's the last you'll ever see of me! I can't hardly believe it myself.
115 *Vive la France!*[8] I can't live around here anymore; it's just not my kind of place. They're all so ignorant, and I can't stand that. [*Drinks more cham-*

---

8. Long live France! (French).

pagne.] What are you crying about? If you'd been a nice girl, you wouldn't have anything to cry about.

DUNYÁSHA [*powders her nose in a mirror*] Don't forget to send me a letter from Paris. Because I loved you, Yásha, I really did. I'm a very sensitive person, Yásha, I really am—

YÁSHA Watch it, someone's coming. [*He starts fussing with the luggage, whistling quietly.*]

[*Enter* LIUBÓV, GÁYEV, ÁNYA, *and* CARLOTTA.]

GÁYEV We should be going. We're already a little late. [*Looks at* YÁSHA.] Who smells like herring?

LIUBÓV ANDRÉYEVNA We've only got ten minutes; then we absolutely must start out. [*Glances around the room.*] Goodbye, house! Wonderful old house! Winter's almost here, and come spring you'll be gone. They'll tear you down. Think of everything these walls have seen! [*Kisses* ÁNYA *with great feeling.*] My treasure, look at you! You're radiant today! Your eyes are shining like diamonds! Are you happy? Really happy?

ÁNYA Oh, yes, Mama, really! We're starting a new life!

GÁYEV She's right—everything worked out extremely well. Before the cherry orchard was sold we were at our wit's end—remember how painful it was?—and now everything's finally settled, once and for all, no turning back, and see? We've all calmed down. We're even rather happy. I'm going to work at the bank, I'm about to become a financier! Yellow ball in the side pocket . . . And you look better than you have in a long time, Lyúba; you do, you know.

LIUBÓV ANDRÉYEVNA I know. My nerves have quieted down. You're quite right.

[*Someone holds out her hat and coat.*]

And I sleep much better now. Take my things, Yásha, will you? It's time to go. [*To* ÁNYA] Darling, we'll see each other soon enough. I'm off to Paris—I kept the money your godmother in Yároslavl sent to buy the estate. [*A hard laugh*] Thank God for the old lady! That ought to get me through the winter at least. . . .

ÁNYA And you'll come back soon, won't you? You promise? I'll study hard and get my diploma, and then I'll get a job and help you out. We can read together the way we used to, can't we? [*Kisses her mother's hands.*] We'll spend long autumn evenings together; we'll read lots of books and learn all about the wonderful new world of the future. . . . [*Dreamily*] Don't forget, Mama, you promised. . . .

LIUBÓV ANDRÉYEVNA I will, my angel, I promise. [*Embraces her.*]

[*Enter* LOPÁKHIN. CARLOTTA *hums a tune under her breath.*]

GÁYEV Carlotta must be happy; she's singing!

CARLOTTA [*picks up a bundle that looks like a baby in swaddling clothes*] Here's my little baby. Bye, bye, baby . . .

[*We hear a baby's voice: "Wah! Wah!"*]

Shh, baby, shh, shh . . . good little children don't cry. . . .

[*Again: "Wah! Wah!"*]

I feel so sorry for the poor thing. [*Hurls the bundle to the floor.*] You will find me a job, won't you? I can't go on like this anymore.

LOPÁKHIN Don't worry, Carlotta; we'll take care of you.

GÁYEV   Everybody's just thrown us away. Várya's leaving. . . . All of a sudden
160   we're useless.

CARLOTTA   How can I live in that town of yours? There must be someplace I
can go. . . . [*Hums.*] What difference does it make . . . ?

[*Enter* PÍSHCHIK.]

LOPÁKHIN   Here comes the wonder boy.

PÍSHCHIK [*panting*]   Ooh, give me a minute . . . I'm all worn out. Good
165   morning, good morning, good morning. Could I get a drink of water?

GÁYEV [*sarcastic*]   You're sure it isn't money you want? You'll all have to
excuse me if I remove myself from the approaching negotiations.

[*Goes out.*]

PÍSHCHIK   I'm so glad to see you all. . . . Dear lady . . . I've been a stranger,
I know. [*To* LOPÁKHIN] And you're here too. Delighted, delighted, a man I
170   admire, always have. . . . Here. Here. This is for you. [*Gives* LOPÁKHIN
money.] Four hundred. And I still owe you eight hundred and forty.

LOPÁKHIN [*a bewildered shrug*]   I must be dreaming. Where did you get
money?

PÍSHCHIK   Wait a minute; let me cool off. Well, it was an absolutely extra-
175   ordinary thing. These Englishmen showed up, they poked around on my
land, found some kind of white clay. . . . [*To* LIUBÓV] Here . . . Here's the
four hundred. You've been so kind . . . so sweet . . . [*Gives her money.*] And
you'll have the rest before you know it. [*Takes a drink of water.*] You know,
there was a young man on the train just now, he was saying . . . there was
180   this philosopher, he said, who wanted us all to jump off the roof. "Jump!"
he said. "Jump!" That was his whole philosophy. [*Amazed*] Really! I don't
believe it! Give me some more water. . . .

LOPÁKHIN   What Englishmen are you talking about?

PÍSHCHIK   I gave them a lease on the land, the place where the clay is, a
185   twenty-four-year lease. And now excuse me, but I'm off. Lots of people to
see, pay back what I owe. I owe money all over the place. [*Takes a drink of
water.*] Well, I just wanted to say hello. I'll come by again on Thursday.

LIUBÓV ANDRÉYEVNA   But we're leaving for town today. And tomorrow I'm
going back to Paris.

190   PÍSHCHIK   What? [*Astonished*] Leaving for town? Oh, my . . . Oh, of course;
the furniture's gone. And all these trunks. I didn't realize. [*Almost in tears*]
I didn't realize. Great thinkers, these English . . . God bless you all. And be
happy. I didn't realize. Well, all things must come to an end. [*Kisses* LIUBÓV's
hand.] I'll come to an end myself one of these days. And when I do, I want
195   you all to say: "Semyónov-Píshchik . . . he was a good old horse. God bless
him." Wonderful weather we're having. Yes. . . . [*Starts out, overcome with
emotion, stops in the doorway and turns.*] Oh, by the way, Dáshenka says
hello.

[*Goes out.*]

LIUBÓV ANDRÉYEVNA   Now we can go. There are just two things still on my
200   mind. The first is old Firs. [*Looks at her watch.*] We've still got five
minutes. . . .

ÁNYA   Mama, they took Firs to the nursing home this morning. Yásha took
care of it.

LIUBÓV ANDRÉYEVNA   . . . And then there's our Várya. She's used to getting
205   up early and working around here all day long, and now she's . . . out of a

job. Like a fish out of water. Poor thing—she's so nervous, she cries, she's losing weight . . .

[*Pause.*]

You know, Yermolái Alexéyich—well, of course you know—I'd always dreamed . . . always dreamed she'd marry you; you know we all think it's
210   a wonderful idea. . . . [*Whispers to* ÁNYA, *who nods to* CARLOTTA; *they both leave.*] She loves you, you like her. . . . I don't know why, I just don't know why the two of you keep avoiding the issue. Really!

LOPÁKHIN   I don't know why either. It's all a little funny. Well, I don't mind. If there's still time, I'll do it. . . . All right, *basta,*[9] let's just get it over with.
215   But I don't know, I don't think I can propose without you—

LIUBÓV ANDRÉYEVNA   Of course you can. All it takes is a minute. I'll send her right in. . . .

LOPÁKHIN   We've even got some champagne all ready. [*Looks at the tray of empty glasses.*] Or at least we did. Somebody must have drunk it all up.

    [YÁSHA *coughs.*]

220   Guzzled it down, I should say.

LIUBÓV ANDRÉYEVNA   Wonderful! We'll leave you alone. Yásha, *allez!*[1] I'll go call her. [*At the door*] Várya, leave that alone; come here a minute, will you? Come on, dear!

    [*Goes out with* YÁSHA.]

LOPÁKHIN [*looks at his watch*]   Well . . .

    [*Pause. A few stifled laughs and whispers behind the door. Finally* VÁRYA *enters.*]

225 VÁRYA [*examines the luggage; takes her time*]   That's funny, I can't find them. . . .

LOPÁKHIN   What are you looking for?

VÁRYA   I packed them myself, and now I don't remember where.

    [*Pause.*]

LOPÁKHIN   What . . . ah . . . where are you off to, Várya?

VÁRYA   Me? I'm going to work for the Ragúlins. I talked to them about it
230   already; they need a housekeeper. And look after things, you know. . . .

LOPÁKHIN   All the way over there? That's fifty miles away.

    [*Pause.*]

Well, looks like this is the end of things around here. . . .

VÁRYA [*still examining the luggage*]   Where are they . . . ? Or maybe I put them in the trunk. You're right: this is the end of things here. The end of
235   one life—

LOPÁKHIN   I'm going too. To Hárkov. Taking the same train, actually. I've got a million things waiting for me. I'm leaving Yepikhódov, though. Hired him to take charge here.

VÁRYA   You hired *who?*

240 LOPÁKHIN   Last year this time it was snowing already, remember? Today it's still sunny. Nice day. A little chilly, though . . . It was freezing this morning; must have been in the thirties.

VÁRYA   I didn't notice.

    [*Pause.*]

Anyway, the thermometer's broken.

9. Enough (Italian).   1. Go on! (French).

[*Pause. A voice from outside calls: "Lopákhin!"*]

245 LOPÁKHIN [*as if he'd been waiting for the call*] I'm coming!

[*Goes out.*]

[VÁRYA *sits down on the floor, leans her head on a bundle of dresses, and cries. The door opens;* LIUBÓV *enters carefully.*]

LIUBÓV ANDRÉYEVNA Well?

[*Pause.*]

We have to go.

VÁRYA [*already stopped crying, wipes her eyes*] Right, Mama, we have to go. I can get to the Ragúlins' today, if I don't miss the train.

250 LIUBÓV ANDRÉYEVNA Ánya, get your coat on.

[*Enter* ÁNYA, GÁYEV, CARLOTTA. GÁYEV *wears a winter overcoat. Servants and drivers come in to pick up the luggage.* YEPIKHÓDOV *directs the operation.*]

Well, we're ready to start.

ÁNYA [*joyfully*] Ready to start!

GÁYEV My dear friends, my very dear friends! On this occasion, this farewell to our beloved house, I cannot keep still. I feel I must say a few words to

255 express the emotion that overwhelms me, overwhelms us all—

ÁNYA [*pleads*] Uncle, please!

VÁRYA That's enough, Uncle.

GÁYEV [*crushed*] All right . . . Yellow ball in the side pocket . . . I'll keep still.

[*Enter* TROFÍMOV, *then* LOPÁKHIN.]

TROFÍMOV Ladies and gentlemen, time to go! You'll be late!

260 LOPÁKHIN Yepikhódov, get my coat.

LIUBÓV ANDRÉYEVNA Let me stay a little minute longer. I never really noticed these walls before, or the ceilings. I want a last look, one last long look. . . .

GÁYEV I remember when I was six, I was watching out that window, right over there. It was a holy day, Trinity Sunday,[2] I think, and I saw Father on

265 his way to church. . . .

LIUBÓV ANDRÉYEVNA Have we got everything?

LOPÁKHIN I guess so. [*To* YEPIKHÓDOV, *who helps him on with his coat*] You keep an eye on things, Yepikhódov.

YEPIKHÓDOV [*loud, businesslike tone*] You can count on me, Yermolái

270 Alexéyich!

LOPÁKHIN Why are you talking like that all of a sudden?

YEPIKHÓDOV I just had a drink—water. . . . It went down the wrong way.

YÁSHA [*with contempt*] Dumb hick!

LIUBÓV ANDRÉYEVNA We're all going away. There won't be a soul left on the

275 place. . . .

LOPÁKHIN But wait till you see what happens here come spring!

[VÁRYA *grabs an umbrella from the luggage, as if she were going to hit him.* LOPÁKHIN *pretends to be terrified.*]

VÁRYA Don't get excited. It was just a joke.

TROFÍMOV You've all got to get moving! It's time to go! You'll miss your train!

---

2. A celebration of the Christian doctrine of the Trinity (the belief that the Father, Son, and Holy Spirit exist together in God); in Eastern Christianity it falls on Pentecost (seven weeks after Easter).

VÁRYA   Here's your galoshes, Pétya, behind this suitcase. [*With tears in her*
280   *eyes*] Smelly old things . . .

TROFÍMOV [*puts them on*]   It's time to go!

GÁYEV [*deeply moved, afraid he'll start crying*]   Yes, the train . . . mustn't miss
the train . . . Yellow ball in the side pocket, white in the corner . . .

LIUBÓV ANDRÉYEVNA   Let's go!

285   LOPÁKHIN   Everybody here? Nobody left? [*Closes and locks the door, left.*]
Got to lock up; I've got a few things stored here. All right, let's go!

ÁNYA   Goodbye, house! Goodbye, old life!

TROFÍMOV   No, hello, new life!

[*Goes out with Ánya.*]

[VÁRYA *looks around the room again; she's not eager to go.* YÁSHA *goes out
with* CARLOTTA *and her little dog.*]

LOPÁKHIN   So. Until next spring. Come on, let's go, everybody. Goodbye!

[LIUBÓV *and* GÁYEV *are left alone. It's as if they'd been waiting for this
moment. They throw their arms around each other and burst out crying,
but try to keep the others outside from hearing.*]

290   GÁYEV [*in despair*]   Oh, sister, sister . . .

LIUBÓV ANDRÉYEVNA   Oh, my orchard, my beautiful orchard! My life, my
youth, my happiness, goodbye! Goodbye! Goodbye!

[ÁNYA's *voice, joyful:* "Mama!" TROFÍMOV's *voice, joyful, excited:*
"Yoo-hoo!"]

These walls, these windows, for the last time . . . And Mama loved this
room . . .

295   GÁYEV   Oh, sister, sister . . .

[ÁNYA: "*Mama!*" TROFÍMOV: "*Yoo-hoo!*"]

LIUBÓV ANDRÉYEVNA   We're coming!

[*They leave.*]

[*The stage is empty. We hear the sound of the door being locked, then the
carriages as they drive away. It grows very quiet. In the silence, we hear
the occasional sound of an ax chopping down the cherry trees, a mournful, lonely sound. Then we hear steps. Enter* FIRS *from the door, right. He
wears his usual butler's livery, but with bedroom slippers. He's very ill.*]

FIRS [*goes to the door, tries the handle*]   Locked. They're gone. [*Sits on the
sofa.*] They forgot about me. That's all right; I'll just sit here for a bit. . . .
300   And Leoníd Andréyich probably forgot his winter coat. [*A worried sigh*] I
should have looked. . . . He's still all wet, that one. . . . [*Mumbles something we can't make out.*] Well, it's all over now, and I never even had a life
to live. . . . [*Lies back.*] I'll just lie here for a bit. . . . No strength left, nothing left, not a thing . . . Oh, you. You young flibbertigibbet. [*Lies there, no
longer moving.*]

[*In the distance we hear a sound that seems to come from the sky, a sad
sound, like a string snapping. It dies away. Everything grows quiet. We
can hear the occasional sound of an ax on a tree.*]

Curtain.

GEORGE BERNARD SHAW

1856–1950

IN the history of English drama, George Bernard Shaw stands second only to SHAKESPEARE as the playwright with the most profound influence on his own era and beyond. Winner of the Nobel Prize for Literature in 1925, Shaw was not only the most famous author of his time but also a highly regarded social critic, routinely sought after for his responses to world events and political issues. Although in the latter part of his career he was best known globally as a public intellectual, his theatrical writing was responsible for his place, long after his death in 1950, as one of the leading cultural forces of the twentieth century. Shaw's plays are still regularly revived and continue to strike audiences as relevant and compelling. This "timeliness" in his work in part reflects how little has changed at the very core of modern civilization over the past century; Shaw's tireless dissection of social ills and insightful grasp of human motivations and foibles also enable his plays to speak to each generation anew. Yet the truthfulness and acuity of his vision would not matter much to audiences if the plays themselves were not such exemplars of theatrical craftsmanship. Shaw's ability to interweave captivating narratives and memorable characters with social critique and, above all, humor sets him apart in the pantheon of modern drama. *PYGMALION* (1913) is one of the most popular, and arguably among the very finest, of Shaw's comedies. Gently poking fun at the pretensions of the lower class, and the idiosyncrasies of the upper class, *Pygmalion* entrances us with fairy-tale transformations and the possibility of romance; at the same time, it exposes the very real economic and gender inequities that continue to plague our modern world.

Shaw was born in 1856 to an Irish Protestant family that had more aspirations to social position than their father's income—reduced by his alcoholism—could sustain. George Carr Shaw cut short his son's formal education at age fifteen and sent him to work to help support his mother and two older sisters. Shaw spent five years as a clerk in a land agency, experience he would later use in his first play, *Widowers' Houses* (1892), which considers the hypocrisies of slum landlords. Shaw's mother, Lucinda Elizabeth Gurly Shaw, a talented singer, focused much of her time and energy on her music and, apparently, on her voice teacher, George J. Vandeleur Lee, with whom she may have been romantically involved. In 1873, Shaw's mother followed Lee to London, taking her two daughters with her. Shaw joined them in 1876. His first employment there was as a ghostwriter of music reviews for Lee, and he parlayed what he learned into lifelong journalistic work as a music, art, theater, and social critic. But Shaw desired a literary career, and he drafted a novel, *Immaturity* (written 1879), that he hoped would establish him both professionally and financially. Over the next four years, he composed four additional novels, only one of which, *Cashel Byron's Profession* (1886; rev. ed., 1901), saw any real success.

In 1884, Shaw discovered the newly organized Fabian Society, a socialist organization named after the Roman general Fabius Cunctator (the Delayer); its guiding principle was the idea that the best way to accomplish political and social reform was through the calculated, gradual infiltration of established channels of power. In the late nineteenth century and into the first decades of the twentieth, the Fabian Society came to have increasing influence on English politics, attracting into its ranks some of the foremost figures of the era—including its leaders, Sidney and Beatrice Webb, and the novelist H. G. Wells. Through the Fabians Shaw also met Charlotte Payne Townshend, whom he married in 1898. Shaw's writing skills and lecturing acumen soon made him the most visible member of this elite group dedicated to the pursuit of what Shaw deemed its "Socialist and Democratic objects."

In 1890, Shaw began to draw together his passionate commitment to the arts and to socialism by delivering a series of lectures for the Society on HENRIK IBSEN, whose dramas had recently been translated into English by Shaw's friend William Archer. As these plays began to be produced on the London stage, they galvanized broader public debate, especially about marriage and the role of women in modern society. Shaw published his talks the following year as *The Quintessence of Ibsenism*, and his analysis of these pioneering works of the modern theater helped him discover his own vocation as a dramatist.

The timing of these events could not have been more auspicious. Shaw emerged as a playwright just as theatrical modernism was beginning to coalesce as a movement across Europe. Shaw championed the arrival of the "New Drama" in England, leading a theatrical revolution that sought to replace formulaic native melodrama and Continental well-made plays with works closely engaged with the pressing issues of the day. Shaw also quickly learned that humor was a highly effective vehicle for social critique, and he exploited its didactic potential throughout his career. A remarkably prolific author, Shaw generated new plays and essays annually through the early 1920s and was still writing steadily through World War II.

Pygmalion brings together many of Shaw's lifelong concerns: class and economic structures, shifting gender roles, and England's global influence and power, among others. The play's opening scene, set in London's Covent Garden, provides an opportunity for Shaw to introduce a cross section of character types and ranks in English society. As members of the upper class search for taxis to take them home from an evening at the theater, a "poor girl," Eliza Doolittle, tries to earn her meager income selling bunches of flowers to the passersby. Henry Higgins, a professor of phonetics who frequents the area to study its range of English idioms, hears Eliza, whose Cockney speech interests him. Quite by accident, he also encounters an amateur linguist, Colonel Pickering, an expert in Indian dialects who has come to London to meet him, and Higgins invites Pickering to his home. Eliza overhears Higgins giving out his address, and she shows up the next day to ask Higgins to teach her "genteel" speech so that she will be qualified to work in a flower shop instead of on the streets. Higgins bets Pickering that he can teach Eliza convincingly to speak as a member of the upper class and comport herself as a duchess. But what will it mean for Eliza to appear to be what she is not? What happens when one is removed from one's "natural" place in the social order? While in its plot *Pygmalion* echoes such tales as "The Ugly Duckling," Shaw's transformation narrative also reflects the real and pressing concerns faced by working-class women with severely limited financial options to improve their lives.

Shaw took his title from a classical myth, best known today in the version that appears in book 10 of Ovid's *Metamorphoses*. Pygmalion, "revolted by the many faults which nature has implanted in the female sex," carves a statue "lovelier than any woman born." He promptly falls in love with his creation and prays to the goddess of love for a wife like his "ivory maid" (translation by Mary M. Innes). Venus brings the statue to life, and Pygmalion immediately marries and impregnates Galatea. Such stories of male construction of idealized womanhood pervade Western literature, and Shaw could have drawn on many versions of this myth, including W. S. Gilbert's theatrical extravaganza *Pygmalion and Galatea* (1871). Higgins's claim "I said I'd make a woman of you; and I have," coupled with his assertion (also in act 5) that he has "created this thing out of the squashed cabbage leaves of Covent Garden," indisputably connects him to this tradition. Shaw's rendition may also have been influenced by even darker variants of such tales, such as Mary Shelley's gothic novel *Frankenstein* (1818), which depicts the uncontrollability of creations once they are brought to life. Echoing Shelley's label for Frankenstein's monster, Higgins refers to Eliza as "the creature," ultimately damning his "own folly in having lavished hard-earned knowledge and the treasure of [his] regard" on her.

Shaw weaves together this creation myth with another equally powerful narrative, a tale of a girl magically transformed, as was Cinderella, from rags to riches. By assert-ing that he can make a "duchess" from a "draggle-tailed guttersnipe," Higgins presents himself as the modern-day fairy godfather who will provide Eliza with clothes fit for an ambassador's party and with rides in a taxi, almost as magical to her as a pumpkin coach. But here, too, Shaw introduces a darker tone by also depicting Higgins as the evil stepfather/witch out of a story like "Snow White," tempting Eliza with sweets and munching on an apple taken from the same dessert stand.

For audiences *Pygmalion*'s enduring appeal clearly lies in part in the teasingly undefined and unresolved relationship of Higgins and Eliza. Shaw builds the comedy, which he subtitled a "A Romance in Five Acts," around Higgins's disavowals of romantic interest in Eliza as well as Eliza's need for "a little kindness" and her "right to be loved." Eliza maintains that "the sort of feeling" she wants from Higgins is not the same as that experienced by men such as the poor but aristocratic Freddy Eynsford Hill, who writes "sheets and sheets" of love letters to her. Shaw always insisted that his subtitle should suggest an older sense of the term *romance*—the sense in which it is applied to the late plays of Shakespeare, which similarly depict mythic transfor-

Left to right: Edmund Gurney as Alfred Doolittle, Stella Campbell as his daughter, Eliza Doolittle, and Herbert Beerbohm Tree as Professor Henry Higgins in the original 1914 production of *Pygmalion*.

mations and adventures beyond the everyday. Nevertheless, the agonistic dynamic between Higgins and Eliza has struck many audiences and critics as the verbal equivalent of sexual foreplay, in the tradition of Beatrice and Benedick in Shakespeare's *Much Ado about Nothing* (ca. 1598) or Mirabel and Millimant in William Congreve's *The Way of the World* (1700). From the first production of *Pygmalion* forward, Shaw had to fight both actors' inclinations and audiences' expectations that the comedy end conventionally, in marriage. In that legendary first staging, Herbert Beerbohm Tree (Higgins) got around Shaw by tossing flowers to Stella Campbell (Eliza) right before the final curtain to signal the pair's ultimate union. Well aware of theatergoers' delight at this gesture, Tree told the irate Shaw, "My ending makes money; you ought to be grateful." Shaw responded, "Your ending is damnable: you ought to be shot."

The critical and theatrical controversy that erupted over the play's lack of narrative closure has perennially overshadowed explorations of other social and political issues raised in the play. It is certainly possible that Shaw perceived the amatory dynamic at work in *Pygmalion* but actively sought to expose the darker realities behind such romantic fantasies. Shortly before Shaw conceived the play, the London periodical *Pall Mall Gazette* featured an exposé of white slavery that prompted a public debate over sexual predation and may have contributed to the drama's aura of barely disguised sexual threat. The journal's revelations of the sexual availability and vulnerability of young working-class women, and their exploitation by men in more economically privileged positions, would certainly have been familiar to Shaw's audiences. That Stella Campbell, for whom Shaw created the role of Eliza, was already known to audiences through her prior star turns in highly sexualized "fallen woman" roles, such as in Arthur Pinero's *The Second Mrs. Tanqueray* (1893), only complicated their perception of her and the reception of *Pygmalion*.

Shaw uses details of language—what he calls "phonetics"—to explore class boundaries and their potential malleability. He overtly links economics with dialect and grammar by suggesting that class position is culturally bound to speech. Through Higgins (whom Shaw partly modeled on Henry Sweet, a noted philologist he had met in 1880), Shaw states that the lower class's acquisition of "new speech"—by which he means what came to be known as Standard British English—can "fil[l] up the deepest gulf that separates class from class and soul from soul." He sets up this major arc of the play in act 1, when Higgins remarks: "You see this creature with her kerbstone English: the English that will keep her in the gutter to the end of her days. . . . [I]n three months I could pass that girl off as a duchess. . . . I could even get her a place as lady's maid or shop assistant, which requires better English." In Higgins's idealized vision, once the marker of lower-class status is removed from speech, individuals not only will be

Stella Campbell, for whom Shaw created the role of Eliza.

able to move upward through social ranks, they will also be able to realize their full potential economically, intellectually, and spiritually.

The juxtaposition of two branches of linguistic inquiry undertaken by Higgins and Pickering—one rooted in the British class system, the other emerging from its imperial endeavors—cannot be accidental. Shaw had already anonymously written the manifesto *Fabianism and the Empire* (1900) for the Fabian Society and had dramatized the familiar parallel of the British and Roman empires in *Caesar and Cleopatra* (written 1898). In *Pygmalion* Shaw demonstrates how language can be used either to perpetuate or to level social distinctions both at home and, by extension, in the colonies. He combines the established idea that British English should be the vehicle for the education and enculturation of colonized natives with social reformers' notions that Britain's underclass had much in common with its colonial "Others."

Shaw uses a streamlined version of the Elizabethan dramatic structure of main plot and comic subplot to develop his themes of language and class. Eliza's willing transfiguration through speech has its comic counterpart in her father's resistance to his removal from the legions of "the undeserving poor" and forced embrace of "middle-class morality" when he unexpectedly receives a sizable legacy. The character of Alfred Doolittle owes much to earlier Victorian literature, especially the novels of Charles Dickens (1812–1870) and the dramas of T. W. Robertson (1829–1871), with their depictions of colorful laggards and other lowlifes. These Victorian characterological influences emerged in Shaw's earliest plays—including *Widowers' Houses,* which featured the rent collector Lickcheese; in *Pygmalion* Shaw more fully and pointedly uses Doolittle to expose the hypocrisy and pretensions of elevated class position through the resolutely unreformed dustman's lectures on "Moral Reform"—lectures that, under the terms of the will that irrevocably changes his social position, he must deliver.

Some critics have contrasted the "human" comedy of Eliza to the "social" comedy of her father, claiming that only the latter is about class. But Shaw's grounding in socialism was too thorough to allow him to separate an understanding of modern humanity from individuals' placement in a class system. Rather, through the triangulated relations of Eliza, Pickering, and Higgins, we come to realize that class position has both external markers and intrinsic qualities. Eliza learns that "apart from the things anyone can pick up (the dressing and the proper way of speaking, and so on), the difference between a lady and a flower girl is not how she behaves, but how shes treated." Henry's mother sees Eliza's transformation from still another perspective: the tension between the appearance of elevated class position and the economic realities of women's lives. Mrs. Higgins questions her son's having taught Eliza "the manners and habits that disqualify a fine lady from earning her own living without giving her a fine lady's income." Eliza pointedly comes to understand the price of class standing for women without independent means—the necessity of finding a husband in a society that still saw marriage as the only "profession" appropriate to real ladies: "I sold flowers. I didnt sell myself. Now youve made a lady of me I'm not fit to sell anything else."

Though Shaw's postscript spells out Eliza's later career in some detail, his play's intentionally ambiguous ending leaves unclear whether she will marry the impecunious Freddy Eynsford Hill, "as soon as hes able to support me," or teach phonetics. It could well be that the financial and emotional independence she craves if she "cant have kindness" proved too threatening to dramatize fully at that time. Tree's conventionally romantic gesture at the final curtain reassured his audiences—members of a society that could not yet accept women's suffrage and other struggles for human equality—that the social problems Shaw placed within the spotlight could be easily resolved. Yet the continued theatrical appeal of *Pygmalion* suggests that the issues Shaw depicts are with us still. Not only can we appreciate the value of complexity and indeterminacy, but such ambiguity may well affirm, better than any pat ending, the realities of our lives.

J.E.G.

Pygmalion
A Romance in Five Acts

CHARACTERS

CLARA EYNSFORD HILL

MRS. EYNSFORD HILL

FREDDY EYNSFORD HILL

ELIZA DOOLITTLE

COLONEL PICKERING

HENRY HIGGINS

MRS. PEARCE

ALFRED DOOLITTLE

MRS. HIGGINS

A PARLOR-MAID

BYSTANDERS

Act 1

[*Covent Garden*[1] *at 11.15 p.m. Torrents of heavy summer rain. Cab whistles blowing frantically in all directions. Pedestrians running for shelter into the market and under the portico of St. Paul's Church, where there are already several people, among them a lady and her daughter in evening dress. They are all peering out gloomily at the rain, except one man with his back turned to the rest, who seems wholly preoccupied with a notebook in which he is writing busily.*

The church clock strikes the first quarter.]

THE DAUGHTER [*in the space between the central pillars, close to the one on her left*] I'm getting chilled to the bone. What can Freddy be doing all this time? Hes[2] been gone twenty minutes.

THE MOTHER [*on her daughter's right*] Not so long. But he ought to have got us a cab by this.

5 A BYSTANDER [*on the lady's right*] He wont get no cab not until half-past eleven, missus, when they come back after dropping their theatre fares.

THE MOTHER But we must have a cab. We cant stand here until half-past eleven. It's too bad.

THE BYSTANDER Well, it aint my fault, missus.

10 THE DAUGHTER If Freddy had a bit of gumption, he would have got one at the theatre door.

THE MOTHER What could he have done, poor boy?

THE DAUGHTER Other people got cabs. Why couldnt he?

[*FREDDY rushes in out of the rain from the Southampton Street side, and comes between them closing a dripping umbrella. He is a young man of twenty, in evening dress, very wet around the ankles.*]

THE DAUGHTER Well, havnt you got a cab?

15 FREDDY Theres not one to be had for love or money.

---

1. The site of London's main produce and flower market from the 1600s until 1974, in Westminster; also the site of major entertainment venues, including the Royal Opera House and the Drury Lane Theatre.

2. An example of one of the spelling reforms advocated by Shaw, who argued that the apostrophe was unnecessary in most contractions (he also insisted on dropping the final *e* from Shakespeare).

THE MOTHER   Oh, Freddy, there must be one. You cant have tried.

THE DAUGHTER   It's too tiresome. Do you expect us to go and get one ourselves?

FREDDY   I tell you theyre all engaged. The rain was so sudden: nobody was
20   prepared; and everybody had to take a cab. Ive been to Charing Cross one way and nearly to Ludgate Circus the other;[3] and they were all engaged.

THE MOTHER   Did you try Trafalgar Square?[4]

FREDDY   There wasnt one at Trafalgar Square.

THE DAUGHTER   Did you try?

25   FREDDY   I tried as far as Charing Cross Station. Did you expect me to walk to Hammersmith?[5]

THE DAUGHTER   You havnt tried at all.

THE MOTHER   You really are very helpless, Freddy. Go again; and dont come back until you have found a cab.

30   FREDDY   I shall simply get soaked for nothing.

THE DAUGHTER   And what about us? Are we to stay here all night in this draught, with next to nothing on. You selfish pig—

FREDDY   Oh, very well: I'll go, I'll go.

[*He opens his umbrella and dashes off Strandwards,[6] but comes into collision with a flower girl, who is hurrying in for shelter, knocking her basket out of her hands. A blinding flash of lightning, followed instantly by a rattling peal of thunder, orchestrates the incident.*]

THE FLOWER GIRL   Nah then, Freddy: look wh' y' gowin, deah.

35   FREDDY   Sorry.

[*He rushes off.*]

THE FLOWER GIRL   [*picking up her scattered flowers and replacing them in the basket*]   Theres menners f' yer! Te-oo banches o voylets trod into the mad.

[*She sits down on the plinth of the column, sorting her flowers, on the lady's right. She is not at all an attractive person. She is perhaps eighteen, perhaps twenty, hardly older. She wears a little sailor hat of black straw that has long been exposed to the dust and soot of London and has seldom if ever been brushed. Her hair needs washing rather badly: its mousy color can hardly be natural. She wears a shoddy black coat that reaches nearly to her knees and is shaped to her waist. She has a brown skirt with a coarse apron. Her boots are much the worse for wear. She is no doubt as clean as she can afford to be; but compared to the ladies she is very dirty. Her features are no worse than theirs; but their condition leaves something to be desired; and she needs the services of a dentist.*]

THE MOTHER   How do you know that my son's name is Freddy, pray?

THE FLOWER GIRL   Ow, eez ye-ooa san, is e? Wal, fewd dan y' de-ooty bawmz a mather should, eed now bettern to spawl a pore gel's flahrzn than ran awy
40   athaht[7] pyin. Will ye-oo py me f'them? [*Here, with apologies, this desperate*

---

3. Freddy has walked more than a half mile in different directions: first southwest to Charing Cross, the busy intersection of a number of major Westminster thoroughfares, and then east to Ludgate Circus, near the entrance to the old City of London.
4. A large plaza near Charing Cross.

5. The westernmost of the inner London boroughs, several miles beyond Charing Cross.
6. That is, toward the Strand, a street in Westminster south of Covent Garden where many theaters were located.
7. Without. *Fewd dan y' de-ooty bawmz:* if you'd done your duty by him.

attempt to represent her dialect without a phonetic alphabet must be abandoned as unintelligible outside London.][8]

THE DAUGHTER   Do nothing of the sort, mother. The idea!

THE MOTHER   Please allow me, Clara. Have you any pennies?

THE DAUGHTER   No. I've nothing smaller than sixpence.[9]

THE FLOWER GIRL [*hopefully*]   I can give you change for a tanner,[1] kind lady.

45   THE MOTHER [*to* CLARA]   Give it to me. [CLARA *parts reluctantly.*] Now [*To the* GIRL] This is for your flowers.

THE FLOWER GIRL   Thank you kindly, lady.

THE DAUGHTER   Make her give you the change. These things are only a penny a bunch.

50   THE MOTHER   Do hold your tongue, Clara. [*To the* GIRL] You can keep the change.

THE FLOWER GIRL   Oh, thank you, lady.

THE MOTHER   Now tell me how you know that young gentleman's name.

THE FLOWER GIRL   I didnt.

55   THE MOTHER   I heard you call him by it. Dont try to deceive me.

THE FLOWER GIRL [*protesting*]   Whos trying to deceive you? I called him Freddy or Charlie same as you might yourself if you was talking to a stranger and wished to be pleasant. [*She sits down beside her basket.*]

THE DAUGHTER   Sixpence thrown away! Really, mamma, you might have

60   spared Freddy that. [*She retreats in disgust behind the pillar.*]

[*An elderly gentleman of the amiable military type rushes into shelter, and closes a dripping umbrella. He is in the same plight as* FREDDY, *very wet about the ankles. He is in evening dress, with a light overcoat. He takes the place left vacant by the daughter's retirement.*]

THE GENTLEMAN   Phew!

THE MOTHER [*to the* GENTLEMAN]   Oh, sir, is there any sign of its stopping?

THE GENTLEMAN   I'm afraid not. It started worse than ever about two min-

utes ago. [*He goes to the plinth beside the flower girl; puts up his foot on it; and stoops to turn down his trouser ends.*]

65   THE MOTHER   Oh, dear! [*She retires sadly and joins her daughter.*]

THE FLOWER GIRL [*taking advantage of the military gentleman's proximity to establish friendly relations with him*]   If it's worse it's a sign it's nearly over. So cheer up, Captain; and buy a flower off a poor girl.

THE GENTLEMAN   I'm sorry, I havnt any change.

THE FLOWER GIRL   I can give you change, Captain.

70   THE GENTLEMAN   For a sovereign?[2] Ive nothing less.

THE FLOWER GIRL   Garn! Oh do buy a flower off me, Captain. I can change half-a-crown.[3] Take this for tuppence.[4]

THE GENTLEMAN   Now dont be troublesome: theres a good girl. [*Trying his pockets*] I really havnt any change—Stop: heres three hapence,[5] if thats

75   any use to you. [*He retreats to the other pillar.*]

---

8. Shaw's note.
9. That is, six pennies, roughly equivalent in value to $2 today. Before the decimalization of U.K. currency in 1971, the pound was worth twenty shillings, and each shilling was worth twelve pence.
1. Nickname for a sixpence coin.

2. A coin worth one pound, roughly equivalent to $80 today.
3. Go on!
4. Two pence (a single coin). *Half-a-crown*: a coin worth two and a half shillings, roughly equivalent to $10 today.
5. Half-penny coins.

THE FLOWER GIRL [*disappointed, but thinking three halfpence better than nothing*]   Thank you, sir.

THE BYSTANDER [*to the girl*]   You be careful: give him a flower for it. Theres a bloke[6] here behind taking down every blessed word youre saying. [*All turn to the man who is taking notes.*]

THE FLOWER GIRL [*springing up terrified*]   I aint done nothing wrong by speak-
80   ing to the gentleman. Ive a right to sell flowers if I keep off the kerb.[7] [*Hysterically*] I'm a respectable girl: so help me, I never spoke to him except to ask him to buy a flower off me. [*General hubbub, mostly sympathetic to the* FLOWER GIRL, *but deprecating her excessive sensibility. Cries of* Dont start hollerin. Whos hurting you? Nobody's going to touch you. Whats the good of fussing? Steady on. Easy, easy, etc., *come from the elderly staid spectators, who pat her comfortingly. Less patient ones bid her shut her head,[8] or ask her roughly what is wrong with her. A remoter group, not knowing what the matter is, crowd in and increase the noise with question and answer:* Whats the row? What she do? Where is he? A tec[9] taking her down. What! him? Yes: him over there: Took money off the gentleman, etc. *The* FLOWER GIRL, *distraught and mobbed, breaks through them to the gentleman, crying wildly.*] Oh, sir, dont let him charge me. You dunno what it means to me. Theyll take away my
85   character[1] and drive me on the streets for speaking to gentlemen. They—

THE NOTE TAKER [*coming forward on her right, the rest crowding after him*]   There, there, there, there! whos hurting you, you silly girl? What do you take me for?

THE BYSTANDER   It's all right: hes a gentleman: look at his boots. [*Explaining to the* NOTE TAKER] She thought you was a copper's nark, sir.

90   THE NOTE TAKER [*with quick interest*]   Whats a copper's nark?

THE BYSTANDER [*inapt at definition*]   It's a—well, it's a copper's nark, as you might say. What else would you call it? A sort of informer.

THE FLOWER GIRL [*still hysterical*]   I take my Bible oath I never said a word—

THE NOTE TAKER [*overbearing but good-humored*]   Oh, shut up, shut up. Do I
95   look like a policeman?

THE FLOWER GIRL [*far from reassured*]   Then what did you take down my words for? How do I know whether you took me down right? You just shew[2] me what youve wrote about me. [*The* NOTE TAKER *opens his book and holds it steadily under her nose, though the pressure of the mob trying to read it over his shoulders would upset a weaker man.*] Whats that? That aint proper
100   writing. I cant read that.

THE NOTE TAKER   I can. [*Reads, reproducing her pronunciation exactly.*] "Cheer ap, Keptin; n' baw ya flahr orf a pore gel."

THE FLOWER GIRL [*much distressed*]   It's because I called him Captain. I meant no harm. [*To the* GENTLEMAN] Oh, sir, dont let him lay a charge
105   agen[3] me for a word like that. You—

THE GENTLEMAN   Charge! I make no charge. [*To the* NOTE TAKER] Really, sir, if you are a detective, you need not begin protecting me against molestation by young women until I ask you. Anybody could see that the girl meant no harm.

6. Man.
7. Curb.
8. That is, shut up.
9. Detective (slang).
1. Testimony about an employee's qualities, provided by the employer; more generally,

reputation. A woman who lost her reputation, and who therefore was unable to find legal work, was in danger of being driven into prostitution ("on the streets").
2. Show.
3. Against.

THE BYSTANDERS GENERALLY [*demonstrating against police espionage*] Course
110 they could. What business is it of yours? You mind your own affairs. He
wants promotion, he does. Taking down people's words! Girl never said a
word to him. What harm if she did? Nice thing a girl cant shelter from the
rain without being insulted, etc., etc., etc. [*She is conducted by the more
sympathetic demonstrators back to her plinth, where she resumes her seat
and struggles with her emotion.*]

THE BYSTANDER He aint a tec. Hes a blooming busybody: thats what he is. I
115 tell you, look at his boots.

THE NOTE TAKER [*turning on him genially*] And how are all your people down
at Selsey?[4]

THE BYSTANDER [*suspiciously*] Who told you my people come from Selsey?

THE NOTE TAKER Never you mind. They did. [*To the* GIRL] How do you come
120 to be up so far east? You were born in Lisson Grove.[5]

THE FLOWER GIRL [*appalled*] Oh, what harm is there in my leaving Lisson
Grove? It wasnt fit for a pig to live in; and I had to pay four-and-six[6] a week.
[*In tears*] Oh, boo—hoo—oo—

THE NOTE TAKER Live where you like; but stop that noise.

125 THE GENTLEMAN [*to the* GIRL] Come, come! he cant touch you: you have a
right to live where you please.

A SARCASTIC BYSTANDER [*thrusting himself between the* NOTE TAKER *and the*
GENTLEMAN] Park Lane, for instance. Id like to go into the Housing
Question[7] with you, I would.

THE FLOWER GIRL [*subsiding into a brooding melancholy over her basket, and
talking very low-spiritedly to herself*] I'm a good girl, I am.

130 THE SARCASTIC BYSTANDER [*not attending to her*] Do you know where I come
from?

THE NOTE TAKER [*promptly*] Hoxton.[8]

[*Titterings. Popular interest in the* NOTE TAKER'S *performance increases.*]

THE SARCASTIC ONE [*amazed*] Well, who said I didnt? Bly me![9] You know
everything, you do.

135 THE FLOWER GIRL [*still nursing her sense of injury*] Aint no call to meddle
with me, he aint.

THE BYSTANDER [*to her*] Of course he aint. Dont you stand it from him. [*To
the* NOTE TAKER] See here: what call have you to know about people what
never offered to meddle with you? Wheres your warrant?

140 SEVERAL BYSTANDERS [*encouraged by this seeming point of law*] Yes: wheres
your warrant?

THE FLOWER GIRL Let him say what he likes. I dont want to have no truck
with him.

THE BYSTANDER You take us for dirt under your feet, dont you? Catch you
145 taking liberties with a gentleman!

4. A town on the coast of England, directly south of London.
5. A district of northwest London notorious in Shaw's day for slums, crime, and prostitution.
6. That is, four shillings and sixpence (the standard form of expressing amounts of these currencies).
7. The early twentieth-century debate over the need to provide adequate, affordable housing for the working classes. *Park Lane:* one of the most fashionable streets in London, about a mile west of Covent Garden.
8. A district of central London known for its theaters and music halls as well as its overcrowding and slums.
9. That is, blimey, a shortened form of "gorblimey" (God blind me!), an exclamation of surprise.

THE SARCASTIC BYSTANDER Yes: tell him where he come from if you want to go fortune-telling.

THE NOTE TAKER Cheltenham, Harrow, Cambridge, and India.[1]

THE GENTLEMAN Quite right. [*Great laughter. Reaction in the* NOTE TAKER'S *favor. Exclamations of* He knows all about it. Told him proper. Hear him tell

150   the toff[2] where he come from? etc.] May I ask, sir, do you do this for your living at a music hall?

THE NOTE TAKER Ive thought of that. Perhaps I shall some day.

[*The rain has stopped; and the persons on the outside of the crowd begin to drop off.*]

THE FLOWER GIRL [*resenting the reaction*] Hes no gentleman, he aint, to interfere with a poor girl.

THE DAUGHTER [*out of patience, pushing her way rudely to the front and displacing the* GENTLEMAN, *who politely retires to the other side of the pillar*]

155   What on earth is Freddy doing? I shall get pneumonia if I stay in this draught any longer.

THE NOTE TAKER [*to himself, hastily making a note of her pronunciation of* "*monia*"] Earlscourt.[3]

THE DAUGHTER [*violently*] Will you please keep your impertinent remarks to yourself?

160 THE NOTE TAKER Did I say that out loud? I didnt mean to. I beg your pardon. Your mother's Epsom,[4] unmistakeably.

THE MOTHER [*advancing between her* DAUGHTER *and the* NOTE TAKER] How very curious! I was brought up in Largelady Park, near Epsom.

THE NOTE TAKER [*uproariously amused*] Ha! ha! What a devil of a name!

165   Excuse me. [*To the* DAUGHTER] You want a cab, do you?

THE DAUGHTER Dont dare speak to me.

THE MOTHER Oh, please, please Clara. [*Her* DAUGHTER *repudiates her with an angry shrug and retires haughtily.*] We should be so grateful to you, sir, if you found us a cab. [*The* NOTE TAKER *produces a whistle.*] Oh, thank you. [*She joins her* DAUGHTER.]

[*The* NOTE TAKER *blows a piercing blast.*]

170 THE SARCASTIC BYSTANDER There! I knowed he was a plain-clothes copper.

THE BYSTANDER That aint a police whistle: thats a sporting whistle.

THE FLOWER GIRL [*still preoccupied with her wounded feelings*] Hes no right to take away my character. My character is the same to me as any lady's.

THE NOTE TAKER I dont know whether youve noticed it; but the rain stopped

175   about two minutes ago.

THE BYSTANDER So it has. Why didnt you say so before? and us losing our time listening to your silliness. [*He walks off towards the Strand.*]

THE SARCASTIC BYSTANDER I can tell where you come from. You come from Anwell. Go back there.

1. In effect, a summary of the gentleman's life: born in Cheltenham, a town in Gloucestershire, west of London; educated first at Harrow, a prestigious private school for boys in a borough of London, and then at Cambridge University, in Cambridge; and finally embarked on a career in India, which, as a large part of the British Empire, required the services of many British army officers and administrators.
2. Slightly derogatory slang term for a well-dressed gentleman.
3. That is, Earls Court, a well-to-do section of west London.
4. A suburb on the western periphery of greater London, known for horseracing.

180 THE NOTE TAKER [*helpfully*] Hanwell.[5]

THE SARCASTIC BYSTANDER [*affecting great distinction of speech*] Thenk you, teacher. Haw haw! So long.

[*He touches his hat with mock respect and strolls off.*]

THE FLOWER GIRL Frightening people like that! How would he like it himself.

THE MOTHER It's quite fine now, Clara. We can walk to a motor bus. Come.

[*She gathers her skirts above her ankles and hurries off towards the Strand.*]

185 THE DAUGHTER But the cab—[*Her mother is out of hearing.*] Oh, how tiresome!

[*She follows angrily.*]

[*All the rest have gone except the* NOTE TAKER, *the* GENTLEMAN, *and the* FLOWER GIRL, *who sits arranging her basket, and still pitying herself in murmurs.*]

THE FLOWER GIRL Poor girl! Hard enough for her to live without being worried and chivied.[6]

THE GENTLEMAN [*returning to his former place on the* NOTE TAKER'*s left*] How
190 do you do it, if I may ask?

THE NOTE TAKER Simply phonetics. The science of speech. Thats my profession: also my hobby. Happy is the man who can make a living by his hobby! You can spot an Irishman or a Yorkshireman by his brogue. *I* can place any man within six miles. I can place him within two miles in London. Some-
195 times within two streets.

THE FLOWER GIRL Ought to be ashamed of himself, unmanly coward!

THE GENTLEMAN But is there a living in that?

THE NOTE TAKER Oh yes. Quite a fat one. This is an age of upstarts. Men begin in Kentish Town with £80 a year, and end in Park Lane with a
200 hundred thousand.[7] They want to drop Kentish Town; but they give themselves away every time they open their mouths. Now I can teach them—

THE FLOWER GIRL Let him mind his own business and leave a poor girl—

THE NOTE TAKER [*explosively*] Woman: cease this detestable boohooing
205 instantly; or else seek the shelter of some other place of worship.

THE FLOWER GIRL [*with feeble defiance*] Ive a right to be here if I like, same as you.

THE NOTE TAKER A woman who utters such depressing and disgusting sounds has no right to be anywhere—no right to live. Remember that you are a
210 human being with a soul and the divine gift of articulate speech: that your native language is the language of Shakespear and Milton and The Bible;[8] and dont sit there crooning like a bilious pigeon.

5. Dropped *h*s are typical of Cockney pronunciation. Hanwell, a working-class precinct of western London, contained a lunatic asylum founded in 1831.
6. That is, worried and hounded.
7. That is, men rise from grim working-class beginnings (Kentish Town is in northwest London) to become millionaires.
8. Three of the greatest literary influences on the English language: the playwright William Shakespeare (1564–1616), the poet John Milton (1608–1674), and the translation of the Bible commissioned by King James (1611).

THE FLOWER GIRL [*quite overwhelmed, and looking up at him in mingled wonder and deprecation without daring to raise her head*] Ah-ah-ah-ow-ow-ow-oo!

215 THE NOTE TAKER [*whipping out his book*] Heavens! what a sound! [*He writes; then holds out the book and reads, reproducing her vowels exactly.*] Ah-ah-ah-ow-ow-ow-oo!

THE FLOWER GIRL [*tickled by the performance, and laughing in spite of herself*] Garn!

THE NOTE TAKER You see this creature with her kerbstone English: the English that will keep her in the gutter to the end of her days. Well, sir, in

220 three months I could pass that girl off as a duchess at an ambassador's garden party. I could even get her a place as lady's maid or shop assistant, which requires better English. Thats the sort of thing I do for commercial millionaires. And on the profits of it I do genuine scientific work in phonetics, and a little as a poet on Miltonic lines.

225 THE GENTLEMAN I am myself a student of Indian dialects; and—

THE NOTE TAKER [*eagerly*] Are you? Do you know Colonel Pickering, the author of Spoken Sanscrit?

THE GENTLEMAN I am Colonel Pickering. Who are you?

THE NOTE TAKER Henry Higgins, author of Higgins's Universal Alphabet.

230 PICKERING [*with enthusiasm*] I came from India to meet you.

HIGGINS I was going to India to meet you.

PICKERING Where do you live?

HIGGINS 27A Wimpole Street.[9] Come and see me tomorrow.

PICKERING I'm at the Carlton.[1] Come with me now and lets have a jaw over

235 some supper.

HIGGINS Right you are.

THE FLOWER GIRL [*to PICKERING, as he passes her*] Buy a flower, kind gentleman. I'm short for my lodging.

PICKERING I really havnt any change. I'm sorry.

[*He goes away.*]

240 HIGGINS [*shocked at girl's mendacity*] Liar. You said you could change half-a-crown.

THE FLOWER GIRL [*rising in desperation*] You ought to be stuffed with nails, you ought. [*Flinging the basket at his feet*] Take the whole blooming basket for sixpence.

[*The church clock strikes the second quarter.*]

HIGGINS [*hearing in it the voice of God, rebuking him for his Pharisaic[2] want of

245 charity to the poor girl*] A reminder.

[*He raises his hat solemnly; then throws a handful of money into the basket and follows PICKERING.*]

THE FLOWER GIRL [*picking up a half-crown*] Ah-ow-ooh! [*Picking up a couple of florins*] Aaah-ow-ooh! [*Picking up several coins*] Aaaaaah-ow-ooh! [*Picking up a half-sovereign*][3] Aaaaaaaaaaaah-ow-ooh!!!

---

9. A street in Westminster; its most famous resident was Elizabeth Barrett, who eloped with Robert Browning from her family's home at 50 Wimpole St. in 1846.
1. An elegant London hotel on Haymarket,

near Piccadilly Circus.
2. That is, self-righteous and hypocritical, like the Pharisees as depicted in the New Testament.
3. A half-pound coin. *Florins*: two-shilling coins.

FREDDY [*springing out of a taxicab*]   Got one at last. Hallo! [*To the* GIRL]
250   Where are the two ladies that were here?

THE FLOWER GIRL   They walked to the bus when the rain stopped.

FREDDY   And left me with a cab on my hands. Damnation!

THE FLOWER GIRL [*with grandeur*]   Never you mind, young man. I'm going
home in a taxi. [*She sails off to the cab. The driver puts his hand behind him
and holds the door firmly shut against her. Quite understanding his mistrust,*
255   *she shews him her handful of money.*] Eightpence aint no object to me,
Charlie. [*He grins and opens the door.*] Angel Court, Drury Lane,[4] round
the corner of Micklejohn's oil shop. Lets see how fast you can make her
hop it.[5] [*She gets in and pulls the door to with a slam as the taxicab starts.*]

FREDDY   Well, I'm dashed![6]

Act 2

[*Next day at 11 a.m.* HIGGINS's *laboratory in Wimpole Street. It is a room on the first
floor, looking on the street, and was meant for the drawing-room. The double doors
are in the middle of the back wall; and persons entering find in the corner to their
right two tall file cabinets at right angles to one another against the walls. In this
corner stands a flat writing-table, on which are a phonograph, a laryngoscope,[7] a row
of tiny organ pipes with a bellows, a set of lamp chimneys for singeing flames with
burners attached to a gas plug in the wall by an indiarubber tube, several tuning-
forks of different sizes, a life-size image of half a human head, showing in section the
vocal organs, and a box containing a supply of wax cylinders for the phonograph.*

*Further down the room, on the same side, is a fireplace, with a comfortable
leather-covered easy-chair at the side of the hearth nearest the door, and a coal-
scuttle. There is a clock on the mantelpiece. Between the fireplace and the phonograph table is a stand for newspapers.*

*On the other side of the central door, to the left of the visitor, is a cabinet of shallow
drawers. On it is a telephone and the telephone directory. The corner beyond, and
most of the side wall, is occupied by a grand piano, with the keyboard at the end fur-
thest from the door, and a bench for the player extending the full length of the keyboard. On the piano is a dessert dish heaped with fruit and sweets, mostly chocolates.*

*The middle of the room is clear. Besides the easy-chair, the piano bench, and two
chairs at the phonograph table, there is one stray chair. It stands near the fireplace.
On the walls, engravings; mostly Piranesis[8] and mezzotint portraits. No paintings.*

PICKERING *is seated at the table, putting down some cards and a tuning-fork
which he has been using.* HIGGINS *is standing up near him, closing two or three file
drawers which are hanging out. He appears in the morning light as a robust, vital,
appetizing sort of man of forty or thereabouts, dressed in a professional-looking
black frock-coat with a white linen collar and black silk tie. He is of the energetic,
scientific type, heartily, even violently interested in everything that can be studied as
a scientific subject, and careless about himself and other people, including their
feelings. He is, in fact, but for his years and size, rather like a very impetuous baby
"taking notice"[9] eagerly and loudly, and requiring almost as much watching to keep
him out of unintended mischief. His manner varies from genial bullying when he is*]

4. A street close to Covent Garden; once
fashionable, by the nineteenth century it
became one of London's worst slums.
5. Go away quickly.
6. That is, "I'll be damned!"
7. An instrument for examining the larynx,
invented in the mid-19th century.

8. Reproductions of works by Giovanni Bat-
tista Piranesi (1720–1778), an Italian print-
maker known for his depictions of classical
and contemporary Roman sites.
9. Showing signs of intelligent observation (a
phrase used specifically of babies).

in a good humor to stormy petulance when anything goes wrong; but he is so entirely frank and void of malice that he remains likeable even in his least reasonable moments.]

HIGGINS [*as he shuts the last drawer*]   Well, I think thats the whole show.

PICKERING   It's really amazing. I havnt taken half of it in, you know.

HIGGINS   Would you like to go over any of it again?

PICKERING [*rising and coming to the fireplace, where he plants himself with his back to the fire*]   No, thank you; not now. I'm quite done up for this morning.

5 HIGGINS [*following him, and standing beside him on his left*]   Tired of listening to sounds?

PICKERING   Yes. It's a fearful strain. I rather fancied myself because I can pronounce twenty-four distinct vowel sounds; but your hundred and thirty beat me. I cant hear a bit of difference between most of them.

10 HIGGINS [*chuckling, and going over to the piano to eat sweets*]   Oh, that comes with practice. You hear no difference at first; but you keep on listening, and presently you find theyre all as different as A from B. [MRS. PEARCE *looks in: she is* HIGGINS's *housekeeper.*] Whats the matter?

MRS. PEARCE [*hesitating, evidently perplexed*]   A young woman wants to see
15 you, sir.

HIGGINS   A young woman! What does she want?

MRS. PEARCE   Well, sir, she says youll be glad to see her when you know what shes come about. Shes quite a common girl, sir. Very common indeed. I should have sent her away, only I thought perhaps you wanted her to talk
20 into your machines. I hope Ive not done wrong; but really you see such queer people sometimes—youll excuse me, I'm sure, sir—

HIGGINS   Oh, thats all right, Mrs. Pearce. Has she an interesting accent?

MRS. PEARCE   Oh, something dreadful, sir, really. I dont know how you can take an interest in it.

25 HIGGINS [*to* PICKERING]   Lets have her up. Shew her up, Mrs. Pearce. [*He rushes across to his working table and picks out a cylinder to use on the phonograph.*]

MRS. PEARCE [*only half resigned to it*]   Very well, sir. It's for you to say.
    [*She goes downstairs.*]

HIGGINS   This is rather a bit of luck. I'll shew you how I make records. We'll set her talking; and I'll take it down first in Bell's Visible Speech, then in broad Romic,[1] and then we'll get her on the phonograph so that you can
30 turn her on as often as you like with the written transcript before you.

MRS. PEARCE [*returning*]   This is the young woman, sir.

    [*The* FLOWER GIRL *enters in state. She has a hat with three ostrich feathers, orange, sky-blue, and red. She has a nearly clean apron, and the shoddy coat has been tidied a little. The pathos of this deplorable figure,*

---

1. The system of phonetic notation—a precursor of the International Phonetic Alphabet (IPA) used today—devised by Henry Sweet (1845–1912), a linguist on whose career Shaw drew in creating Higgins and who defined a "broad" transcription as less detailed (and less scientific) than a narrow one. Bell's

Visible Speech: a system of notation created a decade earlier than Sweet's by the educator Alexander Melville Bell (1819–1905), the father of the inventor Alexander Graham Bell; it attempts to represent the position of the vocal organs as individual sounds are produced.

with its innocent vanity and consequential air, touches PICKERING, *who has already straightened himself in the presence of* MRS. PEARCE. *But as to* HIGGINS, *the only distinction he makes between men and women is that when he is neither bullying nor exclaiming to the heavens against some featherweight cross, he coaxes women as a child coaxes its nurse when it wants to get anything out of her.*]

HIGGINS [*brusquely, recognizing her with unconcealed disappointment, and at once, babylike, making an intolerable grievance of it*]   Why, this is the girl I jotted down last night. Shes no use: Ive got all the records I want of the Lisson Grove lingo; and I'm not going to waste another cylinder on it. [*To*
35 *the* GIRL] Be off with you: I dont want you.

THE FLOWER GIRL   Dont you be so saucy. You aint heard what I come for yet. [*To* MRS. PEARCE, *who is waiting at the door for further instruction*] Did you tell him I come in a taxi?

MRS. PEARCE   Nonsense, girl! what do you think a gentleman like Mr. Hig-
40 gins cares what you came in?

THE FLOWER GIRL   Oh, we are proud! He aint above giving lessons, not him: I heard him say so. Well, I aint come here to ask for any compliment; and if my money's not good enough I can go elsewhere.

HIGGINS   Good enough for what?

45 THE FLOWER GIRL   Good enough for ye-oo. Now you know, dont you? I'm come to have lessons, I am. And to pay for em too: make no mistake.

HIGGINS [*stupent*]²   Well ! ! ! [*Recovering his breath with a gasp*] What do you expect me to say to you?

THE FLOWER GIRL   Well, if you was a gentleman, you might ask me to sit
50 down, I think. Dont I tell you I'm bringing you business?

HIGGINS   Pickering: shall we ask this baggage to sit down or shall we throw her out of the window?

THE FLOWER GIRL [*running away in terror to the piano, where she turns at bay*] Ah-ah-ah-ow-ow-ow-oo! [*Wounded and whimpering*] I wont be called a baggage when Ive offered to pay like any lady.

[*Motionless, the two men stare at her from the other side of the room, amazed.*]

55 PICKERING [*gently*]   What is it you want, my girl?

THE FLOWER GIRL   I want to be a lady in a flower shop stead of selling at the corner of Tottenham Court Road.³ But they wont take me unless I can talk more genteel. He said he could teach me. Well, here I am ready to pay him—not asking any favor—and he treats me as if I was dirt.

60 MRS. PEARCE   How can you be such a foolish ignorant girl as to think you could afford to pay Mr. Higgins?

THE FLOWER GIRL   Why shouldnt I? I know what lessons cost as well as you do; and I'm ready to pay.

HIGGINS   How much?

65 THE FLOWER GIRL [*coming back to him, triumphant*]   Now youre talking! I thought youd come off it when you saw a chance of getting back a bit of what you chucked at me last night. [*Confidentially*] Youd had a drop in,⁴ hadnt you?

---

2. In a state of stupefied amazement.
3. A busy central London shopping street,
within a half mile of Covent Garden.
4. That is, you'd had something to drink.

HIGGINS [*peremptorily*]   Sit down.

70 THE FLOWER GIRL   Oh, if youre going to make a compliment of it—

HIGGINS [*thundering at her*]   Sit down.

MRS. PEARCE [*severely*]   Sit down, girl. Do as youre told. [*She places the stray chair near the hearthrug between* HIGGINS *and* PICKERING, *and stands behind it waiting for the girl to sit down.*]

THE FLOWER GIRL   Ah-ah-ah-ow-ow-oo! [*She stands, half rebellious, half bewildered.*]

PICKERING [*very courteous*]   Wont you sit down?

75 THE FLOWER GIRL [*coyly*]   Dont mind if I do. [*She sits down.* PICKERING *returns to the hearthrug.*]

HIGGINS   Whats your name?

THE FLOWER GIRL   Liza Doolittle.

HIGGINS [*declaiming gravely*]

> Eliza, Elizabeth, Betsy and Bess,
> They went to the woods to get a birds nes':

80 PICKERING   They found a nest with four eggs in it:

HIGGINS   They took one apiece, and left three in it.

They laugh heartily at their own wit.

LIZA   Oh, dont be silly.

MRS. PEARCE   You mustnt speak to the gentleman like that.

LIZA   Well, why wont he speak sensible to me?

85 HIGGINS   Come back to business. How much do you propose to pay me for the lessons?

LIZA   Oh, I know whats right. A lady friend of mine gets French lessons for eighteenpence an hour from a real French gentleman. Well, you wouldnt have the face to ask me the same for teaching me my own lan-

90 guage as you would for French; so I wont give more than a shilling. Take it or leave it.

HIGGINS [*walking up and down the room, rattling his keys and his cash in his pockets*]   You know, Pickering, if you consider a shilling, not as a simple shilling, but as a percentage of this girl's income, it works out as fully equivalent to sixty or seventy guineas[5] from a millionaire.

95 PICKERING   How so?

HIGGINS   Figure it out. A millionaire has about £150 a day. She earns about half-a-crown.

LIZA [*haughtily*]   Who told you I only—

HIGGINS [*continuing*]   She offers me two-fifths of her day's income for a les-

100 son. Two-fifths of a millionaire's income for a day would be somewhere about £60. It's handsome. By George, it's enormous! it's the biggest offer I ever had.

LIZA [*rising, terrified*]   Sixty pounds! What are you talking about? I never offered you sixty pounds. Where would I get—

105 HIGGINS   Hold your tongue.

LIZA [*weeping*]   But I aint got sixty pounds. Oh—

MRS. PEARCE   Dont cry, you silly girl. Sit down. Nobody is going to touch your money.

---

5. Roughly equivalent to $6,000 today; a guinea is a gold coin worth twenty-one shillings.

HIGGINS   Somebody is going to touch you, with a broomstick, if you dont
110   stop snivelling. Sit down.

LIZA [*obeying slowly*]   Ah-ah-ah-ow-oo-o! One would think you was my father.

HIGGINS   If I decide to teach you, I'll be worse than two fathers to you. Here!
[*He offers her his silk handkerchief.*]

LIZA   Whats this for?

115   HIGGINS   To wipe your eyes. To wipe any part of your face that feels moist.
Remember: thats your handkerchief; and thats your sleeve. Dont mistake
the one for the other if you wish to become a lady in a shop.
[LIZA, *utterly bewildered, stares helplessly at him.*]

MRS. PEARCE   It's no use talking to her like that, Mr. Higgins: she doesnt
understand you. Besides, youre quite wrong: she doesnt do it that way at
120   all. [*She takes the handkerchief.*]

LIZA [*snatching it*]   Here! You give me that handkerchief. He give it to me,
not to you.

PICKERING [*laughing*]   He did. I think it must be regarded as her property,
Mrs. Pearce.

125   MRS. PEARCE [*resigning herself*]   Serve you right, Mr. Higgins.

PICKERING   Higgins: I'm interested. What about the ambassador's garden party?
I'll say youre the greatest teacher alive if you make that good. I'll bet you all
the expenses of the experiment you cant do it. And I'll pay for the lessons.

LIZA   Oh, you are real good. Thank you, Captain.

130   HIGGINS [*tempted, looking at her*]   It's almost irresistible. Shes so deliciously
low—so horribly dirty—

LIZA [*protesting extremely*]   Ah-ah-ah-ah-ow-ow-oo-oo!!! I aint dirty: I washed
my face and hands afore I come, I did.

PICKERING   Youre certainly not going to turn her head with flattery, Higgins.

135   MRS. PEARCE [*uneasy*]   Oh, dont say that, sir: theres more ways than one of
turning a girl's head; and nobody can do it better than Mr. Higgins, though
he may not always mean it. I do hope, sir, you wont encourage him to do
anything foolish.

HIGGINS [*becoming excited as the idea grows on him*]   What is life but a series
140   of inspired follies? The difficulty is to find them to do. Never lose a chance:
it doesnt come every day. I shall make a duchess of this draggle-tailed
guttersnipe.

LIZA [*strongly deprecating this view of her*]   Ah-ah-ah-ow-ow-oo!

HIGGINS [*carried away*]   Yes: in six months—in three if she has a good ear
145   and a quick tongue—I'll take her anywhere and pass her off as anything.
We'll start today: now! this moment! Take her away and clean her, Mrs.
Pearce. Monkey Brand,[6] if it wont come off any other way. Is there a good
fire in the kitchen?

MRS. PEARCE [*protesting*]   Yes; but—

150   HIGGINS [*storming on*]   Take all her clothes off and burn them. Ring up
Whiteley[7] or somebody for new ones. Wrap her up in brown paper til they
come.

LIZA   Youre no gentleman, youre not, to talk of such things. I'm a good girl, I
am; and I know what the like of you are, I do.

---

6. A popular brand of scouring soap.   7. A large department store in London.

155 HIGGINS We want none of your Lisson Grove prudery here, young woman. Youve got to learn to behave like a duchess. Take her away, Mrs. Pearce. If she gives you any trouble wallop her.

LIZA [*springing up and running between* PICKERING *and* MRS. PEARCE *for protection*] No! I'll call the police, I will.

MRS. PEARCE But Ive no place to put her.

160 HIGGINS Put her in the dustbin.

LIZA Ah-ah-ah-ow-ow-oo!

PICKERING Oh come, Higgins! be reasonable.

MRS. PEARCE [*resolutely*] You must be reasonable, Mr. Higgins: really you must. You cant walk over everybody like this.

[HIGGINS, *thus scolded, subsides. The hurricane is succeeded by a zephyr of amiable surprise.*]

165 HIGGINS [*with professional exquisiteness of modulation*] I walk over everybody! My dear Mrs. Pearce, my dear Pickering, I never had the slightest intention of walking over anyone. All I propose is that we should be kind to this poor girl. We must help her to prepare and fit herself for her new station in life. If I did not express myself clearly it was because I did not wish

170 to hurt her delicacy, or yours.

[LIZA, *reassured, steals back to her chair.*]

MRS. PEARCE [*to* PICKERING] Well, did you ever hear anything like that, sir?

PICKERING [*laughing heartily*] Never, Mrs. Pearce: never.

HIGGINS [*patiently*] Whats the matter?

MRS. PEARCE Well, the matter is, sir, that you cant take a girl up like that as

175 if you were picking up a pebble on the beach.

HIGGINS Why not?

MRS. PEARCE Why not! But you dont know anything about her. What about her parents? She may be married.

LIZA Garn!

180 HIGGINS There! As the girl very properly says, Garn! Married indeed! Dont you know that a woman of that class looks a worn out drudge of fifty a year after shes married.

LIZA Whood marry me?

HIGGINS [*suddenly resorting to the most thrillingly beautiful low tones in his best elocutionary style*] By George, Eliza, the streets will be strewn with

185 the bodies of men shooting themselves for your sake before Ive done with you.

MRS. PEARCE Nonsense, sir. You mustnt talk like that to her.

LIZA [*rising and squaring herself determinedly*] I'm going away. He's off his chump, he is. I dont want no balmies[8] teaching me.

HIGGINS [*wounded in his tenderest point by her insensibility to his elocution*]

190 Oh, indeed! I'm mad, am I? Very well, Mrs. Pearce: you neednt order the new clothes for her. Throw her out.

LIZA [*whimpering*] Nah-ow. You got no right to touch me.

MRS. PEARCE You see now what comes of being saucy. [*Indicating the door*] This way, please.

195 LIZA [*almost in tears*] I didnt want no clothes. I wouldnt have taken them. [*She throws away the handkerchief.*] I can buy my own clothes.

---

8. Crazies, madmen (slang). *Off his chump:* out of his senses (*chump* is slang for "head").

HIGGINS [*deftly retrieving the handkerchief and intercepting her on her reluc-tant way to the door*]   Youre an ungrateful wicked girl. This is my return for offering to take you out of the gutter and dress you beautifully and make a lady of you.

200 MRS. PEARCE   Stop, Mr. Higgins. I wont allow it. It's you that are wicked. Go home to your parents, girl; and tell them to take better care of you.

LIZA   I aint got no parents. They told me I was big enough to earn my own living and turned me out.

MRS. PEARCE   Wheres your mother?

205 LIZA   I aint got no mother. Her that turned me out was my sixth stepmother. But I done without them. And I'm a good girl, I am.

HIGGINS   Very well, then, what on earth is all this fuss about? The girl doesnt belong to anybody—is no use to anybody but me. [*He goes to* MRS. PEARCE *and begins coaxing.*] You can adopt her, Mrs. Pearce: I'm sure a daughter

210 would be a great amusement to you. Now dont make any more fuss. Take her downstairs; and—

MRS. PEARCE   But whats to become of her? Is she to be paid anything? Do be sensible, sir.

HIGGINS   Oh, pay her whatever is necessary: put it down in the housekeeping

215 book. [*Impatiently*] What on earth will she want with money? She'll have her food and her clothes. She'll only drink if you give her money.

LIZA [*turning on him*]   Oh you are a brute. It's a lie: nobody ever saw the sign of liquor on me. [*She goes back to her chair and plants herself there defiantly.*]

PICKERING [*in good-humored remonstrance*]   Does it occur to you, Higgins,

220 that the girl has some feelings?

HIGGINS [*looking critically at her*]   Oh no, I dont think so. Not any feelings that we need bother about. [*Cheerily*] Have you, Eliza?

LIZA   I got my feelings same as anyone else.

HIGGINS [*to* PICKERING, *reflectively*]   You see the difficulty?

225 PICKERING   Eh? What difficulty?

HIGGINS   To get her to talk grammar. The mere pronunciation is easy enough.

LIZA   I dont want to talk grammar. I want to talk like a lady.

MRS. PEARCE   Will you please keep to the point, Mr. Higgins. I want to know

230 on what terms the girl is to be here. Is she to have any wages? And what is to become of her when youve finished your teaching? You must look ahead a little.

HIGGINS [*impatiently*]   Whats to become of her if I leave her in the gutter? Tell me that, Mrs. Pearce.

235 MRS. PEARCE   Thats her own business, not yours, Mr. Higgins.

HIGGINS   Well, when Ive done with her, we can throw her back into the gut-ter; and then it will be her own business again; so thats all right.

LIZA   Oh, youve no feeling heart in you: you dont care for nothing but your-self. [*She rises and takes the floor resolutely.*] Here! Ive had enough of this. I'm

240 going. [*Making for the door*] You ought to be ashamed of yourself, you ought.

HIGGINS [*snatching a chocolate cream from the piano, his eyes suddenly begin-ning to twinkle with mischief*]   Have some chocolates, Eliza.

LIZA [*halting, tempted*]   How do I know what might be in them? Ive heard of girls being drugged by the like of you.

[HIGGINS *whips out his penknife; cuts a chocolate in two; puts one half into his mouth and bolts it; and offers her the other half.*]

HIGGINS Pledge of good faith, Eliza. I eat one half: you eat the other. [LIZA
245   *opens her mouth to retort: he pops the half chocolate into it.*] You shall have
boxes of them, barrels of them, every day. You shall live on them. Eh?

LIZA [*who has disposed of the chocolate after being nearly choked by it*] I
wouldnt have ate it, only I'm too ladylike to take it out of my mouth.

HIGGINS Listen, Eliza. I think you said you came in a taxi.

250 LIZA Well, what if I did? Ive as good a right to take a taxi as anyone else.

HIGGINS You have, Eliza; and in future you shall have as many taxis as you
want. You shall go up and down and round the town in a taxi every day.
Think of that, Eliza.

MRS. PEARCE Mr. Higgins: youre tempting the girl. It's not right. She should
255   think of the future.

HIGGINS At her age! Nonsense! Time enough to think of the future when
you havnt any future to think of. No, Eliza: do as this lady does: think of
other people's futures; but never think of your own. Think of chocolates,
and taxis, and gold, and diamonds.

260 LIZA No: I dont want no gold and no diamonds. I'm a good girl, I am. [*She
sits down again, with an attempt at dignity.*]

HIGGINS You shall remain so, Eliza, under the care of Mrs. Pearce. And you
shall marry an officer in the Guards, with a beautiful moustache: the son
of a marquis, who will disinherit him for marrying you, but will relent when
he sees your beauty and goodness—

265 PICKERING Excuse me, Higgins; but I really must interfere. Mrs. Pearce is
quite right. If this girl is to put herself in your hands for six months for an
experiment in teaching, she must understand thoroughly what shes doing.

HIGGINS How can she? Shes incapable of understanding anything. Besides,
do any of us understand what we are doing? If we did, would we ever do it?

270 PICKERING Very clever, Higgins; but not sound sense. [*To* ELIZA] Miss
Doolittle—

LIZA [*overwhelmed*] Ah-ah-ow-oo!

HIGGINS There! Thats all you get out of Eliza. Ah-ah-ow-oo! No use explaining. As a military man you ought to know that. Give her her orders: thats
275   what she wants. Eliza: you are to live here for the next six months, learning
how to speak beautifully, like a lady in a florist's shop. If youre good and do
whatever youre told, you shall sleep in a proper bedroom, and have lots to
eat, and money to buy chocolates and take rides in taxis. If youre naughty
and idle you will sleep in the back kitchen among the black beetles, and be
280   walloped by Mrs. Pearce with a broomstick. At the end of six months you
shall go to Buckingham Palace in a carriage, beautifully dressed. If the
King finds out youre not a lady, you will be taken by the police to the Tower
of London, where your head will be cut off as a warning to other presumptuous flower girls. If you are not found out, you shall have a present of
285   seven-and-sixpence to start life with as a lady in a shop. If you refuse this
offer you will be a most ungrateful and wicked girl; and the angels will
weep for you. [*To* PICKERING] Now are you satisfied, Pickering? [*To* MRS.
PEARCE] Can I put it more plainly and fairly, Mrs. Pearce?

MRS. PEARCE [*patiently*] I think youd better let me speak to the girl properly
290   in private. I dont know that I can take charge of her or consent to the
arrangement at all. Of course I know you dont mean her any harm; but
when you get what you call interested in people's accents, you never think
or care what may happen to them or you. Come with me, Eliza.

HIGGINS Thats all right. Thank you, Mrs. Pearce. Bundle her off to the
bath-room.

LIZA [*rising reluctantly and suspiciously*] Youre a great bully, you are. I wont
stay here if I dont like. I wont let nobody wallop me. I never asked to go to
Bucknam Palace, I didnt. I was never in trouble with the police, not me.
I'm a good girl—

MRS. PEARCE Dont answer back, girl. You dont understand the gentleman.
Come with me. [*She leads the way to the door, and holds it open for* ELIZA.]

LIZA [*as she goes out*] Well, what I say is right. I wont go near the king, not if
I'm going to have my head cut off. If I'd known what I was letting myself in
for, I wouldnt have come here. I always been a good girl; and I never
offered to say a word to him; and I dont owe him nothing; and I dont care;
and I wont be put upon; and I have my feelings the same as anyone else—

> [MRS. PEARCE *shuts the door; and* ELIZA's *plaints are no longer audible.*
> PICKERING *comes from the hearth to the chair and sits astride it with his
> arms on the back.*]

PICKERING Excuse the straight question, Higgins. Are you a man of good
character where women are concerned?

HIGGINS [*moodily*] Have you ever met a man of good character where women
are concerned?

PICKERING Yes: very frequently.

HIGGINS [*dogmatically, lifting himself on his hands to the level of the piano, and
sitting on it with a bounce*] Well, I havnt. I find that the moment I let a
woman make friends with me, she becomes jealous, exacting, suspicious,
and a damned nuisance. I find that the moment I let myself make friends
with a woman, I become selfish and tyrannical. Women upset everything.
When you let them into your life, you find that the woman is driving at one
thing and youre driving at another.

PICKERING At what, for example?

HIGGINS [*coming off the piano restlessly*] Oh, Lord knows! I suppose the
woman wants to live her own life; and the man wants to live his; and each
tries to drag the other on to the wrong track. One wants to go north and
the other south; and the result is that both have to go east, though they
both hate the east wind. [*He sits down on the bench at the keyboard.*] So
here I am, a confirmed old bachelor, and likely to remain so.

PICKERING [*rising and standing over him gravely*] Come, Higgins! You know
what I mean. If I'm to be in this business I shall feel responsible for that
girl. I hope it's understood that no advantage is to be taken of her position.

HIGGINS What! That thing! Sacred, I assure you. [*Rising to explain*] You see,
she'll be a pupil; and teaching would be impossible unless pupils were
sacred. Ive taught scores of American millionairesses how to speak English:
the best looking women in the world. I'm seasoned. They might as well be
blocks of wood. *I* might as well be a block of wood. It's—

> [MRS. PEARCE *opens the door. She has* ELIZA's *hat in her hand.* PICKERING
> *retires to the easy-chair at the hearth and sits down.*]

HIGGINS [*eagerly*] Well, Mrs. Pearce: is it all right?

MRS. PEARCE [*at the door*] I just wish to trouble you with a word, if I may,
Mr. Higgins.

HIGGINS Yes, certainly. Come in. [*She comes forward.*] Dont burn that, Mrs.
Pearce. I'll keep it as a curiosity. [*He takes the hat.*]

MRS. PEARCE Handle it carefully, sir, please. I had to promise her not to burn it; but I had better put it in the oven for a while.

340 HIGGINS [*putting it down hastily on the piano*] Oh! thank you. Well, what have you to say to me?

PICKERING Am I in the way?

MRS. PEARCE Not at all, sir. Mr. Higgins: will you please be very particular what you say before the girl?

345 HIGGINS [*sternly*] Of course. I'm always particular about what I say. Why do you say this to me?

MRS. PEARCE [*unmoved*] No, sir: youre not at all particular when youve mislaid anything or when you get a little impatient. Now it doesnt matter before me: I'm used to it. But you really must not swear before the girl.

350 HIGGINS [*indignantly*] I swear! [*Most emphatically*] I never swear. I detest the habit. What the devil do you mean?

MRS. PEARCE [*stolidly*] Thats what I mean, sir. You swear a great deal too much. I dont mind your damning and blasting, and what the devil and where the devil and who the devil—

355 HIGGINS Mrs. Pearce: this language from your lips! Really!

MRS. PEARCE [*not to be put off*] —but there is a certain word I must ask you not to use. The girl has just used it herself because the bath was too hot. It begins with the same letter as bath.[9] She knows no better: she learnt it at her mother's knee. But she must not hear it from your lips.

360 HIGGINS [*loftily*] I cannot charge myself with having ever uttered it, Mrs. Pearce. [*She looks at him steadfastly. He adds, hiding an uneasy conscience with a judicial air.*] Except perhaps in a moment of extreme and justifiable excitement.

MRS. PEARCE Only this morning, sir, you applied it to your boots, to the butter, and to the brown bread.

365

HIGGINS Oh, that! Mere alliteration, Mrs. Pearce, natural to a poet.

MRS. PEARCE Well, sir, whatever you choose to call it, I beg you not to let the girl hear you repeat it.

HIGGINS Oh, very well, very well. Is that all?

370 MRS. PEARCE No, sir. We shall have to be very particular with this girl as to personal cleanliness.

HIGGINS Certainly. Quite right. Most important.

MRS. PEARCE I mean not to be slovenly about her dress or untidy in leaving things about.

375 HIGGINS [*going to her solemnly*] Just so. I intended to call your attention to that. [*He passes on to* PICKERING, *who is enjoying the conversation immensely.*] It is these little things that matter, Pickering. Take care of the pence and the pounds will take care of themselves is as true of personal habits as of money. [*He comes to anchor on the hearthrug, with the air of a man in an unassailable position.*]

380 MRS. PEARCE Yes, sir. Then might I ask you not to come down to breakfast in your dressing-gown, or at any rate not to use it as a napkin to the extent you do, sir. And if you would be so good as not to eat everything off the same plate, and to remember not to put the porridge saucepan out of your

9. That is, "bloody," a colloquial intensifier that came to be considered highly offensive and profane (folk etymology linked it to the oath "God's blood!").

hand on the clean tablecloth, it would be a better example to the girl. You
385   know you nearly choked yourself with a fishbone in the jam only last week.

HIGGINS [*rounded from the hearthrug and drifting back to the piano*] I may
do these things sometimes in absence of mind; but surely I dont do them
habitually. [*Angrily*] By the way: my dressing-gown smells most damnably
of benzine.[1]

390 MRS. PEARCE No doubt it does, Mr. Higgins. But if you will wipe your
fingers—

HIGGINS [*yelling*] Oh very well, very well: I'll wipe them in my hair in future.

MRS. PEARCE I hope youre not offended, Mr. Higgins.

HIGGINS [*shocked at finding himself thought capable of an unamiable sentiment*] Not at all, not at all. Youre quite right, Mrs. Pearce: I shall be par-
395   ticularly careful before the girl. Is that all?

MRS. PEARCE No, sir. Might she use some of those Japanese dresses you
brought from abroad? I really cant put her back into her old things.

HIGGINS Certainly. Anything you like. Is that all?

MRS. PEARCE Thank you, sir. Thats all. [*She goes out.*]

400 HIGGINS You know, Pickering, that woman has the most extraordinary ideas
about me. Here I am, a shy, diffident sort of man. Ive never been able to
feel really grown-up and tremendous, like other chaps. And yet shes firmly
persuaded that I'm an arbitrary overbearing bossing kind of person. I cant
account for it.

       [MRS. PEARCE *returns.*]

405 MRS. PEARCE If you please, sir, the trouble's beginning already. Theres a
dustman[2] downstairs, Alfred Doolittle, wants to see you. He says you have
his daughter here.

PICKERING [*rising*] Phew! I say! [*He retreats to the hearthrug.*]

HIGGINS [*promptly*] Send the blackguard up.

410 MRS. PEARCE Oh, very well, sir. [*She goes out.*]

PICKERING He may not be a blackguard, Higgins.

HIGGINS Nonsense. Of course hes a blackguard.

PICKERING Whether he is or not, I'm afraid we shall have some trouble with
him.

415 HIGGINS [*confidently*] Oh no: I think not. If theres any trouble he shall have
it with me, not I with him. And we are sure to get something interesting out
of him.

PICKERING About the girl?

HIGGINS No. I mean his dialect.

420 PICKERING Oh!

MRS. PEARCE [*at the door*] Doolittle, sir. [*She admits* DOOLITTLE *and retires.*]

       [ALFRED DOOLITTLE *is an elderly but vigorous dustman, clad in the cos-
tume of his profession, including a hat with a back brim covering his
neck and shoulders. He has well marked and rather interesting features, and seems equally free from fear and conscience. He has a
remarkably expressive voice, the result of a habit of giving vent to his
feelings without reserve. His present pose is that of wounded honor and
stern resolution.*]

1. A solvent used to remove grease spots.   2. Garbage collector.

DOOLITTLE [*at the door, uncertain which of the two gentlemen is his man*] Professor Higgins?

HIGGINS Here. Good morning. Sit down.

DOOLITTLE Morning, Governor. [*He sits down magisterially.*] I come about a
425 very serious matter, Governor.

HIGGINS [*to* PICKERING] Brought up in Hounslow.[3] Mother Welsh, I should think. [DOOLITTLE *opens his mouth, amazed.* HIGGINS *continues.*] What do you want, Doolittle?

DOOLITTLE [*menacingly*] I want my daughter: thats what I want. See?

430 HIGGINS Of course you do. Youre her father, arnt you? You dont suppose anyone else wants her, do you? I'm glad to see you have some spark of family feeling left. Shes upstairs. Take her away at once.

DOOLITTLE [*rising, fearfully taken aback*] What!

HIGGINS Take her away. Do you suppose I'm going to keep your daughter for
435 you?

DOOLITTLE [*remonstrating*] Now, now, look here, Governor. Is this reasonable? Is it fairity[4] to take advantage of a man like this? The girl belongs to me. You got her. Where do I come in? [*He sits down again.*]

HIGGINS Your daughter had the audacity to come to my house and ask me to
440 teach her how to speak properly so that she could get a place in a flowershop. This gentleman and my housekeeper have been here all the time. [*Bullying him*] How dare you come here and attempt to blackmail me? You sent her here on purpose.

DOOLITTLE [*protesting*] No, Governor.

445 HIGGINS You must have. How else could you possibly know that she is here?

DOOLITTLE Dont take a man up like that, Governor.

HIGGINS The police shall take you up. This is a plant—a plot to extort money by threats. I shall telephone for the police. [*He goes resolutely to the telephone and opens the directory.*]

DOOLITTLE Have I asked you for a brass farthing?[5] I leave it to the gentle-
450 man here: have I said a word about money?

HIGGINS [*throwing the book aside and marching down on* DOOLITTLE *with a poser*] What else did you come for?

DOOLITTLE [*sweetly*] Well, what would a man come for? Be human, Governor.

HIGGINS [*disarmed*] Alfred: did you put her up to it?

DOOLITTLE So help me, Governor, I never did. I take my Bible oath I aint
455 seen the girl these two months past.

HIGGINS Then how did you know she was here?

DOOLITTLE [*"most musical, most melancholy"*[6]] I'll tell you, Governor, if youll only let me get a word in. I'm willing to tell you. I'm wanting to tell you. I'm waiting to tell you.

460 HIGGINS Pickering: this chap has a certain natural gift of rhetoric. Observe the rhythm of his native wood-notes wild.[7] "I'm willing to tell you: I'm

3. A working-class suburb west of central London.
4. Fair (Doolittle's fanciful coinage).
5. An expression equivalent to "one red cent"; a farthing is one-quarter of a penny, and "brass" here is emphatic.

6. From John Milton's poem "Il Penseroso" (ca. 1631), line 62.
7. A quotation from Milton's "L'Allegro" (ca. 1631), line 134; in the poem (a companion piece to "Il Penseroso"), the phrase refers to Shakespeare.

wanting to tell you: I'm waiting to tell you." Sentimental rhetoric! thats the
Welsh strain in him. It also accounts for his mendacity and dishonesty.

PICKERING   Oh, please, Higgins: I'm west country[8] myself. [*To* DOOLITTLE]
465   How did you know the girl was here if you didnt send her?

DOOLITTLE   It was like this, Governor. The girl took a boy in the taxi to give
him a jaunt. Son of her landlady, he is. He hung about on the chance of her
giving him another ride home. Well, she sent him back for her luggage
when she heard you was willing for her to stop here. I met the boy at the
470   corner of Long Acre and Endell Street.

HIGGINS   Public house.[9] Yes?

DOOLITTLE   The poor man's club, Governor: why shouldnt I?

PICKERING   Do let him tell his story, Higgins.

DOOLITTLE   He told me what was up. And I ask you, what was my feelings
475   and my duty as a father? I says to the boy, "You bring me the luggage," I says—

PICKERING   Why didnt you go for it yourself?

DOOLITTLE   Landlady wouldnt have trusted me with it, Governor. Shes that
kind of woman: you know. I had to give the boy a penny afore he trusted me
with it, the little swine. I brought it to her just to oblige you like, and make
480   myself agreeable. Thats all.

HIGGINS   How much luggage?

DOOLITTLE   Musical instrument, Governor. A few pictures, a trifle of jewelry,
and a bird-cage. She said she didnt want no clothes. What was I to think
from that, Governor? I ask you as a parent what was I to think?

485   HIGGINGS   So you came to rescue her from worse than death, eh?

DOOLITTLE   [*appreciatively: relieved at being so well understood*]   Just so, Governor. Thats right.

PICKERING   But why did you bring her luggage if you intended to take her
away?

490   DOOLITTLE   Have I said a word about taking her away? Have I now?

HIGGINS   [*determinedly*]   Youre going to take her away, double quick. [*He
crosses to the hearth and rings the bell.*]

DOOLITTLE   [*rising*]   No, Governor. Dont say that. I'm not the man to stand in
my girl's light. Heres a career opening for her, as you might say; and—

[MRS. PEARCE *opens the door and awaits orders.*]

HIGGINS   Mrs. Pearce: this is Eliza's father. He has come to take her away.
495   Give her to him. [*He goes back to the piano, with an air of washing his hands
of the whole affair.*]

DOOLITTLE   No. This is a misunderstanding. Listen here—

MRS. PEARCE   He cant take her away, Mr. Higgins: how can he? You told me
to burn her clothes.

DOOLITTLE   Thats right. I cant carry the girl through the streets like a bloom-
500   ing monkey, can I? I put it to you.

HIGGINS   You have put it to me that you want your daughter. Take your
daughter. If she has no clothes go out and buy her some.

DOOLITTLE   [*desperate*]   Wheres the clothes she come in? Did I burn them or
did your missus here?

8. The southwestern counties of England—
Somerset, Dorset, Devon, and Cornwall. The
inhabitants of Cornwall and Wales are connected by their related languages, and the

English long regarded (and often denigrated)
them as separate cultural groups.
9. That is, a pub.

505 MRS. PEARCE I am the housekeeper, if you please. I have sent for some clothes for your girl. When they come you can take her away. You can wait in the kitchen. This way, please.

[DOOLITTLE, *much troubled, accompanies her to the door; then hesitates; finally turns confidentially to* HIGGINS.]

DOOLITTLE Listen here, Governor. You and me is men of the world, aint we?

HIGGINS Oh! Men of the world, are we? Youd better go, Mrs. Pearce.

510 MRS. PEARCE I think so, indeed, sir.

[*She goes, with dignity.*]

PICKERING The floor is yours, Mr. Doolittle.

DOOLITTLE [*to* PICKERING] I thank you, Governor. [*To* HIGGINS, *who takes refuge on the piano bench, a little overwhelmed by the proximity of his visitor; for* DOOLITTLE *has a professional flavor of dust about him*] Well, the truth is, Ive taken a sort of fancy to you, Governor; and if you want the girl, I'm
515 not so set on having her back home again but what I might be open to an arrangement. Regarded in the light of a young woman, shes a fine handsome girl. As a daughter shes not worth her keep; and so I tell you straight. All I ask is my rights as a father; and youre the last man alive to expect me to let her go for nothing; for I can see youre one of the straight sort, Gov-
520 ernor. Well, whats a five pound note to you? And whats Eliza to me? [*He returns to his chair and sits down judicially.*]

PICKERING I think you ought to know, Doolittle, that Mr. Higgins's intentions are entirely honorable.

DOOLITTLE Course they are, Governor. If I thought they wasnt, Id ask fifty.

HIGGINS [*revolted*] Do you mean to say, you callous rascal, that you would
525 sell your daughter for £50?

DOOLITTLE Not in a general way I wouldnt; but to oblige a gentleman like you I'd do a good deal, I do assure you.

PICKERING Have you no morals, man?

DOOLITTLE [*unabashed*] Cant afford them, Governor. Neither could you if
530 you was as poor as me. Not that I mean any harm, you know. But if Liza is going to have a bit out of this, why not me too?

HIGGINS [*troubled*] I dont know what to do, Pickering. There can be no question that as a matter of morals it's a positive crime to give this chap a farthing. And yet I feel a sort of rough justice in his claim.

535 DOOLITTLE Thats it, Governor. Thats all I say. A father's heart, as it were.

PICKERING Well, I know the feeling; but really it seems hardly right—

DOOLITTLE Dont say that, Governor. Dont look at it that way. What am I, Governors both? I ask you, what am I? I'm one of the undeserving poor: thats what I am. Think of what that means to a man. It means that hes up
540 agen[1] middle class morality all the time. If theres anything going, and I put in for a bit of it, it's always the same story: "Youre undeserving; so you cant have it." But my needs is as great as the most deserving widow's that ever got money out of six different charities in one week for the death of the same husband. I dont need less than a deserving man: I need more. I dont
545 eat less hearty than him; and I drink a lot more. I want a bit of amusement, cause I'm a thinking man. I want cheerfulness and a song and a band when I feel low. Well, they charge me just the same for everything as they charge

1. Against.

the deserving. What is middle class morality? Just an excuse for never giving me anything. Therefore, I ask you, as two gentlemen, not to play that
550 game on me. I'm playing straight with you. I aint pretending to be deserving. I'm undeserving; and I mean to go on being undeserving. I like it; and
thats the truth. Will you take advantage of a man's nature to do him out of
the price of his own daughter what hes brought up and fed and clothed by
the sweat of his brow until shes growed big enough to be interesting to
555 you two gentlemen? Is five pounds unreasonable? I put it to you; and I
leave it to you.

HIGGINS [rising, and going over to PICKERING] Pickering: if we were to take
this man in hand for three months, he could choose between a seat in the
Cabinet and a popular pulpit in Wales.

560 PICKERING What do you say to that, Doolittle?

DOOLITTLE Not me, Governor, thank you kindly. Ive heard all the preachers
and all the prime ministers—for I'm a thinking man and game for politics
or religion or social reform same as all the other amusements—and I tell
you it's a dog's life anyway you look at it. Undeserving poverty is my line.
565 Taking one station in society with another, it's—it's—well, it's the only one
that has any ginger in it, to my taste.

HIGGINS I suppose we must give him a fiver.

PICKERING He'll make a bad use of it, I'm afraid.

DOOLITTLE Not me, Governor, so help me I wont. Dont you be afraid that
570 I'll save it and spare it and live idle on it. There wont be a penny of it left by
Monday: I'll have to go to work same as if I'd never had it. It wont pauper-
ize me, you bet. Just one good spree for myself and the missus, giving pleasure to ourselves and employment to others, and satisfaction to you to
think it's not been throwed away. You couldnt spend it better.

HIGGINS [taking out his pocket book and coming between DOOLITTLE and the
575 piano] This is irresistible. Lets give him ten. [He offers two notes to the
dustman.]

DOOLITTLE No, Governor. She wouldnt have the heart to spend ten; and
perhaps I shouldnt neither. Ten pounds is a lot of money: it makes a man
feel prudent like: and then good-bye to happiness. You give me what I ask
you, Governor: not a penny more, and not a penny less.

580 PICKERING Why dont you marry that missus of yours? I rather draw the line
at encouraging that sort of immorality.

DOOLITTLE Tell her so, Governor: tell her so. I'm willing. It's me that suffers
by it. Ive no hold on her. I got to be agreeable to her. I got to give her presents. I got to buy her clothes something sinful. I'm a slave to that woman,
585 Governor, just because I'm not her lawful husband. And she knows it too.
Catch her marrying me! Take my advice, Governor: marry Eliza while shes
young and dont know no better. If you dont youll be sorry for it after. If you
do, she'll be sorry for it after; but better you than her, because youre a man,
and shes only a woman and dont know how to be happy anyhow.

590 HIGGINS Pickering: if we listen to this man another minute, we shall have
no convictions left. [To DOOLITTLE] Five pounds I think you said.

DOOLITTLE Thank you kindly, Governor.

HIGGINS Youre sure you wont take ten?

DOOLITTLE Not now. Another time, Governor.

595 HIGGINS [handing him a five-pound note] Here you are.

DOOLITTLE   Thank you, Governor. Good morning.

[*He hurries to the door, anxious to get away with his booty. When he opens it he is confronted with a dainty and exquisitely clean young Japanese lady in a simple blue cotton kimono printed cunningly with small white jasmine blossoms.* MRS. PEARCE *is with her. He gets out of her way deferentially and apologizes.*]

Beg pardon, miss.

THE JAPANESE LADY   Garn! Dont you know your own daughter?

600   DOOLITTLE ⎱
       HIGGINS   ⎰   *exclaiming*   ⎱ Bly me! it's Eliza!
       PICKERING ⎰   *simultaneously* ⎰ Whats that! This!
                                       ⎰ By Jove!

LIZA   Dont I look silly?

HIGGINS   Silly?

MRS. PEARCE [*at the door*]   Now, Mr. Higgins, please dont say anything to
605   make the girl conceited about herself.

HIGGINS [*conscientiously*]   Oh! Quite right, Mrs. Pearce. [*To* ELIZA] Yes:
       damned silly.

MRS. PEARCE   Please, sir.

HIGGINS [*correcting himself*]   I mean extremely silly.

610   LIZA   I should look all right with my hat on. [*She takes up her hat; puts it on;
       and walks across the room to the fireplace with a fashionable air.*]

HIGGINS   A new fashion, by George! And it ought to look horrible!

DOOLITTLE [*with fatherly pride*]   Well, I never thought she'd clean up as good
       looking as that, Governor. Shes a credit to me, aint she?

615   LIZA   I tell you, it's easy to clean up here. Hot and cold water on tap, just as
       much as you like, there is. Woolly towels, there is; and a towel horse[2] so
       hot, it burns your fingers. Soft brushes to scrub yourself, and a wooden
       bowl of soap smelling like primroses. Now I know why ladies is so clean.
       Washing's a treat for them. Wish they saw what it is for the like of me!

HIGGINS   I'm glad the bath-room met with your approval.

620   LIZA   It didnt: not all of it; and I dont care who hears me say it. Mrs. Pearce
       knows.

HIGGINS   What was wrong, Mrs. Pearce?

MRS. PEARCE [*blandly*]   Oh, nothing, sir. It doesnt matter.

LIZA   I had a good mind to break it. I didnt know which way to look. But I
625   hung a towel over it, I did.

HIGGINS   Over what?

MRS. PEARCE   Over the looking-glass, sir.

HIGGINS   Doolittle: you have brought your daughter up too strictly.

DOOLITTLE   Me! I never brought her up at all, except to give her a lick of a
630   strap now and again. Dont put it on me, Governor. She aint accustomed to
       it, you see: thats all. But she'll soon pick up your free-and-easy ways.

LIZA   I'm a good girl, I am; and I wont pick up no free and easy ways.

HIGGINS   Eliza: if you say again that youre a good girl, your father shall take
       you home.

635   LIZA   Not him. You dont know my father. All he come here for was to touch
       you for some money to get drunk on.

---

2. A towel rack, in this case apparently a metal pipe filled with hot water (usually such racks were made of wood).

DOOLITTLE   Well, what else would I want money for? To put into the plate in church, I suppose. [*She puts out her tongue at him. He is so incensed by this that* PICKERING *presently finds it necessary to step between them.*] Dont
640   you give me none of your lip; and dont let me hear you giving this gentleman any of it neither, or youll hear from me about it. See?

HIGGINS   Have you any further advice to give her before you go, Doolittle? Your blessing, for instance.

DOOLITTLE   No, Governor: I aint such a mug[3] as to put up my children to
645   all I know myself. Hard enough to hold them in without that. If you want Eliza's mind improved, Governor, you do it yourself with a strap. So long, gentlemen. [*He turns to go.*]

HIGGINS [*impressively*]   Stop. Youll come regularly to see your daughter. It's your duty, you know. My brother is a clergyman; and he could help you in
650   your talks with her.

DOOLITTLE [*evasively*]   Certainly. I'll come, Governor. Not just this week, because I have a job at a distance. But later on you may depend on me. Afternoon, gentlemen. Afternoon, maam.

> [*He takes off his hat to* MRS. PEARCE, *who disdains the salutation and goes out. He winks at* HIGGINS, *thinking him probably a fellow-sufferer from* MRS. PEARCE's *difficult disposition, and follows her.*]

LIZA   Dont you believe the old liar. He'd as soon you set a bull-dog on him as
655   a clergyman. You wont see him again in a hurry.

HIGGINS   I dont want to, Eliza. Do you?

LIZA   Not me. I dont want never to see him again, I dont. Hes a disgrace to me, he is, collecting dust, instead of working at his trade.

PICKERING   What is his trade, Eliza?

660   LIZA   Talking money out of other people's pockets into his own. His proper trade's a navvy;[4] and he works at it sometimes too—for exercise—and earns good money at it. Aint you going to call me Miss Doolittle any more?

PICKERING   I beg your pardon, Miss Doolittle. It was a slip of the tongue.

LIZA   Oh, I dont mind; only it sounded so genteel. I should just like to take a
665   taxi to the corner of Tottenham Court Road and get out there and tell it to wait for me, just to put the girls in their place a bit. I wouldnt speak to them, you know.

PICKERING   Better wait til we get you something really fashionable.

HIGGINS   Besides, you shouldnt cut[5] your old friends now that you have risen
670   in the world. Thats what we call snobbery.

LIZA   You dont call the like of them my friends now, I should hope. Theyve took it out of me often enough with their ridicule when they had the chance; and now I mean to get a bit of my own back. But if I'm to have fashionable clothes, I'll wait. I should like to have some. Mrs. Pearce says
675   youre going to give me some to wear in bed at night different to what I wear in the daytime; but it do seem a waste of money when you could get something to shew. Besides, I never could fancy changing into cold things on a winter night.

MRS. PEARCE [*coming back*]   Now, Eliza. The new things have come for you
680   to try on.

---

3. Fool.
4. An unskilled laborer who digs earth.

5. Break off acquaintance with; pretend not to know.

LIZA Ah-ow-oo-ooh!

[*She rushes out.*]

MRS. PEARCE [*following her*] Oh, dont rush about like that, girl.

[*She shuts the door behind her.*]

HIGGINS Pickering: we have taken on a stiff job.

PICKERING [*with conviction*] Higgins: we have.

Act 3

[*It is* MRS. HIGGINS's *at-home day.*[6] *Nobody has yet arrived. Her drawing-room, in a flat on Chelsea Embankment,*[7] *has three windows looking on the river; and the ceiling is not so lofty as it would be in an older house of the same pretension. The windows are open, giving access to a balcony with flowers in pots. If you stand with your face to the windows, you have the fireplace on your left and the door in the right-hand wall close to the corner nearest the windows.*

MRS. HIGGINS *was brought up on Morris and Burne Jones,*[8] *and her room, which is very unlike her son's room in Wimpole Street, is not crowded with furniture and little tables and nicknacks. In the middle of the room there is a big ottoman; and this, with the carpet, the Morris wall-papers, and the Morris chintz windows curtains and brocade covers of the ottoman and its cushions, supply all the ornament, and are much too handsome to be hidden by odds and ends of useless things. A few good oil-paintings from the exhibitions in the Grosvenor Gallery thirty years ago (the Burne Jones, not the Whistler side of them)*[9] *are on the walls. The only landscape is a Cecil Lawson on the scale of a Rubens.*[1] *There is a portrait of* MRS. HIGGINS *as she was when she defied fashion in her youth in one of the beautiful Rossettian*[2] *costumes which, when caricatured by people who did not understand, let to the absurdities of popular estheticism in the eighteen-seventies.*

In the corner diagonally opposite the door MRS. HIGGINS, *now over sixty and long past taking the trouble to dress out of the fashion, sits writing at an elegantly simple writing-table with a bell button within reach of her hand. There is a Chippendale*[3] *chair further back in the room between her and the window nearest her side. At the other side of the room, further forward, is an Elizabethan chair roughly carved in the taste of Inigo Jones.*[4] *On the same side a piano in a decorated case. The corner between the fireplace and the window is occupied by a divan cushioned in Morris chintz.*

It is between four and five in the afternoon.

The door is opened violently; and Higgins enters with his hat on.]

6. In middle- and upper-class society, a set time each week for receiving visitors.

7. A roadway along the north bank of the Thames in central London, developed in the late 19th century with residences for the well-to-do.

8. Two highly influential Victorian artists and designers, who were friends and colleagues. William Morris (1834–1896), associated with the Pre-Raphaelites, was one of the founders of the Arts and Crafts movement and is especially well-known for his wallpaper and fabric designs; Edward Burne-Jones (1833–1898), known for his medieval-style paintings, came under the influence of the Pre-Raphaelites at about the same time as Morris.

9. An allusion to an 1877 exhibition; the painting by the American artist James McNeill Whistler (1834–1903) was so severely attacked in a review by John Ruskin (who praised Burne-Jones's work) that Whistler sued for libel.

1. Peter Paul Rubens (1577–1640), a Flemish artist identified with the baroque style and known for very large paintings. Lawson (1851–1882), an English landscape painter whose early works included a number of studies of Chelsea.

2. In the style of Dante Gabriel Rossetti (1828–1882), an English poet and painter who was a founding member of the Pre-Raphaelite Brotherhood; many of his works depict idealized, sensuous women in flowing garments.

3. A popular 18th-century furniture style, graceful and often ornate; it was named for the English cabinetmaker Thomas Chippendale (1718–1779).

4. The founder of English classical architecture (1573–1652); he designed stage sets as well as buildings.

MRS. HIGGINS [*dismayed*]   Henry! [*Scolding him*] What are you doing here to-day? It is my at-home day: you promised not to come. [*As he bends to kiss her, she takes his hat off, and presents it to him.*]

HIGGINS   Oh bother! [*He throws the hat down on the table.*]

MRS. HIGGINS   Go home at once.

5   HIGGINS [*kissing her*]   I know, mother. I came on purpose.

MRS. HIGGINS   But you mustnt. I'm serious, Henry. You offend all my friends: they stop coming whenever they meet you.

HIGGINS   Nonsense! I know I have no small talk; but people dont mind. [*He sits on the settee.*]

MRS. HIGGINS   Oh! dont they? Small talk indeed! What about your large talk?
10   Really, dear, you mustnt stay.

HIGGINS   I must. Ive a job for you. A phonetic job.

MRS. HIGGINS   No use, dear. I'm sorry; but I cant get round your vowels; and though I like to get pretty postcards in your patent shorthand, I always have to read the copies in ordinary writing you so thoughtfully send me.

15   HIGGINS   Well, this isnt a phonetic job.

MRS. HIGGINS   You said it was.

HIGGINS   Not your part of it. Ive picked up a girl.

MRS. HIGGINS   Does that mean that some girl has picked you up?

HIGGINS   Not at all. I dont mean a love affair.

20   MRS. HIGGINS   What a pity!

HIGGINS   Why?

MRS. HIGGINS   Well, you never fall in love with anyone under forty-five. When will you discover that there are some rather nice-looking young women about?

25   HIGGINS   Oh, I cant be bothered with young women. My idea of a loveable woman is something as like you as possible. I shall never get into the way of seriously liking young women: some habits lie too deep to be changed. [*Rising abruptly and walking about, jingling his money and his keys in his trouser pockets*] Besides, theyre all idiots.

MRS. HIGGINS   Do you know what you would do if you really loved me, Henry?

30   HIGGINS   Oh bother! What? Marry, I suppose?

MRS. HIGGINS   No. Stop fidgeting and take your hands out of your pockets. [*With a gesture of despair, he obeys and sits down again.*] Thats a good boy. Now tell me about the girl.

HIGGINS   Shes coming to see you.

35   MRS. HIGGINS   I dont remember asking her.

HIGGINS   You didnt. *I* asked her. If youd known her you wouldnt have asked her.

MRS. HIGGINS   Indeed! Why?

HIGGINS   Well, it's like this. Shes a common flower girl. I picked her off the kerbstone.

40   MRS. HIGGINS   And invited her to my at-home!

HIGGINS [*rising and coming to her to coax her*]   Oh, thatll be all right. Ive taught her to speak properly; and she has strict orders as to her behavior. Shes to keep to two subjects: the weather and everybody's health—Fine day and How do you do, you know—and not to let herself go on things in
45   general. That will be safe.

MRS. HIGGINS   Safe! To talk about our health! about our insides! perhaps about our outsides! How could you be so silly, Henry?

HIGGINS [*impatiently*]   Well, she must talk about something. [*He controls himself and sits down again.*] Oh, she'll be all right: dont you fuss. Pickering
50 is in it with me. Ive a sort of bet on that I'll pass her off as a duchess in six months. I started on her some months ago; and shes getting on like a house on fire. I shall win my bet. She has a quick ear; and shes been easier to teach than my middle-class pupils because shes had to learn a complete new language. She talks English almost as you talk French.

55 MRS. HIGGINS   Thats satisfactory, at all events.

HIGGINS   Well, it is and it isnt.

MRS. HIGGINS   What does that mean?

HIGGINS   You see, Ive got her pronunciation all right; but you have to considernotonlyhowagirlpronounces,butwhatshepronounces;andthatswhere—

    [*They are interrupted by the* PARLOR-MAID, *announcing guests.*]

60 THE PARLOR-MAID   Mrs. and Miss Eynsford Hill.

    [*She withdraws.*]

HIGGINS   Oh Lord! [*He rises; snatches his hat from the table; and makes for the door; but before he reaches it his mother introduces him.*]

    [MRS. *and* MISS EYNSFORD HILL *are the mother and daughter who sheltered from the rain in Covent Garden. The mother is well bred, quiet, and has the habitual anxiety of straitened means. The daughter has acquired a gay air of being very much at home in society: the bravado of genteel poverty.*]

MRS. EYNSFORD HILL [*to* MRS. HIGGINS]   How do you do? [*They shake hands.*]

MISS EYNSFORD HILL   How d'you do? [*She shakes.*]

MRS. HIGGINS [*introducing*]   My son Henry.

65 MRS. EYNSFORD HILL   Your celebrated son! I have so longed to meet you, Professor Higgins.

HIGGINS [*glumly, making no movement in her direction*]   Delighted. [*He backs against the piano and bows brusquely.*]

MISS EYNSFORD HILL [*going to him with confident familiarity*]   How do you do?

HIGGINS [*staring at her*]   Ive seen you before somewhere. I havnt the ghost of
70 a notion where; but Ive heard your voice. [*Drearily*] It doesnt matter. Youd better sit down.

MRS. HIGGINS   I'm sorry to say that my celebrated son has no manners. You mustnt mind him.

MISS EYNSFORD HILL [*gaily*]   I dont. [*She sits in the Elizabethan chair.*]

75 MRS. EYNSFORD HILL [*a little bewildered*]   Not at all. [*She sits on the ottoman between her daughter and* MRS. HIGGINS, *who has turned her chair away from the writing-table.*]

HIGGINS   Oh, have I been rude? I didnt mean to be.

    [*He goes to the central window, through which, with his back to the company, he contemplates the river and the flowers in Battersea Park on the opposite bank as if they were a frozen desert.*]

    [*The* PARLOR-MAID *returns, ushering in* PICKERING.]

THE PARLOR-MAID   Colonel Pickering.

    [*She withdraws.*]

PICKERING How do you do, Mrs. Higgins?

MRS. HIGGINS So glad youve come. Do you know Mrs. Eynsford Hill—Miss
80   Eynsford Hill? [*Exchange of bows. The* COLONEL *brings the Chippendale
chair a little forward between* MRS. HILL *and* MRS. HIGGINS, *and sits down.*]

PICKERING Has Henry told you what weve come for?

HIGGINS [*over his shoulder*] We were interrupted: damn it!

MRS. HIGGINS Oh Henry, Henry, really!

MRS. EYNSFORD HILL [*half rising*] Are we in the way?

85   MRS. HIGGINS [*rising and making her sit down again*] No, no. You couldnt
have come more fortunately: we want you to meet a friend of ours.

HIGGINS [*turning hopefully*] Yes, by George! We want two or three people.
Youll do as well as anybody else.

                    [*The* PARLOR-MAID *returns, ushering* FREDDY.]

THE PARLOR-MAID Mr. Eynsford Hill.

90   HIGGINS [*almost audibly, past endurance*] God of Heaven! another of them.

FREDDY [*shaking hands with* MRS. HIGGINS] Ahdedo?[5]

MRS. HIGGINS Very good of you to come. [*Introducing*] Colonel Pickering.

FREDDY [*bowing*] Ahdedo?

MRS. HIGGINS I dont think you know my son, Professor Higgins.

95   FREDDY [*going to Higgins*] Ahdedo?

HIGGINS [*looking at him much as if he were a pickpocket*] I'll take my oath
Ive met you before somewhere. Where was it?

FREDDY I dont think so.

HIGGINS [*resignedly*] It dont matter, anyhow. Sit down.

            [*He shakes* FREDDY's *hand, and almost slings him on the ottoman with his
            face to the windows; then comes round to the other side of it.*]

100   HIGGINS Well, here we are, anyhow! [*He sits down on the ottoman next* MRS.
EYNSFORD HILL, *on her left.*] And now, what the devil are we going to talk
about until Eliza comes?

MRS. HIGGINS Henry: you are the life and soul of the Royal Society's[6] soi-
rées; but really youre rather trying on more commonplace occasions.

105   HIGGINS Am I? Very sorry. [*Beaming suddenly*] I suppose I am, you know.
[*Uproariously*] Ha, ha!

MISS EYNSFORD HILL [*who considers* HIGGINS *quite eligible matrimonially*] I
sympathize. I havnt any small talk. If people would only be frank and say
what they really think!

110   HIGGINS [*relapsing into gloom*] Lord forbid!

MRS. EYNSFORD HILL [*taking up her daughter's cue*] But why?

HIGGINS What they think they ought to think is bad enough, Lord knows;
but what they really think would break up the whole show. Do you suppose
it would be really agreeable if I were to come out now with what *I* really
think?

115   MISS EYNSFORD HILL [*gaily*] Is it so very cynical?

HIGGINS Cynical! Who the dickens said it was cynical? I mean it wouldnt be
decent.

MRS. EYNSFORD HILL [*seriously*] Oh! I'm sure you dont mean that, Mr. Higgins.

5. That is, "How do you do?"

6. An independent academy of science in the
United Kingdom (formally named in its 1663

charter "The Royal Society of London for
Improving Natural Knowledge").

898 | GEORGE BERNARD SHAW

HIGGINS   You see, we're all savages, more or less. We're supposed to be civi-
120   lized and cultured—to know all about poetry and philosophy and art and
science, and so on; but how many of us know even the meanings of these
names? [*To* MISS HILL] What do you know of poetry? [*To* MRS. HILL] What
do you know of science? [*Indicating* FREDDY] What does he know of art or
science or anything else? What the devil do you imagine I know of
philosophy?

125 MRS. HIGGINS [*warningly*]   Or of manners, Henry?

THE PARLOR-MAID [*opening the door*]   Miss Doolittle. [*She withdraws.*]

HIGGINS [*rising hastily and running to* MRS. HIGGINS]   Here she is, mother.
[*He stands on tiptoe and makes signs over his mother's head to* ELIZA *to indicate to her which lady is her hostess.*]

> [ELIZA, *who is exquisitely dressed, produces an impression of such remark-
> able distinction and beauty as she enters that they all rise, quite fluttered.
> Guided by* HIGGINS's *signals, she comes to* MRS. HIGGINS *with studied grace.*]

LIZA [*speaking with pedantic correctness of pronunciation and great beauty of
tone*]   How do you do, Mrs. Higgins? [*She gasps slightly in making sure of
the H in Higgins, but is quite successful.*] Mr. Higgins told me I might come.

130 MRS. HIGGINS [*cordially*]   Quite right: I'm very glad indeed to see you.

PICKERING   How do you do, Miss Doolittle?

LIZA [*shaking hands with him*]   Colonel Pickering, is it not?

MRS. EYNSFORD HILL   I feel sure we have met before, Miss Doolittle. I
remember your eyes.

135 LIZA   How do you do? [*She sits down on the ottoman gracefully in the place
just left vacant by* HIGGINS.]

MRS. EYNSFORD HILL [*introducing*]   My daughter Clara.

LIZA   How do you do?

CLARA [*impulsively*]   How do you do? [*She sits down on the ottoman beside
ELIZA, *devouring her with her eyes.*]

FREDDY [*coming to their side of the ottoman*]   Ive certainly had the pleasure.

140 MRS. EYNSFORD HILL [*introducing*]   My son Freddy.

LIZA   How do you do?

> [FREDDY *bows and sits down in the Elizabethan chair, infatuated.*]

HIGGINS [*suddenly*]   By George, yes: it all comes back to me! [*They stare at
him.*] Covent Garden! [*Lamentably*] What a damned thing!

MRS. HIGGINS   Henry, please! [*He is about to sit on the edge of the table.*]

145   Dont sit on my writing-table: youll break it.

HIGGINS [*sulkily*]   Sorry.

> [*He goes to the divan, stumbling into the fender*[7] *and over the fire-irons
> on his way; extricating himself with muttered imprecations; and finishing
> his disastrous journey by throwing himself so impatiently on the divan
> that he almost breaks it. Mrs. Higgins looks at him, but controls herself
> and says nothing.*]

> [*A long and painful pause ensues.*]

MRS. HIGGINS [*at last, conversationally*]   Will it rain, do you think?

LIZA   The shallow depression in the west of these islands is likely to move
slowly in an easterly direction. There are no indications of any great
150   change in the barometrical situation.

---

7. A low metal fire screen.

FREDDY   Ha! ha! how awfully funny!

LIZA   What is wrong with that, young man? I bet I got it right.

FREDDY   Killing!

MRS. EYNSFORD HILL   I'm sure I hope it wont turn cold. Theres so much
155   influenza about. It runs right through our whole family regularly every
spring.

LIZA [*darkly*]   My aunt died of influenza: so they said.

MRS. EYNSFORD HILL [*clicks her tongue sympathetically*]   !!!

LIZA [*in the same tragic tone*]   But it's my belief they done the old woman in.

160   MRS. HIGGINS [*puzzled*]   Done her in?

LIZA   Y-e-e-e-es, Lord love you! Why should she die of influenza? She come
through diphtheria right enough the year before. I saw her with my own
eyes. Fairly blue with it, she was. They all thought she was dead; but my
father he kept ladling gin down her throat til she came to so sudden that
165   she bit the bowl off the spoon.

MRS. EYNSFORD HILL [*startled*]   Dear me!

LIZA [*piling up the indictment*]   What call would a woman with that strength
in her have to die of influenza? What become of her new straw hat that
should have come to me? Somebody pinched it; and what I say is, them as
170   pinched it done her in.

MRS. EYNSFORD HILL   What does doing her in mean?

HIGGINS [*hastily*]   Oh, thats the new small talk. To do a person in means to
kill them.

MRS. EYNSFORD HILL [*to* ELIZA, *horrified*]   You surely dont believe that your
175   aunt was killed?

LIZA   Do I not! Them she lived with would have killed her for a hat-pin, let
alone a hat.

MRS. EYNSFORD HILL   But it cant have been right for your father to pour spirits down her throat like that. It might have killed her.

180   LIZA   Not her. Gin was mother's milk to her. Besides, he'd poured so much
down his own throat that he knew the good of it.

MRS. EYNSFORD HILL   Do you mean that he drank?

LIZA   Drank! My word! Something chronic.

MRS. EYNSFORD HILL   How dreadful for you!

185   LIZA   Not a bit. It never did him no harm what I could see. But then he did
not keep it up regular. [*Cheerfully*] On the burst,[8] as you might say, from
time to time. And always more agreeable when he had a drop in. When he
was out of work, my mother used to give him fourpence and tell him to go
out and not come back until he'd drunk himself cheerful and loving-like.
190   Theres lots of women has to make their husbands drunk to make them fit
to live with. [*Now quite at her ease*] You see, it's like this. If a man has a bit
of a conscience, it always takes him when he's sober; and then it makes
him low-spirited. A drop of booze just takes that off and makes him happy.
[*To* FREDDY, *who is in convulsions of suppressed laughter*] Here! what are you
195   sniggering at?

FREDDY   The new small talk. You do it so awfully well.

LIZA   If I was doing it proper, what was you laughing at? [*To* HIGGINS] Have I
said anything I oughtnt?

---

8. A bout of drunkenness; a binge.

MRS. HIGGINS [*interposing*] Not at all, Miss Doolittle.

200 LIZA Well, thats a mercy, anyhow. [*Expansively*] What I always say is—

HIGGINS [*rising and looking at his watch*] Ahem!

LIZA [*looking round at him; taking the hint; and rising*] Well: I must go. [*They all rise.* FREDDY *goes to the door.*] So pleased to have met you. Good-bye. [*She shakes hands with* MRS. HIGGINS.]

205 MRS. HIGGINS. Good-bye.

LIZA Good-bye, Colonel Pickering.

PICKERING Good-bye, Miss Doolittle. [*They shake hands.*]

LIZA [*nodding to the others*] Good-bye, all.

FREDDY [*opening the door for her*] Are you walking across the Park, Miss
210 Doolittle? If so—

LIZA Walk! Not bloody likely. [*Sensation*] I am going in a taxi. [*She goes out.*]

[PICKERING *gasps and sits down.* FREDDY *goes out on the balcony to catch another glimpse of* ELIZA.]

MRS. EYNSFORD HILL [*suffering from shock*] Well, I really cant get used to the new ways.

CLARA [*throwing herself discontentedly into the Elizabethan chair*] Oh, it's all
215 right, mamma, quite right. People will think we never go anywhere or see anybody if you are so old-fashioned.

MRS. EYNSFORD HILL I daresay I am very old-fashioned; but I do hope you wont begin using that expression, Clara. I have got accustomed to hear you talking about men as rotters, and calling everything filthy and beastly;
220 though I do think it horrible and unladylike. But this last is really too much. Dont you think so, Colonel Pickering?

PICKERING Dont ask me. Ive been away in India for several years; and manners have changed so much that I sometimes dont know whether I'm at a respectable dinner-table or in a ship's forecastle.

225 CLARA It's all a matter of habit. Theres no right or wrong in it. Nobody means anything by it. And it's so quaint, and gives such a smart emphasis to things that are not in themselves very witty. I find the new small talk delightful and quite innocent.

MRS. EYNSFORD HILL [*rising*] Well, after that, I think it's time for us to go.

[PICKERING *and* HIGGINS *rise.*]

230 CLARA [*rising*] Oh yes: we have three at-homes to go to still. Good-bye, Mrs. Higgins. Good-bye, Colonel Pickering. Good-bye, Professor Higgins.

HIGGINS [*coming grimly at her from the divan, and accompanying her to the door*] Good-bye. Be sure you try on that small talk at the three at-homes. Dont be nervous about it. Pitch it in strong.

235 CLARA [*all smiles*] I will. Good-bye. Such nonsense, all this early Victorian prudery!

HIGGINS [*tempting her*] Such damned nonsense!

CLARA Such bloody nonsense!

MRS. EYNSFORD HILL [*convulsively*] Clara!

CLARA. Ha! ha!

[*She goes out radiant, conscious of being thoroughly up to date, and is heard descending the stairs in a stream of silvery laughter.*]

240 FREDDY [*to the heavens at large*] Well, I ask you—[*He gives it up, and comes to* MRS. HIGGINS]. Good-bye.

MRS. HIGGINS [*shaking hands*]   Good-bye. Would you like to meet Miss Doolittle again?

FREDDY [*eagerly*]   Yes, I should, most awfully.

245   MRS. HIGGINS   Well, you know my days.

FREDDY   Yes. Thanks awfully. Good-bye. [*He goes out.*]

MRS. EYNSFORD HILL   Good-bye, Mr. Higgins.

HIGGINS   Good-bye. Good-bye.

MRS. EYNSFORD HILL [*to* PICKERING]   It's no use. I shall never be able to bring
250   myself to use that word.

PICKERING   Dont. It's not compulsory, you know. Youll get on quite well without it.

MRS. EYNSFORD HILL   Only, Clara is so down on me if I am not positively
reeking with the latest slang. Good-bye.

255   PICKERING   Good-bye. [*They shake hands.*]

MRS. EYNSFORD HILL [*to* MRS. HIGGINS]   You mustnt mind Clara. [PICKERING,
catching from her lowered tone that this is not meant for him to hear, discreetly joins HIGGINS *at the window.*] We're so poor! and she gets so few
parties, poor child! She doesnt quite know. [MRS. HIGGINS, *seeing that her
eyes are moist, takes her hand sympathetically and goes with her to the door.*]
260   But the boy is nice. Dont you think so?

MRS. HIGGINS   Oh, quite nice. I shall always be delighted to see him.

MRS. EYNSFORD HILL   Thank you, dear. Good-bye.

[*She goes out.*]

HIGGINS [*eagerly*]   Well? Is Eliza presentable? [*He swoops on his mother and
drags her to the ottoman, where she sits down in* ELIZA's *place with her son on
her left.*]

[PICKERING *returns to his chair on her right.*]

MRS. HIGGINS   You silly boy, of course shes not presentable. Shes a triumph
265   of your art and of her dressmaker's; but if you suppose for a moment that
she doesnt give herself away in every sentence she utters, you must be perfectly cracked about[9] her.

PICKERING   But dont you think something might be done? I mean something
to eliminate the sanguinary element[1] from her conversation.

270   MRS. HIGGINS   Not as long as she is in Henry's hands.

HIGGINS [*aggrieved*]   Do you mean that my language is improper?

MRS. HIGGINS   No, dearest: it would be quite proper—say on a canal barge;
but it would not be proper for her at a garden party.

HIGGINS [*deeply injured*]   Well I must say—

275   PICKERING [*interrupting him*]   Come, Higgins: you must learn to know yourself. I havnt heard such language as yours since we used to review the volunteers[2] in Hyde Park twenty years ago.

HIGGINS [*sulkily*]   Oh, well, if you say so, I suppose I dont always talk like a
bishop.

280   MRS. HIGGINS [*quieting* HENRY *with a touch*]   Colonel Pickering: will you tell
me what is the exact state of things in Wimpole Street?

9. Infatuated with.
1. That is, the word "bloody."
2. Inspect the troops. Hyde Park, a large park
in central London northwest of Buckingham
Palace, was frequently used for large-scale
military reviews in the 19th century.

PICKERING [*cheerfully: as if this completely changed the subject*]   Well, I have come to live there with Henry. We work together at my Indian Dialects; and we think it more convenient—

285 MRS. HIGGINS   Quite so. I know all about that: it's an excellent arrangement. But where does this girl live?

HIGGINS   With us, of course. Where would she live?

MRS. HIGGINS   But on what terms? Is she a servant? If not, what is she?

PICKERING [*slowly*]   I think I know what you mean, Mrs. Higgins.

290 HIGGINS   Well, dash me if *I* do! Ive had to work at the girl every day for months to get her to her present pitch. Besides, shes useful. She knows where my things are, and remembers my appointments and so forth.

MRS. HIGGINS   How does your housekeeper get on with her?

HIGGINS   Mrs. Pearce? Oh, shes jolly glad to get so much taken off her
295   hands; for before Eliza came, she used to have to find things and remind me of my appointments. But shes got some silly bee in her bonnet about Eliza. She keeps saying "You dont think, sir": doesnt she, Pick?

PICKERING   Yes: thats the formula. "You dont think, sir." Thats the end of every conversation about Eliza.

300 HIGGINS   As if I ever stop thinking about the girl and her confounded vowels and consonants. I'm worn out, thinking about her, and watching her lips and her teeth and her tongue, not to mention her soul, which is the quaintest of the lot.

MRS. HIGGINS   You certainly are a pretty pair of babies, playing with your live
305   doll.

HIGGINS   Playing! The hardest job I ever tackled: make no mistake about that, mother. But you have no idea how frightfully interesting it is to take a human being and change her into a quite different human being by creating a new speech for her. It's filling up the deepest gulf that separates class from class and soul from soul.

310 PICKERING [*drawing his chair closer to* MRS. HIGGINS *and bending over to her eagerly*]   Yes: it's enormously interesting. I assure you, Mrs. Higgins, we take Eliza very seriously. Every week—every day almost—there is some new change. [*Closer again*] We keep records of every stage—dozens of gramophone disks and photographs—

315 HIGGINS [*assailing her at the other ear*]   Yes, by George: it's the most absorbing experiment I ever tackled. She regularly fills our lives up; doesnt she, Pick?

PICKERING   We're always talking Eliza.

HIGGINS   Teaching Eliza.

PICKERING   Dressing Eliza.

320 MRS. HIGGINS   What!

HIGGINS   Inventing new Elizas.

HIGGINS	[*speaking together*]	You know, she has the most extraordinary quickness of ear:
PICKERING		I assure you, my dear Mrs. Higgins, that girl
325 HIGGINS		just like a parrot. Ive tried her with every
PICKERING		is a genius. She can play the piano quite beautifully.
HIGGINS		possible sort of sound that a human being
		can make—

PICKERING · We have taken her to classical concerts and to music
330 HIGGINS · Continental dialects, African dialects, Hottentot
PICKERING · halls; and it's all the same to her: she plays every-
thing
HIGGINS · clicks,[3] things it took me years to get hold of; and
PICKERING · she hears right off when she comes home, whether
335 it's
HIGGINS · she picks them up like a shot, right away, as if she
had
PICKERING · Beethoven and Brahms or Lehar and Lionel
Monckton;[4]
340 HIGGINS · been at it all her life.
PICKERING · though six months ago, she'd never as much as
touched a piano—

MRS. HIGGINS [putting her fingers in her ears, as they are by this time shouting one another down with an intolerable noise] Sh-sh-sh—sh! [They stop.]

PICKERING I beg your pardon. [He draws his chair back apologetically.]

345 HIGGINS Sorry. When Pickering starts shouting nobody can get a word in edgeways.

MRS. HIGGINS Be quiet, Henry. Colonel Pickering: dont you realize that when Eliza walked into Wimpole Street, something walked in with her?

PICKERING Her father did. But Henry soon got rid of him.

350 MRS. HIGGINS It would have been more to the point if her mother had. But as her mother didnt something else did.

PICKERING But what?

MRS. HIGGINS [unconsciously dating herself by the word] A problem.

PICKERING Oh, I see. The problem of how to pass her off as a lady.

355 HIGGINS I'll solve that problem. Ive half solved it already.

MRS. HIGGINS No, you two infinitely stupid male creatures: the problem of what is to be done with her afterwards.

HIGGINS I dont see anything in that. She can go her own way, with all the advantages I have given her.

360 MRS. HIGGINS The advantages of that poor woman who was here just now! The manners and habits that disqualify a fine lady from earning her own living without giving her a fine lady's income! Is that what you mean?

PICKERING [indulgently, being rather bored] Oh, that will be all right, Mrs. Higgins. [He rises to go.]

365 HIGGINS [rising also] We'll find her some light employment.

PICKERING Shes happy enough. Dont you worry about her. Good-bye. [He shakes hands as if he were consoling a frightened child, and makes for the door.]

HIGGINS Anyhow, theres no good bothering now. The things done. Good-bye, mother. [He kisses her, and follows PICKERING.]

3. *Hottentot clicks:* implosive consonant sounds used in a number of languages of southern Africa.

4. Examples of composers featured in classical concerts—the Germans Ludwig van Beethoven (1770–1827) and Johannes Brahms (1833–1897)—and those celebrated for more popular fare, the Hungarian Franz Lehár (1870–1948), known for his operettas, and the English Lionel Monckton (1861–1924), who wrote many hit songs for musical theater.

PICKERING [*turning for a final consolation*] There are plenty of openings.
370 We'll do whats right. Good-bye.

HIGGINS [*to* PICKERING *as they go out together*] Let's take her to the Shakespear exhibition at Earls Court.

PICKERING Yes: lets. Her remarks will be delicious.

HIGGINS She'll mimic all the people for us when we get home.

375 PICKERING Ripping.

[*Both are heard laughing as they go downstairs.*]

MRS. HIGGINS [*rises with an impatient bounce, and returns to her work at the writing-table. She sweeps a litter of disarranged papers out of her way; snatches a sheet of paper from her stationery case; and tries resolutely to write. At the third line she gives it up; flings down her pen; grips the table angrily and exclaims.*] Oh, men! men!! men!!!

Act 4

[*The Wimpole Street laboratory. Midnight. Nobody in the room. The clock on the mantelpiece strikes twelve. The fire is not alight: it is a summer night.*

Presently HIGGINS *and* PICKERING *are heard on the stairs.*]

HIGGINS [*calling down to* PICKERING] I say, Pick: lock up, will you. I shant be going out again.

PICKERING Right. Can Mrs. Pearce go to bed? We dont want anything more, do we?

5 HIGGINS Lord, no!

[ELIZA *opens the door and is seen on the lighted landing in opera cloak, brilliant evening dress, and diamonds, with fan, flowers, and all accessories. She comes to the hearth, and switches on the electric lights there. She is tired: her pallor contrasts strongly with her dark eyes and hair; and her expression is almost tragic. She takes off her cloak; puts her fan and flowers on the piano; and sits down on the bench, brooding and silent.* HIGGINS, *in evening dress, with overcoat and hat, comes in, carrying a smoking jacket[5] which he has picked up downstairs. He takes off the hat and overcoat; throws them carelessly on the newspaper stand; disposes of his coat in the same way; puts on the smoking jacket; and throws himself wearily into the easy-chair at the hearth.* PICKERING *similarly attired, comes in. He also takes off his hat and overcoat, and is about to throw them on* HIGGINS's *when he hesitates.*]

PICKERING I say: Mrs. Pearce will row[6] if we leave these things lying about in the drawing-room.

HIGGINS Oh, chuck them over the bannisters into the hall. She'll find them there in the morning and put them away all right. She'll think we were drunk.

10 PICKERING We are, slightly. Are there any letters?

HIGGINS I didnt look. [PICKERING *takes the overcoats and hats and goes downstairs. Higgins begins half singing half yawning an air from La Fanciulla del Golden West.[7] Suddenly he stops and exclaims*] I wonder where the devil my slippers are!

---

5. A casual jacket worn at home, usually in the evening.
6. That is, start a quarrel.

7. That is, *La Fanciulla del West* (*The Girl of the Golden West,* 1910), an opera by Giacomo Puccini.

[ELIZA *looks at him darkly; then rises suddenly and leaves the room.*]

[HIGGINS *yawns again, and resumes his song.*]

[PICKERING *returns, with the contents of the letter-box in his hand.*]

PICKERING   Only circulars, and this coroneted billet-doux[8] for you. [*He throws the circulars into the fender, and posts himself on the hearthrug, with his back to the grate.*]

15 HIGGINS [*glancing at the billet-doux*]   Money-lender. [*He throws the letter after the circulars.*]

[ELIZA *returns with a pair of large down-at-heel slippers. She places them on the carpet before* HIGGINS, *and sits as before without a word.*]

HIGGINS [*yawning again*]   Oh Lord! What an evening! What a crew! What a silly tomfoollery! [*He raises his shoe to unlace it, and catches sight of the slippers. He stops unlacing and looks at them as if they had appeared there of their own accord.*] Oh! theyre there, are they?

PICKERING [*stretching himself*]   Well, I feel a bit tired. It's been a long day.
20 The garden party, a dinner party, and the opera! Rather too much of a good thing. But youve won your bet, Higgins. Eliza did the trick, and something to spare, eh?

HIGGINS [*fervently*]   Thank God it's over!

[ELIZA *flinches violently; but they take no notice of her; and she recovers herself and sits stonily as before.*]

PICKERING   Were you nervous at the garden party? *I* was. Eliza didnt seem a
25 bit nervous.

HIGGINS   Oh, she wasnt nervous. I knew she'd be all right. No: it's the strain of putting the job through all these months that has told on me. It was interesting enough at first, while we were at the phonetics; but after that I got deadly sick of it. If I hadnt backed myself to do it I should have chucked
30 the whole thing up two months ago. It was a silly notion: the whole thing has been a bore.

PICKERING   Oh come! the garden party was frightfully exciting. My heart began beating like anything.

HIGGINS   Yes, for the first three minutes. But when I saw we were going to
35 win hands down, I felt like a bear in a cage, hanging about doing nothing. The dinner was worse: sitting gorging there for over an hour, with nobody but a damned fool of a fashionable woman to talk to! I tell you, Pickering, never again for me. No more artificial duchesses. The whole thing has been simple purgatory.

40 PICKERING   Youve never been broken in properly to the social routine. [*Strolling over to the piano*] I rather enjoy dipping into it occasionally myself: it makes me feel young again. Anyhow, it was a great success: an immense success. I was quite frightened once or twice because Eliza was doing it so well. You see, lots of the real people cant do it at all: theyre such fools that
45 they think style comes by nature to people in their position; and so they never learn. Theres always something professional about doing a thing superlatively well.

HIGGINS   Yes: thats what drives me mad: the silly people dont know their own silly business. [*Rising*] However, it's over and done with; and now I can go
50 to bed at last without dreading tomorrow.

---

8. A love letter on fine stationery (coronets signify nobility).

[ELIZA's *beauty becomes murderous.*]

PICKERING   I think I shall turn in too. Still, it's been a great occasion: a triumph for you. Good-night.

[*He goes.*]

HIGGINS [*following him*]   Good-night. [*Over his shoulder, at the door*] Put out the lights, Eliza; and tell Mrs. Pearce not to make coffee for me in the
55   morning: I'll take tea.

[*He goes out.*]

[ELIZA *tries to control herself and feel indifferent as she rises and walks
across to the hearth to switch off the lights. By the time she gets there she
is on the point of screaming. She sits down in* HIGGINS's *chair and holds
on hard to the arms. Finally she gives way and flings herself furiously on
the floor raging.*]

HIGGINS [*in despairing wrath outside*]   What the devil have I done with my slippers? [*He appears at the door.*]

LIZA [*snatching up the slippers, and hurling them at him one after the other
with all her force*]   There are your slippers. And there. Take your slippers;
and may you never have a day's luck with them!

60   HIGGINS [*astounded*]   What on earth—! [*He comes to her.*] Whats the matter? Get up. [*He pulls her up.*] Anything wrong?

LIZA [*breathless*]   Nothing wrong—with you. Ive won your bet for you, havnt I? That enough for you. *I* dont matter, I suppose.

HIGGINS   You won my bet! You! Presumptuous insect! *I* won it. What did you
65   throw those slippers at me for?

LIZA   Because I wanted to smash your face. I'd like to kill you, you selfish brute. Why didnt you leave me where you picked me out of—in the gutter? You thank God it's all over, and that now you can throw me back again there, do you? [*She crisps*⁹ *her fingers frantically.*]

70   HIGGINS [*looking at her in cool wonder*]   The creature is nervous, after all.

LIZA [*gives a suffocated scream of fury, and instinctively darts her nails at his
face*]   !!

HIGGINS [*catching her wrists*]   Ah! would you? Claws in, you cat. How dare you shew your temper to me? Sit down and be quiet. [*He throws her roughly
into the easy-chair.*]

LIZA [*crushed by superior strength and weight*]   Whats to become of me?
75   Whats to become of me?

HIGGINS   How the devil do I know whats to become of you? What does it matter what becomes of you?

LIZA   You dont care. I know you dont care. You wouldnt care if I was dead. I'm nothing to you—not so much as them slippers.

80   HIGGINS [*thundering*]   Those slippers.

LIZA [*with bitter submission*]   Those slippers. I didnt think it made any difference now.

[*A pause.* ELIZA *hopeless and crushed.* HIGGINS *a little uneasy.*]

HIGGINS [*in his loftiest manner*]   Why have you begun going on like this? May I ask whether you complain of your treatment here?

85   LIZA   No.

HIGGINS   Has anybody behaved badly to you? Colonel Pickering? Mrs. Pearce? Any of the servants?

9. Curls.

LIZA No.

HIGGINS I presume you dont pretend that *I* have treated you badly.

90 LIZA No.

HIGGINS I am glad to hear it. [*He moderates his tone.*] Perhaps youre tired after the strain of the day. Will you have a glass of champagne? [*He moves towards the door.*]

LIZA No. [*Recollecting her manners*] Thank you.

HIGGINS [*good-humored again*] This has been coming on you for some days.

95 I suppose it was natural for you to be anxious about the garden party. But thats all over now. [*He pats her kindly on the shoulder. She writhes.*] Theres nothing more to worry about.

LIZA No. Nothing more for you to worry about. [*She suddenly rises and gets away from him by going to the piano bench, where she sits and hides her face.*] Oh God! I wish I was dead.

100 HIGGINS [*staring after her in sincere surprise*] Why? in heaven's name, why? [*Reasonably, going to her*] Listen to me, Eliza. All this irritation is purely subjective.

LIZA I dont understand. I'm too ignorant.

HIGGINS It's only imagination. Low spirits and nothing else. Nobody's hurt-

105 ing you. Nothing's wrong. You go to bed like a good girl and sleep it off. Have a little cry and say your prayers: that will make you comfortable.

LIZA I heard your prayers. "Thank God it's all over!"

HIGGINS [*impatiently*] Well, dont you thank God it's all over? Now you are free and can do what you like.

110 LIZA [*pulling herself together in desperation*] What am I fit for? What have you left me fit for? Where am I to go? What am I to do? Whats to become of me?

HIGGINS [*enlightened, but not at all impressed*] Oh, thats whats worrying you, is it? [*He thrusts his hands into his pockets, and walks about in his usual manner, rattling the contents of his pockets, as if condescending to a trivial subject out of pure kindness.*] I shouldnt bother about it if I were you. I

115 should imagine you wont have much difficulty in settling yourself some-where or other, though I hadnt quite realized that you were going away. [*She looks quickly at him: he does not look at her, but examines the dessert stand on the piano and decides that he will eat an apple.*] You might marry, you know. [*He bites a large piece out of the apple, and munches it noisily.*] You see, Eliza, all men are not confirmed old bachelors like me and the

120 Colonel. Most men are the marrying sort (poor devils!); and youre not bad-looking; it's quite a pleasure to look at you sometimes—not now, of course, because youre crying and looking as ugly as the very devil; but when youre all right and quite yourself, youre what I should call attractive. That is, to the people in the marrying line, you understand. You go to bed and have a

125 good nice rest; and then get up and look at yourself in the glass; and you wont feel so cheap.

[ELIZA *again looks at him, speechless, and does not stir.*]

[*The look is quite lost on him: he eats his apple with a dreamy expression of happiness, as it is quite a good one.*]

HIGGINS [*a genial afterthought occurring to him*] I daresay my mother could find some chap or other who would do very well.

LIZA We were above that at the corner of Tottenham Court Road.

130 HIGGINS [*waking up*] What do you mean?

LIZA I sold flowers. I didnt sell myself. Now youve made a lady of me I'm not
fit to sell anything else. I wish youd left me where you found me.

HIGGINS [*slinging the core of the apple decisively into the grate*] Tosh, Eliza.
Dont you insult human relations by dragging all this cant about buying and
135   selling into it. You neednt marry the fellow if you dont like him.

LIZA What else am I to do?

HIGGINS Oh, lots of things. What about your old idea of a florist's shop?
Pickering could set you up in one: hes lots of money. [*Chuckling*] He'll
have to pay for all those togs you have been wearing today; and that, with
140   the hire of the jewellery, will make a big hole in two hundred pounds. Why,
six months ago you would have thought it the millennium to have a flower
shop of your own. Come! youll be all right. I must clear off to bed: I'm devilish sleepy. By the way, I came down for something: I forget what it was.

LIZA Your slippers.

145 HIGGINS Oh yes, of course. You shied them at me. [*He picks them up, and is
going out when she rises and speaks to him.*]

LIZA Before you go, sir—

HIGGINS [*dropping the slippers in his surprise at her calling him* Sir] Eh?

LIZA Do my clothes belong to me or to Colonel Pickering?

HIGGINS [*coming back into the room as if her question were the very climax of
unreason*] What the devil use would they be to Pickering?

150 LIZA He might want them for the next girl you pick up to experiment on.

HIGGINS [*shocked and hurt*] Is that the way you feel towards us?

LIZA I dont want to hear anything more about that. All I want to know is
whether anything belongs to me. My own clothes were burnt.

HIGGINS But what does it matter? Why need you start bothering about that
155   in the middle of the night?

LIZA I want to know what I may take away with me. I dont want to be accused
of stealing.

HIGGINS [*now deeply wounded*] Stealing! You shouldnt have said that, Eliza.
That shews a want of feeling.

160 LIZA I'm sorry. I'm only a common ignorant girl; and in my station I have to
be careful. There cant be any feelings between the like of you and the like
of me. Please will you tell me what belongs to me and what doesn't?

HIGGINS [*very sulky*] You may take the whole damned houseful if you like.
Except the jewels. Theyre hired. Will that satisfy you? [*He turns on his heel
and is about to go in extreme dudgeon.*]

LIZA [*drinking in his emotion like nectar, and nagging him to provoke a fur-
165   ther supply*] Stop, please. [*She takes off her jewels.*] Will you take these
to your room and keep them safe? I dont want to run the risk of their
being missing.

HIGGINS [*furious*] Hand them over. [*She puts them into his hands.*] If these
belonged to me instead of to the jeweler, I'd ram them down your ungrate-
170   ful throat. [*He perfunctorily thrusts them into his pockets, unconsciously
decorating himself with the protruding ends of the chains.*]

LIZA [*taking a ring off*] This ring isnt the jeweler's: it's the one you bought
me in Brighton.[1] I dont want it now. [*Higgins dashes the ring violently into
the fireplace, and turns on her so threateningly that she crouches over the
piano with her hands over her face, and exclaims.*] Don't you hit me.

---

1. A seaside resort on the English Channel, about 50 miles south of London.

HIGGINS Hit you! You infamous creature, how dare you accuse me of such a
175   thing? It is you who have hit me. You have wounded me to the heart.

LIZA [*thrilling with hidden joy*] I'm glad. Ive got a little of my own back, anyhow.

HIGGINS [*with dignity, in his finest professional style*] You have caused me to
lose my temper: a thing that has hardly ever happend to me before. I prefer
180   to say nothing more tonight. I am going to bed.

LIZA [*pertly*] Youd better leave a note for Mrs. Pearce about the coffee; for
she wont be told by me.

HIGGINS [*formally*] Damn Mrs. Pearce; and damn the coffee; and damn you;
and damn my own folly in having lavished hard-earned knowledge and the
185   treasure of my regard and intimacy on a heartless guttersnipe.

[*He goes out with impressive decorum, and spoils it by slamming the door
savagely.*]

[ELIZA *smiles for the first time; expresses her feelings by a wild pantomime
in which an imitation of* HIGGINS's *exit is confused with her own triumph; and finally goes down on her knees on the hearthrug to look for
the ring.*]

Act 5

[*Mrs.* HIGGINS's *drawing-room. She is at her writing-table as before. The* PARLOR-
MAID *comes in.*]

THE PARLOR-MAID [*at the door*] Mr. Henry, mam, is downstairs with Colonel
Pickering.

MRS. HIGGINS Well, shew them up.

THE PARLOR-MAID Theyre using the telephone, mam. Telephoning to the
5   police, I think.

MRS. HIGGINS What!

THE PARLOR-MAID [*coming further in and lowering her voice*] Mr. Henry's in
a state, mam. I thought I'd better tell you.

MRS. HIGGINS If you had told me that Mr. Henry was not in a state it would
10   have been more surprising. Tell them to come up when theyve finished
with the police. I suppose hes lost something.

THE PARLOR-MAID Yes, mam. [*Going*]

MRS. HIGGINS Go upstairs and tell Miss Doolittle that Mr. Henry and the
Colonel are here. Ask her not to come down till I send for her.

15 THE PARLOR-MAID Yes, mam.

[HIGGINS *bursts in. He is, as the* PARLOR-MAID *has said, in a state.*]

HIGGINS Look here, mother: heres a confounded thing!

MRS. HIGGINS Yes, dear. Good-morning. [*He checks his impatience and kisses
her, whilst the* PARLOR-MAID *goes out.*] What is it?

HIGGINS Eliza's bolted.

20 MRS. HIGGINS [*calmly continuing her writing*] You must have frightened her.

HIGGINS Frightened her! nonsense! She was left last night, as usual, to turn
out the lights and all that; and instead of going to bed she changed her
clothes and went right off: her bed wasnt slept in. She came in a cab for
her things before seven this morning; and that fool Mrs. Pearce let her
25   have them without telling me a word about it. What am I to do?

MRS. HIGGINS Do without, I'm afraid, Henry. The girl has a perfect right to
leave if she chooses.

HIGGINS [*wandering distractedly across the room*] But I cant find anything. I dont know what appointments Ive got. I'm— [PICKERING *comes in.* MRS. HIGGINS *puts down her pen and turns away from the writing-table.*]

30 PICKERING [*shaking hands*] Good-morning, Mrs. Higgins. Has Henry told you? [*He sits down on the ottoman.*]

HIGGINS What does that ass of an inspector say? Have you offered a reward?

MRS. HIGGINS [*rising in indignant amazement*] You dont mean to say you have set the police after Eliza?

35 HIGGINS Of course. What are the police for? What else could we do? [*He sits in the Elizabethan chair.*]

PICKERING The inspector made a lot of difficulties. I really think he suspected us of some improper purpose.

MRS. HIGGINS Well, of course he did. What right have you to go to the police and give the girl's name as if she were a thief, or a lost umbrella, or some-

40 thing? Really! [*She sits down again, deeply vexed.*]

HIGGINS But we want to find her.

PICKERING We cant let her go like this, you know, Mrs. Higgins. What were we to do?

MRS. HIGGINS You have no more sense, either of you, than two children.

45 Why—

[*The* PARLOR-MAID *comes in and breaks off the conversation.*]

THE PARLOR-MAID Mr. Henry: a gentleman wants to see you very particular. Hes been sent on from Wimpole Street.

HIGGINS Oh, bother! I cant see anyone now. Who is it?

THE PARLOR-MAID A Mr. Doolittle, sir.

50 PICKERING Doolittle! Do you mean the dustman?

THE PARLOR-MAID Dustman! Oh no, sir: a gentleman.

HIGGINS [*springing up excitedly*] By George, Pick, it's some relative of hers that shes gone to. Somebody we know nothing about. [*To the* PARLOR-MAID] Send him up, quick.

55 THE PARLOR-MAID Yes, sir.

[*She goes.*]

HIGGINS [*eagerly, going to his mother*] Genteel relatives! now we shall hear something. [*He sits down in the Chippendale chair.*]

MRS. HIGGINS Do you know any of her people?

PICKERING Only her father: the fellow we told you about.

60 THE PARLOR-MAID [*announcing*] Mr. Doolittle.

[*She withdraws.*]

[DOOLITTLE *enters. He is brilliantly dressed in a new fashionable frock-coat, with white waistcoat and grey trousers. A flower in his buttonhole, a dazzling silk hat, and patent leather shoes complete the effect. He is too concerned with the business he has come on to notice* MRS. HIGGINS. *He walks straight to* HIGGINS, *and accosts him with vehement reproach.*]

DOOLITTLE [*indicating his own person*] See here! Do you see this? You done this.

HIGGINS Done what, man?

DOOLITTLE This, I tell you. Look at it. Look at this hat. Look at this coat.

65 PICKERING Has Eliza been buying you clothes?

DOOLITTLE Eliza! not she. Not half. Why would she buy me clothes?

MRS. HIGGINS   Good-morning, Mr. Doolittle. Wont you sit down?

DOOLITTLE [*taken aback as he becomes conscious that he has forgotten his host-ess*] Asking your pardon, maam. [*He approaches her and shakes her prof-fered hand.*] Thank you. [*He sits down on the ottoman, on Pickering's right.*]
70   I am that full of what has happened to me that I cant think of anything else.

HIGGINS   What the dickens has happened to you?

DOOLITTLE   I shouldnt mind if it had only happened to me: anything might happen to anybody and nobody to blame but Providence, as you might say. But this is something that you done to me: yes, you, Henry Higgins.

75 HIGGINS   Have you found Eliza? Thats the point.

DOOLITTLE   Have you lost her?

HIGGINS   Yes.

DOOLITTLE   You have all the luck, you have. I aint found her; but she'll find me quick enough now after what you done to me.

80 MRS. HIGGINS   But what has my son done to you, Mr. Doolittle?

DOOLITTLE   Done to me! Ruined me. Destroyed my happiness. Tied me up and delivered me into the hands of middle class morality.

HIGGINS [*rising intolerantly and standing over Doolittle*]   Youre raving. Youre drunk. Youre mad. I gave you five pounds. After that I had two conversa-
85   tions with you, at half-a-crown an hour. Ive never seen you since.

DOOLITTLE   Oh! Drunk! am I? Mad! am I? Tell me this. Did you or did you not write a letter to an old blighter in America that was giving five millions to found Moral Reform Societies all over the world, and that wanted you to invent a universal language for him?

90 HIGGINS   What! Ezra D. Wannafeller![2] Hes dead. [*He sits down again carelessly.*]

DOOLITTLE   Yes: hes dead; and I'm done for. Now did you or did you not write a letter to him to say that the most original moralist at present in England, to the best of your knowledge, was Alfred Doolittle, a common dustman.

HIGGINS   Oh, after your last visit I remember making some silly joke of the
95   kind.

DOOLITTLE   Ah! you may well call it a silly joke. It put the lid on me right enough. Just give him the chance he wanted to shew that Americans is not like us: that they recognize and respect merit in every class of life, however humble. Them words is in his blooming will, in which, Henry Higgins,
100   thanks to your silly joking, he leaves me a share in his Pre-digested Cheese Trust worth three thousand a year[3] on condition that I lecture for his Wan-nafeller Moral Reform World League as often as they ask me up to six times a year.

HIGGINS   The devil he does! Whew! [*Brightening suddenly*] What a lark!

105 PICKERING   A safe thing for you, Doolittle. They wont ask you twice.

DOOLITTLE   It aint the lecturing I mind. I'll lecture them blue in the face, I will, and not turn a hair. It's making a gentleman of me that I object to. Who asked him to make a gentleman of me? I was happy. I was free. I touched pretty nigh everybody for money when I wanted it, same as I
110   touched you, Henry Higgins. Now I am worrited; tied neck and heels; and everybody touches me for money. It's a fine thing for you, says my solicitor.

2. Shaw conflates the names of two actual American millionaires, the merchant John Wanamaker (1838–1922) and the industrial- ist John D. Rockefeller (1839–1937).
3. Roughly equivalent to $250,000 today.

Is it? says I. You mean it's a good thing for you, I says. When I was a poor man and had a solicitor once when they found a pram in the dust cart, he got me off, and got shut of[4] me and got me shut of him as quick as he could. Same with the doctors: used to shove me out of the hospital before I could hardly stand on my legs, and nothing to pay. Now they finds out that I'm not a healthy man and cant live unless they looks after me twice a day. In the house I'm not let do a hand's turn for myself: somebody else must do it and touch me for it. A year ago I hadnt a relative in the world except two or three that wouldnt speak to me. Now Ive fifty, and not a decent week's wages among the lot of them. I have to live for others and not for myself: thats middle class morality. You talk of losing Eliza. Dont you be anxious: I bet shes on my doorstep by this: she that could support herself easy by selling flowers if I wasnt respectable. And the next one to touch me will be you, Henry Higgins. I'll have to learn to speak middle class language from you, instead of speaking proper English. Thats where youll come in; and I daresay thats what you done it for.

MRS. HIGGINS But, my dear Mr. Doolittle, you need not suffer all this if you are really in earnest. Nobody can force you to accept this bequest. You can repudiate it. Isnt that so, Colonel Pickering?

PICKERING I believe so.

DOOLITTLE [*softening his manner in deference to her sex*] Thats the tragedy of it, maam. It's easy to say chuck it; but I havent the nerve. Which of us has? We're all intimidated. Intimidated, maam: thats what we are. What is there for me if I chuck it but the workhouse in my old age? I have to dye my hair[5] already to keep my job as a dustman. If I was one of the deserving poor, and had put by a bit, I could chuck it; but then why should I, acause[6] the deserving poor might as well be millionaires for all the happiness they ever has. They dont know what happiness is. But I, as one of the undeserving poor, have nothing between me and the pauper's uniform but this here blasted three thousand a year that shoves me into the middle class. (Excuse the expression, maam: youd use it yourself if you had my provocation.) Theyve got you every way you turn: it's a choice between the Skilly of the workhouse and the Char Bydis of the middle class;[7] and I havnt the nerve for the workhouse. Intimidated: thats what I am. Broke. Bought up. Happier men than me will call for my dust, and touch me for their tip; and I'll look on helpless, and envy them. And thats what your son has brought me to. [*He is overcome by emotion.*]

MRS. HIGGINS Well, I'm very glad youre not going to do anything foolish, Mr. Doolittle. For this solves the problem of Eliza's future. You can provide for her now.

DOOLITTLE [*with melancholy resignation*] Yes, maam: I'm expected to provide for everyone now, out of three thousand a year.

HIGGINS [*jumping up*] Nonsense! he cant provide for her. He shant provide for her. She doesnt belong to him. I paid him five pounds for her. Doolittle: either youre an honest man or a rogue.

---

4. Rid of.
5. That is, to keep from being fired because of his advancing age (no laws prevented such firing).
6. Because.

7. That is, between two equal dangers. In Greek mythology, Scylla and Charybdis are two monsters (who become a rock and whirlpool, respectively) that endanger sailors between Sicily and Italy.

DOOLITTLE [*tolerantly*]   A little of both, Henry, like the rest of us: a little of both.

HIGGINS   Well, you took that money for the girl; and you have no right to
160   take her as well.

MRS. HIGGINS   Henry: dont be absurd. If you really want to know where Eliza is, she is upstairs.

HIGGINS [*amazed*]   Upstairs!!! Then I shall jolly soon fetch her downstairs. [*He makes resolutely for the door.*]

MRS. HIGGINS [*rising and following him*]   Be quiet, Henry. Sit down.

165   HIGGINS   I—

MRS. HIGGINS   Sit down, dear; and listen to me.

HIGGINS   Oh very well, very well, very well. [*He throws himself ungraciously on the ottoman, with his face towards the windows.*] But I think you might have told me this half an hour ago.

170   MRS. HIGGINS   Eliza came to me this morning. She passed the night partly walking about in a rage, partly trying to throw herself into the river and being afraid to, and partly in the Carlton Hotel. She told me of the brutal way you two treated her.

HIGGINS [*bounding up again*]   What!

175   PICKERING [*rising also*]   My dear Mrs. Higgins, shes been telling you stories. We didnt treat her brutally. We hardly said a word to her; and we parted on particularly good terms. [*Turning on* HIGGINS] Higgins: did you bully her after I went to bed?

HIGGINS   Just the other way about. She threw my slippers in my face. She
180   behaved in the most outrageous way. I never gave her the slightest provocation. The slippers came bang into my face the moment I entered the room—before I had uttered a word. And used perfectly awful language.

PICKERING [*astonished*]   But why? What did we do to her?

MRS. HIGGINS   I think I know pretty well what you did. The girl is naturally
185   rather affectionate, I think. Isnt she, Mr. Doolittle?

DOOLITTLE   Very tender-hearted, maam. Takes after me.

MRS. HIGGINS   Just so. She had become attached to you both. She worked very hard for you, Henry! I dont think you quite realize what anything in the nature of brain work means to a girl like that. Well, it seems that when
190   the great day of trial came, and she did this wonderful thing for you without making a single mistake, you two sat there and never said a word to her, but talked together of how glad you were that it was all over and how you had been bored with the whole thing. And then you were surprised because she threw your slippers at you! *I* should have thrown the fire-
195   irons at you.

HIGGINS   We said nothing except that we were tired and wanted to go to bed. Did we, Pick?

PICKERING [*shrugging his shoulders*]   That was all.

MRS. HIGGINS [*ironically*]   Quite sure?

200   PICKERING   Absolutely. Really, that was all.

MRS. HIGGINS   You didn't thank her, or pet her, or admire her, or tell her how splendid she'd been.

HIGGINS [*impatiently*]   But she knew all about that. We didnt make speeches to her, if thats what you mean.

205   PICKERING [*conscience stricken*]   Perhaps we were a little inconsiderate. Is she very angry?

MRS. HIGGINS [*returning to her place at the writing-table*] Well, I'm afraid she wont go back to Wimpole Street, especially now that Mr. Doolittle is able to keep up the position you have thrust on her; but she says she is
210 quite willing to meet you on friendly terms and to let bygones be bygones.

HIGGINS [*furious*] Is she, by George? Ho!

MRS. HIGGINS If you promise to behave yourself, Henry, I'll ask her to come down. If not, go home; for you have taken up quite enough of my time.

HIGGINS Oh, all right. Very well. Pick: you behave yourself. Let us put on
215 our best Sunday manners for this creature that we picked out of the mud. [*He flings himself sulkily into the Elizabethan chair.*]

DOOLITTLE [*remonstrating*] Now, now, Henry Higgins! have some consideration for my feelings as a middle class man.

MRS. HIGGINS Remember your promise, Henry. [*She presses the bell-button on the writing-table.*] Mr. Doolittle: will you be so good as to step out on
220 the balcony for a moment. I dont want Eliza to have the shock of your news until she has made it up with these two gentlemen. Would you mind?

DOOLITTLE As you wish, lady. Anything to help Henry to keep her off my hands. [*He disappears through the window.*]

[*The* PARLOR-MAID *answers the bell.* PICKERING *sits down in Doolittle's place.*]

MRS. HIGGINS Ask Miss Doolittle to come down, please.
225 THE PARLOR-MAID Yes, mam. [*She goes out.*]

MRS. HIGGINS Now, Henry: be good.

HIGGINS I am behaving myself perfectly.

PICKERING He is doing his best, Mrs. Higgins.

[*A pause.* HIGGINS *throws back his head; stretches out his legs; and begins to whistle.*]

MRS. HIGGINS Henry, dearest, you dont look at all nice in that attitude.
230 HIGGINS [*pulling himself together*] I was not trying to look nice, mother.

MRS. HIGGINS It doesnt matter, dear. I only wanted to make you speak.

HIGGINS Why?

MRS. HIGGINS Because you cant speak and whistle at the same time.

[HIGGINS *groans. Another very trying pause.*]

HIGGINS [*springing up, out of patience*] Where the devil is that girl? Are we
235 to wait here all day?

[ELIZA *enters, sunny, self-possessed, and giving a staggeringly convincing exhibition of ease of manner. She carries a little work-basket, and is very much at home.* PICKERING *is too much taken aback to rise.*]

LIZA How do you do, Professor Higgins? Are you quite well?

HIGGINS [*choking*] Am I— [*He can say no more*].

LIZA But of course you are: you are never ill. So glad to see you again, Colonel Pickering. [*He rises hastily; and they shake hands.*] Quite chilly this
240 morning, isnt it? [*She sits down on his left. He sits beside her.*]

HIGGINS Dont you dare try this game on me. I taught it to you; and it doesnt take me in. Get up and come home; and dont be a fool.

[ELIZA *takes a piece of needlework from her basket, and begins to stitch at it, without taking the least notice of this outburst.*]

MRS. HIGGINS Very nicely put, indeed, Henry. No woman could resist such an invitation.

245 HIGGINS You let her alone, mother. Let her speak for herself. You will jolly soon see whether she has an idea that I havnt put into her head or a word that I havnt put into her mouth. I tell you I have created this thing out of the squashed cabbage leaves of Covent Garden; and now she pretends to play the fine lady with me.

250 MRS. HIGGINS [*placidly*] Yes, dear; but youll sit down, wont you?

[HIGGINS *sits down again, savagely.*]

LIZA [*to* PICKERING, *taking no apparent notice of* HIGGINS, *and working away deftly*] Will you drop me altogether now that the experiment is over, Colonel Pickering?

PICKERING Oh dont. You mustnt think of it as an experiment. It shocks me, somehow.

255 LIZA Oh, I'm only a squashed cabbage leaf—

PICKERING [*impulsively*] No.

LIZA [*continuing quietly*] —but I owe so much to you that I should be very unhappy if you forgot me.

PICKERING It's very kind of you to say so, Miss Doolittle.

260 LIZA It's not because you paid for my dresses. I know you are generous to everybody with money. But it was from you that I learnt really nice manners; and that is what makes one a lady, isnt it? You see it was so very difficult for me with the example of Professor Higgins always before me. I was brought up to be just like him, unable to control myself, and using

265 bad language on the slightest provocation. And I should never have known that ladies and gentlemen didnt behave like that if you hadnt been there.

HIGGINS Well!!

PICKERING Oh, thats only his way, you know. He doesnt mean it.

270 LIZA Oh, *I* didnt mean it either, when I was a flower girl. It was only my way. But you see I did it; and thats what makes the difference after all.

PICKERING No doubt. Still, he taught you to speak; and I couldnt have done that, you know.

LIZA [*trivially*] Of course: that is his profession.

275 HIGGINS Damnation!

LIZA [*continuing*] It was just like learning to dance in the fashionable way: there was nothing more than that in it. But do you know what began my real education?

PICKERING What?

280 LIZA [*stopping her work for a moment*] Your calling me Miss Doolittle that day when I first came to Wimpole Street. That was the beginning of self-respect for me. [*She resumes her stitching.*] And there were a hundred little things you never noticed, because they came naturally to you. Things about standing up and taking off your hat and opening door—

285 PICKERING Oh, that was nothing.

LIZA Yes: things that shewed you thought and felt about me as if I were something better than a scullery-maid; though of course I know you would have been just the same to a scullery-maid if she had been let in the drawing-room. You never took off your boots in the dining room when I was

290 there.

PICKERING You mustnt mind that. Higgins takes off his boots all over the place.

LIZA I know. I am not blaming him. It is his way, isnt it? But it made such a difference to me that you didnt do it. You see, really and truly, apart from the things anyone can pick up (the dressing and the proper way of speaking, and so on), the difference between a lady and a flower girl is not how she behaves, but how shes treated. I shall always be a flower girl to Professor Higgins, because he always treats me as a flower girl, and always will; but I know I can be a lady to you, because you always treat me as a lady, and always will.

MRS. HIGGINS Please dont grind your teeth, Henry.

PICKERING Well, this is really very nice of you, Miss Doolittle.

LIZA I should like you to call me Eliza, now, if you would.

PICKERING Thank you. Eliza, of course.

LIZA And I should like Professor Higgins to call me Miss Doolittle.

HIGGINS I'll see you damned first.

MRS. HIGGINS Henry! Henry!

PICKERING [laughing] Why dont you slang back[8] at him? Dont stand it. It would do him a lot of good.

LIZA I cant. I could have done it once; but now I cant go back to it. Last night, when I was wandering about, a girl spoke to me; and I tried to get back into the old way with her; but it was no use. You told me, you know, that when a child is brought to a foreign country, it picks up the language in a few weeks, and forgets its own. Well, I am a child in your country. I have forgotten my own language, and can speak nothing but yours. Thats the real break-off with the corner of Tottenham Court Road. Leaving Wimpole Street finishes it.

PICKERING [much alarmed] Oh! but youre coming back to Wimpole Street, arnt you? Youll forgive Higgins?

HIGGINS [rising] Forgive! Will she, by George! Let her go. Let her find out how she can get on without us. She will relapse into the gutter in three weeks without me at her elbow.

[DOOLITTLE appears at the centre window. With a look of dignified reproach at HIGGINS, he comes slowly and silently to his daughter, who, with her back to the window, is unconscious of his approach.]

PICKERING Hes incorrigible, Eliza. You wont relapse, will you?

LIZA No: Not now. Never again. I have learnt my lesson. I dont believe I could utter one of the old sounds if I tried. [DOOLITTLE touches her on her left shoulder. She drops her work, losing her self-possession utterly at the spectacle of her father's splendor.] A-a-a-a-a-ah-ow-ooh!

HIGGINS [with a crow of triumph] Aha! Just so. A-a-a-a-ahowooh! A-a-a-a-ahowooh! A-a-a-a-ahowooh! Victory! Victory! [He throws himself on the divan, folding his arms, and spraddling arrogantly.]

DOOLITTLE Can you blame the girl? Dont look at me like that, Eliza. It aint my fault. Ive come into some money.

LIZA You must have touched a millionaire this time, dad.

DOOLITTLE I have. But I'm dressed something special today. I'm going to St. George's,[9] Hanover Square. Your stepmother is going to marry me.

8. That is, respond with equal abuse.
9. A church in Mayfair, a fashionable area of Westminster.

LIZA [*angrily*]   Youre going to let yourself down to marry that low common woman!

PICKERING [*quietly*]   He ought to, Eliza. [*To* DOOLITTLE] Why has she changed her mind?

DOOLITTLE [*sadly*]   Intimidated, Governor. Intimidated. Middle class morality claims its victim. Wont you put on your hat, Liza, and come and see me turned off?

LIZA   If the Colonel says I must, I—I'll [*Almost sobbing*] I'll demean myself. And get insulted for my pains, like enough.

DOOLITTLE   Dont be afraid: she never comes to words with anyone now, poor woman! respectability has broke all the spirit out of her.

PICKERING [*squeezing* ELIZA's *elbow gently*]   Be kind to them, Eliza. Make the best of it.

LIZA [*forcing a little smile for him through her vexation*]   Oh well, just to shew theres no ill feeling. I'll be back in a moment. [*She goes out.*]

DOOLITTLE [*sitting down beside* PICKERING]   I feel uncommon nervous about the ceremony, Colonel. I wish youd come and see me through it.

PICKERING   But youve been through it before, man. You were married to Eliza's mother.

DOOLITTLE   Who told you that, Colonel?

PICKERING   Well, nobody told me. But I concluded—naturally—

DOOLITTLE   No: that aint the natural way, Colonel: it's only the middle class way. My way was always the undeserving way. But dont say nothing to Eliza. She dont know: I always had a delicacy about telling her.

PICKERING   Quite right. We'll leave it so, if you dont mind.

DOOLITTLE   And youll come to the church, Colonel, and put me through straight?

PICKERING   With pleasure. As far as a bachelor can.

MRS. HIGGINS   May I come, Mr. Doolittle? I should be very sorry to miss your wedding.

DOOLITTLE   I should indeed be honored by your condescension,[1] maam; and my poor old woman would take it as a tremenjous compliment. Shes been very low, thinking of the happy days that are no more.

MRS. HIGGINS [*rising*]   I'll order the carriage and get ready. [*The men rise, except* HIGGINS.] I shant be more than fifteen minutes. [*As she goes to the door* ELIZA *comes in, hatted and buttoning her gloves.*] I'm going to the church to see your father married, Eliza. You had better come in the brougham[2] with me. Colonel Pickering can go on with the bridegroom.

[MRS. HIGGINS *goes out.* ELIZA *comes to the middle of the room between the centre window and the ottoman.* PICKERING *joins her.*]

DOOLITTLE   Bridegroom! What a word! It makes a man realize his position, somehow. [*He takes up his hat and goes towards the door.*]

PICKERING   Before I go, Eliza, do forgive him and come back to us.

LIZA   I dont think papa would allow me. Would you, dad?

DOOLITTLE [*sad but magnanimous*]   They played you off very cunning, Eliza, them two sportsmen. If it had been only one of them, you could have nailed him. But you see, there was two; and one of them chaperoned the

---

1. Here, courteous disregard of differences in rank (without the negative connotation common in today's usage).

2. A one-horse closed carriage, which holds two or four.

other, as you might say. [*To* PICKERING] It was artful of you, Colonel; but I
380 bear no malice: I should have done the same myself. I been the victim of
one woman after another all my life; and I dont grudge you two getting the
better of Eliza. I shant interfere. It's time for us to go, Colonel. So long,
Henry. See you in St. George's, Eliza.

[*He goes out.*]

PICKERING [*coaxing*]   Do stay with us, Eliza.

[*He follows* DOOLITTLE.]

[ELIZA *goes out on the balcony to avoid being alone with* HIGGINS. *He
rises and joins her there. She immediately comes back into the room and
makes for the door; but he goes along the balcony quickly and gets his
back to the door before she reaches it.*]

385 HIGGINS   Well, Eliza, youve had a bit of your own back, as you call it. Have
you had enough? and are you going to be reasonable? Or do you want any
more?

LIZA   You want me back only to pick up your slippers and put up with your
tempers and fetch and carry for you.

390 HIGGINS   I havnt said I wanted you back at all.

LIZA   Oh, indeed. Then what are we talking about?

HIGGINS   About you, not about me. If you come back I shall treat you just as
I have always treated you. I cant change my nature; and I dont intend
to change my manners. My manners are exactly the same as Colonel
395 Pickering's.

LIZA   Thats not true. He treats a flower girl as if she was a duchess.

HIGGINS   And I treat a duchess as if she was a flower girl.

LIZA   I see. [*She turns away composedly, and sits on the ottoman, facing the
window.*] The same to everybody.

400 HIGGINS   Just so.

LIZA   Like father.

HIGGINS [*grinning, a little taken down*[3]]   Without accepting the comparison
at all points, Eliza, it's quite true that your father is not a snob, and that he
will be quite at home in any station of life to which his eccentric destiny
405 may call him. [*Seriously*] The great secret, Eliza, is not having bad manners
or good manners or any other particular sort of manners, but having the
same manner for all human souls: in short, behaving as if you were in
Heaven, where there are no third-class carriages, and one soul is as good as
another.

410 LIZA   Amen. You are a born preacher.

HIGGINS [*irritated*]   The question is not whether I treat you rudely, but
whether you ever heard me treat anyone else better.

LIZA [*with sudden sincerity*]   I dont care how you treat me. I dont mind your
swearing at me. I dont mind a black eye: Ive had one before this. But
415 [*Standing up and facing him*] I wont be passed over.[4]

HIGGINS   Then get out of my way; for I wont stop for you. You talk about me
as if I were a motor bus.

LIZA   So you are a motor bus: all bounce and go, and no consideration for
anyone. But I can do without you: dont think I cant.

420 HIGGINS   I know you can. I told you you could.

---

3. Humbled.   4. Ignored.

LIZA [*wounded, getting away from him to the other side of the ottoman with her face to the hearth*]   I know you did, you brute. You wanted to get rid of me.

HIGGINS   Liar.

LIZA   Thank you. [*She sits down with dignity.*]

HIGGINS   You never asked yourself, I suppose, whether *I* could do without
425   you.

LIZA [*earnestly*]   Dont you try to get round me.[5] Youll have to do without me.

HIGGINS [*arrogant*]   I can do without anybody. I have my own soul: my own
spark of divine fire. But [*With sudden humility*] I shall miss you, Eliza. [*He
sits down near her on the ottoman.*] I have learnt something from your idi-
430   otic notions: I confess that humbly and gratefully. And I have grown accustomed to your voice and appearance. I like them, rather.

LIZA   Well, you have both of them on your gramophone and in your book of
photographs. When you feel lonely without me, you can turn the machine
on. It's got no feelings to hurt.

435 HIGGINS   I cant turn your soul on. Leave me those feelings; and you can take
away the voice and the face. They are not you.

LIZA   Oh, you are a devil. You can twist the heart in a girl as easy as some
could twist her arms to hurt her. Mrs. Pearce warned me. Time and again
she has wanted to leave you; and you always got round her at the last
440   minute. And you dont care a bit for her. And you dont care a bit for me.

HIGGINS   I care for life, for humanity; and you are a part of it that has come
my way and been built into my house. What more can you or anyone ask?

LIZA   I wont care for anybody that doesnt care for me.

HIGGINS   Commercial principles, Eliza. Like [*Reproducing her Covent Gar-
445   den pronunciation with professional exactness*] s'yollin voylets [selling vio-
lets], isnt it?

LIZA   Dont sneer at me. It's mean to sneer at me.

HIGGINS   I have never sneered in my life. Sneering doesnt become either the
human face or the human soul. I am expressing my righteous contempt for
450   Commercialism. I dont and wont trade in affection. You call me a brute
because you couldnt buy a claim on me by fetching my slippers and finding
my spectacles. You were a fool: I think a woman fetching a man's slippers is
a disgusting sight: did I ever fetch your slippers? I think a good deal more
of you for throwing them in my face. No use slaving for me and then saying
455   you want to be cared for: who cares for a slave? If you come back, come
back for the sake of good fellowship; for youll get nothing else. Youve had a
thousand times as much out of me as I have out of you; and if you dare to
set up your little dog's tricks of fetching and carrying slippers against my
creation of a Duchess Eliza, I'll slam the door in your silly face.

460 LIZA   What did you do it for if you didnt care for me?

HIGGINS [*heartily*]   Why, because it was my job.

LIZA   You never thought of the trouble it would make for me.

HIGGINS   Would the world ever have been made if its maker had been afraid
of making trouble? Making life means making trouble. Theres only one
465   way of escaping trouble; and thats killing things. Cowards, you notice, are
always shrieking to have troublesome people killed.

LIZA   I'm no preacher: I dont notice things like that. I notice that you dont
notice me.

5. That is, don't try to deceive or outsmart me.

HIGGINS [*jumping up and walking about intolerantly*]   Eliza: youre an idiot. I
470   waste the treasures of my Miltonic mind by spreading them before you.
Once for all, understand that I go my way and do my work without caring
twopence what happens to either of us. I am not intimidated, like your
father and your stepmother. So you can come back or go to the devil: which
you please.

475 LIZA   What am I to come back for?

HIGGINS [*bouncing up on his knees on the ottoman and leaning over it to her*]
For the fun of it. Thats why I took you on.

LIZA [*with averted face*]   And you may throw me out tomorrow if I dont do
everything you want me to?

HIGGINS   Yes; and you may walk out tomorrow if I dont do everything you
480   want me to.

LIZA   And live with my stepmother?

HIGGINS   Yes, or sell flowers.

LIZA   Oh! if I only could go back to my flower basket! I should be independent of both you and father and all the world! Why did you take my inde-
485   pendence from me? Why did I give it up? I'm a slave now, for all my fine
clothes.

HIGGINS   Not a bit. I'll adopt you as my daughter and settle money on you if
you like. Or would you rather marry Pickering?

LIZA [*looking fiercely round at him*]   I wouldnt marry you if you asked me;
490   and youre nearer my age than what he is.

HIGGINS [*gently*]   Than he is: not "than what he is."

LIZA [*losing her temper and rising*]   I'll talk as I like. Youre not my teacher
now.

HIGGINS [*reflectively*]   I dont suppose Pickering would, though. Hes as con-
495   firmed an old bachelor as I am.

LIZA   Thats not what I want; and dont you think it. Ive always had chaps
enough wanting me that way. Freddy Hill writes to me twice and three
times a day,[6] sheets and sheets.

HIGGINS [*disagreeably surprised*]   Damn his impudence! [*He recoils and finds
himself sitting on his heels.*]

500 LIZA   He has a right to if he likes, poor lad. And he does love me.

HIGGINS [*getting off the ottoman*]   You have no right to encourage him.

LIZA   Every girl has a right to be loved.

HIGGINS   What! By fools like that?

LIZA   Freddy's not a fool. And if hes weak and poor and wants me, may be
505   hed make me happier than my betters that bully me and dont want me.

HIGGINS   Can he make anything of you? Thats the point.

LIZA   Perhaps I could make something of him. But I never thought of us
making anything of one another; and you never think of anything else. I
only want to be natural.

510 HIGGINS   In short, you want me to be as infatuated about you as Freddy? Is
that it?

LIZA   No I dont. Thats not the sort of feeling I want from you. And dont you
be too sure of yourself or of me. I could have been a bad girl if I'd liked. Ive
seen more of some things than you, for all your learning. Girls like me can

6. At the time, most places in England had two or three mail deliveries daily, and London had
even more.

515 drag gentlemen down to make love to[7] them easy enough. And they wish each other dead the next minute.

HIGGINS Of course they do. Then what in thunder are we quarrelling about?

LIZA [*much troubled*] I want a little kindness. I know I'm a common igno-rant girl, and you a book-learned gentleman; but I'm not dirt under your

520 feet. What I done [*Correcting herself*] what I did was not for the dresses and the taxis: I did it because we were pleasant together and I come— came—to care for you; not to want you to make love to me, and not forget-ting the difference between us, but more friendly like.

HIGGINS Well, of course. Thats just how I feel. And how Pickering feels.

525 Eliza: youre a fool.

LIZA Thats not a proper answer to give me. [*She sinks on the chair at the writing-table in tears.*]

HIGGINS It's all youll get until you stop being a common idiot. If youre going to be a lady, youll have to give up feeling neglected if the men you know dont spend half their time snivelling over you and the other half giving you

530 black eyes. If you cant stand the coldness of my sort of life, and the strain of it, go back to the gutter. Work til you are more a brute than a human being; and then cuddle and squabble and drink til you fall asleep. Oh, it's a fine life, the life of the gutter. It's real: it's warm: it's violent: you can feel it through the thickest skin: you can taste it and smell it without any training

535 or any work. Not like Science and Literature and Classical Music and Phi-losophy and Art. You find me cold, unfeeling, selfish, dont you? Very well: be off with you to the sort of people you like. Marry some sentimental hog or other with lots of money, and a thick pair of lips to kiss you with and a thick pair of boots to kick you with. If you cant appreciate what youve got,

540 youd better get what you can appreciate.

LIZA [*desperate*] Oh, you are a cruel tyrant. I cant talk to you: you turn everything against me: I'm always in the wrong. But you know very well all the time that youre nothing but a bully. You know I cant go back to the gut-ter, as you call it, and that I have no real friends in the world but you and

545 the Colonel. You know well I couldnt bear to live with a low common man after you two; and it's wicked and cruel of you to insult me by pretending I could. You think I must go back to Wimpole Street because I have nowhere else to go but father's. But dont you be too sure that you have me under your feet to be trampled on and talked down. I'll marry Freddy, I will, as

550 soon as hes able to support me.

HIGGINS [*sitting down beside her*] Rubbish! you shall marry an ambassador. You shall marry the Governor-General of India or the Lord-Lieutenant of Ireland, or somebody who wants a deputy-queen. I'm not going to have my masterpiece thrown away on Freddy.

555 LIZA You think I like you to say that. But I havnt forgot what you said a min-ute ago; and I wont be coaxed round as if I was a baby or a puppy. If I cant have kindness, I'll have independence.

HIGGINS Independence? Thats middle class blasphemy. We are all depen-dent on one another, every soul of us on earth.

560 LIZA [*rising determinedly*] I'll let you see whether I'm dependent on you. If you can preach, I can teach. I'll go and be a teacher.

7. To pay amorous attention to, to court.

HIGGINS   Whatll you teach, in heaven's name?

LIZA   What you taught me. I'll teach phonetics.

HIGGINS   Ha! Ha! Ha!

565 LIZA   I'll offer myself as an assistant to Professor Nepean.

HIGGINS [*rising in a fury*]   What! That impostor! that humbug! that toadying ignoramus! Teach him my methods! my discoveries! You take one step in his direction and I'll wring your neck. [*He lays hands on her.*] Do you hear?

LIZA [*defiantly non-resistant*]   Wring away. What do I care? I knew youd
570 strike me some day. [*He lets her go, stamping with rage at having forgotten himself, and recoils so hastily that he stumbles back into his seat on the ottoman.*] Aha! Now I know how to deal with you. What a fool I was not to think of it before! You cant take away the knowledge you gave me. You said I had a finer ear than you. And I can be civil and kind to people, which is more than you can. Aha! Thats done[8] you, Henry Higgins, it has. Now I
575 dont care that [*Snapping her fingers*] for your bullying and your big talk. I'll advertize it in the papers that your duchess is only a flower girl that you taught, and that she'll teach anybody to be a duchess just the same in six months for a thousand guineas. Oh, when I think of myself crawling under your feet and being trampled on and called names, when all the
580 time I had only to lift up my finger to be as good as you, I could just kick myself.

HIGGINS [*wondering at her*]   You damned impudent slut, you! But it's better than snivelling; better than fetching slippers and finding spectacles, isnt it? [*Rising*] By George, Eliza, I said I'd make a woman of you; and I have. I like
585 you like this.

LIZA   Yes: you turn round and make up to me now that I'm not afraid of you, and can do without you.

HIGGINS   Of course I do, you little fool. Five minutes ago you were like a millstone round my neck. Now youre a tower of strength: a consort[9] battle-
590 ship. You and I and Pickering will be three old bachelors together instead of only two men and a silly girl.

[MRS. HIGGINS *returns, dressed for the wedding.* ELIZA *instantly becomes cool and elegant.*]

MRS. HIGGINS   The carriage is waiting, Eliza. Are you ready?

LIZA   Quite. Is the Professor coming?

MRS. HIGGINS   Certainly not. He cant behave himself in church. He makes
595 remarks out loud all the time on the clergyman's pronunciation.

LIZA   Then I shall not see you again, Professor. Good-bye. [*She goes to the door.*]

MRS. HIGGINS [*coming to* HIGGINS]   Good-bye, dear.

HIGGINS   Good-bye, mother. [*He is about to kiss her, when he recollects something.*] Oh, by the way, Eliza, order a ham and a Stilton cheese, will you?
600 And buy me a pair of reindeer gloves, number eights, and a tie to match that new suit of mine, at Eale & Binman's. You can choose the color. [*His cheerful, careless, vigorous voice shows that he is incorrigible.*]

LIZA [*disdainfully*]   Buy them yourself.

[*She sweeps out.*]

---

8. Defeated.   9. A ship sailing in company with another.

MRS. HIGGINS   I'm afraid youve spoiled that girl, Henry. But never mind, dear: I'll buy you the tie and gloves.

605   HIGGINS [*sunnily*]   Oh, dont bother. She'll buy em all right enough. Goodbye.

> [*They kiss.* MRS. HIGGINS *runs out.* HIGGINS, *left alone, rattles his cash in his pocket; chuckles; and disports himself in a highly self-satisfied manner.*]

*   *   *   *   *

The rest of the story need not be shown in action, and indeed, would hardly need telling if our imaginations were not so enfeebled by their lazy dependence on the ready-mades and reach-me-downs of the ragshop[1] in which Romance keeps its stock of "happy endings" to misfit all stories. Now, the history of Eliza Doolittle, though called a romance because of the transfiguration it records seems exceedingly improbable, is common enough. Such transfigurations have been achieved by hundreds of resolutely ambitious young women since Nell Gwynne[2] set them the example by playing queens and fascinating kings in the theatre in which she began by selling oranges. Nevertheless, people in all directions have assumed, for no other reason than that she became the heroine of a romance, that she must have married the hero of it. This is unbearable, not only because her little drama, if acted on such a thoughtless assumption, must be spoiled, but because the true sequel is patent to anyone with a sense of human nature in general, and of feminine instinct in particular.

Eliza, in telling Higgins she would not marry him if he asked her, was not coquetting: she was announcing a well-considered decision. When a bachelor interests, and dominates, and teaches, and becomes important to a spinster, as Higgins with Eliza, she always, if she has character enough to be capable of it, considers very seriously indeed whether she will play for becoming that bachelor's wife, especially if he is so little interested in marriage that a determined and devoted woman might capture him if she set herself resolutely to do it. Her decision will depend a good deal on whether she is really free to choose; and that, again, will depend on her age and income. If she is at the end of her youth, and has no security for her livelihood, she will marry him because she must marry anybody who will provide for her. But at Eliza's age a good-looking girl does not feel that pressure: she feels free to pick and choose. She is therefore guided by her instinct in the matter. Eliza's instinct tells her not to marry Higgins. It does not tell her to give him up. It is not in the slightest doubt as to his remaining one of the strongest personal interests in her life. It would be very sorely strained if there was another woman likely to supplant her with him. But as she feels sure of him on that last point, she has no doubt at all as to her course, and would not have any, even if the difference of twenty years in age, which seems so great to youth, did not exist between them.

As our own instincts are not appealed to by her conclusion, let us see whether we cannot discover some reason in it. When Higgins excused his indifference to young women on the ground that they had an irresistible rival in his mother, he gave the clue to his inveterate old-bachelordom. The case is uncommon only to the extent that remarkable mothers are uncommon. If an imaginative boy has a sufficiently rich mother who has intelligence, personal grace, dignity of character without harshness, and a cultivated sense of the best art of her time to enable her to make her house beautiful, she sets a standard for him against which very few women can struggle, besides effecting for him a disengagement of his affections, his sense of beauty, and his idealism from his specifically sexual impulses. This makes him a standing puzzle to the huge number of uncultivated people who have been brought up in tasteless

---

1. That is, a shop selling cheap mass-produced and secondhand clothing ("ready-mades and reach-me-downs").

2. Eleanor Gwynn (1650–1687), one of the first prominent English actresses and a mistress of King Charles II.

homes by commonplace or disagreeable parents, and to whom, consequently, litera- ture, painting, sculpture, music, and affectionate personal relations come as modes of sex if they come at all. The word passion means nothing else to them; and that Higgins could have a passion for phonetics and idealize his mother instead of Eliza, would seem to them absurd and unnatural. Nevertheless, when we look round and see that hardly anyone is too ugly or disagreeable to find a wife or a husband if he or she wants one, whilst many old maids and bachelors are above the average in quality and culture, we cannot help suspecting that the disentanglement of sex from the associations with which it is so commonly confused, a disentanglement which per- sons of genius achieve by sheer intellectual analysis, is sometimes produced or aided by parental fascination.

Now, though Eliza was incapable of thus explaining to herself Higgins's formida- ble powers of resistance to the charm that prostrated Freddy at the first glance, she was instinctively aware that she could never obtain a complete grip of him, or come between him and his mother (the first necessity of the married woman). To put it shortly, she knew that for some mysterious reason he had not the makings of a mar- ried man in him, according to her conception of a husband as one to whom she would be his nearest and fondest and warmest interest. Even had there been no mother-rival, she would still have refused to accept an interest in herself that was secondary to philosophic interests. Had Mrs. Higgins died, there would still have been Milton and the Universal Alphabet. Landor's[3] remark that to those who have the greatest power of loving, love is a secondary affair, would not have recommended Landor to Eliza. Put that along with her resentment of Higgins's domineering supe- riority, and her mistrust of his coaxing cleverness in getting round her and evading her wrath when he had gone too far with his impetuous bullying, and you will see that Eliza's instinct had good grounds for warning her not to marry her Pygmalion.

And now, whom did Eliza marry? For if Higgins was a predestinate old bachelor, she was most certainly not a predestinate old maid. Well, that can be told very shortly to those who have not guessed it from the indications she has herself given them.

Almost immediately after Eliza is stung into proclaiming her considered determi- nation not to marry Higgins, she mentions the fact that young Mr. Frederick Eyns- ford Hill is pouring out his love for her daily through the post. Now Freddy is young, practically twenty years younger than Higgins: he is a gentleman (or, as Eliza would qualify him, a toff), and speaks like one; he is nicely dressed, is treated by the Colo- nel as an equal, loves her unaffectedly, and is not her master, nor ever likely to domi- nate her in spite of his advantage of social standing. Eliza has no use for the foolish romantic tradition that all women love to be mastered, if not actually bullied and beaten. "When you go to women," says Nietzsche, "take your whip with you."[4] Sen- sible despots have never confined that precaution to women: they have taken their whips with them when they have dealt with men, and been slavishly idealized by the men over whom they have flourished the whip much more than by women. No doubt there are slavish women as well as slavish men; and women, like men, admire those that are stronger than themselves. But to admire a strong person and to live under that strong person's thumb are two different things. The weak may not be admired and hero-worshipped; but they are by no means disliked or shunned; and they never seem to have the least difficulty in marrying people who are too good for them. They may fail in emergencies; but life is not one long emergency: it is mostly a string of situations for which no exceptional strength is needed, and with which even rather

3. The English poet Walter Savage Landor (1775–1864); in "Roger Ascham and the Lady Jane Grey," in *Imaginary Conversations of Lit- erary Men and Statesmen* (1824), he wrote, "Love is a secondary passion in those who love most, a primary in those who love least."

4. Spoken by a fictional old woman in *Thus Spoke Zarathustra* (1883), by the German phi- losopher Friedrich Nietzsche (1844–1900).

weak people can cope if they have a stronger partner to help them out. Accordingly, it is a truth everywhere in evidence that strong people, masculine or feminine, not only do not marry stronger people, but do not shew any preference for them in selecting their friends. When a lion meets another with a louder roar "the first lion thinks the last a bore."[5] The man or woman who feels strong enough for two, seeks for every other quality in a partner than strength.

The converse is also true. Weak people want to marry strong people who do not frighten them too much; and this often leads them to make the mistake we describe metaphorically as "biting off more than they can chew." They want too much for too little; and when the bargain is unreasonable beyond all bearing, the union becomes impossible: it ends in the weaker party being either discarded or borne as a cross, which is worse. People who are not only weak, but silly or obtuse as well, are often in these difficulties.

This being the state of human affairs, what is Eliza fairly sure to do when she is placed between Freddy and Higgins? Will she look forward to a lifetime of fetching Higgins's slippers or to a lifetime of Freddy fetching hers? There can be no doubt about the answer. Unless Freddy is biologically repulsive to her, and Higgins biologically attractive to a degree that overwhelms all her other instincts, she will, if she marries either of them, marry Freddy.

And that is just what Eliza did.

Complications ensued; but they were economic, not romantic. Freddy had no money and no occupation. His mother's jointure, a last relic of the opulence of Largelady Park, had enabled her to struggle along in Earlscourt with an air of gentility, but not to procure any serious secondary education for her children, much less give the boy a profession. A clerkship at thirty shillings a week was beneath Freddy's dignity, and extremely distasteful to him besides. His prospects consisted of a hope that if he kept up appearances somebody would do something for him. The something appeared vaguely to his imagination as a private secretaryship or a sinecure of some sort. To his mother it perhaps appeared as a marriage to some lady of means who could not resist her boy's niceness. Fancy her feelings when he married a flower girl who had become déclassée under extraordinary circumstances which were now notorious!

It is true that Eliza's situation did not seem wholly ineligible. Her father, though formerly a dustman, and now fantastically disclassed, had become extremely popular in the smartest society by a social talent which triumphed over every prejudice and every disadvantage. Rejected by the middle class, which he loathed, he had shot up at once into the highest circles by his wit, his dustmanship (which he carried like a banner), and his Nietzschean transcendence of good and evil.[6] At intimate ducal dinners he sat on the right hand of the Duchess; and in country houses he smoked in the pantry and was made much of by the butler when he was not feeding in the dining-room and being consulted by cabinet ministers. But he found it almost as hard to do all this on four thousand a year as Mrs. Eynsford Hill to live in Earlscourt on an income so pitiably smaller that I have not the heart to disclose its exact figure. He absolutely refused to add the last straw to his burden by contributing to Eliza's support.

Thus Freddy and Eliza, now Mr. and Mrs. Eynsford Hill, would have spent a penniless honeymoon but for a wedding present of £500[7] from the Colonel to Eliza. It lasted a long time because Freddy did not know how to spend money, never having had any to spend, and Eliza, socially trained by a pair of old bachelors, wore her

5. Shaw slightly misquotes the popular comic opera *Bombastes Furioso* (1810), by English dramatist William Barnes Rhodes: "So have I heard on Afric's burning shore / Another lion give a grievous roar; / And the first lion thought the last a bore."

6. A well-known work by Nietzsche is titled *Beyond Good and Evil* (1886).

7. Roughly equivalent to $40,000 today.

clothes as long as they held together and looked pretty, without the least regard to their being many months out of fashion. Still, £500 will not last two young people for ever; and they both knew, and Eliza felt as well, that they must shift for themselves in the end. She could quarter herself on Wimpole Street because it had come to be her home; but she was quite aware that she ought not to quarter Freddy there, and that it would not be good for his character if she did.

Not that the Wimpole Street bachelors objected. When she consulted them, Higgins declined to be bothered about her housing problem when that solution was so simple. Eliza's desire to have Freddy in the house with her seemed of no more importance than if she had wanted an extra piece of bedroom furniture. Pleas as to Freddy's character, and the moral obligation on him to earn his own living, were lost on Higgins. He denied that Freddy had any character, and declared that if he tried to do any useful work some competent person would have the trouble of undoing it: a procedure involving a net loss to the community; and great unhappiness to Freddy himself, who was obviously intended by Nature for such light work as amusing Eliza, which, Higgins declared, was a much more useful and honorable occupation than working in the city.[8] When Eliza referred again to her project of teaching phonetics, Higgins abated not a jot of his violent opposition to it. He said she was not within ten years of being qualified to meddle with his pet subject; and as it was evident that the Colonel agreed with him, she felt she could not go against them in this grave matter, and that she had no right, without Higgins's consent, to exploit the knowledge he had given her; for his knowledge seemed to her as much his private property as his watch: Eliza was no communist. Besides, she was superstitiously devoted to them both, more entirely and frankly after her marriage than before it.

It was the Colonel who finally solved the problem, which had cost him much perplexed cogitation. He one day asked Eliza, rather shyly, whether she had quite given up her notion of keeping a flower shop. She replied that she had thought of it, but had put it out of her head, because the Colonel had said, that day at Mrs. Higgins's, that it would never do. The Colonel confessed that when he said that, he had not quite recovered from the dazzling impression of the day before. They broke the matter to Higgins that evening. The sole comment vouchsafed by him very nearly led to a serious quarrel with Eliza. It was to the effect that she would have in Freddy an ideal errand boy.

Freddy himself was next sounded on the subject. He said he had been thinking of a shop himself; though it had presented itself to his pennilessness as a small place in which Eliza should sell tobacco at one counter whilst he sold newspapers at the opposite one. But he agreed that it would be extraordinarily jolly to go early every morning with Eliza to Covent Garden and buy flowers on the scene of their first meeting: a sentiment which earned him many kisses from his wife. He added that he had always been afraid to propose anything of the sort, because Clara would make an awful row about a step that must damage her matrimonial chances, and his mother could not be expected to like it after clinging for so many years to that step of the social ladder on which retail trade is impossible.

This difficulty was removed by an event highly unexpected by Freddy's mother. Clara, in the course of her incursions into those artistic circles which were the highest within her reach, discovered that her conversational qualifications were expected to include a grounding in the novels of Mr. H. G. Wells.[9] She borrowed them in various directions so energetically that she swallowed them all within two months. The result was a conversion of a kind quite common today. A modern Acts of the Apostles would fill fifty whole Bibles if anyone were capable of writing it.

8. That is, working in London's finance district.
9. The English writer Herbert George Wells (1866–1946), a prominent member of the

socialist Fabian Society and the author not only of science-fiction novels such as The War of the Worlds (1898) but also novels of social criticism such as Tono-Bungay (1908).

Poor Clara, who appeared to Higgins and his mother as a disagreeable and ridiculous person, and to her own mother as in some inexplicable way a social failure, had never seen herself in either light; for, though to some extent ridiculed and mimicked in West Kensington[1] like everybody else there, she was accepted as a rational and normal—or shall we say inevitable?—sort of human being. At worst they called her The Pusher;[2] but to them no more than to herself had it ever occurred that she was pushing the air, and pushing it in a wrong direction. Still, she was not happy. She was growing desperate. Her one asset, the fact that her mother was what the Epsom greengrocer called a carriage lady had no exchange value, apparently. It had prevented her from getting educated, because the only education she could have afforded was education with the Earlscourt greengrocer's daughter. It had led her to seek the society of her mother's class; and that class simply would not have her, because she was much poorer than the greengrocer, and, far from being able to afford a maid,[3] could not afford even a housemaid, and had to scrape along at home with an illiberally treated general servant. Under such circumstances nothing could give her an air of being a genuine product of Largelady Park. And yet its tradition made her regard a marriage with anyone within her reach as an unbearable humiliation. Commercial people and professional people in a small way were odious to her. She ran after painters and novelists; but she did not charm them; and her bold attempts to pick up and practise artistic and literary talk irritated them. She was, in short, an utter failure, an ignorant, incompetent, pretentious, unwelcome, penniless, useless little snob; and though she did not admit these disqualifications (for nobody ever faces unpleasant truths of this kind until the possibility of a way out dawns on them) she felt their effects too keenly to be satisfied with her position.

Clara had a startling eyeopener when, on being suddenly wakened to enthusiasm by a girl of her own age who dazzled her and produced in her a gushing desire to take her for a model, and gain her friendship, she discovered that this exquisite apparition had graduated from the gutter in a few months' time. It shook her so violently, that when Mr. H. G. Wells lifted her on the point of his puissant pen, and placed her at the angle of view from which the life she was leading and the society to which she clung appeared in its true relation to real human needs and worthy social structure, he effected a conversion and a conviction of sin comparable to the most sensational feats of General Booth or Gypsy Smith.[4] Clara's snobbery went bang. Life suddenly began to move with her. Without knowing how or why, she began to make friends and enemies. Some of the acquaintances to whom she had been a tedious or indifferent or ridiculous affliction, dropped her: others became cordial. To her amazement she found that some "quite nice" people were saturated with Wells, and that this accessibility to ideas was the secret of their niceness. People she had thought deeply religious, and had tried to conciliate on that tack with disastrous results, suddenly took an interest in her, and revealed a hostility to conventional religion which she had never conceived possible except among the most desperate characters. They made her read Galsworthy;[5] and Galsworthy exposed the vanity of Largelady Park and finished her. It exasperated her to think that the dungeon in which she had languished for so many unhappy years had been unlocked all the time, and that the impulses she had so carefully struggled with and stifled for the sake of keeping well with society, were precisely those by which alone she could have come into any sort of sincere human contact. In the radiance of these discoveries, and the tumult of

---

1. An area of London at the western edge of the inner suburbs.

2. That is, The Social Climber.

3. A personal attendant, as distinct from a general servant who does housework.

4. That is, feats of religious conversion. William Booth (1829–1912), a Methodist revivalist, founded the Salvation Army; Rodney Smith (1860–1947), briefly a captain in the Salvation Army, became an internationally renowned evangelist.

5. John Galsworthy (1867–1933), an English playwright and novelist whose writings cast a realistic and critical light on the upper middle class.

their reaction, she made a fool of herself as freely and conspicuously as when she so rashly adopted Eliza's expletive in Mrs. Higgins's drawing-room; for the new-born Wellsian had to find her bearings almost as ridiculously as a baby; but nobody hates a baby for its ineptitudes, or thinks the worse of it for trying to eat the matches; and Clara lost no friends by her follies. They laughed at her to her face this time; and she had to defend herself and fight it out as best she could.

When Freddy paid a visit to Earlscourt (which he never did when he could possibly help it) to make the desolating announcement that he and his Eliza were thinking of blackening the Largelady scutcheon[6] by opening a shop, he found the little household already convulsed by a prior announcement from Clara that she also was going to work in an old furniture shop in Dover Street, which had been started by a fellow Wellsian. This appointment Clara owed, after all, to her old social accomplishment of Push. She had made up her mind that, cost what it might, she would see Mr. Wells in the flesh; and she had achieved her end at a garden party. She had better luck than so rash an enterprise deserved. Mr. Wells came up to her expectations. Age had not withered him, nor could custom stale his infinite variety in half an hour.[7] His pleasant neatness and compactness, his small hands and feet, his teeming ready brain, his unaffected accessibility, and a certain fine apprehensiveness which stamped him as susceptible from his topmost hair to his tipmost toe, proved irresistible. Clara talked of nothing else for weeks and weeks afterwards. And as she happened to talk to the lady of the furniture shop, and that lady also desired above all things to know Mr. Wells and sell pretty things to him, she offered Clara a job on the chance of achieving that end through her.

And so it came about that Eliza's luck held, and the expected opposition to the flower shop melted away. The shop is in the arcade of a railway station not very far from the Victoria and Albert Museum; and if you live in that neighborhood you may go there any day and buy a buttonhole[8] from Eliza.

Now here is a last opportunity for romance. Would you not like to be assured that the shop was an immense success, thanks to Eliza's charms and her early business experience in Covent Garden? Alas! the truth is the truth: the shop did not pay for a long time, simply because Eliza and her Freddy did not know how to keep it. True, Eliza had not to begin at the very beginning: she knew the names and prices of the cheaper flowers; and her elation was unbounded when she found that Freddy, like all youths educated at cheap, pretentious, and thoroughly inefficient schools, knew a little Latin. It was very little, but enough to make him appear to her a Porson or Bentley,[9] and to put him at his ease with botanical nomenclature. Unfortunately he knew nothing else; and Eliza, though she could count money up to eighteen shillings or so, and had acquired a certain familiarity with the language of Milton from her struggles to qualify herself for winning Higgins's bet, could not write out a bill without utterly disgracing the establishment. Freddy's power of stating in Latin that Balbus built a wall and that Gaul was divided into three parts[1] did not carry with it the slightest knowledge of accounts or business: Colonel Pickering had to explain to him what a cheque book and a bank account meant. And the pair were by no means easily teachable. Freddy backed up Eliza in her obstinate refusal to believe that they could save money by engaging a bookkeeper with some knowledge of the business. How, they argued, could you possibly save money by going to extra expense when you already could not make both ends meet? But the Colonel, after making the ends meet over and over again, at last gently insisted; and Eliza, humbled to the dust by

6. Reputation (literally, a heraldic shield).
7. An allusion to the description of Cleopatra in Shakespeare's *Antony and Cleopatra* (1606–07): "Age cannot wither her, nor custom stale / Her infinite variety" (2.2.240–41).
8. A flower worn in the buttonhole of a lapel.

9. A great classicist, such as the English scholars Richard Porson (1759–1808) and Richard Bentley (1662–1742).
1. Phrases from standard Latin exercise books (the second is the opening of Caesar's *Gallic War* [ca. 50 B.C.E.]).

having to beg from him so often, and stung by the uproarious derision of Higgins, to whom the notion of Freddy succeeding at anything was a joke that never palled, grasped the fact that business, like phonetics, has to be learned.

On the piteous spectacle of the pair spending their evenings in shorthand schools and polytechnic classes, learning bookkeeping and typewriting with incipient junior clerks, male and female, from the elementary schools, let me not dwell. There were even classes at the London School of Economics, and a humble personal appeal to the director of that institution to recommend a course bearing on the flower business. He, being a humorist, explained to them the method of the celebrated Dickensian essay on Chinese Metaphysics by the gentleman who read an article on China and an article on Metaphysics and combined the information.[2] He suggested that they should combine the London School with Kew Gardens. Eliza, to whom the procedure of the Dickensian gentleman seemed perfectly correct (as in fact it was) and not in the least funny (which was only her ignorance) took his advice with entire gravity. But the effort that cost her the deepest humiliation was a request to Higgins, whose pet artistic fancy, next to Milton's verse, was caligraphy, and who himself wrote a most beautiful Italian hand, that he would teach her to write. He declared that she was congenitally incapable of forming a single letter worthy of the least of Milton's words; but she persisted; and again he suddenly threw himself into the task of teaching her with a combination of stormy intensity, concentrated patience, and occasional bursts of interesting disquisition on the beauty and nobility, the august mission and destiny, of human handwriting. Eliza ended by acquiring an extremely uncommercial script which was a positive extension of her personal beauty, and spending three times as much on stationery as anyone else because certain qualities and shapes of paper became indispensable to her. She could not even address an envelope in the usual way because it made the margins all wrong.

Their commercial school days were a period of disgrace and despair for the young couple. They seemed to be learning nothing about flower shops. At last they gave it up as hopeless, and shook the dust of the shorthand schools, and the polytechnics, and the London School of Economics from their feet for ever. Besides, the business was in some mysterious way beginning to take care of itself. They had somehow forgotten their objections to employing other people. They came to the conclusion that their own way was the best, and that they had really a remarkable talent for business. The Colonel, who had been compelled for some years to keep a sufficient sum on current account at his bankers to make up their deficits, found that the provision was unnecessary: the young people were prospering. It is true that there was not quite fair play between them and their competitors in trade. Their week-ends in the country cost them nothing, and saved them the price of their Sunday dinners; for the motor car was the Colonel's; and he and Higgins paid the hotel bills. Mr. F. Hill, florist and greengrocer (they soon discovered that there was money in asparagus; and asparagus led to other vegetables), had an air which stamped the business as classy; and in private life he was still Frederick Eynsford Hill, Esquire. Not that there was any swank about him: nobody but Eliza knew that he had been christened Frederick Challoner. Eliza herself swanked like anything.

That is all. That is how it has turned out. It is astonishing how much Eliza still manages to meddle in the housekeeping at Wimpole Street in spite of the shop and her own family. And it is notable that though she never nags her husband, and frankly loves the Colonel as if she were his favorite daughter, she has never got out of the habit of nagging Higgins that was established on the fatal night when she won his bet for him. She snaps his head off on the faintest provocation, or on none. He no longer dares to tease her by assuming an abysmal inferiority of Freddy's mind to his own. He storms and bullies and derides; but she stands up to him so ruthlessly that the Colonel has to ask her from time to time to be kinder to Higgins; and it is the

2. An allusion to *The Pickwick Papers* (1836–37), a novel by Charles Dickens.

only request of his that brings a mulish expression into her face. Nothing but some emergency or calamity great enough to break down all likes and dislikes, and throw them both back on their common humanity—and may they be spared any such trial!—will ever alter this. She knows that Higgins does not need her, just as her father did not need her. The very scrupulousness with which he told her that day that he had become used to having her there, and dependent on her for all sorts of little services, and that he should miss her if she went away (it would never have occurred to Freddy or the Colonel to say anything of the sort) deepens her inner certainty that she is "no more to him than them slippers," yet she has a sense, too, that his indifference is deeper than the infatuation of commoner souls. She is immensely interested in him. She has even secret mischievous moments in which she wishes she could get him alone, on a desert island, away from all ties and with nobody else in the world to consider, and just drag him off his pedestal and see him making love like any common man. We all have private imaginations of that sort. But when it comes to business, to the life that she really leads as distinguished from the life of dreams and fancies, she likes Freddy and she likes the Colonel; and she does not like Higgins and Mr. Doolittle. Galatea never does quite like Pygmalion: his relation to her is too godlike to be altogether agreeable.[3]

3. In classical mythology, Pygmalion was a legendary king of Cyprus who fell in love with an ivory statue of a woman that he had carved. In answer to his prayers, Aphrodite (called Venus by the Romans), the goddess of love, gave it life and they married; the most familiar version of the story is found in Ovid, *Metamorphoses* (ca. 10 c.e.), 10.243–97.

SUSAN GLASPELL

1876–1948

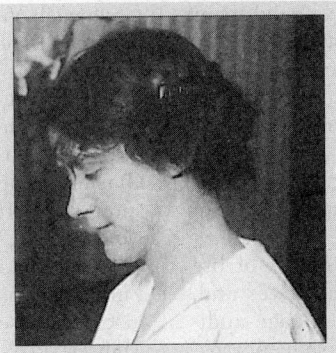

THE rediscovery of Susan Glaspell's writing by feminist critics and theater artists has, over the past few decades, exposed new generations of readers and audiences to this groundbreaking American playwright, novelist, and short story author, who received the Pulitzer Prize for drama in 1931. Glaspell came of age in the late nineteenth century, during the heyday of the "local color" movement in American literature. Works in this tradition—such as those of Glaspell's fellow Davenport, Iowa, resident Alice French (writing as Octave Thanet, 1850–1934)—celebrated regional American life and exposed its idiosyncrasies. By the early twentieth century, however, writers were increasingly focusing on the cultural, economic, and political differences growing between the country's burgeoning urban centers and its established rural locales. Glaspell and her contemporaries felt compelled to share with the nation their large and probing questions about American beliefs, values, and goals. In their creative endeavors, they framed these questions through the lenses of the Progressive era and their modern age, most notably the recent discoveries about human psychology. Glaspell's writing—especially her plays—reflects her keen engagement with the pressing issues of her day: how to foster a democratic and equitable society, what to think about the evolving roles of men and women, and how to honor the nation's founding principles while embracing the spirit of modernism. Artists like Glaspell were also engaged in formal experimentation, and their works reveal a sense of creative excitement as they sought new ways, structurally and aesthetically, to represent these cogent contemporary themes. Glaspell's 1916 play *TRIFLES* has emerged as a canonical text precisely because it exemplifies these intertwining artistic and social goals within American modernism.

Like many American modernists, Glaspell grew up in the nation's heartland. Her father, Elmer Glaspell, was a feed dealer; her mother, born Alice Keating, had been a schoolteacher before her marriage. Glaspell began her career as a journalist, writing a society column for her local paper before leaving home to attend Drake University. After graduation, she secured a post with the *Des Moines Daily News* as a statehouse and legislative reporter, but after two years, she decided to devote herself to fiction. She quickly had success writing short stories, which she placed in such national magazines as *McClure's* and *Harper's*. Following in the local-color tradition, Glaspell based many of her narratives on her experiences growing up in and around Davenport. But she interlaced these intimate portraits of midwestern life with the sharper edge of social critique that epitomizes her evolution as a Progressive and modernist artist. She published her first novel in 1909 and her second in 1911, as she continued to write short fiction. Following her marriage to George Cram "Jig" Cook in 1913, she and her new husband moved to Greenwich Village, as did many other young writers and artists of their generation. They were drawn to New York's bohemian lifestyle and creative freedom, which they felt were unattainable in the Midwest.

During this early twentieth-century moment, a growing number of American modernists recognized the potential of the stage to convey vivid images of life in the contemporary United States and, even more importantly, to engage audiences directly with larger social concerns. Eschewing the commercial theater and its devotion to profit-making entertainment, they sought to create a new kind of theater that would foster the development of a distinctly American culture. As a cofounder of the influential Provincetown Players—the company originally based in Provincetown, Massachusetts, that first produced the work of EUGENE O'NEILL during summer vacations—Glaspell played a central role in this movement. With Cook and other friends and colleagues such as John Reed, Djuna Barnes, Edna St. Vincent Millay, Theodore Dreiser, and Wallace Stevens, Glaspell participated in establishing a national theater dedicated to artistically innovative and political drama reflecting the explosive arrival of modernism in the United States.

For financial, practical, and philosophical reasons, most of the works produced by the Provincetown Players in their early years were one acts. Having been influenced by a U.S. tour of what was still called the Irish Players—the group founded in 1899 by the poet William Butler Yeats, Lady Gregory, and others that in 1904 became the Abbey Theatre—Cook believed that their repertoire of one-act plays had great impact as both artistic and nationalist creations, and he encouraged the Provincetown dramatists to use this form. Glaspell wrote eleven plays, seven of which were one acts (two written with Cook), for the Provincetown group between 1915 and 1922. Glaspell and Cook then departed from New York for Greece, leaving the

Provincetown Players to reconfigure themselves under others' leadership. After Cook died unexpectedly in 1924, Glaspell chose to return to their home on Cape Cod rather than renew her life in the bohemian Greenwich Village milieu. She also chose to return to her first creative form, fiction, producing six new novels and a children's tale. Glaspell did not abandon the theater however. With her new companion Norman Matson, with whom she lived until 1932, Glaspell wrote *The Comic Artist* (1927); soon thereafter she composed *Alison's House* (1930), based on the life and family of Emily Dickinson, for which she won the Pulitzer Prize. From 1936 to 1938 she lived in Chicago, serving as the director of the Midwest Play Bureau of the Federal Theater Project. Glaspell wrote one additional play, *Springs Eternal* (written 1944), which was neither published nor produced. She died in Provincetown in 1948.

Glaspell's first play, *Trifles,* was quickly identified by critics as an exemplar of one-act dramaturgy, and it was soon both widely produced and anthologized. Although Glaspell had initially conceived the piece as another short story, her husband persuaded her to write it first as a play; its short story version, "A Jury of Her Peers," was equally praised on its publication the following year. *Trifles* established Glaspell as a dramatist of real power; like all her short dramatic pieces, it displays her skill at constructing tight plots and using distinctive images in the service of theme. Like her American modernist contemporaries, Glaspell experimented freely with the various "isms" that defined the period, including realism, symbolism, and expressionism, often combining these approaches to achieve a specific thematic or stylistic effect. She demonstrated the effectiveness of both comedy and tragedy as vehicles for social critique. And she capitalized on the power of live theater to examine issues of particular concern to women, placing female characters and their struggles at the center of her dramaturgy. *The Outside* (1917), set in a lifesaving station on Cape Cod, epitomizes her method of integrating the symbolism of her setting with the play's action, as she portrays characters literally and figuratively in need of salvation. Such one acts as *Woman's Honor*

(1918) showcase Glaspell's gifts as a comic playwright, particularly her ability to depict the foibles of all her characters equally, as she introduces a group of allegorical women responding to what they take to be a demonstration of chivalry. This evenhandedness in her dramaturgical technique gives her plays a sense of balance, which is especially important when her theme is politically charged. Her ability to represent differing ideological perspectives is clearly displayed in *Inheritors* (1921), a full-length play that explores the Espionage Act (1917) and the Sedition Act (1918), which were intended to silence opposition to U.S. involvement in World War I. Other longer dramas, such as her highly regarded *The Verge* (1921), feature Glaspell's engagement with questions of gender identity and feminist consciousness as well as stylistic experimentation with realism and expressionism. Though some earlier critics faulted Glaspell for what they perceived as inconsistencies in style or thematic focus, more recently this variety and breadth have been championed as integral to the modernist movement in America and its willingness to engage with many facets of contemporary life.

Between December 1900 and April 1901, while working as a journalist, Glaspell had written a series of articles on the murder case that became the genesis for *Trifles*: the story of an Iowa farmer named Hossack whose wife was accused of killing him with an axe, and her subsequent trial and conviction. Glaspell transformed the details disclosed in the trial into a dramatic work of remarkable power, economy, and artistry. *Trifles* is set in the kitchen of "the now abandoned farmhouse" of John and Minnie Wright. We soon learn that shortly after the murder, a neighbor, Lewis Hale, discovered John strangled in his bed upstairs and Minnie dazedly rocking in her kitchen. With the body removed and the accused wife in jail, the play opens with the arrival of Hale; the sheriff, Henry Peters; and the county prosecutor, George Henderson, to inspect the crime scene. The wives of the sheriff and the neighbor, Mrs. Peters and Mrs. Hale, remain in the kitchen area to collect a few things Minnie has requested from prison. Glaspell's choice to identify them only by their married names underscores the traditional assumption that women have significance only through their relation to their husbands. Once the men leave the room, however, the women begin to explore the domestic space on their own. As they interact with the stage environment, the two women discover clues to the couple's personalities as well as potential evidence in the case. Despite their absence from the scene, Minnie and John Wright become vivid figures for us via the dialogue and actions of Mrs. Hale and Mrs. Peters. Glaspell's technique of building a plot around these absent centers is a hallmark of her dramaturgy, recurring in *Bernice* (1919) and *Alison's House*, among other plays. This device enables her to show that identity is as much constructed as innate. Moreover, it creates a distance between the audience and these characters that thwarts identification, thus making it possible for theatergoers to see them and their reported actions from multiple points of view. The irony that Glaspell emphasizes throughout the play (and in its very title) is the inconsequentiality—to the men who are empowered to solve the crime—of the domestic details these women embrace. The "trifles" of women's lives and work that the men dismiss hold great significance for the women who understand how to read their import empathically. Although the women do not really know each other at the beginning of the play, they come to find they have much in common, just as they do with the absent Minnie. Recognizing a sense of responsibility for and community with this other woman, Mrs. Hale exclaims: "I might have known she needed help! I know how things can be—for women. . . . We all go through the same things—it's all just a different kind of the same thing."

By reversing the narrative conventions that place men at the center of a plot as figures of power and knowledge, Glaspell guides her audience toward the recognition that different perspectives and values are essential to appreciate women's lives. The short story's title, "A Jury of Her Peers," adds another layer of irony by highlighting the impossibility of a woman facing such a jury at a time when women were

The 1916 production of *Trifles* by the Washington Square Players at the Comedy Theater. Pictured, from left to right, are Marjorie Vonnegut (Mrs. Peters), Elinor M. Cox (Mrs. Hale), John King (Lewis Hale), Arthur E. Hohl (Henry Peters), and T. W. Gibson (George Henderson).

systematically denied the right to be jurors. In effect, Mrs. Peters and Mrs. Hale (played by Glaspell in the first production) try Minnie Wright in an alternative venue, using a process that reveals details of her experience and possible motives—aspects of the case that the men's investigation will never discover. While Minnie's ultimate fate is left unresolved at the play's end, we sense that these women have come to their own verdict, one that exonerates Minnie and makes the audience wonder who in the couple was the victim.

Part of the ongoing appeal of *Trifles* surely stems from its reliance on the conventions of the murder mystery. Glaspell capitalized on the growing interest in this form of narrative, a genre that was popularized first in the United States by Edgar Allan Poe (1809–1849) and that gained an even wider readership with the Sherlock Holmes stories of England's Arthur Conan Doyle (1859–1930). Like many writers of mysteries, Glaspell uses amateur detectives—the two women—who turn out to be more perceptive than the male

experts investigating the case. Glaspell involves her audience in the process of discovery and deduction intrinsic to the form. Her employment of the mystery genre thus advances her feminist agenda: all members of the audience, regardless of sex, come to understand each piece of the puzzle through the perspectives of the women sleuths as they grapple with the evidence. As feminist critics point out, Glaspell's play teaches its viewers to see as women, to resist the conventions that have dominated the Western theater since its inception.

Glaspell's deft layering of imagery, her poignant representation of her midwestern locale, and the specificity of her characterizations and dialect in such a brief work all point to her mastery of the one-act form and her significance as an American dramatist. During her period of greatest productivity, she was considered by many to be one of the country's two most important dramatists—O'Neill being the other. The prominent cultural critic Ludwig Lewisohn wrote in 1932, "Susan Glaspell was followed by Eugene O'Neill.

The rest was silence; the rest is silence still." Though recent critical attention has focused on Glaspell primarily as a feminist writer, her dramatic work reflects a number of compelling aesthetic and political concerns. She made important contributions to the development of American modernism, and her writing reflects a forceful commitment to the country's foundational principles of democracy and personal liberty. For those wishing to grasp essential nuances of our cultural and political heritage, Susan Glaspell provides eloquent renditions of our nation a century ago.

J.E.G.

Trifles
A Play in One Act

CHARACTERS

GEORGE HENDERSON, county attorney

HENRY PETERS, sheriff

LEWIS HALE, a neighboring farmer

MRS. PETERS

MRS. HALE

SCENE: *The kitchen in the now abandoned farmhouse of* JOHN WRIGHT, *a gloomy kitchen, and left without having been put in order—unwashed pans under the sink, a loaf of bread outside the breadbox, a dish towel on the table—other signs of incompleted work.*

[*At the rear the outer door opens and the* SHERIFF *comes in followed by the* COUNTY ATTORNEY *and* HALE. *The* SHERIFF *and* HALE *are men in middle life, the* COUNTY ATTORNEY *is a young man; all are much bundled up and go at once to the stove. They are followed by the two women—the* SHERIFF's *wife first; she is a slight wiry woman, a thin nervous face.* MRS. HALE *is larger and would ordinarily be called more comfortable[1] looking, but she is disturbed now and looks fearfully about as she enters. The women have come in slowly, and stand close together near the door.*]

COUNTY ATTORNEY [*rubbing his hands*]   This feels good. Come up to the fire, ladies.

MRS. PETERS [*after taking a step forward*]   I'm not—cold.

5   SHERIFF [*unbuttoning his overcoat and stepping away from the stove as if to mark the beginning of official business*]   Now, Mr. Hale, before we move things about, you explain to Mr. Henderson just what you saw when you came here yesterday morning.

COUNTY ATTORNEY   By the way, has anything been moved? Are things just as you left them yesterday?

SHERIFF [*looking about*]   It's just the same. When it dropped below zero last
10   night I thought I'd better send Frank out this morning to make a fire for us—no use getting pneumonia with a big case on, but I told him not to touch anything except the stove—and you know Frank.

---

1. That is, appearing more relaxed.

COUNTY ATTORNEY   Somebody should have been left here yesterday.

SHERIFF   Oh—yesterday. When I had to send Frank to Morris Center for
15   that man who went crazy—I want you to know I had my hands full yesterday. I knew you could get back from Omaha by today and as long as I went
over everything here myself—

COUNTY ATTORNEY   Well, Mr. Hale, tell just what happened when you came
here yesterday morning.

20   HALE   Harry and I had started to town with a load of potatoes. We came
along the road from my place and as I got here I said, "I'm going to see if I
can't get John Wright to go in with me on a party telephone."[2] I spoke to
Wright about it once before and he put me off, saying folks talked too
much anyway, and all he asked was peace and quiet—I guess you know
25   about how much he talked himself; but I thought maybe if I went to the
house and talked about it before his wife, though I said to Harry that I
didn't know as what his wife wanted made much difference to John—

COUNTY ATTORNEY   Let's talk about that later, Mr. Hale. I do want to talk
about that, but tell now just what happened when you got to the house.

30   HALE   I didn't hear or see anything; I knocked at the door, and still it was all
quiet inside. I knew they must be up, it was past eight o'clock. So I
knocked again, and I thought I heard somebody say, "Come in." I wasn't
sure, I'm not sure yet, but I opened the door—this door [indicating the
door by which the two women are still standing] and there in that rocker—
35   [pointing to it] sat Mrs. Wright.

                    [They all look at the rocker.]

COUNTY ATTORNEY   What—was she doing?

HALE   She was rockin' back and forth. She had her apron in her hand and
was kind of—pleating it.

COUNTY ATTORNEY   And how did she—look?

40   HALE   Well, she looked queer.

COUNTY ATTORNEY   How do you mean—queer?

HALE   Well, as if she didn't know what she was going to do next. And kind of
done up.[3]

COUNTY ATTORNEY   How did she seem to feel about your coming?

45   HALE   Why, I don't think she minded—one way or other. She didn't pay
much attention. I said, "How do, Mrs. Wright, it's cold, ain't it?" And she
said, "Is it?"—and went on kind of pleating at her apron. Well, I was surprised; she didn't ask me to come up to the stove, or to set down, but just
sat there, not even looking at me, so I said, "I want to see John." And then
50   she—laughed. I guess you would call it a laugh. I thought of Harry and the
team outside, so I said a little sharp: "Can't I see John?" "No," she says,
kind o' dull like. "Ain't he home?" says I. "Yes," says she, "he's home."
"Then why can't I see him?" I asked her, out of patience. "'Cause he's
dead," says she. "Dead?" says I. She just nodded her head, not getting a bit
55   excited, but rockin' back and forth. "Why—where is he?" says I, not knowing what to say. She just pointed upstairs—like that [himself pointing to the
room above]. I got up, with the idea of going up there. I walked from there
to here—then I says, "Why, what did he die of?" "He died of a rope round
his neck," says she, and just went on pleatin' at her apron. Well, I went out

---

2. That is, a single telephone line shared by   3. Worn out.
two or four households.

60 and called Harry. I thought I might—need help. We went upstairs and
    there he was lyin'—
    COUNTY ATTORNEY I think I'd rather have you go into that upstairs, where
    you can point it all out. Just go on now with the rest of the story.
    HALE Well, my first thought was to get that rope off. It looked . . . [*Stops, his*
65 *face twitches.*] . . . but Harry, he went up to him, and he said, "No, he's
    dead all right, and we'd better not touch anything." So we went back down
    stairs. She was still sitting that same way. "Has anybody been notified?" I
    asked. "No," says she, unconcerned. "Who did this, Mrs. Wright?" said
    Harry. He said it business-like—and she stopped pleatin' of her apron. "I
70 don't know," she says. "You don't *know?*" says Harry. "No," says she.
    "Weren't you sleepin' in the bed with him?" says Harry. "Yes," says she, "but
    I was on the inside." "Somebody slipped a rope round his neck and stran-
    gled him and you didn't wake up?" says Harry. "I didn't wake up," she said
    after him. We must 'a looked as if we didn't see how that could be, for after
75 a minute she said, "I sleep sound." Harry was going to ask her more ques-
    tions but I said maybe we ought to let her tell her story first to the coroner,
    or the sheriff, so Harry went fast as he could to Rivers' place, where there's
    a telephone.
    COUNTY ATTORNEY And what did Mrs. Wright do when she knew that you
80 had gone for the coroner?
    HALE She moved from that chair to this one over here [*pointing to a small
    chair in the corner*] and just sat there with her hands held together and
    looking down. I got a feeling that I ought to make come conversation, so I
    said I had come in to see if John wanted to put in a telephone, and at that
85 she started to laugh, and then she stopped and looked at me—scared. [*The
    COUNTY ATTORNEY, who has had his notebook out, makes a note.*] I dunno,
    maybe it wasn't scared. I wouldn't like to say it was. Soon Harry got back,
    and then Dr. Lloyd came, and you, Mr. Peters, and so I guess that's all I
    know that you don't.
90 COUNTY ATTORNEY [*looking around*] I guess we'll go upstairs first—and then
    out to the barn and around there. [*To the* SHERIFF] You're convinced that
    there was nothing important here—nothing that would point to any motive.
    SHERIFF Nothing here but kitchen things.
    [*The* COUNTY ATTORNEY, *after again looking around the kitchen, opens
    the door of a cupboard closet. He gets up on a chair and looks on a shelf.
    Pulls his hand away, sticky.*]
    COUNTY ATTORNEY Here's a nice mess.
    [*The women draw nearer.*]
95 MRS. PETERS [*to the other woman*] Oh, her fruit; it did freeze. [*To the* LAW-
    YER] She worried about that when it turned so cold. She said the fire'd go
    out and her jars would break.
    SHERIFF Well, can you beat the women! Held for murder and worryin' about
    her preserves.
100 COUNTY ATTORNEY I guess before we're through she may have something
    more serious than preserves to worry about.
    HALE Well, women are used to worrying over trifles.
    [*The two women move a little closer together.*]
    COUNTY ATTORNEY [*with the gallantry of a young politician*] And yet, for all
    their worries, what would we do without the ladies? [*The women do not
    unbend. He goes to the sink, takes a dipperful of water from the pail and*

pouring it into a basin, washes his hands. Starts to wipe them on the roller
105   *towel, turns it for a cleaner place.*] Dirty towels! [*Kicks his foot against the
       pans under the sink.*] Not much of a housekeeper, would you say, ladies?
       MRS. HALE [*stiffly*]   There's a great deal of work to be done on a farm.
       COUNTY ATTORNEY   To be sure. And yet [*with a little bow to her*] I know there
       are some Dickson county farmhouses which do not have such roller
       towels.

            [*He gives it a pull to expose its full length again.*]

110   MRS. HALE   Those towels get dirty awful quick. Men's hands aren't always as
       clean as they might be.
       COUNTY ATTORNEY   Ah, loyal to your sex, I see. But you and Mrs. Wright were
       neighbors. I suppose you were friends, too.
       MRS. HALE [*shaking her head*]   I've not seen much of her of late years. I've
115   not been in this house—it's more than a year.
       COUNTY ATTORNEY   And why was that? You didn't like her?
       MRS. HALE   I liked her all well enough. Farmers' wives have their hands full,
       Mr. Henderson. And then—
       COUNTY ATTORNEY   Yes—?
120   MRS. HALE [*looking about*]   It never seemed a very cheerful place.
       COUNTY ATTORNEY   No—it's not cheerful. I shouldn't say she had the home-
       making instinct.
       MRS. HALE   Well, I don't know as Wright had, either.
       COUNTY ATTORNEY   You mean that they didn't get on very well?
125   MRS. HALE   No, I don't mean anything. But I don't think a place'd be any
       cheerfuller for John Wright's being in it.
       COUNTY ATTORNEY   I'd like to talk more of that a little later. I want to get the
       lay of things upstairs now.

            [*He goes to the left, where three steps lead to a stair door.*]

       SHERIFF   I suppose anything Mrs. Peters does'll be all right. She was to take
130   in some clothes for her, you know, and a few little things. We left in such a
       hurry yesterday.
       COUNTY ATTORNEY   Yes, but I would like to see what you take, Mrs. Peters,
       and keep an eye out for anything that might be of use to us.
       MRS. PETERS   Yes, Mr. Henderson.

            [*The women listen to the men's steps on the stairs, then look about the
            kitchen.*]

135   MRS. HALE   I'd hate to have men coming into my kitchen, snooping around
       and criticising.

            [*She arranges the pans under sink which the* LAWYER *had shoved out of
            place.*]

       MRS. PETERS   Of course it's no more than their duty.
       MRS. HALE   Duty's all right, but I guess that deputy sheriff that came out to
       make the fire might have got a little of this on. [*Gives the roller towel a
140   pull.*] Wish I'd thought of that sooner. Seems mean to talk about her for
       not having things slicked up when she had to come away in such a hurry.
       MRS. PETERS [*who has gone to a small table in the left rear corner of the room,
       and lifted one end of a towel that covers a pan*]   She had bread set.
            [*Stands still.*]
       MRS. HALE [*Eyes fixed on a loaf of bread beside the bread box, which is on a low
       shelf at the other side of the room. Moves slowly toward it.*]   She was going

to put this in there. [*Picks up loaf, then abruptly drops it. In a manner of*
145   *returning to familiar things.*] It's a shame about her fruit. I wonder if it's all
        gone. [*Gets up on the chair and looks.*] I think there's some here that's all
        right, Mrs. Peters. Yes—here; [*holding it toward the window*] this is cher-
        ries, too. [*Looking again*] I declare I believe that's the only one. [*Gets down,
        bottle in her hand. Goes to the sink and wipes it off on the outside.*] She'll
150   feel awful bad after all her hard work in the hot weather. I remember the
        afternoon I put up my cherries last summer.

> [*She puts the bottle on the big kitchen table, center of the room. With a
> sigh, is about to sit down in the rocking chair. Before she is seated realizes
> what chair it is; with a slow look at it, steps back. The chair which she
> has touched rocks back and forth.*]

MRS. PETERS   Well, I must get those things from the front room closet. [*She
goes to the door at the right, but after looking into the other room, steps
back.*] You coming with me, Mrs. Hale? You could help me carry them.

> [*They go in the other room; reappear,* MRS. PETERS *carrying a dress and
> skirt,* MRS. HALE *following with a pair of shoes.*]

MRS. PETERS   My, it's cold in there.

> [*She puts the clothes on the big table, and hurries to the stove.*]

155   MRS. HALE [*examining the skirt*]   Wright was close.[4] I think maybe that's why
        she kept so much to herself. She didn't even belong to the Ladies Aid. I
        suppose she felt she couldn't do her part, and then you don't enjoy things
        when you feel shabby. She used to wear pretty clothes and be lively, when
        she was Minnie Foster, one of the town girls singing in the choir. But
160   that—oh, that was thirty years ago. This all you was to take in?

MRS. PETERS   She said she wanted an apron. Funny thing to want, for there
        isn't much to get you dirty in jail, goodness knows. But I suppose just to
        make her feel more natural. She said they was in the top drawer in this
        cupboard. Yes, here. And then her little shawl that always hung behind the
165   door. [*Opens stair door and looks.*] Yes, here it is.

> [*Quickly shuts door leading upstairs.*]

MRS. HALE [*abruptly moving toward her*]   Mrs. Peters?

MRS. PETERS   Yes, Mrs. Hale?

MRS. HALE   Do you think she did it?

MRS. PETERS [*in a frightened voice*]   Oh, I don't know.

170   MRS. HALE   Well, I don't think she did. Asking for an apron and her little
        shawl. Worrying about her fruit.

MRS. PETERS [*starts to speak, glances up, where footsteps are heard in the room
        above. In a low voice*]   Mr. Peters says it looks bad for her. Mr. Henderson
        is awful sarcastic in a speech and he'll make fun of her sayin' she didn't
        wake up.

175   MRS. HALE   Well, I guess John Wright didn't wake when they was slipping
        that rope under his neck.

MRS. PETERS   No, it's strange. It must have been done awful crafty and still.
        They say it was such a—funny way to kill a man, rigging it all up like that.

MRS. HALE   That's just what Mr. Hale said. There was a gun in the house. He
180   says that's what he can't understand.

MRS. PETERS   Mr. Henderson said coming out that what was needed for the
        case was a motive; something to show anger, or—sudden feeling.

4. Stingy.

MRS. HALE [*who is standing by the table*]   Well, I don't see any signs of anger around here. [*She puts her hand on the dish towel which lies on the table, stands looking down at table, one half of which is clean, the other half messy.*]
185 It's wiped to here. [*Makes a move as if to finish work, then turns and looks at loaf of bread outside the breadbox. Drops towel. In that voice of coming back to familiar things*] Wonder how they are finding things upstairs. I hope she had it a little more red-up[5] up there. You know, it seems kind of *sneaking*. Locking her up in town and then coming out here and trying to get her own house to turn against her!
190 MRS. PETERS   But Mrs. Hale, the law is the law.
MRS. HALE   I s'pose 'tis. [*Unbuttoning her coat*] Better loosen up your things, Mrs. Peters. You won't feel them when you go out.
[MRS. PETERS *takes off her fur tippet, goes to hang it on hook at back of room, stands looking at the under part of the small corner table.*]
MRS. PETERS   She was piecing a quilt.
[*She brings the large sewing basket and they look at the bright pieces.*]
MRS. HALE   It's log cabin pattern. Pretty, isn't it? I wonder if she was goin' to
195 quilt it or just knot it?
[*Footsteps have been heard coming down the stairs. The* SHERIFF *enters followed by* HALE *and the* COUNTY ATTORNEY.]
SHERIFF   They wonder if she was going to quilt it or just knot it!
[*The men laugh, the women look abashed.*]
COUNTY ATTORNEY [*rubbing his hands over the stove*]   Frank's fire didn't do much up there, did it? Well, let's go out to the barn and get that cleared up.
[*The men go outside.*]
MRS. HALE [*resentfully*]   I don't know as there's anything so strange, our
200 takin' up our time with little things while we're waiting for them to get the evidence. [*She sits down at the big table smoothing out a block with decision.*] I don't see as it's anything to laugh about.
MRS. PETERS [*apologetically*]   Of course they've got awful important things on their minds.
[*Pulls up a chair and joins* MRS. HALE *at the table.*]
205 MRS. HALE [*examining another block*]   Mrs. Peters, look at this one. Here, this is the one she was working on, and look at the sewing! All the rest of it has been so nice and even. And look at this! It's all over the place! Why, it looks as if she didn't know what she was about!
[*After she has said this they look at each other, then start to glance back at the door. After an instant* MRS. HALE *has pulled at a knot and ripped the sewing.*
MRS. PETERS   Oh, what are you doing, Mrs. Hale?
210 MRS. HALE [*mildly*]   Just pulling out a stitch or two that's not sewed very good. [*Threading a needle*] Bad sewing always made me fidgety.
MRS. PETERS [*nervously*]   I don't think we ought to touch things.
MRS. HALE   I'll just finish up this end. [*Suddenly stopping and leaning forward*] Mrs. Peters?
215 MRS. PETERS   Yes, Mrs. Hale?
MRS. HALE   What do you suppose she was so nervous about?

5. Tidied up.

MRS. PETERS   Oh—I don't know. I don't know as she was nervous. I sometimes
sew awful queer when I'm just tired. [MRS. HALE *starts to say something, looks
at* MRS. PETERS, *then goes on sewing.*] Well I must get these things wrapped
220   up. They may be through sooner than we think. [*Putting apron and other
things together*] I wonder where I can find a piece of paper, and string.
MRS. HALE   In that cupboard, maybe.
MRS. PETERS [*looking in cupboard*]   Why, here's a bird-cage. [*Holds it up.*]
Did she have a bird, Mrs. Hale?
225   MRS. HALE   Why, I don't know whether she did or not—I've not been here for
so long. There was a man around last year selling canaries cheap, but I
don't know as she took one; maybe she did. She used to sing real pretty
herself.
MRS. PETERS [*glancing around*]   Seems funny to think of a bird here. But she
must have had one, or why would she have a cage? I wonder what hap-
230   pened to it.
MRS. HALE   I s'pose maybe the cat got it.
MRS. PETERS   No, she didn't have a cat. She's got that feeling some people
have about cats—being afraid of them. My cat got in her room and she was
real upset and asked me to take it out.
235   MRS. HALE   My sister Bessie was like that. Queer, ain't it?
MRS. PETERS [*examining the cage*]   Why, look at this door. It's broke. One
hinge is pulled apart.
MRS. HALE [*looking too*]   Looks as if someone must have been rough with it.
MRS. PETERS   Why, yes.
        [*She brings the cage forward and puts it on the table.*]
240   MRS. HALE   I wish if they're going to find any evidence they'd be about it. I
don't like this place.
MRS. PETERS   But I'm awful glad you came with me, Mrs. Hale. It would be
lonesome for me sitting here alone.
MRS. HALE   It would, wouldn't it? [*Dropping her sewing*] But I tell you what I
245   do wish, Mrs. Peters. I wish I had come over sometimes when *she* was here.
I—[*looking around the room*]—wish I had.
MRS. PETERS   But of course you were awful busy, Mrs. Hale—your house and
your children.
MRS. HALE   I could've come. I stayed away because it weren't cheerful—and
250   that's why I ought to have come. I—I've never liked this place. Maybe
because it's down in a hollow and you don't see the road. I dunno what it
is, but it's a lonesome place and always was. I wish I had come over to see
Minnie Foster sometimes. I can see now—[*Shakes her head.*]
MRS. PETERS   Well, you mustn't reproach yourself, Mrs. Hale. Somehow we
255   just don't see how it is with other folks until—something comes up.
MRS. HALE   Not having children makes less work—but it makes a quiet
house, and Wright out to work all day, and no company when he did come
in. Did you know John Wright, Mrs. Peters?
MRS. PETERS   Not to know him; I've seen him in town. They say he was a
260   good man.
MRS. HALE   Yes—good; he didn't drink, and kept his word as well as most, I
guess, and paid his debts. But he was a hard man, Mrs. Peters. Just to pass
the time of day with him— [*Shivers.*] Like a raw wind that gets to the bone.
[*Pauses, her eye falling on the cage.*] I should think she would 'a wanted a
265   bird. But what do you suppose went with it?

MRS. PETERS   I don't know, unless it got sick and died.

[*She reaches over and swings the broken door, swings it again, both women watch it.*]

MRS. HALE   You weren't raised round here, were you? [MRS. PETERS *shakes her head.*] You didn't know—her?

MRS. PETERS   Not till they brought her yesterday.

270 MRS. HALE   She—come to think of it, she was kind of like a bird herself— real sweet and pretty, but kind of timid and—fluttery. How—she—did— change. [*Silence; then as if struck by a happy thought and relieved to get back to everyday things.*] Tell you what, Mrs. Peters, why don't you take the quilt in with you? It might take up her mind.

275 MRS. PETERS   Why, I think that's a real nice idea, Mrs. Hale. There couldn't possibly be any objection to it, could there? Now, just what would I take? I wonder if her patches are in here—and her things.

[*They look in the sewing basket.*]

MRS. HALE   Here's some red. I expect this has got sewing things in it. [*Brings out a fancy box.*] What a pretty box. Looks like something somebody would
280 give you. Maybe her scissors are in here. [*Opens box. Suddenly puts her hand to her nose.*] Why — [MRS. PETERS *bends nearer, then turns her face away.*] There's something wrapped up in this piece of silk.

MRS. PETERS   Why, this isn't her scissors.

MRS. HALE [*lifting the silk*]   Oh, Mrs. Peters—it's—

[MRS. PETERS *bends closer.*]

285 MRS. PETERS   It's the bird.

MRS. HALE [*jumping up*]   But, Mrs. Peters—look at it! It's neck! Look at its neck! It's all—other side *to.*[6]

MRS. PETERS   Somebody—wrung—its—neck.

[*Their eyes meet. A look of growing comprehension, of horror, Steps are heard outside.* MRS. HALE *slips box under quilt pieces, and sinks into her chair. Enter* SHERIFF *and* COUNTY ATTORNEY. MRS. PETERS *rises.*]

COUNTY ATTORNEY [*as one turning from serious things to little pleasantries*] Well, ladies, have you decided whether she was going to quilt it or knot it?

290 MRS. PETERS   We think she was going to—knot it.

COUNTY ATTORNEY   Well, that's interesting, I'm sure. [*Seeing the birdcage*] Has the bird flown?

MRS. HALE [*putting more quilt pieces over the box*]   We think the—cat got it.

COUNTY ATTORNEY [*preoccupied*]   Is there a cat?

[MRS. HALE *glances in a quick covert way at* MRS. PETERS.]

295 MRS. PETERS   Well, not *now*. They're superstitious, you know. They leave.

COUNTY ATTORNEY [*to* SHERIFF PETERS, *continuing an interrupted conversation*] No sign at all of anyone having come from the outside. Their own rope. Now let's go up again and go over it piece by piece. [*They start upstairs.*] It would have to have been someone who knew just the—

[MRS. PETERS *sits down. The two women sit there not looking at one another, but as if peering into something and at the same time holding back. When they talk now it is in the manner of feeling their way over*

6. Twisted around.

*strange ground, as if afraid of what they are saying, but as if they cannot
help saying it.*]

MRS. HALE   She liked the bird. She was going to bury it in that pretty box.

300 MRS. PETERS [*in a whisper*]   When I was a girl—my kitten—there was a boy
took a hatchet, and before my eyes—and before I could get there—[*covers
her face an instant*] If they hadn't held me back I would have—[*catches
herself, looks upstairs where steps are heard, falters weakly.*]—hurt him.

MRS. HALE [*with a slow look around her*]   I wonder how it would seem never
305 to have had any children around. [*Pause*] No, Wright wouldn't like the bird
— a thing that sang. She used to sing. He killed that, too.

MRS. PETERS [*moving uneasily*]   We don't know who killed the bird.

MRS. HALE   I knew John Wright.

MRS. PETERS   It was an awful thing was done in this house that night, Mrs.
310 Hale. Killing a man while he slept, slipping a rope around his neck that
choked the life out of him.

MRS. HALE   His neck. Choked the life out of him.

[*Her hand goes out and rests on the birdcage.*]

MRS. PETERS [*with rising voice*]   We don't know who killed him. We don't
know.

315 MRS. HALE [*her own feeling not interrupted*]   If there'd been years and years
of nothing, then a bird to sing to you, it would be awful—still, after the
bird was still.

MRS. PETERS [*something within her speaking*]   I know what stillness is. When
we homesteaded in Dakota, and my first baby died—after he was two years
320 old, and me with no other then—

MRS. HALE [*moving*]   How soon do you suppose they'll be through, looking
for the evidence?

MRS. PETERS   I know what stillness is. [*Pulling herself back*] The law has got
to punish crime, Mrs. Hale.

325 MRS. HALE [*not as if answering that*]   I wish you'd seen Minnie Foster when
she wore a white dress with blue ribbons and stood up there in the choir
and sang. [*A look around the room*] Oh, I wish I'd come over here once in a
while! That was a crime! That was a crime! Who's going to punish that?

MRS. PETERS [*looking upstairs*]   We mustn't—take on.

330 MRS. HALE   I might have known she needed help! I know how things can
be—for women. I tell you, it's queer, Mrs. Peters. We live close together
and we live far apart. We all go through the same things—it's all just a different kind of the same thing. [*Brushes her eyes, noticing the bottle of fruit,
reaches out for it.*] If I was you I wouldn't tell her her fruit was gone. Tell
335 her it *ain't.* Tell her it's all right. Take this in to prove it to her. She—she
may never know whether it was broke or not.

MRS. PETERS [*Takes the bottle, looks about for something to wrap it in; takes
petticoat from the clothes brought from the other room, very nervously begins
winding this around the bottle. In a false voice.*]   My, it's a good thing the
men couldn't hear us. Wouldn't they just laugh! Getting all stirred up over
a little thing like a—dead canary. As if that could have anything to do
340 with—with—wouldn't they *laugh!*

[*The men are heard coming down stairs.*]

MRS. HALE [*under her breath*]   Maybe they would—maybe they wouldn't.

COUNTY ATTORNEY   No, Peters, it's all perfectly clear except a reason for doing it. But you know juries when it comes to women. If there was some definite thing. Something to show—something to make a story about—a

345   thing that would connect up with this strange way of doing it—

[*The women's eyes meet for an instant. Enter* HALE *from outer door.*]

HALE   Well, I've got the team around. Pretty cold out there.

COUNTY ATTORNEY   I'm going to stay here a while by myself. [*To the* SHERIFF] You can send Frank out for me, can't you? I want to go over everything. I'm not satisfied that we can't do better.

350   SHERIFF   Do you want to see what Mrs. Peters is going to take in?

[*The* LAWYER *goes to the table, picks up the apron, laughs.*]

COUNTY ATTORNEY   Oh, I guess they're not very dangerous things the ladies have picked out. [*Moves a few things about, disturbing the quilt pieces which cover the box. Steps back.*] No, Mrs. Peters doesn't need supervising. For that matter, a sheriff's wife is married to the law. Ever think of it that

355   way, Mrs. Peters?

MRS. PETERS   Not—just that way.

SHERIFF [*chuckling*]   Married to the law. [*Moves toward the other room.*] I just want you to come in here a minute, George. We ought to take a look at these windows.

360   COUNTY ATTORNEY [*scoffingly*]   Oh, windows!

SHERIFF   We'll be right out, Mr. Hale.

[HALE *goes outside. The* SHERIFF *follows the* COUNTY ATTORNEY *into the other room. Then* MRS. HALE *rises, hands tight together, looking intensely at* MRS. PETERS, *whose eyes make a slow turn, finally meeting* MRS. HALE'S. *A moment* MRS. HALE *holds her, then her own eyes point the way to where the box is concealed. Suddenly* MRS. PETERS *throws back quilt pieces and tries to put the box in the bag she is wearing. It is too big. She opens box, starts to take bird out, cannot touch it, goes to pieces, stands there helpless. Sound of a knob turning in the other room.* MRS. HALE *snatches the box and puts it in the pocket of her big coat. Enter* COUNTY ATTORNEY *and* SHERIFF.]

COUNTY ATTORNEY [*facetiously*]   Well, Henry, at least we found out that she was not going to quilt it. She was going to—what is it you call it, ladies?

MRS. HALE [*her hand against her pocket*]   We call it—knot it, Mr. Henderson.

Curtain.

LUIGI PIRANDELLO

1867–1937

W HEN Pirandello received the Nobel
Prize in Literature in 1934, at the
age of sixty-seven, he was widely known as
the author of intricate philosophical comedies. One in particular, SIX CHARACTERS
IN SEARCH OF AN AUTHOR (1921), had catapulted him onto the international scene
in the early 1920s, leading to acclaimed
performances all over Europe and the
Americas. Like his contemporaries GEORGE
BERNARD SHAW for the English-speaking
world and Maurice Maeterlinck for the
French-speaking world, Pirandello became
the Italian representative of the New
Drama. Pirandello's worldwide success
occurred relatively late in his life, at the
end of a busy writing career that included
hundreds of short stories, dozens of early
plays, and a handful of novels as well as
essays, a dissertation in linguistics, and
several film scripts. Outside Italy, however, Pirandello's name remained tied to
the invention of a new, intellectual drama
thriving on arguments, paradoxes, and
inversions. These plays, of which *Six
Characters* is the best known, apply their
wit to the theater itself, turning actors,
directors, and dramatic authors into the
material from which to fashion outrageous
plots and farfetched conceits. Somehow,
Pirandello managed to transform himself
from an author of local and rather traditional novellas and plays into the most

fashionable and advanced European dramatist of his age.

Luigi Pirandello was born into a
nineteenth-century Sicily where a small
landowning class lorded over impoverished
peasants. It was a society with many lingering feudal structures and a deeply traditional literature and culture to go with it.
Pirandello himself was rather fortunate,
since his father was quite wealthy and was
therefore capable of financing Pirandello's
studies in Rome, his doctorate at the University of Bonn, and his early career as a
writer. Despite his cosmopolitan education, however, Pirandello did not reject
the social values of Sicily and agreed to
an arranged marriage to Antonietta Por-
tulano, the daughter of one of his father's
business partners, whom he barely knew.
His marriage of 1894, business interests,
the sulfur mine—these were the pillars of
Pirandello's life. But they did not last. His
father's fortune and his wife's dowry were
heavily invested in a mine that was flooded
in 1903, and everything was lost. In the
meantime, Pirandello had begun teaching
at a women's college in Rome, an occupation he continued until his international
breakthrough in the early twenties. Just as
the economic foundations of his life crum-
bled, so did the personal ones. His wife was
subject to increasingly pathological fits of
jealousy and other delusional behavior,

and Pirandello retired more and more from social life, maintaining his three children and suffering from an untenable domestic arrangement until Antonietta was eventually committed to a mental institution in 1914.

In the early twentieth century, Pirandello withdrew from life, but he also became a prolific writer of short stories, with which he supplemented his teacher's income. Over the years, he perfected his command of the genre and reissued selected short stories in a collection, *Novellas for a Year* (15 vols., 1922–37), that still enjoys great popularity in Italy. Pirandello's later mastery of drama can be traced back to these works. Like drama, the short story is a genre that requires economy and constraint and is often built around very few scenes and exchanges. Pirandello would frequently recycle his short stories in his dramas, including *Six Characters*.

The world in which Pirandello had grown up had fallen to pieces, but it continued to make itself felt in his literary work. His short stories, novels, and plays often revolve around closed family structures made insufferable by arranged marriages, jealousy, and betrayal. They are set in deeply patriarchal worlds in which women are seen as mothers, virgins, or whores. Even when Pirandello shows the extent to which these roles lead to pathologies, he held on to them to the end. His acclaimed comedies, such as *Six Characters* and *Henry IV* (1922), with their plays-within-the-play, philosophizing characters, and modern structures, contain under their surface the traditional plots of marriage and fertility, jealousy and adultery that are premised on the most traditional of family roles. Pirandello could never quite let go of Sicily—even during his time in Germany, when he studied philology and philosophy at Bonn, he chose as his dissertation subject the Sicilian dialects of his home region.

A similar fascination with Sicily also prompted Pirandello to turn from the short story to drama. After having become acquainted with a Sicilian dialect theater group headed by the charismatic Angelo Musco, Pirandello started writing dialect plays of high passion and melodrama. It was a traditionalist and provincial begin-ning for the future modern dramatist, but it gave him a first taste of the pleasures of the theater, which would come to full fruition in his most successful plays. Musco's group acted in a style reminiscent of the commedia dell'arte, the tradition of improvised theater based on fixed types that are often accentuated with masks. Pirandello continued to use this technique later in his career: for example, in *Six Characters,* where a number of actors wear such masks. Indeed, it was Carlo Goldoni (1707–1793), the playwright most closely associated with commedia dell'arte, rather than HENRIK IBSEN, Shaw, or any of the other modern dramatists, who was Pirandello's favorite playwright. Pirandello's best and best-known dialect play, *Liolà* (1916), whose plot is taken entirely from the first chapters of his novel *The Late Mattia Pascal* (1904), is representative of this phase of his work in that it revolves around fertility, adultery, and the necessity of producing an heir. Yet all these subjects are presented in a particular form of comedy. In a long essay written to qualify for his teaching position, Pirandello had defined humor as the collision of ideals and harsh reality, as a sentiment of contradiction, as a moment when one position merges with its opposite, and as an art of quick reversals and inversions. This theory of humor underlies much of Pirandello's later drama.

Despite some considerable success in the theater, however, Pirandello still viewed it as a secondary art form. He put actors in the same category as illustrators of novels or translators—merely necessary but lamentable vehicles for bringing works of literature to the public. But over time, he became more interested in theatrical representation as well as in modernist forms of literature and drama. The first of his modernist plays, *It Is So! (If You Think So)* (1917), introduced the philosophizing *raisonneur*—a character that comments on the main action of the play, expressing skepticism about the truth of appearances. More important than the validity of this skepticism as a philosophical position is its close relation to Pirandello's theory of humor, which is premised on sudden reversals and quick changes from one appearance to the next. Many of his later plays, including *Six Characters,*

Henry IV, and *Each in His Own Way* (1923), exploit philosophical relativism as a vehicle for a comedy, and they often rely on the figure of the *raisonneur*. Because of the prominence of this figure in many of his plays, Pirandello's works are sometimes considered too theoretical or intellectual, too dependent on words and conceits. But in his most successful plays, Pirandello manages to draw these explanatory figures into the action, exposing their own blindness, missteps, and mistakes. After decades of writing more or less realistic literature set in Sicily and Rome, Pirandello found that the theater formed the perfect setting and subject matter for his art.

The best-known and most cunning of these plays about theater is *Six Characters*. Here Pirandello highlights the difference between the fixed dramatic text and its ever-changing performances by staging a conflict between two groups: a set of characters and the actors who want to impersonate these characters according to the traditions and rules of theatrical representation. Even though the charac-

ters are putatively searching for an author who will write down their story, that story already exists within them. The real conflict breaks out not over how to transform these characters into a play but over how to bring the story that they represent onto the stage. The title, in this sense, is a misnomer, one that can be explained by the history of the play's composition; like many of Pirandello's dramas, it originated as a short story. In fact, it originated as three short stories, all of which featured "characters" appearing before an author and demanding to be turned into literature: "Character" (1906), "A Character's Tragedy" (1911), and "Interview of Characters" (1915). But once this conceit is transported to the theater, characters and actors engage in a struggle over the question of what it means to stage a play. While the characters demand absolute fidelity to their story, the director and the actors recast that story into one suitable for the theater. They simplify the plot, reduce the number of scenes, and do everything necessary for an audience to be able to follow the play.

A production of *Six Characters in Search of an Author* at the Young Vic Theatre, London, 2001. Pictured here are (left to right) Darrel D'Silva as the Director, Liza Sadovy as the Leading Lady, and Dale Rapley as the Leading Man.

Having characters appear onstage as characters and not as full-fledged persons creates a number of interesting problems and conundrums, which Pirandello exploits to the full. Since the story is enclosed inside these characters, they have to tell their story to the director and the actors so that it can be brought to the stage. Most of the narration is done by the father, another version of Pirandello's *raisonneur* figure; he also explains the predicament of the actors, who are caught in their roles and hope to find release through an author. Far from being detached observers, however, these characters, including the father, are fully immersed in their story and therefore lack the capacity to tell it coherently and succinctly. Every time they begin to narrate what happened and how it happened, they "fall into character," as the common theatrical idiom has it—that is, they stop narrating and start feeling and enacting their plight. Indeed, they are entirely trapped inside their story and are forced to live it over and over again. It is only at the very end of the play, after many conflicts between characters and actors, that the audience can surmise that story's contours.

But living the story is one thing, playing it is another. While the characters *feel* their passions, the actors need to *represent* them. The director and the actors in this play argue directly against the common critique of acting as falsifying the author's intentions (a position Pirandello himself had maintained early in his career)—or, more precisely, they prove the necessity of such falsifications in the interest of art. *Six Characters* is thus essentially a play about acting, about theater, about the rules and integrity of theatrical representation. As eccentric and unusual as this piece of metatheater may be, the actual story inside the characters is strikingly traditional. It is precisely the kind of story that had populated Pirandello's earlier works, featuring an adulterous affair, a separation between husband and wife, the threat of incest, and rivalries between stepsiblings, as well as hatred and shame. *Six Characters* is metatheater, but metatheater with a traditional, melodramatic core.

The difference between the unchanging eternal play to which the characters are tied and its variations every time they

relive it on the stage was something Pirandello had absorbed from the Italian critic Adriano Tilgher. Tilgher supplied Pirandello with an aesthetic philosophy, borrowed from such theorists as Henri Bergson (1859–1941) and Friedrich Nietzsche (1844–1900), according to which life is a perpetual chaos onto which the human mind seeks to impose order and form. Art, in Tilgher's view, is the highest imposition of form onto life, connecting the ever-changing with eternal and ideal forms. Pirandello realized that this difference between eternal works of art and ever-changing life corresponded directly to the relation between a fixed literary text and its ever-new performances through live actors. This insight was put into practice most brilliantly in Pirandello's plays about the theater. Some of these metatheatrical pieces—*Six Characters, Each in His Own Way,* and *Tonight We Improvise* (1930)—actually take place in the theater, but many others that draw on the same aesthetic theory do not.

Six Characters, and Pirandello's metatheater more generally, has a more sinister, political side, which is often ignored: it supplied the language in which Pirandello formulated his strong and unwavering allegiance to Benito Mussolini and Italian fascism. Pirandello favored a powerful leader who could stand above the chaos of democratic multiplicity and lead the country with a strong and fatherly hand. In Mussolini he got precisely the leader he was looking for. He met Mussolini in 1923 and immediately began to heap praise on him in the right-wing press, in the precise terms of his aesthetic doctrine—namely, as a strong leader capable of imposing onto the chaos of the nation a single and eternal form. Pirandello thus envisioned Mussolini as the artist of the Italian nation. The playwright who often declared that his art had nothing to do with his politics here treated politics as if it were nothing but an extension of art.

Pirandello's antidemocratic and profascist sympathies were not isolated moments of enthusiasm but were deeply felt. Indeed, he made his strongest gesture of support for fascism at a time of the movement's greatest weakness, after fascist supporters had brutally murdered a socialist member of parliament, Giacomo Matteotti. Rather than being outraged at this level of brutality, as many otherwise sympathetic to fascism were, Pirandello publicly declared his allegiance to the National Fascist Party and finally applied for membership. This political dimension may also account for a somewhat puzzling aspect of Pirandello's work: its violence. Even and especially his most philosophical and metatheatrical plays end with acts of extreme violence; *Six Characters*, for instance, culminates in two sudden deaths, one a suicide. This unexpectedly violent turn in an otherwise talkative and intellectual play corresponds structurally to the fascist doctrine of action: talking is what democracy practices in parliament and it must be ended by pure and bloody acts. It is as if Pirandello felt that his verbose and witty plays likewise needed to be concluded with bloodshed so that mere talking could stop and real action could start.

In addition to Pirandello's genuine attraction to fascism, there was also a mercenary element to his relationship with Mussolini—he hoped that the fascist leader would establish a national theater and place him in charge of it. After his success with *Six Characters*, which received multiple stagings by Europe's most innovative directors, Pirandello founded a theater of his own, the Teatro d'Arte. Although Mussolini never gave sufficient funds to satisfy Pirandello's ambitious plans for a national

theater, he supplied enough to enable Pirandello's theater company to tour Europe and the Americas with *Six Characters* and other plays, thereby functioning, as Pirandello never tired of telling Mussolini, as cultural ambassadors for fascist Italy. These tours also exposed Pirandello to Europe's most innovative directors, such as the Russian Nikolai Evreinov and the Austrian Max Reinhardt, who had perfected new forms of spectacular theater. Indeed, one of Pirandello's last pieces of metatheater set in a theater, *Tonight We Improvise*, contains a parody of Max Reinhardt as a director disrespectful of the playwright and interested only in creating spectacles.

It was during his own work as director and producer that Pirandello in 1925 met the young actress Marta Abba, whom he fell in love with and continued to adore for the rest of his life. It was for her that he wrote his final plays, all of which feature strong female protagonists, such as the utopian *The New Colony* (1928) or his last play, *The Mountain Giants* (1937), a metatheatrical work that features a group of actors and magicians living in a remote mountain region. After a tumultuous life of personal tragedy, political entanglement, and artistic fame, Pirandello ended with a eulogy to the art that he had first rejected but that turned out to be his calling: the theater.   M.P.

Six Characters in Search of an Author[1]

CHARACTERS OF THE PLAY-IN-THE-MAKING

The FATHER
The MOTHER
The SON, aged 22
The STEPDAUGHTER, 18

The BOY, 14
The LITTLE GIRL, 4
(these two last do not speak)
Then, called into being:
MADAM PACE

1. Translated by Eric Bentley.

ACTORS IN THE COMPANY

The DIRECTOR	STAGE MANAGER
(DIRETTORE-CAPOCOMICO)[2]	PROMPTER
LEADING LADY	PROPERTY MAN
LEADING MAN	TECHNICIAN
SECOND ACTRESS	Director's SECRETARY
INGENUE	STAGE DOOR MAN
JUVENILE LEAD	STAGE CREW
Other actors and actresses	

THE PLACE: *The stage of a playhouse.*[3]

When the audience arrives in the theater, the curtain is raised; and the stage, as normally in the daytime, is without wings or scenery and almost completely dark and empty. From the beginning we are to receive the impression of an unrehearsed performance.

Two stairways, left and right respectively, connect the stage with the auditorium. Onstage the dome of the prompter's box[4] has been placed on one side of the box itself. On the other side, at the front of the stage, a small table and an armchair with its back to the audience, for the DIRETTORE-CAPOCOMICO [DIRECTOR].

Two other small tables of different sizes with several chairs around them have also been placed at the front of the stage, ready as needed for the rehearsal. Other chairs here and there, left and right, for the actors, and at the back, a piano, on one side and almost hidden.

As soon as the houselights dim, the TECHNICIAN *is seen entering at the door onstage. He is wearing a blue shirt, and a tool bag hangs from his belt. From a corner at the back he takes several stage braces,[5] then arranges them on the floor downstage, and kneels down to hammer some nails in. At the sound of the hammering, the* STAGE MANAGER *comes running from the door that leads to the dressing rooms.*

STAGE MANAGER   Oh! What are you doing?

TECHNICIAN   What am I doing? Hammering.

STAGE MANAGER   At this hour? [*He looks at the clock.*] It's ten-thirty already. The Director will be here any moment. For the rehearsal.

5 TECHNICIAN   I gotta have time to work, too, see.

STAGE MANAGER   You will have. But not now.

TECHNICIAN   When?

STAGE MANAGER   Not during rehearsal hours. Now move along, take all this stuff away, and let me set the stage for the second act of, um, *The Game of*
10   *Role Playing.*[6]

---

2. Pirandello here combines the modern 20th-century role of director (*direttore* in Italian) with the older position of actor-manager (or "chief actor," *capocomico* in Italian), who fulfilled the function of supervising a theatrical production.

3. The play has neither acts nor scenes. The performance should be interrupted twice; first—without any lowering of the curtain—when the Director and the chief among the Characters retire to put the scenario together and the Actors leave the stage; second when the Technician lets the curtain down by mistake [Pirandello's note].

4. A box in the apron or on the side of a stage, opening toward the actors, that houses someone with a script (sitting below the stage) who is ready to prompt the actors when they forget their lines.

5. Braces used to support a stage set from behind.

6. *Il Gioco delle Parti* (1918), a stage adaptation of Pirandello's own novella.

[*Muttering, grumbling, the* TECHNICIAN *picks up the stage braces and goes away. Meanwhile, from the door onstage, the* ACTORS OF THE COMPANY *start coming in, both men and women, one at a time at first, then in twos, at random, nine or ten of them, the number one would expect as the cast in rehearsals of Pirandello's play "The Game of Role Playing," which is the order of the day. They enter, greet the* STAGE MANAGER *and each other, all saying good-morning to all. Several go to their dressing rooms. Others, among them the* PROMPTER, *who has a copy of the script rolled up under his arm, stay onstage, waiting for the* DIRECTOR *to begin the rehearsal. Meanwhile, either seated in conversational groups, or standing, they exchange a few words among themselves. One lights a cigarette, one complains about the part he has been assigned, one reads aloud to his companions items of news from a theater journal. It would be well if both the Actresses and the Actors wore rather gay and brightly colored clothes and if this first improvised scene [*scena a soggetto*] combined vivacity with naturalness. At a certain point, one of the actors can sit down at the piano and strike up a dance tune. The younger actors and actresses start dancing.*]

STAGE MANAGER [*clapping his hands to call them to order*]   All right, that's enough of that. The Director's here.

[*The noise and the dancing stop at once. The Actors turn and look toward the auditorium from the door of which the* DIRECTOR *is now seen coming. A bowler hat on his head, a walking stick under his arm, and a big cigar in his mouth, he walks down the aisle and, greeted by the Actors, goes onstage by one of the two stairways. The* SECRETARY *hands him his mail: several newspapers and a script in a wrapper.*]

DIRECTOR   Letters?

SECRETARY   None. That's all the mail there is.

15 DIRECTOR [*handing him the script*]   Take this to my room. [*Then, looking around and addressing himself to the* STAGE MANAGER]   We can't see each other in here. Want to give us a little light?

STAGE MANAGER   OK.

[*He goes to give the order, and shortly afterward, the whole left side of the stage where the Actors are is lit by a vivid white light. Meanwhile, the* PROMPTER *has taken up his position in his box. He uses a small lamp and has the script open in front of him.*]

DIRECTOR [*clapping his hands*]   Very well, let's start. [*To the* STAGE MANAGER]

20 Someone missing?

STAGE MANAGER   The Leading Lady.

DIRECTOR   As usual! [*He looks at the clock.*] We're ten minutes late already. Fine her for that, would you, please? Then she'll learn to be on time.

[*He has not completed his rebuke when the voice of the* LEADING LADY *is heard from the back of the auditorium.*]

LEADING LADY   No, no, for heaven's sake! I'm here! I'm here! [*She is dressed all in white with a big, impudent hat on her head and a cute little dog in her arms. She runs down the aisle and climbs one of the sets of stairs in great haste.*]

25 DIRECTOR   You've sworn an oath always to keep people waiting.

LEADING LADY   You must excuse me. Just couldn't find a taxi. But you haven't even begun, I see. And I'm not on right away. [*Then, calling the* STAGE MANAGER *by name, and handing the little dog over to him*] Would you please shut him in my dressing room?

30 DIRECTOR [*grumbling*]   And the little dog to boot! As if there weren't enough
dogs around here. [*He claps his hands again and turns to the* PROMPTER.]
Now then, the second act of *The Game of Role Playing*. [*As he sits down in
his armchair*] Quiet, gentlemen. Who's onstage?

> [*The Actresses and Actors clear the front of the stage and go and sit on
> one side, except for the three who will start the rehearsal and the* LEAD-
> ING LADY *who, disregarding the* DIRECTOR's *request, sits herself down at
> one of the two small tables.*]

DIRECTOR [*to the* LEADING LADY]   You're in this scene, are you?

35 LEADING LADY   Me? No, no.

DIRECTOR [*irritated*]   Then how about getting up, for Heaven's sake?

> [*The* LEADING LADY *rises and goes and sits beside the other Actors who
> have already gone to one side.*]

DIRECTOR [*to the* PROMPTER]   Start, start.

PROMPTER [*reading from the script*]   "In the house of Leone Gala. A strange
room, combined study and dining room."

40 DIRECTOR [*turning to the* STAGE MANAGER]   We'll use the red room.

STAGE MANAGER [*making a note on a piece of paper*]   Red room. Very good.

PROMPTER [*continuing to read from the script*]   "The table is set and the desk
has books and papers on it. Shelves with books on them, and cupboards
with lavish tableware. Door in the rear through which one goes to Leone's

45 bedroom. Side door on the left through which one goes to the kitchen. The
main entrance is on the right."

DIRECTOR [*rising and pointing*]   All right, now listen carefully. That's the main
door. This is the way to the kitchen. [*Addressing himself to the Actor playing
the part of Socrates*] You will come on and go out on this side. [*To the* STAGE

50 MANAGER] The compass at the back. And curtains. [*He sits down again.*]

STAGE MANAGER [*making a note*]   Very good.

PROMPTER [*reading as before*]   "Scene One. Leone Gala, Guido Venanzi,
Filippo called Socrates." [*To the* DIRECTOR] Am I supposed to read the stage
directions, too?

55 DIRECTOR   Yes, yes, yes! I've told you that a hundred times!

PROMPTER [*reading as before*]   "At the rise of the curtain, Leone Gala, wearing a chef's hat and apron, is intent on beating an egg in a saucepan with a
wooden spoon. Filippo, also dressed as a cook, is beating another egg.
Guido Venanzi, seated, is listening."

60 LEADING ACTOR [*to the* DIRECTOR]   Excuse me, but do I really have to wear a
chef's hat?

DIRECTOR [*annoyed by this observation*]   I should say so! It's in the script.
[*And he points at it.*]

LEADING ACTOR   But it's ridiculous, if I may say so.

DIRECTOR [*leaping to his feet, furious*]   "Ridiculous, ridiculous!" What do you

65 want me to do? We never get a good play from France any more, so we're
reduced to producing plays by Pirandello, a fine man and all that, but neither the actors, the critics, nor the audience are ever happy with his plays,
and if you ask me, he does it all on purpose. [*The Actors laugh. And now he
rises and coming over to the* LEADING ACTOR *shouts.*] A cook's hat, yes, my

70 dear man! And you beat eggs. And you think you have nothing more on
your hands than the beating of eggs? Guess again. You symbolize the shell
of those eggs. [*The Actors resume their laughing, and start making ironical*

comments among themselves.] Silence! And pay attention while I explain. [*Again addressing himself to the* LEADING ACTOR] Yes, the shell: that is to say, the empty *form* of reason without the *content* of instinct, which is blind. You are reason, and your wife is instinct in the game of role playing. You play the part assigned you, and you're your own puppet—of your own free will. Understand?

LEADING ACTOR [*extending his arms, palms upward*]   Me? No.

DIRECTOR [*returning to his place*]   Nor do I. Let's go on. Wait and see what I do with the ending. [*In a confidential tone*] I suggest you face three-quarters front. Otherwise, what with the abstruseness of the dialogue, and an audience that can't hear you, good-bye play! [*Again clapping*] Now, again, order! Let's go.

PROMPTER   Excuse me, sir, may I put the top back on the prompter's box? There's rather a draft.

DIRECTOR   Yes, yes, do that.

[*The* STAGE DOOR MAN *has entered the auditorium in the meanwhile, his braided cap on his head. Proceeding down the aisle, he goes up onstage to announce to the* DIRECTOR *the arrival of the Six Characters, who have also entered the auditorium, and have started following him at a certain distance, a little lost and perplexed, looking around them.*

Whoever is going to try and translate this play into scenic terms must take all possible measures not to let these Six Characters get confused with the Actors of the Company. Placing both groups correctly, in accordance with the stage directions, once the Six are onstage, will certainly help, as will lighting the two groups in contrasting colors. But the most suitable and effective means to be suggested here is the use of special masks for the Characters: masks specially made of material which doesn't go limp when sweaty and yet masks which are not too heavy for the Actors wearing them, cut out and worked over so they leave eyes, nostrils, and mouth free. This will also bring out the inner significance of the play. The Characters in fact should not be presented as ghosts but as created realities, unchanging constructs of the imagination, and therefore more solidly real than the Actors with their fluid naturalness. The masks will help to give the impression of figures constructed by art, each one unchangeably fixed in the expression of its own fundamental sentiment, thus:

remorse in the case of the FATHER*; revenge in the case of the* STEP-DAUGHTER*; disdain in the case of the* SON*; grief in the case of the* MOTHER*, who should have wax tears fixed in the rings under her eyes and on her cheeks, as with the sculpted and painted images of the mater dolorosa*[7] *in church. Their clothes should be of special material and design, without extravagance, with rigid, full folds like a statue, in short not suggesting a material you might buy at any store in town, cut out and tailored at any dressmaker's.*

The FATHER *is a man of about fifty, hair thin at the temples, but not bald, thick mustache coiled round a still youthful mouth that is often open in an uncertain, pointless smile. Pale, most notably on his broad forehead: blue eyes, oval, very clear and piercing; dark jacket and light trousers: at times gentle and smooth, at times he has hard, harsh outbursts.*

The MOTHER *seems scared and crushed by an intolerable weight of shame and self-abasement. Wearing a thick black crepe widow's veil, she*

---

7. Grieving mother (Latin); specifically, Mary, mother of Jesus, grieving over the body of her dead son.

[*is modestly dressed in black, and when she lifts the veil, the face does not show signs of suffering, and yet seems made of wax. Her eyes are always on the ground.*

The STEPDAUGHTER, *eighteen, is impudent, almost insolent. Very beautiful, and also in mourning, but mourning of a showy elegance. She shows contempt for the timid, afflicted, almost humiliated manner of her little brother, rather a mess of a* BOX, *fourteen, also dressed in black, but a lively tenderness for her little sister, a* LITTLE GIRL *of around four, dressed in white with a black silk sash round her waist.*

The SON, *twenty-two, tall, almost rigid with contained disdain for the* FATHER *and supercilious indifference toward the* MOTHER, *wears a mauve topcoat and a long green scarf wound round his neck.*]

STAGE DOOR MAN [*beret in hand*]   Excuse me, your honor.

DIRECTOR [*rudely jumping on him*]   What is it now?

90 STAGE DOOR MAN [*timidly*]   There are some people here asking for you.

[*The* DIRECTOR *and the Actors turn in astonishment to look down into the auditorium.*]

DIRECTOR [*furious again*]   But I'm rehearsing here! And you know perfectly well no one can come in during rehearsal! [*Turning again toward the house*] Who are these people? What do they want?

THE FATHER [*stepping forward, followed by the others, to one of the two little stairways to the stage*]   We're here in search of an author.

95 DIRECTOR [*half angry, half astounded*]   An author? What author?

FATHER   Any author, sir.

DIRECTOR   There's no author here at all. It's not a new play we're rehearsing.

STEPDAUGHTER [*very vivaciously as she rushes up the stairs*]   Then so much the better, sir! We can be your new play!

100 ONE OF THE ACTORS [*among the racy comments and laughs of the others*]   Did you hear that?

FATHER [*following the* STEPDAUGHTER *onstage*]   Certainly, but if the author's not here . . . [*To the* DIRECTOR] Unless you'd like to be the author?

[*The* MOTHER, *holding the* LITTLE GIRL *by the hand, and the* BOY *climb the first steps of the stairway and remain there waiting. The* SON *stays morosely below.*]

DIRECTOR   Is this your idea of a joke?

105 FATHER   Heavens, no! Oh, sir, on the contrary: we bring you a painful drama.

STEPDAUGHTER   We can make your fortune for you.

DIRECTOR   Do me a favor, and leave. We have no time to waste on madmen.

FATHER [*wounded, smoothly*]   Oh, sir, you surely know that life is full of infinite absurdities which, brazenly enough, do not need to appear probable, 110 because they're true.

DIRECTOR   What in God's name are you saying?

FATHER   I'm saying it can actually be considered madness, sir, to force oneself to do the opposite: that is, to give probability to things so they will seem true. But permit me to observe that, if this is madness, it is also the 115 *raison d'être* of your profession.

[*The Actors become agitated and indignant.*]

DIRECTOR [*rising and looking him over*]   It is, is it? It seems to you an affair for madmen, our profession?

FATHER   Well, to make something seem true which is not true . . . without
any need, sir: just for fun . . . Isn't it your job to give life onstage to crea-
120   tures of fantasy?

DIRECTOR [*immediately, making himself spokesman for the growing indignation
of his Actors*]   Let me tell you something, my good sir. The actor's profession is a very noble one. If, as things go nowadays, our new playwrights give
us nothing but stupid plays, with puppets in them instead of men, it is our
boast, I'd have you know, to have given life—on these very boards—to
125   immortal works of art.

[*Satisfied, the Actors approve and applaud their* DIRECTOR.]

FATHER [*interrupting and bearing down hard*]   Exactly! That's just it. You
have created living beings—*more* alive than those that breathe and wear
clothes! Less real, perhaps; but more true! We agree completely!

[*The Actors look at each other, astounded.*]

DIRECTOR   What? You were saying just now . . .

130   FATHER   No, no, don't misunderstand me. You shouted that you hadn't time
to waste on madmen. So I wanted to tell you that no one knows better than
you that Nature employs the human imagination to carry her work of creation on to a higher plane!

DIRECTOR   All right, all right. But what are you getting at, exactly?

135   FATHER   Nothing, sir. I only wanted to show that one may be born to this life
in many modes, in many forms: as tree, as rock, water or butterfly . . . or
woman. And that . . . characters are born too.

DIRECTOR [*his amazement ironically feigned*]   And you—with these companions of yours—were born a character?

140   FATHER   Right, sir. And alive, as you see.

[*The* DIRECTOR *and the Actors burst out laughing as at a joke.*]

FATHER [*wounded*]   I'm sorry to hear you laugh, because, I repeat, we carry a
painful drama within us, as you all might deduce from the sight of that lady
there, veiled in black.

[*As he says this, he gives his hand to the* MOTHER *to help her up the last
steps and, still holding her by the hand, he leads her with a certain tragic
solemnity to the other side of the stage, which is suddenly bathed in fantastic light. The* LITTLE GIRL *and the* BOY *follow the* MOTHER; *then the*
SON, *who stands on one side at the back; then the* STEPDAUGHTER *who
also detaches herself from the others—downstage and leaning against the
proscenium arch. At first astonished at this development, then overcome
with admiration, the Actors now burst into applause as at a show performed for their benefit.*]

DIRECTOR [*bowled over at first, then indignant*]   Oh, stop this! Silence please!
145   [*Then, turning to the Characters*] And you, leave! Get out of here! [*To the*
STAGE MANAGER] For God's sake, get them out!

STAGE MANAGER [*stepping forward but then stopping, as if held back by a
strange dismay*]   Go! Go!

FATHER [*to the* DIRECTOR]   No, look, we, um—

DIRECTOR [*shouting*]   I tell you we've got to work!

150   LEADING MAN   It's not right to fool around like this . . .

FATHER [*resolute, stepping forward*]   I'm amazed at your incredulity! You're
accustomed to seeing the created characters of an author spring to life,

aren't you, right here on this stage, the one confronting the other? Perhaps
the trouble is there's no script *there* [*Pointing to the* PROMPTER's *box*] with
us in it?

155 STEPDAUGHTER [*going right up to the* DIRECTOR, *smiling, coquettish*]   Believe
me, we really are six characters, sir. Very interesting ones at that. But lost.
Adrift.

FATHER [*brushing her aside*]   Very well: lost, adrift. [*Going right on*] In the
sense, that is, that the author who created us, made us live, did not wish,
160 or simply and materially was not able, to place us in the world of art. And
that was a real crime, sir, because whoever has the luck to be born a living
character can also laugh at death. He will never die! The man will die, the
writer, the instrument of creation; the creature will never die! And to have
eternal life it doesn't even take extraordinary gifts, nor the performance of
165 miracles. Who was Sancho Panza? Who was Don Abbondio?[8] But they live
forever because, as live germs, they have the luck to find a fertile matrix, an
imagination which knew how to raise and nourish them, make them live
through all eternity!

DIRECTOR   That's all well and good. But what do you people want here?

170 FATHER   We want to live, sir.

DIRECTOR [*ironically*]   Through all eternity?

FATHER   No, sir. But for a moment at least. In you.

AN ACTOR   Well, well, well!

LEADING LADY   They want to live in us.

175 JUVENILE LEAD [*pointing to the* STEPDAUGHTER]   Well, I've no objection, so
long as I get that one.

FATHER   Now look, look. The play is still in the making. [*To the* DIRECTOR]
But if you wish, and your actors wish, we can make it right away. Acting in
concert.

180 LEADING MAN [*annoyed*]   Concert? We don't put on concerts! We do plays,
dramas, comedies!

FATHER   Very good. That's why we came.

DIRECTOR   Well, where's the script?

FATHER   Inside us, sir. [*The Actors laugh.*] The drama is inside us. It *is* us.
185 And we're impatient to perform it. According to the dictates of the passion
within us.

STEPDAUGHTER [*scornful, with treacherous grace, deliberate impudence*]   My
passion—if you only knew, sir! My passion—for him! [*She points to the*
FATHER *and makes as if to embrace him but then breaks into a strident
laugh.*]

FATHER [*an angry interjection*]   You keep out of this now. And please don't
190 laugh that way!

STEPDAUGHTER   No? Then, ladies and gentlemen, permit me. A two months'
orphan, I shall dance and sing for you all. Watch how! [*She mischievously
starts to sing "Beware of Chu Chin Chow" by Dave Stamper, reduced to foxtrot or slow one-step by Francis Salabert:*[9] *the first verse, accompanied by a*

---

8. A rural priest in Alessandro Manzoni's
novel *I Promessi sposi* (*The Betrothed*, 1825–
27). *Sancho Panza:* the servant and companion of the title character in Miguel de
Cervantes' novel *Don Quixote* (1605, 1615).
9. A French music publisher (1884–1946);

his company released numerous recordings of
dance music in the 1920s and 1930s. "Beware
of Chu Chin Chow" (1917), with music by
Dave Stamper (1883–1963) and words by
Gene Buck and Charles Wilmott, was a popular novelty song.

*step or two of dancing. While she sings and dances, the Actors, especially the
young ones, as if drawn by some strange fascination, move toward her and
half raise their hands as if to take hold of her. She runs away and when the
Actors burst into applause she just stands there, remote, abstracted, while the
DIRECTOR protests.*]

ACTORS and ACTRESSES [*laughing and clapping*]   Brava![1] Fine! Splendid!

DIRECTOR [*annoyed*]   Silence! What do you think this is, a night spot? [*Taking the* FATHER *a step or two to one side, with a certain amount of consterna-*
195   *tion*] Tell me something. Is she crazy?

FATHER   Crazy? Of course not. It's much worse than that.

STEPDAUGHTER [*running over at once to the* DIRECTOR]   Worse! Worse! Not
crazy but worse! Just listen: I'll play it for you right now, this drama, and at
a certain point you'll see me—when this dear little thing—[*She takes the*
LITTLE GIRL *who is beside the* MOTHER *by the hand and leads her to the*
200   DIRECTOR.]—isn't she darling? [*Takes her in her arms and kisses her.*]
Sweetie! Sweetie! [*Puts her down again and adds with almost involuntary
emotion.*] Well, when God suddenly takes this little sweetheart away from
her poor mother, and that idiot there—[*Thrusting the* BOY *forward, rudely
seizing him by a sleeve*] does the stupidest of things, like the nitwit that he
205   is, [*With a shove she drives him back toward the* MOTHER] then you will see
me take to my heels. Yes, ladies and gentlemen, take to my heels! I can
hardly wait for that moment. For after what happened between him and
me—[*She points to the* FATHER *with a horrible wink.*] something very intimate, you understand—I can't stay in such company any longer, witnessing
210   the anguish of our mother on account of that fool there—[*She points to the*
SON.] Just look at him, look at him!—how indifferent, how frozen, because
he is the legitimate son, that's what he is, full of contempt for me, for him
[*the* BOY], and for that little creature [*the* LITTLE GIRL], because we three
are bastards, d'you see? Bastards. [*Goes to the* MOTHER *and embraces her.*]
215   And this poor mother, the common mother of us all, he—well, he doesn't
want to acknowledge her as *his* mother too, and he looks down on her,
that's what he does, looks on her as only the mother of us three bastards,
the wretch! [*She says this rapidly in a state of extreme excitement. Her voice
swells to the word: "bastards!" and descends again to the final "wretch,"
almost spitting it out.*]

MOTHER [*to the* DIRECTOR, *with infinite anguish*]   In the name of these two
220   small children, sir, I implore you . . . [*She grows faint and sways.*] Oh,
heavens . . .

FATHER [*rushing over to support her with almost all the Actors, who are astonished and scared*]   Please! Please, a chair, a chair for this poor widow!

ACTORS [*rushing over*]   —Is it true then?—She's *really* fainting?

DIRECTOR   A chair!

[*One of the Actors proffers a chair. The others stand around, ready to
help. The* MOTHER, *seated, tries to stop the* FATHER *from lifting the veil
that hides her face.*]

225   FATHER [*to the* DIRECTOR]   Look at her, look at her . . .

MOTHER   Heavens, no, stop it!

---

1. An Italian exclamation of approval, used when applauding a woman (as *bravo* is used of a
man).

FATHER   Let them see you. [*He lifts her veil.*]

MOTHER [*rising and covering her face with her hands, desperate*]   Oh, sir, please stop this man from carrying out his plan. It's horrible for me!

230   DIRECTOR [*surprised, stunned*]   I don't know where we're at! What's this all about? [*To the* FATHER] Is this your wife?

FATHER [*at once*]   Yes, sir, my wife.

DIRECTOR   Then how is she a widow, if you're alive?

[*The Actors relieve their astonishment in a loud burst of laughter.*]

FATHER [*wounded, with bitter resentment*]   Don't laugh! Don't laugh like
235   that! Please! Just that is her drama, sir. She had another man. Another man who should be here!

MOTHER [*with a shout*]   No! No!

STEPDAUGHTER   He had the good luck to die. Two months ago, as I told you. We're still in mourning as you see.

240   FATHER   But he's absent, you see, not just because he's dead. He's absent—take a look at her, sir, and you will understand at once!—Her drama wasn't in the love of two men for whom she was incapable of feeling anything—except maybe a little gratitude [not to me, but to him]—She is not a woman, she is a mother!—And her drama—a powerful one, very powerful—is in
245   fact all in those four children which she bore to her two men.

MOTHER   *My* men? Have you the gall to say I wanted two men? It was him, sir. He forced the other man on me. Compelled—yes, compelled—me to go off with him!

STEPDAUGHTER [*cutting in, roused*]   It's not true!

250   MOTHER [*astounded*]   How d'you mean, not true?

STEPDAUGHTER   It's not true! It's not true!

MOTHER   And what can you know about it?

STEPDAUGHTER   It's not true. [*To the* DIRECTOR] Don't believe it. Know why she says it? For his sake. [*Pointing to the* SON] His indifference tortures her,
255   destroys her. She wants him to believe that, if she abandoned him when he was two, it was because he [*the* FATHER] compelled her to.

MOTHER [*with violence*]   He did compel me, he did compel me, as God is my witness! [*To the* DIRECTOR] Ask him if that isn't true. [*Her husband*] Make him tell him. [*The* SON] She couldn't know anything about it.

260   STEPDAUGHTER   With my father, while he lived, I know you were always happy and content. Deny it if you can.

MOTHER   I don't deny it, I don't . . .

STEPDAUGHTER   He loved you, he cared for you! [*To the* BOY, *with rage*] Isn't that so? Say it! Why don't you speak, you dope?

265   MOTHER   Leave the poor boy alone. Why d'you want to make me out ungrateful, daughter? I have no wish to offend your father! I told him [*the* FATHER] I didn't abandon my son and my home for my own pleasure. It wasn't my fault.

FATHER   That's true, sir. It was mine.

[*Pause.*]

270   LEADING MAN [*to his companions*]   What a show!

LEADING LADY   And *they* put it on—for us.

JUVENILE LEAD   Quite a change!

DIRECTOR [*who is now beginning to get very interested*]   Let's listen to this, let's listen! [*And saying this, he goes down one of the stairways into the auditorium, and stands in front of the stage, as if to receive a spectator's impression of the show.*]

275 SON [*without moving from his position, cold, quiet, ironic*]   Oh yes, you can now listen to the philosophy lecture. He will tell you about the Demon of Experiment.

FATHER   You are a cynical idiot, as I've told you a hundred times. [*To the* DIRECTOR, *now in the auditorium*] He mocks me, sir, on account of that
280   phrase I found to excuse myself with.

SON [*contemptuously*]   Phrases!

FATHER   Phrases! Phrases! As if they were not a comfort to everyone: in the face of some unexplained fact, in the face of an evil that eats into us, to find a word that says nothing but at least quiets us down!

285 STEPDAUGHTER   Quiets our guilt feelings too. That above all.

FATHER   Our guilt feelings? Not so. I have never quieted my guilt feelings with words alone.

STEPDAUGHTER   It took a little money as well, didn't it, it took a little dough! The hundred lire[2] he was going to pay me, ladies and gentlemen!

[*Movement of horror among the Actors.*]

290 SON [*with contempt toward the* STEPDAUGHTER]   That's filthy.

STEPDAUGHTER   Filthy? The dough was there. In a small pale blue envelope on the mahogany table in the room behind the shop. Madam Pace's [*she pronounces it "Pah-chay"*] shop. One of those Madams who lure us poor girls from good families into their *ateliers* under the pretext of selling *Robes*
295   *et Manteaux*.[3]

SON   And with those hundred lire he was going to pay she has bought the right to tyrannize over us all. Only it so happens—I'd have you know—that he never actually incurred the debt.

STEPDAUGHTER   Oh, oh, but we were really going to it, I assure you! [*She bursts out laughing.*]

300 MOTHER [*rising in protest*]   Shame, daughter! Shame!

STEPDAUGHTER [*quickly*]   Shame? It's my revenge! I am frantic, sir, frantic to live it, live that scene! The room . . . here's the shop window with the coats in it; there's the bed-sofa; the mirror; a screen; and in front of the window the little mahogany table with the hundred lire in the pale blue envelope. I
305   can see it. I could take it. But you men should turn away now: I'm almost naked. I don't blush anymore. It's he that blushes now. [*Points to the* FATHER.] But I assure you he was very pale, very pale, at that moment. [*To the* DIRECTOR] You must believe me, sir.

DIRECTOR   You lost me some time ago.

310 FATHER   Of course! Getting it thrown at you like that! Restore a little order, sir, and let *me* speak. And never mind this ferocious girl. She's trying to heap opprobrium on me by withholding the relevant explanations!

STEPDAUGHTER   This is no place for long-winded narratives!

FATHER   I said—explanations.

2. Equivalent to about $50 today.
3. Dressing gowns and coats (French). *Ateliers:* workshops (French).

315 STEPDAUGHTER   Oh, certainly. Those that suit your turn.

[*At this point, the* DIRECTOR *returns to the stage to restore order.*]

FATHER   But that's the whole root of the evil. Words. Each of us has, inside
him, a world of things—to everyone, his world of things. And how can we
understand each other, sir, if, in the words I speak, I put the sense and value
of things as they are inside me, whereas the man who hears them inevitably
320 receives them in the sense and with the value they have for him, the sense
and value of the world inside him? We think we understand each other but
we never do. Consider: the compassion, all the compassion I feel for this
woman [*the* MOTHER] has been received by her as the most ferocious of
cruelties!

325 MOTHER   You ran me out of the house.

FATHER   Hear that? Ran her out. It *seemed to her* that I ran her out.

MOTHER   You can talk; I can't . . . But, look, sir, after he married me . . . and
who knows why he did? I was poor, of humble birth . . .

FATHER   And that's why I married you for your . . . humility. I loved you for
330 it, believing . . . [*He breaks off, seeing her gestured denials; seeing the impossibility of making himself understood by her, he opens his arms wide in a
gesture of despair, and turns to the* DIRECTOR.] See that? She says No. It's
scarifying, isn't it, sir, scarifying, this deafness of hers, this mental deafness! She has a heart, oh yes, where her children are concerned! But she's
deaf, deaf in the brain, deaf, sir, to the point of desperation!

335 STEPDAUGHTER [*to the* DIRECTOR]   All right, but now make him tell you what
his intelligence has ever done for us.

FATHER   If we could only foresee all the evil that can result from the good we
believe we're doing!

[*At this point, the* LEADING LADY, *who has been on hot coals seeing the*
LEADING MAN *flirt with the* STEPDAUGHTER, *steps forward and asks of the*
DIRECTOR:]

LEADING LADY   Excuse me, is the rehearsal continuing?

340 DIRECTOR   Yes, of course! But let me listen a moment.

JUVENILE LEAD   This is something quite new.

INGENUE   Very interesting!

LEADING LADY   If that sort of thing interests you. [*And she darts a look at the*
LEADING MAN.]

DIRECTOR [*to the* FATHER]   But you must give us *clear* explanations. [*He goes
and sits down.*]

345 FATHER   Right. Yes. Listen. There was a man working for me. A poor man. As
my secretary. Very devoted to me. Understood *her* [*the* MOTHER] very well.
There was mutual understanding between them. Nothing wrong in it. They
thought no harm at all. Nothing off-color about it. No, no, he knew his
place, as she did. They didn't do anything wrong. Didn't even think it.

350 STEPDAUGHTER   So he thought it *for* them. And did it.

FATHER   It's not true! I wanted to do them some good. And myself too, oh
yes, I admit. I'd got to this point, sir: I couldn't say a word to either of them
but they would exchange a significant look. The one would consult the eyes
of the other, asking how what I had said should be taken, if they didn't
355 want to put me in a rage. That sufficed, you will understand, to keep me
continually in a rage, in a state of unbearable exasperation.

DIRECTOR   Excuse me, why didn't you fire him, this secretary?

FATHER   Good question! That's what I did do, sir. But then I had to see that
poor woman remain in my house, a lost soul. Like an animal without a
360   master that one takes pity on and carries home.

MOTHER   No, no, it's—

FATHER   [at once, turning to her to get it in first]   Your son? Right?

MOTHER   He'd already snatched my son from me.

FATHER   But not from cruelty. Just so he'd grow up strong and healthy. In
365   touch with the soil.

STEPDAUGHTER   [pointing at the latter, ironic]   And just look at him!

FATHER   [at once]   Uh? Is it also my fault if he then grew up this way? I sent
him to a wet nurse, sir, in the country, a peasant woman. I didn't find her
[the MOTHER] strong enough, despite her humble origin. I'd married her for
370   similar reasons, as I said. All nonsense maybe, but there we are. I always
had these confounded aspirations toward a certain solidity, toward what is
morally sound. [Here the STEPDAUGHTER bursts out laughing.] Make her
stop that! It's unbearable!

DIRECTOR   Stop it. I can't hear, for Heaven's sake!

> [Suddenly, again, as the DIRECTOR rebukes her, she is withdrawn and
> remote, her laughter cut off in the middle. The DIRECTOR goes down
> again from the stage to get an impression of the scene.]

375   FATHER   I couldn't bear to be with that woman anymore. [Points to the
MOTHER] Not so much, believe me, because she irritated me, and even
made me feel physically ill, as because of the pain—a veritable anguish—
that I felt on her account.

MOTHER   And he sent me away!

380   FATHER.   Well provided for. And to that man. Yes, sir. So she could be free of
me.

MOTHER   And so he could be free.

FATHER   That, too. I admit it. And much evil resulted. But I intended good.
And more for her than for me, I swear it! [He folds his arms across his chest.
385   Then, suddenly, turning to the MOTHER] I never lost sight of you, never lost
sight of you till, from one day to the next, unbeknown to me, he carried you
off to another town. He noticed I was interested in her, you see, but that
was silly, because my interest was absolutely pure, absolutely without ulte-
rior motive. The interest I took in her new family, as it grew up, had an
390   unbelievable tenderness to it. Even she should bear witness to that! [He
points to the STEPDAUGHTER.]

STEPDAUGHTER   Oh, very much so! I was a little sweetie. Pigtails over my
shoulders. Panties coming down a little bit below my skirt. A little sweetie.
He would see me coming out of school, at the gate. He would come and
see me as I grew up . . .

395   FATHER   This is outrageous. You're betraying me!

STEPDAUGHTER   I'm not! What do you mean?

FATHER   Outrageous. Outrageous. [Immediately, still excited, he continues in
a tone of explanation, to the DIRECTOR.] My house, sir, when she had left it,
at once seemed empty. [Points to the MOTHER.] She was an incubus. But she
400   filled my house for me. Left alone, I wandered through these rooms like a
fly without a head. This fellow here [the SON] was raised away from home.
Somehow, when he got back, he didn't seem mine anymore. Without a
mother between me and him, he grew up on his own, apart, without any

relationship to me, emotional or intellectual. And then—strange, sir, but
405 true—first I grew curious, then I was gradually attracted toward *her* family,
which I had brought into being. The thought of *this* family began to fill the
void around me. I had to—really had to—believe she was at peace, absorbed
in the simplest cares of life, lucky to be away and far removed from the
complicated torments of my spirit. And to have proof of this, I would go
410 and see that little girl at the school gate.
STEPDAUGHTER Correct! He followed me home, smiled at me and, when I
was home, waved to me, like this! I would open my eyes wide and look at
him suspiciously. I didn't know who it was. I told mother. And she guessed
right away it was him. [*The* MOTHER *nods.*] At first she didn't want to send
415 me back to school for several days. When I did go, I saw him again at the
gate—the clown!—with a brown paper bag in his hand. He came up to me,
caressed me, and took from the bag a lovely big Florentine straw hat with a
ring of little May roses round it—for me!
DIRECTOR You're making too long a story of this.
420 SON [*contemptuously*] Story is right! Fiction! Literature!
FATHER Literature? This is life, sir. Passion!
DIRECTOR Maybe! But not actable!
FATHER I agree. This is all preliminary. I wouldn't *want* you to act it. As
you see, in fact, she [*the* STEPDAUGHTER] is no longer that little girl with
425 pigtails—
STEPDAUGHTER —and the panties showing below her skirt!
FATHER The drama comes now, sir. Novel, complex—
STEPDAUGHTER [*gloomy, fierce, steps forward*] —What my father's death
meant for us was—
430 FATHER [*not giving her time to continue*] —poverty, sir. They returned, unbeknownst to me. She's so thickheaded. [*Pointing to the* MOTHER] It's true she
can hardly write herself, but she could have had her daughter write, or her
son, telling me they were in need!
MOTHER But, sir, how could I have guessed he felt the way he did?
435 FATHER Which is just where you always went wrong. You could never guess
how I felt about anything!
MOTHER After so many years of separation, with all that had happened . . .
FATHER And is it my fault if that fellow carried you off as he did? [*Turning to
the* DIRECTOR] From one day to the next, as I say. He'd found some job
440 someplace. I couldn't even trace them. Necessarily, then, my interest dwin-
dled, with the years. The drama breaks out, sir, unforeseen and violent, at
their return. When I, alas, was impelled by the misery of my still-living
flesh . . . Oh, and what misery that is for a man who is alone, who has not
wanted to form debasing relationships, not yet old enough to do without a
445 woman, and no longer young enough to go and look for one without
shame! Misery? It's horror, horror, because no woman can give him love
anymore.—Knowing this, one should go without! Well, sir, on the outside,
when other people are watching, each man is clothed in dignity: but, on
the inside, he knows what unconfessable things are going on within him.
450 One gives way, gives way to temptation, to rise again, right afterward, of
course, in a great hurry to put our dignity together again, complete, solid, a
stone on a grave that hides and buries from our eyes every sign of our
shame and even the very memory of it! It's like that with everybody. Only
the courage to say it is lacking—to say certain things.

455 STEPDAUGHTER The courage to do them, though—everybody's got that.

FATHER Everybody. But in secret. That's why it takes more courage to say them. A man only has to say them and it's all over: he's labeled a cynic. But, sir, he isn't! He's just like everybody else. Better! He's better because he's not afraid to reveal, by the light of intelligence, the red stain of shame,
460 there, in the human beast, which closes its eyes to it. Woman—yes, woman—what is she like, actually? She looks at us, inviting, tantalizing. You take hold of her. She's no sooner in your arms than she shuts her eyes. It is the sign of her submission. The sign with which she tells the man: Blind yourself for I am blind.

465 STEPDAUGHTER How about when she no longer keeps them shut? When she no longer feels the need to hide the red stain of shame from herself by closing her eyes, and instead, her eyes now dry and impassive, sees the shame of the man, who has blinded himself even without love? They make me vomit, all those intellectual elaborations, this philosophy that begins
470 by revealing the beast and then goes on to excuse it and save its soul . . . I can't bear to hear about it! Because when a man feels obliged to *reduce* life this way, reduce it all to "the beast," throwing overboard every vestige of the truly human, every aspiration after chastity, all feelings of purity, of the ideal, of duties, of modesty, of shame, then nothing is more con-
475 temptible, more nauseating than his wretched guilt feelings! Crocodile tears!

DIRECTOR Let's get to the facts, to the facts! This is just discussion.

FATHER Very well. But a fact is like a sack. When it's empty, it won't stand up. To make it stand up you must first pour into it the reasons and feelings
480 by which it exists. I couldn't know that—when that man died and they returned here in poverty—she went out to work as a dressmaker to support the children, nor that the person she went to work for was that . . . that Madam Pace!

STEPDAUGHTER A high-class dressmaker, if you'd all like to know! To all
485 appearances, she serves fine ladies, but then she arranges things so that the fine ladies serve *her* . . . without prejudice to ladies not so fine!

MOTHER Believe me, sir, I never had the slightest suspicion that that old witch hired me because she had her eye on my daughter . . .

STEPDAUGHTER Poor mama! Do you know, sir, what the woman did when I
490 brought her my mother's work? She would point out to me the material she'd ruined by giving it to my mother to sew. And she deducted for that, she deducted. And so, you understand, *I* paid, while that poor creature thought she was making sacrifices for me and those two by sewing, even at night, Madam Pace's material!

[*Indignant movements and exclamations from the Actors.*]

495 DIRECTOR [*without pause*] And there, one day, you met—

STEPDAUGHTER [*pointing to the* FATHER] —him, him, yes sir! An old client! Now there's a scene for you to put on! Superb!

FATHER Interrupted by her—the mother—

STEPDAUGHTER [*without pause, treacherously*] —almost in time!—

500 FATHER [*shouting*] No, no, *in* time! Because, luckily, I recognized the girl in time. And I took them all back, sir, into my home. Now try to visualize my situation and hers, the one confronting the other—she as you see her now, myself unable to look her in the face anymore.

STEPDAUGHTER   It's too absurd! But—afterward—was it possible for me to be
505   a modest little miss, virtuous and well-bred, in accordance with those confounded aspirations toward a certain solidity, toward what is morally sound?
FATHER   And therein lies the drama, sir, as far as I'm concerned: in my awareness that each of us thinks of himself as *one* but that, well, it's not true,
each of us is many, oh so many, sir, according to the possibilities of being
510   that are in us. We are one thing for this person, another for that! Already
two utterly different things! And with it all, the illusion of being always one
thing for all men, and always this one thing in every single action. It's not
true! Not true! We realize as much when, by some unfortunate chance, in
one or another of our acts, we find ourselves suspended, hooked. We see, I
515   mean, that we are not wholly in that act, and that therefore it would be
abominably unjust to judge us by that act alone, to hold us suspended,
hooked, in the pillory, our whole life long, as if our life were summed up in
that act! Now do you understand this girl's treachery? She surprised me in
a place, in an act, in which she should never have had to know me—I
520   couldn't be that way for her. And she wants to give me a reality such as I
could never had expected I would have to assume for her, the reality of a
fleeting moment, a shameful one, in my life! This, sir, this is what I feel
most strongly. And you will see that the drama will derive tremendous value
from this. But now add the situation of the others! His . . . [*He points to the*
SON.]
525   SON   [*shrugging contemptuously*]   Leave me out of this! It's none of my
business.
FATHER   What? None of your business?
SON   None. And I *want* to be left out. I wasn't made to be one of you, and
you know it.
530   STEPDAUGHTER   We're common, aren't we?—And he's so refined.—But from
time to time I give him a hard, contemptuous look, and he looks down at
the ground. You may have noticed that, sir. He looks down at the ground.
For he knows the wrong he's done me.
SON   [*hardly looking at her*]   Me?
535   STEPDAUGHTER   You! You! I'm on the streets because of you! [*A movement of
horror from the Actors*] Did you or did you not, by your attitude, deny us—I
won't say the intimacy of home but even the hospitality which puts guests
at their ease? We were the intruders, coming to invade the kingdom of your
legitimacy! I'd like to have you see, sir, certain little scenes between just
540   him and me! He says I tyrannized over them all. But it was entirely because
of his attitude that I started to exploit the situation he calls filthy, a situation which had brought me into his home with my mother, who is also *his*
mother, *as its mistress!*
SON   [*coming slowly forward*]   They can't lose, sir, three against one, an easy
545   game. But figure to yourself a son, sitting quietly at home, who one fine
day sees a young woman arrive, an impudent type with her nose in the air,
asking for his father, with whom she has heaven knows what business; and
then he sees her return, in the same style, accompanied by that little girl
over there; and finally he sees her treat his father—who can say why?—in
550   a very ambiguous and cool manner, demanding money, in a tone that takes
for granted that he *has* to give it, has to, is obligated—
FATHER   —but I *am* obligated: it's for your mother!

SON   How would I know? When, sir, [*To the* DIRECTOR] have I ever seen her? When have I ever heard her spoken of? One day I see her arrive with her
555   [*the* STEPDAUGHTER], with that boy, with that little girl. They say to me: "It's your mother too, know that?" I manage to figure out from her carryings-on [*Pointing at the* STEPDAUGHTER] why they arrived in our home from one day to the next . . . What I'm feeling and experiencing I can't put into words, and wouldn't want to. I wouldn't want to confess it, even to myself. It can-
560   not therefore result in any action on my part. You can see that. Believe me, sir, I'm a character that, dramatically speaking, remains unrealized. I'm out of place in their company. So please leave me out of it all!

FATHER   What? But it's just because you're so—

SON [*in violent exasperation*]   —I'm so what? How would *you* know? When
565   did you ever care about me?

FATHER   *Touché! Touché!* But isn't even that a dramatic situation? This with-drawnness of yours, so cruel to me, and to your mother who, on her return home is seeing you almost for the first time, a grown man she doesn't rec-ognize, though she knows you're her son . . . [*Pointing out the* MOTHER *to*
570   *the* DIRECTOR] Just look at her, she's crying.

STEPDAUGHTER [*angrily, stamping her foot*]   Like the fool she is!

FATHER [*pointing her out to the* DIRECTOR]   And she can't abide him, you know. [*Again referring to the* SON]—He says it's none of his business. The truth is he's almost the pivot of the action. Look at that little boy, clinging
575   to his mother all the time, scared, humiliated . . . It's all because of *him* [*the* SON]. Perhaps the most painful situation of all is that little boy's: he feels alien, more than all the others, and the poor little thing is so morti-fied, so anguished at being taken into our home—out of charity, as it were . . . [*Confidentially*] He's just like his father: humble, doesn't say
580   anything . . .

DIRECTOR   He won't fit anyway. You've no idea what a nuisance children are onstage.

FATHER   But he wouldn't be a nuisance for long. Nor would the little girl, no, she's the first to go . . .

585   DIRECTOR   Very good, yes! The whole thing interests me very much indeed. I have a hunch, a definite hunch, that there's material here for a fine play!

STEPDAUGHTER [*trying to inject herself*]   With a character like me in it!

FATHER [*pushing her to one side in his anxiety to know what the* DIRECTOR *will decide*]   You be quiet!

590   DIRECTOR   [*going right on, ignoring the interruption*]   Yes, it's new stuff . . .

FATHER   Very new!

DIRECTOR   You had some gall, though, to come and throw it at me this way . . .

FATHER   Well, you see, sir, born as we are to the stage . . .

595   DIRECTOR   You're amateurs, are you?

FATHER   No. I say: "born to the stage" because . . .

DIRECTOR   Oh, come on, you must have done some acting!

FATHER   No, no, sir, only as every man acts the part assigned to him—by himself or others—in this life. In me you see passion itself, which—in
600   almost all people, as it rises—invariably becomes a bit theatrical . . .

DIRECTOR   Well, never mind! Never mind about that!—You see, my dear sir, without the author . . . I could direct you to an author . . .

FATHER   No, no, look: you be the author!

DIRECTOR   Me? What are you talking about?

605 FATHER   Yes, you. You. Why not?

DIRECTOR   Because I've never been an author, that's why not!

FATHER   Couldn't you be one now, hm? There's nothing to it. Everyone's doing it. And your job is made all the easier by the fact that you have us—here—alive—right in front of your nose!

610 DIRECTOR   It wouldn't be enough.

FATHER   Not enough? Seeing us live our own drama . . .

DIRECTOR   I know, but you always need someone to write it!

FATHER   No. Just someone to take it down, maybe, since you have us here—in action—scene by scene. It'll be enough if we piece together a rough sketch

615 for you, then you can rehearse it.

DIRECTOR   [tempted, goes up onstage again] Well, I'm almost, almost tempted . . . Just for kicks . . . We could actually rehearse . . .

FATHER   Of course you could! What scenes you'll see emerge! I can list them for you right away.

620 DIRECTOR   I'm tempted . . . I'm tempted . . . Let's give it a try . . . Come to my office. [Turns to the Actors.] Take a break, will you? But don't go away. We'll be back in fifteen or twenty minutes. [To the FATHER] Let's see what we can do . . . Maybe we can get something very extraordinary out of all this . . .

FATHER   We certainly can. Wouldn't it be better to take them along? [He points to the Characters.]

625 DIRECTOR   Yes, let them all come. [Starts going off, then comes back to address the Actors.] Now don't forget. Everyone on time. Fifteen minutes.

[DIRECTOR and Six Characters cross the stage and disappear. The Actors stay there and look at one another in amazement.]

LEADING MAN   Is he serious? What's he going to do?

JUVENILE   This is outright insanity.

A THIRD ACTOR   We have to improvise a drama right off the bat?

630 JUVENILE LEAD   That's right. Like Commedia dell'Arte.[4]

LEADING LADY   Well, if he thinks I'm going to lend myself to that sort of thing . . .

INGENUE   Count me out.

A FOURTH ACTOR   [alluding to the Characters] I'd like to know who those people are.

635 THE THIRD ACTOR   Who would they be? Madmen or crooks!

JUVENILE LEAD   And he's going to pay attention to them?

INGENUE   Carried away by vanity! Wants to be an author now . . .

LEADING MAN   It's out of this world. If this is what the theater is coming to, my friends . . .

640 A FIFTH ACTOR   I think it's rather fun.

THE THIRD ACTOR   Well! We shall see. We shall see. [And chatting thus among themselves, the Actors leave the stage, some using the little door at the back, others returning to their dressing rooms.]

The curtain remains raised. The performance is interrupted by a twenty-minute intermission.

Bells ring. The performance is resumed.

4. A traditional form of Italian comedy featuring stock characters, some in masks, who improvise dialogue.

[*From dressing rooms, from the door, and also from the house, the Actors, the* STAGE MANAGER, *the* TECHNICIAN, *the* PROMPTER, *the* PROPERTY MAN *return to the stage; at the same time the* DIRECTOR *and the Six Characters emerge from the office.*

As soon as the house lights are out, the stage lighting is as before.]

DIRECTOR   Let's go, everybody! Is everyone here? Quiet! We're beginning. [*Calls the* TECHNICIAN *by name.*]

TECHNICIAN   Here!

DIRECTOR   Set the stage for the parlor scene. Two wings and a backdrop with
645   a door in it will do, quickly please!

[*The* TECHNICIAN *at once runs to do the job, and does it while the* DIRECTOR *works things out with the* STAGE MANAGER, *the* PROPERTY MAN, *the* PROMPTER, *and the Actors. This indication of a set consists of two wings, a drop with a door in it, all in pink and gold stripes.*]

DIRECTOR [*to the* PROPERTY MAN]   See if we have some sort of bed-sofa in the prop room.

PROPERTY MAN   Yes, sir, there's the green one.

STEPDAUGHTER   No, no, not green! It was yellow, flowered, plush, and very
650   big. Extremely comfortable.

PROPERTY MAN   Well, we have nothing like that.

DIRECTOR   But it doesn't matter. Bring the one you have.

STEPDAUGHTER   Doesn't matter? Madam Pace's famous chaise longue!

DIRECTOR   This is just for rehearsal. Please don't meddle! [*To the* STAGE MAN-
655   AGER] See if we have a display case—long and rather narrow.

STEPDAUGHTER   The table, the little mahogany table for the pale blue envelope!

STAGE MANAGER [*to the* DIRECTOR]   There's the small one. Gilded.

DIRECTOR   All right. Get that one.

FATHER   A large mirror.

660   STEPDAUGHTER   And the screen. A screen, please, or what'll I do?

STAGE MANAGER   Yes, ma'am, we have lots of screens, don't worry.

DIRECTOR [*to the* STEPDAUGHTER]   A few coat hangers?

STEPDAUGHTER   A great many, yes.

DIRECTOR [*to the* STAGE MANAGER]   See how many we've got, and have them
665   brought on.

STAGE MANAGER   Right, sir, I'll see to it.

[*The* STAGE MANAGER *also hurries to do his job and while the* DIRECTOR *goes on talking with the* PROMPTER *and then with the Characters and the Actors, has the furniture carried on by stagehands and arranges it as he thinks fit.*]

DIRECTOR [*to the* PROMPTER]   Meanwhile you can get into position. Look: this is the outline of the scenes, act by act. [*He gives him several sheets of paper.*] You'll have to be a bit of a virtuoso today.

670   PROMPTER   Shorthand?

DIRECTOR [*pleasantly surprised*]   Oh, good! You know shorthand?

PROMPTER   I may not know prompting, but shorthand . . . [*Turning to a stage-hand*] Get me some paper from my room—quite a lot—all you can find!

[*The stagehand runs off and returns a little later with a wad of paper which he gives to the* PROMPTER.]

DIRECTOR [*going right on, to the* PROMPTER]   Follow the scenes line by line as
675   we play them, and try to pin down the speeches, at least the most important

ones. [*Then, turning to the Actors*] Clear the stage please, everyone! Yes, come over to this side and pay close attention. [*He indicates the left.*]

LEADING LADY   Excuse me but—

DIRECTOR [*forestalling*]   There'll be no improvising, don't fret.

680 LEADING MAN   Then what are we to do?

DIRECTOR   Nothing. For now, just stop, look, and listen. Afterward you'll be given written parts. Right now we'll rehearse. As best we can. With them doing the rehearsing for us. [*He points to the Characters.*]

FATHER [*amid all the confusion onstage, as if he'd fallen from the clouds*] We're rehearsing? How d'you mean?

685 DIRECTOR   Yes, for them. You rehearse for them. [*Indicates the Actors.*]

FATHER   But if we are the characters . . .

DIRECTOR   All right, you're characters, but, my dear sir, characters don't perform here, actors perform here. The characters are there, in the script [*He points to the* PROMPTER's *box.*]—when there is a script!

690 FATHER   Exactly! Since there isn't, and you gentlemen have the luck to have them right here, alive in front of you, those characters . . .

DIRECTOR   Oh, great! Want to do it all yourselves? Appear before the public, do the acting yourselves?

FATHER   Of course. Just as we are.

695 DIRECTOR [*ironically*]   I'll bet you'd put on a splendid show!

LEADING MAN   Then what's the use of staying?

DIRECTOR [*without irony, to the Characters*]   Don't run away with the idea that you can act! That's laughable . . . [*And in fact the Actors laugh.*] Hear that? They're laughing. [*Coming back to the point*] I was forgetting. I must

700 cast the show. It's quite easy. It casts itself. [*To the* SECOND ACTRESS] You, ma'am, will play the Mother. [*To the* FATHER] You'll have to find her a name.

FATHER   Amalia, sir.

DIRECTOR   But that's this lady's real name. We wouldn't want to call her by her real name!

705 FATHER   Why not? If that is her name . . . But of course, if it's to be this lady . . . [*He indicates the* SECOND ACTRESS *with a vague gesture.*] To me she [*the* MOTHER] is Amalia. But suit yourself . . . [*He is getting more and more confused.*] I don't know what to tell you . . . I'm beginning to . . . oh, I don't know . . . to find my own words ringing false, they sound different somehow.

710 DIRECTOR   Don't bother about that, just don't bother about it. We can always find the right sound. As for the name, if you say Amalia, Amalia it shall be; or we'll find another. For now, we'll designate the characters thus: [*To the* JUVENILE LEAD] You're the Son. [*To the* LEADING LADY] You, ma'am, are of course the Stepdaughter.

715 STEPDAUGHTER [*excitedly*]   What, what? That one there is me? [*She bursts out laughing.*]

DIRECTOR [*mad*]   What is there to laugh at?

LEADING LADY [*aroused*]   No one has ever dared laugh at me! I insist on respect—or I quit!

STEPDAUGHTER   But, excuse me, I'm not laughing at you.

720 DIRECTOR [*to the* STEPDAUGHTER]   You should consider yourself honored to be played by . . .

LEADING LADY [*without pause, contemptuously*]   —"That one there!"

STEPDAUGHTER   But I wasn't speaking of you, believe me. I was speaking of
me. I don't see me in you, that's all. I don't know why . . . I guess you're just
725   not like me!

FATHER   That's it, exactly, my dear sir! What is *expressed* in us . . .

DIRECTOR   Expression, expression! You think that's your business? Not at all!

FATHER   Well, but what *we* express . . .

DIRECTOR   But you don't. You don't express. You provide us with raw mate-
730   rial. The actors give it body and face, voice and gesture. They've given
expression to much loftier material, let me tell you. Yours is on such a small
scale that, if it stands up onstage at all, the credit, believe me, should all go
to my actors.

FATHER   I don't dare contradict you, sir, but it's terribly painful for us who
735   are as you see us—with these bodies, these faces—

DIRECTOR [*cutting in, out of patience*]   —that's where makeup comes in, my
dear sir, for whatever concerns the face, the remedy is makeup!

FATHER   Yes. But the voice, gesture—

DIRECTOR   Oh, for Heaven's sake! You can't exist here! Here the actor acts
740   you, and that's that!

FATHER   I understand, sir. But now perhaps I begin to guess also why our
author who saw us, alive as we are, did not want to put us onstage. I don't
want to offend your actors. God forbid! But I feel that seeing myself
acted . . . I don't know by whom . . .

LEADING MAN [*rising with dignity and coming over, followed by the gay young
745   Actresses who laugh*]   By me, if you've no objection.

FATHER [*humble, smooth*]   I'm very honored, sir. [*He bows.*] But however
much art and willpower the gentleman puts into absorbing me into himself . . . [*He is bewildered now.*]

LEADING MAN   Finish. Finish.

[*The Actresses laugh.*]

750   FATHER   Well, the performance he will give, even forcing himself with
makeup to resemble me, well, with that figure [*All the Actors laugh.*] he can
hardly play me as I am. I shall rather be—even apart from the face—what
he interprets me to be, as he feels I am—if he feels I am anything—and not
as I feel myself inside myself. And it seems to me that whoever is called
755   upon to judge us should take this into account.

DIRECTOR   So now you're thinking of what the critics will say? And I was still
listening! Let the critics say what they want. We will concentrate on putting
on your play! [*He walks away a little, and looks around.*] Come on, come on.
Is the set ready? [*To the Actors and the Characters*] Don't clutter up the stage,
760   I want to be able to see! [*He goes down from the stage.*] Let's not lose any
more time! [*To the STEPDAUGHTER*] Does the set seem pretty good to you?

STEPDAUGHTER   Oh! But I can't recognize it!

DIRECTOR   Oh my God, don't tell me we should reconstruct Madam Pace's
back room for you! [*To the FATHER*] Didn't you say a parlor with flowered
765   wallpaper?

FATHER   Yes, sir. White.

DIRECTOR   It's not white. Stripes. But it doesn't matter. As for furniture we're
in pretty good shape. That little table—bring it forward a bit! [*Stagehands
do this. To the PROPERTY MAN*] Meanwhile you get an envelope, possibly a
770   light blue one, and give it to the gentleman. [*Indicating the FATHER*]

PROPERTY MAN   A letter envelope?

DIRECTOR and FATHER   Yes, a letter envelope.

PROPERTY MAN   I'll be right back.

> [*He exits.*]

DIRECTOR   Come on, come on. It's the young lady's scene first. [*The* LEADING
775   LADY *comes forward.*] No, no, wait. I said the young lady. [*Indicating the*
STEPDAUGHTER] You will just watch—

STEPDAUGHTER [*adding, without pause*]   —watch me live it!

LEADING LADY [*resenting this*]   I'll know how to live it too, don't worry, once I
put myself in the role!

780   DIRECTOR [*raising his hands to his head*]   Please! No more chatter! Now,
scene one. The Young Lady with Madam Pace. Oh, and how about this
Madam Pace? [*Bewildered, looking around him, he climbs back onstage.*]

FATHER   She isn't with us, sir.

DIRECTOR   Then what do we do?

785   FATHER   But she's alive. She's alive too.

DIRECTOR   Fine. But where?

FATHER   I'll tell you. [*Turning to the Actresses*] If you ladies will do me the
favor of giving me your hats for a moment.

THE ACTRESSES [*surprised a little, laughing a little, in chorus*]   —What?—Our
790   hats?—What does he say?—Why?—Oh, dear!

DIRECTOR   What are you going to do with the ladies' hats?

> [*The Actors laugh.*]

FATHER   Oh, nothing. Just put them on these coathooks for a minute. And
would some of you be so kind as to take your coats off too?

ACTORS [*as before*]   Their coats too?—And then?—He's nuts!

795   AN ACTRESS OR TWO [*as above*]   —But why?—Just the coats?

FATHER   Just so they can be hung there for a moment. Do me this favor. Will
you?

ACTRESSES [*taking their hats off, and one or two of them their coats, too, continuing to laugh, and going to hang the hats here and there on the coathooks*]
—Well, why not?—There!—This is getting to be really funny!—Are we to
put them on display?

FATHER   Exactly! That's just right, ma'am: on display!

800   DIRECTOR   May one inquire *why* you are doing this?

FATHER   Yes, sir. If we set the stage better, who knows but she may come to
us, drawn by the objects of her trade . . . [*Inviting them to look toward the
entrance at the back*] Look! Look!

> [*The entrance at the back opens, and* MADAM PACE *walks a few paces
> downstage, a hag of enormous fatness with a pompous wig of carrot-
> colored wool and a fiery red rose on one side of it, à l'espagnole,[5] heavily
> made up, dressed with gauche elegance in garish red silk, a feathered fan
> in one hand and the other hand raised to hold a lighted cigarette between
> two fingers. At the sight of this apparition, the* DIRECTOR *and the Actors at
> once dash off the stage with a yell of terror, rushing down the stairs and
> making as if to flee up the aisle. The* STEPDAUGHTER, *on the other hand
> runs to* MADAM PACE—*deferentially, as to her boss.*]

5. Spanish-style (French).

STEPDAUGHTER [*running to her*]   Here she is, here she is!

805 FATHER [*beaming*]   It's she! What did I tell you? Here she is!

DIRECTOR [*overcoming his first astonishment, and incensed now*]   What tricks are these?

[*The next four speeches are more or less simultaneous.*]

LEADING MAN   What goes on around here?

JUVENILE LEAD   Where on earth did she come from?

810 INGENUE   They must have been holding her in reserve.

LEADING LADY   Hocus pocus! Hocus pocus!

FATHER [*dominating these protests*]   Excuse me, though! Why, actually, would you want to destroy this prodigy in the name of vulgar truth, this miracle of a reality that is born of the stage itself—called into being by the stage,
815 drawn here by the stage, and shaped by the stage—and which has more right to live on the stage than you have because it is much truer? Which of you actresses will later re-create Madam Pace? This lady *is* Madam Pace. You must admit that the actress who re-creates her will be less true than this lady—who is Madam Pace. Look: my daughter recognized her, and
820 went right over to her. Stand and watch the scene!

[*Hesitantly, the* DIRECTOR *and the Actors climb back onstage. But the scene between the* STEPDAUGHTER *and* MADAM PACE *has begun during the protest of the Actors and the* FATHER's *answer: sotto voce,*[6] *very quietly, in short naturally—as would never be possible on a stage. When, called to order by the* FATHER, *the Actors turn again to watch, they hear* MADAM PACE, *who has just placed her hand under the* STEPDAUGHTER's *chin in order to raise her head, talk unintelligibly. After trying to hear for a moment, they just give up.*]

DIRECTOR   Well?

LEADING MAN   What's she saying?

LEADING LADY   One can't hear a thing.

JUVENILE LEAD   Louder!

STEPDAUGHTER [*leaving* MADAM PACE, *who smiles a priceless smile, and walking*
825 *down toward the Actors*]   Louder, huh? How d'you mean: louder? These aren't things that can be said louder. *I* was able to say them loudly—to shame him [*Indicating the* FATHER]—that was my revenge. For Madam, it's different, my friends: it would mean—jail.

DIRECTOR   Oh my God! It's like that, is it? But, my dear young lady, in the
830 theater one must be heard. And even we couldn't hear you, right here on the stage. How about an audience out front? There's a scene to be done. And anyway you *can* speak loudly—it's just between yourselves, we won't be standing here listening like now. Pretend you're alone. In a room. The back room of the shop. No one can hear you. [*The* STEPDAUGHTER *charmingly and with a mischievous smile tells him No with a repeated movement of*
835 *the finger.*] Why not?

STEPDAUGHTER [*sotto voce, mysteriously*]   There's someone who'll hear if she [MADAM PACE] speaks loudly.

DIRECTOR [*in consternation*]   Is someone else going to pop up now?

[*The Actors make as if to quit the stage again.*]

---

6. Under the voice (Italian); that is, spoken very softly, under the breath.

FATHER   No, no, sir. She means me. I'm to be there—behind the door—
840   waiting. And Madam knows. So if you'll excuse me. I must be ready for my
entrance. [*He starts to move.*]

DIRECTOR [*stopping him*]   No, wait. We must respect the exigencies of the
theater. Before you get ready—

STEPDAUGHTER [*interrupting him*]   Let's get on with it! I tell you I'm dying
845   with desire to live it, to live that scene! If he's ready, I'm more than ready!

DIRECTOR [*shouting*]   But first we have to get that scene out of you and her!
[*Indicating* MADAM PACE] Do you follow me?

STEPDAUGHTER   Oh dear, oh dear, she was telling me things you already
know—that my mother's work had been badly done once again, the mate-
850   rial is ruined, and I'm going to have to bear with her if I want her to go on
helping us in our misery.

MADAM PACE [*coming forward with a great air of importance*]   Sí, sí, señor,
porque yo[7] no want profit. No advantage, no.

DIRECTOR [*almost scared*]   What, what? She talks like *that?!*
[*All the Actors loudly burst out laughing.*]

855   STEPDAUGHTER [*also laughing*]   Yes, sir, she talks like that—halfway between
Spanish and English—very funny, isn't it?

MADAM PACE   Now that is not good manners, no, that you laugh at me! Yo
hablo[8] the English as good I can, señor!

DIRECTOR   And it *is* good! Yes! Do talk that way, ma'am! It's a surefire effect!
860   There couldn't be anything better to, um, soften the crudity of the situation! Do talk that way! It's fine!

STEPDAUGHTER   Fine! Of course! To have certain propositions put to you in a
lingo like that. Surefire, isn't it? Because, sir, it seems almost a joke. When
I hear there's "an old señor" who wants to "have good time conmigo,"[9] I
865   start to laugh—don't I, Madam Pace?

MADAM PACE   Old, viejo, no. Viejito—leetle beet old, sí, darling? Better like
that: if he no give you fun, he bring you prudencia.[1]

MOTHER [*jumping up, to the stupefaction and consternation of all the Actors,
who had been taking no notice of her, and who now respond to her shouts
with a start and, smiling, try to restrain her, because she has grabbed* MADAM
PACE's *wig and thrown it on the floor*]   Witch! Witch! Murderess! My
daughter!

870   STEPDAUGHTER [*running over to restrain her* MOTHER]   No, no, mama, no,
please!

FATHER [*running over too at the same time*]   Calm down, calm down! Sit
here.

MOTHER   Then send that woman away!

STEPDAUGHTER [*to the* DIRECTOR, *who also has run over*]   It's not possible, not
875   possible that my mother should be here!

FATHER [*also to the* DIRECTOR]   They can't be together. That's why, you see,
the woman wasn't with us when we came. Their being together would spoil
it, you understand.

DIRECTOR   It doesn't matter, doesn't matter at all. This is just a preliminary
880   sketch. Everything helps. However confusing the elements, I'll piece them

7. Yes, yes, yes, Mister, because I . . . (Span-   8. I speak (Spanish).
ish). In Pirandello's original Italian text,   9. With me (Spanish).
Madam Pace mixes Spanish and Italian.   1. Care, caution (Spanish).

together somehow. [*Turning to the* MOTHER *and sitting her down again in her place*] Come along, come along, ma'am, calm down: sit down again.

STEPDAUGHTER [*who meanwhile has moved center stage again. Turning to* MADAM PACE] All right, let's go!

MADAM PACE Ah, no! No thank you! Yo aquí no do nada² with your mother
885 present.

STEPDAUGHTER Oh, come on! Bring in that old señor who wants to have good time conmigo! [*Turning imperiously to all the others*] Yes, we've got to have it, this scene!—Come on, let's go! [*To* MADAM PACE] You may leave.

MADAM PACE Ah sí, I go, I go, go seguramente³ . . . [*She makes her exit furiously, putting her wig back on, and looking haughtily at the Actors who applaud mockingly.*]

890 STEPDAUGHTER [*to the* FATHER] And you can make your entrance. No need to go out and come in again. Come here. Pretend, you're already in. Right. Now I'm here with bowed head, modest, huh? Let's go! Speak up! With a different voice, the voice of someone just in off the street: "Hello, miss."

DIRECTOR [*by this time out front again*] Now look: are you directing this, or
895 am I? [*To the* FATHER *who looks undecided and perplexed.*] Do it, yes. Go to the back. Don't leave the stage, though. And then come forward.

> [*The* FATHER *does it, almost dismayed. Very pale; but already clothed in the reality of his created life, he smiles as he approaches from the back, as if still alien to the drama which will break upon him. The Actors now pay attention to the scene which is beginning.*]

DIRECTOR [*softly, in haste, to the* PROMPTER *in the box*] And you, be ready now, ready to write!

THE SCENE

FATHER [*coming forward, with a different voice*] Hello, miss.
900 STEPDAUGHTER [*with bowed head and contained disgust*] Hello.

FATHER [*scrutinizing her under her hat which almost hides her face and noting that she is very young, exclaims, almost to himself, a little out of complaisance and a little out of fear of compromising himself in a risky adventure*] Oh . . . —Well, I was thinking, it wouldn't be the first time, hm? The first time you came here.

STEPDAUGHTER [*as above*] No, sir.

FATHER You've been here other times? [*And when the* STEPDAUGHTER *nods*]
905 More than once? [*He waits a moment for her to answer, then again scrutinizes her under her hat; smiles; then says*] Well then, hm . . . it shouldn't any longer be so . . . May I take this hat off for you?

STEPDAUGHTER [*without pause, to forestall him, not now containing her disgust*] No, sir, I will take it off! [*And she does so in haste, convulsed.*]

> [*The* MOTHER, *watching the scene with the* SON *and with the two others, smaller and more her own, who are close to her all the time, forming a group at the opposite side of the stage from the Actors, is on tenterhooks as she follows the words and actions of* FATHER *and* STEPDAUGHTER *with varied expression: grief, disdain, anxiety, horror, now hiding her face, now emitting a moan.*]

MOTHER Oh God! My God!

---

2. I do nothing here (Spanish and English).   3. Certainly (Spanish).

FATHER [*is momentarily turned to stone by the moaning; then he reassumes the*
910   *previous tone*]   Now give it to me: I'll hang it up for you. [*He takes the hat
from her hands.*] But I could wish for a little hat worthier of such a dear,
lovely little head! Would you like to help me choose one? From the many
Madam has?—You wouldn't?

INGENUE [*interrupting*]   Oh now, come on, those are *our* hats!

915 DIRECTOR [*without pause, very angry*]   Silence, for Heaven's sake, don't try to
be funny!—This is the stage. [*Turning back to the* STEPDAUGHTER] Would
you begin again, please?

STEPDAUGHTER [*beginning again*]   No, thank you, sir.

FATHER   Oh, come on now, don't say no. Accept one from me. To please
920   me . . . There are some lovely ones you know. And we would make Madam
happy. Why else does she put them on display?

STEPDAUGHTER   No, no, sir, look: I wouldn't even be able to wear it.

FATHER   You mean because of what the family would think when they saw
you come home with a new hat on? Think nothing of it. Know how to han-
925   dle that? What to tell them at home?

STEPDAUGHTER [*breaking out, at the end of her rope*]   But that's not why, sir. I
couldn't wear it because I'm . . . as you see me. You might surely have
noticed! [*Points to her black attire.*]

FATHER   In mourning, yes. Excuse me. It's true: I do see it. I beg your par-
930   don. I'm absolutely mortified, believe me.

STEPDAUGHTER [*forcing herself and plucking up courage to conquer her contempt and nausea*]   Enough! Enough! It's for me to thank you, it is not for
you to be mortified or afflicted. Please pay no more attention to what I
said. Even for me, you understand . . . [*She forces herself to smile and adds*]
I need to forget I am dressed like this.

DIRECTOR [*interrupting, addressing himself to the* PROMPTER *in his box, and
935   going up onstage again*]   Wait! Wait! Don't write. Leave that last sentence
out, leave it out! [*Turning to the* FATHER *and* STEPDAUGHTER] It's going very
well indeed. [*Then to the* FATHER *alone*] This is where you go into the part
we prepared. [*To the Actors*] Enchanting, that little hat scene, don't you
agree?

940 STEPDAUGHTER   Oh, but the best is just coming. Why aren't we continuing?

DIRECTOR   Patience one moment. [*Again addressing himself to the Actors*]
Needs rather delicate handling, of course . . .

LEADING MAN   —With a certain *ease*—

LEADING LADY   Obviously. But there's nothing to it. [*To the* LEADING MAN] We
945   can rehearse it at once, can't we?

LEADING MAN   As far as I'm . . . Very well, I'll go out and make my entrance.
[*And he does go out by the back door, ready to reenter.*]

DIRECTOR [*to the* LEADING LADY]   And so, look, your scene with that Madam
Pace is over. I'll write it up later. You are standing . . . Hey, where are you
going?

950 LEADING LADY   Wait. I'm putting my hat back on . . . [*She does so, taking the
hat from the hook.*]

DIRECTOR   Oh yes, good.—Now, you're standing here with your head bowed.

STEPDAUGHTER [*amused*]   But she's not wearing black!

LEADING LADY   *I shall* wear black! And I'll carry it better than you!

DIRECTOR [*to the* STEPDAUGHTER]   Keep quiet, please! Just watch. You can
learn something. [*Claps his hands.*] Get going, get going! The entrance!
[*And he goes back out front to get an impression of the stage.*]

    [*The door at the back opens, and the* LEADING MAN *comes forward, with
the relaxed, waggish manner of an elderly Don Juan.*[4] *From the first
speeches, the performance of the scene by the Actors is quite a different
thing, without, however, having any element of parody in it—rather, it
seems corrected, set to rights. Naturally, the* STEPDAUGHTER *and the*
FATHER, *being quite unable to recognize themselves in this* LEADING LADY
and LEADING MAN *but hearing them speak their own words express in
various ways, now with gestures, now with smiles, now with open protests, their surprise, their wonderment, their suffering, etc., as will be
seen forthwith.*

    The PROMPTER's *voice is clearly heard from the box.*]

LEADING MAN   Hello, miss.

FATHER [*without pause, unable to contain himself*]   No, no!

    [*The* STEPDAUGHTER, *seeing how the* LEADING MAN *makes his entrance,
has burst out laughing.*]

DIRECTOR [*coming from the proscenium, furious*]   Silence here! And stop that
laughing at once! We can't go ahead till it stops.

STEPDAUGHTER [*coming from the proscenium*]   How can I help it? This lady
[*the* LEADING LADY] just stands there. If she's supposed to be me, let me tell
you that if anyone said hello to me in that manner and that tone of voice,
I'd burst out laughing just as I actually did!

FATHER [*coming forward a little too*]   That's right . . . the manner, the tone . . .

DIRECTOR   Manner! Tone! Stand to one side now, and let me see the
rehearsal.

LEADING MAN [*coming forward*]   If I'm to play an old man entering a house of
ill—

DIRECTOR   Oh, pay no attention, please. Just begin again. It was going fine.
[*Waiting for the Actor to resume*] Now then . . .

LEADING MAN   Hello, miss.

LEADING LADY   Hello.

LEADING MAN [*re-creating the* FATHER's *gesture of scrutinizing her under her
hat, but then expressing very distinctly first the complaisance and then the
fear*]   Oh . . . Well . . . I was thinking it wouldn't be the first time, I
hope . . .

FATHER [*unable to help correcting him*]   Not "I hope." "Would it?" "Would
it?"

DIRECTOR   He says: "would it?" A question.

LEADING MAN [*pointing to the* PROMPTER]   I heard: "I hope."

DIRECTOR   Same thing! "Would it." Or: "I hope." Continue, continue.—Now,
maybe a bit less affected . . . Look, I'll do it for you. Watch me . . . [*Returns
to the stage, then repeats the bit since the entrance*]—Hello, miss.

LEADING LADY   Hello.

DIRECTOR   Oh, well . . . I was thinking . . . [*Turning to the* LEADING MAN *to have
him note how he has looked at the* LEADING LADY *under her hat*] Surprise . . .

---

4. That is, a great lover or seducer of women (from the legendary Spaniard of that name).

fear and complaisance. [*Then, going on, and turning to the* LEADING LADY] It
985 wouldn't be the first time, would it? The first time you came here. [*Again
turning to the* LEADING MAN *with an inquiring look*] Clear? [*To the* LEADING
LADY] Then you say: No, sir. [*Back to the* LEADING MAN] How shall I put it?
Plasticity! [*Goes back out front.*]

LEADING LADY No, sir.

LEADING MAN You came here other times? More than once?

990 DIRECTOR No, no, wait. [*Indicating the* LEADING LADY] First let her nod. "You
came here other times?"

        [*The* LEADING LADY *raises her head a little, closes her eyes painfully as if
in disgust, then nods twice at the word "Down" from the* DIRECTOR.]

STEPDAUGHTER [*involuntarily*] Oh, my God! [*And she at once puts her hand
on her mouth to keep the laughter in.*]

DIRECTOR [*turning round*] What is it?

STEPDAUGHTER [*without pause*] Nothing, nothing.

995 DIRECTOR [*to the* LEADING MAN That's your cue. Go straight on.

LEADING MAN More than once? Well then, hm . . . it shouldn't any longer be
so . . . May I take this little hat off for you?

        [*The* LEADING MAN *says this last speech in such a tone and accompanies
it with such a gesture that the* STEPDAUGHTER, *her hands on her mouth,
much as she wants to hold herself in, cannot contain her laughter, which
comes bursting out through her fingers irresistibly and very loud.*]

LEADING LADY [*returning to her place, enraged*] Now look, I'm not going to
be made a clown of by that person!

1000 LEADING MAN Nor am I. Let's stop.

DIRECTOR [*to the* STEPDAUGHTER, *roaring*] Stop it! Stop it!

STEPDAUGHTER Yes, yes. Forgive me, forgive me . . .

DIRECTOR You have no manners! You're presumptuous! So there!

FATHER [*seeking to intervene*] That's true, yes, that's true, sir, but
forgive . . .

1005 DIRECTOR [*onstage again*] Forgive nothing! It's disgusting!

FATHER Yes, sir. But believe me, it has such a strange effect—

DIRECTOR Strange? Strange? What's strange about it?

FATHER I admire your actors, sir, I really admire them, this gentleman
[LEADING MAN] and that lady [LEADING LADY] but assuredly . . . well, they're
1010 not us . . .

DIRECTOR So what? How *could* they be you, if they're the actors?

FATHER Exactly, the actors! And they play our parts well, both of them. But
of course, to us, they seem something else—that tries to be the same but
simply isn't!

1015 DIRECTOR How d'you mean: isn't? What is it then?

FATHER Something that . . . becomes theirs. And stops being ours.

DIRECTOR Necessarily! I explained that to you!

FATHER Yes. I understand, I do under—

DIRECTOR Then that will be enough! [*Turning to the Actors*] We'll be rehears-
1020 ing by ourselves as we usually do. Rehearsing with authors present has
always been hell, in my experience. There's no satisfying them. [*Turning to
the* FATHER *and the* STEPDAUGHTER] Come along then. Let's resume. And
let's hope you find it possible not to laugh this time.

STEPDAUGHTER   Oh, no, I won't be laughing this time around. My big
1025   moment comes up now. Don't worry!

DIRECTOR   Very well, when she says: "Please pay no more attention to what I
said . . . Even for me—you understand . . ." [*Turning to the* FATHER] You'll
have to cut right in with: "I understand, oh yes, I understand . . ." and ask
her right away—

1030   STEPDAUGHTER [*interrupting*]   Oh? Ask me what?

DIRECTOR   —why she is in mourning.

STEPDAUGHTER   No, no, look: when I told him I needed to forget I was
dressed like this, do you know what his answer was? "Oh, good! Then let's
take that little dress right off, shall we?"

1035   DIRECTOR   Great! Terrific! It'll knock 'em right out of their seats!

STEPDAUGHTER   But it's the truth.

DIRECTOR   Truth, is it? Well, well, well. This is the theater! Our motto is:
truth up to a certain point!

STEPDAUGHTER   Then what would you propose?

1040   DIRECTOR   You'll see. You'll see it. Just leave me alone.

STEPDAUGHTER   Certainly not. From my nausea—from all the reasons one
more cruel than another why I am what I am, why I am "that one there"—
you'd like to cook up some romantic, sentimental concoction, wouldn't
you? He asks me why I'm in mourning, and I tell him, through my tears,
1045   that Papa died two months ago! No, my dear sir! He has to say what he did
say: "Then let's take that little dress right off, shall we?" And I, with my
two-months mourning in my heart, went back there—you see? behind that
screen—and—my fingers quivering with shame, with loathing—I took off
my dress, took off my corset . . .

1050   DIRECTOR [*running his hands through his hair*]   Good God, what are you
saying?

STEPDAUGHTER [*shouting frantically*]   The truth, sir, the truth!

DIRECTOR   Well, yes, of course, that must be the truth . . . and I quite understand your horror, young lady. Would you try to understand that all that is
1055   impossible *on the stage?*

STEPDAUGHTER   Impossible? Then, thanks very much, I'm leaving.

DIRECTOR   No, no, look . . .

STEPDAUGHTER   I'm leaving, I'm leaving! You went in that room, you two, didn't
you, and figured out "what is possible on the stage"? Thanks very much. I see
1060   it all. He wants to skip to the point where he can act out his [*Exaggerating*]
spiritual travail! But I want to play *my* drama. Mine!

DIRECTOR [*annoyed, and shrugging haughtily*]   Oh well, *your* drama. This is
not just your drama, if I may say so. How about the drama of the others?
His drama [*the* FATHER], hers [*the* MOTHER]? We can't let one character hog
1065   the limelight, just taking the whole stage over, and overshadowing all the
others! Everything must be placed within the frame of one harmonious
picture! We must perform only what is performable! I know as well as you
do that each of us has a whole life of his own inside him and would like to
bring it all out. But the difficult thing is this: to bring out only as much as
1070   is needed—in relation to the others—and in this to *imply* all the rest, *suggest* what remains inside! Oh, it would be nice if every character could
come down to the footlights and tell the audience just what is brewing

inside him—in a fine monologue or, if you will, a lecture! [*Good-natured, conciliatory*] Miss, you will have to *contain yourself*. And it will be in your
1075 interest. It could make a bad impression—let me warn you—this tearing fury, this desperate disgust—since, if I may say so, you confessed having been with others at Madam Pace's—before him—more than once!

STEPDAUGHTER [*lowering her head, pausing to recollect, a deeper note in her voice*] It's true. But to me the others are also *him*, all of them equally!

DIRECTOR [*not getting it*] The others? How d'you mean?

1080 STEPDAUGHTER People "go wrong." And wrong follows on the heels of wrong. Who is responsible, if not whoever it was who first brought them down? Isn't that always the case? And for me that is him. Even before I was born. Look at him, and see if it isn't so.

DIRECTOR Very good. And if he has so much to feel guilty about, can't you
1085 appreciate how it must weigh him down? So let's at least permit him to act it out.

STEPDAUGHTER And how, may I ask, how could he act out all that "noble" guilt, all those so "moral" torments, if you propose to spare him the horror of one day finding in his arms—after having bade her take off the black
1090 clothes that marked her recent loss—a woman now, and already gone wrong—that little girl, sir, that little girl whom he used to go watch coming out of school?

[*She says these last words in a voice trembling with emotion. The* MOTHER, *hearing her say this, overcome with uncontrollable anguish, which comes out first in suffocated moans and subsequently bursts out in bitter weeping. The emotion takes hold of everyone. Long pause.*]

STEPDAUGHTER [*as soon as the* MOTHER *gives signs of calming down, somber, determined*] We're just among ourselves now. Still unknown to the public. Tomorrow you will make of us the show you have in mind. You will put
1095 it together in your way. But would you like to really see—our drama? Have it explode—the real thing?

DIRECTOR Of course. Nothing I'd like better. And I'll use as much of it as I possibly can!

STEPDAUGHTER Very well. Have this Mother here go out.

1100 MOTHER [*ceasing to weep, with a loud cry*] No, no! Don't allow this, don't allow it!

DIRECTOR I only want to take a look, ma'am.

MOTHER I can't, I just can't!

DIRECTOR But if it's already happened? Excuse me but I just don't get it.

1105 MOTHER No, no, it's happening now. It's always happening. My torment is not a pretense! I am alive and present—always, in every moment of my torment—it keeps renewing itself, it too is alive and always present. But those two little ones over there—have you heard them speak? They cannot speak, sir, not anymore! They still keep clinging to me—to keep my tor-
1110 ment alive and present. For themselves they don't exist, don't exist any longer. And she [*the* STEPDAUGHTER], she just fled, ran away from me, she's lost, lost . . . . If I see her before me now, it's for the same reason: to renew the torment, keep it always alive and present forever—the torment I've suffered on her account too—forever!

1115 FATHER [*solemn*] The eternal moment, sir, as I told you. She [*the* STEP-DAUGHTER] is here to catch me, fix me, hold me there in the pillory, hanging there forever, hooked, in that single fleeting shameful moment of my life! She cannot give it up. And, actually, sir, *you* cannot spare me.

DIRECTOR   But I didn't say I wouldn't use that. On the contrary, it will be the
1120   nucleus of the whole first act. To the point where she [*the* MOTHER] surprises you.

FATHER   Yes, exactly. Because that is the sentence passed upon me: all our passion which has to culminate in her [*the* MOTHER's] final cry!

STEPDAUGHTER   It still rings in my ears. It's driven me out of my mind, that
1125   cry!—You can present me as you wish, sir, it doesn't matter. Even dressed. As long as at least my arms—just my arms—are bare. Because it was like this. [*She goes to the* FATHER *and rests her head on his chest.*] I was standing like this with my head on his chest and my arms round his neck like this. Then I saw something throbbing right here on my arm. A vein. Then, as if
1130   it was just this living vein that disgusted me, I jammed my eyes shut, like this, d'you see? and buried my head on his chest. [*Turning to the* MOTHER] Scream, scream, mama! [*Buries her head on the* FATHER's *chest and with her shoulders raised as if to avoid hearing the scream she adds in a voice stifled with torment.*] Scream as you screamed then!

MOTHER   [*rushing forward to part them*]   No! My daughter! My daughter!
1135   [*Having pulled her from him*] Brute! Brute! It's my daughter, don't you see—my daughter!

DIRECTOR   [*the outburst having sent him reeling to the footlights, while the Actors show dismay*]   Fine! Splendid! And now: curtain, curtain!

FATHER   [*running to him, convulsed*]   Right! Yes! Because that, sir, is how it actually was!

1140   DIRECTOR   [*in admiration and conviction*]   Yes, yes, of course! Curtain! Curtain!

     [*Hearing this repeated cry of the* DIRECTOR, *the* TECHNICIAN *lets down the curtain, trapping the* DIRECTOR *and the* FATHER *between curtain and footlights.*]

DIRECTOR   [*looking up, with raised arms*]   What an idiot! I say Curtain, meaning that's how the act should end, and they let down the actual curtain! [*He lifts a corner of the curtain so he can get back onstage. To the* FATHER]
1145   Yes, yes, fine, splendid! Absolutely surefire! Has to end that way. I can vouch for the first act. [*Goes behind the curtain with the* FATHER.]

     [*When the curtain rises we see that the stagehands have struck that first "indication of a set," and have put onstage in its stead a small garden fountain. On one side of the stage, the Actors are sitting in a row, and on the other are the Characters. The* DIRECTOR *is standing in the middle of the stage, in the act of meditating with one hand, fist clenched, on his mouth.*]

DIRECTOR   [*shrugging after a short pause*]   Yes, well then, let's get to the second act. Just leave it to me as we agreed beforehand and everything will be all right.

1150   STEPDAUGHTER   Our entrance into his house [*the* FATHER] in spite of him [*the* SON].

DIRECTOR   [*losing patience*]   Very well. But leave it all to me, I say.

STEPDAUGHTER   In spite of him. Just let that be clear.

MOTHER   [*shaking her head from her corner*]   For all the good that's come out of it . . .

1155 STEPDAUGHTER [*turning quickly on her*] It doesn't matter. The more damage to us, the more guilt feelings for him.

DIRECTOR [*still out of patience*] I understand, I understand. All this will be taken into account, especially at the beginning. Rest assured.

MOTHER [*supplicatingly*] Do make them understand, I beg you, sir, for my
1160 conscience' sake, for I tried in every possible way—

STEPDAUGHTER [*continuing her* MOTHER's *speech, contemptuously*] To placate me, to advise me not to give him trouble. [*To the* DIRECTOR] Do what she wants, do it because it's true. I enjoy the whole thing very much because, look: the more she plays the suppliant and tries to gain entrance
1165 into his heart, the more he holds himself aloof: he's an absentee! How I relish this!

DIRECTOR We want to get going—on the second act, don't we?

STEPDAUGHTER I won't say another word. But to play it all in the garden, as you want to, won't be possible.

1170 DIRECTOR Why won't it be possible?

STEPDAUGHTER Because he [*the* SON] stays shut up in his room, on his own. Then again we need the house for the part about this poor bewildered little boy, as I told you.

DIRECTOR Quite right. But on the other hand, we can't change the scenery
1175 in view of the audience three or four times in one act, nor can we stick up signs—

LEADING MAN They used to at one time . . .

DIRECTOR Yes, when the audiences were about as mature as that little girl.

LEADING LADY They got the illusion more easily.

1180 FATHER [*suddenly, rising*] The illusion, please don't say illusion! Don't use that word! It's especially cruel to us.

DIRECTOR [*astonished*] And why, if I may ask?

FATHER Oh yes, cruel, cruel! You should understand that.

DIRECTOR What word would you have us use anyway? The illusion of creat-
1185 ing here for our spectators—

LEADING MAN —By our performance—

DIRECTOR —the illusion of a reality.

FATHER I understand, sir, but perhaps you do not understand us. Because, you see, for you and for your actors all this—quite rightly—is a game—

1190 LEADING LADY [*indignantly interrupting*] Game! We are not children, sir. We act in earnest.

FATHER I don't deny it. I just mean the game of your art which, as this gentleman rightly says, must provide a perfect illusion of reality.

DIRECTOR Yes, exactly.

1195 FATHER But consider this. We [*He quickly indicates himself and the other five Characters.*], we have no reality outside this illusion.

DIRECTOR [*astonished, looking at his Actors who remain bewildered and lost*] And that means?

FATHER [*after observing them briefly, with a pale smile*] Just that, ladies and gentlemen. How should we have any other reality? What for you is an illu-
1200 sion, to be created, is for us our unique reality. [*Short pause. He takes several short steps toward the* DIRECTOR, *and adds*] But not for us alone, of course. Think a moment. [*He looks into his eyes.*] Can you tell me who you are? [*And he stands there pointing his first finger at him.*]

DIRECTOR [*upset, with a half-smile*] How do you mean, who I am? I am I.

1205 FATHER   And if I told you that wasn't true because you are me?

DIRECTOR   I would reply that you are out of your mind. [*The Actors laugh.*]

FATHER   You are right to laugh: because this is a game. [*To the* DIRECTOR] And you can object that it's only in a game that that gentleman there [LEADING MAN], who is himself, must be me, who am *myself*. I've caught

1210 you in a trap, do you see that?

[*Actors start laughing again.*]

DIRECTOR [*annoyed*]   You said all this before. Why repeat it?

FATHER   I won't—I didn't intend to say that. I'm inviting you to emerge from this game. [*He looks at the* LEADING LADY *as if to forestall what she might say.*] This game of art which you are accustomed to play here with your

1215 actors. Let me again ask quite seriously: Who are you?

DIRECTOR [*turning to the Actors, amazed and at the same time irritated*]   The gall of this fellow! Calls himself a character and comes here to ask me who I am!

FATHER [*dignified, but not haughty*]   A character, sir, can always ask a man

1220 who he is. Because a character really has his own life, marked with his own characteristics, by virtue of which he is always someone. Whereas, a man— I'm not speaking of you now—*a man* can be no one.

DIRECTOR   Oh sure. But you are asking me! And I am the manager, understand?

1225 FATHER [*quite softly with mellifluous modesty*]   Only in order to know, sir, if you as you now are see yourself . . . for example, at a distance in time. Do you see the man you once were, with all the illusions you had then, with everything, inside you and outside, as it seemed then—as it was then for you?—Well sir, thinking back to those illusions which you don't have anymore, to all those

1230 things which no longer seem to be what at one time they were for you, don't you feel, not just the boards of this stage, but the very earth beneath slipping away from you? For will not all that you feel yourself to be now, your whole reality of today, as it is now, inevitably seem an illusion tomorrow?

DIRECTOR [*who has not followed exactly, but has been staggered by the plausi-bilities of the argument*]   Well, well, what do you want to prove?

1235 FATHER   Oh nothing, sir. I just wanted to make you see that if *we* [*pointing again at himself and the other Characters*] have no reality outside of illu-sion, it would be well if you should distrust your reality because, though you breathe it and touch it today, it is destined like that of yesterday to stand revealed to you tomorrow as illusion.

1240 DIRECTOR [*deciding to mock him*]   Oh splendid! And you'll be telling me next that you and this play that you have come to perform for me are truer and more real than I am.

FATHER [*quite seriously*]   There can be no doubt of that, sir.

DIRECTOR   Really?

1245 FATHER   I thought you had understood that from the start.

DIRECTOR   More real than me?

FATHER   If your reality can change overnight . . .

DIRECTOR   Of course it can, it changes all the time, like everyone else's.

FATHER [*with a cry*]   But ours does not, sir. You see, that is the difference. It

1250 does not change, it cannot ever change or be otherwise because it is already fixed, it is what is, just that, forever—a terrible thing, sir!—an immutable reality. You should shudder to come near us.

DIRECTOR [*suddenly struck by a new idea, he steps in front of the* FATHER]
I should like to know, however, when anyone ever saw a character get out
of his part and set about expounding and explicating it, delivering lectures
1255   on it. Can you tell me? I have never seen anything like that.

FATHER   You have never seen it, sir, because authors generally hide the travail of their creations. When characters are alive and turn up, living, before
their author, all that author does is follow the words and gestures which
they propose to him. He has to want them to be as they themselves want to
1260   be. Woe betide him if he doesn't! When a character is born, he at once
acquires such an independence, even of his own author, that the whole
world can imagine him in innumerable situations other than those the
author thought to place him in. At times he acquires a meaning that the
author never dreamt of giving him.

1265   DIRECTOR   Certainly, I know that.

FATHER   Then why all this astonishment at us? Imagine what a misfortune it
is for a character such as I described to you—given life in the imagination
of an author who then wished to deny him life—and tell me frankly: isn't
such a character, given life and left without life, isn't he right to set about
1270   doing just what we are doing now as we stand here before you, after having
done just the same—for a very long time, believe me—before *him,* trying to
persuade him, trying to push him . . . I would appear before him sometimes, sometimes she [*looks at* STEPDAUGHTER] would go to him, sometimes
that poor mother . . .

1275   STEPDAUGHTER [*coming forward as if in a trance*]   It's true. I too went there,
sir, to tempt him, many times, in the melancholy of that study of his, at the
twilight hour, when he would sit stretched out in his armchair, unable to
make up his mind to switch the light on, and letting the evening shadows
invade the room, knowing that these shadows were alive with us and that
1280   we were coming to tempt him . . . [*As if she saw herself still in that study
and felt only annoyance at the presence of all of these Actors*] Oh, if only you
would all go away! Leave us alone! My mother there with her son—I with
this little girl—the boy there always alone—then I with him [*the* FATHER]—
then I by myself, I by myself . . . in those shadows. [*Suddenly she jumps up
as if she wished to take hold of herself in the vision she has of herself lighting
1285   up the shadows and alive.*] Ah, my life! What scenes, what scenes we went
there to propose to him: I, I tempted him more than the others.

FATHER   Right, but perhaps that was the trouble: you insisted too much. You
thought you could seduce him.

STEPDAUGHTER   Nonsense. He wanted me that way. [*She comes up to the
1290   DIRECTOR to tell him as in confidence.*] If you ask me, sir, it was because he
was so depressed, or because he despised the theater the public knows and
wants . . .

DIRECTOR   Let's continue. Let's continue, for heaven's sake. Enough theories, I'd like some facts. Give me some facts.

1295   STEPDAUGHTER   It seems to me that we have already given you more facts
than you can handle—with our entry into his [*the* FATHER's] house! You said
you couldn't change the scene every five minutes or start hanging signs.

DIRECTOR   Nor can we, of course not, we have to combine the scenes and
group them in one simultaneous close-knit action. Not your idea at all.
1300   You'd like to see your brother come home from school and wander through

the house like a ghost, hiding behind the doors, and brooding on a plan which—how did you put it—?

STEPDAUGHTER —shrivels him up, sir, completely shrivels him up, sir.

DIRECTOR "Shrivels!" What a word! All right then: his growth was stunted except for his eyes. Is that what you said?

STEPDAUGHTER Yes, sir. Just look at him. [*She points him out next to the* MOTHER.]

DIRECTOR Good girl. And then at the same time you want this little girl to be playing in the garden, dead to the world. Now, the boy in the house, the girl in the garden, is that possible?

STEPDAUGHTER Happy in the sunshine! Yes, that is my only reward, her pleasure, her joy in that garden! After the misery, the squalor of a horrible room where we slept, all four of us, she with me: just think, of the horror of my contaminated body next to hers! She held me tight, oh so tight with her loving innocent little arms! In the garden she would run and take my hand as soon as she saw me. She did not see the big flowers, she ran around looking for the teeny ones and wanted to show them to me, oh the joy of it!

[*Saying this and tortured by the memory she breaks into prolonged desperate sobbing, dropping her head onto her arms which are spread out on the work table. Everyone is overcome by her emotion. The* DIRECTOR *goes to her almost paternally and says to comfort her*]

DIRECTOR We'll do the garden. We'll do the garden, don't worry, and you'll be very happy about it. We'll bring all the scenes together in the garden. [*Calling a* STAGEHAND *by name*] Hey, drop me a couple of trees, will you, two small cypress trees, here in front of the fountain.

[*Two small cypress trees are seen descending from the flies.*[5] A STAGEHAND *runs on to secure them with nails and a couple of braces.*]

DIRECTOR [*to the* STEPDAUGHTER] Something to go on with anyway. Gives us an idea. [*Again calling the* STAGEHAND *by name*] Hey, give me a bit of sky.

STAGEHAND [*from above*] What?

DIRECTOR Bit of sky, a backcloth, to go behind that fountain. [*A white backdrop is seen descending from the flies.*] Not white, I said sky. It doesn't matter, leave it, I'll take care of it. [*Shouting*] Hey, Electrician, put these lights out. Let's have a bit of atmosphere, lunar atmosphere, blue background, and give me a blue spot on that backcloth. That's right. That's enough. [*At his command a mysterious lunar scene is created which induces the Actors to talk and move as they would on an evening in the garden beneath the moon.*] [*To* STEPDAUGHTER] You see? And now instead of hiding behind doors in the house the boy could move around here in the garden and hide behind trees. But it will be difficult, you know, to find a little girl to play the scene where she shows you the flowers. [*Turning to the* BOY] Come down this way a bit. Let's see how this can be worked out. [*And when the* BOY *doesn't move*] Come on, come on. [*Then dragging him forward he tries to make him hold his head up but it falls down again every time.*] Oh dear, another problem, this boy . . . What *is* it? . . . My God, he'll have to say something . . . [*He goes up to him, puts a hand on his shoulder and leads him behind one of the tree drops.*] Come on. Come on. Let me see. You can hide a bit here . . . Like this . . . You can stick your head out a bit to look . . . [*He goes to one*

---

5. The space over the stage from which scenery and equipment can be lowered.

side to see the effect. The BOY *has scarcely run through the actions when the Actors are deeply affected; and they remain quite overwhelmed.*] Ah! Fine!

1340 Splendid! [*He turns again to the* STEPDAUGHTER.] If the little girl surprises him looking out and runs over to him, don't you think she might drag a few words out of him too?

STEPDAUGHTER [*jumping to her feet*] Don't expect him to speak while *he's* here. [*She points to the* SON.] You have to send *him* away first.

1345 SON [*going resolutely toward one of the two stairways*] Suits me. Glad to go. Nothing I want more.

DIRECTOR [*immediately calling him*] No. Where are you going? Wait.

[*The* MOTHER *rises, deeply moved, in anguish at the thought that he is really going. She instinctively raises her arms as if to halt him, yet without moving away from her position.*]

SON [*arriving at the footlights, where the* DIRECTOR *stops him*] I have absolutely nothing to do here. So let me go please. Just let me go.

1350 DIRECTOR How do you mean, you have nothing to do?

STEPDAUGHTER [*placidly, with irony*] Don't hold him! He won't go.

FATHER He has to play the terrible scene in the garden with his mother.

SON [*unhesitating, resolute, proud*] I play nothing. I said so from the start. [*To the* DIRECTOR] Let me go.

STEPDAUGHTER [*running to the* DIRECTOR *to get him to lower his arms so that he 1355 is no longer holding the* SON *back*] Let him go. [*Then turning to the* SON *as soon as the* DIRECTOR *has let him go*] Very well, go. [*The* SON *is all set to move toward the stairs but, as if held by some occult power, he cannot go down the steps. While the Actors are both astounded and deeply troubled, he moves slowly across the footlights straight to the other stairway. But having arrived there he remains poised for the descent but unable to descend. The* STEP- DAUGHTER, *who has followed him with her eyes in an attitude of defiance, bursts out laughing.*] He can't, you see. He can't. He has to stay here, has to. Bound by a chain, indissolubly. But if I who do take flight, sir, when that happens which has to happen, and precisely because of the hatred I 1360 feel for him, precisely so as not to see him again—very well, if *I* am still here and can bear the sight of him and his company—you can imagine whether *he* can go away. He who really must, must remain here with that fine father of his and that mother there who no longer has any other children. [*Turning again to the* MOTHER] Come on, Mother, come on. [*Turning 1365 again to the* DIRECTOR *and pointing to the* MOTHER] Look, she got up to hold him back. [*To the* MOTHER, *as if exerting a magical power over her*] Come. Come . . . [*Then to the* DIRECTOR] You can imagine how little she wants to display her love in front of your actors. But so great is her desire to get at him that—look, you see—she is even prepared to live her scene.

[*In fact the* MOTHER *has approached and no sooner has the* STEPDAUGH- TER *spoken her last words than she spreads her arms to signify consent.*]

SON [*without pause*] But *I* am not, *I* am not. If I cannot go I will stay here, 1370 but I repeat: I will play nothing.

FATHER [*to the* DIRECTOR, *enraged*] You can force him, sir.

SON No one can force me.

FATHER I will force you.

STEPDAUGHTER Wait, wait. First the little girl must be at the fountain. [*She runs to take the* LITTLE GIRL, *drops on her knees in front of her, takes her*

1375   *little face in her hands.*] My poor little darling, you look bewildered with
those lovely big eyes of yours. Who knows where you think you are? We are
on a stage my dear. What is a stage? It is a place where you play at being
serious, a place for playacting, where we will now playact. But seriously!
For real! You too . . . [*She embraces her, presses her to her bosom, and rocks*
1380   *her a little.*] Oh, little darling, little darling, what an ugly play you will
enact! What a horrible thing has been planned for you, the garden, the
fountain . . . All pretense, of course, that's the trouble, my sweet, everything is make-believe here, but perhaps for you, my child, a make-believe
fountain is nicer than a real one for playing in, hmm? It will be a game for
1385   the others, but not for you, alas, because you are real, my darling, and are
actually playing in a fountain that is real, beautiful, big, green with many
bamboo plants reflected in it and giving it shade. Many, many ducklings
can swim in it, breaking the shade to bits. You want to take hold of one of
these ducklings . . . [*With a shout that fills everyone with dismay*] No! No,
1390   my Rosetta! Your mother is not looking after you because of that beast of a
son. A thousand devils are loose in my head . . . and he . . . [*She leaves the*
LITTLE GIRL *and turns with her usual hostility to the* BOY.] And what are you
doing here, always looking like a beggar child? It will be your fault too if
this little girl drowns—with all your standing around like that. As if I hadn't
1395   paid for everybody when I got you all into this house. [*Grabbing one of his*
arms to force him to take a hand out of his pocket] What have you got there?
What are you hiding? Let's see this hand. [*Tears his hand out of his pocket,*
and to the horror of everyone discovers that it holds a small revolver. She
looks at it for a moment as if satisfied and then says] Ah! Where did you get
that and how? [*And as the* BOY *in his confusion, with his eyes staring and*
1400   *vacant all the time, does not answer her*] Idiot, if I were you I wouldn't have
killed myself, I would have killed one of those two—or both of them—the
father and the son! [*She hides him behind the small cypress tree from which*
he had been looking out, and she takes the LITTLE GIRL *and hides her in the*
fountain, having her lie down in it in such a way as to be quite hidden.
Finally, the STEPDAUGHTER *goes down on her knees with her face in her*
hands, which are resting on the rim of the fountain.]

DIRECTOR   Splendid! [*Turning to the* SON] And at the same time . . .

SON [*with contempt*]   And at the same time, nothing. It is not true, sir. There
1405   was never any scene between me and her. [*He points to the* MOTHER.] Let
her tell you herself how it was.

                [*Meanwhile the* SECOND ACTRESS *and the* JUVENILE LEAD *have detached*
                themselves from the group of Actors. The former has started to observe
                the MOTHER, *who is opposite her, very closely. And the other has started*
                to observe the SON. *Both are planning how they will re-create the*
                roles.]

MOTHER   Yes, it is true, sir. I had gone to his room.

SON   My room, did you hear that? Not the garden.

DIRECTOR   That is of no importance. We have to rearrange the action, I told
1410   you that.

SON [*noticing that the* JUVENILE LEAD *is observing him*]   What do *you* want?

JUVENILE LEAD   Nothing. I am observing you.

SON [*turning to the other side where the* SECOND ACTRESS *is*]   Ah, and here we
have you to re-create the role, eh? [*He points to the* MOTHER.]

1415 DIRECTOR   Exactly, exactly. You should be grateful, it seems to me, for the attention they are giving you.

SON   Oh yes, thank you. But you still haven't understood that you cannot do this drama. We are not inside you, not in the least, and your actors are looking at us from the outside. Do you think it's possible for us to live
1420 before a mirror which, not content to freeze us in the fixed image it provides of our expression, also throws back at us an unrecognizable grimace purporting to be ourselves?

FATHER   That is true. That is true. You must see that.

DIRECTOR [to the JUVENILE LEAD and the SECOND ACTRESS]   Very well, get
1425 away from here.

SON   No good. I won't cooperate.

DIRECTOR   Just be quiet a minute and let me hear your mother. [To the MOTHER]   Well? You went into his room?

MOTHER   Yes sir, into his room. I was at the end of my tether. I wanted to
1430 pour out all of the anguish which was oppressing me. But as soon as he saw me come in—

SON   —There was no scene. I went away. I went away so there would be no scene. Because I have never made scenes, never, understand?

MOTHER   That's true. That's how it was. Yes.

1435 DIRECTOR   But now there's got to be a scene between you and him. It is indispensable.

MOTHER   As for me, sir, I am ready. If only you could find some way to have me speak to him for one moment, to have me say what is in my heart.

FATHER [going right up to the SON, very violent]   You will do it! For your
1440 mother! For your mother!

SON [more decisively than ever]   I will do nothing!

FATHER [grabbing him by the chest and shaking him]   By God, you will obey! Can't you hear how she is talking to you? Aren't you her son?

SON [grabbing his FATHER]   No! No! Once and for all let's have done with it!

[General agitation. The MOTHER, terrified, tries to get between them to separate them.]

1445 MOTHER [as before]   Please, please!

FATHER [without letting go of the SON]   You must obey, you must obey!

SON [wrestling with his FATHER and in the end throwing him to the ground beside the little stairway, to the horror of everyone]   What's this frenzy that's taken hold of you? To show your shame and ours to everyone? Have you no restraint? I won't cooperate, I won't cooperate! And that is how I interpret
1450 the wishes of the man who did not choose to put us onstage.

DIRECTOR   But you came here.

SON [pointing to his FATHER]   He came here—not me!

DIRECTOR   But aren't you here too?

SON   It was he who wanted to come, dragging the rest of us with him, and
1455 then getting together with you to plot not only what really happened, but also—as if that did not suffice—what did not happen.

DIRECTOR   Then tell me. Tell me what did happen. Just tell me. You came out of your room without saying a thing?

SON [after a moment of hesitation]   Without saying a thing. In order not to
1460 make a scene.

DIRECTOR [driving him on]   Very well, and then, what did you do then?

SON [*while everyone looks on in anguished attention, he moves a few steps on the front part of the stage*] Nothing . . . crossing the garden . . . [*He stops, gloomy, withdrawn.*]

DIRECTOR [*always driving him on to speak, impressed by his reticence*] Very well, crossing the garden?

SON [*desperate, hiding his face with one arm*] Why do you want to make me
1465 say it, sir? It is horrible.

> [*The* MOTHER *trembles all over, and stifles groans, looking toward the fountain.*]

DIRECTOR [*softly, noticing this look of hers, turning to the* SON, *with growing apprehension*] The little girl?

SON [*looking out into the auditorium*] Over there—in the fountain . . .

FATHER [*on the ground, pointing compassionately toward the* MOTHER] And she followed him, sir.

1470 DIRECTOR [*to the* SON, *anxiously*] And then you . . .

SON [*slowly, looking straight ahead all the time*] I ran out. I started to fish her out . . . but all of a sudden I stopped. Behind those trees I saw something that froze me: the boy, the boy was standing there, quite still. There was madness in the eyes. He was looking at his drowned sister in the fountain. [*The* STEPDAUGHTER, *who has been bent over the fountain, hiding the* LITTLE
1475 GIRL, *is sobbing desperately, like an echo from the bottom. Pause.*] I started to approach and then . . .

> [*From behind the trees where the* BOY *has been hiding, a revolver shot rings out.*]

MOTHER [*running up with a tormented shout, accompanied by the* SON *and all the Actors in a general tumult*] Son! My son! [*And then amid the hubbub and the disconnected shouts of the others*] Help! Help!

DIRECTOR [*amid the shouting, trying to clear a space while the* BOY *is lifted by his head and feet and carried away behind the backcloth*] Is he wounded, is he wounded, really?

> [*Everyone except the* DIRECTOR *and the* FATHER, *who has remained on the ground beside the steps, has disappeared behind the backcloth which has served for a sky, where they can still be heard for a while whispering anxiously. Then from one side and the other of this curtain, the Actors come back onstage.*]

1480 LEADING LADY [*reentering from the right, very much upset*] He's dead! Poor boy! He's dead! What a terrible thing!

LEADING MAN [*reentering from the left, laughing*] How do you mean, dead? Fiction, fiction, one doesn't believe such things.

OTHER ACTORS [*on the right*] Fiction? Reality! Reality! He is dead!

1485 OTHER ACTORS [*on the left*] No! Fiction! Fiction!

FATHER [*rising, and crying out to them*] Fiction indeed! Reality, reality, gentlemen, reality! [*Desperate, he too disappears at the back.*]

DIRECTOR [*at the end of his rope*] Fiction! Reality! To hell with all of you! Lights, lights, lights! [*At a single stroke the whole stage and auditorium is flooded with very bright light. The* DIRECTOR *breathes again, as if freed from an incubus, and they all look each other in the eyes, bewildered and lost.*] Things like this don't happen to me, they've made me lose a whole day. [*He looks at his watch.*] Go, you can all go. What could we do now anyway? It is
1490 too late to pick up the rehearsal where we left off. See you this evening. [*As

soon as the Actors have gone he talks to the ELECTRICIAN *by name.*] Hey, Electrician, lights out. [*He has hardly said the words when the theater is plunged for a moment into complete darkness.*] Hey, for God's sake, leave me at least one light! I like to see where I am going!

[*Immediately, from behind the backcloth, as if the wrong switch had been pulled, a green light comes on which projects the silhouettes, clear-cut and large, of the Characters, minus the* BOY *and the* LITTLE GIRL. *Seeing the silhouettes, the* DIRECTOR, *terrified, rushes from the stage. At the same time the light behind the backcloth goes out and the stage is again lit in nocturnal blue as before.*

Slowly, from the right side of the curtain, the SON *comes forward first, followed by the* MOTHER *with her arms stretched out toward him; then from the left side, the* FATHER. *They stop in the middle of the stage and stay there as if in a trance. Last of all from the right, the* STEPDAUGHTER *comes out and runs toward the two stairways. She stops on the first step, to look for a moment at the other three, and then breaks into a harsh laugh before throwing herself down the steps; she runs down the aisle between the rows of seats; she stops one more time and again laughs, looking at the three who are still onstage; she disappears from the auditorium, and from the lobby her laughter is still heard. Shortly thereafter the curtain falls.*]

SOPHIE TREADWELL

1885–1970

IN the early-morning hours of March 20, 1927, Albert Snyder was murdered in his Queens, New York, home. His wife, Ruth, and her lover, Judd Gray, were accused of the crime, tried, and convicted. An all-male jury sentenced them both to death, and when Ruth Snyder was executed, on January 12, 1928, she became the first woman to die in the electric chair in the state of New York. Considered one of the most sensational events of the era, the murder, the arrests, the trial, the sentences, and the executions all made headlines. Almost two hundred reporters, from the mainstream press and the tabloids alike, were assigned to cover various aspects of the case. By early May 1927, these journalists had already filed approximately 1,500,000 words over the wires; the *New York Times* alone published a story, often on the front page, almost daily from the revelation of the murder through the announcement of the executions. The trial, which was the first to use microphones and speakers in the courtroom, was observed by over 1,500 people, including a number of prominent writers, artists, and public figures. The *New York Times* described the spectators as "a typical Broadway audience," and other reports used similarly theatrical images and language to depict the trial. Author Damon Runyon is said to have deemed it "the best show in town." Thus it should not surprise us that the murder and its perpetrators became infamously popular culture referents for decades thereafter and that the crime spawned any number of fictionalizations, including the films *Double Indemnity* (1944) and *Body Heat* (1981). Journalist Sophie Treadwell, while not formally assigned to cover the story, chose to attend the proceedings; her analysis of the trial and its reportage in the media inspired her theatrical triumph, MACHINAL,[1] the first major creative work based on the Snyder murder, which premiered on Broadway in September 1928. Far from a dramatization of the case as spectacle, however, *Machinal* presents the murder as a response to modern culture and indicts life in the machine age, especially for women, as warping, oppressive, and deadly.

Sophia Anita Treadwell was born in Stockton, California, in 1885. Her father, Alfred, was of English, Spanish, and Mexican ancestry and had spent his childhood in Mexico; her mother, Nettie, had emigrated with her family to the United States

---

1. The definitive pronunciation of this title remains unclear. While some critics believe Treadwell was using the French word meaning *mechan-* *ical* or *unconscious,* pronounced "ma'-shin-al," others argue for "mak'-i-nal" or "ma-shin'-al."

from Scotland. When Sophie was very young, Alfred left Nettie and moved to San Francisco, where he held several judicially related elected offices. Despite efforts to reunite with Alfred, Nettie was left alone to provide for herself and her daughter. These early, troubled impressions of marital and economic instability made a profound impression on the young Sophie. Yet she also felt drawn to her father and her Mexican heritage, and through his influence, she was introduced to the theater and the study of language, interests she pursued as an undergraduate at the University of California at Berkeley. During college, Sophie acted in student theatrical productions, co-edited a campus humor magazine, served as a campus reporter for the *San Francisco Examiner,* and began to experiment with creative writing in addition to pursuing her degree in French. But Treadwell also had to hold multiple jobs to pay for her education, and she suffered the first of a series of breakdowns from the strain and exhaustion of juggling all these undertakings. Indeed, Treadwell's early life was punctuated by periods of productivity and collapse, through which she may have gained an understanding of how external pressures can affect us both psychologically and physiologically—an understanding that shapes *Machinal.*

Treadwell wrote her first full-length drama, *Le Grand Prix,* in 1906–07. On the strength of this writing she received an introduction to the famous actress Helena Modjeska. The star hired Sophie to assist with the writing of her memoirs and instilled in her protégée an understanding of the importance of creative integrity for artists. Treadwell then secured a post as a feature writer and theater critic for the *San Francisco Bulletin.* While working for the paper she met fellow journalist William O. McGeehan; they married in 1910. In 1914 McGeehan took a job with the *New York Evening Journal.* When McGeehan moved east, Treadwell remained in San Francisco to pursue a major assignment: she was convinced by her editor to use her acting as well as her writing skills to go undercover as a homeless prostitute to explore what resources the city would offer her. The resulting serial, "An Outcast at the Christian Door," caused a sensation

and no doubt contributed to Treadwell's expanding feminist consciousness. In 1915 Treadwell traveled to France as one of the first accredited female journalists to cover World War I. Denied access to the front because of her gender, however, she decided to join McGeehan in New York, where she embraced a number of important feminist movements of the era, including the fight for women's suffrage and the campaign for legalized birth control. Treadwell continued to work as a theater critic and also briefly joined the Provincetown Players, home to dramatists SUSAN GLASPELL and EUGENE O'NEILL. With the Players, Treadwell participated in play selection and directed one of their productions in 1917. But she had set her dramaturgical sights on Broadway, maintaining an uncompromising commitment to playwriting for the commercial theater that incorporated formal experimentation, feminist and other progressive political concerns, and timely narratives.

In 1920–21 Treadwell covered the final phases of the Mexican Revolution for the *New York Tribune,* including an exclusive interview with revolutionary leader Pancho Villa, which provided the foundation for her first Broadway play, *Gringo* (1922). A qualified success critically, *Gringo* may have proven too complex politically for audiences or reviewers to fully appreciate. With this play, as with her later *Hope for a Harvest* (1941), Treadwell considered controversial issues still highly relevant today, including America's attitudes toward Mexico and Mexicans and its ambivalence about immigrants. Her creation of Hispanic characters and engagement with the relationship between the United States and Mexico are only now being recognized as evidence of Treadwell's early contributions to the Chicana literary tradition.

Treadwell's investment in current events and sociocultural concerns, combined with her theatrical and journalistic sensibilities, facilitated the expeditious writing of *Machinal* in early 1928. Finishing the script just a few months after the executions, Treadwell was able to take advantage of audiences' continued fixation on the recent, lurid murder. Utilizing core elements of the Snyder case, she created a piece that would be narratively familiar yet thematically and stylistically innovative. In a series of discrete scenes, *Machinal* follows the life of a young woman, whom we come to know as Helen Jones, who works in an office to support herself and her mother. Stifled by the pressures of urban life, she reluctantly accepts her employer's proposal of marriage, deciding that it may be her only alternative to a life of drudgery. The young woman soon realizes that a loveless marriage is equally suffocating, however, and she experiences a fleeting sense of freedom only in an illicit affair. Her naive efforts to secure lasting freedom fail; it is impossible for her to escape the confines of patriarchal law and society. Focusing on the young woman's efforts to untangle the thoughts and feelings she is discovering, Treadwell employed the latest trends in modernist stagecraft, engaged public fascination with emerging concepts in human psychology, and endeavored—as her manuscript notes suggest—also to reach into her spectators' "still secret places," their "consciousness."

America's interest in psychology and psychoanalysis had been piqued when Sigmund Freud and Carl Jung visited Clark University in 1909 to give a series of lectures. Jung returned to the United States in 1912 to give further lectures at Fordham University. These clinicians' theories about dreams, sexuality, the conscious and unconscious mind, and the psychiatric condition known as "hysteria"[2] were soon being disseminated, although not always accurately, in the popular media. Modernist artists and writers quickly latched on to these new notions of the psyche as resonant with their own efforts to better express human thoughts and feelings. Discussions of psychoanalysis and experiments in depicting characters' mental states soon occupied the theater. Some early dramatic efforts, such as Alice Gerstenberg's *Overtones* (1915), sought to demonstrate repressed ideas and emotions by staging characters as split selves, one "cultured," the other "primitive," played by two actors. Susan Glaspell's *The Verge* (1921) featured a central female character diagnosed with

hysteria, represented chillingly by her fractured speech and by the angles and shadows in the lighting and scenic design of her "thwarted tower" room. Eugene O'Neill's *Strange Interlude,* drafted in 1923, utilized lengthy soliloquies to express his characters' psychic struggles; the play premiered on Broadway in January 1928 and won the Pulitzer Prize for drama. *Machinal*, like *The Verge* and *Strange Interlude*, features a woman grappling with the strictures of modern life, and like Glaspell and O'Neill Treadwell sought both a dramaturgical form and a theatrical style that would complement her protagonist's sense of entrapment and desperation and represent her psychic distress.

Precisely because these efforts to represent characters' inner lives necessitated new modes of dramatic writing and staging, some American theater artists now rejected the realist style of stage impresarios like David Belasco, who was famous for the elaborate and authentic physical details of his productions' settings, and gravitated instead toward sparer modernist techniques developed in Europe. A number of international artists, writers, and intellectuals traveled to or lived in exile in New York during the war years; many Americans also encountered modernist artistry while abroad during the war. Discrete European modernist styles, which included symbolism, cubism, fauvism, and surrealism, were often interwoven by the Americans to generate new, hybrid forms. Treadwell participated in the creative fervor of the New York artists who sought to craft through these diverse stylistic influences a uniquely American avant-garde.

Following the war, American artists found in expressionism an aesthetic particularly suited to the representation of modern life. The stage version of this avant-garde form sought to externalize the subjective and internal dimensions of character, complemented by design schema that reflected this subjectivity, often by way of distorted, fragmented, or abstract sounds and images; we find these techniques readily apparent in *Machinal*. There were also

2. Frequently diagnosed in women, hysteria manifested in a range of symptoms and disorders, both physical and psychological, that are now believed to reflect the severe sexual and social restrictions of patriarchal culture.

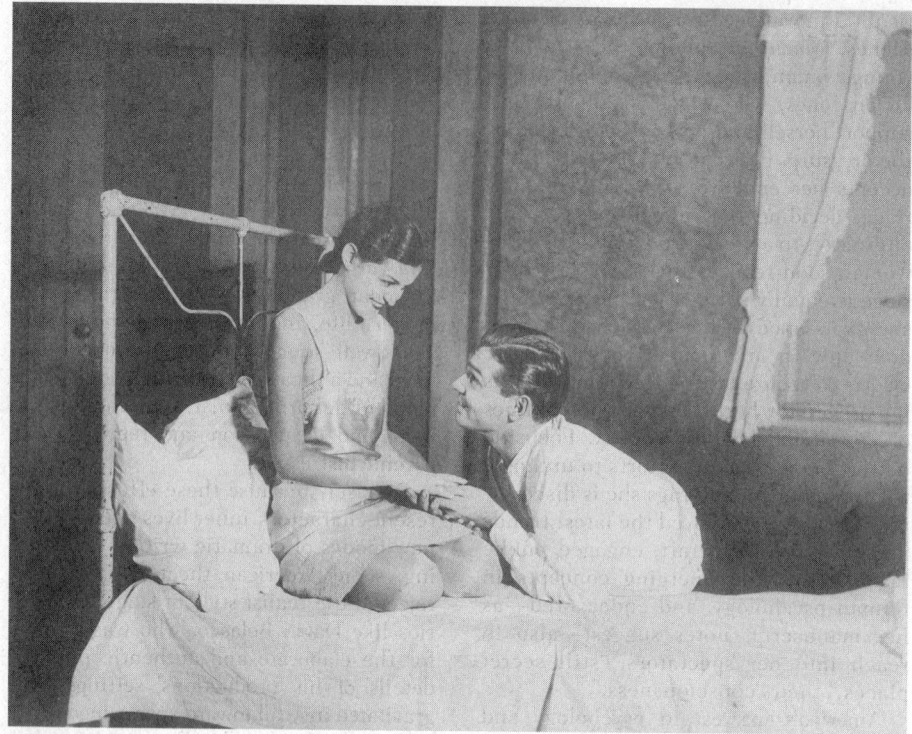

Zita Johann as Helen Jones and Clark Gable as Richard Roe in the original 1928 production of *Machinal* at the Plymouth Theater (New York).

influential expressionist productions of classical works, such as HAMLET, by directors who discovered in older plays psychic strains that were still relevant for their contemporary moment. Some initial reviewers of *Machinal*, as well as later theater historians, have suggested that Treadwell's play, rather than expanding the scope of the modernist theater, merely imitated Elmer Rice's *The Adding Machine* (1923), which utilized expressionist techniques to depict the world of Mr. Zero, a bookkeeper who kills his employer in retaliation for being replaced by an adding machine. Whereas many American expressionist productions in the 1920s were staged by noncommercial theaters, Rice's play remains important for its use of expressionism on Broadway to tell a story critical of American culture and industry. Yet the dismissal of Treadwell's work as simply derivative of Rice's is typical of the undervaluing of women's dramaturgy and creative innovation in the professional theater. Despite its artistic and commercial

success, with productions in France, Germany, England, and the Soviet Union following the Broadway premier, *Machinal* later fell into critical neglect, perhaps exacerbated by Treadwell's inability to duplicate its impact with any of her subsequent productions. Although Treadwell wrote thirty-nine plays, seven of which appeared on Broadway between 1922 and 1941, by the time of her death in 1970 her work for the theater was virtually unknown.

Scholarly efforts to identify forgotten women writers—aided immeasurably by the revival of *Machinal* at New York's Public Theatre in 1990—returned Treadwell to critical attention in the late twentieth century. This notable production then prompted a revival at the Royal National Theatre in London in 1993, and interest in Treadwell and *Machinal* blossomed. Now championed as an important feminist drama, *Machinal* has also reemerged as a pivotal text for the twentieth-century American theater. Treadwell's complex interweaving of cultural critique and stylistic innovation, coupled with her wrenching portrait of a young woman trapped in mechanized, depersonalized urban life, exemplifies the modernist notion of the *gesamtkunstwerk*, or total work of art, that in the theater reflects a synergy of narrative and theme, dramaturgical form, and production style.

Treadwell signals her affinity with expressionist techniques in the script's introductory information. The list of nameless characters, designated only by generic terms, resonates with the impersonal world they inhabit. Treadwell tells us that her central figure, the young woman, could be "any woman," suggesting that her feelings and actions are not unique; indeed, this female figure becomes threatening precisely because she is "ordinary," and thus many others could be like her. At the same time, her repeated calls for "somebody" point to the isolation of the modern individual: we are like each other, but we are also all alone.

Treadwell shifts us away from the thrall to traditional narrative by telling us what will occur: "The plot is the story of a woman who murders her husband." By so doing, Treadwell refocuses our attention to how and why this happens—questions more conducive to our active participation in the drama. *Machinal's* episodic structure also resists that of traditional realist narrative; even more significantly, each scene occurs either before or following what in conventional plots would be considered the dramatic events: a proposal, a wedding, a birth, a moment of sexual passion, a killing. This dramaturgical strategy enables Treadwell to explore the psychic impact of such moments on her Everywoman.

In this regard Treadwell was not only sidestepping the traditional well-made play form, she was also directly critiquing the media's sensationalization of the Snyder murder. In particular, Treadwell recognized how Ruth Snyder became a product of the media, denied any personal agency or voice in her representation. Through each episode of *Machinal*, Treadwell similarly demonstrates how her protagonist is constructed by others and how modern, patriarchal culture systematically precludes any opportunity for the young woman to experience true freedom or independence.

One of the signal strengths of the play is Treadwell's ability to create this character fully despite her relative inarticulateness. In this regard, we might look to Treadwell's own recent contact with new methods in actor training as central to her dramaturgy in *Machinal*. From 1923 to 1925 Treadwell worked with Richard Boleslavski, a pupil of Konstantin Stanislavski who brought the master's acting techniques from Russia to the United States. Stanislavski's "system" provided actors with the means to decipher and then truthfully represent characters' motivations and actions. Through this training Treadwell may have grasped the critical synergy between actor and script and learned how what is unscripted, or unspoken, in the dialogue—what is otherwise known as the "subtext"—must nevertheless be clear if the actor is to understand and embody a character.

One of the hallmarks of Treadwell's expressionist concept for *Machinal* is her notion of a soundscape—the antithesis of a traditional musical score—that accompanies the dialogue and action and, perhaps even more strategically, provides the transitions between scenes. This aural text—every bit as important as the dialogic text to the play's overall theatrical effect—both complements the action and comments on it, especially as words fade out and sounds fill their place. Treadwell believed that sound has an "inherent emotional effect" in addition to its ability to foster atmosphere. In *Machinal* these are, moreover, everyday sounds, as generic as the characters who share the stage with them. Treadwell's dramatic language is everyday as well; she uses colloquial speech and current slang to create an urban American milieu easily recognizable for her Broadway audience. Yet she eschews traditional dialogic forms to strategic effect: words may be used as one part of the larger soundscape, as with the office workers' overlapping staccato speech, mechanical in its rapid-fire articulation, accompanied by the noise of the office equipment in "To Business"; or words may synecdochically reflect, as in the young woman's soliloquized syntactic gaps, the impossibility of full expression of any kind.

The play's scenic environment is generic as well, with only a minimum of furniture and props placed for each episode within a basic stage space. The set is demarcated by a larger, and then a smaller, window and by two, and then only one, entrance as the young woman's world closes in around her. Treadwell understood that lighting would also be integral to the work's impact. The unpublished production script for *Machinal* details the closing moment of the play, which some critics described as a distinct, wordless final scene following the execution and blackout: *Pause—overhead lights come on cyclorama first faint blue—then red—then pink—then amber—they are thrown up full . . . PAUSE, then . . . Curtain.*

This visual evocation of dawn must have provided some emotional balm at the same time that it left audiences with a final image of the complex interplay of technology, culture, and nature in the modern world. Almost a century later Treadwell's urgent questioning of the social, legal, and economic forces that may constrain our lives remains valid and critically important. To learn more about the staging of *Machinal* and to view photographs from select performances of the play, see the "Plays in Performance" color insert near the center of this volume.

J.E.G.

Machinal

CHARACTERS

YOUNG WOMAN	MAN
TELEPHONE GIRL	ANOTHER MAN
STENOGRAPHER	WAITER
FILING CLERK	JUDGE
ADDING CLERK	LAWYER FOR DEFENSE
MOTHER	LAWYER FOR PROSECUTION
HUSBAND	COURT REPORTER
BELLBOY	BAILIFF
NURSE	REPORTER
DOCTOR	SECOND REPORTER
YOUNG MAN	THIRD REPORTER
GIRL	JAILER
MAN	MATRON
BOY	PRIEST

PLAYWRIGHT'S NOTES

THE PLOT is the story of a woman who murders her husband—an ordinary young woman, any woman.

THE PLAN is to tell this story by showing the different phases of life that the woman comes in contact with, and in none of which she finds any place, any peace. The woman is essentially soft, tender, and the life around her is essentially hard, mechanized. Business, home, marriage, having a child, seeking pleasure—all are difficult for her—mechanical, nerve nagging. Only in an illicit love does she find anything with life in it for her, and when she loses this, the desperate effort to win free to it again is her undoing.

The story is told in nine scenes. In the dialogue of these scenes there is the attempt to catch the rhythm of our common city speech, its brassy sound, its trick of repetition, etc.

Then there is, also, the use of many different sounds chosen primarily for their inherent emotional effect (steel rivetting, a priest chanting, a Negro singing, jazz band, etc.), but contributing also to the creation of a background, an atmosphere.

THE HOPE is to create a stage production that will have "style," and at the same time, by the story's own innate drama, by the directness of its telling, by the variety and quick changingness of its scenes, and the excitement of its sounds, to create an interesting play.

SCENICALLY this play is planned to be handled in two basic sets (or in one set with two backs)

The first division—(The first Four Episodes)—needs an entrance at one side, and a back having a door and a large window. The door gives, in

Episode 1—to Vice President's office.
" 2— " hall.
" 3— " bathroom.
" 4— " corridor.
And the window shows, in
" 1—An opposite office.
" 2—An inner apartment court.
" 3—Window of a dance casino opposite.
" 4—Steel girders.
(Of these, only the casino window is important. Sky could be used for the others.)

The second division—(the last Five Episodes)—has the same side entrance, but the back has only one opening—for a small window (barred).

Episode 5, window is masked by electric piano.
" 6, " " disclosed (sidewalk outside).
" 7, " " curtained.
" 8, " " masked by Judge's bench.
" 9, " " disclosed (sky outside).

There is a change of furniture, and props for each episode—(only essential things, full of character).

For Episode 9, the room is closed in from the sides, and there is a place with bars and a door in it, put straight across stage down front (back far enough to leave a clear passageway in front of it.)

LIGHTING concentrated and intense.—Light and shadow—bright light and darkness.—This darkness, already in the scene, grows and blacks out the light for dark stage when the scene changes are made.

OFFSTAGE VOICES

Characters in the Background
Heard, but Unseen

A Janitor
A Baby
A Boy and a Girl
A Husband and Wife
A Husband and Wife
A Radio Announcer
A Negro Singer

MECHANICAL
OFFSTAGE SOUNDS

A small jazz band
A hand organ
Steel rivetting
Telegraph instruments
Aeroplane engine

MECHANICAL ONSTAGE SOUNDS

Office Machines (Typewriters, telephones, etc.)
Electric piano.

CHARACTERS

In the Background
Seen, Not Heard

(Seen, off the main set; i.e., through a window or door)

Couples of men and women dancing
A Woman in a bathrobe
A Woman in a wheel chair

A Nurse with a covered basin
A Nurse with a tray
The feet of men and women passing in the street.

Episode One

TO BUSINESS

SCENE: *An Office.*
A Switchboard
Filing Cabinet
Adding Machine
Typewriter and Table
Manifold Machine[1]

SOUNDS: *Office Machines.*
Typewriters
Adding Machine
Manifold
Telephone Bells
Buzzers

CHARACTERS AND THEIR MACHINES:

A YOUNG WOMAN [*Typewriter*]
A STENOGRAPHER [*Typewriter*]
A FILING CLERK [*Filing cabinet and manifold*]
AN ADDING CLERK [*Adding Machine*]
TELEPHONE OPERATOR [*Switchboard*]

[BEFORE THE CURTAIN—*Sounds of Machines going. They continue throughout the scene, and accompany the Young Woman's thoughts after the scene is blacked out*]

[AT THE RISE OF THE CURTAIN: *All the Machines are disclosed, and all the characters with the exception of* THE YOUNG WOMAN]

Of these characters, THE YOUNG WOMAN, *going any day to any business. Ordinary. The confusion of her own inner thoughts, emotions, desires, dreams cuts her off from any actual adjustment to the routine of work. She gets through this routine with a very small surface of her consciousness. She is not homely and she is not pretty. She is preoccupied with herself—with her person. She has well kept hands, and a trick of constantly arranging her hair over her ears.*

The STENOGRAPHER *is the faded, efficient woman office worker. Drying, dried.*

The ADDING CLERK *is her male counterpart.*

The FILING CLERK *is a boy not grown, callow adolescence.*

The TELEPHONE GIRL, *young, cheap and amorous.*

Lights come up on office scene. Two desks R. *and* L. *Telephone booth back* R.C. *Filing cabinet back of* C. *Adding machine back* L.C.

ADDING CLERK [*in the monotonous voice of his monotonous thoughts; at his adding machine*] 2490, 28, 76, 123, 36842, 1, ¼, 37, 804, 23½, 982.

FILING CLERK [*in the same way—at his filing desk*] Accounts—A. Bonds—B. Contracts—C. Data—D. Earnings—E.

STENOGRAPHER [*in the same way—Left*] Dear Sir—in re—your letter—recent
5   date—will state—

TELEPHONE GIRL   Hello—Hello—George H. Jones Company good morning—hello hello—George H. Jones Company good morning—hello.

1. Copying machine.

FILING CLERK   Market—M. Notes—N. Output—O. Profits—P.—! [*Suddenly.*] What's the matter with Q?

10 TELEPHONE GIRL   Matter with it—Mr. J.—Mr. K. wants you— What you mean matter? Matter with what?

FILING CLERK   Matter with Q.

TELEPHONE GIRL   Well—what is? Spring 1726?

FILING CLERK   I'm asking yuh——

15 TELEPHONE GIRL   WELL?

FILING CLERK   Nothing filed with it——

TELEPHONE GIRL   Well?

FILING CLERK   Look at A. Look at B. What's the matter with Q?

TELEPHONE GIRL   Ain't popular. Hello—Hello—George H. Jones Company.

20 FILING CLERK   Hot dog! Why ain't it?

ADDING CLERK   Has it personality?

STENOGRAPHER   Has it Halitosis?[2]

TELEPHONE GIRL   Has it got it?

FILING CLERK   Hot dog!

25 TELEPHONE GIRL   What number do you want? [*Recognizing but not pleased.*] Oh—hello—sure I know who it is—tonight? Uh, uh— [*Negative, but each with a different inflection.*]—you heard me—No!

FILING CLERK   Don't you like him?

STENOGRAPHER   She likes 'em all.

30 TELEPHONE GIRL   I do not!

STENOGRAPHER   Well—pretty near all!

TELEPHONE GIRL   What number do you want? Wrong number. Hello— hello—George H. Jones Company. Hello, hello—

STENOGRAPHER   Memorandum—attention Mr. Smith—at a conference

35 of——

ADDING CLERK   125—83¾—22—908—34—¼—28593——

FILING CLERK   Report—R, Sales—S, Trade—T.

TELEPHONE GIRL   Shh—! Yes, Mr. J.—? No—Miss A. ain't in yet—I'll tell her, Mr. J.—just the minute she gets in.

40 STENOGRAPHER   She's late again, huh?

TELEPHONE GIRL   Out with her sweetie last night, huh?

FILING CLERK   Hot dog.

ADDING CLERK   She ain't got a sweetie.

STENOGRAPHER   How do you know?

45 ADDING CLERK   I know.

FILING CLERK   Hot dog.

ADDING CLERK   She lives alone with her mother.

TELEPHONE GIRL   Spring 1876? Hello—Spring 1876. Spring! Hello, Spring 1876? 1876! Wrong number! Hello! Hello!

50 STENOGRAPHER   Director's meeting semi-annual report card.

FILING CLERK   Shipments—Sales—Schedules—S.

ADDING CLERK   She doesn't belong in an office.

TELEPHONE GIRL   Who does?

STENOGRAPHER   I do!

55 ADDING CLERK   You said it!

FILING CLERK   Hot dog!

2. Bad breath.

TELEPHONE GIRL   Hello—hello—George H. Jones Company—hello—hello—
STENOGRAPHER   I'm efficient. She's inefficient.
FILING CLERK   She's inefficient.
TELEPHONE GIRL   She's got J. going.
60 STENOGRAPHER   Going?
TELEPHONE GIRL   Going and coming.
FILING CLERK   Hot dog.

[Enter JONES.]

JONES   Good morning, everybody.
TELEPHONE GIRL   Good morning.
65 FILING CLERK   Good morning.
ADDING CLERK   Good morning.
STENOGRAPHER   Good morning, Mr. J.
JONES   Miss A. isn't in yet?
TELEPHONE GIRL   Not yet, Mr. J.
70 FILING CLERK   Not yet.
ADDING CLERK   Not yet.
STENOGRAPHER   She's late.
JONES   I just wanted her to take a letter.
STENOGRAPHER   I'll take the letter.
75 JONES   One thing at a time and that done well.
ADDING CLERK [yessing]   Done well.
STENOGRAPHER   I'll finish it later.
JONES   Hew to the line.
ADDING CLERK   Hew to the line.
80 STENOGRAPHER   Then I'll hurry.
JONES   Haste makes waste.
ADDING CLERK   Waste.
STENOGRAPHER   But if you're in a hurry.
JONES   I'm never in a hurry— That's how I get ahead! [Laughs. They all laugh.]
85   First know you're right—then go ahead.
ADDING CLERK   Ahead.
JONES [to TELEPHONE GIRL]   When Miss A. comes in tell her I want her to take a letter. [Turns to go in—then.] It's important.
TELEPHONE GIRL [making a note]   Miss A.—important.
90 JONES [starts up—then]   And I don't want to be disturbed.
TELEPHONE GIRL   You're in conference?
JONES   I'm in conference. [Turns—then] Unless it's A.B.—of course.
TELEPHONE GIRL   Of course—A.B.
JONES [starts—turns again; attempts to be facetious]   Tell Miss A. the early
95   bird catches the worm.

[Exit JONES.]

TELEPHONE GIRL   The early worm gets caught.
ADDING CLERK   He's caught.
TELEPHONE GIRL   Hooked.
ADDING CLERK   In the pan.
100 FILING CLERK   Hot dog.
STENOGRAPHER   We beg leave to announce——

[Enter YOUNG WOMAN. Goes behind telephone booth to desk R.]

STENOGRAPHER   You're late!

FILING CLERK   You're late.

ADDING CLERK   You're late.

105 STENOGRAPHER   And yesterday!

FILING CLERK   The day before.

ADDING CLERK   And the day before.

STENOGRAPHER   You'll lose your job.

YOUNG WOMAN   No!

110 STENOGRAPHER   No?

[WORKERS *exchange glances.*]

YOUNG WOMAN   I can't!

STENOGRAPHER   Can't?

[*Same business.*]

FILING CLERK   Rent—bills—installments—miscellaneous.

ADDING CLERK   A dollar ten—ninety-five—3.40—35—12.60.

115 STENOGRAPHER   Then why are you late?

YOUNG WOMAN   Why?

STENOGRAPHER   Excuse!

ADDING CLERK   Excuse!

FILING CLERK   Excuse.

120 TELEPHONE GIRL   Excuse it, please.

STENOGRAPHER   Why?

YOUNG WOMAN   The subway?

TELEPHONE GIRL   Long distance?

FILING CLERK   Old stuff!

125 ADDING CLERK   That stall!

STENOGRAPHER   Stalled?

YOUNG WOMAN   No——

STENOGRAPHER   What?

YOUNG WOMAN   I had to get out!

130 ADDING CLERK   Out!

FILING CLERK   Out?

STENOGRAPHER   Out where?

YOUNG WOMAN   In the air!

STENOGRAPHER   Air?

135 YOUNG WOMAN   All those bodies pressing.

FILING CLERK   Hot dog!

YOUNG WOMAN   I thought I would faint! I had to get out in the air!

FILING CLERK   Give her the air.

ADDING CLERK   Free air—

140 STENOGRAPHER   Hot air.

YOUNG WOMAN   Like I'm dying.

STENOGRAPHER   Same thing yesterday. [*Pause.*] And the day before.

YOUNG WOMAN   Yes—what am I going to do?

ADDING CLERK   Take a taxi!

[THEY *laugh.*]

145 FILING CLERK   Call a cop!

TELEPHONE GIRL   Mr. J. wants you.

YOUNG WOMAN   Me?

TELEPHONE GIRL   You!

YOUNG WOMAN [*rises*]   Mr. J.!

150 STENOGRAPHER   Mr. J.

TELEPHONE GIRL   He's bellowing for you!

[YOUNG WOMAN *gives last pat to her hair—goes off into door—back.*]

STENOGRAPHER [*after her*]   Get it just right.

FILING CLERK   She's always doing that to her hair.

TELEPHONE GIRL   It gives a line—it gives a line—[3]

155 FILING CLERK   Hot dog.

ADDING CLERK   She's artistic.

STENOGRAPHER   She's inefficient.

FILING CLERK   She's inefficient.

STENOGRAPHER   Mr. J. knows she's inefficient.

160 ADDING CLERK   46-23-84-2-2-2-1,492—678.

TELEPHONE GIRL   Hello—hello—George H. Jones Company—hello—Mr. Jones? He's in conference.

STENOGRAPHER [*sarcastic*]   Conference!

ADDING CLERK   Conference.

165 FILING CLERK   Hot dog!

TELEPHONE GIRL   Do you think he'll marry her?

ADDING CLERK   If she'll have him.

STENOGRAPHER   If she'll have him!

FILING CLERK   Do you think she'll have him?

170 TELEPHONE GIRL   How much does he get?

ADDING CLERK   Plenty—5,000—10,000—15,000—20,000—25,000.

STENOGRAPHER   And plenty put away.

ADDING CLERK   Gas Preferred—4's—steel—5's—oil—6's.

FILING CLERK   Hot dog.

175 STENOGRAPHER   Will she have him? Will she have him? This agreement entered into—party of the first part—party of the second part—will he have her?

TELEPHONE GIRL   Well, I'd hate to get into bed with him. [*Familiar melting voice.*] Hello—humhum—hum—hum—hold the line a minute—will you—hum hum. [*Professional voice.*] Hell, hello—A.B., just a minute, Mr.

180 A.B.—Mr. J.? Mr. A.B.—go ahead, Mr. A.B. [*Melting voice.*] We were interrupted—huh—huh—huh-huhuh—hum—hum.

[*Enter* YOUNG WOMAN—*she goes to her chair, sits with folded hands.*]

FILING CLERK   That's all you ever say to a guy—

STENOGRAPHER   Hum—hum—or uh huh— [*Negative.*]

TELEPHONE GIRL   That's all you have to. [*To phone.*] Hum—hum—hum
185 hum—hum hum—

STENOGRAPHER   Mostly hum hum.

ADDING CLERK   You've said it!

FILING CLERK   Hot dog.

TELEPHONE GIRL   Hum hum huh hum humhumhum—tonight? She's got a
190 date—she told me last night—humhumhuh—hum—all right. [*Disconnects.*] Too bad—my boy friend's got a friend—but my girl friend's got a date.

YOUNG WOMAN   You have a good time.

TELEPHONE GIRL   Big time.

STENOGRAPHER   Small time.

195 ADDING CLERK   A big time on the small time.

3. The slant or line of a woman's bobbed haircut was one of its notable features.

TELEPHONE GIRL   I'd ask you, kid, but you'd be up to your neck!

STENOGRAPHERS   Neckers!

ADDING CLERK   Petters!

FILING CLERK   Sweet papas.

200 TELEPHONE GIRL   Want to come?

YOUNG WOMAN   Can't.

TELEPHONE GIRL   Date?

YOUNG WOMAN   My mother.

STENOGRAPHER   Worries?

205 TELEPHONE GIRL   Nags—hello—George H. Jones Company—Oh hello—

[YOUNG WOMAN sits *before her machine—hands in lap, looking at them.*]

STENOGRAPHER   Why don't you get to work?

YOUNG WOMAN [*dreaming*]   What?

ADDING CLERK   Work!

YOUNG WOMAN   Can't.

210 STENOGRAPHER   Can't?

YOUNG WOMAN   My machine's out of order.

STENOGRAPHER   Well, fix it!

YOUNG WOMAN   I can't—got to get somebody.

STENOGRAPHER   Somebody! Somebody! Always somebody! Here, sort the

215 mail, then!

YOUNG WOMAN [*rises*]   All right.

STENOGRAPHER   And hurry! You're late.

YOUNG WOMAN [*sorting letters*]   George H. Jones & Company—George H.

Jones Inc. George H. Jones—

220 STENOGRAPHER   You're always late.

ADDING CLERK   You'll lose your job.

YOUNG WOMAN [*hurrying*]   George H. Jones—George H. Jones Personal—

TELEPHONE GIRL   Don't let 'em get your goat, kid—tell 'em where to get off.

YOUNG WOMAN   What?

225 TELEPHONE GIRL   Ain't it all set?

YOUNG WOMAN   What?

TELEPHONE GIRL   You and Mr. J.

STENOGRAPHER   You and the boss.

FILING CLERK   You and the big chief.

230 ADDING CLERK   You and the big cheese.

YOUNG WOMAN   Did he tell you?

TELEPHONE GIRL   I told you!

ADDING CLERK   I told you!

STENOGRAPHER   I don't believe it.

235 ADDING CLERK   5,000—10,000—15,000.

FILING CLERK   Hot dog.

YOUNG WOMAN   No—it isn't so.

STENOGRAPHER   Isn't it?

YOUNG WOMAN   No.

240 TELEPHONE GIRL   Not yet.

ADDING CLERK   But soon.

FILING CLERK   Hot dog.

[Enter JONES.]

TELEPHONE GIRL [*busy*]   George H. Jones Company—Hello—Hello.

STENOGRAPHER   Awaiting your answer—
245 ADDING CLERK   5,000—10,000—15,000—
JONES [*crossing to* YOUNG WOMAN—*puts hand on her shoulder,* ALL *stop and stare*]   That letter done?
YOUNG WOMAN   No. [*She pulls away.*]
JONES   What's the matter?
STENOGRAPHER   She hasn't started.
250 JONES   O.K.—want to make some changes.
YOUNG WOMAN   My machine's out of order.
JONES   O.K.—use the one in my room.
YOUNG WOMAN   I'm sorting the mail.
STENOGRAPHER [*sarcastic*]   One thing at a time!
255 JONES [*retreating—goes back* c.]   O.K. [*To* YOUNG WOMAN] When you're finished. [*Starts back to his room.*]
STENOGRAPHER   Haste makes waste.
JONES [*at door*]   O.K.—don't hurry.
            [*Exits.*]
STENOGRAPHER   Hew to the line!
260 TELEPHONE GIRL   He's hewing.
FILING CLERK   Hot dog.
TELEPHONE GIRL   Why did you flinch, kid?
YOUNG WOMAN   Flinch?
TELEPHONE GIRL   Did he pinch?
265 YOUNG WOMAN   No!
TELEPHONE GIRL   Then what?
YOUNG WOMAN   Nothing!— Just his hand.
TELEPHONE GIRL   Oh—just his hand—[*Shakes her head thoughtfully.*] Uhhuh. [*Negative.*] Uhhuh. [*Decisively.*] No! Tell him no.
270 STENOGRAPHER   If she does she'll lose her job.
ADDING CLERK   Fired.
FILING CLERK   The sack!
TELEPHONE GIRL [*on the defensive*]   And if she doesn't?
ADDING CLERK   She'll come to work in a taxi!
275 TELEPHONE GIRL   Work?
FILING CLERK   No work.
STENOGRAPHER   No worry.
ADDING CLERK   Breakfast in bed.
STENOGRAPHER [*sarcastic*]   Did Madame ring?
280 FILING CLERK   Lunch in bed!
TELEPHONE GIRL   A double bed! [*In phone.*] Yes, Mr. J. [*To* YOUNG WOMAN] J. wants you.
YOUNG WOMAN [*starts to get to her feet—but doesn't*]   I can't—I'm not ready—In a minute. [*Sits staring ahead of her.*]
285 ADDING CLERK   5,000—10,000—15,000—
FILING CLERK   Profits—plans—purchase—
STENOGRAPHER   Call your attention our prices are fixed.
TELEPHONE GIRL   Hello—hello—George H. Jones Company—hello—hello—
YOUNG WOMAN [*thinking her thoughts aloud—to the subdued accompaniment of the office sounds and voices*]   Marry me—wants to marry me—
290 George H. Jones—George H. Jones and Company—Mrs. George H.

Jones—Mrs. George H. Jones. Dear Madame—marry—do you take this man to be your wedded husband—I do—to love honor and to love—kisses— no—I can't—George H. Jones—How would you like to marry me—What do you say—Why Mr. Jones I—let me look at your little hands—you have such
295   pretty little hands—let me hold your pretty little hands—George H. Jones— Fat hands—flabby hands—don't touch me—please—fat hands are never weary—please don't—married—all girls—most girls—married—babies—a baby—curls—little curls all over its head—George H. Jones—straight— thin—bald—don't touch me—please—no—can't—must—somebody—
300   something—no rest—must rest—no rest—must rest—no rest—late today—yesterday—before—late—subway—air—pressing—bodies pressing—bodies—trembling—air—stop—air—late—job—no job—fired— late—alarm clock—alarm clock—alarm clock—hurry—job—ma—nag— nag—nag—ma—hurry—job—no job—no money—installments due—no
305   money—money—George H. Jones—money—Mrs. George H. Jones— money—no work—no worry—free!—rest—sleep till nine—sleep till ten— sleep till noon—now you take a good rest this morning—don't get up till you want to—thank you—oh thank you—oh don't!—please don't touch me—I want to rest—no rest—earn—got to earn—married—earn—no—yes—
310   earn—all girls—most girls—ma—pa—ma—all women—most women—I can't—must—maybe—must—somebody—something—ma—pa—ma—can I, ma? Tell me, ma—something—somebody.

BLACK OUT

[*The sounds of the office machines continue until the scene lights into Episode 2,— and the office sounds become the sound of a radio (offstage).*]

Episode Two

AT HOME

SCENE: *A Kitchen.*
    Table—chairs—plates and food—Garbage can—a pair of rubber gloves.
    The door at the back now opens on a hall—the window, on an apartment house court.

CHARACTERS:
   YOUNG WOMAN
   MOTHER
OUTSIDE VOICES: *Characters heard, but not seen:*
   A JANITOR
   A BABY
   A MOTHER AND A SMALL BOY
   A YOUNG BOY AND YOUNG GIRL
   A HUSBAND AND A WIFE
   ANOTHER HUSBAND AND A WIFE
SOUNDS:
   Buzzer
   Radio [*Voice of Announcer*]
       [*Music and Singer*]
AT RISE:
   YOUNG WOMAN *and* MOTHER *eating—Radio offstage—Radio stops.*

YOUNG WOMAN   Ma—I want to talk to you.

MOTHER   Aren't you eating a potato?

YOUNG WOMAN   No.

MOTHER   Why not?

5 YOUNG WOMAN   I don't want one.

MOTHER   That's no reason. Here! Take one.

YOUNG WOMAN   I don't want it.

MOTHER   Potatoes go with stew—here!

YOUNG WOMAN   Ma, I don't want it!

10 MOTHER   Want it! Take it!

YOUNG WOMAN   But I—oh, all right. [*Takes it—then.*] Ma, I want to ask you
   something.

MOTHER   Eat your potato.

YOUNG WOMAN [*takes a bite—then*]   Ma, there's something I want to ask
15   you—something important.

MOTHER   Is it mealy?

YOUNG WOMAN   S'all right. Ma—tell me.

MOTHER   Three pounds for a quarter.

YOUNG WOMAN   Ma—tell me—
   [*Buzzer.*]

20 MOTHER [*her dull voice brightening*]   There's the garbage. [*Goes to door—or
   dumbwaiter*[4]—*opens it.*]
   [*Stop radio.*]

JANITOR'S VOICE [*offstage*]   Garbage.

MOTHER [*pleased—busy*]   All right. [*Gets garbage can—puts it out.* YOUNG
   WOMAN *walks up and down.*] What's the matter now?

YOUNG WOMAN   Nothing.

25 MOTHER   That jumping up from the table every night the garbage is collected! You act like you're crazy.

YOUNG WOMAN   Ma, do all women—

MOTHER   I suppose you think you're too nice for anything so common! Well,
   let me tell you, my lady, that it's a very important part of life.

30 YOUNG WOMAN   I know, but, Ma, if you—

MOTHER   If it weren't for garbage cans where would we be? Where would we
   all be? Living in filth—that's what! Filth! I should think you'd be glad! I
   should think you'd be grateful!

YOUNG WOMAN   Oh, Ma!

35 MOTHER   Well, are you?

YOUNG WOMAN   Am I what?

MOTHER   Glad! Grateful.

YOUNG WOMAN   Yes!

MOTHER   You don't act like it!

40 YOUNG WOMAN   Oh, Ma, don't talk!

MOTHER   You just said you wanted to talk.

YOUNG WOMAN   Well now—I want to think. I got to think.

MOTHER   Aren't you going to finish your potato?

YOUNG WOMAN   Oh, Ma!

45 MOTHER   Is there anything the matter with it?

YOUNG WOMAN   No—

4. Small elevator system used to move food or other goods between floors of a building.

MOTHER   Then why don't you finish it?

YOUNG WOMAN   Because I don't want it.

MOTHER   Why don't you?

50 YOUNG WOMAN   Oh, Ma! Let me alone!

MOTHER   Well, you've got to eat! If you don't eat—

YOUNG WOMAN   Ma! Don't nag!

MOTHER   Nag! Just because I try to look out for you—nag! Just because I try
to care for you—nag! Why, you haven't sense enough to eat! What would
55 become of you I'd like to know—if I didn't nag!

[*Offstage—a sound of window opening—all these offstage sounds come
in through the court window at the back.*]

WOMAN'S VOICE   Johnny—Johnny—come in now!

A SMALL BOY'S VOICE   Oh, Ma!

WOMAN VOICE   It's getting cold.

A SMALL BOY'S VOICE   Oh, Ma!

60 WOMAN'S VOICE   You heard me! [*Sound of window slamming.*]

YOUNG WOMAN   I'm grown up, Ma.

MOTHER   Grown up! What do you mean by that?

YOUNG WOMAN   Nothing much—I guess. [*Offstage sound of baby crying.*
MOTHER *rises, clatters dishes.*] Let's not do the dishes right away, Ma. Let's
65 talk—I gotta.

MOTHER   Well, I can't talk with dirty dishes around—you may be able to
but—[*Clattering—clattering.*]

YOUNG WOMAN   Ma! Listen! Listen!—There's a man wants to marry me.

MOTHER [*stops clattering—sits*]   What man?

70 YOUNG WOMAN   He says he fell in love with my hands.

MOTHER   In love! Is that beginning again! I thought you were over that!

[*Offstage* BOY'S VOICE—*whistles—*GIRL'S VOICE *answers.*]

BOY'S VOICE   Come on out.

GIRL'S VOICE   Can't.

BOY'S VOICE   Nobody'll see you.

75 GIRL'S VOICE   I can't.

BOY'S VOICE   It's dark now—come on.

GIRL'S VOICE   Well—just for a minute.

BOY'S VOICE   Meet you round the corner.

YOUNG WOMAN   I got to get married, Ma.

80 MOTHER   What do you mean?

YOUNG WOMAN   I gotta.

MOTHER   You haven't got in trouble, have you?

YOUNG WOMAN   Don't talk like that!

MOTHER   Well, you say you got to get married—what do you mean?

85 YOUNG WOMAN   Nothing.

MOTHER   Answer me!

YOUNG WOMAN   All women get married, don't they?

MOTHER   Nonsense!

YOUNG WOMAN   You got married, didn't you?

90 MOTHER   Yes, I did!

[*Offstage voices.*]

WOMAN'S VOICE   Where you going?

MAN'S VOICE   Out.

WOMAN'S VOICE   You were out last night.

MAN'S VOICE   Was I?

95 WOMAN'S VOICE   You're always going out.

MAN'S VOICE   Am I?

WOMAN'S VOICE   Where you going?

MAN'S VOICE   Out.

[End of offstage voices.]

MOTHER   Who is he? Where did you come to know him?

100 YOUNG WOMAN   In the office.

MOTHER   In the office!

YOUNG WOMAN   It's Mr. J.

MOTHER   Mr. J.?

YOUNG WOMAN   The Vice-President.

105 MOTHER   Vice-President! His income must be— Does he know you've got a
mother to support?

YOUNG WOMAN   Yes.

MOTHER   What does he say?

YOUNG WOMAN   All right.

110 MOTHER   How soon you going to marry him?

YOUNG WOMAN   I'm not going to.

MOTHER   Not going to!

YOUNG WOMAN   No! I'm not going to.

MOTHER   But you just said—

115 YOUNG WOMAN   I'm not going to.

MOTHER   Are you crazy?

YOUNG WOMAN   I can't, Ma! I can't!

MOTHER   Why can't you?

YOUNG WOMAN   I don't love him.

120 MOTHER   Love!—what does that amount to! Will it clothe you? Will it feed
you? Will it pay the bills?

YOUNG WOMAN   No! But it's real just the same!

MOTHER   Real!

YOUNG WOMAN   If it isn't—what can you count on in life?

125 MOTHER   I'll tell you what you can count on! You can count that you've got to
eat and sleep and get up and put clothes on your back and take 'em off
again—that you got to get old—and that you got to die. That's what you
can count on! All the rest is in your head!

YOUNG WOMAN   But Ma—didn't you love Pa?

130 MOTHER   I suppose I did—I don't know—I've forgotten—what difference
does it make—now?

YOUNG WOMAN   But then!—oh Ma, tell me!

MOTHER   Tell you what?

YOUNG WOMAN   About all that—love!

[Offstage voices.]

135 WIFE'S VOICE   Don't.

HUSBAND'S VOICE   What's the matter—don't you want me to kiss you?

WIFE'S VOICE   Not like that.

HUSBAND'S VOICE   Like what?

WIFE'S VOICE   That silly kiss!

140 HUSBAND'S VOICE   Silly kiss?

WIFE'S VOICE   You look so silly—oh I know what's coming when you look like that—and kiss me like that—don't—go away—

[*End of off stage voices.*]

MOTHER   He's a decent man, isn't he?

YOUNG WOMAN   I don't know. How should I know—yet.

145 MOTHER   He's a Vice-President—of course he's decent.

YOUNG WOMAN   I don't care whether he's decent or not. I won't marry him.

MOTHER   But you just said you wanted to marry—

YOUNG WOMAN   Not him.

MOTHER   Who?

150 YOUNG WOMAN   I don't know—I don't know—I haven't found him yet!

MOTHER   You talk like you're crazy!

YOUNG WOMAN   Oh, Ma—tell me!

MOTHER   Tell you what?

YOUNG WOMAN   Tell me— [*Words suddenly pouring out.*] Your skin oughtn't

155 to curl—ought it—when he just comes near you—ought it? That's wrong, ain't it? You don't get over that, do you—ever, do you or do you? How is it, Ma—do you?

MOTHER   Do you what?

YOUNG WOMAN   Do you get used to, it—so after a while it doesn't matter? Or

160 don't you? Does it always matter? You ought to be in love, oughtn't you, Ma? You must be in love, mustn't you, Ma? That changes everything, doesn't it—or does it? Maybe if you just like a person it's all right—is it? When he puts a hand on me, my blood turns cold. But your blood oughtn't to run cold, ought it? His hands are—his hands are—fat, Ma—don't you

165 see—his hands are fat—and they sort of press—and they're fat—don't you see?—Don't you see?

MOTHER [*stares at her bewildered*]   See what?

YOUNG WOMAN [*rushing on*]   I've always thought I'd find somebody— somebody young—and—and attractive—with wavy hair—wavy hair—I

170 always think of children with curls—little curls all over their head— somebody young—and attractive—that I'd like—that I'd love— But I haven't found anybody like that yet—I haven't found anybody— I've hardly known anybody—you'd never let me go with anybody and—

MOTHER   Are you throwing it up to me that—

175 YOUNG WOMAN   No—let me finish, Ma! No—let me finish! I just mean I've never found anybody—anybody—nobody's ever asked me—till now—he's the only man that's ever asked me— And I suppose I got to marry somebody—all girls do—

MOTHER   Nonsense.

180 YOUNG WOMAN   But, I can't go on like this, Ma—I don't know why—but I can't—it's like I'm all tight inside—sometimes I feel like I'm stifling!— You don't know—stifling. [*Walks up and down.*] I can't go on like this much longer—going to work—coming home—going to work—coming home—I can't— Sometimes in the subway I think I'm going to die—sometimes even

185 in the office if something don't happen—I got to do something—I don't know—it's like I'll all tight inside.

MOTHER   You're crazy.

YOUNG WOMAN   Oh, Ma!

MOTHER You're crazy!

190 YOUNG WOMAN Ma—if you tell me that again I'll kill you! I'll kill you!

MOTHER If that isn't crazy!

YOUNG WOMAN I'll kill you— Maybe I am crazy— I don't know. Sometimes I think I am—the thoughts that go on in my mind—sometimes I think I am—I can't help it if I am—I do the best I can—I do the best I can and I'm

195 nearly crazy! [MOTHER *rises and sits.*] Go away! Go away! You don't know anything about anything! And you haven't got any pity—no pity—you just take it for granted that I go to work every day—and come home every night and bring my money every week—you just take it for granted—you'd let me go on forever—and never feel any pity—

[*Offstage* RADIO—*a voice singing a sentimental Mother song or popular home song.*]

[MOTHER *begins to cry—crosses to chair Left—sits.*]

200 YOUNG WOMAN Oh Ma—forgive me! Forgive me!

MOTHER My own child! To be spoken to like that by my own child!

YOUNG WOMAN I didn't mean it, Ma—I didn't mean it!

[*She goes to her mother—crosses to Left.*]

MOTHER [*clinging to her hand*] You're all I've got in the world—and you don't want me—you want to kill me.

205 YOUNG WOMAN No—no, I don't, Ma! I just said that!

MOTHER I've worked for you and slaved for you!

YOUNG WOMAN I know, Ma.

MOTHER I brought you into the world.

YOUNG WOMAN I know, Ma.

210 MOTHER You're flesh of my flesh and—

YOUNG WOMAN I know, Ma, I know.

MOTHER And—

YOUNG WOMAN You rest, now, Ma—you rest—

MOTHER [*struggling*] I got to do the dishes.

215 YOUNG WOMAN I'll do the dishes— You listen to the music, Ma—I'll do the dishes.

[MA *sits.*]

[YOUNG WOMAN *crosses to behind screen.*]

[*Takes a pair of rubber gloves and begins to put them on.*]

[*The* MOTHER *sees them—they irritate her—there is a return of her characteristic mood.*]

MOTHER Those gloves! I've been washing dishes for forty years and I never wore gloves! But my lady's hands! My lady's hands!

YOUNG WOMAN Sometimes you talk to me like you're jealous, Ma.

220 MOTHER Jealous?

YOUNG WOMAN It's my hands got me a husband.

MOTHER A husband? So you're going to marry him now!

YOUNG WOMAN I suppose so.

MOTHER If you ain't the craziest—

[*The scene blacks out.*]

[*In the darkness, the* MOTHER *song goes into jazz—very faint—as the scene lights into*]

Episode Three
HONEYMAN

SCENE: *Hotel Bedroom.*
Bed, chair, mirror.
The door at the back now opens on a bathroom; the window, on a dancing casino opposite.

CHARACTERS:
YOUNG WOMAN
HUSBAND
BELLBOY

OFFSTAGE:
Seen but not heard—MEN *and* WOMEN *dancing in couples.*

SOUNDS:
A small jazz band [violin, piano, saxophone—very dim, at first, then louder].

AT RISE:
Set dark.
BELLBOY, HUSBAND, *and* YOUNG WOMAN *enter.* BELLBOY *carries luggage. He switches on light by door.*
Stop music.

HUSBAND   Well, here we are.
[*Throws hat on bed.*]
[BELLBOY *puts luggage down, crosses to window, raises shade three inches, opens window three inches.*]
[*Sounds of jazz music louder. Offstage.*]

BELLBOY [*comes to man for tip*]   Anything else, Sir?
[*Receives tip. Exits.*]

HUSBAND   Well, here we are.

YOUNG WOMAN   Yes, here we are.

5 HUSBAND   Aren't you going to take your hat off—stay a while? [YOUNG WOMAN *looks around as though looking for a way out, then takes off her hat, pulls the hair automatically around her ears.*] This is all right, isn't it? Huh? Huh?

YOUNG WOMAN   It's very nice.

HUSBAND   Twelve bucks a day![5] They know how to soak you in these pleasure resorts. Twelve bucks! [*Music.*] Well—we'll get our money's worth out of it

10 all right. [*Goes toward bathroom.*] I'm going to wash up. [*Stops at door.*] Don't you want to wash up? [YOUNG WOMAN *shakes head "No".*] I do! It was a long trip! I want to wash up! [*Goes off—closes door. Sings in bathroom.* YOUNG WOMAN *goes to window—raises shade—sees the dancers going round and round in couples. Music is louder. Re-enter* HUSBAND.] Say, pull that blind down! They can see in!

15 YOUNG WOMAN   I thought you said there'd be a view of the ocean!

HUSBAND   Sure there is.

YOUNG WOMAN   I just see people—dancing.

HUSBAND   The ocean's beyond.

---

5. Approximately $160 in current value; in 1928 luxury hotel room rates began at $4 to $6 per night, so a $12 room rate would have been for the finest accommodations possible.

YOUNG WOMAN [*desperately*]   I was counting on seeing it!

20 HUSBAND   You'll see it tomorrow—what's eating you? We'll take in the board-walk[6]— Don't you want to wash up?

YOUNG WOMAN   No!

HUSBAND   It was a long trip. Sure you don't? [YOUNG WOMAN *shakes her head "No." * HUSBAND *takes off his coat—puts it over chair.*] Better make yourself at

25 home. I'm going to. [*She stares at him—moves away from the window.*] Say, pull down that blind! [*Crosses to chair down* L*—sits.*]

YOUNG WOMAN   It's close—don't you think it's close?

HUSBAND   Well—you don't want people looking in, do you? [*Laughs.*] Huh—huh?

30 YOUNG WOMAN   No.

HUSBAND [*laughs*]   I guess not. Huh? [*Takes off shoes.* YOUNG WOMAN *leaves the window, and crosses down to the bed.*] Say—you look a little white around the gills! What's the matter?

YOUNG WOMAN   Nothing.

35 HUSBAND   You look like you're scared.

YOUNG WOMAN   No.

HUSBAND   Nothing to be scared of. You're with your husband, you know.
      [*Takes her to chair, left.*]

YOUNG WOMAN   I know.

HUSBAND   Happy?

40 YOUNG WOMAN   Yes.

HUSBAND [*sitting*]   Then come here and give us a kiss. [*He puts her on his knee.*] That's the girlie. [*He bends her head down, and kisses her along the back of her neck.*] Like that? [*She tries to get to her feet.*] Say—stay there! What you moving for? —You know—you got to learn to relax, little girl—

45 [*Dancers go off. Dim lights. Pinches her above knee.*] Say, what you got under there?

YOUNG WOMAN   Nothing.

HUSBAND   Nothing! [*Laughs.*] That's a good one! Nothing, huh? Huh? That reminds me of the story of the pullman porter and the—what's the matter—

50 did I tell you that one?
      [*Music dims off and out.*]

YOUNG WOMAN   I don't know.

HUSBAND   The pullman porter and the tart?

YOUNG WOMAN   No.

HUSBAND   It's a good one—well—the train was just pulling out and the

55 tart—

YOUNG WOMAN   You did tell that one!

HUSBAND   About the—

YOUNG WOMAN   Yes! Yes! I remember now!

HUSBAND   About the—

60 YOUNG WOMAN   Yes!

HUSBAND   All right—if I did. You're sure it was the one about the—

YOUNG WOMAN   I'm sure.

---

6. Although Treadwell does not specify locations in the play, this reference to a boardwalk would have suggested Atlantic City, New Jersey, a popular tourist location accessible from New York City by train.

HUSBAND   When he asked her what she had underneath her seat and she
said—

65 YOUNG WOMAN   Yes! Yes! That one!

HUSBAND   All right— But I don't believe I did. [SHE *tries to get up again, as* HE
holds her.] You know you have got something under there—what is it?

YOUNG WOMAN   Nothing—just—just my garter.

HUSBAND   Your garter! Your garter! Say did I tell you the one about—

70 YOUNG WOMAN   Yes! Yes!

HUSBAND [*with dignity*]   How do you know which one I meant?

YOUNG WOMAN   You told me them all!

HUSBAND [*pulling her back to his knee*]   No, I didn't! Not by a jugful! I got a
lot of 'em up my sleeve yet—that's part of what I owe my success to—my

75 ability to spring a good story— You know— you got to learn to relax, little
girl—haven't you?

YOUNG WOMAN   Yes.

HUSBAND   That's one of the biggest things to learn in life. That's part of
what I owe my success to. Now you go and get those heavy things off—

80 and relax.

YOUNG WOMAN   They're not heavy.

HUSBAND   You haven't got much on—have you? But you'll feel better with
'em off. [*Gets up.*] Want me to help you?

YOUNG WOMAN   No.

85 HUSBAND   I'm your husband, you know.

YOUNG WOMAN   I know.

HUSBAND   You aren't afraid of your husband, are you?

YOUNG WOMAN   No—of course not—but I thought maybe—can't we go out
for a little while?

90 HUSBAND   Out? What for?

YOUNG WOMAN   Fresh air—walk—talk.

HUSBAND   We can talk here—I'll tell you all about myself. Go along now.
[YOUNG WOMAN *goes toward bathroom door—gets bag.*] Where are you going?

YOUNG WOMAN   In here.

95 HUSBAND   I thought you'd want to wash up.

YOUNG WOMAN   I just want to—get ready.

HUSBAND   You don't have to go in there to take your clothes off!

YOUNG WOMAN   I want to.

HUSBAND   What for?

100 YOUNG WOMAN   I always do.

HUSBAND   What?

YOUNG WOMAN   Undress by myself.

HUSBAND   You've never been married till now—have you? [*Laughs.*] Or have
you been putting something over on me?

105 YOUNG WOMAN   No.

HUSBAND   I understand—kind of modest—huh? Huh?

YOUNG WOMAN   Yes.

HUSBAND   I understand women— [*Indulgently.*] Go along. [*She goes off—
starts to close door.* YOUNG WOMAN *exits.*] Don't close the door—thought you

110 wanted to talk. [*He looks around the room with satisfaction—after a pause—
Rises—takes off his collar.*] You're awful quiet—what are you doing in there?

YOUNG WOMAN   Just—getting ready—

HUSBAND [*still in his mood of satisfaction*] I'm going to enjoy life from now
on— I haven't had such an easy time of it. I got where I am by hard work
and self denial—now I'm going to enjoy life—I'm going to enjoy life—I'm
going to make up for all I missed—aren't you about ready?

YOUNG WOMAN Not yet.

HUSBAND Next year maybe we'll go to Paris. You can buy a lot of that French
underwear—and Switzerland—all my life I've wanted a Swiss watch—that
I bought right there— I coulda' got a Swiss watch here, but I always
wanted one that I bought right there— Isn't that funny—huh? Isn't it?
Huh? Huh?

YOUNG WOMAN Yes.

HUSBAND All my life I've wanted a Swiss watch that I bought right there. All
my life I've counted on having that some day—more than anything—except
one thing—you know what?

YOUNG WOMAN No.

HUSBAND Guess.

YOUNG WOMAN I can't.

HUSBAND Then I'm coming in and tell you.

YOUNG WOMAN No! Please! Please don't.

HUSBAND Well hurry up then! I thought you women didn't wear much of
anything these days—huh? Huh? I'm coming in!

YOUNG WOMAN No—no! Just a minute!

HUSBAND All right. Just a minute!

[YOUNG WOMAN *is silent.*]

HUSBAND [*laughs and takes out watch*] 13—14— I'm counting the seconds
on you—that's what you said, didn't you—just a minute!—49—50—51—
52—53—

[*Enter* YOUNG WOMAN.]

YOUNG WOMAN [*at the door*] Here I am.

[*She wears a little white gown that hangs very straight. She is very still,
but her eyes are wide with a curious, helpless, animal terror.*]

HUSBAND [*starts toward her—stops. The room is in shadow except for one dim
light by the bed. Sound of* GIRL *weeping*]. You crying? [*Sound of weeping.*]
What you crying for? [*Crosses to her.*]

YOUNG WOMAN [*crying out*] Ma! Ma! I want my mother!

HUSBAND I thought you were glad to get away from her.

YOUNG WOMAN I want her now—I want somebody.

HUSBAND You got me, haven't you?

YOUNG WOMAN Somebody—somebody—

HUSBAND There's nothing to cry about. There's nothing to cry about.

BLACK OUT

[*The music continues until the lights go up for* EPISODE FOUR.]

[*Rhythm of the music is gradually replaced by the sound of steel riveting for* EPISODE
FOUR.]

Episode Four
MATERNAL

SCENE: *A room in a hospital. The door in the back now opens on a corridor; the window on a tall building going up.*
  Bed. Chair.

CHARACTERS IN THE SCENE:
  YOUNG WOMAN
  DOCTORS
  NURSES
  HUSBAND

OUTSIDE—CORRIDOR LIFE:

CHARACTERS SEEN BUT NOT HEARD:
  WOMAN IN WHEEL CHAIR
  WOMAN IN BATHROBE
  STRETCHER WAGON
  NURSE WITH TRAY
  NURSE WITH COVERED BASIN

SOUNDS:
  [*outside window*]
    Riveting.

AT RISE:
  YOUNG WOMAN *lies still in bed.*
  The door is open.
  In the corridor, a stretcher wagon goes by.
  Enter NURSE.

———————

NURSE   How are you feeling today? [*No response from* YOUNG WOMAN.] Better? [*No response.*] No pain? [*No response.* NURSE *takes her watch in one hand,* YOUNG WOMAN'S *wrist in the other—stands, then goes to chart at foot of bed—writes.*] You're getting along fine. [*No response.*] Such a sweet baby you have, too. [*No response.*] Aren't you glad it's a girl? [YOUNG WOMAN
5 *makes sign with her head, "No".*] You're not! Oh, my! That's no way to talk! Men want boys—women ought to want girls. [*No response.*] Maybe you didn't want either, eh? [YOUNG WOMAN *signs "No". Riveting machine.*] You'll feel different when it begins to nurse. You'll just love it then. Your milk hasn't come yet—has it? [*Sign—"No".*] It will [*Sign—"No".*] Oh, you don't
10 know Doctor! [*Goes to door—turns.*] Anything else you want? [YOUNG WOMAN *points to window.*] Draft? [*Sign—"No".*] The noise? [YOUNG WOMAN *signs "Yes".*] Oh, that can't be helped. Hospital's got to have a new wing. We're the biggest Maternity Hospital in the world. I'll close the window, though. [YOUNG WOMAN *signs "No".*] No?
15 YOUNG WOMAN [*whispers*]   I smell everything then.
NURSE [*starting out the door—riveting machine*]   Here's your man!
      [*Enter* HUSBAND *with large bouquet. Crosses to bed.*]
HUSBAND   Well, how are we today?
      [YOUNG WOMAN—*no response.*]
NURSE   She's getting stronger!
HUSBAND   Of course she is!
20 NURSE [*taking flowers*]   See what your husband brought you.

HUSBAND   Better put 'em in water right away. [*Exit* NURSE.] Everything O.K.?
[YOUNG WOMAN *signs* "No".] Now see here, my dear, you've got to brace up,
you know! And—and face things! Everybody's got to brace up and face
things! That's what makes the world go round. I know all you've been
25   through but— [YOUNG WOMAN *signs* "No".] Oh, yes I do! I know all about it!
I was right outside all the time! [YOUNG WOMAN *makes violent gesture of*
"No". Ignoring.] Oh yes! But you've got to brace up now! Make an effort!
Pull yourself together! Start the uphill climb! Oh I've been down—but I
haven't stayed down. I've been licked but I haven't stayed licked! I've pulled
30   myself up by my own bootstraps, and that's what you've got to do! Will
power! That's what conquers! Look at me! Now you've got to brace up!
Face the music! Stand the gaff![7] Take life by the horns! Look it in the face!
—Having a baby's natural! Perfectly natural thing—why should—

> [YOUNG WOMAN *chokes—points wildly to door. Enter* NURSE *with flowers*
> *in a vase.*]

NURSE   What's the matter?
35   HUSBAND   She's got that gagging again—like she had the last time I was here.

> [YOUNG WOMAN *gestures him out.*]

NURSE   Better go, sir.
HUSBAND [*at door*]   I'll be back.

> [YOUNG WOMAN *gasping and gesturing.*]

NURSE   She needs rest.
HUSBAND   Tomorrow then. I'll be back tomorrow—tomorrow and every
40   day—goodbye.

> [*Exits.*]

NURSE   You got a mighty nice husband, I guess you know that? [*Writes on*
chart.] Gagging.

> [*Corridor life—*WOMAN IN BATHROBE *passes door. Enter* DOCTOR, YOUNG
> DOCTOR, NURSE *wheeling surgeon's wagon with bottles, instruments, etc.*]

DOCTOR   How's the little lady today?

> [*Crosses to bed.*]

NURSE   She's better, Doctor.
45   DOCTOR   Of course she's better! She's all right—aren't you? [YOUNG WOMAN
does not respond.] What's the matter? Can't you talk?

> [*Drops her hand—takes chart.*]

NURSE   She's a little weak yet, Doctor.
DOCTOR [*at chart*]   Milk hasn't come yet?
NURSE   No, Doctor.
50   DOCTOR   Put the child to breast. [YOUNG WOMAN—"*No—no!*" — *Riveting*
machine.] No? Don't you want to nurse your baby? [YOUNG WOMAN *signs*
"No".] Why not? [*No response.*] These modern neurotic[8] women, eh, Doctor? What are we going to do with 'em? [YOUNG DOCTOR *laughs.* NURSE
smiles.] Bring the baby!
55   YOUNG WOMAN   No!
DOCTOR   Well—that's strong enough. I thought you were too weak to talk—
that's better. You don't want your baby?

---

7. Harsh treatment, abuse.
8. Hysteria and neuroses were seen as mod-   ern women's psychological conditions; see
introduction.

YOUNG WOMAN No.

DOCTOR What do you want?

60 YOUNG WOMAN Let alone—let alone.

DOCTOR Bring the baby.

NURSE Yes, Doctor—she's behaved very badly every time, Doctor—very upset—maybe we better not.

DOCTOR I decide what we better and better not here, Nurse!

65 NURSE Yes, Doctor.

DOCTOR Bring the baby.

NURSE Yes, Doctor.

DOCTOR [with chart] Gagging—you mean nausea.

NURSE Yes, Doctor, but—

70 DOCTOR No buts, nurse.

NURSE Yes, Doctor.

DOCTOR Nausea!— Change her diet!—What is her diet?

NURSE Liquids.

DOCTOR Give her solids.

75 NURSE Yes, Doctor. She says she can't swallow solids.

DOCTOR Give her solids.

NURSE Yes, Doctor. [Starts to go.]

[Riveting machine.]

DOCTOR Wait—I'll change her medicine [Takes pad and writes prescription in Latin. Hands it to NURSE.] After meals. [To door.] Bring her baby.

[Exit DOCTOR, followed by YOUNG DOCTOR and NURSE with surgeon's wagon.]

80 NURSE Yes, Doctor.

[Exits.]

YOUNG WOMAN [alone] Let me alone—let me alone—let me alone—I've submitted to enough—I won't submit to any more—crawl off—crawl off in the dark—Vixen crawled under the bed—way back in the corner under the bed—they were all drowned—puppies don't go to heaven—heaven—golden

85 stairs—long stairs—long—too long—long golden stairs—climb those golden stairs—stairs—stairs—climb—tired—too tired—dead—no matter— nothing matters—dead—stairs—long stairs—all the dead going up—going up to be in heaven—heaven—golden stairs—all the children coming down—coming down to be born—dead going up—children coming down—

90 going up—coming down—going up—coming down—going up—coming down—going up—stop—stop—no—no traffic cop—no—no traffic cop in heaven—traffic cop—traffic cop—can't you give us a smile—tired—too tired—no matter—it doesn't matter—St. Peter—St. Peter at the gate—you can't come in—no matter—it doesn't matter—I'll rest—I'll lie down—

95 down—all written down—down in a big book[9]—no matter—it doesn't matter—I'll lie down—it weighs me—it's over me—it weighs—weighs—it's heavy—it's a heavy book—no matter—lie still—don't move—can't move— rest—forget—they say you forget—a girl—aren't you glad it's a girl—a little

_____

9. Matthew 16:19 provides the Biblical source for popularized images of St. Peter as the keeper of the gates to heaven; Peter is often depicted with keys and with a book that lists who has earned entrance through good deeds during life.

girl—with no hair—none—little curls all over his head—a little bald girl—
100 curls—curls all over his head—what kind of hair has God? no matter—it
doesn't matter—everybody loves God—they've got to—got to—got to love
God—God is love—even if he's bad they got to love him—even if he's got
fat hands—fat hands—no no—he wouldn't be God—His hands make you
well—He lays on his hands—well—and happy—no matter—doesn't matter—
105 far—too far—tired—too tired Vixen crawled off under bed—eight—there
were eight—a woman crawled off under the bed—a woman has one—two
three four—one two three four—one two three four—two plus two is
four—two times two is four—two times four is eight Vixen had eight—one
two three four five six seven eight—eight—Puffie had eight—all drowned—
110 drowned—drowned in blood—blood—oh God! God—God never had
one—Mary had one—in a manger—the lowly manger—God's on a high
throne—far—too far—no matter—it doesn't matter—God Mary Mary God
Mary—Virgin Mary—Mary had one—the Holy Ghost—the Holy Ghost—
George H. Jones—oh don't—please don't! Let me rest—now I can rest—the
115 weight is gone—inside the weight is gone—it's only outside—outside—all
around—weight—I'm under it—Vixen crawled under the bed—there were
eight—I'll not submit any more—I'll not submit—I'll not submit—

> [*The scene* BLACKS OUT. *The sound of riveting continues until it goes into
> the sound of an electric piano and the scene lights up for* EPISODE FIVE.]

Episode Five

PROHIBITED[1]

SCENE: *Bar—Bottles—Tables—Chairs—Electric piano.*
SOUND: *Electric piano.*
CHARACTERS:
  MAN *behind the bar*
  POLICEMAN *at bar*
  WAITER
  At Table 1. A MAN *and a* WOMAN
  At Table 2. A MAN *and a* BOY
  At Table 3. TWO MEN *waiting for* TWO GIRLS, *who are*
  TELEPHONE GIRL *of Episode One and* YOUNG WOMAN.

AT RISE. *Everyone except the* GIRLS *on. Of the characters, the* MAN *and* WOMAN *at
  Table* 1 *are an ordinary man and woman.* THE MAN *at Table* 2 *is a middle-aged
  fairy;*[2] *the* BOY *is young, untouched. At Table* 3, IST MAN *is pleasing, common,
  vigorous. He has coarse wavy hair.* 2ND MAN *is an ordinary salesman type.*

IST MAN [*at Table* 3] I'm going to beat it.
2ND MAN Oh, for the love of Mike.

1. The period known as Prohibition, 1919–33, began with the ratification of the Eighteenth Amendment to the U.S. Constitution, which prohibited the sale or transport of alcohol, and ended with its repeal by the Twenty-first Amendment. During this period illegal bars known as "speakeasies" sprang up around the country, especially in urban areas. Treadwell slyly signals how inconsistently the law was enforced by placing a policeman at the bar, flouting the law he was supposed to uphold.
2. Term used to describe an effeminate homosexual male; at the time, such usage was not necessarily derogatory.

IST MAN They ain't going to show.

2ND MAN Sure they'll show.

5 IST MAN How do you know they'll show?

2ND MAN I tell you you can't keep that baby away from me—just got to—[*Snaps fingers.*]—She comes running.

IST MAN Looks like it.

2ND MAN [*to* WAITER—*makes sign "2", with his fingers.*] The same.

[WAITER *goes to the bar.*]

10 MAN [*at Table 2*] Oh, I'm sorry I brought you here.

BOY Why?

MAN This Purgatory of noise! I brought you here to give you pleasure—let you taste pleasure. This sherry they have here is bottled—heaven. Wait till you taste it.

15 BOY But I don't drink.

MAN Drink! This isn't drink! Real amontillado[3] is sunshine and orange groves—it's the Mediterranean and blue moonlight and—love? Have you ever been in love?

BOY No.

20 MAN Never in love with—a woman?

BOY No—not really.

MAN What do you mean—really?

BOY Just—that.

MAN Ah! [*Makes sign to* WAITER.] Two—you know what I want—Two.

[WAITER *goes to the bar.*]

25 MAN [*at Table 1*] Well, are you going through with it, or ain't you?

WOMAN That's what I want to do—go through with it.

MAN But you can't.

WOMAN Why can't I?

MAN How can yuh? [*Silence.*] It's nothing—most women don't think

30 anything about it—they just—Bert told me a doctor to go to—gave me the address—

WOMAN Don't talk about it!

MAN Got to talk about it—you got to get out of this. [*Silence*—MAN *makes sign to* WAITER.] What you having?

35 WOMAN Nothing—I don't want anything. I had enough.

MAN Do you good. The same?

WOMAN I suppose so.

MAN [*makes sign "2" to* WAITER] The same.

[WAITER *goes to the bar.*]

———

[*At Table 3.*]

IST MAN I'm going to beat it.

40 2ND MAN Oh say, listen! I'm counting on you to take the other one off my hands.

IST MAN I'm going to beat it.

2ND MAN For the love of Mike have a heart! Listen—as a favor to me—I got to be home by six—I promised my wife—sure. That don't leave me no time

———

3. Type of dry sherry.

45   at all if we got to hang around—entertain some dame. You got to take her off my hands.

IST MAN   Maybe she won't fall for me.

2ND MAN   Sure she'll fall for you! They all fall for you—even my wife likes you—tries to kid herself it's your brave exploits, but I know what it is—sure
50   she'll fall for you.

          [*Enter two girls—*TELEPHONE GIRL *and* YOUNG WOMAN.]

GIRL [*coming to Table.*]   Hello—

2ND MAN [*grouch*]   Good night.

GIRL   Good night? What's eatin' yuh?

2ND MAN [*same*]   Nothin's eatin' me—thought somethin' musta swallowed
55   you.

GIRL   Why?

2ND MAN   You're late!

GIRL [*unimpressed*]   Oh—[*Brushing it aside.*]—Mrs. Jones—Mr. Smith.

2ND MAN   Meet my friend, Mr. Roe. [*They all sit. To the* WAITER.] The same,
60   and two more.

          [WAITER *goes.*]

GIRL   So we kept you waiting, did we?

2ND MAN   Only about an hour.

YOUNG WOMAN   Was it that long?

2ND MAN   We been here that long—ain't we, Dick?

65 IST MAN   Just about, Harry.

2ND MAN   For the love of God what delayed yuh?

GIRL   Tell Helen that one.

2ND MAN [*to* YOUNG WOMAN]   The old Irish woman that went to her first race? Bet on the skate that came in last—she went up to the jockey and asked
70   him, "For the love of God, what delayed yuh?" [*All laugh.*]

YOUNG WOMAN   Why, that's kinda funny!

2ND MAN   Kinda!—What do you mean kinda?

YOUNG WOMAN   I just mean there are not many of 'em that are funny at all.

2ND MAN   Not if you haven't heard the funny ones.

75 YOUNG WOMAN   Oh I've heard 'em all.

IST MAN   Not a laugh in a carload, eh?

GIRL   Got a cigarette?

2ND MAN [*with package*]   One of these?

GIRL [*taking one*]   Uhhuh.

          [*He offers the package to* YOUNG WOMAN.]

80 YOUNG WOMAN [*taking one*]   Uhhuh.

2ND MAN [*to* IST MAN]   One of these?

IST MAN [*showing his own package*]   Thanks—I like these. [*He lights* YOUNG WOMAN's *cigarette.*]

2ND MAN [*lighting* GIRL's *cigarette*]   Well—baby—how they comin', huh?

GIRL   Couldn't be better.

85 2ND MAN   How's every little thing?

GIRL   Just great.

2ND MAN   Miss me?

GIRL   I'll say so—when did you get in?

2ND MAN   Just a coupla hours ago.

90 GIRL   Miss me?

2ND MAN   Did I? You don't know the half of it.

YOUNG WOMAN [*interrupting restlessly*]   Can we dance here?

2ND MAN   Not here.

YOUNG WOMAN   Where do we go from here?

95 2ND MAN   Where do we go from here! You just got here!

1ST MAN   What's the hurry?

2ND MAN   What's the rush?

YOUNG WOMAN   I don't know.

GIRL   Helen wants to dance.

100 YOUNG WOMAN   I just want to keep moving.

1ST MAN [*smiling*]   You want to keep moving, huh?

2ND MAN   You must be one of those restless babies! Where do we go from here!

YOUNG WOMAN   It's only some days—I want to keep moving.

105 1ST MAN   You want to keep moving, huh? [*He is staring at her smilingly.*]

YOUNG WOMAN [*nods*]   Uhhuh.

1ST MAN [*quietly*]   Stick around a while.

2ND MAN   Where do we go from here! Say, what kind of a crowd do you run with, anyway?

110 GIRL   Helen don't run with any crowd—do you, Helen?

YOUNG WOMAN [*embarrassed*]   No.

1ST MAN   Well, I'm not a crowd—run with me.

2ND MAN [*gratified*]   All set, huh?—Dick was about ready to beat it.

1ST MAN   That's before I met the little lady.

[WAITER *serves drinks.*]

115 1ST MAN   Here's how.

2ND MAN   Here's to you.

GIRL   Here's looking at you.

YOUNG WOMAN   Here's—happy days.

[*They all drink.*]

1ST MAN   That's good stuff!

120 2ND MAN   Off a boat.

1ST MAN   Off a boat?

2ND MAN   They get all their stuff here—off a boat.

GIRL   That's what *they* say.

2ND MAN   No! Sure! Sure they do! Sure!

125 GIRL   It's all right with me.

2ND MAN   But they do! Sure!

GIRL   I believe you, darling!

2ND MAN   Did you miss me?

GIRL   Uhhuh. [*Affirmative.*]

130 2ND MAN   Any other daddies?

GIRL   Uhhuh. [*Negative.*]

2ND MAN   Love any daddy but daddy?

GIRL   Uhhuh. [*Negative.*]

2ND MAN   Let's beat it!

135 GIRL [*a little self-conscious before* YOUNG WOMAN]   We just got here.

2ND MAN   Don't I know it—Come on!

GIRL   But—[*Indicates* YOUNG WOMAN.]

2ND MAN [*not understanding*]   They're all set—aren't you?

1ST MAN [*to* YOUNG WOMAN.]   Are we? [*She doesn't answer.*]

140 2ND MAN   I got to be out to the house by six—come on—[*Rising—to* GIRL.] Come on, kid—let's us beat it! [GIRL *indicates* YOUNG WOMAN.] [*Now understanding—very elaborate.*] Business is business, you know! I got a lot to do yet this afternoon—thought you might go along with me—help me out—how about it?

145 GIRL [*rising, her dignity preserved*]   Sure—I'll go along with you—help you out. [*Both rise.*]

2ND MAN   All right with you folks?

1ST MAN   All right with me.

2ND MAN   All right with you? [*To* YOUNG WOMAN.]

YOUNG WOMAN   All right with me.

150 2ND MAN   Come on, kid. [*They rise.*] Where's the damage?[4]

1ST MAN   Go on!

2ND MAN   No!

1ST MAN   Go on!

2ND MAN   I'll match you.

155 YOUNG WOMAN   Heads win!

GIRL   Heads I win—tails you lose.

2ND MAN [*impatiently*]   He's matching me.

1ST MAN   Am I matching you or you matching me?

2ND MAN   I'm matching you. [*They match.*] You're stung!

160 1ST MAN [*contentedly*]   Not so you can notice it. [*Smiles at* YOUNG WOMAN.]

GIRL   That's for you, Helen.

2ND MAN   She ain't dumb! Come on.

GIRL [*to* 1ST MAN]   You be nice to her now. She's very fastidious. —Goodbye. [*Exit* 2ND MAN *and* GIRL.]

YOUNG WOMAN   I know what business is like.

165 1ST MAN   You do—do yuh?

YOUNG WOMAN   I used to be a business girl myself before—

1ST MAN   Before what?

YOUNG WOMAN   Before I quit.

1ST MAN   What did you quit for?

170 YOUNG WOMAN   I just quit.

1ST MAN   You're married, huh?

YOUNG WOMAN   Yes—I am.

1ST MAN   All right with me.

YOUNG WOMAN   Some men don't seem to like a woman after she's married— [WAITER *comes to the table.*]

175 1ST MAN   What's the difference?

YOUNG WOMAN   Depends on the man, I guess.

1ST MAN   Depends on the woman, I guess. [*To* WAITER, *makes sign of "2".*] The same. [WAITER *goes to the bar.*]

---

4. The bill, or charge for the drinks.

[*At Table 1.*]

MAN   It don't amount to nothing. God! Most women just—

180 WOMAN   I know—I know—I know.

MAN   They don't think nothing of it. They just—

WOMAN   I know—I know—I know.

[*Re-enter* 2ND MAN *and* GIRL. *They go to Table* 3.]

2ND MAN   Say, I forgot—I want you to do something for me, will yuh?

1ST MAN   Sure—what is it?

185 2ND MAN   I want you to telephone me out home tomorrow—and ask me to come into town—will yuh?

1ST MAN   Sure—why not?

2ND MAN   You know—business—get me?

1ST MAN   I get you.

190 2ND MAN   I've worked the telegraph gag to death—and my wife likes you.

1ST MAN   What's your number?

2ND MAN   I'll write it down for you.

[*Writes.*]

1ST MAN   How is your wife?

2ND MAN   She's fine.

195 1ST MAN   And the kid?

2ND MAN   Great. [*Hands him the card.*] Come on, kid. [*To* GIRL. *Turns back to* YOUNG WOMAN.] Get this bird to tell you about himself.

GIRL   Keep him from it.

2ND MAN   Get him to tell you how he killed a couple a spig[5] down in Mexico.

200 GIRL   You been in Mexico?

2ND MAN   He just came up from there.

GIRL   Can you teach us the tango?

YOUNG WOMAN   You killed a man?

2ND MAN   Two of 'em! With a bottle! Get him to tell you—with a bottle.

205 Come on, kid. Goodbye.

[*Exit* 2ND MAN *and* GIRL.]

YOUNG WOMAN   Why did you?

1ST MAN   What?

YOUNG WOMAN   Kill 'em?

1ST MAN   To get free.

210 YOUNG WOMAN   Oh.

[*At Table 2.*]

MAN   You really must taste this—just taste it. It's a real amontillado, you know.

BOY   Where do they get it here?

MAN   It's always down the side streets one finds the real pleasures, don't you

215 think?

BOY   I don't know.

---

5. Derogatory term, alternate of "spic," used to describe Spanish speakers or those speaking English with a Spanish accent.

MAN   Learn. Come, taste this! Amontillado! Or don't you like amontillado?

BOY   I don't know. I never had any before.

MAN   Your first taste! How I envy you! Come, taste it! Taste it! And die.

[BOY *tastes wine—finds it disappointing.*]

220   MAN [*gilding it*]   Poe was a lover of amontillado. He returns to it continually, you remember—or are you a lover of Poe?[6]

BOY   I've read a lot of him.

MAN   But are you a lover?

———————

[*At Table 3.*]

1ST MAN   There were a bunch of bandidos—bandits, you know, took me into
225   the hills—holding me there—what was I to do? I got the two birds that guarded me drunk one night, and then I filled the empty bottle with small stones—and let 'em have it!

YOUNG WOMAN   Oh!

1ST MAN   I had to get free, didn't I? I let 'em have it—

230   YOUNG WOMAN   Oh—then what did you do?

1ST MAN   Then I beat it.

YOUNG WOMAN   Where to—?

1ST MAN   Right here. [*Pause*] Glad?

YOUNG WOMAN [*nods*]   Yes.

235   1ST MAN [*makes sign to* WAITER *of "2"*]   The same.

[WAITER *goes to bar.*]

———————

[*At Table 1.*]

MAN   You're just scared because this is the first time and—

WOMAN   I'm not scared.

MAN   Then what are you for Christ's sake?

WOMAN   I'm not scared. I want it—I want to have it—that ain't being scared,
240   is it?

MAN   It's being goofy.

WOMAN   I don't care.

MAN   What about your folks?

WOMAN   I don't care.

245   MAN   What about your job? [*Silence.*] You got to keep your job, haven't you?
[*Silence.*] Haven't you?

WOMAN   I suppose so.

MAN   Well—there you are!

WOMAN [*silence—then*]   All right—let's go now— You got the address?

250   MAN   Now you're coming to.

[*They get up and go off.*]

[*Exit* MAN *and* WOMAN.]

———————

6. Edgar Allan Poe (1809–1849), American short story writer and poet, perhaps best known today for his contributions to the mystery genre, although here the emphasis appears to be on his verse. To be a lover of Poe, in this context, may also be code for homosexuality.

[*At Table* 3.]

YOUNG WOMAN A bottle like that? [*She picks it up.*]

1ST MAN Yeah—filled with pebbles.

YOUNG WOMAN What kind of pebbles?

1ST MAN Pebbles! Off the ground.

255 YOUNG WOMAN Oh.

1ST MAN Necessity, you know, mother of invention. [*As* YOUNG WOMAN *handles the bottle.*] Ain't a bad weapon—first you got a sledge hammer—then you got a knife.

YOUNG WOMAN Oh. [*Puts bottle down.*]

260 1ST MAN Women don't like knives, do they? [*Pours drink.*]

YOUNG WOMAN No.

1ST MAN Don't mind a hammer so much, though, do they?

YOUNG WOMAN No—

1ST MAN I didn't like it myself—any of it—but I had to get free, didn't I?

265 Sure I had to get free, didn't I? [*Drinks.*] Now I'm damn glad I did.

YOUNG WOMAN Why?

1ST MAN You know why. [*He puts his hand over hers.*]

_____

[*At Table* 2.]

MAN Let's go to my rooms—and I'll show them to you—I have a first edition of Verlaine[7] that will simply make your mouth water. [*They stand up.*]

270 Here—there's just a sip at the bottom of my glass— [BOY *takes it.*] That last sip that's sweetest— Wasn't it?

BOY [*laughs*] And I always thought that was dregs.

[*Exit* MAN *followed by* BOY.]

_____

[*At Table* 3.]

[*The* MAN *is holding her hand across the table.*]

YOUNG WOMAN When you put your hand over mine! When you just touch me!

1ST MAN Yeah? [*Pause.*] Come on, kid, let's go!

275 YOUNG WOMAN Where?

1ST MAN You haven't been around much, have you, kid?

YOUNG WOMAN No.

1ST MAN I could tell that just to look at you.

YOUNG WOMAN You could?

280 1ST MAN Sure I could. What are you running around with a girl like that other one for?

YOUNG WOMAN I don't know. She seems to have a good time.

1ST MAN So that's it?

YOUNG WOMAN Don't she?

285 1ST MAN Don't you?

YOUNG WOMAN No.

1ST MAN Never?

YOUNG WOMAN Never.

1ST MAN What's the matter?

7. Paul Verlaine (1844–1896), French symbolist poet.

290 YOUNG WOMAN   Nothing—just me, I guess.

IST MAN   You're all right.

YOUNG WOMAN   Am I?

IST MAN   Sure. You just haven't met the right guy—that's all—a girl like you—
you got to meet the right guy.

295 YOUNG WOMAN   I know.

IST MAN   You're different from girls like that other one—any guy'll do her.
You're different.

YOUNG WOMAN   I guess I am.

IST MAN   You didn't fall for that business gag—did you—when they went off?

300 YOUNG WOMAN   Well, I thought they wanted to be alone probably, but—

IST MAN   And how!

YOUNG WOMAN   Oh—so that's it.

IST MAN   That's it. Come along—let's go—

YOUNG WOMAN   Oh, I couldn't! Like this?

305 IST MAN   Don't you like me?

YOUNG WOMAN   Yes.

IST MAN   Then what's the matter?

YOUNG WOMAN   Do—you—like me?

IST MAN   Like yuh? You don't know the half of it—listen—you know what
310   you seem like to me?

YOUNG WOMAN   What?

IST MAN   An angel. Just like an angel.

YOUNG WOMAN   I do?

IST MAN   That's what I said! Let's go!

315 YOUNG WOMAN   Where?

IST MAN   Where do you live?

YOUNG WOMAN   Oh, we can't go to my place.

IST MAN   Then come to my place.

YOUNG WOMAN   Oh I couldn't—is it far?

320 IST MAN   Just a step—come on—

YOUNG WOMAN   Oh I couldn't—what is it—a room?

IST MAN   No—an apartment—a one-room apartment.

YOUNG WOMAN   That's different.

IST MAN   On the ground floor—no one will see you—coming or going.

325 YOUNG WOMAN   [getting up]   I couldn't.

IST MAN   [rises]   Wait a minute—I got to pay the damage—and I'll get a bottle
of something to take along.

YOUNG WOMAN   No—don't.

IST MAN   Why not?

330 YOUNG WOMAN   Well—don't bring any pebbles.

IST MAN   Say—forget that! Will you?

YOUNG WOMAN   I just meant I don't think I'll need anything to drink.

IST MAN   [leaning to her eagerly]   You like me—don't you, kid?

YOUNG WOMAN   Do you me?

335 IST MAN   Wait!

[He goes to the bar. SHE remains, her hands outstretched on the table
staring ahead.]

[Enter a MAN and a GIRL. They go to one of the empty tables. The WAITER
goes to them.]

MAN [to GIRL]   What do you want?

GIRL   Same old thing.

MAN [to the WAITER]   The usual. [Makes a sign "2".]

[The 1ST MAN crosses to YOUNG WOMAN with a wrapped bottle under his arm. SHE rises and starts out with him. As they pass the piano, HE stops and puts in a nickel—the music starts as they exit.]

BLACK OUT

[The music of the electric piano continues until the lights go up for EPISODE SIX, and the music has become the music of a hand organ, very very faint.]

Episode Six

INTIMATE

SCENE: A dark room.

SOUNDS: A hand organ. Footbeats, of passing feet.

CHARACTERS:

MAN

YOUNG WOMAN

AT RISE:

DARKNESS. Nothing can be discerned. From the outside comes the sound of a hand organ, very faint, and the irregular rhythm of passing feet.

The hand organ is playing "Cielito Lindo,"[8] that Spanish song that has been on every hand organ lately.

———

MAN   You're awful still, honey. What you thinking about?

WOMAN   About sea shells. [The sound of her voice is beautiful.]

MAN   Sheshells? Gee! I can't say it!

WOMAN   When I was little my grandmother used to have a big pink sea shell
5   on the mantle behind the stove. When we'd go to visit her they'd let me hold it, and listen. That's what I was thinking about now.

MAN   Yeah?

WOMAN   You can hear the sea in 'em, you know.

MAN   Yeah, I know.

10 WOMAN   I wonder why that is?

MAN   Search me. [Pause.]

WOMAN. You going?

[He has moved.]

MAN   No. I just want a cigarette.

WOMAN [glad, relieved]   Oh.

15 MAN   Want one?

WOMAN   No. [Taking the match.] Let me light it for you.

MAN   You got mighty pretty hands, honey. [The match is out.] This little pig went to market. This little pig stayed home. This little pig went—

WOMAN [laughs]   Diddle diddle dee.

[Laughs again.]

20 MAN   You got awful pretty hands.

8. Famous Mexican folk song; the title is a term of endearment meaning "little heaven."

WOMAN   I used to have. But I haven't taken much care of them lately. I will now— [*Pause. The music gets clearer.*] What's that?

MAN   What?

WOMAN   That music?

25 MAN   A dago[9] hand organ. I gave him two bits the first day I got here—so he comes every day.

WOMAN   I mean—what's that he's playing?

MAN   Cielito Lindo.

WOMAN   What does that mean?

30 MAN   Little Heaven?

WOMAN   Little Heaven?

MAN   That's what lovers call each other in Spain.

WOMAN   Spain's where all the castles are, ain't it?

MAN   Yeah.

35 WOMAN   Little Heaven—sing it!

MAN   [*singing to the music of the hand organ*]   De la sierra morena viene, bajando, viene, bajando; un par de ojitos negros—cielito lindo—da contrabando.[1]

WOMAN   What does it mean?

MAN   From the high dark mountains.

40 WOMAN   From the high dark mountains—?

MAN   Oh it doesn't mean anything. It doesn't make sense. It's love. [*Taking up the song.*] Ay-ay-ay-ay.

WOMAN   I know what that means.

MAN   What?

45 WOMAN   Ay-ay-ay-ay.

[*They laugh.*]

MAN   [*taking up the song*]   Canta non llores— Sing don't cry—

WOMAN   [*taking up song*]   La-la-la-la-la-la-la-la-la-la—Little Heaven!

MAN   You got a nice voice, honey.

WOMAN   Have I?

[*Laughs—tickles him.*]

50 MAN   You bet you have—hey!

WOMAN   [*laughing*]   You ticklish?

MAN   Sure I am! Hey! [*They laugh.*] Go on, honey, sing something.

WOMAN   I couldn't.

MAN   Go on—you got a fine voice.

WOMAN   [*laughs and sings*]

55   Hey, diddle, diddle, the cat and the fiddle,
      The cow jumped over the moon
      The little dog laughed to see the sport
      And the dish ran away with the spoon—[*Both laugh.*] I never thought that had any sense before—now I get it.

60 MAN   You got me beat.

WOMAN   It's you and me.—La—lalalalalala—lalalalalalala—Little Heaven. You're the dish and I'm the spoon.

MAN   You're a little spoon all right.

---

9. Slang term, usually for someone of Italian or Spanish origin.
1. "A pair of sweet little black eyes, my dar-ling, is being smuggled down from the Sierra Morena mountain range, my darling."

WOMAN And I guess I'm the little cow that jumped over the moon. [*A pause.*]
65 Do you believe in sorta guardian angels?

MAN What?

WOMAN Guardian angels?

MAN I don't know. Maybe.

WOMAN I do. [*Taking up the song again.*] Lalalalala-lalalalala-lalalala—Little
70 Heaven. [*Talking.*] There must be something that looks out for you and brings
you your happiness, at last—look at us! How did we both happen to go to
that place today if there wasn't something!

MAN Maybe you're right.

WOMAN Look at us!

75 MAN Everything's us to you, kid—ain't it?

WOMAN Ain't it?

MAN All right with me.

WOMAN We belong together! We belong together! And we're going to stick
together, ain't we?

80 MAN Sing something else.

WOMAN I tell you I can't sing!

MAN Sure you can!

WOMAN I tell you I hadn't thought of singing since I was a little bit of a girl.

MAN Well sing anyway.

85 WOMAN [*singing*] And every little wavelet had its night cap on—its night cap
on—its night cap on—and every little wave had its night cap on—so very
early in the morning.[2] [*Talking.*] Did you used to sing that when you were a
little kid?

MAN Nope.

90 WOMAN Didn't you? We used to—in the first grade—little kids—we used to
go round and round in a ring—and flop our hands up and down—supposed
to be the waves. I remember it used to confuse me—because we did just
the same thing to be little angels.

MAN Yeah?

95 WOMAN You know why I came here?

MAN I can make a good guess.

WOMAN Because you told me I looked like an angel to you! That's why I came.

MAN Jeez, honey, all women look like angels to me—all white women. I ain't
been seeing nothing but Indians, you know, for the last couple a years.
100 Gee, when I got off the boat here the other day—and saw all the women—
gee I pretty near went crazy—talk about looking like angels—why—

WOMAN You've had a lot of women, haven't you?

MAN Not so many—real ones.

WOMAN Did you—like any of 'em—better than me?

105 MAN Nope—there wasn't one of 'em any sweeter than you, honey—not as
sweet—no—not as sweet.

WOMAN I like to hear you say it. Say it again—

MAN [*protesting good humoredly*] Oh—

WOMAN Go on—tell me again!

110 MAN Here! [*Kisses her.*] Does that tell you?

WOMAN Yes. [*Pause.*] We're going to stick together—always—aren't we?

2. Excerpt from "A Song for Hal" by Laura Elizabeth Howe Richards, from the collection *In My
Nursery* (1890).

MAN [*honestly*] I'll have to be moving on, kid—some day, you know.

WOMAN When?

MAN Quien sabe?

115 WOMAN What does that mean?

MAN Quien sabe? You got to learn that, kid, if you're figuring on coming with me. It's the answer to everything—below the Rio Grande.[3]

WOMAN What does it mean?

MAN It means—who knows?

120 WOMAN Keen sabe?

MAN Yep—don't forget it—now.

WOMAN I'll never forget it!

MAN Quien sabe?

WOMAN And I'll never get to use it.

125 MAN Quien sabe.

WOMAN I'll never get—below the Rio Grande—I'll never get out of here.

MAN Quien sabe.

WOMAN [*change of mood*] That's right! Keen sabe? Who knows?

MAN That's the stuff.

130 WOMAN You must like it down there.

MAN I can't live anywhere else—for long.

WOMAN Why not?

MAN Oh—you're free down there! You're free!

[*A Street Light is lit outside. The outlines of a window take form against this light. There are bars across it, and from outside it, the sidewalk cuts across almost at the top. (It is a basement room.) The constant going and coming of passing feet, (mostly feet of couples) can be dimly seen. Inside, on the ledge, there is a lily blooming in a bowl of rocks and water.*]

WOMAN What's that?

135 MAN Just the street light going on.

WOMAN Is it as late as that?

MAN Late as what?

WOMAN Dark.

MAN It's been dark for hours—didn't you know that?

140 WOMAN No!—I must go! [*Rises.*]

MAN Wait—the moon will be up in a little while—full moon.

WOMAN It isn't that! I'm late! I must go! [SHE *comes into the light. She wears a white chemise that might be the tunic of a dancer, and as she comes into the light she fastens about her waist a little skirt. She really wears almost exactly the clothes that women wear now, but the finesse of their cut, and the grace and ease with which she puts them on, must turn this episode of her dressing into a personification, an idealization of a woman clothing herself. All her gestures must be unconscious, innocent, relaxed, sure and full of natural grace. As she sits facing the window pulling on a stocking.*] What's that?

MAN What?

WOMAN On the window ledge.

145 MAN A flower.

WOMAN Who gave it to you?

MAN Nobody gave it to me. I bought it.

WOMAN For yourself?

3. River marking the border between Texas and Mexico.

MAN Yeah—why not?

150 WOMAN I don't know.

MAN In Chinatown—made me think of Frisco where I was a kid—so I bought it.

WOMAN Is that where you were born—Frisco?

MAN Yep. Twin Peaks.

WOMAN What's that?

155 MAN A couple hills—together.

WOMAN One for you and one for me.

MAN I bet you'd like Frisco.

WOMAN I know a woman went out there once!

MAN The bay and the hills! Jeez, that's the life! Every Saturday we used to
160   cross the Bay—get a couple nags[4] and just ride—over the hills. One would
       have a blanket on the saddle—the other, the grub. At night, we'd make a
       little fire and eat—and then roll up in the old blanket and—

WOMAN Who? Who was with you?

MAN [indifferently] Anybody. [Enthusiastically.] Jeez, that dry old grass out
165   there smells good at night—full of tar weed—you know—

WOMAN Is that a good smell?

MAN Tar weed? Didn't you ever smell it? [She shakes her head, "No".] Sure
       it's a good smell! The Bay and the hills. [She goes to the mirror of the dresser,
       to finish dressing. She has only a dress to put on that is in one piece—with
       one fastening on the side. Before slipping it on, she stands before the mirror
       and stretches. Appreciatively but indifferently.] You look in good shape, kid.
170   A couple of months riding over the mountains with me, you'd be great.

WOMAN Can I?

MAN What?

WOMAN Some day—ride mountains with you?

MAN Ride mountains? Ride donkeys!

175 WOMAN It's the same thing!—with you!—Can I—some day? The high dark
       mountains?

MAN Who knows?

WOMAN It must be great!

MAN You ever been off like that, kid?—high up? On top of the world?

180 WOMAN Yes.

MAN When?

WOMAN Today.

MAN You're pretty sweet.

WOMAN I never knew anything like this way! I never knew that I could feel
185   like this! So,—so purified! Don't laugh at me!

MAN I ain't laughing, honey.

WOMAN Purified.

MAN It's a hell of a word—but I know what you mean. That's the way it
       is—sometimes.

190 WOMAN [she puts on a little hat, then turns to HIM] Well—goodbye.

MAN Aren't you forgetting something? [Rises.]

WOMAN [she looks toward him, then throws her head slowly back, lifts her right
       arm—this gesture that is in so many statues of women [Volupte][5]—He comes

---

4. Horses.
5. Such imagery had recently become popular
through its depiction by French painter Henri

Matisse (1869–1954) in his work Luxe,
Calme, et Volupté (1904).

out of the shadow, puts his arm around her, kisses her. Her head and arm go further back,—then she brings her arm around with a wide encircling gesture, her hand closes over his head, her fingers spread. Her fingers are protective, clutching. When he releases her, her eyes are shining with tears. She turns away. She looks back at him—and the room—and her eyes fasten on the lily]. Can I have that?

MAN Sure—why not?

> [*She takes it—goes. As she opens the door, the music is louder. The scene blacks out.*]

WOMAN Goodbye. And— [*Hesitates.*] And—thank you.

MUSIC—CURTAIN—BLACK OUT

[*The music continues until the Curtain goes up for* EPISODE SEVEN— *It goes up on silence.*]

Episode Seven

DOMESTIC

SCENE: *A Sitting Room* [*A divan—a telephone—a window.*]
CHARACTERS:

> HUSBAND
> YOUNG WOMAN

They are seated on opposite ends of the divan. They are both reading papers—to themselves.

HUSBAND Record production.
YOUNG WOMAN Girl turns on gas.
HUSBAND Sale hits a million—
YOUNG WOMAN Woman leaves all for love—
5 HUSBAND Market trend steady—
YOUNG WOMAN Young wife disappears—
HUSBAND Owns a life interest— [*Phone rings.* YOUNG WOMAN *looks toward it.*] That's for me. [*In phone.*] Hello—oh hello, A.B. It's all settled?—Everything signed? Good. Good! Tell R.A. to call me up. [*Closes phone—to*
10 YOUNG WOMAN.] Well, it's all settled. They signed!—aren't you interested? Aren't you going to ask me?
YOUNG WOMAN [*by rote*] Did you put it over?
HUSBAND Sure I put it over.
YOUNG WOMAN Did you swing it?
15 HUSBAND Sure I swung it.
YOUNG WOMAN Did they come through?
HUSBAND Sure they came through.
YOUNG WOMAN Did they sign?
HUSBAND I'll say they signed.
20 YOUNG WOMAN On the dotted line?
HUSBAND On the dotted line.
YOUNG WOMAN The property's yours?
HUSBAND The property's mine. I'll put a first mortgage. I'll put a second mortgage and the property's mine. Happy?

25 YOUNG WOMAN [*by rote*]   Happy.

HUSBAND [*going to her*]   The property's mine! It's not all that's mine! [*Pinching her cheek—happy and playful.*] I got a first mortgage on her—I got a second mortgage on her—and she's mine! [YOUNG WOMAN *pulls away swiftly.*] What's the matter?

30 YOUNG WOMAN   Nothing—what?

HUSBAND   You flinched when I touched you.

YOUNG WOMAN   No.

HUSBAND   You haven't done that in a long time.

YOUNG WOMAN   Haven't I?

35 HUSBAND   You used to do it every time I touched you.

YOUNG WOMAN   Did I?

HUSBAND   Didn't know that, did you?

YOUNG WOMAN [*unexpectedly*]   Yes. Yes, I know it.

HUSBAND   Just purity.

40 YOUNG WOMAN   No.

HUSBAND   Oh, I liked it. Purity.

YOUNG WOMAN   No.

HUSBAND   You're one of the purest women that ever lived.

YOUNG WOMAN   I'm just like anybody else only— [*Stops.*]

45 HUSBAND   Only what?

YOUNG WOMAN [*a pause*]   Nothing.

HUSBAND   It must be something.

[*Phone rings.*]

[*She gets up and goes to window.*]

HUSBAND [*in phone*]   Hello—hello, R.A.—well, I put it over—yeah, I swung it—sure they came through—did they sign? On the dotted line! The prop-

50 erty's mine. I made the proposition. I sold them the idea. Now watch me. Tell D.D. to call me up. [*Hangs up.*] That was R.A. What are you looking at?

YOUNG WOMAN   Nothing.

HUSBAND   You must be looking at something.

YOUNG WOMAN   Nothing—the moon.

55 HUSBAND   The moon's something, isn't it?

YOUNG WOMAN   Yes.

HUSBAND   What's it doing?

YOUNG WOMAN   Nothing.

HUSBAND   It must be doing something.

60 YOUNG WOMAN   It's moving—moving—

[*She comes down restlessly.*]

HUSBAND   Pull down the shade, my dear.

YOUNG WOMAN   Why?

HUSBAND   People can look in. [*Phone rings.*] Hello—hello D.D.—Yes—I put it over—they came across—I put it over on them—yep—yep—yep—I'll say

65 I am—yep—on the dotted line— Now you watch me—yep. Yep yep. Tell B.M. to phone me. [*Hangs up.*] That was D.D. [*To* YOUNG WOMAN *who has come down to davenport and picked up a paper.*] Aren't you listening?

YOUNG WOMAN   I'm reading.

HUSBAND   What you reading?

70 YOUNG WOMAN   Nothing.

HUSBAND   Must be something. [*He sits and picks up his paper.*]

YOUNG WOMAN [*reading*]   Prisoner escapes—lifer breaks jail—shoots way to freedom—

HUSBAND   Don't read that stuff—listen—here's a first rate editorial. I agree
75   with this. I agree absolutely. Are you listening?

YOUNG WOMAN   I'm listening.

HUSBAND [*importantly*]   All men are born free and entitled to the pursuit of happiness. [YOUNG WOMAN *gets up.*] My, you're nervous tonight.

YOUNG WOMAN   I try not to be.

80   HUSBAND   You inherit that from your mother. She was in the office today.

YOUNG WOMAN   Was she?

HUSBAND   To get her allowance.

YOUNG WOMAN   Oh—

HUSBAND   Don't you know it's the *first*.

85   YOUNG WOMAN   Poor Ma.

HUSBAND   What would she do without me?

YOUNG WOMAN   I know. You're very good.

HUSBAND   One thing—she's grateful.

YOUNG WOMAN   Poor Ma—poor Ma.

90   HUSBAND   She's got to have care.

YOUNG WOMAN   Yes. She's got to have care.

HUSBAND   A mother's a very precious thing—a good mother.

YOUNG WOMAN [*excitedly*]   I try to be a good mother.

HUSBAND   Of course you're a good mother.

95   YOUNG WOMAN   I try! I try!

HUSBAND   A mother's a very precious thing— [*Resuming his paper.*] And a child's a very precious thing. Precious jewels.

YOUNG WOMAN [*reading*]   Sale of jewels and precious stones. [YOUNG WOMAN *puts her hand to throat.*]

HUSBAND   What's the matter?

100   YOUNG WOMAN   I feel as though I were drowning.

HUSBAND   Drowning?

YOUNG WOMAN   With stones around my neck.

HUSBAND   You just imagine that.

YOUNG WOMAN   Stifling.

105   HUSBAND   You don't breathe deep enough—breathe now—look at me. [*He breathes.*] Breath is life. Life is breath.

YOUNG WOMAN [*suddenly*]   And what is death?

HUSBAND [*smartly*]   Just—no breath!

YOUNG WOMAN [*to herself*]   Just no breath! [*Takes up paper.*]

110   HUSBAND   All right?

YOUNG WOMAN   All right.

HUSBAND [*reads as she stares at her paper. Looks up after a pause*]   I feel cold air, my dear.

YOUNG WOMAN   Cold air?

115   HUSBAND   Close the window, will you?

YOUNG WOMAN   It isn't open.

HUSBAND   Don't you feel cold air?

YOUNG WOMAN   No—you just imagine it.

HUSBAND   I never imagine anything. [YOUNG WOMAN *is staring at the paper.*]
120   What are you reading?

YOUNG WOMAN   Nothing.

HUSBAND   You must be reading something.

YOUNG WOMAN   Woman finds husband dead.

HUSBAND   [*uninterested*]   Oh. [*Interested.*] Here's a man says "I owe my suc-
125   cess to a yeast cake a day—my digestion is good—I sleep very well—and—
[*His wife gets up, goes toward door.*] Where you going?

YOUNG WOMAN   No place.

HUSBAND   You must be going some place.

YOUNG WOMAN   Just—to bed.

130 HUSBAND   It isn't eleven yet. Wait.

YOUNG WOMAN   Wait?

HUSBAND   It's only ten-forty-six—wait! [*Holds out his arms to her.*] Come
here!

YOUNG WOMAN   [*takes a step toward him—recoils*]   Oh—I want to go away!

135 HUSBAND   Away? Where?

YOUNG WOMAN   Anywhere—away.

HUSBAND   Why, what's the matter?

YOUNG WOMAN   I'm scared.

HUSBAND   What of?

140 YOUNG WOMAN   I can't sleep—I haven't slept.

HUSBAND   That's nothing.

YOUNG WOMAN   And the moon—when it's a full moon.

HUSBAND   That's nothing.

YOUNG WOMAN   I can't sleep.

145 HUSBAND   Of course not. It's the light.

YOUNG WOMAN   I don't see it! I feel it! I'm afraid.

HUSBAND   [*kindly*]   Nonsense—come here.

YOUNG WOMAN   I want to go away.

HUSBAND   But I can't get away now.

150 YOUNG WOMAN   Alone!

HUSBAND   You've never been away alone.

YOUNG WOMAN   I know.

HUSBAND   What would you do?

YOUNG WOMAN   Maybe I'd sleep.

155 HUSBAND   Now you wait.

YOUNG WOMAN   [*desperately*]   Wait?

HUSBAND   We'll take a trip—we'll go to Europe—I'll get my watch—I'll get
my Swiss watch—I've always wanted a Swiss watch that I bought right
there—isn't that funny? Wait—wait. [YOUNG WOMAN *comes down to*
160 *davenport—sits.* HUSBAND *resumes his paper.*] Another revolution below the
Rio Grande.

YOUNG WOMAN   Below the Rio Grande?

HUSBAND   Yes—another—

YOUNG WOMAN   Anyone—hurt?

165 HUSBAND   No.

YOUNG WOMAN   Any Prisoners?

HUSBAND   No.

YOUNG WOMAN   All free?

HUSBAND   All free.

    [*He resumes his paper.*]

[YOUNG WOMAN *sits, staring ahead of her—The music of the hand-organ sounds off very dimly, playing Cielito Lindo. Voices begin to sing it—'Ay-ay-ay-ay'—and then the words—the music and voices get louder.*]

170 THE VOICE OF HER LOVER They were a bunch of bandidos—bandits you know—holding me there—what was I to do—I had to get free—didn't I? I had to get free—

VOICES Free—free—free—

LOVER I filled an empty bottle with small stones—

175 VOICES Stones—stones—precious stones—millstones—stones—stones— millstones—

LOVER Just a bottle with small stones.

VOICES Stones—stones—small stones—

LOVER You only need a bottle with small stones.

180 VOICES Stones—stones—small stones—

VOICE OF A HUCKSTER Stones for sale—stones—stones—small stones— precious stones—

VOICES Stones—stones—precious stones—

LOVER Had to get free, didn't I? Free?

185 VOICES Free? Free?

LOVER Quien sabe? Who knows? Who knows?

VOICES Who'd know? Who'd know? Who'd know?

HUCKSTER Stones—stones—small stones—big stones—millstones—cold stones—head stones—

190 VOICES Head stones—head stones—head stones.

[*The music,—the voices—mingle—increase—the* YOUNG WOMAN *flies from her chair and cries out in terror.*]

YOUNG WOMAN Oh! Oh!

[*The scene* BLACKS OUT—*the music and the dim voices, "Stones—stones— stones," continue until the scene lights for* EPISODE EIGHT.]

Episode Eight
THE LAW

SCENE: *Courtroom.*

SOUNDS: *Clicking of telegraph instruments offstage.*

CHARACTERS:

JUDGE

JURY

LAWYERS

SPECTATORS

REPORTERS

MESSENGER BOYS

LAW CLERKS

BAILIFF

COURT REPORTER

YOUNG WOMAN

The words and movements of all these people except the YOUNG WOMAN *are routine— mechanical— Each is going through the motions of his own game.*

AT RISE: ALL *assembled, except* JUDGE.

[*Enter* JUDGE.]

BAILIFF [*mumbling*]   Hear ye—hear ye—hear ye!

[ALL *rise.* JUDGE *sits.* ALL *sit.*]

[LAWYER FOR DEFENSE *gets to his feet—He is the verbose, 'eloquent'—typical criminal defense lawyer.*]

[JUDGE *signs to him to wait—turns to* LAW CLERKS, *grouped at foot of the bench.*]

IST CLERK [*handing up a paper—routine voice*]   State versus Kling—stay of execution.

JUDGE   Denied.

[IST CLERK *goes.*]

5   2ND CLERK   Bing vs. Ding—demurrer.[6]

[JUDGE *signs.*]

[2ND CLERK *goes.*]

3RD CLERK   Case of John King—habeas corpus.[7]

[JUDGE *signs.*]

[3RD CLERK *goes.*]

[JUDGE *signs to* BAILIFF.]

BAILIFF [*mumbling*]   People of the State of————versus Helen Jones.

JUDGE [*to* LAWYER FOR THE DEFENSE]   Defense ready to proceed?

LAWYER FOR DEFENSE   We're ready, your Honor.

10   JUDGE   Proceed.

LAWYER FOR DEFENSE   Helen Jones.

BAILIFF   HELEN JONES!

[YOUNG WOMAN *rises.*]

LAWYER FOR DEFENSE   Mrs. Jones, will you take the stand?

[YOUNG WOMAN *goes to witness stand.*]

IST REPORTER [*writing rapidly*]   The defense sprang a surprise at the opening

15   of court this morning by putting the accused woman on the stand. The prosecution was swept off its feet by this daring defense strategy and—

[*Instruments get louder.*]

2ND REPORTER   Trembling and scarcely able to stand, Helen Jones, accused murderess, had to be almost carried to the witness stand this morning when her lawyer—

20   BAILIFF [*mumbling—with Bible*]   Do you swear to tell the truth, the whole truth and nothing but the truth—so help you God?

YOUNG WOMAN   I do.

JUDGE   You may sit.

[*She sits in witness chair.*]

COURT REPORTER   What is your name?

25   YOUNG WOMAN   Helen Jones.

COURT REPORTER   Your age?

YOUNG WOMAN [*hesitates—then*]   Twenty-nine.

COURT REPORTER   Where do you live?

YOUNG WOMAN   In prison.

6. Form of legal objection.
7. In law, method of releasing someone from unlawful restraint.

30   LAWYER FOR DEFENSE   This is my client's legal address. [*Hands a scrap of paper.*]

    LAWYER FOR PROSECUTION [*jumping to his feet*]   I object to this insinuation on the part of counsel on any illegality in the holding of this defendant in jail when the law—

    LAWYER FOR DEFENSE   I made no such insinuation.

35   LAWYER FOR PROSECUTION   You implied it—

    LAWYER FOR DEFENSE   I did not!

    LAWYER FOR PROSECUTION   You're a—

    JUDGE   Order!

    BAILIFF   Order!

40   LAWYER FOR DEFENSE   Your Honor, I object to counsel's constant attempt to—

    LAWYER FOR PROSECUTION   I protest—I—

    JUDGE   Order!

    BAILIFF   Order!

    JUDGE   Proceed with the witness.

45   LAWYER FOR DEFENSE   Mrs. Jones, you are the widow of the late George H. Jones, are you not?

    YOUNG WOMAN   Yes.

    LAWYER FOR DEFENSE   How long were you married to the late George H. Jones before his demise?

50   YOUNG WOMAN   Six years.

    LAWYER FOR DEFENSE   Six years! And it was a happy marriage, was it not? [YOUNG WOMAN *hesitates.*] Did you quarrel?

    YOUNG WOMAN   No, sir.

    LAWYER FOR DEFENSE   Then it was a happy marriage, wasn't it?

55   YOUNG WOMAN   Yes, sir.

    LAWYER FOR DEFENSE   In those six years of married life with your late husband, the late George H. Jones, did you EVER have a quarrel?

    YOUNG WOMAN   No, sir.

    LAWYER FOR DEFENSE   Never one quarrel?

60   LAWYER FOR PROSECUTION   The witness has said—

    LAWYER FOR DEFENSE   Six years without one quarrel! Six years! Gentlemen of the jury, I ask you to consider this fact! Six years of married life without a quarrel. [*The* JURY *grins.*] I ask you to consider it seriously! Very seriously! Who of us—and this is not intended as any reflection on the sacred institu-

65   tion of marriage—no—but!

    JUDGE   Proceed with your witness.

    LAWYER FOR DEFENSE   You have one child—have you not, Mrs. Jones?

    YOUNG WOMAN   Yes, sir.

    LAWYER FOR DEFENSE   A little girl, is it not?

70   YOUNG WOMAN.   Yes, sir.

    LAWYER FOR DEFENSE   How old is she?

    YOUNG WOMAN   She's five—past five.

    LAWYER FOR DEFENSE   A little girl of past five. Since the demise of the late Mr. Jones you are the only parent she has living, are you not?

75   YOUNG WOMAN   Yes, sir.

    LAWYER FOR DEFENSE   Before your marriage to the late Mr. Jones, you worked and supported your mother, did you not?

    LAWYER FOR PROSECUTION   I object, your honor! Irrelevant—immaterial—and—

80   JUDGE   Objection sustained!

LAWYER FOR DEFENSE   In order to support your mother and yourself as a girl, you worked, did you not?

YOUNG WOMAN   Yes, sir.

LAWYER FOR DEFENSE   What did you do?

85 YOUNG WOMAN   I was a stenographer.

LAWYER FOR DEFENSE   And since your marriage you have continued as her sole support, have you not?

YOUNG WOMAN   Yes, sir.

LAWYER FOR DEFENSE   A devoted daughter, gentlemen of the jury! As well as
90 a devoted wife and a devoted mother!

LAWYER FOR PROSECUTION   Your Honor!

LAWYER FOR DEFENSE [quickly]   And now, Mrs. Jones, I will ask you—the law expects me to ask you—it demands that I ask you—did you—or did you not—on the night of June 2nd last or the morning of June 3rd last—kill
95 your husband, the late George H. Jones—did you, or did you not?

YOUNG WOMAN   I did not.

LAWYER FOR DEFENSE   You did not?

YOUNG WOMAN   I did not.

LAWYER FOR DEFENSE   Now, Mrs. Jones, you have heard the witnesses for the
100 State—They were not many—and they did not have much to say—

LAWYER FOR PROSECUTION   I object.

JUDGE   Sustained.

LAWYER FOR DEFENSE   You have heard some police and you have heard some doctors. None of whom was present! The prosecution could not furnish
105 any witness to the crime—not one witness!

LAWYER FOR PROSECUTION   Your Honor!

LAWYER FOR DEFENSE   Nor one motive.

LAWYER FOR PROSECUTION   Your Honor—I protest! I—

JUDGE   Sustained.

110 LAWYER FOR DEFENSE   But such as these witnesses were, you have heard them try to accuse you of deliberately murdering your own husband, this husband with whom, by your own statement, you had never had a quarrel— not one quarrel in six years of married life, murdering him, I say, or rather they say, while he slept, by brutally hitting him over the head with a bot-
115 tle—a bottle filled with small stones—Did you, I repeat this, or did you not?

YOUNG WOMAN   I did not.

LAWYER FOR DEFENSE   You did not! Of course you did not! [Quickly.] Now, Mrs. Jones, will you tell the jury in your own words exactly what happened
120 on the night of June 2nd or the morning of June 3rd last, at the time your husband was killed.

YOUNG WOMAN   I was awakened by hearing somebody—something—in the room, and I saw two men standing by my husband's bed.

LAWYER FOR DEFENSE   Your husband's bed—that was also your bed, was it
125 not, Mrs. Jones?

YOUNG WOMAN   Yes.

LAWYER FOR DEFENSE   You hadn't the modern idea of separate beds, had you, Mrs. Jones?

YOUNG WOMAN   Mr. Jones objected.

130 LAWYER FOR DEFENSE   I mean you slept in the same bed, did you not?

YOUNG WOMAN   Yes.

LAWYER FOR DEFENSE   Then explain just what you meant by saying 'my husband's bed.'

YOUNG WOMAN   Well—I—

135   LAWYER FOR DEFENSE   You meant his side of the bed, didn't you?

YOUNG WOMAN   Yes. His side.

LAWYER FOR DEFENSE   That is what I thought, but I wanted the jury to be clear on that point. [*To the* JURY.] Mr. and Mrs. Jones slept in the same bed. [*To her.*] Go on, Mrs. Jones. [*As she is silent.*] You heard a noise and—

140   YOUNG WOMAN   I heard a noise and I awoke and saw two men standing beside my husband's side of the bed.

LAWYER FOR DEFENSE   Two men?

YOUNG WOMAN   Yes.

LAWYER FOR DEFENSE   Can you describe them?

145   YOUNG WOMAN   Not, very well—I couldn't see them very well.

LAWYER FOR DEFENSE   Could you say whether they were big or small—light or dark, thin or—

YOUNG WOMAN   They were big dark looking men.

LAWYER FOR DEFENSE   Big dark looking men?

150   YOUNG WOMAN   Yes.

LAWYER FOR DEFENSE   And what did you do, Mrs. Jones, when you suddenly awoke and saw two big dark looking men standing beside your bed?

YOUNG WOMAN   I didn't do anything!

LAWYER FOR DEFENSE   You didn't have time to do anything—did you?

155   YOUNG WOMAN   No. Before I could do anything—one of them raised—something in his hand and struck Mr. Jones over the head with it.

LAWYER FOR DEFENSE   And what did Mr. Jones do?

[SPECTATORS *laugh.*]

JUDGE   Silence.

BAILIFE   Silence.

160   LAWYER FOR DEFENSE   What did Mr. Jones do, Mrs. Jones?

YOUNG WOMAN   He gave a sort of groan and tried to raise up.

LAWYER FOR DEFENSE   Tried to raise up!

YOUNG WOMAN   Yes!

LAWYER FOR DEFENSE   And then what happened?

165   YOUNG WOMAN   The man struck him again and he fell back.

LAWYER FOR DEFENSE   I see. What did the men do then? The big dark looking men.

YOUNG WOMAN   They turned and ran out of the room.

LAWYER FOR DEFENSE   I see. What did you do then, Mrs. Jones?

170   YOUNG WOMAN   I saw Mr. Jones was bleeding from the temple. I got towels and tried to stop it, and then I realized he had—passed away—

LAWYER FOR DEFENSE   I see. What did you do then?

YOUNG WOMAN   I didn't know what to do. But I thought I'd better call the police. So I went to the telephone and called the police.

175   LAWYER FOR DEFENSE   What happened then.

YOUNG WOMAN   Nothing. Nothing happened.

LAWYER FOR DEFENSE   The police came, didn't they?

YOUNG WOMAN   Yes—they came.

LAWYER FOR DEFENSE   [*quickly*]   And that is all you know concerning the

180   death of your husband in the late hours of June 2nd or the early hours of June 3rd last, isn't it?

YOUNG WOMAN   Yes sir.

LAWYER FOR DEFENSE   All?

YOUNG WOMAN   Yes sir.

185 LAWYER FOR DEFENSE [*to* LAWYER FOR PROSECUTION]   Take the witness.

1ST REPORTER [*writing*]   The accused woman told a straightforward story of—

2ND REPORTER   The accused woman told a rambling, disconnected story of—

LAWYER FOR PROSECUTION   You made no effort to cry out, Mrs. Jones, did
   you, when you saw those two big dark men standing over your helpless
190   husband, did you?

YOUNG WOMAN   No sir. I didn't. I—

LAWYER FOR PROSECUTION   And when they turned and ran out of the room,
   you made no effort to follow them or cry out after them, did you?

YOUNG WOMAN   No sir.

195 LAWYER FOR PROSECUTION   Why didn't you?

YOUNG WOMAN   I saw Mr. Jones was hurt.

LAWYER FOR PROSECUTION   Ah! You saw Mr. Jones was hurt! You saw this—
   how did you see it?

YOUNG WOMAN   I just saw it.

200 LAWYER FOR PROSECUTION   Then there was a light in the room?

YOUNG WOMAN   A sort of light.

LAWYER FOR PROSECUTION   What do you mean—a sort of light? A bed light?

YOUNG WOMAN   No. No, there was no light on.

LAWYER FOR PROSECUTION   Then where did it come from—this sort of light?

205 YOUNG WOMAN   I don't know.

LAWYER FOR PROSECUTION   Perhaps—from the window.

YOUNG WOMAN   Yes—from the window.

LAWYER FOR PROSECUTION   Oh, the shade was up!

YOUNG WOMAN   No—no, the shade was down.

210 LAWYER FOR PROSECUTION   You're sure of that?

YOUNG WOMAN   Yes. Mr. Jones always wanted the shade down.

LAWYER FOR PROSECUTION   The shade was down—there was no light in the
   room—but the room was light—how do you explain this?

YOUNG WOMAN   I don't know.

215 LAWYER FOR PROSECUTION   You don't know!

YOUNG WOMAN   I think where the window was open—under the shade—light
   came in—

LAWYER FOR PROSECUTION   There is a street light there?

YOUNG WOMAN   No—there's no street light.

220 LAWYER FOR PROSECUTION   Then where did this light come from—that came
   in under the shade?

YOUNG WOMAN [*desperately*]   From the moon!

LAWYER FOR PROSECUTION   The moon!

YOUNG WOMAN   Yes! It was bright moon!

225 LAWYER FOR PROSECUTION   It was bright moon—you are sure of that!

YOUNG WOMAN   Yes.

LAWYER FOR PROSECUTION   How are you sure?

YOUNG WOMAN   I couldn't sleep—I never can sleep in the bright moon. I
   never can.

230 LAWYER FOR PROSECUTION   It was bright moon. Yet you could not see two big
   dark looking men—but you could see your husband bleeding from the
   temple.

YOUNG WOMAN   Yes sir.

LAWYER FOR PROSECUTION   And did you call a doctor?

235 YOUNG WOMAN   No.

LAWYER FOR PROSECUTION   Why didn't you?

YOUNG WOMAN   The police did.

LAWYER FOR PROSECUTION   But you didn't?

YOUNG WOMAN   No.

240 LAWYER FOR PROSECUTION   What didn't you? [*No answer.*] Why didn't you?

YOUNG WOMAN [*whispers*]   I saw it was—useless.

LAWYER FOR PROSECUTION   Ah! You saw that! You saw that—very clearly.

YOUNG WOMAN   Yes.

LAWYER FOR PROSECUTION   And you didn't call a doctor.

245 YOUNG WOMAN   It was—useless.

LAWYER FOR PROSECUTION   What did you do?

YOUNG WOMAN   It was useless—there was no use of anything.

LAWYER FOR PROSECUTION   I asked you what you did?

YOUNG WOMAN   Nothing.

250 LAWYER FOR PROSECUTION   Nothing!

YOUNG WOMAN   I just sat there.

LAWYER FOR PROSECUTION   You sat there! A long while, didn't you?

YOUNG WOMAN   I don't know.

LAWYER FOR PROSECUTION   You don't know? [*Showing her the neck of a bro-*
255   *ken bottle.*] Mrs. Jones, did you ever see this before?

YOUNG WOMAN   I think so.

LAWYER FOR PROSECUTION   You think so.

YOUNG WOMAN   Yes.

LAWYER FOR PROSECUTION   What do you think it is?

260 YOUNG WOMAN   It think it's the bottle that was used against Mr. Jones.

LAWYER FOR PROSECUTION   Used against him—yes—that's right. You've
   guessed right. This neck and these broken pieces and these pebbles were
   found on the floor and scattered over the bed. There were no fingerprints,
   Mrs. Jones, on this bottle. None at all. Doesn't that seem strange to you?

265 YOUNG WOMAN   No.

LAWYER FOR PROSECUTION   It doesn't seem strange to you that this bottle
   held in the big dark hand of one of those big dark men left no mark! No
   print! That doesn't seem strange to you?

YOUNG WOMAN   No.

270 LAWYER FOR PROSECUTION   You are in the habit of wearing rubber gloves at
   night, Mrs. Jones—are you not? To protect—to soften your hands—are you
   not?

YOUNG WOMAN   I used to.

LAWYER FOR PROSECUTION   Used to—when was that?

275 YOUNG WOMAN   Before I was married.

LAWYER FOR PROSECUTION   And after your marriage you gave it up?

YOUNG WOMAN   Yes.

LAWYER FOR PROSECUTION   Why?

YOUNG WOMAN   Mr. Jones did not like the feeling of them.

280 LAWYER FOR PROSECUTION   You always did everything Mr. Jones wanted?

YOUNG WOMAN   I tried to—Anyway I didn't care any more—so much—about
   my hands.

LAWYER FOR PROSECUTION   I see—so after your marriage you never wore gloves at night any more?

285 YOUNG WOMAN   No.

LAWYER FOR PROSECUTION   Mrs. Jones, isn't it true that you began wearing your rubber gloves again—in spite of your husband's expressed dislike—about a year ago—a year ago this spring?

YOUNG WOMAN   No.

290 LAWYER FOR PROSECUTION   You did not suddenly begin to care particularly for your hands again—about a year ago this spring?

YOUNG WOMAN   No.

LAWYER FOR PROSECUTION   You're quite sure of that?

YOUNG WOMAN   Yes.

295 LAWYER FOR PROSECUTION   Quite sure?

YOUNG WOMAN   Yes.

LAWYER FOR PROSECUTION   Then you did not have in your possession, on the night of June 2nd last, a pair of rubber gloves?

YOUNG WOMAN [shakes her head]   No.

300 LAWYER FOR PROSECUTION [to JUDGE]   I'd like to introduce these gloves as evidence at this time, your Honor.

JUDGE   Exhibit 24.

LAWYER FOR PROSECUTION   I'll return to them later—now, Mrs. Jones—this nightgown—you recognize it, don't you?

305 YOUNG WOMAN   Yes.

LAWYER FOR PROSECUTION   Yours, is it not?

YOUNG WOMAN   Yes.

LAWYER FOR PROSECUTION   The one you were wearing the night your husband was murdered, isn't it?

310 YOUNG WOMAN   The night he died,—yes.

LAWYER FOR PROSECUTION   Not the one you wore under your peignoir—I believe that is what you call it, isn't it? A peignoir? When you received the police—but the one you wore before that—isn't it?

YOUNG WOMAN   Yes.

315 LAWYER FOR PROSECUTION   This was found—not where the gloves were found—no—but at the bottom of the soiled clothes hamper in the bathroom—rolled up and wet—why was it wet, Mrs. Jones?

YOUNG WOMAN   I had tried to wash it.

LAWYER FOR PROSECUTION   Wash it? I thought you had just sat?

320 YOUNG WOMAN   First—I tried to make things clean.

LAWYER FOR PROSECUTION   Why did you want to make this—clean—as you say?

YOUNG WOMAN   There was blood on it.

LAWYER FOR PROSECUTION   Spattered on it?

YOUNG WOMAN   Yes.

325 LAWYER FOR PROSECUTION   How did that happen?

YOUNG WOMAN   The bottle broke—and the sharp edge cut.

LAWYER FOR PROSECUTION   Oh, the bottle broke and the sharp edge cut!

YOUNG WOMAN   Yes. That's what they told me afterwards.

LAWYER FOR PROSECUTION   Who told you?

330 YOUNG WOMAN   The police—that's what they say happened.

LAWYER FOR PROSECUTION   Mrs. Jones, why did you try so desperately to wash that blood away—before you called the police?

LAWYER FOR DEFENSE I object!

JUDGE Objection overruled.

335 LAWYER FOR PROSECUTION Why, Mrs. Jones?

YOUNG WOMAN I don't know. It's what anyone would have done, wouldn't they?

LAWYER FOR PROSECUTION That depends, doesn't it? [*Suddenly taking up bottle.*] Mrs. Jones—when did you first see this?

340 YOUNG WOMAN The night my husband was—done away with.

LAWYER FOR PROSECUTION Done away with! You mean killed?

YOUNG WOMAN Yes.

LAWYER FOR PROSECUTION Why don't you say killed?

YOUNG WOMAN It sounds so brutal.

345 LAWYER FOR PROSECUTION And you never saw this before then?

YOUNG WOMAN No sir.

LAWYER FOR PROSECUTION You're quite sure of that?

YOUNG WOMAN Yes.

LAWYER FOR PROSECUTION And these stones—when did you first see them?

350 YOUNG WOMAN The night my husband was done away with.

LAWYER FOR PROSECUTION Before that night your husband was murdered—you never saw them? Never before then?

YOUNG WOMAN No sir.

LAWYER FOR PROSECUTION You are quite sure of that!

355 YOUNG WOMAN Yes.

LAWYER FOR PROSECUTION Mrs. Jones, do you remember about a year ago, a year ago this spring, bringing home to your house—a lily, a Chinese water lily?

YOUNG WOMAN No—I don't think I do.

LAWYER FOR PROSECUTION You don't think you remember bringing home a
360 water lily growing in a bowl filled with small stones?

YOUNG WOMAN No—No I don't.

LAWYER FOR PROSECUTION I'll show you this bowl, Mrs. Jones. Does that refresh your memory?

YOUNG WOMAN I remember the bowl—but I don't remember—the lily.

365 LAWYER FOR PROSECUTION You recognize the bowl then?

YOUNG WOMAN Yes.

LAWYER FOR PROSECUTION It is yours, isn't it?

YOUNG WOMAN It was in my house—yes.

LAWYER FOR PROSECUTION How did it come there?

370 YOUNG WOMAN How did it come there?

LAWYER FOR PROSECUTION Yes—where did you get it?

YOUNG WOMAN I don't remember.

LAWYER FOR PROSECUTION You don't remember?

YOUNG WOMAN No.

375 LAWYER FOR PROSECUTION You don't remember about a year ago bringing this bowl into your bedroom filled with small stones and some water and a lily? You don't remember tending very carefully that lily till it died? And when it died you don't remember hiding the bowl full of little stones away on the top shelf of your closet—and keeping it there until—you don't
380 remember?

YOUNG WOMAN No, I don't remember.

LAWYER FOR PROSECUTION You may have done so?

YOUNG WOMAN   No—no—I didn't! I didn't! I don't know anything about all that.

385   LAWYER FOR PROSECUTION   But you do remember the bowl?

YOUNG WOMAN   Yes. It was in my house—you found it in my house.

LAWYER FOR PROSECUTION   But you don't remember the lily or the stones?

YOUNG WOMAN   No—No I don't!

[LAWYER FOR PROSECUTION *turns to look among his papers in a brief case.*]

1ST REPORTER [*writing*]   Under the heavy artillery fire of the State's attorney's
390   brilliant cross-questioning, the accused woman's defense was badly rid-
dled. Pale and trembling she—

2ND REPORTER [*writing*]   Undaunted by the Prosecution's machine-gun
attack, the defendant was able to maintain her position of innocence in the
face of rapid-fire questioning that threatened, but never seriously menaced
395   her defense. Flushed but calm she—

LAWYER FOR PROSECUTION [*producing paper*]   Your Honor, I'd like to introduce this paper in evidence at this time.

JUDGE   What is it?

LAWYER FOR PROSECUTION   It is an affidavit taken in the State of Guanajato,
400   Mexico.

LAWYER FOR DEFENSE   Mexico? Your Honor, I protest. A Mexican affidavit! Is
this the United States of America or isn't it?

LAWYER FOR PROSECUTION   It's properly executed—sworn to before a notary—
and certified to by an American Consul.

405   LAWYER FOR DEFENSE   Your Honor! I protest! In the name of this great
United States of America—I protest—are we to permit our sacred institutions to be thus—

JUDGE   What is the purpose of this document—who signed it?

LAWYER FOR PROSECUTION   It is signed by one Richard Roe, and its purpose
410   is to refresh the memory of the witness on the point at issue—and incidentally supply a motive for this murder—this brutal and cold-blooded murder
of a sleeping man by—

LAWYER FOR DEFENSE   I protest, your Honor! I object!

JUDGE   Objection sustained. Let me see the document. [*Takes paper which is
415   handed up to him—looks at it.*] Perfectly regular. Do you offer this affidavit
as evidence at this time for the purpose of refreshing the memory of the
witness at this time?

LAWYER FOR PROSECUTION   Yes, your Honor.

JUDGE   You may introduce the evidence.

420   LAWYER FOR DEFENSE   I object! I object to the introduction of this evidence
at this time as irrelevant, immaterial, illegal, biased, prejudicial, and—

JUDGE   Objection overruled.

LAWYER FOR DEFENSE   Exception.

JUDGE   Exception noted. Proceed.

425   LAWYER FOR PROSECUTION   I wish to read the evidence to the jury at this
time.

JUDGE   Proceed.

LAWYER FOR DEFENSE   I object.

JUDGE   Objection overruled.

430   LAWYER FOR DEFENSE   Exception.

JUDGE Noted.

LAWYER FOR DEFENSE Why is this witness himself not brought into court— so he can be cross-questioned?

LAWYER FOR PROSECUTION The witness is a resident of the Republic of
435 Mexico and as such not subject to subpoena as a witness to this court.

LAWYER FOR DEFENSE If he was out of the jurisdiction of this court how did you get this affidavit out of him?

LAWYER FOR PROSECUTION This affidavit was made voluntarily by the deponent in the furtherance of justice.

440 LAWYER FOR DEFENSE I suppose you didn't threaten him with extradition on some other trumped-up charge so that—

JUDGE Order!

BAILIFF Order!

JUDGE Proceed with the evidence.

445 LAWYER FOR PROSECUTION [*reading*] In the matter of the State of——vs. Helen Jones, I Richard Roe, being of sound mind, do herein depose and state that I know the accused, Helen Jones, and have known her for a period of over one year immediately preceding the date of the signature on this affidavit. That I first met the said Helen Jones in a so-called speak-easy
450 somewhere in the West 40s in New York City. That on the day I met her, she went with me to my room, also somewhere in the West 40s in New York City, where we had intimate relations—

YOUNG WOMAN [*moans*] Oh!

LAWYER FOR PROSECUTION [*continues reading*] —and where I gave her a
455 blue bowl filled with pebbles, also containing a flowering lily. That from the first day we met until I departed for Mexico in the Fall, the said Helen Jones was an almost daily visitor to my room where we continued to—

YOUNG WOMAN. No! No!
[*Moans.*]

LAWYER FOR PROSECUTION What is it, Mrs. Jones—what is it?

460 YOUNG WOMAN Don't read any more! No more!

LAWYER FOR PROSECUTION Why not?

YOUNG WOMAN I did it! I did it! I did it!

LAWYER FOR PROSECUTION You confess?

YOUNG WOMAN Yes—I did it!

465 LAWYER FOR DEFENSE I object, your Honor.

JUDGE You confess you killed your husband?

YOUNG WOMAN I put him out of the way—yes.

JUDGE Why?

YOUNG WOMAN To be free.

470 JUDGE To be free? Is that the only reason?

YOUNG WOMAN Yes.

JUDGE If you just wanted to be free—why didn't you divorce him?

YOUNG WOMAN Oh I couldn't do that!! I couldn't hurt him like that!

[*Burst of laughter from* ALL *in the court. The* YOUNG WOMAN *stares out at them, and then seems to go rigid.*]

JUDGE Silence!

475 BAILIFF Silence!

[*There is a gradual silence.*]

JUDGE Mrs. Jones, why— [YOUNG WOMAN *begins to moan—suddenly—as though the realization of her enormity and her isolation had just come upon her. It is a sound of desolation, of agony, of human woe. It continues until the end of the scene.*] Why—?

[YOUNG WOMAN *cannot speak.*]

LAWYER FOR DEFENSE Your Honor, I ask a recess to—

JUDGE Court's adjourned.

[SPECTATORS *begin to file out. The* YOUNG WOMAN *continues in the witness box, unseeing, unheeding.*]

480 1ST REPORTER Murderess confesses.

2ND REPORTER Paramour brings confession.

3RD REPORTER I did it! Woman cries!

[*There is a great burst of speed from the telegraphic instruments. They keep up a constant accompaniment to the* WOMAN'S *moans.*

The scene BLACKS OUT *as the courtroom empties and* TWO POLICEMEN *go to stand by the woman.*]

BLACK OUT

[*The sound of the telegraph instruments continues until the scene lights into* EPISODE NINE—*and the prayers of the* PRIEST.]

Episode Nine

A MACHINE

SCENE: *A Prison Room. The front bars face the audience.* [*They are set back far enough to permit a clear passageway across the stage.*]

SOUNDS: *The voice of a Negro singing. The whir of an aeroplane flying.*

CHARACTERS:

    YOUNG WOMAN

    A PRIEST

    A JAILER

    TWO BARBERS

    A MATRON

    MOTHER

    TWO GUARDS

AT RISE:

In front of the bars, at one side, sits a MAN; *at the opposite side, a* WOMAN. [*The* JAILER *and the* MATRON.]

Inside the bars, a MAN *and a* WOMAN. [*The* YOUNG WOMAN *and a* PRIEST.] *The* YOUNG WOMAN *sits still with folded hands. The* PRIEST *is praying.*

PRIEST Hear, oh Lord, my prayer; and let me cry come to Thee. Turn not away Thy face from me; in the day when I am in trouble, incline Thy ear to me. In what day soever I shall call upon Thee, hear me speedily. For my days are vanished like smoke; and my bones are grown dry, like fuel for the

5 fire. I am smitten as grass, and my heart is withered; because I forgot to eat my bread. Through the voice of my groaning, my bone hath cleaved to my flesh. I am become like to a pelican of the wilderness. I am like a night raven in the house. I have watched and become as a sparrow all alone on

the housetop. All the day long my enemies reproach me; and they that
10 praised me did swear against me. My days have declined like a shadow, and
I am withered like grass. But Thou, oh Lord, end rest forever.[8] Thou shalt
arise and have mercy, for it is time to have mercy. The time is come.

[*Voice of* NEGRO *offstage—Begins to sing a Negro spiritual.*]

PRIEST The Lord hath looked upon the earth, that He might hear the
groans of them that are in fetters, that He might release the children
15 of—[9]

[VOICE OF NEGRO *grown louder.*]

JAILER Stop that nigger yelling.
YOUNG WOMAN No, let him sing. He helps me.
MATRON You can't hear the Father.
YOUNG WOMAN He helps me.
20 PRIEST Don't I help you, daughter?
YOUNG WOMAN I understand him. He is condemned. I understand him.

[THE VOICE OF THE NEGRO SINGER *goes on louder, drowning out the voice
of the* PRIEST.]

PRIEST [*chanting in Latin*] Gratiam tuum, quaesumus, Domine, metibus nostris infunde, ut qui, angelo nuntiante, Christifilii tui incarnationem cognovi-
mus, per passionem eius et crucem ad ressurectionis gloriam perducamus.
25 Per eudem Christum Dominum nostrum.!

[*Enter* TWO BARBERS. *There is a rattling of keys.*]

1ST BARBER. How is she?
MATRON Calm.
JAILER Quiet.
YOUNG WOMAN [*rising*] I am ready.
30 1ST BARBER Then sit down.
YOUNG WOMAN [*in a steady voice*] Aren't you the death guard come to take
me?
1ST BARBER No, we ain't the death guard. We're the barbers.
YOUNG WOMAN The barbers.
35 MATRON Your hair must be cut.
JAILER Must be shaved.
BARBER Just a patch. [*The* BARBERS *draw near her.*]
YOUNG WOMAN No!
PRIEST Daughter, you're ready. You know you are ready.
40 YOUNG WOMAN [*crying out*] Not for this! Not for this!
MATRON The rule.
JAILER Regulations.
BARBER Routine. [*The* BARBERS *take her by the arms.*]
YOUNG WOMAN No! No! Don't touch me—touch me! [THEY *take her and put
45 her down in the chair, cut a patch from her hair.*] I will not be submitted—

8. Psalm 102.1–13, known as the Fifth Penitential Psalm. "End rest forever" more commonly reads "sit enthroned forever."
9. Ibid., verses 19–20.
1. Excerpt from a Catholic prayer sequence
known as the *Angelus*: "Pour out, we pray

Lord, your grace on our hearts, so that we,
who came to know the incarnation of Christ
your Son through the angel's message, might
come, through His passion and cross, to the
glory of the resurrection. Through the same
Christ our Lord."

this indignity! No! I will not be submitted!—Leave me alone! Oh my God am I never to be let alone! Always to have to submit—to submit! No more— not now—I'm going to die—I won't submit! Not now!

BARBER [*finishing cutting a patch from her hair*]   You'll submit, my lady. Right
50   to the end, you'll submit! There, and a neat job too.

JAILER   Very neat.

MATRON   Very neat.

[*Exit* BARBERS.]

YOUNG WOMAN [*her calm shattered*]   Father, Father! Why was I born?

PRIEST   I came forth from the Father and have come into the world—I leave
55   the world and go into the Father.[2]

YOUNG WOMAN [*weeping*]   Submit! Submit! Is nothing mine? The hair on my head! The very hair on my head—

PRIEST   Praise God.

YOUNG WOMAN   Am I never to be let alone! Never to have peace! When I'm
60   dead, won't I have peace?

PRIEST   Ye shall indeed drink of my cup.[3]

YOUNG WOMAN   Won't I have peace tomorrow?

PRIEST   I shall raise Him up at the last day.[4]

YOUNG WOMAN   Tomorrow! Father! Where shall I be tomorrow?

65   PRIEST   Behold the hour cometh. Yea, is now come. Ye shall be scattered every man to his own.[5]

YOUNG WOMAN   In Hell! Father! Will I be in Hell?

PRIEST   I am the Resurrection and the Life.[6]

YOUNG WOMAN   Life has been hell to me, Father!

70   PRIEST   Life has been hell to you, daughter, because you never knew God! Gloria in excelsis Deo.[7]

YOUNG WOMAN   How could I know Him, Father? He never was around me.

PRIEST   You didn't seek Him, daughter. Seek and ye shall find.[8]

YOUNG WOMAN   I sought something—I was always seeking something.

75   PRIEST   What? What were you seeking?

YOUNG WOMAN   Peace. Rest and peace. Will I find it tonight, Father? Will I find it?

PRIEST   Trust in God.

[*A shadow falls across the passage in the front of the stage—and there is a shirring sound.*]

YOUNG WOMAN   What is that? Father! Jailer! What is that?

80   JAILER   An aeroplane.

MATRON   Aeroplane.

PRIEST   God in His Heaven.

YOUNG WOMAN   Look, Father! A man flying! He has wings! But he is not an angel!

85   JAILER   Hear his engine.

MATRON   Hear the engine.

2. John 16.28.
3. Matthew 20.23.
4. John 6.54.
5. John 16.32.
6. John 11.25.
7. "Glory to God in the highest."
8. Matthew 7.7.

YOUNG WOMAN   He has wings—but he isn't free! I've been free, Father! For one moment—down here on earth—I have been free! When I did what I did I was free! Free and not afraid! How is that, Father? How can that be?
90   A great sin—a mortal sin—for which I must die and go to hell—but it made me free! One moment I was free! How is that, Father? Tell me that?

PRIEST   Your sins are forgiven.

YOUNG WOMAN   And that other sin—that other sin—that sin of love— That's all I ever knew of Heaven—heaven on earth! How is that, Father? How can
95   that be—a sin—a mortal sin—all I know of heaven?

PRIEST   Confess to Almighty God.

YOUNG WOMAN   Oh, Father, pray for me—a prayer—that I can understand!

PRIEST   I will pray for you, daughter, the prayer of desire. Behind the King of Heaven, behold Thy Redeemer and God, Who is even now coming; pre-
100   pare thyself to receive Him with love, invite him with the ardor of thy desire; come, oh my Jesus, come to thy soul which desires Thee! Before Thou givest Thyself to me, I desire to give Thee my miserable heart. Do Thou accept it, and come quickly to take possession of it! Come my God, hasten! Delay no longer! My only and Infinite Good, my Treasure, my Life,
105   my Paradise, my Love, my all, my wish is to receive Thee with the love with which—[9]

[Enter the MOTHER. She comes along the passage way and stops before the bars.]

YOUNG WOMAN [recoiling]   Who's that woman?

JAILER   Your mother.

MATRON   Your mother.

110   YOUNG WOMAN   She's a stranger—take her away—she's a stranger.

JAILER   She's come to say goodbye to you—

MATRON   To say goodbye.

YOUNG WOMAN   But she's never known me—never known me—ever— [To the MOTHER.] Go away! You're a stranger! Stranger! Stranger! [MOTHER
115   turns and starts away. Reaching out her hands to her.] Oh Mother! Mother!

[They embrace through the bars.]

[Enter TWO GUARDS.]

PRIEST   Come, daughter.

1ST GUARD   It's time.

2ND GUARD   Time.

YOUNG WOMAN   Wait! Mother, my child; my little strange child! I never knew
120   her! She'll never know me! Let her live, Mother. Let her live! Live! Tell her—

PRIEST   Come, daughter.

YOUNG WOMAN   Wait! wait! Tell her—

[The JAILER takes the MOTHER away.]

GUARD   It's time.

YOUNG WOMAN   Wait! Wait! Tell her! Wait! Just a minute more! There's so
125   much I want to tell her— Wait—

[The JAILER takes the MOTHER off.]

9. Excerpt from St. Alphonsus Liguori, *Visits to the Blessed Sacrament and the Blessed Virgin Mary* (1835); "Behind the King of Heaven" may be a mistranscription of "Behold the King of Heaven," found in some versions of this text.

[*The* TWO GUARDS *take the* YOUNG WOMAN *by the arms, and start through the door in the bars and down the passage, across stage and off.*
The PRIEST *follows; the* MATRON *follows the* PRIEST; *the* PRIEST *is praying. The scene* BLACKS OUT.

The voice of the PRIEST *gets dimmer and dimmer.*]

PRIEST   Lord have mercy—Christ have mercy—Lord have mercy—Christ hear us! God the Father of Heaven! God the Son, Redeemer of the World, God the Holy Ghost—Holy Trinity one God—Holy Mary—Holy Mother of God—Holy Virgin of Virgins—St. Michael—St. Gabriel—St. Raphael—

[*His voice dies out.*]

[*Out of the darkness come the voices of* REPORTERS.]

130 1ST REPORTER   What time is it now?

2ND REPORTER   Time now.

3RD REPORTER   Hush.

1ST REPORTER   Here they come.

3D REPORTER   Hush.

135 PRIEST [*his voice sounds dimly—gets louder—continues until the end*]   St. Peter pray for us—St. Paul pray for us—St. James pray for us—St. John pray for us—all ye holy Angels and Archangels—all ye blessed orders of holy spirits—St. Joseph—St. John the Baptist—St. Thomas—

1ST REPORTER   Here they are!

140 2ND REPORTER   How little she looks! She's gotten smaller.

3RD REPORTER   Hush.

PRIEST   St. Phillip pray for us. All ye Holy Patriarchs and prophets—St. Phillip—St. Matthew—St. Simon—St. Thaddeus—All ye holy apostles—all ye holy disciples—all ye holy innocents—Pray for us—Pray for us—Pray for

145 us.—

1ST REPORTER   Suppose the machine shouldn't work!

2ND REPORTER   It'll work!—It always works!

3RD REPORTER   Hush!

PRIEST   Saints of God make intercession for us—Be merciful—Spare us, oh

150 Lord—be merciful—

1ST REPORTER   Her lips are moving—what is she saying?

2ND REPORTER   Nothing.

3RD REPORTER   Hush!

PRIEST   Oh Lord deliver us from all evil—from all sin—from Thy wrath—

155 from the snares of the devil—from anger and hatred and every evil will—from—

1ST REPORTER   Did you see that? She fixed her hair under the cap—pulled her hair out under the cap.

3RD REPORTER   Hush!

160 PRIEST   —Beseech Thee—hear us—that Thou would'st spare us—that Thou would'st pardon us—Holy Mary—pray for us—

2ND REPORTER   There—

YOUNG WOMAN [*calling out*]   Somebody! Somebod—

[*Her voice is cut off.*]

PRIEST   Christ have mercy—Lord have mercy—Christ have mercy—

CURTAIN

BERTOLT BRECHT

1898–1956

ARGUABLY the most influential dramatist of the twentieth century, Bertolt
Brecht developed and popularized a provocative form of theater that has changed
the course of theater history. Through
dozens of plays and adaptations, elaborate theories of acting, and a whole new
approach to theatrical performance, Brecht
touched every aspect of theater making
and imposed on it his distinct style and
method. Collaborating with leading musicians, writers, actors, and designers, such
as the composers Kurt Weill and Hanns
Eisler, the writer Elisabeth Hauptmann,
the actor Helene Weigel (Brecht's wife),
and the designer Caspar Neher, Brecht
sought to combine these different arts into
a new and jarring theatrical experience. He
was also intrigued by radio and film, the
newest media at the time, and sought to
transform the theater in their light, making
sure that it would remain "up to date," as
he liked to put it. Brecht wanted to create
new theater fit for an age dominated by science and progress. The product also of an
intensely felt political and social vision,
Brecht's reform sought above all to change
the relation between theater and its audience, seeking to instill in the audience a
critical and analytical attitude. The lasting impact of his work can be measured by
the fact that the adjective *Brechtian* has
long ceased to refer to Brecht's particular

reforms and practices, and often stands for
much modernist theater in general.

Born in the city of Augsburg in southern Germany, Brecht studied philosophy
and medicine in Munich; but in 1924, he
left Munich in order to work with Max
Reinhardt, the acclaimed director of the
Deutsches Theater in Berlin. By that time,
he had already won some recognition with
a number of plays, including *Baal* (1922),
Drums in the Night (1922), and *In the
Jungle of Cities* (1923; 1927). Influenced by
the episodic structures and jagged style of
German expressionist playwrights such
as Ernst Toller (1893–1939) and Georg
Kaiser (1878–1945), these plays are set in
a world whose social fabric has broken
down; even the language spoken by the
characters is ruptured, shifting abruptly
from colloquial speech to abstract metaphysical and religious terms, never resting
in a single, stable idiom.

In the course of the 1920s, Brecht gradually moved away from the topics and the
characteristic language of his early expressionist plays, although he retained their episodic structure. Increasingly, his theater
became a vehicle for understanding, analyzing, and criticizing the social world. *Man
Equals Man* (1926) is a good example of this
change, focused as it is on the analysis of a
single problem: the transformation of a porter, Galy Gay, into a cold-blooded soldier,

or rather into a "human fighting machine," as the play puts it. A similar purpose of critical analysis informs *The Rise and Fall of the City of Mahagonny* (1927; 1930), which identifies different forms of greed and consumption in a capitalist Sodom and Gomorrah. Brecht's greatest success during this period was *The Threepenny Opera* (1928), inspired by John Gay's *Beggar's Opera* (1728). *The Threepenny Opera* depicts a reality as cold as that of *Mahagonny*: the criminal underworld of London, where the king of the beggars, Peachum, and a crook, Macheath, fight for Peachum's daughter. This criminal sphere itself is not the main object of critique, however; instead, it functions as a metaphor for the criminality of capitalism. Though never a member of the Communist Party, Brecht shared with Marxist intellectuals an interest in power relations, and he sought to expose, through his plays, the hidden mechanisms of exploitation. Theater for him had become part of the struggle for a better society.

Even though the subject matter of Brecht's plays had grown more sober during the 1920s, their form and style remained exuberant. *Man Equals Man, Mahagonny,* and *The Threepenny Opera*—as well as many subsequent works, including THE GOOD WOMAN OF SETZUAN (1943)—were conceived as musical plays. In some cases, the music has come to overshadow the plays themselves. The popularity of *The Threepenny Opera,* perhaps the most entertaining work of them all, was due mostly to Kurt Weill's catchy songs; the best known is "Mack the Knife," which hit the top of the American charts after being recorded in the 1950s by Louis Armstrong and by Bobby Darin. Onstage, however, Brecht did not so much use the conventions of musical theater as transform them. Rather than being smoothly integrated into these plays, the music was deliberately set apart. The same was true of the other elements of performance—dialogue, acting, set design. Brecht called this technique the

The 1957 Berliner Ensemble production of *The Good Person of Szechwan.*

"separation of the elements"; it was an attempt to use the different components of performance in such a way that they would interrupt one another rather than work in unison. Brecht and his collaborators thought of the resulting productions as antioperas: operas whose components had been pulled apart and put back together in a new and startling manner.

The result was the *Verfremdungseffekt* or the "estrangement effect," the attempt to "make strange" the entire experience of watching theater (an alternate translation sometimes used, "alienation effect," misleadingly implies an alienation from nature rather than the defamiliarization emphasized by Brecht). This was the heart of the theory of drama that made Brecht famous. Instead of enchanting the audience through well-integrated, harmonious spectacles, Brecht and his collaborators meant to disentangle the different sensory experiences associated with music, acting, scene design, language, and suspenseful plots and to set them against one another. Ultimately, they envisioned estrangement as the foundation of a new relation between theatrical performance and the audience, aimed at making the audience pause, examine, reflect, and criticize—that is, to look at the performance as if from a distance. Brecht once compared this attitude to that displayed by spectators at a boxing match or a similar sporting event; such audiences examine the skill of the players, appreciating their strategies and techniques from a critical distance, rather than being drawn unreflectively into a simulated world.

The technique of estrangement also extended to acting. Whereas traditionally the actor was supposed to inhabit the role completely, Brecht wanted his actors to remind the audience that they were only playing, that they were pretending to be another person for the duration of the performance. Put in the language of the theater, this meant that actor and role were to be clearly distinguished. Accomplishing this separation was a difficult task, but Brecht helped the actors by often having them speak about the character they are impersonating in the third person— commenting on the role as if from the outside. To illustrate his ideal of estranged acting, Brecht used the example of a court-room in which witnesses are asked to demonstrate to the jury how a particular accident occurred. They take on different roles, Brecht explains, and go through the action, but do not seek to become completely absorbed in their performance. They never lose sight of their specific purpose. To encourage playgoers to shift their attention from the "what" (what happened) to the "how" (how did it happen), Brecht often gave away the plot at the beginning of each scene, sometimes writing a brief summary on a half-curtain. The audience (the "jury") was meant to analyze the events depicted onstage, focusing on how they had taken place and how they could be altered, rather than be engrossed by the suspense.

The final dimension of estrangement Brecht employed was geographic. Many of his plays are set in non-European locales: America (*Jungle of Cities; Mahagonny; St. Joan of the Stockyards* [1932]), South Asia (*Man Equals Man*), China (*The Good Woman of Setzuan*), Japan (*The Yea Sayer* [1930]). Brecht's goal here was not to represent, as accurately as possible, these different cultures. Instead he used settings that were foreign (to his German audience) to facilitate a distanced, analytical attitude toward the events depicted onstage, rather than one complicated by familiar investments and opinions. At the same time, however, Brecht was genuinely influenced by the tradition of Chinese acting and by the Japanese noh theater; his play *The Yea Sayer*, for example, is based on the noh play *Taniko* (fifteenth century).

The geographic displacement of the plays was mirrored by Brecht's later life. Fearing the rise of National Socialism, he fled first to Denmark in 1933 and then to the United States in 1941, where he tried and mostly failed to produce his plays or make a living by writing Hollywood screenplays. In 1947, as the McCarthyite anticommunist witch hunts began, Brecht was called before the House Un-American Activities Committee (HUAC); he left the United States directly after the harrowing experience, going first to Switzerland and then, in 1949, to East Germany, where he built the Berliner Ensemble into one of the premier theaters of the world. It was during the years in exile that he wrote not only some of his best-known plays, including *Mother Courage* (1941), *The Life of*

Galileo Galilei (1943), and *The Good Woman of Setzuan*, but also his adaptation of Aeschylus's *Antigone* (1948; his other famous adaptation, of SHAKESPEARE's *Coriolanus,* was written and left incomplete in 1952). In his last years, Brecht withdrew from the public eye, though he was accompanied, as he had been throughout his life, not only by his wife, Helene Weigel, but also by a number of lovers; indeed, many of his plays were collaborations with lovers (especially Elisabeth Hauptmann). He died in East Berlin in 1956, having become the most important cultural representative of socialist East Germany.

The Good Woman of Setzuan, written between 1930 and 1942 but not published until 1953, combines many of Brecht's characteristic techniques. It is set in a remote locale, the Chinese province of Sichuan (spelled "Sezuan" by Brecht and "Szechwan" in the following translation). A prelude, interludes, and the play's scenes are organized episodically and not into a tightly constructed plot; the play is also scattered with songs, written by Paul Dessau, that interrupt the flow of the action. In accordance with Brecht's theory of acting, actors address the audience directly, commenting on the action and explaining their problems and thus destroying any illusion of realism. Brecht worked on this play over a long period of time—precisely the period in which he formulated the tenets of his theory of estrangement. It therefore became the chief representative of estranged theater, or what Brecht himself preferred to call "epic theater."

Like many of Brecht's plays, *The Good Woman of Setzuan* presents a relatively simple dilemma: the inability of the female protagonist, Shen Teh, to be good in the world as it is. Brecht even uses a didactic genre, the parable, to drive this point home: three gods visit Szechwan in order to find a single good person. The only good person they can find, the only one to offer them shelter, is the prostitute Shen Teh, whom they reward by giving her a considerable sum of money. They then leave her to her own devices, urging her only to remain good. Doing so, however, is not all that easy. Shen Teh uses the money to buy a tobacco store. As a good person, she soon begins taking in all kinds of people in need and distributing food to the poor, until

finally the tobacco store itself is in danger of failing. It is at this point that she calls on the services of Shui Ta, her hard-nosed cousin, to keep her business afloat. Immediately, Shui Ta cuts down on Shen Teh's philanthropy and thus restores her business to a sound economic footing. Therein lies the play's central concern: being a good person and getting by in this world are mutually incompatible goals.

The play presents this point through an intriguing variation on the estrangement technique—Shen Teh and Shui Ta are the same person and are played by the same actor. The device is revealed to the audience relatively early, when the change in costume occurs in front of the spectators' eyes; yet all but one of the other characters on the stage remain in the dark. Brecht thereby ensures that the audience has more information at its disposal than the characters and can thus observe their motivations and actions. No attention is wasted on a state of suspense, trying to discover this identity (the "what"); the focus instead is entirely on understanding why Shen Teh depends on Shui Ta. Brecht employs a split character to show not psychological conflict but social conflict.

Another source of dramatic conflict is the demand made by the gods that Shen Teh must be good, which fails to take into account whether she can afford goodness. The state of the world, the fact that the world as it is does not allow a person to be good and survive, does not concern them. This discrepancy between the world and the gods is mediated by a man named Wang, a water carrier. No angel himself, Wang knows what this world requires and how it forces those who live in it to behave. At the same time, he honors the gods, striving to please them as best he can, even as he recognizes the impossibility of their demands. He seeks shelter for them and tries to hide most people's indifference toward them. He is a figure of compromise and attempts to mediate the clash between the gods and the harsh realities of the world—with limited success.

Fueling this clash is not just the gods' disinterest in the world but ultimately their ignorance of it. Wang first recognizes them because their very appearance bears no traces of labor; they are creatures of leisure who know nothing of the world's

Jane Horrocks as Shen Teh / Shui Ta in a 2008 production (under the alternate title *The Good Soul of Szechuan*) staged at the Young Vic Theatre, London.

hard realities; their conception of goodness is merely a lofty ideal. In particular, the gods refuse to interfere in the area of economics, assuming instead that morality and economics have nothing to do with one another. They cling to Shen Teh's goodness without recognizing that it depends on the constant interventions of her harder self, of which the gods disapprove. By revealing to the audience that Shui Ta is just the other side of Shen Teh, Brecht constructs a disjunction between the audience and the gods of which only the audience is aware. The gods are thus in a position of ignorance and the audience, of knowledge.

Like Brecht's other didactic plays, *The Good Woman of Setzuan* does not offer, or preach, a particular solution to the dilemma it presents, such as a socialist society or a new conception of goodness. What it does do, however, is suggest a problem or a set of contradictions, here between the conception of goodness imposed by the gods and the (economic) requisites of the world. It is clear that such a contradiction offers two lines of attack: to get rid of the gods or to get rid of the economic system that does not allow for goodness.

These two consequences are suggested throughout, but they come to the fore in the final scene, which is a trial. Now the contradictions on which the entire play is built are brought into the open: the audience, both onstage and offstage, has to make up its mind. Indeed, trial scenes can be found frequently in Brecht's works, for they offer an opportunity to expose false morals, false laws, and other abuses. At the same time, trial scenes resonate with Brecht's ideal audience: an audience willing to make its own judgments and to come to its own conclusions.

Brecht's theater shaped many of the most important theater makers of the twentieth century, including the German experimental writers Heiner Müller and Peter Weiss, the British feminist playwright CARYL CHURCHILL, and the Brazilian political dramatist Augusto Boal. That they, despite their enormous differences, all refer to Brecht as their primary influence testifies to the long and varied impact he has had on contemporary theater the world over. This unparalleled influence was due to Brecht's ability to institute a coherent theater reform in every dimension of performance, a reform that other artists could then adopt, alter, or rebel against. But despite all his fame, Brecht did not achieve—or at least he did not fully achieve—his ultimate end: namely, to transform the theater from a vehicle of entertainment into a vehicle of critical thought. His legacy is thus an ambiguous one: he single-handedly changed the course of theater history, and yet this change fell short of his grand goal.   M.P.

The Good Woman of Setzuan[1]

CHARACTERS

WONG, *a water seller*
THREE GODS
SHEN TE, *a prostitute, later a shopkeeper*
MRS. SHIN, *former owner of Shen Te's shop*
A family of eight (HUSBAND, WIFE, BROTHER, SISTER-IN-LAW, GRANDFATHER, NEPHEW, NIECE, BOY)
An UNEMPLOYED MAN
A CARPENTER
MRS. MI TZU, *Shen Te's landlady*

Mr. SHUI TA
YANG SUN, *an unemployed pilot, later a factory manager*
An OLD WHORE
A POLICEMAN
An OLD MAN
An OLD WOMAN, *his wife*
Mr. SHU FU, *a barber*
MRS. YANG, *mother of Yang Sun*
GENTLEMEN, VOICES, PRIEST, WAITER, *children (three), etc.*

Prologue

At the gates of the half-Westernized city of Setzuan. Evening. WONG *the water seller[2] introduces himself to the audience.*

WONG   I sell water here in the city of Setzuan. It isn't easy. When water is scarce, I have long distances to go in search of it, and when it is plentiful,

1. Translated by Eric Bentley.
2. The "city of Setzuan" is Chengdu, the capital of Sichuan (Setzuan), a province in Western China. However, the Chinese setting of this play is drawn largely from Brecht's imagination, not from historical or geographical fact.

I have no income. But in our part of the world there is nothing unusual about poverty. Many people think only the gods can save the situation. And I hear from a cattle merchant—who travels a lot—that some of the highest gods are on their way here at this very moment. Informed sources have it that heaven is quite disturbed at all the complaining. I've been coming out here to the city gates for three days now to bid these gods welcome. I want to be the first to greet them. What about those fellows over there? No, no, they *work*. And that one there has ink on his fingers, he's no god, he must be a clerk from the cement factory. *Those* two are another story. They look as though they'd like to beat you. But gods don't need to beat you, do they? [THREE GODS *appear*.] What about those three? Old-fashioned clothes—dust on their feet—they *must* be gods! [*He throws himself at their feet.*] Do with me what you will, illustrious ones!

FIRST GOD [*With an ear trumpet.*]   Ah! [*He is pleased.*] So we were expected?

WONG [*Giving them water.*]   Oh, yes. And I *knew* you'd come.

FIRST GOD   We need somewhere to stay the night. You know of a place?

WONG   The whole town is at your service, illustrious ones! What sort of a place would you like?

[*The* GODS *eye each other.*]

FIRST GOD   Just try the first house you come to, my son.

WONG   That would be Mr. Fo's place.

FIRST GOD   Mr. Fo.

WONG   One moment! [*He knocks at the first house.*]

VOICE FROM MR. FO'S   No!

[WONG *returns a little nervously.*]

WONG   It's too bad. Mr. Fo isn't in. And his servants don't dare do a thing without his consent. He'll have a fit when he finds out who they turned away, won't he?

FIRST GOD [*Smiling.*]   He will, won't he?

WONG   One moment! The next house is Mr. Cheng's. Won't he be thrilled!

FIRST GOD   Mr. Cheng.

[WONG *knocks.*]

VOICE FROM MR. CHENG'S   Keep your gods. We have our own troubles!

WONG [*Back with the* GODS.]   Mr. Cheng is very sorry, but he has a houseful of relations. I think some of them are a bad lot, and naturally, he wouldn't like you to see them.

THIRD GOD   Are we so terrible?

WONG   Well, only with bad people, of course. Everyone knows the province of Kwan is always having floods.

SECOND GOD   Really? How's that?

WONG   Why, because they're so irreligious.

SECOND GOD   Rubbish. It's because they neglected the dam.

FIRST GOD [*To* SECOND.]   Sh! [*To* WONG.] You're still in hopes, aren't you, my son?

WONG   Certainly. All Setzuan is competing for the honor! What happened up to now is pure coincidence. I'll be back. [*He walks away, but then stands undecided.*]

SECOND GOD   What did I tell you?

THIRD GOD   It *could* be pure coincidence.

SECOND GOD   The same coincidence in Shun, Kwan, and Setzuan? People just aren't religious any more, let's face the fact. Our mission has failed!

50 FIRST GOD   Oh come, we might run into a good person any minute.

THIRD GOD   How did the resolution read? [*Unrolling a scroll and reading from it.*] "The world can stay as it is if enough people are found [*At the word "found" he unrolls it a little more*] living lives worthy of human beings." Good people, that is. Well, what about this water seller himself? *He's* good,

55 or I'm very much mistaken.

SECOND GOD   You're very much mistaken. When he gave us a drink, I had the impression there was something odd about the cup. Well, look! [*He shows the cup to the* FIRST GOD.]

FIRST GOD   A false bottom!

SECOND GOD   The man is a swindler.

60 FIRST GOD   Very well, count *him* out. That's one man among millions. And as a matter of fact, we only need one on *our* side. These atheists are saying, "The world must be changed because no one can *be* good and *stay* good." No one, eh? I say: let us find one—just one—and we have those fellows where we want them!

65 THIRD GOD [*To* WONG.]   Water seller, is it so hard to find a place to stay?

WONG   Nothing could be easier. It's just me. I don't go about it right.

THIRD GOD   Really?

[*He returns to the others. A* GENTLEMAN *passes by.*]

WONG   Oh dear, they're catching on. [*He accosts the* GENTLEMAN.] Excuse the intrusion, dear sir, but three gods have just turned up. Three of the very highest. They need a place for the night. Seize this rare opportunity—to

70 have real gods as your guests!

GENTLEMAN [*laughing*]   A new way of finding free rooms for a gang of crooks. [*Exit* GENTLEMAN.]

WONG [*shouting at him.*]   Godless rascal! Have you no religion, gentlemen of Setzuan? [*Pause.*] Patience, illustrious ones! [*Pause.*] There's only one person

75 left. Shen Te, the prostitute. She *can't* say no. [*Calls up to a window.*] Shen Te!

[SHEN TE *opens the shutters and looks out.*]

WONG   Shen Te, it's Wong. *They're* here, and nobody wants them. Will you take them?

SHEN TE   Oh, no, Wong, I'm expecting a gentleman.

WONG   Can't you forget about him for tonight?

80 SHEN TE   The rent has to be paid by tomorrow or I'll be out on the street.

WONG   This is no time for calculation, Shen Te.

SHEN TE   Stomachs rumble even on the Emperor's birthday, Wong.

WONG   Setzuan is one big dung hill!

SHEN TE   Oh, very well! I'll hide till my gentleman has come and gone. Then

85 I'll take them. [*She disappears.*]

WONG   They mustn't see her gentleman or they'll know what she is.

FIRST GOD [*Who hasn't heard any of this.*]   I think it's hopeless.

[*They approach* WONG.]

WONG [*Jumping, as he finds them behind him.*]   A room has been found, illustrious ones! [*He wipes sweat off his brow.*]

90 SECOND GOD   Oh, good.

THIRD GOD   Let's see it.

WONG [*Nervously.*]   Just a minute. It has to be tidied up a bit.

THIRD GOD   Then we'll sit down here and wait.

WONG [*Still more nervous.*]   No, no! [*Holding himself back.*] Too much traf
95   fic, you know.

THIRD GOD [*With a smile.*]   Of course, if you *want* us to move.

[*They retire a little. They sit on a doorstep.* WONG *sits on the ground.*]

WONG [*After a deep breath.*]   You'll be staying with a single girl—the finest
human being in Setzuan!

THIRD GOD   That's nice.

100   WONG [*To the audience.*]   They gave me such a look when I picked up my
cup just now.

THIRD GOD   You're worn out, Wong.

WONG   A little, maybe.

FIRST GOD   Do people here have a hard time of it?

105   WONG   The good ones do.

FIRST GOD   What about yourself?

WONG   You mean I'm not good. That's true. And I don't have an easy time either!

[*During this dialogue, a* GENTLEMAN *has turned up in front of Shen Te's
House, and has whistled several times. Each time* WONG *has given a
start.*]

THIRD GOD [*To* WONG, *softly.*]   Psst! I think he's gone now.

WONG [*Confused and surprised.*]   Ye-e-es.

[*The* GENTLEMAN *has left now, and* SHEN TE *has come down to the street.*]

110   SHEN TE [*Softly.*]   Wong!

[*Getting no answer, she goes off down the street.* WONG *arrives just too
late, forgetting his carrying pole.*]

WONG [*Softly.*]   Shen Te! Shen Te! [*To himself.*] So she's gone off to earn the
rent. Oh dear, I can't go to the gods *again* with no room to offer them. Having failed in the service of the gods, I shall run to my den in the sewer pipe
down by the river and hide from their sight!

[*He rushes off.* SHEN TE *returns, looking for him, but finding the* GODS.
She stops in confusion.]

115   SHEN TE   You are the illustrious ones? My name is Shen Te. It would please
me very much if my simple room could be of use to you.

THIRD GOD   Where is the water seller, Miss . . . Shen Te?

SHEN TE   I missed him, somehow.

FIRST GOD   Oh, he probably thought you weren't coming, and was afraid of
120   telling us.

THIRD GOD [*Picking up the carrying pole.*]   We'll leave this with you. He'll be
needing it.

[*Led by* SHEN TE, *they go into the house. It grows dark, then light. Dawn.
Again escorted by* SHEN TE, *who leads them through the half-light with a
little lamp, the* GODS *take their leave.*]

FIRST GOD   Thank you, thank you, dear Shen Te, for your elegant hospitality!
We shall not forget! And give our thanks to the water seller—he showed us
125   a good human being.

SHEN TE   Oh, *I'm* not good. Let me tell you something: when Wong asked me
to put you up, I hesitated.

FIRST GOD   It's all right to hesitate if you then go ahead! And in giving us that room you did much more than you knew. You proved that good people still
130   exist, a point that has been disputed of late—even in heaven. Farewell!

SECOND GOD   Farewell!

THIRD GOD   Farewell!

SHEN TE   Stop, illustrious ones! I'm not sure you're right. I'd like to be good, it's true, but there's the rent to pay. And that's not all: I sell myself for a living.
135   Even so I can't make ends meet, there's too much competition. I'd like to honor my father and mother and speak nothing but the truth and not covet my neighbor's house. I should love to stay with one man. But how? How is it done? Even breaking a few of your commandments, I can hardly manage.

FIRST GOD   [Clearing his throat.]   These thoughts are but, um, the misgivings
140   of an unusually good woman!

THIRD GOD   Good-bye, Shen Te! Give our regards to the water seller!

SECOND GOD   And above all: be good! Farewell!

FIRST GOD   Farewell!

THIRD GOD   Farewell!

[They start to wave good-bye.]

145   SHEN TE   But everything is so expensive, I don't feel sure I can do it!

SECOND GOD   That's not in our sphere. We never meddle with economics.

THIRD GOD   One moment. [They stop.] Isn't it true she might do better if she had more money?

SECOND GOD   Come, come! How could we ever account for it Up Above?

150   FIRST GOD   Oh, there are ways. [They put their heads together and confer in dumb show. To SHEN TE, with embarrassment.] As you say you can't pay your rent, well, um, we're not paupers, so of course we insist on paying for our room. [Awkwardly thrusting money into her hands.] There! [Quickly.] But don't tell anyone! The incident is open to misinterpretation.

155   SECOND GOD   It certainly is!

FIRST GOD   [Defensively.]   But there's no law against it! It was never decreed that a god mustn't pay hotel bills!

[The GODS leave.]

1

A small tobacco shop. The shop is not as yet completely furnished and hasn't started doing business.

SHEN TE   [To the audience.]   It's three days now since the gods left. When they said they wanted to pay for the room, I looked down at my hand, and there was more than a thousand silver dollars! I bought a tobacco shop with the money, and moved in yesterday. I don't own the building, of course, but
5   I can pay the rent, and I hope to do a lot of good here. Beginning with Mrs. Shin, who's just coming across the square with her pot. She had the shop before me, and yesterday she dropped in to ask for rice for her children. [Enter MRS. SHIN. Both women bow.] How do you do, Mrs. Shin.

MRS. SHIN   How do you do, Miss Shen Te. You like your new home?

10   SHEN TE   Indeed, yes. Did your children have a good night?

MRS. SHIN   In that hovel? The youngest is coughing already.

SHEN TE   Oh, dear!

MRS. SHIN   You're going to learn a thing or two in these slums.

SHEN TE   Slums? That's not what you said when you sold me the shop!

15   MRS. SHIN   Now don't start nagging! Robbing me and my innocent children of their home and then calling it a slum! That's the limit!

[*She weeps.*]

SHEN TE [*Tactfully.*]   I'll get your rice.

MRS. SHIN   And a little cash while you're at it.

SHEN TE   I'm afraid I haven't sold anything yet.

20   MRS. SHIN [*Screeching.*]   I've got to have it. Strip the clothes from my back and then cut my throat, will you? I know what I'll do: I'll dump my children on your doorstep! [*She snatches the pot out of* SHEN TE's *hands.*]

SHEN TE   Please don't be angry. You'll spill the rice.

[*Enter an elderly* HUSBAND *and* WIFE *with their shabbily dressed* NEPHEW.]

WIFE   Shen Te, dear! You've come into money, they tell me. And we haven't a

25   roof over our heads! A tobacco shop. We had one too. But it's gone. Could we spend the night here, do you think?

NEPHEW [*Appraising the shop.*]   Not bad!

WIFE   He's our nephew. We're inseparable!

MRS. SHIN   And who are these . . . ladies and gentlemen?

30   SHEN TE   They put me up when I first came in from the country. [*To the audience.*] Of course, when my small purse was empty, they put me out on the street, and they may be afraid I'll do the same to them. [*To the newcomers, kindly.*] Come in, and welcome, though I've only one little room for you— it's behind the shop.

35   HUSBAND   That'll do. Don't worry.

WIFE [*Bringing* SHEN TE *some tea.*]   We'll stay over here, so we won't be in your way. Did you make it a tobacco shop in memory of your first real home? We can certainly give you a hint or two! That's one reason we came.

MRS. SHIN [*To* SHEN TE.]   Very nice! As long as you have a few customers too!

40   HUSBAND   Sh! A customer!

[*Enter an* UNEMPLOYED MAN, *in rags.*]

UNEMPLOYED MAN   Excuse me. I'm unemployed.

[MRS. SHIN *laughs.*]

SHEN TE   Can I help you?

UNEMPLOYED MAN   Have you any damaged cigarettes? I thought there might be some damage when you're unpacking.

45   WIFE   What nerve, begging for tobacco! [*Rhetorically.*] Why don't they ask for bread?

UNEMPLOYED MAN   Bread is expensive. One cigarette butt and I'll be a new man.

SHEN TE [*Giving him cigarettes.*]   That's very important—to be a new man.

50   You'll be my first customer and bring me luck.

[*The* UNEMPLOYED MAN *quickly lights a cigarette, inhales, and goes off, coughing.*]

WIFE   Was that right, Shen Te, dear?

MRS. SHIN   If this is the opening of a shop, you can hold the closing at the end of the week.

HUSBAND   I bet he had money on him.

55   SHEN TE   Oh, no, he said he hadn't!

NEPHEW   How d'you know he wasn't lying?

SHEN TE [*Angrily*.]   How do you know he was?

WIFE [*Wagging her head*.]   You're too good, Shen Te, dear. If you're going to keep this shop, you'll have to learn to say no.

60 HUSBAND   Tell them the place isn't yours to dispose of. Belongs to . . . some relative who insists on all accounts being strictly in order . . .

MRS. SHIN   That's right! What do you think you are—a philanthropist?

SHEN TE [*Laughing*.]   Very well, suppose I ask you for my rice back, Mrs. Shin?

WIFE [*Combatively, at* MRS. SHIN.]   So that's *her* rice?

[*Enter the* CARPENTER, *a small man*.]

65 MRS. SHIN [*Who, at the sight of him, starts to hurry away*.]   See you tomorrow, Miss Shen Te! [*Exit* MRS. SHIN.]

CARPENTER   Mrs. Shin, it's you I want!

WIFE [*To* SHEN TE.]   Has she some claim on you?

SHEN TE   She's hungry. That's a claim.

70 CARPENTER   Are you the new tenant? And filling up the shelves already? Well, they're not yours till they're paid for, ma'am. I'm the carpenter, so I should know.

SHEN TE   I took the shop "furnishings included."

CARPENTER   You're in league with that Mrs. Shin, of course. All right. I demand

75 my hundred silver dollars.

SHEN TE   I'm afraid I haven't got a hundred silver dollars.

CARPENTER   Then you'll find it. Or I'll have you arrested.

WIFE [*Whispering to* SHEN TE.]   That relative: make it a cousin.

SHEN TE   Can't it wait till next month?

80 CARPENTER   No!

SHEN TE   Be a little patient, Mr. Carpenter, I can't settle all claims at once.

CARPENTER   Who's patient with me? [*He grabs a shelf from the wall*.]   Pay up—or I take the shelves back!

WIFE   Shen Te! Dear! Why don't you let your . . . cousin settle this affair? [*To*

85 CARPENTER.]   Put your claim in writing. Shen Te's cousin will see you get paid.

CARPENTER [*Derisively*.]   Cousin, eh?

HUSBAND   Cousin, yes.

CARPENTER   I know these cousins!

90 NEPHEW   Don't be silly. He's a personal friend of mine.

HUSBAND   What a man! Sharp as a razor!

CARPENTER   All right. I'll put my claim in writing. [*Puts shelf on floor, sits on it, writes out bill*.]

WIFE [*To* SHEN TE.]   He'd tear the dress off your back to get his shelves. Never recognize a claim! That's my motto.

95 SHEN TE   He's done a job, and wants something in return. It's shameful that I can't give it to him. What will the gods say?

HUSBAND   You did your bit when you took *us* in.

[*Enter the* BROTHER, *limping, and the* SISTER-IN-LAW, *pregnant*.]

BROTHER [*To* HUSBAND *and* WIFE.]   So this is where you're hiding out! There's family feeling for you! Leaving us on the corner!

100 WIFE [*Embarrassed, to* SHEN TE.]   It's my brother and his wife. [*To them*.] Now stop grumbling, and sit quietly in that corner. [*To* SHEN TE.] It can't be helped. She's in her fifth month.

SHEN TE   Oh yes. Welcome!

WIFE [*To the couple.*]   Say thank you. [*They mutter something.*] The cups are
105   there. [*To* SHEN TE.] Lucky you bought this shop when you did!

SHEN TE [*Laughing and bringing tea.*]   Lucky indeed!

[*Enter* MRS. MI TZU, *the landlady.*]

MRS. MI TZU   Miss Shen Te? I am Mrs. Mi Tzu, your landlady. I hope our rela-
    tionship will be a happy one. I like to think I give my tenants modern, per-
    sonalized service. Here is your lease. [*To the others, as* SHEN TE *reads the lease.*]
110   There's nothing like the opening of a little shop, is there? A moment of true
    beauty! [*She is looking around.*] Not very much on the shelves, of course.
    But everything in the gods' good time! Where are your references, Miss
    Shen Te?

SHEN TE   Do I *have* to have references?

115 MRS. MI TZU   After all, I haven't a notion who you are!

HUSBAND   Oh, *we'd* be glad to vouch for Miss Shen Te! We'd go through fire
    for her!

MRS. MI TZU   And who may *you* be?

HUSBAND [*Stammering.*]   Ma Fu, tobacco dealer.

120 MRS. MI TZU   Where is your shop, Mr. . . . . Ma Fu?

HUSBAND   Well, um, I haven't got a shop—I've just sold it.

MRS. MI TZU   I see. [*To* SHEN TE.] Is there no one else that knows you?

WIFE [*Whispering to* SHEN TE.]   Your cousin! Your cousin!

MRS. MI TZU   This is a respectable house, Miss Shen Te. I never sign a lease
125   without certain assurances.

SHEN TE [*Slowly, her eyes downcast.*]   I have . . . a cousin.

MRS. MI TZU   On the square? Let's go over and see him. What does he do?

SHEN TE [*As before.*]   He lives . . . in another city.

WIFE [*Prompting.*]   Didn't you say he was in Shung?

130 SHEN TE   That's right. Shung.

HUSBAND [*Prompting.*]   I had his name on the tip of my tongue, Mr. . . . .

SHEN TE [*With an effort.*]   Mr. . . . . Shui . . . Ta.

HUSBAND   That's it! Tall, skinny fellow!

SHEN TE   Shui Ta!

135 NEPHEW [*To* CARPENTER.]   *You* were in touch with him, weren't you? About
    the shelves?

CARPENTER [*Surlily.*]   Give him this bill. [*He hands it over.*] I'll be back in the
    morning. [*Exit* CARPENTER.]

NEPHEW [*Calling after him, but with his eyes on* MRS. MI TZU.]   Don't worry!
140   Mr. Shui Ta pays on the nail!

MRS. MI TZU [*Looking closely at* SHEN TE.]   I'll be happy to make his acquain-
    tance, Miss Shen Te. [*Exit* MRS. MI TZU.]

[*Pause.*]

WIFE   By tomorrow morning she'll know more about you than you do yourself.

SISTER-IN-LAW [*To nephew.*]   This thing isn't built to last.

[*Enter* GRANDFATHER.]

145 WIFE   It's Grandfather! [*To* SHEN TE.] Such a good old soul!

[*The* BOY *enters.*]

BOY [*Over his shoulder.*]   Here they are!

WIFE   And the boy, how he's grown! But he always could eat enough for ten.

[*Enter the* NIECE.]

WIFE [*To* SHEN TE.]   Our little niece from the country. There are more of us
now than in your time. The less we had, the more there were of us; the
150   more there were of us, the less we had. Give me the key. We must protect
ourselves from unwanted guests. [*She takes the key and locks the door.*] Just
make yourself at home. I'll light the little lamp.

NEPHEW [*A big joke.*]   I hope her cousin doesn't drop in tonight! The strict
Mr. Shui Ta!

[SISTER-IN-LAW *laughs.*]

155   BROTHER [*Reaching for a cigarette.*]   One cigarette more or less . . .

HUSBAND   One cigarette more or less.

[*They pile into the cigarettes. The* BROTHER *hands a jug of wine round.*]

NEPHEW   Mr. Shui Ta'll pay for it!

GRANDFATHER [*Gravely, to* SHEN TE.]   How do you do?

[SHEN TE, *a little taken aback by the belatedness of the greeting, bows.
She has the carpenter's bill in one hand, the landlady's lease in the
other.*]

WIFE   How about a bit of a song? To keep Shen Te's spirits up?

160   NEPHEW   Good idea. Grandfather: you start!

SONG OF THE SMOKE

GRANDFATHER

I used to think (before old age beset me)
That brains could fill the pantry of the poor.
But where did all my cerebration get me?
I'm just as hungry as I was before.
165   So what's the use?
See the smoke float free
Into ever colder coldness!
It's the same with me.

HUSBAND

The straight and narrow path leads to disaster
170   And so the crooked path I tried to tread.
That got me to disaster even faster.
(They say we shall be happy when we're dead.)
So what's the use?
See the smoke float free
175   Into ever colder coldness!
It's the same with me.

NIECE

You older people, full of expectation,
At any moment now you'll walk the plank!
The future's for the younger generation!
180   Yes, even if that future is a blank.
So what's the use?
See the smoke float free
Into ever colder coldness!
It's the same with me.

185   NEPHEW [*To the* BROTHER.]   Where'd you get that wine?

SISTER-IN-LAW [*Answering for the* BROTHER.]   He pawned the sack of tobacco.

HUSBAND [*Stepping in.*]   What? That tobacco was all we had to fall back on! You pig!

BROTHER   You'd call a man a pig because your wife was frigid! Did you refuse
190   to drink it?

[*They fight. The shelves fall over.*]

SHEN TE [*Imploringly.*]   Oh don't! Don't break everything! Take it, take it all, but don't destroy a gift from the gods!

WIFE [*Disparagingly.*]   This shop isn't big enough. I should never have mentioned it to Uncle and the others. When *they* arrive, it's going to be disgust-
195   ingly overcrowded.

SISTER-IN-LAW   And did you hear our gracious hostess? She cools off quick!

[*Voices outside. Knocking at the door.*]

UNCLE'S VOICE   Open the door!

WIFE   Uncle? Is that you, Uncle?

UNCLE'S VOICE   Certainly, it's me. Auntie says to tell you she'll have the chil-
200   dren here in ten minutes.

WIFE [*To* SHEN TE.]   I'll have to let him in.

SHEN TE [*Who scarcely hears her.*]

> The little lifeboat is swiftly sent down
> Too many men too greedily
205 > Hold on to it as they drown.

1a

Wong's den in a sewer pipe.

WONG [*Crouching there.*]   All quiet! It's four days now since I left the city. The gods passed this way on the second day. I heard their steps on the bridge over there. They must be a long way off by this time, so I'm safe. [*Breathing a sigh of relief, he curls up and goes to sleep. In his dream the pipe becomes transparent, and the* GODS *appear. Raising an arm, as if in self-defense.*] I know, I know, illustrious ones! I found no one to give you a
5   room—not in all Setzuan! There, it's out. Please continue on your way!

FIRST GOD [*Mildly.*]   But you did find someone. Someone who took us in for the night, watched over us in our sleep, and in the early morning lighted us down to the street with a lamp.

WONG   It was . . . Shen Te that took you in?

10 THIRD GOD   Who else?

WONG   And I ran away! "She isn't coming," I thought, "she just can't afford it."

GODS [*Singing.*]

> O you feeble, well-intentioned, and yet feeble chap
> Where there's need the fellow thinks there is no goodness!
> When there's danger he thinks courage starts to ebb away!
15 > Some people only see the seamy side!
> What hasty judgment! What premature desperation!

WONG   I'm *very* ashamed, illustrious ones.

FIRST GOD   Do us a favor, water seller. Go back to Setzuan. Find Shen Te, and give us a report on her. We hear that she's come into a little money.
20   Show interest in her goodness—for no one can be good for long if goodness is not in demand. Meanwhile we shall continue the search, and find

other good people. After which, the idle chatter about the impossibility of goodness will stop!

[*The* GODS *vanish.*]

2

A knocking.

WIFE   Shen Te! Someone at the door. Where is she anyway?

NEPHEW   She must be getting the breakfast. Mr. Shui Ta will pay for it.

[*The* WIFE *laughs and shuffles to the door. Enter Mr.* SHUI TA *and the* CARPENTER.]

WIFE   Who is it?

SHUI TA   I am Miss Shen Te's cousin.

5 WIFE   What??

SHUI TA   My name is Shui Ta.

WIFE   Her cousin?

NEPHEW   Her cousin?

NIECE   But that was a joke. She hasn't got a cousin.

10 HUSBAND   So early in the morning?

BROTHER   What's all the noise?

SISTER-IN-LAW   This fellow says he's her cousin.

BROTHER   Tell him to prove it.

NEPHEW   Right. If you're Shen Te's cousin, prove it by getting the breakfast.

SHUI TA [*Whose regime begins as he puts out the lamp to save oil; loudly, to all*
15   *present, asleep or awake.*]   Would you all please get dressed! Customers will be coming! I wish to open my shop!

HUSBAND   *Your* shop? Doesn't it belong to our good friend Shen Te?

[SHUI TA *shakes his head.*]

SISTER-IN-LAW   So we've been cheated. Where *is* the little liar?

SHUI TA   Miss Shen Te has been delayed. She wishes me to tell you there will
20   be nothing she can do—now I am here.

WIFE [*Bowled over.*]   I thought she was good!

NEPHEW   Do you have to believe *him*?

HUSBAND   I don't.

NEPHEW   Then do something.

25 HUSBAND   Certainly! I'll send out a search party at once. You, you, you, and you, go out and look for Shen Te. [*As the* GRANDFATHER *rises and makes for the door*] Not you, Grandfather, you and I will hold the fort.

SHUI TA   You won't find Miss Shen Te. She has suspended her hospitable activity for an unlimited period. There are too many of you. She asked me to
30   say: this is a tobacco shop, not a gold mine.

HUSBAND   Shen Te never said a thing like that. Boy, food! There's a bakery on the corner. Stuff your shirt full when they're not looking!

SISTER-IN-LAW   Don't overlook the raspberry tarts.

HUSBAND   And don't let the policeman see you.

[*The* BOY *leaves.*]

35 SHUI TA   Don't you depend on this shop now? Then why give it a bad name by stealing from the bakery?

NEPHEW   Don't listen to him. Let's find Shen Te. She'll give him a piece of her mind.

SISTER-IN-LAW   Don't forget to leave us some breakfast.

[BROTHER, SISTER-IN-LAW *and* NEPHEW *leave.*]

40 SHUI TA [*To the* CARPENTER.]   You see, Mr. Carpenter, nothing has changed since the poet, eleven hundred years ago, penned these lines:

> A governor was asked what was needed
> To save the freezing people in the city.
> He replied:
45 "A blanket ten thousand feet long
> To cover the city and all its suburbs."

[*He starts to tidy up the shop.*]

CARPENTER   Your cousin owes me money. I've got witnesses. For the shelves.

SHUI TA   Yes, I have your bill. [*He takes it out of his pocket.*] Isn't a hundred silver dollars rather a lot?

50 CARPENTER   No deductions! I have a wife and children.

SHUI TA   How many children?

CARPENTER   Three.

SHUI TA   I'll make you an offer. Twenty silver dollars.

[*The* HUSBAND *laughs.*]

CARPENTER   You're crazy. Those shelves are real walnut.

55 SHUI TA   Very well, Take them away.

CARPENTER   What?

SHUI TA   They cost too much. Please take them away.

WIFE   Not bad! [*And she, too, is laughing.*]

CARPENTER [*A little bewildered.*]   Call Shen Te, someone! [*To* SHUI TA.] She's
60 good!

SHUI TA   Certainly. She's ruined.

CARPENTER [*Provoked into taking some of the shelves.*]   All right, you can keep your tobacco on the floor.

SHUI TA [*To the* HUSBAND.]   Help him with the shelves.

HUSBAND [*Grins and carries one shelf over to the door where the* CARPENTER
65 *now is.*]   Good-bye, shelves!

CARPENTER [*To the* HUSBAND.]   You dog! You want my family to starve?

SHUI TA   I repeat my offer. I have no desire to keep my tobacco on the floor. Twenty silver dollars.

CARPENTER [*With desperate aggressiveness.*]   One hundred!

[SHUI TA *shows indifference, looks through the window. The* HUSBAND *picks up several shelves.*]

70 CARPENTER [*To* HUSBAND.]   You needn't smash them against the doorpost, you idiot! [*To* SHUI TA.] These shelves were made to measure. They're no use anywhere else!

SHUI TA   Precisely.

[*The* WIFE *squeals with pleasure.*]

CARPENTER [*Giving up, sullenly.*]   Take the shelves. Pay what you want to pay.

75 SHUI TA [*Smoothly.*]   Twenty silver dollars.

[*He places two large coins on the table. The* CARPENTER *picks them up.*]

HUSBAND [*Brings the shelves back in.*]   And quite enough too!

CARPENTER [*Slinking off.*]   Quite enough to get drunk on.

HUSBAND [*Happily.*]   Well, we got rid of *him!*

WIFE [*Weeping with fun, gives a rendition of the dialogue just spoken.*] "Real
80   walnut," says he. "Very well, take them away," says his lordship. "I have
three children," says he. "Twenty silver dollars," says his lordship. "They're
no use anywhere else," says he. "Pre-cisely," said his lordship! [*She dissolves
into shrieks of merriment.*]

SHUI TA   And now: go!

HUSBAND   What's that?

85 SHUI TA   You're thieves, parasites. I'm giving you this chance. Go!

HUSBAND [*Summoning all his ancestral dignity.*]   That sort deserves no
answer. Besides, one should never shout on an empty stomach.

WIFE   Where's that boy?

SHUI TA   Exactly. The boy. I want no stolen goods in this shop. [*Very loudly.*]
90   I strongly advise you to leave! [*But they remain seated, noses in the air. Quietly.*] As you wish. [SHUI TA *goes to the door. A* POLICEMAN *appears.* SHUI TA
bows.] I am addressing the officer in charge of this precinct?

POLICEMAN   That's right, Mr., um, what was the name, sir?

SHUI TA   Mr. Shui Ta.

95 POLICEMAN   Yes, of course, sir.

       [*They exchange a smile.*]

SHUI TA   Nice weather we're having.

POLICEMAN   A little on the warm side, sir.

SHUI TA   Oh, a little on the warm side.

HUSBAND [*Whispering to the* WIFE.]   If he keeps it up till the boy's back, we're
100   done for. [*Tries to signal* SHUI TA.]

SHUI TA [*Ignoring the signal.*]   Weather, of course, is one thing indoors,
another out on the dusty street!

POLICEMAN   Oh, quite another, sir!

WIFE [*To the* HUSBAND.]   It's all right as long as he's standing in the doorway—
105   the boy will see him.

SHUI TA   Step inside for a moment! It's quite cool indoors. My cousin and I
have just opened the place. And we attach the greatest importance to being
on good terms with the, um, authorities.

POLICEMAN [*Entering.*]   Thank you, Mr. Shui Ta. It *is* cool!

110 HUSBAND [*Whispering to the* WIFE.]   And now the boy *won't* see him.

SHUI TA [*Showing* HUSBAND *and* WIFE *to the* POLICEMAN.]   Visitors, I think my
cousin knows them. They were just leaving.

HUSBAND [*Defeated.*]   Ye-e-es, we were . . . just leaving.

SHUI TA   I'll tell my cousin you couldn't wait.

       [*Noise from the street. Shouts of "Stop, Thief!"*]

115 POLICEMAN   What's that?

       [*The* BOY *is in the doorway with cakes and buns and rolls spilling out of
his shirt. The* WIFE *signals desperately to him to leave. He gets the idea.*]

POLICEMAN   No, you don't. [*He grabs the* BOY *by the collar.*] Where's all this
from?

BOY [*Vaguely pointing.*]   Down the street.

POLICEMAN [*Grimly.*]   So that's it. [*Prepares to arrest the* BOY.]

120 WIFE [*Stepping in.*]   And *we* knew nothing about it. [*To the* BOY.] Nasty little
thief!

POLICEMAN [*Dryly.*]   Can you clarify the situation, Mr. Shui Ta?

       [SHUI TA *is silent.*]

POLICEMAN [*Who understands silence.*] Aha. You're all coming with me—to the station.

125 SHUI TA I can hardly say how sorry I am that *my* establishment . . .

WIFE Oh, he saw the boy leave not ten minutes ago!

SHUI TA And to conceal the theft asked a policeman in?

POLICEMAN Don't listen to her, Mr. Shui Ta, I'll be happy to relieve you of their presence one and all! [*To all three.*] Out!

[*He drives them before him.*]

130 GRANDFATHER [*Leaving last, gravely.*] Good morning!

POLICEMAN Good morning!

[SHUI TA, *left alone, continues to tidy up.* MRS. MI TZU *breezes in.*]

MRS. MI TZU You're her cousin, are you? Then have the goodness to explain what all this means—police dragging people from a respectable house! By what right does your Miss Shen Te turn my property into a house of
135 assignation?—Well, as you see, I know all!

SHUI TA Yes. My cousin has the worst possible reputation: that of being poor.

MRS. MI TZU No sentimental rubbish, Mr. Shui Ta. Your cousin was a common . . .

SHUI TA Pauper. Let's use the uglier word.

140 MRS. MI TZU I'm speaking of her conduct, not her earnings. But there must have *been* earnings, or how did she buy all this? Several elderly gentlemen took care of it, I suppose. I repeat: this is a respectable house! I have tenants who prefer not to live under the same roof with such a person.

SHUI TA [*Quietly.*] How much do you want?

145 MRS. MI TZU [*He is ahead of her now.*] I beg your pardon.

SHUI TA To reassure yourself. To reassure your tenants. How much will it cost?

MRS. MI TZU You're a cool customer.

SHUI TA [*Picking up the lease.*] The rent is high. [*He reads on.*] I assume it's payable by the month?

150 MRS. MI TZU Not in her case.

SHUI TA [*Looking up.*] What?

MRS. MI TZU Six months' rent payable in advance. Two hundred silver dollars.

SHUI TA Six . . . ! Sheer usury! And where am I to find it?

MRS. MI TZU You should have thought of that before.

155 SHUI TA Have you no heart, Mrs. Mi Tzu? It's true Shen Te acted foolishly, being kind to all those people, but she'll improve with time. I'll see to it she does. She'll work her fingers to the bone to pay her rent, and all the time be as quiet as a mouse, as humble as a fly.

MRS. MI TZU Her social background . . .

160 SHUI TA Out of the depths! She came out of the depths! And before she'll go back there, she'll work, sacrifice, shrink from nothing. . . . Such a tenant is worth her weight in gold, Mrs. Mi Tzu.

MRS. MI TZU It's silver we were talking about, Mr. Shui Ta. Two hundred silver dollars or . . .

[*Enter the* POLICEMAN.]

165 POLICEMAN Am I intruding, Mr. Shui Ta?

MRS. MI TZU This tobacco shop is well known to the police, I see.

POLICEMAN Mr. Shui Ta has done us a service, Mrs. Mi Tzu. I am here to present our official felicitations!

MRS. MI TZU That means less than nothing to me, sir. Mr. Shui Ta, all I can
170   say is: I hope your cousin will find my terms acceptable. Good day, gentlemen. [*Exit.*]

SHUI TA Good day, ma'am.

    [*Pause.*]

POLICEMAN Mrs. Mi Tzu a bit of a stumbling block, sir?

SHUI TA She wants six months' rent in advance.

175 POLICEMAN And you haven't got it, eh? [SHUI TA *is silent.*] But surely you can
get it, sir? A man like you?

SHUI TA What about a woman like Shen Te?

POLICEMAN You're not staying, sir?

SHUI TA No, and I won't be back. Do you smoke?

180 POLICEMAN [*Taking two cigars, and placing them both in his pocket.*] Thank
you, sir—I see your point, Miss Shen Te—let's mince no words—Miss
Shen Te lived by selling herself. "What else could she have done?" you ask.
"How else was she to pay the rent?" True. But the fact remains, Mr. Shui
Ta, it is not respectable. Why not? A very deep question. But, in the first
185   place, love—love isn't bought and sold like cigars, Mr. Shui Ta. In the second place, it isn't respectable to go waltzing off with someone that's paying
his way, so to speak—it must be for love! Thirdly and lastly, as the proverb
has it: not for a handful of rice but for love! [*Pause. He is thinking hard.*]
"Well," you may say, "and what good is all this wisdom if the milk's already
190   spilt?" Miss Shen Te is what she is. Is *where* she is. We have to face the fact
that if she doesn't get hold of six months' rent pronto, she'll be back on the
streets. The question then as I see it—everything in this world is a matter
of opinion—the question as I see it is: *how* is she to get hold of this rent?
How? Mr. Shui Ta: I don't know. [*Pause.*] I take that back, sir. It's just come
195   to me. A husband. We must find her a husband!

    [*Enter a little* OLD WOMAN.]

OLD WOMAN A good cheap cigar for my husband, we'll have been married
forty years tomorrow and we're having a little celebration.

SHUI TA Forty years? And you still want to celebrate?

OLD WOMAN As much as we can afford to. We have the carpet shop across
200   the square. We'll be good neighbors, I hope?

SHUI TA I hope so too.

POLICEMAN [*Who keeps making discoveries.*] Mr. Shui Ta, you know what we
need? We need capital. And how do we acquire capital? We get married.

SHUI TA [*To* OLD WOMAN.] I'm afraid I've been pestering this gentleman with
205   my personal worries.

POLICEMAN [*Lyrically.*] We can't pay six months' rent, so what do we do? We
marry money.

SHUI TA That might not be easy.

POLICEMAN Oh, I don't know. She's a good match. Has a nice, growing busi-
210   ness. [*To the* OLD WOMAN.] What do you think?

OLD WOMAN [*Undecided.*] Well—

POLICEMAN Should she put an ad in the paper?

OLD WOMAN [*Not eager to commit herself.*] Well, if *she* agrees—

POLICEMAN I'll write it for her. *You* lend us a hand, and *we* write an ad for
215   you! [*He chuckles away to himself, takes out his notebook, wets the stump of
a pencil between his lips, and writes away.*]

SHUI TA [*Slowly.*]   Not a bad idea.

POLICEMAN   "What . . . *respectable* . . . man . . . with small capital . . . widower . . . not excluded . . . desires . . . marriage . . . into flourishing . . . tobacco shop?" And now let's add: "Am . . . pretty . . ." No! . . . "Prepossessing appearance."

220

SHUI TA   If you don't think that's an exaggeration?

OLD WOMAN   Oh, not a bit. I've seen her.

[*The* POLICEMAN *tears the page out of his notebook, and hands it over to* SHUI TA.]

SHUI TA [*With horror in his voice.*]   How much luck we need to keep our heads above water! How many ideas! How many friends! [*To the* POLICE-MAN.] Thank you, sir, I think I see my way clear.

225

3

Evening in the municipal park. Noise of a plane overhead. YANG SUN, *a young man in rags, is following the plane with his eyes: one can tell that the machine is describing a curve above the park.* YANG SUN *then takes a rope out of his pocket, looking anxiously about him as he does so. He moves toward a large willow. Enter two prostitutes, one old, the other the* NIECE *whom we have already met.*

NIECE   Hello. Coming with me?

YANG SUN [*Taken aback.*]   If you'd like to buy me a dinner?

OLD WHORE   Buy you a dinner! [*To the* NIECE.] Oh, we know him—it's the unemployed pilot. Waste no time on him!

5   NIECE   But he's the only man left in the park. And it's going to rain.

OLD WHORE   Oh, how do you know?

[*And they pass by.* YANG SUN *again looks about him, again takes his rope, and this time throws it round a branch of the willow tree. Again he is interrupted. It is the two prostitutes returning—and in such a hurry they don't notice him.*]

NIECE   It's going to pour!

[*Enter* SHEN TE.]

OLD WHORE   There's that *gorgon* Shen Te! That *drove* your family out into the cold!

10   NIECE   It wasn't her. It was that cousin of hers. She offered to pay for the cakes. I've nothing against her.

OLD WHORE   I have, though. [*So that* SHEN TE *can hear.*] Now where could the little lady be off to? She may be rich now but that won't stop her snatching our young men, will it?

15   SHEN TE   I'm going to the tearoom by the pond.

NIECE   Is it true what they say? You're marrying a widower—with three children?

SHEN TE   Yes. I'm just going to see him.

YANG SUN [*His patience at breaking point.*]   Move on there! This is a park, not a whorehouse!

20

OLD WHORE   Shut your mouth!

[*But the two prostitutes leave.*]

YANG SUN   Even in the farthest corner of the park, even when it's raining, you can't get rid of them! [*He spits.*]

SHEN TE [*Overhearing this.*]   And what right have you to scold them? [*But at
25   this point she sees the rope.*] Oh!
YANG SUN   Well, what are you staring at?
SHEN TE   That rope. What is it for?
YANG SUN   Think! Think! I haven't a penny. Even if I had, I wouldn't spend it
   on you. I'd buy a drink of water.
   [*The rain starts.*]
30   SHEN TE [*Still looking at the rope.*]   What is the rope for? You mustn't!
YANG SUN   What's it to you? Clear out!
SHEN TE [*Irrelevantly.*]   It's raining.
YANG SUN   Well, don't try to come under this tree.
SHEN TE   Oh, no. [*She stays in the rain.*]
35   YANG SUN   Now go away. [*Pause.*] For one thing, I don't like your looks, you're
   bowlegged.
SHEN TE [*Indignantly.*]   That's not true!
YANG SUN   Well, don't show 'em to me. Look, it's raining. You better come
   under this tree.
   [*Slowly, she takes shelter under the tree.*]
40   SHEN TE   Why did you want to do it?
YANG SUN   You really want to know? [*Pause.*] To get rid of you! [*Pause.*] You
   know what a flyer is?
SHEN TE   Oh yes, I've met a lot of pilots. At the tearoom.
YANG SUN   You call *them* flyers? Think they know what a machine is? Just
45   'cause they have leather helmets? They gave the airfield director a bribe,
   that's the way *those* fellows got up in the air! Try one of them out sometime.
   "Go up to two thousand feet," tell him, "then let it fall, then pick it up
   again with a flick of the wrist at the last moment." Know what he'll say to
   that? "It's not in my contract." Then again, there's the landing problem. It's
50   like landing on your own backside. It's no different, planes are human.
   Those fools don't understand. [*Pause.*] And I'm the biggest fool for reading
   the book on flying in the Peking[3] school and skipping the page where it
   says: "We've got enough flyers and we don't need you." I'm a mail pilot with
   no mail. You understand that?
55   SHEN TE [*Shyly.*]   Yes, I do.
YANG SUN   No, you don't. You'd never understand that.
SHEN TE   When we were little we had a crane with a broken wing. He made
   friends with us and was very good-natured about our jokes. He would strut
   along behind us and call out to stop us going too fast for him. But every
60   spring and autumn when the cranes flew over the villages in great swarms,
   he got quite restless. [*Pause.*] I understand that.
   [*She bursts out crying.*]
YANG SUN   Don't!
SHEN TE [*Quieting down.*]   No.
YANG SUN   It's bad for the complexion.
65   SHEN TE [*Sniffing.*]   I've stopped.

3. That is, Beijing, the capital of China.

[*She dries her tears on her big sleeve. Leaning against the tree, but not looking at her, he reaches for her face.*]

YANG SUN   You can't even wipe your own face. [*He is wiping it for her with his handkerchief. Pause.*]

SHEN TE [*Still sobbing.*]   I don't know *anything*!

YANG SUN   You interrupted me! What for?

SHEN TE   It's such a rainy day. You only wanted to do . . . *that* because it's
70   such a rainy day. [*To the audience.*]

> In our country
> The evenings should never be somber
> High bridges over rivers
> The gray hour between night and morning
75 > And the long, long winter:
> Such things are dangerous
> For, with all the misery,
> A very little is enough
> And men throw away an unbearable life.

[*Pause.*]

80 YANG SUN   Talk about yourself for a change.

SHEN TE   What about me? I have a shop.

YANG SUN [*Incredulous.*]   You have a shop, have you? Never thought of walking the streets?

SHEN TE   I did walk the streets. Now I have a shop.

85 YANG SUN [*Ironically.*]   A gift of the gods, I suppose!

SHEN TE   How did you know?

YANG SUN [*Even more ironical.*]   One fine evening the gods turned up saying: here's some money!

SHEN TE [*Quickly.*]   One fine morning.

90 YANG SUN [*Fed up.*]   This isn't much of an entertainment.

[*Pause.*]

SHEN TE   I can play the zither a little. [*Pause.*] And I can mimic men. [*Pause.*] I got the shop, so the first thing I did was to give my zither away. I can be as stupid as a fish now, I said to myself, and it won't matter.

> I'm rich now, I said
95 > I walk alone, I sleep alone
> For a whole year, I said
> I'll have nothing to do with a man.

YANG SUN   And now you're marrying one! The one at the tearoom by the pond? [SHEN TE *is silent.*]

YANG SUN   What do you know about love?

100 SHEN TE   Everything.

YANG SUN   Nothing. [*Pause.*] Or d'you just mean you enjoyed it?

SHEN TE   No.

YANG SUN [*Again without turning to look at her, he strokes her cheek with his hand.*]   You like that?

SHEN TE   Yes.

105 YANG SUN [*Breaking off.*]   You're easily satisfied, I must say. [*Pause.*] What a town!

SHEN TE   You have no friends?

YANG SUN [*Defensively.*]   Yes, I have! [*Change of tone.*] But they don't want to hear I'm still unemployed. "What?" they ask. "Is there still water in the
110   sea?" You have friends?

SHEN TE [*Hesitating.*]   Just a . . . cousin.

YANG SUN   Watch him carefully.

SHEN TE   He only came once. Then he went away. He won't be back. [YANG SUN *is looking away.*] But to be without hope, they say, is to be without goodness!
        [*Pause.*]

115 YANG SUN   Go on talking. A voice is a voice.

SHEN TE   Once, when I was a little girl, I fell, with a load of brushwood. An old man picked me up. He gave me a penny too. Isn't it funny how people who don't have very much like to give some of it away? They must like to show what they can do, and how could they show it better than by being
120 kind? Being wicked is just like being clumsy. When we sing a song, or build a machine, or plant some rice, we're being kind. You're kind.

YANG SUN   You make it sound easy.

SHEN TE   Oh, no. [*Little pause.*] Oh! A drop of rain!

YANG SUN   Where'd you feel it?

125 SHEN TE   Between the eyes.

YANG SUN   Near the right eye? Or the left?

SHEN TE   Near the left eye.

YANG SUN   Oh, good. [*He is getting sleepy.*] So you're through with men, eh?

130 SHEN TE [*With a smile.*]   But I'm not bowlegged.

YANG SUN   Perhaps not.

SHEN TE   Definitely not.
        [*Pause.*]

YANG SUN [*Leaning wearily against the willow.*]   I haven't had a drop to drink all day, I haven't eaten anything for *two* days. I couldn't love you if
135 I tried.
        [*Pause.*]

SHEN TE   I like it in the rain.
        [*Enter* WONG *the water seller, singing.*]

THE SONG OF THE WATER SELLER IN THE RAIN

"Buy my water," I am yelling
And my fury restraining
For no water I'm selling
140   'Cause it's raining, 'cause it's raining!
        I keep yelling: "Buy my water!"
        But no one's buying
        Athirst and dying
        And drinking and paying!
145   Buy water!
        Buy water, you dogs!

Nice to dream of lovely weather!
Think of all the consternation

Were there no precipitation
150   Half a dozen years together!
        Can't you hear them shrieking: "Water!"
        Pretending they adore me?
        They all would go down on their knees before me!
        Down on your knees!
155   Go down on your knees, you dogs!

        What are lawns and hedges thinking?
        What are fields and forests saying?
        "At the cloud's breast we are drinking!
        And we've no idea who's paying!"
160   I keep yelling: "Buy my water!"
        But no one's buying
        Athirst and dying
        And drinking and paying!
        Buy water!
165   Buy water, you dogs!

[*The rain has stopped now.* SHEN TE *sees* WONG *and runs toward him.*]

SHEN TE   Wong! You're back! Your carrying pole's at the shop.
WONG   Oh, thank you, Shen Te. And how is life treating *you*?
SHEN TE   I've just met a brave and clever man. And I want to buy him a cup
of your water.
170 WONG [*Bitterly.*]   Throw back your head and open your mouth and you'll
have all the water you need—
SHEN TE [*Tenderly.*]

        I want *your* water, Wong
        The water that has tired you so
        The water that you carried all this way
175   The water that is hard to sell because it's been raining.
        I need it for the young man over there—he's a flyer!

        A flyer is a bold man:
        Braving the storms
        In company with the clouds
180   He crosses the heavens
        And brings to friends in faraway lands
        The friendly mail!

[*She pays* WONG, *and runs over to* YANG SUN *with the cup. But* YANG SUN
is fast asleep.]

SHEN TE [*Calling to* WONG, *with a laugh.*]   He's fallen asleep! Despair and
rain and I have worn him out!

3a

Wong's den. The sewer pipe is transparent, and the GODS *again appear to* WONG *in
a dream.*

WONG [*Radiant*]   I've seen her, illustrious ones! And she hasn't changed!
FIRST GOD   That's good to hear.

WONG   She loves someone.

FIRST GOD   Let's hope the experience gives her the strength to stay good!

5 WONG   It does. She's doing good deeds all the time.

FIRST GOD   Ah? What sort? What sort of good deeds, Wong?

WONG   Well, she has a kind word for everybody.

FIRST GOD [*Eagerly.*]   And then?

WONG   Hardly anyone leaves her shop without tobacco in his pocket—even

10 if he can't pay for it.

FIRST GOD   Not bad at all. Next?

WONG   She's putting up a family of eight.

FIRST GOD [*Gleefully, to the* SECOND GOD.]   Eight! [*To* WONG.] And that's not all, of course!

15 WONG   She bought a cup of water from me even though it was raining.

FIRST GOD   Yes, yes, yes, all these smaller good deeds!

WONG   Even they run into money. A little tobacco shop doesn't make so much.

FIRST GOD [*Sententiously*.]   A prudent gardener works miracles on the smallest plot.

20 WONG   She hands out rice every morning. That eats up half her earnings.

FIRST GOD [*A little disappointed.*]   Well, as a beginning . . .

WONG   They call her the Angel of the Slums—whatever the carpenter may say!

FIRST GOD   What's this? A carpenter speaks ill of her?

WONG   Oh, he only says her shelves weren't paid for in full.

SECOND GOD [*Who has a bad cold and can't pronounce his n's and m's.*]

25 What's this? Not paying a carpenter? Why was that?

WONG   I suppose she didn't have the money.

SECOND GOD [*Severely.*]   One pays what one owes, that's in our book of rules! First the letter of the law, then the spirit.

WONG   But it wasn't Shen Te, illustrious ones, it was her cousin. She called

30 *him* in to help.

SECOND GOD   Then her cousin must never darken her threshold again!

WONG   Very well, illustrious ones! But in fairness to Shen Te, let me say that her cousin is a businessman.

FIRST GOD   Perhaps we should inquire what is customary? I find business

35 quite unintelligible. But everybody's doing it. Business! Did the Seven Good Kings[4] do business? Did Kung the Just sell fish?

SECOND GOD   In any case, such a thing must not occur again!

[*The* GODS *start to leave.*]

THIRD GOD   Forgive us for taking this tone with you, Wong, we haven't been getting enough sleep. The rich recommend us to the poor, and the poor tell

40 us they haven't enough room.

SECOND GOD   Feeble, feeble, the best of them!

FIRST GOD   No great deeds! No heroic daring!

THIRD GOD   On such a *small* scale!

SECOND GOD   Sincere, yes, but what is actually *achieved*?

---

4. K'ung Futzu (Master K'ung), the Chinese philosopher better known by his latinized name, Confucius (551–497 B.C.E.). *Seven Good Kings*: rulers of the first historical dynasty of China (traditionally dated ca. 1766–ca. 1122 B.C.E.), whom the Confucian scholar Mencius called "sage worthies."

[*One can no longer hear them.*]

45 WONG [*Calling after them.*]   I've thought of something, illustrious ones: Perhaps you shouldn't ask—too—much—all—at—once!

4

The square in front of Shen Te's tobacco shop. Besides Shen Te's place, two other shops are seen: the carpet shop and a barber's. Morning. Outside Shen Te's the GRANDFATHER, *the* SISTER-IN-LAW, *the* UNEMPLOYED MAN, *and* MRS. SHIN *stand waiting.*

SISTER-IN-LAW   She's been out all night again.

MRS. SHIN   No sooner did we get rid of that crazy cousin of hers than Shen Te herself starts carrying on! Maybe she does give us an ounce of rice now and then, but can you depend on her? Can you depend on her?

[*Loud voices from the barber's.*]

5 VOICE OF SHU FU   What are you doing in my shop? Get out—at once!
VOICE OF WONG   But sir. They all let me sell . . .

[WONG *comes staggering out of the barber's shop pursued by Mr.* SHU FU, *the barber, a fat man carrying a heavy curling iron.*]

SHU FU   Get out, I said! Pestering my customers with your slimy old water! Get out! Take your cup!

[*He holds out the cup.* WONG *reaches out for it. Mr.* SHU FU *strikes his hand with the curling iron, which is hot.* WONG *howls.*]

SHU FU   You had it coming my man!

[*Puffing, he returns to his shop. The* UNEMPLOYED MAN *picks up the cup and gives it to* WONG.]

10 UNEMPLOYED MAN   You can report that to the police.
WONG   My hand! It's smashed up!
UNEMPLOYED MAN   Any bones broken?
WONG   I can't move my fingers.
UNEMPLOYED MAN   Sit down. I'll put some water on it.

[WONG *sits.*]

15 MRS. SHIN   The water won't cost you anything.
SISTER-IN-LAW   You might have got a bandage from Miss Shen Te till she took to staying out all night. It's a scandal.
MRS. SHIN [*Despondently.*]   If you ask me, she's forgotten we ever existed!

[*Enter* SHEN TE *down the street, with a dish of rice.*]

SHEN TE [*To the audience.*]   How wonderful to see Setzuan in the early
20 morning! I always used to stay in bed with my dirty blanket over my head afraid to wake up. This morning I saw the newspapers being delivered by little boys, the streets being washed by strong men, and fresh vegetables coming in from the country on ox carts. It's a long walk from where Yang Sun lives, but I feel lighter at every step. They say you walk on air when
25 you're in love, but it's even better walking on the rough earth, on the hard cement. In the early morning, the old city looks like a great heap of rubbish! Nice, though, with all its little lights. And the sky, so pink, so transparent, before the dust comes and muddies it! What a lot you miss if you never see your city rising from its slumbers like an honest old craftsman
30 pumping his lungs full of air and reaching for his tools, as the poet says!
[*Cheerfully, to her waiting guests.*]   Good morning, everyone, here's your

rice! [*Distributing the rice, she comes upon* WONG.] Good morning, Wong, I'm quite lightheaded today. On my way over, I looked at myself in all the shop windows. I'd love to be beautiful.

[*She slips into the carpet shop. Mr.* SHU FU *has just emerged from his shop.*]

35 SHU FU [*To the audience.*]   It surprises me how beautiful Miss Shen Te is looking today! I never gave her a passing thought before. But now I've been gazing upon her comely form for exactly three minutes! I begin to suspect I am in love with her. She is overpoweringly attractive! [*Crossly, to* WONG.] Be off with you rascal!

[*He returns to his shop.* SHEN TE *comes back out of the carpet shop with the* OLD MAN, *its proprietor, and his wife—whom we have already met—the* OLD WOMAN. SHEN TE *is wearing a shawl. The* OLD MAN *is holding up a looking glass for her.*]

40 OLD WOMAN   Isn't it lovely? We'll give you a reduction because there's a little hole in it.

SHEN TE [*Looking at another shawl on the old woman's arm.*]   The other one's nice too.

OLD WOMAN [*Smiling.*]   Too bad there's no hole in that!

45 SHEN TE   That's right. My shop doesn't make very much.

OLD WOMAN   And your deeds eat it all up! Be more careful, my dear . . .

SHEN TE [*Trying on the shawl with the hole.*]   Just now, I'm lightheaded! Does the color suit me?

OLD WOMAN   You'd better ask a man.

50 SHEN TE [*To the* OLD MAN.]   Does the color suit me?

OLD MAN   You'd better ask your young friend.

SHEN TE   I'd like to have your opinion.

OLD MAN   It suits you very well. But wear it this way: the dull side out.

[SHEN TE *pays up.*]

OLD WOMAN   If you decide you don't like it, you can exchange it. [*She pulls*
55   SHEN TE *to one side.*]   Has he got money?

SHEN TE [*With a laugh.*]   Yang Sun? Oh, no.

OLD WOMAN   Then how're you going to pay your rent?

SHEN TE   I'd forgotten about that.

OLD WOMAN   And next Monday is the first of the month! Miss Shen Te, I've
60   got something to say to you. After we [*Indicating her husband.*] got to know you, we had our doubts about that marriage ad. We thought it would be better if you'd let *us* help you. Out of our savings. We reckon we could lend you two hundred silver dollars. We don't need anything in writing—you could pledge us your tobacco stock.

65 SHEN TE   You're prepared to lend money to a person like me?

OLD WOMAN   It's folks like you that need it. We'd think twice about lending anything to your cousin.

OLD MAN [*Coming up.*]   All settled, my dear?

SHEN TE   I wish the gods could have heard what your wife was just saying,
70   Mr. Ma. They're looking for good people who're happy—and helping me makes you happy because you know it was love that got me into difficulties!

[*The old couple smile knowingly at each other.*]

OLD MAN   And here's the money, Miss Shen Te.

[*He hands her an envelope.* SHEN TE *takes it. She bows. They bow back. They return to their shop.*]

SHEN TE [*Holding up her envelope.*]   Look, Wong, here's six months' rent! Don't you believe in miracles now? And how do you like my new shawl?

75 WONG   For the young fellow I saw you with in the park?

[SHEN TE *nods.*]

MRS. SHIN   Never mind all that. It's time you took a look at this hand!

SHEN TE   Have you hurt your hand?

MRS. SHIN   That barber smashed it with his hot curling iron. Right in front of our eyes.

80 SHEN TE [*Shocked at herself.*]   And I never noticed! We must get you to a doctor this minute or who knows what will happen?

UNEMPLOYED MAN   It's not a doctor he should see, it's a judge. He can ask for compensation. The barber's filthy rich.

WONG   You think I have a chance?

85 MRS. SHIN [*With relish.*]   If it's really good and smashed. But is it?

WONG   I think so. It's very swollen. Could I get a pension?

MRS. SHIN   You'd need a witness.

WONG   Well, you all saw it. You could all testify.

[*He looks round. The* UNEMPLOYED MAN, *the* GRANDFATHER, *and the* SISTER-IN-LAW *are all sitting against the wall of the shop eating rice. Their concentration on eating is complete.*]

SHEN TE [*To* MRS. SHIN.]   You saw it yourself.

90 MRS. SHIN   I want nothing to do with the police. It's against my principles.

SHEN TE [*To* SISTER-IN-LAW.]   What about you?

SISTER-IN-LAW   Me? I wasn't looking.

SHEN TE [*To the* GRANDFATHER, *coaxingly.*]   Grandfather, *you'll* testify, won't you?

95 SISTER-IN-LAW   And a lot of good that will do. He's simple-minded.

SHEN TE [*To the* UNEMPLOYED MAN.]   You seem to be the only witness left.

UNEMPLOYED MAN   My testimony would only hurt him. I've been picked up twice for begging.

SHEN TE

Your brother is assaulted, and you shut your eyes?

100 He is hit, cries out in pain, and you are silent?

The beast prowls, chooses and seizes his victim, and you say:

"Because we showed no displeasure, he has spared us."

If no one present will be a witness, I will. I'll say *I* saw it.

MRS. SHIN [*Solemnly.*]   The name for that is perjury.

105 WONG   I don't know if I can accept that. Though maybe I'll have to. [*Looking at his hand.*] Is it swollen enough, do you think? The swelling's not going down.

UNEMPLOYED MAN   No, no, the swelling's holding up well.

WONG   Yes. It's *more* swollen if anything. Maybe my wrist is broken after all.

110 I'd better see a judge at once.

[*Holding his hand very carefully, and fixing his eyes on it, he runs off.* MRS. SHIN *goes quickly into the barber's shop.*]

UNEMPLOYED MAN [*Seeing her.*]   She is getting on the right side of Mr. Shu Fu.

SISTER-IN-LAW   You and I can't change the world, Shen Te.

SHEN TE   Go away! Go away all of you! [*The* UNEMPLOYED MAN, *the* SISTER-IN-LAW, *and the* GRANDFATHER *stalk off, eating and sulking. To the audience.*]

They've stopped answering
115 They stay put
They do as they're told
They don't care
Nothing can make them look up
But the smell of food.

[*Enter* MRS. YANG, *Yang Sun's mother, out of breath.*]

120 MRS. YANG   Miss Shen Te. My son has told me everything. I am Mrs. Yang, Sun's mother. Just think. He's got an offer. Of a job as a pilot. A letter has just come. From the director of the airfield in Peking!

SHEN TE   So he can fly again! Isn't that wonderful!

MRS. YANG [*Less breathlessly all the time.*]   They won't give him the job for
125   nothing. They want five hundred silver dollars.

SHEN TE   We can't let money stand in his way, Mrs. Yang!

MRS. YANG   If only you could help him out!

SHEN TE   I have the shop. I can try! [*She embraces* MRS. YANG.] I happen to have two hundred with me now. Take it. [*She gives her the old couple's*
130   *money.*] It was a loan but they said I could repay it with my tobacco stock.

MRS. YANG   And they were calling Sun the Dead Pilot of Setzuan! A friend in need!

SHEN TE   We must find another three hundred.

135 MRS. YANG   How?

SHEN TE   Let me think. [*Slowly.*] I know someone who can help. I didn't want to call on his services again, he's hard and cunning. But a flyer must fly. And I'll make this the last time.

[*Distant sound of a plane.*]

MRS. YANG   If the man you mentioned can do it . . . Oh, look, there's the
140   morning mail plane, heading for Peking!

SHEN TE   The pilot can see us, let's wave!

[*They wave. The noise of the engine is louder.*]

MRS. YANG   You know that pilot up there?

SHEN TE   Wave, Mrs. Yang! I know the pilot who will be up there. He gave up hope. But he'll do it now. One man to raise himself above the misery, above
145   us all. [*To the audience.*]
Yang Sun, my lover:
Braving the storms
In company with the clouds
Crossing the heavens
150   And bringing to friends in faraway lands
The friendly mail!

4a

In front of the inner curtain. Enter SHEN TE , *carrying Shui Ta's mask. She sings.*

THE SONG OF DEFENSELESSNESS

In our country
A useful man needs luck
Only if he finds strong backers

Can he prove himself useful.
5   The good can't defend themselves and
Even the gods are defenseless.

Oh, why don't the gods have their own ammunition
And launch against badness their own expedition
Enthroning the good and preventing sedition
10   And bringing the world to a peaceful condition?

Oh, why don't the gods do the buying and selling
Injustice forbidding, starvation dispelling
Give bread to each city and joy to each dwelling?
Oh, why don't the gods do the buying and selling?

[*She puts on Shui Ta's mask and sings in his voice.*]

15   You can only help one of your luckless brothers
By trampling down a dozen others.

Why is it the gods do not feel indignation
And come down in fury to end exploitation
Defeat all defeat and forbid desperation
20   Refusing to tolerate such toleration?

Why is it?

5

Shen Te's tobacco shop. Behind the counter, Mr. SHUI TA, *reading the paper.* MRS.
SHIN *is cleaning up. She talks and he takes no notice.*

MRS. SHIN   And when certain rumors get about, what *happens* to a little
place like this? It goes to pot. *I* know. So, if you want my advice, Mr. Shui
Ta, find out just what has been going on between Miss Shen Te and that
Yang Sun from Yellow Street. And remember: a certain interest in Miss
5   Shen Te has been expressed by the barber next door, a man with twelve
houses and only one wife,[5] who, for that matter, is likely to drop off at any
time. A certain interest has been expressed. He was even inquiring about
her means and, if *that* doesn't prove a man is getting serious, what would?
[*Still getting no response, she leaves with her bucket.*]
YANG SUN'S VOICE   Is that Miss Shen Te's tobacco shop?
10   MRS. SHIN'S VOICE   Yes, it is, but it's Mr. Shui Ta who's here today.
[SHUI TA *runs to the mirror with the short, light steps of* SHEN TE, *and is
just about to start primping, when he realizes his mistake, and turns
away, with a short laugh. Enter* YANG SUN. MRS. SHIN *enters behind him
and slips into the back room to eavesdrop.*]
YANG SUN   I am Yang Sun. [SHUI TA *bows.*] Is Shen Te in?
SHUI TA   No.
YANG SUN   I guess you know our relationship? [*He is inspecting the stock.*]
Quite a place! And I thought she was just talking big. I'll be flying again, all
15   right. [*He takes a cigar, solicits and receives a light from* SHUI TA.] You think
we can squeeze the other three hundred out of the tobacco stock?

5. Ancient Chinese law permitted a man to have more than one wife.

SHUI TA   May I ask if it is your intention to sell at once?

YANG SUN   It was decent of her to come out with the two hundred but they aren't much use with the other three hundred still missing.

20 SHUI TA   Shen Te was overhasty promising so much. She might have to sell the shop itself to raise it. Haste, they say, is the wind that blows the house down.

YANG SUN   Oh, she isn't a girl to keep a man waiting. For one thing or the other, if you take my meaning.

25 SHUI TA   I take your meaning.

YANG SUN   [Leering.]   Uh, huh.

SHUI TA   Would you explain what the five hundred silver dollars are for?

YANG SUN   Want to sound me out? Very well. The director of the Peking airfield is a friend of mine from flying school. I give him five hundred: he gets
30 me the job.

SHUI TA   The price is high.

YANG SUN   Not as these things go. He'll have to fire one of the present pilots—for negligence. Only the man he has in mind isn't negligent. Not easy, you understand. You needn't mention that part of it to Shen Te.

35 SHUI TA   [Looking intently at YANG SUN.]   Mr. Yang Sun, you are asking my cousin to give up her possessions, leave her friends, and place her entire fate in your hands. I presume you intend to marry her?

YANG SUN   I'd be prepared to.

[Slight pause.]

SHUI TA   Those two hundred silver dollars would pay the rent here for six
40 months. If you were Shen Te wouldn't you be tempted to continue in business?

YANG SUN   What? Can you imagine Yang Sun the flyer behind a counter? [In an oily voice.] "A strong cigar or a mild one, worthy sir?" Not in this century!

45 SHUI TA   My cousin wishes to follow the promptings of her heart, and, from her own point of view, she may even have what is called the right to love. Accordingly, she has commissioned me to help you to this post. There is nothing here that I am not empowered to turn immediately into cash. Mrs. Mi Tzu, the landlady, will advise me about the sale.

[Enter MRS. MI TZU.]

50 MRS. MI TZU   Good morning, Mr. Shui Ta, you wish to see me about the rent? As you know it falls due the day after tomorrow.

SHUI TA   Circumstances have changed, Mrs. Mi Tzu: my cousin is getting married. Her future husband here, Mr. Yang Sun, will be taking her to Peking. I am interested in selling the tobacco stock.

55 MRS. MI TZU   How much are you asking, Mr. Shui Ta?

YANG SUN   Three hundred sil—

SHUI TA   Five hundred silver dollars.

MRS. MI TZU   How much did she pay for it, Mr. Shui Ta?

SHUI TA   A thousand. And very little has been sold.

60 MRS. MI TZU   She was robbed. But I'll make you a special offer if you'll promise to be out by the day after tomorrow. Three hundred silver dollars.

YANG SUN   [Shrugging.]   Take it, man, take it.

SHUI TA   It is not enough.

YANG SUN   Why not? Why not? Certainly, it's enough.

65 SHUI TA   Five hundred silver dollars.
YANG SUN   But why? We only need three!
SHUI TA [*To* MRS. MI TZU.]   Excuse me. [*Takes* YANG SUN *on one side.*] The
tobacco stock is pledged to the old couple who gave my cousin the two
hundred.
70 YANG SUN   Is it in writing?
SHUI TA   No.
YANG SUN [*To* MRS. MI TZU.]   Three hundred will do.
MRS. MI TZU   Of course, I need an assurance that Miss Shen Te is not in debt.
YANG SUN   Mr. Shui Ta?
75 SHUI TA   She is not in debt.
YANG SUN   When can you let us have the money?
MRS. MI TZU   The day after tomorrow. And remember: I'm doing this because
I have a soft spot in my heart for young lovers! [*Exit.*]
YANG SUN [*Calling after her.*]   Boxes, jars and sacks—three hundred for the
80 lot and the pain's over! [*To* SHUI TA.] Where else can we raise money by the
day after tomorrow?
SHUI TA   Nowhere. Haven't you enough for the trip and the first few weeks?
YANG SUN   Oh, certainly.
85 SHUI TA   How much, exactly.
YANG SUN   Oh, I'll dig it up, even if I have to steal it.
SHUI TA   I see.
YANG SUN   Well, don't fall off the roof. I'll get to Peking somehow.
SHUI TA   Two people can't travel for nothing.
90 YANG SUN [*Not giving* SHUI TA *a chance to answer.*]   I'm leaving *her* behind.
No millstones round *my* neck!
SHUI TA   Oh.
YANG SUN   Don't look at me like that!
SHUI TA   How precisely is my cousin to live?
95 YANG SUN   Oh, you'll think of something.
SHUI TA   A small request, Mr. Yang Sun. Leave the two hundred silver dollars
here until you can show me two tickets for Peking.
YANG SUN   You learn to mind your own business, Mr. Shui Ta.
SHUI TA   I'm afraid Miss Shen Te may not wish to sell the shop when she
100 discovers that . . .
YANG SUN   You don't know women. She'll want to. Even then.
SHUI TA [*A slight outburst.*]   She is a human being, sir! And not devoid of
common sense!
YANG SUN   Shen Te is a woman: she *is* devoid of common sense. I only have
105 to lay my hand on her shoulder, and church bells ring.
SHUI TA [*With difficulty.*]   Mr. Yang Sun!
YANG SUN   Mr. Shui Whatever-it-is!
SHUI TA   My cousin is devoted to you . . . because . . .
YANG SUN   Because I have my hands on her breasts. Give me a cigar. [*He
takes one for himself, stuffs a few more in his pocket, then changes his mind
110 and takes the whole box.*] Tell her I'll marry her, then bring me the three
hundred. Or let her bring it. One or the other. [*Exit.*]
MRS. SHIN [*Sticking her head out of the back room.*]   Well, he has your cousin
under his thumb, and doesn't care if all Yellow Street knows it!
SHUI TA [*Crying out.*]   I've lost my shop! And he doesn't love me! [*He runs
berserk through the room, repeating these lines incoherently. Then stops sud-*

115 *denly, and addresses* MRS. SHIN.] Mrs. Shin, you grew up in the gutter, like
me. Are we lacking in hardness? I doubt it. If you steal a penny from me,
I'll take you by the throat till you spit it out! You'd do the same to me. The
times are bad, this city is hell, but we're like ants, we keep coming, up and
up the walls, however smooth! Till bad luck comes. Being in love, for
120 instance. One weakness is enough, and love is the deadliest.

MRS. SHIN [*Emerging from the back room.*]   You should have a little talk with
Mr. Shu Fu, the barber. He's a real gentleman and just the thing for your
cousin. [*She runs off.*]

SHUI TA

> A caress becomes a stranglehold
125 > A sigh of love turns to a cry of fear
> Why are there vultures circling in the air?
> A girl is going to meet her lover.

[SHUI TA *sits down and Mr.* SHU FU *enters with* MRS. SHIN.]

SHUI TA   Mr. Shu Fu?
SHU FU   Mr. Shui Ta.
[*They both bow.*]

130 SHUI TA   I am told that you have expressed a certain interest in my cousin
Shen Te. Let me set aside all propriety and confess: she is at this moment
in grave danger.

SHU FU   Oh, dear!

SHUI TA   She has lost her shop, Mr. Shu Fu.

135 SHU FU   The charm of Miss Shen Te, Mr. Shui Ta, derives from the goodness, not of her shop, but of her heart. Men call her the Angel of the
Slums.

SHUI TA   Yet her goodness has cost her two hundred silver dollars in a single
day: we must put a stop to it.

140 SHU FU   Permit me to differ, Mr. Shui Ta. Let us, rather, open wide the gates
to such goodness! Every morning, with pleasure tinged by affection, I watch
her charitable ministrations. For they are hungry, and she giveth them to
eat! Four of them, to be precise. Why only four? I ask. Why not four hundred? I hear she has been seeking shelter for the homeless. What about my
145 humble cabins behind the cattle run? They are at her disposal. And so
forth. And so on. Mr. Shui Ta, do you think Miss Shen Te could be persuaded to listen to certain ideas of mine? Ideas like these?

SHUI TA   Mr. Shu Fu, she would be honored.

[*Enter* WONG *and the* POLICEMAN. *Mr.* SHU FU *turns abruptly away and
studies the shelves.*]

WONG   Is Miss Shen Te here?
150 SHUI TA   No.

WONG   I am Wong the water seller. You are Mr. Shui Ta?

SHUI TA   I am.

WONG   I am a friend of Shen Te's.

SHUI TA   An intimate friend, I hear.

155 WONG [*To the* POLICEMAN.]   You see? [*To* SHUI TA.] It's because of my hand.

POLICEMAN   He hurt his hand, sir, that's a fact.

SHUI TA [*Quickly.*]   You need a sling, I see. [*He takes a shawl from the back
room, and throws it to* WONG.]

WONG   But that's her new shawl!

SHUI TA   She has no more use for it.
160 WONG   But she bought it to please someone!
SHUI TA   It happens to be no longer necessary.
WONG [*Making the sling.*]   She is my only witness.
POLICEMAN   Mr. Shui Ta, your cousin is supposed to have seen the barber hit the water seller with a curling iron.
165 SHUI TA   I'm afraid my cousin was not present at the time.
WONG   But she was, sir! Just ask her! Isn't she in?
SHUI TA [*Gravely.*]   Mr. Wong, my cousin has her own troubles. You wouldn't wish her to add to them by committing perjury?
WONG   But it was she that told me to go to the judge!
170 SHUI TA   Was the judge supposed to heal your hand?

[*Mr.* SHU FU *turns quickly around.* SHUI TA *bows to* SHU FU, *and vice versa.*]

WONG [*Taking the sling off, and putting it back.*]   I see how it is.
POLICEMAN   Well, I'll be on my way. [*To* WONG.] And you be careful. If Mr. Shu Fu wasn't a man who tempers justice with mercy, as the saying is, you'd be in jail for libel. Be off with you!

[*Exit* WONG *followed by* POLICEMAN.]

175 SHUI TA   Profound apologies, Mr. Shu Fu.
SHU FU   Not at all, Mr. Shui Ta. [*Pointing to the shawl.*] The episode is over?
SHUI TA   It may take her time to recover. There are some fresh wounds.
SHU FU   We shall be discreet. Delicate. A short vacation could be arranged . . .
SHUI TA   First of course, you and she would have to talk things over.
180 SHU FU   At a small supper in a small, but high-class, restaurant.
SHUI TA   I'll go and find her. [*Exit into back room.*]
MRS. SHIN [*Sticking her head in again.*]   Time for congratulations, Mr. Shu Fu?
SHU FU   Ah, Mrs. Shin! Please inform Miss Shen Te's guests they may take
185 shelter in the cabins behind the cattle run!

[MRS. SHIN *nods, grinning.*]

SHU FU [*To the audience.*]   Well? What do you think of me, ladies and gentlemen? What could a man do more? Could he be less selfish? More farsighted? A small supper in a small but . . . Does that bring rather vulgar and clumsy thoughts into your mind? Ts, ts, ts. Nothing of the sort will
190 occur. She won't even be touched. Not even accidentally while passing the salt. An exchange of ideas only. Over the flowers on the table—white chrysanthemums, by the way [*He writes down a note of this.*]—yes, over the white chrysanthemums, two young souls will . . . shall I say "find each other"? We shall NOT exploit the misfortune of others. Understanding? Yes.
195 An offer of assistance? Certainly. But quietly. Almost inaudibly. Perhaps with a single glance. A glance that could also—mean more.
MRS. SHIN [*Coming forward.*]   Everything under control, Mr. Shu Fu?
SHU FU   Oh, Mrs. Shin, what do you know about this worthless rascal Yang Sun?
200 MRS. SHIN   Why, he's the most worthless rascal . . .
SHU FU   Is he really? You're sure? [*As she opens her mouth.*] From now on, he doesn't exist! Can't be found anywhere!

[*Enter* YANG SUN.]

YANG SUN   What's been going on here?

MRS. SHIN   Shall I call Mr. Shui Ta, Mr. Shu Fu? He wouldn't want strangers
205   in here!

SHU FU   Mr. Shui Ta is in conference with Miss Shen Te. Not to be disturbed!

YANG SUN   Shen Te here? I didn't see her come in. What kind of conference?

SHU FU [*Not letting him enter the back room.*]   Patience, dear sir! And if by
chance I have an inkling who you are, pray take note that Miss Shen Te
210   and I are about to announce our engagement.

YANG SUN   What?

MRS. SHIN   You didn't expect that, did you?

[YANG SUN *is trying to push past the barber into the back room when*
SHEN TE *comes out.*]

SHU FU   My dear Shen Te, ten thousand apologies! Perhaps you . . .

YANG SUN   What is it, Shen Te? Have you gone crazy?

215   SHEN TE [*Breathless.*]   My cousin and Mr. Shu Fu have come to an understanding. They wish me to hear Mr. Shu Fu's plans for helping the poor.

YANG SUN   Your cousin wants to part us.

SHEN TE   Yes.

YANG SUN   And you've agreed to it?

220   SHEN TE   Yes.

YANG SUN   They told you I was bad. [SHEN TE *is silent.*] And suppose I am.
Does that make me need you less? I'm low, Shen Te, I have no money, I
don't do the right thing but at least I put up a fight! [*He is near her now, and
speaks in an undertone.*] Have you no eyes? Look at him. Have you forgot-
225   ten already?

SHEN TE   No.

YANG SUN   How it was raining?

SHEN TE   No.

YANG SUN   How you cut me down from the willow tree? Bought me water?
230   Promised me money to fly with?

SHEN TE [*Shakily.*]   Yang Sun, what do you want?

YANG SUN   I want you to come with me.

SHEN TE [*In a small voice.*]   Forgive me, Mr. Shu Fu, I want to go with Mr.
Yang Sun.

235   YANG SUN   We're lovers, you know. Give me the key to the shop. [SHEN TE
takes the key from around her neck. YANG SUN *puts it on the counter. To* MRS.
SHIN.] Leave it under the mat when you're through. Let's go, Shen Te.

SHU FU   But this is rape! Mr. Shui Ta!!

YANG SUN [*To* SHEN TE.]   Tell him not to shout.

SHEN TE   Please don't shout for my cousin, Mr. Shu Fu. He doesn't agree
240   with me, I know, but he's wrong. [*To the audience.*]

I want to go with the man I love
I don't want to count the cost
I don't want to consider if it's wise
I don't want to know if he loves me
245   I want to go with the man I love.

YANG SUN   That's the spirit.

[*And the couple leave.*]

5a

In front of the inner curtain. SHEN TE *in her wedding clothes, on the way to her wedding.*

SHEN TE   Something terrible has happened. As I left the shop with Yang Sun, I found the old carpet dealer's wife waiting on the street, trembling all over. She told me her husband had taken to his bed—sick with all the worry and excitement over the two hundred silver dollars they lent me. She said it would be best if I gave it back now. Of course, I had to say I would. She said she couldn't quite trust my cousin Shui Ta or even my fiancé, Yang Sun. There were tears in her eyes. With my emotions in an uproar, I threw myself into Yang Sun's arms, I couldn't resist him. The things he'd said to Shui Ta had taught Shen Te nothing. Sinking into his arms, I said to myself:

> To let no one perish, not even oneself
> To fill everyone with happiness, even oneself
> Is so good

How could I have forgotten those two old people? Yang Sun swept me away like a small hurricane. But he's not a bad man, and he loves me. He'd rather work in the cement factory than owe his flying to a crime. Though, of course, flying *is* a great passion with Sun. Now, on the way to my wedding, I waver between fear and joy.

6

The "private dining room" on the upper floor of a cheap restaurant in a poor section of town. With SHEN TE: *the* GRANDFATHER, *the* SISTER-IN-LAW, *the* NIECE, MRS. SHIN, *the* UNEMPLOYED MAN. *In a corner, alone, a* PRIEST.[6] *A* WAITER *pouring wine. Downstage,* YANG SUN *talking to his mother. He wears a dinner jacket.*

YANG SUN   Bad news, Mamma. She came right out and told me she can't sell the shop for me. Some idiot is bringing a claim because he lent her the two hundred she gave you.

MRS. YANG   What did you say? Of course, you can't marry her now.

YANG SUN   It's no use saying anything to *her*. I've sent for her cousin, Mr. Shui Ta. He said there was nothing in writing.

MRS. YANG   Good idea. I'll go out and look for him. Keep an eye on things.

[*Exit* MRS. YANG. SHEN TE *has been pouring wine.*]

SHEN TE   [*To the audience, pitcher in hand.*]   I wasn't mistaken in him. He's bearing up well. Though it must have been an awful blow—giving up flying. I do love him so. [*Calling across the room to him.*] Sun, you haven't drunk a toast with the bride!

YANG SUN   What do we drink to?

SHEN TE   Why, to the future!

YANG SUN   When the bridegroom's dinner jacket won't be a hired one!

SHEN TE   But when the bride's dress will still get rained on sometimes!

YANG SUN   To everything we ever wished for!

SHEN TE   May all our dreams come true!

[*They drink.*]

6. A Buddhist monk or priest.

YANG SUN [*With loud conviviality.*] And now, friends, before the wedding gets under way, I have to ask the bride a few questions. I've no idea what
20 kind of a wife she'll make, and it worries me. [*Wheeling on* SHEN TE.] For example. Can you make five cups of tea with three tea leaves?

SHEN TE   No.

YANG SUN   So I won't be getting very much tea. Can you sleep on a straw mattress the size of that book? [*He points to the large volume the* PRIEST *is reading.*]

25 SHEN TE   The two of us?

YANG SUN   The one of you.

SHEN TE   In that case, no.

YANG SUN   What a wife! I'm shocked!

[*While the audience is laughing, his mother returns. With a shrug of her shoulders, she tells* SUN *the expected guest hasn't arrived. The* PRIEST *shuts the book with a bang, and makes for the door.*]

MRS. YANG   Where are *you* off to? It's only a matter of minutes.

30 PRIEST [*Watch in hand.*]   Time goes on, Mrs. Yang, and I've another wedding to attend to. Also a funeral.

MRS. YANG [*Irately.*]   D'you think we planned it this way? I was hoping to manage with one pitcher of wine, and we've run through two already. [*Points to empty pitcher. Loudly.*] My dear Shen Te, I don't know where
35 your cousin can be keeping himself!

SHEN TE   My cousin?!

MRS. YANG   Certainly. I'm old-fashioned enough to think such a close relative should attend the wedding.

SHEN TE   Oh, Sun, is it the three hundred silver dollars?

40 YANG SUN [*Not looking her in the eye.*]   Are you deaf? Mother says she's old-fashioned. And I say I'm considerate. We'll wait another fifteen minutes.

HUSBAND   Another fifteen minutes.

MRS. YANG [*Addressing the company.*]   Now you all know, don't you, that my son is getting a job as a mail pilot?

45 SISTER-IN-LAW   In Peking, too, isn't it?

MRS. YANG   In Peking, too! The two of us are moving to Peking!

SHEN TE   Sun, tell your mother Peking is out of the question now.

YANG SUN   Your cousin'll tell her. If he agrees. I don't agree.

SHEN TE [*Amazed, and dismayed.*]   Sun!

50 YANG SUN   I hate this godforsaken Setzuan. What people! Know what they look like when I half close my eyes? Horses! Whinnying, fretting, stamping, screwing their necks up! [*Loudly.*] And what is it the thunder says? They are su-per-flu-ous! [*He hammers out the syllables.*] They've run their last race! They can go trample themselves to death! [*Pause.*] I've got to get out
55 of here.

SHEN TE   But I've promised the money to the old couple.

YANG SUN   And since you always do the wrong thing, it's lucky your cousin's coming. Have another drink.

SHEN TE [*Quietly.*]   My cousin can't be coming.

60 YANG SUN   How d'you mean?

SHEN TE   My cousin can't be where I am.

YANG SUN   Quite a conundrum!

SHEN TE [*Desperately.*]   Sun, I'm the one that loves you. Not my cousin. He
was thinking of the job in Peking when he promised you the old couple's
65   money—

YANG SUN   Right. And that's why he's bringing the three hundred silver dollars. Here—to my wedding.

SHEN TE   He is not bringing the three hundred silver dollars.

YANG SUN   Huh? What makes you think that?

70   SHEN TE [*Looking into his eyes.*]   He says you only bought one ticket to
Peking.

[*Short pause.*]

YANG SUN   That was yesterday. [*He pulls two tickets part way out of his inside
pocket, making her look under his coat.*] Two tickets. I don't want Mother
to know. She'll get left behind. I sold her furniture to buy these tickets, so
75   you see . . .

SHEN TE   But what's to become of the old couple?

YANG SUN   What's to become of me? Have another drink. Or do you believe
in moderation? If I drink, I fly again. And if you drink, you may learn to
understand me.

80   SHEN TE   You want to fly. But I can't help you.

YANG SUN   "Here's a plane, my darling—but it's only got one wing!"

[*The* WAITER *enters.*]

WAITER   Mrs. Yang!

MRS. YANG   Yes?

WAITER   Another pitcher of wine, ma'am?

85   MRS. YANG   We have enough, thanks. Drinking makes me sweat.

WAITER   Would you mind paying, ma'am?

MRS. YANG [*To everyone.*]   Just be patient a few moments longer, everyone,
Mr. Shui Ta is on his way over! [*To the* WAITER.] Don't be a spoilsport.

WAITER   I can't let you leave till you've paid your bill, ma'am.

90   MRS. YANG   But they know me here!

WAITER   That's just it.

PRIEST [*Ponderously getting up.*]   I humbly take my leave. [*And he does.*]

MRS. YANG [*To the others, desperately.*]   Stay where you are, everybody! The
priest says he'll be back in two minutes!

95   YANG SUN   It's no good Mamma. Ladies and gentlemen, Mr. Shui Ta still
hasn't arrived and the priest has gone home. We won't detain you any
longer.

[*They are leaving now.*]

GRANDFATHER [*In the doorway, having forgotten to put his glass down.*]   To the
bride! [*He drinks, puts down the glass, and follows the others.*]

[*Pause.*]

100   SHEN TE   Shall I go too?

YANG SUN   You? Aren't you the bride? Isn't this your wedding? [*He drags her
across the room, tearing her wedding dress.*] If we can wait, you can wait.
Mother calls me her falcon. She wants to see me in the clouds. But I think
it may be St. Nevercome's Day before she'll go to the door and see my
105   plane thunder by. [*Pause. He pretends the guests are still present.*] Why such
a lull in the conversation, ladies and gentlemen? Don't you like it here?
The ceremony is only slightly postponed—because an important guest is

expected at any moment. Also because the bride doesn't know what love is. While we're waiting, the bridegroom will sing a little song. [*He does so.*]

THE SONG OF ST. NEVERCOME'S DAY

110   On a certain day, as is generally known,
        One and all will be shouting: Hooray, hooray!
    For the beggar maid's son has a solid-gold throne
        And the day is St. Nevercome's Day
    On St. Nevercome's, Nevercome's, Nevercome's Day
115   He'll sit on his solid-gold throne

    Oh, hooray, hooray! That day goodness will pay!
        That day badness will cost you your head!
    And merit and money will smile and be funny
        While exchanging salt and bread
120   On St. Nevercome's, Nevercome's, Nevercome's Day
        While exchanging salt and bread

    And the grass, oh, the grass will look down at the sky
        And the pebbles will roll up the stream
    And all men will be good without batting an eye
125   They will make of our earth a dream
    On St. Nevercome's, Nevercome's, Nevercome's Day
        They will make of our earth a dream

    And as for me, that's the day I shall be
        A flyer and one of the best
130   Unemployed man, you will have work to do
        Washerwoman, you'll get your rest
    On St. Nevercome's, Nevercome's, Nevercome's Day
        Washerwoman, you'll get your rest

MRS. YANG   It looks like he's not coming.
    [*The three of them sit looking at the door.*]

6a

Wong's den. The sewer pipe is again transparent and again the GODS *appear to* WONG *in a dream.*

WONG   I'm so glad you've come, illustrious ones. It's Shen Te. She's in great trouble from following the rule about loving thy neighbor. Perhaps she's *too* good for this world!

FIRST GOD   Nonsense! You are eaten up by lice and doubts!

5 WONG   Forgive me, illustrious one, I only meant you might deign to intervene.

FIRST GOD   Out of the question! My colleague here intervened in some squabble or other only yesterday. [*He points to the* THIRD GOD, *who has a black eye.*] The results are before us!

10 WONG   She had to call on her cousin again. But not even he could help. I'm afraid the shop is done for.

THIRD GOD [*A little concerned.*]   Perhaps we should help after all?

FIRST GOD   The gods help those that help themselves.

WONG   What if we *can't* help ourselves, illustrious ones?

   [*Slight pause.*]

15 SECOND GOD   Try, anyway! Suffering ennobles!

FIRST GOD   Our faith in Shen Te is unshaken!

THIRD GOD   We certainly haven't found any *other* good people. You can see where we spend our nights from the straw on our clothes.

WONG   You might help her find her way by—

20 FIRST GOD   The good man finds his own way here below!

SECOND GOD   The good woman too.

FIRST GOD   The heavier the burden, the greater her strength!

THIRD GOD   We're only onlookers, you know.

FIRST GOD   And everything will be all right in the end, O ye of little faith!

   [*They are gradually disappearing through these last lines.*]

7

The yard behind Shen Te's shop. A few articles of furniture on a cart. SHEN TE *and* MRS. SHIN *are taking the washing off the line.*

MRS. SHIN   If you ask me, you should fight tooth and nail to keep the shop.

SHEN TE   How can I? I have to sell the tobacco to pay back the two hundred silver dollars today.

MRS. SHIN   No husband, no tobacco, no house and home! What are you
5 going to live on?

SHEN TE   I can work. I can sort tobacco.

MRS. SHIN   Hey, look, Mr. Shui Ta's trousers! He must have left here stark naked!

SHEN TE   Oh, he may have another pair, Mrs. Shin.

10 MRS. SHIN   But if he's gone for good as you say, why has he left his pants behind?

SHEN TE   Maybe he's thrown them away.

MRS. SHIN   Can I take them?

SHEN TE   Oh, no.

   [*Enter Mr.* SHU FU, *running.*]

15 SHU FU   Not a word! Total silence! I know all. You have sacrificed your own love and happiness so as not to hurt a dear old couple who had put their trust in you! Not in vain does this district—for all its malevolent tongues— call you the Angel of the Slums! That young man couldn't rise to your level, so you left him. And now, when I see you closing up the little shop, that
20 veritable haven of rest for the multitude, well, I cannot, I cannot let it pass. Morning after morning I have stood watching in the doorway not unmoved—while you graciously handed out rice to the wretched. Is that never to happen again? Is the good woman of Setzuan to disappear? If only you would allow *me* to assist you! Now don't say anything! No assurances,
25 no exclamations of gratitude! [*He has taken out his checkbook.*] Here! A blank check. [*He places it on the cart.*] Just my signature. Fill it out as you wish. Any sum in the world. I herewith retire from the scene, quietly, unobtrusively, making no claims, on tiptoe, full of veneration, absolutely selflessly . . . [*He has gone.*]

30 MRS. SHIN   Well! You're saved. There's always some idiot of a man. . . . Now hurry! Put down a thousand silver dollars and let me fly to the bank before he comes to his senses.

SHEN TE   I can pay you for the washing without any check.

MRS. SHIN   What? You're not going to cash it just because you might have to
35 marry him? Are you crazy? Men like him *want* to be led by the nose! Are you still thinking of that flyer? All Yellow Street knows how he treated you!

SHEN TE   When I heard his cunning laugh, I was afraid
            But when I saw the holes in his shoes, I loved him dearly.

MRS. SHIN   Defending that good-for-nothing after all that's happened!

40 SHEN TE [*Staggering as she holds some of the washing.*] Oh!

MRS. SHIN [*Taking the washing from her, dryly.*]   So you feel dizzy when you stretch and bend? There couldn't be a little visitor on the way? If that's it, you can forget Mr. Shu Fu's blank check: it wasn't meant for a christening present!

      [*She goes to the back with a basket. Shen Te's eyes follow* MRS. SHIN *for a moment. Then she looks down at her own body, feels her stomach, and a great joy comes into her eyes.*]

45 SHEN TE   O joy! A new human being is on the way. The world awaits him. In the cities the people say: he's got to be reckoned with, this new human being! [*She imagines a little boy to be present, and introduces him to the audience.*] This is my son, the well-known flyer!

      Say: Welcome
50   To the conqueror of unknown mountains and unreachable regions
      Who brings us our mail across the impassable deserts!
      [*She leads him up and down by the hand.*]

Take a look at the world, my son. That's a tree. Tree, yes. Say: "Hello, tree!" And bow. Like this. [*She bows.*] Now you know each other. And, look, here comes the water seller. He's a friend, give him your hand. A cup of fresh
55 water for my little son, please. Yes, it *is* a warm day. [*Handing the cup.*] Oh dear, a policeman, we'll have to make a circle round *him*. Perhaps we can pick a few cherries over there in the rich Mr. Pung's garden. But we mustn't be seen. You want cherries? Just like children with fathers. No, no, you can't go straight at them like that. Don't pull. We must learn to be
60 reasonable. Well, have it your own way. [*She has let him make for the cherries.*] Can you reach? Where to put them? Your mouth is the best place. [*She tries one herself.*] Mmm, they're good. But the policeman, we must run! [*They run.*] Yes, back to the street. Calm now, so no one will notice us. [*Walking the street with her child, she sings.*]
            Once a plum—'twas in Japan—
65   Made a conquest of a man
            But the man's turn soon did come
            For he gobbled up the plum
      [*Enter* WONG, *with a child by the hand. He coughs.*]

SHEN TE   Wong!

WONG   It's about the carpenter, Shen Te. He's lost his shop, and he's been
70 drinking. His children are on the streets. This is one. Can you help?

SHEN TE [*To the child.*]   Come here, little man. [*Takes him down to the footlights. To the audience.*]

You there! A man is asking you for shelter!

A man of tomorrow says: what about today?

His friend the conqueror, whom you know,

75   Is his advocate!

[*To* WONG.] He can live in Mr. Shu Fu's cabins. I may have to go there
myself. I'm going to have a baby. That's a secret—don't tell Yang
Sun—we'd only be in his way. Can you find the carpenter for me?

80 WONG   I knew you'd think of something. [*To the child.*] Good-bye, son, I'm
going for your father.

SHEN TE   What about your hand, Wong? I wanted to help, but my cousin . . .

WONG   Oh, I can get along with one hand, don't worry. [*He shows how he can
handle his pole with his left hand alone.*]

SHEN TE   But your right hand! Look, take this cart, sell everything that's on
85 it, and go to the doctor with the money . . .

WONG   She's still good. But first I'll bring the carpenter. I'll pick up the cart
when I get back. [*Exit* WONG.]

SHEN TE [*To the child.*]   Sit down over here, son, till your father comes.

[*The child sits crosslegged on the ground. Enter the* HUSBAND *and* WIFE,
each dragging a large, full sack.]

WIFE [*Furtively.*]   You're alone, Shen Te, dear?

[SHEN TE *nods. The* WIFE *beckons to the* NEPHEW *offstage. He comes on
with another sack.*]

90 WIFE   Your cousin's away? [SHEN TE *nods.*] He's not coming back?

SHEN TE   No. I'm giving up the shop.

WIFE   That's why we're here. We want to know if we can leave these things in
your new home. Will you do us this favor?

SHEN TE   Why, yes, I'd be glad to.

95 HUSBAND [*Cryptically.*]   And if anyone asks about them, say they're yours.

SHEN TE   Would anyone ask?

WIFE [*With a glance back at her husband.*]   Oh, someone might. The police,
for instance. They don't seem to like us. Where can we put it?

SHEN TE   Well, I'd rather not get in any more trouble . . .

100 WIFE   Listen to her! The good woman of Setzuan!

[SHEN TE *is silent.*]

HUSBAND   There's enough tobacco in those sacks to give us a new start in
life. We could have our own tobacco factory!

SHEN TE [*Slowly.*]   You'll have to put them in the back room.

[*The sacks are taken offstage, while the child is alone. Shyly glancing
about him, he goes to the garbage can, starts playing with the contents,
and eating some of the scraps. The others return.*]

WIFE   We're counting on you, Shen Te!

105 SHEN TE   Yes. [*She sees the child and is shocked.*]

HUSBAND   We'll see you in Mr. Shu Fu's cabins.

NEPHEW   The day after tomorrow.

SHEN TE   Yes. Now, go. Go! I'm not feeling well.

[*Exeunt all three, virtually pushed off.*]

He is eating the refuse in the garbage can!
110   Only look at his little gray mouth!

[*Pause. Music.*]

As this is the world *my* son will enter
I will study to defend him.
To be good to you, my son,
I shall be a tigress to all others
115   If I have to.
And I shall have to.

[*She starts to go*]

One more time, then. I hope really the last.

[*Exit* SHEN TE, *taking Shui Ta's trousers.* MRS. SHIN *enters and watches her with marked interest. Enter the* SISTER-IN-LAW *and the* GRANDFATHER.]

SISTER-IN-LAW   So it's true, the shop has closed down. And the furniture's in the back yard. It's the end of the road!

120 MRS. SHIN [*Pompously.*]   The fruit of high living, selfishness, and sensuality! Down the primrose path to Mr. Shu Fu's cabins—with you!

SISTER-IN-LAW   Cabins? Rat holes! He gave them to us because his soap supplies only went moldy there!

[*Enter the* UNEMPLOYED MAN.]

UNEMPLOYED MAN   Shen Te is moving?

125 SISTER-IN-LAW   Yes. She was sneaking away.

MRS. SHIN   She's ashamed of herself, and no wonder!

UNEMPLOYED MAN   Tell her to call Mr. Shui Ta or she's done for this time!

SISTER-IN-LAW   Tell her to call Mr. Shui Ta or *we're* done for this time!

[*Enter* WONG *and* CARPENTER, *the latter with a child on each hand.*]

CARPENTER   So we'll have a roof over our heads for a change!

130 MRS. SHIN   Roof? Whose roof?

CARPENTER   Mr. Shu Fu's cabins. And we have little Feng to thank for it. [*Feng, we find, is the name of the child already there; his father now takes him. To the other two.*] Bow to your little brother, you two!

[*The* CARPENTER *and the two new arrivals bow to Feng. Enter* SHUI TA.]

UNEMPLOYED MAN   Sst! Mr. Shui Ta!

[*Pause.*]

SHUI TA   And what is this crowd here for, may I ask?

135 WONG   How do you do, Mr. Shui Ta. This is the carpenter. Miss Shen Te promised him space in Mr. Shu Fu's cabins.

SHUI TA   That will not be possible.

CARPENTER   We can't go there after all?

SHUI TA   All the space is needed for other purposes.

140 SISTER-IN-LAW   You mean we have to get out? But we've got nowhere to go.

SHUI TA   Miss Shen Te finds it possible to provide employment. If the proposition interests you, you may stay in the cabins.

SISTER-IN-LAW [*With distaste.*]   You mean *work*? Work for Miss Shen Te?

SHUI TA   Making tobacco, yes. There are three bales here already. Would you
145 like to get them?

SISTER-IN-LAW [*Trying to bluster.*]   We have our own tobacco! We were in the tobacco business before you were born!

SHUI TA [*To the* CARPENTER *and the* UNEMPLOYED MAN] You *don't* have your own tobacco. What about you?

[*The* CARPENTER *and the* UNEMPLOYED MAN *get the point, and go for the sacks. Enter* MRS. MI TZU.]

150 MRS. MI TZU Mr. Shui Ta? I've brought you your three hundred silver dollars.

SHUI TA I'll sign your lease instead. I've decided not to sell.

MRS. MI TZU What? You don't need the money for that flyer?

SHUI TA No.

MRS. MI TZU And you can pay six months' rent?

155 SHUI TA [*Takes the barber's blank check from the cart and fills it out.*] Here is a check for ten thousand silver dollars. On Mr. Shu Fu's account. Look. [*He shows her the signature on the check.*] Your six months' rent will be in your hands by seven this evening. And now, if you'll excuse me.

MRS. MI TZU So it's Mr. Shu Fu now. The flyer has been given his walking
160 papers. These modern girls! In my day they'd have said she was flighty. That poor, deserted Mr. Yang Sun!

[*Exit* MRS. MI TZU. *The* CARPENTER *and the* UNEMPLOYED MAN *drag the three sacks back on the stage.*]

CARPENTER [*To* SHUI TA.] I don't know why I'm doing this for you.

SHUI TA Perhaps your children want to eat, Mr. Carpenter.

SISTER-IN-LAW [*Catching sight of the sacks.*] Was my brother-in-law here?

165 MRS. SHIN Yes, he was.

SISTER-IN-LAW I thought as much. I know those sacks! That's our tobacco!

SHUI TA Really? I thought it came from my back room! Shall we consult the police on the point?

SISTER-IN-LAW [*Defeated.*] No.

170 SHUI TA Perhaps you will show me the way to Mr. Shu Fu's cabins?

[*Taking Feng by the hand,* SHUI TA *goes off, followed by the* CARPENTER *and his two older children, the* SISTER-IN-LAW, *the* GRANDFATHER, *and the* UNEMPLOYED MAN. *Each of the last three drags a sack. Enter* OLD MAN *and* OLD WOMAN.]

MRS. SHIN A pair of pants—missing from the clothes line one minute—and next minute on the honorable backside of Mr. Shui Ta.

OLD WOMAN We thought Miss Shen Te was here.

MRS. SHIN [*Preoccupied.*] Well, she's not.

175 OLD MAN There was something she was going to give us.

WONG She was going to help me too. [*Looking at his hand.*] It'll be too late soon. But she'll be back. This cousin has never stayed long.

MRS. SHIN [*Approaching a conclusion.*] No, he hasn't, has he?

7a

The Sewer Pipe: WONG *asleep. In his dream, he tells the* GODS *his fears. The* GODS *seem tired from all their travels. They stop for a moment and look over their shoulders at the water seller.*

WONG Illustrious ones. I've been having a bad dream. Our beloved Shen Te was in great distress in the rushes down by the river—the spot where the bodies of suicides are washed up. She kept staggering and holding her head down as if she was carrying something and it was dragging her down into
5 the mud. When I called out to her, she said she had to take your Book of

Rules[7] to the other side, and not get it wet, or the ink would all come off. You had talked to her about the virtues, you know, the time she gave you shelter in Setzuan.

THIRD GOD   Well, but what do you suggest, my dear Wong?

10 WONG   Maybe a little relaxation of the rules, Benevolent One, in view of the bad times.

THIRD GOD   As for instance?

WONG   Well, um, good-will, for instance, might do instead of love?

THIRD GOD   I'm afraid that would create new problems.

15 WONG   Or, instead of justice, good sportsmanship?

THIRD GOD   That would only mean more work.

WONG   Instead of honor, outward propriety?

THIRD GOD   Still more work! No, no! The rules will have to stand, my dear Wong!

[*Wearily shaking their heads, all three journey on.*]

8

Shui Ta's tobacco factory in Shu Fu's cabins. Huddled together behind bars, several families, mostly women and children. Among these people the SISTER-IN-LAW, *the* GRANDFATHER, *the* CARPENTER, *and his three children. Enter* MRS. YANG *followed by* YANG SUN.

MRS. YANG [*To the audience.*]   There's something I just *have* to tell you: strength and wisdom are wonderful things. The strong and wise Mr. Shui Ta has transformed my son from a dissipated good-for-nothing into a model citizen. As you may have heard, Mr. Shui Ta opened a small tobacco factory

5 near the cattle runs. It flourished. Three months ago—I shall never forget it—I asked for an appointment, and Mr. Shui Ta agree to see us—me and my son. I can see him now as he came through the door to meet us. . . .

[*Enter* SHUI TA, *from a door.*]

SHUI TA   What can I do for you, Mrs. Yang?

MRS. YANG   This morning the police came to the house. We find you've brought

10 an action for breach of promise of marriage. In the name of Shen Te. You also claim that Sun came by two hundred silver dollars by improper means.

SHUI TA   That is correct.

MRS. YANG   Mr. Shui Ta, the money's all gone. When the Peking job didn't materialize, he ran through it all in three days. I know he's a good-for-nothing.

15 He sold my furniture. He was moving to Peking without me. Miss Shen Te thought highly of him at one time.

SHUI TA   What do *you* say, Mr. Yang Sun?

YANG SUN   The money's gone.

SHUI TA [*To* MRS. YANG.]   Mrs. Yang, in consideration of my cousin's incom

20 prehensible weakness for your son, I am prepared to give him another chance. He can have a job—here. The two hundred silver dollars will be taken out of his wages.

YANG SUN   So it's the factory or jail?

SHUI TA   Take your choice.

25 YANG SUN   May I speak with Shen Te?

7. Reference to neo-Confucianist commentator's rigid and prescriptive interpretation of Confucius's *Analects*, especially regarding the role of women.

SHUI TA   You may not.

[*Pause.*]

YANG SUN [*Sullenly.*]   Show me where to go.

MRS. YANG   Mr. Shui Ta, you are kindness itself: the gods will reward you! [*To* YANG SUN.] And honest work will make a man of you, my boy. [YANG SUN *follows* SHUI TA *into the factory.* MRS. YANG *comes down again to the footlights.*]

30   Actually, honest work didn't agree with him—at first. And he got no opportunity to distinguish himself till—in the third week—when the wages were being paid . . .

[SHUI TA *has a bag of money. Standing next to his foreman—the former* UNEMPLOYED MAN—*he counts out the wages. It is Yang Sun's turn.*]

UNEMPLOYED MAN [*Reading.*]   Carpenter, six silver dollars. Yang Sun, six silver dollars.

35 YANG SUN [*Quietly.*]   Excuse me, sir. I don't think it can be more than five. May I see? [*He takes the foreman's list.*] It says six working days. But that's a mistake, sir. I took a day off for court business. And I won't take what I haven't earned, however miserable the pay is!

UNEMPLOYED MAN   Yang Sun. Five silver dollars. [*To* SHUI TA.] A rare case,
40   Mr. Shui Ta!

SHUI TA   How is it the book says six when it should say five?

UNEMPLOYED MAN   I must've made a mistake, Mr. Shui Ta. [*With a look at* YANG SUN.] It won't happen again.

SHUI TA [*Taking* YANG SUN *aside.*]   You don't hold back, do you? You give your
45   all to the firm. You're even honest. Do the foreman's mistakes always favor the workers?

YANG SUN   He does have . . . friends.

SHUI TA   Thank you. May I offer you any little recompense?

YANG SUN   Give me a trial period of one week, and I'll prove my intelligence
50   is worth more to you than my strength.

MRS. YANG [*Still down at the footlights.*]   Fighting words, fighting words! That evening, I said to Sun: "If you're a flyer, then fly, my falcon! Rise in the world!" And he got to be foreman. Yes, in Mr. Shui Ta's tobacco factory, he worked real miracles.

[*We see* YANG SUN *with his legs apart standing behind the workers, who are handing along a basket of raw tobacco above their heads.*]

55 YANG SUN   Faster! Faster! You, there, d'you think you can just stand around, now you're not foreman any more? It'll be your job to lead us in song. Sing!

[UNEMPLOYED MAN *starts singing. The others join in the refrain.*]

SONG OF THE EIGHTH ELEPHANT

Chang had seven elephants—all much the same—
But then there was Little Brother
The seven, they were wild, Little Brother, he was tame
60   And to guard them Chang chose Little Brother
Run faster!
Mr. Chang has a forest park
Which must be cleared before tonight
And already it's growing dark!

65　　　When the seven elephants cleared that forest park
　　　　　Mr. Chang rode high on Little Brother
　　　While the seven toiled and moiled till dark
　　　　　On his big behind sat Little Brother
　　　　　　Dig faster!
70　　　　　Mr. Chang has a forest park
　　　　　Which must be cleared before tonight
　　　　　And already it's growing dark!

　　　And the seven elephants worked many an hour
　　　　　Till none of them could work another
75　　　Old Chang, he looked sour, on the seven he did glower
　　　　　But gave a pound of rice to Little Brother
　　　　　　What was that?
　　　　　Mr. Chang has a forest park
　　　　　Which must be cleared before tonight
80　　　　　And already it's growing dark!

　　　And the seven elephants hadn't any tusks
　　　　　The one that had the tusks was Little Brother
　　　Seven are no match for one, if the one has a gun!
　　　　　How old Chang did laugh at Little Brother!
85　　　　　　Keep on digging!
　　　　　Mr. Chang has a forest park
　　　　　Which must be cleared before tonight
　　　　　And already it's growing dark!

[Smoking a cigar, SHUI TA strolls by. YANG SUN, laughing, has joined in
the refrain of the third stanza and speeded up the tempo of the last stanza
by clapping his hands.]

MRS. YANG　And that's why I say: strength and wisdom are wonderful things.
90　It took the strong and wise Mr. Shui Ta to bring out the best in Yang Sun.
　A real superior man is like a bell. If you ring it, it rings, and if you don't, it
　don't, as the saying is.[8]

9

Shen Te's shop, now an office with club chairs and fine carpets. It is raining. SHUI
TA, now fat, is just dismissing the OLD MAN and OLD WOMAN. MRS. SHIN, in obviously
new clothes, looks on, smirking.

SHUI TA　No! I cannot tell you when we expect her back.
OLD WOMAN　The two hundred silver dollars came today. In an envelope.
　There was no letter, but it must be from Shen Te. We want to write and
　thank her. May we have her address?
5 SHUI TA　I'm afraid I haven't got it.
OLD MAN [Pulling Old Woman's sleeve.]　Let's be going.
OLD WOMAN　She's got to come back some time!
　　　[They move off, uncertainly, worried. SHUI TA bows.]

8. A saying by the Chinese philosopher Mo-tzu (470–391 B.C.E.).

MRS. SHIN   They lost the carpet shop because they couldn't pay their taxes. The money arrived too late.

10 SHUI TA   They could have come to me.

MRS. SHIN   People don't like coming to you.

SHUI TA [*Sits suddenly, one hand to his head.*]   I'm dizzy.

MRS. SHIN   After all, you *are* in your seventh month. But old Mrs. Shin will be there in your hour of trial! [*She cackles feebly.*]

15 SHUI TA [*In a stifled voice.*]   Can I count on that?

MRS. SHIN   We all have our price, and mine won't be too high for the great Mr. Shui Ta! [*She opens Shui Ta's collar.*]

SHUI TA   It's for the child's sake. All of this.

MRS. SHIN   "All for the child," of course.

20 SHUI TA   I'm so fat. People must notice.

MRS. SHIN   Oh no, they think it's 'cause you're rich.

SHIU TA [*More feelingly.*]   What will happen to the child?

MRS. SHIN   You ask that nine times a day. Why, it'll have the best that money can buy!

25 SHUI TA   He must never see Shui Ta.

MRS. SHIN   Oh, no. Always Shen Te.

SHUI TA   What about the neighbors? There are rumors, aren't there?

MRS. SHIN   As long as Mr. Shu Fu doesn't find out, there's nothing to worry about. Drink this.

[*Enter* YANG SUN *in a smart business suit, and carrying a businessman's briefcase.* SHUI TA *is more or less in Mrs. Shin's arms.*]

30 YANG SUN [*Surprised.*]   I guess I'm in the way.

SHUI TA [*Ignoring this, rises with an effort.*]   Till tomorrow, Mrs. Shin.

[MRS. SHIN *leaves with a smile, putting on her new gloves.*]

YANG SUN   Gloves now! She couldn't be fleecing you? And since when did *you* have a private life? [*Taking a paper from the briefcase.*] You haven't been at your best lately, and things are getting out of hand. The police want to

35 close us down. They say that at the most they can only permit twice the lawful number of workers.

SHUI TA [*Evasively.*]   The cabins are quite good enough.

YANG SUN   For the workers maybe, not for the tobacco. They're too damp. We must take over some of Mrs. Mi Tzu's buildings.

40 SHUI TA   Her price is double what I can pay.

YANG SUN   Not unconditionally. If she has me to stroke her knees she'll come down.

SHUI TA   I'll never agree to that.

YANG SUN   What's wrong? Is it the rain? You get so irritable whenever it rains.

45 SHUI TA   Never! I will never . . .

YANG SUN   Mrs. Mi Tzu'll be here in five minutes. *You* fix it. And Shu Fu will be with her. . . . What's all that noise?

[*During the above dialogue,* WONG *is heard offstage, calling: "The good Shen Te, where is she? Which of you has seen Shen Te, good people? Where is Shen Te?" A knock. Enter* WONG.]

WONG   Mr. Shui Ta, I've come to ask when Miss Shen Te will be back, it's six months now. . . . There are rumors. People say something's happened to

50 her.

SHUI TA   I'm busy. Come back next week.

WONG [*Excited.*]   In the morning there was always rice on her doorstep—for the needy. It's been there again lately!

SHUI TA   And what do people conclude from this?

55 WONG   That Shen Te is still in Setzuan! She's been . . . [*He breaks off.*]

SHUI TA   She's been what? Mr. Wong, if you're Shen Te's friend, talk a little less about her, that's my advice to you.

WONG   I don't want your advice! Before she disappeared, Miss Shen Te told me something very important—she's pregnant!

60 YANG SUN   What? What was that?

SHUI TA [*Quickly.*]   The man is lying.

WONG   A good woman isn't so easily forgotten, Mr. Shui Ta.

[*He leaves.* SHUI TA *goes quickly into the back room.*]

YANG SUN [*To the audience.*]   Shen Te pregnant? So that's why. Her cousin sent her away, so I wouldn't get wind of it. I have a son, a Yang appears on

65 the scene, and what happens? Mother and child vanish into thin air! That scoundrel, that unspeakable . . . [*The sound of sobbing is heard from the back room.*] What was that? Someone sobbing? Who was it? Mr. Shui Ta the Tobacco King doesn't weep his heart out. And where does the rice come from that's on the doorstep in the morning? [SHUI TA *returns. He goes*

70 *to the door and looks out into the rain.*] Where is she?

SHUI TA   Sh! It's nine o'clock. But the rain's so heavy, you can't hear a thing.

YANG SUN   What do you want to hear?

SHUI TA   The mail plane.

YANG SUN   What?!

75 SHUI TA   I've been told *you* wanted to fly at one time. Is that all forgotten?

YANG SUN   Flying mail is night work. I prefer the daytime. And the firm is very dear to me—after all it belongs to my ex-fiancée, even if she's not around. And she's not, is she?

SHUI TA   What do you mean by that?

80 YANG SUN   Oh, well, let's say I haven't altogether—lost interest.

SHUI TA   My cousin might like to know that.

YANG SUN   I might not be indifferent—if I found she was being kept under lock and key.

SHUI TA   By whom?

85 YANG SUN   By you.

SHUI TA   What could you do about it?

YANG SUN   I could submit for discussion—my position in the firm.

SHUI TA   You are now my manager. In return for a more . . . appropriate position, you might agree to drop the inquiry into your ex-fiancée's whereabouts?

90 YANG SUN   I might.

SHUI TA   What position *would* be more appropriate?

YANG SUN   The one at the top.

SHUI TA   My own? [*Silence.*] And if I preferred to throw you out on your neck?

95 YANG SUN   I'd come back on my feet. With suitable escort.

SHUI TA   The police?

YANG SUN   The police.

SHUI TA   And when the police found no one?

YANG SUN   I might ask them not to overlook the back room. [*Ending the pre-*

100 *tense.*] In short, Mr. Shui Ta, my interest in this young woman has not been

officially terminated. I should like to see more of her. [*Into Shui Ta's face.*] Besides, she's pregnant and needs a friend. [*He moves to the door.*] I shall talk about it with the water seller.

> [*Exit.* SHUI TA *is rigid for a moment, then he quickly goes into the back room. He returns with Shen Te's belongings: underwear, etc. He takes a long look at the shawl of the previous scene. He then wraps the things in a bundle, which, upon hearing a noise, he hides under the table. Enter* MRS. MI TZU *and Mr.* SHU FU. *They put away their umbrellas and galoshes.*]

MRS. MI TZU   I thought your manager was here, Mr. Shui Ta. He combines
105 charm with business in a way that can only be to the advantage of all of us.

SHU FU   You sent for us, Mr. Shui Ta?

SHUI TA   The factory is in trouble.

SHU FU   It always is.

SHUI TA   The police are threatening to close us down unless I can show that
110 the extension of our facilities is imminent.

SHU FU   Mr. Shui Ta, I'm sick and tired of your constantly expanding projects. I place cabins at your cousin's disposal; you make a factory of them. I hand your cousin a check; you present it. Your cousin disappears; you find the cabins too small and start talking of yet more—

115 SHUI TA   Mr. Shu Fu, I'm authorized to inform you that Miss Shen Te's return is now imminent.

SHU FU   Imminent? It's becoming his favorite word.

MRS. MI TZU   Yes, what does it mean?

SHUI TA   Mrs. Mi Tzu, I can pay you exactly half what you asked for your
120 buildings. Are you ready to inform the police that I am taking them over?

MRS. MI TZU   Certainly, if I can take over your manager.

SHU FU   What?

MRS. MI TZU   He's so efficient.

SHUI TA   I'm afraid I need Mr. Yang Sun.

125 MRS. MI TZU   So do I.

SHUI TA   He will call on you tomorrow.

SHU FU   So much the better. With Shen Te likely to turn up at any moment, the presence of that young man is hardly in good taste.

SHUI TA   So we have reached a settlement. In what was once the good Shen
130 Te's little shop we are laying the foundations for the great Mr. Shui Ta's twelve magnificent super tobacco markets. You will bear in mind that though they call me the Tobacco King of Setzuan, it is my cousin's interests that have been served . . .

VOICES [*Off.*]   The police, the police! Going to the tobacco shop! Something
135 must have happened!

> [*Enter* YANG SUN, WONG, *and the* POLICEMAN.]

POLICEMAN   Quiet there, quiet, quiet! [*They quiet down.*] I'm sorry, Mr. Shui Ta, but there's a report that you've been depriving Miss Shen Te of her freedom. Not that I believe all I hear, but the whole city's in an uproar.

SHUI TA   That's a lie.

140 POLICEMAN   Mr. Yang Sun has testified that he heard someone sobbing in the back room.

SHU FU   Mrs. Mi Tzu and myself will testify that no one here has been sobbing.

MRS. MI TZU We have been quietly smoking our cigars.

145 POLICEMAN Mr. Shui Ta, I'm afraid I shall have to take a look at that room. [*He does so. The room is empty.*] No one there, of course, sir.

YANG SUN But I heard sobbing. What's that?

[*He finds the clothes.*]

WONG Those are Shen Te's things. [*To crowd.*] Shen Te's clothes are here!

VOICES [*Off, in sequence.*] Shen Te's clothes!

150 —They've been found under the table!

—Body of murdered girl still missing!

—Tobacco King suspected!

POLICEMAN Mr. Shui Ta, unless you can tell us where the girl is, I'll have to ask you to come along.

155 SHUI TA I do not know.

POLICEMAN I can't say how sorry I am, Mr. Shui Ta. [*He shows him the door.*]

SHUI TA Everything will be cleared up in no time. There are still judges in Setzuan.

YANG SUN I heard sobbing!

9a

Wong's den. For the last time, the GODS *appear to the water seller in his dream. They have changed and show signs of a long journey, extreme fatigue, and plenty of mishaps. The* FIRST *no longer has a hat; the* THIRD *has lost a leg; all three are barefoot.*

WONG Illustrious ones, at last you're here. Shen Te's been gone for months and today her cousin's been arrested. They think he murdered her to get the shop. But I had a dream and in this dream Shen Te said her cousin was keeping her prisoner. You must find her for us, illustrious ones!

5 FIRST GOD We've found very few good people anywhere, and even they didn't keep it up. Shen Te is still the only one that stayed good.

SECOND GOD If she *has* stayed good.

WONG Certainly she has. But she's vanished.

FIRST GOD That's the last straw. All is lost!

10 SECOND GOD A little moderation, dear colleague!

FIRST GOD [*Plaintively.*] What's the good of moderation now? If she can't be found, we'll have to resign! The world is a terrible place! Nothing but misery, vulgarity, and waste! Even the countryside isn't what it used to be. The trees are getting their heads chopped off by telephone wires, and there's such a noise from all the gunfire, and I can't stand those heavy clouds of smoke, and—

15

THIRD GOD The place is absolutely unlivable! Good intentions bring people to the brink of the abyss, and good deeds push them over the edge. I'm afraid our book of rules is destined for the scrap heap—

20 SECOND GOD It's people! They're a worthless lot!

THIRD GOD The world is too cold!

SECOND GOD It's people! They're too weak!

FIRST GOD Dignity, dear colleagues, dignity! Never despair! As for this world, didn't we agree that we only have to find one human being who can stand the place? Well, we found her. True, we lost her again. We must find her again, that's all! And at once!

25

[*They disappear.*]

10

Courtroom. Groups: SHU FU *and* MRS. MI TZU; YANG SUN *and* MRS. YANG; WONG, *the* CARPENTER, *the* GRANDFATHER, *the* NIECE, *the* OLD MAN, *the* OLD WOMAN; MRS. SHIN, *the* POLICEMAN; *the* UNEMPLOYED MAN, *the* SISTER-IN-LAW.

OLD MAN So much power isn't good for one man.

UNEMPLOYED MAN And he's going to open twelve super tobacco markets!

WIFE One of the judges is a friend of Mr. Shu Fu's.

SISTER-IN-LAW Another one accepted a present from Mr. Shui Ta only last
5   night. A great fat goose.

OLD WOMAN [*To* WONG] And Shen Te is nowhere to be found.

WONG Only the gods will ever know the truth.

POLICEMAN Order in the court! My lords the judges!

> [*Enter the* THREE GODS *in judges' robes. We overhear their conversation
> as they pass along the footlights to their bench.*]

THIRD GOD We'll never get away with it, our certificates were so badly forged.

10 SECOND GOD My predecessor's "sudden indigestion" will certainly cause
    comment.

FIRST GOD But he *had* just eaten a whole goose.

UNEMPLOYED MAN Look at that! *New* judges.

WONG New judges. And what good ones!

> [*The* THIRD GOD *hears this, and turns to smile at* WONG. *The* GODS *sit.
> The* FIRST GOD *beats on the bench with his gavel. The* POLICEMAN *brings
> in* SHUI TA, *who walks with lordly steps. He is whistled[9] at.*]

15 POLICEMAN [*To* SHUI TA.] Be prepared for a surprise. The judges have been
    changed.

> [SHUI TA *turns quickly round, looks at them, and staggers.*]

NIECE What's the matter now?

WIFE The great Tobacco King nearly fainted.

HUSBAND Yes, as soon as he saw the new judges.

20 WONG Does *he* know who they are?

> [SHUI TA *picks himself up, and the proceedings open.*]

FIRST GOD Defendant Shui Ta, you are accused of doing away with your
    cousin Shen Te in order to take possession of her business. Do you plead
    guilty or not guilty?

SHUI TA Not guilty, my lord.

25 FIRST GOD [*Thumbing through the documents of the case.*] The first witness
    is the policeman. I shall ask him to tell us something of the respective
    reputations of Miss Shen Te and Mr. Shui Ta.

POLICEMAN Miss Shen Te was a young lady who aimed to please, my lord.
    She liked to live and let live, as the saying goes. Mr. Shui Ta, on the other
30 hand, is a man of principle. Though the generosity of Miss Shen Te forced
    him at times to abandon half measures, unlike the girl he was always on
    the side of the law, my lord. One time, he even unmasked a gang of thieves
    to whom his too trustful cousin had given shelter. The evidence, in short,
    my lord, proves that Mr. Shui Ta was *incapable* of the crime of which he
35 stands accused!

9. Hissed.

FIRST GOD I see. And are there others who could testify along, shall we say, the same lines?

[SHU FU *rises.*]

POLICEMAN [*Whispering to* GODS.] Mr. Shu Fu—a very important person.

FIRST GOD [*Inviting him to speak.*] Mr. Shu Fu!

40 SHU FU Mr. Shui Ta is a businessman, my lord. Need I say more?

FIRST GOD Yes.

SHU FU Very well, I will. He is Vice President of the Council of Commerce and is about to be elected a Justice of the Peace. [*He returns to his seat.*

MRS. MI TZU *rises.*]

WONG Elected! *He* gave him the job!

[*With a gesture the* FIRST GOD *asks who* MRS. MI TZU *is.*]

45 POLICEMAN Another very important person. Mrs. Mi Tzu.

FIRST GOD [*Inviting her to speak.*] Mrs. Mi Tzu!

MRS. MI TZU My lord, as Chairman of the Committee on Social Work, I wish to call attention to just a couple of eloquent facts: Mr. Shui Ta not only has erected a model factory with model housing in our city, he is a regular con-
50 tributor to our home for the disabled. [*She returns to her seat.*]

POLICEMAN [*Whispering.*] And she's a great friend of the judge that ate the goose!

FIRST GOD [*To the* POLICEMAN.] Oh, thank you. What next? [*To the Court, genially.*] Oh, yes. We should find out if any of the evidence is less favorable
55 to the defendant.

[WONG, *the* CARPENTER, *the* OLD MAN, *the* OLD WOMAN, *the* UNEMPLOYED MAN, *the* SISTER-IN-LAW, *and the* NIECE *come forward.*]

POLICEMAN [*Whispering.*] Just the riffraff, my lord.

FIRST GOD [*Addressing the "riffraff."*] Well, um, riffraff—do you know anything of the defendant, Mr. Shui Ta?

WONG Too much, my lord.

60 UNEMPLOYED MAN What don't we know, my lord.

CARPENTER He ruined us.

SISTER-IN-LAW He's a cheat.

NIECE Liar.

WIFE Thief.

65 BOY Blackmailer.

BROTHER Murderer.

FIRST GOD Thank you. We should now let the defendant state his point of view.

SHUI TA I only came on the scene when Shen Te was in danger of losing
70 what I had understood was a gift from the gods. Because I did the filthy jobs which someone had to do, they hate me. My activities were restricted to the minimum, my lord.

SISTER-IN-LAW He had us arrested!

SHUI TA Certainly. You stole from the bakery!

75 SISTER-IN-LAW Such concern for the bakery! You didn't want the shop for yourself, I suppose!

SHUI TA I didn't want the shop overrun with parasites.

SISTER-IN-LAW We had nowhere else to go.

SHUI TA There were too many of you.

80 WONG What about this old couple: Were *they* parasites?

OLD MAN   We lost our shop because of you!

OLD WOMAN   And we gave your cousin money!

SHUI TA   My cousin's fiancé was a flyer. The money had to go to *him.*

WONG   Did you care whether he flew or not? Did you care whether she mar-
85   ried him or not? You wanted her to marry someone else!

[*He points to* SHU FU.]

SHUI TA   The flyer unexpectedly turned out to be a scoundrel.

YANG SUN [*Jumping up.*]   Which was the reason you made him your manager?

SHUI TA   Later on he improved.

WONG   And when he improved, you sold him to her? [*He points out* MRS. MI
TZU.]

90   SHUI TA   She wouldn't let me have her premises unless she had him to stroke
her knees!

MRS. MI TZU   What? The man's a pathological liar. [*To him.*] Don't mention
my property to me as long as you live! Murderer! [*She rustles off, in high
dudgeon.*]

YANG SUN [*Pushing in.*]   My lord, I wish to speak for the defendant.

95   SISTER-IN-LAW   Naturally. He's your employer.

UNEMPLOYED MAN   And the worst slave driver in the country.

MRS. YANG   That's a lie! My lord, Mr. Shui Ta is a great man. He . . .

YANG SUN   He's this and he's that, but he is not a murderer, my lord. Just
fifteen minutes before his arrest I heard Shen Te's voice in his own back
100   room.

FIRST GOD   Oh? Tell us more!

YANG SUN   I heard sobbing, my lord!

FIRST GOD   But lots of women sob, we've been finding.

YANG SUN   Could I fail to recognize her voice?

105   SHU FU   No, you made her sob so often yourself, young man!

YANG SUN   Yes. But I also made her happy. Till he [*Pointing at* SHUI TA.]
decided to sell her to you!

SHUI TA   Because you didn't love her.

WONG   Oh, no: it was for the money, my lord!

110   SHUI TA   And what was the money for, my lord? For the poor! And for Shen
Te so she could go on being good!

WONG   For the poor? That he sent to his sweatshops? And why didn't you let
Shen Te be good when you signed the big check?

SHUI TA   For the child's sake, my lord.

115   CARPENTER   What about *my* children? What did he do about them?

[SHUI TA *is silent.*]

WONG   The shop was to be a fountain of goodness. That was the gods' idea.
You came and spoiled it!

SHUI TA   If I hadn't, it would have run dry!

MRS. SHIN   There's a lot in that, my lord.

120   WONG   What have you done with the good Shen Te, bad man? She *was* good,
my lords, she was, I swear it! [*He raises his hand in an oath.*]

THIRD GOD   What's happened to your hand, water seller?

WONG [*Pointing to* SHUI TA.]   It's all his fault, my lord, *she* was going to send
me to a doctor— [*To* SHUI TA.] You were her worst enemy!

125   SHUI TA   I was her only friend!

WONG   Where is she then? Tell us where your good friend is!
      [*The excitement of this exchange has run through the whole crowd.*]
ALL   Yes, where is she? Where is Shen Te? [*Etc.*]
SHUI TA   Shen Te . . . had to go.
WONG   Where? Where to?
130 SHUI TA   I cannot tell you! I cannot tell you!
ALL   Why? Why did she have to go away? [*Etc.*]
WONG   [*Into the din with the first words, but talking on beyond the others.*]
    Why not, why not? Why did she have to go away?
SHUI TA   [*Shouting.*]   Because you'd all have torn her to shreds, that's why!
    My lords, I have a request. Clear the court! When only the judges remain,
135   I will make a confession.
ALL   [*Except* WONG, *who is silent, struck by the new turn of events.*]   So he's
    guilty? He's confessing! [*Etc.*]
FIRST GOD   [*Using the gavel.*]   Clear the court!
POLICEMAN   Clear the court!
140 WONG   Mr. Shui Ta has met his match this time.
MRS. SHIN   [*With a gesture toward the judges.*]   You're in for a little surprise.
      [*The court is cleared. Silence.*]
SHUI TA   Illustrious ones!
      [*The* GODS *look at each other, not quite believing their ears.*]
SHUI TA   Yes, I recognize you!
SECOND GOD   [*Taking matters in hand, sternly.*]   What have you done with our
145   good woman of Setzuan?
SHUI TA   I have a terrible confession to make: I am she! [*He takes off his
    mask, and tears away his clothes.* SHEN TE *stands there.*]
SECOND GOD   Shen Te!
SHEN TE   Shen Te, yes. Shui Ta *and* Shen Te. Both.

      Your injunction
150   To be good and yet to live
      Was a thunderbolt:
      It has torn me in two
      I can't tell how it was
      But to be good to others
155   And myself at the same time
      I could not do it
      Your world is not an easy one, illustrious ones!
      When we extend our hand to a beggar, he tears it off for us
      When we help the lost, we are lost ourselves
160   And so
      Since not to eat is to die
      Who can long refuse to be bad?
      As I lay prostrate beneath the weight of good intentions
      Ruin stared me in the face
165   It was when I was unjust that I ate good meat
      And hobnobbed with the mighty
      Why?
      Why are bad deeds rewarded?

Good ones punished?
170 I enjoyed giving
I truly wished to be the Angel of the Slums
But washed by a foster-mother in the water of the gutter
I developed a sharp eye
The time came when pity was a thorn in my side
175 And, later, when kind words turned to ashes in my mouth
And anger took over
I became a wolf
Find me guilty, then, illustrious ones,
But know:
180 All that I have done I did
To help my neighbor
To love my lover
And to keep my little one from want
For your great, godly deeds, I was too poor, too small.
[*Pause.*]

185 FIRST GOD [*Shocked.*] Don't go on making yourself miserable, Shen Te! We're overjoyed to have found you!

SHEN TE I'm telling you I'm the bad man who committed all those crimes!

FIRST GOD [*Using—or failing to use—his ear trumpet.*] The good woman who did all those good deeds?

190 SHEN TE Yes, but the bad man too!

FIRST GOD [*As if something had dawned.*] Unfortunate coincidences! Heartless neighbors!

THIRD GOD [*Shouting in his ear.*] But how is she to continue?

FIRST GOD Continue? Well, she's a strong, healthy girl . . .

195 SECOND GOD You didn't hear what she said!

FIRST GOD I heard every word! She is confused, that's all! [*He begins to bluster.*] And what about this book of rules—we can't renounce our rules, can we? [*More quietly.*] Should the world be changed? How? By whom? The world should *not* be changed! [*At a sign from him, the lights turn pink, and music plays.*]

200 And now the hour of parting is at hand.
Dost thou behold, Shen Te, yon fleecy cloud?
It is our chariot. At a sign from me
'Twill come and take us back from whence we came
Above the azure vault and silver stars. . . .

205 SHEN TE No! Don't go, illustrious ones!

FIRST GOD
Our cloud has landed now in yonder field
From which it will transport us back to heaven.
Farewell, Shen Te, let not thy courage fail thee. . . .
[*Exeunt* GODS.]

SHEN TE What about the old couple? They've lost their shop! What about the
210 water seller and his hand? And I've got to defend myself against the barber, because I don't love him! And against Sun, because I do love him! How? How?
[*Shen Te's eyes follow the* GODS *as they are imagined to step into a cloud, which rises and moves forward over the orchestra and up beyond the balcony.*]

FIRST GOD [*From on high.*]   We have faith in you, Shen Te!

SHEN TE   There'll be a child. And he'll have to be fed. I can't stay here. Where shall I go?

215 FIRST GOD   Continue to be good, good woman of Setzuan!

SHEN TE   I need my bad cousin!

FIRST GOD   But not very often!

SHEN TE   Once a week at least!

FIRST GOD   Once a month will be quite enough!

220 SHEN TE [*Shrieking.*]   No, no! Help!

[*But the cloud continues to recede as the* GODS *sing.*]

VALEDICTORY HYMN

What rapture, oh, it is to know
A good thing when you see it
And having seen a good thing, oh,
What rapture 'tis to flee it

225 Be good, sweet maid of Setzuan
Let Shui Ta be clever
Departing, we forget the man
Remember your endeavor

Because through all the length of days
230 Her goodness faileth never
Sing hallelujah! Make Shen Te's
Good name live on forever!

SHEN TE   Help!

Epilogue

You're thinking, aren't you, that this is no right
235 Conclusion to the play you've seen tonight?
After a tale, exotic, fabulous,
A nasty ending was slipped up on us.
We feel deflated too. We too are nettled
To see the curtain down and nothing settled.
240 How could a better ending be arranged?
Could one change people? Can the world be changed?
Would new gods do the trick? Will atheism?
Moral rearmament? Materialism?
It is for you to find a way, my friends,
245 To help good men arrive at happy ends.
You write the happy ending to the play!
There must, there must, there's got to be a way!

EUGENE O'NEILL

1888–1953

Ever since his breakthrough in the 1920s, Eugene O'Neill has been regarded as the first truly modern playwright of the United States—a status confirmed in 1936, when he became the first American dramatist to receive the Nobel Prize in Literature. O'Neill made full use of the cultural and artistic achievements of modernism. We find in his oeuvre the vernacular voices of working-class characters, typical of naturalism; the exaggerated, shrill voices of expressionism; the eruptions of repressed feelings associated with Freudian psychology; the chorus and masks of ancient tragedy that were being revived in the early twentieth century; and the multiple voices and open structures of modern ensemble pieces that have no main protagonist. In bringing the new experimental dramas of modernism to America, O'Neill drew on a panoply of styles, thereby providing in effect a condensed history of the various stages of modern drama. At the same time, however, O'Neill did more than merely channel artistic and intellectual trends invented elsewhere. He managed to create out of them original plays that capture the forces of the modern world through unusual dramatic structures as well as through deeply felt and often tragic characters. For many, O'Neill remains not only the founder of modern drama in America but also its most distinguished representative.

O'Neill was born into an Irish American family, with a dominating father who was a successful actor and a doting mother from a wealthy family. While his father's career in the theater would prove an important inspiration for the dramatist, it was also a cautionary tale. James O'Neill, born in Ireland and raised in poverty in America, had once been a rising star. Then he was offered the title role in a melodrama that would dominate the rest of his life: *The Count of Monte Cristo* (1846). He bought the rights to the work and played its wrongly accused hero more than 5,000 times, only to find that the role and its endless performances had blunted his talent, bringing him fame and financial rewards but thwarting his true artistic achievement. For much of his youth, Eugene seemed to be rebelling against parental expectations—failing to complete his freshman year at Princeton, working odd jobs, and marrying a respectable young woman, Kathleen Jenkins, against his father's wishes. Leaving behind his wife and infant son, he then went to sea as a crewman on a cargo ship; he spent considerable time on a number of freighters and passenger liners. When he returned to New York, he and his wife divorced, and he began working for the New London *Telegraph,* writing both news stories and occasional verse. Soon thereafter he was diagnosed with a life-threatening case of tuberculosis. During the months he spent at a sanatorium, 1912–13, O'Neill found a new focus: he decided to become a playwright.

His first significant teacher and champion was George Pierce Baker of Harvard University, a pioneer in offering workshop-like courses in modern dramatic literature; O'Neill attended his seminar in 1914–15. Another early supporter was the influential New York theater critic George Jean Nathan, who became O'Neill's close friend. Equally if not more important for his success was a group that formed as an experimental summer theater in Provincetown on Cape Cod and later relocated to New York City. The Provincetown Players, founded in 1915, was devoted to fostering a new American theater; under the leadership of George Cram (Jig) Cook and SUSAN GLASPELL, the group—which had its first New York City season in 1916—helped establish off-Broadway theaters as essential venues for serious drama. One of the plays featured in that first season was O'Neill's Bound East for Cardiff (1916); over the next ten years, the Provincetown Players staged many of his plays, some of which later moved to Broadway.

Even during this relatively stable and highly productive period of his life, O'Neill was restless. He had married Agnes Boulton in 1918, and they moved between Provincetown and New York before taking up residence in a series of houses purchased on Cape Cod, in Connecticut, and finally in Bermuda. But in 1927 he left Agnes and their two children for Carlotta Monterey, whom he married in Paris in 1929. After living in France for two years, they returned to the United States, living first in Georgia and then in California. His final decades were marred by declining health as well as by disappointment in and estrangement from his children; his eldest child, Eugene Jr., an alcoholic who failed to live up to his early promise, committed suicide in 1950; his other son, Shane, became a heroin addict; and he disowned his eighteen-year-old daughter, Oona, in 1943, after she married Charlie Chaplin, who was three times her age and was widely reputed to be a womanizer. As early as the mid-1930s O'Neill was showing signs of physical weakness, no doubt exac-

erbated by his lifelong struggles with depression and alcohol; he was too ill to attend his own Nobel Prize ceremony. By 1940, hand tremors were making it difficult for him to hold a pencil—the Parkinson-like shaking was caused by the degenerative neurological disease that ultimately led to his death at the age of sixty-five. He had stopped writing ten years earlier, in 1943. Yet in his last years of work, he produced his finest plays, The Iceman Cometh (written 1939; produced 1946) and LONG DAY'S JOURNEY INTO NIGHT (written 1941; produced 1956).

O'Neill's early plays drew extensively on his life at sea. The one-act plays Bound East for Cardiff and The Moon of the Caribbees (1918), as well as the full-length drama Anna Christie (1921), are set on ships, and many of his mature later works also pay homage to the sea. These plays brought O'Neill recognition, and soon he began writing the plays with which he staked his claim to be the first modernist playwright in the United States. In The Hairy Ape (1922), he channeled the themes of his early one acts into an expressionistic play about a stoker who identifies himself with the powerful engine of a steamship. A second expressionist play, The Emperor Jones (1920), is set on an island in the West Indies; it revolves around a megalomaniac ruler, with a plot inspired by Joseph Conrad's modernist story Heart of Darkness (1902). Indeed, O'Neill frequently drew on the techniques of novels, as is clear from his long and descriptive stage directions and characterizations. More specifically, in having characters express their secret thoughts through long asides, as he did in Strange Interlude (1928), he sought to introduce the new stream-of-consciousness technique of James Joyce and Virginia Woolf to drama. In some plays—such as The Great God Brown (1926), whose title character is an architect who ultimately assumes the persona of his rival—O'Neill relied on masks to help reveal characters' innermost thoughts and express hidden conflicts.

Though O'Neill worked with an astonishing range of theatrical styles, he concentrated on modern tragedy, a thrust that culminated in his great late plays. O'Neill owed his tragic worldview in part to his enthusiasm for the writings of Friedrich Nietzsche, who in *The Birth of Tragedy* (1872) advocated a revival of Greek tragedy, a project to which O'Neill remained dedicated throughout his career as a dramatist. Several of his most significant plays are rewritings of specific Greek tragedies; for example, *Desire under the Elms* (1924) transfers the story of the love felt for Hippolytus by his young stepmother, Phaedra, to a New England farm, and O'Neill's magisterial trilogy, *Mourning Becomes Electra* (1931), is a modern version of Aeschylus's plays about the house of Atreus.

The high point of O'Neill's oeuvre is *Long Day's Journey into Night*, perhaps the finest tragedy written in the twentieth century, which draws on his lifelong work in this form. At the same time, it differs from most of his important plays in that it is unabashedly autobiographical. In fact, it is so closely interwoven with his own family history that O'Neill kept it secret throughout his life and demanded it not be published or performed until twenty-five years after his death. When Carlotta nevertheless allowed its premiere in Stockholm in 1956, it cast a new light on his entire career. Audiences and critics sought out autobiographical elements and figures

in O'Neill's other plays as well, and soon biographers began using the play as a unique window onto his formative years. Like O'Neill's father, James Tyrone has made his name and fortune playing the title role in a commercially successful but artistically mediocre play. Like O'Neill's mother, Mary Tyrone is unhappy in the itinerant life forced on her by her husband's tours across the United States, and she too becomes addicted to morphine while recovering from childbirth. Like O'Neill's older brother, Jamie Tyrone leads a life devoted to the bar and the whorehouse, remaining financially dependent on his wealthy but stingy father. And like O'Neill himself, Edmund Tyrone is an aspiring poet, immersed in Nietzsche and Baudelaire, who is about to be sent to a cheap state sanatorium to treat his tuberculosis. Finally, the whole play is set in a summer residence in Connecticut of the kind the O'Neills possessed and which his mother could never bring herself to regard as a proper home.

The close connection between the play and the O'Neill family is remarkable, but it does not explain the play's unique power. Indeed, those of O'Neill's early works, such as *Bread and Butter* (written 1914), that are based on particular family

Scene from the world premiere, in February 1956, of *Long Day's Journey into Night* at the Royal Dramatic Theatre, Stockholm.

members and that contain a poet figure with whom the author clearly identifies are among O'Neill's weakest plays. *Long Day's Journey into Night* is a masterpiece of twentieth-century tragedy not because of but despite its autobiographical elements. O'Neill may have used some events and family structures he knew from his childhood and adolescence, but he significantly compressed and altered them, imposing on them a carefully balanced dramatic form.

The play conforms to the neoclassical unities of time, space, and action: the time is confined to one evening, and the entire play takes place in the living room of the Tyrone household. The quality of its dramatic action is more difficult to grasp, for unlike most tragedies, *Long Day's Journey into Night* presents the audience with little action, onstage or (as in Greek tragedy) offstage. Nothing seems to happen except the talking of characters who slowly but surely descend into drunken or drugged reverie. The rhythms of speech vary, as periods of introspection and silence are followed by heated exchanges, accusations, and monologues, and as characters enter and exit. But the net effect is their inexorable movement into the night evoked in the play's title.

The dearth of action on the stage does not mean that *Long Day's Journey into Night* lacks development, turning points, or suspense. On the contrary, the play contains plenty of action, but it has all happened in the past. What occurs on the stage is the gradual discovery of that past, as words lay bare hidden events, emotions, and relations. O'Neill borrowed this technique from the most important but also most unusual of Greek tragedies, SOPHOCLES' *Oedipus the King* (ca. 428 B.C.E.). Rather than presenting confrontations and dilemmas as they arise in the present, *Oedipus* reveals the true meaning of what has already happened. O'Neill is among a number of modern writers and thinkers, from HENRIK IBSEN to Sigmund Freud, who saw *Oedipus* as the most modern of Greek tragedies.

Out of his studies in tragedy and selected elements of his own life, O'Neill creates a network of relations among characters hopelessly tangled in a web of guilt and dependence, love and hate—all the human passions. There is not a single innocent figure in this play, which constantly shifts blame from one to the next. James Tyrone speculates in real estate, but he is too tightfisted to provide a real home of the kind his wife dreams of. In addition, his stinginess is at least partially responsible for his wife's morphine addiction, which began when he sought medical advice on the cheap. Yet Tyrone himself, no less than his family, is a victim of his desire for financial security—a desire he has pursued at the expense of his larger artistic ambitions. And on another level, Mary's addiction was caused not by his cheapness but by the pain of Edmund's difficult birth, which the morphine originally was treating. Though Edmund clearly bears no direct responsibility, there is unquestionably a link between his existence and his mother's condition. Nor can Mary herself be viewed simply as a victim. By insisting on the Tyrones' social superiority to others in town, she has isolated herself; and by idolizing her father, she has intensified her dissatisfaction with her husband. It seems that in her eyes no home could ever equal the one in which she grew up. O'Neill cruelly knots his characters together so that the more they attack one another, the more tightly the bonds tie them.

The power of *Long Day's Journey into Night* lies in O'Neill's subtle unveiling of a terrible history. The past, which determines the inner quality of these figures and their relationships, must be made visible in the present. In part, this revelation is accomplished through long confessional speeches, embellished with quotes from SHAKESPEARE, made by increasingly drunk characters. Yet these declarations are not always trustworthy, skewed as they are by a toxic mixture of guilt, self-justification, and self-deception. This blend of confession and dissimulation becomes manifest onstage though characters' habits, poses, and tics, as well as stage props. The living room is barely lit, because James Tyrone tries to save every penny. And when one of his sons insists on turning on a few lights upon reentering the house, an argument ensues. O'Neill here uses a significant element of the theater—lighting—to capture a character trait and to trigger one of the conflicts whose progression will reveal

David Suchet as James Tyrone and Laurie Metcalf as Mary Cavan Tyrone in the 2012 Apollo Theatre (London) production of *Long Day's Journey into Night*.

another piece of the past, another knot of causation and guilt.

More significant than stage props are the physiognomy and gestures of these characters, whose present actions are driven entirely by past events, becoming in effect symptoms through which their histories can be read. The most legible, and the most closely scrutinized, are Mary's. The audience and the other characters on the stage constantly examine her appearance and gestures to determine whether she has gone back to using drugs. We learn that Mary once aspired to become a pianist and prided herself on her fine hands. Now, however, they are crippled with rheumatism and shake nervously, a result of the detoxification she has just undergone; her husband desperately tries to still them. They are quieted only by the several doses of morphine she takes over the course of the play. Similarly, James's mode of speech and acting are mere extensions of his roles on the stage, but he cannot escape them: grand gestures and grandiose speech have become his second nature. Nor can Jamie stop his cynical invectives, the product of a long and bitter fight against his own failure. When the play begins, it appears to be firmly rooted in a single day in 1912 as it reaches back in time; by its end, the present has almost disappeared, overwhelmed by the past that holds these characters in its grip.

Long Day's Journey into Night is O'Neill's most compelling play because it uniquely balances such externals as the shabbiness of the house, the significance of each stage prop, and the symptomatic quality of each gesture, habit, and tic as the characters interact. It displays impressive elegance of form, whose elements function like interwoven signs and signals that reveal the past. Through such simple and economical means, Long Day's Journey into Night develops characters that are complex and internally divided, drifting through violence and silence into the abysmal darkness of the play's close.   M.P.

Long Day's Journey into Night

For Carlotta, on our 12th Wedding Anniversary

Dearest: I give you the original script of this play of old sorrow, written in tears and blood. A sadly inappropriate gift, it would seem, for a day celebrating happiness. But you will understand. I mean it as a tribute to your love and tenderness which gave me the faith in love that enabled me to face my dead at last and write this play—write it with deep pity and understanding and forgiveness for all the four haunted Tyrones.

These twelve years, Beloved One, have been a Journey into Light—into love. You know my gratitude. And my love!   GENE

Tao House
July 22, 1941.

CHARACTERS

JAMES TYRONE
MARY CAVAN TYRONE, his wife
JAMES TYRONE, JR., their elder son

EDMUND TYRONE, their younger son
CATHLEEN, second girl

Act 1

SCENE: *Living room of James Tyrone's summer home on a morning in August, 1912.*

At rear are two double doorways with portieres.[1] The one at right leads into a front parlor with the formally arranged, set appearance of a room rarely occupied. The other opens on a dark, windowless back parlor, never used except as a passage from living room to dining room. Against the wall between the doorways is a small bookcase, with a picture of Shakespeare above it, containing novels by Balzac, Zola, Stendhal, philosophical and sociological works by Schopenhauer, Nietzsche, Marx, Engels, Kropotkin, Max Stirner, plays by Ibsen, Shaw, Strindberg, poetry by Swinburne, Rossetti, Wilde, Ernest Dawson, Kipling, etc.

In the right wall, rear, is a screen door leading out on the porch which extends halfway around the house. Farther forward, a series of three windows looks over the front lawn to the harbor and the avenue that runs along the waterfront. A small wicker table and an ordinary oak desk are against the wall, flanking the windows.

In the left wall, a similar series of windows looks out on the grounds in back of the house. Beneath them is a wicker couch with cushions, its head toward rear. Farther back is a large, glassed-in bookcase with sets of Dumas, Victor Hugo, Charles Lever, three sets of Shakespeare, The World's Best Literature *in fifty large volumes,* Hume's History of England, Thiers' History of the Consulate and Empire, Smollett's History of England, Gibbon's Roman Empire, *and miscellaneous volumes of old plays, poetry, and several histories of Ireland. The astonishing thing about these sets is that all the volumes have the look of having been read and reread.*

The hardwood floor is nearly covered by a rug, inoffensive in design and color. At center is a round table with a green-shaded reading lamp, the cord plugged in one of the four sockets in the chandelier above. Around the table within reading-light range are four chairs, three of them wicker armchairs, the fourth (at right front of table) a varnished oak rocker with leather bottom.

It is around 8:30. Sunshine comes through the windows at right.

As the curtain rises, the family have just finished breakfast. MARY TYRONE *and her husband enter together from the back parlor, coming from the dining room.*

MARY *is fifty-four, about medium height. She still has a young, graceful figure, a trifle plump, but showing little evidence of middle-aged waist and hips, although she is not tightly corseted. Her face is distinctly Irish in type. It must once have been extremely pretty, and is still striking. It does not match her healthy figure but is thin and pale with the bone structure prominent. Her nose is long and straight, her mouth wide with full, sensitive lips. She uses no rouge or any sort of makeup. Her high forehead is framed by thick pure white hair. Accentuated by her pallor and white hair, her dark brown eyes appear black. They are unusually large and beautiful, with black brows and long curling lashes.*

---

1. Heavy curtains hung over the doorway.

What strikes one immediately is her extreme nervousness. Her hands are never still. They were once beautiful hands, with long, tapering fingers, but rheumatism has knotted the joints and warped the fingers, so that now they have an ugly crippled look. One avoids looking at them, the more so because one is conscious she is sensitive about their appearance and humiliated by her inability to control the nervousness which draws attention to them.

She is dressed simply but with a sure sense of what becomes her. Her hair is arranged with fastidious care. Her voice is soft and attractive. When she is merry, there is a touch of Irish lilt in it.

Her most appealing quality is the simple, unaffected charm of a shy convent-girl youthfulness she has never lost—an innate unworldly innocence.

JAMES TYRONE *is sixty-five but looks ten years younger. About five feet eight, broad-shouldered and deep-chested, he seems taller and slenderer because of his bearing, which has a soldierly quality of head up, chest out, stomach in, shoulders squared. His face has begun to break down but he is still remarkably good-looking—a big, finely shaped head, a handsome profile, deep-set light-brown eyes. His grey hair is thin with a bald spot like a monk's tonsure.*

The stamp of his profession is unmistakably on him. Not that he indulges in any of the deliberate temperamental posturings of the stage star. He is by nature and preference a simple, unpretentious man, whose inclinations are still close to his humble beginnings and his Irish farmer forebears. But the actor shows in all his unconscious habits of speech, movement, and gesture. These have the quality of belonging to a studied technique. His voice is remarkably fine, resonant and flexible, and he takes great pride in it.

His clothes, assuredly, do not costume any romantic part. He wears a threadbare, ready-made, grey sack suit[2] and shineless black shoes, a collarless shirt with a thick white handkerchief knotted loosely around his throat. There is nothing picturesquely careless about this get-up. It is commonplace shabby. He believes in wearing his clothes to the limit of usefulness, is dressed now for gardening, and doesn't give a damn how he looks.

He has never been really sick a day in his life. He has no nerves. There is a lot of stolid, earthy peasant in him, mixed with streaks of sentimental melancholy and rare flashes of intuitive sensibility.

TYRONE's *arm is around his wife's waist as they appear from the back parlor. Entering the living room he gives her a playful hug.*

TYRONE You're a fine armful now, Mary, with those twenty pounds you've gained.

MARY [*smiles affectionately*] I've gotten too fat, you mean, dear. I really ought to reduce.

5 TYRONE None of that, my lady! You're just right. We'll have no talk of reducing. Is that why you ate so little breakfast?

MARY So little? I thought I ate a lot.

TYRONE You didn't. Not as much as I'd like to see, anyway.

MARY [*teasingly*] Oh you! expect everyone to eat the enormous breakfast you
10 do. No one else in the world could without dying of indigestion.

[*She comes forward to stand by the right of table.*]

TYRONE [*following her*] I hope I'm not as big a glutton as that sounds. [*With hearty satisfaction*] But thank God, I've kept my appetite and I've the digestion of a young man of twenty, if I am sixty-five.

---

2. A suit with a straight, loose-fitting jacket.

MARY   You surely have, James. No one could deny that.

> [*She laughs and sits in the wicker armchair at right rear of table. He comes around in back of her and selects a cigar from a box on the table and cuts off the end with a little clipper. From the dining room* JAMIE's *and* EDMUND's *voices are heard.* MARY *turns her head that way.*]

15   Why did the boys stay in the dining room, I wonder? Cathleen must be waiting to clear the table.

TYRONE   [*jokingly but with an undercurrent of resentment*]   It's a secret confab they don't want me to hear, I suppose. I'll bet they're cooking up some new scheme to touch the Old Man.[3]

> [*She is silent on this, keeping her head turned toward their voices. Her hands appear on the table top, moving restlessly. He lights his cigar and sits down in the rocker at right of table, which is his chair, and puffs contentedly.*]

20   There's nothing like the first after-breakfast cigar, if it's a good one, and this new lot have the right mellow flavor. They're a great bargain, too. I got them dead cheap. It was McGuire put me on to them.

MARY   [*a trifle acidly*]   I hope he didn't put you on to any new piece of property at the same time. His real estate bargains don't work out so well.

25   TYRONE   [*defensively*]   I wouldn't say that, Mary. After all, he was the one who advised me to buy that place on Chestnut Street and I made a quick turnover on it for a fine profit.

MARY   [*smiles now with teasing affection*]   I know. The famous one stroke of good luck. I'm sure McGuire never dreamed— [*Then she pats his hand.*]

30   Never mind, James. I know it's a waste of breath trying to convince you you're not a cunning real estate speculator.

TYRONE   [*huffily*]   I've no such idea. But land is land, and it's safer than the stocks and bonds of Wall Street swindlers. [*Then placatingly*] But let's not argue about business this early in the morning.

> [*A pause. The boys' voices are again heard and one of them has a fit of coughing.* MARY *listens worriedly. Her fingers play nervously on the table top.*]

35   MARY   James, it's Edmund you ought to scold for not eating enough. He hardly touched anything except coffee. He needs to eat to keep up his strength. I keep telling him that but he says he simply has no appetite. Of course, there's nothing takes away your appetite like a bad summer cold.

TYRONE   Yes, it's only natural. So don't let yourself get worried—

40   MARY   [*quickly*]   Oh, I'm not. I know he'll be all right in a few days if he takes care of himself. [*As if she wanted to dismiss the subject but can't.*] But it does seem a shame he should have to be sick right now.

TYRONE   Yes, it is bad luck. [*He gives her a quick, worried look.*] But you mustn't

45   let it upset you, Mary. Remember, you've got to take care of yourself, too.

MARY   [*quickly*]   I'm not upset. There's nothing to be upset about. What makes you think I'm upset?

TYRONE   Why, nothing, except you've seemed a bit high-strung the past few days.

50   MARY   [*forcing a smile*]   I have? Nonsense, dear. It's your imagination. [*With sudden tenseness*] You really must not watch me all the time, James. I mean, it makes me self-conscious.

---

3. That is, to get money from their father.

TYRONE [*putting a hand over one of her nervously playing ones*] Now, now, Mary. That's your imagination. If I've watched you it was to admire how fat
55 and beautiful you looked. [*His voice is suddenly moved by deep feeling.*] I can't tell you the deep happiness it gives me, darling, to see you as you've been since you came back to us, your dear old self again.

> [*He leans over and kisses her cheek impulsively—then turning back adds with a constrained air.*]

So keep up the good work, Mary.

MARY [*has turned her head away*] I will, dear.

> [*She gets up restlessly and goes to the windows at right.*]

60 Thank heavens, the fog is gone. [*She turns back.*] I do feel out of sorts this morning. I wasn't able to get much sleep with that awful foghorn going all night long.

TYRONE Yes, it's like having a sick whale in the backyard. It kept me awake, too.

65 MARY [*affectionately amused*] Did it? You had a strange way of showing your restlessness. You were snoring so hard I couldn't tell which was the foghorn!

> [*She comes to him, laughing, and pats his cheek playfully.*]

Ten foghorns couldn't disturb you. You haven't a nerve in you. You've never had.

TYRONE [*his vanity piqued—testily*] Nonsense. You always exaggerate about
70 my snoring.

MARY I couldn't. If you could only hear yourself once—

> [*A burst of laughter comes from the dining room. She turns her head, smiling.*]

What's the joke, I wonder?

TYRONE [*grumpily*] It's on me. I'll bet that much. It's always on the Old Man.

MARY [*teasingly*] Yes, it's terrible the way we all pick on you, isn't it? You're so
75 abused!

> [*She laughs—then with a pleased, relieved air.*]

Well, no matter what the joke is about, it's a relief to hear Edmund laugh. He's been so down in the mouth lately.

TYRONE [*ignoring this—resentfully*] Some joke of Jamie's, I'll wager. He's forever making sneering fun of somebody, that one.

80 MARY Now don't start in on poor Jamie, dear. [*Without conviction*] He'll turn out all right in the end, you wait and see.

TYRONE He'd better start soon, then. He's nearly thirty-four.

MARY [*ignoring this*] Good heavens, are they going to stay in the dining room all day?

> [*She goes to the back parlor doorway and calls.*]

85 Jamie! Edmund! Come in the living room and give Cathleen a chance to clear the table.

> [EDMUND *calls back,* "We're coming, Mama." *She goes back to the table.*]

TYRONE [*grumbling*] You'd find excuses for him no matter what he did.

MARY [*sitting down beside him, pats his hand*] Shush.

> [*Their sons* JAMES, JR., *and* EDMUND *enter together from the back parlor. They are both grinning, still chuckling over what had caused their*

laughter, and as they come forward they glance at their father and their grins grow broader.

JAMIE, *the elder, is thirty-three. He has his father's broad-shouldered, deep-chested physique, is an inch taller and weighs less, but appears shorter and stouter because he lacks* TYRONE's *bearing and graceful carriage. He also lacks his father's vitality. The signs of premature disintegration are on him. His face is still good-looking, despite marks of dissipation, but it has never been handsome like* TYRONE's, *although* JAMIE *resembles him rather than his mother. He has fine brown eyes, their color midway between his father's lighter and his mother's darker ones. His hair is thinning and already there is indication of a bald spot like* TYRONE's. *His nose is unlike that of any other member of the family, pronouncedly aquiline. Combined with his habitual expression of cynicism it gives his countenance a Mephistophelian cast.*[4] *But on the rare occasions when he smiles without sneering, his personality possesses the remnant of a humorous, romantic, irresponsible Irish charm—that of the beguiling ne'er-do-well, with a strain of the sentimentally poetic, attractive to women and popular with men.*

He is dressed in an old sack suit, not as shabby as TYRONE's, *and wears a collar and tie. His fair skin is sunburned a reddish, freckled tan.*

EDMUND *is ten years younger than his brother, a couple of inches taller, thin and wiry. Where* JAMIE *takes after his father, with little resemblance to his mother,* EDMUND *looks like both his parents, but is more like his mother. Her big, dark eyes are the dominant feature in his long, narrow Irish face. His mouth has the same quality of hypersensitiveness hers possesses. His high forehead is hers accentuated, with dark brown hair, sun-bleached to red at the ends, brushed straight back from it. But his nose is his father's and his face in profile recalls* TYRONE's. EDMUND's *hands are noticeably like his mother's, with the same exceptionally long fingers. They even have to a minor degree the same nervousness. It is in the quality of extreme nervous sensibility that the likeness of* EDMUND *to his mother is most marked.*

He is plainly in bad health. Much thinner than he should be, his eyes appear feverish and his cheeks are sunken. His skin, in spite of being sunburned a deep brown, has a parched sallowness. He wears a shirt, collar and tie, no coat, old flannel trousers, brown sneakers.]

MARY [*turns smilingly to them, in a merry tone that is a bit forced*]   I've been
90   teasing your father about his snoring. [*To* TYRONE] I'll leave it to the boys,
James. They must have heard you. No, not you, Jamie. I could hear you
down the hall almost as bad as your father. You're like him. As soon as your
head touches the pillow you're off and ten foghorns couldn't wake you.

[*She stops abruptly, catching* JAMIE's *eyes regarding her with an uneasy, probing look. Her smile vanishes and her manner becomes self-conscious.*]

Why are you staring, Jamie? [*Her hands flutter up to her hair.*] Is my hair
95   coming down? It's hard for me to do it up properly now. My eyes are getting
so bad and I never can find my glasses.

JAMIE [*looks away guiltily*]   Your hair's all right, Mama. I was only thinking
how well you look.

---

4. A devilish aspect; that is, resembling Mephistopheles, the devil in the Faust legend.

TYRONE [*heartily*]   Just what I've been telling her, Jamie. She's so fat and
100   sassy, there'll soon be no holding her.

EDMUND   Yes, you certainly look grand, Mama.

> [*She is reassured and smiles at him lovingly. He winks with a kidding grin.*]

I'll back you up about Papa's snoring. Gosh, what a racket!

JAMIE   I heard him, too. [*He quotes, putting on a ham-actor manner.*] "The Moor, I know his trumpet."[5]

> [*His mother and brother laugh.*]

105   TYRONE [*scathingly*]   If it takes my snoring to make you remember Shake-speare instead of the dope sheet[6] on the ponies, I hope I'll keep on with it.

MARY   Now, James! You mustn't be so touchy.

> [JAMIE *shrugs his shoulders and sits down in the chair on her right.*]

EDMUND [*irritably*]   Yes, for Pete's sake, Papa! The first thing after breakfast! Give it a rest, can't you?

> [*He slumps down in the chair at left of table next to his brother. His father ignore him.*]

110   MARY [*reprovingly*]   Your father wasn't finding fault with you. You don't have to always take Jamie's part. You'd think you were the one ten years older.

JAMIE [*boredly*]   What's all the fuss about? Let's forget it.

TYRONE [*contemptuously*]   Yes, forget! Forget everything and face nothing! It's a convenient philosophy if you've no ambition in life except to—

115   MARY   James, do be quiet.

> [*She puts an arm around his shoulder—coaxingly.*]

You must have gotten out of the wrong side of the bed this morning. [*To the boys, changing the subject*] What were you two grinning about like Cheshire cats[7] when you came in? What was the joke?

TYRONE [*with a painful effort to be a good sport*]   Yes, let us in on it, lads. I
120   told your mother I knew damned well it would be one on me, but never mind that, I'm used to it.

JAMIE [*dryly*]   Don't look at me. This is the Kid's story.

EDMUND [*grins*]   I meant to tell you last night, Papa, and forgot it. Yesterday when I went for a walk I dropped in at the Inn—

125   MARY [*worriedly*]   You shouldn't drink now, Edmund.

EDMUND [*ignoring this*]   And who do you think I met there, with a beautiful bun on,[8] but Shaughnessy, the tenant on that farm of yours.

MARY [*smiling*]   That dreadful man! But he is funny.

TYRONE [*scowling*]   He's not so funny when you're his landlord. He's a wily
130   Shanty Mick,[9] that one. He could hide behind a corkscrew. What's he com-plaining about now, Edmund—for I'm damned sure he's complaining. I sup-pose he wants his rent lowered. I let him have the place for almost nothing, just to keep someone on it, and he never pays that till I threaten to evict him.

EDMUND   No, he didn't beef about anything. He was so pleased with life he
135   even bought a drink, and that's practically unheard of. He was delighted

---

5. Quoting Iago, from William Shakespeare's *Othello* (1604), 2.1.177.
6. A piece of paper containing information about racehorses.
7. That is, like the broadly grinning cat (as

drawn by John Tenniel) in *Alice's Adventures in Wonderland* (1865), by Lewis Carroll.
8. That is, highly intoxicated.
9. Derogatory term for a lower-class Irish immigrant.

because he'd had a fight with your friend, Harker, the Standard Oil[1] millionaire, and won a glorious victory.

MARY [with amused dismay]   Oh, Lord! James, you'll really have to do something—

140 TYRONE   Bad luck to Shaughnessy, anyway!

JAMIE [maliciously]   I'll bet the next time you see Harker at the Club and give him the old respectful bow, he won't see you.

EDMUND   Yes. Harker will think you're no gentleman for harboring a tenant who isn't humble in the presence of a king of America.

145 TYRONE   Never mind the Socialist gabble. I don't care to listen—

MARY [tactfully]   Go on with your story, Edmund.

EDMUND [grins at his father provocatively]   Well, you remember, Pap, the ice pond on Harker's estate is right next to the farm, and you remember Shaughnessy keeps pigs. Well, it seems there's a break in the fence and the

150 pigs have been bathing in the millionaire's ice pond, and Harker's foreman told him he was sure Shaughnessy had broken the fence on purpose to give his pigs a free wallow.

MARY [shocked and amused]   Good heavens!

TYRONE [sourly, but with a trace of admiration]   I'm sure he did, too, the dirty

155 scallywag. It's like him.

EDMUND   So Harker came in person to rebuke Shaughnessy. [He chuckles.] A very bonehead play! If I needed any further proof that our ruling plutocrats, especially the ones who inherited their boodle, are not mental giants, that would clinch it.

160 TYRONE [with appreciation, before he thinks]   Yes, he'd be no match for Shaughnessy. [Then he growls.] Keep your damned anarchist remarks to yourself. I won't have them in my house. [But he is full of eager anticipation.] What happened?

EDMUND   Harker had as much chance as I would with Jack Johnson.[2]

165 Shaughnessy got a few drinks under his belt and was waiting at the gate to welcome him. He told me he never gave Harker a chance to open his mouth. He began by shouting that he was no slave Standard Oil could trample on. He was a King of Ireland, if he had his rights, and scum was scum to him, no matter how much money it had stolen from the poor.

170 MARY   Oh, Lord! [But she can't help laughing.]

EDMUND   Then he accused Harker of making his foreman break down the fence to entice the pigs into the ice pond in order to destroy them. The poor pigs, Shaughnessy yelled, had caught their death of cold. Many of them were dying of pneumonia, and several others had been taken down

175 with cholera from drinking the poisoned water. He told Harker he was hiring a lawyer to sue him for damages. And he wound up by saying that he had to put up with poison ivy, ticks, potato bugs, snakes and skunks on his farm, but he was an honest man who drew the line somewhere, and he'd be damned if he'd stand for a Standard Oil thief trespassing. So would Harker

180 kindly remove his dirty feet from the premises before he sicked the dog on him. And Harker did!

---

1. The oil company founded by John D. Rockefeller and forced to break up in 1911 because it was a monopoly. (Its successor companies, some of which originally had "Standard Oil" in their names, continue to dominate the U.S. oil industry.)

2. African American boxer (1878–1946); in 1908, he became the first black world heavyweight champion.

[*He and* JAMIE *laugh.*]

MARY [*shocked but giggling*]   Heavens, what a terrible tongue that man has!

TYRONE [*admiringly before he thinks*]   The damned old scoundrel! By God, you can't beat him!

[*He laughs—then stops abruptly and scowls.*]

185   The dirty blackguard! He'll get me in serious trouble yet. I hope you told him I'd be mad as hell—

EDMUND   I told him you'd be tickled to death over the great Irish victory, and so you are. Stop faking, Papa.

TYRONE   Well, I'm not tickled to death.

190   MARY [*teasingly*]   You are, too, James. You're simply delighted!

TYRONE   No, Mary, a joke is a joke, but—

EDMUND   I told Shaughnessy he should have reminded Harker that a Standard Oil millionaire ought to welcome the flavor of hog in his ice water as an appropriate touch.

195   TYRONE   The devil you did! [*Frowning*] Keep your damned Socialist anarchist sentiments out of my affairs!

EDMUND   Shaughnessy almost wept because he hadn't thought of that one, but he said he'd include it in a letter he's writing to Harker, along with a few other insults he'd overlooked.

[*He and* JAMIE *laugh.*]

200   TYRONE   What are you laughing at? There's nothing funny— A fine son you are to help that blackguard get me into a lawsuit!

MARY   Now, James, don't lose your temper.

TYRONE [*turns on* JAMIE]   And you're worse than he is, encouraging him. I suppose you're regretting you weren't there to prompt Shaughnessy with a

205   few nastier insults. You've a fine talent for that, if for nothing else.

MARY   James! There's no reason to scold Jamie.

[JAMIE *is about to make some sneering remark to his father, but he shrugs his shoulders.*]

EDMUND [*with sudden nervous exasperation*]   Oh, for God's sake, Papa! If you're starting that stuff again, I'll beat it. [*He jumps up.*] I left my book upstairs, anyway. [*He goes to the front parlor, saying disgustedly*] God, Papa,

210   I should think you'd get sick of hearing yourself—

[*He disappears.* TYRONE *looks after him angrily.*]

MARY   You mustn't mind Edmund, James. Remember he isn't well.

[EDMUND *can be heard coughing as he goes upstairs. She adds nervously.*]

A summer cold makes anyone irritable.

JAMIE [*genuinely concerned*]   It's not just a cold he's got. The Kid is damned sick.

[*His father gives him a sharp warning look but he doesn't see it.*]

215   MARY [*turns on him resentfully*]   Why do you say that? It *is* just a cold! Anyone can tell that! You always imagine things!

TYRONE [*with another warning glance at* JAMIE—*easily*]   All Jamie meant was Edmund might have a touch of something else, too, which makes his cold worse.

220   JAMIE   Sure, Mama. That's all I meant.

TYRONE   Doctor Hardy thinks it might be a bit of malarial fever he caught when he was in the tropics. If it is, quinine will soon cure it.

MARY [*a look of contemptuous hostility flashes across her face*]   Doctor Hardy! I wouldn't believe a thing he said, if he swore on a stack of Bibles! I know what doctors are. They're all alike. Anything, they don't care what, to keep you coming to them.

> [*She stops short, overcome by a fit of acute self-consciousness as she catches their eyes fixed on her. Her hands jerk nervously to her hair. She forces a smile.*]

What is it? What are you looking at? Is my hair—?

TYRONE [*puts his arm around her—with guilty heartiness, giving her a playful hug*]   There's nothing wrong with your hair. The healthier and fatter you get, the vainer you become. You'll soon spend half the day primping before the mirror.

MARY [*half reassured*]   I really should have new glasses. My eyes are so bad now.

TYRONE [*with Irish blarney*]   Your eyes are beautiful, and well you know it.

> [*He gives her a kiss. Her face lights up with a charming, shy embarrassment. Suddenly and startlingly one sees in her face the girl she had once been, not a ghost of the dead, but still a living part of her.*]

MARY   You mustn't be so silly, James. Right in front of Jamie!

TYRONE   Oh, he's on to you, too. He knows this fuss about eyes and hair is only fishing for compliments. Eh, Jamie?

JAMIE [*his face has cleared, too, and there is an old boyish charm in his loving smile at his mother*]   Yes. You can't kid us, Mama.

MARY [*laughs and an Irish lilt comes into her voice*]   Go along with both of you! [*Then she speaks with a girlish gravity.*] But I did truly have beautiful hair once, didn't I, James?

TYRONE   The most beautiful in the world!

MARY   It was a rare shade of reddish brown and so long it came down below my knees. You ought to remember it, too, Jamie. It wasn't until after Edmund was born that I had a single grey hair. Then it began to turn white.

> [*The girlishness fades from her face.*]

TYRONE [*quickly*]   And that made it prettier than ever.

MARY [*again embarrassed and pleased*]   Will you listen to your father, Jamie—after thirty-five years of marriage! He isn't a great actor for nothing, is he? What's come over you, James? Are you pouring coals of fire on my head for teasing you about snoring? Well then, I take it all back. It must have been only the foghorn I heard. [*She laughs, and they laugh with her. Then she changes to a brisk businesslike air.*] But I can't stay with you any longer, even to hear compliments. I must see the cook about dinner and the day's marketing. [*She gets up and sighs with humorous exaggeration.*] Bridget is so lazy. And so sly. She begins telling me about her relatives so I can't get a word in edgeways and scold her. Well, I might as well get it over.

> [*She goes to the back-parlor doorway, then turns, her face worried again.*]

You mustn't make Edmund work on the grounds with you, James, remember. [*Again with the strange obstinate set to her face*] Not that he isn't strong enough, but he'd perspire and he might catch more cold.

> [*She disappears through the back parlor. TYRONE turns on JAMIE condemningly.*]

260 TYRONE   You're a fine lunkhead! Haven't you any sense? The one thing to avoid is saying anything that would get her more upset over Edmund.

JAMIE [*shrugging his shoulders*]   All right. Have it your way. I think it's the wrong idea to let Mama go on kidding herself. It will only make the shock worse when she has to face it. Anyway, you can see she's deliberately fool-

265   ing herself with that summer cold talk. She knows better.

TYRONE   Knows? Nobody knows yet.

JAMIE   Well, I do. I was with Edmund when he went to Doc Hardy on Monday. I heard him pull that touch of malaria stuff. He was stalling. That isn't what he thinks anymore. You know it as well as I do. You talked to him

270   when you went uptown yesterday, didn't you?

TYRONE   He couldn't say anything for sure yet. He's to phone me today before Edmund goes to him.

JAMIE [*slowly*]   He thinks it's consumption,³ doesn't he, Papa?

TYRONE [*reluctantly*]   He said it might be.

275 JAMIE [*moved, his love for his brother coming out*]   Poor kid! God damn it!

[*He turns on his father accusingly.*]

It might never have happened if you'd sent him to a real doctor when he first got sick.

TYRONE   What's the matter with Hardy? He's always been our doctor up here.

280 JAMIE   Everything's the matter with him! Even in this hick burg he's rated third class! He's a cheap old quack!

TYRONE   That's right! Run him down! Run down everybody! Everyone is a fake to you!

JAMIE [*contemptuously*]   Hardy only charges a dollar. That's what makes you

285   think he's a fine doctor!

TYRONE [*stung*]   That's enough! You're not drunk now! There's no excuse—

[*He controls himself—a bit defensively.*]

If you mean I can't afford one of the fine society doctors who prey on the rich summer people—

JAMIE   Can't afford? You're one of the biggest property owners around here.

290 TYRONE   That doesn't mean I'm rich. It's all mortgaged—

JAMIE   Because you always buy more instead of paying off mortgages. If Edmund was a lousy acre of land you wanted, the sky would be the limit!

TYRONE   That's a lie! And your sneers against Doctor Hardy are lies! He doesn't put on frills, or have an office in a fashionable location, or drive

295   around in an expensive automobile. That's what you pay for with those other five-dollars-to-look-at-your-tongue fellows, not their skill.

JAMIE [*with a scornful shrug of his shoulders*]   Oh, all right. I'm a fool to argue. You can't change the leopard's spots.

TYRONE [*with rising anger*]   No, you can't. You've taught me that lesson only

300   too well. I've lost all hope you will ever change yours. You dare tell me what I can afford? You've never known the value of a dollar and never will! You've never saved a dollar in your life! At the end of each season you're penniless! You've thrown your salary away every week on whores and whiskey!

JAMIE   My salary! Christ!

---

3. A wasting disease, especially pulmonary tuberculosis.

305 TYRONE It's more than you're worth, and you couldn't get that if it wasn't for me. If you weren't my son, there isn't a manager in the business who would give you a part, your reputation stinks so. As it is, I have to humble my pride and beg for you, saying you've turned over a new leaf, although I know it's a lie!

310 JAMIE I never wanted to be an actor. You forced me on the stage.

TYRONE That's a lie! You made no effort to find anything else to do. You left it to me to get you a job and I have no influence except in the theater. Forced you! You never wanted to do anything except loaf in barrooms! You'd have been content to sit back like a lazy lunk and sponge on me for the rest

315 of your life! After all the money I'd wasted on your education, and all you did was get fired in disgrace from every college you went to!

JAMIE Oh, for God's sake, don't drag up that ancient history!

TYRONE It's not ancient history that you have to come home every summer to live on me.

320 JAMIE I earn my board and lodging working on the grounds. It saves you hiring a man.

TYRONE Bah! You have to be driven to do even that much! [*His anger ebbs into a weary complaint.*] I wouldn't give a damn if you ever displayed the slightest sign of gratitude. The only thanks is to have you sneer at me for a

325 dirty miser, sneer at my profession, sneer at every damned thing in the world—except yourself.

JAMIE [*wryly*] That's not true, Papa. You can't hear me talking to myself, that's all.

TYRONE [*stares at him puzzledly, then quotes mechanically*] "Ingratitude, the

330 vilest weed that grows"![4]

JAMIE I could see that line coming! God, how many thousand times—! [*He stops, bored with their quarrel, and shrugs his shoulders.*] All right, Papa. I'm a bum. Anything you like, so long as it stops the argument.

TYRONE [*with indignant appeal now*] If you'd get ambition in your head

335 instead of folly! You're young yet. You could still make your mark. You had the talent to become a fine actor! You have it still. You're my son—!

JAMIE [*boredly*] Let's forget me. I'm not interested in the subject. Neither are you.

[TYRONE *gives up.* JAMIE *goes on casually.*]

What started us on this? Oh, Doc Hardy. When is he going to call you up

340 about Edmund?

TYRONE Around lunch time [*He pauses—then defensively.*] I couldn't have sent Edmund to a better doctor. Hardy's treated him whenever he was sick up here, since he was knee high. He knows his constitution as no other doctor could. It's not a question of my being miserly, as you'd like to make

345 out. [*Bitterly*] And what could the finest specialist in America do for Edmund, after he's deliberately ruined his health by the mad life he's led ever since he was fired from college? Even before that when he was in prep school, he began dissipating and playing the Broadway sport to imitate you, when he's never had your constitution to stand it. You're a healthy hulk like

350 me—or you were at his age—but he's always been a bundle of nerves like

4. Perhaps Tyrone's own adaptation of a line from *King Edward III* (1596), a play sometimes attributed to Shakespeare: "Ingratitude, the basest weed that grows" (2.1.165).

his mother. I've warned him for years his body couldn't stand it, but he wouldn't heed me, and now it's too late.

JAMIE [*sharply*]   What do you mean, too late? You talk as if you thought—

TYRONE [*guiltily explosive*]   Don't be a damned fool! I meant nothing but
355   what's plain to anyone! His health has broken down and he may be an invalid for a long time.

JAMIE [*stares at his father, ignoring his explanation*]   I know it's an Irish peasant idea consumption is fatal. It probably is when you live in a hovel on a bog, but over here, with modern treatment—

360   TYRONE   Don't I know that! What are you gabbing about, anyway? And keep your dirty tongue off Ireland, with your sneers about peasants and bogs and hovels! [*Accusingly*] The less you say about Edmund's sickness, the better for your conscience! You're more responsible than anyone!

JAMIE [*stung*]   That's a lie! I won't stand for that, Papa!

365   TYRONE   It's the truth! You've been the worst influence for him. He grew up admiring you as a hero! A fine example you set him! If you ever gave him advice except in the ways of rottenness, I've never heard of it! You made him old before his time, pumping him full of what you consider worldly wisdom, when he was too young to see that your mind was so poisoned by
370   your own failure in life, you wanted to believe every man was a knave with his soul for sale, and every woman who wasn't a whore was a fool!

JAMIE [*with a defensive air of weary indifference again*]   All right. I did put Edmund wise to things, but not until I saw he'd started to raise hell, and knew he'd laugh at me if I tried the good advice, older brother stuff. All I
375   did was make a pal of him and be absolutely frank so he'd learn from my mistakes that— [*He shrugs his shoulders—cynically.*] Well, that if you can't be good you can at least be careful.

> [*His father snorts contemptuously. Suddenly* JAMIE *becomes really moved.*]

That's a rotten accusation, Papa. You know how much the Kid means to me, and how close we've always been—not like the usual brothers! I'd do
380   anything for him.

TYRONE [*impressed—mollifyingly*]   I know you may have thought it was for the best, Jamie. I didn't say you did it deliberately to harm him.

JAMIE   Besides it's damned rot! I'd like to see anyone influence Edmund more than he wants to be. His quietness fools people into thinking they
385   can do what they like with him. But he's stubborn as hell inside and what he does is what he wants to do, and to hell with anyone else! What had I to do with all the crazy stunts he's pulled in the last few years—working his way all over the map as a sailor and all that stuff. I thought that was a damned fool idea, and I told him so. You can't imagine me getting fun out
390   of being on the beach in South America, or living in filthy dives, drinking rotgut, can you? No, thanks! I'll stick to Broadway, and a room with a bath, and bars that serve bonded Bourbon.[5]

TYRONE   You and Broadway! It's made you what you are! [*With a touch of pride*] Whatever Edmund's done, he's had the guts to go off on his own,
395   where he couldn't come whining to me the minute he was broke.

5. That is, good bourbon. Bonded whiskey is   in Bond Act of 1897; it must be at least four
aged, bottled, and stored under government   years old and bottled at 100 proof.
supervision, in accordance with the Bottled

JAMIE [*stung into sneering jealousy*]   He's always come home broke finally, hasn't he? And what did his going away get him? Look at him now! [*He is suddenly shamefaced.*] Christ! That's a lousy thing to say. I don't mean that.

TYRONE [*decides to ignore this*]   He's been doing well on the paper. I was hop-
400   ing he'd found the work he wants to do at last.

JAMIE [*sneering jealously again*]   A hick town rag! Whatever bull they hand you, they tell me he's a pretty bum reporter. If he weren't your son— [*Ashamed again*] No, that's not true! They're glad to have him, but it's the special stuff that gets him by. Some of the poems and parodies he's written
405   are damned good. [*Grudgingly again*] Not that they'd ever get him any-where on the big time. [*Hastily*] But he's certainly made a damned good start.

TYRONE   Yes. He's made a start. You used to talk about wanting to become a newspaperman but you were never willing to start at the bottom. You
410   expected—

JAMIE   Oh, for Christ's sake, Papa! Can't you lay off me!

TYRONE [*stares at him—then looks away—after a pause*]   It's damnable luck Edmund should be sick right now. It couldn't have come at a worse time for him. [*He adds, unable to conceal an almost furtive uneasiness.*] Or for
415   your mother. It's damnable she should have this to upset her, just when she needs peace and freedom from worry. She's been so well in the two months since she came home. [*His voice grows husky and trembles a little.*] It's been heaven to me. This home has been a home again. But I needn't tell you, Jamie.

> [*His son looks at him, for the first time with an understanding sympathy. It is as if suddenly a deep bond of common feeling existed between them in which their antagonisms could be forgotten.*]

420   JAMIE [*almost gently*]   I've felt the same way, Papa.

TYRONE   Yes, this time you can see how strong and sure of herself she is. She's a different woman entirely from the other times. She has control of her nerves—or she had until Edmund got sick. Now you can feel her grow-ing tense and frightened underneath. I wish to God we could keep the
425   truth from her, but we can't if he has to be sent to a sanatorium. What makes it worse is her father died of consumption. She worshiped him and she's never forgotten. Yes, it will be hard for her. But she can do it! She has the willpower now! We must help her, Jamie, in every way we can!

JAMIE [*moved*]   Of course, Papa. [*Hesitantly*] Outside of nerves, she seems
430   perfectly all right this morning.

TYRONE [*with hearty confidence now*]   Never better. She's full of fun and mis-chief. [*Suddenly he frowns at Jamie suspiciously.*] Why do you say, seems? Why shouldn't she be all right? What the hell do you mean?

JAMIE   Don't start jumping down my throat! God, Papa, this ought to be one
435   thing we can talk over frankly without a battle.

TYRONE   I'm sorry, Jamie. [*Tensely*] But go on and tell me—

JAMIE   There's nothing to tell. I was all wrong. It's just that last night— Well, you know how it is, I can't forget the past. I can't help being suspicious. Any more than you can. [*Bitterly*] That's the hell of it. And it makes it hell
440   for Mama! She watches us watching her—

TYRONE [*sadly*]   I know. [*Tensely*] Well, what was it? Can't you speak out?

JAMIE   Nothing, I tell you. Just my damned foolishness. Around three o'clock this morning, I woke up and heard her moving around in the spare room.

Then she went to the bathroom. I pretended to be asleep. She stopped in
445   the hall to listen, as if she wanted to make sure I was.

TYRONE [*with forced scorn*] For God's sake, is that all? She told me herself
the foghorn kept her awake all night, and every night since Edmund's been
sick she's been up and down, going to his room to see how he was.

JAMIE [*eagerly*] Yes, that's right, she did stop to listen outside his room.
450   [*Hesitantly again*] It was her being in the spare room that scared me. I
couldn't help remembering that when she starts sleeping alone in there, it
has always been a sign—

TYRONE It isn't this time! It's easily explained. Where else could she go last
night to get away from my snoring? [*He gives way to a burst of resentful*
455   *anger.*] By God, how you can live with a mind that sees nothing but the
worst motives behind everything is beyond me!

JAMIE [*stung*] Don't pull that! I've just said I was all wrong. Don't you suppose I'm as glad of that as you are!

TYRONE [*mollifyingly*] I'm sure you are, Jamie.

        [*A pause. His expression becomes somber. He speaks slowly with a super-*
        stitious dread.]

460   It would be like a curse she can't escape if worry over Edmund—It was in
her long sickness after bringing him into the world that she first—

JAMIE She didn't have anything to do with it!

TYRONE I'm not blaming her.

JAMIE [*bitingly*] Then who are you blaming? Edmund, for being born?
465 TYRONE You damned fool! No one was to blame.

JAMIE The bastard of a doctor was! From what Mama's said, he was another
cheap quack like Hardy! You wouldn't pay for a first-rate—

TYRONE That's a lie! [*Furiously*] So I'm to blame! That's what you're driving
at, is it? You evil-minded loafer!

470 JAMIE [*warningly as he hears his mother in the dining room*] Ssh!

        [TYRONE *gets hastily to his feet and goes to look out the windows at right.*
        JAMIE *speaks with a complete change of tone.*]

Well, if we're going to cut the front hedge today, we'd better go to work.

        [MARY *comes in from the back parlor. She gives a quick, suspicious glance*
        from one to the other, her manner nervously self-conscious.]

TYRONE [*turns from the window—with an actor's heartiness*] Yes, it's too fine
a morning to waste indoors arguing. Take a look out the window, Mary.
There's no fog in the harbor. I'm sure the spell of it we've had is over now.

475 MARY [*going to him*] I hope so, dear. [*To* JAMIE, *forcing a smile*] Did I actually
hear you suggesting work on the front hedge, Jamie? Wonders will never
cease! You must want pocket money badly.

JAMIE [*kiddingly*] When don't I? [*He winks at her, with a derisive glance at*
his father.] I expect a salary of at least one large iron man[6] at the end of the
480   week—to carouse on!

MARY [*does not respond to his humor—her hands fluttering over the front of her*
dress] What were you two arguing about?

JAMIE [*shrugs his shoulders*] The same old stuff.

MARY I heard you say something about a doctor, and your father accusing
you of being evil-minded.

6. A dollar (slang).

485 JAMIE [*quickly*] Oh, that. I was saying again Doc Hardy isn't my idea of the world's greatest physician.

MARY [*knows he is lying—vaguely*] Oh. No, I wouldn't say he was, either. [*Changing the subject—forcing a smile*] That Bridget! I thought I'd never get away. She told me all about her second cousin on the police force in St.

490 Louis. [*Then with nervous irritation*] Well, if you're going to work on the hedge why don't you go? [*Hastily*] I mean, take advantage of the sunshine before the fog comes back. [*Strangely, as if talking aloud to herself*] Because I know it will. [*Suddenly she is self-consciously aware that they are both staring fixedly at her—flurriedly, raising her hands.*] Or I should say, the rheumatism

495 in my hands knows. It's a better weather prophet than you are, James. [*She stares at her hands with fascinated repulsion.*] Ugh! How ugly they are! Who'd ever believe they were once beautiful?

[*They stare at her with a growing dread.*]

TYRONE [*takes her hands and gently pushes them down*] Now, now, Mary. None of that foolishness. They're the sweetest hands in the world.

[*She smiles, her face lighting up, and kisses him gratefully. He turns to his son.*]

500 Come on Jamie. Your mother's right to scold us. The way to start work is to start work. The hot sun will sweat some of that booze fat off your middle.

[*He opens the screen door and goes out on the porch and disappears down a flight of steps leading to the ground. JAMIE rises from his chair and, taking off his coat, goes to the door. At the door he turns back but avoids looking at her, and she does not look at him.*]

JAMIE [*with an awkward, uneasy tenderness*] We're all so proud of you, Mama, so darned happy.

[*She stiffens and stares at him with a frightened defiance. He flounders on.*]

But you've still got to be careful. You mustn't worry so much about Edmund.
505 He'll be all right.

MARY [*with a stubborn, bitterly resentful look*] Of course, he'll be all right. And I don't know what you mean, warning me to be careful.

JAMIE [*rebuffed and hurt, shrugs his shoulders*] All right, Mama. I'm sorry I spoke.

[*He goes out on the porch. She waits rigidly until he disappears down the steps. Then she sinks down in the chair he had occupied, her face betraying a frightened, furtive desperation, her hands roving over the tabletop, aimlessly moving objects around. She hears EDMUND descending the stairs in the front hall. As he nears the bottom he has a fit of coughing. She springs to her feet, as if she wanted to run away from the sound, and goes quickly to the windows at right. She is looking out, apparently calm, as he enters from the front parlor, a book in one hand. She turns to him, her lips set in a welcoming, motherly smile.*]

510 MARY Here you are. I was just going upstairs to look for you.

EDMUND I waited until they went out. I don't want to mix up in any arguments. I feel too rotten.

MARY [*almost resentfully*] Oh, I'm sure you don't feel half as badly as you make out. You're such a baby. You like to get us worried so we'll make a fuss

515 over you. [*Hastily*] I'm only teasing, dear. I know how miserably uncomfortable you must be. But you feel better today, don't you? [*Worriedly, taking*

his arm] All the same, you've grown much too thin. You need to rest all you can. Sit down and I'll make you comfortable.

[*He sits down in the rocking chair and she puts a pillow behind his back.*]

There. How's that?

520 EDMUND   Grand. Thanks, Mama.

MARY [*kisses him—tenderly*]   All you need is your mother to nurse you. Big as you are, you're still the baby of the family to me, you know.

EDMUND [*takes her hand—with deep seriousness*]   Never mind me. You take care of yourself. That's all that counts.

525 MARY [*evading his eyes*]   But I am, dear. [*Forcing a laugh.*] Heavens, don't you see how fat I've grown! I'll have to have all my dresses let out.

[*She turns away and goes to the windows at right. She attempts a light, amused tone.*]

They've started clipping the hedge. Poor Jamie! How he hates working in front where everyone passing can see him. There go the Chatfields in their new Mercedes. It's a beautiful car, isn't it? Not like our secondhand 530 Packard.[7] Poor Jamie! He bent almost under the hedge so they wouldn't notice him. They bowed to your father and he bowed back as if he were taking a curtain call. In that filthy old suit I've tried to make him throw away. [*Her voice has grown bitter.*] Really, he ought to have more pride than to make such a show of himself.

535 EDMUND   He's right not to give a damn what anyone thinks. Jamie's a fool to care about the Chatfields. For Pete's sake, who ever heard of them outside this hick burg?

MARY [*with satisfaction*]   No one. You're quite right, Edmund. Big frogs in a small puddle. It is stupid of Jamie. [*She pauses, looking out the window— then with an undercurrent of lonely yearning.*] Still, the Chatfields and 540 people like them stand for something. I mean they have decent, present-able homes they don't have to be ashamed of. They have friends who enter-tain them and whom they entertain. They're not cut off from everyone. [*She turns back from the window.*] Not that I want anything to do with 545 them. I've always hated this town and everyone in it. You know that. I never wanted to live here in the first place, but your father liked it and insisted on building this house, and I've had to come here every summer.

EDMUND   Well, it's better than spending the summer in a New York hotel, isn't it? And this town's not so bad. I like it well enough. I suppose because 550 it's the only home we've had.

MARY   I've never felt it was my home. It was wrong from the start. Everything was done in the cheapest way. Your father would never spend the money to make it right. It's just as well we haven't any friends here. I'd be ashamed to have them step in the door. But he's never wanted family friends. He hates 555 calling on people, or receiving them. All he likes is to hobnob with men at the Club or in a barroom. Jamie and you are the same way, but you're not to blame. You've never had a chance to meet decent people here. I know you both would have been so different if you'd been able to associate with nice girls instead of— You'd never have disgraced yourselves as you have, so that 560 now no respectable parents will let their daughters be seen with you.

---

7. A brand of American luxury automobile (manufactured from 1899 to 1958).

EDMUND [*irritably*]   Oh, Mama, forget it! Who cares? Jamie and I would be bored stiff. And about the Old Man, what's the use of talking? You can't change him.

MARY [*mechanically rebuking*]   Don't call your father the Old Man. You
565   should have more respect. [*Then dully*] I know it's useless to talk. But sometimes I feel so lonely. [*Her lips quiver and she keeps her head turned away.*]

EDMUND   Anyway, you've got to be fair, Mama. It may have been all his fault in the beginning, but you know that later on, even if he'd wanted to, we couldn't have had people here— [*He flounders guiltily.*] I mean, you
570   wouldn't have wanted them.

MARY [*wincing—her lips quivering pitifully*]   Don't. I can't bear having you remind me.

EDMUND   Don't take it that way! Please, Mama! I'm trying to help. Because it's bad for you to forget. The right way is to remember. So you'll always be
575   on your guard. You know what's happened before. [*Miserably*] God, Mama, you know I hate to remind you. I'm doing it because it's been so wonderful having you home the way you've been, and it would be terrible—

MARY [*strickenly*]   Please, dear. I know you mean it for the best, but— [*A defensive uneasiness comes into her voice again.*] I don't understand why
580   you should suddenly say such things. What put it in your mind this morning?

EDMUND [*evasively*]   Nothing. Just because I feel rotten and blue, I suppose.

MARY   Tell me the truth. Why are you so suspicious all of a sudden?

EDMUND   I'm not!

585   MARY   Oh, yes you are. I can feel it. Your father and Jamie, too—particularly Jamie.

EDMUND   Now don't start imagining things, Mama.

MARY [*her hands fluttering*]   It makes it so much harder, living in this atmosphere of constant suspicion, knowing everyone is spying on me, and none
590   of you believe in me, or trust me.

EDMUND   That's crazy, Mama. We do trust you.

MARY   If there was only some place I could go to get away for a day, or even an afternoon, some woman friend I could talk to—not about anything serious, simply laugh and gossip and forget for a while—someone besides the
595   servants—that stupid Cathleen!

EDMUND [*gets up worriedly and puts his arm around her*]   Stop it, Mama. You're getting yourself worked up over nothing.

MARY   Your father goes out. He meets his friends in barrooms or at the Club. You and Jamie have the boys you know. You go out. But I am alone. I've
600   always been alone.

EDMUND [*soothingly*]   Come now! You know that's a fib. One of us always stays around to keep you company, or goes with you in the automobile when you take a drive.

MARY [*bitterly*]   Because you're afraid to trust me alone! [*She turns on him—
605   sharply.*] I insist you tell me why you act so differently this morning—why you felt you had to remind me—

EDMUND [*hesitates—then blurts out guiltily*]   It's stupid. It's just that I wasn't asleep when you came in my room last night. You didn't go back to your and Papa's room. You went in the spare room for the rest of the night.

610 MARY Because your father's snoring was driving me crazy! For heaven's sake, haven't I often used the spare room as my bedroom? [*Bitterly*] But I see what you thought. That was when—

EDMUND [*too vehemently*] I didn't think anything!

MARY So you pretended to be asleep in order to spy on me!

615 EDMUND No! I did it because I knew if you found out I was feverish and couldn't sleep, it would upset you.

MARY Jamie was pretending to be asleep, too, I'm sure, and I suppose your father—

EDMUND Stop it, Mama!

620 MARY Oh, I can't bear it, Edmund, when even you—!

[*Her hands flutter up to pat her hair in their aimless, distracted way. Suddenly a strange undercurrent of revengefulness comes into her voice.*]

It would serve all of you right if it was true!

EDMUND Mama! Don't say that! That's the way you talk when—

MARY Stop suspecting me! Please, dear! You hurt me! I couldn't sleep because I was thinking about you. That's the real reason! I've been so worried ever

625 since you've been sick.

[*She puts her arms around him and hugs him with a frightened, protective tenderness.*]

EDMUND [*soothingly*] That's foolishness. You know it's only a bad cold.

MARY Yes, of course, I know that!

EDMUND But listen, Mama. I want you to promise me that even if it should turn out to be something worse, you'll know I'll soon be all right again, anyway,

630 and you won't worry yourself sick, and you'll keep on taking care of yourself—

MARY [*frightenedly*] I won't listen when you're so silly! There's absolutely no reason to talk as if you expected something dreadful! Of course, I promise you. I give you my sacred word of honor! [*Then with a sad bitterness*] But I

635 suppose you're remembering I've promised before on my word of honor.

EDMUND No!

MARY [*her bitterness receding into a resigned helplessness*] I'm not blaming you, dear. How can you help it? How can any one of us forget? [*Strangely*] That's what makes it so hard—for all of us. We can't forget.

640 EDMUND [*grabs her shoulder*] Mama! Stop it!

MARY [*forcing a smile*] All right, dear. I didn't mean to be so gloomy. Don't mind me. Here. Let me feel your head. Why, it's nice and cool. You certainly haven't any fever now.

EDMUND Forget! It's you—

645 MARY But I'm quite all right, dear. [*With a quick, strange, calculating, almost sly glance at him*] Except I naturally feel tired and nervous this morning, after such a bad night. I really ought to go upstairs and lie down until lunch time and take a nap.

[*He gives her an instinctive look of suspicion—then, ashamed of himself, looks quickly away. She hurries on nervously.*]

What are you going to do? Read here? It would be much better for you to

650 go out in the fresh air and sunshine. But don't get overheated, remember. Be sure and wear a hat.

[*She stops, looking straight at him now. He avoids her eyes. There is a tense pause. Then she speaks jeeringly.*]

Or are you afraid to trust me alone?

EDMUND [*tormentedly*]   No! Can't you stop talking like that! I think you ought to take a nap. [*He goes to the screen door—forcing a joking tone.*] I'll go
655   down and help Jamie bear up. I love to lie in the shade and watch him work.

> [*He forces a laugh in which she makes herself join. Then he goes out on the porch and disappears down the steps. Her first reaction is one of relief. She appears to relax. She sinks down in one of the wicker armchairs at rear of table and leans her head back, closing her eyes. But suddenly she grows terribly tense again. Her eyes open and she strains forward, seized by a fit of nervous panic. She begins a desperate battle with herself. Her long fingers, warped and knotted by rheumatism, drum on the arms of the chair, driven by an insistent life of their own, without her consent.*]

Curtain.

Act 2, Scene 1

SCENE: *The same. It is around quarter to one. No sunlight comes into the room now through the windows at right. Outside the day is still fine but increasingly sultry, with a faint haziness in the air which softens the glare of the sun.*

EDMUND *sits in the armchair at left of table, reading a book. Or rather he is trying to concentrate on it but cannot. He seems to be listening for some sound from upstairs. His manner is nervously apprehensive and he looks more sickly than in the previous act.*

The second girl, CATHLEEN, *enters from the back parlor. She carries a tray on which is a bottle of bonded Bourbon, several whiskey glasses, and a pitcher of ice water. She is a buxom Irish peasant, in her early twenties, with a red-cheeked comely face, black hair and blue eyes—amiable, ignorant, clumsy, and possessed by a dense, well-meaning stupidity. She puts the tray on the table.* EDMUND *pretends to be so absorbed in his book he does not notice her, but she ignores this.*

CATHLEEN [*with garrulous familiarity*]   Here's the whiskey. It'll be lunchtime soon. Will I call your father and Mister Jamie, or will you?
EDMUND [*without looking up from his book*]   You do it.
CATHLEEN   It's a wonder your father wouldn't look at his watch once in a
5   while. He's a divil for making the meals late, and then Bridget curses me as if I was to blame. But he's a grand handsome man, if he is old. You'll never see the day you're as good-looking—nor Mister Jamie, either. [*She chuckles.*] I'll wager Mister Jamie wouldn't miss the time to stop work and have his drop of whiskey if he had a watch to his name!
10   EDMUND [*gives up trying to ignore her and grins*]   You win that one.
CATHLEEN   And here's another I'd win, that you're making me call them so you can sneak a drink before they come.
EDMUND   Well, I hadn't thought of that—
CATHLEEN   Oh no, not you! Butter wouldn't melt in your mouth, I suppose.
15   EDMUND   But now you suggest it—
CATHLEEN [*suddenly primly virtuous*]   I'd never suggest a man or a woman touch drink, Mister Edmund. Sure, didn't it kill an uncle of mine in the old country. [*Relenting*] Still, a drop now and then is no harm when you're in low spirits, or have a bad cold.
20   EDMUND   Thanks for handing me a good excuse. [*Then with forced casualness*] You'd better call my mother, too.
CATHLEEN   What for? She's always on time without any calling. God bless her, she has some consideration for the help.

EDMUND   She's been taking a nap.

25 CATHLEEN   She wasn't asleep when I finished my work upstairs a while back. She was lying down in the spare room with her eyes wide open. She'd a terrible headache, she said.

EDMUND [*his casualness more forced*]   Oh well then, just call my father.

CATHLEEN [*goes to the screen door, grumbling good-naturedly*]   No wonder my
30   feet kill me each night. I won't walk out in this heat and get sunstroke. I'll call from the porch.

[*She goes out on the side porch, letting the screen door slam behind her, and disappears on her way to the front porch. A moment later she is heard shouting.*]

Mister Tyrone! Mister Jamie! It's time!

[EDMUND, *who has been staring frightenedly before him, forgetting his book, springs to his feet nervously.*]

EDMUND   God, what a wench!

[*He grabs the bottle and pours a drink, adds ice water and drinks. As he does so, he hears someone coming in the front door. He puts the glass hastily on the tray and sits down again, opening his book. Jamie comes in from the front parlor, his coat over his arm. He has taken off collar[8] and tie and carries them in his hand. He is wiping sweat from his forehead with a handkerchief. Edmund looks up as if his reading was interrupted. Jamie takes one look at the bottle and glasses and smiles cynically.*]

JAMIE   Sneaking one, eh? Cut out the bluff, Kid. You're a rottener actor than
35   I am.

EDMUND [*grins*]   Yes, I grabbed one while the going was good.

JAMIE [*puts a hand affectionately on his shoulder*]   That's better. Why kid me? We're pals, aren't we?

EDMUND   I wasn't sure it was you coming.

40 JAMIE   I made the Old Man look at his watch. I was halfway up the walk when Cathleen burst into song. Our wild Irish lark! She ought to be a train announcer.

EDMUND   That's what drove me to drink. Why don't you sneak one while you've got a chance?

45 JAMIE   I was thinking of that little thing.

[*He goes quickly to the window at right.*]

The Old Man was talking to old Captain Turner. Yes, he's still at it.

[*He comes back and takes a drink.*]

And now to cover up from his eagle eye. He memorizes the level in the bottle after every drink.

[*He measures two drinks of water and pours them in the whiskey bottle and shakes it up.*]

There. That fixes it.

[*He pours water in the glass and sets it on the table by* EDMUND.]

50   And here's the water you've been drinking.

EDMUND   Fine! You don't think it will fool him, do you?

JAMIE   Maybe not, but he can't prove it. [*Putting on his collar and tie*] I hope he doesn't forget lunch listening to himself talk. I'm hungry. [*He sits across*

---

8. Detachable collars—of starched linen or paper and celluloid—were common from the mid-19th century until after World War I.

the table from Edmund—irritably.] That's what I hate about working down
55   in front. He puts on an act for every damned fool that comes along.

EDMUND [gloomily]   You're in luck to be hungry. The way I feel I don't care if
    I ever eat again.

JAMIE [gives him a glance of concern]   Listen, Kid. You know me. I've never
    lectured you, but Doctor Hardy was right when he told you to cut out the
60   red-eye.[9]

EDMUND   Oh, I'm going to after he hands me the bad news this afternoon. A
    few before then won't make any difference.

JAMIE [hesitates—then slowly]   I'm glad you've got your mind prepared for
    bad news. It won't be such a jolt. [He catches EDMUND staring at him.] I
65   mean, it's a cinch you're really sick, and it would be wrong dope to kid
    yourself.

EDMUND [disturbed]   I'm not. I know how rotten I feel, and the fever and
    chills I get at night are no joke. I think Doctor Hardy's last guess was right.
    It must be the damned malaria come back on me.

70 JAMIE   Maybe, but don't be too sure.

EDMUND   Why? What do you think it is?

JAMIE   Hell, how would I know? I'm no doc. [Abruptly] Where's Mama?

EDMUND   Upstairs.

JAMIE [looks at him sharply]   When did she go up?

75 EDMUND   Oh, about the time I came down to the hedge, I guess. She said
    she was going to take a nap.

JAMIE   You didn't tell me—

EDMUND [defensively]   Why should I? What about it? She was tired out. She
    didn't get much sleep last night.

80 JAMIE   I know she didn't.

            [A pause. The brothers avoid looking at each other.]

EDMUND   That damned foghorn kept me awake, too.

            [Another pause.]

JAMIE   She's been upstairs alone all morning, eh? You haven't seen her?

EDMUND   No. I've been reading here. I wanted to give her a chance to sleep.

JAMIE   Is she coming down to lunch?

85 EDMUND   Of course.

JAMIE [dryly]   No of course about it. She might not want any lunch. Or she
    might start having most of her meals alone upstairs. That's happened,
    hasn't it?

EDMUND [with frightened resentment]   Cut it out, Jamie! Can't you think
90   anything but—? [Persuasively] You're all wrong to suspect anything. Cath-
    leen saw her not long ago. Mama didn't tell her she wouldn't be down to
    lunch.

JAMIE   Then she wasn't taking a nap?

EDMUND   Not right then, but she was lying down, Cathleen said.

95 JAMIE   In the spare room?

EDMUND   Yes. For Pete's sake, what of it?

JAMIE [bursts out]   You damned fool! Why did you leave her alone so long?
    Why didn't you stick around?

9. Cheap whiskey.

EDMUND   Because she accused me—and you and Papa—of spying on her all
the time and not trusting her. She made me feel ashamed. I know how rotten it must be for her. And she promised on her sacred word of honor—

JAMIE [*with a bitter weariness*]   You ought to know that doesn't mean anything.

EDMUND   It does this time!

JAMIE   That's what we thought the other times. [*He leans over the table to
give his brother's arm an affectionate grasp.*] Listen, Kid, I know you think
I'm a cynical bastard, but remember I've seen a lot more of this game than
you have. You never knew what was really wrong until you were in prep
school. Papa and I kept it from you. But I was wise ten years or more before
we had to tell you. I know the game backwards and I've been thinking all
morning of the way she acted last night when she thought we were asleep.
I haven't been able to think of anything else. And now you tell me she got
you to leave her alone upstairs all morning.

EDMUND   She didn't! You're crazy!

JAMIE [*placatingly*]   All right, Kid. Don't start a battle with me. I hope as
much as you do I'm crazy. I've been as happy as hell because I'd really
begun to believe that this time— [*He stops—looking through the front parlor toward the hall—lowering his voice, hurriedly.*] She's coming downstairs.
You win on that. I guess I'm a damned suspicious louse.

[*They grow tense with a hopeful, fearful expectancy. Jamie mutters.*]

Damn! I wish I'd grabbed another drink.

EDMUND   Me, too.

[*He coughs nervously and this brings on a real fit of coughing.* JAMIE
glances at him with worried pity. MARY *enters from the front parlor. At
first one notices no change except that she appears to be less nervous, to
be more as she was when we first saw her after breakfast, but then one
becomes aware that her eyes are brighter, and there is a peculiar detachment in her voice and manner, as if she were a little withdrawn from her
words and actions.*]

MARY [*goes worriedly to* EDMUND *and puts her arm around him*]   You mustn't
cough like that. It's bad for your throat. You don't want to get a sore throat
on top of your cold.

[*She kisses him. He stops coughing and gives her a quick apprehensive
glance, but if his suspicious are aroused her tenderness makes him
renounce them and he believes what he wants to believe for the moment.
On the other hand,* JAMIE *knows after one probing look at her that his
suspicions are justified. His eyes fall to stare at the floor, his face sets in an
expression of embittered, defensive cynicism.* MARY *goes on, half sitting
on the arm of* EDMUND's *chair, her arm around him, so her face is above
and behind his and he cannot look into her eyes.*]

But I seem to be always picking on you, telling you don't do this and don't
do that. Forgive me, dear. It's just that I want to take care of you.

EDMUND   I know, Mama. How about you? Do you feel rested?

MARY   Yes, ever so much better. I've been lying down ever since you went out.
It's what I needed after such a restless night. I don't feel nervous now.

EDMUND   That's fine.

[*He pats her hand on his shoulder.* JAMIE *gives him a strange, almost contemptuous glance, wondering if his brother can really mean this.* EDMUND
does not notice but his mother does.]

130 MARY [*in a forced teasing tone*]   Good heavens, how down in the mouth you look, Jamie. What's the matter now?

JAMIE [*without looking at her*]   Nothing.

MARY   Oh, I'd forgotten you've been working on the front hedge. That accounts for your sinking into the dumps, doesn't it?

135 JAMIE   If you want to think so, Mama.

MARY [*keeping her tone*]   Well, that's the effect it always has, isn't it? What a big baby you are! Isn't he, Edmund?

EDMUND   He's certainly a fool to care what anyone thinks.

MARY [*strangely*]   Yes, the only way is to make yourself not care.

[*She catches* JAMIE *giving her a bitter glance and changes the subject.*]

140   Where is your father? I heard Cathleen call him.

EDMUND   Gabbing with old Captain Turner, Jamie says. He'll be late, as usual.

[JAMIE *gets up and goes to the windows at right, glad of an excuse to turn his back.*]

MARY   I've told Cathleen time and again she must go wherever he is and tell him. The idea of screaming as if this were a cheap boardinghouse!

145 JAMIE [*looking out the window*]   She's down there now. [*Sneeringly*] Interrupting the famous Beautiful Voice! She should have more respect.

MARY [*sharply—letting her resentment toward him come out*]   It's you who should have more respect! Stop sneering at your father! I won't have it! You ought to be proud you're his son! He may have his faults. Who hasn't? But

150   he's worked hard all his life. He made his way up from ignorance and poverty to the top of his profession! Everyone else admires him and you should be the last one to sneer—you, who, thanks to him, have never had to work hard in your life!

[*Stung,* JAMIE *has turned to stare at her with accusing antagonism. Her eyes waver guiltily and she adds in a tone which begins to placate.*]

Remember your father is getting old, Jamie. You really ought to show more

155   consideration.

JAMIE   *I* ought to?

EDMUND [*uneasily*]   Oh, dry up, Jamie!

[JAMIE *looks out the window again.*]

And, for Pete's sake, Mama, why jump on Jamie all of a sudden?

MARY [*bitterly*]   Because he's always sneering at someone else, always look-

160   ing for the worst weakness in everyone. [*Then with a strange, abrupt change to a detached, impersonal tone*] But I suppose life has made him like that, and he can't help it. None of us can help the things life has done to us. They're done before you realize it, and once they're done they make you do other things until at last everything comes between you and what you'd

165   like to be, and you've lost your true self forever.

[EDMUND *is made apprehensive by her strangeness. He tries to look up in her eyes but she keeps them averted.* JAMIE *turns to her—then looks quickly out of the window again.*]

JAMIE [*dully*]   I'm hungry. I wish the Old Man would get a move on. It's a rotten trick the way he keeps meals waiting, and then beefs because they're spoiled.

MARY [*with a resentment that has a quality of being automatic and on the surface while inwardly she is indifferent*]   Yes, it's very trying, Jamie. You don't

170 know how trying. You don't have to keep house with summer servants who don't care because they know it isn't a permanent position. The really good servants are all with people who have homes and not merely summer places. And your father won't even pay the wages the best summer help ask. So every year I have stupid, lazy greenhorns to deal with. But you've

175 heard me say this a thousand times. So has he, but it goes in one ear and out the other. He thinks money spent on a home is money wasted. He's lived too much in hotels. Never the best hotels, of course. Second-rate hotels. He doesn't understand a home. He doesn't feel at home in it. And yet, he wants a home. He's even proud of having this shabby place. He

180 loves it here. [*She laughs—a hopeless and yet amused laugh.*] It's really funny, when you come to think of it. He's a peculiar man.

EDMUND [*again attempting uneasily to look up in her eyes*]   What makes you ramble on like that, Mama?

MARY [*quickly casual—patting his cheek*]   Why, nothing in particular, dear. It

185 is foolish.

　　　　[*As she speaks,* CATHLEEN *enters from the back parlor.*]

CATHLEEN [*volubly*]   Lunch is ready, Ma'am, I went down to Mister Tyrone, like you ordered, and he said he'd come right away, but he kept on talking to that man, telling him of the time when—

MARY [*indifferently*]   All right, Cathleen. Tell Bridget I'm sorry but she'll have

190 to wait a few minutes until Mister Tyrone is here.

　　　　[CATHLEEN *mutters,* "Yes, Ma'am," *and goes off through the back parlor, grumbling to herself.*]

JAMIE   Damn it! Why don't you go ahead without him? He's told us to.

MARY [*with a remote, amused smile*]   He doesn't mean it. Don't you know your father yet? He'd be so terribly hurt.

EDMUND [*jumps up—as if he was glad of an excuse to leave*]   I'll make him get

195 a move on.

　　　　[*He goes out on the side porch. A moment later he is heard calling from the porch exasperatedly.*]

Hey! Papa! Come on! We can't wait all day!

　　　　[MARY *has risen from the arm of the chair. Her hands play restlessly over the tabletop. She does not look at* JAMIE *but she feels the cynically appraising glance he gives her face and hands.*]

MARY [*tensely*]   Why do you stare like that?

JAMIE   You know.

　　　　[*He turns back to the window.*]

MARY   I don't know.

200 JAMIE   Oh, for God's sake, do you think you can fool me, Mama? I'm not blind.

MARY [*looks directly at him now, her face set again in an expression of blank, stubborn denial*]   I don't know what you're talking about.

JAMIE   No? Take a look at your eyes in the mirror!

EDMUND [*coming in from the porch*]   I got Papa moving. He'll be here in a

205 minute. [*With a glance from one to the other, which his mother avoids— uneasily*] What's happened? What's the matter, Mama?

MARY [*disturbed by his coming, gives way to a flurry of guilty, nervous excitement*]   Your brother ought to be ashamed of himself. He's been insinuating I don't know what.

EDMUND [*turns on* JAMIE] God damn you!

[*He takes a threatening step toward him.* JAMIE *turns his back with a shrug and looks out the window.*]

210 MARY [*more upset, grabs* EDMUND's *arm—excitedly*] Stop this at once, do you hear me? How dare you use such language before me! [*Abruptly her tone and manner change to the strange detachment she has shown before.*] It's wrong to blame your brother. He can't help being what the past has made him. Any more than your father can. Or you. Or I.

215 EDMUND [*frightenedly—with a desperate hoping against hope*] He's a liar! It's a lie, isn't it, Mama?

MARY [*keeping her eyes averted*] What is a lie? Now you're talking in riddles like Jamie.

[*Then her eyes meet his stricken, accusing look. She stammers.*]

Edmund! Don't! [*She looks away and her manner instantly regains the qual-*
220 *ity of strange detachment—calmly.*] There's your father coming up the steps now. I must tell Bridget.

[*She goes through the back parlor.* EDMUND *moves slowly to his chair. He looks sick and hopeless.*]

JAMIE [*from the window, without looking around*] Well?

EDMUND [*refusing to admit anything to his brother yet—weakly defiant*] Well, what? You're a liar.

[JAMIE *again shrugs his shoulders. The screen door on the front porch is heard closing.* EDMUND *says dully*]

225 Here's Papa. I hope he loosens up with the old bottle.

[TYRONE *comes in through the front parlor. He is putting on his coat.*]

TYRONE Sorry I'm late. Captain Turner stopped to talk and once he starts gabbing you can't get away from him.

JAMIE [*without turning—dryly*] You mean once he starts listening.

[*His father regards him with dislike. He comes to the table with a quick measuring look at the bottle of whiskey. Without turning,* JAMIE *senses this.*]

It's all right. The level in the bottle hasn't changed.

230 TYRONE I wasn't noticing that. [*He adds caustically.*] As if it proved anything with you around. I'm on to your tricks.

EDMUND [*dully*] Did I hear you say, let's all have a drink?

TYRONE [*frowns at him*] Jamie is welcome after his hard morning's work, but I won't invite you. Doctor Hardy—

235 EDMUND To hell with Doctor Hardy! One isn't going to kill me. I feel—all in,[1] Papa.

TYRONE [*with a worried look at him—putting on a fake heartiness*] Come along, then. It's before a meal and I've always found that good whiskey, taken in moderation as an appetizer, is the best of tonics.

[EDMUND *gets up as his father passes the bottle to him. He pours a big drink.* TYRONE *frowns admonishingly.*]

240 I said, in moderation.

[*He pours his own drink and passes the bottle to* JAMIE, *grumbling.*]

It'd be a waste of breath mentioning moderation to you.

---

1. Exhausted.

[*Ignoring the hint,* JAMIE *pours a big drink. His father scowls—then, giving it up, resumes his hearty air, raising his glass.*]

Well, here's health and happiness!

[EDMUND *gives a bitter laugh.*]

EDMUND   That's a joke!

TYRONE   What is?

245 EDMUND   Nothing. Here's how.

[*They drink.*]

TYRONE [*becoming aware of the atmosphere*]   What's the matter here? There's gloom in the air you could cut with a knife. [*Turns on* JAMIE *resentfully.*] You got the drink you were after, didn't you? Why are you wearing that gloomy look on your mug?

250 JAMIE [*shrugging his shoulders*]   You won't be singing a song yourself soon.

EDMUND   Shut up, Jamie.

TYRONE [*uneasy now—changing the subject*]   I thought lunch was ready. I'm hungry as a hunter. Where is your mother?

MARY [*returning through the back parlor, calls*]   Here I am.

[*She comes in. She is excited and self-conscious. As she talks, she glances everywhere except at any of their faces.*]

255 I've had to calm down Bridget. She's in a tantrum over your being late again, and I don't blame her. If your lunch is dried up from waiting in the oven, she said it served you right, you could like it or leave it for all she cared. [*With increasing excitement*] Oh, I'm so sick and tired of pretending this is a home! You won't help me! You won't put yourself out the least bit! You don't know how to act in a home! You don't really want one! You never

260 have wanted one—never since the day we were married! You should have remained a bachelor and lived in second-rate hotels and entertained your friends in barrooms! [*She adds strangely, as if she were now talking aloud to herself rather than to* TYRONE] Then nothing would ever have happened.

[*They stare at her.* TYRONE *knows now. He suddenly looks a tired, bitterly sad old man.* EDMUND *glances at his father and sees that he knows, but he still cannot help trying to warn his mother.*]

265 EDMUND   Mama! Stop talking. Why don't we go in to lunch.

MARY [*starts and at once the quality of unnatural detachment settles on her face again. She even smiles with an ironical amusement to herself.*]   Yes, it is inconsiderate of me to dig up the past, when I know your father and Jamie must be hungry. [*Putting her arm around Edmund's shoulder—with a fond solicitude which is at the same time remote*] I do hope you have an appetite,

270 dear. You really must eat more. [*Her eyes become fixed on the whiskey glass on the table beside him—sharply.*] Why is that glass there? Did you take a drink? Oh, how can you be such a fool? Don't you know it's the worst thing?

[*She turns on* TYRONE.] You're to blame, James. How could you let him?

275 Do you want to kill him? Don't you remember my father? He wouldn't stop after he was stricken. He said doctors were fools! He thought, like you, that whiskey is a good tonic! [*A look of terror comes into her eyes and she stammers.*] But, of course, there's no comparison at all. I don't know why I—Forgive me for scolding you, James. One small drink won't hurt Edmund.

280 It might be good for him, if it gives him an appetite.

[*She pats* EDMUND's *cheek playfully, the strange detachment again in her manner. He jerks his head away. She seems not to notice, but she moves instinctively away.*]

JAMIE [*roughly, to hide his tense nerves*]   For God's sake, let's eat. I've been work-ing in the damned dirt under the hedge all morning. I've earned my grub.

[*He comes around in back of his father, not looking at his mother, and grabs* EDMUND's *shoulder.*]

Come on, Kid. Let's put on the feed bag.

[EDMUND *gets up, keeping his eyes averted from his mother. They pass her, heading for the back parlor.*]

TYRONE [*dully*]   Yes, you go in with your mother, lads. I'll join you in a second.

[*But they keep on without waiting for her. She looks at their backs with a helpless hurt and, as they enter the back parlor, starts to follow them.* TYRONE's *eyes are on her, sad and condemning. She feels them and turns sharply without meeting his stare.*]

MARY   Why do you look at me like that? [*Her hands flutter up to pat her hair.*]
Is it my hair coming down? I was so worn out from last night. I thought I'd
285   better lie down this morning. I drowsed off and had a nice refreshing nap.
But I'm sure I fixed my hair again when I woke up. [*Forcing a laugh*]
Although, as usual, I couldn't find my glasses. [*Sharply*] Please stop star-ing! One would think you were accusing me— [*Then pleadingly*] James!
You don't understand!

290   TYRONE [*with dull anger*]   I understand that I've been a God-damned fool to
believe in you!

[*He walks away from her to pour himself a big drink.*]

MARY [*her face again sets in stubborn defiance*]   I don't know what you mean
by "believing in me." All I've felt was distrust and spying and suspicion.
[*Then accusingly*] Why are you having another drink? You never have more
295   than one before lunch. [*Bitterly*] I know what to expect. You will be drunk
tonight. Well, it won't be the first time, will it—or the thousandth? [*Again
she bursts out pleadingly.*] Oh, James, please! You don't understand! I'm so
worried about Edmund! I'm so afraid he—

TYRONE   I don't want to listen to your excuses, Mary.

300   MARY [*strickenly*]   Excuses? You mean—? Oh, you can't believe that of me!
You mustn't believe that, James! [*Then slipping away into her strange
detachment—quite casually*] Shall we not go into lunch, dear? I don't want
anything but I know you're hungry.

[*He walks slowly to where she stands in the doorway. He walks like an old
305   man. As he reaches her she bursts out piteously.*]

James! I tried so hard! I tried so hard! Please believe—!

TYRONE [*moved in spite of himself—helplessly*]   I suppose you did, Mary.
[*Then grief-strickenly*] For the love of God, why couldn't you have the
strength to keep on?

MARY [*her face setting into that stubborn denial again*]   I don't know what
you're talking about. Have the strength to keep on what?

310   TYRONE [*hopelessly*]   Never mind. It's no use now.

[*He moves on and she keeps beside him as they disappear in the back
parlor.*]

Curtain.

Act 2, Scene 2

SCENE: *The same, about a half hour later. The tray with the bottle of whiskey has been removed from the table. The family are returning from lunch as the curtain rises.* MARY *is the first to enter from the back parlor. Her husband follows. He is not with her as he was in the similar entrance after breakfast at the opening of Act 1. He avoids touching her or looking at her. There is condemnation in his face, mingled now with the beginning of an old weary, helpless resignation.* JAMIE *and* EDMUND *follow their father.* JAMIE's *face is hard with defensive cynicism.* EDMUND *tries to copy this defense but without success. He plainly shows he is heartsick as well as physically ill.*

MARY *is terribly nervous again, as if the strain of sitting through lunch with them had been too much for her. Yet at the same time, in contrast to this, her expression shows more of that strange aloofness which seems to stand apart from her nerves and the anxieties which harry them.*

She is talking as she enters—a stream of words that issues casually, in a routine of family conversation, from her mouth. She appears indifferent to the fact that their thoughts are not on what she is saying any more than her own are. As she talks, she comes to the left of the table and stands, facing front, one hand fumbling with the bosom of her dress, the other playing over the tabletop. TYRONE *lights a cigar and goes to the screen door, staring out.* JAMIE *fills a pipe from a jar on top of the bookcase at rear. He lights it as he goes to look out the window at right.* EDMUND *sits in a chair by the table, turned half away from his mother so he does not have to watch her.*

MARY   It's no use finding fault with Bridget. She doesn't listen. I can't threaten her, or she'd threaten she'd leave. And she does do her best at times. It's too bad they seem to be just the times you're sure to be late, James. Well, there's this consolation: it's difficult to tell from her cooking whether she's doing
5   her best or her worst. [*She gives a little laugh of detached amusement— indifferently.*] Never mind. The summer will soon be over, thank goodness. Your season will open again and we can go back to second-rate hotels and trains. I hate them, too, but at least I don't expect them to be like a home, and there's no housekeeping to worry about. It's unreasonable to expect
10   Bridget or Cathleen to act as if this was a home. They know it isn't as well as we know it. It never has been and it never will be.
TYRONE [*bitterly without turning around*]   No, it never can be now. But it was once, before you—
MARY [*her face instantly set in blank denial*]   Before I what?
       [*There is a dead silence. She goes on with a return of her detached air.*]
15   No, no. Whatever you mean, it isn't true, dear. It was never a home. You've always preferred the Club or a barroom. And for me it's always been as lonely as a dirty room in a one-night-stand hotel. In a real home one is never lonely. You forget I know from experience what a home is like. I gave up one to marry you—my father's home.
       [*At once, through an association of ideas she turns to* EDMUND. *Her manner becomes tenderly solicitous, but there is the strange quality of detachment in it.*]
20   I'm worried about you, Edmund. You hardly touched a thing at lunch. That's no way to take care of yourself. It's all right for me not to have an appetite. I've been growing too fat. But you must eat. [*Coaxingly maternal*] Promise me you will, dear, for my sake.
EDMUND [*dully*]   Yes, Mama.

25 MARY [*pats his cheek as he tries not to shrink away*]   That's a good boy.

> [*There is another pause of dead silence. Then the telephone in the front hall rings and all of them stiffen startledly.*]

TYRONE [*hastily*]   I'll answer. McGuire said he'd call me.

> [*He goes out through the front parlor.*]

MARY [*indifferently*]   McGuire. He must have another piece of property on his list that no one would think of buying except your father. It doesn't matter any more, but it's always seemed to me your father could afford to

30 keep on buying property but never to give me a home. [*She stops to listen as* TYRONE's *voice is heard from the hall.*]

TYRONE   Hello. [*With forced heartiness*] Oh, how are you, Doctor?

> [JAMIE *turns from the window.* MARY's *fingers play more rapidly on the tabletop.* TYRONE's *voice, trying to conceal, reveals that he is hearing bad news.*]

I see— [*Hurriedly*] Well, you'll explain all about it when you see him this afternoon. Yes, he'll be in without fail. Four o'clock. I'll drop in myself and have a talk with you before that. I have to go uptown on business, anyway.

35 Goodbye, Doctor.

EDMUND [*dully*]   That didn't sound like glad tidings.

> [JAMIE *gives him a pitying glance—then looks out the window again.* MARY's *face is terrified and her hands flutter distractedly.* TYRONE *comes in. The strain is obvious in his casualness as he addresses* EDMUND.]

TYRONE   It was Doctor Hardy. He wants you to be sure and see him at four.

EDMUND [*dully*]   What did he say? Not that I give a damn now.

MARY [*bursts out excitedly*]   I wouldn't believe him if he swore on a stack of

40 Bibles. You mustn't pay attention to a word he says, Edmund.

TYRONE [*sharply*]   Mary!

MARY [*more excitedly*]   Oh, we all realize why you like him, James! Because he's cheap! But please don't try to tell me! I know all about Doctor Hardy. Heaven knows I ought to after all these years. He's an ignorant fool! There

45 should be a law to keep men like him from practicing. He hasn't the slightest idea— When you're in agony and half insane, he sits and holds your hand and delivers sermons on willpower!

> [*Her face is drawn in an expression of intense suffering by the memory. For the moment, she loses all caution. With bitter hatred.*]

He deliberately humiliates you! He makes you beg and plead! He treats you like a criminal! He understands nothing! And yet it was exactly the same

50 type of cheap quack who first gave you the medicine—and you never knew what it was until too late! [*Passionately*] I hate doctors! They'll do anything— anything to keep you coming to them. They'll sell their souls! What's worse, they'll sell yours, and you never know it till one day you find yourself in hell!

55 EDMUND   Mama! For God's sake, stop talking.

TYRONE [*shakenly*]   Yes, Mary, it's no time—

MARY [*suddenly is overcome by guilty confusion—stammers*]   I— Forgive me, dear. You're right. It's useless to be angry now.

> [*There is again a pause of dead silence. When she speaks again, her face has cleared and is calm, and the quality of uncanny detachment is in her voice and manner.*]

I'm going upstairs for a moment, if you'll excuse me. I have to fix my hair.

60 [*She adds smilingly.*] That is if I can find my glasses. I'll be right down.

TYRONE [*as she starts through the doorway—pleading and rebuking*] Mary!

MARY [*turns to stare at him calmly*] Yes, dear? What is it?

TYRONE [*helplessly*] Nothing.

MARY [*with a strange derisive smile*] You're welcome to come up and watch
65 me if you're so suspicious.

TYRONE As if that could do any good! You'd only postpone it. And I'm not
your jailor. This isn't a prison.

MARY No. I know you can't help thinking it's a home. [*She adds quickly with
a detached contrition.*] I'm sorry, dear. I don't mean to be bitter. It's not your
70 fault.

> [*She turns and disappears through the back parlor. The three in the room
> remain silent. It is as if they were waiting until she got upstairs before
> speaking.*]

JAMIE [*cynically brutal*] Another shot in the arm!

EDMUND [*angrily*] Cut out that kind of talk!

TYRONE Yes! Hold your foul tongue and your rotten Broadway loafer's lingo!
Have you no pity or decency? [*Losing his temper*] You ought to be kicked
75 out in the gutter! But if I did it, you know damned well who'd weep and
plead for you, and excuse you and complain till I let you come back.

JAMIE [*a spasm of pain crosses his face*] Christ, don't I know that? No pity? I
have all the pity in the world for her. I understand what a hard game to
beat she's up against—which is more than you ever have! My lingo didn't
80 mean I had no feeling. I was merely putting bluntly what we all know, and
have to live with now, again. [*Bitterly*] The cures are no damned good
except for a while. The truth is there is no cure and we've been saps to
hope— [*Cynically*] They never come back!

EDMUND [*scornfully parodying his brother's cynicism*] They never come back!
85 Everything is in the bag! It's all a frame-up! We're all fall guys and suckers
and we can't beat the game! [*Disdainfully*] Christ, if I felt the way you do—!

JAMIE [*stung for a moment—then shrugging his shoulders, dryly*] I thought
you did. Your poetry isn't very cheery. Nor the stuff you read and claim you
admire. [*He indicates the small bookcase at rear.*] Your pet with the unpro-
90 nounceable name, for example.

EDMUND Nietzsche.[2] You don't know what you're talking about. You haven't
read him.

JAMIE Enough to know it's a lot of bunk!

TYRONE Shut up, both of you! There's little choice between the philosophy
95 you learned from Broadway loafers, and the one Edmund got from his
books. They're both rotten to the core. You've both flouted the faith you
were born and brought up in—the one true faith of the Catholic Church—
and your denial has brought nothing but self-destruction!

> [*His two sons stare at him contemptuously. They forget their quarrel and
> are as one against him on this issue.*]

EDMUND That's the bunk, Papa!

100 JAMIE We don't pretend, at any rate. [*Caustically*] I don't notice you've worn
any holes in the knees of your pants going to Mass.

---

2. Friedrich Nietzsche (1844–1900), the German philosopher who, in such works as *Thus Spake Zarathustra* (1883–85), challenged religion and conventional philosophy. He also influenced modern dramatists such as August Strindberg and O'Neill with his theory of tragedy, as put forth in *The Birth of Tragedy* (1872).

TYRONE   It's true I'm a bad Catholic in the observance, God forgive me. But I believe! [*Angrily*] And you're a liar! I may not go to church but every night and morning of my life I get on my knees and pray!

105 EDMUND [*bitingly*]   Did you pray for Mama?

TYRONE   I did. I've prayed to God these many years for her.

EDMUND   Then Nietzsche must be right. [*He quotes from* Thus Spake Zarathustra.] "God is dead: of His pity for man hath God died."

TYRONE [*ignores this*]   If your mother had prayed, too— She hasn't denied

110 her faith, but she's forgotten it, until now there's no strength of the spirit left in her to fight against her curse. [*Then dully resigned*] But what's the good of talk? We've lived with this before and now we must again. There's no help for it. [*Bitterly*] Only I wish she hadn't led me to hope this time. By God, I never will again!

115 EDMUND   That's a rotten thing to say, Papa! [*Defiantly*] Well, I'll hope! She's just started. It can't have got a hold on her yet. She can still stop. I'm going to talk to her.

JAMIE [*shrugs his shoulders*]   You can't talk to her now. She'll listen but she won't listen. She'll be here but she won't be here. You know the way she

120 gets.

TYRONE   Yes, that's the way the poison acts on her always. Every day from now on, there'll be the same drifting away from us until by the end of each night—

EDMUND [*miserably*]   Cut it out, Papa! [*He jumps up from his chair.*] I'm

125 going to get dressed. [*Bitterly, as he goes*] I'll make so much noise she can't suspect I've come to spy on her.

[*He disappears through the front parlor and can be heard stamping noisily upstairs.*]

JAMIE [*after a pause*]   What did Doc Hardy say about the Kid?

TYRONE [*dully*]   It's what you thought. He's got consumption.

JAMIE   God damn it!

130 TYRONE   There is no possible doubt, he said.

JAMIE   He'll have to go to a sanatorium.

TYRONE   Yes, and the sooner the better, Hardy said, for him and everyone around him. He claims that in six months to a year Edmund will be cured, if he obeys orders. [*He sighs—gloomily and resentfully.*] I never thought a

135 child of mine— It doesn't come from my side of the family. There wasn't one of us that didn't have lungs as strong as an ox.

JAMIE   Who gives a damn about that part of it! Where does Hardy want to send him?

TYRONE   That's what I'm to see him about.

140 JAMIE   Well, for God's sake, pick out a good place and not some cheap dump!

TYRONE [*stung*]   I'll send him wherever Hardy thinks best!

JAMIE   Well, don't give Hardy your old over-the-hills-to-the-poorhouse song about taxes and mortgages.

TYRONE   I'm no millionaire who can throw money away! Why shouldn't I tell

145 Hardy the truth?

JAMIE   Because he'll think you want him to pick a cheap dump, and because he'll know it isn't the truth—especially if he hears afterwards you've seen McGuire and let that flannel-mouth, gold-brick merchant sting you with another piece of bum property!

150 TYRONE [*furiously*]   Keep your nose out of my business!

JAMIE   This is Edmund's business. What I'm afraid of is, with your Irish bog-trotter[3] idea that consumption is fatal, you'll figure it would be a waste of money to spend any more than you can help.

TYRONE   You liar!

155 JAMIE   All right. Prove I'm a liar. That's what I want. That's why I brought it up.

TYRONE [*his rage still smouldering*]   I have every hope Edmund will be cured. And keep your dirty tongue off Ireland! You're a fine one to sneer, with the map of it on your face!

160 JAMIE   Not after I wash my face. [*Then before his father can react to this insult to the Old Sod, he adds dryly, shrugging his shoulders.*] Well, I've said all I have to say. It's up to you. [*Abruptly*] What do you want me to do this afternoon, now you're going uptown? I've done all I can do on the hedge until you cut more of it. You don't want me to go ahead with your clipping,

165 I know that.

TYRONE   No. You'd get it crooked, as you get everything else.

JAMIE   Then I'd better go uptown with Edmund. The bad news coming on top of what's happened to Mama may hit him hard.

TYRONE [*forgetting his quarrel*]   Yes, go with him, Jamie. Keep up his spirits,

170 if you can. [*He adds caustically.*] If you can without making it an excuse to get drunk!

JAMIE   What would I use for money? The last I heard they were still selling booze, not giving it away. [*He starts for the front-parlor doorway.*] I'll get dressed.

[*He stops in the doorway as he sees his mother approaching from the hall, and moves aside to let her come in. Her eyes look brighter, and her manner is more detached. This change becomes more marked as the scene goes on.*]

175 MARY [*vaguely*]   You haven't seen my glasses anywhere, have you, Jamie?

[*She doesn't look at him. He glances away, ignoring her question but she doesn't seem to expect an answer. She comes forward, addressing her husband without looking at him.*]

You haven't seen them, have you, James?

[*Behind her JAMIE disappears through the front parlor.*]

TYRONE [*turns to look out the screen door*]   No, Mary.

MARY   What's the matter with Jamie? Have you been nagging at him again? You shouldn't treat him with such contempt all the time. He's not to blame.

180   If he'd been brought up in a real home, I'm sure he would have been different. [*She comes to the windows at right—lightly.*] You're not much of a weather prophet, dear. See how hazy it's getting. I can hardly see the other shore.

TYRONE [*trying to speak naturally*]   Yes, I spoke too soon. We're in for another

185 night of fog, I'm afraid.

MARY   Oh, well, I won't mind it tonight.

TYRONE   No, I don't imagine you will, Mary.

MARY [*flashes a glance at him—after a pause*]   I don't see Jamie going down to the hedge. Where did he go?

3. A derogatory nickname for the Irish.

190 TYRONE He's going with Edmund to the doctor's. He went up to change his clothes. [*Then, glad of an excuse to leave her*] I'd better do the same or I'll be late for my appointment at the Club.

[*He makes a move toward the front-parlor doorway, but with a swift impulsive movement she reaches out and clasps his arm.*]

MARY [*a note of pleading in her voice*] Don't go yet, dear. I don't want to be alone. [*Hastily*] I mean, you have plenty of time. You know you boast you
195 can dress in one-tenth the time it takes the boys. [*Vaguely*] There is something I wanted to say. What is it? I've forgotten. I'm glad Jamie is going uptown. You didn't give him any money, I hope.

TYRONE I did not.

MARY He'd only spend it on drink and you know what a vile, poisonous
200 tongue he has when he's drunk. Not that I would mind anything he said tonight, but he always manages to drive you into a rage, especially if you're drunk, too, as you will be.

TYRONE [*resentfully*] I won't. I never get drunk.

MARY [*teasing indifferently*] Oh, I'm sure you'll hold it well. You always have.
205 It's hard for a stranger to tell, but after thirty-five years of marriage—

TYRONE I've never missed a performance in my life. That's the proof! [*Then bitterly*] If I did get drunk it is not you who should blame me. No man has ever had a better reason.

MARY Reason? What reason? You always drink too much when you go to the
210 Club, don't you? Particularly when you meet McGuire. He sees to that. Don't think I'm finding fault, dear. You must do as you please. I won't mind.

TYRONE I know you won't [*He turns toward the front parlor, anxious to escape.*] I've got to get dressed.

MARY [*again she reaches out and grasps his arm—pleadingly*] No, please wait
215 a little while, dear. At least, until one of the boys comes down. You will all be leaving me so soon.

TYRONE [*with bitter sadness*] It's you who are leaving us, Mary.

MARY I? That's a silly thing to say, James. How could I leave? There is nowhere I could go. Who would I go to see? I have no friends.

220 TYRONE It's your own fault— [*He stops and sighs helplessly—persuasively.*] There's surely one thing you can do this afternoon that will be good for you, Mary. Take a drive in the automobile. Get away from the house. Get a little sun and fresh air. [*Injuredly*] I bought the automobile for you. You know I don't like the damned things. I'd rather walk any day, or take a trol-
225 ley. [*With growing resentment*] I had it here waiting for you when you came back from the sanatorium. I hoped it would give you pleasure and distract your mind. You used to ride in it every day, but you've hardly used it at all lately. I paid a lot of money I couldn't afford, and there's the chauffeur I have to board and lodge and pay high wages whether he drives you or not.
230 [*Bitterly*] Waste! The same old waste that will land me in the poorhouse in my old age! What good did it do you? I might as well have thrown the money out the window.

MARY [*with detached calm*] Yes, it was a waste of money, James. You shouldn't have bought a secondhand automobile. You were swindled again as you
235 always are, because you insist on secondhand bargains in everything.

TYRONE It's one of the best makes! Everyone says it's better than any of the new ones!

MARY [*ignoring this*]   It was another waste to hire Smythe, who was only a
helper in a garage and had never been a chauffeur. Oh, I realize his wages
240   are less than a real chauffeur's, but he more than makes up for that, I'm
sure, by the graft he gets from the garage on repair bills. Something is
always wrong. Smythe sees to that, I'm afraid.

TYRONE   I don't believe it! He may not be a fancy millionaire's flunky but he's
honest! You're as bad as Jamie, suspecting everyone!

245   MARY   You mustn't be offended, dear. I wasn't offended when you gave me
the automobile. I knew you didn't mean to humiliate me. I knew that was
the way you had to do everything. I was grateful and touched. I knew buying the car was a hard thing for you to do, and it proved how much you
loved me, in your way, especially when you couldn't really believe it would
250   do me any good.

TYRONE   Mary! [*He suddenly hugs her to him—brokenly.*] Dear Mary! For the
love of God, for my sake and the boys' sake and your own, won't you stop
now?

MARY [*stammers in guilty confusion for a second*]   I— James! Please! [*Her
255   strange, stubborn defense comes back instantly.*] Stop what? What are you
talking about?

[*He lets his arm fall to his side brokenly. She impulsively puts her arm
around him.*]

James! We've loved each other! We always will! Let's remember only that,
and not try to understand what we cannot understand, or help things that
cannot be helped—the things life has done to us we cannot excuse or
260   explain.

TYRONE [*as if he hadn't heard—bitterly*]   You won't even try?

MARY [*her arms drop hopelessly and she turns away—with detachment*]   Try to
go for a drive this afternoon, you mean? Why, yes, if you wish me to,
although it makes me feel lonelier than if I stayed here. There is no one I
265   can invite to drive with me, and I never know where to tell Smythe to go. If
there was a friend's house where I could drop in and laugh and gossip
awhile. But, of course, there isn't. There never has been. [*Her manner
becoming more and more remote*] At the Convent I had so many friends.
Girls whose families lived in lovely homes. I used to visit them and they'd
270   visit me in my father's home. But, naturally, after I married an actor—you
know how actors were considered in those days—a lot of them gave me the
cold shoulder. And then, right after we were married, there was the scandal
of that woman who had been your mistress, suing you. From then on, all
my old friends either pitied me or cut me dead.[4] I hated the ones who cut
275   me much less than the pitiers.

TYRONE [*with guilty resentment*]   For God's sake, don't dig up what's long
forgotten. If you're that far gone in the past already, when it's only the
beginning of the afternoon, what will you be tonight?

MARY [*stares at him defiantly now*]   Come to think of it, I do have to drive
280   uptown. There's something I must get at the drugstore.

TYRONE [*bitterly scornful*]   Leave it to you to have some of the stuff hidden,
and prescriptions for more! I hope you'll lay in a good stock ahead so we'll
never have another night like the one when you screamed for it, and ran

---

4. Pretended not to know her; broke off their acquaintance.

out of the house in your nightdress half crazy, to try and throw yourself off
285   the dock!

MARY [*tries to ignore this*]   I have to get tooth powder and toilet soap and cold
cream— [*She breaks down pitiably.*] James! You mustn't remember! You
mustn't humiliate me so!

TYRONE [*ashamed*]   I'm sorry. Forgive me, Mary!

290   MARY [*defensively detached again*]   It doesn't matter. Nothing like that ever
happened. You must have dreamed it.

[*He stares at her hopelessly. Her voice seems to drift farther and farther
away.*]

I was so healthy before Edmund was born. You remember, James. There
wasn't a nerve in my body. Even traveling with you season after season,
with week after week of one-night stands, in trains without Pullmans,[5] in
295   dirty rooms of filthy hotels, eating bad food, bearing children in hotel rooms,
I still kept healthy. But bearing Edmund was the last straw. I was so sick
afterwards, and that ignorant quack of a cheap hotel doctor— All he knew
was I was in pain. It was easy for him to stop the pain.

TYRONE   Mary! For God's sake, forget the past!

300   MARY [*with strange objective calm*]   Why? How can I? The past is the present, isn't it? It's the future, too. We all try to lie out of that but life won't let
us. [*Going on*] I blame only myself. I swore after Eugene died I would
never have another baby. I was to blame for his death. If I hadn't left him
with my mother to join you on the road, because you wrote telling me you
305   missed me and were so lonely, Jamie would never have been allowed, when
he still had measles, to go in the baby's room. [*Her face hardening*] I've
always believed Jamie did it on purpose. He was jealous of the baby. He
hated him. [*As Tyrone starts to protest.*] Oh, I know Jamie was only seven,
but he was never stupid. He'd been warned it might kill the baby. He knew.
310   I've never been able to forgive him for that.

TYRONE [*with bitter sadness*]   Are you back with Eugene now? Can't you let
our dead baby rest in peace?

MARY [*as if she hadn't heard him*]   It was my fault. I should have insisted on
staying with Eugene and not have let you persuade me to join you, just
315   because I loved you. Above all, I shouldn't have let you insist I have another
baby to take Eugene's place, because you thought that would make me
forget his death. I knew from experience by then that children should have
homes to be born in, if they are to be good children, and women need
homes, if they are to be good mothers. I was afraid all the time I carried
320   Edmund. I knew something terrible would happen. I knew I'd proved by
the way I'd left Eugene that I wasn't worthy to have another baby, and that
God would punish me if I did. I never should have borne Edmund.

TYRONE [*with an uneasy glance through the front parlor*]   Mary! Be careful
with your talk. If he heard you he might think you never wanted him. He's
325   feeling bad enough already without—

MARY [*violently*]   It's a lie! I did want him! More than anything in the world!
You don't understand! I meant, for his sake. He has never been happy. He
never will be. Nor healthy. He was born nervous and too sensitive, and

5. Sleeping cars.

that's my fault. And now, ever since he's been so sick I've kept remembering
330   Eugene and my father and I've been so frightened and guilty— [*Then,
catching herself, with an instant change to stubborn denial*] Oh, I know it's
foolish to imagine dreadful things when there's no reason for it. After all,
everyone has colds and gets over them.

[*TYRONE stares at her and sighs helplessly. He turns away toward the front
parlor and sees EDMUND coming down the stairs in the hall.*]

TYRONE [*sharply, in a low voice*]   Here's Edmund. For God's sake try and be
335   yourself—at least until he goes! You can do that much for him!

[*He waits, forcing his face into a pleasantly paternal expression. She
waits frightenedly, seized again by a nervous panic, her hands fluttering
over the bosom of her dress, up to her throat and hair, with a distracted
aimlessness. Then, as EDMUND approaches the doorway, she cannot face
him. She goes swiftly away to the windows at left and stares out with her
back to the front parlor. EDMUND enters. He has changed to a ready-made
blue serge suit, high stiff collar and tie, black shoes.*]

[*With an actor's heartiness*] Well! You look spic and span. I'm on my way up
to change, too.

[*He starts to pass him.*]

EDMUND [*dryly*]   Wait a minute, Papa. I hate to bring up disagreeable topics,
but there's the matter of carfare. I'm broke.

340 TYRONE [*starts automatically on a customary lecture*]   You'll always be broke
until you learn the value— [*Checks himself guiltily, looking at his son's sick
face with worried pity.*] But you've been learning, lad. You worked hard
before you took ill. You've done splendidly. I'm proud of you.

[*He pulls out a small roll of bills from his pants pocket and carefully
selects one. EDMUND takes it. He glances at it and his face expresses
astonishment. His father again reacts customarily—sarcastically.*]

Thank you. [*He quotes.*] "How sharper than a serpent's tooth it is—"
345 EDMUND   "To have a thankless child."[6] I know. Give me a chance, Papa. I'm
knocked speechless. This isn't a dollar. It's a ten spot.

TYRONE [*embarrassed by his generosity*]   Put it in your pocket. You'll probably
meet some of your friends uptown and you can't hold your end up and be
sociable with nothing in your jeans.

350 EDMUND   You meant it? Gosh, thank you, Papa. [*He is genuinely pleased and
grateful for a moment—then he stares at his father's face with uneasy suspicion.*] But why all of a sudden—? [*Cynically*] Did Doc Hardy tell you I was
going to die? [*Then he sees his father is bitterly hurt.*] No! That's a rotten
crack. I was only kidding, Papa.

[*He puts an arm around his father impulsively and gives him an affectionate hug.*]

I'm very grateful. Honest, Papa.
355 TYRONE [*touched, returns his hug*]   You're welcome, lad.

MARY [*suddenly turns to them in a confused panic of frightened anger*]   I won't
have it! [*She stamps her foot.*] Do you hear, Edmund! Such morbid nonsense! Saying you're going to die! It's the books you read! Nothing but sadness and death! Your father shouldn't allow you to have them. And some of

---

6. Quoting Lear, from Shakespeare's *King Lear* (1605), 1.4.251–52.

360 the poems you've written yourself are even worse! You'd think you didn't want to live! A boy of your age with everything before him! It's just a pose you get out of books! You're not really sick at all!

TYRONE   Mary! Hold your tongue!

MARY [*instantly changing to a detached tone*]   But, James, it's absurd of Edmund
365 to be so gloomy and make such a great to-do about nothing. [*Turning to* EDMUND *but avoiding his eyes—teasingly affectionate*] Never mind, dear. I'm on to you. [*She comes to him.*] You want to be petted and spoiled and made a fuss over, isn't that it? You're still such a baby.

> [*She puts her arm around him and hugs him. He remains rigid and unyielding. Her voice begins to tremble.*]

But please don't carry it too far, dear. Don't say horrible things. I know it's fool-
370 ish to take them seriously but I can't help it. You've got me—so frightened.

> [*She breaks and hides her face on his shoulder, sobbing.* EDMUND *is moved in spite of himself. He pats her shoulder with an awkward tenderness.*]

EDMUND   Don't, mother. [*His eyes meet his father's.*]

TYRONE [*huskily—clutching at hopeless hope*]   Maybe if you asked your mother now what you said you were going to— [*He fumbles with his*
375 *watch.*] By God, look at the time! I'll have to shake a leg.

> [*He hurries away through the front parlor.* MARY *lifts her head. Her manner is again one of detached motherly solicitude. She seems to have forgotten the tears which are still in her eyes.*]

MARY   How do you feel, dear? [*She feels his forehead.*] Your head is a little hot, but that's just from going out in the sun. You look ever so much better than you did this morning. [*Taking his hand*] Come and sit down. You mustn't stand on your feet so much. You must learn to husband your
380 strength.

> [*She gets him to sit and she sits sideways on the arm of his chair, an arm around his shoulder, so he cannot meet her eyes.*]

EDMUND [*starts to blurt out the appeal he now feels is quite hopeless*]   Listen, Mama—

MARY [*interrupting quickly*]   Now, now! Don't talk. Lean back and rest. [*Persuasively*] You know, I think it would be much better for you if you stayed
385 home this afternoon and let me take care of you. It's such a tiring trip uptown in the dirty old trolley on a hot day like this. I'm sure you'd be much better off here with me.

EDMUND [*dully*]   You forget I have an appointment with Hardy. [*Trying again to get his appeal started*] Listen, Mama—

390 MARY [*quickly*]   You can telephone and say you don't feel well enough. [*Excitedly*] It's simply a waste of time and money seeing him. He'll only tell you some lie. He'll pretend he's found something serious the matter because that's his bread and butter. [*She gives a hard sneering little laugh.*] The old idiot! All he knows about medicine is to look solemn and preach willpower!

395 EDMUND [*trying to catch her eyes*]   Mama! Please listen! I want to ask you something! You— You're only just started. You can still stop. You've got the willpower! We'll all help you. I'll do anything! Won't you, Mama?

MARY [*stammers pleadingly*]   Please don't—talk about things you don't understand!

400 EDMUND [*dully*]   All right, I give up. I knew it was no use.

MARY [*in blank denial now*]   Anyway, I don't know what you're referring to. But I do know you should be the last one— Right after I returned from the sanatorium, you began to be ill. The doctor there had warned me I must have peace at home with nothing to upset me, and all I've done is worry

405 about you. [*Then distractedly*] But that's no excuse! I'm only trying to explain. It's not an excuse! [*She hugs him to her—pleadingly.*] Promise me, dear, you won't believe I made you an excuse.

EDMUND [*bitterly*]   What else can I believe?

MARY [*slowly takes her arm away—her manner remote and objective again*] Yes, I suppose you can't help suspecting that.

410 EDMUND [*ashamed but still bitter*]   What do you expect?

MARY   Nothing, I don't blame you. How could you believe me—when I can't believe myself? I've become such a liar. I never lied about anything once upon a time. Now I have to lie, especially to myself. But how can you understand, when I don't myself. I've never understood anything about it,

415 except that one day long ago I found I could no longer call my soul my own. [*She pauses—then lowering her voice to a strange tone of whispered confidence.*] But someday, dear, I will find it again—someday when you're all well, and I see you healthy and happy and successful, and I don't have to feel guilty anymore—someday when the Blessed Virgin Mary forgives me and gives me back the faith in Her love and pity I used to have in my con-

420 vent days, and I can pray to Her again—when She sees no one in the world can believe in me even for a moment anymore, then She will believe in me, and with Her help it will be so easy. I will hear myself scream with agony, and at the same time I will laugh because I will be so sure of myself. [*Then as Edmund remains hopelessly silent, she adds sadly.*] Of course, you can't

425 believe that, either.

[*She rises from the arm of his chair and goes to stare out the windows at right with her back to him—casually.*]

Now I think of it, you might as well go uptown. I forgot I'm taking a drive. I have to go to the drugstore. You would hardly want to go there with me. You'd be so ashamed.

EDMUND [*brokenly*]   Mama! Don't!

430 MARY   I suppose you'll divide that ten dollars your father gave you with Jamie. You always divide with each other, don't you? Like good sports. Well, I know what he'll do with his share. Get drunk someplace where he can be with the only kind of woman he understands or likes. [*She turns to him, pleading frightenedly.*] Edmund! Promise me you won't drink! It's so dan-

435 gerous! You know Doctor Hardy told you—

EDMUND [*bitterly*]   I thought he was an old idiot. Anyway, by tonight, what will you care?

MARY [*pitifully*]   Edmund!

[*JAMIE's voice is heard from the front hall, "Come on, Kid, let's beat it."*]

[*MARY's manner at once becomes detached again.*]

Go on, Edmund. Jamie's waiting.

[*She goes to the front-parlor doorway.*]

440 There comes your father downstairs, too.

[*TYRONE's voice calls, "Come on, Edmund."*]

EDMUND [*jumping up from his chair*]   I'm coming.

[*He stops beside her—without looking at her.*]
Goodbye, Mama.

MARY [*kisses him with detached affection*]   Goodbye, dear. If you're coming home for dinner, try not to be late. And tell your father. You know what
445   Bridget is.

[*He turns and hurries away.* TYRONE *calls from the hall,* "*Goodbye, Mary,*" *and then* JAMIE, "*Goodbye, Mama.*"]

[*She calls back.*] Goodbye.

[*The front screen door is heard closing after them. She comes and stands by the table, one hand drumming on it, the other fluttering up to pat her hair. She stares about the room with frightened, forsaken eyes and whispers to herself.*]

It's so lonely here. [*Then her face hardens into bitter self-contempt.*] You're lying to yourself again. You wanted to get rid of them. Their contempt and disgust aren't pleasant company. You're glad they're gone. [*She gives a little*
450   *despairing laugh.*] Then Mother of God, why do I feel so lonely?

Curtain.

Act 3

SCENE: *The same. It is around half past six in the evening. Dusk is gathering in the living room, an early dusk due to the fog which has rolled in from the Sound*[7] *and is like a white curtain drawn down outside the windows. From a lighthouse beyond the harbor's mouth, a foghorn is heard at regular intervals, moaning like a mournful whale in labor, and from the harbor itself, intermittently, comes the warning ringing of bells on yachts at anchor.*

The tray with the bottle of whiskey, glasses, and pitcher of ice water is on the table, as it was in the pre-luncheon scene of the previous act.

MARY *and the second girl,* CATHLEEN, *are discovered. The latter is standing at left of table. She holds an empty whiskey glass in her hand as if she'd forgotten she had it. She shows the effects of drink. Her stupid, good-humored face wears a pleased and flattered simper.*

MARY *is paler than before and her eyes shine with unnatural brilliance. The strange detachment in her manner has intensified. She has hidden deeper within herself and found refuge and release in a dream where present reality is but an appearance to be accepted and dismissed unfeelingly—even with a hard cynicism—or entirely ignored. There is at times an uncanny gay, free youthfulness in her manner, as if in spirit she were released to become again, simply and without self-consciousness, the naive, happy, chattering schoolgirl of her convent days. She wears the dress into which she had changed for her drive to town, a simple, fairly expensive affair, which would be extremely becoming if it were not for the careless, almost slovenly way she wears it. Her hair is no longer fastidiously in place. It has a slightly disheveled, lopsided look. She talks to* CATHLEEN *with a confiding familiarity, as if the second girl were an old, intimate friend. As the curtain rises, she is standing by the screen door looking out. A moan of the foghorn is heard.*

7. Long Island Sound.

MARY [amused—girlishly]   That foghorn! Isn't it awful, Cathleen?

CATHLEEN [talks more familiarly than usual but never with intentional impertinence because she sincerely likes her mistress]   It is indeed, Ma'am. It's like
a banshee.[8]

MARY [goes on as if she hadn't heard. In nearly all the following dialogue there
is the feeling that she has CATHLEEN with her merely as an excuse to keep
talking.]   I don't mind it tonight. Last night it drove me crazy. I lay awake
5   worrying until I couldn't stand it anymore.

CATHLEEN   Bad cess[9] to it. I was scared out of my wits riding back from town.
I thought that ugly monkey, Smythe, would drive us in a ditch or against a
tree. You couldn't see your hand in front of you. I'm glad you had me sit in
back with you, Ma'am. If I'd been in front with that monkey— He can't keep
10   his dirty hands to himself. Give him half a chance and he's pinching me on
the leg or you-know-where—asking your pardon, Ma'am, but it's true.

MARY [dreamily]   It wasn't the fog I minded, Cathleen. I really love fog.

CATHLEEN   They say it's good for the complexion.

MARY   It hides you from the world and the world from you. You feel that
15   everything has changed, and nothing is what it seemed to be. No one can
find or touch you anymore.

CATHLEEN   I wouldn't care so much if Smythe was a fine, handsome man
like some chauffeurs I've seen—I mean, if it was all in fun, for I'm a decent
girl. But for a shriveled runt like Smythe—! I've told him, you must think
20   I'm hard up that I'd notice a monkey like you. I've warned him, one day I'll
give a clout that'll knock him into next week. And so I will!

MARY   It's the foghorn I hate. It won't let you alone. It keeps reminding you,
and warning you, and calling you back. [She smiles strangely.] But it can't
tonight. It's just an ugly sound. It doesn't remind me of anything. [She gives
25   a teasing, girlish laugh.] Except, perhaps, Mr. Tyrone's snores. I've always
had such fun teasing him about it. He has snored ever since I can remember, especially when he's had too much to drink, and yet he's like a child, he
hates to admit it. [She laughs, coming to the table.] Well, I suppose I snore
at times, too, and I don't like to admit it. So I have no right to make fun of
30   him, have I?

[She sits in the rocker at right of table.]

CATHLEEN   Ah, sure, everybody healthy snores. It's a sign of sanity, they say.
[Then, worriedly] What time is it, Ma'am? I ought to go back in the kitchen.
The damp is in Bridget's rheumatism and she's like a raging divil. She'll
bite my head off.

[She puts her glass on the table and makes a movement toward the back
parlor.]

35   MARY [with a flash of apprehension]   No, don't go, Cathleen. I don't want to
be alone, yet.

CATHLEEN   You won't be for long. The Master and the boys will be home
soon.

MARY   I doubt if they'll come back for dinner. They have too good an excuse
40   to remain in the barrooms where they feel at home.

[CATHLEEN stares at her, stupidly puzzled. MARY goes on smilingly.]

---

8. In Irish folklore, a female spirit whose   9. That is, bad luck (a chiefly Irish curse).
wailing cry warns of an impending death.

Don't worry about Bridget. I'll tell her I kept you with me, and you can take a big drink of whiskey to her when you go. She won't mind then.

CATHLEEN [*grins—at her ease again*]   No, Ma'am. That's the one thing can make her cheerful. She loves her drop.

45   MARY   Have another drink yourself, if you wish, Cathleen.

CATHLEEN   I don't know if I'd better, Ma'am. I can feel what I've had already. [*Reaching for the bottle*] Well, maybe one more won't harm. [*She pours a drink.*] Here's your good health, Ma'am.

[*She drinks without bothering about a chaser.*]

MARY [*dreamily*]   I really did have good health once, Cathleen. But that was 50   long ago.

CATHLEEN [*worried again*]   The Master's sure to notice what's gone from the bottle. He has the eye of a hawk for that.

MARY [*amusedly*]   Oh, we'll play Jamie's trick on him. Just measure a few drinks of water and pour them in.

55   CATHLEEN [*does this—with a silly giggle*]   God save me, it'll be half water. He'll know by the taste.

MARY [*indifferently*]   No, by the time he comes home he'll be too drunk to tell the difference. He has such a good excuse, he believes, to drown his sorrows.

60   CATHLEEN [*philosophically*]   Well, it's a good man's failing. I wouldn't give a trauneen[1] for a teetotaler. They've no high spirits. [*Then, stupidly puzzled*] Good excuse? You mean Master Edmund, Ma'am? I can tell the Master is worried about him.

MARY [*stiffens defensively—but in a strange way the reaction has a mechanical quality, as if it did not penetrate to real emotion*]   Don't be silly, Cathleen.

65   Why should he be? A touch of grippe[2] is nothing. And Mr. Tyrone never is worried about anything, except money and property and the fear he'll end his days in poverty. I mean, deeply worried. Because he cannot really understand anything else. [*She gives a little laugh of detached, affectionate amusement.*] My husband is a very peculiar man, Cathleen.

70   CATHLEEN [*vaguely resentful*]   Well, he's a fine, handsome, kind gentleman just the same, Ma'am. Never mind his weakness.

MARY   Oh, I don't mind. I've loved him dearly for thirty-six years. That proves I know he's lovable at heart and can't help being what he is, doesn't it?

CATHLEEN [*hazily reassured*]   That's right, Ma'am. Love him dearly, for any 75   fool can see he worships the ground you walk on. [*Fighting the effect of her last drink and trying to be soberly conversational*] Speaking of acting, Ma'am, how is it you never went on the stage?

MARY [*resentfully*]   I? What put that absurd notion in your head? I was brought up in a respectable home and educated in the best convent in the 80   Middle West. Before I met Mr. Tyrone I hardly knew there was such a thing as a theater. I was a very pious girl. I even dreamed of becoming a nun. I've never had the slightest desire to be an actress.

CATHLEEN [*bluntly*]   Well, I can't imagine you a holy nun, Ma'am. Sure, you never darken the door of a church, God forgive you.

85   MARY [*ignores this*]   I've never felt at home in the theater. Even though Mr. Tyrone has made me go with him on all his tours, I've had little to do with

---

1. Long, thin blade of grass (Irish Gaelic).   2. Influenza.

the people in his company, or with anyone on the stage. Not that I have anything against them. They have always been kind to me, and I to them. But I've never felt at home with them. Their life is not my life. It has always
90 stood between me and— [*She gets up—abruptly.*] But let's not talk of old things that couldn't be helped.

> [*She goes to the porch door and stares out.*]

How thick the fog is. I can't see the road. All the people in the world could pass by and I would never know. I wish it was always that way. It's getting dark already. It will soon be night, thank goodness. [*She turns back—*
95 *vaguely.*] It was kind of you to keep me company this afternoon, Cathleen. I would have been lonely driving uptown alone.

CATHLEEN Sure, wouldn't I rather ride in a fine automobile than stay here and listen to Bridget's lies about her relations? It was like a vacation, Ma'am. [*She pauses—then stupidly.*] There was only one thing I didn't like.
100 MARY [*vaguely*] What was that, Cathleen?

CATHLEEN The way the man in the drugstore acted when I took in the prescription for you. [*Indignantly*] The impidence of him!

MARY [*with stubborn blankness*] What are you talking about? What drugstore? What prescription? [*Then hastily, as Cathleen stares in stupid amaze-*
105 *ment*] Oh, of course, I'd forgotten. The medicine for the rheumatism in my hands. What did the man say? [*Then with indifference*] Not that it matters, as long as he filled the prescription.

CATHLEEN It mattered to me, then! I'm not used to being treated like a thief. He gave me a long look and says insultingly, "Where did you get hold of
110 this?" and I says, "It's none of your damned business, but if you must know, it's for the lady I work for, Mrs. Tyrone, who's sitting out in the automobile." That shut him up quick. He gave a look out at you and said, "Oh," and went to get the medicine.

MARY [*vaguely*] Yes, he knows me.

> [*She sits in the armchair at right rear of table. She adds in a calm, detached voice.*]

115 It's a special kind of medicine. I have to take it because there is no other that can stop the pain—*all* the pain—I mean, in my hands.

> [*She raises her hands and regards them with melancholy sympathy. There is no tremor in them now.*]

Poor hands! You'd never believe it, but they were once one of my good points, along with my hair and eyes, and I had a fine figure, too. [*Her tone has become more and more far-off and dreamy.*] They were a musician's
120 hands. I used to love the piano. I worked so hard at my music in the Convent—if you can call it work when you do something you love. Mother Elizabeth and my music teacher both said I had more talent than any student they remembered. My father paid for special lessons. He spoiled me. He would do anything I asked. He would have sent me to Europe to study
125 after I graduated from the Convent. I might have gone—if I hadn't fallen in love with Mr. Tyrone. Or I might have become a nun. I had two dreams. To be a nun, that was the more beautiful one. To become a concert pianist, that was the other.

> [*She pauses, regarding her hands fixedly. Cathleen blinks her eyes to fight off drowsiness and a tipsy feeling.*]

I haven't touched a piano in so many years. I couldn't play with such crip-
130   pled fingers, even if I wanted to. For a time after my marriage I tried to
keep up my music. But it was hopeless. One-night stands, cheap hotels,
dirty trains, leaving children, never having a home— [*She stares at her
hands with fascinated disgust.*] See, Cathleen, how ugly they are! So maimed
and crippled! You would think they'd been through some horrible accident!
135   [*She gives a strange little laugh.*] So they have, come to think of it. [*She suddenly thrusts her hands behind her back.*] I won't look at them. They're worse
than the foghorn for reminding me— [*Then with defiant self-assurance*]
But even they can't touch me now. [*She brings her hands from behind
her back and deliberately stares at them—calmly.*] They're far away. I see
140   them, but the pain has gone.

CATHLEEN [*stupidly puzzled*]   You've taken some of the medicine? It made
you act funny, Ma'am. If I didn't know better, I'd think you'd a drop taken.

MARY [*dreamily*]   It kills the pain. You go back until at last you are beyond its
reach. Only the past when you were happy is real.

> [*She pauses—then as if her words had been an evocation which called
> back happiness she changes in her whole manner and facial expression.
> She looks younger. There is a quality of an innocent convent girl about
> her, and she smiles shyly.*]

145   If you think Mr. Tyrone is handsome now, Cathleen, you should have seen
him when I first met him. He had the reputation of being one of the best-
looking men in the country. The girls in the Convent who had seen him
act, or seen his photographs, used to rave about him. He was a great matinee idol then, you know. Women used to wait at the stage door just to see
150   him come out. You can imagine how excited I was when my father wrote
me he and James Tyrone had become friends, and that I was to meet him
when I came home for Easter vacation. I showed the letter to all the girls,
and how envious they were! My father took me to see him act first. It was a
play about the French Revolution and the leading part was a nobleman.[3] I
155   couldn't take my eyes off him. I wept when he was thrown in prison—and
then was so mad at myself because I was afraid my eyes and nose would be
red. My father had said we'd go backstage to his dressing room right after
the play, and so we did. [*She gives a little excited, shy laugh.*] I was so bashful all I could do was stammer and blush like a little fool. But he didn't
160   seem to think I was a fool. I know he liked me the first moment we were
introduced. [*Coquettishly*] I guess my eyes and nose couldn't have been
red, after all. I was really very pretty then, Cathleen. And he was hand-
somer than my wildest dream, in his makeup and his nobleman's costume
that was so becoming to him. He was different from all ordinary men, like
165   someone from another world. At the same time he was simple, and kind,
and unassuming, not a bit stuck-up or vain. I fell in love right then. So did
he, he told me afterwards. I forgot all about becoming a nun or a concert
pianist. All I wanted was to be his wife. [*She pauses, staring before her with
unnaturally bright, dreamy eyes, and a rapt, tender, girlish smile.*] Thirty-six
170   years ago, but I can see it as clearly as if it were tonight! We've loved each

---

3. O'Neill's Irish-born father, James O'Neill,   a melodrama adapted from Alexandre Dumas's
spent years touring the United States playing   novel (1844–45).
the lead in *The Count of Monte Cristo* (1846),

other ever since. And in all those thirty-six years, there has never been a breath of scandal about him. I mean, with any other woman. Never since he met me. That has made me very happy, Cathleen. It has made me forgive so many other things.

175 CATHLEEN [*fighting tipsy drowsiness—sentimentally*] He's a fine gentleman and you're a lucky woman. [*Then, fidgeting*] Can I take the drink to Bridget, Ma'am? It must be near dinnertime and I ought to be in the kitchen helping her. If she don't get something to quiet her temper, she'll be after me with the cleaver.

180 MARY [*with a vague exasperation at being brought back from her dream*] Yes, yes, go. I don't need you now.

CATHLEEN [*with relief*] Thank you, Ma'am.

[*She pours out a big drink and starts for the back parlor with it.*]

You won't be alone long. The Master and the boys—

MARY [*impatiently*] No, no, they won't come. Tell Bridget I won't wait. You

185 can serve dinner promptly at half past six. I'm not hungry but I'll sit at the table and we'll get it over with.

CATHLEEN You ought to eat something, Ma'am. It's a queer medicine if it takes away your appetite.

MARY [*has begun to drift into dreams again—reacts mechanically*] What med-

190 icine? I don't know what you mean. [*In dismissal*] You better take the drink to Bridget.

CATHLEEN Yes, Ma'am.

[*She disappears through the back parlor.* MARY *waits until she hears the pantry door close behind her. Then she settles back in relaxed dreaminess, staring fixedly at nothing. Her arms rest limply along the arms of the chair, her hands with long, warped, swollen-knuckled, sensitive fingers drooping in complete calm. It is growing dark in the room. There is a pause of dead quiet. Then from the world outside comes the melancholy moan of the foghorn, followed by a chorus of bells, muffled by the fog, from the anchored craft in the harbor.* MARY'S *face gives no sign she has heard, but her hands jerk and the fingers automatically play for a moment on the air. She frowns and shakes her head mechanically as if a fly had walked across her mind. She suddenly loses all the girlish quality and is an aging, cynically sad, embittered woman.*]

MARY [*bitterly*] You're a sentimental fool. What is so wonderful about that first meeting between a silly romantic schoolgirl and a matinee idol? You

195 were much happier before you knew he existed, in the Convent when you used to pray to the Blessed Virgin. [*Longingly*] If I could only find the faith I lost, so I could pray again! [*She pauses—then begins to recite the Hail Mary in a flat, empty tone.*] "Hail, Mary, full of grace! The Lord is with Thee; blessed art Thou among women." [*Sneeringly*] You expect the

200 Blessed Virgin to be fooled by a lying dope fiend reciting words! You can't hide from her!

[*She springs to her feet. Her hands fly up to pat her hair distractedly.*]

I must go upstairs. I haven't taken enough. When you start again you never know exactly how much you need.

[*She goes toward the front parlor—then stops in the doorway as she hears the sound of voices from the front path. She starts guiltily.*]

That must be them—

[*She hurries back to sit down. Her face sets in stubborn defensiveness—resentfully.*]

205 Why are they coming back? They don't want to. And I'd much rather be alone.

[*Suddenly her whole manner changes. She becomes pathetically relieved and eager.*]

Oh, I'm so glad they've come! I've been so horribly lonely!

[*The front door is heard closing and Tyrone calls uneasily from the hall.*]

TYRONE Are you there, Mary?

[*The light in the hall is turned on and shines through the front parlor to fall on* MARY.]

MARY [*rises from her chair, her face lighting up lovingly—with excited eagerness*] I'm here, dear. In the living room. I've been waiting for you.

[TYRONE *comes in through the front parlor.* EDMUND *is behind him.* TYRONE *has had a lot to drink but beyond a slightly glazed look in his eyes and a trace of blur in his speech, he does not show it.* EDMUND *has also had more than a few drinks without much apparent effect, except that his sunken cheeks are flushed and his eyes look bright and feverish. They stop in the doorway to stare appraisingly at her. What they see fulfills their worst expectations. But for the moment* MARY *is unconscious of their condemning eyes. She kisses her husband and then* EDMUND. *Her manner is unnaturally effusive. They submit shrinkingly. She talks excitedly.*]

210 I'm so happy you've come. I had given up hope. I was afraid you wouldn't come home. It's such a dismal, foggy evening. It must be much more cheerful in the barrooms uptown, where there are people you can talk and joke with. No, don't deny it. I know how you feel. I don't blame you a bit. I'm all the more grateful to you for coming home. I was sitting here so
215 lonely and blue. Come and sit down.

[*She sits at left rear of table,* EDMUND *at left of table, and* TYRONE *in the rocker at right of it.*]

Dinner won't be ready for a minute. You're actually a little early. Will wonders never cease. Here's the whiskey, dear. Shall I pour a drink for you? [*Without waiting for a reply she does so.*] And you, Edmund? I don't want to encourage you, but one before dinner, as an appetizer, can't do any harm.

[*She pours a drink for him. They make no move to take the drinks. She talks on as if unaware of their silence.*]

220 Where's Jamie? But, of course, he'll never come home so long as he has the price of a drink left. [*She reaches out and clasps her husband's hand—sadly.*] I'm afraid Jamie has been lost to us for a long time, dear. [*Her face hardens.*] But we mustn't allow him to drag Edmund down with him, as he'd like to do. He's jealous because Edmund has always been the baby—just as
225 he used to be of Eugene. He'll never be content until he makes Edmund as hopeless a failure as he is.

EDMUND [*miserably*] Stop talking, Mama.

TYRONE [*dully*] Yes, Mary, the less you say now— [*Then to Edmund, a bit tipsily*] All the same there's truth in your mother's warning. Beware of that
230 brother of yours, or he'll poison life for you with his damned sneering serpent's tongue!

EDMUND [*as before*] Oh, cut it out, Papa.

MARY [*goes on as if nothing had been said*]   It's hard to believe, seeing Jamie
as he is now, that he was ever my baby. Do you remember what a healthy,
235   happy baby he was, James? The one-night stands and filthy trains and
cheap hotels and bad food never made him cross or sick. He was always
smiling or laughing. He hardly ever cried. Eugene was the same, too, happy
and healthy, during the two years he lived before I let him die through my
neglect.

240   TYRONE   Oh, for the love of God! I'm a fool for coming home!

EDMUND   Papa! Shut up!

MARY [*smiles with detached tenderness at* EDMUND]   It was Edmund who was
the crosspatch when he was little, always getting upset and frightened
about nothing at all. [*She pats his hand—teasingly.*] Everyone used to say,
245   dear, you'd cry at the drop of a hat.

EDMUND [*cannot control his bitterness*]   Maybe I guessed there was a good
reason not to laugh.

TYRONE [*reproving and pitying*]   Now, now, lad. You know better than to pay
attention—

250   MARY [*as if she hadn't heard—sadly again*]   Who would have thought Jamie
would grow up to disgrace us. You remember, James, for years after he went
to boarding school, we received such glowing reports. Everyone liked him.
All his teachers told us what a fine brain he had, and how easily he learned
his lessons. Even after he began to drink and they had to expel him, they
255   wrote us how sorry they were, because he was so likable and such a brilliant student. They predicted a wonderful future for him if he would only
learn to take life seriously. [*She pauses—then adds with a strange, sad
detachment.*] It's such a pity. Poor Jamie! It's hard to understand—

[*Abruptly a change comes over her. Her face hardens and she stares at
her husband with accusing hostility.*]

No, it isn't at all. You brought him up to be a boozer. Since he first opened
260   his eyes, he's seen you drinking. Always a bottle on the bureau in the cheap
hotel rooms! And if he had a nightmare when he was little, or a stomach-
ache, your remedy was to give him a teaspoonful of whiskey to quiet him.

TYRONE [*stung*]   So I'm to blame because that lazy hulk has made a drunken
loafer of himself? Is that what I came home to listen to? I might have
265   known! When you have the poison in you, you want to blame everyone but
yourself!

EDMUND   Papa! You told me not to pay attention. [*Then, resentfully*] Anyway
it's true. You did the same thing with me. I can remember that teaspoonful
270   of booze every time I woke up with a nightmare.

MARY [*in a detached reminiscent tone*]   Yes, you were continually having
nightmares as a child. You were born afraid. Because I was so afraid to
bring you into the world. [*She pauses—then goes on with the same detachment.*] Please don't think I blame your father, Edmund. He didn't know any
275   better. He never went to school after he was ten. His people were the most
ignorant kind of poverty-stricken Irish. I'm sure they honestly believed
whiskey is the healthiest medicine for a child who is sick or frightened.

[TYRONE *is about to burst out in angry defense of his family but* EDMUND
intervenes.]

EDMUND [*sharply*]   Papa! [*Changing the subject*] Are we going to have this
drink, or aren't we?

280 TYRONE [*controlling himself—dully*] You're right. I'm a fool to take notice. [*He picks up his glass listlessly.*] Drink hearty, lad.

> [EDMUND *drinks but* TYRONE *remains staring at the glass in his hand.* EDMUND *at once realizes how much the whiskey has been watered. He frowns, glancing from the bottle to his mother—starts to say something but stops.*]

MARY [*in a changed tone—repentently*] I'm sorry if I sounded bitter, James. I'm not. It's all so far away. But I did feel a little hurt when you wished you hadn't come home. I was so relieved and happy when you came, and grate-
285 ful to you. It's very dreary and sad to be here alone in the fog with night falling.

TYRONE [*moved*] I'm glad I came, Mary, when you act like your real self.

MARY I was so lonesome I kept Cathleen with me just to have someone to talk to. [*Her manner and quality drift back to the shy convent girl again.*] Do
290 you know what I was telling her, dear? About the night my father took me to your dressing room and I first fell in love with you. Do you remember?

TYRONE [*deeply moved—his voice husky*] Can you think I'd ever forget, Mary?

> [EDMUND *looks away from them, sad and embarrassed.*]

MARY [*tenderly*] No. I know you still love me, James, in spite of everything.

TYRONE [*his face works and he blinks back tears—with quiet intensity*] Yes! As
295 God is my judge! Always and forever, Mary!

MARY And I love you, dear, in spite of everything.

> [*There is a pause in which* EDMUND *moves embarrassedly. The strange detachment comes over her manner again as if she were speaking imper- sonally of people seen from a distance.*]

But I must confess, James, although I couldn't help loving you, I would never have married you if I'd known you drank so much. I remember the first night your barroom friends had to help you up to the door of our hotel
300 room, and knocked and then ran away before I came to the door. We were still on our honeymoon, do you remember?

TYRONE [*with guilty vehemence*] I don't remember! It wasn't on our honey- moon! And I never in my life had to be helped to bed, or missed a performance!

305 MARY [*as though he hadn't spoken*] I had waited in that ugly hotel room hour after hour. I kept making excuses for you. I told myself it must be some business connected with the theater. I knew so little about the theater. Then I became terrified. I imagined all sorts of horrible accidents. I got on my knees and prayed that nothing had happened to you—and then they
310 brought you up and left you outside the door. [*She gives a little, sad sigh.*] I didn't know how often that was to happen in the years to come, how many times I was to wait in ugly hotel rooms. I became quite used to it.

EDMUND [*bursts out with a look of accusing hate at his father*] Christ! No wonder—! [*He controls himself—gruffly.*] When is dinner, Mama? It must
315 be time.

TYRONE [*overwhelmed by shame which he tries to hide, fumbles with his watch*] Yes. It must be. Let's see.

> [*He stares at his watch without seeing it. Pleadingly.*]

Mary! Can't you forget—?

MARY [*with detached pity*]   No, dear. But I forgive. I always forgive you. So don't look so guilty. I'm sorry I remembered out loud. I don't want to be
320 sad, or to make you sad. I want to remember only the happy part of the past. [*Her manner drifts back to the shy, gay convent girl.*] Do you remember our wedding, dear? I'm sure you've completely forgotten what my wedding gown looked like. Men don't notice such things. They don't think they're important. But it was important to me, I can tell you! How I
325 fussed and worried! I was so excited and happy! My father told me to buy anything I wanted and never mind what it cost. The best is none too good, he said. I'm afraid he spoiled me dreadfully. My mother didn't. She was very pious and strict. I think she was a little jealous. She didn't approve of my marrying—especially an actor. I think she hoped I would
330 become a nun. She used to scold my father. She'd grumble, "You never tell me, never mind what it costs, when I buy anything! You've spoiled that girl so, I pity her husband if she ever marries. She'll expect him to give her the moon. She'll never make a good wife." [*She laughs affectionately.*] Poor mother! [*She smiles at* TYRONE *with a strange, incongruous*
335 *coquetry.*] But she was mistaken, wasn't she, James? I haven't been such a bad wife, have I?

TYRONE [*huskily, trying to force a smile*]   I'm not complaining, Mary.

MARY [*a shadow of vague guilt crosses her face*]   At least, I've loved you dearly, and done the best I could—under the circumstances. [*The shadow
340 vanishes and her shy, girlish expression returns.*] That wedding gown was nearly the death of me and the dressmaker, too! [*She laughs.*] I was so particular. It was never quite good enough. At last she said she refused to touch it anymore or she might spoil it, and I made her leave so I could be alone to examine myself in the mirror. I was so pleased and vain. I
345 thought to myself, "Even if your nose and mouth and ears are a trifle too large, your eyes and hair and figure, and your hands, make up for it. You're just as pretty as any actress he's ever met, and you don't have to use paint." [*She pauses, wrinkling her brow in an effort of memory.*] Where is my wedding gown now, I wonder? I kept it wrapped up in tissue paper
350 in my trunk. I used to hope I would have a daughter and when it came time for her to marry— She couldn't have bought a lovelier gown, and I knew, James, you'd never tell her, never mind the cost. You'd want her to pick up something at a bargain. It was made of soft, shimmering satin, trimmed with wonderful old duchesse lace, in tiny ruffles around the
355 neck and sleeves, and worked in with the folds that were draped round in a bustle effect at the back. The basque was boned[4] and very tight. I remember I held my breath when it was fitted, so my waist would be as small as possible. My father even let me have duchesse lace on my white satin slippers, and lace with the orange blossoms in my veil. Oh, how I
360 loved that gown! It was so beautiful! Where is it now, I wonder? I used to take it out from time to time when I was lonely, but it always made me cry, so finally a long while ago— [*She wrinkles her forehead again.*] I wonder where I hid it? Probably in one of the old trunks in the attic. Someday I'll have to look.

4. That is, the bodice was stiffened with whalebone.

[*She stops, staring before her.* TYRONE *sighs, shaking his head hopelessly, and attempts to catch his son's eye, looking for sympathy, but* EDMUND *is staring at the floor.*]

365 TYRONE [*forces a casual tone*] Isn't it dinner time, dear? [*With a feeble attempt at teasing*] You're forever scolding me for being late, but now I'm on time for once, it's dinner that's late.

[*She doesn't appear to hear him. He adds, still pleasantly.*]

Well, if I can't eat yet, I can drink. I'd forgotten I had this.

[*He drinks his drink.* EDMUND *watches him.* TYRONE *scowls and looks at his wife with sharp suspicion—roughly.*]

Who's been tampering with my whiskey? The damned stuff is half water!
370 Jamie's been away and he wouldn't overdo his trick like this, anyway. Any fool could tell—Mary, answer me! [*With angry disgust*] I hope to God you haven't taken to drink on top of—

EDMUND Shut up, Papa! [*To his mother, without looking at her*] You treated Cathleen and Bridget, isn't that it, Mama?

375 MARY [*with indifferent casualness*] Yes, of course. They work hard for poor wages. And I'm the housekeeper, I have to keep them from leaving. Besides, I wanted to treat Cathleen because I had her drive uptown with me, and sent her to get my prescription filled.

EDMUND For God's sake, Mama! You can't trust her! Do you want everyone
380 on earth to know?

MARY [*her face hardening stubbornly*] Know what? That I suffer from rheumatism in my hands and have to take medicine to kill the pain? Why should I be ashamed of that? [*Turns on* EDMUND *with a hard, accusing antagonism—almost a revengeful enmity.*] I never knew what rheumatism
385 was before you were born! Ask your father!

[EDMUND *looks away, shrinking into himself.*]

TYRONE Don't mind her, lad. It doesn't mean anything. When she gets to the stage where she gives the old crazy excuse about her hands she's gone far away from us.

MARY [*turns on him—with a strangely triumphant, taunting smile*] I'm glad
390 you realize that, James! Now perhaps you'll give up trying to remind me, you and Edmund! [*Abruptly, in a detached, matter-of-fact tone*] Why don't you light the light, James? It's getting dark. I know you hate to, but Edmund has proved to you that one bulb burning doesn't cost much. There's no sense letting your fear of the poorhouse make you too stingy.

395 TYRONE [*reacts mechanically*] I never claimed one bulb cost much! It's having them on, one here and one there, that makes the Electric Light Company rich.

[*He gets up and turns on the reading lamp—roughly.*]

But I'm a fool to talk reason to you. [*To* EDMUND] I'll get a fresh bottle of whiskey, lad, and we'll have a real drink.

[*He goes through the back parlor.*]

400 MARY [*with detached amusement*] He'll sneak around to the outside cellar door so the servants won't see him. He's really ashamed of keeping his whiskey padlocked in the cellar. Your father is a strange man, Edmund. It took many years before I understood him. You must try to understand and

forgive him, too, and not feel contempt because he's close-fisted. His
405 father deserted his mother and their six children a year or so after they
came to America. He told them he had a premonition he would die soon,
and he was homesick for Ireland, and wanted to go back there to die. So he
went and he did die. He must have been a peculiar man, too. Your father
had to go to work in a machine shop when he was only ten years old.

410 EDMUND [protests dully] Oh, for Pete's sake, Mama. I've heard Papa tell that
machine shop story ten thousand times.

MARY Yes, dear, you've had to listen, but I don't think you've ever tried to
understand.

EDMUND [ignoring this—miserably] Listen, Mama! You're not so far gone yet
415 you've forgotten everything. You haven't asked me what I found out this
afternoon. Don't you care a damn?

MARY [shakenly] Don't say that! You hurt me, dear!

EDMUND What I've got is serious, Mama. Doc Hardy knows for sure now.

MARY [stiffens into scornful, defensive stubbornness] That lying old quack! I
420 warned you he'd invent—!

EDMUND [miserably dogged] He called in a specialist to examine me, so he'd
be absolutely sure.

MARY [ignoring this] Don't tell me about Hardy! If you heard what the doctor at the sanatorium, who really knows something, said about how he'd
425 treated me! He said he ought to be locked up! He said it was a wonder I
hadn't gone mad! I told him I had once, that time I ran down in my nightdress to throw myself off the dock. You remember that, don't you? And yet
you want me to pay attention to what Doctor Hardy says. Oh, no!

EDMUND [bitterly] I remember, all right. It was right after that Papa and
430 Jamie decided they couldn't hide it from me anymore. Jamie told me. I
called him a liar! I tried to punch him in the nose. But I knew he wasn't
lying. [His voice trembles, his eyes begin to fill with tears.] God, it made
everything in life seem rotten!

MARY [pitiably] Oh, don't. My baby! You hurt me so dreadfully!

435 EDMUND [dully] I'm sorry, Mama. It was you who brought it up. [Then with
a bitter, stubborn persistence] Listen, Mama. I'm going to tell you whether
you want to hear or not. I've got to go to a sanatorium.

MARY [dazedly, as if this was something that had never occurred to her] Go
away? [Violently] No! I won't have it! How dare Doctor Hardy advise such
440 a thing without consulting me! How dare your father allow him! What right
has he? You are my baby! Let him attend to Jamie! [More and more excited
and bitter] I know why he wants you sent to a sanatorium. To take you from
me! He's always tried to do that. He's been jealous of every one of my
babies! He kept finding ways to make me leave them. That's what caused
445 Eugene's death. He's been jealous of you most of all. He knew I loved you
most because—

EDMUND [miserably] Oh, stop talking crazy, can't you, Mama! Stop trying to
blame him. And why are you so against my going away now? I've been away
a lot, and I've never noticed it broke your heart!

450 MARY [bitterly] I'm afraid you're not very sensitive, after all. [Sadly] You
might have guessed, dear, that after I knew you knew—about me—I had to
be glad whenever you were where you couldn't see me.

EDMUND [*brokenly*] Mama! Don't!

[*He reaches out blindly and takes her hand—but he drops it immediately, overcome by bitterness again.*]

All this talk about loving me—and you won't even listen when I try to tell
455 you how sick—

MARY [*with an abrupt transformation into a detached bullying motherliness*]
Now, now. That's enough! I don't care to hear because I know it's nothing
but Hardy's ignorant lies.

[*He shrinks back into himself. She keeps on in a forced, teasing tone but
with an increasing undercurrent of resentment.*]

You're so like your father, dear. You love to make a scene out of nothing so
you can be dramatic and tragic. [*With a belittling laugh*] If I gave you the
460 slightest encouragement, you'd tell me next you were going to die—

EDMUND People do die of it. Your own father—

MARY [*sharply*] Why do you mention him? There's no comparison at all with
you. He had consumption. [*Angrily*] I hate you when you become gloomy
and morbid! I forbid you to remind me of my father's death, do you hear
465 me?

EDMUND [*his face hard—grimly*] Yes, I hear you, Mama. I wish to God I didn't!

[*He gets up from his chair and stands staring condemningly at her—
bitterly.*]

It's pretty hard to take at times, having a dope fiend for a mother!

[*She winces—all life seeming to drain from her face, leaving it with the
appearance of a plaster cast. Instantly* EDMUND *wishes he could take back
what he has said. He stammers miserably.*]

Forgive me, Mama. I was angry. You hurt me.

[*There is a pause in which the foghorn and the ships' bells are heard.*]

MARY [*goes slowly to the windows at right like an automaton—looking out, a
blank, far-off quality in her voice*] Just listen to that awful foghorn. And
470 the bells. Why is it fog makes everything sound so sad and lost, I wonder?

EDMUND [*brokenly*] I—I can't stay here. I don't want any dinner.

[*He hurries away through the front parlor. She keeps staring out the window until she hears the front door close behind him. Then she comes
back and sits in her chair, the same blank look on her face.*]

MARY [*vaguely*] I must go upstairs. I haven't taken enough. [*She pauses—
then longingly*] I hope, sometime, without meaning it, I will take an over-
dose. I never could do it deliberately. The Blessed Virgin would never
475 forgive me, then.

[*She hears* TYRONE *returning and turns as he comes in, through the back
parlor, with a bottle of whiskey he has just uncorked. He is fuming.*]

TYRONE [*wrathfully*] The padlock is all scratched. That drunken loafer has
tried to pick the lock with a piece of wire, the way he's done before. [*With
satisfaction, as if this was a perpetual battle of wits with his elder son*] But
I've fooled him this time. It's a special padlock a professional burglar
480 couldn't pick. [*He puts the bottle on the tray and suddenly is aware of
EDMUND's absence.*] Where's Edmund?

MARY [*with a vague far-away air*] He went out. Perhaps he's going uptown
again to find Jamie. He still has some money left, I suppose, and it's burning a hole in his pocket. He said he didn't want any dinner. He doesn't

485 seem to have any appetite these days. [*Then stubbornly*] But it's just a summer cold.

> [TYRONE *stares at her and shakes his head helplessly and pours himself a big drink and drinks it. Suddenly it is too much for her and she breaks out and sobs.*]

Oh, James, I'm so frightened!

> [*She gets up and throws her arms around him and hides her face on his shoulder—sobbingly.*]

I know he's going to die!

TYRONE Don't say that! It's not true! They promised me in six months he'd 490 be cured.

MARY You don't believe that! I can tell when you're acting! And it will be my fault. I should never have borne him. It would have been better for his sake. I could never hurt him then. He wouldn't have had to know his mother was a dope fiend—and hate her!

495 TYRONE [*his voice quivering*] Hush, Mary, for the love of God! He loves you. He knows it was a curse put on you without your knowing or willing it. He's proud you're his mother! [*Abruptly as he hears the pantry door opening*] Hush, now! Here comes Cathleen. You don't want her to see you crying.

> [*She turns quickly away from him to the windows at right, hastily wiping her eyes. A moment later* CATHLEEN *appears in the back-parlor doorway. She is uncertain in her walk and grinning woozily.*]

CATHLEEN [*starts guiltily when she sees Tyrone—with dignity*] Dinner is 500 served, Sir. [*Raising her voice unnecessarily*] Dinner is served, Ma'am. [*She forgets her dignity and addresses* TYRONE *with good-natured familiarity.*] So you're here, are you? Well, well. Won't Bridget be in a rage! I told her the Madame said you wouldn't be home. [*Then reading accusation in his eye*] Don't be looking at me that way. If I've a drop taken, I didn't steal it. I was 505 invited.

> [*She turns with huffy dignity and disappears through the back parlor.*]

TYRONE [*sighs—then summoning his actor's heartiness*] Come along, dear. Let's have our dinner. I'm hungry as a hunter.

MARY [*comes to him—her face is composed in plaster again and her tone is remote*] I'm afraid you'll have to excuse me, James. I couldn't possibly eat anything. My hands pain me dreadfully. I think the best thing for me is to 510 go to bed and rest. Good night, dear.

> [*She kisses him mechanically and turns toward the front parlor.*]

TYRONE [*harshly*] Up to take more of that God-damned poison, is that it? You'll be like a mad ghost before the night's over!

MARY [*starts to walk away—blankly*] I don't know what you're talking about, James. You say such mean, bitter things when you've drunk too much. 515 You're as bad as Jamie or Edmund.

> [*She moves off through the front parlor. He stands a second as if not knowing what to do. He is a sad, bewildered, broken old man. He walks wearily off through the back parlor toward the dining room.*]

Curtain.

Act 4

SCENE: *The same. It is around midnight. The lamp in the front hall has been turned out, so that now no light shines through the front parlor. In the living room only the reading lamp on the table is lighted. Outside the windows the wall of fog appears denser than ever. As the curtain rises, the foghorn is heard, followed by the ships' bells from the harbor.*

TYRONE *is seated at the table. He wears his pince-nez, and is playing solitaire. He has taken off his coat and has on an old brown dressing gown. The whiskey bottle on the tray is three-quarters empty. There is a fresh full bottle on the table, which he has brought from the cellar so there will be an ample reserve at hand. He is drunk and shows it by the owlish, deliberate manner in which he peers at each card to make certain of its identity, and then plays it as if he wasn't certain of his aim. His eyes have a misted, oily look and his mouth is slack. But despite all the whiskey in him, he has not escaped, and he looks as he appeared at the close of the preceding act, a sad, defeated old man, possessed by hopeless resignation.*

As the curtain rises, he finishes a game and sweeps the cards together. He shuffles them clumsily, dropping a couple on the floor. He retrieves them with difficulty, and starts to shuffle again, when he hears someone entering the front door. He peers over his pince-nez through the front parlor.

TYRONE [*his voice thick*] Who's that? Is it you, Edmund?

> [EDMUND's *voice answers curtly, "Yes." Then he evidently collides with something in the dark hall and can be heard cursing. A moment later the hall lamp is turned on.* TYRONE *frowns and calls.*]

Turn that light out before you come in.

> [*But* EDMUND *doesn't. He comes in through the front parlor. He is drunk now, too, but like his father he carries it well, and gives little physical sign of it except in his eyes and a chip-on-the-shoulder aggressiveness in his manner.* TYRONE *speaks, at first with a warm, relieved welcome.*]

I'm glad you've come, lad. I've been damned lonely. [*Then resentfully*] You're a fine one to run away and leave me to sit alone here all night when
5   you know— [*with sharp irritation*] I told you to turn out that light! We're not giving a ball. There's no reason to have the house ablaze with electricity at this time of night, burning up money!

EDMUND [*angrily*] Ablaze with electricity! One bulb! Hell, everyone keeps a light on in the front hall until they go to bed. [*He rubs his knee.*] I damned
10   near busted my knee on the hat stand.

TYRONE The light from here shows in the hall. You could see your way well enough if you were sober.

EDMUND If *I* was sober? I like that!

TYRONE I don't give a damn what other people do. If they want to be waste-
15   ful fools, for the sake of show, let them be!

EDMUND One bulb! Christ, don't be such a cheapskate! I've proved by figures if you left the lightbulb on all night it wouldn't be as much as one drink!

TYRONE To hell with your figures! The proof is in the bills I have to pay!

EDMUND [*sits down opposite his father—contemptuously*] Yes, facts don't
20   mean a thing, do they? What you want to believe, that's the only truth! [*Derisively*] Shakespeare was an Irish Catholic,[5] for example.

---

5. Few biographical facts are known about Shakespeare; according to one theory, which scholars have generally dismissed, he was secretly a practicing Catholic (secrecy would have been necessary, because Roman Catholics were persecuted during the reign of Elizabeth I). Tyrone may be alone in believing the playwright to have been Irish.

TYRONE [*stubbornly*]   So he was. The proof is in his plays.

EDMUND   Well he wasn't, and there's no proof of it in his plays, except to you! [*Jeeringly*] The Duke of Wellington,[6] there was another good Irish Catholic!

TYRONE   I never said he was a good one. He was a renegade but a Catholic just the same.

EDMUND   Well, he wasn't. You just want to believe no one but an Irish Catholic general could beat Napoleon.[7]

TYRONE   I'm not going to argue with you. I asked you to turn out that light in the hall.

EDMUND   I heard you, and as far as I'm concerned it stays on.

TYRONE   None of your damned insolence! Are you going to obey me or not?

EDMUND   Not! If you want to be a crazy miser put it out yourself!

TYRONE [*with threatening anger*]   Listen to me! I've put up with a lot from you because from the mad things you've done at times I've thought you weren't quite right in your head. I've excused you and never lifted my hand to you. But there's a straw that breaks the camel's back. You'll obey me and put out that light or, big as you are, I'll give you a thrashing that'll teach you—! [*Suddenly he remembers* EDMUND's *illness and instantly becomes guilty and shamefaced.*] Forgive me, lad. I forgot— You shouldn't goad me into losing my temper.

EDMUND [*ashamed himself now*]   Forget it, Papa. I apologize, too. I had no right being nasty about nothing. I am a bit soused, I guess. I'll put out the damned light.

[*He starts to get up.*]

TYRONE   No, stay where you are. Let it burn.

[*He stands up abruptly—and a bit drunkenly—and begins turning on the three bulbs in the chandelier, with a childish, bitterly dramatic self-pity.*]

We'll have them all on! Let them burn! To hell with them! The poorhouse is the end of the road, and it might as well be sooner as later! [*He finishes turning on the lights.*]

EDMUND [*has watched this proceeding with an awakened sense of humor—now he grins, teasing affectionately*]   That's a grand curtain. [*He laughs.*] You're a wonder, Papa.

TYRONE [*sits down sheepishly—grumbles pathetically*]   That's right, laugh at the old fool! The poor old ham! But the final curtain will be in the poorhouse just the same, and that's not comedy! [*Then as Edmund is still grinning, he changes the subject.*] Well, well, let's not argue. You've got brains in that head of yours, though you do your best to deny them. You'll live to learn the value of a dollar. You're not like your damned tramp of a brother. I've given up hope he'll ever get sense. Where is he, by the way?

EDMUND   How would I know?

TYRONE   I thought you'd gone back uptown to meet him.

6. Arthur Wellesley, first duke of Wellington (1769–1852), a statesman and military hero. Although born in Ireland, he was a member of the Anglo-Irish aristocracy and thus Protestant, not Roman Catholic.
7. Napoléon Bonaparte (1769–1821), the French military leader who became emperor of France; one of the greatest military strategists of history, he was overcome by the European countries allied against him and suffered his final defeat at the hands of British forces under Wellington's command at Waterloo (in Belgium) in 1815.

60 EDMUND No. I walked out to the beach. I haven't seen him since this afternoon.

TYRONE Well, if you split the money I gave you with him, like a fool—

EDMUND Sure I did. He's always staked me when he had anything.

TYRONE Then it doesn't take a soothsayer to tell he's probably in the whore-
65 house.

EDMUND What of it if he is? Why not?

TYRONE [contemptuously] Why not, indeed. It's the fit place for him. If he's ever had a loftier dream than whores and whiskey, he's never shown it.

EDMUND Oh, for Pete's sake, Papa! If you're going to start that stuff, I'll beat it.

[He starts to get up.]

70 TYRONE [placatingly] All right, all right, I'll stop. God knows, I don't like the subject either. Will you join me in a drink?

EDMUND Ah! Now you're talking!

TYRONE [passes the bottle to him—mechanically] I'm wrong to treat you. You've had enough already.

75 EDMUND [pouring a big drink—a bit drunkenly] Enough is not as good as a feast.

[He hands back the bottle.]

TYRONE It's too much in your condition.

EDMUND Forget my condition! [He raises his glass.] Here's how.

TYRONE Drink hearty. [They drink.] If you walked all the way to the beach
80 you must be damp and chilled.

EDMUND Oh, I dropped in at the Inn on the way out and back.

TYRONE It's not a night I'd pick for a long walk.

EDMUND I loved the fog. It was what I needed. [He sounds more tipsy and looks it.]

TYRONE You should have more sense than to risk—

85 EDMUND To hell with sense! We're all crazy. What do we want with sense? [He quotes from Dowson sardonically.]

> "They are not long, the weeping and the laughter,
> Love and desire and hate:
> I think they have no portion in us after
> We pass the gate.

90
> They are not long, the days of wine and roses:
> Out of a misty dream
> Our path emerges for a while, then closes
> Within a dream."[8]

[Staring before him] The fog was where I wanted to be. Halfway down the
95 path you can't see this house. You'd never know it was here. Or any of the other places down the avenue. I couldn't see but a few feet ahead. I didn't meet a soul. Everything looked and sounded unreal. Nothing was what it is. That's what I wanted—to be alone with myself in another world where truth is untrue and life can hide from itself. Out beyond the harbor, where
100 the road runs along the beach, I even lost the feeling of being on land. The fog and the sea seemed part of each other. It was like walking on the bottom of the sea. As if I had drowned long ago. As if I was a ghost belong-

8. "They Are Not Long" (1896), by the English poet Ernest Dowson (1867–1900).

ing to the fog, and the fog was the ghost of the sea. It felt damned peaceful to be nothing more than a ghost within a ghost.

[*He sees his father staring at him with mingled worry and irritated disapproval. He grins mockingly.*]

105 Don't look at me as if I'd gone nutty. I'm talking sense. Who wants to see life as it is, if they can help it? It's the three Gorgons[9] in one. You look in their faces and turn to stone. Or it's Pan.[1] You see him and you die—that is, inside you—and have to go on living as a ghost.

TYRONE [*impressed and at the same time revolted*]   You have a poet in you but
110 it's a damned morbid one! [*Forcing a smile*] Devil take your pessimism. I feel low-spirited enough. [*He sighs.*] Why can't you remember your Shakespeare and forget the third-raters. You'll find what you're trying to say in him—as you'll find everything else worth saying. [*He quotes, using his fine voice.*] "We are such stuff as dreams are made on, and our little life is
115 rounded with a sleep."[2]

EDMUND [*ironically*]   Fine! That's beautiful. But I wasn't trying to say that. We are such stuff as manure is made on, so let's drink up and forget it. That's more my idea.

TYRONE [*disgustedly*]   Ach! Keep such sentiments to yourself. I shouldn't
120 have given you that drink.

EDMUND   It did pack a wallop, all right. On you, too. [*He grins with affectionate teasing.*] Even if you've never missed a performance! [*Aggressively*] Well, what's wrong with being drunk? It's what we're after, isn't it? Let's not kid each other, Papa. Not tonight. We know what we're trying to for-
125 get. [*Hurriedly*] But let's not talk about it. It's no use now.

TYRONE [*dully*]   No. All we can do is try to be resigned—again.

EDMUND   Or be so drunk you can forget.

[*He recites, and recites well, with bitter, ironical passion, the Symons' translation of Baudelaire's prose poem.*]

"Be always drunken. Nothing else matters: that is the only question. If you would not feel the horrible burden of Time weighing on your shoulders and
130 crushing you to the earth, be drunken continually.

"Drunken with what? With wine, with poetry, or with virtue, as you will. But be drunken.

"And if sometimes, on the stairs of a palace, or on the green side of a ditch, or in the dreary solitude of your own room, you should awaken and the
135 drunkenness be half or wholly slipped away from you, ask of the wind, or of the wave, or of the star, or of the bird, or of the clock, of whatever flies, or sighs, or rocks, or sings, or speaks, ask what hour it is; and the wind, wave, star, bird, clock, will answer you: 'It is the hour to be drunken! Be drunken, if you would not be martyred slaves of Time; be drunken continually! With
140 wine, with poetry, or with virtue, as you will.'"[3]

[*He grins at his father provocatively.*]

---

9. In Greek mythology, three snake-haired sisters, the sight of whom turned all who looked at them to stone.
1. The Greek god of pastures, flocks, and wild places, who had horns and goat's feet; he was also believed responsible for irrational terrors that seize animals and humans (i.e., panic).

2. Quoting Prospero, from Shakespeare's *The Tempest* (1611), 4.1.156–58.
3. Quoted from the prose poem "Get Drunk" (1862), by the French poet Charles Baudelaire (1821–1867). The poet Arthur Symons (1865–1945) translated and introduced to England Baudelaire and many other French poets associated with symbolism and decadence.

TYRONE [*thickly humorous*] I wouldn't worry about the virtue part of it, if I were you. [*Then disgustedly*] Pah! It's morbid nonsense! What little truth is in it you'll find nobly said in Shakespeare. [*Then appreciatively*] But you recited it well, lad. Who wrote it?

145 EDMUND Baudelaire.

TYRONE Never heard of him.

EDMUND [*grins provocatively*] He also wrote a poem about Jamie and the Great White Way.

TYRONE That loafer! I hope to God he misses the last car and has to stay 150 uptown!

EDMUND [*goes on, ignoring this*] Although he was French and never saw Broadway and died before Jamie was born. He knew him and Little Old New York just the same.

[*He recites the Symons' translation of Baudelaire's "Epilogue."*[4]]

"With heart at rest I climbed the citadel's
155   Steep height, and saw the city as from a tower,
            Hospital, brothel, prison, and such hells,

"Where evil comes up softly like a flower.
            Thou knowest, O Satan, patron of my pain,
            Not for vain tears I went up at that hour;

160   "But like an old sad faithful lecher, fain[5]
            To drink delight of that enormous trull
            Whose hellish beauty makes me young again.

"Whether thou sleep, with heavy vapours full,
            Sodden with day, or, new apparelled, stand
165   In gold-laced veils of evening beautiful,

"I love thee, infamous city! Harlots and
            Hunted have pleasures of their own to give,
            The vulgar herd can never understand."

TYRONE [*with irritable disgust*] Morbid filth! Where the hell do you get your 170 taste in literature? Filth and despair and pessimism! Another atheist, I suppose. When you deny God, you deny hope. That's the trouble with you. If you'd get down on your knees—

EDMUND [*as if he hadn't heard—sardonically*] It's a good likeness of Jamie, don't you think, hunted by himself and whiskey, hiding in a Broadway hotel room 175 with some fat tart—he likes them fat—reciting Dowson's Cynara to her.

[*He recites derisively, but with deep feeling.*]

"All night upon mine heart I felt her warm heart beat,
            Night-long within mine arms in love and sleep she lay;
            Surely the kisses of her bought red mouth were sweet;
            But I was desolate and sick of an old passion,
180   When I awoke and found the dawn was gray:
            I have been faithful to thee, Cynara! in my fashion."[6]

---

4. The final poem in *Petits poèmes en prose* (1862), the volume in which "Get Drunk" appeared.

5. Eager.

6. The third stanza of "Cynara" (1891).

[*Jeeringly*] And the poor fat burlesque queen doesn't get a word of it, but suspects she's being insulted! And Jamie never loved any Cynara, and was never faithful to a woman in his life, even in his fashion! But he lies there, kidding himself he is superior and enjoys pleasures "the vulgar herd can never understand"! [*He laughs.*] It's nuts—completely nuts!

TYRONE [*vaguely—his voice thick*] It's madness, yes. If you'd get on your knees and pray. When you deny God, you deny sanity.

EDMUND [*ignoring this*] But who am I to feel superior? I've done the same damned thing. And it's no more crazy than Dowson himself, inspired by an absinthe[7] hangover, writing it to a dumb barmaid, who thought he was a poor crazy souse, and gave him the gate[8] to marry a waiter! [*He laughs—then soberly, with genuine sympathy.*] Poor Dowson. Booze and consumption got him.

[*He starts and for a second looks miserable and frightened. Then with defensive irony.*]

Perhaps it would be tactful of me to change the subject.

TYRONE [*thickly*] Where you get your taste in authors— That damned library of yours! [*He indicates the small bookcase at rear.*] Voltaire, Rousseau, Schopenhauer, Nietzsche, Ibsen![9] Atheists, fools, and madmen! And your poets! This Dowson, and this Baudelaire, and Swinburne and Oscar Wilde, and Whitman and Poe![1] Whoremongers and degenerates! Pah! When I've three good sets of Shakespeare there [*he nods at the large bookcase*] you could read.

EDMUND [*provocatively*] They say he was a souse, too.

TYRONE They lie! I don't doubt he liked his glass—it's a good man's failing—but he knew how to drink so it didn't poison his brain with morbidness and filth. Don't compare him with the pack you've got in there. [*He indicates the small bookcase again.*] Your dirty Zola! And your Dante Gabriel Rossetti[2] who was a dope fiend! [*He starts and looks guilty.*]

EDMUND [*with defensive dryness*] Perhaps it would be wise to change the subject.

[*A pause.*]

You can't accuse me of not knowing Shakespeare. Didn't I win five dollars from you once when you bet me I couldn't learn a leading part of his in a week, as you used to do in stock in the old days. I learned Macbeth and recited it letter perfect, with you giving me the cues.

TYRONE [*approvingly*] That's true. So you did. [*He smiles teasingly and sighs.*] It was a terrible ordeal, I remember, hearing you murder the lines. I kept wishing I'd paid over the bet without making you prove it.

[*He chuckles and EDMUND grins. Then he starts as he hears a sound from upstairs—with dread.*]

7. A green liqueur distilled from herbs (including wormwood), highly popular in late 19th-century Paris; it was alleged to be an addictive hallucinogen.
8. That is, rejected or dismissed him.
9. All philosophers, except for the Norwegian dramatist Henrik Ibsen (1828–1906).
1. The writers Algernon Charles Swinburne (1837–1909), Oscar Wilde (1854–1900), Walt Whitman (1819–1892), and Edgar Allan Poe (1809–1849) were all attacked for sexual deviancy, on various grounds.
2. The English poet (1828–1882) became increasingly morbid toward the end of his life, when he was addicted to the sedative chloral. The French novelist Émile Zola (1840–1902) was a leading proponent of naturalism; his scientific observations of working-class French life struck many readers as sordid.

1172 | EUGENE O'NEILL

Did you hear? She's moving around. I was hoping she'd gone to sleep.

EDMUND   Forget it! How about another drink?

[*He reaches out and gets the bottle, pours a drink and hands it back. Then with a strained casualness, as his father pours a drink.*]

220   When did Mama go to bed?

TYRONE   Right after you left. She wouldn't eat any dinner. What made you run away?

EDMUND   Nothing. [*Abruptly raising his glass*] Well, here's how.

TYRONE [*mechanically*]   Drink hearty, lad.

[*They drink.* TYRONE *again listens to sounds upstairs—with dread.*]

225   She's moving around a lot. I hope to God she doesn't come down.

EDMUND [*dully*]   Yes. She'll be nothing but a ghost haunting the past by this time. [*He pauses—then miserably.*] Back before I was born—

TYRONE   Doesn't she do the same with me? Back before she ever knew me. You'd think the only happy days she's ever known were in her father's

230   home, or at the Convent, praying and playing the piano. [*Jealous resentment in his bitterness*] As I've told you before, you must take her memories with a grain of salt. Her wonderful home was ordinary enough. Her father wasn't the great, generous, noble Irish gentleman she makes out. He was a nice enough man, good company and a good talker. I liked him and he

235   liked me. He was prosperous enough, too, in his wholesale grocery business, an able man. But he had his weakness. She condemns my drinking but she forgets his. It's true he never touched a drop till he was forty, but after that he made up for lost time. He became a steady champagne drinker, the worst kind. That was his grand pose, to drink only champagne. Well, it

240   finished him quick—that and the consumption—

[*He stops with a guilty glance at his son.*]

EDMUND [*sardonically*]   We don't seem able to avoid unpleasant topics, do we?

TYRONE [*sighs sadly*]   No. [*Then with a pathetic attempt at heartiness*] What do you say to a game or two of Casino,[3] lad?

245   EDMUND   All right.

TYRONE [*shuffling the cards clumsily*]   We can't lock up and go to bed till Jamie comes on the last trolley—which I hope he won't—and I don't want to go upstairs, anyway, till she's asleep.

EDMUND   Neither do I.

250   TYRONE [*keeps shuffling the cards fumblingly, forgetting to deal them*]   As I was saying, you must take her tales of the past with a grain of salt. The piano playing and her dream of becoming a concert pianist. That was put in her head by the nuns flattering her. She was their pet. They loved her for being so devout. They're innocent women, anyway, when it comes to the

255   world. They don't know that not one in a million who shows promise ever rises to concert playing. Not that your mother didn't play well for a schoolgirl, but that's no reason to take it for granted she could have—

EDMUND [*sharply*]   Why don't you deal, if we're going to play.

TYRONE   Eh? I am. [*Dealing with very uncertain judgment of distance*] And

260   the idea she might have become a nun. That's the worst. Your mother was

---

3. A card game in which players capture cards exposed on the table by matching them with cards from their own hands.

one of the most beautiful girls you could ever see. She knew it, too. She was a bit of a rogue and a coquette, God bless her, behind all her shyness and blushes. She was never made to renounce the world. She was bursting with health and high spirits and the love of loving.

265 EDMUND   For God's sake, Papa! Why don't you pick up your hand?

TYRONE [picks it up—dully]   Yes, let's see what I have here.

[They both stare at their cards unseeingly. Then they both start. TYRONE whispers.]

Listen!

EDMUND   She's coming downstairs.

TYRONE [hurriedly]   We'll play our game. Pretend not to notice and she'll
270 soon go up again.

EDMUND [staring through the front parlor—with relief]   I don't see her. She must have started down and then turned back.

TYRONE   Thank God.

EDMUND   Yes. It's pretty horrible to see her the way she must be now. [With
275 bitter misery] The hardest thing to take is the blank wall she builds around her. Or it's more like a bank of fog in which she hides and loses herself. Deliberately, that's the hell of it! You know something in her does it deliberately—to get beyond our reach, to be rid of us, to forget we're alive! It's as if, in spite of loving us, she hated us!

280 TYRONE [remonstrates gently]   Now, now, lad. It's not her. It's the damned poison.

EDMUND [bitterly]   She takes it to get that effect. At least, I know she did this time! [Abruptly] My play, isn't it? Here. [He plays a card.]

TYRONE [plays mechanically—gently reproachful]   She's been terribly fright-
285 ened about your illness, for all her pretending. Don't be too hard on her, lad. Remember she's not responsible. Once that cursed poison gets a hold on anyone—

EDMUND [his face grows hard and he stares at his father with bitter accusation]   It never should have gotten a hold on her! I know damned well she's not to blame! And I know who is! You are! Your damned stinginess! If you'd spent
290 money for a decent doctor when she was so sick after I was born, she'd never have known morphine existed! Instead you put her in the hands of a hotel quack who wouldn't admit his ignorance and took the easiest way out, not giving a damn what happened to her afterwards! All because his fee was cheap! Another one of your bargains!

295 TYRONE [stung—angrily]   Be quiet! How dare you talk of something you know nothing about! [Trying to control his temper.] You must try to see my side of it, too, lad. How was I to know he was that kind of a doctor? He had a good reputation—

EDMUND   Among the souses in the hotel bar, I suppose!

300 TYRONE   That's a lie! I asked the hotel proprietor to recommend the best—

EDMUND   Yes! At the same time crying poorhouse and making it plain you wanted a cheap one! I know your system! By God, I ought to after this afternoon!

TYRONE [guiltily defensive]   What about this afternoon?

305 EDMUND   Never mind now. We're talking about Mama! I'm saying no matter how you excuse yourself you know damned well your stinginess is to blame—

TYRONE   And I say you're a liar! Shut your mouth right now, or—

EDMUND [*ignoring this*] After you found out she'd been made a morphine
310 addict, why didn't you send her to a cure then, at the start, while she still
had a chance? No, that would have meant spending some money! I'll bet
you told her all she had to do was use a little willpower! That's what you
still believe in your heart, in spite of what doctors, who really know something about it, have told you!

315 TYRONE You lie again! I know better than that now! But how was I to know
then? What did I know of morphine? It was years before I discovered what
was wrong. I thought she'd never got over her sickness, that's all. Why
didn't I send her to a cure, you say? [*Bitterly*] Haven't I? I've spent thousands upon thousands in cures! A waste. What good have they done her?
320 She always started again.

EDMUND Because you've never given her anything that would help her want
to stay off it! No home except this summer dump in a place she hates and
you've refused even to spend money to make this look decent, while you
keep buying more property, and playing sucker for every con man with a gold
325 mine, or a silver mine, or any kind of get-rich-quick swindle! You've dragged
her around on the road, season after season, on one-night stands, with no
one she could talk to, waiting night after night in dirty hotel rooms for you
to come back with a bun on after the bars closed! Christ, is it any wonder
she didn't want to be cured. Jesus, when I think of it I hate your guts!

330 TYRONE [*strickenly*] Edmund! [*Then in a rage*] How dare you talk to your
father like that, you insolent young cub! After all I've done for you.

EDMUND We'll come to that, what you're doing for me!

TYRONE [*looking guilty again—ignores this*] Will you stop repeating your
mother's crazy accusations, which she never makes unless it's the poison
335 talking? I never dragged her on the road against her will. Naturally, I
wanted her with me. I loved her. And she came because she loved me and
wanted to be with me. That's the truth, no matter what she says when she's
not herself. And she needn't have been lonely. There was always the members of my company to talk to, if she'd wanted. She had her children, too,
340 and I insisted, in spite of the expense, on having a nurse to travel with her.

EDMUND [*bitterly*] Yes, your one generosity, and that because you were jealous of her paying too much attention to us, and wanted us out of your way!
It was another mistake, too! If she'd had to take care of me all by herself,
and had that to occupy her mind, maybe she'd have been able—

345 TYRONE [*goaded into vindictiveness*] Or for that matter, if you insist on judging things by what she says when she's not in her right mind, if you hadn't
been born she'd never— [*He stops ashamed.*]

EDMUND [*suddenly spent and miserable*] Sure. I know that's what she feels,
Papa.

350 TYRONE [*protests penitently*] She doesn't! She loves you as dearly as ever
mother loved a son! I only said that because you put me in such a God-
damned rage, raking up the past, and saying you hate me—

EDMUND [*dully*] I didn't mean it, Papa. [*He suddenly smiles—kidding a bit
drunkenly.*] I'm like Mama, I can't help liking you, in spite of everything.

355 TYRONE [*grins a bit drunkenly in return*] I might say the same of you. You're
no great shakes as a son. It's a case of "A poor thing but mine own."[4]

---

4. A shortened version of what Touchstone   "A poor virgin, sir, an ill-favoured thing, sir,
says in Shakespeare's *As You Like It* (1599):   but mine own" (5.4.55–56).

[*They both chuckle with real, if alcoholic, affection.* TYRONE *changes the subject.*]

What's happened to our game? Whose play is it?

EDMUND   Yours, I guess.

[TYRONE *plays a card which* EDMUND *takes and the game gets forgotten again.*]

TYRONE   You mustn't let yourself be too downhearted, lad, by the bad news
360   you had today. Both the doctors promised me, if you obey orders at this
place you're going, you'll be cured in six months, or a year at most.

EDMUND   [*his face hard again*]   Don't kid me. You don't believe that.

TYRONE   [*too vehemently*]   Of course I believe it! Why shouldn't I believe it
when both Hardy and the specialist—?

365   EDMUND   You think I'm going to die.

TYRONE   That's a lie! You're crazy!

EDMUND   [*more bitterly*]   So why waste money? That's why you're sending me
to a state farm—

TYRONE   [*in guilty confusion*]   What state farm? It's the Hilltown Sanatorium,
370   that's all I know, and both doctors said it was the best place for you.

EDMUND   [*scathingly*]   For the money! That is, for nothing, or practically
nothing. Don't lie, Papa! You know damned well Hilltown Sanatorium is a
state institution! Jamie suspected you'd cry poorhouse to Hardy and he
wormed the truth out of him.

375   TYRONE   [*furiously*]   That drunken loafer! I'll kick him out in the gutter! He's
poisoned your mind against me ever since you were old enough to listen!

EDMUND   You can't deny it's the truth about the state farm, can you?

TYRONE   It's not true the way you look at it! What if it is run by the state?
That's nothing against it. The state has the money to make a better place
380   than any private sanatorium. And why shouldn't I take advantage of it? It's
my right—and yours. We're residents. I'm a property owner. I help to support it. I'm taxed to death—

EDMUND   [*with bitter irony*]   Yes, on property valued at a quarter of a million.

TYRONE   Lies! It's all mortgaged!

385   EDMUND   Hardy and the specialist know what you're worth. I wonder what
they thought of you when they heard you moaning poorhouse and showing
you wanted to wish me on charity!

TYRONE   It's a lie! All I told them was I couldn't afford any millionaire's sanatorium because I was land-poor.[5] That's the truth!

390   EDMUND   And then you went to the Club to meet McGuire and let him stick
you with another bum piece of property! [*As* TYRONE *starts to deny*] Don't lie
about it! We met McGuire in the hotel bar after he left you. Jamie kidded
him about hooking you, and he winked and laughed!

TYRONE   [*lying feebly*]   He's a liar if he said—

395   EDMUND   Don't lie about it! [*With gathering intensity*] God, Papa, ever since
I went to sea and was on my own, and found out what hard work for little
pay was, and what it felt like to be broke, and starve, and camp on park
benches because I had no place to sleep, I've tried to be fair to you because
I knew what you'd been up against as a kid. I've tried to make allowances.
400   Christ, you have to make allowances in this damned family or go nuts! I
have tried to make allowances for myself when I remember all the rotten

5. That is, short on cash because his wealth is tied up in the ownership of unprofitable land.

stuff I've pulled! I've tried to feel like Mama that you can't help being what you are where money is concerned. But God Almighty, this last stunt of yours is too much! It makes me want to puke! Not because of the rotten
405 way you're treating me. To hell with that! I've treated you rottenly, in my way, more than once. But to think when it's a question of your son having consumption, you can show yourself up before the whole town as such a stinking old tightwad! Don't you know Hardy will talk and the whole damned town will know! Jesus, Papa, haven't you any pride or shame?
410 [*Bursting with rage*] And don't think I'll let you get away with it! I won't go to any damned state farm just to save you a few lousy dollars to buy more bum property with! You stinking old miser—!

> [*He chokes huskily, his voice trembling with rage, and then is shaken by a fit of coughing.*]

TYRONE [*has shrunk back in his chair under this attack, his guilty contrition greater than his anger. He stammers*]   Be quiet! Don't say that to me! You're drunk! I won't mind you. Stop coughing, lad. You've got yourself worked up
415 over nothing. Who said you had to go to this Hilltown place? You can go anywhere you like. I don't give a damn what it costs. All I care about is to have you get well. Don't call me a stinking miser, just because I don't want doctors to think I'm a millionaire they can swindle.

> [EDMUND *has stopped coughing. He looks sick and weak. His father stares at him frightenedly.*]

You look weak, lad. You'd better take a bracer.
420 EDMUND [*grabs the bottle and pours his glass brimfull—weakly*]   Thanks. [*He gulps down the whiskey.*]
TYRONE [*pours himself a big drink, which empties the bottle, and drinks it. His head bows and he stares dully at the cards on the table—vaguely.*]   Whose play is it? [*He goes on dully, without resentment.*] A stinking old miser. Well, maybe you're right. Maybe I can't help being, although all my life since I had anything I've thrown money over the bar to buy drinks for everyone in
425 the house, or loaned money to sponges I knew would never pay it back— [*With a loose-mouthed sneer of self-contempt*] But, of course, that was in barrooms, when I was full of whiskey. I can't feel that way about it when I'm sober in my home. It was at home I first learned the value of a dollar and the fear of the poorhouse. I've never been able to believe in my luck
430 since. I've always feared it would change and everything I had would be taken away. But still, the more property you own, the safer you think you are. That may not be logical, but it's the way I have to feel. Banks fail, and your money's gone, but you think you can keep land beneath your feet. [*Abruptly his tone becomes scornfully superior*] You said you realized what
435 I'd been up against as a boy. The hell you do! How could you? You've had everything—nurses, schools, college, though you didn't stay there. You've had food, clothing. Oh, I know you had a fling of hard work with your back and hands, a bit of being homeless and penniless in a foreign land, and I respect you for it. But it was a game of romance and adventure to you. It
440 was play.
EDMUND [*dully sarcastic*]   Yes, particularly the time I tried to commit suicide at Jimmie the Priest's, and almost did.
TYRONE   You weren't in your right mind. No son of mine would ever— You were drunk.

445 EDMUND   I was stone cold sober. That was the trouble. I'd stopped to think too long.

TYRONE [*with drunken peevishness*]   Don't start your damned atheist morbidness again! I don't care to listen. I was trying to make plain to you— [*Scornfully*] What do you know of the value of a dollar? When I was ten my
450 father deserted my mother and went back to Ireland to die. Which he did soon enough, and deserved to, and I hope he's roasting in hell. He mistook rat poison for flour, or sugar, or something. There was gossip it wasn't by mistake but that's a lie. No one in my family ever—

EDMUND   My bet is, it wasn't by mistake.

455 TYRONE   More morbidness! Your brother put that in your head. The worst he can suspect is the only truth for him. But never mind. My mother was left, a stranger in a strange land,[6] with four small children, me and a sister a little older and two younger than me. My two older brothers had moved to other parts. They couldn't help. They were hard put to it to keep them-
460 selves alive. There was no damned romance in our poverty. Twice we were evicted from the miserable hovel we called home, with my mother's few sticks of furniture thrown out in the street, and my mother and sisters crying. I cried, too, though I tried hard not to, because I was the man of the family. At ten years old! There was no more school for me. I worked twelve
465 hours a day in a machine shop, learning to make files. A dirty barn of a place where rain dripped through the roof, where you roasted in summer, and there was no stove in winter, and your hands got numb with cold, where the only light came through two small filthy windows, so on grey days I'd have to sit bent over with my eyes almost touching the files in
470 order to see! You talk of work! And what do you think I got for it? Fifty cents a week! It's the truth! Fifty cents a week! And my poor mother washed and scrubbed for the Yanks by the day, and my older sister sewed, and my two younger stayed at home to keep the house. We never had clothes enough to wear, nor enough food to eat. Well I remember one
475 Thanksgiving, or maybe it was Christmas, when some Yank in whose house mother had been scrubbing gave her a dollar extra for a present, and on the way home she spent it all on food. I can remember her hugging and kissing us and saying with tears of joy running down her tired face: "Glory be to God, for once in our lives we'll have enough for each of us!"
480 [*He wipes tears from his eyes.*] A fine, brave, sweet woman. There never was a braver or finer.

EDMUND [*moved*]   Yes, she must have been.

TYRONE   Her one fear was she'd get old and sick and have to die in the poorhouse. [*He pauses—then adds with grim humor.*] It was in those days I
485 learned to be a miser. A dollar was worth so much then. And once you've learned a lesson, it's hard to unlearn it. You have to look for bargains. If I took this state farm sanatorium for a good bargain, you'll have to forgive me. The doctors did tell me it's a good place. You must believe that, Edmund. And I swear I never meant you to go there if you didn't want to.
490 [*Vehemently*] You can choose any place you like! Never mind what it costs! Any place I can afford. Any place you like—within reason.

6. A phrase from Exodus 2.22.

[*At this qualification, a grin twitches* EDMUND's *lips. His resentment has gone. His father goes on with an elaborately offhand, casual air.*]

There was another sanatorium the specialist recommended. He said it had a record as good as any place in the country. It's endowed by a group of millionaire factory owners, for the benefit of their workers principally, but
495 you're eligible to go there because you're a resident. There's such a pile of money behind it, they don't have to charge much. It's only seven dollars a week but you get ten times that value. [*Hastily*] I don't want to persuade you to anything, understand. I'm simply repeating what I was told.

EDMUND [*concealing his smile—casually*]   Oh, I know that. It sounds like a
500 good bargain to me. I'd like to go there. So that settles that. [*Abruptly he is miserably desperate again—dully.*] It doesn't matter a damn now, anyway. Let's forget it! [*Changing the subject*] How about our game? Whose play is it?

TYRONE [*mechanically*]   I don't know. Mine, I guess. No, it's yours.

[EDMUND *plays a card. His father takes it. Then about to play from his hand, he again forgets the game.*]

Yes, maybe life overdid the lesson for me, and made a dollar worth too
505 much, and the time came when that mistake ruined my career as a fine actor. [*Sadly*] I've never admitted this to anyone before, lad, but tonight I'm so heartsick I feel at the end of everything, and what's the use of fake pride and pretense. That God-damned play I bought for a song and made such a great success in—a great money success—it ruined me with its promise of
510 an easy fortune. I didn't want to do anything else, and by the time I woke up to the fact I'd become a slave to the damned thing and did try other plays, it was too late. They had identified me with that one part, and didn't want me in anything else. They were right, too. I'd lost the great talent I once had through years of easy repetition, never learning a new part, never
515 really working hard. Thirty-five to forty thousand dollars net profit a season like snapping your fingers! It was too great a temptation. Yet before I bought the damned thing I was considered one of the three or four young actors with the greatest artistic promise in America. I'd worked like hell. I'd left a good job as a machinist to take supers' parts[7] because I loved the the-
520 ater. I was wild with ambition. I read all the plays ever written. I studied Shakespeare as you'd study the Bible. I educated myself. I got rid of an Irish brogue you could cut with a knife. I loved Shakespeare. I would have acted in any of his plays for nothing, for the joy of being alive in his great poetry. And I acted well in him. I felt inspired by him. I could have been a
525 great Shakespearean actor, if I'd kept on. I know that! In 1874 when Edwin Booth[8] came to the theater in Chicago where I was leading man, I played Cassius to his Brutus one night, Brutus to his Cassius the next, Othello to his Iago, and so on.[9] The first night I played Othello, he said to our manager, "That young man is playing Othello better than I ever did!" [*Proudly*]
530 That from Booth, the greatest actor of his day or any other! And it was true! And I was only twenty-seven years old! As I look back on it now, that night was the high spot in my career. I had life where I wanted it! And for a time

7. That is, to be an extra; supernumerary roles are nonspeaking parts.
8. The foremost American actor of the 19th century (1833–1893) and the first to gain international fame (especially for his interpretations of Shakespeare).
9. Cassius and Brutus are principal roles in Shakespeare's *Julius Caesar* (1599); Othello and Iago are principal roles in *Othello*.

after that I kept on upward with ambition high. Married your mother. Ask
her what I was like in those days. Her love was an added incentive to ambi-
535 tion. But a few years later my good bad luck made me find the big money-
maker. It wasn't that in my eyes at first. It was a great romantic part I knew
I could play better than anyone. But it was a great box office success from
the start—and then life had me where it wanted me—at from thirty-five to
forty thousand net profit a season! A fortune in those days—or even in
540 these. [*Bitterly*] What the hell was it I wanted to buy, I wonder, that was
worth— Well, no matter. It's a late day for regrets. [*He glances vaguely at
his cards.*] My play, isn't it?

EDMUND [*moved, stares at his father with understanding—slowly*] I'm glad
you've told me this, Papa. I know you a lot better now.

545 TYRONE [*with a loose, twisted smile*] Maybe I shouldn't have told you. Maybe
you'll only feel more contempt for me. And it's a poor way to convince you
of the value of a dollar.

> [*Then as if this phrase automatically aroused an habitual association in
> his mind, he glances up at the chandelier disapprovingly.*]

The glare from those extra lights hurts my eyes. You don't mind if I turn
them out, do you? We don't need them, and there's no use making the
550 Electric Company rich.

EDMUND [*controlling a wild impulse to laugh—agreeably*] No, sure not. Turn
them out.

TYRONE [*gets heavily and a bit waveringly to his feet and gropes uncertainly for
the lights—his mind going back to its line of thought*] No, I don't know
what the hell it was I wanted to buy. [*He clicks out one bulb.*] On my sol-
555 emn oath, Edmund, I'd gladly face not having an acre of land to call my
own, nor a penny in the bank— [*He clicks out another bulb.*] I'd be willing
to have no home but the poorhouse in my old age if I could look back now
on having been the fine artist I might have been.

> [*He turns out the third bulb, so only the reading lamp is on, and sits
> down again heavily. EDMUND suddenly cannot hold back a burst of
> strained, ironical laughter. TYRONE is hurt.*]

What the devil are you laughing at?

560 EDMUND Not at you, Papa. At life. It's so damned crazy.

TYRONE [*growls*] More of your morbidness! There's nothing wrong with life.
It's we who— [*He quotes.*] "The fault, dear Brutus, is not in our stars, but
in ourselves that we are underlings."[1] [*He pauses—then sadly.*] The praise
Edwin Booth gave my Othello. I made the manager put down his exact
565 words in writing. I kept it in my wallet for years. I used to read it every once
in a while until finally it made me feel so bad I didn't want to face it any
more. Where is it now, I wonder? Somewhere in this house. I remember I
put it away carefully—

EDMUND [*with a wry ironical sadness*] It might be in an old trunk in the attic,
570 along with Mama's wedding dress. [*Then as his father stares at him, he adds
quickly.*] For Pete's sake, if we're going to play cards, let's play.

> [*He takes the card his father had played and leads. For a moment, they
> play the game, like mechanical chess players. Then TYRONE stops, listen-
> ing to a sound upstairs.*]

---

1. Quoting Cassius, from Shakespeare's *Julius Caesar*, 1.2.141–42.

TYRONE   She's still moving around. God knows when she'll go to sleep.

EDMUND [*pleads tensely*]   For Christ's sake, Papa, forget it!

[*He reaches out and pours a drink.* TYRONE *starts to protest, then gives it up.* EDMUND *drinks. He puts down the glass. His expression changes. When he speaks it is as if he were deliberately giving way to drunkenness and seeking to hide behind a maudlin manner.*]

575   Yes, she moves above and beyond us, a ghost haunting the past, and here we sit pretending to forget, but straining our ears listening for the slightest sound, hearing the fog drip from the eaves like the uneven tick of a run-down, crazy clock—or like the dreary tears of a trollop spattering in a puddle of stale beer on a honky-tonk tabletop! [*He laughs with maudlin appreciation.*] Not so bad, that last, eh? Original, not Baudelaire. Give me credit!

580   [*Then with alcoholic talkativeness*] You've just told me some high spots in your memories. Want to hear mine? They're all connected with the sea. Here's one. When I was on the Squarehead square-rigger,[2] bound for Buenos Aires. Full moon in the Trades. The old hooker[3] driving fourteen knots. I lay on the bowsprit, facing astern, with the water foaming into spume

585   under me, the masts with every sail white in the moonlight, towering high above me. I became drunk with the beauty and singing rhythm of it, and for a moment I lost myself—actually lost my life. I was set free! I dissolved in the sea, became white sails and flying spray, became beauty and rhythm, became moonlight and the ship and the high dim-starred sky! I belonged,

590   without past or future, within peace and unity and a wild joy, within something greater than my own life, or the life of Man, to Life itself! To God, if you want to put it that way. Then another time, on the American Line,[4] when I was lookout on the crow's nest in the dawn watch. A calm sea, that time. Only a lazy ground swell and a slow drowsy roll of the ship. The pas-

595   sengers asleep and none of the crew in sight. No sound of man. Black smoke pouring from the funnels behind and beneath me. Dreaming, not keeping lookout, feeling alone, and above, and apart, watching the dawn creep like a painted dream over the sky and sea which slept together. Then the moment of ecstatic freedom came. The peace, the end of the quest, the

600   last harbor, the joy of belonging to a fulfillment beyond men's lousy, pitiful, greedy fears and hopes and dreams! And several other times in my life, when I was swimming far out, or lying alone on a beach, I have had the same experience. Became the sun, the hot sand, green seaweed anchored to a rock, swaying in the tide. Like a saint's vision of beatitude. Like the veil of

605   things as they seem drawn back by an unseen hand. For a second you see—and seeing the secret, are the secret. For a second there is meaning! Then the hand lets the veil fall and you are alone, lost in the fog again, and you stumble on toward nowhere, for no good reason! [*He grins wryly.*] It was a great mistake, my being born a man, I would have been much more suc-

610   cessful as a seagull or a fish. As it is, I will always be a stranger who never feels at home, who does not really want and is not really wanted, who can never belong, who must always be a little in love with death!

TYRONE [*stares at him—impressed*]   Yes, there's the makings of a poet in you all right. [*Then protesting uneasily*] But that's morbid craziness about not

615   being wanted and loving death.

---

2. A large sailing vessel with square sails on two or more masts.
3. An affectionate term for an older ship.

4. The American Steamship Line, which provided transatlantic passenger service in the late 19th century.

EDMUND [*sardonically*] The *makings* of a poet. No, I'm afraid I'm like the guy who is always panhandling for a smoke. He hasn't even got the makings. He's got only the habit. I couldn't touch what I tried to tell you just now. I just stammered. That's the best I'll ever do, I mean, if I live. Well, it will be faithful realism, at least. Stammering is the native eloquence of us fog people.

[*A pause. Then they both jump startledly as there is a noise from outside the house, as if someone had stumbled and fallen on the front steps.* EDMUND *grins.*]

Well, that sounds like the absent brother. He must have a peach of a bun on.

TYRONE [*scowling*] That loafer! He caught the last car, bad luck to it. [*He gets to his feet.*] Get him to bed, Edmund. I'll go out on the porch. He has a tongue like an adder when he's drunk. I'd only lose my temper.

[*He goes out the door to the side porch as the front door in the hall bangs shut behind* JAMIE. EDMUND *watches with amusement* JAMIE's *wavering progress through the front parlor.* JAMIE *comes in. He is very drunk and woozy on his legs. His eyes are glassy, his face bloated, his speech blurred, his mouth slack like his father's, a leer on his lips.*]

JAMIE [*swaying and blinking in the doorway—in a loud voice*] What ho! What ho!

EDMUND [*sharply*] Nix on the loud noise!

JAMIE [*blinks at him*] Oh, hello, Kid. [*With great seriousness*] I'm as drunk as a fiddler's bitch.

EDMUND [*dryly*] Thanks for telling me your great secret.

JAMIE [*grins foolishly*] Yes. Unneshesary information Number One, eh? [*He bends and slaps at the knees of his trousers.*] Had serious accident. The front steps tried to trample on me. Took advantage of fog to waylay me. Ought to be a lighthouse out there. Dark in here, too. [*Scowling*] What the hell is this, the morgue? Lesh have some light on subject.

[*He sways forward to the table, reciting Kipling.*]

"Ford, ford, ford o' Kabul river,
Ford o' Kabul river in the dark!
Keep the crossing-stakes beside you, an' they will surely guide you
'Cross the ford o' Kabul river in the dark."[5]

[*He fumbles at the chandelier and manages to turn on the three bulbs.*]

Thash more like it. To hell with old Gaspard.[6] Where is the old tightwad?

EDMUND Out on the porch.

JAMIE Can't expect us to live in the Black Hole of Calcutta.[7] [*His eyes fix on the full bottle of whiskey.*] Say! Have I got the d.t.'s? [*He reaches out fumblingly and grabs it.*] By God, it's real. What's matter with the Old Man tonight? Must be ossified to forget he left this out. Grab opportunity by the forelock. Key to my success.

[*He slops a big drink into a glass.*]

EDMUND You're stinking now. That will knock you stiff.

5. From "Ford o' Kabul River" (1892), by the English poet and novelist Rudyard Kipling (1865–1936).
6. A miserly character who cheats two heirs out of their inheritance in the 1877 operetta *Les cloches de Corneville* (*The Bells of Corneville*), by Louis Clairville and Charles Gabet.
7. The small, stifling room into which, in 1756, captured British soldiers were packed so tightly that most did not survive the night.

650 JAMIE   Wisdom from the mouth of babes. Can the wise stuff, Kid. You're still
wet behind the ears.

[*He lowers himself into a chair, holding the drink carefully aloft.*]

EDMUND   All right. Pass out if you want to.

JAMIE   Can't, that's trouble. Had enough to sink a ship, but can't sink. Well,
here's hoping. [*He drinks.*]

655 EDMUND   Shove over the bottle. I'll have one, too.

JAMIE [*with sudden, big-brotherly solicitude, grabbing the bottle*]   No, you
don't. Not while I'm around. Remember doctor's orders. Maybe no one else
gives a damn if you die, but I do. My kid brother. I love your guts, Kid.
Everything else is gone. You're all I've got left. [*Pulling bottle closer to him.*]
660 So no booze for you, if I can help it. [*Beneath his drunken sentimentality
there is a genuine sincerity.*]

EDMUND [*irritably*]   Oh, lay off it.

JAMIE [*is hurt and his face hardens*]   You don't believe I care, eh? Just
drunken bull. [*He shoves the bottle over.*] All right. Go ahead and kill
yourself.

665 EDMUND [*seeing he is hurt—affectionately*]   Sure I know you care, Jamie, and
I'm going on the wagon. But tonight doesn't count. Too many damned
things have happened today. [*He pours a drink.*] Here's how. [*He drinks.*]

JAMIE [*sobers up momentarily and with a pitying look*]   I know, Kid. It's been
a lousy day for you. [*Then with sneering cynicism*] I'll bet old Gaspard
670 hasn't tried to keep you off booze. Probably give you a case to take with you
to the state farm for pauper patients. The sooner you kick the bucket, the
less expense. [*With contemptuous hatred*] What a bastard to have for a
father! Christ, if you put him in a book, no one would believe it!

EDMUND [*defensively*]   Oh, Papa's all right, if you try to understand him—-
675 and keep your sense of humor.

JAMIE [*cynically*]   He's been putting on the old sob act for you, eh? He can
always kid you. But not me. Never again. [*Then slowly*] Although, in a way,
I do feel sorry for him about one thing. But he has even that coming to
him. He's to blame. [*Hurriedly*] But to hell with that. [*He grabs the bottle
680 and pours another drink, appearing very drunk again.*] That lash drink's getting me. This one ought to put the lights out. Did you tell Gaspard I got it
out of Doc Hardy this sanatorium is a charity dump?

EDMUND [*reluctantly*]   Yes. I told him I wouldn't go there. It's all settled now.
He said I can go anywhere I want. [*He adds, smiling without resentment.*]
685 Within reason, of course.

JAMIE [*drunkenly imitating his father*]   Of course, lad. Anything within reason. [*Sneering*] That means another cheap dump. Old Gaspard, the miser
in "The Bells," that's a part he can play without makeup.

EDMUND [*irritably*]   Oh, shut up, will you. I've heard that Gaspard stuff a
690 million times.

JAMIE [*shrugs his shoulders—thickly*]   Aw right, if you're shatisfied—let him
get away with it. It's your funeral—I mean, I hope it won't be.

EDMUND [*changing the subject*]   What did you do uptown tonight? Go to
Mamie Burns?

695 JAMIE [*very drunk, his head nodding*]   Sure thing. Where else could I find
suitable feminine companionship? And love. Don't forget love. What is a
man without a good woman's love? A God-damned hollow shell.

EDMUND [*chuckles tipsily, letting himself go now and be drunk*]   You're a nut.

JAMIE [*quotes with gusto from Oscar Wilde's "The Harlot's House"*]

700
> "Then, turning to my love, I said,
> 'The dead are dancing with the dead,
> The dust is whirling with the dust.'

> But she—she heard the violin,
> And left my side and entered in:
> Love passed into the house of lust.

705
> Then suddenly the tune went false,
> The dancers wearied of the waltz . . ."[8]

[*He breaks off, thickly.*] Not strictly accurate. If my love was with me, I didn't notice it. She must have been a ghost. [*He pauses.*] Guess which one of Mamie's charmers I picked to bless me with her woman's love. It'll hand

710 you a laugh, Kid. I picked Fat Violet.

EDMUND [*laughs drunkenly*]   No, honest? Some pick! God, she weighs a ton. What the hell for, a joke?

JAMIE   No joke. Very serious. By the time I hit Mamie's dump I felt very sad about myself and all the other poor bums in the world. Ready for a weep on

715 any old womanly bosom. You know how you get when John Barleycorn[9] turns on the soft music inside you. Then, soon as I got in the door, Mamie began telling me all her troubles. Beefed how rotten business was, and she was going to give Fat Violet the gate. Customers didn't fall for Vi. Only reason she'd kept her was she could play the piano. Lately Vi's gone on

720 drunks and been too boiled to play, and was eating her out of house and home, and although Vi was a goodhearted dumbbell, and she felt sorry for her because she didn't know how the hell she'd make a living, still business was business, and she couldn't afford to run a home for fat tarts. Well, that made me feel sorry for Fat Violet, so I squandered two bucks of your dough

725 to escort her upstairs. With no dishonorable intentions whatever. I like them fat, but not that fat. All I wanted was a little heart-to-heart talk concerning the infinite sorrow of life.

EDMUND [*chuckles drunkenly*]   Poor Vi! I'll bet you recited Kipling and Swinburne and Dowson and gave her "I have been faithful to thee, Cynara, in

730 my fashion."

JAMIE [*grins loosely*]   Sure—with the Old Master, John Barleycorn, playing soft music. She stood it for a while. Then she got good and sore. Got the idea I took her upstairs for a joke. Gave me a grand bawling out. Said she was better than a drunken bum who recited poetry. Then she began to cry.

735 So I had to say I loved her because she was fat, and she wanted to believe that, and I stayed with her to prove it, and that cheered her up, and she kissed me when I left, and said she'd fallen hard for me, and we both cried a little more in the hallway, and everything was fine, except Mamie Burns thought I'd gone bughouse.

---

8. This 1881 poem is said to have been inspired by a night Wilde spent with a French prostitute.
9. That is, alcohol. In an English folk song

John Barleycorn is the personification of barley and the alcoholic beverages made from it, beer and whiskey.

740 EDMUND [*quotes derisively*]   "Harlots and

        Hunted have pleasures of their own to give,
        The vulgar herd can never understand."[1]

JAMIE [*nods his head drunkenly*] Egzactly! Hell of a good time, at that. You should have stuck around with me, Kid. Mamie Burns inquired after you.
745 Sorry to hear you were sick. She meant it, too. [*He pauses—then with maudlin humor, in a ham-actor tone.*] This night has opened my eyes to a great career in store for me, my boy! I shall give the art of acting back to the performing seals, which are its most perfect expression. By applying my natural God-given talents in their proper sphere, I shall attain the pinnacle of
750 success! I'll be the lover of the fat woman in Barnum and Bailey's circus![2]

    [EDMUND *laughs.* JAMIE's *mood changes to arrogant disdain.*]

Pah! Imagine me sunk to the fat girl in a hick town hooker shop! Me! Who have made some of the best-lookers on Broadway sit up and beg!

    [*He quotes from Kipling's "Sestina of the Tramp-Royal."*]

      "Speakin' in general, I 'ave tried 'em all,
      The 'appy roads that take you o'er the world."[3]

755 [*With sodden melancholy*] Not so apt. Happy roads is bunk. Weary roads is right. Get you nowhere fast. That's where I've got—nowhere. Where everyone lands in the end, even if most of the suckers won't admit it.

EDMUND [*derisively*] Can it! You'll be crying in a minute.

JAMIE [*starts and stares at his brother for a second with bitter hostility—thickly*] Don't get—too damned fresh. [*Then abruptly*] But you're right.
760 To hell with repining! Fat Violet's a good kid. Glad I stayed with her. Christian act. Cured her blues. Hell of a good time. You should have stuck with me, Kid. Taken your mind off your troubles. What's the use coming home to get the blues over what can't be helped. All over—finished now—not a hope!

    [*He stops, his head nodding drunkenly, his eyes closing—then suddenly he looks up, his face hard, and quotes jeeringly.*]

765   "If I were hanged on the highest hill,
      Mother o' mine, O mother o' mine!
    I know whose love would follow me still . . ."[4]

EDMUND [*violently*] Shut up!

JAMIE [*in a cruel, sneering tone with hatred in it*] Where's the hophead?
770 Gone to sleep?

    [EDMUND *jerks as if he'd been struck. There is a tense silence.* EDMUND's *face looks stricken and sick. Then in a burst of rage he springs from his chair.*]

EDMUND You dirty bastard!

    [*He punches his brother in the face, a blow that glances off the cheekbone. For a second* JAMIE *reacts pugnaciously and half rises from his chair*]

1. From Baudelaire's "Epilogue" (see above.)
2. The circuses owned by P. T. Barnum (1810–1891) and James Bailey (1847–1906) merged in 1881, becoming America's most celebrated circus.
3. Kipling's 1896 poem, written in Cockney dialect, celebrates the life of the itinerant seaman.
4. Lines from the dedication poem to Kipling's novel *The Light That Failed* (1890).

*to do battle, but suddenly he seems to sober up to a shocked realization of
what he has said and he sinks back limply.*]

JAMIE [*miserably*] Thanks, Kid. I certainly had that coming. Don't know
what made me—booze talking—You know me, Kid.

EDMUND [*his anger ebbing*] I know you'd never say that unless— But God,
775 Jamie, no matter how drunk you are, it's no excuse! [*He pauses—miserably.*]
I'm sorry I hit you. You and I never scrap—that bad.

[*He sinks back on his chair.*]

JAMIE [*huskily*] It's all right. Glad you did. My dirty tongue. Like to cut it
out. [*He hides his face in his hands—dully.*] I suppose it's because I feel so
damned sunk. Because this time Mama had me fooled. I really believed she
780 had it licked. She thinks I always believe the worst, but this time I believed
the best. [*His voice flutters.*] I suppose I can't forgive her—yet. It meant so
much. I'd begun to hope, if she'd beaten the game, I could, too.

[*He begins to sob, and the horrible part of his weeping is that it appears
sober, not the maudlin tears of drunkenness.*]

EDMUND [*blinking back tears himself*] God, don't I know how you feel! Stop
it, Jamie!

785 JAMIE [*trying to control his sobs*] I've known about Mama so much longer
than you. Never forget the first time I got wise. Caught her in the act with
a hypo. Christ, I'd never dreamed before that any women but whores took
dope! [*He pauses.*] And then this stuff of you getting consumption. It's got
me licked. We've been more than brothers. You're the only pal I've ever
790 had. I love your guts. I'd do anything for you.

EDMUND [*reaches out and pats his arm*] I know that, Jamie.

JAMIE [*his crying over—drops his hands from his face—with a strange bitterness*] Yet I'll bet you've heard Mama and old Gaspard spill so much bunk
about my hoping for the worst, you suspect right now I'm thinking to
myself that Papa is old and can't last much longer, and if you were to die,
795 Mama and I would get all he's got, and so I'm probably hoping—

EDMUND [*indignantly*] Shut up, you damned fool! What the hell put that in
your nut? [*He stares at his brother accusingly.*] Yes, that's what I'd like to
know. What put that in your mind?

JAMIE [*confusedly—appearing drunk again*] Don't be a dumbbell! What I
800 said! Always suspected of hoping for the worst. I've got so I can't help —
[*Then drunkenly resentful*] What are you trying to do, accuse me? Don't
play the wise guy with me! I've learned more of life than you'll ever know!
Just because you've read a lot of highbrow junk, don't think you can fool
me! You're only an overgrown kid! Mama's baby and Papa's pet! The family
805 White Hope![5] You've been getting a swelled head lately. About nothing!
About a few poems in a hick town newspaper! Hell, I used to write better
stuff for the Lit magazine in college! You better wake up! You're setting no
rivers on fire! You let hick town boobs flatter you with bunk about your future—

[*Abruptly his tone changes to disgusted contrition.* EDMUND *has looked
away from him, trying to ignore this tirade.*]

Hell, Kid, forget it. That goes for Sweeny.[6] You know I don't mean it. No
810 one hopes more than I do you'll knock 'em all dead. No one is prouder

5. That is, the person on whom hopes are
centered (first used of the unknown white
boxer who might defeat Jack Johnson).

6. An early 20th-century catchphrase meaning "forget it" or "pay no attention."

you've started to make good. [*Drunkenly assertive*] Why shouldn't I be proud? Hell, it's purely selfish. You reflect credit on me. I've had more to do with bringing you up than anyone. I wised you up about women, so you'd never be a fall guy, or make any mistakes you didn't want to make! And who steered
815 you on to reading poetry first? Swinburne, for example? I did! And because I once wanted to write, I planted it in your mind that someday you'd write! Hell, you're more than my brother. I made you! You're my Frankenstein![7]

[*He has risen to a note of drunken arrogance.* EDMUND *is grinning with amusement now.*]

EDMUND   All right, I'm your Frankenstein. So let's have a drink. [*He laughs.*] You crazy nut!

820 JAMIE [*thickly*]   I'll have a drink. Not you. Got to take care of you.

[*He reaches out with a foolish grin of doting affection and grabs his brother's hand.*]

Don't be scared of this sanatorium business. Hell, you can beat that standing on your head. Six months and you'll be in the pink. Probably haven't got consumption at all. Doctors lot of fakers. Told me years ago to cut out booze or I'd soon be dead—and here I am. They're all con men. Anything to
825 grab your dough. I'll bet this state farm stuff is political graft game. Doctors get a cut for every patient they send.

EDMUND [*disgustedly amused*]   You're the limit! At the Last Judgment, you'll be around telling everyone it's in the bag.

JAMIE   And I'll be right. Slip a piece of change to the Judge and be saved, but
830 if you're broke you can go to hell!

[*He grins at this blasphemy and* EDMUND *has to laugh.* JAMIE *goes on.*]

"Therefore put money in thy purse."[8] That's the only dope. [*Mockingly*] The secret of my success! Look what it's got me!

[*He lets* EDMUND's *hand go to pour a big drink, and gulps it down. He stares at his brother with bleary affection—takes his hand again and begins to talk thickly but with a strange, convincing sincerity.*]

Listen, Kid, you'll be going away. May not get another chance to talk. Or might not be drunk enough to tell you truth. So got to tell you now. Some-
835 thing I ought to have told you long ago—for your own good.

[*He pauses—struggling with himself.* EDMUND *stares, impressed and uneasy.* JAMIE *blurts out.*]

Not drunken bull, but "in vino veritas"[9] stuff. You better take it seriously. Want to warn you—against me. Mama and Papa are right. I've been rotten bad influence. And worst of it is, I did it on purpose.

EDMUND [*uneasily*]   Shut up! I don't want to hear—

840 JAMIE   Nix, Kid! You listen! Did it on purpose to make a bum of you. Or part of me did. A big part. That part that's been dead so long. That hates life. My putting you wise so you'd learn from my mistakes. Believed that myself at times, but it's a fake. Made my mistakes look good. Made getting drunk romantic. Made whores fascinating vampires instead of poor, stupid, dis-
845 eased slobs they really are. Made fun of work as sucker's game. Never wanted you succeed and make me look even worse by comparison. Wanted

7. That is, his creation, like the unnamed monster brought to life by Victor Frankenstein in Mary Shelley's novel *Frankenstein: or, The Modern Prometheus* (1818).

8. Quoting Iago from Shakespeare's *Othello,* 1.3.343–44. The phrase means "you can believe me" (cf. "you can bank on it").

9. "In wine [lies] truth" (Latin proverb).

you to fail. Always jealous of you. Mama's baby, Papa's pet! [*He stares at* EDMUND *with increasing enmity.*] And it was your being born that started Mama on dope. I know that's not your fault, but all the same, God damn
850 you, I can't help hating your guts— !

EDMUND [*almost frightenedly*] Jamie! Cut it out! You're crazy!

JAMIE But don't get wrong idea, Kid. I love you more than I hate you. My saying what I'm telling you now proves it. I run the risk you'll hate me— and you're all I've got left. But I didn't mean to tell you that last stuff—go
855 that far back. Don't know what made me. What I wanted to say is, I'd like to see you become the greatest success in the world. But you'd better be on your guard. Because I'll do my damnedest to make you fail. Can't help it. I hate myself. Got to take revenge. On everyone else. Especially you. Oscar Wilde's "Reading Gaol"[1] has the dope twisted. The man was dead and so he
860 had to kill the thing he loved. That's what it ought to be. The dead part of me hopes you won't get well. Maybe he's even glad the game has got Mama again! He wants company, he doesn't want to be the only corpse around the house! [*He gives a hard, tortured laugh.*]

EDMUND Jesus, Jamie! You really have gone crazy!

865 JAMIE Think it over and you'll see I'm right. Think it over when you're away from me in the sanatorium. Make up your mind you've got to tie a can to me—get me out of your life—think of me as dead—tell people, "I had a brother, but he's dead." And when you come back, look out for me. I'll be waiting to welcome you with that "my old pal" stuff, and give you the glad
870 hand, and at the first good chance I get stab you in the back.

EDMUND Shut up! I'll be God-damned if I'll listen to you anymore—

JAMIE [*as if he hadn't heard*] Only don't forget me. Remember I warned you—for your sake. Give me credit. Greater love hath no man than this, that he saveth his brother from himself.[2] [*Very drunkenly, his head bobbing*]
875 That's all. Feel better now. Gone to confession. Know you absolve me, don't you, Kid? You understand. You're a damned fine kid. Ought to be. I made you. So go and get well. Don't die on me. You're all I've got left. God bless you, Kid. [*His eyes close. He mumbles.*] That last drink—the old K.O.[3]

> [*He falls into a drunken doze, not completely asleep.* EDMUND *buries his face in his hands miserably.* TYRONE *comes in quietly through the screen door from the porch, his dressing gown wet with fog, the collar turned up around his throat. His face is stern and disgusted but at the same time pitying.* EDMUND *does not notice his entrance.*]

TYRONE [*In a low voice*] Thank God he's asleep.

> [EDMUND *looks up with a start.*]

880 I thought he'd never stop talking. [*He turns down the collar of his dressing gown.*] We'd better let him stay where he is and sleep it off.

> [EDMUND *remains silent.* TYRONE *regards him—then goes on.*]

I heard the last part of his talk. It's what I've warned you. I hope you'll heed the warning, now it comes from his own mouth.

> [EDMUND *gives no sign of having heard.* TYRONE *adds pityingly*]

---

1. "The Ballad of Reading Gaol," which Wilde wrote upon his 1897 release from prison ("gaol") in Reading, England; the poem's most famous line is "Yet each man kills the thing he loves."

2. See John 15.13: "Greater love hath no man than this, that a man lay down his life for his friends."
3. Knockout.

But don't take it too much to heart, lad. He loves to exaggerate the worst of
885 himself when he's drunk. He's devoted to you. It's the one good thing left in
him. [*He looks down on* JAMIE *with a bitter sadness.*] A sweet spectacle for
me! My first-born, who I hoped would bear my name in honor and dignity,
who showed such brilliant promise!

EDMUND [*miserably*]   Keep quiet, can't you, Papa?

890 TYRONE [*pours a drink*]   A waste! A wreck, a drunken hulk, done with and
finished!

> [*He drinks.* JAMIE *has become restless, sensing his father's presence, strug-
> gling up from his stupor. Now he gets his eyes open to blink up at* TYRONE.
> *The latter moves back a step defensively, his face growing hard.*]

JAMIE [*suddenly points a finger at him and recites with dramatic emphasis*]

> "Clarence is come, false, fleeting, perjured Clarence,
> That stabbed me in the field by Tewksbury.
> Seize on him, Furies, take him into torment."[4]

895 [*Then resentfully*] What the hell are you staring at?

> [*He recites sardonically from Rossetti.*]

> "Look in my face. My name is Might-Have-Been;
> I am also called No More, Too Late, Farewell."[5]

TYRONE   I'm well aware of that, and God knows I don't want to look at it.

EDMUND   Papa! Quit it!

900 JAMIE [*derisively*]   Got a great idea for you, Papa. Put on revival of "The
Bells" this season. Great part in it you can play without makeup. Old Gaspard, the miser!

> [TYRONE *turns away, trying to control his temper.*]

EDMUND   Shut up, Jamie!

JAMIE [*jeeringly*]   I claim Edwin Booth never saw the day when he could give
905 as good a performance as a trained seal. Seals are intelligent and honest.
They don't put up any bluffs about the Art of Acting. They admit they're
just hams earning their daily fish.

TYRONE [*stung, turns on him in a rage*]   You loafer!

EDMUND   Papa! Do you want to start a row that will bring Mama down?
910 Jamie, go back to sleep! You've shot off your mouth too much already.

> [TYRONE *turns away.*]

JAMIE [*thickly*]   All right, Kid. Not looking for argument. Too damned sleepy.

> [*He closes his eyes, his head nodding.* TYRONE *comes to the table and sits
> down, turning his chair so he won't look at* JAMIE. *At once he becomes
> sleepy, too.*]

TYRONE [*heavily*]   I wish to God she'd go to bed so that I could, too. [*Drows-
ily*] I'm dog tired. I can't stay up all night like I used to. Getting old—old
and finished. [*With a bone-cracking yawn*] Can't keep my eyes open. I think
915 I'll catch a few winks. Why don't you do the same, Edmund? It'll pass the
time until she—

> [*His voice trails off. His eyes close, his chin sags, and he begins to breathe
> heavily through his mouth.* EDMUND *sits tensely. He hears something and*

4. Quoting Clarence from Shakespeare's
Richard III (1592–93), 1.4.55–57.

5. The opening lines of sonnet 97, "A Super-
scription," from *The House of Life* (1870).

jerks nervously forward in his chair, staring through the front parlor into the hall. He jumps up with a hunted, distracted expression. It seems for a second he is going to hide in the back parlor. Then he sits down again and waits, his eyes averted, his hands gripping the arms of his chair. Suddenly all five bulbs of the chandelier in the front parlor are turned on from a wall switch, and a moment later someone starts playing the piano in there—the opening of one of Chopin's simpler waltzes, done with a forgetful, stiff-fingered groping, as if an awkward schoolgirl were practicing it for the first time. TYRONE *starts to wide-awakeness and sober dread, and* JAMIE's *head jerks back and his eyes open. For a moment they listen frozenly. The playing stops as abruptly as it began, and* MARY *appears in the doorway. She wears a sky-blue dressing gown over her nightdress, dainty slippers with pompons on her bare feet. Her face is paler than ever. Her eyes look enormous. They glisten like polished black jewels. The uncanny thing is that her face now appears so youthful. Experience seems ironed out of it. It is a marble mask of girlish innocence, the mouth caught in a shy smile. Her white hair is braided in two pigtails which hang over her breast. Over one arm, carried neglectfully, trailing on the floor, as if she had forgotten she held it, is an old-fashioned white satin wedding gown, trimmed with duchesse lace. She hesitates in the doorway, glancing round the room, her forehead puckered puzzledly, like someone who has come to a room to get something but has become absent-minded on the way and forgotten what it was. They stare at her. She seems aware of them merely as she is aware of other objects in the room, the furniture, the windows, familiar things she accepts automatically as naturally belonging there but which she is too preoccupied to notice.*]

JAMIE [*breaks the cracking silence—bitterly, self-defensively sardonic*] The Mad Scene. Enter Ophelia![6]

[*His father and brother both turn on him fiercely.* EDMUND *is quicker. He slaps* JAMIE *across the mouth with the back of his hand.*]

TYRONE [*his voice trembling with suppressed fury*] Good boy, Edmund. The
920 dirty blackguard! His own mother!

JAMIE [*mumbles guiltily, without resentment*] All right, Kid. Had it coming. But I told you how much I'd hoped—

[*He puts his hands over his face and begins to sob.*]

TYRONE I'll kick you out in the gutter tomorrow, so help me God.

[*But* JAMIE's *sobbing breaks his anger, and he turns and shakes his shoulder, pleading.*]

Jamie, for the love of God, stop it!

[*Then* MARY *speaks, and they freeze into silence again, staring at her. She has paid no attention whatever to the incident. It is simply a part of the familiar atmosphere of the room, a background which does not touch her preoccupation; and she speaks aloud to herself, not to them.*]

925 MARY I play so badly now. I'm all out of practice. Sister Theresa will give me a dreadful scolding. She'll tell me it isn't fair to my father when he spends so much money for extra lessons. She's quite right, it isn't fair, when he's so good and generous, and so proud of me. I'll practice every day from now on. But something horrible has happened to my hands. The fingers have
930 gotten so stiff— [*She lifts her hands to examine them with a frightened*

6. In Shakespeare's *Hamlet* (ca. 1600), 4.5, Ophelia enters—apparently mad, but conveying a good deal of matter in her distracted words.

puzzlement.] The knuckles are all swollen. They're so ugly. I'll have to go to the Infirmary and show Sister Martha. [*With a sweet smile of affectionate trust.*] She's old and a little cranky, but I love her just the same, and she has things in her medicine chest that'll cure anything. She'll give me some-
935 thing to rub on my hands, and tell me to pray to the Blessed Virgin, and they'll be well again in no time.

> [*She forgets her hands and comes into the room, the wedding gown trailing on the floor. She glances around vaguely, her forehead puckered again.*]

Let me see. What did I come here to find? It's terrible, how absent-minded I've become. I'm always dreaming and forgetting.

TYRONE [*in a stifled voice*]   What's that she's carrying, Edmund?

940 EDMUND [*dully*]   Her wedding gown, I suppose.

TYRONE   Christ!

> [*He gets to his feet and stands directly in her path—in anguish.*]

Mary! Isn't it bad enough—? [*Controlling himself—gently persuasive*] Here, let me take it, dear. You'll only step on it and tear it and get it dirty dragging it on the floor. Then you'd be sorry afterwards.

> [*She lets him take it, regarding him from somewhere far away within herself, without recognition, without either affection or animosity.*]

MARY [*with the shy politeness of a well-bred young girl toward an elderly gentle-
945 man who relieves her of a bundle*]   Thank you. You are very kind. [*She regards the wedding gown with a puzzled interest.*] It's a wedding gown. It's very lovely, isn't it? [*A shadow crosses her face and she looks vaguely uneasy.*] I remember now. I found it in the attic hidden in a trunk. But I don't know what I wanted it for. I'm going to be a nun—that is, if I can only find—
950 [*She looks around the room, her forehead puckered again.*] What is it I'm looking for? I know it's something I lost.

> [*She moves back from TYRONE, aware of him now only as some obstacle in her path.*]

TYRONE [*in hopeless appeal*]   Mary!

> [*But it cannot penetrate her preoccupation. She doesn't seem to hear him. He gives up helplessly, shrinking into himself, even his defensive drunkenness taken from him, leaving him sick and sober. He sinks back on his chair, holding the wedding gown in his arms with an unconscious clumsy, protective gentleness.*]

JAMIE [*drops his hand from his face, his eyes on the tabletop. He has suddenly sobered up, too—dully.*]   It's no good, Papa.

> [*He recites from Swinburne's "A Leave-taking" and does it well, simply but with a bitter sadness.*]

"Let us rise up and part; she will not know.
955   Let us go seaward as the great winds go,
Full of blown sand and foam; what help is here?
There is no help, for all these things are so,
And all the world is bitter as a tear.
And how these things are, though ye strove to show,
960   She would not know."[7]

---

7. The second stanza of the 1866 poem (he then quotes the first stanza, followed by the sixth, and final, stanza).

MARY [*looking around her*]   Something I miss terribly. It can't be altogether lost.

[*She starts to move around in back of* JAMIE'S *chair.*]

JAMIE [*turns to look up into her face—and cannot help appealing pleadingly in his turn*]   Mama!

[*She does not seem to hear. He looks away hopelessly.*]

Hell! What's the use? It's no good.

[*He recites from "A Leave-taking" again with increased bitterness.*]

965   "Let us go hence, my songs; she will not hear.
           Let us go hence together without fear;
           Keep silence now, for singing-time is over,
           And over all old things and all things dear.
           She loves not you nor me as all we love her.
970   Yea, though we sang as angels in her ear,
           She would not hear."

MARY [*looking around her*]   Something I need terribly. I remember when I had it I was never lonely nor afraid. I can't have lost it forever, I would die if I thought that. Because then there would be no hope.

[*She moves like a sleepwalker, around the back of* JAMIE'S *chair, then forward toward left front, passing behind* EDMUND.]

EDMUND [*turns impulsively and grabs her arm. As he pleads he has the quality of a bewilderedly hurt little boy.*]   Mama! It isn't a summer cold! I've got consumption!

MARY [*for a second he seems to have broken through to her. She trembles and her expression becomes terrified. She calls distractedly, as if giving a command to herself.*]   No!

[*And instantly she is far away again. She murmurs gently but impersonally.*]

You must not try to touch me. You must not try to hold me. It isn't right, when I am hoping to be a nun.

[*He lets his hand drop from her arm. She moves left to the front end of the sofa beneath the windows and sits down, facing front, her hands folded in her lap, in a demure schoolgirlish pose.*]

980 JAMIE [*gives* EDMUND *a strange look of mingled pity and jealous gloating*]   You damned fool. It's no good.

[*He recites again from the Swinburne poem.*]

           "Let us go hence, go hence; she will not see.
           Sing all once more together; surely she,
           She too, remembering days and words that were,
985   Will turn a little toward us, sighing; but we,
           We are hence, we are gone, as though we had not been there.
           Nay, and though all men seeing had pity on me,
           She would not see."

TYRONE [*trying to shake off his hopeless stupor*]   Oh, we're fools to pay any 990 attention. It's the damned poison. But I've never known her to drown herself in it as deep as this. [*Gruffly*] Pass me that bottle, Jamie. And stop reciting that damned morbid poetry. I won't have it in my house!

[JAMIE *pushes the bottle toward him. He pours a drink without disarranging the wedding gown he holds carefully over his other arm and on his lap, and shoves the bottle back.* JAMIE *pours his and passes the bottle to* EDMUND, *who, in turn, pours one.* TYRONE *lifts his glass and his sons follow suit mechanically, but before they can drink* MARY *speaks and they slowly lower their drinks to the table, forgetting them.*]

MARY [*staring dreamily before her. Her face looks extraordinarily youthful and innocent. The shyly eager, trusting smile is on her lips as she talks aloud to herself.*]   I had a talk with Mother Elizabeth. She is so sweet and good. A saint on earth. I love her dearly. It may be sinful of me but I love her better

995 than my own mother. Because she always understands, even before you say a word. Her kind blue eyes look right into your heart. You can't keep any secrets from her. You couldn't deceive her, even if you were mean enough to want to. [*She gives a little rebellious toss of her head—with girlish pique.*] All the same, I don't think she was so understanding this time. I told her I

1000 wanted to be a nun. I explained how sure I was of my vocation, that I had prayed to the Blessed Virgin to make me sure, and to find me worthy. I told Mother I had had a true vision when I was praying in the shrine of Our Lady of Lourdes,[8] on the little island in the lake. I said I knew, as surely as I knew I was kneeling there, that the Blessed Virgin had smiled and blessed me with

1005 her consent. But Mother Elizabeth told me I must be more sure than that, even, that I must prove it wasn't simply my imagination. She said, if I was so sure, then I wouldn't mind putting myself to a test by going home after I graduated, and living as other girls lived, going out to parties and dances and enjoying myself; and then if after a year or two I still felt sure, I could come

1010 back to see her and we would talk it over again. [*She tosses her head—indignantly.*] I never dreamed Holy Mother would give me such advice! I was really shocked. I said, of course, I would do anything she suggested, but I knew it was simply a waste of time. After I left her, I felt all mixed up, so I went to the shrine and prayed to the Blessed Virgin and found peace again

1015 because I knew she heard my prayer and would always love me and see no harm ever came to me so long as I never lost my faith in her.

[*She pauses and a look of growing uneasiness comes over her face. She passes a hand over her forehead as if brushing cobwebs from her brain—vaguely.*]

That was in the winter of senior year. Then in the spring something happened to me. Yes, I remember. I fell in love with James Tyrone and was so happy for a time.

[*She stares before her in a sad dream.* TYRONE *stirs in his chair.* EDMUND *and* JAMIE *remain motionless.*]

Curtain.

Tao House
September 20, 1940

---

8. The town of Lourdes, in southwestern France, has been a major destination for Christian pilgrims since 1858, when Berna- dette Soubirous reported seeing apparitions of the Virgin Mary

TENNESSEE WILLIAMS

1911–1983

W HEN Tennessee Williams's play *The Glass Menagerie* premiered in 1944, American drama found itself at a crossroads. EUGENE O'NEILL, whose plays helped establish the American theater as a serious artistic medium, had been absent from the stage since 1934, and the drama of social protest that dominated the 1930s was eclipsed by the outbreak of World War II. American society was undergoing a transition, as traditional values and institutions were shaken by the mid-twentieth century's accelerating economic and social transformations. In this theatrical and social climate, the plays of Williams and ARTHUR MILLER restored the centrality of theater to the nation's cultural life. But whereas Miller's *All My Sons* (1947) and *DEATH OF A SALESMAN* (1949) concentrated on the ethical conflicts of individuals and society, Williams's drama explored the deeper (and often darker) regions of America's psyche: the psychological fault lines between convention and romantic individualism; the dynamics of sexuality, violence, and alienation; and the place of art and the artist's visionary temperament in a society seen as increasingly hostile to the imagination. Drawn to characters who cling to failing illusions—outsiders who have difficulty fitting in the modern world—Williams pioneered a lyrical dramatic style that confronted but also transcended the harsh

realities of contemporary life. In plays such as *The Glass Menagerie*, A STREETCAR NAMED DESIRE (1947), and *Cat on a Hot Tin Roof* (1955), the clash of cultures, generations, and psyches is marked by a lyricism reminiscent of the works of ANTON CHEKHOV (1860–1904) and Federico García Lorca (1898–1936). After Williams's death, the playwright DAVID MAMET called these plays "the greatest dramatic poetry in the American language."

Williams was, before all else, a Southern writer; like his fellow twentieth-century authors William Faulkner, Eudora Welty, and Flannery O'Connor, he explored the region's self-defining myths and codes of behavior, its changing economy, and its multiple—often conflicting—cultures. The playwright was born Thomas Lanier Williams III on March 26, 1911, in Columbus, Mississippi, to Edwina Dakin Williams, the daughter of an Episcopal minister, and Cornelius Coffin Williams, a shoe salesman from east Tennessee. (The playwright would later change his first name to Tennessee in recognition of his paternal ancestors.) Although he suffered a near-fatal bout of diphtheria at the age of five that kept him out of school, his childhood in Mississippi was an idyllic one. But the idyll ended in 1918 when his father moved the family to St. Louis to take a managerial position at the International Shoe Company. Living in what he later recalled as "a perpetually dim little apartment in a wilderness of identical brick and concrete structures with no grass and no trees nearer than the park," mocked by other children for their southern accents, Williams and his sister Rose (with whom he was very close) found themselves isolated and unhappy in this harsh urban setting. The situation at home was hardly better: his parents quarreled frequently, and his relationship with his father was strained.

Williams began writing at the age of twelve and saw his first article published in a popular magazine at the age of sixteen. He attended the University of Missouri from 1929 to 1932 and majored in journalism, but his father withdrew him from college after he failed a mandatory ROTC course. For the next several years, he worked at his father's company while writing stories at night. Williams eventually attended Washington University in St. Louis and the University of Iowa, where he earned a B.A. in English in 1938. During these years Williams turned his attention to playwriting. A year after his first play—a farce about sailors titled *Cairo! Shanghai! Bombay!*—was produced in a backyard theater in 1935, Williams became involved with the Mummers, a semiprofessional St. Louis theater group specializing in plays of social protest. The country was in the throes of the Depression, and the theater had become an outlet for expressing social and political discontent. Clifford Odets's *Waiting for Lefty* took the theater world by storm in 1935, and the Federal Theatre Project (part of the New Deal's Works Progress Administration) was popularizing the multimedia "Living Newspaper" format as a way of commenting on poverty and other social issues. Reflecting this theatrical climate, Williams's drama during these years was socially and politically engaged. In 1937 the Mummers produced *Candles to the Sun*, a play about Alabama coal miners, and *Fugitive Kind*, which explored the hardships of Depression America through a group of characters living in a St. Louis flophouse. Williams also completed *Not About Nightingales*, a play about prison conditions that he had started at the University of Iowa; the Mummers considered this play, but it would not be produced until 1998.

Buoyed by the local success of these plays, Williams submitted three works to a playwriting competition sponsored by the Group Theater, one of the leading American theater companies of the 1930s. He also moved to New Orleans for two months, a city to which he would return throughout his career and to which he would later refer as his "spiritual home." Williams received a special prize from the Group Theater for a collection of one-act plays and subsequently won a Rockefeller Foundation fellowship, which he used to write *The Battle of Angels*. The Theater Guild of New York produced this play in Boston in 1940, but the production was condemned by spectators and critics.

Over the next four years Williams held a variety of jobs, including a two-month scriptwriting stint for MGM in Hollywood, and he worked on a number of other writing projects. One of these, a play titled *The Gentleman Caller*, would earn Williams the fame that had eluded him in Boston. Under the revised title *The Glass Menagerie*, this play opened in Chicago in December 1944. Response was initially lukewarm, but the glowing review by a prominent Chicago theater critic led to sold-out houses. After transferring to Broadway in March 1945, the play ran for 561 performances and won the New York Drama Critics' Circle Award for Best Play. Williams's most deeply autobiographical drama—its narrator, Tom Wingfield, is modeled on Williams himself, and Tom's sister Laura is a portrait of Rose Williams—*The Glass Menagerie* was important to American theater (and to the playwright's subsequent career) as much for its technical and stylistic innovations as for its subject matter. Seeking to express the fluidity of memory in theatrical terms, Williams employs setting, music, and light in ways that blur the lines between realism and expressionism. The playwright's production notes to *The Glass Menagerie* call for "a new, plastic theatre which must take the place of the exhausted theatre of realistic conventions if the theatre is to resume vitality as a part of our culture." Such a theater must not escape reality; rather, the use of expressionistic and poetic devices allows fuller access to the truth. "[T]ruth, life, or reality," Williams wrote, "is an organic thing which the poetic imagination can represent or suggest, in essence, only through transformation, through changing into other forms than those which were merely present in appearance."

The success of *The Glass Menagerie* catapulted Williams to the forefront of public attention and generated a celebrity toward which he remained profoundly ambivalent. His reputation as one of America's leading dramatists was underscored by the success of his next play, *A Streetcar Named Desire*. Williams had conceived the play's outlines in the early 1940s and had written a number of early versions: *Blanche's Chair on the Moon*, *The Moth*, *The Primary Colors*, and *The Poker Night* were among the titles he tried. The completed *Streetcar Named Desire* opened on December 3, 1947, at the Ethel Barrymore Theater in New York in a production directed by Elia Kazan. Starring a little-known actor, Marlon Brando, in the role of Stanley Kowalski, the play ran for 855 performances over the next two years and was awarded a Pulitzer Prize and the New York Drama Critics' Circle Award. The 1951 film version of *Streetcar* (also directed by Kazan) was equally celebrated. In addition to receiving a number of major revivals, *A Streetcar Named Desire* has been translated into nearly twenty-five languages and staged around the world.

During the decade and a half after *A Streetcar Named Desire*, Williams had a string of plays produced on Broadway: *The Rose Tattoo* (1951), *Camino Real* (1953), *Cat on a Hot Tin Roof* (1955, Pulitzer Prize), *Orpheus Descending* (1957), *Suddenly Last Summer* (1958), *Sweet Bird of Youth* (1959), and *The Night of the Iguana* (1961). Although Williams continued to write plays in the 1960s and 1970s— including *In the Bar of a Tokyo Hotel* (1969), *The Two-Character Play/Out Cry* (1967, 1971), *The Red Devil Battery Sign* (1975), and *Clothes for a Summer Hotel* (1980)—his dramatic work after *Night of the Iguana* failed to receive the acclaim of his earlier plays. Convinced for most of his life that he would die young, Tennessee Williams passed away at the age of seventy-one on February 25, 1983.

Final scene from the original 1947 Broadway production of *A Streetcar Named Desire*.

A *Streetcar Named Desire* is set in the French Quarter of New Orleans, a city known for its international influences (French, Spanish, Caribbean) as well as its theatricalized ceremonies and celebrations and its bohemian subculture. The play is full of references to the city's sites and institutions; indeed, the streetcar named Desire, which brings Blanche DuBois to her sister's apartment in the play's opening scene, did run through the French Quarter in the 1940s. At the same time, Williams's New Orleans is as much an atmosphere as an actual location. Like the blues music rising from a nearby bar, the turquoise evening sky that opens the play "invests the scene with a kind of lyricism and gracefully attenuates the atmosphere of decay." Throughout *A Streetcar Named Desire,* the play's setting embodies moods and states of mind, accentuating points of crisis and imbuing realism with expressionism's more subjective reach. The apartment of Stanley and Stella Kowalski reflects this shifting border between inside and outside. Obscured in darkness when the play's action takes place outside, it appears as an interior acting space when the lighting changes. Its back wall consists of a scrim (or see-through fabric), which appears solid when lit from the front but transparent when lit from behind, allowing a view of the alley beyond the apartment.

Reviewers and scholars who have written about *A Streetcar Named Desire* have focused, for the most part, on the characters of Stanley and Blanche. While such an emphasis risks obscuring the important roles of other characters (particularly Stella and Stanley's friend Mitch), the interaction between Stanley and Blanche represents one of the great *agones,* or dramatic conflicts, in Western drama. The two characters are, in many ways, dramatic antitheses. From his initial appearance, Stanley is defined by his rough manners, working-class pride, and sexual confidence. Polish American by birth, he inhabits a neighbor-

Vivien Leigh as Blanche DuBois and Marlon Brando as Stanley Kowalski in Elia Kazan's 1951 film adaptation of *A Streetcar Named Desire.*

hood defined by its relaxed—at times violent—behavior and its ethnic and racial mix. Stanley's is a male-centered world of poker nights, Jax beer, and sexual pleasure; as Williams writes in introducing the character, "Since earliest manhood the center of his being has been pleasure with women, the giving and taking of it, not with weak indulgence, dependently, but with the power and pride of a richly feathered male bird among hens." Given to explosive outbursts but also a man of shrewdness and calculation, he defends his territory with a fierceness that masks an awareness of his own limitations. His charismatic yet threatening presence in Williams's play derives from the aggressive masculinity that he wears like a badge. In this mode of interacting with others he contrasts markedly with Mitch, a man of sensitivity and deep emotional attachments who lives with his mother.

Unlike Stanley, Blanche comes from a plantation world of landed wealth, breeding, and sexual decorum, a world (encapsulated in the plantation's name, Belle Reve—French for "beautiful dream") that was, in reality, already yielding in the 1940s to a newly industrializing South. With her white suit, bodice, and gloves, Blanche's mothlike appearance in the opening scene is incongruous with her urban surroundings. Whereas Stanley represents the vitality, dynamism, and swagger of a country emerging from World War II, Blanche represents more traditional ideals of culture, civilization, and manners. Yet even as Blanche articulates these ideals, the audience is aware that they have failed her. Belle Reve has been lost to the sexual appetites and financial improvidence of its inhabitants, and the history of decline and death that Blanche recounts is gothic in tone. Traumatized by the suicide of her homosexual husband years earlier, Blanche has led a life of promiscuity and fleeting encounters. As age begins to threaten her attractiveness, her efforts to maintain the southern belle image that she was raised to project grow more strained. Standing as the centerpiece of Williams's theatrical world, Blanche becomes stage manager in her own right, controlling the lighting by which she is seen and adding music, decorating the Kowalski apartment, and dressing herself and applying makeup in order to play the starring role in her interactions with others. "I don't want realism. I want magic!" she tells Mitch, and these words capture her increasingly desperate faith in the compensatory power of illusion. Her attempts to maintain this illusion and the accompanying struggle to hold together the different parts of her personality break down the lines between her subjective life and the ever more hostile surroundings in which she finds herself. Of all the characters, it is Blanche who is most closely linked to the expressionistic devices of *A Streetcar Named Desire*. In the play's early scenes she hears the Varsouviana polka that was playing the night her husband shot himself; and as the play progresses, the lighting and sound effects of the stage increasingly mirror her mental and emotional turmoil.

In the aftermath of Stanley's violent outburst at the poker night he hosts for his friends in scene 3, Blanche pleads with Stella to choose tenderness and civilization over the bestiality and violence that Stanley embodies: "*Don't—don't hang back with the brutes!*" By framing the choice of values so explicitly, Blanche seeks to triumph over Stanley in the battle for Stella's love and allegiance. But the claims presented by the characters engage the audience's sympathies as well. Though scholars and reviewers have often sided with Stanley or Blanche in their assessments of the play's central confrontation, such judgments violate the complex balances and counterpoints that Williams establishes. In their sympathies, audiences must come to terms with competing social and moral codes, and they must deal with the fact that Williams's character portrayals amplify and change as the play progresses. For his part, while Williams condemned what he called "the ravishment of the tender, the sensitive, the delicate, by the savage and brutal forces of modern society," his sympathies extended in both directions: "[Blanche] was broken on the rock of the world; I find her a sympathetic character, but I also find Stanley sympathetic."

With its exploration of traditional and contemporary gender roles and its juxtaposition of the old South with the new, *A Streetcar Named Desire* offers a powerful portrait of the changing social landscape of postwar America. In keeping with this achievement, its characters, actions, and lines of dialogue became potent cultural symbols in the decades that followed. Brando's Stanley—memorialized by the widely successful film adaptation—became an image of masculinity for a generation that also worshipped such male icons as John Wayne, Elvis Presley, and James Dean. Subsequent actors playing Stanley have had to work to free their role from this mesmerizing performance. But the figure of Blanche DuBois—introduced on stage by Jessica Tandy and popularized on screen by Vivien Leigh—may be more resonant in the latter half of the twentieth century and the early years of the twenty-first. Embodying the strains in female social roles during the supposed return to normalcy following World War II, Blanche serves as an image of the conflicted place of both women and men in a society in which expected ideals and behaviors no longer match the realities of contemporary gender relations. Like Stanley, she deals with the realities of desire—physical and emotional—that fly in the face of death itself. That she cannot control her journey on the streetcar named Desire says as much about the society she inhabits as it does her precarious psyche. Though the contemporary world is no longer that of postwar America, issues of sexuality remain pressing in both traditional and cosmopolitan societies. When the drag queen Prior Walters quotes Blanche in TONY KUSHNER's *Angels in America* (1991–92), he acknowledges the line between Williams's female protagonist—trapped between roles—and a more contemporary field of sexual identities. To learn more about the staging of *A Streetcar Named Desire* and to view photographs from select performances of the play, see the "Plays in Performance" color insert near the center of this volume.   S.G.

A Streetcar Named Desire

And so it was I entered the broken world
To trace the visionary company of love, its voice
An instant in the wind (I know not whither hurled)
But not for long to hold each desperate choice.
                    "The Broken Tower" by Hart Crane[1]

CHARACTERS

BLANCHE	PABLO
STELLA	A NEGRO WOMAN
STANLEY	A DOCTOR
MITCH	A NURSE
EUNICE	A YOUNG COLLECTOR
STEVE	A MEXICAN WOMAN

1. American poet (1899–1932); "The Broken Tower" was the last poem Crane wrote before committing suicide at the age of 32.

Scene 1

The exterior of a two-story corner building on a street in New Orleans which is named Elysian Fields and runs between the L & N tracks[2] and the river. The section is poor but, unlike corresponding sections in other American cities, it has a raffish charm. The houses are mostly white frame, weathered grey, with rickety outside stairs and galleries and quaintly ornamented gables. This building contains two flats, upstairs and down. Faded white stairs ascend to the entrances of both.

It is first dark of an evening early in May. The sky that shows around the dim white building is a peculiarly tender blue, almost a turquoise, which invests the scene with a kind of lyricism and gracefully attenuates the atmosphere of decay. You can almost feel the warm breath of the brown river beyond the river warehouses with their faint redolences of bananas and coffee. A corresponding air is evoked by the music of Negro entertainers at a barroom around the corner. In this part of New Orleans you are practically always just around the corner, or a few doors down the street, from a tinny piano being played with the infatuated fluency of brown fingers. This "blue piano" expresses the spirit of the life which goes on here.

Two women, one white and one colored, are taking the air on the steps of the building. The white woman is EUNICE, *who occupies the upstairs flat; the colored woman a neighbor, for New Orleans is a cosmopolitan city where there is a relatively warm and easy intermingling of races in the old part of town.*

Above the music of the "blue piano" the voices of people on the street can be heard overlapping.

> [*Two men come around the corner,* STANLEY KOWALSKI *and* MITCH. *They are about twenty-eight or thirty years old, roughly dressed in blue denim work clothes.* STANLEY *carries his bowling jacket and a red-stained package from a butcher's. They stop at the foot of the steps.*]

STANLEY [*bellowing*] Hey, there! Stella, baby!

> [STELLA *comes out on the first floor landing, a gentle young woman, about twenty-five, and of a background obviously quite different from her husband's.*]

STELLA [*mildly*] Don't holler at me like that. Hi, Mitch.

STANLEY Catch!

STELLA What?

5 STANLEY Meat!

> [*He heaves the package at her. She cries out in protest but manages to catch it: then she laughs breathlessly. Her husband and his companion have already started back around the corner.*]

STELLA [*calling after him*] Stanley! Where are you going?

STANLEY Bowling!

STELLA Can I come watch?

STANLEY Come on.

> [*He goes out.*]

10 STELLA Be over soon. [*To the white woman*] Hello, Eunice. How are you?

EUNICE I'm all right. Tell Steve to get him a poor boy's sandwich[3] 'cause nothing's left here.

---

2. Tracks used by trains of the Louisville and Nashville Railroad—formerly a major freight and passenger company in the southeastern United States. *Elysian Fields:* a street just north of the French Quarter, the oldest neigh-

borhood of New Orleans; also, in classical mythology, the abode of the blessed dead.
3. A po'boy, the Gulf Coast version of a submarine sandwich, featuring beef, shrimp, or other fillings in a hollowed-out loaf of French bread.

[*They all laugh; the* COLORED WOMAN *does not stop.* STELLA *goes out.*]

COLORED WOMAN   What was that package he th'ew at 'er? [*She rises from steps, laughing louder.*]

EUNICE   You hush, now!

15 NEGRO WOMAN   Catch *what!*

[*She continues to laugh.* BLANCHE *comes around the corner, carrying a valise. She looks at a slip of paper, then at the building, then again at the slip and again at the building. Her expression is one of shocked disbelief. Her appearace is incongruous to this setting. She is daintily dressed in a white suit with a fluffy bodice, necklace and earrings of pearl, white gloves and hat, looking as if she were arriving at a summer tea or cocktail party in the garden district.[4] She is about five years older than* STELLA. *Her delicate beauty must avoid a strong light. There is something about her uncertain manner, as well as her white clothes, that suggests a moth.*]

EUNICE [*finally*]   What's the matter, honey? Are you lost?

BLANCHE [*with faintly hysterical humor*]   They told me to take a streetcar named Desire, and then transfer to one called Cemeteries[5] and ride six blocks and get off at—Elysian Fields!

20 EUNICE   That's where you are now.

BLANCHE   At Elysian Fields?

EUNICE   This here is Elysian Fields.

BLANCHE   They mustn't have—understood—what number I wanted . . .

EUNICE   What number you lookin' for?

[BLANCHE *wearily refers to the slip of paper.*]

25 BLANCHE   Six thirty-two.

EUNICE   You don't have to look no further.

BLANCHE [*uncomprehendingly*]   I'm looking for my sister, Stella DuBois. I mean—Mrs. Stanley Kowalski.

EUNICE   That's the party.—You just did miss her, though.

30 BLANCHE   This—can this be—her home?

EUNICE   She's got the downstairs here and I got the up.

BLANCHE   Oh. She's—out?

EUNICE   You noticed that bowling alley around the corner?

BLANCHE   I'm—not sure I did.

35 EUNICE   Well, that's where she's at, watchin' her husband bowl. [*There is a pause.*] You want to leave your suitcase here an' go find her?

BLANCHE   No.

NEGRO WOMAN   I'll go tell her you come.

BLANCHE   Thanks.

40 NEGRO WOMAN   You welcome.

[*She goes out.*]

EUNICE   She wasn't expecting you?

BLANCHE   No. No, not tonight.

EUNICE   Well, why don't you just go in and make yourself at home till they get back.

45 BLANCHE   How could I—do that?

EUNICE   We own this place so I can let you in.

---

4. An elegant New Orleans neighborhood known for its Greek Revival and Italianate architecture.
5. Streetcar routes in New Orleans at the time the play was written; the Desire line, which went through the French Quarter, was replaced by a bus in 1948.

[*She gets up and opens the downstairs door. A light goes on behind the blind, turning it light blue.* BLANCHE *slowly follows her into the downstairs flat. The surrounding areas dim out as the interior is lighted.*]

[*Two rooms can be seen, not too clearly defined. The one first entered is primarily a kitchen but contains a folding bed to be used by* BLANCHE. *The room beyond this is a bedroom. Off this room is a narrow door to a bathroom.*]

EUNICE [*defensively, noticing* BLANCHE's *look*] It's sort of messed up right now but when it's clean it's real sweet.

BLANCHE Is it?

50 EUNICE Uh-huh, I think so. So you're Stella's sister?

BLANCHE Yes. [*Wanting to get rid of her*] Thanks for letting me in.

EUNICE *Por nada,*[6] as the Mexicans say, *por nada!* Stella spoke of you.

BLANCHE Yes?

EUNICE I think she said you taught school.

55 BLANCHE Yes.

EUNICE And you're from Mississippi, huh?

BLANCHE Yes.

EUNICE She showed me a picture of your home-place, the plantation.

BLANCHE Belle Reve?[7]

60 EUNICE A great big place with white columns.

BLANCHE Yes . . .

EUNICE A place like that must be awful hard to keep up.

BLANCHE If you will excuse me, I'm just about to drop.

EUNICE Sure, honey. Why don't you set down?

65 BLANCHE What I meant was I'd like to be left alone.

EUNICE [*offended*] Aw. I'll make myself scarce, in that case.

BLANCHE I didn't mean to be rude, but—

EUNICE I'll drop by the bowling alley an' hustle her up.

[*She goes out the door.*]

[BLANCHE *sits in a chair very stiffly with her shoulders slightly hunched and her legs pressed close together and her hands tightly clutching her purse as if she were quite cold. After a while the blind look goes out of her eyes and she begins to look slowly around. A cat screeches. She catches her breath with a startled gesture. Suddenly she notices something in a half-opened closet. She springs up and crosses to it, and removes a whiskey bottle. She pours a half tumbler of whiskey and tosses it down. She carefully replaces the bottle and washes out the tumbler at the sink. Then she resumes her seat in front of the table.*]

BLANCHE [*faintly to herself*] I've got to keep hold of myself!

[STELLA *comes quickly around the corner of the building and runs to the door of the downstairs flat.*]

70 STELLA [*calling out joyfully*] Blanche!

[*For a moment they stare at each other. Then* BLANCHE *springs up and runs to her with a wild cry.*]

BLANCHE Stella, oh, Stella, Stella! Stella for Star![8]

[*She begins to speak with feverish vivacity as if she feared for either of them to stop and think. They catch each other in a spasmodic embrace.*]

6. It's nothing (Spanish).
7. Beautiful Dream (French).

8. *Stella* means "star" in Latin.

BLANCHE Now, then, let me look at you. But don't you look at me, Stella, no, no, no, not till later, not till I've bathed and rested! And turn that over-light off! Turn that off! I won't be looked at in this merciless glare! [STELLA laughs and complies.] Come back here now! Oh, my baby! Stella! Stella for Star! [She embraces her again.] I thought you would never come back to this horrible place! What am I saying? I didn't mean to say that. I meant to be nice about it and say—Oh, what a convenient location and such—Ha-a-ha! Precious lamb! You haven't said a word to me.

STELLA You haven't given me a chance to, honey! [She laughs, but her glance at BLANCHE is a little anxious.]

BLANCHE Well, now you talk. Open your pretty mouth and talk while I look around for some liquor! I know you must have some liquor on the place! Where could it be, I wonder? Oh, I spy, I spy!

[She rushes to the closet and removes the bottle; she is shaking all over and panting for breath as she tries to laugh. The bottle nearly slips from her grasp.]

STELLA [noticing] Blanche, you sit down and let me pour the drinks. I don't know what we've got to mix with. Maybe a coke's[9] in the icebox. Look'n see, honey, while I'm—

BLANCHE No coke, honey, not with my nerves tonight! Where—where— where is—?

STELLA Stanley? Bowling! He loves it. They're having a—found some soda!—tournament . . .

BLANCHE Just water, baby, to chase it! Now don't get worried, your sister hasn't turned into a drunkard, she's just all shaken up and hot and tired and dirty! You sit down, now, and explain this place to me! What are you doing in a place like this?

STELLA Now, Blanche—

BLANCHE Oh, I'm not going to be hypocritical, I'm going to be honestly critical about it! Never, never, never in my worst dreams could I picture— Only Poe! Only Mr. Edgar Allan Poe!—could do it justice! Out there I suppose is the ghoul-haunted woodland of Weir![1] [She laughs.]

STELLA No, honey, those are the L & N tracks.

BLANCHE No, now seriously, putting joking aside. Why didn't you tell me, why didn't you write me, honey, why didn't you let me know?

STELLA [carefully, pouring herself a drink] Tell you what, Blanche?

BLANCHE Why, that you had to live in these conditions!

STELLA Aren't you being a little intense about it? It's not that bad at all! New Orleans isn't like other cities.

BLANCHE This has got nothing to do with New Orleans. You might as well say—forgive me, blessed baby! [She suddenly stops short.] The subject is closed!

STELLA [a little drily] Thanks.

[During the pause, BLANCHE stares at her. She smiles at BLANCHE.]

BLANCHE [looking down at her glass, which shakes in her hand] You're all I've got in the world, and you're not glad to see me!

9. In the South, coke is often used as a generic term for any soft drink.
1. The setting of the gothic ballad "Ulalume"

(1847), by Poe, the American short story writer and poet (1809–1849).

STELLA [*sincerely*]   Why, Blanche, you know that's not true.

BLANCHE   No?—I'd forgotten how quiet you were.

115 STELLA   You never did give me a chance to say much, Blanche. So I just got in the habit of being quiet around you.

BLANCHE [*vaguely*]   A good habit to get into . . . [*Then, abruptly*] You haven't asked me how I happened to get away from the school before the spring term ended.

120 STELLA   Well, I thought you'd volunteer that information—if you wanted to tell me.

BLANCHE   You thought I'd been fired?

STELLA   No, I—thought you might have—resigned . . .

BLANCHE   I was so exhausted by all I'd been through my—nerves broke.

125 [*Nervously tamping cigarette*] I was on the verge of—lunacy, almost! So Mr. Graves—Mr. Graves is the high school superintendent—he suggested I take a leave of absence. I couldn't put all of those details into the wire[2] . . . [*She drinks quickly.*] Oh, this buzzes right through me and feels so *good!*

130 STELLA   Won't you have another?

BLANCHE   No, one's my limit.

STELLA   Sure?

BLANCHE   You haven't said a word about my appearance.

STELLA   You look just fine.

135 BLANCHE   God love you for a liar! Daylight never exposed so total a ruin! But you—you've put on some weight, yes, you're just as plump as a little partridge! And it's so becoming to you!

STELLA   Now, Blanche—

BLANCHE   Yes, it is, it is or I wouldn't say it! You just have to watch around

140 the hips a little. Stand up.

STELLA   Not now.

BLANCHE   You hear me? I said stand up! [STELLA *complies reluctantly.*] You messy child, you, you've spilt something on that pretty white lace collar! About your hair—you ought to have it cut in a feather bob with your dainty

145 features. Stella, you have a maid, don't you?

STELLA   No. With only two rooms it's—

BLANCHE   What? *Two* rooms, did you say?

STELLA   This one and— [*She is embarrassed.*]

BLANCHE   The other one? [*She laughs sharply. There is an embarrassed

150 silence.*] I am going to take just one little tiny nip more, sort of to put the stopper on, so to speak. . . . Then put the bottle away so I won't be tempted. [*She rises.*] I want you to look at *my* figure! [*She turns around.*] You know I haven't put on one ounce in ten years, Stella? I weigh what I weighed the summer you left Belle Reve. The summer Dad died and you

155 left us . . .

STELLA [*a little wearily*]   It's just incredible, Blanche, how well you're looking.

[*They both laugh uncomfortably.*]

BLANCHE   But, Stella, there's only two rooms, I don't see where you're going to put me!

160 STELLA   We're going to put you in here.

2. Telegram.

BLANCHE   What kind of bed's this—one of those collapsible things?
   [*She sits on it.*]

STELLA   Does it feel all right?

BLANCHE [*dubiously*]   Wonderful, honey. I don't like a bed that gives much.
   But there's no door between the two rooms, and Stanley—will it be decent?

165 STELLA   Stanley is Polish, you know.

BLANCHE   Oh, yes. They're something like Irish, aren't they?

STELLA   Well—

BLANCHE   Only not so—highbrow? [*They both laugh again in the same way.*]
   I brought some nice clothes to meet all your lovely friends in.

170 STELLA   I'm afraid you won't think they are lovely.

BLANCHE   What are they like?

STELLA   They're Stanley's friends.

BLANCHE   Polacks?

STELLA   They're a mixed lot, Blanche.

175 BLANCHE   Heterogeneous—types?

STELLA   Oh, yes. Yes, types is right!

BLANCHE   Well—anyhow—I brought nice clothes and I'll wear them. I guess
   you're hoping I'll say I'll put up at a hotel, but I'm not going to put up at a
   hotel. I want to be *near* you, got to be *with* somebody, I *can't* be *alone!*

180   Because—as you must have noticed—I'm—*not* very *well* . . . [*Her voice
   drops and her look is frightened.*]

STELLA   You seem a little bit nervous or overwrought or something.

BLANCHE   Will Stanley like me, or will I be just a visiting in-law, Stella? I
   couldn't stand that.

STELLA   You'll get along fine together, if you'll just try not to—well—compare
185   him with men that we went out with at home.

BLANCHE   Is he so—different?

STELLA   Yes. A different species.

BLANCHE   In what way; what's he like?

STELLA   Oh, you can't describe someone you're in love with! Here's a picture
190   of him! [*She hands a photograph to* BLANCHE.]

BLANCHE   An officer?

STELLA   A Master Sergeant in the Engineers' Corps.[3] Those are decorations!

BLANCHE   He had those on when you met him?

STELLA   I assure you I wasn't just blinded by all the brass.

195 BLANCHE   That's not what I—

STELLA   But of course there were things to adjust myself to later on.

BLANCHE   Such as his civilian background! [STELLA *laughs uncertainly.*] How
   did he take it when you said I was coming?

STELLA   Oh, Stanley doesn't know yet.

200 BLANCHE [*frightened*]   You—haven't told him?

STELLA   He's on the road a good deal.

BLANCHE   Oh. Travels?

STELLA   Yes.

BLANCHE   Good. I mean—isn't it?

205 STELLA [*half to herself*]   I can hardly stand it when he is away for a night . . .

---

3. A branch of the U.S. Army that provides construction and engineering services in support of
combat soldiers and federal agencies.

BLANCHE   Why, Stella!

STELLA   When he's away for a week I nearly go wild!

BLANCHE   Gracious!

STELLA   And when he comes back I cry on his lap like a baby . . . [*She smiles to herself.*]

210 BLANCHE   I guess that is what is meant by being in love . . . [STELLA *looks up with a radiant smile.*] Stella—

STELLA   What?

BLANCHE   [*in an uneasy rush*]   I haven't asked you the things you probably thought I was going to ask. And so I'll expect you to be understanding 215   about what I have to tell *you*.

STELLA   What, Blanche? [*Her face turns anxious.*]

BLANCHE   Well, Stella—you're going to reproach me, I know that you're bound to reproach me—but before you do—take into consideration—you left! I stayed and struggled! You came to New Orleans and looked out for 220   yourself! *I* stayed at *Belle Reve* and tried to hold it together! I'm not meaning this in any reproachful way, but *all* the burden descended on *my* shoulders.

STELLA   The best I could do was make my own living, Blanche.

[*Blanche begins to shake again with intensity.*]

BLANCHE   I know, I know. But you are the one that abandoned Belle Reve, 225   not I! I stayed and fought for it, bled for it, almost died for it!

STELLA   Stop this hysterical outburst and tell me what's happened? What do you mean fought and bled? What kind of—

BLANCHE   I knew you would, Stella. I knew you would take this attitude about it!

230 STELLA   About—what?—please!

BLANCHE   [*slowly*]   The loss—the loss . . .

STELLA   Belle Reve? Lost, is it? No!

BLANCHE   Yes, Stella.

[*They stare at each other across the yellow-checked linoleum of the table. BLANCHE slowly nods her head and STELLA looks slowly down at her hands folded on the table. The music of the "blue piano" grows louder. BLANCHE touches her handkerchief to her forehead.*]

STELLA   But how did it go? What happened?

230 BLANCHE   [*springing up*]   You're a fine one to ask me how it went!

STELLA   Blanche!

BLANCHE   You're a fine one to sit there *accusing me* of it!

STELLA   *Blanche!*

BLANCHE   I, I, I took the blows in my face and my body! All of those deaths! 240   The long parade to the graveyard! Father, Mother! Margaret, that dreadful way! So big with it, it couldn't be put in a coffin! But had to be burned like rubbish! You just came home in time for the funerals, Stella. And funerals are pretty compared to deaths. Funerals are quiet, but deaths—not always. Sometimes their breathing is hoarse, and sometimes it rattles, and some-245   times they even cry out to you, "Don't let me go!" Even the old, sometimes, say, "Don't let me go." As if you were able to stop them! But funerals are quiet, with pretty flowers. And, oh, what gorgeous boxes they pack them away in! Unless you were there at the bed when they cried out, "Hold me!" you'd never suspect there was the struggle for breath and bleeding. You

250   didn't dream, but I saw! *Saw! Saw!* And now you sit there telling me with
your eyes that I let the place go! How in hell do you think all that sickness
and dying was paid for? Death is expensive, Miss Stella! And old Cousin
Jessie's right after Margaret's, hers! Why, the Grim Reaper had put up his
tent on our doorstep! . . . Stella. Belle Reve was his headquarters! Honey—

255   that's how it slipped through my fingers! Which of them left us a fortune?
Which of them left a cent of insurance even? Only poor Jessie—one hundred to pay for her coffin. That was all, Stella! And I with my pitiful salary
at the school. Yes, accuse me! Sit there and stare at me, thinking I let the
place go! *I* let the place go? Where were *you!* In bed with your—Polack!

260   STELLA [*springing*]   Blanche! You be still! That's enough! [*She starts out.*]

   BLANCHE   Where are you going?

   STELLA   I'm going into the bathroom to wash my face.

   BLANCHE   Oh, Stella, Stella, you're crying!

   STELLA   Does that surprise you?

265   BLANCHE   Forgive me—I didn't mean to—

      [*The sound of men's voices is heard.* STELLA *goes into the bathroom, clos-
ing the door behind her. When the men appear, and* BLANCHE *realizes it
must be* STANLEY *returning, she moves uncertainly from the bathroom
door to the dressing table, looking apprehensively toward the front door.*
STANLEY *enters, followed by* STEVE *and* MITCH. STANLEY *pauses near his
door,* STEVE *by the foot of the spiral stair, and* MITCH *is slightly above and
to the right of them, about to go out. As the men enter, we hear some of
the following dialogue.*]

   STANLEY   Is that how he got it?

   STEVE   Sure that's how he got it. He hit the old weather-bird for 300 bucks
on a six-number-ticket.[4]

   MITCH   Don't tell him those things; he'll believe it.

      [MITCH *starts out.*]

270   STANLEY [*restraining* MITCH]   Hey, Mitch—come back here.

      [BLANCHE, *at the sound of voices, retires in the bedroom. She picks up*
STANLEY's *photo from dressing table, looks at it, puts it down. When* STAN-
LEY *enters the apartment, she darts and hides behind the screen at the
head of bed.*]

   STEVE [*to* STANLEY *and* MITCH]   Hey, are we playin' poker tomorrow?

   STANLEY   Sure—at Mitch's.

   MITCH [*hearing this, returns quickly to the stair rail*]   No—not at my place.
My mother's still sick!

275   STANLEY   Okay, at my place . . . [MITCH *starts out again.*] But you bring the
beer!

      [MITCH *pretends not to hear—calls out "Goodnight, all," and goes out,
singing.*]

   EUNICE [*heard from above*]   Break it up down there! I made the spaghetti
dish and ate it myself.

   STEVE [*going upstairs*]   I told you and phoned you we was playing. [*To the*

280   *men*] Jax beer![5]

---

4. That is, he won $300 on a six-number lottery
ticket. *Hit the old weather-bird:* got extraordinarily lucky (as one would have to be to shoot
at and hit an ornamental weather vane, which

traditionally was shaped like a rooster).
5. Made by the Jackson Brewing Company of
New Orleans until 1974. The brewery sponsored a bowling team in nearby St. Charles.

EUNICE You never phoned me once.

STEVE I told you at breakfast—and phoned you at lunch . . .

EUNICE Well, never mind about that. You just get yourself home here once in a while.

285 STEVE You want it in the papers?

[*More laughter and shouts of parting come from the men.* STANLEY *throws the screen door of the kitchen open and comes in. He is of medium height, about five feet eight or nine, and strongly, compactly built. Animal joy in his being is implicit in all his movements and attitudes. Since earliest manhood the center of his life has been pleasure with women, the giving and taking of it, not with weak indulgence, dependently, but with the power and pride of a richly feathered male bird among hens. Branching out from this complete and satisfying center are all the auxiliary channels of his life, such as his heartiness with men, his appreciation of rough humor, his love of good drink and food and games, his car, his radio, everything that is his, that bears his emblem of the gaudy seed-bearer. He sizes women up at a glance, with sexual classifications, crude images flashing into his mind and determining the way he smiles at them.*]

BLANCHE [*drawing involuntarily back from his stare*] You must be Stanley. I'm Blanche.

STANLEY Stella's sister?

BLANCHE Yes.

290 STANLEY H'lo. Where's the little woman?

BLANCHE In the bathroom.

STANLEY Oh. Didn't know you were coming in town.

BLANCHE I—uh—

STANLEY Where you from, Blanche?

295 BLANCHE Why, I—live in Laurel.[6]

[*He has crossed to the closet and removed the whiskey bottle.*]

STANLEY In Laurel, huh? Oh, yeah. Yeah, in Laurel, that's right. Not in my territory. Liquor goes fast in hot weather.

[*He holds the bottle to the light to observe its depletion.*]

Have a shot?

BLANCHE No, I—rarely touch it.

300 STANLEY Some people rarely touch it, but it touches them often.

BLANCHE [*faintly*] Ha-ha.

STANLEY My clothes're stickin' to me. Do you mind if I make myself comfortable? [*He starts to remove his shirt.*]

BLANCHE Please, please do.

305 STANLEY Be comfortable is my motto.

BLANCHE It's mine, too. It's hard to stay looking fresh. I haven't washed or even powdered my face and—here you are!

STANLEY You know you can catch cold sitting around in damp things, especially when you been exercising hard like bowling is. You're a teacher, aren't

310 you?

BLANCHE Yes.

STANLEY What do you teach, Blanche?

BLANCHE English.

6. A town in southeast Mississippi, about 135 miles from New Orleans.

STANLEY   I never was a very good English student. How long you here for,
315   Blanche?

BLANCHE   I—don't know yet.

STANLEY   You going to shack up here?

BLANCHE   I thought I would if it's not inconvenient for you all.

STANLEY   Good.

320   BLANCHE   Traveling wears me out.

STANLEY   Well, take it easy.

[*A cat screeches near the window.* BLANCHE *spring up.*]

BLANCHE   What's that?

STANLEY   Cats . . . Hey, Stella!

STELLA [*faintly, from the bathroom*]   Yes, Stanley.

325   STANLEY   Haven't fallen in, have you? [*He grins at* BLANCHE. *She tries unsuccessfully to smile back. There is a silence.*] I'm afraid I'll strike you as being
the unrefined type. Stella's spoke of you a good deal. You were married
once, weren't you?

[*The music of the polka rises up, faint in the distance.*]

BLANCHE   Yes. When I was quite young.

330   STANLEY   What happened?

BLANCHE   The boy—the boy died. [*She sinks back down.*] I'm afraid I'm—
going to be sick!

[*Her head falls on her arms.*]

Scene 2

It is six o'clock the following evening. BLANCHE *is bathing.* STELLA *is completing her
toilette.* BLANCHE's *dress, a flowered print, is laid out on* STELLA's *bed.*

STANLEY *enters the kitchen from outside, leaving the door open on the perpetual
"blue piano" around the corner.*

STANLEY   What's all this monkey doings?

STELLA   Oh, Stan! [*She jumps up and kisses him, which he accepts with lordly
composure.*] I'm taking Blanche to Galatoire's[7] for supper and then to a
show, because it's your poker night.

5   STANLEY   How about my supper, huh? I'm not going to no Galatoire's for
supper!

STELLA   I put you a cold plate on ice.

STANLEY   Well, isn't that just dandy!

STELLA   I'm going to try to keep Blanche out till the party breaks up because
10   I don't know how she would take it. So we'll go to one of the little places in
the Quarter[8] afterward and you'd better give me some money.

STANLEY   Where is she?

STELLA   She's soaking in a hot tub to quiet her nerves. She's terribly upset.

STANLEY   Over what?

15   STELLA   She's been through such an ordeal.

STANLEY   Yeah?

STELLA   Stan, we've—lost Belle Reve!

STANLEY   The place in the country?

7. An elegant restaurant on Bourbon Street,   8. The French Quarter.
specializing in French Creole cuisine.

STELLA Yes.

20 STANLEY How?

STELLA [*vaguely*] Oh, it had to be—sacrificed or something. [*There is a pause while* STANLEY *considers.* STELLA *is changing into her dress.*] When she comes in be sure to say something nice about her appearance. And, oh! Don't mention the baby. I haven't said anything yet, I'm waiting until she

25 gets in a quieter condition.

STANLEY [*ominously*] So?

STELLA And try to understand her and be nice to her, Stan.

BLANCHE [*singing in the bathroom*] "From the land of the sky blue water, They brought a captive maid!"[9]

30 STELLA She wasn't expecting to find us in such a small place. You see I'd tried to gloss things over a little in my letters.

STANLEY So?

STELLA And admire her dress and tell her she's looking wonderful. That's important with Blanche. Her little weakness!

35 STANLEY Yeah. I get the idea. Now let's skip back a little to where you said the country place was disposed of.

STELLA Oh!—yes . . .

STANLEY How about that? Let's have a few more details on that subjeck.

STELLA It's best not to talk much about it until she's calmed down.

40 STANLEY So that's the deal, huh? Sister Blanche cannot be annoyed with business details right now!

STELLA You saw how she was last night.

STANLEY Uh-hum, I saw how she was. Now let's have a gander at the bill of sale.

45 STELLA I haven't seen any.

STANLEY She didn't show you no papers, no deed of sale or nothing like that, huh?

STELLA It seems like it wasn't sold.

STANLEY Well, what in hell was it then, give away? To charity?

50 STELLA Shhh! She'll hear you.

STANLEY I don't care if she hears me. Let's see the papers!

STELLA There weren't any papers, she didn't show any papers, I don't care about papers.

STANLEY Have you ever heard of the Napoleonic code?[1]

55 STELLA No, Stanley, I haven't heard of the Napoleonic code and if I have, I don't see what it—

STANLEY Let me enlighten you on a point or two, baby.

STELLA Yes?

STANLEY In the state of Louisiana we have the Napoleonic code according

60 to which what belongs to the wife belongs to the husband and vice versa. For instance if I had a piece of property, or you had a piece of property—

9. From "From the Land of the Sky-Blue Water" (1908), by Nelle Richmond Eberhart and Charles Wakefield Cadman, a song popularized by the Andrews Sisters in the late 1930s.

1. The civil law code established in France under Napoleon in 1804 and adopted by most other European countries. In 1808, after Louisiana had been purchased from France but before it became a state, it adopted a version of the Napoleonic code; all other U.S. states follow the British common law model.

STELLA   My head is swimming!

STANLEY   All right. I'll wait till she gets through soaking in a hot tub and then
   I'll inquire if *she* is acquainted with the Napoleonic code. It looks to me
65   like you have been swindled, baby, and when you're swindled under the
   Napoleonic code I'm swindled *too*. And I don't like to be *swindled.*

STELLA   There's plenty of time to ask her questions later but if you do now
   she'll go to pieces again. I don't understand what happened to Belle Reve
   but you don't know how ridiculous you are being when you suggest that my
70   sister or I or anyone of our family could have perpetrated a swindle on anyone else.

STANLEY   Then where's the money if the place was sold?

STELLA   Not sold—*lost, lost!*

   [*He stalks into bedroom, and she follows him.*]

   Stanley!

   [*He pulls open the wardrobe trunk standing in middle of room and jerks
   out an armful of dresses.*]

75   STANLEY   Open your eyes to this stuff! You think she got them out of a
   teacher's pay?

STELLA   Hush!

STANLEY   Look at these feathers and furs that she come here to preen herself
   in! What's this here? A solid-gold dress, I believe! And this one! What is
80   these here? Fox-pieces! [*He blows on them.*] Genuine fox fur-pieces, a half
   a mile long! Where are your fox-pieces, Stella? Bushy snow-white ones, no
   less! Where are your white fox-pieces?

STELLA   Those are inexpensive summer furs that Blanche has had a long
   time.

STANLEY   I got an acquaintance who deals in this sort of merchandise. I'll
85   have him in here to appraise it. I'm willing to bet you there's thousands of
   dollars invested in this stuff here!

STELLA   Don't be such an idiot, Stanley!

   [*He hurls the furs to the day bed. Then he jerks open small drawer in the
   trunk and pulls up a fistful of costume jewelry.*]

STANLEY   And what have we here? The treasure chest of a pirate!

STELLA   Oh, Stanley!

90   STANLEY   Pearls! Ropes of them! What is this sister of yours, a deep-sea
   diver? Bracelets of solid gold, too! Where are your pearls and gold
   bracelets?

STELLA   Shhh! Be still, Stanley!

STANLEY   And diamonds! A crown for an empress!

95   STELLA   A rhinestone tiara she wore to a costume ball.

STANLEY   What's rhinestone?

STELLA   Next door to glass.

STANLEY   Are you kidding? I have an acquaintance that works in a jewelry
   store. I'll have him in here to make an appraisal of this. Here's your planta-
100   tion, or what was left of it, here!

STELLA   You have no idea how stupid and horrid you're being! Now close that
   trunk before she comes out of the bathroom!

   [*He kicks the trunk partly closed and sits on the kitchen table.*]

STANLEY   The Kowalskis and the DuBoises have different notions.

STELLA [*angrily*]   Indeed they have, thank heavens!—*I'm* going outside.
> [*She snatches up her white hat and gloves and crosses to the outside door.*]

105   You come out with me while Blanche is getting dressed.
STANLEY   Since when do you give me orders?
STELLA   Are you going to stay here and insult her?
STANLEY   You're damn tootin' I'm going to stay here.
> [STELLA *goes out to the porch.* BLANCHE *comes out of the bathroom in a red satin robe.*]

BLANCHE [*airily*]   Hello, Stanley! Here I am, all freshly bathed and scented,
110   and feeling like a brand-new human being!
> [*He lights a cigarette.*]

STANLEY   That's good.
BLANCHE [*drawing the curtains at the windows*]   Excuse me while I slip on my pretty new dress!
STANLEY   Go right ahead, Blanche.
> [*She closes the drapes between the rooms.*]

115   BLANCHE   I understand there's to be a little card party to which we ladies are cordially *not* invited!
STANLEY [*ominously*]   Yeah?
> [BLANCHE *throws off her robe and slips into a flowered print dress.*]

BLANCHE   Where's Stella?
STANLEY   Out on the porch.
120   BLANCHE   I'm going to ask a favor of you in a moment.
STANLEY   What could that be, I wonder?
BLANCHE   Some buttons in back! You may enter!
> [*He crosses through drapes with a smoldering look.*]

How do I look?
STANLEY   You look all right.
125   BLANCHE   Many thanks! Now the buttons!
STANLEY   I can't do nothing with them.
BLANCHE   You men with your big clumsy fingers. May I have a drag on your cig?
STANLEY   Have one for yourself.
BLANCHE   Why, thanks! . . . It looks like my trunk has exploded.
130   STANLEY   Me an' Stella were helping you unpack.
BLANCHE   Well, you certainly did a fast and thorough job of it!
STANLEY   It looks like you raided some stylish shops in Paris.
BLANCHE   Ha-ha! Yes—clothes are my passion!
STANLEY   What does it cost for a string of fur-pieces like that?
135   BLANCHE   Why, those were a tribute from an admirer of mine!
STANLEY   He must have had a lot of—admiration!
BLANCHE   Oh, in my youth I excited some admiration. But look at me now!
[*She smiles at him radiantly.*] Would you think it possible that I was once considered to be—attractive?
140   STANLEY   Your looks are okay.
BLANCHE   I was fishing for a compliment, Stanley.
STANLEY   I don't go in for that stuff.
BLANCHE   What—stuff?

STANLEY   Compliments to women about their looks. I never met a woman
145   that didn't know if she was good-looking or not without being told, and
some of them give themselves credit for more than they've got. I once went
out with a doll who said to me, "I am the glamorous type, I am the glamorous type!" I said, "So what?"

BLANCHE   And what did she say then?

150   STANLEY   She didn't say nothing. That shut her up like a clam.

BLANCHE   Did it end the romance?

STANLEY   It ended the conversation—that was all. Some men are took in by
this Hollywood glamor stuff and some men are not.

BLANCHE   I'm sure you belong in the second category.

155   STANLEY   That's right.

BLANCHE   I cannot imagine any witch of a woman casting a spell over you.

STANLEY   That's—right.

BLANCHE   You're simple, straightforward and honest, a little bit on the primitive side I should think. To interest you a woman would have to— [*She
pauses with an indefinite gesture.*]

160   STANLEY [*slowly*]   Lay . . . her cards on the table.

BLANCHE [*smiling*]   Well, I never cared for wishy-washy people. That was
why, when you walked in here last night, I said to myself—"My sister has
married a man!"—Of course that was all that I could tell about you.

STANLEY [*booming*]   Now let's cut the re-bop![2]

165   BLANCHE [*pressing hands to her ears*]   Ouuuuu!

STELLA [*calling from the steps*]   Stanley! You come out here and let Blanche
finish dressing!

BLANCHE   I'm through dressing, honey.

STELLA   Well, you come out, then.

170   STANLEY   Your sister and I are having a little talk.

BLANCHE [*lightly*]   Honey, do me a favor. Run to the drugstore and get me a
lemon Coke with plenty of chipped ice in it!—Will you do that for me,
sweetie?

STELLA [*uncertainly*]   Yes.

[*She goes around the corner of the building.*]

175   BLANCHE   The poor little thing was out there listening to us, and I have an
idea she doesn't understand you as well as I do. . . . All right; now, Mr.
Kowalski, let us proceed without any more double-talk. I'm ready to answer
all questions. I've nothing to hide. What is it?

180   STANLEY   There is such a thing in this state of Louisiana as the Napoleonic
code, according to which whatever belongs to my wife is also mine—and
vice versa.

BLANCHE   My, but you have an impressive judicial air!

[*She sprays herself with her atomizer; then playfully sprays him with it.
He seizes the atomizer and slams it down on the dresser. She throws back
her head and laughs.*]

STANLEY   If I didn't know that you was my wife's sister I'd get ideas about
you!

185   BLANCHE   Such as what!

---

2. Nonsense (a variant of *bebop* or *bop,* the virtuosic jazz of the late 1940s and a term meaning
"glib or deceptive talk").

STANLEY Don't play so dumb. You know what!

BLANCHE [*she puts the atomizer on the table*] All right. Cards on the table. That suits me. [*She turns to* STANLEY.] I know I fib a good deal. After all, a woman's charm is fifty per cent illusion, but when a thing is important I
190 tell the truth, and this is the truth: I haven't cheated my sister or you or anyone else as long as I have lived.

STANLEY Where's the papers? In the trunk?

BLANCHE Everything that I own is in that trunk.

> [STANLEY *crosses to the trunk, shoves it roughly open and begins to open compartments.*]

BLANCHE What in the name of heaven are you thinking of! What's in the
195 back of that little boy's mind of yours? That I am absconding with something, attempting some kind of treachery on my sister?—Let me do that! It will be faster and simpler . . . [*She crosses to the trunk and takes out a box.*] I keep my papers mostly in this tin box. [*She opens it.*]

STANLEY What's them underneath? [*He indicates another sheaf of paper.*]

200 BLANCHE These are love-letters, yellowing with antiquity, all from one boy. [*He snatches them up. She speaks fiercely.*] Give those back to me!

STANLEY I'll have a look at them first!

BLANCHE The touch of your hands insults them!

STANLEY Don't pull that stuff!

> [*He rips off the ribbon and starts to examine them.* BLANCHE *snatches them from him, and they cascade to the floor.*]

205 BLANCHE Now that you've touched them I'll burn them!

STANLEY [*staring, baffled*] What in hell are they?

BLANCHE [*on the floor gathering them up*] Poems a dead boy wrote. I hurt him the way that you would like to hurt me, but you can't! I'm not young and vulnerable any more. But my young husband was and I—never mind
210 about that! Just give them back to me!

STANLEY What do you mean by saying you'll have to burn them?

BLANCHE I'm sorry, I must have lost my head for a moment. Everyone has something he won't let others touch because of their—intimate nature . . .

> [*She now seems faint with exhaustion and she sits down with the strong box and puts on a pair of glasses and goes methodically through a large stack of papers.*]

Ambler & Ambler. Hmmmmm. . . . Crabtree. . . . More Ambler & Ambler.

215 STANLEY What is Ambler & Ambler?

BLANCHE A firm that made loans on the place.

STANLEY Then it *was* lost on a mortgage?

BLANCHE [*touching her forehead*] That must've been what happened.

STANLEY I don't want no ifs, ands or buts! What's all the rest of them papers?

> [*She hands him the entire box. He carries it to the table and starts to examine the papers.*]

220 BLANCHE [*picking up a large envelope containing more papers*] There are thousands of papers, stretching back over hundreds of years, affecting Belle Reve as, piece by piece, our improvident grandfathers and father and uncles and brothers exchanged the land for their epic fornications—to put it plainly! [*She removes her glasses with an exhausted laugh.*] The four-letter
225 word deprived us of our plantation, till finally all that was left—and Stella can verify that!—was the house itself and about twenty acres of ground,

including a graveyard, to which now all but Stella and I have retreated. [*She pours the contents of the envelope on the table.*] Here all of them are, all papers! I hereby endow you with them! Take them, peruse them—
230 commit them to memory, even! I think it's wonderfully fitting that Belle Reve should finally be this bunch of old papers in your big, capable hands! . . . I wonder if Stella's come back with my lemon Coke . . . [*She leans back and closes her eyes.*]

STANLEY I have a lawyer acquaintance who will study these out.

BLANCHE Present them to him with a box of aspirin tablets.

235 STANLEY [*becoming somewhat sheepish*] You see, under the Napoleonic code—a man has to take an interest in his wife's affairs—especially now that she's going to have a baby.

[BLANCHE *opens her eyes. The "blue piano" sounds louder.*]

BLANCHE Stella? Stella going to have a baby? [*Dreamily*] I didn't know she was going to have a baby!

[*She gets up and crosses to the outside door.* STELLA *appears around the corner with a carton from the drugstore.*]

[STANLEY *goes into the bedroom with the envelope and the box.*]

[*The inner rooms fade to darkness and the outside wall of the house is visible.* BLANCHE *meets* STELLA *at the foot of the steps to the sidewalk.*]

240 BLANCHE Stella, Stella for Star! How lovely to have a baby! It's all right. Everything's all right.

STELLA I'm sorry he did that to you.

BLANCHE Oh, I guess he's just not the type that goes for jasmine perfume, but maybe he's what we need to mix with our blood now that we've lost
245 Belle Reve. We thrashed it out. I feel a bit shaky, but I think I handled it nicely, I laughed and treated it all as a joke. [STEVE *and* PABLO *appear, carrying a case of beer.*] I called him a little boy and laughed and flirted. Yes, I was flirting with your husband! [*As the men approach*] The guests are gathering for the poker party. [*The two men pass between them, and enter the*
250 *house.*] Which way do we go now, Stella—this way?

STELLA No, this way. [*She leads* BLANCHE *away.*]

BLANCHE [*laughing*] The blind are leading the blind![3]

[*A tamale* VENDOR *is heard calling.*]

VENDOR'S VOICE Red-hot!

Scene 3
The Poker Night[4]

*There is a picture of Van Gogh's of a billiard-parlor at night.[5] The kitchen now suggests that sort of lurid nocturnal brilliance, the raw colors of childhood's spectrum. Over the yellow linoleum of the kitchen table hangs an electric bulb with a vivid green glass shade. The poker players—*STANLEY, STEVE, MITCH, *and* PABLO—*wear colored shirts, solid blue, a purple, a red-and-white check, a light green, and they are men at the peak of their physical manhood, as coarse and direct and powerful as the primary colors. There are vivid slices of watermelon on the table, whiskey bottles*

3. See Matthew 15.14: "And if the blind lead the blind, both shall fall into the ditch."
4. "The Poker Night" was Williams's working title for *A Streetcar Named Desire*.
5. *The Night Café* (1888), by the Dutch painter Vincent Van Gogh (1853–1890).

and glasses. The bedroom is relatively dim with only the light that spills between the portieres[6] and through the wide window on the street. For a moment, there is absorbed silence as a hand is dealt.

STEVE Anything wild this deal?

PABLO One-eyed jacks are wild.

STEVE Give me two cards.

PABLO You, Mitch?

5 MITCH I'm out.

PABLO One.

MITCH Anyone want a shot?

STANLEY Yeah. Me.

PABLO Why don't somebody go to the Chinaman's and bring back a load of
10 chop suey?

STANLEY When I'm losing you want to eat! Ante up! Openers? Openers! Get y'r ass off the table, Mitch. Nothing belongs on a poker table but cards, chips, and whiskey.

[*He lurches up and tosses some watermelon rinds to the floor.*]

MITCH Kind of on your high horse, ain't you?

15 STANLEY How many?

STEVE Give me three.

STANLEY One.

MITCH I'm out again. I oughta go home pretty soon.

STANLEY Shut up.

20 MITCH I gotta sick mother. She don't go to sleep until I come in at night.

STANLEY Then why don't you stay home with her?

MITCH She says to go out, so I go, but I don't enjoy it. All the while I keep wondering how she is.

STANLEY Aw, for the sake of Jesus, go home, then!

25 PABLO What've you got?

STEVE Spade flush.

MITCH You all are married. But I'll be alone when she goes.—I'm going to the bathroom.

STANLEY Hurry back and we'll fix you a sugar-tit.[7]

30 MITCH Aw, go rut. [*He crosses through the bedroom into the bathroom.*]

STEVE [*dealing a hand*] Seven card stud. [*Telling his joke as he deals.*] This ole farmer is out in back of his house sittin' down th'owing corn to the chickens when all at once he hears a loud cackle and this young hen comes lickety split around the side of the house with the rooster right behind her
35 and gaining on her fast.

STANLEY [*impatient with the story*] Deal!

STEVE But when the rooster catches sight of the farmer th'owing the corn he puts on the brakes and lets the hen get away and starts pecking corn. And the old farmer says, "Lord God, I hopes I never gits *that* hongry!"

[STEVE *and* PABLO *laugh. The sisters appear around the corner of the building.*]

40 STELLA The game is still going on.

BLANCHE How do I look?

STELLA Lovely, Blanche.

6. Heavy curtains hung across a doorway. 7. A pacifier dipped in sugar.

BLANCHE   I feel so hot and frazzled. Wait till I powder before you open the
   door. Do I look done in?

45 STELLA   Why no. You are as fresh as a daisy.

BLANCHE   One that's been picked a few days.

   [STELLA *opens the door and they enter.*]

STELLA   Well, well, well. I see you boys are still at it!

STANLEY   Where you been?

STELLA   Blanche and I took in a show. Blanche, this is Mr. Gonzales and Mr.
50   Hubbell.

BLANCHE   Please don't get up.

STANLEY   Nobody's going to get up, so don't be worried.

STELLA   How much longer is this game going to continue?

STANLEY   Till we get ready to quit.

55 BLANCHE   Poker is so fascinating. Could I kibitz?

STANLEY   You could not. Why don't you women go up and sit with Eunice?

STELLA   Because it is nearly two-thirty. [BLANCHE *crosses into the bedroom and
   partially closes the portieres.*] Couldn't you call it quits after one more hand?

   [*A chair scrapes.* STANLEY *gives a loud whack of his hand on her thigh.*]

STELLA [*sharply*]   That's not fun, Stanley.

   [*The men laugh.* STELLA *goes into the bedroom.*]

60 STELLA   It makes me so mad when he does that in front of people.

BLANCHE   I think I will bathe.

STELLA   Again?

BLANCHE   My nerves are in knots. Is the bathroom occupied?

STELLA   I don't know.

   [BLANCHE *knocks.* MITCH *opens the door and comes out, still wiping his
   hands on a towel.*]

65 BLANCHE   Oh!—good evening.

MITCH   Hello. [*He stares at her.*]

STELLA   Blanche, this is Harold Mitchell. My sister, Blanche DuBois.

MITCH [*with awkward courtesy*]   How do you do, Miss DuBois.

STELLA   How is your mother now, Mitch?

70 MITCH   About the same, thanks. She appreciated your sending over that
   custard.—Excuse me, please.

   [*He crosses slowly back into the kitchen, glancing back at* BLANCHE *and
   coughing a little shyly. He realizes he still has the towel in his hands and
   with an embarrassed laugh hands it to* STELLA. BLANCHE *looks after him
   with a certain interest.*]

BLANCHE   That one seems—superior to the others.

STELLA   Yes, he is.

BLANCHE   I thought he had a sort of sensitive look.

75 STELLA   His mother is sick.

BLANCHE   Is he married?

STELLA   No.

BLANCHE   Is he a wolf?

STELLA   Why, Blanche! [BLANCHE *laughs.*] I don't think he would be.

80 BLANCHE   What does—what does he do?

   [*She is unbuttoning her blouse.*]

STELLA   He's on the precision bench in the spare parts department. At the plant Stanley travels for.

BLANCHE   Is that something much?

STELLA   No. Stanley's the only one of his crowd that's likely to get anywhere.

85   BLANCHE   What makes you think Stanley will?

STELLA   Look at him.

BLANCHE   I've looked at him.

STELLA   Then you should know.

BLANCHE   I'm sorry, but I haven't noticed the stamp of genius even on Stan-
90   ley's forehead.

> [*She takes off the blouse and stands in her pink silk brassiere and white skirt in the light through the portieres. The game has continued in undertones.*]

STELLA   It isn't on his forehead and it isn't genius.

BLANCHE   Oh. Well, what is it, and where? I would like to know.

STELLA   It's a drive that he has. You're standing in the light, Blanche!

BLANCHE   Oh, am I!

> [*She moves out of the yellow streak of light. Stella has removed her dress and put on a light blue satin kimona.*[8]]

95   STELLA [*with girlish laughter*]   You ought to see their wives.

BLANCHE [*laughingly*]   I can imagine. Big, beefy things, I suppose.

STELLA   You know that one upstairs? [*More laughter*] One time [*Laughing*] the plaster—[*Laughing*] cracked—

STANLEY   You hens cut out that conversation in there!

100   STELLA   You can't hear us.

STANLEY   Well, you can hear me and I said to hush up!

STELLA   This is my house and I'll talk as much as I want to!

BLANCHE   Stella, don't start a row.

STELLA   He's half drunk!—I'll be out in a minute.

> [*She goes into the bathroom.* BLANCHE *rises and crosses leisurely to a small white radio and turns it on.*]

105   STANLEY   Awright, Mitch, you in?

MITCH   What? Oh!—No, I'm out!

> [BLANCHE *moves back into the streak of light. She raises her arms and stretches, as she moves indolently back to the chair.*]

> [*Rhumba music comes over the radio.* MITCH *rises at the table.*]

STANLEY   Who turned that on in there?

BLANCHE   I did. Do you mind?

STANLEY   Turn it off!

110   STEVE   Aw, let the girls have their music.

PABLO   Sure, that's good, leave it on!

STEVE   Sounds like Xavier Cugat![9]

> [STANLEY *jumps up and, crossing to the radio, turns it off. He stops short at the sight of* BLANCHE *in the chair. She returns his look without flinching. Then he sits again at the poker table.*]

> [*Two of the men have started arguing hotly.*]

8. Kimono.
9. The Cuban American bandleader (1900–   1990) whose hits of the 1930s won him the nickname "Rhumba King."

STEVE   I didn't hear you name it.

PABLO   Didn't I name it, Mitch?

115 MITCH   I wasn't listenin'.

PABLO   What were you doing, then?

STANLEY   He was looking through them drapes. [*He jumps up and jerks roughly at curtains to close them.*] Now deal the hand over again and let's play cards or quit. Some people get ants[1] when they win.

[*MITCH rises as STANLEY returns to his seat.*]

120 STANLEY [*yelling*]   Sit down!

MITCH   I'm going to the "head."[2] Deal me out.

PABLO   Sure he's got ants now. Seven five-dollar bills in his pants pocket folded up tight as spitballs.

STEVE   Tomorrow you'll see him at the cashier's window getting them
125 changed into quarters.

STANLEY   And when he goes home he'll deposit them one by one in a piggy bank his mother give him for Christmas. [*Dealing*] This game is Spit in the Ocean.

[*MITCH laughs uncomfortably and continues through the portieres. He stops just inside.*]

BLANCHE [*softly*]   Hello! The Little Boys' Room is busy right now.

130 MITCH   We've—been drinking beer.

BLANCHE   I hate beer.

MITCH   It's—a hot weather drink.

BLANCHE   Oh, I don't think so; it always makes me warmer. Have you got any cigs? [*She has slipped on the dark red satin wrapper.*]

135 MITCH   Sure.

BLANCHE   What kind are they?

MITCH   Luckies.

BLANCHE   Oh, good. What a pretty case. Silver?

MITCH   Yes. Yes; read the inscription.

140 BLANCHE   Oh, is there an inscription? I can't make it out. [*He strikes a match and moves closer.*] Oh! [*Reading with feigned difficulty.*]

"And if God choose,
I shall but love thee better—after—death!"

Why, that's from my favorite sonnet by Mrs. Browning![3]

145 MITCH   You know it?

BLANCHE   Certainly I do!

MITCH   There's a story connected with that inscription.

BLANCHE   It sounds like a romance.

MITCH   A pretty sad one.

150 BLANCHE   Oh?

MITCH   The girl's dead now.

BLANCHE [*in a tone of deep sympathy*]   *Oh!*

---

1. Antsy.
2. Navy slang for a ship's toilet.
3. The English poet Elizabeth Barrett Browning (1806–1861). She is best known for her *Sonnets from the Portuguese* (1850), a sequence of love poems written before her marriage to Robert Browning; Blanche quotes from the most famous of them, Sonnet XLIII ("How do I love thee? Let me count the ways").

MITCH   She knew she was dying when she give me this. A very strange girl, very sweet—very!

155 BLANCHE   She must have been fond of you. Sick people have such deep, sincere attachments.

MITCH   That's right, they certainly do.

BLANCHE   Sorrow makes for sincerity, I think.

MITCH   It sure brings it out in people.

160 BLANCHE   The little there is belongs to people who have experienced some sorrow.

MITCH   I believe you are right about that.

BLANCHE   I'm positive that I am. Show me a person who hasn't known any sorrow and I'll show you a shuperficial—Listen to me! My tongue is a

165   little—thick! You boys are responsible for it. The show let out at eleven and we couldn't come home on account of the poker game so we had to go somewhere and drink. I'm not accustomed to having more than one drink. Two is the limit—and *three*! [*She laughs.*] Tonight I had three.

STANLEY   Mitch!

170 MITCH   Deal me out. I'm talking to Miss—

BLANCHE   DuBois.

MITCH   Miss DuBois?

BLANCHE   It's a French name. It means woods and Blanche means white, so the two together mean white woods. Like an orchard in spring! You can

175   remember it by that.

MITCH   You're French?

BLANCHE   We are French by extraction. Our first American ancestors were French Huguenots.[4]

MITCH   You are Stella's sister, are you not?

180 BLANCHE   Yes, Stella is my precious little sister. I call her little in spite of the fact she's somewhat older than I. Just slightly. Less than a year. Will you do something for me?

MITCH   Sure. What?

BLANCHE   I bought this adorable little colored paper lantern at a Chinese

185   shop on Bourbon.[5] Put it over the light bulb! Will you, please?

MITCH   Be glad to.

BLANCHE   I can't stand a naked light bulb, any more than I can a rude remark or a vulgar action.

MITCH [*adjusting the lantern*]   I guess we strike you as being a pretty rough

190   bunch.

BLANCHE   I'm very adaptable—to circumstances.

MITCH   Well, that's a good thing to be. You are visiting Stanley and Stella?

BLANCHE   Stella hasn't been so well lately, and I came down to help her for a while. She's very run down.

195 MITCH   You're not—?

BLANCHE   Married? No, no. I'm an old maid schoolteacher!

MITCH   You may teach school but you're certainly not an old maid.

4. French Protestants, repeatedly persecuted by the Catholic monarchy. Many Huguenots emigrated to the American colonies after Louis XIV's Edict of Fontainebleau declared Protestantism illegal in 1685.
5. Bourbon Street, the center of the French Quarter's nightlife.

BLANCHE   Thank you, sir! I appreciate your gallantry!

MITCH   So you are in the teaching profession?

200   BLANCHE   Yes. Ah, yes . . .

MITCH   Grade school or high school or—

STANLEY [*bellowing*]   Mitch!

MITCH   Coming!

BLANCHE   Gracious, what lung-power! . . . I teach high school. In Laurel.

205   MITCH   What do you teach? What subject?

BLANCHE   Guess!

MITCH   I bet you teach art or music? [BLANCHE *laughs delicately.*] Of course I could be wrong. You might teach arithmetic.

BLANCHE   Never arithmetic, sir; never arithmetic! [*With a laugh*] I don't even
210   know my multiplication tables! No, I have the misfortune of being an English instructor. I attempt to instill a bunch of bobby-soxers and drug-store Romeos with reverence for Hawthorne and Whitman and Poe![6]

MITCH   I guess that some of them are more interested in other things.

BLANCHE   How very right you are! Their literary heritage is not what most of
215   them treasure above all else! But they're sweet things! And in the spring, it's touching to notice them making their first discovery of love! As if nobody had ever known it before!

[*The bathroom door opens and* STELLA *comes out.* BLANCHE *continues talking to* MITCH.]

Oh! Have you finished? Wait—I'll turn on the radio.

[*She turns the knobs on the radio and it begins to play "Wien, Wien, nur du allein."*[7] BLANCHE *waltzes to the music with romantic gestures.* MITCH *is delighted and moves in awkward imitation like a dancing bear.*]

[STANLEY *stalks fiercely through the portieres into the bedroom. He crosses to the small white radio and snatches it off the table. With a shouted oath, he tosses the instrument out the window.*]

STELLA   Drunk—drunk—animal thing, you! [*She rushes through to the poker*
220   *table.*] All of you—please go home! If any of you have one spark of decency in you—

BLANCHE [*wildly*]   Stella, watch out, he's—

[STANLEY *charges after* STELLA.]

MEN [*feebly*]   Take it easy, Stanley. Easy, fellow.—Let's all—

STELLA   You lay your hands on me and I'll—

[*She backs out of sight. He advances and disappears. There is the sound of a blow.* STELLA *cries out.* BLANCHE *screams and runs into the kitchen. The men rush forward and there is grappling and cursing. Something is overturned with a crash.*]

225   BLANCHE [*shrilly*]   My sister is going to have a baby!

MITCH   This is terrible.

6. Classic American authors: Nathaniel Haw-thorne (1804–1864), Walt Whitman (1819–1892), and Edgar Allan Poe. *Bobby-soxers and drugstore Romeos*: teenage boys and girls. "Bobby-soxer" was a term first applied to the girls in ankle socks who cried and swooned at Frank Sinatra's concerts in the early 1940s; and boys were "drugstore Romeos" because drugstores usually had soda fountains, where teenagers socialized.
7. "Vienna, Vienna, only you alone" (German); from the popular waltz "Wien, du Stadt meiner Träume" ("Vienna, You City of My Dreams," 1914), by the Austrian composer Rudolf Sieczynski.

BLANCHE   Lunacy, absolute lunacy!

MITCH   Get him in here, men.

> [STANLEY *is forced, pinioned by the two men, into the bedroom. He nearly throws them off. Then all at once he subsides and is limp in their grasp.*]
>
> [*They speak quietly and lovingly to him and he leans his face on one of their shoulders.*]

230 STELLA [*in a high, unnatural voice, out of sight*]   I want to go away, I want to go away!

MITCH   Poker shouldn't be played in a house with women.

> [BLANCHE *rushes into the bedroom.*]

BLANCHE   I want my sister's clothes! We'll go to that woman's upstairs!

MITCH   Where is the clothes?

BLANCHE [*opening the closet*]   I've got them! [*She rushes through to* STELLA.]

235 Stella, Stella, precious! Dear, dear little sister, don't be afraid!

> [*With her arms around* STELLA, BLANCHE *guides her to the outside door and upstairs.*]

STANLEY [*dully*]   What's the matter; what's happened?

MITCH   You just blew your top, Stan.

PABLO   He's okay, now.

STEVE   Sure, my boy's okay!

240 MITCH   Put him on the bed and get a wet towel.

PABLO   I think coffee would do him a world of good, now.

STANLEY [*thickly*]   I want water.

MITCH   Put him under the shower!

> [*The men talk quietly as they lead him to the bathroom.*]

STANLEY   Let the rut go of me, you sons of bitches!

> [*Sounds of blows are heard. The water goes on full tilt.*]

245 STEVE   Let's get quick out of here!

> [*They rush to the poker table and sweep up their winings on their way out.*]

MITCH [*sadly but firmly*]   Poker should not be played in a house with women.

> [*The door closes on them and the place is still. The Negro entertainers in the bar around the corner play "Paper Doll"*[8] *slow and blue. After a moment Stanley comes out of the bathroom dripping water and still in his clinging wet polka-dot drawers.*]

STANLEY   Stella! [*There is a pause.*] My baby doll's left me!

> [*He breaks into sobs. Then he goes to the phone and dials, still shuddering with sobs.*]

Eunice? I want my baby! [*He waits a moment; then he hangs up and dials again.*] Eunice! I'll keep on ringin' until I talk with my baby!

> [*An indistinguishable shrill voice is heard. He hurls phone to floor. Dissonant brass and piano sounds as the rooms dim out to darkness and the outer walls appear in the night light. The "blue piano" plays for a brief interval.*]
>
> [*Finally,* STANLEY *stumbles half-dressed out to the porch and down the wooden steps to the pavement before the building. There he throws back his head like a baying hound and bellows his wife's name: "Stella! Stella, sweetheart! Stella!"*]

---

8. A song written by Johnny S. Black in 1915; the Mills Brothers' 1943 version was a huge hit.

250 STANLEY Stell-*lahhhhh!*

EUNICE [*calling down from the door of her upper apartment*] Quit that howling out there an' go back to bed!

STANLEY I want my baby down here. Stella, Stella!

EUNICE She ain't comin' down so you quit! Or you'll git th' law on you!

255 STANLEY Stella!

EUNICE You can't beat on a woman an' then call 'er back! She won't come!
And her goin' t' have a baby! . . . You stinker! You whelp of a Polack, you! I
hope they do haul you in and turn the fire hose on you, same as the last
time!

STANLEY [*humbly*] Eunice, I want my girl to come down with me!

260 EUNICE Hah! [*She slams her door.*]

STANLEY [*with heaven-splitting violence*] STELL-LAHHHHH!

[*The low-tone clarinet moans. The door upstairs opens again.* STELLA
*slips down the rickety stairs in her robe. Her eyes are glistening with tears
and her hair loose about her throat and shoulders. They stare at each
other. Then they come together with low, animal moans. He falls to his
knees on the steps and presses his face to her belly, curving a little with
maternity. Her eyes go blind with tenderness as she catches his head and
raises him level with her. He snatches the screen door open and lifts her
off her feet and bears her into the dark flat.*]

[BLANCHE *comes out on the upper landing in her robe and slips fearfully
down the steps.*]

BLANCHE Where is my little sister? Stella? Stella?

[*She stops before the dark entrance of her sister's flat. Then catches her
breath as if struck. She rushes down to the walk before the house. She
looks right and left as if for a sanctuary.*]

[*The music fades away.* MITCH *appears from around the corner.*]

MITCH Miss DuBois?

BLANCHE Oh!

265 MITCH All quiet on the Potomac[9] now?

BLANCHE She ran downstairs and went back in there with him.

MITCH Sure she did.

BLANCHE I'm terrified!

270 MITCH Ho-ho! There's nothing to be scared of. They're crazy about each
other.

BLANCHE I'm not used to such—

MITCH Naw, it's a shame this had to happen when you just got here. But
don't take it serious.

BLANCHE Violence! Is so—

275 MITCH Set down on the steps and have a cigarette with me.

BLANCHE I'm not properly dressed.

MITCH That don't make no difference in the Quarter.

BLANCHE Such a pretty silver case.

MITCH I showed you the inscription, didn't I?

9. Because of the inaction of the Union general George McClellan in 1861–62, newspaper correspondents frequently reported "All
quiet on the Potomac"; it became a bitter
catchphrase, featured in ballads and a popular song.

280 BLANCHE Yes. [*During the pause, she looks up at the sky.*] There's so much—so much confusion in the world . . . [*He coughs diffidently.*] Thank you for being so kind! I need kindness now.

Scene 4

It is early the following morning. There is a confusion of street cries like a choral chant.

STELLA *is lying down in the bedroom. Her face is serene in the early morning sunlight. One hand rests on her belly, rounding slightly with new maternity. From the other dangles a book of colored comics. Her eyes and lips have that almost narcotized tranquility that is in the faces of Eastern idols.*

The table is sloppy with remains of breakfast and the debris of the preceding night, and STANLEY'S *gaudy pyjamas lie across the threshold of the bathroom. The outside door is slightly ajar on a sky of summer brilliance.*

BLANCHE *appears at this door. She has spent a sleepless night and her appearance entirely contrasts with* STELLA's. *She presses her knuckles nervously to her lips as she looks through the door, before entering.*

BLANCHE Stella?

STELLA [*stirring lazily*] Hmmh?

[BLANCHE *utters a moaning cry and runs into the bedroom, throwing herself down beside* STELLA *in a rush of hysterical tenderness.*]

BLANCHE Baby, my baby sister!

STELLA [*drawing away from her*] Blanche, what is the matter with you?

[BLANCHE *straightens up slowly and stands beside the bed looking down at her sister with knuckles pressed to her lips.*]

5 BLANCHE He's left?

STELLA Stan? Yes.

BLANCHE Will he be back?

STELLA He's gone to get the car greased. Why?

BLANCHE Why! I've been half crazy, Stella! When I found out you'd been
10 insane enough to come back in here after what happened—I started to rush in after you!

STELLA I'm glad you didn't.

BLANCHE What were you thinking of? [STELLA *makes an indefinite gesture.*] Answer me! What? What?

15 STELLA Please, Blanche! Sit down and stop yelling.

BLANCHE All right, Stella. I will repeat the question quietly now. How could you come back in this place last night? Why, you must have slept with him!

[STELLA *gets up in a calm and leisurely way.*]

STELLA Blanche, I'd forgotten how excitable you are. You're making much too much fuss about this.

20 BLANCHE Am I?

STELLA Yes, you are, Blanche. I know how it must have seemed to you and I'm awful sorry it had to happen, but it wasn't anything as serious as you seem to take it. In the first place, when men are drinking and playing poker anything can happen. It's always a powder-keg. He didn't know what he
25 was doing. . . . He was as good as a lamb when I came back and he's really very, very ashamed of himself.

BLANCHE   And that—that makes it all right?

STELLA   No, it isn't all right for anybody to make such a terrible row, but—people do sometimes. Stanley's always smashed things. Why, on our wedding night—soon as we came in here—he snatched off one of my slippers and rushed about the place smashing light bulbs with it.

BLANCHE   He did—*what*?

STELLA   He smashed all the light bulbs with the heel of my slipper! [*She laughs.*]

BLANCHE   And you—you *let* him? Didn't *run*, didn't *scream*?

STELLA   I was—sort of—thrilled by it. [*She waits for a moment.*] Eunice and you had breakfast?

BLANCHE   Do you suppose I wanted any breakfast?

STELLA   There's some coffee left on the stove.

BLANCHE   You're so—matter-of-fact about it, Stella.

STELLA   What other can I be? He's taken the radio to get it fixed. It didn't land on the pavement so only one tube[1] was smashed.

BLANCHE   And you are standing there smiling!

STELLA   What do you want me to do?

BLANCHE   Pull yourself together and face the facts.

STELLA   What are they, in your opinion?

BLANCHE   In my opinion? You're married to a madman!

STELLA   No!

BLANCHE   Yes, you are, your fix is worse than mine is! Only you're not being sensible about it. I'm going to *do* something. Get hold of myself and make myself a new life!

STELLA   Yes?

BLANCHE   But you've given in. And that isn't right, you're not old! You can get out.

STELLA   [*slowly and emphatically*]   I'm not in anything I want to get out of.

BLANCHE   [*incredulously*]   What—Stella?

STELLA   I said I am not in anything that I have a desire to get out of. Look at the mess in this room! And those empty bottles! They went through two cases last night! He promised this morning that he was going to quit having these poker parties, but you know how long such a promise is going to keep. Oh, well, it's his pleasure, like mine is movies and bridge. People have got to tolerate each other's habits, I guess.

BLANCHE   I don't understand you. [STELLA *turns toward her.*] I don't understand your indifference. Is this a Chinese philosophy you've—cultivated?

STELLA   Is what—what?

BLANCHE   This—shuffling about and mumbling—'One tube smashed—beer bottles—mess in the kitchen!'—as if nothing out of the ordinary has happened! [STELLA *laughs uncertainly and picking up the broom, twirls it in her hands.*]

BLANCHE   Are you deliberately shaking that thing in my face?

STELLA   No.

BLANCHE   Stop it. Let go of that broom. I won't have you cleaning up for him!

STELLA   Then who's going to do it? Are you?

BLANCHE   I? I!

---

1. Vacuum tube (used in radios before the invention of transistors).

STELLA   No, I didn't think so.

75 BLANCHE   Oh, let me think, if only my mind would function! We've got to get hold of some money, that's the way out!

STELLA   I guess that money is always nice to get hold of.

BLANCHE   Listen to me. I have an idea of some kind. [*Shakily she twists a cigarette into her holder.*] Do you remember Shep Huntleigh? [STELLA

80   *shakes her head.*] Of course you remember Shep Huntleigh. I went out with him at college and wore his pin[2] for a while. Well—

STELLA   Well?

BLANCHE   I ran into him last winter. You know I went to Miami during the Christmas holidays?

85 STELLA   No.

BLANCHE   Well, I did. I took the trip as an investment, thinking I'd meet someone with a million dollars.

STELLA   Did you?

BLANCHE   Yes. I ran into Shep Huntleigh—I ran into him on Biscayne Bou-

90   levard, on Christmas Eve, about dusk . . . getting into his car—Cadillac convertible; must have been a block long!

STELLA   I should think it would have been—inconvenient in traffic!

BLANCHE   You've heard of oil wells?

STELLA   Yes—remotely.

95 BLANCHE   He has them, all over Texas. Texas is literally spouting gold in his pockets.

STELLA   My, my.

BLANCHE   Y'know how indifferent I am to money. I think of money in terms of what it does for you. But he could do it, he could certainly do it!

100 STELLA   Do what, Blanche?

BLANCHE   Why—set us up in a—shop!

STELLA   What kind of a shop?

BLANCHE   Oh, a—shop of some kind! He could do it with half what his wife throws away at the races.

105 STELLA   He's married?

BLANCHE   Honey, would I be here if the man weren't married? [STELLA *laughs a little.* BLANCHE *suddenly springs up and crosses to phone. She speaks shrilly.*] How do I get Western Union?[3]—Operator! Western Union!

STELLA   That's a dial phone,[4] honey.

BLANCHE   I can't dial, I'm too—

110 STELLA   Just dial O.

BLANCHE   O?

STELLA   Yes, "O" for Operator! [BLANCHE *considers a moment; then she puts the phone down.*]

BLANCHE   Give me a pencil. Where is a slip of paper? I've got to write it down first—the message, I mean . . .

[*She goes to the dressing table, and grabs up a sheet of Kleenex and an eyebrow pencil for writing equipment.*]

---

2. A fraternity pin, worn as a sign that a couple were "going steady."

3. The dominant American telegraph company for most of the twentieth century.

4. Though dial telephones came into use in the 1930s, in some parts of the country (rural Mississippi presumably among them) operators placed all calls for another decade or more.

115   Let me see now . . . [*She bites the pencil.*] 'Darling Shep. Sister and I in
       desperate situation.'

STELLA   I beg your pardon!

BLANCHE   'Sister and I in desperate situation. Will explain details later.
       Would you be interested in—?' [*She bites the pencil again.*] 'Would you
120   be—interested—in . . .' [*She smashes the pencil on the table and springs
       up.*] You never get anywhere with direct appeals!

STELLA [*with a laugh*]   Don't be so ridiculous, darling!

BLANCHE   But I'll think of something, I've *got* to think of—*something*! Don't,
       don't laugh at me, Stella! Please, please don't—I—I want you to look at the
125   contents of my purse! Here's what's in it! [*She snatches her purse open.*]
       Sixty-five measly cents in coin of the realm!

STELLA [*crossing to bureau*]   Stanley doesn't give me a regular allowance, he
       likes to pay bills himself, but—this morning he gave me ten dollars to
       smooth things over. You take five of it, Blanche, and I'll keep the rest.

130 BLANCHE   Oh, no. No, Stella.

STELLA [*insisting*]   I know how it helps your morale just having a little pocket
       money on you.

BLANCHE   No, thank you—I'll take to the streets!

STELLA   Talk sense! How did you happen to get so low on funds?

135 BLANCHE   Money just goes—it goes places. [*She rubs her forehead.*] Some-
       time today I've got to get hold of a Bromo![5]

STELLA   I'll fix you one now.

BLANCHE   Not yet—I've got to keep thinking!

STELLA   I wish you'd just let things go, at least for a—while . . .

140 BLANCHE   Stella, I can't live with him! You can, he's your husband. But how
       could I stay here with him, after last night, with just those curtains between
       us?

STELLA   Blanche, you saw him at his worst last night.

BLANCHE   On the contrary, I saw him at his best! What such a man has to
145   offer is animal force and he gave a wonderful exhibition of that! But the
       only way to live with such a man is to—go to bed with him! And that's your
       job—not mine!

STELLA   After you've rested a little, you'll see it's going to work out. You don't
       have to worry about anything while you're here. I mean—expenses . . .

150 BLANCHE   I have to plan for us both, to get us both—out!

STELLA   You take it for granted that I am in something that I want to get out of.

BLANCHE   I take it for granted that you still have sufficient memory of Belle
       Reve to find this place and these poker players impossible to live with.

STELLA   Well, you're taking entirely too much for granted.

155 BLANCHE   I can't believe you're in earnest.

STELLA   No?

BLANCHE   I understand how it happened—a little. You saw him in uniform,
       an officer, not here but—

STELLA   I'm not sure it would have made any difference where I saw him.

160 BLANCHE   Now don't say it was one of those mysterious electric things
       between people! If you do I'll laugh in your face.

---

5. Bromo-Seltzer, a headache remedy and antacid introduced in 1891; its effervescent granules
are dissolved in water.

STELLA   I am not going to say anything more at all about it!

BLANCHE   All right, then, don't!

STELLA   But there are things that happen between a man and a woman in

165   the dark—that sort of make everything else seem—unimportant. [*Pause*]

BLANCHE   What you are talking about is brutal desire—just—Desire!—the name of that rattletrap streetcar that bangs through the Quarter, up one old narrow street and down another . . .

STELLA   Haven't you ever ridden on that streetcar?

170   BLANCHE   It brought me here.—Where I'm not wanted and where I'm ashamed to be . . .

STELLA   Then don't you think your superior attitude is a bit out of place?

BLANCHE   I am not being or feeling at all superior, Stella. Believe me I'm not! It's just this. This is how I look at it. A man like that is someone to go out

175   with—once—twice—three times when the devil is in you. But live with? Have a child by?

STELLA   I have told you I love him.

BLANCHE   Then I *tremble* for you! I just—*tremble* for you. . . .

STELLA   I can't help your trembling if you insist on trembling!

[*There is a pause.*]

180   BLANCHE   May I—speak—*plainly*?

STELLA   Yes, do. Go ahead. As plainly as you want to.

[*Outside, a train approaches. They are silent till the noise subsides. They are both in the bedroom.*]

[*Under cover of the train's noise* STANLEY *enters from outside. He stands unseen by the women, holding some packages in his arms, and overhears their following conversation. He wears an undershirt and grease-stained seersucker pants.*]

BLANCHE   Well—if you'll forgive me—he's *common*!

STELLA   Why, yes, I suppose he is.

BLANCHE   Suppose! You can't have forgotten that much of our bringing up,

185   Stella, that you just *suppose* that any part of a gentleman's in his nature! *Not one particle, no!* Oh, if he was just—*ordinary*! Just *plain*—but good and wholesome, but—*no*. There's something downright—*bestial*—about him! You're hating me saying this, aren't you?

STELLA [*coldly*]   Go on and say it all, Blanche.

190   BLANCHE   He acts like an animal, has an animal's habits! Eats like one, moves like one, talks like one! There's even something—subhuman—something not quite to the stage of humanity yet! Yes, something—apelike about him, like one of those pictures I've seen in—anthropological studies! Thousands and thousands of years have passed him right by, and there he is—

195   Stanley Kowalski—survivor of the Stone Age! Bearing the raw meat home from the kill in the jungle! And you—*you* here—*waiting* for him! Maybe he'll strike you or maybe grunt and kiss you! That is, if kisses have been discovered yet! Night falls and the other apes gather! There in the front of the cave, all grunting like him, and swilling and gnawing and hulking! His

200   poker night!—you call it—this party of apes! Somebody growls—some creature snatches at something—the fight is on! *God!* Maybe we are a long way from being made in God's image, but Stella—my sister—there has been *some* progress since then! Such things as art—as poetry and music— such kinds of new light have come into the world since then! In some kinds

205 of people some tenderer feelings have had some little beginning! That we have got to make *grow!* And *cling* to, and hold as our flag! In this dark march toward whatever it is we're approaching. . . . *Don't—don't hang back with the brutes!*

> [*Another train passes outside.* STANLEY *hesitates, licking his lips. Then suddenly he turns stealthily about and withdraws through front door. The women are still unaware of his presence. When the train has passed he calls through the closed front door.*]

STANLEY   Hey! Hey, Stella!

210 STELLA [*who has listened gravely to* BLANCHE]   Stanley!

BLANCHE   Stell, I—

> [*But* STELLA *has gone to the front door.* STANLEY *enters casually with his packages.*]

STANLEY   Hiyuh, Stella. Blanche back?

STELLA   Yes, she's back.

STANLEY   Hiyuh, Blanche. [*He grins at her.*]

215 STELLA   You must've got under the car.

STANLEY   Them darn mechanics at Fritz's don't know their ass fr'm—Hey!

> [STELLA *has embraced him with both arms, fiercely, and full in the view of* BLANCHE. *He laughs and clasps her head to him. Over her head he grins through the curtains at* BLANCHE.]

> [*As the lights fade away, with a lingering brightness on their embrace, the music of the "blue piano" and trumpet and drums is heard.*]

Scene 5

BLANCHE *is seated in the bedroom fanning herself with a palm leaf as she reads over a just-completed letter. Suddenly she bursts into a peal of laughter.* STELLA *is dressing in the bedroom.*

STELLA   What are you laughing at, honey?

BLANCHE   Myself, myself, for being such a liar! I'm writing a letter to Shep. [*She picks up the letter.*] "Darling Shep. I am spending the summer on the wing, making flying visits here and there. And who knows, perhaps I shall
5 take a sudden notion to *swoop* down on *Dallas!* How would you feel about that? Ha-ha! [*She laughs nervously and brightly, touching her throat as if actually talking to Shep.*] Forewarned is forearmed, as they say!"—How does that sound?

STELLA   Uh-huh . . .

10 BLANCHE [*going on nervously*]   "Most of my sister's friends go north in the summer but some have homes on the Gulf and there has been a continued round of entertainments, teas, cocktails, and luncheons—"

> [*A disturbance is heard upstairs at the Hubbells' apartment.*]

STELLA   Eunice seems to be having some trouble with Steve.

> [EUNICE's *voice shouts in terrible wrath.*]

EUNICE   I heard about you and that blonde!

15 STEVE   That's a damn lie!

EUNICE   You ain't pulling the wool over my eyes! I wouldn't mind if you'd stay down at the Four Deuces, but you always going up.

STEVE   Who ever seen me up?

EUNICE   I seen you chasing her 'round the balcony—I'm gonna call the vice
20 squad!

STEVE   Don't you throw that at me!

EUNICE [*shrieking*]   You hit me! I'm gonna call the police!

[*A clatter of aluminum striking a wall is heard, followed by a man's angry roar, shouts and overturned furniture. There is a crash; then a relative hush.*]

BLANCHE [*brightly*]   Did he *kill* her?

[EUNICE *appears on the steps in daemonic disorder.*]

STELLA   No! She's coming downstairs.

25 EUNICE   Call the police, I'm going to call the police! [*She rushes around the corner.*]

[*They laugh lightly.* STANLEY *comes around the corner in his green and scarlet silk bowling shirt. He trots up the steps and bangs into the kitchen.* BLANCHE *registers his entrance with nervous gestures.*]

STANLEY   What's a matter with Eun-uss?

STELLA   She and Steve had a row. Has she got the police?

STANLEY   Naw. She's gettin' a drink.

STELLA   That's much more practical!

[STEVE *comes down nursing a bruise on his forehead and looks in the door.*]

30 STEVE   She here?

STANLEY   Naw, naw. At the Four Deuces.

STEVE   That rutting hunk! [*He looks around the corner a bit timidly, then turns with affected boldness and runs after her.*]

BLANCHE   I must jot that down in my notebook. Ha-ha! I'm compiling a notebook of quaint little words and phrases I've picked up here.

35 STANLEY   You won't pick up nothing here you ain't heard before.

BLANCHE   Can I count on that?

STANLEY   You can count on it up to five hundred.

BLANCHE   That's a mighty high number. [*He jerks open the bureau drawer, slams it shut and throws shoes in a corner. At each noise* BLANCHE *winces slightly. Finally she speaks.*] What sign were you born under?

40 STANLEY [*while he is dressing*]   Sign?

BLANCHE   Astrological sign. I bet you were born under Aries. Aries people are forceful and dynamic. They dote on noise! They love to bang things around! You must have had lots of banging around in the army and now that you're out, you make up for it by treating inanimate objects with such

45 a fury!

[STELLA *has been going in and out of closet during this scene. Now she pops her head out of the closet.*]

STELLA   Stanley was born just five minutes after Christmas.

BLANCHE   Capricorn—the Goat!

STANLEY   What sign were *you* born under?

BLANCHE   Oh, my birthday's next month, the fifteenth of September; that's

50 under Virgo.

STANLEY   What's Virgo?

BLANCHE   Virgo is the Virgin.

STANLEY [*contemptuously*]   Hah! [*He advances a little as he knots his tie.*] Say, do you happen to know somebody named Shaw?

[*Her face expresses a faint shock. She reaches for the cologne bottle and dampens her handkerchief as she answers carefully.*]

55 BLANCHE   Why, everybody knows somebody named Shaw!

STANLEY   Well, this somebody named Shaw is under the impression he met you in Laurel, but I figure he must have got you mixed up with some other party because this other party is someone he met at a hotel called the Flamingo.

[BLANCHE *laughs breathlessly as she touches the cologne-dampened handkerchief to her temples.*]

60 BLANCHE   I'm afraid he does have me mixed up with this "other party." The Hotel Flamingo is not the sort of establishment I would dare to be seen in!

STANLEY   You know of it?

BLANCHE   Yes, I've seen it and smelled it.

65 STANLEY   You must've got pretty close if you could smell it.

BLANCHE   The odor of cheap perfume is penetrating.

STANLEY   That stuff you use is expensive?

BLANCHE   Twenty-five dollars an ounce! I'm nearly out. That's just a hint if you want to remember my birthday! [*She speaks lightly but her voice has a note of fear.*]

70 STANLEY   Shaw must've got you mixed up. He goes in and out of Laurel all the time so he can check on it and clear up any mistake.

[*He turns away and crosses to the portieres.* BLANCHE *closes her eyes as if faint. Her hand trembles as she lifts the handkerchief again to her forehead.*]

[STEVE *and* EUNICE *come around corner.* STEVE's *arm is around* EUNICE's *shoulder and she is sobbing luxuriously and he is cooing love-words. There is a murmur of thunder as they go slowly upstairs in a tight embrace.*]

STANLEY [*to* STELLA]   I'll wait for you at the Four Deuces!

STELLA   Hey! Don't I rate one kiss?

STANLEY   Not in front of your sister.

[*He goes out.* BLANCHE *rises from her chair. She seems faint; looks about her with an expression of almost panic.*]

75 BLANCHE   Stella! What have you heard about me?

STELLA   Huh?

BLANCHE   What have people been telling you about me?

STELLA   Telling?

BLANCHE   You haven't heard any—unkind—gossip about me?

80 STELLA   Why, no, Blanche, of course not!

BLANCHE   Honey, there was—a good deal of talk in Laurel.

STELLA   About *you*, Blanche?

BLANCHE   I wasn't so good the last two years or so, after Belle Reve had started to slip through my fingers.

85 STELLA   All of us do things we—

BLANCHE   I never was hard or self-sufficient enough. When people are soft—soft people have got to shimmer and glow—they've got to put on soft colors, the colors of butterfly wings, and put a—paper lantern over the light. . . . It isn't enough to be soft. You've got to be soft *and attractive*. And I—I'm

90 fading now! I don't know how much longer I can turn the trick.

[*The afternoon has faded to dusk.* STELLA *goes into the bedroom and turns on the light under the paper lantern. She holds a bottled soft drink in her hand.*]

BLANCHE   Have you been listening to me?

STELLA   I don't listen to you when you are being morbid! [*She advances with the bottled Coke.*]

BLANCHE [*with abrupt change to gaiety*]   Is that Coke for me?

STELLA   Not for anyone else!

95 BLANCHE   Why, you precious thing, you! Is it just Coke?

STELLA [*turning*]   You mean you want a shot in it!

BLANCHE   Well, honey, a shot never does a Coke any harm! Let me! You mustn't wait on me!

STELLA   I like to wait on you, Blanche. It makes it seem more like home. [*She goes into the kitchen, finds a glass and pours a shot of whiskey into it.*]

100 BLANCHE   I have to admit I love to be waited on . . .

> [*She rushes into the bedroom.* STELLA *goes to her with the glass.* BLANCHE *suddenly clutches* STELLA's *free hand with a moaning sound and presses the hand to her lips.* STELLA *is embarrassed by her show of emotion.* BLANCHE *speaks in a choked voice.*]

You're—you're—so *good* to me! And I—

STELLA   Blanche.

BLANCHE   I know, I won't! You hate me to talk sentimental! But honey, *believe* I feel things more than I *tell* you! I *won't* stay long! I won't, I *promise* I—

105 STELLA   Blanche!

BLANCHE [*hysterically*]   I won't, I promise, *I'll* go! Go *soon*! I will *really*! I *won't* hang around until he—throws me out . . .

STELLA   Now will you stop talking foolish?

BLANCHE   Yes, honey. Watch how you pour—that fizzy stuff foams over!

> [BLANCHE *laughs shrilly and grabs the glass, but her hand shakes so it almost slips from her grasp.* STELLA *pours the Coke into the glass. It foams over and spills.* BLANCHE *gives a piercing cry.*]

110 STELLA [*shocked by the cry*]   Heavens!

BLANCHE   Right on my pretty white skirt!

STELLA   Oh . . . Use my hanky. Blot gently.

BLANCHE [*slowly recovering*]   I know—gently—gently . . .

STELLA   Did it stain?

115 BLANCHE   Not a bit. Ha-ha! Isn't that lucky? [*She sits down shakily, taking a grateful drink. She holds the glass in both hands and continues to laugh a little.*]

STELLA   Why did you scream like that?

BLANCHE   I don't know why I screamed! [*Continuing nervously*] Mitch—Mitch is coming at seven. I guess I am just feeling nervous about our relations. [*She begins to talk rapidly and breathlessly.*] He hasn't gotten a thing
120 but a good-night kiss, that's all I have given him, Stella. I want his respect. And men don't want anything they get too easy. But on the other hand men lose interest quickly. Especially when the girl is over—thirty. They think a girl over thirty ought to—the vulgar term is—"put out." . . . And I—I'm not "putting out." Of course he—he doesn't know—I mean I haven't informed
125 him—of my real age!

STELLA   Why are you sensitive about your age?

BLANCHE   Because of hard knocks my vanity's been given. What I mean is— he thinks I'm sort of—prim and proper, you know! [*She laughs out sharply.*] I want to *deceive* him enough to make him—want me . . .

130 STELLA   Blanche, do you want *him*?

BLANCHE   I want to *rest!* I want to breathe quietly again! Yes—I *want* Mitch . . . *very badly!* Just think! If it happens! I can leave here and not be anyone's problem . . .

[STANLEY *comes around the corner with a drink under his belt.*]

STANLEY [*bawling*]   Hey, Steve! Hey, Eunice! Hey, Stella!

[*There are joyous calls from above. Trumpet and drums are heard from around the corner.*]

135 STELLA [*kissing* BLANCHE *impulsively*]   It *will* happen!

BLANCHE [*doubtfully*]   It will?

STELLA   It *will!* [*She goes across into the kitchen, looking back at* BLANCHE.] It will, honey, *it will.* . . . But don't take another drink! [*Her voice catches as she goes out the door to meet her husband.*]

[BLANCHE *sinks faintly back in her chair with her drink.* EUNICE *shrieks with laughter and runs down the steps.* STEVE *bounds after her with goat-like screeches and chases her around corner.* STANLEY *and* STELLA *twine arms as they follow, laughing.*]

[*Dusk settles deeper. The music from the Four Deuces is slow and blue.*]

BLANCHE   Ah, me, ah, me, ah, me . . .

[*Her eyes fall shut and the palm leaf fan drops from her fingers. She slaps her hand on the chair arm a couple of times. There is a little glimmer of lightning about the building.*]

[*A* YOUNG MAN *comes along the street and rings the bell.*]

140 BLANCHE   Come in.

[*The* YOUNG MAN *appears through the portieres. She regards him with interest.*]

BLANCHE   Well, well! What can I do for *you?*

YOUNG MAN   I'm collecting for *The Evening Star.*

BLANCHE   I didn't know that stars took up collections.

YOUNG MAN   It's the paper.

145 BLANCHE   I know, I was joking—feebly! Will you—have a drink?

YOUNG MAN   No, ma'am. No, thank you. I can't drink on the job.

BLANCHE   Oh, well, now, let's see. . . . No, I don't have a dime! I'm not the lady of the house. I'm her sister from Mississippi. I'm one of those poor relations you've heard about.

150 YOUNG MAN   That's all right. I'll drop by later. [*He starts to go out. She approaches a little.*]

BLANCHE   Hey! [*He turns back shyly. She puts a cigarette in a long holder.*] Could you give me a light? [*She crosses toward him. They meet at the door between the two rooms.*]

YOUNG MAN   Sure. [*He takes out a lighter.*] This doesn't always work.

BLANCHE   It's temperamental? [*It flares.*] Ah!—thank you. [*He starts away again.*] Hey! [*He turns again, still more uncertainly. She goes close to him.*]
155 Uh—what time is it?

YOUNG MAN   Fifteen of seven, ma'am.

BLANCHE   So late? Don't you just love these long rainy afternoons in New Orleans when an hour isn't just an hour—but a little piece of eternity
160 dropped into your hands—and who knows what to do with it? [*She touches his shoulders.*] You—uh—didn't get wet in the rain?

YOUNG MAN   No, ma'am. I stepped inside.

BLANCHE   In a drugstore? And had a soda?

YOUNG MAN   Uh-huh.

165   BLANCHE   Chocolate?

YOUNG MAN   No, ma'am. Cherry.

BLANCHE [*laughing*]   Cherry!

YOUNG MAN   A cherry soda.

BLANCHE   You make my mouth water. [*She touches his cheek lightly, and smiles. Then she goes to the trunk.*]

170   YOUNG MAN   Well, I'd better be going—

BLANCHE [*stopping him*]   Young man!

[*He turns. She takes a large, gossamer scarf from the trunk and drapes it about her shoulders.*]

[*In the ensuing pause, the "blue piano" is heard. It continues through the rest of this scene and the opening of the next. The young man clears his throat and looks yearningly at the door.*]

Young man! Young, young, young man! Has anyone ever told you that you look like a young Prince out of the Arabian Nights?[6]

[*The* YOUNG MAN *laughs uncomfortably and stands like a bashful kid.* BLANCHE *speaks softly to him.*]

Well, you do, honey lamb! Come here. I want to kiss you, just once, softly
175   and sweetly on your mouth!

[*Without waiting for him to accept, she crosses quickly to him and presses her lips to his.*]

Now run along, now, quickly! It would be nice to keep you, but I've got to be good—and keep my hands off children.

[*He stares at her a moment. She opens the door for him and blows a kiss at him as he goes down the steps with a dazed look. She stands there a little dreamily after he has disappeared. Then* MITCH *appears around the corner with a bunch of roses.*]

BLANCHE [*gaily*]   Look who's coming! My Rosenkavalier! Bow to me first . . . now present them! *Ahhhh—Merciiii!*[7]

[*She looks at him over them, coquettishly pressing them to her lips. He beams at her self-consciously.*]

Scene 6

It is about two A.M. *on the same evening. The outer wall of the building is visible.*
BLANCHE *and* MITCH *come in. The utter exhaustion which only a neurasthenic personality*[8] *can know is evident in* BLANCHE'*s voice and manner.* MITCH *is stolid but depressed. They have probably been out to the amusement park on Lake Pontchartrain, for* MITCH *is bearing, upside down, a plaster statuette of Mae West,*[9] *the sort of prize won at shooting galleries and carnival games of chance.*

6. That is, *The Thousand and One Nights*, a collection of ancient tales in Arabic, arranged in its present form in the 15th century.

7. Thank you (French). *Rosenkavalier*: literally, "Knight of the Rose" (German), an allusion to Richard Strauss's romantic opera *Der Rosenkavalier* (1911).

8. Someone suffering from neurasthenia, a psychological disorder characterized by ner-

vous exhaustion. A common clinical diagnosis during the late 19th century, the term is no longer in scientific use.

9. An American actress of burlesque shows, stage, and screen (1893–1980), famous for her sexual double entendres. *Lake Pontchartrain*: the large, shallow lake immediately north of New Orleans.

BLANCHE [*stopping lifelessly at the steps*]   Well—
    [MITCH *laughs uneasily.*]
  Well . . .

MITCH   I guess it must be pretty late—and you're tired.

BLANCHE   Even the hot tamale man has deserted the street, and he hangs on
5   till the end. [MITCH *laughs uneasily again.*] How will you get home?

MITCH   I'll walk over to Bourbon and catch an owl-car.[1]

BLANCHE [*laughing grimly*]   Is that streetcar named Desire still grinding
along the tracks at this hour?

MITCH [*heavily*]   I'm afraid you haven't gotten much fun out of this evening,
10   Blanche.

BLANCHE   I spoiled it for *you*.

MITCH   No, you didn't, but I felt all the time that I wasn't giving you
much—entertainment.

BLANCHE   I simply couldn't rise to the occasion. That was all. I don't think
15   I've ever tried so hard to be gay and made such a dismal mess of it. I get ten
points for trying!—I *did* try.

MITCH   Why did you try if you didn't feel like it, Blanche?

BLANCHE   I was just obeying the law of nature.

MITCH   Which law is that?

20   BLANCHE   The one that says the lady must entertain the gentleman—or no
dice! See if you can locate my door key in this purse. When I'm so tired my
fingers are all thumbs!

MITCH [*rooting in her purse*]   This it?

BLANCHE   No, honey, that's the key to my trunk which I must soon be
25   packing.

MITCH   You mean you are leaving here soon?

BLANCHE   I've outstayed my welcome.

MITCH   This it?

    [*The music fades away.*]

BLANCHE   Eureka! Honey, you open the door while I take a last look at the
30   sky. [*She leans on the porch rail. He opens the door and stands awkwardly
behind her.*] I'm looking for the Pleiades, the Seven Sisters,[2] but these girls
are not out tonight. Oh, yes they are, there they are! God bless them! All in
a bunch going home from their little bridge party. . . . Y' get the door open?
Good boy! I guess you—want to go now . . .

    [*He shuffles and coughs a little.*]

35   MITCH   Can I—uh—kiss you—good night?

BLANCHE   Why do you always ask me if you may?

MITCH   I don't know whether you want me to or not.

BLANCHE   Why should you be so doubtful?

MITCH   That night when we parked by the lake and I kissed you, you—

40   BLANCHE   Honey, it wasn't the kiss I objected to. I liked the kiss very much.
It was the other little—familiarity—that I—felt obliged to—discourage. . . .
I didn't resent it! Not a bit in the world! In fact, I was somewhat flattered
that you—desired me! But, honey, you know as well as I do that a single

---

1. A late-night streetcar (i.e., for "night owls").
2. In Greek mythology, the Pleiades are the seven daughters of Atlas who were changed

into a cluster of stars in the constellation Taurus.

girl, a girl alone in the world, has got to keep a firm hold on her emotions
45 or she'll be lost!

MITCH [*solemnly*] Lost?

BLANCHE I guess you are used to girls that like to be lost. The kind that get lost immediately, on the first date!

MITCH I like you to be exactly the way that you are, because in all my—
50 experience—I have never known anyone like you.

> [BLANCHE *looks at him gravely; then she bursts into laughter and then claps a hand to her mouth.*]

MITCH Are you laughing at me?

BLANCHE No, honey. The lord and lady of the house have not yet returned, so come in. We'll have a nightcap. Let's leave the lights off. Shall we?

MITCH You just—do what you want to.

> [BLANCHE *precedes him into the kitchen. The outer wall of the building disappears and the interiors of the two rooms can be dimly seen.*]

55 BLANCHE [*remaining in the first room*] The other room's more comfortable—go on in. This crashing around in the dark is my search for some liquor.

MITCH You want a drink?

BLANCHE I want *you* to have a drink! You have been so anxious and solemn all evening, and so have I; we have both been anxious and solemn and now
60 for these few last remaining moments of our lives together—I want to create—*joie de vivre*![3] I'm lighting a candle.

MITCH That's good.

BLANCHE We are going to be very Bohemian. We are going to pretend that we are sitting in a little artists' cafe on the Left Bank[4] in Paris! [*She lights a*
65 *candle stub and puts it in a bottle.*] *Je suis la Dame aux Camellias! Vous êtes—Armand!*[5] Understand French?

MITCH [*heavily*] Naw. Naw, I—

BLANCHE *Voulez-vous couchez avec moi ce soir? Vous ne comprenez pas? Ah, quelle dommage!*[6] I mean it's a damned good thing. . . . I've found some
70 liquor! Just enough for two shots without any dividends, honey . . .

MITCH [*heavily*] That's—good.

> [*She enters the bedroom with the drinks and the candle.*]

BLANCHE Sit down! Why don't you take off your coat and loosen your collar?

MITCH I better leave it on.

BLANCHE No. I want you to be comfortable.

75 MITCH I am ashamed of the way I perspire. My shirt is sticking to me.

BLANCHE Perspiration is healthy. If people didn't perspire they would die in five minutes. [*She takes his coat from him.*] This is a nice coat. What kind of material is it?

MITCH They call that stuff alpaca.

3. Joy of life (French).
4. A neighborhood on the western ("left") bank of the river Seine, known for cultural and intellectual activities.
5. I am the Lady of the Camellias. You are— Armand! (French). The reference is to Alexandre Dumas's novel *La Dame aux camélias* (1848), the tragic story of Marguerite Gautier, a Parisian courtesan who falls in love with Armand Duval, a respectable member of middle-class society, and dies of consumption. Dumas's 1852 theatrical adaptation of this novel (often titled *Camille* in English) was highly popular with late 19th-century audiences.
6. Would you like to go to bed with me tonight? You don't understand? Ah, what a shame! (French).

80 BLANCHE Oh. Alpaca.

MITCH It's very light-weight alpaca.

BLANCHE Oh. Light-weight alpaca.

MITCH I don't like to wear a wash-coat[7] even in summer because I sweat through it.

85 BLANCHE Oh.

MITCH And it don't look neat on me. A man with a heavy build has got to be careful of what he puts on him so he don't look too clumsy.

BLANCHE You are not too heavy.

MITCH You don't think I am?

90 BLANCHE You are not the delicate type. You have a massive bone-structure and a very imposing physique.

MITCH Thank you. Last Christmas I was given a membership to the New Orleans Athletic Club.

BLANCHE Oh, good.

95 MITCH It was the finest present I ever was given. I work out there with the weights and I swim and I keep myself fit. When I started there, I was getting soft in the belly but now my belly is hard. It is so hard now that a man can punch me in the belly and it don't hurt me. Punch me! Go on! See? [She pokes lightly at him.]

BLANCHE Gracious. [Her hand touches her chest.]

100 MITCH Guess how much I weigh, Blanche?

BLANCHE Oh, I'd say in the vicinity of—one hundred and eighty?

MITCH Guess again.

BLANCHE Not that much?

MITCH No. More.

105 BLANCHE Well, you're a tall man and you can carry a good deal of weight without looking awkward.

MITCH I weigh two hundred and seven pounds and I'm six feet one and one half inches tall in my bare feet—without shoes on. And that is what I weigh stripped.

110 BLANCHE Oh, my goodness, me! It's awe-inspiring.

MITCH [embarrassed] My weight is not a very interesting subject to talk about. [He hesitates for a moment.] What's yours?

BLANCHE My weight?

MITCH Yes.

115 BLANCHE Guess!

MITCH Let me lift you.

BLANCHE Samson![8] Go on, lift me. [He comes behind her and puts his hands on her waist and raises her lightly off the ground.] Well?

MITCH You are light as a feather.

120 BLANCHE Ha-ha! [He lowers her but keeps his hands on her waist. BLANCHE speaks with an affectation of demureness.] You may release me now.

MITCH Huh?

BLANCHE [gaily] I said unhand me, sir. [He fumblingly embraces her. Her voice sounds gently reproving.] Now, Mitch. Just because Stanley and Stella

125 aren't at home is no reason why you shouldn't behave like a gentleman.

---

7. A light washable jacket, here made of a silky wool.

8. An Israelite hero of great strength (see Judges 13–16).

MITCH   Just give me a slap whenever I step out of bounds.

BLANCHE   That won't be necessary. You're a natural gentleman, one of the very few that are left in the world. I don't want you to think that I am severe and old maid school-teacherish or anything like that. It's just—well—

130 MITCH   Huh?

BLANCHE   I guess it is just that I have—old-fashioned ideals! [*She rolls her eyes, knowing he cannot see her face.* MITCH *goes to the front door. There is a considerable silence between them.* BLANCHE *sighs and* MITCH *coughs self-consciously.*]

MITCH [*finally*]   Where's Stanley and Stella tonight?

BLANCHE   They have gone out. With Mr. and Mrs. Hubbell upstairs.

MITCH   Where did they go?

135 BLANCHE   I think they were planning to go to a midnight prevue at Loew's State.

MITCH   We should all go out together some night.

BLANCHE   No. That wouldn't be a good plan.

MITCH   Why not?

140 BLANCHE   You are an old friend of Stanley's?

MITCH   We was together in the Two-forty-first.[9]

BLANCHE   I guess he talks to you frankly?

MITCH   Sure.

BLANCHE   Has he talked to you about me?

145 MITCH   Oh—not very much.

BLANCHE   The way you say that, I suspect that he has.

MITCH   No, he hasn't said much.

BLANCHE   But what he *has* said. What would you say his attitude toward me was?

150 MITCH   Why do you want to ask that?

BLANCHE   Well—

MITCH   Don't you get along with him?

BLANCHE   What do you think?

MITCH   I don't think he understands you.

155 BLANCHE   That is putting it mildly. If it weren't for Stella about to have a baby, I wouldn't be able to endure things here.

MITCH   He isn't—nice to you?

BLANCHE   He is insufferably rude. Goes out of his way to offend me.

MITCH   In what way, Blanche?

160 BLANCHE   Why, in every conceivable way.

MITCH   I'm surprised to hear that.

BLANCHE   Are you?

MITCH   Well, I—don't see how anybody could be rude to you.

BLANCHE   It's really a pretty frightful situation. You see, there's no privacy
165 here. There's just these portieres between the two rooms at night. He stalks through the rooms in his underwear at night. And I have to ask him to close the bathroom door. That sort of commonness isn't necessary. You probably wonder why I don't move out. Well, I'll tell you frankly. A teacher's salary is barely sufficient for her living expenses. I didn't save a penny last year and
170 so I had to come here for the summer. That's why I have to put up with my

9. The 241st Battalion of the Army Corps of Engineers.

sister's husband. And he has to put up with me, apparently so much against his wishes. . . . Surely he must have told you how much he hates me!

MITCH   I don't think he hates you.

BLANCHE   He hates me. Or why would he insult me? The first time I laid
175   eyes on him I thought to myself, that man is my executioner! That man will destroy me, unless—

MITCH   Blanche—

BLANCHE   Yes, honey?

MITCH   Can I ask you a question?

180   BLANCHE   Yes. What?

MITCH   How old are you?

[She makes a nervous gesture.]

BLANCHE   Why do you want to know?

MITCH   I talked to my mother about you and she said, "How old is Blanche?" And I wasn't able to tell her. [There is another pause.]

185   BLANCHE   You talked to your mother about me?

MITCH   Yes.

BLANCHE   Why?

MITCH   I told my mother how nice you were, and I liked you.

BLANCHE   Were you sincere about that?

190   MITCH   You know I was.

BLANCHE   Why did your mother want to know my age?

MITCH   Mother is sick.

BLANCHE   I'm sorry to hear it. Badly?

MITCH   She won't live long. Maybe just a few months.

195   BLANCHE   Oh.

MITCH   She worries because I'm not settled.

BLANCHE   Oh.

MITCH   She wants me to be settled down before she—[His voice is hoarse and he clears his throat twice, shuffling nervously around with his hands in and out of his pockets.]

BLANCHE   You love her very much, don't you?

200   MITCH   Yes.

BLANCHE   I think you have a great capacity for devotion. You will be lonely when she passes on, won't you? [MITCH clears his throat and nods.] I understand what that is.

MITCH   To be lonely?

205   BLANCHE   I loved someone, too, and the person I loved I lost.

MITCH   Dead? [She crosses to the window and sits on the sill, looking out. She pours herself another drink.] A man?

BLANCHE   He was a boy, just a boy, when I was a very young girl. When I was sixteen, I made the discovery—love. All at once and much, much too com-
210   pletely. It was like you suddenly turned a blinding light on something that had always been half in shadow, that's how it struck the world for me. But I was unlucky. Deluded. There was something different about the boy, a nervousness, a softness and tenderness which wasn't like a man's, although he wasn't the least bit effeminate-looking—still—that thing was there. . . .
215   He came to me for help. I didn't know that. I didn't find out anything till after our marriage when we'd run away and come back and all I knew was I'd failed him in some mysterious way and wasn't able to give the help he

needed but couldn't speak of! He was in the quicksands and clutching at me—but I wasn't holding him out, I was slipping in with him! I didn't know that. I didn't know anything except I loved him unendurably but without being able to help him or help myself. Then I found out. In the worst of all possible ways. By coming suddenly into a room that I thought was empty— which wasn't empty, but had two people in it . . . the boy I had married and an older man who had been his friend for years . . .

[*A locomotive is heard approaching outside. She claps her hands to her ears and crouches over. The headlight of the locomotive glares into the room as it thunders past. As the noise recedes she straightens slowly and continues speaking.*]

Afterward we pretended that nothing had been discovered. Yes, the three of us drove out to Moon Lake Casino,[1] very drunk and laughing all the way.

[*Polka music sounds, in a minor key faint with distance.*]

We danced the Varsouviana![2] Suddenly in the middle of the dance the boy I had married broke away from me and ran out of the casino. A few moments later—a shot!

[*The polka stops abruptly.*]

[BLANCHE *rises stiffly. Then, the polka resumes in a major key.*]

I ran out—all did!—all ran and gathered about the terrible thing at the edge of the lake! I couldn't get near for the crowding. Then somebody caught my arm. "Don't go any closer! Come back! You don't want to see!" See? See what! Then I heard voices say—Allan! Allan! The Grey boy! He'd stuck the revolver into his mouth, and fired—so that the back of his head had been—blown away!

[*She sways and covers her face.*]

It was because—on the dance floor—unable to stop myself—I'd suddenly said—"I saw! I know! You disgust me . . ." And then the searchlight which had been turned on the world was turned off again and never for one moment since has there been any light that's stronger than this—kitchen— candle . . .

[MITCH *gets up awkwardly and moves toward her a little. The polka music increases.* MITCH *stands beside her.*]

MITCH [*drawing her slowly into his arms*] You need somebody. And I need somebody, too. Could it be—you and me, Blanche?

[*She stares at him vacantly for a moment. Then with a soft cry huddles in his embrace. She makes a sobbing effort to speak but the words won't come. He kisses her forehead and her eyes and finally her lips. The polka tune fades out. Her breath is drawn and released in long, grateful sobs.*]

BLANCHE Sometimes—there's God—so quickly!

Scene 7

It is late afternoon in mid-September.

The portieres are open and a table is set for a birthday supper, with cake and flowers. STELLA *is completing the decorations as* STANLEY *comes in.*

---

1. A popular night spot and casino during the 1940s, located in Dundee, Mississippi.   2. A jaunty polka dance.

STANLEY   What's all this stuff for?

STELLA   Honey, it's Blanche's birthday.

STANLEY   She here?

STELLA   In the bathroom.

5 STANLEY [*mimicking*]   "Washing out some things"?

STELLA   I reckon so.

STANLEY   How long she been in there?

STELLA   All afternoon.

STANLEY [*mimicking*]   "Soaking in a hot tub"?

10 STELLA   Yes.

STANLEY   Temperature 100 on the nose, and she soaks herself in a hot tub.

STELLA   She says it cools her off for the evening.

STANLEY   And you run out an' get her cokes, I suppose? And serve 'em to Her Majesty in the tub? [STELLA *shrugs*.] Set down here a minute.

15 STELLA   Stanley, I've got things to do.

STANLEY   Set down! I've got th' dope on your big sister, Stella.

STELLA   Stanley, stop picking on Blanche.

STANLEY   That girl calls *me* common!

STELLA   Lately you been doing all you can think of to rub her the wrong way,
20   Stanley, and Blanche is sensitive and you've got to realize that Blanche and I grew up under very different circumstances than you did.

STANLEY   So I been told. And told and told and told! You know she's been feeding us a pack of lies here?

STELLA   No, I don't, and—

25 STANLEY   Well, she has, however. But now the cat's out of the bag! I found out some things!

STELLA   What—things?

STANLEY   Things I already suspected. But now I got proof from the most reliable sources—which I have checked on!

[BLANCHE *is singing in the bathroom a saccharine popular ballad which is used contrapuntally with Stanley's speech.*]

30 STELLA [*to* STANLEY]   Lower your voice!

STANLEY   Some canary bird, huh!

STELLA   Now please tell me quietly what you think you've found out about my sister.

STANLEY   Lie Number One: All this squeamishness she puts on! You should
35   just know the line she's been feeding to Mitch. He thought she had never been more than kissed by a fellow! But Sister Blanche is no lily! Ha-ha! Some lily she is!

STELLA   What have you heard and who from?

STANLEY   Our supply-man down at the plant has been going through Laurel
40   for years and he knows all about her and everybody else in the town of Laurel knows all about her. She is as famous in Laurel as if she was the President of the United States, only she is not respected by any party! This supply-man stops at a hotel called the Flamingo.

BLANCHE [*singing blithely*]

   "Say, it's only a paper moon, Sailing over a cardboard sea—But it
45   wouldn't be make-believe If you believed in me!"[3]

---

3. From "It's Only a Paper Moon" (lyrics by Yip Harburg and Billy Rose, music by Harold Arlen), used in the film *Take a Chance* (1933).

STELLA What about the—Flamingo?

STANLEY She stayed there, too.

STELLA My sister lived at Belle Reve.

STANLEY This is after the home-place had slipped through her lily-white fin-
50 gers! She moved to the Flamingo! A second-class hotel which has the advantage of not interfering in the private social life of the personalities there! The
Flamingo is used to all kinds of goings-on. But even the management of the
Flamingo was impressed by Dame Blanche! In fact they was so impressed by
Dame Blanche that they requested her to turn in her room key—for perma-
55 nently! This happened a couple of weeks before she showed here.

BLANCHE [singing]

"It's a Barnum and Bailey world,[4] Just as phony as it can be—
But it wouldn't be make-believe If you believed in me!"

STELLA What—contemptible—lies!

STANLEY Sure, I can see how you would be upset by this. She pulled the
60 wool over your eyes as much as Mitch's!

STELLA It's pure invention! There's not a word of truth in it and if I were a
man and this creature had dared to invent such things in my presence—

BLANCHE [singing]

"Without your love,
It's a honky-tonk parade!
65 Without your love,
It's a melody played In a penny arcade . . ."

STANLEY Honey, I told you I thoroughly checked on these stories! Now wait
till I finished. The trouble with Dame Blanche was that she couldn't put on
her act any more in Laurel! They got wised up after two or three dates with
70 her and then they quit, and she goes on to another, the same old line, same
old act, same old hooey! But the town was too small for this to go on forever! And as time went by she became a town character. Regarded as not
just different but downright loco—nuts.

[STELLA draws back.]

And for the last year or two she has been washed up like poison. That's why
75 she's here this summer, visiting royalty, putting on all this act—because
she's practically told by the mayor to get out of town! Yes, did you know
there was an army camp near Laurel and your sister's was one of the places
called "Out-of-Bounds"?

BLANCHE

"It's only a paper moon, Just as phony as it can be—
80 But it wouldn't be make-believe If you believed in me!"

STANLEY Well, so much for her being such a refined and particular type of
girl. Which brings us to Lie Number Two.

STELLA I don't want to hear any more!

STANLEY She's not going back to teach school! In fact I am willing to bet
85 you that she never had no idea of returning to Laurel! She didn't resign

---

4. That is, a circus performance. P. T. Barnum (1810–1891) and James A. Bailey (1847–1906)
merged their circuses in 1881.

temporarily from the high school because of her nerves! No, siree, Bob! She didn't. They kicked her out of that high school before the spring term ended—and I hate to tell you the reason that step was taken! A seventeen-year-old boy—she'd gotten mixed up with!

BLANCHE

90   "It's a Barnum and Bailey world, Just as phony as it can be—"

[*In the bathroom the water goes on loud; little breathless cries and peals of laughter are heard as if a child were frolicking in the tub.*]

STELLA   This is making me—sick!

STANLEY   The boy's dad learned about it and got in touch with the high school superintendent. Boy, oh, boy, I'd like to have been in that office when Dame Blanche was called on the carpet! I'd like to have seen her try-

95   ing to squirm out of that one! But they had her on the hook good and proper that time and she knew that the jig was all up! They told her she better move on to some fresh territory. Yep, it was practickly a town ordinance passed against her!

[*The bathroom door is opened and* BLANCHE *thrusts her head out, holding a towel about her hair.*]

BLANCHE   Stella!

100 STELLA [*faintly*]   Yes, Blanche?

BLANCHE   Give me another bath-towel to dry my hair with. I've just washed it.

STELLA   Yes, Blanche. [*She crosses in a dazed way from the kitchen to the bathroom door with a towel.*]

BLANCHE   What's the matter, honey?

STELLA   Matter? Why?

105 BLANCHE   You have such a strange expression on your face!

STELLA   Oh—[*She tries to laugh.*] I guess I'm a little tired!

BLANCHE   Why don't you bathe, too, soon as I get out?

STANLEY [*calling from the kitchen*]   How soon is that going to be?

BLANCHE   Not so terribly long! Possess your soul in patience![5]

110 STANLEY   It's not my soul, it's my kidneys I'm worried about!

[BLANCHE *slams the door.* STANLEY *laughs harshly.* STELLA *comes slowly back into the kitchen.*]

STANLEY   Well, what do you think of it?

STELLA   I don't believe all of those stories and I think your supply-man was

115   mean and rotten to tell them. It's possible that some of the things he said are partly true. There are things about my sister I don't approve of—things that caused sorrow at home. She was always—flighty!

STANLEY   Flighty!

STELLA   But when she was young, very young, she married a boy who wrote poetry. . . . He was extremely good-looking. I think Blanche didn't just love him but worshipped the ground he walked on! Adored him and thought

120   him almost too fine to be human! But then she found out—

STANLEY   What?

STELLA   This beautiful and talented young man was a degenerate. Didn't your supply-man give you that information?

STANLEY   All we discussed was recent history. That must have been a pretty

125   long time ago.

5. "In your patience possess ye your souls" (Luke 21.19).

STELLA   Yes, it was—a pretty long time ago . . .

[STANLEY *comes up and takes her by the shoulders rather gently. She gently withdraws from him. Automatically she starts sticking little pink candles in the birthday cake.*]

STANLEY   How many candles you putting in that cake?

STELLA   I'll stop at twenty-five.

STANLEY   Is company expected?

130 STELLA   We asked Mitch to come over for cake and ice-cream.

[STANLEY *looks a little uncomfortable. He lights a cigarette from the one he has just finished.*]

STANLEY   I wouldn't be expecting Mitch over tonight.

[STELLA *pauses in her occupation with candles and looks slowly around at* STANLEY.]

STELLA   *Why?*

STANLEY   Mitch is a buddy of mine. We were in the same outfit together—Two-forty-first Engineers. We work in the same plant and now on the same 135 bowling team. You think I could face him if—

STELLA   Stanley Kowalski, did you—did you repeat what that—?

STANLEY   You're goddam right I told him! I'd have that on my conscience the rest of my life if I knew all that stuff and let my best friend get caught!

STELLA   Is Mitch through with her?

140 STANLEY   Wouldn't you be if—?

STELLA   I said, *Is Mitch through with her?*

[BLANCHE's *voice is lifted again, serenely as a bell. She sings "But it wouldn't be make-believe If you believed in me."*]

STANLEY   No, I don't think he's necessarily through with her—just wised up!

STELLA   Stanley, she thought Mitch was—going to—going to marry her. I was hoping so, too.

145 STANLEY   Well, he's not going to marry her. Maybe he *was*, but he's not going to jump in a tank with a school of sharks—now! [*He rises.*] Blanche! Oh, Blanche! Can I please get in my bathroom? [*There is a pause.*]

BLANCHE   Yes, indeed, sir! Can you wait one second while I dry?

STANLEY   Having waited one hour I guess one second ought to pass in a hurry.

150 STELLA   And she hasn't got her job? Well, what will she do!

STANLEY   She's not stayin' here after Tuesday. You know that, don't you? Just to make sure I bought her ticket myself. A bus ticket?

STELLA   In the first place, Blanche wouldn't go on a bus.

STANLEY   She'll go on a bus and like it.

155 STELLA   No, she won't, no, she won't, Stanley!

STANLEY   *She'll go!* Period. P.S. She'll go *Tuesday!*

STELLA [*slowly*]   What'll—she—do? What on earth will she—*do!*

STANLEY   Her future is mapped out for her.

STELLA   What do you mean?

[BLANCHE *sings.*]

160 STANLEY   Hey, canary bird! Toots! Get *OUT* of the *BATHROOM!*

[*The bathroom door flies open and* BLANCHE *emerges with a gay peal of laughter, but as* STANLEY *crosses past her, a frightened look appears in her face, almost a look of panic. He doesn't look at her but slams the bathroom door shut as he goes in.*]

BLANCHE [*snatching up a hairbrush*] Oh, I feel so good after my long, hot bath, I feel so good and cool and—rested!

STELLA [*sadly and doubtfully from the kitchen*] Do you, Blanche?

BLANCHE [*brushing her hair vigorously*] Yes, I do, so refreshed! [*She tinkles her highball glass.*] A hot bath and a long, cold drink always give me a brand new outlook on life! [*She looks through the portieres at* STELLA, *standing between them, and slowly stops brushing.*] Something has happened!—What is it?

STELLA [*turning away quickly*] Why, nothing has happened, Blanche.

BLANCHE You're lying! Something has!

> [*She stares fearfully at* STELLA, *who pretends to be busy at the table. The distant piano goes into a hectic breakdown.*]

Scene 8

Three-quarters of an hour later.

The view through the big windows is fading gradually into a still-golden dusk. A torch of sunlight blazes on the side of a big water-tank or oil-drum across the empty lot toward the business district which is now pierced by pinpoints of lighted windows or windows reflecting the sunset.

The three people are completing a dismal birthday supper. STANLEY *looks sullen.* STELLA *is embarrassed and sad.* BLANCHE *has a tight, artificial smile on her drawn face. There is a fourth place at the table which is left vacant.*

BLANCHE [*suddenly*] Stanley, tell us a joke, tell us a funny story to make us all laugh. I don't know what's the matter, we're all so solemn. Is it because I've been stood up by my beau?

> [STELLA *laughs feebly.*]

It's the first time in my entire experience with men, and I've had a good deal of all sorts, that I've actually been stood up by anybody! Ha-ha! I don't know how to take it. . . . Tell us a funny little story, Stanley! Something to help us out.

STANLEY I didn't think you liked my stories, Blanche.

BLANCHE I like them when they're amusing but not indecent.

STANLEY I don't know any refined enough for your taste.

BLANCHE Then let me tell one.

STELLA Yes, you tell one, Blanche. You used to know lots of good stories.

> [*The music fades.*]

BLANCHE Let me see, now. . . . I must run through my repertoire! Oh, yes—I love parrot stories! Do you all like parrot stories? Well, this one's about the old maid and the parrot. This old maid, she had a parrot that cursed a blue streak and knew more vulgar expressions than Mr. Kowalski!

STANLEY Huh.

BLANCHE And the only way to hush the parrot up was to put the cover back on its cage so it would think it was night and go back to sleep. Well, one morning the old maid had just uncovered the parrot for the day—when who should she see coming up the front walk but the preacher! Well, she rushed back to the parrot and slipped the cover back on the cage and then she let in the preacher. And the parrot was perfectly still, just as quiet as a mouse, but just as she was asking the preacher how much sugar he wanted in his coffee—the parrot broke the silence with a loud—[*She whistles.*]—and said—"God *damn*, but that was a short day!"

[*She throws back her head and laughs.* STELLA *also makes an ineffectual effort to seem amused.* STANLEY *pays no attention to the story but reaches way over the table to spear his fork into the remaining chop which he eats with his fingers.*]

BLANCHE   Apparently Mr. Kowalski was not amused.

STELLA   Mr. Kowalski is too busy making a pig of himself to think of anything else!

30   STANLEY   That's right, baby.

STELLA   Your face and your fingers are disgustingly greasy. Go and wash up and then help me clear the table.

[*He hurls a plate to the floor.*]

STANLEY   That's how I'll clear the table! [*He seizes her arm.*] Don't ever talk that way to me! "Pig—Polack—disgusting—vulgar—greasy!"—them kind
35   of words have been on your tongue and your sister's too much around here! What do you two think you are? A pair of queens? Remember what Huey Long said—"Every Man is a King!"[6] And I am the king around here, so don't forget it! [*He hurls a cup and saucer to the floor.*] My place is cleared! You want me to clear your places?

[STELLA *begins to cry weakly.* STANLEY *stalks out on the porch and lights a cigarette.*]

[*The Negro entertainers around the corner are heard.*]

40   BLANCHE   What happened while I was bathing? What did he tell you, Stella?

STELLA   Nothing, nothing, nothing!

BLANCHE   I think he told you something about Mitch and me! You know why Mitch didn't come but you won't tell me! [STELLA *shakes her head helplessly.*] I'm going to call him!

45   STELLA   I wouldn't call him, Blanche.

BLANCHE   I am, I'm going to call him on the phone.

STELLA   [*miserably*]   I wish you wouldn't.

BLANCHE   I intend to be given some explanation from someone!

[*She rushes to the phone in the bedroom.* STELLA *goes out on the porch and stares reproachfully at her husband. He grunts and turns away from her.*]

STELLA   I hope you're pleased with your doings. I never had so much trouble
50   swallowing food in my life, looking at that girl's face and the empty chair! [*She cries quietly.*]

BLANCHE   [*at the phone*]   Hello. Mr. Mitchell, please. . . . Oh. . . . I would like to leave a number if I may. Magnolia 9047. And say it's important to call. . . . Yes, very important. . . . Thank you. [*She remains by the phone with a lost, frightened look.*]

[STANLEY *turns slowly back toward his wife and takes her clumsily in his arms.*]

STANLEY   Stell, it's gonna be all right after she goes and after you've had the
55   baby. It's gonna be all right again between you and me the way that it was. You remember that way that it was? Them nights we had together? God, honey, it's gonna be sweet when we can make noise in the night the way

6. The slogan used by the populist Democrat Long (1893–1935) in his successful campaigns for governor of and then senator from Louisiana.

that we used to and get the colored lights going with nobody's sister behind the curtains to hear us!

[*Their upstairs neighbors are heard in bellowing laughter at something.* STANLEY *chuckles.*]

60 Steve an' Eunice . . .

STELLA Come on back in. [*She returns to the kitchen and starts lighting the candles on the white cake.*] Blanche?

BLANCHE Yes. [*She returns from the bedroom to the table in the kitchen.*] Oh, those pretty, pretty little candles! Oh, don't burn them, Stella.

65 STELLA I certainly will.

[STANLEY *comes back in.*]

BLANCHE You ought to save them for baby's birthdays. Oh, I hope candles are going to glow in his life and I hope that his eyes are going to be like candles, like two blue candles lighted in a white cake!

STANLEY [*sitting down*] What poetry!

70 BLANCHE [*she pauses reflectively for a moment*] I shouldn't have called him.

STELLA There's lots of things could have happened.

BLANCHE There's no excuse for it, Stella. I don't have to put up with insults. I won't be taken for granted.

STANLEY Goddamn, it's hot in here with the steam from the bathroom.

75 BLANCHE I've said I was sorry three times. [*The piano fades out.*] I take hot baths for my nerves. Hydrotherapy, they call it. You healthy Polack, without a nerve in your body, of course you don't know what anxiety feels like!

STANLEY I am not a Polack. People from Poland are Poles, not Polacks. But what I am is a one-hundred-per-cent American, born and raised in the great-
80 est country on earth and proud as hell of it, so don't ever call me a Polack.

[*The phone rings.* BLANCHE *rises expectantly.*]

BLANCHE Oh, that's for me, I'm sure.

STANLEY *I'm* not sure. Keep your seat. [*He crosses leisurely to phone.*] H'lo. Aw, yeh, hello, Mac.

[*He leans against wall, staring insultingly in at* BLANCHE. *She sinks back in her chair with a frightened look.* STELLA *leans over and touches her shoulder.*]

BLANCHE Oh, keep your hands off me, Stella. What is the matter with you?
85 Why do you look at me with that pitying look?

STANLEY [*bawling*] QUIET IN THERE!—We've got a noisy woman on the place.—Go on, Mac. At Riley's? No, I don't wanta bowl at Riley's. I had a little trouble with Riley last week. I'm the team captain, ain't I? All right, then, we're not gonna bowl at Riley's, we're gonna bowl at the West Side or
90 the Gala! All right, Mac. See you!

[*He hangs up and returns to the table.* BLANCHE *fiercely controls herself, drinking quickly from her tumbler of water. He doesn't look at her but reaches in a pocket. Then he speaks slowly and with false amiability.*]

Sister Blanche, I've got a little birthday remembrance for you.

BLANCHE Oh, have you, Stanley? I wasn't expecting any, I—I don't know why Stella wants to observe my birthday! I'd much rather forget it—when you—reach twenty-seven! Well—age is a subject that you'd prefer
95 to—ignore!

STANLEY Twenty-seven?

BLANCHE [*quickly*]   What is it? Is it for *me*?

[*He is holding a little envelope toward her.*]

STANLEY   Yes, I hope you like it!

BLANCHE   Why, why—Why, it's a—

100 STANLEY   Ticket! Back to Laurel! On the Greyhound![7] Tuesday!

[*The Varsouviana music steals in softly and continues playing.* STELLA *rises abruptly and turns her back.* BLANCHE *tries to smile. Then she tries to laugh. Then she gives both up and springs from the table and runs into the next room. She clutches her throat and then runs into the bathroom. Coughing, gagging sounds are heard.*]

Well!

STELLA   You didn't need to do that.

STANLEY   Don't forget all that I took off her.

STELLA   You needn't have been so cruel to someone alone as she is.

105 STANLEY   Delicate piece she is.

STELLA   She is. She was. You didn't know Blanche as a girl. Nobody, nobody, was tender and trusting as she was. But people like you abused her, and forced her to change.

[*He crosses into the bedroom, ripping off his shirt, and changes into a brilliant silk bowling shirt. She follows him.*]

Do you think you're going bowling now?

110 STANLEY   Sure.

STELLA   You're not going bowling. [*She catches hold of his shirt.*] Why did you do this to her?

STANLEY   I done nothing to no one. Let go of my shirt. You've torn it.

STELLA   I want to know why. Tell me why.

115 STANLEY   When we first met, me and you, you thought I was common. How right you was, baby. I was common as dirt. You showed me the snapshot of the place with the columns. I pulled you down off them columns and how you loved it, having them colored lights going! And wasn't we happy together, wasn't it all okay till she showed here?

[STELLA *makes a slight movement. Her look goes suddenly inward as if some interior voice had called her name. She begins a slow, shuffling progress from the bedroom to the kitchen, leaning and resting on the back of the chair and then on the edge of a table with a blind look and listening expression. Stanley, finishing with his shirt, is unaware of her reaction.*]

120 And wasn't we happy together? Wasn't it all okay? Till she showed here. Hoity-toity, describing me as an ape. [*He suddenly notices the change in* STELLA.] Hey, what is it, Stell? [*He crosses to her.*]

STELLA [*quietly*]   Take me to the hospital.

[*He is with her now, supporting her with his arm, murmuring indistinguishably as they go outside.*]

Scene 9

A while later that evening. BLANCHE *is seated in a tense hunched position in a bedroom chair that she has recovered with diagonal green and white stripes. She has on her scarlet satin robe. On the table beside chair is a bottle of liquor and a glass. The rapid, feverish polka tune, the "Varsouviana," is heard. The music is in her mind;*

7. That is, the long-distance bus.

she is drinking to escape it and the sense of disaster closing in on her, and she seems to whisper the words of the song. An electric fan is turning back and forth across her.

MITCH *comes around the corner in work clothes: blue denim shirt and pants. He is unshaven. He climbs the steps to the door and rings.* BLANCHE *is startled.*

BLANCHE   Who is it, please?

MITCH [*hoarsely*]   Me. Mitch.

[*The polka tune stops.*]

BLANCHE   Mitch!—Just a minute.

[*She rushes about frantically, hiding the bottle in a closet, crouching at the mirror and dabbing her face with cologne and powder. She is so excited that her breath is audible as she dashes about. At last she rushes to the door in the kitchen and lets him in.*]

Mitch!—Y'know, I really shouldn't let you in after the treatment I have
5   received from you this evening! So utterly uncavalier! But hello, beautiful!

[*She offers him her lips. He ignores it and pushes past her into the flat. She looks fearfully after him as he stalks into the bedroom.*]

My, my, what a cold shoulder! And such uncouth apparel! Why, you haven't even shaved! The unforgivable insult to a lady! But I forgive you. I forgive you because it's such a relief to see you. You've stopped that polka tune that I had caught in my head. Have you ever had anything caught in your head?
10   No, of course you haven't, you dumb angel-puss, you'd never get anything awful caught in your head!

[*He stares at her while she follows him while she talks. It is obvious that he has had a few drinks on the way over.*]

MITCH   Do we have to have that fan on?

BLANCHE   No!

MITCH   I don't like fans.

15   BLANCHE   Then let's turn it off, honey. I'm not partial to them!

[*She presses the switch and the fan nods slowly off. She clears her throat uneasily as* MITCH *plumps himself down on the bed in the bedroom and lights a cigarette.*]

I don't know what there is to drink. I—haven't investigated.

MITCH   I don't want Stan's liquor.

BLANCHE   It isn't Stan's. Everything here isn't Stan's. Some things on the premises are actually mine! How is your mother? Isn't your mother well?

20   MITCH   Why?

BLANCHE   Something's the matter tonight, but never mind. I won't cross-examine the witness. I'll just—[*She touches her forehead vaguely. The polka tune starts up again.*]—pretend I don't notice anything different about you! That—music again . . .

25   MITCH   What music?

BLANCHE   The "Varsouviana"! The polka tune they were playing when Allan—Wait!

[*A distant revolver shot is heard.* BLANCHE *seems relieved.*]

There now, the shot! It always stops after that.

[*The polka music dies out again.*]

Yes, now it's stopped.

30   MITCH   Are you boxed out of your mind?

BLANCHE   I'll go and see what I can find in the way of—[*She crosses into the closet, pretending to search for the bottle.*] Oh, by the way, excuse me for not being dressed. But I'd practically given you up! Had you forgotten your invitation to supper?

35 MITCH   I wasn't going to see you anymore.

BLANCHE   Wait a minute. I can't hear what you're saying and you talk so little that when you do say something, I don't want to miss a single syllable of it. . . . What am I looking around here for? Oh, yes—liquor! We've had so much excitement around here this evening that I *am* boxed out of my

40 mind! [*She pretends suddenly to find the bottle. He draws his foot up on the bed and stares at her contemptuously.*] Here's something. Southern Comfort![8] What is that, I wonder?

MITCH   If you don't know, it must belong to Stan.

BLANCHE   Take your foot off the bed. It has a light cover on it. Of course you

45 boys don't notice things like that. I've done so much with this place since I've been here.

MITCH   I bet you have.

BLANCHE   You saw it before I came. Well, look at it now! This room is almost—dainty! I want to keep it that way. I wonder if this stuff ought to be

50 mixed with something? Ummm, it's sweet, so sweet! It's terribly, terribly sweet! Why, it's a *liqueur*, I believe! Yes, that's what it *is*, a liqueur! [MITCH *grunts*.] I'm afraid you won't like it, but try it, and maybe you will.

MITCH   I told you already I don't want none of his liquor and I mean it. You ought to lay off his liquor. He says you been lapping it up all summer like a

55 wild cat!

BLANCHE   What a fantastic statement! Fantastic of him to say it, fantastic of you to repeat it! I won't descend to the level of such cheap accusations to answer them, even!

MITCH   Huh.

60 BLANCHE   What's in your mind? I see something in your eyes!

MITCH [*getting up*]   It's dark in here.

BLANCHE   I like it dark. The dark is comforting to me.

MITCH   I don't think I ever seen you in the light. [BLANCHE *laughs breathlessly.*] That's a fact!

65 BLANCHE   Is it?

MITCH   I've never seen you in the afternoon.

BLANCHE   Whose fault is that?

MITCH   You never want to go out in the afternoon.

BLANCHE   Why, Mitch, you're at the plant in the afternoon!

70 MITCH   Not Sunday afternoon. I've asked you to go out with me sometimes on Sundays but you always make an excuse. You never want to go out till after six and then it's always some place that's not lighted much.

BLANCHE   There is some obscure meaning in this but I fail to catch it.

MITCH   What it means is I've never had a real good look at you, Blanche.

75 Let's turn the light on here.

BLANCHE [*fearfully*]   Light? Which light? What for?

MITCH   This one with the paper thing on it. [*He tears the paper lantern off the light bulb. She utters a frightened gasp.*]

---

8. A flavored whiskey liqueur.

BLANCHE   What did you do that for?

MITCH   So I can take a look at you good and plain!

80 BLANCHE   Of course you don't really mean to be insulting!

MITCH   No, just realistic.

BLANCHE   I don't want realism. I want magic! [MITCH *laughs.*] Yes, yes, magic!
I try to give that to people. I misrepresent things to them. I don't tell truth,
I tell what *ought* to be truth. And if that is sinful, then let me be damned
85   for it!—*Don't turn the light on!*

> [MITCH *crosses to the switch. He turns the light on and stares at her. She*
> *cries out and covers her face. He turns the light off again.*]

MITCH [*slowly and bitterly*]   I don't mind you being older than what I thought.
But all the rest of it—Christ! That pitch about your ideals being so old-
fashioned and all the malarkey that you've dished out all summer. Oh, I
knew you weren't sixteen anymore. But I was a fool enough to believe you
90   was straight.

BLANCHE   Who told you I wasn't—"straight"? My loving brother-in-law. And
you believed him.

MITCH   I called him a liar at first. And then I checked on the story. First I
asked our supply-man who travels through Laurel. And then I talked directly
95   over long-distance to this merchant.

BLANCHE   Who is this merchant?

MITCH   Kiefaber.

BLANCHE   The merchant Kiefaber of Laurel! I know the man. He whistled at
me. I put him in his place. So now for revenge he makes up stories about
100   me.

MITCH   Three people, Kiefaber, Stanley, and Shaw, swore to them!

BLANCHE   Rub-a-dub-dub, three men in a tub![9] And such a filthy tub!

MITCH   Didn't you stay at a hotel called The Flamingo?

BLANCHE   Flamingo? No! Tarantula was the name of it! I stayed at a hotel
105   called The Tarantula Arms!

MITCH [*stupidly*]   Tarantula?

BLANCHE   Yes, a big spider! That's where I brought my victims. [*She pours*
herself another drink.] Yes, I had many intimacies with strangers. After the
death of Allan—intimacies with strangers was all I seemed able to fill my
110   empty heart with. . . . I think it was panic, just panic, that drove me from
one to another, hunting for some protection—here and there, in the most—
unlikely places—even, at last, in a seventeen-year-old boy but—somebody
wrote the superintendent about it—"This woman is morally unfit for her
position!"

> [*She throws back her head with convulsive, sobbing laughter. Then she*
> *repeats the statement, gasps, and drinks.*]

115   True? Yes, I suppose—unfit somehow—anyway. . . . So I came here. There
was nowhere else I could go. I was played out. You know what played out
is? My youth was suddenly gone up the water-spout, and—I met you. You
said you needed somebody. Well, I needed somebody, too. I thanked God
for you, because you seemed to be gentle—a cleft in the rock of the world
120   that I could hide in! But I guess I was asking, hoping—too much! Kiefaber,
Stanley, and Shaw have tied an old tin can to the tail of the kite.

9. A reference to the nursery rhyme.

[*There is a pause.* MITCH *stares at her dumbly.*]

MITCH   You lied to me, Blanche.

BLANCHE   Don't say I lied to you.

MITCH   Lies, lies, inside and out, all lies.

125 BLANCHE   Never inside, I didn't lie in my heart . . .

[*A vendor comes around the corner. She is a blind* MEXICAN WOMAN *in a dark shawl, carrying bunches of those gaudy tin flowers that lower-class Mexicans display at funerals and other festive occasions. She is calling barely audibly. Her figure is only faintly visible outside the building.*]

MEXICAN WOMAN   Flores. Flores. Flores para los muertos.[1] Flores. Flores.

BLANCHE   What? Oh! Somebody outside . . . [*She goes to the door, opens it and stares at the* MEXICAN WOMAN.]

MEXICAN WOMAN   [*she is at the door and offers* BLANCHE *some of her flowers*] Flores? Flores para los muertos?

BLANCHE   [*frightened*]   No, no! Not now! Not now!

[*She darts back into the apartment, slamming the door.*]

130 MEXICAN WOMAN   [*she turns away and starts to move down the street*]   Flores para los muertos.

[*The polka tune fades in.*]

BLANCHE   [*as if to herself*]   Crumble and fade and—regrets—recriminations . . . "If you'd done this, it wouldn't've cost me that!"

MEXICAN WOMAN   Corones[2] para los muertos. Corones . . .

135 BLANCHE   Legacies! Huh. . . . And other things such as bloodstained pillowslips—"Her linen needs changing"—"Yes, Mother. But couldn't we get a colored girl to do it?" No, we couldn't of course. Everything gone but the—

MEXICAN WOMAN   Flores.

BLANCHE   Death—I used to sit here and she used to sit over there and death
140 was as close as you are. . . . We didn't dare even admit we had ever heard of it!

MEXICAN WOMAN   Flores para los muertos, flores—flores . . .

BLANCHE   The opposite is desire. So do you wonder? How could you possibly wonder! Not far from Belle Reve, before we had lost Belle Reve, was a
145 camp where they trained young soldiers. On Saturday nights they would go in town to get drunk—

MEXICAN WOMAN   [*softly*]   Corones . . .

BLANCHE   —and on the way back they would stagger onto my lawn and call—"Blanche! Blanche!"—the deaf old lady remaining suspected noth-
150 ing. But sometimes I slipped outside to answer their calls. . . . Later the paddy-wagon would gather them up like daisies . . . the long way home . . .

[*The* MEXICAN WOMAN *turns slowly and drifts back off with her soft mournful cries.* BLANCHE *goes to the dresser and leans forward on it. After a moment,* MITCH *rises and follows her purposefully. The polka music fades away. He places his hands on her waist and tries to turn her about.*]

BLANCHE   What do you want?

MITCH   [*fumbling to embrace her*]   What I been missing all summer.

BLANCHE   Then marry me, Mitch!

155 MITCH   I don't think I want to marry you anymore.

BLANCHE   No?

---

1. Flowers for the dead (Spanish).   2. Crowns (Spanish); wreaths of flowers.

MITCH [*dropping his hands from her waist*] You're not clean enough to bring in the house with my mother.

BLANCHE Go away, then. [*He stares at her.*] Get out of here quick before I

160 start screaming fire! [*Her throat is tightening with hysteria.*] Get out of here quick before I start screaming fire.

> [*He still remains staring. She suddenly rushes to the big window with its pale blue square of the soft summer light and cries wildly.*]

Fire! Fire! Fire!

> [*With a startled gasp,* MITCH *turns and goes out the outer door, clatters awkwardly down the steps and around the corner of the building.* BLANCHE *staggers back from the window and falls to her knees. The distant piano is slow and blue.*]

Scene 10

It is a few hours later that night.

BLANCHE *has been drinking fairly steadily since* MITCH *left. She has dragged her wardrobe trunk into the center of the bedroom. It hangs open with flowery dresses thrown across it. As the drinking and packing went on, a mood of hysterical exhilaration came into her and she has decked herself out in a somewhat soiled and crumpled white satin evening gown and a pair of scuffed silver slippers with brilliants[3] set in their heels.*

Now she is placing the rhinestone tiara on her head before the mirror of the dressing-table and murmuring excitedly as if to a group of spectral admirers.

BLANCHE How about taking a swim, a moonlight swim at the old rock quarry? If anyone's sober enough to drive a car! Ha-ha! Best way in the world to stop your head buzzing! Only you've got to be careful to dive where the deep pool is—if you hit a rock you don't come up till tomorrow. . . .

> [*Tremblingly she lifts the hand mirror for a closer inspection. She catches her breath and slams the mirror face down with such violence that the glass cracks. She moans a little and attempts to rise.*]

> [STANLEY *appears around the corner of the building. He still has on the vivid green silk bowling shirt. As he rounds the corner the honky-tonk music is heard. It continues softly throughout the scene.*]

> [*He enters the kitchen, slamming the door. As he peers in at* BLANCHE, *he gives a low whistle. He has had a few drinks on the way and has brought some quart beer bottles home with him.*]

5 BLANCHE How is my sister?

STANLEY She is doing okay.

BLANCHE And how is the baby?

STANLEY [*grinning amiably*] The baby won't come before morning so they told me to go home and get a little shut-eye.

10 BLANCHE Does that mean we are to be alone in here?

STANLEY Yep. Just me and you, Blanche. Unless you got somebody hid under the bed. What've you got on those fine feathers for?

BLANCHE Oh, that's right. You left before my wire came.

STANLEY You got a wire?

15 BLANCHE I received a telegram from an old admirer of mine.

3. Sparkling gems.

STANLEY Anything good?

BLANCHE I think so. An invitation.

STANLEY What to? A fireman's ball?

BLANCHE [*throwing back her head*] A cruise of the Caribbean on a yacht!

20 STANLEY Well, well. What do you know?

BLANCHE I have never been so surprised in my life.

STANLEY I guess not.

BLANCHE It came like a bolt from the blue!

STANLEY Who did you say it was from?

25 BLANCHE An old beau of mine.

STANLEY The one that give you the white fox-pieces?

BLANCHE Mr. Shep Huntleigh. I wore his ATO[4] pin my last year at college. I
hadn't seen him again until last Christmas. I ran in to him on Biscayne
Boulevard. Then—just now—this wire—inviting me on a cruise of the
30   Caribbean! The problem is clothes. I tore into my trunk to see what I have
that's suitable for the tropics!

STANLEY And come up with that—gorgeous—diamond—tiara?

BLANCHE This old relic? Ha-ha! It's only rhinestones.

STANLEY Gosh. I thought it was Tiffany diamonds.[5] [*He unbuttons his shirt.*]

35 BLANCHE Well, anyhow, I shall be entertained in style.

STANLEY Uh-huh. It goes to show, you never know what is coming.

BLANCHE Just when I thought my luck had begun to fail me—

STANLEY Into the picture pops this Miami millionaire.

BLANCHE This man is not from Miami. This man is from Dallas.

40 STANLEY This man is from Dallas?

BLANCHE Yes, this man is from Dallas where gold spouts out of the ground!

STANLEY Well, just so he's from somewhere! [*He starts removing his shirt.*]

BLANCHE Close the curtains before you undress any further.

STANLEY [*amiably*] This is all I'm going to undress right now. [*He rips the
45   sack off a quart beer bottle.*] Seen a bottle-opener?

[*She moves slowly toward the dresser, where she stands with her hands
knotted together.*]

I used to have a cousin who could open a beer bottle with his teeth. [*Pounding the bottle cap on the corner of table.*] That was his only accomplishment,
all he could do—he was just a human bottle-opener. And then one time, at
a wedding party, he broke his front teeth off! After that he was so ashamed
50   of himself he used t' sneak out of the house when company came . . .

[*The bottle cap pops off and a geyser of foam shoots up.* STANLEY *laughs
happily, holding up the bottle over his head.*]

Ha-ha! Rain from heaven! [*He extends the bottle toward her.*] Shall we bury
the hatchet and make it a loving-cup? Huh?

BLANCHE No, thank you.

STANLEY Well, it's a red-letter night for us both. You having an oil millionaire
55   and me having a baby.

[*He goes to the bureau in the bedroom and crouches to remove something from the bottom drawer.*]

---

4. The fraternity Alpha Tau Omega.

5. That is, diamonds from the famous jewelry store in New York.

BLANCHE [*drawing back*]   What are you doing in here?

STANLEY   Here's something I always break out on special occasions like this. The silk pyjamas I wore on my wedding night!

BLANCHE   Oh.

60 STANLEY   When the telephone rings and they say, "You've got a son!" I'll tear this off and wave it like a flag! [*He shakes out a brilliant pyjama coat.*] I guess we are both entitled to put on the dog.[6] [*He goes back to the kitchen with the coat over his arm.*]

BLANCHE   When I think of how divine it is going to be to have such a thing as privacy once more—I could weep with joy!

65 STANLEY   This millionaire from Dallas is not going to interfere with your privacy any?

BLANCHE   It won't be the sort of thing you have in mind. This man is a gentleman and he respects me. [*Improvising feverishly.*] What he wants is my companionship. Having great wealth sometimes makes people lonely! A
70 cultivated woman, a woman of intelligence and breeding, can enrich a man's life—immeasurably! I have those things to offer, and this doesn't take them away. Physical beauty is passing. A transitory possession. But beauty of the mind and richness of the spirit and tenderness of the heart—and I have all of those things—aren't taken away, but grow! Increase with
75 the years! How strange that I should be called a destitute woman! When I have all of these treasures locked in my heart. [*A choked sob comes from her.*] I think of myself as a very, very rich woman! But I have been foolish—casting my pearls before swine![7]

STANLEY   Swine, huh?

80 BLANCHE   Yes, swine! Swine! And I'm thinking not only of you but of your friend, Mr. Mitchell. He came to see me tonight. He dared to come here in his work clothes! And to repeat slander to me, vicious stories that he had gotten from you! I gave him his walking papers. . . .

STANLEY   You did, huh?

85 BLANCHE   But then he came back. He returned with a box of roses to beg my forgiveness! He implored my forgiveness. But some things are not forgivable. Deliberate cruelty is not forgivable. It is the one unforgivable thing in my opinion and it is the one thing of which I have never, never been guilty. And so I told him, I said to him, "Thank you," but it was foolish of me to
90 think that we could ever adapt ourselves to each other. Our ways of life are too different. Our attitudes and our backgrounds are incompatible. We have to be realistic about such things. So farewell, my friend! And let there be no hard feelings . . .

STANLEY   Was this before or after the telegram came from the Texas oil
95 millionaire?

BLANCHE   What telegram? No! No, after! As a matter of fact, the wire came just as—

STANLEY   As a matter of fact there wasn't no wire at all!

BLANCHE   Oh, oh!

100 STANLEY   There isn't no millionaire! And Mitch didn't come back with roses 'cause I know where he is—

BLANCHE   Oh!

6. That is, put on uncharacteristic stylishness, show off.

7. An allusion to Jesus's Sermon on the Mount (Matthew 7.6).

STANLEY   There isn't a goddam thing but imagination!

BLANCHE   Oh!

105   STANLEY   And lies and conceit and tricks!

BLANCHE   Oh!

STANLEY   And look at yourself! Take a look at yourself in that worn-out Mardi Gras[8] outfit, rented for fifty cents from some rag-picker! And with the crazy crown on! What queen do you think you are?

110   BLANCHE   Oh—God . . .

STANLEY   I've been on to you from the start! Not once did you pull any wool over this boy's eyes! You come in here and sprinkle the place with powder and spray perfume and cover the lightbulb with a paper lantern, and lo and behold the place has turned into Egypt and you are the Queen of the Nile!

115   Sitting on your throne and swilling down my liquor! I say—*Ha!—Ha!* Do you hear me? *Ha—ha—ha!* [*He walks into the bedroom.*]

BLANCHE   Don't come in here!

[*Lurid reflections appear on the walls around* BLANCHE. *The shadows are of a grotesque and menacing form. She catches her breath, crosses to the phone and jiggles the hook.* STANLEY *goes into the bathroom and closes the door.*]

Operator, operator! Give me long-distance, please. . . . I want to get in touch with Mr. Shep Huntleigh of Dallas. He's so well known he doesn't

120   require any address. Just ask anybody who—Wait!!—No, I couldn't find it right now. . . . Please understand, I—No! No, wait! . . . One moment! Someone is—Nothing! Hold on, please!

[*She sets the phone down and crosses warily into the kitchen. The night is filled with inhuman voices like cries in a jungle.*]

[*The shadows and lurid reflections move sinuously as flames along the wall spaces.*]

[*Through the back wall of the rooms, which have become transparent, can be seen the sidewalk. A prostitute has rolled[9] a drunkard. He pursues her along the walk, overtakes her and there is a struggle. A policeman's whistle breaks it up. The figures disappear.*]

[*Some moments later the* NEGRO WOMAN *appears around the corner with a sequined bag which the prostitute had dropped on the walk. She is rooting excitely through it.*]

[BLANCHE *presses her knuckles to her lips and returns slowly to the phone. She speaks in a hoarse whisper.*]

BLANCHE   Operator! Operator! Never mind long-distance. Get Western Union. There isn't time to be—Western—Western Union!

[*She waits anxiously.*]

125   Western Union? Yes! I—want to—Take down this message! "In desperate, desperate circumstances! Help me! Caught in a trap. Caught in—" Oh!

[*The bathroom door is thrown open and* STANLEY *comes out in the brilliant silk pyjamas. He grins at her as he knots the tasseled sash about his waist. She gasps and backs away from the phone. He stares at her for a*

8. Fat Tuesday (French), or Shrove Tuesday, the final day before Lent, traditionally a time of penitence and prayer for Christians, begins. In many places it is celebrated with merrymaking and parades; the festivities are particularly famous and extensive in New Orleans.

9. Robbed (by going through the pockets of someone drunk, unconscious, or asleep).

[*count of ten. Then a clicking becomes audible from the telephone, steady and rasping.*]

STANLEY You left th' phone off th' hook.

[*He crosses to it deliberately and sets it back on the hook. After he has replaced it, he stares at her again, his mouth slowly curving into a grin, as he weaves between* BLANCHE *and the outer door.*]

[*The barely audible "blue piano" begins to drum up louder. The sound of it turns into the roar of an approaching locomotive.* BLANCHE *crouches, pressing her fists to her ears until it has gone by.*]

BLANCHE [*finally straightening*] Let me—let me get by you!

STANLEY Get by me? Sure. Go ahead. [*He moves back a pace in the doorway.*]

130 BLANCHE You—you stand over there! [*She indicates a further position.*]

STANLEY [*grinning*] You got plenty of room to walk by me now.

BLANCHE Not with you there! But I've got to get out somehow!

STANLEY You think I'll interfere with you? Ha-ha!

[*The "blue piano" goes softly. She turns confusedly and makes a faint gesture. The inhuman jungle voices rise up. He takes a step toward her, biting his tongue which protrudes between his lips.*]

STANLEY [*softly*] Come to think of it—maybe you wouldn't be bad to—
135 interfere with . . .

[BLANCHE *moves backward through the door into the bedroom.*]

BLANCHE Stay back! Don't you come toward me another step or I'll—

STANLEY What?

BLANCHE Some awful thing will happen! It will!

STANLEY What are you putting on now?

[*They are now both inside the bedroom.*]

140 BLANCHE I warn you, don't, I'm in danger!

[*He takes another step. She smashes a bottle on the table and faces him, clutching the broken top.*]

STANLEY What did you do that for?

BLANCHE So I could twist the broken end in your face!

STANLEY I bet you would do that!

BLANCHE I would! I will if you—

145 STANLEY Oh! So you want some roughhouse! All right, let's have some roughhouse!

[*He springs toward her, overturning the table. She cries out and strikes at him with the bottle top but he catches her wrist.*]

Tiger—tiger! Drop the bottle-top! Drop it! We've had this date with each other from the beginning!

[*She moans. The bottle-top falls. She sinks to her knees. He picks up her inert figure and carries her to the bed. The hot trumpet and drums from the Four Deuces sound loudly.*]

Scene 11

It is some weeks later. STELLA *is packing* BLANCHE's *things. Sound of water can be heard running in the bathroom.*

*The portieres are partly open on the poker players—*STANLEY, STEVE, MITCH, *and* PABLO—*who sit around the table in the kitchen. The atmosphere of the kitchen is now the same raw, lurid one of the disastrous poker night.*

The building is framed by the sky of turquoise. STELLA *has been crying as she arranges the flowery dresses in the open trunk.*

EUNICE *comes down the steps from her flat above and enters the kitchen. There is an outburst from the poker table.*

STANLEY   Drew to an inside straight and made it, by God.

PABLO   *Maldita sea tu suerto!*

STANLEY   Put it in English, greaseball.

PABLO   I am cursing your rutting luck.

5   STANLEY   [*prodigiously elated*]   You know what luck is? Luck is believing you're lucky. Take at Salerno.[1] I believed I was lucky. I figured that 4 out of 5 would not come through but I would . . . and I did. I put that down as a rule. To hold front position in this rat race you've got to believe you are lucky.

10   MITCH   You . . . you . . . you. . . . Brag . . . brag . . . bull . . . bull.

[STELLA *goes into the bedroom and starts folding a dress.*]

STANLEY   What's the matter with him?

EUNICE   [*walking past the table*]   I always did say that men are callous things with no feelings, but this does beat anything. Making pigs of yourselves. [*She comes through the portieres into the bedroom.*]

STANLEY   What's the matter with her?

15   STELLA   How is my baby?

EUNICE   Sleeping like a little angel. Brought you some grapes. [*She puts them on a stool and lowers her voice.*] Blanche?

STELLA   Bathing.

EUNICE   How is she?

20   STELLA   She wouldn't eat anything but asked for a drink.

EUNICE   What did you tell her?

STELLA   I—just told her that—we'd made arrangements for her to rest in the country. She's got it mixed in her mind with Shep Huntleigh.

[BLANCHE *opens the bathroom door slightly.*]

BLANCHE   Stella.

25   STELLA   Yes, Blanche?

BLANCHE   If anyone calls while I'm bathing take the number and tell them I'll call right back.

STELLA   Yes.

BLANCHE   That cool yellow silk—the bouclé.[2] See if it's crushed. If it's not

30   too crushed I'll wear it and on the lapel that silver and turquoise pin in the shape of a seahorse. You will find them in the heart-shaped box I keep my accessories in. And Stella . . . Try and locate a bunch of artificial violets in that box, too, to pin with the seahorse on the lapel of the jacket.

[*She closes the door.* STELLA *turns to* EUNICE.]

STELLA   I don't know if I did the right thing.

35   EUNICE   What else could you do?

STELLA   I couldn't believe her story and go on living with Stanley.

EUNICE   Don't ever believe it. Life has got to go on. No matter what happens, you've got to keep on going.

1. A city in southern Italy on the Gulf of Salerno, an important beachhead in the Allied invasion of Italy during World War II.

2. A rough-textured fabric made of looped yarn.

[*The bathroom door opens a little.*]

BLANCHE [*looking out*] Is the coast clear?

40 STELLA Yes, Blanche. [*To* EUNICE] Tell her how well she's looking.

BLANCHE Please close the curtains before I come out.

STELLA They're closed.

STANLEY —How many for you?

PABLO —Two.

45 STEVE —Three.

[BLANCHE *appears in the amber light of the door. She has a tragic radiance in her red satin robe following the sculptural lines of her body. The "Varsouviana" rises audibly as* BLANCHE *enters the bedroom.*]

BLANCHE [*with faintly hysterical vivacity*] I have just washed my hair.

STELLA Did you?

BLANCHE I'm not sure I got the soap out.

EUNICE Such fine hair!

50 BLANCHE [*accepting the compliment*] It's a problem. Didn't I get a call?

STELLA Who from, Blanche?

BLANCHE Shep Huntleigh . . .

STELLA Why, not yet, honey!

BLANCHE How strange! I—

[*At the sound of* BLANCHE's *voice* MITCH's *arm supporting his cards has sagged and his gaze is dissolved into space.* STANLEY *slaps him on the shoulder.*]

55 STANLEY Hey, Mitch, come to!

[*The sound of this new voice shocks* BLANCHE. *She makes a shocked gesture, forming his name with her lips.* STELLA *nods and looks quickly away.* BLANCHE *stands quite still for some moments—the silver-backed mirror in her hand and a look of sorrowful perplexity as though all human experience shows on her face.* BLANCHE *finally speaks but with sudden hysteria.*]

BLANCHE What's going on here?

[*She turns from* STELLA *to* EUNICE *and back to* STELLA. *Her rising voice penetrates the concentration of the game.* MITCH *ducks his head lower but* STANLEY *shoves back his chair as if about to rise.* STEVE *places a restraining hand on his arm.*]

BLANCHE [*continuing*] What's happened here? I want an explanation of what's happened here.

STELLA [*agonizingly*] Hush! Hush!

60 EUNICE Hush! Hush! Honey.

STELLA Please, Blanche.

BLANCHE Why are you looking at me like that? Is something wrong with me?

EUNICE You look wonderful, Blanche. Don't she look wonderful?

STELLA Yes.

65 EUNICE I understand you are going on a trip.

STELLA Yes, Blanche *is*. She's going on a vacation.

EUNICE I'm green with envy.

BLANCHE Help me, help me get dressed!

STELLA [*handing her dress*] Is this what you—

70 BLANCHE Yes, it will do! I'm anxious to get out of here—this place is a trap!

EUNICE What a pretty blue jacket.

STELLA It's lilac colored.

BLANCHE   You're both mistaken. It's Della Robbia blue.[3] The blue of the robe in the old Madonna pictures. Are these grapes washed?

[*She fingers the bunch of grapes which* EUNICE *had brought in.*]

75 EUNICE   Huh?

BLANCHE   Washed, I said. Are they washed?

EUNICE   They're from the French Market.[4]

BLANCHE   That doesn't mean they've been washed. [*The cathedral bells chime.*] Those cathedral bells—they're the only clean thing in the Quarter.

80 Well, I'm going now. I'm ready to go.

EUNICE [*whispering*]   She's going to walk out before they get here.

STELLA   Wait, Blanche.

BLANCHE   I don't want to pass in front of those men.

EUNICE   Then wait'll the game breaks up.

85 STELLA   Sit down and . . .

[BLANCHE *turns weakly, hesitantly about. She lets them push her into a chair.*]

BLANCHE   I can smell the sea air. The rest of my time I'm going to spend on the sea. And when I die, I'm going to die on the sea. You know what I shall die of? [*She plucks a grape.*] I shall die of eating an unwashed grape one day out on the ocean. I will die—with my hand in the hand of some nice-

90 looking ship's doctor, a very young one with a small blond mustache and a big silver watch. "Poor lady," they'll say, "the quinine[5] did her no good. That unwashed grape has transported her soul to heaven." [*The cathedral chimes are heard.*] And I'll be buried at sea sewn up in a clean white sack and dropped overboard—at noon—in the blaze of summer—and into an ocean

95 as blue as [*Chimes again*] my first lover's eyes!

[*A* DOCTOR *and a* MATRON *have appeared around the corner of the building and climbed the steps to the porch. The gravity of their profession is exaggerated—the unmistakable aura of the state institution with its cynical detachment. The* DOCTOR *rings the doorbell. The murmur of the game is interrupted.*]

EUNICE [*whispering to* STELLA]   That must be them.

[STELLA *presses her fists to her lips.*]

BLANCHE [*rising slowly*]   What is it?

EUNICE [*affectedly casual*]   Excuse me while I see who's at the door.

STELLA   Yes.

[EUNICE *goes into the kitchen.*]

100 BLANCHE [*tensely*]   I wonder if it's for me.

[*A whispered colloquy takes place at the door.*]

EUNICE [*returning, brightly*]   Someone is calling for Blanche.

BLANCHE   It is for me, then! [*She looks fearfully from one to the other and then to the portieres. The "Varsouviana" faintly plays.*] Is it the gentleman I was expecting from Dallas?

105 EUNICE   I think it is, Blanche.

---

3. The distinctive blue backgrounds of the reliefs made first by the Florentine sculptor Luca della Robbia (ca. 1400–1482) and then by his descendants. The color blue is symbolic of heaven and is associated with fidelity, chastity, and modesty.

4. A city market—partly open-air, partly enclosed—in the French Quarter, on the bank of the Mississippi, since 1791.

5. A salt used to treat malaria and reduce fever.

BLANCHE   I'm not quite ready.

STELLA   Ask him to wait outside.

BLANCHE   I . . .

[EUNICE *goes back to the portieres. Drums sound very softly.*]

STELLA   Everything packed?

110 BLANCHE   My silver toilet articles are still out.

STELLA   Ah!

EUNICE [*returning*]   They're waiting in front of the house.

BLANCHE   They! Who's "they"?

EUNICE   There's a lady with him.

115 BLANCHE   I cannot imagine who this "lady" could be! How is she dressed?

EUNICE   Just—just a sort of a—plain-tailored outfit.

BLANCHE   Possibly she's— [*Her voice dies out nervously.*]

STELLA   Shall we go, Blanche?

BLANCHE   Must we go through that room?

120 STELLA   I will go with you.

BLANCHE   How do I look?

STELLA   Lovely.

EUNICE [*echoing*]   Lovely.

[BLANCHE *moves fearfully to the portieres.* EUNICE *draws them open for her.* BLANCHE *goes into the kitchen.*]

BLANCHE [*to the men*]   Please don't get up. I'm only passing through.

[*She crosses quickly to outside door.* STELLA *and* EUNICE *follow. The poker players stand awkwardly at the table—all except* MITCH, *who remains seated, looking down at the table.* BLANCHE *steps out on a small porch at the side of the door. She stops short and catches her breath.*]

125 DOCTOR   How do you do?

BLANCHE   You are not the gentleman I was expecting. [*She suddenly gasps and starts back up the steps. She stops by* STELLA, *who stands just outside the door, and speaks in a frightening whisper.*] That man isn't Shep Huntleigh.

[*The "Varsouviana" is playing distantly.*]

[STELLA *stares back at* BLANCHE. EUNICE *is holding* STELLA's *arm. There is a moment of silence—no sound but that of* STANLEY *steadily shuffling the cards.*]

[BLANCHE *catches her breath again and slips back into the flat. She enters the flat with a peculiar smile, her eyes wide and brilliant. As soon as her sister goes past her,* STELLA *closes her eyes and clenches her hands.* EUNICE *throws her arms comfortingly about her. Then she starts up to her flat.* BLANCHE *stops just inside the door.* MITCH *keeps staring down at his hands on the table, but the other men look at her curiously. At last she starts around the table toward the bedroom. As she does,* STANLEY *suddenly pushes back his chair and rises as if to block her way. The* MATRON *follows her into the flat.*]

STANLEY   Did you forget something?

BLANCHE [*shrilly*]   Yes! Yes, I forgot something!

[*She rushes past him into the bedroom. Lurid reflections appear on the walls in odd, sinuous shapes. The "Varsouviana" is filtered into a weird distortion, accompanied by the cries and noises of the jungle.* BLANCHE *seizes the back of a chair as if to defend herself.*]

130 STANLEY [*sotto voce*[6]]   Doc, you better go in.

DOCTOR [*sotto voce, motioning to the* MATRON]   Nurse, bring her out.

> [*The* MATRON *advances on one side,* STANLEY *on the other. Divested of all the softer properties of womanhood, the* MATRON *is a peculiarly sinister figure in her severe dress. Her voice is bold and toneless as a fire-bell.*]

MATRON   Hello, Blanche.

> [*The greeting is echoed and re-echoed by other mysterious voices behind the walls, as if reverberated through a canyon of rock.*]

STANLEY   She says that she forgot something.

> [*The echo sounds in threatening whispers.*]

MATRON   That's all right.

135 STANLEY   What did you forget, Blanche?

BLANCHE   I—I—

MATRON   It don't matter. We can pick it up later.

STANLEY   Sure. We can send it along with the trunk.

BLANCHE [*retreating in panic*]   I don't know you—I don't know you. I want to
140   be—left alone—please!

MATRON   Now, Blanche!

ECHOES [*rising and falling*]   Now, Blanche—now, Blanche—now, Blanche!

STANLEY   You left nothing here but spilt talcum and old empty perfume
bottles—unless it's the paper lantern you want to take with you. You want
145   the lantern?

> [*He crosses to dressing table and seizes the paper lantern, tearing it off the light bulb, and extends it toward her. She cries out as if the lantern was herself. The* MATRON *steps boldly toward her. She screams and tries to break past the* MATRON. *All the men spring to their feet.* STELLA *runs out to the porch, with* EUNICE *following to comfort her, simultaneously with the confused voices of the men in the kitchen.* STELLA *rushes into* EUNICE's *embrace on the porch.*]

STELLA   Oh, my God, Eunice help me! Don't let them do that to her, don't let
them hurt her! Oh, God, oh, please God, don't hurt her! What are they
doing to her? What are they doing? [*She tries to break from* EUNICE's *arms.*]

EUNICE   No, honey, no, no, honey. Stay here. Don't go back in there. Stay
150   with me and don't look.

STELLA   What have I done to my sister? Oh, God, what have I done to my
sister?

EUNICE   You done the right thing, the only thing you could do. She couldn't
stay here; there wasn't no other place for her to go.

> [*While* STELLA *and* EUNICE *are speaking on the porch the voices of the men in the kitchen overlap them.* MITCH *has started toward the bedroom.* STANLEY *crosses to block him.* STANLEY *pushes him aside.* MITCH *lunges and strikes at* STANLEY. STANLEY *pushes* MITCH *back. Mitch collapses at the table, sobbing.*]

> [*During the preceding scenes, the* MATRON *catches hold of* BLANCHE's *arm and prevents her flight.* BLANCHE *turns wildly and scratches at the* MATRON. *The heavy woman pinions her arms.* BLANCHE *cries out hoarsely and slips to her knees.*]

---

6. Under his breath, in an undertone (Italian).

155 MATRON   These fingernails have to be trimmed. [*The* DOCTOR *comes into the room and she looks at him.*] Jacket,[7] Doctor?

DOCTOR   Not unless necessary.

[*He takes off his hat and now he becomes personalized. The unhuman quality goes. His voice is gentle and reassuring as he crosses to* BLANCHE *and crouches in front of her. As he speaks her name, her terror subsides a little. The lurid reflections fade from the walls, the inhuman cries and noises die out and her own hoarse crying is calmed.*]

DOCTOR   Miss DuBois.

[*She turns her face to him and stares at him with desperate pleading. He smiles; then he speaks to the* MATRON.]

It won't be necessary.

160 BLANCHE [*faintly*]   Ask her to let go of me.

DOCTOR [*to the* MATRON]   Let go.

[*The* MATRON *releases her.* BLANCHE *extends her hands toward the* DOCTOR. *He draws her up gently and supports her with his arm and leads her through the portieres.*]

BLANCHE [*holding tight to his arm*]   Whoever you are—I have always depended on the kindness of strangers.

[*The poker players stand back as* BLANCHE *and the* DOCTOR *cross the kitchen to the front door. She allows him to lead her as if she were blind. As they go out on the porch,* STELLA *cries out her sister's name from where she is crouched a few steps up on the stairs.*]

STELLA   Blanche! Blanche, Blanche!

[BLANCHE *walks on without turning, followed by the* DOCTOR *and the* MATRON. *They go around the corner of the building.*]

[EUNICE *descends to* STELLA *and places the child in her arms. It is wrapped in a pale blue blanket. Stella accepts the child, sobbingly.* EUNICE *continues downstairs and enters the kitchen where the men, except for* STANLEY, *are returning silently to their places about the table.* STANLEY *has gone out on the porch and stands at the foot of the steps looking at* STELLA.]

165 STANLEY [*a bit uncertainly*]   Stella?

[*She sobs with inhuman abandon. There is something luxurious in her complete surrender to crying now that her sister is gone.*]

STANLEY [*voluptuously, soothingly*]   Now, honey. Now, love. Now, now, love. [*He kneels beside her and his fingers find the opening of her blouse.*] Now, now, love. Now, love. . . .

[*The luxurious sobbing, the sensual murmur fade away under the swelling music of the "blue piano" and the muted trumpet.*]

STEVE   This game is seven-card stud.

Curtain.

7. Straitjacket.

ARTHUR MILLER
1915–2005

IN A career that lasted sixty-one years and garnered national and international acclaim, Arthur Miller established himself as one of the American theater's most visible and publicly engaged playwrights. He was born two years before the United States' entry into World War I, and his political and artistic convictions were forged in the crucible of national crisis: the Great Depression, World War II, McCarthyism. While Miller felt the impact of these turbulent years in very personal ways—like EUGENE O'NEILL and TENNESSEE WILLIAMS, he is a deeply autobiographical playwright—his plays situate the personal within social realms where the individual is defined as an ethical and moral agent. The son of an Eastern European Jewish immigrant, Miller grew up in a country struggling to come to terms with its national identity, with the social contracts that underlie this identity, and with the increasing tension between its various animating myths and ideologies. Following what the playwright called "the age-old tradition of theatre as a civic art," Miller's plays trace the fault lines running through social psyche of twentieth-century America.

In plays such as *DEATH OF A SALESMAN* (1949), Miller determined many of the directions that postwar American drama would follow. But the roots of his drama and the central experiences to which it gives form lie in the century's earlier decades. Miller was born in Manhattan on October 17, 1915, to Isadore Miller, a clothing manufacturer, and his wife, Augusta Barnett Miller. The family lived in an apartment on the edge of Harlem overlooking Central Park and enjoyed an affluent life during Miller's childhood. When his father's business failed in 1928, however, they were forced to move to a small house in Brooklyn. The stock market crash in 1929 and the Depression years that followed deepened the future playwright's awareness of the narrow line separating success and failure and the discrepancy between myth and reality in the American capitalist system. Attending high school in Brooklyn, Miller played on the football team but was an average student; for two years after he graduated he held a series of jobs, including deliveryman for his father and sales clerk in an auto parts warehouse in Manhattan. Having saved enough money to attend college, Miller applied and was accepted to the University of Michigan in 1934.

In Ann Arbor, Miller wrote for the school newspaper, majored in English, and began writing drama. He studied playwriting with the English professor Kenneth Rowe and became aware of Clifford Odets, the author of *Waiting for Lefty*

(1935), and other dramatists who made the theater an instrument of social protest during the 1930s. His first two plays won the university's prestigious Avery Hopwood Award in drama in successive years, and he won the Theatre Guild Bureau of New Plays award in 1937. After graduating in June of that year, Miller went to New York to work with the Federal Theatre Project, which was established in 1935 to offer employment to promising young playwrights as part of the New Deal's Works Progress Administration. When the program was abolished by Congress in 1939, he worked in a series of jobs, sold a number of radio scripts, and published *Situation Normal* (1944), a work of military reportage, and *Focus* (1945), a novel dealing with anti-Semitism. At that time, he was living in Brooklyn Heights with his first wife, Mary Grace Slattery, and their two children.

Miller's emergence onto the New York theater scene came in November 1944, when his play *The Man Who Had All the Luck* was produced on Broadway. Although this production received some favorable notice, most reviews were negative, and it closed after only four performances. Three more years would elapse before Miller found Broadway success with *All My Sons* (1947). This play—which is about Joe Keller, a manufacturer of airplane engines, and the disclosure that he had sold defective airplane parts that led to the death of twenty-one pilots and, indirectly, his eldest son—won the New York Drama Critics' Circle Award and was made into a movie in 1948. Its critical and financial success would pale, of course, next to the acclaim that greeted Miller's next play. After a brief preview run in Philadelphia, *Death of a Salesman* opened on February 10, 1949, at Broadway's Morosco Theater in a production directed by Elia Kazan (who had also directed *All My Sons*) and starring Lee J. Cobb as the aging salesman Willy Loman. Hailed by many reviewers as one of the finest plays to emerge in the American theater, *Salesman* won the Critics' Circle Award and the inaugural Pulitzer Prize for Drama. The play ran for 742 productions on Broadway, and by early

1950 eleven foreign productions had opened in Europe, South America, and Israel.

The success of *Salesman* catapulted Miller into the ranks of America's leading writers. But the country itself, growing increasingly obsessed with what it perceived as the Communist threat to its way of life, was undergoing a different kind of transformation. In response to the heightened paranoia of the postwar Red Scare, Miller wrote a play about the 1692 witch persecutions in Salem, Massachusetts. *The Crucible* (1953) is the story of John Proctor, a Salem individualist who struggles with questions of guilt, responsibility, and moral conduct as the witch hunt develops and he is accused. Miller himself was subpoenaed to appear before the House Un-American Activities Committee in June 1956; and while he was forthright in answering questions concerning his own brief involvement with so-called subversive organizations during the war, he, like Proctor, refused to provide the names of others who attended meetings of Communist writers. As a result, he was found guilty of contempt of Congress in May 1957, a conviction that was reversed the following year by the U.S. Court of Appeals.

In the decade after *The Crucible*, Miller wrote several important plays for the theater, including *A View from the Bridge* (1955), *After the Fall* (1964), and *Incident at Vichy* (1964). *After the Fall*, Miller's most autobiographical play, drew on the playwright's often troubled marriage (1956–61) with his second wife, the film star Marilyn Monroe. He married Inge Morath, an Austrian-born photographer, in 1962 (they had two children, and they remained together until Inge's death in 2002). After a four-year break from playwriting—during which he was appointed president of PEN, an international organization that fights censorship and other political pressures on writers—Miller returned to the theater in 1968 with *The Price*, which ran on Broadway for more than a year. But the American theater was changing, and in ways that proved less hospitable to Miller's drama of the individual, society, and the ethical life. Miller wrote a number of plays after *The*

The set, designed by Jo Mielziner, for the original 1949 Broadway production of *Death of a Salesman* at the Morosco Theater in New York.

Price—including *The Creation of the World and Other Business* (1972), *The Archbishop's Ceiling* (1977), *The American Clock* (1980), *The Last Yankee* (1991; 1993), *The Ride Down Mt. Morgan* (1991), *Broken Glass* (1994), *Mr. Peters' Connections* (1998), and *Resurrection Blues* (2002)—but these later works received a mixed reception from American reviewers.

Death of a Salesman is one of the most widely known and influential plays of the twentieth-century theater, and in its narrative techniques and stagecraft, it represents an important development in Miller's career. His preceding play, *All My Sons*, which hinges on the gradual revelation of past events, follows the cause-and-effect structure of discovery and consequence that he admired in the plays of HENRIK IBSEN. In *Salesman*, in contrast, the playwright sought to capture the lived experience of time, with its fluid boundaries between past and present, inner world and outer world. He wanted a play, he later wrote, that would "cut through time like a knife through a layer cake or a road through a mountain revealing its geologic layers, and instead of one incident in one time-frame succeeding another, display past and present concurrently, with neither one ever coming to a stop." Miller's initial image of the set was of a face as tall as the proscenium arch that would open up to reveal the inside of a man's head, a conception captured in his early working title: *The Inside of His Head.* But as the play developed—and as he incorporated the theatrical contributions of Kazan and the stage designer, Jo Mielziner—Miller abandoned such an expressionistic approach for the mode of subjective realism that Mielziner had pioneered in productions of Tennessee Williams's *A Glass Menagerie* (1945) and *A STREETCAR NAMED DESIRE* (1947).

By drawing on realist stagecraft while simultaneously transcending it, subjective realism renders porous the boundaries between internal and external reality.

Death of a Salesman takes place in the house and backyard of the Loman family in midcentury Brooklyn. Surrounding this area, marked by a harsh orange glow, loom the towering shapes of city buildings. The house itself, which creates an impression of fragility, is indicated only in outline, with imaginary walls, a one-dimensional roofline, and minimal furnishings. An apron that curves into the audience provides the setting for other city scenes and for Willy Loman's memories and imaginings. When the play's action takes place in the present, characters observe the conventions of realistic time and space, entering the house only through its doors. When the scene shifts to the past, however, characters walk through the imaginary walls as if they didn't exist. In keeping with Willy's memories of a more pastoral Brooklyn when the neighborhood was covered with elms, the surrounding buildings recede and the stage is lit with a pattern of leaves during those scenes when Willy relives his past.

Even before Miller wrote *Death of a Salesman* in the spring of 1948, the figure of the salesman occupied an important place in his life and imagination. His father had worked as a salesman for Miller's grandfather's company, traveling around the country selling coats, and two of his uncles—both of whom lived with their families in Brooklyn, where Miller visited them before his own family moved to the borough—were career salesmen. The traveling salesmen whom Miller knew embodied the entrepreneurial dreams and haunting failures that marked American capitalism. "[T]hese men lived like artists," Miller declared, "like actors whose product is first of all themselves, forever imagining triumphs in a world that either ignores them or denies their presence altogether." While working for his father in the early 1930s, Miller wrote a short story, "In Memoriam," that was based on a salesman in his father's business who had committed suicide by throwing himself in front of a New York elevated train.

In the twenty-four hours during which the play takes place, Willy Loman searches for some way of reconciling the aspirations that have shaped his life with what he fears is the failure of that life. More than sixty years old, he can no longer earn his keep as a traveling salesman, his sons have not fulfilled the dreams he held for them, and the contradictions that have defined his personality are becoming increasingly apparent. Faced with a desperate present, he seeks refuge in a past that is the product more of nostalgia than of accurate recall. The "remembered" scenes with his family a quarter century earlier, in which he basks in his sons' adoration, are clearly idealized, polished and buffed like his old car. The glow of this past is the glow of an America with a limitless panorama of opportunity and promise, a place where the sky's the limit and all things are possible for a man with personal magnetism. This America has roots in the nineteenth-century frontier: specifically, the American West, where Willy's father sold flutes with his family in a covered wagon, and the territories—Alaska and Africa—where his brother Ben earned a fortune. "[T] hat's the wonder, the wonder of this country," Willy rhapsodizes, "that a man can end with diamonds here on the basis of being liked!" These myths of individualism and success are epitomized in Dave Singleman, a salesman of the previous generation who, after a successful career spent crisscrossing the country, winning customers and making friends, dies "the death of a salesman"—in green velvet slippers in the smoking car of a train—and is fondly remembered by hundreds of salesmen and buyers at his funeral.

Willy holds fiercely to this entrepreneurial dream and all it entails—competition, consumerism, status, the marketing of oneself as a commodity—as if his faith in the American dream guaranteed him a place within it. His slogans about success and popularity are repeated like mantras. But the discrepancies between myth and reality, as well as the contradictions between different facets of the myth itself, create powerful ironies. Willy buys the refrigerator that has the "biggest ads" but finds it in constant need of repairs. He boasts of his popularity on the road—"I can park my car in any street in New England, and the cops protect it like their own"—but minutes later confides to his wife that prospective customers laugh at him behind his back. Willy champions his sons Biff and Happy over their neighbor Bernard, but it is the latter who achieves economic and social success. Once a promising high school football star, Biff drifts from job to job, compulsively stealing things in a self-destructive flight from himself. And the ironically named Happy, who works as an assistant manager, womanizes as a way of bolstering his self-image. Willy has tried to imbue his sons with the secrets of success, but what they inherit from him are the pathological undersides of the ethic he advocates.

To the director and drama critic Harold Clurman, *Death of a Salesman* represents a challenge to the American dream, or at least the capitalist version of it: "[S]ince the Civil War, and particularly since 1900, the American dream has become distorted by the dream of business success." From a Marxist perspective, Willy's tragedy reflects the logic of commodification, whereby the value of something is what it can sell for. Alienated from the work of his hands and the genuineness of relationships, this salesman is worth, in the end, only the dollar amount of the insurance policy on his life. Reacting to this component of Miller's critique, one right-wing publication called *Death of a Salesman* "a time bomb expertly placed under the edifice of Americanism." But Miller's attitude toward the capitalist culture that produced Willy Loman was ambivalent. As he himself pointed out, the most decent person in the play is Charley, a successful businessman, and the dreams that he and his son hold come to pass, as far as we can see. And while Biff Loman finds himself by rejecting his father's aspirations—"He had the wrong dreams"—Charley offers an alternative perspective: "A salesman is got to dream, boy. It comes with the territory."

Willy Loman (played by Lee Cobb, center) in a "memory" scene with his boys Happy (left; played by Cameron Mitchell) and Biff (right; played by Arthur Kennedy), from the 1949 Broadway production of *Death of a Salesman*.

The last words in *Salesman* belong to Linda Loman, and her presence underscores the centrality of family to Miller's tragedy. *Death of a Salesman* was written and produced in the years immediately after World War II, and its dramatic concerns reflect pressures on the institution of the family that mounted in the postwar United States: urbanization, the emergence (and increasing isolation) of the nuclear family, and a hardening of gender roles that would continue into the 1950s. Miller registers the impact of these forces on the relationships within the Loman family, particularly those between fathers and sons. The sense of need that drives Willy—he confesses to feeling "kind of temporary about [him]self"—is linked to his having been abandoned by his father at an early age, and he turns to his brother Ben as a surrogate for that missing paternal presence. Looking to the generation ahead, he seeks to consolidate through his two sons what identity he does possess. Despite the heightened images of male accomplishment throughout the play— high school football hero, wilderness explorer, business tycoon, ladies' man— masculinity, for Miller, is a source of anxiety, and the struggles, exaggerations, and rule breaking in which Willy engages are compensations for his failure to live up to these images. Emphasizing this dynamic, feminists and other analysts have drawn attention to Linda's role within the play. Some critics view her as a source of Willy's problems, arguing that she fails to understand him, encourages him in self-deception or illusion, or interjects materialistic values of her own. Others see her as a source of strength, acting forcefully at a number of moments while trying to balance the claims of reality with her husband's need for self-esteem. In the eyes of one of the play's early reviewers, the single-mindedness of Linda's love holds the play together; more recently, a number of feminist critics have contended that her characterization is circumscribed by the roles available to her in the masculine value system that dominates Miller's play.

In a 1999 essay commemorating the play's fiftieth anniversary, Miller described what he considered to be the power of *Death of a Salesman*: "Being human—a father, mother, son—is something most of us fail at most of the time, and a little mercy is eminently in order given the societies we live in, which purport to be stable and sound as mountains when in fact they are all trembling in a fast wind blowing mindlessly around the earth." In countries as remote from postwar America as Communist China (where *Salesman* was produced to great acclaim in 1983), the play has spoken to the dreams and anxieties of the late twentieth- and early twenty-first-century world. Indeed, as national economies become part of an ever-expanding global capitalism—and developed nations deal with outsourced labor, international finance markets, and the loss of blue-collar jobs—its insistence on the dignity of the individual is as urgent as ever.   S.G.

Death of a Salesman

CHARACTERS

WILLY LOMAN	UNCLE BEN
LINDA	HOWARD WAGNER
BIFF	JENNY
HAPPY	STANLEY
BERNARD	MISS FORSYTHE
THE WOMAN	LETTA
CHARLEY	

The action takes place in Willy Loman's house and yard and in various places he visits in the New York and Boston of today.

Act 1

A melody is heard, played upon a flute. It is small and fine, telling of grass and trees and the horizon. The curtain rises.

Before us is the Salesman's house. We are aware of towering, angular shapes behind it, surrounding it on all sides. Only the blue light of the sky falls upon the house and forestage; the surrounding area shows an angry glow of orange. As more light appears, we see a solid vault of apartment houses around the small, fragile-seeming home. An air of the dream clings to the place, a dream rising out of reality. The kitchen at center seems actual enough, for there is a kitchen table with three chairs, and a refrigerator. But no other fixtures are seen. At the back of the kitchen there is a draped entrance, which leads to the living room. To the right of the kitchen, on a level raised two feet, is a bedroom furnished only with a brass bedstead and a straight chair. On a shelf over the bed a silver athletic trophy stands. A window opens onto the apartment house at the side.

Behind the kitchen, on a level raised six and a half feet, is the boys' bedroom, at present barely visible. Two beds are dimly seen, and at the back of the room a dormer window. (This bedroom is above the unseen living room.) At the left a stairway curves up to it from the kitchen.

The entire setting is wholly, or, in some places, partially transparent. The roofline of the house is one-dimensional; under and over it we see the apartment buildings. Before the house lies an apron,[1] curving beyond the forestage into the orchestra. This forward area serves as the backyard as well as the locale of all WILLY's imaginings and of his city scenes. Whenever the action is in the present the actors observe the imaginary wall-lines, entering the house only through its door at the left. But in the scenes of the past these boundaries are broken, and characters enter or leave a room by stepping "through" a wall onto the forestage.

From the right, WILLY LOMAN, the Salesman, enters, carrying two large sample cases. The flute plays on. He hears but is not aware of it. He is past sixty years of age, dressed quietly. Even as he crosses the stage to the doorway of the house, his

---

1. The foremost part of the stage, in front of the proscenium arch.

*exhaustion is apparent. He unlocks the door, comes into the kitchen, and thank-
fully lets his burden down, feeling the soreness of his palms. A word-sigh escapes his
lips—it might be "Oh, boy, oh, boy." He closes the door, then carries his cases out
into the living room, through the draped kitchen doorway.*

LINDA, *his wife, has stirred in her bed at the right. She gets out and puts on a
robe, listening. Most often jovial, she has developed an iron repression of her
exceptions to Willy's behavior—she more than loves him, she admires him, as
though his mercurial nature, his temper, his massive dreams and little cruelties,
served her only as sharp reminders of the turbulent longings within him, longings
which she shares but lacks the temperament to utter and follow to their end.*

LINDA [*hearing* WILLY *outside the bedroom, calls with some trepidation*]   Willy!

WILLY   It's all right. I came back.

LINDA   Why? What happened? [*Slight pause*] Did something happen, Willy?

WILLY   No, nothing happened.

5 LINDA   You didn't smash the car, did you?

WILLY [*with casual irritation*]   I said nothing happened. Didn't you hear me?

LINDA   Don't you feel well?

WILLY   I'm tired to the death. [*The flute has faded away. He sits on the bed
beside her, a little numb.*] I couldn't make it. I just couldn't make it, Linda.

10 LINDA [*very carefully, delicately*]   Where were you all day? You look terrible.

WILLY   I got as far as a little above Yonkers. I stopped for a cup of coffee.
Maybe it was the coffee.

LINDA   What?

WILLY [*after a pause*]   I suddenly couldn't drive anymore. The car kept going

15 off onto the shoulder, y'know?

LINDA [*helpfully*]   Oh. Maybe it was the steering again. I don't think Angelo
knows the Studebaker.

WILLY   No, it's me, it's me. Suddenly I realize I'm goin' sixty miles an hour
and I don't remember the last five minutes. I'm—I can't seem to—keep my

20 mind to it.

LINDA   Maybe it's your glasses. You never went for your new glasses.

WILLY   No, I see everything. I came back ten miles an hour. It took me nearly
four hours from Yonkers.

LINDA [*resigned*]   Well, you'll just have to take a rest, Willy, you can't

25 continue this way.

WILLY   I just got back from Florida.

LINDA   But you didn't rest your mind. Your mind is overactive, and the mind
is what counts, dear.

WILLY   I'll start out in the morning. Maybe I'll feel better in the morning.

30 [*She is taking off his shoes.*] These goddam arch supports are killing me.

LINDA   Take an aspirin. Should I get you an aspirin? It'll soothe you.

WILLY [*with wonder*]   I was driving along, you understand? And I was fine. I
was even observing the scenery. You can imagine, me looking at scenery, on
the road every week of my life. But it's so beautiful up there, Linda, the

35 trees are so thick, and the sun is warm. I opened the windshield and just let
the warm air bathe over me. And then all of a sudden I'm goin' off the road!
I'm tellin' ya, I absolutely forgot I was driving. If I'd've gone the other way
over the white line I might've killed somebody. So I went on again—and
five minutes later I'm dreamin' again, and I nearly—[*He presses two fingers

40 against his eyes.*] I have such thoughts, I have such strange thoughts.

LINDA   Willy, dear. Talk to them again. There's no reason why you can't work
in New York.

WILLY   They don't need me in New York. I'm the New England man. I'm vital
in New England.

45   LINDA   But you're sixty years old. They can't expect you to keep traveling
every week.

WILLY   I'll have to send a wire to Portland. I'm supposed to see Brown and
Morrison tomorrow morning at ten o'clock to show the line. Goddammit, I
could sell them! [*He starts putting on his jacket.*]

50   LINDA   [*taking the jacket from him*]   Why don't you go down to the place
tomorrow and tell Howard you've simply got to work in New York? You're
too accommodating, dear.

WILLY   If old man Wagner was alive I'd a been in charge of New York now!
That man was a prince, he was a masterful man. But that boy of his, that

55   Howard, he don't appreciate. When I went north the first time, the Wagner
Company didn't know where New England was!

LINDA   Why don't you tell those things to Howard, dear?

WILLY   [*encouraged*]   I will, I definitely will. Is there any cheese?

LINDA   I'll make you a sandwich.

60   WILLY   No, go to sleep. I'll take some milk. I'll be up right away. The boys in?

LINDA   They're sleeping. Happy took Biff on a date tonight.

WILLY   [*interested*]   That so?

LINDA   It was so nice to see them shaving together, one behind the other, in
the bathroom. And going out together. You notice? The whole house smells

65   of shaving lotion.

WILLY   Figure it out. Work a lifetime to pay off a house. You finally own it,
and there's nobody to live in it.

LINDA   Well, dear, life is a casting off. It's always that way.

WILLY   No, no, some people—some people accomplish something. Did Biff

70   say anything after I went this morning?

LINDA   You shouldn't have criticized him, Willy, especially after he just got
off the train. You mustn't lose your temper with him.

WILLY   When the hell did I lose my temper? I simply asked him if he was
making any money. Is that a criticism?

75   LINDA   But, dear, how could he make any money?

WILLY   [*worried and angered*]   There's such an undercurrent in him. He
became a moody man. Did he apologize when I left this morning?

LINDA   He was crestfallen, Willy. You know how he admires you. I think if he
finds himself, then you'll both be happier and not fight any more.

80   WILLY   How can he find himself on a farm? Is that a life? A farmhand? In the
beginning, when he was young, I thought, well, a young man, it's good for
him to tramp around, take a lot of different jobs. But it's more than ten
years now and he has yet to make thirty-five dollars[2] a week!

LINDA   He's finding himself, Willy.

85   WILLY   Not finding yourself at the age of thirty-four is a disgrace!

LINDA   Shh!

WILLY   The trouble is he's lazy, goddammit!

LINDA   Willy, please!

---

2. The equivalent of about $325 in 2008.

WILLY   Biff is a lazy bum!

90 LINDA   They're sleeping. Get something to eat. Go on down.

WILLY   Why did he come home? I would like to know what brought him home.

LINDA   I don't know. I think he's still lost, Willy. I think he's very lost.

WILLY   Biff Loman is lost. In the greatest country in the world a young man
95   with such—personal attractiveness, gets lost. And such a hard worker.
There's one thing about Biff—he's not lazy.

LINDA   Never.

WILLY [*with pity and resolve*]   I'll see him in the morning; I'll have a nice talk
with him. I'll get him a job selling. He could be big in no time. My God!
100   Remember how they used to follow him around in high school? When he
smiled at one of them their faces lit up. When he walked down the
street . . . [*He loses himself in reminiscences.*]

LINDA [*trying to bring him out of it*]   Willy, dear, I got a new kind of American-
type cheese today. It's whipped.

105 WILLY   Why do you get American when I like Swiss?

LINDA   I just thought you'd like a change—

WILLY   I don't want a change! I want Swiss cheese. Why am I always being
contradicted?

LINDA [*with a covering laugh*]   I thought it would be a surprise.

110 WILLY   Why don't you open a window in here, for God's sake?

LINDA [*with infinite patience*]   They're all open, dear.

WILLY   The way they boxed us in here. Bricks and windows, windows and
bricks.

LINDA   We should've bought the land next door.

115 WILLY   The street is lined with cars. There's not a breath of fresh air in the
neighborhood. The grass don't grow anymore, you can't raise a carrot in the
backyard. They should've had a law against apartment houses. Remember
those two beautiful elm trees out there? When I and Biff hung the swing
between them?

120 LINDA   Yeah, like being a million miles from the city.

WILLY   They should've arrested the builder for cutting those down. They
massacred the neighborhood. [*Lost*] More and more I think of those days,
Linda. This time of year it was lilac and wisteria. And then the peonies
would come out, and the daffodils. What fragrance in this room!

125 LINDA   Well, after all, people had to move somewhere.

WILLY   No, there's more people now.

LINDA   I don't think there's more people. I think—

WILLY   There's more people! That's what's ruining this country! Population is
getting out of control. The competition is maddening! Smell the stink from
130   that apartment house! And another one on the other side . . . How can they
whip cheese?

[*On* WILLY's *last line,* BIFF *and* HAPPY *raise themselves up in their beds,
listening.*]

LINDA   Go down, try it. And be quiet.

WILLY [*turning to* LINDA, *guiltily*]   You're not worried about me, are you,
sweetheart?

135 BIFF   What's the matter?

HAPPY   Listen!

LINDA   You've got too much on the ball to worry about.

WILLY   You're my foundation and my support, Linda.

LINDA   Just try to relax, dear. You make mountains out of molehills.

140 WILLY   I won't fight with him anymore. If he wants to go back to Texas, let him go.

LINDA   He'll find his way.

WILLY   Sure. Certain men just don't get started till later in life. Like Thomas Edison, I think. Or B. F. Goodrich.[3] One of them was deaf. [*He starts for*
145   *the bedroom doorway.*] I'll put my money on Biff.

LINDA   And Willy—if it's warm Sunday we'll drive in the country. And we'll open the windshield, and take lunch.

WILLY   No, the windshields don't open on the new cars.

LINDA   But you opened it today.

150 WILLY   Me? I didn't. [*He stops.*] Now isn't that peculiar! Isn't that a remarkable—[*He breaks off in amazement and fright as the flute is heard distantly.*]

LINDA   What, darling?

WILLY   That is the most remarkable thing.

LINDA   What, dear?

155 WILLY   I was thinking of the Chevvy. [*Slight pause*] Nineteen twenty-eight . . . when I had that red Chevvy—[*Breaks off.*] That funny? I coulda sworn I was driving that Chevvy today.

LINDA   Well, that's nothing. Something must've reminded you.

WILLY   Remarkable. Ts. Remember those days? The way Biff used to simo-
160   nize[4] that car? The dealer refused to believe there was eighty thousand miles on it. [*He shakes his head.*] Heh! [*To* LINDA] Close your eyes, I'll be right up. [*He walks out of the bedroom.*]

HAPPY [*to* BIFF]   Jesus, maybe he smashed up the car again!

LINDA [*calling after* WILLY]   Be careful on the stairs, dear! The cheese is on
165   the middle shelf! [*She turns, goes over to the bed, takes his jacket, and goes out of the bedroom.*]

[*Light has risen on the boys' room. Unseen,* WILLY *is heard talking to himself, "Eighty thousand miles," and a little laugh.* BIFF *gets out of bed, comes downstage a bit, and stands attentively.* BIFF *is two years older than his brother* HAPPY, *well built, but in these days bears a worn air and seems less self-assured. He has succeeded less, and his dreams are stronger and less acceptable than* HAPPY's. HAPPY *is tall, powerfully made. Sexuality is like a visible color on him, or a scent that many women have discovered. He, like his brother, is lost, but in a different way, for he has never allowed himself to turn his face toward defeat and is thus more confused and hard-skinned, although seemingly more content.*]

HAPPY [*getting out of bed*]   He's going to get his license taken away if he keeps that up. I'm getting nervous about him, y'know, Biff?

BIFF   His eyes are going.

3. An American industrialist (1851–1888); his first investment venture into rubber manufacturing failed, but in 1870 he helped form the company that soon bore only his name. The legendary American inventor Edison (1847–1931) is most famous for creating the phonograph and the first commercially viable incandescent lightbulb; his rapid rise to success and early hearing loss are well-known chapters in his life story.
4. To polish (the Simoniz brand of car wax was first sold in 1935).

HAPPY   No, I've driven with him. He sees all right. He just doesn't keep his
170   mind on it. I drove into the city with him last week. He stops at a green
   light and then it turns red and he goes. [*He laughs.*]
BIFF   Maybe he's color-blind.
HAPPY   Pop? Why he's got the finest eye for color in the business. You know
   that.
175   BIFF   [*sitting down on his bed*]   I'm going to sleep.
HAPPY   You're not still sour on Dad, are you, Biff?
BIFF   He's all right, I guess.
WILLY   [*underneath them, in the living room*]   Yes, sir, eighty thousand miles—
   eighty-two thousand!
180   BIFF   You smoking?
HAPPY   [*holding out a pack of cigarettes*]   Want one?
BIFF   [*taking a cigarette*]   I can never sleep when I smell it.
WILLY   What a simonizing job, heh!
HAPPY   [*with deep sentiment*]   Funny, Biff, y'know? Us sleeping in here again?
185   The old beds. [*He pats his bed affectionately.*] All the talk that went across
   those two beds, huh? Our whole lives.
BIFF   Yeah. Lotta dreams and plans.
HAPPY   [*with a deep and masculine laugh*]   About five hundred women would
   like to know what was said in this room.
   [*They share a soft laugh.*]
190   BIFF   Remember that big Betsy something—what the hell was her name—
   over on Bushwick Avenue?[5]
HAPPY   [*combing his hair*]   With the collie dog!
BIFF   That's the one. I got you in there, remember?
HAPPY   Yeah, that was my first time—I think. Boy, there was a pig! [*They
195   laugh, almost crudely.*] You taught me everything I know about women.
   Don't forget that.
BIFF   I bet you forgot how bashful you used to be. Especially with girls.
HAPPY   Oh, I still am, Biff.
BIFF   Oh, go on.
200   HAPPY   I just control it, that's all. I think I got less bashful and you got more
   so. What happened, Biff? Where's the old humor, the old confidence? [*He
   shakes* BIFF'*s knee.* BIFF *gets up and moves restlessly about the room.*] What's
   the matter?
BIFF   Why does Dad mock me all the time?
205   HAPPY   He's not mocking you, he—
BIFF   Everything I say there's a twist of mockery on his face. I can't get near
   him.
HAPPY   He just wants you to make good, that's all. I wanted to talk to you
   about Dad for a long time, Biff. Something's—happening to him. He—
210   talks to himself.
BIFF   I noticed that this morning. But he always mumbled.
HAPPY   But not so noticeable. It got so embarrassing I sent him to Florida.
   And you know something? Most of the time he's talking to you.
BIFF   What's he say about me?

5. A major thoroughfare in Brooklyn, New York.

215 HAPPY   I can't make it out.

BIFF   What's he say about me?

HAPPY   I think the fact that you're not settled, that you're still kind of up in the air . . .

BIFF   There's one or two other things depressing him, Happy.

220 HAPPY   What do you mean?

BIFF   Never mind. Just don't lay it all to me.

HAPPY   But I think if you just got started—I mean—is there any future for you out there?

BIFF   I tell ya, Hap, I don't know what the future is. I don't know—what I'm
225 supposed to want.

HAPPY   What do you mean?

BIFF   Well, I spent six or seven years after high school trying to work myself up. Shipping clerk, salesman, business of one kind or another. And it's a measly manner of existence. To get on that subway on the hot mornings in
230 summer. To devote your whole life to keeping stock, or making phone calls, or selling or buying. To suffer fifty weeks of the year for the sake of a two-week vacation, when all you really desire is to be outdoors, with your shirt off. And always to have to get ahead of the next fella. And still—that's how you build a future.

235 HAPPY   Well, you really enjoy it on a farm? Are you content out there?

BIFF [*with rising agitation*]   Hap, I've had twenty or thirty different kinds of jobs since I left home before the war, and it always turns out the same. I just realized it lately. In Nebraska when I herded cattle, and the Dakotas, and Arizona, and now in Texas. It's why I came home now, I guess,
240 because I realized it. This farm I work on, it's spring there now, see? And they've got about fifteen new colts. There's nothing more inspiring or—beautiful than the sight of a mare and a new colt. And it's cool there now, see? Texas is cool now, and it's spring. And whenever spring comes to where I am, I suddenly get the feeling, my God, I'm not gettin' anywhere!
245 What the hell am I doing, playing around with horses, twenty-eight dollars a week! I'm thirty-four years old, I oughta be makin' my future. That's when I come running home. And now, I get here, and I don't know what to do with myself. [*After a pause*] I've always made a point of not wasting my life, and every time I come back here I know that all I've done is to waste
250 my life.

HAPPY   You're a poet, you know that, Biff? You're a—you're an idealist!

BIFF   No, I'm mixed up very bad. Maybe I oughta get married. Maybe I oughta get stuck into something. Maybe that's my trouble. I'm like a boy. I'm not married, I'm not in business, I just—I'm like a boy. Are you content,
255 Hap? You're a success, aren't you? Are you content?

HAPPY   Hell, no!

BIFF   Why? You're making money, aren't you?

HAPPY [*moving about with energy, expressiveness*]   All I can do now is wait for the merchandise manager to die. And suppose I get to be merchandise
260 manager? He's a good friend of mine, and he just built a terrific estate on Long Island. And he lived there about two months and sold it, and now he's building another one. He can't enjoy it once it's finished. And I know that's just what I would do. I don't know what the hell I'm workin' for. Sometimes

I sit in my apartment—all alone. And I think of the rent I'm paying. And it's
265 crazy. But then, it's what I always wanted. My own apartment, a car, and
plenty of women. And still, goddammit, I'm lonely.

BIFF [with enthusiasm]   Listen, why don't you come out West with me?

HAPPY   You and I, heh?

BIFF   Sure, maybe we could buy a ranch. Raise cattle, use our muscles. Men
270 built like we are should be working out in the open.

HAPPY [avidly]   The Loman Brothers, heh?

BIFF [with vast affection]   Sure, we'd be known all over the counties!

HAPPY [enthralled]   That's what I dream about, Biff. Sometimes I want to
just rip my clothes off in the middle of the store and outbox that goddam
275 merchandise manager. I mean I can outbox, outrun, and outlift anybody in
that store, and I have to take orders from those common, petty sons-of-
bitches till I can't stand it anymore.

BIFF   I'm tellin' you, kid, if you were with me I'd be happy out there.

HAPPY [enthused]   See, Biff, everybody around me is so false that I'm con-
280 stantly lowering my ideals . . .

BIFF   Baby, together we'd stand up for one another, we'd have someone to
trust.

HAPPY   If I were around you—

BIFF   Hap, the trouble is we weren't brought up to grub for money. I don't
285 know how to do it.

HAPPY   Neither can I!

BIFF   Then let's go!

HAPPY   The only thing is—what can you make out there?

290 BIFF   But look at your friend. Builds an estate and then hasn't the peace of
mind to live in it.

HAPPY   Yeah, but when he walks into the store the waves part in front of him.
That's fifty-two thousand dollars a year coming through the revolving door,
and I got more in my pinky finger than he's got in his head.

BIFF   Yeah, but you just said—

295 HAPPY   I gotta show some of those pompous, self-important executives over
there that Hap Loman can make the grade. I want to walk into the store
the way he walks in. Then I'll go with you, Biff. We'll be together yet,
I swear. But take those two we had tonight. Now weren't they gorgeous
creatures?

300 BIFF   Yeah, yeah, most gorgeous I've had in years.

HAPPY   I get that anytime I want, Biff. Whenever I feel disgusted. The only
trouble is, it gets like bowling or something. I just keep knockin' them over
and it doesn't mean anything. You still run around a lot?

BIFF   Naa. I'd like to find a girl—steady, somebody with substance.

305 HAPPY   That's what I long for.

BIFF   Go on! You'd never come home.

HAPPY   I would! Somebody with character, with resistance! Like Mom,
y'know? You're gonna call me a bastard when I tell you this. That girl Charlotte I was with tonight is engaged to be married in five weeks. [He tries on
his new hat.]

310 BIFF   No kiddin'!

HAPPY   Sure, the guy's in line for the vice-presidency of the store. I don't
know what gets into me, maybe I just have an overdeveloped sense of

competition or something, but I went and ruined her, and furthermore I can't get rid of her. And he's the third executive I've done that to. Isn't that

315 a crummy characteristic? And to top it all, I go to their weddings! [*Indignantly, but laughing*] Like I'm not supposed to take bribes. Manufacturers offer me a hundred-dollar bill now and then to throw an order their way. You know how honest I am, but it's like this girl, see. I hate myself for it. Because I don't want the girl, and, still, I take it and—I love it!

320 BIFF   Let's go to sleep.

HAPPY   I guess we didn't settle anything, heh?

BIFF   I just got one idea that I think I'm going to try.

HAPPY   What's that?

BIFF   Remember Bill Oliver?

325 HAPPY   Sure, Oliver is very big now. You want to work for him again?

BIFF   No, but when I quit he said something to me. He put his arm on my shoulder, and he said, "Biff, if you ever need anything, come to me."

HAPPY   I remember that. That sounds good.

BIFF   I think I'll go to see him. If I could get ten thousand or even seven or

330 eight thousand dollars I could buy a beautiful ranch.

HAPPY   I bet he'd back you. 'Cause he thought highly of you, Biff. I mean, they all do. You're well liked, Biff. That's why I say to come back here, and we both have the apartment. And I'm tellin' you, Biff, any babe you want . . .

335 BIFF   No, with a ranch I could do the work I like and still be something. I just wonder though. I wonder if Oliver still thinks I stole that carton of basketballs.

HAPPY   Oh, he probably forgot that long ago. It's almost ten years. You're too sensitive. Anyway, he didn't really fire you.

340 BIFF   Well, I think he was going to. I think that's why I quit. I was never sure whether he knew or not. I know he thought the world of me, though. I was the only one he'd let lock up the place.

WILLY [*below*]   You gonna wash the engine, Biff?

HAPPY   Shh!

      [BIFF *looks at* HAPPY, *who is gazing down, listening.* WILLY *is mumbling in the parlor.*]

345 HAPPY   You hear that?

      [*They listen.* WILLY *laughs warmly.*]

BIFF [*growing angry*]   Doesn't he know Mom can hear that?

WILLY   Don't get your sweater dirty, Biff!

      [*A look of pain crosses* BIFF's *face.*]

HAPPY   Isn't that terrible? Don't leave again, will you? You'll find a job here. You gotta stick around. I don't know what to do about him, it's getting

350 embarrassing.

WILLY   What a simonizing job!

BIFF   Mom's hearing that!

WILLY   No kiddin', Biff, you got a date? Wonderful!

HAPPY   Go on to sleep. But talk to him in the morning, will you?

355 BIFF [*reluctantly getting into bed*]   With her in the house. Brother!

HAPPY [*getting into bed*]   I wish you'd have a good talk with him.

      [*The light on their room begins to fade.*]

BIFF [*to himself in bed*]   That selfish, stupid . . .

HAPPY   Sh . . . Sleep, Biff.

> [*Their light is out. Well before they have finished speaking,* WILLY's *form is dimly seen below in the darkened kitchen. He opens the refrigerator, searches in there, and takes out a bottle of milk. The apartment houses are fading out, and the entire house and surroundings become covered with leaves. Music insinuates itself as the leaves appear.*]

360 WILLY   Just wanna be careful with those girls, Biff, that's all. Don't make any promises. No promises of any kind. Because a girl, y'know, they always believe what you tell 'em, and you're very young, Biff, you're too young to be talking seriously to girls.

> [*Light rises on the kitchen.* WILLY, *talking, shuts the refrigerator door and comes downstage to the kitchen table. He pours milk into a glass. He is totally immersed in himself, smiling faintly.*]

WILLY   Too young entirely, Biff. You want to watch your schooling first. Then when you're all set, there'll be plenty of girls for a boy like you. [*He smiles*
365 *broadly at a kitchen chair.*] That so? The girls pay for you? [*He laughs.*] Boy, you must really be makin' a hit.

> [WILLY *is gradually addressing—physically—a point offstage, speaking through the wall of the kitchen, and his voice has been rising in volume to that of a normal conversation.*]

WILLY   I been wondering why you polish the car so careful. Ha! Don't leave the hubcaps, boys. Get the chamois to the hubcaps. Happy, use newspaper on the windows, it's the easiest thing. Show him how to do it, Biff! You see,
370 Happy? Pad it up, use it like a pad. That's it, that's it, good work. You're doin' all right, Hap. [*He pauses, then nods in approbation for a few seconds, then looks upward.*] Biff, first thing we gotta do when we get time is clip that big branch over the house. Afraid it's gonna fall in a storm and hit the roof. Tell you what. We get a rope and sling her around, and then we climb
375 up there with a couple of saws and take her down. Soon as you finish the car, boys, I wanna see ya. I got a surprise for you, boys.

BIFF [*offstage*]   Whatta ya got, Dad?

WILLY   No, you finish first. Never leave a job till you're finished—remember that. [*Looking toward the "big trees"*] Biff, up in Albany I saw a beautiful
380 hammock. I think I'll buy it next trip, and we'll hang it right between those two elms. Wouldn't that be something? Just swingin' there under those branches. Boy, that would be . . .

> [YOUNG BIFF *and* YOUNG HAPPY *appear from the direction* WILLY *was addressing.* HAPPY *carries rags and a pail of water.* BIFF, *wearing a sweater with a block "S," carries a football.*]

BIFF [*pointing in the direction of the car offstage*]   How's that, Pop, professional?

385 WILLY   Terrific. Terrific job, boys. Good work, Biff.

HAPPY   Where's the surprise, Pop?

WILLY   In the back seat of the car.

HAPPY   Boy! [*He runs off.*]

BIFF   What is it, Dad? Tell me, what'd you buy?

390 WILLY [*laughing, cuffs him*]   Never mind, something I want you to have.

BIFF [*turns and starts off*]   What is it, Hap?

HAPPY [*offstage*]   It's a punching bag!

BIFF   Oh, Pop!

WILLY   It's got Gene Tunney's[6] signature on it!

[HAPPY *runs onstage with a punching bag.*]

395   BIFF   Gee, how'd you know we wanted a punching bag?

WILLY   Well, it's the finest thing for the timing.

HAPPY   [*lies down on his back and pedals with his feet*]   I'm losing weight, you notice, Pop?

WILLY   [*to* HAPPY]   Jumping rope is good too.

400   BIFF   Did you see the new football I got?

WILLY   [*examining the ball*]   Where'd you get a new ball?

BIFF   The coach told me to practice my passing.

WILLY   That so? And he gave you the ball, heh?

BIFF   Well, I borrowed it from the locker room. [*He laughs confidentially.*]

405   WILLY   [*laughing with him at the theft*]   I want you to return that.

HAPPY   I told you he wouldn't like it!

BIFF   [*angrily*]   Well, I'm bringing it back!

WILLY   [*stopping the incipient argument, to* HAPPY]   Sure, he's gotta practice with a regulation ball, doesn't he? [*To* BIFF] Coach'll probably congratulate

410   you on your initiative!

BIFF   Oh, he keeps congratulating my initiative all the time, Pop.

WILLY   That's because he likes you. If somebody else took that ball there'd be an uproar. So what's the report, boys, what's the report?

BIFF   Where'd you go this time, Dad? Gee, we were lonesome for you.

415   WILLY   [*pleased, puts an arm around each boy and they come down to the apron*]   Lonesome, heh?

BIFF   Missed you every minute.

WILLY   Don't say? Tell you a secret, boys. Don't breathe it to a soul. Someday I'll have my own business, and I'll never have to leave home anymore.

HAPPY   Like Uncle Charley, heh?

420   WILLY   Bigger than Uncle Charley! Because Charley is not—liked. He's liked, but he's not—well liked.

BIFF   Where'd you go this time, Dad?

WILLY   Well, I got on the road, and I went north to Providence. Met the Mayor.

425   BIFF   The Mayor of Providence!

WILLY   He was sitting in the hotel lobby.

BIFF   What'd he say?

WILLY   He said, "Morning!" And I said, "You got a fine city here, Mayor." And then he had coffee with me. And then I went to Waterbury. Waterbury is a

430   fine city. Big clock city, the famous Waterbury clock. Sold a nice bill[7] there. And then Boston—Boston is the cradle of the Revolution. A fine city. And a couple of other towns in Mass., and on to Portland and Bangor and straight home!

BIFF   Gee, I'd love to go with you sometime, Dad.

435   WILLY   Soon as summer comes.

HAPPY   Promise?

---

6. James Joseph Tunney (1897–1978), an American boxer who was undefeated world heavyweight champion, 1926–28.

7. That is, a bill of goods; a consignment of merchandise.

WILLY   You and Hap and I, and I'll show you all the towns. America is full of beautiful towns and fine, upstanding people. And they know me, boys, they know me up and down New England. The finest people. And when I bring
440   you fellas up, there'll be open sesame for all of us, 'cause one thing, boys: I have friends. I can park my car in any street in New England, and the cops protect it like their own. This summer, heh?

BIFF and HAPPY [*together*]   Yeah! You bet!

WILLY   We'll take our bathing suits.

445 HAPPY   We'll carry your bags, Pop!

WILLY   Oh, won't that be something! Me comin' into the Boston stores with you boys carryin' my bags. What a sensation!

[BIFF *is prancing around, practicing passing the ball.*]

WILLY   You nervous, Biff, about the game?

BIFF   Not if you're gonna be there.

450 WILLY   What do they say about you in school, now that they made you captain?

HAPPY   There's a crowd of girls behind him every time the classes change.

BIFF [*taking* WILLY's *hand*]   This Saturday, Pop, this Saturday—just for you, I'm going to break through for a touchdown.

455 HAPPY   You're supposed to pass.

BIFF   I'm takin' one play for Pop. You watch me, Pop, and when I take off my helmet, that means I'm breakin' out. Then you watch me crash through that line!

WILLY [*kisses* BIFF]   Oh, wait'll I tell this in Boston!

[BERNARD *enters in knickers. He is younger than* BIFF, *earnest and loyal, a worried boy.*]

460 BERNARD   Biff, where are you? You're supposed to study with me today.

WILLY   Hey, looka Bernard. What're you lookin' so anemic about, Bernard?

BERNARD   He's gotta study, Uncle Willy. He's got Regents[8] next week.

HAPPY [*tauntingly, spinning* BERNARD *around*]   Let's box, Bernard!

BERNARD   Biff! [*He gets away from* HAPPY.] Listen, Biff, I heard Mr. Birnbaum
465   say that if you don't start studyin' math he's gonna flunk you, and you won't graduate. I heard him!

WILLY   You better study with him, Biff. Go ahead now.

BERNARD   I heard him!

BIFF   Oh, Pop, you didn't see my sneakers! [*He holds up a foot for* WILLY *to look at.*]

470 WILLY   Hey, that's a beautiful job of printing!

BERNARD [*wiping his glasses*]   Just because he printed University of Virginia on his sneakers doesn't mean they've got to graduate him, Uncle Willy!

WILLY [*angrily*]   What're you talking about? With scholarships to three universities they're gonna flunk him?

475 BERNARD   But I heard Mr. Birnbaum say—

WILLY   Don't be a pest, Bernard! [*To his boys*]   What an anemic!

BERNARD   Okay, I'm waiting for you in my house, Biff.

[BERNARD *goes off. The Lomans laugh.*]

WILLY   Bernard is not well liked, is he?

8. That is, Regents examinations: tests in specific subject areas administered by the state of New York to all students in public high schools.

BIFF   He's liked, but he's not well liked.

480 HAPPY   That's right, Pop.

WILLY   That's just what I mean. Bernard can get the best marks in school, y'understand, but when he gets out in the business world, y'understand, you are going to be five times ahead of him. That's why I thank Almighty God you're both built like Adonises.[9] Because the man who makes an
485 appearance in the business world, the man who creates personal interest, is the man who gets ahead. Be liked and you will never want. You take me, for instance. I never have to wait in line to see a buyer. "Willy Loman is here!" That's all they have to know, and I go right through.

BIFF   Did you knock them dead, Pop?

490 WILLY   Knocked 'em cold in Providence, slaughtered 'em in Boston.

HAPPY   [on his back, pedaling again]   I'm losing weight, you notice, Pop?
        [LINDA enters, as of old, a ribbon in her hair, carrying a basket of washing.]

LINDA   [with youthful energy]   Hello, dear!

WILLY   Sweetheart!

LINDA   How'd the Chevvy run?

495 WILLY   Chevrolet, Linda, is the greatest car ever built. [To the boys] Since when do you let your mother carry wash up the stairs?

BIFF   Grab hold there, boy!

HAPPY   Where to, Mom?

LINDA   Hang them up on the line. And you better go down to your friends,
500 Biff. The cellar is full of boys. They don't know what to do with themselves.

BIFF   Ah, when Pop comes home they can wait!

WILLY   [laughs appreciatively]   You better go down and tell them what to do, Biff.

BIFF   I think I'll have them sweep out the furnace room.

505 WILLY   Good work, Biff.

BIFF   [goes through wall-line of kitchen to doorway at back and calls down] Fellas! Everybody sweep out the furnace room! I'll be right down!

VOICES   All right! Okay, Biff.

BIFF   George and Sam and Frank, come out back! We're hangin' up the wash! Come on, Hap, on the double! [He and HAPPY carry out the basket.]

510 LINDA   The way they obey him!

WILLY   Well, that's training, the training. I'm tellin' you, I was sellin' thousands and thousands, but I had to come home.

LINDA   Oh, the whole block'll be at that game. Did you sell anything?

WILLY   I did five hundred gross in Providence and seven hundred gross in
515 Boston.

LINDA   No! Wait a minute, I've got a pencil. [She pulls pencil and paper out of her apron pocket.] That makes your commission . . . Two hundred—my God! Two hundred and twelve dollars!

WILLY   Well, I didn't figure it yet, but . . .

520 LINDA   How much did you do?

WILLY   Well, I—I did—about a hundred and eighty gross in Providence. Well, no—it came to—roughly two hundred gross on the whole trip.

LINDA   [without hesitation]   Two hundred gross. That's . . . [She figures.]

9. In Greek mythology, Adonis was a beautiful youth.

WILLY   The trouble was that three of the stores were half closed for inventory
525   in Boston. Otherwise I woulda broke records.
LINDA   Well, it makes seventy dollars and some pennies. That's very good.
WILLY   What do we owe?
LINDA   Well, on the first there's sixteen dollars on the refrigerator—
WILLY   Why sixteen?
530   LINDA   Well, the fan belt broke, so it was a dollar eighty.
WILLY   But it's brand new.
LINDA   Well, the man said that's the way it is. Till they work themselves in,
   y'know.

[*They move through the wall-line into the kitchen.*]

WILLY   I hope we didn't get stuck on that machine.
535   LINDA   They got the biggest ads of any of them!
WILLY   I know, it's a fine machine. What else?
LINDA   Well, there's nine-sixty for the washing machine. And for the vacuum
   cleaner there's three and a half due on the fifteenth. Then the roof, you got
   twenty-one dollars remaining.
540   WILLY   It don't leak, does it?
LINDA   No, they did a wonderful job. Then you owe Frank for the carburetor.
WILLY   I'm not going to pay that man! That goddam Chevrolet, they ought to
   prohibit the manufacture of that car!
LINDA   Well, you owe him three and a half. And odds and ends, comes to
545   around a hundred and twenty dollars by the fifteenth.
WILLY   A hundred and twenty dollars! My God, if business don't pick up I
   don't know what I'm gonna do!
LINDA   Well, next week you'll do better.
WILLY   Oh, I'll knock 'em dead next week. I'll go to Hartford. I'm very well
550   liked in Hartford. You know, the trouble is, Linda, people don't seem to
   take to me.

[*They move onto the forestage.*]

LINDA   Oh, don't be foolish.
WILLY   I know it when I walk in. They seem to laugh at me.
LINDA   Why? Why would they laugh at you? Don't talk that way, Willy.

[WILLY *moves to the edge of the stage.* LINDA *goes into the kitchen and
   starts to darn stockings.*]

555   WILLY   I don't know the reason for it, but they just pass me by. I'm not noticed.
LINDA   But you're doing wonderful, dear. You're making seventy to a hundred
   dollars a week.
WILLY   But I gotta be at it ten, twelve hours a day. Other men—I don't
   know—they do it easier. I don't know why—I can't stop myself—I talk too
560   much. A man oughta come in with a few words. One thing about Charley.
   He's a man of few words, and they respect him.
LINDA   You don't talk too much, you're just lively.
WILLY   [*smiling*]   Well, I figure, what the hell, life is short, a couple of jokes.
   [*To himself*] I joke too much! [*The smile goes.*]
565   LINDA   Why? You're—
WILLY   I'm fat. I'm very—foolish to look at, Linda. I didn't tell you, but
   Christmastime I happened to be calling on F. H. Stewart's, and a salesman
   I know, as I was going in to see the buyer I heard him say something

about—walrus. And I—I cracked him right across the face. I won't take
570　that. I simply will not take that. But they do laugh at me. I know that.

LINDA　Darling . . .

WILLY　I gotta overcome it. I know I gotta overcome it. I'm not dressing to
advantage, maybe.

LINDA　Willy, darling, you're the handsomest man in the world—

575　WILLY　Oh, no, Linda.

LINDA　To me you are. [*Slight pause*] The handsomest.

> [*From the darkness is heard the laughter of a woman.* WILLY *doesn't turn
> to it, but it continues through* LINDA's *lines.*]

LINDA　And the boys, Willy. Few men are idolized by their children the way
you are.

> [*Music is heard as behind a scrim, to the left of the house,* THE WOMAN,
> *dimly seen, is dressing.*]

WILLY [*with great feeling*]　You're the best there is, Linda, you're a pal, you
580　know that? On the road—on the road I want to grab you sometimes and
just kiss the life outa you.

> [*The laughter is loud now, and he moves into a brightening area at the
> left, where* THE WOMAN *has come from behind the scrim and is standing,
> putting on her hat, looking into a "mirror" and laughing.*]

WILLY　'Cause I get so lonely—especially when business is bad and there's
nobody to talk to. I get the feeling that I'll never sell anything again, that I
won't make a living for you, or a business, a business for the boys. [*He talks
through* THE WOMAN's *subsiding laughter;* THE WOMAN *primps at the "mir-*
585　*ror."*] There's so much I want to make for—

THE WOMAN　Me? You didn't make me, Willy. I picked you.

WILLY [*pleased*]　You picked me?

THE WOMAN [*who is quite proper-looking,* WILLY's *age*]　I did. I've been sitting
at that desk watching all the salesmen go by, day in, day out. But you've got
590　such a sense of humor, and we do have such a good time together, don't
we?

WILLY　Sure, sure. [*He takes her in his arms.*] Why do you have to go now?

THE WOMAN　It's two o'clock . . .

WILLY　No, come on in! [*He pulls her.*]

595　THE WOMAN　. . . my sisters'll be scandalized. When'll you be back?

WILLY　Oh, two weeks about. Will you come up again?

THE WOMAN　Sure thing. You do make me laugh. It's good for me. [*She
squeezes his arm, kisses him.*] And I think you're a wonderful man.

WILLY　You picked me, heh?

600　THE WOMAN　Sure. Because you're so sweet. And such a kidder.

WILLY　Well, I'll see you next time I'm in Boston.

THE WOMAN　I'll put you right through to the buyers.

WILLY [*slapping her bottom*]　Right. Well, bottoms up!

THE WOMAN [*slaps him gently and laughs*]　You just kill me, Willy. [*He sud-*
605　*denly grabs her and kisses her roughly.*] You kill me. And thanks for the
stockings. I love a lot of stockings. Well, good night.

WILLY　Good night. And keep your pores open!

THE WOMAN　Oh, Willy!

> [THE WOMAN *bursts out laughing, and* LINDA's *laughter blends in.* THE
> WOMAN *disappears into the dark. Now the area at the kitchen table*

brightens. LINDA *is sitting where she was at the kitchen table, but now is mending a pair of her silk stockings.*]

LINDA   You are, Willy. The handsomest man. You've got no reason to feel that—

610 WILLY [*coming out of* THE WOMAN's *dimming area and going over to* LINDA]   I'll make it all up to you, Linda, I'll—

LINDA   There's nothing to make up, dear. You're doing fine, better than—

WILLY [*noticing her mending*]   What's that?

LINDA   Just mending my stockings. They're so expensive—

615 WILLY [*angrily, taking them from her*]   I won't have you mending stockings in this house! Now throw them out!

[LINDA *puts the stockings in her pocket.*]

BERNARD [*entering on the run*]   Where is he? If he doesn't study!

WILLY [*moving to the forestage, with great agitation*]   You'll give him the answers!

620 BERNARD   I do, but I can't on a Regents! That's a state exam! They're liable to arrest me!

WILLY   Where is he? I'll whip him, I'll whip him!

LINDA   And he'd better give back that football, Willy, it's not nice.

WILLY   Biff! Where is he? Why is he taking everything?

625 LINDA   He's too rough with the girls, Willy. All the mothers are afraid of him!

WILLY   I'll whip him!

BERNARD   He's driving the car without a license!

[THE WOMAN's *laugh is heard.*]

WILLY   Shut up!

LINDA   All the mothers—

630 WILLY   Shut up!

BERNARD [*backing quietly away and out*]   Mr. Birnbaum says he's stuck up.

WILLY   Get outa here!

BERNARD   If he doesn't buckle down he'll flunk math! [*He goes off.*]

LINDA   He's right, Willy, you've gotta—

635 WILLY [*exploding at her*]   There's nothing the matter with him! You want him to be a worm like Bernard? He's got spirit, personality . . .

[*As he speaks,* LINDA, *almost in tears, exits into the living room.* WILLY *is alone in the kitchen, wilting and staring. The leaves are gone. It is night again, and the apartment houses look down from behind.*]

WILLY   Loaded with it. Loaded! What is he stealing? He's giving it back, isn't he? Why is he stealing? What did I tell him? I never in my life told him anything but decent things.

[HAPPY *in pajamas has come down the stairs;* WILLY *suddenly becomes aware of* HAPPY's *presence.*]

640 HAPPY   Let's go now, come on.

WILLY [*sitting down at the kitchen table*]   Huh! Why did she have to wax the floors herself? Everytime she waxes the floors she keels over. She knows that!

HAPPY   Shh! Take it easy. What brought you back tonight?

645 WILLY   I got an awful scare. Nearly hit a kid in Yonkers. God! Why didn't I go to Alaska with my brother Ben that time! Ben! That man was a genius, that man was success incarnate! What a mistake! He begged me to go.

HAPPY   Well, there's no use in—

WILLY   You guys! There was a man started with the clothes on his back and
650   ended up with diamond mines!

HAPPY   Boy, someday I'd like to know how he did it.

WILLY   What's the mystery? The man knew what he wanted and went out and
got it! Walked into a jungle, and comes out, the age of twenty-one, and he's
rich! The world is an oyster, but you don't crack it open on a mattress!

655 HAPPY   Pop, I told you I'm gonna retire you for life.

WILLY   You'll retire me for life on seventy goddam dollars a week? And your
women and your car and your apartment, and you'll retire me for life!
Christ's sake, I couldn't get past Yonkers today! Where are you guys, where
are you? The woods are burning! I can't drive a car!

[CHARLEY *has appeared in the doorway. He is a large man, slow of speech,
laconic, immovable. In all he says, despite what he says, there is pity, and,
now, trepidation. He has a robe over pajamas, slippers on his feet. He
enters the kitchen.*]

660 CHARLEY   Everything all right?

HAPPY   Yeah, Charley, everything's . . .

WILLY   What's the matter?

CHARLEY   I heard some noise. I thought something happened. Can't we do
something about the walls? You sneeze in here, and in my house hats blow
665   off.

HAPPY   Let's go to bed, Dad. Come on.

[CHARLEY *signals to* HAPPY *to go.*]

WILLY   You go ahead, I'm not tired at the moment.

HAPPY [*to* WILLY]   Take it easy, huh? [*He exits.*]

WILLY   What're you doin' up?

670 CHARLEY [*sitting down at the kitchen table opposite* WILLY]   Couldn't sleep
good. I had a heartburn.

WILLY   Well, you don't know how to eat.

CHARLEY   I eat with my mouth.

WILLY   No, you're ignorant. You gotta know about vitamins and things like
675   that.

CHARLEY   Come on, let's shoot. Tire you out a little.

WILLY [*hesitantly*]   All right. You got cards?

CHARLEY [*taking a deck from his pocket*]   Yeah, I got them. Someplace. What
is it with those vitamins?

680 WILLY [*dealing*]   They build up your bones. Chemistry.

CHARLEY   Yeah, but there's no bones in a heartburn.

WILLY   What are you talkin' about? Do you know the first thing about it?

CHARLEY   Don't get insulted.

WILLY   Don't talk about something you don't know anything about.

[*They are playing. Pause.*]

685 CHARLEY   What're you doin' home?

WILLY   A little trouble with the car.

CHARLEY   Oh. [*Pause*] I'd like to take a trip to California.

WILLY   Don't say.

CHARLEY   You want a job?

690 WILLY   I got a job, I told you that. [*After a slight pause*] What the hell are you
offering me a job for?

CHARLEY   Don't get insulted.

WILLY   Don't insult me.

CHARLEY   I don't see no sense in it. You don't have to go on this way.

695 WILLY   I got a good job. [*Slight pause*] What do you keep comin' in here for?

CHARLEY   You want me to go?

WILLY [*after a pause, withering*]   I can't understand it. He's going back to Texas again. What the hell is that?

CHARLEY   Let him go.

700 WILLY   I got nothin' to give him, Charley, I'm clean, I'm clean.

CHARLEY   He won't starve. None a them starve. Forget about him.

WILLY   Then what have I got to remember?

CHARLEY   You take it too hard. To hell with it. When a deposit bottle is broken you don't get your nickel back.

705 WILLY   That's easy enough for you to say.

CHARLEY   That ain't easy for me to say.

WILLY   Did you see the ceiling I put up in the living room?

CHARLEY   Yeah, that's a piece of work. To put up a ceiling is a mystery to me. How do you do it?

710 WILLY   What's the difference?

CHARLEY   Well, talk about it.

WILLY   You gonna put up a ceiling?

CHARLEY   How could I put up a ceiling?

WILLY   Then what the hell are you bothering me for?

715 CHARLEY   You're insulted again.

WILLY   A man who can't handle tools is not a man. You're disgusting.

CHARLEY   Don't call me disgusting. Willy.

[UNCLE BEN, *carrying a valise and an umbrella, enters the forestage from around the right corner of the house. He is a stolid man, in his sixties, with a mustache and an authoritative air. He is utterly certain of his destiny, and there is an aura of far places about him. He enters exactly as* WILLY *speaks.*]

WILLY   I'm getting awfully tired, Ben.

[BEN's *music is heard.* BEN *looks around at everything.*]

CHARLEY   Good, keep playing; you'll sleep better. Did you call me Ben?

[BEN *looks at his watch.*]

720 WILLY   That's funny. For a second there you reminded me of my brother Ben.

BEN   I only have a few minutes. [*He strolls, inspecting the place.* WILLY *and* CHARLEY *continue playing.*]

CHARLEY   You never heard from him again, heh? Since that time?

WILLY   Didn't Linda tell you? Couple of weeks ago we got a letter from his wife in Africa. He died.

725 CHARLEY   That so.

BEN [*chuckling*]   So this is Brooklyn, eh?

CHARLEY   Maybe you're in for some of his money.

WILLY   Naa, he had seven sons. There's just one opportunity I had with that man . . .

730 BEN   I must make a train, William. There are several properties I'm looking at in Alaska.

WILLY   Sure, sure! If I'd gone with him to Alaska that time, everything would've been totally different.

CHARLEY   Go on, you'd froze to death up there.

735 WILLY What're you talking about?

BEN Opportunity is tremendous in Alaska, William. Surprised you're not up there.

WILLY Sure, tremendous.

CHARLEY Heh?

740 WILLY There was the only man I ever met who knew the answers.

CHARLEY Who?

BEN How are you all?

WILLY [*taking a pot,*[1] *smiling*] Fine, fine.

CHARLEY Pretty sharp tonight.

745 BEN Is Mother living with you?

WILLY No, she died a long time ago.

CHARLEY Who?

BEN That's too bad. Fine specimen of a lady, Mother.

WILLY [*to Charley*] Heh?

750 BEN I'd hoped to see the old girl.

CHARLEY Who died?

BEN Heard anything from Father, have you?

WILLY [*unnerved*] What do you mean, who died?

CHARLEY [*taking a pot*] What're you talkin' about?

755 BEN [*looking at his watch*] William, it's half-past eight!

WILLY [*as though to dispel his confusion he angrily stops* CHARLEY'S *hand*] That's my build![2]

CHARLEY I put the ace—

WILLY If you don't know how to play the game I'm not gonna throw my money away on you!

760 CHARLEY [*rising*] It was my ace, for God's sake!

WILLY I'm through, I'm through!

BEN When did Mother die?

WILLY Long ago. Since the beginning you never knew how to play cards.

CHARLEY [*picks up the cards and goes to the door*] All right! Next time I'll
765 bring a deck with five aces.

WILLY I don't play that kind of game!

CHARLEY [*turning to him*] You ought to be ashamed of yourself!

WILLY Yeah?

CHARLEY Yeah! [*He goes out.*]

770 WILLY [*slamming the door after him*] Ignoramus!

BEN [*as* WILLY *comes toward him through the wall-line of the kitchen*] So you're William.

WILLY [*shaking* BEN'S *hand*] Ben! I've been waiting for you so long! What's the answer? How did you do it?

775 BEN Oh, there's a story in that.

[LINDA *enters the forestage, as of old, carrying the wash basket.*]

LINDA Is this Ben?

BEN [*gallantly*] How do you do, my dear.

LINDA Where've you been all these years? Willy's always wondered why you—

---

1. The bets at stake in a hand of casino, the card game they are playing.

2. Casino players must take in builds (cards that combine to form a declared total) to win.

780 WILLY [*pulling* BEN *away from her impatiently*]   Where is Dad? Didn't you
follow him? How did you get started?

BEN   Well, I don't know how much you remember.

WILLY   Well, I was just a baby, of course, only three or four years old—

BEN   Three years and eleven months.

785 WILLY   What a memory, Ben!

BEN   I have many enterprises, William, and I have never kept books.

WILLY   I remember I was sitting under the wagon in—was it Nebraska?

BEN   It was South Dakota, and I gave you a bunch of wild flowers.

WILLY   I remember you walking away down some open road.

790 BEN [*laughing*]   I was going to find Father in Alaska.

WILLY   Where is he?

BEN   At that age I had a very faulty view of geography, William. I discovered
after a few days that I was heading due south, so instead of Alaska, I ended
up in Africa.

795 LINDA   Africa!

WILLY   The Gold Coast!³

BEN   Principally diamond mines.

LINDA   Diamond mines!

BEN   Yes, my dear. But I've only a few minutes—

800 WILLY   No! Boys! Boys! [YOUNG BIFF *and* HAPPY *appear*.] Listen to this. This is
your Uncle Ben, a great man! Tell my boys, Ben!

BEN   Why, boys, when I was seventeen I walked into the jungle, and when I
was twenty-one I walked out. [*He laughs.*] And by God I was rich.

WILLY [*to the boys*]   You see what I been talking about? The greatest things
805 can happen!

BEN [*glancing at his watch*]   I have an appointment in Ketchikan Tuesday
week.⁴

WILLY   No, Ben! Please tell about Dad. I want my boys to hear. I want them
to know the kind of stock they spring from. All I remember is a man with a
810 big beard, and I was in Mamma's lap, sitting around a fire, and some kind
of high music.

BEN   His flute. He played the flute.

WILLY   Sure, the flute, that's right!

[*New music is heard, a high, rollicking tune.*]

BEN   Father was a very great and a very wild-hearted man. We would start in
815 Boston, and he'd toss the whole family into the wagon, and then he'd drive
the team right across the country; through Ohio, and Indiana, Michigan,
Illinois, and all the Western states. And we'd stop in the towns and sell the
flutes that he'd made on the way. Great inventor, Father. With one gadget
he made more in a week than a man like you could make in a lifetime.

820 WILLY   That's just the way I'm bringing them up, Ben—rugged, well liked,
all-around.

BEN   Yeah? [*To* BIFF] Hit that, boy—hard as you can. [*He pounds his
stomach.*]

BIFF   Oh, no, sir!

---

3. The region of West Africa that is now
Ghana (still a British colony in 1949); industrial diamonds are one of its major exports.

4. That is, in Ketchikan, Alaska, one week
from Tuesday.

BEN [*taking boxing stance*]   Come on, get to me! [*He laughs.*]

825 WILLY   Go to it, Biff! Go ahead, show him!

BIFF   Okay! [*He cocks his fists and starts in.*]

LINDA [*to* WILLY]   Why must he fight, dear?

BEN [*sparring with* BIFF]   Good boy! Good boy!

WILLY   How's that, Ben, heh?

830 HAPPY   Give him the left, Biff!

LINDA   Why are you fighting?

BEN   Good boy! [*Suddenly comes in, trips* BIFF, *and stands over him, the point of his umbrella poised over* BIFF's *eye.*]

LINDA   Look out, Biff!

BIFF   Gee!

835 BEN [*patting* BIFF's *knee*]   Never fight fair with a stranger, boy. You'll never get out of the jungle that way. [*Taking* LINDA's *hand and bowing*] It was an honor and a pleasure to meet you, Linda.

LINDA [*withdrawing her hand coldly, frightened*]   Have a nice—trip.

BEN [*to* WILLY]   And good luck with your—what do you do?

840 WILLY   Selling.

BEN   Yes. Well . . . [*He raises his hand in farewell to all.*]

WILLY   No, Ben, I don't want you to think . . . [*He takes* BEN's *arm to show him.*] It's Brooklyn, I know, but we hunt too.

BEN   Really, now.

845 WILLY   Oh, sure, there's snakes and rabbits and—that's why I moved out here. Why, Biff can fell any one of these trees in no time! Boys! Go right over to where they're building the apartment house and get some sand. We're gonna rebuild the entire front stoop right now! Watch this, Ben!

BIFF   Yes, sir! On the double, Hap!

850 HAPPY [*as he and* BIFF *run off*]   I lost weight, Pop, you notice?

[CHARLEY *enters in knickers, even before the boys are gone.*]

CHARLEY   Listen, if they steal any more from that building the watchman'll put the cops on them!

LINDA [*to* Willy]   Don't let Biff . . .

[BEN *laughs lustily.*]

WILLY   You shoulda seen the lumber they brought home last week. At least a
855   dozen six-by-tens worth all kinds a money.

CHARLEY   Listen, if that watchman—

WILLY   I gave them hell, understand. But I got a couple of fearless characters there.

CHARLEY   Willy, the jails are full of fearless characters.

860 BEN [*clapping* WILLY *on the back, with a laugh at* CHARLEY]   And the stock exchange, friend!

WILLY [*joining in Ben's laughter*]   Where are the rest of your pants?

CHARLEY   My wife bought them.

WILLY   Now all you need is a golf club and you can go upstairs and go to
865   sleep. [*To* BEN] Great athlete! Between him and his son Bernard they can't hammer a nail!

BERNARD [*rushing in*]   The watchman's chasing Biff!

WILLY [*angrily*]   Shut up! He's not stealing anything!

LINDA [*alarmed, hurrying off left*]   Where is he? Biff, dear! [*She exits.*]

870 WILLY [*moving toward the left, away from* BEN] There's nothing wrong. What's the matter with you?

BEN Nervy boy. Good!

WILLY [*laughing*] Oh, nerves of iron, that Biff!

CHARLEY Don't know what it is. My New England man comes back and he's
875 bleedin', they murdered him up there.

WILLY It's contacts, Charley, I got important contacts!

CHARLEY [*sarcastically*] Glad to hear it, Willy. Come in later, we'll shoot a little casino. I'll take some of your Portland money. [*He laughs at Willy and exits.*]

WILLY [*turning to* BEN] Business is bad, it's murderous. But not for me, of
880 course.

BEN I'll stop by on my way back to Africa.

WILLY [*longingly*] Can't you stay a few days? You're just what I need, Ben, because I—I have a fine position here, but I—well, Dad left when I was such a baby and I never had a chance to talk to him and I still feel—kind of
885 temporary about myself.

BEN I'll be late for my train.

[*They are at opposite ends of the stage.*]

WILLY Ben, my boys—can't we talk? They'd go into the jaws of hell for me, see, but I—

BEN William, you're being first-rate with your boys. Outstanding, manly
890 chaps!

WILLY [*hanging on to his words*] Oh, Ben, that's good to hear! Because sometimes I'm afraid that I'm not teaching them the right kind of—Ben, how should I teach them?

BEN [*giving great weight to each word, and with a certain vicious audacity*] William, when I walked into the jungle, I was seventeen. When I walked
895 out I was twenty-one. And, by God, I was rich! [*He goes off into the darkness around the right corner of the house.*]

WILLY . . . was rich! That's just the spirit I want to imbue them with! To walk into a jungle! I was right! I was right! I was right!

[BEN *is gone, but* WILLY *is still speaking to him as* LINDA, *in nightgown and robe, enters the kitchen, glances around for* WILLY, *then goes to the door of the house, looks out and sees him. Comes down to his left. He looks at her.*]

LINDA Willy, dear? Willy?

WILLY I was right!

900 LINDA Did you have some cheese? [*He can't answer.*] It's very late, darling. Come to bed, heh?

WILLY [*looking straight up*] Gotta break your neck to see a star in this yard.

LINDA You coming in?

WILLY Whatever happened to that diamond watch fob? Remember? When
905 Ben came from Africa that time? Didn't he give me a watch fob with a diamond in it?

LINDA You pawned it, dear. Twelve, thirteen years ago. For Biff's radio correspondence course.

WILLY Gee, that was a beautiful thing. I'll take a walk.

910 LINDA But you're in your slippers.

WILLY [*starting to go around the house at the left*] I was right! I was! [*Half to* LINDA, *as he goes, shaking his head*] What a man! There was a man worth talking to. I was right!

LINDA [*calling after* WILLY] But in your slippers, Willy!

[WILLY *is almost gone when* BIFF, *in his pajamas, comes down the stairs and enters the kitchen.*]

915 BIFF What is he doing out there?

LINDA Sh!

BIFF God Almighty, Mom, how long has he been doing this?

LINDA Don't, he'll hear you.

BIFF What the hell is the matter with him?

920 LINDA It'll pass by morning.

BIFF Shouldn't we do anything?

LINDA Oh, my dear, you should do a lot of things, but there's nothing to do, so go to sleep.

[HAPPY *comes down the stair and sits on the steps.*]

HAPPY I never heard him so loud, Mom.

925 LINDA Well, come around more often; you'll hear him. [*She sits down at the table and mends the lining of* WILLY's *jacket.*]

BIFF Why didn't you ever write me about this, Mom?

LINDA How would I write to you? For over three months you had no address.

BIFF I was on the move. But you know I thought of you all the time. You know that, don't you, pal?

930 LINDA I know, dear, I know. But he likes to have a letter. Just to know that there's still a possibility for better things.

BIFF He's not like this all the time, is he?

LINDA It's when you come home he's always the worst.

BIFF When I come home?

935 LINDA When you write you're coming, he's all smiles, and talks about the future, and—he's just wonderful. And then the closer you seem to come, the more shaky he gets, and then, by the time you get here, he's arguing, and he seems angry at you. I think it's just that maybe he can't bring him-self to—to open up to you. Why are you so hateful to each other? Why is

940 that?

BIFF [*evasively*] I'm not hateful, Mom.

LINDA But you no sooner come in the door than you're fighting!

BIFF I don't know why. I mean to change. I'm tryin', Mom, you understand?

LINDA Are you home to stay now?

945 BIFF I don't know. I want to look around, see what's doin'.

LINDA Biff, you can't look around all your life, can you?

BIFF I just can't take hold, Mom. I can't take hold of some kind of a life.

LINDA Biff, a man is not a bird, to come and go with the springtime.

BIFF Your hair . . . [*He touches her hair.*] Your hair got so gray.

950 LINDA Oh, it's been gray since you were in high school. I just stopped dyeing it, that's all.

BIFF Dye it again, will ya? I don't want my pal looking old. [*He smiles.*]

LINDA You're such a boy! You think you can go away for a year and . . . You've got to get it into your head now that one day you'll knock on this door and

955 there'll be strange people here—

BIFF   What are you talking about? You're not even sixty, Mom.

LINDA   But what about your father?

BIFF [*lamely*]   Well, I meant him too.

HAPPY   He admires Pop.

960 LINDA   Biff, dear, if you don't have any feeling for him, then you can't have any feeling for me.

BIFF   Sure I can, Mom.

LINDA   No. You can't just come to see me, because I love him. [*With a threat, but only a threat, of tears*] He's the dearest man in the world to me, and I

965 won't have anyone making him feel unwanted and low and blue. You've got to make up your mind now, darling, there's no leeway any more. Either he's your father and you pay him that respect, or else you're not to come here. I know he's not easy to get along with—nobody knows that better than me—but . . .

970 WILLY [*from the left, with a laugh*]   Hey, hey, Biffo!

BIFF [*starting to go out after* WILLY]   What the hell is the matter with him? [HAPPY *stops him.*]

LINDA   Don't—don't go near him!

BIFF   Stop making excuses for him! He always, always wiped the floor with you. Never had an ounce of respect for you.

975 HAPPY   He's always had respect for—

BIFF   What the hell do you know about it?

HAPPY [*surlily*]   Just don't call him crazy!

BIFF   He's got no character—Charley wouldn't do this. Not in his own house—spewing out that vomit from his mind.

980 HAPPY·   Charley never had to cope with what he's got to.

BIFF   People are worse off than Willy Loman. Believe me, I've seen them!

LINDA   Then make Charley your father, Biff. You can't do that, can you? I don't say he's a great man. Willy Loman never made a lot of money. His name was never in the paper. He's not the finest character that ever lived.

985 But he's a human being, and a terrible thing is happening to him. So attention must be paid. He's not to be allowed to fall into his grave like an old dog. Attention, attention must be finally paid to such a person. You called him crazy—

BIFF   I didn't mean—

LINDA   No, a lot of people think he's lost his—balance. But you don't have to

990 be very smart to know what his trouble is. The man is exhausted.

HAPPY   Sure!

LINDA   A small man can be just as exhausted as a great man. He works for a company thirty-six years this March, opens up unheard-of territories to their trademark, and now in his old age they take his salary away.

995 HAPPY [*indignantly*]   I didn't know that, Mom.

LINDA   You never asked, my dear! Now that you get your spending money someplace else you don't trouble your mind with him.

HAPPY   But I gave you money last—

LINDA   Christmastime, fifty dollars! To fix the hot water it cost ninety-seven

1000 fifty! For five weeks he's been on straight commission, like a beginner, an unknown!

BIFF   Those ungrateful bastards!

LINDA   Are they any worse than his sons? When he brought them business,
when he was young, they were glad to see him. But now his old friends, the
1005   old buyers that loved him so and always found some order to hand him in
a pinch—they're all dead, retired. He used to be able to make six, seven
calls a day in Boston. Now he takes his valises out of the car and puts them
back and takes them out again and he's exhausted. Instead of walking he
talks now. He drives seven hundred miles, and when he gets there no one
1010   knows him anymore, no one welcomes him. And what goes through a
man's mind, driving seven hundred miles home without having earned a
cent? Why shouldn't he talk to himself? Why? When he has to go to Charley and borrow fifty dollars a week and pretend to me that it's his pay? How
long can that go on? How long? You see what I'm sitting here and waiting
1015   for? And you tell me he has no character? The man who never worked a day
but for your benefit? When does he get the medal for that? Is this his
reward—to turn around at the age of sixty-three and find his sons, who he
loved better than his life, one a philandering bum—
HAPPY   Mom!
1020   LINDA   That's all you are, my baby! [*To* BIFF] And you! What happened to the
love you had for him? You were such pals! How you used to talk to him on
the phone every night! How lonely he was till he could come home to you!
BIFF   All right, Mom. I'll live here in my room, and I'll get a job. I'll keep
away from him, that's all.
1025   LINDA   No, Biff. You can't stay here and fight all the time.
BIFF   He threw me out of this house, remember that.
LINDA   Why did he do that? I never knew why.
BIFF   Because I know he's a fake and he doesn't like anybody around who
knows!
1030   LINDA   Why a fake? In what way? What do you mean?
BIFF   Just don't lay it all at my feet. It's between me and him—that's all I
have to say. I'll chip in from now on. He'll settle for half my paycheck. He'll
be all right. I'm going to bed. [*He starts for the stairs.*]
LINDA   He won't be all right.
1035   BIFF   [*turning on the stairs, furiously*]   I hate this city and I'll stay here. Now
what do you want?
LINDA   He's dying, Biff.
[HAPPY *turns quickly to her, shocked.*]
BIFF   [*after a pause*]   Why is he dying?
LINDA   He's been trying to kill himself.
1040   BIFF   [*with great horror*]   How?
LINDA   I live from day to day.
BIFF   What're you talking about?
LINDA   Remember I wrote you that he smashed up the car again? In February?
BIFF   Well?
1045   LINDA   The insurance inspector came. He said that they have evidence. That
all these accidents in the last year—weren't—weren't—accidents.
HAPPY   How can they tell that? That's a lie.
LINDA   It seems there's a woman . . . [*She takes a breath as*]
BIFF   [*sharply but contained*]   What woman?   }
1050   LINDA   [*simultaneously*]   . . . and this woman . . . ʃ

LINDA What?

BIFF Nothing. Go ahead.

LINDA What did you say?

BIFF Nothing. I just said what woman?

1055 HAPPY What about her?

LINDA Well, it seems she was walking down the road and saw his car. She says that he wasn't driving fast at all, and that he didn't skid. She says he came to that little bridge, and then deliberately smashed into the railing, and it was only the shallowness of the water that saved him.

1060 BIFF Oh, no, he probably just fell asleep again.

LINDA I don't think he fell asleep.

BIFF Why not?

LINDA Last month . . . [*With great difficulty*] Oh, boys, it's so hard to say a thing like this! He's just a big stupid man to you, but I tell you there's more

1065 good in him than in many other people. [*She chokes, wipes her eyes.*] I was looking for a fuse. The lights blew out, and I went down the cellar. And behind the fuse box—it happened to fall out—was a length of rubber pipe—just short.

HAPPY No kidding?

1070 LINDA There's a little attachment on the end of it. I knew right away. And sure enough, on the bottom of the water heater there's a new little nipple on the gas pipe.

HAPPY [*angrily*] That—jerk.

BIFF Did you have it taken off?

1075 LINDA I'm—I'm ashamed to. How can I mention it to him? Every day I go down and take away that little rubber pipe. But, when he comes home, I put it back where it was. How can I insult him that way? I don't know what to do. I live from day to day, boys. I tell you, I know every thought in his mind. It sounds so old-fashioned and silly, but I tell you he put his whole

1080 life into you and you've turned your backs on him. [*She is bent over in the chair, weeping, her face in her hands.*] Biff, I swear to God! Biff, his life is in your hands!

HAPPY [*to* BIFF] How do you like that damned fool!

BIFF [*kissing her*] All right, pal, all right. It's all settled now. I've been remiss.

1085 I know that, Mom. But now I'll stay, and I swear to you, I'll apply myself. [*Kneeling in front of her, in a fever of self-reproach*] It's just—you see, Mom, I don't fit in business. Not that I won't try. I'll try, and I'll make good.

HAPPY Sure you will. The trouble with you in business was you never tried to please people.

1090 BIFF I know, I—

HAPPY Like when you worked for Harrison's. Bob Harrison said you were tops, and then you go and do some damn fool thing like whistling whole songs in the elevator like a comedian.

BIFF [*against* HAPPY] So what? I like to whistle sometimes.

1095 HAPPY You don't raise a guy to a responsible job who whistles in the elevator!

LINDA Well, don't argue about it now.

HAPPY Like when you'd go off and swim in the middle of the day instead of taking the line around.

1100 BIFF [*his resentment rising*] Well, don't you run off? You take off sometimes, don't you? On a nice summer day?

HAPPY Yeah, but I cover myself!

LINDA Boys!

HAPPY If I'm going to take a fade[5] the boss can call any number where I'm
1105 supposed to be and they'll swear to him that I just left. I'll tell you something that I hate to say, Biff, but in the business world some of them think
you're crazy.

BIFF [angered] Screw the business world!

HAPPY All right, screw it! Great, but cover yourself!

1110 LINDA Hap, Hap!

BIFF I don't care what they think! They've laughed at Dad for years, and you
know why? Because we don't belong in this nuthouse of a city! We should
be mixing cement on some open plain, or—or carpenters. A carpenter is
allowed to whistle!

[WILLY walks in from the entrance of the house, at left.]

1115 WILLY Even your grandfather was better than a carpenter. [Pause. They
watch him.] You never grew up. Bernard does not whistle in the elevator, I
assure you.

BIFF [as though to laugh WILLY out of it] Yeah, but you do, Pop.

WILLY I never in my life whistled in an elevator! And who in the business
1120 world thinks I'm crazy?

BIFF I didn't mean it like that, Pop. Now don't make a whole thing out of it,
will ya?

WILLY Go back to the West! Be a carpenter, a cowboy, enjoy yourself!

LINDA Willy, he was just saying—

1125 WILLY I heard what he said!

HAPPY [trying to quiet WILLY] Hey, Pop, come on now . . .

WILLY [continuing over HAPPY's line] They laugh at me, heh? Go to Filene's,
go to the Hub,[6] go to Slattery's, Boston. Call out the name Willy Loman
and see what happens! Big shot!

1130 BIFF All right, Pop.

WILLY Big!

BIFF All right!

WILLY Why do you always insult me?

BIFF I didn't say a word. [To LINDA] Did I say a word?

1135 LINDA He didn't say anything, Willy.

WILLY [going to the doorway of the living room] All right, good night, good
night.

LINDA Willy, dear, he just decided . . .

WILLY [to BIFF] If you get tired hanging around tomorrow, paint the ceiling I
1140 put up in the living room.

BIFF I'm leaving early tomorrow.

HAPPY He's going to see Bill Oliver, Pop.

WILLY [interestedly] Oliver? For what?

BIFF [with reserve, but trying, trying] He always said he'd stake me. I'd like to
1145 go into business, so maybe I can take him up on it.

LINDA Isn't that wonderful?

WILLY Don't interrupt. What's wonderful about it? There's fifty men in the
City of New York who'd stake him. [To BIFF] Sporting goods?

5. Disappear.
6. Boston (label given the Massachusetts State House in 1858 by Oliver Wendell Holmes).

BIFF   I guess so. I know something about it and—

1150 WILLY   He knows something about it! You know sporting goods better than Spalding,[7] for God's sake! How much is he giving you?

BIFF   I don't know, I didn't even see him yet, but—

WILLY   Then what're you talkin' about?

BIFF   [getting angry]   Well, all I said was I'm gonna see him, that's all!

1155 WILLY   [turning away]   Ah, you're counting your chickens again.

BIFF   [starting left for the stairs]   Oh, Jesus, I'm going to sleep!

WILLY   [calling after him]   Don't curse in this house!

BIFF   [turning]   Since when did you get so clean?

HAPPY   [trying to stop them]   Wait a . . .

1160 WILLY   Don't use that language to me! I won't have it!

HAPPY   [grabbing BIFF, shouts]   Wait a minute! I got an idea. I got a feasible idea. Come here, Biff, let's talk this over now, let's talk some sense here. When I was down in Florida last time, I thought of a great idea to sell sporting goods. It just came back to me. You and I, Biff—we have a line,

1165 the Loman Line. We train a couple of weeks, and put on a couple of exhibitions, see?

WILLY   That's an idea!

HAPPY   Wait! We form two basketball teams, see? Two water-polo teams. We play each other. It's a million dollars' worth of publicity. Two brothers, see?

1170 The Loman Brothers. Displays in the Royal Palms—all the hotels. And banners over the ring and the basketball court: "Loman Brothers." Baby, we could sell sporting goods!

WILLY   That is a one-million-dollar idea!

LINDA   Marvelous!

1175 BIFF   I'm in great shape as far as that's concerned.

HAPPY   And the beauty of it is, Biff, it wouldn't be like a business. We'd be out playin' ball again . . .

BIFF   [enthused]   Yeah, that's . . .

WILLY   Million-dollar . . .

1180 HAPPY   And you wouldn't get fed up with it, Biff. It'd be the family again. There'd be the old honor, and comradeship, and if you wanted to go off for a swim or somethin'—well, you'd do it! Without some smart cooky gettin' up ahead of you!

WILLY   Lick the world! You guys together could absolutely lick the civilized

1185 world.

BIFF   I'll see Oliver tomorrow. Hap, if we could work that out . . .

LINDA   Maybe things are beginning to—

WILLY   [wildly enthused, to LINDA]   Stop interrupting! [To BIFF] But don't wear sport jacket and slacks when you see Oliver.

1190 BIFF   No, I'll—

WILLY   A business suit, and talk as little as possible, and don't crack any jokes.

BIFF   He did like me. Always liked me.

LINDA   He loved you!

7. The sporting goods company named after the American baseball star A. G. Spalding (1850–1915), who founded it.

1195 WILLY [*to* LINDA]   Will you stop! [*To* BIFF] Walk in very serious. You are not
applying for a boy's job. Money is to pass. Be quiet, fine, and serious.
Everybody likes a kidder, but nobody lends him money.

HAPPY   I'll try to get some myself, Biff. I'm sure I can.

WILLY   I see great things for you kids, I think your troubles are over. But
1200 remember, start big and you'll end big. Ask for fifteen. How much you
gonna ask for?

BIFF   Gee, I don't know—

WILLY   And don't say "Gee." "Gee" is a boy's word. A man walking in for fifteen thousand dollars does not say "Gee!"

1205 BIFF   Ten, I think, would be top though.

WILLY   Don't be so modest. You always started too low. Walk in with a big
laugh. Don't look worried. Start off with a couple of your good stories to
lighten things up. It's not what you say, it's how you say it—because personality always wins the day.

1210 LINDA   Oliver always thought the highest of him—

WILLY   Will you let me talk?

BIFF   Don't yell at her, Pop, will ya?

WILLY [*angrily*]   I was talking, wasn't I?

BIFF   I don't like you yelling at her all the time, and I'm tellin' you, that's all.

1215 WILLY   What're you, takin' over this house?

LINDA   Willy—

WILLY [*turning on her*]   Don't take his side all the time, goddammit!

BIFF [*furiously*]   Stop yelling at her!

WILLY [*suddenly pulling on his cheek, beaten down, guilt ridden*]   Give my
1220 best to Bill Oliver—he may remember me. [*He exits through the living room
doorway.*]

LINDA [*her voice subdued*]   What'd you have to start that for? [BIFF *turns
away.*] You see how sweet he was as soon as you talked hopefully? [*She goes
over to* BIFF.] Come up and say good night to him. Don't let him go to bed
that way.

1225 HAPPY   Come on, Biff, let's buck him up.

LINDA   Please, dear. Just say good night. It takes so little to make him happy.
Come. [*She goes through the living room doorway, calling upstairs from
within the living room.*] Your pajamas are hanging in the bathroom, Willy!

HAPPY [*looking toward where* LINDA *went out*]   What a woman! They broke
1230 the mold when they made her. You know that, Biff?

BIFF   He's off salary. My God, working on commission!

HAPPY   Well, let's face it: he's no hot-shot selling man. Except that sometimes, you have to admit, he's a sweet personality.

BIFF [*deciding*]   Lend me ten bucks, will ya? I want to buy some new ties.

1235 HAPPY   I'll take you to a place I know. Beautiful stuff. Wear one of my striped
shirts tomorrow.

BIFF   She got gray. Mom got awful old. Gee, I'm gonna go in to Oliver tomorrow and knock him for a—

HAPPY   Come on up. Tell that to Dad. Let's give him a whirl. Come on.

1240 BIFF [*steamed up*]   You know, with ten thousand bucks, boy!

HAPPY [*as they go into the living room*]   That's the talk, Biff, that's the first
time I've heard the old confidence out of you! [*From within the living room,*

fading off] You're gonna live with me, kid, and any babe you want just say the word . . . [*The last lines are hardly heard. They are mounting the stairs to their parents' bedroom.*]

1245 LINDA [*entering her bedroom and addressing* WILLY, *who is in the bathroom. She is straightening the bed for him.*] Can you do anything about the shower? It drips.

WILLY [*from the bathroom*] All of a sudden everything falls to pieces! Goddam plumbing, oughta be sued, those people. I hardly finished putting it in and the thing . . . [*His words rumble off.*]

1250 LINDA I'm just wondering if Oliver will remember him. You think he might?

WILLY [*coming out of the bathroom in his pajamas*] Remember him? What's the matter with you, you crazy? If he'd've stayed with Oliver he'd be on top by now! Wait'll Oliver gets a look at him. You don't know the average caliber any more. The average young man today—[*He is getting into bed.*]—is

1255 got a caliber of zero. Greatest thing in the world for him was to bum around.

[BIFF *and* HAPPY *enter the bedroom. Slight pause.*]

WILLY [*stops short, looking at* BIFF] Glad to hear it, boy.

HAPPY He wanted to say good night to you, sport.

WILLY [*to* BIFF] Yeah. Knock him dead, boy. What'd you want to tell me?

1260 BIFF Just take it easy, Pop. Good night. [*He turns to go.*]

WILLY [*unable to resist*] And if anything falls off the desk while you're talking to him—like a package or something—don't you pick it up. They have office boys for that.

LINDA I'll make a big breakfast—

1265 WILLY Will you let me finish? [*To* BIFF] Tell him you were in the business in the West. Not farm work.

BIFF All right, Dad.

LINDA I think everything—

WILLY [*going right through her speech*] And don't undersell yourself. No less

1270 than fifteen thousand dollars.

BIFF [*unable to bear him*] Okay. Good night, Mom. [*He starts moving.*]

WILLY Because you got a greatness in you, Biff, remember that. You got all kinds a greatness . . . [*He lies back, exhausted.* BIFF *walks out.*]

LINDA [*calling after Biff*] Sleep well, darling!

1275 HAPPY I'm gonna get married, Mom. I wanted to tell you.

LINDA Go to sleep, dear.

HAPPY [*going*] I just wanted to tell you.

WILLY Keep up the good work. [HAPPY *exits.*] God . . . remember that Ebbets Field[8] game? The championship of the city?

1280 LINDA Just rest. Should I sing to you?

WILLY Yeah. Sing to me. [LINDA *hums a soft lullaby.*] When that team came out—he was the tallest, remember?

LINDA Oh, yes. And in gold.

[BIFF *enters the darkened kitchen, takes a cigarette, and leaves the house. He comes downstage into a golden pool of light. He smokes, staring at the night.*]

---

8. Brooklyn's baseball stadium, home of the Dodgers before the team's move to Los Angeles in 1957. Football was also played there.

1285 WILLY   Like a young god. Hercules[9]—something like that. And the sun, the sun all around him. Remember how he waved to me? Right up from the field, with the representatives of three colleges standing by? And the buyers I brought, and the cheers when he came out—Loman, Loman, Loman! God Almighty, he'll be great yet. A star like that, magnificent, can never really fade away!

[*The light on* WILLY *is fading. The gas heater begins to glow through the kitchen wall, near the stairs, a blue flame beneath red coils.*]

1290 LINDA [*timidly*]   Willy dear, what has he got against you?

WILLY   I'm so tired. Don't talk anymore.

[BIFF *slowly returns to the kitchen. He stops, stares toward the heater.*]

LINDA   Will you ask Howard to let you work in New York?

WILLY   First thing in the morning. Everything'll be all right.

[BIFF *reaches behind the heater and draws out a length of rubber tubing. He is horrified and turns his head toward* WILLY'S *room, still dimly lit, from which the strains of* LINDA'S *desperate but monotonous humming rise.*]

WILLY [*staring through the window into the moonlight*]   Gee, look at the moon moving between the buildings!

[BIFF *wraps the tubing around his hand and quickly goes up the stairs.*]

Curtain.

Act 2

Music is heard, gay and bright. The curtain rises as the music fades away. WILLY, *in shirt sleeves, is sitting at the kitchen table, sipping coffee, his hat in his lap.* LINDA *is filling his cup when she can.*

WILLY   Wonderful coffee. Meal in itself.

LINDA   Can I make you some eggs?

WILLY   No. Take a breath.

LINDA   You look so rested, dear.

5 WILLY   I slept like a dead one. First time in months. Imagine, sleeping till ten on a Tuesday morning. Boys left nice and early, heh?

LINDA   They were out of here by eight o'clock.

WILLY   Good work!

LINDA   It was so thrilling to see them leaving together. I can't get over the

10   shaving lotion in this house!

WILLY [*smiling*]   Mmm—

LINDA   Biff was very changed this morning. His whole attitude seemed to be hopeful. He couldn't wait to get downtown to see Oliver.

WILLY   He's heading for a change. There's no question, there simply are cer-

15   tain men that take longer to get—solidified. How did he dress?

LINDA   His blue suit. He's so handsome in that suit. He could be a—anything in that suit!

[WILLY *gets up from the table.* LINDA *holds his jacket for him.*]

WILLY   There's no question, no question at all. Gee, on the way home tonight I'd like to buy some seeds.

---

9. In classical mythology, the greatest of all heroes (a son of Zeus, king of the gods, and the mortal Alcmene).

20 LINDA [*laughing*]   That'd be wonderful. But not enough sun gets back there. Nothing'll grow anymore.

WILLY   You wait, kid, before it's all over we're gonna get a little place out in the country, and I'll raise some vegetables, a couple of chickens . . .

LINDA   You'll do it yet, dear.

[WILLY *walks out of his jacket.* LINDA *follows him.*]

25 WILLY   And they'll get married, and come for a weekend. I'd build a little guest house. 'Cause I got so many fine tools, all I'd need would be a little lumber and some peace of mind.

LINDA [*joyfully*]   I sewed the lining . . .

WILLY   I could build two guest houses, so they'd both come. Did he decide
30   how much he's going to ask Oliver for?

LINDA [*getting him into the jacket*]   He didn't mention it, but I imagine ten or fifteen thousand. You going to talk to Howard today?

WILLY   Yeah. I'll put it to him straight and simple. He'll just have to take me off the road.

35 LINDA   And Willy, don't forget to ask for a little advance, because we've got the insurance premium. It's the grace period now.

WILLY   That's a hundred . . . ?

LINDA   A hundred and eight, sixty-eight. Because we're a little short again.

WILLY   Why are we short?

40 LINDA   Well, you had the motor job on the car . . .

WILLY   That goddam Studebaker!

LINDA   And you got one more payment on the refrigerator . . .

WILLY   But it just broke again!

LINDA   Well, it's old, dear.

45 WILLY   I told you we should've bought a well-advertised machine. Charley bought a General Electric and it's twenty years old and it's still good, that son-of-a-bitch.

LINDA   But, Willy—

WILLY   Whoever heard of a Hastings refrigerator? Once in my life I would
50   like to own something outright before it's broken! I'm always in a race with the junkyard! I just finished paying for the car and it's on its last legs. The refrigerator consumes belts like a goddam maniac. They time those things. They time them so when you finally paid for them, they're used up.

LINDA [*buttoning up his jacket as he unbuttons it*]   All told, about two hun-
55   dred dollars would carry us, dear. But that includes the last payment on the mortgage. After this payment, Willy, the house belongs to us.

WILLY   It's twenty-five years!

LINDA   Biff was nine years old when we bought it.

WILLY   Well, that's a great thing. To weather a twenty-five year mortgage is—
60 LINDA   It's an accomplishment.

WILLY   All the cement, the lumber, the reconstruction I put in this house! There ain't a crack to be found in it anymore.

LINDA   Well, it served its purpose.

WILLY   What purpose? Some stranger'll come along, move in, and that's that.
65   If only Biff would take this house, and raise a family . . . [*He starts to go.*] Good-by, I'm late.

LINDA [*suddenly remembering*]   Oh, I forgot! You're supposed to meet them for dinner.

WILLY   Me?

70   LINDA   At Frank's Chop House on Forty-eighth near Sixth Avenue.

WILLY   Is that so! How about you?

LINDA   No, just the three of you. They're gonna blow you to a big meal![1]

WILLY   Don't say! Who thought of that?

LINDA   Biff came to me this morning, Willy, and he said, "Tell Dad, we want

75   to blow him to a big meal." Be there six o'clock. You and your two boys are going to have dinner.

WILLY   Gee whiz! That's really somethin'. I'm gonna knock Howard for a loop, kid. I'll get an advance, and I'll come home with a New York job. Goddammit, now I'm gonna do it!

80   LINDA   Oh, that's the spirit, Willy!

WILLY   I will never get behind a wheel the rest of my life!

LINDA   It's changing, Willy, I can feel it changing!

WILLY   Beyond a question. G'by, I'm late. [He starts to go again.]

LINDA   [calling after him as she runs to the kitchen table for a handkerchief] You got your glasses?

85   WILLY   [feels for them, then comes back in]   Yeah, yeah, got my glasses.

LINDA   [giving him the handkerchief]   And a handkerchief.

WILLY   Yeah, handkerchief.

LINDA   And your saccharine?

WILLY   Yeah, my saccharine.

90   LINDA   Be careful on the subway stairs.

[She kisses him, and a silk stocking is seen hanging from her hand. WILLY notices it.]

WILLY   Will you stop mending stockings? At least while I'm in the house. It gets me nervous. I can't tell you. Please.

[LINDA hides the stocking in her hand as she follows WILLY across the forestage in front of the house.]

LINDA   Remember, Frank's Chop House.

WILLY   [passing the apron]   Maybe beets would grow out there.

95   LINDA   [laughing]   But you tried so many times.

WILLY   Yeah. Well, don't work hard today. [He disappears around the right corner of the house.]

LINDA   Be careful!

[As WILLY vanishes, Linda waves to him. Suddenly the phone rings. She runs across the stage and into the kitchen and lifts it.]

LINDA   Hello? Oh, Biff! I'm so glad you called, I just . . . Yes, sure, I just told him. Yes, he'll be there for dinner at six o'clock, I didn't forget. Listen, I was

100   just dying to tell you. You know that little rubber pipe I told you about? That he connected to the gas heater? I finally decided to go down the cellar this morning and take it away and destroy it. But it's gone! Imagine? He took it away himself, it isn't there! [She listens]. When? Oh, then you took it. Oh—nothing, it's just that I'd hoped he'd taken it away himself. Oh, I'm

105   not worried, darling, because this morning he left in such high spirits, it was like the old days! I'm not afraid anymore. Did Mr. Oliver see you? . . . Well, you wait there then. And make a nice impression on him, darling. Just don't perspire too much before you see him. And have a nice time with

1. That is, treat him to dinner, spending extravagantly on it.

Dad. He may have big news too! . . . That's right, a New York job. And be
110   sweet to him tonight, dear. Be loving to him. Because he's only a little boat
looking for a harbor. [*She is trembling with sorrow and joy.*] Oh, that's wonderful, Biff, you'll save his life. Thanks, darling. Just put your arm around
him when he comes into the restaurant. Give him a smile. That's the
boy . . . Good-by, dear. . . . You got your comb? . . . That's fine. Good-by,
115   Biff dear.

> [*In the middle of her speech,* HOWARD WAGNER, *thirty-six, wheels in a
> small typewriter table on which is a wire-recording machine*[2] *and pro-
> ceeds to plug it in. This is on the left forestage. Light slowly fades on*
> LINDA *as it rises on* HOWARD. HOWARD *is intent on threading the machine
> and only glances over his shoulder as* WILLY *appears.*]

WILLY   Pst! Pst!

HOWARD   Hello, Willy, come in.

WILLY   Like to have a little talk with you, Howard.

HOWARD   Sorry to keep you waiting. I'll be with you in a minute.

120   WILLY   What's that, Howard?

HOWARD   Didn't you ever see one of these? Wire recorder.

WILLY   Oh. Can we talk a minute?

HOWARD   Records things. Just got delivery yesterday. Been driving me crazy,
the most terrific machine I ever saw in my life. I was up all night with it.

125   WILLY   What do you do with it?

HOWARD   I bought it for dictation, but you can do anything with it. Listen
to this. I had it home last night. Listen to what I picked up. The first one
is my daughter. Get this. [*He flicks the switch and "Roll out the Barrel"*[3] *is
heard being whistled.*] Listen to that kid whistle.

130   WILLY   That is lifelike, isn't it?

HOWARD   Seven years old. Get that tone.

WILLY   Ts, ts. Like to ask a little favor if you . . .

> [*The whistling breaks off, and the voice of* HOWARD's *daughter is heard.*]

HIS DAUGHTER   "Now you, Daddy."

HOWARD   She's crazy for me! [*Again the same song is whistled.*] That's me!
135   Ha! [*He winks.*]

WILLY   You're very good!

> [*The whistling breaks off again. The machine runs silent for a moment.*]

HOWARD   Sh! Get this now, this is my son.

HIS SON   "The capital of Alabama is Montgomery; the capital of Arizona is
Phoenix; the capital of Arkansas is Little Rock; the capital of California is
140   Sacramento . . ." [*And on, and on.*]

HOWARD [*holding up five fingers*]   Five years old, Willy!

WILLY   He'll make an announcer some day!

HIS SON [*continuing*]   "The capital . . ."

HOWARD   Get that—alphabetical order! [*The machine breaks off suddenly.*]
145   Wait a minute. The maid kicked the plug out.

WILLY   It certainly is a—

HOWARD   Sh, for God's sake!

---

2. The earliest practical magnetic sound recording machine, first commercially available after World War II (soon made obsolete by the tape recorder).

3. "The Beer Barrel Polka" (music written 1927; English lyrics written 1939), a song that became very popular during World War II.

HIS SON   "It's nine o'clock, Bulova watch time.[4] So I have to go to sleep."

WILLY   That really is—

150 HOWARD   Wait a minute! The next is my wife.

[*They wait.*]

HOWARD'S VOICE   "Go on, say something." [*Pause*] "Well, you gonna talk?"

HIS WIFE   "I can't think of anything."

HOWARD'S VOICE   "Well, talk—it's turning."

HIS WIFE [*shyly, beaten*]   "Hello." [*Silence*] "Oh, Howard, I can't talk into
155   this . . ."

HOWARD [*snapping the machine off*]   That was my wife.

WILLY   That is a wonderful machine. Can we—

HOWARD   I tell you, Willy, I'm gonna take my camera, and my bandsaw, and
all my hobbies, and out they go. This is the most fascinating relaxation I
160   ever found.

WILLY   I think I'll get one myself.

HOWARD   Sure, they're only a hundred and a half. You can't do without it.
Supposing you wanna hear Jack Benny,[5] see? But you can't be at home at
that hour. So you tell the maid to turn the radio on when Jack Benny
165   comes on, and this automatically goes on with the radio . . .

WILLY   And when you come home you . . .

HOWARD   You can come home twelve o'clock, one o'clock, anytime you like,
and you get yourself a Coke and sit yourself down, throw the switch, and
there's Jack Benny's program in the middle of the night!

170 WILLY   I'm definitely going to get one. Because lots of time I'm on the road,
and I think to myself, what I must be missing on the radio!

HOWARD   Don't you have a radio in the car?

WILLY   Well, yeah, but who ever thinks of turning it on?

HOWARD   Say, aren't you supposed to be in Boston?

175 WILLY   That's what I want to talk to you about, Howard. You got a minute?
[*He draws a chair in from the wing.*]

HOWARD   What happened? What're you doing here?

WILLY   Well . . .

HOWARD   You didn't crack up again, did you?

WILLY   Oh, no. No . . .

180 HOWARD   Geez, you had me worried there for a minute. What's the trouble?

WILLY   Well, tell you the truth, Howard. I've come to the decision that I'd
rather not travel any more.

HOWARD   Not travel! Well, what'll you do?

WILLY   Remember, Christmastime, when you had the party here? You said
185   you'd try to think of some spot for me here in town.

HOWARD   With us?

WILLY   Well, sure.

HOWARD   Oh, yeah, yeah. I remember. Well, I couldn't think of anything for
you, Willy.

190 WILLY   I tell ya, Howard. The kids are all grown up, y'know. I don't need
much anymore. If I could take home—well, sixty-five dollars a week, I
could swing it.

---

4. A phrase used for years in Bulova's radio
advertisements, beginning in 1926.
5. American comedian and actor (Benjamin

Kubelsky, 1894–1974), host of a popular
comedy show on radio (1932–55) and television (1950–65).

HOWARD   Yeah, but Willy, see I—

WILLY   I tell ya why, Howard. Speaking frankly and between the two of us,
195   y'know—I'm just a little tired.

HOWARD   Oh, I could understand that, Willy. But you're a road man, Willy,
    and we do a road business. We've only got a half-dozen salesmen on the
    floor here.

WILLY   God knows, Howard, I never asked a favor of any man. But I was with
200   the firm when your father used to carry you in here in his arms.

HOWARD   I know that, Willy, but—

WILLY   Your father came to me the day you were born and asked me what I
    thought of the name of Howard, may he rest in peace.

HOWARD   I appreciate that, Willy, but there just is no spot here for you. If I
205   had a spot I'd slam you right in, but I just don't have a single solitary spot.

         [*He looks for his lighter.* WILLY *has picked it up and gives it to him.*
         Pause.]

WILLY [*with increasing anger*]   Howard, all I need to set my table is fifty dol-
    lars a week.

HOWARD   But where am I going to put you, kid?

WILLY   Look, it isn't a question of whether I can sell merchandise, is it?

210 HOWARD   No, but it's a business, kid, and everybody's gotta pull his own
    weight.

WILLY [*desperately*]   Just let me tell you a story, Howard—

HOWARD   'Cause you gotta admit, business is business.

WILLY [*angrily*]   Business is definitely business, but just listen for a minute.
215   You don't understand this. When I was a boy—eighteen, nineteen—I was
    already on the road. And there was a question in my mind as to whether
    selling had a future for me. Because in those days I had a yearning to go to
    Alaska. See, there were three gold strikes in one month in Alaska, and I felt
    like going out. Just for the ride, you might say.

220 HOWARD [*barely interested*]   Don't say.

WILLY   Oh, yeah, my father lived many years in Alaska. He was an adventur-
    ous man. We've got quite a little streak of self-reliance in our family. I
    thought I'd go out with my older brother and try to locate him, and maybe
    settle in the North with the old man. And I was almost decided to go, when
225   I met a salesman in the Parker House.[6] His name was Dave Singleman.
    And he was eighty-four years old, and he'd drummed merchandise in
    thirty-one states. And old Dave, he'd go up to his room, y'understand, put
    on his green velvet slippers—I'll never forget—and pick up his phone and
    call the buyers, and without ever leaving his room, at the age of eighty-four,
230   he made his living. And when I saw that, I realized that selling was the
    greatest career a man could want. 'Cause what could be more satisfying
    than to be able to go, at the age of eighty-four, into twenty or thirty differ-
    ent cities, and pick up a phone, and be remembered and loved and helped
    by so many different people? Do you know? when he died—and by the way
235   he died the death of a salesman, in his green velvet slippers in the smoker[7]
    of the New York, New Haven and Hartford, going into Boston—when he
    died, hundreds of salesmen and buyers were at his funeral. Things were

6. A venerable Boston luxury hotel.
7. The smoking car on a train (Willy names the specific railroad).

sad on a lotta trains for months after that. [*He stands up.* HOWARD *has not looked at him.*] In those days there was personality in it, Howard. There was respect, and comradeship, and gratitude in it. Today, it's all cut and dried, and there's no chance for bringing friendship to bear—or personality. You see what I mean? They don't know me anymore.

HOWARD [*moving away, to the right*]   That's just the thing, Willy.

WILLY   If I had forty dollars a week—that's all I'd need. Forty dollars, Howard.

HOWARD   Kid, I can't take blood from a stone, I—

WILLY [*desperation is on him now*]   Howard, the year Al Smith was nominated,[8] your father came to me and—

HOWARD [*starting to go off*]   I've got to see some people, kid.

WILLY [*stopping him*]   I'm talking about your father! There were promises made across this desk! You mustn't tell me you've got people to see—I put thirty-four years into this firm, Howard, and now I can't pay my insurance! You can't eat the orange and throw the peel away—a man is not a piece of fruit! [*After a pause*] Now pay attention. Your father—in 1928 I had a big year. I averaged a hundred and seventy dollars a week in commissions.

HOWARD [*impatiently*]   Now, Willy, you never averaged—

WILLY [*banging his hand on the desk*]   I averaged a hundred and seventy dollars a week in the year of 1928! And your father came to me—or rather, I was in the office here—it was right over this desk—and he put his hand on my shoulder—

HOWARD [*getting up*]   You'll have to excuse me, Willy, I gotta see some people. Pull yourself together. [*Going out*] I'll be back in a little while.

[*On* HOWARD's *exit, the light on his chair grows very bright and strange.*]

WILLY   Pull myself together! What the hell did I say to him? My God, I was yelling at him! How could I! [WILLY *breaks off, staring at the light, which occupies the chair, animating it. He approaches this chair, standing across the desk from it.*] Frank, Frank, don't you remember what you told me that time? How you put your hand on my shoulder, and Frank . . . [*He leans on the desk and as he speaks the dead man's name he accidentally switches on the recorder, and instantly.*]

HOWARD'S SON   ". . . of New York is Albany. The capital of Ohio is Cincinnati, the capital of Rhode Island is . . ." [*The recitation continues.*]

WILLY [*leaping away with fright, shouting*]   Ha! Howard! Howard! Howard!

HOWARD [*rushing in*]   What happened?

WILLY [*pointing at the machine, which continues nasally, childishly, with the capital cities*]   Shut it off! Shut it off!

HOWARD [*pulling the plug out*]   Look, Willy . . .

WILLY [*pressing his hands to his eyes*]   I gotta get myself some coffee. I'll get some coffee . . .

[WILLY *starts to walk out.* HOWARD *stops him.*]

HOWARD [*rolling up the cord*]   Willy, look . . .

WILLY   I'll go to Boston.

HOWARD   Willy, you can't go to Boston for us.

WILLY   Why can't I go?

8. That is, in 1928; Smith (1873–1944) was the Democratic Party's presidential nominee.

HOWARD   I don't want you to represent us. I've been meaning to tell you for
280   a long time now.

WILLY   Howard, are you firing me?

HOWARD   I think you need a good long rest, Willy.

WILLY   Howard—

HOWARD   And when you feel better, come back, and we'll see if we can work
285   something out.

WILLY   But I gotta earn money, Howard. I'm in no position to—

HOWARD   Where are your sons? Why don't your sons give you a hand?

WILLY   They're working on a very big deal.

HOWARD   This is no time for false pride, Willy. You go to your sons and you
290   tell them that you're tired. You've got two great boys, haven't you?

WILLY   Oh, no question, no question, but in the meantime . . .

HOWARD   Then that's that, heh?

WILLY   All right, I'll go to Boston tomorrow.

HOWARD   No, no.

295   WILLY   I can't throw myself on my sons. I'm not a cripple!

HOWARD   Look, kid, I'm busy this morning.

WILLY   [grasping HOWARD's arm]   Howard, you've got to let me go to Boston!

HOWARD   [hard, keeping himself under control]   I've got a line of people to see
this morning. Sit down, take five minutes, and pull yourself together, and
300   then go home, will ya? I need the office, Willy. [He starts to go, turns, remembering the recorder, starts to push off the table holding the recorder.] Oh,
yeah. Whenever you can this week, stop by and drop off the samples. You'll
feel better, Willy, and then come back and we'll talk. Pull yourself together,
kid, there's people outside.

> [HOWARD exits, pushing the table off left. WILLY stares into space,
> exhausted. Now the music is heard—BEN's music—first distantly, then
> closer, closer. As WILLY speaks, BEN enters from the right. He carries valise
> and umbrella.]

WILLY   Oh, Ben, how did you do it? What is the answer? Did you wind up
305   the Alaska deal already?

BEN   Doesn't take much time if you know what you're doing. Just a short
business trip. Boarding ship in an hour. Wanted to say good-by.

WILLY   Ben, I've got to talk to you.

BEN   [glancing at his watch]   Haven't the time, William.

310   WILLY   [crossing the apron to Ben]   Ben, nothing's working out. I don't know
what to do.

BEN   Now, look here, William. I've bought timberland in Alaska and I need a
man to look after things for me.

WILLY   God, timberland! Me and my boys in those grand outdoors!

315   BEN   You've a new continent at your doorstep, William. Get out of these cities, they're full of talk and time payments and courts of law. Screw on your
fists and you can fight for a fortune up there.

WILLY   Yes, yes! Linda, Linda!

> [LINDA enters as of old, with the wash.]

LINDA   Oh, you're back?

320   BEN   I haven't much time.

WILLY   No, wait! Linda, he's got a proposition for me in Alaska.

LINDA   But you've got—[To BEN] He's got a beautiful job here.

WILLY But in Alaska, kid, I could—

LINDA You're doing well enough, Willy!

325 BEN [*to* LINDA] Enough for what, my dear?

LINDA [*frightened of* BEN *and angry at him*] Don't say those things to him! Enough to be happy right here, right now. [*To* WILLY, *while* BEN *laughs*] Why must everybody conquer the world? You're well liked, and the boys love you, and someday—[*To* BEN]—why, old man Wagner told him just the other day

330 that if he keeps it up he'll be a member of the firm, didn't he, Willy?

WILLY Sure, sure. I am building something with this firm, Ben, and if a man is building something he must be on the right track, mustn't he?

BEN What are you building? Lay your hand on it. Where is it?

WILLY [*hesitantly*] That's true, Linda, there's nothing.

335 LINDA Why? [*To* BEN] There's a man eighty-four years old—

WILLY That's right, Ben, that's right. When I look at that man I say, what is there to worry about?

BEN Bah!

WILLY It's true, Ben. All he has to do is go into any city, pick up the phone,

340 and he's making his living and you know why?

BEN [*picking up his valise*] I've got to go.

WILLY [*holding* BEN *back*] Look at this boy!

[BIFF, *in his high school sweater, enters carrying suitcase.* HAPPY *carries* BIFF's *shoulder guards, gold helmet, and football pants.*]

WILLY Without a penny to his name, three great universities are begging for him, and from there the sky's the limit, because it's not what you do, Ben.

345 It's who you know and the smile on your face! It's contacts, Ben, contacts! The whole wealth of Alaska passes over the lunch table at the Commodore Hotel, and that's the wonder, the wonder of this country, that a man can end with diamonds here on the basis of being liked! [*He turns to* BIFF.] And that's why when you get out on that field today it's important. Because

350 thousands of people will be rooting for you and loving you. [*To* BEN, *who has again begun to leave*] And Ben! when he walks into a business office his name will sound out like a bell and all the doors will open to him! I've seen it, Ben, I've seen it a thousand times! You can't feel it with your hand like timber, but it's there!

355 BEN Good-by, William.

WILLY Ben, am I right? Don't you think I'm right? I value your advice.

BEN There's a new continent at your doorstep, William. You could walk out rich. Rich! [*He is gone.*]

WILLY We'll do it here, Ben! You hear me? We're gonna do it here!

[YOUNG BERNARD *rushes in. The gay music of the Boys is heard.*]

360 BERNARD Oh, gee, I was afraid you left already!

WILLY Why? What time is it?

BERNARD It's half-past one!

WILLY Well, come on, everybody! Ebbets Field next stop! Where's the pennants? [*He rushes through the wall-line of the kitchen and out into the living room.*]

365 LINDA [*to* BIFF] Did you pack fresh underwear?

BIFF [*who has been limbering up*] I want to go!

BERNARD Biff, I'm carrying your helmet, ain't I?

HAPPY No, I'm carrying the helmet.

BERNARD   Oh, Biff, you promised me.

370 HAPPY   I'm carrying the helmet.

BERNARD   How am I going to get in the locker room?

LINDA   Let him carry the shoulder guards. [*She puts her coat and hat on in the kitchen.*]

BERNARD   Can I, Biff? 'Cause I told everybody I'm going to be in the locker room.

375 HAPPY   In Ebbets Field it's the clubhouse.

BERNARD   I meant the clubhouse. Biff!

HAPPY   Biff!

BIFF [*grandly, after a slight pause*]   Let him carry the shoulder guards.

HAPPY [*as he gives* BERNARD *the shoulder guards*]   Stay close to us now.

[WILLY *rushes in with the pennants.*]

380 WILLY [*handing them out*]   Everybody wave when Biff comes out on the field. [HAPPY *and* BERNARD *run off.*] You set now, boy?

[*The music has died away.*]

BIFF   Ready to go, Pop. Every muscle is ready.

WILLY [*at the edge of the apron*]   You realize what this means?

BIFF   That's right, Pop.

385 WILLY [*feeling* BIFF's *muscle*]   You're comin' home this afternoon captain of the All-Scholastic Championship Team of the City of New York.

BIFF   I got it, Pop. And remember, pal, when I take off my helmet, that touchdown is for you.

WILLY   Let's go! [*He is starting out, with his arm around Biff, when* CHARLEY

390 *enters, as of old, in knickers.*] I got no room for you, Charley.

CHARLEY   Room? For what?

WILLY   In the car.

CHARLEY   You goin' for a ride? I wanted to shoot some casino.

WILLY [*furiously*]   Casino! [*Incredulously*] Don't you realize what today is?

395 LINDA   Oh, he knows, Willy. He's just kidding you.

WILLY   That's nothing to kid about!

CHARLEY   No. Linda, what's goin' on?

LINDA   He's playing in Ebbets Field.

CHARLEY   Baseball in this weather?

400 WILLY   Don't talk to him. Come on, come on! [*He is pushing them out.*]

CHARLEY   Wait a minute, didn't you hear the news?

WILLY   What?

CHARLEY   Don't you listen to the radio? Ebbets Field just blew up.

WILLY   You go to hell! [CHARLEY *laughs. Pushing them out*] Come on, come

405 on! We're late.

CHARLEY [*as they go*]   Knock a homer, Biff, knock a homer!

WILLY [*the last to leave, turning to* CHARLEY]   I don't think that was funny, Charley. This is the greatest day of his life.

CHARLEY   Willy, when are you going to grow up?

410 WILLY   Yeah, heh? When this game is over, Charley, you'll be laughing out of the other side of your face. They'll be calling him another Red Grange.[9] Twenty-five thousand a year.

9. Harold Edward Grange (1903–1991), a football player who was a three-time All-American halfback at the University of Illi- nois (1923–25); after starting for the Chicago Bears, he became a sportscaster.

CHARLEY [*kidding*]   Is that so?

WILLY   Yeah, that's so.

415 CHARLEY   Well, then, I'm sorry, Willy. But tell me something.

WILLY   What?

CHARLEY   Who is Red Grange?

WILLY   Put up your hands. Goddam you, put up your hands!

[CHARLEY, *chuckling, shakes his head and walks away, around the left corner of the stage.* WILLY *follows him. The music rises to a mocking frenzy.*]

WILLY   Who the hell do you think you are, better than everybody else? You
420 don't know everything, you big, ignorant, stupid . . . Put up your hands!

[*Light rises, on the right side of the forestage, on a small table in the reception room of* CHARLEY's *office. Traffic sounds are heard.* BERNARD, *now mature, sits whistling to himself. A pair of tennis rackets and an overnight bag are on the floor beside him.*]

WILLY [*offstage*]   What are you walking away for? Don't walk away! If you're going to say something say it to my face! I know you laugh at me behind my back. You'll laugh out of the other side of your goddam face after this game. Touchdown! Touchdown! Eighty thousand people! Touchdown! Right
425 between the goal posts.

[BERNARD *is a quiet, earnest, but self-assured young man.* WILLY's *voice is coming from right upstage now.* BERNARD *lowers his feet off the table and listens.* JENNY, *his father's secretary, enters.*]

JENNY [*distressed*]   Say, Bernard, will you go out in the hall?

BERNARD   What is that noise? Who is it?

JENNY   Mr. Loman. He just got off the elevator.

BERNARD [*getting up*]   Who's he arguing with?

430 JENNY   Nobody. There's nobody with him. I can't deal with him any more, and your father gets all upset everytime he comes. I've got a lot of typing to do, and your father's waiting to sign it. Will you see him?

WILLY [*entering*]   Touchdown! Touch—[*He sees* JENNY.] Jenny, Jenny, good to see you. How're ya? Workin'? Or still honest?

435 JENNY   Fine. How've you been feeling?

WILLY   Not much anymore, Jenny. Ha, ha! [*He is surprised to see the rackets.*]

BERNARD   Hello, Uncle Willy.

WILLY [*almost shocked*]   Bernard! Well, look who's here! [*He comes quickly, guiltily, to* BERNARD *and warmly shakes his hand.*]

BERNARD   How are you? Good to see you.

440 WILLY   What are you doing here?

BERNARD   Oh, just stopped by to see Pop. Get off my feet till my train leaves. I'm going to Washington in a few minutes.

WILLY   Is he in?

BERNARD   Yes, he's in his office with the accountant. Sit down.

445 WILLY [*sitting down*]   What're you going to do in Washington?

BERNARD   Oh, just a case I've got there, Willy.

WILLY   That so? [*Indicating the rackets*] You going to play tennis there?

BERNARD   I'm staying with a friend who's got a court.

WILLY   Don't say. His own tennis court. Must be fine people, I bet.

450 BERNARD   They are, very nice. Dad tells me Biff's in town.

WILLY [*with a big smile*]   Yeah, Biff's in. Working on a very big deal, Bernard.

BERNARD   What's Biff doing?

WILLY   Well, he's been doing very big things in the West. But he decided to establish himself here. Very big. We're having dinner. Did I hear your wife
455   had a boy?
BERNARD   That's right. Our second.
WILLY   Two boys! What do you know!
BERNARD   What kind of a deal has Biff got?
WILLY   Well, Bill Oliver—very big sporting-goods man—he wants Biff very
460   badly. Called him in from the West. Long distance, carte blanche, special deliveries. Your friends have their own private tennis court?
BERNARD   You still with the old firm, Willy?
WILLY   [after a pause]   I'm—I'm overjoyed to see how you made the grade, Bernard, overjoyed. It's an encouraging thing to see a young man really—
465   really—Looks very good for Biff—very—[He breaks off, then] Bernard—[He is so full of emotion, he breaks off again.]
BERNARD   What is it, Willy?
WILLY   [small and alone]   What—what's the secret?
BERNARD   What secret?
WILLY   How—how did you? Why didn't he ever catch on?
470   BERNARD   I wouldn't know that, Willy.
WILLY   [confidentially, desperately]   You were his friend, his boyhood friend. There's something I don't understand about it. His life ended after that Ebbets Field game. From the age of seventeen nothing good ever happened to him.
475   BERNARD   He never trained himself for anything.
WILLY   But he did, he did. After high school he took so many correspondence courses. Radio mechanics; television; God knows what, and never made the slightest mark.
BERNARD   [taking off his glasses]   Willy, do you want to talk candidly?
480   WILLY   [rising, faces BERNARD]   I regard you as a very brilliant man, Bernard. I value your advice.
BERNARD   Oh, the hell with the advice, Willy. I couldn't advise you. There's just one thing I've always wanted to ask you. When he was supposed to graduate, and the math teacher flunked him—
485   WILLY   Oh, that son-of-a-bitch ruined his life.
BERNARD   Yeah, but, Willy, all he had to do was go to summer school and make up that subject.
WILLY   That's right, that's right.
BERNARD   Did you tell him not to go to summer school?
490   WILLY   Me? I begged him to go. I ordered him to go!
BERNARD   Then why wouldn't he go?
WILLY   Why? Why! Bernard, that question has been trailing me like a ghost for the last fifteen years. He flunked the subject, and laid down and died like a hammer hit him!
495   BERNARD   Take it easy, kid.
WILLY   Let me talk to you—I got nobody to talk to. Bernard, Bernard, was it my fault? Y'see? It keeps going around in my mind, maybe I did something to him. I got nothing to give him.
BERNARD   Don't take it so hard.
500   WILLY   Why did he lay down? What is the story there? You were his friend!
BERNARD   Willy, I remember, it was June, and our grades came out. And he'd flunked math.

WILLY That son-of-a-bitch!

505 BERNARD No, it wasn't right then. Biff just got very angry, I remember, and he was ready to enroll in summer school.

WILLY [*surprised*] He was?

BERNARD He wasn't beaten by it at all. But then, Willy, he disappeared from the block for almost a month. And I got the idea that he'd gone up to New

510 England to see you. Did he have a talk with you then?

[WILLY *stares in silence.*]

BERNARD Willy?

WILLY [*with a strong edge of resentment in his voice*] Yeah, he came to Boston. What about it?

BERNARD Well, just that when he came back—I'll never forget this, it always

515 mystifies me. Because I'd thought so well of Biff, even though he'd always taken advantage of me. I loved him, Willy, y'know? And he came back after that month and took his sneakers—remember those sneakers with "University of Virginia" printed on them? He was so proud of those, wore them every day. And he took them down in the cellar, and burned them up in the

520 furnace. We had a fist fight. It lasted at least half an hour. Just the two of us, punching each other down the cellar, and crying right through it. I've often thought of how strange it was that I knew he'd given up his life. What happened in Boston, Willy?

[WILLY *looks at him as at an intruder.*]

BERNARD I just bring it up because you asked me.

525 WILLY [*angrily*] Nothing. What do you mean, "What happened?" What's that got to do with anything?

BERNARD Well, don't get sore.

WILLY What are you trying to do, blame it on me? If a boy lays down is that my fault?

530 BERNARD Now, Willy, don't get—

WILLY Well, don't—don't talk to me that way! What does that mean, "What happened?"

[CHARLEY *enters. He is in his vest, and he carries a bottle of bourbon.*]

CHARLEY Hey, you're going to miss that train. [*He waves the bottle.*]

BERNARD Yeah, I'm going. [*He takes the bottle.*] Thanks, Pop. [*He picks up*

535 *his rackets and bag.*] Good-by, Willy, and don't worry about it. You know, "If at first you don't succeed . . ."

WILLY Yes, I believe in that.

BERNARD But sometimes, Willy, it's better for a man just to walk away.

WILLY Walk away?

540 BERNARD That's right.

WILLY But if you can't walk away?

BERNARD [*after a slight pause*] I guess that's when it's tough. [*Extending his hand*] Good-by, Willy.

WILLY [*shaking* BERNARD's *hand*] Good-by, boy.

545 CHARLEY [*an arm on* BERNARD's *shoulder*] How do you like this kid? Gonna argue a case in front of the Supreme Court.

BERNARD [*protesting*] Pop!

WILLY [*genuinely shocked, pained, and happy*] No! The Supreme Court!

BERNARD I gotta run. 'By, Dad!

550 CHARLEY Knock 'em dead, Bernard!

[BERNARD *goes off.*]

WILLY [*as* CHARLEY *takes out his wallet*] The Supreme Court! And he didn't even mention it!

CHARLEY [*counting out money on the desk*] He don't have to—he's gonna do it.

WILLY And you never told him what to do, did you? You never took any inter-
555 est in him.

CHARLEY My salvation is that I never took any interest in anything. There's some money—fifty dollars. I got an accountant inside.

WILLY Charley, look . . . [*With difficulty*] I got my insurance to pay. If you can manage it—I need a hundred and ten dollars.

[CHARLEY *doesn't reply for a moment; merely stops moving.*]

560 WILLY I'd draw it from my bank but Linda would know, and I . . .

CHARLEY Sit down, Willy.

WILLY [*moving toward the chair*] I'm keeping an account of everything, remember. I'll pay every penny back. [*He sits.*]

CHARLEY Now listen to me, Willy.

565 WILLY I want you to know I appreciate . . .

CHARLEY [*sitting down on the table*] Willy, what're you doin'? What the hell is goin' on in your head?

WILLY Why? I'm simply . . .

CHARLEY I offered you a job. You can make fifty dollars a week. And I won't
570 send you on the road.

WILLY I've got a job.

CHARLEY Without pay? What kind of a job is a job without pay? [*He rises.*] Now, look, kid, enough is enough. I'm no genius but I know when I'm being insulted.

575 WILLY Insulted!

CHARLEY Why don't you want to work for me?

WILLY What's the matter with you? I've got a job.

CHARLEY Then what're you walkin' in here every week for?

WILLY [*getting up*] Well, if you don't want me to walk in here—
580 CHARLEY I am offering you a job.

WILLY I don't want your goddam job!

CHARLEY When the hell are you going to grow up?

WILLY [*furiously*] You big ignoramus, if you say that to me again I'll rap you one! I don't care how big you are! [*He's ready to fight.*]

[*Pause.*]

585 CHARLEY [*kindly, going to him*] How much do you need, Willy?

WILLY Charley, I'm strapped, I'm strapped. I don't know what to do. I was just fired.

CHARLEY Howard fired you?

WILLY That snotnose. Imagine that? I named him. I named him Howard.

590 CHARLEY Willy, when're you gonna realize that them things don't mean anything? You named him Howard, but you can't sell that. The only thing you got in this world is what you can sell. And the funny thing is that you're a salesman, and you don't know that.

WILLY I've always tried to think otherwise, I guess. I always felt that if a man
595 was impressive, and well liked, that nothing—

CHARLEY Why must everybody like you? Who liked J. P. Morgan?[1] Was he impressive? In a Turkish bath he'd look like a butcher. But with his pockets on he was very well liked. Now listen, Willy, I know you don't like me, and nobody can say I'm in love with you, but I'll give you a job because—just 600 for the hell of it, put it that way. Now what do you say?

WILLY   I—I just can't work for you, Charley.

CHARLEY   What're you, jealous of me?

WILLY   I can't work for you, that's all, don't ask me why.

CHARLEY [*angered, takes out more bills*]   You been jealous of me all your life, 605 you damned fool! Here, pay your insurance. [*He puts the money in* WILLY's *hand.*]

WILLY   I'm keeping strict accounts.

CHARLEY   I've got some work to do. Take care of yourself. And pay your insurance.

WILLY [*moving to the right*]   Funny, y'know? After all the highways, and the 610 trains, and the appointments, and the years, you end up worth more dead than alive.

CHARLEY   Willy, nobody's worth nothin' dead. [*After a slight pause*] Did you hear what I said?

[WILLY *stands still, dreaming.*]

CHARLEY   Willy!

615 WILLY   Apologize to Bernard for me when you see him. I didn't mean to argue with him. He's a fine boy. They're all fine boys, and they'll end up big—all of them. Someday they'll all play tennis together. Wish me luck, Charley. He saw Bill Oliver today.

CHARLEY   Good luck.

620 WILLY [*on the verge of tears*]   Charley, you're the only friend I got. Isn't that a remarkable thing? [*He goes out.*]

CHARLEY   Jesus!

[CHARLEY *stares after him a moment and follows. All light blacks out. Suddenly raucous music is heard, and a red glow rises behind the screen at right.* STANLEY, *a young waiter, appears, carrying a table, followed by* HAPPY, *who is carrying two chairs.*]

STANLEY [*putting the table down*]   That's all right, Mr. Loman, I can handle it myself. [*He turns and takes the chairs from* HAPPY *and places them at the table.*]

625 HAPPY [*glancing around*]   Oh, this is better.

STANLEY   Sure, in the front there you're in the middle of all kinds a noise. Whenever you got a party, Mr. Loman, you just tell me and I'll put you back here. Y'know, there's a lotta people they don't like it private, because when they go out they like to see a lotta action around them because they're sick 630 and tired to stay in the house by theirself. But I know you, you ain't from Hackensack.[2] You know what I mean?

HAPPY [*sitting down*]   So how's it coming, Stanley?

STANLEY   Ah, it's a dog's life. I only wish during the war they'd a took me in the Army. I coulda been dead by now.

635 HAPPY   My brother's back, Stanley.

STANLEY   Oh, he come back, heh? From the Far West.

---

1. American financier, industrialist, and philanthropist (1837–1913); he amassed an enormous fortune.

2. A mainly working-class town in northern New Jersey, several miles from Manhattan.

HAPPY   Yeah, big cattle man, my brother, so treat him right. And my father's coming too.

STANLEY   Oh, your father too!

640   HAPPY   You got a couple of nice lobsters?

STANLEY   Hundred per cent, big.

HAPPY   I want them with the claws.

STANLEY   Don't worry, I don't give you no mice. [HAPPY *laughs*.] How about some wine? It'll put a head on the meal.

645   HAPPY   No. You remember, Stanley, that recipe I brought you from overseas? With the champagne in it?

STANLEY   Oh, yeah, sure. I still got it tacked up yet in the kitchen. But that'll have to cost a buck apiece anyways.

HAPPY   That's all right.

650   STANLEY   What'd you, hit a number[3] or somethin'?

HAPPY   No, it's a little celebration. My brother is—I think he pulled off a big deal today. I think we're going into business together.

STANLEY   Great! That's the best for you. Because a family business, you know what I mean?—that's the best.

655   HAPPY   That's what I think.

STANLEY   'Cause what's the difference? Somebody steals? It's in the family. Know what I mean? [*Sotto voce*[4]] Like this bartender here. The boss is goin' crazy what kinda leak he's got in the cash register. You put it in but it don't come out.

660   HAPPY   [*raising his head*]   Sh!

STANLEY   What?

HAPPY   You notice I wasn't lookin' right or left, was I?

STANLEY   No.

HAPPY   And my eyes are closed.

665   STANLEY   So what's the—?

HAPPY   Strudel's comin'.

STANLEY   [*catching on, looks around*]   Ah, no, there's no—

[*He breaks off as a furred, lavishly dressed girl enters and sits at the next table. Both follow her with their eyes.*]

STANLEY   Geez, how'd ya know?

HAPPY   I got radar or something. [*Staring directly at her profile*]   Oooooooo . . .

670   Stanley.

STANLEY   I think that's for you, Mr. Loman.

HAPPY   Look at that mouth. Oh, God. And the binoculars.

STANLEY   Geez, you got a life, Mr. Loman.

HAPPY   Wait on her.

675   STANLEY   [*going to the girl's table*]   Would you like a menu, ma'am?

GIRL   I'm expecting someone, but I'd like a—

HAPPY   Why don't you bring her—excuse me, miss, do you mind? I sell champagne, and I'd like you to try my brand. Bring her a champagne, Stanley.

680   GIRL   That's awfully nice of you.

3. That is, win in an illegal lottery.
4. Under the voice (Italian); that is, spoken very softly, under the breath.

HAPPY   Don't mention it. It's all company money. [*He laughs.*]

GIRL   That's a charming product to be selling, isn't it?

HAPPY   Oh, gets to be like everything else. Selling is selling, y'know.

GIRL   I suppose.

685 HAPPY   You don't happen to sell, do you?

GIRL   No, I don't sell.

HAPPY   Would you object to a compliment from a stranger? You ought to be on a magazine cover.

GIRL   [*looking at him a little archly*]   I have been.

[STANLEY *comes in with a glass of champagne.*]

690 HAPPY   What'd I say before, Stanley? You see? She's a cover girl.

STANLEY   Oh, I could see, I could see.

HAPPY   [*to the* GIRL]   What magazine?

GIRL   Oh, a lot of them. [*She takes the drink.*] Thank you.

HAPPY   You know what they say in France, don't you? "Champagne is the
695   drink of the complexion"—Hya, Biff!

[BIFF *has entered and sits with* HAPPY.]

BIFF   Hello, kid. Sorry I'm late.

HAPPY   I just got here. Uh, Miss—?

GIRL   Forsythe.

HAPPY   Miss Forsythe, this is my brother.

700 BIFF   Is Dad here?

HAPPY   His name is Biff. You might've heard of him. Great football player.

GIRL   Really? What team?

HAPPY   Are you familiar with football?

GIRL   No, I'm afraid I'm not.

705 HAPPY   Biff is quarterback with the New York Giants.

GIRL   Well, that is nice, isn't it? [*She drinks.*]

HAPPY   Good health.

GIRL   I'm happy to meet you.

HAPPY   That's my name. Hap. It's really Harold, but at West Point they called
710   me Happy.

GIRL   [*now really impressed*]   Oh, I see. How do you do? [*She turns her profile.*]

BIFF   Isn't Dad coming?

HAPPY   You want her?

BIFF   Oh, I could never make that.

715 HAPPY   I remember the time that idea would never come into your head. Where's the old confidence, Biff?

BIFF   I just saw Oliver—

HAPPY   Wait a minute. I've got to see that old confidence again. Do you want her? She's on call.[5]

720 BIFF   Oh, no. [*He turns to look at the* GIRL.]

HAPPY   I'm telling you. Watch this. [*Turning to the* GIRL] Honey? [*She turns to him.*] Are you busy?

GIRL   Well, I am . . . but I could make a phone call.

___

5. That is, a call girl, a prostitute.

HAPPY   Do that, will you, honey? And see if you can get a friend. We'll be
725   here for a while. Biff is one of the greatest football players in the country.
GIRL [*standing up*]   Well, I'm certainly happy to meet you.
HAPPY   Come back soon.
GIRL   I'll try.
HAPPY   Don't try, honey, try hard.

> [*The* GIRL *exits.* STANLEY *follows, shaking his head in bewildered
> admiration.*]

730   HAPPY   Isn't that a shame now? A beautiful girl like that? That's why I can't
get married. There's not a good woman in a thousand. New York is loaded
with them, kid!
BIFF   Hap, look—
HAPPY   I told you she was on call!
735   BIFF [*strangely unnerved*]   Cut it out, will ya? I want to say something to you.
HAPPY   Did you see Oliver?
BIFF   I saw him all right. Now look, I want to tell Dad a couple of things and
I want you to help me.
HAPPY   What? Is he going to back you?
740   BIFF   Are you crazy? You're out of your goddam head, you know that?
HAPPY   Why? What happened?
BIFF [*breathlessly*]   I did a terrible thing today, Hap. It's been the strangest
day I ever went through. I'm all numb, I swear.
HAPPY   You mean he wouldn't see you?
745   BIFF   Well, I waited six hours for him, see? All day. Kept sending my name in.
Even tried to date his secretary so she'd get me to him, but no soap.
HAPPY   Because you're not showin' the old confidence, Biff. He remembered
you, didn't he?
BIFF [*stopping* HAPPY *with a gesture*]   Finally, about five o'clock, he comes
750   out. Didn't remember who I was or anything. I felt like such an idiot, Hap.
HAPPY   Did you tell him my Florida idea?
BIFF   He walked away. I saw him for one minute. I got so mad I could've torn
the walls down! How the hell did I ever get the idea I was a salesman there?
I even believed myself that I'd been a salesman for him! And then he gave
755   me one look and—I realized what a ridiculous lie my whole life has been!
We've been talking in a dream for fifteen years. I was a shipping clerk.
HAPPY   What'd you do?
BIFF [*with great tension and wonder*]   Well, he left, see. And the secretary
went out. I was all alone in the waiting-room. I don't know what came over
760   me, Hap. The next thing I know I'm in his office—paneled walls, every-
thing. I can't explain it. I—Hap, I took his fountain pen.
HAPPY   Geez, did he catch you?
BIFF   I ran out. I ran down all eleven flights. I ran and ran and ran.
HAPPY   That was an awful dumb—what'd you do that for?
765   BIFF [*agonized*]   I don't know, I just—wanted to take something, I don't
know. You gotta help me, Hap, I'm gonna tell Pop.
HAPPY   You crazy? What for?
BIFF   Hap, he's got to understand that I'm not the man somebody lends that
kind of money to. He thinks I've been spiting him all these years and it's
770   eating him up.

HAPPY   That's just it. You tell him something nice.

BIFF   I can't.

HAPPY   Say you got a lunch date with Oliver tomorrow.

BIFF   So what do I do tomorrow?

775   HAPPY   You leave the house tomorrow and come back at night and say Oliver is thinking it over. And he thinks it over for a couple of weeks, and gradually it fades away and nobody's the worse.

BIFF   But it'll go on forever!

HAPPY   Dad is never so happy as when he's looking forward to something!

[WILLY *enters.*]

780   HAPPY   Hello, scout!

WILLY   Gee, I haven't been here in years!

[STANLEY *has followed* WILLY *in and sets a chair for him.* STANLEY *starts off but* HAPPY *stops him.*]

HAPPY   Stanley!

[STANLEY *stands by, waiting for an order.*]

BIFF [*going to* WILLY *with guilt, as to an invalid*]   Sit down, Pop. You want a drink?

WILLY   Sure, I don't mind.

785   BIFF   Let's get a load on.

WILLY   You look worried.

BIFF   N-no. [*To* STANLEY] Scotch all around. Make it doubles.

STANLEY   Doubles, right. [*He goes.*]

WILLY   You had a couple already, didn't you?

790   BIFF   Just a couple, yeah.

WILLY   Well, what happened, boy? [*Nodding affirmatively, with a smile*] Everything go all right?

BIFF [*takes a breath, then reaches out and grasps* WILLY's *hand*]   Pal . . . [*He is smiling bravely, and* WILLY *is smiling too.*] I had an experience today.

795   HAPPY   Terrific, Pop.

WILLY   That so? What happened?

BIFF [*high, slightly alcoholic, above the earth*]   I'm going to tell you everything from first to last. It's been a strange day. [*Silence. He looks around, composes himself as best he can, but his breath keeps breaking the rhythm of his voice.*] I had to wait quite a while for him, and—

800   WILLY   Oliver?

BIFF   Yeah, Oliver. All day, as a matter of cold fact. And a lot of—instances—facts, Pop, facts about my life came back to me. Who was it, Pop? Who ever said I was a salesman with Oliver?

WILLY   Well, you were.

805   BIFF   No, Dad, I was a shipping clerk.

WILLY   But you were practically—

BIFF [*with determination*]   Dad, I don't know who said it first, but I was never a salesman for Bill Oliver.

WILLY   What're you talking about?

810   BIFF   Let's hold on to the facts tonight, Pop. We're not going to get anywhere bullin' around. I was a shipping clerk.

WILLY [*angrily*]   All right, now listen to me—

BIFF   Why don't you let me finish?

WILLY   I'm not interested in stories about the past or any crap of that kind
815   because the woods are burning, boys, you understand? There's a big blaze
going on all around. I was fired today.

BIFF [*shocked*]   How could you be?

WILLY   I was fired, and I'm looking for a little good news to tell your mother,
because the woman has waited and the woman has suffered. The gist of it
820   is that I haven't got a story left in my head, Biff. So don't give me a lecture
about facts and aspects. I am not interested. Now what've you got to say to
me?

[STANLEY *enters with three drinks. They wait until he leaves.*]

WILLY   Did you see Oliver?

BIFF   Jesus, Dad!

825   WILLY   You mean you didn't go up there?

HAPPY   Sure he went up there.

BIFF   I did. I—saw him. How could they fire you?

WILLY [*on the edge of his chair*]   What kind of a welcome did he give you?

BIFF   He won't even let you work on commission?

830   WILLY   I'm out! [*Driving*] So tell me, he gave you a warm welcome?

HAPPY   Sure, Pop, sure!

BIFF [*driven*]   Well, it was kind of—

WILLY   I was wondering if he'd remember you. [*To* HAPPY] Imagine, man
doesn't see him for ten, twelve years and gives him that kind of a
835   welcome!

HAPPY   Damn right!

BIFF [*trying to return to the offensive*]   Pop, look—

WILLY   You know why he remembered you, don't you? Because you impressed
him in those days.

840   BIFF   Let's talk quietly and get this down to the facts, huh?

WILLY [*as though* BIFF *had been interrupting*]   Well, what happened? It's
great news, Biff. Did he take you into his office or'd you talk in the waiting
room?

BIFF   Well, he came in, see, and—

845   WILLY [*with a big smile*]   What'd he say? Betcha he threw his arm around
you.

BIFF   Well, he kinda—

WILLY   He's a fine man. [*To* HAPPY] Very hard man to see, y'know.

HAPPY [*agreeing*]   Oh, I know.

850   WILLY [*to Biff*]   Is that where you had the drinks?

BIFF   Yeah, he gave me a couple of—no, no!

HAPPY [*cutting in*]   He told him my Florida idea.

WILLY   Don't interrupt. [*To* BIFF] How'd he react to the Florida idea?

BIFF   Dad, will you give me a minute to explain?

855   WILLY   I've been waiting for you to explain since I sat down here! What happened? He took you into his office and what?

BIFF   Well—I talked. And—and he listened, see.

WILLY   Famous for the way he listens, y'know. What was his answer?

BIFF   His answer was—[*He breaks off, suddenly angry.*] Dad, you're not let-
860   ting me tell you what I want to tell you!

WILLY [*accusing, angered*]   You didn't see him, did you?

BIFF   I did see him!

WILLY   What'd you insult him or something? You insulted him, didn't you?

BIFF   Listen, will you let me out of it, will you just let me out of it!

865 HAPPY   What the hell!

WILLY   Tell me what happened!

BIFF [to HAPPY]   I can't talk to him!

[A single trumpet note jars the ear. The light of green leaves stains the house, which holds the air of night and a dream. YOUNG BERNARD enters and knocks on the door of the house.]

YOUNG BERNARD [frantically]   Mrs. Loman, Mrs. Loman!

HAPPY   Tell him what happened!

870 BIFF [to HAPPY]   Shut up and leave me alone!

WILLY   No, no! You had to go and flunk math!

BIFF   What math? What're you talking about?

YOUNG BERNARD   Mrs. Loman, Mrs. Loman!

[LINDA appears in the house, as of old.]

WILLY [wildly]   Math, math, math!

875 BIFF   Take it easy, Pop!

YOUNG BERNARD   Mrs. Loman!

WILLY [furiously]   If you hadn't flunked you'd've been set by now!

BIFF   Now, look, I'm gonna tell you what happened, and you're going to listen to me.

880 YOUNG BERNARD   Mrs. Loman!

BIFF   I waited six hours—

HAPPY   What the hell are you saying?

BIFF   I kept sending in my name but he wouldn't see me. So finally he . . .

[He continues unheard as light fades low on the restaurant.]

YOUNG BERNARD   Biff flunked math!

885 LINDA   No!

YOUNG BERNARD   Birnbaum flunked him! They won't graduate him!

LINDA   But they have to. He's gotta go to the university. Where is he? Biff! Biff!

YOUNG BERNARD   No, he left. He went to Grand Central.[6]

890 LINDA   Grand—You mean he went to Boston!

YOUNG BERNARD   Is Uncle Willy in Boston?

LINDA   Oh, maybe Willy can talk to the teacher. Oh, the poor, poor boy!

[Light on house area snaps out.]

BIFF [at the table, now audible, holding up a gold fountain pen]   . . . so I'm washed up with Oliver, you understand? Are you listening to me?

895 WILLY [at a loss]   Yeah, sure. If you hadn't flunked—

BIFF   Flunked what? What're you talking about?

WILLY   Don't blame everything on me! I didn't flunk math—you did! What pen?

HAPPY   That was awful dumb, Biff, a pen like that is worth—

900 WILLY [seeing the pen for the first time]   You took Oliver's pen?

BIFF [weakening]   Dad, I just explained it to you.

WILLY   You stole Bill Oliver's fountain pen!

BIFF   I didn't exactly steal it! That's just what I've been explaining to you!

6. Grand Central Terminal, one of New York City's two main railroad stations.

HAPPY   He had it in his hand and just then Oliver walked in, so he got ner-
905   vous and stuck it in his pocket!

WILLY   My God, Biff!

BIFF   I never intended to do it, Dad!

OPERATOR'S VOICE   Standish Arms, good evening!

WILLY [*shouting*]   I'm not in my room!

910   BIFF [*frightened*]   Dad, what's the matter? [*He and* HAPPY *stand up.*]

OPERATOR   Ringing Mr. Loman for you!

WILLY   I'm not there, stop it!

BIFF [*horrified, gets down on one knee before* WILLY]   Dad, I'll make good, I'll
   make good. [WILLY *tries to get to his feet.* BIFF *holds him down.*] Sit down
915   now.

WILLY   No, you're no good, you're no good for anything.

BIFF   I am, Dad, I'll find something else, you understand? Now don't worry
   about anything. [*He holds up* WILLY'*s face.*] Talk to me, Dad.

OPERATOR   Mr. Loman does not answer. Shall I page him?

920   WILLY [*attempting to stand, as though to rush and silence the* OPERATOR]   No,
   no, no!

HAPPY   He'll strike something, Pop.

WILLY   No, no . . .

BIFF [*desperately, standing over* WILLY]   Pop, listen! Listen to me! I'm telling
925   you something good. Oliver talked to his partner about the Florida idea.
   You listening? He—he talked to his partner, and he came to me . . . I'm
   going to be all right, you hear? Dad, listen to me, he said it was just a question of the amount!

WILLY   Then you . . . got it?

930   HAPPY   He's gonna be terrific, Pop!

WILLY [*trying to stand*]   Then you got it, haven't you? You got it! You got it!

BIFF [*agonized, holds* WILLY *down*]   No, no. Look, Pop. I'm supposed to have
   lunch with them tomorrow. I'm just telling you this so you'll know that I
   can still make an impression, Pop. And I'll make good somewhere, but I
935   can't go tomorrow, see?

WILLY   Why not? You simply—

BIFF   But the pen, Pop!

WILLY   You give it to him and tell him it was an oversight!

HAPPY   Sure, have lunch tomorrow!

940   BIFF   I can't say that—

WILLY   You were doing a crosswood puzzle and accidentally used his pen!

BIFF   Listen, kid, I took those balls years ago, now I walk in with his fountain
   pen? That clinches it, don't you see? I can't face him like that! I'll try
   elsewhere.

945   PAGE'S VOICE   Paging Mr. Loman!

WILLY   Don't you want to be anything?

BIFF   Pop, how can I go back?

WILLY   You don't want to be anything, is that what's behind it?

BIFF [*now angry at* WILLY *for not crediting his sympathy*]   Don't take it that
950   way! You think it was easy walking into that office after what I'd done to
   him? A team of horses couldn't have dragged me back to Bill Oliver!

WILLY   Then why'd you go?

BIFF   Why did I go? Why did I go! Look at you! Look at what's become of you!

[*Off left,* THE WOMAN *laughs.*]

WILLY   Biff, you're going to go to that lunch tomorrow, or—

955   BIFF   I can't go. I've got no appointment!

HAPPY   Biff, for . . . !

WILLY   Are you spiting me?

BIFF   Don't take it that way! Goddammit!

WILLY [*strikes* BIFF *and falters away from the table*]   You rotten little louse! Are
960   you spiting me?

THE WOMAN   Someone's at the door, Willy!

BIFF   I'm no good, can't you see what I am?

HAPPY [*separating them*]   Hey, you're in a restaurant! Now cut it out, both of
   you! [*The girls enter.*] Hello, girls, sit down.

[THE WOMAN *laughs, off left.*]

965   MISS FORSYTHE   I guess we might as well. This is Letta.

THE WOMAN   Willy, are you going to wake up?

BIFF [*ignoring* WILLY]   How're ya, miss, sit down. What do you drink?

MISS FORSYTHE   Letta might not be able to stay long.

LETTA   I gotta get up very early tomorrow. I got jury duty. I'm so excited!
970   Were you fellows ever on a jury?

BIFF   No, but I been in front of them! [*The girls laugh.*] This is my father.

LETTA   Isn't he cute? Sit down with us, Pop.

HAPPY   Sit him down, Biff!

BIFF [*going to him*]   Come on, slugger, drink us under the table. To hell with
975   it! Come on, sit down, pal.

[*On* BIFF's *last insistence,* WILLY *is about to sit.*]

THE WOMAN [*now urgently*]   Willy, are you going to answer the door!

[THE WOMAN's *call pulls* WILLY *back. He starts right, befuddled.*]

BIFF   Hey, where are you going?

WILLY   Open the door.

BIFF   The door?

980   WILLY   The washroom . . . the door . . . where's the door?

BIFF [*leading* WILLY *to the left*]   Just go straight down.

[WILLY *moves left.*]

THE WOMAN   Willy, Willy, are you going to get up, get up, get up, get up?

[WILLY *exits left.*]

LETTA   I think it's sweet you bring your daddy along.

MISS FORSYTHE   Oh, he isn't really your father!

985   BIFF [*at left, turning to her resentfully*]   Miss Forsythe, you've just seen a
   prince walk by. A fine, troubled prince. A hard-working, unappreciated
   prince. A pal, you understand? A good companion. Always for his boys.

LETTA   That's so sweet.

HAPPY   Well, girls, what's the program? We're wasting time. Come on, Biff.
990   Gather round. Where would you like to go?

BIFF   Why don't you do something for him?

HAPPY   Me!

BIFF   Don't you give a damn for him, Hap?

HAPPY   What're you talking about? I'm the one who—

995   BIFF   I sense it, you don't give a good goddam about him. [*He takes the
   rolled-up hose from his pocket and puts it on the table in front of* HAPPY.]

Look what I found in the cellar, for Christ's sake. How can you bear to let it go on?

HAPPY   Me? Who goes away? Who runs off and—

BIFF   Yeah, but he doesn't mean anything to you. You could help him—I
1000   can't! Don't you understand what I'm talking about? He's going to kill himself, don't you know that?

HAPPY   Don't I know it! Me!

BIFF   Hap, help him! Jesus . . . help him . . . Help me, help me, I can't bear
to look at his face! [*Ready to weep, he hurries out, up right.*]

1005   HAPPY [*starting after him*]   Where are you going?

MISS FORSYTHE   What's he so mad about?

HAPPY   Come on, girls, we'll catch up with him.

MISS FORSYTHE [*as Happy pushes her out*]   Say, I don't like that temper of his!

HAPPY   He's just a little overstrung, he'll be all right!

1010   WILLY [*off left, as* THE WOMAN *laughs*]   Don't answer! Don't answer!

LETTA   Don't you want to tell your father—

HAPPY   No, that's not my father. He's just a guy. Come on, we'll catch Biff,
and, honey, we're going to paint this town! Stanley, where's the check! Hey,
Stanley!

[*They exit.* STANLEY *looks toward left.*]

1015   STANLEY [*calling to* HAPPY *indignantly*]   Mr. Loman! Mr. Loman!

[STANLEY *picks up a chair and follows them off. Knocking is heard off
left.* THE WOMAN *enters, laughing.* WILLY *follows her. She is in a black
slip; he is buttoning his shirt. Raw, sensuous music accompanies their
speech.*]

WILLY   Will you stop laughing? Will you stop?

THE WOMAN   Aren't you going to answer the door? He'll wake the whole hotel.

WILLY   I'm not expecting anybody.

THE WOMAN   Whyn't you have another drink, honey, and stop being so damn
1020   self-centered?

WILLY   I'm so lonely.

THE WOMAN   You know you ruined me, Willy? From now on, whenever you
come to the office, I'll see that you go right through to the buyers. No waiting at my desk anymore, Willy. You ruined me.

1025   WILLY   That's nice of you to say that.

THE WOMAN   Gee, you are self-centered! Why so sad? You are the saddest,
self-centeredest soul I ever did see-saw. [*She laughs. He kisses her.*] Come
on inside, drummer[7] boy. It's silly to be dressing in the middle of the night.
[*As knocking is heard*] Aren't you going to answer the door?

1030   WILLY   They're knocking on the wrong door.

THE WOMAN   But I felt the knocking. And he heard us talking in here. Maybe
the hotel's on fire!

WILLY [*his terror rising*]   It's a mistake.

THE WOMAN   Then tell him to go away!

1035   WILLY   There's nobody there.

THE WOMAN   It's getting on my nerves, Willy. There's somebody standing out
there and it's getting on my nerves!

7. A commercial traveler, a salesman.

WILLY [*pushing her away from him*] All right, stay in the bathroom here, and don't come out. I think there's a law in Massachusetts about it,[8] so 1040 don't come out. It may be that new room clerk. He looked very mean. So don't come out. It's a mistake, there's no fire.

> [*The knocking is heard again. He takes a few steps away from her, and she vanishes into the wing. The light follows him, and now he is facing* YOUNG BIFF, *who carries a suitcase. Biff steps toward him. The music is gone.*]

BIFF Why didn't you answer?

WILLY Biff! What are you doing in Boston?

BIFF Why didn't you answer? I've been knocking for five minutes, I called 1045 you on the phone—

WILLY I just heard you. I was in the bathroom and had the door shut. Did anything happen home?

BIFF Dad—I let you down.

WILLY What do you mean?

1050 BIFF Dad . . .

WILLY Biffo, what's this about? [*Putting his arm around* BIFF] Come on, let's go downstairs and get you a malted.

BIFF Dad, I flunked math.

WILLY Not for the term?

1055 BIFF The term. I haven't got enough credits to graduate.

WILLY You mean to say Bernard wouldn't give you the answers?

BIFF He did, he tried, but I only got a sixty-one.

WILLY And they wouldn't give you four points?

BIFF Birnbaum refused absolutely. I begged him, Pop, but he won't give me 1060 those points. You gotta talk to him before they close the school. Because if he saw the kind of man you are, and you just talked to him in your way, I'm sure he'd come through for me. The class came right before practice, see, and I didn't go enough. Would you talk to him? He'd like you, Pop. You know the way you could talk.

1065 WILLY You're on. We'll drive right back.

BIFF Oh, Dad, good work! I'm sure he'll change it for you!

WILLY Go downstairs and tell the clerk I'm checkin' out. Go right down.

BIFF Yes, sir! See, the reason he hates me, Pop—one day he was late for class so I got up at the blackboard and imitated him. I crossed my eyes and 1070 talked with a lithp.

WILLY [*laughing*] You did? The kids like it?

BIFF They nearly died laughing!

WILLY Yeah? What'd you do?

BIFF The thquare root of thixthy twee is . . . [WILLY *bursts out laughing;* BIFF 1075 *joins him.*] And in the middle of it he walked in!

> [WILLY *laughs and* THE WOMAN *joins in offstage.*]

WILLY [*without hesitation*] Hurry downstairs and—

BIFF Somebody in there?

WILLY No, that was next door.

> [THE WOMAN *laughs offstage.*]

---

8. That is, adultery, which is a felony in Massachusetts, though this law was rarely enforced even in the 1940s.

BIFF   Somebody got in your bathroom!

1080 WILLY   No, it's the next room, there's a party—

THE WOMAN [*enters, laughing. She lisps this*]   Can I come in? There's something in the bathtub, Willy, and it's moving!

> [WILLY *looks at* BIFF, *who is staring open-mouthed and horrified at* THE WOMAN.]

WILLY   Ah—you better go back to your room. They must be finished painting by now. They're painting her room so I let her take a shower here. Go back,
1085 go back . . . [*He pushes her.*]

THE WOMAN [*resisting*]   But I've got to get dressed, Willy, I can't—

WILLY   Get out of here! Go back, go back . . . [*Suddenly striving for the ordinary*] This is Miss Francis, Biff, she's a buyer. They're painting her room. Go back, Miss Francis, go back . . .

1090 THE WOMAN   But my clothes, I can't go out naked in the hall!

WILLY [*pushing her offstage*]   Get outa here! Go back, go back!

> [BIFF *slowly sits down on his suitcase as the argument continues offstage.*]

THE WOMAN   Where's my stockings? You promised me stockings, Willy!

WILLY   I have no stockings here!

THE WOMAN   You had two boxes of size nine sheers for me, and I want them!

1095 WILLY   Here, for God's sake, will you get outa here!

THE WOMAN [*enters holding a box of stockings*]   I just hope there's nobody in the hall. That's all I hope. [*To* BIFF] Are you football or baseball?

BIFF   Football.

THE WOMAN [*angry, humiliated*]   That's me too. G'night. [*She snatches her clothes from* WILLY, *and walks out.*]

1100 WILLY [*after a pause*]   Well, better get going. I want to get to the school first thing in the morning. Get my suits out of the closet. I'll get my valise. [BIFF *doesn't move.*] What's the matter? [BIFF *remains motionless, tears falling.*] She's a buyer. Buys for J. H. Simmons. She lives down the hall—they're painting. You don't imagine—[*He breaks off. After a pause*] Now listen, pal,
1105 she's just a buyer. She sees merchandise in her room and they have to keep it looking just so . . . [*Pause. Assuming command*] All right, get my suits. [BIFF *doesn't move.*] Now stop crying and do as I say. I gave you an order. Biff, I gave you an order! Is that what you do when I give you an order? How dare you cry! [*Putting his arm around Biff*] Now look, Biff, when you
1110 grow up you'll understand about these things. You mustn't—you mustn't overemphasize a thing like this. I'll see Birnbaum first thing in the morning.

BIFF   Never mind.

WILLY [*getting down beside* BIFF]   Never mind! He's going to give you those
1115 points. I'll see to it.

BIFF   He wouldn't listen to you.

WILLY   He certainly will listen to me. You need those points for the U. of Virginia.

BIFF   I'm not going there.

1120 WILLY   Heh? If I can't get him to change that mark you'll make it up in summer school. You've got all summer to—

BIFF [*his weeping breaking from him*]   Dad . . .

WILLY [*infected by it*]   Oh, my boy . . .

BIFF Dad . . .

1125 WILLY She's nothing to me, Biff. I was lonely, I was terribly lonely.

BIFF You—you gave her Mama's stockings! [*His tears break through and he rises to go.*]

WILLY [*grabbing for* BIFF] I gave you an order!

BIFF Don't touch me, you—liar!

WILLY Apologize for that!

1130 BIFF You fake! You phony little fake! You fake! [*Overcome, he turns quickly and weeping fully goes out with his suitcase.* WILLY *is left on the floor on his knees.*]

WILLY I gave you an order! Biff, come back here or I'll beat you! Come back here! I'll whip you!

[STANLEY *comes quickly in from the right and stands in front of* WILLY.]

WILLY [*shouts at Stanley*] I gave you an order . . .

STANLEY Hey, let's pick it up, pick it up, Mr. Loman. [*He helps* WILLY *to his
1135 feet.*] Your boys left with the chippies.[9] They said they'll see you home.

[*A second waiter watches some distance away.*]

WILLY But we were supposed to have dinner together.

[*Music is heard,* WILLY'S *theme.*]

STANLEY Can you make it?

WILLY I'll—sure, I can make it. [*Suddenly concerned about his clothes*] Do I—I look all right?

1140 STANLEY Sure, you look all right. [*He flicks a speck off* WILLY'S *lapel.*]

WILLY Here—here's a dollar.

STANLEY Oh, your son paid me. It's all right.

WILLY [*putting it in* STANLEY'S *hand*] No, take it. You're a good boy.

STANLEY Oh, no, you don't have to . . .

1145 WILLY Here—here's some more, I don't need it anymore. [*After a slight pause*] Tell me—is there a seed store in the neighborhood?

STANLEY Seeds? You mean like to plant?

[*As* WILLY *turns,* STANLEY *slips the money back into his jacket pocket.*]

WILLY Yes. Carrots, peas . . .

STANLEY Well, there's hardware stores on Sixth Avenue, but it may be too
1150 late now.

WILLY [*anxiously*] Oh, I'd better hurry, I've got to get some seeds. [*He starts off to the right.*] I've got to get some seeds, right away. Nothing's planted. I don't have a thing in the ground.

[WILLY *hurries out as the light goes down.* STANLEY *moves over to the right after him, watches him off. The other waiter has been staring at* WILLY.]

STANLEY [*to the waiter*] Well, whatta you looking at?

[*The waiter picks up the chairs and moves off right.* STANLEY *takes the table and follows him. The light fades on this area. There is a long pause, the sound of the flute coming over. The light gradually rises on the kitchen, which is empty.* HAPPY *appears at the door of the house, followed by* BIFF. HAPPY *is carrying a large bunch of long-stemmed roses. He enters the kitchen, looks around for* LINDA. *Not seeing her, he turns to* BIFF, *who is just outside the house door, and makes a gesture with his hands, indicating "Not here, I guess." He looks into the living room and freezes.*]

9. Tramps, prostitutes.

Inside, Linda, unseen, is seated, WILLY's *coat on her lap. She rises ominously and quietly and moves toward* HAPPY, *who backs up into the kitchen, afraid.*]

1155 HAPPY   Hey, what're you doing up? [LINDA *says nothing but moves toward him implacably.*] Where's Pop? [*He keeps backing to the right, and now* LINDA *is in full view in the doorway to the living room.*] Is he sleeping?

LINDA   Where were you?

HAPPY [*trying to laugh it off*]   We met two girls, Mom, very fine types. Here,
1160   we brought you some flowers. [*Offering them to her*] Put them in your room, Ma.

[*She knocks them to the floor at* BIFF's *feet. He has now come inside and closed the door behind him. She stares at* BIFF, *silent.*]

HAPPY   Now what'd you do that for? Mom, I want you to have some flowers—

LINDA [*cutting* HAPPY *off, violently to* BIFF]   Don't you care whether he lives or dies?

1165 HAPPY [*going to the stairs*]   Come upstairs, Biff.

BIFF [*with a flare of disgust, to* HAPPY]   Go away from me! [*To* LINDA] What do you mean, lives or dies? Nobody's dying around here, pal.

LINDA   Get out of my sight! Get out of here!

BIFF   I wanna see the boss.

1170 LINDA   You're not going near him!

BIFF   Where is he? [*He moves into the living room and* LINDA *follows.*]

LINDA [*shouting after* BIFF]   You invite him for dinner. He looks forward to it all day—[BIFF *appears in his parents' bedroom, looks around, and exits.*]—and then you desert him there. There's no stranger you'd do that to!

1175 HAPPY   Why? He had a swell time with us. Listen, when I—[LINDA *comes back into the kitchen.*]—desert him I hope I don't outlive the day!

LINDA   Get out of here!

HAPPY   Now look, Mom . . .

LINDA   Did you have to go to women tonight? You and your lousy rotten
1180   whores!

[BIFF *reenters the kitchen.*]

HAPPY   Mom, all we did was follow Biff around trying to cheer him up! [*To* BIFF] Boy, what a night you gave me!

LINDA   Get out of here, both of you, and don't come back! I don't want you tormenting him anymore. Go on now, get your things together! [*To* BIFF]
1185   You can sleep in his apartment. [*She starts to pick up the flowers and stops herself.*] Pick up this stuff, I'm not your maid anymore. Pick it up, you bum, you!

[HAPPY *turns his back to her in refusal.* BIFF *slowly moves over and gets down on his knees, picking up the flowers.*]

LINDA   You're a pair of animals! Not one, not another living soul would have had the cruelty to walk out on that man in a restaurant!

1190 BIFF [*not looking at her*]   Is that what he said?

LINDA   He didn't have to say anything. He was so humiliated he nearly limped when he came in.

HAPPY   But, Mom, he had a great time with us—

BIFF [*cutting him off violently*]   Shut up!

[*Without another word,* HAPPY *goes upstairs.*]

1195 LINDA   You! You didn't even go in to see if he was all right!

BIFF [*still on the floor in front of* LINDA, *the flowers in his hand; with self-loathing*]   No. Didn't. Didn't do a damned thing. How do you like that, heh? Left him babbling in a toilet.

LINDA   You louse. You . . .

BIFF   Now you hit it on the nose! [*He gets up, throws the flowers in the waste-*
1200   *basket.*] The scum of the earth, and you're looking at him!

LINDA   Get out of here!

BIFF   I gotta talk to the boss, Mom. Where is he?

LINDA   You're not going near him. Get out of this house!

BIFF [*with absolute assurance, determination*]   No. We're gonna have an
1205   abrupt conversation, him and me.

LINDA   You're not talking to him!

[*Hammering is heard from outside the house, off right.* BIFF *turns toward the noise.*]

LINDA [*suddenly pleading*]   Will you please leave him alone?

BIFF   What's he doing out there?

LINDA   He's planting the garden!

1210   BIFF [*quietly*]   Now? Oh, my God!

[BIFF *moves outside,* LINDA *following. The light dies down on them and comes up on the center of the apron as* WILLY *walks into it. He is carrying a flashlight, a hoe, and a handful of seed packets. He raps the top of the hoe sharply to fix it firmly, and then moves to the left, measuring off the distance with his foot. He holds the flashlight to look at the seed packets, reading off the instructions. He is in the blue of night.*]

WILLY   Carrots . . . quarter-inch apart. Rows . . . one-foot rows. [*He measures it off.*] One foot. [*He puts down a package and measures off.*] Beets. [*He puts down another package and measures again.*] Lettuce. [*He reads the package, puts it down.*] One foot—[*He breaks off as* BEN *appears at the right*
1215   *and moves slowly down to him.*] What a proposition, ts, ts. Terrific, terrific. 'Cause she's suffered, Ben, the woman has suffered. You understand me? A man can't go out the way he came in, Ben, a man has got to add up to something. You can't, you can't—[BEN *moves toward him as though to interrupt.*] You gotta consider, now. Don't answer so quick. Remember, it's a
1220   guaranteed twenty-thousand-dollar proposition. Now look, Ben, I want you to go through the ins and outs of this thing with me. I've got nobody to talk to, Ben, and the woman has suffered, you hear me?

BEN [*standing still, considering*]   What's the proposition?

WILLY   It's twenty thousand dollars on the barrelhead. Guaranteed, gilt-
1225   edged, you understand?

BEN   You don't want to make a fool of yourself. They might not honor the policy.

WILLY   How can they dare refuse? Didn't I work like a coolie to meet every premium on the nose? And now they don't pay off? Impossible!

1230   BEN   It's called a cowardly thing, William.

WILLY   Why? Does it take more guts to stand here the rest of my life ringing up a zero?

BEN [*yielding*]   That's a point, William. [*He moves, thinking, turns.*] And twenty thousand—that *is* something one can feel with the hand, it is there.

1235   WILLY [*now assured, with rising power*]   Oh, Ben, that's the whole beauty of it! I see it like a diamond, shining in the dark, hard and rough, that I can pick up and touch in my hand. Not like—like an appointment! This would

not be another damned-fool appointment, Ben, and it changes all the aspects. Because he thinks I'm nothing, see and so he spites me. But the
1240 funeral—[*Straightening up*] Ben, that funeral will be massive! They'll come from Maine, Massachusetts, Vermont, New Hampshire! All the old-timers with the strange license plates—that boy will be thunder-struck, Ben, because he never realized—I am known! Rhode Island, New York, New Jersey—I am known, Ben, and he'll see it with his eyes once and for all.
1245 He'll see what I am, Ben! He's in for a shock, that boy!

BEN [*coming down to the edge of the garden*] He'll call you a coward.

WILLY [*suddenly fearful*] No, that would be terrible.

BEN Yes. And a damned fool.

WILLY No, no, he mustn't, I won't have that! [*He is broken and desperate.*]
1250 BEN He'll hate you, William.

[*The gay music of the Boys is heard.*]

WILLY Oh, Ben, how do we get back to all the great times? Used to be so full of light, and comradeship, the sleigh-riding in winter, and the ruddiness on his cheeks. And always some kind of good news coming up, always some-thing nice coming up ahead. And never even let me carry the valises in the
1255 house, and simonizing, simonizing that little red car! Why, why can't I give him something and not have him hate me?

BEN Let me think about it. [*He glances at his watch.*] I still have a little time. Remarkable proposition, but you've got to be sure you're not making a fool of yourself.

[BEN *drifts off upstage and goes out of sight.* BIFF *comes down from the left.*]

WILLY [*suddenly conscious of* BIFF, *turns and looks up at him, then begins pick-*
1260 *ing up the packages of seeds in confusion*] Where the hell is that seed? [*Indignantly*] You can't see nothing out here! They boxed in the whole god-dam neighborhood!

BIFF There are people all around here. Don't you realize that?

WILLY I'm busy. Don't bother me.

1265 BIFF [*taking the hoe from* WILLY] I'm saying good-by to you, Pop. [WILLY *looks at him, silent, unable to move.*] I'm not coming back anymore.

WILLY You're not going to see Oliver tomorrow?

BIFF I've got no appointment, Dad.

WILLY He put his arm around you, and you've got no appointment?

1270 BIFF Pop, get this now, will you? Everytime I've left it's been a fight that sent me out of here. Today I realized something about myself and I tried to explain it to you and I—I think I'm just not smart enough to make any sense out of it for you. To hell with whose fault it is or anything like that. [*He takes* WILLY's *arm.*] Let's just wrap it up, heh? Come on in, we'll tell
1275 Mom. [*He gently tries to pull* WILLY *to left.*]

WILLY [*frozen, immobile, with guilt in his voice*] No, I don't want to see her.

BIFF Come on! [*He pulls again, and* WILLY *tries to pull away.*]

WILLY [*highly nervous*] No, no, I don't want to see her.

BIFF [*tries to look into* WILLY's *face, as if to find the answer there*] Why don't
1280 you want to see her?

WILLY [*more harshly now*] Don't bother me, will you?

BIFF What do you mean, you don't want to see her? You don't want them calling you yellow, do you? This isn't your fault; it's me, I'm a bum. Now come inside! [WILLY *strains to get away.*] Did you hear what I said to you?

[WILLY *pulls away and quickly goes by himself into the house.* BIFF *follows.*]

1285 LINDA [*to* WILLY]   Did you plant, dear?

BIFF [*at the door, to* LINDA]   All right, we had it out. I'm going and I'm not writing anymore.

LINDA [*going to* WILLY *in the kitchen*]   I think that's the best way, dear. 'Cause there's no use drawing it out, you'll just never get along.

[WILLY *doesn't respond.*]

1290 BIFF   People ask where I am and what I'm doing, you don't know, and you don't care. That way it'll be off your mind and you can start brightening up again. All right? That clears it, doesn't it? [WILLY *is silent, and* BIFF *goes to him.*] You gonna wish me luck, scout? [*He extends his hand.*] What do you say?

1295 LINDA   Shake his hand, Willy.

WILLY [*turning to her, seething with hurt*]   There's no necessity to mention the pen at all, y'know.

BIFF [*gently*]   I've got no appointment, Dad.

WILLY [*erupting fiercely*]   He put his arm around . . . ?

1300 BIFF   Dad, you're never going to see what I am, so what's the use of arguing? If I strike oil I'll send you a check. Meantime forget I'm alive.

WILLY [*to* LINDA]   Spite, see?

BIFF   Shake hands, Dad.

WILLY   Not my hand.

1305 BIFF   I was hoping not to go this way.

WILLY   Well, this is the way you're going. Good-by.

[BIFF *looks at him a moment, then turns sharply and goes to the stairs.*]

WILLY [*stops him with*]   May you rot in hell if you leave this house!

BIFF [*turning*]   Exactly what is it that you want from me?

WILLY   I want you to know, on the train, in the mountains, in the valleys,
1310   wherever you go, that you cut down your life for spite!

BIFF   No, no.

WILLY   Spite, spite, is the word of your undoing! And when you're down and out, remember what did it. When you're rotting somewhere beside the rail-road tracks, remember, and don't you dare blame it on me!

1315 BIFF   I'm not blaming it on you!

WILLY   I won't take the rap for this, you hear?

[HAPPY *comes down the stairs and stands on the bottom step, watching.*]

BIFF   That's just what I'm telling you!

WILLY [*sinking into a chair at the table, with full accusation*]   You're trying to put a knife in me—don't think I don't know what you're doing!

1320 BIFF   All right, phony! Then let's lay it on the line. [*He whips the rubber tube out of his pocket and puts it on the table.*]

HAPPY   You crazy—

LINDA   Biff! [*She moves to grab the hose, but* BIFF *holds it down with his hand.*]

BIFF   Leave it there! Don't move it!

WILLY [*not looking at it*]   What is that?

1325 BIFF   You know goddam well what that is.

WILLY [*caged, wanting to escape*]   I never saw that.

BIFF You saw it. The mice didn't bring it into the cellar! What is this supposed to do, make a hero out of you? This supposed to make me sorry for
you?

1330 WILLY Never heard of it.

BIFF There'll be no pity for you, you hear it? No pity!

WILLY [to LINDA] You hear the spite!

BIFF No, you're going to hear the truth—what you are and what I am!

LINDA Stop it!

1335 WILLY Spite!

HAPPY [coming down toward BIFF] You cut it now!

BIFF [to HAPPY] The man don't know who we are! The man is gonna know!
[To WILLY] We never told the truth for ten minutes in this house!

HAPPY We always told the truth!

1340 BIFF [turning on him] You big blow, are you the assistant buyer? You're one
of the two assistants to the assistant, aren't you?

HAPPY Well, I'm practically—

BIFF You're practically full of it! We all are! And I'm through with it. [To
WILLY] Now hear this, Willy, this is me.

1345 WILLY I know you!

BIFF You know why I had no address for three months? I stole a suit in Kansas City and I was in jail. [To LINDA, who is sobbing] Stop crying. I'm
through with it.

[LINDA turns away from them, her hands covering her face.]

WILLY I suppose that's my fault!

1350 BIFF I stole myself out of every good job since high school!

WILLY And whose fault is that?

BIFF And I never got anywhere because you blew me so full of hot air I
could never stand taking orders from anybody! That's whose fault it is!

WILLY I hear that!

1355 LINDA Don't, Biff!

BIFF It's goddam time you heard that! I had to be boss big shot in two weeks,
and I'm through with it!

WILLY Then hang yourself! For spite, hang yourself!

BIFF No! Nobody's hanging himself, Willy! I ran down eleven flights with a
1360 pen in my hand today. And suddenly I stopped, you hear me? And in the
middle of that office building, do you hear this? I stopped in the middle of
that building and I saw—the sky. I saw the things that I love in this world.
The work and the food and time to sit and smoke. And I looked at the pen
and said to myself, what the hell am I grabbing this for? Why am I trying to
1365 become what I don't want to be? What am I doing in an office, making a
contemptuous, begging fool of myself, when all I want is out there, waiting
for me the minute I say I know who I am! Why can't I say that, Willy? [He
tries to make WILLY face him, but WILLY pulls away and moves to the left.]

WILLY [with hatred, threateningly] The door of your life is wide open!

BIFF Pop! I'm a dime a dozen, and so are you!

1370 WILLY [turning on him now in an uncontrolled outburst] I am not a dime a
dozen! I am Willy Loman, and you are Biff Loman!

[BIFF starts for WILLY, but is blocked by HAPPY. In his fury, BIFF seems on
the verge of attacking his father.]

BIFF   I am not a leader of men, Willy, and neither are you. You were never anything but a hard-working drummer who landed in the ash can like all the rest of them! I'm one dollar an hour, Willy! I tried seven states and
1375   couldn't raise it. A buck an hour! Do you gather my meaning? I'm not bringing home any prizes anymore, and you're going to stop waiting for me to bring them home!

WILLY [*directly to* BIFF]   You vengeful, spiteful mut!

[BIFF *breaks from* HAPPY. WILLY, *in fright, starts up the stairs.* BIFF *grabs him.*]

BIFF [*at the peak of his fury*]   Pop, I'm nothing! I'm nothing, Pop. Can't you
1380   understand that? There's no spite in it anymore. I'm just what I am, that's all.

[BIFF'*s fury has spent itself, and he breaks down, sobbing, holding on to* WILLY, *who dumbly fumbles for* BIFF'*s face.*]

WILLY [*astonished*]   What're you doing? What're you doing? [*To* LINDA] Why is he crying?

BIFF [*crying, broken*]   Will you let me go, for Christ's sake? Will you take that
1385   phony dream and burn it before something happens? [*Struggling to contain himself, he pulls away and moves to the stairs.*] I'll go in the morning. Put him—put him to bed. [*Exhausted,* BIFF *moves up the stairs to his room.*]

WILLY [*after a long pause, astonished, elevated*]   Isn't that—isn't that remarkable? Biff—he likes me!

1390   LINDA   He loves you, Willy!

HAPPY [*deeply moved*]   Always did, Pop.

WILLY   Oh, Biff! [*Staring wildly*] He cried! Cried to me. [*He is choking with his love, and now cries out his promise*] That boy—that boy is going to be magnificent!

[BEN *appears in the light just outside the kitchen.*]

1395   BEN   Yes, outstanding, with twenty thousand behind him.

LINDA [*sensing the racing of his mind, fearfully, carefully*]   Now come to bed, Willy. It's all settled now.

WILLY [*finding it difficult not to rush out of the house*]   Yes, we'll sleep. Come on. Go to sleep, Hap.

1400   BEN   And it does take a great kind of a man to crack the jungle.

[*In accents of dread,* BEN'*s idyllic music starts up.*]

HAPPY [*his arm around* LINDA]   I'm getting married, Pop, don't forget it. I'm changing everything. I'm gonna run that department before the year is up. You'll see, Mom. [*He kisses her.*]

BEN   The jungle is dark but full of diamonds, Willy.

[WILLY *turns, moves, listening to* BEN.]

1405   LINDA   Be good. You're both good boys, just act that way, that's all.

HAPPY   Night, Pop. [*He goes upstairs.*]

LINDA [*to* WILLY]   Come, dear.

BEN [*with greater force*]   One must go in to fetch a diamond out.

WILLY [*to* LINDA, *as he moves slowly along the edge of the kitchen, toward the door*]   I just want to get settled down, Linda. Let me sit alone for a little.

1410   LINDA [*almost uttering her fear*]   I want you upstairs.

WILLY [*taking her in his arms*]   In a few minutes, Linda. I couldn't sleep right now. Go on, you look awful tired. [*He kisses her.*]

BEN   Not like an appointment at all. A diamond is rough and hard to the touch.

1415 WILLY   Go on now. I'll be right up.

LINDA   I think this is the only way, Willy.

WILLY   Sure, it's the best thing.

BEN   Best thing!

WILLY   The only way. Everything is gonna be—go on, kid, get to bed. You

1420 look so tired.

LINDA   Come right up.

WILLY   Two minutes.

[LINDA *goes into the living room, then reappears in her bedroom.* WILLY *moves just outside the kitchen door.*]

WILLY   Loves me. [*Wonderingly*] Always loved me. Isn't that a remarkable thing? Ben, he'll worship me for it!

1425 BEN [*with promise*]   It's dark there, but full of diamonds.

WILLY   Can you imagine that magnificence with twenty thousand dollars in his pocket?

LINDA [*calling from her room*]   Willy! Come up!

WILLY [*calling into the kitchen*]   Yes! Yes. Coming! It's very smart, you realize

1430 that, don't you, sweetheart? Even Ben sees it. I gotta go, baby. 'By! 'By! [*Going over to Ben, almost dancing*] Imagine? When the mail comes he'll be ahead of Bernard again!

BEN   A perfect proposition all around.

WILLY   Did you see how he cried to me? Oh, if I could kiss him, Ben!

1435 BEN   Time, William, time!

WILLY   Oh, Ben, I always knew one way or another we were gonna make it, Biff and I!

BEN [*looking at his watch*]   The boat. We'll be late. [*He moves slowly off into the darkness.*]

WILLY [*elegiacally, turning to the house*]   Now when you kick off, boy, I want

1440 a seventy-yard boot, and get right down the field under the ball, and when you hit, hit low and hit hard, because it's important, boy. [*He swings around and faces the audience.*] There's all kinds of important people in the stands, and the first thing you know . . . [*Suddenly realizing he is alone*] Ben! Ben, where do I . . . ? [*He makes a sudden movement of search.*] Ben, how do

1445 I . . . ?

LINDA [*calling*]   Willy, you coming up?

WILLY [*uttering a gasp of fear, whirling about as if to quiet her*]   Sh! [*He turns around as if to find his way; sounds, faces, voices, seem to be swarming in upon him and he flicks at them, crying*] Sh! Sh! [*Suddenly music, faint and high, stops him. It rises in intensity, almost to an unbearable scream. He goes up and down on his toes, and rushes off around the house.*] Shhh!

1450 LINDA   Willy?

[*There is no answer.* LINDA *waits.* BIFF *gets up off his bed. He is still in his clothes.* HAPPY *sits up.* BIFF *stands listening.*]

LINDA [*with real fear*]   Willy, answer me! Willy!

[*There is the sound of a car starting and moving away at full speed.*]

LINDA   No!

BIFF [*rushing down the stairs*]   Pop!

[*As the car speeds off, the music crashes down in a frenzy of sound, which becomes the soft pulsation of a single cello string.* BIFF *slowly returns to his bedroom. He and* HAPPY *gravely don their jackets.* LINDA *slowly walks out of her room. The music has developed into a dead march. The leaves of day are appearing over everything.* CHARLEY *and* BERNARD, *somberly dressed, appear and knock on the kitchen door.* BIFF *and* HAPPY *slowly descend the stairs to the kitchen as* CHARLEY *and* BERNARD *enter. All stop a moment when* LINDA, *in clothes of mourning, bearing a little bunch of roses, comes through the draped doorway into the kitchen. She goes to* CHARLEY *and takes his arm. Now all move toward the audience, through the wall-line of the kitchen. At the limit of the apron,* LINDA *lays down the flowers, kneels, and sits back on her heels. All stare down at the grave.*]

Requiem[1]

CHARLEY   It's getting dark, Linda.

[LINDA *doesn't react. She stares at the grave.*]

BIFF   How about it, Mom? Better get some rest, heh? They'll be closing the gate soon.

[LINDA *makes no move. Pause.*]

HAPPY [*deeply angered*]   He had no right to do that. There was no necessity
5   for it. We would've helped him.

CHARLEY [*grunting*]   Hmmm.

BIFF   Come along, Mom.

LINDA   Why didn't anybody come?

CHARLEY   It was a very nice funeral.

10   LINDA   But where are all the people he knew? Maybe they blame him.

CHARLEY   Naa. It's a rough world, Linda. They wouldn't blame him.

LINDA   I can't understand it. At this time especially. First time in thirty-five
years we were just about free and clear. He only needed a little salary. He
was even finished with the dentist.

15   CHARLEY   No man only needs a little salary.

LINDA   I can't understand it.

BIFF   There were a lot of nice days. When he'd come home from a trip; or on
Sundays, making the stoop; finishing the cellar; putting on the new porch;
when he built the extra bathroom; and put up the garage. You know some-
20   thing, Charley, there's more of him in that front stoop than in all the sales
he ever made.

CHARLEY   Yeah. He was a happy man with a batch of cement.

LINDA   He was so wonderful with his hands.

BIFF   He had the wrong dreams. All, all, wrong.

25   HAPPY [*almost ready to fight* BIFF]   Don't say that!

BIFF   He never knew who he was.

CHARLEY [*stopping* HAPPY's *movement and reply. To* BIFF]   Nobody dast blame
this man. You don't understand: Willy was a salesman. And for a salesman,
there is no rock bottom to the life. He don't put a bolt to a nut, he don't tell
30   you the law or give you medicine. He's a man way out there in the blue,
riding on a smile and a shoeshine. And when they start not smiling back—

---

1. In Roman Catholicism, a special mass for the repose of departed souls; also, a musical setting for such a mass, and by extension any solemn dirge or chant for the dead.

that's an earthquake. And then you get yourself a couple of spots on your hat, and you're finished. Nobody dast blame this man. A salesman is got to dream, boy. It comes with the territory.

35 BIFF   Charley, the man didn't know who he was.

HAPPY [*infuriated*]   Don't say that!

BIFF   Why don't you come with me, Happy?

HAPPY   I'm not licked that easily. I'm staying right in this city, and I'm gonna beat this racket! [*He looks at* BIFF, *his chin set.*] The Loman Brothers!

40 BIFF   I know who I am, kid.

HAPPY   All right, boy. I'm gonna show you and everybody else that Willy Loman did not die in vain. He had a good dream. It's the only dream you can have—to come out number-one man. He fought it out here, and this is where I'm gonna win it for him.

45 BIFF [*with a hopeless glance at* HAPPY, *bends toward his mother*]   Let's go, Mom.

LINDA   I'll be with you in a minute. Go on, Charley. [*He hesitates.*] I want to, just for a minute. I never had a chance to say good-by.

> [CHARLEY *moves away, followed by* HAPPY. BIFF *remains a slight distance up and left of* LINDA. *She sits there, summoning herself. The flute begins, not far away, playing behind her speech.*]

LINDA   Forgive me, dear. I can't cry. I don't know what it is, but I can't cry. I
50 don't understand it. Why did you ever do that? Help me, Willy, I can't cry. It seems to me that you're just on another trip. I keep expecting you. Willy, dear, I can't cry. Why did you do it? I search and search and I search, and I can't understand it, Willy. I made the last payment on the house today. Today, dear. And there'll be nobody home. [*A sob rises in her throat.*] We're
55 free and clear. [*Sobbing more fully, released*] We're free. [BIFF *comes slowly toward her.*] We're free . . . We're free . . .

> [BIFF *lifts her to her feet and moves out up right with her in his arms.* LINDA *sobs quietly.* BERNARD *and* CHARLEY *come together and follow them, followed by* HAPPY. *Only the music of the flute is left on the darkening stage as over the house the hard towers of the apartment buildings rise into sharp focus, and*]

The curtain falls.

TAWFIQ AL-HAKIM
1898–1987

COMMONLY regarded as the founder of modern Egyptian drama, Tawfiq al-Hakim is a towering literary figure in Egypt and the Arab world. His diverse literary output includes plays, short stories, poems, autobiographies, essays, and novels, but his reputation rests mostly on his dramatic work. Driven by what he called a "creative panic" to explore new artistic terrain and new modes of expression, al-Hakim continuously examined fresh perspectives and challenged the social and artistic status quo. Throughout his long life, al-Hakim was also involved in the intellectual and political ferment of his country, and by the 1980s, he was widely revered as a sage and elder statesman as well as one of the most prominent Arab writers. Produced domestically and internationally, such plays as SONG OF DEATH (1950) address the shifting cultural and political landscapes of twentieth-century Egypt and the broader Arab world.

Born to a rural upper-middle-class family, al-Hakim was pushed by his parents to become a lawyer. In 1920, he was sent to live with his uncles in Cairo to finish his undergraduate studies in law, but al-Hakim spent this unsupervised time attending plays and getting to know Cairo's theatrical community. Before long, he started writing musicals and farces—the most popular theatrical forms at that time—for the well-known 'Ukasha Brothers Troupe. Between 1920 and 1925, he wrote four plays: three of them were adaptations of French plays and the fourth, *al-Mar'ah al-Jadida* (*The Modern Woman*, 1923), was an original play inspired by the nascent feminist movement in Egypt. Though al-Hakim had assumed a pseudonym, hoping to avoid his parents' disapproval, they discovered his increasingly active participation in Cairo's theater world. After al-Hakim finished his *licence en droit* (bachelor's in law) in 1925 at Cairo University, his father attempted to break his son's attachment to the theater by sending him to France to obtain a doctorate in law. But the move only encouraged the young playwright, for in Paris al-Hakim had the opportunity to attend the plays of such modern European dramatists as HENRIK IBSEN, Maurice Maeterlinck, GEORGE BERNARD SHAW, Jean Cocteau, and LUIGI PIRANDELLO. He found himself drawn to the intellectual content in these plays and to the craftsmanship of the European stage. Al-Hakim also read widely during this time in philosophy, poetry, and fiction. Among the writers who affected him deeply were Lope de Vega, Johann Wolfgang von Goethe, Edgar Allan Poe, Arthur Rimbaud, Friedrich Nietzsche, and Andre Gide. Al-Hakim's time in Paris profoundly expanded his aesthetic and creative consciousness, transforming him into a full-fledged writer and intellectual.

Realizing after a few years that his son was not going to earn his doctorate, al-Hakim's father summoned him back to Cairo and encouraged him to become a public prosecutor in the Egyptian provinces. Upon his return to Cairo in 1928, al-Hakim embarked on an important new stage in his playwriting career, as he ceased to collaborate with popular theater troupes. Determined that Arab theater not remain an ephemeral art form, al-Hakim set out to write serious plays that would help establish an Arab dramatic literary heritage. In choosing this path, he was consciously working against the long-held belief in Egypt and the Arab world more generally that theater was a popular form, not high literature, and that plays therefore need not be preserved for future generations or even published at all. Most of Egypt's theater producers were convinced that to achieve commercial success, they must stage popular drama, in colloquial language. At the same time, Egypt's cultural elite scorned any texts not written in classical Arabic, a language in which few were proficient; they viewed colloquial texts as beneath the dignity of the Arabic literary canon. Consequently, though theater was a vital part of popular culture, Egypt had no written dramatic literary tradition to speak of.

In choosing to write plays in a literary mode, al-Hakim thus filled a glaring gap in modern Arabic literature. His plays of the 1930s were inspired by history, Greek and Arab mythology, folklore, and religion and were written in the classical Arabic known as *Fusha*: they belonged to what he called the "theater of ideas" (or "theater of the mind"). Al-Hakim considered these plays—among them *Ahl al-Kahf* (*People of the Cave*, 1933), *Shahrazad* (1934), *Praxagora* (1939; enlarged, 1954), *Pygmalion* (1942), *Sulayman al-Hakim* (*Solomon the Wise*, 1943), and *Al-Malik Udib* (*King Oedipus*, 1949)—works to be read, not staged; he insisted that they should be categorized as dramatic literature, not theatrical pieces.

The earliest of these plays, *People of the Cave*, was both a turning point in al-Hakim's career and a milestone in Egyptian and Arab drama. Based on a Christian tale retold in the Qur'an, *People of the Cave* tells the story of three Christian converts who seek refuge in a cave in order to escape the wrath of a brutal king who is persecuting converts. The three characters and a dog sleep there for three hundred years. When they rise from their long slumber, they realize that the world around them has changed. Overwhelmed by these changes and aware that they have become representatives of the past, the characters decide to retreat to the cave. Addressed to Egyptians unsure of how to respond to a rapidly changing modern world, al-Hakim's play suggests that if nations do not modernize, they perish. The intellectual content of this play (as well as others that al-Hakim wrote during the early 1930s) and the classical Arabic language in which it was written gained the approval of Egypt's literary and intellectual elite, who praised al-Hakim for winning drama a place in the canon of Arabic literature. In recognition of its importance, *People of the Cave* was the first play staged at Egypt's National Theater when it opened in 1935. Though the play's use of classical Arabic—and its division into four very long acts—guaranteed that *People of the Cave* would not appeal to a broad audience, it remains a touchstone in Egyptian cultural memory.

Al-Hakim continued to compose philosophy-steeped plays through the 1940s, but in the 1950s, he started to write in a more populist vein. This shift in al-Hakim's career was tied in part to political changes in the country. In 1952, a peaceful coup d'état led by Gamal Abdel Nasser transformed Egypt from a 150-year-old monarchy into a socialist republic. Nasser and his allies instituted educational and cultural reforms designed to publicize and promote the socialist principles of the new republic. Many Egyptian authors, including the novelist Naguib Mahfouz (who would win the Nobel Prize in Literature in 1988), supported Nasser's reforms and embraced a "social realist" style that reflected his ideology.

Under the leadership of the Ministry of Culture, those engaged in the performance arts turned away from the adaptations of Western plays, musicals, and farces that had dominated the pre-Nasser period and directed their efforts toward establishing a national literacy dramatic canon. While the National Theater continued to provide a venue for classic Arab plays and world classics in translation, additional theaters were built that featured other kinds of performance: the Puppet Theater for children's drama, the Pocket Theater for experimental drama, the Balloon Theater for ballet and folkloric dance, and the Modern Theater for contemporary texts. A number of new initiatives were also undertaken to support artists, such as artist-in-residence programs, and prizes were granted to honor excellence in the arts. Al-Hakim himself received two important playwriting awards in the 1950s.

During this decade of social and political reform, both Nasser's government and the creative community were mainly concerned with giving artistic expression to the lives of the masses. The young playwrights who emerged in the postrevolutionary period with the state's encouragement and financial support generally advocated commitment to social change. The dramas (and films) that they produced during this period focused on social issues, the family, and the place of the new postcolonial Egyptian in the world, and did so in a realist and naturalistic vein. Playwrights and intellectuals during the 1950s paid equal attention to the remaking of Egyptian theater arts and of Arab theater more generally. For most Egyptian intellectuals, this work of creating a uniquely Arab theater depended on their establishing a connection to the Arab past—a period of intellectual and cultural flowering that, they believed, was cut off by European colonialism. As part of this cultural effort, many playwrights, including al-Hakim, incorporated Arab history and folklore into their plays.

The issue of language played a central role in this nationalist project. Wanting both to reach a wide audience and to help shape the identity of Egyptian and Arab theater, al-Hakim realized that the long-standing dispute over the use of classical versus colloquial language in drama had to be resolved if Arab theater was to continue developing at all. His solution was a new stage language, which he called "the third language." He proposed that writers compose plays in a style that could both entertain and serve literature, accessible to the layperson as well as the intellectual; such a style could accommodate realist topics and express a variety of themes, including tragic ones. The language of these plays was similar to classical Arabic, or *Fusha*, but with some concessions to everyday speech. By writing in this modified version of *Fusha* rather than the local Egyptian dialect, al-Hakim also ensured that his plays could be understood in all of the Standard Arabic–speaking countries that constitute the Arab world. Al-Hakim's approach could easily be adapted to Arabic's many local dialects, and by the 1960s, the period many consider the heyday of Arab drama, a number of other playwrights had taken it up.

In his introduction to *Masrah al-Mujtama* (*Theater of Social Themes*, 1950), a collection of short plays from this period that contains some of his most widely read and produced works, al-Hakim emphasizes that every play in the volume—even ones whose plots seem to be far-fetched—authentically reflects Egyptian social realities in the 1940s and 1950s. One central reality is the place of women in traditional Arab society. Three plays in the collection underscore women's power and represent female characters in nonstereotypical ways: *Urid Hadha'l-Rajul* (*I Want This Man*), *al-Na'iba al-Muhtarama* (*The Honorable Lady Member of Parliament*), and *Ughiniyyat al-Mawt* (*Song of Death*), which is included here. In keeping with the dictates of social realism, al-Hakim wished to depict the opportunities for education and work that became increasingly available to women during the 1940s and 1950s. Although feminist and other critics have taken issue with aspects of his representation of women—arguing, for instance, that these characters are given to irrationality and often pursue domestic bliss more avidly than independence—the works in this collection explore the social, familial, and psychological demands with which Arab women contend and the conflicting roles they have traditionally assumed.

No play of al-Hakim's more powerfully captures the pressures of tradition on women—and on Egyptian society as a whole—than *Song of Death*, whose well-crafted structure and poignant, tragic tone have won it praise as one of the finest modern Arabic plays. An unsparing critique of brutal village customs and the tyranny of traditional gender roles, Song of Death takes as its subject the long-standing peasant tradition of blood revenge. For centuries, cycles of blood revenge were the undisputed law of the land for country folk in Egypt, and since the beginning of the twentieth century, governments have combated the deeply ingrained belief that the murder of a family member should be punished privately, not by the state's justice system. As a public prosecutor who had confronted this provincial mind-set directly, al-Hakim strongly believed that private vengeance was a barbaric and regressive custom—a tradition that had to end if society was to move forward. Song of Death was his attempt in dramatic form to address his professional and humanistic concerns about this destructive tradition.

Al-Hakim's play takes place in a peasant house in Upper Egypt, the region of the Nile Valley that stretches south of Cairo. Asakir, a widow, has spent seventeen years yearning for retribution for the death of her husband, murdered by a member of a rival family as part of a generations-long blood feud. As the play opens, she is awaiting the arrival of her son, Ilwan, who was sent away as a child and raised as a student at one of Cairo's oldest theology schools (housed in an ancient mosque), with the expectation that he will take the weapon with which his father was killed and exact vengeance. When Ilwan arrives and challenges the cycle of violence, maintaining that the law is more important, his refusal to meet traditional expectations precipitates an equally devastating tragedy, and Asakir must face the consequences of her commitment to retribution and family honor. Song of Death embeds its story of vengeance and loss in the images and remembered sounds of rural Egyptian life: a reference to walls painted in mud, the joyful trilling of women, ritual gestures.

Hard and single-minded, the figure of Asakir dominates the play. With "a memory that can never forget and a heart that cannot relent," she has put her implacable fantasy of revenge before maternal and other feelings. The events of the past have

shaped her view of the world, but the hardness to which she has given herself also reflects the social role that she, as woman and mother, has been asked to assume. The deliberately masculine name Asakir (which means "soldiers" in Arabic) indicates that although she is a woman, she is expected to act as a man. In peasant societies, such as the one depicted in the play, masculinity has historically signified strength and status; thus, sons have been valued more than daughters. This power imbalance forces women to act in conformity with masculine ways—to teach their sons to be "men" and to inspire their daughters to become more like men (by giving them ruthless-sounding names, for instance). Women in such communities are responsible for upholding the laws of their village and passing them down to their children. As Song of Death illustrates, women also play central roles in preserving and defending family honor.

But such hardening comes with a price. What makes Asakir such a richly dramatic figure is the conflict between her consuming desire for vengeance and the emotional bond that connects her, despite her struggles to escape it, to her son, Ilwan. Asakir is portrayed as both nurturing and controlling, but her excessive determination to take revenge for her husband's murder turns her into a tragic figure: her single-minded focus on killing drives all tenderness from her motherly love, leaving her with nothing but hatred on her mind and in her heart. By upholding the code that requires sons to avenge their fathers, she places the imperatives of the past over life in the present. In the play's climactic scene, as her desires pull her in opposite directions, Asakir confronts the grim logic of her vengeance in a growing spectacle of loss.

Song of Death delves deeply into the particularities of Egyptian rural life and exposes universal human flaws, such as excessive hatred, adherence to illogical traditions, and the blindness caused by anger and pride. Its themes are as relevant to our contemporary world as to al-Hakim's Egypt in 1950. Because of its poignant message—its insistence on the need to put an end to violence between nations and to the cycles of grievance that perpetuate this violence—it continues to be staged by Arab directors. The local and universal layers of *Song of Death* suggest why al-Hakim's name remains synonymous with modern Arab theater and why his concerns, vision, and tireless experimentation are still points of reference for emerging dramatic voices in the Arab world.   DINA AHMED AMIN

Song of Death[1]

CHARACTERS[2]

ASAKIR, a widowed peasant woman
MABRUKA, her sister-in-law
SIMEIDA, son of Mabruka
ILWAN, son of Asakir

[*A peasant hut in an Upper Egyptian village.*[3] ASAKIR *and* MABRUKA, *both dressed in black, are sitting near the entrance, with heads bowed in silence. Close by them a calf and a kid are seen eating herbage and dried clover. The whistle of a train is heard.*]

MABRUKA [*raising her head*]   There's the train.

ASAKIR [*without moving*]   Do you think he has come on it?

MABRUKA   Didn't he say he would, in his letter? Sheikh[4] Isnawi, the schoolteacher, read it out for us yesterday.

5   ASAKIR   Are you sure you've told no one at all that he's my son?

MABRUKA   Do you think I've gone mad? Your son Ilwan died when he was a mere child of two. He was drowned in the sluice of the waterwheel.[5] The whole village knows that.

ASAKIR   But *they* no longer believe it.

10   MABRUKA   Who are "they"? The Tahawis?

ASAKIR   Didn't your son Simeida tell you what he heard in the market the other day?

MABRUKA   No. What did he hear?

ASAKIR   He heard someone say to a group of people, "Either the Azizes have
15   no more men left among them or else they're concealing a man in order to take revenge, a man closer to the victim then his nephew Simeida." And who but a man's own son can be any closer than his nephew?

1. Translated by Mustafa Badawi; revised by Andrew Parkin and Mahmoud Manzalaoui.
2. The characters' names in this play, like most Arabic names, have specific meanings: *Asakir*, "army of soldiers"; *Mabruka*, "blessed"; *Simeida*, "stiff" or "stonelike"; *Ilwan*, "transcendent" or "sublime."
3. That is, a village in the less populous southern region of Egypt, up the Nile River from Cairo.
4. An honorary title given to teachers in provincial religious schools (and to graduates of al-Azhar University). The local schoolteacher reads the letter to Asakir and Mabruka because they are illiterate.
5. An irrigation device.

MABRUKA   Oh yes: Simeida told me about that. If it hadn't been for this
rumor he would never have been able to hold up his head in the village.

20 ASAKIR   Well, let them know now that the dead man's son is still alive. We've
no fear for him now that he's a grown man. I'm not the one who is afraid
now. It's them that fear keeps awake of a night. Hurry up, train, and bring
him soon. I've waited a long time—seventeen years, I've counted them
hour by hour. Seventeen whole years and I've milked them out of Time's
25 udders, drop after drop, with all the hard tugging you'd need if you were
milking a cow that's far gone in her age.

MABRUKA [listening to a far-off sound]   There's the train arrived in the station.
He'll find my son Simeida waiting to meet him.

ASAKIR [as if talking to herself]   That's right.

30 MABRUKA [turning to her]   What's the matter with you, Asakir? You're
trembling.

ASAKIR [as if to herself]   Simeida's song will tell me.

MABRUKA   Tell you?

ASAKIR   That he's come.

35 MABRUKA   Did you tell my son to sing as a sign that Ilwan was here?

ASAKIR   Yes, as soon as they set foot across the village bounds.

MABRUKA   Patience, Asakir. Be patient. The worst is over now.

ASAKIR   It's not fear nor weakness that I'm feeling now.

MABRUKA   The fearsome days have now gone. Gone forever, they are. I shan't
40 ever forget the day when you hid your son Ilwan—and he a mere child of
two then—hid him in the flour basket and carried him under cover of darkness out of the village. Took him all the way to Cairo, and gave him into the
care of that kinsman of yours, the flour merchant who kept shop in the
spice dealer's row near the mosque of our blessed Hussein.[6]

45 ASAKIR   Bring him up as a butcher, I said to him. Let him learn to use the
knife like a master.

MABRUKA   But he never did as you asked him.

ASAKIR   He did that! Soon as he was seven years old he placed him in a
butcher's shop. But run away, he did, some time later.

50 MABRUKA   And went into the Holy al-Azhar[7] as a student.

ASAKIR   That's it. When I visited him last year I saw him in his gown and
turban[8] looking most dignified. I said to him, "If only your father could
have seen you looking like that, he'd have been mighty proud." But they
didn't spare him to enjoy watching his son grow up.

55 MABRUKA   Wouldn't it have been better if he'd stayed on in the butcher's
shop?

ASAKIR   What makes you say that, Mabruka?

MABRUKA   I don't know. It's only a thought that came into my head.

ASKIR   I reckon I know your thought.

60 MABRUKA   What is it, then, Asakir?

6. That is, the ancient mosque and shrine of
Hussein (also spelled al-Husayn, ca. 629–
680), the grandson of the Prophet Muhammad, in the heart of old Cairo.
7. That is, Cairo's al-Azhar University; estab-

lished in 975, it is one of the oldest universities in the world and a leading center for the
study of Islam and the Arabic language.
8. Attire worn by students and graduates of al-
Azhar, highly respected as clerics and scholars.

ASAKIR   It grieves you to see my son in gown and turban while yours goes on
wearing his woolly skull cap and his smock.[9]

MABRUKA   By the memory of the dear departed, I give you my oath, nothing
of the kind was in my mind.

65   ASAKIR   Why then don't you like Ilwan to be at the Holy al-Azhar?

MABRUKA   I give you my oath, it isn't that I don't like it, it's just that I'm
afraid . . .

ASAKIR   Afraid?

MABRUKA   That he might not be such a master at wielding his knife.

70   ASAKIR   Set your mind at rest, Mabruka. When you see Ilwan now, a full-
grown man, you'll realize that he has the lean, strong-thewed arm of the
Aziz family.

MABRUKA   [listening to the train whistle]   The train's moving out of the station
now.

75   ASAKIR   Let it go where it will, so long as it's brought us Ilwan to force the
murderer's soul out of his body, and to leave him for the farm dogs in scattered gobbets of flesh.

MABRUKA   What if he hasn't come?

ASAKIR   Why do you say that, Mabruka?

80   MABRUKA   I don't know. Just a feeling I've got.

ASAKIR   What would stop him coming?

MABRUKA   What would drive him to leave Cairo and the city life and the
Holy al-Azhar and come to this—?

ASAKIR   This is where he was born, where blood is calling out to him.

85   MABRUKA   Our village is a long, long way away from Cairo! Can blood make
itself heard as far as the cities?

ASAKIR   Do you really think he hasn't come?

MABRUKA   I know no more about it than you do.

ASAKIR   And what about the letter that the schoolmaster read out to us?

90   MABRUKA   Don't you recall his words: "I hope to come if my circumstances
allow it." Who knows whether or not his circumstances have allowed it?

ASAKIR   Don't dampen my spirits, Mabruka. Don't dash my hope. I've just
heard the train whistle turning into trills[1] of joy in my heart, announcing
that the end of this long mourning is near. Ilwan not come? What would
95   become of me if that were true? And how much longer would I have to wait
then?

MABRUKA   The station isn't so far from here, nor the main road. If he'd
arrived, Simeida would be singing now.

ASAKIR   Perhaps they're taking their time, chatting. After all, they haven't
100   seen each other for more than three years . . . since your son was in Cairo
last during the Fair of the Blessed Hussein.[2]

MABRUKA   If he'd come my son's heart would have brimmed over with joy
and he'd have started his singing even before he'd reached the main road.

ASAKIR   Perhaps he's forgotten to sing.

105   MABRUKA   It's impossible: he can't forget.

9. That is, wearing attire typical of peasants.
1. High-pitched sounds traditionally made by
women to express joy on such happy occasions as weddings, pregnancy announce-
ments, and the births of children.
2. In the Islamic world, fairs are popular festivals in honor of venerated religious figures.

ASAKIR [*listening*]   I can hear no one singing.

MABRUKA [*listening*]   Nor I neither.

ASAKIR [*continuing to listen*]   There's no one singing, not even a shepherd
lad. There's not a single creature singing, not even the owl over in the
110   ruins. You're right, Mabruka. He hasn't come.

MABRUKA [*as if to herself*]   My heart tells me things.

ASAKIR   No, not yours—mine. Mine, that's as secret as the grave, as hard as
rock, is now beginning to tell me things.

MABRUKA   What things?

115   ASAKIR   Things that will happen.

MABRUKA   Do tell me.

ASAKIR [*listening intently*]   Hush! Listen, listen. Can you not hear, Mabruka?
Can you not hear?

MABRUKA   Simeida singing.

120   ASAKIR   The heavens be thanked for that!

[*They listen for a while to* SIMEIDA's *song, which grows increasingly clear.*]

SIMEIDA [*sings*]

> O my dear one,
> Your bitter voice accuses:
> Repentance and excuses
> Were all I ever gave!
125
> You reproached me then the more,
> And out of grief
> My clothes
> To shreds I tore.
> When they told me of your father,
130
> It was my silent shame
> Which set unmanly cheeks aflame,
> Where eyes ran dry
> And made a desert of my face.

ASAKIR   He's come, Ilwan is here! And now it's off with the shirt of my shame
135   and on with my garment of honor.

MABRUKA   And now we can hold the true rites[3] over the body of the dear
one—and may he rest in peace.

ASAKIR   And sacrifice to his spirit the kid and the calf.

MABRUKA   O joy! O happiness! [*Makes as though to give out a loud trill.*]

140   ASAKIR [*restrains her*]   Not now. Otherwise we'll be known to the world too
early.

MABRUKA   Your hours are numbered, Suweilam Tahawi![4]

[*A knock on the door.* ASAKIR *rushes to open it:* SIMEIDA *appears carrying
a bag.*]

SIMEIDA   I have brought you Sheikh Ilwan. [*Puts the bag on the floor and is
soon followed in by* ILWAN.]

ASAKIR [*with open arms*]   Ilwan, my son.

145   ILWAN [*kisses her head*]   Mother.

---

3. By village custom, a person killed in a
blood feud is not officially mourned until his
family has avenged his death.

4. Either the man or the son of the man who
killed Asakir's husband.

ASAKIR [to her son]   Say your greetings to your Aunt Mabruka.

ILWAN [turns to MABRUKA]   Are you well, Aunt Mabruka?

MABRUKA   You can see for yourself, Ilwan. You are our only hope now.

SIMEIDA   Let us go home now, Mother.

150 MABRUKA   Come. It's close now, Asakir—the hour of relief.

[MABRUKA and SIMEIDA go out.]

ASAKIR   You must be hungry, Ilwan. I've a bowl of sour milk.

ILWAN   Thank you, Mother. No, I'm not hungry. I had some hard-boiled eggs
and some barley cake on the train.

ASAKIR   You'll be thirsty then?

155 ILWAN   No, not thirsty either.

ASAKIR   Of course you haven't come here for food or drink. You've come to
eat of his flesh and drink of his blood.

ILWAN [as if in a trance]   I have come here to do something truly great,
Mother.

160 ASAKIR   I know, I know, my son. Wait till I bring you something: something
you've never set your eyes on before. [Rushes to an inner room where she
disappears for a while.]

ILWAN [casting a look around the room]   My eyes can still see animals and
their droppings in your houses. The dirty water jar, firewood, and dried
stalks of maize forming a shaky roof.

ASAKIR [emerges from the inner room holding a saddlebag which she lays before
165 her son]   Here. For seventeen years I have kept these things for you.

ILWAN [looks at the saddlebag without moving]   What is this?

ASAKIR   The saddlebag that your father's body was sent to me in, carried on
his donkey. In this pouch I found his severed head, and in the other one
the rest of his body, hacked to pieces. With his own knife they stabbed him
170 to death—the knife he was carrying, then they put knife and body in the
saddlebag. See, here is the knife. I left the blood on it until it's turned to
rust as you can see. As for the donkey that brought me the body of your
murdered father, tracing its steps back to this house by force of habit, with
its head bowed down, as if it was grieving over its master—I couldn't keep
175 it alive for you. It couldn't endure for all these years: it's died.

ILWAN   Who did this?

ASAKIR   Suweilam Tahawi.

ILWAN   How do you know?

ASAKIR   The whole village knows.

180 ILWAN   I know you've told me that. You've told that name to me over and over
again, whenever you came to visit me in Cairo. I was too young to think
then or to argue. But now my reason needs to be satisfied. What's the evidence? Did the police ever look into the crime?

ASAKIR   Look into the crime?

185 ILWAN   Yes. What did you say to the Public Prosecutor?

ASAKIR   Public Prosecutor? The shame of it! We say anything to the Public
Prosecutor? We the Azizes do that? Did even the Tahawis ever do that?

ILWAN   Didn't the Public Prosecutor ask you any questions?

ASAKIR   Of course. But we said we knew nothing about the business, that
190 we'd seen no corpse. Meantime we had buried your father in secret under
cover of darkness.

ILWAN [*as if addressing himself*]   So that we may exact requital with our own hands.

ASAKIR   With the selfsame knife that stabbed your father.

195 ILWAN   And the murderer?

ASAKIR   Alive and hearty. There's not a saint or a holy man in the neighborhood but whose shrine I visited. I held on to the railings of their sanctuary, uncovered my head and heaped dust from their ground over my hair,[5] and I prayed to them to beseech our God for me that He might prolong the

200   slayer's days until you, my son, should take his life—with your own hands

ILWAN   Are you sure, Mother, that he was the murderer?

ASAKIR   We've no enemies beside the Tahawis.

ILWAN   But how do you know it was Suweilam himself who did it?

ASAKIR   Because he believed it was your father who'd murdered his father.

205 ILWAN   And is that true? Did my father kill his father?

ASAKIR   God alone knows.

ILWAN   But what started this family feud in the first place?

ASAKIR   I don't know. Nobody knows. It's something far gone in the past. All that we know is that there's always been blood spilt between us.

210 ILWAN   The cause may well be that one of our calves happened to drink from a water-channel in a field that belonged to their ancestors!

ASAKIR   God alone knows. As for us mortals, all that we know is that between the Azizes and Tahawis rivers of blood have flowed.

ILWAN   Rivers that water neither crop nor fruit.

215 ASAKIR   Rivers that stopped flowing only with the death of your father. And that because of your tender age. Years then went past dry as the thirsty season, and people whispered lies and false rumors, while I was writhing in the flames of my hidden anger, waiting for this hour. And now the hour has come, so get up, son, and put out my fire and slake my thirst for the blood

220   of Suweilam Tahawi.

ILWAN   Has this Suweilam Tahawi got a son?

ASAKIR   Yes. Fourteen years old.

ILWAN   So I have no more than another four or five years to live.

ASAKIR   What is it you are saying?

225 ILWAN   . . . Only until he grows strong enough to do to me what I am supposed to do to his father.

ASAKIR   Do you fear for your life, Ilwan?

ILWAN   And what about you, Mother? Do you fear for my life?

ASAKIR   The Lord be my witness, how I fear for every hair on your head.

230 ILWAN   You really care about my life, Mother?

ASAKIR   Has my life any worth without yours? Or for that matter, the lives of all the Azizes? It's your life alone has made it possible for every one of us to live through the past seventeen years.

ILWAN [*bows his head*]   I see.

235 ASAKIR   How often we suffered shame and humiliation. But as soon as your image crossed our minds our energy would revive, our resolution would strengthen and we were united in the hope that we placed upon you.

ILWAN [*his head still bowed and as if talking to himself*]   You certainly need my life.

5. A traditional gesture of abasement and supplication.

240 ASAKIR Even your father's funeral waits for you, Ilwan. These sacrifices here
are ready for the slaughter. My lamentation which I've been choking down
in my throat all these years is waiting for you to set it free. My frock, which
I've kept myself from tearing open all that time, is waiting for you,[6] too.
Everything in our existence is dead. Stagnant. Looking to you to breathe
245 life into it.

ILWAN Is this how life is breathed into you?

ASAKIR Yes, Ilwan. Bring the appointed hour closer. Be quick, for we've been
waiting for it for so long.

ILWAN [in wonder] The appointed hour?

250 ASAKIR I've forgotten nothing. Even the stone to whet the rusty knife I've
brought for you and hidden in this room.

ILWAN But how am I to know this Suweilam? I've never set eyes on him in
the whole of my life.

ASAKIR Simeida will show you where to find him. He'll point him out to you.

255 ILWAN [looks at his clothes] Am I to commit this deed while I'm dressed in
this way?

ASAKIR Take off those clothes. I've a cloak that belonged to your father. I've
kept it for you. [She turns to go into the inner room.]

ILWAN [stops her] Just a minute, Mother. Why the hurry?

260 ASAKIR Every breath Suweilam draws while you are here is a gift which you
are granting to him.

ILWAN And what harm is there in that?

ASAKIR It's taken from our breaths; it's drawn out of our well-being. Against
our wishes we were forced to extend his life by as much as nearly brought
265 us to the grave. Look at your mother, Ilwan. I was a young woman when
your father died. But look what all those years have done to me. It is as if
they were forty years, not seventeen. The sap of my youth has dried up and
my bones have grown weak. All I have left is a memory that can never forget and a heart that cannot relent.

270 ILWAN [as if to himself] What a price it costs to avenge one's blood.

ASAKIR [uncomprehending] What did you say, Ilwan?

ILWAN I said that God the Mighty Avenger is merciful to us: He offers to
relive us of this burden without any cost to us.

ASAKIR [in a suspicious tone] What do you mean?

275 ILWAN Nothing, Mother, nothing.

ASAKIR [decisively] Take off those clothes. I'll bring you the cloak and
sharpen the knife for you myself.

ILWAN Isn't there a mosque nearby?

ASAKIR We've only a little chapel next to Sheikh Isnawi's schoolhouse.

280 ILWAN [moving] I'll go there and say my evening prayers.

ASAKIR At this hour?

ILWAN I think the sun is about to set.[7]

ASAKIR Do you want to be seen in the mosque by everyone in the village?

ILWAN That would be the best opportunity for my purpose.

285 ASAKIR [stares him in the face] Have you gone mad, Ilwan?

---

6. In Egyptian villages, the tearing of one's
outer garments is a ritualized expression of
extreme grief.
7. Every healthy adult Muslim is required to

pray five times daily—at dawn, at midday, in
late afternoon, at sunset, and at night before
retiring—and it is better to pray in a mosque
than alone.

ILWAN It's most important for me to meet the villagers. Haven't I just told you that I have come to do something truly great?

ASAKIR [*as if mocking him*] I shouldn't imagine you'll want to reveal to the village the reason for your coming here?

290 ILWAN It's essential to let them all hear what I have to tell.

ASAKIR Ilwan, my son! What is it that I hear you say? Are you serious? Are you in your right mind? What is it that you want to tell them?

ILWAN [*as if in a dream*] I'll tell them what I have come here to say. I have often thought about my village and its people, in spite of the long time I've
295 been away from it. There, at al-Azhar, when the classes were over, we—the students, that is—we'd gather together and read the newspapers. And we'd think of the places we'd come from. We were very homesick. And we often worried about when our people in the countryside would be able to live like human beings, in clean houses where they wouldn't share their meals with
300 animals. When the roofs of their houses would be something better than dry stalks of cotton and maize, and the walls painted with something better than mud and the droppings of their beasts. When the water pot would disappear and there would be clean piped water in the house. When electric lights would replace the oil lamp. Was that too much to ask for our
305 people? Don't they have the same rights as others?

ASAKIR [*as if uncomprehending*] What is all this you're saying, Ilwan?

ILWAN This is what the people of the village ought to know. And those of us who were educated in Cairo—it's our duty to make them see and realize their human rights. It shouldn't be difficult for them to achieve this aim: if
310 only they would unite, join hands, and co-operate. They ought to set up a council. Elect a council, that's it, from amongst themselves. And they could tax those who had money enough to pay. They'd form a team of able-bodied men to spend those long hours when there's nothing doing in making dykes and bridges and other constructive things. Not wasting time in
315 squabbles and feuds. Why, if they worked together like that, if they would only make the effort, we'd make this a model village. And it would soon be an example for all the other villages in the country to follow.

ASAKIR You're talking the language of books. You can keep that for later. For when you have your evening talk with Sheikh Muhammad Isnawi. He can
320 understand it—I can't. As for the present, there's something more important that we've to do, Ilwan.

ILWAN [*shocked*] What is it that's more important?

ASAKIR No. Don't go to the mosque to pray tonight. Else our plan might fail. Pray here tonight, if you wish to. Go and take off those clothes. I'll fetch water from the water pot for you to prepare for your prayers.[8] Put on the
325 cloak and help me sharpen the knife.

ILWAN [*his head bowed, whispers*] Your mercy, O God, Your favor and forgiveness!

ASAKIR What are you saying, Ilwan?

330 ILWAN [*raises his head*] I am saying that I have come here only to make you see and realize what life is, to bring you life.

ASAKIR And that's exactly what we've been waiting for patiently for all these long nights. For seventeen years all the Azizes have been dead, waiting for your return to bring life back to them.

8. In Islam, ritual washing before prayer is obligatory.

335 ILWAN [*whispers with his head bowed down*] God! What am I to do with
these people?

ASAKIR What is wrong with you, Ilwan? You keep bowing your head. Come
on. Get up. Don't waste any more time.

ILWAN [*raises his head and takes courage*] Mother, I will not kill.

340 ASAKIR [*tries to conceal her distress*] What do I hear?

ILWAN I will not kill.

ASAKIR [*in a rough voice*] The blood of your father!

ILWAN It's you yourselves who left it spilt and wasted by hiding the crime
from the government. It's up to the authorities to punish.

345 ASAKIR [*beside herself*] The blood of your father!

ILWAN My hand wasn't made to destroy a human being.

ASAKIR [*as if in a trance*] The blood of your father!

ILWAN [*alarmed at her condition*] Mother, Mother: what is the matter with
you?

350 ASAKIR [*as if she can see nobody in front of her*] The blood of your father!
Seventeen years. The blood of your father. Seventeen years . . . !

ILWAN Mother, calm yourself. Of course it's a shock to you. But you must
realize that I could never be an assassin and use my knife on a man.

ASAKIR [*whispers as if out of her mind*] Seventeen years . . . Vengeance for
355 your father's murder . . . Seventeen years . . .

ILWAN [*as if to himself*] Mother, I know that you've stood it patiently for so
long. If only this patience and endurance of yours were given up to a useful
cause you would perform miracles! But you must understand that I—

ASAKIR [*with a quaver in her throat*] The blood of your father!

360 ILWAN [*rushes towards her, alarmed*] Mother! Mother! Mother!

ASAKIR [*recovers awareness of her surroundings*] Who are you?

ILWAN Your son, Ilwan. Your son.

ASAKIR [*screams*] Son? *My* son? No, no! Never, never, never!

ILWAN [*astonished*] Mother!

365 ASAKIR I'm not your mother. I don't know you. No son has ever been born
out of my womb. No son have I ever given birth to.

ILWAN [*pleading*] Please, Mother! Try to understand that I—

ASAKIR Out of my house . . . God's curse be upon you to the Day of Judgment. Out of my house.

370 ILWAN Mother!

ASAKIR [*screams*] Out of my house . . . or else I'll ask the help of our men to
throw you out. We still have men. There are still men among the Azizes.
But you—you're not one of them. Out of my house with you.

375 ILWAN [*picks up his bag*] I'll go to the station and go back to where I came
from. And I'll pray to God that your disturbed soul may find peace, and that
I may see you in Cairo soon to explain my way of looking at things, in quiet,
far away from here. Goodbye, Mother.

[*He leaves. His mother remains motionless in her place. After a while,*
SIMEIDA *enters, first putting his head round the door, then gently pushing
it open.*]

SIMEIDA Was it you screaming, Aunt Asakir?

380 ASAKIR [*with determination: she is fully recovered now*] Come here, Simeida.

SIMEIDA [*looks round*] Where's Ilwan? Where's your son?

ASAKIR I have no son. I never bore a son.

SIMEIDA   What are you saying, Aunt Asakir?

ASAKIR   If I had a son he'd now be avenging his father's murder.

385 SIMEIDA   Where has he gone?

ASAKIR   To the station. On his way back to Cairo.

SIMEIDA   My mother was right. As soon as she saw him just now, she said, as
we were leaving, "That turbaned preacher will never kill Suweilam Tahawi."

ASAKIR   I wish my womb had been torn to shreds before it brought such a
390   son into the world!

SIMEIDA   Don't upset yourself, Aunt. There are still men among the Azizes.

ASAKIR   Our hope is now in you, Simeida.

SIMEIDA   A nephew can stand in for a son.

ASAKIR   But in this case the son's alive. It's his duty before anybody else, to
395   avenge the shedding of his father's blood. He's alive. Alive. He's about
amongst the living.

SIMEIDA   Just try to tell yourself that he's dead.

ASAKIR   I wish he had really died, drowned in the sluice of the waterwheel
when he was a child. We would then never have had to wait all those years,
400   writhing and roasting on the live coals of our pent-up anger, waiting to no
purpose. I wish he had truly died. We would have been able to live honor-
ably then, and not be wearing our garment of shame. But he is alive, and it
has been broadcast in the market places and in the whole neighborhood
that he is alive. Oh, the shame. The ignominy. The disgrace!

405 SIMEIDA   Aunt, don't be so upset.

ASAKIR   It's impossible not to be upset by a disgrace like this. Carrying such
a shame, life will be impossible. How can I go on living in this village now
that people know that I have a son like this. How many a mouth'll spit
whenever his name is mentioned. From all directions the cry will be heard:
410   "Cursed be the womb that brought him forth!" Yes, this womb [*striking her
belly hard and wildly*]. A curse on this womb. All the women of the village
will mock it: even the ugly, the dim-witted, the barren. This womb . . . this
womb . . . this womb.

SIMEIDA   [*tries to stop her*]   Aunt Asakir, don't punish yourself so!

415 ASAKIR   Fetch the knife, Simeida, fetch the knife, and rip it open.

SIMEIDA   Have you gone mad?

ASAKIR   [*screams*]   Simeida: are you a man?

SIMEIDA   [*looks at her intently*]   What is it you want?

ASAKIR   Stop your cousin's disgrace.

420 SIMEIDA   Ilwan's?

ASAKIR   And his mother's, your Aunt Asakir's. Prevent her shame.

SIMEIDA   How?

ASAKIR   [*takes the knife from the saddle bag*]   Kill him with this knife.

SIMEIDA   Kill who?

425 ASAKIR   Ilwan. Dig this knife into his heart.

SIMEIDA   I kill Ilwan? Your son?

ASAKIR   Yes. Kill him. Send him to join the dead.

SIMEIDA   Pull yourself together, Aunt.

ASAKIR   Do this, Simeida . . . for my sake and for his!

430 SIMEIDA   For his sake!

ASAKIR   Yes. Better for him and better for me that it should be said he was
killed, than for folk to say that he fled from his duty of avenging his father's
murder.

SIMEIDA   My own cousin!

435 ASAKIR   If you're a man, Simeida, you must never let him bring shame upon
the Azizes. Never again will you be able to carry yourself like a man. Men
will whisper and laugh behind their hands at you and point at you in the
marketplace, and say: "There goes no more than a woman and one who's
given shelter to another mere woman, at that."

440 SIMEIDA   [to himself]   A woman!

ASAKIR   If the Tahawis had such a son they'd never have let him live for an
hour.

SIMEIDA   [to himself]   A woman—giving shelter to another woman!

ASAKIR   Yes, that's so; that'll be you if you allow him to behave as he means
445 to.

SIMEIDA   [stretches out his hand resolutely]   Give me the knife.

ASAKIR   [hands him the knife]   Here it is. But wait till I wash the dried blood
and the rust off its blade.

SIMEIDA   [impatiently]   Give it to me, before he slips away by the evening
450 train.

ASAKIR   [gives him the knife eagerly and forcefully]   Take it. Let his blood
wash away the blood of his father that's dried upon the blade.

SIMEIDA   [goes off with the knife]   If I manage to kill him, you'll at hear my
voice raised in song at the outskirts of the village, Aunt.

[Exit quickly. ASAKIR remains alone, fixed to the spot like a statue, gazing
motionless and absently. After a while, MABRUKA appears, carrying a
water pitcher on her head.]

455 MABRUKA   [puts down the pitcher]   I've brought some dried fish for Sheikh
Ilwan.

ASAKIR   [turns to her slowly]   May your life be longer than his,[9] Mabruka.

MABRUKA   Who are you talking about?

ASAKIR   Ilwan.

460 MABRUKA   Your son?

ASAKIR   He's no longer mine; he belongs to the dust.

MABRUKA   What are you saying, Asakir? I left him with you only a moment
ago. Where is he?

ASAKIR   Gone to the station on his way back to where he came from. Giving
465 his back to the duty of avenging his father's murder.

MABRUKA   [her head bowed down]   Just as my heart has been telling me.

ASAKIR   Your prophecy has come true, Mabruka.

MABRUKA   If only he had never come.

ASAKIR   Seventeen years we've been waiting.

470 MABRUKA   Every year you used to say, "He's growing." You measured him by
the handspan as if he were a shoot of maize. But then, when he grew tall
and his cob was ripe, you stripped him, only to find that there was no grain
on the cob.

ASAKIR   It wouldn't have been such a disaster if he were no more than a bare
475 cob. We never expected any material gain through him. We expected him
to give us back our dignity—that was all. How proud I was of him, Mabruka,
how often I boasted about him to you. I thought I'd brought forth the son
who'd cleanse the stain off the honor of the family. And how has he turned

9. According to funeral etiquette throughout   deceased family; the customary response is
the Arab world, the blessing "May you live   "May your life be longer than his."
long after the departed one" is directed to the

out now? The very son I've given birth to, the son I took great care to hide
480 like a treasure in a crock of clay—he's no more than a stain on our tree, like
a blight overtaking a cotton plant. God's mercy be on your soul, my husband: they spilt your blood and it has not been avenged. I've given you a
son who brings comfort to your enemies and makes them gloat.

MABRUKA   Oh shame, shame on the Azizes!

485 ASAKIR   If he stays alive. But before long he'll be buried in the earth.

MABRUKA   [*turns round suddenly*]   Where's Simeida?

       [*The whistling of a train is heard.*]

ASAKIR   [*listening intently*]   Hush! There's the evening train entering the
station.

MABRUKA   Asakir, where's Simeida?

490 ASAKIR   [*still listening intently*]   Be quiet. Now, at this instant, at this very
instant.

MABRUKA   [*astonished*]   What happens at this instant?

ASAKIR   [*as if to herself*]   Do you think the train has carried him off? Or has
he been carried off by—

495 MABRUKA   If he's gone to the station, as you say, he must have got on the
train. All these curses you are heaping on his head will do no good.

ASAKIR   Do you really think he has got on the train?

MABRUKA   What could have stopped him?

ASAKIR   [*slipping out the answer*]   Simeida!

500 MABRUKA   Simeida? Did he go after him to stop him leaving?

ASAKIR   Yes.

MABRUKA   When did he go?

ASAKIR   A short while before you came.

MABRUKA   I shouldn't think he could have overtaken him.

505 ASAKIR   [*sighs in relief*]   Do you really think so?

MABRUKA   Unless he ran very fast.

       [*The train whistle is heard again.*]

ASAKIR   [*listens intently*]   There, the train is leaving the station.

MABRUKA   [*stares at her*]   What's wrong with you, Asakir? Why have you gone
so pale?

510 ASAKIR   What does your heart tell you, Mabruka?

MABRUKA   It tells me that he has gone.

ASAKIR   Gone. Gone—where?

MABRUKA   Where he came from.

ASAKIR   What do you mean?

515 MABRUKA   [*watches her*]   Why is your breast heaving like that?

ASAKIR   [*in a whisper, her eyes wandering*]   Gone where he came from!

MABRUKA   Do you still hope for some good from him?

ASAKIR   No.

MABRUKA   You must think of him as if he'd never been.

520 ASAKIR   [*as if to herself*]   Yes. His death is less shameful than his life.

MABRUKA   And thank God that he's far away.

ASAKIR   [*to herself*]   Is he on the train now?

MABRUKA   Who knows? Perhaps Simeida was able to catch him up and persuade him not to go: perhaps he'll bring him back now.

525 ASAKIR   [*as if dreaming*]   Bring him back now?

MABRUKA   Why not? If Simeida ran really fast he wouldn't have missed the
   train.
ASAKIR [*whispers*]   . . . Was able to catch him up . . .
MABRUKA   And it may not be long before we see them coming back again
530   together.
ASAKIR [*to herself*]   No. This time Simeida will be coming alone.
MABRUKA [*watches her anxiously*]   Your face, Asakir: it fills me with terror.
ASAKIR [*listens intently*]   Hush! Listen! Listen! Can't you hear anything?
MABRUKA   No. What do you want me to hear?
535 ASAKIR   Singing.
MABRUKA   No, I cannot hear any singing.
ASAKIR [*with relief*]   Nor can I.
MABRUKA   Did Simeida tell you he was going to sing?
ASAKIR [*to herself, anxiously*]   Perhaps he hasn't reached the edge of the vil-
540   lage yet.
MABRUKA   I should imagine he has, by now.
ASAKIR [*breathing more freely*]   And he is not singing!
MABRUKA   Now the blood has come back to your cheeks.
ASAKIR [*whispers*]   He hasn't caught him up.
545 MABRUKA   You'd rather he didn't come back, Asakir, wouldn't you? You'd
   rather the train carried him away from this village. So would I. I'd much
   rather he returned to his Cairo, to his preachers and the other students.
   He doesn't belong to us, nor we to him. He's done well to leave us so soon,
   before the people of the village could meet him and get to know what we
550   know about him. [ASAKIR *listens to a distant sound.*] You're not listening to
   me, Asakir. Don't you think I'm right?
ASAKIR [*in a rough, alarmed voice*]   No, no, I can't hear anything!
MABRUKA [*listens*]   It is Simeida singing. [*Turns, alarmed, to* ASAKIR, *whose
   eyes have glazed over.*] Asakir! Asakir! What's wrong? You scare me!
SIMEIDA [*outside, sings*]

555   *O my dear one,*
                          Your bitter voice accuses:
                          Repentance and excuses
                          Were all I ever gave!
                          You reproached me then the more,
560   *And out of grief*
                          My clothes
                          To shreds I tore.
                          When they told me of your father,
                          It was my silent shame
565   *Which set unmanly cheeks aflame,*
                          Where eyes ran dry
                          And made a desert of my face.

ASAKIR [*pulls herself together, to stop herself from collapsing, but lets slip a faint
   choking cry like a death rattle*]   My son!

                              Curtain.

SAMUEL BECKETT

1906–1989

THE career of Samuel Beckett, one of the modern period's most influential dramatists, bridges the most important artistic currents of the early and late twentieth century. A member of the novelist James Joyce's literary circle in Paris during the late 1920s and early 1930s, Beckett was one of the last of the high modernists, and his drama and fiction mark the twilight of a movement that produced such works as Joyce's *Ulysses* and T. S. Eliot's *The Waste Land* (both published in 1922). A writer who lived in France most of his life (and who often composed in French), he also continued a tradition of modern Irish playwriting that flourished in the plays of William Butler Yeats and John Millington Synge. Even as they are rooted in the past, however, Beckett's works opened paths for later twentieth-century writers. His trailblazing is particularly evident in the theater, whose boundaries Beckett's plays extended in radically individual ways. WAITING FOR GODOT, which premiered in Paris in 1953 and became a symbol of the crisis of meaning in post–World War II Europe, stands as the landmark play of contemporary drama. With its drama of nonaction announcing the exhaustion of traditional dramatic structures, *Waiting for Godot*—like Beckett's other plays—inaugurated new theatrical possibilities for dramatists as diverse

as HAROLD PINTER, Sam Shepard, ATHOL FUGARD, and CARYL CHURCHILL.

Samuel Barclay Beckett was born in 1906 to an affluent Protestant family who lived in the Dublin suburb of Foxrock. His date of birth is listed on his birth certificate as May 13, though he was actually born on April 13 (Beckett relished the fact that this date coincided not only with Friday the thirteenth but also with Good Friday). Beckett was educated in Portora Royal School in County Fermanagh, the alma mater of his fellow Irish writer OSCAR WILDE, and Trinity College, Dublin, where he excelled as a student while studying Dante as well as English and French literature. Upon graduation, Beckett taught French in Belfast for two terms; he then was chosen to represent Trinity as *lecteur* in English at the Ecole Normale Supérieure in Paris, and he began this two-year position in 1928. It was in Paris that Beckett met Joyce, who was at work on his final novel, *Finnegans Wake* (1939), and who became a powerful influence on the younger Irishman. Beckett's own career as a writer was launched with an essay on Joyce's work (published in 1929 as the lead essay in a collection of essays on *Finnegans Wake,* then known as *Work in Progress*) and a poetic parody of the seventeenth-century French philosopher Descartes titled *Whoroscope*, which was published in 1930. In 1930, Beckett also wrote a study of Marcel Proust, the French author whose novel *Remembrance of Things Past* (1913–27) explores questions of time, memory, and human consciousness that would prove central to Beckett's later writing.

After completing his term as *lecteur*, Beckett spent seven years living in Dublin, Paris, and London before returning to France for good in 1937. In addition to *Proust*, which appeared in 1931, these years saw the publication of a collection of short stories, *More Kicks Than Pricks* (1934), and the novel *Murphy* (1938). Twenty years after the end of World War I, war was on the horizon again; and when Germany invaded France in 1940 Beckett joined the French Resistance, typing and translating information concerning German troop movements. As a result of his activities he was forced to flee Paris in 1942; he spent the rest of the war in hiding in Roussillon, in the Vichy-controlled south of France, where he wrote the novel *Watt* (published in 1953).

The period immediately after World War II was, for Beckett, a time of enormous creativity. In fiction, Beckett wrote a trilogy that helped revolutionize the novel form: *Molloy* (1951), *Malone Dies* (1951), and *The Unnamable* (1953). Composed originally in French, then translated (primarily by Beckett) into English, these novels establish deeply self-referential narrative worlds; they explore the limits of fiction, as consciousness engages in an increasingly urgent struggle with the language in which it seeks to articulate itself. It was in part to escape the constrictions of language in these novels that Beckett turned to the stage. In 1948–49, between completing the second and third novels in his trilogy, Beckett wrote *En attendant Godot*—soon to be translated by the author himself as *Waiting for Godot*—"as a relaxation, to get away from the awful prose I was writing at the time." It was not his first play. *Eleuthéria*, a drawing room play that was written in January 1947 but never published or produced during Beckett's lifetime, gave little indication of what he would achieve less than two years later. When *Godot* opened at the 230-seat Théâtre de Babylone in Paris on January 5, 1953, audiences were confronted by a radically new

The cast and set of the original 1953 production of *Waiting for Godot* at the Théâtre de Babylone. From left to right, Jean Martin as Lucky, Lucien Raimbourg as Vladimir, Pierre Latour as Estragon, and Roger Blin (the director of the production) as Pozzo.

conception of drama. Over the course of two acts that mix vaudeville routines with metaphysical speculation, two tramps wait on a country road for a figure—referred to as Godot—who never arrives. *Waiting for Godot,* which ran for more than 100 performances, became an immediate cause célèbre, and critics struggled to come to terms with its reduced but undeniably powerful dramatic vision. Beckett's "tragicomedy" was soon produced in Berlin (1953), London (1955), and Miami (the United States premiere, 1956); in the decades since, it has received theatrical productions all over the world.

In the plays that followed *Godot,* Beckett continued his theatrical innovations as he explored the human predicament. The action of *Endgame* (1957), one of Beckett's most bleakly comic plays, is restricted to a room set against a postapocalyptic landscape; its characters, positioned like pieces in the terminal stage of a chess match, play out their diminished existence within a world that is winding down. *Krapp's Last Tape* (1958) explores the existence of the individual in time as its lone protagonist plays the recorded voices of his earlier selves. In *Happy Days* (1961), a woman buried in a mound up to her waist—then neck—plays with the objects and words that are all that is left of her world. *Play* (1963) offers one of Beckett's most arresting stage images: three characters, entombed up to their necks in urns, recount the details of a love triangle in alternating confessional fragments. In the late 1950s and early 1960s, he also wrote several plays for radio—including *All That Fall,* which was broadcast by the British Broadcasting Company in 1957—that allowed him to experiment with the staging of disembodied voices.

Following the principle that less is more, Beckett's drama from *Godot* to *Play* is increasingly minimalistic, with its characters progressively immobilized and its dialogue transformed into interiorized monologues. Through that process, this drama laid the foundation for his remarkable plays of the 1970s and 1980s, where character and setting are more radically reduced and even the human body is subject to fragmentation. The protagonist of

Not I (1972) is a mouth: illuminated at a height of eight feet above the stage floor, it narrates the disconnected pieces of a life that it refuses to acknowledge as its own. A companion play, *That Time* (1976), features a suspended head listening to the voices of intersecting memories. Inhabiting an increasingly spectral space, the figures who people these and other late Beckett plays—*Footfalls* (1976), *Rockaby* (1981), *Ohio Impromptu* (1981), and *What Where* (1983), to name some of the most prominent—encounter the voices of their own ghosted lives within a field of emptiness and silence. This deepening minimalism also characterizes Beckett's late plays for television, a medium whose dramatic possibilities first interested him in the 1960s. His television plays of the 1970s and 1980s—including *Ghost Trio* (1977), . . . *but the clouds . . .* (1977), and *Nacht und Träume* (1983)—exploit the medium's technical possibilities in order to achieve unearthly, and deeply lyrical, visual landscapes. By the 1970s, Beckett's dramatic writing—and his continuing work in fiction—had garnered an international reputation; he received the Nobel Prize in Literature in 1969, and he was revered as one of the greatest living writers until his death in 1989. Since then, his plays have continued to be produced around the world.

Waiting for Godot, the play that launched Beckett's career in the theater, reflects the intellectual and artistic climate of a Europe still recovering from the devastation of World War II. In the aftermath of the war's unprecedented horrors, a number of Continental dramatists rejected dramatic coherence and logic and the centuries-old tradition of rationality on which they stood. In 1961 the critic Martin Esslin coined the influential phrase "Theater of the Absurd" to describe the drama of Beckett, Eugène Ionesco, Jean Genet, and others. Philosophically akin to the writings of Albert Camus, Jean-Paul Sartre, and other existential philosophers who were writing about human existence in a world without meaning, the Theater of the Absurd, according to Esslin, sought to convey this human condition in nontraditional dramatic forms. In *The Myth of Sisyphus* (1942), Albert Camus wrote:

A world that can be explained by reasoning, however faulty, is a familiar world. But in a universe that is suddenly deprived of illusions and of light, man feels a stranger. His is an irremediable exile, because he is deprived of memories of a lost homeland as much as he lacks the hope of a promised land to come. This divorce between man and his life, the actor and his setting, truly constitutes the feeling of Absurdity.

Playing out the implications of Camus' theatrical metaphor, Beckett dismantles the elements, or meaning structures, that have sustained and defined dramatic literature. In place of a plot that might organize onstage incidents in relation to each other and that generates movement toward a conclusion, *Waiting for Godot* is organized around activities—pacing, speaking, remembering, falling down— that refuse to cohere into a beginning, middle, and end. Instead of presenting dramatic action, Beckett dramatizes the condition of waiting, a quintessential

nonaction that depends on forces and events beyond the acting subject. Time, for its part, loses what claim it has to linearity and becomes disconnected and unknowable. The amount of time that elapses between acts 1 and 2 of *Godot* remains mysterious: the latter act seems to take place the next day, but the lone onstage tree has sprouted leaves—a change that suggests a longer temporal span—and neither Vladimir (Didi) nor Estragon (Gogo), the play's protagonists, can determine how much time has passed. The play's minimalist setting—"A country road. A tree."—is equally indeterminate. Unlike the coherent settings of such modern dramatists as HENRIK IBSEN or GEORGE BERNARD SHAW, Beckett's setting is a kind of nonplace. Uncongenial, not humanized in any way, it is obviously a stage, and an empty one at that. The world beyond the stage is even more frightening and unknown. The characters make references to more idyllic times and places—climbing the Eiffel Tower in the 1890s, grape harvesting near the Rhône—but it is barely conceivable that these realms could be

The second act of *Waiting for Godot* in the 1961 Paris Odeon production. The tree was designed by Beckett's friend, the Italian sculptor Alberto Giacometti.

continuous with the inert, radically reduced world the text describes.

Like all of Beckett's characters, Vladimir and Estragon try to understand this world and to come to terms with their own being (or nonbeing) as its inhabitants. Waiting for a figure whose arrival might give meaning to their lives, the two ponder their condition while devising strategies to pass the time. It is worth noting, in this regard, that the play's original French title—*En attendant Godot*—translates into English more accurately as "While waiting for Godot," a participial phrase that shifts attention from the act of waiting to what one does to kill time during that time of waiting. Didi and Gogo develop routines—putting on boots, engaging in crosstalk "canters," even (they fantasize) hanging themselves—that provide distractions from the tedium of waiting. Much of the crosstalk and many of the routines that these tramps devise recall vaudeville and music hall entertainment, clown performances, and the silent films of Charlie Chaplin; indeed, the many visual gags (pants falling down, pratfalls, exchanges of hats) of *Waiting for Godot* help explain why this play has attracted many of the theater's finest comic actors. But there is no mistaking either the urgency of the characters' attempts to distract themselves through such activities or the high stakes for these figures whose very reality and purpose elude their grasp. As Estragon says to Vladimir, "We always find something, eh Didi, to give us the impression we exist?" The absurdity of their predicament and the meaninglessness of their existence repeatedly interrupt their attempts at play, particularly at those times when language gives way to silence. In such moments, as Beckett wrote in his study of Proust, "the boredom of living is replaced by the suffering of being." After one particularly long silence, Vladimir's anguish is undisguisable: "Say something! . . . Say anything at all!"

The two tramps' greatest distraction in each of the two acts is the arrival and departure of Pozzo and Lucky, whose master-slave relationship is reflected in the rope that connects them. Pozzo, a former landowner, seeks to dominate the stage and those around him with oratorical declamations and physical assertions of power. The ironically named Lucky, his servant,

carries his bags like a packhorse and submits to Pozzo's abuse. Lucky remains silent until commanded to "think" near the end of the first act, at which point he delivers a disjointed monologue consisting of quasi-philosophical and quasi-theological discourse, arcane and invented references, and sexual/scatological wordplay. This monologue, which teases the audience with fragmentary structures and half-meanings amid its barrage of apparent nonsense, offers a mock-academic portrayal of an intellectual tradition whose religious and rational frameworks have imploded. The very notion of an originative thinking subject is undermined by Lucky's performance. His torrent of words issues forth—involuntarily, it seems—like water from a faucet, and it is turned off just as mechanically when Vladimir wrestles away his hat.

Pozzo and Lucky cross the stage in each act, moving on a linear course between unknown points. In this regard, they differ from Vladimir and Estragon, who return to the same point each evening, who mark the boundaries of their familiar space by marking the edges of the stage, and whose existence is one of familiarities and recurrences. Pozzo and Lucky undergo catastrophic changes between acts—Pozzo becomes blind, and Lucky loses the ability to speak—while the two tramps seem largely unchanged. Like the German drinking song that Vladimir sings to open it—in which a dog's death is recounted in an endlessly repeating narrative—the play's second act recapitulates many of the situations, actions, and changes of the first act. At the same time, it is not an exact repetition. The scholar Vivian Mercier may have characterized *Godot*, famously, as "a play in which nothing happens, twice," but the shape and feel of nothing assume different forms in the two acts. The second act is noticeably darker than the first, the comic efforts of its central figures more strained. Time for Didi and Gogo is a process of diminishment, in which "lessness" (to borrow a title from one of Beckett's late prose pieces) makes itself felt with increasing force. The carrot of act 1 is gone in act 2. Even memory seems to weaken between acts. The two characters labor to remember what happened in act 1, and the uncertainty that they confront renders their lives even more out of their control.

And what about Godot, the object of their waiting? Scholars have speculated on the origins of this name—Godeau is the name of an absent character in a Balzac novel, and *godillot* and *godasse* are French slang terms for "boot"—but whatever echoes the name may carry, the identity of this figure remains, in the end, unknowable. A frequent assumption by spectators, readers, and critics is that Godot represents the Christian God and that his absence marks the twentieth-century historical moment when the Age of Faith had passed and the idea of God no longer served, in the minds of leading artists and intellectuals, as the foundation of moral order. The play is filled, to be sure, with Christian references and allusions: Didi and Gogo speak of the two thieves who were crucified on either side of Jesus, and references to crucifixion, salvation, and other Christian motifs occur throughout. But the name "Godot" is not linguistically identical with "God"; and as Beckett himself noted, this resemblance is wholly absent from the text in

Patrick Stewart (left) as Vladimir and Ian McKellen as Estragon in the 2009 production of *Waiting for Godot* at the Theatre Royal Haymarket (London), directed by Sean Mathias.

French, the play's original language. Beckett also said that if he knew who Godot was, he would have said so in the play. In the absence of such direct identification, we can conclude little more than the following: Godot is that for which Didi and Gogo wait, the absent promise on which they pin their desires for meaningfulness and purpose. Does he really exist? Though his repeated failure to arrive may suggest that he doesn't, the entrance of a boy who brings a message from him at the end of each act undermines even this potential certainty. Beckett once stated, not surprisingly, that his favorite word was "perhaps."

Against their uncertainty and disappointment, the dignity of these two tramps lies in their insistence on keeping their appointment and their refusal to succumb to despair, close though they may come to it. They also have the presence of each other and their shared familiarity, which keeps them together even though they ask themselves, in moments of weariness, whether they should part. Finally, they have the consolation of language, which finds poetry in the most painful of recognitions: "Astride of a grave and a difficult birth. Down in the hole, lingeringly, the grave-digger puts on the forceps. We have time to grow old. The air is full of our cries." In its gritty lyricism and daringly innovative use of the stage, this most original of plays offers a theatrically rich portrayal of boredom, anguish, hope, and resiliency. In urging his London audience to see *Waiting for Godot,* Harold Hobson, one of the play's first English reviewers, captured its haunting power for a generation that had experienced nothing like it: "At the worst you will discover a curiosity, a four-leaved clover, a black tulip; at the best, something that will securely lodge in a corner of your mind for as long as you live."   S.G.

Waiting for Godot
A Tragicomedy in Two Acts[1]

CHARACTERS

ESTRAGON	POZZO
VLADIMIR	A BOY
LUCKY	

Act 1

A country road. A tree.
Evening.

> [ESTRAGON, *sitting on a low mound, is trying to take off his boot. He pulls at it with both hands, panting. He gives up, exhausted, rests, tries again. As before.*]
>
> [*Enter* VLADIMIR.]

ESTRAGON [*giving up again*]   Nothing to be done.
VLADIMIR [*advancing with short, stiff strides, legs wide apart*]   I'm beginning to come round to that opinion. All my life I've tried to put it from me, saying,

---

1. Translated from the original French text by the author.

Vladimir, be reasonable, you haven't yet tried everything. And I resumed the
5   struggle. [*He broods, musing on the struggle. Turning to* ESTRAGON.] So there
you are again.

ESTRAGON   Am I?

VLADIMIR   I'm glad to see you back. I thought you were gone for ever.

ESTRAGON   Me too.

10 VLADIMIR   Together again at last! We'll have to celebrate this. But how? [*He
reflects.*] Get up till I embrace you.

ESTRAGON [*irritably*]   Not now, not now.

VLADIMIR [*hurt, coldly*]   May one enquire where His Highness spent the night?

15 ESTRAGON   In a ditch.

VLADIMIR [*admiringly*]   A ditch! Where?

ESTRAGON [*without gesture*]   Over there.

VLADIMIR   And they didn't beat you?

ESTRAGON   Beat me? Certainly they beat me.

20 VLADIMIR   The same lot as usual?

ESTRAGON   The same? I don't know.

VLADIMIR   When I think of it . . . all these years . . . but for me . . . where
would you be . . . [*Decisively*] You'd be nothing more than a little heap of
bones at the present minute, no doubt about it.

25 ESTRAGON   And what of it?

VLADIMIR [*gloomily*]   It's too much for one man. [*Pause. Cheerfully.*] On the
other hand what's the good of losing heart now, that's what I say. We should
have thought of it a million years ago, in the nineties.[2]

ESTRAGON   Ah stop blathering and help me off with this bloody thing.

30 VLADIMIR   Hand in hand from the top of the Eiffel Tower, among the first.
We were respectable in those days. Now it's too late. They wouldn't even let
us up. [ESTRAGON *tears at his boot.*] What are you doing?

ESTRAGON   Taking off my boot. Did that never happen to you?

VLADIMIR   Boots must be taken off every day, I'm tired telling you that. Why
35   don't you listen to me?

ESTRAGON [*feebly*]   Help me!

VLADIMIR   It hurts?

ESTRAGON [*angrily*]   Hurts! He wants to know if it hurts!

VLADIMIR [*angrily*]   No one ever suffers but you. I don't count. I'd like to
40   hear what you'd say if you had what I have.

ESTRAGON   It hurts?

VLADIMIR [*angrily*]   Hurts! He wants to know if it hurts!

ESTRAGON [*pointing*]   You might button it all the same.

VLADIMIR [*stooping*]   True. [*He buttons his fly.*] Never neglect the little things
45   of life.

ESTRAGON   What do you expect, you always wait till the last moment.

VLADIMIR [*musingly*]   The last moment . . . [*He meditates.*] Hope deferred
maketh the something sick, who said that?[3]

ESTRAGON   Why don't you help me?

50 VLADIMIR   Sometimes I feel it coming all the same. Then I go all queer. [*He
takes off his hat, peers inside it, feels about inside it, shakes it, puts it on*

---

2. That is, the 1890s.

3. "Hope deferred maketh the heart sick: but
when the desire cometh, it is a tree of life"
(Proverbs 13.12).

again.] How shall I say? Relieved and at the same time . . . [*He searches for the word.*] . . . appalled. [*With emphasis*] AP-PALLED. [*He takes off his hat again, peers inside it.*] Funny. [*He knocks on the crown as though to dislodge a foreign body, peers into it again, puts it on again.*] Nothing to be done. [ESTRAGON *with a supreme effort succeeds in pulling off his boot. He peers inside it, feels about inside it, turns it upside down, shakes it, looks on the ground to see if anything has fallen out, finds nothing, feels inside it again,*
55 *staring sightlessly before him.*] Well?

ESTRAGON   Nothing.

VLADIMIR   Show.

ESTRAGON   There's nothing to show.

VLADIMIR   Try and put it on again.

60 ESTRAGON [*examining his foot*]   I'll air it for a bit.

VLADIMIR   There's man all over for you, blaming on his boots the faults of his feet. [*He takes off his hat again, peers inside it, feels about inside it, knocks on the crown, blows into it, puts it on again.*] This is getting alarming. [*Silence. Vladimir deep in thought, Estragon pulling at his toes.*] One of the thieves
65 was saved.[4] [*Pause*] It's a reasonable percentage. [*Pause*] Gogo.

ESTRAGON   What?

VLADIMIR   Suppose we repented.

ESTRAGON   Repented what?

VLADIMIR   Oh . . . [*He reflects.*] We wouldn't have to go into the details.

70 ESTRAGON   Our being born?

[VLADIMIR *breaks into a hearty laugh which he immediately stifles, his hand pressed to his pubis, his face contorted.*]

VLADIMIR   One daren't even laugh any more.

ESTRAGON   Dreadful privation.

VLADIMIR   Merely smile. [*He smiles suddenly from ear to ear, keeps smiling, ceases as suddenly.*] It's not the same thing. Nothing to be done. [*Pause*]
75 Gogo.

ESTRAGON [*irritably*]   What is it?

VLADIMIR   Did you ever read the Bible?

ESTRAGON   The Bible . . . [*He reflects.*] I must have taken a look at it.

VLADIMIR   Do you remember the Gospels?

80 ESTRAGON   I remember the maps of the Holy Land. Coloured they were. Very pretty. The Dead Sea[5] was pale blue. The very look of it made me thirsty. That's where we'll go, I used to say, that's where we'll go for our honeymoon. We'll swim. We'll be happy.

VLADIMIR   You should have been a poet.

85 ESTRAGON   I was. [*Gesture towards his rags*] Isn't that obvious?

[*Silence.*]

VLADIMIR   Where was I . . . How's your foot?

ESTRAGON   Swelling visibly.

VLADIMIR   Ah yes, the two thieves. Do you remember the story?

---

4. That is, one of the two thieves crucified at the same time as Jesus. One of the Gospels describes one thief railing at him and the other asking to be remembered in heaven. To the second thief Jesus replied, "Verily I say unto thee, today shalt thou be with me in paradise" (Luke 23.43).

5. A salt lake, about 45 miles long and up to 10 miles wide, on the boundary between Israel and Jordan.

ESTRAGON No.

90 VLADIMIR Shall I tell it to you?

ESTRAGON No.

VLADIMIR It'll pass the time. [*Pause*] Two thieves, crucified at the same time as our Saviour. One—

ESTRAGON Our what?

95 VLADIMIR Our Saviour. Two thieves. One is supposed to have been saved and the other . . . [*He searches for the contrary of saved.*] . . . damned.

ESTRAGON Saved from what?

VLADIMIR Hell.

ESTRAGON I'm going.

[*He does not move.*]

100 VLADIMIR And yet . . . [*Pause*] . . . how is it—this is not boring you I hope— how is it that of the four Evangelists only one speaks of a thief being saved. The four of them were there—or thereabouts—and only one speaks of a thief being saved. [*Pause*] Come on, Gogo, return the ball, can't you, once in a way?

105 ESTRAGON [*with exaggerated enthusiasm*] I find this really most extraordinarily interesting.

VLADIMIR One out of four. Of the other three two don't mention any thieves at all and the third says that both of them abused him.[6]

ESTRAGON Who?

110 VLADIMIR What?

ESTRAGON What's all this about? Abused who?

VLADIMIR The Saviour.

ESTRAGON Why?

VLADIMIR Because he wouldn't save them.

115 ESTRAGON From hell?

VLADIMIR Imbecile! From death.

ESTRAGON I thought you said hell.

VLADIMIR From death, from death.

ESTRAGON Well what of it?

120 VLADIMIR Then the two of them must have been damned.

ESTRAGON And why not?

VLADIMIR But one of the four says that one of the two was saved.

ESTRAGON Well? They don't agree and that's all there is to it.

VLADIMIR But all four were there. And only one speaks of a thief being 125 saved. Why believe him rather than the others?

ESTRAGON Who believes him?

VLADIMIR Everybody. It's the only version they know.

ESTRAGON People are bloody ignorant apes.

[*He rises painfully, goes limping to extreme left, halts, gazes into distance off with his hand screening his eyes, turns, goes to extreme right, gazes into distance.* VLADIMIR *watches him, then goes and picks up the boot, peers into it, drops it hastily.*]

VLADIMIR Pah!

[*He spits.* ESTRAGON *moves to center, halts with his back to auditorium.*]

6. See Matthew 27.44. Both Mark (15.27) and John (who calls them simply "two others"; 19.18) mention the thieves.

130 ESTRAGON   Charming spot. [*He turns, advances to front, halts facing auditorium.*] Inspiring prospects. [*He turns to* VLADIMIR.] Let's go.

VLADIMIR   We can't.

ESTRAGON   Why not?

VLADIMIR   We're waiting for Godot.

135 ESTRAGON [*despairingly*]   Ah! [*Pause*] You're sure it was here?

VLADIMIR   What?

ESTRAGON   That we were to wait.

VLADIMIR   He said by the tree. [*They look at the tree.*] Do you see any others?

ESTRAGON   What is it?

140 VLADIMIR   I don't know. A willow.[7]

ESTRAGON   Where are the leaves?

VLADIMIR   It must be dead.

ESTRAGON   No more weeping.

VLADIMIR   Or perhaps it's not the season.

145 ESTRAGON   Looks to me more like a bush.

VLADIMIR   A shrub.

ESTRAGON   A bush.

VLADIMIR   A—. What are you insinuating? That we've come to the wrong place?

150 ESTRAGON   He should be here.

VLADIMIR   He didn't say for sure he'd come.

ESTRAGON   And if he doesn't come?

VLADIMIR   We'll come back tomorrow.

ESTRAGON   And then the day after tomorrow.

155 VLADIMIR   Possibly.

ESTRAGON   And so on.

VLADIMIR   The point is—

ESTRAGON   Until he comes.

VLADIMIR   You're merciless.

160 ESTRAGON   We came here yesterday.

VLADIMIR   Ah no, there you're mistaken.

ESTRAGON   What did we do yesterday?

VLADIMIR   What did we do yesterday?

ESTRAGON   Yes.

165 VLADIMIR   Why . . . [*Angrily*] Nothing is certain when you're about.

ESTRAGON   In my opinion we were here.

VLADIMIR [*looking round*]   You recognize the place?

ESTRAGON   I didn't say that.

VLADIMIR   Well?

170 ESTRAGON   That makes no difference.

VLADIMIR   All the same . . . that tree . . . [*Turning towards auditorium*] that bog . . .

ESTRAGON   You're sure it was this evening?

VLADIMIR   What?

175 ESTRAGON   That we were to wait.

VLADIMIR   He said Saturday. [*Pause*] I think.

7. A tree associated with mourning.

ESTRAGON   You think.

VLADIMIR   I must have made a note of it. [*He fumbles in his pockets, bursting with miscellaneous rubbish.*]

ESTRAGON [*very insidious*]   But what Saturday? And is it Saturday? Is it not
180   rather Sunday? [*Pause*] Or Monday? [*Pause*] Or Friday?

VLADIMIR [*looking wildly about him, as though the date was inscribed in the landscape*]   It's not possible!

ESTRAGON   Or Thursday?

VLADIMIR   What'll we do?

ESTRAGON   If he came yesterday and we weren't here you may be sure he
185   won't come again today.

VLADIMIR   But you say we were here yesterday.

ESTRAGON   I may be mistaken. [*Pause*] Let's stop talking for a minute, do you mind?

VLADIMIR [*feebly*]   All right. [ESTRAGON *sits down on the mound.* VLADIMIR *paces agitatedly to and fro, halting from time to time to gaze into distance off.*
190   ESTRAGON *falls asleep.* VLADIMIR *halts finally before* ESTRAGON.] Gogo! . . . Gogo! . . . GOGO!

[ESTRAGON *wakes with a start.*]

ESTRAGON [*restored to the horror of his situation*]   I was asleep! [*Despairingly*] Why will you never let me sleep?

VLADIMIR   I felt lonely.

195 ESTRAGON   I had a dream.

VLADIMIR   Don't tell me!

ESTRAGON   I dreamt that—

VLADIMIR   DON'T TELL ME!

ESTRAGON [*gesture towards the universe*]   This one is enough for you?
200   [*Silence*] It's not nice of you, Didi. Who am I to tell my private nightmares to if I can't tell them to you?

VLADIMIR   Let them remain private. You know I can't bear that.

ESTRAGON [*coldly*]   There are times when I wonder if it wouldn't be better for us to part.

205 VLADIMIR   You wouldn't go far.

ESTRAGON   That would be too bad, really too bad. [*Pause*] Wouldn't it, Didi, be really too bad? [*Pause*] When you think of the beauty of the way. [*Pause*] And the goodness of the wayfarers. [*Pause. Wheedling.*] Wouldn't it, Didi?

VLADIMIR   Calm yourself.

210 ESTRAGON [*voluptuously*]   Calm . . . calm . . . The English say cawm. [*Pause*] You know the story of the Englishman in the brothel?

VLADIMIR   Yes.

ESTRAGON   Tell it to me.

VLADIMIR   Ah stop it!

215 ESTRAGON   An Englishman having drunk a little more than usual proceeds to a brothel. The bawd asks him if he wants a fair one, a dark one or a red-haired one. Go on.

VLADIMIR   STOP IT!

[*Exit* VLADIMIR *hurriedly.* ESTRAGON *gets up and follows him as far as the limit of the stage. Gestures of* ESTRAGON *like those of a spectator encouraging a pugilist. Enter* VLADIMIR. *He brushes past* ESTRAGON, *crosses the stage with bowed head.* ESTRAGON *takes a step towards him, halts.*]

ESTRAGON [*gently*]   You wanted to speak to me? [*Silence.* ESTRAGON *takes a*
220   *step forward.*] You had something to say to me? [*Silence. Another step for-*
       ward.] Didi . . .

VLADIMIR [*without turning*]   I've nothing to say to you.

ESTRAGON [*step forward*]   You're angry? [*Silence. Step forward.*] Forgive me.
       [*Silence. Step forward.* ESTRAGON *lays his hand on* VLADIMIR'S *shoulder.*]
       Come, Didi. [*Silence*] Give me your hand. [VLADIMIR *half turns.*] Embrace
225   me! [VLADIMIR *stiffens.*] Don't be stubborn! [VLADIMIR *softens. They embrace.*
       ESTRAGON *recoils.*] You stink of garlic!

VLADIMIR   It's for the kidneys. [*Silence.* ESTRAGON *looks attentively at the*
       tree.] What do we do now?

ESTRAGON   Wait.

230 VLADIMIR   Yes, but while waiting.

ESTRAGON   What about hanging ourselves?

VLADIMIR   Hmm. It'd give us an erection.

ESTRAGON [*highly excited*]   An erection!

VLADIMIR   With all that follows. Where it[8] falls mandrakes grow. That's why
235   they shriek when you pull them up. Did you not know that?

ESTRAGON   Let's hang ourselves immediately!

VLADIMIR   From a bough? [*They go towards the tree.*] I wouldn't trust it.

ESTRAGON   We can always try.

VLADIMIR   Go ahead.

240 ESTRAGON   After you.

VLADIMIR   No no, you first.

ESTRAGON   Why me?

VLADIMIR   You're lighter than I am.

ESTRAGON   Just so!

245 VLADIMIR   I don't understand.

ESTRAGON   Use your intelligence, can't you?

       [VLADIMIR *uses his intelligence.*]

VLADIMIR [*finally*]   I remain in the dark.

ESTRAGON   This is how it is. [*He reflects.*] The bough . . . the bough . . .
       [*Angrily*] Use your head, can't you?

250 VLADIMIR   You're my only hope.

ESTRAGON [*with effort*]   Gogo light—bough not break—Gogo dead. Didi
       heavy—bough break—Didi alone. Whereas—

VLADIMIR   I hadn't thought of that.

ESTRAGON   If it hangs you it'll hang anything.

255 VLADIMIR   But am I heavier than you?

ESTRAGON   So you tell me. I don't know. There's an even chance. Or nearly.

VLADIMIR   Well? What do we do?

ESTRAGON   Don't let's do anything. It's safer.

VLADIMIR   Let's wait and see what he says.

260 ESTRAGON   Who?

VLADIMIR   Godot.

ESTRAGON   Good idea.

8. That is, semen. The mandrake, whose root sometimes splits in a way that resembles a man's body, was long believed to be inhabited by a demon (its shriek at being uprooted was said to be fatal). The idea that mandrakes grow from the semen of hanged men was widespread in Europe in the Middle Ages.

VLADIMIR	Let's wait till we know exactly how we stand.
ESTRAGON	On the other hand it might be better to strike the iron before it

265 freezes.[9]

VLADIMIR	I'm curious to hear what he has to offer. Then we'll take it or leave

it.

ESTRAGON	What exactly did we ask him for?
VLADIMIR	Were you not there?
270 ESTRAGON	I can't have been listening.
VLADIMIR	Oh . . . Nothing very definite.
ESTRAGON	A kind of prayer.
VLADIMIR	Precisely.
ESTRAGON	A vague supplication.
275 VLADIMIR	Exactly.
ESTRAGON	And what did he reply?
VLADIMIR	That he'd see.
ESTRAGON	That he couldn't promise anything.
VLADIMIR	That he'd have to think it over.
280 ESTRAGON	In the quiet of his home.
VLADIMIR	Consult his family.
ESTRAGON	His friends.
VLADIMIR	His agents.
ESTRAGON	His correspondents.
285 VLADIMIR	His books.
ESTRAGON	His bank account.
VLADIMIR	Before taking a decision.[1]
ESTRAGON	It's the normal thing.
VLADIMIR	Is it not?
290 ESTRAGON	I think it is.
VLADIMIR	I think so too.

[Silence.]

ESTRAGON [anxious]	And we?
VLADIMIR	I beg your pardon?
ESTRAGON	I said, And we?
295 VLADIMIR	I don't understand.
ESTRAGON	Where do we come in?
VLADIMIR	Come in?
ESTRAGON	Take your time.
VLADIMIR	Come in? On our hands and knees.
300 ESTRAGON	As bad as that?
VLADIMIR	Your Worship wishes to assert his prerogatives?
ESTRAGON	We've no rights any more?

[Laugh of VLADIMIR, stifled as before, less the smile.]

VLADIMIR	You'd make me laugh if it wasn't prohibited.
ESTRAGON	We've lost our rights?
305 VLADIMIR [distinctly]	We got rid of them.

---

9. A version of the proverb "Strike while the iron is hot," whose earliest attribution is to Publilius Syrus (1st c. B.C.E.).

1. That is, making a decision (a British idiom).

[*Silence. They remain motionless, arms dangling, heads sunk, sagging at the knees.*]

ESTRAGON [*feebly*]   We're not tied? [*Pause*] We're not—

VLADIMIR   Listen!

[*They listen, grotesquely rigid.*]

ESTRAGON   I hear nothing.

VLADIMIR   Hsst! [*They listen.* ESTRAGON *loses his balance, almost falls. He clutches the arm of* VLADIMIR *who totters. They listen, huddled together.*]

310   Nor I.

[*Sighs of relief. They relax and separate.*]

ESTRAGON   You gave me a fright.

VLADIMIR   I thought it was he.

ESTRAGON   Who?

VLADIMIR   Godot.

315 ESTRAGON   Pah! The wind in the reeds.

VLADIMIR   I could have sworn I heard shouts.

ESTRAGON   And why would he shout?

VLADIMIR   At his horse.

[*Silence.*]

ESTRAGON [*violently*]   I'm hungry!

320 VLADIMIR   Do you want a carrot?

ESTRAGON   Is that all there is?

VLADIMIR   I might have some turnips.

ESTRAGON   Give me a carrot. [VLADIMIR *rummages in his pockets, takes out a turnip and gives it to* ESTRAGON *who takes a bite out of it. Angrily.*] It's a

325   turnip!

VLADIMIR   Oh pardon! I could have sworn it was a carrot. [*He rummages again in his pockets, finds nothing but turnips.*] All that's turnips. [*He rummages.*] You must have eaten the last. [*He rummages.*] Wait, I have it. [*He brings out a carrot and gives it to* ESTRAGON.] There, dear fellow. [ESTRAGON

330   *wipes the carrot on his sleeve and begins to eat it.*] Make it last, that's the end of them.

ESTRAGON [*chewing*]   I asked you a question.

VLADIMIR   Ah.

ESTRAGON   Did you reply?

335 VLADIMIR   How's the carrot?

ESTRAGON   It's a carrot.

VLADIMIR   So much the better, so much the better. [*Pause.*] What was it you wanted to know?

ESTRAGON   I've forgotten. [*Chews.*] That's what annoys me. [*He looks at the

340   carrot appreciatively, dangles it between finger and thumb.*] I'll never forget this carrot. [*He sucks the end of it meditatively.*] Ah yes, now I remember.

VLADIMIR   Well?

ESTRAGON [*his mouth full, vacuously*]   We're not tied?

VLADIMIR   I don't hear a word you're saying.

345 ESTRAGON [*chews, swallows*]   I'm asking you if we're tied.

VLADIMIR   Tied?

ESTRAGON   Ti-ed.

VLADIMIR   How do you mean tied?

ESTRAGON Down.

350 VLADIMIR But to whom? By whom?

ESTRAGON To your man.

VLADIMIR To Godot? Tied to Godot! What an idea! No question of it. [*Pause*] For the moment.

ESTRAGON His name is Godot?

355 VLADIMIR I think so.

ESTRAGON Fancy that. [*He raises what remains of the carrot by the stub of leaf, twirls it before his eyes.*] Funny, the more you eat the worse it gets.

VLADIMIR With me it's just the opposite.

ESTRAGON In other words?

360 VLADIMIR I get used to the muck as I go along.

ESTRAGON [*after prolonged reflection*] Is that the opposite?

VLADIMIR Question of temperament.

ESTRAGON Of character.

VLADIMIR Nothing you can do about it.

365 ESTRAGON No use struggling.

VLADIMIR One is what one is.

ESTRAGON No use wriggling.

VLADIMIR The essential doesn't change.

ESTRAGON Nothing to be done. [*He proffers the remains of the carrot to*
370 VLADIMIR.] Like to finish it?

[*A terrible cry, close at hand.* ESTRAGON *drops the carrot. They remain motionless, then together make a sudden rush towards the wings.* ESTRAGON *stops halfway, runs back, picks up the carrot, stuffs it in his pocket, runs to rejoin* VLADIMIR *who is waiting for him, stops again, runs back, picks up his boot, runs to rejoin* VLADIMIR. *Huddled together, shoulders hunched, cringing away from the menace, they wait.*]

[*Enter* POZZO *and* LUCKY. POZZO *drives* LUCKY *by means of a rope passed round his neck, so that* LUCKY *is the first to enter, followed by the rope which is long enough to let him reach the middle of the stage before* POZZO *appears.* LUCKY *carries a heavy bag, a folding stool, a picnic basket and a greatcoat,* POZZO *a whip.*]

POZZO [*off*] On! [*Crack of whip.* POZZO *appears. They cross the stage.* LUCKY *passes before* VLADIMIR *and* ESTRAGON *and exit.* POZZO *at the sight of* VLADIMIR *and* ESTRAGON *stops short. The rope tautens.* POZZO *jerks at it violently.*] Back!

[*Noise of* LUCKY *falling with all his baggage.* VLADIMIR *and* ESTRAGON *turn towards him, half wishing half fearing to go to his assistance.* VLADIMIR *takes a step towards Lucky,* ESTRAGON *holds him back by the sleeve.*]

VLADIMIR Let me go!

ESTRAGON Stay where you are!

375 POZZO Be careful! He's wicked. [VLADIMIR *and* ESTRAGON *turn towards* POZZO.] With strangers.

ESTRAGON [*undertone*] Is that him?

VLADIMIR Who?

ESTRAGON [*trying to remember the name*] Er . . .

380 VLADIMIR Godot?

ESTRAGON Yes.

POZZO I present myself: Pozzo.

VLADIMIR [*to* ESTRAGON]   Not at all!

ESTRAGON   He said Godot.

385 VLADIMIR   Not at all!

ESTRAGON [*timidly, to* POZZO]   You're not Mr. Godot, Sir?

POZZO [*terrifying voice*]   I am Pozzo! [*Silence*] Pozzo! [*Silence*] Does that name mean nothing to you? [*Silence*] I say does that name mean nothing to you?

[VLADIMIR *and* ESTRAGON *look at each other questioningly.*]

390 ESTRAGON [*pretending to search*]   Bozzo . . . Bozzo . . .

VLADIMIR [*ditto*]   Pozzo . . . Pozzo . . .

POZZO   PPPOZZZO!

ESTRAGON   Ah! Pozzo . . . let me see . . . Pozzo . . .

VLADIMIR   Is it Pozzo or Bozzo?

395 ESTRAGON   Pozzo . . . no . . . I'm afraid I . . . no . . . I don't seem to . . .

[POZZO *advances threateningly.*]

VLADIMIR [*conciliating*]   I once knew a family called Cozzo. The mother had the clap.[2]

ESTRAGON [*hastily*]   We're not from these parts, Sir.

POZZO [*halting*]   You are human beings none the less. [*He puts on his glasses.*]

400 As far as one can see. [*He takes off his glasses.*] Of the same species as myself. [*He bursts into an enormous laugh.*] Of the same species as Pozzo! Made in God's image!

VLADIMIR   Well you see—

POZZO [*peremptory*]   Who is Godot?

405 ESTRAGON   Godot?

POZZO   You took me for Godot.

VLADIMIR   Oh no, Sir, not for an instant, Sir.

POZZO   Who is he?

VLADIMIR   Oh he's a . . . he's a kind of acquaintance.

410 ESTRAGON   Nothing of the kind, we hardly know him.

VLADIMIR   True . . . we don't know him very well . . . but all the same . . .

ESTRAGON   Personally I wouldn't even know him if I saw him.

POZZO   You took me for him.

ESTRAGON [*recoiling before* POZZO]   That's to say . . . you understand . . . the

415 dusk . . . the strain . . . waiting . . . I confess . . . I imagined . . . for a second . . .

POZZO   Waiting? So you were waiting for him?

VLADIMIR   Well you see—

POZZO   Here? On my land?

420 VLADIMIR   We didn't intend any harm.

ESTRAGON   We meant well.

POZZO   The road is free to all.

VLADIMIR   That's how we looked at it.

POZZO   It's a disgrace. But there you are.

425 ESTRAGON   Nothing we can do about it.

POZZO [*with magnanimous gesture*]   Let's say no more about it. [*He jerks the rope.*] Up pig! [*Pause*] Every time he drops he falls asleep. [*Jerks the rope.*] Up hog! [*Noise of* LUCKY *getting up and picking up his baggage.* POZZO *jerks*

2. Gonorrhea (slang).

430 *the rope.*] Back! [*Enter* LUCKY *backwards.*] Stop! [LUCKY *stops.*] Turn! [LUCKY *turns. To* VLADIMIR *and* ESTRAGON, *affably.*] Gentlemen, I am happy to have met you. [*Before their incredulous expression*] Yes yes, sincerely happy. [*He jerks the rope.*] Closer! [LUCKY *advances.*] Stop! [LUCKY *stops.*] Yes, the road seems long when one journeys all alone for . . . [*He consults his watch.*] . . . yes . . . [*He calculates.*] . . . yes, six hours, that's right, six hours on end,

435 and never a soul in sight. [*To* LUCKY] Coat! [LUCKY *puts down the bag, advances, gives the coat, goes back to his place, takes up the bag.*] Hold that! [POZZO *holds out the whip.* LUCKY *advances and, both his hands being occupied, takes the whip in his mouth, then goes back to his place.* POZZO *begins to put on his coat, stops.*] Coat! [LUCKY *puts down bag, basket and stool, advances, helps* POZZO *on with his coat, goes back to his place and takes up bag, basket and stool.*] Touch of autumn in the air this evening. [POZZO *finishes buttoning his coat, stoops, inspects himself, straightens up.*] Whip! [LUCKY *advances, stoops,* POZZO *snatches the whip from his mouth,* LUCKY

440 *goes back to his place.*] Yes, gentlemen, I cannot go for long without the society of my likes [*He puts on his glasses and looks at the two likes.*] even when the likeness is an imperfect one. [*He takes off his glasses.*] Stool! [LUCKY *puts down bag and basket, advances, opens stool, puts it down, goes back to his place, takes up bag and basket.*] Closer! [LUCKY *puts down bag and basket, advances, moves stool, goes back to his place, takes up bag and basket.* POZZO *sits down, places the butt of his whip against* LUCKY's *chest and pushes.*] Back! [LUCKY *takes a step back.*] Further! [LUCKY *takes another step*

445 *back.*] Stop! [LUCKY *stops. To* VLADIMIR *and* ESTRAGON.] That is why, with your permission, I propose to dally with you a moment, before I venture any further. Basket! [LUCKY *advances, gives the basket, goes back to his place.*] The fresh air stimulates the jaded appetite. [*He opens the basket, takes out a piece of chicken and a bottle of wine.*] Basket! [LUCKY *advances,*

450 *picks up the basket and goes back to his place.*] Further! [LUCKY *takes a step back.*] He stinks. Happy days!

> [*He drinks from the bottle, puts it down and begins to eat. Silence.* VLADIMIR *and* ESTRAGON, *cautiously at first, then more boldly, begin to circle about* LUCKY, *inspecting him up and down.* POZZO *eats his chicken voraciously, throwing away the bones after having sucked them.* LUCKY *sags slowly, until bag and basket touch the ground, then straightens up with a start and begins to sag again. Rhythm of one sleeping on his feet.*]

ESTRAGON   What ails him?

VLADIMIR   He looks tired.

ESTRAGON   Why doesn't he put down his bags?

455 VLADIMIR   How do I know? [*They close in on him.*] Careful!

ESTRAGON   Say something to him.

VLADIMIR   Look!

ESTRAGON   What?

VLADIMIR [*pointing*]   His neck!

460 ESTRAGON [*looking at the neck*]   I see nothing.

VLADIMIR   Here.

> [ESTRAGON *goes over beside* VLADIMIR.]

ESTRAGON   Oh I say!

VLADIMIR   A running sore!

ESTRAGON   It's the rope.

465 VLADIMIR It's the rubbing.

ESTRAGON It's inevitable.

VLADIMIR It's the knot.

ESTRAGON It's the chafing.

[*They resume their inspection, dwell on the face.*]

VLADIMIR [*grudgingly*] He's not bad looking.

470 ESTRAGON [*shrugging his shoulders, wry face*] Would you say so?

VLADIMIR A trifle effeminate.

ESTRAGON Look at the slobber.

VLADIMIR It's inevitable.

ESTRAGON Look at the slaver.[3]

475 VLADIMIR Perhaps he's a halfwit.

ESTRAGON A cretin.

VLADIMIR [*looking closer*] Looks like a goiter.

ESTRAGON [*ditto*] It's not certain.

VLADIMIR He's panting.

480 ESTRAGON It's inevitable.

VLADIMIR And his eyes!

ESTRAGON What about them?

VLADIMIR Goggling out of his head.

ESTRAGON Looks at his last gasp to me.

485 VLADIMIR It's not certain. [*Pause*] Ask him a question.

ESTRAGON Would that be a good thing?

VLADIMIR What do we risk?

ESTRAGON [*timidly*] Mister . . .

VLADIMIR Louder.

490 ESTRAGON [*louder*] Mister . . .

POZZO Leave him in peace! [*They turn towards* POZZO *who, having finished eating, wipes his mouth with the back of his hand.*] Can't you see he wants to rest? Basket! [*He strikes a match and begins to light his pipe.* ESTRAGON *sees the chicken bones on the ground and stares at them greedily. As* LUCKY *does not move* POZZO *throws the match angrily away and jerks the rope.*] Basket! [LUCKY *starts, almost falls, recovers his senses, advances, puts the bottle in the basket and goes back to his place.* ESTRAGON *stares at the bones.* POZZO

495 *strikes another match and lights his pipe.*] What can you expect, it's not his job. [*He pulls at his pipe, stretches out his legs.*] Ah! That's better.

ESTRAGON [*timidly*] Please Sir . . .

POZZO What is it, my good man?

ESTRAGON Er . . . you've finished with the . . . er . . . you don't need the . . .

500 er . . . bones, Sir?

VLADIMIR [*scandalized*] You couldn't have waited?

POZZO No no, he does well to ask. Do I need the bones? [*He turns them over with the end of his whip.*] No, personally I do not need them any more. [ESTRAGON *takes a step towards the bones.*] But . . . [ESTRAGON *stops*

505 *short.*] . . . but in theory the bones go to the carrier. He is therefore the one to ask. [ESTRAGON *turns towards* LUCKY, *hesitates.*] Go on, go on, don't be afraid, ask him, he'll tell you.

3. Saliva falling from the mouth.

[ESTRAGON *goes towards* LUCKY, *stops before him.*]

ESTRAGON   Mister . . . excuse me, Mister . . .

POZZO   You're being spoken to, pig! Reply! [*To* ESTRAGON] Try him again.

510 ESTRAGON   Excuse me, Mister, the bones, you won't be wanting the bones?

[LUCKY *looks long at* ESTRAGON.]

POZZO [*in raptures*]   Mister! [LUCKY *bows his head.*] Reply! Do you want them
or don't you? [*Silence of* LUCKY. *To* ESTRAGON.] They're yours. [ESTRAGON
makes a dart at the bones, picks them up and begins to gnaw them.] I don't
like it. I've never known him refuse a bone before. [*He looks anxiously at*
515 LUCKY.] Nice business it'd be if he fell sick on me! [*He puffs at his pipe.*]

VLADIMIR [*exploding*]   It's a scandal!

[*Silence. Flabbergasted,* ESTRAGON *stops gnawing, looks at* POZZO *and*
VLADIMIR *in turn.* POZZO *outwardly calm.* VLADIMIR *embarrassed.*]

POZZO [*to* VLADIMIR]   Are you alluding to anything in particular?

VLADIMIR [*stutteringly resolute*]   To treat a man . . . [*Gesture towards*
LUCKY] . . . like that . . . I think that . . . no . . . a human being . . . no . . .
520 it's a scandal!

ESTRAGON [*not to be outdone*]   A disgrace! [*He resumes his gnawing.*]

POZZO   You are severe. [*To* VLADIMIR] What age are you, if it's not a rude
question? [*Silence*] Sixty? Seventy? [*To* ESTRAGON] What age would you say
he was?

525 ESTRAGON   Eleven.

POZZO   I am impertinent. [*He knocks out his pipe against the whip, gets up.*]
I must be getting on. Thank you for your society. [*He reflects.*] Unless
I smoke another pipe before I go. What do you say? [*They say nothing.*] Oh
I'm only a small smoker, a very small smoker, I'm not in the habit of smok-
530 ing two pipes one on top of the other, it makes [*Hand to heart, sighing*] my
heart go pit-a-pat. [*Silence*] It's the nicotine, one absorbs it in spite of one's
precautions. [*Sighs*] You know how it is. [*Silence*] But perhaps you don't
smoke? Yes? No? It's of no importance. [*Silence*] But how am I to sit down
now, without affectation, now that I have risen? Without appearing to—
535 how shall I say—without appearing to falter. [*To* VLADIMIR] I beg your pardon? [*Silence*] Perhaps you didn't speak? [*Silence*] It's of no importance.
Let me see . . . [*He reflects.*]

ESTRAGON   Ah! That's better. [*He puts the bones in his pocket.*]

VLADIMIR   Let's go.

540 ESTRAGON   So soon?

POZZO   One moment! [*He jerks the rope.*] Stool! [*He points with his whip.*
LUCKY *moves the stool.*] More! There! [*He sits down.* LUCKY *goes back to his*
place.] Done it! [*He fills his pipe.*]

VLADIMIR [*vehemently*]   Let's go!

545 POZZO   I hope I'm not driving you away. Wait a little longer, you'll never
regret it.

ESTRAGON [*sensing charity*]   We're in no hurry.

POZZO [*having lit his pipe*]   The second is never so sweet . . . [*He takes the*
pipe out of his mouth, contemplates it.] . . . as the first I mean. [*He puts the*
550 *pipe back in his mouth.*] But it's sweet just the same.

VLADIMIR   I'm going.

POZZO   He can no longer endure my presence. I am perhaps not particularly
human, but who cares? [*To* VLADIMIR] Think twice before you do anything

rash. Suppose you go now while it is still day, for there is no denying it is
555   still day. [*They all look up at the sky.*] Good. [*They stop looking at the sky.*]
What happens in that case—[*He takes the pipe out of his mouth, examines
it.*]—I'm out—[*He relights his pipe.*]—in that case—[*Puff*]—in that case—
[*Puff*]—what happens in that case to your appointment with this . . .
Godet . . . Godot . . . Godin . . . anyhow you see who I mean, who has your
560   future in his hands . . . [*Pause*] . . . at least your immediate future?

VLADIMIR   Who told you?

POZZO   He speaks to me again! If this goes on much longer we'll soon be old
friends.

ESTRAGON   Why doesn't he put down his bags?

565 POZZO   I too would be happy to meet him. The more people I meet the happier I become. From the meanest creature one departs wiser, richer, more
conscious of one's blessings. Even you . . . [*He looks at them ostentatiously
in turn to make it clear they are both meant.*] . . . even you, who knows, will
have added to my store.

570 ESTRAGON   Why doesn't he put down his bags?

POZZO   But that would surprise me.

VLADIMIR   You're being asked a question.

POZZO [*delighted*]   A question! Who? What? A moment ago you were calling
me Sir, in fear and trembling. Now you're asking me questions. No good
575   will come of this!

VLADIMIR [*to* ESTRAGON]   I think he's listening.

ESTRAGON [*circling about* LUCKY]   What?

VLADIMIR   You can ask him now. He's on the alert.

ESTRAGON   Ask him what?

580 VLADIMIR   Why he doesn't put down his bags.

ESTRAGON   I wonder.

VLADIMIR   Ask him, can't you?

POZZO [*who has followed these exchanges with anxious attention, fearing lest
the question get lost*]   You want to know why he doesn't put down his bags,
as you call them.

585 VLADIMIR   That's it.

POZZO [*to* ESTRAGON]   You are sure you agree with that?

ESTRAGON   He's puffing like a grampus.[4]

POZZO   The answer is this. [*To* ESTRAGON] But stay still, I beg of you, you're
making me nervous!

590 VLADIMIR   Here.

ESTRAGON   What is it?

VLADIMIR   He's about to speak.

[ESTRAGON *goes over beside* VLADIMIR. *Motionless, side by side, they wait.*]

POZZO   Good. Is everybody ready? Is everybody looking at me? [*He looks at*
LUCKY, *jerks the rope.* LUCKY *raises his head.*] Will you look at me, pig!
595   [LUCKY *looks at him.*] Good. [*He puts the pipe in his pocket, takes out a little
vaporizer and sprays his throat, puts back the vaporizer in his pocket, clears
his throat, spits, takes out the vaporizer again, sprays his throat again, puts
back the vaporizer in his pocket.*] I am ready. Is everybody listening? Is
everybody ready? [*He looks at them all in turn, jerks the rope.*] Hog! [LUCKY

4. A variety of dolphin.

raises his head.] I don't like talking in a vacuum. Good. Let me see. [*He reflects.*]

600 ESTRAGON   I'm going.

POZZO   What was it exactly you wanted to know?

VLADIMIR   Why he—

POZZO [*angrily*]   Don't interrupt me! [*Pause. Calmer.*] If we all speak at once we'll never get anywhere. [*Pause.*] What was I saying? [*Pause. Louder.*] What was I saying?

[VLADIMIR *mimics one carrying a heavy burden.* POZZO *looks at him, puzzled.*]

605 ESTRAGON [*forcibly*]   Bags. [*He points at* LUCKY.] Why? Always hold. [*He sags, panting.*] Never put down. [*He opens his hands, straightens up with relief.*] Why?

POZZO   Ah! Why couldn't you say so before? Why he doesn't make himself comfortable? Let's try and get this clear. Has he not the right to? Certainly

610 he has. It follows that he doesn't want to. There's reasoning for you. And why doesn't he want to? [*Pause*] Gentlemen, the reason is this.

VLADIMIR [*to* ESTRAGON]   Make a note of this.

POZZO   He wants to impress me, so that I'll keep him.

ESTRAGON   What?

615 POZZO   Perhaps I haven't got it quite right. He wants to mollify me, so that I'll give up the idea of parting with him. No, that's not exactly it either.

VLADIMIR   You want to get rid of him?

POZZO   He wants to cod[5] me, but he won't.

VLADIMIR   You want to get rid of him?

620 POZZO   He imagines that when I see how well he carries I'll be tempted to keep him on in that capacity.

ESTRAGON   You've had enough of him?

POZZO   In reality he carries like a pig. It's not his job.

VLADIMIR   You want to get rid of him?

625 POZZO   He imagines that when I see him indefatigable I'll regret my decision. Such is his miserable scheme. As though I were short of slaves! [*All three look at* LUCKY.] Atlas, son of Jupiter![6] [*Silence*] Well, that's that I think. Anything else?

[*Vaporizer.*]

VLADIMIR   You want to get rid of him?

630 POZZO   Remark that I might just as well have been in his shoes and he in mine. If chance had not willed otherwise. To each one his due.

VLADIMIR   You waagerrim?

POZZO   I beg your pardon?

VLADIMIR   You want to get rid of him?

635 POZZO   I do. But instead of driving him away as I might have done, I mean instead of simply kicking him out on his arse, in the goodness of my heart I am bringing him to the fair, where I hope to get a good price for him. The truth is you can't drive such creatures away. The best thing would be to kill them.

---

5. Play a joke on, tease; or, perhaps, a shortened version of *coddle*.
6. In classical mythology, Atlas's father was the Titan Iapetus, not Jupiter; as punishment

for leading the Titans in their war against the Olympian gods, Atlas was condemned to hold the heavens on his shoulders.

[LUCKY *weeps.*]

640 ESTRAGON He's crying!

POZZO Old dogs have more dignity. [*He proffers his handkerchief to* ESTRAGON.] Comfort him, since you pity him. [ESTRAGON *hesitates.*] Come on. [ESTRAGON *takes the handkerchief.*] Wipe away his tears, he'll feel less forsaken.

[ESTRAGON *hesitates.*]

645 VLADIMIR Here, give it to me, I'll do it.

[ESTRAGON *refuses to give the handkerchief. Childish gestures.*]

POZZO Make haste, before he stops. [ESTRAGON *approaches* LUCKY *and makes to wipe his eyes.* LUCKY *kicks him violently in the shins.* ESTRAGON *drops the handkerchief, recoils, staggers about the stage howling with pain.*] Hanky!

[LUCKY *puts down bag and basket, picks up handkerchief and gives it to* POZZO, *goes back to his place, picks up bag and basket.*]

ESTRAGON Oh the swine! [*He pulls up the leg of his trousers.*] He's crippled me!

650 POZZO I told you he didn't like strangers.

VLADIMIR [*to* ESTRAGON] Show. [ESTRAGON *shows his leg. To* POZZO, *angrily*] He's bleeding!

POZZO It's a good sign.

ESTRAGON [*on one leg*] I'll never walk again!

655 VLADIMIR [*tenderly*] I'll carry you. [*Pause*] If necessary.

POZZO He's stopped crying. [*To* ESTRAGON] You have replaced him as it were. [*Lyrically*] The tears of the world are a constant quantity. For each one who begins to weep somewhere else another stops. The same is true of the laugh. [*He laughs.*] Let us not then speak ill of our generation, it is not any

660 unhappier than its predecessors. [*Pause*] Let us not speak well of it either. [*Pause*] Let us not speak of it at all. [*Pause. Judiciously.*] It is true the population has increased.

VLADIMIR Try and walk.

[ESTRAGON *takes a few limping steps, stops before* LUCKY *and spits on him, then goes and sits down on the mound.*]

POZZO Guess who taught me all these beautiful things. [*Pause. Pointing to*
665 LUCKY] My Lucky!

VLADIMIR [*looking at the sky*] Will night never come?

POZZO But for him all my thoughts, all my feelings, would have been of common things. [*Pause. With extraordinary vehemence.*] Professional worries! [*Calmer*] Beauty, grace, truth of the first water,[7] I knew they were all
670 beyond me. So I took a knook.[8]

VLADIMIR [*startled from his inspection of the sky*] A knook?

POZZO That was nearly sixty years ago . . . [*He consults his watch.*] . . . yes, nearly sixty. [*Drawing himself up proudly*] You wouldn't think it to look at me, would you? Compared to him I look like a young man, no? [*Pause*] Hat!

---

7. Of the highest quality (formerly, a technical term used of diamonds).
8. A coinage of Beckett's, possibly echoing *knut* (the Russian word for "whip"). In a passage from the original French version that Beckett did not include in his English translation, Pozzo expounds on the word to Vladimir as follows: "You are not from these parts. Are you so out of touch with the times? Years ago people used to have jesters. Now they have knooks. Those who are able to afford them."

[LUCKY *puts down the basket and takes off his hat. His long white hair falls*
₆₇₅ *about his face. He puts his hat under his arm and picks up the basket.*] Now
look. [POZZO *takes off his hat.*[9] *He is completely bald. He puts on his hat
again.*] Did you see?

VLADIMIR   And now you turn him away? Such an old and faithful servant!

ESTRAGON   Swine!

[POZZO *more and more agitated.*]

₆₈₀ VLADIMIR   After having sucked all the good out of him you chuck him away
like a . . . like a banana skin. Really . . .

POZZO [*groaning, clutching his head*]   I can't bear it . . . any longer . . . the
way he goes on . . . you've no idea . . . it's terrible . . . he must go . . . [*He
waves his arms.*] . . . I'm going mad . . . [*He collapses, his head in his
₆₈₅ hands.*] . . . I can't bear it . . . any longer . . .

[*Silence. All look at* POZZO.]

VLADIMIR   He can't bear it.

ESTRAGON   Any longer.

VLADIMIR   He's going mad.

ESTRAGON   It's terrible.

₆₉₀ VLADIMIR [*to* LUCKY]   How dare you! It's abominable! Such a good master!
Crucify him like that! After so many years! Really!

POZZO [*sobbing*]   He used to be so kind . . . so helpful . . . and entertaining . . . my good angel . . . and now . . . he's killing me.

ESTRAGON [*to* VLADIMIR]   Does he want to replace him?

₆₉₅ VLADIMIR   What?

ESTRAGON   Does he want someone to take his place or not?

VLADIMIR   I don't think so.

ESTRAGON   What?

VLADIMIR   I don't know.

₇₀₀ ESTRAGON   Ask him.

POZZO [*calmer*]   Gentlemen, I don't know what came over me. Forgive me.
Forget all I said. [*More and more his old self*] I don't remember exactly what
it was, but you may be sure there wasn't a word of truth in it. [*Drawing
himself up, striking his chest*] Do I look like a man that can be made to suf-
₇₀₅ fer? Frankly? [*He rummages in his pockets.*] What have I done with my
pipe?

VLADIMIR   Charming evening we're having.

ESTRAGON   Unforgettable.

VLADIMIR   And it's not over.

₇₁₀ ESTRAGON   Apparently not.

VLADIMIR   It's only beginning.

ESTRAGON   It's awful.

VLADIMIR   Worse than the pantomime.

ESTRAGON   The circus.

₇₁₅ VLADIMIR   The music-hall.

ESTRAGON   The circus.

POZZO   What can I have done with that briar?[1]

ESTRAGON   He's a scream. He's lost his dudeen.[2] [*Laughs noisily.*]

---

9. All four wear bowlers [Beckett's note].
1. That is, his pipe made from briar wood.

2. A short-stemmed clay tobacco pipe (Irish
Gaelic).

VLADIMIR   I'll be back. [*He hastens towards the wings.*]
720 ESTRAGON   End of the corridor, on the left.
VLADIMIR   Keep my seat. [*Exit* VLADIMIR.]
POZZO [*on the point of tears*]   I've lost my Kapp and Peterson![3]
ESTRAGON [*convulsed with merriment*]   He'll be the death of me!
POZZO   You didn't see by any chance—. [*He misses* VLADIMIR.] Oh! He's gone!
725   Without saying goodbye! How could he! He might have waited!
ESTRAGON   He would have burst.
POZZO   Oh! [*Pause*] Oh well then of course in that case . . .
ESTRAGON   Come here.
POZZO   What for?
730 ESTRAGON   You'll see.
POZZO   You want me to get up?
ESTRAGON   Quick! [POZZO *gets up and goes over beside* ESTRAGON. ESTRAGON *points off.*] Look!
POZZO [*having put on his glasses*]   Oh I say!
735 ESTRAGON   It's all over.

>   [*Enter* VLADIMIR, *somber. He shoulders* LUCKY *out of his way, kicks over the stool, comes and goes agitatedly.*]

POZZO   He's not pleased.
ESTRAGON [*to* VLADIMIR]   You missed a treat. Pity.

>   [VLADIMIR *halts, straightens the stool, comes and goes, calmer.*]

POZZO   He subsides. [*Looking round*] Indeed all subsides. A great calm descends. [*Raising his hand*] Listen! Pan sleeps.[4]
740 VLADIMIR   Will night never come?

>   [*All three look at the sky.*]

POZZO   You don't feel like going until it does?
ESTRAGON   Well you see—
POZZO   Why it's very natural, very natural. I myself in your situation, if I had an appointment with a Godin . . . Godet . . . Godot . . . anyhow you see
745   who I mean, I'd wait till it was black night before I gave up. [*He looks at the stool.*] I'd very much like to sit down, but I don't quite know how to go about it.
ESTRAGON   Could I be of any help?
POZZO   If you asked me perhaps.
750 ESTRAGON   What?
POZZO   If you asked me to sit down.
ESTRAGON   Would that be a help?
POZZO   I fancy so.
ESTRAGON   Here we go. Be seated, Sir, I beg of you.
755 POZZO   No no, I wouldn't think of it! [*Pause. Aside.*] Ask me again.
ESTRAGON   Come come, take a seat I beseech you, you'll get pneumonia.
POZZO   You really think so?
ESTRAGON   Why it's absolutely certain.

---

3. A brand of pipe. Kapp and Peterson were Dublin's most renowned manufacturers and purveyors of smoking pipes and other tobacco products.

4. Pan, the Greek god of pastures, flocks, and wild places, was said to sleep at noon; to accommodate him, all of nature fell quiet.

POZZO   No doubt you are right. [*He sits down.*] Done it again! [*Pause*] Thank
760   you, dear fellow. [*He consults his watch.*] But I must really be getting along,
if I am to observe my schedule.

VLADIMIR   Time has stopped.

POZZO   [*cuddling his watch to his ear*] Don't you believe it, Sir, don't you
believe it. [*He puts his watch back in his pocket.*] Whatever you like, but
765   not that.

ESTRAGON   [*to* POZZO]   Everything seems black to him today.

POZZO   Except the firmament. [*He laughs, pleased with this witticism.*] But I
see what it is, you are not from these parts, you don't know what our twi-
lights can do. Shall I tell you? [*Silence.* ESTRAGON *is fiddling with his boot*
770   *again,* VLADIMIR *with his hat.*] I can't refuse you. [*Vaporizer*] A little attention, if you please. [VLADIMIR *and* ESTRAGON *continue their fiddling,* LUCKY
is half asleep. POZZO *cracks his whip feebly.*] What's the matter with this
whip? [*He gets up and cracks it more vigorously, finally with success.* LUCKY
jumps. VLADIMIR'*s hat,* ESTRAGON'*s boot,* LUCKY'*s hat, fall to the ground.* POZZO
throws down the whip.] Worn out, this whip. [*He looks at* VLADIMIR *and*
775   ESTRAGON.] What was I saying?

VLADIMIR   Let's go.

ESTRAGON   But take the weight off your feet, I implore you, you'll catch your
death.

POZZO   True. [*He sits down. To* ESTRAGON.] What is your name?

780 ESTRAGON   Adam.

POZZO   [*who hasn't listened*] Ah yes! The night. [*He raises his head.*] But be a
little more attentive, for pity's sake, otherwise we'll never get anywhere.
[*He looks at the sky.*] Look! [*All look at the sky except* LUCKY *who is dozing off
again.* POZZO *jerks the rope.*] Will you look at the sky, pig! [LUCKY *looks at the*
785   *sky.*] Good, that's enough. [*They stop looking at the sky.*] What is there so
extraordinary about it? Qua[5] sky. It is pale and luminous like any sky at this
hour of the day. [*Pause*] In these latitudes. [*Pause*] When the weather is
fine. [*Lyrical*] An hour ago [*He looks at his watch, prosaic.*] roughly [*Lyrical*]
after having poured forth even since [*He hesitates, prosaic.*] say ten o'clock
790   in the morning [*Lyrical*] tirelessly torrents of red and white light it begins
to lose its effulgence, to grow pale [*Gesture of the two hands lapsing by
stages*] pale, ever a little paler, a little paler until [*Dramatic pause, ample
gesture of the two hands flung wide apart*] pppfff! finished! it comes to rest.
But—[*Hand raised in admonition*]—but behind this veil of gentleness and
795   peace night is charging [*Vibrantly*] and will burst upon us [*Snaps his fingers.*] pop! like that! [*His inspiration leaves him.*] just when we least expect
it. [*Silence. Gloomily.*] That's how it is on this bitch of an earth.

   [*Long silence.*]

ESTRAGON   So long as one knows.

VLADIMIR   One can bide one's time.

800 ESTRAGON   One knows what to expect.

VLADIMIR   No further need to worry.

ESTRAGON   Simply wait.

5. As (a term common in philosophical discourse).

VLADIMIR   We're used to it. [*He picks up his hat, peers inside it, shakes it, puts it on.*]

POZZO   How did you find me? [VLADIMIR *and* ESTRAGON *look at him blankly.*]
805   Good? Fair? Middling? Poor? Positively bad?

VLADIMIR [*first to understand*]   Oh very good, very very good.

POZZO [*to* ESTRAGON]   And you, Sir?

ESTRAGON   Oh tray bong, tray tray tray bong.[6]

POZZO [*fervently*]   Bless you, gentlemen, bless you! [*Pause*] I have such need
810   of encouragement! [*Pause*] I weakened a little towards the end, you didn't
       notice?

VLADIMIR   Oh perhaps just a teeny weeny little bit.

ESTRAGON   I thought it was intentional.

POZZO   You see my memory is defective.

       [*Silence.*]

815 ESTRAGON   In the meantime nothing happens.

POZZO   You find it tedious?

ESTRAGON   Somewhat.

POZZO [*to* VLADIMIR]   And you, Sir?

VLADIMIR   I've been better entertained.

       [*Silence.* POZZO *struggles inwardly.*]

820 POZZO   Gentlemen, you have been . . . civil to me.

ESTRAGON   Not at all!

VLADIMIR   What an idea!

POZZO   Yes yes, you have been correct. So that I ask myself is there anything
       I can do in my turn for these honest fellows who are having such a dull,
825   dull time.

ESTRAGON   Even ten francs would be a help.

VLADIMIR   We are not beggars!

POZZO   Is there anything I can do, that's what I ask myself, to cheer them
       up? I have given them bones, I have talked to them about this and that, I
830   have explained the twilight, admittedly. But is it enough, that's what tor-
       tures me, is it enough?

ESTRAGON   Even five.

VLADIMIR [*to* ESTRAGON, *indignantly*]   That's enough!

ESTRAGON   I couldn't accept less.

835 POZZO   Is it enough? No doubt. But I am liberal. It's my nature. This eve-
       ning. So much the worse for me. [*He jerks the rope.* LUCKY *looks at him.*]
       For I shall suffer, no doubt about that. [*He picks up the whip.*] What do you
       prefer? Shall we have him dance, or sing, or recite, or think, or—

ESTRAGON   Who?

840 POZZO   Who! You know how to think, you two?

VLADIMIR   He thinks?

POZZO   Certainly. Aloud. He even used to think very prettily once, I could
       listen to him for hours. Now . . . [*He shudders.*] So much the worse for me.
       Well, would you like him to think something for us?

6. "Oui! Tray bong!" (which plays on the French phrase *oui très bon*—"yes, very good") was the title of a late 19th-century song made popular in English music halls by Charles Chaplin Sr., father of the famous film actor.

845 ESTRAGON   I'd rather he'd dance, it'd be more fun.

POZZO   Not necessarily.

ESTRAGON   Wouldn't it, Didi, be more fun?

VLADIMIR   I'd like well to hear him think.

ESTRAGON   Perhaps he could dance first and think afterwards, if it isn't too
850   much to ask him.

VLADIMIR [to POZZO]   Would that be possible?

POZZO   By all means, nothing simpler. It's the natural order. [He laughs
briefly.]

VLADIMIR   Then let him dance.

[Silence.]

POZZO   Do you hear, hog?

855 ESTRAGON   He never refuses?

POZZO   He refused once. [Silence] Dance, misery!

[LUCKY puts down bag and basket, advances towards front, turns to
POZZO. LUCKY dances. He stops.]

ESTRAGON   Is that all?

POZZO   Encore!

[LUCKY executes the same movements, stops.]

ESTRAGON   Pooh! I'd do as well myself. [He imitates LUCKY, almost falls.] With
860   a little practice.

POZZO   He used to dance the farandole, the fling, the brawl, the jig, the fan-
dango and even the hornpipe.[7] He capered. For joy. Now that's the best he
can do. Do you know what he calls it?

ESTRAGON   The Scapegoat's Agony.

865 VLADIMIR   The Hard Stool.

POZZO   The Net. He thinks he's entangled in a net.

VLADIMIR [squirming like an aesthete]   There's something about it . . .

[LUCKY makes to return to his burdens.]

POZZO   Woaa!

[LUCKY stiffens.]

ESTRAGON   Tell us about the time he refused.

870 POZZO   With pleasure, with pleasure. [He fumbles in his pockets.] Wait. [He
· fumbles.] What have I done with my spray? [He fumbles.] Well now isn't
that . . . [He looks up, consternation on his features. Faintly.] I can't find my
pulverizer![8]

ESTRAGON [faintly]   My left lung is very weak! [He coughs feebly. In ringing
875   tones.] But my right lung is as sound as a bell!

POZZO [normal voice]   No matter! What was I saying. [He ponders.] Wait.
[Ponders.] Well now isn't that . . . [He raises his head.] Help me!

ESTRAGON   Wait!

VLADIMIR   Wait!

880 POZZO   Wait!

[All three take off their hats simultaneously, press their hands to their
foreheads, concentrate.]

---

7. All energetic dances, associated (respectively) with Provence, the Scottish highlands,
France, Ireland, Spain, and England.
8. That is, his vaporizer, mentioned earlier.

ESTRAGON [*triumphantly*]   Ah!

VLADIMIR   He has it.

POZZO [*impatient*]   Well?

ESTRAGON   Why doesn't he put down his bags?

885 VLADIMIR   Rubbish!

POZZO   Are you sure?

VLADIMIR   Damn it haven't you already told us?

POZZO   I've already told you?

ESTRAGON   He's already told us?

890 VLADIMIR   Anyway he has put them down.

ESTRAGON [*glance at Lucky*]   So he has. And what of it?

VLADIMIR   Since he has put down his bags it is impossible we should have asked why he does not do so.

POZZO   Stoutly reasoned!

895 ESTRAGON   And why has he put them down?

POZZO   Answer us that.

VLADIMIR   In order to dance.

ESTRAGON   True!

POZZO   True!

[*Silence. They put on their hats.*]

900 ESTRAGON   Nothing happens, nobody comes, nobody goes, it's awful!

VLADIMIR [*to* POZZO]   Tell him to think.

POZZO   Give him his hat.

VLADIMIR   His hat?

POZZO   He can't think without his hat.

905 VLADIMIR [*to* ESTRAGON]   Give him his hat.

ESTRAGON   Me! After what he did to me! Never!

VLADIMIR   I'll give it to him. [*He does not move.*]

ESTRAGON [*to* POZZO]   Tell him to go and fetch it.

POZZO   It's better to give it to him.

910 VLADIMIR   I'll give it to him.

[*He picks up the hat and tenders it at arm's length to* LUCKY, *who does not move.*]

POZZO   You must put it on his head.

ESTRAGON [*to* POZZO]   Tell him to take it.

POZZO   It's better to put it on his head.

VLADIMIR   I'll put it on his head.

[*He goes round behind* LUCKY, *approaches him cautiously, puts the hat on his head and recoils smartly.* LUCKY *does not move. Silence.*]

915 ESTRAGON   What's he waiting for?

POZZO   Stand back! [VLADIMIR *and* ESTRAGON *move away from* LUCKY. POZZO *jerks the rope.* LUCKY *looks at* POZZO.] Think, pig! [*Pause.* LUCKY *begins to dance.*] Stop! [LUCKY *stops.*] Forward! [LUCKY *advances.*] Stop! [LUCKY *stops.*] Think!

[*Silence.*]

920 LUCKY   On the other hand with regard to—

POZZO   Stop! [LUCKY *stops.*] Back! [LUCKY *moves back.*] Stop! [LUCKY *stops.*] Turn! [LUCKY *turns towards auditorium.*] Think!

LUCKY   Given the existence as uttered forth in the public works of Puncher
and Wattmann[9] of a personal God quaquaquaqua with white beard
925   quaquaquaqua outside time without extension who from the heights of
divine apathia divine athambia divine aphasia[1] loves us dearly with some
exceptions for reasons unknown but time will tell and

[VLADIMIR   suffers like the divine Miranda[2] with those who for reasons
    and   unknown but time will tell are plunged in torment plunged in
930 ESTRAGON   fire whose fire flames if that continues and who can doubt it will
    all   fire the firmament that is to say blast hell to heaven so blue still
attention,   and calm so calm with a calm which even though intermittent
POZZO   is better than nothing but not so fast and considering what is
dejected   more that as a result of the labors left unfinished crowned by the
935   and   Acacacacademy of Anthropopopometry of Essy-in-Possy[3] of
disgusted.]   Testew and Cunard it is established beyond all doubt all other
    doubt than that which clings to the labors of men that as a
[VLADIMIR   result of the labors unfinished of Testew and Cunard it is
    and   established as hereinafter but not so fast for reasons unknown
940 ESTRAGON   that as a result of the public works of Puncher and Wattmann
begin to   it is established beyond all doubt that in view of the labors of
protest,   Fartov and Belcher left unfinished for reasons unknown of
POZZO's   Testew and Cunard left unfinished it is established what many
sufferings   deny that man in Possy of Testew and Cunard that man in Essy
945 increase.]   that man in short that man in brief in spite of the strides of
    alimentation and defecation wastes and pines wastes and pines
[VLADIMIR   and concurrently simultaneously what is more for reasons
    and   unknown in spite of the strides of physical culture the practice
ESTRAGON   of sports such as tennis football running cycling swimming
950 attentive   flying floating riding gliding conating camogie[4] skating tennis of
again,   all kinds dying flying sports of all sorts autumn summer winter
POZZO   winter tennis of all kinds hockey of all sorts penicillin and
more and   succedanea[5] in a word I resume flying gliding golf over nine
more   and eighteen holes tennis of all sorts in a word for reasons
955 agitated   unknown in Feckham Peckham Fulham Clapham[6] namely
    and   concurrently simultaneously what is more for reasons unknown
groaning.]   but time will tell fades away I resume Fulham Clapham in a
    word the dead loss per head since the death of Bishop

9. Fictitious academics, as are "Testew and Cunard," "Fartov and Belcher," "Steinweg and Peterman," and so on, below. Mixing quasi-philosophical discourse, arcane language, and sexual/scatological wordplay, this speech uses invented and altered proper names, technical terms, and allusions to create half-meanings amid apparent nonsense.
1. Of the three Greek words employed here—apatheia (freedom from emotion), athambia (freedom from fear or surprise), and aphasia (lack or loss of speech)—only the last is actually used in English.
2. The character in William Shakespeare's The Tempest (1611) who agonizes over a ship-wreck she has witnessed: "O, I have suffered / With those that I saw suffer!" (1.2.5–6).
3. An echo of the Latin verbs esse (to be) and posse (to be able to). Acacacademy: in several Romance languages, including French, caca is a child's word for excrement. Anthropopopometry: that is, anthropometry (the study of measurement of the human body).
4. A Celtic team sport played with sticks and a ball (the women's version of hurling). Conating: desiring, attempting (Beckett's back-formation from conation).
5. Substitutes.
6. Three areas of south London, preceded by an obscene pun on them.

Berkeley[7] being to the tune of one inch four ounce per head

960

approximately by and large more or less to the nearest decimal

[VLADIMIR good measure round figures stark naked in the stockinged feet

and in Connemara[8] in a word for reasons unknown no matter what

ESTRAGON matter the facts are there and considering what is more much

protest more grave that in the light of the labors lost of Steinweg

965 *violently.* and Peterman it appears what is more much more grave that

POZZO in the light the light the light of the labors lost of Steinweg

jumps up, and Peterman that in the plains in the mountains by the

pulls on seas by the rivers running water running fire the air is the

the rope. same and then the earth namely the air and then the earth

970 *General* in the great cold the great dark the air and the earth abode

outcry. of stones in the great cold alas alas in the year of their Lord

LUCKY *pulls* six hundred and something the air the earth the sea the earth

on the rope, abode of stones in the great deeps the great cold on sea on

staggers, land and in the air I resume for reasons unknown in spite of the

975 *shouts his* tennis the facts are there but time will tell I resume alas alas

text. All on on in short in fine on on abode of stones who can doubt it I

three throw resume but not so fast I resume the skull fading fading fading

themselves and concurrently simultaneously what is more for reasons

on LUCKY unknown in spite of the tennis on on the beard the flames

980 *who* the tears the stones so blue so calm alas alas on on the skull

struggles the skull the skull the skull in Connemara in spite of the

and shouts tennis the labors abandoned left unfinished graver still abode

his text.] of stones in a word I resume alas alas abandoned unfinished

the skull the skull in Connemara in spite of the tennis the skull

985 alas the stones Cunard [*Mêlée, final vociferations*] tennis . . . the

stones . . . so calm . . . Cunard . . . unfinished . . .

POZZO His hat!

> [VLADIMIR *seizes* LUCKY'*s hat. Silence of* LUCKY. *He falls. Silence. Panting of the victors.*]

ESTRAGON Avenged!

> [VLADIMIR *examines the hat, peers inside it.*]

POZZO Give me that! [*He snatches the hat from* VLADIMIR, *throws it on the*

990 *ground, tramples on it.*] There's an end to his thinking!

VLADIMIR But will he be able to walk?

POZZO Walk or crawl! [*He kicks* LUCKY.] Up pig!

ESTRAGON Perhaps he's dead.

VLADIMIR You'll kill him.

995 POZZO Up scum! [*He jerks the rope.*] Help me!

VLADIMIR How?

POZZO Raise him up!

> [VLADIMIR *and* ESTRAGON *hoist* LUCKY *to his feet, support him an instant, then let him go. He falls.*]

ESTRAGON He's doing it on purpose!

---

7. George Berkeley (1685–1753), Irish idealist philosopher and bishop in the Church
of Ireland. Berkeley's theory, which held that
the world exists only insofar as it is per-

ceived by the senses, is summed up in his
Latin dictum *Esse est percipi* (To be is to be
perceived).
8. A region of Galway in western Ireland.

POZZO   You must hold him. [*Pause*] Come on, come on, raise him up.

1000 ESTRAGON   To hell with him!

VLADIMIR   Come on, once more.

ESTRAGON   What does he take us for?

[*They raise* LUCKY, *hold him up.*]

POZZO   Don't let him go! [VLADIMIR *and* ESTRAGON *totter.*] Don't move! [POZZO *fetches bag and basket and brings them towards* LUCKY.] Hold him tight! [*He* 1005 *puts the bag in* LUCKY's *hand.* LUCKY *drops it immediately.*] Don't let him go! [*He puts back the bag in* LUCKY's *hand. Gradually, at the feel of the bag,* LUCKY *recovers his senses and his fingers finally close round the handle.*] Hold him tight! [*As before with basket*] Now! You can let him go. [VLADIMIR *and* ESTRAGON *move away from* LUCKY *who totters, reels, sags, but succeeds in remaining on his feet, bag and basket in his hands.* POZZO *steps back, cracks his whip.*] Forward! [LUCKY *totters forward.*] Back! [LUCKY *totters back.*] Turn! [LUCKY *turns.*] Done it! He can walk. [*Turning to* VLADIMIR *and* 1010 ESTRAGON] Thank you, gentlemen, and let me . . . [*He fumbles in his pockets*] . . . let me wish you . . . [*Fumbles.*] . . . wish you . . . [*Fumbles.*] . . . what have I done with my watch? [*Fumbles.*] A genuine half-hunter, gentlemen, with deadbeat escapement![9] [*Sobbing.*] Twas my granpa gave it to me! [*He searches on the ground,* VLADIMIR *and* ESTRAGON *likewise.* POZZO *turns over with his foot the remains of* LUCKY's *hat.*] Well now isn't that just—

1015 VLADIMIR   Perhaps it's in your fob.[1]

POZZO   Wait! [*He doubles up in an attempt to apply his ear to his stomach, listens. Silence.*] I hear nothing. [*He beckons them to approach.* VLADIMIR *and* ESTRAGON *go over to him, bend over his stomach.*] Surely one should hear the tick-tick.

1020 VLADIMIR   Silence!

[*All listen, bent double.*]

ESTRAGON   I hear something.

POZZO   Where?

VLADIMIR   It's the heart.

POZZO [*disappointed*]   Damnation!

1025 VLADIMIR   Silence!

ESTRAGON   Perhaps it has stopped.

[*They straighten up.*]

POZZO   Which of you smells so bad?

ESTRAGON   He has stinking breath and I have stinking feet.

POZZO   I must go.

1030 ESTRAGON   And your half-hunter?

POZZO   I must have left it at the manor.

[*Silence.*]

ESTRAGON   Then adieu.

POZZO   Adieu.

VLADIMIR   Adieu.

1035 POZZO   Adieu.

9. The mechanism in watches that regulates the movement of the hands, here "deadbeat" because it does not recoil. *Half-hunter:* a kind of pocket watch featuring a metal case with a small glass window through which the hands are visible.
1. A small pocket, originally in the waistband (also known as a "watch pocket").

[*Silence. No one moves.*]

VLADIMIR Adieu.

POZZO Adieu.

ESTRAGON Adieu.

[*Silence.*]

POZZO And thank you.

1040 VLADIMIR Thank *you*.

POZZO Not at all.

ESTRAGON Yes yes.

POZZO No no.

VLADIMIR Yes yes.

1045 ESTRAGON No no.

[*Silence.*]

POZZO I don't seem to be able . . . [*Long hesitation*] . . . to depart.

ESTRAGON Such is life.

[POZZO *turns, moves away from* LUCKY *towards the wings, paying out the rope as he goes.*]

VLADIMIR You're going the wrong way.

POZZO I need a running start. [*Having come to the end of the rope, i.e. off*

1050 *stage, he stops, turns and cries.*] Stand back! [VLADIMIR *and* ESTRAGON *stand back, look towards* POZZO. *Crack of whip.*] On! On!

ESTRAGON On!

VLADIMIR On!

[LUCKY *moves off.*]

POZZO Faster! [*He appears, crosses the stage preceded by* LUCKY. VLADIMIR *and*

1055 ESTRAGON *wave their hats. Exit* LUCKY.] On! On! [*On the point of disappearing in his turn he stops and turns. The rope tautens. Noise of* LUCKY *falling off.*] Stool! [VLADIMIR *fetches stool and gives it to* POZZO *who throws it to* LUCKY.] Adieu!

VLADIMIR ⎫
ESTRAGON ⎭ [*waving*] Adieu! Adieu!

POZZO Up! Pig! [*Noise of* LUCKY *getting up.*] On! [*Exit* POZZO.] Faster! On!

1060 Adieu! Pig! Yip! Adieu!

[*Long silence.*]

VLADIMIR That passed the time.

ESTRAGON It would have passed in any case.

VLADIMIR Yes, but not so rapidly.

[*Pause.*]

ESTRAGON What do we do now?

1065 VLADIMIR I don't know.

ESTRAGON Let's go.

VLADIMIR We can't.

ESTRAGON Why not?

VLADIMIR We're waiting for Godot.

1070 ESTRAGON [*despairingly*] Ah!

[*Pause.*]

VLADIMIR How they've changed!

ESTRAGON Who?

VLADIMIR   Those two.

ESTRAGON   That's the idea, let's make a little conversation.

1075 VLADIMIR   Haven't they?

ESTRAGON   What?

VLADIMIR   Changed.

ESTRAGON   Very likely. They all change. Only we can't.

VLADIMIR   Likely! It's certain. Didn't you see them?

1080 ESTRAGON   I suppose I did. But I don't know them.

VLADIMIR   Yes you do know them.

ESTRAGON   No I don't know them.

VLADIMIR   We know them, I tell you. You forget everything. [*Pause. To himself.*] Unless they're not the same . . .

1085 ESTRAGON   Why didn't they recognize us then?

VLADIMIR   That means nothing. I too pretended not to recognize them. And then nobody ever recognizes us.

ESTRAGON   Forget it. What we need—ow! [VLADIMIR *does not react.*] Ow!

VLADIMIR [*to himself*]   Unless they're not the same . . .

1090 ESTRAGON   Didi! It's the other foot! [*He goes hobbling towards the mound.*]

VLADIMIR   Unless they're not the same . . .

BOY [*off*]   Mister!

[ESTRAGON *halts. Both look towards the voice.*]

ESTRAGON   Off we go again.

VLADIMIR   Approach, my child.

[*Enter* BOY, *timidly. He halts.*]

1095 BOY   Mister Albert . . . ?

VLADIMIR   Yes.

ESTRAGON   What do you want?

VLADIMIR   Approach!

[*The* BOY *does not move.*]

ESTRAGON [*forcibly*]   Approach when you're told, can't you?

[*The* BOY *advances timidly, halts.*]

1100 VLADIMIR   What is it?

BOY   Mr. Godot . . .

VLADIMIR   Obviously . . . [*Pause*] Approach.

ESTRAGON [*violently*]   Will you approach! [*The* BOY *advances timidly.*] What kept you so late?

1105 VLADIMIR   You have a message from Mr. Godot?

BOY   Yes Sir.

VLADIMIR   Well, what is it?

ESTRAGON   What kept you so late?

[*The* BOY *looks at them in turn, not knowing to which he should reply.*]

VLADIMIR [*to* ESTRAGON]   Let him alone.

1110 ESTRAGON [*violently*]   You let me alone. [*Advancing, to the* BOY] Do you know what time it is?

BOY [*recoiling*]   It's not my fault, Sir.

ESTRAGON   And whose is it? Mine?

BOY   I was afraid, Sir.

1115 ESTRAGON   Afraid of what? Of us? [*Pause*] Answer me!

VLADIMIR   I know what it is, he was afraid of the others.

ESTRAGON   How long have you been here?

BOY   A good while, Sir.

VLADIMIR   You were afraid of the whip?

1120 BOY   Yes Sir.

VLADIMIR   The roars?

BOY   Yes Sir.

VLADIMIR   The two big men.

BOY   Yes Sir.

1125 VLADIMIR   Do you know them?

BOY   No Sir.

VLADIMIR   Are you a native of these parts? [*Silence*] Do you belong to these parts?

BOY   Yes Sir.

1130 ESTRAGON   That's all a pack of lies. [*Shaking the* BOY *by the arm*] Tell us the truth!

BOY [*trembling*]   But it is the truth, Sir!

VLADIMIR   Will you let him alone! What's the matter with you? [ESTRAGON *releases the* BOY, *moves away, covering his face with his hands.* VLADIMIR *and the* BOY *observe him.* ESTRAGON *drops his hands. His face is convulsed.*] What's the matter with you?

1135 ESTRAGON   I'm unhappy.

VLADIMIR   Not really! Since when?

ESTRAGON   I'd forgotten.

VLADIMIR   Extraordinary the tricks that memory plays!

[ESTRAGON *tries to speak, renounces, limps to his place, sits down and begins to take off his boots. To* BOY]

Well?

1140 BOY   Mr. Godot—

VLADIMIR   I've seen you before, haven't I?

BOY   I don't know, Sir.

VLADIMIR   You don't know me?

BOY   No Sir.

1145 VLADIMIR   It wasn't you came yesterday?

BOY   No Sir.

VLADIMIR   This is your first time?

BOY   Yes Sir.

[*Silence.*]

VLADIMIR   Words words. [*Pause*] Speak.

1150 BOY [*in a rush*]   Mr. Godot told me to tell you he won't come this evening but surely tomorrow.

[*Silence.*]

VLADIMIR   Is that all?

BOY   Yes Sir.

[*Silence.*]

VLADIMIR   You work for Mr. Godot?

1155 BOY   Yes Sir.

VLADIMIR   What do you do?

BOY   I mind the goats, Sir.

VLADIMIR   Is he good to you?

BOY Yes Sir.
1160 VLADIMIR He doesn't beat you?
BOY No Sir, not me.
VLADIMIR Whom does he beat?
BOY He beats my brother, Sir.
VLADIMIR Ah, you have a brother?
1165 BOY Yes Sir.
VLADIMIR What does he do?
BOY He minds the sheep, Sir.
VLADIMIR And why doesn't he beat you?
BOY I don't know, Sir.
1170 VLADIMIR He must be fond of you.
BOY I don't know, Sir.
        [Silence.]
VLADIMIR Does he give you enough to eat? [The BOY hesitates.] Does he feed
    you well?
BOY Fairly well, Sir.
1175 VLADIMIR You're not unhappy? [The BOY hesitates.] Do you hear me?
BOY Yes Sir.
VLADIMIR Well?
BOY I don't know, Sir.
VLADIMIR You don't know if you're unhappy or not?
1180 BOY No Sir.
VLADIMIR You're as bad as myself. [Silence] Where do you sleep?
BOY In the loft, Sir.
VLADIMIR With your brother?
BOY Yes Sir.
1185 VLADIMIR In the hay?
BOY Yes Sir.
        [Silence.]
VLADIMIR All right, you may go.
BOY What am I to tell Mr. Godot, Sir?
VLADIMIR Tell him . . . [He hesitates.] . . . tell him you saw us. [Pause] You
1190   did see us, didn't you?
BOY Yes Sir.
        [He steps back, hesitates, turns and exits running. The light suddenly
        fails. In a moment it is night. The moon rises at back, mounts in the sky,
        stands still, shedding a pale light on the scene.]
VLADIMIR At last! [ESTRAGON gets up and goes towards VLADIMIR, a boot in
    each hand. He puts them down at edge of stage, straightens and contemplates
    the moon.] What are you doing?
ESTRAGON Pale for weariness.
1195 VLADIMIR Eh?
ESTRAGON Of climbing heaven and gazing on the likes of us.
VLADIMIR Your boots, what are you doing with your boots?
ESTRAGON [turning to look at the boots] I'm leaving them there. [Pause]
    Another will come, just as . . . as . . . as me, but with smaller feet, and
1200   they'll make him happy.
VLADIMIR But you can't go barefoot!

ESTRAGON   Christ did.

VLADIMIR   Christ! What has Christ got to do with it? You're not going to compare yourself to Christ!

1205   ESTRAGON   All my life I've compared myself to him.

VLADIMIR   But where he lived it was warm, it was dry!

ESTRAGON   Yes. And they crucified quick.

[*Silence.*]

VLADIMIR   We've nothing more to do here.

ESTRAGON   Nor anywhere else.

1210   VLADIMIR   Ah Gogo, don't go on like that. Tomorrow everything will be
better.

ESTRAGON   How do you make that out?

VLADIMIR   Did you not hear what the child said?

ESTRAGON   No.

VLADIMIR   He said that Godot was sure to come tomorrow. [*Pause*] What do
1215   you say to that?

ESTRAGON   Then all we have to do is to wait on here.

VLADIMIR   Are you mad? We must take cover. [*He takes* ESTRAGON *by the
arm.*] Come on.

[*He draws* ESTRAGON *after him.* ESTRAGON *yields, then resists. They halt.*]

ESTRAGON   [*looking at the tree*]   Pity we haven't got a bit of rope.

1220   VLADIMIR   Come on. It's cold.

[*He draws* ESTRAGON *after him. As before.*]

ESTRAGON   Remind me to bring a bit of rope tomorrow.

VLADIMIR   Yes. Come on.

[*He draws him after him. As before.*]

ESTRAGON   How long have we been together all the time now?

VLADIMIR   I don't know. Fifty years maybe.

1225   ESTRAGON   Do you remember the day I threw myself into the Rhône?[2]

VLADIMIR   We were grape harvesting.

ESTRAGON   You fished me out.

VLADIMIR   That's all dead and buried.

ESTRAGON   My clothes dried in the sun.

1230   VLADIMIR   There's no good harking back on that. Come on.

[*He draws him after him. As before.*]

ESTRAGON   Wait!

VLADIMIR   I'm cold!

ESTRAGON   Wait! [*He moves away from* VLADIMIR.] I sometimes wonder if we
wouldn't have been better off alone, each one for himself. [*He crosses the
1235   stage and sits down on the mound.*] We weren't made for the same road.

VLADIMIR   [*without anger*]   It's not certain.

ESTRAGON   No, nothing is certain.

[VLADIMIR *slowly crosses the stage and sits down beside* ESTRAGON.]

VLADIMIR   We can still part, if you think it would be better.

ESTRAGON   It's not worthwhile now.

[*Silence.*]

2. A major river in southeastern France.

1240   VLADIMIR   No, it's not worthwhile now.

         [*Silence.*]

  ESTRAGON   Well, shall we go?

  VLADIMIR   Yes, let's go.

         [*They do not move.*]

Curtain.

Act 2

Next day. Same time.
Same place.

         [ESTRAGON's *boots front center, heels together, toes splayed.* LUCKY's *hat at same place.*]

         [*The tree has four or five leaves.*]

         [*Enter* VLADIMIR *agitatedly. He halts and looks long at the tree, then suddenly begins to move feverishly about the stage. He halts before the boots, picks one up, examines it, sniffs it, manifests disgust, puts it back carefully. Comes and goes. Halts extreme right and gazes into distance off, shading his eyes with his hand. Comes and goes. Halts extreme left, as before. Comes and goes. Halts suddenly and begins to sing loudly.*]

  VLADIMIR   A dog came in—

         [*Having begun too high he stops, clears his throat, resumes.*]

         A dog came in the kitchen
         And stole a crust of bread.
         Then cook up with a ladle
5   And beat him till he was dead.

         Then all the dogs came running
         And dug the dog a tomb—

         [*He stops, broods, resumes.*]

         Then all the dogs came running
         And dug the dog a tomb
10   And wrote upon the tombstone
         For the eyes of dogs to come:

         A dog came in the kitchen
         And stole a crust of bread.
         Then cook up with a ladle
15   And beat him till he was dead.

         Then all the dogs came running
         And dug the dog a tomb—

         [*He stops, broods, resumes.*]

         Then all the dogs came running
         And dug the dog a tomb—

         [*He stops, broods. Softly.*]

20   And dug the dog a tomb . . .

[*He remains a moment silent and motionless, then begins to move fever-ishly about the stage. He halts before the tree, comes and goes, before the boots, comes and goes, halts extreme right, gazes into distance, extreme left, gazes into distance. Enter* ESTRAGON *right, barefoot, head bowed. He slowly crosses the stage.* VLADIMIR *turns and sees him.*]

VLADIMIR   You again! [ESTRAGON *halts but does not raise his head.* VLADIMIR *goes towards him.*] Come here till I embrace you.

ESTRAGON   Don't touch me!

[VLADIMIR *holds back, pained.*]

VLADIMIR   Do you want me to go away? [*Pause*] Gogo! [*Pause.* VLADIMIR
25   *observes him attentively.*] Did they beat you? [*Pause*] Gogo! [ESTRAGON *remains silent, head bowed.*] Where did you spend the night?

ESTRAGON   Don't touch me! Don't question me! Don't speak to me! Stay with me!

VLADIMIR   Did I ever leave you?

30 ESTRAGON   You let me go.

VLADIMIR   Look at me. [ESTRAGON *does not raise his head. Violently.*] Will you look at me!

[ESTRAGON *raises his head. They look long at each other, then suddenly embrace, clapping each other on the back. End of the embrace.* ESTRAGON, *no longer supported, almost falls.*]

ESTRAGON   What a day!

VLADIMIR   Who beat you? Tell me.

35 ESTRAGON   Another day done with.

VLADIMIR   Not yet.

ESTRAGON   For me it's over and done with, no matter what happens. [*Silence*] I heard you singing.

VLADIMIR   That's right, I remember.

40 ESTRAGON   That finished me. I said to myself, He's all alone, he thinks I'm gone for ever, and he sings.

VLADIMIR   One is not master of one's moods. All day I've felt in great form. [*Pause*] I didn't get up in the night, not once!

ESTRAGON [*sadly*]   You see, you piss better when I'm not there.

45 VLADIMIR   I missed you . . . and at the same time I was happy. Isn't that a queer thing?

ESTRAGON [*shocked*]   Happy?

VLADIMIR   Perhaps it's not quite the right word.

ESTRAGON   And now?

50 VLADIMIR   Now? . . . [*Joyous*] There you are again . . . [*Indifferent*] There we are again . . . [*Gloomy*] There I am again.

ESTRAGON   You see, you feel worse when I'm with you. I feel better alone too.

VLADIMIR [*vexed*]   Then why do you always come crawling back?

ESTRAGON   I don't know.

55 VLADIMIR   No, but I do. It's because you don't know how to defend yourself. I wouldn't have let them beat you.

ESTRAGON   You couldn't have stopped them.

VLADIMIR   Why not?

ESTRAGON   There was ten of them.

60 VLADIMIR   No, I mean before they beat you. I would have stopped you from doing whatever it was you were doing.

ESTRAGON   I wasn't doing anything.

VLADIMIR   Then why did they beat you?

ESTRAGON   I don't know.

65 VLADIMIR   Ah no, Gogo, the truth is there are things escape you that don't escape me, you must feel it yourself.

ESTRAGON   I tell you I wasn't doing anything.

VLADIMIR   Perhaps you weren't. But it's the way of doing it that counts, the way of doing it, if you want to go on living.

70 ESTRAGON   I wasn't doing anything.

VLADIMIR   You must be happy too, deep down, if you only knew it.

ESTRAGON   Happy about what?

VLADIMIR   To be back with me again.

ESTRAGON   Would you say so?

75 VLADIMIR   Say you are, even if it's not true.

ESTRAGON   What am I to say?

VLADIMIR   Say, I am happy.

ESTRAGON   I am happy.

VLADIMIR   So am I.

80 ESTRAGON   So am I.

VLADIMIR   We are happy.

ESTRAGON   We are happy. [*Silence*] What do we do now, now that we are happy?

VLADIMIR   Wait for Godot. [ESTRAGON *groans. Silence.*] Things have changed
85 here since yesterday.

ESTRAGON   And if he doesn't come.

VLADIMIR   [*after a moment of bewilderment*]   We'll see when the time comes. [*Pause*] I was saying that things have changed here since yesterday.

ESTRAGON   Everything oozes.

90 VLADIMIR   Look at the tree.

ESTRAGON   It's never the same pus from one second to the next.

VLADIMIR   The tree, look at the tree.

[ESTRAGON *looks at the tree.*]

ESTRAGON   Was it not there yesterday?

VLADIMIR   Yes of course it was there. Do you not remember? We nearly
95 hanged ourselves from it. But you wouldn't. Do you not remember?

ESTRAGON   You dreamt it.

VLADIMIR   Is it possible you've forgotten already?

ESTRAGON   That's the way I am. Either I forget immediately or I never forget.

VLADIMIR   And Pozzo and Lucky, have you forgotten them too?

100 ESTRAGON   Pozzo and Lucky?

VLADIMIR   He's forgotten everything!

ESTRAGON   I remember a lunatic who kicked the shins off me. Then he played the fool.

VLADIMIR   That was Lucky.

105 ESTRAGON   I remember that. But when was it?

VLADIMIR   And his keeper, do you not remember him?

ESTRAGON   He gave me a bone.

VLADIMIR   That was Pozzo.

ESTRAGON   And all that was yesterday, you say?

110 VLADIMIR   Yes of course it was yesterday.

ESTRAGON   And here where we are now?

VLADIMIR   Where else do you think? Do you not recognize the place?

ESTRAGON [*suddenly furious*]   Recognize! What is there to recognize? All my lousy life I've crawled about in the mud! And you talk to me about scenery!

115 [*Looking wildly about him*] Look at this muckheap! I've never stirred from it!

VLADIMIR   Calm yourself, calm yourself.

ESTRAGON   You and your landscapes! Tell me about the worms!

VLADIMIR   All the same, you can't tell me that this [*Gesture*] bears any resemblance to . . . [*He hesitates.*] . . . to the Mâcon country[3] for example. You

120 can't deny there's a big difference.

ESTRAGON   The Mâcon country! Who's talking to you about the Mâcon country?

VLADIMIR   But you were there yourself, in the Mâcon country.

ESTRAGON   No I was never in the Mâcon country! I've puked my puke of a

125 life away here, I tell you! Here! In the Cackon country!

VLADIMIR   But we were there together, I could swear to it! Picking grapes for a man called . . . [*He snaps his fingers.*] . . . can't think of the name of the man, at a place called . . . [*Snaps his fingers.*] . . . can't think of the name of the place, do you not remember?

130 ESTRAGON [*a little calmer*]   It's possible. I didn't notice anything.

VLADIMIR   But down there everything is red!

ESTRAGON [*exasperated*]   I didn't notice anything, I tell you!

    [*Silence.* VLADIMIR *sighs deeply.*]

VLADIMIR   You're a hard man to get on with, Gogo.

ESTRAGON   It'd be better if we parted.

135 VLADIMIR   You always say that and you always come crawling back.

ESTRAGON   The best thing would be to kill me, like the other.

VLADIMIR   What other? [*Pause*] What other?

ESTRAGON   Like billions of others.

VLADIMIR [*sententious*]   To every man his little cross. [*He sighs.*] Till he dies.

140 [*Afterthought*] And is forgotten.

ESTRAGON   In the meantime let us try and converse calmly, since we are incapable of keeping silent.

VLADIMIR   You're right, we're inexhaustible.

ESTRAGON   It's so we won't think.

145 VLADIMIR   We have that excuse.

ESTRAGON   It's so we won't hear.

VLADIMIR   We have our reasons.

ESTRAGON   All the dead voices.

VLADIMIR   They make a noise like wings.

150 ESTRAGON   Like leaves.

VLADIMIR   Like sand.

ESTRAGON   Like leaves.

    [*Silence.*]

VLADIMIR   They all speak at once.

ESTRAGON   Each one to itself.

    [*Silence.*]

3. A wine-producing district in the Bourgogne region of east-central France.

155	VLADIMIR	Rather they whisper.
	ESTRAGON	They rustle.
	VLADIMIR	They murmur.
	ESTRAGON	They rustle.

[Silence.]

	VLADIMIR	What do they say?
160	ESTRAGON	They talk about their lives.
	VLADIMIR	To have lived is not enough for them.
	ESTRAGON	They have to talk about it.
	VLADIMIR	To be dead is not enough for them.
	ESTRAGON	It is not sufficient.

[Silence.]

165	VLADIMIR	They make a noise like feathers.
	ESTRAGON	Like leaves.
	VLADIMIR	Like ashes.
	ESTRAGON	Like leaves.

[Long silence.]

	VLADIMIR	Say something!
170	ESTRAGON	I'm trying.

[Long silence.]

	VLADIMIR	*[in anguish]* Say anything at all!
	ESTRAGON	What do we do now?
	VLADIMIR	Wait for Godot.
	ESTRAGON	Ah!

[Silence.]

175	VLADIMIR	This is awful!
	ESTRAGON	Sing something.
	VLADIMIR	No no! *[He reflects.]* We could start all over again perhaps.
	ESTRAGON	That should be easy.
	VLADIMIR	It's the start that's difficult.
180	ESTRAGON	You can start from anything.
	VLADIMIR	Yes, but you have to decide.
	ESTRAGON	True.

[Silence.]

	VLADIMIR	Help me!
	ESTRAGON	I'm trying.

[Silence.]

185	VLADIMIR	When you seek you hear.
	ESTRAGON	You do.
	VLADIMIR	That prevents you from finding.
	ESTRAGON	It does.
	VLADIMIR	That prevents you from thinking.
190	ESTRAGON	You think all the same.
	VLADIMIR	No no, impossible.
	ESTRAGON	That's the idea, let's contradict each other.
	VLADIMIR	Impossible.
	ESTRAGON	You think so?
195	VLADIMIR	We're in no danger of ever thinking any more.

ESTRAGON	Then what are we complaining about?
VLADIMIR	Thinking is not the worst.
ESTRAGON	Perhaps not. But at least there's that.
VLADIMIR	That what?
200 ESTRAGON	That's the idea, let's ask each other questions.
VLADIMIR	What do you mean, at least there's that?
ESTRAGON	That much less misery.
VLADIMIR	True.
ESTRAGON	Well? If we gave thanks for our mercies?
205 VLADIMIR	What is terrible is to *have* thought.
ESTRAGON	But did that ever happen to us?
VLADIMIR	Where are all these corpses from?
ESTRAGON	These skeletons.
VLADIMIR	Tell me that.
210 ESTRAGON	True.
VLADIMIR	We must have thought a little.
ESTRAGON	At the very beginning.
VLADIMIR	A charnel-house! A charnel-house!⁴
ESTRAGON	You don't have to look.
215 VLADIMIR	You can't help looking.
ESTRAGON	True.
VLADIMIR	Try as one may.
ESTRAGON	I beg your pardon?
VLADIMIR	Try as one may.
220 ESTRAGON	We should turn resolutely towards Nature.
VLADIMIR	We've tried that.
ESTRAGON	True.
VLADIMIR	Oh it's not the worst, I know.
ESTRAGON	What?
225 VLADIMIR	To have thought.
ESTRAGON	Obviously.
VLADIMIR	But we could have done without it.
ESTRAGON	Que voulez-vous?⁵
VLADIMIR	I beg your pardon?
230 ESTRAGON	Que voulez-vous.
VLADIMIR	Ah! que voulez-vous. Exactly.
	[*Silence.*]
ESTRAGON	That wasn't such a bad little canter.
VLADIMIR	Yes, but now we'll have to find something else.
235 ESTRAGON	Let me see. [*He takes off his hat, concentrates.*]
VLADIMIR	Let me see. [*He takes off his hat, concentrates. Long silence.*] Ah! [*They put on their hats, relax.*]
ESTRAGON	Well?
VLADIMIR	What was I saying, we could go on from there.
ESTRAGON	What were you saying when?
VLADIMIR	At the very beginning.

4. A building or vault in which the bodies or bones of the dead are placed.

5. What do you want? (French).

240 ESTRAGON The very beginning of WHAT?

VLADIMIR This evening . . . I was saying . . . I was saying . . .

ESTRAGON I'm not a historian.

VLADIMIR Wait . . . we embraced . . . we were happy . . . happy . . . what do
we do now that we're happy . . . go on waiting . . . waiting . . . let me
245 think . . . it's coming . . . go on waiting . . . now that we're happy . . . let
me see . . . ah! The tree!

ESTRAGON The tree?

VLADIMIR Do you not remember?

ESTRAGON I'm tired.

250 VLADIMIR Look at it.

[*They look at the tree.*]

ESTRAGON I see nothing.

VLADIMIR But yesterday evening it was all black and bare. And now it's covered with leaves.

ESTRAGON Leaves?

255 VLADIMIR In a single night.

ESTRAGON It must be the Spring.

VLADIMIR But in a single night!

ESTRAGON I tell you we weren't here yesterday. Another of your nightmares.

VLADIMIR And where were we yesterday evening according to you?

260 ESTRAGON How would I know? In another compartment. There's no lack of
void.

VLADIMIR [*sure of himself*] Good. We weren't here yesterday evening. Now
what did we do yesterday evening?

ESTRAGON Do?

265 VLADIMIR Try and remember.

ESTRAGON Do . . . I suppose we blathered.

VLADIMIR [*controlling himself*] About what?

ESTRAGON Oh . . . this and that I suppose, nothing in particular. [*With
assurance*] Yes, now I remember, yesterday evening we spent blathering
270 about nothing in particular. That's been going on now for half a century.

VLADIMIR You don't remember any fact, any circumstance?

ESTRAGON [*weary*] Don't torment me, Didi.

VLADIMIR The sun. The moon. Do you not remember?

ESTRAGON They must have been there, as usual.

275 VLADIMIR You didn't notice anything out of the ordinary?

ESTRAGON Alas!

VLADIMIR And Pozzo? And Lucky?

ESTRAGON Pozzo?

VLADIMIR The bones.

280 ESTRAGON They were like fishbones.

VLADIMIR It was Pozzo gave them to you.

ESTRAGON I don't know.

VLADIMIR And the kick.

ESTRAGON That's right, someone gave me a kick.

285 VLADIMIR It was Lucky gave it to you.

ESTRAGON And all that was yesterday?

VLADIMIR Show your leg.

ESTRAGON   Which?

VLADIMIR   Both. Pull up your trousers. [ESTRAGON *gives a leg to* VLADIMIR,
290   *staggers.* VLADIMIR *takes the leg. They stagger.*] Pull up your trousers.

ESTRAGON   I can't.

[VLADIMIR *pulls up the trousers, looks at the leg, lets it go.* ESTRAGON
almost falls.]

VLADIMIR   The other. [ESTRAGON *gives the same leg.*] The other, pig! [ESTRAGON
gives the other leg. Triumphantly.] There's the wound! Beginning to fester!

295   ESTRAGON   And what about it?

VLADIMIR   [*letting go the leg*]   Where are your boots?

ESTRAGON   I must have thrown them away.

VLADIMIR   When?

ESTRAGON   I don't know.

300   VLADIMIR   Why?

ESTRAGON   [*exasperated*]   I don't know why I don't know!

VLADIMIR   No, I mean why did you throw them away?

ESTRAGON   [*exasperated*]   Because they were hurting me!

VLADIMIR   [*triumphantly, pointing to the boots*]   There they are! [ESTRAGON
305   *looks at the boots.*] At the very spot where you left them yesterday!

[ESTRAGON *goes towards the boots, inspects them closely.*]

ESTRAGON   They're not mine.

VLADIMIR   [*stupefied*]   Not yours!

ESTRAGON   Mine were black. These are brown.

VLADIMIR   You're sure yours were black?

310   ESTRAGON   Well they were a kind of grey.

VLADIMIR   And these are brown. Show.

ESTRAGON   [*picking up a boot*]   Well they're a kind of green.

VLADIMIR   Show. [ESTRAGON *hands him the boot.* VLADIMIR *inspects it, throws
it down angrily.*] Well of all the—

315   ESTRAGON   You see, all that's a lot of bloody—

VLADIMIR   Ah! I see what it is. Yes, I see what's happened.

ESTRAGON   All that's a lot of bloody—

VLADIMIR   It's elementary. Someone came and took yours and left you his.

ESTRAGON   Why?

320   VLADIMIR   His were too tight for him, so he took yours.

ESTRAGON   But mine were too tight.

VLADIMIR   For you. Not for him.

ESTRAGON   [*having tried in vain to work it out*]   I'm tired! [*Pause*] Let's go.

VLADIMIR   We can't.

325   ESTRAGON   Why not?

VLADIMIR   We're waiting for Godot.

ESTRAGON   Ah! [*Pause. Despairing*] What'll we do, what'll we do!

VLADIMIR   There's nothing we can do.

ESTRAGON   But I can't go on like this!

330   VLADIMIR   Would you like a radish?

ESTRAGON   Is that all there is?

VLADIMIR   There are radishes and turnips.

ESTRAGON   Are there no carrots?

VLADIMIR   No. Anyway you overdo it with your carrots.

335 ESTRAGON   Then give me a radish. [VLADIMIR *fumbles in his pockets, finds nothing but turnips, finally brings out a radish and hands it to* ESTRAGON *who examines it, sniffs it.*] It's black!

VLADIMIR   It's a radish.

ESTRAGON   I only like the pink ones, you know that!

VLADIMIR   Then you don't want it?

340 ESTRAGON   I only like the pink ones!

VLADIMIR   Then give it back to me. [ESTRAGON *gives it back.*]

ESTRAGON   I'll go and get a carrot. [*He does not move.*]

VLADIMIR   This is becoming really insignificant.

ESTRAGON   Not enough.

     [*Silence.*]

345 VLADIMIR   What about trying them.

ESTRAGON   I've tried everything.

VLADIMIR   No, I mean the boots.

ESTRAGON   Would that be a good thing?

VLADIMIR   It'd pass the time. [ESTRAGON *hesitates.*] I assure you, it'd be an 350 occupation.

ESTRAGON   A relaxation.

VLADIMIR   A recreation.

ESTRAGON   A relaxation.

VLADIMIR   Try.

355 ESTRAGON   You'll help me?

VLADIMIR   I will of course.

ESTRAGON   We don't manage too badly, eh Didi, between the two of us?

VLADIMIR   Yes yes. Come on, we'll try the left first.

ESTRAGON   We always find something, eh Didi, to give us the impression we 360 exist?

VLADIMIR   [*impatiently*] Yes yes, we're magicians. But let us persevere in what we have resolved, before we forget. [*He picks up a boot.*] Come on, give me your foot. [ESTRAGON *raises his foot.*] The other, hog! [ESTRAGON *raises the other foot.*] Higher! [*Wreathed together they stagger about the* 365 *stage.* VLADIMIR *succeeds finally in getting on the boot.*] Try and walk. [ESTRAGON *walks.*] Well?

ESTRAGON   It fits.

VLADIMIR   [*taking string from his pocket*] We'll try and lace it.

ESTRAGON   [*vehemently*] No no, no laces, no laces!

370 VLADIMIR   You'll be sorry. Let's try the other. [*As before*] Well?

ESTRAGON   [*grudgingly*] It fits too.

VLADIMIR   They don't hurt you?

ESTRAGON   Not yet.

VLADIMIR   Then you can keep them.

375 ESTRAGON   They're too big.

VLADIMIR   Perhaps you'll have socks some day.

ESTRAGON   True.

VLADIMIR   Then you'll keep them?

ESTRAGON   That's enough about these boots.

380 VLADIMIR   Yes, but—

ESTRAGON   [*violently*] Enough! [*Silence*] I suppose I might as well sit down. [*He looks for a place to sit down, then goes and sits down on the mound.*]

VLADIMIR   That's where you were sitting yesterday evening.
ESTRAGON   If I could only sleep.
VLADIMIR   Yesterday you slept.
385 ESTRAGON   I'll try. [*He resumes his foetal posture, his head between his knees.*]
VLADIMIR   Wait. [*He goes over and sits down beside* ESTRAGON *and begins to sing in a loud voice.*]

> Bye bye bye bye
> Bye bye—

ESTRAGON [*looking up angrily*]   Not so loud!
VLADIMIR [*softly*]

390
> Bye bye bye bye
> Bye bye bye bye
> Bye bye bye bye
> Bye bye . . .

[ESTRAGON *sleeps.* VLADIMIR *gets up softly, takes off his coat and lays it across* ESTRAGON's *shoulders, then starts walking up and down, swinging his arms to keep himself warm.* ESTRAGON *wakes with a start, jumps up, casts about wildly.* VLADIMIR *returns to him, puts his arms round him.*]

There . . . there . . . Didi is there . . . don't be afraid . . .
395 ESTRAGON   Ah!
VLADIMIR   There . . . there . . . it's all over.
ESTRAGON   I was falling—
VLADIMIR   It's all over, it's all over.
ESTRAGON   I was on top of a—
400 VLADIMIR   Don't tell me! Come, we'll walk it off.
[*He takes* ESTRAGON *by the arm and walks him up and down until* ESTRAGON *refuses to go any further.*]
ESTRAGON   That's enough. I'm tired.
VLADIMIR   You'd rather be stuck there doing nothing?
ESTRAGON   Yes.
VLADIMIR   Please yourself.
[*He releases* ESTRAGON, *picks up his coat and puts it on.*]
405 ESTRAGON   Let's go.
VLADIMIR   We can't.
ESTRAGON   Why not?
VLADIMIR   We're waiting for Godot.
ESTRAGON   Ah! [VLADIMIR *walks up and down.*] Can you not stay still?
410 VLADIMIR   I'm cold.
ESTRAGON   We came too soon.
VLADIMIR   It's always at nightfall.
ESTRAGON   But night doesn't fall.
VLADIMIR   It'll fall all of a sudden, like yesterday.
415 ESTRAGON   Then it'll be night.
VLADIMIR   And we can go.

ESTRAGON   Then it'll be day again. [*Pause. Despairing.*] What'll we do, what'll we do!

VLADIMIR [*halting, violently*]   Will you stop whining! I've had about my belly-
420   ful of your lamentations!

ESTRAGON   I'm going.

VLADIMIR [*seeing* LUCKY's *hat*]   Well!

ESTRAGON   Farewell.

VLADIMIR   Lucky's hat. [*He goes towards it.*] I've been here an hour and never
425   saw it. [*Very pleased*] Fine!

ESTRAGON   You'll never see me again.

VLADIMIR   I knew it was the right place. Now our troubles are over. [*He picks up the hat, contemplates it, straightens it.*] Must have been a very fine hat. [*He puts it on in place of his own which he hands to* ESTRAGON.] Here.

430   ESTRAGON   What?

VLADIMIR   Hold that.

[ESTRAGON *takes* VLADIMIR's *hat.* VLADIMIR *adjusts* LUCKY's *hat on his head.* ESTRAGON *puts on* VLADIMIR's *hat in place of his own which he hands to* VLADIMIR. VLADIMIR *takes* ESTRAGON's *hat.* ESTRAGON *adjusts* VLADIMIR's *hat on his head.* VLADIMIR *puts on* ESTRAGON's *hat in place of* LUCKY's *which he hands to* ESTRAGON. ESTRAGON *takes* LUCKY's *hat.* VLAD-IMIR *adjusts* ESTRAGON's *hat on his head.* ESTRAGON *puts on* LUCKY's *hat in place of* VLADIMIR's *which he hands to* VLADIMIR. VLADIMIR *takes his hat.* ESTRAGON *adjusts* LUCKY's *hat on his head.* VLADIMIR *puts on his hat in place of* ESTRAGON's *which he hands to* ESTRAGON. ESTRAGON *takes his hat.* VLADIMIR *adjusts his hat on his head.* ESTRAGON *puts on his hat in place of* LUCKY's *which he hands to* VLADIMIR. VLADIMIR *takes* LUCKY's *hat.* ESTRAGON *adjusts his hat on his head.* VLADIMIR *puts on* LUCKY's *hat in place of his own which he hands to* ESTRAGON. ESTRAGON *takes* VLADI-MIR's *hat.* VLADIMIR *adjusts* LUCKY's *hat on his head.* ESTRAGON *hands* VLADIMIR's *hat back to* VLADIMIR *who takes it and hands it back to* ESTRAGON *who takes it and hands it back to* VLADIMIR *who takes it and throws it down.*]

How does it fit me?

ESTRAGON   How would I know?

VLADIMIR   No, but how do I look in it? [*He turns his head coquettishly to and fro, minces like a mannequin.*]

435   ESTRAGON   Hideous.

VLADIMIR   Yes, but not more so than usual?

ESTRAGON   Neither more nor less.

VLADIMIR   Then I can keep it. Mine irked me. [*Pause*] How shall I say? [*Pause*] It itched me. [*He takes off* LUCKY's *hat, peers into it, shakes it, knocks on the crown, puts it on again.*]

440   ESTRAGON   I'm going.

[*Silence.*]

VLADIMIR   Will you not play?

ESTRAGON   Play at what?

VLADIMIR   We could play at Pozzo and Lucky.

ESTRAGON   Never heard of it.

445   VLADIMIR   I'll do Lucky, you do Pozzo. [*He imitates* LUCKY *sagging under the weight of his baggage.* ESTRAGON *looks at him with stupefaction.*] Go on.

ESTRAGON   What am I to do?

VLADIMIR   Curse me!

ESTRAGON [*after reflection*]   Naughty!

450 VLADIMIR   Stronger!

ESTRAGON   Gonococcus! Spirochete![6]

[VLADIMIR *sways back and forth, doubled in two.*]

VLADIMIR   Tell me to think.

ESTRAGON   What?

VLADIMIR   Say, Think, pig!

455 ESTRAGON   Think, pig!

[*Silence.*]

VLADIMIR   I can't!

ESTRAGON   That's enough of that.

VLADIMIR   Tell me to dance.

ESTRAGON   I'm going.

460 VLADIMIR   Dance, hog! [*He writhes. Exit* ESTRAGON *left, precipitately.*] I can't!
[*He looks up, misses* ESTRAGON.] Gogo! [*He moves wildly about the stage.
Enter* ESTRAGON *left, panting. He hastens towards* VLADIMIR, *falls into his
arms.*] There you are again at last!

ESTRAGON   I'm accursed!

VLADIMIR   Where were you? I thought you were gone for ever.

465 ESTRAGON   They're coming!

VLADIMIR   Who?

ESTRAGON   I don't know.

VLADIMIR   How many?

ESTRAGON   I don't know.

470 VLADIMIR [*triumphantly*]   It's Godot! At last! Gogo! It's Godot! We're saved!
Let's go and meet him! [*He drags* ESTRAGON *towards the wings.* ESTRAGON
resists, pulls himself free, exit right.] Gogo! Come back! [VLADIMIR *runs to
extreme left, scans the horizon. Enter* ESTRAGON *right, he hastens towards*
VLADIMIR, *falls into his arms.*] There you are again again!

ESTRAGON   I'm in hell!

475 VLADIMIR   Where were you?

ESTRAGON   They're coming there too!

VLADIMIR   We're surrounded! [ESTRAGON *makes a rush towards back.*] Imbecile! There's no way out there. [*He takes* ESTRAGON *by the arm and drags
him towards front. Gesture towards front.*] There! Not a soul in sight! Off
480 you go! Quick! [*He pushes* ESTRAGON *towards auditorium.* ESTRAGON *recoils
in horror.*] You won't? [*He contemplates auditorium.*] Well I can understand
that. Wait till I see. [*He reflects.*] Your only hope left is to disappear.

ESTRAGON   Where?

VLADIMIR   Behind the tree. [ESTRAGON *hesitates.*] Quick! Behind the tree.
[ESTRAGON *goes and crouches behind the tree, realizes he is not hidden,
485 comes out from behind the tree.*] Decidedly this tree will not have been the
slightest use to us.

---

6. Bacteria that cause venereal diseases. The gonococcus bacterium is associated with gonorrhea; the spirochete, with syphilis as well as other diseases.

ESTRAGON [*calmer*]   I lost my head. Forgive me. It won't happen again. Tell me what to do.

VLADIMIR   There's nothing to do.

490 ESTRAGON   You go and stand there. [*He draws* VLADIMIR *to extreme right and places him with his back to the stage.*] There, don't move, and watch out. [VLADIMIR *scans horizon, screening his eyes with his hand.* ESTRAGON *runs and takes up same position extreme left. They turn their heads and look at each other.*] Back to back like in the good old days. [*They continue to look at each other for a moment, then resume their watch. Long silence.*] Do you see anything coming?

495 VLADIMIR [*turning his head.*]   What?

ESTRAGON [*louder*]   Do you see anything coming?

VLADIMIR   No.

ESTRAGON   Nor I.

[*They resume their watch. Silence.*]

VLADIMIR   You must have had a vision.

500 ESTRAGON [*turning his head*]   What?

VLADIMIR [*louder*]   You must have had a vision.

ESTRAGON   No need to shout!

[*They resume their watch. Silence.*]

VLADIMIR ⎱
ESTRAGON ⎰ [*turning simultaneously*]   Do you—

VLADIMIR   Oh pardon!

505 ESTRAGON   Carry on.

VLADIMIR   No no, after you.

ESTRAGON   No no, you first.

VLADIMIR   I interrupted you.

ESTRAGON   On the contrary.

[*They glare at each other angrily.*]

510 VLADIMIR   Ceremonious ape!

ESTRAGON   Punctilious pig!

VLADIMIR   Finish your phrase, I tell you!

ESTRAGON   Finish your own!

[*Silence. They draw closer, halt.*]

VLADIMIR   Moron!

515 ESTRAGON   That's the idea, let's abuse each other.

[*They turn, move apart, turn again and face each other.*]

VLADIMIR   Moron!

ESTRAGON   Vermin!

VLADIMIR   Abortion!

ESTRAGON   Morpion![7]

520 VLADIMIR   Sewer-rat!

ESTRAGON   Curate!

VLADIMIR   Cretin!

ESTRAGON [*with finality*]   Crritic!

VLADIMIR   Oh! [*He wilts, vanquished, and turns away.*]

---

7. Crab louse (a French word, obsolete in English).

525 ESTRAGON   Now let's make it up.
VLADIMIR   Gogo!
ESTRAGON   Didi!
VLADIMIR   Your hand!
ESTRAGON   Take it!
530 VLADIMIR   Come to my arms!
ESTRAGON   Your arms?
VLADIMIR   My breast!
ESTRAGON   Off we go!

[*They embrace. They separate. Silence.*]

VLADIMIR   How time flies when one has fun!

[*Silence.*]

535 ESTRAGON   What do we do now?
VLADIMIR   While waiting.
ESTRAGON   While waiting.

[*Silence.*]

VLADIMIR   We could do our exercises.
ESTRAGON   Our movements.
540 VLADIMIR   Our elevations.
ESTRAGON   Our relaxations.
VLADIMIR   Our elongations.
ESTRAGON   Our relaxations.
VLADIMIR   To warm us up.
545 ESTRAGON   To calm us down.
VLADIMIR   Off we go.

[VLADIMIR *hops from one foot to the other.* ESTRAGON *imitates him.*]

ESTRAGON [*stopping*]   That's enough. I'm tired.
VLADIMIR [*stopping*]   We're not in form. What about a little deep breathing?
ESTRAGON   I'm tired breathing.
550 VLADIMIR   You're right. [*Pause*] Let's just do the tree, for the balance.
ESTRAGON   The tree?

[VLADIMIR *does the tree, staggering about on one leg.*]

VLADIMIR [*stopping*]   Your turn.

[ESTRAGON *does the tree, staggers.*]

ESTRAGON   Do you think God sees me?
VLADIMIR   You must close your eyes.

[ESTRAGON *closes his eyes, staggers worse.*]

555 ESTRAGON [*stopping, brandishing his fists, at the top of his voice*]   God have
pity on me!
VLADIMIR [*vexed*]   And me?
ESTRAGON   On me! On me! Pity! On me!

[*Enter* POZZO *and* LUCKY. POZZO *is blind.* LUCKY *burdened as before. Rope
as before, but much shorter, so that* POZZO *may follow more easily.* LUCKY
wearing a different hat. At the sight of VLADIMIR *and* ESTRAGON *he stops
short.* POZZO, *continuing on his way, bumps into him.*]

VLADIMIR   Gogo!
560 POZZO [*clutching on to* LUCKY *who staggers*]   What is it? Who is it?

[LUCKY *falls, drops everything and brings down* POZZO *with him. They lie helpless among the scattered baggage.*]

ESTRAGON   Is it Godot?

VLADIMIR   At last! [*He goes towards the heap.*] Reinforcements at last!

POZZO   Help!

ESTRAGON   Is it Godot?

565 VLADIMIR   We were beginning to weaken. Now we're sure to see the evening out.

POZZO   Help!

ESTRAGON   Do you hear him?

VLADIMIR   We are no longer alone, waiting for the night, waiting for Godot,
570 waiting for . . . waiting. All evening we have struggled, unassisted. Now it's over. It's already tomorrow.

POZZO   Help!

VLADIMIR   Time flows again already. The sun will set, the moon rise, and we away . . . from here.

575 POZZO   Pity!

VLADIMIR   Poor Pozzo!

ESTRAGON   I knew it was him.

VLADIMIR   Who?

ESTRAGON   Godot.

580 VLADIMIR   But it's not Godot.

ESTRAGON   It's not Godot?

VLADIMIR   It's not Godot.

ESTRAGON   Then who is it?

VLADIMIR   It's Pozzo.

585 POZZO   Here! Here! Help me up!

VLADIMIR   He can't get up.

ESTRAGON   Let's go.

VLADIMIR   We can't.

ESTRAGON   Why not?

590 VLADIMIR   We're waiting for Godot.

ESTRAGON   Ah!

VLADIMIR   Perhaps he has another bone for you.

ESTRAGON   Bone?

VLADIMIR   Chicken. Do you not remember?

595 ESTRAGON   It was him?

VLADIMIR   Yes.

ESTRAGON   Ask him.

VLADIMIR   Perhaps we should help him first.

ESTRAGON   To do what?

600 VLADIMIR   To get up.

ESTRAGON   He can't get up?

VLADIMIR   He wants to get up.

ESTRAGON   Then let him get up.

VLADIMIR   He can't.

605 ESTRAGON   Why not?

VLADIMIR   I don't know.

[POZZO *writhes, groans, beats the ground with his fists.*]

ESTRAGON   We should ask him for the bone first. Then if he refuses we'll leave him there.

VLADIMIR   You mean we have him at our mercy?

610 ESTRAGON   Yes.

VLADIMIR   And that we should subordinate our good offices to certain conditions?

ESTRAGON   What?

VLADIMIR   That seems intelligent all right. But there's one thing I'm afraid of.

615 POZZO   Help!

ESTRAGON   What?

VLADIMIR   That Lucky might get going all of a sudden. Then we'd be ballocksed.[8]

ESTRAGON   Lucky?

620 VLADIMIR   The one that went for you yesterday.

ESTRAGON   I tell you there was ten of them.

VLADIMIR   No, before that, the one that kicked you.

ESTRAGON   Is he there?

VLADIMIR   As large as life. [*Gesture towards* LUCKY.] For the moment he is
625   inert. But he might run amuck any minute.

POZZO   Help!

ESTRAGON   And suppose we gave him a good beating the two of us?

VLADIMIR   You mean if we fell on him in his sleep?

ESTRAGON   Yes.

630 VLADIMIR   That seems a good idea all right. But could we do it? Is he really
   asleep? [*Pause*] No, the best would be to take advantage of Pozzo's calling
   for help—

POZZO   Help!

VLADIMIR   To help him—

635 ESTRAGON   *We* help *him*?

VLADIMIR   In anticipation of some tangible return.

ESTRAGON   And suppose he—

VLADIMIR   Let us not waste our time in idle discourse! [*Pause. Vehemently.*]
   Let us do something, while we have the chance! It is not every day that we
640   are needed. Not indeed that we personally are needed. Others would meet
   the case equally well, if not better. To all mankind they were addressed,
   those cries for help still ringing in our ears! But at this place, at this
   moment of time, all mankind is us, whether we like it or not. Let us make
   the most of it, before it is too late! Let us represent worthily for once the
645   foul brood to which a cruel fate consigned us! What do you say? [ESTRAGON
   says nothing.] It is true that when with folded arms we weigh the pros and
   cons we are no less a credit to our species. The tiger bounds to the help of
   his congeners[9] without the least reflexion, or else he slinks away into the
   depths of the thickets. But that is not the question. What are we doing
650   here, *that* is the question. And we are blessed in this, that we happen to
   know the answer. Yes, in this immense confusion one thing alone is clear.
   We are waiting for Godot to come—

ESTRAGON   Ah!

POZZO   Help!

8. Ruined, screwed (slang).   9. Members of his class or kind.

655 VLADIMIR   Or for night to fall. [*Pause*] We have kept our appointment and
    that's an end to that. We are not saints, but we have kept our appointment.
    How many people can boast as much?

ESTRAGON   Billions.

VLADIMIR   You think so?

660 ESTRAGON   I don't know.

VLADIMIR   You may be right.

POZZO   Help!

VLADIMIR   All I know is that the hours are long, under these conditions, and
    constrain us to beguile them with proceedings which—how shall I say—
665   which may at first sight seem reasonable, until they become a habit. You
    may say it is to prevent our reason from foundering. No doubt. But has it
    not long been straying in the night without end of the abyssal depths?
    That's what I sometimes wonder. You follow my reasoning?

ESTRAGON   [*aphoristic for once*]   We are all born mad. Some remain so.

670 POZZO   Help! I'll pay you!

ESTRAGON   How much?

POZZO   One hundred francs!

ESTRAGON   It's not enough.

VLADIMIR   I wouldn't go so far as that.

675 ESTRAGON   You think it's enough?

VLADIMIR   No, I mean so far as to assert that I was weak in the head when I
    came into the world. But that is not the question.

POZZO   Two hundred!

VLADIMIR   We wait. We are bored. [*He throws up his hand.*] No, don't protest,
680   we are bored to death, there's no denying it. Good. A diversion comes along
    and what do we do? We let it go to waste. Come, let's get to work! [*He
    advances towards the heap, stops in his stride.*] In an instant all will vanish
    and we'll be alone once more, in the midst of nothingness! [*He broods.*]

POZZO   Two hundred!

685 VLADIMIR   We're coming!

    [*He tries to pull* POZZO *to his feet, fails, tries again, stumbles, falls, tries to
    get up, fails.*]

ESTRAGON   What's the matter with you all?

VLADIMIR   Help!

ESTRAGON   I'm going.

VLADIMIR   Don't leave me! They'll kill me!

690 POZZO   Where am I?

VLADIMIR   Gogo!

POZZO   Help!

VLADIMIR   Help!

ESTRAGON   I'm going.

695 VLADIMIR   Help me up first, then we'll go together.

ESTRAGON   You promise?

VLADIMIR   I swear it!

ESTRAGON   And we'll never come back?

VLADIMIR   Never!

700 ESTRAGON   We'll go to the Pyrenees.[1]

1. The mountain range on the border between Spain and France, extending from the Atlantic
Ocean to the Mediterranean Sea.

VLADIMIR   Wherever you like.

ESTRAGON   I've always wanted to wander in the Pyrenees.

VLADIMIR   You'll wander in them.

ESTRAGON [*recoiling*]   Who farted?

705 VLADIMIR   Pozzo.

POZZO   Here! Here! Pity!

ESTRAGON   It's revolting!

VLADIMIR   Quick! Give me your hand!

ESTRAGON   I'm going. [*Pause. Louder.*] I'm going.

710 VLADIMIR   Well I suppose in the end I'll get up by myself. [*He tries, fails.*] In the fullness of time.

ESTRAGON   What's the matter with you?

VLADIMIR   Go to hell.

ESTRAGON   Are you staying there?

715 VLADIMIR   For the time being.

ESTRAGON   Come on, get up, you'll catch a chill.

VLADIMIR   Don't worry about me.

ESTRAGON   Come on, Didi, don't be pig-headed!

[*He stretches out his hand which* VLADIMIR *makes haste to seize.*]

VLADIMIR   Pull!

[ESTRAGON *pulls, stumbles, falls. Long silence.*]

720 POZZO   Help!

VLADIMIR   We've arrived.

POZZO   Who are you?

VLADIMIR   We are men.

[*Silence.*]

ESTRAGON   Sweet mother earth!

725 VLADIMIR   Can you get up?

ESTRAGON   I don't know.

VLADIMIR   Try.

ESTRAGON   Not now, not now.

[*Silence.*]

POZZO   What happened?

730 VLADIMIR [*violently*]   Will you stop it, you! Pest! He can think of nothing but himself!

ESTRAGON   What about a little snooze?

VLADIMIR   Did you hear him? He wants to know what happened!

ESTRAGON   Don't mind him. Sleep.

[*Silence.*]

735 POZZO   Pity! Pity!

ESTRAGON [*with a start*]   What is it?

VLADIMIR   Were you asleep?

ESTRAGON   I must have been.

VLADIMIR   It's this bastard Pozzo at it again.

740 ESTRAGON   Make him stop it. Kick him in the crotch.

VLADIMIR [*striking Pozzo*]   Will you stop it! Crablouse! [POZZO *extricates himself with cries of pain and crawls away. He stops, saws the air blindly, calling*

for help. VLADIMIR, *propped on his elbow, observes his retreat.*] He's off!
[POZZO *collapses.*] He's down!

ESTRAGON   What do we do now?

745 VLADIMIR   Perhaps I could crawl to him.

ESTRAGON   Don't leave me!

VLADIMIR   Or I could call to him.

ESTRAGON   Yes, call to him.

VLADIMIR   Pozzo! [*Silence*] Pozzo! [*Silence*] No reply.

750 ESTRAGON   Together.

VLADIMIR   } Pozzo! Pozzo!
ESTRAGON

VLADIMIR   He moved.

ESTRAGON   Are you sure his name is Pozzo?

VLADIMIR [*alarmed*]   Mr. Pozzo! Come back! We won't hurt you!

[*Silence.*]

755 ESTRAGON   We might try him with other names.

VLADIMIR   I'm afraid he's dying.

ESTRAGON   It'd be amusing.

VLADIMIR   What'd be amusing?

ESTRAGON   To try him with other names, one after the other. It'd pass the
760   time. And we'd be bound to hit on the right one sooner or later.

VLADIMIR   I tell you his name is Pozzo.

ESTRAGON   We'll soon see. [*He reflects.*] Abel! Abel!

POZZO   Help!

ESTRAGON   Got it in one!

765 VLADIMIR   I begin to weary of this motif.

ESTRAGON   Perhaps the other is called Cain.[2] Cain! Cain!

POZZO   Help!

ESTRAGON   He's all humanity. [*Silence*] Look at the little cloud.

VLADIMIR [*raising his eyes*]   Where?

770 ESTRAGON   There. In the zenith.[3]

VLADIMIR   Well? [*Pause*] What is there so wonderful about it?

[*Silence.*]

ESTRAGON   Let's pass on now to something else, do you mind?

VLADIMIR   I was just going to suggest it.

ESTRAGON   But to what?

775 VLADIMIR   Ah!

[*Silence.*]

ESTRAGON   Suppose we got up to begin with?

VLADIMIR   No harm trying.

[*They get up.*]

ESTRAGON   Child's play.

VLADIMIR   Simple question of will-power.

780 ESTRAGON   And now?

2. In the Bible, the first murderer (a son of
Adam and Eve); after Cain killed his brother
Abel, God made him "a fugitive and a vaga-
bond" (Genesis 4.12).
3. Literally, the point of the sky directly
overhead.

POZZO   Help!

ESTRAGON   Let's go.

VLADIMIR   We can't.

ESTRAGON   Why not?

785 VLADIMIR   We're waiting for Godot.

ESTRAGON   Ah! [*Despairing*] What'll we do, what'll we do!

POZZO   Help!

VLADIMIR   What about helping him?

ESTRAGON   What does he want?

790 VLADIMIR   He wants to get up.

ESTRAGON   Then why doesn't he?

VLADIMIR   He wants us to help him to get up.

ESTRAGON   Then why don't we? What are we waiting for?

[*They help* POZZO *to his feet, let him go. He falls.*]

VLADIMIR   We must hold him. [*They get him up again.* POZZO *says between*
795   *them, his arms round their necks.*] Feeling better?

POZZO   Who are you?

VLADIMIR   Do you not recognize us?

POZZO   I am blind.

[*Silence.*]

ESTRAGON   Perhaps he can see into the future.

800 VLADIMIR   Since when?

POZZO   I used to have wonderful sight—but are you friends?

ESTRAGON [*laughing noisily*]   He wants to know if we are friends!

VLADIMIR   No, he means friends of his.

ESTRAGON   Well?

805 VLADIMIR   We've proved we are, by helping him.

ESTRAGON   Exactly. Would we have helped him if we weren't his friends?

VLADIMIR   Possibly.

ESTRAGON   True.

VLADIMIR   Don't let's quibble about that now.

810 POZZO   You are not highwaymen?

ESTRAGON   Highwaymen! Do we look like highwaymen?

VLADIMIR   Damn it can't you see the man is blind!

ESTRAGON   Damn it so he is. [*Pause*] So he says.

POZZO   Don't leave me!

815 VLADIMIR   No question of it.

ESTRAGON   For the moment.

POZZO   What time is it?

VLADIMIR [*inspecting the sky*]   Seven o'clock . . . eight o'clock . . .

ESTRAGON   That depends what time of year it is.

820 POZZO   Is it evening?

[*Silence.* VLADIMIR *and* ESTRAGON *scrutinize the sunset.*]

ESTRAGON   It's rising.

VLADIMIR   Impossible.

ESTRAGON   Perhaps it's the dawn.

VLADIMIR   Don't be a fool. It's the west over there.

825 ESTRAGON   How do you know?

POZZO [*anguished*]   Is it evening?

VLADIMIR   Anyway it hasn't moved.

ESTRAGON   I tell you it's rising.

POZZO   Why don't you answer me?

830 ESTRAGON   Give us a chance.

VLADIMIR [*reassuring*]   It's evening, Sir, it's evening, night is drawing nigh. My friend here would have me doubt it and I must confess he shook me for a moment. But it is not for nothing I have lived through this long day and I can assure you it is very near the end of its repertory. [*Pause*] How do you
835 feel now?

ESTRAGON   How much longer are we to cart him around. [*They half release him, catch him again as he falls.*] We are not caryatids![4]

VLADIMIR   You were saying your sight used to be good, if I heard you right.

POZZO   Wonderful! Wonderful, wonderful sight!

[*Silence.*]

840 ESTRAGON [*irritably*]   Expand! Expand!

VLADIMIR   Let him alone. Can't you see he's thinking of the days when he was happy. [*Pause*] *Memoria praeteritorum bonorum*[5]—that must be unpleasant.

ESTRAGON   We wouldn't know.

845 VLADIMIR   And it came on you all of a sudden?

POZZO   Quite wonderful!

VLADIMIR   I'm asking you if it came on you all of a sudden.

POZZO   I woke up one fine day as blind as Fortune.[6] [*Pause*] Sometimes I wonder if I'm not still asleep.

850 VLADIMIR   And when was that?

POZZO   I don't know.

VLADIMIR   But no later than yesterday—

POZZO [*violently*]   Don't question me! The blind have no notion of time. The things of time are hidden from them too.

855 VLADIMIR   Well just fancy that! I could have sworn it was just the opposite.

ESTRAGON   I'm going.

POZZO   Where are we?

VLADIMIR   I couldn't tell you.

POZZO   It isn't by any chance the place known as the Board?[7]

860 VLADIMIR   Never heard of it.

POZZO   What is it like?

VLADIMIR [*looking round*]   It's indescribable. It's like nothing. There's nothing. There's a tree.

POZZO   Then it's not the Board.

865 ESTRAGON [*sagging*]   Some diversion!

POZZO   Where is my menial?

VLADIMIR   He's about somewhere,

POZZO   Why doesn't he answer when I call?

VLADIMIR   I don't know. He seems to be sleeping. Perhaps he's dead.

870 POZZO   What happened exactly?

ESTRAGON   Exactly!

---

4. In architecture, draped female figures that act as supporting columns.

5. Memory of past goods (Latin); a phrase quoted from St. Thomas Aquinas, *Summa Theologica* (1269–73), 2.2.36.1.

6. The Roman goddess Fortuna, the personification of fortune, was sometimes depicted wearing a blindfold.

7. The stage itself is often referred to as "the boards."

VLADIMIR   The two of you slipped. [*Pause*] And fell.

POZZO   Go and see is he hurt.

VLADIMIR   We can't leave you.

875 POZZO   You needn't both go.

VLADIMIR [*to* ESTRAGON]   You go.

ESTRAGON   After what he did to me? Never!

POZZO   Yes yes, let your friend go, he stinks so. [*Silence.*] What is he waiting
    for?

880 VLADIMIR   What you waiting for?

ESTRAGON   I'm waiting for Godot.

    [*Silence.*]

VLADIMIR   What exactly should he do?

POZZO   Well to begin with he should pull on the rope, as hard as he likes so
    long as he doesn't strangle him. He usually responds to that. If not he
885   should give him a taste of his boot, in the face and the privates as far as
    possible.

VLADIMIR [*to* ESTRAGON]   You see, you've nothing to be afraid of. It's even an
    opportunity to revenge yourself.

ESTRAGON   And if he defends himself?

890 POZZO   No no, he never defends himself.

VLADIMIR   I'll come flying to the rescue.

ESTRAGON   Don't take your eyes off me. [*He goes towards* LUCKY.]

VLADIMIR   Make sure he's alive before you start. No point in exerting your-
    self if he's dead.

895 ESTRAGON [*bending over* LUCKY]   He's breathing.

VLADIMIR   Then let him have it.

    [*With sudden fury* ESTRAGON *starts kicking* LUCKY, *hurling abuse at him
    as he does so. But he hurts his foot and moves away, limping and groan-
    ing.* LUCKY *stirs.*]

ESTRAGON   Oh the brute!

    [*He sits down on the mound and tries to take off his boot. But he soon
    desists and disposes himself for sleep, his arms on his knees and his head
    on his arms.*]

POZZO   What's gone wrong now?

VLADIMIR   My friend has hurt himself

900 POZZO   And Lucky?

VLADIMIR   So it is he?

POZZO   What?

VLADIMIR   It is Lucky?

POZZO   I don't understand.

905 VLADIMIR   And you are Pozzo?

POZZO   Certainly I am Pozzo.

VLADIMIR   The same as yesterday?

POZZO   Yesterday?

VLADIMIR   We met yesterday. [*Silence*] Do you not remember?

910 POZZO   I don't remember having met anyone yesterday. But tomorrow I won't
    remember having met anyone today. So don't count on me to enlighten
    you.

VLADIMIR   But—

POZZO   Enough! Up pig!

915   VLADIMIR   You were bringing him to the fair to sell him. You spoke to us. He danced. He thought. You had your sight.

POZZO   As you please. Let me go! [VLADIMIR *moves away.*] Up! [LUCKY *gets up, gathers up his burdens.*]

VLADIMIR   Where do you go from here.

POZZO   On. [LUCKY, *laden down, takes his place before* POZZO.] Whip! [LUCKY *puts everything down, looks for whip, finds it, puts it into* POZZO's *hand, takes*

920   *up everything again.*] Rope!

[LUCKY *puts everything down, puts end of rope into* POZZO's *hand, takes up everything again.*]

VLADIMIR   What is there in the bag?

POZZO   Sand. [*He jerks the rope.*] On!

VLADIMIR   Don't go yet.

POZZO   I'm going.

925   VLADIMIR   What do you do when you fall far from help?

POZZO   We wait till we can get up. Then we go on. On!

VLADIMIR   Before you go tell him to sing.

POZZO   Who?

VLADIMIR   Lucky.

930   POZZO   To sing?

VLADIMIR   Yes. Or to think. Or to recite.

POZZO   But he is dumb.

VLADIMIR   Dumb!

POZZO   Dumb. He can't even groan.

935   VLADIMIR   Dumb! Since when?

POZZO   [*suddenly furious*]   Have you not done tormenting me with your accursed time! It's abominable! When! When! One day, is that not enough for you, one day he went dumb, one day I went blind, one day we'll go deaf, one day we were born, one day we shall die, the same day, the same second,

940   is that not enough for you? [*Calmer*] They give birth astride of a grave, the light gleams an instant, then it's night once more. [*He jerks the rope.*] On!

[*Exeunt*[8] *Pozzo and Lucky. Vladimir follows them to the edge of the stage, looks after them. The noise of falling, reinforced by mimic of Vladimir, announces that they are down again. Silence. Vladimir goes towards Estragon, contemplates him a moment, then shakes him awake.*]

ESTRAGON   [*wild gestures, incoherent words. Finally*]   Why will you never let me sleep?

VLADIMIR   I felt lonely.

945   ESTRAGON   I was dreaming I was happy.

VLADIMIR   That passed the time.

ESTRAGON   I was dreaming that—

VLADIMIR   [*violently*]   Don't tell me! [*Silence*] I wonder is he really blind.

ESTRAGON   Blind? Who?

950   VLADIMIR   Pozzo.

ESTRAGON   Blind?

VLADIMIR   He told us he was blind.

8. [They] exit (Latin).

ESTRAGON   Well what about it?

VLADIMIR   It seemed to me he saw us.

955 ESTRAGON   You dreamt it. [*Pause*] Let's go. We can't. Ah! [*Pause*] Are you sure it wasn't him?

VLADIMIR   Who?

ESTRAGON   Godot.

VLADIMIR   But who?

960 ESTRAGON   Pozzo.

VLADIMIR   Not at all! [*Less sure*] Not at all! [*Still less sure*] Not at all!

ESTRAGON   I suppose I might as well get up. [*He gets up painfully.*] Ow! Didi!

VLADIMIR   I don't know what to think any more.

ESTRAGON   My feet! [*He sits down again and tries to take off his boots.*] Help
965 me!

VLADIMIR   Was I sleeping, while the others suffered? Am I sleeping now? Tomorrow, when I wake, or think I do, what shall I say of today? That with Estragon my friend, at this place, until the fall of night, I waited for Godot? That Pozzo passed, with his carrier, and that he spoke to us? Probably. But
970 in all that what truth will there be? [ESTRAGON, *having struggled with his boots in vain, is dozing off again.* VLADIMIR *looks at him.*] He'll know nothing. He'll tell me about the blows he received and I'll give him a carrot. [*Pause*] Astride of a grave and a difficult birth. Down in the hole, lingeringly, the grave-digger puts on the forceps.[9] We have time to grow old. The
975 air is full of our cries. [*He listens.*] But habit is a great deadener. [*He looks again at* ESTRAGON.] At me too someone is looking, of me too someone is saying, He is sleeping, he knows nothing, let him sleep on. [*Pause*] I can't go on! [*Pause*] What have I said?

> [*He goes feverishly to and fro, halts finally at extreme left, broods. Enter* BOY *right. He halts. Silence.*]

BOY   Mister . . . [VLADIMIR *turns.*] Mister Albert . . .

980 VLADIMIR   Off we go again. [*Pause*] Do you not recognize me?

BOY   No Sir.

VLADIMIR   It wasn't you came yesterday.

BOY   No Sir.

VLADIMIR   This is your first time.

985 BOY   Yes Sir.

> [*Silence.*]

VLADIMIR   You have a message from Mr. Godot.

BOY   Yes Sir.

VLADIMIR   He won't come this evening.

BOY   No Sir.

990 VLADIMIR   But he'll come tomorrow.

BOY   Yes Sir.

VLADIMIR   Without fail.

BOY   Yes Sir.

> [*Silence.*]

VLADIMIR   Did you meet anyone?

995 BOY   No Sir.

---

9. An instrument for grasping (obstetrical forceps help pull a baby from the birth canal).

VLADIMIR   Two other . . . [*He hesitates.*] . . . men?

BOY   I didn't see anyone, Sir.

      [*Silence.*]

VLADIMIR   What does he do, Mr. Godot? [*Silence*] Do you hear me?

BOY   Yes Sir.

1000 VLADIMIR   Well?

BOY   He does nothing, Sir.

      [*Silence*]

VLADIMIR   How is your brother?

BOY   He's sick, Sir.

VLADIMIR   Perhaps it was he came yesterday.

1005 BOY   I don't know, Sir.

      [*Silence*]

VLADIMIR [*softly*]   Has he a beard, Mr. Godot?

BOY   Yes Sir.

VLADIMIR   Fair or . . . [*He hesitates.*] . . . or black?

BOY   I think it's white, Sir.

      [*Silence.*]

1010 VLADIMIR   Christ have mercy on us!

      [*Silence.*]

BOY   What am I to tell Mr. Godot, Sir?

VLADIMIR   Tell him . . . [*He hesitates.*] . . . tell him you saw me and that . . . [*He hesitates.*] . . . that you saw me. [*Pause.* VLADIMIR *advances, the* BOY *recoils.* VLADIMIR *halts, the* BOY *halts. With sudden violence.*] You're sure you

1015   saw me, you won't come and tell me tomorrow that you never saw me!

      [*Silence.* VLADIMIR *makes a sudden spring forward, the* BOY *avoids him and exit running. Silence. The sun sets, the moon rises. As in Act 1.* VLADIMIR *stands motionless and bowed.* ESTRAGON *wakes, takes off his boots, gets up with one in each hand and goes and puts them down center front, then goes towards* VLADIMIR.]

ESTRAGON   What's wrong with you?

VLADIMIR   Nothing.

ESTRAGON   I'm going.

VLADIMIR   So am I.

1020 ESTRAGON   Was I long asleep?

VLADIMIR   I don't know.

      [*Silence.*]

ESTRAGON   Where shall we go?

VLADIMIR   Not far.

ESTRAGON   Oh yes, let's go far away from here.

1025 VLADIMIR   We can't.

ESTRAGON   Why not?

VLADIMIR   We have to come back tomorrow.

ESTRAGON   What for?

VLADIMIR   To wait for Godot.

1030 ESTRAGON   Ah! [*Silence.*] He didn't come?

VLADIMIR   No.

ESTRAGON   And now it's too late.

VLADIMIR   Yes, now it's night.

ESTRAGON   And if we dropped him? [*Pause*] If we dropped him?
1035 VLADIMIR   He'd punish us. [*Silence. He looks at the tree.*] Everything's dead but the tree.
ESTRAGON   [*looking at the tree*]   What is it?
VLADIMIR   It's the tree.
ESTRAGON   Yes, but what kind?
1040 VLADIMIR   I don't know. A willow.

[ESTRAGON *draws* VLADIMIR *towards the tree. They stand motionless before it. Silence.*]

ESTRAGON   Why don't we hang ourselves?
VLADIMIR   With what?
ESTRAGON   You haven't got a bit of rope?
VLADIMIR   No.
1045 ESTRAGON   Then we can't.

[*Silence.*]

VLADIMIR   Let's go.
ESTRAGON   Wait, there's my belt.
VLADIMIR   It's too short.
ESTRAGON   You could hang on to my legs.
1050 VLADIMIR   And who'd hang on to mine?
ESTRAGON   True.
VLADIMIR   Show all the same. [ESTRAGON *loosens the cord that holds up his trousers which, much too big for him, fall about his ankles. They look at the cord.*] It might do at a pinch. But is it strong enough?
ESTRAGON   We'll soon see. Here.

[*They each take an end of the cord and pull. It breaks. They almost fall.*]

1055 VLADIMIR   Not worth a curse.

[*Silence.*]

ESTRAGON   You say we have to come back tomorrow?
VLADIMIR   Yes.
ESTRAGON   Then we can bring a good bit of rope.
VLADIMIR   Yes.

[*Silence.*]

1060 ESTRAGON   Didi.
VLADIMIR   Yes.
ESTRAGON   I can't go on like this.
VLADIMIR   That's what you think.
ESTRAGON   If we parted? That might be better for us.
1065 VLADIMIR   We'll hang ourselves tomorrow. [*Pause*] Unless Godot comes.
ESTRAGON   And if he comes?
VLADIMIR   We'll be saved.

[VLADIMIR *takes off his hat* (LUCKY's), *peers inside it, feels about inside it, shakes it, knocks on the crown, puts it on again.*]

ESTRAGON   Well? Shall we go?
VLADIMIR   Pull on your trousers.
1070 ESTRAGON   What?
VLADIMIR   Pull on your trousers.
ESTRAGON   You want me to pull off my trousers?

VLADIMIR Pull ON your trousers.
ESTRAGON [*realizing his trousers are down*] True. [*He pulls up his trousers.*]
1075 VLADIMIR Well? Shall we go?
ESTRAGON Yes, let's go.
  [*They do not move.*]

Curtain.

HAROLD PINTER

1930–2008

HAROLD Pinter, who won the Nobel Prize in Literature in 2005, is, in the opinion of many, the most important British dramatist since GEORGE BERNARD SHAW. Despite the obvious differences between the playwrights, they shared a similar relationship to the theater and society of their times. An Irishman and outsider to the English stage at the turn of the twentieth century, Shaw turned one of its dominant genres, the well-made play, into a mode of ironic social drama recalling the socially conscious realist plays of HENRIK IBSEN that he had championed. Likewise Pinter, a Jewish, working-class outsider from London's East End, remade the dominant conventions of the London stage after World War II—those of psychological realism and the drawing-room play—into vehicles of modern tragicomedy. Although both the playwright and his work lacked Shaw's didacticism, Pinter became a leading figure in the movement for a new British drama in the late 1950s and 1960s. More than those of any other playwright associated with that movement, Pinter's plays moved the British theater nearer to the Absurdist vision of SAMUEL BECKETT and the Continental avant-garde.

Beginning with his first play, *The Room* (1957), and continuing with *The Birthday Party* (1958), *The Caretaker* (1960), and *THE HOMECOMING* (1965), Pinter developed a dramaturgy so distinctive it has earned the label "Pinteresque." Employing a mix of familiar and indecipherable dramatic events, the Pinteresque is associated with the following elements: a sparsely furnished room; an ongoing and precarious balance of power—physical, verbal, and psychological—between the inhabitants of the room; and the entrance of an outsider who disturbs the balance, provoking power struggles that issue in a violent or near-violent denouement. The term "Pinteresque" also refers to Pinter's characteristic use of dramatic language. In Pinter's plays, every line (and every silence) serves to maintain, disturb, or renegotiate the balance of power between characters. Speech often reflects a need for dominance and displaces a physical violence that would break out if that need were not contained or redirected. The dialogue is marked by patterns of verbal repetition, crosstalk (characters speaking "past" or "around" each other), outbursts of uneasy garrulity (trivial banter, jokes, anecdotes, philosophical ruminations), and, above all, Pinter's signature pauses and silences. The patterns emerge from what Pinter called the "desire for verification"—the speaker's desire to have an assertion, and often his or her very sense of identity, affirmed by the other character. Silence is pivotal in this cat-and-mouse game as characters refuse or become unable to say what they think or feel or to verify what their interlocutor has asserted. Early in his career, Pinter wrote: "The speech we hear . . . is a necessary avoidance, a violent, sly, and anguished or mocking smoke screen which keeps the other in its place. When true silence falls we are still left with the echo but are nearer nakedness. One way of looking at speech is to say that it is a constant stratagem to cover nakedness."

The facts of Pinter's early life provide clues to his obsession with violence and the power of language to embody and repress it. Born in 1930, Pinter grew up in Hackney, a run-down working-class area in London's East End. His father was a women's tailor, and his ancestors were Jews who had escaped pogroms in Poland and Ukraine. At the start of World War II, the ten-year-old Pinter was sent to the countryside to escape the German bombing of London, though he returned home a year later and experienced the Blitz firsthand. While Pinter was a teenager, a fascist movement led by Sir Oswald Mosley was active in the East End. Pinter and his friends, many of whom were Jewish, regularly encountered gangs of young toughs who were roaming the streets with broken milk bottles and threatening to attack Jews and Communists. They escaped assault by engaging gang members in verbal banter, using language to defer violence in a manner that would become typical in Pinter's plays.

During 1944–47 Pinter attended Hackney Downs, the local all-boys grammar school, where he was an accomplished runner, cricketer, and soccer player. He also wrote poetry, acted in productions of Shakespeare, and developed a close circle of friends who shared his interests in art and literature. After graduation, Pinter trained as an actor at the Royal Academy of Dramatic Art (RADA) and the Central School of Speech and Drama, both in London. In the 1950s, he acted in provincial repertory theaters, most notably Andrew McMaster's Shakespearean touring company; there he met his first wife, Vivien Merchant, who became a leading interpreter of his female characters in the 1960s and early 1970s. (They divorced in 1980, and Pinter married the novelist and historian Lady Antonia Fraser.) During

this time, Pinter wrote steadily: poems, short stories, and a semiautobiographical novel, *The Dwarfs* (published 1990). He turned to playwriting in 1957 after being invited to write a play for the Bristol University Drama Department. The resulting one act, *The Room*, was performed in the Sunday Times Student Drama Festival and received an enthusiastic review from the influential *Times* critic Harold Hobson. The review brought Pinter to the attention of the West End producer Michael Codron, who staged Pinter's first full-length play, *The Birthday Party*, in 1958. The daily reviewers (with the exception of Hobson) attacked the play, but it caught the interest of critics and directors in the United States and Germany as well as in Britain. In 1959–60 Pinter premiered two additional works: a one act, *The Dumb Waiter* (1959), and a second full-length play, *The Caretaker*. More naturalistic than his previous plays, *The Caretaker* was Pinter's first critical success, winning prestigious prizes in London and New York and solidifying his reputation as a major if controversial dramatist.

In the late 1950s and early 1960s several other young authors—most notably John Osborne, Arnold Wesker, and John Arden—received widespread critical attention for plays that decried the rise of social affluence and complacency in Britain after the war. Dubbed the "Angry Young Men" by the press, these playwrights offered both innovative naturalistic depictions of British working-class life and epic historical dramas that used the past to mirror present-day political concerns. Unlike the Angry Young Men, Pinter never sought to lead a theatrical movement or advocate a new kind of drama. Pinter's early plays reflect the realities of working-class life in their settings, characters, and language; yet social class is not so much a dramatic focus of the plays as an aspect of the sense of identity over which Pinter's characters struggle. Although Pinter himself was a man of strong political beliefs—a conscientious objector during the Cold War, he published scathing essays on American and British military interventions in the Balkans and the Middle East during the 1990s and 2000s—it was not until the 1980s that Pinter's plays expressed explicitly political subjects. Even then, though, the political represents one facet of a power dynamic that operates at all levels of human relationship—physical, emotional, and psychological as well as political.

Both *The Room* and *The Birthday Party* present mundane situations that disintegrate into scenes of ominous danger. The latter opens with a breakfast at a seaside boardinghouse, as the landlady fusses over her husband and a young boarder. The domestic scene is disturbed when two men visit the boarder and interrogate him with unanswerable questions; in the end, they take him away. These plays turn a seemingly familiar situation into something mystifying and inexplicable: characters and their pasts are not revealed but instead are shown to be perplexing, beyond explanation. In *The Caretaker,* and to even greater effect in *The Homecoming,* the tensions between the familiar and the inexplicable remain constant while the dramatic action grows more complex. In *The Caretaker,* a young man takes in an elderly homeless man to serve as "caretaker" of the apartment that the young man shares with his brother; the three men become entwined in a territorial struggle that ends when one of them is evicted and humiliated. In *The Homecoming,* a philosophy professor returns from an American university to his working-class home in London, where he introduces his father, brothers, and uncle to his English-born wife. The struggles that ensue among the men are heightened by sexual tension between the men and the wife, by the couple's deployment of the higher social position to which they have risen, and by the tough "male" occupations (boxer, pimp) of the brothers. In both plays, the territorial struggle for dominance within the room is wedded to intricate psychological encounters that occur over issues of class, education, age, sex, and gender.

This deepening of Pinter's psychological exploration in *The Caretaker* and *The Homecoming* anticipated the tone and focus of Pinter's major plays of the 1970s: *Old Times* (1971), *No Man's Land* (1975), and *Betrayal* (1978). Abandoning the physically menacing environments of the earlier works, these plays dwell more deeply on the remembered past and the impor-

tance of memory to self-identity. Though they are grounded in realistic portrayals of the English middle class, the plays unfold in a fragmented, dreamlike manner. *Betrayal,* for example, traces the relationship between two old university friends and a woman who is the wife of one and the lover of the other. The play presents the development of these relationships over many years but does so in reverse chronological order; it thereby highlights the duplicities, both small and large, on which friendship, marriage, and infidelity are founded. In their use of time-jumping and time-eliding strategies more common to film, these plays exhibit the impact of Pinter's work as a screenwriter on his playwriting. That career included screen adaptations of his plays and novels by other authors (notably, John Fowles's *The French Lieutenant's Woman* [1969; film, 1981] and Margaret Atwood's *The Handmaid's Tale* [1985; film, 1990]). In bringing works of fiction to the screen, Pinter exploited the structural flexibility of film to find a cinematic equivalent of the novel's complex point of view and use of time. The playwright's foremost achievement in this regard is his adaptation of *Remembrance of Things Past* (1913–27), Marcel Proust's fictional reminiscence of childhood, love, and sexual awakening, on which Pinter worked in the years between *Old Times* and *No Man's Land.* While this film was never produced, a dramatic adaptation was staged in 2000 at the Royal National Theatre in London.

Although Pinter's exploration of memory continued in *Family Voices* (1981), *Victoria Station* (1982), and *A Kind of Alaska* (1982), the 1980s saw a shift in his dramatic writing to more directly political situations and issues. In *One for the Road* (1984), *Mountain Language* (1988), and *Party Time* (1991), which deal with government torture, class inequality, and other human rights abuses, the violence that lurks beneath the surface of Pinter's earlier plays is given specific institutional contexts. Pinter's final plays—*Moonlight* (1993), *Ashes to Ashes* (1996), and *Celebration* (1999)—revisit the subject of memory while conveying the political overtones that marked his work in the 1980s. As these very different plays indicate, the "Pinteresque" is a resilient and adaptable dramatic mode, and Pinter's dramaturgy of minimal words and maximal silence continues, like that of Beckett, to speak to the anxieties of contemporary life.

The Homecoming is Harold Pinter's best-known play. Initially produced by the Royal Shakespeare Company at London's Aldwych Theatre on June 3, 1965, the play has been staged a number of times over the years, including a 1967 Broadway production (which won four Tony Awards) and a highly acclaimed New York revival forty years later. Since its opening, The Homecoming has also been one of Pinter's most analyzed plays, as critics, theater artists, audiences, and readers try to come to terms with its unexpected, often shocking, action. Teddy, a professor of philosophy, brings his wife, Ruth, from the United States, where they live with three children, to introduce her to his North London family. But the family he rejoins is anything but benign. On the play's emotionally barren set, his father, Max, a former butcher, lashes out bitterly against his other two sons—Lenny, a small-time pimp, and Joey, an aspiring boxer—and against his brother Sam, who

works as a chauffeur. Throughout the play's opening scenes, the four seek dominance over each other with aggressive, animal-like territoriality. When Ruth arrives with Teddy, the men alternate between treating her as a target of hostility and welcoming her as "kith" and "kin." Under the eye of her impassive husband, the males make increasingly open sexual advances on Ruth and end with the proposition that she stay with them as part of the family. The terms of this proposition, Ruth's response to it, and Teddy's calm departure represent the final outrages in this disturbing, savagely funny play.

As the metaphors of butchering and boxing indicate, The Homecoming is pervaded with violence and the threat of violence. Max lectures Joey on boxing: "[Y]ou've got to learn how to defend yourself, and you've got to learn how to attack." But with the exception of one explosive onstage moment this violence is exerted through language. As Austin Quigley notes in his influential study The Pinter Problem, the dialogue in a play like The Homecoming is "interrelational" rather than referential. Words (and their absence), in other words, are a form of

A 2011 production of The Homecoming at the American Conservatory Theatre (San Francisco), featuring (left to right) Andrew Polk as Lenny, Anthony Fusco as Teddy, and René Augesen as Ruth.

action taken on others rather than a medium for referring to reality. When Max attempts to talk with Lenny in the play's opening scene, his silence in response to much of what he is told has the effect of leaving his father unacknowledged and exposed. Their subsequent conversation shifts the balance of power with the precision of a sparring match. When Sam enters, followed by Joey, the dynamics change yet again. Sam boasts about his reputation as a chauffeur, but Max changes the subject in order to target his brother's vulnerability: "It's funny you never got married, isn't it? A man with all your gifts." Reading and acting out exchanges such as this, one needs to pay attention to the subtextual meaning of words, to the intentions beneath what is spoken that accomplish something other than what the words purport to say. One should also pay attention to the pauses and silences, those moments when characters are brought up short, words fail, and the hostile intimacy that binds these characters is open to view.

Underlying the play's territorial struggles is the assertion of masculine power: power over women, power over other men, power over each other. Max, a failing patriarch, claims to have been one of the "worst hated men in the West End of London" when he prowled the city in his prime with his friend MacGregor. In the play's second act Lenny recounts the story that he and Joey picked up two women, chased away their escorts, and had sex with them, bordering on rape, in the rubble of a bombed site. But their pose of aggressive, even violent, masculinity masks a much more complex psychodynamic terrain, one defined—indeed dominated—by the memory of Max's deceased wife, Jessie. What kind of wife and mother Jessie was is difficult to determine: Max remembers her at one point as a woman "with a will of iron, a heart of gold, and a mind" but shortly after refers to her as "a slutbitch of a wife." Sam, we learn, drove Jessie and MacGregor around in the backseat of his car, and in his references to this he taunts Max with what he claims to know. Remembered in the conflicting roles of mother and whore, the absent Jessie embodies an

unsteady emotional landscape of domesticity, maternal love, sexuality, and betrayal. The family that remains negotiates this landscape with a male assertiveness made all the fiercer by the wounds they harbor.

This is the world that Ruth enters when she and Teddy arrive in the play's first act. The details of Ruth's past are themselves sketchy. She refers to having worked as a photographic "model for the body," but exactly what this entailed and how she met Teddy are never disclosed. She is clearly unhappy with her life as a professor's wife in the United States, and she seems on more familiar ground when she takes a walk alone at night after they arrive. She is also surprisingly adept at dealing with the reception she receives. When Lenny encounters Ruth alone after her walk, he questions the nature of her relationship with his brother, refers to the fact that he's in his pajamas and she's fully dressed, and subjects her to two long stories that end with physical violence to women. In addition, when Max finds out that she spent the night in his house, he refers to her as a "stinking pox-ridden slut." But Ruth skillfully establishes her control of these situations. In a series of brilliant moves, she turns the tables on Lenny in their nighttime exchange, asserting her sexuality and calling his bluff as a misogynistic aggressor. And in her interactions with Max and the others she quickly asserts her role as a member of the family, occupying the place vacated by the deceased Jessie. While her decision at the end of the play comes as a shock, it is consistent with her newfound authority. Like the Old Testament Ruth, who returned with her mother-in-law, Naomi, to Bethlehem after the death of her husband and remarried one of Naomi's kinsmen, she undergoes a homecoming of her own.

As *The Homecoming*'s interactions take their course, no character appears more enigmatic than Teddy. Why does Teddy bring his wife home to this environment, and why does he respond to the play's developments as he does? When the subject of his critical works comes up, he characterizes them in terms of an intellectual stance that doesn't get lost in the objects and encounters of the world: "It's a question of how far you can operate on things and not in things." Teddy's seeming detachment from the events that transpire represents, in his eyes, a triumph in the play's survival-of-the-fittest struggle. But passivity can be its own form of aggres-sion, and Teddy is very much a product of this violent, wounded family. As *The Homecoming* moves to its almost inconceivable conclusion, one wonders if Teddy and his own three sons are destined to repeat the cycle he knows so well.

ART BORRECA, S.G.

The Homecoming

CHARACTERS

MAX, *a man of seventy*
LENNY, *a man in his early thirties*
SAM, *a man of sixty-three*

JOEY, *a man in his middle twenties*
TEDDY, *a man in his middle thirties*
RUTH, *a woman in her early thirties*

An old house in North London.[1]
   A large room, extending the width of the stage.
   The back wall, which contained the door, has been removed. A square arch shape remains. Beyond it, the hall. In the hall a staircase, ascending U.L., *well in view. The front door* U.R. *A coatstand, hooks, etc.*
   In the room a window, R. *Odd tables, chairs. Two large armchairs. A large sofa,* L. *Against* R. *wall a large sideboard,[2] the upper half of which contains a mirror.* U.L., *a radiogram.[3]*

Act One

Evening.
   LENNY *is sitting on the sofa with a newspaper, a pencil in his hand. He wears a dark suit. He makes occasional marks on the back page.*
   MAX *comes in, from the direction of the kitchen. He goes to sideboard, opens top drawer, rummages in it, closes it.*
   He wears an old cardigan[4] and a cap, and carries a stick.[5]
   He walks downstage, stands, looks about the room.

MAX   What have you done with the scissors?
   [*Pause.*]

---

1. Area of London north of the River Thames. Demographically diverse, North London includes well-established Jewish and nonwhite communities.
2. Piece of furniture, typically placed against a wall, that is used for serving and displaying food.
3. Piece of furniture that combines a radio and a gramophone (record player).
4. Sweater that fastens in the front.
5. That is, walking stick or cane.

I said I'm looking for the scissors. What have you done with them?

[*Pause.*]

Did you hear me? I want to cut something out of the paper.

LENNY   I'm reading the paper.

5   MAX   Not that paper. I haven't even read that paper. I'm talking about last Sunday's paper. I was just having a look at it in the kitchen.

[*Pause.*]

Do you hear what I'm saying? I'm talking to you! Where's the scissors?

LENNY [*looking up, quietly*]   Why don't you shut up, you daft prat?[6]

[MAX *lifts his stick and points it at him.*]

MAX   Don't you talk to me like that. I'm warning you.

[*He sits in large armchair.*]

10   There's an advertisement in the paper about flannel vests. Cut price. Navy surplus. I could do with a few of them.

[*Pause.*]

I think I'll have a fag.[7] Give me a fag.

[*Pause.*]

I just asked you to give me a cigarette.

[*Pause.*]

Look what I'm lumbered[8] with.

[*He takes a crumpled cigarette from his pocket.*]

15   I'm getting old, my word of honour.

[*He lights it.*]

You think I wasn't a tearaway?[9] I could have taken care of you, twice over. I'm still strong. You ask your Uncle Sam what I was. But at the same time I always had a kind heart. Always.

[*Pause.*]

I used to knock about with[1] a man called MacGregor. I called him Mac.

20   You remember Mac? Eh?

[*Pause.*]

Huhh! We were two of the worst hated men in the West End of London.[2] I tell you, I still got the scars. We'd walk into a place, the whole room'd stand up, they'd make way to let us pass. You never heard such silence. Mind you, he was a big man, he was over six foot tall. His family were all

25   MacGregors, they came all the way from Aberdeen,[3] but he was the only one they called Mac.

[*Pause.*]

He was very fond of your mother, Mac was. Very fond. He always had a good word for her.

---

6. Idiot or fool (British), originally slang for "buttocks."
7. Cigarette (slang).
8. Burdened or encumbered.
9. Petty thief or hooligan (British slang).
1. Associate with.

2. Fashionable area of central London known for its government buildings and monuments, upscale shopping, theaters, and other cultural attractions.
3. City in northeast Scotland.

[*Pause.*]

Mind you, she wasn't such a bad woman. Even though it made me sick just
30   to look at her rotten stinking face, she wasn't such a bad bitch. I gave her
the best bleeding years of my life, anyway.

LENNY   Plug it, will you, you stupid sod,[4] I'm trying to read the paper.

MAX   Listen! I'll chop your spine off, you talk to me like that! You understand? Talking to your lousy filthy father like that!

35 LENNY   You know what, you're getting demented.

[*Pause.*]

What do you think of Second Wind for the three-thirty?[5]

MAX   Where?

LENNY   Sandown Park.[6]

MAX   Don't stand a chance.

40 LENNY   Sure he does.

MAX   Not a chance.

LENNY   He's the winner.

[LENNY *ticks the paper.*]

MAX   He talks to me about horses.

[*Pause.*]

I used to live on the course. One of the loves of my life. Epsom? I knew it
45   like the back of my hand. I was one of the best-known faces down at the
paddock. What a marvellous open-air life.

[*Pause.*]

He talks to me about horses. You only read their names in the papers.
But I've stroked their manes, I've held them, I've calmed them down
before a big race. I was the one they used to call for. Max, they'd say,
50   there's a horse here, he's highly strung, you're the only man on the
course who can calm him. It was true. I had a . . . I had an instinctive
understanding of animals. I should have been a trainer. Many times I
was offered the job—you know, a proper post, by the Duke of . . . I forget his name . . . one of the Dukes. But I had family obligations, my
55   family needed me at home.

[*Pause.*]

The times I've watched those animals thundering past the post. What an
experience. Mind you, I didn't lose, I made a few bob[7] out of it, and you
know why? Because I always had the smell of a good horse. I could smell
him. And not only the colts but the fillies. Because the fillies are more
60   highly strung than the colts, they're more unreliable, did you know that?
No, what do you know? Nothing. But I was always able to tell a good filly
by one particular trick. I'd look her in the eye. You see? I'd stand in front of
her and look her straight in the eye, it was a kind of hypnotism, and by the

4. That is, "sodomite," or homosexual (British
slang).
5. Name of a racehorse running in the 3:30
P.M. race.
6. Like Epsom Downs, referred to several
lines later, a horse-racing track on the outskirts of London.
7. Shilling. Before the decimalization of British currency in 1971, a shilling was equivalent to 12 pence (or pennies), and one pound
was equivalent to 20 shillings.

look deep down in her eye I could tell whether she was a stayer[8] or not. It
was a gift. I had a gift.

    [*Pause.*]

And he talks to me about horses.

LENNY Dad, do you mind if I change the subject?

    [*Pause.*]

I want to ask you something. That dinner we had before, what was the
name of it? What do you call it?

    [*Pause.*]

Why don't you buy a dog? You're a dog cook. Honest. You think you're cooking for a lot of dogs.

MAX If you don't like it get out.

LENNY I am going out. I'm going out to buy myself a proper dinner.

MAX Well, get out! What are you waiting for?

    [LENNY *looks at him.*]

LENNY What did you say?

MAX I said shove off out of it, that's what I said.

LENNY You'll go before me, Dad, if you talk to me in that tone of voice.

MAX Will I, you bitch?

    [MAX *grips his stick.*]

LENNY Oh, Daddy, you're not going to use your stick on me, are you? Eh?
Don't use your stick on me, Daddy. No, please. It wasn't my fault, it was one
of the others. I haven't done anything wrong, Dad, honest. Don't clout[9] me
with that stick, Dad.

    [*Silence.*]

    [MAX *sits hunched.* LENNY *reads the paper.*]

    [SAM *comes in the front door. He wears a chauffeur's uniform. He hangs
his hat on a hook in the hall and comes into the room. He goes to a chair,
sits in it and sighs.*]

Hullo, Uncle Sam.

SAM Hullo.

LENNY How are you, Uncle?

SAM Not bad. A bit tired.

LENNY Tired? I bet you're tired. Where you been?

SAM I've been to London Airport.[1]

LENNY All the way up to London Airport? What, right up the M4?[2]

SAM Yes, all the way up there.

LENNY Tch, tch, tch. Well, I think you're entitled to be tired, Uncle.

SAM Well, it's the drivers.

LENNY I know. That's what I'm talking about. I'm talking about the drivers.

SAM Knocks you out.

    [*Pause.*]

MAX I'm here, too, you know.

---

8. Horse-racing term for a horse that races
well over long distances.
9. Strike or hit.
1. Heathrow Airport was known as the Lon-

don Airport until 1966.
2. A major motorway (highway) that runs
east-west between London and South
Wales.

[SAM *looks at him.*]

I said I'm here, too. I'm sitting here.

SAM   I know you're here.

[*Pause.*]

SAM   I took a Yankee[3] out there today . . . to the Airport.

LENNY   Oh, a Yankee, was it?

100 SAM   Yes, I been with him all day. Picked him up at the Savoy at half past twelve, took him to the Caprice[4] for his lunch. After lunch I picked him up again, took him down to a house in Eaton Square[5]—he had to pay a visit to a friend there—and then round about tea-time[6] I took him right the way out to the Airport.

105 LENNY   Had to catch a plane there, did he?

SAM   Yes. Look what he gave me. He gave me a box of cigars.

[SAM *takes a box of cigars from his pocket.*]

MAX   Come here. Let's have a look at them.

[SAM *shows* MAX *the cigars.* MAX *takes one from the box, pinches it and sniffs it.*[7]]

It's a fair cigar.

SAM   Want to try one?

[MAX *and* SAM *light cigars.*]

110 You know what he said to me? He told me I was the best chauffeur he'd ever had. The best one.

MAX   From what point of view?

SAM   Eh?

MAX   From what point of view?

115 LENNY   From the point of view of his driving, Dad, and his general sense of courtesy, I should say.

MAX   Thought you were a good driver, did he, Sam? Well, he gave you a first-class cigar.

SAM   Yes, he thought I was the best he'd ever had. They all say that, you 120 know. They won't have anyone else, they only ask for me. They say I'm the best chauffeur in the firm.

LENNY   I bet the other drivers tend to get jealous, don't they, Uncle?

SAM   They do get jealous. They get very jealous.

MAX   Why?

[*Pause.*]

125 SAM   I just told you.

MAX   No, I just can't get it clear, Sam. Why do the other drivers get jealous?

SAM   Because (a) I'm the best driver, and because . . . (b) I don't take liberties.

[*Pause.*]

---

3. That is, American.
4. Le Caprice is an upscale restaurant, and the Savoy is a well-known luxury hotel. Both are located in London's West End.
5. Residential square in London's West End that is one of the city's most exclusive and fashionable neighborhoods.

6. Small meal taken in the afternoon, traditionally consisting of tea and lighter fare such as small sandwiches, scones, or small cakes.
7. Pinching a cigar is the most common method of testing the cigar's quality. The feel of the cigar can indicate whether or not it has been stored at the proper humidity.

I don't press myself on people, you see. These big businessmen, men of
130 affairs, they don't want the driver jawing[8] all the time, they like to sit in the
back, have a bit of peace and quiet. After all, they're sitting in a Humber
Super Snipe,[9] they can afford to relax. At the same time, though, this is
what really makes me special . . . I do know how to pass the time of day
when required.

[*Pause.*]

135 For instance, I told this man today I was in the second world war. Not the
first. I told him I was too young for the first. But I told him I fought in the
second.

[*Pause.*]

So did he, it turned out.

[LENNY *stands, goes to the mirror and straightens his tie.*]

LENNY   He was probably a colonel, or something, in the American Air Force.
140 SAM   Yes.
LENNY   Probably a navigator, or something like that, in a Flying Fortress.[1]
Now he's most likely a high executive in a worldwide group of aeronautical
engineers.
SAM   Yes.
145 LENNY   Yes, I know the kind of man you're talking about.

[LENNY *goes out, turning to his right.*]

SAM   After all, I'm experienced. I was driving a dust cart[2] at the age of nineteen. Then I was in long-distance haulage. I had ten years as a taxi-driver
and I've had five as a private chauffeur.
MAX   It's funny you never got married, isn't it? A man with all your gifts.

[*Pause.*]

150 Isn't it? A man like you?
SAM   There's still time.
MAX   Is there?

[*Pause.*]

SAM   You'd be surprised.
MAX   What you been doing, banging away at your lady customers, have you?
155 SAM   Not me.
MAX   In the back of the Snipe? Been having a few crafty reefs[3] in a layby,
have you?[4]
SAM   Not me.
MAX   On the back seat? What about the armrest, was it up or down?
160 SAM   I've never done that kind of thing in my car.
MAX   Above all that kind of thing, are you, Sam?
SAM   Too true.
MAX   Above having a good bang on the back seat, are you?
SAM   Yes, I leave that to others.

8. Speaking aimlessly or babbling.
9. Six-cylinder luxury vehicle produced in
England by Humber Motor Cars between
1938 and 1967.
1. American-designed bomber aircraft. "Flying
Fortress" bombers were instrumental in World
War II campaigns against German targets.

2. Garbage truck.
3. Fondling, petting, or groping (British
slang). The term also has homosexual
connotations.
4. Paved area next to a major roadway where
travelers can park and rest. On larger roadways
these areas can include public facilities.

165 MAX   You leave it to others? What others? You paralysed prat!

SAM   I don't mess up my car! Or my . . . my boss's car! Like other people.

MAX   Other people? What other people?

> [*Pause.*]

What other people?

> [*Pause.*]

SAM   Other people.

> [*Pause.*]

170 MAX   When you find the right girl, Sam, let your family know, don't forget, we'll give you a number one send-off, I promise you. You can bring her to live here, she can keep us all happy. We'd take it in turns to give her a walk round the park.

SAM   I wouldn't bring her here.

175 MAX   Sam, it's your decision. You're welcome to bring your bride here, to the place where you live, or on the other hand you can take a suite at the Dorchester.[5] It's entirely up to you.

SAM   I haven't got a bride.

> [SAM *stands, goes to the sideboard, takes an apple from the bowl, bites into it.*]

Getting a bit peckish.[6]

> [*He looks out of the window.*]

180 Never get a bride like you had, anyway. Nothing like your bride . . . going about these days. Like Jessie.

> [*Pause.*]

After all, I escorted her once or twice, didn't I? Drove her round once or twice in my cab. She was a charming woman.

> [*Pause.*]

All the same, she was your wife. But still . . . they were some of the most
185 delightful evenings I've ever had. Used to just drive her about. It was my pleasure.

MAX   [*softly, closing his eyes*]   Christ.

SAM   I used to pull up at a stall[7] and buy her a cup of coffee. She was a very nice companion to be with.

> [*Silence.*]
> [JOEY *comes in the front door. He walks into the room, takes his jacket off, throws it on a chair and stands.*]
> [*Silence.*]

190 JOEY   Feel a bit hungry.

SAM   Me, too.

MAX   Who do you think I am, your mother? Eh? Honest. They walk in here every time of the day and night like bloody[8] animals. Go and find yourself a mother.

> [LENNY *walks into the room, stands.*]

195 JOEY   I've been training down at the gym.

SAM   Yes, the boy's been working all day and training all night.

---

5. Another luxury hotel in the West End of London.
6. Hungry.

7. Stand where food and beverages are sold.
8. A mild oath, usually used as an intensifier (British).

MAX   What do you want, you bitch? You spend all the day sitting on your arse
at London Airport, buy yourself a jamroll.[9] You expect me to sit here wait-
ing to rush into the kitchen the moment you step in the door? You've been
200   living sixty-three years, why don't you learn to cook?
SAM   I can cook.
MAX   Well, go and cook!
        [*Pause.*]
LENNY   What the boys want, Dad, is your own special brand of cooking, Dad.
That's what the boys look forward to. The special understanding of food,
205   you know, that you've got.
MAX   Stop calling me Dad. Just stop all that calling me Dad, do you under-
stand?
LENNY   But I'm your son. You used to tuck me up in bed every night. He
tucked you up, too, didn't he, Joey?
        [*Pause.*]
210   He used to like tucking up his sons.
        [LENNY *turns and goes towards the front door.*]
MAX   Lenny.
LENNY [*turning*]   What?
MAX   I'll give you a proper tuck up one of these nights, son. You mark my word.
        [*They look at each other.*]
        [LENNY *opens the front door and goes out.*]
        [*Silence.*]
JOEY   I've been training with Bobby Dodd.[1]
        [*Pause.*]
215   And I had a good go at the bag as well.[2]
        [*Pause.*]
I wasn't in bad trim.[3]
MAX   Boxing's a gentleman's game.
        [*Pause.*]
I'll tell you what you've got to do. What you've got to do is you've got to
learn how to defend yourself, and you've got to learn how to attack. That's
220   your only trouble as a boxer. You don't know how to defend yourself, and
you don't know how to attack.
        [*Pause.*]
Once you've mastered those arts you can go straight to the top.
        [*Pause.*]
JOEY   I've got a pretty good idea . . . of how to do that.
        [JOEY *looks round for his jacket, picks it up, goes out of the room and up
        the stairs.*]
        [*Pause.*]
MAX   Sam . . . why don't you go, too, eh? Why don't you just go upstairs?
225   Leave me quiet. Leave me alone.
SAM   I want to make something clear about Jessie, Max. I want to. I do.
When I took her out in the cab, round the town, I was taking care of her,

9. That is, jelly roll.   2. Punching bag.
1. Unknown reference.   3. That is, in bad physical condition.

for you. I was looking after her for you, when you were busy, wasn't I? I was showing her the West End.

    [*Pause.*]

230 You wouldn't have trusted any of your other brothers. You wouldn't have trusted Mac, would you? But you trusted me. I want to remind you.

    [*Pause.*]

Old Mac died a few years ago, didn't he? Isn't he dead?

    [*Pause.*]

He was a lousy stinking rotten loudmouth. A bastard uncouth sodding[4] runt. Mind you, he was a good friend of yours.

    [*Pause.*]

235 MAX Eh, Sam . . .

SAM What?

MAX Why do I keep you here? You're just an old grub.

SAM Am I?

MAX You're a maggot.

240 SAM Oh yes?

MAX As soon as you stop paying your way here, I mean when you're too old to pay your way, you know what I'm going to do? I'm going to give you the boot.

SAM You are, eh?

245 MAX Sure. I mean, bring in the money and I'll put up with you. But when the firm gets rid of you—you can flake off.

SAM This is my house as well, you know. This was our mother's house.

MAX One lot after the other. One mess after the other.

SAM Our father's house.

250 MAX Look what I'm lumbered with. One cast-iron bunch of crap after another. One flow of stinking pus after another.

    [*Pause.*]

Our father? I remember him. Don't worry. You kid yourself. He used to come over to me and look down at me. My old man did. He'd bend right over me, then he'd pick me up. I was only that big. Then he'd dandle[5] me. Give me the
255 bottle. Wipe me clean. Give me a smile. Pat me on the bum. Pass me around, pass me from hand to hand. Toss me up in the air. Catch me coming down. I remember my father.

    [BLACKOUT.]

    [LIGHTS UP.]

    [*Night.*]

    [TEDDY *and* RUTH *stand at the threshold of the room.*]

    [*They are both well dressed in light summer suits and light raincoats.*]

    [*Two suitcases are by their side.*]

    [*They look at the room.* TEDDY *tosses the key in his hand, smiles.*]

TEDDY Well, the key worked.

    [*Pause.*]

They haven't changed the lock.

    [*Pause.*]

---

4. An oath, derived from "sod."   5. Playfully bounce up and down on one knee.

260 RUTH No one's here.

TEDDY [*looking up*] They're asleep.

     [*Pause.*]

RUTH Can I sit down?

TEDDY Of course.

RUTH I'm tired.

     [*Pause.*]

265 TEDDY Then sit down.

     [*She does not move.*]

  That's my father's chair.

RUTH That one?

TEDDY [*smiling*] Yes, that's it. Shall I go up and see if my room's still there?

RUTH It can't have moved.

270 TEDDY No, I mean if my bed's still there.

RUTH Someone might be in it.

TEDDY No. They've got their own beds.

     [*Pause.*]

RUTH Shouldn't you wake someone up? Tell them you're here?

TEDDY Not at this time of night. It's too late.

     [*Pause.*]

275 Shall I go up?

     [*He goes into the hall, looks up the stairs, comes back.*]

  Why don't you sit down?

     [*Pause.*]

  I'll just go up . . . have a look.

     [*He goes up the stairs, stealthily.*]
     [RUTH *stands, then slowly walks across the room.*]
     [TEDDY *returns.*]

  It's still there. My room. Empty. The bed's there. What are you doing?

     [*She looks at him.*]

  Blankets, no sheets. I'll find some sheets. I could hear snores. Really.
280 They're all still here, I think. They're all snoring up there. Are you cold?

RUTH No.

TEDDY I'll make something to drink, if you like. Something hot.

RUTH No, I don't want anything.

     [TEDDY *walks about.*]

TEDDY What do you think of the room? Big, isn't it? It's a big house. I mean,
285 it's a fine room, don't you think? Actually there was a wall, across there . . .
with a door. We knocked it down . . . years ago . . . . to make an open living
area. The structure wasn't affected, you see. My mother was dead.

     [RUTH *sits.*]

  Tired?

RUTH Just a little.

290 TEDDY We can go to bed if you like. No point in waking anyone up now. Just go
to bed. See them all in the morning . . . see my father in the morning. . . .

     [*Pause.*]

RUTH Do you want to stay?

TEDDY   Stay?

     [*Pause.*]

We've come to stay. We're bound to stay . . . for a few days.

295 RUTH   I think . . . the children . . . might be missing us.

TEDDY   Don't be silly.

RUTH   They might.

TEDDY   Look, we'll be back in a few days, won't we?

     [*He walks about the room.*]

Nothing's changed. Still the same.

     [*Pause.*]

300   Still, he'll get a surprise in the morning, won't he? The old man. I think
you'll like him very much. Honestly. He's a . . . well, he's old, of course.
Getting on.

     [*Pause.*]

I was born here, do you realize that?

RUTH   I know.

     [*Pause.*]

305 TEDDY   Why don't you go to bed? I'll find some sheets. I feel . . . wide awake,
isn't it odd? I think I'll stay up for a bit. Are you tired?

RUTH   No.

TEDDY   Go to bed. I'll show you the room.

RUTH   No, I don't want to.

310 TEDDY   You'll be perfectly all right up there without me. Really you will. I
mean, I won't be long. Look, it's just up there. It's the first door on the landing. The bathroom is right next door. You . . . need some rest, you know.

     [*Pause.*]

I just want to . . . walk about for a few minutes. Do you mind?

RUTH   Of course I don't.

315 TEDDY   Well . . . Shall I show you the room?

RUTH   No, I'm happy at the moment.

TEDDY   You don't have to go to bed. I'm not saying you have to. I mean, you
can stay up with me. Perhaps I'll make a cup of tea or something. The only
thing is we don't want to make too much noise, we don't want to wake any-
320 one up.

RUTH   I'm not making any noise.

TEDDY   I know you're not.

     [*He goes to her.*]

[*Gently.*] Look, it's all right, really. I'm here. I mean . . . I'm with you. There's
no need to be nervous. Are you nervous?

325 RUTH   No.

TEDDY   There's no need to be.

     [*Pause.*]

They're very warm people, really. Very warm. They're my family. They're not
ogres.

     [*Pause.*]

Well, perhaps we should go to bed. After all, we have to be up early, see
330 Dad. Wouldn't be quite right if he found us in bed, I think. [*He chuckles.*]
Have to be up before six, come down, say hullo.

[*Pause.*]

RUTH I think I'll have a breath of air.

TEDDY Air?

[*Pause.*]

What do you mean?

335 RUTH [*standing*] Just a stroll.

TEDDY At this time of night? But we've . . . only just got here. We've got to go to bed.

RUTH I just feel like some air.

TEDDY But I'm going to bed.

340 RUTH That's all right.

TEDDY But what am I going to do?

[*Pause.*]

The last thing I want is a breath of air. Why do you want a breath of air?

RUTH I just do.

TEDDY But it's late.

345 RUTH I won't go far. I'll come back.

[*Pause.*]

TEDDY I'll wait up for you.

RUTH Why?

TEDDY I'm not going to bed without you.

RUTH Can I have the key?

[*He gives it to her.*]

350 Why don't you go to bed?

[*He puts his arms on her shoulders and kisses her.*]
[*They look at each other, briefly. She smiles.*]

I won't be long.

[*She goes out of the front door.*]
[*TEDDY goes to the window, peers out after her, half turns from the window, stands, suddenly chews his knuckles.*]
[*LENNY walks into the room from U.L. He stands. He wears pyjamas and dressing-gown.[6] He watches TEDDY.*]
[*TEDDY turns and sees him.*]
[*Silence.*]

TEDDY Hullo, Lenny.

LENNY Hullo, Teddy.

[*Pause.*]

TEDDY I didn't hear you come down the stairs.

355 LENNY I didn't.

[*Pause.*]

I sleep down here now. Next door. I've got a kind of study, workroom cum[7] bedroom next door now, you see.

TEDDY Oh. Did I . . . wake you up?

LENNY No. I just had an early night tonight. You know how it is. Can't sleep.

360 Keep waking up.

[*Pause.*]

6. Robe or housecoat.   7. With (Latin).

TEDDY How are you?

LENNY Well, just sleeping a bit restlessly, that's all. Tonight, anyway.

TEDDY Bad dreams?

LENNY No, I wouldn't say I was dreaming. It's not exactly a dream. It's just
365 that something keeps waking me up. Some kind of tick.

TEDDY A tick?

LENNY Yes.

TEDDY Well, what is it?

LENNY I don't know.

[*Pause.*]

370 TEDDY Have you got a clock in your room?

LENNY Yes.

TEDDY Well, maybe it's the clock.

LENNY Yes, could be, I suppose.

[*Pause.*]

Well, if it's the clock I'd better do something about it. Stifle it in some way,
375 or something.

[*Pause.*]

TEDDY I've . . . just come back for a few days.

LENNY Oh yes? Have you?

[*Pause.*]

TEDDY How's the old man?

LENNY He's in the pink.[8]

[*Pause.*]

380 TEDDY I've been keeping well.

LENNY Oh, have you?

[*Pause.*]

Staying the night then, are you?

TEDDY Yes.

LENNY Well, you can sleep in your old room.

385 TEDDY Yes, I've been up.

LENNY Yes, you can sleep there.

[LENNY *yawns.*]

Oh well.

TEDDY I'm going to bed.

LENNY Are you?

390 TEDDY Yes, I'll get some sleep.

LENNY Yes, I'm going to bed, too.

[TEDDY *picks up the cases.*]

I'll give you a hand.

TEDDY No, they're not heavy.

[TEDDY *goes into the hall with the cases.*]
[LENNY *turns out the light in the room.*]
[*The light in the hall remains on.*]
[LENNY *follows into the hall.*]

LENNY Nothing you want?

---

8. In perfect health and high spirits.

395 TEDDY   Mmmm?

LENNY   Nothing you might want, for the night? Glass of water, anything like that?

TEDDY   Any sheets anywhere?

LENNY   In the sideboard in your room.

400 TEDDY   Oh, good.

LENNY   Friends of mine occasionally stay there, you know, in your room, when they're passing through this part of the world.

[LENNY *turns out the hall light and turns on the first landing*[9] *light.*]

[TEDDY *begins to walk up the stairs.*]

TEDDY   Well, I'll see you at breakfast, then.

LENNY   Yes, that's it. Ta-ta.

[TEDDY *goes upstairs.*]
[LENNY *goes off* L.]
[*Silence.*]
[*The landing light goes out.*]
[*Slight night light in the hall and room.*]
[LENNY *comes back into the room, goes to the window and looks out.*]
[*He leaves the window and turns on a lamp.*]
[*He is holding a small clock.*]
[*He sits, places the clock in front of him, lights a cigarette and sits.*]
[RUTH *comes in the front door.*]
[*She stands still.* LENNY *turns his head, smiles. She walks slowly into the room.*]

405 LENNY   Good evening.

RUTH   Morning, I think.

LENNY   You're right there.

[*Pause.*]

My name's Lenny. What's yours?

RUTH   Ruth.

[*She sits, puts her coat collar around her.*]

410 LENNY   Cold?

RUTH   No.

LENNY   It's been a wonderful summer, hasn't it? Remarkable.

[*Pause.*]

Would you like something? Refreshment of some kind? An aperitif,[1] anything like that?

415 RUTH   No, thanks.

LENNY   I'm glad you said that. We haven't got a drink in the house. Mind you, I'd soon get some in, if we had a party or something like that. Some kind of celebration . . . you know.

[*Pause.*]

You must be connected with my brother in some way. The one who's been

420 abroad.

RUTH   I'm his wife.

---

9. That is, the light at the top of the first stairwell.

1. Drink served before a meal and typically intended to whet the appetite.

LENNY Eh listen, I wonder if you can advise me. I've been having a bit of a rough time with this clock. The tick's been keeping me up. The trouble is I'm not all that convinced it was the clock. I mean there are lots of things which tick in the night, don't you find that? All sorts of objects, which, in the day, you wouldn't call anything else but commonplace. They give you no trouble. But in the night any given one of a number of them is liable to start letting out a bit of a tick. Whereas you look at these objects in the day and they're just commonplace. They're as quiet as mice during the daytime. So . . . all things being equal . . . this question of me saying it was the clock that woke me up, well, that could very easily prove something of a false hypothesis.

[*He goes to the sideboard, pours from a jug into a glass, takes the glass to* RUTH.]

Here you are. I bet you could do with this.

RUTH What is it?

LENNY Water.

[*She takes it, sips, places the glass on a small table by her chair.*]
[LENNY *watches her.*]

Isn't it funny? I've got my pyjamas on and you're fully dressed?

[*He goes to the sideboard and pours another glass of water.*]

Mind if I have one? Yes, it's funny seeing my old brother again after all these years. It's just the sort of tonic my Dad needs, you know. He'll be chuffed[2] to his bollocks[3] in the morning, when he sees his eldest son. I was surprised myself when I saw Teddy, you know. Old Ted. I thought he was in America.

RUTH We're on a visit to Europe.

LENNY What, both of you?

RUTH Yes.

LENNY What, you sort of live with him over there, do you?

RUTH We're married.

LENNY On a visit to Europe, eh? Seen much of it?

RUTH We've just come from Italy.

LENNY Oh, you went to Italy first, did you? And then he brought you over here to meet the family, did he? Well, the old man'll be pleased to see you, I can tell you.

RUTH Good.

LENNY What did you say?

RUTH Good.

[*Pause.*]

LENNY Where'd you go to in Italy?

RUTH Venice.

LENNY Not dear old Venice? Eh? That's funny. You know, I've always had a feeling that if I'd been a soldier in the last war—say in the Italian campaign[4]—I'd probably have found myself in Venice. I've always had that

2. Pleased.
3. Testicles (slang).
4. Pivotal World War II campaign (1943–45) in which British, American, and Canadian forces converged upon and defeated German forces in Italy.

460 feeling. The trouble was I was too young to serve, you see. I was only a
child, I was too small, otherwise I've got a pretty shrewd idea I'd probably
have gone through Venice. Yes, I'd almost certainly have gone through it
with my battalion. Do you mind if I hold your hand?

RUTH Why?

465 LENNY Just a touch.

[He stands and goes to her.]

Just a tickle.

RUTH Why?

[He looks down at her.]

LENNY I'll tell you why.

[Slight pause.]

One night, not too long ago, one night down by the docks, I was standing
470 alone under an arch, watching all the men jibbing the boom,[5] out in the
harbour, and playing about with the yardarm,[6] when a certain lady came up
to me and made me a certain proposal. This lady had been searching for
me for days. She'd lost track of my whereabouts. However, the fact was she
eventually caught up with me, and when she caught up with me she made
475 me this certain proposal. Well, this proposal wasn't entirely out of order
and normally I would have subscribed to it. I mean I would have subscribed to it in the normal course of events. The only trouble was she was
falling apart with the pox.[7] So I turned it down. Well, this lady was very
insistent and started taking liberties with me down under this arch, liber-
480 ties which by any criterion I couldn't be expected to tolerate, the facts
being what they were, so I clumped her one.[8] It was on my mind at the
time to do away with her, you know, to kill her, and the fact is, that as kill-
ings go, it would have been a simple matter, nothing to it. Her chauffeur,
who had located me for her, he'd popped round the corner to have a drink,
485 which just left this lady and myself, you see, alone, standing underneath
this arch, watching all the steamers steaming up, no one about, all quiet on
the Western Front,[9] and there she was up against this wall—well, just sliding down the wall, following the blow I'd given her. Well, to sum up, everything was in my favour, for a killing. Don't worry about the chauffeur. The
490 chauffeur would never have spoken. He was an old friend of the family.
But . . . in the end I thought . . . Aaah, why go to all the bother . . . you
know, getting rid of the corpse and all that, getting yourself into a state of
tension. So I just gave her another belt in the nose and a couple of turns of
the boot and sort of left it at that.

495 RUTH How did you know she was diseased?

LENNY How did I know?

5. Nautical term that describes shifting the
sail of a sailboat so that the wind hits the sail
from the opposite side, thereby causing the
boom (the bar on the bottom of the sail) to
swing to the other side and the boat to change
directions.
6. Horizontal bar perpendicular to the main
mast from which sails are hung.

7. Syphilis (slang).
8. Hit her.
9. Title of a 1929 novel by German World
War I veteran Erich Maria Remarque, which
details the horrors of combat trauma endured
by soldiers of war as they try to reenter civilian life. "Western Front" refers to the battle
line in western Europe.

[*Pause.*]

I decided she was.

[*Silence.*]

You and my brother are newly-weds, are you?

RUTH   We've been married six years.

500 LENNY   He's always been my favourite brother, old Teddy. Do you know that? And my goodness we are proud of him here, I can tell you. Doctor of Philosophy and all that . . . leaves quite an impression. Of course, he's a very sensitive man, isn't he? Ted. Very. I've often wished I was as sensitive as he is.

505 RUTH   Have you?

LENNY   Oh yes. Oh yes, very much so. I mean, I'm not saying I'm not sensitive. I am. I could just be a bit more so, that's all.

RUTH   Could you?

LENNY   Yes, just a bit more so, that's all.

[*Pause.*]

510 I mean, I am very sensitive to atmosphere, but I tend to get desensitized, if you know what I mean, when people make unreasonable demands on me. For instance, last Christmas I decided to do a bit of snow-clearing for the Borough Council,[1] because we had a heavy snow over here that year in Europe. I didn't have to do this snow-clearing—I mean I wasn't financially 515 embarrassed in any way—it just appealed to me, it appealed to something inside me. What I anticipated with a good deal of pleasure was the brisk cold bite in the air in the early morning. And I was right. I had to get my snowboots on and I had to stand on a corner, at about five-thirty in the morning, to wait for the lorry[2] to pick me up, to take me to the allotted 520 area. Bloody freezing. Well, the lorry came, I jumped on the tailboard,[3] headlights on, dipped,[4] and off we went. Got there, shovels up, fags on, and off we went, deep into the December snow, hours before cockcrow.[5] Well, that morning, while I was having my mid-morning cup of tea in a neighbouring cafe, the shovel standing by my chair, an old lady approached 525 me and asked me if I would give her a hand with her iron mangle.[6] Her brother-in-law, she said, had left it for her, but he'd left it in the wrong room, he'd left it in the front room. Well, naturally, she wanted it in the back room. It was a present he'd given her, you see, a mangle, to iron out the washing. But he'd left it in the wrong room, he'd left it in the front room, 530 well that was a silly place to leave it, it couldn't stay there. So I took time off to give her a hand. She only lived up the road. Well, the only trouble was when I got there I couldn't move this mangle. It must have weighed about half a ton. How this brother-in-law got it up there in the first place I can't even begin to envisage. So there I was, doing a bit of shoulders on with the 535 mangle, risking a rupture, and this old lady just standing there, waving me on,

1. Local authority.
2. Truck (British).
3. Board on the back of a truck, usually attached by hinges, intended to assist in loading and unloading.
4. Lowered (British). Headlight beams are generally lowered at night or during inclem-
ent weather in order to avoid glare.
5. That is, dawn.
6. A laundry machine with heavy rollers, designed to wring water from laundered items. An iron mangle can also serve as a heavy-service flatiron.

not even lifting a little finger to give me a helping hand. So after a few minutes I said to her, now look here, why don't you stuff this iron mangle up your
arse? Anyway, I said, they're out of date, you want to get a spin drier. I had a
good mind to give her a workover there and then, but as I was feeling jubilant
with the snow-clearing I just gave her a short-arm jab to the belly and jumped
on a bus outside. Excuse me, shall I take this ashtray out of your way?

RUTH   It's not in my way.

LENNY   It seems to be in the way of your glass. The glass was about to fall. Or
the ashtray. I'm rather worried about the carpet. It's not me, it's my father.
He's obsessed with order and clarity. He doesn't like mess. So, as I don't
believe you're smoking at the moment, I'm sure you won't object if I move the
ashtray.

[*He does so.*]

And now perhaps I'll relieve you of your glass.

RUTH   I haven't quite finished.

LENNY   You've consumed quite enough, in my opinion.

RUTH   No, I haven't.

LENNY   Quite sufficient, in my own opinion.

RUTH   Not in mine, Leonard.

[*Pause.*]

LENNY   Don't call me that, please.

RUTH   Why not?

LENNY   That's the name my mother gave me.
Just give me the glass.

RUTH   No.

[*Pause.*]

LENNY   I'll take it, then.

RUTH   If you take the glass . . . I'll take you.

[*Pause.*]

LENNY   How about me taking the glass without you taking me?

RUTH   Why don't I just take you?

[*Pause.*]

LENNY   You're joking.

[*Pause.*]

You're in love, anyway, with another man. You've had a secret liaison with
another man. His family didn't even know. Then you come here without a
word of warning and start to make trouble.

[*She picks up the glass and lifts it towards him.*]

RUTH   Have a sip. Go on. Have a sip from my glass.

[*He is still.*]

Sit on my lap. Take a long cool sip.

[*She pats her lap. Pause.*]
[*She stands, moves to him with the glass.*]

Put your head back and open your mouth.

LENNY   Take that glass away from me.

RUTH   Lie on the floor. Go on. I'll pour it down your throat.

LENNY   What are you doing, making me some kind of proposal?

[*She laughs shortly, drains the glass.*]

RUTH   Oh, I was thirsty.

[*She smiles at him, puts the glass down, goes into the hall and up the stairs.*]

[*He follows into the hall and shouts up the stairs.*]

LENNY   What was that supposed to be? Some kind of proposal?

[*Silence.*]

[*He comes back into the room, goes to his own glass, drains it.*]

[*A door slams upstairs.*]

[*The landing light goes on.*]

[MAX *comes down the stairs, in pyjamas and cap. He comes into the room.*]

575 MAX   What's going on here? You drunk?

[*He stares at* LENNY.]

What are you shouting about? You gone mad?

[LENNY *pours another glass of water.*]

Prancing about in the middle of the night shouting your head off. What are you, a raving lunatic?

LENNY   I was thinking aloud.

580 MAX   Is Joey down here? You been shouting at Joey?

LENNY   Didn't you hear what I said, Dad? I said I was thinking aloud.

MAX   You were thinking so loud you got me out of bed.

LENNY   Look, why don't you just . . . pop off,[7] eh?

MAX   Pop off? He wakes me up in the middle of the night, I think we got

585 burglars here, I think he's got a knife stuck in him, I come down here, he tells me to pop off.

[LENNY *sits down.*]

He was talking to someone. Who could he have been talking to? They're all asleep. He was having a conversation with someone. He won't tell me who it was. He pretends he was thinking aloud. What are you doing, hiding

590 someone here?

LENNY   I was sleepwalking. Get out of it, leave me alone, will you?

MAX   I want an explanation, you understand? I asked you who you got hiding here.

[*Pause.*]

LENNY   I'll tell you what, Dad, since you're in the mood for a bit of a . . .

595 chat, I'll ask you a question. It's a question I've been meaning to ask you for some time. That night . . . you know . . . the night you got me[8] . . . that night with Mum, what was it like? Eh? When I was just a glint in your eye.[9] What was it like? What was the background to it? I mean, I want to know the real facts about my background. I mean, for instance, is it a fact that

600 you had me in mind all the time, or is it a fact that I was the last thing you had in mind?

[*Pause.*]

I'm only asking this in a spirit of inquiry, you understand that, don't you? I'm curious. And there's lots of people of my age share that curiosity, you know

---

7. Die (slang).

8. That is, when I was conceived.

9. That is, before my conception.

that, Dad? They often ruminate, sometimes singly, sometimes in groups,
605   about the true facts of that particular night—the night they were made in
the image of those two people *at it*.[1] It's a question long overdue, from my
point of view, but as we happen to be passing the time of day here tonight
I thought I'd pop it to you.

     [*Pause.*]

MAX   You'll drown in your own blood.

610 LENNY   If you prefer to answer the question in writing I've got no objection.

     [MAX *stands.*]

I should have asked my dear mother. Why didn't I ask my dear mother?
Now it's too late. She's passed over to the other side.

     [MAX *spits at him.*]

     [LENNY *looks down at the carpet.*]

Now look what you've done. I'll have to Hoover[2] that in the morning, you
know.

     [MAX *turns and walks up the stairs.*]
     [LENNY *sits still.*]
     [BLACKOUT.]
     [LIGHTS UP.]

   Morning.

     JOEY *in front of the mirror. He is doing some slow limbering-up exercises. He
stops, combs his hair, carefully. He then shadowboxes, heavily, watching himself
in the mirror.*

     MAX *comes in from* U.L.

     Both MAX *and* JOEY *are dressed.* MAX *watches* JOEY *in silence.* JOEY *stops shad-
owboxing, picks up a newspaper and sits.*

     Silence.

615 MAX   I hate this room.

     [*Pause.*]

It's the kitchen I like. It's nice in there. It's cosy.

     [*Pause.*]

But I can't stay in there. You know why? Because he's always washing up in
there, scraping the plates, driving me out of the kitchen, that's why.

JOEY   Why don't you bring your tea in here?

620 MAX   I don't want to bring my tea in here. I hate it here. I want to drink my
tea in there.

     [*He goes into the hall and looks towards the kitchen.*]

What's he doing in there?

     [*He returns.*]

What's the time?

JOEY   Half past six.

625 MAX   Half past six.

     [*Pause.*]

I'm going to see a game of football this afternoon.[3] You want to come?

     [*Pause.*]

---

1. Having sexual intercourse.   3. Soccer (British).
2. That is, vacuum.

I'm talking to you.

JOEY   I'm training this afternoon. I'm doing six rounds with Blackie.

MAX   That's not till five o'clock. You've got time to see a game of football
630   before five o'clock. It's the first game of the season.

JOEY   No, I'm not going.

MAX   Why not?

> [*Pause.*]
>
> [MAX *goes into the hall.*]

Sam! Come here!

> [MAX *comes back into the room.*]
>
> [SAM *enters with a cloth.*]

SAM   What?

635   MAX   What are you doing in there?

SAM   Washing up.

MAX   What else?

SAM   Getting rid of your leavings.

MAX   Putting them in the bin,[4] eh?

640   SAM   Right in.

MAX   What point you trying to prove?

SAM   No point.

MAX   Oh yes, you are. You resent making my breakfast, that's what it is, isn't
it? That's why you bang round the kitchen like that, scraping the frying-
645   pan, scraping all the leavings into the bin, scraping all the plates, scraping
all the tea out of the teapot . . . that's why you do that, every single stinking morning. I know. Listen, Sam. I want to say something to you. From
my heart.

> [*He moves closer.*]

I want you to get rid of these feelings of resentment you've got towards me.
650   I wish I could understand them. Honestly, have I ever given you cause?
Never. When Dad died he said to me, Max, look after your brothers. That's
exactly what he said to me.

SAM   How could he say that when he was dead?

MAX   What?

655   SAM   How could he speak if he was dead?

> [*Pause.*]

MAX   Before he died, Sam. Just before. They were his last words. His last
sacred words, Sammy. A split second after he said those words . . . he was a
dead man. You think I'm joking? You think when my father spoke—on his
death-bed—I wouldn't obey his words to the last letter? You hear that, Joey?
660   He'll stop at nothing. He's even prepared to spit on the memory of our Dad.
What kind of a son were you, you wet wick?[5] You spent half your time doing
crossword puzzles! We took you into the butcher's shop, you couldn't even
sweep the dust off the floor. We took MacGregor into the shop, he could
run the place by the end of a week. Well, I'll tell you one thing. I respected
665   my father not only as a man but as a number one butcher! And to prove
it I followed him into the shop. I learned to carve a carcass at his knee. I

---

4. Trashcan.
5. Penis (slang); by extension, feeble or effeminate male.

commemorated his name in blood. I gave birth to three grown men! All on my own bat.[6] What have you done?

[*Pause.*]

What have you done? You tit!

670 SAM   Do you want to finish the washing up? Look, here's the cloth.

MAX   So try to get rid of these feelings of resentment, Sam. After all, we are brothers.

SAM   Do you want the cloth? Here you are. Take it.

[TEDDY *and* RUTH *come down the stairs. They walk across the hall and stop just inside the room.*]
[*The others turn and look at them.* JOEY *stands.*]
[TEDDY *and* RUTH *are wearing dressing-gowns.*]
[*Silence.*]
[TEDDY *smiles.*]

TEDDY   Hullo . . . Dad . . . We overslept.

[*Pause.*]

675   What's for breakfast?

[*Silence.*]
[TEDDY *chuckles.*]

Huh. We overslept.

[MAX *turns to* SAM.]

MAX   Did you know he was here?

SAM   No.

[MAX *turns to* JOEY.]

MAX   Did you know he was here?

[*Pause.*]

680   I asked you if you knew he was here.

JOEY   No.

MAX   Then who knew?

[*Pause.*]

Who knew?

[*Pause.*]

I didn't know.

685 TEDDY   I was going to come down, Dad, I was going to . . . be here, when you came down.

[*Pause.*]

How are you?

[*Pause.*]

Uh . . . look, I'd . . . like you to meet . . .

MAX   How long you been in this house?

690 TEDDY   All night.

MAX   All night? I'm a laughing-stock. How did you get in?

TEDDY   I had my key.

[MAX *whistles and laughs.*]

MAX   Who's this?

6. Through my own efforts.

TEDDY   I was just going to introduce you.

695 MAX   Who asked you to bring tarts[7] in here?

TEDDY   Tarts?

MAX   Who asked you to bring dirty tarts into this house?

TEDDY   Listen, don't be silly—

MAX   You been here all night?

700 TEDDY   Yes, we arrived from Venice—

MAX   We've had a smelly scrubber[8] in my house all night. We've had a stink-ing pox-ridden slut in my house all night.

TEDDY   Stop it! What are you talking about?

MAX   I haven't seen the bitch for six years, he comes home without a word,
705 he brings a filthy scrubber off the street, he shacks up in my house!

TEDDY   She's my wife! We're married!

[Pause.]

MAX   I've never had a whore under this roof before. Ever since your mother died. My word of honour. [To JOEY.] Have you ever had a whore here? Has Lenny ever had a whore here? They come back from America, they bring
710 the slopbucket[9] with them. They bring the bedpan with them. [To TEDDY.] Take that disease away from me. Get her away from me.

TEDDY   She's my wife.

MAX [to JOEY]   Chuck them out.

[Pause.]

A Doctor of Philosophy. Sam, you want to meet a Doctor of Philosophy?
715 [To JOEY.] I said chuck them out.

[Pause.]

What's the matter? You deaf?

JOEY   You're an old man. [To TEDDY.] He's an old man.

[LENNY walks into the room, in a dressing-gown.]
[He stops.]
[They all look round.]
[MAX turns back, hits JOEY in the stomach with all his might. JOEY con-torts, staggers across the stage. MAX, with the exertion of the blow, begins to collapse. His knees buckle. He clutches his stick.]
[SAM moves forward to help him.]
[MAX hits him across the head with his stick. SAM sits, head in hands.]
[JOEY, hands pressed to his stomach, sinks down at the feet of RUTH.]
[She looks down at him.]
[LENNY and TEDDY are still.]
[JOEY slowly stands. He is close to RUTH. He turns from RUTH, looks round at MAX.]
[SAM clutches his head.]
[MAX breathes heavily, very slowly gets to his feet.]
[JOEY moves to him.]
[They look at each other.]
[Silence.]
[MAX moves past JOEY, walks towards RUTH. He gestures with his stick.]

MAX   Miss.

7. Loose or immoral woman; prostitute (slang).
8. Prostitute (slang).
9. Bucket for collecting mud or liquid refuse; also used to collect food waste for pigs or other farm animals.

[RUTH *walks towards him.*]

RUTH   Yes?

[*He looks at her.*]

720   MAX   You a mother?

RUTH   Yes.

MAX   How many you got?

RUTH   Three.

[*He turns to* TEDDY.]

MAX   All yours, Ted?

[*Pause.*]

725   Teddy, why don't we have a nice cuddle and kiss, eh? Like the old days?
What about a nice cuddle and kiss, eh?

TEDDY.   Come on, then.

[*Pause.*]

MAX   You want to kiss your old father? Want a cuddle with your old father?

TEDDY   Come on, then.

[TEDDY *moves a step towards him.*]

730   Come on.

[*Pause.*]

MAX   You still love your old Dad, eh?

[*They face each other.*]

TEDDY   Come on, Dad. I'm ready for the cuddle.

[MAX *begins to chuckle, gurgling.*]

[*He turns to the family and addresses them.*]

MAX   He still loves his father!

Curtain

Act Two

Afternoon.

MAX, TEDDY, LENNY and SAM *are about the stage, lighting cigars.*

JOEY *comes in from* U.L. *with a coffee tray, followed by* RUTH. *He puts the tray
down.* RUTH *hands coffee to all the men. She sits with her cup.* MAX *smiles at
her.*

RUTH   That was a very good lunch.

MAX   I'm glad you liked it. [*To the others.*] Did you hear that? [*To* RUTH.] Well,
I put my heart and soul into it, I can tell you. [*He sips.*] And this is a lovely
cup of coffee.

5   RUTH   I'm glad.

[*Pause.*]

MAX   I've got the feeling you're a first-rate cook.

RUTH   I'm not bad.

MAX   No, I've got the feeling you're a number one cook. Am I right, Teddy?

TEDDY   Yes, she's a very good cook.

[*Pause.*]

10   MAX   Well, it's a long time since the whole family was together, eh? If only
your mother was alive. Eh, what do you say, Sam? What would Jessie say if
she was alive? Sitting here with her three sons. Three fine grown-up lads.

And a lovely daughter-in-law. The only shame is her grandchildren aren't
here. She'd have petted them and cooed over them, wouldn't she, Sam?
15 She'd have fussed over them and played with them, told them stories, tickled them—I tell you she'd have been hysterical. [To RUTH.] Mind you, she
taught those boys everything they know. She taught them all the morality
they know. I'm telling you. Every single bit of the moral code they live by—
was taught to them by their mother. And she had a heart to go with it. What
20 a heart. Eh, Sam? Listen, what's the use of beating round the bush? That
woman was the backbone to this family. I mean, I was busy working twenty-
four hours a day in the shop, I was going all over the country to find meat, I
was making my way in the world, but I left a woman at home with a will of
iron, a heart of gold and a mind. Right, Sam?
        [Pause.]
25 What a mind.
        [Pause.]
Mind you, I was a generous man to her. I never left her short of a few bob. I
remember one year I entered into negotiations with a top-class group of
butchers with continental connections. I was going into association with
them. I remember the night I came home, I kept quiet. First of all I gave
30 Lenny a bath, then Teddy a bath, then Joey a bath. What fun we used to have
in the bath, eh, boys? Then I came downstairs and I made Jessie put her feet
up on a pouffe[1]—what happened to that pouffe, I haven't seen it for years—
she put her feet up on the pouffe and I said to her, Jessie, I think our ship is
going to come home,[2] I'm going to treat you to a couple of items, I'm going
35 to buy you a dress in pale corded blue silk, heavily encrusted in pearls, and
for casual wear, a pair of pantaloons[3] in lilac flowered taffeta.[4] Then I gave
her a drop of cherry brandy. I remember the boys came down, in their pyjamas, all their hair shining, their faces pink, it was before they started shaving, and they knelt down at our feet, Jessie's and mine. I tell you, it was like
40 Christmas.
        [Pause.]
RUTH What happened to the group of butchers?
MAX   The group? They turned out to be a bunch of criminals like everyone
else.
        [Pause.]
This is a lousy cigar.
        [He stubs it out.]
        [He turns to SAM.]
45 What time you going to work?
SAM   Soon.
MAX   You've got a job on this afternoon, haven't you?
SAM   Yes, I know.
MAX   What do you mean, you know? You'll be late. You'll lose your job? What
50 are you trying to do, humiliate me?

---

1. Low-cushioned ottoman or padded seat
without a back.
2. Popular phrase indicating the expectation
of good fortune.

3. Long, loose pants.
4. Light fabric made from silk or synthetic
fibers.

SAM Don't worry about me.

MAX It makes the bile come up in my mouth. The bile—you understand? [*To*
RUTH.] I worked as a butcher all my life, using the chopper and the slab,
the slab, you know what I mean, the chopper and the slab! To keep my
55 family in luxury. Two families! My mother was bedridden, my brothers were
all invalids. I had to earn the money for the leading psychiatrists. I had to
read books! I had to study the disease, so that I could cope with an emergency at every stage. A crippled family, three bastard sons, a slutbitch of a
wife—don't talk to me about the pain of childbirth—I suffered the pain,
60 I've still got the pangs—when I give a little cough my back collapses—and
here I've got a lazy idle bugger of a brother won't even get to work on time.
The best chauffeur in the world. All his life he's sat in the front seat giving
lovely hand signals. You call that work? This man doesn't know his gearbox
from his arse!

65 SAM You go and ask my customers! I'm the only one they ever ask for.

MAX What do the other drivers do, sleep all day?

SAM I can only drive one car. They can't all have me at the same time.

MAX Anyone could have you at the same time. You'd bend over[5] for half a
dollar on Blackfriars Bridge.[6]

70 SAM Me!

MAX For two bob and a toffee apple.[7]

SAM He's insulting me. He's insulting his brother. I'm driving a man to
Hampton Court[8] at four forty-five.

MAX Do you want to know who could drive? MacGregor! MacGregor was a
75 driver.

SAM Don't you believe it.

[MAX *points his stick at* SAM.]

MAX He didn't even fight in the war. This man didn't even fight in the bloody
war!

SAM I did!

80 MAX Who did you kill?

[*Silence.*]

[SAM *gets up, goes to* RUTH, *shakes her hand and goes out of the front
door.*]

[MAX *turns to* TEDDY.]

Well, how you been keeping, son?

TEDDY I've been keeping very well, Dad.

MAX It's nice to have you with us, son.

TEDDY It's nice to be back, Dad.

[*Pause.*]

85 MAX You should have told me you were married, Teddy. I'd have sent you a
present. Where was the wedding, in America?

TEDDY No. Here. The day before we left.

MAX Did you have a big function?

---

5. That is, submit sexually.
6. Bridge spanning the River Thames, open to
pedestrian and motor traffic.
7. Apple covered in toffee on a stick.

8. Sixteenth-century royal palace in the Greater
London county of Middlesex. Hampton Court
Palace is open to the public.

TEDDY   No, there was no one there.

90 MAX   You're mad. I'd have given you a white wedding. We'd have had the cream of the cream here. I'd have been only too glad to bear the expense, my word of honour.

[*Pause.*]

TEDDY   You were busy at the time. I didn't want to bother you.

MAX   But you're my own flesh and blood. You're my first born. I'd have
95   dropped everything. Sam would have driven you to the reception in the Snipe, Lenny would have been your best man, and then we'd have all seen you off on the boat. I mean, you don't think I disapprove of marriage, do you? Don't be daft. [*To* RUTH.] I've been begging my two youngsters for years to find a nice feminine girl with proper credentials—it makes life worth liv-
100   ing. [*To* TEDDY.] Anyway, what's the difference, you did it, you made a wonderful choice, you've got a wonderful family, a marvellous career . . . so why don't we let bygones be bygones?

[*Pause.*]

You know what I'm saying? I want you both to know that you have my blessing.

105 TEDDY   Thank you.

MAX   Don't mention it. How many other houses in the district have got a Doctor of Philosophy sitting down drinking a cup of coffee?

[*Pause.*]

RUTH   I'm sure Teddy's very happy . . . to know that you're pleased with me.

[*Pause.*]

110   I think he wondered whether you would be pleased with me.

MAX   But you're a charming woman.

[*Pause.*]

RUTH   I was . . .

MAX   What?

[*Pause.*]

What she say?

[*They all look at her.*]

115 RUTH   I was . . . different . . . when I met Teddy . . . first.

TEDDY   No you weren't. You were the same.

RUTH   I wasn't.

MAX   Who cares? Listen, live in the present, what are you worrying about? I mean, don't forget the earth's about five thousand million years old, at
120   least. Who can afford to live in the past?

[*Pause.*]

TEDDY   She's a great help to me over there. She's a wonderful wife and mother. She's a very popular woman. She's got lots of friends. It's a great life, at the University . . . you know . . . it's a very good life. We've got a lovely house . . . we've got all . . . we've got everything we want. It's a very stimulating
125   environment.

[*Pause.*]

My department . . . is highly successful.

[*Pause.*]

We've got three boys, you know.

MAX All boys? Isn't that funny, eh? You've got three, I've got three. You've got three nephews, Joey. Joey! You're an uncle, do you hear? You could teach
130   them how to box.

[*Pause.*]

JOEY [*to* RUTH] I'm a boxer. In the evenings, after work. I'm in demolition in the daytime.

RUTH Oh?

JOEY Yes. I hope to be full time, when I get more bouts.

135 MAX [*to* LENNY] He speaks so easily to his sister-in-law, do you notice? That's because she's an intelligent and sympathetic woman.

[*He leans to her.*]

Eh, tell me, do you think the children are missing their mother?

[*She looks at him.*]

TEDDY Of course they are. They love her. We'll be seeing them soon.

[*Pause.*]

LENNY [*to* TEDDY] Your cigar's gone out.

140 TEDDY Oh, yes.

LENNY Want a light?

TEDDY No. No.

[*Pause.*]

So has yours.

LENNY Oh, yes.

[*Pause.*]

145 Eh, Teddy, you haven't told us much about your Doctorship of Philosophy. What do you teach?

TEDDY Philosophy.

LENNY Well, I want to ask you something. Do you detect a certain logical incoherence in the central affirmations of Christian theism?[9]

150 TEDDY That question doesn't fall within my province.[1]

LENNY Well, look at it this way . . . you don't mind my asking you some questions, do you?

TEDDY If they're within my province.

LENNY Well, look at it this way. How can the unknown merit reverence? In
155   other words, how can you revere that of which you're ignorant? At the same time, it would be ridiculous to propose that what we *know* merits reverence. What we know merits any one of a number of things, but it stands to reason reverence isn't one of them. In other words, apart from the known and the unknown, what else is there?

[*Pause.*]

160 TEDDY I'm afraid I'm the wrong person to ask.

LENNY But you're a philosopher. Come on, be frank. What do you make of all this business of being and not-being?[2]

---

9. Christian worldview that centers on the belief in one God.
1. Area of expertise.
2. Reference to Jean-Paul Sartre's 1943 *Being and Nothingness*, which addresses the issues of consciousness and free will. Sartre's treatise was an important work of existential philosophy.

TEDDY What do you make of it?

LENNY Well, for instance, take a table. Philosophically speaking. What is it?

165 TEDDY A table.

LENNY Ah. You mean it's nothing else but a table. Well, some people would
envy your certainty, wouldn't they, Joey? For instance, I've got a couple of
friends of mine, we often sit round the Ritz Bar[3] having a few liqueurs, and
they're always saying things like that, you know, things like: Take a table,
170 take it. All right, I say, *take* it, *take* a table, but once you've taken it, what
you going to do with it? Once you've got hold of it, where you going to take
it?

MAX You'd probably sell it.

LENNY You wouldn't get much for it.

175 JOEY Chop it up for firewood.

> [LENNY *looks at him and laughs.*]

RUTH Don't be too sure though. You've forgotten something. Look at me.
I . . . move my leg. That's all it is. But I wear . . . underwear . . . which
moves with me . . . it . . . captures your attention. Perhaps you misinter-
pret. The action is simple. It's a leg . . . moving. My lips move. Why don't
180 you restrict . . . your observations to that? Perhaps the fact that they move
is more significant . . . than the words which come through them. You
must bear that . . . possibility . . . in mind.

> [Silence.]
> [TEDDY *stands.*]

I was born quite near here.

> [Pause.]

Then . . . six years ago, I went to America.

> [Pause.]

185 It's all rock. And sand. It stretches . . . so far . . . everywhere you look. And
there's lots of insects there.

> [Pause.]

And there's lots of insects there.

> [Silence.]
> [She is still.]
> [MAX *stands.*]

MAX Well, it's time to go to the gym. Time for your workout, Joey.

LENNY [standing] I'll come with you.

> [JOEY *sits looking at* RUTH.]

190 MAX Joe.

> [JOEY *stands. The three go out.*]
> [TEDDY *sits by* RUTH, *holds her hand.*]
> [She smiles at him.]
> [Pause.]

TEDDY I think we'll go back. Mmnn?

---

3. The Ritz Hotel in London's West End is known for its ornate restaurant, bar, and tea room.

[*Pause.*]

    Shall we go home?

RUTH   Why?

TEDDY   Well, we were only here for a few days, weren't we? We might as
195   well . . . cut it short, I think.

RUTH   Why? Don't you like it here?

TEDDY   Of course I do. But I'd like to go back and see the boys now.

    [*Pause.*]

RUTH   Don't you like your family?

TEDDY   Which family?

200 RUTH   Your family here.

TEDDY   Of course I like them. What are you talking about?

    [*Pause.*]

RUTH   You don't like them as much as you thought you did?

TEDDY   Of course I do. Of course I . . . like them. I don't know what you're
talking about.

    [*Pause.*]

205   Listen. You know what time of the day it is there now, do you?

RUTH   What?

TEDDY   It's morning. It's about eleven o'clock.

RUTH   Is it?

TEDDY   Yes, they're about six hours behind us . . . I mean . . . behind
210   the time here. The boys'll be at the pool . . . now . . . swimming. Think
of it. Morning over there. Sun. We'll go anyway, mmnn? It's so clean there.

RUTH   Clean.

TEDDY   Yes.

RUTH   Is it dirty here?

215 TEDDY   No, of course not. But it's cleaner there.

    [*Pause.*]

    Look, I just brought you back to meet the family, didn't I? You've met them,
we can go. The fall semester will be starting soon.

RUTH   You find it dirty here?

TEDDY   I didn't say I found it dirty here.

    [*Pause.*]

220   I didn't say that.

    [*Pause.*]

    Look. I'll go and pack. You rest for a while. Will you? They won't be back
for at least an hour. You can sleep. Rest. Please.

    [*She looks at him.*]

    You can help me with my lectures when we get back. I'd love that. I'd be so
grateful for it, really. We can bathe till October. You know that. Here, there's
225   nowhere to bathe, except the swimming bath[4] down the road. You know
what it's like? It's like a urinal. A filthy urinal!

    [*Pause.*]

    You liked Venice, didn't you? It was lovely, wasn't it? You had a good week.
I mean . . . I took you there. I can speak Italian.

---

4. That is, swimming pool. To "bathe," in this instance, is to swim.

RUTH   But if I'd been a nurse in the Italian campaign I would have been
230   there before.
         [*Pause.*]
TEDDY You just rest. I'll go and pack.
         [TEDDY *goes out and up the stairs.*]
         [*She closes her eyes.*]
         [LENNY *appears from* U.L.]
         [*He walks into the room and sits near her.*]
         [*She opens her eyes.*]
         [*Silence.*]
LENNY Well, the evenings are drawing in.
RUTH   Yes, it's getting dark.
         [*Pause.*]
LENNY Winter'll soon be upon us. Time to renew one's wardrobe.
         [*Pause.*]
235 RUTH That's a good thing to do.
LENNY What?
         [*Pause.*]
RUTH   I always . . .
         [*Pause.*]
    Do you like clothes?
LENNY Oh, yes. Very fond of clothes.
         [*Pause.*]
240 RUTH I'm fond . . .
         [*Pause.*]
    What do you think of my shoes?
LENNY They're very nice.
RUTH   No, I can't get the ones I want over there.
LENNY Can't get them over there, eh?
245 RUTH No . . . you don't get them there.
         [*Pause.*]
    I was a model before I went away.
LENNY Hats?
         [*Pause.*]
    I bought a girl a hat once. We saw it in a glass case, in a shop. I tell you what
    it had. It had a bunch of daffodils on it, tied with a black satin bow, and then
250 it was covered with a cloche[5] of black veiling. A cloche. I'm telling you. She
    was made for it.
RUTH   No . . . I was a model for the body. A photographic model for the body.
LENNY Indoor work?
RUTH   That was before I had . . . all my children.
         [*Pause.*]
255 No, not always indoors.
         [*Pause.*]

5. Close-fitting, bell-shaped woman's hat.

Once or twice we went to a place in the country, by train. Oh, six or seven times. We used to pass a . . . a large white water tower. This place . . . this house . . . was very big . . . the trees . . . there was a lake, you see . . . we used to change and walk down towards the lake . . . we went down a path . . .
260 on stones . . . there were . . . on this path. Oh, just . . . wait . . . yes . . . when we changed in the house we had a drink. There was a cold buffet.

[*Pause.*]

Sometimes we stayed in the house but . . . most often . . . we walked down to the lake . . . and did our modelling there.

[*Pause.*]

Just before we went to America I went down there. I walked from the sta-
265 tion to the gate and then I walked up the drive. There were lights on . . . I stood in the drive . . . the house was very light.

[TEDDY *comes down the stairs with the cases. He puts them down, looks at* LENNY.]

TEDDY   What have you been saying to her?

[*He goes to* RUTH.]

Here's your coat.

[LENNY *goes to the radiogram and puts on a record of slow jazz.*]

Ruth. Come on. Put it on.

270 LENNY [*to* RUTH]   What about one dance before you go?

TEDDY   We're going.

LENNY   Just one.

TEDDY   No. We're going.

LENNY   Just one dance, with her brother-in-law, before she goes.

[LENNY *bends to her.*]

275 Madam?

[RUTH *stands. They dance, slowly.*]
[TEDDY *stands, with* RUTH's *coat.*]
[MAX *and* JOEY *come in the front door and into the room. They stand.*]
[LENNY *kisses* RUTH. *They stand, kissing.*]

JOEY   Christ, she's wide open. Dad, look at that.

[*Pause.*]

She's a tart.

[*Pause.*]

Old Lenny's got a tart in here.

[JOEY *goes to them. He takes* RUTH's *arm. He smiles at* LENNY. *He sits with* RUTH *on the sofa, embraces and kisses her.*]
[*He looks up at* LENNY.]

Just up my street.

[*He leans her back until she lies beneath him. He kisses her.*]
[*He looks up at* TEDDY *and* MAX.]

280 It's better than a rubdown,[6] this.

[LENNY *sits on the arm of the sofa. He caresses* RUTH's *hair as* JOEY *embraces her.*]
[MAX *comes forward, looks at the cases.*]

6. Brisk massage used to increase circulation and relax the muscles, often administered by trainers or therapists.

MAX   You going, Teddy? Already?

　　　[*Pause.*]

Well, when you coming over again, eh? Look, next time you come over, don't forget to let us know beforehand whether you're married or not. I'll always be glad to meet the wife. Honest. I'm telling you.

　　　[JOEY *lies heavily on* RUTH.]
　　　[*They are almost still.*]
　　　[LENNY *caresses her hair.*]

285　Listen, you think I don't know why you didn't tell me you were married? I know why. You were ashamed. You thought I'd be annoyed because you married a woman beneath you. You should have known me better. I'm broad-minded. I'm a broadminded man.

　　　[*He peers to see* RUTH's *face under* JOEY, *turns back to* TEDDY.]

　　　Mind you, she's a lovely girl. A beautiful woman. And a mother too. A
290　mother of three. You've made a happy woman out of her. It's something to be proud of. I mean, we're talking about a woman of quality. We're talking about a woman of feeling.

　　　[JOEY *and* RUTH *roll off the sofa on to the floor.*]
　　　[JOEY *clasps her.* LENNY *moves to stand above them. He looks down on them. He touches* RUTH *gently with his foot.*]
　　　[RUTH *suddenly pushes* JOEY *away.*]
　　　[*She stands up.*]
　　　[JOEY *gets to his feet, stares at her.*]

RUTH   I'd like something to eat. [*To* LENNY.] I'd like a drink. Did you get any drink?

295　LENNY   We've got drink.

RUTH   I'd like one, please.

LENNY   What drink?

RUTH   Whisky.

LENNY   I've got it.

　　　[*Pause.*]

300　RUTH   Well, get it.

　　　[LENNY *goes to the sideboard, takes out bottle and glasses.*]
　　　[JOEY *moves towards her.*]

Put the record off.

　　　[*He looks at her, turns, puts the record off.*]

I want something to eat.

　　　[*Pause.*]

JOEY   I can't cook. [*Pointing to* MAX.] He's the cook.

　　　[LENNY *brings her a glass of whisky.*]

LENNY   Soda on the side?

305　RUTH   What's this glass? I can't drink out of this. Haven't you got a tumbler?[7]

LENNY   Yes.

RUTH   Well, put it in a tumbler.

　　　[*He takes the glass back, pours whisky into a tumbler, brings it to her.*]

---

7. Flat-bottomed drinking glass used for serving whiskey.

LENNY On the rocks? Or as it comes?[8]

310 RUTH Rocks? What do you know about rocks?

LENNY We've got rocks. But they're frozen stiff in the fridge.

[RUTH *drinks.*]

[LENNY *looks round at the others.*]

Drinks all round?

[*He goes to the sideboard and pours drinks.*]

[JOEY *moves closer to* RUTH.]

JOEY What food do you want?

[RUTH *walks round the room.*]

RUTH [*to* TEDDY] Have your family read your critical works?

315 MAX That's one thing I've never done. I've never read one of his critical works.

TEDDY You wouldn't understand them.

[LENNY *hands drinks all round.*]

JOEY What sort of food do you want? I'm not the cook, anyway.

LENNY Soda, Ted? Or as it comes?

320 TEDDY You wouldn't understand my works. You wouldn't have the faintest idea of what they were about. You wouldn't appreciate the points of reference. You're way behind. All of you. There's no point in my sending you my works. You'd be lost. It's nothing to do with the question of intelligence. It's a way of being able to look at the world. It's a question of how far you can
325 operate on things and not in things. I mean it's a question of your capacity to ally the two, to relate the two, to balance the two. To see, to be able to *see*! I'm the one who can see. That's why I can write my critical works. Might do you good . . . have a look at them . . . see how certain people can view . . . things . . . how certain people can maintain . . . intellectual equi-
330 librium. Intellectual equilibrium. You're just objects. You just . . . move about. I can observe it. I can see what you do. It's the same as I do. But you're lost in it. You won't get me being . . . I won't be lost in it.

[BLACKOUT.]
[LIGHTS UP.]
[*Evening.*]
[TEDDY *sitting, in his coat, the cases by him.* SAM.]
[*Pause.*]

SAM Do you remember MacGregor, Teddy?

TEDDY Mac?

335 SAM Yes.

TEDDY Of course I do.

SAM What did you think of him? Did you take to him?

TEDDY Yes. I liked him. Why?

[*Pause.*]

SAM You know, you were always my favourite, of the lads. Always.

[*Pause.*]

---

8. Served without anything else. "On the rocks": over ice. Like "frozen stiff," these phrases carry sexual connotations.

340 When you wrote to me from America I was very touched, you know. I mean you'd written to your father a few times but you'd never written to me. But then, when I got that letter from you . . . well, I was very touched. I never told him. I never told him I'd heard from you.

[*Pause.*]

[*Whispering.*] Teddy, shall I tell you something? You were always your
345 mother's favourite. She told me. It's true. You were always the . . . you were always the main object of her love.

[*Pause.*]

Why don't you stay for a couple more weeks, eh? We could have a few laughs.

[LENNY *comes in the front door and into the room.*]

LENNY   Still here, Ted? You'll be late for your first seminar.

[*He goes to the sideboard, opens it, peers in it, to the right and the left, stands.*]

350 Where's my cheese-roll?[9]

[*Pause.*]

Someone's taken my cheese-roll. I left it there. [*To* SAM.] You been thieving?

TEDDY   I took your cheese-roll, Lenny.

[*Silence.*]

[SAM *looks at them, picks up his hat and goes out of the front door.*]

[*Silence.*]

LENNY   You took my cheese-roll?
355 TEDDY   Yes.

LENNY   I made that roll myself. I cut it and put the butter on. I sliced a piece of cheese and put it in between. I put it on a plate and I put it in the sideboard. I did all that before I went out. Now I come back and you've eaten it.

360 TEDDY   Well, what are you going to do about it?

LENNY   I'm waiting for you to apologize.

TEDDY   But I took it deliberately, Lenny.

LENNY   You mean you didn't stumble on it by mistake?

TEDDY   No, I saw you put it there. I was hungry, so I ate it.

[*Pause.*]

365 LENNY   Barefaced audacity.

[*Pause.*]

What led you to be so . . . vindictive against your own brother? I'm bowled over.[1]

[*Pause.*]

Well, Ted, I would say this is something approaching the naked truth, isn't it? It's a real cards on the table[2] stunt. I mean, we're in the land of no holds
370 barred[3] now. Well, how else can you interpret it? To pinch[4] your younger

---

9. A slice of bread covered in cheese, rolled up, then toasted in the oven or held in place with toothpicks.

1. Surprised, overwhelmed.

brother's specially made cheese-roll when he's out doing a spot of work, that's not equivocal, it's unequivocal.

[*Pause.*]

Mind you, I will say you do seem to have grown a bit sulky during the last six years. A bit sulky. A bit inner. A bit less forthcoming. It's funny, because I'd
375 have thought that in the United States of America, I mean with the sun and all that, the open spaces, on the old campus, in your position, lecturing, in the centre of all the intellectual life out there, on the old campus, all the social whirl, all the stimulation of it all, all your kids and all that, to have fun with, down by the pool, the Greyhound buses and all that, tons of iced
380 water, all the comfort of those Bermuda shorts and all that, on the old cam-pus, no time of the day or night you can't get a cup of coffee or a Dutch gin,[5] I'd have thought you'd have grown more forthcoming, not less. Because I want you to know that you set a standard for us, Teddy. Your family looks up to you, boy, and you know what it does? It does its best to follow the
385 example you set. Because you're a great source of pride to us. That's why we were so glad to see you come back, to welcome you back to your birthplace. That's why.

[*Pause.*]

No, listen, Ted, there's no question that we live a less rich life here than you do over there. We live a closer life. We're busy, of course. Joey's busy with his
390 boxing, I'm busy with my occupation, Dad still plays a good game of poker, and he does the cooking as well, well up to his old standard, and Uncle Sam's the best chauffeur in the firm. But nevertheless we do make up a unit, Teddy, and you're an integral part of it. When we all sit round the backyard having a quiet gander[6] at the night sky, there's always an empty chair stand-
395 ing in the circle, which is in fact yours. And so when you at length return to us, we do expect a bit of grace, a bit of je ne sais quoi,[7] a bit of generosity of mind, a bit of liberality of spirit, to reassure us. We do expect that. But do we get it? Have we got it? Is that what you've given us?

[*Pause.*]

TEDDY Yes.

[JOEY *comes down the stairs and into the room, with a newspaper.*]
400 LENNY [*to* JOEY] How'd you get on?
JOEY Er . . . not bad.
LENNY What do you mean?

[*Pause.*]

What do you mean?
JOEY Not bad.
405 LENNY I want to know what you *mean*—by not bad.
JOEY What's it got to do with you?

2. "Cards on the table" refers to the moment at the end of a card game when players reveal their hand by laying their cards face up on the table. The phrase is commonly used to refer to the moment when a truth is revealed.
3. Wrestling term indicating that all moves will be considered legal.
4. Steal.
5. English term for Jenever, a strong Dutch liqueur flavored with juniper berries.
6. Look.
7. "I don't know what" (French), commonly used to indicate an indescribable special quality.

LENNY Joey, you tell your brother everything.

    [*Pause.*]

JOEY I didn't get all the way.

LENNY You didn't get all the way?

    [*Pause.*]

410   [*With emphasis.*] You didn't get all the way?
But you've had her up there for two hours.

JOEY Well?

LENNY You didn't get all the way and you've had her up there for two hours!

JOEY What about it?

    [LENNY *moves closer to him.*]

415 LENNY What are you telling me?

JOEY What do you mean?

LENNY Are you telling me she's a tease?

    [*Pause.*]

She's a tease!

    [*Pause.*]

What do you think of that, Ted? Your wife turns out to be a tease. He's had
420 her up there for two hours and he didn't go the whole hog.[8]

JOEY I didn't say she was a tease.

LENNY Are you joking? It sounds like a tease to me, don't it to you, Ted?

TEDDY Perhaps he hasn't got the right touch.

LENNY Joey? Not the right touch? Don't be ridiculous. He's had more dolly[9]
425 than you've had cream cakes.[1] He's irresistible. He's one of the few and far
between. Tell him about the last bird[2] you had, Joey.

    [*Pause.*]

JOEY What bird?

LENNY The last bird! When we stopped the car . . .

JOEY Oh, that . . . yes . . . well, we were in Lenny's car one night last week . . .

430 LENNY The Alfa.[3]

JOEY And er . . . bowling down the road . . .

LENNY Up near the Scrubs.[4]

JOEY Yes, up over by the Scrubs . . .

LENNY We were doing a little survey of North Paddington.[5]

435 JOEY And er . . . it was pretty late, wasn't it?

LENNY Yes, it was late. Well?

    [*Pause.*]

JOEY And then we . . . well, by the kerb,[6] we saw this parked car . . . with a
couple of girls in it.

LENNY And their escorts.

440 JOEY Yes, there were two geezers[7] in it. Anyway . . .

    [*Pause.*]

---

8. That is, complete the act of sexual intercourse.
9. Attractive young woman (slang).
1. Cakes filled and often topped with cream
or custard.
2. Woman (slang).
3. Alfa Romeo, an expensive Italian sports car.

4. Wormwood Scrubs is a large area of open
land in West London.
5. Borough in west-central London, located
several miles from Wormwood Scrubs.
6. Curb.
7. Guys, men (British).

What we do then?

LENNY   We stopped the car and got out!

JOEY   Yes . . . we got out . . . and we told the . . . two escorts . . . to go away . . . which they did . . . and then we . . . got the girls out of the car . . .

445 LENNY   We didn't take them over the Scrubs.

JOEY   Oh, no. Not over the Scrubs. Well, the police would have noticed us there . . . you see. We took them over a bombed site.[8]

LENNY   Rubble. In the rubble.

JOEY   Yes, plenty of rubble.

[Pause.]

450 Well . . . you know . . . then we had them.

LENNY   You've missed out the best bit. He's missed out the best bit!

JOEY   What bit?

LENNY [to TEDDY]   His bird says to him, I don't mind, she says, but I've got to have some protection. I've got to have some contraceptive protection. I

455 haven't got any contraceptive protection, old Joey says to her. In that case I won't do it, she says. Yes you will, says Joey, never mind about the contraceptive protection.

[LENNY laughs.]

Even my bird laughed when she heard that. Yes, even she gave out a bit of a laugh. So you can't say old Joey isn't a bit of a knockout when he gets going,

460 can you? And here he is upstairs with your wife for two hours and he hasn't even been the whole hog. Well, your wife sounds like a bit of a tease to me, Ted. What do you make of it, Joey? You satisfied? Don't tell me you're satisfied without going the whole hog?

[Pause.]

JOEY   I've been the whole hog plenty of times. Sometimes . . . you can be

465 happy . . . and not go the whole hog. Now and again . . . you can be happy . . . without going any hog.

[LENNY stares at him.]

[MAX and SAM come in the front door and into the room.]

MAX   Where's the whore? Still in bed? She'll make us all animals.

LENNY   The girl's a tease.

MAX   What?

470 LENNY   She's had Joey on a string.

MAX   What do you mean?

TEDDY   He had her up there for two hours and he didn't go the whole hog.

[Pause.]

MAX   My Joey? She did that to my boy?

[Pause.]

To my youngest son? Tch, tch, tch, tch. How you feeling, son? Are you all

475 right?

JOEY   Sure I'm all right.

MAX [to TEDDY]   Does she do that to you, too?

8. Remnant of the heavy German bombing of London and other British cities during World War II.

TEDDY   No.

LENNY   He gets the gravy.[9]

480   MAX   You think so?

JOEY   No he don't.

[*Pause.*]

SAM   He's her lawful husband. She's his lawful wife.

JOEY   No he don't! He don't get no gravy! I'm telling you. I'm telling all of
you. I'll kill the next man who says he gets the gravy.

485   MAX   Joey . . . what are you getting so excited about? [*To* LENNY.] It's because
he's frustrated. You see what happens?

JOEY   Who is?

MAX   Joey. No one's saying you're wrong. In fact everyone's saying you're right.

[*Pause.*]

[MAX *turns to the others.*]

You know something? Perhaps it's not a bad idea to have a woman in the
490   house. Perhaps it's a good thing. Who knows? Maybe we should keep her.

[*Pause.*]

Maybe we'll ask her if she wants to stay.

[*Pause.*]

TEDDY   I'm afraid not, Dad. She's not well, and we've got to get home to the
children.

MAX   Not well? I told you, I'm used to looking after people who are not so
495   well. Don't worry about that. Perhaps we'll keep her here.

[*Pause.*]

SAM   Don't be silly.

MAX   What's silly?

SAM   You're talking rubbish.

MAX   Me?

500   SAM   She's got three children.

MAX   She can have more! Here. If she's so keen.

TEDDY   She doesn't want any more.

MAX   What do you know about what she wants, eh, Ted?

TEDDY [*smiling*]   The best thing for her is to come home with me, Dad. Really.
505   We're married, you know.

[MAX *walks about the room, clicks his fingers.*]

MAX   We'd have to pay her, of course. You realize that? We can't leave her walking about without any pocket money. She'll have to have a little allowance.

JOEY   Of course we'll pay her. She's got to have some money in her pocket.

MAX   That's what I'm saying. You can't expect a woman to walk about without
510   a few bob to spend on a pair of stockings.

[*Pause.*]

LENNY   Where's the money going to come from?

MAX   Well, how much is she worth? What we talking about, three figures?

LENNY   I asked you where the money's going to come from. It'll be an extra
mouth to feed. It'll be an extra body to clothe. You realize that?

9. Reaps the benefit (here, sexually).

515 JOEY I'll buy her clothes.

LENNY What with?

JOEY I'll put in a certain amount out of my wages.

MAX That's it. We'll pass the hat round. We'll make a donation. We're all grown-up people, we've got a sense of responsibility. We'll all put a little in
520 the hat. It's democratic.

LENNY It'll come to a few quid,[1] Dad.

[*Pause.*]

I mean, she's not a woman who likes walking around in second-hand goods. She's up to the latest fashion. You wouldn't want her walking about in clothes which don't show her off at her best, would you?

525 MAX Lenny, do you mind if I make a little comment? It's not meant to be critical. But I think you're concentrating too much on the economic considerations. There are other considerations. There are the human considerations. You understand what I mean? There are the human considerations. Don't forget them.

530 LENNY I won't.

MAX Well don't.

[*Pause.*]

Listen, we're bound to treat her in something approximating, at least, to the manner in which she's accustomed. After all, she's not someone off the street, she's my daughter-in-law!

535 JOEY That's right.

MAX There you are, you see. Joey'll donate, Sam'll donate. . . .

[SAM *looks at him.*]

I'll put in a few bob out of my pension, Lenny'll cough up. We're laughing. What about you, Ted? How much you going to put in the kitty?[2]

TEDDY I'm not putting anything in the kitty.

540 MAX What? You won't even help to support your own wife? I thought he was a son of mine. You lousy stinkpig. Your mother would drop dead if she heard you take that attitude.

LENNY Eh, Dad.

[LENNY *walks forward.*]

I've got a better idea.

545 MAX What?

LENNY There's no need for us to go to all this expense. I know these women. Once they get started they ruin your budget. I've got a better idea. Why don't I take her with me to Greek Street?[3]

[*Pause.*]

MAX You mean put her on the game?[4]

[*Pause.*]

1. British pounds (currency).
2. In a card game, the pool into which players contribute a pre-agreed-upon amount to begin the betting. The term also refers, as here, to a general pool of money to which the members of a group contribute.
3. Street in the fashionable West End neighborhood of Soho. The street is famous for its restaurants and nightclubs and has been a primary location for London's sex trade. The Street Offences Act of 1959 meant that prostitutes could no longer solicit clients in the street, and as a result, many of the homes and businesses on Greek Street in the 1960s served as a front for brothels.

550　We'll put her on the game. That's a stroke of genius, that's a marvellous idea.
　　You mean she can earn the money herself—on her back?

LENNY　Yes.

MAX　Wonderful. The only thing is, it'll have to be short hours. We don't want
　　her out of the house all night.

555　LENNY　I can limit the hours.

MAX　How many?

LENNY　Four hours a night.

MAX　[dubiously]　Is that enough?

LENNY　She'll bring in a good sum for four hours a night.

560　MAX　Well, you should know. After all, it's true, the last thing we want to do is
　　wear the girl out. She's going to have her obligations this end as well. Where
　　you going to put her in Greek Street?

LENNY　It doesn't have to be right in Greek Street, Dad. I've got a number of
　　flats[5] all around that area.

565　MAX　You have? Well, what about me? Why don't you give me one?

LENNY　You're sexless.

JOEY　Eh, wait a minute, what's all this?

MAX　I know what Lenny's saying. Lenny's saying she can pay her own way.
　　What do you think, Teddy? That'll solve all our problems.

570　JOEY　Eh, wait a minute. I don't want to share her.

MAX　What did you say?

JOEY　I don't want to share her with a lot of yobs![6]

MAX　Yobs! You arrogant git![7] What arrogance. [To LENNY.] Will you be sup-
　　plying her with yobs?

575　LENNY　I've got a very distinguished clientèle, Joey. They're more distinguished
　　than you'll ever be.

MAX　So you can count yourself lucky we're including you in.

JOEY　I didn't think I was going to have to share her!

MAX　Well, you are going to have to share her! Otherwise she goes straight
580　back to America. You understand?

　　　　[Pause.]

　　It's tricky enough as it is, without you shoving your oar in. But there's some-
　　thing worrying me. Perhaps she's not so up to the mark.[8] Eh? Teddy, you're
　　the best judge. Do you think she'd be up to the mark?

　　　　[Pause.]

　　I mean what about all this teasing? Is she going to make a habit of it? That'll
585　get us nowhere.

　　　　[Pause.]

TEDDY　It was just love play . . . I suppose . . . that's all I suppose it was.

MAX　Love play? Two bleeding hours? That's a bloody long time for love play!

LENNY　I don't think we've got anything to worry about on that score, Dad.

MAX　How do you know?

590　LENNY　I'm giving you a professional opinion.

---

4. That is, put her on the market as a prostitute.
5. Apartments or suite of rooms on one floor of a building.
6. Thugs or hooligans (British slang). The word was coined in the 18th century by spelling "boy" backward.
7. Worthless or contemptible person.
8. That is, up to standard.

[LENNY *goes to* TEDDY.]

LENNY Listen, Teddy, you could help us, actually. If I were to send you some
cards, over to America . . . you know, very nice ones, with a name on, and a
telephone number, very discreet, well, you could distribute them . . . to various parties, who might be making a trip over here. Of course, you'd get a
595 little percentage out of it.

MAX I mean, you needn't tell them she's your wife.

LENNY No, we'd call her something else. Dolores, or something.

MAX Or Spanish Jacky.

LENNY No, you've got to be reserved about it, Dad. We could call her some-
600 thing nice . . . like Cynthia . . . or Gillian.

[*Pause.*]

JOEY Gillian.

[*Pause.*]

LENNY No, what I mean, Teddy, you must know lots of professors, heads of
departments, men like that. They pop over here for a week at the Savoy,
they need somewhere they can go to have a nice quiet poke.[9] And of course
605 you'd be in a position to give them inside information.

MAX Sure. You can give them proper data. You know, the kind of thing she's
willing to do. How far she'd be prepared to go with their little whims and fancies. Eh, Lenny? To what extent she's various. I mean if you don't know who
does?

[*Pause.*]

610 I bet you before two months we'd have a waiting list.

LENNY You could be our representative in the States.

MAX Of course. We're talking in international terms! By the time we've finished Pan-American'll[1] give us a discount.

[*Pause.*]

TEDDY She'd get old . . . very quickly.

615 MAX No . . . not in this day and age! With the health service?[2] Old! How
could she get old? She'll have the time of her life.

[RUTH *comes down the stairs, dressed.*]
[*She comes into the room.*]
[*She smiles at the gathering, and sits.*]
[*Silence.*]

TEDDY Ruth . . . the family have invited you to stay, for a little while longer.
As a . . . as a kind of guest. If you like the idea I don't mind. We can manage very easily at home . . . until you come back.

620 RUTH How very nice of them.

[*Pause.*]

MAX It's an offer from our heart.

RUTH It's very sweet of you.

MAX Listen . . . it would be our pleasure.

[*Pause.*]

9. Sexual intercourse (slang).
1. Leading international air carrier that went
bankrupt in 1991.

2. The National Health Service, which was
founded in 1948, provides free access to health
care for residents of the United Kingdom.

RUTH I think I'd be too much trouble.

625 MAX Trouble? What are you talking about? What trouble? Listen, I'll tell you something. Since poor Jessie died, eh, Sam? we haven't had a woman in the house. Not one. Inside this house. And I'll tell you why. Because their mother's image was so dear any other woman would have . . . tarnished it. But you . . . Ruth . . . you're not only lovely and beautiful, but you're kin.[3] You're

630 kith.[4] You belong here.

[*Pause.*]

RUTH I'm very touched.

MAX Of course you're touched. I'm touched.

[*Pause.*]

TEDDY But Ruth, I should tell you . . . that you'll have to pull your weight a little, if you stay. Financially. My father isn't very well off.

635 RUTH [*to* MAX] Oh, I'm sorry.

MAX No, you'd just have to bring in a little, that's all. A few pennies. Nothing much. It's just that we're waiting for Joey to hit the top as a boxer. When Joey hits the top . . . well . . .

[*Pause.*]

TEDDY Or you can come home with me.

640 LENNY We'd get you a flat.

[*Pause.*]

RUTH A flat?

LENNY Yes.

RUTH Where?

LENNY In town.

[*Pause.*]

645 But you'd live here, with us.

MAX Of course you would. This would be your home. In the bosom of the family.

LENNY You'd just pop up to the flat a couple of hours a night, that's all.

MAX Just a couple of hours, that's all. That's all.

650 LENNY And you make enough money to keep you going here.

[*Pause.*]

RUTH How many rooms would this flat have?

LENNY Not many.

RUTH I would want at least three rooms and a bathroom.

LENNY You wouldn't need three rooms and a bathroom.

655 MAX She'd need a bathroom.

LENNY But not three rooms.

[*Pause.*]

RUTH Oh, I would. Really.

LENNY Two would do.

RUTH No. Two wouldn't be enough.

[*Pause.*]

660 I'd want a dressing-room, a rest-room, and a bedroom.

[*Pause.*]

3. Family, blood relations.
4. Acquaintances, friends, or fellow countrymen.

LENNY   All right, we'll get you a flat with three rooms and a bathroom.
RUTH   With what kind of conveniences?
LENNY   All conveniences.
RUTH   A personal maid?
665 LENNY   Of course.

        [*Pause.*]

    We'd finance you, to begin with, and then, when you were established, you
    could pay us back, in instalments.
RUTH   Oh, no, I wouldn't agree to that.
LENNY   Oh, why not?
670 RUTH   You would have to regard your original outlay simply as a capital
    investment.[5]

        [*Pause.*]

LENNY   I see. All right.
RUTH   You'd supply my wardrobe, of course?
LENNY   We'd supply everything. Everything you need.
675 RUTH   I'd need an awful lot. Otherwise I wouldn't be content.
LENNY   You'd have everything.
RUTH   I would naturally want to draw up an inventory of everything I would
    need, which would require your signatures in the presence of witnesses.
LENNY   Naturally.
680 RUTH   All aspects of the agreement and conditions of employment would have
    to be clarified to our mutual satisfaction before we finalized the contract.
LENNY   Of course.

        [*Pause.*]

RUTH   Well, it might prove a workable arrangement.
LENNY   I think so.
685 MAX   And you'd have the whole of your daytime free, of course. You could do
    a bit of cooking here if you wanted to.
LENNY   Make the beds.
MAX   Scrub the place out a bit.
TEDDY   Keep everyone company.

        [SAM *comes forward.*]

690 SAM   [*in one breath*]   MacGregor had Jessie in the back of my cab as I drove
    them along.

        [*He croaks and collapses.*]
        [*He lies still.*]
        [*They look at him.*]

MAX   What's he done? Dropped dead?
LENNY   Yes.
MAX   A corpse? A corpse on my floor? Get him out of here! Clear him out of
695 here!

        [JOEY *bends over* SAM.]

JOEY   He's not dead.
LENNY   He probably was dead, for about thirty seconds.
MAX   He's not even dead!

---

5. One-time expense, or initial outlay, meant to increase a business's assets, as opposed to an
operational expense, which would be the daily cost of maintaining and operating a business.

[LENNY *looks down at* SAM.]

LENNY   Yes, there's still some breath there.

700   MAX [*pointing at* SAM]   You know what that man had?

LENNY   Has.

MAX   Has! A diseased imagination.

[*Pause.*]

RUTH   Yes, it sounds a very attractive idea.

MAX   Do you want to shake on it now, or do you want to leave it till later?

705   RUTH   Oh, we'll leave it till later.

[TEDDY *stands.*]
[*He looks down at* SAM.]

TEDDY   I was going to ask him to drive me to London Airport.

[*He goes to the cases, picks one up.*]

Well, I'll leave your case, Ruth. I'll just go up the road to the Underground.[6]

MAX   Listen, if you go the other way, first left, first right, you remember, you might find a cab passing there.

710   TEDDY   Yes, I might do that.

MAX   Or you can take the tube to Piccadilly Circus,[7] won't take you ten minutes, and pick up a cab from there out to the Airport.

TEDDY   Yes, I'll probably do that.

MAX   Mind you, they'll charge you double fare. They'll charge you for the

715   return trip. It's over the six-mile limit.

TEDDY   Yes. Well, bye-bye, Dad. Look after yourself.

[*They shake hands.*]

MAX   Thanks, son. Listen. I want to tell you something. It's been wonderful to see you.

[*Pause.*]

TEDDY   It's been wonderful to see you.

720   MAX   Do your boys know about me? Eh? Would they like to see a photo, do you think, of their grandfather?

TEDDY   I know they would.

[MAX *brings out his wallet.*]

MAX   I've got one on me. I've got one here. Just a minute. Here you are. Will they like that one?

725   TEDDY [*taking it*]   They'll be thrilled.

[*He turns to* LENNY.]

Good-bye, Lenny.

[*They shake hands.*]

LENNY   Ta-ta, Ted. Good to see you. Have a good trip.

TEDDY   Bye-bye, Joey.

[JOEY *does not move.*]

JOEY   Ta-ta.

[TEDDY *goes to the front door.*]

730   RUTH   Eddie.

---

6. London's major rail transportation system. While some lines have aboveground sections, most of the rail system is underground.

7. Bustling, well-known intersection in London's West End.

[TEDDY *turns.*]
[*Pause.*]

Don't become a stranger.

[TEDDY *goes, shuts the front door.*]
[*Silence.*]
[*The three men stand.*]
[RUTH *sits relaxed in her chair.*]
[SAM *lies still.*]
[JOEY *walks slowly across the room.*]
[*He kneels at her chair.*]
[*She touches his head, lightly.*]
[*He puts his head in her lap.*]
[MAX *begins to move above them, backwards and forwards.*]
[LENNY *stands still.*]
[MAX *turns to* LENNY.]

MAX   I'm too old, I suppose. She thinks I'm an old man.

[*Pause.*]

I'm not such an old man.

[*Pause.*]

[*To* RUTH.] You think I'm too old for you?

[*Pause.*]

735   Listen. You think you're just going to get that big slag[8] all the time? You think you're just going to have him . . . you're going to just have him all the time? You're going to have to work! You'll have to take them on, you understand?

[*Pause.*]

Does she realize that?

[*Pause.*]

Lenny, do you think she understands . . .

[*He begins to stammer.*]

740   What . . . what . . . what . . . we're getting at? What . . . we've got in mind? Do you think she's got it clear?

[*Pause.*]

I don't think she's got it clear.

[*Pause.*]

You understand what I mean? Listen, I've got a funny idea she'll do the dirty on us, you want to bet? She'll use us, she'll make use of us, I can tell
745   you! I can smell it! You want to bet?

[*Pause.*]

She won't . . . be adaptable!

[*He falls to his knees, whimpers, begins to moan and sob.*]
[*He stops sobbing, crawls past* SAM's *body round her chair, to the other side of her.*]

I'm not an old man.

[*He looks up at her.*]

Do you hear me?

[*He raises his face to her.*]

8. Prostitute or promiscuous woman (slang), particularly derogatory when applied, as here, to a man.

Kiss me.

[*She continues to touch* JOEY's *head, lightly.*]
[LENNY *stands, watching.*]

Curtain

WOLE SOYINKA

b. 1934

AN active writer for more than five decades, Wole Soyinka is widely regarded as Africa's foremost dramatist and one of the most compelling contemporary writers in English more generally, a judgment affirmed by his being awarded the Nobel Prize in Literature in 1986. Though he is also an accomplished poet, novelist, and essayist, Soyinka's worldwide acclaim rests mainly on his dramatic oeuvre. His plays make use of the rituals and festivals of Nigeria's Yoruba culture and are marked by Nigeria's volatile history, but they also reflect the influences of other cultures, such as that of classical Greece. Soyinka has been one of the continent's most outspoken critics of abuses of power, in Nigeria and elsewhere, even as he has crafted plays that cannot be tied to a particular political creed. For many, his most significant achievement is the creation of a new form of tragedy that draws on both Western and Yoruba traditions, a form that is perhaps most fully realized in DEATH AND THE KING'S HORSEMAN (1975).

During Soyinka's formative years, Nigeria was in its last decades of British rule. Consequently, Soyinka received a traditional education in English, first at an elite grammar school and then at Government College, Ibadan, where he excelled in the study of various Western literatures, including French and Greek. He continued his education in England, where he studied drama at the University of Leeds. In Leeds and later in London, Soyinka also intensified his engagement with the theater and wrote his first plays, which helped win him a research grant and begin his swift rise as a dramatist. He returned to Nigeria in 1960, the year of its independence from Britain and the start of a period of intense conflict between different regions of the country. Over the next few years, Soyinka founded theater groups; wrote fiction and verse as well as plays for stage, television, and radio; and taught as a university lecturer in English. At the same time, he attempted to prevent the civil war that ultimately broke out in 1967 when the southeast of Nigeria declared its independence as Biafra; these efforts led to his imprisonment. He spent much of his two years of detention in solitary confinement, an experience he later described in one of his autobiographical prose works, *The Man Died: Prison Notes of Wole Soyinka* (1972). His subsequent career has been marked by a series of exiles and returns. Soyinka has taught at the University of Cambridge and Yale University and has directed shows in Europe and the United States, but his most sustained project has been the fostering of Nigeria's literary culture and democracy.

The clearest indications of Soyinka's changing attitude toward nationalism and cultural autonomy can be found in his essays. Writing in the sixties, Soyinka was often critical of those seeking an "authentic" culture that existed before Europeans colonized Africa and focused instead on cultural mixture. By the 1970s, however, he had turned more fully to Yoruba culture—to which he was exposed early, despite his mother's fervent Christianity—as a resource for drama. In the 1980s, as Soyinka once more became disenchanted with Nigeria's political realities, he placed less emphasis on Yoruba culture. His critical writings thus chart a path through the cultural struggles of a former colony dealing with an imposed culture that has now fused with local ones; after the terrible experience of colonialism, Western and indigenous cultures had become permanently intertwined. Soyinka's relation to colonialism was further complicated by his decision to write in English, albeit an English shot through with metaphors, idioms, and sayings from Yoruba. At various times in his career, he advocated the use of Swahili throughout the continent as a lingua franca to replace the languages of Africa's former European colonizers, but this proposal won few followers.

Soyinka's oeuvre oscillates between tradition and modernity. His earliest plays, *The Swamp Dwellers* (1958) and *The Lion and the Jewel* (1959), present a critique of traditional Yoruba practices and social structures as they come under increasing pressure from forces of modernization both from within and from without. Each play contains a village priest or ruler who opposes modernization and who cunningly seeks to hold on to vestiges of power predicated on the old ways. Soyinka clearly does not endorse this defensive rejection of modernization, although he recognizes the pain that accompanied the transformation of the Nigerian hinterland. Ultimately, these plays satirize the attempt to preserve the old at all cost. A similar critique is developed in *The Trials of Brother Jero* (1960) and *Jero's Metamorphosis* (1973), two plays that revolve around a pseudo-prophet who attracts followers solely for his own economic gain and who is ready to employ every trick possible to outsmart his rivals. In other works, Soyinka is more fully concerned with the social reality of the

outcast. In *The Road* (1965), one of his best plays, a number of lowlifes are assembled around a figure called Professor, who is akin to the sham prophet Jero. As Professor ekes out a living by forging documents, he is also engaged in an unlikely quest for spiritual enlightenment. These plays show that modernity is not something imposed onto Yoruba culture from the outside but a force at work within it.

Some of Soyinka's plays aim squarely at Nigerian politics—for example, *From Zia, with Love* (1992), which harshly indicts the dictatorship—but his best-known plays avoid direct political engagement, seeking instead to weave together different cultures and traditions. In his drama, Soyinka has continually insisted on the affinities between Greek and Yoruba tragedy. Most significantly, he has related the Yoruba god Ogun, the deity to whom he himself feels closest, to the Greek god Dionysus, who is connected with the origins of Greek tragedy. This attempt to forge new forms of tragedy out of Western and African traditions led to a long-standing controversy between Soyinka and a group of Nigerian intellectuals and critics—dubbed by Soyinka the "Leftocracy"—who accused him of seeking universal human meaning while ignoring the specifics of Nigeria's political and social situation after independence.

The tensions between political drama and tragedy as well as the tensions between the use of Western and Yoruba traditions are most visible in Soyinka's adaptations of EURIPIDES' *The Bacchae* (406 B.C.E.) and of BERTOLT BRECHT's *The Threepenny Opera* (1928). *The Bacchae of Euripides* (1973) provided Soyinka with an occasion to gauge the similarities and differences between Greek and Yoruba myths. Soyinka's Dionysus is less vindictive than Euripides', and his play displays a broader social range (its chorus is made up of slaves). Yet he shares with Euripides the attempt to connect drama to its lost origin in ritual. Brecht's *Threepenny Opera* is much more overtly political; *Opera Wonyosi* (1977) replaces the underworld of London, which Brecht himself had borrowed from the eighteenth-century British playwright John Gay, with a politically corrupt West Africa. In both adaptations, Soyinka demonstrates the power of translation and transposition, encouraging cultural mixture and cross-fertilization in a way that respects the integrity of different traditions and practices.

Soyinka's project of inventing a new tragic form culminates in *Death and the King's Horseman*, a play based on a historical incident. In 1946, a British colonial district officer interrupted the ritual suicide of a village notable, the King's Horseman—a suicide prescribed by the Yoruba religious and social system—without realizing how his interference would affect the village and, most importantly, the King's Horseman's son, who is also his protégé. This historical incident thus ties the officer, the King's Horseman, and his son in an inextricable and fatal knot. The officer himself is presented as a relatively two-dimensional figure, distinguished mainly by his colonial arrogance: Simon Pilkings interferes with local customs without knowing anything about their role in the social order or their religious significance. As a result, some critics have read the play as a defense of Yoruba customs. In his author's note, however, Soyinka takes issue with all readings that reduce the play to a simple "clash of cultures"; indeed, the play spends considerable energy trying—and failing—to bridge the gulf between them.

The two cultures are connected by various mediating figures, who participate in or have knowledge of both worlds. The officer, for example, depends on his Yoruba employees for information about local customs and religion. While Pilkings, who arrogantly dismisses their culture, often finds it difficult to interpret what his informants say, his wife is somewhat more open-minded and thus more aware of the inescapable cultural clash. The most competent intermediary is Olunde, the son of Elesin, the King's Horseman. Sent by Pilkings to England to study medicine against his father's wishes, Olunde has now returned for his father's burial. Although he is Westernized (as evidenced by the suit he wears), he does not dismiss the requirement that his father commit suicide, knowing how deeply the ritual is woven into the social fabric of the village. In eloquently criticizing the folly of the colonial officer's attempt to stop the ritual, he serves as an authoritative commentator on the play's main conflict. Events take a tragic turn at precisely the moment when the son feels forced to abandon his role as mediator and instead become a participant.

Even as Soyinka emphasizes the significance of the Yoruba custom and Elesin's

British colonial administrators meeting tribal representatives in Lagos, Nigeria, ca. 1900.

social position, he also highlights the customs and social rituals of the British colonizers. Jane, the colonial officer's wife, approvingly recounts the story of a British captain's suicide, condoned because it was deemed heroic. At the same time, Soyinka contrasts Yoruba dances with a masque held by the British, who dress in costumes to attend a ball that evokes European court culture and its rigid hierarchies. Each culture thus has a place for suicide and for masked dance. To intertwine the two cultures even more closely, Soyinka has each imitate the other. At one point, a group of village women and girls mock the idioms and intonation of their colonial rulers. At another, we see the Pilkingses appear in sacred costumes associated with the Yoruba dead, mimicking ritual movements (as best they can) to amuse their European audience.

Soyinka's interest in different forms of ritual is part of an undertaking that informs his entire oeuvre, including *Death and the King's Horseman*: the creation of a total theater. Like many other theater artists of the nineteenth and twentieth centuries, Soyinka employs as many different modes of expression as possible, seeking to bring together song, poetry, dance, speech, ritual, and music. In this play, we encounter a variety of sounds and instruments—for example, the royal drums, which weave together the traditional rhythms of wedding and death and delineate the play's tragic trajectory; different dance interludes, including the gripping suicidal dance of the King's Horseman; and different Western musical pieces, such as the tango blaring from a gramophone at the colonial officer's house and a band playing "Rule Britannia" in honor of the Prince, who is visiting the colony. But unlike some makers of total theater, Soyinka is not interested in unifying these various traditions of music, dance, and theater into one seamless whole. Rather, the play thrives on their collisions, interchanges, and mutual imitations.

The different forms of ceremony, ritual, and dance that make up this complex play are mirrored and reinforced by its unusual language and poetry. Certain Yoruba songs that accompany the play's central event, the ritual suicide, are rendered in poetic English. Like all of the utterances of the non-British characters, they are informed by the syntax, idioms, expressions, proverbs, and metaphors of Yoruba. The result is a multilayered English that takes on deeper meaning as it draws on the Yoruba world—its flora, fauna, social structure, and cosmology. The play juxtaposes and blends different languages as thoroughly as it intermingles different forms of theater and performance.

This commingling is perhaps the most important feature of *Death and the King's Horseman*. For while the play certainly shows the violence that occurs at a moment of cultural contact between the British and Yoruba cultures, it refuses to blame all problems on their clash. Each culture has internal tensions. Thus Yoruba culture, for Soyinka, is never simply an authentic and monolithic given that is then, in a second step, set against the putatively modern British culture. He instead views Yoruba culture as having itself undergone a process of modernization, making it a culture compatible with the international, cosmopolitan world represented by Olunde, the most

A Yoruba tribal leader, 1960.

articulate figure in the play. At the same time, Soyinka points to tradition and even ritualistic aspects of British culture. In this way, both Yoruba culture and British culture are divided between tradition and modernization, though Soyinka never lets us forget which one has suppressed and belittled the other.

The attempt to show the different forms of modernization at work in Yoruba and British culture stands behind the mythic construction of this tragedy, which rests on the assumption that the Yoruba gods and the Greek gods are somehow compatible or comparable. It was a project conceived as a response to the more simplistic forms of postcolonial nationalism, which took shape as incipient nations sought to create distinct national traditions in isolation. At the same time, Soyinka is trying to dismantle the vestiges of colonialism—specifically, the assumption that Western culture has a unique claim to being modern and that in order for Yoruba culture to become modern it would have

to adapt Western customs, religion, and culture.

Death and the King's Horseman has sometimes been accused of nostalgically privileging the Yoruba ritual by contrasting it favorably with the ignorance of the colonial officer, but Soyinka's complex mixing of the different ritualistic practices shows that no false nostalgia is in fact at work. Like many other works of modernism written by former colonizers and colonized alike, his plays display not just a fascination with premodern mythology and ritual but also an awareness that such myths and rituals can never be recovered in the present. Just as Richard Wagner sought to relate his operatic artwork of the future to a mythic German past and James Joyce fashioned his groundbreaking novel after Homer, so Soyinka's play gains its strength by invoking but not embracing different ritual practices. While its characters accept and perform the ritual, Soyinka's play itself is and remains a modern work, albeit one with living roots in the past.   M.P.

Death and the King's Horseman

Dedicated
In Affectionate Greeting
to
My Father, Ayodele
who lately danced, and joined the Ancestors.

Author's Note

This play is based on events which took place in Oyo,[1] ancient Yoruba city of Nigeria, in 1946. That year, the lives of Elesin (Olori Elesin), his son, and the Colonial District Officer intertwined with the disastrous results set out in the play. The changes I have made are in matters of detail, sequence, and of course characterisation. The action has also been set back two or three years to while the war was still on,[2] for minor reasons of dramaturgy.

1. A city in western Nigeria, about 100 miles north of Lagos.

2. That is, World War II.

DEATH AND THE KING'S HORSEMAN | 1473

The factual account still exists in the archives of the British Colonial Administration. It has already inspired a fine play in Yoruba (Oba Wàjà[3]) by Duro Ladipo. It has also misbegotten a film by some German television company.

The bane of themes of this genre is that they are no sooner employed creatively than they acquire the facile tag of 'clash of cultures', a prejudicial label which, quite apart from its frequent misapplication, presupposes a potential equality *in every given situation* of the alien culture and the indigenous, on the actual soil of the latter. (In the area of misapplication, the overseas prize for illiteracy and mental conditioning undoubtedly goes to the blurb-writer for the American edition of my novel *Season of Anomy*[4] who unblushingly declares that this work portrays the 'clash between old values and new ways, between western methods and African traditions'!) It is thanks to this kind of perverse mentality that I find it necessary to caution the would-be producer of this play against a sadly familiar reductionist tendency, and to direct his vision instead to the far more difficult and risky task of eliciting the play's threnodic[5] essence.

One of the more obvious alternative structures of the play would be to make the District Officer the victim of a cruel dilemma. This is not to my taste and it is not by chance that I have avoided dialogue or situation which would encourage this. No attempt should be made in production to suggest it. The Colonial Factor is an incident, a catalytic incident merely. The confrontation in the play is largely metaphysical, contained in the human vehicle which is Elesin and the universe of the Yoruba mind—the world of the living, the dead and the unborn, and the numinous passage which links all: transition. *Death and the King's Horseman* can be fully realised only through an evocation of music from the abyss of transition.   W.S.

CHARACTERS

PRAISE-SINGER
ELESIN, Horseman of the King
IYALOJA, 'Mother' of the market
SIMON PILKINGS, District Officer
JANE PILKINGS, his wife
SERGEANT AMUSA
JOSEPH, houseboy to the Pilkingses
BRIDE
H.R.H. THE PRINCE
THE RESIDENT[6]
AIDE-DE-CAMP
OLUNDE, eldest son of Elesin

DRUMMERS, WOMEN, YOUNG GIRLS, DANCERS AT THE BALL

The play should run without an interval. For rapid scene changes, one adjustable outline set is very appropriate.

3. *The King Is Dead* (1964).
4. Published in New York in 1974 (London, 1973).

5. Resembling a threnody, or song of lament for the dead.
6. The ranking British officer in a province.

Act 1

A passage through a market in its closing stages. The stalls are being emptied, mats folded. A few WOMEN *pass through on their way home, loaded with baskets. On a cloth-stand, bolts of cloth are taken down, display pieces folded and piled on a tray.* ELESIN OBA *enters along a passage before the market, pursued by his* DRUMMERS *and* PRAISE-SINGERS. *He is a man of enormous vitality, speaks, dances, and sings with that infectious enjoyment of life which accompanies all his actions.*

PRAISE-SINGER   Elesin o! Elesin Oba! Howu![7] What tryst is this the cockerel goes to keep with such haste that he must leave his tail behind?

ELESIN [*slows down a bit, laughing*]   A tryst where the cockerel needs no adornment.

5 PRAISE-SINGER   O-oh, you hear that my companions? That's the way the world goes. Because the man approaches a brand-new bride he forgets the long faithful mother of his children.[8]

ELESIN   When the horse sniffs the stable does he not strain at the bridle? The market is the long-suffering home of my spirit and the women are

10 packing up to go. That Esu[9]-harassed day slipped into the stewpot while we feasted. We ate it up with the rest of the meat. I have neglected my women.

PRAISE-SINGER   We know all that. Still it's no reason for shedding your tail on this day of all days. I know the women will cover you in damask and *alari*[1] but when the wind blows cold from behind, that's when the fowl knows his

15 true friends.

ELESIN   Olohun-iyo![2]

PRAISE-SINGER   Are you sure there will be one like me on the other side?

ELESIN   Olohun-iyo!

PRAISE-SINGER   Far be it for me to belittle the dwellers of that place but, a

20 man is either born to his art or he isn't. And I don't know for certain that you'll meet my father, so who is going to sing these deeds in accents that will pierce the deafness of the ancient ones. I have prepared my going—just tell me: Olohun-iyo, I need you on this journey and I shall be behind you.

ELESIN   You're like a jealous wife. Stay close to me, but only on this side. My

25 fame, my honour are legacies to the living; stay behind and let the world sip its honey from your lips.

PRAISE-SINGER   Your name will be like the sweet berry a child places under his tongue to sweeten the passage of food. The world will never spit it out.

ELESIN   Come then. This market is my roost. When I come among the

30 women I am a chicken with a hundred mothers. I become a monarch whose palace is built with tenderness and beauty.

PRAISE-SINGER   They love to spoil you but beware. The hands of women also weaken the unwary.

ELESIN   This night I'll lay my head upon their lap and go to sleep. This night

35 I'll touch feet with their feet in a dance that is no longer of this earth. But the smell of their flesh, their sweat, the smell of indigo[3] on their cloth, this is the last air I wish to breathe as I go to meet my great forebears.

---

7. Why have you come? (Yoruba greeting). *Oba:* king (Yoruba).
8. Traditionally, Yoruba men had multiple wives.
9. The Yoruba trickster god.

1. A rich, woven cloth, brightly coloured [Soyinka]. *Damask:* a lustrous patterned fabric.
2. Praise-singer (Yoruba).
3. A costly blue dye made from plants and used by royalty in Africa.

PRAISE-SINGER   In their time the world was never tilted from its groove, it
    shall not be in yours.
40 ELESIN   The gods have said No.
PRAISE-SINGER   In their time the great wars came and went, the little wars
    came and went; the white slavers came and went, they took away the heart
    of our race, they bore away the mind and muscle of our race. The city fell
    and was rebuilt; the city fell and our people trudged through mountain and
45   forest to found a new home but—Elesin Oba do you hear me?
ELESIN   I hear your voice Olohun-iyo.
PRAISE-SINGER   Our world was never wrenched from its true course.
ELESIN   The gods have said No.
PRAISE-SINGER   There is only one home to the life of a river-mussel; there is
50   only one home to the life of a tortoise; there is only one shell to the soul of
    man; there is only one world to the spirit of our race. If that world leaves its
    course and smashes on boulders of the great void, whose world will give us
    shelter?
ELESIN   It did not in the time of my forebears, it shall not in mine.
55 PRAISE-SINGER   The cockerel must not be seen without his feathers.
ELESIN   Nor will the Not-I bird[4] be much longer without his nest.
PRAISE-SINGER [stopped in his lyric stride]   The Not-I bird, Elesin?
ELESIN   I said, the Not-I bird.
PRAISE-SINGER   All respect to our elders but, is there really such a bird?
60 ELESIN   What! Could it be that he failed to knock on your door?
PRAISE-SINGER [smiling]   Elesin's riddles are not merely the nut in the kernel
    that breaks human teeth; he also buries the kernel in hot embers and dares
    a man's fingers to draw it out.
ELESIN   I am sure he called on you, Olohun-iyo. Did you hide in the loft and
65   push out the servant to tell him you were out?

> [ELESIN executes a brief, half-taunting dance. The DRUMMER moves in
> and draws a rhythm out of his steps. ELESIN dances towards the market-
> place as he chants the story of the Not-I bird, his voice changing dexter-
> ously to mimic his characters. He performs like a born raconteur,
> infecting his retinue with his humour and energy. More WOMEN arrive
> during his recital, including IYALOJA.]

Death came calling.
Who does not know his rasp of reeds?
A twilight whisper in the leaves before
The great araba[5] falls? Did you hear it?
70 Not I! swears the farmer. He snaps
His fingers round his head, abandons
A hard-worn harvest and begins
A rapid dialogue with his legs.

'Not I,' shouts the fearless hunter, 'but—
75 It's getting dark, and this night-lamp
Has leaked out all its oil. I think
It's best to go home and resume my hunt

4. A bird whose call resembles the Yoruba   5. A silk-cotton tree (Yoruba), which yields
phrase that means "not I."   the fiber kapok.

Another day.' But now he pauses, suddenly
Lets out a wail: 'Oh foolish mouth, calling
80   Down a curse on your own head! Your lamp
Has leaked out all its oil, has it?'
Forwards or backwards now he dare not move.
To search for leaves and make *etutu*[6]
On that spot? Or race home to the safety
85   Of his hearth? Ten market-days have passed
My friends, and still he's rooted there
Rigid as the plinth of Orayan.[7]

The mouth of the courtesan barely
Opened wide enough to take a ha'penny *robo*[8]
90   When she wailed: 'Not I.' All dressed she was
To call upon my friend the Chief Tax Officer.
But now she sends her go-between instead:
'Tell him I'm ill: my period has come suddenly
But not—I hope—my time.'

95   Why is the pupil crying?
His hapless head was made to taste
The knuckles of my friend the Mallam.[9]
'If you were then reciting the Koran
Would you have ears for idle noises
100 Darkening the trees, you child of ill omen?'
He shuts down school before its time
Runs home and rings himself with amulets.

And take my good kinsman Ifawomi.
His hands were like a carver's, strong
105 And true. I saw them
Tremble like wet wings of a fowl
One day he cast his time-smoothed *opele*[1]
Across the divination board. And all because
The suppliant looked him in the eye and asked,
110 'Did you hear that whisper in the leaves?'
'Not I,' was his reply; 'perhaps I'm growing deaf—
Good-day.' And Ifa spoke no more that day
The priest locked fast his doors,
Sealed up his leaking roof—but wait!
115 This sudden care was not for Fawomi
But for Osanyin,[2] courier-bird of Ifa's
Heart of wisdom. I did not know a kite
Was hovering in the sky
And Ifa now a twittering chicken in

6. Placatory rites or medicine [Soyinka].
7. A tall landmark in Ile-Ife, ancestral home
of the Yoruba. Orayan was a son of Oduduwa,
first Yoruba king, and progenitor of all subsequent kings.
8. A delicacy made from crushed melon

seeds, fried in tiny balls [Soyinka].
9. A teacher of Islamic doctrine (Hausa).
1. String of beads used in Ifa divination
[Soyinka].
2. Patron deity of diviners. *Fawomi*: a reference to Ifa, the Yoruba god of divination.

120   The brood of Fawomi the Mother Hen.

Ah, but I must not forget my evening
Courier from the abundant palm, whose groan
Became Not I, as he constipated down
A wayside bush. He wonders if Elegbara[3]
125   Has tricked his buttocks to discharge
Against a sacred grove. Hear him
Mutter spells to ward off penalties
For an abomination he did not intend.
If any here
130   Stumbles on a gourd of wine, fermenting
Near the road, and nearby hears a stream
Of spells issuing from a crouching form,
Brother to a *sigidi*,[4] bring home my wine,
Tell my tapper[5] I have ejected
135   Fear from home and farm. Assure him,
All is well.

PRAISE-SINGER   In your time we do not doubt the peace of farmstead and home,
    the peace of road and hearth, we do not doubt the peace of the forest.
ELESIN   There was fear in the forest too.
140   Not-I was lately heard even in the lair
Of beasts. The hyena cackled loud Not I,
The civet[6] twitched his fiery tail and glared:
Not I. Not-I became the answering-name
Of the restless bird, that little one
145   Whom Death found nesting in the leaves
When whisper of his coming ran
Before him on the wind. Not-I
Has long abandoned home. This same dawn
I heard him twitter in the gods' abode.
150   Ah, companions of this living world
What a thing this is, that even those
We call immortal
Should fear to die.
IYALOJA   But you, husband of multitudes?
155 ELESIN   I, when that Not-I bird perched
Upon my roof, bade him seek his nest again,
Safe, without care or fear. I unrolled
My welcome mat for him to see. Not-I
Flew happily away, you'll hear his voice
160   No more in this lifetime—You all know
What I am.
PRAISE-SINGER   That rock which turns its open lodes
    Into the path of lightning. A gay

---

3. Another name for Esu, the trickster god.
4. A squat, carved figure, endowed with the powers of an incubus [Soyinka], which is a demon that lies on people in their sleep.

5. The person who collects the sap of palm trees, which is fermented into wine.
6. A weasel-like carnivorous mammal (especially the species native to Africa).

Thoroughbred whose stride disdains
165   To falter though an adder reared
Suddenly in his path.
ELESIN   My rein is loosened.
I am master of my Fate. When the hour comes
Watch me dance along the narrowing path
170   Glazed by the soles of my great precursors.
My soul is eager. I shall not turn aside.
WOMEN   You will not delay?
ELESIN   Where the storm pleases, and when, it directs
The giants of the forest. When friendship summons
175   Is when the true comrade goes.
WOMEN   Nothing will hold you back?
ELESIN   Nothing. What! Has no one told you yet?
I go to keep my friend and master company.
Who says the mouth does not believe in
180   'No, I have chewed all that before?' I say I have.
The world is not a constant honey-pot.
Where I found little I made do with little.
Where there was plenty I gorged myself.
My master's hands and mine have always
185   Dipped together and, home or sacred feast,
The bowl was beaten bronze, the meats
So succulent our teeth accused us of neglect.
We shared the choicest of the season's
Harvest of yams. How my friend would read
190   Desire in my eyes before I knew the cause—
However rare, however precious, it was mine.
WOMEN   The town, the very land was yours.
ELESIN   The world was mine. Our joint hands
Raised houseposts of trust that withstood
195   The siege of envy and the termites of time.
But the twilight hour brings bats and rodents—
Shall I yield them cause to foul the rafters?
PRAISE-SINGER   Elesin Oba! Are you not that man who
Looked out of doors that stormy day
200   The god of luck limped by, drenched
To the very lice that held
His rags together? You took pity upon
His sores and wished him fortune.
Fortune was footloose this dawn, he replied,
205   Till you trapped him in a heartfelt wish
That now returns to you. Elesin Oba!
I say you are that man who
Chanced upon the calabash[7] of honour
You thought it was palm wine and
210   Drained its contents to the final drop.
ELESIN   Life has an end. A life that will outlive

---

7. A drinking vessel made from a gourd.

Fame and friendship begs another name.
What elder takes his tongue to his plate,
Licks it clean of every crumb? He will encounter
215 Silence when he calls on children to fulfill
The smallest errand! Life is honour.
It ends when honour ends.

WOMEN We know you for a man of honour.

ELESIN Stop! Enough of that!

WOMEN [*puzzled, they whisper among themselves, turning mostly to* IYALOJA]
220 What is it? Did we say something to give offence? Have we slighted him in
some way?

ELESIN Enough of that sound I say. Let me hear no more in that vein. I've
heard enough.

IYALOJA We must have said something wrong. [*Comes forward a little.*]
225 Elesin Oba, we ask forgiveness before you speak.

ELESIN I am bitterly offended.

IYALOJA Our unworthiness has betrayed us. All we can do is ask your forgiveness. Correct us like a kind father.

ELESIN This day of all days . . .

230 IYALOJA It does not bear thinking. If we offend you now we have mortified
the gods. We offend heaven itself. Father of us all, tell us where we went
astray. [*She kneels, the other women follow.*]

ELESIN Are you not ashamed? Even a tear-veiled
Eye preserves its function of sight.
235 Because my mind was raised to horizons
Even the boldest man lowers his gaze
In thinking of, must my body here
Be taken for a vagrant's?

IYALOJA Horseman of the King, I am more baffled than ever.

240 PRAISE-SINGER The strictest father unbends his brow when the child is penitent, Elesin. When time is short, we do not spend it prolonging the riddle.
Their shoulders are bowed with the weight of fear lest they have marred
your day beyond repair. Speak now in plain words and let us pursue the ailment to the home of remedies.

245 ELESIN Words are cheap. 'We know you for
A man of honour.' Well tell me, is this how
A man of honour should be seen?
Are these not the same clothes in which
I came among you a full half-hour ago?

[*He roars with laughter and the* WOMEN, *relieved, rise and rush into stalls
to fetch rich cloths.*]

250 WOMEN The gods are kind. A fault soon remedied is soon forgiven. Elesin
Oba, even as we match our words with deed, let your heart forgive us
completely.

ELESIN You who are breath and giver of my being
How shall I dare refuse you forgiveness
Even if the offence were real.

IYALOJA [*dancing round him. Sings*]
255 He forgives us. He forgives us.
What a fearful thing it is when

The voyager sets forth
But a curse remains behind.
WOMEN   For a while we truly feared
260   Our hands had wrenched the world adrift
In emptiness.
IYALOJA   Richly, richly, robe him richly
The cloth of honour is *alari*
Sanyan is the band of friendship
265   Boa-skin[8] makes slippers of esteem
WOMEN   For a while we truly feared
Our hands had wrenched the world adrift
In emptiness.
PRAISE-SINGER   He who must, must voyage forth
270   The world will not roll backwards
It is he who must, with one
Great gesture overtake the world.
WOMEN   For a while we truly feared
Our hands had wrenched the world
275   In emptiness.
PRAISE-SINGER   The gourd you bear is not for shirking.
The gourd is not for setting down
At the first crossroad or wayside grove.
Only one river may know its contents.
280 WOMEN   We shall all meet at the great market[9]
We shall all meet at the great market
He who goes early takes the best bargains
But we shall meet, and resume our banter.
        [ELESIN *stands resplendent in rich clothes, cap, shawl, etc. His sash is of
        a bright red alari cloth. The* WOMEN *dance round him. Suddenly, his
        attention is caught by an object offstage.*]
ELESIN   The world I know is good.
285 WOMEN   We know you'll leave it so.
ELESIN   The world I know is the bounty
Of hives after bees have swarmed.
No goodness teems with such open hands
Even in the dreams of deities.
290 WOMEN   And we know you'll leave it so.
ELESIN   I was born to keep it so. A hive
Is never known to wander. An anthill
Does not desert its roots. We cannot see
The still great womb of the world—
295   No man beholds his mother's womb—
Yet who denies it's there? Coiled
To the navel of the world is that
Endless cord that links us all
To the great origin. If I lose my way

8. That is, snakeskin. *Sanyan*: a richly valued   9. That is, in the afterlife.
woven cloth [Soyinka].

300   The trailing cord will bring me to the roots.

WOMEN   The world is in your hands.

[*The earlier distraction, a beautiful* YOUNG GIRL, *comes along the passage through which* ELESIN *first made his entry.*]

ELESIN   I embrace it. And let me tell you, women—
I like this farewell that the world designed,
Unless my eyes deceive me, unless
305   We are already parted, the world and I,
And all that breeds desire is lodged
Among our tireless ancestors. Tell me friends,
Am I still earthed in that beloved market
Of my youth? Or could it be my will
310   Has outleapt the conscious act and I have come
Among the great departed?

PRAISE-SINGER   Elesin-Oba why do your eyes roll like a bush-rat who sees his fate like his father's spirit, mirrored in the eye of a snake? And all these questions! You're standing on the same earth you've always stood
315   upon. This voice you hear is mine, Oluhun-iyo, not that of an acolyte in heaven.

ELESIN   How can that be? In all my life
As Horseman of the King, the juiciest
Fruit on every tree was mine. I saw,
320   I touched, I wooed, rarely was the answer No.
The honour of my place, the veneration I
Received in the eye of man or woman
Prospered my suit and
Played havoc with my sleeping hours.
325   And they tell me my eyes were a hawk
In perpetual hunger. Split an iroko[1] tree
In two, hide a woman's beauty in its heartwood
And seal it up again—Elesin, journeying by,
Would make his camp beside that tree
330   Of all the shades in the forest.

PRAISE-SINGER   Who would deny your reputation, snake-on-the-loose in dark passages of the market! Bed-bug who wages war on the mat and receives the thanks of the vanquished! When caught with his bride's own sister he protested—but I was only prostrating myself to her as becomes a grateful in-
335   law. Hunter who carries his powder-horn on the hips and fires crouching or standing! Warrior who never makes that excuse of the whining coward—but how can I go to battle without my trousers?—trouserless or shirtless it's all one to him. Oka[2]-rearing-from-a-camouflage-of-leaves, before he strikes the victim is already prone! Once they told him, Howu, a stallion does not feed
340   on the grass beneath him: he replied, true, but surely he can roll on it!

WOMEN   Ba-a-a-ba O!

PRAISE-SINGER   Ah, but listen yet. You know there is the leaf-nibbling grub and there is the cola-chewing beetle; the leaf-nibbling grub lives on the

1. A large tree of the mulberry family, sometimes called African teak; according to Yoruba
folklore, its denser, multicolored heartwood is
inhabited by an impish spirit.
2. A snake.

1482 | WOLE SOYINKA

leaf, the cola-chewing beetle lives in the colanut. Don't we know what our
345   man feeds on when we find him cocooned in a woman's wrapper?

    ELESIN   Enough, enough, you all have cause
           To know me well. But, if you say this earth
           Is still the same as gave birth to those songs,
           Tell me who was that goddess through whose lips
350   I saw the ivory pebbles of Oya's[3] river-bed.
           Iyaloja, who is she? I saw her enter
           Your stall; all your daughters I know well.
           No, not even Ogun[4]-of-the-farm toiling
           Dawn till dusk on his tuber patch
355   Not even Ogun with the finest hoe he ever
           Forged at the anvil could have shaped
           That rise of buttocks, not though he had
           The richest earth between his fingers.
           Her wrapper was no disguise
360   For thighs whose ripples shamed the river's
           Coils around the hills of Ilesi.[5] Her eyes
           Were new-laid eggs glowing in the dark.
           Her skin . . .

    IYALOJA   Elesin Oba . . .
365   ELESIN   What! Where do you all say I am?
    IYALOJA   Still among the living.
    ELESIN   And that radiance which so suddenly
      Lit up this market I could boast
      I knew so well?
370   IYALOJA   Has one step already in her husband's home. She is betrothed.
    ELESIN [irritated]   Why do you tell me that?

        [IYALOJA falls silent. The WOMEN shuffle uneasily.]

    IYALOJA   Not because we dare give you offence Elesin. Today is your day and
    the whole world is yours. Still, even those who leave town to make a new
    dwelling elsewhere like to be remembered by what they leave behind.
375   ELESIN   Who does not seek to be remembered?
           Memory is Master of Death, the chink
           In his armour of conceit. I shall leave
           That which makes my going the sheerest
           Dream of an afternoon. Should voyagers
380   Not travel light? Let the considerate traveller
           Shed, of his excessive load, all
           That may benefit the living.
    WOMEN [relieved]   Ah Elesin Oba, we knew you for a man of honour.
    ELESIN   Then honour me. I deserve a bed of honour to lie upon.
385   IYALOJA   The best is yours. We know you for a man of honour. You are not one
    who eats and leaves nothing on his plate for children. Did you not say it
    yourself? Not one who blights the happiness of others for a moment's
    pleasure.

---

3. The goddess of the Niger River and of winds.
4. The god of iron and war and patron of
blacksmiths. Soyinka compares him to various
gods and figures from Greek myth—Apollo,
Prometheus, and especially Dionysus, the god
of fertility and wine and patron of theater.
5. A town in western Nigeria.

ELESIN Who speaks of pleasure? O women, listen!
390   Pleasure palls. Our acts should have meaning.
      The sap of the plantain never dries.
      You have seen the young shoot swelling
      Even as the parent stalk begins to wither.
      Women, let my going be likened to
395   The twilight hour of the plantain.
WOMEN What does he mean Iyaloja? This language is the language of our
   elders, we do not fully grasp it.
IYALOJA I dare not understand you yet Elesin.
ELESIN All you who stand before the spirit that dares
400   The opening of the last door of passage,
      Dare to rid my going of regrets! My wish
      Transcends the blotting out of thought
      In one mere moment's tremor of the senses.
      Do me credit. And do me honour.
405   I am girded for the route beyond
      Burdens of waste and longing.
      Then let me travel light. Let
      Seed that will not serve the stomach
      On the way remain behind. Let it take root
410   In the earth of my choice, in this earth
      I leave behind.
IYALOJA [turns to WOMEN] The voice I hear is already touched by the waiting
   fingers of our departed. I dare not refuse.
WOMEN But Iyaloja . . .
415 IYALOJA The matter is no longer in our hands.
WOMAN But she is betrothed to your own son. Tell him.
IYALOJA My son's wish is mine. I did the asking for him, the loss can be remedied. But who will remedy the blight of closed hands on the day when all
   should be openness and light? Tell him, you say! You wish that I burden
420 him with knowledge that will sour his wish and lay regrets on the last
   moments of his mind. You pray to him who is your intercessor to the
   world—don't set this world adrift in your own time; would you rather it was
   my hand whose sacrilege wrenched it loose?
WOMAN Not many men will brave the curse of a dispossessed husband.
425 IYALOJA Only the curses of the departed are to be feared. The claims of one
   whose foot is on the threshold of their abode surpasses even the claims of
   blood. It is impiety even to place hindrances in their ways.
ELESIN What do my mothers say? Shall I step
      Burdened into the unknown?
430 IYALOJA Not we, but the very earth says No. The sap in the plantain does not
   dry. Let grain that will not feed the voyager at his passage drop here and
   take root as he steps beyond this earth and us. Oh you who fill the home
   from hearth to threshold with the voices of children, you who now bestride
   the hidden gulf and pause to draw the right foot across and into the
435 resting-home of the great forebears, it is good that your loins be drained
   into the earth we know, that your last strength be ploughed back into the
   womb that gave you being.

PRAISE-SINGER Iyaloja, mother of multitudes in the teeming market of the world, how your wisdom transfigures you!

440 IYALOJA [smiling broadly, completely reconciled] Elesin, even at the narrow end of the passage I know you will look back and sigh a last regret for the flesh that flashed past your spirit in flight. You always had a restless eye. Your choice has my blessing. [To the WOMEN] Take the good news to our daughter and make her ready. [Some WOMEN go off.]

445 ELESIN Your eyes were clouded at first.

IYALOJA Not for long. It is those who stand at the gateway of the great change to whose cry we must pay heed. And then, think of this—it makes the mind tremble. The fruit of such a union is rare. It will be neither of this world nor of the next. Nor of the one behind us. As if the timelessness of 450 the ancestor world and the unborn have joined spirits to wring an issue of the elusive being of passage . . . Elesin!

ELESIN I am here. What is it?

IYALOJA Did you hear all I said just now?

ELESIN Yes.

455 IYALOJA The living must eat and drink. When the moment comes, don't turn the food to rodents' droppings in their mouth. Don't let them taste the ashes of the world when they step out at dawn to breathe the morning dew.

ELESIN This doubt is unworthy of you Iyaloja.

460 IYALOJA Eating the awusa nut[6] is not so difficult as drinking water afterwards.

ELESIN The waters of the bitter stream are honey to a man
Whose tongue has savoured all.

IYALOJA No one knows when the ants desert their home; they leave the mound intact. The swallow is never seen to peck holes in its nest when it is 465 time to move with the season. There are always throngs of humanity behind the leave-taker. The rain should not come through the roof for them, the wind must not blow through the walls at night.

ELESIN I refuse to take offence.

IYALOJA You wish to travel light. Well, the earth is yours. But be sure the 470 seed you leave in it attracts no curse.

ELESIN You really mistake my person Iyaloja.

IYALOJA I said nothing. Now we must go prepare your bridal chamber. Then these same hands will lay your shrouds.

ELESIN [exasperated] Must you be so blunt? [Recovers.] Well, weave your 475 shrouds, but let the fingers of my bride seal my eyelids with earth and wash my body.

IYALOJA Prepare yourself Elesin.

[She gets up to leave. At that moment the WOMEN return, leading the BRIDE. ELESIN's face glows with pleasure. He flicks the sleeves of his agbada[7] with renewed confidence and steps forward to meet the group. As the girl kneels before IYALOJA, lights fade out on the scene.]

---

6. A walnutlike seed that is eaten or used to produce oil. Raw, it has a bitter flavor.

7. A flowing, wide-sleeved robe worn by important men.

Act 2

The verandah of the District Officer's bungalow. A tango is playing from an old hand-cranked gramophone and, glimpsed through the wide windows and doors which open onto the forestage verandah are the shapes of SIMON PILKINGS *and his wife,* JANE, *tangoing in and out of shadows in the living room. They are wearing what is immediately apparent as some form of fancy dress.*[8] *The dance goes on for some moments and then the figure of a* 'NATIVE ADMINISTRATION' POLICEMAN *emerges and climbs up the steps onto the verandah. He peeps through and observes the dancing couple, reacting with what is obviously a long-standing bewilderment. He stiffens suddenly, his expression changes to one of disbelief and horror. In his excitement he upsets a flowerpot and attracts the attention of the couple. They stop dancing.*

PILKINGS   Is there anyone out there?

JANE   I'll turn off the gramophone.

PILKINGS [*approaching the verandah*]   I'm sure I heard something fall over. [*The* CONSTABLE *retreats slowly, open-mouthed as* PILKINGS *approaches the verandah.*] Oh it's you Amusa. Why didn't you just knock instead of knock-
5   ing things over?

AMUSA [*stammers badly and points a shaky finger at his dress*]   Mista Pirinkin . . . Mista Pirinkin . . .

PILKINGS   What is the matter with you?

JANE [*emerging*]   Who is it dear? Oh, Amusa . . .

10 PILKINGS   Yes it's Amusa, and acting most strangely.

AMUSA [*his attention now transferred to* MRS PILKINGS]   Mammadam . . . you
too!

PILKINGS   What the hell is the matter with you man!

JANE   Your costume darling. Our fancy dress.

15 PILKINGS   Oh hell, I'd forgotten all about that. [*Lifts the face mask over his
head showing his face. His wife follows suit.*]

JANE   I think you've shocked his big pagan heart bless him.

PILKINGS   Nonsense, he's a Moslem. Come on Amusa, you don't believe in
all this nonsense do you? I thought you were a good Moslem.

AMUSA   Mista Pirinkin, I beg you sir, what you think you do with that dress?
20   It belong to dead cult, not for human being.

PILKINGS   Oh Amusa, what a let down you are. I swear by you at the club you
know—thank God for Amusa, he doesn't believe in any mumbo-jumbo.
And now look at you!

AMUSA   Mista Pirinkin, I beg you, take it off. Is not good for man like you to
25   touch that cloth.

PILKINGS   Well, I've got it on. And what's more Jane and I have bet on it we're
taking first prize at the ball. Now, if you can just pull yourself together and
tell me what you wanted to see me about . . .

AMUSA   Sir, I cannot talk this matter to you in that dress. I no fit.

30 PILKINGS   What's that rubbish again?

JANE   He is dead earnest too Simon. I think you'll have to handle this delicately.

---

8. That is, costumes.

PILKINGS   Delicately my . . . ! Look here Amusa, I think this little joke has
gone far enough hm? Let's have some sense. You seem to forget that you
are a police officer in the service of His Majesty's Government. I order you
35   to report your business at once or face disciplinary action.

AMUSA   Sir, it is a matter of death. How can man talk against death to person
in uniform of death? Is like talking against government to person in uniform of police. Please sir, I go and come back.

PILKINGS   [roars] Now! [AMUSA switches his gaze to the ceiling suddenly,
remains mute.]

40   JANE   Oh Amusa, what is there to be scared of in the costume? You saw it
confiscated last month from those egungun⁹ men who were creating trouble
in town. You helped arrest the cult leaders yourself—if the juju¹ didn't harm
you at the time how could it possibly harm you now? And merely by looking
at it?

45   AMUSA   [without looking down] Madam, I arrest the ringleaders who make
trouble but me I no touch egungun. That egungun itself, I no touch. And I
no abuse 'am. I arrest ringleader but I treat egungun with respect.

PILKINGS   It's hopeless. We'll merely end up missing the best part of the ball.
When they get this way there is nothing you can do. It's simply hammering
50   against a brick wall. Write your report or whatever it is on that pad Amusa
and take yourself out of here. Come on Jane. We only upset his delicate
sensibilities by remaining here.

[AMUSA waits for them to leave, then writes in the notebook, somewhat
laboriously. Drumming from the direction of the town wells up. AMUSA
listens, makes a movement as if he wants to recall PILKINGS but changes
his mind. Completes his note and goes. A few moments later PILKINGS
emerges, picks up the pad and reads.]

PILKINGS   Jane!

JANE   [from the bedroom] Coming darling. Nearly ready.

55   PILKINGS   Never mind being ready, just listen to this.

JANE   What is it?

PILKINGS   Amusa's report. Listen. 'I have to report that it come to my information that one prominent chief, namely, the Elesin Oba, is to commit
death tonight as a result of native custom. Because this is criminal offence
60   I await further instruction at charge office. Sergeant Amusa.'

[JANE comes out onto the verandah while he is reading.]

JANE   Did I hear you say commit death?

PILKINGS   Obviously he means murder.

JANE   You mean a ritual murder?

PILKINGS   Must be. You think you've stamped it all out but it's always lurking
65   under the surface somewhere.

JANE   Oh. Does it mean we are not getting to the ball at all?

PILKINGS   No-o. I'll have the man arrested. Everyone remotely involved. In
any case there may be nothing to it. Just rumours.

JANE   Really? I thought you found Amusa's rumours generally reliable.

70   PILKINGS   That's true enough. But who knows what may have been giving
him the scare lately. Look at his conduct tonight.

9. Ancestral masquerade [Soyinka]. The spir-   possess those wearing these costumes.
its of the dead are believed to temporarily   1. Magic associated with fetish objects.

JANE [*laughing*]   You have to admit he had his own peculiar logic. [*Deepens her voice.*] How can man talk against death to person in uniform of death? [*Laughs.*] Anyway, you can't go into the police station dressed like that.

75   PILKINGS   I'll send Joseph with instructions. Damn it, what a confounded nuisance!

JANE   But don't you think you should talk first to the man, Simon?

PILKINGS   Do you want to go to the ball or not?

JANE   Darling, why are you getting rattled? I was only trying to be intelligent. It
80   seems hardly fair just to lock up a man—and a chief at that—simply on the er . . . what is the legal word again?—uncorroborated word of a sergeant.

PILKINGS   Well, that's easily decided. Joseph!

JOSEPH [*from within*]   Yes master.

PILKINGS   You're quite right of course, I am getting rattled. Probably the
85   effect of those bloody drums. Do you hear how they go on and on?

JANE   I wondered when you'd notice. Do you suppose it has something to do with this affair?

PILKINGS   Who knows? They always find an excuse for making a noise . . . [*Thoughtfully*] Even so . . .

90   JANE   Yes Simon?

PILKINGS   It's different Jane. I don't think I've heard this particular—sound— before. Something unsettling about it.

JANE   I thought all bush drumming sounded the same.

PILKINGS   Don't tease me now Jane. This may be serious.

95   JANE   I'm sorry. [*Gets up and throws her arms around his neck. Kisses him. The* HOUSEBOY *enters, retreats and knocks.*]

PILKINGS [*wearily*]   Oh, come in Joseph! I don't know where you pick up all these elephantine notions of tact. Come over here.

JOSEPH   Sir?

PILKINGS   Joseph, are you a Christian or not?

100   JOSEPH   Yessir.

PILKINGS   Does seeing me in this outfit bother you?

JOSEPH   No sir, it has no power.

PILKINGS   Thank God for some sanity at last. Now Joseph, answer me on the honour of a Christian—what is supposed to be going on in town tonight?

105   JOSEPH   Tonight sir? You mean the chief who is going to kill himself?

PILKINGS   What?

JANE   What do you mean, kill himself?

PILKINGS   You do mean he is going to kill somebody don't you?

JOSEPH   No master. He will not kill anybody and no one will kill him. He will
110   simply die.

JANE   But why Joseph?

JOSEPH   It is native law and custom. The King die last month. Tonight is his burial. But before they can bury him, the Elesin must die so as to accompany him to heaven.

115   PILKINGS   I seem to be fated to clash more often with that man than with any of the other chiefs.

JOSEPH   He is the King's Chief Horseman.

PILKINGS [*in a resigned way*]   I know.

JANE   Simon, what's the matter?

120   PILKINGS   It would have to be him!

JANE   Who is he?

PILKINGS   Don't you remember? He's that chief with whom I had a scrap some three or four years ago. I helped his son get to a medical school in England, remember? He fought tooth and nail to prevent it.

125 JANE   Oh now I remember. He was that very sensitive young man. What was his name again?

PILKINGS   Olunde. Haven't replied to his last letter come to think of it. The old pagan wanted him to stay and carry on some family tradition or the other. Honestly I couldn't understand the fuss he made. I literally had to

130   help the boy escape from close confinement and load him onto the next boat. A most intelligent boy, really bright.

JANE   I rather thought he was much too sensitive you know. The kind of person you feel should be a poet munching rose petals in Bloomsbury.[2]

PILKINGS   Well, he's going to make a first-class doctor. His mind is set on

135   that. And as long as he wants my help he is welcome to it.

JANE [after a pause]   Simon.

PILKINGS   Yes?

JANE   This boy, he was the eldest son wasn't he?

PILKINGS   I'm not sure. Who could tell with that old ram?

140 JANE   Do you know, Joseph?

JOSEPH   Oh yes madam. He was the eldest son. That's why Elesin cursed master good and proper. The eldest son is not supposed to travel away from the land.

JANE [giggling]   Is that true Simon? Did he really curse you good and proper?

145 PILKINGS   By all accounts I should be dead by now.

JOSEPH   Oh no, master is white man. And good Christian. Black man juju can't touch master.

JANE   If he was his eldest, it means that he would be the Elesin to the next king. It's a family thing isn't it Joseph?

150 JOSEPH   Yes madam. And if this Elesin had died before the King, his eldest son must take his place.

JANE   That would explain why the old chief was so mad you took the boy away.

PILKINGS   Well it makes me all the more happy I did.

155 JANE   I wonder if he knew.

PILKINGS   Who? Oh, you mean Olunde?

JANE   Yes. Was that why he was so determined to get away? I wouldn't stay if I knew I was trapped in such a horrible custom.

PILKINGS [thoughtfully]   No, I don't think he knew. At least he gave no indi-

160   cation. But you couldn't really tell with him. He was rather close[3] you know, quite unlike most of them. Didn't give much away, not even to me.

JANE   Aren't they all rather close, Simon?

PILKINGS   These natives here? Good gracious. They'll open their mouths and yap with you about their family secrets before you can stop them. Only the

165   other day . . .

---

2. The district of central London in which the British Museum and the University of London are located; it has long been associated with art and literary culture, notably the Pre-Raphaelites in the 19th century and Virginia Woolf and the "Bloomsbury Group" in the 20th.

3. Secretive, taciturn.

JANE But Simon, do they really give anything away? I mean, anything that really counts. This affair for instance, we didn't know they still practised that custom did we?

PILKINGS Ye-e-es, I suppose you're right there. Sly, devious bastards.

170 JOSEPH [*stiffly*] Can I go now master? I have to clean the kitchen.

PILKINGS What? Oh, you can go. Forgot you were still there.

[JOSEPH *goes.*]

JANE Simon, you really must watch your language. Bastard isn't just a simple swear-word in these parts, you know.

175 PILKINGS Look, just when did you become a social anthropologist, that's what I'd like to know.

JANE I'm not claiming to know anything. I just happen to have overheard quarrels among the servants. That's how I know they consider it a smear.

PILKINGS I thought the extended family system took care of all that. Elastic family, no bastards.

180 JANE [*shrugs*] Have it your own way.

[*Awkward silence. The drumming increases in volume.* JANE *gets up suddenly, restless.*]

That drumming Simon, do you think it might really be connected with this ritual? It's been going on all evening.

PILKINGS Let's ask our native guide. Joseph! Just a minute Joseph. [JOSEPH *reenters.*] What's the drumming about?

185 JOSEPH I don't know master.

PILKINGS What do you mean you don't know? It's only two years since your conversion. Don't tell me all that holy water nonsense also wiped out your tribal memory.

JOSEPH [*visibly shocked*] Master!

190 JANE Now you've done it.

PILKINGS What have I done now?

JANE Never mind. Listen Joseph, just tell me this. Is that drumming connected with dying or anything of that nature?

JOSEPH Madam, this is what I am trying to say: I am not sure. It sounds like
195 the death of a great chief and then, it sounds like the wedding of a great chief. It really mix me up.

PILKINGS Oh get back to the kitchen. A fat lot of help you are.

JOSEPH Yes master. [*Goes.*]

JANE Simon . . .

200 PILKINGS Alright, alright. I'm in no mood for preaching.

JANE It isn't my preaching you have to worry about, it's the preaching of the missionaries who preceded you here. When they make converts they really convert them. Calling holy water nonsense to our Joseph is really like insulting the Virgin Mary before a Roman Catholic. He's going to hand in
205 his notice tomorrow you mark my word.

PILKINGS Now you're being ridiculous.

JANE Am I? What are you willing to bet that tomorrow we are going to be without a steward-boy? Did you see his face?

PILKINGS I am more concerned about whether or not we will be one native
210 chief short by tomorrow. Christ! Just listen to those drums. [*He strides up and down, undecided.*]

JANE [*getting up*] I'll change and make us some supper.

PILKINGS What's that?

JANE Simon, it's obvious we have to miss this ball.

PILKINGS Nonsense. It's the first bit of real fun the European club has man-
215 aged to organise for over a year, I'm damned if I'm going to miss it. And it
is a rather special occasion. Doesn't happen every day.

JANE You know this business has to be stopped Simon. And you are the only
man who can do it.

PILKINGS I don't have to stop anything. If they want to throw themselves off
220 the top of a cliff or poison themselves for the sake of some barbaric custom what is that to me? If it were ritual murder or something like that I'd
be duty-bound to do something. I can't keep an eye on all the potential
suicides in this province. And as for that man—believe me it's good
riddance.

225 JANE [laughs] I know you better than that Simon. You are going to have to
do something to stop it—after you've finished blustering.

PILKINGS [shouts after her] And suppose after all it's only a wedding. I'd look
a proper fool if I interrupted a chief on his honeymoon, wouldn't I? [Resumes
his angry stride, slows down.] Ah well, who can tell what those chiefs actually
230 do on their honeymoon anyway? [He takes up the pad and scribbles rapidly on it.] Joseph! Joseph! Joseph! [Some moments later JOSEPH puts in a
sulky appearance.] Did you hear me call you? Why the hell didn't you
answer?

JOSEPH I didn't hear master.

235 PILKINGS You didn't hear me! How come you are here then?

JOSEPH [stubbornly] I didn't hear master.

PILKINGS [controls himself with an effort] We'll talk about it in the morning.
I want you to take this note directly to Sergeant Amusa. You'll find him at
the charge office.[4] Get on your bicycle and race there with it. I expect you
240 back in twenty minutes exactly. Twenty minutes, is that clear?

JOSEPH Yes master. [Going]

PILKINGS Oh er . . . Joseph.

JOSEPH Yes master?

PILKINGS [between gritted teeth] Er . . . forget what I said just now. The holy
245 water is not nonsense. I was talking nonsense.

JOSEPH Yes master. [Goes.]

JANE [pokes her head round the door] Have you found him?

PILKINGS Found who?

JANE Joseph. Weren't you shouting for him?

250 PILKINGS Oh yes, he turned up finally.

JANE You sounded desperate. What was it all about?

PILKINGS Oh nothing. I just wanted to apologise to him. Assure him that the
holy water isn't really nonsense.

JANE Oh? And how did he take it?

255 PILKINGS Who the hell gives a damn! I had a sudden vision of our Very Reverend MacFarlane drafting another letter of complaint to the Resident
about my unchristian language towards his parishioners.

JANE Oh I think he's given up on you by now.

4. Police station.

PILKINGS   Don't be too sure. And anyway, I wanted to make sure Joseph
260   didn't 'lose' my note on the way. He looked sufficiently full of the holy cru-
sade to do some such thing.

JANE   If you've finished exaggerating, come and have something to eat.

PILKINGS   No, put it all away. We can still get to the ball.

JANE   Simon . . .

265 PILKINGS   Get your costume back on. Nothing to worry about. I've instructed
Amusa to arrest the man and lock him up.

JANE   But that station is hardly secure Simon. He'll soon get his friends to help
him escape.

PILKINGS   A-ah, that's where I have out-thought you. I'm not having him put
270   in the station cell. Amusa will bring him right here and lock him up in my
study. And he'll stay with him till we get back. No one will dare come here
to incite him to anything.

JANE   How clever of you darling. I'll get ready.

PILKINGS   Hey.

275 JANE   Yes darling.

PILKINGS   I have a surprise for you. I was going to keep it until we actually
got to the ball.

JANE   What is it?

PILKINGS   You know the Prince[5] is on a tour of the colonies don't you? Well,
280   he docked in the capital only this morning but he is already at the Residency.
He is going to grace the ball with his presence later tonight.

JANE   Simon! Not really.

PILKINGS   Yes he is. He's been invited to give away the prizes and he has
agreed. You must admit old Engleton is the best Club Secretary we ever
285   had. Quick off the mark that lad.

JANE   But how thrilling.

PILKINGS   The other provincials are going to be damned envious.

JANE   I wonder what he'll come as.

PILKINGS   Oh I don't know. As a coat-of-arms perhaps. Anyway it won't be
290   anything to touch this.

JANE   Well that's lucky. If we are to be presented I won't have to start looking
for a pair of gloves. It's all sewn on.

PILKINGS   [laughing]   Quite right. Trust a woman to think of that. Come on,
let's get going.

295 JANE   [rushing off]   Won't be a second. [Stops.] Now I see why you've been so
edgy all evening. I thought you weren't handling this affair with your usual
brilliance—to begin with that is.

PILKINGS   [his mood is much improved]   Shut up woman and get your things
on.

300 JANE   Alright boss, coming.

[PILKINGS suddenly begins to hum the tango to which they were dancing
before. Starts to execute a few practice steps. Lights fade.]

Act 3

A swelling, agitated hum of women's voices rises immediately in the background.
The lights come on and we see the frontage of a converted cloth stall in the market.

5. Prince Henry, duke of Gloucester (1900–1974), the uncle of the future Queen Elizabeth II,
toured Ceylon (Sri Lanka), India, and North Africa in 1942.

The floor leading up to the entrance is covered in rich velvets and woven cloth. The WOMEN *come on stage, borne backwards by the determined progress of Sergeant* AMUSA *and his two* CONSTABLES *who already have their batons out and use them as a pressure against the* WOMEN. *At the edge of the cloth-covered floor however the* WOMEN *take a determined stand and block all further progress of the men. They begin to tease them mercilessly.*

AMUSA   I am tell you women for last time to commot my road.[6] I am here on official business.

WOMAN   Official business you white man's eunuch? Official business is taking place where you want to go and it's a business you wouldn't under-
5   stand.

WOMAN   [*makes a quick tug at the* CONSTABLE'S *baton*]   That doesn't fool any-one you know. It's the one you carry under your government knickers[7] that counts. [*She bends low as if to peep under the baggy shorts. The embarrassed* CONSTABLE *quickly puts his knees together. The* WOMEN *roar.*]

WOMAN   You mean there is nothing there at all?

10   WOMAN   Oh there was something. You know that handbell which the white-man uses to summon his servants . . . ?

AMUSA   [*he manages to preserve some dignity throughout*]   I hope you women know that interfering with officer in execution of his duty is criminal offence.

WOMAN   Interfere? He says we're interfering with him. You foolish man we're
15   telling you there's nothing to interfere with.

AMUSA   I am order you now to clear the road.

WOMAN   What road? The one your father built?

WOMAN   You are a Policeman not so? Then you know what they call trespass-ing in court. Or—[*Pointing to the cloth-lined steps*]—do you think that kind
20   of road is built for every kind of feet.

WOMAN   Go back and tell the white man who sent you to come himself.

AMUSA   If I go I will come back with reinforcement. And we will all return carrying weapons.

WOMAN   Oh, now I understand. Before they can put on those knickers the
25   white man first cuts off their weapons.

WOMAN   What a cheek! You mean you come here to show power to women and you don't even have a weapon.

AMUSA   [*shouting above the laughter*]   For the last time I warn you women to clear the road.

30   WOMAN   To where?

AMUSA   To that hut. I know he dey dere.

WOMAN   Who?

AMUSA   The chief who call himself Elesin Oba.

WOMAN   You ignorant man. It is not he who calls himself Elesin Oba, it is his
35   blood that says it. As it called out to his father before him and will to his son after him. And that is in spite of everything your white man can do.

WOMAN   Is it not the same ocean that washes this land and the white man's land? Tell your white man he can hide our son away as long as he likes. When the time comes for him, the same ocean will bring him back.

---

6. Come out of my road (pidgin English); that is, get out of my way.
7. Woman's underpants; here, a contemptu- ous reference to the khaki shorts worn by colonial policemen.

40 AMUSA The government say dat kin' ting[8] must stop.

WOMAN Who will stop it? You? Tonight our husband and father will prove himself greater than the laws of strangers.

AMUSA I tell you nobody go prove anyting tonight or anytime. Is ignorant and criminal to prove dat kin' prove.

IYALOJA [*entering, from the hut. She is accompanied by a group of* YOUNG GIRLS
45 *who have been attending the* BRIDE] What is it Amusa? Why do you come here to disturb the happiness of others.

AMUSA Madame Iyaloja, I glad you come. You know me, I no like trouble but duty is duty. I am here to arrest Elesin for criminal intent. Tell these women to stop obstructing me in the performance of my duty.

50 IYALOJA And you? What gives you the right to obstruct our leader of men in the performance of his duty?

AMUSA What kin' duty be dat one Iyaloja.

IYALOJA What kin' duty? What kin' duty does a man have to his new bride?

AMUSA [*bewildered, looks at the* WOMEN *and at the entrance to the hut*] Iyaloja, is it wedding you call dis kin' ting?

55 IYALOJA You have wives haven't you? Whatever the white man has done to you he hasn't stopped you having wives. And if he has, at least he is married. If you don't know what a marriage is, go and ask him to tell you.

AMUSA This no to wedding.

IYALOJA And ask him at the same time what he would have done if anyone
60 had come to disturb him on his wedding night.

AMUSA Iyaloja, I say dis no to wedding.

IYALOJA You want to look inside the bridal chamber? You want to see for yourself how a man cuts the virgin knot?

AMUSA Madam . . .

65 WOMAN Perhaps his wives are still waiting for him to learn.

AMUSA Iyaloja, make you tell dese women make den no insult me again. If I hear dat kin' insult once more . . .

GIRL [*pushing her way through*] You will do what?

GIRL He's out of his mind. It's our mothers you're talking to, do you know
70 that? Not to any illiterate villager you can bully and terrorise. How dare you intrude here anyway?

GIRL What a cheek, what impertinence!

GIRL You've treated them too gently. Now let them see what it is to tamper with the mothers of this market.

75 GIRL Your betters dare not enter the market when the women say no!

GIRL Haven't you learnt that yet, you jester in khaki and starch?

IYALOJA Daughters . . .

GIRL No no Iyaloja, leave us to deal with him. He no longer knows his mother, we'll teach him.

[*With a sudden movement they snatch the batons of the two* CONSTABLES. *They begin to hem them in.*]

80 GIRL What next? We have your batons? What next? What are you going to do?

[*With equally swift movements they knock off their hats.*]

GIRL Move if you dare. We have your hats, what will you do about it? Didn't the white man teach you to take off your hats before women?

IYALOJA It's a wedding night. It's a night of joy for us. Peace . . .

8. That kind of thing (pidgin English).

GIRL Not for him. Who asked him here?

85 GIRL Does he dare go to the Residency without an invitation?

GIRL Not even where the servants eat the left-overs.

GIRL [*in turn. In an 'English' accent*] Well well it's Mister Amusa. Were you invited? [*Play-acting to one another. The older* WOMEN *encourage them with their titters.*]

—Your invitation card please?

90 —Who are you? Have we been introduced?

—And who did you say you were?

—Sorry, I didn't quite catch your name.

—May I take your hat?

—If you insist. May I take yours? [*Exchanging the* POLICEMEN's *hats*]

95 —How very kind of you.

—Not at all. Won't you sit down?

—After you.

—Oh no.

—I insist.

100 —You're most gracious.

—And how do you find the place?

—The natives are alright.

—Friendly?

—Tractable.

105 —Not a teeny-weeny bit restless?

—Well, a teeny-weeny bit restless.

—One might even say, difficult?

—Indeed one might be tempted to say, difficult.

—But you do manage to cope?

110 —Yes indeed I do. I have a rather faithful ox called Amusa.

—He's loyal?

—Absolutely.

—Lay down his life for you what?

—Without a moment's thought.

115 —Had one like that once. Trust him with my life.

—Mostly of course they are liars.

—Never known a native to tell the truth.

—Does it get rather close[9] around here?

—It's mild for this time of the year.

120 —But the rains may still come.

—They are late this year aren't they?

—They are keeping African time.

—Ha ha ha ha

—Ha ha ha ha

125 —The humidity is what gets me.

—It used to be whisky.

—Ha ha ha ha

—Ha ha ha ha

—What's your handicap old chap?

130 —Is there racing by golly?

9. Stifling, hot.

—Splendid golf course, you'll like it.

—I'm beginning to like it already.

—And a European club, exclusive.

—You've kept the flag flying.

135 —We do our best for the old country.

—It's a pleasure to serve.

—Another whisky old chap?

—You are indeed too too kind.

—Not at all sir. Where is that boy? [*With a sudden bellow*] Sergeant!

140 AMUSA [*snaps to attention*]   Yessir!

        [*The* WOMEN *collapse with laughter.*]

GIRL   Take your men out of here.

AMUSA [*realising the trick, he rages from loss of face*]   I'm give you warning . . .

GIRL   Alright then. Off with his knickers! [*They surge slowly forward.*]

IYALOJA   Daughters, please.

145 AMUSA [*squaring himself for defence*]   The first woman wey touch me . . .

IYALOJA   My children, I beg of you . . .

GIRL   Then tell him to leave this market. This is the home of our mothers. We don't want the eater of white left-overs at the feast their hands have prepared.

150 IYALOJA   You heard them Amusa. You had better go.

GIRL   Now!

AMUSA [*commencing his retreat*]   We dey go now, but make you no say we no warn you.

GIRL   Now!

155 GIRL   Before we read the riot act[1]—you should know all about that.

AMUSA   Make we go. [*They depart, more precipitately.*]

        [*The* WOMEN *strike their palms across in the gesture of wonder.*]

WOMEN   Do they teach you all that at school?

WOMAN   And to think I nearly kept Apinke away from the place.

WOMAN   Did you hear them? Did you see how they mimicked the white

160 man?

WOMAN   The voices exactly. Hey, there are wonders in this world!

IYALOJA   Well, our elders have said it: Dada may be weak, but he has a younger sibling who is truly fearless.[2]

WOMAN   The next time the white man shows his face in this market I will set

165 Wuraola[3] on his tail.

        [*A* WOMAN *bursts into song and dance of euphoria—'Tani l'awa o l'ogbeja? Kayi! A l'ogbeja. Omo Kekere l'ogbeja.*[4] *The rest of the* WOMEN *join in, some placing the* GIRLS *on their back like infants, others dancing round them. The dance becomes general, mounting in excitement.* ELESIN *appears, in wrapper only. In his hands a white velvet cloth folded loosely as if it held some delicate object. He cries out.*]

---

1. The act of Parliament (1716) that enabled local authorities to declare a group unlawfully assembled; before the law could be enforced, a proclamation ordering them to disperse had to be read.

2. Dada, the mythical king of Oyo and god of vegetables, abdicated in favor of his fierce younger brother Shango, who was god of lightning.

3. A common Yoruba girl's name; it means "rich gold."

4. Who says we haven't a defender? Silence! We have our defenders. Little children are our champions [Soyinka's translation].

ELESIN   Oh you mothers of beautiful brides! [*The dancing stops. They turn
and see him, and the object in his hands.* IYALOJA *approaches and gently takes
the cloth from him.*] Take it. It is no mere virgin stain, but the union of life
and the seeds of passage. My vital flow, the last from this flesh is inter-
mingled with the promise of future life. All is prepared. Listen! [*A steady*
170   *drum-beat from the distance.*] Yes. It is nearly time. The King's dog has been
killed. The King's favourite horse is about to follow his master. My brother
chiefs know their task and perform it well. [*He listens again.*]

[*The* BRIDE *emerges, stands shyly by the door. He turns to her.*]

Our marriage is not yet wholly fulfilled. When earth and passage wed, the
consummation is complete only when there are grains of earth on the eye-
175   lids of passage. Stay by me till then. My faithful drummers, do me your last
service. This is where I have chosen to do my leave-taking, in this heart of
life, this hive which contains the swarm of the world in its small compass.
This is where I have known love and laughter away from the palace. Even
the richest food cloys when eaten days on end; in the market, nothing ever
180   cloys. Listen. [*They listen to the drums.*] They have begun to seek out the
heart of the King's favourite horse. Soon it will ride in its bolt of raffia[5] with
the dog at its feet. Together they will ride on the shoulders of the King's
grooms through the pulse centres of the town. They know it is here I shall
await them. I have told them. [*His eyes appear to cloud. He passes his hand
185   over them as if to clear his sight. He gives a faint smile.*] It promises well; just
then I felt my spirit's eagerness. The kite[6] makes for wide spaces and the
wind creeps up behind its tail; can the kite say less than—thank you, the
quicker the better? But wait a while my spirit. Wait. Wait for the coming of
the courier of the King. Do you know, friends, the horse is born to this one
190   destiny, to bear the burden that is man upon its back. Except for this night,
this night alone when the spotless stallion will ride in triumph on the back of
man. In the time of my father I witnessed the strange sight. Perhaps tonight
also I shall see it for the last time. If they arrive before the drums beat for
me, I shall tell them to let the Alafin[7] know I follow swiftly. If they come
195   after the drums have sounded, why then, all is well for I have gone ahead.
Our spirits shall fall in step along the great passage. [*He listens to the drums.
He seems again to be falling into a state of semi-hypnosis; his eyes scan the sky
but it is in a kind of daze. His voice is a little breathless.*] The moon has fed,
a glow from its full stomach fills the sky and air, but I cannot tell where is
that gateway through which I must pass. My faithful friends, let our feet
200   touch together this last time, lead me into the other market with sounds
that cover my skin with down yet make my limbs strike earth like a thoroughbred. Dear mothers, let me dance into the passage even as I have lived
beneath your roofs. [*He comes down progressively among them. They make
way for him, the* DRUMMERS *playing. His dance is one of solemn, regal
motions, each gesture of the body is made with a solemn finality. The* WOMEN
join him, their steps a somewhat more fluid version of his. Beneath the PRAISE-
SINGER'*s exhortations the women dirge 'Alẹ lẹ lẹ, awo mi lọ.'*[8]]

5. The fiber of raffia palms, used to fringe the
masks of *egungun* and make their skirts.
6. One of a number of birds in the family that
includes hawks.
7. The title of the paramount king of the Yor-

uba (that is, the deceased king); thus "Elesin
Alafin," below, means "King's Horseman."
8. Night has fallen, the seasoned initiate is
leaving (Yoruba).

205 PRAISE-SINGER Elesin Alafin, can you hear my voice?

ELESIN Faintly, my friend, faintly.

PRAISE-SINGER Elesin Alafin, can you hear my call?

ELESIN Faintly my king, faintly.

PRAISE-SINGER Is your memory sound Elesin?

Shall my voice be a blade of grass and

210 Tickle the armpit of the past?

ELESIN My memory needs no prodding but

What do you wish to say to me?

PRAISE-SINGER Only what has been spoken. Only what concerns

The dying wish of the father of all.

215 ELESIN It is buried like seed-yam in my mind.

This is the season of quick rains, the harvest

Is this moment due for gathering.

PRAISE-SINGER If you cannot come, I said, swear

You'll tell my favourite horse. I shall

220 Ride on through the gates alone.

ELESIN Elesin's message will be read

Only when his loyal heart no longer beats.

PRAISE-SINGER If you cannot come Elesin, tell my dog.

I cannot stay the keeper too long

225 At the gate.

ELESIN A dog does not outrun the hand

That feeds it meat. A horse that throws its rider

Slows down to a stop. Elesin Alafin

Trusts no beasts with messages between

230 A king and his companion.

PRAISE-SINGER If you get lost my dog will track

The hidden path to me.

ELESIN The seven-way crossroads[9] confuses

Only the stranger. The Horseman of the King

235 Was born in the recesses of the house.

PRAISE-SINGER I know the wickedness of men. If there is

Weight on the loose end of your sash, such weight

As no mere man can shift; if your sash is earthed

By evil minds who mean to part us at the last . . .

240 ELESIN My sash is of the deep purple *alari*;

It is no tethering-rope. The elephant

Trails no tethering-rope; that king

Is not yet crowned who will peg an elephant—

Not even you my friend and King.

245 PRAISE-SINGER And yet this fear will not depart from me

The darkness of this new abode is deep—

Will your human eyes suffice?

ELESIN In a night which falls before our eyes

However deep, we do not miss our way.

250 PRAISE-SINGER Shall I now not acknowledge I have stood

Where wonders met their end? The elephant deserves

9. A symbol of confusion; in Yoruba folklore, the trickster god, Esu Elegba, is often found at such
a crossroads.

Better than that we say 'I have caught
A glimpse of something'. If we see the tamer
Of the forest let us say plainly, we have seen
255   An elephant.

ELESIN [*his voice is drowsy*]
I have freed myself of earth and now
It's getting dark. Strange voices guide my feet.

PRAISE-SINGER   The river is never so high that the eyes
Of a fish are covered. The night is not so dark
260   That the albino[1] fails to find his way. A child
Returning homewards craves no leading by the hand.
Gracefully does the mask regain his grove at the end of the day . . .
Gracefully. Gracefully does the mask dance
Homeward at the end of the day, gracefully . . .

[ELESIN's *trance appears to be deepening, his steps heavier.*]

265 IYALOJA   It is the death of war that kills the valiant,
Death of water is how the swimmer goes
It is the death of markets that kills the trader
And death of indecision takes the idle away
The trade of the cutlass blunts its edge
270   And the beautiful die the death of beauty.
It takes an Elesin to die the death of death . . .
Only Elesin . . . dies the unknowable death of death . . .
Gracefully, gracefully does the horseman regain
The stables at the end of day, gracefully . . .

275 PRAISE-SINGER   How shall I tell what my eyes have seen? The Horseman gal-
lops on before the courier, how shall I tell what my eyes have seen? He says
a dog may be confused by new scents of beings he never dreamt of, so he
must precede the dog to heaven. He says a horse may stumble on strange
boulders and be lamed, so he races on before the horse to heaven. It is
280   best, he says, to trust no messenger who may falter at the outer gate; oh
how shall I tell what my ears have heard? But do you hear me still Elesin,
do you hear your faithful one?

[ELESIN *in his motions appears to feel for a direction of sound, subtly, but
he only sinks deeper into his trance-dance.*]

285 Elesin Alafin, I no longer sense your flesh. The drums are changing now
but you have gone far ahead of the world. It is not yet noon in heaven; let
those who claim it is begin their own journey home. So why must you rush
like an impatient bride: why do you race to desert your Olohun-iyo?

[ELESIN *is now sunk fully deep in his trance, there is no longer sign of any
awareness of his surroundings.*]

Does the deep voice of *gbedu*[2] cover you then, like the passage of royal elephants? Those drums that brook no rivals, have they blocked the passage to
your ears that my voice passes into wind, a mere leaf floating in the night?
290   Is your flesh lightened Elesin, is that lump of earth I slid between your
slippers to keep you longer slowly sifting from your feet? Are the drums on

---

1. Yoruba view albinism as a handicap (while
believing that handicapped people are sacred
to the creator of humans).
2. A deep-timbred royal drum [Soyinka].

the other side now tuning skin to skin with ours in *osugbo*?[3] Are there sounds there I cannot hear, do footsteps surround you which pound the earth like *gbedu*, roll like thunder round the dome of the world? Is the darkness gathering in your head Elesin? Is there now a streak of light at the end of the passage, a light I dare not look upon? Does it reveal whose voices we often heard, whose touches we often felt, whose wisdoms come suddenly into the mind when the wisest have shaken their heads and murmured: It cannot be done? Elesin Alafin, don't think I do not know why your lips are heavy, why your limbs are drowsy as palm oil in the cold of harmattan.[4] I would call you back but when the elephant heads for the jungle, the tail is too small a handhold for the hunter that would pull him back. The sun that heads for the sea no longer heeds the prayers of the farmer. When the river begins to taste the salt of the ocean, we no longer know what deity to call on, the river-god or Olokun.[5] No arrow flies back to the string, the child does not return through the same passage that gave it birth. Elesin Oba, can you hear me at all? Your eyelids are glazed like a courtesan's, is it that you see the dark groom and master of life? And will you see my father? Will you tell him that I stayed with you to the last? Will my voice ring in your ears awhile, will you remember Olohun-iyo even if the music on the other side surpasses his mortal craft? But will they know you over there? Have they eyes to gauge your worth, have they the heart to love you, will they know what thoroughbred prances towards them in caparisons[6] of honour? If they do not Elesin, if any there cuts your yam with a small knife, or pours you wine in a small calabash, turn back and return to welcoming hands. If the world were not greater than the wishes of Olohun-iyo, I would not let you go . . .

[*He appears to break down.* ELESIN *dances on, completely in a trance. The dirge wells up louder and stronger.* ELESIN'*s dance does not lose its elasticity but his gestures become, if possible, even more weighty. Lights fade slowly on the scene.*]

Act 4

A Masque.[7] *The front side of the stage is part of a wide corridor around the great hall of the Residency extending beyond vision into the rear and wings. It is redolent of the tawdry decadence of a far-flung but key imperial frontier. The couples in a variety of fancy-dress are ranged around the walls, gazing in the same direction. The guest-of-honour is about to make an appearance. A portion of the local police brass band with its white conductor is just visible. At last, the entrance of Royalty. The band plays 'Rule Britannia',*[8] *badly, beginning long before he is visible. The couples bow and curtsey as he passes by them. Both he and his companions are dressed in seventeenth-century European costume. Following behind are the* RESIDENT *and his partner similarly attired. As they gain the end of the hall where the orchestra dais begins the music comes to an end. The* PRINCE *bows to the guests. The band strikes up a Viennese waltz and the* PRINCE *formally opens the floor. Several bars later the*

3. Secret "executive" cult of the Yoruba; its meeting place [Soyinka].
4. A dry, dust-bearing seasonal wind that blows into West Africa from the Sahara Desert.
5. The god of the ocean.
6. Ornamental cloths spread over the saddle or harness of horses.
7. That is, a masquerade, or elaborate masked ball (a European entertainment).
8. A patriotic song (1740); its words, taken from James Thomson's poem of the same title, are set to music by Thomas Arne.

RESIDENT *and his companion follow suit. Others follow in appropriate pecking order. The orchestra's waltz rendition is not of the highest musical standard.*

Some time later the PRINCE *dances again into view and is settled into a corner by the* RESIDENT *who then proceeds to select couples as they dance past for introduction, sometimes threading his way through the dancers to tap the lucky couple on the shoulder. Desperate efforts from many to ensure that they are recognised in spite of, perhaps, their costume. The ritual of introductions soon takes in* PILKINGS *and his wife. The* PRINCE *is quite fascinated by their costume and they demonstrate the adaptations they have made to it, pulling down the mask to demonstrate how the egungun normally appears, then showing the various press-button controls they have innovated for the face flaps, the sleeves, etc. They demonstrate the dance steps and the guttural sounds made by the egungun, harass other dancers in the hall,* MRS PILKINGS *playing the 'restrainer'[9] to* PILKINGS' *manic darts. Everyone is highly entertained, the Royal Party especially who lead the applause.*

At this point a liveried footman comes in with a note on a salver and is intercepted almost absent-mindedly by the RESIDENT *who takes the note and reads it. After polite coughs he succeeds in excusing the* PILKINGS *from the* PRINCE *and takes them aside. The* PRINCE *considerately offers the* RESIDENT's *wife his hand and dancing is resumed.*

On their way out the RESIDENT *gives an order to his* AIDE-DE-CAMP. *They come into the side corridor where the* RESIDENT *hands the note to* PILKINGS.

RESIDENT   As you see it says 'emergency' on the outside. I took the liberty of opening it because His Highness was obviously enjoying the entertainment. I didn't want to interrupt unless really necessary.

PILKINGS   Yes, yes of course, sir.

5   RESIDENT   Is it really as bad as it says? What's it all about?

PILKINGS   Some strange custom they have sir. It seems because the King is dead some important chief has to commit suicide.

RESIDENT   The King? Isn't it the same one who died nearly a month ago?

PILKINGS   Yes sir.

10   RESIDENT   Haven't they buried him yet?

PILKINGS   They take their time about these things, sir. The preburial ceremonies last nearly thirty days. It seems tonight is the final night.

RESIDENT   But what has it got to do with the market women? Why are they rioting? We've waived that troublesome tax haven't we?

15   PILKINGS   We don't quite know that they are exactly rioting yet sir. Sergeant Amusa is sometimes prone to exaggerations.

RESIDENT   He sounds desperate enough. That comes out even in his rather quaint grammar. Where is the man anyway? I asked my aide-de-camp to bring him here.

20   PILKINGS   They are probably looking in the wrong verandah. I'll fetch him myself.

RESIDENT   No no you stay here. Let your wife go and look for them. Do you mind my dear . . . ?

JANE   Certainly not, your Excellency. [*Goes.*]

25   RESIDENT   You should have kept me informed, Pilkings. You realise how disastrous it would have been if things had erupted while His Highness was here.

PILKINGS   I wasn't aware of the whole business until tonight sir.

---

9. The person who exercises a restraining influence on the wild movements of the main dancer.

RESIDENT Nose to the ground Pilkings, nose to the ground. If we all let
these little things slip past us where would the empire be eh? Tell me that.
Where would we all be?

PILKINGS [*low voice*] Sleeping peacefully at home I bet.

RESIDENT What did you say Pilkings?

PILKINGS It won't happen again sir.

RESIDENT It mustn't Pilkings. It mustn't. Where is that damned sergeant? I
ought to get back to His Highness as quickly as possible and offer him
some plausible explanation for my rather abrupt conduct. Can you think of
one, Pilkings?

PILKINGS You could tell him the truth, sir.

RESIDENT I could? No no no Pilkings, that would never do. What! Go and
tell him there is a riot just two miles away from him? This is supposed to be
a secure colony of His Majesty, Pilkings.

PILKINGS Yes, sir.

RESIDENT Ah, there they are. No, these are not our native police. Are these
the ring-leaders of the riot?

PILKINGS Sir, these are my police officers.

RESIDENT Oh, I beg your pardon officers. You do look a little . . . I say, isn't
there something missing in their uniform? I think they used to have some
rather colourful sashes. If I remember rightly I recommended them myself
in my young days in the service. A bit of colour always appeals to the
natives, yes, I remember putting that in my report. Well well well, where
are we? Make your report man.

PILKINGS [*moves close to* AMUSA, *between his teeth*] And let's have no more
superstitious nonsense from you Amusa or I'll throw you in the guardroom
for a month and feed you pork![1]

RESIDENT What's that? What has pork to do with it?

PILKINGS Sir, I was just warning him to be brief. I'm sure you are most anxious to hear his report.

RESIDENT Yes yes yes of course. Come on man, speak up. Hey, didn't we
give them some colourful fez hats with all those wavy things, yes, pink
tassels . . .

PILKINGS Sir, I think if he was permitted to make his report we might find
that he lost his hat in the riot.

RESIDENT Ah yes indeed. I'd better tell His Highness that. Lost his hat in the
riot, ha ha. He'll probably say well, as long as he didn't lose his head.
[*Chuckles to himself.*] Don't forget to send me a report first thing in the
morning young Pilkings.

PILKINGS No sir.

RESIDENT And whatever you do, don't let things get out of hand. Keep a cool
head and—nose to the ground Pilkings. [*Wanders off in the general direction of the hall.*]

PILKINGS Yes, sir.

AIDE-DE-CAMP Would you be needing me sir?

PILKINGS No thanks Bob. I think His Excellency's need of you is greater
than ours.

AIDE-DE-CAMP We have a detachment of soldiers from the capital sir. They
accompanied His Highness up here.

1. The eating of pork is forbidden to Muslims by the Qur'an.

PILKINGS I doubt if it will come to that but, thanks, I'll bear it in mind. Oh, could you send an orderly with my cloak.

AIDE-DE-CAMP Very good sir. [*Goes.*]

80 PILKINGS Now sergeant.

AMUSA Sir . . . [*Makes an effort, stops dead. Eyes to the ceiling.*]

PILKINGS Oh, not again.

AMUSA I cannot against death to dead cult. This dress get power of dead.

PILKINGS Alright, let's go. You are relieved of all further duty Amusa. Report

85   to me first thing in the morning.

JANE Shall I come Simon?

PILKINGS No, there's no need for that. If I can get back later I will. Otherwise get Bob to bring you home.

JANE Be careful Simon . . . I mean, be clever.

90 PILKINGS Sure I will. You two, come with me. [*As he turns to go, the clock in the Residency begins to chime.* PILKINGS *looks at his watch then turns, horror-stricken, to stare at his wife. The same thought clearly occurs to her. He swallows hard. An orderly brings his cloak.*] It's midnight. I had no idea it was that late.

JANE But surely . . . they don't count the hours the way we do. The moon, or something . . .

95 PILKINGS I am . . . not so sure.

[*He turns and breaks into a sudden run. The two* CONSTABLES *follow, also at a run.* AMUSA, *who has kept his eyes on the ceiling throughout waits until the last of the footsteps has faded out of hearing. He salutes suddenly, but without once looking in the direction of the woman.*]

AMUSA Goodnight madam.

JANE Oh. [*She hesitates.*] Amusa . . . [*He goes off without seeming to have heard.*] Poor Simon . . . [*A figure emerges from the shadows, a young black man dressed in a sober western suit. He peeps into the hall, trying to make out the figures of the dancers.*] Who is that?

100 OLUNDE [*emerging into the light*] I didn't mean to startle you madam. I am looking for the District Officer.

JANE Wait a minute . . . don't I know you? Yes, you are Olunde, the young man who . . .

OLUNDE Mrs Pilkings! How fortunate. I came here to look for your husband.

105 JANE Olunde! Let's look at you. What a fine young man you've become. Grand but solemn. Good God, when did you return? Simon never said a word. But you do look well Olunde. Really!

OLUNDE You are . . . well, you look quite well yourself Mrs Pilkings. From what little I can see of you.

110 JANE Oh, this. It's caused quite a stir I assure you, and not all of it very pleasant. You are not shocked I hope?

OLUNDE Why should I be? But don't you find it rather hot in there? Your skin must find it difficult to breathe.

JANE Well, it is a little hot I must confess, but it's all in a good cause.

115 OLUNDE What cause Mrs Pilkings?

JANE All this. The ball. And His Highness being here in person and all that.

OLUNDE [*mildly*] And that is the good cause for which you desecrate an ancestral mask?

JANE Oh, so you are shocked after all. How disappointing.

120 OLUNDE   No I am not shocked Mrs Pilkings. You forget that I have now spent
        four years among your people. I discovered that you have no respect for
        what you do not understand.

JANE   Oh. So you've returned with a chip on your shoulder. That's a pity
        Olunde. I am sorry.

        [*An uncomfortable silence follows.*]

125   I take it then that you did not find your stay in England altogether edifying.

OLUNDE   I don't say that. I found your people quite admirable in many ways,
        their conduct and courage in this war[2] for instance.

JANE   Ah yes, the war. Here of course it is all rather remote. From time to
        time we have a black-out drill just to remind us that there is a war on. And
130   the rare convoy passes through on its way somewhere or on manoeuvres.
        Mind you there is the occasional bit of excitement like that ship that was
        blown up in the harbour.[3]

OLUNDE   Here? Do you mean through enemy action?

JANE   Oh no, the war hasn't come that close. The captain did it himself. I
135   don't quite understand it really. Simon tried to explain. The ship had to be
        blown up because it had become dangerous to the other ships, even to the
        city itself. Hundreds of the coastal population would have died.

OLUNDE   Maybe it was loaded with ammunition and had caught fire. Or
        some of those lethal gases they've been experimenting on.

140 JANE   Something like that. The captain blew himself up with it. Deliberately.
        Simon said someone had to remain on board to light the fuse.

OLUNDE   It must have been a very short fuse.

JANE [*shrugs*]   I don't know much about it. Only that there was no other way
        to save lives. No time to devise anything else. The captain took the decision
145   and carried it out.

OLUNDE   Yes . . . I quite believe it. I met men like that in England.

JANE   Oh just look at me! Fancy welcoming you back with such morbid
        news. Stale too. It was at least six months ago.

OLUNDE   I don't find it morbid at all. I find it rather inspiring. It is an affir-
150   mative commentary on life.

JANE   What is?

OLUNDE   That captain's self-sacrifice.

JANE   Nonsense. Life should never be thrown deliberately away.

OLUNDE   And the innocent people round the harbour?

155 JANE   Oh, how does one know? The whole thing was probably exaggerated
        anyway.

OLUNDE   That was a risk the captain couldn't take. But please Mrs Pilkings,
        do you think you could find your husband for me? I have to talk to him.

JANE   Simon? Oh. [*As she recollects for the first time the full significance of
160   OLUNDE's presence.*] Simon is . . . there is a little problem in town. He was
        sent for. But . . . when did you arrive? Does Simon know you're here?

OLUNDE [*suddenly earnest*]   I need your help Mrs Pilkings. I've always found
        you somewhat more understanding than your husband. Please find him for
        me and when you do, you must help me talk to him.

---

2. That is, World War II.
3. Perhaps a reference to a tragic incident that involved no heroism: on December 5, 1942, when three British naval trawlers were moored in the harbor at Lagos, an oil spill caught fire. The ships exploded, killing about 200 men.

165 JANE   I'm afraid I don't quite . . . follow you. Have you seen my husband already?

OLUNDE   I went to your house. Your houseboy told me you were here. [*He smiles.*] He even told me how I would recognise you and Mr Pilkings.

JANE   Then you must know what my husband is trying to do for you.

170 OLUNDE   For me?

JANE   For you. For your people. And to think he didn't even know you were coming back! But how do you happen to be here? Only this evening we were talking about you. We thought you were still four thousand miles away.

OLUNDE   I was sent a cable.

175 JANE   A cable? Who did? Simon? The business of your father didn't begin till tonight.

OLUNDE   A relation sent it weeks ago, and it said nothing about my father. All it said was, Our King is dead. But I knew I had to return home at once so as to bury my father. I understood that.

180 JANE   Well, thank God you don't have to go through that agony. Simon is going to stop it.

OLUNDE   That's why I want to see him. He's wasting his time. And since he has been so helpful to me I don't want him to incur the enmity of our people. Especially over nothing.

185 JANE [*sits down open-mouthed*]   You . . . you Olunde!

OLUNDE   Mrs Pilkings, I came home to bury my father. As soon as I heard the news I booked my passage home. In fact we were fortunate. We travelled in the same convoy as your Prince, so we had excellent protection.

JANE   But you don't think your father is also entitled to whatever protection
190   is available to him?

OLUNDE   How can I make you understand? He *has* protection. No one can undertake what he does tonight without the deepest protection the mind can conceive. What can you offer him in place of his peace of mind, in place of the honour and veneration of his own people? What would you
195   think of your Prince if he refused to accept the risk of losing his life on this voyage? This . . . showing-the-flag tour of colonial possessions.

JANE   I see. So it isn't just medicine you studied in England.

OLUNDE   Yet another error into which your people fall. You believe that everything which appears to make sense was learnt from you.

200 JANE   Not so fast Olunde. You have learnt to argue I can tell that, but I never said you made sense. However clearly you try to put it, it is still a barbaric custom. It is even worse—it's feudal! The king dies and a chieftain must be buried with him. How feudalistic can you get!

OLUNDE [*waves his hand towards the background. The* PRINCE *is dancing past again—to a different step—and all the guests are bowing and curtseying as he passes*]   And this? Even in the midst of a devastating war, look at that.
205   What name would you give to that?

JANE   Therapy, British style. The preservation of sanity in the midst of chaos.

OLUNDE   Others would call it decadence. However, it doesn't really interest me. You white races know how to survive; I've seen proof of that. By all logical and natural laws this war should end with all the white races wiping
210   out one another, wiping out their so-called civilisation for all time and reverting to a state of primitivism the like of which has so far only existed

in your imagination when you thought of us. I thought all that at the beginning. Then I slowly realised that your greatest art is the art of survival. But at least have the humility to let others survive in their own way.

215 JANE   Through ritual suicide?

OLUNDE   Is that worse than mass suicide? Mrs Pilkings, what do you call what those young men are sent to do by their generals in this war? Of course you have also mastered the art of calling things by names which don't remotely describe them.

220 JANE   You talk! You people with your long-winded, roundabout way of making conversation.

OLUNDE   Mrs Pilkings, whatever we do, we never suggest that a thing is the opposite of what it really is. In your newsreels I heard defeats, thorough, murderous defeats described as strategic victories. No wait, it wasn't just
225   on your newsreels. Don't forget I was attached to hospitals all the time. Hordes of your wounded passed through those wards. I spoke to them. I spent long evenings by their bedsides while they spoke terrible truths of the realities of that war. I know now how history is made.

JANE   But surely, in a war of this nature, for the morale of the nation you
230   must expect . . .

OLUNDE   That a disaster beyond human reckoning be spoken of as a triumph? No. I mean, is there no mourning in the home of the bereaved that such blasphemy is permitted?

JANE [after a moment's pause]   Perhaps I can understand you now. The time
235   we picked for you was not really one for seeing us at our best.

OLUNDE   Don't think it was just the war. Before that even started I had plenty of time to study your people. I saw nothing, finally, that gave you the right to pass judgement on other peoples and their ways. Nothing at all.

240 JANE [hesitantly]   Was it the . . . colour thing? I know there is some discrimination.

OLUNDE   Don't make it so simple, Mrs Pilkings. You make it sound as if when I left, I took nothing at all with me.

JANE   Yes . . . and to tell the truth, only this evening, Simon and I agreed that
245   we never really knew what you left with.

OLUNDE   Neither did I. But I found out over there. I am grateful to your country for that. And I will never give it up.

JANE   Olunde please . . . promise me something. Whatever you do, don't throw away what you have started to do. You want to be a doctor. My hus-
250   band and I believe you will make an excellent one, sympathetic and competent. Don't let anything make you throw away your training.

OLUNDE [genuinely surprised]   Of course not. What a strange idea. I intend to return and complete my training. Once the burial of my father is over.

JANE   Oh, please . . . !

255 OLUNDE   Listen! Come outside. You can't hear anything against that music.

JANE   What is it?

OLUNDE   The drums. Can you hear the changes? Listen.
   [The drums come over, still distant but more distinct. There is a change of rhythm, it rises to a crescendo and then, suddenly, it is cut off. After a silence, a new beat begins, slow and resonant.]

There, it's all over.

JANE   You mean he's . . .

260   OLUNDE   Yes, Mrs Pilkings, my father is dead. His will-power has always been enormous; I know he is dead.

JANE [*screams*]   How can you be so callous! So unfeeling! You announce your father's own death like a surgeon looking down on some strange . . . stranger's body! You're just a savage like all the rest.

265   AIDE-DE-CAMP [*rushing out*]   Mrs Pilkings. Mrs Pilkings. [*She breaks down, sobbing.*] Are you all right, Mrs Pilkings?

OLUNDE   She'll be all right. [*Turns to go.*]

AIDE-DE-CAMP   Who are you? And who the hell asked your opinion?

OLUNDE   You're quite right, nobody. [*Going*]

270   AIDE-DE-CAMP   What the hell! Did you hear me ask you who you were?

OLUNDE   I have business to attend to.

AIDE-DE-CAMP   I'll give you business in a moment you impudent nigger. Answer my question!

OLUNDE   I have a funeral to arrange. Excuse me. [*Going*]

275   AIDE-DE-CAMP   I said stop! Orderly!

JANE   No, no, don't do that. I'm alright. And for heaven's sake don't act so foolishly. He's a family friend.

AIDE-DE-CAMP   Well he'd better learn to answer civil questions when he's asked them. These natives put a suit on and they get high opinions of

280   themselves.

OLUNDE   Can I go now?

JANE   No no don't go. I must talk to you. I'm sorry about what I said.

OLUNDE   It's nothing, Mrs Pilkings. And I'm really anxious to go. I couldn't see my father before, it's forbidden for me, his heir and successor, to set

285   eyes on him from the moment of the King's death. But now . . . I would like to touch his body while it is still warm.

JANE   You will. I promise I shan't keep you long. Only, I couldn't possibly let you go like that. Bob, please excuse us.

AIDE-DE-CAMP   If you're sure . . .

290   JANE   Of course I'm sure. Something happened to upset me just then, but I'm alright now. Really.

[*The* AIDE-DE-CAMP *goes, somewhat reluctantly.*]

OLUNDE   I mustn't stay long.

JANE   Please, I promise not to keep you. It's just that . . . oh you saw yourself what happens to one in this place. The Resident's man thought he was

295   being helpful, that's the way we all react. But I can't go in among that crowd just now and if I stay by myself somebody will come looking for me. Please, just say something for a few moments and then you can go. Just so I can recover myself.

OLUNDE   What do you want me to say?

300   JANE   Your calm acceptance for instance, can you explain that? It was so unnatural. I don't understand that at all. I feel a need to understand all I can.

OLUNDE   But you explained it yourself. My medical training perhaps. I have seen death too often. And the soldiers who returned from the front, they died on our hands all the time.

305   JANE   No. It has to be more than that. I feel it has to do with the many things we don't really grasp about your people. At least you can explain.

OLUNDE   All these things are part of it. And anyway, my father has been dead in my mind for nearly a month. Ever since I learnt of the King's death. I've lived with my bereavement so long now that I cannot think of him alive.

310   On that journey on the boat, I kept my mind on my duties as the one who must perform the rites over his body. I went through it all again and again in my mind as he himself had taught me. I didn't want to do anything wrong, something which might jeopardise the welfare of my people.

JANE   But he had disowned you. When you left he swore publicly you were

315   no longer his son.

OLUNDE   I told you, he was a man of tremendous will. Sometimes that's another way of saying stubborn. But among our people, you don't disown a child just like that. Even if I had died before him I would still be buried like his eldest son. But it's time for me to go.

320 JANE   Thank you. I feel calmer. Don't let me keep you from your duties.

OLUNDE   Goodnight, Mrs Pilkings.

JANE   Welcome home. [*She holds out her hand. As he takes it footsteps are heard approaching the drive. A short while later a woman's sobbing is also heard.*]

PILKINGS [*off*]   Keep them here till I get back. [*He strides into view, reacts at the sight of* OLUNDE *but turns to his wife.*] Thank goodness you're still here.

325 JANE   Simon, what happened?

PILKINGS   Later Jane, please. Is Bob still here?

JANE   Yes, I think so. I'm sure he must be.

PILKINGS   Try and get him out here as quickly as you can. Tell him it's urgent.

JANE   Of course. Oh Simon, you remember . . .

330 PILKINGS   Yes yes. I can see who it is. Get Bob out here. [*She runs off.*] At first I thought I was seeing a ghost.

OLUNDE   Mr Pilkings, I appreciate what you tried to do. I want you to believe that. I can tell you it would have been a terrible calamity if you'd succeeded.

335 PILKINGS [*opens his mouth several times, shuts it*]   You . . . said what?

OLUNDE   A calamity for us, the entire people.

PILKINGS [*sighs*]   I see. Hm.

OLUNDE   And now I must go. I must see him before he turns cold.

PILKINGS   Oh ah . . . em . . . but this is a shock to see you. I mean er think-

340   ing all this while you were in England and thanking God for that.

OLUNDE   I came on the mail boat. We travelled in the Prince's convoy.

PILKINGS   Ah yes, a-ah, hm . . . er well . . .

OLUNDE   Goodnight. I can see you are shocked by the whole business. But you must know by now there are things you cannot understand—or help.

345 PILKINGS   Yes. Just a minute. There are armed policemen that way and they have instructions to let no one pass. I suggest you wait a little. I'll er . . . give you an escort.

OLUNDE   That's very kind of you. But do you think it could be quickly arranged?

PILKINGS   Of course. In fact, yes, what I'll do is send Bob over with some

350   men to the er . . . place. You can go with them. Here he comes now. Excuse me a minute.

AIDE-DE-CAMP   Anything wrong sir?

PILKINGS [*takes him to one side*]   Listen Bob, that cellar in the disused annexe of the Residency, you know, where the slaves were stored before

355   being taken down to the coast . . .

AIDE-DE-CAMP   Oh yes, we use it as a storeroom for broken furniture.

PILKINGS   But it's still got the bars on it?

AIDE-DE-CAMP   Oh yes, they are quite intact.

PILKINGS   Get the keys please. I'll explain later. And I want a strong guard
360   over the Residency tonight.

AIDE-DE-CAMP   We have that already. The detachment from the coast . . .

PILKINGS   No, I don't want them at the gates of the Residency. I want you to
   deploy them at the bottom of the hill, a long way from the main hall so they
   can deal with any situation long before the sound carries to the house.

365 AIDE-DE-CAMP   Yes of course.

PILKINGS   I don't want His Highness alarmed.

AIDE-DE-CAMP   You think the riot will spread here?

PILKINGS   It's unlikely but I don't want to take a chance. I made them believe
   I was going to lock the man up in my house, which was what I had planned
370   to do in the first place. They are probably assailing it by now. I took a
   roundabout route here so I don't think there is any danger at all. At least
   not before dawn. Nobody is to leave the premises of course—the native
   employees I mean. They'll soon smell something is up and they can't keep
   their mouths shut.

375 AIDE-DE-CAMP   I'll give instructions at once.

PILKINGS   I'll take the prisoner down myself. Two policemen will stay with
   him throughout the night. Inside the cell.

AIDE-DE-CAMP   Right sir. [Salutes and goes off at the double.]

PILKINGS   Jane. Bob is coming back in a moment with a detachment. Until
380   he gets back please stay with Olunde. [He makes an extra warning gesture
   with his eyes.]

OLUNDE   Please, Mr Pilkings . . .

PILKINGS   I hate to be stuffy old son, but we have a crisis on our hands. It
   has to do with your father's affair if you must know. And it happens also at
   a time when we have His Highness here. I am responsible for security so
385   you'll simply have to do as I say. I hope that's understood. [Marches off
   quickly, in the direction from which he made his first appearance.]

OLUNDE   What's going on? All this can't be just because he failed to stop my
   father killing himself.

JANE   I honestly don't know. Could it have sparked off a riot?

OLUNDE   No. If he'd succeeded that would be more likely to start the riot.
390   Perhaps there were other factors involved. Was there a chieftancy dispute?

JANE   None that I know of.

ELESIN [an animal bellow from off]   Leave me alone! Is it not enough that
   you have covered me in shame! White man, take your hand from my body!
      [OLUNDE stands frozen to the spot. JANE, understanding at last, tries to
      move him.]

JANE   Let's go in. It's getting chilly out here.

395 PILKINGS [off]   Carry him.

ELESIN   Give me back the name you have taken away from me you ghost
   from the land of the nameless!

PILKINGS   Carry him! I can't have a disturbance here. Quickly! stuff up his
   mouth.

400 JANE   Oh God! Let's go in. Please Olunde. [OLUNDE does not move.]

ELESIN   Take your albino's[4] hand from me you . . .

---

4. A term of abuse when applied to a white person.

[*Sounds of a struggle. His voice chokes as he is gagged.*]

OLUNDE [*quietly*]   That was my father's voice.

JANE   Oh you poor orphan, what have you come home to?

[*There is a sudden explosion of rage from offstage and powerful steps come running up the drive.*]

PILKINGS   You bloody fools, after him!

[*Immediately* ELESIN, *in handcuffs, comes pounding in the direction of* JANE *and* OLUNDE, *followed some moments afterwards by* PILKINGS *and the* CONSTABLES. ELESIN, *confronted by the seeming statue of his son, stops dead.* OLUNDE *stares above his head into the distance. The* CONSTABLES *try to grab him.* JANE *screams at them.*]

405   JANE   Leave him alone! Simon, tell them to leave him alone.

PILKINGS   All right, stand aside you. [*Shrugs.*] Maybe just as well. It might help to calm him down.

[*For several moments they hold the same position.* ELESIN *moves a step forward, almost as if he's still in doubt.*]

ELESIN   Olunde? [*He moves his head, inspecting him from side to side.*] Olunde! [*He collapses slowly at* OLUNDE'*s feet.*] Oh son, don't let the sight of

410   your father turn you blind!

OLUNDE [*he moves for the first time since he heard his voice, brings his head slowly down to look on him*]   I have no father, eater of left-overs.

[*He walks slowly down the way his father had run. Light fades out on* ELESIN, *sobbing into the ground.*]

Act 5

A wide iron-barred gate stretches almost the whole width of the cell in which ELE-SIN *is imprisoned. His wrists are encased in thick iron bracelets, chained together; he stands against the bars, looking out. Seated on the ground to one side on the outside is his recent bride, her eyes bent perpetually to the ground. Figures of the two* GUARDS *can be seen deeper inside the cell, alert to every movement* ELESIN *makes.* PILKINGS *now in a police officer's uniform, enters noiselessly, observes him a while. Then he coughs ostentatiously and approaches. Leans against the bars near a corner, his back to* ELESIN. *He is obviously trying to fall in mood with him. Some moments' silence.*

PILKINGS   You seem fascinated by the moon.

ELESIN [*after a pause*]   Yes, ghostly one. Your twin-brother up there engages my thoughts.

PILKINGS   It is a beautiful night.

5   ELESIN   Is that so?

PILKINGS   The light on the leaves, the peace of the night . . .

ELESIN   The night is not at peace, District Officer.

PILKINGS   No? I would have said it was. You know, quiet . . .

ELESIN   And does quiet mean peace for you?

10   PILKINGS   Well, nearly the same thing. Naturally there is a subtle difference . . .

ELESIN   The night is not at peace, ghostly one. The world is not at peace. You have shattered the peace of the world for ever. There is no sleep in the world tonight.

15   PILKINGS   It is still a good bargain if the world should lose one night's sleep as the price of saving a man's life.

ELESIN   You did not save my life, District Officer. You destroyed it.

PILKINGS   Now come on . . .

ELESIN   And not merely my life but the lives of many. The end of the night's
20   work is not over. Neither this year nor the next will see it. If I wished you
well, I would pray that you do not stay long enough on our land to see the
disaster you have brought upon us.

PILKINGS   Well, I did my duty as I saw it. I have no regrets.

ELESIN   No. The regrets of life always come later.

[Some moments' pause.]

25   You are waiting for dawn white man. I hear you saying to yourself: only so
many hours until dawn and then the danger is over. All I must do is to keep
him alive tonight. You don't quite understand it all but you know that
tonight is when what ought to be must be brought about. I shall ease your
mind even more, ghostly one. It is not an entire night but a moment of the
30   night, and that moment is past. The moon was my messenger and guide.
When it reached a certain gateway in the sky, it touched that moment for
which my whole life has been spent in blessings. Even I do not know the
gateway. I have stood here and scanned the sky for a glimpse of that door
but, I cannot see it. Human eyes are useless for a search of this nature. But
35   in the house of *osugbo*, those who keep watch through the spirit recognised the moment, they sent word to me through the voice of our sacred
drums to prepare myself. I heard them and I shed all thoughts of earth. I
began to follow the moon to the abode of the gods . . . servant of the white
king, that was when you entered my chosen place of departure on feet of
40   desecration.

PILKINGS   I'm sorry, but we all see our duty differently.

ELESIN   I no longer blame you. You stole from me my first-born, sent him to
your country so you could turn him into something in your own image. Did
you plan it all beforehand? There are moments when it seems part of a
45   larger plan. He who must follow my footsteps is taken from me, sent across
the ocean. Then, in my turn, I am stopped from fulfilling my destiny. Did
you think it all out before, this plan to push our world from its course and
sever the cord that links us to the great origin?

PILKINGS   You don't really believe that. Anyway, if that was my intention with
50   your son, I appear to have failed.

ELESIN   You did not fail in the main thing ghostly one. We know the roof covers the rafters, the cloth covers blemishes; who would have known that the
white skin covered our future, preventing us from seeing the death our
enemies had prepared for us. The world is set adrift and its inhabitants are
55   lost. Around them, there is nothing but emptiness.

PILKINGS   Your son does not take so gloomy a view.

ELESIN   Are you dreaming now, white man? Were you not present at the
reunion of shame? Did you not see when the world reversed itself and the
father fell before his son, asking forgiveness?

60   PILKINGS   That was in the heat of the moment. I spoke to him and . . . if you
want to know, he wishes he could cut out his tongue for uttering the words
he did.

ELESIN   No. What he said must never be unsaid. The contempt of my own
son rescued something of my shame at your hands. You have stopped me in
65   my duty but I know now that I did give birth to a son. Once I mistrusted

him for seeking the companionship of those my spirit knew as enemies of
our race. Now I understand. One should seek to obtain the secrets of his
enemies. He will avenge my shame, white one. His spirit will destroy you
and yours.

70 PILKINGS   That kind of talk is hardly called for. If you don't want my
consolation . . .

ELESIN   No white man, I do not want your consolation.

PILKINGS   As you wish. Your son, anyway, sends his consolation. He asks your
forgiveness. When I asked him not to despise you his reply was: I cannot
75   judge him, and if I cannot judge him, I cannot despise him. He wants to
come to you and say goodbye and to receive your blessing.

ELESIN   Goodbye? Is he returning to your land?

PILKINGS   Don't you think that's the most sensible thing for him to do? I
advised him to leave at once, before dawn, and he agrees that is the right
80   course of action.

ELESIN   Yes, it is best. And even if I did not think so, I have lost the father's
place of honour. My voice is broken.

PILKINGS   Your son honours you. If he didn't he would not ask your
blessing.

85 ELESIN   No. Even a thoroughbred is not without pity for the turf he strikes
with his hoof. When is he coming?

PILKINGS   As soon as the town is a little quieter. I advised it.

ELESIN   Yes white man, I am sure you advised it. You advise all our lives
although on the authority of what gods, I do not know.

90 PILKINGS   [opens his mouth to reply, then appears to change his mind. Turns to
go. Hesitates and stops again]   Before I leave you, may I ask just one thing
of you?

ELESIN   I am listening.

PILKINGS   I wish to ask you to search the quiet of your heart and tell me—do
95   you not find great contradictions in the wisdom of your own race?

ELESIN   Make yourself clear, white one.

PILKINGS   I have lived among you long enough to learn a saying or two. One
came to my mind tonight when I stepped into the market and saw what
was going on. You were surrounded by those who egged you on with song
100   and praises. I thought, are these not the same people who say: the elder
grimly approaches heaven and you ask him to bear your greetings yonder;
do you really think he makes the journey willingly? After that, I did not
hesitate.

[A pause. ELESIN sighs. Before he can speak a sound of running feet is
heard.]

JANE   [off]   Simon! Simon!

105 PILKINGS   What on earth . . . !   [Runs off.]

[ELESIN turns to his new wife, gazes on her for some moments.]

ELESIN   My young bride, did you hear the ghostly one? You sit and sob in
your silent heart but say nothing to all this. First I blamed the white man,
then I blamed my gods for deserting me. Now I feel I want to blame you for
the mystery of the sapping of my will. But blame is a strange peace offering
110   for a man to bring a world he has deeply wronged, and to its innocent
dwellers. Oh little mother, I have taken countless women in my life but you
were more than a desire of the flesh. I needed you as the abyss across

which my body must be drawn, I filled it with earth and dropped my seed
in it at the moment of preparedness for my crossing. You were the final gift
115 of the living to their emissary to the land of the ancestors, and perhaps
your warmth and youth brought new insights of this world to me and
turned my feet leaden on this side of the abyss. For I confess to you, daughter, my weakness came not merely from the abomination of the white man
who came violently into my fading presence, there was also a weight of
120 longing on my earth-held limbs. I would have shaken it off, already my foot
had begun to lift but then, the white ghost entered and all was defiled.

[*Approaching voices of* PILKINGS *and his wife.*]

JANE   Oh Simon, you will let her in won't you?

PILKINGS   I really wish you'd stop interfering.

[*They come into view.* JANE *is in a dressing-gown.* PILKINGS *is holding a
note to which he refers from time to time.*]

JANE   Good gracious, I didn't initiate this. I was sleeping quietly, or trying to
125 anyway, when the servant brought it. It's not my fault if one can't sleep
undisturbed even in the Residency.

PILKINGS   He'd have done the same thing if we were sleeping at home so
don't sidetrack the issue. He knows he can get round⁵ you or he wouldn't
send you the petition in the first place.

130 JANE   Be fair Simon. After all he was thinking of your own interests. He is
grateful you know, you seem to forget that. He feels he owes you something.

PILKINGS   I just wish they'd leave this man alone tonight, that's all.

JANE   Trust him Simon. He's pledged his word it will all go peacefully.

PILKINGS   Yes, and that's the other thing. I don't like being threatened.

135 JANE   Threatened? [*Takes the note.*] I didn't spot any threat.

PILKINGS   It's there. Veiled, but it's there. The only way to prevent serious
rioting tomorrow—what a cheek!

JANE   I don't think he's threatening you Simon.

PILKINGS   He's picked up the idiom alright. Wouldn't surprise me if he's been
140 mixing with commies or anarchists over there. The phrasing sounds too good
to be true. Damn! If only the Prince hadn't picked this time for his visit.

JANE   Well, even so Simon, what have you got to lose? You don't want a riot
on your hands, not with the Prince here.

PILKINGS [*going up to* ELESIN]   Let's see what he has to say. Chief Elesin,
145 there is yet another person who wants to see you. As she is not a next-of-
kin I don't really feel obliged to let her in. But your son sent a note with
her, so it's up to you.

ELESIN   I know who that must be. So she found out your hiding-place. Well,
it was not difficult. My stench of shame is so strong, it requires no hunter's
150 dog to follow it.

PILKINGS   If you don't want to see her, just say so and I'll send her packing.

ELESIN   Why should I not want to see her? Let her come. I have no more
holes in my rag of shame. All is laid bare.

PILKINGS   I'll bring her in. [*Goes off.*]

155 JANE [*hesitates, then goes to* ELESIN]   Please, try and understand. Everything
my husband did was for the best.

5. That is, circumvent, cajole.

ELESIN [*he gives her a long strange stare, as if he is trying to understand who she is*] You are the wife of the District Officer?

JANE Yes. My name, is Jane.

ELESIN That is my wife sitting down there. You notice how still and silent she
160   sits? My business is with your husband.

[PILKINGS *returns with* IYALOJA.]

PILKINGS Here she is. Now first I want your word of honour that you will try
nothing foolish.

ELESIN Honour? White one, did you say you wanted my word of honour?

PILKINGS I know you to be an honourable man. Give me your word of honour
165   you will receive nothing from her.

ELESIN But I am sure you have searched her clothing as you would never
dare touch your own mother. And there are these two lizards of yours who
roll their eyes even when I scratch.

PILKINGS And I shall be sitting on that tree trunk watching even how you
170   blink. Just the same I want your word that you will not let her pass anything to you.

ELESIN You have my honour already. It is locked up in that desk in which
you will put away your report of this night's events. Even the honour of my
people you have taken already; it is tied together with those papers of
175   treachery which make you masters in this land.

PILKINGS Alright. I am trying to make things easy but if you must bring in
politics we'll have to do it the hard way. Madam, I want you to remain
along this line and move no nearer to the cell door. Guards! [*They spring to
attention.*] If she moves beyond this point, blow your whistle. Come on
180   Jane. [*They go off.*]

IYALOJA How boldly the lizard struts before the pigeon when it was the eagle
itself he promised us he would confront.

ELESIN I don't ask you to take pity on me Iyaloja. You have a message for me or
you would not have come. Even if it is the curses of the world, I shall listen.

185 IYALOJA You made so bold with the servant of the white king who took your
side against death. I must tell your brother chiefs when I return how
bravely you waged war against him. Especially with words.

ELESIN I more than deserve your scorn.

IYALOJA [*with sudden anger*] I warned you, if you must leave a seed behind,
190   be sure it is not tainted with the curses of the world. Who are you to open
a new life when you dared not open the door to a new existence? I say who
are you to make so bold? [*The* BRIDE *sobs and* IYALOJA *notices her. Her contempt noticeably increases as she turns back to* ELESIN.] Oh you self-vaunted
stem of the plantain, how hollow it all proves. The pith is gone in the par-
195   ent stem, so how will it prove with the new shoot? How will it go with that
earth that bears it? Who are you to bring this abomination on us!

ELESIN My powers deserted me. My charms, my spells, even my voice
lacked strength when I made to summon the powers that would lead me
over the last measure of earth into the land of the fleshless. You saw it,
200   Iyaloja. You saw me struggle to retrieve my will from the power of the
stranger whose shadow fell across the doorway and left me floundering and
blundering in a maze I had never before encountered. My senses were
numbed when the touch of cold iron came upon my wrists. I could do nothing to save myself.

205 IYALOJA   You have betrayed us. We fed you sweetmeats such as we hoped
awaited you on the other side. But you said No, I must eat the world's left-
overs. We said you were the hunter who brought the quarry down; to you
belonged the vital portions of the game. No, you said, I am the hunter's dog
and I shall eat the entrails of the game and the faeces of the hunter. We
210 said you were the hunter returning home in triumph, a slain buffalo pressing down on his neck; you said wait, I first must turn up this cricket hole
with my toes. We said yours was the doorway at which we first spy the tapper when he comes down from the tree, yours was the blessing of the twilight wine, the purl[6] that brings night spirits out of doors to steal their
215 portion before the light of day. We said yours was the body of wine whose
burden shakes the tapper like a sudden gust on his perch. You said, No, I
am content to lick the dregs from each calabash when the drinkers are
done. We said, the dew on earth's surface was for you to wash your feet
along the slopes of honour. You said No, I shall step in the vomit of cats
220 and the droppings of mice; I shall fight them for the left-overs of the world.
ELESIN   Enough Iyaloja, enough.
IYALOJA   We called you leader and oh, how you led us on. What we have no
intention of eating should not be held to the nose.
ELESIN   Enough, enough. My shame is heavy enough.
225 IYALOJA   Wait. I came with a burden.
ELESIN   You have more than discharged it.
IYALOJA   I wish I could pity you.
ELESIN   I need neither your pity nor the pity of the world. I need understanding. Even I need to understand. You were present at my defeat. You were
230 part of the beginnings. You brought about the renewal of my tie to earth,
you helped in the binding of the cord.
IYALOJA   I gave you warning. The river which fills up before our eyes does not
sweep us away in its flood.
ELESIN   What were warnings beside the moist contact of living earth between
235 my fingers? What were warnings beside the renewal of famished embers
lodged eternally in the heart of man. But even that, even if it overwhelmed
one with a thousandfold temptations to linger a little while, a man could
overcome it. It is when the alien hand pollutes the source of will, when a
stranger force of violence shatters the mind's calm resolution, this is when
240 a man is made to commit the awful treachery of relief, commit in his
thought the unspeakable blasphemy of seeing the hand of the gods in this
alien rupture of his world. I know it was this thought that killed me, sapped
my powers and turned me into an infant in the hands of unnamable
strangers. I made to utter my spells anew but my tongue merely rattled in
245 my mouth. I fingered hidden charms and the contact was damp; there was
no spark left to sever the life-strings that should stretch from every fingertip. My will was squelched in the spittle of an alien race, and all because I
had committed this blasphemy of thought—that there might be the hand
of the gods in a stranger's intervention.
250 IYALOJA   Explain it how you will, I hope it brings you peace of mind. The
bush-rat fled his rightful cause, reached the market and set up a lamenta-

---

6. A liquor made by infusing bitter herbs in beer or ale. *Twilight wine:* that is, the finest wine;
palm wine tapped before dawn is believed to be especially fresh and potent.

tion. 'Please save me!'—are these fitting words to hear from an ancestral mask? 'There's a wild beast at my heels' is not becoming language from a hunter.

255 ELESIN   May the world forgive me.

IYALOJA   I came with a burden I said. It approaches the gates which are so well guarded by those jackals whose spittle will from this day be on your food and drink. But first, tell me, you who were once Elesin Oba, tell me, you who know so well the cycle of the plantain: is it the parent shoot which

260   withers to give sap to the younger or, does your wisdom see it running the other way?

ELESIN   I don't see your meaning Iyaloja?

IYALOJA   Did I ask you for a meaning? I asked a question. Whose trunk withers to give sap to the other? The parent shoot or the younger?

265 ELESIN   The parent.

IYALOJA   Ah. So you do know that. There are sights in this world which say different Elesin. There are some who choose to reverse the cycle of our being. Oh, you emptied bark that the world once saluted for a pith-laden being, shall I tell you what the gods have claimed of you?

[*In her agitation she steps beyond the line indicated by* PILKINGS *and the air is rent by piercing whistles. The two* GUARDS *also leap forward and place safe-guarding hands on* ELESIN. IYALOJA *stops, astonished.* PILKINGS *comes racing in, followed by* JANE.]

270 PILKINGS   What is it? Did they try something?

GUARD   She stepped beyond the line.

ELESIN [*in a broken voice*]   Let her alone. She meant no harm.

IYALOJA   Oh Elesin, see what you've become. Once you had no need to open your mouth in explanation because evil-smelling goats, itchy of hand and

275   foot, had lost their senses. And it was a brave man indeed who dared lay hands on you because Iyaloja stepped from one side of the earth onto another. Now look at the spectacle of your life. I grieve for you.

PILKINGS   I think you'd better leave. I doubt you have done him much good by coming here. I shall make sure you are not allowed to see him again. In

280   any case we are moving him to a different place before dawn, so don't bother to come back.

IYALOJA   We foresaw that. Hence the burden I trudged here to lay beside your gates.

PILKINGS   What was that you said?

285 IYALOJA   Didn't our son explain? Ask that one. He knows what it is. At least we hope the man we once knew as Elesin remembers the lesser oaths he need not break.

PILKINGS   Do you know what she is talking about?

ELESIN   Go to the gates, ghostly one. Whatever you find there, bring it to me.

290 IYALOJA   Not yet. It drags behind me on the slow, weary feet of women. Slow as it is Elesin, it has long overtaken you. It rides ahead of your laggard will.

PILKINGS   What is she saying now? Christ! Must your people forever speak in riddles?

ELESIN   It will come white man, it will come. Tell your men at the gates to let

295   it through.

PILKINGS [*dubiously*]   I'll have to see what it is.

IYALOJA   You will. [*Passionately*] But this is one oath he cannot shirk. White
one, you have a king here, a visitor from your land. We know of his presence here. Tell me, were he to die would you leave his spirit roaming rest
300   lessly on the surface of earth? Would you bury him here among those you
consider less than human? In your land have you no ceremonies of the
dead?

PILKINGS   Yes. But we don't make our chiefs commit suicide to keep him
company.

305 IYALOJA   Child, I have not come to help your understanding. [*Points to* ELE-
SIN.] This is the man whose weakened understanding holds us in bondage
to you. But ask him if you wish. He knows the meaning of a king's passage;
he was not born yesterday. He knows the peril to the race when our dead
father, who goes as intermediary, waits and waits and knows he is betrayed.
310   He knows when the narrow gate was opened and he knows it will not stay
for laggards who drag their feet in dung and vomit, whose lips are reeking
of the left-overs of lesser men. He knows he has condemned our King to
wander in the void of evil with beings who are enemies of life.

PILKINGS   Yes er . . . but look here . . .

315 IYALOJA   What we ask is little enough. Let him release our King so he can
ride on homewards alone. The messenger is on his way on the backs of
women. Let him send word through the heart that is folded up within the
bolt. It is the least of all his oaths, it is the easiest fulfilled.

[*The* AIDE-DE-CAMP *runs in.*]

PILKINGS   Bob?

320 AIDE-DE-CAMP   Sir, there's a group of women chanting up the hill.

PILKINGS [*rounding on* IYALOJA]   If you people want trouble . . .

JANE   Simon, I think that's what Olunde referred to in his letter.

PILKINGS   He knows damned well I can't have a crowd here! Damn it, I
explained the delicacy of my position to him. I think it's about time I got
325   him out of town. Bob, send a car and two or three soldiers to bring him in.
I think the sooner he takes his leave of his father and gets out the better.

IYALOJA   Save your labour white one. If it is the father of your prisoner you
want, Olunde, he who until this night we knew as Elesin's son, he comes
soon himself to take his leave. He has sent the women ahead, so let them in.

[PILKINGS *remains undecided.*]

330 AIDE-DE-CAMP   What do we do about the invasion? We can still stop them far
from here.

PILKINGS   What do they look like?

AIDE-DE-CAMP   They're not many. And they seem quite peaceful.

PILKINGS   No men?

335 AIDE-DE-CAMP   Mm, two or three at the most.

JANE   Honestly, Simon, I'd trust Olunde. I don't think he'll deceive you about
their intentions.

PILKINGS   He'd better not. Alright then, let them in Bob. Warn them to control themselves. Then hurry Olunde here. Make sure he brings his baggage
340   because I'm not returning him into town.

AIDE-DE-CAMP   Very good, sir. [*Goes.*]

PILKINGS [*to* IYALOJA]   I hope you understand that if anything goes wrong it
will be on your head. My men have orders to shoot at the first sign of
trouble.

345 IYALOJA To prevent one death you will actually make other deaths? Ah, great
is the wisdom of the white race. But have no fear. Your Prince will sleep
peacefully. So at long last will ours. We will disturb you no further, servant
of the white King. Just let Elesin fulfil his oath and we will retire home and
pay homage to our King.

350 JANE I believe her Simon, don't you?

PILKINGS Maybe.

ELESIN Have no fear ghostly one. I have a message to send my King and
then you have nothing more to fear.

IYALOJA Olunde would have done it. The chiefs asked him to speak the
355 words but he said no, not while you lived.

ELESIN Even from the depths to which my spirit has sunk, I find some joy
that this little has been left to me.

[The WOMEN enter, intoning the dirge 'Alẹ lẹ lẹ' and swaying from side to
side. On their shoulders is borne a longish object roughly like a cylindrical bolt, covered in cloth. They set it down on the spot where IYALOJA
had stood earlier, and form a semi-circle round it. The PRAISE-SINGER
and DRUMMER stand on the inside of the semi-circle but the drum is
not used at all. The DRUMMER intones under the PRAISE-SINGER's
invocations.]

PILKINGS [as they enter] What is that?

IYALOJA The burden you have made white one, but we bring it in peace.

360 PILKINGS I said what is it?

ELESIN White man, you must let me out. I have a duty to perform.

PILKINGS I most certainly will not.

ELESIN There lies the courier of my King. Let me out so I can perform what
is demanded of me.

365 PILKINGS You'll do what you need to do from inside there or not at all. I've
gone as far as I intend to with this business.

ELESIN The worshipper who lights a candle in your church to bear a message
to his god bows his head and speaks in a whisper to the flame. Have I not
seen it ghostly one? His voice does not ring out to the world. Mine are no
370 words for anyone's ears. They are not words even for the bearers of this
load. They are words I must speak secretly, even as my father whispered
them in my ears and I in the ears of my first-born. I cannot shout them to
the wind and the open night-sky.

JANE Simon . . .

375 PILKINGS Don't interfere. Please!

IYALOJA They have slain the favourite horse of the King and slain his dog.
They have borne them from pulse to pulse centre of the land receiving
prayers for their King. But the rider has chosen to stay behind. Is it too
much to ask that he speak his heart to heart of the waiting courier? [PILK-
380 INGS turns his back on her.] So be it, Elesin Oba, you see how even the
mere leavings are denied you. [She gestures to the PRAISE-SINGER.]

PRAISE-SINGER Elesin Oba! I call you by that name only this last time.
Remember when I said, if you cannot come, tell my horse. [Pause.] What?
I cannot hear you? I said, if you cannot come, whisper in the ears of my
385 horse. Is your tongue severed from the roots Elesin? I can hear no response.
I said, if there are boulders you cannot climb, mount my horse's back, this
spotless black stallion, he'll bring you over them. [Pauses.] Elesin Oba,

once you had a tongue that darted like a drummer's stick. I said, if you get lost my dog will track a path to me. My memory fails me but I think you
390 replied: My feet have found the path, Alafin.

[*The dirge rises and falls.*]

I said at the last, if evil hands hold you back, just tell my horse there is weight on the hem of your smock. I dare not wait too long.

[*The dirge rises and falls.*]

There lies the swiftest-ever messenger of a king, so set me free with the errand of your heart. There lie the head and heart of the favourite of the
395 gods, whisper in his ears. Oh my companion, if you had followed when you should, we would not say that the horse preceded its rider. If you had followed when it was time, we would not say the dog has raced beyond and left his master behind. If you had raised your will to cut the thread of life at the summons of the drums, we would not say your mere shadow fell
400 across the gateway and took its owner's place at the banquet. But the hunter, laden with slain buffalo, stayed to root in the cricket's hole with his toes. What now is left? If there is a dearth of bats, the pigeon must serve us for the offering. Speak the words over your shadow which must now serve in your place.

405 ELESIN   I cannot approach. Take off the cloth. I shall speak my message from heart to heart of silence.

IYALOJA [*moves forward and removes the covering*]   Your courier Elesin, cast your eyes on the favoured companion of the King.

[*Rolled up in the mat, his head and feet showing at either end, is the body of* OLUNDE.]

There lies the honour of your household and of our race. Because he could
410 not bear to let honour fly out of doors, he stopped it with his life. The son has proved the father, Elesin, and there is nothing left in your mouth to gnash but infant gums.

PRAISE-SINGER   Elesin, we placed the reins of the world in your hands yet you watched it plunge over the edge of the bitter precipice. You sat with
415 folded arms while evil strangers tilted the world from its course and crashed it beyond the edge of emptiness—you muttered, there is little that one man can do, you left us floundering in a blind future. Your heir has taken the burden on himself. What the end will be, we are not gods to tell. But this young shoot has poured its sap into the parent stalk, and we know this is
420 not the way of life. Our world is tumbling in the void of strangers, Elesin.

[ELESIN *has stood rock-still, his knuckles taut on the bars, his eyes glued to the body of his son. The stillness seizes and paralyses everyone, including* PILKINGS *who has turned to look. Suddenly* ELESIN *flings one arm round his neck, once, and with the loop of the chain, strangles himself in a swift, decisive pull. The* GUARDS *rush forward to stop him but they are only in time to let his body down.* PILKINGS *has leapt to the door at the same time and struggles with the lock. He rushes within, fumbles with the handcuffs and unlocks them, raises the body to a sitting position while he tries to give resuscitation. The* WOMEN *continue their dirge, unmoved by the sudden event.*]

IYALOJA   Why do you strain yourself? Why do you labour at tasks for which no one, not even the man lying there, would give you thanks? He is gone at last into the passage but oh, how late it all is. His son will feast on the meat

and throw him bones. The passage is clogged with droppings from the
425 King's stallion; he will arrive all stained in dung.

PILKINGS [*in a tired voice*]   Was this what you wanted?

IYALOJA   No child, it is what you brought to be, you who play with strangers'
lives, who even usurp the vestments of our dead, yet believe that the stain
of death will not cling to you. The gods demanded only the old expired
430 plantain but you cut down the sap-laden shoot to feed your pride. There is
your board, filled to overflowing. Feast on it. [*She screams at him suddenly,
seeing that* PILKINGS *is about to close* ELESIN's *staring eyes.*] Let him alone!
However sunk he was in debt he is no pauper's carrion abandoned on the
road. Since when have strangers donned clothes of indigo before the
435 bereaved cries out his loss?

[*She turns to the* BRIDE *who has remained motionless throughout.*]

Child.

[*The girl takes up a little earth, walks calmly into the cell and closes
ELESIN's eyes. She then pours some earth over each eyelid and comes out
again.*]

IYALOJA   Now forget the dead, forget even the living. Turn your mind only to
the unborn.

[*She goes off, accompanied by the* BRIDE. *The dirge rises in volume and
the* WOMEN *continue their sway. Lights fade to a black-out.*]

The End

CARYL CHURCHILL

b. 1938

IN May 1982, shortly before English dramatist Caryl Churchill won the OBIE
Award[1] for Best Playwriting for *CLOUD
NINE* (1979), *Ms.* magazine published a
feature story on the socialist feminist writer
and her enthusiastically received play—a
groundbreaking, antic exposé of patriarchal culture and imperialist ideology in
both the Victorian and contemporary
eras. Just over a year later, having earned
the same accolade for *Top Girls* (1982)—a
clear-eyed examination of feminism and
women's lives in the "me decade"—
Churchill agreed to be interviewed for
Vogue magazine. There, she was dubbed
"Britain's top girl playwright," albeit with
less irony than was embedded in Churchill's
own use of the phrase. These two articles
from the early 1980s, printed in ideologi-
cally antithetical locations, nevertheless
demonstrated Churchill's burgeoning international prominence as a writer and public figure; they also spoke to the growing
appeal of her perennially topical dramaturgy to disparate audiences. At the same
time, the features confirmed that feminism was a movement of note for those
with serious sociopolitical commitments
as well as those with an interest in current

cultural trends. Indeed, following the volatile suffrage and women's rights campaigns
of the late nineteenth through early twentieth centuries, the final two decades of
the twentieth century were marked globally by the rise of and attention to what is
now called "second wave" feminism. These
more recent struggles reflect women's
renewed efforts to achieve greater financial, educational, legal, and social equality. Through this movement, we have come
to recognize the existence of multiple
"feminisms," which embrace the range of
women's racial and ethnic identities, gender roles and sexual orientations, and
class positions, all of which inform their
relationship to society. Churchill's plays
from this period compellingly dramatize
women's historical conflicts with and current resistance to patriarchal culture.
They brought a female playwright's voice
into a theater dominated by male dramatists and also helped launch the influential field of feminist theater theory and
criticism. Her subsequent writing has
expanded her topical and stylistic reach
even further; she remains among the most
influential, productive, and innovative of
contemporary dramatists, consistently
challenging theater artists and audiences
alike since the 1970s with her politically
charged and technically adventurous
dramaturgy.

1. The OBIE Awards are given annually by *The
Village Voice* for excellence in off-Broadway
theater.

Caryl Churchill came of age at a potent, transitional period in English theater, the era of the "angry young men" like John Osborne, whose *Look Back in Anger* (1956) voiced hostility toward the British class system. Born in London in 1938, Churchill spent part of her childhood in Canada but returned to England in 1955; in 1957 she went to Oxford, studying English language and literature. At the university she began writing plays that were produced by student theater groups. Shortly after graduation she married David Harter, a lawyer. The couple had three children in the 1960s, and Churchill speaks frankly of her struggles in attempting simultaneously to continue writing and to fulfill her family obligations. She was initially politicized not by the broader social movements of that tumultuous era but by "being discontent with [her] own way of life—of being a barrister's wife and just being at home with small children." She started composing radio plays, because working in that form afforded her both the flexibility required by her family life and a respectable outlet for her work that was relatively accessible. As Churchill later noted in an interview, it was a time when world-renowned dramatist "[SAMUEL] BECKETT was on the radio" and when the medium was perceived as "the way to break in" to professional playwriting.

In 1972 the first of Churchill's several television plays was produced and *Owners* was staged at London's Royal Court Theatre, a venue known for its commitment to new playwrights. Two years later Churchill became the first woman to be offered a playwriting residency with the Royal Court; more than a dozen of her plays have premiered there, including *Top Girls, Serious Money* (1987), and *A Number* (2002). Another professional relationship that was to profoundly influence Churchill's work began in 1976, when she became involved with the Joint Stock Company. This theater collective was committed to a collaborative production process and creative political engagement, and Churchill's affiliation with it facilitated the creation of *Cloud Nine*, her first commercially successful play.

During the late 1970s Churchill also worked closely with the socialist-feminist theater group Monstrous Regiment, which took its name from a sixteenth-century misogynist pamphlet by John Knox that inveighs against the "monstrous regiment of women." The group collaborated with her in staging several pieces; one of these was *Vinegar Tom* (1976), a gripping historical drama about the persecution of women accused of witchcraft. Over the next decade, Churchill catapulted to international renown; *Top Girls, Cloud Nine, Fen* (1983), and *Serious Money* were among her plays produced throughout the English-speaking world as well as in Europe, Asia, and Latin America. She received the Susan Smith Blackburn Prize for both *Fen* and *Serious Money* and the Laurence Olivier Award (the British equivalent of the Tony Award) for *Serious Money*.

Churchill has repeatedly harnessed the power of live performance to engage audiences in meaningful political debate. Together with Mark Wing-Davey, the artistic director of London's Central School of Speech and Drama, she brought students from that professional conservatory to Romania to work with students from the Caragiale Institute of Theatre and Cinema in Bucharest in developing a piece dealing with the fall of Nicolae Ceauşescu and the impact of his policies on the lives of Romanian citizens. The resulting drama, *Mad Forest* (1990), captures the complexities of life under and after an oppressive political regime. *The Skriker* (1994) weaves the dark world of folktale magic together with a hard-edged consideration of contemporary female adolescence and our natural environment as it blurs the boundaries of drama and dance. In *Far Away* (2000) Churchill creates an apocalyptic vision of a land torn apart by conflict so profound it beggars description. And *A Number* brings us into a frightening and all-too-conceivable world where scientific advances challenge long-held assumptions about individuals' autonomy and humanity. Working in a country where theater has long reflected and affected national culture and discourse, Churchill has embraced the stage for expressing her deeply held social convictions. For decades, her plays have conveyed with growing urgency and intensity the potential devastation—sociological, economic, environmental, and political—

that those with power can wreak on the individual and on society.

Cloud Nine exemplifies these concerns through its interweaving of the past and the present (as of 1979). While its two acts are set a century apart, many of the characters we meet in act 1 also appear in act 2, having aged only twenty-five years. Churchill uses this chronological compression to demonstrate both the tenacity of historical perspectives and the potential for their gradual change. She simultaneously distances her audiences from both eras, allowing for greater objectivity and critique. Churchill scholars have identified this device as a form of Brechtian estrangement, referencing the techniques BERTOLT BRECHT championed for a politically engaged theater. While Churchill has not explicitly identified Brecht as an influence for *Cloud Nine*, she has acknowledged that English theater artists of the 1970s had absorbed his ideas, which became more widely known there following the tour of Brecht's Berliner Ensemble in 1956. A number of Brecht's plays were then staged in England in the 1960s, and British theater artists—especially those who shared Brecht's socialist beliefs—soon began to utilize Brechtian acting and dramaturgical techniques in their own work. Critics suggest that, both performatively and thematically, *Cloud Nine* engages Brechtian theatrical strategies.

Employing the conceit of the family as a microcosm of society, Churchill explores in *Cloud Nine* the nexus of the personal and the political as she traces the lives of Clive, a British colonial administrator, his wife, Betty, their children, Edward and Victoria, and their household staff, extended family, and friends. Throughout, the characters negotiate their relations with each other in a culture defined by white male supremacy and heteronormativity—a culture resisted more strongly as the play progresses. Act 1, set in Africa, provides comically exaggerated, yet still disturbing, images of compulsory heterosexuality and British imperial practices. We watch *paterfamilias* Clive blithely embody the sexual double standard and impose traditional gender roles on all around him, while he simultaneously endeavors to suppress native resistance to British rule. Act 2, set in England, shows less parodically the lingering influence of such oppression as Betty, Edward, and Victoria struggle toward independent identities and new notions of what constitutes a family.

A number of Churchill's early dramatic themes, especially her critique of patriarchy and its construction and control of female identity, emerged through the creation of *Cloud Nine*. Some of her signature dramaturgical techniques coalesced at this time as well, including her nonnaturalistic and nonlinear narrative style and her use of cross-gender/race casting and double casting. In act 1, for example, Betty is played by a male actor because, as she explains, "I am a man's creation as you see, / And what men want is what I want to be." Their black servant, Joshua, is played by a white actor for comparable reasons: "My skin is black but oh my soul is white. / I hate my tribe. My master is my light." *Cloud Nine*'s seven actors all play multiple roles, but Churchill provides options as to how this doubling occurs. Which roles the actors portray thus affects how we see the characters and their interrelationships; this happens because, for the audience, the actors will carry from one role to the next a resonance of their previous characters. Thus if the actor playing Clive in act 1 becomes the child Cathy in act 2, that will impact the audience differently than if the actor who played Joshua in act 1 becomes this same little girl.

The origins of these noteworthy components of Churchill's playwriting can be traced to various theatrical influences explored with the Joint Stock Theatre Company during its creative process. Logistical constraints with the company, such as the fact that it had no black actors at the time, were also significant: Churchill, the actors, and Joint Stock's director, Max Stafford-Clark, began with a workshop involving research, improvisation, and discussion around the topic of sexual politics. Churchill then used the fruits of that exploratory process to draft her script. The play's title emerged from an interview with an older woman who employed the phrase to describe physical intimacy with her husband, while some of the actors' discoveries about themselves and their attitudes toward gender roles

Bo Poraj as Betty and James Fleet as Clive in the 2007 Almeida Theatre (London) production of *Cloud Nine.*

and sexual identities helped give shape to the plot. According to Churchill, Kate Millet's groundbreaking feminist literary study *Sexual Politics* (1970) informed their thinking, as did the work of French dramatist Jean Genet, whose plays *The Maids* (1947), *The Balcony* (1957), *The Blacks* (1958), and *The Screens* (1961), already published in English, had also all been revived in England in the 1970s. Churchill credits Genet with articulating "the parallel between colonial and sexual repression"—one of the main themes in *Cloud Nine. The Screens*, Genet's critique of French colonialism, may have been important both thematically and theatrically, as it requires actors "to play five or six roles, male or female." In other writing, Genet envisioned his female characters "performed by adolescent boys." He also stated that he "would bring this [casting] to the attention of the spectators by means of a placard which would remain nailed to . . . the sets during the entire performance." Such directives, similar to Brecht's alienation effect, not only disrupt any semblance of theatrical realism but also call audiences' attention to the separation between actor and role. The English theater, of course, also has a long history of cross-gender casting, which includes performances by the all-male troupes of Shakespeare's day. The Victorian tradition of an actress playing a young male character, known as a "principal boy," still defines the casting of Peter Pan and similarly shapes the portrayal of *Cloud Nine*'s Edward. Similarly, the tradition of "dame" roles, which use male actors for comic portraits of female characters, may have informed the creation of Cathy in Churchill's so-called "reversal" of Edward.[2]

In *The Blacks*, subtitled "a clown show," Genet instructs some of the characters in the all-black cast to wear white masks to highlight the dominant culture's notions of racial identity. In this regard Genet, like Churchill and the Joint Stock Company, was influenced by Francophone writer Frantz Fanon (1925–61), whose seminal work *Black Skin, White Masks* (1952) suggests that "what is called the black soul is a construction by white folk." Thus the embodiment of Joshua by a white actor in *Cloud Nine* neatly wedded Fanon's theory with theatrical necessity. But because the colonial context in Africa is so strongly defined by issues of race, Churchill's effort to create a synergy with the colonial context of Northern Ireland in act 2 has not always been seen as successful. In particular, she has been criticized for a simplified notion of racial identity, her failure to consider the complex position of black women experiencing both imperial and patriarchal oppression, and her generalizing of African colonization. Her critique of England's ongoing imperialist enterprise, embodied by the ghost of a British soldier just killed in Belfast, only briefly informs the second act. Rather, as critics have noted, Churchill's use of colonialism as a metaphor for sex and gender repression emerges as the dominant structuring device for *Cloud Nine* overall.

Through the Joint Stock workshop process Churchill discovered that many of the actors had experienced, during their childhoods and young adulthoods, the tenacity of Victorian ideas about gender and sexuality. Traditional notions of what it means to be the ideal wife and mother, for example—what Coventry Patmore (1823–96) famously called "The Angel in the House" in his poem of that title (1854/1862)—can create conflicts for women who experience other kinds of desires or may have different life goals. Churchill's script both satirizes and critiques such proscriptive notions of femininity and masculinity at the same time that she demonstrates the challenges of breaking free of their constraints. When it premiered, *Cloud Nine* also stood out for its frank and objective depiction of gay and lesbian sexualities. Yet critics have subsequently noted how, in performance, *Cloud Nine* may actually, albeit unintentionally, reinforce heteronormativity. When in act 1 the governess Ellen expresses her love and desire for Betty, or the explorer Harry accepts the sexual overtures of Edward, the attractions the audience observes occur between a man and a woman—the sexes of the actors in those roles. Moreover, the casting of Edward may mirror stereotypical notions of gay male identity as feminine. Any sexual encounters between homosexual characters played by actors of the same sex, such as that between Harry and Joshua, only happen offstage. Such critical realizations exemplify the challenges facing artists who wish to tackle complex theoretical and sociological precepts while they also craft creative, innovative work. Yet despite these valid concerns, *Cloud Nine* remains one of the most influential of Churchill's plays and among her most widely produced. Indeed, precisely because of her standing in the contemporary theater, Churchill's dramas continue to fascinate artists and scholars alike. Her works provide vivid characters and memorable narratives that bring to life her social and political convictions. For over forty years Caryl Churchill has offered audiences worldwide plays that stimulate, provoke, and entertain.

J.E.G

2. Dame roles are, traditionally, older female figures, but Churchill's comedic style with Cathy is comparable.

Cloud Nine

Except for Cathy, characters in Act Two are played by actors of their own sex.

Act One takes place in a British colony in Africa in Victorian times. Act Two takes place in London in 1979. But for the characters it is twenty-five years later.

Act One

SCENE ONE: *Low bright sun. Veranda. Flagpole with Union Flag. The family*—CLIVE, BETTY, EDWARD, VICTORIA, MAUD, ELLEN, JOSHUA.

ALL [*sing*]   Come gather, sons of England, come gather in your pride.
      Now meet the world united, now face it side by side;
      Ye who the earth's wide corners, from veldt to prairie, roam.
      From bush and jungle muster all who call old England 'home'.
5   Then gather round for England,
      Rally to the flag,
      From north and south and east and west
      Come one and all for England![1]
  CLIVE   This is my family. Though far from home
10   We serve the Queen wherever we may roam.
      I am a father to the natives here,
      And father to my family so dear.
        [*He presents* BETTY. *She is played by a man.*]
      My wife is all I dreamt a wife should be,
      And everything she is she owes to me.
15 BETTY   I live for Clive. The whole aim of my life
      Is to be what he looks for in a wife.

---

1. Lyric from 1902, by Anthony Wilkin.

I am a man's creation as you see,
And what men want is what I want to be.

[CLIVE *presents* JOSHUA. *He is played by a white.*]

CLIVE   My boy's a jewel. Really has the knack.
20   You'd hardly notice that the fellow's black.

JOSHUA   My skin is black but oh my soul is white.
I hate my tribe. My master is my light.
I only live for him. As you can see,
What white men want is what I want to be.

[CLIVE *presents* EDWARD. *He is played by a woman.*]

25   CLIVE   My son is young. I'm doing all I can
To teach him to grow up to be a man.

EDWARD   What father wants I'd dearly like to be.
I find it rather hard as you can see.

[CLIVE *presents* VICTORIA, *who is a dummy,* MAUD, *and* ELLEN.]

CLIVE   No need for any speeches by the rest.
30   My daughter, mother-in-law, and governess.

ALL [*sing*]   O'er countless numbers she, our Queen,
Victoria reigns supreme;
O'er Africa's sunny plains, and o'er
Canadian frozen stream;
35   The forge of war shall weld the chains of brotherhood secure;
So to all time in ev'ry clime our Empire shall endure.

Then gather round for England,
Rally to the flag,
From north and south and east and west
40   Come one and all for England!

[*All go except* BETTY. CLIVE *comes.*]

BETTY   Clive?

CLIVE   Betty. Joshua!

[JOSHUA *comes with a drink for* CLIVE.]

BETTY   I thought you would never come. The day's so long without you.

CLIVE   Long ride in the bush.

45   BETTY   Is anything wrong? I heard drums.

CLIVE   Nothing serious. Beauty is a damned good mare. I must get some new
boots sent from home. These ones have never been right. I have a blister.

BETTY   My poor dear foot.

CLIVE   It's nothing.

50   BETTY   Oh but it's sore.

CLIVE   We are not in this country to enjoy ourselves. Must have ridden fifty
miles. Spoke to three different headmen who would all gladly chop off
each other's heads and wear them round their waists.

BETTY   Clive!

55   CLIVE   Don't be squeamish, Betty, let me have my joke. And what has my little
dove done today?

BETTY   I've read a little.

CLIVE   Good. Is it good?

BETTY   It's poetry.

60	CLIVE	You're so delicate and sensitive.
	BETTY	And I played the piano. Shall I send for the children?
	CLIVE	Yes, in a minute. I've a piece of news for you.
	BETTY	Good news?
	CLIVE	You'll certainly think it's good. A visitor.
65	BETTY	From home?
	CLIVE	No. Well of course originally from home.
	BETTY	Man or woman?
	CLIVE	Man.
	BETTY	I can't imagine.
70	CLIVE	Something of an explorer. Bit of a poet. Odd chap but brave as a lion. And a great admirer of yours.
	BETTY	What do you mean? Whoever can it be?
	CLIVE	With an H and a B. And does conjuring tricks for little Edward.
	BETTY	That sounds like Mr Bagley.
75	CLIVE	Harry Bagley.
	BETTY	He certainly doesn't admire me, Clive, what a thing to say. How could I possibly guess from that. He's hardly explored anything at all, he's just been up a river, he's done nothing at all compared to what you do. You should have said a heavy drinker and a bit of a bore.
80	CLIVE	But you like him well enough. You don't mind him coming?
	BETTY	Anyone at all to break the monotony.
	CLIVE	But you have your mother. You have Ellen.
	BETTY	Ellen is a governess. My mother is my mother.
	CLIVE	I hoped when she came to visit she would be company for you.
85	BETTY	I don't think mother is on a visit. I think she lives with us.
	CLIVE	I think she does.
	BETTY	Clive you are so good.
	CLIVE	But are you bored my love?
	BETTY	It's just that I miss you when you're away. We're not in this country to
90		enjoy ourselves. If I lack society that is my form of service.
	CLIVE	That's a brave girl. So today has been, all right? No fainting? No hysteria?[2]
	BETTY	I have been very tranquil.
	CLIVE	Ah what a haven of peace to come home to. The cool, the calm, the
95		beauty.
	BETTY	There is one thing, Clive, if you don't mind.
	CLIVE	What can I do for you, my dear?
	BETTY	It's about Joshua.
	CLIVE	I wouldn't leave you alone here with a quiet mind if it weren't for
100		Joshua.
	BETTY	Joshua doesn't like me.
	CLIVE	Joshua has been my boy for eight years. He has saved my life. I have saved his life. He is devoted to me and to mine. I have said this before.
	BETTY	He is rude to me. He doesn't do what I say. Speak to him.
105	CLIVE	Tell me what happened.
	BETTY	He said something improper.
	CLIVE	Well, what?

2. Churchill alludes here parodically to Sigmund Freud (1856–1939), whose theory of female hysteria influenced feminist notions of the patriarchal suppression of women.

BETTY   I don't like to repeat it.

CLIVE   I must insist.

110 BETTY   I had left my book inside on the piano. I was in the hammock. I asked him to fetch it.

CLIVE   And did he not fetch it?

BETTY   Yes, he did eventually.

CLIVE   And what did he say?

115 BETTY   Clive.

CLIVE   Betty.

BETTY   He said Fetch it yourself. You've got legs under that dress.

CLIVE   Joshua!

[JOSHUA comes.]

Joshua, madam says you spoke impolitely to her this afternoon.

120 JOSHUA   Sir?

CLIVE   When she asked you to pass her book from the piano.

JOSHUA   She has the book, sir.

BETTY   I have the book now, but when I told you

CLIVE   Betty, please, let me handle this. You didn't pass it at once?

125 JOSHUA   No sir, I made a joke first.

CLIVE   What was that?

JOSHUA   I said my legs were tired, sir. That was funny because the book was very near, it would not make my legs tired to get it.

BETTY   That's not true.

130 JOSHUA   Did madam hear me wrong?

CLIVE   She heard something else.

JOSHUA   What was that, madam?

BETTY   Never mind.

CLIVE   Now Joshua, it won't do you know. Madam doesn't like that kind of

135   joke. You must do what madam says, just do what she says and don't answer back. You know your place, Joshua. I don't have to say any more.

JOSHUA   No sir.

BETTY   I expect an apology.

JOSHUA   I apologise, madam.

140 CLIVE   There now. It won't happen again, my dear. I'm very shocked Joshua, very shocked.

[CLIVE winks at JOSHUA, unseen by BETTY.]

[JOSHUA goes.]

CLIVE   I think another drink, and send for the children, and isn't that Harry riding down the hill? Wave, wave. Just in time before dark. Cuts it fine, the blighter. Always a hothead, Harry.

145 BETTY   Can he see us?

CLIVE   Stand further forward. He'll see your white dress. There, he waved back.

BETTY   Do you think so? I wonder what he saw. Sometimes sunset is so terrifying I can't bear to look.

150 CLIVE   It makes me proud. Elsewhere in the empire the sun is rising.

BETTY   Harry looks so small on the hillside.

[ELLEN comes.]

ELLEN   Shall I bring the children?

BETTY   Shall Ellen bring the children?

CLIVE   Delightful.

155 BETTY   Yes, Ellen, make sure they're warm. The night air is deceptive. Victoria was looking pale yesterday.

CLIVE   My love.

[MAUD *comes from inside the house.*]

MAUD   Are you warm enough Betty?

BETTY   Perfectly.

160 MAUD   The night air is deceptive.

BETTY   I'm quite warm. I'm too warm.

MAUD   You're not getting a fever, I hope? She's not strong, you know, Clive. I don't know how long you'll keep her in this climate.

CLIVE   I look after Her Majesty's domains. I think you can trust me to look

165   after my wife.

[ELLEN *comes carrying* VICTORIA, *aged 2.*]
[EDWARD, *aged 9, lags behind.*]

BETTY   Victoria, my pet, say good evening to Papa.

[CLIVE *takes* VICTORIA *on his knee.*]

CLIVE   There's my sweet little Vicky. What have we done today?

BETTY   She wore Ellen's hat.

CLIVE   Did she wear Ellen's big hat like a lady. What a pretty.

170 BETTY   And Joshua gave her a piggy back. Tell Papa. Horsey with Joshy?

ELLEN   She's tired.

CLIVE   Nice Joshy played horsey. What a big strong Joshy. Did you have a gallop? Did you make him stop and go? Not very chatty tonight are we?

BETTY   Edward, say good evening to Papa.

175 CLIVE   Edward my boy. Have you done your lessons well?

EDWARD   Yes Papa.

CLIVE   Did you go riding?

EDWARD   Yes Papa.

CLIVE   What's that you're holding?

180 BETTY   It's Victoria's doll. What are you doing with it, Edward?

EDWARD   Minding her.

BETTY   Well I should give it to Ellen quickly. You don't want Papa to see you with a doll.

CLIVE   No, we had you with Victoria's doll once before, Edward.

185 ELLEN   He's minding it for Vicky. He's not playing with it.

BETTY   He's not playing with it, Clive. He's minding it for Vicky.

CLIVE   Ellen minds Victoria, let Ellen mind the doll.

ELLEN   Come, give it to me.

[ELLEN *takes the doll.*]

EDWARD   Don't pull her about. Vicky's very fond of her. She likes me to have

190   her.

BETTY   He's a very good brother.

CLIVE   Yes, it's manly of you Edward, to take care of your little sister. We'll say no more about it. Tomorrow I'll take you riding with me and Harry Bagley. Would you like that?

195 EDWARD   Is he here?

CLIVE   He's just arrived. There Betty, take Victoria now. I must go and welcome Harry.

[CLIVE *tosses* VICTORIA *to* BETTY, *who gives her to* ELLEN.]

EDWARD   Can I come, Papa?

BETTY   Is he warm enough?

200 EDWARD   Am I warm enough?

CLIVE   Never mind the women, Ned. Come and meet Harry.

[*They go. The women are left. There is a silence.*]

MAUD   I daresay Mr Bagley will be out all day and we'll see nothing of him.

BETTY   He plays the piano. Surely he will sometimes stay at home with

205 us.

MAUD   We can't expect it. The men have their duties and we have ours.

BETTY   He won't have seen a piano for a year. He lives a very rough life.

ELLEN   Will it be exciting for you, Betty?

MAUD   Whatever do you mean, Ellen?

210 ELLEN   We don't have very much society.

BETTY   Clive is my society.

MAUD   It's time Victoria went to bed.

ELLEN   She'd like to stay up and see Mr Bagley.

MAUD   Mr Bagley can see her tomorrow.

[ELLEN *goes.*]

215 MAUD   You let that girl forget her place, Betty.

BETTY   Mother, she is governess to my son. I know what her place is. I think my friendship does her good. She is not very happy.

MAUD   Young women are never happy.

BETTY   Mother, what a thing to say.

220 MAUD   Then when they're older they look back and see that comparatively speaking they were ecstatic.

BETTY   I'm perfectly happy.

MAUD   You are looking very pretty tonight. You were such a success as a young girl. You have made a most fortunate marriage. I'm sure you will be

225 an excellent hostess to Mr Bagley.

BETTY   I feel quite nervous at the thought of entertaining.

MAUD   I can always advise you if I'm asked.

BETTY   What a long time they're taking. I always seem to be waiting for the men.

230 MAUD   Betty you have to learn to be patient. I am patient. My mama was very patient.

[CLIVE *approaches, supporting* MRS SAUNDERS.]

CLIVE   It is a pleasure. It is an honour. It is positively your duty to seek my help. I would be hurt, I would be insulted by any show of independence. Your husband would have been one of my dearest friends if he had lived.

235 Betty, look who has come, Mrs Saunders. She has ridden here all alone, amazing spirit. What will you have? Tea or something stronger? Let her lie down, she is overcome. Betty, you will know what to do.

[MRS SAUNDERS *lies down.*]

MAUD   I knew it. I heard drums. We'll be killed in our beds.

CLIVE   Now, please, calm yourself.

240 MAUD   I am perfectly calm. I am just outspoken. If it comes to being killed I shall take it as calmly as anyone.

CLIVE   There is no cause for alarm. Mrs Saunders has been alone since her husband died last year, amazing spirit. Not surprisingly, the strain has told. She has come to us as her nearest neighbours.

245 MAUD   What happened to make her come?

CLIVE   This is not an easy country for a woman.

MAUD   Clive, I heard drums. We are not children.

CLIVE   Of course you heard drums. The tribes are constantly at war, if the term is not too grand to grace their squabbles. Not unnaturally Mrs

250 Saunders would like the company of white women. The piano. Poetry.

BETTY   We are not her nearest neighbours.

CLIVE   We are among her nearest neighbours and I was a dear friend of her late husband. She knows that she will find a welcome here. She will not be disappointed. She will be cared for.

255 MAUD   Of course we will care for her.

BETTY   Victoria is in bed. I must go and say goodnight. Mother, please, you look after Mrs Saunders.

CLIVE   Harry will be here at once.

[BETTY goes.]

MAUD   How rash to go out after dark without a shawl.

260 CLIVE   Amazing spirit. Drink this.

MRS SAUNDERS   Where am I?

MAUD   You are quite safe.

MRS SAUNDERS   Clive? Clive? Thank God. This is very kind. How do you do? I am sorry to be a nuisance. Charmed. Have you a gun? I have a gun.

265 CLIVE   There is no need for guns I hope. We are all friends here.

MRS SAUNDERS   I think I will lie down again.

[HARRY BAGLEY and EDWARD have approached.]

MAUD   Ah, here is Mr Bagley.

EDWARD   I gave his horse some water.

CLIVE   You don't know Mrs Saunders, do you Harry? She has at present col-

270 lapsed, but she is recovering thanks to the good offices of my wife's mother who I think you've met before. Betty will be along in a minute. Edward will go home to school shortly. He is quite a young man since you saw him.

HARRY   I hardly knew him.

MAUD   What news have you for us, Mr Bagley?

275 CLIVE   Do you know Mrs Saunders, Harry? Amazing spirit.

EDWARD   Did you hardly know me?

HARRY   Of course I knew you. I mean you have grown.

EDWARD   What do you expect?

HARRY   That's quite right, people don't get smaller.

280 MAUD   Edward. You should be in bed.

EDWARD   No, I'm not tired, I'm not tired am I Uncle Harry?

HARRY   I don't think he's tired.

CLIVE   He is overtired. It is past his bedtime. Say goodnight.

EDWARD   Goodnight, sir.

285 CLIVE   And to your grandmother.

EDWARD   Goodnight, Grandmother.

[EDWARD goes.]

MAUD   Shall I help Mrs Saunders indoors? I'm afraid she may get a chill.

CLIVE   Shall I give her an arm?

MAUD   How kind of you Clive. I think I am strong enough.

[MAUD *helps* MRS SAUNDERS *into the house.*]

290   CLIVE   Not a word to alarm the women.

HARRY   Absolutely.

CLIVE   I did some good today I think. Kept up some alliances. There's a lot of affection there.

HARRY   They're affectionate people. They can be very cruel of course.

295   CLIVE   Well they are savages.

HARRY   Very beautiful people many of them.

CLIVE   Joshua! [*To* HARRY.] I think we should sleep with guns.

HARRY   I haven't slept in a house for six months. It seems extremely safe.

[JOSHUA *comes.*]

CLIVE   Joshua, you will have gathered there's a spot of bother. Rumours of
300   this and that. You should be armed I think.

JOSHUA   There are many bad men, sir. I pray about it. Jesus will protect us.

CLIVE   He will indeed and I'll also get you a weapon. Betty, come and keep
Harry company. Look in the barn, Joshua, every night.

[CLIVE *and* JOSHUA *go.* BETTY *comes.*]

HARRY   I wondered where you were.

305   BETTY   I was singing lullabies.

HARRY   When I think of you I always think of you with Edward in your lap.

BETTY   Do you think of me sometimes then?

HARRY   You have been thought of where no white woman has ever been
thought of before.

310   BETTY   It's one way of having adventures. I suppose I will never go in person.

HARRY   That's up to you.

BETTY   Of course it's not. I have duties.

HARRY   Are you happy, Betty?

BETTY   Where have you been?

315   HARRY   Built a raft and went up the river. Stayed with some people. The king
is always very good to me. They have a lot of skulls around the place but not
white men's I think. I made up a poem one night. If I should die in this forsaken spot, There is a loving heart without a blot, Where I will live—and so on.

BETTY   When I'm near you it's like going out into the jungle. It's like going up
320   the river on a raft. It's like going out in the dark.

HARRY   And you are safety and light and peace and home.

BETTY   But I want to be dangerous.

HARRY   Clive is my friend.

BETTY   I am your friend.

325   HARRY   I don't like dangerous women.

BETTY   Is Mrs Saunders dangerous?

HARRY   Not to me. She's a bit of an old boot.

[JOSHUA *comes, unobserved.*]

BETTY   Am I dangerous?

HARRY   You are rather.

330   BETTY   Please like me.

HARRY   I worship you.

BETTY   Please want me.

HARRY   I don't want to want you. Of course I want you.

BETTY   What are we going to do?

335 HARRY   I should have stayed on the river. The hell with it.

[*He goes to take her in his arms, she runs away into the house.* HARRY *stays where he is. He becomes aware of* JOSHUA.]

HARRY   Who's there?

JOSHUA   Only me sir.

HARRY   Got a gun now have you?

JOSHUA   Yes sir.

340 HARRY   Where's Clive?

JOSHUA   Going round the boundaries sir.

HARRY   Have you checked there's nobody in the barns?

JOSHUA   Yes sir.

HARRY   Shall we go in a barn and fuck? It's not an order.

345 JOSHUA   That's all right, yes.

[*They go off.*]

SCENE TWO: *An open space some distance from the house.* MRS SAUNDERS *alone, breathless. She is carrying a riding crop.* CLIVE *arrives.*

CLIVE   Why? Why?

MRS SAUNDERS   Don't fuss, Clive, it makes you sweat.

CLIVE   Why ride off now? Sweat, you would sweat if you were in love with somebody as disgustingly capricious as you are. You will be shot with poi-

350   soned arrows. You will miss the picnic. Somebody will notice I came after you.

MRS SAUNDERS   I didn't want you to come after me. I wanted to be alone.

CLIVE   You will be raped by cannibals.

MRS SAUNDERS   I just wanted to get out of your house.

355 CLIVE   My God, what women put us through. Cruel, cruel. I think you are the sort of woman who would enjoy whipping somebody. I've never met one before.

MRS SAUNDERS   Can I tell you something, Clive?

CLIVE   Let me tell you something first. Since you came to the house I have

360   had an erection twenty-four hours a day except for ten minutes after the time we had intercourse.

MRS SAUNDERS   I don't think that's physically possible.

CLIVE   You are causing me appalling physical suffering. Is this the way to treat a benefactor?

365 MRS SAUNDERS   Clive, when I came to your house the other night I came because I was afraid. The cook was going to let his whole tribe in through the window.

CLIVE   I know that, my poor sweet. Amazing—

MRS SAUNDERS   I came to you although you are not my nearest neighbour—

370 CLIVE   Rather than to the old major of seventy-two.

MRS SAUNDERS   Because the last time he came to visit me I had to defend myself with a shotgun and I thought you would take no for an answer.

CLIVE   But you've already answered yes.

MRS SAUNDERS   I answered yes once. Sometimes I want to say no.

375 CLIVE   Women, my God. Look the picnic will start, I have to go to the picnic. Please Caroline—

MRS SAUNDERS   I think I will have to go back to my own house.

CLIVE   Caroline, if you were shot with poisoned arrows do you know what
I'd do? I'd fuck your dead body and poison myself. Caroline, you smell
380   amazing. You terrify me. You are dark like this continent. Mysterious.
Treacherous. When you rode to me through the night. When you fainted
in my arms. When I came to you in your bed, when I lifted the mosquito
netting, when I said let me in, let me in. Oh don't shut me out, Caroline,
let me in.

[*He has been caressing her feet and legs. He disappears completely under
her skirt.*]

385   MRS SAUNDERS   Please stop. I can't concentrate. I want to go home. I wish
I didn't enjoy the sensation because I don't like you, Clive. I do like
living in your house where there's plenty of guns. But I don't like you at
all. But I do like the sensation. Well I'll have it then. I'll have it, I'll have
it—

[*Voices are heard singing 'The First Noel'.*]

390   Don't stop. Don't stop.

[CLIVE *comes out from under her skirt.*]

CLIVE   The Christmas picnic. I came.

MRS SAUNDERS   I didn't.

CLIVE   I'm all sticky.

MRS SAUNDERS   What about me? Wait.

395   CLIVE   All right, are you? Come on. We mustn't be found.

MRS SAUNDERS   Don't go now.

CLIVE   Caroline, you are so voracious. Do let go. Tidy yourself up. There's a
hair in my mouth.

[CLIVE *and* MRS SAUNDERS *go off.* BETTY *and* MAUD *come, with* JOSHUA
carrying hamper.]

MAUD   I never would have thought a guinea fowl could taste so like a
400   turkey.

BETTY   I had to explain to Cook three times.

MAUD   You did very well dear.

[JOSHUA *sits apart with gun.* EDWARD *and* HARRY *with* VICTORIA *on his
shoulder, singing 'The First Noel'.* MAUD *and* BETTY *are unpacking the
hamper.* CLIVE *arrives separately.*]

MAUD   This tablecloth was one of my mama's.

BETTY   Uncle Harry playing horsey.

405   EDWARD   Crackers crackers.[3]

BETTY   Not yet, Edward.

CLIVE   And now the moment we have all been waiting for.

[CLIVE *opens champagne. General acclaim.*]

Oh dear, stained my trousers, never mind.

EDWARD   Can I have some?

410   MAUD   Oh no Edward, not for you.

CLIVE   Give him half a glass.

MAUD   If your father says so.

---

3. Traditional British Christmas favor made
of stiff paper tubes filled with a paper crown
and small toys, covered with colored paper.
When the paper wrapping is pulled at both
ends, the tube makes a cracking noise and
splits open to release the contents.

CLIVE   All rise please. To Her Majesty Queen Victoria, God bless her, and
    her husband and all her dear children.
415 ALL   The Queen.
EDWARD   Crackers crackers.
    [*General cracker pulling, hats.* CLIVE *and* HARRY *discuss champagne.*]
HARRY   Excellent, Clive, wherever did you get it?
CLIVE   I know a chap in French Equatorial Africa.
EDWARD   I won, I won Mama.
    [ELLEN *arrives.*]
420 BETTY   Give a hat to Joshua, he'd like it.
    [EDWARD *takes hat to* JOSHUA. BETTY *takes a ball from the hamper and
    plays catch with* ELLEN. *Murmurs of surprise and congratulation from
    the men as they catch the ball.*]
EDWARD   Mama, don't play. You know you can't catch a ball.
BETTY   He's perfectly right. I can't throw either.
    [BETTY *sits down.* ELLEN *has the ball.*]
EDWARD   Ellen, don't you play either. You're no good. You spoil it.
    [EDWARD *takes* VICTORIA *from* HARRY *and gives her to* ELLEN. *He takes the
    ball and throws it to* HARRY. HARRY, CLIVE *and* EDWARD *play ball.*]
BETTY   Ellen come and sit with me. We'll be spectators and clap.
    [EDWARD *misses the ball.*]
425 CLIVE   Butterfingers.
EDWARD   I'm not.
HARRY   Throw straight now.
EDWARD   I did, I did.
CLIVE   Keep your eye on the ball.
430 EDWARD   You can't throw.
CLIVE   Don't be a baby.
EDWARD   I'm not, throw a hard one, throw a hard one—
CLIVE   Butterfingers. What will Uncle Harry think of you?
EDWARD   It's your fault. You can't throw. I hate you.
    [*He throws the ball wildly in the direction of* JOSHUA.]
435 CLIVE   Now you've lost the ball. He's lost the ball.
EDWARD   It's Joshua's fault. Joshua's butterfingers.
CLIVE   I don't think I want to play any more. Joshua, find the ball will you?
EDWARD   Yes, please play. I'll find the ball. Please play.
CLIVE   You're so silly and you can't catch. You'll be no good at cricket.
440 MAUD   Why don't we play hide-and-seek?
EDWARD   Because it's a baby game.
BETTY   You've hurt Edward's feelings.
CLIVE   A boy has no business having feelings.
HARRY   Hide-and-seek. I'll be it. Everybody must hide. This is the base, you
445   have to get home to base.
EDWARD   Hide-and-seek, hide-and-seek.
HARRY   Can we persuade the ladies to join us?
MAUD   I'm playing. I love games.
BETTY   I always get found straight away.
450 ELLEN   Come on, Betty, do. Vicky wants to play.

EDWARD   You won't find me ever.

[*They all go except* CLIVE, HARRY, JOSHUA.]

HARRY   It is safe, I suppose?

CLIVE   They won't go far. This is very much my territory and it's broad daylight. Joshua will keep an open eye.

455 HARRY   Well I must give them a hundred. You don't know what this means to
me, Clive. A chap can only go on so long alone. I can climb mountains and
go down rivers, but what's it for? For Christmas and England and games and
women singing. This is the empire, Clive. It's not me putting a flag in new
lands. It's you. The empire is one big family. I'm one of its black sheep, Clive.
460 And I know you think my life is rather dashing. But I want you to know I
admire you. This is the empire, Clive, and I serve it. With all my heart.

CLIVE   I think that's about a hundred.

HARRY   Ready or not, here I come!

[*He goes.*]

CLIVE   Harry Bagley is a fine man, Joshua. You should be proud to know him.
465 He will be in history books.

JOSHUA   Sir, while we are alone.

CLIVE   Joshua of course, what is it? You always have my ear. Any time.

JOSHUA   Sir, I have some information. The stable boys are not to be trusted.
They whisper. They go out at night. They visit their people. Their people
470 are not my people. I do not visit my people.

CLIVE   Thank you, Joshua. They certainly look after Beauty. I'll be sorry to
have to replace them.

JOSHUA   They carry knives.

CLIVE   Thank you, Joshua.

475 JOSHUA   And, sir.

CLIVE   I appreciate this, Joshua, very much.

JOSHUA   Your wife.

CLIVE   Ah, yes?

JOSHUA   She also thinks Harry Bagley is a fine man.

480 CLIVE   Thank you, Joshua.

JOSHUA   Are you going to hide?

CLIVE   Yes, yes I am. Thank you. Keep your eyes open Joshua.

JOSHUA   I do, sir.

[CLIVE *goes.* JOSHUA *goes.* HARRY *and* BETTY *race back to base.*]

BETTY   I can't run, I can't run at all.

485 HARRY   There, I've caught you.

BETTY   Harry, what are we going to do?

HARRY   It's impossible, Betty.

BETTY   Shall we run away together?

[MAUD *comes.*]

MAUD   I give up. Don't catch me. I have been stung.

490 HARRY   Nothing serious I hope.

MAUD   I have ointment in my bag. I always carry ointment. I shall just sit
down and rest. I am too old for all this fun. Hadn't you better be seeking,
Harry?

[HARRY *goes.* MAUD *and* BETTY *are alone for some time. They don't speak.*]
[HARRY *and* EDWARD *race back.*]

EDWARD   I won, I won, you didn't catch me.

495 HARRY   Yes I did.

EDWARD   Mama, who was first?

BETTY   I wasn't watching. I think it was Harry.

EDWARD   It wasn't Harry. You're no good at judging. I won, didn't I Grandma?

MAUD   I expect so, since it's Christmas.

500 EDWARD   I won, Uncle Harry. I'm better than you.

BETTY   Why don't you help Uncle Harry look for the others?

EDWARD   Shall I?

HARRY   Yes, of course.

BETTY   Run along then. He's just coming.

     [EDWARD goes.]

505 Harry, I shall scream.

HARRY   Ready or not here I come.

     [HARRY runs off.]

BETTY   Why don't you go back to the house, Mother, and rest your insect bite?

MAUD   Betty, my duty is here. I don't like what I see. Clive wouldn't like it,

510   Betty. I am your mother.

BETTY   Clive gives you a home because you are my mother.

     [HARRY comes back.]

HARRY   I can't find anyone else. I'm getting quite hot.

BETTY   Sit down a minute.

HARRY   I can't do that I'm he. How's your sting?

515 MAUD   It seems to be swelling up.

BETTY   Why don't you go home and rest? Joshua will go with you. Joshua!

HARRY   I could take you back.

MAUD   That would be charming.

BETTY   You can't go. You're he.

     [JOSHUA comes.]

520 BETTY   Joshua, my mother wants to go back to the house. Will you go with her please.

JOSHUA   Sir told me I have to keep an eye.

BETTY   I am telling you to go back to the house. Then you can come back here and keep an eye.

525 MAUD   Thank you Betty. I know we have our little differences, but I always want what is best for you.

     [JOSHUA and MAUD go.]

HARRY   Don't give way. Keep calm.

BETTY   I shall kill myself.

HARRY   Betty, you are a star in my sky. Without you I would have no sense of

530   direction. I need you, and I need you where you are, I need you to be Clive's wife. I need to go up rivers and know you are sitting here thinking of me.

BETTY   I want more than that. Is that wicked of me?

HARRY   Not wicked, Betty. Silly.

     [EDWARD calls in the distance.]

535 EDWARD   Uncle Harry, where are you?

BETTY   Can't we ever be alone?

HARRY   You are a mother. And a daughter. And a wife.

BETTY   I think I shall go and hide again.

[BETTY *goes.* HARRY *goes.* CLIVE *chases* MRS SAUNDERS *across the stage.*]
[EDWARD *and* HARRY *call in the distance.*]

EDWARD   Uncle Harry!

540 HARRY   Edward!

[EDWARD *comes.*]

EDWARD   Uncle Harry!

[HARRY *comes.*]

There you are. I haven't found anyone have you?

HARRY   I wonder where they all are.

EDWARD   Perhaps they're lost for ever. Perhaps they're dead. There's trouble

545 going on isn't there, and nobody says because of not frightening the women
and children.

HARRY   Yes, that's right.

EDWARD   Do you think we'll be killed in our beds?

HARRY   Not very likely.

550 EDWARD   I can't sleep at night. Can you?

HARRY   I'm not used to sleeping in a house.

EDWARD   If I'm awake at night can I come and see you? I won't wake you up.
I'll only come in if you're awake.

HARRY   You should try to sleep.

555 EDWARD   I don't mind being awake because I make up adventures. Once we
were on a raft going down to the rapids. We've lost the paddles because we
used them to fight off the crocodiles. A crocodile comes at me and I stab it
again and again and the blood is everywhere and it tips up the raft and it
has you by the leg and it's biting your leg right off and I take my knife and

560 stab it in the throat and rip open its stomach and it lets go of you but it
bites my hand but it's dead. And I drag you onto the river bank and I'm
almost fainting with pain and we lie there in each other's arms.

HARRY   Have I lost my leg?

EDWARD   I forgot about the leg by then.

565 HARRY   Hadn't we better look for the others?

EDWARD   Wait I've got something for you. It was in Mama's box but she
never wears it.

[EDWARD *gives* HARRY *a necklace.*]

You don't have to wear it either but you might like it to look at.

HARRY   It's beautiful. But you'll have to put it back.

570 EDWARD   I wanted to give it to you.

HARRY   You did. It can go back in the box. You still gave it to me. Come on
now, we have to find the others.

EDWARD   Harry, I love you.

HARRY   Yes I know. I love you too.

575 EDWARD   You know what we did when you were here before. I want to do it
again. I think about it all the time. I try to do it to myself but it's not as
good. Don't you want to any more?

HARRY   I do, but it's a sin and a crime and it's also wrong.

EDWARD   But we'll do it anyway won't we?

580   HARRY   Yes of course.

EDWARD   I wish the others would all be killed. Take it out now and let me see it.

HARRY   No.

EDWARD   Is it big now?

HARRY   Yes.

585   EDWARD   Let me touch it.

HARRY   No.

EDWARD   Just hold me.

HARRY   When you can't sleep.

EDWARD   We'd better find the others then. Come on.

590   HARRY   Ready or not, here we come.

       [*They go out with whoops and shouts.* BETTY *and* ELLEN *come.*]

BETTY   Ellen, I don't want to play any more.

ELLEN   Nor do I, Betty.

BETTY   Come and sit here with me. Oh Ellen, what will become of me?

ELLEN   Betty, are you crying? Are you laughing?

595   BETTY   Tell me what you think of Harry Bagley.

ELLEN   He's a very fine man.

BETTY   No, Ellen, what you really think.

ELLEN   I think you think he's very handsome.

BETTY   And don't you think he is? Oh Ellen, you're so good and I'm so wicked.

600   ELLEN   I'm not so good as you think.

       [EDWARD *comes.*]

EDWARD   I've found you.

ELLEN   We're not hiding Edward.

EDWARD   But I found you.

ELLEN   We're not playing, Edward, now run along.

605   EDWARD   Come on, Ellen, do play. Come on, Mama.

ELLEN   Edward, don't pull your mama like that.

BETTY   Edward, you must do what your governess says. Go and play with Uncle Harry.

EDWARD   Uncle Harry!

       [EDWARD *goes.*]

610   BETTY   Ellen, can you keep a secret?

ELLEN   Oh yes, yes please.

BETTY   I love Harry Bagley. I want to go away with him. There, I've said it, it's true.

ELLEN   How do you know you love him?

615   BETTY   I kissed him.

ELLEN   Betty.

BETTY   He held my hand like this. Oh I want him to do it again. I want him to stroke my hair.

ELLEN   Your lovely hair. Like this, Betty?

620   BETTY   I want him to put his arm around my waist.

ELLEN   Like this, Betty?

BETTY   Yes, oh I want him to kiss me again.

ELLEN   Like this Betty?

       [ELLEN *kisses* BETTY.]

BETTY   Ellen, whatever are you doing? It's not a joke.

625   ELLEN   I'm sorry, Betty. You're so pretty. Harry Bagley doesn't deserve you. You wouldn't really go away with him?

BETTY   Oh Ellen, you don't know what I suffer. You don't know what love is. Everyone will hate me, but it's worth it for Harry's love.

ELLEN   I don't hate you, Betty, I love you.

630   BETTY   Harry says we shouldn't go away. But he says he worships me.

ELLEN   I worship you Betty.

BETTY   Oh Ellen, you are my only friend.

[*They embrace. The others have all gathered together.*]
[MAUD *has rejoined the party, and* JOSHUA.]

CLIVE   Come along everyone, you mustn't miss Harry's conjuring trick.

[BETTY *and* ELLEN *go to join the others.*]

MAUD   I didn't want to spoil the fun by not being here.

635   HARRY   What is it that flies all over the world and is up my sleeve?

[HARRY *produces a Union Flag from up his sleeve.*[4] *General acclaim.*]

CLIVE   I think we should have some singing now. Ladies, I rely on you to lead the way.

ELLEN   We have a surprise for you. I have taught Joshua a Christmas carol. He has been singing it at the piano but I'm sure he can sing it unaccompa-

640   nied, can't you, Joshua?

JOSHUA   In the deep midwinter
Frosty wind made moan,
Earth stood hard as iron,
Water like a stone.
645   Snow had fallen snow on snow
Snow on snow,
In the deep midwinter
Long long ago.
What can I give him
650   Poor as I am?
If I were a shepherd
I would bring a lamb.
If I were a wise man
I would do my part.
655   What I can I give him?
Give my heart.[5]

SCENE THREE: *Inside the house.* BETTY, MRS SAUNDERS, MAUD *with* VICTORIA. *The blinds are down so the light isn't bright though it is day outside.* CLIVE *looks in.*

CLIVE   Everything all right? Nothing to be frightened of.

[CLIVE *goes. Silence.*]

4. The flag of England, also known as the Union Jack.
5. Excerpt from a Christina Rossetti (1830–1894) lyric, "A Christmas Carol" (1872), set to music in 1906 by Gustav Holst (1874–1934).

MAUD Clap hands, Daddy comes, with his pockets full of plums. All for
Vicky.

[Silence.]

660 MRS SAUNDERS Who actually does the flogging?

MAUD I don't think we want to imagine.

MRS SAUNDERS I imagine Joshua.

BETTY Yes I think it would be Joshua. Or would Clive do it himself?

MRS SAUNDERS Well we can ask them afterwards.

665 MAUD I don't like the way you speak of it, Mrs Saunders.

MRS SAUNDERS How should I speak of it?

MAUD The men will do it in the proper way, whatever it is. We have our own
part to play.

MRS SAUNDERS Harry Bagley says they should just be sent away. I don't think

670 he likes to see them beaten.

BETTY Harry is so tender-hearted. Perhaps he is right.

MAUD Harry Bagley is not altogether— He has lived in this country a long
time without any responsibilities. It is part of his charm but it hasn't
improved his judgement. If the boys were just sent away they would go back

675 to the village and make more trouble.

MRS SAUNDERS And what will they say about us in the village if they've been
flogged?

BETTY Perhaps Clive should keep them here.

MRS SAUNDERS That is never wise.

680 BETTY Whatever shall we do?

MAUD I don't think it is up to us to wonder. The men don't tell us what is
going on among the tribes, so how can we possibly make a judgement?

MRS SAUNDERS I know a little of what is going on.

BETTY Tell me what you know. Clive tells me nothing.

685 MAUD You would not want to be told about it, Betty. It is enough for you that
Clive knows what is happening. Clive will know what to do. Your father
always knew what to do.

BETTY Are you saying you would do something different, Caroline?

MRS SAUNDERS I would do what I did at my own home. I left. I can't see any

690 way out except to leave. I will leave here. I will keep leaving everywhere I
suppose.

MAUD Luckily this household has a head. I am squeamish myself. But luckily Clive is not.

BETTY You are leaving here then, Caroline?

695 MRS SAUNDERS Not immediately. I'm sorry.

[Silence.]

I wonder if it's over.

[EDWARD comes in.]

BETTY Shouldn't you be with the men, Edward?

EDWARD I didn't want to see any more. They got what they deserved. Uncle
Harry said I could come in.

700 MRS SAUNDERS I never allowed the servants to be beaten in my own house.
I'm going to find out what's happening.

[MRS SAUNDERS goes out.]

BETTY Will she go and look?

MAUD   Let Mrs Saunders be a warning to you, Betty. She is alone in the
    world. You are not, thank God. Since your father died, I know what it is to
705 be unprotected. Vicky is such a pretty little girl. Clap hands, Daddy comes,
    with his pockets full of plums. All for Vicky.

> [EDWARD, *meanwhile, has found the doll and is playing clap hands with*
> *her.*]

BETTY   Edward, what have you got there?
EDWARD   I'm minding her.
BETTY   Edward, I've told you before, dolls are for girls.
710 MAUD   Where is Ellen? She should be looking after Edward. [*She goes to the*
    door.] Ellen! Betty, why do you let that girl mope about in her own room?
    That's not what she's come to Africa for.
BETTY   You must never let the boys at school know you like dolls. Never,
    never. No one will talk to you, you won't be on the cricket team, you won't
715 grow up to be a man like your papa.
EDWARD   I don't want to be like Papa. I hate Papa.
MAUD   Edward! Edward!
BETTY   You're a horrid wicked boy and Papa will beat you. Of course you
    don't hate him, you love him. Now give Victoria her doll at once.
720 EDWARD   She's not Victoria's doll, she's my doll. She doesn't love Victoria
    and Victoria doesn't love her. Victoria never even plays with her.
MAUD   Victoria will learn to play with her.
EDWARD   She's mine and she loves me and she won't be happy if you take her
    away, she'll cry, she'll cry, she'll cry.

> [BETTY *takes the doll away, slaps him, bursts into tears.*]
> [ELLEN *comes in.*]

725 BETTY   Ellen, look what you've done. Edward's got the doll again. Now,
    Ellen, will you please do your job.
ELLEN   Edward, you are a wicked boy. I am going to lock you in the nursery
    until supper time. Now go upstairs this minute.

> [*She slaps* EDWARD, *who bursts into tears and goes out.*]

I do try to do what you want. I'm so sorry.

> [ELLEN *bursts into tears and goes out.*]

730 MAUD   There now, Vicky's got her baby back. Where did Vicky's naughty baby
    go? Shall we smack her? Just a little smack. [MAUD *smacks the doll hard.*]
    There, now she's a good baby. Clap hands, Daddy comes, with his pockets
    full of plums. All for Vicky's baby. When I was a child we honoured our
    parents. My mama was an angel.

> [JOSHUA *comes in. He stands without speaking.*]

735 BETTY   Joshua?
JOSHUA   Madam?
BETTY   Did you want something?
JOSHUA   Sent to see the ladies are all right, madam.

> [MRS SAUNDERS *comes in.*]

MRS SAUNDERS   We're very well thank you, Joshua, and how are you?
740 JOSHUA   Very well thank you, Mrs Saunders.
MRS SAUNDERS   And the stable boys?
JOSHUA   They have had justice, madam.
MRS SAUNDERS   So I saw. And does your arm ache?

MAUD   This is not a proper conversation, Mrs Saunders.

745   MRS SAUNDERS   You don't mind beating your own people?

JOSHUA   Not my people, madam.

MRS SAUNDERS   A different tribe?

JOSHUA   Bad people.

[HARRY *and* CLIVE *come in.*]

CLIVE   Well this is all very gloomy and solemn. Can we have the shutters
750   open? The heat of the day has gone, we could have some light, I think. And
cool drinks on the verandah, Joshua. Have some lemonade yourself. It is
most refreshing. [*Sunlight floods in as the shutters are opened.*]

[EDWARD *comes.*]

EDWARD   Papa, Papa, Ellen tried to lock me in the nursery. Mama is going to
tell you of me. I'd rather tell you myself. I was playing with Vicky's doll
755   again and I know it's very bad of me. And I said I didn't want to be like you
and I said I hated you. And it's not true and I'm sorry, I'm sorry and please
beat me and forgive me.

CLIVE   Well there's a brave boy to own up. You should always respect and
love me, Edward, not for myself, I may not deserve it, but as I respected
760   and loved my own father, because he was my father. Through our father we
love our Queen and our God, Edward.[6] Do you understand? It is something men understand.

EDWARD   Yes Papa.

CLIVE   Then I forgive you and shake you by the hand. You spend too much
765   time with the women. You may spend more time with me and Uncle Harry,
little man.

EDWARD   I don't like women. I don't like dolls Papa, and I love you, Uncle
Harry.

CLIVE   There's a fine fellow. Let us go out onto the verandah.

[*They all start to go.* EDWARD *takes* HARRY'S *hand and goes with him.*
CLIVE *draws* BETTY *back. They embrace.*]

770   BETTY   Poor Clive.

CLIVE   It was my duty to have them flogged. For you and Edward and Victoria, to keep you safe.

BETTY   It is terrible to feel betrayed.

CLIVE   You can tame a wild animal only so far. They revert to their true
775   nature and savage your hand. Sometimes I feel the natives are the enemy. I
know that is wrong. I know I have a responsibility towards them, to care for
them and bring them all to be like Joshua. But there is something dangerous. Implacable. This whole continent is my enemy. I am pitching my
whole mind and will and reason and spirit against it to tame it, and I some-
780   times feel it will break over me and swallow me up.

BETTY   Clive, Clive, I am here. I have faith in you.

CLIVE   Yes, I can show you my moments of weakness, Betty, because you are
my wife and because I trust you. I trust you, Betty, and it would break my

6. Churchill alludes here to the notion of the
"Great Chain of Being," explicated by E. M. W.
Tillyard in *The Elizabethan World Picture*
(1943). Tillyard traces this notion of continuous ties from the lowest forms on earth up to
God back to the medieval period and establishes its flourishing in Renaissance culture.

heart if you did not deserve that trust. Harry Bagley is my friend. It would
785 break my heart if he did not deserve my trust.

BETTY   I'm sorry, I'm sorry. Forgive me. It is not Harry's fault, it is all mine.
Harry is noble. He has rejected me. It is my wickedness. I get bored, I get
restless, I imagine things. There is something so wicked in me, Clive.

CLIVE   I have never thought of you having the weakness of your sex, only the
790 good qualities.

BETTY   I am bad, bad, bad—

CLIVE   You are thoughtless, Betty, that's all. Women can be treacherous and
evil. They are darker and more dangerous than men. The family protects us
from that, you protect me from that. You are not that sort of woman. You
795 are not unfaithful to me, Betty. I can't believe you are. It would hurt me so
much to cast you off. That would be my duty.

BETTY   No, no, no.

CLIVE   Joshua has seen you kissing.

BETTY   Forgive me.

800 CLIVE   But I don't want to know about it. I don't want to know. I wonder of
course, I wonder constantly. If Harry Bagley was not my friend I would
shoot him. If I shot you every British man and woman would applaud
me. But no. It was a moment of passion such as women are too weak to
resist. But you must resist it, Betty, or it will destroy us. We must fight
805 against it. We must resist this dark female lust, Betty, or it will swallow
us up.[7]

BETTY   I do, I do resist. Help me. Forgive me.

CLIVE   Yes I do forgive you. But I can't feel the same about you as I did. You
are still my wife and we still have duties to the household.

[They go out arm in arm. As soon as they have gone EDWARD *sneaks back
to get the doll, which has been dropped on the floor. He picks it up and
comforts it.* JOSHUA *comes through with a tray of drinks.]*

810 JOSHUA   Baby. Sissy. Girly.

*[*JOSHUA *goes.* BETTY *calls from off.]*

BETTY   Edward?

*[*BETTY *comes in.]*

There you are my darling. Come, Papa wants us all to be together. Uncle
Harry is going to tell how he caught a crocodile. Mama's sorry she smacked
you.

[They embrace. JOSHUA *comes in again, passing through.]*

815 BETTY   Joshua, fetch me some blue thread from my sewing box. It is on the
piano.

JOSHUA   You've got legs under that skirt.

BETTY   Joshua.

JOSHUA   And more than legs.

820 BETTY   Edward, are you going to stand there and let a servant insult your
mother?

EDWARD   Joshua, get my mother's thread.

JOSHUA   Oh little Eddy, playing at master. It's only a joke.

EDWARD   Don't speak to my mother like that again.

---

7. Churchill alludes here parodically to traditional Western patriarchal notions of female lascivi-
ousness, which originate with the story of Eve in the Book of Genesis.

825 JOSHUA   Ladies have no sense of humour. You like a joke with Joshua.

EDWARD   You fetch her sewing at once, do you hear me? You move when I speak to you, boy.

JOSHUA   Yes sir, master Edward sir.

[JOSHUA *goes.*]

BETTY   Edward, you were wonderful.

[*She goes to embrace him but he moves away.*]

830 EDWARD   Don't touch me.

ALL [*sing 'A Boy's Best Friend'*]

While plodding on our way, the toilsome road of life,
How few the friends that daily there we meet.
Not many will stand by in trouble and strife,
With counsel and affection ever sweet.
835   But there is one whose smile will ever on us beam,
Whose love is dearer far than any other;
And wherever we may turn
This lesson we will learn
A boy's best friend is his mother.

840   Then cherish her with care
And smooth her silv'ry hair,
When gone you will never get another.
And wherever we may turn
This lesson we shall learn,
845   A boy's best friend is his mother.[8]

SCENE FOUR: *The verandah as in Scene One. Early morning. Nobody there.* JOSHUA *comes out of the house slowly and stands for some time doing nothing.* EDWARD *comes out.*

EDWARD   Tell me another bad story, Joshua. Nobody else is even awake yet.

JOSHUA   First there was nothing and then there was the great goddess. She was very large and she had golden eyes and she made the stars and the sun and the earth. But soon she was miserable and lonely and she cried like a
850   great waterfall and her tears made all the rivers in the world. So the great spirit sent a terrible monster, a tree with hundreds of eyes and a long green tongue, and it came chasing after her and she jumped into a lake and the tree jumped in after her, and she jumped right up into the sky. And the tree couldn't follow, he was stuck in the mud. So he picked up a big handful of
855   mud and he threw it at her, up among the stars, and it hit her on the head. And she fell down onto the earth into his arms and the ball of mud is the moon in the sky. And then they had children which is all of us.

EDWARD   It's not true, though.

JOSHUA   Of course it's not true. It's a bad story. Adam and Eve is true. God
860   made man white like him and gave him the bad woman who liked the snake and gave us all this trouble.

[CLIVE *and* HARRY *come out.*]

CLIVE   Run along now, Edward. No, you may stay. You mustn't repeat anything you hear to your mother or your grandmother or Ellen.

EDWARD   Or Mrs Saunders?

8. Lyric from 1897, by Joseph D. Skelly.

865 CLIVE Mrs Saunders is an unusual woman and does not require protection
in the same way. Harry, there was trouble last night where we expected it.
But it's all over now. Everything is under control but nobody should leave
the house today I think.

HARRY Casualties?

870 CLIVE No, none of the soldiers hurt thank God. We did a certain amount of
damage, set a village on fire and so forth.

HARRY Was that necessary?

CLIVE Obviously, it was necessary, Harry, or it wouldn't have happened. The
army will come and visit, no doubt. You'll like that, eh, Joshua, to see the
875 British army? And a treat for you, Edward, to see the soldiers. Would you
like to be a soldier?

EDWARD I'd rather be an explorer.

CLIVE Ah, Harry, like you, you see. I didn't know an explorer at his age.
Breakfast, I think, Joshua.

[CLIVE and JOSHUA go in. HARRY is following.]

880 EDWARD Uncle.

[HARRY stops.]

Harry, why won't you talk to me?

HARRY Of course I'll talk to you.

EDWARD If you won't be nice to me I'll tell father.

HARRY Edward, no, not a word, never, not to your mother, nobody, please.
885 Edward, do you understand? Please.

EDWARD I won't tell. I promise I'll never tell. I've cut my finger and sworn.

HARRY There's no need to get so excited Edward. We can't be together all
the time. I will have to leave soon anyway, and go back to the river.

EDWARD You can't, you can't go. Take me with you.

890 ELLEN Edward!

HARRY I have my duty to the Empire.

[HARRY goes in. ELLEN comes out.]

ELLEN Edward, breakfast time. Edward.

EDWARD I'm not hungry.

ELLEN Betty, please come and speak to Edward.

[BETTY comes.]

895 BETTY Why, what's the matter?

ELLEN He won't come in for breakfast.

BETTY Edward, I shall call your father.

EDWARD You can't make me eat.

[He goes in. BETTY is about to follow.]

ELLEN Betty.

[BETTY stops.]

900 Betty, when Edward goes to school will I have to leave?

BETTY Never mind, Ellen dear, you'll get another place. I'll give you an excellent reference.

ELLEN I don't want another place, Betty. I want to stay with you for ever.

BETTY If you go back to England you might get married, Ellen. You're quite
905 pretty, you shouldn't despair of getting a husband.

ELLEN I don't want a husband. I want you.

BETTY Children of your own, Ellen, think.

ELLEN I don't want children, I don't like children. I just want to be alone with you, Betty, and sing for you and kiss you because I love you, Betty.

910 BETTY I love you too, Ellen. But women have their duty as soldiers have. You must be a mother if you can.

ELLEN Betty, Betty, I love you so much. I want to stay with you for ever, my love for you is eternal, stronger than death. I'd rather die than leave you, Betty.

BETTY No you wouldn't, Ellen, don't be silly. Come, don't cry. You don't feel 915 what you think you do. It's the loneliness here and the climate is very confusing. Come and have breakfast, Ellen dear, and I'll forget all about it.

[ELLEN goes. CLIVE comes.]

BETTY Clive, please forgive me.

CLIVE Will you leave me alone?

[BETTY goes back into the house. HARRY comes.]

Women, Harry. I envy you going into the jungle, a man's life.

920 HARRY I envy you.

CLIVE Harry, I know you do. I have spoken to Betty.

HARRY I assure you, Clive—

CLIVE Please say nothing about it.

HARRY My friendship for you—

925 CLIVE Absolutely. I know the friendship between us, Harry, is not something that could be spoiled by the weaker sex. Friendship between men is a fine thing. It is the noblest form of relationship.

HARRY I agree with you.

CLIVE There is the necessity of reproduction. The family is all important. 930 And there is the pleasure. But what we put ourselves through to get the pleasure, Harry. When I heard about our fine fellows last night fighting those savages to protect us I thought yes, that is what I aspire to. I tell you Harry, in confidence, I suddenly got out of Mrs Saunders' bed and came out here on the verandah and looked at the stars.

935 HARRY I couldn't sleep last night either.

CLIVE There is something dark about women, that threatens what is best in us. Between men that light burns brightly.

HARRY I didn't know you felt like that.

CLIVE Women are irrational, demanding, inconsistent, treacherous, lustful, 940 and they smell different from us.

HARRY Clive—

CLIVE Think of the comradeship of men, Harry, sharing adventures, sharing danger, risking their lives together.

[HARRY takes hold of CLIVE.]

CLIVE What are you doing?

945 HARRY Well, you said—

CLIVE I said what?

HARRY Between men.

[CLIVE is speechless.]

I'm sorry, I misunderstood, I would never have dreamt, I thought—

CLIVE My God, Harry, how disgusting.

950 HARRY You will not betray my confidence.

CLIVE I feel contaminated.

HARRY I struggle against it. You cannot imagine the shame. I have tried everything to save myself.

CLIVE The most revolting perversion. Rome fell, Harry, and this sin can 955 destroy an empire.[9]

HARRY It is not a sin, it is a disease.

CLIVE A disease more dangerous than diphtheria. Effeminacy is contagious. How I have been deceived. Your face does not look degenerate.[1] Oh Harry, how did you sink to this?

960 HARRY Clive, help me, what am I to do?

CLIVE You have been away from England too long,

HARRY Where can I go except into the jungle to hide?

CLIVE You don't do it with the natives, Harry? My God, what a betrayal of the Queen.

965 HARRY Clive, I am like a man born crippled. Please help me.

CLIVE You must repent.

HARRY I have thought of killing myself.

CLIVE That is a sin too.

HARRY There is no way out. Clive, I beg of you, do not betray my confidence.

970 CLIVE I cannot keep a secret like this. Rivers will be named after you, it's unthinkable. You must save yourself from depravity. You must get married. You are not unattractive to women. What a relief that you and Betty were not after all—good God, how disgusting. Now Mrs Saunders. She's a woman of spirit, she could go with you on your expeditions.

975 HARRY I suppose getting married wouldn't be any worse than killing myself.

CLIVE Mrs Saunders! Mrs Saunders! Ask her now, Harry. Think of England.

[MRS SAUNDERS comes. CLIVE withdraws.]

[HARRY goes up to MRS SAUNDERS.]

HARRY Mrs Saunders, will you marry me?

MRS SAUNDERS Why?

980 HARRY We are both alone.

MRS SAUNDERS I choose to be alone, Mr Bagley. If I can look after myself, I'm sure you can. Clive, I have something important to tell you. I've just found Joshua putting earth on his head. He tells me his parents were killed last night by the British soldiers. I think you owe him an apology on behalf 985 of the Queen.

CLIVE Joshua! Joshua!

MRS SAUNDERS Mr Bagley, I could never be a wife again. There is only one thing about marriage that I like.

[JOSHUA comes.]

CLIVE Joshua, I am horrified to hear what has happened. Good God.

990 MRS SAUNDERS His father was shot. His mother died in the blaze.

[MRS SAUNDERS goes.]

CLIVE Joshua, do you want a day off? Do you want to go to your people?

9. Allusion to Edward Gibbon's *The History of the Decline and Fall of the Roman Empire* (1776–89), which chronicled the end of Roman supremacy through moral decay and ebbing manliness.

1. Allusion to Max Nordau's influential study *Degeneration* (1892), translated from German to English in 1895.

JOSHUA   Not my people, sir.

CLIVE   But you want to go to your parents' funeral?

JOSHUA   No sir.

995 CLIVE   Yes, Joshua, yes, your father and mother. I'm sure they were loyal to the Crown. I'm sure it was all a terrible mistake.

JOSHUA   My mother and father were bad people.

CLIVE   Joshua, no.

JOSHUA   You are my father and mother.

1000 CLIVE   Well really. I don't know what to say. That's very decent of you. Are you sure there's nothing I can do? You can have the day off you know.

[BETTY *comes out followed by* EDWARD.]

BETTY   What's the matter? What's happening?

CLIVE   Something terrible has happened. No, I mean some relatives of Joshua's met with an accident.

1005 JOSHUA   May I go sir?

CLIVE   Yes, yes of course. Good God, what a terrible thing. Bring us a drink will you Joshua?

[JOSHUA *goes.*]

EDWARD   What? What?

BETTY   Edward, go and do your lessons.

1010 EDWARD   What is it, Uncle Harry?

HARRY   Go and do your lessons.

ELLEN   Edward, come in here at once.

EDWARD   What's happened, Uncle Harry?

[HARRY *has moved aside.* EDWARD *follows him.*]

[ELLEN *comes out.*]

HARRY   Go away. Go inside. Ellen!

1015 ELLEN   Go inside, Edward. I shall tell your mother.

BETTY   Go inside, Edward at once. I shall tell your father.

CLIVE   Go inside, Edward. And Betty you go inside too.

[BETTY, EDWARD *and* ELLEN *go.* MAUD *comes out.*]

Go inside. And Ellen, you come outside.

[ELLEN *comes out.*]

Mr Bagley has something to say to you.

1020 HARRY   Ellen. I don't suppose you would marry me?

ELLEN   What if I said yes?

CLIVE   Run along now, you two want to be alone.

[HARRY *and* ELLEN *go out.* JOSHUA *brings* CLIVE *a drink.*]

JOSHUA   The governess and your wife, sir.

CLIVE   What's that, Joshua?

1025 JOSHUA   She talks of love to your wife, sir. I have seen them. Bad women.

CLIVE   Joshua, you go too far. Get out of my sight.

SCENE FIVE: *The verandah. A table with a white cloth. A wedding cake and a large knife. Bottles and glasses.* JOSHUA *is putting things on the table.* EDWARD *has the doll.* JOSHUA *sees him with it. He holds out his hand.* EDWARD *gives him the doll.* JOSHUA *takes the knife and cuts the doll open and shakes the sawdust out of it.* JOSHUA *throws the doll under the table.*

MAUD   Come along Edward, this is such fun.

[*Everyone enters, triumphal arch for* HARRY *and* ELLEN.]

Your mama's wedding was a splendid occasion, Edward. I cried and cried.

[ELLEN *and* BETTY *go aside.*]

1030   ELLEN   Betty, what happens with a man? I don't know what to do.

BETTY   You just keep still.

ELLEN   And what does he do?

BETTY   Harry will know what to do.

ELLEN   And is it enjoyable?

1035   BETTY   Ellen, you're not getting married to enjoy yourself.

ELLEN   Don't forget me, Betty.

[ELLEN *goes.*]

BETTY   I think my necklace has been stolen Clive. I did so want to wear it at the wedding.

EDWARD   It was Joshua. Joshua took it.

1040   CLIVE   Joshua?

EDWARD   He did, he did, I saw him with it.

HARRY   Edward, that's not true.

EDWARD   It is, it is.

HARRY   Edward, I'm afraid you took it yourself.

1045   EDWARD   I did not.

HARRY   I have seen him with it.

CLIVE   Edward, is that true? Where is it? Did you take your mother's necklace? And to try and blame Joshua, good God.

[EDWARD *runs off.*]

BETTY   Edward, come back. Have you got my necklace?

1050   HARRY   I should leave him alone. He'll bring it back.

BETTY   I wanted to wear it. I wanted to look my best at your wedding.

HARRY   You always look your best to me.

BETTY   I shall get drunk.

[MRS SAUNDERS *comes.*]

MRS SAUNDERS   The sale of my property is completed. I shall leave tomorrow.

1055   CLIVE   That's just as well. Whose protection will you seek this time?

MRS SAUNDERS   I shall go to England and buy a farm there. I shall introduce threshing machines.

CLIVE   Amazing spirit.

[*He kisses her.* BETTY *launches herself on* MRS SAUNDERS. *They fall to the ground.*]

Betty—Caroline—I don't deserve this—Harry, Harry.

[HARRY *and* CLIVE *separate them.* HARRY *holding* MRS SAUNDERS, CLIVE BETTY.]

1060   Mrs Saunders, how can you abuse my hospitality? How dare you touch my wife? You must leave here at once.

BETTY   Go away, go away. You are a wicked woman.

MAUD   Mrs Saunders, I am shocked. This is your hostess.

CLIVE   Pack your bags and leave the house this instant.

1065 MRS SAUNDERS   I was leaving anyway. There's no place for me here. I have made arrangements to leave tomorrow, and tomorrow is when I will leave. I wish you joy, Mr Bagley.

        [MRS SAUNDERS *goes.*]

CLIVE   No place for her anywhere I should think. Shocking behaviour.

BETTY   Oh Clive, forgive me, and love me like you used to.

1070 CLIVE   Were you jealous my dove? My own dear wife!

MAUD   Ah, Mr Bagley, one flesh, you see.

        [EDWARD *comes back with the necklace.*]

CLIVE   Good God, Edward, it's true.

EDWARD   I was minding it for Mama because of the troubles.

CLIVE   Well done, Edward, that was very manly of you. See Betty? Edward
1075 was protecting his mama's jewels from the rebels. What a hysterical fuss over nothing. Well done, little man. It is quite safe now. The bad men are dead. Edward, you may do up the necklace for Mama.

        [EDWARD *does up* BETTY'*s necklace, supervised by* CLIVE. JOSHUA *is drinking steadily.* ELLEN *comes back.*]

MAUD   Ah, here's the bride. Come along, Ellen, you don't cry at your own wedding, only at other people's.

1080 CLIVE   Now, speeches, speeches. Who is going to make a speech? Harry, make a speech.

HARRY   I'm no speaker. You're the one for that.

ALL   Speech, speech.

HARRY   My dear friends—what can I say—the empire—the family—the
1085 married state to which I have always aspired—your shining example of domestic bliss—my great good fortune in winning Ellen's love—happiest day of my life.

        [*Applause.*]

CLIVE   Cut the cake, cut the cake.

        [HARRY *and* ELLEN *take the knife to cut the cake.* HARRY *steps on the doll under the table.*]

HARRY   What's this?

1090 ELLEN   Oh look.

BETTY   Edward.

EDWARD   It was Joshua. It was Joshua. I saw him.

CLIVE   Don't tell lies again.

        [*He hits* EDWARD *across the side of the head.*]

Unaccustomed as I am to public speaking—
        [*Cheers.*]

1095 Harry, my friend. So brave and strong and supple. Ellen, from 'neath her veil so shyly peeking. I wish you joy. A toast— the happy couple. Dangers are past. Our enemies are killed. Put your arm around her, Harry, have a kiss— All murmuring of discontent is stilled. Long may you live in peace and joy and bliss.

        [*While he is speaking,* JOSHUA *raises his gun to shoot* CLIVE. *Only* EDWARD *sees. He does nothing to warn the others. He put his hands over his ears.*]

        [BLACK.]

Act Two

SCENE ONE

GERRY The train from Victoria to Clapham still has those compartments without a corridor. As soon as I got on the platform I saw who I wanted. Slim hips, tense shoulders, trying not to look at anyone. I put my hand on my packet just long enough so that he couldn't miss it. The train came in.
5   You don't want to get in too fast or some straight dumbo might get in with you. I sat by the window. I couldn't see where the fuck he'd got to. Then just as the whistle went he got in. Great. It's a six-minute journey so you can't start anything you can't finish. I stared at him and he unzipped his flies. Then he stopped. So I stood up and took my cock out. He took me in
10   his mouth and shut his eyes tight. He was sort of mumbling it about as if he wasn't sure what to do, so I said, A bit tighter son and he said Sorry and then got on with it. He was jerking off with his left hand, and I could see he'd got a fair-sized one. I wished he'd keep still so I could see his watch. I was getting really turned on. What if we pulled into Clapham Junction
15   now. Of course by the time we sat down again the train was just slowing up. I felt wonderful. Then he started talking. It's better if nothing is said. Once you find he's a librarian in Walthamstow[2] with a special interest in science fiction and lives with his aunt, then forget it. He said I hope you don't think I do this all the time. I said I hope you will from now on. He
20   said he would if I was on the train, but why don't we go out for a meal? I opened the door before the train stopped. I told him I lived with somebody. I don't want to know. He was jogging sideways to keep up. He said What's your phone number, you're my ideal physical type, what sign of the zodiac are you? Where do you live? Where are you going now? It's not fair. I saw
25   him at Victoria a couple of months later and I went straight down to the end of the platform and I picked up somebody really great who never said a word, just smiled.

Winter afternoon. Inside the hut of a one o'clock club,[3] a children's play centre in a park, VICTORIA *and* LIN, *mothers.* CATHY, LIN's *daughter, aged 4, played by a man, clinging to* LIN. VICTORIA *reading a book.*

CATHY Yum yum bubblegum.
       Stick it up your mother's bum.
30   When it's brown
       Pull it down
       Yum yum bubblegum.
LIN   Like your shoes, Victoria.
CATHY Jack be nimble, Jack be quick,
35   Jack jump over the candlestick.
       Silly Jack, he should jump higher,
       Goodness gracious, great balls of fire.
LIN   Cathy, do stop. Do a painting.
CATHY You do a painting.
40 LIN You do a painting.

2. Suburban community in the northeast part of London.
3. Public spaces, often connected with parks or recreation centers, where parents or caregivers can bring young children for play and supervised activities.

CATHY What shall I paint?

LIN Paint a house.

CATHY No.

LIN Princess.

45 CATHY No.

LIN Pirates.

CATHY Already done that.

LIN Spacemen.

CATHY I never paint spacemen. You know I never.

50 LIN Paint a car crash and blood everywhere.

CATHY No, don't tell me. I know what to paint.

LIN Go on then. You need an apron, where's an apron. Here.

CATHY Don't want an apron.

LIN Lift up your arms. There's a good girl.

55 CATHY I don't want to paint.

LIN Don't paint. Don't paint.

CATHY What shall I do? You paint. What shall I do Mum?

VICTORIA There's nobody on the big bike, Cathy, quick.

[CATHY *goes out.* VICTORIA *is watching the children playing outside.*]

VICTORIA Tommy, it's Jimmy's gun. Let him have it. What the hell.

[*She goes on reading. She reads while she talks.*]

60 LIN I don't know how you can concentrate.

VICTORIA You have to or you never do anything.

LIN Yeah well. It's really warm in here, that's one thing. It's better than standing out there. I got chilblains[4] last winter.

VICTORIA It is warm.

65 LIN I suppose Tommy doesn't let you read much. I expect he talks to you while you're reading.

VICTORIA Yes, he does.

LIN I didn't get very far with that book you lent me.

VICTORIA That's all right.

70 LIN I was glad to have it, though. I sit with it on my lap while I'm watching telly. Well, Cathy's off. She's frightened I'm going to leave her. It's the baby-minder[5] didn't work out when she was two, she still remembers. You can't get them used to other people if you're by yourself. It's no good blaming me. She clings round my knees every morning up the nursery[6] and they don't say anything but they make you feel you're making her do it. But I'm desperate for her to go to school. I did cry when I left her the first day. You wouldn't, you're too fucking sensible. You'll call the teacher by her first name. I really fancy you.

75

VICTORIA What?

80 LIN Put your book down will you for five minutes. You didn't hear a word I said.

VICTORIA I don't get much time to myself.

LIN Do you ever go to the movies?

VICTORIA Tommy's very funny who he's left with. My mother babysits sometimes.

85

4. Inflammation from exposure to cold.
5. Babysitter.

6. As in nursery school or preschool.

LIN   Your husband could babysit.

VICTORIA   But then we couldn't go to the movies.

LIN   You could go to the movies with me.

VICTORIA   Oh I see.

90 LIN   Couldn't you?

VICTORIA   Well yes, I could.

LIN   Friday night?

VICTORIA   What film are we talking about?

LIN   Does it matter what film?

95 VICTORIA   Of course it does.

LIN   You choose then. Friday night.

> [CATHY *comes in with gun, shoots them saying kiou kiou kiou, and runs off again.*]

Not in a foreign language, OK. You don't go to the movies to read.

> [LIN *watches the children playing outside.*]

Don't hit him, Cathy, kill him. Point the gun, kiou, kiou, kiou. That's the way.

VICTORIA   They've just banned war toys in Sweden.

100 LIN   The kids'll just hit each other more.

VICTORIA   Well, psychologists do differ in their opinions as to whether or not aggression is innate.

LIN   Yeah?

VICTORIA   I'm afraid I do let Tommy play with guns and just hope he'll get it

105 out of his system and not end up in the army.

LIN   I've got a brother in the army.

VICTORIA   Oh I'm sorry. Whereabouts is he stationed?

LIN   Belfast.[7]

VICTORIA   Oh dear.

110 LIN   I've got a friend who's Irish and we went on a Troops Out march.[8] Now my dad won't speak to me.

VICTORIA   I don't get on too well with my father either.

LIN   And your husband? How do you get on with him?

VICTORIA   Oh, fine. Up and down. You know. Very well. He helps with the

115 washing up and everything.

LIN   I left mine two years ago. He let me keep Cathy and I'm grateful for that.

VICTORIA   You shouldn't be grateful.

LIN   I'm a lesbian.

120 VICTORIA   You still shouldn't be grateful.

LIN   I'm grateful he didn't hit me harder than he did.

VICTORIA   I suppose I'm very lucky, with Martin.

LIN   Don't get at me about how I bring up Cathy, OK?

VICTORIA   I didn't.

125 LIN   Yes you did. War toys. I'll give her a rifle for Christmas and blast Tommy's pretty head off for a start.

> [VICTORIA *goes back to her book.*]

I hate men.

---

7. Capital of Northern Ireland, central to the ongoing conflict between loyalist forces that support the British government and republi- can forces that support an end to British rule.
8. Movement supporting the end of British military involvement in Northern Ireland.

VICTORIA You have to look at it in a historical perspective in terms of learnt behaviour since the industrial revolution.

130 LIN I just hate the bastards.

VICTORIA Well it's a point of view.

[*By now* CATHY *has come back in and started painting in many colours, without an apron.* EDWARD *comes in.*]

EDWARD Victoria, mother's in the park. She's walking round all the paths very fast.

VICTORIA By herself.

135 EDWARD I told her you were here.

VICTORIA Thanks.

EDWARD Come on.

VICTORIA Ten minutes talking to my mother and I have to spend two hours in a hot bath.

[VICTORIA *goes out.*]

140 LIN Shit, Cathy, what about an apron. I don't mind you having paint on your frock but if it doesn't wash off just don't tell me you can't wear a frock with paint on, OK?

CATHY OK.

LIN You're gay, aren't you?

145 EDWARD I beg your pardon?

LIN I really fancy your sister. I thought you'd understand. You do but you can go on pretending you don't, I don't mind. That's lovely Cathy, I like the green bit.

EDWARD Don't go around saying that. I might lose my job.

150 LIN The last gardener was ever so straight. He used to flash at all the little girls.

EDWARD I wish you hadn't said that about me. It's not true.

LIN It's not true and I never said it and I never thought it and I never will think it again.

155 EDWARD Someone might have heard you.

LIN Shut up about it then.

[BETTY *and* VICTORIA *come up.*]

BETTY It's quite a nasty bump.

VICTORIA He's not even crying.

BETTY I think that's very worrying. You and Edward always cried. Perhaps
160 he's got concussion.

VICTORIA Of course he hasn't Mummy.

BETTY That other little boy was very rough. Should you speak to somebody about him?

VICTORIA Tommy was hitting him with a spade.

165 BETTY Well he's a real little boy. And so brave not to cry. You must watch him for signs of drowsiness. And nausea. If he's sick in the night, phone an ambulance. Well, you're looking very well darling, a bit tired, a bit peaky. I think the fresh air agrees with Edward. He likes the open-air life because of growing up in Africa. He misses the sunshine, don't you, darling? We'll
170 soon have Edward back on his feet. What fun it is here.

VICTORIA This is Lin. And Cathy.

BETTY Oh Cathy what a lovely painting. What is it? Well I think it's a house on fire. I think all that red is a fire. Is that right? Or do I see legs, is it a

175 horse? Can I have the lovely painting or is it for Mummy? Children have such imagination, it makes them so exhausting. [*To* LIN.] I'm sure you're wonderful, just like Victoria. I had help with my children. One does need help. That was in Africa of course so there wasn't the servant problem. This is my son Edward. This is—

EDWARD   Lin.

180 BETTY   Lin, this is Lin. Edward is doing something such fun, he's working in the park as a gardener. He does look exactly like a gardener.

EDWARD   I am a gardener.

BETTY   He's certainly making a stab at it. Well it will be a story to tell. I expect he will write a novel about it, or perhaps a television series. Well what a
185 pretty child Cathy is. Victoria was a pretty child just like a little doll—you can't be certain how they'll grow up. I think Victoria's very pretty but she doesn't make the most of herself, do you darling, it's not the fashion I'm told but there are still women who dress out of *Vogue*, well we hope that's not what Martin looks for, though in many ways I wish it was, I don't know
190 what it is Martin looks for and nor does he I'm afraid poor Martin. Well I am rattling on. I like your skirt dear but your shoes won't do at all. Well do they have lady gardeners, Edward, because I'm going to leave your father and I think I might need to get a job, not a gardener really of course. I haven't got green fingers I'm afraid, everything I touch shrivels straight up. Vicky gave
195 me a poinsettia last Christmas and the leaves all fell off on Boxing Day.[9] Well good heavens, look what's happened to that lovely painting.

[CATHY *has slowly and carefully been going over the whole sheet with black paint. She has almost finished.*]

LIN   What you do that for silly? It was nice.

CATHY   I like your earrings.

VICTORIA   Did you say you're leaving Daddy?

200 BETTY   Do you darling? Shall I put them on you? My ears aren't pierced, I never wanted that, they just clip on the lobe.

LIN   She'll get paint on you, mind.

BETTY   There's a pretty girl. It doesn't hurt does it? Well you'll grow up to know you have to suffer a little bit for beauty.

205 CATHY   Look mum I'm pretty, I'm pretty, I'm pretty.

LIN   Stop showing off Cathy.

VICTORIA   It's time we went home. Tommy, time to go home. Last go then, all right.

EDWARD   Mum did I hear you right just now?

210 CATHY   I want my ears pierced.

BETTY   Ooh, not till you're big.

CATHY   I know a girl got her ears pierced and she's three. She's got real gold.

BETTY   I don't expect she's English, darling. Can I give her a sweetie? I know they're not very good for the teeth, Vicky gets terribly cross with me. What
215 does Mummy say?

LIN   Just one, thank you very much.

CATHY   I like your beads.

BETTY   Yes they are pretty. Here you are.

[*It is the necklace from Act One.*]

9. December 26; traditionally, the day for boxing up Christmas gifts.

CATHY   Look at me, look at me. Vicky, Vicky look at me.

220 LIN   You look lovely, come on now.

CATHY   And your hat, and your hat.

LIN   No, that's enough.

BETTY   Of course she can have my hat.

CATHY   Yes, yes, hat, hat. Look look look.

225 LIN   That's enough, please, stop it now. Hat off, bye-bye hat.

CATHY   Give me my hat.

LIN   Bye-bye beads.

BETTY   It's just fun.

LIN   It's very nice of you.

230 CATHY   I want my beads.

LIN   Where's the other earring?

CATHY   I want my beads.

> [CATHY *has the other earring in her hand. Meanwhile* VICTORIA *and*
> EDWARD *look for it.*]

EDWARD   Is it on the floor?

VICTORIA   Don't step on it.

235 EDWARD   Where?

CATHY   I want my beads. I want my beads.

LIN   You'll have a smack.

> [LIN *gets the earring from* CATHY.]

CATHY   I want my beads.

BETTY   Oh dear oh dear. Have you got the earring? Thank you darling.

240 CATHY   I want my beads, you're horrid, I hate you, Mum, you smell.

BETTY   This is the point you see where one had help. Well it's been lovely
seeing you dears and I'll be off again on my little walk.

VICTORIA   You're leaving him? Really?

BETTY   Yes you hear a'right, Vicky, yes. I'm finding a little flat, that will be
245 fun. Bye-bye Tommy, Granny's going now. Tommy don't hit that little girl,
say goodbye to Granny.

> [BETTY *goes.*]

VICTORIA   Fucking hell.

EDWARD   Puking Jesus.

LIN   That was news was it, leaving your father?

250 EDWARD   They're going to want so much attention.

VICTORIA   Does everybody hate their mothers?

EDWARD   Mind you, I wouldn't live with him.

LIN   Stop snivelling, pigface. Where's your coat? Be quiet now and we'll have
doughnuts for tea and if you keep on we'll have dogshit on toast.

> [CATHY *laughs so much she lies on the floor.*]

255 VICTORIA   Tommy, you've had two last goes. Last last last last go.

LIN   Not that funny, come on, coat on.

EDWARD   Can I have your painting?

CATHY   What for?

EDWARD   For a friend of mine.

260 CATHY   What's his name?

EDWARD   Gerry.

CATHY   How old is he?

EDWARD   Thirty-two.

CATHY   You can if you like. I don't care. Kiou kiou kiou kiou.

[CATHY *goes out.* EDWARD *takes the painting and goes out.*]

265 LIN   Will you have sex with me?

VICTORIA   I don't know what Martin would say. Does it count as adultery with a woman?

LIN   You'd enjoy it.

SCENE TWO: *Spring. Swing, bench, pond nearby.* EDWARD *is gardening.* GERRY *is sitting on a bench.*

EDWARD   I sometimes pretend we don't know each other. And you've come to
270   the park to eat your sandwiches and look at me.

GERRY   That would be more interesting, yes. Come and sit down.

EDWARD   If the superintendent comes I'll be in trouble. It's not my dinner time yet. Where were you last night? I think you owe me an explanation. We always do tell each other everything.

275 GERRY   Is that a rule?

EDWARD   It's what we agreed.

GERRY   It's a habit we've got into. Look, I was drunk. I woke up at four o'clock on somebody's floor. I was sick. I hadn't any money for a cab. I went back to sleep.

280 EDWARD   You could have phoned.

GERRY   There wasn't a phone.

EDWARD   Sorry.

GERRY   There was a phone and I didn't phone you. Leave it alone, Eddy, I'm warning you.

285 EDWARD   What are you going to do to me, then?

GERRY   I'm going to the pub.

EDWARD   I'll join you in ten minutes.

GERRY   I didn't ask you to come.

[EDWARD *goes.* CATHY *is on the swing.*]

CATHY   Batman and Robin
290   Had a batmobile.
Robin done a fart
And paralysed the wheel.
The wheel couldn't take it,
The engine fell apart,
295   All because of Robin
And his supersonic fart.

[CATHY *goes.* MARTIN, VICTORIA *and* BETTY *walking slowly.*]

MARTIN   Tom!

BETTY   He'll fall in.

VICTORIA   No he won't.

300 MARTIN   Don't go too near the edge, Tom. Throw the bread from there. The ducks can get it.

BETTY   I'll never be able to manage. If I can't even walk down the street by myself. Everything looks so fierce.

VICTORIA   Just watch Tommy feeding the ducks.

305 BETTY   He's going to fall in. Make Martin make him move back.

VICTORIA   He's not going to fall in.

BETTY   It's since I left your father.

VICTORIA   Mummy, it really was the right decision.

BETTY   Everything comes at me from all directions. Martin despises me.

310 VICTORIA   Of course he doesn't Mummy.

BETTY   Of course he does.

MARTIN   Throw the bread. That's the way. The duck can get it. Quack quack quack quack quack.

BETTY   I don't want to take pills. Lin says you can't trust doctors.

315 VICTORIA   You're not taking pills. You're doing very well.

BETTY   But I'm so frightened.

VICTORIA   What are you frightened of?

BETTY   Victoria, you always ask that as if there was suddenly going to be an answer.

320 VICTORIA   Are you all right sitting there?

BETTY   Yes, yes. Go and be with Martin.

[VICTORIA *joins* MARTIN. BETTY *stays sitting on the bench.*]

MARTIN   You take the job, you go to Manchester. You turn it down, you stay in London. People are making decisions like this every day of the week. It needn't be for more than a year. You get long vacations. Our relationship
325   might well stand the strain of that, and if it doesn't we're better out of it. I don't want to put any pressure on you. I'd just like to know so we can sell the house. I think we're moving into an entirely different way of life if you go to Manchester because it won't end there. We could keep the house as security for Tommy but he might as well get used to the fact that life nowadays is
330   insecure. You should ask your mother what she thinks and then do the opposite. I could just take that room in Barbara's house, and then we could baby-sit for each other. You think that means I want to fuck Barbara. I don't. Well I do, but I won't. And even if I did, what's a fuck between friends? Who are we meant to do it with, strangers? Whatever you want to do, I'll be delighted.
335   If you could just let me know what it is I'm to be delighted about. Don't cry again, Vicky, I'm not the sort of man who makes women cry.

[LIN *has come in and sat down with* BETTY.]

[CATHY *joins them. She is wearing a pink dress and carrying a rifle.*]

LIN   I've bought her three new frocks. She won't wear jeans to school any more because Tracy and Mandy called her a boy.

CATHY   Tracy's got a perm.

340 LIN   You should have shot them.

CATHY   They're coming to tea and we've got to have trifle. Not trifle you make, trifle out of a packet.[1] And you've got to wear a skirt. And tights.

LIN   Tracy's mum wears jeans.

CATHY   She does not. She wears velvet.

345 BETTY   Well I think you look very pretty. And if that gun has caps in it please take it a long way away.

---

1. Traditional English layered dessert made with sponge cake, jam, custard, and whipped cream. The packet version includes cake and mixes for the other components.

CATHY   It's got red caps. They're louder.

MARTIN   Do you think you're well enough to do this job? You don't have to do
it. No one's going to think any the less of you if you stay here with me.
350   There's no point being so liberated you make yourself cry all the time. You
stay and we'll get everything sorted out. What it is about sex, when we talk
while it's happening I get to feel it's like a driving lesson. Left, right, a little
faster, carry on, slow down—

    [CATHY shoots VICTORIA.]

CATHY   You're dead Vicky.

355 VICTORIA   Aaaargh.

CATHY   Fall over.

VICTORIA   I'm not falling over, the ground's wet.

CATHY   You're dead.

VICTORIA   Yes, I'm dead.

360 CATHY   The Dead Hand Gang fall over. They said I had to fall over in the
mud or I can't play. That duck's a mandarin.

MARTIN   Which one? Look, Tommy?

CATHY   That's a diver. It's got a yellow eye and it dives. That's a goose. Tommy
doesn't know it's a goose, he thinks it's a duck. The babies get eaten by wea-
365   sels. Kiou kiou.

    [CATHY goes.]

MARTIN   So I lost my erection last night, not because I'm not prepared to
talk, it's just that taking in technical information is a different part of the
brain and also I don't like to feel that you do it better to yourself. I have
read the Hite Report.[2] I do know that women have to learn to get their
370   pleasure despite our clumsy attempts at expressing undying devotion and
ecstasy, and that what we spent our adolescence thinking was an animal
urge we had to suppress is in fact a fine art we have to acquire. I'm not like
whatever percentage of American men have become impotent as a direct
result of women's liberation, which I am totally in favour of, more I some-
375   times think than you are yourself. Nor am I one of your villains who sticks
it in, bangs away, and falls asleep. My one aim is to give you pleasure. My
one aim is to give you rolling orgasms like I do other women. So why the
hell don't you have them? My analysis for what it's worth is that despite all
my efforts you still feel dominated by me. I in fact think it's very sad that
380   you don't feel able to take that job. It makes me feel very guilty. I don't want
you to do it just because I encourage you to do it. But don't you think you'd
feel better if you did take the job? You're the one who's talked about freedom. You're the one who's experimenting with bisexuality, and I don't stop
you, I think women have something to give each other. You seem to need
385   the mutual support. You find me too overwhelming. So follow it through,
go away, leave me and Tommy alone for a bit, we can manage perfectly well
without you. I'm not putting any pressure on you but I don't think you're
being a whole person. God knows I do everything I can to make you stand
on your own two feet. Just be yourself. You don't seem to realise how
390   insulting it is to me that you can't get yourself together.

    [MARTIN and VICTORIA go.]

2. Shere Hite's influential 1976 study of female sexuality.

BETTY You must be very lonely yourself with no husband. You don't miss him?

LIN Not really, no.

BETTY Maybe you like being on your own.

395 LIN I'm seeing quite a lot of Vicky. I don't live alone. I live with Cathy.

BETTY I would have been frightened when I was your age. I thought, the poor children, their mother all alone.

LIN I've a lot of friends.

BETTY I find when I'm making tea I put out two cups. It's strange not having
400 a man in the house. You don't know who to do things for.

LIN Yourself.

BETTY Oh, that's very selfish.

LIN Have you any women friends?

BETTY I've never been so short of men's company that I've had to bother
405 with women.

LIN Don't you like women?

BETTY They don't have such interesting conversations as men. There has never been a woman composer of genius. They don't have a sense of humour. They spoil things for themselves with their emotions. I can't say I do like
410 women very much, no.

LIN But you're a woman.

BETTY There's nothing says you have to like yourself.

LIN Do you like me?

BETTY There's no need to take it personally, Lin.

  [MARTIN and VICTORIA come back.]

415 MARTIN Do you know if you put cocaine on your prick you can keep up it all night? The only thing is of course it goes numb so you don't feel anything. But you would, that's the main thing. I just want to make you happy.

BETTY Vicky, I'd like to go home.

VICTORIA Yes, Mummy, of course.

420 BETTY I'm sorry, dear.

VICTORIA I think Tommy would like to stay out a bit longer.

LIN Hello, Martin. We do keep out of each other's way.

MARTIN I think that's the best thing to do.

BETTY Perhaps you'd walk home with me, Martin. I do feel safer with a man.
425 The park is so large the grass seems to tilt.

MARTIN Yes, I'd like to go home and do some work. I'm writing a novel about women from the women's point of view.

  [MARTIN and BETTY go. LIN and VICTORIA are alone. They embrace.]

VICTORIA Why the hell can't he just be a wife and come with me? Why does Martin make me tie myself in knots? No wonder we can't just have a simple
430 fuck. No, not Martin, why do I make myself tie myself in knots. It's got to stop, Lin. I'm not like that with you. Would you love me if I went to Manchester?

LIN Yes.

VICTORIA Would you love me if I went on a climbing expedition in the Andes
435 mountains?

LIN Yes.

VICTORIA Would you love me if my teeth fell out?

LIN Yes.

VICTORIA Would you love me if I loved ten other people?
440 LIN And me?
VICTORIA Yes.
LIN Yes.
VICTORIA And I feel apologetic for not being quite so subordinate as I was. I am more intelligent than him. I am brilliant.
445 LIN Leave him Vic. Come and live with me.
VICTORIA Don't be silly
LIN Silly, Christ, don't then. I'm not asking because I need to live with someone. I'd enjoy it, that's all, we'd both enjoy it. Fuck you. Cathy, for fuck's sake stop throwing stones at the ducks. The man's going to get you.
450 VICTORIA What man? Do you need a man to frighten your child with?
LIN My mother said it.
VICTORIA You're so inconsistent, Lin.
LIN I've changed who I sleep with, I can't change everything.
VICTORIA Like when I had to stop you getting a job in a boutique and col-
455 laborating with sexist consumerism.
LIN I should have got that job, Cathy would have liked it. Why shouldn't I have some decent clothes? I'm sick of dressing like a boy, why can't I look sexy, wouldn't you love me?
VICTORIA Lin, you've no analysis.
460 LIN No but I'm good at kissing aren't I? I give Cathy guns, my mum didn't give me guns. I dress her in jeans, she wants to wear dresses. I don't know. I can't work it out I don't want to. You read too many books, you get at me all the time, you're worse to me than Martin is to you, you piss me off, my brother's been killed. I'm sorry to win the argument that way but there
465 it is.
VICTORIA What do you mean win the argument?
LIN I mean be nice to me.
VICTORIA In Belfast?
LIN I heard this morning. Don't don't start. I've hardly seen him for two
470 years. I rung my father. You'd think I shot him myself. He doesn't want me to go to the funeral.
    [CATHY approaches.]
VICTORIA What will you do?
LIN Go of course.
CATHY What is it? Who's killed? What?
475 LIN It's Bill. Your uncle. In the army. Bill that gave you the blue teddy.
CATHY Can I have his gun?
LIN It's time we went home. Time you went to bed.
CATHY No it's not.
LIN We go home and you have tea and you have a bath and you go to bed.
480 CATHY Fuck off.
LIN Cathy, shut up.
VICTORIA It's only half past five, why don't we—
LIN I'll tell you why she has to go to bed—
VICTORIA She can come home with me.
485 LIN Because I want her out the fucking way.
VICTORIA She can come home with me.
CATHY I'm not going to bed.

LIN   I want her home with me not home with you, I want her in bed, I want
today over.

490   CATHY   I'm not going to bed.

[LIN *hits* CATHY, CATHY *cries.*]

LIN   And shut up or I'll give you something to cry for.

CATHY   I'm not going to bed.

VICTORIA   Cathy—

LIN   You keep out of it.

495   VICTORIA   Lin for God's sake.

[*They are all shouting.* CATHY *runs off.* LIN *and* VICTORIA *are silent. Then
they laugh and embrace.*]

LIN   Where's Tommy?

VICTORIA   What? Didn't he go with Martin?

LIN   Did he?

VICTORIA   God oh God.

500   LIN   Cathy! Cathy!

VICTORIA   I haven't thought about him. How could I not think about him?
Tommy!

LIN   Cathy! Come on, quick, I want some help.

VICTORIA   Tommy! Tommy!

[CATHY *comes back.*]

505   LIN   Where's Tommy? Have you seen him? Did he go with Martin? Do you
know where he is?

CATHY   I showed him the goose. We went in the bushes.

LIN   Then what?

CATHY   I came back on the swing.

510   VICTORIA   And Tommy? Where was Tommy?

CATHY   He fed the ducks.

LIN   No that was before.

CATHY   He did a pee in the bushes. I helped him with his trousers.

VICTORIA   And after that?

515   CATHY   He fed the ducks.

VICTORIA   No no.

CATHY   He liked the ducks. I expect he fell in.

LIN   Did you see him fall in?

VICTORIA   Tommy! Tommy!

520   LIN   What's the last time you saw him?

CATHY   He did a pee.

VICTORIA   Mummy said he would fall in. Oh God, Tommy!

LIN   We'll go round the pond. We'll go opposite ways round the pond.

ALL   [*shout*]   Tommy!

[VICTORIA *and* LIN *go off opposite sides.* CATHY *climbs the bench.*]

525   CATHY   Georgie Best superstar
Walks like a woman and wears a bra.
There he is! I see him! Mum! Vicky! There he is!
He's in the bushes.

[LIN *comes back.*]

LIN   Come on Cathy love, let's go home.

530   CATHY   Vicky's got him.

LIN   Come on.

CATHY   Is she cross?

LIN   No. Come on.

CATHY   I found him.

535   LIN   Yes. Come on.

[CATHY *gets off the bench.* CATHY *and* LIN *hug.*]

CATHY   I'm watching telly.

LIN   OK.

CATHY   After the news.

LIN   OK.

540   CATHY   I'm not going to bed.

LIN   Yes you are.

CATHY   I'm not going to bed now.

LIN   Not now but early.

CATHY   How early?

545   LIN   Not late.

CATHY   How not late?

LIN   Early.

CATHY   How early?

LIN   Not late.

[*They go off together.* GERRY *comes on. He waits.* EDWARD *comes.*]

550   EDWARD   I've got some fish for dinner. I thought I'd make a cheese sauce.

GERRY   I won't be in.

EDWARD   Where are you going?

GERRY   For a start I'm going to a sauna. Then I'll see.

EDWARD   All right. What time will you be back? We'll eat then.

555   GERRY   You're getting like a wife.

EDWARD   I don't mind that.

GERRY   Why don't I do the cooking some time?

EDWARD   You can if you like. You're just not as good at it that's all. Do it tonight.

560   GERRY   I won't be in tonight.

EDWARD   Do it tomorrow. If we can't eat it we can always go to a restaurant.

GERRY   Stop it.

EDWARD   Stop what?

GERRY   Just be yourself.

565   EDWARD   I don't know what you mean. Everyone's always tried to stop me being feminine and now you are too.

GERRY   You're putting it on.

EDWARD   I like doing the cooking. I like being fucked. You do like me like this really.

570   GERRY   I'm bored, Eddy.

EDWARD   Go to the sauna.

GERRY   And you'll stay home and wait up for me.

EDWARD   No, I'll go to bed and read a book.

GERRY   Or knit. You could knit me a pair of socks.

575   EDWARD   I might knit. I like knitting.

GERRY   I don't mind if you knit. I don't want to be married.

EDWARD   I do.

GERRY   Well I'm divorcing you.

EDWARD   I wouldn't want to keep a man who wants his freedom.

580 GERRY   Eddy, do stop playing the injured wife, it's not funny.

EDWARD   I'm not playing. It's true.

GERRY   I'm not the husband so you can't be the wife.

EDWARD   I'll always be here, Gerry, if you want to come back. I know you
men like to go off by yourselves. I don't think I could love deeply more than
585 once. But I don't think I can face life on my own so don't leave it too long
or it may be too late.

GERRY   What are you trying to turn me into?

EDWARD   A monster, darling, which is what you are.

GERRY   I'll collect my stuff from the flat in the morning.

[GERRY goes. EDWARD sits on the bench. It gets darker. VICTORIA comes.]

590 VICTORIA   Tommy dropped a toy car somewhere, you haven't seen it? It's red.
He says it's his best one. Oh the hell with it. Martin's reading him a story.
There, isn't it quiet?

[They sit on the bench, holding hands.]

EDWARD   I like women.

VICTORIA   That should please Mother.

595 EDWARD   No listen Vicky. I'd rather be a woman. I wish I had breasts like
that, I think they're beautiful. Can I touch them?

VICTORIA   What, pretending they're yours?

EDWARD   No, I know it's you.

VICTORIA   I think I should warn you I'm enjoying this.

600 EDWARD   I'm sick of men.

VICTORIA   I'm sick of men.

EDWARD   I think I'm a lesbian.

SCENE THREE: *The park. Summer night.* VICTORIA, LIN *and* EDWARD *drunk.*

LIN   Where are you?

VICTORIA   Come on.

605 EDWARD   Do we sit in a circle?

VICTORIA   Sit in a triangle.

EDWARD   You're good at mathematics. She's good at mathematics.

VICTORIA   Give me your hand. We all hold hands.

EDWARD   Do you know what to do?

610 LIN   She's making it up.

VICTORIA   We start off by being quiet.

EDWARD   What?

LIN   Hush.

EDWARD   Will something appear?

615 VICTORIA   It was your idea.

EDWARD   It wasn't my idea. It was your book.

LIN   You said call up the goddess.

EDWARD   I don't remember saying that.

LIN   We could have called her on the telephone.

620 EDWARD   Don't be so silly, this is meant to be frightening.

LIN   Kiss me.

VICTORIA   Are we going to do it?

LIN   We're doing it.

VICTORIA   A ceremony.

625 LIN   It's very sexy, you said it is. You said the women were priests in the temples and fucked all the time. I'm just helping.

VICTORIA   As long as it's sacred.

LIN   It's very sacred.

VICTORIA   Innin, Innana, Nana, Nut, Anat, Anahita, Istar, Isis.[3]

630 LIN   I can't remember all that.

VICTORIA   Lin! Innin, Innana, Nana, Nut, Anat, Anahita, Istar, Isis.

> [LIN *and* EDWARD *join in and continue the chant under* VICTORIA's *speech.*]

Goddess of many names, oldest of the old, who walked in chaos and created life, hear us calling you back through time, before Jehovah, before Christ, before men drove you out and burnt your temples, hear us, Lady, 635 give us back what we were, give us the history we haven't had, make us the women we can't be.

ALL   Innin, Innana, Nana, Nut, Anat, Anahita, Istar, Isis.

> [*Chant continues under other speeches.*]

LIN   Come back, goddess.

VICTORIA   Goddess of the sun and the moon her brother, little goddess of 640 Crete with snakes in your hands.

LIN   Goddess of breasts.

VICTORIA   Goddess of cunts.

LIN   Goddess of fat bellies and babies. And blood blood blood.

> [*Chant continues.*]

I see her.

645 EDWARD   What?

> [*They stop chanting.*]

LIN   I see her. Very tall. Snakes in her hands. Light light light—look out! Did I give you a fright?

EDWARD   I was terrified.

VICTORIA   Don't spoil it Lin.

650 LIN   It's all out of a book.

VICTORIA   Innin Innana I can't do it now. I was really enjoying myself.

LIN   She won't appear with a man here.

VICTORIA   They had men, they had sons and lovers.

EDWARD   They had eunuchs.

655 LIN   Don't give us ideas.

VICTORIA   There's Attis and Tammuz, they're torn to pieces.[4]

EDWARD   Tear me to pieces, Lin.

VICTORIA   The priestess chose a lover for a year and he was king because she chose him and then he was killed at the end of the year.

660 EDWARD   Hurray.

---

3. Mythological goddesses from various ancient cultures. Innin, Innana, and Nana are all names for the Sumerian goddess of fertility and sexual love; Istar is the Akkadian name and Anahita the Persian name for the same goddess. Anat is the Egyptian war goddess; Isis is the Egyptian mother goddess; and Nut is the Egyptian sky goddess.

4. Attis was a Phrygian semideity associated with castration; he was also a vegetation god. Tammuz was his Sumerran counterpart, consort of Innana.

VICTORIA   And the women had the children and nobody knew it was done by fucking so they didn't know about their fathers and nobody cared who the father was and the property was passed down through the maternal line—

LIN   Don't turn it into a lecture, Vicky, it's meant to be an orgy.

665 VICTORIA   It never hurts to understand the theoretical background. You can't separate fucking and economics.

LIN   Give us a kiss.

EDWARD   Shut up, listen.

LIN   What?

670 EDWARD   There's somebody there.

LIN   Where?

EDWARD   There.

VICTORIA   The priestesses used to make love to total strangers.

LIN   Go on then, I dare you.

675 EDWARD   Go on, Vicky.

VICTORIA   He won't know it's a sacred rite in honour of the goddess.

EDWARD   We'll know.

LIN   We can tell him.

EDWARD   It's not what he thinks, it's what we think.

680 LIN   Don't tell him till after, he'll run a mile.

VICTORIA   Hello. We're having an orgy. Do you want me to suck your cock?

[*The stranger approaches. It is* MARTIN.]

MARTIN   There you are. I've been looking everywhere. What the hell are you doing. Do you know what the time is? You're all pissed out of your minds.

[*They leap on* MARTIN, *and pull him down and start to make love to him.*]

Well that's all right. If all we're talking about is having a lot of sex there's no
685 problem. I was all for the sixties when liberation just meant fucking.

[*Another stranger approaches.*]

LIN   Hey you, come here. Come and have sex with us.

VICTORIA   Who is it?

[*The stranger is a* SOLDIER.]

LIN   It's my brother.

EDWARD   Lin, don't.

690 LIN   It's my brother.

VICTORIA   It's her sense of humour, you get used to it.

LIN   Shut up Vicky, it's my brother. Isn't it? Bill?

SOLDIER   Yes it's me.

LIN   And you are dead.

695 SOLDIER   Fucking dead all right yeah.

LIN   Have you come back to tell us something?

SOLDIER   No I've come for a fuck. That was the worst thing in the fucking army. Never fucking let out. Can't fucking talk to Irish girls. Fucking bored out of my fucking head. That or shit scared. For five minutes I'd be glad I
700 wasn't bored, then I was fucking scared. Then we'd come in and I'd be glad I wasn't scared and then I was fucking bored. Spend the day reading fucking porn and the fucking night wanking. Man's nicking life in the fucking army? No fun when the fucking kids hate you. I got so I fucking wanted to kill someone and I got fucking killed myself and I want a fuck.

705 LIN   I miss you. Bill. Bill.

[LIN *collapses.* SOLDIER *goes.* VICTORIA *comforts* LIN.]

EDWARD   Let's go home.

LIN   Victoria, come home with us. Victoria's coming to live with me and Edward.

MARTIN   Tell me about it in the morning.

710   LIN   It's true.

VICTORIA   It is true.

MARTIN   Tell me when you're sober.

[EDWARD, LIN, VICTORIA *go off together.*]
[MARTIN *goes off alone.* GERRY *comes on.*]

GERRY   I come here sometimes at night and pick somebody up. Sometimes I come here at night and don't pick anybody up. I do also enjoy walking

715   about at night. There's never any trouble finding someone. I can have sex any time. You might not find the type you most fancy every day of the week, but there's plenty of people about who just enjoy having a good time. I quite like living alone. If I live with someone I get annoyed with them. Edward always put on Capital Radio[5] when he got up. The silence gets wasted. I wake up

720   at four o'clock sometimes. Birds. Silence. If I bring somebody home I never let them stay the night. Edward! Edward!

[EDWARD *from Act One comes on.*]

EDWARD   Gerry, I love you.

GERRY   Yes, I know. I love you, too.

EDWARD   You know what we did? I want to do it again. I think about it all the

725   time. Don't you want to any more?

GERRY   Yes, of course.

ALL [*sing 'Cloud Nine'*]

It'll be fine when you reach Cloud Nine.

Mist was rising and the night was dark.
Me and my baby took a walk in the park.

730   He said Be mine and you're on Cloud Nine.

Better watch out when you're on Cloud Nine.

Smoked some dope on the playground swings
Higher and higher on true love's wings
He said Be mine and you're on Cloud Nine.

735   Twenty-five years on the same Cloud Nine.

Who did she meet on her first blind date?
The guys were no surprise but the lady was great
They were women in love, they were on Cloud Nine.

Two the same, they were on Cloud Nine.

740   The bride was sixty-five, the groom was seventeen,
They fucked in the back of the black limousine.
It was divine in the silver Cloud Nine.

Simply divine in their silver Cloud Nine.

The wife's lover's children and my lover's wife,

5. United Kingdom hit music station.

745   Cooking in my kitchen, confusing my life.
        And it's upside down when you reach Cloud Nine.

        Upside down when you reach Cloud Nine.[6]

SCENE FOUR: *The park. Afternoon in late summer.* MARTIN, CATHY, EDWARD.

CATHY   Under the bramble bushes,
        Under the sea boom boom boom,
750   True love for you my darling,
        True love for me my darling,
        When we are married,
        We'll raise a family.
        Boy for you, girl for me,
755   Boom tiddley oom boom.[7]
        SEXY.

EDWARD   You'll have Tommy and Cathy tonight then OK? Tommy's still on
antibiotics, do make him finish the bottle, he takes it in Ribena.[8] It's no
good in orange, he spits it out. Remind me to give you Cathy's swimming
760 things.

CATHY   I did six strokes, didn't I Martin? Did I do a width? How many strokes
is a length? How many miles is a swimming pool? I'm going to take my
bronze and silver and gold and diamond.

MARTIN   Is Tommy still wetting the bed?

765 EDWARD   Don't get angry with him about it.

MARTIN   I just need to go to the launderette so I've got a spare sheet. Of course
I don't get fucking angry, Eddy, for God's sake. I don't like to say he is my
son but he is my son. I'm surprised I'm not wetting the bed myself.

CATHY   I don't wet the bed ever. Do you wet the bed Martin?

770 MARTIN   No.

CATHY   You said you did.

        [BETTY *comes.*]

BETTY   I do miss the sun living in England but today couldn't be more beautiful. You appreciate the weekend when you're working. Betty's been at work
this week, Cathy. It's terribly tiring, Martin, I don't know how you've done it
775 all these years. And the money, I feel like a child with money, Clive always
paid everything but I do understand it perfectly well. Look, Cathy, let me
show you my money.

CATHY   I'll count it. Let me count it. What's that?

BETTY   Five pounds. Five and five is—?

780 CATHY   One two three—

BETTY   Five and five is ten, and five—

CATHY   If I get it right can I have one?

EDWARD   No you can't.

        [CATHY *goes on counting the money.*]

BETTY   I never like to say anything, Martin, or you'll think I'm being a
785 mother-in-law.

EDWARD   Which you are.

---

6. Churchill and Andy Roberts composed this song for the play.
7. Traditional English children's rhymed clap- ping game.
8. Popular British fruit beverage, traditionally made from black currants.

BETTY Thank you, Edward, I'm not talking to you. Martin, I think you're being wonderful. Vicky will come back. Just let her stay with Lin till she sorts herself out. It's very nice for a girl to have a friend, I had friends at
790 school, that was very nice. But I'm sure Lin and Edward don't want her with them all the time. I'm not at all shocked that Lin and Edward aren't married and she already has a child, we all know first marriages don't always work out. But really Vicky must be in the way. And poor little Tommy. I hear he doesn't sleep properly and he's had a cough.
795 MARTIN No, he's fine, Betty, thank you.
CATHY My bed's horrible. I want to sleep in the big bed with Lin and Vicky and Eddy and I do get in if I've got a bad dream, and my bed's got a bump right in my back. I want to sleep in a tent.
BETTY Well Tommy has got a nasty cough, Martin, whatever you say.
800 EDWARD He's over that. He's got some medicine.
MARTIN He takes it in Ribena.
BETTY Well I'm glad to hear it. Look what a lot of money, Cathy, and I sit behind a desk on my own and I answer the telephone and keep the doctor's appointment book and it really is great fun.
805 CATHY Can we go camping, Martin, in a tent? We could take the Dead Hand Gang.
BETTY Not those big boys, Cathy? They're far too big and rough for you. They climb back into the park after dark. I'm sure Mummy doesn't let you play with them, does she Edward? Well I don't know.

[Ice-cream bells.]

810 CATHY Ice cream. Martin you promised. I'll have a double ninety-nine. No I'll have a shandy lolly.[9] Betty, you have a shandy lolly and I'll have a lick. No, you have a double ninety-nine and I'll have the chocolate.

[MARTIN, CATHY and BETTY go, leaving EDWARD. GERRY comes.]

GERRY Hello, Eddy. Thought I might find you here.
EDWARD Gerry.
815 GERRY Not working today then?
EDWARD I don't work here any more.
GERRY Your mum got you into a dark suit?
EDWARD No of course not. I'm on the dole.[1] I am working, though, I do housework.
820 GERRY Whose wife are you now then?
EDWARD Nobody's. I don't think like that any more. I'm living with some women.
GERRY What women?
EDWARD It's my sister, Vic, and her lover. They go out to work and I look
825 after the kids.
GERRY I thought for a moment you said you were living with women.
EDWARD We do sleep together, yes.
GERRY I was passing the park anyway so I thought I'd look in. I was in the sauna the other night and I saw someone who looked like you but it wasn't.
830 I had sex with him anyway.

9. Nonalcoholic beer and lemon-flavored popsicle; a double ninety-nine is a vanilla soft-serve cone with two flaky chocolate bars inserted.
1. Public assistance or welfare.

EDWARD   I do go to the sauna sometimes.

[CATHY *comes, gives* EDWARD *an ice cream, goes.*]

GERRY   I don't think I'd like living with children. They make a lot of noise don't they?

EDWARD   I tell them to shut up and they shut up. I wouldn't want to leave
835   them at the moment.

GERRY   Look why don't we go for a meal some time?

EDWARD   Yes I'd like that. Where are you living now?

GERRY   Same place.

EDWARD   I'll come round for you tomorrow night about 7.30.

840 GERRY   Great.

[EDWARD *goes.* HARRY *comes.* HARRY *and* GERRY *pick each other up. They go off.* BETTY *comes back.*]

BETTY   No, the ice cream was my treat, Martin. Off you go. I'm going to have a quiet sit in the sun.

[MAUD *comes.*]

MAUD   Let Mrs Saunders be a warning to you, Betty. I know what it is to be unprotected.

845 BETTY   But Mother, I have a job. I earn money.

MAUD   I know we have our little differences but I always want what is best for you.

[ELLEN *comes.*]

ELLEN   Betty, what happens with a man?

BETTY   You just keep still.

850 ELLEN   And is it enjoyable? Don't forget me, Betty.

[MAUD *and* ELLEN *go.*]

BETTY   I used to think Clive was the one who liked sex. But then I found I missed it. I used to touch myself when I was very little, I thought I'd invented something wonderful. I used to do it to go to sleep with or to cheer myself up, and one day it was raining and I was under the kitchen table, and my
855   mother saw me with my hand under my dress rubbing away, and she dragged me out so quickly I hit my head and it bled and I was sick, and nothing was said, and I never did it again till this year. I thought if Clive wasn't looking at me there wasn't a person there. And one night in bed in my flat I was so frightened I started touching myself. I thought my hand might go through
860   into space. I touched my face, it was there, my arm, my breast, and my hand went down where I thought it shouldn't, and I thought well there is somebody there. It felt very sweet, it was a feeling from very long ago, it was very soft, just barely touching, and I felt myself gathering together more and more and I felt angry with Clive and angry with my mother and I went on and on
865   defying them, and there was this vast feeling growing in me and all round me and they couldn't stop me and no one could stop me and I was there and coming and coming. Afterwards I thought I'd betrayed Clive. My mother would kill me. But I felt triumphant because I was a separate person from them. And I cried because I didn't want to be. But I don't cry about it any
870   more. Sometimes I do it three times in one night and it really is great fun.

[VICTORIA *and* LIN *come in.*]

VICTORIA   So I said to the professor, I don't think this is an occasion for invoking the concept of structural causality—oh hello Mummy.

BETTY   I'm going to ask you a question, both of you. I have a little money
from your grandmother. And the three of you are living in that tiny flat with
875   two children. I wonder if we could get a house and all live in it together? It
would give you more room.

VICTORIA   But I'm going to Manchester anyway.

LIN   We'd have a garden, Vicky.

BETTY   You do seem to have such fun all of you.

880   VICTORIA   I don't want to.

BETTY   I didn't think you would.

LIN   Come on, Vicky, she knows we sleep together, and Eddy.

BETTY   I think I've known for quite a while but I'm not sure. I don't usually
think about it, so I don't know if I know about it or not.

885   VICTORIA   I don't want to live with my mother.

LIN   Don't think of her as your mother, think of her as Betty.

VICTORIA   But she thinks of herself as my mother.

BETTY   I am your mother.

VICTORIA   But Mummy we don't even like each other.

890   BETTY   We might begin to.

[CATHY *comes on howling with a nosebleed.*]

LIN   Oh Cathy what happened?

BETTY   She's been assaulted.

VICTORIA   It's a nosebleed.

CATHY   Took my ice cream.

895   LIN   Who did?

CATHY   Took my money.

[MARTIN *comes.*]

MARTIN   Is everything all right?

LIN   I thought you were looking after her.

CATHY   They hit me. I can't play. They said I'm a girl.

900   BETTY   Those dreadful boys, the gang, the Dead Hand.

MARTIN   What do you mean you thought I was looking after her?

LIN   Last I saw her she was with you getting an ice cream. It's your
afternoon.

MARTIN   Then she went off to play. She goes off to play. You don't keep an eye
905   on her every minute.

LIN   She doesn't get beaten up when I'm looking after her.

CATHY   Took my money.

MARTIN   Why the hell should I look after your child anyway? I just want
Tommy. Why should he live with you and Vicky all week?

910   LIN   I don't mind if you don't want to look after her but don't say you will and
then this happens.

VICTORIA   When I get to Manchester everything's going to be different anyway, Lin's staying here, and you're staying here, we're all going to have to
sit down and talk it through.

915   MARTIN   I'd really enjoy that.

CATHY   Hit me on the face.

LIN   You were the one looking after her and look at her now, that's all.

MARTIN   I've had enough of you telling me.

LIN   Yes you know it all.

920 MARTIN   Now stop it. I work very hard at not being like this, I could do with
  some credit.

LIN   OK you're quite nice, try and enjoy it. Don't make me sorry for you,
  Martin, it's hard for me too. We've better things to do than quarrel. I've got
  to go and sort those little bastards out for a start. Where are they, Cathy?

925 CATHY   Don't kill them, Mum, hit them. Give them a nosebleed, Mum.

  [LIN *goes.*]

VICTORIA   Tommy's asleep in the pushchair. We'd better wake him up or he
  won't sleep tonight.

MARTIN   Sometimes I keep him up watching television till he falls asleep on
  the sofa so I can hold him. Come on, Cathy, we'll get another ice cream.

930 CATHY   Chocolate sauce and nuts.

VICTORIA   Betty, would you like an ice cream?

BETTY   No thank you, the cold hurts my teeth, but what a nice thought,
  Vicky, thank you.

  [VICTORIA *goes.* BETTY *alone.* GERRY *comes.*]

  I think you used to be Edward's flatmate.

935 GERRY   You're his mother. He's talked about you.

BETTY   Well never mind children are always wrong about their parents. It's a
  great problem knowing where to live and who to share with. I live by myself
  just now.

GERRY   Good, so do I. You can do what you like.

940 BETTY   I don't really know what I like.

GERRY   You'll soon find out.

BETTY   What do you like?

GERRY   Waking up at four in the morning.

BETTY   I like listening to music in bed and sometimes for supper I just have
945 a big piece of bread and dip it in very hot lime pickle. So you don't get
  lonely by yourself? Perhaps you have a lot of visitors. I've been thinking I
  should have some visitors, I could give a little dinner party. Would you
  come? There wouldn't just be bread and lime pickle.

GERRY   Thank you very much.

950 BETTY   Or don't wait to be asked to dinner. Just drop in informally. I'll give
  you the address shall I? I don't usually give strange men my address but
  then you're not a strange man, you're a friend of Edward's. I suppose I
  seem a different generation to you but you are older than Edward. I was
  married for so many years it's quite hard to know how to get acquainted.
955 But if there isn't a right way to do things you have to invent one. I always
  thought my mother was far too old to be attractive but when you get to an
  age yourself it feels quite different.

GERRY   I think you could be quite attractive.

BETTY   If what?

960 GERRY   If you stop worrying.

BETTY   I think when I do more about things I worry about them less. So perhaps you could help me do more.

GERRY   I might be going to live with Edward again.

BETTY   That's nice, but I'm rather surprised if he wants to share a flat. He's
965 rather involved with a young woman he lives with, or two young women, I
  don't understand Edward but never mind.

GERRY   I'm very involved with him.

1574 | CARYL CHURCHILL

BETTY   I think Edward did try to tell me once but I didn't listen. So what I'm
being told now is that Edward is 'gay' is that right? And you are too. And
970   I've been making rather a fool of myself. But Edward does also sleep with
women.

GERRY   He does, yes, I don't.

BETTY   Well people always say it's the mother's fault but I don't intend to
start blaming myself. He seems perfectly happy.

975   GERRY   I could still come and see you.

BETTY   So you could, yes. I'd like that. I've never tried to pick up a man
before.

GERRY   Not everyone's gay.

BETTY   No, that's lucky isn't it.

[GERRY *goes.* CLIVE *comes.*]

980   CLIVE   You are not that sort of woman, Betty. I can't believe you are. I can't
feel the same about you as I did. And Africa is to be Communist I suppose.
I used to be proud to be British. There was a high ideal. I came out onto
the verandah and looked at the stars.

[CLIVE *goes.* BETTY *from Act One comes.* BETTY *and* BETTY *embrace.*]

ATHOL FUGARD

b. 1932

IN Athol Fugard's *Sorrows and Rejoicings* (2001), a poet's death gives his friends an occasion to ponder the conflicted role of the white, liberal writer in contemporary South Africa. One character observes that the late author "was meant to be a poet, not a politician," but another disagrees: "And he would have told you that in this country you can't separate the two." Fugard might have been describing himself, for the politics of South Africa—specifically, his opposition to the practice of racial segregation known as apartheid—cannot be separated from his life's work; it has driven his creativity. Though critics may disagree on the political impact and efficacy of Fugard's dramaturgy, especially in a post-apartheid era, all acknowledge Fugard's place as one of the leading dramatists of the late twentieth century: a writer whose work has been produced to acclaim around the world and who has fostered global understanding of his country and its people.

Harold Athol Lannigan Fugard (called "Hally" as a boy) describes himself as being of "mixed descent." His mother, Elizabeth Magdalena Potgieter, was of Afrikaner heritage—that is, she was descended from the Dutch who were the original European settlers in South Africa—while his father, Harold David, was of Anglo-Irish stock. Fugard grew up in a polyglot environment, speaking both Afrikaans (one of the coun-

try's official languages, derived from Dutch) and English, and he was also exposed to African languages (mainly Xhosa). He writes in English but uses a South African idiom richly peppered with words and phrases from other tongues in the region.

In 1935, Fugard's family moved to Port Elizabeth, a coastal city in the Eastern Cape. Fugard's father, a musician who had been crippled in youth and who suffered from chronic pain and alcoholism, became incapable of supporting his family. Fugard's mother, their financial mainstay, first ran the Jubilee Hotel (a small boardinghouse) and then the Saint George's Park Tea Room, both of which feature in "*MASTER HAROLD*" . . . *AND THE BOYS* (1982). At the Port Elizabeth Technical College, Fugard studied automobile mechanics and experimented with amateur dramatics and creative writing. He won a scholarship to the University of Cape Town; there he pursued studies in social anthropology and philosophy and first encountered the existentialist writings of Albert Camus and Jean-Paul Sartre, both of whom have strongly influenced his dramaturgy. In 1953, he decided to hitchhike with a friend north through Africa, and he left the university without a degree. Arriving penniless in Port Sudan, he signed on as the captain's personal servant aboard a British tramp steamer. Fugard maintains that his experience as the only white crew member, living and working closely with men of other races, liberated him from his boyhood prejudices.

Upon his return to South Africa in 1954, Fugard wrote briefly for the *Port Elizabeth Evening Post* before settling in Cape Town to work in broadcast journalism. There he met Sheila Meiring, an actor (and later a poet and novelist); they married in 1956. Meiring encouraged his latent interest in theater and directed some of his early one-act plays for amateur groups. Watching productions of imported English dramas, Fugard had recognized the need for writers to tell South Africa's own stories on stage. In notebooks (published in 1983), in which he recorded ideas for future writing and thoughts about his experiences, he explained that he believes his "life's work was possibly just to witness as truthfully as I could, the nameless and destitute (desperate) of this one little corner of the world." By "witness," Fugard means not just to observe but also to provide oral or written evidence of what he has observed—sharing with others faithful images of his region and those who live there.

The couple moved to Johannesburg in 1958. Working as a clerk in a local court, where violations of South Africa's "pass law" were tried, Fugard saw the apartheid system in action. During this same period, his encounter with the artists and culture of Sophiatown, a black township on the outskirts of Johannesburg that was "open"—that is, it could be entered by whites without a special permit—proved instrumental in the development of his dramaturgy. Fugard wrote his first full-length plays, *No-Good Friday* (1958) and *Nongogo* (1959), about blacks living in Johannesburg and its environs. The plays were performed by amateur casts and directed by the playwright. Both featured the actor Zakes Mokae, whom Fugard had met in Sophiatown and who soon became one of his most important collaborators and closest friends. Fugard would later cast Mokae as Sam in the world premiere of *"MASTER HAROLD" . . . and the boys.*

Several years later, Fugard co-founded an amateur theater group called the Serpent Players, based in the black township near Port Elizabeth. Fugard directed its productions of Machiavelli (*The Man-*

drake), Georg Büchner, Camus, Sartre, SAMUEL BECKETT, and WOLE SOYINKA, all amid increasing police scrutiny of its activities. When two black actors were arrested and sent to Robben Island, a jail for political dissidents, one of them chose to perform there a version of SOPHOCLES' *Antigone* (ca. 441 B.C.E.)—an incident that inspired a series of original pieces developed by Fugard and the Serpent Players. *Sizwe Bansi Is Dead* (1972) and *The Island* (1973), both co-written with John Kani and Winston Ntshona, soon provided international audiences gripping representations of the inequities and inhumanity of the apartheid regime. Fugard's growing international reputation helped foster strong ties with several theater companies abroad, including London's National Theatre and New Haven's Yale Repertory Theatre. He turned to the latter when, in 1982, he chose for the first time to stage the world premiere of one of his works outside South Africa. According to Fugard, *"MASTER HAROLD" . . . and the boys*—a play based on memories of his childhood relationships with his family and with a black man who worked for them—was too personal for him to produce at home before testing the work's broader appeal elsewhere.

Set on a rainy afternoon in the Saint George's Park Tea Room, *"MASTER HAROLD"* opens on the daily routine of two black employees, Sam and Willie, who await the arrival from school of the white owner's teenage son, Hally. Sam and Willie are practicing for an upcoming ballroom dance competition—an event that Hally later will realize could serve as the topic of an assigned school essay. As Hally settles in, doing his homework and reminiscing with the men about their years of service to his family, he receives a phone call from his mother: his father, a disabled alcoholic, is unexpectedly being discharged from the hospital. Hally's ambivalence about this news and the impact his father's release will have on his family life triggers emotions he cannot control and actions that will haunt him ever after. Simultaneously establishing their own dignity and maturity, as well as their deep affection for the troubled youth, the black men serve as witnesses for Hally, whose struggle to decide what kind of man he will be has just begun.

The 1982 New York production of *"MASTER HAROLD" . . . and the boys* at the Lyceum Theatre, featuring Danny Glover (foreground) as Willie, Zakes Mokae as Sam, and Lonny Price as Hally.

Fugard's ability to truthfully represent the motivations and perspectives of each of his characters at critical junctures—no matter how difficult or ugly—is a hallmark of his dramaturgy. He creates great intimacy with small casts, a technique that is often compared to that of Beckett. Most of Fugard's plays feature only two or three characters, reflecting as well a stylistic predilection for the "poor theatre" championed by Jerzy Grotowski, whose theory Fugard explicitly embraces, along with Grotowski's concept of an actor-centered theater devoid of the trappings of the commercial stage. In finally writing this autobiographical drama—this portrait of the artist as a young man (or, as he has said, a young fool)—Fugard explores the universal tropes of conflict between fathers and sons and exposes personal and political realities specific to his native country.

Fugard places *"MASTER HAROLD"* in 1950, just when the South African government enacted the Population Registration Act and the Group Areas Act, legislation that classified and separated its residents by race. Although the autobiographical events chronicled by the play had actually occurred earlier, his decision to advance Hally's age from boyhood to adolescence allows Fugard to set him at the cusp of adulthood—the moment when an individual's identity and ideas about the world solidify—at a time of enormous political change. The play's title—and Fugard has been extremely clear about the importance of his capitalization and punctuation—highlights the ironies inherent in the ages and races of these characters as individuals and as South Africans. Hally has yet to grasp, for example, that Willie's agonizing choice between using his coins to play music to which he can practice ballroom dancing or to pay for bus fare home has everything to do with the laws that forced blacks to live in areas far removed from their places of employment. Fugard wants us to see this pivotal historic moment as having both microcosmic and macrocosmic consequences—we cannot separate the story of these three people from the world we now inhabit.

Fugard weaves together these stories of individuals and a nation in three scenes demarcated by two telephone calls. The play is, structurally, a long one act, running about 100 minutes in performance, with no intermission to relieve its growing tension. Confined to a single set, the action onstage occurs in real time; neither the audience nor the characters can escape the inexorable momentum of the conflict. Fugard also frames the action with separate glimpses of the lives of Sam and Willie; as characters, the men must have the independence and agency necessary to resist both the political context that would deny them those capacities and the narrative traditions that normalize blacks' marginality.

As the three characters discuss "social reformers" and "men of magnitude" from Hally's lessons, such men as Abraham Lincoln and Charles Darwin, the first scene foregrounds historic figures whose achievements resonate with the play's own societal concerns. This conversation later intertwines with Hally's personal memories, especially the story of a kite that Sam once made for him. Sam emerges as an unheralded man of magnitude for the troubled boy—someone who has affected him profoundly but whose story would not appear in any textbook. Fugard uses this same tale to develop Hally's conflicting allegiance to his two "fathers" and, ultimately, his passage from youthful obliviousness to a more mature recognition of the significance of apartheid. Sam interprets for Hally the current meaning of the whites-only area in which the boy had rested after their kite flying: "You don't *have* to sit up there by yourself. You know what that bench means now, and you can leave it any time you choose. All

you've got to do is stand up and walk away from it."

Hally cannot walk away from his conflicted relationship to his biological father, however, and Fugard uses the trope of mobility to connect Hally's personal dilemma with the metaphoric narratives of the kite and the ballroom competition. The miracle of the kite's flight and the beauty of the dancers' movement stand in stark contrast to Hally's perceptions of his father's disability, yet we also see these same stories of physical triumph from the perspectives of Sam and Willie, who are crippled by social forces beyond their control. In the play's closing moments, Fugard may be using ballroom dance to suggest hope not only on a global but also on a local scale. A final glimpse of Sam and Willie dancing a slow foxtrot seems to hint at a better future if South Africa's disenfranchised majority can work together to bring it about. Such an interpretation may account for why the play was initially banned from production in South Africa. While officials pointed to what they called obscene language in the script and not its political content in justifying their decision, they also maintained that they did not know the drama was by Fugard, despite the wide publicity surrounding its premiere and its enthusiastic critical reception in the United States. Because of the work's literary merit, the ban was soon lifted; ironically, this governmental response to *"MASTER HAROLD"* had the immediate effect of drawing international attention to the work and its contemporary relevance.

Fugard no longer considers himself a dissident writer, driven by the necessity to give voice to a silenced majority. Yet he feels a continuing challenge to "witness" his country and its people as they confront new questions about their identity and their past. He holds fast to the idea that the theater can be a force for change and maintains his commitment "to entertain in order to make a difference" worldwide.   J.E.G.

"Master Harold"
. . . and the boys

CHARACTERS

HALLY
SAM
WILLIE

The St. George's Park Tea Room on a wet and windy Port Elizabeth[1] afternoon.

Tables and chairs have been cleared and are stacked on one side except for one which stands apart with a single chair. On this table a knife, fork, spoon, and side plate in anticipation of a simple meal, together with a pile of comic books.

Other elements: a serving counter with a few stale cakes under glass and a not very impressive display of sweets, cigarettes and cool drinks, etc.; a few cardboard advertising handouts—Cadbury's Chocolate, Coca-Cola—and a blackboard on which an untrained hand has chalked up the prices of Tea, Coffee, Scones, Milkshakes—all flavors—and Cool Drinks; a few sad ferns in pots; a telephone; an old-style jukebox.

There is an entrance on one side and an exit into a kitchen on the other.

Leaning on the solitary table, his head cupped in one hand as he pages through one of the comic books, is SAM. *A black man in his mid-forties. He wears the white coat of a waiter. Behind him on his knees, mopping down the floor with a bucket of water and a rag, is* WILLIE. *Also black and about the same age as* SAM. *He has his sleeves and trousers rolled up.*

The year: 1950.

WILLIE [*singing as he works*]
"She was scandalizin' my name,[2]
She took my money
She called me honey
But she was scandalizin' my name.
5   Called it love but was playin' a game . . ."

[*He gets up and moves the bucket. Stands thinking for a moment, then, raising his arms to hold an imaginary partner, he launches into an intricate ballroom dance step. Although a mildly comic figure, he reveals a reasonable degree of accomplishment.*]

Hey, Sam.

[SAM, *absorbed in the comic book, does not respond.*]

Hey, Boet[3] Sam!

1. A city on the southeastern coast of South Africa; it has been Fugard's primary residence since 1935 and is the setting for a number of his plays.
2. "Scandalizing My Name," recorded by Thomas Wayne (1959); a rhythm-and-blues version of "Scandalize My Name," a black gospel song recorded by Paul Robeson in the 1930s.
3. Brother (Afrikaans), a term here used in the sense of friendship.

[SAM *looks up.*]

I'm getting it. The quickstep. Look now and tell me. [*He repeats the step.*]
Well?

10 SAM [*encouragingly*]   Show me again.

WILLIE   Okay, count for me.

SAM   Ready?

WILLIE   Ready.

SAM   Five, six, seven, eight . . . [WILLIE *starts to dance.*] A-n-d one two three
15   four . . . and one two three four. . . . [*Ad libbing as* WILLIE *dances*] Your
shoulders, Willie . . . your shoulders! Don't look down! Look happy, Willie!
Relax, Willie!

WILLIE [*desperate but still dancing*]   I am relax.

SAM   No, you're not.

20 WILLIE [*he falters*]   Ag no man, Sam! Mustn't talk. You make me make
mistakes.

SAM   But you're too stiff.

WILLIE   Yesterday I'm not straight . . . today I'm too stiff!

SAM   Well, you are. You asked me and I'm telling you.

25 WILLIE   Where?

SAM   Everywhere. Try to glide through it.

WILLIE   Glide?

SAM   Ja,[4] make it smooth. And give it more style. It must look like you're
enjoying yourself.

30 WILLIE [*emphatically*]   I wasn't.

SAM   Exactly.

WILLIE   How can I enjoy myself? Not straight, too stiff and now it's also
glide, give it more style, make it smooth. . . . Haai! Is hard to remember all
those things, Boet Sam.

35 SAM   That's your trouble. You're trying too hard.

WILLIE   I try hard because it *is* hard.

SAM   But don't let me see it. The secret is to make it look easy. Ballroom
must look happy, Willie, not like hard work. It must . . . Ja! . . . it must look
like romance.

40 WILLIE   Now another one! What's romance?

SAM   Love story with happy ending. A handsome man in tails, and in his
arms, smiling at him, a beautiful lady in evening dress!

WILLIE   Fred Astaire, Ginger Rogers.[5]

SAM   You got it. Tapdance or ballroom, it's the same. Romance. In two weeks'
45   time when the judges look at you and Hilda, they must see a man and a
woman who are dancing their way to a happy ending. What I saw was you
holding her like you were frightened she was going to run away.

WILLIE   Ja! Because that is what she wants to do! I got no romance left for
Hilda anymore, Boet Sam.

50 SAM   Then pretend. When you put your arms around Hilda, imagine she is
Ginger Rogers.

WILLIE   With no teeth? You try.

---

4. Yes (Afrikaans).
5. Famous dance partners in movie musicals;
the American actors Astaire (1899–1987) and
Rogers (1911–1995) starred together in ten
films (1933–39, 1949).

SAM   Well, just remember, there's only two weeks left.

WILLIE   I know, I know! [*To the jukebox*] I do it better with music. You got
55   sixpence for Sarah Vaughan?[6]

SAM   That's a slow foxtrot. You're practicing the quickstep.

WILLIE   I'll practice slow foxtrot.

SAM [*shaking his head*]   It's your turn to put money in the jukebox.

WILLIE   I only got bus fare to go home. [*He returns disconsolately to his
60   work.*] Love story and happy ending! She's doing it all right, Boet Sam, but
is not me she's giving happy endings. Fuckin' whore! Three nights now she
doesn't come practice. I wind up gramophone, I get record ready and I sit
and wait. What happens? Nothing. Ten o'clock I start dancing with my pillow. You try and practice romance by yourself, Boet Sam. Struesgod,[7] she
65   doesn't come tonight I take back my dress and ballroom shoes and I find
me new partner. Size twenty-six. Shoes size seven. And now she's also making trouble for me with the baby again. Reports me to Child Wellfed, that
I'm not giving her money. She lies! Every week I am giving her money for
milk. And how do I know is my baby? Only his hair looks like me. She's fuck-
70   ing around all the time I turn my back. Hilda Samuels is a bitch! [*Pause*] Hey,
Sam!

SAM   Ja.

WILLIE   You listening?

SAM   Ja.

75   WILLIE   So what you say?

SAM   About Hilda?

WILLIE   Ja.

SAM   When did you last give her a hiding?

WILLIE [*reluctantly*]   Sunday night.

80   SAM   And today is Thursday.

WILLIE [*he knows what's coming*]   Okay.

SAM   Hiding on Sunday night, then Monday, Tuesday and Wednesday she
doesn't come to practice . . . and you are asking me why?

WILLIE   I said okay, Boet Sam!

85   SAM   You hit her too much. One day she's going to leave you for good.

WILLIE   So? She makes me the hell-in[8] too much.

SAM [*emphasizing his point*]   *Too* much and *too* hard. You had the same trouble with Eunice.

WILLIE   Because she also make the hell-in, Boet Sam. She never got the
90   steps right. Even the waltz.

SAM   Beating her up every time she makes a mistake in the waltz? [*Shaking
his head*] No, Willie! That takes the pleasure out of ballroom dancing.

WILLIE   Hilda is not too bad with the waltz, Boet Sam. Is the quickstep
where the trouble starts.

95   SAM [*teasing him gently*]   How's your pillow with the quickstep?

WILLIE [*ignoring the tease*]   Good! And why? Because it got no legs. That's
her trouble. She can't move them quick enough, Boet Sam. I start the

---

6. An American jazz vocalist and pianist (1924–1990).
7. As true as God (Afrikaans); that is, "I swear."

8. That is, she drives me crazy (South African slang).

record and before halfway Count Basie[9] is already winning. Only time we catch up with him is when gramophone runs down.

[SAM *laughs.*]

100 Haaikona,[1] Boet Sam, is not funny.

SAM [*snapping his fingers*] I got it! Give her a handicap.

WILLIE What's that?

SAM Give her a ten-second start and then let Count Basie go. Then I put my money on her. Hot favorite in the Ballroom Stakes: Hilda Samuels ridden
105 by Willie Malopo.

WILLIE [*turning away*] I'm not talking to you no more.

SAM [*relenting*] Sorry, Willie . . .

WILLIE It's finish between us.

SAM Okay, okay . . . I'll stop.

110 WILLIE You can also fuck off.

SAM Willie, listen! I want to help you!

WILLIE No more jokes?

SAM I promise.

WILLIE Okay. Help me.

115 SAM [*his turn to hold an imaginary partner*] Look and learn. Feet together. Back straight. Body relaxed. Right hand placed gently in the small of her back and wait for the music. Don't start worrying about making mistakes or the judges or the other competitors. It's just you, Hilda, and the music, and you're going to have a good time. What Count Basie do you play?

120 WILLIE "You the cream in my coffee, you the salt in my stew."[2]

SAM Right. Give it to me in strict tempo.[3]

WILLIE Ready?

SAM Ready.

WILLIE A-n-d . . . [*Singing*]

125 "You the cream in my coffee.
You the salt in my stew.
You will always be my necessity.
I'd be lost without you. . . ." (*etc.*)

[SAM *launches into the quickstep. He is obviously a much more accomplished dancer than* WILLIE. HALLY *enters. A seventeen-year-old white boy. Wet raincoat and school case. He stops and watches* SAM. *The demonstration comes to an end with a flourish. Applause from* HALLY *and* WILLIE.]

HALLY Bravo! No question about it. First place goes to Mr. Sam Semela.

130 WILLIE [*in total agreement*] You was gliding with style, Boet Sam.

HALLY [*cheerfully*] How's it, chaps?

SAM Okay, Hally.

WILLIE [*springing to attention like a soldier and saluting*] At your service, Master[4] Harold!

---

9. William "Count" Basie (1904–1984), American pianist, arranger, and composer who was one of the most influential bandleaders of the 20th century.
1. An exclamation of strong negation (Xhosa).
2. From "You're the Cream in My Coffee" (1928; music by Ray Henderson, lyrics by Buddy G. DeSylva and Lew Brown).
3. That is, with an unvarying beat, so that it can be danced to more easily.
4. In Britain, the traditional courtesy title of a young gentleman not considered old enough to be called "Mister."

135 HALLY   Not long to the big event, hey!

SAM   Two weeks.

HALLY   You nervous?

SAM   No.

HALLY   Think you stand a chance?

140 SAM   Let's just say I'm ready to go out there and dance.

HALLY   It looked like it. What about you, Willie?

[WILLIE *groans*.]

What's the matter?

SAM   He's got leg trouble.

HALLY [*innocently*]   Oh, sorry to hear that, Willie.

145 WILLIE   Boet Sam! You promised. [WILLIE *returns to his work*.]

[HALLY *deposits his school case and takes off his raincoat. His clothes are a little neglected and untidy: black blazer with school badge, gray flannel trousers in need of an ironing, khaki shirt and tie, black shoes.* SAM *has fetched a towel for* HALLY *to dry his hair*.]

HALLY   God, what a lousy bloody day. It's coming down cats and dogs out there. Bad for business, chaps . . . [*Conspiratorial whisper*] . . . but it also means we're in for a nice quiet afternoon.

SAM   You can speak loud. Your Mom's not here.

150 HALLY   Out shopping?

SAM   No. The hospital.

HALLY   But it's Thursday. There's no visiting on Thursday afternoons. Is my Dad okay?

SAM   Sounds like it. In fact, I think he's going home.

155 HALLY [*stopped short by* SAM's *remark*]   What do you mean?

SAM   The hospital phoned.

HALLY   To say what?

SAM   I don't know. I just heard your Mom talking.

HALLY   So what makes you say he's going home?

160 SAM   It sounded as if they were telling her to come and fetch him.

[HALLY *thinks about what* SAM *has said for a few seconds*.]

HALLY   When did she leave?

SAM   About an hour ago. She said she would phone you. Want to eat?

[HALLY *doesn't respond*.]

Hally, want your lunch?

HALLY   I suppose so. [*His mood has changed*.] What's on the menu? . . . as if

165 I don't know.

SAM   Soup, followed by meat pie and gravy.

HALLY   Today's?

SAM   No.

HALLY   And the soup?

170 SAM   Nourishing pea soup.

HALLY   Just the soup. [*The pile of comic books on the table*] And these?

SAM   For your Dad. Mr. Kempston brought them.

HALLY   You haven't been reading them, have you?

SAM   Just looking.

175 HALLY [*examining the comics*]   Jungle Jim . . . Batman and Robin . . . Tarzan . . . God, what rubbish! Mental pollution. Take them away.

[SAM *exits waltzing into the kitchen.* HALLY *turns to* WILLIE.]

HALLY   Did you hear my Mom talking on the telephone, Willie?

WILLIE   No, Master Hally. I was at the back.

HALLY   And she didn't say anything to you before she left?

180 WILLIE   She said I must clean the floors.

HALLY   I mean about my Dad.

WILLIE   She didn't say nothing to me about him, Master Hally.

HALLY [*with conviction*]   No! It can't be. They said he needed at least another three weeks of treatment. Sam's definitely made a mistake. [*Rummages through his school case, finds a book and settles down at the table to read.*]

185   So, Willie!

WILLIE   Yes, Master Hally! Schooling okay today?

HALLY   Yes, okay. . . . [*He thinks about it.*] . . . No, not really. Ag, what's the difference? I don't care. And Sam says you've got problems.

WILLIE   Big problems.

190 HALLY   Which leg is sore?

[WILLIE *groans.*]

Both legs.

WILLIE   There is nothing wrong with my legs. Sam is just making jokes.

HALLY   So then you *will* be in the competition.

WILLIE   Only if I can find me a partner.

195 HALLY   But what about Hilda?

SAM [*returning with a bowl of soup*]   She's the one who's got trouble with her legs.

HALLY   What sort of trouble, Willie?

SAM   From the way he describes it, I think the lady has gone a bit lame.

200 HALLY   Good God! Have you taken her to see a doctor?

SAM   I think a vet would be better.

HALLY   What do you mean?

SAM   What do you call it again when a racehorse goes very fast?

HALLY   Gallop?

205 SAM   That's it!

WILLIE   Boet Sam!

HALLY   "A gallop down the homestretch to the winning post." But what's that got to do with Hilda?

SAM   Count Basie always gets there first.

[WILLIE *lets fly with his slop rag. It misses* SAM *and hits* HALLY.]

210 HALLY [*furious*]   For Christ's sake, Willie! What the hell do you think you're doing!

WILLIE   Sorry, Master Hally, but it's him. . . .

HALLY   Act your bloody age! [*Hurls the rag back at* WILLIE.] Cut out the nonsense now and get on with your work. And you too, Sam. Stop fooling around.

[SAM *moves away.*]

215   No. Hang on. I haven't finished! Tell me exactly what my Mom said.

SAM   I have. "When Hally comes, tell him I've gone to the hospital and I'll phone him."

HALLY   She didn't say anything about taking my Dad home?

SAM   No. It's just that when she was talking on the phone . . .

220 HALLY [*interrupting him*] No, Sam. They can't be discharging him. She would have said so if they were. In any case, we saw him last night and he wasn't in good shape at all. Staff nurse even said there was talk about taking more X-rays. And now suddenly today he's better? If anything, it sounds more like a bad turn to me . . . which I sincerely hope it isn't. Hang on . . .
225 how long ago did you say she left?

SAM Just before two . . . [*His wristwatch*] . . . hour and a half.

HALLY I know how to settle it. [*Behind the counter to the telephone. Talking as he dials*] Let's give her ten minutes to get to the hospital, ten minutes to load him up, another ten, at the most, to get home, and another ten to get
230 him inside. Forty minutes. They should have been home for at least half an hour already. [*Pause—he waits with the receiver to his ear.*] No reply, chaps. And you know why? Because she's at his bedside in hospital helping him pull through a bad turn. You definitely heard wrong.

SAM Okay.

> [*As far as* HALLY *is concerned, the matter is settled. He returns to his table, sits down and divides his attention between the book and his soup.* SAM *is at his school case and picks up a textbook.*]

235 *Modern Graded Mathematics for Standards*[5] *Nine and Ten.* [*Opens it at random and laughs at something he sees.*] Who is this supposed to be?

HALLY Old fart-face Prentice.

SAM Teacher?

HALLY Thinks he is. And believe me, that is not a bad likeness.

240 SAM Has he seen it?

HALLY Yes.

SAM What did he say?

HALLY Tried to be clever, as usual. Said I was no Leonardo da Vinci[6] and that bad art had to be punished. So, six of the best, and his are bloody
245 good.

SAM On your bum?

HALLY Where else? The days when I got them on my hands are gone forever, Sam.

SAM With your trousers down!

250 HALLY No. He's not quite that barbaric.

SAM That's the way they do it in jail.

HALLY [*flicker of morbid interest*] Really?

SAM Ja. When the magistrate sentences you to "strokes with a light cane."

HALLY Go on.

255 SAM They make you lie down on a bench. One policeman pulls down your trousers and holds your ankles, another one pulls your shirt over your head and holds your arms . . .

HALLY Thank you! That's enough.

SAM . . . and the one that gives you the strokes talks to you gently and for a
260 long time between each one. [*He laughs.*]

HALLY I've heard enough, Sam! Jesus! It's a bloody awful world when you come to think of it. People can be real bastards.

---

5. That is, grades.
6. Italian artist (1452–1519), famous for his

precisely rendered drawings as well as his paintings.

SAM   That's the way it is, Hally.

HALLY   It doesn't *have* to be that way. There is something called progress,
265   you know. We don't exactly burn people at the stake anymore.

SAM   Like Joan of Arc.[7]

HALLY   Correct. If she was captured today, she'd be given a fair trial.

SAM   And then the death sentence.

HALLY   [*a world-weary sigh*]   I know, I know! I oscillate between hope and
270   despair for this world as well, Sam. But things will change, you wait and
see. One day somebody is going to get up and give history a kick up the
backside and get it going again.

SAM   Like who?

HALLY   [*after thought*]   They're called social reformers. Every age, Sam, has
275   got its social reformer. My history book is full of them.

SAM   So where's ours?

HALLY   Good question. And I hate to say it, but the answer is: I don't know.
Maybe he hasn't even been born yet. Or is still only a babe in arms at his
mother's breast. God, what a thought.

280   SAM   So we just go on waiting.

HALLY   Ja, looks like it. [*Back to his soup and the book*]

SAM   [*reading from the textbook*]   "Introduction: In some mathematical problems only the magnitude . . ." [*He mispronounces the word "magnitude."*]

HALLY   [*correcting him without looking up*]   Magnitude.

285   SAM   What's it mean?

HALLY   How big it is. The size of the thing.

SAM   [*reading*]   ". . . magnitude of the quantities is of importance. In other
problems we need to know whether these quantities are negative or positive. For example, whether there is a debit or credit bank balance . . ."

290   HALLY   Whether you're broke or not.

SAM   ". . . whether the temperature is above or below Zero . . ."

HALLY   Naught degrees. Cheerful state of affairs! No cash and you're freezing to death. Mathematics won't get you out of that one.

SAM   "All these quantities are called . . ." [*Spelling the word*] . . . s-c-a-l . . .

295   HALLY   Scalars.

SAM   Scalars! [*Shaking his head with a laugh*] You understand all that?

HALLY   [*turning a page*]   No. And I don't intend to try.

SAM   So what happens when the exams come?

HALLY   Failing a maths exam isn't the end of the world, Sam. How many
300   times have I told you that examination results don't measure intelligence?

SAM   I would say about as many times as you've failed one of them.

HALLY   [*mirthlessly*]   Ha, ha, ha.

SAM   [*simultaneously*]   Ha, ha, ha.

HALLY   Just remember Winston Churchill[8] didn't do particularly well at
305   school.

SAM   You've also told me that one many times.

HALLY   Well, it just so happens to be the truth.

---

7. The French saint and national heroine
(ca. 1412–1431); she successfully led French
troops against the English, but was captured
and burned at the stake after being charged
with heresy and witchcraft.

8. British statesman and author (1874–1965);
as prime minister (1940–45, 1951–55) he
was a highly effective leader during World
War II.

SAM [*enjoying the word*] Magnitude! Magnitude! Show me how to use it.

HALLY [*after thought*] An intrepid social reformer will not be daunted by the
310   magnitude of the task he has undertaken.

SAM [*impressed*] Couple of jaw-breakers in there!

HALLY I gave you three for the price of one. Intrepid, daunted, and magnitude. I did that once in an exam. Put five of the words I had to explain in
one sentence. It was half a page long.

315 SAM Well, I'll put my money on you in the English exam.

HALLY Piece of cake. Eighty percent without even trying.

SAM [*another textbook from* HALLY's *case*] And history?

HALLY So-so. I'll scrape through. In the fifties if I'm lucky.

SAM You didn't do too badly last year.

320 HALLY Because we had World War One. That at least had some action. You
try to find that in the South African Parliamentary system.

SAM [*reading from the history textbook*] "Napoleon[9] and the principle of
equality." Hey! This sounds interesting. "After concluding peace with Britain in 1802, Napoleon used a brief period of calm to in-sti-tute . . ."

325 HALLY Introduce.

SAM ". . . many reforms. Napoleon regarded all people as equal before the
law and wanted them to have equal opportunities for advancement. All ves-
ti-ges of the feu-dal system with its oppression of the poor were abolished."
Vestiges, feudal system, and abolished. I'm all right on oppression.

330 HALLY I'm thinking. He swept away . . . abolished . . . the last remains . . .
vestiges . . . of the bad old days . . . feudal system.

SAM Ha! There's the social reformer we're waiting for. He sounds like a man
of some magnitude.

HALLY I'm not so sure about that. It's a damn good title for a book, though.
335 A man of magnitude!

SAM He sounds pretty big to me, Hally.

HALLY Don't confuse historical significance with greatness. But maybe I'm
being a bit prejudiced. Have a look in there and you'll see he's two chapters
long. And hell! . . . has he only got dates, Sam, all of which you've got to
340 remember! This campaign and that campaign, and then, because of all the
fighting, the next thing is we get Peace Treaties all over the place. And
what's the end of the story? Battle of Waterloo, which he loses. Wasn't
worth it. No, I don't know about him as a man of magnitude.

SAM Then who would you say was?

345 HALLY To answer that, we need a definition of greatness, and I suppose that
would be somebody who . . . somebody who benefited all mankind.

SAM Right. But like who?

HALLY [*he speaks with total conviction*] Charles Darwin.[1] Remember him?
That big book from the library. *The Origin of the Species.*

350 SAM Him?

HALLY Yes. For his Theory of Evolution.

SAM You didn't finish it.

---

9. Napoléon Bonaparte (1769–1821), the
French general who in 1804 declared himself
emperor of France; he undertook domestic
reforms as well as military conquest (he was
finally defeated at Waterloo in 1815).

1. British naturalist (1809–1882), author of
the groundbreaking treatise *On the Origin of
Species by Means of Natural Selection* (1859).
Chapter 3 of the work is titled "Struggle for
Existence."

HALLY   I ran out of time. I didn't finish it because my two weeks was up. But
         I'm going to take it out again after I've digested what I read. It's safe. I've
355   hidden it away in the Theology section. Nobody ever goes in there. And
         anyway who are you to talk? You hardly even looked at it.

SAM   I tried. I looked at the chapters in the beginning and I saw one called
         "The Struggle for an Existence." Ah ha, I thought. At last! But what did I
         get? Something called the mistiltoe which needs the apple tree and there's
360   too many seeds and all are going to die except one . . . !² No, Hally.

HALLY   [intellectually outraged]   What do you mean, No! The poor man had
         to start somewhere. For God's sake, Sam, he revolutionized science. Now
         we know.

SAM   What?

365 HALLY   Where we come from and what it all means.

SAM   And that's a benefit to mankind? Anyway, I still don't believe it.

HALLY   God, you're impossible. I showed it to you in black and white.

SAM   Doesn't mean I got to believe it.

HALLY   It's the likes of you that kept the Inquisition³ in business. It's called
370   bigotry. Anyway, that's my man of magnitude. Charles Darwin! Who's
         yours?

SAM   [without hesitation]   Abraham Lincoln.⁴

HALLY   I might have guessed as much. Don't get sentimental, Sam. You've
         never been a slave, you know. And anyway we freed your ancestors here in
375   South Africa long before the Americans. But if you want to thank some-
         body on their behalf, do it to Mr. William Wilberforce.⁵ Come on. Try again.
         I want a real genius. [Now enjoying himself, and so is SAM. HALLY goes behind
         the counter and helps himself to a chocolate.]

SAM   William Shakespeare.

HALLY   [no enthusiasm]   Oh. So you're also one of them,⁶ are you? You're bas-
380   ing that opinion on only one play, you know. You've only read my Julius
         Caesar and even I don't understand half of what they're talking about. They
         should do what they did with the old Bible: bring the language up to date.

SAM   That's all you've got. It's also the only one you've read.

HALLY   I know. I admit it. That's why I suggest we reserve our judgment until
385   we've checked up on a few others. I've got a feeling, though, that by the
         end of this year one is going to be enough for me, and I can give you the
         names of twenty-nine other chaps in the Standard Nine class of the Port
         Elizabeth Technical College who feel the same. But if you want him, you
         can have him. My turn now. [Pacing] This is a damned good exercise, you

2. In two dense sentences, Darwin mentions
mistletoe and apple trees to distinguish para-
sitism and competition.
3. A tribunal of the Roman Catholic Church,
established in 1233 to investigate heresy;
over the centuries, a number of philosophers
and scientists (including Galileo) were tried
by its officers.
4. The sixteenth president of the United States
(1809–1865; president, 1861–65), known as
the "Great Emancipator" because of his proclamation freeing the slaves who were living in

states that were in rebellion against the federal
government.
5. British politician and opponent of slavery
(1759–1833); days before his death, Parliament passed an act outlawing slavery throughout most of the British Empire, including the
Cape Colony (later to become part of South
Africa).
6. That is, one of the many who regard Shakespeare (1564–1616) as the greatest dramatist
of all time. Julius Caesar was first performed in
1599.

390   know! It started off looking like a simple question and here it's got us really
      probing into the intellectual heritage of our civilization.

SAM   So who is it going to be?

HALLY   My next man . . . and he gets the title on two scores: social reform
      and literary genius . . . is Leo Nikolaevich Tolstoy.[7]

395 SAM   That Russian.

HALLY   Correct. Remember the picture of him I showed you?

SAM   With the long beard.

HALLY   [*trying to look like Tolstoy*] And those burning, visionary eyes. My
      God, the face of a social prophet if ever I saw one! And remember my words

400   when I showed it to you? Here's a *man*, Sam!

SAM   Those were words, Hally.

HALLY   Not many intellectuals are prepared to shovel manure with the peas-
      ants and then go home and write a "little book" called *War and Peace*. Inci-
      dentally, Sam, he was somebody else who, to quote, ". . . did not distinguish

405   himself scholastically."

SAM   Meaning?

HALLY   He was also no good at school.

SAM   Like you and Winston Churchill.

HALLY   [*mirthlessly*] Ha, ha, ha.

410 SAM   [*simultaneously*] Ha, ha, ha.

HALLY   Don't get clever, Sam. That man freed his serfs of his own free will.

SAM   No argument. He was a somebody, all right. I accept him.

HALLY   I'm sure Count Tolstoy will be very pleased to hear that. Your turn.
      Shoot. [*Another chocolate from behind the counter*] I'm waiting, Sam.

415 SAM   I've got him.

HALLY   Good. Submit your candidate for examination.

SAM   Jesus.

HALLY   [*stopped dead in his tracks*] Who?

SAM   Jesus Christ.

420 HALLY   Oh, come on, Sam!

SAM   The Messiah.

HALLY   Ja, but still . . . No, Sam. Don't let's get started on religion. We'll just
      spend the whole afternoon arguing again. Suppose I turn around and say
      Mohammed?

425 SAM   All right.

HALLY   You can't have them both on the same list!

SAM   Why not? You like Mohammed, I like Jesus.

HALLY   I *don't* like Mohammed. I never have. I was merely being hypotheti-
      cal. As far as I'm concerned, the Koran is as bad as the Bible. No. Religion

430   is out! I'm not going to waste my time again arguing with you about the
      existence of God. You know perfectly well I'm an atheist . . . and I've got
      homework to do.

SAM   Okay, I take him back.

HALLY   You've got time for one more name.

---

7. Russian novelist and philosopher (1828–1910), born into the nobility (he inherited an estate
that included hundreds of serfs); one of his masterpieces is *War and Peace* (1863–69).

435 SAM [*after thought*]   I've got one I know we'll agree on. A simple straightfor-
       ward great Man of Magnitude . . . and no arguments. And *he* really *did*
       benefit all mankind.

     HALLY   I wonder. After your last contribution I'm beginning to doubt whether
       anything in the way of an intellectual agreement is possible between the
440   two of us. Who is he?

     SAM   Guess.

     HALLY   Socrates? Alexandre Dumas? Karl Marx? Dostoevsky? Nietzsche?[8]
       [SAM *shakes his head after each name.*]
       Give me a clue.

     SAM   The letter P is important . . .

445 HALLY   Plato!

     SAM   . . . and his name begins with an F.

     HALLY   I've got it. Freud[9] and Psychology.

     SAM   No. I didn't understand him.

     HALLY   That makes two of us.

450 SAM   Think of mouldy apricot jam.

     HALLY [*after a delighted laugh*]   Penicillin and Sir Alexander Fleming![1] And
       the title of the book: *The Microbe Hunters.* [*Delighted.*] Splendid, Sam!
       Splendid. For once we are in total agreement. The major breakthrough in
       medical science in the Twentieth Century. If it wasn't for him, we might
455   have lost the Second World War. It's deeply gratifying, Sam, to know that I
       haven't been wasting my time in talking to you. [*Strutting around proudly*]
       Tolstoy may have educated his peasants, but I've educated you.

     SAM   Standard Four to Standard Nine.

     HALLY   Have we been at it as long as that?

460 SAM   Yep. And my first lesson was geography.

     HALLY [*intrigued*]   Really? I don't remember.

     SAM   My room there at the back of the old Jubilee Boarding House. I had
       just started working for your Mom. Little boy in short trousers walks in one
       afternoon and asks me seriously: "Sam, do you want to see South Africa?"
465   Hey man! Sure I wanted to see South Africa!

     HALLY   Was that me?

     SAM   . . . So the next thing I'm looking at a map you had just done for home-
       work. It was your first one and you were very proud of yourself.

     HALLY   Go on.

470 SAM   Then came my first lesson. "Repeat after me, Sam: Gold in the Trans-
       vaal, mealies in the Free State, sugar in Natal and grapes in the Cape."[2] I
       still know it!

---

8. A mixture of philosophers—the Greek
Socrates (469–399 B.C.E.), who is featured in
the dialogues of Plato (427–347 B.C.E.), and
the Germans Karl Marx (1818–1883) and
Friedrich Nietzsche (1844–1900)—and novelists: the French Dumas père (1802–1870)
and fils (1824–1895), and the Russian Fyodor
Dostoyevsky (1821–1881).
9. Sigmund Freud (1856–1939), the Austrian
founder of psychoanalysis.

1. A Scottish bacteriologist (1881–1955); in
1928, he discovered penicillin, the first effective antibiotic. Fleming is one of the scientists
featured in Paul de Kruif's *Microbe Hunters*
(1926).
2. In 1950, the four provinces of South Africa
were the Transvaal, the Orange Free State,
Natal, and the Cape Province. *Mealies* (U.S.
corn): maize, the principal staple of southern
Africa.

HALLY   Well, I'll be buggered.[3] So that's how it all started.

SAM   And your next map was one with all the rivers and the mountains they
475   came from. The Orange, the Vaal, the Limpopo, the Zambezi . . .

HALLY   You've got a phenomenal memory!

SAM   You should be grateful. That is why you started passing your exams. You
tried to be better than me.

[*They laugh together.* WILLIE *is attracted by the laughter and joins them.*]

HALLY   The old Jubilee Boarding House. Sixteen rooms with board and lodg-
480   ing, rent in advance and one week's notice. I haven't thought about it for
donkey's years[4] . . . and I don't think that's an accident. God, was I glad
when we sold it and moved out. Those years are not remembered as the
happiest ones of an unhappy childhood.

WILLIE [*knocking on the table and trying to imitate a woman's voice*]   "Hally,
485   are you there?"

HALLY   Who's that supposed to be?

WILLIE   "What you doing in there, Hally? Come out at once!"

HALLY [*to* SAM]   What's he talking about?

SAM   Don't you remember?

490   WILLIE   "Sam, Willie . . . is he in there with you boys?"

SAM   Hiding away in our room when your mother was looking for you.

HALLY [*another good laugh*]   Of course! I used to crawl and hide under your
bed! But finish the story, Willie. Then what used to happen? You chaps
would give the game away by telling her I was in there with you. So much
495   for friendship.

SAM   We couldn't lie to her. She knew.

HALLY   Which meant I got another rowing[5] for hanging around the "servants'
quarters." I think I spent more time in there with you chaps than anywhere
else in that dump. And do you blame me? Nothing but bloody misery wher-
500   ever you went. Somebody was always complaining about the food, or my
mother was having a fight with Micky Nash because she'd caught her with
a petty officer in her room. Maud Meiring was another one. Remember
those two? They were prostitutes, you know. Soldiers and sailors from the
troopships. Bottom fell out of the business when the war ended. God, the
505   flotsam and jetsam that life washed up on our shores! No joking, if it wasn't
for your room, I would have been the first certified[6] ten-year-old in medical
history. Ja, the memories are coming back now. Walking home from school
and thinking: "What can I do this afternoon?" Try out a few ideas, but
sooner or later I'd end up in there with you fellows. I bet you I could still
510   find my way to your room with my eyes closed. [*He does exactly that.*] Down
the corridor . . . telephone on the right, which my Mom keeps locked
because somebody is using it on the sly and not paying . . . past the kitchen
and unappetizing cooking smells . . . around the corner into the backyard,
hold my breath again because there are more smells coming when I pass
515   your lavatory, then into that little passageway, first door on the right and
into your room. How's that?

SAM   Good. But, as usual, you forgot to knock.

---

3. That is, I'll be damned (slang).   5. Scolding.
4. That is, a very long time (British slang).   6. Officially declared insane.

HALLY   Like that time I barged in and caught you and Cynthia . . . at it. Remember? God, was I embarrassed! I didn't know what was going on at first.

520 SAM   Ja, that taught you a lesson.

HALLY   And about a lot more than knocking on doors, I'll have you know, and I don't mean geography either. Hell, Sam, couldn't you have waited until it was dark?

SAM   No.

525 HALLY   Was it that urgent?

SAM   Yes, and if you don't believe me, wait until your time comes.

HALLY   No, thank you. I am not interested in girls. [*Back to his memories . . . Using a few chairs he re-creates the room as he lists the items.*] A gray little room with a cold cement floor. Your bed against that wall . . . and I now
530   know why the mattress sags so much! . . . Willie's bed . . . it's propped up on bricks because one leg is broken . . . that wobbly little table with the washbasin and jug of water . . . Yes! . . . stuck to the wall above it are some pin-up pictures from magazines. Joe Louis[7] . . .

WILLIE   Brown Bomber. World Title. [*Boxing pose*] Three rounds and knockout.

535 HALLY   Against who?

SAM   Max Schmeling.

HALLY   Correct. I can also remember Fred Astaire and Ginger Rogers, and Rita Hayworth[8] in a bathing costume which always made me hot and bothered when I looked at it. Under Willie's bed is an old suitcase with all his
540   clothes in a mess, which is why I never hide there. Your things are neat and tidy in a trunk next to your bed, and on it there is a picture of you and Cynthia in your ballroom clothes, your first silver cup for third place in a competition and an old radio which doesn't work anymore. Have I left out anything?

545 SAM   No.

HALLY   Right, so much for the stage directions. Now the characters. [SAM *and* WILLIE *move to their appropriate positions in the bedroom.*] Willie is in bed, under his blankets with his clothes on, complaining nonstop about something, but we can't make out a word of what he's saying because he's
550   got his head under the blankets as well. You're on your bed trimming your toenails with a knife—not a very edifying sight—and as for me . . . What am I doing?

SAM   You're sitting on the floor giving Willie a lecture about being a good loser while you get the checkerboard and pieces ready for a game. Then
555   you go to Willie's bed, pull off the blankets and make him play with you first because you know you're going to win, and that gives you the second game with me.

HALLY   And you certainly were a bad loser, Willie!

WILLIE   Haai!

560 HALLY   Wasn't he, Sam? And so slow! A game with you almost took the whole afternoon. Thank God I gave up trying to teach you how to play chess.

WILLIE   You and Sam cheated.

---

7. A black American boxer (1914–1981); he was world heavyweight champion when he knocked out the German champion, Max Schmeling (1905–2005), in the first round of their celebrated 1938 rematch (Schmeling had knocked him out in a 1936 fight).
8. American movie star (1918–1987), a leading sex symbol of the 1940s.

HALLY   I never saw Sam cheat, and mine were mostly the mistakes of youth.

WILLIE   Then how is it you two was always winning?

565 HALLY   Have you ever considered the possibility, Willie, that it was because we were better than you?

WILLIE   Every time better?

HALLY   Not every time. There were occasions when we deliberately let you win a game so that you would stop sulking and go on playing with us. Sam

570   used to wink at me when you weren't looking to show me it was time to let you win.

WILLIE   So then you two didn't play fair.

HALLY   It was for your benefit, Mr. Malopo, which is more than being fair. It was an act of self-sacrifice. [To SAM] But you know what my best memory

575   is, don't you?

SAM   No.

HALLY   Come on, guess. If your memory is so good, you must remember it as well.

SAM   We got up to a lot of tricks in there, Hally.

580 HALLY   This one was special, Sam.

SAM   I'm listening.

HALLY   It started off looking like another of those useless nothing-to-do afternoons. I'd already been down to Main Street looking for adventure, but nothing had happened. I didn't feel like climbing trees in the Donkin

585   Park[9] or pretending I was a private eye and following a stranger . . . so as usual: See what's cooking in Sam's room. This time it was you on the floor. You had two thin pieces of wood and you were smoothing them down with a knife. It didn't look particularly interesting, but when I asked you what you were doing, you just said, "Wait and see, Hally. Wait . . . and see" . . .

590   in that secret sort of way of yours, so I knew there was a surprise coming. You teased me, you bugger, by being deliberately slow and not answering my questions!

[SAM laughs.]

And whistling while you worked away! God, it was infuriating! I could have brained you! It was only when you tied them together in a cross and put

595   that down on the brown paper that I realized what you were doing. "Sam is making a kite?" And when I asked you and you said "Yes" . . . ! [Shaking his head with disbelief] The sheer audacity of it took my breath away. I mean, seriously, what the hell does a black man know about flying a kite? I'll be honest with you, Sam, I had no hopes for it. If you think I was excited and

600   happy, you got another guess coming. In fact, I was shit-scared that we were going to make fools of ourselves. When we left the boarding house to go up onto the hill, I was praying quietly that there wouldn't be any other kids around to laugh at us.

SAM [enjoying the memory as much as HALLY]   Ja, I could see that.

605 HALLY   I made it obvious, did I?

SAM   Ja. You refused to carry it.

HALLY   Do you blame me? Can you remember what the poor thing looked like? Tomato-box wood and brown paper! Flour and water for glue! Two of

9. That is, the Donkin Reserve, a park established in Port Elizabeth in 1820.

my mother's old stockings for a tail, and then all those bits and pieces of
610   string you made me tie together so that we could fly it! Hell, no, that was
now only asking for a miracle to happen.

SAM   Then the big argument when I told you to hold the string and run with
it when I let go.

HALLY   I was prepared to run, all right, but straight back to the boarding
615   house.

SAM   [knowing what's coming]   So what happened?

HALLY   Come on, Sam, you remember as well as I do.

SAM   I want to hear it from you.

[HALLY pauses. He wants to be as accurate as possible.]

HALLY   You went a little distance from me down the hill, you held it up ready
620   to let it go. . . . "This is it," I thought. "Like everything else in my life, here
comes another fiasco." Then you shouted, "Go, Hally!" and I started to run.
[Another pause] I don't know how to describe it, Sam. Ja! The miracle happened! I was running, waiting for it to crash to the ground, but instead suddenly there was something alive behind me at the end of the string, tugging
625   at it as if it wanted to be free. I looked back . . . [Shakes his head.] . . . I still
can't believe my eyes. It was flying! Looping around and trying to climb
even higher into the sky. You shouted to me to let it have more string. I did,
until there was none left and I was just holding that piece of wood we had
tied it to. You came up and joined me. You were laughing.

630   SAM   So were you. And shouting, "It works, Sam! We've done it!"

HALLY   And we had! I was so proud of us! It was the most splendid thing I
had ever seen. I wished there were hundreds of kids around to watch us.
The part that scared me, though, was when you showed me how to make it
dive down to the ground and then just when it was on the point of crash-
635   ing, swoop up again!

SAM   You didn't want to try yourself.

HALLY   Of course not! I would have been suicidal if anything had happened
to it. Watching you do it made me nervous enough. I was quite happy just
to see it up there with its tail fluttering behind it. You left me after that,
640   didn't you? You explained how to get it down, we tied it to the bench so that
I could sit and watch it, and you went away. I wanted you to stay, you know.
I was a little scared of having to look after it by myself.

SAM   [quietly]   I had work to do, Hally.

HALLY   It was sort of sad bringing it down, Sam. And it looked sad again
645   when it was lying there on the ground. Like something that had lost its
soul. Just tomato-box wood, brown paper and two of my mother's old stockings! But, hell, I'll never forget that first moment when I saw it up there. I
had a stiff neck the next day from looking up so much.

[SAM laughs. HALLY turns to him with a question he never thought of asking before.]

Why did you make that kite, Sam?

650   SAM   [evenly]   I can't remember.

HALLY   Truly?

SAM   Too long ago, Hally.

HALLY   Ja, I suppose it was. It's time for another one, you know.

SAM   Why do you say that?

655   HALLY   Because it feels like that. Wouldn't be a good day to fly it, though.

SAM   No. You can't fly kites on rainy days.

HALLY [*he studies* SAM. *Their memories have made him conscious of the man's presence in his life*]   How old are you, Sam?

SAM   Two score and five.

HALLY   Strange, isn't it?

660 SAM   What?

HALLY   Me and you.

SAM   What's strange about it?

HALLY   Little white boy in short trousers and a black man old enough to be his father flying a kite. It's not every day you see that.

665 SAM   But why strange? Because the one is white and the other black?

HALLY   I don't know. Would have been just as strange, I suppose, if it had been me and my Dad . . . cripple man and a little boy! Nope! There's no chance of me flying a kite without it being strange. [*Simple statement of fact—no self-pity*] There's a nice little short story there. "The Kite-Flyers."

670 But we'd have to find a twist in the ending.

SAM   Twist?

HALLY   Yes. Something unexpected. The way it ended with us was too straightforward . . . me on the bench and you going back to work. There's no drama in that.

675 WILLIE   And me?

HALLY   You?

WILLIE   Yes me.

HALLY   You want to get into the story as well, do you? I got it! Change the title: "Afternoons in Sam's Room" . . . expand it and tell all the stories. It's on

680 its way to being a novel. Our days in the old Jubilee. Sad in a way that they're over. I almost wish we were still in that little room.

SAM   We're still together.

HALLY   That's true. It's just that life felt the right size in there . . . not too big and not too small. Wasn't so hard to work up a bit of courage. It's got so

685 bloody complicated since then.

[*The telephone rings.* SAM *answers it.*]

SAM   St. George's Park Tea Room . . . Hello, Madam . . . Yes, Madam, he's here. . . . Hally, it's your mother.

HALLY   Where is she phoning from?

SAM   Sounds like the hospital. It's a public telephone.

690 HALLY [*relieved*]   You see! I told you. [*The telephone*] Hello, Mom . . . Yes . . . Yes no fine. Everything's under control here. How's things with poor old Dad? . . . Has he had a bad turn? . . . What? . . . Oh, God! . . . Yes, Sam told me, but I was sure he'd made a mistake. But what's this all about, Mom? He didn't look at all good last night. How can he get better so quickly? . . .

695 Then very obviously you must say no. Be firm with him. You're the boss. . . . You know what it's going to be like if he comes home. . . . Well then, don't blame me when I fail my exams at the end of the year. . . . Yes! How am I expected to be fresh for school when I spend half the night massaging his gammy[1] leg? . . . So am I! . . . So tell him a white lie. Say Dr. Colley wants

700 more X-rays of his stump. Or bribe him. We'll sneak in double tots of brandy in future. . . . What? . . . Order him to get back into bed at once! If

---

1. Game; lame.

he's going to behave like a child, treat him like one. . . . All right, Mom! I
was just trying to . . . I'm sorry. . . . I said I'm sorry. . . . Quick, give me your
number. I'll phone you back. [*He hangs up and waits a few seconds.*] Here
705   we go again! [*He dials.*] I'm sorry, Mom. . . . Okay . . . But now listen to me
carefully. All it needs is for you to put your foot down. Don't take no for an
answer. . . . Did you hear me? And whatever you do, don't discuss it with
him. . . . Because I'm frightened you'll give in to him. . . . Yes, Sam gave me
lunch. . . . I ate all of it! . . . No, Mom not a soul. It's still raining here. . . .
710   Right, I'll tell them. I'll just do some homework and then lock up. . . . But
remember now, Mom. Don't listen to anything he says. And phone me back
and let me know what happens. . . . Okay. Bye, Mom. [*He hangs up. The
men are staring at him.*] My Mom says that when you're finished with the
floors you must do the windows. [*Pause*] Don't misunderstand me, chaps.
715   All I want is for him to get better. And if he was, I'd be the first person to
say: "Bring him home." But he's not, and we can't give him the medical
care and attention he needs at home. That's what hospitals are there for.
[*Brusquely*] So don't just stand there! Get on with it!

         [SAM *clears* HALLY's *table.*]

You heard right. My Dad wants to go home.
720   SAM   Is he better?

HALLY [*sharply*]   No! How the hell can he be better when last night he was
groaning with pain? This is not an age of miracles!

SAM   Then he should stay in hospital.

HALLY [*seething with irritation and frustration*]   Tell me something I don't
725   know, Sam. What the hell do you think I was saying to my Mom? All I can
say is fuck-it-all.

SAM   I'm sure he'll listen to your Mom.

HALLY   You don't know what she's up against. He's already packed his shaving kit and pajamas and is sitting on his bed with his crutches, dressed and
730   ready to go. I know him when he gets in that mood. If she tries to reason
with him, we've had it. She's no match for him when it comes to a battle of
words. He'll tie her up in knots. [*Trying to hide his true feelings*]

SAM   I suppose it gets lonely for him in there.

HALLY   With all the patients and nurses around? Regular visits from the Sal
735   vation Army? Balls! It's ten times worse for him at home. I'm at school and
my mother is here in the business all day.

SAM   He's at least got you at night.

HALLY [*before he can stop himself*]   And we've got him! Please! I don't want
to talk about it anymore. [*Unpacks his school case, slamming down books on
740   the table.*] Life is just a plain bloody mess, that's all. And people are fools.

SAM   Come on, Hally.

HALLY   Yes, they are! They bloody well deserve what they get.

SAM   Then don't complain.

HALLY   Don't try to be clever, Sam. It doesn't suit you. Anybody who thinks
745   there's nothing wrong with this world needs to have his head examined.
Just when things are going along all right, without fail someone or something will come along and spoil everything. Somebody should write that
down as a fundamental law of the Universe. The principle of perpetual disappointment. If there is a God who created this world, he should scrap it
750   and try again.

SAM   All right, Hally, all right. What you got for homework?

HALLY   Bullshit, as usual. [*Opens an exercise book and reads.*] "Write five hundred words describing an annual event of cultural or historical significance."

755 SAM   That should be easy enough for you.

HALLY   And also plain bloody boring. You know what he wants, don't you? One of their useless old ceremonies. The commemoration of the landing of the 1820 Settlers,[2] or if it's going to be culture, Carols by Candlelight every Christmas.

760 SAM   It's an impressive sight. Make a good description, Hally. All those candles glowing in the dark and the people singing hymns.

HALLY   And it's called religious hysteria. [*Intense irritation*] Please, Sam! Just leave me alone and let me get on with it. I'm not in the mood for games this afternoon. And remember my Mom's orders . . . you're to help Willie with
765 the windows. Come on now, I don't want any more nonsense in here.

SAM   Okay, Hally, okay.

> [HALLY *settles down to his homework; determined preparations . . . pen, ruler, exercise book, dictionary, another cake . . . all of which will lead to nothing.*]

[SAM *waltzes over to* WILLIE *and starts to replace tables and chairs. He practices a ballroom step while doing so.* WILLIE *watches. When* SAM *is finished,* WILLIE *tries.*] Good! But just a little bit quicker on the turn and only move in to her after she's crossed over. What about this one?

> [*Another step. When* SAM *is finished,* WILLIE *again has a go.*]

Much better. See what happens when you just relax and enjoy yourself?
770 Remember that in two weeks' time and you'll be all right.

WILLIE   But I haven't got partner, Boet Sam.

SAM   Maybe Hilda will turn up tonight.

WILLIE   No, Boet Sam. [*Reluctantly*] I gave her a good hiding.

SAM   You mean a bad one.

775 WILLIE   Good bad one.

SAM   Then you mustn't complain either. Now you pay the price for losing your temper.

WILLIE   I also pay two pounds ten shilling entrance fee.

SAM   They'll refund you if you withdraw now.

780 WILLIE   [*appalled*]   You mean, don't dance?

SAM   Yes.

WILLIE   No! I wait too long and I practice too hard. If I find me new partner, you think I can be ready in two weeks? I ask Madam for my leave now and we practice every day.

785 SAM   Quickstep non-stop for two weeks. World record, Willie, but you'll be mad at the end.

WILLIE   No jokes, Boet Sam.

SAM   I'm not joking.

WILLIE   So then what?

790 SAM   Find Hilda. Say you're sorry and promise you won't beat her again.

WILLIE   No.

---

2. That is, the founders of Port Elizabeth, which was established to strengthen the Cape Colony against the Xhosa people to the east.

SAM   Then withdraw. Try again next year.

WILLIE   No.

SAM   Then I give up.

795   WILLIE   Haaikona, Boet Sam, you can't.

SAM   What do you mean, I can't? I'm telling you: I give up.

WILLIE   [adamant] No! [Accusingly] It was you who start me ballroom
dancing.

SAM   So?

WILLIE   Before that I use to be happy. And is you and Miriam who bring me
800   to Hilda and say here's partner for you.

SAM   What are you saying, Willie?

WILLIE   You!

SAM   But me what? To blame?

WILLIE   Yes.

805   SAM   Willie . . . ? [Bursts into laughter.]

WILLIE   And now all you do is make jokes at me. You wait. When Miriam
leaves you is my turn to laugh. Ha! Ha! Ha!

SAM   [he can't take WILLIE seriously any longer] She can leave me tonight! I
know what to do. [Bowing before an imaginary partner] May I have the
810   pleasure? [He dances and sings.]
    "Just a fellow with his pillow . . .
    Dancin' like a willow . . .
    In an autumn breeze . . ."

WILLIE   There you go again!

    [SAM goes on dancing and singing.]

815   Boet Sam!

SAM   There's the answer to your problem! Judges' announcement in two
weeks' time: "Ladies and gentlemen, the winner in the open section . . .
Mr. Willie Malopo and his pillow!"

    [This is too much for a now really angry WILLIE. He goes for SAM, but the
    latter is too quick for him and puts HALLY's table between the two of
    them.]

HALLY   [exploding] For Christ's sake, you two!

820   WILLIE   [still trying to get at SAM] I donner[3] you, Sam! Struesgod!

SAM   [still laughing] Sorry, Willie . . . Sorry . . .

HALLY   Sam! Willie! [Grabs his ruler and gives WILLIE a vicious whack on the
bum.] How the hell am I supposed to concentrate with the two of you
behaving like bloody children!

825   WILLIE   Hit him too!

HALLY   Shut up, Willie.

WILLIE   He started jokes again.

HALLY   Get back to your work. You too, Sam. [His ruler] Do you want
another one, Willie?

    [SAM and WILLIE return to their work. HALLY uses the opportunity to
    escape from his unsuccessful attempt at homework. He struts around like
    a little despot, ruler in hand, giving vent to his anger and frustration.]

830   Suppose a customer had walked in then? Or the Park Superintendent. And
seen the two of you behaving like a pair of hooligans. That would have

3. Beat up (slang).

been the end of my mother's license, you know. And your jobs! Well, this is the end of it. From now on there will be no more of your ballroom non-sense in here. This is a business establishment, not a bloody New Brighton[4] dancing school. I've been far too lenient with the two of you. [*Behind the counter for a green cool drink and a dollop of ice cream. He keeps up his tirade as he prepares it.*] But what really makes me bitter is that I allow you chaps a little freedom in here when business is bad and what do you do with it? The foxtrot! Specially you, Sam. There's more to life than trotting around a dance floor and I thought at least you knew it.

SAM   It's a harmless pleasure, Hally. It doesn't hurt anybody.

HALLY   It's also a rather simple one, you know.

SAM   You reckon so? Have you ever tried?

HALLY   Of course not.

SAM   Why don't you? Now.

HALLY   What do you mean? Me dance?

SAM   Yes. I'll show you a simple step—the waltz—then you try it.

HALLY   What will that prove?

SAM   That it might not be as easy as you think.

HALLY   I didn't say it was easy. I said it was simple—like in simple-minded, meaning mentally retarded. You can't exactly say it challenges the intellect.

SAM   It does other things.

HALLY   Such as?

SAM   Make people happy.

HALLY   [*the glass in his hand*]   So do American cream sodas with ice cream. For God's sake, Sam, you're not asking me to take ballroom dancing seri-ous, are you?

SAM   Yes.

HALLY   [*sigh of defeat*]   Oh, well, so much for trying to give you a decent edu-cation. I've obviously achieved nothing.

SAM   You still haven't told me what's wrong with admiring something that's beautiful and then trying to do it yourself.

HALLY   Nothing. But we happen to be talking about a foxtrot, not a thing of beauty.

SAM   But that is just what I'm saying. If you were to see two champions doing, two masters of the art . . . !

HALLY   Oh, God, I give up. So now it's also art!

SAM   Ja.

HALLY   There's a limit, Sam. Don't confuse art and entertainment.

SAM   So then what is art?

HALLY   You want a definition?

SAM   Ja.

HALLY   [*he realizes he has got to be careful. He gives the matter a lot of thought before answering*]   Philosophers have been trying to do that for centuries. What is Art? What is Life? But basically I suppose it's . . . the giving of meaning to matter.

SAM   Nothing to do with beautiful?

HALLY   It goes beyond that. It's the giving of form to the formless.

SAM   Ja, well, maybe it's not art, then. But I still say it's beautiful.

4. A suburb of Port Elizabeth (a black township).

HALLY   I'm sure the word you mean to use is entertaining.

SAM   [*adamant*]   No. Beautiful. And if you want proof, come along to the
880   Centenary Hall in New Brighton in two weeks' time.

[*The mention of the Centenary Hall draws* WILLIE *over to them.*]

HALLY   What for? I've seen the two of you prancing around in here often
enough.

SAM   [*he laughs*]   This isn't the real thing, Hally. We're just playing around in
here.

885   HALLY   So? I can use my imagination.

SAM   And what do you get?

HALLY   A lot of people dancing around and having a so-called good time.

SAM   That all?

HALLY   Well, basically it is that, surely.

890   SAM   No, it isn't. Your imagination hasn't helped you at all. There's a lot more
to it than that. We're getting ready for the championships, Hally, not just
another dance. There's going to be a lot of people, all right, and they're
going to have a good time, but they'll only be spectators, sitting around and
watching. It's just the competitors out there on the dance floor. Party dec-
895   orations and fancy lights all around the walls! The ladies in beautiful evening
dresses!

HALLY   My mother's got one of those, Sam, and, quite frankly, it's an embarrassment every time she wears it.

SAM   [*undeterred*]   Your imagination left out the excitement.

[HALLY *scoffs.*]

900   Oh, yes. The finalists are not going to be out there just to have a good time.
One of those couples will be the 1950 Eastern Province Champions. And
your imagination left out the music.

WILLIE   Mr. Elijah Gladman Guzana and his Orchestral Jazzonions.

SAM   The sound of the big band, Hally. Trombone, tenor and alto
905   sax. And then, finally, your imagination also left out the climax of the evening when the dancing is finished, the judges have stopped whispering
among themselves and the Master of Ceremonies collects their scorecards
and goes up onto the stage to announce the winners.

HALLY   All right. So you make it sound like a bit of a do. It's an occasion.
910   Satisfied?

SAM   [*victory*]   So you admit that!

HALLY   Emotionally yes, intellectually no.

SAM   Well, I don't know what you mean by that, all I'm telling you is that it is
going to be *the* event of the year in New Brighton. It's been sold out for two
915   weeks already. There's only standing room left. We've got competitors coming from Kingwilliamstown, East London, Port Alfred.[5]

[HALLY *starts pacing thoughtfully.*]

HALLY   Tell me a bit more.

SAM   I thought you weren't interested . . . intellectually.

HALLY   [*mysteriously*]   I've got my reasons.

920   SAM   What do you want to know?

HALLY   It takes place every year?

5. East London is a coastal city, not far from King William's Town and about 150 miles east of
Port Elizabeth; Port Alfred is a small town halfway between East London and Port Elizabeth.

SAM   Yes. But only every third year in New Brighton. It's East London's turn to have the championships next year.

HALLY   Which, I suppose, makes it an even more significant event.

925 SAM   Ah ha! We're getting somewhere. Our "occasion" is now a "significant event."

HALLY   I wonder.

SAM   What?

HALLY   I wonder if I would get away with it.

930 SAM   But what?

HALLY   [to the table and his exercise book]   "Write five hundred words describing an annual event of cultural or historical significance." Would I be stretching poetic license a little too far if I called your ballroom championships a cultural event?

935 SAM   You mean . . . ?

HALLY   You think we could get five hundred words out of it, Sam?

SAM   Victor Sylvester[6] has written a whole book on ballroom dancing.

WILLIE   You going to write about it, Master Hally?

HALLY   Yes, gentlemen, that is precisely what I am considering doing. Old Doc
940 Bromely—he's my English teacher—is going to argue with me, of course. He doesn't like natives. But I'll point out to him that in strict anthropological terms the culture of a primitive black society includes its dancing and singing. To put my thesis in a nutshell: The war-dance has been replaced by the waltz. But it still amounts to the same thing: the release of primitive
945 emotions through movement. Shall we give it a go?

SAM   I'm ready.

WILLIE   Me also.

HALLY   Ha! This will teach the old bugger a lesson. [Decision taken[7]] Right. Let's get ourselves organized. [This means another cake on the table. He sits.]
950 I think you've given me enough general atmosphere, Sam, but to build the tension and suspense I need facts. [Pencil poised]

WILLIE   Give him facts, Boet Sam.

HALLY   What you called the climax . . . how many finalists?

SAM   Six couples.

955 HALLY   [making notes]   Go on. Give me the picture.

SAM   Spectators seated right around the hall. [WILLIE becomes a spectator.]

HALLY   . . . and it's a full house.

SAM   At one end, on the stage, Gladman and his Orchestral Jazzonions. At the other end is a long table with the three judges. The six finalists go onto
960 the dance floor and take up their positions. When they are ready and the spectators have settled down, the Master of Ceremonies goes to the microphone. To start with, he makes some jokes to get the people laughing . . .

HALLY   Good touch! [As he writes] ". . . creating a relaxed atmosphere which will change to one of tension and drama as the climax is approached."

965 SAM   [onto a chair to act out the M.C.]   "Ladies and gentlemen, we come now to the great moment you have all been waiting for this evening. . . . The finals of the 1950 Eastern Province Open Ballroom Dancing Champion-

6. An English dancer and bandleader (1900–1978), who helped popularize ballroom dancing worldwide—notably, in Modern Ballroom

Dancing (1927); by 1952, it was already in its 45th edition.
7. Made.

ships. But first let me introduce the finalists! Mr. and Mrs. Welcome Tcha-
balala from Kingwilliamstown . . ."

970 WILLIE [*he applauds after every name*] Is when the people clap their hands
and whistle and make a lot of noise, Master Hally.

SAM "Mr. Mulligan Njikelane and Miss Nomhle Nkonyeni of Grahamstown;
Mr. and Mrs. Norman Nchinga from Port Alfred; Mr. Fats Bokolane and Miss
Dina Plaatjies from East London; Mr. Sipho Dugu and Mrs. Mable Magada
975 from Peddie; and from New Brighton our very own Mr. Willie Malopo and
Miss Hilda Samuels."

[WILLIE *can't believe his ears. He abandons his role as spectator and
scrambles into position as a finalist.*]

WILLIE Relaxed and ready to romance!

SAM The applause dies down. When everybody is silent, Gladman lifts up
his sax, nods at the Orchestral Jazzonions . . .

980 WILLIE Play the jukebox please, Boet Sam!

SAM I also only got bus fare, Willie.

HALLY Hold it, everybody. [*Heads for the cash register behind the counter.*]
How much is in the till, Sam?

SAM Three shillings. Hally . . . your Mom counted it before she left.

[HALLY *hesitates.*]

985 HALLY Sorry, Willie. You know how she carried on the last time I did it. We'll
just have to pool our combined imaginations and hope for the best. [*Returns
to the table.*] Back to work. How are the points scored, Sam?

SAM Maximum of ten points each for individual style, deportment, rhythm,
and general appearance.

990 WILLIE Must I start?

HALLY Hold it for a second, Willie. And penalties?

SAM For what?

HALLY For doing something wrong. Say you stumble or bump into somebody . . . do they take off any points?

995 SAM [*aghast*] Hally . . . !

HALLY When you're dancing. If you and your partner collide into another
couple.

[HALLY *can get no further.* SAM *has collapsed with laughter. He explains
to* WILLIE.]

SAM If me and Miriam bump into you and Hilda . . .

[WILLIE *joins him in another good laugh.*]

Hally, Hally . . . !

1000 HALLY [*perplexed*] Why? What did I say?

SAM There's no collisions out there, Hally. Nobody trips or stumbles or
bumps into anybody else. That's what that moment is all about. To be one
of those finalists on that dance floor is like . . . like being in a dream about
a world in which accidents don't happen.

1005 HALLY [*genuinely moved by* SAM's *image*] Jesus, Sam! That's beautiful!

WILLIE [*can endure waiting no longer*] I'm starting! [WILLIE *dances while*
SAM *talks.*]

SAM Of course it is. That's what I've been trying to say to you all afternoon.
And it's beautiful because that is what we want life to be like. But instead,
like you said, Hally, we're bumping into each other all the time. Look at the

1010   three of us this afternoon: I've bumped into Willie, the two of us have
          bumped into you, you've bumped into your mother, she bumping into your
          Dad. . . . None of us knows the steps and there's no music playing. And it
          doesn't stop with us. The whole world is doing it all the time. Open a news-
          paper and what do you read? America has bumped into Russia, England is
1015   bumping into India, rich man bumps into poor man. Those are big colli-
          sions, Hally. They make for a lot of bruises. People get hurt in all that
          bumping, and we're sick and tired of it now. It's been going on for too long.
          Are we never going to get it right? . . . Learn to dance life like champions
          instead of always being just a bunch of beginners at it?

1020 HALLY [deep and sincere admiration of the man]   You've got a vision, Sam!
      SAM   Not just me. What I'm saying to you is that everybody's got it. That's
          why there's only standing room left for the Centenary Hall in two weeks'
          time. For as long as the music lasts, we are going to see six couples get it
          right, the way we want life to be.
1025 HALLY   But is that the best we can do, Sam . . . watch six finalists dreaming
          about the way it should be?
      SAM   I don't know. But it starts with that. Without the dream we won't know
          what we're going for. And anyway I reckon there are a few people who have
          got past just dreaming about it and are trying for something real. Remem-
1030   ber that thing we read once in the paper about the Mahatma Gandhi?[8]
          Going without food to stop those riots in India?
      HALLY   You're right. He certainly was trying to teach people to get the steps
          right.
      SAM   And the Pope.
1035 HALLY   Yes, he's another one. Our old General Smuts[9] as well, you know.
          He's also out there dancing. You know, Sam, when you come to think of it,
          that's what the United Nations boils down to . . . a dancing school for
          politicians!
      SAM   And let's hope they learn.
      HALLY [a little surge of hope]   You're right. We mustn't despair. Maybe there's
1040   some hope for mankind after all. Keep it up, Willie. [Back to his table with
          determination] This is a lot bigger than I thought. So what have we got?
          Yes, our title: "A World Without Collisions."
      SAM   That sounds good! "A World Without Collisions."
      HALLY   Subtitle: "Global Politics on the Dance Floor." No. A bit too heavy,
1045   hey? What about "Ballroom Dancing as a Political Vision"?
                [The telephone rings. SAM answers it.]
      SAM   St. George's Park Tea Room . . . Yes, Madam . . . Hally, it's your Mom.
      HALLY [back to reality]   Oh, God, yes! I'd forgotten all about that. Shit!
          Remember my words, Sam? Just when you're enjoying yourself, someone
          or something will come along and wreck everything.

---

8. Indian political activist and religious leader
(1869–1948) who used nonviolent resistance
and fasting in his struggle against British
imperial rule; when violence between Muslims and Hindus erupted before the partition
of the Indian subcontinent into India and
Pakistan, he undertook lengthy fasts (the last
ended with his assassination).

9. Jan Christian Smuts (1870–1950), a South
African statesman and soldier who helped
found the Union of South Africa (1910) as a
self-governing nation within the British Commonwealth. He twice served as its prime
minister (1919–24, 1939–48), and he championed the creation of both the League of
Nations and the United Nations.

1050 SAM   You haven't heard what she's got to say yet.
      HALLY   Public telephone?
      SAM   No.
      HALLY   Does she sound happy or unhappy?
      SAM   I couldn't tell. [*Pause*] She's waiting, Hally.
1055 HALLY   [*to the telephone*]   Hello, Mom . . . No, everything is okay here. Just
      doing my homework. . . . What's your news? . . . You've what? . . . [*Pause.*
      He takes the receiver away from his ear for a few seconds. In the course of
      HALLY's *telephone conversation*, SAM *and* WILLIE *discretely position the*
      stacked tables and chairs. HALLY *places the receiver back to his ear.*] Yes, I'm
      still here. Oh, well, I give up now. Why did you do it, Mom? . . . Well, I just
      hope you know what you've let us in for. . . . [*Loudly*] I said I hope you
1060 know what you've let us in for! It's the end of the peace and quiet we've
      been having. [*Softly*] Where is he? [*Normal voice*] He can't hear us from in
      there. But for God's sake, Mom, what happened? I told you to be firm with
      him. . . . Then you and the nurses should have held him down, taken his
      crutches away. . . . I know only too well he's my father! . . . I'm not being
1065 disrespectful, but I'm sick and tired of emptying stinking chamberpots full
      of phlegm and piss. . . . Yes, I do! When you're not there, he asks *me* to do
      it. . . . If you really want to know the truth, that's why I've got no appetite
      for my food. . . . Yes! There's a lot of things you don't know about. For your
      information, I still haven't got that science textbook I need. And you know
1070 why? He borrowed the money you gave me for it. . . . Because I didn't want
      to start another fight between you two. . . . He says that every time. . . . All
      right, Mom! [*Viciously*] Then just remember to start hiding your bag away
      again, because he'll be at your purse before long for money for booze. And
      when he's well enough to come down here, you better keep an eye on the
1075 till as well, because that is also going to develop a leak. . . . Then don't
      complain to me when he starts his old tricks. . . . Yes, you do. I get it from
      you on one side and from him on the other, and it makes life hell for me.
      I'm not going to be the peacemaker anymore. I'm warning you now: when
      the two of you start fighting again, I'm leaving home. . . . Mom, if you start
1080 crying, I'm going to put down the receiver. . . . Okay . . . [*Lowering his*
      voice to a vicious whisper] Okay, Mom. I heard you. [*Desperate*] No. . . .
      Because I don't want to. I'll see him when I get home! Mom! . . . [*Pause.*
      When he speaks again, his tone changes completely. It is not simply pretense.
      We sense a genuine emotional conflict.] Welcome home, chum! . . . What's
      that? . . . Don't be silly, Dad. You being home is just about the best news in
1085 the world. . . . I bet you are. Bloody depressing there with everybody going
      on about their ailments, hey! . . . How you feeling? . . . Good . . . Here as
      well, pal. Coming down cats and dogs. . . . That's right. Just the day for a
      kip and a toss in your old Uncle Ned.[1] . . . Everything's just hunky-dory on
      my side, Dad. . . . Well, to start with, there's a nice pile of comics for you
1090 on the counter. . . . Yes, old Kemple brought them in. *Batman and Robin,*
      Submariner . . . just your cup of tea . . . I will. . . . Yes, we'll spin a few
      yarns tonight. . . . Okay, chum, see you in a little while. . . . No, I promise.
      I'll come straight home. . . . [*Pause—his mother comes back on the phone.*]
      Mom? Okay. I'll lock up now. . . . What? . . . Oh, the brandy . . . Yes, I'll

---

1. That is, a nap (kip, toss) in your bed ("Uncle Ned" in Cockney rhyming slang).

1095   remember! . . . I'll put it in my suitcase now, for God's sake. I know well
        enough what will happen if he doesn't get it. . . . [*Places a bottle of brandy
        on the counter.*] I *was* kind to him, Mom. I didn't say anything nasty! . . . All
        right. Bye. [*End of telephone conversation. A desolate* HALLY *doesn't move. A
        strained silence.*]

SAM [*quietly*]   That sounded like a bad bump, Hally.

HALLY [*having a hard time controlling his emotions. He speaks carefully*]
1100   Mind your own business, Sam.

SAM   Sorry. I wasn't trying to interfere. Shall we carry on? Hally? [*He indi-
        cates the exercise book. No response from* HALLY.]

WILLIE [*also trying*]   Tell him about when they give out the cups, Boet Sam.

SAM   Ja! That's another big moment. The presentation of the cups after the
        winners have been announced. You've got to put that in.

            [*Still no response from* HALLY.]

1105 WILLIE   A big silver one, Master Hally, called floating trophy for the champions.

SAM   We always invite some big-shot personality to hand them over. Guest of
        honor this year is going to be His Holiness Bishop Jabulani of the All Afri-
        can Free Zionist Church.

            [HALLY *gets up abruptly, goes to his table and tears up the page he was
            writing on.*]

HALLY   So much for a bloody world without collisions.

1110 SAM   Too bad. It was on its way to being a good composition.

HALLY   Let's stop bullshitting ourselves, Sam.

SAM   Have we been doing that?

HALLY   Yes! That's what all our talk about a decent world has been . . . just so
        much bullshit.

1115 SAM   We did say it was still only a dream.

HALLY   And a bloody useless one at that. Life's a fuck-up and it's never going
        to change.

SAM   Ja, maybe that's true.

HALLY   There's no maybe about it. It's a blunt and brutal fact. All we've done
1120   this afternoon is waste our time.

SAM   Not if we'd got your homework done.

HALLY   I don't give a shit about my homework, so, for Christ's sake, just shut
        up about it. [*Slamming books viciously into his school case*] Hurry up now
        and finish your work. I want to lock up and get out of here. [*Pause*] And
1125   then go where? Home-sweet-fucking-home. Jesus, I hate that word.

            [HALLY *goes to the counter to put the brandy bottle and comics in his
            school case. After a moment's hesitation, he smashes the bottle of brandy.
            He abandons all further attempts to hide his feelings.* SAM *and* WILLIE
            work away as unobtrusively as possible.]

        Do you want to know what is really wrong with your lovely little dream,
        Sam? It's not just that we are all bad dancers. That does happen to be per-
        fectly true, but there's more to it than just that. You left out the cripples.

SAM   Hally!

1130 HALLY [*now totally reckless*]   Ja! Can't leave them out, Sam. That's why we
        always end up on our backsides on the dance floor. They're also out there
        dancing . . . like a bunch of broken spiders trying to do the quickstep! [*An
        ugly attempt at laughter*] When you come to think of it, it's a bloody comi-
        cal sight. I mean, it's bad enough on two legs . . . but one and a pair of

1606 | ATHOL FUGARD

1135   crutches! Hell, no, Sam. That's guaranteed to turn that dance floor into a
shambles. Why you shaking your head? Picture it, man. For once this afternoon let's use our imaginations sensibly.

SAM   Be careful, Hally.

HALLY   Of what? The truth? I seem to be the only one around here who is
1140   prepared to face it. We've had the pretty dream, it's time now to wake up
and have a good long look at the way things really are. Nobody knows the
steps, there's no music, the cripples are also out there tripping up everybody and trying to get into the act, and it's all called the All-Comers-How-
to-Make-a-Fuckup-of-Life Championships. [*Another ugly laugh*] Hang on,
1145   Sam! The best bit is still coming. Do you know what the winner's trophy is?
A beautiful big chamber-pot with roses on the side, and it's full to the brim
with piss. And guess who I think is going to be this year's winner.

SAM [*almost shouting*]   Stop now!

HALLY [*suddenly appalled by how far he has gone*]   Why?

1150 SAM   Hally? It's your father you're talking about.

HALLY   So?

SAM   Do you know what you've been saying?

      [HALLY *can't answer. He is rigid with shame.* SAM *speaks to him sternly.*]

    No, Hally, you mustn't do it. Take back those words and ask for forgiveness!
It's a terrible sin for a son to mock his father with jokes like that. You'll
1155   be punished if you carry on. Your father is your father, even if he is a . . .
cripple man.

WILLIE   Yes, Master Hally. Is true what Sam say.

SAM   I understand how you are feeling, Hally, but even so . . .

HALLY   No, you don't!

1160 SAM   I think I do.

HALLY   And I'm telling you you don't. Nobody does. [*Speaking carefully as his
shame turns to rage at* SAM] It's your turn to be careful, Sam. Very careful!
You're treading on dangerous ground. Leave me and my father alone.

SAM   I'm not the one who's been saying things about him.

1165 HALLY   What goes on between me and my Dad is none of your business!

SAM   Then don't tell me about it. If that's all you've got to say about him, I
don't want to hear.

      [*For a moment* HALLY *is at loss for a response.*]

HALLY   Just get on with your bloody work and shut up.

SAM   Swearing at me won't help you.

1170 HALLY   Yes, it does! Mind your own fucking business and shut up!

SAM   Okay. If that's the way you want it, I'll stop trying.

      [*He turns away. This infuriates* HALLY *even more.*]

HALLY   Good. Because what you've been trying to do is meddle in something
you know nothing about. All that concerns you in here, Sam, is to try and
do what you get paid for—keep the place clean and serve the customers. In
1175   plain words, just get on with your job. My mother is right. She's always
warning me about allowing you to get too familiar. Well, this time you've
gone too far. It's going to stop right now.

      [*No response from* SAM.]

    You're only a servant in here, and don't forget it.

      [*Still no response.* HALLY *is trying hard to get one.*]

And as far as my father is concerned, all you need to remember is that he
1180   is your boss.

SAM [*needled at last*]   No, he isn't. I get paid by your mother.

HALLY   Don't argue with me, Sam!

SAM   Then don't say he's my boss.

HALLY   He's a white man and that's good enough for you.

1185   SAM   I'll try to forget you said that.

HALLY   Don't! Because you won't be doing me a favor if you do. I'm telling
   you to remember it.

   [*A pause.* SAM *pulls himself together and makes one last effort.*]

SAM   Hally, Hally . . . ! Come on now. Let's stop before it's too late. You're
   right. We *are* on dangerous ground. If we're not careful, somebody is going
1190   to get hurt.

HALLY   It won't be me.

SAM   Don't be so sure.

HALLY   I don't know what you're talking about, Sam.

SAM   Yes, you do.

1195   HALLY [*furious*]   Jesus, I wish you would stop trying to tell me what I do and
   what I don't know.

   [SAM *gives up. He turns to* WILLIE.]

SAM   Let's finish up.

HALLY   Don't turn your back on me! I haven't finished talking.

   [*He grabs* SAM *by the arm and tries to make him turn around.* SAM *reacts
   with a flash of anger.*]

SAM   Don't do that, Hally! [*Facing the boy*] All right, I'm listening. Well?
1200   What do you want to say to me?

HALLY [*pause as* HALLY *looks for something to say*]   To begin with, why don't
   you also start calling me Master Harold, like Willie.

SAM   Do you mean that?

HALLY   Why the hell do you think I said it?

1205   SAM   And if I don't?

HALLY   You might just lose your job.

SAM [*quietly and very carefully*]   If you make me say it once, I'll never call
   you anything else again.

HALLY   So? [*The boy confronts the man.*] Is that meant to be a threat?

1210   SAM   Just telling you what will happen if you make me do that. You must
   decide what it means to you.

HALLY   Well, I have. It's good news. Because that is exactly what Master
   Harold wants from now on. Think of it as a little lesson in respect, Sam,
   that's long overdue, and I hope you remember it as well as you do your geo-
1215   graphy. I can tell you now that somebody who will be glad to hear I've
   finally given it to you will be my Dad. Yes! He agrees with my Mom. He's
   always going on about it as well. "You must teach the boys to show you
   more respect, my son."

SAM   So now you can stop complaining about going home. Everybody is
1220   going to be happy tonight.

HALLY   That's perfectly correct. You see, you mustn't get the wrong idea
   about me and my Dad, Sam. We also have our good times together. Some
   bloody good laughs. He's got a marvelous sense of humor. Want to know

what our favorite joke is? He gives out a big groan, you see, and says: "It's
not fair, is it, Hally?" Then I have to ask: "What, chum?" And then he says:
"A nigger's arse"[2] . . . and we both have a good laugh.

> [*The men stare at him with disbelief.*]

What's the matter, Willie? Don't you catch the joke? You always were a bit
slow on the uptake. It's what is called a pun. You see, fair means both light
in color and to be just and decent. [*He turns to* SAM.] I thought *you* would
catch it, Sam.

SAM   Oh ja, I catch it all right.

HALLY   But it doesn't appeal to your sense of humor.

SAM   Do you really laugh?

HALLY   Of course.

SAM   To please him? Make him feel good?

HALLY   No, for heaven's sake! I laugh because I think it's a bloody good joke.

SAM   You're really trying hard to be ugly, aren't you? And why drag poor old
Willie into it? He's done nothing to you except show you the respect you
want so badly. That's also not being fair, you know . . . and *I* mean just or
decent.

WILLIE   It's all right, Sam. Leave it now.

SAM   It's me you're after. You should just have said "Sam's arse" . . . because
that's the one you're trying to kick. Anyway, how do you know it's not fair?
You've never seen it. Do you want to? [*He drops his trousers and underpants
and presents his backside for* HALLY's *inspection.*] Have a good look. A real
Basuto[3] arse . . . which is about as nigger as they can come. Satisfied?
[*Trousers up*] Now you can make your Dad even happier when you go home
tonight. Tell him I showed you my arse and he is quite right. It's not fair.
And if it will give him an even better laugh next time, I'll also let *him* have
a look. Come, Willie, let's finish up and go.

> [SAM *and* WILLIE *start to tidy up the tea room.* HALLY *doesn't move. He
> waits for a moment when* SAM *passes him.*]

HALLY [*quietly*]   Sam . . .

> [SAM *stops and looks expectantly at the boy.* HALLY *spits in his face. A long
> and heartfelt groan from* WILLIE. *For a few seconds* SAM *doesn't move.*]

SAM [*taking out a handkerchief and wiping his face*]   It's all right, Willie.

> [*To* HALLY.]

Ja, well, you've done it . . . Master Harold. Yes, I'll start calling you that
from now on. It won't be difficult anymore. You've hurt yourself, Master
Harold. I saw it coming. I warned you, but you wouldn't listen. You've just
hurt yourself *bad*. And you're a coward, Master Harold. The face you
should be spitting in is your father's . . . but you used mine, because you
think you're safe inside your fair skin . . . and this time I don't mean just or
decent. [*Pause, then moving violently towards* HALLY] Should I hit him,
Willie?

WILLIE [*stopping* SAM]   No, Boet Sam.

SAM [*violently*]   Why not?

WILLIE   It won't help, Boet Sam.

---

2. In editions and performances outside the
United States, Fugard replaces "nigger's" with
"kaffir's," a term that in South Africa conveys
comparable insult and contempt.
3. One of the principal tribal groups of southern Africa.

SAM   I don't want to help! I want to hurt him.

1265 WILLIE   You also hurt yourself.

SAM   And if he had done it to you, Willie?

WILLIE   Me? Spit at me like I was a dog? [*A thought that had not occurred to him before. He looks at* HALLY.] Ja. Then I want to hit him. I want to hit him hard!

[*A dangerous few seconds as the men stand staring at the boy.* WILLIE *turns away, shaking his head.*]

1270 But maybe all I do is go cry at the back. He's little boy, Boet Sam. Little *white* boy. Long trousers now, but he's still little boy.

SAM   [*his violence ebbing away into defeat as quickly as it flooded*] You're right. So go on, then: groan again, Willie. You do it better than me. [*To* HALLY] You don't know all of what you've just done . . . Master Harold. It's

1275 not just that you've made me feel dirtier than I've ever been in my life . . . I mean, how do I wash off yours and your father's filth? . . . I've also failed. A long time ago I promised myself I was going to try and do something, but you've just shown me . . . Master Harold . . . that I've failed. [*Pause*] I've also got a memory of a little white boy when he was still wearing short

1280 trousers and a black man, but they're not flying a kite. It was the old Jubilee days,[4] after dinner one night. I was in my room. You came in and just stood against the wall, looking down at the ground, and only after I'd asked you what you wanted, what was wrong, I don't know how many times, did you speak and even then so softly I almost didn't hear you. "Sam, please

1285 help me to go and fetch my Dad." Remember? He was dead drunk on the floor of the Central Hotel Bar. They'd phoned for your Mom, but you were the only one at home. And do you remember how we did it? You went in first by yourself to ask permission for me to go into the bar. Then I loaded him onto my back like a baby and carried him back to the boarding house

1290 with you following behind carrying his crutches. [*Shaking his head as he remembers*] A crowded Main Street with all the people watching a little white boy following his drunk father on a nigger's back! I felt for that little boy . . . Master Harold. I felt for him. After that we still had to clean him up, remember? He'd messed in his trousers, so we had to clean him up and

1295 get him into bed.

HALLY   [*great pain*]   I love him, Sam.

SAM   I know you do. That's why I tried to stop you from saying these things about him. It would have been so simple if you could have just despised him for being a weak man. But he's your father. You love him and you're

1300 ashamed of him. You're ashamed of so much! . . . And now that's going to include yourself. That was the promise I made to myself: to try and stop that happening. [*Pause*] After we got him to bed you came back with me to my room and sat in a corner and carried on just looking down at the ground. And for days after that! You hadn't done anything wrong, but you

1305 went around as if you owed the world an apology for being alive. I didn't like seeing that! That's not the way a boy grows up to be a man! . . . But the one person who should have been teaching you what that means was the cause of your shame. If you really want to know, that's why I made you that kite. I wanted you to look up, be proud of something, of yourself . . . [*Bitter*

4. That is, when they were living in the old Jubilee Boarding House.

1310 *smile at the memory]* . . . and you certainly were that when I left you with it
up there on the hill. Oh, ja . . . something else! . . . If you ever do write it
as a short story, there *was* a twist in our ending. I couldn't sit down there
and stay with you. It was a "Whites Only" bench. You were too young, too
excited to notice then. But not anymore. If you're not careful . . . Master
1315 Harold . . . you're going to be sitting up there by yourself for a long time to
come, and there won't be a kite in the sky. [SAM *has got nothing more to say.
He exits into the kitchen, taking off his waiter's jacket.*]

WILLIE   Is bad. Is all all bad in here now.

HALLY [*looks into his school case, raincoat on*] Willie . . . [*It is difficult to
speak.*] Will you lock up for me and look after the keys?

1320 WILLIE   Okay.

          [SAM *returns.* HALLY *goes behind the counter and collects the few coins in
          the cash register. As he starts to leave . . .*]

SAM   Don't forget the comic books.

          [HALLY *returns to the counter and puts them in his case. He starts to leave
          again.*]

SAM [*to the retreating back of the boy*]   Stop . . . Hally . . .

          [HALLY *stops, but doesn't turn to face him.*]

       Hally . . . I've got no right to tell you what being a man means if I don't
       behave like one myself, and I'm not doing so well at that this afternoon.
1325   Should we try again, Hally?

HALLY   Try what?

SAM   Fly another kite, I suppose. It worked once, and this time I need it as
       much as you do.

HALLY   It's still raining, Sam. You can't fly kites on rainy days, remember.

1330 SAM   So what do we do? Hope for better weather tomorrow?

HALLY [*helpless gesture*]   I don't know. I don't know anything anymore.

SAM   You sure of that, Hally? Because it would be pretty hopeless if that was
       true. It would mean nothing has been learnt in here this afternoon, and
       there was a hell of a lot of teaching going on . . . one way or the other. But
1335   anyway, I don't believe you. I reckon there's one thing you know. You don't
       have to sit up there by yourself. You know what that bench means now, and
       you can leave it any time you choose. All you've got to do is stand up and
       walk away from it.

          [HALLY *leaves.* WILLIE *goes up quietly to* SAM.]

WILLIE   Is okay, Boet Sam. You see. Is . . . [*He can't find any better words.*] . . .
1340   is going to be okay tomorrow. [*Changing his tone*] Hey, Boet Sam! [*He is
       trying hard.*] You right. I think about it and you right. Tonight I find Hilda
       and say sorry. And make promise I won't beat her no more. You hear me,
       Boet Sam?

SAM   I hear you, Willie.

1345 WILLIE   And when we practice I relax and romance with her from beginning to
       end. Non-stop! You watch! Two weeks' time: "First prize for promising new-
       comers: Mr. Willie Malopo and Miss Hilda Samuels." [*Sudden impulse*] To
       hell with it! I walk home. [*He goes to the jukebox, puts in a coin and selects a
       record. The machine comes to life in the gray twilight, blushing its way through
       a spectrum of soft, romantic colors.*] How did you say it, Boet Sam? Let's
1350   dream. [WILLIE *sways with the music and gestures for* SAM *to dance.*]

[*Sarah Vaughan sings.*[5]]
"Little man you're crying,
I know why you're blue,
    Someone took your kiddy car away;
    Better go to sleep now,
Little man you've had a busy day." [*etc. etc.*]

1355

        You lead. I follow.
        [*The men dance together.*]
"Johnny won your marbles,
    Tell you what we'll do;
    Dad will get you new ones right away;
    Better go to sleep now,
    Little man you've had a busy day."

1360

5. "Little Man You've Had a Busy Day" (1934; by Al Hoffman, Maurice Sigler, and Mabel Wayne), recorded by Sarah Vaughan and the Count Basie Orchestra in 1961.

AUGUST WILSON

1945–2005

OF the many African American dramatists who have written for the theater since Lorraine Hansberry's acclaimed *A Raisin in the Sun* (1959), none has enjoyed more popular and critical success than August Wilson. *Ma Rainey's Black Bottom* (1984), the first of Wilson's plays to reach Broadway, won the New York Drama Critics' Circle Award for best new play; FENCES (1985) received numerous honors, including the Tony Award for Best Play and the Pulitzer Prize; and *The Piano Lesson* (1987) won Wilson another Drama Critics' Circle Award and a second Pulitzer. Subsequent plays, which continued Wilson's stated project of dramatizing African American history throughout the twentieth century one decade at a time, have also received widespread acclaim. Few dramatists, white or black, have matched Wilson's historical and sociological ambition or so minutely examined the dynamics, memories, and traumas that constitute the twentieth-century African American community.

Wilson was born Frederick August Kittel on April 27, 1945, in the Hill District, a largely African American neighborhood of Pittsburgh, where all but one of his major plays are set. The fourth of six children, he was the son of a black mother and a white German baker who was absent throughout his childhood. The family had little money, relying mainly on welfare and on Daisy Wilson Kittel's earnings as a janitor. When his father, whose name he bore, died in 1965, the future writer began calling himself August Wilson, thereby choosing to identify with the African American side of his family. By that point in his life, Wilson had had ample opportunity to learn what such an identity meant in the civil rights– era United States. In 1959 his mother and her second husband, a black man named David Bedford who worked in the city Sewer Department and would provide a model for Troy in *Fences,* had moved the family to a predominantly white neighborhood. Wilson's teenage years took him from one high school to another until, the target of racist remarks and ostracism, he dropped out of school for good in tenth grade when a teacher accused him of plagiarism, insisting that his paper on Napoleon was so good that one of his sisters must have written it.

Unwilling to tell his parents what he had done, Wilson spent much of his free time in a public library; there, in the "Negro Section," he discovered the works of such African American writers as Langston Hughes, Ralph Ellison, and James Baldwin. Wilson later recalled in an interview that he derived comfort from the fact that black people wrote books, adding that he "used to dream about being part of the Harlem Renaissance." After serving one year in the U.S. Army and spending two years working odd jobs, he took major steps toward realizing his ambition in 1965 when he moved from his mother's house into a rooming house back in the Hill District, bought himself a typewriter, and changed his name. The move immersed Wilson in a culturally and socially vibrant African American community, and from the musicians, artists, ex-convicts, and workers he encountered he absorbed the personalities, behaviors, and stories that would later appear in his plays. Wilson also learned the rich and varied vernacular of this black community, marked by cadences and idioms that mixed northern and southern, urban and rural.

Wilson's early years as a writer coincided with a shift in politics and culture as the forms of social and artistic protest that characterized the late 1950s and early 1960s were replaced by the more radicalized politics of black separatism, cultural nationalism, and the black power movement. By 1965 the playwright Amiri Baraka, who had begun his career as the Beat poet LeRoi Jones, had written such incendiary plays as *Dutchman* (1964) and *The Slave* (1964) and was calling for a "Black Revolutionary Theater." Wilson was deeply influenced by black cultural nationalism and its project of celebrating African American culture and developing institutions where this culture could be nurtured and shared within the black community. In 1968 he co-founded the Black Horizons Theater in Pittsburgh to raise black consciousness and help politicize the community. The new theater put on the plays of Baraka and other playwrights of the Black Arts movement, and Wilson tried his hand at playwriting for the first time.

These attempts at one-act dramas were not successful; indeed, not until the mid-1970s would Wilson devote himself seriously to the theater. A 1976 work based on the life and death of 1920s blues musician Blind Lemon Jefferson, *The Homecoming*, became Wilson's first produced play, and other playscripts followed; they included a 1977 musical satire about the white nineteenth-century rustler Black Bart and *Jitney!* (1979), a play set in a gypsy cab station in his native Pittsburgh. In 1978 Wilson moved to St. Paul, Minnesota, where he became associated with the Playwright's

Center in Minneapolis; among other jobs, he wrote short educational plays for a theater troupe affiliated with the Science Museum of Minnesota. The breakthrough for this relatively unknown playwright came when he developed early material he had written on Ma Rainey into *Ma Rainey's Black Bottom* and submitted the completed play to the Eugene O'Neill Theater Center's Playwright's Conference in Connecticut. The play was accepted for staged reading, and Wilson was introduced to Lloyd Richards, who would serve as his mentor and director in subsequent projects. After a process of workshop revisions, *Ma Rainey* premiered at the Yale Repertory Theatre in April 1984 and moved to Broadway in October of the same year.

As *Ma Rainey* was winning praise among the theatergoing public, Wilson's *Fences* and an early version of *Joe Turner's Come and Gone* had already been presented in staged readings and workshops. By that time, Wilson was fully embarked on the project that he would complete twenty years later: tracing the history of twentieth-century black America through a cycle of ten plays set in each decade of the century. The result is a remarkable panorama of modern African American history. *Ma Rainey's Black Bottom,* the only play in the cycle not set in Pittsburgh, takes place in a Chicago recording studio in 1927. Most of the action of *Fences* takes place in Troy Maxson's backyard in 1957, while *Joe Turner's Come and Gone* (1986) is set in a boardinghouse in 1911. *The Piano Lesson* (1987), which deals with the conflict between brother and sister over a 135-year-old piano that has been central to their family's history, takes place in 1936. *Two Trains Running* (1990) is set in a Pittsburgh restaurant in 1969; *Seven Guitars* (1996) deals with the causes and repercussions of a young guitar player's death in 1948. A revised version of *Jitney* (which premiered in 1996), takes place in 1977, and *King Hedley II* (1999) explores the breakdown of the black family and community in the 1980s. *Gem of the Ocean* (2003), which is set in 1904, is dominated by the figure of Aunt Ester, a 287-year-old community elder and seer who arrived on the first shipload of American slaves in 1619. *Radio Golf,* which premiered six months before Wilson's death from cancer in 2005, centers on a plan to redevelop Pittsburgh's Hill District proposed in the 1990s.

With its broad historical ambitions, Wilson's history of a people invites comparison to the cycle plays of the medieval mystery guilds presented at York, Wakefield, and elsewhere. Wilson's plays similarly stand firmly on their own yet acquire wider meanings when viewed or read in relation to each other. The historical backdrop, or metanarrative, of these plays is certainly epic in scope. Like Hansberry, Wilson takes on the legacy of the Great Migration—the movement of black Americans who left the poverty and economic limitations of the Mississippi Delta and other parts of the South for Chicago, Cleveland, New York, and other northern cities in the largest demographic shift in U.S. history. Though this migration spanned the years between 1900 and 1970 (the year that black Americans started returning to the South), its peak came during World War I and the 1920s. In his brief introduction to *Fences*, Wilson describes how the "descendants of African slaves," pursuing the same hopes and dreams as European immigrants, found a very different reception in the cities of the North and how hard they worked to make their lives, now spent "in shallow, ramshackle houses made of sticks and tar paper," into something free and dignified. Plays such as *Joe Turner's Come and Gone, Fences,* and *The Piano Lesson* examine the impact of the Great Migration on the generations that undertook it and those that followed. In doing so, they also look back to a past whose traumas and histories constitute the horizons of urban African American racial memory: the life of southern sharecroppers during Reconstruction, when the hopes of emancipation confronted the realities of socialized racism; the uncountable brutalities of slavery; the hardships of the Middle Passage; and, at the farthest reach, Africa and its forms of community, culture, and identity. As Wilson himself has commented, "When your back is pressed to the wall you go to the deepest part of yourself, and there's a response—it's your great ancestors talking. It's blood memory."

Their identities fragmented to varying degrees, Wilson's characters carry this history with them in the form of conflicting needs, drives, and behaviors. Such conflicts particularly affect Wilson's male characters. Negotiating their way through a society uncomfortable with their presence, they move, often compulsively, from place to place, relationship to relationship, seeking a haven in the world and some balm for their restless psyches. They fall in and out of jobs and end up so regularly in jail (or the "workhouse") that being arrested becomes a kind of initiation ritual. All of Wilson's characters, male and female, are haunted by the experiences of their parents and ancestors, and they seek, in sometimes self-defeating and contradictory ways, to escape or redeem this inheritance. In *The Piano Lesson*, Berniece and Boy Willie struggle for control of the family piano, each with a different understanding of what its painful history means to the present: Boy Willie wants to sell the piano and put the money toward purchasing the plantation where their great-grandparents had worked as slaves, while Berniece is equally determined to preserve the representations of family members that their great-grandfather had carved into the piano's legs after the relatives had been sold away. The siblings' struggle with the past comes to a head when Boy Willie fights the ghost of Sutter, the slave owner who controlled their ancestors' fate, in the play's final scene.

Wilson's dual interests in the present and the historical memories that inform it have driven certain stylistic and formal choices in the composition of his plays. Though he was influenced by Baraka's writing, Wilson chose not to employ the confrontational aesthetic of the Black Revolutionary Theater movement in his own drama. Nor has he pursued the antitheatrical styles and techniques through which some other contemporary black playwrights (such as Adrienne Kennedy, Ntozake Shange, and SUZAN-LORI PARKS) subvert the representational conventions that have traditionally governed the staging of African Americans. Wilson's drama draws on realism as an aesthetic; stylistically, his plays resemble those of EUGENE O'NEILL, ARTHUR MILLER, and others in the American mainstream. Yet at the same time that Wilson's plays display an almost ethnographic attention to the lives of his characters, detailing their material world and social codes with a range and specificity that recall the nineteenth-century realist novel, their realism is neither simple nor seamless. Wilson's settings—a backyard, a drawing room, a cab station—are based in the everyday, but they are invested with memory, history, and myth. For one thing, the dramatic present of Wilson's plays is expanded through the act of storytelling as characters narrate individual and family history, legends, and dreams. Several scholars have noted the similarities between Wilson's raconteurs and the West African griot, or storyteller, who preserved and transmitted the oral tradition of families and communities. In their access to traumatic memory and visionary revelation, these characters—such as Herald Loomis in *Joe Turner's Come and Gone,* with his trancelike vision of bones rising from the ocean waves and re-forming as bodies on the shore—introduce myth and the supernatural to Wilson's plays. In this respect, they are related to other figures created by Wilson whose presence unsettles the boundaries of realism—characters such as Aunt Ester, the centuries-old seer who has a presence, onstage and off, in several of his plays; Hedley in *Seven Guitars,* who is obsessed by visions about his dead father and the belief that he will father the Messiah; and Troy Maxson's brother Gabe in *Fences,* who, having suffered a brain injury in World War II, carries a trumpet and believes that he is the archangel Gabriel. Traversed by characters such as these, history in August Wilson's twentieth-century chronicle becomes actual and mythic at the same time.

There is certainly something mythic and outsized about the protagonist of *Fences,* Wilson's most widely known play. The name "Troy" calls to mind the embattled city of Homer's *Iliad,* while "Maxson" (Max-son) evokes the idea of patrilineal succession so central to heroic sagas. Like Babe Ruth, Josh Gibson, and the other baseball legends in whose company he places himself, Troy is larger than life; as Wilson notes, "[t]ogether with his blackness, his largeness informs his sensibilities and the choices he has made in his life." In a play profoundly concerned with space, ownership, and boundaries, Troy's presence dominates the stage even when he is absent from a particular scene; as a glance at the character list indicates, the

other characters are defined primarily in terms of their relationship to him. Boasting that he "wrestled with Death" when he was seriously ill in the hospital, Troy displays the same indomitability in his job as a garbage collector, confronting his boss to ask why only whites drive the trucks while blacks lift the garbage. His passions in life are women and baseball, and it is not always clear which comes first. Troy learned baseball while in prison for killing a man, and upon his release he played in the Negro League, the circuit of teams for black ballplayers; none played in the major leagues until Jackie Robinson joined the Brooklyn Dodgers in 1947. Negro League teams, which often drew crowds as large as those that watched their white counterparts, featured some of the best players in the history of the

James Earl Jones as Troy in the world premiere of *Fences* at the Yale Repertory Theatre, 1985.

sport—including Josh Gibson, the so-called black Babe Ruth, who played for the powerful Homestead Grays, based in a steel mill town adjacent to Pittsburgh. As the archetypal American pastime, baseball serves as a powerful symbol in *Fences* of the exclusion of black Americans from the country's social and cultural institutions. Unfortunately for Troy, by the time baseball's color line had been breached and black players gradually began playing for major league teams, he was too old to be one of them. At age fifty-three, he carries his baseball past with him as a bitter reminder of racial oppression and as a metaphor of his battles against an antagonistic life: for him, "Death ain't nothing but a fastball on the outside corner."

Troy's personality was forged in his relationship with his father, an embittered and abusive sharecropper who towered over his children and drove Troy away with a particularly ugly explosion of violence. From his father Troy learns responsibility, but it is a responsibility born of hardness, not love. When applied to his two sons, it is accompanied by a rigid sense of authority and a demand that they live their lives with the pressure-forged self-denial he has been forced to accept in his. In different ways, both Lyons (who aspires to be a musician) and Cory (a high school football star) resist this narrow definition of life's possibilities. Cory's desire to win a scholarship to play football in college reflects the changing place of black athletes in American sports: in 1957, the year the play opens, the running back Jim Brown was declared the National Football League's Most Valuable Player and the Milwaukee Braves won the World Series, defeating the New York Yankees behind the hitting of Hank Aaron (who would eventually break Babe Ruth's revered lifetime home run record). As Troy's wife Rose explains to him, "The world's changing around you and you can't even see it." But Troy is the product of a different world. Unable to perceive an alternative to the father-son struggle that he himself was forced to endure and scarred by the deprivations he faced, Troy becomes the father he ran away from, standing in the way of a younger generation's new opportunities and driving away those he loves. Resenting the self-sacrifice, suffering, and disappoint-

ment that he has nonetheless worked into a code of living, he betrays his younger son, wife, and brother.

With its psychologically embattled patriarch, urban backyard setting, and other details of plot and action, *Fences* bears more than casual resemblance to ARTHUR MILLER's *Death of a Salesman* (1949). Like the earlier play, *Fences* revolves around questions of masculinity: what the social performance of maleness consists of, how it is transmitted (or not transmitted) from fathers to sons, how it relates to social models of femaleness. Their economic and social disempowerment has made the task of fulfilling traditional male roles particularly fraught for African American men. Like Biff Loman, Cory must negotiate the boundaries of his own identity and thereby become a man, in the shadow of his father's frustrated and defensive masculinity: "It would wrap around you and lay there until you couldn't tell which one was you anymore." He is not alone in struggling against Troy. Rose, one of only two female characters in the play, must confront her failure to meet all of her husband's needs and affirm, in the process, her own need for selfhood. Critics have been divided over the status of the women Wilson created, who inhabit a dramatic world whose orientation is largely determined by male preoccupations. To what extent is Rose's character defined in terms of and limited by the support—psychological, domestic, sexual—that she provides her husband? To what extent, conversely, does she succeed in articulating an autonomous set of experiences, desires, and identity boundaries?

Against these psychological and sociological backdrops, the play's title resonates in complex ways. Designed both to keep people in and to keep them out, the backyard fence represents the many ways in which society and the human mind establish boundaries around psyches, social units, races, genders. The play's principal characters think about fences differently. Rose, who builds fences in order to "keep people in," desires a space where her family can remain protected and whole. Troy, on the other hand, constructs fences against those aspects of life that threaten his view of the world and himself. In so doing, he establishes barriers between himself and those who love him, denying himself the possibilities of growth, intimacy, and pride in the son who has tried so hard to live up to his expectations. Alone in the play's penultimate scene, all Troy can do is swing his bat, hoping to clear the fences— hit a home run—in one last act of solitary heroism.   S.G

Fences

When the sins of our fathers visit us
We do not have to play host.
We can banish them with forgiveness
As God, in His Largeness and Laws.
—AUGUST WILSON

CHARACTERS

TROY MAXSON
JIM BONO, Troy's friend
ROSE, Troy's wife
LYONS, Troy's oldest son by previous marriage
GABRIEL, Troy's brother
CORY, Troy and Rose's son
RAYNELL, Troy's daughter

Setting

The setting is the yard which fronts the only entrance to the MAXSON household, an ancient two-story brick house set back off a small alley in a big-city neighborhood. The entrance to the house is gained by two or three steps leading to a wooden porch badly in need of paint.

A relatively recent addition to the house and running its full width, the porch lacks congruence. It is a sturdy porch with a flat roof. One or two chairs of dubious value sit at one end where the kitchen window opens onto the porch. An old-fashioned icebox stands silent guard at the opposite end.

The yard is a small dirt yard, partially fenced, except for the last scene, with a wooden sawhorse, a pile of lumber, and other fence-building equipment set off to the side. Opposite is a tree from which hangs a ball made of rags. A baseball bat leans against the tree. Two oil drums serve as garbage receptacles and sit near the house at right to complete the setting.

The Play

Near the turn of the century, the destitute of Europe sprang on the city with tenacious claws and an honest and solid dream. The city devoured them. They swelled its belly until it burst into a thousand furnaces and sewing machines, a thousand butcher shops and bakers' ovens, a thousand churches and hospitals and funeral parlors and moneylenders. The city grew. It nourished itself and offered each man a partnership limited only by his talent, his guile, and his willingness and capacity for hard work. For the immigrants of Europe, a dream dared and won true.

The descendants of African slaves were offered no such welcome or participation. They came from places called the Carolinas and the Virginias, Georgia, Alabama, Mississippi, and Tennessee. They came strong, eager, searching. The city rejected them and they fled and settled along the riverbanks and under bridges in shallow, ramshackle houses made of sticks and tar paper. They collected rags and wood. They sold the use of their muscles and their bodies. They cleaned houses and washed clothes, they shined shoes, and in quiet desperation and vengeful pride, they stole, and lived in pursuit of their own dream. That they could breathe free, finally, and stand to meet life with the force of dignity and whatever eloquence the heart could call upon.

By 1957, the hard-won victories of the European immigrants had solidified the industrial might of America. War had been confronted and won with new energies that used loyalty and patriotism as its fuel. Life was rich, full, and flourishing. The Milwaukee Braves won the World Series, and the hot winds of change that would make the sixties a turbulent, racing, dangerous, and provocative decade had not yet begun to blow full.

1.1

It is 1957. TROY *and* BONO *enter the yard, engaged in conversation.* TROY *is fifty-three years old, a large man with thick, heavy hands; it is this largeness that he strives to fill out and make an accommodation with. Together with his blackness, his largeness informs his sensibilities and the choices he has made in his life.*

Of the two men, BONO *is obviously the follower. His commitment to their friendship of thirty-odd years is rooted in his admiration of* TROY's *honesty, capacity for hard work, and his strength, which* BONO *seeks to emulate.*

It is Friday night, payday, and the one night of the week the two men engage in a ritual of talk and drink. TROY *is usually the most talkative and at times he can be crude and almost vulgar, though he is capable of rising to profound heights of expression. The men carry lunch buckets and wear or carry burlap aprons and are dressed in clothes suitable to their jobs as garbage collectors.*

BONO   Troy, you ought to stop that lying!

TROY   I ain't lying! The nigger had a watermelon this big. [*He indicates with his hands.*] Talking about . . . "What watermelon, Mr. Rand?" I liked to fell out![1] "What watermelon, Mr. Rand?" . . . And it sitting there big as life.

5   BONO   What did Mr. Rand say?

TROY   Ain't said nothing. Figure if the nigger too dumb to know he carrying a watermelon, he wasn't gonna get much sense out of him. Trying to hide that great big old watermelon under his coat. Afraid to let the white man see him carry it home.

10   BONO   I'm like you . . . I ain't got no time for them kind of people.

TROY   Now what he look like getting mad cause he see the man from the union talking to Mr. Rand?

BONO   He come to me talking about . . . "Maxson gonna get us fired." I told him to get away from me with that. He walked away from me calling you a

15   troublemaker. What Mr. Rand say?

TROY   Ain't said nothing. He told me to go down the Commissioner's office next Friday. They called me down there to see them.

BONO   Well, as long as you got your complaint filed, they can't fire you. That's what one of them white fellows tell me.

20   TROY   I ain't worried about them firing me. They gonna fire me cause I asked a question? That's all I did. I went to Mr. Rand and asked him, "Why? Why

---

1. I nearly fell out of my tree; that is, I was amazed.

you got the white mens driving and the colored lifting?" Told him, "What's the matter, don't I count? You think only white fellows got sense enough to drive a truck. That ain't no paper job! Hell, anybody can drive a truck. How come you got all whites driving and the colored lifting? He told me, "Take it to the union." Well, hell, that's what I done! Now they wanna come up with this pack of lies.

BONO   I told Brownie if the man come and ask him any questions . . . just tell the truth! It ain't nothing but something they done trumped up on you cause you filed a complaint on them.

TROY   Brownie don't understand nothing. All I want them to do is change the job description. Give everybody a chance to drive the truck. Brownie can't see that. He ain't got that much sense.

BONO   How you figure he be making out with that gal be up at Taylors' all the time . . . that Alberta gal?

TROY   Same as you and me. Getting just as much as we is. Which is to say nothing.

BONO   It is, huh? I figure you doing a little better than me . . . and I ain't saying what I'm doing.

TROY   Aw, nigger, look here . . . I know you. If you had got anywhere near that gal, twenty minutes later you be looking to tell somebody. And the first one you gonna tell . . . that you gonna want to brag to . . . is gonna be me.

BONO   I ain't saying that. I see where you be eyeing her.

TROY   I eye all the women. I don't miss nothing. Don't never let nobody tell you Troy Maxson don't eye the women.

BONO   You been doing more than eyeing her. You done bought her a drink or two.

TROY   Hell yeah, I bought her a drink! What that mean? I bought you one, too. What that mean cause I buy her a drink? I'm just being polite.

BONO   It's alright to buy her one drink. That's what you call being polite. But when you wanna be buying two or three . . . that's what you call eyeing her.

TROY   Look here, as long as you known me . . . you ever known me to chase after women?

BONO   Hell yeah! Long as I done known you. You forgetting I knew you when.

TROY   Naw, I'm talking about since I been married to Rose?

BONO   Oh, not since you been married to Rose. Now, that's the truth, there. I can say that.

TROY   Alright then! Case closed.

BONO   I see you be walking up around Alberta's house. You supposed to be at Taylors' and you be walking up around there.

TROY   What you watching where I'm walking for? I ain't watching after you.

BONO   I seen you walking around there more than once.

TROY   Hell, you liable to see me walking anywhere! That don't mean nothing cause you see me walking around there.

BONO   Where she come from anyway? She just kinda showed up one day.

TROY   Tallahassee. You can look at her and tell she one of them Florida gals. They got some big healthy women down there. Grow them right up out the ground. Got a little bit of Indian in her. Most of them niggers down in Florida got some Indian in them.

BONO   I don't know about that Indian part. But she damn sure big and healthy. Woman wear some big stockings. Got them great big old legs and hips as wide as the Mississippi River.

TROY   Legs don't mean nothing. You don't do nothing but push them out of the way. But them hips cushion the ride!

75 BONO   Troy, you ain't got no sense.

TROY   It's the truth! Like you riding on Goodyears![2]

> [ROSE *enters from the house. She is ten years younger than* TROY, *her devotion to him stems from her recognition of the possibilities of her life without him: a succession of abusive men and their babies, a life of partying and running the streets, the Church, or aloneness with its attendant pain and frustration. She recognizes* TROY's *spirit as a fine and illuminating one and she either ignores or forgives his faults, only some of which she recognizes. Though she doesn't drink, her presence is an integral part of the Friday night rituals. She alternates between the porch and the kitchen, where supper preparations are under way.*]

ROSE   What you all out here getting into?

TROY   What you worried about what we getting into for? This is men talk, woman.

80 ROSE   What I care what you all talking about? Bono, you gonna stay for supper?

BONO   No, I thank you, Rose. But Lucille say she cooking up a pot of pigfeet.

TROY   Pigfeet! Hell, I'm going home with you! Might even stay the night if

85 you got some pigfeet. You got something in there to top them pigfeet, Rose?

ROSE   I'm cooking up some chicken. I got some chicken and collard greens.

TROY   Well, go on back in the house and let me and Bono finish what we was talking about. This is men talk. I got some talk for you later. You know what kind of talk I mean. You go on and powder it up.

90 ROSE   Troy Maxson, don't you start that now!

TROY   [*puts his arm around her*]   Aw, woman . . . come here. Look here, Bono . . . when I met this woman . . . I got out that place, say, "Hitch up my pony, saddle up my mare . . . there's a woman out there for me somewhere. I looked here. Looked there. Saw Rose and latched on to her." I

95 latched on to her and told her—I'm gonna tell you the truth—I told her, "Baby, I don't wanna marry, I just wanna be your man." Rose told me . . . tell him what you told me, Rose.

ROSE   I told him if he wasn't the marrying kind, then move out the way so the marrying kind could find me.

100 TROY   That's what she told me. "Nigger, you in my way. You blocking the view! Move out the way so I can find me a husband." I thought it over two or three days. Come back—

ROSE   Ain't no two or three days nothing. You was back the same night.

TROY   Come back, told her . . . "Okay, baby . . . but I'm gonna buy me a

105 banty[3] rooster and put him out there in the backyard . . . and when he see a stranger come, he'll flap his wings and crow . . ." Look here, Bono, I could watch the front door by myself . . . it was that back door I was worried about.

ROSE   Troy, you ought not talk like that. Troy ain't doing nothing but telling

110 a lie.

TROY   Only thing is . . . when we first got married . . . forget the rooster . . . we ain't had no yard!

---

2. That is, on automobile tires.

3. That is, bantam, or small (a term applied to several breeds of domestic fowl).

BONO   I hear you tell it. Me and Lucille was staying down there on Logan Street. Had two rooms with the outhouse in the back. I ain't mind the out-
115   house none. But when that goddamn wind blow through there in the winter . . . that's what I'm talking about! To this day I wonder why in the hell I ever stayed down there for six long years. But see, I didn't know I could do no better. I thought only white folks had inside toilets and things.

ROSE   There's a lot of people don't know they can do no better than they doing
120   now. That's just something you got to learn. A lot of folks still shop at Bella's.

TROY   Ain't nothing wrong with shopping at Bella's. She got fresh food.

ROSE   I ain't said nothing about if she got fresh food. I'm talking about what she charge. She charge ten cents more than the A&P.[4]

TROY   The A&P ain't never done nothing for me. I spends my money where
125   I'm treated right. I go down to Bella, say, "I need a loaf of bread, I'll pay you Friday." She give it to me. What sense that make when I got money to go and spend it somewhere else and ignore the person who done right by me? That ain't in the Bible.

ROSE   We ain't talking about what's in the Bible. What sense it make to shop
130   there when she overcharge?

TROY   You shop where you want to. I'll do my shopping where the people been good to me.

ROSE   Well, I don't think it's right for her to overcharge. That's all I was saying.

BONO   Look here . . . I got to get on. Lucille going be raising all kind of hell.
135   TROY   Where you going, nigger? We ain't finished this pint. Come here, finish this pint.

BONO   Well, hell, I am . . . if you ever turn the bottle loose.

TROY   [hands him the bottle]   The only thing I say about the A&P is I'm glad Cory got that job down there. Help him take care of his school clothes and
140   things. Gabe done moved out and things getting tight around here. He got that job. . . . He can start to look out for himself.

ROSE   Cory done went and got recruited by a college football team.

TROY   I told that boy about that football stuff. The white man ain't gonna let him get nowhere with that football. I told him when he first come to me
145   with it. Now you come telling me he done went and got more tied up in it. He ought to go and get recruited in how to fix cars or something where he can make a living.

ROSE   He ain't talking about making no living playing football. It's just something the boys in school do. They gonna send a recruiter by to talk to you.
150   He'll tell you he ain't talking about making no living playing football. It's a honor to be recruited.

TROY   It ain't gonna get him nowhere. Bono'll tell you that.

BONO   If he be like you in the sports . . . he's gonna be alright. Ain't but two men ever played baseball as good as you. That's Babe Ruth and Josh Gib
155   son.[5] Them's the only two men ever hit more home runs than you.

---

4. The dominant U.S. supermarket chain in the 1950s.
5. Respectively, the most famous white and black hitters of the 20th century. Ruth (1895–1948), who played with the N.Y. Yankees for most of his career (1914–35), held the major-league record for home runs in a season (60) for 34 years and the lifetime home run record (714) for 39; Gibson (1911–1947; catcher, 1930–46), who played mainly for the Homestead Grays (near Pittsburgh) in the Negro League, was known as "the black Babe Ruth"; it is estimated that in his career he hit more than 800 home runs, 75 of them in a single season.

TROY   What it ever get me? Ain't got a pot to piss in or a window to throw it out of.

ROSE   Times have changed since you was playing baseball, Troy. That was before the war. Times have changed a lot since then.

160 TROY   How in hell they done changed?

ROSE   They got lots of colored boys playing ball now.[6] Baseball and football.

BONO   You right about that, Rose. Times have changed, Troy. You just come along too early.

TROY   There ought not never have been no time called too early! Now you
165 take that fellow . . . what's that fellow they had playing right field for the Yankees back then? You know who I'm talking about, Bono. Used to play right field for the Yankees.

ROSE   Selkirk?[7]

TROY   Selkirk! That's it! Man batting .269, understand? .269. What kind of
170 sense that make? I was hitting .432 with thirty-seven home runs! Man batting .269 and playing right field for the Yankees! I saw Josh Gibson's daughter yesterday. She walking around with raggedy shoes on her feet. Now I bet you Selkirk's daughter ain't walking around with raggedy shoes on her feet! I bet you that!

175 ROSE   They got a lot of colored baseball players now. Jackie Robinson was the first. Folks had to wait for Jackie Robinson.

TROY   I done seen a hundred niggers play baseball better than Jackie Robinson. Hell, I know some teams Jackie Robinson couldn't even make! What you talking about Jackie Robinson. Jackie Robinson wasn't nobody.[8] I'm
180 talking about if you could play ball then they ought to have let you play. Don't care what color you were. Come telling me I come along too early. If you could play . . . then they ought to have let you play.

[TROY *takes a long drink from the bottle.*]

ROSE   You gonna drink yourself to death. You don't need to be drinking like that.

185 TROY   Death ain't nothing. I done seen him. Done wrassled with him. You can't tell me nothing about death. Death ain't nothing but a fastball on the outside corner. And you know what I'll do to that! Lookee here, Bono . . . am I lying? You get one of them fastballs, about waist high, over the outside corner of the plate where you can get the meat of the bat on it . . . and
190 good god! You can kiss it goodbye. Now, am I lying?

BONO   Naw, you telling the truth there. I seen you do it.

TROY   If I'm lying . . . that 450 feet worth of lying![9] [*Pause*] That's all death is to me. A fastball on the outside corner.

6. Until 1947, when Jackie Robinson (1919–1972) began playing for the Brooklyn Dodgers, no "colored" athletes had been allowed to play in baseball's minor or major leagues since the late 19th century. Initially, professional football had a few black players (1920–34), but none subsequently played for the National Football League until 1946, when four were signed.
7. George Selkirk (1908–1987), who became the Yankee's right fielder in 1935 after Ruth

retired; he batted .269 in 1940 (his average was above .300 five times in the 1930s).
8. Robinson was in fact Rookie of the Year, a six-time All-Star, and the 1949 National League MVP, outstanding as both a fielder and a hitter with a career batting average of .311.
9. A ball hit this distance would be an impressive home run in any ballpark (at its deepest, no fence is more than 435 feet from home plate).

ROSE   I don't know why you want to get on talking about death.

195 TROY   Ain't nothing wrong with talking about death. That's part of life. Everybody gonna die. You gonna die, I'm gonna die. Bono's gonna die. Hell, we
all gonna die.

ROSE   But you ain't got to talk about it. I don't like to talk about it.

TROY   You the one brought it up. Me and Bono was talking about base
200 ball . . . you tell me I'm gonna drink myself to death. Ain't that right, Bono?
You know I don't drink this but one night out of the week. That's Friday
night. I'm gonna drink just enough to where I can handle it. Then I cuts it
loose. I leave it alone. So don't you worry about me drinking myself to
death. 'Cause I ain't worried about Death. I done seen him. I done wrestled
205 with him.

Look here, Bono . . . I looked up one day and Death was marching
straight at me. Like Soldiers on Parade! The Army of Death was marching
straight at me. The middle of July, 1941. It got real cold just like it be winter. It seem like Death himself reached out and touched me on the shoul-
210 der. He touch me just like I touch you. I got cold as ice and Death standing
there grinning at me.

ROSE   Troy, why don't you hush that talk.

TROY   I say . . . What you want, Mr. Death? You be wanting me? You done
brought your army to be getting me? I looked him dead in the eye. I wasn't
215 fearing nothing. I was ready to tangle. Just like I'm ready to tangle now.
The Bible say be ever vigilant.[1] That's why I don't get but so drunk. I got to
keep watch.

ROSE   Troy was right down there in Mercy Hospital. You remember he had
pneumonia? Laying there with a fever talking plumb out of his head.

220 TROY   Death standing there staring at me . . . carrying that sickle in his
hand. Finally he say, "You want bound over for another year?" See, just like
that . . . "You want bound over[2] for another year?" I told him, "Bound over
hell! Let's settle this now!"

It seem like he kinda fell back when I said that, and all the cold went out
225 of me. I reached down and grabbed that sickle and threw it just as far as I
could throw it . . . and me and him commenced to wrestling.

We wrestled for three days and three nights. I can't say where I found the
strength from. Every time it seemed like he was gonna get the best of
me, I'd reach way down deep inside myself and find the strength to do
230 him one better.

ROSE   Every time Troy tell that story he find different ways to tell it. Different things to make up about it.

TROY   I ain't making up nothing. I'm telling you the facts of what happened.
I wrestled with Death for three days and three nights and I'm standing here
235 to tell you about it.

[Pause.]

Alright. At the end of the third night we done weakened each other to
where we can't hardly move. Death stood up, throwed on his robe . . . had
him a white robe with a hood on it. He throwed on that robe and went off

1. "Be sober, be vigilant; because your adver-
sary the devil, as a roaring lion, walketh about,
seeking whom he may devour" (1 Peter 5.8).

2. That is, agreeing to one more year of servitude, as if he were a sharecropper.

to look for his sickle. Say, "I'll be back." Just like that. "I'll be back." I told
240   him, say, "Yeah, but . . . you gonna have to find me!" I wasn't no fool. I
        wasn't going looking for him. Death ain't nothing to play with. And I know
        he's gonna get me. I know I got to join his army . . . his camp followers. But
        as long as I keep my strength and see him coming . . . as long as I keep up
        my vigilance . . . he's gonna have to fight to get me. I ain't going easy.
245 BONO   Well, look here, since you got to keep up your vigilance . . . let me
        have the bottle.
    TROY   Aw hell, I shouldn't have told you that part. I should have left out that
        part.
    ROSE   Troy be talking that stuff and half the time don't even know what he
250   be talking about.
    TROY   Bono know me better than that.
    BONO   That's right. I know you. I know you got some Uncle Remus[3] in your
        blood. You got more stories than the devil got sinners.
    TROY   Aw hell, I done seen him too! Done talked with the devil.
255 ROSE   Troy, don't nobody wanna be hearing all that stuff.

        [LYONS *enters the yard from the street. Thirty-four years old,* TROY's *son by
        a previous marriage, he sports a neatly trimmed goatee, sport coat, white
        shirt, tieless and buttoned at the collar. Though he fancies himself a musi-
        cian, he is more caught up in the rituals and "idea" of being a musician
        than in the actual practice of the music. He has come to borrow money
        from* TROY, *and while he knows he will be successful, he is uncertain as to
        what extent his lifestyle will be held up to scrutiny and ridicule.*]

    LYONS   Hey, Pop.
    TROY   What you come "Hey, Popping" me for?
    LYONS   How you doing, Rose?
        [*He kisses her.*]
        Mr. Bono. How you doing?
260 BONO   Hey, Lyons . . . how you been?
    TROY   He must have been doing alright. I ain't seen him around here last
        week.
    ROSE   Troy, leave your boy alone. He come by to see you and you wanna start
        all that nonsense.
265 TROY   I ain't bothering Lyons. [*Offers him the bottle.*] Here . . . get you a
        drink. We got an understanding. I know why he come by to see me and he
        know I know.
    LYONS   Come on, Pop . . . I just stopped by to say hi . . . see how you was
        doing.
270 TROY   You ain't stopped by yesterday.
    ROSE   You gonna stay for supper, Lyons? I got some chicken cooking in the
        oven.
    LYONS   No, Rose . . . thanks. I was just in the neighborhood and thought I'd
        stop by for a minute.
275 TROY   You was in the neighborhood alright, nigger. You telling the truth
        there. You was in the neighborhood cause it's my payday.
    LYONS   Well, hell, since you mentioned it . . . let me have ten dollars.

3. The fictional narrator of popular black folktales compiled by the white humorist Joel Chandler
Harris, beginning with *Uncle Remus: His Songs and Sayings* (1881).

TROY   I'll be damned! I'll die and go to hell and play blackjack with the devil before I give you ten dollars.

280 BONO   That's what I wanna know about . . . that devil you done seen.

LYONS   What . . . Pop done seen the devil? You too much, Pops.

TROY   Yeah, I done seen him. Talked to him too!

ROSE   You ain't seen no devil. I done told you that man ain't had nothing to do with the devil. Anything you can't understand, you want to call it the

285 devil.

TROY   Look here, Bono . . . I went down to see Hertzberger about some furniture. Got three rooms for two-ninety-eight. That what it say on the radio. "Three rooms . . . two-ninety-eight." Even made up a little song about it. Go down there . . . man tell me I can't get no credit. I'm working every day

290 and can't get no credit. What to do? I got an empty house with some raggedy furniture in it. Cory ain't got no bed. He's sleeping on a pile of rags on the floor. Working every day and can't get no credit. Come back here—Rose'll tell you—madder than hell. Sit down . . . try to figure what I'm gonna do. Come a knock on the door. Ain't been living here but three

295 days. Who know I'm here? Open the door . . . devil standing there bigger than life. White fellow . . . got on good clothes and everything. Standing there with a clipboard in his hand. I ain't had to say nothing. First words come out of his mouth was . . . "I understand you need some furniture and can't get no credit." I liked to fell over. He say "I'll give you all the credit you

300 want, but you got to pay the interest on it." I told him, "Give me three rooms worth and charge whatever you want." Next day a truck pulled up here and two men unloaded them three rooms. Man what drove the truck give me a book. Say send ten dollars, first of every month to the address in the book and everything will be alright. Say if I miss a payment the devil

305 was coming back and it'll be hell to pay. That was fifteen years ago. To this day . . . the first of the month I send my ten dollars, Rose'll tell you.

ROSE   Troy lying.

TROY   I ain't never seen that man since. Now you tell me who else that could have been but the devil? I ain't sold my soul or nothing like that, you

310 understand. Naw, I wouldn't have truck with the devil about nothing like that. I got my furniture and pays my ten dollars the first of the month just like clockwork.

BONO   How long you say you been paying this ten dollars a month?

TROY   Fifteen years!

315 BONO   Hell, ain't you finished paying for it yet? How much the man done charged you?

TROY   Aw hell, I done paid for it. I done paid for it ten times over! The fact is I'm scared to stop paying it.

ROSE   Troy lying. We got that furniture from Mr. Glickman. He ain't paying

320 no ten dollars a month to nobody.

TROY   Aw hell, woman. Bono know I ain't that big a fool.

LYONS   I was just getting ready to say . . . I know where there's a bridge for sale.[4]

---

4. To sell the Brooklyn Bridge proverbially demonstrates both the seller's powers of persuasion and the buyer's gullibility (a couple of turn-of-the-century confidence men did manage to pull off this swindle).

TROY   Look here, I'll tell you this . . . it don't matter to me if he was the devil.
325   It don't matter if the devil give credit. Somebody has got to give it.

ROSE   It ought to matter. You going around talking about having truck with
the devil . . . God's the one you gonna have to answer to. He's the one
gonna be at the Judgment.

LYONS   Yeah, well, look here, Pop . . . let me have that ten dollars. I'll give it
330   back to you. Bonnie got a job working at the hospital.

TROY   What I tell you, Bono? The only time I see this nigger is when he
wants something. That's the only time I see him.

LYONS   Come on, Pop, Mr. Bono don't want to hear all that. Let me have the
ten dollars. I told you Bonnie working.

335 TROY   What that mean to me? "Bonnie working." I don't care if she working.
Go ask her for the ten dollars if she working. Talking about "Bonnie working." Why ain't you working?

LYONS   Aw, Pop, you know I can't find no decent job. Where am I gonna get
a job at? You know I can't get no job.

340 TROY   I told you I know some people down there. I can get you on the rubbish if you want to work. I told you that the last time you came by here
asking me for something.

LYONS   Naw, Pop . . . thanks. That ain't for me. I don't wanna be carrying
nobody's rubbish. I don't wanna be punching nobody's time clock.

345 TROY   What's the matter, you too good to carry people's rubbish? Where you
think that ten dollars you talking about come from? I'm just supposed to
haul people's rubbish and give my money to you cause you too lazy to work.
You too lazy to work and wanna know why you ain't got what I got.

ROSE   What hospital Bonnie working at? Mercy?

350 LYONS   She's down at Passavant working in the laundry.

TROY   I ain't got nothing as it is. I give you that ten dollars and I got to eat
beans the rest of the week. Naw . . . you ain't getting no ten dollars here.

LYONS   You ain't got to be eating no beans. I don't know why you wanna say
that.

355 TROY   I ain't got no extra money. Gabe done moved over to Miss Pearl's paying her the rent and things done got tight around here. I can't afford to be
giving you every payday.

LYONS   I ain't asked you to give me nothing. I asked you to loan me ten dollars. I know you got ten dollars.

360 TROY   Yeah, I got it. You know why I got it? Cause I don't throw my money
away out there in the streets. You living the fast life . . . wanna be a musician . . . running around in them clubs and things . . . then, you learn to
take care of yourself. You ain't gonna find me going and asking nobody for
nothing. I done spent too many years without.

365 LYONS   You and me is two different people, Pop.

TROY   I done learned my mistake and learned to do what's right by it. You still
trying to get something for nothing. Life don't owe you nothing. You owe it
to yourself. Ask Bono. He'll tell you I'm right.

LYONS   You got your way of dealing with the world . . . I got mine. The only
370   thing that matters to me is the music.

TROY   Yeah, I can see that! It don't matter how you gonna eat . . . where your
next dollar is coming from. You telling the truth there.

LYONS   I know I got to eat. But I got to live too. I need something that gonna
help me to get out of the bed in the morning. Make me feel like I belong in
375   the world. I don't bother nobody. I just stay with my music cause that's the
only way I can find to live in the world. Otherwise there ain't no telling
what I might do. Now I don't come criticizing you and how you live. I just
come by to ask you for ten dollars. I don't wanna hear all that about how I
live.

380   TROY   Boy, your mama did a hell of a job raising you.

LYONS   You can't change me, Pop. I'm thirty-four years old. If you wanted to
change me, you should have been there when I was growing up. I come by
to see you . . . ask for ten dollars and you want to talk about how I was
raised. You don't know nothing about how I was raised.

385   ROSE   Let the boy have ten dollars, Troy.

TROY [to LYONS]   What the hell you looking at me for? I ain't got no ten dollars. You know what I do with my money. [To ROSE] Give him ten dollars if
you want him to have it.

ROSE   I will. Just as soon as you turn it loose.

390   TROY [handing ROSE the money]   There it is. Seventy-six dollars and forty-two
cents. You see this, Bono? Now, I ain't gonna get but six of that back.

ROSE   You ought to stop telling that lie. Here, Lyons.

[She hands him the money.]

LYONS   Thanks, Rose. Look . . . I got to run . . . I'll see you later.

TROY   Wait a minute. You gonna say, "Thanks, Rose," and ain't gonna look to
395   see where she got that ten dollars from? See how they do me, Bono?

LYONS   I know she got it from you, Pop. Thanks. I'll give it back to you.

TROY   There he go telling another lie. Time I see that ten dollars . . . he'll be
owing me thirty more.

LYONS   See you, Mr. Bono.

400   BONO   Take care, Lyons!

LYONS   Thanks, Pop. I'll see you again.

[LYONS exits the yard.]

TROY   I don't know why he don't go and get him a decent job and take care of
that woman he got.

BONO   He'll be alright, Troy. The boy is still young.

405   TROY   The boy is thirty-four years old.

ROSE   Let's not get off into all that.

BONO   Look here . . . I got to be going. I got to be getting on. Lucille gonna
be waiting.

TROY [puts his arm around ROSE]   See this woman, Bono? I love this woman.
410   I love this woman so much it hurts. I love her so much . . . I done run out
of ways of loving her. So I got to go back to basics. Don't you come by my
house Monday morning talking about time to go to work . . .'cause I'm still
gonna be stroking!

ROSE   Troy! Stop it now!

415   BONO   I ain't paying him no mind, Rose. That ain't nothing but gin-talk. Go
on, Troy. I'll see you Monday.

TROY   Don't you come by my house, nigger! I done told you what I'm gonna
be doing.

[The lights go down to black.]

1.2

The lights come up on ROSE *hanging up clothes. She hums and sings softly to herself. It is the following morning.*

ROSE [*sings*]

Jesus, be a fence all around me every day

Jesus, I want you to protect me as I travel on my way.

Jesus, be a fence all around me every day.[5]

[TROY *enters from the house.*]

ROSE [*continued*]

Jesus, I want you to protect me

5   As I travel on my way.

[*To* TROY] 'Morning. You ready for breakfast? I can fix it soon as I finish hanging up these clothes?

TROY   I got the coffee on. That'll be alright. I'll just drink some of that this morning.

10 ROSE   That 651 hit yesterday.[6] That's the second time this month. Miss Pearl hit for a dollar . . . seem like those that need the least always get lucky. Poor folks can't get nothing.

TROY   Them numbers don't know nobody. I don't know why you fool with them. You and Lyons both.

15 ROSE   It's something to do.

TROY   You ain't doing nothing but throwing your money away.

ROSE   Troy, you know I don't play foolishly. I just play a nickel here and a nickel there.

TROY   That's two nickels you done thrown away.

20 ROSE   Now I hit sometimes . . . that makes up for it. It always comes in handy when I do hit. I don't hear you complaining then.

TROY   I ain't complaining now. I just say it's foolish. Trying to guess out of six hundred ways which way the number gonna come. If I had all the money niggers, these Negroes, throw away on numbers for one week—just one

25   week—I'd be a rich man.

ROSE   Well, you wishing and calling it foolish ain't gonna stop folks from playing numbers. That's one thing for sure. Besides . . . some good things come from playing numbers. Look where Pope done bought him that restaurant off of numbers.

30 TROY   I can't stand niggers like that. Man ain't had two dimes to rub together. He walking around with his shoes all run over bumming money for cigarettes. Alright. Got lucky there and hit the numbers . . .

ROSE   Troy, I know all about it.

TROY   Had good sense, I'll say that for him. He ain't throwed his money away.

35   I seen niggers hit the numbers and go through two thousand dollars in four days. Man brought him that restaurant down there . . . fixed it up real nice . . . and then didn't want nobody to come in it! A Negro go in there

5. Traditional gospel song.
6. A reference to playing the numbers, a form of illegal gambling that was popular before the advent of legal state-run lotteries.

and can't get no kind of service. I seen a white fellow come in there and
order a bowl of stew. Pope picked all the meat out the pot for him. Man ain't
40   had nothing but a bowl of meat! Negro come behind him and ain't got
nothing but the potatoes and carrots. Talking about what numbers do for
people, you picked a wrong example. Ain't done nothing but make a worser
fool out of him than he was before.

ROSE   Troy, you ought to stop worrying about what happened at work
45   yesterday.

TROY   I ain't worried. Just told me to be down there at the Commissioner's
office on Friday. Everybody think they gonna fire me. I ain't worried about
them firing me. You ain't got to worry about that.

[*Pause.*]

Where's Cory? Cory in the house? [*Calls.*] Cory?

50   ROSE   He gone out.

TROY   Out, huh? He gone out cause he know I want him to help me with this
fence. I know how he is. That boy scared of work.

[GABRIEL *enters. He comes halfway down the alley and, hearing* TROY's
voice, stops.]

TROY [*continues*]   He ain't done a lick of work in his life.

ROSE   He had to go to football practice. Coach wanted them to get in a little
55   extra practice before the season start.

TROY   I got his practice . . . running out of here before he get his chores
done.

ROSE   Troy, what is wrong with you this morning? Don't nothing set right
with you. Go on back in there and go to bed . . . get up on the other side.

60   TROY   Why something got to be wrong with me? I ain't said nothing wrong
with me.

ROSE   You got something to say about everything. First it's the numbers . . .
then it's the way the man runs his restaurant . . . then you done got on
Cory. What's it gonna be next? Take a look up there and see if the weather
65   suits you . . . or is it gonna be how you gonna put up the fence with the
clothes hanging in the yard.

TROY   You hit the nail on the head then.

ROSE   I know you like I know the back of my hand. Go on in there and get
you some coffee . . . see if that straighten you up. Cause you ain't right this
70   morning.

[TROY *starts into the house and sees* GABRIEL. GABRIEL *starts singing.*
TROY's *brother, he is seven years younger than* TROY. *Injured in World War
II, he has a metal plate in his head. He carries an old trumpet tied
around his waist and believes with every fiber of his being that he is the
Archangel Gabriel. He carries a chipped basket*[7] *with an assortment of
discarded fruits and vegetables he has picked up in the strip district and
which he attempts to sell.*]

GABRIEL [*singing*]

Yes, ma'am, I got plums
You ask me how I sell them
Oh ten cents apiece

---

7. That is, a chip basket, made from roughly joined strips of split wood.

Three for a quarter
75   Come and buy now
'Cause I'm here today
And tomorrow I'll be gone

[GABRIEL *enters.*]

Hey, Rose!
ROSE   How you doing, Gabe?
80 GABRIEL   There's Troy . . . Hey, Troy!
    TROY   Hey, Gabe.

[*Exit into kitchen.*]

ROSE [*to* GABRIEL]   What you got there?
GABRIEL   You know what I got, Rose. I got fruits and vegetables.
ROSE [*looking in basket*]   Where's all these plums you talking about?
85 GABRIEL   I ain't got no plums today, Rose. I was just singing that. Have some
    tomorrow. Put me in a big order for plums. Have enough plums tomorrow
    for St. Peter and everybody.

[TROY *reenters from kitchen, crosses to steps.*]

[*To* ROSE] Troy's mad at me.
    TROY   I ain't mad at you. What I got to be mad at you about? You ain't done
90   nothing to me.
    GABRIEL   I just moved over to Miss Pearl's to keep out from in your way. I
    ain't mean no harm by it.
    TROY   Who said anything about that? I ain't said anything about that.
    GABRIEL   You ain't mad at me, is you?
95 TROY   Naw . . . I ain't mad at you, Gabe. If I was mad at you I'd tell you
    about it.
    GABRIEL   Got me two rooms. In the basement. Got my own door too. Wanna
    see my key? [*He holds up a key.*] That's my own key! Ain't nobody else got a
    key like that. That's my key! My two rooms!
100 TROY   Well, that's good, Gabe. You got your own key . . . that's good.
    ROSE   You hungry, Gabe? I was just fixing to cook Troy his breakfast.
    GABRIEL   I'll take some biscuits. You got some biscuits? Did you know when
    I was in heaven . . . every morning me and St. Peter would sit down by the
    gate and eat some big fat biscuits? Oh, yeah! We had us a good time. We'd
105   sit there and eat us them biscuits and then St. Peter would go off to sleep
    and tell me to wake him up when it's time to open the gates for the
    judgment.
    ROSE   Well, come on . . . I'll make up a batch of biscuits.

[ROSE *exits into the house.*]

    GABRIEL   Troy . . . St. Peter got your name in the book. I seen it. It say . . .
110   Troy Maxson. I say . . . I know him! He got the same name like what I got.
    That's my brother!
    TROY   How many times you gonna tell me that, Gabe?
    GABRIEL   Ain't got my name in the book. Don't have to have my name. I done
    died and went to heaven. He got your name though. One morning St. Peter
115   was looking at his book . . . marking it up for the judgment . . . and he let
    me see your name. Got it in there under M. Got Rose's name . . . I ain't seen
    it like I seen yours . . . but I know it's in there. He got a great big book. Got

everybody's name what was ever been born. That's what he told me. But I seen your name. Seen it with my own eyes.

120 TROY Go on in the house there. Rose going to fix you something to eat.

GABRIEL Oh, I ain't hungry. I done had breakfast with Aunt Jemimah.[8] She come by and cooked me up a whole mess of flapjacks. Remember how we used to eat them flapjacks?

TROY Go on in the house and get you something to eat now.

125 GABRIEL I got to go sell my plums. I done sold some tomatoes. Got me two quarters. Wanna see? [*He shows* TROY *his quarters.*] I'm gonna save them and buy me a new horn so St. Peter can hear me when it's time to open the gates.

[GABRIEL *stops suddenly. Listens.*]

Hear that? That's the hellhounds. I got to chase them out of here. Go on
130 get out of here! Get out!

[GABRIEL *exits singing.*]

> Better get ready for the judgment
> Better get ready for the judgment
> My Lord is coming down

[ROSE *enters from the house.*]

TROY He gone off somewhere.

GABRIEL [*offstage*]

135
> Better get ready for the judgment
> Better get ready for the judgment morning
> Better get ready for the judgment
> My God is coming down

ROSE He ain't eating right. Miss Pearl say she can't get him to eat nothing.

140 TROY What you want me to do about it, Rose? I done did everything I can for the man. I can't make him get well. Man got half his head blown away . . . what you expect?

ROSE Seem like something ought to be done to help him.

TROY Man don't bother nobody. He just mixed up from that metal plate he
145 got in his head. Ain't no sense for him to go back into the hospital.

ROSE Least he be eating right. They can help him take care of himself.

TROY Don't nobody wanna be locked up, Rose. What you wanna lock him up for? Man go over there and fight the war . . . messin' around with them Japs, get half his head blown off . . . and they give him a lousy three thou
150 sand dollars. And I had to swoop down on that.

ROSE Is you fixing to go into that again?

TROY That's the only way I got a roof over my head . . . cause of that metal plate.

ROSE Ain't no sense you blaming yourself for nothing. Gabe wasn't in no
155 condition to manage that money. You done what was right by him. Can't nobody say you ain't done what was right by him. Look how long you took

---

8. Stereotypical "mammy" from a minstrel song; in 1893 the name and image were trademarked by a pancake mix company, which for decades hired women to portray the character.

care of him . . . till he wanted to have his own place and moved over there with Miss Pearl.

TROY   That ain't what I'm saying, woman! I'm just stating the facts. If my
160   brother didn't have that metal plate in his head . . . I wouldn't have a pot to piss in or a window to throw it out of. And I'm fifty-three years old. Now see if you can understand that!

[TROY *gets up from the porch and starts to exit the yard.*]

ROSE   Where you going off to? You been running out of here every Saturday for weeks. I thought you was gonna work on this fence?
165   TROY   I'm gonna walk down to Taylors'. Listen to the ball game. I'll be back in a bit. I'll work on it when I get back.

[*He exits the yard. The lights go to black.*]

1.3

The lights come up on the yard. It is four hours later. ROSE *is taking down the clothes from the line.* CORY *enters carrying his football equipment.*

ROSE   Your daddy like to had a fit with you running out of here this morning without doing your chores.
CORY   I told you I had to go to practice.
ROSE   He say you were supposed to help him with this fence.
5   CORY   He been saying that the last four or five Saturdays, and then he don't never do nothing, but go down to Taylors'. Did you tell him about the recruiter?
ROSE   Yeah, I told him.
CORY   What he say?
10   ROSE   He ain't said nothing too much. You get in there and get started on your chores before he gets back. Go on and scrub down them steps before he gets back here hollering and carrying on.
CORY   I'm hungry. What you got to eat, Mama?
ROSE   Go on and get started on your chores. I got some meat loaf in there.
15   Go on and make you a sandwich . . . and don't leave no mess in there.

[CORY *exits into the house,* ROSE *continues to take down the clothes.* TROY *enters the yard and sneaks up and grabs her from behind.*]

Troy! Go on, now. You liked to scared me to death. What was the score of the game? Lucille had me on the phone and I couldn't keep up with it.
TROY   What I care about the game? Come here, woman. [*He tries to kiss her.*]
ROSE   I thought you went down Taylors' to listen to the game. Go on, Troy!
20   You supposed to be putting up this fence.
TROY [*attempting to kiss her again.*]   I'll put it up when I finish with what is at hand.
ROSE   Go on, Troy. I ain't studying you.[9]
TROY [*chasing after her*]   I'm studying you . . . fixing to do my homework!
25   ROSE   Troy, you better leave me alone.
TROY   Where's Cory? That boy brought his butt home yet?
ROSE   He's in the house doing his chores.
TROY [*calling*]   Cory! Get your butt out here, boy!

---

9. That is, paying any attention to you.

[ROSE *exits into the house with the laundry.* TROY *goes over to the pile of wood, picks up a board, and starts sawing.* CORY *enters from the house.*]

TROY   You just now coming in here from leaving this morning?

30   CORY   Yeah, I had to go to football practice.

TROY   Yeah, what?

CORY   Yessir.

TROY   I ain't but two seconds off you noway. The garbage sitting in there overflowing . . . you ain't done none of your chores . . . and you come in

35   here talking about "Yeah."

CORY   I was just getting ready to do my chores now, Pop . . .

TROY   Your first chore is to help me with this fence on Saturday. Everything else come after that. Now get that saw and cut them boards.

[CORY *takes the saw and begins cutting the boards.* TROY *continues working. There is a long pause.*]

CORY   Hey, Pop . . . why don't you buy a TV?

40   TROY   What I want with a TV? What I want one of them for?

CORY   Everybody got one. Earl, Ba Bra . . . Jesse!

TROY   I ain't asked you who had one. I say what I want with one?

CORY   So you can watch it. They got lots of things on TV. Baseball games and everything. We could watch the World Series.

45   TROY   Yeah . . . and how much this TV cost?

CORY   I don't know. They got them on sale for around two hundred dollars.[1]

TROY   Two hundred dollars, huh?

CORY   That ain't that much, Pop.

TROY   Naw, it's just two hundred dollars. See that roof you got over your

50   head at night? Let me tell you something about that roof. It's been over ten years since that roof was last tarred. See now . . . the snow come this winter and sit up there on that roof like it is . . . and it's gonna seep inside. It's just gonna be a little bit . . . ain't gonna hardly notice it. Then the next thing you know, it's gonna be leaking all over the house. Then the wood rot

55   from all that water and you gonna need a whole new roof. Now, how much you think it cost to get that roof tarred?

CORY   I don't know.

TROY   Two hundred and sixty-four dollars . . . cash money. While you thinking about a TV, I got to be thinking about the roof . . . and whatever else go

60   wrong around here. Now if you had two hundred dollars, what would you do . . . fix the roof or buy a TV?

CORY   I'd buy a TV. Then when the roof started to leak . . . when it needed fixing . . . I'd fix it.

TROY   Where you gonna get the money from? You done spent it for a TV. You

65   gonna sit up and watch the water run all over your brand new TV.

CORY   Aw, Pop. You got money. I know you do.

TROY   Where I got it at, huh?

CORY   You got it in the bank.

TROY   You wanna see my bankbook? You wanna see that seventy-three dollars

70   and twenty-two cents I got sitting up in there?

CORY   You ain't got to pay for it all at one time. You can put a down payment on it and carry it on home with you.

1. Equivalent to about $1,650 in 2013.

TROY   Not me. I ain't gonna owe nobody nothing if I can help it. Miss a payment and they come and snatch it right out your house. Then what you
75   got? Now, soon as I get two hundred dollars clear, then I'll buy a TV. Right
now, as soon as I get two hundred and sixty-four dollars, I'm gonna have
this roof tarred.

CORY   Aw . . . Pop!

TROY   You go on and get you two hundred dollars and buy one if ya want it. I
80   got better things to do with my money.

CORY   I can't get no two hundred dollars. I ain't never seen two hundred
dollars.

TROY   I'll tell you what . . . you get you a hundred dollars and I'll put the
other hundred with it.

85   CORY   Alright, I'm gonna show you.

TROY   You gonna show me how you can cut them boards right now.

[CORY *begins to cut the boards. There is a long pause.*]

CORY   The Pirates won today. That makes five in a row.

TROY   I ain't thinking about the Pirates. Got an all-white team. Got that
boy . . . that Puerto Rican boy . . . Clemente.[2] Don't even half-play him.
90   That boy could be something if they give him a chance. Play him one day
and sit him on the bench the next.

CORY   He gets a lot of chances to play.

TROY   I'm talking about playing regular. Playing every day so you can get your
timing. That's what I'm talking about.

95   CORY   They got some white guys on the team that don't play every day. You
can't play everybody at the same time.

TROY   If they got a white fellow sitting on the bench . . . you can bet your last
dollar he can't play! The colored guy got to be twice as good before he get
on the team. That's why I don't want you to get all tied up in them sports.
100   Man on the team and what it get him? They got colored on the team and
don't use them. Same as not having them. All them teams the same.

CORY   The Braves got Hank Aaron and Wes Covington.[3] Hank Aaron hit two
home runs today. That makes forty-three.

TROY   Hank Aaron ain't nobody. That's what you supposed to do. That's how
105   you supposed to play the game. Ain't nothing to it. It's just a matter of timing . . . getting the right follow-through. Hell, I can hit forty-three home
runs right now!

CORY   Not off no major-league pitching, you couldn't.

TROY   We had better pitching in the Negro leagues. I hit seven home runs off
110   of Satchel Paige.[4] You can't get no better than that!

2. Roberto Clemente (1934–1972), a Hall of
Fame outfielder who played for the Pittsburgh Pirates between 1955 and his death in
a plane crash; he was a twelve-time All-Star
and four-time National League batting champion. He played in 111 (of 162) games in
1957.
3. Aaron (b. 1934), who spent all but the last
two years of his major-league career (1954–76)
with the Milwaukee (later Atlanta) Braves,
was one of the greatest baseball players of all

time; his best-known achievement was breaking Ruth's lifetime home run record, eventually hitting 755; in 1957 he hit 44 home runs.
Covington (b. 1932), who played for the
Braves (1956–61) and five other teams (1961–
66), was integral to the Braves' 1957 run to
the World Series.
4. The legendary Negro League pitcher (1906–
1982); he began playing in the mid-1920s,
and between 1948 and 1965 played for several major-league teams.

CORY Sandy Koufax.[5] He's leading the league in strikeouts.

TROY I ain't thinking of no Sandy Koufax.

CORY You got Warren Spahn and Lew Burdette.[6] I bet you couldn't hit no home runs off of Warren Spahn.

115 TROY I'm through with it now. You go on and cut them boards. [*Pause*] Your mama tell me you done got recruited by a college football team? Is that right?

CORY Yeah. Coach Zellman say the recruiter gonna be coming by to talk to you. Get you to sign the permission papers.

120 TROY I thought you supposed to be working down there at the A&P. Ain't you suppose to be working down there after school?

CORY Mr. Stawicki say he gonna hold my job for me until after the football season. Say starting next week I can work weekends.

TROY I thought we had an understanding about this football stuff? You sup
125 pose to keep up with your chores and hold that job down at the A&P. Ain't been around here all day on a Saturday. Ain't none of your chores done . . . and now you telling me you done quit your job.

CORY I'm gonna be working weekends.

TROY You damn right you are! And ain't no need for nobody coming around
130 here to talk to me about signing nothing.

CORY Hey, Pop . . . you can't do that. He's coming all the way from North Carolina.

TROY I don't care where he coming from. The white man ain't gonna let you get nowhere with that football noway. You go on and get your book-learning
135 so you can work yourself up in that A&P or learn how to fix cars or build houses or something, get you a trade. That way you have something can't nobody take away from you. You go on and learn how to put your hands to some good use. Besides hauling people's garbage.

CORY I get good grades, Pop. That's why the recruiter wants to talk with you.
140 You got to keep up your grades to get recruited. This way I'll be going to college. I'll get a chance . . .

TROY First you gonna get your butt down there to the A&P and get your job back.

CORY Mr. Stawicki done already hired somebody else cause I told him I was
145 playing football.

TROY You a bigger fool than I thought . . . to let somebody take away your job so you can play some football. Where you gonna get your money to take out your girlfriend and whatnot? What kind of foolishness is that to let somebody take away your job?

150 CORY I'm still gonna be working weekends.

TROY Naw . . . naw. You getting your butt out of here and finding you another job.

---

5. A Hall of Fame pitcher (b. 1935), for the Brooklyn (later Los Angeles) Dodgers (1955–66).
6. The Braves' left-handed and right-handed pitching aces in 1957. Spahn (1921–2003), a Hall of Famer, played all but the final year of his career (1942–65) with the Boston (later Milwaukee) Braves; Burdette (1926–2007), the MVP of the 1957 World Series, played mainly for the Braves (1951–63) but for four other teams as well (1950, 1963–67).

CORY Come on, Pop! I got to practice. I can't work after school and play football too. The team needs me. That's what Coach Zellman say . . .

155 TROY I don't care what nobody else say. I'm the boss . . . you understand? I'm the boss around here. I do the only saying what counts.

CORY Come on, Pop!

TROY I asked you . . . did you understand?

CORY Yeah . . .

160 TROY What?!

CORY Yessir.

TROY You go on down there to that A&P and see if you can get your job back. If you can't do both . . . then you quit the football team. You've got to take the crookeds with the straights.

165 CORY Yessir. [*Pause*] Can I ask you a question?

TROY What the hell you wanna ask me? Mr. Stawicki the one you got the questions for.

CORY How come you ain't never liked me?

TROY Liked you? Who the hell say I got to like you? What law is there say I

170 got to like you? Wanna stand up in my face and ask a damn fool-ass question like that. Talking about liking somebody. Come here, boy, when I talk to you.

    [CORY *comes over to where* TROY *is working. He stands slouched over and* TROY *shoves him on his shoulder.*]

Straighten up, goddammit! I asked you a question . . . what law is there say I got to like you?

175 CORY None.

TROY Well, alright then! Don't you eat every day? [*Pause*] Answer me when I talk to you! Don't you eat every day?

CORY Yeah.

TROY Nigger, as long as you in my house, you put that sir on the end of it

180 when you talk to me!

CORY Yes . . . sir.

TROY You eat every day.

CORY Yessir!

TROY Got a roof over your head.

185 CORY Yessir!

TROY Got clothes on your back.

CORY Yessir.

TROY Why you think that is?

CORY Cause of you.

190 TROY Aw, hell I know it's 'cause of me . . . but why do you think that is?

CORY [*hesitant*] Cause you like me.

TROY Like you? I go out of here every morning . . . bust my butt . . . putting up with them crackers[7] every day . . . cause I like you? You about the biggest fool I ever saw. [*Pause*] It's my job. It's my responsibility! You under-

195 stand that? A man got to take care of his family. You live in my house . . . sleep you behind on my bedclothes . . . fill you belly up with my food . . . cause you my son. You my flesh and blood. Not 'cause I like you! Cause it's

---

7. Poor whites (derogatory term).

my duty to take care of you. I owe a responsibility to you! Let's get this straight right here . . . before it go along any further . . . I ain't got to like you. Mr. Rand don't give me my money come payday cause he likes me. He gives me cause he owe me. I done give you everything I had to give you. I gave you your life! Me and your mama worked that out between us. And liking your black ass wasn't part of the bargain. Don't you try and go through life worrying about if somebody like you or not. You best be mak

205   ing sure they doing right by you. You understand what I'm saying, boy?

CORY   Yessir.

TROY   Then get the hell out of my face, and get on down to that A&P.

[ROSE *has been standing behind the screen door for much of the scene. She enters as* CORY *exits.*]

ROSE   Why don't you let the boy go ahead and play football, Troy? Ain't no harm in that. He's just trying to be like you with the sports.

210   TROY   I don't want him to be like me! I want him to move as far away from my life as he can get. You the only decent thing that ever happened to me. I wish him that. But I don't wish him a thing else from my life. I decided seventeen years ago that boy wasn't getting involved in no sports. Not after what they did to me in the sports.

215   ROSE   Troy, why don't you admit you was too old to play in the major leagues? For once . . . why don't you admit that?

TROY   What do you mean too old? Don't come telling me I was too old. I just wasn't the right color. Hell, I'm fifty-three years old and can do better than Selkirk's .269 right now!

220   ROSE   How's was you gonna play ball when you were over forty? Sometimes I can't get no sense out of you.

TROY   I got good sense, woman. I got sense enough not to let my boy get hurt over playing no sports. You been mothering that boy too much. Worried about if people like him.

225   ROSE   Everything that boy do . . . he do for you. He wants you to say "Good job, son." That's all.

TROY   Rose, I ain't got time for that. He's alive. He's healthy. He's got to make his own way. I made mine. Ain't nobody gonna hold his hand when he get out there in that world.

230   ROSE   Times have changed from when you was young, Troy. People change. The world's changing around you and you can't even see it.

TROY   [*slow, methodical*]   Woman . . . I do the best I can do. I come in here every Friday. I carry a sack of potatoes and a bucket of lard. You all line up at the door with your hands out. I give you the lint from my pockets. I give

235   you my sweat and my blood. I ain't got no tears.[8] I done spent them. We go upstairs in that room at night . . . and I fall down on you and try to blast a hole into forever. I get up Monday morning . . . find my lunch on the table. I go out. Make my way. Find my strength to carry me through to the next Friday. [*Pause*] That's all I got, Rose. That's all I got to give. I can't give

240   nothing else.

[TROY *exits into the house. The lights go down to black.*]

---

8. An allusion to a famous wartime declaration to the British Parliament by Prime Minister Winston Churchill in May 1940: "I have nothing to offer but blood, toil, tears, and sweat."

1.4

It is Friday. Two weeks later. CORY *starts out of the house with his football equipment. The phone rings.*

CORY [*calling*] I got it! [*He answers the phone and stands in the screen door talking.*] Hello? Hey, Jesse. Naw . . . I was just getting ready to leave now.

ROSE [*calling*] Cory!

CORY I told you, man, them spikes is all tore up. You can use them if you
5 want, but they ain't no good. Earl got some spikes.

ROSE [*calling*] Cory!

CORY [*calling to* ROSE] Mam? I'm talking to Jesse. [*Into phone*] When she say that? [*Pause*] Aw, you lying, man. I'm gonna tell her you said that.

ROSE [*calling*] Cory, don't you go nowhere!

10 CORY I got to go to the game, Ma! [*Into the phone*] Yeah, hey, look, I'll talk to you later. Yeah, I'll meet you over Earl's house. Later. Bye, Ma.

[CORY *exists the house and starts out the yard.*]

ROSE Cory, where you going off to? You got that stuff all pulled out and thrown all over your room.

CORY [*in the yard*] I was looking for my spikes. Jesse wanted to borrow my
15 spikes.

ROSE Get up there and get that cleaned up before your daddy get back in here.

CORY I got to go to the game! I'll clean it up *when I get back.*

[CORY *exits.*]

ROSE That's all he need to do is see that room all messed up.

[ROSE *exits into the house.* TROY *and* BONO *enter the yard.* TROY *is dressed in clothes other than his work clothes.*]

20 BONO He told him the same thing he told you. Take it to the union.

TROY Brownie ain't got that much sense. Man wasn't thinking about nothing. He wait until I confront them on it . . . then he wanna come crying seniority. [*Calls*] Hey, Rose!

BONO I wish I could have seen Mr. Rand's face when he told you.

25 TROY He couldn't get it out of his mouth! Liked to bit his tongue! When they called me down there to the Commissioner's office . . . he thought they was gonna fire me. Like everybody else.

BONO I didn't think they was gonna fire you. I thought they was gonna put you on the warning paper.

30 TROY Hey, Rose! [*To* BONO] Yeah, Mr. Rand like to bit his tongue.

[TROY *breaks the seal on the bottle, takes a drink, and hands it to* BONO.]

BONO I see you run right down to Taylors' and told that Alberta gal.

TROY [*calling*] Hey Rose! [*To* BONO] I told everybody. Hey, Rose! I went down there to cash my check.

ROSE [*entering from the house*] Hush all that hollering, man! I know you out
35 here. What they say down there at the Commissioner's office?

TROY You supposed to come when I call you, woman. Bono'll tell you that. [*To* BONO] Don't Lucille come when you call her?

ROSE Man, hush your mouth. I ain't no dog . . . talk about "come when you call me."

40 TROY [*puts his arm around* ROSE]   You hear this, Bono? I had me an old dog
used to get uppity like that. You say, "C'mere, Blue!" . . . and he just lay
there and look at you. End up getting a stick and chasing him away trying
to make him come.

ROSE   I ain't studying you and your dog. I remember you used to sing that
45 old song.

TROY [*he sings*]

Hear it ring! Hear it ring!
I had a dog his name was Blue.[9]

ROSE   Don't nobody wanna hear you sing that old song.

TROY [*sings*]   You know Blue was mighty true.

50 ROSE   Used to have Cory running around here singing that song.

BONO   Hell, I remember that song myself.

TROY [*sings*]

You know Blue was a good old dog.
Blue treed a possum in a hollow log.

That was my daddy's song. My daddy made up that song.

55 ROSE   I don't care who made it up. Don't nobody wanna hear you sing it.

TROY [*makes a song like calling a dog*]   Come here, woman.

ROSE   You come in here carrying on, I reckon they ain't fired you. What they
say down there at the Commissioner's office?

TROY   Look here, Rose . . . Mr. Rand called me into his office today when I
60 got back from talking to them people down there . . . it come from up
top . . . he called me in and told me they was making me a driver.

ROSE   Troy, you kidding!

TROY   No I ain't. Ask Bono.

ROSE   Well, that's great, Troy. Now you don't have to hassle them people no
65 more.

[LYONS *enters from the street.*]

TROY   Aw hell, I wasn't looking to see you today. I thought you was in jail.
Got it all over the front page of the *Courier*[1] about them raiding Sefus'
place . . . where you be hanging out with all them thugs.

LYONS   Hey, Pop . . . that ain't got nothing to do with me. I don't go down
70 there gambling. I go down there to sit in with the band. I ain't got nothing
to do with the gambling part. They got some good music down there.

TROY   They got some rogues . . . is what they got.

LYONS   How you been, Mr. Bono? Hi, Rose.

BONO   I see where you playing down at the Crawford Grill tonight.

75 ROSE   How come you ain't brought Bonnie like I told you. You should have
brought Bonnie with you, she ain't been over in a month of Sundays.

LYONS   I was just in the neighborhood . . . thought I'd stop by.

TROY   Here he come . . .

BONO   Your daddy got a promotion on the rubbish. He's gonna be the first

9. A variation on "Old Blue," a traditional
African American folk song.
1. The *Pittsburgh Courier*, one of the top-
selling African American newspapers in the
mid-20th century.

80   colored driver. Ain't got to do nothing but sit up there and read the paper like them white fellows.

LYONS   Hey, Pop . . . if you knew how to read you'd be alright.

BONO   Naw . . . naw . . . you mean if the nigger knew how to drive he'd be all right. Been fighting with them people about driving and ain't even got a

85   license. Mr. Rand know you ain't got no driver's license?

TROY   Driving ain't nothing. All you do is point the truck where you want it to go. Driving ain't nothing.

BONO   Do Mr. Rand know you ain't got no driver's license? That's what I'm talking about. I ain't asked if driving was easy. I asked if Mr. Rand know you

90   ain't got no driver's license.

TROY   He ain't got to know. The man ain't got to know my business. Time he find out, I have two or three driver's licenses.

LYONS [*going into his pocket*]   Say, look here, Pop . . .

TROY   I knew it was coming. Didn't I tell you, Bono? I know what kind of

95   "Look here, Pop" that was. The nigger fixing to ask me for some money. It's Friday night. It's my payday. All them rogues down there on the avenue . . . the ones that ain't in jail . . . and Lyons is hopping in his shoes to get down there with them.

LYONS   See, Pop . . . if you give somebody else a chance to talk sometime,

100   you'd see that I was fixing to pay you back your ten dollars like I told you. Here . . . I told you I'd pay you when Bonnie got paid.

TROY   Naw . . . you go ahead and keep that ten dollars. Put it in the bank. The next time you feel like you wanna come by here and ask me for something . . . you go on down there and get that.

105 LYONS   Here's your ten dollars, Pop. I told you I don't want you to give me nothing. I just wanted to borrow ten dollars.

TROY   Naw . . . you go on and keep that for the next time you want to ask me.

LYONS   Come on, Pop . . . here go your ten dollars.

ROSE   Why don't you go on and let the boy pay you back, Troy?

110 LYONS   Here you go, Rose. If you don't take it I'm gonna have to hear about it for the next six months.

    [*He hands her the money.*]

ROSE   You can hand yours over here too, Troy.

TROY   You see this, Bono. You see how they do me.

BONO   Yeah, Lucille do me the same way.

    [GABRIEL *is heard singing offstage. He enters.*]

115 GABRIEL   Better get ready for the Judgment! Better get ready for . . . Hey! . . . Hey! . . . There's Troy's boy!

LYONS   How you doing, Uncle Gabe?

GABRIEL   Lyons . . . The King of the Jungle! Rose . . . hey, Rose. Got a flower for you. [*He takes a rose from his pocket.*] Picked it myself. That's the same

120   rose like you is!

ROSE   That's right nice of you, Gabe.

LYONS   What you been doing, Uncle Gabe?

GABRIEL   Oh, I been chasing hellhounds and waiting on the time to tell St. Peter to open the gates.

125 LYONS   You been chasing hellhounds, huh? Well . . . you doing the right thing, Uncle Gabe. Somebody got to chase them.

GABRIEL   Oh, yeah . . . I know it. The devil's strong. The devil ain't no push-
over. Hellhounds snipping at everybody's heels. But I got my trumpet waiting on the judgment time.

130 LYONS   Waiting on the Battle of Armageddon,[2] huh?

GABRIEL   Ain't gonna be too much of a battle when God get to waving that
Judgment sword. But the people's gonna have a hell of a time trying to get
into heaven if them gates ain't open.

LYONS [putting his arm around GABRIEL]   You hear this, Pop. Uncle Gabe,
135 you alright!

GABRIEL [laughing with LYONS]   Lyons! King of the Jungle.

ROSE   You gonna stay for supper, Gabe. Want me to fix you a plate?

GABRIEL   I'll take a sandwich, Rose. Don't want no plate. Just wanna eat with
my hands. I'll take a sandwich.

140 ROSE   How about you, Lyons? You staying? Got some short ribs cooking.

LYONS   Naw, I won't eat nothing till after we finished playing. [Pause] You
ought to come down and listen to me play, Pop.

TROY   I don't like that Chinese music. All that noise.

ROSE   Go on in the house and wash up, Gabe . . . I'll fix you a sandwich.

145 GABRIEL [to LYONS, as he exits]   Troy's mad at me.

LYONS   What you mad at Uncle Gabe for, Pop?

ROSE   He thinks Troy's mad at him cause he moved over to Miss Pearl's.

TROY   I ain't mad at the man. He can live where he want to live at.

LYONS   What he move over there for? Miss Pearl don't like nobody.

150 ROSE   She don't mind him none. She treats him real nice. She just don't
allow all that singing.

TROY   She don't mind that rent he be paying . . . that's what she don't mind.

ROSE   Troy, I ain't going through that with you no more. He's over there
cause he want to have his own place. He can come and go as he please.

155 TROY   Hell, he could come and go as he please here. I wasn't stopping him. I
ain't put no rules on him.

ROSE   It ain't the same thing, Troy. And you know it.

[GABRIEL comes to the door.]

Now, that's the last I wanna hear about that. I don't wanna hear nothing
else about Gabe and Miss Pearl. And next week . . .

160 GABRIEL   I'm ready for my sandwich, Rose.

ROSE   And next week . . . when that recruiter come from that school . . . I
want you to sign that paper and go on and let Cory play football. Then
that'll be the last I have to hear about that.

TROY [to ROSE as she exits into the house]   I ain't thinking about Cory nothing.

165 LYONS   What . . . Cory got recruited? What school he going to?

TROY   That boy walking around here smelling his piss . . . thinking he's
grown. Thinking he's gonna do what he want, irrespective of what I say.
Look here, Bono . . . I left the Commissioner's office and went down to the
A&P . . . that boy ain't working down there. He lying to me. Telling me he
170 got his job back . . . telling me he working weekends . . . telling me he working after school . . . Mr. Stawicki tell me he ain't working down there at all!

---

2. The final battle between the forces of God and of evil, as described in the New Testament's
book of Revelation (see 16.16).

LYONS   Cory just growing up. He's just busting at the seams trying to fill out your shoes.

TROY   I don't care what he's doing. When he get to the point where he wanna
175   disobey me . . . then it's time for him to move on. Bono'll tell you that. I bet he ain't never disobeyed his daddy without paying the consequences.

BONO   I ain't never had a chance. My daddy came on through . . . but I ain't never knew him to see him . . . or what he had on his mind or where he went. Just moving on through. Searching out the New Land. That's what
180   the old folks used to call it. See a fellow moving around from place to place . . . woman to woman . . . called it searching out the New Land. I can't say if he ever found it. I come along, didn't want no kids. Didn't know if I was gonna be in one place long enough to fix on them right as their daddy. I figured I was going searching too. As it turned out I been hooked
185   up with Lucille near about as long as your daddy been with Rose. Going on sixteen years.

TROY   Sometimes I wish I hadn't known my daddy. He ain't cared nothing about no kids. A kid to him wasn't nothing. All he wanted was for you to learn how to walk so he could start you to working. When it come time for
190   eating . . . he ate first. If there was anything left over, that's what you got. Man would sit down and eat two chickens and give you the wing.

LYONS   You ought to stop that, Pop. Everybody feed their kids. No matter how hard times is . . . everybody care about their kids. Make sure they have something to eat.

195   TROY   The only thing my daddy cared about was getting them bales of cotton in to Mr. Lubin. That's the only thing that mattered to him. Sometimes I used to wonder why he was living. Wonder why the devil hadn't come and got him. "Get them bales of cotton in to Mr. Lubin" and find out he owe him money[3] . . .

200   LYONS   He should have just went on and left when he saw he couldn't get nowhere. That's what I would have done.

TROY   How he gonna leave with eleven kids? And where he gonna go? He ain't knew how to do nothing but farm. No, he was trapped and I think he knew it. But I'll say this for him . . . he felt a responsibility toward us.
205   Maybe he ain't treated us the way I felt he should have . . . but without that responsibility he could have walked off and left us . . . made his own way.

BONO   A lot of them did. Back in those days what you talking about . . . they walk out their front door and just take on down one road or another and
210   keep on walking.

LYONS   There you go! That's what I'm talking about.

BONO   Just keep on walking till you come to something else. Ain't you never heard of nobody having the walking blues? Well, that's what you call it when you just take off like that.

215   TROY   My daddy ain't had them walking blues! What you talking about? He stayed right there with his family. But he was just as evil as he could be. My

---

3. Under the sharecropping system that arose in the South after the Civil War, tenant farmers received their seed, tools, food and clothing, and housing on credit from landowners; after harvesting the cotton, they had to repay these charges from their share of the value of the crop.

mama couldn't stand him. Couldn't stand that evilness. She run off when I was about eight. She sneaked off one night after he had gone to sleep. Told me she was coming back for me. I ain't never seen her no more. All his
220 women run off and left him. He wasn't good for nobody.

When my turn come to head out, I was fourteen and got to sniffing around Joe Canewell's daughter. Had us an old mule we called Greyboy. My daddy sent me out to do some plowing and I tied up Greyboy and went to fooling around with Joe Canewell's daughter. We done found us a nice
225 little spot, got real cozy with each other. She about thirteen and we done figured we was grown anyway . . . so we down there enjoying ourselves . . . ain't thinking about nothing. We didn't know Greyboy had got loose and wandered back to the house and my daddy was looking for me. We down there by the creek enjoying ourselves when my daddy come up on us. Sur-
230 prised us. He had them leather straps off the mule and commenced to whupping me like there was no tomorrow. I jumped up, mad and embarrassed. I was scared of my daddy. When he commenced to whupping on me . . . quite naturally I run to get out of the way.

[*Pause.*]

Now I thought he was mad cause I ain't done my work. But I see where he
235 was chasing me off so he could have the gal for himself. When I see what the matter of it was, I lost all fear of my daddy. Right there is where I become a man . . . at fourteen years of age.

[*Pause.*]

Now it was my turn to run him off. I picked up them same reins that he had used on me. I picked up them reins and commenced to whupping on
240 him. The gal jumped up and run off . . . and when my daddy turned to face me, I could see why the devil had never come to get him . . . cause he was the devil himself. I don't know what happened. When I woke up, I was laying right there by the creek, and Blue . . . this old dog we had . . . was licking my face. I thought I was blind. I couldn't see nothing. Both my eyes
245 were swollen shut. I layed there and cried. I didn't know what I was gonna do. The only thing I knew was the time had come for me to leave my daddy's house. And right there the world suddenly got big. And it was a long time before I could cut it down to where I could handle it.

Part of that cutting down was when I got to the place where I could feel
250 him kicking in my blood and knew that the only thing that separated us was the matter of a few years.

[GABRIEL *enters from the house with a sandwich.*]

LYONS   What you got there, Uncle Gabe?

GABRIEL   Got me a ham sandwich. Rose gave me a ham sandwich.

TROY   I don't know what happened to him. I done lost touch with everybody
255 except Gabriel. But I hope he's dead. I hope he found some peace.

LYONS   That's a heavy story, Pop. I didn't know you left home when you was fourteen.

TROY   And didn't know nothing. The only part of the world I knew was the forty-two acres of Mr. Lubin's land. That's all I knew about life.

260 LYONS   Fourteen's kinda young to be out on your own. [*Phone rings.*] I don't even think I was ready to be out on my own at fourteen. I don't know what I would have done.

TROY   I got up from the creek and walked on down to Mobile. I was through
with farming. Figured I could do better in the city. So I walked the two
265   hundred miles to Mobile.

LYONS   Wait a minute . . . you ain't walked no two hundred miles, Pop. Ain't
nobody gonna walk no two hundred miles. You talking about some walking
there.

BONO   That's the only way you got anywhere back in them days.

270   LYONS   Shhh. Damn if I wouldn't have hitched a ride with somebody!

TROY   Who you gonna hitch it with? They ain't had no cars and things like
they got now. We talking about 1918.

ROSE [entering]   What you all out here getting into?

TROY [to ROSE]   I'm telling Lyons how good he got it. He don't know nothing
275   about this I'm talking.

ROSE   Lyons, that was Bonnie on the phone. She say you supposed to pick
her up.

LYONS   Yeah, okay, Rose.

TROY   I walked on down to Mobile and hitched up with some of them fellows
280   that was heading this way. Got up here and found out . . . not only couldn't
you get a job . . . you couldn't find no place to live. I thought I was in freedom. Shhh. Colored folks living down there on the riverbanks in whatever
kind of shelter they could find for themselves. Right down there under the
Brady Street Bridge. Living in shacks made of sticks and tar paper. Messed
285   around there and went from bad to worse. Started stealing. First it was
food. Then I figured, hell, if I steal money I can buy me some food. Buy me
some shoes too! One thing led to another. Met your mama. I was young
and anxious to be a man. Met your mama and had you. What I do that for?
Now I got to worry about feeding you and her. Got to steal three times as
290   much. Went out one day looking for somebody to rob . . . that's what I was,
a robber. I'll tell you the truth. I'm ashamed of it today. But it's the truth.
Went to rob this fellow . . . pulled out my knife . . . and he pulled out a
gun. Shot me in the chest. It felt just like somebody had taken a hot brand-
ing iron and laid it on me. When he shot me I jumped at him with my
295   knife. They told me I killed him and they put me in the penitentiary and
locked me up for fifteen years. That's where I met Bono. That's where I
learned how to play baseball. Got out that place and your mama had taken
you and went on to make life without me. Fifteen years was a long time for
her to wait. But that fifteen years cured me of that robbing stuff. Rose'll tell
300   you. She asked me when I met her if I had gotten all that foolishness out of
my system. And I told her, "Baby, it's you and baseball all what count with
me." You hear me, Bono? I meant it too. She say, "Which one comes first?"
I told her, "Baby, ain't no doubt it's baseball . . . but you stick and get old
with me and we'll both outlive this baseball." Am I right, Rose? And it's true.

305   ROSE   Man, hush your mouth. You ain't said no such thing. Talking about,
"Baby, you know you'll always be number one with me." That's what you
was talking.

TROY   You hear that, Bono. That's why I love her.

BONO   Rose'll keep you straight. You get off the track, she'll straighten you up.

310   ROSE   Lyons, you better get on up and get Bonnie. She waiting on you.

LYONS [gets up to go]   Hey, Pop, why don't you come on down to the Grill and
hear me play?

TROY   I ain't going down there. I'm too old to be sitting around in them clubs.

BONO   You got to be good to play down at the Grill.

315 LYONS   Come on, Pop . . .

TROY   I got to get up in the morning.

LYONS   You ain't got to stay long.

TROY   Naw, I'm gonna get my supper and go on to bed.

LYONS   Well, I got to go. I'll see you again.

320 TROY   Don't you come around my house on my payday.

ROSE   Pick up the phone and let somebody know you coming. And bring Bonnie with you. You know I'm always glad to see her.

LYONS   Yeah, I'll do that, Rose. You take care now. See you, Pop. See you, Mr. Bono. See you, Uncle Gabe.

325 GABRIEL   Lyons! King of the Jungle!

[LYONS *exits.*]

TROY   Is supper ready, woman? Me and you got some business to take care of. I'm gonna tear it up too.

ROSE   Troy, I done told you now!

TROY   [*puts his arm around* BONO] Aw hell, woman . . . this is Bono. Bono

330   like family. I done known this nigger since . . . how long I done know you?

BONO   It's been a long time.

TROY   I done known this nigger since Skippy was a pup.[4] Me and him done been through some times.

BONO   You sure right about that.

335 TROY   Hell, I done know him longer than I known you. And we still standing shoulder to shoulder. Hey, look here, Bono . . . a man can't ask for no more than that. [*Drinks to him.*] I love you, nigger.

BONO   Hell, I love you too . . . but I got to get home see my woman. You got yours in hand. I got to go get mine.

[BONO *starts to exit as* CORY *enters the yard, dressed in his football uniform. He gives* TROY *a hard, uncompromising look.*]

340 CORY   What you do that for, Pop?

[*He throws his helmet down in the direction of* TROY.]

ROSE   What's the matter? Cory . . . what's the matter?

CORY   Papa done went up to the school and told Coach Zellman I can't play football no more. Wouldn't even let me play the game. Told him to tell the recruiter not to come.

345 ROSE   Troy . . .

TROY   What you Troying me for. Yeah, I did it. And the boy know why I did it.

CORY   Why you wanna do that to me? That was the one chance I had.

ROSE   Ain't nothing wrong with Cory playing football, Troy.

TROY   The boy lied to me. I told the nigger if he wanna play football . . . to

350   keep up his chores and hold down that job at the A&P. That was the conditions. Stopped down there to see Mr. Stawicki . . .

CORY   I can't work after school during the football season, Pop! I tried to tell you that Mr. Stawicki's holding my job for me. You don't never want to listen to nobody. And then you wanna go and do this to me!

---

4. That is, for a very long time (folk expression).

355   TROY   I ain't done nothing to you. You done it to yourself.

      CORY   Just cause you didn't have a chance! You just scared I'm gonna be better than you, that's all.

      TROY   Come here.

      ROSE   Troy . . .

          [CORY *reluctantly crosses over to* TROY.]

360   TROY   Alright! See. You done made a mistake.

      CORY   I didn't even do nothing!

      TROY   I'm gonna tell you what your mistake was. See . . . you swung at the ball and didn't hit it. That's strike one. See, you in the batter's box now. You swung and you missed. That's strike one. Don't you strike out!

          [*Lights fade to black.*]

2.1

The following morning. CORY *is at the tree hitting the ball with the bat. He tries to mimic* TROY, *but his swing is awkward, less sure.* ROSE *enters from the house.*

      ROSE   Cory, I want you to help me with this cupboard.

      CORY   I ain't quitting the team. I don't care what Poppa say.

      ROSE   I'll talk to him when he gets back. He had to go see about your Uncle Gabe. The police done arrested him. Say he was disturbing the peace. He'll
5   be back directly. Come on in here and help me clean out the top of this cupboard.

          [CORY *exits into the house.* ROSE *sees* TROY *and* BONO *coming down the alley.*]

      Troy . . . what they say down there?

      TROY   Ain't said nothing. I give them fifty dollars and they let him go. I'll talk to you about it. Where's Cory?

10   ROSE   He's in there helping me clean out these cupboards.

      TROY   Tell him to get his butt out here.

          [TROY *and* BONO *go over to the pile of wood.* BONO *picks up the saw and begins sawing.*]

      TROY [*to* BONO]   All they want is the money. That makes six or seven times I done went down there and got him. See me coming they stick out their hands.

15   BONO   Yeah. I know what you mean. That's all they care about . . . that money. They don't care about what's right. [*Pause*] Nigger, why you got to go and get some hard wood? You ain't doing nothing but building a little old fence. Get you some soft pine wood. That's all you need.

      TROY   I know what I'm doing. This is outside wood. You put pine wood inside
20   the house. Pine wood is inside wood. This here is outside wood. Now you tell me where the fence is gonna be?

      BONO   You don't need this wood. You can put it up with pine wood and it'll stand as long as you gonna be here looking at it.

      TROY   How you know how long I'm gonna be here, nigger? Hell, I might just
25   live forever. Live longer than old man Horsely.

      BONO   That's what Magee used to say.

      TROY   Magee's a damn fool. Now you tell me who you ever heard of gonna pull their own teeth with a pair of rusty pliers.

BONO   The old folks . . . my granddaddy used to pull his teeth with pliers.
30   They ain't had no dentists for the colored folks back then.
TROY   Get clean pliers! You understand? Clean pliers! Sterilize them! Besides
we ain't living back then. All Magee had to do was walk over to Doc
Goldblum's.
BONO   I see where you and that Tallahassee gal . . . that Alberta . . . I see
35   where you all done got tight.
TROY   What you mean "got tight"?
BONO   I see where you be laughing and joking with her all the time.
TROY   I laughs and jokes with all of them, Bono. You know me.
BONO   That ain't the kind of laughing and joking I'm talking about.

[CORY *enters from the house.*]

40   CORY   How you doing, Mr. Bono?
TROY   Cory? Get that saw from Bono and cut some wood. He talking about
the wood's too hard to cut. Stand back there, Jim, and let that young boy
show you how it's done.
BONO   He's sure welcome to it.

[CORY *takes the saw and begins to cut the wood.*]

45   Whew-e-e! Look at that. Big old strong boy. Look like Joe Louis.[5] Hell,
must be getting old the way I'm watching that boy whip through that wood.
CORY   I don't see why Mama want a fence around the yard noways.
TROY   Damn if I know either. What the hell she keeping out with it? She ain't
got nothing nobody want.
50   BONO   Some people build fences to keep people out . . . and other people
build fences to keep people in. Rose wants to hold on to you all. She loves
you.
TROY   Hell, nigger, I don't need nobody to tell me my wife loves me, Cory . . .
go on in the house and see if you can find that other saw.
55   CORY   Where's it at?
TROY   I said find it! Look for it till you find it!

[CORY *exists into the house.*]

    What's that supposed to mean? Wanna keep us in?
BONO   Troy . . . I done known you seem like damn near my whole life. You
and Rose both. I done know both of you all for a long time. I remember
60   when you met Rose. When you was hitting them baseball out the park. A
lot of them old gals was after you then. You had the pick of the litter. When
you picked Rose, I was happy for you. That was the first time I knew you
had any sense. I said . . . My man Troy knows what he's doing . . . I'm
gonna follow this nigger . . . he might take me somewhere. I been follow-
65   ing you too. I done learned a whole heap of things about life watching you.
I done learned how to tell where the shit lies. How to tell it from the
alfalfa. You done learned me a lot of things. You showed me how to not
make the same mistakes . . . to take life as it comes along and keep putting
one foot in front of the other. [*Pause*] Rose a good woman, Troy.
70   TROY   Hell, nigger, I know she a good woman. I been married to her for eighteen years. What you got on your mind, Bono?

5. American boxer (1914–1981); as world heavyweight champion (1937–49), he was the most
famous black man in the United States.

BONO   I just say she a good woman. Just like I say anything. I ain't got to have nothing on my mind.

TROY   You just gonna say she a good woman and leave it hanging out there like that? Why you telling me she a good woman?

BONO   She loves you, Troy. Rose loves you.

TROY   You saying I don't measure up. That's what you trying to say. I don't measure up cause I'm seeing this other gal. I know what you trying to say.

BONO   I know what Rose means to you, Troy. I'm just trying to say I don't want to see you mess up.

TROY   Yeah, I appreciate that, Bono. If you was messing around on Lucille I'd be telling you the same thing.

BONO   Well, that's all I got to say. I just say that because I love you both.

TROY   Hell, you know me . . . I wasn't out there looking for nothing. You can't find a better woman than Rose. I know that. But seems like this woman just stuck onto me where I can't shake her loose. I done wrestled with it, tried to throw her off me . . . but she just stuck on tighter. Now she's stuck on for good.

BONO   You's in control . . . that's what you tell me all the time. You responsible for what you do.

TROY   I ain't ducking the responsibility of it. As long as it sets right in my heart . . . then I'm okay. Cause that's all I listen to. It'll tell me right from wrong every time. And I ain't talking about doing Rose no bad turn. I love Rose. She done carried me a long ways and I love and respect her for that.

BONO   I know you do. That's why I don't want to see you hurt her. But what you gonna do when she find out? What you got then? If you try and juggle both of them . . . sooner or later you gonna drop one of them. That's common sense.

TROY   Yeah, I hear what you saying, Bono. I been trying to figure a way to work it out.

BONO   Work it out right, Troy. I don't want to be getting all up between you and Rose's business . . . but work it so it come out right.

TROY   Aw hell, I get all up between you and Lucille's business. When you gonna get that woman that refrigerator she been wanting? Don't tell me you ain't got no money now. I know who your banker is. Mellon[6] don't need that money bad as Lucille want that refrigerator. I'll tell you that.

BONO   Tell you what I'll do . . . when you finish building this fence for Rose . . . I'll buy Lucille that refrigerator.

TROY   You done stuck your foot in your mouth now!

[TROY grabs up a board and begins to saw. BONO starts to walk out the yard.]

Hey, nigger . . . where you going?

BONO   I'm going home. I know you don't expect me to help you now. I'm protecting my money. I wanna see you put that fence up by yourself. That's what I want to see. You'll be here another six months without me.

TROY   Nigger, you ain't right.

BONO   When it comes to my money . . . I'm right as fireworks on the Fourth of July.

TROY   Alright, we gonna see now. You better get out your bankbook.

[BONO exits, and TROY continues to work. ROSE enters from the house.]

6. Mellon National Bank, founded in Pittsburgh in 1870 by Thomas Mellon.

ROSE   What they say down there? What's happening with Gabe?

TROY   I went down there and got him out. Cost me fifty dollars. Say he was
120   disturbing the peace. Judge set up a hearing for him in three weeks. Say to
      show cause why he shouldn't be recommitted.

ROSE   What was he doing that cause them to arrest him?

TROY   Some kids was teasing him and he run them off home. Say he was
      howling and carrying on. Some folks seen him and called the police. That's
125   all it was.

ROSE   Well, what's you say? What'd you tell the judge?

TROY   Told him I'd look after him. It didn't make no sense to recommit the
      man. He stuck out his big greasy palm and told me to give him fifty dollars
      and take him on home.

130 ROSE   Where's he at now? Where'd he go off to?

TROY   He's gone on about his business. He don't need nobody to hold his
      hand.

ROSE   Well, I don't know. Seem like that would be the best place for him if
      they did put him into the hospital. I know what you're gonna say. But that's
135   what I think would be best.

TROY   The man done had his life ruined fighting for what? And they wanna
      take and lock him up. Let him be free. He don't bother nobody.

ROSE   Well, everybody got their own way of looking at it I guess. Come on
      and get your lunch. I got a bowl of lima beans and some cornbread in the
140   oven. Come on get something to eat. Ain't no sense you fretting over Gabe.

        [ROSE *turns to go into the house.*]

TROY   Rose . . . got something to tell you.

ROSE   Well, come on . . . wait till I get this food on the table.

TROY   Rose!

        [*She stops and turns around.*]

      I don't know how to say this. [*Pause*] I can't explain it none. It just sort of
145   grows on you till it gets out of hand. It starts out like a little bush . . . and
      the next think you know it's a whole forest.

ROSE   Troy . . . what is you talking about?

TROY   I'm talking, woman, let me talk. I'm trying to find a way to tell you . . .
      I'm gonna be a daddy. I'm gonna be somebody's daddy.

150 ROSE   Troy . . . you're not telling me this? You're gonna be . . . what?

TROY   Rose . . . now . . . see . . .

ROSE   You telling me you gonna be somebody's daddy? You telling your *wife*
      this?

        [GABRIEL *enters from the street. He carries a rose in his hand.*]

GABRIEL   Hey, Troy! Hey, Rose!

155 ROSE   I have to wait eighteen years to hear something like this.

GABRIEL   Hey, Rose . . . I got a flower for you. [*He hands it to her.*] That's a
      rose. Same rose like you is.

ROSE   Thanks, Gabe.

GABRIEL   Troy, you ain't mad at me is you? Them bad mens come and put me
160   away. You ain't mad at me is you?

TROY   Naw, Gabe, I ain't mad at you.

ROSE   Eighteen years and you wanna come with this.

GABRIEL [*takes a quarter out of his pocket*]   See what I got? Got a brand new
      quarter.

165 TROY   Rose . . . it's just . . .

ROSE   Ain't nothing you can say, Troy. Ain't no way of explaining that.

GABRIEL   Fellow that give me this quarter had a whole mess of them. I'm gonna keep this quarter till it stop shining.

ROSE   Gabe, go on in the house there. I got some watermelon in the frigidaire.
170   Go on and get you a piece.

GABRIEL   Say, Rose . . . you know I was chasing hellhounds and them bad mens come and get me and take me away. Troy helped me. He come down there and told them they better let me go before he beat them up. Yeah, he did!

175 ROSE   You go on and get you a piece of watermelon, Gabe. Them bad mens is gone now.

GABRIEL   Okay, Rose . . . gonna get me some watermelon. The kind with the stripes on it.

[GABRIEL *exits into the house.*]

ROSE   Why, Troy? Why? After all these years to come dragging this in to me
180   now. It don't make no sense at your age. I could have expected this ten or fifteen years ago, but not now.

TROY   Age ain't got nothing to do with it, Rose.

ROSE   I done tried to be everything a wife should be. Everything a wife could be. Been married eighteen years and I got to live to see the day you tell me
185   you been seeing another woman and done fathered a child by her. And you know I ain't never wanted no half nothing in my family. My whole family is half. Everybody got different fathers and mothers . . . my two sisters and my brother. Can't hardly tell who's who. Can't never sit down and talk about Papa and Mama. It's your papa and your mama and my papa and my
190   mama . . .

TROY   Rose . . . stop it now.

ROSE   I ain't never wanted that for none of my children. And now you wanna drag your behind in here and tell me something like this.

TROY   You ought to know. It's time for you to know.

195 ROSE   Well, I don't want to know, goddamn it!

TROY   I can't just make it go away. It's done now. I can't wish the circumstance of the thing away.

ROSE   And you don't want to either. Maybe you want to wish me and my boy away. Maybe that's what you want? Well, you can't wish us away. I've got
200   eighteen years of my life invested in you. You ought to have stayed upstairs in my bed where you belong.

TROY   Rose . . . now listen to me . . . we can get a handle on this thing. We can talk this out . . . come to an understanding.

ROSE   All of a sudden it's "we." Where was "we" at when you was down there
205   rolling around with some godforsaken woman? "We" should have come to an understanding before you started making a damn fool of yourself. You're a day late and a dollar short when it comes to an understanding with me.

TROY   It's just . . . She gives me a different idea . . . a different understanding about myself. I can step out of this house and get away from the pressures
210   and problems . . . be a different man. I ain't got to wonder how I'm gonna pay the bills or get the roof fixed. I can just be a part of myself that I ain't never been.

ROSE   What I want to know . . . is do you plan to continue seeing her. That's all you can say to me.

215 TROY   I can sit up in her house and laugh. Do you understand what I'm say-
         ing. I can laugh out loud . . . and it feels good. It reaches all the way down
         to the bottom of my shoes. [*Pause*] Rose, I can't give that up.

    ROSE   Maybe you ought to go on and stay down there with her . . . if she a
         better woman than me.

220 TROY   It ain't about nobody being a better woman or nothing. Rose, you ain't
         the blame. A man couldn't ask for no woman to be a better wife than you've
         been. I'm responsible for it. I done locked myself into a pattern trying to
         take care of you all that I forgot about myself.

    ROSE   What the hell was I there for? That was my job, not somebody else's.

225 TROY   Rose, I done tried all my life to live decent . . . to live a clean . . .
         hard . . . useful life. I tried to be a good husband to you. In every way I
         knew how. Maybe I come into the world backwards, I don't know. But . . .
         you born with two strikes on you before you come to the plate. You got to
         guard it closely . . . always looking for the curve ball on the inside corner.
230   You can't afford to let none get past you. You can't afford a call strike.[7]
         If you going down . . . you going down swinging. Everything lined up
         against you. What you gonna do. I fooled them, Rose. I bunted. When I
         found you and Cory and a halfway decent job . . . I was safe. Couldn't
         nothing touch me. I wasn't gonna strike out no more. I wasn't going back
235   to the penitentiary. I wasn't gonna lay in the streets with a bottle of wine. I
         was safe. I had me a family. A job. I wasn't gonna get that last strike. I was
         on first looking for one of them boys to knock me in. To get me home.

    ROSE   You should have stayed in my bed, Troy.

    TROY   Then when I saw that gal . . . she firmed up my backbone. And I got to
240   thinking that if I tried . . . I just might be able to steal second. Do you
         understand after eighteen years I wanted to steal second.

    ROSE   You should have held me tight. You should have grabbed me and held
         on.

    TROY   I stood on first base for eighteen years and I thought . . . well, god
245   damn it . . . go on for it!

    ROSE   We're not talking about baseball! We're talking about you going off to
         lay in bed with another woman . . . and then bring it home to me. That's
         what we're talking about. We ain't talking about no baseball.

    TROY   Rose, you're not listening to me. I'm trying the best I can to explain it
250   to you. It's not easy for me to admit that I been standing in the same place
         for eighteen years.

    ROSE   I been standing with you! I been right here with you, Troy. I got a life
         too. I gave eighteen years of my life to stand in the same spot with you.
         Don't you think I ever wanted other things? Don't you think I had dreams
255   and hopes? What about my life? What about me? Don't you think it ever
         crossed my mind to want to know other men? That I wanted to lay up
         somewhere and forget about my responsibilities? That I wanted someone
         to make me laugh so I could feel good? You not the only one who's got
         wants and needs. But I held on to you, Troy. I took all my feelings, my
260   wants and needs, my dreams . . . and I buried them inside you. I planted a
         seed and watched and prayed over it. I planted myself inside you and

---

7. That is, a called strike: a pitch at which the batter fails to swing that the umpire judges to have
been within the strike zone.

waited to bloom. And it didn't take me no eighteen years to find out the soil was hard and rocky and it wasn't never gonna bloom.

265   But I held on to you, Troy. I held you tighter. You was my husband. I owed you everything I had. Every part of me I could find to give you. And upstairs in that room . . . with the darkness falling in on me . . . I gave everything I had to try and erase the doubt that you wasn't the finest man in the world. And wherever you was going . . . I wanted to be there with you. Cause you was my husband. Cause that's the only way I was gonna

270   survive as your wife. You always talking about what you give . . . and what you don't have to give. But you take too. You take . . . and don't even know nobody's giving!

[ROSE *turns to exit into the house;* TROY *grabs her arm.*]

TROY   You say I take and don't give!
ROSE   Troy! You're hurting me!
275 TROY   You say I take and don't give.
ROSE   Troy . . . you're hurting my arm! Let go!
TROY   I done give you everything I got. Don't you tell that lie on me.
ROSE   Troy!
TROY   Don't you tell that lie on me!

[CORY *enters from the house.*]

280 CORY   Mama!
ROSE   Troy. You're hurting me.
TROY   Don't you tell me about no taking and giving.

[CORY *comes up behind* TROY *and grabs him.* TROY, *surprised, is thrown off balance just as* CORY *throws a glancing blow that catches him on the chest and knocks him down.* TROY *is stunned, as is* CORY.]

ROSE   Troy. Troy. No!

[TROY *gets to his feet and starts at* CORY.]

Troy . . . no. Please! Troy!

[ROSE *pulls on* TROY *to hold him back.* TROY *stops himself.*]

285 TROY [*to* CORY]   Alright. That's strike two. You stay away from around me, boy. Don't you strike out. You living with a full count. Don't you strike out.

[TROY *exits out the yard as the lights go down.*]

2.2

It is six months later, early afternoon. TROY *enters from the house and starts to exit the yard.* ROSE *enters from the house.*

ROSE   Troy, I want to talk to you.
TROY   All of a sudden, after all this time, you want to talk to me, huh? You ain't wanted to talk to me for months. You ain't wanted to talk to me last night. You ain't wanted no part of me then. What you wanna talk to me

5   about now?
ROSE   Tomorrow's Friday.
TROY   I know what day tomorrow is. You think I don't know tomorrow's Friday? My whole life I ain't done nothing but look to see Friday coming and you got to tell me it's Friday.

10 ROSE   I want to know if you're coming home.

TROY   I always come home, Rose. You know that. There ain't never been a
       night I ain't come home.
ROSE   That ain't what I mean . . . and you know it. I want to know if you're
       coming straight home after work.
15 TROY I figure I'd cash my check . . . hang out at Taylors' with the boys . . .
       maybe play a game of checkers . . .
ROSE   Troy, I can't live like this. I won't live like this. You livin' on borrowed
       time with me. It's been going on six months now you ain't been coming
       home.
20 TROY I be here every night. Every night of the year. That's 365 days.
ROSE   I want you to come home tomorrow after work.
TROY   Rose . . . I don't mess up my pay. You know that now. I take my pay and
       I give it to you. I don't have no money but what you give me back. I just
       want to have a little time to myself . . . a little time to enjoy life.
25 ROSE What about me? When's my time to enjoy life?
TROY   I don't know what to tell you, Rose. I'm doing the best I can.
ROSE   You ain't been home from work but time enough to change your
       clothes and run out . . . and you wanna call that the best you can do?
TROY   I'm going over to the hospital to see Alberta. She went into the hospital
30   this afternoon. Look like she might have the baby early. I won't be gone long.
ROSE   Well, you ought to know. They went over to Miss Pearl's and got Gabe
       today. She said you told them to go ahead and lock him up.
TROY   I ain't said no such thing. Whoever told you that is telling a lie. Pearl
       ain't doing nothing but telling a big fat lie.
35 ROSE She ain't had to tell me. I read it on the papers.
TROY   I ain't told them nothing of the kind.
ROSE   I saw it right there on the papers.
TROY   What it say, huh?
ROSE   It said you told them to take him.
40 TROY Then they screwed that up, just the way they screw up everything. I
       ain't worried about what they got on the paper.
ROSE   Say the government send part of his check to the hospital and the
       other part to you.
TROY   I ain't got nothing to do with that if that's the way it works. I ain't
45   made up the rules about how it work.
ROSE   You did Gabe just like you did Cory. You wouldn't sign the paper for
       Cory . . . but you signed for Gabe. You signed that paper.
       [*The telephone is heard ringing inside the house.*]
TROY   I told you I ain't signed nothing, woman! The only thing I signed was
       the release form. Hell, I can't read, I don't know what they had on that
50   paper! I ain't signed nothing about sending Gabe away.
ROSE   I said send him to the hospital . . . you said let him be free . . . now
       you done went down there and signed him to the hospital for half his
       money. You went back on yourself, Troy. You gonna have to answer for that.
TROY   See now . . . you been over there talking to Miss Pearl. She done got
55   mad cause she ain't getting Gabe's rent money. That's all it is. She's liable
       to say anything.
ROSE   Troy, I seen where you signed the paper.
TROY   You ain't seen nothing I signed. What she doing got papers on my
       brother anyway? Miss Pearl telling a big fat lie. And I'm gonna tell her

60   about it too! You ain't seen nothing I signed. Say . . . you ain't seen nothing
      I signed.

              [ROSE *exits into the house to answer the telephone. Presently she returns.*]

      ROSE   Troy . . . that was the hospital. Alberta had the baby.
      TROY   What she have? What is it?
      ROSE   It's a girl.
65   TROY   I better get on down to the hospital to see her.
      ROSE   Troy . . .
      TROY   Rose . . . I got to go see her now. That's only right . . . what's the mat-
              ter . . . the baby's alright, ain't it?
      ROSE   Alberta died having the baby.
70   TROY   Died . . . you say she's dead? Alberta's dead?
      ROSE   They said they done all they could. They couldn't do nothing for her.
      TROY   The baby? How's the baby?
      ROSE   They say it's healthy. I wonder who's gonna bury her.
      TROY   She had family, Rose. She wasn't living in the world by herself.
75   ROSE   I know she wasn't living in the world by herself.
      TROY   Next thing you gonna want to know if she had any insurance.
      ROSE   Troy, you ain't got to talk like that.
      TROY   That's the first thing that jumped out your mouth. "Who's gonna bury
              her?" Like I'm fixing to take on that task for myself.
80   ROSE   I am your wife. Don't push me away.
      TROY   I ain't pushing nobody away. Just give me some space. That's all. Just
              give me some room to breathe.

              [ROSE *exits into the house.* TROY *walks about the yard.*]

      TROY [*with a quiet rage that threatens to consume him*]   Alright . . . Mr.
              Death. See now . . . I'm gonna tell you what I'm gonna do. I'm gonna take
85   and build me a fence around this yard. See? I'm gonna build me a fence
              around what belongs to me. And then I want you to stay on the other
              side. See? You stay over there until you're ready for me. Then you come on.
              Bring your army. Bring your sickle. Bring your wrestling clothes. I ain't
              gonna fall down on my vigilance this time. You ain't gonna sneak up on me
90   no more. When you ready for me . . . when the top of your list say Troy
              Maxson . . . that's when you come around here. You come up and knock on
              the front door. Ain't nobody else got nothing to do with this. This is
              between you and me. Man to man. You stay on the other side of that fence
              until you ready for me. Then you come up and knock on the front door.
95   Anytime you want. I'll be ready for you.

              [*The lights go down to black.*]

2.3

The lights come up on the porch. It is late evening three days later. ROSE *sits listening to the ball game waiting for* TROY. *The final out of the game is made and* ROSE
switches off the radio. TROY *enters the yard carrying an infant wrapped in blankets.
He stands back from the house and calls.*

              [ROSE *enters and stands on the porch. There is a long, awkward silence,
              the weight of which grows heavier with each passing second.*]

      TROY   Rose . . . I'm standing here with my daughter in my arms. She ain't
              but a wee bittie little old thing. She don't know nothing about grownups'
              business. She innocent . . . and she ain't got no mama.

ROSE   What you telling me for, Troy?

[*She turns and exits into the house.*]

5 TROY   Well . . . I guess we'll just sit out here on the porch.

[*He sits down on the porch. There is an awkward indelicateness about the way he handles the baby. His largeness engulfs and seems to swallow it. He speaks loud enough for* ROSE *to hear.*]

A man's got to do what's right for him. I ain't sorry for nothing I done. It felt right in my heart.

[*To the baby*]

What you smiling at? Your daddy's a big man. Got these great big old hands. But sometimes he's scared. And right now your daddy's scared cause
10 we sitting out here and ain't got no home. Oh, I been homeless before. I ain't had no little baby with me. But I been homeless. You just be out on the road by your lonesome and you see one of them trains coming and you just kinda go like this . . .

[*He sings as a lullaby.*]

Please, Mr. Engineer let a man ride the line
15 Please, Mr. Engineer let a man ride the line
I ain't got no ticket please let me ride the blinds[8]

[ROSE *enters from the house.* TROY *hearing her steps behind him, stands and faces her.*]

She's my daughter, Rose. My own flesh and blood. I can't deny her no more than I can deny them boys. [*Pause*] You and them boys is my family. You and them and this child is all I got in the world. So I guess what I'm saying
20 is . . . I'd appreciate it if you'd help me take care of her.

ROSE   Okay, Troy . . . you're right. I'll take care of your baby for you . . . cause . . . like you say . . . she's innocent . . . and you can't visit the sins of the father upon the child. A motherless child has got a hard time.

[*She takes the baby from him.*]

From right now . . . this child got a mother. But you a womanless man.

[ROSE *turns and exits into the house with the baby. Lights go down to black.*]

2.4

It is two months later. LYONS *enters from the street. He knocks on the door and calls.*

LYONS   Hey, Rose! [*Pause*] Rose!

ROSE [*from inside the house*]   Stop that yelling. You gonna wake up Raynell. I just got her to sleep.

LYONS   I just stopped by to pay Papa this twenty dollars I owe him. Where's
5 Papa at?

ROSE   He should be here in a minute. I'm getting ready to go down to the church. Sit down and wait on him.

LYONS   I got to go pick up Bonnie over her mother's house.

ROSE   Well, sit it down there on the table. He'll get it.

8. Baggage cars with no end doors. This is a traditional blues song, with lyrics adapted by Wilson.

10 LYONS [*enters the house and sets the money on the table*] Tell Papa I said thanks. I'll see you again.

ROSE Alright, Lyons. We'll see you.

[LYONS *starts to exit as* CORY *enters.*]

CORY Hey, Lyons.

LYONS What's happening, Cory. Say man, I'm sorry I missed your gradua-
15 tion. You know I had a gig and couldn't get away. Otherwise, I would have been there, man. So what you doing?

CORY I'm trying to find a job.

LYONS Yeah I know how that go, man. It's rough out here. Jobs are scarce.

CORY Yeah, I know.

20 LYONS Look here, I got to run. Talk to Papa . . . he know some people. He'll be able to help get you a job. Talk to him . . . see what he say.

CORY Yeah . . . alright, Lyons.

LYONS You take care. I'll talk to you soon. We'll find some time to talk.

[LYONS *exits the yard.* CORY *wanders over to the tree, picks up the bat and assumes a batting stance. He studies an imaginary pitcher and swings. Dissatisfied with the result, he tries again.* TROY *enters. They eye each other for a beat.* CORY *puts the bat down and exits the yard.* TROY *starts into the house as* ROSE *exits with* RAYNELL. *She is carrying a cake.*]

TROY I'm coming in and everybody's going out.

25 ROSE I'm taking this cake down to the church for the bakesale. Lyons was by to see you. He stopped by to pay you your twenty dollars. It's laying in there on the table.

TROY [*going into his pocket*] Well . . . here go this money.

ROSE Put it in there on the table, Troy. I'll get it.

30 TROY What time you coming back?

ROSE Ain't no use in you studying me. It don't matter what time I come back.

TROY I just asked you a question, woman. What's the matter . . . can't I ask you a question?

ROSE Troy, I don't want to go into it. Your dinner's in there on the stove. All
35 you got to do is heat it up. And don't you be eating the rest of them cakes in there. I'm coming back for them. We having a bakesale at the church tomorrow.

[ROSE *exits the yard.* TROY *sits down on the steps, takes a pint bottle from his pocket, opens it and drinks. He begins to sing.*]

TROY
Hear it ring! Hear it ring!
Had an old dog his name was Blue
40 You know Blue was mighty true
You know Blue as a good old dog
Blue trees a possum in a hollow log
You know from that he was a good old dog

[BONO *enters the yard.*]

BONO Hey, Troy.

45 TROY Hey, what's happening, Bono?

BONO I just thought I'd stop by to see you.

TROY What you stop by and see me for? You ain't stopped by in a month of Sundays. Hell, I must owe you money or something.

BONO   Since you got your promotion I can't keep up with you. Used to see
50   you everyday. Now I don't even know what route you working.

TROY   They keep switching me around. Got me out in Greentree[9] now . . .
hauling white folks' garbage.

BONO   Greentree, huh? You lucky, at least you ain't got to be lifting them barrels. Damn if they ain't getting heavier. I'm gonna put in my two years and
55   call it quits.

TROY   I'm thinking about retiring myself.

BONO   You got it easy. You can *drive* for another five years.

TROY   It ain't the same, Bono. It ain't like working the back of the truck. Ain't
got nobody to talk to . . . feel like you working by yourself. Naw, I'm think-
60   ing about retiring. How's Lucille?

BONO   She alright. Her arthritis get to acting up on her sometime. Saw Rose
on my way in. She going down to the church, huh?

TROY   Yeah, she took up going down there. All them preachers looking for
somebody to fatten their pockets. [*Pause*] Got some gin here.

65   BONO   Naw, thanks. I just stopped by to say hello.

TROY   Hell, nigger . . . you can take a drink. I ain't never known you to say no
to a drink. You ain't got to work tomorrow.

BONO   I just stopped by. I'm fixing to go over to Skinner's. We got us a domino game going over his house every Friday.

70   TROY   Nigger, you can't play no dominoes. I used to whup you four games
out of five.

BONO   Well, that learned me. I'm getting better.

TROY   Yeah? Well, that's alright.

BONO   Look here . . . I got to be getting on. Stop by sometime, huh?

75   TROY   Yeah, I'll do that, Bono. Lucille told Rose you bought her a new
refrigerator.

BONO   Yeah, Rose told Lucille you had finally built your fence . . . so I figured we'd call it even.

TROY   I knew you would.

80   BONO   Yeah . . . okay. I'll be talking to you.

TROY   Yeah, take care, Bono. Good to see you. I'm gonna stop over.

BONO   Yeah. Okay, Troy.

[BONO *exits.* TROY *drinks from the bottle.*]

TROY
Old Blue died and I dig his grave
Let him down with a golden chain
85   Every night when I hear old Blue bark
I know Blue treed a possum in Noah's Ark.
Hear it ring! Hear it ring!

[CORY *enters the yard. They eye each other for a beat.* TROY *is sitting in the
middle of the steps.* CORY *walks over.*]

CORY   I got to get by.

TROY   Say what? What's you say?

90   CORY   You in my way. I got to get by.

---

9. That is, Green Tree, an affluent suburb of Pittsburgh.

TROY   You got to get by where? This is my house. Bought and paid for. In full. Took me fifteen years. And if you wanna go in my house and I'm sitting on the steps . . . you say excuse me. Like your mama taught you.

CORY   Come on, Pop . . . I got to get by.

[CORY *starts to maneuver his way past* TROY. TROY *grabs his leg and shoves him back.*]

95   TROY   You just gonna walk over top of me?

CORY   I live here too!

TROY [*advancing toward him*]   You just gonna walk over top of me in my own house?

CORY   I ain't scared of you.

100   TROY   I ain't asked if you was scared of me. I asked you if you was fixing to walk over top of me in my own house? That's the question. You ain't gonna say excuse me? You just gonna walk over top of me?

CORY   If you wanna put it like that.

TROY   How else am I gonna put it?

105   CORY   I was walking by you to go into the house cause you sitting on the steps drunk, singing to yourself. You can put it like that.

TROY   Without saying excuse me???

[CORY *doesn't respond.*]

I asked you a question. Without saying excuse me???

CORY   I ain't got to say excuse me to you. You don't count around here no more.

110   TROY   Oh, I see . . . I don't count around here no more. You ain't got to say excuse me to your daddy. All of a sudden you done got so grown that your daddy don't count around here no more . . . Around here in his own house and yard that he done paid for with the sweat of his brow. You done got so grown to where you gonna take over. You gonna take over my house. Is that

115   right? You gonna wear my pants. You gonna go in there and stretch out on my bed. You ain't got to say excuse me cause I don't count around here no more. Is that right?

CORY   That's right. You always talking this dumb stuff. Now, why don't you just get out my way.

120   TROY   I guess you got someplace to sleep and something to put in your belly. You got that, huh? You got that? That's what you need. You got that, huh?

CORY   You don't know what I got. You ain't got to worry about what I got.

TROY   You right! You one hundred percent right! I done spent the last seventeen years worrying about what you got. Now it's your turn, see? I'll tell you

125   what to do. You grown . . . we done established that. You a man. Now, let's see you act like one. Turn your behind around and walk out this yard. And when you get out there in the alley . . . you can forget about this house. See? Cause this is my house. You go on and be a man and get your own house. You can forget about this. Cause this is mine. You go on and get

130   yours cause I'm through with doing for you.

CORY   You talking about what you did for me . . . what'd you ever give me?

TROY   Them feet and bones! That pumping heart, nigger! I give you more than anybody else is ever gonna give you.

CORY   You ain't never gave me nothing! You ain't never done nothing but hold

135   me back. Afraid I was gonna be better than you. All you ever did was try and make me scared of you. I used to tremble every time you called my

name. Every time I heard your footsteps in the house. Wondering all the time . . . what's Papa gonna say if I do this? . . . What's he gonna say if I do that? . . . What's Papa gonna say if I turn on the radio? And Mama, too . . .
140   she tries . . . but she's scared of you.

TROY   You leave your mama out of this. She ain't got nothing to do with this.

CORY   I don't know how she stand you . . . after what you did to her.

TROY   I told you to leave your mama out of this!

    [*He advances toward* CORY.]

CORY   What you gonna do . . . give me a whupping? You can't whup me no
145   more. You're too old. You just an old man.

TROY   [*shoves him on his shoulder*]   Nigger! That's what you are. You just another nigger on the street to me!

CORY   You crazy! You know that?

TROY   Go on now! You got the devil in you. Get on away from me!

150   CORY   You just a crazy old man . . . talking about I got the devil in me.

TROY   Yeah, I'm crazy! If you don't get on the other side of that yard . . . I'm gonna show you how crazy I am! Go on . . . get the hell out of my yard.

CORY   It ain't your yard. You took Uncle Gabe's money he got from the army to buy this house and then you put him out.

155   TROY   [*advances on* CORY]   Get your black ass out of my yard!

    [TROY's *advance backs* CORY *up against the tree.* CORY *grabs up the bat.*]

CORY   I ain't going nowhere! Come on . . . put me out! I ain't scared of you.

TROY   That's my bat!

CORY   Come on!

TROY   Put my bat down!

160   CORY   Come on, put me out.

    [CORY *swings at* TROY, *who backs across the yard.*]

    What's the matter? You so bad . . . put me out!

    [TROY *advances toward* CORY.]

CORY   [*backing up*]   Come on! Come on!

TROY   You're gonna have to use it! You wanna draw that bat back on me . . . you're gonna have to use it.

165   CORY   Come on! . . . Come on!

    [CORY *swings the bat at* TROY *a second time. He misses.* TROY *continues to advance toward him.*]

TROY   You're gonna have to kill me! You wanna draw that bat back on me. You're gonna have to kill me.

    [CORY, *backed up against the tree, can go no farther.* TROY *taunts him. He sticks out his head and offers him a target.*]

    Come on! Come on!

    [CORY *is unable to swing the bat.* TROY *grabs it.*]

TROY   Then I'll show you.

    [CORY *and* TROY *struggle over the bat. The struggle is fierce and fully engaged.* TROY *ultimately is the stronger, and takes the bat from* CORY *and stands over him ready to swing. He stops himself.*]

170   Go on and get away from around my house.

    [CORY *stung by his defeat, picks himself up, walks slowly out of the yard and up the alley.*]

CORY   Tell Mama I'll be back for my things.

TROY   They'll be on the other side of that fence.

[CORY *exits.*]

TROY   I can't taste nothing. Helluljah! I can't taste nothing no more. [TROY *assumes a batting posture and begins to taunt Death, the fastball on the out-side corner.*] Come on! It's between you and me now! Come on! Anytime
175   you want! Come on! I be ready for you . . . but I ain't gonna be easy.

[*The lights go down on the scene.*]

2.5

The time is 1965. The lights come up in the yard. It is the morning of TROY's *funeral. A funeral plaque with a light hangs beside the door. There is a small garden plot off to the side. There is noise and activity in the house as* ROSE, GABRIEL, *and* BONO *have gathered. The door opens and* RAYNELL, *seven years old, enters dressed in a flannel nightgown. She crosses to the garden and pokes around with a stick.* ROSE *calls from the house.*

ROSE   Raynell!

RAYNELL   Mam?

ROSE   What you doing out there?

RAYNELL   Nothing.

[ROSE *comes to the door.*]

5   ROSE   Girl, get in here and get dressed. What you doing?

RAYNELL   Seeing if my garden growed.

ROSE   I told you it ain't gonna grow overnight. You got to wait.

RAYNELL   It don't look like it never gonna grow. Dag!

ROSE   I told you a watched pot never boils. Get in here and get dressed.

10   RAYNELL   This ain't even no pot, Mama.

ROSE   You just have to give it a chance. It'll grow. Now you come on and do what I told you. We got to be getting ready. This ain't no morning to be playing around. You hear me?

RAYNELL   Yes, mam.

[ROSE *exits into the house.* RAYNELL *continues to poke at her garden with a stick.* CORY *enters. He is dressed in a Marine corporal's uniform, and carries a duffel bag. His posture is that of a military man, and his speech has a clipped sternness.*]

15   CORY [*to* RAYNELL]   Hi. [*Pause*] I bet your name is Raynell.

RAYNELL   Uh huh.

CORY   Is your mama home?

[RAYNELL *runs up on the porch and calls through the screen door.*]

RAYNELL   Mama . . . there's some man out here. Mama?

[ROSE *comes to the door.*]

ROSE   Cory? Lord have mercy! Look here, you all!

[ROSE *and* CORY *embrace in a tearful reunion as* BONO *and* LYONS *enter from the house dressed in funeral clothes.*]

20   BONO   Aw, looka here . . .

ROSE   Done got all grown up!

CORY   Don't cry, Mama. What you crying about?

ROSE   I'm just so glad you made it.

CORY Hey Lyons. How you doing, Mr. Bono.

[LYONS *goes to embrace* CORY.]

25 LYONS Look at you, man. Look at you. Don't he look good, Rose. Got them Corporal stripes.

ROSE What took you so long.

CORY You know how the Marines are, Mama. They got to get all their paper-work straight before they let you do anything.

30 ROSE Well, I'm sure glad you made it. They let Lyons come. Your Uncle Gabe's still in the hospital. They don't know if they gonna let him out or not. I just talked to them a little while ago.

LYONS A Corporal in the United States Marines.

BONO Your daddy knew you had it in you. He used to tell me all the time.

35 LYONS Don't he look good, Mr. Bono?

BONO Yeah, he remind me of Troy when I first met him. [*Pause*] Say, Rose, Lucille's down at the church with the choir. I'm gonna go down and get the pallbearers lined up. I'll be back to get you all.

ROSE Thanks, Jim.

40 CORY See you, Mr. Bono.

LYONS [*with his arm around* RAYNELL] Cory . . . look at Raynell. Ain't she precious? She gonna break a whole lot of hearts.

ROSE Raynell, come and say hello to your brother. This is your brother, Cory. You remember Cory.

45 RAYNELL No, Mam.

CORY She don't remember me, Mama.

ROSE Well, we talk about you. She heard us talk about you. [*To* RAYNELL] This is your brother, Cory. Come on and say hello.

RAYNELL Hi.

50 CORY Hi. So you're Raynell. Mama told me a lot about you.

ROSE You all come on into the house and let me fix you some breakfast. Keep up your strength.

CORY I ain't hungry, Mama.

LYONS You can fix me something, Rose. I'll be in there in a minute.

55 ROSE Cory, you sure you don't want nothing. I know they ain't feeding you right.

CORY No, Mama . . . thanks. I don't feel like eating. I'll get something later.

ROSE Raynell . . . get on upstairs and get that dress on like I told you.

[ROSE *and* RAYNELL *exit into the house.*]

LYONS So . . . I hear you thinking about getting married.

60 CORY Yeah, I done found the right one, Lyons. It's about time.

LYONS Me and Bonnie been split up about four years now. About the time Papa retired. I guess she just got tired of all them changes I was putting her through. [*Pause*] I always knew you was gonna make something out your-self. Your head was always in the right direction. So . . . you gonna stay

65 in . . . make it a career . . . put in your twenty years?[1]

CORY I don't know. I got six already, I think that's enough.

LYONS Stick with Uncle Sam and retire early. Ain't nothing out here. I guess Rose told you what happened with me. They got me down the workhouse. I thought I was being slick cashing other people's checks.

---

1. The minimum years of service required for retirement benefits.

70 CORY How much time you doing?

LYONS They give me three years. I got that beat now. I ain't got but nine more months. It ain't so bad. You learn to deal with it like anything else. You got to take the crookeds with the straights. That's what Papa used to say. He used to say that when he struck out. I seen him strike out three
75 times in a row . . . and the next time up he hit the ball over the grandstand. Right out there in Homestead Field. He wasn't satisfied hitting in the seats . . . he want to hit it over everything! After the game he had two hundred people standing around waiting to shake his hand. You got to take the crookeds with the straights. Yeah, Papa was something else.

80 CORY You still playing?

LYONS Cory . . . you know I'm gonna do that. There's some fellows down there we got us a band . . . we gonna try and stay together when we get out . . . but yeah, I'm still playing. It still helps me to get out of bed in the morning. As long as it do that I'm gonna be right there playing and trying to
85 make some sense out of it.

ROSE [calling] Lyons, I got these eggs in the pan.

LYONS Let me go on and get these eggs, man. Get ready to go bury Papa. [Pause] How you doing? You doing alright?

[CORY nods. LYONS touches him on the shoulder and they share a moment of silent grief. LYONS exits into the house. CORY wanders about the yard. RAYNELL enters.]

RAYNELL Hi.

90 CORY Hi.

RAYNELL Did you used to sleep in my room?

CORY Yeah . . . that used to be my room.

RAYNELL That's what Papa call it. "Cory's room." It got your football in the closet.

[ROSE comes to the door.]

95 ROSE Raynell, get in there and get them good shoes on.

RAYNELL Mama, can't I wear these? Them other one hurt my feet.

ROSE Well, they just gonna have to hurt your feet for a while. You ain't said they hurt your feet when you went down to the store and got them.

RAYNELL They didn't hurt then. My feet done got bigger.

100 ROSE Don't you give me no backtalk now. You get in there and get them shoes on.

[RAYNELL exits into the house.]

Ain't too much changed. He still got that piece of rag tied to that tree. He was out here swinging that bat. I was just ready to go back in the house. He swung that bat and then he just fell over. Seem like he swung it and stood
105 there with this grin on his face . . . and then he just fell over. They carried him on down to the hospital, but I knew there wasn't no need . . . why don't you come on in the house?

CORY Mama . . . I got something to tell you. I don't know how to tell you this . . . but I've got to tell you . . . I'm not going to Papa's funeral.

110 ROSE Boy, hush your mouth. That's your daddy you talking about. I don't want hear that kind of talk this morning. I done raised you to come to this? You standing there all healthy and grown talking about you ain't going to your daddy's funeral?

CORY Mama . . . listen . . .

115 ROSE   I don't want to hear it, Cory. You just get that thought out of your
head.

CORY   I can't drag Papa with me everywhere I go. I've got to say no to him.
One time in my life I've got to say no.

ROSE   Don't nobody have to listen to nothing like that. I know you and your
daddy ain't seen eye to eye, but I ain't got to listen to that kind of talk this
120 morning. Whatever was between you and your daddy . . . the time has
come to put it aside. Just take it and set it over there on the shelf and forget
about it. Disrespecting your daddy ain't gonna make you a man, Cory. You
got to find a way to come to that on your own. Not going to your daddy's
funeral ain't gonna make you a man.

125 CORY   The whole time I was growing up . . . living in his house . . . Papa was
like a shadow that followed you everywhere. It weighed on you and sunk
into your flesh. It would wrap around you and lay there until you couldn't
tell which one was you anymore. That shadow digging in your flesh. Trying
to crawl in. Trying to live through you. Everywhere I looked, Troy Maxson
130 was staring back at me . . . hiding under the bed . . . in the closet. I'm just
saying I've got to find a way to get rid of that shadow, Mama.

ROSE   You just like him. You got him in you good.

CORY   Don't tell me that, Mama.

ROSE   You Troy Maxson all over again.

135 CORY   I don't want to be Troy Maxson. I want to be me.

ROSE   You can't be nobody but who you are, Cory. That shadow wasn't nothing but you growing into yourself. You either got to grow into it or cut it
down to fit you. But that's all you got to make life with. That's all you got to
measure yourself against that world out there. Your daddy wanted you to be
140 everything he wasn't . . . and at the same time he tried to make you into
everything he was. I don't know if he was right or wrong . . . but I do know
he meant to do more good than he meant to do harm. He wasn't always
right. Sometimes when he touched he bruised. And sometimes when he
took me in his arms he cut.

145 When I first met your daddy I thought . . . Here is a man I can lay down
with and make a baby. That's the first thing I thought when I seen him. I
was thirty years old and had done seen my share of men. But when he
walked up to me and said, "I can dance a waltz that'll make you dizzy," I
thought, Rose Lee, here is a man that you can open yourself up to and be
150 filled to bursting. Here is a man that can fill all them empty spaces you
been tipping around the edges of. One of them empty spaces was being
somebody's mother.

I married your daddy and settled down to cooking his supper and keeping clean sheets on the bed. When your daddy walked through the house
155 he was so big he filled it up. That was my first mistake. Not to make him
leave some room for me. For my part in the matter. But at that time I
wanted that. I wanted a house that I could sing in. And that's what your
daddy gave me. I didn't know to keep up his strength I had to give up little
pieces of mine. I did that. I took on his life as mine and mixed up the
160 pieces so that you couldn't hardly tell which was which anymore. It was my
choice. It was my life and I didn't have to live it like that. But that's what
life offered me in the way of being a woman and I took it. I grabbed hold of
it with both hands.

By the time Raynell came into the house, me and your daddy had done
lost touch with one another. I didn't want to make my blessing off of
nobody's misfortune . . . but I took on to Raynell like she was all them
babies I had wanted and never had.

[*The phone rings.*]

Like I'd been blessed to relive a part of my life. And if the Lord see fit to
keep up my strength . . . I'm gonna do her just like your daddy did you . . .
I'm gonna give her the best of what's in me.

RAYNELL [*entering, still with her old shoes*]   Mama . . . Reverend Tollivier on
the phone.

[ROSE *exits into the house.*]

RAYNELL   Hi.

CORY   Hi.

RAYNELL   You in the Army or the Marines?

CORY   Marines.

RAYNELL   Papa said it was the Army. Did you know Blue?

CORY   Blue? Who's Blue?

RAYNELL   Papa's dog what he sing about all the time.

CORY [*singing*]

> Hear it ring! Hear it ring!
> I had a dog his name was Blue
> You know Blue was mighty true
> You know Blue was a good old dog
> Blue treed a possum in a hollow log
> You know from that he was a good old dog.
> Hear it ring! Hear it ring!

[RAYNELL *joins in singing.*]

CORY and RAYNELL

> Blue treed a possum out on a limb
> Blue looked at me and I looked at him
> Grabbed that possum and put him in a sack
> Blue stayed there till I came back
> Old Blue's feets was big and round
> Never allowed a possum to touch the ground.
>
> Old Blue died and I dug his grave
> I dug his grave with a silver spade
> Let him down with a golden chain
> And every night I call his name
> Go on Blue, you good dog you
> Go on Blue, you good dog you

RAYNELL

> Blue laid down and died like a man
> Blue laid down and died . . .

BOTH

> Blue laid down and died like a man
> Now he's treeing possums in the Promised Land
> I'm gonna tell you this to let you know
> Blue's gone where the good dogs go

205 When I hear old Blue bark
When I hear old Blue bark
Blue treed a possum in Noah's Ark.
Blue treed a possum in Noah's Ark.

[ROSE *comes to the screen door.*]

ROSE   Cory, we gonna be ready to go in a minute.

210 CORY [*to* RAYNELL]   You go on in the house and change them shoes like Mama told you so we can go to Papa's funeral.

RAYNELL   Okay, I'll be back.

[RAYNELL *exits into the house.* CORY *gets up and crosses over to the tree.* ROSE *stands in the screen door watching him.* GABRIEL *enters from the alley.*]

GABRIEL [*calling*]   Hey, Rose!

ROSE   Gabe?

215 GABRIEL   I'm here, Rose. Hey Rose, I'm here!

[ROSE *enters from the house.*]

ROSE   Lord . . . Look here, Lyons!

LYONS   See, I told you, Rose . . . I told you they'd let him come.

CORY   How you doing, Uncle Gabe?

LYONS   How you doing, Uncle Gabe?

220 GABRIEL   Hey, Rose. It's time. It's time to tell St. Peter to open the gates. Troy, you ready? You ready, Troy. I'm gonna tell St. Peter to open the gates. You get ready now.

[*Gabriel, with great fanfare, braces himself to blow. The trumpet is without a mouthpiece. He puts the end of it into his mouth and blows with great force, like a man who has been waiting some twenty-odd years for this single moment. No sound comes out of the trumpet. He braces himself and blows again with the same result. A third time he blows. There is a weight of impossible description that falls away and leaves him bare and exposed to a frightful realization. It is a trauma that a sane and normal mind would be unable to withstand. He begins to dance. A slow, strange dance, eerie and life-giving. A dance of atavistic signature and ritual.* LYONS *attempts to embrace him.* GABRIEL *pushes* LYONS *away. He begins to howl in what is an attempt at song, or perhaps a song turning back into itself in an attempt at speech. He finishes his dance and the gates of heaven stand open as wide as God's closet.*]

That's the way that go!

Blackout.

DAVID HENRY HWANG

b. 1957

From the Filipinos who escaped from a Spanish galleon in 1763 and established villages in the Louisiana bayous to the Chinese laborers who built the transcontinental railroad in the nineteenth century to the Cambodians who fled the killing fields of the Khmer Rouge in the 1970s, Asians have come to America and have been an integral part of American history. As the United States expanded westward, a country that had defined itself in relation to Europe (and, through the institution of slavery, to Africa) found itself increasingly engaged with the Pacific region. In the Spanish-American War (1898), the United States annexed Hawaii, was granted protectorship over Guam and the Philippines, and thereby extended a colonial arm across the Pacific Ocean. As American contacts with Asia and its people deepened, popular perceptions of the East vacillated between fascination with the exotic and mysterious "Orient" and fear of the "Yellow Peril" posed by races seemingly alien to American national identity. Even as the vogue for Chinese and Japanese design flourished in the late nineteenth and early twentieth centuries, the U.S. Congress passed laws limiting Asian immigration.

Against this historical backdrop, contemporary Asian Americans—a term that generally includes those who claim origin or ancestry from East Asia, Southeast Asia, or the Indian subcontinent—have often found themselves caught between identities. Racially linked to countries with which those in later generations have had little or no contact, they inhabit a culture that has traditionally represented Asians and those of Asian descent through stereotypes: submissive lotus blossom, dragon lady, evil genius, exotic dancer, obedient servant, warmonger. In recent years Asian American writers have challenged these stereotypes by depicting the experience of themselves and their communities in its human complexity, and the drama of David Henry Hwang and other Asian American playwrights has given this experience a powerful voice in the American theater. Since Hwang first came to the attention of the theatrical world in the late 1970s, he has written plays exploring the complicated relationship of Chinese Americans to their familial, cultural, and spiritual roots. With his 1988 play *M. BUTTERFLY*—the most critically and commercially successful play ever written by an Asian American—Hwang broadened his gaze to include the intricate (mis)perceptions that characterize the East in the Western imagination.

David Henry Hwang (pronounced "Wong") was born on August 11, 1957, in San Gabriel, California, a wealthy suburb of Los Angeles. His father, who emigrated from Shanghai and—later—Taiwan, was a successful accountant and businessman, and his mother, who was born in southern China to a family that had been converted to fundamentalist Christianity and was raised in the Philippines, was a talented pianist. Hwang would explore this family heritage in his 1996 play *Golden Child,* which is based on the story of his great-grandfather who brought Christianity to his family in China. Because of his mother's religious background and his father's desire to assimilate in his adopted country, the family did not celebrate Chinese holidays or raise their children with an awareness of their Chinese heritage. It wasn't until he was a college student that Hwang became interested in knowing more about his roots. As a child Hwang studied violin and excelled in debating, and his talents earned him admission to an exclusive preparatory school in Hollywood Hills. Hwang would later credit music and debate as important influences on his playwriting: "Music really helps in terms of developing structure and dramatic growth, and jazz in particular helps with theatrical improvisation. . . . And my early interest in debate no doubt contributed to my theatrical interest in the opposition of ideas and the interplay of ideas in many plays."

Hwang enrolled at Stanford University in 1975 in order to study law, but by his sophomore year he decided that he wanted to write plays. When his creative writing professor explained to him that he lacked an adequate understanding of theater, he immersed himself in drama by attending the theater and reading as many plays as he could. He was particularly drawn to the drama of Sam Shepard, several of whose plays premiered during this time at the Magic Theater in nearby San Francisco. In 1978 Hwang had the opportunity to study playwriting with Shepard and the Cuban American playwright Maria Irene Fornes at the Padua Hills Playwrights Festival workshop in Claremont, California; it was during this workshop that he conceived the idea of his first play, *FOB.* The play, whose title is the acronym popularly applied to new immigrants—standing for the condescending label "fresh off the boat"—centers on the interaction of three characters: Grace, a first-generation Chi-

nese American; her cousin Dale, a second-generation Chinese American; and Steve, a wealthy immigrant who has just arrived from Hong Kong. Set in the back room of a California restaurant, *FOB* explores the conflicts that immigrants experience as they struggle to assimilate into their new country while also retaining their cultural identity. Though its dialogue and action are clearly influenced by Shepard's plays of the 1970s, the play reveals a highly original dramatic sensibility. In addition to offering carefully drawn psychological portraits, the play dramatizes the confrontation between realism and myth. Steve imagines himself to be the Chinese god Gwan Gung, while Grace identifies with Fa Mu Lan, the mythic "woman warrior" who is the spiritual center of Maxine Hong Kingston's 1976 novel by the same name. When the two engage in a ritualized battle in the play's second act, the realistic present gives way to the timeless space of myth.

FOB was first performed in the lounge of Hwang's Stanford dorm in March 1979 as part of a festival of student plays and musicals. Hwang also submitted the play to the Eugene O'Neill National Playwrights Conference in Connecticut, where it was selected and produced that summer. After attracting the interest of Joseph Papp, producer of the off-Broadway New York Public Theater, *FOB* was produced in New York the following year and received enthusiastic reviews. As the play moved from its college production to the Public Theater, it underwent a significant change in its theatrical style. Papp and others who read the play felt that the ritualized sequence in the play's second act should be staged using the movements and visual approach of the Peking (or Beijing) Opera, a highly stylized form of Chinese theater involving drama, music, mime, dance, and acrobatics. The addition of stage conventions from Chinese opera established a theatrical equivalent to the confrontation of East and West within the play's action, and it launched Hwang's interest in the fusion of Eastern and Western theatrical traditions that would culminate seven years later in *M. Butterfly.*

After the success of *FOB,* which won an Obie Award for Best New American Play, Hwang spent a year in the Yale School of

Drama graduate playwriting program. During that time he wrote *The Dance and the Railroad*, which was produced in New York in 1981. Set during an 1867 strike by Chinese laborers working on the first transcontinental railroad, this two-character play dramatizes the plight of early immigrants who pursued the promise of America while living as "coolies" in an alien land. Through the character of Lone, who trained in Chinese opera and practices his craft on a mountainside at the end of each day's work, the play also expands Hwang's use of Asian theatrical traditions to explore the clash of East and West. *The Dance and the Railroad*, which enjoyed widespread critical acclaim, was followed by a series of plays whose reviews were more mixed: *Family Devotions* (1981); *The House of Sleeping Beauties* and *The Sound of a Voice*, two one-act plays produced in 1983 under the title *Sound and Beauty*; and *Rich Relations* (1986). Hwang's next play, however, would overshadow all his earlier triumphs and disappointments. After a brief preview at the National Theater in Washington, D.C., *M. Butterfly* opened at Broadway's Eugene O'Neill Theatre on March 20, 1988. Lavishly staged, the play was an enormous popular and critical success; indeed, it became one of the most commercially successful nonmusical plays in Broadway history and won a number of awards, including the Tony, Drama Desk, and Outer Critics Circle awards for Best Play. In the years since *M. Butterfly*, Hwang has done collaborative work—including a musical drama titled *1000 Airplanes on the Roof* (1988) with the composer Philip Glass—produced television scripts, and written a number of screenplays and libretti. In 2001 Hwang's updated text for the 1958 Richard Rodgers and Oscar Hammerstein II's musical *Flower Drum Song* was staged in Los Angeles before moving to Broadway. He has also continued to write dramatic works. In 1996 Hwang received an Obie Award for *Golden Child* (discussed above). Recent plays include *Yellow Face* (2007), which addresses the issue of cross-racial casting, and *Chinglish* (2011), a comedy about an American businessman in China. The latter was named Best New American Play of the year by *TIME* magazine.

M. Butterfly, like many of Hwang's other plays, is characterized by a blending of history and imagination. In May 1986 Hwang heard about an incident reported earlier that month in the *New York Times*. A former French diplomat named Bernard Boursicot and a Chinese opera star named Shi Pei Pu had been arrested and tried for espionage in Paris after a twenty-year sexual relationship during which Boursicot passed government information to Shi, who then passed it on to the Communist Chinese government. During the trial it was revealed that Boursicot had believed his lover—a man who played women's roles in Chinese and Western opera—was a woman and had conducted what he thought was a heterosexual affair. Boursicot explained that he had never seen "her" naked: "He was very shy. I thought it was a Chinese custom." Intrigued by the theatrical possibilities of so incredible a story, Hwang began working on a play. The crucial moment in conceiving this new work came when he realized that the French diplomat had fallen in love not with a person but with a stereotype of Asian women. "I was driving down Santa Monica Boulevard one afternoon, and asked myself, 'What did Boursicot think he was getting in this Chinese actress?' The answer came to me clearly: 'He probably thought he had found Madame Butterfly.'"

Although Hwang had not yet seen or listened to Giacomo Puccini's opera by that name, he was familiar with the stereotype represented by its delicate, self-sacrificing heroine. *Madame Butterfly* (*Madama* in the original Italian), which premiered in Milan in 1904, was based on a 1900 one-act play by the American playwright and producer David Belasco that Puccini had seen in London (Belasco's play was itself based on a 1898 short story by John Luther Long). Both play and opera tell the story of Cio-Cio-San, a Japanese geisha known as Madame Butterfly, and the American naval lieutenant named Pinkerton who marries her during one of his tours of duty to Japan. He then leaves with his ship, and although he fails to return the following year as promised, Cio-Cio-San waits faithfully, refusing the marriage proposal of a wealthy Japanese man. When Pinkerton finally does come

John Lithgow, center, as Rene Gallimard, and B. D. Wong, right, as Song Liling, in the 1988 Broadway production of *M. Butterfly*.

back to Japan, several years later, he is accompanied by a new American wife; Butterfly takes her own life, leaving behind a child that Pinkerton and his wife will bring back to the United States. In its portrait of a submissive and feminized Asia, *Madame Butterfly* exemplifies the Western fantasy of the East as an exotic realm that displays its mysteries for the West to admire, collect, and dominate. Such a conception of the "Orient," as Edward Said argued in his influential book *Orientalism* (1978), is a Western invention, reflecting an "imaginative geography" rather than the actual sociocultural geography of Asia and its peoples. The operations of such myths, Said claimed, can be felt not only in

the representations of Asians by Europeans and North Americans but in the military and political relationships between West and East that form part of the history of imperialism.

In writing what he has called a "deconstructivist *Madame Butterfly*," Hwang established a series of parallels and counterpoints between Puccini's opera, contemporary history, and a fictionalized version of the Boursicot story. Rene Gallimard, the diplomat of Hwang's play, relives the events of his past from the cell of a Paris prison, a nightly ritual in which he seeks the understanding, and perhaps envy, of his audience for having loved and been loved by "the Perfect Woman." In order to justify his belief and the actions, he recounts the story of *Madame Butterfly*— the opera in which he first saw the singer Song Liling perform—and identifies himself with Puccini's Pinkerton in his quest for the feminine ideal of beauty and submissiveness. The power of this myth is only deepened when Song challenges its premises: "It's one of your favorite fantasies, isn't it? The submissive Oriental woman and the cruel white man." In the following scenes Gallimard pursues the fantasy of Pinkerton and Butterfly, exulting in his apparent power over his mistress and in his initiation, after an unpromising sexual past, into the privileges of maleness.

One of the central themes of *M. Butterfly*, Hwang suggested in a 1989 interview, is "the nature of seduction, in the sense that to some degree we seduce ourselves." On the collective as well as the individual level, the West's self-seducing perceptions of the East are intimately connected to male perceptions of the female. As Song explains when he is asked about Gallimard's delusion by a Paris judge, "One, . . . when he finally met his fantasy woman, he wanted more than anything to believe that she was, in fact, a woman. And second, I am an Oriental. And being an Oriental, I could never be completely a man." Such thinking, the play suggests, accounts for the West's historic diplomatic and military failings in its encounters with the East. Advising the French ambassador about the Americans' prospects in neighboring Vietnam, Gallimard offers the disastrously misguided prediction that "Orientals will always submit to a greater force."

Hwang's exploration of seduction and misperception also extends to the play's interaction with its audience. On the level of theatrical form, *M. Butterfly* achieves an intricate counterpointing of Eastern and Western characters, impersonations, and styles. A French diplomat taking on the role of an American lieutenant interacts with a Chinese performer playing a Japanese heroine from an opera written by an Italian. Visually and aurally, the play juxtaposes the operatic traditions of Europe with the stage conventions and music of Chinese opera, complicating the audience's point of view with a sometimes jarring cultural fusion of East and West. Moreover, as a commentary on the fluidity of roles and identities, *M. Butterfly* challenges the seemingly clear-cut categories of male and female. Hwang replaced the *Madame* of Puccini's title with the letter *M.*, which stands for *Monsieur* in French but in English is more ambiguous in its gender reference. Even spectators who know the story on which the play is based can find themselves seduced by Song's performance as a woman. Accordingly, when Song removes "her" costume and makeup near the play's end, the audience witnesses the uncanny crossing of gender boundaries. When, in the play's unexpected final scene, Gallimard turns the tables on Song and rescues his fantasy from the harsh light of reality, these boundaries are rendered even more fluid and indeterminate.

M. Butterfly has not been without its critics in the Asian American community, a number of whom have charged Hwang with falling into stereotypes of his own concerning the East and indulging the theatrical exoticism that his play otherwise faults. Yet despite such critiques, the play established Hwang as one of the leading American playwrights of his generation and the most successful figure in Asian American theater. By bringing the lives and experiences of Asian Americans into the theatrical mainstream, he has helped expose the prejudices, misconceptions, and idealized images that have limited the representations of Asianness within and beyond the borders of the United States. Just as importantly, he has served as the voice of a new generation of Asian Americans who find themselves pulled between cultures and who must come to terms with their histories, myths, and traditions while making their lives in a country half a world away from their ancestors' home.   S.G.

M. Butterfly

CHARACTERS

KUROGO[1]
RENE GALLIMARD / PINKERTON
SONG LILING / BUTTERFLY
WOMAN at party
MAN 1
MAN 2
MARC / CONSUL SHARPLESS

GIRL in magazine
COMRADE CHIN / SUZUKI
HELGA
SHU-FANG
M. TOULON
RENEE
JUDGE

Playwright's Notes

A former French diplomat and a Chinese opera singer have been sentenced to six years in jail for spying for China after a two-day trial that traced a story of clandestine love and mistaken sexual identity. . . . Mr. Boursicot was accused of passing information to China after he fell in love with Mr. Shi, whom he believed for twenty years to be a woman.
—The New York Times, May 11, 1986

This play was suggested by international newspaper accounts of a recent espionage trial. For purposes of dramatization, names have been changed, characters created, and incidents devised or altered, and this play does not purport to be a factual record of real events or real people.

> *I could escape this feeling*
> *With my China girl . . .* [2]
> —DAVID BOWIE & IGGY POP

SETTING: *The action of the play takes place in a Paris prison in the present, and in recall, during the decade 1960 to 1970 in Beijing, and from 1966 to the present in Paris.*

1.1

M. GALLIMARD's *prison cell. Paris. Present.*

Lights fade up to reveal RENE GALLIMARD, 65, *in a prison cell. He wears a comfortable bathrobe, and looks old and tired. The sparsely furnished cell contains a wooden crate upon which sits a hot plate with a kettle, and a portable tape recorder.* GALLIMARD *sits on the crate staring at the recorder, a sad smile on his face.*

1. In traditional Japanese theater, black-clad stage attendants (treated as invisible).
2. From "China Girl," co-written by the English rock musician David Bowie (b. 1947) and the American rock singer Iggy Pop (b. 1947); first released on Pop's album *The Idiot* (1977), it became a hit on Bowie's album *Let's Dance* (1983).

Upstage SONG, *who appears as a beautiful woman in traditional Chinese garb, dances a traditional piece from the Peking Opera,[3] surrounded by the percussive clatter of Chinese music.*

Then, slowly, lights and sound cross-fade; the Chinese opera music dissolves into a Western opera, the "Love Duet" from Puccini's Madame Butterfly.[4] SONG *continues dancing, now to the Western accompaniment. Though her movements are the same, the difference in music now gives them a balletic quality.*

GALLIMARD *rises, and turns upstage towards the figure of* SONG, *who dances without acknowledging him.*

GALLIMARD   Butterfly, Butterfly . . .

> [*He forces himself to turn away, as the image of* SONG *fades out, and talks to us.*]

GALLIMARD   The limits of my cell are as such: four-and-a-half meters by five. There's one window against the far wall; a door, very strong, to protect me from autograph hounds. I'm responsible for the tape recorder, the hot
5   plate, and this charming coffee table.

     When I want to eat, I'm marched off to the dining room—hot, steaming slop appears on my plate. When I want to sleep, the lightbulb turns itself off—the work of fairies. It's an enchanted space I occupy. The French—we know how to run a prison.

10   But, to be honest, I'm not treated like an ordinary prisoner. Why? Because I'm a celebrity. You see, I make people laugh.

     I never dreamed this day would arrive. I've never been considered witty or clever. In fact, as a young boy, in an informal poll among my grammar school classmates, I was voted "least likely to be invited to a party." It's a title
15   I managed to hold onto for many years. Despite some stiff competition.

     But now, how the tables turn! Look at me: the life of every social function in Paris. Paris? Why be modest? My fame has spread to Amsterdam, London, New York. Listen to them! In the world's smartest parlors. I'm the one who lifts their spirits!

> [*With a flourish,* GALLIMARD *directs our attention to another part of the stage.*]

1.2

A party. Present.

Lights go up on a chic-looking parlor, where a well-dressed trio, two men and one woman, make conversation. GALLIMARD *also remains lit; he observes them from his cell.*

WOMAN   And what of Gallimard?
MAN 1   Gallimard?
MAN 2   Gallimard!
GALLIMARD [*to us*]   You see? They're all determined to say my name, as if it
5   were some new dance.
WOMAN   He still claims not to believe the truth.

---

3. Chinese opera is a highly stylized art form involving drama, song, mime, dance, and acrobatics. *Peking*: former Westernization of Beijing.
4. That is, *Madama Butterfly* (1904), an Italian opera composed by Giacomo Puccini (1858–1924) with a libretto by Luigi Illica (1857–1919) and Giuseppi Giacosa (1847–1906); it is one of the most frequently performed of all operas.

MAN 1   What? Still? Even since the trial?

WOMAN   Yes. Isn't it mad?

MAN 2   [*laughing*]   He says . . . it was dark . . . and she was very modest!

[*The trio break into laughter.*]

10   MAN 1   So—what? He never touched her with his hands?

MAN 2   Perhaps he did, and simply misidentified the equipment. A compelling case for sex education in the schools.

WOMAN   To protect the National Security—the Church can't argue with that.

MAN 1   That's impossible! How could he not know?

15   MAN 2   Simple ignorance.

MAN 1   For twenty years?

MAN 2   Time flies when you're being stupid.

WOMAN   Well, I thought the French were ladies' men.

MAN 2   It seems Monsieur Gallimard was overly anxious to live up to his

20   national reputation.

WOMAN   Well, he's not very good-looking.

MAN 1   No, he's not.

MAN 2   Certainly not.

WOMAN   Actually, I feel sorry for him.

25   MAN 2   A toast! To Monsieur Gallimard!

WOMAN   Yes! To Gallimard!

MAN 1   To Gallimard!

MAN 2   Vive la différence!⁵

[*They toast, laughing. Lights down on them.*]

1.3

M. GALLIMARD's *cell.*

GALLIMARD   [*smiling*]   You see? They toast me. I've become patron saint of the socially inept. Can they really be so foolish? Men like that—they should be scratching at my door, begging to learn my secrets! For I, Rene Gallimard, you see, I have known, and been loved by . . . the Perfect Woman.

5   Alone in this cell, I sit night after night, watching our story play through my head, always searching for a new ending, one which redeems my honor, where she returns at last to my arms. And I imagine you—my ideal audience— who come to understand and even, perhaps just a little, to envy me.

[*He turns on his tape recorder. Over the house speakers, we hear the opening phrases of Madame Butterfly.*]

GALLIMARD   In order for you to understand what I did and why, I must intro-

10   duce you to my favorite opera: *Madame Butterfly.* By Giacomo Puccini. First produced at La Scala, Milan, in 1904, it is now beloved throughout the Western world.

[*As GALLIMARD describes the opera, the tape segues in and out to sections he may be describing.*]

GALLIMARD   And why not? Its heroine, Cio-Cio-San, also known as Butterfly, is a feminine ideal, beautiful and brave. And its hero, the man for whom

---

5. Long live the difference (French), an expression that specifically celebrates the difference between the sexes.

15 she gives up everything, is—[*He pulls out a naval officer's cap from under his crate, pops it on his head, and struts about.*]—not very good-looking, not too bright, and pretty much a wimp: Benjamin Franklin Pinkerton of the U.S. Navy. As the curtain rises, he's just closed on two great bargains: one on a house, the other on a woman—call it a package deal.

20 Pinkerton purchased the rights to Butterfly for one hundred yen—in modern currency, equivalent to about . . . sixty-six cents. So, he's feeling pretty pleased with himself as Sharpless, the American consul, arrives to witness the marriage.

[MARC, *wearing an official cap to designate* SHARPLESS, *enters and plays the character.*]

SHARPLESS/MARC   Pinkerton!

25 PINKERTON/GALLIMARD   Sharpless! How's it hangin'? It's a great day, just great. Between my house, my wife, and the rickshaw[6] ride in from town, I've saved nineteen cents just this morning.

SHARPLESS   Wonderful. I can see the inscription on your tombstone already: "I saved a dollar, here I lie." [*He looks around.*] Nice house.

30 PINKERTON   It's artistic. Artistic, don't you think? Like the way the shoji[7] screens slide open to reveal the wet bar and disco mirror ball? Classy, huh? Great for impressing the chicks.

SHARPLESS   "Chicks"? Pinkerton, you're going to be a married man!

PINKERTON   Well, sort of.

35 SHARPLESS   What do you mean?

PINKERTON   This country—Sharpless, it is okay. You got all these geisha[8] girls running around—

SHARPLESS   I know! I live here!

PINKERTON   Then, you know the marriage laws, right? I split for one month,

40 it's annulled!

SHARPLESS   Leave it to you to read the fine print. Who's the lucky girl?

PINKERTON   Cio-Cio-San. Her friends call her Butterfly. Sharpless, she eats out of my hand!

SHARPLESS   She's probably very hungry.

45 PINKERTON   Not like American girls. It's true what they say about Oriental girls. They want to be treated bad!

SHARPLESS   Oh, please!

PINKERTON   It's true!

SHARPLESS   Are you serious about this girl?

50 PINKERTON   I'm marrying her, aren't I?

SHARPLESS   Yes—with generous trade-in terms.

PINKERTON   When I leave, she'll know what it's like to have loved a real man. And I'll even buy her a few nylons.

SHARPLESS   You aren't planning to take her with you?

55 PINKERTON   Huh? Where?

SHARPLESS   Home!

PINKERTON   You mean, America? Are you crazy? Can you see her trying to buy rice in St. Louis?

SHARPLESS   So, you're not serious.

---

6. That is, *jinrikisha* (Japanese), a light, two-wheeled passenger vehicle drawn by one or two men.
7. Paper screens used as walls, partitions, or sliding doors (Japanese).
8. In traditional Japanese society, professional women trained from childhood to entertain men with singing, dancing, and conversation.

[Pause.]

60 PINKERTON/GALLIMARD [*as* PINKERTON] Consul, I am a sailor in port. [*As* GAL-
LIMARD] They then proceed to sing the famous duet, "The Whole World
Over."[9]

> [*The duet plays on the speakers.* GALLIMARD, *as* PINKERTON, *lip-syncs his
> lines from the opera.*]

GALLIMARD To give a rough translation: "The whole world over, the Yankee
travels, casting his anchor wherever he wants. Life's not worth living unless
65 he can win the hearts of the fairest maidens, then hotfoot it off the premises ASAP." [*He turns towards* MARC.] In the preceding scene, I played
Pinkerton, the womanizing cad, and my friend Marc from school . . . [MARC
bows grandly for our benefit.] played Sharpless, the sensitive soul of reason.
In life, however, our positions were usually—no, always—reversed.

1.4

Ecole Nationale. Aix-en-Provence.[1] *1947.*

GALLIMARD No, Marc, I think I'd rather stay home.
MARC Are you crazy?! We are going to Dad's condo in Marseille![2] You know
what happened last time?
GALLIMARD Of course I do.
5 MARC Of course you don't! You never know. . . . They stripped, Rene!
GALLIMARD Who stripped?
MARC The girls!
GALLIMARD Girls? Who said anything about girls?
MARC Rene, we're a buncha university guys goin' up to the woods. What are
10 we gonna do—talk philosophy?
GALLIMARD What girls? Where do you get them?
MARC Who cares? The point is, they come. On trucks. Packed in like sardines. The back flips open, babes hop out, we're ready to roll.
GALLIMARD You mean, they just—?
15 MARC Before you know it, every last one of them—they're stripped and
splashing around my pool. There's no moon out, they can't see what's going
on, their boobs are flapping, right? You close your eyes, reach out—it's grab
bag, get it? Doesn't matter whose ass is between whose legs, whose teeth
are sinking into who. You're just in there, going at it, eyes closed, on and on
20 for as long as you can stand. [*Pause*] Some fun, huh?
GALLIMARD What happens in the morning?
MARC In the morning, you're ready to talk some philosophy. [*Beat*[3]] So how
'bout it?
GALLIMARD Marc, I can't . . . I'm afraid they'll say no—the girls. So I never
25 ask.
MARC You don't have to ask! That's the beauty—don't you see? They don't
have to say yes. It's perfect for a guy like you, really.
GALLIMARD You go ahead . . . I may come later.

9. "Dovunque al mondo" is in fact an aria sung
by Pinkerton.
1. A city in southern France, about 20 miles
north of Marseille. Among its universities is
the École Nationale Supérieure d'Arts et
Métiers (National School of Arts and Trades),
an elite school of engineering.
2. France's second-largest city, an important
commercial and industrial center on the
Mediterranean coast.
3. Pause (theater term).

MARC   Hey, Rene—it doesn't matter that you're clumsy and got zits—they're
30   not looking!
GALLIMARD   Thank you very much.
MARC   Wimp.

[MARC *walks over to the other side of the stage, and starts waving and smiling at women in the audience.*]

GALLIMARD [*to us*]   We now return to my version of *Madame Butterfly* and the events leading to my recent conviction for treason.

[GALLIMARD *notices* MARC *making lewd gestures.*]

35   GALLIMARD   Marc, what are you doing?
MARC   Huh? [*Sotto voce*[4]] Rene, there're a lotta great babes out there. They're probably lookin' at me and thinking, "What a dangerous guy."
GALLIMARD   Yes—how could they help but be impressed by your cool sophistication?

[GALLIMARD *pops the* SHARPLESS *cap on* MARC's *head, and points him off-stage.* MARC *exits, leering.*]

1.5

M. GALLIMARD's *cell.*

GALLIMARD   Next, Butterfly makes her entrance. We learn her age—fifteen . . . but very mature for her years.

[*Lights come up on the area where we saw* SONG *dancing at the top of the play. She appears there again, now dressed as Madame* BUTTERFLY, *moving to the "Love Duet."*[5] GALLIMARD *turns upstage slightly to watch, transfixed.*]

GALLIMARD   But as she glides past him, beautiful, laughing softly behind her fan, don't we who are men sigh with hope? We, who are not handsome, nor
5   brave, nor powerful, yet somehow believe, like Pinkerton, that we deserve a Butterfly. She arrives with all her possessions in the folds of her sleeves, lays them all out, for her man to do with as he pleases. Even her life itself—she bows her head as she whispers that she's not even worth the hundred yen he paid for her. He's already given too much, when we know
10   he's really had to give nothing at all.

[*Music and lights on* SONG *out.* GALLIMARD *sits at his crate.*]

GALLIMARD   In real life, women who put their total worth at less than sixty-six cents are quite hard to find. The closest we come is in the pages of these magazines. [*He reaches into his crate, pulls out a stack of girlie magazines, and begins flipping through them.*] Quite a necessity in prison. For
15   three or four dollars, you get seven or eight women.
I first discovered these magazines at my uncle's house. One day, as a boy of twelve. The first time I saw them in his closet . . . all lined up—my body shook. Not with lust—no, with power. Here were women—a shelfful—who would do exactly as I wanted.

[*The "Love Duet" creeps in over the speakers. Special*[6] *comes up, revealing, not* SONG *this time, but a pinup girl in a sexy negligee, her back to us.* GALLIMARD *turns upstage and looks at her.*]

4. Under the voice (Italian); that is, spoken very softly, under the breath.
5. "Viene la sera" ("Evening Is Falling"), a duet sung by Pinkerton and Butterfly at the
end of act 1 of *Madama Butterfly*.
6. A stage light used at designated moments during a play for specific, highly theatrical effects.

20 GIRL   I know you're watching me.

GALLIMARD   My throat . . . it's dry.

GIRL   I leave my blinds open every night before I go to bed.

GALLIMARD   I can't move.

GIRL   I leave my blinds open and the lights on.

25 GALLIMARD   I'm shaking. My skin is hot, but my penis is soft. Why?

GIRL   I stand in front of the window.

GALLIMARD   What is she going to do?

GIRL   I toss my hair, and I let my lips part . . . barely.

GALLIMARD   I shouldn't be seeing this. It's so dirty. I'm so bad.

30 GIRL   Then, slowly, I lift off my nightdress.

GALLIMARD   Oh, god. I can't believe it. I can't—

GIRL   I toss it to the ground.

GALLIMARD   Now, she's going to walk away. She's going to—

GIRL   I stand there, in the light, displaying myself.

35 GALLIMARD   No. She's—why is she naked?

GIRL   To you.

GALLIMARD   In front of a window? This is wrong. No—

GIRL   Without shame.

GALLIMARD   No, she must . . . like it.

40 GIRL   I like it.

GALLIMARD   She . . . she wants me to see.

GIRL   I want you to see.

GALLIMARD   I can't believe it! She's getting excited!

GIRL   I can't see you. You can do whatever you want.

45 GALLIMARD   I can't do a thing. Why?

GIRL   What would you like me to do . . . next?

[*Lights go down on her. Music off. Silence, as* GALLIMARD *puts away his magazines. Then he resumes talking to us.*]

GALLIMARD   Act Two begins with Butterfly staring at the ocean. Pinkerton's been called back to the U.S., and he's given his wife a detailed schedule of his plans. In the column marked "return date," he's written "when the

50   robins nest." This failed to ignite her suspicions. Now, three years have passed without a peep from him. Which brings a response from her faithful servant, Suzuki.

[COMRADE CHIN *enters, playing* SUZUKI.]

SUZUKI   Girl, he's a loser. What'd he ever give you? Nineteen cents and those ugly Day-Glo stockings? Look, it's finished! Kaput! Done! And you should

55   be glad! I mean, the guy was a woofer![7] He tried before, you know—before he met you, he went down to geisha central and plunked down his spare change in front of the usual candidates—everyone else gagged! These are hungry prostitutes, and they were not interested, get the picture? Now, stop slathering when an American ship sails in, and let's make some

60   bucks—I mean, yen! We are broke!

Now, what about Yamadori? Hey, hey—don't look away—the man is a prince—figuratively, and, what's even better, literally. He's rich, he's handsome, he says he'll die if you don't marry him—and he's even willing to overlook the little fact that you've been deflowered all over the place by a

65   foreign devil. What do you mean, "But he's Japanese?" You're Japanese! You

7. That is, a dog, an ugly person (slang).

think you've been touched by the whitey god? He was a sailor with dirty hands!

[SUZUKI *stalks offstage.*]

GALLIMARD   She's also visited by Consul Sharpless, sent by Pinkerton on a minor errand.

[MARC *enters, as* SHARPLESS.]

SHARPLESS   I hate this job.

70 GALLIMARD   This Pinkerton—he doesn't show up personally to tell his wife he's abandoning her. No, he sends a government diplomat . . . at taxpayer's expense.

SHARPLESS   Butterfly? Butterfly? I have some bad—I'm going to be ill. But-terfly, I came to tell you—

75 GALLIMARD   Butterfly says she knows he'll return and if he doesn't she'll kill herself rather than go back to her own people. [*Beat*] This causes a lull in the conversation.

SHARPLESS   Let's put it this way . . .

GALLIMARD   Butterfly runs into the next room, and returns holding—

[*Sound cue: a baby crying.* SHARPLESS, *"seeing" this, backs away.*]

80 SHARPLESS   Well, good. Happy to see things going so well. I suppose I'll be going now. Ta ta. Ciao. [*He turns away. Sound cue out.*] I hate this job. [*He exits.*]

GALLIMARD   At that moment, Butterfly spots in the harbor an American ship—the *Abramo Lincoln!*[8]

[*Music cue: "The Flower Duet."*[9] SONG, *still dressed as* BUTTERFLY, *changes into a wedding kimono, moving to the music.*]

GALLIMARD   This is the moment that redeems her years of waiting. With
85 Suzuki's help, they cover the room with flowers—

[CHIN, *as* SUZUKI, *trudges onstage and drops a lone flower without much enthusiasm.*]

GALLIMARD   —and she changes into her wedding dress to prepare for Pinker-ton's arrival.

[SUZUKI *helps* BUTTERFLY *change.* HELGA *enters, and helps* GALLIMARD *change into a tuxedo.*]

GALLIMARD   I married a woman older than myself—Helga.

HELGA   My father was ambassador to Australia. I grew up among criminals
90 and kangaroos.[1]

GALLIMARD   Hearing that brought me to the altar—

[HELGA *exits.*]

GALLIMARD   —where I took a vow renouncing love. No fantasy woman would ever want me, so, yes, I would settle for a quick leap up the career ladder. Passion, I banish, and in its place—practicality!

95   But my vows had long since lost their charm by the time we arrived in China. The sad truth is that all men want a beautiful woman, and the uglier the man, the greater the want.

8. Abraham Lincoln (Italian).
9. "Tutti i fior?" ("All the Flowers"), a duet sung by Butterfly and her servant Suzuki in act 2 of *Madama Butterfly* at the point in the story narrated here by Gallimard.

1. Australia was originally used by Great Brit-ain as a penal colony, and a sizable portion of the early settlers were convicts transported between 1788 and 1868.

[SUZUKI *makes final adjustments of* BUTTERFLY's *costume, as does* GALLI-MARD *of his tuxedo.*]

GALLIMARD   I married late, at age thirty-one. I was faithful to my marriage for eight years. Until the day when, as a junior-level diplomat in puritanical
100   Peking, in a parlor at the German ambassador's house, during the "Reign of a Hundred Flowers,"[2] I first saw her . . . singing the death scene from *Madame Butterfly*.

[SUZUKI *runs offstage.*]

1.6

German ambassador's house. Beijing. 1960.

*The upstage special area now becomes a stage. Several chairs face upstage, repre-senting seating for some twenty guests in the parlor. A few "diplomats"—*RENEE, MARC, TOULON—*in formal dress enter and take seats.*

GALLIMARD *also sits down, but turns towards us and continues to talk. Orchestral accompaniment on the tape is now replaced by a simple piano.* SONG *picks up the death scene from the point where* BUTTERFLY *uncovers the hara-kiri[3] knife.*

GALLIMARD   The ending is pitiful. Pinkerton, in an act of great courage, stays home and sends his American wife to pick up Butterfly's child. The truth, long deferred, has come up to her door.

[SONG, *playing* BUTTERFLY, *sings the lines from the opera in her own voice—which, though not classical, should be decent.*]

SONG   "Con onor muore / chi non puo serbar / vita con onore."
5 GALLIMARD [*simultaneously*]   "Death with honor / Is better than life / Life with dishonor."

[*The stage is illuminated; we are now completely within an elegant dip-lomat's residence.* SONG *proceeds to play out an abbreviated death scene. Everyone in the room applauds.* SONG, *shyly, takes her bows. Others in the room rush to congratulate her.* GALLIMARD *remains with us.*]

GALLIMARD   They say in opera the voice is everything. That's probably why I'd never before enjoyed opera. Here . . . here was a Butterfly with little or no voice—but she had the grace, the delicacy . . . I believed this girl. I believed
10   her suffering. I wanted to take her in my arms—so delicate, even I could protect her, take her home, pamper her until she smiled.

[*Over the course of the preceding speech,* SONG *has broken from the upstage crowd and moved directly upstage of* GALLIMARD.]

SONG   Excuse me. Monsieur . . . ?

[GALLIMARD *turns upstage, shocked.*]

GALLIMARD   Oh! Gallimard. Mademoiselle . . . ? A beautiful . . .
SONG   Song Liling.
15 GALLIMARD   A beautiful performance.
SONG   Oh, please.
GALLIMARD   I usually—
SONG   You make me blush. I'm no opera singer at all.
GALLIMARD   I usually don't like *Butterfly*.

2. The so-called Hundred Flowers Campaign, a brief period (1956–57) during which the Communist authorities allowed intellectuals greater freedom of thought and speech.
3. Ritual suicide by disembowelment (Japanese).

20 SONG   I can't blame you in the least.

GALLIMARD   I mean, the story—

SONG   Ridiculous.

GALLIMARD   I like the story, but . . . what?

SONG   Oh, you like it?

25 GALLIMARD   I . . . what I mean is, I've always seen it played by huge women in so much bad makeup.

SONG   Bad makeup is not unique to the West.

GALLIMARD   But, who can believe them?

SONG   And you believe me?

30 GALLIMARD   Absolutely. You were utterly convincing. It's the first time—

SONG   Convincing? As a Japanese woman? The Japanese used hundreds of our people for medical experiments during the war,[4] you know. But I gather such an irony is lost on you.

GALLIMARD   No! I was about to say, it's the first time I've seen the beauty of

35 the story.

SONG   Really?

GALLIMARD   Of her death. It's a . . . a pure sacrifice. He's unworthy, but what can she do? She loves him . . . so much. It's a very beautiful story.

SONG   Well, yes, to a Westerner.

40 GALLIMARD   Excuse me?

SONG   It's one of your favorite fantasies, isn't it? The submissive Oriental woman and the cruel white man.

GALLIMARD   Well, I didn't quite mean . . .

SONG   Consider it this way: what would you say if a blonde homecoming

45 queen fell in love with a short Japanese businessman? He treats her cruelly, then goes home for three years, during which time she prays to his picture and turns down marriage from a young Kennedy.[5] Then, when she learns he has remarried, she kills herself. Now, I believe you would consider this girl to be a deranged idiot, correct? But because it's an Oriental who kills

50 herself for a Westerner—ah!—you find it beautiful.

[Silence.]

GALLIMARD   Yes . . . well . . . I see your point . . .

SONG   I will never do Butterfly again, Monsieur Gallimard. If you wish to see some real theatre, come to the Peking Opera sometime. Expand your mind.

[SONG walks offstage.]

GALLIMARD [to us]   So much for protecting her in my big Western arms.

1.7

M. GALLIMARD's apartment. Beijing. 1960.

GALLIMARD changes from his tux into a casual suit. HELGA enters.

GALLIMARD   The Chinese are an incredibly arrogant people.

HELGA   They warned us about that in Paris, remember?

4. The Japanese conducted gruesome medical experiments on Chinese prisoners and civilians during their World War II–era occupation of China (1937–45).
5. A member of the Massachusetts political family whose best-known members are President John F. Kennedy (1917–1963), Senator Robert F. Kennedy (1925–1968), and Senator Edward Kennedy (1932–2009).

GALLIMARD   Even Parisians consider them arrogant. That's a switch.

HELGA   What is it that Madame Su says? "We are a very old civilization." I
5   never know if she's talking about her country or herself.

GALLIMARD   I walk around here, all I hear every day, everywhere is how *old*
this culture is. The fact that "old" may be synonymous with "senile" doesn't
occur to them.

HELGA   You're not going to change them. "East is east, west is west, and . . ."[6]
10   whatever that guy said.

GALLIMARD   It's just that—silly. I met . . . at Ambassador Koening's tonight—
you should've been there.

HELGA   Koening? Oh god, no. Did he enchant you all again with the history
of Bavaria?[7]

15 GALLIMARD   No. I met, I suppose, the Chinese equivalent of a diva.[8] She's a
singer in the Chinese opera.

HELGA   They have an opera, too? Do they sing in Chinese? Or maybe—in
Italian?

GALLIMARD   Tonight, she did sing in Italian.

20 HELGA   How'd she manage that?

GALLIMARD   She must've been educated in the West before the Revolution.[9]
Her French is very good also. Anyway, she sang the death scene from
Madame Butterfly.

HELGA   *Madame Butterfly!* Then I should have come. [*She begins humming,*
25   *floating around the room as if dragging long kimono sleeves.*] Did she have a
nice costume? I think it's a classic piece of music.

GALLIMARD   That's what *I* thought, too. Don't let her hear you say that.

HELGA   What's wrong?

GALLIMARD   Evidently the Chinese hate it.

30 HELGA   She hated it, but she performed it anyway? Is she perverse?

GALLIMARD   They hate it because the white man gets the girl. Sour grapes if
you ask me.

HELGA   Politics again? Why can't they just hear it as a piece of beautiful
music? So, what's in their opera?

35 GALLIMARD   I don't know. But, whatever it is, I'm sure it must be *old.*

[HELGA *exits.*]

1.8

Chinese opera house and the streets of Beijing. 1960.

The sound of gongs clanging fills the stage.

GALLIMARD   My wife's innocent question kept ringing in my ears. I asked
around, but no one knew anything about the Chinese opera. It took four
weeks, but my curiosity overcame my cowardice. This Chinese diva—this
unwilling Butterfly—what did she do to make her so proud?

6. "Oh, East is East, and West is West, and
never the twain shall meet," from the poem
"The Ballad of East and West" (1889) by the
British writer Rudyard Kipling (1865–1936).
7. Germany's southernmost state, which was
an independent kingdom until 1871.
8. A female opera star of the most glamorous

and imperious sort (literally, "goddess";
Italian).
9. The civil war between the Nationalist government, led by Chiang Kai-shek, and the
Communist rebels, led by Mao Zedong, which
ended with the establishment of the People's
Republic of China under Mao in 1949.

5   The room was hot, and full of smoke. Wrinkled faces, old women, teeth missing—a man with a growth on his neck, like a human toad. All smiling, pipes falling from their mouths, cracking nuts between their teeth, a live chicken pecking at my foot—all looking, screaming, gawking . . . at her.

> [*The upstage area is suddenly hit with a harsh white light. It has become the stage for the Chinese opera performance. Two dancers enter, along with* SONG. GALLIMARD *stands apart, watching.* SONG *glides gracefully amidst the two dancers. Drums suddenly slam to a halt.* SONG *strikes a pose, looking straight at* GALLIMARD. *Dancers exit. Light change. Pause, then* SONG *walks right off the stage and straight up to* GALLIMARD.]

SONG   Yes. You. White man. I'm looking straight at you.

10 GALLIMARD   Me?

SONG   You see any other white men? It was too easy to spot you. How often does a man in my audience come in a tie?

> [SONG *starts to remove her costume. Underneath, she wears simple baggy clothes. They are now backstage. The show is over.*]

SONG   So, you are an adventurous imperialist?

GALLIMARD   I . . . thought it would further my education.

15 SONG   It took you four weeks. Why?

GALLIMARD   I've been busy.

SONG   Well, education has always been undervalued in the West, hasn't it?

GALLIMARD [*laughing*]   I don't think it's true.

SONG   No, you wouldn't. You're a Westerner. How can you objectively judge

20 your own values?

GALLIMARD   I think it's possible to achieve some distance.

SONG   Do you? [*Pause*] It stinks in here. Let's go.

GALLIMARD   These are the smells of your loyal fans.

SONG   I love them for being my fans, I hate the smell they leave behind. I too

25 can distance myself from my people. [*She looks around, then whispers in his ear.*] "Art for the masses"[1] is a shitty excuse to keep artists poor. [*She pops a cigarette in her mouth.*] Be a gentleman, will you? And light my cigarette.

> [GALLIMARD *fumbles for a match.*]

GALLIMARD   I don't . . . smoke.

SONG [*lighting her own*]   Your loss. Had you lit my cigarette, I might have

30 blown a puff of smoke right between your eyes. Come.

> [*They start to walk about the stage. It is a summer night on the Beijing streets. Sounds of the city play on the house speakers.*]

SONG   How I wish there were even a tiny cafe to sit in. With cappuccinos, and men in tuxedos and bad expatriate jazz.

GALLIMARD   If my history serves me correctly, you weren't even allowed into the clubs in Shanghai[2] before the Revolution.

35 SONG   Your history serves you poorly, Monsieur Gallimard. True, there were signs reading "No dogs and Chinamen." But a woman, especially a delicate Oriental woman—we always go where we please. Could you imagine it otherwise? Clubs in China filled with pasty, big-thighed white women, while

---

1. A Communist slogan advocating a proletarian (working-class) art in place of the so-called elite art of Western capitalism.
2. The largest city in China; as one of the five ports opened to foreign trade and to foreign residents in the 19th century, it became the country's economic and cultural center until investment from overseas was halted by the Communist victory.

thousands of slender lotus blossoms[3] wait just outside the door? Never. The
40 clubs would be empty. [*Beat*] We have always held a certain fascination for
you Caucasian men, have we not?

GALLIMARD But . . . that fascination is imperialist, or so you tell me.

SONG Do you believe everything I tell you? Yes. It is always imperialist. But
sometimes . . . sometimes, it is also mutual. Oh—this is my flat.

45 GALLIMARD I didn't even—

SONG Thank you. Come another time and we will further expand your mind.

> [SONG *exits.* GALLIMARD *continues roaming the streets as he speaks to us.*]

GALLIMARD What was that? What did she mean, "Sometimes . . . it is mutual?"
Women do not flirt with me. And I normally can't talk to them. But tonight,
I held up my end of the conversation.

1.9

GALLIMARD's *bedroom. Beijing. 1960.*

> HELGA *enters.*

HELGA You didn't tell me you'd be home late.

GALLIMARD I didn't intend to. Something came up.

HELGA Oh? Like what?

GALLIMARD I went to the . . . to the Dutch ambassador's home.

5 HELGA Again?

GALLIMARD There was a reception for a visiting scholar. He's writing a six-
volume treatise on the Chinese revolution. We all gathered that meant he'd
have to live here long enough to actually write six volumes, and we all
expressed our deepest sympathies.

10 HELGA Well, I had a good night too. I went with the ladies to a martial arts
demonstration. Some of those men—when they break those thick boards—
[*She mimes fanning herself.*] whoo-whoo!

> [HELGA *exits. Lights dim.*]

GALLIMARD I lied to my wife. Why? I've never had any reason to lie before.
But what reason did I have tonight? I didn't do anything wrong. That night, I
15 had a dream. Other people, I've been told, have dreams where angels appear.
Or dragons, or Sophia Loren[4] in a towel. In my dream, Marc from school
appeared.

> [MARC *enters, in a nightshirt and cap.*]

MARC Rene! You met a girl!

> [GALLIMARD *and* MARC *stumble down the Beijing streets. Night sounds
> over the speakers.*]

GALLIMARD It's not that amazing, thank you.

20 MARC No! It's so monumental, I heard about it halfway around the world in
my sleep!

GALLIMARD I've met girls before, you know.

MARC Name one. I've come across time and space to congratulate you. [*He
hands* GALLIMARD *a bottle of wine.*]

---

3. That is, Asian women. The lotus blossom
symbolized the practice of footbinding, which
was highly eroticized in traditional Chinese
culture.

4. An Italian actress (b. 1934), famous for her
beauty and viewed as an international sex
symbol.

GALLIMARD   Marc, this is expensive.

25   MARC   On those rare occasions when you become a formless spirit, why not steal the best?

[MARC *pops open the bottle, begins to share it with* GALLIMARD.]

GALLIMARD   You embarrass me. She . . . there's no reason to think she likes me.

MARC   "Sometimes, it is mutual"?

30   GALLIMARD   Oh.

MARC   "Mutual"? "Mutual"? What does that mean?

GALLIMARD   You heard!

MARC   It means the money is in the bank, you only have to write the check!

GALLIMARD   I am a married man!

35   MARC   And an excellent one too. I cheated after . . . six months. Then again and again, until now—three hundred girls in twelve years.

GALLIMARD   I don't think we should hold that up as a model.

MARC   Of course not! My life—it is disgusting! Phooey! Phooey! But, you— you are the model husband.

40   GALLIMARD   Anyway, it's impossible. I'm a foreigner.

MARC   Ah, yes. She cannot love you, it is taboo, but something deep inside her heart . . . she cannot help herself . . . she must surrender to you. It is her destiny.

GALLIMARD   How do you imagine all this?

45   MARC   The same way you do. It's an old story. It's in our blood. They fear us, Rene. Their women fear us. And their men—their men hate us. And, you know something? They are all correct.

[*They spot a light in a window.*]

MARC   There! There, Rene!

GALLIMARD   It's her window.

50   MARC   Late at night—it burns. The light—it burns for you.

GALLIMARD   I won't look. It's not respectful.

MARC   We don't have to be respectful. We're foreign devils.

[*Enter* SONG, *in a sheer robe. The "One Fine Day"*[5] *aria creeps in over the speakers. With her back to us,* SONG *mimes attending to her toilette. Her robe comes loose, revealing her white shoulders.*]

MARC   All your life you've waited for a beautiful girl who would lay down for you. All your life you've smiled like a saint when it's happened to every 55   other man you know. And you see them in magazines and you see them in movies. And you wonder, what's wrong with me? Will anyone beautiful ever want me? As the years pass, your hair thins and you struggle to hold onto even your hopes. Stop struggling, Rene. The wait is over. [*He exits.*]

GALLIMARD   Marc? Marc?

[*At that moment,* SONG, *her back still towards us, drops her robe. A second of her naked back, then a sound cue: a phone ringing, very loud. Blackout, followed in the next beat by a special up on the bedroom area, where a phone now sits.* GALLIMARD *stumbles across the stage and picks up the phone. Sound cue out. Over the course of his conversation, area lights fill in the vicinity of his bed. It is the following morning.*]

5. "Un bel dì vedremo" ("One Fine Day We Shall See"), an aria sung by Butterfly in act 2 of *Madama Butterfly.*

60 GALLIMARD Yes? Hello?
SONG [*offstage*] Is it very early?
GALLIMARD Why, yes.
SONG [*offstage*] How early?
GALLIMARD It's . . . it's 5:30. Why are you—?
65 SONG [*offstage*] But it's light outside. Already.
GALLIMARD It is. The sun must be in confusion today.

[*Over the course of* SONG's *next speech, her upstage special comes up again. She sits in a chair, legs crossed, in a robe, telephone to her ear.*]

SONG I waited until I saw the sun. That was as much discipline as I could manage for one night. Do you forgive me?
GALLIMARD Of course . . . for what?
70 SONG Then I'll ask you quickly. Are you really interested in the opera?
GALLIMARD Why, yes. Yes I am.
SONG Then come again next Thursday. I am playing *The Drunken Beauty.*[6] May I count on you?
GALLIMARD Yes. You may.
75 SONG Perfect. Well, I must be getting to bed. I'm exhausted. It's been a very long night for me.

[SONG *hangs up; special on her goes off.* GALLIMARD *begins to dress for work.*]

1.10

SONG LILING's *apartment. Beijing. 1960.*

GALLIMARD I returned to the opera that next week, and the week after that . . . she keeps our meetings so short—perhaps fifteen, twenty minutes at most. So I am left each week with a thirst which is intensified. In this way, fifteen weeks have gone by. I am starting to doubt the words of my
5 friend Marc. But no, not really. In my heart, I know she has . . . an interest in me. I suspect this is her way. She is outwardly bold and outspoken, yet her heart is shy and afraid. It is the Oriental in her at war with her Western education.
SONG [*offstage*] I will be out in an instant. Ask the servant for anything you
10 want.
GALLIMARD Tonight, I have finally been invited to enter her apartment. Though the idea is almost beyond belief, I believe she is afraid of me.

[GALLIMARD *looks around the room. He picks up a picture in a frame, studies it. Without his noticing,* SONG *enters, dressed elegantly in a black gown from the twenties. She stands in the doorway looking like Anna May Wong.*[7]]

SONG That is my father.
GALLIMARD [*surprised*] Mademoiselle Song . . .

[*She glides up to him, snatches away the picture.*]

6. A traditional Chinese opera about an imperial concubine during the Tang dynasty (set ca. 750 C.E.). Enraged that the emperor has chosen to visit a new concubine, his previous favorite drinks herself into a state of gaiety and then despondency. *The Drunken Beauty* (or *The Drunken Concubine*) was made famous by the Beijing Opera star Mei Lanfang (1894–1961), a man who specialized in female roles.
7. A Chinese American actress (1905–1961), the first Asian woman to become a film star; she often played temptresses or exotic villainesses in the 1920s and '30s.

15 SONG   It is very good that he did not live to see the Revolution. They would, no doubt, have made him kneel on broken glass.[8] Not that he didn't deserve such a punishment. But he is my father. I would've hated to see it happen.

GALLIMARD   I'm very honored that you've allowed me to visit your home.

[SONG *curtsies*.]

SONG   Thank you. Oh! Haven't you been poured any tea?

20 GALLIMARD   I'm really not—

SONG   [*to her offstage servant*]   Shu-Fang! Cha! Kwai-lah![9] [*To* GALLIMARD]   I'm sorry. You want everything to be perfect—

GALLIMARD   Please.

SONG   —and before the evening even begins—

25 GALLIMARD   I'm really not thirsty.

SONG   —It's ruined.

GALLIMARD [*sharply*]   Mademoiselle Song!

[SONG *sits down*.]

SONG   I'm sorry.

GALLIMARD   What are you apologizing for now?

[*Pause;* SONG *starts to giggle*.]

30 SONG   I don't know!

[GALLIMARD *laughs*.]

GALLIMARD   Exactly my point.

SONG   Oh, I am silly. Lightheaded. I promise not to apologize for anything else tonight, do you hear me?

GALLIMARD   That's a good girl.

[SHU-FANG, *a servant girl, comes out with a tea tray and starts to pour*.]

35 SONG [*to* SHU-FANG]   No! I'll pour myself for the gentleman!

[SHU-FANG, *staring at* GALLIMARD, *exits*.]

SONG   No, I . . . I don't even know why I invited you up.

GALLIMARD   Well, I'm glad you did.

[SONG *looks around the room*.]

SONG   There is an element of danger to your presence.

GALLIMARD   Oh?

40 SONG   You must know.

GALLIMARD   It doesn't concern me. We both know why I'm here.

SONG   It doesn't concern me either. No . . . well perhaps . . .

GALLIMARD   What?

SONG   Perhaps I am slightly afraid of scandal.

45 GALLIMARD   What are we doing?

SONG   I'm entertaining you. In my parlor.

GALLIMARD   In France, that would hardly—

SONG   France. France is a country living in the modern era. Perhaps even ahead of it. China is a nation whose soul is firmly rooted two thousand

50 years in the past. What I do, even pouring the tea for you now . . . it has . . . implications. The walls and windows say so. Even my own heart, strapped inside this Western dress . . . even it says things—things I don't care to hear.

8. A punishment inflicted by the Communists on those viewed as "class enemies."   9. Tea, quickly, please! (Chinese).

[SONG *hands* GALLIMARD *a cup of tea.* GALLIMARD *puts his hand over both the teacup and* SONG's *hand.*]

GALLIMARD   This is a beautiful dress.

55 SONG   Don't.

GALLIMARD   What?

SONG   I don't even know if it looks right on me.

GALLIMARD   Believe me—

SONG   You are from France. You see so many beautiful women.

60 GALLIMARD   France? Since when are the European women—?

SONG   Oh! What am I trying to do, anyway?!

[SONG *runs to the door, composes herself, then turns towards* GALLIMARD.]

SONG   Monsieur Gallimard, perhaps you should go.

GALLIMARD   But . . . why?

SONG   There's something wrong about this.

65 GALLIMARD   I don't see what.

SONG   I feel . . . I am not myself.

GALLIMARD   No. You're nervous.

SONG   Please. Hard as I try to be modern, to speak like a man, to hold a
Western woman's strong face up to my own . . . in the end, I fail. A small,
70 frightened heart beats too quickly and gives me away. Monsieur Gallimard,
I'm a Chinese girl. I've never . . . never invited a man up to my flat before.
The forwardness of my actions makes my skin burn.

GALLIMARD   What are you afraid of? Certainly not me, I hope.

SONG   I'm a modest girl.

75 GALLIMARD   I know. And very beautiful. [*He touches her hair.*]

SONG   Please—go now. The next time you see me, I shall again be myself.

GALLIMARD   I like you the way you are right now.

SONG   You are a cad.

GALLIMARD   What do you expect? I'm a foreign devil.

[GALLIMARD *walks downstage.* SONG *exits.*]

80 GALLIMARD [*to us*]   Did you hear the way she talked about Western women?
Much differently than the first night. She does—she feels inferior to them—
and to me.

1.11

The French embassy. Beijing. 1960.

GALLIMARD *moves towards a desk.*

GALLIMARD   I determined to try an experiment. In *Madame Butterfly,* Cio-
Cio-San fears that the Western man who catches a butterfly will pierce its
heart with a needle, then leave it to perish. I began to wonder: had I, too,
caught a butterfly who would writhe on a needle?

[MARC *enters, dressed as a bureaucrat, holding a stack of papers. As* GAL-
LIMARD *speaks,* MARC *hands papers to him. He peruses, then signs,
stamps, or rejects them.*]

5 GALLIMARD   Over the next five weeks, I worked like a dynamo. I stopped
going to the opera, I didn't phone or write her. I knew this little flower was
waiting for me to call, and, as I wickedly refused to do so, I felt for the first
time that rush of power—the absolute power of a man.

[MARC *continues acting as the bureaucrat, but he now speaks as himself.*]

MARC   Rene! It's me!

10 GALLIMARD   Marc—I hear your voice everywhere now. Even in the midst of work.

MARC   That's because I'm watching you—all the time.

GALLIMARD   You were always the most popular guy in school.

MARC   Well, there's no guarantee of failure in life like happiness in high
15 school. Somehow I knew I'd end up in the suburbs working for Renault[1]
and you'd be in the Orient picking exotic women off the trees. And they say there's no justice.

GALLIMARD   That's why you were my friend?

MARC   I gave you a little of my life, so that now you can give me some of
20 yours. [*Pause*] Remember Isabelle?

GALLIMARD   Of course I remember! She was my first experience.

MARC   We all wanted to ball her. But she only wanted me.

GALLIMARD   I had her.

MARC   Right. You balled her.

25 GALLIMARD   You were the only one who ever believed me.

MARC   Well, there's a good reason for that. [*Beat*] C'mon. You must've guessed.

GALLIMARD   You told me to wait in the bushes by the cafeteria that night.
The next thing I knew, she was on me. Dress up in the air.

MARC   She never wore underwear.

30 GALLIMARD   My arms were pinned to the dirt.

MARC   She loved the superior position. A girl ahead of her time.

GALLIMARD   I looked up, and there was this woman . . . bouncing up and
down on my loins.

MARC   Screaming, right?

35 GALLIMARD   Screaming, and breaking off the branches all around me, and
pounding my butt up and down into the dirt.

MARC   Huffing and puffing like a locomotive.

GALLIMARD   And in the middle of all this, the leaves were getting into my
mouth, my legs were losing circulation, I thought, "God. So this is *it*?"

40 MARC   You thought that?

GALLIMARD   Well, I was worried about my legs falling off.

MARC   You didn't have a good time?

GALLIMARD   No, that's not what I—I had a great time!

MARC   You're sure?

45 GALLIMARD   Yeah. Really.

MARC   'Cuz I wanted you to have a good time.

GALLIMARD   I did.

[*Pause.*]

MARC   Shit. [*Pause*] When all is said and done, she was kind of a lousy lay,
wasn't she? I mean, there was a lot of energy there, but you never knew
50 what she was doing with it. Like when she yelled "I'm coming!"—hell, it
was so loud, you wanted to go "Look, it's not that big a deal."

GALLIMARD   I got scared. I thought she meant someone was actually coming.
[*Pause*] But, Marc?

MARC   What?

1. A French automobile manufacturing company.

55 GALLIMARD Thanks.

MARC Oh, don't mention it.

GALLIMARD It was my first experience.

MARC Yeah. You got her.

GALLIMARD I got her.

60 MARC Wait! Look at that letter again!

[GALLIMARD *picks up one of the papers he's been stamping, and rereads it.*]

GALLIMARD [*to us*] After six weeks, they began to arrive. The letters.

[*Upstage special on* SONG, *as Madame* BUTTERFLY. *The scene is underscored by the "Love Duet."*]

SONG Did we fight? I do not know. Is the opera no longer of interest to you? Please come—my audiences miss the white devil in their midst.

[GALLIMARD *looks up from the letter, towards us.*]

GALLIMARD [*to us*] A concession, but much too dignified. [*Beat; he discards 65 the letter.*] I skipped the opera again that week to complete a position paper on trade.

[*The bureaucrat hands him another letter.*]

SONG Six weeks have passed since last we met. Is this your practice—to leave friends in the lurch? Sometimes I hate you, sometimes I hate myself, but always I miss you.

70 GALLIMARD [*to us*] Better, but I don't like the way she calls me "friend." When a woman calls a man her "friend," she's calling him a eunuch or a homosexual. [*Beat; he discards the letter.*] I was absent from the opera for the seventh week, feeling a sudden urge to clean out my files.

[*Bureaucrat hands him another letter.*]

SONG Your rudeness is beyond belief. I don't deserve this cruelty. Don't 75 bother to call. I'll have you turned away at the door.

GALLIMARD [*to us*] I didn't. [*He discards the letter; bureaucrat hands him another.*] And then finally, the letter that concluded my experiment.

SONG I am out of words. I can hide behind dignity no longer. What do you want? I have already given you my shame.

[GALLIMARD *gives the letter back to* MARC, *slowly. Special on* SONG *fades out.*]

80 GALLIMARD [*to us*] Reading it, I became suddenly ashamed. Yes, my experiment had been a success. She was turning on my needle. But the victory seemed hollow.

MARC Hollow?! Are you crazy?

GALLIMARD Nothing, Marc. Please go away.

85 MARC [*exiting, with papers*] Haven't I taught you anything?

GALLIMARD "I have already given you my shame." I had to attend a reception that evening. On the way, I felt sick. If there is a God, surely he would punish me now. I had finally gained power over a beautiful woman, only to abuse it cruelly. There must be justice in the world. I had the strange feel-90 ing that the ax would fall this very evening.

1.12

Ambassador TOULON's *residence. Beijing. 1960.*

Sound cue: party noises. Light change. We are now in a spacious residence. TOULON, *the French ambassador, enters and taps* GALLIMARD *on the shoulder.*

TOULON Gallimard? Can I have a word? Over here.

GALLIMARD [to us] Manuel Toulon. French ambassador to China. He likes to think of us all as his children. Rather like God.

TOULON Look, Gallimard, there's not much to say. I've liked you. From the
5 day you walked in. You were no leader, but you were tidy and efficient.

GALLIMARD Thank you, sir.

TOULON Don't jump the gun. Okay, our needs in China are changing. It's embarrassing that we lost Indochina.[2] Someone just wasn't on the ball there. I don't mean you personally, of course.

10 GALLIMARD Thank you, sir.

TOULON We're going to be doing a lot more information-gathering in the future. The nature of our work here is changing. Some people are just going to have to go. It's nothing personal.

GALLIMARD Oh.

15 TOULON Want to know a secret? Vice-Consul LeBon is being transferred.

GALLIMARD [to us] My immediate superior!

TOULON And most of his department.

GALLIMARD [to us] Just as I feared! God has seen my evil heart—

TOULON But not you.

20 GALLIMARD [to us] —and he's taking her away just as . . . [To TOULON] Excuse me, sir?

TOULON Scare you? I think I did. Cheer up, Gallimard. I want you to replace LeBon as vice-consul.

GALLIMARD You—? Yes, well, thank you, sir.

25 TOULON Anytime.

GALLIMARD I . . . accept with great humility.

TOULON Humility won't be part of the job. You're going to coordinate the revamped intelligence division. Want to know a secret? A year ago, you would've been out. But the past few months, I don't know how it hap-
30 pened, you've become this new aggressive confident . . . thing. And they also tell me you get along with the Chinese. So I think you're a lucky man, Gallimard. Congratulations.

[They shake hands. TOULON exits. Party noises out. GALLIMARD stumbles across a darkened stage.]

GALLIMARD Vice-consul? Impossible! As I stumbled out of the party, I saw it written across the sky: There is no God. Or, no—say that there is a God.
35 But that God . . . understands. Of course! God who creates Eve to serve Adam, who blesses Solomon with his harem but ties Jezebel to a burning bed[3]—that God is a man. And he understands! At age thirty-nine, I was suddenly initiated into the way of the world.

2. That is, French Indochina, a colony established in the late 19th century that comprised present-day Laos, Cambodia, and Vietnam. It was "lost" with the French defeat at the Battle of Dien Bien Phu in 1954, ending an insurgency that had begun with Vietnam's declaration of independence in 1945.

3. A series of biblical references: see Genesis 2.21–23 and 1 Corinthians 11.8–9 (the creation of Eve), 1 Kings 11.1–3 (Solomon's wives and concubines), and Revelation 2.20–23 (the punishment of Jezebel for harlotry, as described here).

1.13

SONG LILING's *apartment. Beijing. 1960.*

SONG *enters, in a sheer dressing gown.*

SONG   Are you crazy?
GALLIMARD   Mademoiselle Song—
SONG   To come here—at this hour? After . . . after eight weeks?
GALLIMARD   It's the most amazing—
5 SONG   You bang on my door? Scare my servants, scandalize the neighbors?
GALLIMARD   I've been promoted. To vice-consul.
　　　　　[*Pause.*]
SONG   And what is that supposed to mean to me?
GALLIMARD   Are you my Butterfly?
SONG   What are you saying?
10 GALLIMARD   I've come tonight for an answer: are you my Butterfly?
SONG   Don't you know already?
GALLIMARD   I want you to say it.
SONG   I don't want to say it.
GALLIMARD   So, that is your answer?
15 SONG   You know how I feel about—
GALLIMARD   I do remember one thing.
SONG   What?
GALLIMARD   In the letter I received today.
SONG   Don't.
20 GALLIMARD   "I have already given you my shame."
SONG   It's enough that I even wrote it.
GALLIMARD   Well, then—
SONG   I shouldn't have it splashed across my face.
GALLIMARD   —if that's all true—
25 SONG   Stop!
GALLIMARD   Then what is one more short answer?
SONG   I don't want to!
GALLIMARD   Are you my Butterfly? [*Silence; he crosses the room and begins to touch her hair.*] I want from you honesty. There should be nothing false
30 between us. No false pride.
　　　　　[*Pause.*]
SONG   Yes, I am. I am your Butterfly.
GALLIMARD   Then let me be honest with you. It is because of you that I was promoted tonight. You have changed my life forever. My little Butterfly, there should be no more secrets: I love you.
　　　　　[*He starts to kiss her roughly. She resists slightly.*]
35 SONG   No . . . no . . . gently . . . please, I've never . . .
GALLIMARD   No?
SONG   I've tried to appear experienced, but . . . the truth is . . . no.
GALLIMARD   Are you cold?
SONG   Yes. Cold.
40 GALLIMARD   Then we will go very, very slowly.
　　　　　[*He starts to caress her; her gown begins to open.*]
SONG   No . . . let me . . . keep my clothes . . .

GALLIMARD But . . .

SONG Please . . . it all frightens me. I'm a modest Chinese girl.

GALLIMARD My poor little treasure.

45 SONG I am your treasure. Though inexperienced, I am not . . . ignorant. They teach us things, our mothers, about pleasing a man.

GALLIMARD Yes?

SONG I'll do my best to make you happy. Turn off the lights.

[GALLIMARD *gets up and heads for a lamp.* SONG, *propped up on one elbow, tosses her hair back and smiles.*]

SONG Monsieur Gallimard?

50 GALLIMARD Yes, Butterfly?

SONG "Vieni, vieni!"[4]

GALLIMARD "Come, darling."

SONG "Ah! Dolce notte!"

GALLIMARD "Beautiful night."

55 SONG "Tutto estatico d'amor ride il ciel!"

GALLIMARD "All ecstatic with love, the heavens are filled with laughter."

[*He turns off the lamp. Blackout.*]

2.1

M. GALLIMARD's *cell. Paris. Present.*

Lights up on GALLIMARD. *He sits in his cell, reading from a leaflet.*

GALLIMARD This, from a contemporary critic's commentary on *Madame Butterfly*: "Pinkerton suffers from . . . being an obnoxious bounder whom every man in the audience itches to kick." Bully for us men in the audience! Then, in the same note: "Butterfly is the most irresistibly appealing of Puccini's 'Little Women.' Watching the succession of her humiliations is like watching a child under torture." [*He tosses the pamphlet over his shoulder.*] I suggest that, while we men may all want to kick Pinkerton, very few of us would pass up the opportunity to *be* Pinkerton.

[GALLIMARD *moves out of his cell.*]

2.2

GALLIMARD *and* BUTTERFLY's *flat. Beijing. 1960.*

We are in a simple but well-decorated parlor. GALLIMARD *moves to sit on a sofa, while* SONG, *dressed in a chong sam,[5] enters and curls up at his feet.*

GALLIMARD [*to us*] We secured a flat on the outskirts of Peking. Butterfly, as I was calling her now, decorated our "home" with Western furniture and Chinese antiques. And there, on a few stolen afternoons or evenings each week, Butterfly commenced her education.

5 SONG The Chinese men—they keep us down.

GALLIMARD Even in the "New Society"?[6]

---

4. Song's Italian lines ending this scene, translated by Gallimard, are drawn from the "Love Duet" finale of act 1 of *Madama Butterfly*.

5. That is, a cheongsam (literally, "long gown"), a traditional Chinese dress with a high collar and a slit skirt.

6. In his essay "On New Democracy" (1940), Mao Zedong called for "a new society and a new state for the Chinese nation."

SONG   In the "New Society," we are all kept ignorant equally. That's one of the exciting things about loving a Western man. I know you are not threatened by a woman's education.

10 GALLIMARD   I'm no saint, Butterfly.

SONG   But you come from a progressive society.

GALLIMARD   We're not always reminding each other how "old" we are, if that's what you mean.

SONG   Exactly. We Chinese—once, I suppose, it is true, we ruled the world.
15   But so what? How much more exciting to be part of the society ruling the world today. Tell me—what's happening in Vietnam?[7]

GALLIMARD   Oh, Butterfly—you want me to bring my work home?

SONG   I want to know what you know. To be impressed by my man. It's not the particulars so much as the fact that you're making decisions which
20   change the shape of the world.

GALLIMARD   Not the world. At best, a small corner.

[TOULON *enters, and sits at a desk upstage.*]

2.3

French embassy. Beijing. 1961.

GALLIMARD *moves downstage, to* TOULON's *desk.* SONG *remains upstage,* *watching.*

TOULON   And a more troublesome corner is hard to imagine.

GALLIMARD   So, the Americans plan to begin bombing?

TOULON   This is very secret, Gallimard: yes. The Americans don't have an embassy here.[8] They're asking us to be their eyes and ears. Say Jack Ken-
5   nedy signed an order to bomb North Vietnam, Laos.[9] How would the Chinese react?

GALLIMARD   I think the Chinese will squawk—

TOULON   Uh-huh.

GALLIMARD   —but, in their hearts, they don't even like Ho Chi Minh.[1]

[*Pause.*]

10 TOULON   What a bunch of jerks. Vietnam was *our* colony. Not only didn't the Americans help us fight to keep them, but now, seven years later, they've come back to grab the territory for themselves. It's very irritating.

GALLIMARD   With all due respect, sir, why should the Americans have won our war for us back in '54 if we didn't have the will to win it ourselves?

7. On gaining its independence in 1954, Vietnam was divided into two countries: the Communist-controlled Democratic Republic of Vietnam (North Vietnam) and the U.S.-backed Republic of Vietnam (South Vietnam). In the late 1950s Communist insurgents in the South (the Viet Cong), aided by the North, launched a guerrilla war seeking the reunification of Vietnam.
8. The United States did not establish official diplomatic relations with the People's Republic of China until 1979.
9. While campaigning for the presidency in 1960, Kennedy pledged to increase U.S. military assistance to South Vietnam in its struggle against the armed insurgency supported by the North. In 1961 his administration signed a military and economic aid treaty with South Vietnam, leading to large increases in the number of U.S. military advisers in the country (U.S. air strikes against North Vietnam and Laos would not begin until 1964).
1. Vietnamese nationalist (1890–1969), a Communist who led the struggle for independence; after the country's partition in 1954, he became president of North Vietnam. In the early 1950s China had sent military advisers and weapons to the Vietnamese insurgents, and it supported the North in its war with the South.

15 TOULON   You're kidding, aren't you?

[*Pause.*]

GALLIMARD   The Orientals simply want to be associated with whoever shows the most strength and power. You live with the Chinese, sir. Do you think they like Communism?

TOULON   I live in China. Not with the Chinese.

20 GALLIMARD   Well, I—

TOULON   *You* live with the Chinese.

GALLIMARD   Excuse me?

TOULON   I can't keep a secret.

GALLIMARD   What are you saying?

25 TOULON   Only that I'm not immune to gossip. So, you're keeping a native mistress. Don't answer. It's none of my business. [*Pause*] I'm sure she must be gorgeous.

GALLIMARD   Well . . .

TOULON   I'm impressed. You have the stamina to go out into the streets and
30   hunt one down. Some of us have to be content with the wives of the expatriate community.

GALLIMARD   I do feel . . . fortunate.

TOULON   So, Gallimard, you've got the inside knowledge—what *do* the Chinese think?

35 GALLIMARD   Deep down, they miss the old days. You know, cappuccinos, men in tuxedos—

TOULON   So what do we tell the Americans about Vietnam?

GALLIMARD   Tell them there's a natural affinity between the West and the Orient.

40 TOULON   And that you speak from experience?

GALLIMARD   The Orientals are people too. They want the good things we can give them. If the Americans demonstrate the will to win, the Vietnamese will welcome them into a mutually beneficial union.

TOULON   I don't see how the Vietnamese can stand up to American
45   firepower.

GALLIMARD   Orientals will always submit to a greater force.

TOULON   I'll note your opinions in my report. The Americans always love to hear how "welcome" they'll be. [*He starts to exit.*]

GALLIMARD   Sir?

50 TOULON   Mmmm?

GALLIMARD   This . . . rumor you've heard.

TOULON   Uh-huh?

GALLIMARD   How . . . widespread do you think it is?

TOULON   It's only widespread within this embassy. Where nobody talks
55   because everybody is guilty. We were worried about you, Gallimard. We thought you were the only one here without a secret. Now you go and find a lotus blossom . . . and top us all. [*He exits.*]

GALLIMARD [*to us*]   Toulon knows! And he approves! I was learning the benefits of being a man. We form our own clubs, sit behind thick doors,
60   smoke—and celebrate the fact that we're still boys. [*He starts to move downstage, towards* SONG.] So, over the—

[*Suddenly* COMRADE CHIN *enters.* GALLIMARD *backs away.*]

GALLIMARD [*to* SONG]   No! Why does she have to come in?

SONG   Rene, be sensible. How can they understand the story without her?
Now, don't embarrass yourself.

[GALLIMARD *moves down center.*]

65 GALLIMARD [*to us*]   Now, you will see why my story is so amusing to so many
people. Why they snicker at parties in disbelief. Please—try to understand
it from my point of view. We are all prisoners of our time and place. [*He
exits.*]

2.4

GALLIMARD *and* BUTTERFLY's *flat. Beijing. 1961.*

SONG [*to us*]   1961. The flat Monsieur Gallimard rented for us. An evening
after he has gone.

CHIN   Okay, see if you can find out when the Americans plan to start bombing Vietnam. If you can find out what cities, even better.

5 SONG   I'll do my best, but I don't want to arouse his suspicions.

CHIN   Yeah, sure, of course. So, what else?

SONG   The Americans will increase troops in Vietnam to 170,000 soldiers
with 120,000 militia and 11,000 American advisors.

CHIN [*writing*]   Wait, wait. 120,000 militia and—

10 SONG   —11,000 American—

CHIN   —American advisors. [*Beat*] How do you remember so much?

SONG   I'm an actor.

CHIN   Yeah. [*Beat*] Is that how come you dress like that?

SONG   Like what, Miss Chin?

15 CHIN   Like that dress! You're wearing a dress. And every time I come here,
you're wearing a dress. Is that because you're an actor? Or what?

SONG   It's a . . . disguise, Miss Chin.

CHIN   Actors, I think they're all weirdos. My mother tells me actors are like
gamblers or prostitutes or—

20 SONG   It helps me in my assignment.

[*Pause.*]

CHIN   You're not gathering information in any way that violates Communist
Party principles, are you?

SONG   Why would I do that?

CHIN   Just checking. Remember: when working for the Great Proletarian
25 State, you represent our Chairman Mao[2] in every position you take.

SONG   I'll try to imagine the Chairman taking my positions.

CHIN   We all think of him this way. Good-bye, comrade.[3] [*She starts to exit.*]
Comrade?

SONG   Yes?

30 CHIN   Don't forget: there is no homosexuality in China!

SONG   Yes, I've heard.

CHIN   Just checking. [*She exits.*]

2. Mao Zedong (1893–1976) was chairman
of the Central Committee of the Chinese
Communist Party from 1945 until his death.
Proletarian state: a transitional stage in the
proletarian (i.e., working-class) revolution
that Karl Marx and Friedrich Engels, in *Man-*
ifesto of the Communist Party (1848), envisioned as necessary to overthrow capitalism
and bring about a classless society.
3. Customary form of address among
Communists.

SONG [*to us*]   What passes for a woman in modern China.

[GALLIMARD *sticks his head out from the wings.*]

GALLIMARD   Is she gone?

35 SONG   Yes, Rene. Please continue in your own fashion.

2.5

Beijing. 1961–63.

GALLIMARD *moves to the couch where* SONG *still sits. He lies down in her lap, and she strokes his forehead.*

GALLIMARD [*to us*]   And so, over the years 1961, '62, '63, we settled into our routine, Butterfly and I. She would always have prepared a light snack and then, ever so delicately, and only if I agreed, she would start to pleasure me. With her hands, her mouth . . . too many ways to explain, and too sad, given
5   my present situation. But mostly we would talk. About my life. Perhaps there is nothing more rare than to find a woman who passionately listens.

[SONG *remains upstage, listening, as* HELGA *enters and plays a scene downstage with* GALLIMARD.]

HELGA   Rene, I visited Dr. Bolleart this morning.

GALLIMARD   Why? Are you ill?

HELGA   No, no. You see, I wanted to ask him . . . that question we've been
10   discussing.

GALLIMARD   And I told you, it's only a matter of time. Why did you bring a doctor into this? We just have to keep trying—like a crapshoot, actually.

HELGA   I went, I'm sorry. But listen: he says there's nothing wrong with me.

GALLIMARD   You see? Now, will you stop—?

15 HELGA   Rene, he says he'd like you to go in and take some tests.

GALLIMARD   Why? So he can find there's nothing wrong with both of us?

HELGA   Rene, I don't ask for much. One trip! One visit! And then, whatever you want to do about it—you decide.

20 GALLIMARD   You're assuming he'll find something defective!

HELGA   No! Of course not! Whatever he finds—if he finds nothing, we decide what to do about nothing! But go!

GALLIMARD   If he finds nothing, we keep trying. Just like we do now.

HELGA   But at least we'll know! [*Pause*] I'm sorry. [*She starts to exit.*]

25 GALLIMARD   Do you really want me to see Dr. Bolleart?

HELGA   Only if you want a child, Rene. We have to face the fact that time is running out. Only if you want a child. [*She exits.*]

GALLIMARD [*to* SONG]   I'm a modern man, Butterfly. And yet, I don't want to go. It's the same old voodoo. I feel like God himself is laughing at me if I
30   can't produce a child.

SONG   You men of the West—you're obsessed by your odd desire for equality. Your wife can't give you a child, and *you're* going to the doctor?

GALLIMARD   Well, you see, she's already gone.

SONG   And because this incompetent can't find the defect, you now have to
35   subject yourself to him? It's unnatural.

GALLIMARD   Well, what is the "natural" solution?

SONG   In Imperial China, when a man found that one wife was inadequate, he turned to another—to give him his son.

GALLIMARD   What do you—? I can't . . . marry you, yet.

40 SONG   Please. I'm not asking you to be my husband. But I am already your wife.

GALLIMARD   Do you want to . . . have my child?

SONG   I thought you'd never ask.

GALLIMARD   But, your career . . . your—

SONG   Phooey on my career! That's your Western mind, twisting itself into
45   strange shapes again. Of course I love my career. But what would I love
most of all? To feel something inside me—day and night—something I
know is yours. [*Pause*] Promise me . . . you won't go to this doctor. Who is
this Western quack to set himself as judge over the man I love? I know who
is a man, and who is not. [*She exits.*]

50 GALLIMARD [*to us*]   Dr. Bolleart? Of course I didn't go. What man would?

2.6

Beijing. 1963.

Party noises over the house speakers. RENEE *enters, wearing a revealing gown.*

GALLIMARD   1963. A party at the Austrian embassy. None of us could
remember the Austrian ambassador's name, which seemed somehow
appropriate. [*To* RENEE] So, I tell the Americans, Diem[4] must go. The U.S.
wants to be respected by the Vietnamese, and yet they're propping up this
5   nobody seminarian as her president. A man whose claim to fame is his
sister-in-law[5] imposing fanatic "moral order" campaigns? Oriental women—
when they're good, they're very good, but when they're bad, they're
Christians.

RENEE   Yeah.

10 GALLIMARD   And what do you do?

RENEE   I'm a student. My father exports a lot of useless stuff to the Third
World.

GALLIMARD   How useless?

RENEE   You know. Squirt guns, confectioner's sugar, hula hoops[6] . . .

15 GALLIMARD   I'm sure they appreciate the sugar.

RENEE   I'm here for two years to study Chinese.

GALLIMARD   Two years?

RENEE   That's what everybody says.

GALLIMARD   When did you arrive?

20 RENEE   Three weeks ago.

GALLIMARD   And?

RENEE   I like it. It's primitive, but . . . well, this is the place to learn Chinese,
so here I am.

GALLIMARD   Why Chinese?

25 RENEE   I think it'll be important someday.

4. Ngo Dinh Diem (1901–1963); as a boy, he studied in a French Catholic school and briefly entered a monastery. With U.S. support, he became prime minister of Vietnam in 1954 and president of South Vietnam in 1955. His authoritarian and corrupt rule made him widely unpopular, and he was ousted and murdered by a group of generals who had been assured that the United States would not interfere with a coup.
5. Tran Le Xian (1924–2011), the wife of Diem's brother and chief adviser, Ngo Dinh Nhu; she was known as Madame Nhu. Because Diem was unmarried, she was in effect the country's first lady. A passionate convert to Roman Catholicism, she worked for laws banning divorce, contraception, brothels, and the like and encouraged the persecution of Buddhists.
6. Hula Hoops were a brief U.S. craze in 1958, when 25 million were sold in four months.

GALLIMARD You do?

RENEE Don't ask me when, but . . . that's what I think.

GALLIMARD Well, I agree with you. One hundred percent. That's very farsighted.

30 RENEE Yeah. Well of course, my father thinks I'm a complete weirdo.

GALLIMARD He'll thank you someday.

RENEE Like when the Chinese start buying hula hoops?

GALLIMARD There're a billion bellies out there.

RENEE And if they end up taking over the world—well, then I'll be lucky to
35 know Chinese too, right?

[Pause.]

GALLIMARD At this point, I don't see how the Chinese can possibly take—

RENEE You know what I *don't* like about China?

GALLIMARD Excuse me? No—what?

RENEE Nothing to do at night.

40 GALLIMARD You come to parties at embassies like everyone else.

RENEE Yeah, but they get out at ten. And then what?

GALLIMARD I'm afraid the Chinese idea of a dance hall is a dirt floor and a man with a flute.

RENEE Are you married?

45 GALLIMARD Yes. Why?

RENEE You wanna . . . fool around?

[Pause.]

GALLIMARD Sure.

RENEE I'll wait for you outside. What's your name?

GALLIMARD Gallimard. Rene.

50 RENEE Weird. I'm Renee too. [*She exits.*]

GALLIMARD [*to us*] And so, I embarked on my first extra-extramarital affair. Renee was picture perfect. With a body like those girls in the magazines. If I put a tissue paper over my eyes, I wouldn't have been able to tell the difference. And it was exciting to be with someone who wasn't afraid to be
55 seen completely naked. But is it possible for a woman to be *too* uninhibited, *too* willing, so as to seem almost too . . . masculine?

[*Chuck Berry*[7] *blares from the house speakers, then comes down in volume as* RENEE *enters, toweling her hair.*]

RENEE You have a nice weenie.

GALLIMARD What?

RENEE Penis. You have a nice penis.

60 GALLIMARD Oh. Well, thank you. That's very . . .

RENEE What—can't take a compliment?

GALLIMARD No, it's very . . . reassuring.

RENEE But most girls don't come out and say it, huh?

GALLIMARD And also . . . what did you call it?

65 RENEE Oh. Most girls don't call it a "weenie," huh?

GALLIMARD It sounds very—

RENEE Small, I know.

---

7. An African American songwriter, guitarist, and singer (b. 1926), a pioneer of rock music whose hits include "Roll Over Beethoven" (1956) and "Johnny B. Goode" (1958).

GALLIMARD   I was going to say, "young."

RENEE   Yeah. Young, small, same thing. Most guys are pretty, uh, sensitive
70   about that. Like, you know, I had a boyfriend back home in Denmark. I got
mad at him once and called him a little weeniehead. He got so mad! He
said at least I should call him a great big weeniehead.

GALLIMARD   I suppose I just say "penis."

RENEE   Yeah. That's pretty clinical. There's "cock," but that sounds like a
75   chicken. And "prick" is painful, and "dick" is like you're talking about
someone who's not in the room.

GALLIMARD   Yes. It's a . . . bigger problem than I imagined.

RENEE   I—I think maybe it's because I really don't know what to do with
them—that's why I call them "weenies."

80   GALLIMARD   Well, you did quite well with . . . mine.

RENEE   Thanks, but I mean, really *do* with them. Like, okay, have you ever
looked at one? I mean, really?

GALLIMARD   No, I suppose when it's part of you, you sort of take it for
granted.

85   RENEE   I guess. But, like, it just hangs there. This little . . . flap of flesh. And
there's so much fuss that we make about it. Like, I think the reason we
fight wars is because we wear clothes. Because no one knows—between
the men, I mean—who has the bigger . . . weenie. So, if I'm a guy with a
small one, I'm going to build a really big building or take over a really big
90   piece of land or write a really long book so the other men don't know, right?
But, see, it never really works, that's the problem. I mean, you conquer the
country, or whatever, but you're still wearing clothes, so there's no way to
prove absolutely whose is bigger or smaller. And that's what we call a civilized society. The whole world run by a bunch of men with pricks the size
95   of pins. [*She exits.*]

GALLIMARD   [*to us*]   This was simply not acceptable.

[*A high-pitched chime rings through the air.* SONG, *dressed as* BUTTERFLY,
*appears in the upstage special. She is obviously distressed. Her body
swoons as she attempts to clip the stems of flowers she's arranging in a
vase.*]

GALLIMARD   But I kept up our affair, wildly, for several months. Why? I
believe because of Butterfly. She knew the secret I was trying to hide. But,
unlike a Western woman, she didn't confront me, threaten, even pout. I
100   remembered the words of Puccini's *Butterfly*:

SONG   "Noi siamo gente avvezza / alle piccole cose / umili e silenziose."[8]

GALLIMARD   "I come from a people / Who are accustomed to little / Humble
and silent." I saw Pinkerton and Butterfly, and what she would say if he
were unfaithful . . . nothing. She would cry, alone, into those wildly soft
105   sleeves, once full of possessions, now empty to collect her tears. It was her
tears and her silence that excited me, every time I visited Renee.

TOULON   [*offstage*]   Gallimard!

[TOULON *enters.* GALLIMARD *turns towards him. During the next section,*
SONG, *up center, begins to dance with the flowers. It is a drunken dance,
where she breaks small pieces off the stems.*]

8. Lines from the aria "Vogliatemi bene" ("Ah, Love Me a Little"), sung by Butterfly in the opera's
first act.

TOULON   They're killing him.

GALLIMARD   Who? I'm sorry? What?

110   TOULON   Bother you to come over at this late hour?

GALLIMARD   No . . . of course not.

TOULON   Not after you hear my secret. Champagne?

GALLIMARD   Um . . . thank you.

TOULON   You're surprised. There's something that you've wanted, Gallimard.

115   No, not a promotion. Next time. Something in the world. You're not aware of this, but there's an informal gossip circle among intelligence agents. And some of ours heard from some of the Americans—

GALLIMARD   Yes?

TOULON   That the U.S. will allow the Vietnamese generals to stage a coup . . .

120   and assassinate President Diem.[9]

> [*The chime rings again.* TOULON *freezes.* GALLIMARD *turns upstage and looks at* BUTTERFLY, *who slowly and deliberately clips a flower off its stem.* GALLIMARD *turns back towards* TOULON.]

GALLIMARD   I think . . . that's a very wise move!

> [TOULON *unfreezes.*]

TOULON   It's what you've been advocating. A toast?

GALLIMARD   Sure. I consider this a vindication.

TOULON   Not exactly. "To the test. Let's hope you pass."

> [*They drink. The chime rings again.* TOULON *freezes.* GALLIMARD *turns upstage, and* SONG *clips another flower.*]

125   GALLIMARD [*to* TOULON]   The test?

TOULON [*unfreezing*]   It's a test of everything you've been saying. I personally think the generals probably will stop the Communists. And you'll be a hero. But if anything goes wrong, then your opinions won't be worth a pig's ear. I'm sure that won't happen. But sometimes it's easier when they don't listen to you.

130   GALLIMARD   They're your opinions too, aren't they?

TOULON   Personally, yes.

GALLIMARD   So we agree.

TOULON   But my opinions aren't on that report. Yours are. Cheers.

> [TOULON *turns away from* GALLIMARD *and raises his glass. At that instant* SONG *picks up the vase and hurls it to the ground. It shatters.* SONG *sinks down amidst the shards of the vase, in a calm, childlike trance. She sings softly, as if reciting a child's nursery rhyme.*]

SONG [*repeat as necessary*]   "The whole world over, the white man travels,

135   setting anchor, wherever he likes. Life's not worth living, unless he finds, the finest maidens, of every land . . ."[1]

> [GALLIMARD *turns downstage towards us.* SONG *continues singing.*]

GALLIMARD   I shook as I left his house. That coward! That worm! To put the burden for his decisions on my shoulders!

I started for Renee's. But no, that was all I needed. A schoolgirl who

140   would question the role of the penis in modern society. What I wanted was

---

9. See the first note of this scene.

1. A translation of lines sung by Pinkerton in the first act of *Madama Butterfly*.

revenge. A vessel to contain my humiliation. Though I hadn't seen her in several weeks, I headed for Butterfly's.

[GALLIMARD *enters* SONG's *apartment.*]

SONG   Oh! Rene . . . I was dreaming!

GALLIMARD   You've been drinking?

145 SONG   If I can't sleep, then yes, I drink. But then, it gives me these dreams which—Rene, it's been almost three weeks since you visited me last.

GALLIMARD   I know. There's been a lot going on in the world.

SONG   Fortunately I am drunk. So I can speak freely. It's not the world, it's you and me. And an old problem. Even the softest skin becomes like

150 leather to a man who's touched it too often. I confess I don't know how to stop it. I don't know how to become another woman.

GALLIMARD   I have a request.

SONG   Is this a solution? Or are you ready to give up the flat?

GALLIMARD   It may be a solution. But I'm sure you won't like it.

155 SONG   Oh well, that's very important. "Like it?" Do you think I "like" lying here alone, waiting, always waiting for your return? Please—don't worry about what I may not "like."

GALLIMARD   I want to see you . . . naked.

[*Silence.*]

SONG   I thought you understood my modesty. So you want me to—what—

160 strip? Like a big cowboy girl? Shiny pasties on my breasts? Shall I fling my kimono over my head and yell "ya-hoo" in the process? I thought you respected my shame!

GALLIMARD   I believe you gave me your shame many years ago.

SONG   Yes—and it is just like a white devil to use it against me. I can't believe

165 it. I thought myself so repulsed by the passive Oriental and the cruel white man. Now I see—we are always most revolted by the things hidden within us.

GALLIMARD   I just mean—

SONG   Yes?

170 GALLIMARD   —that it will remove the only barrier left between us.

SONG   No, Rene. Don't couch your request in sweet words. Be yourself—a cad—and know that my love is enough, that I submit—submit to the worst you can give me. [*Pause*] Well, come. Strip me. Whatever happens, know that you have willed it. Our love, in your hands. I'm helpless before my man.

[GALLIMARD *starts to cross the room.*]

175 GALLIMARD   Did I not undress her because I knew, somewhere deep down, what I would find? Perhaps. Happiness is so rare that our mind can turn somersaults to protect it.

At the time, I only knew that I was seeing Pinkerton stalking towards his Butterfly, ready to reward her love with his lecherous hands. The image

180 sickened me, pulled me to my knees, so I was crawling towards her like a worm. By the time I reached her, Pinkerton . . . had vanished from my heart. To be replaced by something new, something unnatural, that flew in the face of all I'd learned in the world—something very close to love.

[*He grabs her around the waist; she strokes his hair.*]

GALLIMARD   Butterfly, forgive me.

185 SONG   Rene . . .

GALLIMARD   For everything. From the start.

SONG   I'm . . .

GALLIMARD   I want to—

SONG   I'm pregnant. [*Beat*] I'm pregnant. [*Beat*] I'm pregnant.
[*Beat.*]

190 GALLIMARD   I want to marry you!

2.7

GALLIMARD *and* BUTTERFLY's *flat. Beijing. 1963.*

Downstage, SONG *paces as* COMRADE CHIN *reads from her notepad. Upstage,* GAL-
LIMARD *is still kneeling. He remains on his knees throughout the scene, watching
it.*

SONG   I need a baby.

CHIN [*from pad*]   He's been spotted going to a dorm.

SONG   I need a baby.

CHIN   At the Foreign Language Institute.

5 SONG   I need a baby.

CHIN   The room of a Danish girl . . . What do you mean, you need a baby?!

SONG   Tell Comrade Kang—last night, the entire mission, it could've ended.

CHIN   What do you mean?

SONG   Tell Kang—he told me to strip.

10 CHIN   *Strip?!*

SONG   Write!

CHIN   I tell you, I don't understand nothing about this case anymore.
Nothing.

SONG   He told me to strip, and I took a chance. Oh, we Chinese, we know

15   how to gamble.

CHIN [*writing*]   ". . . told him to strip."

SONG   My palms were wet, I had to make a split-second decision.

CHIN   Hey! Can you slow down?!
[*Pause.*]

SONG   You write faster, I'm the artist here. Suddenly, it hit me—"All he wants

20   is for her to submit. Once a woman submits, a man is always ready to
become 'generous.'"

CHIN   You're just gonna end up with rough notes.

SONG   And it worked! He gave in! Now, if I can just present him with a baby.
A Chinese baby with blond hair—he'll be mine for life!

25 CHIN   Kang will never agree! The trading of babies has to be a counterrevolutionary[2] act!

SONG   Sometimes, a counterrevolutionary act is necessary to counter a
counterrevolutionary act.
[*Pause.*]

CHIN   Wait.

30 SONG   I need one . . . in seven months. Make sure it's a boy.

CHIN   This doesn't sound like something the Chairman would do. Maybe
you'd better talk to Comrade Kang yourself.

2. That is, undermining the goals of the Revolution of 1949.

SONG   Good. I will.

      [CHIN *gets up to leave.*]

SONG   Miss Chin? Why, in the Peking Opera, are women's roles played by
35   men?

CHIN   I don't know. Maybe, a reactionary remnant of male—

SONG   No. [*Beat*] Because only a man knows how a woman is supposed to
    act.

      [CHIN *exits.* SONG *turns upstage, towards* GALLIMARD.]

GALLIMARD   [*calling after* CHIN]   Good riddance! [*To* SONG] I could forget all
40   that betrayal in an instant, you know. If you'd just come back and become
    Butterfly again.

SONG   Fat chance. You're here in prison, rotting in a cell. And I'm on a plane,
    winging my way back to China. Your President pardoned me of our treason,
    you know.

45 GALLIMARD   Yes, I read about that.

SONG   Must make you feel . . . lower than shit.

GALLIMARD   But don't you, even a little bit, wish you were here with me?

SONG   I'm an artist, Rene. You were my greatest . . . acting challenge. [*She
    laughs.*] It doesn't matter how rotten I answer, does it? You still adore me.
50   That's why I love you, Rene. [*She points to us.*] So—you were telling your
    audience about the night I announced I was pregnant.

      [GALLIMARD *puts his arms around* SONG's *waist. He and* SONG *are in the
      positions they were in at the end of Scene 6.*]

2.8

Same.

GALLIMARD   I'll divorce my wife. We'll live together here, and then later in
    France.

SONG   I feel so . . . ashamed.

GALLIMARD   Why?

5 SONG   I had begun to lose faith. And now, you shame me with your
    generosity.

GALLIMARD   Generosity? No, I'm proposing for very selfish reasons.

SONG   Your apologies only make me feel more ashamed. My outburst a
    moment ago!

10 GALLIMARD   Your outburst? What about my request?!

SONG   You've been very patient dealing with my . . . eccentricities. A Western
    man, used to women freer with their bodies—

GALLIMARD   It was sick! Don't make excuses for me.

SONG   I have to. You don't seem willing to make them for yourself.

      [*Pause.*]

15 GALLIMARD   You're crazy.

SONG   I'm happy. Which often looks like crazy.

GALLIMARD   Then make me crazy. Marry me.

      [*Pause.*]

SONG   No.

GALLIMARD   What?

20 SONG   Do I sound silly, a slave, if I say I'm not worthy?

GALLIMARD   Yes. In fact you do. No one has loved me like you.

SONG   Thank you. And no one ever will. I'll see to that.

GALLIMARD   So what is the problem?

SONG   Rene, we Chinese are realists. We understand rice, gold, and guns.
25   You are a diplomat. Your career is skyrocketing. Now, what would happen if
you divorced your wife to marry a Communist Chinese actress?

GALLIMARD   That's not being realistic. That's defeating yourself before you
begin.

SONG   We must conserve our strength for the battles we can win.

30 GALLIMARD   That sounds like a fortune cookie!

SONG   Where do you think fortune cookies come from?

GALLIMARD   I don't care.

SONG   You do. So do I. And we should. That is why I say I'm not worthy. I'm
worthy to love and even to be loved by you. But I am not worthy to end the
35   career of one of the West's most promising diplomats.

GALLIMARD   It's not that great a career! I made it sound like more than it is!

SONG   Modesty will get you nowhere. Flatter yourself, and you flatter me.
I'm flattered to decline your offer. [*She exits.*]

GALLIMARD [*to us*]   Butterfly and I argued all night. And, in the end, I left,
40   knowing I would never be her husband. She went away for several
months—to the countryside, like a small animal. Until the night I received
her call.

[*A baby's cry from offstage.* SONG *enters, carrying a child.*]

SONG   He looks like you.

GALLIMARD   Oh! [*Beat; he approaches the baby.*] Well, babies are never very
45   attractive at birth.

SONG   Stop!

GALLIMARD   I'm sure he'll grow more beautiful with age. More like his
mother.

SONG   "Chi vide mai / a bimbo del Giappon . . ."[3]

50 GALLIMARD   "What baby, I wonder, was ever born in Japan"—or China, for
that matter—

SONG   ". . . occhi azzurrini?"

GALLIMARD   "With azure eyes"—they're actually sort of brown, wouldn't you
say?

55 SONG   "E il labbro."

GALLIMARD: "And such lips!" [*He kisses* SONG.] And such lips.

SONG   "E i ricciolini d'oro schietto?"

GALLIMARD   "And such a head of golden"—if slightly patchy—"curls?"

SONG   I'm going to call him "Peepee."

60 GALLIMARD   Darling, could you repeat that because I'm sure a rickshaw just
flew by overhead.

SONG   You heard me.

GALLIMARD   "Song Peepee"? May I suggest Michael, or Stephan, or Adolph?

SONG   You may, but I won't listen.

65 GALLIMARD   You can't be serious. Can you imagine the time this child will
have in school?

SONG   In the West, yes.

3. These lines and those that follow are sung by Butterfly in act 2 of *Madama Butterfly.*

GALLIMARD   It's worse than naming him Ping Pong or Long Dong[4] or—

SONG   But he's never going to live in the West, is he?

[*Pause.*]

70   GALLIMARD   That wasn't my choice.

SONG   It is mine. And this is my promise to you: I will raise him, he will be our child, but he will never burden you outside of China.

GALLIMARD   Why do you make these promises? I want to be burdened! I want a scandal to cover the papers!

75   SONG [*to us*]   Prophetic.

GALLIMARD   I'm serious.

SONG   So am I. His name is as I registered it. And he will never live in the West.

[SONG *exits with the child.*]

GALLIMARD [*to us*]   It is possible that her stubbornness only made me want

80   her more. That drawing back at the moment of my capitulation was the most brilliant strategy she could have chosen. It is possible. But it is also possible that by this point she could have said, could have done . . . anything, and I would have adored her still.

2.9

Beijing. 1966.

A driving rhythm of Chinese percussion fills the stage.

GALLIMARD   And then, China began to change. Mao became very old, and his cult became very strong. And, like many old men, he entered his second childhood. So he handed over the reins of state to those with minds like his own. And children ruled the Middle Kingdom[5] with complete caprice. The

5   doctrine of the Cultural Revolution[6] implied continuous anarchy. Contact between Chinese and foreigners became impossible. Our flat was confiscated. Her fame and my money now counted against us.

[*Two dancers in Mao suits and red-starred caps enter, and begin crudely mimicking revolutionary violence, in an agitprop[7] fashion.*]

GALLIMARD   And somehow the American war went wrong too. Four hundred thousand dollars were being spent for every Viet Cong killed; so General

10   Westmoreland's[8] remark that the Oriental does not value life the way

4. Penis (slang).

5. The Chinese name for China (in Mandarin, *Zongguo*, "central state"), first used in the 11th century.

6. The Great Proletarian Cultural Revolution (1966–76), a campaign launched by Mao to rekindle revolutionary fervor by removing so-called counterrevolutionary elements from the Communist Party and society in general. Repeated purges led by the Red Guards—a mass movement composed mainly of students and of young people from the countryside, who subscribed wholeheartedly to Mao's new cult of personality—were aimed at bureaucrats, teachers and intellectuals, and

writers and artists. The result was factionalism, violence, and chaos.

7. Agitation and propaganda, usually on behalf of communism and conveyed through the arts or literature (from the name of the department of the Russian Communist Party responsible for such activities).

8. William Westmoreland (1914–2005), commander of American military operations in Vietnam (1964–68) and U.S. Army chief of staff (1968–72); in the documentary *Hearts and Minds* (1974) he said, "The Oriental doesn't put the same high price on life as does the Westerner. Life is plentiful, life is cheap in the Orient."

Americans do was oddly accurate. Why weren't the Vietnamese people giving in? Why were they content instead to die and die and die again?

[TOULON *enters.*]

TOULON   Congratulations, Gallimard.

GALLIMARD   Excuse me, sir?

15 TOULON   Not a promotion. That was last time. You're going home.

GALLIMARD   What?

TOULON   Don't say I didn't warn you.

GALLIMARD   I'm being transferred . . . because I was wrong about the American war?[9]

20 TOULON   Of course not. We don't care about the Americans. We care about your mind. The quality of your analysis. In general, everything you've predicted here in the Orient . . . just hasn't happened.

GALLIMARD   I think that's premature.

TOULON   Don't force me to be blunt. Okay, you said China was ready to open

25 to Western trade. The only thing they're trading out there are Western heads. And, yes, you said the Americans would succeed in Indochina. You were kidding, right?

GALLIMARD   I think the end is in sight.

TOULON   Don't be pathetic. And don't take this personally. You were wrong.

30 It's not your fault.

GALLIMARD   But I'm going home.

TOULON   Right. Could I have the number of your mistress? [*Beat*] Joke! Joke! Eat a croissant for me.

[TOULON *exits.* SONG, *wearing a Mao suit,*[1] *is dragged in from the wings as part of the upstage dance. They "beat" her, then lampoon the acrobatics of the Chinese opera, as she is made to kneel onstage.*]

GALLIMARD [*simultaneously*]   I don't care to recall how Butterfly and I said our

35 hurried farewell. Perhaps it was better to end our affair before it killed her.

[GALLIMARD *exits.* COMRADE CHIN *walks across the stage with a banner reading: "The Actor Renounces His Decadent Profession!" She reaches the kneeling* SONG. *Percussion stops with a thud. Dancers strike poses.*]

CHIN   Actor-oppressor, for years you have lived above the common people and looked down on their labor. While the farmer ate millet—

SONG   I ate pastries from France and sweetmeats from silver trays.

CHIN   And how did you come to live in such an exalted position?

40 SONG   I was a plaything for the imperialists!

CHIN   What did you do?

SONG   I shamed China by allowing myself to be corrupted by a foreigner . . .

CHIN   What does this mean? The People demand a full confession!

SONG   I engaged in the lowest perversions with China's enemies!

9. After the Tonkin Gulf Resolution (1964) gave the president authority to "take all necessary measures" to defend U.S. forces "and to prevent further aggression," the first U.S. combat troops arrived in South Vietnam, joining 16,000 military advisers. By the end of 1966 close to 400,000 troops were in Vietnam; troop strength peaked in 1968 at 540,000. The last American forces left in 1973, and South Vietnam fell to the North in 1975.

1. A suit like that worn by Mao at the ceremony founding the People's Republic of China—with a high, buttoned collar and four external pockets. It was especially common during the Cultural Revolution.

45 CHIN What perversions? Be more clear!

SONG I let him put it up my ass!

        [Dancers look over, disgusted.]

CHIN Aaaa-ya! How can you use such sickening language?!

SONG My language . . . is only as foul as the crimes I committed . . .

CHIN Yeah. That's better. So—what do you want to do now?

50 SONG I want to serve the people.

        [Percussion starts up, with Chinese strings.]

CHIN What?

SONG I want to serve the people!

        [Dancers regain their revolutionary smiles, and begin a dance of victory.]

CHIN What?!

SONG I want to serve the people!!

        [Dancers unveil a banner: "The Actor Is Rehabilitated!" SONG *remains kneeling before* CHIN, *as the dancers bounce around them, then exit. Music out.]*

2.10

A commune. Hunan Province.[2] 1970.

CHIN How you planning to do that?

SONG I've already worked four years in the fields of Hunan, Comrade Chin.[3]

CHIN So? Farmers work all their lives. Let me see your hands.

        *[*SONG *holds them out for her inspection.]*

CHIN Goddamn! Still so smooth! How long does it take to turn you actors
5   into good anythings? Hunh. You've just spent too many years in luxury to
    be any good to the Revolution.

SONG I served the Revolution.

CHIN Serve the Revolution? Bullshit! You wore dresses! Don't tell me—I was
    there. I saw you! You and your white vice-consul! Stuck up there in your
10   flat, living off the People's Treasury! Yeah, I knew what was going on! You
    two . . . homos! Homos! Homos! *[Pause; she composes herself.]* Ah! Well . . .
    you will serve the people, all right. But not with the Revolution's money.
    This time, you use your own money.

SONG I have no money.

15 CHIN Shut up! And you won't stink up China anymore with your pervert
    stuff. You'll pollute the place where pollution begins—the West.

SONG What do you mean?

CHIN Shut up! You're going to France. Without a cent in your pocket. You
    find your consul's house, you make him pay your expenses—

20 SONG No.

CHIN And you give us weekly reports! Useful information!

SONG That's crazy. It's been four years.

CHIN Either that, or back to rehabilitation center!

2. In southern China. *Commune:* the basic unit of China's collectivized system of agriculture (introduced in 1958 and abandoned in 1981).
3. During the Cultural Revolution, many deemed counterrevolutionary were sent to the countryside in order to be "rehabilitated" through hard labor and political reindoctrination.

SONG   Comrade Chin, he's not going to support me! Not in France! He's a
25   white man! I was just his plaything—

CHIN   Oh yuck! Again with the sickening language? Where's my stick?

SONG   You don't understand the mind of a man.

[*Pause.*]

CHIN   Oh no? No I don't? Then how come I'm married, huh? How come I
got a man? Five, six years ago, you always tell me those kind of things, I felt
30   very bad. But not now! Because what does the Chairman say? He tells us
I'm now the smart one, you're now the nincompoop! *You're* the blackhead,
the harebrain, the nitwit! You think you're so smart? You understand "The
Mind of a Man"? Good! Then *you* go to France and be a pervert for Chairman Mao!

[CHIN *and* SONG *exit in opposite directions.*]

2.11

Paris. 1968–70.

GALLIMARD *enters.*

GALLIMARD   And what was waiting for me back in Paris? Well, better Chinese
food than I'd eaten in China. Friends and relatives. A little accounting,
regular schedule, keeping track of traffic violations in the suburbs. . . . And
the indignity of students shouting the slogans of Chairman Mao at me—in
5   French.[4]

HELGA   Rene? Rene? [*She enters, soaking wet.*] I've had a . . . a problem.
[*She sneezes.*]

GALLIMARD   You're wet.

HELGA   Yes, I . . . coming back from the grocer's. A group of students, waving
red flags, they—

[GALLIMARD *fetches a towel.*]

10   HELGA   —they ran by, I was caught up along with them. Before I knew what
was happening—

[GALLIMARD *gives her the towel.*]

HELGA   Thank you. The police started firing water cannons at us. I tried to
shout, to tell them I was the wife of a diplomat, but—you know how it
is . . . [*Pause*] Needless to say, I lost the groceries. Rene, what's happening
15   to France?

GALLIMARD   What's—? Well, nothing, really.

HELGA   Nothing?! The storefronts are in flames, there's glass in the streets,
buildings are toppling—and I'm wet!

GALLIMARD   Nothing! . . . that I care to think about.

20   HELGA   And is that why you stay in this room?

GALLIMARD   Yes, in fact.

HELGA   With the incense burning? You know something? I hate incense. It
smells so sickly sweet.

GALLIMARD   Well, I hate the French. Who just smell—period!

4. In May 1968 student demonstrations
against the French government's heavy-
handed response to earlier protests grew into
a massive uprising, joined by a general strike
of millions of workers, seeking to end the
administration of President Charles de
Gaulle. The students were a mixture of radicals and leftists, including anarchists, Marx-
ists, Trotskyites, and Maoists.

25 HELGA   And the Chinese were better?

GALLIMARD   Please—don't start.

HELGA   When we left, this exact same thing, the riots—

GALLIMARD   No, no . . .

HELGA   Students screaming slogans, smashing down doors—

30 GALLIMARD   Helga—

HELGA   It was all going on in China, too. Don't you remember?!

GALLIMARD   Helga! Please! [*Pause*] You have never understood China, have you? You walk in here with these ridiculous ideas, that the West is falling apart, that China was spitting in our faces. You come in, dripping of the
35 streets, and you leave water all over my floor. [*He grabs* HELGA'*s towel, begins mopping up the floor.*]

HELGA   But it's the truth!

GALLIMARD   Helga, I want a divorce.

[*Pause;* GALLIMARD *continues, mopping the floor.*]

HELGA   I take it back. China is . . . beautiful. Incense, I like incense.

GALLIMARD   I've had a mistress.

40 HELGA   So?

GALLIMARD   For eight years.

HELGA   I knew you would. I knew you would the day I married you. And now what? You want to marry her?

GALLIMARD   I can't. She's in China.

45 HELGA   I see. You want to leave. For someone who's not here, is that right?

GALLIMARD   That's right.

HELGA   You can't live with her, but still you don't want to live with me.

GALLIMARD   That's right.

[*Pause.*]

HELGA   Shit. How terrible that I can figure that out. [*Pause.*] I never thought
50 I'd say it. But, in China, I was happy. I knew, in my own way, I knew that you were not everything you pretended to be. But the pretense—going on your arm to the embassy ball, visiting your office and the guards saying, "Good morning, good morning, Madame Gallimard"—the pretense . . . was very good indeed. [*Pause*] I hope everyone is mean to you for the rest
55 of your life. [*She exits.*]

GALLIMARD   [*to us*]   Prophetic.

[MARC *enters with two drinks.*]

GALLIMARD   [*to* MARC]   In China, I was different from all other men.

MARC   Sure. You were white. Here's your drink.

GALLIMARD   I felt . . . touched.

60 MARC   In the head? Rene, I don't want to hear about the Oriental love goddess. Okay? One night—can we just drink and throw up without a lot of conversation?

GALLIMARD   You still don't believe me, do you?

MARC   Sure I do. She was the most beautiful, et cetera, et cetera, blasé blasé.

[*Pause.*]

65 GALLIMARD   My life in the West has been such a disappointment.

MARC   Life in the West is like that. You'll get used to it. Look, you're driving me away. I'm leaving. Happy, now? [*He exits, then returns.*] Look, I have a date tomorrow night. You wanna come? I can fix you up with—

GALLIMARD   Of course. I would love to come.

    [*Pause.*]

70 MARC   Uh—on second thought, no. You'd better get ahold of yourself first.

    [*He exits;* GALLIMARD *nurses his drink.*]

GALLIMARD [*to us*]   This is the ultimate cruelty, isn't it? That I can talk and talk and to anyone listening, it's only air—too rich a diet to be swallowed by a mundane world. Why can't anyone understand? That in China, I once loved, and was loved by, very simply, the Perfect Woman.

    [SONG *enters, dressed as* BUTTERFLY *in wedding dress.*]

75 GALLIMARD [*to* SONG]   Not again. My imagination is hell. Am I asleep this time? Or did I drink too much?

SONG   Rene?

GALLIMARD   God, it's too painful! That you speak?

SONG   What are you talking about? Rene—touch me.

80 GALLIMARD   Why?

SONG   I'm real. Take my hand.

GALLIMARD   Why? So you can disappear again and leave me clutching at the air? For the entertainment of my neighbors who—?

    [SONG *touches* GALLIMARD.]

SONG   Rene?

    [GALLIMARD *takes* SONG's *hand. Silence.*]

85 GALLIMARD   Butterfly? I never doubted you'd return.

SONG   You hadn't . . . forgotten—?

GALLIMARD   Yes, actually, I've forgotten everything. My mind, you see—there wasn't enough room in this hard head—not for the world *and* for you. No, there was only room for one. [*Beat*] Come, look. See? Your bed has been

90 waiting, with the Klimt[5] poster you like, and—see? The xiang lu [incense burner] you gave me?

SONG   I . . . I don't know what to say.

GALLIMARD   There's nothing to say. Not at the end of a long trip. Can I make you some tea?

95 SONG   But where's your wife?

GALLIMARD   She's by my side. She's by my side at last.

    [GALLIMARD *reaches to embrace* SONG. SONG *sidesteps, dodging him.*]

GALLIMARD   Why?!

SONG [*to us*]   So I did return to Rene in Paris. Where I found—

GALLIMARD   Why do you run away? Can't we show them how we embraced

100 that evening?

SONG   Please. I'm talking.

GALLIMARD   You have to do what I say! I'm conjuring you up in *my* mind!

SONG   Rene, I've never done what you've said. Why should it be any different in your mind? Now split—the story moves on, and I must change.

105 GALLIMARD   I welcomed you into my home! I didn't have to, you know! I could've left you penniless on the streets of Paris! But I took you in!

SONG   Thank you.

GALLIMARD   So . . . please . . . don't change.

---

5. Gustav Klimt (1862–1918), an Austrian painter associated with exoticism and eroticism.

SONG   You know I have to. You know I will. And anyway, what difference does
110   it make? No matter what your eyes tell you, you can't ignore the truth. You
         already know too much.

[GALLIMARD *exits.* SONG *turns to us.*]

SONG   The change I'm going to make requires about five minutes. So I
         thought you might want to take this opportunity to stretch your legs, enjoy
         a drink, or listen to the musicians. I'll be here, when you return, right
115   where you left me.

[SONG *goes to a mirror in front of which is a wash basin of water. She starts*
to remove her makeup as stagelights go to half and houselights come up.]

3.1

A courthouse in Paris. 1986.

As he promised, SONG *has completed the bulk of his transformation, onstage by*
the time the houselights go down and the stagelights come up full. He removes his
wig and kimono, leaving them on the floor. Underneath, he wears a well-cut suit.

SONG   So I'd done my job better than I had a right to expect. Well, give him
         some credit, too. He's right—I was in a fix when I arrived in Paris. I walked
         from the airport into town, then I located, by blind groping, the Chinatown
         district. Let me make one thing clear: whatever else may be said about the
5   Chinese, they are stingy! I slept in doorways three days until I could find a
         tailor who would make me this kimono on credit. As it turns out, maybe I
         didn't even need it. Maybe he would've been happy to see me in a simple
         shift and mascara. But . . . better safe than sorry.
             That was 1970, when I arrived in Paris. For the next fifteen years, yes, I
10   lived a very comfy life. Some relief, believe me, after four years on a fuck-
         ing commune in Nowheresville, China. Rene supported the boy and me,
         and I did some demonstrations around the country as part of my "cultural
         exchange" cover. And then there was the spying.

[SONG *moves upstage, to a chair.* TOULON *enters as a judge, wearing the*
appropriate wig and robes. He sits near SONG. *It's 1986, and* SONG *is tes-*
tifying in a courtroom.]

SONG   Not much at first. Rene had lost all his high-level contacts. Comrade
15   Chin wasn't very interested in parking-ticket statistics. But finally, at my
         urging, Rene got a job as a courier, handling sensitive documents. He'd
         photograph them for me, and I'd pass them on to the Chinese embassy.
JUDGE Did he understand the extent of his activity?
SONG   He didn't ask. He knew that I needed those documents, and that was
20   enough.
JUDGE But he must've known he was passing classified information.
SONG   I can't say.
JUDGE He never asked what you were going to do with them?
SONG   Nope.

[*Pause.*]

25 JUDGE There is one thing that the court—indeed, that all of France—would
         like to know.
SONG   Fire away.
JUDGE Did Monsieur Gallimard know you were a man?

SONG   Well, he never saw me completely naked. Ever.

30   JUDGE   But surely, he must've . . . how can I put this?

SONG   Put it however you like. I'm not shy. He must've felt around?

JUDGE   Mmmmm.

SONG   Not really. I did all the work. He just laid back. Of course we did enjoy more . . . complete union, and I suppose he *might* have wondered why I was

35   always on my stomach, but. . . . But what you're thinking is: "Of course a wrist must've brushed . . . a hand hit . . . over twenty years!" Yeah. Well, Your Honor, it was my job to make him think I was a woman. And chew on this: it wasn't all that hard. See, my mother was a prostitute along the Bundt[6] before the Revolution. And, uh, I think it's fair to say she learned a

40   few things about Western men. So I borrowed her knowledge. In service to my country.

JUDGE   Would you care to enlighten the court with this secret knowledge? I'm sure we're all very curious.

SONG   I'm sure you are. [*Pause*] Okay, Rule One is: Men always believe what

45   they want to hear. So a girl can tell the most obnoxious lies and the guys will believe them every time—"This is my first time"—"That's the biggest I've ever seen"—or *both*, which, if you really think about it, is not possible in a single lifetime. You've maybe heard those phrases a few times in your own life, yes, Your Honor?

50   JUDGE   It's not my life, Monsieur Song, which is on trial today.

SONG   Okay, okay, just trying to lighten up the proceedings. Tough room.

JUDGE   Go on.

SONG   Rule Two: As soon as a Western man comes into contact with the East—he's already confused. The West has sort of an international rape

55   mentality towards the East. Do you know rape mentality?

JUDGE   Give us your definition, please.

SONG   Basically, "Her mouth says no, but her eyes say yes."

The West thinks of itself as masculine—big guns, big industry, big money—so the East is feminine—weak, delicate, poor . . . but good at art,

60   and full of inscrutable wisdom—the feminine mystique.

Her mouth says no, but her eyes say yes. The West believes the East, deep down, *wants* to be dominated—because a woman can't think for herself.

JUDGE   What does this have to do with my question?

SONG   You expect Oriental countries to submit to your guns, and you expect

65   Oriental women to be submissive to your men. That's why you say they make the best wives.

JUDGE   But why would that make it possible for you to fool Monsieur Galli-mard? Please—get to the point.

SONG   One, because when he finally met his fantasy woman, he wanted

70   more than anything to believe that she was, in fact, a woman. And second, I am an Oriental. And being an Oriental, I could never be completely a man.

[*Pause.*]

JUDGE   Your armchair political theory is tenuous, Monsieur Song.

6. That is, the Bund, a thoroughfare along the Huangpu River in the former Shanghai International Settlement; before the Revolution, it was lined with financial institutions, hotels, and clubs as well as wharves (*bund* is the name often given in the Far East to an embanked street along a river or sea).

SONG   You think so? That's why you'll lose in all your dealings with the East.
75 JUDGE   Just answer my question: did he know you were a man?

[*Pause.*]

SONG   You know, Your Honor, I never asked.

3.2

Same.

Music from the "Death Scene" from Butterfly blares over the house speakers. It is the loudest thing we've heard in this play.

GALLIMARD enters, crawling towards SONG's wig and kimono.

GALLIMARD   Butterfly? Butterfly?

[SONG *remains a man, in the witness box, delivering a testimony we do not hear.*]

GALLIMARD   [*to us*]   In my moment of greatest shame, here, in this courtroom—with that . . . person up there, telling the world. . . . What strikes me especially is how shallow he is, how glib and obsequious . . .
5   completely . . . without substance! The type that prowls around discos with a gold medallion, stinking of garlic. So little like my Butterfly.

    Yet even in this moment my mind remains agile, flip-flopping like a man on a trampoline. Even now, my picture dissolves, and I see that . . . witness . . . talking to me.

[SONG *suddenly stands straight up in his witness box, and looks at* GALLIMARD.]

10 SONG   Yes. You. White man.

[SONG *steps out of the witness box, and moves downstage towards* GALLIMARD. *Light change.*]

GALLIMARD   [*to* SONG]   Who? Me?
SONG   Do you see any other white men?
GALLIMARD   Yes. There're white men all around. This is a French courtroom.
SONG   So you are an adventurous imperialist. Tell me, why did it take you so
15   long? To come back to this place?
GALLIMARD   What place?
SONG   This theatre in China. Where we met many years ago.
GALLIMARD   [*to us*]   And once again, against my will, I am transported.

[*Chinese opera music comes up on the speakers.* SONG *begins to do opera moves, as he did the night they met.*]

SONG   Do you remember? The night you gave your heart?
20 GALLIMARD   It was a long time ago.
SONG   Not long enough. A night that turned your world upside down.
GALLIMARD   Perhaps.
SONG   Oh, be honest with me. What's another bit of flattery when you've already given me twenty years' worth? It's a wonder my head hasn't swollen
25   to the size of China.
GALLIMARD   Who's to say it hasn't?
SONG   Who's to say? And what's the shame? In pride? You think I could've pulled this off if I wasn't already full of pride when we met? No, not just pride. Arrogance. It takes arrogance, really—to believe you can will, with
30   your eyes and your lips, the destiny of another. [*He dances.*] C'mon. Admit it. You still want me. Even in slacks and a button-down collar.

GALLIMARD I don't see what the point of—

SONG You don't? Well maybe, Rene, just maybe—I want you.

GALLIMARD You do?

35 SONG Then again, maybe I'm just playing with you. How can you tell? [*Reprising his feminine character, he sidles up to* GALLIMARD.] "How I wish there were even a small cafe to sit in. With men in tuxedos, and cappuccinos, and bad expatriate jazz." Now you want to kiss me, don't you?

GALLIMARD [*pulling away*] What makes you—?

40 SONG —so sure? See? I take the words from your mouth. Then I wait for you to come and retrieve them. [*He reclines on the floor.*]

GALLIMARD Why?! Why do you treat me so cruelly?

SONG Perhaps I *was* treating you cruelly. But now—I'm being nice. Come here, my little one.

45 GALLIMARD I'm not your little one!

SONG My mistake. It's I who am *your* little one, right?

GALLIMARD Yes, I—

SONG So come get your little one. If you like. I may even let you strip me.

GALLIMARD I mean, you were! Before . . . but not like this!

50 SONG I was? Then perhaps I still am. If you look hard enough. [*He starts to remove his clothes.*]

GALLIMARD What—what are you doing?

SONG Helping you to see through my act.

GALLIMARD Stop that! I don't want to! I don't—

SONG Oh, but you asked me to strip, remember?

55 GALLIMARD What? That was years ago! And I took it back!

SONG No. You postponed it. Postponed the inevitable. Today, the inevitable has come calling.

[*From the speakers, cacophony:* BUTTERFLY *mixed in with Chinese gongs.*]

GALLIMARD No! Stop! I don't want to see!

SONG Then look away.

60 GALLIMARD You're only in my mind! All this is in my mind! I order you! To stop!

SONG To what? To strip? That's just what I'm—

GALLIMARD No! Stop! I want you—!

SONG You want me?

65 GALLIMARD To stop!

SONG You know something, Rene? Your mouth says no, but your eyes say yes. Turn them away. I dare you.

GALLIMARD I don't have to! Every night, you say you're going to strip, but then I beg you and you stop!

70 SONG I guess tonight is different.

GALLIMARD Why? Why should that be?

SONG Maybe I've become frustrated. Maybe I'm saying "Look at me, you fool!" Or maybe I'm just feeling . . . sexy. [*He is down to his briefs.*]

GALLIMARD Please. This is unnecessary. I know what you are.

75 SONG Do you? What am I?

GALLIMARD A—a man.

SONG You don't really believe that.

GALLIMARD Yes I do! I knew all the time somewhere that my happiness was temporary, my love a deception. But my mind kept the knowledge at bay. To

80 make the wait bearable.

SONG   Monsieur Gallimard—the wait is over.

[SONG *drops his briefs. He is naked. Sound cue out. Slowly, we and* SONG *come to the realization that what we had thought to be* GALLIMARD's *sobbing is actually his laughter.*]

GALLIMARD   Oh god! What an idiot! Of course!

SONG   Rene—what?

GALLIMARD   Look at you! You're a man! [*He bursts into laughter again.*]

85 SONG   I fail to see what's so funny!

GALLIMARD   "You fail to see—!" I mean, you never did have much of a sense of humor, did you? I just think it's ridiculously funny that I've wasted so much time on just a man!

SONG   Wait. I'm not "just a man."

90 GALLIMARD   No? Isn't that what you've been trying to convince me of?

SONG   Yes, but what I mean—

GALLIMARD   And now, I finally believe you, and you tell me it's not true? I think you must have some kind of identity problem.

SONG   Will you listen to me?

95 GALLIMARD   Why?! I've been listening to you for twenty years. Don't I deserve a vacation?

SONG   I'm not just any man!

GALLIMARD   Then, what exactly are you?

SONG   Rene, how can you ask—? Okay, what about this?

[*He picks up* BUTTERFLY's *robes, starts to dance around. No music.*]

100 GALLIMARD   Yes, that's very nice. I have to admit.

[SONG *holds out his arm to* GALLIMARD.]

SONG   It's the same skin you've worshiped for years. Touch it.

GALLIMARD   Yes, it does feel the same.

SONG   Now—close your eyes.

[SONG *covers* GALLIMARD's *eyes with one hand. With the other,* SONG *draws* GALLIMARD's *hand up to his face.* GALLIMARD, *like a blind man, lets his hands run over* SONG's *face.*]

GALLIMARD   This skin, I remember. The curve of her face, the softness of her
105 cheek, her hair against the back of my hand . . .

SONG   I'm your Butterfly. Under the robes, beneath everything, it was always me. Now, open your eyes and admit it—you adore me. [*He removes his hand from* GALLIMARD's *eyes.*]

GALLIMARD   You, who knew every inch of my desires—how could you, of all people, have made such a mistake?

110 SONG   What?

GALLIMARD   You showed me your true self. When all I loved was the lie. A perfect lie, which you let fall to the ground—and now, it's old and soiled.

SONG   So—you never really loved me? Only when I was playing a part?

GALLIMARD   I'm a man who loved a woman created by a man. Everything
115 else—simply falls short.

[*Pause.*]

SONG   What am I supposed to do now?

GALLIMARD   You were a fine spy, Monsieur Song, with an even finer accomplice. But now I believe you should go. Get out of my life!

SONG   Go where? Rene, you can't live without me. Not after twenty years.

120 GALLIMARD   I certainly can't live with you—not after twenty years of betrayal.

SONG   Don't be so stubborn! Where will you go?

GALLIMARD   I have a date . . . with my Butterfly.

SONG   So, throw away your pride. And come . . .

125 GALLIMARD   Get away from me! Tonight, I've finally learned to tell fantasy from reality. And, knowing the difference, I choose fantasy.

SONG   *I'm* your fantasy!

GALLIMARD   You? You're as real as hamburger. Now get out! I have a date with my Butterfly and I don't want your body polluting the room! [*He tosses* SONG's *suit at him.*] Look at these—you dress like a pimp.

130 SONG   Hey! These are Armani slacks[7] and—! [*He puts on his briefs and slacks.*] Let's just say . . . I'm disappointed in you, Rene. In the crush of your adoration, I thought you'd become something more. More like . . . a woman.

But no. Men. You're like the rest of them. It's all in the way we dress, and 135 make up our faces, and bat our eyelashes. You really have so little imagination!

GALLIMARD   You, Monsieur Song? Accuse me of too little imagination? You, if anyone, should know—I am pure imagination. And in imagination I will remain. Now get out!

[GALLIMARD *bodily removes* SONG *from the stage, taking his kimono.*]

140 SONG   Rene! I'll never put on those robes again! You'll be sorry!

GALLIMARD [*to* SONG]   I'm already sorry! [*Looking at the kimono in his hands*] Exactly as sorry . . . as a Butterfly.

3.3

M. GALLIMARD's *prison cell. Paris. Present.*

GALLIMARD   I've played out the events of my life night after night, always searching for a new ending to my story, one where I leave this cell and return forever to my Butterfly's arms.

Tonight I realize my search is over. That I've looked all along in the 5 wrong place. And now, to you, I will prove that my love was not in vain—by returning to the world of fantasy where I first met her.

[*He picks up the kimono; dancers enter.*]

GALLIMARD   There is a vision of the Orient that I have. Of slender women in chong sams and kimonos who die for the love of unworthy foreign devils. Who are born and raised to be the perfect women. Who take whatever 10 punishment we give them, and bounce back, strengthened by love, unconditionally. It is a vision that has become my life.

[*Dancers bring the wash basin to him and help him make up his face.*]

GALLIMARD   In public, I have continued to deny that Song Liling is a man. This brings me headlines, and is a source of great embarrassment to my French colleagues, who can now be sent into a coughing fit by the mere 15 mention of Chinese food. But alone, in my cell, I have long since faced the truth.

And the truth demands a sacrifice. For mistakes made over the course of a lifetime. My mistakes were simple and absolute—the man I loved was a

---

7. That is, expensive designer clothing. Giorgio Armani (b. 1934) is an Italian designer of relaxed but luxurious clothes for men and women.

cad, a bounder. He deserved nothing but a kick in the behind, and instead I gave him . . . all my love.

Yes—love. Why not admit it all? That was my undoing, wasn't it? Love warped my judgment, blinded my eyes, rearranged the very lines on my face . . . until I could look in the mirror and see nothing but . . . a woman.

[*Dancers help him put on the* BUTTERFLY *wig.*]

GALLIMARD   I have a vision. Of the Orient. That, deep within its almond eyes, there are still women. Women willing to sacrifice themselves for the love of a man. Even a man whose love is completely without worth.

[*Dancers assist* GALLIMARD *in donning the kimono. They hand him a knife.*]

GALLIMARD   Death with honor is better than life . . . life with dishonor. [*He sets himself center stage, in a seppuku*[8] *position.*] The love of a Butterfly can withstand many things—unfaithfulness, loss, even abandonment. But how can it face the one sin that implies all others? The devastating knowledge that, underneath it all, the object of her love was nothing more, nothing less than . . . a man. [*He sets the tip of the knife against his body.*] It is 19__. And I have found her at last. In a prison on the outskirts of Paris. My name is Rene Gallimard—also known as Madame Butterfly.

[GALLIMARD *turns upstage and plunges the knife into his body, as music from the "Love Duet" blares over the speakers. He collapses into the arms of the dancers, who lay him reverently on the floor. The image holds for several beats. Then a tight special up on* SONG, *who stands as a man, staring at the dead* GALLIMARD. *He smokes a cigarette; the smoke filters up through the lights. Two words leave his lips.*]

SONG   Butterfly? Butterfly?

[*Smoke rises as lights fade slowly to black.*]

8. Ritual suicide by disembowelment (Japanese); synonymous with hara-kiri.

TONY KUSHNER

b. 1956

WHEN MILLENNIUM APPROACHES, Part One of ANGELS IN AMERICA, opened on Broadway in 1993, Tony Kushner was hailed as the savior of serious American theater. Since the 1970s skyrocketing production costs had made it all but impossible for an ambitious nonmusical drama to survive on Broadway. Not only did Kushner defy those odds, he did so with a work of enormous scope and ambition. *Angels in America* is a two-part epic drama exploring personal identity, sexual orientation, political responsibility, AIDS, Mormonism, Judaism, and Reagan-era conservatism within an eclectic dramaturgy that mixes realism, surrealism, and the spectacular. *Millennium Approaches* received numerous awards, including the Tony Award for Best Play and the Pulitzer Prize for Drama; not surprisingly, its sequel, *Perestroika*, was similarly acclaimed. Critics compared the play to such landmark works as TENNESSEE WILLIAMS's *A Streetcar Named Desire* (1947) and ARTHUR MILLER's *Death of a Salesman* (1949). In the ensuing years, additional North American and European productions of *Angels in America* have established Kushner's reputation as the preeminent American dramatist of his generation.

The success of *Angels* also made Kushner one of the most widely known gay artists and activists of the 1990s and early 2000s. Born in 1956 in New York City to parents who were classical musicians and raised in Lake Charles, Louisiana, Kushner became aware of his homosexuality by the age of ten. Because of the social stigma attached to being gay, he felt unable to acknowledge his sexual orientation openly, even to his politically liberal parents. Like Joe in *Angels,* Kushner came out to his mother in a telephone call—made from a pay phone on the morning of his first graduate class at New York University (where he completed a master of fine arts in directing in 1984). Kushner's mentor at NYU was Carl Weber, a highly reputed scholar, director, and former assistant of BERTOLT BRECHT's at the Berliner Ensemble. After graduation Kushner worked as a director at the Repertory Theatre of St. Louis and the New York Theatre Workshop. His first major play, *A Bright Room Called Day*, premiered in San Francisco in 1987 and was produced by the New York Shakespeare Festival in 1991. In 1990 Kushner received a commission to develop *Angels in America* for the Eureka Theatre in San Francisco, where *Millennium Approaches* premiered in 1991. The play subsequently moved to the Mark Taper Forum in Los Angeles, where it was performed with *Perestroika* in 1992. Both plays were produced in London at the National Theater in 1992; in New York,

Millennium Approaches opened in 1993 and *Perestroika* in 1994. In the years following the success of *Angels in America* Kushner wrote a number of adaptations and plays, including *Slavs! Thinking About the Longstanding Problems of Virtue and Happiness* (1994), which features scenes that the playwright had originally intended for *Angels; Henry Box Brown, or The Mirror of Slavery* (1998), the story of an American slave who mailed himself to freedom in 1848; and the musical *Caroline, or Change* (2002). Kushner's 2001 play *Homebody/Kabul* is set in Afghanistan in 1998, during the rule of the oppressive Taliban government. *Angels in America* was made into a highly acclaimed film for television in 2003. His translation of Bertolt Brecht's *Mother Courage and Her Children* premiered in 2006, and his play *The Intelligent Homosexual's Guide to Capitalism and Socialism with a Key to the Scriptures* opened at the Guthrie Theater in Minneapolis in 2009.

Labeled by Kushner "a gay fantasia on national themes," *Angels* joined a number of other plays that deal with the experience of gay men in contemporary America. Although issues of homosexuality pervade the drama of Williams and Edward Albee, the emergence of openly gay drama can be dated to 1968 and the off-Broadway production of Mart Crowley's *The Boys in the Band*. Crowley's play gave the mainstream theater its first view inside "the closet" of gay life: in this case, a Manhattan birthday party at which a group of gay men descend into alcohol-fueled self-loathing. The writing and production of gay plays accelerated in the wake of two events: the Stonewall Riots of June 1969 and the onset of the AIDS crisis in the early 1980s. In the 1960s the police in New York often raided bars frequented by homosexuals—who were arrested for being "disorderly"—but late on June 26, 1969, gay and lesbian patrons of Greenwich Village's Stonewall Inn resisted arrest, spawning a riot; violent protests followed for several more nights. This uprising was instrumental in sparking a new phase of the gay rights movement; its emergence was accompanied by plays that depicted the personal and sexual struggles of gay male characters. Key works of the time include Martin Sherman's *Passing By* (1974) and *Bent* (1979),

Lanford Wilson's *Fifth of July* (1978), Robert Patrick's *T-Shirts* (1978), and Harvey Fierstein's *Torch Song Trilogy* (1981).

In the 1980s "AIDS plays" expanded on the conventions of earlier gay drama to explore the impact on individuals, relationships, and families of a new and devastating epidemic. Works such as Larry Kramer's *The Normal Heart* (1985) and William Hoffman's *As Is* (1985) were aggressive in expressing their anger at the relative lack of concern displayed by the Reagan administration and by Americans generally. Even more forcefully than the plays of the 1970s, AIDS plays challenged heterosexual audiences to empathize with gay characters as individuals entitled to equal rights and opportunities within society.

Despite their dramatic power, none of these plays received the attention won by *Angels in America*. The particular acclaim that greeted Kushner's play resulted, in part, from the way in which its characters, themes, and issues address the question of American national identity. This focus on Americanness invites comparison between *Angels* and Miller's *Death of a Salesman*. Produced just four years after the end of World War II, *Salesman* exposed the false myths of the "American Dream" and the vulnerability of the self-made man whose success in business and access to the good life rest on his personal charm. Produced near the end of the twentieth century, *Angels in America* likewise reveals a fundamental social betrayal—in this case, of America's founding ideals of freedom and equality. Miller's play is grounded in the history of European immigration to the United States and in the Great Depression; Kushner's is tied to the legacy of the civil rights movement in the 1960s, the rise of the gay rights movement, and the conservative backlash against both in the 1980s and early 1990s.

Yet whereas *Salesman* critiques American society through the lens of liberal humanism, *Angels* explores how those in power legislate and enforce normative assumptions about sex and sexuality, gender, race, and class. In its affirmation of social pluralism, the play embraces a decidedly postmodern understanding of identity and history. Narratives, myths,

and themes that have traditionally constituted "America"—the Founding Fathers,
manifest destiny, "the melting pot," the
American family—no longer fit the changing demographics and experiences of contemporary life as Kushner dramatizes
them. In one of the opening scenes of *Millennium Approaches*, Harper Pitt—one
of the play's visionaries—speaks of "beautiful systems dying, old fixed orders spiraling apart." Characters in *Angels in
America* must rethink their identities and
that of their nation within new relationships and psychological frameworks, rein-
terpreting the myths of America in light
of more pluralistic social realities. On the
eve of the third millennium, Kushner
suggests, the question of what it means to
be an American must be answered in
ways that are at once collective and deeply
individual.

The political and social breadth of
Angels in America is matched by its stylistic
expansiveness. Whereas *Death of a Salesman* helped define the tradition of American poetic realism, innovatively combining
naturalistic and expressionistic elements,
Angels employs an extraordinary collage of
theatrical styles—from realism to surrealism, tragedy to farce, Brechtian political
theater to the gay performance traditions
of camp and drag. Ranging from the
broadly political to the intensely personal
and spiritual, the play balances intimately
crafted scenes with an overarching epic
structure, blending psychological realism
together with nonrealistic dream scenes
and heightened theatrical spectacle. While
interweaving these styles and structures,
the play also intercuts story lines cinemati-
cally, thereby encouraging the audience to
see the life of each character in relation to
society and to understand that such supposedly "personal" matters as sex and love
are inherently political. Coining the label
"Theatre of the Fabulous" for this stylistic
collage, Kushner has stressed the theatrical nature of the play's scenes and effects.
In his "playwright's notes," he comments,
"The moments of magic . . . are to be fully
realized, as bits of wonderful *theatrical*
illusion—which means it's OK if the wires
show, and maybe it's good that they do, but
the magic should at the same time be thoroughly amazing."

Even as *Angels in America* has one foot
in the miraculous, its other is firmly
planted in the actual. Kushner's play is set
in the mid-1980s during the Reagan presidency, and its cast includes characters
drawn from modern American history.
Most important among these is Roy Cohn,
who served as chief counsel to Senator
Joseph McCarthy during the Senate's anticommunist investigations of the 1950s and
who, earlier, as an assistant U.S. attorney
in New York, played a key role in the most
sensational and controversial case of the
decade's Red Scare: the prosecution of
Julius and Ethel Rosenberg, a Jewish couple accused of helping to pass secrets of
American nuclear research to the Soviet
Union. They were convicted in 1951 and
executed in 1953. Though Cohn's investi-
gative methods were ultimately exposed
as unethical, and perhaps illegal, he went
on to become a powerful attorney in Washington, D.C., and New York, giving behind-
the-scenes advice to FBI Chief J. Edgar
Hoover as well as to judges, mayors, and
presidents. Throughout his career he repu-
diated his familial and cultural roots, striving to become the reverse of what he was:
the son of a Jewish, liberal, Democratic
New York state supreme court judge. Cohn
died from AIDS in 1986 but sought, to the
very end, to hide his homosexuality, insisting that his ailment was "liver cancer."

Kushner juxtaposes Cohn's life with the
lives of two fictional couples, one homosexual and the other heterosexual, who
represent ordinary, young middle-class
Americans living in New York in the mid-
1980s. The homosexual couple are Louis,
who works as a word processor in an office
located in Roy's building, and Prior, a drag
queen who has recently learned he is HIV-
positive. When Prior develops full-blown
AIDS, Louis's commitment to him and to
their relationship shrinks as he confronts
his fears of death and emotional pain. The
heterosexual couple are Joe and Harper,
Mormons who have moved from Utah to
New York City to further Joe's legal career;
Joe has become Roy's protégé, the object
of his professional mentoring and almost
paternal love. Joe and Harper's marriage
is brought to a crisis by Roy's offer to place
Joe in a job in Washington, D.C.—a position that will enable him to block Roy's

threatened disbarment—and by Joe's homosexuality, with which he has struggled all his life and which he must eventually acknowledge to himself and his wife. As the play unfolds, shifting focus from one story to another, the choices and actions of these characters shed light on each other. The audience sees Prior's experience of AIDS against Roy's denial of the disease, Joe's personal and professional integrity against Roy's dishonesty, Louis's abandonment of his partner against Joe's rejection of Harper, and Joe's emerging awareness of

his homosexuality against Roy's repression of his own. By thus placing characters side by side, Kushner reveals their social interconnectedness and makes them symbolic of contradictions at the heart of the United States as a nation.

Joe's and Harper's Mormonism serves as one of a number of intellectual and spiritual backdrops to *Angels in America*. The one Christian religion indigenous to the United States, the Church of Jesus Christ of Latter-day Saints was founded in response to what its adherents view as a

The 2003 miniseries of *Angels in America*, produced by HBO and directed by Mike Nichols, managed to translate the play's theatricality onto the small screen.

revelation that revised established Christian belief; it developed fully only after its first members journeyed to the edges of the frontier in search of the Promised Land. The metaphor of building on a past, of migrating, of crossing personal and ideological boundaries on the way to some anticipated rebirth or revelation recurs throughout *Angels:* in the opening monologue on Jewish emigration to the United States, in Joe's awakening to his sexuality, in Louis's movement away from Prior and toward Joe, and in Harper's and Prior's visions. Indeed, Kushner makes the stage itself a frontier, filling it with diverse styles that he synthesizes into a vision of social theater. As it moves between realism and nonrealism, between epic theater and spectacle, the play explores the limits of theatrical representation; at the outer reaches of those limits are the play's split scenes and dream scenes, which address social and spiritual dissolution and redemption.

Written as the cold war ended and in the waning years of the twentieth century, *Millennium Approaches* is charged with millenarian apprehension toward an unknown future. Apocalyptic foreboding occurs throughout the play, from Harper's fears about the vanishing ozone layer to terror at the pestilential specter of AIDS. *Perestroika,* the concluding part of *Angels in America,* lightens this tone somewhat, as it affirms life, community, and the possibility of personal, social, and spiritual progress. Like Kushner himself, who found himself anointed as a theatrical prophet while he moved steadily on with his writing and his activism, the play's characters seek ways to confront the world's problems while cultivating a vision of humanity's underlying grace. But though the two-part drama moves in the direction of healing, the most memorable moment in Kushner's theatrical epic is the spectacular conclusion of *Millennium Approaches.* Terrifying, beautiful, yet ambiguous, this final scene reflects the longings and fears, the restless spirituality, and the sense of the unknown that mark the turn of the millennium. To learn more about the staging of *Angels in America* and to view photographs from select performances of the play, see the "Plays in Performance" color insert near the center of this volume.   ART BORRECA

Angels in America
A Gay Fantasia on National Themes

PART ONE:

MILLENNIUM APPROACHES

CHARACTERS

ROY M. COHN,[1] a successful New York lawyer and unofficial power broker.
JOSEPH PORTER PITT, chief clerk for Justice Theodore Wilson of the Federal Court of Appeals, Second Circuit.
HARPER AMATY PITT, Joe's wife, an agoraphobic with a mild Valium[2] addiction.

1. A Jewish, New York–born lawyer (1927–1986) who attracted public attention and controversy throughout his career, most notoriously as chief counsel (1953–54) to the Permanent Subcommittee on Investigations, which, under the chairmanship of Senator Joseph McCarthy, hunted for Communists in the government and U.S. Army.
2. Diazepam (trademark), a tranquilizer that in the 1980s was the most frequently prescribed drug in the United States.

LOUIS IRONSON, a word processor working for the Second Circuit Court of Appeals.

PRIOR WALTER, Louis's boyfriend. Occasionally works as a club designer or caterer, otherwise lives very modestly but with great style off a small trust fund.

HANNAH PORTER PITT, Joe's mother, currently residing in Salt Lake City, living off her deceased husband's army pension.

BELIZE, a former drag queen and former lover of Prior's. A registered nurse. Belize's name was originally Norman Arriaga; Belize is a drag name that stuck.

THE ANGEL, four divine emanations, Fluor, Phosphor, Lumen, and Candle;[3] manifest in One: the Continental Principality of America. She has magnificent steel-gray wings.

Other Characters in Part One

RABBI ISIDOR CHEMELWITZ, an orthodox Jewish rabbi, played by the actor playing HANNAH.

MR. LIES, Harper's imaginary friend, a travel agent, who in style of dress and speech suggests a jazz musician; he always wears a large lapel badge emblazoned "IOTA" (The International Order of Travel Agents). He is played by the actor playing BELIZE.

THE MAN IN THE PARK, played by the actor playing PRIOR.

THE VOICE, the voice of THE ANGEL.

HENRY, ROY's doctor, played by the actor playing HANNAH.

EMILY, a nurse, played by the actor playing THE ANGEL.

MARTIN HELLER, a Reagan Administration Justice Department flackman, played by the actor playing HARPER.

SISTER ELLA CHAPTER, a Salt Lake City real estate saleswoman, played by the actor playing THE ANGEL.

PRIOR 1, the ghost of a dead Prior Walter from the 13th century, played by the actor playing JOE. He is a blunt, gloomy medieval farmer with a guttural Yorkshire accent.

PRIOR 2, the ghost of a dead Prior Walter from the 17th century, played by the actor playing ROY. He is a Londoner, sophisticated, with a High British accent.

THE ESKIMO, played by the actor playing JOE.

THE WOMAN IN THE SOUTH BRONX, played by the actor playing THE ANGEL.

ETHEL ROSENBERG,[4] played by the actor playing HANNAH.

Playwright's Notes

A DISCLAIMER: Roy M. Cohn, the character, is based on the late Roy M. Cohn (1927–1986), who was all too real; for the most part the acts attributed to the character Roy, such as his illegal conferences with Judge Kaufman during the trial of Ethel Rosenberg, are to be found in the historical record. But this Roy is a work of dramatic fiction; his words are my invention, and liberties have been taken.

3. All terms having to do with light: *fluor,* or fluorite, is a mineral whose crystals can exhibit luminescence; *phosphor,* or phosphorus, also emits light; and *lumen* (literally, "light" in Latin) and *candle* are both measures of light (of its intensity and flux, respectively).

4. A Jewish, New York–born Communist (1915–1953); along with her husband, Julius, she was tried and executed for conspiring to give the Soviet Union information about the atomic bomb. As an assistant in the U.S. Attorney's office in New York, Roy Cohn played a prominent role in her 1951 trial.

A NOTE ABOUT THE STAGING: The play benefits from a pared-down style of presentation, with minimal scenery and scene shifts done rapidly (no blackouts!), employing the cast as well as stagehands—which makes for an actor-driven event, as this must be. The moments of magic—the appearance and disappearance of Mr. Lies and the ghosts, the Book hallucination, and the ending—are to be fully realized, as bits of wonderful *theatrical illusion*—which means it's OK if the wires show, and maybe it's good that they do, but the magic should at the same time be thoroughly amazing.

> In a murderous time
> the heart breaks and breaks
> and lives by breaking.
> —Stanley Kunitz[5]
> "The Testing-Tree"

Act 1: Bad News

[October–November 1985]

Scene 1

[*The last days of October.* RABBI ISIDOR CHEMELWITZ *alone onstage with a small coffin. It is a rough pine box with two wooden pegs, one at the foot and one at the head, holding the lid in place. A prayer shawl embroidered with a Star of David is draped over the lid, and by the head a yarzheit[6] candle is burning.*]

RABBI ISIDOR CHEMELWITZ [*he speaks sonorously, with a heavy Eastern European accent, unapologetically consulting a sheet of notes for the family names*] Hello and good morning. I am Rabbi Isidor Chemelwitz of the Bronx Home for Aged Hebrews. We are here this morning to pay respects at the passing of Sarah Ironson, devoted wife of Benjamin Ironson, also deceased, loving and caring mother of her sons Morris, Abraham, and Samuel, and her
5   daughters Esther and Rachel; beloved grandmother of Max, Mark, Louis, Lisa, Maria . . . uh . . . Lesley, Angela, Doris, Luke, and Eric. [*Looks more closely at paper.*] Eric? This is a Jewish name? [*Shrugs.*] Eric. A large and loving family. We assemble that we may mourn collectively this good and righteous woman. [*He looks at the coffin.*]
10   This woman. I did not know this woman. I cannot accurately describe her attributes, nor do justice to her dimensions. She was . . . Well, in the Bronx Home of Aged Hebrews are many like this, the old, and to many I speak but not to be frank with this one. She preferred silence. So I do not know her and yet I know her. She was . . . [*He touches the coffin.*] . . . not a
15   person but a whole kind of person, the ones who crossed the ocean, who brought with us to America the villages of Russia and Lithuania—and how we struggled, and how we fought, for the family, for the Jewish home, so that you would not grow up *here*, in this strange place, in the melting pot where nothing melted. Descendants of this immigrant woman, you do not

---

5. An American poet (1905–2006); "The Testing-Tree" is the title poem of a collection published in 1971.
6. Anniversary (Yiddish); on the anniversary of a relative's death, observant Jews light a memorial candle at home and in their synagogue.

20 grow up in America, you and your children and their children with the
goyische[7] names. You do not live in America. No such place exists. Your
clay is the clay of some Litvak shtetl,[8] your air the air of the steppes—
because she carried the old world on her back across the ocean, in a boat,
and she put it down on Grand Concourse Avenue, or in Flatbush,[9] and she
25 worked that earth into your bones, and you pass it to your children, this
ancient, ancient culture and home. [*Little pause*]

You can never make that crossing that she made, for such Great Voyages
in this world do not anymore exist. But every day of your lives the miles
that voyage between that place and this one you cross. Every day. You
30 understand me? In you that journey is.

So . . .

She was the last of the Mohicans,[1] this one was. Pretty soon . . . all the
old will be dead.

Scene 2

[*Same day.* ROY *and* JOE *in* ROY's *office.* ROY *at an impressive desk, bare
except for a very elaborate phone system, rows and rows of flashing buttons which bleep and beep and whistle incessantly, making chaotic music
underneath* ROY's *conversations.* JOE *is sitting, waiting.* ROY *conducts
business with great energy, impatience, and sensual abandon: gesticulat-
ing, shouting, cajoling, crooning, playing the phone, receiver and hold
button, with virtuosity and love.*]

ROY [*hitting a button*]   Hold. [*To* JOE] I wish I was an octopus, a fucking octopus. Eight loving arms and all those suckers. Know what I mean?

JOE   No, I . . .

ROY [*gesturing to a deli platter of little sandwiches on his desk*]   You want
lunch?

5 JOE   No, that's OK really I just . . .

ROY [*hitting a button*]   Ailene? Roy Cohn. Now what kind of a greeting
is. . . . I thought we were friends, Ai . . . Look Mrs. Soffer you don't have to
get . . . You're upset. You're yelling. You'll aggravate your condition, you
shouldn't yell, you'll pop little blood vessels in your face if you yell. . . . No
10 that was a joke, Mrs. Soffer, I was joking. . . . I already apologized sixteen
times for that, Mrs. Soffer, you . . . [*While she's fulminating,* ROY *covers the
mouthpiece with his hand and talks to* JOE.] This'll take a minute, *eat* already,
what is this tasty sandwich here it's— [*He takes a bite of a sandwich.*]
Mmmmm, liver or some . . . Here.

[*He pitches the sandwich to* JOE, *who catches it and returns it to the
platter.*]

15 ROY [*back to Mrs. Soffer*]   Uh huh, uh huh. . . . No, I already told you, it
wasn't a vacation, it was business, Mrs. Soffer, I have clients in Haiti, Mrs.
Soffer, I . . . Listen, Ailene, YOU THINK I'M THE ONLY GODDAM
LAWYER IN HISTORY EVER MISSED A COURT DATE? Don't make
such a big fucking . . . Hold. [*He hits the hold button.*] You HAG!

---

7. Non-Jewish, Gentile (Yiddish; sometimes
pejorative).
8. Lithuanian village (Yiddish).
9. Two middle-class areas of New York City to
which Jews moved in large numbers in the

1920s and '30s (in the Bronx and in Brooklyn, respectively).
1. That is, the last of her kind—an allusion to
James Fenimore Cooper's novel *The Last of
the Mohicans* (1826).

20 JOE   If this is a bad time . . .

ROY   *Bad* time? This is a *good* time! [*Button*] Baby doll, get me . . . Oh fuck,
wait . . . [*Button, button*] Hello? Yah. Sorry to keep you holding, Judge
Hollins, I . . . Oh Mrs. Hollins, sorry dear deep voice you got. Enjoying
your visit? [*Hand over mouthpiece again, to* JOE] She sounds like a truck-
25   driver and he sounds like Kate Smith,[2] very confusing. Nixon[3] appointed
him, all the geeks are Nixon appointees . . . [*To Mrs. Hollins*] Yeah yeah
right good so how many tickets dear? Seven. For what, *Cats, 42nd Street*,
what? No you wouldn't like *La Cage*,[4] trust me, I know. Oh for godsake . . .
Hold. [*Button, button*] Baby doll, seven for *Cats* or something, anything
30   hard to get, I don't give a fuck what and neither will they. [*Button; to* JOE]
You see *La Cage*?

JOE   No, I . . . .

ROY   Fabulous. Best thing on Broadway. Maybe ever. [*Button*] Who? Aw,
Jesus H. Christ, Harry, *no*, Harry, Judge John Francis Grimes, Manhattan
35   Family Court. Do I have to do every goddam thing myself? *Touch* the bastard, Harry, and don't call me on this line again, I told you not to . . .

JOE [*starting to get up*]   Roy, uh, should I wait outside or . . .

ROY [*to* JOE]   Oh sit. [*To Harry*] You hold. I pay you to hold fuck you Harry
you jerk. [*Button*] Half-wit dick-brain. [*Instantly philosophical*] I see the
40   universe, Joe, as a kind of sandstorm in outer space with winds of mega-
hurricane velocity, but instead of grains of sand it's shards and splinters of
glass. You ever feel that way? Ever have one of those days?

JOE   I'm not sure I . . .

ROY   So how's life in Appeals?[5] How's the Judge?

45 JOE   He sends his best.

ROY   He's a good man. Loyal. Not the brightest man on the bench, but he
has manners. And a nice head of silver hair.

JOE   He gives me a lot of responsibility.

ROY   Yeah, like writing his decisions and signing his name.

50 JOE   Well . . .

ROY   He's a nice guy. And you cover admirably.

JOE   Well, thanks, Roy, I . . .

ROY [*button*]   Yah? Who is *this*? Well who the fuck are *you*? Hold— [*Button*]
Harry? Eighty-seven grand, something like that. Fuck him. Eat me. New
55   Jersey, chain of porno film stores in, uh, Weehawken.[6] That's—Harry, that's
the beauty of the law. [*Button*] So, baby doll, what? *Cats*? Bleah. [*Button*]

---

2. A popular American singer (1907–1986),
best known for her rendition of Irving Berlin's "God Bless America" (1918); her career
peaked in the 1940s, but her robust voice
made her a star of radio and television from
the 1930s to the 1960s.
3. Richard M. Nixon (1913–1994), thirty-
seventh president of the United States (1969–
74); Nixon rose to national prominence in the
1940s as an ardently anticommunist Republican congressman on the House Committee
on Un-American Activities.
4. Long-running musicals on Broadway in the
1980s: *Cats* (1982–2000; lyrics by T. S. Eliot

and Trevor Nunn, music by Andrew Lloyd
Webber); *42nd Street* (1980–89; book by
Mark Bramble and Michael Stewart, lyrics by
Al Dubin, music by Harry Warren); and *La
Cage aux Folles* (1983–87; book by Harvey
Fierstein, lyrics and music by Jerry Herman),
which presents the interactions between a
gay couple (the manager and the star of a
drag nightclub), the manager's son, and the
conservative parents of the son's fiancée.
5. The U.S. Court of Appeals, where Joe is a
lawyer holding a senior administrative position.
6. A town directly across the Hudson River
from New York City.

Cats! It's about cats. Singing cats, you'll love it. Eight o'clock, the theatre's always at eight. [*Button*] Fucking tourists. [*Button, then to* JOE] Oh live a little, Joe, *eat* something for Christ sake—

60 JOE Um, Roy, could you . . .

ROY What? [*To Harry*] Hold a minute. [*Button*] Mrs. Soffer? Mrs. . . . [*Button*] God-fucking-dammit to hell, where is . . .

JOE [*overlapping*] Roy, I'd really appreciate it if . . .

ROY [*overlapping*] Well she was here a minute ago, baby doll, see if . . .

[*The phone starts making three different beeping sounds, all at once.*]

65 ROY [*smashing buttons*] Jesus fuck this goddam thing . . .

JOE [*overlapping*] I really wish you wouldn't . . .

ROY [*overlapping*] Baby doll? Ring the *Post*[7] get me Suzy see if . . .

[*The phone starts whistling loudly.*]

ROY CHRIST!

JOE Roy.

70 ROY [*into receiver*] Hold. [*Button; to* JOE] What?

JOE Could you please not take the Lord's name in vain? [*Pause*] I'm sorry. But please. At least while I'm . . .

ROY [*laughs, then*] Right. Sorry. Fuck.

Only in America. [*Punches a button.*] Baby doll, tell 'em all to fuck off.

75 Tell 'em I died. You handle Mrs. Soffer. Tell her it's on the way. Tell her I'm schtupping[8] the judge. I'll call her back. I *will* call her. I *know* how much I borrowed. She's got four hundred times that stuffed up her . . . Yeah, tell her I said that. [*Button. The phone is silent.*]

So, Joe.

80 JOE I'm sorry Roy, I just . . .

ROY No no no no, principles count, I respect principles, I'm not religious but I like God and God likes me. Baptist, Catholic?

JOE Mormon.

ROY Mormon. Delectable. Absolutely. Only in America. So, Joe. Whattya

85 think?

JOE It's . . . well . . .

ROY Crazy life.

JOE Chaotic.

ROY Well but God bless chaos. Right?

90 JOE Ummm . . .

ROY Huh. Mormons. I knew Mormons, in, um, Nevada.

JOE Utah, mostly.

ROY No, these Mormons were in Vegas.

So. So, how'd you like to go to Washington and work for the Justice

95 Department?

JOE Sorry?

ROY How'd you like to go to Washington and work for the Justice Department? All I gotta do is pick up the phone, talk to Ed, and you're in.

JOE In . . . what, exactly?

---

7. The *New York Post*, which by the 1980s had become a conservative tabloid.

8. Aggressively pushing, ingratiating himself with; fucking (from Yiddish).

100 ROY Associate Assistant Something Big. Internal Affairs, heart of the woods, something nice with clout.

JOE Ed . . . ?

ROY Meese.[9] The Attorney General.

JOE Oh.

105 ROY I just have to pick up the phone . . .

JOE I have to think.

ROY Of course. [*Pause*]
It's a great time to be in Washington, Joe.

JOE Roy, it's incredibly exciting . . .

110 ROY And it would mean something to me. You understand?

[*Little pause.*]

JOE I . . . can't say how much I appreciate this Roy, I'm sort of . . . well, stunned, I mean . . . Thanks, Roy. But I have to give it some thought. I have to ask my wife.

ROY Your wife. Of course.

115 JOE But I really appreciate . . .

ROY Of course. Talk to your wife.

Scene 3

[*Later that day.* HARPER *at home, alone. She is listening to the radio and talking to herself, as she often does. She speaks to the audience.*]

HARPER People who are lonely, people left alone, sit talking nonsense to the air, imagining . . . beautiful systems dying, old fixed orders spiraling apart . . .
   When you look at the ozone layer, from outside, from a spaceship, it looks like a pale blue halo, a gentle, shimmering aureole encircling the atmosphere encircling the earth. Thirty miles above our heads, a thin layer of three-atom oxygen molecules, product of photosynthesis, which explains the fussy vegetable preference for visible light, its rejection of darker rays and emanations. Danger from without. It's a kind of gift, from God, the crowning touch to the creation of the world: guardian angels, hands linked, make a spherical net, a blue-green nesting orb, a shell of safety for life itself. But everywhere, things are collapsing, lies surfacing, systems of defense giving way.[1] . . . This is why, Joe, this is why I shouldn't be left alone. [*Little pause*]
   I'd like to go traveling. Leave you behind to worry. I'll send postcards with strange stamps and tantalizing messages on the back. "Later maybe."
15 "Nevermore . . ."

[MR. LIES, *a travel agent, appears.*]

HARPER Oh! You startled me!

MR. LIES Cash, check, or credit card?

HARPER I remember you. You're from Salt Lake. You sold us the plane tickets when we flew here. What are you doing in Brooklyn?

9. Edwin Meese III (b. 1931), who served as attorney general (1985–88) under President Ronald Reagan (1911–2004; 40th president, 1981–89).

1. Beginning in the 1970s, scientists began to warn that industrial pollutants such as chlorofluorocarbons (CFCs) might concentrate in the stratosphere and deplete the ozone there, which affords protection against harmful high-energy radiation. The first "ozone hole"—a seasonal depletion—was discovered above Antarctica in 1985, and subsequent research confirmed the widespread loss of ozone.

20 MR. LIES   You said you wanted to travel . . .

HARPER   And here you are. How thoughtful.

MR. LIES   Mr. Lies. Of the International Order of Travel Agents. We mobilize the globe, we set people adrift, we stir the populace and send nomads eddying across the planet. We are adepts of motion, acolytes of the flux.
25   Cash, check, or credit card. Name your destination.

HARPER   Antarctica, maybe. I want to see the hole in the ozone. I heard on the radio . . .

MR. LIES [*he has a computer terminal in his briefcase*]   I can arrange a guided tour. Now?

30 HARPER   Soon. Maybe soon. I'm not safe here you see. Things aren't right with me. Weird stuff happens . . .

MR. LIES   Like?

HARPER   Well, like you, for instance. Just appearing. Or last week . . . well never mind.
35   People are like planets, you need a thick skin. Things get to me, Joe stays away and now. . . . Well look. My dreams are talking back to me.

MR. LIES   It's the price of rootlessness. Motion sickness. The only cure: to keep moving.

HARPER   I'm undecided. I feel . . . that something's going to give. It's 1985.
40   Fifteen years till the third millennium. Maybe Christ will come again. Maybe seeds will be planted, maybe there'll be harvests then, maybe early figs to eat, maybe new life, maybe fresh blood, maybe companionship and love and protection, safety from what's outside, maybe the door will hold, or maybe . . . maybe the troubles[2] will come, and the end will come, and the
45   sky will collapse and there will be terrible rains and showers of poison light, or maybe my life is really fine, maybe Joe loves me and I'm only crazy thinking otherwise, or maybe not, maybe it's even worse than I know, maybe . . . I want to know, maybe I don't. The suspense, Mr. Lies, it's killing me.

MR. LIES   I suggest a vacation.

50 HARPER [*hearing something*]   That was the elevator. Oh God, I should fix myself up, I . . . You have to go, you shouldn't be here . . . you aren't even real.

MR. LIES   Call me when you decide . . .

HARPER   Go!

[*The travel agent vanishes as* JOE *enters.*]

JOE   Buddy?
55   Buddy? Sorry I'm late. I was just . . . out. Walking. Are you mad?

HARPER   I got a little anxious.

JOE   Buddy kiss.

[*They kiss.*]

JOE   Nothing to get anxious about.
   So. So how'd you like to move to Washington?

---

2. That is, the apocalyptic "end times" foretold in the New Testament's book of Revelation.

Scene 4

[*Same day.* LOUIS *and* PRIOR *outside the funeral home, sitting on a bench, both dressed in funereal finery, talking. The funeral service for Sarah Ironson has just concluded and* LOUIS *is about to leave for the cemetery.*]

LOUIS My grandmother actually saw Emma Goldman[3] speak. In Yiddish. But all Grandma could remember was that she spoke well and wore a hat. What a weird service. That rabbi . . .

PRIOR A definite find. Get his number when you go to the graveyard. I want
5   him to bury me.

LOUIS Better head out there. Everyone gets to put dirt on the coffin once it's lowered in.

PRIOR Oooh. Cemetery fun. Don't want to miss that.

LOUIS It's an old Jewish custom to express love. Here, Grandma, have a
10   shovelful. Latecomers run the risk of finding the grave completely filled.
     She was pretty crazy. She was up there in that home for ten years, talking to herself. I never visited. She looked too much like my mother.

PRIOR [*hugs him*] Poor Louis. I'm sorry your grandma is dead.

LOUIS Tiny little coffin, huh?
15   Sorry I didn't introduce you to. . . . I always get so closety[4] at these fam-
     ily things.

PRIOR Butch.[5] You get butch. [*Imitating*] "Hi Cousin Doris, you don't remember me I'm Lou, Rachel's boy." Lou, not Louis, because if you say Louis they'll hear the sibilant S.

20 LOUIS I don't have a . . .

PRIOR I don't blame you, hiding. Bloodlines. Jewish curses are the worst. I personally would dissolve if anyone ever looked me in the eye and said "Feh."[6] Fortunately WASPs don't say "Feh." Oh and by the way, darling, cousin Doris is a dyke.

25 LOUIS No.
     Really?

PRIOR You don't notice anything. If I hadn't spent the last four years fellat-
     ing you I'd swear you were straight.

LOUIS You're in a pissy mood. Cat still missing?

     [*Little pause.*]

30 PRIOR Not a furball in sight. It's your fault.

LOUIS It is?

PRIOR I warned you, Louis. Names are important. Call an animal "Little
     Sheba"[7] and you can't expect it to stick around. Besides, it's a dog's name.

LOUIS I wanted a dog in the first place, not a cat. He sprayed my books.

35 PRIOR He was a female cat.

---

3. A Lithuanian-born American anarchist and writer (1869–1940); she championed socialism and women's rights in the United States, Russia, and Britain. Though Goldman's primary languages were Russian and German, she gave speeches in Yiddish—the lingua franca of Jews from central and eastern Europe—to reach the largest audience possible.

4. That is, secretive about his homosexuality.
5. Assertively masculine.
6. A Yiddish interjection that expresses disgust or displeasure.
7. A reference to *Come Back, Little Sheba,* a 1952 film (dir. Daniel Mann) based on William Inge's 1950 play, which takes its title from the call for a lost dog.

LOUIS   Cats are stupid, high-strung predators. Babylonians sealed them up in bricks. Dogs have brains.

PRIOR   Cats have intuition.

LOUIS   A sharp dog is as smart as a really dull two-year-old child.

40   PRIOR   Cats know when something's wrong.

LOUIS   Only if you stop feeding them.

PRIOR   They know. That's why Sheba left, because she knew.

LOUIS   Knew what?

> [Pause.]

PRIOR   I did my best Shirley Booth[8] this morning, floppy slippers, housecoat,

45   curlers, can of Little Friskies; "Come back, Little Sheba, come back. . . ." To no avail. Le chat, elle ne reviendra jamais, jamais[9] . . .

> [He removes his jacket, rolls up his sleeve, shows LOUIS a dark-purple spot on the underside of his arm near the shoulder.] See.

LOUIS   That's just a burst blood vessel.

PRIOR   Not according to the best medical authorities.

LOUIS   What? [Pause]

50   Tell me.

PRIOR   K.S.,[1] baby. Lesion number one. Lookit. The wine-dark kiss of the angel of death.

LOUIS [very softly, holding PRIOR's arm]   Oh please . . .

PRIOR   I'm a lesionnaire. The Foreign Lesion. The American Lesion.

55   Lesionnaire's disease.

LOUIS   Stop.

PRIOR   My troubles are lesion.

LOUIS   Will you stop.

PRIOR   Don't you think I'm handling this well?

60   I'm going to die.

LOUIS   Bullshit.

PRIOR   Let go of my arm.

LOUIS   No.

PRIOR   Let go.

LOUIS [grabbing PRIOR, embracing him ferociously]   No.

65   PRIOR   I can't find a way to spare you baby. No wall like the wall of hard scientific fact. K.S. Wham. Bang your head on that.

LOUIS   Fuck you. [Letting go] Fuck you fuck you fuck you.

PRIOR   Now that's what I like to hear. A mature reaction.

Let's go see if the cat's come home.

70   Louis?

LOUIS   When did you find this?

PRIOR   I couldn't tell you.

LOUIS   Why?

PRIOR   I was scared, Lou.

75   LOUIS   Of what?

PRIOR   That you'll leave me.

LOUIS   Oh.

---

8. An American actor (1898–1992); she starred in the stage and film versions of *Come Back, Little Sheba.*
9. The cat, she will never, ever come back

(French).
1. That is, Kaposi's sarcoma, a type of lesion associated with AIDS; it was one of the first recognized signs of HIV infection.

[*Little pause.*]

PRIOR   Bad timing, funeral and all, but I figured as long as we're on the subject of death . . .

80 LOUIS   I have to go bury my grandma.

PRIOR   Lou?

[*Pause.*]

Then you'll come home?

LOUIS   Then I'll come home.

Scene 5

[*Same day, later on. Split scene:* JOE *and* HARPER *at home;* LOUIS *at the cemetery with* RABBI ISIDOR CHEMELWITZ *and the little coffin.*]

HARPER   Washington?

JOE   It's an incredible honor, buddy, and . . .

HARPER   I have to think.

JOE   Of course.

5 HARPER   Say no.

JOE   You said you were going to think about it.

HARPER   I don't want to move to Washington.

JOE   Well I do.

HARPER   It's a giant cemetery, huge white graves and mausoleums everywhere.

10 JOE   We could live in Maryland. Or Georgetown.

HARPER   We're happy here.

JOE   That's not really true, buddy, we . . .

HARPER   Well happy enough! Pretend-happy. That's better than nothing.

JOE   It's time to make some changes, Harper.

15 HARPER   No changes. Why?

JOE   I've been chief clerk for four years. I make twenty-nine thousand dollars a year. That's ridiculous. I graduated fourth in my class and I make less than anyone I know. And I'm . . . I'm tired of being a clerk, I want to go where something good is happening.

20 HARPER   Nothing good happens in Washington. We'll forget church teachings and buy furniture at . . . at *Conran's* and become yuppies.[2] I have too much to do here.

JOE   Like what?

HARPER   I *do* have things . . .

25 JOE   What things?

HARPER   I have to finish painting the bedroom.

JOE   You've been painting in there for over a year.

HARPER   I know, I . . . It just isn't done because I never get time to finish it.

JOE   Oh that's . . . that doesn't make sense. You have all the time in the
30   world. You could finish it when I'm at work.

HARPER   I'm afraid to go in there alone.

JOE   Afraid of what?

HARPER   I heard someone in there. Metal scraping on the wall. A man with a knife, maybe.

2. A term that came into widespread use in the 1980s. *Conran's*: New York retailer of contemporary home furnishings marketed to young urban professionals.

35 JOE   There's no one in the bedroom, Harper.

HARPER   Not now.

JOE   Not this morning either.

HARPER   How do you know? You were at work this morning. There's something creepy about this place. Remember *Rosemary's Baby?*[3]

40 JOE   *Rosemary's Baby?*

HARPER   Our apartment looks like that one. Wasn't that apartment in
Brooklyn?

JOE   No, it was . . .

HARPER   Well, it looked like this. It did.

45 JOE   Then let's move.

HARPER   Georgetown's worse. *The Exorcist* was in Georgetown.[4]

JOE   The devil, everywhere you turn, huh, buddy.

HARPER   Yeah. Everywhere.

JOE   How many pills today, buddy?

50 HARPER   None. One. Three. Only three.

LOUIS [*pointing at the coffin*]   Why are there just two little wooden pegs
holding the lid down?

RABBI ISIDOR CHEMELWITZ   So she can get out easier if she wants to.

LOUIS   I hope she stays put.

55   I pretended for years that she was already dead. When they called to say
she had died it was a surprise. I abandoned her.

RABBI ISIDOR CHEMELWITZ   "Sharfer vi di tson fun a shlang iz an umdankbar
kind!"

LOUIS   I don't speak Yiddish.

60 RABBI ISIDOR CHEMELWITZ   Sharper than the serpent's tooth is the ingratitude of children. Shakespeare. *Kenig Lear.*[5]

LOUIS   Rabbi, what does the Holy Writ say about someone who abandons
someone he loves at a time of great need?

RABBI ISIDOR CHEMELWITZ   Why would a person do such a thing?

65 LOUIS   Because he has to.
        Maybe because this person's sense of the world, that it will change for
the better with struggle, maybe a person who has this neo-Hegelian positivist sense of constant historical progress towards happiness or perfection or
something,[6] who feels very powerful because he feels connected to these
70   forces, moving uphill all the time . . . maybe that person can't, um, incorporate sickness into his sense of how things are supposed to go. Maybe

3. A horror film directed by Roman Polanski
(1968), based on a best-selling novel by Ira
Levin (1967), in which a young couple move
into a Manhattan apartment building inhabited by Satan worshippers.

4. An affluent neighborhood in Washington,
D.C., that was the setting of *The Exorcist*
(1973; dir. William Friedkin), a horror film
adapted from William Peter Blatty's best-
selling novel (1971) about a twelve-year-old
girl possessed by the devil.

5. That is, *King Lear* (Yiddish); the line
paraphrases Shakespeare's play (1605),
1.4.265–66.

6. The German philosopher Georg Wilhelm
Friedrich Hegel (1770–1831), who saw in
culture and civilization the logical development of consciousness, has traditionally been
viewed as an idealist (i.e., his theory is not
connected to external reality or the senses);
but his belief in the dialectical process—that
a thesis inevitably generates its antithesis,
and their interaction results in a new
synthesis—can lead to such positivist philosophies (i.e., systems of thought focused on
observable phenomena) as the dialectical
materialism connected with Marxism.

vomit . . . and sores and disease . . . really frighten him, maybe . . . he isn't
so good with death.

RABBI ISIDOR CHEMELWITZ   The Holy Scriptures have nothing to say about
75   such a person.

LOUIS   Rabbi, I'm afraid of the crimes I may commit.

RABBI ISIDOR CHEMELWITZ   Please, mister. I'm a sick old rabbi facing a long
drive home to the Bronx. You want to confess, better you should find a
priest.

LOUIS   But I'm not a Catholic, I'm a Jew.

80   RABBI ISIDOR CHEMELWITZ   Worse luck for you, bubbulah.[7] Catholics believe
in forgiveness. Jews believe in Guilt. [He pats the coffin tenderly.]

LOUIS   You just make sure those pegs are in good and tight.

RABBI ISIDOR CHEMELWITZ   Don't worry, mister. The life she had, she'll stay
put. She's better off.

85   JOE   Look, I know this is scary for you. But try to understand what it means
to me. Will you try?

HARPER   Yes.

JOE   Good. Really try.
I think things are starting to change in the world.

90   HARPER   But I don't want . . .

JOE   Wait. For the good. Change for the good. America has rediscovered itself.
Its sacred position among nations. And people aren't ashamed of that like
they used to be. This is a great thing. The truth restored. Law restored.
That's what President Reagan's done, Harper. He says "Truth exists and can
95   be spoken proudly." And the country responds to him. We become better.
More good. I need to be a part of that, I need something big to lift me up. I
mean, six years ago the world seemed in decline, horrible, hopeless, full of
unsolvable problems and crime and confusion and hunger and . . .

HARPER   But it still seems that way. More now than before. They say the
100   ozone layer is . . .

JOE   Harper . . .

HARPER   And today out the window on Atlantic Avenue there was a schizo-
phrenic traffic cop who was making these . . .

JOE   Stop it! I'm trying to make a point.

105   HARPER   So am I.

JOE   You aren't even making sense, you . . .

HARPER   My point is the world seems just as . . .

JOE   It only seems that way to you because you never go out in the world,
Harper, and you have emotional problems.

110   HARPER   I do so get out in the world.

JOE   You don't. You stay in all day, fretting about imaginary . . .

HARPER   I get out. I do. You don't know what I do.

JOE   You don't stay in all day.

HARPER   No.

115   JOE   Well. . . . Yes you do.

HARPER   That's what you think.

JOE   Where do you go?

HARPER   Where do you go? When you walk.

7. Literally, "little grandmother" (Yiddish); a term of endearment, often applied to children.

[*Pause, then angrily*] And I DO NOT have emotional problems.

120 JOE   I'm sorry.

HARPER   And if I do have emotional problems it's from living with you. Or . . .

JOE   I'm sorry buddy, I didn't mean to . . .

HARPER   Or if you do think I do then you should never have married me. You

125   have all these secrets and lies.

JOE   I want to be married to you, Harper.

HARPER   You shouldn't. You never should. [*Pause*]
        Hey buddy. Hey buddy.

JOE   Buddy kiss . . .
        [*They kiss.*]

130 HARPER   I heard on the radio how to give a blowjob.

JOE   What?

HARPER   You want to try?

JOE   You really shouldn't listen to stuff like that.

HARPER   Mormons can give blowjobs.

135 JOE   *Harper.*

HARPER   [*imitating his tone*]   *Joe.*
        It was a little Jewish lady with a German accent.[8]
        This is a good time. For me to make a baby.
        [*Little pause. JOE turns away.*]

HARPER   Then they went on to a program about holes in the ozone layer.
140   Over Antarctica. Skin burns, birds go blind, icebergs melt. The world's
        coming to an end.

Scene 6

[*First week of November. In the men's room of the offices of the Brooklyn Federal Court of Appeals; LOUIS is crying over the sink; JOE enters.*]

JOE   Oh, um . . . Morning.

LOUIS   Good morning, counselor.

JOE   [*he watches LOUIS cry*]   Sorry, I . . . I don't know your name.

LOUIS   Don't bother. Word processor. The lowest of the low.

5 JOE   [*holding out hand*]   Joe Pitt. I'm with Justice Wilson . . .

LOUIS   Oh, I know that. Counselor Pitt. Chief Clerk.

JOE   Were you . . . are you OK?

LOUIS   Oh, yeah. Thanks. What a nice man.

JOE   Not so nice.

10 LOUIS   What?

JOE   Not so nice. Nothing. You sure you're . . .

LOUIS   Life sucks shit. Life . . . just sucks shit.

JOE   What's wrong?

LOUIS   Run in my nylons.

15 JOE   Sorry . . . ?

LOUIS   Forget it. Look, thanks for asking.

8. Ruth Westheimer (b. 1928), the German-born psychologist and sex therapist who, as "Dr. Ruth," began hosting the radio call-in program *Sexually Speaking* in New York in 1980; it became hugely successful and was soon followed by a cable television program, *The Dr. Ruth Show.*

JOE   Well . . .

LOUIS   I mean it really is nice of you. [*He starts crying again.*]
 Sorry, sorry, sick friend . . .

20 JOE   Oh, I'm sorry.

LOUIS   Yeah, yeah, well, that's sweet.
 Three of your colleagues have preceded you to this baleful sight and
 you're the first one to ask. The others just opened the door, saw me, and
 fled. I hope they had to pee real bad.

25 JOE   [*handing him a wad of toilet paper*]   They just didn't want to intrude.

LOUIS   Hah. Reaganite heartless macho asshole lawyers.⁹

JOE   Oh, that's unfair.

LOUIS   What is? Heartless? Macho? Reaganite? Lawyer?

JOE   I voted for Reagan.

30 LOUIS   You did?

JOE   Twice.

LOUIS   Twice? Well, oh boy. A Gay Republican.

JOE   Excuse me?

LOUIS   Nothing.

35 JOE   I'm not . . .
 Forget it.

LOUIS   Republican? Not Republican? Or . . .

JOE   What?

LOUIS   What?

40 JOE   Not gay. I'm not gay.

LOUIS   Oh. Sorry.
 [*Blows his nose loudly.*] It's just . . .

JOE   Yes?

LOUIS   Well, sometimes you can tell from the way a person sounds that . . . I
 mean you *sound* like a . . .

45 JOE   No I don't. Like what?

LOUIS   Like a Republican.
  [*Little pause.* JOE *knows he's being teased;* LOUIS *knows he knows.* JOE
  decides to be a little brave.]

JOE   [*making sure no one else is around*]   Do I? Sound like a . . . ?

LOUIS   What? Like a . . . ? Republican, or . . . ? Do I?

JOE   Do you what?

50 LOUIS   Sound like a . . . ?

JOE   Like a . . . ?
 I'm . . . confused.

LOUIS   Yes.
 My name is Louis. But all my friends call me Louise. I work in Word
55 Processing. Thanks for the toilet paper.
  [LOUIS *offers* JOE *his hand,* JOE *reaches,* LOUIS *feints and pecks* JOE *on the
  cheek, then exits.*]

---

9. Court of appeals judges and district court judges are presidential appointees who, after confirmation, hold their positions for life, and they generally hire subordinates who share their legal philosophies. During his two terms as president, Reagan appointed almost 400 federal judges.

Scene 7

[*A week later. Mutual dream scene.* PRIOR *is at a fantastic makeup table, having a dream, applying the face.* HARPER *is having a pill-induced hallucination. She has these from time to time. For some reason,* PRIOR *has appeared in this one. Or* HARPER *has appeared in* PRIOR'*s dream. It is bewildering.*]

PRIOR [*alone, putting on makeup, then examining the results in the mirror; to the audience*] "I'm ready for my closeup, Mr. DeMille."[1]
One wants to move through life with elegance and grace, blossoming infrequently but with exquisite taste, and perfect timing, like a rare bloom, a zebra orchid. . . . One wants. . . . But one so seldom gets what one wants, does one? No. One does not. One gets fucked. Over. One . . . dies at thirty, robbed of . . . decades of majesty.
Fuck this shit. Fuck this shit.
[*He almost crumbles; he pulls himself together; he studies his handiwork in the mirror.*] I look like a corpse. A corpsette. Oh my queen; you know you've hit rock-bottom when even drag is a drag.
[HARPER *appears.*]

HARPER   Are you. . . . Who are you?

PRIOR   Who are you?

HARPER   What are you doing in my hallucination?

PRIOR   I'm not in your hallucination. You're in my dream.

HARPER   You're wearing makeup.

PRIOR   So are you.

HARPER   But you're a man.

PRIOR [*feigning dismay, shock, he mimes slashing his throat with his lipstick and dies, fabulously tragic. Then*]   The hands and feet give it away.

HARPER   There must be some mistake here. I don't recognize you. You're not. . . . Are you my . . . some sort of imaginary friend?

PRIOR   No. Aren't you too old to have imaginary friends?

HARPER   I have emotional problems. I took too many pills. Why are you wearing makeup?

PRIOR   I was in the process of applying the face, trying to make myself feel better—I swiped the new fall colors at the Clinique counter at Macy's.[2] [*Showing her*]

HARPER   You stole these?

PRIOR   I was out of cash; it was an emotional emergency!

HARPER   Joe will be so angry. I promised him. No more pills.

PRIOR   These pills you keep alluding to?

HARPER   Valium. I take Valium. Lots of Valium.

PRIOR   And you're dancing as fast as you can.[3]

HARPER   I'm not *addicted*. I don't believe in addiction, and I never . . . well, I *never* drink. And I *never* take drugs.

---

1. The final line of *Sunset Boulevard* (1950; dir. Billy Wilder), spoken by Gloria Swanson as the delusional former silent-movie star Norma Desmond, is "All right, Mr. DeMille, I'm ready for my closeup." The pioneering film director Cecil B. DeMille (1881–1959) plays himself in the film.

2. A chain of department stores; its flagship store is in New York City at Herald Square. *Clinique:* an upscale brand of cosmetics.
3. A play on *I'm Dancing as Fast as I Can* (1982; dir. Jack Hofsiss), a film adapted from Barbara Gordon's best-selling 1972 memoir about Valium addiction.

PRIOR   Well, smell *you,* Nancy Drew.[4]

HARPER   Except Valium.

35 PRIOR   Except Valium; in wee fistfuls.

HARPER   It's terrible. Mormons are not supposed to be addicted to anything. I'm a Mormon.

PRIOR   I'm a homosexual.

HARPER   Oh! In my church we don't believe in homosexuals.

40 PRIOR   In my church we don't believe in Mormons.

HARPER   What church do . . . oh! [*She laughs.*] I get it.

I don't understand this. If I didn't ever see you before and I don't think I did then I don't think you should be here, in this hallucination, because in my experience the mind, which is where hallucinations come from,
45 shouldn't be able to make up anything that wasn't there to start with, that didn't enter it from experience, from the real world. Imagination can't create anything new, can it? It only recycles bits and pieces from the world and reassembles them into visions. . . . Am I making sense right now?

PRIOR   Given the circumstances, yes.

50 HARPER   So when we think we've escaped the unbearable ordinariness and, well, untruthfulness of our lives, it's really only the same old ordinariness and falseness rearranged into the appearance of novelty and truth. Nothing unknown is knowable. Don't you think it's depressing?

PRIOR   The limitations of the imagination?

55 HARPER   Yes.

PRIOR   It's something you learn after your second theme party: It's All Been Done Before.

HARPER   The world. Finite. Terribly, terribly. . . . Well . . .

This is the most depressing hallucination I've ever had.

60 PRIOR   Apologies. I do try to be amusing.

HARPER   Oh, well, don't apologize, you . . . I can't expect someone who's really sick to entertain me.

PRIOR   How on earth did you know . . .

HARPER   Oh that happens. This is the very threshhold of revelation some-
65 times. You can see things . . . how sick you are. Do you see anything about me?

PRIOR   Yes.

HARPER   What?

PRIOR   You are amazingly unhappy.

70 HARPER   Oh big deal. You meet a Valium addict and you figure out she's unhappy. That doesn't count. Of course I . . . Something else. Something surprising.

PRIOR   Something surprising.

HARPER   Yes.

75 PRIOR   Your husband's a homo.

[*Pause.*]

HARPER   Oh, ridiculous.

[*Pause, then very quietly*] Really?

PRIOR [*shrugs*]   Threshhold of revelation.

---

4. A schoolyard taunt; Nancy Drew, a wholesome teenage detective, is the heroine of a popular series that the Stratemeyer syndicate began publishing in 1930.

HARPER   Well I don't like your revelations. I don't think you intuit well at all.
Joe's a very normal man, he . . .

80 Oh God. Oh God. He . . . Do homos take, like, lots of long walks?

PRIOR   Yes. We do. In stretch pants with lavender coifs. I just looked at you,
and there was . . .

HARPER   A sort of blue streak of recognition.

PRIOR   Yes.

85 HARPER   Like you knew me incredibly well.

PRIOR   Yes.

HARPER   Yes.

I have to go now, get back, something just . . . fell apart.
Oh God, I feel so sad . . .

90 PRIOR   I . . . I'm sorry. I usually say, "Fuck the truth," but mostly, the truth
fucks you.

HARPER   I see something else about you . . .

PRIOR   Oh?

HARPER   Deep inside you, there's a part of you, the most inner part, entirely

95 free of disease. I can see that.

PRIOR   Is that . . . That isn't true.

HARPER   Threshhold of revelation.

Home . . .

[She vanishes.]

PRIOR   People come and go so quickly here . . .

100 [To himself in the mirror] I don't think there's any uninfected part of me.
My heart is pumping polluted blood. I feel dirty.

[He begins to wipe makeup off with his hands, smearing it around. A
large gray feather falls from up above. PRIOR stops smearing the makeup
and looks at the feather. He goes to it and picks it up.]

A VOICE [it is an incredibly beautiful voice]   Look up!

PRIOR [looking up, not seeing anyone]   Hello?

A VOICE   Look up!

105 PRIOR   Who is that?

A VOICE   Prepare the way!

PRIOR   I don't see any . . .

[There is a dramatic change in lighting, from above.]

A VOICE

Look up, look up,
prepare the way

110 the infinite descent
A breath in air
floating down
Glory to . . .

[Silence.]

PRIOR   Hello? Is that it? Helloooo!

115 What the fuck . . . ? [He holds himself.]

Poor me. Poor poor me. Why me? Why poor poor me? Oh I don't feel
good right now. I really don't.

Scene 8

[*That night. Split scene:* HARPER *and* JOE *at home;* PRIOR *and* LOUIS *in bed.*]

HARPER   Where were you?

JOE   Out.

HARPER   Where?

JOE   Just out. Thinking.

5 HARPER   It's late.

JOE   I had a lot to think about.

HARPER   I burned dinner.

JOE   Sorry.

HARPER   Not my dinner. My dinner was fine. Your dinner. I put it back in the
10 oven and turned everything up as high as it could go and I watched till it
    burned black. It's still hot. Very hot. Want it?

JOE   You didn't have to do that.

HARPER   I know. It just seemed like the kind of thing a mentally deranged
    sex-starved pill-popping housewife would do.

15 JOE   Uh huh.

HARPER   So I did it. Who knows anymore what I have to do?

JOE   How many pills?

HARPER   A bunch. Don't change the subject.

JOE   I won't talk to you when you . . .

20 HARPER   No. No. Don't do that! I'm . . . I'm fine, pills are not the problem,
    not our problem, I WANT TO KNOW WHERE YOU'VE BEEN! I WANT
    TO KNOW WHAT'S GOING ON!

JOE   Going on with what? The job?

HARPER   Not the job.

25 JOE   I said I need more time.

HARPER   Not the job!

JOE   Mr. Cohn, I talked to him on the phone, he said I had to hurry . . .

HARPER   Not the . . .

JOE   But I can't get you to talk sensibly about anything so . . .

30 HARPER   SHUT UP!

JOE   Then what?

HARPER   Stick to the subject.

JOE   I don't know what that is. You have something you want to ask me? Ask
    me. Go.

35 HARPER   I . . . can't. I'm scared of you.

JOE   I'm tired, I'm going to bed.

HARPER   Tell me without making me ask. Please.

JOE   This is crazy, I'm not . . .

HARPER   When you come through the door at night your face is never exactly
40 the way I remembered it. I get surprised by something . . . mean and hard
    about the way you look. Even the weight of you in the bed at night, the way
    you breathe in your sleep seems unfamiliar.
       You terrify me.

JOE [*cold*]   I know who you are.

45 HARPER   Yes. I'm the enemy. That's easy. That doesn't change.
       You think you're the only one who hates sex; I do; I hate it with you; I do.
    I dream that you batter away at me till all my joints come apart, like wax,

and I fall into pieces. It's like a punishment. It was wrong of me to marry you. I knew you . . . [*She stops herself.*] It's a sin, and it's killing us both.

50 JOE I can always tell when you've taken pills because it makes you red-faced and sweaty and frankly that's very often why I don't want to . . .

HARPER Because . . .

JOE Well, you aren't pretty. Not like this.

HARPER I have something to ask you.

55 JOE Then ASK! ASK! What in hell are you . . .

HARPER Are you a homo? [*Pause*]
Are you? If you try to walk out right now I'll put your dinner back in the oven and turn it up so high the whole building will fill with smoke and everyone in it will asphyxiate. So help me God I will.

60   Now answer the question.

JOE What if I . . .
[*Small pause.*]

HARPER Then tell me, please. And we'll see.

JOE No. I'm not.
I don't see what difference it makes.

65 LOUIS Jews don't have any clear textual guide to the afterlife; even that it exists. I don't think much about it. I see it as a perpetual rainy Thursday afternoon in March. Dead leaves.

PRIOR Eeeugh. Very Greco-Roman.[5]

LOUIS Well, for us it's not the verdict that counts, it's the act of judgment.
70   That's why I could never be a lawyer. In court all that matters is the verdict.

PRIOR You could never be a lawyer because you are oversexed. You're too distracted.

LOUIS Not distracted; *ab*stracted. I'm trying to make a point:

PRIOR Namely:

75 LOUIS It's the judge in his or her chambers, weighing, books open, pondering the evidence, ranging freely over categories: good, evil, innocent, guilty; the judge in the chamber of circumspection, not the judge on the bench with the gavel. The shaping of the law, not its execution.

PRIOR The point, dear, the point . . .

80 LOUIS That it should be the questions and shape of a life, its total complexity gathered, arranged, and considered, which matters in the end, not some stamp of salvation or damnation which disperses all the complexity in some unsatisfying little decision—the balancing of the scales . . .

PRIOR I like this; very zen; it's . . . reassuringly incomprehensible and use-
85   less. We who are about to die thank you.[6]

LOUIS You are not about to die.

PRIOR It's not going well, really . . . two new lesions. My leg hurts. There's protein in my urine, the doctor says, but who knows what the fuck that portends. Anyway it shouldn't be there, the protein. My butt is chapped
90   from diarrhea and yesterday I shat blood.

LOUIS I really hate this. You don't tell me . . .

5. An adjective apparently intended to evoke stoicism and austerity.
6. An echo of "We who are about to die greet you," popularly believed to be the salute of Roman gladiators to the emperor. *Zen:* exhibiting the calm associated with this meditative Japanese school of Buddhism.

PRIOR   You get too upset, I wind up comforting you. It's easier . . .
LOUIS   Oh thanks.
PRIOR   If it's bad I'll tell you.
95 LOUIS   Shitting blood sounds bad to me.
PRIOR   And I'm telling you.
LOUIS   And I'm handling it.
PRIOR   Tell me some more about justice.
LOUIS   I *am* handling it.
100 PRIOR   Well Louis you win Trooper of the Month.

[LOUIS *starts to cry.*]

PRIOR   I take it back. You aren't Trooper of the Month.
        This isn't working . . .
        Tell me some more about justice.
LOUIS   You are not about to die.
105 PRIOR   Justice . . .
LOUIS   . . . is an immensity, a confusing vastness. Justice is God.
        Prior?
PRIOR   Hmmm?
LOUIS   You love me.
110 PRIOR   Yes.
LOUIS   What if I walked out on this?
        Would you hate me forever?

[PRIOR *kisses* LOUIS *on the forehead.*]

PRIOR   Yes.
JOE   I think we ought to pray. Ask God for help. Ask him together . . .
115 HARPER   God won't talk to me. I have to make up people to talk to me.
JOE   You have to keep asking.
HARPER   I forgot the question.
        Oh yeah. God, is my husband a . . .
JOE [*scary*]   Stop it. Stop it. I'm warning you.
120   Does it make any difference? That I might be one thing deep within, no
        matter how wrong or ugly that thing is, so long as I have fought, with every-
        thing I have, to kill it. What do you want from me? What do you want from
        me, Harper? More than that? For God's sake, there's nothing left, I'm a
        shell. There's nothing left to kill.
125   As long as my behavior is what I know it has to be. Decent. Correct. That
        alone in the eyes of God.
HARPER   No, no, not that, that's Utah talk, Mormon talk, I hate it, Joe, tell
        me, say it . . .
JOE   All I will say is that I am a very good man who has worked very hard to
130   become good and you want to destroy that. You want to destroy me, but I
        am not going to let you do that.

[*Pause.*]

HARPER   I'm going to have a baby.
JOE   Liar.
HARPER   You liar.
135   A baby born addicted to pills. A baby who does not dream but who hal-
        lucinates, who stares up at us with big mirror eyes and who does not know
        who we are.

[*Pause.*]

JOE   Are you really . . .

HARPER   No. Yes. No. Yes. Get away from me.

140   Now we both have a secret.

PRIOR   One of my ancestors was a ship's captain who made money bringing
whale oil to Europe and returning with immigrants—Irish mostly, packed
in tight, so many dollars per head. The last ship he captained foundered off
the coast of Nova Scotia in a winter tempest and sank to the bottom. He
145   went down with the ship—*la Grande Geste*[7]—but his crew took seventy
women and kids in the ship's only longboat, this big, open rowboat, and
when the weather got too rough, and they thought the boat was overcrowded, the crew started lifting people up and hurling them into the sea.
Until they got the ballast right. They walked up and down the longboat,
150   eyes to the waterline, and when the boat rode low in the water they'd grab
the nearest passenger and throw them into the sea. The boat was leaky,
see; seventy people; they arrived in Halifax with nine people on board.

LOUIS   Jesus.

PRIOR   I think about that story a lot now. People in a boat, waiting, terrified,
155   while implacable, unsmiling men, irresistibly strong, seize . . . maybe the
person next to you, maybe you, and with no warning at all, with time only
for a quick intake of air you are pitched into freezing, turbulent water and
salt and darkness to drown.

   I like your cosmology, baby. While time is running out I find myself
160   drawn to anything that's suspended, that lacks an ending—but it seems to
me that it lets you off scot-free.

LOUIS   What do you mean?

PRIOR   No judgment, no guilt or responsibility.

LOUIS   For me.

165 PRIOR   For anyone. It was an editorial "you."

LOUIS   Please get better. Please.

   Please don't get any sicker.

Scene 9

[Third week in November. ROY and HENRY, his doctor, in HENRY's office.]

HENRY   Nobody knows what causes it. And nobody knows how to cure it. The
best theory is that we blame a retrovirus, the Human Immunodeficiency
Virus. Its presence is made known to us by the useless antibodies which
appear in reaction to its entrance into the bloodstream through a cut, or an
5   orifice. The antibodies are powerless to protect the body against it. Why, we
don't know. The body's immune system ceases to function. Sometimes the
body even attacks itself. At any rate it's left open to a whole horror house of
infections from microbes which it usually defends against.

   Like Kaposi's sarcomas. These lesions. Or your throat problem. Or the
10   glands.

   We think it may also be able to slip past the blood-brain barrier[8] into the
brain. Which is of course very bad news.

7. The grand gesture (French); by tradition, the captain is the last to leave a sinking ship.
8. The physical structure and system of cel- lular transport mechanisms that prevent harmful chemicals in the bloodstream from reaching the brain.

And it's fatal in we don't know what percent of people with suppressed immune responses.

[*Pause.*]

15 ROY This is very interesting, Mr. Wizard,[9] but why the fuck are you telling me this?

[*Pause.*]

HENRY Well, I have just removed one of three lesions which biopsy results will probably tell us is a Kaposi's sarcoma lesion. And you have a pronounced swelling of glands in your neck, groin, and armpits—lymphadenopathy[1] is

20 another sign. And you have oral candidiasis[2] and maybe a little more fungus under the fingernails of two digits on your right hand. So that's why . . .

ROY This disease . . .

HENRY Syndrome.

ROY Whatever. It afflicts mostly homosexuals and drug addicts.

25 HENRY Mostly. Hemophiliacs are also at risk.

ROY Homosexuals and drug addicts. So why are you implying that I . . .

[*Pause*]

What are you implying, Henry?

HENRY I don't . . .

ROY I'm not a drug addict.

30 HENRY Oh come on Roy.

ROY What, what, come on Roy what? Do you think I'm a junkie, Henry, do you see tracks?

HENRY This is absurd.

ROY Say it.

35 HENRY Say what?

ROY Say, "Roy Cohn, you are a . . ."

HENRY Roy.

ROY "You are a . . ." Go on. Not "Roy Cohn you are a drug fiend." "Roy Marcus Cohn, you are a . . ."

40 Go on, Henry, it starts with an "H."

HENRY Oh I'm not going to . . .

ROY *With an "H,"* Henry, and it isn't "Hemophiliac." Come on . . .

HENRY What are you doing, Roy?

ROY No, say it. I mean it. Say: "Roy Cohn, you are a homosexual." [*Pause*]

45 And I will proceed, systematically, to destroy your reputation and your practice and your career in New York State, Henry. Which you know I can do.

[*Pause.*]

HENRY Roy, you have been seeing me since 1958. Apart from the facelifts I have treated you for everything from syphilis . . .

ROY From a whore in Dallas.

50 HENRY From syphilis to venereal warts. In your rectum. Which you may have gotten from a whore in Dallas, but it wasn't a female whore.

[*Pause.*]

ROY So say it.

---

9. The host of *Watch Mr. Wizard* (1951–65), a television show that explained science to children (revived on cable as *Mr. Wizard's World,* 1983–90).

1. An abnormal enlargement of the lymph nodes.
2. An infection of the mouth by the yeastlike fungus *Candida albicans.*

HENRY   Roy Cohn, you are . . .
        You have had sex with men, many many times, Roy, and one of them, or
55   any number of them, has made you very sick. You have AIDS.[3]
ROY   AIDS.
        Your problem, Henry, is that you are hung up on words, on labels, that
        you believe they mean what they seem to mean. AIDS. Homosexual. Gay.
        Lesbian. You think these are names that tell you who someone sleeps with,
60   but they don't tell you that.
HENRY   No?
ROY   No. Like all labels they tell you one thing and one thing only: where does
        an individual so identified fit in the food chain, in the pecking order? Not ide-
        ology, or sexual taste, but something much simpler: clout. Not who I fuck or
65   who fucks me, but who will pick up the phone when I call, who owes me favors.
        This is what a label refers to. Now to someone who does not understand this,
        homosexual is what I am because I have sex with men. But really this is wrong.
        Homosexuals are not men who sleep with other men. Homosexuals are men
        who in fifteen years of trying cannot get a pissant antidiscrimination bill
70   through City Council. Homosexuals are men who know nobody and who
        nobody knows. Who have zero clout. Does this sound like me, Henry?
HENRY   No.
ROY   No. I have clout. A lot. I can pick up this phone, punch fifteen num-
        bers, and you know who will be on the other end in under five minutes,
75   Henry?
HENRY   The President.
ROY   Even better, Henry. His wife.
HENRY   I'm impressed.
ROY   I don't want you to be impressed. I want you to understand. This is not
80   sophistry. And this is not hypocrisy. This is reality. I have sex with men. But
        unlike nearly every other man of whom this is true, I bring the guy I'm
        screwing to the White House and President Reagan smiles at us and
        shakes his hand. Because *what* I am is defined entirely by *who* I am. Roy
        Cohn is not a homosexual. Roy Cohn is a heterosexual man, Henry, who
85   fucks around with guys.
HENRY   OK, Roy.
ROY   And what is my diagnosis, Henry?
HENRY   You have AIDS, Roy.
ROY   No, Henry, no. AIDS is what homosexuals have. I have liver cancer.
        [*Pause.*]
90   HENRY   Well, whatever the fuck you have, Roy, it's very serious, and I haven't
        got a damn thing for you. The NIH in Bethesda has a new drug called AZT[4]
        with a two-year waiting list that not even I can get you onto. So get on the
        phone, Roy, and dial the fifteen numbers, and tell the First Lady you need
        in on an experimental treatment for liver cancer, because you can call it
95   any damn thing you want, Roy, but what it boils down to is very bad news.

---

3. Acquired immune deficiency syndrome was first recognized in 1981.
4. Azidothymidine or zidovudine, an antiviral drug that was the first approved (in 1987) to treat AIDS; that the government accelerate the testing process required for its approval was a major demand of early AIDS activists. NIH: the National Institutes of Health, the federal agency primarily responsible for supporting and conducting medical research; its headquarters are in Bethesda, Maryland.

Act 2: In Vitro

[December 1985–January 1986]

Scene 1

[*Night, the third week in December.* PRIOR *alone on the floor of his bedroom; he is much worse.*]

PRIOR   Louis, Louis, please wake up, oh God.

   [*Louis runs in.*]

PRIOR   I think something horrible is wrong with me I can't breathe . . .

LOUIS [*starting to exit*]   I'm calling the ambulance.

PRIOR   No, wait, I . . .

5   LOUIS   *Wait?* Are you fucking crazy? Oh God you're on fire, your head is on fire.

PRIOR   It hurts, it hurts . . .

LOUIS   I'm calling the ambulance.

PRIOR   I don't want to go to the hospital, I don't want to go to the hospital

10   please let me lie here, just . . .

LOUIS   No, no, God, Prior, stand up . . .

PRIOR   DON'T TOUCH MY LEG!

LOUIS   We have to . . . oh God this is so crazy.

PRIOR   I'll be OK if I just lie here Lou, really, if I can only sleep a little . . .

   [LOUIS *exits.*]

15   PRIOR   Louis?

   NO! NO! Don't call, you'll send me there and I won't come back, please, please Louis I'm begging, baby, please . . .

   [*Screams.*] LOUIS!!

LOUIS [*from off; hysterical*]   WILL YOU SHUT THE FUCK UP!

20   PRIOR [*trying to stand*]   Aaah. I have . . . to go to the bathroom. Wait. Wait, just . . . oh. Oh God. [*He shits himself.*]

LOUIS [*Entering*]   Prior? They'll be here in . . .

   Oh my God.

PRIOR   I'm sorry, I'm sorry.

25   LOUIS   What did . . . ? What?

PRIOR   I had an accident.

   [*Louis goes to him.*]

LOUIS   This is blood.

PRIOR   Maybe you shouldn't touch it . . . me. . . . I . . . [*He faints.*]

LOUIS [*quietly*]   Oh help. Oh help. Oh God oh God oh God help me I can't I

30   can't I can't.

Scene 2

[*Same night.* HARPER *is sitting at home, all alone, with no lights on. We can bare ly see her.* JOE *enters, but he doesn't turn on the lights.*]

JOE   Why are you sitting in the dark? Turn on the light.

HARPER   *No.* I heard the sounds in the bedroom again. I know someone was in there.

JOE   No one was.

5   HARPER   Maybe actually in the bed, under the covers with a knife.

Oh, boy. Joe. I, um, I'm thinking of going away. By which I mean: I think
I'm going off again. You . . . you know what I mean?

JOE   Please don't. Stay. We can fix it. I pray for that. This is my fault, but I
can correct it. You have to try too . . .

[*He turns on the light. She turns it off again.*]

10 HARPER   When you pray, what do you pray for?

JOE   I pray for God to crush me, break me up into little pieces and start all
over again.

HARPER   Oh. Please. Don't pray for that.

JOE   I had a book of Bible stories when I was a kid. There was a picture I'd
15   look at twenty times every day: Jacob wrestles with the angel.[5] I don't really
remember the story, or why the wrestling—just the picture. Jacob is young
and very strong. The angel is . . . a beautiful man, with golden hair and
wings, of course. I still dream about it. Many nights. I'm . . . It's me. In that
struggle. Fierce, and unfair. The angel is not human, and it holds nothing
20   back, so how could anyone human win, what kind of a fight is that? It's not
just. Losing means your soul thrown down in the dust, your heart torn out
from God's. But you can't not lose.

HARPER   In the whole entire world, you are the only person, the only person
I love or have ever loved. And I love you terribly. Terribly. That's what's so
25   awfully, irreducibly real. I can make up anything but I can't dream that
away.

JOE   Are you . . . are you really going to have a baby?

HARPER   It's my time, and there's no blood. I don't really know. I suppose it
wouldn't be a great thing. Maybe I'm just not bleeding because I take too
30   many pills. Maybe I'll give birth to a pill. That would give a new meaning to
pill-popping, huh?
   I think you should go to Washington. Alone. Change, like you said.

JOE   I'm not going to leave you, Harper.

HARPER   Well maybe not. But I'm going to leave you.

Scene 3

[*One AM, the next morning. LOUIS and a nurse, EMILY, are sitting in*
PRIOR's *room in the hospital.*]

EMILY   He'll be all right now.

LOUIS   No he won't.

EMILY   No. I guess not. I gave him something that makes him sleep.

LOUIS   Deep asleep?

5 EMILY   Orbiting the moons of Jupiter.

LOUIS   A good place to be.

EMILY   Anyplace better than here. You his . . . uh?

LOUIS   Yes. I'm his uh.

EMILY   This must be hell for you.

10 LOUIS   It is. Hell. The After Life. Which is not at all like a rainy afternoon in
March, by the way, Prior. A lot more vivid than I'd expected. Dead leaves,
but the crunchy kind. Sharp, dry air. The kind of long, luxurious dying feeling that breaks your heart.

EMILY   Yeah, well we all get to break our hearts on this one.

5. See Genesis 32.24–30.

15   He seems like a nice guy. Cute.

LOUIS   Not like this.

Yes, he is. Was. Whatever.

EMILY   Weird name. Prior Walter. Like, "The Walter before this one."

LOUIS   Lots of Walters before this one. Prior is an old old family name in an
20   old old family. The Walters go back to the Mayflower and beyond. Back to
        the Norman Conquest. He says there's a Prior Walter stitched into the
        Bayeux tapestry.[6]

EMILY   Is that impressive?

LOUIS   Well, it's old. Very old. Which in some circles equals impressive.

25 EMILY   Not in my circle. What's the name of the tapestry?

LOUIS   The Bayeux tapestry. Embroidered by La Reine Mathilde.[7]

EMILY   I'll tell my mother. She embroiders. Drives me nuts.

LOUIS   Manual therapy for anxious hands.

EMILY   Maybe you should try it.

30 LOUIS   Mathilde stitched while William the Conqueror was off to war. She
        was capable of . . . more than loyalty. Devotion.

        She waited for him, she stitched for years. And if he had come back bro-
        ken and defeated from war, she would have loved him even more. And if he
        had returned mutilated, ugly, full of infection and horror, she would still
35   have loved him; fed by pity, by a sharing of pain, she would love him even
        more, and even more, and she would never, never have prayed to God,
        please let him die if he can't return to me whole and healthy and able to live
        a normal life. . . . If he had died, she would have buried her heart with him.

        So what the fuck is the matter with me? [Little pause]
40   Will he sleep through the night?

EMILY   At least.

LOUIS   I'm going.

EMILY   It's one AM. Where do you have to go at . . .

LOUIS   I know what time it is. A walk. Night air, good for the . . . . The park.

45 EMILY   Be careful.

LOUIS   Yeah. Danger.

        Tell him, if he wakes up and you're still on, tell him goodbye, tell him I
        had to go.

Scene 4

[An hour later. Split scene: JOE and ROY in a fancy [straight] bar; LOUIS
and a MAN in the Rambles[8] in Central Park. JOE and ROY are sitting at the
bar; the place is brightly lit. JOE has a plate of food in front of him but he
isn't eating. ROY occasionally reaches over the table and forks small bites
off JOE's plate. ROY is drinking heavily, JOE not at all. LOUIS and the MAN
are eyeing each other, each alternating interest and indifference.]

JOE   The pills were something she started when she miscarried or . . . no,
        she took some before that. She had a really bad time at home, when she

6. An embroidery, 230 feet long, that chronicles the invasion and conquest of England by
the Normans in 1066 (preserved in the Bayeux Museum in northern France). *Mayflower*: the ship that in 1620 brought the
English founders of the Plymouth Colony to
Massachusetts.
7. Queen Matilda (French; ca. 1031–1083),

the wife of William the Conqueror (ca. 1028–
1087); the tradition that attributes the creation of the Bayeux tapestry to her has little
foundation.
8. A wooded section in New York's Central
Park, designed as a wild garden; for much of
the 20th century, the Ramble was notorious
as an area for homosexual cruising.

was a kid, her home was really bad. I think a lot of drinking and physical
stuff. She doesn't talk about that, instead she talks about . . . the sky falling
5   down, people with knives hiding under sofas. Monsters. Mormons. Everyone thinks Mormons don't come from homes like that, we aren't supposed
to behave that way, but we do. It's not lying, or being two-faced. Everyone
tries very hard to live up to God's strictures, which are very . . . um . . .

ROY   Strict.

10 JOE   I shouldn't be bothering you with this.

ROY   No, please. Heart to heart. Want another. . . . What is that, seltzer?[9]

JOE   The failure to measure up hits people very hard. From such a strong
desire to be good they feel very far from goodness when they fail.
What scares me is that maybe what I really love in her is the part of her
15   that's farthest from the light, from God's love; maybe I was drawn to that in
the first place. And I'm keeping it alive because I need it.

ROY   Why would you need it?

JOE   There are things. . . . I don't know how well we know ourselves. I mean,
what if? I know I married her because she . . . because I loved it that she
20   was always wrong, always doing something wrong, like one step out of step.
In Salt Lake City that stands out. I never stood out, on the outside, but
inside, it was hard for me. To pass.

ROY   Pass?

JOE   Yeah.

25 ROY   Pass as what?

JOE   Oh. Well. . . . As someone cheerful and strong. Those who love God with
an open heart unclouded by secrets and struggles are cheerful; God's easy
simple love for them shows in how strong and happy they are. The saints.[1]

ROY   But you had secrets? Secret struggles . . .

30 JOE   I wanted to be one of the elect, one of the Blessed. You feel you ought
to be, that the blemishes are yours by choice, which of course they aren't.
Harper's sorrow, that really deep sorrow, she didn't choose that. But it's
there.

ROY   You didn't put it there.

35 JOE   No.

ROY   You sound like you think you did.

JOE   I am responsible for her.

ROY   Because she's your wife.

JOE   That. And I do love her.

40 ROY   Whatever. She's your wife. And so there are obligations. To her. But
also to yourself.

JOE   She'd fall apart in Washington.

ROY   Then let her stay here.

JOE   She'll fall apart if I leave her.

45 ROY   Then bring her to Washington.

JOE   I just can't, Roy. She needs me.

ROY   Listen, Joe. I'm the best divorce lawyer in the business.

[*Little pause.*]

JOE   Can't Washington wait?

9. Observant Mormons do not drink alcohol
or caffeine (or smoke).
1. That is, Mormons, members of what is

officially called the Church of Jesus Christ of
Latter-day Saints (the LDS Church).

ROY You do what you need to do, Joe. What *you* need. *You.* Let her life go
50   where it wants to go. You'll both be better for that. *Somebody* should get
      what they want.
MAN What do you want?
LOUIS I want you to fuck me, hurt me, make me bleed.
MAN I want to.
55 LOUIS Yeah?
MAN I want to hurt you.
LOUIS Fuck me.
MAN Yeah?
LOUIS Hard.
60 MAN Yeah? You been a bad boy?
           [*Pause.* LOUIS *laughs, softly.*]
LOUIS Very bad. Very bad.
MAN You need to be punished, boy?
LOUIS Yes. I do.
MAN Yes what?
           [*Little pause.*]
65 LOUIS Um, I . . .
MAN Yes *what*, boy?
LOUIS Oh. Yes sir.
MAN I want you to take me to your place, boy.
LOUIS No, I can't do that.
70 MAN No *what*?
LOUIS No sir, I can't, I . . .
      I don't live alone, sir.
MAN Your lover know you're out with a man tonight, boy?
LOUIS No sir, he . . .
75   My lover doesn't know.
MAN Your lover know you . . .
LOUIS Let's change the subject, OK? Can we go to your place?
MAN I live with my parents.
LOUIS Oh.

80 ROY Everyone who makes it in this world makes it because somebody older
      and more powerful takes an interest. The most precious asset in life, I
      think, is the ability to be a good son. You have that, Joe. Somebody who can
      be a good son to a father who pushes them farther than they would other-
      wise go. I've had many fathers, I owe my life to them, powerful, powerful
85   men. Walter Winchell, Edgar Hoover. Joe McCarthy most of all.[2] He val-

2. The historical Cohn, through his work on
the Permanent Subcommittee on Investigations, is most closely identified with McCarthy (1908–1957), who as senator from
Wisconsin (1947–57) gained national attention with his sensational and unsubstantiated
claims that the State Department and other
parts of the government had been infiltrated
by Communists. Winchell (1897–1972) wrote
a hugely popular gossip column (begun in
1924); he lost influence after he allied himself
with McCarthy's anticommunist witch hunt.

Hoover (1895–1972), early in his career (during the first Red Scare, 1919–20), was placed
in charge of investigating suspected alien radicals; in 1924, he became director of the
Bureau of Investigation (renamed the Federal
Bureau of Investigation in 1935), amassing
enormous and virtually unchecked power
during his forty-eight years in that position.
A believer in a worldwide communist conspiracy, he too was an ally of McCarthy;
rumors that he was a homosexual circulated
for decades.

ued me because I am a good lawyer, but he loved me because I was and am a good son. He was a very difficult man, very guarded and cagey; I brought out something tender in him. He would have died for me. And me for him. Does this embarrass you?

90 JOE I had a hard time with my father.

ROY Well sometimes that's the way. Then you have to find other fathers, substitutes, I don't know. The father-son relationship is central to life. Women are for birth, beginning, but the father is continuance. The son offers the father his life as a vessel for carrying forth his father's dream.

95 Your father's living?

JOE Um, dead.

ROY He was . . . what? A difficult man?

JOE He was in the military. He could be very unfair. And cold.

ROY But he loved you.

100 JOE I don't know.

ROY No, no, Joe, he did, I know this. Sometimes a father's love has to be very, very hard, unfair even, cold to make his son grow strong in a world like this. This isn't a good world.

MAN Here, then.

105 LOUIS I. . . . Do you have a rubber?

MAN I don't use rubbers.

LOUIS You should. [*He takes one from his coat pocket.*] Here.

MAN I don't use them.

LOUIS Forget it, then. [*He starts to leave.*]

110 MAN No, wait.
Put it on me. Boy.

LOUIS Forget it, I have to get back. Home. I must be going crazy.

MAN Oh come on please he won't find out.

LOUIS It's cold. Too cold.

115 MAN It's never too cold, let me warm you up. Please?
[*They begin to fuck.*]

MAN Relax.

LOUIS [*a small laugh*] Not a chance.

MAN It . . .

LOUIS What?

120 MAN I think it broke. The rubber. You want me to keep going?
[*Little pause*] Pull out? Should I . . .

LOUIS Keep going.
Infect me.
I don't care. I don't care.
[*Pause. The* MAN *pulls out.*]

125 MAN I . . . um, look, I'm sorry, but I think I want to go.

LOUIS Yeah.
Give my best to mom and dad.
[*The* MAN *slaps him.*]

LOUIS Ow!
[*They stare at each other.*]

LOUIS It was a joke.
[*The* MAN *leaves.*]

130 ROY How long have we known each other?

JOE Since 1980.

ROY Right. A long time. I feel close to you, Joe. Do I advise you well?

JOE You've been an incredible friend, Roy, I . . .

ROY I want to be family. Familia, as my Italian friends call it. La Familia. A
135   lovely word. It's important for me to help you, like I was helped.

JOE I owe practically everything to you, Roy.

ROY I'm dying, Joe. Cancer.

JOE Oh my God.

ROY Please. Let me finish.

140   Few people know this and I'm telling you this only because . . . I'm not
afraid of death. What can death bring that I haven't faced? I've lived; life is
the worst. [*Gently mocking himself*] Listen to me, I'm a philosopher.

     Joe. You must do this. You must must must. Love; that's a trap. Respon-
sibility; that's a trap too. Like a father to a son I tell you this: Life is full of
145   horror; nobody escapes, nobody; save yourself. Whatever pulls on you,
whatever needs from you, threatens you. Don't be afraid; people are so
afraid; don't be afraid to live in the raw wind, naked, alone. . . . Learn at
least this: What you are capable of. Let nothing stand in your way.

Scene 5

[*Three days later.* PRIOR *and* BELIZE *in* PRIOR's *hospital room.* PRIOR *is
very sick but improving.* BELIZE *has just arrived.*]

PRIOR Miss Thing.

BELIZE Ma cherie bichette.[3]

PRIOR Stella.

BELIZE Stella for star.[4] Let me see. [*Scrutinizing* PRIOR] You look like shit,
5   why yes indeed you do, comme la merde![5]

PRIOR Merci.[6]

BELIZE [*taking little plastic bottles from his bag, handing them to* PRIOR] Not
to despair, Belle Reeve.[7] Lookie! Magic goop!

PRIOR [*opening a bottle, sniffing*] Pooh! What kinda crap is that?

10 BELIZE Beats me. Let's rub it on your poor blistered body and see what it does.

PRIOR This is not Western medicine, these bottles . . .

BELIZE Voodoo cream. From the botanica 'round the block.

PRIOR And you a registered nurse.

BELIZE [*sniffing it*] Beeswax and cheap perfume. Cut with Jergen's Lotion.
15   Full of good vibes and love from some little black Cubana witch in
Miami.

PRIOR Get that trash away from me, I am immune-suppressed.

BELIZE I *am* a health professional. I *know* what I'm doing.

PRIOR It stinks. Any word from Louis?

     [*Pause.* BELIZE *starts giving* PRIOR *a gentle massage.*]

20 PRIOR Gone.

---

3. My dear little darling (French).
4. A line spoken by Blanche DuBois to her sister Stella in Tennessee Williams's *A Street-car Named Desire* (1947). (*Stella* means "star" in Latin.)
5. Like shit! (French).
6. Thanks (French).
7. In *A Streetcar Named Desire*, Belle Reve (Beautiful Dream; French) is the name of Blanche and Stella's ancestral home.

BELIZE He'll be back. I know the type. Likes to keep a girl on edge.

PRIOR It's been . . .

> [*Pause.*]

BELIZE [*trying to jog his memory*] How long?

PRIOR I don't remember.

25 BELIZE How long have you been here?

PRIOR [*getting suddenly upset*] I don't remember, I don't give a fuck. I want
Louis. I want my fucking boyfriend, where the fuck is he? I'm dying, I'm
dying, where's Louis?

BELIZE Shhhh, shhh . . .

30 PRIOR This is a very strange drug, this drug. Emotional lability, for starters.

BELIZE Save a tab or two for me.

PRIOR Oh no, not this drug, ce n'est pas pour la joyeux noël et la bonne
année, this drug she is serious poisonous chemistry, ma pauvre bichette.[8]
And not just disorienting. I hear things. Voices.

35 BELIZE Voices.

PRIOR A voice.

BELIZE Saying what?

> [*Pause.*]

PRIOR I'm not supposed to tell.

BELIZE You better tell the doctor. Or I will.

40 PRIOR No no don't. Please. I want the voice; it's wonderful. It's all that's
keeping me alive. I don't want to talk to some intern about it.
You know what happens? When I hear it, I get hard.

BELIZE Oh my.

PRIOR Comme ça.[9] [*He uses his arm to demonstrate.*] And you know I am
45 slow to rise.

BELIZE My jaw aches at the memory.

PRIOR And would you deny me this little solace—betray my concupiscence
to Florence Nightingale's storm troopers?[1]

BELIZE Perish the thought, ma bébé.[2]

50 PRIOR They'd change the drug just to spoil the fun.

BELIZE You and your boner can depend on me.

PRIOR Je t'adore, ma belle nègre.[3]

BELIZE All this girl-talk shit is politically incorrect, you know. We should
have dropped it back when we gave up drag.

55 PRIOR I'm sick, I get to be politically incorrect if it makes me feel better. You
sound like Lou. [*Little pause*]
Well, at least I have the satisfaction of knowing he's in anguish somewhere. I loved his anguish. Watching him stick his head up his asshole and
eat his guts out over some relatively minor moral conundrum—it was the
60 best show in town. But Mother warned me: if they get overwhelmed by the
little things . . .

BELIZE They'll be belly-up bustville when something big comes along.

PRIOR Mother warned me.

---

8. It doesn't give you a merry Christmas and a
happy New Year . . . my poor little darling
(French).
9. Like that (French).
1. That is, nurses; Nightingale (1820–1910),
an English reformer whose work organizing a
unit of nurses during the Crimean War won
her international fame, is credited with
founding modern nursing.
2. My baby, my child (French).
3. I adore you, my beautiful Negro (French).

BELIZE And they do come along.

65 PRIOR But I didn't listen.

BELIZE No. [*Doing Hepburn*][4] Men are beasts.

PRIOR [*also Hepburn*] The absolute lowest.

BELIZE I have to go. If I want to spend my whole lonely life looking after white people I can get underpaid to do it.

70 PRIOR You're just a Christian martyr.

BELIZE Whatever happens, baby, I will be here for you.

PRIOR Je t'aime.[5]

BELIZE Je t'aime. Don't go crazy on me, girlfriend, I already got enough crazy queens for one lifetime. For two. I can't be bothering with dementia.

75 PRIOR I promise.

BELIZE [*touching him; softly*] Ouch.

PRIOR Ouch. Indeed.

BELIZE Why'd they have to pick on you?

And eat more, girlfriend, you really do look like shit.

[BELIZE *leaves.*]

80 PRIOR [*after waiting a beat*] He's gone.

Are you still . . .

VOICE I can't stay. I will return.

PRIOR Are you one of those "Follow me to the other side" voices?

VOICE No. I am no nightbird. I am a messenger . . .

85 PRIOR You have a beautiful voice, it sounds . . . like a viola, like a perfectly tuned, tight string, balanced, the truth. . . . Stay with me.

VOICE Not now. Soon I will return, I will reveal myself to you; I am glorious, glorious; my heart, my countenance, and my message. You must prepare.

PRIOR For what? I don't want to . . .

90 VOICE No death, no:

A marvelous work and a wonder[6] we undertake, an edifice awry we sink plumb and straighten, a great Lie we abolish, a great error correct, with the rule, sword, and broom of Truth!

PRIOR What are you talking about, I . . .

VOICE

95 I am on my way; when I am manifest, our Work begins:

Prepare for the parting of the air,

The breath, the ascent,

Glory to . . .

Scene 6

[*The second week of January.* MARTIN, ROY, *and* JOE *in a fancy Manhattan restaurant.*]

MARTIN It's a revolution in Washington, Joe. We have a new agenda and finally a real leader. They got back the Senate[7] but we have the courts. By the nineties the Supreme Court will be block-solid Republican appointees, and the Federal bench—Republican judges like land mines, everywhere,

4. That is, the American stage and film star Katharine Hepburn (1907–2003), who often portrayed independent women.
5. I love you (French).
6. See Isaiah 29.14.

7. Majority control of the U.S. Senate shifted to the Democrats in the 1986 election (Republicans gained majorities in both the House and the Senate in 1994).

5   everywhere they turn. Affirmative action? Take it to court. Boom! Land
mine. And we'll get our way on just about everything: abortion, defense,
Central America, family values, a live investment climate. We have the
White House locked till the year 2000. And beyond. A permanent fix on the
Oval Office? It's possible. By '92 we'll get the Senate back, and in ten years
10   the South is going to give us the House. It's really the end of Liberalism.
The end of New Deal Socialism.[8] The end of ipso facto secular humanism.[9] The dawning of a genuinely American political personality. Modeled
on Ronald Wilson Reagan.

JOE   It sounds great, Mr. Heller.

15 MARTIN   Martin. And Justice is the hub. Especially since Ed Meese took
over. He doesn't specialize in Fine Points of the Law. He's a flatfoot, a cop.
He reminds me of Teddy Roosevelt.[1]

JOE   I can't wait to meet him.

MARTIN   Too bad, Joe, he's been dead for sixty years!

    [*There is a little awkwardness.* JOE *doesn't respond.*]

20 MARTIN   Teddy Roosevelt. You said you wanted to. . . . Little joke. It reminds
me of the story about the . . .

ROY [*smiling, but nasty*]   Aw shut the fuck up Martin.

    [*To* JOE] You see that? Mr. Heller here is one of the mighty, Joseph, in
D.C. he sitteth on the right hand of the man who sitteth on the right hand
25   of The Man.[2] And yet I can say "shut the fuck up" and he will take no
offense. Loyalty. He . . .

    Martin?

MARTIN   Yes, Roy?

ROY   Rub my back.

30 MARTIN   Roy . . .

ROY   No no really, a sore spot, I get them all the time now, these . . . Rub it
for me darling, would you do that for me?

    [MARTIN *rubs* ROY's *back. They both look at* JOE.]

ROY [*to* JOE]   How do you think a handful of Bolsheviks turned St. Petersburg into Leningrad in one afternoon? *Comrades*. Who do for each other.
35   Marx and Engels. Lenin and Trotsky. Josef Stalin and Franklin Delano
Roosevelt.[3]

    [MARTIN *laughs.*]

8. That is, the government programs promoting
economic and social welfare (and thus labeled
"socialist" by opponents) of the type first instituted during the New Deal, the name given by
Franklin Delano Roosevelt (1882–1945; 32nd
president, 1933–45) to his domestic reform initiatives. These programs include Social Security, banking reform, and the minimum wage.
9. A philosophy that locates value in human
reason and interests, rejecting religion and
the supernatural.
1. Theodore Roosevelt (1858–1919), twenty-
sixth president of the United States (1901–
09); between 1895 and 1897, he served as
president of the New York City Board of
Police Commissioners.
2. Compare Colossians 3.1 ("Christ sitteth on
the right hand of God").
3. That is, symbiosis—even between sup-

posed adversaries—is the key to success. The
German political philosopher Karl Marx
(1818–1883) and the German socialist Friedrich Engels (1820–1895) co-wrote the *Manifesto of the Communist Party* (1848); the
Russian revolutionaries Vladimir Lenin
(1870–1924) and Leon Trotsky (1879–1940)
led the Bolshevik faction of socialists that triumphed in the October Revolution of 1917
(Saint Petersburg, which was a focal point of
revolutionary activity, had been given the less
Germanic name Petrograd in 1914; it was
renamed Leningrad after Lenin died, but its
original name was restored in 1991); the dic-
tator Joseph Stalin (1879–1953), who controlled the Soviet Union from Lenin's death
until his own death, and President Roosevelt
became allies in World War II. *Comrades*:
form of address used among Communists.

ROY *Comrades*, right Martin?

MARTIN This man, Joe, is a Saint of the Right.

JOE I know, Mr. Heller, I . . .

40 ROY And you see what I mean, Martin? He's special, right?

MARTIN Don't embarrass him, Roy.

ROY Gravity, decency, smarts! His strength is as the strength of ten because his heart is pure![4] *And* he's a Royboy, one hundred percent.

MARTIN We're on the move, Joe. On the move.

45 JOE Mr. Heller, I . . .

MARTIN [*ending backrub*] We can't wait any longer for an answer.

[*Little pause.*]

JOE Oh. Um, I . . .

ROY Joe's a married man, Martin.

MARTIN Aha.

50 ROY With a wife. She doesn't care to go to D.C., and so Joe cannot go. And keeps us dangling. We've seen that kind of thing before, haven't we? These men and their wives.

MARTIN Oh yes. Beware.

JOE I really can't discuss this under . . .

55 MARTIN Then *don't* discuss. Say yes, Joe.

ROY Now.

MARTIN Say yes I will.

ROY Now.

Now. I'll hold my breath till you do, I'm turning blue waiting. . . . *Now*,
60 goddammit!

MARTIN Roy, calm down, it's not . . .

ROY Aw, fuck it. [*He takes a letter from his jacket pocket, hands it to* JOE.] Read. Came today.

[JOE *reads the first paragraph, then looks up.*]

JOE Roy. This is . . . Roy, this is terrible.

65 ROY You're telling me.

A letter from the New York State Bar Association, Martin. They're gonna try and disbar me.

MARTIN Oh my.

JOE Why?

70 ROY Why, Martin?

MARTIN Revenge.

ROY The whole Establishment. Their little rules. Because I know no rules. Because I don't see the Law as a dead and arbitrary collection of anti-quated dictums, thou shall, thou shalt not, because, because I know the
75 Law's a pliable, breathing, sweating . . . *organ*, because, because . . .

MARTIN Because he borrowed half a million from one of his clients.[5]

ROY Yeah, well, there's that.

MARTIN *And* he forgot to *return* it.

JOE Roy, that's . . . You borrowed money from a client?

80 ROY I'm deeply ashamed.

---

4. Paraphrase of a couplet from "Sir Galahad" (1842), by Alfred, Lord Tennyson.
5. Cohn was in fact disbarred in 1986 for unethical conduct, which included borrowing $109,000 from a client and not repaying her.

[*Little pause.*]

JOE [*very sympathetic*]   Roy, you know how much I admire you. Well I mean I know you have unorthodox ways, but I'm sure you only did what you thought at the time you needed to do. And I have faith that . . .

ROY   Not so damp, please. I'll deny it was a loan. She's got no paperwork.
85   Can't prove a fucking thing.

[*Little pause.* MARTIN *studies the menu.*]

JOE [*handing back the letter, more official in tone*]   Roy I really appreciate your telling me this, and I'll do whatever I can to help.

ROY [*holding up a hand, then, carefully*]   I'll tell you what you can do.

I'm about to be tried, Joe, by a jury that is not a jury of my peers. The
90   disbarment committee: genteel gentleman Brahmin[6] lawyers, country-club men. I offend them, to these men . . . I'm what, Martin, some sort of filthy little Jewish troll?

MARTIN   Oh well, I wouldn't go so far as . . .

ROY   Oh well I would.
95   Very fancy lawyers, these disbarment committee lawyers, fancy lawyers with fancy corporate clients and complicated cases. Antitrust suits. Deregulation. Environmental control. Complex cases like these need Justice Department cooperation like flowers need the sun. Wouldn't you say that's an accurate assessment, Martin?

100   MARTIN   I'm not here, Roy. I'm not hearing any of this.

ROY   No. Of course not.

Without the light of the sun, Joe, these cases, and the fancy lawyers who represent them, will wither and die.

A well-placed friend, someone in the Justice Department, say, can turn
105   off the sun. Cast a deep shadow on my behalf. Make them shiver in the cold. If they overstep. They would fear that.

[*Pause.*]

JOE   Roy. I don't understand.

ROY   You do.

[*Pause.*]

JOE   You're not asking me to . . .
110   ROY   Ssssshhhh. Careful.

JOE [*a beat,*[7] *then*]   Even if I said yes to the job, it would be illegal to interfere. With the hearings. It's unethical. No. I can't.

ROY   Un-ethical.

Would you excuse us, Martin?
115   MARTIN   Excuse you?

ROY   Take a walk, Martin. For real.

[MARTIN *leaves.*]

ROY   Un-ethical. Are you trying to embarrass me in front of my friend?

JOE   Well it is unethical, I can't . . .

ROY   Boy, you are really something. What the fuck do you think this is, Sun-
120   day School?

JOE   No, but Roy this is . . .

6. That is, of high social standing (Brahmans are Hindus of the highest caste).   7. Pause (theater term).

ROY   This is . . . this is gastric juices churning, this is enzymes and acids, this
is intestinal is what this is, bowel movement and blood-red meat—this
stinks, this is *politics*, Joe, the game of being alive. And you think you're. . . .
125   What? Above that? Above alive is what? Dead! In the clouds! You're on
earth, goddammit! Plant a foot, stay awhile.
   I'm sick. They smell I'm weak. They want blood this time. I must have
eyes in Justice. In Justice you will protect me.
JOE   Why can't Mr. Heller . . .
130   ROY   Grow up, Joe. The administration can't get involved.
JOE   But I'd be part of the administration. The same as him.
ROY   Not the same. Martin's Ed's man. And Ed's Reagan's man. So Martin's
Reagan's man.
   And you're mine. [*Little pause. He holds up the letter.*] This will never be.
135   Understand me? [*He tears the letter up.*]
   I'm gonna be a lawyer, Joe, I'm gonna be a lawyer, Joe, I'm gonna be a
goddam motherfucking legally licensed member of the bar lawyer, just like
my daddy was,[8] till my last bitter day on earth, Joseph, until the day I die.
   [*Martin returns.*]
ROY   Ah, Martin's back.
140   MARTIN   So are we agreed?
ROY   Joe?
   [*Little pause.*]
JOE   I will think about it.
   [*To* ROY.] I will.
ROY   Huh.
145   MARTIN   It's the fear of what comes after the doing that makes the doing
hard to do.
ROY   Amen.
MARTIN   But you can almost always live with the consequences.

Scene 7

[*That afternoon. On the granite steps outside the Hall of Justice, Brooklyn. It is cold and sunny. A Sabrett[9] wagon is selling hot dogs. Louis, in a
shabby overcoat, is sitting on the steps contemplatively eating one. Joe
enters with three hot dogs and a can of Coke.*]

JOE   Can I . . . ?
LOUIS   Oh sure. Sure. Crazy cold sun.
JOE   [*sitting*]   Have to make the best of it.
   How's your friend?
5   LOUIS   My . . . ? Oh. He's worse. My friend is worse.
JOE   I'm sorry.
LOUIS   Yeah, well. Thanks for asking. It's nice. You're nice. I can't believe you
voted for Reagan.
JOE   I hope he gets better.
10   LOUIS   Reagan?
JOE   Your friend.
LOUIS   He won't. Neither will Reagan.

8. Albert Cohn (1885–1959) was a New York
state supreme court justice, appointed by
Governor Franklin Delano Roosevelt.
9. A New York–based hot dog company.

JOE   Let's not talk politics, OK?

LOUIS [*pointing to* JOE's *lunch*] You're eating *three* of those?

15 JOE   Well . . . I'm . . . hungry.

LOUIS They're really terrible for you. Full of rat-poo and beetle legs and wood shavings 'n' shit.

JOE   Huh.

LOUIS And . . . um . . . irridium, I think. Something toxic.[1]

20 JOE   You're eating one.

LOUIS Yeah, well, the shape, I can't help myself, plus I'm *trying* to commit suicide, what's your excuse?

JOE   I don't have an excuse. I just have Pepto-Bismol.[2]

       [JOE *takes a bottle of Pepto-Bismol and chugs it.* LOUIS *shudders audibly.*]

JOE   Yeah I know but then I wash it down with Coke.

       [*He does this.* LOUIS *mimes barfing in* JOE's *lap.* JOE *pushes* LOUIS's *head away.*]

25 JOE   Are you *always* like this?

LOUIS I've been worrying a lot about his kids.

JOE   Whose?

LOUIS Reagan's. Maureen and Mike and little orphan Patti and Miss Ron Reagan Jr.,[3] the you-should-pardon-the-expression heterosexual.

30 JOE   Ron Reagan Jr. is *not* . . . You shouldn't just make these assumptions about people. How do you know? About him? What he is? You don't know.

LOUIS [*doing Tallulah*[4]] Well darling he never sucked *my* cock but . . .

JOE   Look, if you're going to get vulgar . . .

LOUIS No no really I mean . . . What's it like to be the child of the Zeitgeist?
35   To have the American Animus as your dad? It's not really a *family*, the Reagans, I read *People*,[5] there aren't any connections there, no love, they don't ever even speak to each other except through their agents. So what's it like to be Reagan's kid? Enquiring minds want to know.

JOE   You can't believe everything you . . .

40 LOUIS [*looking away*] But . . . I think we all know what that's like. Nowadays. No connections. No responsibilities. All of us . . . falling through the cracks that separate what we owe to our selves and . . . and what we owe to love.

JOE   You just. . . . Whatever you feel like saying or doing, you don't care, you just . . . do it.

45 LOUIS Do what?

JOE   It. Whatever. Whatever it is you want to do.

LOUIS Are you trying to tell me something?

       [*Little pause, sexual. They stare at each other.* JOE *looks away.*]

JOE   No, I'm just observing that you . . .

LOUIS Impulsive.

1. Many hot dogs contain preservatives that can be toxic in large quantities (*iridium* is a rare metallic element).

2. A product used to treat various kinds of minor digestive distress.

3. Ronald Reagan's children from his first marriage, to Jane Wyman (Maureen [1941–2001] and Michael [b. 1945]), and his second marriage, to Nancy Davis (Patti [b. 1952] and Ron [b. 1958]). Patti's estrangement from her parents made her an "orphan."

4. Imitating the husky, drawled "darling" with which the American stage and film star Tallulah Bankhead (1902–1968) customarily addressed people.

5. An American magazine that focuses on celebrities and human interest stories; it began publication in 1974.

50 JOE   Yes, I mean it must be scary, you . . .

LOUIS [*Shrugs*]   Land of the free. Home of the brave. Call me irresponsible.[6]

JOE   It's kind of terrifying.

LOUIS   Yeah, well, freedom is. Heartless, too.

JOE   Oh you're not heartless.

55 LOUIS   You don't know.

Finish your weenie.

[*He pats* JOE *on the knee, starts to leave.*]

JOE   Um . . .

[LOUIS *turns, looks at him.* JOE *searches for something to say.*]

JOE   Yesterday was Sunday but I've been a little unfocused recently and I thought it was Monday. So I came here like I was going to work. And the
60   whole place was empty. And at first I couldn't figure out why, and I had this moment of incredible . . . fear and also . . . It just flashed through my mind: The whole Hall of Justice, it's empty, it's deserted, it's gone out of business. Forever. The people that make it run have up and abandoned it.

LOUIS [*looking at the building*]   Creepy.

65 JOE   Well yes but. I felt that I was going to scream. Not because it was creepy, but because the emptiness felt so *fast*.

And . . . well, good. A . . . happy scream.

I just wondered what a thing it would be . . . if overnight everything you owe anything to, justice, or love, had really gone away. Free.

70   It would be . . . heartless terror. Yes. Terrible, and . . .

Very great. To shed your skin, every old skin, one by one and then walk away, unencumbered, into the morning. [*Little pause. He looks at the building.*]

I can't go in there today.

75 LOUIS   Then don't.

JOE [*not really hearing* LOUIS]   I can't go in, I need . . .

[*He looks for what he needs. He takes a swig of Pepto-Bismol.*] I can't *be* this anymore. I need . . . a change, I should just . . .

LOUIS [*not a come-on, necessarily; he doesn't want to be alone*]   Want some
80   company? For whatever?

[*Pause.* JOE *looks at* LOUIS *and looks away, afraid.* LOUIS *shrugs.*]

LOUIS   Sometimes, even if it scares you to death, you have to be willing to break the law. Know what I mean?

[*Another little pause.*]

JOE   Yes.

[*Another little pause.*]

LOUIS   I moved out. I moved out on my . . .

85   I haven't been sleeping well.

JOE   Me neither.

[LOUIS *goes up to* JOE, *licks his napkin and dabs at* JOE's *mouth.*]

LOUIS   Antacid moustache.

[*Points to the building.*]   Maybe the court won't convene. Ever again. Maybe we are free. To do whatever.

6. The opening phrase and the title of a 1963 song (music by Jimmy Van Heusen, lyrics by Sammy Cahn). "O'er the land of the free, and the home of the brave" is the closing phrase of the refrain of "The Star-Spangled Banner," the U.S. national anthem (words by Francis Scott Key, 1814).

90 Children of the new morning, criminal minds. Selfish and greedy and loveless and blind. Reagan's children.

You're scared. So am I. Everybody is in the land of the free. God help us all.

Scene 8

[*Late that night.* JOE *at a payphone phoning* HANNAH *at home in Salt Lake City.*]

JOE Mom?

HANNAH Joe?

JOE Hi.

HANNAH You're calling from the street. It's . . . it must be four in the morning.
5 What's happened?

JOE Nothing, nothing, I . . .

HANNAH It's Harper. Is Harper. . . . Joe? Joe?

JOE Yeah, hi. No, Harper's fine. Well, no, she's . . . not fine. How are you, Mom?

10 HANNAH What's happened?

JOE I just wanted to talk to you. I, uh, wanted to try something out on you.

HANNAH Joe, you haven't . . . have you been drinking, Joe?

JOE Yes ma'am. I'm drunk.

HANNAH That isn't like you.

15 JOE No. I mean, who's to say?

HANNAH Why are you out on the street at four AM? In that crazy city. It's dangerous.

JOE Actually, Mom, I'm not on the street. I'm near the boathouse in the park.

HANNAH What park?

20 JOE Central Park.

HANNAH CENTRAL PARK! Oh my Lord. What on earth are you doing in Central Park at this time of night? Are you . . .

Joe, I think you ought to go home right now. Call me from home. [*Little pause*] Joe?

25 JOE I come here to watch, Mom. Sometimes. Just to watch.

HANNAH Watch what? What's there to watch at four in the . . .

JOE Mom, did Dad love me?

HANNAH What?

JOE Did he?

30 HANNAH You ought to go home and call from there.

JOE Answer.

HANNAH Oh now really. This is maudlin. I don't like this conversation.

JOE Yeah, well, it gets worse from here on.

[*Pause.*]

HANNAH Joe?

35 JOE Mom. Momma. I'm a homosexual, Momma.

Boy, did that come out awkward. [*Pause*] Hello? Hello?

I'm a homosexual. [*Pause*] Please, Momma. Say something.

HANNAH You're old enough to understand that your father didn't love you without being ridiculous about it.

40 JOE What?

HANNAH You're ridiculous. You're being ridiculous.

JOE I'm . . .

What?

HANNAH   You really ought to go home now to your wife. I need to go to bed.
45   This phone call. . . . We will just forget this phone call.

JOE   Mom.

HANNAH   No more talk. Tonight. This . . .

[*Suddenly very angry*] Drinking is a sin! A sin! I raised you better than that. [*She hangs up.*]

Scene 9

[*The following morning, early. Split scene:* HARPER *and* JOE *at home;* LOUIS *and* PRIOR *in* PRIOR'S *hospital room.* JOE *and* LOUIS *have just entered. This should be fast and obviously furious; overlapping is fine; the proceedings may be a little confusing but not the final results.*]

HARPER   Oh God. Home. The moment of truth has arrived.

JOE   Harper.

LOUIS   I'm going to move out.

PRIOR   The fuck you are.

5   JOE   Harper. Please listen. I still love you very much. You're still my best buddy; I'm not going to leave you.

HARPER   No, I don't like the sound of this. I'm leaving.

LOUIS   I'm leaving.
I already have.

10   JOE   Please listen. Stay. This is really hard. We have to talk.

HARPER   We are talking. Aren't we. Now please shut up. OK?

PRIOR   Bastard. Sneaking off while I'm flat out here, that's low. If I could get up now I'd beat the holy shit out of you.

JOE   Did you take pills? How many?

15   HARPER   No pills. Bad for the . . . [*Pats stomach.*]

JOE   You aren't pregnant. I called your gynecologist.

HARPER   I'm seeing a new gynecologist.

PRIOR   You have no right to do this.

LOUIS   Oh, that's ridiculous.

20   PRIOR   No right. It's criminal.

JOE   Forget about that. Just listen. You want the truth. This is the truth.
I knew this when I married you. I've known this I guess for as long as I've known anything, but . . . I don't know, I thought maybe that with enough effort and will I could change myself . . . but I can't . . .

25   PRIOR   Criminal.

LOUIS   There oughta be a law.

PRIOR   There is a law. You'll see.

JOE   I'm losing ground here, I go walking, you want to know where I walk,
I . . . go to the park, or up and down 53rd Street, or places where . . . And
30   I keep swearing I won't go walking again, but I just can't.

LOUIS   I need some privacy.

PRIOR   That's new.

LOUIS   Everything's new, Prior.

JOE   I try to tighten my heart into a knot, a snarl, I try to learn to live dead,
35   just numb, but then I see someone I want, and it's like a nail, like a hot spike right through my chest, and I know I'm losing.

PRIOR   Apartment too small for three? Louis and Prior comfy but not Louis and Prior and Prior's disease?

LOUIS   Something like that.

40   I won't be judged by you. This isn't a crime, just—the inevitable consequence of people who run out of—whose limitations . . .

PRIOR   Bang bang bang. The court will come to order.

LOUIS   I mean let's talk practicalities, schedules; I'll come over if you want, spend nights with you when I can, I can . . .

45   PRIOR   Has the jury reached a verdict?

LOUIS   I'm doing the best I can.

PRIOR   Pathetic. Who cares?

JOE   My whole life has conspired to bring me to this place, and I can't despise my whole life. I think I believed when I met you I could save you, you at
50   least if not myself, but . . .
        I don't have any sexual feelings for you, Harper. And I don't think I ever did.

        [*Little pause.*]

HARPER   I think you should go.

JOE   Where?

55   HARPER   Washington. Doesn't matter.

JOE   What are you talking about?

HARPER   Without me.
        Without me, Joe. Isn't that what you want to hear?

        [*Little pause.*]

JOE   Yes.

60   LOUIS   You can love someone and fail them. You can love someone and not be able to . . .

PRIOR   You *can,* theoretically, yes. A person can, maybe an editorial "you" can love, Louis, but not *you,* specifically you, I don't know, I think you are excluded from that general category.

65   HARPER   You were going to save me, but the whole time you were spinning a lie. I just don't understand that.

PRIOR   A person could theoretically love and maybe many do but we both know now you can't.

LOUIS   I do.

70   PRIOR   You can't even say it.

LOUIS   I love you, Prior.

PRIOR   I repeat. Who cares?

HARPER   This is so scary, I want this to stop, to go back . . .

PRIOR   We have reached a verdict, your honor. This man's heart is deficient.
75   He loves, but his love is worth nothing.

JOE   Harper . . .

HARPER   Mr. Lies, I want to get away from here. Far away. Right now. Before he starts talking again. Please, please . . .

JOE   As long as I've known you Harper you've been afraid of . . . of men hid-
80   ing under the bed, men hiding under the sofa, men with knives.

PRIOR   [*shattered; almost pleading; trying to reach him*]   I'm dying! You stupid fuck! Do you know what that is! Love! Do you know what love means? We lived together four-and-a-half years, you animal, you idiot.

LOUIS   I have to find some way to save myself.

85   JOE   Who are these men? I never understood it. Now I know.

HARPER   What?

JOE   It's me.

HARPER   It is?

PRIOR   GET OUT OF MY ROOM!

90   JOE   I'm the man with the knives.

HARPER   You are?

PRIOR   If I could get up now I'd kill you. I would. Go away. Go away or I'll
scream.

HARPER   Oh God . . .

95   JOE   I'm sorry . . .

HARPER   It is you.

LOUIS   Please don't scream.

PRIOR   Go.

HARPER   I recognize you now.

100   LOUIS   Please . . .

JOE   Oh. Wait, I . . . Oh!

[*He covers his mouth with his hand, gags, and removes his hand, red with
blood.*] I'm bleeding.

[PRIOR *screams.*]

HARPER   Mr. Lies.

MR. LIES [*appearing, dressed in Antarctic explorer's apparel*]   Right here.

105   HARPER   I want to go away. I can't see him anymore.

MR. LIES   Where?

HARPER   Anywhere. Far away.

MR. LIES   Absolutamento.

[HARPER *and* MR. LIES *vanish.* JOE *looks up, sees that she's gone.*]

PRIOR [*closing his eyes*]   When I open my eyes you'll be gone.

[LOUIS *leaves.*]

110   JOE   Harper?

PRIOR [*opening his eyes*]   Huh. It worked.

JOE [*calling*]   Harper?

PRIOR   I hurt all over. I wish I was dead.

Scene 10

[*The same day, sunset.* HANNAH *and* SISTER ELLA CHAPTER, *a real estate
saleswoman,* HANNAH PITT's *closest friend, in front of* HANNAH's *house in
Salt Lake City.*]

SISTER ELLA CHAPTER   Look at that view! A view of heaven. Like the living
city of heaven,[7] isn't it, it just fairly glimmers in the sun.

HANNAH   Glimmers.

SISTER ELLA CHAPTER   Even the stone and brick it just glimmers and glitters

5   like heaven in the sunshine. Such a nice view you get, perched up on a
canyon rim. Some kind of beautiful place.

HANNAH   It's just Salt Lake, and you're selling the house *for* me, not *to* me.

7. As the headquarters of the LDS Church, Salt Lake City contains an enormous temple and
many church-related buildings.

SISTER ELLA CHAPTER   I like to work up an enthusiasm for my properties.

HANNAH   Just get me a good price.

10 SISTER ELLA CHAPTER   Well, the market's off.

HANNAH   At least fifty.

SISTER ELLA CHAPTER   Forty'd be more like it.

HANNAH   Fifty.

SISTER ELLA CHAPTER   Wish you'd wait a bit.

15 HANNAH   Well I can't.

SISTER ELLA CHAPTER   Wish you would. You're about the only friend I got.

HANNAH   Oh well now.

SISTER ELLA CHAPTER   Know why I decided to like you? I decided to like you
'cause you're the only unfriendly Mormon I ever met.

20 HANNAH   Your wig is crooked.

SISTER ELLA CHAPTER   Fix it.

[HANNAH *straightens* SISTER ELLA's *wig.*]

SISTER ELLA CHAPTER   New York City. All they got there is tiny rooms.
I always thought: People ought to stay put. That's why I got my license to
sell real estate. It's a way of saying: Have a house! Stay put! It's a way of
25 saying traveling's no good. Plus I needed the cash. [*She takes a pack of cigarettes out of her purse, lights one, offers pack to* HANNAH.]

HANNAH   Not out here, anyone could come by.
There's been days I've stood at this ledge and thought about stepping over.
It's a hard place, Salt Lake: baked dry. Abundant energy; not much intel-
ligence. That's a combination that can wear a body out. No harm looking
30 someplace else. I don't need much room.
My sister-in-law Libby thinks there's radon gas[8] in the basement.

SISTER ELLA CHAPTER   Is there gas in the . . .

HANNAH   Of course not. Libby's a fool.

SISTER ELLA CHAPTER   'Cause I'd have to include that in the description.

35 HANNAH   There's no gas, Ella. [*Little pause.*] Give a puff. [*She takes a furtive
drag of* ELLA's *cigarette.*] Put it away now.

SISTER ELLA CHAPTER   So I guess it's goodbye.

HANNAH   You'll be all right, Ella, I wasn't ever much of a friend.

SISTER ELLA CHAPTER   I'll say something but don't laugh, OK?
40 This is the home of saints, the godliest place on earth, they say, and I
think they're right. That mean there's no evil here? No. Evil's everywhere.
Sin's everywhere. But this . . . is the spring of sweet water in the desert, the
desert flower. Every step a Believer takes away from here is a step fraught
with peril. I fear for you, Hannah Pitt, because you are my friend. Stay put.
45 This is the right home of saints.

HANNAH   Latter-day saints.

SISTER ELLA CHAPTER   Only kind left.

HANNAH   But still. Late in the day . . . for saints and everyone. That's all.
That's all.
50 Fifty thousand dollars for the house, Sister Ella Chapter; don't undersell. It's an impressive view.

---

8. A naturally occurring radioactive gas that can cause lung cancer.

Act 3: Not-Yet-Conscious, Forward Dawning

[January 1986]

Scene 1

[Late night, three days after the end of Act 2. The stage is completely dark. PRIOR is in bed in his apartment, having a nightmare. He wakes up, sits up, and switches on a nightlight. He looks at his clock. Seated by the table near the bed is a man dressed in the clothing of a 13th-century British squire.]

PRIOR [terrified] Who are you?

PRIOR 1 My name is Prior Walter.

[Pause.]

PRIOR My name is Prior Walter.

PRIOR 1 I know that.

5 PRIOR Explain.

PRIOR 1 You're alive. I'm not. We have the same name. What do you want me to explain?

PRIOR A ghost?

PRIOR 1 An ancestor.

10 PRIOR Not the Prior Walter? The Bayeux tapestry Prior Walter?

PRIOR 1 His great-great grandson. The fifth of the name.

PRIOR I'm the thirty-fourth, I think.

PRIOR 1 Actually the thirty-second.

PRIOR Not according to Mother.

15 PRIOR 1 She's including the two bastards, then; I say leave them out. I say no room for bastards. The little things you swallow . . .

PRIOR Pills.

PRIOR 1 Pills. For the pestilence. I too . . .

PRIOR Pestilence. . . . You too what?

20 PRIOR 1 The pestilence[9] in my time was much worse than now. Whole villages of empty houses. You could look outdoors and see Death walking in the morning, dew dampening the ragged hem of his black robe. Plain as I see you now.

PRIOR You died of the plague.

25 PRIOR 1 The spotty monster. Like you, alone.

PRIOR I'm not alone.

PRIOR 1 You have no wife, no children.

PRIOR I'm gay.

PRIOR 1 So? Be gay, dance in your altogether for all I care, what's that to do 30 with not having children?

PRIOR Gay homosexual, not bonny, blithe and[1] . . . never mind.

PRIOR 1 I had twelve. When I died.

[The second ghost appears, this one dressed in the clothing of an elegant 17th-century Londoner.]

PRIOR 1 [pointing to PRIOR 2] And I was three years younger than him.

[PRIOR sees the new ghost, screams.]

9. Bubonic plague, or the Black Death; it killed more than one-third of the population of Asia and Europe in the 1300s.
1. An allusion to the nursery rhyme that begins "Monday's child is fair of face"; one version ends "But the child born on the Sabbath Day / Is bonny and blithe and good and gay."

PRIOR   Oh God another one.

35 PRIOR 2   Prior Walter. Prior to you by some seventeen others.

PRIOR 1   He's counting the bastards.

PRIOR   Are we having a convention?

PRIOR 2   We've been sent to declare her fabulous incipience. They love a well-paved entrance with lots of heralds, and . . .

40 PRIOR 1   The messenger come. Prepare the way. The infinite descent, a breath in air . . .

PRIOR 2   They chose us, I suspect, because of the mortal affinities. In a family as long-descended as the Walters there are bound to be a few carried off by plague.

45 PRIOR 1   The spotty monster.

PRIOR 2   Black Jack.[2] Came from a water pump, half the city of London, can you imagine? His came from fleas. Yours, I understand, is the lamentable consequence of venery . . .

PRIOR 1   Fleas on rats, but who knew that?

50 PRIOR   Am I going to die?

PRIOR 2   We aren't allowed to discuss . . .

PRIOR 1   When you do, you don't get ancestors to help you through it. You may be surrounded by children but you die alone.

PRIOR   I'm afraid.

55 PRIOR 1   You should be. There aren't even torches, and the path's rocky, dark, and steep.

PRIOR 2   Don't alarm him. There's good news before there's bad.
    We two come to strew rose petal and palm leaf before the triumphal procession. Prophet. Seer. Revelator. It's a great honor for the family.

60 PRIOR 1   He hasn't got a family.

PRIOR 2   I meant for the Walters, for the family in the larger sense.

PRIOR [singing]
    All I want is a room somewhere,
    Far away from the cold night air . . . [3]

PRIOR 2 [putting a hand on PRIOR's forehead]   Calm, calm, this is no brain
65 fever . . .

    [PRIOR calms down, but keeps his eyes closed. The lights begin to change. Distant Glorious Music.]

PRIOR 1 [low chant]
    Adonai, Adonai,
    Olam ha-yichud,
    Zefirot, Zazahot,
    Ha-adam, ha-gadol[4]
70 Daughter of Light,

2. Another name for bubonic plague. The worst epidemic to devastate London killed up to 100,000, or one-fifth of the city's population, in 1665–66.
3. The opening lines of "Wouldn't It Be Loverly?"—a song from Alan Jay Lerner and Frederick Loewe's musical *My Fair Lady* (1956).
4. Hebrew terms associated with the Kabbalah, a tradition of mystical interpretation of the Hebrew Bible, though *Adonai* is a com-

mon way of referring to the Lord. *Olam hayichud*: the world of unification (i.e., unified by God); *Zefirot*: the divine emanations that represent the aspects of God visible in the world (usually *sefirot*); *Zazahot*: the three "brightnesses" (*Tzachtzachot*, often called the "splendors") that precede and govern the emanations of the sefirot; *Ha-adam, ha-gadol*: the heavenly man (literally, "the great man"; see Joshua 14.15).

Daughter of Splendors,
Fluor! Phosphor!
Lumen! Candle!
PRIOR 2 [*simultaneously*]
Even now,
75   From the mirror-bright halls of heaven,
Across the cold and lifeless infinity of space,
The Messenger comes
Trailing orbs of light,
Fabulous, incipient,
80   Oh Prophet,
To you . . .
PRIOR 1 and PRIOR 2
Prepare, prepare,
The Infinite Descent,
A breath, a feather,
85   Glory to . . .
[*They vanish.*]

Scene 2

[*The next day. Split scene:* LOUIS *and* BELIZE *in a coffee shop.* PRIOR *is at the outpatient clinic at the hospital with* EMILY, *the nurse; she has him on a pentamidine[5] IV drip.*]

LOUIS Why has democracy succeeded in America? Of course by succeeded I
mean comparatively, not literally, not in the present, but what makes for
the prospect of some sort of radical democracy spreading outward and
growing up? Why does the power that was once so carefully preserved at
5   the top of the pyramid by the original framers of the Constitution seem
drawn inexorably downward and outward in spite of the best effort of the
Right to stop this? I mean it's the really hard thing about being Left in this
country, the American Left can't help but trip over all these petrified little
fetishes: freedom, that's the worst; you know, *Jeane Kirkpatrick*[6] for God's
10   sake will go on and on about freedom and so what does that mean, the
word freedom, when she talks about it, or human rights; you have Bush[7]
talking about human rights, and so what are these people talking about,
they might as well be talking about the mating habits of Venusians, these
people don't begin to know what, ontologically, freedom is or human rights,
15   like they see these bourgeois property-based Rights-of-Man-type rights[8]
but that's not enfranchisement, not democracy, not what's implicit, what's
potential within the idea, not the idea with blood in it. That's just liberalism, the worst kind of liberalism, really, bourgeois tolerance, and what I

5. Pentamidine isethionate, a drug that fights
AIDS-related pneumonia.
6. An American professor of political science
(1926–2006), selected by Reagan to be U.S.
ambassador to the United Nations (1981–
85); she criticized the Carter administration's emphasis on human rights, arguing for
U.S. support of authoritarian regimes that
oppose revolutionary totalitarian (Commu-

nist) regimes.
7. George H. W. Bush (b. 1924), vice president under Ronald Reagan (1981–89) and
president (1989–93).
8. An allusion to the property-based political
theory of the British philosopher John Locke
(1632–1704), which influenced the framers
of the U.S. Constitution.

think is that what AIDS shows us is the limits of tolerance, that it's not
20   enough to be tolerated, because when the shit hits the fan you find out
how much tolerance is worth. Nothing. And underneath all the tolerance is
intense, passionate hatred.

BELIZE   Uh huh.

LOUIS   Well don't you think that's true?

25   BELIZE   Uh huh. It is.

LOUIS   *Power* is the object, not being tolerated. Fuck assimilation. But I
mean in spite of all this the thing about America, I think, is that ultimately
we're different from every other nation on earth, in that, with people here
of every race, we can't. . . . Ultimately what defines us isn't race, but poli-
30   tics. Not like any European country where there's an insurmountable fact
of a kind of racial, or ethnic, monopoly, or monolith, like all Dutchmen, I
mean Dutch people, are well, Dutch, and the Jews of Europe were never
Europeans, just a small problem. Facing the monolith. But here there are
so many small problems, it's really just a collection of small problems, the
35   monolith is missing. Oh, I mean, of course I suppose there's the monolith
of White America. White Straight Male America.

BELIZE   Which is not unimpressive, even among monoliths.

LOUIS   Well, no, but when the race thing gets taken care of, and I don't mean
to minimalize how major it is, I mean I know it is, this is a really, really
40   incredibly racist country but it's like, well, the British. I mean, all these
blue-eyed pink people. And it's just weird, you know, I mean I'm not all that
Jewish-looking, or . . . well, maybe I am but, you know, in New York, everyone is . . . well, not everyone, but so many are but so but in England, in
London I walk into bars and I feel like Sid the Yid, you know I mean like
45   Woody Allen in *Annie Hall*, with the payess and the gabardine coat,[9] like
never, never anywhere so much—I mean, not actively despised, not like
they're Germans, who I think are still terribly anti-Semitic, and racist too,
I mean black-racist, they pretend otherwise but, anyway, in London, there's
just . . . and at one point I met this black gay guy from Jamaica who talked
50   with a lilt but he said his family'd been living in London since before the
Civil War—the American one[1]—and how the English never let him forget
for a minute that he wasn't blue-eyed and pink and I said yeah, me too,
these people are anti-Semites and he said yeah but the British Jews have
the clothing business all sewed up and blacks there can't get a foothold.
55   And it was an incredibly awkward moment of just . . . I mean here we were,
in this bar that was gay but it was a *pub,* you know, the beams and the plaster and those horrible little, like, two-day-old fish and egg sandwiches—
and just so British, so *old,* and I felt, well, there's no way out of this
because both of us are, right now, too much immersed in this history, hope
60   is dissolved in the sheer age of this place, where race is what counts and
there's no real hope of change—it's the racial destiny of the Brits that matters to them, not their political destiny, whereas in America . . .

BELIZE   Here in America race doesn't count.

9. In *Annie Hall* (1977), directed by and starring Allen (b. 1935), a Jew born in New York
City, Allen's character imagines that his girlfriend's midwestern family sees him as a
Hasid, wearing the tight-woven wool coat and

payess (side curls; Yiddish) characteristic of
that ultraorthodox Jewish sect. *Yid:* Jew
(pejorative).
1. That is, not the English Civil War
(1642–48).

LOUIS No, no, that's not . . . I mean you *can't* be hearing that . . .

65 BELIZE I . . .

LOUIS It's—look, race, yes, but ultimately race here is a political question, right? Racists just try to use race here as a tool in a political struggle. It's not really about race. Like the spiritualists try to use that stuff, are you enlightened, are you centered, channeled, whatever, this reaching out for a

70 spiritual past in a country where no indigenous spirits exist—only the Indians, I mean Native American spirits and we killed them off so now, there are no gods here, no ghosts and spirits in America, there are no angels in America, no spiritual past, no racial past, there's only the political, and the decoys and the ploys to maneuver around the inescapable battle of politics,

75 the shifting downwards and outwards of political power to the people . . .

BELIZE POWER to the People![2] AMEN! [*Looking at his watch*] OH MY GOODNESS! Will you look at the time, I gotta . . .

LOUIS Do you. . . . You think this is, what, racist or naive or something?

BELIZE Well it's certainly *something*. Look, I just remembered I have an

80 appointment . . .

LOUIS What? I mean I really don't want to, like, speak from some position of privilege and . . .

BELIZE I'm sitting here, thinking, eventually he's *got* to run out of steam, so I let you rattle on and on saying about maybe seven or eight things I find

85 really offensive.

LOUIS What?

BELIZE But I know you, Louis, and I know the guilt fueling this peculiar tirade is obviously already swollen bigger than your hemorrhoids.

LOUIS I don't have hemorrhoids.

90 BELIZE I hear different. May I finish?

LOUIS Yes, but I don't have hemorrhoids.

BELIZE So finally, when I . . .

LOUIS Prior told you, he's an asshole, he shouldn't have . . .

BELIZE You promised, Louis. Prior is not a subject.

95 LOUIS You brought him up.

BELIZE I brought up hemorrhoids.

LOUIS So it's indirect. Passive-aggressive.

BELIZE Unlike, I suppose, banging me over the head with your theory that America doesn't have a race problem.

100 LOUIS Oh be fair I never said that.

BELIZE Not exactly, but . . .

LOUIS I said . . .

BELIZE . . . but it was close enough, because if it'd been that blunt I'd've just walked out and . . .

105 LOUIS You deliberately misinterpreted! I . . .

BELIZE Stop interrupting! I haven't been able to . . .

LOUIS Just let me . . .

BELIZE NO! What, *talk*? You've been running your mouth nonstop since I got here, yaddadda yaddadda blah blah blah, up the hill, down the hill,

110 playing with your MONOLITH . . .

---

2. A slogan of the 1960s, associated both with student protesters and with the militant Black Panthers.

LOUIS [*overlapping*] Well, you could have joined in at any time instead of . . .

BELIZE [*continuing over* LOUIS] . . . and girlfriend it is truly an *awesome* spectacle but I got better things to do with my time than sit here listening
115 to this racist bullshit just because I feel sorry for you that . . .

LOUIS I am not a racist!

BELIZE Oh come on . . .

LOUIS So maybe I am a racist but . . .

BELIZE Oh I really hate that! It's no fun picking on you Louis; you're so
120 guilty, it's like throwing darts at a glob of jello, there's no satisfying hits, just quivering, the darts just blop in and vanish.

LOUIS I just think when you are discussing lines of oppression it gets very complicated and . . .

BELIZE Oh is that a fact? You know, we black drag queens have a rather inti-
125 mate knowledge of the complexity of the lines of . . .

LOUIS *Ex*–black drag queen.

BELIZE Actually ex-ex.

LOUIS You're doing drag again?

BELIZE I don't . . . Maybe. I don't have to tell you. Maybe.

130 LOUIS I think it's sexist.

BELIZE I didn't ask you.

LOUIS Well it is. The gay community, I think, has to adopt the same attitude towards drag as black women have to take towards black women blues singers.

135 BELIZE Oh my we *are* walking dangerous tonight.

LOUIS Well, it's all internalized oppression, right, I mean the masochism, the stereotypes, the . . .

BELIZE Louis, are you deliberately trying to make me hate you?

LOUIS No, I . . .

140 BELIZE I mean, are you deliberately transforming yourself into an arrogant, sexual-political Stalinist-slash-racist flag-waving thug for my benefit?

[*Pause.*]

LOUIS You know what I think?

BELIZE What?

145 LOUIS You hate me because I'm a Jew.

BELIZE I'm leaving.

LOUIS It's true.

BELIZE You have no basis except your . . .

     Louis, it's good to know you haven't changed; you are still an honorary
150 citizen of the Twilight Zone,[3] and after your pale, pale white polemics on behalf of racial insensitivity you have a flaming *fuck* of a lot of nerve calling me an anti-Semite. Now I really gotta go.

LOUIS You called me Lou the Jew.

BELIZE That was a joke.

155 LOUIS I didn't think it was funny. It was hostile.

BELIZE It was three years ago.

LOUIS So?

BELIZE You just called yourself Sid the Yid.

3. That is, in the fantasy world of *The Twilight Zone* (1959–64), Rod Serling's television series.

LOUIS That's not the same thing.

160 BELIZE Sid the Yid is different from Lou the Jew.

LOUIS Yes.

BELIZE Someday you'll have to explain that to me, but right now . . .
You hate me because you hate black people.

LOUIS I do not. But I do think most black people are anti-Semitic.

165 BELIZE "Most black people." *That's* racist, Louis, and *I* think most Jews . . .

LOUIS Louis Farrakhan.[4]

BELIZE Ed Koch.[5]

LOUIS Jesse Jackson.[6]

BELIZE Jackson. Oh really, Louis, this is . . .

170 LOUIS Hymietown! Hymietown!

BELIZE Louis, you voted for Jesse Jackson. You send checks to the Rainbow
Coalition.

LOUIS I'm ambivalent. The checks bounced.

BELIZE All your checks bounce, Louis; you're ambivalent about everything.

175 LOUIS What's that supposed to mean?

BELIZE You may be dumber than shit but I refuse to believe you can't figure
it out. Try.

LOUIS I was never ambivalent about Prior. I love him. I do. I really do.

BELIZE Nobody said different.

180 LOUIS Love and ambivalence are . . . Real love isn't ambivalent.

BELIZE "Real love isn't ambivalent." I'd swear that's a line from my favorite
bestselling paperback novel, *In Love with the Night Mysterious*,[7] except I
don't think you ever read it.

[*Pause.*]

LOUIS I never read it, no.

185 BELIZE You ought to. Instead of spending the rest of your life trying to get
through *Democracy in America*.[8] It's about this white woman whose Daddy
owns a plantation in the Deep South in the years before the Civil War—the
American one—and her name is Margaret, and she's in love with her
Daddy's number-one slave, and his name is Thaddeus, and she's married
190 but her white slave-owner husband has AIDS: Antebellum Insufficiently
Developed Sexorgans. And there's a lot of hot stuff going down when Margaret and Thaddeus can catch a spare torrid ten under the cotton-picking
moon, and then of course the Yankees come, and they set the slaves free,
and the slaves string up old Daddy, and so on. Historical fiction. Some-
195 where in there I recall Margaret and Thaddeus find the time to discuss the

Footnotes.

4. A black religious leader (b. 1933), who in
1977 became leader of the Nation of Islam
(Black Muslims); beginning in the 1980s, he
received public censure for statements viewed
as anti-Semitic and antiwhite.
5. Jewish New York politician (1924–2013);
though popular as mayor (1978–89), early in
his administration he angered black political
leaders by reorganizing the city's poverty programs, and in the 1980s he became a vocal
critic of Farrakhan and Jesse Jackson.
6. A black civil rights leader (b. 1941), who ran
for president in 1984 and 1988; the 1984 revelation that he had called New York "Hymi-

etown," together with his association—soon
disavowed—with Farrakhan, damaged his reputation with Jews. After the 1984 campaign,
he turned his informal "rainbow coalition" of
minorities into a national social justice
organization.
7. A line from Cole Porter's 1948 song "So in
Love" (whose refrain begins "So taunt me
and hurt me, / Deceive me, desert me, / I'm
yours 'til I die"); no such novel exists.
8. Alexis de Tocqueville's classic study of
Americans and their system of government (2
vols., 1835–40).

nature of love; her face is reflecting the flames of the burning plantation—
you know, the way white people do—and his black face is dark in the night
and she says to him, "Thaddeus, real love isn't ever ambivalent."

[*Little pause.* EMILY *enters and turns off IV drip.*]

BELIZE   Thaddeus looks at her; he's contemplating her thesis; and he isn't
200   sure he agrees.

EMILY   [*removing IV drip from* PRIOR's *arm*]   Treatment number . . . [*Consulting chart*] four.

PRIOR   Pharmaceutical miracle. Lazarus[9] breathes again.

LOUIS   Is he. . . . How bad is he?

205   BELIZE   You want the laundry list?

EMILY   Shirt off, let's check the . . .

[PRIOR *takes his shirt off. She examines his lesions.*]

BELIZE   There's the weight problem and the shit problem and the morale
problem.

EMILY   Only six. That's good. Pants.

[*He drops his pants. He's naked. She examines.*]

210   BELIZE   And. He thinks he's going crazy.

EMILY   Looking good. What else?

PRIOR   Ankles sore and swollen, but the leg's better. The nausea's mostly
gone with the little orange pills. BM's pure liquid but not bloody anymore,
for now, my eye doctor says everything's OK, for now, my dentist says
215   "Yuck!" when he sees my fuzzy tongue, and now he wears little condoms on
his thumb and forefinger. And a mask. So what? My dermatologist is in
Hawaii and my mother . . . well leave my mother out of it. Which is usually
where my mother is, out of it. My glands are like walnuts, my weight's
holding steady for week two, and a friend died two days ago of bird tuber-
220   culosis;[1] bird tuberculosis; that scared me and I didn't go to the funeral
today because he was an Irish Catholic and it's probably open casket and
I'm afraid of . . . something, the bird TB or seeing him or . . . So I guess
I'm doing OK. Except for of course I'm going nuts.

EMILY   We ran the toxoplasmosis series[2] and there's no indication . . .

225   PRIOR   I know, I know, but I feel like something terrifying is on its way, you
know, like a missile from outer space, and it's plummeting down towards
the earth, and I'm ground zero, and . . . I am generally known where I am
known as one cool, collected queen. And I am ruffled.

EMILY   There's really nothing to worry about. I think that shochen bamro-
230   mim hamtzeh menucho nechono al kanfey haschino.[3]

PRIOR   What?

EMILY   Everything's fine. Bemaalos k'doshim ut'horim kezohar horokeea
mazhirim . . .

---

9. Jesus's resurrection of Lazarus from the dead is described in John 11.1–44.

1. A hard-to-treat form of tuberculosis that is common in AIDS patients.

2. A series of tests for toxoplasmosis, one of the infections commonly associated with AIDS; it often affects the brain.

3. This line begins transliterated Hebrew taken from the prayer traditionally recited at funerals for the soul of the departed; the translation is "[God, full of compassion,] who dwells on high, grant true rest upon the wings of your Divine Presence, in the exalted spheres of the holy and pure, who shine as the brightness of the heavens, to the soul of Prior, who has gone to his eternal rest, for charity has been donated in remembrance of his soul."

PRIOR Oh I don't understand what you're . . .

235 EMILY Es nishmas Prior sheholoch leolomoh, baavur shenodvoo z'dokoh b'ad hazkoras nishmosoh.

PRIOR Why are you doing that?! Stop it! Stop it!

EMILY Stop what?

PRIOR You were just . . . weren't you just speaking in Hebrew or something.

240 EMILY *Hebrew?* [*Laughs.*] I'm basically Italian-American. No. I didn't speak in Hebrew.

PRIOR Oh no, oh God please I really think I . . .

EMILY Look, I'm sorry, I have a waiting room full of . . . I think you're one of the lucky ones, you'll live for years, probably—you're pretty healthy for 245 someone with no immune system. Are you seeing someone? Loneliness is a danger. A therapist?

PRIOR No, I don't need to see anyone, I just . . .

EMILY Well think about it. You aren't going crazy. You're just under a lot of stress. No wonder . . . [*She starts to write in his chart.*]

[*Suddenly there is an astonishing blaze of light, a huge chord sounded by a gigantic choir, and a great book with steel pages mounted atop a molten-red pillar pops up from the stage floor. The book opens; there is a large Aleph[4] inscribed on its pages, which bursts into flames. Immediately the book slams shut and disappears instantly under the floor as the lights become normal again.* EMILY *notices none of this, writing.* PRIOR *is agog.*]

250 EMILY [*laughing, exiting*] Hebrew . . .

[*Prior flees.*]

LOUIS Help me.

BELIZE I beg your pardon?

LOUIS You're a nurse, give me something, I . . . don't know what to do any-255 more, I . . . Last week at work I screwed up the Xerox machine like perma-nently and so I . . . then I tripped on the subway steps and my glasses broke and I cut my forehead, here, see, and now I can't see much and my forehead . . . it's like the Mark of Cain,[5] stupid, right, but it won't heal and every morning I see it and I think, Biblical things, Mark of Cain, Judas Iscariot and his silver and his noose,[6] people who . . . in betraying what 260 they love betray what's truest in themselves, I feel . . . nothing but cold for myself, just cold, and every night I miss him, I miss him so much but then . . . those sores, and the smell and . . . where I thought it was going. . . . I could be . . . I could be sick too, maybe I'm sick too. I don't know.

Belize. Tell him I love him. Can you do that?

265 BELIZE I've thought about it for a very long time, and I still don't understand what love is. Justice is simple. Democracy is simple. Those things are unambivalent. But love is very hard. And it goes bad for you if you violate the hard law of love.

LOUIS I'm dying.

4. The first letter of the Hebrew alphabet.
5. According to Genesis (4.1–16), the first son of Adam and Eve, whose forehead was marked by God after he killed Abel, his brother.

6. For the story of the betrayal of Jesus by Judas Iscariot, his disciple, for thirty pieces of silver, and Judas's subsequent suicide by hanging, see Matthew 26.14–15, 27.3–5.

270 BELIZE   He's dying. You just wish you were.

Oh cheer up, Louis. Look at that heavy sky out there.

LOUIS   Purple.

BELIZE   *Purple?* Boy, what kind of a homosexual are you, anyway? That's not purple, Mary, that color up there is [*Very grand*] *mauve.*

275   All day today it's felt like Thanksgiving. Soon, this . . . ruination will be blanketed white. You can smell it—can you smell it?

LOUIS   Smell what?

BELIZE   Softness, compliance, forgiveness, grace.

LOUIS   No . . .

280 BELIZE   I can't help you learn that. I can't help you, Louis. You're not my business. [*He exits.*]

[*Louis puts his head in his hands, inadvertently touching his cut forehead.*]

LOUIS   Ow FUCK! [*He stands slowly, looks towards where* BELIZE *exited.*] Smell what?

[*He looks both ways to be sure no one is watching, then inhales deeply, and is surprised.*] Huh. Snow.

Scene 3

[*Same day.* HARPER *in a very white, cold place, with a brilliant blue sky above; a delicate snowfall. She is dressed in a beautiful snowsuit. The sound of the sea, faint.*]

HARPER   Snow! Ice! Mountains of ice! Where am I? I . . .

I feel better, I do,

I . . . feel better. There are ice crystals in my lungs, wonderful and sharp. And the snow smells like cold, crushed peaches. And there's something . . .

5   some current of blood in the wind, how strange, it has that iron taste.

MR. LIES   Ozone.

HARPER   Ozone! Wow! Where am I?

MR. LIES   The Kingdom of Ice, the bottommost part of the world.

HARPER [*looking around, then realizing*]   Antarctica. This is Antarctica!

10 MR. LIES   Cold shelter for the shattered. No sorrow here, tears freeze.

HARPER   Antarctica, Antarctica, oh boy oh boy, LOOK at this, I . . . Wow, I must've really snapped the tether, huh?

MR. LIES   Apparently . . .

HARPER   That's great. I want to stay here forever. Set up camp. Build things.

15   Build a city, an enormous city made up of frontier forts, dark wood and green roofs and high gates made of pointed logs and bonfires burning on every street corner. I should build by a river. Where are the forests?

MR. LIES   No timber here. Too cold. Ice, no trees.

HARPER   Oh details! I'm sick of details! I'll plant them and grow them. I'll live

20   off caribou fat, I'll melt it over the bonfires and drink it from long, curved goat-horn cups. It'll be great. I want to make a new world here. So that I never have to go home again.

MR. LIES   As long as it lasts. Ice has a way of melting . . .

HARPER   No. Forever. I can have anything I want here—maybe even com-

25   panionship, someone who has . . . desire for me. You, maybe.

MR. LIES   It's against the by-laws of the International Order of Travel Agents to get involved with clients. Rules are rules. Anyway, I'm not the one you really want.

HARPER   There isn't anyone . . . maybe an Eskimo. Who could ice-fish for
30   food. And help me build a nest for when the baby comes.

MR. LIES   There are no Eskimo in Antarctica. And you're not really pregnant.
You made that up.

HARPER   Well all of this is made up. So if the snow feels cold I'm pregnant.
Right? Here, I can be pregnant. And I can have any kind of a baby I want.

35   MR. LIES   This is a retreat, a vacuum, its virtue is that it lacks everything;
deep-freeze for feelings. You can be numb and safe here, that's what you
came for. Respect the delicate ecology of your delusions.

HARPER   You mean like no Eskimo in Antarctica.

MR. LIES   Correcto. Ice and snow, no Eskimo. Even hallucinations have laws.

40   HARPER   Well then who's that?

[*The Eskimo appears.*]

MR. LIES   An Eskimo.

HARPER   An antarctic Eskimo. A fisher of the polar deep.

MR. LIES   There's something wrong with this picture.

[*The Eskimo beckons.*]

HARPER   I'm going to like this place. It's my own National Geographic Spe-
45   cial![7] Oh! Oh! [*She holds her stomach.*] I think . . . I think I felt her kicking.
Maybe I'll give birth to a baby covered with thick white fur, and that way
she won't be cold. My breasts will be full of hot cocoa so she doesn't get
chilly. And if it gets really cold, she'll have a pouch I can crawl into. Like a
marsupial. We'll mend together. That's what we'll do; we'll mend.

Scene 4

[*Same day. An abandoned lot in the South Bronx. A homeless* WOMAN *is
standing near an oil drum in which a fire is burning. Snowfall. Trash
around.* HANNAH *enters dragging two heavy suitcases.*]

HANNAH   Excuse me? I said excuse me? Can you tell me where I am? Is this
Brooklyn? Do you know a Pineapple Street?[8] Is there some sort of bus or
train or . . . ?
    I'm lost, I just arrived from Salt Lake. City. Utah? I took the bus that I
5   was told to take and I got off—well it was the very last stop, so I had to get
off, and I *asked* the driver was this Brooklyn, and he nodded yes but he was
from one of those foreign countries where they think it's good manners to
nod at everything even if you have no idea what it is you're nodding at, and
in truth I think he spoke no English at all, which I think would make him
10   ineligible for employment on public transportation. The public being
English-speaking, mostly. Do you speak English?

[*The* WOMAN *nods.*]

HANNAH   I was supposed to be met at the airport by my son. He didn't show
and I don't wait more than three and three-quarters hours for *anyone.* I
should have been patient, I guess, I . . . Is this . . .

15   WOMAN   Bronx.

HANNAH   Is that . . . The *Bronx?* Well how in the name of Heaven did I get to
the Bronx when the bus driver said . . .

7. That is, like the television programs—
mainly documentaries featuring the exploration of the natural world—produced by the
National Geographic Society since 1964.
8. A street in Brooklyn Heights, a historic
district of Brooklyn.

WOMAN [*talking to herself*]   Slurp slurp slurp will you STOP that disgusting
slurping! YOU DISGUSTING SLURPING FEEDING ANIMAL! Feeding
20   yourself, just feeding yourself, what would it matter, to you or to ANYONE,
if you just stopped. Feeding. And DIED?

[*Pause.*]

HANNAH   Can you just tell me where I . . .

WOMAN   Why was the Kosciuszko Bridge[9] named after a Polack?

HANNAH   I don't know what you're . . .

25   WOMAN   That was a joke.

HANNAH   Well what's the punchline?

WOMAN   I don't know.

HANNAH [*looking around desperately*]   Oh for pete's sake, is there anyone else
who . . .

30   WOMAN [*again, to herself*]   Stand further off you fat loathsome whore, you
can't have any more of this soup, slurp slurp slurp you animal, and the—I
know you'll just go pee it all away and where will you do that? Behind what
bush? It's FUCKING COLD out here and I . . .
Oh that's right, because it was supposed to have been a tunnel!
35   That's not very funny.
Have you read the prophecies of Nostradamus?[1]

HANNAH   Who?

WOMAN   Some guy I went out with once somewhere, Nostradamus. Prophet,
outcast, eyes like . . . Scary shit, he . . .

40   HANNAH   Shut up. Please. Now I want you to stop jabbering for a minute and
pull your wits together and tell me how to get to Brooklyn. Because you
know! And you are going to tell me! Because there is no one else around to
tell me and I am wet and cold and I am very angry! So I am sorry you're
psychotic but just make the effort—take a deep breath—DO IT!

[HANNAH *and the* WOMAN *breathe together.*]

45   HANNAH   That's good. Now exhale.

[*They do.*]

HANNAH   Good. Now how do I get to Brooklyn?

WOMAN   Don't know. Never been. Sorry. Want some soup?

HANNAH   Manhattan? Maybe you know . . . I don't suppose you know the
location of the Mormon Visitor's[2] . . .

50   WOMAN   65th and Broadway.

HANNAH   How do you . . .

WOMAN   Go there all the time. Free movies. Boring, but you can stay all day.

HANNAH   Well. . . . So how do I . . .

WOMAN   Take the D Train.[3] Next block make a right.

55   HANNAH   Thank you.

WOMAN   Oh yeah. In the new century I think we will all be insane.

9. A bridge that connects the Bronx and
Queens (a borough that, like Brooklyn, is on
Long Island); it is named for Tadeusz
Kościuszko (1746–1817), a Polish military
engineer who fought with distinction in
America's Continental Army in the Revolu-
tionary War.
1. Michel de Nostredame (1503–1566), a

French astrologer and physician whose
Prophesies (1555), a collection of predictions
about the future, has long found a receptive
audience.
2. The Mormon Visitors' Center.
3. A subway line that, in the Bronx, runs
along the Grand Concourse; it extends to
Brooklyn.

Scene 5

[*Same day.* JOE *and* ROY *in the study of* ROY's *brownstone.* ROY *is wearing an elegant bathrobe. He has made a considerable effort to look well. He isn't well, and he hasn't succeeded much in looking it.*]

JOE   I can't. The answer's no. I'm sorry.

ROY   Oh, well, apologies . . .

I can't see that there's anyone asking for apologies.

[*Pause.*]

JOE   I'm sorry, Roy.

5 ROY   Oh, well, apologies.

JOE   My wife is missing, Roy. My mother's coming from Salt Lake to . . . to help look, I guess. I'm supposed to be at the airport now, picking her up but . . . I just spent two days in a hospital, Roy, with a bleeding ulcer, I was spitting up blood.

10 ROY   Blood, huh? Look, I'm very busy here and . . .

JOE   It's just a job.

ROY   A job? A *job? Washington!* Dumb Utah Mormon hick shit!

JOE   Roy . . .

ROY   *WASHINGTON!* When Washington called me I was younger than you,
15   you think I said "Aw fuck no I can't go I got two fingers up my asshole and a little moral nosebleed to boot!" When Washington calls you my pretty young punk friend you go or you can go fuck yourself sideways 'cause the train has pulled out of the station, and you are *out*, nowhere, out in the cold. Fuck you, Mary Jane, get outta here.

20 JOE   Just let me . . .

ROY   Explain? Ephemera. You broke my heart. Explain that. Explain that.

JOE   I love you. Roy.

There's so much that I want, to be . . . what you see in me, I want to be a participant in the world, in your world, Roy, I want to be capable of that,
25   I've tried, really I have but . . . I can't do this. Not because I don't believe in you, but because I believe in you so much, in what you stand for, at heart, the order, the decency. I would give anything to protect you, but . . . There are laws I can't break. It's too ingrained. It's not me. There's enough damage I've already done.

30   Maybe you were right, maybe I'm dead.

ROY   You're not dead, boy, you're a sissy.

You love me; that's moving, I'm moved. It's nice to be loved. I warned you about her, didn't I, Joe? But you don't listen to me, why, because you say Roy is smart and Roy's a friend but Roy . . . well, he isn't nice, and you
35   wanna be nice. Right? A nice, nice man! [*Little pause*]

You know what my greatest accomplishment was, Joe, in my life, what I am able to look back on and be proudest of? And I have helped make Presidents and unmake them and mayors and more goddam judges than anyone in NYC ever—AND several million dollars, tax-free—and what do you
40   think means the most to me?

You ever hear of Ethel Rosenberg? Huh, Joe, huh?

JOE   Well, yeah, I guess I . . . Yes.

ROY   Yes. Yes. You have heard of Ethel Rosenberg. Yes. Maybe you even read about her in the history books.

45 If it wasn't for me, Joe, Ethel Rosenberg would be alive today, writing some personal-advice column for *Ms.* magazine.[4] She isn't. Because during the trial, Joe, I was on the phone every day, talking with the judge . . .

JOE Roy . . .

ROY Every day, doing what I do best, talking on the telephone, making sure
50 that timid Yid nebbish[5] on the bench did his duty to America, to history. That sweet unprepossessing woman, two kids, boo-hoo-hoo, reminded us all of our little Jewish mamas—she came this close to getting life; I pleaded till I wept to put her in the chair.[6] Me. I did that. I would have fucking pulled the switch if they'd have let me. Why? Because I fucking hate trai-
55 tors. Because I fucking hate communists. Was it legal? Fuck legal. Am I a nice man? Fuck nice. They say terrible things about me in the *Nation.*[7] Fuck the *Nation.* You want to be Nice, or you want to be Effective? Make the law, or subject to it. Choose. Your wife chose. A week from today, she'll be back. SHE knows how to get what SHE wants. Maybe I ought to send
60 *her* to Washington.

JOE I don't believe you.

ROY Gospel.

JOE You can't possibly mean what you're saying.
    Roy, you were the Assistant United States Attorney on the Rosenberg
65 case, ex-parte[8] communication with the judge during the trial would be . . . censurable, at least, probably conspiracy and . . . in a case that resulted in execution, it's . . .

ROY What? Murder?

JOE You're not well is all.

70 ROY What do you mean, not well? Who's not well?
    [*Pause.*]

JOE You said . . .

ROY No I didn't. I said what?

JOE Roy, you have cancer.

ROY No I don't.
    [*Pause.*]

75 JOE You told me you were dying.

ROY What the fuck are you talking about, Joe? I never said that. I'm in per-fect health. There's not a goddam thing wrong with me. [*He smiles.*]
    Shake?
    [JOE *hesitates. He holds out his hand to* ROY. ROY *pulls* JOE *into a close, strong clinch.*]

80 ROY [*more to himself than to* JOE] It's OK that you hurt me because I love you, baby Joe. That's why I'm so rough on you.
    [ROY *releases* JOE. JOE *backs away a step or two.*]

---

4. An American feminist magazine that appeared monthly from 1972 to 1987; it resumed publication in 2001.
5. A nonentity, a loser (Yiddish); the presiding judge in the Rosenbergs' trial was Irving R. Kaufman (1910–1992).
6. The electric chair, used to execute the Rosenbergs.

7. A left-liberal American journal of culture and politics, published weekly since 1865.
8. In law, proceedings conducted in the absence of and without notice to one party, a practice that is normally prohibited (literally, "from [one] side"; Latin); see Playwright's Notes.

ROY Prodigal son.[9] The world will wipe its dirty hands all over you.

JOE It already has, Roy.

ROY Now go.

> [ROY *shoves* JOE, *hard.* JOE *turns to leave.* ROY *stops him, turns him around.*]

ROY [*smoothing* JOE's *lapels, tenderly*] I'll always be here, waiting for you . . .

85 [*Then again, with sudden violence, he pulls* JOE *close, violently.*] What did you want from me, what was all this, what do you want, treacherous ungrateful little . . .

> [JOE, *very close to belting* ROY, *grabs him by the front of his robe, and propels him across the length of the room. He holds* ROY *at arm's length, the other arm ready to hit.*]

ROY [*laughing softly, almost pleading to be hit*] Transgress a little, Joseph.

> [JOE *releases* ROY.]

90 ROY There are so many laws; find one you can break.

> [JOE *hesitates, then leaves, backing out. When* JOE *has gone,* ROY *doubles over in great pain, which he's been hiding throughout the scene with* JOE.]

ROY Ah, Christ . . .
Andy! Andy! Get in here! Andy!

> [*The door opens, but it isn't* ANDY. *A small Jewish* WOMAN *dressed modestly in a fifties hat and coat stands in the doorway. The room darkens.*]

ROY Who the fuck are you? The new nurse?

> [*The figure in the doorway says nothing. She stares at* ROY. *A pause.* ROY *looks at her carefully, gets up, crosses to her. He crosses back to the chair, sits heavily.*]

ROY Aw, fuck. Ethel.

95 ETHEL ROSENBERG [*her manner is friendly, her voice is ice-cold*] You don't look good, Roy.

ROY Well, Ethel. I don't feel good.

ETHEL ROSENBERG But you lost a lot of weight. That suits you. You were heavy back then. Zaftig, mit[1] hips.

100 ROY I haven't been that heavy since 1960. We were all heavier back then, before the body thing started. Now I look like a skeleton. They stare.

ETHEL ROSENBERG The shit's really hit the fan, huh, Roy?

> [*Little pause.* ROY *nods.*]

ETHEL ROSENBERG Well the fun's just started.

ROY What is this, Ethel, Halloween? You trying to scare me?

> [ETHEL *says nothing.*]

105 ROY Well you're wasting your time! I'm scarier than you any day of the week! So beat it, Ethel! BOOO! BETTER DEAD THAN RED![2] Somebody trying to shake me up? HAH HAH! From the throne of God in heaven to the belly of hell, you can all fuck yourselves and then go jump in the lake because I'M NOT AFRAID OF YOU OR DEATH OR HELL OR ANYTHING!

---

9. That is, the son who squanders his inheritance but is joyfully welcomed back home (see Luke 15.11–32).

1. Plump, with (Yiddish); *zaftig* usually means "buxom."

2. A slogan used in the 1950s to denounce Communists ("Reds") and leftists.

110 ETHEL ROSENBERG   Be seeing you soon, Roy. Julius[3] sends his regards.

ROY   Yeah, well send this to Julius!

> [*He flips the bird in her direction,[4] stands and moves towards her. Halfway across the room he slumps to the floor, breathing laboriously, in pain.*]

ETHEL ROSENBERG   You're a very sick man, Roy.

ROY   Oh God . . . ANDY!

ETHEL ROSENBERG   Hmmm. He doesn't hear you, I guess. We should call the
115 ambulance.

> [*She goes to the phone.*] Hah! Buttons! Such things they got now.
> What do I dial, Roy?
> [*Pause.* ROY *looks at her, then.*]

ROY   911.

ETHEL ROSENBERG [*dials the phone*]   It sings!
120 [*Imitating dial tones*] La la la . . .
Huh.
Yes, you should please send an ambulance to the home of Mister Roy
Cohn, the famous lawyer.
What's the address, Roy?

125 ROY [*a beat, then*]   244 East 87th.

ETHEL ROSENBERG   244 East 87th Street. No apartment number, he's got the
whole building.
My name? [*A beat*] Ethel Greenglass Rosenberg.
[*Small smile*] Me? No I'm not related to Mr. Cohn. An old friend. [*She
hangs up.*]
130 They said a minute.

ROY   I have all the time in the world.

ETHEL ROSENBERG   You're immortal.

ROY   I'm immortal. Ethel. [*He forces himself to stand.*]
I have *forced* my way into history. I ain't never gonna die.

135 ETHEL ROSENBERG [*a little laugh, then*]   History is about to crack wide open.
Millennium approaches.

Scene 6

> [*Late that night.* PRIOR's *bedroom.* PRIOR 1 *watching* PRIOR *in bed, who is
> staring back at him, terrified. Tonight* PRIOR 1 *is dressed in weird alchemical robes and hat over his historical clothing and he carries a long palm-
> leaf bundle.*]

PRIOR 1   Tonight's the night! Aren't you excited? Tonight she arrives! Right
through the roof! Ha-adam, Ha-gadol . . .

PRIOR 2 [*appearing, similarly attired*]   Lumen! Phosphor! Fluor! Candle! An
unending billowing of scarlet and . . .

5 PRIOR   Look. Garlic. A mirror. Holy water. A crucifix.[5] FUCK OFF! Get the
fuck out of my room! GO!

PRIOR 1 [*to* PRIOR 2]   Hard as a hickory knob, I'll bet.

PRIOR 2   We all tumesce when they approach. We wax full, like moons.

PRIOR 1   Dance.

---

3. Julius Rosenberg (1918–1953), Ethel's
husband.

4. Gives her the finger.
5. All items believed to deter vampires.

10 PRIOR   Dance?

PRIOR 1   Stand up, dammit, give us your hands, dance!

PRIOR 2   Listen . . .

[*A lone oboe begins to play a little dance tune.*]

PRIOR 2   Delightful sound. Care to dance?

PRIOR   Please leave me alone, please just let me sleep . . .

15 PRIOR 2   Ah, he wants someone familiar. A partner who knows his steps. [*To* PRIOR] Close your eyes. Imagine . . .

PRIOR   I don't . . .

PRIOR 2   Hush. Close your eyes.

[PRIOR *does.*]

PRIOR 2   Now open them.

[PRIOR *does.* LOUIS *appears. He looks gorgeous. The music builds gradually into a full-blooded, romantic dance tune.*]

20 PRIOR   Lou.

LOUIS   Dance with me.

PRIOR   I can't, my leg, it hurts at night . . .

Are you . . . a ghost, Lou?

LOUIS   No. Just spectral. Lost to myself. Sitting all day on cold park benches.

25 Wishing I could be with you. Dance with me, babe . . .

[PRIOR *stands up. The leg stops hurting. They begin to dance. The music is beautiful.*]

PRIOR 1   [*to* PRIOR 2]   Hah. Now I see why he's got no children. He's a sodomite.

PRIOR 2   Oh be quiet, you medieval gnome, and let them dance.

PRIOR 1   I'm not interfering, I've done my bit. Hooray, hooray, the messenger's

30 come, now I'm blowing off. I don't like it here.

[PRIOR 1 *vanishes.*]

PRIOR 2   The twentieth century. Oh dear, the world has gotten so terribly, terribly old.

[PRIOR 2 *vanishes.* LOUIS *and* PRIOR *waltz happily. Lights fade back to normal.* LOUIS *vanishes.*

PRIOR *dances alone.*

Then suddenly, the sound of wings fills the room.]

Scene 7

[*Split scene:* PRIOR *alone in his apartment;* LOUIS *alone in the park. Again, a sound of beating wings.*]

PRIOR   Oh don't come in here don't come in . . . LOUIS!!

No. My name is Prior Walter, I am . . . the scion of an ancient line, I am . . . abandoned I . . . no, my name is . . . is . . . Prior and I live . . . *here and now,* and . . . in the dark, in the dark, the Recording Angel opens its

5 hundred eyes and snaps the spine of the Book of Life[6] and . . . hush! Hush! I'm talking nonsense, I . . .

---

6. In Jewish tradition, the symbolic book in which all who lived are sealed each year on the Day of Atonement, Yom Kippur; in the New Testament, it contains the names of those who will not be damned on Judgment Day (Revelation 13.8, 20.12–15).

No more mad scene, hush, hush . . .

[LOUIS *in the park on a bench.* JOE *approaches, stands at a distance. They stare at each other, then* LOUIS *turns away.*]

LOUIS   Do you know the story of Lazarus?

JOE   Lazarus?

10 LOUIS   Lazarus. I can't remember what happens, exactly.

JOE   I don't . . . Well, he was dead, Lazarus, and Jesus breathed life into him. He brought him back from death.

LOUIS   Come here often?

JOE   No. Yes. Yes.

15 LOUIS   Back from the dead. You believe that really happened?

JOE   I don't know anymore what I believe.

LOUIS   This is quite a coincidence. Us meeting.

JOE   I followed you.
    From work. I . . . followed you here.
    [*Pause.*]

20 LOUIS   You followed me.
    You probably saw me that day in the washroom and thought: there's a sweet guy, sensitive, cries for friends in trouble.

JOE   Yes.

LOUIS   You thought maybe I'll cry for you.

25 JOE   Yes.

LOUIS   Well I fooled you. Crocodile tears. Nothing . . . [*He touches his heart, shrugs.*]

    [JOE *reaches tentatively to touch* LOUIS's *face.*]

LOUIS [*pulling back*]   What are you doing? Don't do that.

JOE [*withdrawing his hand*]   Sorry. I'm sorry.

LOUIS   I'm . . . just not . . . I think, if you touch me, your hand might fall off

30   or something. Worse things have happened to people who have touched me.

JOE   Please.
    Oh, boy . . .
    Can I . . .

35   I . . . want . . . to touch you. Can I please just touch you . . . um, here?
    [*He puts his hand on one side of* LOUIS's *face. He holds it there.*]
    I'm going to hell for doing this.

LOUIS   Big deal. You think it could be any worse than New York City?
    [*He puts his hand on* JOE's *hand. He takes* JOE's *hand away from his face, holds it for a moment, then.*] Come on.

JOE   Where?

40 LOUIS   Home. With me.

JOE   This makes no sense. I mean I don't know you.

LOUIS   Likewise.

JOE   And what you do know about me you don't like.

LOUIS   The Republican stuff?

45 JOE   Yeah, well for starters.

LOUIS   I don't not like that. I *hate* that.

JOE   So why on earth should we . . .

    [LOUIS *goes to* JOE *and kisses him.*]

LOUIS Strange bedfellows. I don't know. I never made it with one of the damned before.

50   I would really rather not have to spend tonight alone.

JOE I'm a pretty terrible person, Louis.

LOUIS Lou.

JOE No, I really really am. I don't think I deserve being loved.

LOUIS There? See? We already have a lot in common.

[LOUIS *stands, begins to walk away. He turns, looks back at* JOE. JOE *follows. They exit.*]

[PRIOR *listens. At first no sound, then once again, the sound of beating wings, frighteningly near.*]

55 PRIOR That sound, that sound, it. . . . What is that, like birds or something, like a *really* big bird, I'm frightened, I . . . no, no fear, find the anger, find the . . . anger, my blood is clean, my brain is fine, I can handle pressure, I am a gay man and I am used to pressure, to trouble, I am tough and strong and. . . . Oh. Oh my goodness. I . . . [*He is washed over by an intense sexual*

60 *feeling.*] Ooohhhh. . . . I'm hot, I'm . . . so . . . aw Jeez what is going on here I . . . must have a fever I . . .

[*The bedside lamp flickers wildly as the bed begins to roll forward and back. There is a deep bass creaking and groaning from the bedroom ceiling, like the timbers of a ship under immense stress, and from above a fine rain of plaster dust.*]

PRIOR OH!

PLEASE, OH PLEASE! Something's coming in here, I'm scared, I don't like this at all, something's approaching and I . . . OH!

[*There is a great blaze of triumphal music, heralding. The light turns an extraordinary harsh, cold, pale blue, then a rich, brilliant warm golden color, then a hot, bilious green, and then finally a spectacular royal purple. Then silence.*]

65 PRIOR [*an awestruck whisper*] God almighty . . .
Very Steven Spielberg.[7]

[*A sound, like a plummeting meteor, tears down from very, very far above the earth, hurtling at an incredible velocity towards the bedroom; the light seems to be sucked out of the room as the projectile approaches; as the room reaches darkness, we hear a terrifying CRASH as something immense strikes earth; the whole building shudders and a part of the bedroom ceiling, lots of plaster and lathe and wiring, crashes to the floor. And then in a shower of unearthly white light, spreading great opalescent gray-silver wings, the Angel descends into the room and floats above the bed.*]

ANGEL

Greetings, Prophet;
The Great Work begins:
The Messenger has arrived.

[*Blackout.*]

End of Part One.

7. An American film director (b. 1947), known for his use of special effects in such hits as *Close Encounters of the Third Kind* (1977), *Raiders of the Lost Ark* (1981), and *E.T.: The Extraterrestrial* (1982).

DANIEL DAVID MOSES

b. 1952

WHEN the Lakota Sioux warrior chief Sitting Bull joined Buffalo Bill's Wild West show as a "show Indian" in 1884, he entered a theatrical culture that was fascinated with North America's Native, or indigenous, people. The stereotypes used to represent these people—noble savage, treacherous heathen, idealized Indian princess, loyal sidekick, vanishing primitive— have been staples of theater, film, television, and popular culture over the last two hundred years. Indigenous playwrights and theater artists, First Nations people (as they are referred to in Canada) or Native Americans (as they are referred to in the United States), have been working in the theater since the turn of the twentieth century: Cherokee dramatist Lynn Riggs's 1930 play *Green Grow the Lilacs*, for instance, was the source for the Rodgers and Hammerstein musical *Oklahoma!*, while Chickasaw storyteller and actress Te Ata performed for President Franklin Roosevelt and other heads of state during her long career. But it was not until the 1960s and 1970s that Native people on both sides of the border began organizing theater groups to challenge the stereotypical images of Indians in the mainstream media and to support the

work of Native playwrights, actors, and theater artists who have claimed the stage as a medium for their own experiences, beliefs, histories, and identities. The theater that resulted from these efforts—including the drama of First Nations playwright Daniel David Moses—challenges prevailing histories of Native/non-Native encounters, introduces new aesthetic principles and worldviews, and examines the question of Native identity in powerful and innovative ways.

Daniel David Moses, a registered Delaware (or Lenape) Indian, was born and grew up on a farm on the Six Nations Reserve, a largely Iroquoian community along the Grand River in southern Ontario ("reserves" are the Canadian equivalent of U.S. reservations). He developed a love of language from listening to the liturgy and hymns of the Anglican mission church he attended as a child and reading traditional and contemporary literature in school. He decided in high school to become a writer and pursued this vocation while earning a college degree at York University in Toronto. His earliest writing took the form of poetry, but his passion for spoken language and the interaction of multiple voices led him to playwriting as well. "Whatever idea I have . . . I have to write until the idea can be said by the body entire," he stated in a 1991 essay. "I write words that are meant to be spoken and heard, that mean what they must in the air." While completing the MFA program in creative writing at the University of British Columbia, Moses won the program's prize for playwriting in 1977, and the collection of poetry he submitted for his thesis that year included a one-act play.

Moses's exploration of Native writing and performance deepened when he moved to Toronto in the late 1970s. He volunteered with the Association for Native Development in the Performing and Visual Arts, which had been established in 1974 to support the training of Native playwrights and theater practitioners, and joined a circle of Native writers that formed around the Ojibway writer, storyteller, and Native literature activist Lenore Keeshig-Tobias. In 1982 he met Cree-born playwright Tomson Highway, who was instrumental in the founding of Native Earth Performing Arts (NEPA), Canada's most prominent Native theater company. Along with the De-ba-jeh-mu-jig Theatre Group—a Native company whose name means "storytellers" in Cree and Ojibway and which was founded in 1984 on Manitoulin Island in Lake Huron—NEPA introduced the plays of Native dramatists to Canadian audiences. Prominent among these plays were Highway's *The Rez Sisters* (1986) and *Dry Lips Oughta Move to Kapuskasing* (1989), which received widespread acclaim and helped establish First Nations drama on the international theater scene. Highway served as artistic director of NEPA from 1986 to 1992, while Moses served as co-director from 1998 to 2000.

Moses has described the writer's task as "expressing my 'self' as a twenty-first-century First Nations person, reclaiming and reviving, for myself and my circle, what is still viable in our tradition and inventing whatever else is needed." One of the Native traditions that Moses embraced was the Trickster, a figure who appears in Native folklore under such names as Coyote, Raven, Nanabush, and Weesageechak. The Trickster is a contradictory figure, marked by duplicity as well as moral authority; both hero and fool, the Trickster teaches the lessons of life by positive and negative example. Moses's first play, *Coyote City*, which was produced by Native Earth in 1988 and nominated for the Governor General's Literary Prize in 1991, adapts the Trickster legend to contemporary Native life. It also introduces the relationship between the human and spirit worlds that Moses would return to in later plays. *Coyote City* draws upon a Nez Perce story entitled "Coyote and the Shadow People." In this story Coyote is led by a spirit guide to an open prairie, where he encounters the ghost of his wife at night in a great lodge peopled by the dead. After visiting her and the other departed souls over a series of nights, Coyote tries to bring his wife back to the real world but loses her when he disobeys the spirit guide's instructions not to embrace her. The Coyote City of Moses's play is Toronto, where the character Lena travels to rescue her lover Johnny from the spirit world in the Silver Dollar Bar, where he was killed. The family members and other characters that pursue Lena are sharply drawn personalities, while Johnny appears as a ghostly emissary from the spirit world that looms within their everyday lives. Like Coyote, Lena fails, in the end, to rescue her lover from the realm of the dead.

In subsequent plays Moses explores twentieth- and twenty-first-century Native identities through a range of subjects and dramatic styles. His one-act play *The Dreaming Beauty* (1990) draws on the story of Sleeping Beauty to describe the rebirth of Native identity in a girl, referred to as Beauty, who has forgotten her name and cultural heritage. *Big Buck City* (1991) is the second of Moses's "city plays" exploring contemporary Native urban experience, while the third, *Kyotopolis* (1993), is a space-age fantasia set "at a variety of intersections in the global Indian village, that almost-present dream of the city of tomorrow." With ALMIGHTY VOICE AND HIS WIFE (1991) Moses turned his attention to frontier history—in particular, a bloody confrontation between a young Cree Native and the Royal Canadian Mounted Police in late nineteenth-century western Canada. Moses returned to the frontier and its myths in *The Moon and Dead Indians*

(1993), which won the DuMaurier One-Act Playwriting Competition and was performed with another play, *Angel of the Medicine Show*, under the title *The Indian Medicine Shows* in 1996. The combined plays, which are set in New Mexico in the late nineteenth century, won the James Buller Award for Excellence in Aboriginal Theatre. Moses's 1996 play *Brebeuf's Ghost*, which is inspired by Shakespeare's *Macbeth* and the story of the French missionary Jean de Brébeuf, explores European-Native conflicts during the fur trade wars in seventeenth-century Ontario, while *Red River* (1998), which Moses co-wrote with Jim Millan, is set during the Red River Rebellion in Manitoba in 1869–70. Other works include *The Witch of Niagara* (1998), a mythic play of sickness and rebirth, and *Songs of Love and Medicine* (2005), two one-act plays with songs.

Almighty Voice and His Wife, Moses's best-known play and a staple of the contemporary Canadian repertoire, is an innovative and powerful work of Native theater. The play was first produced in Ottawa in September 1991 by the Great Canadian Theatre Company and in Toronto the following spring by Native Earth Performing Arts. A highly acclaimed revival of the play, also produced by Native Earth, opened in Toronto in 2009; this production was included in an international festival of First Nations drama, film, ceremony, and comedy at London's Riverside Studios that year and toured throughout Canada in 2010 and 2012.

The success of Moses's play about a young Cree man named Almighty Voice who was killed with his two companions in an 1897 shootout with the North-West Mounted Police owes much to its theatrically daring two-act structure. While the stripped-down first act of *Almighty Voice and His Wife* explores the resistance of Native peoples to the dispossession of their lands, lives, and freedoms, the play's theatrical second act—written in the form of a parodic minstrel show—exposes the stereotypes governing non-Native perceptions of Native identity and culture. Bracing and unsettling, the collision of perspectives in *Almighty Voice and His Wife* calls attention to the artificiality of the term "Indian" and

Almighty Voice, ca. 1895.

forces the audience to examine its own racial assumptions and biases.

Moses first encountered the story of Almighty Voice in the late 1970s while working as a researcher at a First Nations educational and cultural center in Brandford, Ontario. The historical Almighty Voice (1875–97), whose Cree name was *Kisse-Manitou-Wayou* but who appears in official records as Jean Baptiste, was raised by John Sounding Sky and Spotted Calf on the One Arrow Reserve a few miles from Batoche near the South Saskatchewan River. Formerly hunters, the One Arrow Cree faced starvation and disease on the reserve, where they had settled as the result of an 1876 land treaty and found themselves ill-suited to the agricultural life. In October 1895 Almighty Voice, then in his twenties, was imprisoned in nearby Duck Lake for poaching a cow—one source says to provide meat for a wedding feast, another to feed his brother's sick child. After a guard joked that he would be hanged for stealing the cow, Almighty Voice escaped from the prison and headed toward his reservation. When he was apprehended by a sergeant in the North-West Mounted Police a week later, he shot and killed the man. Now wanted for murder, he eluded the resulting manhunt for nineteen months before being discovered with two companions on the One Arrow Reserve in May 1897. The three men were pursued and cornered in a bluff of poplar trees, where they held off a siege of rifles and field guns with their own weapons. At the end of this confrontation, six men were dead, including Almighty Voice and his two friends.

When Moses researched the story of the young Cree warrior in the late 1980s, he was struck by the mention, in some accounts of these events, of a girl who accompanied Almighty Voice when he encountered and killed the Mountie. Having also learned that Almighty Voice's fourth wife was the thirteen-year-old daughter of an Indian named Old Dust, Moses decided that these sketchy historical figures represented a single character. This character, he realized, would allow him to tell a love story along the lines of *Bonnie and Clyde* or *Romeo and Juliet* rather than "the renegade Indian one that I'd heard all too often before." Moses gave the character a name—White Girl—and a childhood spent in one of the Indian residential (or industrial) schools that were established in the nineteenth century to assimilate First Nations children into the language, culture, and Christian beliefs of non-Native Canadian society. White Girl struggles with the internalized legacy of this education and with the glass-eyed "Great White God of the ghost-men" to whom she was introduced. Act One of *Almighty Voice and His Wife* presents her relationship with Almighty Voice from their courtship to his death through a series of short scenes identified by projected titles. The staging of this act is lean and lyrical, with images and locales established through language, stage lighting, sound, and movement. The events of recorded history unfold offstage, while the stage itself is the space of more intimate interactions and loss.

Moses designed his first act so that it doesn't end with the violent death of Almighty Voice. One reason for this, he later wrote, was that he didn't want to pro-vide the public with "yet another image of the defeated wild Indian." His original plans for continuing the play beyond the first act were to explore the reasons for Almighty Voice's death through the perspective of the Mounties, soldiers, and settlers responsible for his death. After realizing that his Native actors would have to whiten their faces in order to perform these characters, he decided to make this theatrical device central to the play's second act by employing the structure and conventions of nineteenth-century minstrelsy. Minstrel shows—which enjoyed a vogue in the United States in the 1840s, remained highly popular throughout the century, and were taken on tour to other countries (including Canada)—were formally patterned variety shows featuring songs, dances, and comic dialogues. The typical stage arrangement of these shows featured musicians and singers seated in a semicircle with two "end-men" named Tambo and Bones and an Interlocutor seated in the middle who engaged in verbal back-and-forth with the other two. Minstrel shows portrayed demeaning stereotypes of African Americans, and until later in the nineteenth century, when African American minstrel companies began performing, these stereotypes were performed by white actors whose skin was "blackened" by burnt cork or shoe polish. The tradition of blackface performance that these shows helped popularize survived into the twentieth century, as did the parallel practice of "whiteface," which was used by African American actors and entertainers performing white characters. Whitening one's face, of course, is also a standard practice in clown performance.

Whiteface and the conventions of minstrel shows allowed Moses to shift his focus from the story of Almighty Voice to the ways in which this story—and the story of all Native North Americans—has been appropriated and re-presented by white society. In a theatrical tour de force entitled "Ghost Dance," White Girl and Almighty Voice reappear in the play's second act as minstrel performers: White Girl, dressed as a Mountie, in the role of Interlocutor with the Ghost of Almighty Voice standing in for the missing Tambo and Bones. Their faces whitened, they

Derek Garza as Almighty Voice and P. J. Prudat as White Girl in the 2012 Pi Theatre
(Vancouver) production of *Almighty Voice and His Wife*.

employ a series of traditional minstrel
show routines—overture, baritone solo,
stump speech, walkaround, tenor solo, playlet, duet, stand-up comic exchange, and
finale—in order to confront the play's audience with its equally conventionalized ways
of "seeing" Native people. From their position of symbolic whiteness, they recir-
culate long-standing images of Native
people—cigar store Indians, exotic war
dances, buck and squaw, redcoats and
wild Indians, urban alcoholics, Tonto, Sitting Bull—and revisit the events of the
first act from a series of parodic vantage
points. As Ghost recounts the events of his
final hours in the act's "Overture," Interlocutor sarcastically frames his story as
"the Red and White Victoria Regina Spirit
Revival Show" and "a shocking but true
tale of the frontier." They conduct a "martial interlude" that celebrates the Mounties
responsible for Almighty Voice's death, sing
a parodic Indian love song, and perform a
melodramatic playlet featuring a Native
woman called "Sweet Sioux." The audience
may want to "know the truth, the amazing
details and circumstances behind your savagely beautifully appearance," as Interlocutor tells Ghost, but what they get, instead,

are culturally sanctioned misrepresenta-
tions. At the heart of these distortions is
whiteness itself, that racial category that
depends on racial "others" for its purity. As
Moses has written, "White as a color only
exists because some of us get told we're
black or yellow or Indian. I think my ghosts
exist to probe this white problem, this tonal
confusion, to spook its metaphors. Maybe
my ghosts are like mirrors, but from a
funhouse."

The perceptions of white society pose an
additional problem for the play's two characters. As the abandoned industrial school
that provides the backdrop for the second
act reminds us, whiteness is an internalized phenomenon as well. Underlying the
act's parodic send-up of stereotypes, clichés, and performances is Ghost's attempt
to return White Girl-as-Interlocutor to an
awareness of her Native identity. "This is
what they've done to you," he says at the
end of Scene Two, looking into her eyes.
Seen this way, Interlocutor's minstrel performance is an act of self-hatred that
reflects her acculturation within a white
perspective. The sometimes playful, sometimes painful back-and-forth between the
two is a spiritual wooing in which White

Girl is eventually rescued from the greatest loss of all: herself.

The result of this theatricalized encounter is a brilliant, often searing examination of Native stereotypes, a journey through the funhouse mirror of distorted images. *Almighty Voice and His Wife*, Moses writes, "works like a purging or an exorcism," and in its unique combination of lyricism and grotesque variety-show comedy it seeks to clear the channels through which Native identity is experienced and perceived. Cleansed of the poison of cultural misrepresentation, the play can end with an image of reclamation and rebirth.

Almighty Voice and His Wife

CHARACTERS

ALMIGHTY VOICE[1] At first a young Cree[2] man, early twenties, Kisse-Manitou-Wayou, also known as John Baptist, later his own playful GHOST.

WHITE GIRL At first a young Cree woman, early teens, the daughter of Old Dust and the wife of Almighty Voice, later the INTERLOCUTOR.

The action of Act One incorporates historic events that happened between the end of October 1895 and May of 1897 on the Saskatchewan prairie, at and between the One Arrow and Fort a la Corne reserves.[3] Act Two occurs on the auditorium stage of the abandoned industrial school at Duck Lake.[4]

Act One

A projected title: "Act One: Running with the Moon."

Scene One

The projected title: "Scene One: Her Vision." A drum beats in night's blue darkness. The full moon sweeps down from the sky like a spotlight to show and surround WHITE GIRL, *asleep in a fetal position on the ground. The drum begins a sneak-up*

1. The historical Almighty Voice (1875–1897), a Cree warrior, lived on the One Arrow Reserve in present-day Saskatchewan. Jailed in 1895 for slaughtering a cow, he escaped and killed a member of the North-West Mounted Police (or Mountie) who had apprehended him while on the run. When he was discovered eighteen months later, he fled with his companions Little Salteau and Dubling to a bluff of poplars, where the men engaged in a gun battle with a large force of Mounties and civilians. At the end of the confrontation, six people, including Almighty Voice and his two friends, were dead. "Kisse-Manitou-Wayou" (literally "Voice of the Spirit") is Cree for "Almighty Voice."

Almighty Voice also appears in some records as Jean-Baptiste.
2. The Cree, who have historically ranged across much of North America, are Canada's largest First Nations population.
3. Canadian equivalent of the American term *reservation*. The One Arrow and Fort a la Corne reserves are located to the east and northeast of Duck Lake in central Saskatchewan. In the 1900s the present-day province of Saskatchewan was a territory in western Canada.
4. St. Michael's Indian Industrial School, a school in the Canadian residential school system, opened in the town of Duck Lake in 1892. The school was closed in 1964.

beat, the moon pulses in a similar rhythm. WHITE GIRL *wakes at the quake, gets to her feet, and takes a step. The drum hesitates. A gunshot and a slanting bolt of light stop her and block out the moon. Three more shots and slanting bolts of light come in quick succession, confining her in a spectral teepee. She peers out through its skin of light at* ALMIGHTY VOICE, *a silhouette against the moon. He collapses to the beats of the drum, echoes of the gunshots.* WHITE GIRL *falls to her knees as the teepee fades and the moon bleeds.*

Scene Two

The projected title: "Scene Two: The Proposal." WHITE GIRL *is by the fire, stripping meat for drying.* ALMIGHTY VOICE *loiters at a distance.*

VOICE   Hiya. Hiya. Hey girl, I said, "Hiya."
GIRL   I heard you the first time. I'm working here.
VOICE   Oh ya?
GIRL   I am. And my dad doesn't like it, you talking to me.
5 VOICE   Old Dust? What's he got to worry about? He's winning over there. I'm just talking.
GIRL   It's not your talking he's worried about.
VOICE   What you talking about?
GIRL   You never mind.
10 VOICE   What you talking about, girl? Hey White Girl, what you talking about?
GIRL   My dad says you already got a wife.
VOICE   What's that got to do with anything?
GIRL   I hear you already had two others.[5]
VOICE   You don't have to believe everything you hear. White Girl, you know
15   something? I think you got pretty eyes.
GIRL   I got no time to be told my eyes are pretty.
VOICE   You're pretty fierce for a little girl.
GIRL   You should leave little girls alone, Almighty Voice.
VOICE   You're not that little, little girl.
20 GIRL   I'm working here.
VOICE   You're big enough.
GIRL   Go away.
VOICE   Is that the way they do it at that school? That's not the way my mother does it.
25 GIRL   Spotted Calf doesn't know everything.
VOICE   She knows how to strip meat. Here, let me—
GIRL   You could get cut.
VOICE   You're pretty fierce all right, little girl. You are like Spotted Calf.
GIRL   What?
30 VOICE   My mother's not as pretty as you.
GIRL   Go bother my brother for a while.
VOICE   But he's not as pretty as you.
GIRL   Sure he is. He's my brother. You know what?
VOICE   What is it, White Girl?
35 GIRL   My brother, Young Dust, he likes you.
VOICE   He's my friend.

---

5. Polygamy was a common practice among First Nations peoples.

GIRL   No, Almighty Voice, he likes you. He thinks you are the pretty one. Your wife won't kiss you? Well, my brother will.

VOICE   You're a crazy one.

40 GIRL   You're right. I am a crazy one. As long as you know. But my brother does want to kiss—

VOICE   I don't want to talk about your brother.

GIRL   Look, he's coming this way.

VOICE   What? No he's not.

45 GIRL   But Young Dust does like you.

VOICE   And I like you.

GIRL   I'm just a little girl, Almighty Voice.

VOICE   A little girl working away.

GIRL   You could get cut.

50 VOICE   I want to kiss you, White Girl.

GIRL   My father's looking at you. He sees you talking to me.

VOICE   Let him.

GIRL   You got to talk to him first, you know.

VOICE   I don't want to break that hand game up. All right, I'll go talk to him

55 first.

GIRL   Then we'll talk.

VOICE   Just talk? What will we talk about?

GIRL   The wife you have now.

VOICE   What wife?

60 GIRL   The Rump's Daughter.

VOICE   Oh ya.

GIRL   You're going to send her home to her father.

VOICE   She won't go.

GIRL   She will go. I'm going to be your wife now. Your only wife. You can't

65 feed us both. Well then, my father's waiting to talk to you. Go on.

VOICE   Crazy.

Scene Three

A projected title: "Scene Three: The Wedding Night." A second fire in night's blue. A gunshot and a slanting bolt of light. The reverberations become a social dance beat on a drum and bring up the rest of the teepee of light. WHITE GIRL *enters it and sits. Then* ALMIGHTY VOICE *enters. The drum and teepee fade.*

VOICE   Hiya, wife. I said, "Hiya, wife."

GIRL   What can I do for my husband?

VOICE   Come here. Look at me. Leave that be.

GIRL   Does my husband want some tea?

5 VOICE   Your husband wants his blanket.

GIRL   There. Your blanket's ready for you. It's snowing out. Shall I go for wood to build the fire up?

VOICE   Can't you be quiet, girl?

GIRL   Shall I tell your friends to be quiet? Shall I tell them to go away?

10 VOICE   They'll go when they're full.

GIRL   Do you want more to eat, husband? I'll go get some more.

VOICE   Stay here with me. Look at me, White Girl.

GIRL   That was a wonderful cow you brought for the feast. It was so fat.

VOICE   You didn't eat much.

15 GIRL   I'm stuffed full. I have never eaten so well before, husband. Now my father will have to admit his daughter is well-fed. You are such a hunter.

VOICE   It was only a stupid cow. What's wrong, White Girl?

GIRL   I was thinking about my mother. She would have made him come. And your father. How could the Mounties take him? The day before our wedding.

20 VOICE   They're stupid. Look at me, wife.

GIRL   I don't want to be a wife. I don't want to be a woman. That school—I don't know how. I'm only thirteen. I'm crazy.

VOICE   You're not crazy.

GIRL   I am. I am.

25 VOICE   Come here. Let me hold you.

GIRL   No, it's too dangerous.

VOICE   It's not dangerous. Hey, come on, pretend I'm your brother.

GIRL   No, you're my husband. I don't want you to die.

VOICE   You're not going to kill me. You're going to kiss me.

30 GIRL   I have bad medicine in me. I went to that school.[6] The treaty agent[7] took me.

VOICE   But you got away, girl.

GIRL   School's a strange place. All made out of stone. The wind tries to get in, and can't, and cries. It's so hot and dry, your throat gets sore. You cough

35   a lot, too. I used to even cough blood. And they won't let you talk. They try to make you talk like they do. It's like stones in your mouth.

VOICE   You're here now.

GIRL   I liked it there.

VOICE   How could you like that?

40 GIRL   They said I could live there forever.

VOICE   What are you talking about?

GIRL   They said everybody at home had died of the smallpox.[8] They said I could live forever but I had to marry their god.

VOICE   Hey, you're my wife now and I'm alive. Everybody's alive.

45 GIRL   He's going to kill you. He's a jealous god.

VOICE   He's another one of their lies.

GIRL   They say he's everywhere. He can see everything.

VOICE   He's got nothing better to do than watch us?

GIRL   They say he's like a ghost.

50 VOICE   Hey little girl, even your dad didn't know for sure about us and he watched you like a hawk.

GIRL   Or a white bird. They say he's like a white bird.

VOICE   A white bird? A white bird in here?

GIRL   He made the smallpox.

6. Reference to the Canadian Indian residential school system, which was established in the 19th century to assimilate First Nations children into the language, culture, and Christian beliefs of Euro-Canadian society. In 1884 attendance at these schools, which were run by churches of different denominations, became mandatory for children under the age of 16.

7. Government representative appointed to implement the terms of the treaties signed between the reigning monarch of Canada and First Nations peoples. While government-native relations had been conducted through treaties since the mid-1700s, the so-called "numbered treaties" affecting western Canada were signed during the years 1871–1921.

8. Smallpox, which was brought to the Americas by European settlers, ravaged Canada's First Nations population during the 19th century.

55 VOICE   Let's get that bird out of here! Where is it?

GIRL   You crazy, he'll kill you.

VOICE   Hey, little girl, I found it! [*He mocks flatulence.*]

GIRL   Stop that. You're crazy.

VOICE   Oh ya? Both of us? Made for each other. [*He kisses and caresses her.*]

60   Little girl, my White Girl.

GIRL   Wait, husband, wait. I'm afraid.

VOICE   Don't be. I'm brave now I got you for my wife.

GIRL   But I'm afraid.

VOICE   What is it now, girl?

65 GIRL   It's the bad medicine. They gave me another name when I married
their god.

VOICE   Shut up about their god! I don't want to hear it!

GIRL   They called me Marrie. It's the name of their god's mother.

VOICE   What's wrong with White Girl? White Girl's a good name. They're so
70   stupid. That agent has to call me John Baptist[9] so I can get my treaty money.

GIRL   John Baptist. That's the name of one of their ghosts.

VOICE   I'm no ghost. I'm Almighty Voice. Why can't they say Almighty Voice?

GIRL   I'll call you John Baptist too.

VOICE   You're not the agent! You're my wife.

75 GIRL   It's so he'll kill the ghost instead of you, husband. That god won't know
it's us if we use their names.

VOICE   So I have to call my wife Marrie?

GIRL   Yes. Their god won't be able to touch us. Just call me Marrie.

VOICE   My crazy White Girl.

80 GIRL   Call me Marrie, husband.

VOICE   Marrie. Marrie, will you kiss me now?

GIRL   Yes, husband.

[*They kiss, caress, and begin to undress.*]

VOICE   Crazy Marrie.

GIRL   John Baptist.

85 VOICE   My little girl.

Scene Four

The projected title: "Scene Four: Flight." A drum beats in darkness. WHITE GIRL
pretends to sleep by the second fire. ALMIGHTY VOICE *enters at a run, drops to his
knees. The drum fades.*

VOICE   White Girl, wake up.

GIRL   Go away. I'm sleeping here.

VOICE   Where's my Winchester?[1]

GIRL   How should I know?

5 VOICE   Did my mother take it?

GIRL   Where have you been?

VOICE   I'll be right back.

GIRL   Have you been with the Rump's Daughter?

VOICE   I got to get my Winchester.

---

9. The historical Almighty Voice was listed on
government records as Jean-Baptiste.
1. Repeating rifle widely used throughout
western Canada and the United States during
the 19th century.

10 GIRL   Have you been with the Rump's Daughter?

VOICE   I'll go wake my mother.

GIRL   Answer me!

VOICE   What?

GIRL   I'm your wife now. Your only wife.

15 VOICE   White Girl, I was with your brother.

GIRL   You weren't with the Rump's Daughter?

VOICE   We were in jail.

GIRL   Jail?

VOICE   That sergeant over at Duck Lake, he threw us in the guard house.

20 GIRL   But you went for treaty money.[2]

VOICE   Well the sergeant has it now. Somebody told them that cow I shot belonged to somebody.

GIRL   You're all wet. Here. Get warm.

VOICE   Hey girl, I been swimming.

25 GIRL   You got away.

VOICE   In the freezing Saskatchewan.[3]

GIRL   What about Young Dust?

VOICE   He said it was warm there.

GIRL   You shouldn't have left him there. They threw you in jail for killing that

30   cow.

VOICE   That cow belonged to the Great White Mother. This half-breed told me the guard said no way would I rot in jail like my dirty chief of a father. The guard said I'd hang for killing that cow!

GIRL   But that's crazy. They don't hang people over meat.

35 VOICE   I'm not going back to that guard house, White Girl.

GIRL   They can't take you there.

VOICE   They always come after you. My dad's in jail at Prince Albert[4] over the pieces of a plough. He hates their stupid farming, this stupid reserve. They even turn the prairie into a jail.

40 GIRL   They can't put the wind in prison.

VOICE   Sounding Sky used to mean warrior. Now it's hard labour.

GIRL   Here. Dry yourself. Get warm.

VOICE   But I got to go get my Winchester.

GIRL   You rest while I find you your Winchester. They can't cross the river so

45   quick. And you need to take some of that beef with you.

VOICE   They'll catch me with it.

GIRL   You got to eat. And the Mounties aren't going to catch us.

VOICE   But you can't come.

GIRL   I'm coming with my husband.

50 VOICE   You'll slow me down.

GIRL   No I won't.

VOICE   But there's snow coming.

GIRL   Better for us. Two can be warmer than one. You know that. Lie down. Lie down, John Baptist. I'll get your Winchester.

55 VOICE   But White Girl, crazy one—

---

2. Annual payments made to First Nations people according to land treaties made with the Canadian government.

3. South Saskatchewan River.

4. City in central Saskatchewan, located 44 kilometers (27 miles) north of Duck Lake.

GIRL   Lie down, John Baptist, rest. I'll be ready soon. No, rest. Listen, John
   Baptist, I'm a better shot than your mother Spotted Calf. I got better eyes.
VOICE   This is crazy, girl.
GIRL   Both of us. Remember?

Scene Five

The projected title: "Scene Five: The Killing." ALMIGHTY VOICE *and* WHITE GIRL *sit
by the third fire. A drifting beat comes and goes on the drum.*

GIRL   It's all gone. The beef's all gone.
VOICE   I don't really like beef.
GIRL   What's wrong? I didn't burn it.
VOICE   No. Cattle aren't like real meat. They're stupid.
5 GIRL   They're not buffalo.
VOICE   That's for sure. They don't taste right.
GIRL   I like it. It makes me feel full.
VOICE   I'll get something else soon. My wife's not going hungry.
GIRL   It's good to be hungry.
10 VOICE   It's better to be full.
GIRL   It reminds you you're alive. That's what my mother used to say.
VOICE   What's wrong?
GIRL   Young Dust said the snow was too deep. The treaty agent wouldn't
   send the supplies out. Last winter. My mother wouldn't eat. She wouldn't
15   eat. While I was away at that school. She used to like the way I cook.
VOICE   I do too, White Girl.
GIRL   I would have cooked for her.
VOICE   Cook for me now, White Girl.
GIRL   I didn't really want to be there. We had to eat this mush made out of
20   grass seeds.
VOICE   No meat?
GIRL   Mush.
VOICE   How about some tea then? It's hot enough. It'll make you feel full.
GIRL   That's all there is.
25 VOICE   Can we go see your father now? He likes his tea. He always has sugar.
GIRL   The ice was almost too thick this morning. I was afraid we'd have to
   melt snow.
VOICE   We better go soon.
GIRL   Snow takes too long.
30 VOICE   That sergeant's not as stupid as he looks. He'll see we doubled back.
GIRL   Do you know what glass is? Like thin ice?
VOICE   What are you talking about, White Girl?
GIRL   Some of the walls at the school were made out of it.
VOICE   Made out of what?
35 GIRL   Glass. A wall you can see through. I didn't know it was there at first, the
   wall. I tried to crawl through. I saw the sky, the grass moving. Out there. I
   banged my face. The glass broke. Sharp pieces, too. That's what this is
   from.
VOICE   A place to kiss.
40 GIRL   You know what, John Baptist? I dreamed about you. I knew you would
   come.
VOICE   What's the matter?

GIRL   I was looking at you far away. Through a glass wall!

VOICE   The soldiers, they have these clear beads they look through. Far away
45   comes real close. All the walking in between seems to disappear.

GIRL   It was like that. It was. But it was also like I was waiting in my father's
teepee. I could see you coming, I saw the moonlight on the barrel of your
Winchester.

VOICE   I was bringing meat, I bet, buffalo meat for my wife.

50   GIRL   No you weren't. No! Let go.

VOICE   What's the matter, White Girl?

GIRL   You shot and the teepee broke. All the sharp pieces fell down on you,
worse than hail. I think it hurt you, I think you got hurt.

VOICE   Stop it, White Girl, stop it. Don't be afraid. I'm all right.

55   GIRL   That god. That god. I'm afraid.

VOICE   That stupid god can't hurt me. That god belongs in that place, in the
school. You're here now, I'm here now. He's not.

GIRL   He's everywhere!

VOICE   I told you he's a lie.

60   GIRL   He's like the glass. He's hard. He cuts you down.

VOICE   I'm your husband now. I won't let him hurt you. He doesn't deserve
you.

GIRL   I'm sorry. I'm sorry.

VOICE   Listen, crazy one. You married Almighty Voice, who's not afraid to say
65   his name. Let your glass god hear it. Almighty Voice!—who has listened to
our fathers and heard what they say. Almighty Voice, who remembers our
Creator and our people's ways. Almighty Voice knows how to fight for you.
Do you hear what I'm saying? Do you?

GIRL   Yes. Yes, I do.

70   VOICE   Who is saying it?

GIRL   Almighty Voice.

VOICE   Remember who you are. Remember what your mother taught you.

GIRL   Almighty Voice, the husband of White Girl!

VOICE   I'll break your glass god for you.

75   GIRL   Keep your bad medicine!

VOICE   It's just a bad smell. A stink. Come on. I'll get the horse. Your father
has the tea ready for us.

GIRL   Husband, look!

VOICE   Give me my Winchester. My wife'll have rabbit for breakfast.

    [*He loads and exits.* WHITE GIRL *watches him go, then builds up the fire.
She hears a noise from another direction and looks and stops. A shot. She
runs toward the place where* ALMIGHTY VOICE *exited. He enters, dead rabbit in hand.*]

80   [*laughing*] Look how fat! This'll make you full.

GIRL   Husband, be quiet.

    [ALMIGHTY VOICE *drops the rabbit.*]

    It's the god. See his glass eye.

VOICE   It's the sergeant, White Girl. Just the stupid sergeant. What's he say?

GIRL   I can't understand him.

85   VOICE   That's that stupid half-breed with him. Stay behind me, girl.

GIRL   He wants to make peace. There's the sign.

VOICE   Get down. He's got a gun.

GIRL   Where's the half-breed going?

VOICE   Stay where you are!

90 GIRL   What about the horse?

VOICE   No time. Stay there! Where's the other one?

GIRL   I can't see. Over there.

VOICE   Circling around. Don't come any closer. [*He reloads his Winchester.*]

GIRL   Leave us alone! Go away!

95 VOICE   I'm warning you!

GIRL   Husband—

VOICE   This gun's loaded!

GIRL   —the half-breed's behind us.

VOICE   Keep close. I'm warning you! Stop there! Stay there! [*shooting*] You
100   stupid!

GIRL   One shot. One shot, Almighty Voice!

VOICE   The other one?

GIRL   I told you glass breaks.

VOICE   Gone. Scared his horse, too. He'll bring more Mounties. There will
105   be more from now on.

GIRL   Glass breaks so easily.

VOICE   Wife, look at me.

GIRL   I'm all right, husband.

VOICE   Come on.

110 GIRL   No. There will be more from now on. I'll slow you down.

VOICE   I can't leave you, girl.

GIRL   They won't hurt me. They'll be afraid to now.

VOICE   White Girl, look at me.

GIRL   They'll have to take me home. I'll tell everyone how it happened, how
115   he wouldn't listen. They'll just take me home. I'll just slow them down. We
can meet at my mother's—I mean your mother's house. My mother's gone.
She died of hunger last winter. But I'm all right, Almighty Voice. And I
know I have to go talk to your mother soon.

VOICE   What about?

120 GIRL   I want us to make her a grandchild. She has to tell me how to get ready.
Women's stuff. I know I have to eat. [*She goes and picks up the rabbit.*] You
better go now.

[ALMIGHTY VOICE *exits.* WHITE GIRL *takes the rabbit to the fire.*]

Scene Six

*The projected title: "Scene Six: Mid-Winter Moon." A martial beat on the drum as
the bloody moon rises. Then silence.* WHITE GIRL *sits near the second fire while*
ALMIGHTY VOICE *wanders between the fires.*

GIRL   Mister. Mister! Mister God! I see your glass eye. Eye-eye! Stinky
breath. It's me. Marrie! Marrie, your wife. Wife wife wife! God, look at me
like before. How they taught me at school. How how. Here's my hair. Look.
Here's my skin. How how, husband god, see what a little girl I am. Great
5   White God of the ghost men,[5] mother is here. Blood blood blood between
my thighs. Yes, gimme, gimme, gimme something sweet. Oh yes, yes, you're
rotten, rotten meat, but wifey wife will eat you up. Mister God, god, stupid

5. Men with pale skin (that is, Caucasians).

god, this is what you want! Come on! Come on, don't leave! I'm your little squaw.[6] Eye-eye! See! Eye-eye, Mister God. Eye-eye!

10 VOICE   Don't talk, cousin. You're being stupid. No one would mistake you for a warrior. And your woman, she's so skinny, no one would call you a hunter either. Or a lover. Could your woman do what my woman has? Could she look those white men in the eyes? They took her back to Duck Lake and kept her in that guard house and she gave them lies for their lies. "Run,

15 husband. We will meet later." She said that to me. Is it a surprise I think about her? I believe what she says. If she is crazy, we all should be. Not a word, Little Salteau! Who's the one who killed a Mountie.[7]

GIRL   I am the wife of Almighty Voice. You don't know my name. You don't even wonder if I have one. I'm only a crazy squaw. You're watching me but

20 you expect to see my husband. His is a name you know. Almighty Voice. John Baptist. You say these names of his over and over again, like the prayers you say to your glass-eyed god for the grace of your Great White Mother Victoria.[8] But your prayers won't make him come. Mister God Mountie, you don't know what his name means.

25 VOICE   Your sister, Young Dust, she makes me remember how my father used to talk about the buffalo. Maybe because she likes meat so much. I'd like to feed her till she's fat. My father said everyone used to be like that. Everyone used to follow the buffalo. He hates farming. A man shouldn't be a bag of bones. My mother says he gets no meat. In Prince Albert. John Sound-

30 ing Sky is in jail because his son mistook a Mountie for a cow!

GIRL   You're laughing with that half-breed.[9] "Let the crazy squaw go home. Easy to keep an eye on her there." So he unlocks the door, walks away to the fire where you play with your silver coin, your dollar. That's what you want to trade my husband's blood for. Why? What is its power? A coin is

35 not the moon. Can't you see it's dead, Mister Mountie? Cold as the bullet my husband kills rabbits or enemies with.

VOICE   So my mother Spotted Calf is alone still, running things, hating it. She says there are too many women now. I think there aren't enough men. It's like a war but no one will say so, so there's never any peace. How many

40 of our brothers are there still in Stoney Mountain?[1] How many come home in the spring? My mother says it makes her children crazy, living on snow. Maybe she's right. Come on. Let's go make some blood flow tonight!

GIRL   You've got a bad look on your face, a blindness, a glassy gaze. What are you staring at? Your silver dollar? The fire? My husband's bullet. You'll stare

45 till they all turn to glass. And what will you see through them then? That forever place you want to live,[2] the one they promised me in school? I turn here in the wind toward the river and the moon is there, a woman with better things to do. She slips away from you, going home.

---

6. Native woman or wife.
7. Member of the North-West Mounted Police. The NWMP was established in 1873 to maintain order in Canada's Northwest Territories, which included the present-day province of Saskatchewan.
8. Queen Victoria I (1819–1901), who ruled the United Kingdom of Great Britain and Ireland from 1836 to 1901. Under the British

North America Act, which established the Dominion of Canada in 1867, Victoria continued to serve as the country's monarch.
9. Member of the Métis, an aboriginal people of mixed European and Native ancestry.
1. Penitentiary established in 1877 in the present-day province of Manitoba.
2. The Christian heaven.

Scene Seven

The projected title: "Scene Seven: Honeymoon." The drum beats. The full moon sweeps down from the sky like a spotlight to show and surround the lovers, lying together on the ground.

GIRL   Almighty Voice, come on.

VOICE   Not again.

GIRL   I want to be sure.

VOICE   Let me sleep.

5   GIRL   This is the time to do it. Your mother said so.

VOICE   I don't want to know that. I don't want to do it for my mother.

GIRL   Do it for me. It's the best time now.

VOICE   I don't want to know that stuff.

GIRL   Young Dust dreamed we had a son.

10   VOICE   This is none of your brother's business.

GIRL   Come on, John Baptist.

VOICE   White Girl, we got to sleep.

GIRL   Almighty Voice, do you like my hand there?

VOICE   Don't. You keep this up, we'll fall asleep on the horse later.

15   GIRL   You fall off, you can fall on me.

VOICE   White Girl, we got to move on tonight. Little Salteau said those stupid Mounties are just south of here.

GIRL   They're hunting quail, not us. I like it here. I like how flat it is. Like your belly.

20   VOICE   White Girl, stop it.

GIRL   Come on, Almighty Voice.

VOICE   Do as your husband says. And don't laugh.

GIRL   The Mounties don't know we're here. Why worry?

VOICE   Go to sleep.

25   GIRL   They'll forget about you.

VOICE   I killed a Mountie. They don't give up.

GIRL   But he would have killed you.

VOICE   I know.

GIRL   Spring comes, the snow goes. Too many other things to do. Cows running away through the grass. Fresh meat, husband.

30

VOICE   Can't you be quiet, girl?

GIRL   Isn't this grass moving in the wind here on your flat prairie?

VOICE   I'm your husband, White Girl.

GIRL   Oh, your wife likes to run in the grass, Almighty Voice.

35   VOICE   Stop it. Go to sleep.

GIRL   They can't see you as long as you're with me.

VOICE   We can't hide in that grass, little girl.

GIRL   We can hide. With me you're in the dark of the moon. It's what your mother talks about. When we're together, it's like we're inside a bead of glass made of wind. They can't get at us. It's my medicine, husband. In the dream—you were in the dream. That's all I can tell you.

40

VOICE   You fasted? When?

GIRL   The last blizzard. Your mother took me out. In that wind.

VOICE   The moon was dark then.

45   GIRL   She took me down to the river. I built a fire on the ice. She visited me every morning. And she sang to me.

VOICE   And she serves tea to the priest!

GIRL   And laughs at him. He expects her to give you away. That priest wants her to marry his god too.

50   VOICE   That's crazy.

GIRL   Instead she gets news of your father in Prince Albert.

VOICE   I didn't know. What does she say about my father? Is his cough any better? When One Arrow[3] got back from the jail at Stoney Mountain, he was old. He told my father that the visions of warriors have no more power

55   against the soldiers.

GIRL   He was old, husband. He was tired.

VOICE   Not even Riel's vision,[4] and he was part white.

GIRL   It's the jail, husband. They watch you all the time. You can't move.

VOICE   I was there when he said it.

60   GIRL   And it's all stone.

VOICE   He gave away his rifle.

GIRL   You can't see anything but stones. You can't see anything, husband. You forget everything.

VOICE   How can you forget everything and be a man?

65   GIRL   You're not a man then. You're like a ghost. You're lost.

VOICE   I want to see my father. I'm going to Prince Albert.

GIRL   That's crazy.

VOICE   The Mounties won't know I'm there. Why worry?

GIRL   Your mother says someone's always watching him. You don't know that

70   place.

VOICE   I'm going to talk to him.

GIRL   You have to hide. Your mother said so.

VOICE   Shut up about my mother! I don't want to hear it.

GIRL   She won't let you go.

75   VOICE   Am I a child again? Hiding behind women. How can you look at me?

GIRL   You're my husband.

VOICE   My father is a man. John Sounding Sky still means warrior. But Almighty Voice?

GIRL   He's a warrior.

80   VOICE   Does a warrior run away? Almighty Voice is a stupid old man, a ghost. He's here, there, nowhere.

GIRL   You can't go.

VOICE   I should be in Prince Albert. John Sounding Sky should be at home with Spotted Calf.

85   GIRL   They ache to hang Almighty Voice.

VOICE   What good am I here?

GIRL   I need you.

VOICE   What good am I to you, White Girl?

GIRL   I don't want to be alone.

90   VOICE   You can stay with my mother.

3. One Arrow (ca. 1815–1886), chief of the Willow Cree band that settled on the One Arrow reservation. One Arrow was imprisoned after participating in the unsuccessful North West Rebellion of 1885.
4. Louis Riel (1844–1885), who claimed to have had a vision in which God anointed him a prophet, led two armed rebellions against the Canadian government on behalf of the Métis, an aboriginal people of mixed European and Native ancestry. Riel himself is said to have had one-eighth Native blood.

GIRL   Two women old with no men? Your mother will die like my mother did. You can't leave me too.

VOICE   Your father will take you.

GIRL   You're sending me home?

95 VOICE   He'll get you a better husband.

GIRL   He'll get me a worse one.

VOICE   Who? Who could that be?

GIRL   Any ghost man will do. You want me to die.

VOICE   You won't die!

100 GIRL   I will. For years. Kill me now. Be good to me, husband. Kill me now and then you can go, go and be hanged.

VOICE   You're pretty fierce, all right.

GIRL   Let go of me.

VOICE   For a little girl.

105 GIRL   I'll get you your Winchester.

VOICE   Stay here with me.

GIRL   You can kill me, husband. We'll both be dead.

VOICE   That's stupid. White Girl who has visions, stay here with me.

GIRL   What about your father?

110 VOICE   We'll find a way. My mother will help.

GIRL   You won't leave me?

VOICE   Hey, I'm here with you. In the dark of the moon. They can't get at us.

GIRL   Almighty Voice—

VOICE   Can't you be quiet, girl? Your husband doesn't want to sleep anymore.

115   He likes your hand here.

Scene Eight

A projected title: "Scene Eight: The Hunting Moon." A gunshot. The social drum. Three more shots. ALMIGHTY VOICE *with his Winchester at the last fire, the dead one.* WHITE GIRL *with a baby-sized bundle in her arms, still illuminated by the moon.*

GIRL   You brought me home to your mother. It was time. Spotted Calf expected me. She took me into her new house. Other women were waiting. "Go away," she said. "Young Dust will bring you news." Someone, the Rump's Daughter, might tell. It was dangerous. The Mounties—it was dan-
5   gerous. You wanted to hide under the floor, under her bed like last winter. But she made you go. "You men shouldn't know women's stuff." You men. Little Salteau and Dubling came along. I heard you laughing. Off you rode to hunt somewhere, the grass new, blue-green. I saw you through the glass in the window of that house. Going.

10 VOICE   Has he come? Tell him, wife, tell him how good a season it was every-where along the Saskatchewan the winter before he was born. Tell him I always found game, never got cold. Till now. Say the ghost men shivered in their huts, too afraid of the wind to fire a shot. Tell him it can be like that again. Tell him, girl. Do you hear me? I wish you did.

15   Tell him how we visited and people would give his mother more to eat. Even people in the woods far up north. An old bull buffalo, chewy but sweet. You worried it might be their last one but ate anyway. Tell him Old Dust gave in, gave us lots of sugar for our tea, called me son, when he saw how fat you were. One day I remember. Cold, bright. Leather stiff as

20 wood. Your belly had begun to curve. Your breath feathers,[5] or smoke that fell, hugged the ground. I teased you, your belly like the iron stove at the store at Duck Lake. Tight as a drum. I felt him kick then. What a thump! I knew I had a son. I wanted to dance.

> [ALMIGHTY VOICE *dances with the drum in celebration. Then, as* WHITE GIRL *speaks, his steps turn into a war dance and then into stillness. The moon around* WHITE GIRL *turns bloody.*]

GIRL They tell me you came across another cow. They say you wanted to feast
25 me and the baby. So you shot the stupid thing. Some farmer heard your guns, didn't mind his own business. Him and his sons gave chase. I can hear you laughing, leading them into this bluff[6] of poplars. And suddenly there's Mounties, soldiers, farmers everywhere. And someone shoots someone. I hope it was that farmer. They tell me you got no food, no water all day. They
30 say someone else got shot. Maybe a Mountie. Young Dust said he heard you singing. War songs. He says you were dancing. There were ghost men all around that night. Farmers, soldiers, priests of the glass god. Over a hundred against Little Salteau, Dubling, and Almighty Voice by the end. And two big iron guns.[7] I saw them myself the second day. Spotted Calf and I stood
35 watching. I wanted you to be anywhere else. Young Dust held the baby, reminded me to feed his nephew. I didn't notice I was full, aching. I have no milk now. [*She puts her bundle down.*] That night I saw my husband Almighty Voice again against that moon I had tried to forget. Then those two guns started firing and firing. Firing and firing. It was cold and the smoke would
40 not go away. I seemed to see you sometime in the night, in the smoke, but even before morning broke, your mother was singing her death song.[8]

Scene Nine

A projected title: "Scene Nine: His Vision." The drum beats in the night. The moon is low in the sky, pulsing. ALMIGHTY VOICE *lies by the dead fire, his leg badly wounded. The spectral teepee appears and the drum goes silent. Inside the teepee are* WHITE GIRL *and her baby, mother and child, a destination.* ALMIGHTY VOICE *rises and uses his Winchester as a crutch to come to the teepee.* WHITE GIRL *comes out and shows him the baby and the baby cries. The moon turns white.* ALMIGHTY VOICE *dies.*

Act Two

A follow spot finds a title placard: "Act Two: Ghost Dance."

Scene One

The spot shifts to a second title placard:[9] "Scene One: Overture," then fades. Spectral light from the dead fire. ALMIGHTY VOICE, *now in whiteface[1] as his own* GHOST, *continues his dance of celebration around the fire inside the last crescent of the moon. Scattered around the moon's half-circle are mined stools three of which are still sturdy enough to be useful. On the one upright at the crescent's midpoint, a*

5. Downy feathers of an eagle or other bird, often used for ceremonial purposes. These are referred to as "breath feathers" because they move under the slightest breeze.
6. Dense grove of trees.
7. Mounted artillery guns.
8. Song sung by Native individuals, especially warriors, at the approach of death.

9. This and the following scene titles refer to parts of a minstrel show, a popular 19th-century American entertainment form that featured music, song, and comic dialogue and offered stereotypical representations of African Americans.
1. Makeup applied to make a nonwhite performer appear white.

searching spot finds a seated figure and, finding its head, discovers white-gloved hands hiding its face. As the crescent moon fades, the hands open to reveal the white-face that masks WHITE GIRL *into the role of the* INTERLOCUTOR,[2] *a Mountie and the Master of Ceremonies. In a glance their eyes meet. Sudden light shift to variety-show lights, both the* GHOST *and the* INTERLOCUTOR *in follow spots. The* INTERLOCUTOR *adjusts her monocle.*

INTERLOCUTOR   Here, here? I said, "Here, here." Hey dead man? Hey red man! Hey Indian!

GHOST   *Awas. Si-pwete.* [*Go away. Go on.*]

INTERLOCUTOR   "Here, here," I said. What's the meaning of this? Come on,
5   use the queen's tongue,[3] or I'll sell you to a cigar store.[4]

GHOST   *Awas kititin ni-nimihiton oma ota.* [*Go away. I'm dancing here.*]

INTERLOCUTOR   You dare call these furtive foot steps, these frenzied flailings of arms like wings, dancing! Stop it. It s nonsense.

GHOST   *Awena kiya? Kekwiy ka-ayimota-man?* [*Who are you? What are you talking about?*]

10   INTERLOCUTOR   Snap out of it, Chief. [*slapping him with the gloves four times*]

GHOST   Oweeya! Oweeya! Ya! Ya! *Pakitinin awena kiya moya ki-kis-ke yimitin.* [*Ow! Ow! Ow! Ow! Let go of me. Who are you? I don't know you.*]

INTERLOCUTOR   You know very well who the hell I am. I don't have to remind you no show can begin without its master. Here, here. Stop I say. How dare you go faster.

15   GHOST   *Nahkee. Kawiya-[ekosi]. Ponikawin poko ta kisisimoyan.* [*Stop. Let me alone. I have to finish my dance.*]

INTERLOCUTOR   I'll break the other leg for you, Kisse-Manitou-Wayou.

GHOST   *Tansi esi kiskeyitaman ni wiyowin?* [*How do you know my name?*]

INTERLOCUTOR   Names, names, they're all the same. Crees all wear feathers. Dead man, red man. Indian, Kisse-Manitou-Wayou, Almighty Voice. John
20   Baptist! Geronimo,[5] Tonto,[6] Calijah.[7] Or most simply, Mister Ghost.

GHOST   Ghost?

INTERLOCUTOR   Boo! Almighty Ghost, Chief. Now we're speaking English.

GHOST   What? Who are you?

INTERLOCUTOR   How.[8] You're supposed to say "How." You know. Hey Pon-
25   tiac,[9] how's the engine? Can't you stick to the script? You're too new at this ghost schtick[1] to go speaking *ad liberatum.*[2]

---

2. Master of ceremonies in the minstrel show. Sitting at the center of a semicircle featuring musicians and singers, the Interlocutor engaged in comic back-and-forth with Tambo and Bones, his two "endmen."

3. That is, English.

4. Because Native Americans introduced tobacco to European settlers, wooden representations of American Indians were used as advertisements on tobacconists' shops. These figures were often referred to as "cigar store Indians."

5. Apache Indian leader (1829–1909) who fought against Mexico and the United States during the Apache Wars (1849–86).

6. Native American companion of the Lone Ranger in the mid-20th century *Lone Ranger* radio and television series.

7. "Kaw-Liga," a song about a wooden display Indian who falls in love with an Indian maid in a nearby antique shop but is too stubborn to let her know, was written by Hank Williams and Fred Rose in 1952. The song was released in January 1953 after Williams's death and spent fourteen weeks at the top of the *Billboard* country chart.

8. The word "how," which derives from interjections used by Plains Indians tribes, became a stereotypical Indian greeting in popular cinema and television.

9. Leader of the Ottawa tribe (ca. 1720–1769) who led a revolt against the British following the French and Indian War. The war that bears his name—Pontiac's Rebellion—was fought during 1763–66. Until it was discontinued in 2010, Pontiac was also an automobile brand manufactured by General Motors.

1. Stage routine, gag, or gimmick (Yiddish).

2. However you wish (the actual Latin phrase is *ad libitum*).

GHOST   Let me go. I don't know you. Let me dance.

INTERLOCUTOR   Here here. Stop. I say. How dare you! Do I have to remind you this colourful display, these exotic ceremonials, belong later on in the
30   program? Listen to me, Chief. One doesn't begin with a climax, an end. Unmitigated foolishness. I'll have you know. If you begin at the end, then where do you go? Do you know? No. Well? What have you got to say for yourself?

GHOST   How—

35 INTERLOCUTOR   That's more like it!

GHOST   How did I get here? What's going on?

INTERLOCUTOR   What's going on! The show. The Red and White Victoria Regina[3] Spirit Revival show! These fine, kind folks want to know the truth, the amazing details and circumstance behind your savagely beautiful
40   appearance. They also want to be entertained and enlightened and maybe a tiny bit thrilled, just a goose of frightened. They want to laugh and cry. They want to know the facts. And it's up to you and me to try and lie that convincingly. And since all the rest of our company is late for the curtain, this is your chance, your big break for certain.

45 GHOST   No, I won't dance for you.

INTERLOCUTOR   But you have to toe the line. Chief. We all do. Here. Let me smell your breath. Bah! Like death warmed over. I've warned you before. You choose to booze and you're back on the street where I found you.

GHOST   Leave me alone. Go away.

50 INTERLOCUTOR   Don't you realize you could be internationally known, the most acclaimed magic act of the century?

GHOST   What do you mean?

INTERLOCUTOR   The Vanishing Indian!

GHOST   Poof?[4]

55 INTERLOCUTOR   Forget about faggots.

GHOST   I want to know how I got here.

INTERLOCUTOR   Gutter.[5] Does that sound mean anything to you? Gutter?

GHOST   All I remember—

INTERLOCUTOR   Answer me, you sotted[6] fancy dancer.

60 GHOST   My leg was gone.

INTERLOCUTOR   Come on. Chief, be a friend.

GHOST   It was! I used a branch from a sapling.

INTERLOCUTOR   Be a pal, Chiefy, dear.

GHOST   No, it was my gun for a crutch.

65 INTERLOCUTOR   This is a bit much for this early in the proceedings.

GHOST   Sometime in the night—

INTERLOCUTOR   Wait wait wait. I'd like to apologize to the ladies in the audience and suggest that this might be a prime opportunity to make use of our theatre's other facilities. The details of the following story may be not for
70   the faint of heart, are in fact quite gory, and ordinarily it would be our custom to warn you and ask your permission before we proceed. However— how-ever—as you can see, my peer here feels he must thrust the entire tale

---

3. Queen Victoria (Latin).
4. As a verb, to appear or disappear like a puff of air; as a noun, a derogatory term for a homosexual (as is *faggot* in the following line).

5. That is, street gutter. This exchange addresses the stereotype associating Native people with alcoholism.
6. Affected by alcohol.

upon us. Once again, I apologize. Thank you for your attention. All right. Proceed.

75 GHOST   My legs were gone.

INTERLOCUTOR   His leg was gone!

GHOST   I must have screamed.

INTERLOCUTOR   Talk about Wounded Knee.[7]

GHOST   But my throat was too dry.

80 INTERLOCUTOR   The bones were shattered, pulp. Not that that mattered.

GHOST   There was no sound in my mouth.

INTERLOCUTOR   Quite the comedown for Almighty Vocal Cords.

GHOST   I couldn't sing my song.

INTERLOCUTOR   Oh Lord, talented, too!

85 GHOST   My death song. I crawled out of the pit.

INTERLOCUTOR   And we're not talking orchestra pits out here in the sticks.

GHOST   We had dug it in the ground to protect us from the gunfire.

INTERLOCUTOR   Not much good compared to a couple of cannons, was it?

GHOST   There was smoke close to the ground.

90 INTERLOCUTOR   From the fires all around?

GHOST   I thought I might be able to make it across the open space.

INTERLOCUTOR   And was it really over a hundred men by then?

GHOST   Against Little Salteau, Dubling, and me.

INTERLOCUTOR   Imagine. Red coats and wild Indians. What a spectacle! Where
95 are my glasses?

GHOST   It was the middle of the night. I might get by if the watch was asleep.

INTERLOCUTOR   Not on duty? Now that's not very funny.

GHOST   I had seen her watching, many times that day, beyond their lines. I
got halfway across.

100 INTERLOCUTOR   And amazingly, no one saw him then. He might have made
good his escape. Think about that. However—how-ever—he was bleeding
a lot. Red blood oozing from red skin. Oh what a thrill! I'm not offending
you, am I?

GHOST   She came to meet me.

105 INTERLOCUTOR   [à la "Indian Love Call"][8]   When I'm calling you-oo-oo-oo-
oo-oo-oo!

GHOST   No one could see her. My wife had denied their glass-eyed god. It
was her medicine to be invisible.

INTERLOCUTOR   Wish my wife could do that. That's really interesting. Kissy
110 Kisse-Manitou-Wayou? Did you give her some tongue!

GHOST   She told me about my son. She told me I would not be forgotten.

INTERLOCUTOR   How can I put this delicately? Your last meeting, your last
touch. Your life dribbling out of you, hot and sticky. Big strong buck like
you used to be. Was it savage love? Did you have a last quickie?

115 GHOST   I knew I could die then.

INTERLOCUTOR   She was some babe, eh?

GHOST   People would remember me.

INTERLOCUTOR   Give me some of the juicy details, Chief.

---

7. South Dakota creek where more than 200 Lakota Sioux men, women, and children were massacred by U.S. Calvary troops on December 28, 1890.

8. Popular song from the 1924 Broadway musical *Rose-Marie*, which was made into a film starring Nelson Eddie and Jeanette Mac-Donald in 1936.

GHOST My people would remember me.

120 INTERLOCUTOR One must always strive for accuracy. Do you have documentation?

GHOST I knew I could die then.

INTERLOCUTOR Come on, Chief, speak up. Anybody got a cigar? Never mind.

GHOST I could hear my mother, off on the hill, singing her song.

125 INTERLOCUTOR Talent just runs in that family!

GHOST Her death song.

INTERLOCUTOR So does manic depression! Do we feel better now? We do remember you, Mister Almighty Ghost. The angry young man, the passionate lover, the wild and crazy Indian kid. A shocking but true tale of the

130 frontier. Now don't you think this is just too touching, ladies and gentlemen? Too much for my refined sensibilities, that's a certainty. That wasn't too bad, Chief, considering. And now—[*She changes the title placard.*]

Scene Two

The new placard reads "Scene Two: Baritone Solo."

INTERLOCUTOR Ladies and gentlemen, for your further edification and delight, a musical selection. Mister Almighty Ghost, the famous Aboriginal[9] voice, will now render for you the sweet ballad, "Lament of the Redskin Lover." Mister Ghost?

5 GHOST [*in a spotlight*] What are you talking about?

INTERLOCUTOR Go on, Mister Ghost. We wait upon you, sir. Sing. Sing.

GHOST I don't know this.

INTERLOCUTOR No memory at all? Here. It's number two on your lyric sheet, sir.

10 GHOST Who are you?

INTERLOCUTOR This is it, your last show. You're back on the street in the morning. The gutter? Here we go.

[*The* INTERLOCUTOR *stands behind the* GHOST *and guides him through the accompanying mime.*]

GHOST [*to the tune of "Oh! Susanna"*][1]
I track the winter prairie for the little squaw I lost.
I'm missing all the kissing I had afore the frost.

15 I'm moping, oh I'm hoping oh, to hold her hand in mine.
My flower of Saskatchewan, oh we were doing fine.

GHOST & INTERLOCUTOR In our teepee, oh we were so in love,
One Arrow was too narrow for my little squaw and me.

GHOST I had a dream the other night, I saw her on a hill.

20 INTERLOCUTOR My little squaw was shaking, the wind was standing still.

GHOST The bannock bread[2] was in her mouth, and blood was in her eye.
The moon so bright I lost my sight—

INTERLOCUTOR —I pray she didn't die!

GHOST On the prairie, oh how the white does blow!

25 Who makes it through the winter?

---

9. Referring to an original or earliest inhabitant of a land.

1. Popular minstrel song written by Stephen Foster and published in 1848.

2. A fried form of flat quick bread popular among Native North Americans. Also called *fry bread.*

Not my little squaw or me.

INTERLOCUTOR   Nicely done. Thank you, thank you, Mister Ghost. You were almost your spooky self again.

GHOST   Thank you, Mister Interlocutor.

30 INTERLOCUTOR   Buck up, Mister Ghost. Isn't this all familiar? Might not, say, Buck[3] and Squaw be the latest dance craze?

[*The* INTERLOCUTOR *pulls the* GHOST *into a short Hollywood Indian War Dance. The* GHOST *resists. At the end the* GHOST *grabs the* INTERLOCUTOR *and looks into her eyes.*]

GHOST   This is what they've done to you.

INTERLOCUTOR   Thank you, thank you, Mister Ghost. A most original interpretation of the material. Gentle listeners, Mister Bones[4] will now perform

35 for you—

GHOST   Mister Bones? He the one with the dice?

INTERLOCUTOR   No, Mister Ghost. He s the one who's got rhythm.

GHOST   There's no one like that backstage, sir.

INTERLOCUTOR   No? Perhaps our friend Mister Tambo waits in the wings.

40 GHOST   That the Tamborine Man?[5] Not even in the flies, sir. Nor, sir, is Mister Drum lurking below the trap door.

INTERLOCUTOR   No Mister Drum? Well, Mister Ghost—no! Wait!

[*The* GHOST *changes the placard.*]

Scene Three

The new placard reads "Scene Three: The Stump."

GHOST   Ladies and gentlemen, boys and girls, dogs and cats, we of the Pale-Faced Band of the Sweet Saskatchewaners are pleased to present for your information and concern our own Mister Interlocutor in the role of Mister Drum, a loyal citizen of our territory.

5 INTERLOCUTOR   Wait a moment, Mister Ghost. That is not my part.

GHOST   But you do know it by heart. This is your chance, sir, your big break for certain. Ladies and gentlemen, please welcome Mister Drum.

INTERLOCUTOR   Ahem. Ahem. I come before you this evening, my dear friends, full, full of concern. We have ourselves a problem, dear friends, an

10 Indian problem. Dare I say an indigent Indian problem? Dear friends, the pampered redskins, they are the bad ones. Those tribes that have been cared for as if they were our equals, they, dear friends, are the first to turn and shed the blood of their benefactors. Noisemaker[6] was petted,[7] yes, even feted,[8] my friends, and now raids our farms. Pricky Pinecone was paid

15 to come up to our fine territory and what, dear friends, is his pursuit nowadays? Carnage! Large Prairie Dog, who for years has sharpened his teeth by chewing on the bone of idleness, shows his gratitude by killing his priests for their holy wine. That is not communion, friends. Little Dump, a non-

3. Native male.
4. The minstrel characters, Tambo and Bones, are named for the instruments they played (a clacking folk instrument called "bones" and a tambourine). These characters, who sat on the end of the semicircle of singers and musicians, engaged in comic banter with each other and with the Interlocutor).
5. Bob Dylan's song "Mr. Tambourine Man" was recorded and released in 1965.
6. Noisemaker: Noisemaker, Pricky Pinecone, Large Prairie Dog, and Little Dump are invented names.
7. That is, pampered and indulged.
8. Feasted (French).

20 treaty Indian, has been, friends, provisioned with all necessaries and so gets to spend all his days gallivanting about the territory, shouting loudly and plotting mischief. And now, my dear friends, this Almighty Gas character joins in on the season's carnival of ruin. Oh friends, the petted Indians have proved the bad ones and this gives weight to the wise adage, friends, that the only good Indians are the dead ones.

25 GHOST   Bravo! Bravo, Mister Interlocutor, sir. Mister Drum could not have said it better.

INTERLOCUTOR   Thank you. Mister Ghost.

GHOST   No, thank you. Mister Interlocutor. I take your words to heart. My heart soars! We all thank you, sir. Don't we, ladies and gentles? Never a truer

30 word was said. It is to our great benefit to know of this dread red threat to our well-beings and livelihoods, this deadly hood, this Almighty Fart character. Dead Indians would be even better, sir, if they didn't stink that way.

INTERLOCUTOR   Thank you again, Mister Ghost, thank you again. I thank you too, ladies and gentle sirs. We will now return to the sequence of events as

35 listed in your programs.

GHOST   But sir, there's still no sign of Messers Bone. Tambo, Drum, or any one. The entire company, sir, seems to be running on Indian Time![9]

INTERLOCUTOR   Would you now consider performing, Mister Ghost, for our attentive friends, that charming curiosity you called a dance?

40 GHOST   No.

INTERLOCUTOR   Surely. Mister Ghost—

GHOST   Call me the late Almighty Voice. Call me an early redman. Call me, yes, even call me a ghost—but don't call me Shirley![1]

INTERLOCUTOR   You're the most spirited ghost I've ever met.

45 GHOST   You better believe it. There's a stir of dissatisfaction, sir, in the audience. Perhaps number seven?

INTERLOCUTOR   An excellent suggestion. Mister Ghost. An excellent selection, I assure you, my friends.

GHOST   But, sir, it calls for the entire company. And we, sir, are the skeleton

50 crew!

Scene Four

The INTERLOCUTOR *changes the title placard to "Scene Four: The Walkaround."*

INTERLOCUTOR   Ladies and gentlemen, for your delight and encouragement, Mister Ghost and Yours Truly will now present a martial interlude. In honour of all our heroic boys in uniform!

GHOST   I'll even honour those boys out of uniform.

5 INTERLOCUTOR   I appear first in the role of Mister Allan,[2] Leading the charge through the bluff. After the renegade!

GHOST   Hurrah! We're beating the bushes.

INTERLOCUTOR   Where are the cowards?

9. The traditional Native notion of time is nonlinear; the joke here is that the company's performers cannot follow a clock.
1. Reference to a comic exchange in the 1980 movie *Airplane*, starring Lesley Nielsen: "Surely you can't be serious." "I am serious. And don't call me Shirley."
2. Inspector John B. "Bronco Jack" Allan

and Sergeant Charles Raven were wounded in the attack on the poplar bluff where Almighty Voice and his two companions were holed up. Corporal Charles Home Sterling Hockin, Postmaster Ernest Grundy, and Constable J. R. Kerr were killed during this assault.

GHOST   Moo? Pow, pow!

10 INTERLOCUTOR   Ambush, vicious ambush!

GHOST   It appears Mister Allan's fallen off his horse!

INTERLOCUTOR   A bullet! A bullet shattered my arm.

GHOST   Bull! The bottle did him in.

INTERLOCUTOR   Then I take the part of the brave second-in-command, Mis-
15   ter Raven.

GHOST   Already shot on the wing.

INTERLOCUTOR   What?

GHOST   In his private parts!

INTERLOCUTOR   Not my leg?

20 GHOST   Groin, groin, gone!

INTERLOCUTOR   Oh where is the rest of my happy company?

GHOST   Retreat! Retreat! Buck up, my friend, there are but three of them.

INTERLOCUTOR   We've got them outnumbered. I, Mister Hockin, take charge.
   Surround the bluff!

25 GHOST   But are you nine and the settlers enough?

INTERLOCUTOR   Postmaster Grundy here, volunteer, sir. We'll all of us beat
   them bushes again.

GHOST   March then. March south, men. They can't hide from you.

INTERLOCUTOR   Where have they gone? We had them surrounded.

30 GHOST   This could be embarrassing.

INTERLOCUTOR   East to west now. Shoulder to shoulder.

GHOST   Nothing. No one. Again?

INTERLOCUTOR   Here we go. These darn trees.

GHOST   Unpopular poplars?

35 INTERLOCUTOR   If they weren't so green. Fire would force them out.

GHOST   Say again.

INTERLOCUTOR   Fire!

GHOST   Bang bang! Bang bang, bang bang, bang bang! The mail comes late.

INTERLOCUTOR   Why?

40 GHOST   Postmaster Grundy got shot in the gut.

INTERLOCUTOR   What about Hockin?

GHOST   His heart got broken.

INTERLOCUTOR   And Kerr?

GHOST   Sorry, sir. Retreat! Retreat!

45 INTERLOCUTOR   I don't want to wait all day and all night.

GHOST   Too late.

INTERLOCUTOR   I could have got them.

GHOST   Reinforcements arrive!

INTERLOCUTOR   I could have got them alive!

50 GHOST   So can I play the one little, two little dozen Mounties?

INTERLOCUTOR   I'll take the roles of the two big guns?

GHOST   Bang bang? Boom boom. Doom doom!

INTERLOCUTOR   As well as the crowd of concerned civilians, including the
   disappointed—

55 GHOST   —I do so much for those ungrateful wretches—

INTERLOCUTOR   —farm instructor and his friend the ever hopeful—

GHOST   —Spare the rod and spoil the child!—[3]

3. Traditional saying that reflects the belief that corporal discipline encourages proper child behavior.

INTERLOCUTOR   —missionary priest. Well?

60 GHOST   It will be the least I can do then and an honour to represent the man's wife and mother as well as others from the One Arrow Reserve, Treaty Number Six.[4]

INTERLOCUTOR   Perhaps, then, you will do the parts then of the young man and his ill-fated companions? Yes?

GHOST   No.

65 INTERLOCUTOR   Mister Ghost, sure—please listen to me and consider—

GHOST   Fuck you. I'm not going through that again for your entertainment.

INTERLOCUTOR   Mister Ghost—

GHOST   You do it.

INTERLOCUTOR [*to the tune of "Derry Down"*][5]   Who is fighting the battle
70   for everyone—

GHOST   —is fighting the battle for everyone—

INTERLOCUTOR   —fights bloodthirsty redskins and wears a grin—

GHOST   —not afeard of anything?—

GHOST & INTERLOCUTOR
    Who rides high in the saddle and shoots a gun,
75   rides high in the saddle and shoots a gun,
    shoots bloodthirsty redskins and wears a grin,
    not afeard of anything?
    We have the guns, the guts, the wit.
    We know that you are stinking shit.
80   We did it to the buffalo.
    Want to be next? Yes or no?
    We are the men with guns and bucks.
    We know that you are stupid fucks.
    We did it to the buffalo.
85   Want to be next? Yes or no?

INTERLOCUTOR
    Who is fighting the battle for everyone,
    is fighting the battle for everyone,
    shoots bloodthirsty redskins and wears a grin,
    not afeard of anything?

90 GHOST   We have the guns, the guts, the wit.
    We know that you are stupid shit.
    We did it to the buffalo.
    Want to be next? Yes or no?

GHOST & INTERLOCUTOR
    We are the men,
95   well let's say it again,
    to get them heathen Indians.
    We are the ones,
    oh let's do it with guns,
    let's kill them stinking Indians.

---

4. An 1876 treaty between the Canadian monarchy and the Plains and Woods Cree tribes of central Manitoba and Saskatchewan whereby land rights to large areas of First Nations lands were ceded to the federal government. In return the government provided money, 11.5 square kilometers of land for each family of five, farming tools, fishing and hunting rights, schools on reserves, and a medicine chest for use of the tribes.
5. English folk song.

100 　　We are the ones,
　　　　well let's do it with rum,
　　　　let's get them redskin Indians.
　　　　We are the men,
　　　　oh let's say it again,
105 　　to kill them damn dead Indians.
GHOST 　Who rides high in the saddle and shoots a gun,
　　　　rides high in the saddle and shoots a gun,
　　　　shoots bloodthirsty redskins and wears a grin,
　　　　not afeard of anything?
INTERLOCUTOR
110 　　We have the guns, the guts, the wit.
　　　　We know that you are stinking shit.
　　　　We did it to the buffalo.
　　　　Want to be next? Yes or No?
GHOST & INTERLOCUTOR
　　　　We have the bucks and you do not.
115 　　Is it a wonder that you got shot?
　　　　We have the bucks and you do not.
　　　　Is it a wonder that you got shot?
　　　　We have the bucks and you do not.
　　　　Is it a wonder that you got shot?
120 　　We have the bucks and you do not.
　　　　Is it a wonder that you got shot?

　　　　We have the blankets and the rum.
　　　　Oh did you say that you want some?

GHOST 　Well, Mister Interlocutor, how do you feel now?
125 INTERLOCUTOR 　No, Mister Ghost, how do you feel now?
GHOST 　Well, Mister Interlocutor, I feel somewhat like a newspaper.
INTERLOCUTOR 　You feel like a newspaper? How is that, Mister Ghost?
GHOST 　I'm pale as a sheet of paper.
INTERLOCUTOR 　A sheet of paper? With black eyes, Mister Ghost?
130 GHOST 　Every one dotted, sir.
　　　　　[*The* INTERLOCUTOR *hits the* GHOST.]
　　　And ultimately, sir, I am like a newspaper in that I am read all over[6]—the
　　　countryside.
INTERLOCUTOR 　Red all over, sir? A most colourful conceit. Bloody good, as
　　　our cousins would have it. Newspapers are our pass to an understanding of
135 　the reserve and the life of its denizens.·
GHOST 　And we don't have to go to the Indian agent to get them. The passes.
INTERLOCUTOR 　Are you making one at me, sir? [*hitting him*] Did you read
　　　how we're teaching our primitive friends agriculture?
GHOST 　That'll bring them down to earth.
140 INTERLOCUTOR 　And we're giving them the benefit of our modern tongue.
GHOST 　They'll need no other one, our kingdom come.
INTERLOCUTOR 　Did you read how tranquil and subordinate they've become
　　　under our wise and humane government?

6. What's black and white and red all over? Answer (playing on the homophone red/read): a
newspaper.

[*The* GHOST *claps a "gunshot."*]

Was that a gun? A shot?

145 GHOST   Likely not. The Indian agent won't give them any more ammunition until they put in a crop.

INTERLOCUTOR   What will they eat in the meantime?

GHOST [*hitting himself*]   Off to the hoose-gow[7] with them! Lazy is as lazy does. So it says in the newspaper. Or the Bible. [*reprising "Derry Down"*]

150   Who is shooting in battle at every one,
             is shooting in battle at everyone—

GHOST & INTERLOCUTOR

             —fights bloodthirsty redskins and wears a grin,
             not afeard of anything?—

GHOST   —We have the words, the pens, the laws.
155   We know that treaties are for fools.
             We did it to the buffalo.
             You want to be next?

Scene Five

The GHOST *reveals the next placard: "Scene Five: Tenor Solo."*

GHOST   And now, for the particular delectation of the ladies in the audience—

INTERLOCUTOR   What are you doing?

GHOST   —Mister Interlocutor will render in his most famous transvestatory manner—

5 INTERLOCUTOR   I won't do this.

GHOST   —as the Princess Porkly Haunches,[8] he now sings "The Sioux Song."

INTERLOCUTOR   This is not a regular part of the program, ladies and gentlemen.

GHOST   And therefore we must show our gratitude to the princess. Let us
10   further encourage her, ladies and gentle sirs.

INTERLOCUTOR [*to the tune of "Amazing Grace"*][9]

             How beautiful
             A man the moon.
             I am what I am.
             I'm not above
15   A buck for love.
             What good is it? Sioux me.

             A sparkling place
             The city is.
             My face is my face.
20   I must go far
             Below zero.
             What good is it? Sioux me.
             My name is Sioux.
             What did I do?
25   I never ever said

---

7. Jail (slang).
8. Invented name.
9. Widely known hymn, written by English poet and clergyman John Newton in 1779. Its lyrics speak of sin, forgiveness, and redemption.

That red is what
I want to drink.
It goes right to my head.

30 How beautiful
A place the past.
We are where we are.
The redskin race
Finishes last.
What good is it? Sioux me.

35 GHOST Thank you, thank you, Mister Interlocutor. An astonishingly touching masquerade. It seemed almost real. Is this a tear here, washing the war paint?[1]

INTERLOCUTOR Unhand me, sir. I'm not afraid of you.

GHOST Boo is no go then. So how do you feel, Mister Interlocutor?

40 INTERLOCUTOR I'm the Interlocutor here!

GHOST How do you feel now?

INTERLOCUTOR I know what to do. I know the order of the show.

GHOST You do, do you?

INTERLOCUTOR I want my happy company.

45 GHOST They're even later than I am, sir. It's curtains for all of us!

INTERLOCUTOR No, the show must go on.

GHOST The audience is waiting. Mister Interlocutor?

INTERLOCUTOR The playlet.

Scene Six

The INTERLOCUTOR *reveals the placard: "Scene Six: The Playlet."*

GHOST The playlet!

INTERLOCUTOR Ladies and gentlemen, as a public service to the citizens at the forefront of our civilization, we now present a short drama of spiritual significance.

5 GHOST Mister Interlocutor, in the continued absence of Mister Bones, will now render the role of Sweet Sioux.

INTERLOCUTOR I dream. I dream, I do, of the bright lights of the city. Regina,[2] she's the finest, the queen city of my dreams. But I promised Daddy, Daddy dear, I would keep up the homestead, I would be his little
10 red pioneer. This on his deathbed. Sigh. Gangrene from an arrow. Oh horror!

GHOST Shot by me, ha ha, in error. Oops!

INTERLOCUTOR Mister Ghost now appears, in the infelicitous absence of Mister Tambo, in the role of the villainous Chief Magistrate.

15 GHOST Ahem. Ahem. Give me some rum or I'll shoot you in the bum. I need firewater for a starter. Then off I go on a hunt or to court. Order, order, I say to the buffalo. Right between the eyes, I warn the prisoners. Tonight it's too late, too late for her.

1. Paint applied to a warrior's face and body before a battle.
2. Named in 1882 for Queen Victoria, this southern Saskatchewan city served as capital of the Canadian Northwest Territories until 1903, when it became the capital of the province of Saskatchewan.

INTERLOCUTOR It is the eleventh hour. It is beyond my power to pay the
20 mortgage on my daddy's farm. Oh I am losing courage.

GHOST Knocka knocka, Sweet Sioux.

INTERLOCUTOR Who's there? At this hour.

GHOST Knocka knocka.

INTERLOCUTOR What would Daddy do?

25 GHOST Answer the door.

INTERLOCUTOR You think so?

GHOST Knocka knocka, Sioux!

INTERLOCUTOR Hello. Who's there?

GHOST It is I, my dear. Your sweetheart, Chief Magistrate.

30 INTERLOCUTOR You're no sweetheart to me.

GHOST She's not all there up here. Sometimes she believes me.

INTERLOCUTOR Stay away. What is it you want?

GHOST The time is short. The deed on this land is about to come due. I was
worried, my dear, about you.

35 INTERLOCUTOR You were? Really?

GHOST Do you have the necessary dollars?

INTERLOCUTOR No—

GHOST —Hooray!—

INTERLOCUTOR —I'm sorry to say.

40 GHOST I mean to say I'm here to help you.

INTERLOCUTOR But at what price? A chief doesn't become magistrate without vice.

GHOST Oh Sweet Sioux.

INTERLOCUTOR What's a girl to do?

45 GHOST Oh sweet Sweet Sioux.

INTERLOCUTOR Oh, no, Chief Magistrate. I couldn't do that.

GHOST Why not, my dear? She's done it before.

INTERLOCUTOR I'm not that kind of girl. I only do it for love and/or
marriage.

50 GHOST Why buy the moo cow?

INTERLOCUTOR I won't do it for meat anymore.

GHOST I'll give the deed to you.

INTERLOCUTOR Oh no. I couldn't do that. That would make me one of those
women, nothing more than a squaw.

55 GHOST A squaw? You mean like Buck and Squaw?

[The GHOST pulls the INTERLOCUTOR into a reprise of the Hollywood
Indian War Dance. The INTERLOCUTOR complies but keeps it short.]

INTERLOCUTOR Midnight is about to strike!

GHOST There goes the farm.

INTERLOCUTOR But I keep my honour.

GHOST Midnight strikes. The farm is mine. And what the hell, so are you!

60 INTERLOCUTOR Oh no no! That would be—rape!

GHOST Right you are! You're more intelligent than you appear.

INTERLOCUTOR Rape, oh no!

GHOST Oh yes, yes. Sweet Sioux! Talk about the Almighty Buck.

INTERLOCUTOR Corporal? Corporal Coat? Mister Tambo? Mister Drum!

65 Anybody!

GHOST There's no one here to come to your aid.

INTERLOCUTOR   Stop! Stop, I know. It is I, I, Corporal Red Coat of the Mounted Police—[3]

GHOST   —Aye, aye!—

70 INTERLOCUTOR   —cleverly disguised as Sweet Sioux in order to tempt the evil Chief Magistrate to show his true colours.

GHOST   Blast you, Corporal Red Coat. Talk about an Indian giver. Your feminine innocence, your eyes, had me completely convinced.

INTERLOCUTOR   It is now my duty to arrest you, Chief Magistrate.

75 GHOST   Corporal Coat, could I make you an offer?

INTERLOCUTOR   Oh more villainy. You're trying to bribe me.

GHOST   I offer you the deed to the farm for a taste of your feminine charms.

INTERLOCUTOR   How dare you, sir! Bang bang!

GHOST   Oh I am wounded, I am dying, mortifying, I am dead.

80 INTERLOCUTOR   Oh Corporal Coat.

GHOST   As my soul slips toward hell, I repent. Is it too late?

INTERLOCUTOR   Call me Red, miss.

GHOST   What a sorry end this is!

INTERLOCUTOR   I want to thank you.

85 GHOST   Jesus loves me!

INTERLOCUTOR   We can talk about that later on, Sioux.

GHOST   And suddenly my skin is white.

INTERLOCUTOR   Oh, Red, may I offer you some apple cider?

GHOST   Oh miracle! I'm heaven-sent!

90 INTERLOCUTOR   I love you.

GHOST   Or are those wedding bells I hear?

INTERLOCUTOR   I love you, too, my dear. I'm beside myself with love.

GHOST   And as I say adieu to those two united souls, choirs of angels remind me how true it is said that the only good Indians are the ones who are
95   sainted.

INTERLOCUTOR   Bravo, Mister Ghost. What a wonderful halo.

GHOST   It's old paint, Mister Interlocutor. Bravo to you, too, sir. I love your Sweet Sioux.

INTERLOCUTOR   As you were. Thank you, thank you, ladies and gentlemen.
100   You're too kind.

GHOST   They're deaf, dumb, and blinded by the light of the heavenly Ghost, sir.

INTERLOCUTOR   We hope our tale encouraged all and offended none.

GHOST   There ain't no nuns I can see out there, sir.

105 INTERLOCUTOR   We give you laughter and tears. We give hope to all who toil and are laden.

GHOST   For every girl, there is a guy.

INTERLOCUTOR   For every man, a maiden.

GHOST   For every nun, a holy Ghost.

Scene Seven

The GHOST, *on his way to the footlights, bumps into the placard stand and "Scene Seven: Duet" turns up.*

GHOST   Hi, my name's Almighty. Do you come here much?

3. The North-West Mounted Police wore red uniform coats.

INTERLOCUTOR   Mister Ghost, where are you going?

GHOST   I want to get in touch with the audience.

INTERLOCUTOR   Our final curtain has yet to descend, Mister Ghost.

5 GHOST   Speak for yourself. I want to make some new friends in the pit.

INTERLOCUTOR   You can't leave me too.

GHOST   Hiya. Will you help me down?

INTERLOCUTOR   Mister Ghost, I implore you.

GHOST   Mister Interlocutor, sir, or madam, I was forgetting about you.

10 INTERLOCUTOR   You can't go. I mean, we do have some few ensuing numbers, Mister Ghost.

GHOST   The two of us? Go on without me.

INTERLOCUTOR   None of the rest of our happy company has come along.

GHOST   Look me in the eyes and ask.

15 INTERLOCUTOR   Please, Mister Ghost. Please.

GHOST   Mister Interlocutor, sir, how do you feel?

INTERLOCUTOR   How do I feel? With my hands! No, Mister Ghost, I feel this
evening like the moon.

GHOST   You feel like the moon, Mister Interlocutor. How is that?

20 INTERLOCUTOR   Envious and pale of face and alone, Mister Ghost.

GHOST   I know how you feel, but you are mistaken.

INTERLOCUTOR   How am I mistaken, Mister Ghost?

GHOST   The Moon's an old woman. We call her Grandmother.[4] [to the tune of
"God Save The Queen"][5]

The Moon's an old woman

25   A very wise woman.

She's made of light!

GHOST & INTERLOCUTOR

She watches over us,

Over the children

Each of us is a child again

30   In the coldest night.

INTERLOCUTOR

The Moon's a young woman

A very new woman

Made out of dark

She's waiting for the light

35   Just as a child might

Wrapped warmly in a blanket and

Not at all afraid.

GHOST   Well how do you feel now, Mister Interlocutor? Mister?

Scene Eight

The INTERLOCUTOR, *fleeing the* GHOST, *bumps into the placard stand. "Scene Eight:
Stand-up" turns up.*

GHOST   Sir!

INTERLOCUTOR   Did you know, Mister Ghost, that marriage is an institution?

4. Grandmother Moon, who watches over the
earth, is an important figure in Native spiritual beliefs.

5. Royal anthem of the United Kingdom and
its territories since the 1700s.

GHOST   Yes, sir, I had heard that said.

INTERLOCUTOR   Well, sir, so is an insane asylum! Did you know, Mister
5   Ghost, that love makes the world go round? Well, sir, so does a sock in the
jaw! Which reminds me, sir. An Indian from Batoche[6] came up to me the
other day and said he hadn't had a bite in days. So I bit him! Do you know,
sir, how many Indians it takes to screw in a light bulb?

GHOST   What's a light bulb?

10   INTERLOCUTOR   Good one, Mister Ghost, a very good one. Well then, sir, if
it's nighttime here, it must be winter in Regina. Nothing could be finah
than Regina in the wintah, sir. Am I making myself clear? Does this bear
repeating? Does this buffalo repeating? Almighty Gas, you say! Answer me,
Mister Ghost. Answer! What! A fine time to demand a medium! It's very
15   small of you, sir. I promise you I will large this in your face if you do not
choose to co-operate. Tell me, is it true that the Indian brave will marry his
wife's sister so he doesn't have to break in a new mother-in-law? Does it
therefore follow, sir, that our good and great Queen Victoria keeps her
Prince Albert in a can?[7] That's where she keeps the Indians! Hear ye, hear
20   ye! Don't knock off her bonnet and stick her in her royal rump with a
sword, sir. The word, sir, is treason. Or are you drunk? Besotted! Be seated,
sir. No! Stand up! You, sir, you, I recognize you now. You're that redskin!
You're that wagon burner! That feather head, Chief Bullshit. No, Chief
Shitting Bull![8] Oh, no, no. Bloodthirsty savage. Yes, you're primitive, unciv-
25   ilized, a cantankerous cannibal! Unruly redman, you lack human intelligence! Stupidly stoic, sick, demented, foaming at the maws! Weirdly mad
and dangerous, alcoholic, diseased, dirty, filthy, stinking, ill-fated degenerate race, vanishing, dying, lazy, mortifying, fierce, fierce and crazy, crazy,
shit, shit, shit, shit . . .

30   GHOST   What's a light bulb?

INTERLOCUTOR   Who are you? Who the hell are you?

GHOST   I'm a dead Indian. I eat crow instead of buffalo.

INTERLOCUTOR   That's good. That's very good.

Scene Nine

*The lights shift from variety to spectral as the spotlight finds the placard: "Scene
Nine: Finale."*

INTERLOCUTOR   Who am I? Do you know?

GHOST   I recognized you by your eyes.

INTERLOCUTOR   Who am I?

GHOST   White Girl, my White Girl.

6. The Battle of Batoche in central Saskatchewan concluded the 1885 Northwest Rebellion. This series of skirmishes between the
Métis—mixed-race people of First Nations
and European descent—and Canadian government forces resulted in the defeat of the
Métis forces.
7. American brand of tobacco first introduced
in 1907. The name refers to King Edward VII
(reigned 1901–10), who was known as Prince
Albert before his coronation. The availability
of Prince Albert in tins later provided the subject for a well-known practical joke, in which
a phone caller calls a store and asks, "Do you
have Prince Albert in a can?" When the person on the other line answers yes, the caller
retorts, "Well, let him out!"
8. Sitting Bull, Lakota Sioux Indian chief (ca.
1831–1890) who led resistance against U.S.
military and civilian encroachment on Native
lands.

5 INTERLOCUTOR Who? Who is that?

GHOST My fierce, crazy little girl. My wife. *Ni-wikimakan*. [*My wife.*]

> [*The* INTERLOCUTOR *touches her face with her gloved hands as the* GHOST *embraces and releases her. The spotlight finds her face as her gloved hands begin to wipe the whiteface off, unmasking the woman inside. The* GHOST *removes one glove and throws it on the dead fire, she does the same with the other. The fire rekindles.*]

   Piko ta-ta-wi kisisomoyan ekwo. [*I have to go finish dancing now.*]

INTERLOCUTOR *Patima, Kisse-Manitou-Wayou*. [*Goodbye, Almighty Voice.*]

> [*The* GHOST *goes and dances in celebration to a drum. The woman removes the rest of the whiteface and costume, becoming* WHITE GIRL *again. She gathers the costume in her arms as the spotlight drifts away to become a full moon in the night.* WHITE GIRL *lifts a baby-sized bundle to the audience as the* GHOST *continues to dance in the fading lights.*]

   The end.

SUZAN-LORI PARKS

b. 1964

WHEN Suzan-Lori Parks was a senior at Mount Holyoke College, she wrote her first play, *The Sinner's Place*. Because, as Parks later recalled, the play's setting consisted of "a lot of dirt on stage which was being dug at," the Theater Department rejected it for production. By the time she was awarded a Pulitzer Prize in 2002 for her play *Topdog/Underdog*, however, Parks's fascination with digging—turning over the topsoil of cultural myths, sifting through the artifacts of history, unearthing the buried voices of African Americans within history—had established her as one of the American theater's foremost archaeologists. "The responsibility of a writer," the novelist James Baldwin once remarked, "is to excavate the experience of the people who produced him." Deeply concerned with forebears and inheritances, Parks's drama uncovers this experience by examining its traces and absences in the American historical imagination. "Because so much of African American history has been unrecorded, dismembered, washed out," Parks writes, "one of my tasks as playwright is to—through literature and the special strange relationship between theater and real-life—locate the ancestral burial ground, dig for bones, find bones, hear the bones sing, write it down." By "remembering" history in the double sense of retrieving and remaking it, Parks offers new theatrical possibilities for staging the dialogue between past, present, and future. Innovative (often challenging) in language, dramatic structure, and performance, her drama remains among the most startlingly original in the contemporary American theater.

Suzan-Lori Parks was born in Fort Knox, Kentucky. The daughter of an Army colonel, she moved frequently as a child and considered a number of places home: Texas, California, North Carolina, Maryland, Vermont, and Germany, where she attended German schools rather than those for the children of American military personnel. This experience of changing location—of moving between places with divergent regional and national histories and of negotiating language differences—clearly contributed to her interest in language and in the relationships between geography, history, and identity. As an undergraduate at Mount Holyoke she took a short story writing class with James Baldwin; after she gave an animated in-class reading of one of her stories, he suggested that she consider playwriting. The turn to drama was a natural one: as she explained in a 2000 interview, she felt while writing short stories that her characters were in the room with her, "standing right behind me, talking. Not telling the story, but acting it out—doing it." Despite the Theater Department's rejection of *The Sinner's Place*, Parks decided to pursue her interest in dramatic writing. Encouraged by one of her English professors, she read the plays of two pioneering African American women playwrights: Adrienne Kennedy, whose *Funnyhouse of a Negro* (1962) dramatized its protagonist's haunted consciousness on a dreamlike stage reminiscent of the stages of AUGUST STRINDBERG and Jean Genet, and Ntozake Shange, who has explored the relationship of drama, poetry, dance, and female African American identity in *for colored girls who have considered suicide / when the rainbow is enuf* (1975) and other plays. After graduating from college in 1985 with majors in English and German, Parks studied acting for a year in London.

Upon her return to the United States, Parks quickly established herself as a playwright of note. *Betting on the Dust Commander* (1987) was produced in New York, as was *Imperceptible Mutabilities in the Third Kingdom* (1989). The latter play received an Obie (off-Broadway) Award for Best New American Play and was widely praised by critics; indeed, after seeing the play, Mel Gussow of the *New York Times* called Parks "the year's most promising playwright." *The Death of the Last Black Man in the Whole Entire World* opened the following year at the same theater, and *Devotees in the Garden of Love* was produced at the Humana Festival in Louisville in 1992. Parks's next drama, THE AMERICA PLAY, was given workshop productions in Washington and Dallas in 1993 before opening at the Yale Repertory Theatre and the New York Public Theater in 1994. In 1996, her play *Venus*—based on the life of Saartjie Baartman, a Khoisan African woman who, because of her large buttocks, was exhibited in the early 1800s in London and Paris as the "Hottentot Venus"—was produced at the Public Theatre in New York and received an Obie Award for Playwriting. *In the Blood* was produced in New York in 1999, and *Fucking A* premiered in Houston in 2000; both plays were inspired by Nathaniel Hawthorne's novel *The Scarlet Letter* (1850). The Pulitzer Prize–winning *Topdog/Underdog*, which features two brothers named Lincoln and Booth, opened at the Public Theater in New York in 2001 and was subsequently taken to

Broadway. Parks's most ambitious theatrical project began in 2002, when the playwright decided to write one play every day for a year. The completed plays—some less than a page in length, others considerably longer—were performed by theater groups across the United States in 2006–07 as part of a cycle titled *365 Days/365 Plays*. More recent plays include *Father Comes Home from the Wars (Parts 1, 8 & 9)* (2009) and *The Book of Grace* (2010). Her adaptation of George and Ira Gershwin's opera *Porgy and Bess* for the musical-theater stage premiered in 2011. Parks has also written the screenplay for the film *Girl 6* (1996, directed by Spike Lee) and an adaptation of Zora Neale Hurston's 1937 novel *Their Eyes Were Watching God*, which was televised in 2005. Parks's novel *Getting Mother's Body* was published in 2003.

Intricate (sometimes dense) in texture and meaning, Parks's plays have received widespread attention for their distinctive, highly theatricalized conception of language, character, and dramatic form. As befits a dramatist whose favorite writers include the modernists William Faulkner, Virginia Woolf, and James Joyce, Parks makes intricate, highly self-conscious use of the acoustic and semantic qualities of dramatic speech. Words, Parks insists, are "spells in our mouths." Driven by the cadences, syntax, and word forms of African American dialect, distinguished by frequent wordplay and by multiple meanings, the language of Parks's drama reflects her characters' complex lives and inheritance. When one of the characters in *Imperceptible Mutabilities* says "Last night I dreamed of where I comed from. But where I comed from diduhnt look like nowhere like I been," his words evoke a collective experience of migration, relocation, and lost origins. How do contemporary African Americans, descendants of those who endured the Middle Passage in the holds of slave ships, bridge the gap between Africa and North America, between the present and the history that informs it? Like the words that Parks uses, with their "thrilling histories" and "fabulous etymologies," the characters who people her plays are indelibly marked by history. They bear names such as those in *Death of the Last Black Man in the Whole Entire World:* Black Man with Watermelon, Yes and Greens Black-Eyed Peas Cornbread, And Bigger and Bigger and Bigger, Before Columbus, and Queen-then-Pharaoh-Hatshepsut. Drawing together racial stereotypes, African history, soul food, and literary references (the character And Bigger and Bigger and Bigger, for example, is named after Bigger Thomas, the protagonist of Richard Wright's 1940 novel *Native Son*), these figures embody many of the ways in which black Americans have been represented in American history and culture.

While Parks's dramatic characters are rooted in real lives and relationships, they also function as improvised meditations, or riffs, on cultural themes and images. Not surprisingly, music—in the form of jazz, classical music, opera, and hip-hop—has played an important role in the language and structure of Parks's drama. Rejecting the linear form of traditional drama, in which action proceeds with a clear beginning, middle, and end, Parks experiments with alternative ways of structuring dramatic incidents. One of her signature

devices is "repetition and revision"—the technique, popular with jazz composers and musicians (and echoing the cadence of African American oral traditions, including preaching), of repeating a phrase over and over again while varying it slightly each time. In Parks's drama, words, exchanges, and situations return with hypnotic regularity, establishing connections and counterpoints that build with a logic as much circular as linear. "Characters refigure their words," Parks declares, "and through a refiguring of language show us that they are experiencing their situation anew." The phrase that supplies the title of *The Death of the Last Black Man in the Whole Entire World*, for instance, is spoken at a number of points in the play, and this repetition mirrors that of the action, in which the central protagonist—representing one black man and every black man—is murdered over and over again. Only in the burial scene that ends the play does this repetitive cycle in African American history attain closure.

Repetition, doubling, and, again, the remembering of history are central to *The America Play*, Parks's most frequently per-

Rhonnie Washington (left) as The Foundling Father in a 2008 production of *The America Play* staged by the Thick Description Theater Company (San Francisco).

formed work. The play is set in a "great hole" somewhere in the American West, "an exact replica" (the stage direction indicates) "of the Great Hole of History," a fictional theme park located back East where a parade of historical figures emerge and march by for the audience's entertainment. The play's protagonist, an African American man identified by his stage name, The Foundling Father, was so entranced with the marvels of history when he visited the Great Park on his honeymoon that he became determined to re-create it. After being told that he resembled Abraham Lincoln—the two "were dead ringers, more or less"—he took to reciting speeches by the famous president in costume. When someone observed that "he played Lincoln so well that he ought to be shot," The Foundling Father devised just such an act: customers pay a penny to shoot him as he sits in Ford's Theater. One after another, they select a pistol, stand in position, and, after shooting him in the head, jump to the stage yelling "Thus to the tyrants!" or other exclamations attributed to Lincoln's assassin John Wilkes Booth (and others). The assassination is replayed over and over again while The Foundling Father recounts to the play's audience his past and his peculiar vocation.

All history repeats itself, Karl Marx famously observed: "the first time as tragedy, the second time as farce." But in an age of historical theme parks, Revolutionary and Civil War reenactments, and interactive museums (such as the Abraham Lincoln Presidential Museum in Springfield, Illinois, which opened in 2005), history is just as likely to repeat itself as theater. In *The America Play*, Parks explores the many ways in which American history—the images, texts, performances, commemorations with which we tell the story of our collective past—writes itself into the present. The Foundling Father is flanked by a pasteboard cutout and bust of Lincoln, to which he frequently gestures; he collects the pennies that bear Lincoln's profile; and he carries with him the props by which the legendary president is identified in the popular imagination: black coat, stovepipe hat, and an assortment of beards (including a blond one, which he rarely wears because

it undermines the illusion). The Foundling Father quotes from the Gettysburg Address and retells the events of the fateful night in Ford's Theater, though the account he provides is based as much on tradition and hearsay as historical fact. Parks plays with the idea of historical accuracy in her footnotes to the play, which include humorous or speculative information (including a line that Mary Todd Lincoln "might have said . . . that night") as well as documented facts. In a play that features an actor impersonating a historical figure, a replay of this performance on television (in the play's second act), and scenes from the play that Lincoln was watching (*Our American Cousin* [1858] by Tom Taylor), history becomes the site of multiple performances and competing imitations. At times, original and copy seem indistinguishable from one another. Even the Great Hole of History reappears as a theme park somewhere else.

With its parade of well-known historical figures and deeds, the Great Hole provides a spectacle of American history as it has traditionally circulated and been known. But this hole in the ground also signals its absences and elisions. Reversing the nineteenth-century tradition of blackface—white actors blackening their faces in order to play African American characters—The Foundling Father's impersonation of Abraham Lincoln foregrounds the absence or marginalization of African Americans from this history. As he refers to himself as the "Lesser Known," in contrast to the "Great Man," The Foundling Father reflects on the discrepancy between the latter's fame and his own anonymity. A "digger" by trade, he discovers a more elevated calling by following in the Great Man's footsteps. Yet the reflected glory that he acquires by impersonating Lincoln only underscores the historical invisibility to which his racial identity has otherwise consigned him. Lincoln may have freed the slaves—but the idea of America that he represents has largely excluded African Americans from its originating myths as well as from the prevailing national identity. The Foundling Father may assume the mantle of one of his country's forefathers—but as Parks's play on his name signifies, his is an illegitimate inheritance (a *foundling* is a child of unknown parentage). When one of his customers, a woman, yells "LIES!" after jumping to the stage, her accusation strikes at the heart of the national myth—the idea of America as "a new nation, conceived in Liberty, and dedicated to the proposition that all men are created equal"—that Lincoln represents.

The search for (fore)fathers in *The America Play* extends into the play's second act, set years later, when The Foundling Father's wife, Lucy, and son Brazil look for traces of him after his death.

Marked by the rituals of grief, this act is pervaded with a sense of mourning, yet it also conveys a tone of affirmation. The Foundling Father may have "fall[en] in love with the wrong person, fall[en] in love with the wrong dream" (as Parks suggests), but his deconstructive performance of American history has been celebratory as well. By showing this history to itself through the mirror of blackness, he has claimed a space, however small, in the performance of national identity.   S.G.

The America Play

THE ROLES

Act 1:   THE FOUNDLING FATHER, AS ABRAHAM LINCOLN
           A VARIETY OF VISITORS
Act 2:   LUCY
           BRAZIL
           THE FOUNDLING FATHER, AS ABRAHAM LINCOLN
           2 ACTORS
           The Visitors in Act 1 are played by the 2 Actors who assume
           the roles in the passages from *Our American Cousin* in Act 2.
Place   A great hole. In the middle of nowhere. The hole is an exact
           replica of The Great Hole of History.

SYNOPSIS OF ACTS AND SCENES

Act 1: Lincoln Act
Act 2: The Hall of Wonders
  A. Big Bang   E. Spadework
  B. Echo   F. Echo
  C. Archeology   G. The Great Beyond
  D. Echo

Brackets in the text indicate optional cuts for production.

In the beginning, all the world was America.
                                    —JOHN LOCKE[1]

1. English philosopher and political theorist (1632–1704); the quotation is from *Two Treatises of Government* (1689).

Act 1: Lincoln Act

A great hole. In the middle of nowhere. The hole is an exact replica of the Great Hole of History.

THE FOUNDLING FATHER AS ABRAHAM LINCOLN   "To stop too fearful and too faint to go."[2]

[*Rest.*[3]]

"He digged the hole and the whole held him."

[*Rest.*]

"I cannot dig, to beg I am ashamed."[4]

[*Rest.*]

5   "He went to the theatre but home went she."[5]

[*Rest.*]

Goatee. Goatee. What he sported when he died. Its not my favorite.

[*Rest.*]

"He digged the hole and the whole held him." Huh.

[*Rest.*]

There was once a man who was told that he bore a strong resemblance to Abraham Lincoln.[6] He was tall and thinly built just like the Great Man.
10   His legs were the longer part just like the Great Mans legs. His hands and feet were large as the Great Mans were large. The Lesser Known had several beards which he carried around in a box. The beards were his although he himself had not grown them on his face but since he'd secretly bought the hairs from his barber and arranged their beard shapes and since the
15   procurement and upkeep of his beards took so much work he figured that the beards were completely his. Were as authentic as he was, so to speak. His beard box was of cherry wood and lined with purple velvet. He had the initials "A.L." tooled in gold on the lid.

[*Rest.*]

While the Great Mans livelihood kept him in Big Town the Lesser Knowns
20   work kept him in Small Town. The Great Man by trade was a President. The Lesser Known was a Digger by trade. From a family of Diggers. Digged graves. He was known in Small Town to dig his graves quickly and neatly. This brought him a steady business.

[*Rest.*]

2. An example of chiasmus, by Oliver Goldsmith, cited under "chiasmus" in *Webster's Ninth New Collegiate Dictionary* (Springfield, MA: Merriam-Webster, Inc., 1983) p. 232. Notes 4 and 5 also refer to examples of chiasmus [Parks's note]. *Chiasmus:* the syntactic inversion of the second of two parallel clauses (a rhetorical figure). The example is from "The Traveller; or, A Prospect of Society" (1794), by Goldsmith (ca. 1730–1774), an Irish-born novelist, poet, and playwright.
3. Pause.
4. *A Dictionary of Modern English Usage,* H. W. Fowler (New York: Oxford University Press, 1983) p. 86 [Parks's note]. The quotation is from Luke 16.3.
5. *The New American Heritage Dictionary of the English Language,* William Morris, ed. (Boston: Houghton Mifflin Co., 1981) p. 232 [Parks's note].
6. The sixteenth president of the United States (1809–1865; president, 1861–65), a lawyer and legislator from Illinois who was born in backwoods Kentucky; he has been acclaimed for his leadership during the Civil War (1861–65) and for his role in ending slavery.

A wink to Mr. Lincolns pasteboard cutout. [*Winks at Lincoln's pasteboard cutout.*]

[*Rest.*]

25   It would be helpful to our story if when the Great Man died in death he were to meet the Lesser Known. It would be helpful to our story if, say, the Lesser Known were summoned to Big Town by the Great Mans wife: "*Emergency oh, Emergency,* please put the Great Man in the ground"[7] (they say the Great Mans wife was given to hysterics: one young son dead

30   others sickly:[8] even the Great Man couldnt save them: a war on then off and surrendered to: "Play Dixie I always liked that song":[9] the brother against the brother: a new nation all conceived and ready to be hatched: the Great Man takes to guffawing guffawing at thin jokes in bad plays: "You sockdologizing old man-trap!"[1] haw haw haw because he wants so very

35   badly to laugh at something and one moment guffawing and the next moment the Great Man is gunned down. In his rocker. "Useless Useless."[2] And there were bills to pay.) "*Emergency,* oh *Emergency* please put the Great Man in the ground."

[*Rest.*]

It is said that the Great Mans wife did call out and it is said that the Lesser

40   Known would [sneak away from his digging and stand behind a tree where he couldnt be seen or get up and] leave his wife and child after the blessing had been said and [the meat carved during the distribution of the vegetables it is said that he would leave his wife and his child and] standing in the kitchen or sometimes out in the yard [between the right angles of the

45   house] stand out there where he couldnt be seen standing with his ear cocked. "*Emergency,* oh *Emergency,* please put the Great Man in the ground."

[*Rest.*]

It would help if she had called out and if he had been summoned been given a ticket all bought and paid for and boarded a train in his look-alike

50   black frock coat bought on time and already exhausted. Ridiculous. If he had been summoned. [Been summoned between the meat and the vegetables and boarded a train to Big Town where he would line up and gawk at

7. Possibly the words of Mary Todd Lincoln [1818–1882] after the death of her husband [Parks's note].
8. Of the Lincolns' four sons—Robert (1843–1926), Edward (1846–1850), William (1850–1862), and Thomas, nicknamed Tad (1853–1871)—only Robert survived into adulthood. Mary Todd Lincoln has often been described as mentally unstable.
9. At the end of the Civil War, President Lincoln told his troops to play "Dixie," the song of the South, in tribute to the Confederacy [Parks's note]. The song was published in 1860 by the Ohio-born Daniel Decatur Emmett, who wrote songs for his blackface minstrel troupe, but his claim of authorship is disputed.
1. A very funny line from the play *Our American Cousin.* As the audience roared with

laughter, Booth entered Lincoln's box and shot him dead [Parks's note]. *Our American Cousin* (1858), a comedy by the English dramatist and writer Tom Taylor. John Wilkes Booth (1838–1865), a renowned Shakespearean actor and a Southern sympathizer who led the conspiracy to assassinate Lincoln as he attended a performance less than a week after the Civil War ended.
2. The last words of President Lincoln's assassin, John Wilkes Booth [Parks's note]. After shooting Lincoln, Booth leaped to the stage and broke his leg but escaped on horseback. After soldiers and detectives found him hiding in a barn in Virginia, about 75 miles southwest of Washington, he either was shot or shot himself and died shortly thereafter.

the Great Mans corpse along with the rest of them.[3]] But none of this was
meant to be.

[*Rest.*]

55 A nod to the bust of Mr. Lincoln. [*Nods to the bust of Lincoln.*] But none of
this was meant to be. For the Great Man had been murdered long before
the Lesser Known had been born. How uhboutthat. [So that any calling
that had been done he couldnt hear, any summoning he had hoped for he
couldnt answer but somehow not even unheard and unanswered because
60 he hadnt even been there] although you should note that he talked about
the murder and the mourning that followed as if he'd been called away on
business at the time and because of the business had missed it. Living
regretting he hadnt arrived sooner. Being told from birth practically that he
and the Great Man were dead ringers, more or less, and knowing that he,
65 if he had been in the slightest vicinity back then, would have had at least a
chance at the great honor of digging the Great Mans grave.

[*Rest.*]

This beard I wear for the holidays. I got shoes to match. Rarely wear em
together. It's a little *much.*

[*Rest.*]

[His son named in a fit of meanspirit after the bad joke about fancy nuts[4]
70 and old mens toes his son looked like a nobody. Not Mr. Lincoln or the
father or the mother either for that matter although the father had assumed
the superiority of his own blood and hadnt really expected the mother to
exert any influence.]

[*Rest.*]

Sunday. Always slow on Sunday. I'll get thuh shoes. Youll see. A wink to Mr.
75 Lincolns pasteboard cutout. [*Winks at Lincoln's cutout.*]

[*Rest.*]

Everyone who has ever walked the earth has a shape around which their
entire lives and their posterity shapes itself. The Great Man had his log
cabin into which he was born, the distance between the cabin and Big
Town multiplied by the half-life, the staying power of his words and image,
80 being the true measurement of the Great Mans stature. The Lesser Known
had a favorite hole. A chasm, really. Not a hole he had digged but one he'd
visited. Long before the son was born. When he and his Lucy were newly
wedded. Lucy kept secrets for the dead. And they figured what with his digging and her Confidence work[5] they could build a mourning business. The
85 son would be a weeper.[6] Such a long time uhgo. So long uhgo. When he
and his Lucy were newly wedded and looking for some postnuptial excitement: A Big Hole. A theme park. With historical parades. The size of the
hole itself was enough to impress any Digger but it was the Historicity of
the place the order and beauty of the pageants which marched by them the
90 Greats on parade in front of them. From the sidelines he'd be calling
"Ohwayohwhyohwayoh" and "Hello" and waving and saluting. The Hole

3. Thousands viewed Lincoln's body lying
in state in the U.S. Capitol, and thousands
more watched the train bearing him home to
Springfield, Illinois, where he was buried.
4. That is, Brazil nuts, which were long
known in some regions of the United States
as "nigger toes."
5. That is, her work as someone entrusted
with confidential communications.
6. A hired mourner.

and its Historicity and the part he played in it all gave a shape to the life and posterity of the Lesser Known that he could never shake.

[*Rest.*]

95 Here they are. I wont put them on. I'll just hold them up. See. Too much. Told ya. [Much much later when the Lesser Known had made a name for himself he began to record his own movements. He hoped he'd be of interest to posterity. As in the Great Mans footsteps.]

[*Rest.*]

Traveling home again from the honeymoon at the Big Hole riding the train with his Lucy: wife beside him the Reconstructed Historicities he has wit-
100 nessed continue to march before him in his minds eye as they had at the Hole. Cannons wicks were lit and the rockets did blare and the enemy was slain and lay stretched out and smoldering for dead and rose up again to take their bows. On the way home again the histories paraded again on past him although it wasnt on past him at all it wasnt something he could
105 expect but again like Lincolns life not "on past" but *past. Behind him.* Like an echo in his head.

[*Rest.*]

When he got home again he began to hear the summoning. At first they thought it only an echo. Memories sometimes stuck like that and he and his Lucy had both seen visions. But after a while it only called to him. And it
110 became louder not softer but louder louder as if he were moving toward it.

[*Rest.*]

This is my fancy beard. Yellow. Mr. Lincolns hair was dark so I dont wear it much. If you deviate too much they wont get their pleasure. Thats my experience. Some inconsistencies are perpetuatable because theyre good for business. But not the yellow beard. Its just my fancy. Every once and a
115 while. Of course, his hair was dark.

[*Rest.*]

The Lesser Known left his wife and child and went out West finally. [Between the meat and the vegetables. A monumentous journey. Enduring all the elements. Without a friend in the world. And the beasts of the forest took him in. He got there and he got his plot he staked his claim he tried
120 his hand at his own Big Hole.] As it had been back East everywhere out West he went people remarked on his likeness to Lincoln. How, in a limited sort of way, taking into account of course his natural God-given limitations, how he was identical to the Great Man in gait and manner how his legs were long and torso short. The Lesser Known had by this time taken to
125 wearing a false wart on his cheek in remembrance of the Great Mans wart. When the Westerners noted his wart they pronounced the 2 men in virtual twinship.

[*Rest.*]

Goatee. Huh. Goatee.

[*Rest.*]

"He digged the Hole and the Whole held him."

[*Rest.*]

130 "I cannot dig, to beg I am ashamed."

[*Rest.*]

The Lesser Known had under his belt a few of the Great Mans words and after a day of digging, in the evenings, would stand in his hole reciting. But the Lesser Known was a curiosity at best. None of those who spoke of his virtual twinship with greatness would actually pay money to watch him be
135 that greatness. One day he tacked up posters inviting them to come and throw old food at him while he spoke. This was a moderate success. People began to save their old food "for Mr. Lincoln" they said. He took to traveling playing small towns. Made money. And when someone remarked that he played Lincoln so well that he ought to be shot, it was as if the Great
140 Mans footsteps had been suddenly revealed:
  [Rest.]
The Lesser Known returned to his hole and, instead of speeching, his act would now consist of a single chair, a rocker, in a dark box. The public was invited to pay a penny, choose from the selection of provided pistols, enter the darkened box and "Shoot Mr. Lincoln." The Lesser Known became
145 famous overnight.
  [A MAN, as John Wilkes Booth, enters. He takes a gun and "stands in position": at the left side of THE FOUNDLING FATHER, as Abraham LINCOLN, pointing the gun at THE FOUNDLING FATHER's head]
A MAN Ready.
THE FOUNDLING FATHER Haw Haw Haw Haw
  [Rest.]
  HAW HAW HAW HAW
  [BOOTH shoots. LINCOLN "slumps in his chair." BOOTH jumps.]
A MAN [theatrically] "Thus to the tyrants!"[7]
  [Rest.]
150 Hhhh. [Exits.]
THE FOUNDLING FATHER Most of them do that, thuh "Thus to the tyrants!"— what they say the killer said. "Thus to the tyrants!" The killer was also heard to say "The South is avenged!"[8] Sometimes they yell that.
  [A man, the same man as before, enters again, again as John Wilkes Booth. He takes a gun and "stands in position": at the left side of THE FOUNDLING FATHER, as Abraham LINCOLN, pointing the gun at THE FOUNDLING FATHER's head.]
A MAN Ready.
155 THE FOUNDLING FATHER Haw Haw Haw Haw
  [Rest.]
  HAW HAW HAW HAW
  [BOOTH shoots. LINCOLN "slumps in his chair." BOOTH jumps.]
A MAN [theatrically] "The South is avenged!"
  [Rest.]

7. Or "Sic semper tyrannis." Purportedly, Booth's words after he slew Lincoln and leapt from the presidential box to the stage of Ford's Theatre in Washington, D.C. on 14 April 1865, not only killing the President but also interrupting a performance of *Our American Cousin,* starring Miss Laura Keene [Parks's note]. *Sic semper tyrannis:* Thus always to tyrants (Latin), adopted in 1776 as the state motto of Virginia (whose capital, Richmond, became the capital of the Confederacy). Keene (ca. 1826–1873), a London-born actress who became well-known in the United States on the stage and as a theater manager. 8. Allegedly, Booth's words [Parks's note].

Hhhh.

[*Rest.*]

Thank you.

160 THE FOUNDLING FATHER Pleasures mine.

A MAN Till next week.

THE FOUNDLING FATHER Till next week.

[A MAN *exits.*]

THE FOUNDLING FATHER Comes once a week that one. Always chooses the
Derringer[9] although we've got several styles he always chooses the Der-
165 ringer. Always "The tyrants" and then "The South avenged." The ones who
choose the Derringer are the ones for History. He's one for History. As it
Used to Be. Never wavers. No frills. By the book. Nothing excessive.

[*Rest.*]

A nod to Mr. Lincolns bust. [*Nods to Lincoln's bust.*]

[*Rest.*]

I'll wear this one. He sported this style in the early war years. Years of
170 uncertainty. When he didnt know if the war was right when it could be said
he didnt always know which side he was on not because he was a stupid man
but because it was sometimes not 2 different sides at all but one great side
surging toward something beyond either Northern or Southern. A beard of
uncertainty. The Lesser Known meanwhile living his life long after all this
175 had happened and not knowing much about it until he was much older [(as
a boy "The Civil War" was an afterschool game and his folks didnt mention
the Great Mans murder for fear of frightening him)] knew only that he was
a dead ringer in a family of Diggers and that he wanted to grow and have
others think of him and remove their hats and touch their hearts and look
180 up into the heavens and say something about the freeing of the slaves. That
is, he wanted to make a great impression as he understood Mr. Lincoln to
have made.

[*Rest.*]

And so in his youth the Lesser Known familiarized himself with all aspects
of the Great Mans existence. What interested the Lesser Known most was
185 the murder and what was most captivating about the murder was the 20
feet—

[A WOMAN, *as* BOOTH, *enters.*]

A WOMAN Excuse me.

THE FOUNDLING FATHER Not at all.

[A WOMAN, *as* BOOTH, "*stands in position.*"]

THE FOUNDLING FATHER Haw Haw Haw Haw

[*Rest.*]

190 HAW HAW HAW HAW

[BOOTH *shoots.* LINCOLN "*slumps in his chair.*" BOOTH *jumps.*]

A WOMAN "Strike the tent."[1] [*Exits.*]

---

9. A small, easily concealed pistol with a large
bore, invented ca. 1852 by the American gun-
smith Henry Deringer; Booth used a derringer to shoot Lincoln in the back of the head.

1. The last words of General Robert E. Lee
[1807–1870], Commander of the Confeder-
ate Army [Parks's note].

THE FOUNDLING FATHER   What interested the Lesser Known most about the
Great Mans murder was the 20 feet which separated the presidents box
from the stage. In the presidents box sat the president his wife and their 2
friends.[2] On the stage that night was *Our American Cousin* starring Miss
Laura Keene. The plot of this play is of little consequence to our story. Suf-
fice it to say that it was thinly comedic and somewhere in the 3rd Act a
man holds a gun to his head—something about despair—
[*Rest.*]
Ladies and Gentlemen: *Our American Cousin*—
[B WOMAN, *as* BOOTH, *enters. She "stands in position."*]

200 B WOMAN   Go ahead.
THE FOUNDLING FATHER   Haw Haw Haw Haw
[*Rest.*]
HAW HAW HAW HAW
[BOOTH *shoots.* LINCOLN *"slumps in his chair."* BOOTH *jumps.*]
B WOMAN [*rest*]   LIES!
[*Rest.*]
L I I I I I I I I I I I I I I I I I I I I I I I I I E S !
[*Rest.*]

205 L I I I I I I I I I I I I I I I I I A R R R R R R R R R R R R R R S !
[*Rest.*]
Lies.
[*Rest. Exits. Reenters. Steps downstage. Rest.*]
LIES!
[*Rest.*]
L I I I I I I I I I I I I I I I I I I I I I I I I E S !
[*Rest.*]
L I I I I I I I I I I I I I I I I I I A R R R R R R R R R R R R R R S !
[*Rest.*]

210 Lies.
[*Rest. Exits.*]
THE FOUNDLING FATHER [*rest*]   I think I'll wear the yellow beard. Variety.
Works like uh tonic.
[*Rest.*]
Some inaccuracies are good for business. Take the stovepipe hat! Never
really worn indoors but people dont like their Lincoln hatless.
[*Rest.*]

215 Mr. Lincoln my apologies. [*Nods to the bust and winks to the cutout.*]
[*Rest.*]
[Blonde. Not bad if you like a stretch. Hmmm. Let us pretend for a
moment that our beloved Mr. Lincoln was a blonde. "The sun on his fair
hair looked like the sun itself."[3]—. Now. What interested our Mr. Lesser
Known most was those feet between where the Great *Blonde* Man sat, in

2. Clara Harris (1845–1883), the daughter of
a U.S. senator, and her fiancée, Major Henry
Rathbone (1837–1911).

3. From "The Sun," a composition by The
Foundling Father, unpublished [Parks's note].

220   his rocker, the stage, the time it took the murderer to cross that expanse, and how the murderer crossed it. He jumped. Broke his leg in the jumping. It was said that the Great Mans wife then began to scream. (She was given to hysterics several years afterward in fact declared insane did you know she ran around Big Town poor desperate for money trying to sell her cloth-

225   ing? On that sad night she begged her servant: "Bring in Taddy, Father will speak to Taddy."[4] But Father died instead unconscious. And she went mad from grief. Off her rocker. Mad Mary claims she hears her dead men. Summoning. The older son, Robert, he locked her up.[5] "*Emergency, oh, Emergency* please put the Great Man in the ground.")

   [*Enter* B MAN, *as* BOOTH. *He "stands in position."*]

230 THE FOUNDLING FATHER   Haw Haw Haw Haw
   [*Rest.*]

   HAW HAW HAW HAW
   [BOOTH *shoots.* LINCOLN *"slumps in his chair."* BOOTH *jumps.*]

   B MAN   "Now he belongs to the ages."[6]
   [*Rest.*]

   Blonde?

   THE FOUNDLING FATHER   (I only talk with the regulars.)
235 B MAN   He wasnt blonde. [*Exits.*]

   THE FOUNDLING FATHER   A slight deafness in this ear other than that there are no side effects.
   [*Rest.*]

   Hhh. Clean-shaven for a while. The face needs air. Clean-shaven as in his youth. When he met his Mary. —. Hhh. Blonde.
   [*Rest.*]

240   6 feet under is a long way to go. Imagine. When the Lesser Known left to find his way out West he figured he had dug over 7 hundred and 23 graves. 7 hundred and 23. Excluding his Big Hole. Excluding the hundreds of shallow holes he later digs the hundreds of shallow holes he'll use to bury his faux-historical knickknacks when he finally quits this business. Not

245   including those. 7 hundred and 23 graves.

   [C MAN *and* C WOMAN *enter.*]

   C MAN   You allow 2 at once?

   THE FOUNDLING FATHER
   [*Rest.*]

   C WOMAN   We're just married. You know: newlyweds. We hope you dont mind. Us both at once.

   THE FOUNDLING FATHER
   [*Rest.*]

4. Mary Todd Lincoln, wanting her dying husband to speak to their son Tad, might have said this that night [Parks's note]. After he was shot, Lincoln was carried to a home across the street from the theater; he died the next morning.
5. In 1875 Robert had his mother committed to an insane asylum, but she was later declared

legally competent. *Hears her dead men*: from the 1850s onward, Mary Todd Lincoln became increasingly interested in spiritualism, or communication with the dead (usually attempted with the help of a medium).
6. The words of Secretary of War Edwin Stanton [1814–1869], as Lincoln died [Parks's note].

C MAN   We're just married.
250 C WOMAN   Newlyweds.
THE FOUNDLING FATHER
          [Rest.]
          [Rest.]
          [They "stand in position." Both hold one gun.]
C MAN AND C WOMAN   Shoot.
THE FOUNDLING FATHER   Haw Haw Haw Haw
          [Rest.]
    HAW HAW HAW HAW
          [Rest.]
          [Rest.]
    HAW HAW HAW HAW
          [They shoot. LINCOLN "slumps in his chair." They jump.]
255 C MAN   Go on.
    C WOMAN [theatrically]   "Theyve killed the president!"[7]
          [Rest. They exit.]
THE FOUNDLING FATHER   Theyll have children and theyll bring their children
    here. A slight deafness in this ear other than that there are no side effects.
    Little ringing in the ears. Slight deafness. I cant complain.
          [Rest.]
260 The passage of time. The crossing of space. [The Lesser Known recorded
    his every movement.] He'd hoped he'd be of interest in his posterity. [Once
    again riding in the Great Mans footsteps.] A nod to the presidents bust.
    [Nods.]
          [Rest.]
          [Rest.]
    The Great Man lived in the past that is was an inhabitant of time imme-
    morial and the Lesser Known out West alive a resident of the present. And
265 the Great Mans deeds had transpired during the life of the Great Man
    somewhere in past-land that is somewhere "back there" and all this while
    the Lesser Known digging his holes bearing the burden of his resemblance
    all the while trying somehow to equal the Great Man in stature, word and
    deed going forward with his lesser life trying somehow to follow in the
270 Great Mans footsteps footsteps that were of course behind him. The
    Lesser Known trying somehow to catch up to the Great Man all this while
    and maybe running too fast in the wrong direction. Which is to say that
    maybe the Great Man had to catch him. Hhhh. Ridiculous.
          [Rest.]
    Full fringe. The way he appears on the money.
          [Rest.]
275 A wink to Mr. Lincolns pasteboard cutout. A nod to Mr. Lincolns bust.
          [Rest. Time passes. Rest.]

7. The words of Mary Todd, just after Lincoln was shot [Parks's note].

When someone remarked that he played Lincoln so well that he ought to be shot it was as if the Great Mans footsteps had been suddenly revealed: instead of making speeches his act would now consist of a single chair, a rocker, in a dark box. The public was cordially invited to pay a penny,
280 choose from a selection of provided pistols enter the darkened box and "Shoot Mr. Lincoln." The Lesser Known became famous overnight.

> [A MAN, *as John Wilkes* BOOTH, *enters. He takes a gun and "stands in position": at the left side of* THE FOUNDLING FATHER, *as Abraham* LINCOLN, *pointing the gun at* THE FOUNDLING FATHER's *head.*]

THE FOUNDLING FATHER   Mmm. Like clockwork.

A MAN   Ready.

THE FOUNDLING FATHER   Haw Haw Haw Haw

> [*Rest.*]

285   HAW HAW HAW HAW

> [BOOTH *shoots.* LINCOLN *"slumps in his chair."* BOOTH *jumps.*]

A MAN [*theatrically*]   "Thus to the tyrants!"

> [*Rest.*]

Hhhh.

LINCOLN
BOOTH
LINCOLN
BOOTH
LINCOLN
BOOTH
LINCOLN
BOOTH
LINCOLN[8]

> [BOOTH *jumps.*]

A MAN [*theatrically*]   "The South is avenged!"

> [*Rest.*]

Hhhh.

> [*Rest.*]

290   Thank you.

THE FOUNDLING FATHER   Pleasures mine.

A MAN   Next week then. [*Exits.*]

THE FOUNDLING FATHER   Little ringing in the ears. Slight deafness.

> [*Rest.*]

Little ringing in the ears.

> [*Rest.*]

295   A wink to the Great Mans cutout. A nod to the Great Mans bust. Once again striding in the Great Mans footsteps. Riding on in. Riding to the rescue the way they do. They both had such long legs. Such big feet. And the Greater Man had such a lead although of course somehow still "back there." If the Lesser Known had slowed down stopped moving completely

---

8. The repetition of characters' names without dialogue indicates an extended pause, or what Parks has elsewhere described as "an elongated and heightened (rest)."

300 gone in reverse died maybe the Greater Man could have caught up. Woulda had a chance. Woulda sneaked up behind him the Greater Man would have sneaked up behind the Lesser Known unbeknownst and wrestled him to the ground. Stabbed him in the back. In revenge. "Thus to the tyrants!" Shot him maybe. The Lesser Known forgets who he is and just crumples. His
305 bones cannot be found. The Greater Man continues on.

> [Rest.]

"Emergency, oh Emergency, please put the Great Man in the ground."

> [Rest.]

Only a little ringing in the ears. Thats all. Slight deafness.

> [Rest.]

> [He puts on the blonde beard.]

Huh. Whatdoyou say I wear the blonde.

> [Rest.]

> [A gunshot echoes. Softly. And echoes.]

Act 2: The Hall of Wonders

A gunshot echoes. Loudly. And echoes.
They are in a great hole. In the middle of nowhere. The hole is an exact replica
of The Great Hole of History.
A gunshot echoes. Loudly. And echoes. LUCY with ear trumpet circulates. BRAZIL
digs.

A. BIG BANG

LUCY Hear that?
BRAZIL Zit him?
LUCY No.
BRAZIL Oh.

> [A gunshot echoes. Loudly. And echoes.]

5 LUCY Hear?
BRAZIL Zit him?!
LUCY Nope. Ssuhecho.
BRAZIL Ssuhecho.
LUCY Uh echo uh huhn. Of gunplay. Once upon uh time somebody had uh
10 little gunplay and now thuh gun goes on playing: KER-BANG! KERBANG-
Kerbang-kerbang-(kerbang)-((kerbang)).
BRAZIL Thuh echoes.

> [Rest.]

> [Rest.]

LUCY Youre stopped.
BRAZIL Mmlistenin.
15 LUCY Dig on, Brazil. Cant stop diggin till you dig up somethin. Your Daddy
was uh Digger.
BRAZIL Uh huhnnn.

LUCY

BRAZIL

> [*A gunshot echoes. Loudly. And echoes. Rest. A gunshot echoes. Loudly. And echoes. Rest.*]

[LUCY   Itssalways been important in my line to distinguish. Tuh know thuh
difference. Not like your Fathuh. Your Fathuh became confused. His lonely
20   death and lack of proper burial is our embarrassment. Go on: dig. Now me
I need tuh know thuh real thing from thuh echo. Thuh truth from thuh
hearsay.

> [*Rest.*]

Bram Price for example. His dear ones and relations told me his dying
words but Bram Price hisself of course told me something quite different.

25   BRAZIL   I wept forim.

LUCY   Whispered his true secrets to me and to me uhlone.

BRAZIL   Then he died.

LUCY   Then he died.

> [*Rest.*]

Thuh things he told me I will never tell. Mr. Bram Price. Huh.

> [*Rest.*]

30   Dig on.

BRAZIL

LUCY

BRAZIL

LUCY   Little Bram Price Junior.

BRAZIL   Thuh fat one?

LUCY   Burned my eardrums. Just like his Dad did.

BRAZIL   I wailed forim.

35   LUCY   Ten days dead wept over and buried and that boy comes back. Not him
though. His echo. Sits down tuh dinner and eats up everybodys food just
like he did when he was livin.

> [*Rest.*]

> [*Rest.*]

Little Bram Junior. Burned my eardrums. Miz Penny Price his mother.
Thuh things she told me I will never tell.

> [*Rest.*]

40   You remember her.

BRAZIL   Wore red velvet in August.

LUCY   When her 2 Brams passed she sold herself, son.

BRAZIL   O.

LUCY   Also lost her mind. —. She finally went. Like your Fathuh went, per-
45   haps. Foul play.

BRAZIL   I gnashed for her.

LUCY   You did.

BRAZIL   Couldnt choose between wailin or gnashin. Weepin sobbin or
moanin. Went for gnashing. More to it. Gnashed for her and hers like I
50   have never gnashed. I woulda tore at my coat but thats extra. Chipped uh
tooth. One in thuh front.

LUCY   You did your job son.

BRAZIL   I did my job.

LUCY   Confidence. Huh. Thuh things she told me I will never tell. Miz Penny

55   Price. Miz Penny Price.

[*Rest.*]

Youre stopped.

BRAZIL   Mmlistenin.

LUCY   Dig on, Brazil.

BRAZIL

LUCY

BRAZIL   We arent from these parts.

60   LUCY   No. We're not.

BRAZIL   Daddy iduhnt[9] either.

LUCY   Your Daddy iduhnt either.

[*Rest.*]

Dig on, son. —. Cant stop diggin till you dig up somethin. You dig that
something up you brush that something off you give that something uh

65   designated place. Its own place. Along with thuh other discoveries. In thuh
Hall of Wonders. Uh place in the Hall of Wonders right uhlong with thuh
rest of thuh Wonders hear?

BRAZIL   Uh huhn.

[*Rest.*]

LUCY   Bram Price Senior, son. Bram Price Senior was not thuh man he

70   claimed tuh be. Huh. Nope. Was not thuh man he claimed tuh be atall.
You ever see him in his stocking feet? Or barefoot? Course not. I guessed
before he told me. He told me then he died. He told me and I havent told
no one. I'm uh good Confidence. As Confidences go. Huh. One of thuh
best. As Confidence, mmonly contracted tuh keep quiet 12 years. After 12

75   years nobody cares. For 19 years I have kept his secret. In my bosom.

[*Rest.*]

He wore lifts in his shoes, son.

BRAZIL   Lifts?

LUCY   Lifts. Made him seem taller than he was.

BRAZIL   Bram Price Senior?

80   LUCY   Bram Price Senior wore lifts in his shoes yes he did, Brazil. I tell you
just as he told me with his last breaths on his dying bed: "Lifts." Thats all
he said. Then he died. I put thuh puzzle pieces in place. I put thuh puzzle
pieces in place. Couldnt tell no one though. Not even your Pa. "Lifts." I
never told no one son. For 19 years I have kept Brams secret in my bosom.

85   Youre thuh first tuh know. Hhh! Dig on. Dig on.

BRAZIL   Dig on.

LUCY

BRAZIL

LUCY

[*A gunshot echoes. Loudly. And echoes.*]

BRAZIL   [*rest*]   Ff Pa was here weud find his bones.

9. That is, "isn't."

LUCY   Not always.

BRAZIL   Thereud be his bones and thereud be thuh Wonders surrounding his
90   bones.

LUCY   Ive heard of different.

BRAZIL   Thereud be thuh Wonders surrounding his bones and thereud be his
Whispers.

LUCY   Maybe.

95 BRAZIL   Ffhe sspast like they say he'd of parlayed to uh Confidence his last
words and dying wishes. His secrets and his dreams.

LUCY   Thats how we pass[1] back East. They could pass different out here.

BRAZIL   We got Daddys ways Daddyssgot ours. When theres no Confidence
available we just dribble thuh words out. In uh whisper.

100 LUCY   Sometimes.

BRAZIL   Thuh Confidencell gather up thuh whispers when she arrives.

LUCY   Youre uh prize, Brazil. Uh prize.]

BRAZIL

LUCY

BRAZIL

LUCY

BRAZIL   You hear him then? His whispers?

LUCY   Not exactly.

105 BRAZIL   He wuduhnt here then.

LUCY   He was here.

BRAZIL   Ffyou dont hear his whispers he wuduhnt here.

LUCY   Whispers dont always come up right away. Takes time sometimes.
Whispers could travel different out West than they do back East. Maybe
110   slower. Maybe. Whispers are secrets and often shy. We aint seen your Pa in
30 years. That could be part of it. We also could be experiencing some sort
of interference. Or some sort of technical difficulty. Ssard tuh tell.

[Rest.]

So much to live for.

BRAZIL   So much to live for.

115 LUCY   Look on thuh bright side.

BRAZIL   Look on thuh bright side. Look on thuh bright side. Loook onnnnn
thuhhhh briiiiiiight siiiiiiiide!!!!

LUCY   DIIIIIIIIIIIG!

BRAZIL   Dig.

LUCY

BRAZIL

120 LUCY   Helloooo! —. Hellooooo!

BRAZIL

LUCY

BRAZIL   [We're from out East. We're not from these parts.

[Rest.]

My foe-father, her husband, my Daddy, her mate, her man, my Pa come
out here. Out West.

[Rest.]

1. Die.

125   Come out here all uhlone. Cleared thuh path tamed thuh wilderness dug
this whole Hole with his own 2 hands and et cetera.

> [*Rest.*]

Left his family behind. Back East. His Lucy and his child. He waved
"Goodbye." Left us tuh carry on. I was only 5.

> [*Rest.*]

My Daddy was uh Digger. Shes whatcha call uh Confidence. I did thuh
weepin and thuh moanin.

> [*Rest.*]

130   His lonely death and lack of proper burial is our embarrassment.

> [*Rest.*]

Diggin was his livelihood but fakin was his callin. Ssonly natural heud
come out here and combine thuh 2. Back East he was always diggin. He
was uh natural. Could dig uh hole for uh body that passed like no one else.
Digged em quick and they looked good too. This Hole here—this large
135   one—sshis biggest venture to date. So says hearsay.

> [*Rest.*]

Uh exact replica of thuh Great Hole of History!

LUCY Sshhhhhht.

BRAZIL [*rest*] Thuh original ssback East. He and Lucy they honeymooned
there. At thuh original Great Hole. Its uh popular spot. He and Her would
140   sit on thuh lip and watch everybody who was ever anybody parade on by.
Daily parades! Just like thuh Tee Vee. Mr. George Washington, for example, thuh Fathuh of our Country hisself, would rise up from thuh dead and
walk uhround and cross thuh Delaware and say stuff!![2] Right before their
very eyes!!!!

145 LUCY Son?

BRAZIL Huh?

LUCY That iduhnt how it went.

BRAZIL Oh.

LUCY Thuh Mr. Washington me and your Daddy seen was uh lookuhlike of
150   thuh Mr. Washington of history-fame, son.

BRAZIL Oh.

LUCY Thuh original Mr. Washingtonssbeen long dead.

BRAZIL O.

LUCY That Hole back East was uh theme park son. Keep your story to scale.

155 BRAZIL K.[3]

> [*Rest.*]

Him and Her would sit by thuh lip uhlong with thuh others all in uh row
cameras clickin and theyud look down into that Hole and see—ooooo—
you name it. Ever-y-day you could look down that Hole and see—ooooo—
you name it. Amerigo Vespucci hisself made regular appearances. Marcus
160   Garvey. Ferdinand and Isabella. Mary Queen of thuh Scots! Tarzan King of

---

2. Washington (1732–1799), the "Father of
our Country," the first U.S. president (1789–
97), crossed the Delaware from Pennsylvania
on December 25, 1776, to make a surprise
attack on the Hessian forces garrisoned in
Trenton, New Jersey; the attack's success was
an enormous boost to American morale early
in the Revolutionary War.
3. That is, "OK."

thuh Apes! Washington Jefferson Harding and Millard Fillmore. Mistufer Columbus even.[4] Oh they saw all thuh greats. Parading daily in thuh Great Hole of History.

[Rest.]

165 My Fathuh did thuh living and thuh dead. Small-town and big-time. Mr. Lincoln was of course his favorite.

[Rest.]

Not only Mr. Lincoln but Mr. Lincolns last show. His last deeds. His last laughs.

[Rest.]

Being uh Digger of some renown Daddy comes out here tuh build uh like attraction. So says hearsay. Figures theres people out here who'll enjoy
170 amusements such as them amusements He and Her enjoyed. We're all citizens of one country afterall.

[Rest.]

Mmrestin.

[A gunshot echoes. Loudly. And echoes.]

BRAZIL   Woooo! [Drops dead.]
LUCY   Youre fakin Mr. Brazil.
175 BRAZIL   Uh uhnnn.
LUCY   Tryin tuh get you some benefits.
BRAZIL   Uh uhnnnnnnnn.
LUCY   I know me uh faker when I see one. Your Father was uh faker. Huh. One of thuh best. There wuduhnt nobody your Fathuh couldnt do. Did
180 thuh living and thuh dead. Small-town and big-time. Made-up and historical. Fakin was your Daddys callin but diggin was his livelihood. Oh, back East he was always diggin. Was uh natural. Could dig uh hole for uh body that passed like no one else. Digged em quick and they looked good too. You dont remember of course you dont.
185 BRAZIL   I was only 5.
LUCY   You were only 5. When your Fathuh spoke he'd quote thuh Greats. Mister George Washington. Thuh Misters Roosevelt.[5] Mister Millard Fillmore. Huh. All thuh greats. You dont remember of course you dont.
BRAZIL   I was only 5—
190 LUCY   —only 5. Mr. Lincoln was of course your Fathuhs favorite. Wuz. Huh. Wuz. Huh. Heresay says he's past. Your Daddy. Digged this hole then he died. So says hearsay.

4. Brazil names figures who were instrumental in "discovering" America: King Ferdinand (1452–1516) and Queen Isabella (1451–1504), rulers of Aragón and Castile, who underwrote the expeditions of the Italian-born explorer Christopher Columbus (1451–1506), two of which the Italian navigator Amerigo Vespucci (1454–1512)—whose accounts of his voyages to the New World led to the lands being named "America"—helped outfit; he also mentions presidents both lauded—Washington and Thomas Jefferson (1743–1826; 3rd president, 1801–09)—and disparaged: Warren Harding (1865–1923;

29th president, 1921–23) and Millard Fillmore (1800–1874; 13th president, 1850–53). The story of Mary, Queen of Scots (1542–1587; r. 1542–67)—executed, after years of imprisonment, for plotting against England's Elizabeth I—was retold in drama and opera, and Tarzan, a fictional character created by Edgar Rice Burroughs in Tarzan of the Apes (1912), has had a long afterlife in print sequels, film, and comics.
5. Two U.S. presidents named Roosevelt, Theodore (1858–1919; 26th president, 1901–09) and his distant cousin Franklin Delano (1882–1945; 32nd president, 1933–45).

[*Rest.*]

Dig, Brazil.

BRAZIL   My paw—

195   LUCY   Ssonly natural that heud come out here tuh dig out one of his own.
He loved that Great Hole so. He'd stand at thuh lip of that Great Hole:
"OHWAYOHWHYOHWAYOH!"

BRAZIL   "OHWAYOHWHYOHWAYOH!"

LUCY   "OHWAYOHWHYOHWAYOH!" You know: hole talk. Ohwayohwhyo-

200   hwayoh, just tuh get their attention, then: "Hellooo!" He'd shout down to
em. Theyd call back "Helllloooo!" and wave. He loved that Great Hole so.
Came out here. Digged this lookuhlike.

BRAZIL   Then he died?

LUCY   Then he died. Your Daddy died right here. Huh. Oh, he was uh faker.

205   Uh greaaaaat biiiiig faker too. He was your Fathuh. Thats thuh connection.
You take after him.

BRAZIL   I do?

LUCY   Sure. Put your paw back where it belongs. Go on—back on its stump.
—. Poke it on out of your sleeve son. There you go. I'll draw uh X for you.

210   See? Heresuh X. Huh. Dig here.

[*Rest.*]

DIG!

BRAZIL

LUCY

BRAZIL

LUCY   Woah! Woah!

BRAZIL   Whatchaheard?!

LUCY   No tellin, son. Cant say.

[BRAZIL *digs.* LUCY *circulates.*]

215   BRAZIL [*rest. Rest*]   On thuh day he claimed to be the 100th anniversary of
the founding of our country the Father took the Son out into the yard. The
Father threw himself down in front of the Son and bit into the dirt with his
teeth. His eyes leaked. "This is how youll make your mark, Son" the Father
said. The Son was only 2 then. "This is the Wail," the Father said. "There's

220   money init," the Father said. The Son was only 2 then. Quiet. On what he
claimed was the 101st anniversary the Father showed the Son "the Weep"
"the Sob" and "the Moan." How to stand just so what to do with the hands
and feet (to capitalize on what we in the business call "the Mourning
Moment"). Formal stances the Fatherd picked up at the History Hole. The

225   Son studied night and day. By candlelight. No one could best him. The money
came pouring in. On the 102nd anniversary[6] the Son was 5 and the Father
taught him "the Gnash." The day after that the Father left for out West. To
seek his fortune. In the middle of dinnertime. The Son was eating his peas.

LUCY

BRAZIL

LUCY

BRAZIL

LUCY   Hellooooo! Hellooooo!

[*Rest.*]

6. Hearsay [Parks's note].

BRAZIL
LUCY
230 BRAZIL   HO! [*Unearths something.*]
LUCY   Whatcha got?
BRAZIL   Uh Wonder!
LUCY   Uh Wonder!
BRAZIL   Uh Wonder: Ho!
235 LUCY   Dust it off and put it over with thuh rest of thuh Wonders.
BRAZIL   Uh bust.
LUCY   Whose?
BRAZIL   Says "A. Lincoln." A. Lincolns bust. —. Abraham Lincolns bust!!!
LUCY   Howuhboutthat!

[*Rest.*]

[*Rest.*]

240   Woah! Woah!
BRAZIL   Whatchaheard?
LUCY   Uh—. Cant say.
BRAZIL   Whatchaheard?!!
LUCY   SSShhhhhhhhhhhhhhhhhhht!

[*Rest.*]

245   *dig!*

B. ECHO

THE FOUNDLING FATHER   Ladies and Gentlemen: *Our American Cousin*, Act
   III, scene 5:
MR. TRENCHARD[7]   Have you found it?
MISS KEENE   I find no trace of it. [*Discovering*] What is this?!
5 MR. TRENCHARD   This is the place where father kept all the old deeds.
MISS KEENE   Oh my poor muddled brain! What can this mean?!
MR. TRENCHARD [*with difficulty*]   I cannot survive the downfall of my house
   but choose instead to end my life with a pistol to my head!

[*Applause.*]

THE FOUNDLING FATHER   OHWAYOHWHYOHWAYOH!

[*Rest.*]

[*Rest.*]

10   Hellloooooooo!

[*Rest.*]

Hellloooooooo!

[*Rest. Waves.*]

7. Asa Trenchard is the title character of *Our
American Cousin*; Laura Keene played his
cousin, Florence Trenchard. (The exchange
paraphrases one found in scene 6, but Florence is not present and the suicide is threatened in the following scene by another
character, Sir Edward Trenchard.)

C. ARCHEOLOGY

BRAZIL   You hear im?

LUCY   Echo of thuh first sort: thuh sound. (E.g. thuh gunplay.)

> [Rest.]

Echo of thuh 2nd sort: thuh words. Type A: thuh words from thuh dead. Category: Unrelated.

> [Rest.]

5   Echo of thuh 2nd sort, Type B: words less fortunate: thuh Disembodied Voice. Also known as "Thuh Whispers." Category: Related. Like your Fathuhs.

> [Rest.]

Echo of thuh 3rd sort: thuh body itself.

> [Rest.]

BRAZIL   You hear im.

LUCY   Cant say. Cant say, son.

10   BRAZIL   My faux-father. Thuh one who comed out here before us. Thuh one who left us behind. Tuh come out here all uhlone. Tuh do his bit. All them who comed before us—my Daddy. He's one of them.

LUCY

> [Rest.]

> [Rest.]

[BRAZIL: He's one of them. All of them who comed before us—my Daddy.

> [Rest.]

I'd say thuh creation of thuh world must uh been just like thuh clearing off

15   of this plot. Just like him diggin his Hole. i'd say. Must uh been just as dug up. And unfair.

> [Rest.]

Peoples (or thuh what-was), just had tuh hit thuh road. In thuh beginning there was one of those voids here and then "bang" and then *voilà!*[8] And here we is.

> [Rest.]

20   But where did those voids that was here before *we* was here go off to? Hmmm. In thuh beginning there were some of them voids here and then: KERBANG-KERBLAMMO! And now it all belongs tuh us.

LUCY

> [Rest.]

> [Rest.]

BRAZIL   This Hole is our inheritance of sorts. My Daddy died and left it to me and Her. And when She goes, Shes gonna give it all to me!!

25   LUCY   Dig, son.

BRAZIL   I'd rather dust and polish. [Puts something on.]

LUCY   Dust and polish then. —. You dont got tuh put on that tuh do it.

BRAZIL   It helps. Uh Hehm. *Uh Hehm.* WELCOME WELCOME WELCOME TUH THUH HALL OF—

30   LUCY   Sssht.

BRAZIL

8. Literally, "see there" (French).

LUCY

BRAZIL   (welcome welcome welcome to thuh hall. of. wonnndersss: To our
right A Jewel Box made of cherry wood, lined in velvet, letters "A.L." carved
in gold on thuh lid: the jewels have long escaped. Over here one of Mr.
Washingtons bones, right pointer so they say; here is his likeness and here:
35   his wooden teeth.[9] Yes, uh top and bottom pair of nibblers: nibblers, lookin
for uh meal. Nibblin. I iduhnt your lunch. Quit nibblin. Quit that nibblin
you. Quit that nibblin you nibblers you nibblin nibblers you.)

LUCY   Keep it tuh scale.

BRAZIL   (Over here our newest Wonder: uh bust of Mr. Lincoln carved of
40   marble lookin like he looked in life. Right heress thuh bit from thuh mouth
of thuh mount on which some great Someone rode tuh thuh rescue. This
is all thats left. Uh glass tradin bead—one of thuh first. Here are thuh licked boots. Here, uh dried scrap of whales blubber. Uh petrified scrap of uh
great blubberer, servin to remind us that once this land was covered with
45   sea. And blubberers were Kings. In this area here are several documents:
peace pacts, writs, bills of sale, treaties, notices, handbills and circulars,
freein papers, summonses, declarations of war, addresses, title deeds,
obits, long lists of dids. And thuh medals: for bravery and honesty; for
trustworthiness and for standing straight; for standing tall; for standing
50   still. For advancing and retreating. For makin do. For skills in whittlin, for
skills in painting and drawing, for uh knowledge of sewin, of handicrafts
and building things, for leather tannin, blacksmithery, lacemakin, horseback riding, swimmin, croquet, and badminton. Community Service. For
cookin and for cleanin. For bowin and scrapin. Uh medal for fakin? Huh.
55   This could uh been his. Zsis his? This is his! This is his!!!

LUCY   Keep it tuh scale, Brazil.

BRAZIL   This could be his!

LUCY   May well be.

BRAZIL [rest]   Whaddyahear?

60 LUCY   Bits and pieces.

BRAZIL   This could be his.

LUCY   Could well be.

BRAZIL [rest. Rest]   waaaaaahhhhhhhhHHHHHHHHHHHHHH! HUH HEE
HUH HEE HUH HEE HUH.

65 LUCY   There there, Brazil. Dont weep.

BRAZIL   WAHHHHHHHHHHH!—imissim—WAHHHHHHHHHHHHH!

LUCY   It is an honor to be of his line. He cleared this plot for us. He was uh
Digger.

BRAZIL   Huh huh huh. Uh Digger.

70 LUCY   Mr. Lincoln was his favorite.

BRAZIL   I was only 5.

LUCY   He dug this whole Hole.

BRAZIL   Sssnuch.[1] This whole Hole.

LUCY   This whole Hole.

          [Rest.]

BRAZIL

LUCY

9. Washington's famous "wooden teeth" were
in fact dentures made of ivory and of animal
and human teeth.

1. Parks defines "Sssnuch" as "a fast reverse
snort, a big sniff (usually accompanies crying
or sneezing)."

BRAZIL

LUCY

BRAZIL

LUCY

75   I couldnt never deny him nothin.
       I gived intuh him on everything.
       Thuh moon. Thuh stars,
       Thuh bees knees. Thuh cats pyjamas.

          [*Rest.*]

BRAZIL

LUCY

BRAZIL Anything?

80 LUCY Stories too horrible tuh mention.

BRAZIL His stories?

LUCY Nope.

          [*Rest.*]

BRAZIL Mama Lucy?

LUCY Whut.

85 BRAZIL —Imissim—.

LUCY Hhh. ((dig.))

D. ECHO

THE FOUNDLING FATHER Ladies and Gentlemen: *Our American Cousin,* Act
    III, scene 2:

MR. TRENCHARD You crave affection, *you* do. Now I've no fortune, but I'm
    biling over with affections, which I'm ready to pour out to all of you, like
5   apple sass over roast pork.

AUGUSTA Sir, your American talk do woo me.[2]

THE FOUNDLING FATHER [*as Mrs. Mount*] Mr. Trenchard, you will please rec-
    ollect you are addressing my daughter and in my presence.

MR. TRENCHARD Yes, I'm offering her my heart and hand just as she wants
10   them, with nothing in 'em.

THE FOUNDLING FATHER [*as Mrs. Mount*] Augusta dear, to your room.

AUGUSTA Yes, Ma, the nasty beast.

THE FOUNDLING FATHER [*as Mrs. Mount*] I am aware, Mr. Trenchard, that you
    are not used to the manners of good society, and that, alone, will excuse the
15   impertinence of which you have been guilty.

MR. TRENCHARD Don't know the manners of good society, eh? Wal, I guess I
    know enough to turn you inside out, old gal—you sockdologizing old
    man-trap.

          [*Laughter. Applause.*]

THE FOUNDLING FATHER Thanks. Thanks so much. Snyder has always been a
20   very special very favorite town uh mine. Thank you thank you so very
    much. Loverly loverly evening loverly tuh be here loverly tuh be here with
    you with all of you thank you very much.

          [*Rest.*]

    Uh Hehm. I *only* do thuh greats.

2. Parks adds this line to a passage that is otherwise quoted directly from the play.

[*Rest.*]

25 A crowd pleaser: 4score and 7 years ago our fathers brought forth upon this continent a new nation conceived in Liberty and dedicated to the proposition that all men are created equal![3]

[*Applause.*]

Observe!: Indiana? Indianapolis. Louisiana? Baton Rouge. Concord? New Hampshire. Pierre? South Dakota. Honolulu? Hawaii. Springfield? Illinois. Frankfort? Kentucky. Lincoln? Nebraska.[4] Ha! Lickety split!

[*Applause.*]

30 And now, the centerpiece of the evening!!

[*Rest.*]

Uh Hehm. The Death of Lincoln!: —. The watching of the play, the laughter, the smiles of Lincoln and Mary Todd, the slipping of Booth into the presidential box unseen, the freeing of the slaves, the pulling of the trigger, the bullets piercing above the left ear, the bullets entrance into the great
35 head, the bullets lodging behind the great right eye, the slumping of Lincoln, the leaping onto the stage of Booth, the screaming of Todd, the screaming of Todd, the screaming of Keene, the leaping onto the stage of Booth; the screaming of Todd, the screaming of Keene, the shouting of Booth "Thus to the tyrants!," the death of Lincoln! —And the silence of
40 the nation.

[*Rest.*]

Yes. —.The year was way back when. The place: our nations capitol. 4score, back in the olden days, and Mr. Lincolns great head. The the-a-ter was "Fords." The wife "Mary Todd." Thuh freeing of the slaves and thuh great black hole that thuh fatal bullet bored. And how that great head was
45 bleedin. Thuh body stretched crossways acrosst thuh bed. Thuh last words. Thuh last breaths. And how thuh nation mourned.

[*Applause.*]

E. SPADEWORK

LUCY Thats uh hard nut tuh crack uh hard nut tuh crack indeed.
BRAZIL Alaska—?
LUCY Thats uh hard nut tuh crack. Thats uh hard nut tuh crack indeed. —. Huh. Juneau.
5 BRAZIL Good!
LUCY Go uhgain.
BRAZIL —. Texas?
LUCY —. Austin. Wyoming?
BRAZIL —. —. Cheyenne. Florida?
10 LUCY Tallahassee.

[*Rest.*]

Ohio.
BRAZIL Oh. Uh. Well: Columbus. Louisiana?

3. The opening sentence of Lincoln's Gettysburg Address, delivered November 19, 1863, in Gettysburg, Pennsylvania, at the dedication ceremony for a national cemetery on the site of the Civil War's bloodiest battle, fought four months earlier.
4. This list pairs states with their capitals (a pattern that continues in the next scene).

LUCY Baton Rouge. Arkansas.

BRAZIL Little Rock. Jackson.

15 LUCY Mississippi. Spell it.

BRAZIL M-i-s-s-i-s-s-i-p-p-i!

LUCY Huh. Youre good. Montgomery.

BRAZIL Alabama.

LUCY Topeka.

20 BRAZIL Kansas?

LUCY Kansas.

BRAZIL Boise, Idaho?

LUCY Boise, Idaho.

BRAZIL Huh. Nebraska.

25 LUCY Nebraska. Lincoln.

[*Rest.*]

Thuh year was way back when. Thuh place: our nations capitol.

[*Rest.*]

Your Fathuh couldnt get that story out of his head: Mr. Lincolns great head. And thuh hole thuh fatal bullet bored. How that great head was bleedin. Thuh body stretched crossways acrosst thuh bed. Thuh last words.

30 Thuh last breaths. And how thuh nation mourned. Huh. Changed your Fathuhs life.

[*Rest.*]

Couldnt get that story out of his head. Whuduhnt my favorite page from thuh book of Mr. Lincolns life, me myself now I prefer thuh part where he gets married to Mary Todd and she begins to lose her mind (and then of

35 course where he frees all thuh slaves) but shoot, he couldnt get that story out of his head. Hhh. Changed his life.

[*Rest.*]

BRAZIL (wahhhhhhh—)

LUCY There there, Brazil.

BRAZIL (wahhhhhh—)

40 LUCY Dont weep. Got somethin for ya.

BRAZIL (o)?

LUCY Spade. —. Dont scrunch up your face like that, son. Go on. Take it.

BRAZIL Spade?

LUCY Spade. He woulda wanted you tuh have it.

45 BRAZIL Daddys diggin spade? Ssnnuch.

LUCY I swannee⁵ you look more and more and more and more like him every day.

BRAZIL His chin?

LUCY You got his chin.

50 BRAZIL His lips?

LUCY You got his lips.

BRAZIL His teeths?

LUCY Top and bottom. In his youth. He had some. Just like yours. His frock coat. Was just like that. He had hisself uh stovepipe hat which you lack.

55 His medals—yours are for weepin his of course were for diggin.

---

5. A punning combination of *I swan* (i.e., "I declare"; dialect) and *Swannee* (*River*), an allusion to Stephen Foster's 1851 song "Old Folks at Home" (which presents a sentimental view of African American life in the antebellum South).

BRAZIL   And I got his spade.
LUCY   And now you got his spade.
BRAZIL   We could say I'm his spittin image.
LUCY   We could say that.
60 BRAZIL   We could say I just may follow in thuh footsteps of my foe-father.
LUCY   We could say that.
BRAZIL   Look on thuh bright side!
LUCY   Look on thuh bright side!
BRAZIL   So much tuh live for!
65 LUCY   So much tuh live for! Sweet land of—! Sweet land of—?
BRAZIL   Of liberty!
LUCY   Of liberty! Thats it thats it and *"Woah!"* Lets say I hear his words!
BRAZIL   And you could say?
LUCY   And I could say.
70 BRAZIL   Lets say you hear his words!
LUCY   *Woah!*
BRAZIL   Whatwouldhesay?!
LUCY   He'd say: "Hello." He'd say. —. "Hope you like your spade."
BRAZIL   Tell him I do.
75 LUCY   He'd say: "My how youve grown!" He'd say: "Hows your weepin?" He'd
say: —Ha! He's running through his states and capitals! Licketysplit!
BRAZIL   Howuhboutthat!
LUCY   He'd say: "Uh house divided cannot stand!" He'd say: "4score and 7
years uhgoh." Say: "Of thuh people by thuh people and for thuh people."
80 Say: "Malice toward none and charity toward all." Say: "Cheat some of
thuh people some of thuh time."[6] He'd say: (and this is only to be spoken
between you and me and him—)
BRAZIL   K.
LUCY   Lean in. Ssfor our ears and our ears uhlone.
LUCY
BRAZIL
LUCY
BRAZIL
85 BRAZIL   O.
LUCY   Howuhboutthat. And here he comes. Striding on in striding on in and
he surveys thuh situation. And he nods tuh what we found cause he knows
his Wonders. And he smiles. And he tells us of his doins all these years. And
he does his Mr. Lincoln for us. Uh great page from thuh great mans great
90 life! And you n me llsmile, cause then we'll know, more or less, exactly
where he is.
[*Rest.*]

6. Some of the most famous words spoken by or attributed to Lincoln, from, respectively, his speech on June 16, 1858, to the Illinois Republican State Convention in Springfield—"A house divided against itself cannot stand" (an allusion to Mark 3.25); the beginning and the end of the Gettysburg Address—"government of the people, by the people, for the people"; his second Inaugural Address, delivered March 4, 1865—"With malice toward none; with charity for all"; and (with slight variations in wording) a speech of September 8, 1858, in Clinton, Illinois, or a remark made to a caller at the White House—"You may fool all the people some of the time; you can even fool some of the people all the time; but you can't fool all of the people all the time" (this observation, which does not appear in any surviving Lincoln documents, has also been attributed to the 19th-century American showman P. T. Barnum).

BRAZIL Lucy? Where is he?

LUCY Lincoln?

BRAZIL Papa.

95 LUCY Close by, I guess. Huh. Dig.

> [BRAZIL *digs. Times passes.*]

Youre uh Digger. Youre uh Digger. Your Daddy was uh Digger and so are you.

BRAZIL Ho!

LUCY I couldnt never deny him nothin.

100 BRAZIL Wonder: Ho! Wonder: Ho!

LUCY I gived intuh him on everything.

BRAZIL Ssuhtrumpet.

LUCY Gived intuh him on everything.

BRAZIL Ssuhtrumpet, Lucy.

105 LUCY Howboutthat.

BRAZIL Try it out.

LUCY How uh-bout that.

BRAZIL Anythin?

LUCY Cant say, son. Cant say.

> [*Rest.*]

110 I couldnt never deny him nothin.
  I gived intuh him on everything.
  Thuh moon. Thuh stars.

BRAZIL Ho!

LUCY Thuh bees knees. Thuh cats pyjamas.

115 BRAZIL Wonder: Ho! Wonder: Ho!

> [*Rest.*]

Howuhboutthat: Uh bag of pennies. Money, Lucy.

LUCY Howuhboutthat.

> [*Rest.*]

  Thuh bees knees.
  Thuh cats pyjamas.
120 Thuh best cuts of meat.
  My baby teeth.

BRAZIL Wonder: Ho! Wonder: HO!

LUCY

  Thuh apron from uhround my waist.
  Thuh hair from off my head.

125 BRAZIL Huh. Yellow fur.

LUCY My mores and my folkways.

BRAZIL Oh. Uh beard. Howuhboutthat.

> [*Rest.*]

LUCY WOAH. WOAH!

BRAZIL Whatchaheard?

LUCY

> [*Rest.*]
> [*Rest.*]

130 BRAZIL Whatchaheard?!

LUCY You dont wanna know.

BRAZIL
LUCY
BRAZIL
LUCY
BRAZIL Wonder: Ho! Wonder: HO! WONDER: HO!
LUCY
    Thuh apron from uhround my waist.
    Thuh hair from off my head.
135 BRAZIL Huh: uh Tee-Vee.
LUCY Huh.
BRAZIL I'll hold ontooit for uh minit.
    [*Rest.*]

LUCY
    Thuh apron from uhround my waist.
    Thuh hair from off my head.
140   My mores and my folkways.
    My rock and my foundation.
BRAZIL
LUCY
BRAZIL
LUCY My re-memberies—you know—thuh stuff out of my head.
    [*The TV comes on.* THE FOUNDLING FATHER's *face appears.*]
BRAZIL (ho! ho! wonder: ho!)
LUCY
    My spare buttons in their envelopes.
145   Thuh leftovers from all my unmade meals.
    Thuh letter R.
    Thuh key of G.
BRAZIL (ho! ho! wonder: ho!)
LUCY
    All my good jokes. All my jokes that fell flat.
150   Thuh way I walked, cause you liked it so much.
    All my winnin dance steps.
    My teeth when yours runned out.
    My smile.
BRAZIL (ho! ho! wonder: ho!)
155 LUCY Sssssht.
    [*Rest.*]
  Well. Its him.

F. ECHO

A gunshot echoes. Loudly. And echoes.

G. THE GREAT BEYOND

LUCY *and* BRAZIL *watch the TV: a replay of "The Lincoln Act."* THE FOUNDLING
FATHER *has returned. His coffin awaits him.*
LUCY Howuhboutthat!

BRAZIL They just gunned him down uhgain.
LUCY Howuhboutthat.
BRAZIL He's dead but not really.
5 LUCY Howuhboutthat.
BRAZIL Only fakin. Only fakin. See? Hesupuhgain.
LUCY What-izzysayin?
BRAZIL Sound duhnt work.
LUCY Zat right.
   [*Rest.*]
10 THE FOUNDLING FATHER I believe this is the place where I do the Gettysburg
   Address, I believe.
BRAZIL
THE FOUNDLING FATHER
LUCY
BRAZIL Woah!
LUCY Howuhboutthat.
BRAZIL Huh. Well.
   [*Rest.*]
15 Huh. Zit him?
LUCY Its him.
BRAZIL He's dead?
LUCY He's dead.
BRAZIL Howuhboutthat.
   [*Rest.*]
20 Shit.
LUCY
BRAZIL
LUCY
BRAZIL Mail the in-vites?
LUCY I did.
BRAZIL Think theyll come?
LUCY I do. There are hundreds upon thousands who knew of your Daddy,
25 glorified his reputation, and would like to pay their respects.
THE FOUNDLING FATHER Howuhboutthat.
BRAZIL Howuhboutthat!
LUCY Turn that off, son.
   [*Rest.*]
   You gonna get in yr coffin now or later?
30 THE FOUNDLING FATHER I'd like tuh wait uhwhile.
LUCY Youd like tuh wait uhwhile.
BRAZIL Mmgonna gnash for you. You know: teeth in thuh dirt, hands like
   this, then jump up rip my clothes up, you know, you know go all out.
THE FOUNDLING FATHER Howuhboutthat. Open casket or closed?
35 LUCY —. Closed.
   [*Rest.*]
   Turn that off, son.
BRAZIL K.
THE FOUNDLING FATHER Hug me.
BRAZIL Not yet.
40 THE FOUNDLING FATHER You?

LUCY   Gimmieuhminute.

     [*A gunshot echoes. Loudly. And echoes.*]

LUCY   That gunplay. Wierdiduhntit. Comes. And goze.

     [*They ready his coffin. He inspects it.*]

At thuh Great Hole where we honeymooned—son, at thuh Original Great Hole, you could see thuh whole world without goin too far. You could look
45   intuh that Hole and see your entire life pass before you. Not your own life but someones life from history, you know, [someone who'd done somethin of note, got theirselves known somehow, uh President or] somebody who killed somebody important, uh face on uh postal stamp, you know, someone from History. *Like* you, but *not* you. You know: *Known.*

50 THE FOUNDLING FATHER   "*Emergency,* oh, *Emergency,* please put the Great Man in the ground."

LUCY   Go on. Get in. Try it out. Ssnot so bad. See? Sstight, but private. Bought on time but we'll manage. And you got enough height for your hat.

     [*Rest.*]

THE FOUNDLING FATHER   Hug me.

55 LUCY   Not yet.

THE FOUNDLING FATHER   You?

BRAZIL   Gimmieuhminute.

     [*Rest.*]

LUCY   He loved that Great Hole so. Came out here. Digged this lookuhlike.

BRAZIL   Then he died?

60 LUCY   Then he died.

THE FOUNDLING FATHER

BRAZIL

LUCY

THE FOUNDLING FATHER

BRAZIL

LUCY

THE FOUNDLING FATHER   A monumentous occasion. I'd like to say a few words from the grave. Maybe a little conversation: Such a long story. Uhhem. I quit the business. And buried all my things. I dropped anchor: Bottomless. Your turn.

LUCY

BRAZIL

THE FOUNDLING FATHER

65 LUCY [*rest*]   Do your Lincoln for im.

THE FOUNDLING FATHER   Yeah?

LUCY   He was only 5.

THE FOUNDLING FATHER   Only 5. *Uh Hehm.* So very loverly to be here so very very loverly to be here the town of —Wonderville has always been a special
70   favorite of mine always has been a very very special favorite of mine. Now, I *only* do thuh greats. Uh hehm: I was born in a log cabin of humble parentage. But I picked up uh few things. Uh Hehm: 4score and 7 years ago our fathers—ah you know thuh rest. Lets see now. Yes. Uh house divided cannot stand! You can fool some of thuh people some of thuh time! Of
75   thuh people by thuh people and for thuh people! Malice toward none and charity toward all! Ha! The Death of Lincoln! (Highlights): Haw Haw Haw Haw

[*Rest.*]

HAW HAW HAW HAW

[*A gunshot echoes. Loudly. And echoes.* THE FOUNDLING FATHER *"slumps in his chair."*]

THE FOUNDLING FATHER

LUCY

BRAZIL

LUCY

THE FOUNDLING FATHER

BRAZIL [Izzy dead?

80 LUCY Mmlistenin.

BRAZIL Anything?

LUCY Nothin.

BRAZIL [*rest*] As a child it was her luck tuh be in thuh same room with her Uncle when he died. Her family wanted to know what he had said. What
85 his last words had been. Theyre hadnt been any. Only screaming. Or, you know, breath. Didnt have uh shape to it. Her family thought she was holding on to thuh words. For safekeeping. And they proclaimed thuh girl uh Confidence. At the age of 8. Sworn tuh secrecy. She picked up thuh tricks of thuh trade as she went uhlong.]

[*Rest.*]

90 Should I gnash now?

LUCY Better save it for thuh guests. I guess.

[*Rest.*]

Well. Dust and polish, son. I'll circulate.

BRAZIL Welcome Welcome Welcome to thuh hall. Of. Wonders.

[*Rest.*]

To our right A Jewel Box of cherry wood, lined in velvet, letters "A.L."
95 carved in gold on thuh lid. Over here one of Mr. Washingtons bones and here: his wooden teeth. Over here: uh bust of Mr. Lincoln carved of marble lookin like he looked in life. —More or less. And thuh medals: for bravery and honesty; for trustworthiness and for standing straight; for standing tall; for standing still. For advancing and retreating. For makin
100 do. For skills in whittlin, for skills in painting and drawing, for uh knowledge of sewin, of handicrafts and building things, for leather tannin, blacksmithery, lacemakin, horseback riding, swimmin, croquet, and badminton. Community Service. For cookin and for cleanin. For bowin and scrapin. Uh medal for fakin.

[*Rest.*]

105 To my right: our newest Wonder: One of thuh greats Hisself! Note: thuh body sitting propped upright in our great Hole. Note the large mouth opened wide. Note the top hat and frock coat, just like the greats. Note the death wound: thuh great black hole—thuh great black hole in thuh great head. —And how this great head is bleedin. —Note: thuh last words. —
110 And thuh last breaths. —And how thuh nation mourns—

[*Takes his leave.*]

Selected Bibliographies

TAWFIQ AL-HAKIM

In addition to the 1977 translation by M. M. Badawi included here, *Song of Death* has been translated into English by C. W. R. Long (1972) and Denys Johnson-Davies (1973). One of the most comprehensive treatments in English of Tawfiq al-Hakim and his contribution to Egyptian theater is found in Badawi's seminal work *Modern Arabic Drama in Egypt* (1987). In this study, Badawi provides a thorough overview of al-Hakim's different developmental stages as a playwright and traces his dramatic production from its earliest experiments to the last stages. *Tawfiq al-Hakim: A Reader's Guide*, ed. William Maynard Hutchins (2003), discusses al-Hakim's plays, novels, and short stories and includes an excellent annotated biography and chronology of the writer's life and work. Other studies of al-Hakim's drama include Richard Long, *Tawfiq al Hakim, Playwright of Egypt* (1979); Roger Allen, "Egyptian Drama after the Revolution" (1979); Paul Starkey, "Tawfiq Al-Hakim: Leading Playwright of the Arab World" (1989); and Ali al-Ra'i, "Arab Drama Since the Thirties," in *The Cambridge History of Arabic Literature: Modern Arabic Literature*, ed. M. M. Badawi (1992). Those interested in reading more of al-Hakim's works will find Denys Johnson-Davies, ed., *The Essential Tawfiq al-Hakim: Plays, Fiction, Autobiography* (2008) an excellent resource.

ARISTOPHANES

For a detailed description of the competitions and how they were staged, see Sir Arthur Pickard-Cambridge, *The Dramatic Festivals of Athens* (2nd ed., 1968). Eric Csapo and William J. Slater's *The Context of Ancient Drama* (1994) provides further valuable primary resources on all aspects of classical theater in production. Useful overviews of the work of Aristophanes include K. J. Dover, *Aristophanic Comedy* (1972); A. M. Bowie, *Aristophanes: Myth, Ritual and Comedy* (1993); David Konstan, *Greek Comedy and Ideology* (1995) and James Robson, *Aristophanes: An Introduction* (2009). Two thematic studies with particular relevance to *Lysistrata* are Jeffrey Henderson, *The Maculate Muse: Obscene Language in Attic Comedy* (1975; 2nd ed., 1991), and Lauren K. Taaffe, *Aristophanes and Women* (1993). John Vaio's "The Manipulation of Theme and Action in Aristophanes' *Lysistrata*" (1973) and Jeffrey Henderson's "*Lysistrata*: The Play and Its Themes" (1980) provide excellent, detailed readings of the play, while Niall Slater's "Making the Aristophanic Audience" (1999) offers hypotheses about classic comedies in performance. The scholarly translations by Alan H. Sommerstein (2002), Jeffrey Henderson (1996), and Stephen Halliwell (1997) all offer detailed introductions and textual analysis of this complex and challenging text.

SAMUEL BECKETT

Samuel Beckett's plays are published in the United States by Grove/Atlantic and in Britain by Faber and Faber. The most complete biography of Beckett, written with the author's approval, is James Knowlson, *Damned to Fame: The Life of Samuel Beckett* (1996), which has supplemented and, in the view of most Beckett scholars, superseded Deirdre Bair's earlier *Samuel Beckett: A Biography* (1978). Other important biographies written since Beckett's death include Anthony Cronin, *Samuel Beckett: The Last Modernist* (1996), and Lois Gordon, *The World of Samuel Beckett, 1906–1946* (1996). Among the many critical discussions of Beckett's work, the following are particularly useful to students of his plays: Hugh Kenner, *Samuel Beckett: A Critical Study* (1961; new ed., 1968); Eugene Webb, *The Plays of Samuel Beckett* (1972); John Fletcher and John Spurling, *Beckett: A Study of His Plays* (1972; 2d ed., 1978); Ruby Cohn, *Back to Beckett* (1973) and *Just Play: Beckett's Theater* (1980); John Pilling, *Samuel Beckett* (1976); S. E. Gontarski, *The Intent of Undoing in Samuel Beckett's Dramatic Texts* (1985); Steven Connor, *Samuel Beckett: Repetition, Theory and Text* (1988); Andrew K. Kennedy, *Samuel Beckett* (1989); Enoch Brater, *Why Beckett* (1989); David Pattie, *The Complete Critical Guide to Samuel Beckett* (2000); Rónán McDonald, *The Cambridge Introduction to Samuel Beckett* (2006); Jonathan Boulter, *Beckett: A Guide for the Perplexed* (2008); and S. E. Gontarski, ed., *A Companion to Samuel Beckett* (2010). Important collections of essays include Martin Esslin, ed., *Samuel Beckett: A Collection of Critical Essays* (1965); S. E. Gontarski, ed., *On Beckett: Essays and Criticism* (1986); and Lance St. John Butler and Robin J. Davis, eds., *Rethinking Beckett: A Collection of Critical Essays* (1990). Studies of Beckett's plays in performance include Dougald McMillan and Martha Fehsenfeld, *Beckett in the Theatre: The Author as Practical Playwright and Director* (1988), and Jonathan Kalb, *Beckett in Performance* (1989). Linda Ben-Zvi, ed., *Women in Beckett: Performance and Critical Perspectives* (1990), explores issues of gender in Beckett's drama with an emphasis on performance.

Resources for the study of *Waiting for Godot* include the following: Ruby Cohn, ed., *Casebook on "Waiting for Godot"* (1967); Bert O. States, *The Shape of Paradox: An Essay on "Waiting for Godot"* (1978); Lawrence Graver, *Samuel Beckett, "Waiting for Godot,"* (1989; 2nd ed., 2004);

Thomas Cousineau, *"Waiting for Godot": Form in Movement* (1990); Steven Connor, ed., *"Waiting for Godot" and "Endgame,"* by Samuel Beckett (1992); Lois Gordon, *Reading "Godot"* (2002); and Harold Bloom, ed., *Samuel Beckett's "Waiting for Godot"* (2008). David Bradby, *Beckett: "Waiting for Godot"* (2001), and Jonathan Croall, *The Coming of Godot: A Short History of a Masterpiece* (2005), discuss the play's production history. Dougald McMillan and James Knowlson, eds., *The Theatrical Notebooks of Samuel Beckett*, vol. 1, *Waiting for Godot* (1993), contains the working notes that Beckett kept while directing *Godot* at Berlin's Schiller-Theater in 1975 and will be of particular interest to actors and directors of Beckett's play.

APHRA BEHN

Maureen Duffy, *The Passionate Shepherdess: Aphra Behn, 1640–89* (1977); Angeline Goreau, *Reconstructing Aphra: A Social Biography of Aphra Behn* (1980); George Woodcock, *Aphra Behn: The English Sappho* (1989); and Janet Todd, *The Secret Life of Aphra Behn* (1996) are the most recent and authoritative of a series of biographical studies. Todd's *The Sign of Angellica: Women, Writing, and Fiction, 1660–1800* (1989) documents the increasing presence and impact of women writers in England. Todd's edited volume, *Aphra Behn Studies* (1996), provides additional recent perspectives on Behn's work as a dramatist, poet, and fiction writer and further augments the Behn biographies, as does her volume edition with Derek Hughes, *The Cambridge Companion to Aphra Behn* (2004). Heidi Hutner's edited volume, *Rereading Aphra Behn: History, Theory, and Criticism* (1993), contributes other important essays on Behn's writing in all major genres. Individual essays on her work from a range of critical perspectives abound. For comparisons of *The Rover* and *Thomaso*, see especially Jones DeRitter, "The Gypsy, *The Rover*, and the Wanderer: Aphra Behn's Revision of Thomas Killigrew" (1986), and Elaine Hobby, "No Stolen Object, but Her Own: Aphra Behn's *Rover* and Thomas Killigrew's *Thomaso*" (1999). For studies of the setting of the play, see Linda R. Payne, "The Carnivalesque Regeneration of Corrupt Economies in *The Rover*" (1998), and Dagny Boebel, "In the Carnival World of Adam's Garden: Roving and Rape in Behn's *Rover*," in *Broken Boundaries: Women and Feminism in Restoration Drama*, ed. Katherine M. Quinsey (1996). Readings that incorporate important considerations of staging and performance include Elin Diamond, "*Gestus* and Signature in Aphra Behn's *The Rover*" (1989), and John Franceschina, "Shadow and Substance in Aphra Behn's *The Rover*: The Semiotics of Restoration Performance" (1995). Mary Anne O'Donnell has compiled the useful reference volume *Aphra Behn: An Annotated Bibliography of Primary and Secondary Sources* (1986; 2nd ed., 2004). Among the growing body of historical and critical writings on Restoration drama and theater practice, see Robert D. Hume, *The Development of English Drama in the Late Seventeenth Century* (1976) and his *Rakish Stage: Studies in English Drama, 1660–1800* (1983); J. Douglas Canfield and Deborah C. Payne, eds., *Cultural Readings of Restoration and Eighteenth-Century English Theater* (1995); Laura Brown, *English Dramatic Form, 1660–1760: An Essay in Generic History* (1981); J. L. Styan, *Restoration Comedy in Performance* (1986); Mary Anne Schofield and Cecilia Macheski, eds., *Curtain Calls: British and American Women and Theater, 1660–1820* (1991); Jocelyn Powell, *Restoration Theatre Production* (1984); and Deborah Payne Fisk, ed., *The Cambridge Companion to English Restoration Theatre* (2000), which also contains a very useful bibliography. The definitive reference work for documenting performances of the period remains William Van Lennep et al., eds., *The London Stage, 1660–1800: A Calendar of Plays, Entertainments, and Afterpieces, together with Casts, Box-Receipts, and Contemporary Comment*, 5 vols. (1960–68).

BERTOLT BRECHT

Not surprisingly, the critical literature on Brecht's life and work is extensive. The person who introduced Brecht to America was Eric Bentley, who translated many of Brecht's plays, adapted them, and wrote extensively on the author. Although his not always faithful translations have been criticized, his writings on Brecht are important milestones in Brecht criticism; they include *Bentley on Brecht* (1998; 3d ed., 2008) and *The Playwright as Thinker: A Study of Drama in Modern Times* (1967). A good biography of Brecht is still Frederic Ewen's *Bertolt Brecht: His Life, His Art, and His Times* (1967). A more recent biography, John Fuegi's controversial *Brecht and Company: Sex, Politics, and the Making of the Modern Drama* (1994), argues that much of what has been viewed as original in Brecht was noncredited work by a number of others, including several of his lovers. Though exaggerated and shrill in

its claims, the book nevertheless draws needed attention to the collaborative process that was undoubtedly part of Brecht's work. A good and simple introduction to Brecht's work is John Willett's *The Theatre of Bertolt Brecht: A Study from Eight Aspects* (1959; 3d ed., 1967); Martin Esslin's *Brecht: A Choice of Evils: A Critical Study of the Man, His Work, and His Opinions* (1959; 4th ed., 1984) is more ambitious and insightful. On Brecht's exile in and influence on the theater of the United States, see James Lyon's informative *Bertolt Brecht in America* (1980). Brecht's theoretical works are collected and translated by John Willett in *Brecht on Theatre: The Development of an Aesthetic* (1964; 2d ed., 1974); a good recent study of Brecht's theater is John J. White's *Bertolt Brecht's Dramatic Theory* (2004). A theoretically challenging but intriguing discussion of Brecht is Fredric Jameson's *Brecht and Method* (1998). On the use, in *The Good Person of Szechwan*, of a Chinese setting as well as on Brecht's interest in Chinese theater, see Eric Hayot's *Chinese Dreams: Pound, Brecht, Tel Quel* (2004).

Given Brecht's immense influence on modern drama, most classic studies of that period include substantial chapters on Brecht. See, for example, Raymond Williams, *Drama from Ibsen to Brecht* (1969); Richard Gilman, *The Making of Modern Drama* (1972); and Robert Brustein, *The Theatre of Revolt: An Approach to the Modern Drama* (1964). Brecht's paradigm has also shaped studies such as Janelle Reinelt's *After Brecht: British Epic Theater* (1994) and Elin Diamond's *Unmaking Mimesis* (1997).

ANTON CHEKHOV

Numerous translations of Chekhov's plays have appeared in the past forty years, including versions by such playwrights as Michael Frayn, Trevor Griffiths, and David Mamet. While its translations are not as stageworthy as the best of these, Ronald Hingley's nine-volume edition, *The Oxford Chekhov* (1964–80), includes all of Chekhov's plays and most of his stories. Laurence Senelick's Norton Critical Edition, *Anton Chekhov's Selected Plays* (2005), contains useful annotations on *The Cherry Orchard* and other plays. Donald Rayfield's authoritative biography, *Anton Chekhov: A Life* (1997), was the first account of the playwright's life to benefit from the opening of Russian archives after the dissolution of the Soviet Union in 1991. James N. Loehlin, *The Cambridge Introduction to Chekhov* (2010), is a useful introduction to Chekhov's life and work.

The following are useful studies of Chekhov's drama: Maurice Valency, *The Breaking String: The Plays of Anton Chekhov* (1966); J. L. Styan, *Chekhov in Performance: A Commentary on the Major Plays* (1971); Richard Peace, *Chekhov: A Study of the Four Major Plays* (1983); Laurence Senelick, *Anton Chekhov* (1985); Richard Gilman, *Chekhov's Plays: An Opening into Eternity* (1995); and Donald Rayfield, *Understanding Chekhov: A Critical Study of Chekhov's Prose and Drama* (1999). Toby W. Clyman, ed., *A Chekhov Companion* (1985), and Vera Gottlieb and Paul Allain, eds., *The Cambridge Companion to Chekhov* (2000), contain valuable essays on Chekhov, while Harold Bloom, ed., *Anton Chekhov* (1999), reprints a number of previously published essays on Chekhov's fiction and drama. The chapters on Chekhov in Robert Brustein, *The Theatre of Revolt: An Approach to the Modern Drama* (1964), and Richard Gilman, *The Making of Modern Drama* (1974), remain among the best discussions of the playwright's dramatic work. Donald Rayfield, *The Cherry Orchard: Catastrophe and Comedy* (1994), is a book-length study of Chekhov's final play. Laurence Senelick, *The Chekhov Theatre: A Century of the Plays in Performance* (1997), and David Allen, *Performing Chekhov* (2000), examine Chekhov's plays in performance.

CARYL CHURCHILL

Most of Caryl Churchill's produced dramas and radio scripts to date have been published in single and/or collected volumes by Methuen and Nick Hern Books. While Churchill produced a revised version of *Cloud Nine* for its initial New York production, she has stated her preference for the British version used here. Some of her very early, unproduced pieces have not yet been made publicly available. *File on Churchill* (1989), compiled by Linda Fitzsimmons, contains much useful information on Churchill's biography and early career as well as excerpts from reviews, interviews, and other commentary. To date, there is no published biography of Churchill, although she has shared information on her life with interviewers. Among the most useful of these dialogues are Kathleen Betsko and Rachel Koenig's *Interviews with Contemporary Women Playwrights* (1987); Laurie Stone, "Caryl Churchill: Making Room at the Top" (*Village Voice*, 1 March 1983); and Lynne Truss, "A Fair Cop" (*Plays and Players*, January 1984). An interview with Judith Thurman provided the foundation for the *Ms.* article (May

1982), while prominent New York theater critic John Simon interviewed Churchill for *Vogue* (August 1983). Early full-length studies of her work include Geraldine Cousin, *Churchill: The Playwright* (1989), and Amelia Howe Kritzer, *The Plays of Caryl Churchill* (1991). Elaine Aston's *Caryl Churchill* (1997) builds productively on this early criticism. Janelle Reinelt's relevant scholarship includes *After Brecht: British Epic Theater* (1994) and her essay on Churchill in *Modern British Women Playwrights* (2000). Phyllis Randall's edited volume, *Caryl Churchill: A Casebook* (1988); Elaine Aston and Elin Diamond's edited volume, *The Cambridge Companion to Caryl Churchill* (2009); Helene Keyssar's entry in *Feminist Theatre* (1984); Elin Diamond's article in *Making a Spectacle: Feminist Essays on Contemporary Women's Theatre* (1989); Austin Quigley's essay in *Feminine Focus: The New Women Playwrights* (1989); Frances Gray's entry in *British and Irish Drama Since 1960* (1993); and Lisa Merrill's piece in *Modern Dramatists: A Casebook of Major British, Irish, and American Playwrights* (2001) are all worthwhile. For an understanding of Churchill in the context of British feminist theater, see Michelene Wandor, *Carry on Understudies: Theatre and Sexual Politics* (1981); for Churchill and political theater in England, see Catherine Itzin, *Stages in the Revolution: Political Theatre in Britain Since 1968* (1980). Apollo Amoko's "Casting Aside Colonial Occupation: Intersections of Race, Sex, and Gender in *Cloud Nine* and *Cloud Nine* Criticism" (1999) and James Harding's "Cloud Cover: (Re)Dressing Desire and Comfortable Subversions in Caryl Churchill's *Cloud Nine*" (1998) provide important responses to the play's explorations of colonialism and homosexuality.

EURIPIDES
Medea

Donald J. Mastronarde provides a helpful overview of Euripides' dramas in *The Art of Euripides: Dramatic Technique and Social Context* (2010). Other useful sources include the collection of essays *Greek Tragedy*, volume XXV of the *Yale Classical Studies* series, eds. T. F. Gould and C. J. Herington (1977), with essays by B. M. W. Knox ("The *Medea* of Euripides") and P. E. Easterling ("The Infanticide in Euripides' *Medea*). Some of the most significant research on *Medea* has appeared in scholarly journals. Anne Burnett's "*Medea* and the Tragedy of Revenge," published in *Classical Philology* (1973), has been particularly influential. Helene Foley's "Medea's Divided Self," which appeared in *Classical Antiquity* (1989), and Judith Fletcher's "Women and Oaths in Euripides," published in a special issue of *Theatre Journal* devoted to ancient theater (1983), are both worthwhile. Froma Zeitlin's *Playing the Other: Gender and Society in Classical Greek Literature* (1996) is a major study using feminist critical techniques. Anton Powell's edited volume *Euripides, Women, and Sexuality* (1990) also provides analyses of gender and sexuality in a select group of plays; Margaret Williamson's essay "A Woman's Place in Euripides' *Medea*" is an especially valuable contribution. Nancy Sorkin Rabinowitz, *Anxiety Veiled: Euripides and the Traffic in Women* (2003), offers a particularly insightful reading of Medea's character in the context of Euripidean dramaturgy. Several recent English-language translations of *Medea* include highly useful scholarly introductions. Foremost among these are Peter D. Arnott's *Three Greek Plays for the Theatre* (1961), John Harrison's *Medea* (2000), J. Michael Walton and Marianne McDonald's introduction to Walton's *Medea* (2002), and Robin Mitchell-Boysak's introduction to Diane Arnson Svarlien's *Euripides: Alcestis, Medea, Hippolytus* (2007), the source of the translation selected for this anthology. Emma Griffith's *Medea* (2006) offers a historical overview of this mythic figure, while *Medea in Performance, 1500–2000* (2000), ed. Edith Hall, Fiona Macintosh, and Oliver Taplin, provides a comprehensive study of the global appearance and influence of this character in the performing arts. Taplin's *Pots and Plays: Interactions between Tragedy and Greek Vase-Painting of the Fourth Century* (2007) makes a case for the use of vase imagery to understand both the influence of Greek drama on other art forms and its possible staging.

EVERYMAN

A. C. Cawley's 1961 *Everyman* is the most widely cited text of the play; Cawley's introduction to this edition gives valuable background information. A more recent edition of *Everyman* can be found in Douglas Bruster and Eric Rasmussen, eds., *Everyman and Mankind* (2009), which appears in the Arden Early Modern Drama series. *The Mirror of Everyman's Salvation: A Prose Translation of the Original Everyman*, eds. John Conley, Guido de Baere, H. J. C. Schaap,

and W. H. Toppen (1985), includes both the text of *Everyman* and a translation of the Dutch *Elckerlijc*. Important critical studies of *Everyman* include Lawrence V. Ryan, "Doctrine and Dramatic Structure in *Everyman*" (1957); Thomas F. Van Laan, "*Everyman*: A Structural Analysis" (1963); V. A. Kolve, "*Everyman* and the Parable of the Talents" (1972); C. J. Wortham, "*Everyman* and the Reformation" (1981); Carolynn Van Dyke, "The Intangible and Its Image: Allegorical Discourse and the Cast of *Everyman*" (1982); Donald F. Duclow, "*Everyman* and the *Ars moriendi*: Fifteenth-Century Ceremonies of Dying" (1983); Phoebe S. Spinrad, "The Last Temptation of Everyman" (1985); Stanton B. Garner, Jr., "Theatricality in *Mankind* and *Everyman*" (1987); Jacqueline Vanhoutte, "When Elckerlijc Becomes Everyman: Translating Dutch to English, Performance to Print" (1995); David Mills, "The Theaters of *Everyman*" (1995); Elizabeth Harper and Britt Mize, "Material Economy, Spiritual Economy, and Social Critique in *Everyman*" (2006); and Julie Paulson, "Death's Arrival and Everyman's Separation" (2007). Robert Potter's *The English Morality Play: Origins, History and Influence of a Dramatic Tradition* (1975) discusses the influential 1901 revival of *Everyman* and the play's twentieth-century reputation.

ATHOL FUGARD

For a history of South African performance traditions, see Loren Kruger, *The Drama of South Africa: Plays, Pageants and Politics Since 1910* (1999); Martin Orkin, *Drama and the South African State* (1991); and Margarete Seidenspinner, *Exploring the Labyrinth: Athol Fugard's Approach to South African Drama* (1986). Useful bibliographies and resources about Athol Fugard's plays in production include Temple Hauptfleisch, Wilma Vijoen, and Céleste Van Greunen, eds., *Athol Fugard: A Source Guide* (1982); John Read, comp., *Athol Fugard: A Bibliography* (1991); and Stephen Gray, comp., *File on Fugard* (1991). For full-length critical studies of Fugard's work, see Dennis Walder, *Athol Fugard* (1984) and *Athol Fugard* (2003); Alan Shelley, *Athol Fugard: His Plays, People, and Politics: A Critical Overview* (2009); Russell Vandenbroucke, *Truths the Hand Can Touch: The Theatre of Athol Fugard* (1985); and Albert Wertheim, *The Dramatic Art of Athol Fugard: From South Africa to the World* (2000). The work most critical of Fugard as a political writer is Robert Mshengu, "Political Theatre in South

Africa and the Work of Athol Fugard" (1982). For details of Fugard's plays and perspectives post-1994, see Marcia Blumberg and Dennis Walder, eds., *South African Theatre as/and Intervention* (1999).

The standard edition of *"MASTER HAROLD"* is that published by Penguin in 1982. Among the essays of particular relevance to its analysis are Rob Amato, "Fugard's Confessional Analysis: *'MASTER HAROLD'... and the boys*," in *Momentum: On Recent South African Writing*, ed. M. J. Daymond, J. U. Jacobs, and Margaret Lenta (1984); Errol Durbach, "*'MASTER HAROLD'... and the boys*: Athol Fugard and the Psychopathology of Apartheid" (1987); and J. Ellen Gainor, "'A World without Collisions': Ballroom Dance in Athol Fugard's *'MASTER HAROLD'... and the boys*," in *Bodies of the Text: Dance as Theory, Literature as Dance*, ed. Ellen W. Goellner and Jacqueline Shea Murphy (1995). Mel Gussow's "Profiles: Witness" (1982) provides a summary of the play's autobiographical elements as well as Fugard's direction of the play in the context of his career. Fugard's *Notebooks, 1960–1977* (1983) contains details of the play's background from the playwright's perspective.

SUSAN GLASPELL

All of Glaspell's dramatic writing has been collected in *Susan Glaspell: The Complete Plays*, ed. Linda Ben-Zvi and J. Ellen Gainor (2010). C. W. E. Bigsby's selection, *Plays* (1987), reprints several of her major works (including *Trifles*) and contains a worthwhile introduction; his entry on Glaspell for the first volume of his *Critical Introduction to Twentieth-Century American Drama* (1983) is also helpful. Marcia Noe's *Susan Glaspell: Voice from the Heartland* (1983) was the first critical biography of Glaspell. More recent definitive biographies are Linda Ben-Zvi, *Susan Glaspell: Her Life and Times* (2005), and Barbara Ozieblo, *Susan Glaspell: A Critical Biography* (2000). J. Ellen Gainor, *Susan Glaspell in Context: American Theater, Culture, and Politics, 1915–48* (2001), provides readings of Glaspell's dramas within their creative, historical, and critical milieus. Linda Ben-Zvi, ed., *Susan Glaspell: Essay on Her Theater and Fiction* (1995), contains a useful section on *Trifles* and "Jury." Veronica Makowsky, *Susan Glaspell's Century of American Women: A Critical Interpretation of Her Work* (1993), focuses on female characters and themes in Glaspell's fiction and drama, while Kristina

Hinz-Bode, *Susan Glaspell and the Anxiety of Expression: Language and Isolation in the Plays* (2006), examines issues of language and isolation in the playwright's dramas, and Noelia Hernando-Real's *Self and Space in the Theater of Susan Glaspell* (2011) offers a philosophical approach to the plays. Robert Károly Sarlós, *Jig Cook and the Provincetown Players: Theatre in Ferment* (1982), provides the broader historical background to Glaspell's early theatrical career, and Cheryl Black's *The Women of Provincetown, 1915–22* (2002) focuses on the artistry of Glaspell and her female colleagues. In *Midnight Assassin: A Murder in America's Heartland* (2005), Patricia L. Bryan and Thomas Wolf provide a historical analysis of the murder that was the source for Glaspell's play. Mary E. Papke, *Susan Glaspell: A Research and Production Sourcebook* (1993), is the most comprehensive bibliographic resource.

GUAN HANQING

The Yuan text of *Dou E Yuan* has been preserved in a collection of *zaju* plays published three centuries after Guan's lifetime, but there is no single authoritative written version that defines how the play has been experienced by audiences throughout China over the centuries. Like most Chinese drama, *zaju* plays present a traditional core that survives and proliferates in performance. Each *zaju* play has been excerpted, expanded, modified, and appropriated many times throughout the past seven hundred years. No *zaju* play, *Dou E Yuan* included, has a "definitive" text. For example, Ye Xianzu (1566–1641) adapted the third act of the Yuan text of *Dou E Yuan* as part of his play *Story of the Golden Lock*, which was written in the Ming dynasty form known as *chuanqi*. This play in turn has been adapted into numerous forms—song, storytelling, puppetry, and live theater—all of which, at some level, recognizably derive from Guan's creation. Chinese artists and audiences favor appropriating and transforming famous plays, for doing so presents old stories to contemporary audiences. These strategies are seen not as a violation of the playwright's intentions but rather as a means of keeping the text alive. Although Yang Xianyi and Gladys Yang's 1979 translation of *Dou E Yuan* included in this anthology is a nearly complete version based on the Yuan original, its title, *Snow in Midsummer* (*Liuyue xue*), is taken from that given to a number of adaptations of a single act of *Dou E Yuan*. Other versions of Guan's play can be found in *Six Yuan Plays*, trans. Jung-en Liu (1972); *Injustice to Tou O (Tou O Yuan): A Study and Translation*, trans. Chung-wen Shih (1972); and *Monks, Bandits, Lovers, and Immortals: Eleven Early Chinese Plays*, ed. and trans. Stephen H. West and Wilt L. Idema (2010).

Criticism in English on Yuan drama, and more specifically on Guan Hanqing and *Dou E Yuan*, is fairly meager. Stephen H. West's article "A Study in Appropriation: Zang Maoxun's Injustice to Dou E" (1991) contains valuable information regarding the differences between the three published versions of the play. Ching-Hsi Perng's *Double Jeopardy: A Critique of Seven Yüan Courtroom Dramas* (1978) compares the play to others in its genre. Haiping Yan's "Theatricality in Classical Chinese Drama," in *Theatricality*, eds. Tracy C. Davis and Thomas Postlewait (2003), discusses the theatrical aspects of Guan's play. Wu-chi Liu's article "Kuan Han-Ch'ing: The Man and His Life" (1990–92) sorts through the scarce evidence on the life of the playwright. J. I. Crump's *Chinese Theater in the Days of Kublai Khan* (1980) describes the performance conventions and historical context of Yuan drama. Faye Chunfang Fei's *Chinese Theories of Theater and Performance from Confucius to the Present* (1999) contains important excerpts of Chinese dramatic theory relating to Guan Hanqing and Yuan drama in general.

HROTSVIT OF GANDERSHEIM

Major studies of the medieval theater include E. K. Chambers, *The Mediaeval Stage*, 2 vols. (1903); Karl Young, *The Drama of the Medieval Church* (1933); and O. B. Hardison Jr., *Christian Rite and Christian Drama in the Middle Ages: Essays in the Origin and Early History of Modern Drama* (1965). Anne Lyon Haight edited a useful bibliographical volume, *Hroswitha of Gandersheim: Her Life, Time, Works, and a Comprehensive Bibliography* (1965), that includes information on translations, productions, and scholarship. Among the most influential English translations of Hrotsvit are Christopher St. John, *The Plays of Roswitha* (1923); Larissa Bonfante, *The Plays of Hrotswitha of Gandersheim* (1979); and Katharina M. Wilson, *The Plays of Hrotsvit of Gandersheim* (1989), the last of which provides the text used in this anthology. Sister Mary Marguerite Butler's *Hrotsvitha: The Theatricality of Her Plays* (1960) cogently argues for the performative potential of the dramas. Bert Nagel,

"The Dramas of Hrotsvit von Gandersheim" (1970), and Kenneth DeLuca, "Hrotsvit's 'Imitation' of Terence" (1974), are both significant additions to the scholarship. The chapter on Hrotsvit in Peter Dronke's *Women Writers of the Middle Ages: A Critical Study of Texts from Perpetua (d. 203) to Marguerite Porete (d. 1310)* (1984) has proven extremely influential. Feminist approaches to the dramatist include Sue-Ellen Case, "Re-Viewing Hrotsvit" (1983); M. R. Sperberg-McQueen, "Whose Body Is It? Chaste Strategies and the Reinforcement of Patriarchy in Three Plays by Hrotswitha von Gandersheim" (1993); and Patricia Demers, "*In virginea forma*: The Salvific Feminine in the Plays of Hrotsvitha of Gandersheim and Hildegard of Bingen" (1993). Among his many publications on the dramatist, Sandro Sticca's "Sacred Drama and Comic Realism in the Plays of Hrotswitha of Gandersheim" (1979) and "Hrotswitha's 'Dulcitius' and Christian Symbolism" (1970) are particularly valuable. In addition to her fine translation, Katharina M. Wilson has published two other notable volumes, *Hrotsvit of Gandersheim: The Ethics of Authorial Stance* (1988), and another collection of the nun's dramatic and nondramatic writings, *Hrotsvit of Gandersheim: A Florilegium of Her Works* (1998); she also co-edited the volume *Hrotsvit of Gandersheim: Contexts, Identities, Affinities, and Performances* (2004) with Phyllis R. Brown and Linda A. McMillin.

DAVID HENRY HWANG

The standard text of *M. Butterfly* is the New American Library edition (1989), which includes Hwang's afterword on the play and its composition. The acting edition (1988) published by Dramatists Play Service contains the same afterword, as well as a discussion of the play's Broadway production and suggestions for prospective actors, directors, and designers. William C. Boles, *Understanding David Henry Hwang* (2013), is an important book-length study of Hwang's life and work. Douglas Street's brief but useful monograph *David Henry Hwang* (1989) contains biographical information on the playwright and an overview of his dramatic writing through *M. Butterfly*. William C. Boles, *Understanding David Henry Hwang* (2013), is an important book-length study of Hwang's life and work. Miles Xian Liu, ed., *Asian American Playwrights: A Bio-bibliographical Critical Sourcebook* (2002), provides biographical backgrounds, production history, and bibliographical information on the works of Hwang and other Asian American dramatists.

Important articles on *M. Butterfly* include Robert Skloot, "Breaking the Butterfly: The Politics of David Henry Hwang" (1990); Douglas Kerr, "David Henry Hwang and the Revenge of *Madame Butterfly*," in *Asian Voices in English*, ed. Mimi Chan and Roy Harris (1991); Marjorie Garber, "The Occidental Tourist: *M. Butterfly* and the Scandal of Transvestism," in *Nationalities and Sexualities*, ed. Andrew Parker, Mary Russo, Doris Sommer, and Patricia Yaeger (1992); Karen Shimakawa, "'Who's to Say?' or, Making Space for Gender and Ethnicity in *M. Butterfly*" (1993); Foong Ling Kong's "Pulling the Wings Off Butterfly" (1994); and Hsiu-Chen Lin, "Staging Orientalia: Dangerous 'Authenticity' in David Henry Hwang's *M. Butterfly*" (1997). James S. Moy, *Marginal Sights: Staging the Chinese in America* (1993), and Josephine Lee, *Performing Asian America: Race and Ethnicity on the Contemporary Stage* (1997), explore *M. Butterfly* in the context of earlier and contemporary representations of Asian Americans in theater and in American culture.

HENRIK IBSEN

Among the early reactions to Ibsen was George Bernard Shaw's *The Quintessence of Ibsenism* (1891), which emphasizes Ibsen's concern with pressing social and political issues; William Archer's essays, collected by Thomas Postlewait in *William Archer on Ibsen: The Major Essays, 1889–1919* (1984), foreground Ibsen's poetic choices and techniques. The decisive impact of Shaw and Archer is described in detail in Thomas Postlewait's *Prophet of the New Drama: William Archer and the Ibsen Campaign* (1986). Ibsen's third major early supporter was the critic Georg Brandes, who accompanied Ibsen's career with three essays, written in the 1870s, '80s, and '90s, collected in his *Henrik Ibsen: A Critical Study* (1899). Charles Lyons's compilation, *Critical Essays on Henrik Ibsen* (1987), includes landmark essay by Ibsen's modernist admirers, among them James Joyce, E. M. Forster, and Georg Lukàcs. The wider cultural context of Ibsen's European success, as well as a wealth of personal detail, is captured in Michael Meyer's *Ibsen: A Biography* (1971). While there have been a number of excellent studies devoted to Ibsen—for example, Michael Goldman's imaginative reading of Ibsen's subtexts and psychologies in *Ibsen: The*

Dramaturgy of Fear (1999)—the most influential accounts of Ibsen's impact on modern drama are to be found in studies devoted to modern drama more generally, many of which take their point of departure from Ibsen's work. Of these, Raymond Williams's *Drama: From Ibsen to Eliot* (1952; 2nd rev. ed., 1973) is the most important, discussing Ibsen's social drama and modern tragedy. Robert Brustein's *The Theatre of Revolt: An Approach to the Modern Drama* (1964) and Richard Gilman's *The Making of Modern Drama* (1974) are classics in dating the origin of a modern revolt to Ibsen's drama, as is Peter Szondi's *The Theory of the Modern Drama* (1956; trans. 1987), which measures Ibsen against Sophocles' *Oedipus the King*. In *Ibsen and Early Modernist Theatre, 1890–1900* (1997), Kirsten Shepherd-Barr situates Ibsen in the context of theater history, and Joan Templeton's *Ibsen's Women* (1997) is the first in-depth analysis of Ibsen's construction of female characters, including Hedda Gabler. *The Cambridge Companion to Ibsen*, ed. James McFarlane (1994), provides a good introduction to recent scholarship and contemporary approaches. For a detailed comparison of different English translations of *A Doll House*, see Kristian Smidt, *Ibsen Translated: A Report on English Versions of Henrik Ibsen's* Peer Gynt *and* A Doll's House (2000). The best book on Ibsen is Toril Moi's *Henrik Ibsen and the Birth of Modernism: Art, Theater, Philosophy* (2006).

TONY KUSHNER

Angels in America: A Gay Fantasia on National Themes (Theatre Communications Group, 1995) is the standard edition of this two-part play. James Fisher, *The Theater of Tony Kushner: Living Past Hope* (2001) and *Understanding Tony Kushner* (2008), are full-length studies of the development of Kushner's drama in its social, theatrical, and biographical contexts. Robert Vorlicky, ed., *Tony Kushner in Conversation* (1998), is a rich collection of biographical, critical, and backstage interviews with the playwright. Deborah R. Geis and Steven F. Kruger, eds., *Approaching the Millennium: Essays on "Angels in America"* (1997); Per Brask, ed., *Essays on Kushner's "Angels"* (1995); and James Fisher, ed., *Tony Kushner: New Essays on the Art and Politics of His Plays* (2006), provide a range of historical, critical, and theatrical perspectives on the play. In addition to the essays included in the above collections, the following articles are useful: Charles McNulty, "*Angels in America*: Tony Kushner's Theses on the Philosophy of

History" (1996); Jonathan Freedman, "Angels, Monsters, and Jews: Intersections of Queer and Jewish Identity in Kushner's *Angels in America*" (1998); Daryl Ogden, "Cold War Science and the Body Politic: An Immuno/Virological Approach to *Angels in America*" (2000); Ranen Omer-Sherman, "The Fate of the Other in Tony Kushner's *Angels in America*" (2007); and Cristine Hutchinson-Jones, "Center and Periphery: Mormons and American Culture in Tony Kushner's *Angels in America*," in Mark T. Decker and Michael Austin, eds., *Peculiar Portrayals: Mormons on the Page, Stage, and Screen* (2010).

CHRISTOPHER MARLOWE

Readers who are curious about the competing texts of *Doctor Faustus* would do well to consult *Doctor Faustus, 1604–1616: Parallel Texts*, ed. W. W. Greg (1950), and Michael Warren's authoritative essay "*Doctor Faustus:* The Old Man and the Text" (1981). The closest approximation to a standard scholarly text of the play is by Roma Gill (2nd ed., 1989). A modern edition of *The English Faust Book* has been produced by John Henry Jones (1994). Among the classic book-length studies of Marlowe that include excellent discussions of *Doctor Faustus* are Harry Levin, *The Overreacher: A Study of Christopher Marlowe* (1952); Wilbur Sanders, *The Dramatist and the Received Idea: Studies in the Plays of Marlowe and Shakespeare* (1968); and J. B. Steane, *Marlowe: A Critical Study* (1964). More provocative approaches to Marlowe and *Doctor Faustus* can be found in Michael Goldman's "Marlowe and the Histrionics of Ravishment," Stephen J. Greenblatt's "Marlowe and Renaissance Self-Fashioning," and especially Edward A. Snow's "Marlowe's *Doctor Faustus* and the Ends of Desire," all of which appear in *Two Renaissance Mythmakers: Christopher Marlowe and Ben Jonson*, a remarkable collection of essays edited by Alvin Kernan (1977). Lawrence Danson's "Marlowe: The Questioner" (1982) also has special pertinence to *Doctor Faustus*. One of the more controversial and inventive scholarly engagements with *Doctor Faustus* is William Empson's posthumously published *Faustus and the Censor: The English Faust-book and Marlowe's "Doctor Faustus"* (1987). Readers looking for a similar blend of historical scholarship and high-wire speculation in a life of Marlowe should consult Charles Nicholl's *The Reckoning: The Murder of Christopher Marlowe* (1992; rev. ed., 2002). Those in search of a more traditional biography need look no further than David Riggs's *The World of Christopher Marlowe* (2004). *The Cambridge Introduction to Christopher Marlowe*, ed. Tom Rutter (2012), provides a useful overview of Marlowe's life and work, while *Christopher Marlowe the Craftsman: Lives, Stage, and Page*, eds. Sarah K. Scott and M. L. Stapleton (2010), is a valuable collection of essays on Marlowe the working artist.

ARTHUR MILLER

Arthur Miller's *Collected Plays* (1957) contains the playwright's five major plays through 1957; *The Portable Arthur Miller* (1971; rev. ed., 2003) includes a useful selection of plays from throughout his career. Published two years before the playwright's death, Martin Gottfried's *Arthur Miller: His Life and Work* (2003) is a full-length biography of Miller. An engaging overview can also be found in Enoch Brater, *Arthur Miller: A Playwright's Life and Works* (2005). Those who want an in-depth account of the playwright's life and times through the early 1980s can consult his wide-ranging and critically acclaimed autobiography, *Timebends: A Life* (1987). Important studies of Miller's plays include Sheila Huftel, *Arthur Miller: The Burning Glass* (1965); Edward Murray, *Arthur Miller, Dramatist* (1967); Leonard Moss, *Arthur Miller* (1967; rev. ed., 1980); Benjamin Nelson, *Arthur Miller: Portrait of a Playwright* (1970); Dennis Welland, *Miller the Playwright* (1979; 3d ed., 1985); Neil Carson, *Arthur Miller* (1982; 2d ed., 2008); June Schlueter and James K. Flanagan, *Arthur Miller* (1987); David Savran, *Communist, Cowboys, and Queers: The Politics of Masculinity in the Work of Arthur Miller and Tennessee Williams* (1992); Alice Griffin, *Understanding Arthur Miller* (1996); Enoch Brater, ed., *Arthur Miller's Global Theater* (2007); and three books by Christopher Bigsby: *Arthur Miller: A Critical Study* (2005), *Arthur Miller: 1915–1962* (2009), and *Arthur Miller: 1962–2005* (2011). Bigsby, ed., *The Cambridge Companion to Arthur Miller* (1997; 2d ed., 2010) includes a useful collection of essays covering Miller's career as a whole.

Miller wrote and spoke widely on his plays and his career as a writer. Collections of his essays and interviews include *The Theater Essays of Arthur Miller*, ed. Robert A. Martin (1978; rev. ed., 1996); Matthew C. Roudané, ed., *Conversations with Arthur Miller* (1987); *Echoes down the Corridor: Collected Essays, 1944–2000*, ed. Steven R. Centola (2000); and Mel Gussow, *Conver-*

sations with Miller (2002). Stefani Koorey, *Arthur Miller's Life and Literature: An Annotated and Comprehensive Guide* (2000), offers an extensive bibliography of books and articles on Miller's drama as well as information on Miller's life and politics, references to theater reviews, and production information on his plays. Susan C. W. Abbotson's *Critical Companion to Arthur Miller: A Literary Reference to His Life and Work* (2007) is also an important resource.

Among the collections of critical essays on *Death of a Salesman* are *Death of a Salesman: Text and Criticism*, ed. Gerald Weales (1967); Helene Wickham Koon, ed., *Twentieth-Century Interpretations of "Death of a Salesman": A Collection of Critical Essays* (1983); Harold Bloom, ed., *Arthur Miller's "Death of a Salesman"* (1988; updated, 2007) and *Willy Loman* (1991; updated, 2005); Matthew C. Roudané, ed., *Approaches to Teaching Miller's "Death of a Salesman"* (1995); Stephen A. Marino, ed., *"The 'Salesman' Has a Birthday": Essays Celebrating the Fiftieth Anniversary of Arthur Miller's "Death of a Salesman"* (2000); and Eric J. Sterling, ed., *Arthur Miller's "Death of a Salesman"* (2008). Kay Stanton, "Women and the American Dream of *Death of a Salesman*," in *Feminist Rereadings of Modern American Drama*, ed. June Schlueter (1989), is an important feminist reading of Miller's play. Brenda Murphy, *Miller: "Death of a Salesman"* (1995), is a history of *Death of a Salesman* productions during the years 1949–89, while Miller's own *Salesman in Beijing* (1984) discusses his experiences directing the play in the People's Republic of China in 1983.

MOLIÈRE (JEAN-BAPTISTE POQUELIN)

There is, to date, no definitive, complete edition of Molière's works in English, though his plays have regularly been translated into this and many other languages. Among English translations, those of the poet Richard Wilbur have long been admired; others, such as those of Maya Slater, attempt to capture more exactly the form of the French originals. The translation by Haskell M. Block (1985) includes the preface and letters to Louis XIV quoted above. The version of *Tartuffe* created for *The Norton Anthology of Drama* is by the playwright Constance Congdon, who based it on the scholarly translation of Virginia Scott. Scott's biography *Molière: A Theatrical Life* (2000) offers an accessible and balanced portrait of the artist and provides reasoned conjectures about many of the contested and unprovable details of his career. Congdon and

Scott's co-edited Norton Critical Edition of the play, *Tartuffe: A New Verse Translation* (2008), provides valuable contextual materials. Useful introductions to seventeenth-century drama and theater include Henry Carrington Lancaster, *The Period of Molière, 1652–1672*, part 3 of *A History of French Dramatic Literature in the Seventeenth Century* (1936); Peter D. Arnott, *An Introduction to the French Theatre* (1977); John Lough, *Seventeenth-Century French Drama: The Background* (1979); Nicholas Hammond, *Creative Tensions: An Introduction to Seventeenth-Century French Literature* (1997); and Gerry McCarthy, *The Theatres of Molière* (2002). *The Molière Encyclopedia* (2002), edited by James F. Gaines, contains a wealth of useful and succinct information on the dramatist and his works. Richard Parish's edition of the play in French (1994) also includes an informative introduction and notes in English.

Full-length critical studies of Molière abound. Those with particularly helpful discussions for a consideration of *Tartuffe* include David Bradby and Andrew Calder's *Cambridge Companion to Moliere* (2006); James F. Gaines, *Social Structures in Molière's Theater* (1984); Nathan Gross, *From Gesture to Idea—Esthetics and Ethics in Molière's Comedy* (1982); W. D. Howarth, *Molière: A Playwright and His Audience* (1982); J. D. Hubert, *Molière & the Comedy of Intellect* (1962); Michael S. Koppisch, *Rivalry and the Disruption of Order in Molière's Theater* (2004); Gertrud Mander, *Molière* (1967, trans. 1973); and Martin Turnell, *The Classical Moment: Studies of Corneille, Molière and Racine* (1947). Jerry Lewis Kasparek's *Molière's "Tartuffe" and the Traditions of Roman Satire* (1977) explores sources and influences, and John Cairncross's *New Light on Molière: "Tartuffe"; "Elomire hypocondre"* (1956) establishes the arguments for the 1664 performance text accepted by many scholars as definitive. Albert Bermel's *Molière's Theatrical Bounty: A New View of the Plays* (1990) considers some of the more recent, influential productions of *Tartuffe*. Christopher Braider's chapter on *Tartuffe* in his study of French drama, *Indiscernible Counterparts: The Invention of the Text in French Classical Drama* (2002), provides a most elegant and insightful contemporary reading of the play.

DANIEL DAVID MOSES

Almighty Voice and His Wife was originally published in 1992 by Williams-Wallace Publishers; a second edition was Playwrights Canada Press in 2009. The play has also been anthologized in *Staging Coyote's Dream: An Anthology of First Nations Drama in English*, ed. Monique Mojica and Ric Knowles (2003). The fullest biographical account of Moses's life and career can be found in Don Perkins, "Daniel David Moses," in *Twentieth-Century Canadian Writers*, volume 334 of *The Dictionary of Literary Biography* (2007). Important studies of Moses's drama and *Almighty Voice* in particular include Rob Appleford, "The Desire to Crunch Bone: Daniel David Moses and the 'True Real Indian'" (1993); Barbara Goddard, "Writing between Cultures" (1997); Ric Knowles, "'Look. Look again.': Daniel David Moses' Decolonizing Optics" (2002); Helen Gilbert, "Black and White and Re(a)d All Over Again: Indigenous Minstrelsy in Contemporary Canadian and Australian Theatre" (2003); Marc Maufort, *Transgressive Itineraries: Postcolonial Hybridizations of Dramatic Realism* (2003); and Jo-Ann Episkenew, *Taking Back Our Spirits: Indigenous Literature, Public Policy, and Healing* (2009). *Outlaws and Lawmen of Western Canada*, ed. Art Downs (1983), is one of a number of accounts of the historical Almighty Voice. In September 1999 the Canadian Broadcast Channel aired a story entitled "Cree Prisoner Almighty Voice: Hero or Outlaw?"; this story is available in the CBC Digital Archives at www.cbc.ca/archives/categories/society/crime-justice/general-3/almighty-voice-hero-or-outlaw.html.

EUGENE O'NEILL

As befits his stature as the most significant U.S. dramatist, the critical literature on O'Neill is extensive and varied. The autobiographical character of *Long Day's Journey into Night* and other plays has led many critics and commentators to describe O'Neill as the tragic hero of U.S. theater. The two-volume study by Louis Sheaffer, *O'Neill: Son and Playwright* (1968) and *O'Neill: Son and Artist* (1973), remains the most informative of the several biographies, although Stephen Black's *Eugene O'Neill: Beyond Mourning and Tragedy* (1999) usefully takes O'Neill's interest in Freud and psychoanalysis as a point of departure for psychoanalytical readings of O'Neill's life and work. Travis Bogard's *Contour in Time: The Plays of Eugene O'Neill* (1972; rev. ed., 1988) is the best of the earlier analyses of the drama. Many studies tend toward idealizing their subject, presenting O'Neill's work as a heroic quest for artistic excellence. Notable exceptions to this rule are Joel Pfister's *Staging Depth: Eugene O'Neill and the Politics of Psychological Discourse* (1995), which provides historical context for the playwright's interest in psychology and interiority, and Zander Brietzke's excellent *Aesthetics of Failure: Dynamic Structure in the Plays of Eugene O'Neill* (2001), which examines the relation between O'Neill's significant failures and his stunning successes. Also useful are Kurt Eisner's *The Inner Strength of Opposites: O'Neill's Novelistic Drama and the Melodramatic Imagination* (1994), which focuses on O'Neill's novelistic techniques (including his stage directions, asides, and monologues), and Thierry Dubost's *Struggle, Defeat or Rebirth: Eugene O'Neill's Vision of Humanity* (1997).

There is a rich literature on and documentation of O'Neill's view of the theater and the staging of his plays, including *Eugene O'Neill: Comments on the Drama and the Theater: A Source Book*, ed. Ulrich Halfmann (1987), which contains early reviews as well as the playwright's letters to actors, directors, and critics; see also *Conversations with Eugene O'Neill*, ed. Mark W. Estrin (1990), and Yvonne Shafer, *Performing O'Neill: Conversations with Actors and Directors* (2000). Brenda Murphy's *O'Neill: Long Day's Journey into Night* (2001) documents the play's stage history. In addition, there are several valuable collections of essays, such as Michael Manheim, ed., *The Cambridge Companion to Eugene O'Neill* (1998), and Harold Bloom, ed., *Eugene O'Neill's "Long Day's Journey into Night"* (1987).

SUZAN-LORI PARKS

The America Play is published in *The America Play and Other Works* (Theatre Communications Group, 1995). Those interested in further biographical information on Suzan-Lori Parks should consult the entry on her in *Contemporary Authors Online* (Thompson Gale, 2005). Deborah R. Geis, *Suzan-Lori Parks* (2008), is an important and useful full-length study of Parks's plays, and Philip C. Kolin, ed., *Suzan-Lori Parks: Essays on the Plays and Other Works* (2010), provides an interesting collection of critical essays. Important articles on *The America Play* and Parks's career as a whole include the following: Alisa Solomon, "Signifying on the Signifyin'": The Plays of Suzan-Lori Parks" (1990); Katy Ryan, "'No Less Human': Making History in Suzan-Lori Parks's *The America Play*" (1999); Harry Elam and Alice Rayner, "Echoes from the

Black (W)hole: An Examination of *The America Play* by Suzan-Lori Parks," in *Performing America: Cultural Nationalism in American Theater*, ed. Jeffrey D. Mason and J. Ellen Gainor (1999); S. E. Wilmer, "Restaging the Nation: The Work of Suzan-Lori Parks" (2000); Shawn-Marie Garrett, "The Possession of Suzan-Lori Parks" (2000); and Frank Haike, "The Instability of Meaning in Suzan-Lori Parks's *The America Play*" (2002).

HAROLD PINTER

Old Times (Grove, 1971) is the standard edition of the play; it is reprinted in volume 4 of Harold Pinter, *Complete Works* (Grove, 1990). Michael Billington's *Harold Pinter* (2007), published in an earlier edition as *The Life and Work of Harold Pinter* (1996), is the authoritative biography, while Mel Gussow's *Conversations with Pinter* (1994) is an important collection of interviews conducted at different stages of Pinter's career. Martin Esslin, *The Peopled Wound: The Work of Harold Pinter* (1970), revised and updated as *Pinter, the Playwright* (6th ed., 2000), is a classic critical study. Other valuable book-length studies are Austin E. Quigley, *The Pinter Problem* (1975); Elin Diamond, *Pinter's Comic Play* (1985); David T. Thompson, *Pinter: The Player's Playwright* (1985); Susan Hollis Merritt, *Pinter in Play: Critical Strategies and the Plays of Harold Pinter* (1990); Marc Silverstein, *Harold Pinter and the Language of Cultural Power* (1993); Mark Batty, *Harold Pinter* (2001); and Charles Grimes, *Harold Pinter's Politics: A Silence Beyond Echo* (2005). The following collections provide a range of critical approaches: Arthur Ganz, ed., *Pinter: A Collection of Critical Essays* (1972); Steven H. Gale, ed., *Critical Essays on Harold Pinter* (1990); Peter Raby, ed., *The Cambridge Companion to Harold Pinter* (2001); Mark Batty, *Harold Pinter* (2001); Charles Grimes, *Harold Pinter's Politics: A Silence beyond Echo* (2005); and Peter Raby, ed., *The Cambridge Companion to Harold Pinter*, 2d ed. (2009). The website www.haroldpinter.org is a compendium of information about Pinter as playwright, screenwriter, actor, director, and political activist.

John Lahr, ed., *A Casebook on Harold Pinter's The Homecoming* (1971), and Michael Scott, ed., *Harold Pinter: The Birthday Party, The Caretaker, The Homecoming: A Casebook* (1986), contain important reviews and essays on Pinter's play. The former includes revealing interviews with director Peter Hall, designer John Bury, and two actors from the original London production. Other useful essays include Bert O. States, "Pinter's *Homecoming*: The Shock of Nonrecognition" (1968), and Vera M. Jiji, "Pinter's Four Dimensional House: *The Homecoming*" (1974). The 1997–98 issue of the *Pinter Review* includes Pinter's first draft of *The Homecoming* and Francis Gillen's article "Pinter at Work: An Introduction to the First Draft of *The Homecoming* and Its Relationship to the Completed Drama."

LUIGI PIRANDELLO

As a general overview of Pirandello's life, Gaspare Guidice's *Pirandello: A Biography* (1963; abridged trans. 1975) is more measured than Domenico Vittorini's *The Drama of Luigi Pirandello* (1935), written only one year after Pirandello had received the Nobel Prize. Because of Pirandello's place in the canon of modern drama, many of the most important commentators on modern drama have devoted essays or book chapters to his work. Among the classics in the field are Eric Bentley's *The Pirandello Commentaries* (1985) and Francis Fergusson's *The Idea of the Theater, a Study of Ten Plays: The Art of Drama in Changing Perspective* (1949), which places Pirandello in relation to other modern dramatists such as George Bernard Shaw and Bertolt Brecht. The best essay on Pirandello and metatheater is by Maurizio Grande, "Pirandello and the Theatre-within-the-Theatre: Thresholds and Frames in *Cascuno a suo modo*," in *Luigi Pirandello: Contemporary Perspectives*, ed. Gian-Paolo Biasin (1999). Roger W. Oliver's *Dreams of Passion: The Theater of Luigi Pirandello* (1979) focuses on Pirandello's theory of humor and applies it to his best-known plays, including *Six Characters*. The best book-length study of Pirandello in English is Ann Hallamore Caesar's *Characters and Authors in Luigi Pirandello* (1998), which includes detailed discussions of Pirandello's aesthetic theories and also an incisive critique of his patriarchal family structures. Daniela Bini's *Pirandello and His Muse: The Plays for Marta Abba* (1998) takes a similar approach to Pirandello's late plays. Pirandello's work in the theater is captured in *Luigi Pirandello in the Theatre: A Documentary Record*, ed. Susan Bassnett and Jennifer Lorch (1993), and in A. Richard Sogliuzzo's *Luigi Pirandello, Director: The Playwright in the Theatre* (1982). The political aspects of Pirandello's work are articulated especially well by Mary Ann Frese

Witt in *The Search for Modern Tragedy: Aesthetic Fascism in Italy and France* (2001).

WILLIAM SHAKESPEARE

S. Schoenbaum's *William Shakespeare: A Compact Documentary Life* (1977; rev. ed., 1987) and Stephen Greenblatt's *Will in the World: How Shakespeare Became Shakespeare* (2004) are excellent places to learn more about Shakespeare's life and career. A very useful introduction to early modern culture and theatrical practices is Russ McDonald's *Bedford Companion to Shakespeare: An Introduction with Documents* (1996; 2nd ed., 2001).

Hamlet

A. C. Bradley's classic *Shakespearean Tragedy* (1904; 3rd ed., 1992) and Bert O. States's *Hamlet and the Concept of Character* (1992) are very different but equally outstanding investigations of Hamlet as a character. Harold Bloom's *Shakespeare: The Invention of the Human* (1998) offers an accessible and in-depth discussion of the complex and self-reflective nature of the mind of Hamlet. Ernest Jones's *Hamlet and Oedipus* (1949) is a landmark psychoanalytic work that offers a comprehensive explanation for Hamlet's delay. Arthur Kinney's recent edited volume *Hamlet: New Critical Essays* (2002) includes a number of useful articles. Janet Adelman's *Suffocating Mothers: Fantasies of Maternal Origin in Shakespeare's Plays, "Hamlet" to "The Tempest"* (1992) combines feminist concerns with a psychological approach. Jacqueline Rose's "Hamlet—The Mona Lisa of Literature," originally published in 1986 and anthologized in *Shakespeare and Gender: A History*, eds. Deborah Barker and Ivo Kamps (1995), analyzes the influence of gender in interpretations of *Hamlet*.

Michael Cohen's *Hamlet in My Mind's Eye* (1989) offers a sustained, book-length reading of the play with a keen eye to performance possibilities. Stephen Greenblatt's *Hamlet in Purgatory* (2001) is a masterful treatment of the role of religious energies in the play.

Those interested in Shakespeare's representation of madness and its connection to political subversion can turn to Karin S. Coddon's "'Such Strange Designs': Madness, Subjectivity, and Treason in Hamlet and Elizabethan Culture," in *Shakespeare's Tragedies*, ed. Susan Zimmerman (1998). Carol Thomas Neely writes on madness in *Twelfth Night* and *Hamlet* in her historically informed essay "'Documents in Madness': Reading Madness and Gender in Shakespeare's Trag-

edies and Early Modern Culture" (1991). *Marxist Shakespeares* (2001), edited by Jean E. Howard and Scott Cutler Shershow, includes intriguing Marxist readings of *Hamlet*. Gary Taylor's "*Hamlet* in Africa 1607" in *Travel Knowledge: European "Discoveries" in the Early Modern Period*, eds. Ivo Kamps and Jyotsna G. Singh (2001), provides a fascinating account of the first non-European performance of *Hamlet* aboard a ship in Sierra Leone. Tony Howard's fascinating *Women as Hamlet: Performance and Interpretation in Theatre, Film, and Fiction* (2007) discusses the extensive tradition of women actors performing the role of Hamlet. Another excellent study, Margreta de Grazia's *"Hamlet" without Hamlet* (2007), considers Hamlet within the physical and metaphysical worlds he inhabits.

Twelfth Night

For a discussion of Shakespeare's comedies as a form influenced by popular Elizabethan festivals, see C. L. Barber's *Shakespeare's Festive Comedy: A Study of Dramatic Form and Its Relation to Social Custom* (1959). For details of Coleridge's famous interpretations, see Terence Hawkes's collection of them, *Coleridge's Writings on Shakespeare* (1959). Harold Bloom's *Shakespeare: The Invention of the Human* (1998) provides detailed characterological analyses.

Bruce Smith's *Twelfth Night, or, What You Will: Text and Contexts* (2001) offers a number of relevant texts and documents contemporaneous with the play. Jean Howard analyzes the practice of boy actors in female roles in "Cross-Dressing, the Theatre and Gender Struggle in Early Modern England" (1988), reprinted in *The Routledge Reader in Gender and Performance*, ed. Lizbeth Goodman with Jane de Gau (1998). A number of outstanding essays take up questions of gender and sexuality in *Twelfth Night*, including Dympna Callaghan's "'And All Is Semblative a Woman's Part': Body Politics and *Twelfth Night*" (1993); Stephen Greenblatt's "Fiction and Friction," in *Shakespearean Negotiations: The Circulation of Social Energy in Renaissance England* (1988); and Joseph Pequigney's "The Two Antonios and Same-Sex Love in *Twelfth Night* and *The Merchant of Venice*," in *Shakespeare and Gender: A History*, eds. Deborah Barker and Ivo Kamps (1995). Barbara Correll's "Malvolio at Malfi: Managing Desire in Shakespeare and Webster" (2007) offers a compelling study of this darker plotline, while M. J. Kietzmann's "Will Personified: Viola as Actor-Author in *Twelfth*

1868 | SELECTED BIBLIOGRAPHIES

Night" (2012) considers the performative dimensions of the comedy. *Twentieth Century Interpretations of "Twelfth Night": A Collection of Critical Essays,* ed. Walter N. King (1968), contains a number of classic assessments of the play, while James Schiffer's *Twelfth Night: New Critical Essays* (2011) offers more recent insights.

GEORGE BERNARD SHAW

Throughout his lifetime Shaw not only tried to control the presentation of his plays, he also carefully orchestrated his public persona, essentially collaborating with, if not ghostwriting, every attempt at authorized biography. Thus Michael Holroyd's four-volume *Bernard Shaw* (1988–92) may stand for some time as the only definitive and reasonably objective study of his life and work. Shaw repeatedly revised his plays even after publication; Dan Laurence's two-volume *Bernard Shaw: A Bibliography* (1983) meticulously traces Shaw's complete oeuvre. *The Bodley Head Bernard Shaw: Collected Plays with Their Prefaces,* 7 vols. (1970–74), is considered the definitive edition. Laurence also edited Shaw's four-volume *Collected Letters* (1965–88), which shed important light on his plays and other writings; many additional edited volumes of letters between Shaw and individual correspondents have also been published. Shaw published selections from his critical and political writings during his lifetime; scholarly editions of his dramatic, art, and music criticism have appeared more recently. Major Shaw research archives, which include both published and unpublished materials, are located in the British Library, the Berg Collection of the New York Public Library, the Bernard F. Burgunder Collection at Cornell University, and the Harry Ransom Humanities Research Center at the University of Texas at Austin.

Shaw's astounding volume of writing is matched only by the vast body of critical writing about him and his work. The three-volume (to date) *G. B. Shaw: An Annotated Bibliography of Writings about Him,* comp. J. P. Wearing (1986–), provides a helpful starting point for research. *Shaw: The Critical Heritage,* ed. T. F. Evans (1976), includes excerpts from reviews of his plays. *The Cambridge Companion to George Bernard Shaw,* ed. Christopher Innes (1998), includes current essays that provide valuable overviews of major topics in Shaw scholarship and contains extensive bibliographical suggestions. Raymond Mander and Joe Mitchenson's *Theatrical Companion to Shaw: A Pictorial Record of the First Performances of the Plays of George Bernard Shaw* (1954) remains the best record of his works in performance.

Among many full-length studies worth consulting are Eric Bentley, *Bernard Shaw* (1947); Tracy C. Davis, *George Bernard Shaw and the Socialist Theatre* (1994); Bernard F. Dukore, *Bernard Shaw, Playwright: Aspects of Shavian Drama* (1973); J. Ellen Gainor, *Shaw's Daughters: Dramatic and Narrative Constructions of Gender* (1991); Arthur Ganz, *George Bernard Shaw* (1983); Martin Meisel, *Shaw and the Nineteenth-Century Theater* (1963); Margery M. Morgan, *The Shavian Playground: An Exploration of the Art of George Bernard Shaw* (1972); and Alfred Turco Jr., *Shaw's Moral Vision: The Self and Salvation* (1976). Shaw scholarship has also flourished in essay form. There are three journals entirely devoted to Shaw—the *Shavian,* the *Shaw Bulletin,* and *Shaw: The Annual of Bernard Shaw Studies*— but essays abound throughout the periodic literature as well as in anthologies. For discussions of *Pygmalion* in particular, readers may wish to consult Awam Amkpa, "Drama and the Languages of Postcolonial Desire: Bernard Shaw's *Pygmalion*" (1999); Milton Crane, "Pygmalion: Bernard Shaw's Dramatic Theory and Practice" (1951); J. Ellen Gainor, "Bernard Shaw and the Drama of Imperialism," in *The Performance of Power: Theatrical Discourse and Politics,* ed. Sue-Ellen Case and Janelle Reinelt (1991); Celia Marshik, "Parodying the £5 Virgin: Bernard Shaw and the Playing of *Pygmalion*" (2000); and Jean Reynolds, "Deconstructing Henry Higgins, or Eliza as Derridean 'Text'" (1994).

SOPHOCLES

Like all classical Greek tragedies, Sophocles' plays survived through a series of accidents. Generations of scholars have tried to approximate the original text, distorted by scribes, commentators, and adaptors. The recent scholarship on the playwright is extensive; it draws on newly discovered fragments of other plays, new archaeological evidence, and new insights into Greek society and culture. The French scholars Jean-Pierre Vernan and Pierre Vidal-Naquet have been especially successful, for example, in using new anthropological theories in their commentaries on the play. Their essays are collected in *Myth and Tragedy in Ancient Greece* (1972, trans.

1988). The best general introduction to Sophocles is R. P. Winnington-Ingram's *Sophocles: An Interpretation* (1980). An older classic, H. D. Kitto's *Greek Tragedy: A Literary Study* (1939), contains a good discussion of both plays as well as comments on the philosophical outlook of the playwright. However, Mary Whitlock Blundell's *Helping Friends and Harming Enemies: A Study in Sophocles and Greek Ethics* (1989) is a much more searching and sophisticated analysis of Sophocles in the context of Greek ethics and philosophy. The city of Thebes in Greek tragedy, with particular attention to *Antigone* and *King Oedipus*, is discussed by Froma Zeitlin in her essay in Zeitlin and John J. Winkler, eds., *Nothing to Do with Dionysus* (1990). The political dimensions of the two plays are particularly difficult to understand for modern readers and are explained in Michael Vickers, *Sophocles and Alcibiades: Athenian Politics in Ancient Greek Literature* (2008). Charles Segal's *Oedipus Tyrannus: Tragic Heroism and the Limits of Knowledge* (1993) also places *Oedipus the King* in the context of theories of knowledge, while David Seale, in his *Vision and Stagecraft in Sophocles* (1982), emphasizes the metaphor and role of vision and blindness in the play. Particularly influential has been Charles Segal's *Tragedy and Civilization: An Interpretation of Sophocles* (1981), which uses Sophocles to explore the relation of kinship and ritual in Greek society and culture. Both plays have also been important for philosophers, from Aristotle, in his *Poetics* (ca. 330 B.C.E.), through G. W. F. Hegel, in his *Lectures on Aesthetics* (1835–38). *Oedipus the King* was central in the formulation of psychoanalysis, in Sigmund Freud's *Interpretation of Dreams* (1900). For information on Greek theater, Sir Arthur Pickard-Cambridge's *The Dramatic Festivals of Athens* (1968) is still a classic, and Eric Scapo and William J. Slater have made many fragments about Greek theater available in translation in their *The Context of Ancient Drama* (1995). Both plays have been adapted in many different ways for the modern stage; one important example is Seamus Heaney's version of *Antigone*, set in Northern Ireland, *The Burial at Thebes* (2004).

WOLE SOYINKA

For an authoritative text and extensive background readings on *Death and the King's Horseman*, consult the Norton Critical Edition, edited by Simon Gikandi (2003). The general bibliography on Soyinka's work is extensive. Book-length accounts started to appear in the early 1970s—notably, Eldred Duromsimi Jones's *The Writing of Wole Soyinka* (1973; 3d ed., 1988). A more recent study, Derek Wright's *Wole Soyinka Revisited* (1993), provides a more nuanced analysis of the dramatic works; it focuses on the different theatrical categories, particularly ritual, tragedy, and satire, that are central for understanding Soyinka's work. Ketu H. Katrak's *Wole Soyinka and Modern Tragedy* (1986) examines Soyinka's attempt to create a "Yoruba tragedy." By far the best of the critical literature on the playwright is Biodun Jeyifo's *Wole Soyinka: Politics, Poetics and Postcoloniality* (2004), which analyzes the complex relations between colonial culture, independence, and literature that mark his oeuvre. Jeyifo is among those intellectuals with whom Soyinka has heatedly debated the relation between art and politics; see, for example, Soyinka's collection of essays, *Art, Dialogue, and Outrage: Essays on Literature and Culture* (1988; rev. and expanded ed., 1993). Also useful is a collection of interviews, *Conversations with Wole Soyinka*, ed. Biodun Jeyifo (2001). Other major critics to have devoted attention to Soyinka are the philosopher Anthony Appiah, in *In My Father's House: Africa in the Philosophy of Culture* (1992), and Henry Louis Gates Jr., in "Being, the Will, and the Semantics of Death" (1981). Valuable collections of essays on Soyinka include James Gibb, ed., *Critical Perspectives on Wole Soyinka* (1980), and Biodun Jeyifo, ed., *Perspectives on Wole Soyinka: Freedom and Complexity* (2001). Jonathan Peters's *A Dance of Masks: Senghor, Achebe, Soyinka* (1978) and Kole Omotoso's *Achebe or Soyinka? A Study in Contrasts* (1996) are noteworthy comparative studies of Soyinka.

AUGUST STRINDBERG

The best biography available is Michael Meyer's *Strindberg* (1985), which seeks to distinguish between Strindberg's autobiographical novels and plays and the facts of his own life, especially his three marriages. The topic of autobiography receives special focus in Michael Robinson's *Strindberg and Autobiography: Writing and Reading a Life* (1986) and Harry G. Carlson's *Out of Inferno: Strindberg's Reawakening as an Artist* (1996). Particular attention to Strindberg the playwright is paid by Evert Sprinchorn (whose translation of *Miss Julie* in included in this volume) in *Strindberg as Dramatist* (1992) and by Egil Törnqvist, Strindberg's main Swedish interpreter, in *Strindbergian Drama: Themes and Structure* (1982). More interested in the literary and poetic dimensions of Strindberg's drama is another translator of his plays, Harry G. Carlson, in *Strindberg and the Poetry of Myth* (1982). Also commendable is Freddie Rokem's *Strindberg's Secret Codes* (2004). Given Strindberg's influence, most of the classic studies of modern drama dedicate important essays to the playwright, including Robert Brustein's *The Theatre of Revolt: An Approach to the Modern Drama* (1964), which emphasizes Strindberg's revolt against modern life, and Raymond Williams's *Drama from Ibsen to Brecht* (1968), which combines social analysis with an attention to form. An international collection of essays on Strindberg was assembled by Göran Stockenström in *Strindberg's Dramaturgy* (1988) as well as by Michael Robinson in *Studies in Strindberg* (1998). More interested in particular genres is Børge Gedsø Madsen's *Strindberg's Naturalistic Theatre: Its Relation to French Naturalism* (1962), Walter Johnson's *Strindberg and the Historical Drama* (1963), and John Ward's *The Social and Religious Plays of Strindberg* (1980). And Strindberg's influence on expressionist theater is detailed in Michael Robinson and Sven Rossel's collection *Expressionism and Modernism: New Approaches to August Strindberg* (1999). Most thoroughly dedicated to Strindberg on stage is Frederick J. Marker and Lise-Lone Marker's *Strindberg and Modernist Theatre: Post-Inferno Drama on the Stage* (2002). For analysis specifically of *Miss Julie*, see the collection edited by Egil Törnqvist and Barry Jacobs, *Strindberg's "Miss Julie": A Play and Its Transpositions* (1988).

SOPHIE TREADWELL

Machinal was first published in John Gassner's influential anthology, *Twenty-Five Best Plays of the Modern American Theatre, Early Series* (1949). It was reprinted in Judith Barlow's *Plays by American Women, 1900–1930* (1985), the anthology that led to the play's theatrical revival in 1990 and increased scholarly interest in her writing, especially among feminist critics. A number of Treadwell's other plays are now available through the *North American Women's Drama* database, issued by Alexander Street Press. The University of Arizona Library oversees the major archive of Treadwell materials, while the Billy Rose Theatre Collection of the New York Public Library maintains production-related documents and photos.

Theater scholar Jerry Dickey is the leading authority on Sophie Treadwell; he has written extensively on her life and work and serves as the literary advisor to her estate. Among Dickey's valuable publications, see his *Sophie Treadwell: A Research and Production Sourcebook* (1997), which provides a comprehensive bibliography; "The 'Real Lives' of Sophie Treadwell: Expressionism and the Feminist Aesthetic in *Machinal* and *For Saxophone*" in *Speaking the Other Self: American Women Writers*, ed. Jeanne Campbell Reesman (1997); and "The Expressionist Moment: Sophie Treadwell" in *The Cambridge Companion to American Women Playwrights*, ed. Brenda Murphy (1999). With Barbara Ozieblo, Dickey published *Susan Glaspell and Sophie Treadwell* (2008), and with J. Ellen Gainor, he wrote "Susan Glaspell and Sophie Treadwell: Staging Feminism and Modernism, 1915–1941" in *A Companion to Twentieth-Century American Drama*, ed. David Krasner (2005). With Miriam López-Rodríguez, Dickey edited *Broadway's Bravest Woman: Selected Writings of Sophie Treadwell* (2006).

Articles of note by other scholars include Nancy Wynn, "Sophie Treadwell: Author of *Machinal*" in the *Journal of American Drama and Theatre* (1991); Ginger Strand, "Treadwell's Neologism: *Machinal*" in *Theatre Journal* (1992); and Jennifer Jones, "In Defense of the Woman: Sophie Treadwell's *Machinal*" in *Modern Drama* (1994). Useful essays in edited volumes include Barbara L. Bywaters, "Marriage, Madness, and Murder in Sophie Treadwell's *Machinal*" in *Modern American Drama: The Female Canon*, ed. June Schlueter (1990); Kornelia Tancheva, "Sophie Treadwell's Play *Machinal*: Strategies of Reception and Interpretation" in *Experimenters, Rebels, and Disparate Voices: The Theatre of the 1920s Celebrates American Diversity*, eds. Arthur Gewirtz and James J. Kolb (2003); Richard Wattenberg, "Sophie Treadwell and the Frontier Myth: Western Motifs in *Machinal* and *Hope for a Harvest*" in *Staging Difference: Cultural Pluralism in American Theatre and Drama*, ed. Marc Maufort (1995); and Miriam López-Rodríguez, "Sophie Treadwell, Jung, and the Mandala, Acting a Gendered Identity" in *Codifying the National Self: Spectators, Actors and the American Dramatic Text*, eds. Barbara Ozieblo and María Dolores Narbona-Carrión (2006).

Ronald H. Wainscott provides a detailed and informative historical analysis of American expressionist plays and productions in *The Emergence of the Modern American Theater*

1914–1929 (1997). Julia A. Walker offers an additional insightful reading of the play in her book *Expressionism and Modernism in the American Theatre: Bodies, Voices, Words* (2005). Jennifer Parent has researched the original Broadway production in her article, "Arthur Hopkins' Production of Sophie Treadwell's *Machinal*" in *The Drama Review: TDR* (1982).

For information on Ruth Snyder and Judd Gray, see John Kobler, *The Trial of Ruth Snyder and Judd Gray* (1938) and Landis MacKellar, *The "Double Indemnity" Murder: Ruth Snyder, Judd Gray, and New York's Crime of the Century* (2006). Ann Jones's *Women Who Kill* (1980, 2009) offers a compelling feminist historical reading of Ruth Snyder's case, which Jessie Ramey extends through linguistic analysis in "The Bloody Blonde and the Marble Woman: Gender and Power in the Case of Ruth Snyder" in the *Journal of Social History* (2004). W. David Sievers's *Freud on Broadway* (1955) remains a useful resource on psychoanalysis and psychological theory as they are represented in the American theater. For a history of American women journalists, see Ishbel Ross, *Ladies of the Press: The Story of Women in Journalism by an Insider* (1936).

THE WAKEFIELD MASTER
The authoritative text of the *Second Shepherds' Play* can be found in Martin Stevens and A. C. Cawley, eds., *The Towneley Plays* (1994). Stevens and Cawley have also written the introduction to the published facsimile of the Towneley manuscript, *The Towneley Cycle: A Facsimile of the Huntington MS HM 1* (1976). Book-length studies of the Towneley Cycle and the plays of the Wakefield Master include Walter E. Meyers, *A Figure Given: Typology in the Wakefield Plays* (1969); John Gardner, *The Construction of the Wakefield Cycle* (1974); Jeffrey Helterman, *Symbolic Action in the Plays of the Wakefield Master* (1981); Martin Stevens, *Four Middle English Mystery Cycles: Textual, Contextual, and Critical Interpretations* (1987); Liam O. Purdon, *The Wakefield Master's Dramatic Art: A Drama of Spiritual Understanding* (2003); Warren Edminster, *The Preaching Fox: Festive Subversion in the Plays of the Wakefield Master* (2005); and Peter Happé, *The Towneley Cycle: Unity and Diversity* (2007). The introductions to A. C. Cawley, ed., *The Wakefield Pageants in the Towneley Cycle* (1958), and Martial Rose, ed., *The Wakefield Mystery Plays* (1961), contain valuable information on the Wakefield plays as a group, as does

Peter Meredith's chapter on the Towneley cycle in *The Cambridge Companion to Medieval English Theatre*, eds. Richard Beadle and Alan J. Fletcher (1994; 2nd ed., 2008). Important articles include Claude Chidamian, "Mak and the Tossing in the Blanket" (1947); William M. Manly, "Shepherds and Prophets: Religious Unity in the Towneley *Secunda Pastorum*" (1963); Margery M. Morgan, "'High Fraud': Paradox and Double-Plot in the English Shepherds' Plays" (1964); Lawrence J. Ross, "Symbol and Structure in the *Secunda Pastorum*" (1967); Maynard Mack Jr., "The *Second Shepherds' Play*: A Reconsideration" (1978); Regula Meyer Evitt, "Musical Structure in the *Second Shepherds' Play*" (1988–89); and Lisa J. Kiser, "'Mak's Heirs': Sheep and Humans in the Pastoral Ecology of the Towneley *First* and *Second Shepherds' Plays*" (2009). Rosemary Woolf, *The English Mystery Plays* (1972), is one of the finest general studies of the English Corpus Christi cycles.

OSCAR WILDE
While there is no standard edition of Oscar Wilde's plays, *"The Importance of Being Earnest" and Other Plays*, ed. David Raby (1995), is a useful collection. Richard Ellmann, *Oscar Wilde* (1987), is considered the authoritative biography. Studies of Wilde's career include Rodney Shewan, *Oscar Wilde: Art and Egotism* (1977); Regenia Gagnier, *Idylls of the Marketplace: Oscar Wilde and the Victorian Public* (1986); Alan Sinfield, *The Wilde Century: Effeminacy, Oscar Wilde, and the Queer Moment* (1994); Josephine M. Guy and Ian Small, *Oscar Wilde's Profession: Writing and the Culture Industry in the Late Nineteenth Century* (2000); Neil Sammells, *Wilde Style: The Plays and Prose of Oscar Wilde* (2000); John Sloan, *Oscar Wilde* (2003); Paul L. Fortunato, *Modernist Aesthetics and Consumer Culture in the Writings of Oscar Wilde* (2007); Kerry Powell, *Acting Wilde: Victorian Sexuality, Theatre, and Oscar Wilde* (2009); and Ruth Robbins, *Oscar Wilde* (2011). Early critical responses to Wilde's life and work are included in Richard Ellmann, ed., *Oscar Wilde: A Collection of Critical Essays* (1969). C. George Sandulescu, ed., *Rediscovering Oscar Wilde* (1994), and Peter Raby, ed., *The Cambridge Companion to Oscar Wilde* (1997), are valuable collections of essays.

Wilde's drama is the subject of Alan Bird, *The Plays of Oscar Wilde* (1977); Katharine Worth, *Oscar Wilde* (1983); Sos Eltis, *Revising Wilde: Society and Subversion in the Plays of Oscar Wilde* (1996); and Kerry Powell, *Oscar Wilde and* the Theatre of the 1890s (1990). Joseph Donohue and Ruth Berggren, eds., Oscar Wilde's "The Importance of Being Earnest": A Reconstructive Critical Edition of the Text of the First Production at St. James's Theatre, London, 1895 (1995), provides an extensively annotated edition of Wilde's masterpiece with an exhaustive discussion of the play's composition and manuscript history.

TENNESSEE WILLIAMS

The standard collection of Tennessee Williams's plays is The Theatre of Tennessee Williams, published in eight volumes by New Directions (1971–81). Additional plays from Williams's early career have been published separately. Among the several biographies of Williams, the finest is Lyle Leverich's Tom: The Unknown Tennessee Williams (1995), which covers the playwright's life to 1945. Students interested in Williams's life as a whole might consult Ronald Hayman, Tennessee Williams: Everyone Else Is an Audience (1993). Richard F. Leavitt, ed., The World of Tennessee Williams (1978), includes photographs, theater programs, and other documents illustrating Williams's life and career, while Philip Kolin, ed., The Tennessee Williams Encyclopedia (2004), contains valuable information on the playwright's works. Kenneth Holditch and Richard Freeman Leavitt's Tennessee Williams and the South (2002) discusses the profound influence of this region on Williams's work.

The following include valuable critical discussions of Williams's drama: Jac Tharpe, ed., Tennessee Williams: A Tribute (1977); Roger Boxill, Tennessee Williams (1987); Alice Griffin, Understanding Tennessee Williams (1995); Matthew C. Roudané, ed., The Cambridge Companion to Tennessee Williams (1997); Robert A. Martin, ed., Critical Essays on Tennessee Williams (1997); Philip C. Kolin, ed., Tennessee Williams: A Guide to Research and Performance (1998); Nancy M. Tischler, Student Companion to Tennessee Williams (2000); and Judith J. Thompson, Tennessee Williams' Plays: Memory, Myth, and Symbol (1987; rev. ed., 2002). One of the best discussions of Williams's dramatic career can be found in volume 2 of C. W. E. Bigsby, A Critical Introduction to Twentieth-Century American Drama (1984). The influence of Williams's homosexuality on his drama is explored in David Savran, Communists, Cowboys, and Queers: The Politics of Masculinity in the Work of Arthur Miller and Tennessee Williams (1992), and John M. Clum, Acting Gay: Male Homosexuality in Modern Drama (1992; expanded ed., 1994).

The essays in Jordan Y. Miller, ed., Twentieth Century Interpretations of "A Streetcar Named Desire" (1971), are devoted exclusively to Williams's play, as are Thomas P. Adler, "A Streetcar Named Desire": The Moth and the Lantern (1990), and Philip C. Kolin, ed., Confronting Tennessee Williams's "A Streetcar Named Desire": Essays in Critical Pluralism (1993). Philip C. Kolin, Williams: "A Streetcar Named Desire" (2000), provides a history of Streetcar in performance, while Brenda Murphy's Tennessee Williams and Elia Kazan: A Collaboration in the Theatre (1992) examines the productions of Streetcar and other Williams plays directed by Kazan. Kazan's valuable directorial notes on Streetcar are excerpted in the Twentieth Century Interpretations collection mentioned above. Maurice Yacowar's Tennessee Williams and Film (1977) offers a useful discussion of the 1951 film version of Williams's play.

AUGUST WILSON

The plays of August Wilson's twentieth-century cycle were published in 2007 by Theatre Communications Group in a ten-volume collection. The best book-length studies of August Wilson's life and plays are Sandra G. Shannon, The Dramatic Vision of August Wilson (1995); Kim Pereira, August Wilson and the African-American Odyssey (1995); Peter Wolfe, August Wilson (1999); Harry J. Elam Jr., The Past as Present in the Drama of August Wilson (2004); and Mary L. Bogumil, Understanding August Wilson rev. ed., (2011). Harry J. Elam Jr., "August Wilson," in A Companion to Twentieth-Century American Drama, ed. David Krasner (2005), is a general introduction to Wilson's work, while Yvonne Shafer, August Wilson: A Research and Production Sourcebook (1998), and Mary Ellen Snodgrass, August Wilson: A Literary Companion (2004), are valuable resources for the student of Wilson's plays. Jackson R. Bryer and Mary C. Hartig, eds., Conversations with August Wilson (2006), contains Wilson's major interviews. Dana A. Williams and Sandra G. Shannon, eds., August Wilson and Black Aesthetics (2004), examines the cultural politics of Wilson as an African American writer. The essays in Alan Nadel, ed., August Wilson: Completing the Twentieth-Century Cycle (2010), discuss Wilson's final five plays and the overall arc of the cycle as a whole.

Three collections of essays—Marilyn Elkins, ed., *August Wilson: A Casebook* (1994); Alan Nadel, ed., *May All Your Fences Have Gates: Essays on the Drama of August Wilson* (1994); and Christopher Bigsby, ed., *The Cambridge Companion to August Wilson* (2007)—present the range of critical approaches adopted by scholars analyzing Wilson's plays. Not surprising, *Fences* comes in for a large share of their discussion. Joan Fishman, "Developing His Song: August Wilson's *Fences*" (in Elkins), traces the development of Wilson's dramatic text through revisions, staged readings, and productions; Michael Awkward, "'The Crookeds with the Straights': *Fences*, Race, and the Politics of Adaptation" (in Nadel), considers *Fences* in the context of Wilson's well-publicized insistence that any film production of the play be directed by an African American. Susan Koprince, "Baseball as History and Myth in August Wilson's *Fences*" (2006), discusses the role of baseball in the play.

The black feminist scholar bell hooks has challenged the portrayal of women in Wilson's *Fences* in *Yearning: Race, Gender, and Cultural Politics* (1990). Harry J. Elam Jr., "August Wilson's Women," and Missy Dehn Kubitschek, "August Wilson's Gender Lesson" (both in Nadel), address the question of Wilson's women from feminist and other theoretical perspectives. Carla J. McDonough, *Staging Masculinity: Male Identity in Contemporary American Drama* (1997), considers the question of masculinity in Wilson's drama in the context of social issues facing urban black males.

ZEAMI MOTOKIYO

Although Zeami mentions *Atsumori* in his treatises, the earliest extant text is from the early sixteenth century. As a result, it is not possible to pinpoint the date of this play or to know if the text we have has been revised from Zeami's version. *Atsumori* was translated into French by Arthur Arrivet in 1895 but became well known in the West only in 1921 with the translation of Arthur Waley, which has been reprinted in *Masterpieces of the Orient*, ed. G. L. Anderson (1961; enlarged ed., 1977). The translation in Karen Brazell, ed., *Traditional Japanese Theater: An Anthology of Plays* (1997), has fuller stage directions than the version included here and is illustrated. That anthology also includes selections from other plays based on the Atsumori story and general information about Japanese theater. Royall Tyler's translation in *Japanese Nō Dramas* (1992) is also recommended. Zeami's treatises may be found in J. Thomas Rimer and Yamazaki Masakazu, trans., *On the Art of the Noh Drama: The Major Treatises of Zeami* (1984), and Tom Hare, trans., *Zeami: Performance Notes* (2008). Benito Ortolani, *The Japanese Theatre: From Shamanistic Ritual to Contemporary Pluralism* (1990; rev. ed., 1995), is an authoritative history of noh and other Japanese theater traditions, while Kunio Konparu, *The Noh Theatre: Principles and Perspectives* (trans. 1983), contains a useful introductory discussion of noh theater. Thomas Blenham Hare's *Zeami's Style: The Noh Plays of Zeami Motokiyo* (1986) discusses Zeami's dramatic work as a whole; Shelley Fenno Quinn's *Developing Zeami: the Noh Actor's Attunement in Practice* (2005) explores Zeami's dramatic and theatrical writings with a particular emphasis on his theory of acting. *In the Artistry of Aeschylus and Zeami: A Comparative Study of Greek Tragedy and Nō* (1989), Mae J. Smethurst presents interesting similarities in and differences between the genres.

PERMISSIONS ACKNOWLEDGMENTS

TEXT

ILLUSTRATIONS

Index